01/08/01

Sports Illustrated
2001
Sports
Almanac

By the Editors of Sports Illustrated

D1019341

Sports Illustrated
2001
Sports
Almanac

For information about permission to reproduce
selections from this book, please write to:
Permissions
Total Sports Publishing
100 Enterprise Dr.
Kingston, NY 12401
www.totalsportspublishing.com

First Edition
ISBN 1-892129-45-0

Sports Illustrated 2001 Sports Almanac was prepared by
Bishop Books of New York City.

Cover photography credits (clockwise from left):
Tiger Woods: John Biever
Alex Rodriguez: Otto Gruele
Kurt Warner: John W. McDonough

Back cover photography credits (clockwise from left):
Marion Jones: Bill Frakes
Lance Armstrong: Mike Powell/ Allsport
Shaquille O'Neal: John W. McDonough

Title page photography credit: Jon Ferrey/Allsport

10 9 8 7 6 5 4 3 2 1
COM
PRINTED IN THE UNITED STATES OF AMERICA

CONTENTS

SOURCES

In compiling the *Sports Illustrated 2001 Sports Almanac*, the editors would again like to thank the staff of the *Sports Illustrated* library for its invaluable assistance. They would also like to extend their gratitude to the media relations offices of the following organizations for their help in providing information and materials relating to their sports: Major League Baseball; the Canadian Football League; the National Football League; the National Collegiate Athletic Association; the National Basketball Association; the National Hockey League; the Association of Tennis Professionals; the Women's Tennis Association; the U.S. Tennis Association; the U.S. Golf Association; the Ladies Professional Golf Association; the Professional Golfers Association; National Thoroughbred Racing Association; the U.S. Trotting Association; the Breeders' Cup; Churchill Downs; the New York Racing Association, Inc.; the Maryland Jockey Club; Championship Auto Racing Teams; the National Hot Rod Association; the International Motor Sports Association; the National Association for Stock Car Auto Racing; the Professional Bowlers Association; the Ladies Professional Bowlers Tour; the American Professional Soccer League; the National Professional Soccer League; the *Fédération Internationale de Football Association*; the U.S. Soccer Federation; the U.S. Olympic Committee; USA Track & Field; U.S. Swimming; U.S. Diving; U.S. Skiing; U.S. Skating; the U.S. Chess Federation; U.S. Curling; the Iditarod Trail Committee; the International Game Fish Association; the U.S. Gymnastics Federation; U.S. Handball Association; the Lacrosse Foundation; the American Power Boat Association; the Hydroplane Racing Association; the Professional Rodeo Cowboys Association; U.S. Rowing; the American Softball Association; the U.S. Speed Skating Association; U.S. Rugby Football Union; the Triathlon Federation USA; the National Archery Association; USA Wrestling; the U.S. Squash Racquets Association; the U.S. Polo Association; ABC Sports; and the U.S. Volleyball Association.

The following sources were consulted in gathering information:

Baseball   *The Baseball Encyclopedia*, Macmillan Publishing Co., 1990; *Total Baseball*, Viking Penguin, 1995; *Baseballistics*, St. Martin's Press, 1990; *The Book of Baseball Records*, Seymour Siwoff, publisher, 1991; *The Complete Baseball Record Book*, The Sporting News Publishing Co., 1992; *The Sporting News Baseball Guide*, The Sporting News Publishing Co., 1996; *The Sporting News Official Baseball Register*, The Sporting News Publishing Co., 1996; *National League Green Book—1994*, The Sporting News Publishing Co., 1993; *American League Red Book—1994*, The Sporting News Publishing Co., 1993; *The Scouting Report: 1996,* Harper Perennial, 1996.

Pro Football   *The Official 1997 National Football League Record & Fact Book*, The National Football League, 1997; *The Official National Football League Encyclopedia*, New American Library, 1990; *The Sporting News Football Guide*, The Sporting News Publishing Co., 1996; *The Sporting News Football Register*, The Sporting News Publishing Co., 1996; *The 1993 National Football League Record & Fact Book,* Workman Publishing, 1993; *The Football Encyclopedia,* David Neft and Richard Cohen, St. Martin's Press, 1991.

College Football   *1997 NCAA Football*, The National Collegiate Athletic Association, 1997.

Pro Basketball   *The Official NBA Basketball Encyclopedia*, Villard Books, 1994; *The Sporting News Official NBA Guide*, The Sporting News Publishing Co., 1996; *The Sporting News Official NBA Register*, The Sporting News Publishing Co., 1996.

College Basketball   *1997 NCAA Basketball*, The National Collegiate Athletic Association, 1996.

Hockey *The National Hockey League Official Guide & Record Book 1997–98*, The National Hockey League, 1997; *The Sporting News Complete Hockey Book,* The Sporting News Publishing Co., 1993; *The Complete Encyclopedia of Hockey,* Visible Ink Press, 1993.

Tennis *1997 Official USTA Tennis Yearbook*, H.O. Zimman, Inc., 1997; *IBM/ATP Tour 1997 Player Guide*, Association of Tennis Professionals, 1997; *1997 Corel WTA Tour Media Guide*, Corel WTA Tour, 1997.

Golf *PGA Tour Book 1997*, PGA Tour Creative Services, 1997; *LPGA 1997 Player Guide*, LPGA Communications Department, 1997; *Senior PGA Tour Book 1997*, PGA Tour Creative Services, 1997; *USGA Yearbook 1997*, U.S. Golf Association, 1997.

Boxing *The Ring 1986–87 Record Book and Boxing Encyclopedia*, The Ring Publishing Corp., 1987. (To subscribe to *The Ring* magazine, write to P.O. Box 768, Rockville Centre, New York 11571-9905; or call (516) 678-7464); *Computer Boxing Update*, Ralph Citro, Inc., 1992; Bob Yalen, boxing statistician at ESPN.

Horse Racing *The American Racing Manual 1994*, Daily Racing Form, Inc., 1994; *1994 Directory and Record Book*, The Thoroughbred Racing Association, 1994; *The Trotting and Pacing Guide 1994*, United States Trotting Association, 1994; *Breeders' Cup 1993 Statistics*, Breeders' Cup Limited, 1993; *NYRA Media Guide 1993*, The New York Racing Association, 1994; *The 120th Kentucky Derby Media Guide, 1994*, Churchill Downs Public Relations Dept., 1994; *The 120th Preakness Press Guide, 1994*, Maryland Jockey Club, 1994; *Harness Racing News,* Harness Racing Communications.

Motor Sports *The Official NASCAR Yearbook and Press Guide 1997*, UMI Publications, Inc., 1997; *1994 Indianapolis 500 Media Fact Book*, Indy 500 Publications, 1994; *IMSA Yearbook 1995 Season Review*, International Motor Sports Association, 1995; *1994 Winston Drag Racing Series Media Guide*, Sports Marketing Enterprises, 1994.

Bowling *1994 Professional Bowlers Association Press, Radio and Television Guide*, Professional Bowlers Association, Inc., 1994; *The Professional Women's Bowling Association Tour Guide 1997*.

Soccer *Rothmans Football Yearbook 1993–94*, Headline Book Publishing, 1993; *American Professional Soccer League 1992 Media Guide*, APSL Media Relations Department, 1992; The *European Football Yearbook*, Facer Publications Limited, 1988; *Soccer America,* Burling Communications; Dan Goldstein, editor of *Football Europe.*

NCAA Sports *1997–98 National Collegiate Championships*, The National Collegiate Athletic Association, 1998; *1993–94 National Directory of College Athletics,* Collegiate Directories Inc., 1993.

Olympics *The Complete Book of the Olympics*, Little, Brown and Co., 1991; *The Complete Book of the Summer Olympics,* Little, Brown and Co., 1996.

Track and Field *American Athletics Annual 1996*, The Athletics Congress/USA, 1996.

Swimming *6th World Swimming Championships Media Guide*, The World Swimming Championships Organizing Committee, 1991.

Skiing *U.S. Ski Team 1994 Media Guide / USSA Directory*, U.S. Ski Association, 1993; *Ski Racing Annual Competition Guide 1993–94*, Ski Racing International, 1993; *Ski Magazine's Encyclopedia of Skiing*, Harper & Row, 1974; *Caffe Lavazza Ski World Cup Press Kit*, Biorama, 1991.

The Year In Sports

JOHN BIEVER

Year of the Tiger

In a year of dark deeds by sports figures in and out of competition, Tiger Woods was an incandescent counterpoint

BY MERRELL NODEN

WHEN, EXACTLY, did 2000 become the Year of the Tiger? Did it happen as early as June, when Earl Woods's precocious, ferocious son won the U.S. Open at Pebble Beach by a record 15 strokes? Or was it in July, when he traveled to St. Andrews, golf's most hallowed ground, and blew away a strong international field with rounds of 67, 66, 67 and 69? Or was it as late as August, when he appeared simultaneously on the covers of both *Time* and *The New Yorker* (albeit in cartoon likeness), launching his Q rating even higher than his wedge shots?

Most likely, though, it happened later that month, at the PGA Championship, where Woods finally got a real scare—from little-known Bob May, of all people—and showed his mettle by birdieing the final two holes of regulation to get into a three-hole playoff, which he essentially put away with a 20-foot birdie putt on the first hole. *That* was staring down pressure. That was the stuff of legends.

Woods's fellow pros reacted to his dominance with either grumpy defiance or a resigned shrug of acceptance. But in their heart of hearts most had to agree with Mark Calcavecchia, who said, "He's the best who ever played, and he's 24."

If we discount a certain iciness of focus and the fact that he hawked a Nike ball he wasn't using at the time, Woods's only real misstep came at the U.S. Open when, apparently unaware that there was a mike on the 18th tee, he unleashed a string of profanity after hitting his drive out of bounds. Much was made of this spewing, and Woods duly apologized. But to all but the most prissily proper listeners, it was no big deal, a humanizing by-product of the extreme perfectionism that fuels his success. And compared to the behavior of many of his fellow athletes, Tiger's tirade was really quite tame.

This was the year of Men Behaving Badly, in which incident after incident underscored growing questions about the price we are willing to pay for athletic success, the dangerous drugs athletes take and the special dispensations we grant our

Murder charges against Lewis, who became a poster boy for NFL violence, were dropped.

sporting heroes—and, in at least one case, their coaches.

Bad behavior by athletes is nothing new, of course. This year, however, on top of the usual long rap sheet of larceny, sexual exploitation and thuggery, several top athletes were actually charged with murder. Baltimore Ravens linebacker Ray Lewis was at the scene of an early-morning brawl that left two men dead outside an Atlanta nightclub following the Super Bowl. He was charged with murder the day after the NFL's biggest night. Wide receiver Rae Carruth of the Carolina Panthers was alleged to have hired someone to shoot his pregnant girlfriend. (She died; the baby survived.) Murder charges against Lewis were ultimately dropped, and in a plea agreement he received one-year's probation for a misdemeanor obstruction of justice. He rejoined the Ravens before the 2000 season. But the Mecklenberg County (N.C.) district attor-

ney's office announced that it planned to seek the death penalty against Carruth, whose trial began in late October. The two cases made the NFL's ongoing campaign against taunting and excessive celebration seem a bit misplaced and the high-octane ads for the XFL, the new "extreme" football league, seem particularly tasteless. And they made the National Rifle Association's buying ad time on several NFL regional broadcasts in September seem simply absurd.

Not that football players had a monopoly on reprehensible behavior. Virtually every major sport had its share of embarrassment. Baseball had John Rocker, the Atlanta Braves reliever whose bigoted, homophobic rant about New Yorkers to SPORTS ILLUSTRATED writer Jeff Pearlman earned him a two-week suspension at the start of the season and a special security detail when he first appeared at Shea Stadium following the publication of his remarks. The National Hockey League had Marty McSorley, a career goon who wound up in a Vancouver courtroom, charged with assault, for slashing Donald Brashear across the right temple with his hockey stick. College football had Peter Warrick, the talented wide receiver for national champion Florida State, who blew his shot at the Heisman Trophy by accepting too good a deal at a Tallahassee department store. And then there was Bobby Knight, who managed to embarrass not just college basketball, but also Indiana University and higher education in general through acts of bullying that no one could continue to ignore. Even the Olympics, which presented its usual crop of fresh-faced heroes, did so amid a troubling swirl of drug allegations.

With foils like that, Woods stood out like a ray of pure sunlight. His position as arguably the world's top sports figure was all the more impressive in a year that did not lack for exciting new faces. Sure, slam-dunking Vince Carter and goateed Kobe Bryant do not yet possess Michael Jordan's supreme drive to win, but they showed this year that they are capable of the same high-flying wizardry as His Airness. And for examples of extraordinary persistence you had cancer survivor Lance Armstrong dominating the Tour de

France for the second straight year and Kurt Warner, who led the St. Louis Rams to the Super Bowl title five years after he seemed on his way out of football and was forced to support himself by stocking shelves at an Iowa grocery.

The year began with the usual glut of bowl games, some meaningful, some not. The most meaningful was the Sugar Bowl, which featured top-ranked Florida State against No. 2 Virginia Tech. Leading Tech was one of the most electric players in college football, redshirt freshman quarterback Michael Vick. But Warrick outdazzled Vick in New Orleans, finishing with 163 receiving yards and three touchdowns, one of them coming on a 59-yard punt return. Vick performed brilliantly, too, carrying 23 times for 97 yards, throwing for another 225 and providing inspiration to his teammates. But there was no mistaking which was the better team: Florida State won 46–29 to claim the national championship and complete Bobby Bowden's first undefeated season.

The NFL's run of bad tidings began with the off-field troubles of Lewis and Carruth and continued with the sad news of the deaths of two Hall of Famers: Tom Landry, who coached the Dallas Cowboys to 250 regular-season wins and two Super Bowl titles, and former Chicago Bears great Walter Payton, the NFL's alltime rushing leader with 16,726 yards in 13 seasons. Sweetness, as Payton was known, had been suffering for months from a liver ailment. Another terrible shock was the death of Derrick Thomas, the Kansas City Chiefs' All-Pro linebacker, who died from a blood clot caused by injuries he sustained in a car accident.

The league also said goodbye to the playing days of Miami quarterback Dan Marino and 49ers signal-caller Steve Young, both of whom retired in 2000. Marino set countless passing records in his 17-year career, including career yards (61,361) and career touchdowns (420). Young, the NFL's career leader in passing efficiency (96.8), called it quits after suffering the sixth reported concussion of his career.

On the field it was a topsy-turvy season that saw doormats become powerhouses and vice versa. The two-time Super Bowl champion Denver Broncos lost leading rusher Terrell Davis to an injured knee and went just 6–10. Green Bay went 8–8 and failed to reach the playoffs for the first time since 1992. Rushing to fill the vacuum at the top were teams like Jacksonville, which had the league's best regular-season record, 14–2, and Tennessee, Indianapolis and St. Louis, all 13–3.

St. Louis quarterback Warner completed 65.1% of his passes, and the Rams quickly emerged as the league's top offense. Coached by former Philadelphia Eagles coach Dick Vermeil, who had previously retired from coaching in 1982 because of burnout, the Rams went a perfect 8–0 in the NFC West. They rolled all the way to the Super Bowl, where they faced the Tennessee Titans, who were rather lucky to be there. In the first round of the playoffs, Tennessee defeated Buffalo on a wild kickoff-return play for a touchdown in the closing seconds. The play, which involved a handoff and a questionable cross-field lat-

JOHN BIEVER

Role reversal: Brand pointed the finger at Knight, dismissing him after 29 years at IU.

JOHN BIEVER

Super Bowl–MVP Warner was one of several exciting new stars to emerge in 2000.

eral to receiver Kevin Dyson, was dubbed the Music City Miracle and joined the Immaculate Reception as one of the weirdest game-winning plays ever.

The Rams won Super Bowl XXXIV 23–16 when Dyson, having used up his quota of miracles, was stopped one yard short of a touchdown by Rams linebacker Mike Jones on the game's final play. The 62-year-old Vermeil couldn't resist the chance to go out on top and announced soon after the game that he would return to retired life.

Another coach who enhanced his résumé was Zenmeister Phil Jackson, who won six NBA titles with the Chicago Bulls in the 1990s. In June 1999 Jackson signed a five-year, $30 million contract to coach the under-achieving L.A. Lakers, knowing full well that this was a make-or-break situation for his coaching reputation. Many detractors sniped that any coach with Jordan in his lineup would look good. Well, the Lakers were stocked with superstars Shaquille O'Neal and Bryant, and they had made several coaches look *bad* in their unfulfilled quest for a championship. Smart man that he is, Jackson knew that his first priority was to persuade the two superstars to mesh their yin-yang, inside-outside games. They did so and then some, finishing the regular season at 67–15 and then squeaking by Portland in the Western Conference finals before dispatching Indiana in six games for the title. O'Neal had his best season ever, winning the league scoring title (29.7 points per game) as well as the regular-season and Finals MVP awards.

One of the most important events in college hoops occurred in the quarterfinals of the Conference USA tournament, when Cincinnati star Kenyon Martin, the player of the year, broke his leg in a game against St. Louis. The Bearcats lost the game and a sure No. 1 seed in the NCAAs, where they fell to Tulsa in the second round. Martin recovered and was the first pick in the 2000 NBA draft, going to the New Jersey Nets.

On the eve of the tournament CNN/SI aired a report in which former Hoosier player Neil Reed accused Knight of choking him, a charge Knight steadfastly denied. Perhaps distracted by the controversy, Indiana lost badly to Pepperdine in the first round.

Reaching the Final Four were defense-minded Wisconsin; surprising North Carolina (18–13 in the regular season); young, run-and-gun Florida; and Michigan State, whose point guard, Mateen Cleaves, had decided to return for his senior year instead of entering the NBA draft and then broke his foot during the preseason, missing 13 games. But Cleaves eventually got what he came back for—an NCAA title—as he scored 18 points to help the Spartans beat upstart Florida 89–76 in the final. It was MSU's first title since Magic beat Larry in '79.

Soon after that exhilarating scene came the beginning of Knight's fall. Shortly after the tournament CNN/SI obtained a copy of a video that despite its graininess clearly showed Knight placing his hand on Reed's throat during a Hoosier practice. Following an investigation by several trustees, IU president Myles Brand announced that Knight would not be fired but given a final chance with "zero tolerance" for any dubious behavior.

The probationary term ended in September when Knight had an altercation with a 19-year-old IU freshman named Kent Harvey. Knight acknowledged the incident but downplayed its seriousness, saying he never raised his voice above a conversational level. Brand quickly announced Knight's firing, sparking a tidal wave of sympathy from the Hoosier faithful for the irascible coach. Much of it went way too far: Harvey was burned in effigy outside of Brand's home; both Brand and Harvey were threatened. A marked man on campus, Harvey eventually withdrew from IU. Knight's supporters pointed out that the coach ran a clean program and that his players graduated at a much higher rate than those at other schools.

It was widely assumed that Knight would turn up at some other university. McSorley, for his part, almost turned up in jail. He was found guilty of assault with a weapon but given probation instead of jail time—a penalty that surely would have made other players think about the violence that is part of hockey culture. In a physical Stanley Cup final between the New Jersey Devils and the Dallas Stars, the Devils won three road games to win the Cup, and they did so with Petr Sykora, their leading goal scorer in the playoffs, in the hospital after a bone-rattling hit by Dallas's Derian Hatcher.

The first month of the 2000 baseball season was dominated by the saga of John Rocker, but that soon was eclipsed by the astonishing explosion of power hitting. "I don't like to give up home runs, but in this day and age it's not a big deal," said Tim Hudson of the A's. May was a merry month for sluggers, who clouted 1,069 homers, more than in any other single month in baseball history. On May 21 there were six grand slams, a single-day record. Suspicions about a juiced ball were so prevalent that the commissioner's office actually enlisted Jim Sherwood, an engineer at the University of Massachusetts-Lowell, to test the ball independently. His conclusion: the ball was essentially the same as in previous years, though the MLB logo may have made it easier for hitters to pick up.

In the end, though, the power numbers flattened out, while other batting categories ballooned. Red Sox shortstop Nomar Garciaparra batted .372 to win his second straight batting title, while Todd Helton of the Colorado Rockies also batted .372 to win the NL title. The last time both batting champions topped .370 was in 1937, when Joe (Ducky) Medwick hit .374 for St. Louis and Charlie Gehringer hit .371 for Detroit. Poor Darin Erstad of the Angels got 240 hits—a number that hadn't been reached since Wade Boggs did it in 1985—and didn't even win the batting title. All of this made Boston pitcher Pedro Martinez's E.R.A. of 1.74 even more astounding. It beat AL runner-up Roger Clemens by nearly two runs.

The San Francisco Giants had the best record in baseball, with 97 wins. In the American League the surprise team was the resurrected Chicago White Sox. After finishing 1999 in second place in the Central Division, 21 1/2 games behind Cleveland, the White Sox led the American League with 95 wins. Their improvement was due in part to DH Frank Thomas, who finished the season with 43 home runs (a career-best), 143 RBIs and a .328 batting average, sure MVP numbers except that Jason Giambi of the A's went 43-137-.333 and Carlos Delgado of the Blue Jays went 41-137-.344, and they both play first base.

Even tennis had its share of nastiness. At the U.S. Open, Martina Hingis and Lindsay

AP PHOTO/CHUCK STOODY

Davenport joined forces to psych each other up to prevent an all-Williams final between sisters Venus and Serena Williams. They accomplished that but couldn't stop Venus from winning the tournament. The elder Williams sister, who began the year battling tendinitis in both wrists, also won the Wimbledon and Olympic singles titles. The Williams sisters have not yet faced each other in a Grand Slam final, but that day is surely coming.

On the men's side, Pete Sampras defeated Patrick Rafter in the finals of Wimbledon for his record 13th Grand Slam title. But at the U.S. Open, Marat Safin, a handsome, 20-year-old Russian, used a booming serve to beat Sampras in straight sets. Safin looks like an heir apparent to Sampras.

The Sydney Olympics kicked off in grand style on Sept. 15 when 400-meter runner Cathy Freeman, of Aboriginal descent, lit the Olympic torch in an emotional crescendo to a great opening ceremony. These were in almost every way a superb Games, though that fact was lost on those stuck watching NBC's tape-delayed, feature-heavy coverage. Many who went to Sydney called them the best ever. Not only was the city itself gorgeous, but the sports-mad Australians embraced the Games with infectious giddiness.

Still, there was the perception that the Games were awash in performance-enhancing drugs. China left 27 athletes home, most for failing preliminary drug screening; a coach from Uzbekistan was caught carrying human growth hormone through customs at Sydney Airport; and all but one member of the Bulgarian weightlifting team was sent home after three of its members tested positive for steroids. Tiny Andreea Raducan, the all-around women's gymnastics champion, was stripped of her gold medal for testing positive for the mild stimulant pseudoephedrine, which she'd been given for a cold by the Romanian team doctor. Drugs didn't ruin these Games, but they were an unspoken subtext in many sports and openly discussed in others.

But they hardly detracted from the Games' many highlights. Nowhere was the excitement more palpable than at the Aquatic Centre, where the swimming-mad Aussies were able to cheer on national heroes like Ian Thorpe, the 17-year-old with the size-17 paddles for feet. Thorpe won the 400 freestyle in world-record time, as expected, but his greatest moment came on the anchor swim of the 4 x 100 free relay, when he chased down and outtouched the brash American Gary Hall Jr. amid a din that former Boston Celtic John Havlicek called the "loudest noise I've ever heard in an arena." But the U.S. remained the world's swimming power, led by gold medalists Lenny Krayzelburg, the transplanted Ukrainian who won both backstrokes, Megan Quann (100-meter breaststroke) and Brooke Bennett (400 and 800 free).

The brightest swimming star was Inge de Bruijn of the Netherlands, the only swimmer to win three individual events (the 50 and 100 freestyles and the 100 fly), who then had to endure waves of innuendo. "It's sad," said Jacco Verhaeren, who is de Bruijn's coach

Carter and the U.S. Dream Team III struggled to win gold in Sydney.

points of defeating the mighty U.S. in the men's basketball semifinals.

Finally, there was Marion Jones, who was aiming for an unprecedented five gold medals in track and field. She didn't pull it off, but she impressed everyone with her grace under pressure as she won three golds and two bronzes while dealing with the distractions caused by reports that her husband, world shot put champion C.J. Hunter, had tested positive for drugs four times during the summer. Which generated perhaps the biggest mystery of these Games: What exactly did he and Mrs. Jones have going on? Was she dabbling in performance-enhancing substances as well? No evidence to that effect ever surfaced. It is a tribute to Jones's effervescent personality that she seemed to escape the shadow even though the cloud was hovering right above her.

and boyfriend. "If you swim fast, you're treated like a criminal."

There were many upsets. The mighty Cuban baseball team suffered its first Olympic loss, to the Netherlands of all teams, and then was shut out 4–0 in the gold medal game by Tommy Lasorda's U.S. team. Hicham El Guerrouj, the world-record holder in the mile and the 1,500, lost the latter to Noah Ngeny of Kenya. Twenty-nine-year-old Wyoming farm boy Rulon Gardner pulled off the biggest shocker of the Games, defeating the mighty, 6' 4'', 290-pound Alexander Karelin of Russia 1–0 in Greco-Roman wrestling. Karelin had not lost in 14 years of international competition. There was also one near-upset that would have been colossal: Lithuania came within two

In the end, though, 2000 was unquestionably Woods's year. When he signed a five-year, $100 million endorsement deal with Nike in September, no one questioned for an instant whether he was worth it. Perhaps they were recalling the way he'd won the Canadian Open a week earlier by launching yet another "career" shot, this one to beat Grant Waite: a 218-yard six-iron, out of a fairway bunker. Over a greenside pond. Right at the flag. No hesitation. Poor Waite could only shake his head: "The guy fires at the flag with the tournament on the line? I told him, 'You're not supposed to do that.'"

So heave a sigh of relief, pro golfers, as we bid farewell to the Year of the Tiger. Now, what can you do to stop him from owning the next decade, too?

compiled by John Bolster

Baseball

Oct 27, 1999—Miffed over the exclusion of Hall of Famer Roberto Clemente from Major League Baseball's All-Century Team, a group of Latin American journalists selects a Latin American team of the century. Making the cut are such stars as Sammy Sosa, Bernie Williams, Orlando Cepeda and Juan Marichal. The group selects Clemente as the Latin player of the century.

Oct 27—The Chicago Cubs' Sammy Sosa and Manny Ramirez of the Cleveland Indians are the recipients of the inaugural Hank Aaron Award, which henceforth will be presented annually to the top overall batters in the American League and the National League. Ramirez batted .333 with 44 home runs and 165 RBIs; Sosa smacked 63 homers, drove in 141 runs and batted .288.

Nov 1—Former Colorado Rockies skipper Don Baylor signs a four-year, $5.2 million contract to manage the Chicago Cubs, while in Cleveland, the Indians hire Charlie Manuel as manager, and in Anaheim, the Angels name Bill Stoneman as their new general manager.

Nov 2—Seattle superstar Ken Griffey Jr. rejects the Mariners' eight-year, $140 million contract offer and demands to be traded to a team in a city closer to his home in Orlando, Fla. In Texas, the Rangers deal two-time AL MVP Juan Gonzalez to the Detroit Tigers in a blockbuster trade involving nine players.

Nov 4—One day after the Baltimore Orioles hire former Cleveland manager Mike Hargrove to lead their team in 2000, the Milwaukee Brewers sign former LA Dodgers star Davey Lopes as their manager.

Nov 4—Using family trusts in addition to his own capital, Larry Dolan, 68, the managing partner of a law firm in suburban Cleveland, purchases the Cleveland Indians for a record $320 million from Richard Jacobs, who had owned the team since 1986. The sale is approved in January.

Nov 9—After a season in which he became the first rookie in 24 years to both drive in and score 100 runs, Carlos Beltran, a 22-year-old switch hitting outfielder for the Kansas City Royals, is named American League Rookie of the Year. Beltran batted .293 with 22 homers, 108 RBIs and 112 runs scored.

Nov 10—The Cincinnati Reds are doubly honored as skipper Jack McKeon is voted NL Manager of the Year on the same day that reliever Scott Williamson, who won 12 games and saved 19, is named NL Rookie of the Year.

Nov 11—Jimy Williams of the Boston Red Sox is named AL Manager of the Year. Williams led the Sox to a 94–68 record and the AL wild-card berth.

Nov 11—After 18 seasons in the major leagues with Boston, the New York Yankees and the Tampa Bay Devil Rays, third baseman Wade Boggs, 41, announces his retirement. He ends his career with 3,010 hits and a .328 lifetime average.

Nov 15—Arizona lefthander Randy Johnson wins the NL Cy Young Award to become the second pitcher ever to win the award in both leagues. Johnson, who won the award with Seattle in 1995, went 17–9 with a 2.48 ERA in '99, but seven of his losses came in games in which the Diamondbacks scored two runs or fewer.

Nov 16—Pedro Martinez of the Boston Red Sox becomes the third pitcher ever to win the Cy Young Award in both the AL and the NL as he is the unanimous choice for the honor in the AL.

JOHN IACONO

Boggs, a .328 lifetime hitter, called it quits after 3,010 hits and 18 seasons.

Martinez, who won the NL Cy Young Award in 1997 as a Montreal Expo, was 23–4 with 313 strikeouts and a 2.07 ERA. He is the fourth unanimous choice for the award in AL history.

Nov 16—Winning 29 of 32 first-place votes, Atlanta's Chipper Jones is named MVP of the National League. Jones batted .319 with 45 home runs and 110 RBIs.

Nov 17—Baseball's final managerial opening is filled as the Anaheim Angels hire former LA Dodgers catcher Mike Scioscia to lead the team.

Nov 18—Despite receiving fewer first-place votes than Boston ace Pedro Martinez, Texas catcher Ivan (Pudge) Rodriguez is named AL MVP. Martinez received eight first-place votes and 239 points while Rodriguez, who batted .332 with 35 homers, won seven first-place votes and 252 points.

Nov 30—The troubled Montreal Expos franchise, which was about to become the first team to relocate since the 1972 Washington Senators (who moved to Texas), is sold to a group headed by New York art dealer Jeffrey Loria and will

Demand and ye shall receive: Griffey left Seattle for Cincinnati, where he grew up.

TOM DiPACE

remain in Montreal. In New York, major league umpires vote by a 57–35 margin to dissolve their union, ending the 21-year tenure of union head Richie Phillips.

Jan 6, 2000—Baseball commissioner Bud Selig orders Braves closer John Rocker to undergo psychological testing following a series of bigoted remarks about minorities, foreigners and homosexuals the reliever made in a December SPORTS ILLUSTRATED article.

Jan 11—Former Red Sox catcher Carlton Fisk and ex-Cincinnati first baseman Tony Perez are elected to baseball's Hall of Fame.

Jan 19—In a unanimous vote, baseball owners approve several resolutions that will expand the power and authority of the commissioner's office to a breadth not seen since Kennesaw (Mountain) Landis held the office in the 1920s. Under the new rules, the commissioner will have a mandate to ensure competitive balance in the league, and will be able to block trades and redistribute revenue from large-market teams to small-market franchises as deemed necessary.

Jan 24—The Yankees re-sign lefthander Andy Pettitte, a player whom owner George Steinbrenner had wanted to jettison in '99, for three years and $25.5 million.

Jan 31—Commissioner Bud Selig suspends Atlanta reliever John Rocker until May 1 and fines him $20,000 for the pitcher's ugly comments to *SI* reporter Jeff Pearlman. The following day the players' union files a grievance asking that the punishment be rescinded.

Feb 8—After reviewing a study by two Harvard scientists on the effects of androstenedione, a testosterone-boosting dietary supplement, commissioner Bud Selig announces that Major League Baseball will continue to allow players to use the substance, which has been banned by the NCAA, the NFL, the men's and women's tennis tours and the Olympics.

Feb 10—With one year left on his contract in Seattle, All-Star centerfielder Ken Griffey Jr., who as a 10-year veteran has the power to veto any trade, gets his wish as the Mariners ship him to his hometown, Cincinnati, in exchange for centerfielder Mike Cameron, pitcher Brett Tomko, minor league infielder Antonio Perez and minor league reliever Jake Meyer.

Feb 28—Six days after it was revealed that Darryl Strawberry tested positive for cocaine on Jan. 19, commissioner Bud Selig announces the Yankee DH's punishment: a one-year suspension from baseball.

Feb 29—The Veterans Committee elects former manager Sparky Anderson, the only skipper to win the World Series with an AL team (Detroit) and an NL team (Cincinnati), to the baseball Hall of Fame.

Former Pittsburgh slugger Bill Mazeroski misses election by one vote, but joining Anderson in the Hall are second baseman Bid McPhee, who played for the Reds in the 1800s, and Negro league outfielder Norman (Turkey) Stearnes, who batted .359 during 18 seasons in the 1920s and '30s.

March 2—Atlanta's John Rocker re-signs with the Braves on Feb. 29, then joins the team in Florida for spring training on March 2, one day after an arbitrator cuts his suspension from two months to two weeks.

March 8—The Atlanta Braves lose John Smoltz for the 2000 season after he elects to have surgery on a torn ligament in his right elbow.

March 23—The St. Louis Cardinals send pitcher Kent Bottenfield and second baseman Adam Kennedy to the Anaheim Angels for centerfielder Jim Edmonds.

March 29—The sun rises on the 2000 Major League Baseball season as the Cubs and the Mets stage an unprecedented Opening Day in Tokyo. It is the earliest opening day ever and the first regular-season game played outside of North America. The Cubs win 5–3.

April 3—Opening Day in North America features the return of Atlanta first baseman Andres Galarraga, who missed the '99 season to undergo cancer treatment. Galarraga scores the Braves' first run of 2000 as Atlanta defeats Colorado 2–0. The defending champion New York Yankees begin their season with a 3–2 victory over the Angels in Anaheim.

April 10—Cincinnati's Ken Griffey Jr., 30, hits his 400th career home run to become the youngest player in major league history to reach the milestone.

April 16—With his third hit of the game, a single up the middle off Minnesota reliever Hector Carrasco, Cal Ripken Jr. becomes the 24th major league player to join the 3,000-hit club.

April 18—John Rocker of Atlanta returns to baseball following his two-week suspension and pitches a scoreless ninth inning against Philadelphia at Turner Field.

April 23—Yankees centerfielder Bernie Williams and catcher Jorge Posada each hit a lefthanded and a righthanded home run in New York's 10–7 win over Toronto. According to the Elias Sports Bureau, it is a baseball first.

May 2—In his first major league start since he underwent elbow surgery in April 1999, Chicago Cubs righthander Kerry Wood allows only three hits and strikes out four batters in six innings to claim an 11–1 victory over Houston.

May 14—With two home runs in St. Louis's 12–10 win over the Dodgers, the Cards' Mark McGwire passes Jimmie Foxx and ties Mickey Mantle on the career homers list with 536.

May 17—After being released by the Mets four days earlier, veteran leadoff hitter Rickey Henderson, 41, baseball's alltime leader in career steals, signs to play for the Seattle Mariners.

May 21—With two outs in the third inning of a game between Anaheim and Kansas City, the Angels' Garret Anderson smacks a grand slam off the Royals' Chris Fussell; it is the sixth bases-loaded home run of the day in the majors, a record.

May 24—Major League Baseball suspends 16 Dodgers players and three L.A. coaches for their part in a May 16 confrontation with fans at Chicago's Wrigley Field.

May 29—Oakland second baseman Randy Velarde catches a line drive off the bat of New York's Shane Spencer, tags Jorge Posada and steps on second to eliminate Tino Martinez and complete the 10th unassisted triple play in regular-season baseball history.

May 31—The month of May concludes with a 1,069 home runs having been hit, a major league record.

June 4—Atlanta closer John Rocker threatens *SI* reporter Jeff Pearlman in the tunnel at Turner Field, telling the man who wrote the December 1999 article quoting Rocker's disparaging remarks about foreigners, gays and minorities, "This isn't over between us," and "Do you know what I can do to you?" The following day the Braves demote Rocker to their Class AAA affiliate.

June 26—Two-time AL MVP Juan Gonzalez of Detroit, seeking a long-term contract, rejects a one-year offer from the Yankees that would have clinched a trade between the two teams to bring Gonzalez to New York.

June 28—A team of researchers led by UMass-Lowell engineer Jim Sherwood announces after a two-week study that despite the dramatic increase in home runs in 2000, the balls are not "juiced."

July 6—Righthander Orel Hershiser, 41, who pitched a record 59 consecutive scoreless innings in 1988, announces his retirement.

July 8—In an interleague game at Yankee Stadium Yankees fireballer Roger Clemens hits Mets catcher Mike Piazza in the head with a fastball. After the game Piazza, who suffered a slight concussion, accuses Clemens of intentionally throwing at his head.

July 11—Powered by a double and two RBIs from game MVP Derek Jeter, the American League wins the All-Star Game 6–3.

July 12—The 1999 World Series teams make moves to strengthen their pitching staffs as the Yankees acquire lefthander Denny Neagle from Cincinnati for four minor leaguers, and the Braves give up lefthander Bruce Chen and a minor leaguer to get righthander Andy Ashby from Philadelphia.

July 26—Arizona trades utility man Travis Lee and pitchers Omar Daal, Vincent Padilla and Nelson Figueroa to the Phillies for righthanded ace Curt Schilling

July 29—The Yankees trade outfielder Ricky Ledee and two players to be named to Cleveland for outfielder David Justice.

Aug 10—Massachusetts state police, after finding steroids in the car of Boston's Manny Alexander on June 30, begin the process of filing criminal charges against the Red Sox infielder.

Aug 30—The Red Sox trade two minor league pitchers to Cincinnati for slugger Dante Bichette.

Sept 4—Under the auspices of a brand new union, the World Umpires Association, major league umpires announce that they've reached a five-year labor agreement with baseball management.

Sept 10—One day after defeating Boston ace Pedro Martinez, the Yankees rout the Red Sox 6–2 to complete a three-game sweep at Fenway Park and leave the Red Sox nine games back in the AL East standings.

Sept 10—Five days before a bankruptcy deadline for the franchise, San Diego Padres President Larry Lucchino announces that the team has raised the $20 million necessary to stay afloat.

Sept 18—The Braves defeat the Mets 6–3 in Atlanta to run their record at Turner Field against New York to 17–2. In New York, Bartolo Colon one-hits the Yankees while striking out 13 in a 2–0 Indians win.

Sept 24—Despite a 6–5 loss to Minnesota, the White Sox clinch the Central division title as Cleveland, which had won the previous five Central titles, loses to Kansas City.

Sept 26—Atlanta wins its ninth consecutive division title when it clinches the NL East with a 7–1 rout of the Mets. The next day the Mets beat Atlanta 6–2 to secure the NL wild-card berth.

Sept 28—The Brewers close County Stadium, which opened in 1953 and will be replaced in 2001 by Miller Park, with an 8–1 loss to the Reds. Three days later Pittsburgh fans say goodbye to Three Rivers Stadium, which will be replaced by PNC Park in 2001, as the Pirates lose to the Cubs 10–9.

Oct 1—In a wild final day of the regular season, which sees three teams vying for two playoff spots, the A's and the Mariners win to secure the AL West crown and the AL wild-card, respectively. Oakland defeats Texas 3–0 at home while Seattle knocks off the Angels 5–2 in Anaheim. Cleveland also wins at home in its season finale, routing Toronto 11–4, but misses the playoffs due to the Oakland and Seattle victories.

Oct 3—St. Louis lefthander Rick Ankiel, a 21-year-old rookie, comes unglued in the NL Division Series opener against Atlanta, throwing five wild pitches in the third inning, an incidence of wayward pitching not seen since Sept. 15, 1890. Fortunately for Ankiel, the Braves committed two errors in the first and allowed St. Louis to jump out to a 6–0 lead; the Cards win 7–5.

Oct 6—Pinch hitter Carlos Guillen lays down a bunt in the bottom of the ninth, scoring Rickey Henderson and giving wild-card Seattle a 2–1 victory and a three-game sweep of the AL Division Series against Chicago, the AL's top team during the regular season.

Oct 7—The Cardinals rout the Braves 7–1 in Game 3 to complete a sweep of their NL Division Series. St. Louis centerfielder Jim Edmonds goes 8 for 14 in the series with two homers, seven RBIs and a series-record six extra-base hits.

Oct 8—Both New York teams advance to the League Championship series as righthander Bobby J. Jones fires a complete-game one-hitter to lead the Mets to a 4–0 blanking of San Francisco—and a three-games-to-one victory in the NL Division Series—and the Yankees jump out to a 6–0 lead against Oakland in the decisive Game 5 of the ALDS, then hold on for a 7–5 win.

Oct 16—One side of a potential "Subway Series" is set as the Mets ride the momentum of their Division Series triumph over the Giants and dispatch St. Louis in the NLCS with surprising ease, winning the fifth game 7–0 behind Mike Hampton's three-hit performance on the mound.

Oct 17—The first Subway Series in 44 years is set as leftfielder David Justice blasts a three-run homer in the seventh inning to help rally the Yankees from a 4–0 deficit to a 9–7 victory over Seattle in Game 6 of the ALCS. It will be the third consecutive World Series appearance for the Yankees.

Oct 22—The Yankees win Game 2 of the World Series after jumping out to a 6–0 lead behind Roger Clemens's one-hit pitching through eight innings and then holding off a furious, five-run rally by the Mets in the ninth inning. The game is marred by a strange incident in the first inning in which pitcher Roger Clemens hurls a chunk of Mike Piazza's broken bat toward the Mets' catcher as Piazza jogs down the first base line.

Oct 26—The Yankees break a 2–2 tie with two runs in the ninth inning of Game 5 then hold on to win their third consecutive World Series and the 26th in franchise history. With the victory they become only the fourth team in baseball history to win three consecutive World Series.

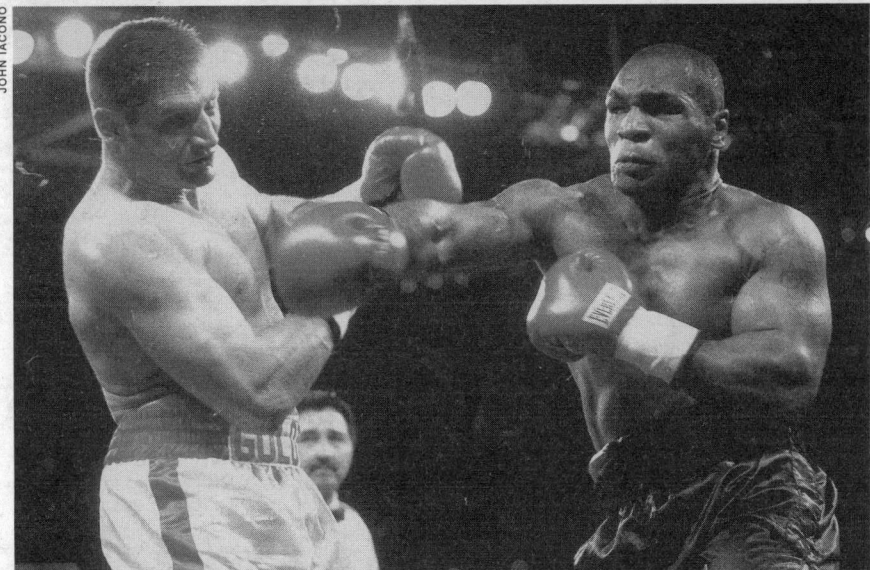

JOHN IACONO

Golota quit after Round 2 of his bout with Tyson at The Palace in Auburn Hills, Mich.

Nov 3, 1999—*The Miami Herald* reports that several fighters claim to have been paid to take dives or to have fallen to avoid injury in fights against George Foreman and Eric (Butterbean) Esch. Tony Fulilangi, who earned $30,000 in his second-round-knockout loss to Foreman on Oct. 27, 1998, tells the paper that he ducked under a punch and dropped to the canvas "just to get the money."

Nov 3—A grand jury indicts President Robert W. Lee and several other IBF officials on charges of accepting bribes to manipulate rankings.

Nov 13—Lennox Lewis wins a unanimous decision over Evander Holyfield in Las Vegas to win the WBA, WBC and IBF titles, unifying the heavyweight division for the first time since Riddick Bowe won all three titles in 1992.

Nov 29—Stevie Johnston of the U.S. retains his WBC lightweight title with a unanimous decision over Billy Schwer of Great Britain at Wembley Stadium.

Jan 13, 2000—With his scheduled bout against Julius Francis in Manchester, England, only 16 days away, Mike Tyson is finally granted permission to enter the UK for the bout. Government officials had threatened to bar the former heavyweight champ because of his 1992 rape conviction.

Jan 15—In the first sporting event ever held at New York City's Radio City Music Hall, Roy Jones Jr. defends his WBC, WBA and IBF light heavyweight titles with a unanimous decision over David Telesco. Jones, who broke his left wrist three and a half weeks before the bout, wins every round on all three judges' scorecards.

Jan 29—Mike Tyson drops Julius Francis five times and KOs him at 1:03 of the second round in their heavyweight bout in Manchester, England.

Feb 26—Five months after suffering the first defeat of his career, a split decision against Felix Trinidad, welterweight Oscar De La Hoya gets back on the winning track with a seventh-round knockout of Derrell Coley.

April 13—U.S. District Judge Lewis Kaplan rules that Lennox Lewis must relinquish his WBA title if he proceeds with plans to fight Michael Grant on April 29. The judge determines that the Grant fight would constitute a breach of Lewis's contract with promoter Don King that provided for the winner of the Nov. 13 Holyfield-Lewis bout to fight John Ruiz, the top WBA contender. The ruling benefits Holyfield, Ruiz and King since the two fighters, both of whom are represented by King, will now fight for the vacant WBA title.

April 15—Fernando Vargas defends his IBF junior middleweight title with a unanimous decision over Ike Quartey in Las Vegas.

April 29—At 6'5", 247 pounds and 6'7", 250 pounds, respectively, Lennox Lewis and Michael

Grant make the heaviest heavyweight title fight pairing ever. Their bout at Madison Square Garden, however, is anticlimactic, as Lewis floors Grant three times in the first round before knocking him out in the second.

May 13—Roy Jones Jr. defends his undisputed light heavyweight title with a 11th-round TKO of Richard Hall in Indianapolis.

June 17—Shane Mosley (35–0) grabs a split decision from Oscar De La Hoya in Los Angeles to win the undisputed world welterweight title

June 24—In a heavyweight bout in Glasgow, Mike Tyson decks Lou Savarese after 12 seconds and finishes him off after 38.

July 15—Lennox Lewis stops Francois Botha at 2:28 of the second round of their WBC and IBF heavywieght title fight.

July 22—Felix Trinidad retains his undisputed super welterweight title with a third-round TKO of Mamadou Thiam in Miami.

July 29—Kostya Tszyu defends his WBC junior welterweight title with a brutal sixth-round TKO of Julio Cesar Chavez, 38, in Phoenix. It is the fifth loss in 110 fights for Chavez, who won six titles in three weight classes during his career.

Aug 5—Junior welterweight Zab Judah retains

his IBF title with a fourth-round TKO of former champion Terronn Millett in Uncasville, Conn.

Aug 12—Evander Holyfield becomes the only man ever to win a portion of the heavyweight title four times when he takes a highly disputed unanimous decision from John Ruiz in their WBA title fight in Las Vegas.

Aug 16—The Nevada Athletic Commission fines promoter Bob Arum $125,000 and suspends him for six months after Arum admits to bribing IBF officials in exchange for favorable rankings for his fighters.

Aug 26—Fernando Vargas defends his IBF junior middleweight title with a fourth-round KO of challenger Ross Thompson in Las Vegas.

Sept 9—Suffering from a torn biceps muscle, light heavyweight challenger Eric Harding fails to come out for the 11th round of his bout against undisputed champion Roy Jones Jr.

Sept 15—Mexico's Jose Luis Castillo defends his WBC lightweight when his bout with Stevie Johnston of the U.S. ends in a draw in Denver.

Oct 20—Andrew Golota quits following the second round of his heavyweight bout with Mike Tyson in suburban Detroit. He suffers a fractured cheekbone and a concussion in the first round.

College Basketball

Oct 26, 1999—In the wake of allegations from a former tutor that she completed more than 400 academic assignments for at least 20 former University of Minnesota basketball players, the school imposes its own sanctions on the Gopher basketball program, announcing a one-year ban on postseason play and an indefinite term of probation. NCAA penalties will follow.

Nov 1—Ed Cota and Terrence Newby are suspended indefinitely from the North Carolina team for their involvement in a fight in Chapel Hill. They are reinstated 11 days later.

Nov 12—Stanford wins the Coaches vs. Cancer Classic with a 72–58 triumph over Iowa at Madison Square Garden.

Nov 14—Eight days before the start of his third season, Tic Jones resigns as coach of Memphis. He is replaced by assistant Johnny Jones, who will be interim coach.

Nov 28—In an early-season matchup of women's basketball powers, fifth-ranked Tennessee defeats No. 4 UCLA 88–77. Tamika Catchings scores 28 points and grabs 13 rebounds for the Vols.

Dec 5—With a 85–62 win at Wisconsin, Tennessee coach Pat Summitt, 47, becomes the

youngest coach and the second woman to achieve 700 career victories.

Dec 18—Unranked Xavier defeats its city rival, No. 1–ranked Cincinnati 66–64, handing the Bearcats their first loss of the season.

Dec 30—In the season's biggest upset to date, Wright State (4–8) stuns No. 8 Michigan State 53–49.

Jan 5, 2000—Two Top 10 teams are upset as Notre Dame knocks off second-ranked Connecticut 75–70 in a Big East opener in Hartford, and Vanderbilt topples No. 6 Florida 87–77 in Nashville.

Jan 18—Returning to Bloomington's Assembly Hall for the first time since he helped Indiana win the 1987 national championship as a player, Iowa coach Steve Alford sees his charges fall to Bob Knight's Hoosiers 74–71.

Jan 27—With his team's 89–61 victory over Wisconsin-Parkdale, Kentucky Wesleyan coach Ray Harper sets an all-division NCAA record by reaching the 100-victory milestone in only his 114th game.

Feb 2—Fourth-ranked Tennessee edges No. 1 Connecticut 72–71 to hand the UConn women (19–1) their first loss of the season.

Feb 7—Syracuse is the last Division I school to fall from the ranks of the unbeaten as it drops its first game of the year (69–67 to Seton Hall) after 19 victories.

Feb 9—Maryland ends Duke's ACC-record 46-game home winning streak with a 98–87 triumph at Cameron Indoor Stadium.

Feb 18—Georgia Tech coach Bobby Cremins, whose Yellow Jackets are 11–13 (3–8 in the ACC), announces his resignation.

Feb 20—The top spots in the polls are reshuffled again as visiting Temple shocks No. 1–ranked Cincinnati 77–69. The Bearcats drop to No. 3 with the loss, while Stanford and Duke are ranked No.1 and No. 2, respectively.

Feb 23—Shooting 68.3% from the field, the UConn women rout West Virginia 100–28.

Feb 26—St. John's edges second-ranked Duke 83–82 in Raleigh, ending the Blue Devils' 64-game home winning streak against unranked opponents.

March 8—Auburn learns that its star forward, Chris Porter, who was suspended in February for allegedly accepting $2,500 from a sports agent,

Mission Accomplished: Cleaves came back to school for a national title and got one.

will most likely miss the tournament as the NCAA declines to restore his eligibility pending the completion of its investigation.

March 9—Kenyon Martin of Cincinnati, the best player on the No. 1–ranked team in the country, breaks his leg in a first-round Conference USA tournament game against Saint Louis, all but dashing the Bearcats' national title hopes and putting in jeopardy Martin's status as a likely No. 1 pick in the June NBA draft. The Bearcats lose the game 68–58.

March 14—CNN/SPORTS ILLUSTRATED broadcasts an interview with former Indiana player Neil Reed in which Reed alleges that Hoosier coach Bob Knight choked him during a 1997 practice.

March 16—There are several close calls but no shockers on the first day of the men's NCAA tournament as Kentucky, LSU, Purdue and Auburn all survive scares from lower seeds. Tenth-seeded Gonzaga pulls the lone upset of the day, defeating No. 7–seed Louisville 77–66.

March 18—For the first time since 1981 the four No. 1 seeds in the NCAA tournament fail to place at least three of their ranks in the Sweet 16, as top seeds Arizona and Stanford are eliminated in the second round. The Wildcats fall to eighth-seeded Wisconsin 69–59 on March 17, while the next day the Cardinal loses to No. 8–seed North Carolina 60–53.

March 19—Tenth-seeded Seton Hall stuns second-seeded Temple 67–65 as reserve guard Ty Shine, who is seven of 11 from three-point range, scores 26 points, including the game-winner in overtime.

March 26—The men's Final Four is set as North Carolina defeats Tulsa 59–54 and Florida upends Oklahoma State 77–65. They will join Michigan State, 75–64 winners over Iowa State, and Wisconsin, which edged Purdue 64–60, in the semis in Indianapolis. It is the first time in tournament history that two No. 8 seeds (Wisconsin and North Carolina) reach the Final Four.

March 27—Top ranked Connecticut defeats LSU 86–71 to advance to the women's Final Four in Philadelphia, where it will be joined by Penn State, which routed No. 1–seed Louisiana Tech 86–65. The other semifinalists are Rutgers, which beat Georgia 59–51 (and whose coach, C. Vivian Stringer, will be taking her third team to the Final Four, an unprecedented achievement), and Tennessee, which knocked off Texas Tech 57–44.

March 30—Wake Forest wins the NIT with a 71–61 victory over Notre Dame in New York City. In Houston, second-year coach Clyde Drexler resigns as coach of the Cougars.

April 2—Connecticut (36–1) avenges its only loss of the season and wins its second women's national title in five years with a 71–52 rout of Tennessee.

April 3—Despite losing its star point guard, Mateen Cleaves, to a sprained ankle for eight minutes of the second half, Michigan State outlasts Florida 89–76 to win the NCAA men's championship.

May 15—Indiana University President Myles Brand fines Hoosier coach Bob Knight and suspends him for three games of the 2000–01 season after concluding the university's investigation into charges that Knight choked former Hoosier Neil Reed (a charge corroborated by video tape) and abused and intimidated other people at IU. Brand also announces that the school has adopted a "zero-tolerance" policy with regard to any further indiscretions by Knight.

June 11—Illinois hires former Tulsa coach Bill Self to replace Lon Kruger, who departed for the NBA's Atlanta Hawks.

June 30—North Carolina coach Bill Guthridge, 62, a member of the Tar Heel staff for 30 years, announces his retirement after leading UNC to two Final Fours in three years as head coach.

July 11—Former UNC guard Matt Doherty, the head coach at Notre Dame, decides to leave South Bend for Chapel Hill, signing a six-year contract to succeed Bill Guthridge as Tar Heel coach.

Sept 6—John Thompson III, the son and namesake of the Hall of Fame former Georgetown coach, is hired as coach at Princeton, replacing Bill Carmody, who leaves to coach Northwestern.

Sept 10—Several days after he is involved in an incident in which he allegedly grabbed and cursed at an IU undergraduate, Indiana coach Bob Knight, who won three national titles in his 29 years in Bloomington, is fired by university president Myles Brand. Two days later he is replaced on an interim basis by former assistant Mike Davis.

Oct 17—Kent Harvey, the Indiana student involved in the incident that led to coach Bob Knight's firing, decides to withdraw from school. He had received several death threats in the days following Knight's dismissal.

College Football

Wisconsin's Dayne rumbled off with the Heisman.

Nov 13—Leading Heisman Trophy candidate Ron Dayne of Wisconsin stakes an undeniable claim to the award as he leads the Badgers to a 41–3 rout of Iowa and a berth in the Rose Bowl. Dayne rushes for 216 yards and a touchdown in the game and is now the alltime leading career rusher in Division I history with 6,397 yards, 118 more than former Texas runner Ricky Williams. All three of the previous D-I career leading rushers—Williams, Tony Dorsett of Pitt and Southern Cal's Charles White—won Heisman Trophies.

Nov 13—Following a 2–8 season in which it lost eight consecutive games for the first time in school history, Louisiana State fires head coach Gerry DiNardo. Assistant coach Hal Hunter will lead the team in its final game, against Arkansas.

Nov 20—Stanford (7–3) clinches its first trip to the Rose Bowl in 28 years with a 31–13 drubbing of Cal.

Oct 28, 1999—Tennessee concludes its internal investigation of its football program and announces it has found no evidence of academic fraud and no violations of NCAA regulations.

Nov 6—Minnesota upsets Penn State 24–23, handing the Nittany Lions (9–1) their first loss of the season and effectively ending their national title hopes. The result leaves three undefeated major college teams: Florida State (9–0), Virginia Tech (8–0) and Kansas State (9–0).

Nov 23—Florida State and Penn State each place three players on the Football Writers All America team. Seminoles kicker Sebastian Janikowski, wide receiver Peter Warrick and defensive tackle Corey Simon make the team along with Nittany Lions defensive end Courtney Brown and linebackers LaVar Arrington and Brandon Short. Virginia Tech DE Corey Moore and Wisconsin fullback Ron Dayne are among others making the first team.

Nov 24—North Carolina State coach Mike O'Cain is fired after his Wolfpack loses its final two games to finish 6–6 and miss a bowl bid.

Nov 28—In the wake of its handling of a questionable fumble call in the game's closing seconds that cost Georgia a chance to win, the entire seven-man officiating crew of the Nov. 27 Georgia Tech–Georgia game is suspended by the Southeastern Conference. Tech won the game 51–48 in overtime after Georgia turned the ball over on the Tech one-yard line with the score tied in the waning seconds of regulation. Replays showed that Bulldog running back Jasper Sanks was down before the ball came loose. The loss jeopardizes Georgia's Cotton Bowl hopes.

Dec 5—Michigan State removes the word "interim" from head coach Bobby Williams's title five days after the former running backs coach was promoted to succeed Nick Saban, who departed for Louisiana State. Williams, who signs a five-year contract, will lead the ninth-ranked Spartans in the Citrus Bowl against No. 10 Florida.

Dec 5—The Bowl Championship Series is set, and the voters, coaches, computer rankings and astrological alignments are nearly unanimous: Florida State (11–0) and Virginia Tech (11–0) are No. 1 and No. 2, respectively, and will play for the national title in the Sugar Bowl. The BCS, which was designed to produce a clear-cut national title game in lieu of playoffs, has done so in the first two years of its existence. Third-ranked Nebraska (11–1) will play No. 6 Tennessee in the Fiesta Bowl.

Dec 8—Following an internal investigation Southern Methodist fires an assistant coach accused of violating NCAA recruiting rules and cuts eight scholarships from the football program for the 2000 and 2001 seasons.

Dec 11—Rowan (N.J.) ends the record 54-game winning streak of three-time defending national champion Mount Union (Ohio) with a 24–17 overtime victory in the Division III semifinals. In Division II, Northwest Missouri State repeats as national champion with a 58–52 quadruple overtime victory over Carson-Newman.

Dec 12—Wisconsin fullback Ron Dayne, the alltime leading rusher in Division I history with 6,397 yards, wins the Heisman Trophy by a nearly 2 to 1 margin, outpointing the runner-up, Georgia Tech quarterback Joe Hamilton, 2,042 to 994.

Dec 17—For the first time in its 113-year history, the Notre Dame football program is disciplined for NCAA violations. The infractions, which involve players' dealings with former booster Kimberly Dunbar, 30, who embezzled more than $1.2 million from her employer and then showered Notre Dame players with gifts, trips

and cash, result in the loss of two scholarships and two years' probation for the program.

Dec 18—The bowl schedule kicks off as Utah edges Fresno State 17–16 in the Las Vegas Bowl, and Hampton routs Jackson State 24–3 in the Heritage Bowl in Atlanta.

Dec 27—In only its third year in Division I-A, Marshall finishes a perfect 13–0 following a 21–3 triumph over Brigham Young in the Motor City Bowl in Pontiac, Mich. The Thundering Herd will be one of only two undefeated teams in the nation.

Dec 28—Penn State, which lost consecutively to Minnesota, Michigan and Michigan State at the end of the season to drop from No. 2 to No. 17 in the polls, avoids the first four-game losing streak in coach Joe Paterno's 34-year career when it blanks No. 13 Texas A&M 24–0 in the Alamo Bowl.

Dec 29—Kansas State defeats Washington 24–20 in the Holiday Bowl to finish 11–1 and place sixth in both national polls.

Jan 1, 2000—Six bowls kick off on New Year's Day, and though none of them has national-title implications, several are stirring games, including Georgia's 28–25 overtime win over Purdue in the Outback Bowl and Michigan's 35–34 nailbiter over Alabama in the Orange Bowl, which is decided, somewhat anticlimactically, when Alabama misses an extra point in overtime. In the Rose Bowl, Wisconsin, which ends up fourth in the national polls, upends Stanford 17–9, while in the Fiesta Bowl the following day Nebraska, which finishes third in the AP poll and second in the coaches' poll, downs Tennessee 31–21.

Jan 4—Virginia Tech pushes Florida State—even rallying to take a 29–28 lead into the fourth quarter—but eventually proves no match for the powerful Seminoles, who pull away to win the Sugar Bowl 46–29 and deliver coach Bobby Bowden the second national title and first undefeated season (12–0) of his 34-year career. Florida State wide receiver Peter Warrick, who scores a Sugar Bowl–record 20 points, six of them on a 64-yard touchdown catch in the first quarter, is named MVP of the game.

Jan 10—Chris Weinke, Florida State's 27-year-old junior quarterback who threw for 329 yards and four touchdowns in the Sugar Bowl, decides to return to school for his senior season rather than enter the NFL draft.

Feb 27—The University of Miami files an appeal with the NCAA to reduce the three-game suspension of Hurricane linebacker Nate Webster, who was penalized for declaring himself eligible for the draft on Jan. 10 and then changing his mind.

May 18—Federal marshals arrest former Ohio State quarterback Art Schlicter, who is wanted on a variety of felony charges, in a restaurant in northeastern Ohio, ending a three-day search.

Aug 17—Brigham Young coach LaVell Edwards, who has more victories (251) than any active major college coach except Penn State's Joe Paterno (317) and Florida State's Bobby Bowden (304), announces that the 2000 season will be his last.

Aug 27—The college football season kicks off as No. 16 Southern California rocks No. 17 Penn State 29–5 in the Kickoff Classic in East Rutherford, N.J. The game between No. 10 Virginia Tech and Georgia Tech is postponed due to a violent thunderstorm.

Aug 31—Hours before the fifth-ranked Badgers are to open their season against Western Michigan, the NCAA suspends 26 Wisconsin players for one to three games for receiving unadvertised discounts at a shoe store. The Badgers nonetheless win their opener 19–7.

Sept 9—Top-ranked Nebraska escapes from South Bend with a 27–24 overtime victory over Notre Dame to preserve its unbeaten record (2–0) and its national title hopes.

Sept 23—Holding on to the top spots in the polls are No. 1 Nebraska, which routs Iowa 42–13, and No. 2 Florida State, which blanks Louisville 31–0. In Division III, Ben Matthews of Bethel (Minn.) ties an all-division record with five interceptions in a 14–3 win over Gustavus (Minn.)

Oct 2—Only three teams remain in the spot they occupied the previous week when the Monday-morning coaches' poll is released: Nebraska (4–0), a 42–24 winner over Missouri, and Florida State (5–0), which steamrolled Maryland 59–7, retain the No. 1 and No. 2 rankings, while UCLA holds onto the No. 17 spot with a 38–31 triumph over Arizona State. Every other place is shuffled. Virginia Tech (4–0) moves up to No. 3 with a 48–34 win over Boston College.

Golf

Oct 28, 1999—In the chilly morning fog prior to the tournament, Tom Lehman leads most of the golfers entered in the Tour Championship in Houston in a somber memorial for Payne Stewart, who was killed in a plane crash in South Dakota on Oct. 25.

Oct 31—Tiger Woods wins the season-ending Tour Championship for his fourth victory in a row, his seventh title of the year and a record $5.6 million in earnings to this point in the season.

Nov 1—The LPGA season ends with a three-way playoff between Se Ri Pak, Karrie Webb and Laura Davies at the PageNet Championship in Las Vegas. Pak birdies the first playoff hole for the win.

Nov 21—With Tiger Woods leading the way, the U.S. wins the 32-team World Cup of golf in Kuala Lumpur. Woods shoots the lowest score in the history of the tournament (21-under 263) and wins the individual title by nine strokes.

Nov 28—Eighteen-year-old Aaron Baddeley becomes the youngest winner in the Australian Open's 95-year history when he shoots a 3-under 69 on Sunday to finish two strokes ahead of Greg Norman and Nick O'Hern.

Dec 8—The Golf Writers Association announces its PGA, LPGA and Senior Tour players of the year: Tiger Woods (eight titles; record $6.6 million in earnings), Juli Inkster (five titles, including two majors; qualified for LPGA Hall of Fame) and Bruce Fleisher (seven titles; seven second-place finishes).

Jan 2, 2000—Tom Lehman ends his four-year victory drought when he birdies five of the final six holes to win the World Challenge invitational in Scottsdale, Ariz., by three strokes over David Duval.

Jan 9—Tiger Woods picks up the 2000 season right where he left off the previous one, with a victory, his fifth in a row, at the Mercedes Championships in Kapalua, Hawaii. Woods eagles the par-5 finishing hole, then birdies the second playoff hole to defeat Ernie Els.

Jan 18—Karrie Webb and Juli Inkster, the LPGA's top two performers in '99, finish one-two at the season-opening Office Depot tournament in West Palm Beach, Fla.

Jan 19—Casey Martin, who suffers from a rare circulatory disease that makes it difficult for him to walk, begins play in the Bob Hope Classic in Palm Springs, where he will be the first PGA player ever to compete using a golf cart. Four days later Jesper Parnevik shoots a fifth-round 65 to win the tournament by one stroke over Rory Sabbatini. Martin misses the cut after the fourth round by three strokes.

Jan 23—Two years after having her left shoulder reconstructed, LPGA veteran Nancy Scranton, 38, wins the Memorial in Naples, Fla.

Feb 7—Trailing Matt Gogel by seven strokes at the Pebble Beach National Pro-Am, Tiger Woods scores three birdies and an eagle over the final seven holes to win by two strokes and claim his sixth victory in a row. Woods's winning streak ties Ben Hogan's 1948 run as the second longest ever.

Feb 13—Phil Mickelson ends Tiger Woods's six-tournament winning streak when he wins the Buick Invitational in La Jolla, Calif., with an 18-under 270.

March 4—The Tiger Woods of the LPGA, Karrie Webb, wins her fourth title in her fourth tournament of the year, defeating Annika Sorenstam in a playoff to claim the Takefuji Classic in Hawaii. The following day Jim Furyk rallies from six shots down with seven holes to play to win the PGA's Doral Open in Miami by two strokes over Franklin Langham.

March 26—Shooting a final-round 70 that includes an ace on No. 5, Karrie Webb wins the Nabisco Championship in Rancho Mirage, Calif. Thirteen-year-old Aree Wongluekiet of Bradenton, Fla., finishes 10th.

March 27—Hal Sutton holds off a late charge from Tiger Woods to win the Players Chamionship in Ponte Vedra Beach, Fla., by one stroke. Sutton's 278 is 10 under par.

April 9—Vijay Singh shoots a final-round 69 to win the Masters by three strokes over Ernie Els. It is the eighth PGA victory of Singh's career.

May 21—At the Colonial in Fort Worth, Tex., Phil Mickelson shoots a final-round 63 to overcome a six-stroke deficit and claim his third title of the season. He defeats Stewart Cink and Davis Love III by two strokes.

June 15—Shigeki Marayuma of Japan breaks the alltime 18-hole record when he shoots a 13-under 58 during U.S. Open qualifying at the Woodmont Country Club in Rockville, Md.

June 18—SPORTS ILLUSTRATED calls it the greatest performance in golf history as Tiger Woods devastates the U.S. Open field at Pebble Beach, scoring four birdies over the final nine holes to win by a record 15 strokes with an Open-record 12-under-par 272.

June 25—In Wilmington, Del., Juli Inkster defends her LPGA Championship title with a one-stroke playoff victory over Stefania Croce.

July 23—Tiger Woods continues to astound as he wins the British Open on the Old Course at St. Andrews, Scotland, with a record 19-under 269.

July 30—The LPGA gets its youngest winner in 25 years when Dorothy Delasin, 19, wins the Giant Eagle Classic in Warren, Ohio, in a playoff over Pat Hurst.

Aug 6—Ernie Els, who has finished second five times in 2000 (four of them to Tiger Woods), wins the International in Castle Rock, Colo.

Aug 14—Meg Mallon defeats Rosie Jones by a stroke to win the final du Maurier Classic in Aylmer, Quebec. The tournament, which will be replaced as an LPGA major by the British Open, is ending due to legislation against tobacco sponsorships.

Aug 20—Holding off a furious challenge from little-known Bob May, Tiger Woods wins the PGA championship by one stroke in a three-hole playoff to become the first player since Ben Hogan in 1953 to win three majors in a single year. The victory also makes Woods the youngest golfer ever to complete a career Grand Slam.

Sept 10—On the final hole at the PGA Tour Canadian Open in Oakville, Ontario, Tiger Woods hits an instant-legend of a shot to win the tournament by one stroke over Grant Waite. Using his 6-iron, Woods blasts out of a bunker, over water and to the back of the green 215 yards away, then birdies the hole. It is his ninth victory of the year, the most in a season since Sam Snead won 11 in 1950.

Oct 1—David Duval wins for the first time in 17 months as he rallies to take the Buick Challenge in Callaway Gardens, Ga., by one stroke over Jeff Maggert.

Oct 22—The U.S. cruises to victory in the Presidents Cup, downing the International Team 21 1/2–10 1/2 in Gainesville, Va.

Hockey

Oct 1, 1999—The National Hockey League drops the puck on the 1999–2000 season as the New York Rangers and the Edmonton Oilers skate to a 1–1 tie. In a ceremony before the game the jersey of superstar Wayne Gretzky, who played for both Edmonton and New York, is retired.

Oct 26—The Calgary Flames, who moved from Atlanta in 1980, return to Georgia to play the expansion Atlanta Thrashers. The Thrashers secure the first home win in franchise history with a 2–1 victory. In North Carolina, contract talks between the Hurricanes and All-Star center Keith Primeau break down, and Primeau decides to depart the U.S. to play for Canada's national team.

Nov 9—Alleging that holdout Alexei Yashin has

breached his contract, the Ottawa Senators suspend the center for the rest of the season.

Dec 4—On the busiest day in league history, with 14 games scheduled, the Mighty Ducks of Anaheim stop the Coyote's eight-game winning streak with a 2–1 victory, the Flames end the New Jersey Devils' 12-game home unbeaten streak with a 4–2 win, and the Nashville Predators get off the schneid, beating the Detroit Red Wings 4–1 to end a seven-game losing streak.

Dec 31—Dallas center Brett Hull scores two goals in the Stars' 5–4 win over Anaheim, giving him 601 career goals. He is the 12th player in NHL history to surpass 600 goals, reaching the milestone in his 900th game; only Wayne Gretzky (718) and Mario Lemieux (719) got there faster.

Jan 13, 2000—New Jersey forward Scott Gomez, the runaway leader in rookie scoring with 42 points in 43 games, is named to the North American team for the All-Star Game. Gomez is the NHL's first latino player.

Jan 23—Keith Primeau's five-month contract dispute with Carolina comes to an end as the Hurricanes trade the rangy center and a fifth-round draft pick to the Philadelphia Flyers for center Rod Brind'Amour, minor league goalie Jean-Marc Pelletier and a second-round pick.

Feb 1—Behind two goals from Martin Straka, Pittsburgh defeats Washington 3–2 to end the Capitals' 11-game unbeaten streak, longest in the league this year.

Feb 6—Pavel Bure scores three goals and makes one assist to lead the World team to a 9–4 win over the North American team in the NHL All-Star Game.

Feb 21—In one of the ugliest incidents in NHL history, Boston defenseman Marty McSorley clubs Vancouver forward Donald Brashear in the side of the head with his stick during a game in Vancouver. Brashear crumples to the ground with a concussion. Vancouver police are investigating the incident and may file criminal charges against McSorley.

Feb 23—The NHL suspends Boston's Marty McSorley for the remaining 23 games (plus the playoffs if the Bruins qualify) for his Feb. 21 slash to the head of the Canucks's Donald Brashear. It is the longest suspension in league history.

March 2—Calgary wing Jarome Iginla, the son of a Nigerian immigrant to Canada, is named player of the month for February. He is the first black player in NHL history to win the honor.

March 6—The Bruins accommodate defenseman Ray Bourque's request for a trade to a contender by dealing him and left wing Dave Andreychuk to Colorado in exchange for winger Brian Rolston, two prospects and a first-round draft pick. Bourque, 39, had spent 21 years in a Boston uniform.

March 7—The British Columbia attorney general's office charges Boston's Marty McSorley with assault with a weapon for his Feb. 21 clubbing of Vancouver's Donald Brashear.

March 21—New Jersey defenseman

Roy became the NHL's alltime leader in victories.

Scott Niedermayer is suspended for 10 games for hitting Florida's Peter Worrell in the head with his stick.

March 22—The Flyers announce that center Eric Lindros will miss six weeks after suffering his fourth concussion in two years.

March 25—Pavel and Valeri Bure set an NHL record for goals scored in a season by brothers when Pavel scores two for the Panthers against the Canadiens. He now has 54 goals and Valeri, of Calgary, has 35; they surpass the 1968–69 season of Bobby and Dennis Hull (58 and 30 goals, respectively).

April 27—Charles Wang and Sanjay Kumar, executives of business-software giant Computer Associates, purchase the New York Islanders for a reported $175 million.

May 4—Eric Lindros's return to the Flyers from a March 4 concussion is delayed when he collides with a minor league opponent during a controlled scrimmage and suffers a bruised lip and a cut requiring 20 stitches. He rejoins the team on date May 24.

May 26—The Devils, who made the controversial move of firing coach Robbie Ftorek with only 20 days remaining in the regular

LOU CAPOZZOLA

season, advance to the Stanley Cup finals with Ftorek's replacement, Larry Robinson, after rallying from a three-games-to-one deficit and knocking off Philadelphia 2–1 in Game 7 of the Eastern Conference finals.

May 27—Dallas defeats Colorado 3–2 in Game 7 of the Western Conference finals to advance to the Stanley Cup for the second year in a row. The victory stymies the Stanley Cup dreams of 21-year veteran Ray Bourque of Colorado, who requested a trade from Boston in March in the hope of winning a title.

June 1—The Rangers hire former Edmonton Oilers coach and G.M. Glen Sather to help revive the sagging franchise as G.M.

June 8—Former Philadelphia coach Roger Neilson, who left the team in mid-February to receive treatment for cancer, is replaced behind the Flyer bench by Craig Ramsay.

June 10—Devils center Jason Arnott scores at 8:20 of the second overtime of Game 6 to give the Devils a 2–1 victory over Dallas and clinch New Jersey's second Stanley Cup title in five years. Devils defenseman Scott Stevens is named MVP of the playoffs. The tense six-game series features four one-goal games, a triple overtime thriller and the double OT finale.

June 15—New York City native Joe Mullen, who learned the game playing roller hockey and is the only U.S.-born NHL veteran with 500 goals, is elected to the Hall of Fame. Denis Savard, who had five 100-point seasons in the NHL, is also elected.

June 15—St. Louis's Chris Pronger becomes the first defenseman to win the Hart Trophy as NHL MVP since Bobby Orr in 1972.

June 19—The Minnesota Wild, one of two expansion teams that will begin play in 2000–01, names former Devils coach Jacques Lemaire as its first coach.

July 5—The expansion Columbus Blue Jackets tap Dave King, who has led Canada's Olympic and national teams in his career, as their first coach.

Sept 5—Alexei Yashin loses his appeal of an arbitrator's decision that he owes Ottawa another season of hockey after refusing to play in 1999–2000.

Oct 6—A British Columbia court finds Bruins defenseman Marty McSorley guilty of assault with a weapon for his Feb. 21 on-ice clubbing of Canucks forward Donald Brashear. McSorley receives probation instead of jail time.

Oct 9—Dallas center Brett Hull passes his father, Bobby, on the alltime goal-scoring list when he finds the net for the 611th time in his career during third period of the Stars' 3–1 victory over the Maple Leafs in Toronto. The goal moves Brett into seventh on the list, two behind Mario Lemieux.

Oct 17—Colorado goalie Patrick Roy becomes the NHL's alltime leader in goaltending victories as the Avalanche defeats the Capitals in Washington 4–3 in overtime. Roy now has 448 career victories, one more than Terry Sawchuck.

Horse Racing

Oct 29, 1999—Harness racing's Breeders Crown in Cambellville, Ontario, yields two huge upsets as Self Possessed, a 1–9 favorite in the three-year-old trot, is overtaken in the stretch by CR Renegade, and Blissfull Hall, the Pacing Triple Crown winner, is chased down in the stretch by Grinfromeartoear, which wins the three-year-old Colt Pace.

Dec 10—Laffit Pincay breaks Bill Shoemaker's career record for wins when he rides Irish Nip to victory at Hollywood Park for his 8,834th triumph in 44,647 mounts and 35 years.

Dec 26—Citing degenerative arthritis in his right knee, three-time Kentucky Derby winner and Hall of Fame jockey Gary Stevens announces his retirement.

Jan 17, 2000—Former claiming horse Charismatic, winner of the Kentucky Derby and Preakness in 1999, is named '99 Horse of the Year.

Feb 7—J.T. Lundy and Gary Matthews, the former president and chief financial officer, respectively, of Calumet Farms, are convicted of conspiracy, fraud and bribery charges in a

bungled scheme to save the thoroughbred stable. The FBI is also investigating the death of the farm's fabled stallion, Alydar, which was insured for $335 million.

March 25—Dubai Millennium, a British-bred four-year-old whose name was changed for the race, wins the Dubai World Cup by six lengths to take home $3.5 million, the world's richest purse.

April 8—Trainer Jenine Sahadi's colt The Deputy, with Chris McCarron up, wins the $1 million Santa Anita Derby by three lengths over the Bob Baffert–trained Captain Steve. Earlier in the week Baffert had insulted Sahadi by asking McCarron if he or Sahadi trained The Deputy.

April 15—Red Bullet finishes second to Derby favorite Fusaichi Pegasus in the Wood Memorial, but two days later his owner, Frank Stronach, announces he will pull the colt from the Derby to preserve its longevity.

May 2—Retired jockey Julie Krone, who won the 1993 Belmont, becomes the first woman ever elected to the National Museum of Racing's Hall of Fame.

May 6—Prerace favorite Fusaichi Pegasus delivers, winning the Kentucky Derby by one and a half lengths over Aptitude.

May 20—Going off a 1–5 favorite at the Preakness, Derby winner Fusaichi Pegasus is unable to fulfill the lofty expectations, getting chased down at the half-mile pole by Red Bullet, who goes on to win by nearly four lengths.

June 10—Even though—for the first time in four years—there is no Triple Crown bid at stake, 67,810 fans attend the Belmont in 95° weather. They see Commendable outdistance the field by one and a half lengths.

June 27—Coolmore Stud, a breeding operation based in Ireland, buys Fusaichi Pegasus for between $60 million and $70 million.

July 15—Gallo Blue Chip, driven by Daniel Dube, wins the $1.15 million Meadowlands Pace. It is the gelding's sixth victory in 11 starts in 2000.

July 29—David Miller drives Magician to victory in the $1 million Breeders Crown trot in East Rutherford, N.J.

Aug 6—Lemon Drop Kid wins the Whitney by two lengths over Cat Thief in Saratoga Springs, while in East Rutherford, Yankee Paco wins trotting's premier race, the Hambletonian.

Aug 7—Julie Krone (*see May 2 entry*) is inducted into the National Museum of Racing Hall of Fame along with Neil Drysdale, a trainer who guided five Eclipse champions and five Breeders Cup winners. Also inducted are the horses A.P. Indy, Winning Colors and Needles

Aug 26—Unshaded overtakes Albert the Great in the stretch to win the Travers Stakes in Saratoga Springs.

Sept 16—At Belmont Park, Lemon Drop Kid wins the $500,000 Woodward Stakes by a head over Behrens.

Sept 21—Astreos holds off the favorite, Gallo Blue Chip, to win the Little Brown Jug in Delaware, Ohio. The race, the second jewel in trotting's Triple Crown, is decided in a run-off.

Oct 1—With Johnny Murtagh up, Sinndar passes Raypour 500 feet from the finish and holds on to win the $800,000 Arc de Triomphe in Paris. Sinndar, owned by Aga Khan, also won the English Derby and the Irish Derby in 2000.

Motor Sports

Oct 28, 1999—Citing business considerations and the ongoing split between the two factions, Goodyear withdraws its sponsorship of both CART and the Indy Racing League.

Oct 31—Colombia's Juan Montoya, 24, becomes the youngest champion in CART's 21-year history when he finishes fourth at the season-ending Marlboro 500 in Fontana, Calif. The placing gives him 212 points for the year, tied with Dario Franchitti of Scotland, but Montoya takes the title because he has seven victories to Franchitti's three. The excitement of the finish is overshadowed by the death of driver Greg Moore in a crash during the race.

Nov 2—With 1,200 mourners in attendance, former CART racer Greg Moore, 24, who was killed in a crash during the season-ending Marlboro 500, is laid to rest in his native British Columbia.

Nov 14—With one race remaining in the NASCAR Winston Cup season, Dale Jarrett, 42, clinches the season points title by finishing fifth at the Pennzoil 400 in Homestead, Fla. It is the first season championship for the 10-year veteran. First-year driver Tony Stewart wins the race for his third victory of the year, a rookie record.

Nov 18—After three years as executive director of the Indy Racing League, Leo Mehl, 63, announces his retirement.

Nov 21—Bobby Labonte, who will finish second in the NASCAR season points race, wins the year-ending Winston Cup race at Altanta Motor Speedway. Dale Jarrett, who clinched the season title the previous week, finishes second in the final race.

Jan 11, 2000—Tobacco giant R.J. Reynolds announces that it will double the NASCAR winnings pot to $10 million for the 2000 season. The season champion, who received $2 million from a $5 million fund in 1999, will receive $3 million in December 2000.

Jan 24—Chrysler taps crew chief Ray Evernham, who helped guide Jeff Gordon to three straight Winston Cup championships, to lead its Dodge Intrepid team for the 2001 NASCAR season.

Feb 14—Former CART driver and longtime owner Tony Bettenhausen is killed in a plane crash along with his wife and two business partners near Leesburg, Ky.

Feb 20—Defending NASCAR champion Dale Jarrett starts off the new season in grand style, winning the Daytona 500 for the third time in eight years. Jarrett scores the victory 24 hours after his car suffers severe damage when it is hit from behind and then rams a car in front during a practice session on the eve of the race.

Motor Sports (Cont.)

March 12—Dale Earnhardt wins the 75th race of his career, edging Bobby Labonte by less than two feet at the Cracker Barrel 500 at Atlanta Motor Speedway. In the season-opening F/1 race at Melbourne, Ferrari teammates Michael Schumacher and Ruben Barrichello finish 1–2.

April 2—Dale Earnhardt Jr. wins his first NASCAR race, taking the DirecTV 500 at Texas Motor Speedway.

May 12—Adam Petty, 19, the fourth generation of NASCAR's famous Petty family, is killed in a crash during practice in Loudon, N.H. The family patriarch, Lee, 86, died on April 5.

May 28—Defending CART champion Juan Montoya endures a three-hour rain delay to win the 84th running of the Indy 500. Montoya, who led for 167 of 200 laps, is the first Indy rookie since Graham Hill in 1966 to win the race.

June 11—NASCAR's Tony Stewart wins for the second week in a row, topping the field at the Michigan 400.

July 7—Fomer open-wheel star Kenny Irwin, 30, who switched to NASCAR in 1997, is killed in a crash during practice for the New England 300.

Aug 6—Bobby Labonte wins the Brickyard 400 in Indianapolis to open up an 87-point lead over Dale Jarrett in the NASCAR Winston Cup season points race.

Aug 13—Making an aggressive pass at the start of the race, F/1 driver Mika Hakkinen takes the lead at the Hungarian Grand Prix and never lets go. The victory gives him a two-point lead over Michael Schumacher in the season standings.

Sept 3—Bobby Labonte wins the Southern 500 in Darlington, S.C., to increase his Winston Cup points lead over Dale Jarrett to 111.

Sept 24—Michael Schumacher wins the first F/1 race held in the U.S. since 1991, cruising to an easy victory in the U.S. Grand Prix in Indianapolis. The triumph is his second in a row and puts him back in the lead over Mika Hakkinen in the season points race.

Olympics

Nov 15, 1999—USA Gymnastics announces that Bela Karolyi will come out of retirement to assist the U.S. women's national team in its preparations for the Sydney Games.

Nov 21—The International Amateur Athletics Federation (IAAF) names sprinters Carl Lewis of the U.S. and Fanny Blankers-Koen of the Netherlands male and female athlete of the century. The IAAF also selects 200-meter world-record holder Michael Johnson of the U.S. and distance runner Gabriela Szabo of Romania as the top athletes of 1999.

Dec 21—The United States Olympic Committee selects cyclist Lance Armstrong, swimmer Jenny Thompson and the U.S. women's soccer team as its sportsman, sportswoman and team of the year.

Jan 5, 2000—USA Basketball extends invitations to the Detroit Pistons' Grant Hill, the Miami Heat's Alonzo Mourning and the Milwaukee Bucks' Ray Allen to join the U.S. men's basketball team that will compete in the Sydney Olympics.

Jan 6—Former University of Connecticut star Kara Wolters, now with the WNBA's Indiana Fever, is added to the U.S. women's basketball team for the Olympic Games in Sydney, leaving one roster spot yet to be filled.

Jan 8—The U.S. men's and women's volleyball teams, neither of which reached the medal round in Atlanta in '96, each qualify for the 2000 Games in Sydney by winning separate four-nation tournaments.

Feb 6—Downing defending world champion Russia 22–9 in the final, the U.S. wins the

World Cup of freestyle wrestling in Fairfax, Va.

March 28—Justin Huish, who won a gold medal in archery at the Atlanta Games in 1996, resigns from the 2000 U.S. Olympic team after pleading not guilty to a Feb. 24 charge of possessing marijuana with intent to sell.

July 20—Tom Welch and David Johnson, former executives for the Salt Lake Olympic Organizing Committee, are indicted in federal court for their roles in a widespread bribery scandal surrounding Salt Lake's successful bid for the 2002 Games.

Aug 22—Olympic arbitrator Richard K. Jeydel upholds U.S. coach Billie Jean King's selection of Serena Williams to the Olympic tennis team for the Sydney Games. The choice had been challenged by Lisa Raymond, who argued that her position as the top doubles player in the world warranted a spot on the team.

Sept 5—According to reports citing unnamed Olympic sources, former U.S. Secretary of State Henry Kissinger will become an "honor member" of the International Olympic Committee. Kissinger was on the commission to revamp the IOC following the bribery scandal of the Salt Lake bid.

Sept 13—Two days before the opening ceremonies of the 2000 Olympic Games in Sydney, the Olympic soccer tournament kicks off in Canberra, the capital of Australia, as the U.S. ties the Czech Republic 2–2, and Cameroon defeats Kuwait 2–1.

Sept 15—Cathy Freeman, Australia's gold medal favorite in the 400-meter run, lights the torch in a stirring opening ceremony in Sydney, and the 2000 Olympics are officially under way.

Sept 16—Highlighting the first weekend of competition at the Sydney Olympics is the men's 4 x 100-meter freestyle relay in which Australia, getting a furious anchor leg from 17-year-old Ian Thorpe, outtouches the U.S. at the wall to win in a world-record 3:13.67.

Sept 16—Halil (Little Dynamo) Mutlu, a 4' 1" weightlifter from Turkey, supplants his countryman Naim (Pocket Hercules) Suleymanoglu as the top pint-sized weightlifter in the world when he hefts a world-record 369.3 pounds (slightly more than three times his body weight) in the clean and jerk at Sydney. Mutlu also sets a world record in the snatch and for total weight as he wins two gold medals. The 33-year-old Suleymanoglu, a three-time Olympic champ who came out of retirement to compete in Sydney, fails to advance out of the snatch competition.

Sept 17—Inge de Bruijn of the Netherlands wins the 100-meter butterfly in a world-record time of 56.61. Finishing nearly 16 seconds behind de Bruijn in 49th place is Tracy-Ann Route, who is the first Olympic competitor from the Federated States of Micronesia, a union of some 600 islands in the Pacific Ocean.

Sept 18—U.S. swimmer Megan Quann takes the gold medal in the 100-meter breaststroke with a world-record swim of 1:07.05.

Sept 19—Pieter van den Hoogenband of the Netherlands sets a world record in the 100-meter freestyle with a swim of 47.84. In the final, he wins the gold medal in 48.30. Van den Hoogenband also wins gold in the 200-meter free, upsetting heavy favorite and Australian hero Ian Thorpe with a world-record-tying swim of 1:45.35.

Sept 21—Inge de Bruijn of the Netherlands shatters the world record in the 100 free, clocking 53.77 in Sydney. She later wins the gold medal in the event.

Sept 22—U.S. swimmer Brooke Bennett wins the 800-meter freestyle in an Olympic-record time of 8:19.67. It is the second gold of the Games for Bennett, who also won the 400 free.

Sept 22—The Netherlands' Inge de Bruijn wins her third gold medal of the Sydney Olympics, taking the 50-meter freestyle with a time of 24.32.

Quann, 16, won the gold medal in the 100-meter breaststroke at Sydney.

BOB MARTIN

Dara Torres of the U.S. wins the bronze in 24.63. De Bruijn had set a world record of 24.13 during the preliminaries, giving her three world records in these Olympics.

Sept 22—Gary Hall Jr. and Anthony Ervin, both of the U.S., touch the wall at the same time in the men's 50-meter freestyle and are declared co-winners. They each get a gold medal.

Sept 23—Marion Jones begins her quest to become the first woman ever to win five gold medals in a single Olympics by blazing to victory in the 100 meters. She finishes in 10.75; Ekaterini Thanou of Greece is second in 11.12.

Sept 23—Jenny Thompson swims the butterfly leg on the victorious U.S. women's 4 x 100 meter medley relay team to win the eighth gold medal of her Olympic career. The team sets a world record of 3:58.30.

Sept 25—The U.S. camp at Sydney is rocked by revelations that shot-putter C.J. Hunter, the husband of sprinter Marion Jones, tested positive for the steroid nandrolone in July. Hunter is not competing in the Games due to a knee injury, but Jones has four events remaining in her quest to become the first woman ever to win five track and field gold medals.

Sept 25—Cathy Freeman, who lit the Olympic flame to start the Sydney Games and who is the first athlete of Aboriginal descent to compete in an Olympics for Australia, wins the gold medal in the 400-meter run, clocking 49.11.

Sept 25—Michael Johnson of the U.S., who won the 200 and the 400 in Atlanta in 1996, becomes the first man ever to repeat as Olympic 400-meter champion when he wins the gold medal in Sydney in 43.84 seconds. Alvin Harrison of the U.S. is second in 44.40.

Sept 26—The U.S. softball team, which suffered three consecutive losses in the tournament (something it had never done in its history), recovers and defeats Japan 2–1 in the gold medal game.

Sept 27—Rulon Gardner, the U.S. heavyweight in Greco-Roman wrestling, pulls off the shocker of the Olympics, stunning Russian legend Alexander Karelin, who was undefeated in 14 years of international competition, with a 1–0 victory to take the gold medal.

Olympics (Cont.)

Sept 27—The United States ends Cuba's 20-year reign atop international baseball when it gets a three-hitter from pitcher Ben Sheets to defeat Cuba 4–0 and win the gold medal. It is the first Olympic gold medal in baseball for the U.S.

Sept 28—Marion Jones wins the 200 meters in 21.84 seconds, outpacing Pauline Davis-Thompson of the Bahamas, who takes silver in 22.27.

Sept 29—Lithuania nearly pulls off a titanic upset, falling to the United States 85–83 in the men's basketball semifinal. Lithuania has the ball with a chance to win or tie in the final seconds but its attempt at a game-winning three-pointer falls short. The U.S. goes on to defeat France in the gold medal game.

Sept 29—Marion Jones's attempt to win five Olympic gold medals falls short when she jumps 22' 8 ½" to claim the bronze in the long jump. She struggles with foot fouls throughout the competition. Jones will go on to win another bronze in the 4 x 100-meter relay and a gold in the 4 x 400-meter relay, bringing her total haul to three golds and two bronzes.

Sept 30—Felix Sávon of Cuba equals the legacy of his famous countryman Teofilo Stevenson when he defeats Russia's Sultanahmed Ibzagimov to win his third consecutive heavyweight boxing gold medal.

Oct 4—Only three days after the closing ceremonies of the Sydney Games, Australia's Olympic minister, Michael Knight, announces his resignation, effective in December.

Pro Basketball

Oct 26, 1999—Magic Johnson, 40, appears in a game in the Swedish League, playing for Magic M7 and leading it to an 84–60 victory over Sallen. The fomer Los Angeles Lakers point guard scores 14 points and grabs 11 rebounds in the game.

Nov 2—The New York Knicks and swingman Latrell Sprewell come to terms on a five-year, $62 million contract for the player. In Texas, Bexar County voters approve the construction of a taxpayer-funded new arena for the NBA's San Antonio Spurs.

Nov 9—The Portland Trail Blazers (4–1) are the final team to fall from the ranks of the unbeaten in the young 1999–2000 NBA season as they lose to the Jazz 92–87 in Utah.

Nov 20—New York's Latrell Sprewell returns to The Arena in Oakland for the first time since his 1997 attack on Warriors coach P.J. Carlesimo. He scores 14 points as the Knicks beat the Warriors 86–79.

Nov 22—The Boston Celtics announce that on Dec. 22 they will replace the famous parquet floor they have used for 53 years in the Boston Garden and the FleetCenter.

Dec 5—Raptors swingman Vince Carter scores a career-high 39 points to lead Toronto to a 98–92 victory over the defending champion Spurs.

Dec 8—NBA commissioner David Stern announces that the slam-dunk contest, absent since 1997, will return to the schedule of events during All-Star weekend in February.

Dec 8—NBA commissioner David Stern announces that the league's All-Star weekend, scheduled for Feb. 12–14 in Philadelphia, will be canceled due to the labor dispute.

Dec 13—Citing a need to spend more time with his family, Phoenix Suns coach Danny Ainge

resigns; he is replaced by fomer assistant Scott Skiles, who, at 35, becomes the youngest head coach in the league.

Dec 14—Dikembe Mutombo of the Hawks pulls down 29 rebounds in Atlanta's 105–94 home victory over the Minnesota Timberwolves. He also scores 27 points in the game.

Dec 15—The LA Clippers set two records they wish they hadn't, scoring three points in the second quarter and 19 in the first half—both NBA lows since the inception of the shot clock in 1954—of a 95–68 loss to the Lakers.

Dec 16—After dropping 18 of their first 22 games, the Vancouver Grizzlies fire coach Brian Hill and replace him with assistant Lionel Hollins.

Dec 27—The Warriors fire coach P.J. Carlesimo, who had led Golden State to a 6–21 record, second-worst in the league.

Jan 10, 2000—Tim Duncan of San Antonio scores a career-high 46 points to lead the Spurs to a 93–86 win over Utah in the Alamodome.

Jan 12—Bobby Phills, 30, a guard for the Hornets, is killed in a car accident after practice in Charlotte.

Jan 16—Phoenix forward Cliff Robinson pours in 50 points as the Suns edge the Denver Nuggets 113–110. Robinson's performance is a career best as well as tops in the NBA this season.

Jan 19—Chicago Bulls legend Michael Jordan announces he has purchased a minority ownership share in the Washington Bullets and will become the team's president of basketball operations.

Jan 29—Karl Malone becomes the third player in NBA history with 30,000 career points during Utah's 96–94 home loss to Minnesota. He scores 35 points in the game to run his career total to 30,023.

The sight of Ewing in Seattle green is sure to provoke double takes from Knicks fans.

Feb 3—Rebounding specialist Dennis Rodman returns to the NBA after an 11-month absence, signing a $470,000 contract with the Dallas Mavericks for the remainder of the season.

Feb 6—Allen Iverson of Philadelphia, the NBA's leading scorer, ties a career high as well as the high in the NBA this season (Cliff Robinson, Jan. 16) with 50 points in the 76ers 119–108 home win over Sacramento.

Feb 12—Toronto's Vince Carter wins the NBA slam-dunk contest at The Arena in Oakland with an astonishing between-the-legs tomahawk jam.

Feb 13—The West defeats the East 137–126 in the NBA All-Star Game in Oakland. The Lakers' Shaquille O'Neal and Tim Duncan of San Antonio are named co-MVPs of the game.

Feb 16—The Bulls trade forward Toni Kukoc, the last player remaining from the Chicago dynasty of the '90s, to Philadelphia in a three-team deal that also sends guard Larry Hughes and forward Billy Owens from the Sixers to Golden State and guard John Starks from the Warriors to the Bulls.

Feb 27—Vince Carter explodes for 51 points, an NBA season high, in the Raptors' 103–102 victory over Phoenix in Toronto.

March 6—The Detroit Pistons (28–30) fire coach Alvin Gentry.

March 7—Shaquille O'Neal scores an NBA season- and career-high 61 points as the Lakers rout their hapless crosstown counterparts, the Clippers, 123–103.

March 8—After a stormy 13-game engagement, the Mavericks release controversial forward Dennis Rodman.

March 14—San Antonio's Sean Elliott, who underwent a kidney transplant in August 1999, makes a stirring comeback to the NBA, starting, scoring two points and grabbing a rebound in the Spurs' 94–79 win over Atlanta in the Alamodome.

March 16—In Washington, the Lakers fall 109–102 to the Wizards, ending their winning streak at 19, the third longest in NBA history.

March 23—Former Suns point guard Kevin Johnson comes out of retirement to replace Jason Kidd, who went down with a broken ankle, on the Phoenix roster.

April 19—Tim Duncan of the Spurs learns he may miss the first round of the playoffs when an MRI shows torn cartilage in his left knee, which he injured on April 11.

April 24—Lenny Wilkens, the NBA's alltime leader in coaching wins, resigns as coach of the Atlanta Hawks, who finished the season 28–54.

JOHN W. McDONOUGH

He will be replaced by former University of Illinois coach Lon Kruger in May.

April 27—After leading the Orlando Magic—a team that traded away four of its five starters from the previous season—to a 41–41 record, Doc Rivers wins the NBA coach of the year award. Rivers, who lined up four players who were not drafted by any NBA team, is the first recipient of the honor not to lead his team to the playoffs.

April 26—X-rays reveal that Detroit swingman Grant Hill has a broken left ankle and will miss the rest of the season. Thinking he had a bone bruise, Hill had played the first two games of the Piston's first-round playoff series against Miami.

May 1—Rodney Rogers of Phoenix wins the NBA's Sixth Man Award after a season in which he averaged 13.8 points and 5.5 rebounds per game and was the only Phoenix player to appear in every Suns game.

May 1—Playing with a swollen right (shooting) elbow, a broken left big toe and a chip fracture in his right ankle, Allen Iverson scores 26 points to lead Philadelphia to a 105–99 victory over Charlotte and a three-games-to-one win in their first-round playoff series.

May 2—The Phoenix Suns eliminate the defending champion San Antonio Spurs, who are playing without injured big man Tim Duncan, with a 89–78 victory in Game 4 of their first-round playoff series.

May 9—Following a season in which he led the league with 29.7 points per game, grabbed 13.6

rebounds per game (second in the league) and helped the Lakers to a 67–15 record, L.A. center Shaquille O'Neal is named league MVP.

May 10—Chicago's Elton Brand and Steve Francis of Houston are named co-winners of the NBA Rookie of the Year award. Brand led all rookies in scoring (20.1 ppg) while Francis led first-year players in assists (6.6 pg).

May 16—Portland eliminates the Jazz with an 81–79 victory in Game 5 of their Western Conference seminfinal series. The Blazers will meet the Lakers, who defeat Phoenix in five games in the conference finals.

May 20—Minnesota guard Malik Sealy is killed when his Range Rover is hit by a pickup truck traveling the wrong way on Highway 100 outside Minneapolis.

May 21—The Knicks eliminate the Heat from the playoffs for third straight year, knocking off the Atlantic Division champs 83–82 in Miami in Game 7 of their Eastern Conference semifinal series. The Knicks will meet the Pacers, who get past Philadelphia in six games, in the conference finals.

May 24—At the head of a class of six inducted into the Basketball Hall of Fame are former Pistons guard Isiah Thomas and University of Tennessee women's coach Pat Summitt. Also inducted are three-time NBA scoring champ Bob McAdoo, DeMatha Catholic (Md.) high school coach Morgan Wootten, University of Kentucky athletic director C.M. Newton and Danny Biasone, who invented the NBA shot clock.

June 2—With a 93–80 victory over the Knicks in Game 6 at Madison Square Garden, the Indiana Pacers advance to the NBA Finals for the first time in their 24-year history in the league.

June 4—The Lakers rally from a 16-point fourth-quarter deficit against Portland in Game 7 of the Western conference finals. They win 89–84 and advance to the NBA Finals for the first time since '92.

June 11—The Sacramento Monarchs hand the Los Angeles Sparks (4–1) their first loss of the new WNBA season, defeating them 75–68 in a nationally televised game.

June 14—Former University of Miami coach Leonard Hamilton accepts a five-year, $10 million offer to coach Washington. In Toronto the Raptors fire coach Butch Carter.

June 19—Shaquille O'Neal scores 41 points and Kobe Bryant chips in 26 as the Lakers defeat Indiana 116–111 in Game 6 to clinch the NBA title. O'Neal, the regular-season MVP, who averages 38.0 points and 16.6 rebounds per game in the series, is named Finals MVP.

June 27—Former NBA star Isiah Thomas, the owner of the Continental Basketball Association, announces his intent to sell the league, to the NBA Players Association, so that he can take the job as coach of the Pacers without a conflict of interest. The Indiana job is vacant because Larry Bird retired after the Pacers' failed NBA title run.

June 28—Former Cincinnati star Kenyon Martin goes first, to New Jersey, at the NBA draft in Minneapolis. It is an eventful day for the Nets, who also announce the retirement of injured big man Jayson Williams—one day after introducing their new coach, former Laker guard Byron Scott. The Vancouver Grizzlies select Stromile Swift out of LSU with the second pick, and the Clippers take East St. Louis (Ill.) high schooler Darius Miles in the third slot.

July 11—Spurs star Tim Duncan, a free agent, announces that he will re-sign with San Antonio.

July 17—Led by game-MVP Tina Thompson's 13 points and 11 rebounds, the West defeats the East 73–61 in the WNBA All-Star Game in Phoenix.

July 20—As expected, former Pistons guard Isiah Thomas accepts the head coaching job in Indiana, signing a four-year, $20 million deal to succeed Larry Bird.

Aug 1—Charlotte and Miami complete a nine-player deal that brings swingman Eddie Jones to the Heat while sending forwards Jamal Mashburn and P.J. Brown to the Hornets.

Aug 3—The Pistons make a sign-and-trade deal with Orlando, sending superstar Grant Hill to the Magic in exchange for guard Chucky Atkins and forward Ben Wallace.

Aug 7—After 40 years with the Lakers as a player and an executive, Hall of Famer Jerry West announces his retirement.

Aug 27—The Houston Comets defeat the New York Liberty 79–73 in overtime of Game 3 to clinch their fourth consecutive WNBA title. Houston guard Cynthia Cooper, who retires after the game, wins her fourth straight Finals MVP award.

Aug 30—The TrailBlazers trade forward Brian Grant to Miami in a three-way deal with Cleveland. Portland receives forward Shawn Kemp from the Cavaliers, who get forwards Chris Gatling and Clarence Weatherspoon, guard Gary Grant and a first-round draft pick.

Sept 21—An era comes to an end in New York as the Knicks, Seattle, the Lakers and Phoenix complete a blockbuster 12-player deal that sends Knicks center Patrick Ewing, the backbone of the franchise for 15 years, to the Sonics. The Knicks get forward Glen Rice from Los Angeles and center Luc Longley from Phoenix, along with four other players. The Suns receive center Chris Dudley from New York and the Lakers pick up forward Horace Grant from the Sonics, along with three other players and a draft pick.

Sept 27—Pacers center Rik Smits, an NBA All-Star in 1998, retires after 12 seasons in the league.

Oct 27, 1999—Leigh Steinberg, one of sports' most powerful agents and representative to many of the NFL's top quarterbacks, sells his company for approximately $120 million.

Nov 1—Walter Payton, the NFL's alltime leading rusher, dies after months of battling a rare liver disease.

Nov 3—The Chargers suspend quarterback Ryan Leaf and fine him $73,530 for an obscenity-laced tirade directed at San Diego general manager Bobby Beathard and members of the team's strength and conditioning staff.

Nov 8—Dallas quarterback Troy Aikman suffers his second concussion in as many weeks as the Vikings handle the Cowboys 27–17 on Monday night.

Nov 12—The 49ers suspend oft-troubled running back Lawrence Phillips for making light of a lecture from head coach Steve Mariucci. Phillips will soon be released outright; he had previously been given his walking papers by the Rams and Dolphins for similar conduct problems.

Nov 16—Cherica Adams, the pregnant girlfriend of Carolina wide receiver Rae Carruth, is shot while driving her car in Charlotte. She dies one month later but the baby survives, and the shooters will later be linked to Carruth.

Nov 21—The 8–2 Rams defeat the 3–7 49ers 23–7 in San Francisco, sweeping the season series for the first time since 1980.

Nov 25—Carolina wide receiver Rae Carruth is arrested on charges of conspiracy to commit first-degree murder, attempted murder and shooting into an occupied vehicle in the shooting of his pregnant girlfriend, Cherica Adams.

Nov 28—The Hamilton Tiger-Cats win the CFL's Grey Cup with a 32–21 victory over the Calgary Stampeders. Former Florida State quarterback Danny McManus passes for two touchdowns and is named the game's outstanding player.

Dec 1—Bears quarterback Jim Miller is suspended for four games by the NFL after testing positive for anabolic steroids.

Dec 15—After Cherica Adams dies in the hospital on Dec. 14 from wounds she suffered in a November drive-by shooting, Rae Carruth is found hiding in the trunk of his car at a hotel in Wildersville, Tenn. Carruth fails to surrender to authorities on charges of plotting the murder of Adams, his girlfriend.

Dec 16—Dolphins running back Cecil Collins is suspended indefinitely after he is arrested on burglary charges.

Dec 19—The Rams clinch home field advantage in the playoffs with a 31–10 win against the Giants, promising the city of St. Louis its first playoff game ever. In Indianapolis, the Colts come from behind to beat the Redskins 24–21 and claim their second AFC East championship in 22 years. In Cleveland, the Jaguars beat the Browns 24–14 to win their 11th game in a row. The game will be remembered for the undecorous actions of Browns tackle Orlando Brown, who shoves a referee to the ground after he is inadvertently hit in the eye with a weighted penalty flag. In Nashville, rookie star Jevon Kearse breaks the NFL rookie record for sacks (13.5) after a two-sack performance against the Falcons.

Dec 26—Titans quarterback Steve McNair tosses a career-high five touchdowns, and Tennessee clobbers the Jaguars 41–14. The Titans will be the only team to beat Jacksonville all season: twice during the regular season and once more in the playoffs.

Jan 3, 2000—Bill Parcells resigns as coach of the Jets and names assistent Bill Belichick as his successor. In Green Bay, Ray Rhodes is fired after only one season with the Packers, and in New England, Pete Carroll is dismissed after an 8–8 season.

Jan 4—One day after being handed the head coaching job, Bill Belichick blindsides the Jets and resigns, citing uncertainties surrounding the Jets franchise.

Jan 5—Mike Ditka, who won a Super Bowl in Chicago and famously exchanged all of his draft picks for Ricky Williams as the coach of the Saints, is fired after three seasons (15–33) in New Orleans.

Jan 8—Trailing the Bills by one in the AFC wild-card game with 20 seconds remaining, the Titans set up a trick play on a kickoff return. Lorenzo Neal fields the squibbed kick at the Titans' 25-yard line. He hands the ball to Frank Wycheck, who runs right, stops and throws the ball the width of the field to Kevin Dyson on the left sideline. Dyson catches the lateral, which appears to some to be a forward pass and thus illegal, and runs 75 yards for the touchdown to stun the Bills. After viewing the replay, officials let the play stand and it enters NFL lore as the Music City Miracle. The Titans advance to the next round of the playoffs. In Washington, the Redskins jump out to a 27-point lead and defeat the Lions 27–13.

Jan 9—In Seattle, Dolphins quarterback Dan Marino completes his 37th career fourth-quarter comeback as Miami edges the Seahawks 20–17. In Minneapolis, Robert Smith rushes for 140 yards and the Vikings eliminate the Cowboys 27–10.

Jan 11—Cowboys coach Chan Gailey, 18–14 in two seasons in Dallas, is fired two days after his team is eliminated from the playoffs by the Vikings.

Jan 11—Robert Wood Johnson IV purchases the Jets from the estate of the late Leon Hess for $635 million.

Jan 15—The Jaguars end the Dolphins' season (and Dan Marino's and Jimmy Johnson's careers) with a 62–7 rout. In nearby Tampa, the Bucs shut down the conference's leading rusher Stephen Davis (37 yards) and advance to the NFC title game with a 14–13 victory.

Jan 16—The Titans travel to Indianapolis for that city's first home playoff game and emerge with a 19–16 victory against the Colts. In St. Louis, the Rams silence their critics with an impressive 49–37 win against the Vikings, as quarterback Kurt Warner tosses five touchdowns.

Jan 18—Former Redskins general manager Charley Casserly, who helped build the Joe Gibbs teams of the 1980s, agrees to become the G.M. of the expansion Houston franchise.

Jan 22—The Titans force six Jaguar turnovers and quarterback Steve McNair runs for 91 yards and two touchdowns as Tennessee beats Jacksonville for the third time of the season. The 33–14 road win makes the Titans the sixth wild-card team to advance to a Super Bowl.

Jan 23—Chiefs linebacker Derrick Thomas is paralyzed and his close friend Michael Tellis is killed in a one-car accident on an icy Interstate 435 in Missouri.

Jan 23—The league's most prolific offense and the league's hardest-hitting defense collide in St. Louis with the NFC title on the line. Tampa Bay's defense is as good as advertised, but the Rams' D is equally stingy. They keep the Bucs out of the end zone and a late Kurt Warner touchdown pass to Ricky Proehl gives the Rams an 11–6 victory.

Jan 27—The Patriots give the Jets a future No. 1 draft pick in exchange for the right to hire former defensive coordinator Bill Belichick, who had rejected the opportunity to succeed the retired Bill Parcells as head coach of the Jets.

Jan 30—Rags-to-riches hero Kurt Warner throws for a Super Bowl–record 414 yards, and Rams linebacker Mike Jones stops Tennessee receiver Kevin Dyson one yard short of the end zone in the game's final play to give St. Louis and head coach Dick Vermeil their first Super

Marino said goodbye after 420 TD passes and 61,361 yards.

Bowl championship, 23–16.

Jan 31—Two men are killed in a brawl outside an Atlanta nightclub after the Super Bowl. Ravens All-Pro linebacker Ray Lewis is later identified as one of the men who participated in the dispute that led to the double murder.

Feb 1—Rams head coach Dick Vermeil, who spent 14 years in the broadcast booth between coaching stints with the Eagles and St. Louis, retires after leading the Rams to their first Super Bowl victory.

Feb 1—Ravens linebacker Ray Lewis is charged with murder in connection with the stabbing deaths of two men outside on Atlanta nightclub after the Super Bowl.

Feb 2—The World Wrestling Federation announces plans for a new professional football league, the XFL, an eight-team league that promises a fast-paced, wide-open game with fewer rules and greater emotion than the NFL.

Feb 3—The Saints hire former Pittsburgh defensive coordinator Jim Haslett to replace Mike Ditka as their new head coach.

Feb 6—The NFC outscores the AFC 51–31 in the Pro Bowl. Randy Moss, who sets records with nine catches and 212 yards, is named the game's MVP.

Feb 8—Chiefs linebacker Derrick Thomas, 33, paralyzed from a car accident in January, dies in the hospital from complications brought on by a blood clot.

Feb 10—Three of the stars that helped the Bills to four Super Bowls—defensive end Bruce Smith, running back Thurman Thomas and wide receiver Andre Reed—are released by the Bills.

Feb 12—Tom Landry, 75, known for his trademark fedora and stoic leadership as head coach of the Dallas Cowboys, dies of leukemia. Landry made the Cowboys into "America's Team," winning 270 games and two Super Bowl championships during his 29-year reign.

Feb 16—Shannon Sharpe, John Elway's favorite target in Denver, becomes the NFL's highest-paid tight end after signing a four-year, $14 million contract with the Ravens.

March 8—ABC Sports fires *Monday Night Football* analyst Boomer Esiason and two members of the production crew. Don Ohlmeyer,

AP/HELEN COMER

Charged with conspiracy to commit murder, Carruth went on trial in October.

who helped make *MNF* a big hit in the 1970s, is recalled as the show's new producer.

March 13—Dan Marino, the NFL's alltime leader in passing yards (61,361) and touchdowns (420) retires after 17 years with the Dolphins.

April 10—Packers tight end Mark Chmura is arrested after the 17-year old girl who babysits Chmura's children accuses him of sexual assault at a party following her prom.

April 12—The Bucs make Keyshawn Johnson the highest-paid wide receiver in football with an eight-year, $56 million contract. The Jets traded Johnson to the Bucs for two first-round draft picks after deciding that his salary demands were more than they could afford.

April 15—The Browns select Penn State defensive lineman Courtney Brown, the school's alltime leader in sacks (33), with the first pick of the NFL Draft. The Redskins select Brown's teammate, linebacker LaVar Arrington, with the second pick.

April 26—After 37 years, seven Super Bowls and four championships, Charger general manager Bobby Beathard retires from the front office.

June 5—Deion Sanders, who won Super Bowls with the 49ers and the Cowboys, signs a seven-year, $56 million contract with the Redskins.

June 5—Ravens linebacker Ray Lewis, charged with the murder of two men at an Atlanta nightclub, enters a plea agreement that exonerates him from six felony counts in exchange for testifying against two associates. Lewis receives one year of probation for obstruction of justice.

June 12—49ers quarterback Steve Young, the NFL's highest-rated passer ever, retires after a string of concussions and with the 49ers facing a massive rebuilding project.

June 22—ABC Sports announces that Dennis Miller, the former *Saturday Night Live* comic, will join the broadcast team for *Monday Night Football*. Miller will be partnered with longtime play-by-play man Al Michaels and former Chargers quarterback Dan Fouts.

June 25—The Rhein Fire defeat the Scottish Claymores 13–10 to win NFL Europe's World Bowl 2000.

July 6—Colts running back Fred Lane is found shot to death in his Charlotte home. His wife, Deidra, is later charged with murder.

July 11—Cowboys wide receiver Michael Irvin, whose final season was cut short by a frightening neck injury on the turf of Philadelphia's Veteran Stadium, announces his retirement. He leaves the game with 750 career catches and 11,904 yards.

July 29—The Pro Football Hall of Fame welcomes Pittsburgh owner Dan Rooney; former 49ers quarterback Joe Montana, who led San Francisco to four Super Bowl titles and won three Super Bowl–MVP trophies; ex-Niners safety Ronnie Lott, the most feared DB of his time; former San Francisco linebacker Dave Wilcox, who dominated offenses in the '70s; and ex-Raiders defensive end Howie Long, an All-Pro pass rusher in the 1980s.

Sept 3—The Bills avenge the previous season's painful playoff loss to the Titans, defeating the defending AFC champions 16–13 in the opening weekend of NFL action. In Philadelphia, the Eagles blast the Cowboys 41–14, as Dallas loses quarterback Troy Aikman to another concussion and wide receiver Joey Galloway to a torn ACL.

Sept 4—Comedian Dennis Miller debuts as a football broadcaster on *Monday Night Football*, presiding over the Rams' 41–36 outgunning of the Broncos.

Sept 6—Owner Bob McNair announces that Houston's new franchise will be called the Texans.

Sept 17—The Jets beat the Bills 27–14 and the Giants defeat the Bears 14–7. Both teams are 3–0, the first time ever that both New York teams have shared that record.

Sept 19—Cleveland releases lineman Orlando Brown, who still hasn't recovered from an injury he suffered last season when a referee's weighted yellow penalty flag struck him in the eye.

Sept 24—The Jets come from behind to beat the Bucs 21–17 in the first "Keyshawn Bowl," as New York receiver Wayne Chrebet, who had been publicly ridiculed by former Jet Keyshawn Johnson in the week preceding the game, catches the game-winning TD pass in the final minute. Johnson catches one pass for one yard.

Sept 25—One day after a 37–0 loss to the Ravens, Bengals coach Bruce Coslet resigns. Dick LeBeau takes over his duties. In San Francisco, 49ers receiver Terrell Owens, who nearly incited a bench-clearing brawl during the previous day's victory over the Cowboys when he danced on the Cowboys logo at the 50-yard line after a touchdown, is supended by his team for one week.

Oct 22—Bengals running back Corey Dillon breaks Walter Payton's single-game rushing record of 275, which had stood for 23 years, when he gains 278 yards on the ground in Cincinnati's 31–21 win over the Broncos.

Oct 22—The defending champion Rams (6–1) lose their first game of the season, falling to Kansas City 54–34 at Arrowhead Stadium. St. Louis quarterback Kurt Warner breaks his finger during the game and will be out at least three weeks. The loss makes Minnesota (7–0), which rallied to beat the Bills 31–27, the NFL's sole remaining unbeaten team. The Vikings defeat Buffalo and Gary Anderson moves past George Blanda and into first place on the NFL's alltime scoring list with a last-minute, 21-yard field goal. Anderson, 41, now has 2,004 career points to Blanda's 2,002.

Oct 23—Jury selection begins in the trial of former Carolina Panthers wide receiver Rae Carruth, who is charged with plotting the murder of his pregnant girlfriend, Cherica Adams. Adams was the victim of a drive-by shooting in November 1999; she died in December but doctors were able to save her baby.

Oct 30—The Minnesota Vikings (7–1) are the last team to fall from the ranks of the NFL's unbeaten, and they do so in spectacular fashion, getting routed 41–13 by NFC Central rival Tampa Bay. The victory moves the Bucs, a preseason favorites to advance to the Super Bowl, to 4–4.

Soccer

Nov 3, 1999—Tony DiCicco, who led the U.S. women's national team to a 103-8-8 record and the 1999 Women's World Cup title in nearly five yerars as its coach, announces his resignation.

Nov 11—With a 3–1 victory over the Dallas Burn in front of 25,703 fans at the Rose Bowl, the Los Angeles Galaxy advances to the Major League Soccer championship game for the second time in three years. Greg Vanney, Carlos Hermosillo and Mauricio Cienfuegos score for L.A.

Nov 13—D.C. United advances to the MLS title game for the fourth consecutive time, blanking the Columbus Crew 4–0 in Game 3 of the Eastern Conference finals at RFK Stadium in Washington. Midfielder Marco Etcheverry has three assists and a goal for D.C.

Nov 21—Before a boisterous crowd of 44,910 in Foxboro, Mass., D.C. United wins its third MLS title in four years, shutting out Los Angeles 2–0. Striker Jaime Moreno and midfielder Ben Olsen, who is named MVP of the game, score for D.C.

Nov 29—The New York/New Jersey MetroStars hire their sixth coach in four years, tapping former Galaxy coach Octavio Zambrano to lead the team in 2000. In New England, the Revolution sign former MetroStars assistant Fernando Clavijo to succeed Walter Zenga as coach.

Nov 30—Columbus striker Stern John, who scored 52 goals in two MLS seasons with the Crew, is sold to Nottingham Forest of the English First Division in a deal that nets Major League Soccer, which owns all player contracts, $2.7 million. That figure could increase to $6 million depending upon how John performs in England.

Jan 11, 2000—The MetroStars, who finished a league-worst 7–25 in 1999, dismiss general manager Charlie Stillitano and replace him with Nick Sakewicz, who was named executive of the year with the Tampa Bay Mutiny in '99.

Jan 13—With all of the players who won the Women's World Cup in '99 boycotting the tournament due to a contract dispute with U.S. Soccer, the women's national team wins the four-team Australia Cup. The U.S. starts six players under the age of 20 but still defeats a full-strength Australia 3-1 in the final.

Jan 16—In an exhibition rematch of the game that eliminated the Yanks from the 1998 World Cup, the U.S. and Iran play to a 1–1 tie in Pasadena. Chris Armas scores for the U.S.

Jan 17—University of Virginia coach April Heinrichs is tapped to succeed Tony DiCicco as head coach of the U.S. women's national team.

Jan 30—Ending a one-month boycott, Mia Hamm and co. sign new five-year contracts with U.S. Soccer.

Feb 16—Cobi Jones scores the lone goal as the U.S. defeats Peru 1–0 in the Gold Cup in Miami. Three days later the U.S. is bounced out of the tournament by Colombia, which wins a penalty-kick shootout after a 2–2 tie.

Feb 29—U.S. Soccer secretary general Hank Steinbrecher resigns after 10 years of service.

March 15—Hristo Stoitchkov, who scored six goals to lead Bulgaria to the semifinals of the 1994 World Cup, signs with Major League Soccer and will be allocated to the Chicago Fire.

Albright (11) and the U.S. Olympic team reached the semis in Sydney.

BOB MARTIN

In San Jose, Earthquakes midfielder Eddie Lewis is sold to Fulham of the English First Division.

March 19—The 2000 MLS season kicks off at the Cotton Bowl as the Dallas Burn defeats Chicago 4–2. Newly acquired Hristo Stoitchkov scores both goals for the Fire.

March 26—Sixteen-year-old Bobby Convey, a member of the U.S. team that finished fourth in the 1999 under-17 World Cup, becomes the youngest player ever to appear in an MLS game, logging 15 minutes in D.C.'s 4–0 loss to Los Angeles. Convey breaks the record set the previous week by Chicago's 17-year-old DaMarcus Beasley, the runner-up MVP of the '99 under-17 World Cup.

March 26—Lothar Matthäus, who led Germany to the 1990 World Cup title, makes his MLS debut, playing all 90 minutes of the MetroStars 3–1 loss to the Miami Fusion. In Columbus, MLS, which has introduced 10-minute, sudden-death overtime to break ties, gets its first overtime victory as the Crew edges San Jose 2–1 on Robert Warzycha's golden goal.

April 1—In front of 27,322 at the Meadowlands, the MetroStars and new signing Lothar Matthäus make their home debut, jumping out to a 3–0 lead and then holding on for a 3–2 victory over D.C. United.

April 29—Kansas City loudly announces that it is not the same team as the doormat that went 8–24 in '99, blasting Colorado 5–0 in Denver to improve its record to 6-0-1.

May 20—Striker Luis Hernandez of Mexico, acquired by MLS for a record $4 million, debuts with the Los Angeles Galaxy in a 2–1 win over D.C. The MetroStars receive midfielder Roy Myers and forward Clint Mathis as part of the deal that brings Hernandez to L.A., and the pair debut in a 3–2 NY/NJ win over Tampa Bay.

May 31—The U.S. women's national team falls to China 1–0 in Canberra, Australia.

June 4—Chicago defeats Kansas City 3–2 at home in front of 36,469 fans to snap the Wizards 12-game unbeaten streak, a 10-0-2 run that ties the 1996 Galaxy for the best start in league history.

June 6—The U.S. men play Ireland to a 1–1 tie in rainy, windy Foxboro, Mass. Ante Razov scores for the Americans.

June 11—Brian McBride, Ante Razov and Frankie Hejduk score as the U.S. blanks Mexico 3–0 in front of 45,008 fans at Giants Stadium in East Rutherford, N.J. In Newcastle, Australia, the U.S. women lift the inaugural Pacific Cup with a 1–0 triumph over Australia.

July 2—France gets a goal from Sylvain Wiltourd in stoppage time and one from David Trezeguet in extra time to complete a dramatic come-from-behind victory over Italy in the final of the European Championship in Rotterdam. The 2–1 triumph makes Les Bleus the only team ever to win the World Cup and the European title in succession.

July 3—The U.S. women blank Brazil 1–0 to win the CONCACAF Gold Cup in Foxboro, Mass.

July 6—FIFA's executive committee, in the closest vote ever, awards the 2006 World Cup to Germany over South Africa. The vote is 12–11 with one abstention.

July 16—The U.S. begins its qualifying campaign for the 2002 World Cup with a 1–1 tie against Guatemala in Mazatanengo, Guatemala. Ante Razov scores for the U.S., which gives up an 88th-minute goal to Carlos Ruiz.

July 23—With the score tied 1–1, referee Peter Prendergast of Jamaica awards Costa Rica a dubious penalty kick in the 93rd minute of its World Cup qualifier with the U.S. in San Jose, Costa Rica. Hernan Medford scores to give the Ticos a 2–1 win.

July 29—The East outguns the West 9–4 in a wide-open MLS All-Star Game in Columbus. Mamadou Diallo of Tampa Bay, who scores two goals and has an assist, is named MVP.

Aug 24—Michelle Akers, arguably the greatest women's soccer player of all time, announces her retirement from the U.S. national team. Akers, 34, who has battled a variety of injuries as well as chronic fatigue syndrome, retires with 103 goals.

Aug 26—MetroStars striker Clint Mathis sets an MLS record with five goals in his team's 6–4 victory over Dallas. The win clinches the Eastern division for the MetroStars, who finished last in MLS in '99.

Sept 3—Brian McBride scores in the 72nd minute to give the U.S. a 1–0 victory over Guatemala in a World Cup qualifier at RFK Stadium in Washington, D.C. The U.S. plays the final 25 minutes shorthanded due to the ejection of midfielder Eddie Lewis.

Sept 8—The MLS playoff picture is set as Colorado striker Paul Bravo scores in overtime to give the Rapids a 1–0 win over Los Angeles. The victory clinches a playoff berth for Colorado and eliminates Columbus and Miami.

Sept 14—FIFA suspends U.S. coach Bruce Arena (three games) and midfielder Claudio Reyna (two games) from World Cup qualifying for their role in harassing referee Peter Pendergrast after the U.S. game against Costa Rica on July 23. Pendergrast awarded Costa Rica a questionable late penalty kick in the game.

Sept 15—Adolfo (el Tren) Valencia scores with four seconds remaining in sudden-death overtime to give the MetroStars a 2–1 victory in Game 1 of their first-round playoff series against Dallas.

Sept 19—The U.S. men's Olympic team defeats Kuwait 3–1 to win its group and advance to the second round of the tournament for the first time in history.

Sept 23—In Sydney, the U.S. men's Olympic team gets by Japan in a penalty-kick shootout to advance to the semifinals of the Olympic tournament. Three days later the Americans lose to Spain 3–1.

Sept 24—Chicago blasts New England 6–0 in Game 3 of their first-round playoff series to advance to a semifinal meeting with the MetroStars, who swept Dallas. The other semifinal matchup pits Los Angeles, which swept Tampa Bay against Kansas City, which outasted Colorado.

Sept 28—The U.S. women's team falls to Norway 3–2 in overtime of the gold medal game at the Sydney Olympics.

Oct 6—Chicago's Ante Razov scores in the 88th minute to give the Fire a 3–2 victory over the MetroStars in Game 3 of their semifinal series at Soldier Field. The Fire will play Kansas City for the title as the Wizards get two goals from striker Miklos Molnar to defeat Los Angeles 1–0 in Game 3, and 1–0 again in a 20-minute sudden-death tiebreaker. Kansas City advances to MLS Cup 2000 a year after finishing 8–24.

Oct 15—Kansas City wins MLS Cup 2000 after striker Miklos Molnar scores in the 11th minute and goalkeeper Tony Meola makes 10 saves to preserve a 1–0 triumph over Chicago. Meola, who led the league with an MLS-record 16 shutouts in the regular season, is named MVP of the game.

Oct 21—Claiming a measure of consolation following its 1–0 loss in the MLS title game, the Chicago Fire edges Miami 2–1 at Soldier Field in the final of the U.S. Open Cup, the nation's oldest tournament.

Tennis

Nov 4, 1999—Andre Agassi, who was ranked No. 141 in the world in 1997, is ensured of finishing 1999 as the world No. 1 when No. 2 Yevgeny Kafelnikov, the only player with a chance to catch Agassi, loses to Lleyton Hewitt at the Paris Open.

Nov 7—Outlasting teenager Marat Safin of Russia 7–6 (7–1), 6–2, 4–6, 6–4, Andre Agassi wins the Paris Open. Agassi had won the French Open in June and the U.S. Open in September.

Nov 14—Lindsay Davenport wins her sixth title of the year, defeating Martina Hingis 6–3, 6–4 in the final of the Advanta Championship in Villanova, Pa.

Nov 21—In the finals of the season-ending Chase Championships at Madison Square Garden, Lindsay Davenport reverses the result of last year's tournament, knocking off top-ranked Martina Hingis 6–4, 6–2 in a scant 61 minutes.

Dec 2—Citing knee problems, MaliVai Washington, 30, who reached the final of

Wimbledon in 1996, announces his retirement.

Jan 10, 2000—Monica Seles withdraws from the Australian Open, a tournament she has won four times, with a recurring foot injury.

Jan 17—On the eve of the Australian Open, tournament officials rename the stadium court in Melbourne the Rod Laver Arena after Australia's Laver, 61, the only man ever to win tennis's Grand Slam twice.

Jan 27—Pete Sampras injures his hip in his marathon 6–4, 3–6, 6–7 (0–7), 7–6 (7–5), 6–1 semifinal loss to Andre Agassi at the Australian Open and will have to withdraw from the United States' upcoming Davis Cup tie with Zimbabwe.

Jan 30—Andre Agassi wins the sixth Grand Slam title of his career, defeating Yevgeny Kafelnikov 3–6, 6–3, 6–2, 6–4 in the final of the Australian Open. In the women's final, Lindsay Davenport downs Martina Hingis 6–1, 7–5.

Feb 6—The United States Davis Cup team edges Zimbabwe 3–2 in Harare, Zimbabwe, to

Triple Triumph: Williams won Wimbledon, the U.S. Open and Olympic gold.

advance to the quarterfinals against the Czech Republic.

Feb 20—Serena Williams steamrolls Denisa Chladkova 6–1, 6–1 in the final of the Faber Grand Prix in Hanover, Germany, to claim her sixth career title.

Feb 27—Playing in her first tournament since September 1999, Monica Seles wins the IGA Tennis Classic in Oklahoma City with a 6–1, 7–6 (7–3) triumph over Nathalie Dechy of France in the final.

March 12—Nineteen-year-old Lleyton Hewitt of Australia wins the fifth title of his career, defeating Britain's Tim Henman 6–4, 7–6 (7–2) in the final of the Franklin Templeton Classic in Scottsdale, Ariz.

March 27—Jennifer Capriati, 24, who was ranked sixth in the world at age 15, continues her comeback with a 7–6 (7–2), 1–6, 6–3 upset of Serena Williams in the third round of the Ericsson Open in Key Biscayne, Fla.

April 1—Martina Hingis breezes past Lindsay Davenport 6–3, 6–2 to win the Ericsson Open. In the men's final the next day, Pete Sampras outlasts Gustavo Kuerten 6–1, 6–7 (2–7), 7–6 (7–5), 7–6 (10–8).

April 9—The United States rallies to beat the Czech Republic 3–2 in the Davis Cup quarterfinals in Inglewood, Calif. Pete Sampras

wins the decisive match, beating Slava Dosedel 6–4, 6–4, 7–6 (7–2).

May 8—Former world No. 1 Jim Courier, 29, who won four Grand Slam titles in the 1990s, announces his retirement.

May 29—For the second time in 11 appearances, Pete Sampras exits the French Open in the first round, losing 4–6, 7–5, 7–6 (7–4), 4–6, 8–6 to Australia's Mark Philippoussis.

June 10—Doubles specialists Mark Woodforde and Todd Woodbridge win the French Open title for their record 58th doubles championship.

June 11—Mary Pierce wins the French Open with a 6–2, 7–5 win over Conchita Martinez in the final. The following day Brazil's Gustavo Kuerten wins the men's title at Roland Garros for the second time in four years, downing Sweden's Magnus Norman 6–2, 6–3, 2–6, 7–6 (8–6) in a 3-hour, 43-minute final.

July 8—Defeating Lindsay Davenport 6–3, 7–6 (7–3) in the Wimbledon final, Venus Williams wins her first Grand Slam title. She and her sister, Serena, who won the U.S. Open in '99, are the only sisters who have both won Grand Slam titles.

July 9—Pete Sampras surpasses Roy Emerson as the alltime leader in Grand Slam titles, winning his 13th career Grand Slam championship with a 6–7 (10–12), 7–6 (7–5), 6–4, 6–2 triumph over Pat Rafter at Wimbledon. It is Sampras's seventh Wimbledon title.

Aug 6—Apparently ignited by her victory at Wimbledon, Venus Williams wins her third tournament in a row, taking the Acura Classic in San Diego with a 6–0, 6–7 (3–7), 6–3 triumph over Monica Seles in the final. Williams defeated Lindsay Davenport in the final of the Bank of the West Classic the previous week.

Aug 13—The Williams sisters continue to dominate the WTA Tour as Serena wins the Estyle.com Classic in Los Angeles with a 4–6, 6–4, 7–6 (7–1) defeat of Lindsay Davenport in the final.

Aug 27—After Martina Hingis interrupts the Williams sisters' four-tournament run of titles on Aug. 20, defeating Serena in the final of the du Maurier, Venus promptly resumes the streak, knocking off Monica Seles 6–2, 6–4 in the final of the Pilot Pen International tournament in New Haven, Conn.

Aug 31—Andre Agassi is eliminated in the second round of the U.S. Open, falling to unseeded frenchman Arnaud Clement 6–3, 6–2, 6–4. He joins world No. 2 and French Open champ Gustavo Kuerten, a first-round victim of unseeded Australian Wayne Arthurs, on the sidelines.

Sept 7—Citing personal reasons, Andre Agassi

announces he will not compete at the Sydney Olympic Games.

Sept 8—In perhaps the best match of the year on the women's tour, Venus Williams rallies to beat Martina Hingis 4–6, 6–3, 7–5 and advance to the final of the U.S. Open.

Sept 9—Venus Williams wins her second Grand Slam of the year, her fifth straight title and her 26th consecutive match as she defeats Lindsay Davenport 6–4, 7–5 in the U.S. Open final.

Sept 10—A 20-year-old Russian with teen-idol good looks and a 136-mph serve, Marat Safin upsets Pete Sampras in the U.S. Open final. Safin's 6–4, 6–3, 6–3 win is the most lopsided defeat of a former Open champ in 25 years.

Sept 18—After winning the U.S. Open the previous week, Marat Safin travels to Tashkent, Uzbekistan, for the President's Cup, which he wins, defeating Davide Sanguinetti of Italy in the final in 62 minutes. His next stop is Sydney for the Olympic Games, but the globe-trotting trek

apparently wears him out as he loses to Fabrice Sontoro of France in the first round on Sept 22.

Sept 27—What was indisputably the year of the Williams sisters in women's tennis ends, appropriately, with a gold medal for Venus in singles and a gold medal for both sisters in doubles at the Sydney Olympic Games. Venus defeats Elena Dementieva 6–2, 6–4 in the singles gold medal match on Sept. 26 to run her consecutive-match victory streak to 32. The Williams team then routs Kristie Boogert and Miriam Oremans of the Netherlands 6–1, 6–1, for the doubles gold medal.

Sept 28—Yevgeny Kafelnikov wins the gold medal in men's tennis at the Sydney Games. He defeats 22-year-old Tommy Haas of Germany 7–6 (7–4), 3–6, 6–2, 4–6, 6–3 in the decisive match.

Oct 1—Jennifer Capriati wins her first title in 17 months, defeating Magdalena Maleeva of Bulgaria 4–6, 6–1, 6–4 in the final of the Luxembourg Open.

Other Sports

Oct 24, 1999—Morocco's Khalid Khannouchi, who will become a U.S. citizen on May 2, 2000, wins the Chicago marathon in 2:05:42, a world record. Moses Tanui of Kenya is second in 2:06:16. Kenya's Joyce Chepchumba wins the women's race in 2:25:59.

Oct 31—Austria's Hermann Maier wins the season-opening event in World Cup skiing, taking the Giant Slalom in Tignes, France. Sonja Nef of Switzerland wins the women's Giant Slalom.

Nov 7—Angler Darrell Robertson of Jay, Okla., wins the M1 Millennium bass fishing tournament in Cypress Gardens, Fla. Robertson catches two bass in the final 15 minutes of the event to claim the record $600,000 purse.

Nov 7—Joseph Chebet of Kenya clocks 2:09:14 to win the New York City marathon by four seconds over Portugal's Domingos Castro. Mexico's Adriana Fernandez wins the women's race by a more comfortable margin, finishing in 2:25:06, two-and-a-half minutes ahead of runner-up Catherine Ndereba of Kenya.

Nov 17—Needing two strikes and seven pins in the last frame, bowler Jason Couch rolls three strikes to win the $100,000 Brunswick World Tournament of Champions in Overland Park, Kans., by four pins over Chris Barnes

Nov 22—Arkansas wins a record tenth NCAA Division I cross-country title, outpointing runner-up Wisconsin. Brigham Young wins the women's crown.

Nov 28—Hermann Maier of Austria wins the

super-G in Beaver Creek, Colo., for his fourth victory in a row on the World Cup circuit. His teammate Stephan Eberharter finishes second. Maier's victory is the 10th super-G win of his career, tying him with Switzerland's Pirmin Zurbriggen for the most ever.

Dec 5—*Stars and Stripes*, the U.S. entry in the America's Cup sailing preliminaries, breaks down before a race against Italy's *Prada Challenger*.

Dec 12—At the National Finals Rodeo in Las Vegas, Fred Whitfield of Hockley, Texas, becomes the first African-American all-around champion in the history of the Professional Rodeo Cowboys Association. Whitfield also wins the calf roping title, the fourth of his career.

Dec 16—Henderson, Nevada's Wendy MacPherson, who won twice and had nine Top 5 finishes, is named Professional Women's Bowling Association player of the year. It is the third time in four years she has won the honor.

Dec 20—Penn State defeats Stanford 3–0 to win the NCAA Division I women's volleyball championship.

Jan 8, 2000—Austria's Hermann Maier wins his sixth World Cup ski race of the season, taking the downhill in Chamonix, France.

Jan 12—Jeremy Wotherspoon of Canada sets a world record in the 1,000 meters clocking 1:08.49 at the Canadian national speed skating championships.

Jan 29—Baseball Hall of Famer Ted Williams joins a second Hall of Fame as he is inducted into the International Game Fishing Association's Fishing Hall of Fame in Dania Beach, Fla. Williams is an avid angler whose favorite pursuits are tarpon, bonefish and Atlantic Salmon.

Feb 6—For the first time since 1851, the U.S. is eliminated from the America's Cup before the final round as Italy's Prada boat defeats Paul Cayard's *AmericaOne* 5–4 on Auckland, New Zealand's Hauraki Gulf. The boat from Italy will now challenge Team New Zealand for the Cup.

Feb 13—In Cleveland, Michelle Kwan wins the fourth U.S. figure skating championship of her career. Fifteen-year-old Sasha Cohen finishes second. Michael Weiss wins the men's title.

March 2—Team New Zealand completes a 5–0 sweep of Italy's Prada boat to win the America's Cup off Auckland. It is the second straight America's Cup victory for New Zealand, whose boat *Black Magic I* triumphed in 1995.

March 4—Daron Rahlves of the U.S. wins the downhill in Kvitjfell, Norway, for his second straight World Cup victory.

March 10—U.S. skier Kristina Koznick wins the World Cup slalom at Sestriere, Italy.

March 14—Musher Doug Swingley of Lincoln, Mont., wins the Iditarod Trail Sled Dog Race in record time, reaching the finish line in Nome, Alaska, after 9 days, 58 minutes. He breaks the previous record of 9 days, 2 hours, 42 minutes, which he set in 1995.

March 15—Kristina Koznick of the U.S. wins the World Cup slalom in Bormio, Italy.

April 2—U.S. figure skating champion Michelle Kwan adds the world title to her list of accomplishments in 2000, defeating Irina Slutskaya and Maria Butyrskaya, both of Russia, in Nice. Russia's Alexei Yagudin wins the men's title. Michael Weiss of the U.S. places third.

April 16—Elijah Lagat of Kenya wins the Boston Marathon in 2:09:47. Kenya's Catherine Ndereba, who finished second in the '99 New York City marathon, wins the women's race in 2:26:11.

May 7—UCLA knocks off Ohio State 3–0 for the NCAA Division I men's volleyball title. The Bruins' Brandon Taliaferro is named MVP of the tournament.

May 30—Syracuse defeats Princeton 13–7 to win the NCAA men's Division I lacrosse title, the seventh in school history.

June 15—Roman Sloudnov of Russia sets a world record in the 100-meter breaststroke, clocking 1:00.36 in Moscow. The following day his countryman Alexander Popov touches the wall in 21.64 for a new world record in the 50-meter freestyle.

June 17—Mike Koivuniemi wins the $35,000 ABC Masters bowling tournament in Albuquerque, edging Pete Weber 236–235 in the championship final.

July 15—In Phoenix, Robert Smith wins the U.S. Open bowling tournament, defeating Norm Duke 202–201 in the championship final to claim the $35,000 purse.

July 23—Lance Armstrong of the U.S. repeats as Tour de France champion. Armstrong, who battled cancer in 1996 and '97, completes the 21-stage race in 92 hours, 33 minutes, 8 seconds.

July 23—U.S. pole vaulter Stacy Dragila sets a world record in Sacramento, clearing 15 ft 2 1/4 inches.

July 30—At the U.S. gymnastic championships, Elise Ray lands a difficult vault in her last attempt to win her first all-around title.

Aug 27—The team from Maracaibo, Venezuela, which came to the tournament with only one bat, defeats U.S. South champion Bellaire (Texas) 3–2 to win the Little League World Series in Williamsport, Pa.

Oct 5—U.S. sprinter Marion Jones, who won three gold and two bronze medals at the Olympics in Sydney, closes her season with a victory in the 100 meters at the Grand Prix in Doha, Qatar. Jones clocks 11.00 to edge U.S. rival Chryste Gaines by 0.09 seconds.

The indomitable Armstrong defended his Tour de France title in convincing fashion.

MARK THOMPSON/ALLSPORT

Baseball

Joe Torre and the
World Series champion
New York Yankees

Express Train

The Yankee dynasty made only one stop as it zipped past the Mets in the first Subway Series in 44 years

BY MARK BECHTEL

It had been 44 years since New York had a World Series all to itself, so Gothamites were more than ready to hype the Mets-Yankees Subway Series as a latter day Civil War, an event of national import that would pit brother against brother. "I was growing up in New York in the '40s and '50s, when the Dodgers and Giants played all the time, and that was wild," Yankees manager Joe Torre said. "I have a feeling that this city is not going to be the same for the next 10 days, and maybe for some time after that. I hope it's going to be a good Series. I hope it's clean. I hope that people behave themselves, because it's going to split a few families up, I think."

As it turned out, the fans behaved famously. The players were a different story. Roger Clemens, possessor of a sizable surly streak, sparked one of the odder imbroglios in Series history when he threw a spiky piece of wood, *Buffy the Vampire Slayer*–style, in the direction of Mike Piazza. He was part Bob Feller, part Sarah Michelle Gellar. It was an improbable turn of events in what was an improbable matchup, not because the

Mets were making their first Fall Classic appearance since 1986, but because the two-time defending champs had made it back to the Series.

It was not a good regular season for the established powers. Last year's AL Central champs, the Cleveland Indians, missed the playoffs. So did the defending West champs, the Texas Rangers, who finished last in the division. The Yankees were the only team to return to the postseason from the American League, and they limped their way in. New York clinched the AL East on the same day it was beaten 13–2 by the Orioles, and the Yankees entered the playoffs on a seven-game losing streak, during which they were outscored 68–15 by lightweights Detroit, Tampa Bay and Baltimore.

So who were the new faces hogging most of the good times? Well, in the American League, it took a supercomputer, some slide rules and a team of MIT graduates to figure out the playoff scenarios as the AL West pennant and the wild-card race came down to the wire. Oakland, with a roster chock full of kids, seized the AL West crown on the

final day of the season, while Seattle, which not only missed the playoffs in '99 but also traded its star, Ken Griffey Jr., to the Reds before this season, took the wild card. And the White Sox—written off as quitters in 1997 when they dumped proven veterans for prospects while still in contention in late July—dominated the Central, a division the Indians had won five years running.

The Tribe ran into all sorts of injury problems in 2000. Their pitching staff was decimated, and they ended up using a Major League–record 32 hurlers. Their best player, rightfielder Manny Ramirez, missed 44 games with an assortment of maladies, and the team went 22–22 without him. That opened the door for the White Sox, who got a dominating first-half performance from the heretofore underachieving pitcher James Baldwin, and plenty of pop from designated hitter Frank Thomas, who batted .328, belted 43 homers and drove in 143 runs. Chicago took first place on April 19 and never let go.

The division may have been out of reach early, but the Indians battled through their injuries to contend for the wild card. Even

Jeter, who batted .409 with two homers in the Subway Series, was its MVP.

though a series of rainouts forced them to play nine games in six days in September—including one each against the White Sox and the Twins on the same day—Cleveland was still running neck-and-neck-and-neck with Oakland and Seattle as the season's final weekend approached. The rainout of a September game between the A's and the Devil Rays threw a giant monkey wrench into the race. Heading into the last weekend, Oakland was a half game behind the Mariners in the West and $1\frac{1}{2}$ ahead of the Indians in the wild-card race.

Not only were there several scenarios in which two of the three teams would have to play a one-game playoff the day after the season ended, but there was also the possibility that Oakland would have to travel to Tampa on Oct. 2 to make up the rained-out game with the Devil Rays after the regular season ended. Further, there was the chance that following the makeup game, the A's still could be tied for either the divi-

V.J. LOVERO

final weekend of the season, beating 20-game winner David Wells in the finale, a development that put the pressure squarely on the Mariners, who played later that afternoon against the Angels. A loss would have put Seattle in a playoff against the Indians to determine the AL wild-card. A win and they were in. The M's delivered a 5–2 comeback victory.

While those three teams provided drama and generally reminded fans of what was so great about baseball, the sport's reigning champs were putting on an amazing display of ineptitude. Father Time seemed to be getting the better of the Bronx Bombers as 37-year-old David Cone went 4–14 with a 6.91 ERA, 34-year-old Scott Brosius hit a meager .230 and who-knows-how-old-but-older-than-he-says Orlando Hernandez went 12–13. Things were so bad that journeyman Glenallen Hill was New York's best player for part of the summer. When they finally sewed up the East, thanks to a Boston loss to Tampa Bay, the Yankees sat around the clubhouse until manager Joe Torre told them to celebrate what they had done over the course of the season and hit the champagne.

The stalwarts of '99 struggled in the National League as well. The Astros, fresh from a 97-win season in the frumpy, spacious Astrodome, *lost* 90 games in their new, state-of-the-art bandbox, Enron Field. The small-market Reds, who as scrappy underdogs fought their way to within one game of the playoffs last year, added arguably the game's greatest player, Griffey Jr., and then finished 10 games out of first in the Central. Hailed as a genius in '99, Cincinnati manager Jack McKeon was dumped at the end of 2000.

Arizona, which essentially bought a division title in '99, added fireballer Curt Schilling for the stretch run in 2000 but never seriously challenged for a playoff spot. The Diamondbacks were replaced in the postseason by San Francisco, which won the NL West in its first season in Pac Bell Park, a beautiful stadium abutting the Bay. MVP candidates second baseman Jeff Kent (.334,

sion or the wild card. That would require—you guessed it—another one-game playoff.

Players didn't know which was worse: the pressure of a playoff race or the headache of trying to figure out the playoff race. "A lot of the guys in this room don't have the college education necessary to follow all that," said A's first baseman Jason Giambi, scanning the Oakland clubhouse. "Sometimes ignorance is bliss."

So is having a player like Giambi, who had a September to remember, hitting .400 with 13 homers and 32 RBIs while racking up a slugging percentage over .800. But more important was his presence in the clubhouse. On most nights the A's fielded a lineup in which seven of the nine players had less than five years of big league experience, and Giambi was their unquestioned leader. Seemingly impervious to pressure, the youthful A's went 22–7 in the season's final month, and when the complicated playoff picture finally came into focus, they needed a victory against Texas on Oct. 1 to win the West. They delivered a 3–0 gem.

Indeed, all of the teams involved in the race took care of business when it mattered most. The Indians swept Toronto over the

33 home runs, 125 RBIs) and leftfielder Barry Bonds (.306, career-high 49 homers, 106 RBIs) led the way for the Giants.

Replacing the Astros atop the NL Central were the Cardinals, who used some clever acquisitions to run away with the division. In an era in which teams rely increasingly on free agency rather than trades to build teams, St. Louis G.M. Walt Jocketty pulled off one great preseason swap after another. Without giving up much of anything, he bolstered his pitching staff with Darryl Kile, Pat Hentgen and Dave Veres. Kile, who had lost 30 games in two years with Colorado, won 20 games for St. Louis and lowered his E.R.A. by 2.70. Hentgen won 15 games for the Cards, and Veres saved 29.

Jocketty also picked up second baseman Fernando Vina, which allowed him to trade prospect Adam Kennedy, along with suddenly expendable starter Kent Bottenfield, to Anaheim for centerfielder Jim Edmonds. Edmonds, who'd become unhappy in Anaheim, smacked 42 homers for St. Louis. And when Mark McGwire went down with a bad knee, Jocketty made a deadline deal for veteran Will Clark, who hit .345 with 12 homers in two months with the team.

McGwire's injury limited him to 89 games, yet he still hit 32 homers. But the home run race, which was close once again, suffered in Big Mac's absence and failed to capture fans' imaginations, though Sammy Sosa did belt 50—the third year in a row he reached that milestone. Instead of being captivated by a home run derby, fans caught .400 fever, as Colorado first baseman Todd Helton flirted with the lofty batting-average barrier before a .267 September dropped him to .372.

In the end, the only run at history that was successful was the Yankees'. No team since the 1972–74 A's had won three consecutive world championships, and the Bronx Bombers' trifecta was even tougher to pull off than Oakland's had been. It came in the free-agent era, when holding a team together is all but impossible. The Yankees are, of course, something of an exception. You can call New York owner George Steinbrenner many things but cheap is not one of them.

The Yankees have the fiscal wherewithal to keep their vital cogs in place—and to acquire spare parts as needed—but it seemed like other forces were aligned against them. Pitching coach Mel Stottlemyre left the team in September after undergoing cancer treatment. Darryl Strawberry, who provided such a spark in the '99 playoffs, couldn't stay out of trouble with the law, and was suspended for the year after testing positive for cocaine. Second baseman Chuck Knoblauch's throwing woes bordered on the clinical. Shane Spencer, a hot bat off the bench the past two years, blew out his knee. Veteran Paul O'Neill could barely run come October.

Say what you want about the amount of money they spent, but the Yanks' 26th World Series win might have been their most impressive, as evidenced by the increasingly emotional state of their usually stoic boss, Torre, as his team clawed through the postseason. The gritty A's almost sent them packing in the Division Series, forcing them to a fifth game. In the ALCS they met the Mariners, who had swept the White Sox in their first round meeting. Seattle stymied the New York bats for long stretches at a time, but when the Yankees got their offense on track, it was deadly. A seven-run eighth inning won Game 2 for the Yanks, and they wrapped up the series with a six-run inning in Game 6.

In the National League the Braves vaunted pitching rotation got shellacked by the Cardinals, who swept Atlanta without the game's greatest slugger, McGwire. St. Louis hammered Greg Maddux and lit up Tom Glavine and the mighty Braves were gone. In the other first-round series, another slugger staged a vanishing act: Barry Bonds was MIA as the Giants bowed out to the Mets in four games. The Mets found a gem in minor-league callup Timo Perez, who replaced the injured Derek Bell in right field and stroked clutch hit after clutch hit. In the NLCS, the Mets rolled over the Cardinals, with Mike Hampton twirling a three-hit shutout in Game 5 to clinch.

That set up the Subway Series, which very nearly lived up to the leviathan hype it gen-

Helton (17) flirted with .400 before finishing at .372 with 42 homers and 147 RBIs.

erated. The Yankees took Game 1 when Mets closer Armando Benitez failed to hold a 3–2 lead in the bottom of the ninth. Benitez was the one player who made Mets fans nervous. He'd blown more than half of the postseason save opportunities of his career, many of them on home runs. The Yankees closer, Mariano Rivera, on the other hand, was on his way to a postseason record for consecutive scoreless innings, a run that stretched back to 1997. Benitez allowed the Yankees to tie the game on a Knoblauch sacrifice fly, and the Bombers won it in the 12th on a base hit by Jose Vizcaino.

As dramatic as the opener was, Game 2 devolved into the realm of the ridiculous before half an inning was in the books. The Mets were wondering which Clemens would show up: the one the A's roughed up in the Division Series or the one who handcuffed the Mariners with a one-hit, 15-strikeout performance in the ALCS. They got the latter, but not without a bizarre prelude. In the top of the first, Clemens faced Piazza, whom he had infamously beaned during a July interleague meeting. As Yankee Stadium throbbed with the tension of not only a World Series but also the

subplot between Piazza and Clemens (Piazza had publicly criticized Clemens in July), Clemens whipped a fastball that Piazza fought off, breaking his bat into three pieces. The largest piece, the jagged barrel head, skittered toward Clemens, who picked it up and—inexplicably—threw it across the first base line directly in front of the path of Piazza, who was running out the foul ball. The broken bat missed Piazza, but both benches cleared and Piazza immediately strolled toward Clemens, asking what in God's name the pitcher was doing.

No punches were thrown, and Clemens settled down to two-hit the Mets for eight innings. After the game, Clemens offered excuses for the incident that were more ridiculous than the act itself. He claimed he thought the bat was actually the ball, which begs the question of why he would throw the ball in the direction of the runner. He also said he never saw Piazza, which seemed unlikely at best. Clemens was fined $50,000 the next day, and almost forgotten was the way he dominated Mets hitters. The Yankees took a 6–0 lead into the ninth before the Mets hit two homers to close to 6–5, the final score.

Two nights later, the Mets finally solved the Yankees, winning 4–2 on Benny Agbayani's eighth inning tie-breaking single. But Jeter hit Bobby Jones' first pitch of Game 4 for a homer, and the Yanks held on for a 3–2 win. They returned to their clubhouse to discover that a main had broken, flooding the locker room with water. The next night, the Yankees flooded it with champagne as second baseman Luis Sojo, whom New York picked up from the Pirates in August, came through with the game-winning base hit off a valiant but exhausted Al Leiter in the ninth. The Yankees bore Torre aloft on their shoulders, and he shed a few tears along the way.

"You never get tired of it," he said later. "It never gets old."

Final Standings

National League

EASTERN DIVISION

Team	Won	Lost	Pct	GB	Home	Away
Atlanta	95	67	.586	—	51–30	44–37
†New York	94	68	.580	1	55–26	39–42
Florida	79	82	.491	15½	43–38	36–44
Montreal	67	95	.414	28	37–44	30–51
Philadelphia	65	97	.401	30	34–47	31–50

CENTRAL DIVISION

Team	Won	Lost	Pct	GB	Home	Away
St. Louis	95	67	.586	—	50–31	45–36
Cincinnati	85	77	.525	10	43–38	42–39
Milwaukee	73	89	.451	22	42–39	31–50
Houston	72	90	.444	23	39–42	33–48
Pittsburgh	69	93	.426	26	37–44	32–49
Chicago	65	97	.401	30	38–43	27–54

WESTERN DIVISION

Team	Won	Lost	Pct	GB	Home	Away
San Francisco	97	65	.599	—	55–26	42–39
Los Angeles	86	76	.531	11	44–37	42–39
Arizona	85	77	.525	12	47–34	38–43
Colorado	82	80	.506	15	48–33	34–47
San Diego	76	86	.469	21	41–40	35–46

†Wild-card team.

American League

EASTERN DIVISION

Team	Won	Lost	Pct	GB	Home	Away
New York	87	74	.540	—	44–36	43–38
Boston	85	77	.525	2½	42–39	43–38
Toronto	83	79	.512	4½	45–36	38–43
Baltimore	74	88	.457	13½	44–37	30–51
Tampa Bay	69	92	.429	18	36–44	33–48

CENTRAL DIVISION

Team	Won	Lost	Pct	GB	Home	Away
Chicago	95	67	.586	—	46–35	49–32
Cleveland	90	72	.556	5	48–33	42–39
Detroit	79	83	.488	16	43–38	36–45
Kansas City	77	85	.475	18	42–39	35–46
Miinnesota	69	93	.426	26	36–45	33–48

WESTERN DIVISION

Team	Won	Lost	Pct	GB	Home	Away
Oakland	91	70	.565	—	47–34	44–36
†Seattle	91	71	.562	½	47–34	44–37
Anaheim	82	80	.506	9½	46–35	36–45
Texas	71	91	.438	20½	42–39	29–52

2000 Playoffs

National League Divisional Playoffs

Oct 3 ....Atlanta 5 at St. Louis 7
Oct 5 ....Atlanta 4 at St. Louis 10

Oct 7 ....St. Louis 7 at Atlanta 1

(St. Louis won series 3–0)

Oct 4 ....New York 1 at San Francisco 5
Oct 5 ....New York 5 at San Francisco 4 (10 inn.)

Oct 7 ....San Francisco 2 at New York 3 (13 inn.)
Oct 8 ....San Francisco 0 at New York 4

(New York won series 3–1)

National League Championship Series

Oct 11 ....New York 6 at St. Louis 2
Oct 12 ....New York 6 at St. Louis 5
Oct 14 ....St. Louis 8 at New York 2

Oct 15 ....St. Louis 6 at New York 10
Oct 16 ....St. Louis 0 at New York 7

(New York won series 4–1)

GAME 1

New York	2	0	0	0	1	0	0	0	3	—6
St. Louis	0	0	0	0	0	0	0	0	2	—2

WP—Hampton. **LP**—Kile. **E**—New York: Agbayani, Abbott, Perez. **LOB**—New York 4, St. Louis 11. **2B**—New York: Perez, Piazza; St. Louis: Clark, Lankford. **HR**—New York: Zeile, Payton. **SF**—New York: Ventura. **GIDP**—New York: Perez. **T**—3:08. **A**—52,255.

Recap: New York ace Mike Hampton pitched seven innings of shutout ball, and Todd Zeile and Jay Payton connected on ninth-inning home runs to put the Cardinals away in Game 1 at Busch Stadium in St. Louis. The Mets extended their postseason scoreless streak to a team-record 26 innings before allowing two unearned runs with two outs in the ninth.

GAME 2

New York	2	0	1	0	0	0	0	2	1	—6
St. Louis	0	1	0	0	2	0	0	2	0	—5

WP—Wendell. **LP**—Timlin. **SV**—Benitez. **E**—St. Louis: Vina, Clark, Edmonds. **LOB**—New York 12, St. Louis 8. **2B**—New York: Agbayani, Zeile; St. Louis: Dunston, Clark, Renteria, Tatis, Drew. **3B**—New York: Piazza. **HR**—New York: Piazza. **Sac**—New York: Agbayani; St. Louis: Dunston. **SF**—New York: Zeile. **SB**—St. Louis: Renteria 3. **T**—3:59. **A**—52,250.

Recap: Jay Payton singled home the winning run in the ninth inning after Cardinals first baseman Will Clark muffed a simple two-hopper from Robin Ventura to prolong the inning. Rookie pitcher Rick Ankiel struggled mightily for the Cards, throwing five of his first 20 pitches past the catcher and to the backstop before being removed with two outs in the first inning.

National League Championship Series (Cont.)

GAME 3

St. Louis	2 0 2	1 3 0	0 0 0	—8
New York	1 0 0	1 0 0	0 0 0	—2

WP—Benes. **LP**—Reed.
E—New York: Ventura. **LOB**—St. Louis 10, New York 7. **2B**—St. Louis: Edmonds, Tatis. **Sac**—St. Louis: Renteria, Benes. **SF**—St. Louis: Tatis. **GIDP:** New York: Piazza, Payton. **T**—3:23. **A**—55,693.
Recap: All nine Cardinals starters had at least one hit and righthander Andy Benes pitched eight strong innings as St. Louis won Game 3 at Shea Stadium in New York. The Cardinals, who struggled offensively against New York's lefthanders in the first two games of the series, exploded on righthander Rick Reed, knocking him out in the fourth inning after he allowed eight hits and five runs.

GAME 4

St. Louis	2 0 0	1 3 0	0 0 0	—6
New York	4 3 0	1 0 2	0 0 x	—10

WP—Rusch. **LP**—Kile.
E—St. Louis: Tatis 2. **LOB**—St. Louis 6, New York 4. **2B**—St. Louis: Vina, Davis; New York: Perez, Alfonzo, Piazza, Ventura, Agbayani, Zeile. **HR**—St. Louis: Edmonds, Clark; New York: Piazza. **Sac**—St. Louis: Renteria; New York: Rusch. **SF**—St. Louis: Renteria; New York: Ventura. **SB**—New York: Perez. **CS**— New York: Perez. **T**—3:14. **A**—55,665.

GAME 4 (CONT.)

Recap: The Cardinals started righthander Darryl Kile on three-days rest and the Mets sent him to the showers early with a parade of doubles. New York set a record with five two-base hits during a four-run first inning. St. Louis inched to within 8–6 after a three-run fifth, but Mets first baseman Todd Kile's defensive gem snuffed out a Cardinals rally in the sixth to help preserve the win. Mets rookie lefthander Glendon Rusch came out of the bullpen to pitch three innings of scoreless relief for the win.

GAME 5

St. Louis	0 0 0	0 0 0	0 0 0	—0
New York	3 0 0	3 0 0	1 0 x	—7

WP—Hampton. **LP**—Hentgen.
E—St. Louis: Hernandez, Clark. **LOB**—St. Louis 4, New York 13. **2B**—New York: Piazza, Zeile. **Sac**—New York: Hampton. **SB**—New York: Perez. **CS**—New York: Perez. **T**—3:17. **A**—55,695.
Recap: NLCS MVP Mike Hampton handcuffed the Cardinals for the second time, tossing a complete-game three-hit shutout to send the Mets to their first World Series since 1986. A three-run first inning ignited by the speedy Timo Perez and a double by Todd Zeile in the fourth gave Hampton all the offense he would need. Perez tied an NLCS record with eight runs.

American League Divisional Playoffs

Oct 3 ....Seattle 7 at Chicago 4
Oct 4 ....Seattle 5 at Chicago 2
Oct 6 ....Chicago 1 at Seattle 2

(Seattle won series 3–0)

Oct 3 ....New York 3 at Oakland 5
Oct 4 ....New York 4 at Oakland 0
Oct 6 ....Oakland 2 at New York 4
Oct 7 ....Oakland 11 at New York 1
Oct 8 ....New York 7 at Oakland 5

(New York won series 3–2)

American League Championship Series

Oct 10 ....Seattle 2 at New York 0
Oct 11 ....Seattle 1 at New York 7
Oct 13 ....New York 8 at Seattle 2
Oct 14 ....New York 5 at Seattle 0
Oct 15 ....New York 2 at Seattle 6
Oct 17 ....Seattle 7 at New York 9

(New York won series 4–2)

GAME 1

Seattle	0 0 0	0 1 1	0 0 0	—2
New York	0 0 0	0 0 0	0 0 0	—0

WP—Garcia. **LP**—Neagle. **SV**—Sasaki.
E—New York: Brosius. **LOB**—Seattle 7, New York 8. **2B**—Seattle: McLemore; New York: Knoblauch. **HR**—Seattle: Rodriguez. **CS**—Seattle: Henderson. **GIDP**—New York: Brosius. **T**—3:45. **A**—54,481.
Recap: The New York Yankees looked like a tired group after a hectic travel schedule and a grueling five-game series with Oakland. Seattle righthander Freddy Garcia pitched 6⅔ innings of three-hit ball and combined with the bullpen to fan 13 Yankees.

GAME 2

Seattle	0 0 1	0 0 0	0 0 0	—1
New York	0 0 0	0 0 0	0 7 x	—7

WP—Hernandez. **LP**—Rhodes.
E—Seattle: McLemore, Wilson. **LOB**—Seattle 7, New York 8. **2B**—Seattle: Martin, McLemore, Olerud; New York: Knoblauch, Justice, Vizcaino. **HR**—New York: Jeter. **SF**—New York: O'Neill. **SB**—Seattle: Cameron; New York: Vizcaino. **CS**—New York: Posada. **GIDP**—Seattle: Olerud; New York: Williams.

GAME 2 (CONT.)

T—3:36. **A**—55,317.
Recap: The Yankees offense awoke just in time, snapping a 21-inning postseason scoreless streak with seven runs in the eighth inning to even the series at one game apiece. New Yorker starter Orlando Hernandez pitched eight solid innings, improving his career postseason record to 7–0.

GAME 3

New York	0 2 1	0 0 1	0 0 4	—8
Seattle	1 0 0	0 1 0	0 0 0	—2

WP—Pettitte. **LP**—Sele. **SV**—Rivera.
E—Seattle: McLemore. **LOB**—New York 6, Seattle 7. **2B**—New York: Justice; Seattle: Henderson. **HR**—New York: Williams, Martinez. **Sac**—Seattle: McLemore. **SF**—New York: Williams. **SB**—New York: Vizcaino; Seattle: Rodriguez. **CS**—New York: Brosius. **GIDP**—New York: Justice; Seattle: Oliver. **T**—3:35. **A**—47,827.
Recap: New York got 13 hits and ripped open the game with four runs in the ninth. Closer Mariano Rivera broke Whitey Ford's record for consecutive scoreless postseason innings (32⅓ IP) while picking up the save.

American League Championship Series (Cont.)

GAME 4

New York	0	0	0	0	3	0	0	2	0	—5
Seattle	0	0	0	0	0	0	0	0	0	—0

WP—Clemens. **LP**—Abbott.
LOB—New York 4, Seattle 3. **2B**—Seattle: Martin. **HR**—New York: Jeter, Justice. **SB**—New York: Williams. **T**—2:59. **A**—47,803.
Recap: Roger Clemens set a nine-inning ALCS record for strikeouts (15) and allowed only a seventh-inning double while pitching the Yankees to within one win of a third consecutive World Series.

GAME 5

New York	0	0	0	2	0	0	0	0	0	—2
Seattle	1	0	0	0	5	0	0	0	0	—6

WP—Garcia. **LP**—Neagle.
LOB—New York 15, Seattle 8. **2B**—New York: Martinez, Sojo, Williams. **HR**—Seattle: Martinez, Olerud. **Sac**—Seattle: Cameron. **SF**—Seattle: Olerud. **SB**—Seattle: Olerud. **T**—4:14. **A**—47,802.
Recap: With his team facing elimination, Alex Rodriguez revived the Mariners with a two-run single in the fifth inning. Edgar Martinez and John Olerud followed with consecutive homers to carry Seattle to a 6–2 win, and send the best-of-seven series back to New York with the Yankees ahead three games to two. Freddy Garcia beat the two-time defending World Series champions for the second time in six days, allowing seven hits in five innings.

GAME 6

Seattle	2	0	0	2	0	0	0	3	0	—7
New York	0	0	0	3	0	0	6	0	x	—9

WP—Hernandez. **LP**—Paniagua.
LOB—Seattle 6, New York 8. **2B**—Seattle: Rodriguez, Martinez, Olerud 2, McLemore; New York: Posada, Martinez. **HR**—Seattle: Guillen, Rodriguez; New York: Justice. **Sac**—New York: Knoblauch. **SF**—New York: Vizcaino. **SB**—New York: Jeter. **CS**—Seattle: Guillen. **GIDP**—New York: Martinez. **T**—4:03. **A**—56,598.
Recap: With Seattle ahead 4–3 in the seventh inning, ALCS MVP David Justice lined a pitch from Arthur Rhodes into the rightfield upper deck for a three-run homer, vaulting New York, which had trailed 4–0, into a 6–4 lead. The Yanks increased that lead to 9–4 before Seattle staged one last rally in the eighth, sparked by an Alex Rodriguez home run, only to fall two runs short.

Composite Box Scores

National League Championship Series

NEW YORK

BATTING	AB	R	H	HR	RBI	Avg
Alfonzo	18	5	8	0	4	.444
Piazza	17	7	7	2	4	.412
Zeile	19	7	7	1	8	.368
Agbayani	17	0	6	0	3	.353
Perez	23	8	7	0	0	.304
Ventura	14	4	3	0	5	.214
Hampton	6	1	1	0	0	.167
Payton	19	1	3	1	3	.158
Bordick	13	2	1	0	0	.077
Trammell	3	0	0	0	0	.000
Abbott	3	0	0	0	0	.000
M. Franco	3	0	0	0	0	.000
Hamilton	2	0	0	0	0	.000
McEwing	0	2	0	0	0	.000
four others	7	0	0	0	0	.000
Totals	164	31	43	4	27	.262

PITCHING	G	IP	H	BB	SO	ERA
Hampton	2	16	9	4	12	0.00
Rusch	2	3⅔	3	0	3	0.00
Benitez	3	3	3	2	2	0.00
Wendell	2	1⅓	1	1	2	0.00
Cook	1	1	1	0	2	0.00
Leiter	1	7	8	0	9	3.86
J. Franco	3	2⅔	3	2	2	6.75
White	1	3	5	1	1	9.00
Reed	1	3⅓	8	1	4	10.80
B.J. Jones	1	4	6	0	2	13.50
Totals	5	45	47	11	39	3.60

ST. LOUIS

BATTING	AB	R	H	HR	RBI	Avg
Hentgen	1	0	1	0	0	1.000
Clark	17	3	7	1	1	.412
Drew	12	2	4	0	1	.333
Lankford	12	1	4	0	1	.333
Dunston	6	1	2	0	0	.333
Benes	3	1	1	0	0	.333
Renteria	20	4	6	0	4	.300
Viña	23	3	6	0	1	.261
Hernandez	16	3	4	0	1	.250
Tatis	13	1	3	0	2	.231
Edmonds	22	1	5	1	5	.227
Davis	10	1	2	0	1	.200
Polanco	5	0	1	0	0	.200
Paquette	6	0	1	0	0	.167
Marrero	4	0	0	0	0	.000
four others	7	0	0	0	0	.000
Totals	177	21	47	2	18	.266

PITCHING	G	IP	H	BB	SO	ERA
Timlin	3	3⅓	1	2	0	0.00
Christiansen	2	2	0	0	1	0.00
Veres	3	2⅓	2	0	3	0.00
Reames	2	6⅓	5	4	6	1.42
Benes	1	8	6	3	5	2.25
Morris	2	3⅔	3	2	2	4.91
Kile	2	10	13	5	3	9.00
Hentgen	1	3⅔	7	5	2	14.73
James	4	2⅓	5	1	0	15.43
Ankiel	2	1⅓	1	5	2	20.25
Totals	5	43	43	27	24	5.86

American League Championship Series

SEATTLE

BATTING	AB	R	H	HR	RBI	Avg
Rodriguez	22	4	9	2	5	.409
Olerud	20	3	7	1	2	.350
McLemore	16	2	4	0	2	.250
Martinez	21	2	5	1	4	.238
Bell	18	0	4	0	0	.222
Henderson	9	2	2	0	1	.222
Guillen	5	1	1	1	2	.200
Buhner	11	0	2	0	0	.182
Martin	11	1	2	0	0	.182
Oliver	6	0	1	0	0	.167
Cameron	18	3	2	0	1	.111
Wilson	11	0	1	0	0	.091
Javier	14	0	1	0	1	.071
Ibanez	9	0	0	0	0	.000
Gipson	0	0	0	0	0	—
Totals	191	18	41	5	18	.215

PITCHING	G	IP	H	BB	SO	ERA
Sasaki	2	2⅔	3	1	3	0.00
Ramsay	2	1⅔	2	0	1	0.00
Garcia	2	11⅔	10	4	11	1.54
Halama	2	9⅓	10	5	3	2.89
Paniagua	5	4⅓	4	1	4	4.15
Abbott	1	5	3	3	3	5.40
Sele	1	6	9	0	4	6.00
Tomko	2	5	3	4	4	7.20
Mesa	3	4⅓	5	3	3	12.46
Rhodes	4	2	8	3	3	31.50
Totals	6	52	57	25	41	5.37

NEW YORK

BATTING	AB	R	H	HR	RBI	Avg
Vizcaino	2	3	2	0	2	1.000
Williams	23	5	10	1	3	.435
Martinez	23	5	8	1	1	.320
Jeter	22	6	7	2	5	.318
Knoblauch	23	3	6	0	2	.261
Sojo	23	1	6	0	2	.261
O'Neill	20	0	5	0	5	.250
Justice	26	4	6	2	8	.231
Brosius	18	2	4	0	0	.222
Posada	19	2	3	0	3	.158
Hill	2	0	0	0	0	.000
Polonia	1	0	0	0	0	.000
Bellinger	0	0	0	0	0	—
Totals	204	31	57	6	31	.279

PITCHING	G	IP	H	BB	SO	ERA
Clemens	1	9	1	2	15	0.00
Gooden	1	2⅓	1	0	1	0.00
Grimsley	2	1	2	3	1	0.00
Cone	1	1	0	0	0	0.00
Choate	1	⅓	0	0	1	0.00
Rivera	3	4⅔	4	0	1	1.93
Pettitte	1	6⅔	9	1	2	2.70
Hernandez	2	15	13	8	14	4.20
Neagle	2	10	6	7	7	4.50
Nelson	3	3	5	0	6	9.00
Totals	6	53	41	21	48	3.06

2000 World Series

Oct 21 ....New York (N) 3 at New York (A) 4
Oct 22 ....New York (N) 5 at New York (A) 6
Oct 24 ....New York (A) 2 at New York (N) 4

Oct 25 ....New York (A) 3 at New York (N) 2
Oct 26 ....New York (A) 4 at New York (N) 2

(New York [A] won series 4–1)

GAME 1

```
New York (N)  0 0 0   0 0 0   3 0 0   0 0 0   —3
New York (A)  0 0 0   0 0 2   0 0 1   0 0 1   —4
```

WP—Stanton. **LP**—Wendell.
LOB—NYM 8, NYY 15. **2B**—NYM: Agbayani, Zeile, Abbott; NYY: Justice, Posada. **Sac**—NYM: Bordick. **SF**—NYY: Knoblauch. **CS**—NYM: Piazza; NYY: Knoblauch. **GIDP**—NYY: O'Neill.
T—4:51. **A**—55,913.
Recap: Jose Vizcaino singled home the winning run with two outs in the 12th inning of the longest World Series game ever in terms of time—4 hours, 51 minutes.

GAME 2

```
New York (N)  0 0 0   0 0 0   0 0 5   —5
New York (A)  2 1 0   0 1 0   1 1 x   —6
```

WP—Clemens. **LP**—Hampton.
E—NYM: Payton, Bordick, Perez; NYY: Clemens.
LOB—NYM 4, NYY 12. **2B**—NYY: Martinez, Jeter 2, O'Neill. **HR**—NYM: Piazza, Payton; NYY: Brosius.
SF—NYY: Brosius. **CS**—NYY: Vizcaino.
T—3:30. **A**—56,059.
Recap: Roger Clemens settled down after a bizarre first-inning incident in which he threw a piece of Mike Piazza's broken bat—which had skittered toward him on the mound—in the direction of Piazza as the Mets' catcher ran down the first base line after a foul

GAME 2 *(CONT.)*

Recap (Cont.): ball. The benches cleared but no punches were thrown. Clemens then pitched eight shutout innings and the Yankees held off the Mets' rally in the ninth for a 6–5 victory.

GAME 3

```
New York (A)  0 0 1   1 0 0   0 0 0   —2
New York (N)  0 1 0   0 0 1   0 2 x   —4
```

WP—Franco. **LP**—Hernandez. **SV**—Benitez.
LOB—NYY 10, NYM 8. **2B**—NYY: O'Neill, Justice; NYM: Ventura, Piazza, Zeile, Agbayani. **3B**—NYY: O'Neill. **HR**—NYM: Ventura. **S**—NYY: Hernandez; NYM: Reed. **SF**—NYM: Trammell.
T—3:39. **A**—55,299.
Recap: Benny Agbayani got Shea Stadium shaking with a go-ahead double in the eighth inning as the Mets handed Orlando Hernandez his first postseason defeat in 10 starts.

GAME 4

```
New York (A)  1 1 1   0 0 0   0 0 0   —3
New York (N)  0 0 2   0 0 0   0 0 0   —2
```

WP—Nelson. **LP**—Jones. **SV**—Rivera.
E—NYM: Trammell. **LOB**—NYY 9, NYM 6. **3B**—NYY: O'Neill, Jeter. **HR**—NYY: Jeter; NYM: Piazza. **SF**—NYY: Brosius. **SB**—NYY: Sojo. **GIDP**—NYY: O'Neill.
T—3:20. **A**—55,290.

GAME 4 *(CONT.)*

Recap: Derek Jeter, batting lead-off for the first time in the Series, set the tone with a home run on the very first pitch of the game. He also hit a triple in the third and scored the third Yankee run. Mike Piazza's two-run home run in the third brought the Mets to within one run, but the Yankee bullpen shut down the National League champs the rest of the way.

GAME 5

New York (A)	0	1	0	0	0	1	0	0	2	—4
New York (N)	0	2	0	0	0	0	0	0	0	—2

WP—Stanton. **LP**—Leiter. **SV**—Rivera.
E—NYY: Pettitte; NYM: Payton. **LOB**—NYY 6, NYM 10. **2B**—NYM: Piazza. **HR**—NYY: Williams, Jeter.
S—NYM: Leiter.
T—3:32. **A**—55,292.

GAME 5 *(CONT.)*

Recap: A taut pitching duel between Andy Pettitte and Al Leiter unraveled in the ninth when Leiter, after striking out Tino Martinez and Paul O'Neill to start the inning, gave up a walk to Jorge Posada and a single to Scott Brosius. The next batter, Luis Sojo, bounced Leiter's 142nd pitch of the night up the middle to score Posada, who was hit by Jay Payton's throw to the plate. The ball got away and Brosius scored as well to give the Yankees a two-run cushion in the bottom of the ninth. In the Mets' last turn at the plate Benny Agbayani hit a single and stole second uncontested. With two out and Agbayani on second, Mike Piazza hit a fly ball to the warning track, where Bernie Williams squeezed it to deliver the Yankees their third consecutive World Series title and 26th in franchise history. The Yankees are the first team since the 1972–74 A's to win three straight World Series.

2000 World Series Composite Box Score

NEW YORK (N)

BATTING	AB	R	H	HR	RBI	Avg
Zeile	20	1	8	0	1	.400
Trammell	5	1	2	0	3	.400
Payton	21	3	7	1	3	.333
Agbayani	18	2	5	0	2	.278
Piazza	22	3	6	2	4	.273
Abbott	8	0	2	0	0	.250
Ventura	20	1	3	1	1	.150
Alfonzo	21	1	3	0	1	.143
Perez	16	1	2	0	0	.125
Bordick	8	0	1	0	0	.125
Hamilton	3	0	0	0	0	.000
Harris	4	1	0	0	0	.000
Pratt	2	1	0	0	0	.000
McEwing	1	1	0	0	0	.000
Franco	1	0	0	0	0	.000
Others	5	0	1	0	0	.200
Totals	175	16	40	4	15	.229

PITCHING	G	IP	H	BB	SO	ERA
Franco	4	3⅓	3	0	1	0.00
Cook	3	⅔	1	3	1	0.00
Rusch	3	4	6	2	2	2.25
Leiter	2	15⅔	12	6	16	2.87
Reed	1	6	6	1	8	3.00
Benitez	3	3	3	2	2	3.00
Jones	1	5	4	3	3	5.40
Wendell	2	1⅔	3	2	2	5.40
Hampton	1	6	8	5	4	6.00
White	1	1⅓	1	1	1	6.75
Totals	5	46⅔	47	25	40	3.47

NEW YORK (A)

BATTING	AB	R	H	HR	RBI	Avg
Polonia	2	0	1	0	0	.500
O'Neill	19	2	9	0	2	.474
Jeter	22	6	9	2	2	.409
Martinez	22	3	8	0	2	.364
Brosius	13	2	4	1	3	.308
Sojo	7	0	2	0	2	.286
Vizcaino	17	0	4	0	1	.235
Posada	18	2	4	0	1	.222
Justice	19	1	3	0	3	.158
Williams	18	2	2	1	1	.111
Knoblauch	10	1	1	0	1	.100
Hill	3	0	0	0	0	.000
Canseco	1	0	0	0	0	.000
Bellinger	0	0	0	0	0	—
Others	8	0	0	0	0	.000
Totals	179	19	47	4	18	.263

PITCHING	G	IP	H	BB	SO	ERA
Clemens	1	8	2	0	9	0.00
Stanton	4	4⅓	0	0	7	0.00
Cone	1	⅓	0	0	0	0.00
Pettitte	2	13⅔	16	4	9	1.98
Rivera	4	6	4	1	7	3.00
Neagle	1	4⅔	4	2	3	3.86
Hernandez	1	7⅓	9	3	12	4.91
Nelson	3	2⅔	5	1	1	10.13
Totals	5	47	40	11	48	2.68

2000 Individual Leaders

National League Batting

BATTING AVERAGE

Todd Helton, Col	.372
Moises Alou, Hou	.355
Vladimir Guerrero, Mtl	.345
Jeffrey Hammonds, Col	.335
Jeff Kent, SF	.334
Luis Castillo, Fla	.334
Jose Vidro, Mtl	.330
Jeff Cirillo, Col	.326
Gary Sheffield, LA	.325
Edgardo Alfonzo, NY	.324

HITS

Todd Helton, Col	216
Jose Vidro, Mtl	200
Andruw Jones, Atl	199
Vladimir Guerrero, Mtl	197
Jeff Kent, SF	196
Jeff Cirillo, Col	195
Sammy Sosa, Chi	193
Luis Gonzalez, Ariz	192
Neifi Perez, Col	187
Jason Kendall, Pitt	185

DOUBLES

Todd Helton, Col	59
Jeff Cirillo, Col	53
Jose Vidro, Mtl	51
Luis Gonzalez, Ariz	47
Shawn Green, LA	44

TRIPLES

Tony Womack, Ariz	14
Neifi Perez, Col	11
Vladimir Guerrero, Mtl	11
Bobby Abreu, Phil	10
Tom Goodwin, LA	9
Ron Belliard, Mil	9

HOME RUNS

Sammy Sosa, Chi	50
Barry Bonds, SF	49
Jeff Bagwell, Hou	47
Richard Hidalgo, Hou	44
Vladimir Guerrero, Mtl	44
Gary Sheffield, LA	43
Todd Helton, Col	42
Jim Edmonds, StL	42
Ken Griffey, Cin	40
Mike Piazza, NY	38

RUNS SCORED

Jeff Bagwell, Hou	152
Todd Helton, Col	138
Barry Bonds, SF	129
Jim Edmonds, StL	129
Andruw Jones, Atl	122
Richard Hidalgo, Hou	118
Chipper Jones, Atl	118
Jeff Kent, SF	114
Jason Kendall, Pitt	112
Brian Giles, Pitt	111

TOTAL BASES

Todd Helton, Col	405
Sammy Sosa, Chi	383
Vladimir Guerrero, Mtl	379
Jeff Bagwell, Hou	363
Richard Hidalgo, Hou	355
Andruw Jones, Atl	355

STOLEN BASES

Luis Castillo, Fla	62
Tom Goodwin, LA	55
Eric Young, Chi	54
Tony Womack, Ariz	45
Rafael Furcal, Atl	40

RUNS BATTED IN

Todd Helton, Col	147
Sammy Sosa, Chi	138
Jeff Bagwell, Hou	132
Jeff Kent, SF	125
Vladimir Guerrero, Mtl	123
Brian Giles, Pitt	123
Richard Hidalgo, Hou	122
Preston Wilson, Fla	121
Ken Griffey, Cinn	118
Jeff Cirillo, Col	115

SLUGGING PERCENTAGE

Todd Helton, Col	.698
Barry Bonds, SF	.688
Vladimir Guerrero, Mtl	.664
Gary Sheffield, LA	.643
Richard Hidalgo, Hou	.636

ON-BASE PERCENTAGE

Todd Helton, Col	.463
Barry Bonds, SF	.440
Gary Sheffield, LA	.438
Brian Giles, Pitt	.432
Edgardo Alfonzo, NY	.425

BASES ON BALLS

Barry Bonds, SF	117
Brian Giles, Pitt	114
Jeff Bagwell, Hou	107
Todd Helton, Col	103
Jim Edmonds, StL	103

National League Pitching

EARNED RUN AVERAGE

Kevin Brown, LA	2.58
Randy Johnson, Ariz	2.64
Jeff D'Amico, Mil	2.66
Greg Maddux, Atl	3.00
Mike Hampton, NY	3.14
Al Leiter, NY	3.20
Chan Ho Park, LA	3.27
Tom Glavine, Atl	3.40
Rick Ankiel, StL	3.50
Robert Person, Phil	3.63

SAVES

Antonio Alfonseca, Fla	45
Trevor Hoffman, SD	43
Robb Nen, SF	41
Armando Benitez, NY	41
Danny Graves, Cinn	30
Dave Veres, StL	29
Rick Aguilera, Chi	29
Jeff Shaw, LA	27
Jose Jimenez, Col	24
John Rocker, Atl	24

WINS

Tom Glavine, Atl	21
Darryl Kile, StL	20
Randy Johnson, Ariz	19
Greg Maddux, Atl	19
Chan Ho Park, LA	18
Scott Elarton, Hou	17
Livan Hernandez, SF	17
Al Leiter, NY	16
Garrett Stephenson, StL	16
Mike Hampton, NY	15

GAMES PITCHED

Steve Kline, Mtl	83
Scott Sullivan, Cin	79
Mike Myers, Col	78
Turk Wendell, NY	77
Armando Benitez, NY	76
Felix Rodriguez, SF	76

INNINGS PITCHED

Jon Lieber, Chi	251
Greg Maddux, Atl	249½
Randy Johnson, Ariz	248⅔
Tom Glavine, Atl	241
Livan Hernandez, SF	240

STRIKEOUTS

Randy Johnson, Ariz	347
Chan Ho Park, LA	217
Kevin Brown, LA	216
Ryan Dempster, Fla	209
Al Leiter, NY	200
Javier Vazquez, Mtl	196
Rick Ankiel, StL	194
Pedro Astacio, Col	193
Jon Lieber, Chi	192
Darryl Kile, StL	192

COMPLETE GAMES

Curt Schilling, Ariz	8
Randy Johnson, Ariz	8
Greg Maddux, Atl	6
Jon Lieber, Chi	6
Three tied with five.	

SHUTOUTS

Greg Maddux, Atl	3
Randy Johnson, Ariz	3
Six tied with two.	

American League Batting

BATTING AVERAGE

Nomar Garciaparra, Bos ... .372
Darin Erstad, Ana .... .355
Manny Ramirez, Clev......... .351
Carlos Delgado, Tor .... .344
Derek Jeter, NY .... .339
David Segui, Clev.............. .334
Jason Giambi, Oak............ .333
Mike Sweeney, KC............. .333
Frank Thomas, Chi............ .328
Johnny Damon, KC............ .327

HITS

Darin Erstad, Ana 240
Johnny Damon, KC..............214
Mike Sweeney, KC...............206
Derek Jeter, NY 201
Nomar Garciaparra, Bos 197
Carlos Delgado, Tor 196
Jermaine Dye, KC................193
David Segui, Clev................192
Frank Thomas, Chi...............191
Roberto Alomar, Clev 189

DOUBLES

Carlos Delgado, Tor 57
Nomar Garciaparra, Bos 51
Deivi Cruz, Det......................46
John Olerud, Sea...................45
Bobby Higginson, Det 44
Matt Lawton, Minn 44
Frank Thomas, Chi................44
Three tied with 41.

TRIPLES

Cristian Guzman, Minn 20
Adam Kennedy, Ana 11
Al Martin, Sea 10
Johnny Damon, KC.................10
Ray Durham, Chi 9

HOME RUNS

Troy Glaus, Ana.....................47
Frank Thomas, Chi.................43
Jason Giambi, Oak.................43
Carlos Delgado, Tor 41
David Justice, NY 41
Tony Batista, Tor....................41
Alex Rodriguez, Sea..............41
Rafael Palmeiro, Tex..............39
Manny Ramirez, Clev.............38
Edgar Martinez, Sea...............37

RUNS SCORED

Johnny Damon, KC.................136
Alex Rodriguez, Sea............134
Ray Durham, Chi 121
Darin Erstad, Ana 121
Troy Glaus, Ana 120
Derek Jeter, NY 119
Frank Thomas, Chi................115
Carlos Delgado, Tor 115
Roberto Alomar, Clev 111
Tim Salmon, Ana..................108

TOTAL BASES

Carlos Delgado, Tor 378
Darin Erstad, Ana 366
Frank Thomas, Chi................364
Troy Glaus, Ana 340
Jermaine Dye, KC................337

STOLEN BASES

Johnny Damon, KC................46
Roberto Alomar, Clev 39
Delino DeShields, Balt...........37
Rickey Henderson, Sea 36
Kenny Lofton, Clev 30
Mark McLemore, Sea 30

RUNS BATTED IN

Edgar Martinez, Sea............145
Mike Sweeney, KC...............144
Frank Thomas, Chi...............143
Jason Giambi, Oak...............137
Carlos Delgado, Tor 137
Alex Rodriguez, Sea............132
Magglio Ordonez, Chi 126
Manny Ramirez, Clev...........122
Bernie Williams, NY 121
Rafael Palmeiro, Tex............120

SLUGGING PERCENTAGE

Manny Ramirez, Clev.......... .697
Carlos Delgado, Tor .... .664
Jason Giambi, Oak.............. .647
Frank Thomas, Chi.............. .625
Alex Rodriguez, Sea........... .606

ON-BASE PERCENTAGE

Jason Giambi, Oak.............. .476
Carlos Delgado, Tor .... .470
Manny Ramirez, Clev.......... .457
Frank Thomas, Chi.............. .436
Nomar Garciaparra, Bos ..... .434

BASES ON BALLS

Jason Giambi, Oak...............137
Carlos Delgado, Tor 123
Jim Thome, Clev 118
Frank Thomas, Chi...............112
Troy Glaus, Ana 112

American League Pitching

EARNED RUN AVERAGE

Pedro Martinez, Bos 1.74
Roger Clemens, NY 3.70
Mike Mussina, Balt..............3.79
Mike Sirotka, Chi.................3.79
Bartolo Colon, Clev.............3.88
David Wells, NY 4.11
Gil Heredia, Oak 4.12
Albie Lopez, TB 4.13
Tim Hudson, Oak.................4.14
Chuck Finley, Clev..............4.17

SAVES

Todd Jones, Det 42
Derek Lowe, Bos 42
Kazuhiro Sasaki, Sea.............37
Mariano Rivera, NY 36
John Wetteland, Tex..............34
Keith Foulke, Clev.................34
Jason Isringhausen, Oak.......33
Billy Koch, Tor.......................33
Roberto Hernandez, TB.........32
Troy Percival, Ana.................32

WINS

David Wells, Tor.....................20
Tim Hudson, Oak...................20
Andy Pettitte, NY....................19
Pedro Martinez, Bos 18
Aaron Sele, Sea.....................17
Chuck Finley, Clev.................16
Dave Burba, Clev 16
Rick Helling, Tex....................16
Denny Neagle, NY 15
Bartolo Colon, Clev................15

GAMES PITCHED

Kelly Wunsch, Chi..................83
Mike Venafro, Tex 77
Mark Guthrie, Minn 76
Bob Wells, Minn.....................76
Mike Trombley, Balt...............75

INNINGS PITCHED

Mike Mussina, Balt 237⅔
David Wells, Tor 229⅔
Kenny Rogers, Tex............227⅓
Brad Radke, Minn 226⅔
Sidney Ponson, Balt............222

STRIKEOUTS

Pedro Martinez, Bos 284
Bartolo Colon, Clev..............212
Mike Mussina, Balt...............210
Chuck Finley, Clev...............189
Roger Clemens, NY 188
Hideo Nomo, Det 181
Dave Burba, Clev 180
Tim Hudson, Oak.................169
David Wells, Tor 166
Eric Milton, Minn 160

COMPLETE GAMES

David Wells, Tor......................9
Pedro Martinez, Bos 7
Mike Mussina, Balt..................6
Sidney Ponson, Balt................6
Brad Radke, Minn....................4
Albie Lopez, TB 4

SHUTOUTS

Pedro Martinez, Bos 4
Aaron Sele, Sea......................2
Tim Hudson, Oak 2
Seven tied with 1.

2000 Team Statistics

National League

TEAM BATTING	BA	AB	R	H	TB	2B	3B	HR	RBI	SB	BB	SO
Colorado	.294	5660	968	1664	2573	320	53	161	905	131	601	907
San Francisco	.278	5519	925	1535	2605	304	44	226	889	79	709	1032
Houston	.278	5570	938	1547	2655	289	36	249	900	114	673	1129
Cincinnati	.274	5635	825	1545	2519	302	36	200	794	99	559	995
Atlanta	.271	5489	810	1490	2353	274	26	179	758	148	595	1010
St. Louis	.270	5478	887	1481	2495	259	25	235	841	87	675	1253
Pittsburgh	.267	5643	793	1506	2392	320	31	168	749	86	564	1032
Montreal	.266	5535	738	1475	2389	310	35	178	705	58	476	1048
Arizona	.265	5527	792	1466	2373	282	44	179	756	97	535	975
New York	.263	5486	807	1445	2360	281	20	198	761	66	675	1037
Florida	.262	5509	731	1441	2253	274	29	160	691	168	540	1184
Los Angeles	.257	5481	798	1408	2362	265	28	211	756	95	668	1083
Chicago	.256	5577	764	1426	2293	272	23	183	722	93	632	1120
San Diego	.254	5560	752	1413	2237	279	37	157	714	131	602	1177
Philadelphia	.251	5511	708	1386	2202	304	40	144	668	102	611	1117
Milwaukee	.246	5563	740	1366	2244	297	25	177	708	72	620	1245

TEAM PITCHING	ERA	W	L	Sho	CG	SV	Inn	H	R	ER	BB	SO
Atlanta	4.05	95	67	9	13	53	1440⅓	1428	714	648	484	1093
Los Angeles	4.10	86	76	11	9	36	1445	1379	729	659	600	1154
New York	4.16	94	68	10	8	49	1450	1398	738	670	574	1164
San Francisco	4.21	97	65	15	9	47	1444⅓	1452	747	675	623	1076
Cincinnati	4.33	85	77	7	8	42	1456⅓	1446	765	700	659	1015
Arizona	4.35	85	77	8	16	38	1443⅔	1441	754	698	500	1220
St. Louis	4.38	95	67	7	10	37	1433⅔	1403	771	698	606	1100
San Diego	4.52	76	86	5	5	46	1459⅓	1443	815	733	649	1071
Florida	4.59	79	82	4	5	48	1429⅔	1477	797	729	650	1051
Milwaukee	4.63	73	89	7	2	29	1466⅓	1501	826	755	728	967
Philadelphia	4.77	65	97	6	8	34	1438⅔	1458	830	763	640	1123
Pittsburgh	4.94	69	93	7	5	27	1449	1554	888	795	711	1070
Montreal	5.13	67	95	7	4	39	1424⅔	1575	902	812	579	1011
Chicago	5.25	65	97	5	10	39	1454⅔	1505	904	849	658	1143
Colorado	5.26	82	80	2	7	33	1430	1568	897	835	588	1001
Houston	5.42	72	90	2	8	30	1437⅔	1596	944	865	598	1064

American League

TEAM BATTING	BA	AB	R	H	TB	2B	3B	HR	RBI	SB	BB	SO
Kansas City	.288	5709	879	1644	2429	281	27	150	831	121	511	840
Cleveland	.288	5683	950	1639	2672	310	30	221	889	113	685	1057
Chicago	.286	5646	978	1615	2654	325	33	216	926	119	591	960
Texas	.283	5648	848	1601	2520	330	35	173	806	69	580	922
Anaheim	.280	5628	864	1574	2659	309	34	236	837	93	608	1024
New York	.277	5556	871	1541	2500	294	25	205	833	99	631	1007
Toronto	.275	5677	861	1562	2664	328	21	244	826	89	526	1026
Detroit	.275	5644	823	1553	2473	307	41	177	785	83	562	982
Baltimore	.272	5549	794	1508	2414	310	22	184	750	126	558	900
Oakland	.270	5560	947	1501	2545	281	23	239	908	40	750	1159
Minnesota	.270	5615	748	1516	2287	325	49	116	711	90	556	1021
Seattle	.269	5497	907	1481	2427	300	26	198	869	122	775	1073
Boston	.267	5630	792	1503	2384	316	32	167	755	43	611	1019
Tampa Bay	.257	5505	733	1414	2197	253	22	162	692	90	559	1022

TEAM PITCHING	ERA	W	L	Sho	CG	SV	Inn	H	R	ER	BB	SO
Boston	4.23	85	77	12	7	46	1452⅔	1433	745	683	499	1121
Seattle	4.49	91	71	10	4	44	1441⅔	1442	780	720	634	998
Oakland	4.58	91	70	11	7	43	1435⅓	1535	813	730	615	963
Chicago	4.66	95	67	7	5	43	1450⅓	1509	839	751	614	1037
Detroit	4.71	79	83	6	6	44	1443⅓	1583	827	755	496	978
New York	4.76	87	74	6	9	40	1424⅓	1458	814	753	577	1040
Cleveland	4.84	90	72	5	6	34	1442⅓	1511	816	775	666	1213
Tampa Bay	4.86	69	92	8	10	38	1431⅓	1553	842	773	533	955
Anaheim	5.00	82	80	3	5	46	1448	1534	869	805	662	846
Minnesota	5.14	69	93	4	6	35	1432⅔	1634	880	819	516	1042
Toronto	5.14	83	79	4	15	37	1437⅓	1615	908	821	560	978
Baltimore	5.37	74	88	6	14	33	1433⅓	1547	913	855	665	1017
Kansas City	5.48	77	85	6	10	29	1439⅓	1585	930	876	693	927
Texas	5.52	71	91	4	3	39	1429	1683	974	876	661	918

Arizona Diamondbacks

BATTING

BATTING	BA	G	AB	R	H	TB	2B	3B	HR	RBI	SB	BB	SO
Craig Counsell	.316	67	152	23	48	64	8	1	2	11	3	20	18
Greg Colbrunn	.313	116	329	48	103	172	22	1	15	57	0	43	45
Luis Gonzalez	.311	162	618	106	192	336	47	2	31	114	2	78	85
Danny Bautista	.285	131	351	54	100	167	20	7	11	59	6	25	50
Steve Finley	.280	152	539	100	151	293	27	5	35	96	12	65	87
Matt Williams	.275	96	371	43	102	160	18	2	12	47	1	20	51
Damian Miller	.275	100	324	43	89	143	24	0	10	44	2	36	74
Tony Womack	.271	146	617	95	167	237	21	14	7	57	45	30	74
Jay Bell	.267	149	565	87	151	247	30	6	18	68	7	70	88
Erubial Durazo	.265	67	196	35	52	87	11	0	8	33	1	34	43
Kelly Stinnett	.217	76	240	22	52	83	7	0	8	33	0	19	56

PITCHING

PITCHING	ERA	W	L	G	GS	CG	SV	INN	H	R	ER	BB	SO
Randy Johnson	2.64	19	7	35	35	8	0	248⅔	202	89	73	76	347
Dan Plesac	3.15	5	1	62	0	0	0	40	34	21	14	26	45
Greg Swindell	3.20	2	6	64	0	0	1	76	71	29	27	20	64
Curt Schilling	3.81	11	12	29	29	8	0	210⅓	204	90	89	45	168
Brian Anderson	4.05	11	7	33	32	2	0	213⅓	226	101	96	39	104
Byung-Hyun Kim	4.46	6	6	61	1	0	14	70⅔	52	39	35	46	111
Matt Mantei	4.57	1	1	47	0	0	17	45⅓	31	24	23	35	53
Mike Morgan	4.87	5	5	60	4	0	5	101⅔	123	55	55	40	56
Todd Stottlemyre	4.91	9	6	18	18	0	0	95⅓	98	55	52	36	76
Russ Springer	5.08	2	4	52	0	0	0	62	63	36	35	34	59
Armando Reynoso	5.27	11	12	31	30	2	0	170⅔	179	102	100	52	89
Geraldo Guzman	5.37	5	4	13	10	0	0	60⅓	66	36	36	22	52

Atlanta Braves

BATTING

BATTING	BA	G	AB	R	H	TB	2B	3B	HR	RBI	SB	BB	SO
Chipper Jones	.311	156	579	118	180	328	38	1	36	111	14	95	64
Quilvio Veras	.309	84	298	56	92	122	15	0	5	37	25	51	50
Andruw Jones	.303	161	656	122	199	355	36	6	36	104	21	59	100
Andres Galarraga	.302	141	494	67	149	260	25	1	28	100	3	36	126
Rafael Furcal	.295	131	455	87	134	174	20	4	4	37	40	73	80
B.J. Surhoff	.291	147	539	69	157	239	36	2	14	68	10	41	58
Javy Lopez	.287	134	481	60	138	233	21	1	24	89	0	35	80
Wally Joyner	.281	119	224	24	63	90	12	0	5	32	0	31	31
Keith Lockhart	.265	113	275	32	73	97	12	3	2	32	4	29	31
Brian Jordan	.264	133	489	71	129	206	26	0	17	77	10	38	80
Walt Weiss	.260	80	192	29	50	60	6	2	0	18	1	26	32
Bobby Bonilla	.255	114	239	23	61	95	13	3	5	28	0	37	51
Reggie Sanders	.232	103	340	43	79	137	23	1	11	37	21	32	78
Paul Bako	.226	81	221	18	50	68	10	1	2	20	0	27	64

PITCHING

PITCHING	ERA	W	L	G	GS	CG	SV	INN	H	R	ER	BB	SO
John Rocker	2.89	1	2	59	0	0	24	53	42	25	17	48	77
Greg Maddux	3.00	19	9	35	35	6	0	249⅓	225	91	83	42	190
Tom Glavine	3.40	21	9	35	35	4	0	241	222	101	91	65	152
Mike Remlinger	3.47	5	3	71	0	0	12	72⅔	55	29	28	37	72
Kerry Ligtenberg	3.61	2	3	59	0	0	12	52⅓	43	21	21	24	51
Kevin Millwood	4.66	10	13	36	35	0	0	212⅔	213	115	110	62	168
John Burkett	4.89	10	6	31	22	0	0	134⅓	162	79	73	51	110
Andy Ashby	4.92	12	13	31	31	0	0	199½	216	124	109	61	106
Terry Mulholland	5.11	9	9	54	20	1	1	156⅔	198	96	89	41	78
Scott Kamieniecki	5.59	3	4	52	0	0	2	58	64	40	36	42	46

Chicago Cubs

BATTING

BATTING	BA	G	AB	R	H	TB	2B	3B	HR	RBI	SB	BB	SO
Sammy Sosa	.320	156	604	106	193	383	38	1	50	138	7	91	168
Rondell White	.311	94	357	59	111	176	26	0	13	61	5	33	79
Eric Young	.297	153	607	98	180	242	40	2	6	47	54	63	39
Mark Grace	.280	143	510	75	143	219	41	1	11	82	1	95	28
Joe Girardi	.278	106	363	47	101	136	15	1	6	40	1	32	61
Ricky Gutierrez	.276	125	449	73	124	180	19	2	11	56	8	66	58
Damon Buford	.251	150	495	64	124	193	18	3	15	48	4	47	118
Shane Andrews	.229	66	192	25	44	91	5	0	14	39	1	27	59
Jeff Reed	.214	90	229	26	49	71	10	0	4	25	0	44	68
Jose Nieves	.212	82	198	17	42	69	6	3	5	24	1	11	43
Willie Greene	.201	105	299	34	60	109	15	2	10	37	4	36	69

National League Team-by-Team Statistical Leaders *(Cont.)*

Chicago Cubs *(Cont.)*

PITCHING	ERA	W	L	G	GS	CG	SV	INN	H	R	ER	BB	SO
Tim Worrell	2.47	3	4	54	0	0	3	62	60	20	17	24	52
Todd Van Poppel	3.75	4	5	51	2	0	2	86⅓	80	38	36	48	77
Steve Rain	4.35	3	4	37	0	0	0	49⅔	46	25	24	27	54
Jon Lieber	4.41	12	11	35	35	6	0	251	248	130	123	54	192
Felix Heredia	4.76	7	3	74	0	0	2	58⅔	46	31	31	33	52
Kerry Wood	4.80	8	7	23	23	1	0	137	112	77	73	87	132
Rick Aguilera	4.91	1	2	54	0	0	29	47⅔	47	28	26	18	38
Kevin Tapani	5.01	8	12	30	30	2	0	195⅔	208	113	109	47	150
Jerry Spradlin	6.00	4	5	58	1	0	7	90	101	64	60	32	67
Daniel Garibay	6.03	2	8	30	8	0	0	74⅔	88	54	50	39	46
Kyle Farnsworth	6.43	2	9	46	5	0	1	77	90	58	55	50	74
Ruben Quevedo	7.47	3	10	21	15	1	0	88	96	81	73	54	65

Cincinnati Reds

BATTING	BA	G	AB	R	H	TB	2B	3B	HR	RBI	SB	BB	SO
Chris Stynes	.334	119	380	71	127	189	24	1	12	40	5	32	54
Alex Ochoa	.316	118	244	50	77	143	21	3	13	58	8	24	27
Sean Casey	.315	133	480	69	151	248	33	2	20	85	1	52	80
Barry Larkin	.313	102	396	71	124	193	26	5	11	41	14	48	31
Dmitri Young	.303	152	548	68	166	269	37	6	18	88	0	36	80
Aaron Boone	.285	84	291	44	83	137	18	0	12	43	6	24	52
Ken Griffey Jr	.271	145	520	100	141	289	22	3	40	118	6	94	117
Eddie Taubensee	.267	81	266	29	71	101	12	0	6	24	0	21	44
Brian L. Hunter	.267	104	240	47	64	74	5	1	1	14	20	27	40
Michael Tucker	.267	148	270	55	72	138	13	4	15	36	13	44	64
Benito Santiago	.262	89	252	22	66	103	11	1	8	45	2	19	45
Pokey Reese	.255	135	518	76	132	200	20	6	12	46	29	45	86
Juan Castro	.241	82	224	20	54	82	12	2	4	23	0	14	33

PITCHING	ERA	W	L	G	GS	CG	SV	INN	H	R	ER	BB	SO
Danny Graves	2.56	10	5	66	0	0	30	91⅓	81	31	26	42	53
Scott Williamson	3.29	5	8	48	10	0	6	112	92	45	41	75	136
Scott Sullivan	3.47	3	6	79	0	0	3	106⅓	87	44	41	38	96
Osvaldo Fernandez	3.62	4	3	15	14	1	0	79⅔	69	33	32	31	36
Elmer Dessens	4.28	11	5	40	16	1	1	147⅓	170	73	70	43	85
Dennys Reyes	4.53	2	1	62	0	0	0	43⅔	43	31	22	29	36
Pete Harnisch	4.74	8	6	22	22	2	0	131	133	76	69	46	71
Steve Parris	4.81	12	17	33	33	0	0	192⅔	227	109	103	71	117
Rob Bell	5.00	7	8	26	26	1	0	140⅓	130	84	78	73	112
Ron Villone	5.43	10	10	35	23	2	0	141	154	95	85	78	77

Colorado Rockies

BATTING	BA	G	AB	R	H	TB	2B	3B	HR	RBI	SB	BB	SO
Todd Helton	.372	160	580	138	216	405	59	2	42	147	5	103	61
Jeffrey Hammonds	.335	122	454	94	152	240	24	2	20	106	14	44	83
Jeff Cirillo	.326	157	598	111	195	285	53	2	11	115	3	67	72
Ben Petrick	.322	52	146	32	47	68	10	1	3	20	1	20	33
Todd Walker	.316	57	171	28	54	93	10	4	7	36	4	20	19
Juan Pierre	.310	51	200	26	62	64	2	0	0	20	7	13	15
Larry Walker	.309	87	314	64	97	159	21	7	9	51	5	46	40
Brent Mayne	.301	117	335	36	101	140	21	0	6	64	1	47	48
Neifi Perez	.287	162	651	92	187	278	39	11	10	71	3	30	63
Todd Hollandsworth	.269	137	428	81	115	192	20	0	19	47	18	41	99
Terry Shumpert	.259	115	263	52	68	120	11	7	9	40	8	28	40

PITCHING	ERA	W	L	G	GS	CG	SV	INN	H	R	ER	BB	SO
Mike Myers	1.99	0	1	78	0	0	1	45⅓	24	10	10	24	41
Gabe White	2.36	11	2	67	0	0	5	84	64	21	20	14	82
Jose Jimenez	3.18	5	2	72	0	0	24	70⅔	63	27	25	28	44
Julian Tavarez	4.43	11	5	51	12	1	1	120	124	68	59	53	62
Brian Bohanan	4.68	12	10	34	26	2	0	177	181	101	92	79	98
Mike DeJean	4.89	4	4	54	0	0	0	53⅓	54	31	29	30	34
Pedro Astacio	5.27	12	9	32	32	3	0	196⅓	217	119	115	77	193
Brian Rose	5.79	7	10	27	24	0	0	116⅔	130	78	75	51	64
Masato Yoshii	5.86	6	15	29	29	0	0	167⅓	201	112	109	53	88
Kevin Jarvis	5.95	3	4	24	19	0	0	115	138	83	76	33	60
Scott Karl	7.68	2	3	17	9	0	0	65⅔	95	56	56	33	29

Florida Marlins

BATTING	BA	G	AB	R	H	TB	2B	3B	HR	RBI	SB	BB	SO
Luis Castillo	.334	136	539	101	180	209	17	3	2	17	62	78	86
Cliff Floyd	.300	121	420	75	126	222	30	0	22	91	24	50	82
Mark Kotsay	.298	152	530	87	158	235	31	5	12	57	19	42	46
Derrek Lee	.281	158	477	70	134	242	18	3	28	70	0	63	123
Mike Lowell	.270	140	508	73	137	241	38	0	22	91	4	54	75
Preston Wilson	.264	161	605	94	160	294	35	3	31	121	36	55	187
Kevin Millar	.259	123	259	36	67	129	14	3	14	42	0	36	47
Henry Rodriguez	.256	112	367	47	94	177	21	1	20	61	1	36	99
Dave Berg	.252	82	210	23	53	72	14	1	1	21	3	25	46
Mike Redmond	.252	87	210	17	53	63	8	1	0	15	0	13	19
Mark Smith	.245	104	192	22	47	72	8	1	5	27	2	17	54
Andy Fox	.232	100	250	29	58	82	8	2	4	20	10	22	53
Alex Gonzalez	.200	109	385	35	77	123	17	4	7	42	7	13	77

PITCHING	ERA	W	L	G	GS	CG	SV	INN	H	R	ER	BB	SO
Chuck Smith	3.23	6	6	19	19	1	0	122⅔	111	53	44	54	118
Ryan Dempster	3.66	14	10	33	33	2	0	226⅓	210	102	92	97	209
Vic Darensbourg	4.06	5	3	56	0	0	0	62	61	32	28	28	59
Antonio Alfonseca	4.24	5	6	68	0	0	45	70	82	35	33	24	47
Manny Aybar	4.31	2	2	54	0	0	0	79½	74	42	38	35	45
Braden Looper	4.41	5	1	73	0	0	2	67⅓	71	41	33	36	29
Ricky Bones	4.54	2	3	56	0	0	0	77⅓	95	43	39	27	59
A.J. Burnett	4.79	3	7	13	13	0	0	82⅔	80	46	44	44	57
Brad Penny	4.81	8	7	23	22	0	0	119⅔	120	70	64	60	80
Reid Cornelius	4.82	4	10	22	21	0	0	125	135	74	67	50	50
Jesus Sanchez	5.34	9	12	32	32	2	0	182	197	118	108	76	123

Houston Astros

BATTING	BA	G	AB	R	H	TB	2B	3B	HR	RBI	SB	BB	SO
Moises Alou	.355	126	454	82	161	283	28	2	30	114	3	52	45
Richard Hidalgo	.314	153	558	118	175	355	42	3	44	122	13	56	110
Jeff Bagwell	.310	159	590	152	183	363	37	1	47	132	9	107	116
Ken Caminiti	.303	59	208	42	63	121	13	0	15	45	3	42	37
Bill Spiers	.301	124	355	41	107	139	17	3	3	43	7	49	38
Mitch Melusky	.300	117	337	47	101	164	21	0	14	69	1	55	74
Lance Berkman	.297	114	353	76	105	198	28	1	21	67	6	56	73
Julio Lugo	.283	116	420	78	119	181	22	5	10	40	22	37	93
Roger Cedeno	.282	74	259	54	73	103	2	5	6	26	25	43	47
Tony Eusabio	.280	74	218	24	61	100	18	0	7	33	0	25	45
Craig Biggio	.268	101	377	67	101	148	13	5	8	35	12	61	73
Chris Truby	.260	78	258	28	67	123	15	4	11	59	2	10	56
Daryle Ward	.258	119	264	36	68	142	10	2	20	47	0	15	61

PITCHING	ERA	W	L	G	GS	CG	SV	INN	H	R	ER	BB	SO
Joe Slusarski	4.21	2	7	54	0	0	3	77	80	36	36	22	54
Scott Elarton	4.81	17	7	30	30	2	0	192⅔	198	117	103	84	131
Marc Valdes	5.08	5	5	53	0	0	2	56⅔	69	41	32	25	35
Wade Miller	5.14	6	6	16	16	2	0	105	104	66	60	42	89
Shane Reynolds	5.22	7	8	22	22	0	0	131	150	86	76	45	93
Chris Holt	5.35	8	16	34	32	3	0	207	247	131	123	75	136
Octavio Dotel	5.40	3	7	50	16	0	16	125	127	80	75	61	142
Jose Cabrera	5.92	2	3	52	0	0	2	59½	74	40	39	17	41
Jose Lima	6.65	7	16	33	33	0	0	196½	251	152	145	68	124

Los Angeles Dodgers

BATTING	BA	G	AB	R	H	TB	2B	3B	HR	RBI	SB	BB	SO
Gary Sheffield	.325	141	501	105	163	322	24	3	43	109	4	101	71
Adrian Beltre	.290	138	510	71	148	242	30	2	20	85	12	56	80
Dave Hansen	.289	102	121	18	35	69	6	2	8	26	0	26	32
Todd Hundley	.284	90	299	49	85	173	16	0	24	70	0	45	69
Mark Grudzielanek	.279	148	617	101	172	240	35	6	7	49	12	45	81
Shawn Green	.269	162	610	98	164	288	44	4	24	99	24	90	121
Chad Kreuter	.264	80	212	32	56	87	13	0	6	28	1	54	48
Tom Goodwin	.263	147	528	94	139	186	11	9	6	58	55	68	117
Bruce Aven	.250	81	168	20	42	74	11	0	7	29	2	8	39
Eric Karros	.250	155	584	84	146	268	29	0	31	106	4	63	122
Alex Cora	.238	109	353	39	84	126	18	6	4	32	4	26	53
Kevin Elster	.227	80	220	29	50	100	8	0	14	32	0	38	52

National League Team-by-Team Statistical Leaders *(Cont.)*

Los Angeles Dodgers *(Cont.)*

PITCHING	ERA	W	L	G	GS	CG	SV	INN	H	R	ER	BB	SO
Kevin Brown	2.58	13	6	33	33	5	0	230	181	76	66	47	216
Matt Herges	3.17	11	3	59	4	0	1	110⅔	100	43	39	40	75
Mike Fetters	3.24	6	2	51	0	0	5	50	35	18	18	25	40
Chan Ho Park	3.27	18	10	34	34	3	0	226	173	92	82	124	217
Terry Adams	3.52	6	9	66	0	0	2	84⅓	80	42	33	39	56
Antonio Osuna	3.74	3	6	46	0	0	0	67⅓	57	30	28	35	70
Darren Dreifort	4.16	12	9	32	32	1	0	192⅔	175	105	89	87	164
Jeff Shaw	4.24	3	4	60	0	0	27	57⅓	61	29	27	16	39
Eric Gagne	5.15	4	6	20	19	0	0	101⅓	106	62	58	60	79
Carlos Perez	5.56	5	8	30	22	0	0	144	192	95	89	33	64
Ismael Valdez	5.64	2	7	21	20	0	0	107	124	69	67	40	74

Milwaukee Brewers

BATTING	BA	G	AB	R	H	TB	2B	3B	HR	RBI	SB	BB	SO
Geoff Jenkins	.303	135	512	100	155	301	36	4	34	94	11	33	135
Mark Loretta	.281	91	352	49	99	143	21	1	7	40	0	37	38
Richie Sexson	.272	148	537	89	146	268	30	1	30	91	2	59	159
Luis Lopez	.264	78	201	24	53	85	14	0	6	27	1	9	35
Ron Belliard	.263	152	571	83	150	222	30	9	8	54	7	82	84
Charlie Hayes	.251	121	370	46	93	137	17	0	9	46	1	57	84
Tyler Houston	.250	101	284	30	71	140	15	0	18	43	2	17	72
Raul Casanova	.247	86	231	20	57	94	13	3	6	36	1	26	48
Jose Hernandez	.244	124	446	51	109	166	22	1	11	59	3	41	125
Marquis Grissom	.244	146	595	67	145	209	18	2	14	62	20	39	99
Henry Blanco	.236	93	284	29	67	112	24	0	7	31	0	36	60
James Mouton	.233	87	159	28	37	52	7	1	2	17	13	30	43
Jeromy Burnitz	.232	161	564	91	131	257	29	2	31	98	6	99	121

PITCHING	ERA	W	L	G	GS	CG	SV	INN	H	R	ER	BB	SO
Curtis Leskanic	2.56	9	3	73	0	0	12	77⅓	58	23	22	51	75
Jeff D'Amico	2.66	12	7	23	23	1	0	162⅓	143	55	48	46	101
Dave Weathers	3.07	3	5	69	0	0	1	76⅓	73	29	26	32	50
Juan Acevedo	3.81	3	7	62	0	0	0	82⅔	77	38	35	31	51
Jamey Wright	4.10	7	9	26	25	0	0	164⅔	157	81	75	88	96
Valerio de los Santos	5.13	2	3	66	2	0	0	73⅔	72	43	42	33	70
Paul Rigdon	5.15	5	5	17	16	0	0	87⅓	89	52	50	35	63
Jimmy Haynes	5.33	12	13	33	33	0	0	199⅓	228	128	118	100	88
Everett Stull	5.82	2	3	20	4	0	0	43⅓	41	30	28	30	33
John Snyder	6.17	3	10	23	23	0	0	127	147	95	87	77	69

Montreal Expos

BATTING	BA	G	AB	R	H	TB	2B	3B	HR	RBI	SB	BB	SO
Vladimir Guerrero	.345	154	571	101	197	379	28	11	44	123	9	58	74
Jose Vidro	.330	153	606	101	200	327	51	2	24	97	5	49	69
Mike Mordecai	.284	86	169	20	48	76	16	0	4	16	2	12	34
Geoff Blum	.283	124	343	40	97	154	20	2	11	45	1	26	60
Fernando Seguignol	.278	76	162	22	45	83	8	0	10	22	0	9	46
Wilton Guerrero	.267	127	288	30	77	94	7	2	2	23	8	19	41
Lee Stevens	.265	123	449	60	119	216	27	2	22	75	0	48	105
Andy Tracy	.260	83	192	29	50	93	8	1	11	32	1	22	61
Terry Jones	.250	108	168	30	42	54	8	2	0	13	7	10	32
Peter Bergeron	.245	148	518	80	127	181	25	7	5	31	11	58	100
Orlando Cabrera	.237	125	422	47	100	166	25	1	13	55	4	25	28
Michael Barrett	.214	89	271	28	58	78	15	1	1	22	0	23	35

PITCHING	ERA	W	L	G	GS	CG	SV	INN	H	R	ER	BB	SO
Scott Strickland	3.00	4	3	49	0	0	9	48	38	18	16	16	48
Carl Pavano	3.06	8	4	15	15	0	0	97	89	40	33	34	64
Steve Kline	3.50	1	5	83	0	0	14	82⅓	88	36	32	27	64
Anthony Telford	3.79	5	4	64	0	0	3	78⅓	76	38	33	23	68
Javier Vasquez	4.05	11	9	33	33	2	0	217⅔	247	104	98	61	196
Tony Armas Jr	4.36	7	9	17	17	0	0	95	74	49	46	50	59
Dustin Hermanson	4.77	12	14	38	30	2	4	198	226	128	105	77	94
Scott Downs	5.29	4	3	19	19	0	0	97	122	62	57	40	63
Felipe Lira	5.40	5	8	53	7	0	0	101⅔	129	71	61	36	51
Julio Santana	5.67	1	5	36	4	0	0	66⅔	69	45	42	33	58
Mike Johnson	6.39	5	6	41	13	0	0	101⅓	107	73	72	53	70
Mike Thurman	6.42	4	9	17	17	0	0	88⅓	112	69	63	46	52

New York Mets

BATTING	BA	G	AB	R	H	TB	2B	3B	HR	RBI	SB	BB	SO
Edgardo Alfonzo	.324	150	544	109	176	295	40	2	25	94	3	95	70
Mike Piazza	.324	136	482	90	156	296	26	0	38	113	4	58	69
Jay Payton	.291	149	488	63	142	218	23	1	17	62	5	30	60
Benny Agbayani	.289	119	350	59	101	168	19	1	15	60	5	54	68
Mike Bordick	.285	156	583	88	166	258	30	1	20	80	9	49	99
Todd Pratt	.275	80	160	33	44	74	6	0	8	25	0	22	31
Todd Zeile	.268	153	544	67	146	254	36	3	22	79	3	74	85
Derek Bell	.266	144	546	87	145	232	31	1	18	69	8	65	125
Bubba Trammell	.265	102	245	28	65	112	13	2	10	45	4	29	49
Lenny Harris	.260	112	223	31	58	85	7	4	4	26	13	20	22
Matt Franco	.239	101	134	9	32	42	4	0	2	14	0	21	22
Robin Ventura	.232	141	469	61	109	206	23	1	24	84	3	75	91
Joe McEwing	.222	87	153	20	34	56	14	1	2	19	3	5	29
Kurt Abbott	.217	79	157	22	34	61	7	1	6	12	1	14	51

PITCHING	ERA	W	L	G	GS	CG	SV	INN	H	R	ER	BB	SO
Armando Benitez	2.61	4	4	76	0	0	41	76	39	24	22	38	106
Mike Hampton	3.14	15	10	33	33	3	0	217⅔	194	89	76	99	151
Al Leiter	3.20	16	8	31	31	2	0	208	176	84	74	76	200
John Franco	3.40	5	4	62	0	0	4	55⅔	46	24	21	26	56
Rick White	3.52	5	9	66	0	0	3	99⅔	83	44	39	38	67
Turk Wendell	3.59	8	6	77	0	0	1	82⅔	60	36	33	41	73
Glendon Rusch	4.01	11	11	31	30	2	0	190¾	196	91	85	44	157
Rick Reed	4.11	11	5	30	30	0	0	184	192	90	84	34	121
Bobby J. Jones	5.06	11	6	27	27	1	0	154⅔	171	90	87	49	85
Dennis Cook	5.34	6	3	68	0	0	2	59	63	35	35	31	53
Pat Mahomes	5.46	5	3	53	5	0	0	94	96	63	57	66	76

Philadelphia Phillies

BATTING	BA	G	AB	R	H	TB	2B	3B	HR	RBI	SB	BB	SO
Bobby Abreu	.316	154	576	103	182	319	42	10	25	79	28	100	116
Scott Rolen	.298	128	483	88	144	266	32	6	26	89	8	51	99
Mike Lieberthal	.278	108	389	55	108	183	30	0	15	71	2	40	53
Doug Glanville	.275	154	637	89	175	238	27	6	8	52	31	31	76
Pat Burrell	.260	111	408	57	106	189	27	1	18	79	0	63	139
Tom Prince	.238	46	122	14	29	44	9	0	2	16	1	13	31
Kevin Sefcik	.235	99	153	15	36	46	6	2	0	10	4	13	19
Travis Lee	.235	128	404	53	95	148	24	1	9	54	8	65	79
Marlon Anderson	.228	41	162	10	37	50	8	1	1	15	2	12	22
Kevin Jordan	.220	109	337	30	74	109	16	2	5	36	0	17	41
Brian R. Hunter	.214	87	140	14	30	55	5	0	8	23	0	20	39
Rob Ducey	.197	112	152	24	30	54	4	1	6	25	1	29	47
Alex Arias	.187	70	155	17	29	44	9	0	2	15	1	16	28

PITCHING	ERA	W	L	G	GS	CG	SV	INN	H	R	ER	BB	SO
Bruce Chen	3.29	7	4	37	15	0	0	134	116	54	49	46	112
Robert Person	3.63	9	7	28	28	1	0	173⅓	144	73	70	95	164
Cliff Politte	3.66	4	3	12	8	0	0	59	55	24	24	27	50
Vicente Padilla	3.72	4	7	55	0	0	2	65⅓	72	33	27	28	51
Chris Brock	4.34	7	8	63	5	0	1	93⅓	85	48	45	41	69
Randy Wolf	4.36	11	9	32	32	1	0	206⅓	210	107	100	83	160
Wayne Gomes	4.40	4	6	65	0	0	7	73⅔	72	41	36	35	49
Kent Bottenfield	5.40	8	10	29	29	1	0	171⅔	185	106	103	77	106
Jeff Brantley	5.86	2	7	55	0	0	23	55⅓	64	36	36	29	57
Omar Daal	6.14	4	19	32	28	0	0	167	208	128	114	72	96
Paul Byrd	6.51	2	9	17	15	0	0	83	89	67	60	35	53

Pittsburgh Pirates

BATTING	BA	G	AB	R	H	TB	2B	3B	HR	RBI	SB	BB	SO
Jason Kendall	.320	152	579	112	185	272	33	6	14	58	22	79	79
Adrian Brown	.315	104	308	64	97	133	18	3	4	28	13	29	34
Brian Giles	.315	156	559	11	176	332	37	7	35	123	6	114	69
John Vander Wal	.299	134	384	74	115	216	29	0	24	94	11	72	92
Keith Osik	.293	46	123	11	36	56	6	1	4	22	3	14	11
Enrique Wilson	.262	80	239	27	70	102	15	1	5	27	2	18	24
Mike Benjamin	.270	93	233	28	63	91	18	2	2	19	5	12	45
Warren Morris	.259	144	528	68	137	181	31	2	3	43	7	65	78
Kevin Young	.258	132	496	77	128	215	27	0	20	88	8	32	96
Aramis Ramirez	.256	73	254	19	65	102	15	2	6	35	0	10	36
Alex Ramirez	.247	84	227	26	56	102	11	2	9	30	2	12	49
Pat Meares	.240	132	462	55	111	176	22	2	13	47	1	36	91
Emil Brown	.218	50	119	13	26	40	5	0	3	16	3	11	34

PITCHING	ERA	W	L	G	GS	CG	SV	INN	H	R	ER	BB	SO
Josias Manzanillo	3.38	2	2	43	0	0	0	58⅔	50	23	22	32	39
Mike Williams	3.50	3	4	72	0	0	24	72	56	34	28	40	71
Kris Benson	3.85	10	12	32	32	2	0	217⅔	206	104	93	86	184
Scott Sauerbeck	4.04	5	4	75	0	0	1	75⅔	76	36	34	61	83
Todd Ritchie	4.81	9	8	31	31	1	0	187	208	111	100	51	124
Marc Wilkins	5.07	4	2	52	0	0	0	60⅓	54	34	34	43	37
Francisco Cordova	5.21	6	8	18	17	0	0	95	107	63	55	38	66
Jimmy Anderson	5.25	5	11	27	26	1	0	144	169	94	84	58	73
Jason Schmidt	5.40	2	5	11	11	0	0	63⅓	71	43	38	41	51
Dan Serafini	5.51	2	5	14	11	0	0	65¼	79	41	40	28	35
Jose Silva	5.56	11	9	51	19	1	0	136	178	96	84	50	98
Bronson Arroyo	6.40	2	6	20	12	0	0	71⅔	88	61	51	36	50

St. Louis Cardinals

BATTING	BA	G	AB	R	H	TB	2B	3B	HR	RBI	SB	BB	SO
Will Clark	.319	130	427	78	136	233	30	2	21	70	5	69	69
Placido Polanco	.316	118	323	50	102	135	12	3	5	39	4	16	26
Mark McGwire	.305	89	236	60	72	176	8	0	32	73	1	76	78
Eric Davis	.303	92	254	38	77	109	14	0	6	40	1	36	60
Fernando Vina	.300	123	487	81	146	194	24	6	4	31	10	36	36
J.D. Drew	.295	135	407	73	120	195	17	2	18	57	17	67	99
Jim Edmonds	.295	152	525	129	155	306	25	0	42	108	10	103	167
Edgar Renteria	.278	150	562	94	156	238	32	1	16	76	21	63	77
Mike Matheny	.261	128	417	43	109	151	21	1	6	47	0	32	96
Carlos Hernandez	.256	75	242	23	62	86	15	0	3	35	2	21	35
Fernando Tatis	.253	96	324	59	82	159	21	1	18	64	2	57	94
Ray Lankford	.253	128	392	73	99	199	16	3	26	65	5	70	148
Shawon Dunston	.250	98	216	28	54	105	11	2	12	43	3	6	47
Craig Paquette	.245	134	384	47	94	167	24	2	15	61	4	27	83
Thomas Howard	.211	86	133	13	28	52	4	1	6	21	1	7	34

PITCHING	ERA	W	L	G	GS	CG	SV	INN	H	R	ER	BB	SO
Dave Veres	2.85	3	5	71	0	0	29	75⅔	65	26	24	25	67
Mike James	3.16	2	2	51	0	0	2	51⅓	40	22	18	24	41
Rick Ankiel	3.50	11	7	31	30	0	0	175	137	80	68	91	194
Matt Morris	3.57	3	3	31	0	0	4	53	53	22	21	17	34
Darryl Kile	3.91	20	9	34	34	5	0	232⅓	215	109	101	58	192
Mike Timlin	4.18	5	4	62	0	0	12	64⅔	67	33	30	35	52
Garrett Stephenson	4.49	16	9	32	31	3	0	200⅓	209	105	100	63	123
Pat Hentgen	4.72	15	12	33	33	1	0	194⅓	202	107	102	89	118
Andy Benes	4.88	12	9	30	27	1	0	166	174	95	90	68	137
Jason Christiansen	5.06	3	8	65	0	0	1	48	41	29	27	27	53

San Diego Padres

BATTING	BA	G	AB	R	H	TB	2B	3B	HR	RBI	SB	BB	SO
Tony Gwynn	.323	36	127	17	41	56	12	0	1	17	0	9	4
Phil Nevin	.303	143	538	87	163	292	34	1	31	107	2	59	121
Eric Owens	.293	145	583	87	171	222	19	7	6	51	29	45	63
Ryan Klesko	.283	145	494	88	140	255	33	2	26	92	23	91	81
Dave Magadan	.273	95	132	13	36	49	7	0	2	21	0	32	23
Mike Darr	.268	58	205	21	55	80	14	4	1	30	9	23	45
Damian Jackson	.255	138	470	68	120	177	27	6	6	37	28	62	108
Bret Boone	.251	127	463	61	116	195	18	2	19	74	8	50	97
Ed Sprague	.243	106	268	30	65	117	16	0	12	36	0	25	58
John Mabry	.235	96	226	35	53	90	13	0	8	32	0	15	69
Wiki Gonzalez	.232	95	284	25	66	98	15	1	5	30	1	30	31
Desi Relaford	.215	128	410	55	88	123	14	3	5	46	13	75	71
Ruben Rivera	.208	135	423	62	88	169	18	6	17	57	8	44	137

PITCHING	ERA	W	L	G	GS	CG	SV	INN	H	R	ER	BB	SO
Trevor Hoffman	2.99	4	7	70	0	0	43	72⅓	61	29	24	11	85
Donne Wall	3.35	5	2	44	0	0	1	53⅔	36	20	20	21	29
Brian Tollberg	3.58	4	5	19	19	1	0	118	126	58	47	35	76
Woody Williams	3.75	10	8	23	23	4	0	168	152	74	70	54	111
Adam Eaton	4.13	7	4	22	22	0	0	135	134	63	62	61	90
Kevin Walker	4.19	7	1	70	0	0	0	66⅔	49	35	31	38	56
Carlos Almanzar	4.39	4	5	62	0	0	0	69⅔	73	35	34	25	56
Sterling Hitchcock	4.93	1	6	11	11	0	0	65⅓	69	38	36	26	61
Heathcliff Slocumb	4.98	2	4	65	0	o	1	68⅔	69	43	38	37	46
Matt Clement	5.14	13	17	34	34	0	0	205	194	131	117	125	170
Jat Witasick	5.64	6	10	33	25	2	0	150	178	107	97	73	121
Todd Erdos	5.93	0	0	36	0	0	2	54⅔	63	38	36	28	34

San Francisco Giants

BATTING	BA	G	AB	R	H	TB	2B	3B	HR	RBI	SB	BB	SO
Ellis Burks	.344	122	393	74	135	238	21	5	24	96	5	56	49
Jeff Kent	.334	159	587	114	196	350	41	7	33	125	12	90	107
Barry Bonds	.306	143	480	129	147	330	28	4	49	106	11	117	77
Ramon Martinez	.302	88	189	30	57	92	13	2	6	25	3	15	22
Felipe Crespo	.290	89	131	17	38	58	6	1	4	29	3	10	23
J.T. Snow	.284	155	536	82	152	246	33	2	19	96	1	66	129
Rich Aurilia	.271	141	509	67	138	226	24	2	20	79	1	54	90
Bill Mueller	.268	153	560	97	150	217	29	4	10	55	4	52	62
Armando Rios	.266	115	233	38	62	117	15	5	10	50	3	31	43
Marvin Benard	.263	149	560	102	147	222	27	6	12	55	22	63	97
Russ Davis	.261	80	180	27	47	79	5	0	9	24	0	9	29
Calvin Murray	.242	108	194	35	47	67	12	1	2	22	9	29	33
Bobby Estalella	.234	106	299	45	70	140	22	3	14	53	3	57	92
Doug Mirabelli	.230	82	230	23	53	85	10	2	6	28	1	36	57

PITCHING	ERA	W	L	G	GS	CG	SV	INN	H	R	ER	BB	SO
Robb Nen	1.50	4	3	68	0	0	41	66	37	15	11	19	92
Felix Rodriguez	2.64	4	2	76	0	0	3	81⅓	65	29	24	42	95
Livan Hernandez	3.75	17	11	33	33	5	0	240	254	114	100	73	165
Doug Henry	3.79	4	4	72	0	0	1	78⅓	57	36	33	49	62
Kirk Reuter	3.96	11	9	32	31	0	0	184	205	92	81	62	71
Mark Gardner	4.05	11	7	30	20	0	0	149	155	72	67	42	92
Shawn Estes	4.26	15	6	30	30	4	0	190½	194	99	90	108	136
Aaron Fultz	4.67	5	2	58	0	0	1	69⅓	67	38	36	28	62
Alan Embree	4.95	3	5	63	0	0	2	60	62	34	33	25	49
Russ Ortiz	5.01	14	12	33	32	0	0	195⅔	192	117	109	112	167
Joe Nathan	5.21	5	2	20	15	0	0	93⅓	89	63	54	63	61

American League Team-by-Team Statistical Leaders

Anaheim Angels

BATTING	BA	G	AB	R	H	TB	2B	3B	HR	RBI	SB	BB	SO
Darin Erstad	.355	157	676	121	240	366	39	6	25	100	28	64	82
Orlando Palmeiro	.300	108	243	38	73	97	20	2	0	25	4	20	38
Tim Salmon	.290	158	568	108	165	307	36	2	34	97	0	104	139
Garret Anderson	.286	159	647	92	185	336	40	3	35	117	7	24	87
Troy Glaus	.284	159	563	120	160	340	37	1	47	102	14	112	163
Bengie Molina	.281	130	473	59	133	199	20	2	14	71	1	23	33
Mo Vaughn	.272	161	614	93	167	306	31	0	36	117	2	79	181
Adam Kennedy	.266	156	598	82	159	241	33	11	9	72	22	28	73
Ron Gant	.249	123	425	69	106	209	19	3	26	54	6	56	91
Scott Spiezio	.242	123	297	47	72	138	11	2	17	49	1	40	56
Benji Gil	.239	110	301	28	72	106	14	1	6	23	10	30	59
Kevin Stocker	.219	110	343	41	75	109	20	4	2	24	1	51	81

PITCHING	ERA	W	L	G	GS	CG	SV	INN	H	R	ER	BB	SO
Mike Fyhrie	2.39	0	0	32	0	0	0	52⅔	54	14	14	15	43
Lou Pote	3.40	1	1	32	1	0	1	50⅓	52	23	18	17	44
Shigetoshi Hasegawa	3.57	10	6	66	0	0	9	95⅔	100	43	38	38	59
Jarrod Washburn	3.74	7	2	14	14	0	0	84⅓	64	38	35	37	49
Al Levine	3.87	3	4	51	5	0	2	95⅓	98	44	41	49	42
Mark Petkovsek	4.22	4	2	64	1	0	2	81	86	39	38	23	31
Troy Percival	4.50	5	5	54	0	0	32	50	42	27	25	30	49
Ramon Ortiz	5.09	8	6	18	18	2	0	111⅓	96	69	63	55	73
Scott Schoeneweis	5.45	7	10	27	27	1	0	170	183	112	103	67	78
Seth Etherton	5.52	5	1	11	11	0	0	60⅓	68	38	37	22	32
Brian Cooper	5.90	4	8	15	15	1	0	87	105	66	57	35	36
Kent Mercker	6.52	1	3	21	7	0	0	48⅓	57	35	35	29	30
Scott Karl	7.42	4	5	23	13	0	0	87⅓	126	77	72	45	38

Baltimore Orioles

BATTING	BA	G	AB	R	H	TB	2B	3B	HR	RBI	SB	BB	SO
Brook Fordryce	.301	93	302	41	91	153	18	1	14	49	0	17	50
Delino DeShields	.296	151	561	84	166	249	43	5	10	86	37	69	82
Jeff Conine	.284	119	409	53	116	179	20	2	13	46	4	36	53
Albert Belle	.281	141	559	71	157	265	37	1	23	103	0	52	68
Melvin Mora	.275	132	414	60	114	170	22	5	8	47	12	35	80
Chris Richard	.265	62	215	39	57	117	14	2	14	37	7	17	40
Brady Anderson	.257	141	506	89	130	213	26	0	19	50	16	92	103
Cal Ripken	.256	83	309	43	79	140	16	0	15	56	0	23	37
Jerry Hairston	.256	49	180	27	46	66	5	0	5	19	8	21	22
Mark Lewis	.253	82	182	20	46	70	18	0	2	24	7	13	34
Luis Matos	.225	72	182	21	41	56	6	3	1	17	13	12	30
Greg Myers	.224	43	125	9	28	43	6	0	3	12	0	8	29

PITCHING	ERA	W	L	G	GS	CG	SV	INN	H	R	ER	BB	SO
Ryan Kohlmeier	2.39	0	1	25	0	0	13	26⅓	30	9	7	15	17
Mike Mussina	3.79	11	15	34	34	6	0	237⅔	236	105	100	46	210
Jose Mercedes	4.02	14	7	36	20	1	0	145⅔	150	71	65	64	70
Mike Trombley	4.13	4	5	75	0	0	4	72	67	34	33	38	72
Chuck McElroy	4.69	3	0	43	2	0	0	63⅓	60	36	33	34	50
Sidney Ponson	4.82	9	13	32	32	6	0	222	223	125	119	83	152
Buddy Groom	4.85	6	3	70	0	0	4	59⅓	63	37	32	21	44
Alan Mills	5.29	4	1	41	0	0	2	49⅓	56	29	29	35	36
Pat Rapp	5.90	9	12	31	31	0	0	174	203	125	114	83	106
Jason Johnson	7.02	1	10	25	13	0	0	107⅔	119	95	84	61	79
Scott Erickson	7.87	5	8	16	16	1	0	92⅔	127	81	81	48	41

American League Team-by-Team Statistical Leaders *(Cont.)*

Boston Red Sox

BATTING	BA	G	AB	R	H	TB	2B	3B	HR	RBI	SB	BB	SO
Nomar Garciaparra	.372	140	529	104	197	317	51	3	21	96	5	61	50
Carl Everett	.300	137	496	82	149	291	32	4	34	108	11	52	113
Dante Bichette	.294	155	575	80	169	274	32	2	23	90	5	49	91
Midre Cummings	.277	98	206	29	57	79	10	0	4	24	0	17	28
Trot Nixon	.276	123	427	66	118	197	27	8	12	60	8	63	85
Scott Hatteberg	.265	92	230	21	61	100	15	0	8	36	0	38	39
Troy O'Leary	.261	138	513	68	134	211	30	4	13	70	0	44	76
Jose Offerman	.255	116	451	73	115	162	14	3	9	41	0	70	70
Jason Varitek	.258	139	448	55	111	174	31	1	10	65	1	60	84
Brian Daubach	.248	142	495	55	123	222	32	2	21	76	1	44	130
Darren Lewis	.241	97	270	44	65	83	12	0	2	17	10	22	34
Mike Lansing	.240	139	504	72	121	184	18	6	11	60	8	38	75
Rico Brogna	.232	81	185	20	43	66	17	0	2	21	1	10	41
Manny Alexander	.211	101	194	30	41	63	4	3	4	19	2	13	41

PITCHING	ERA	W	L	G	GS	CG	SV	INN	H	R	ER	BB	SO
Pedro Martinez	1.74	18	6	29	29	7	0	217	128	44	42	32	284
Derek Lowe	2.56	4	4	74	0	0	42	91⅓	90	27	26	22	79
Tomo Ohka	3.12	3	6	13	12	0	0	69⅓	70	25	24	26	40
Rich Garces	3.25	8	1	64	0	0	1	74⅔	64	28	27	23	69
Hipolito Pichardo	3.46	6	3	38	1	0	1	65	63	29	25	26	37
Rheal Cormier	4.61	3	3	64	0	0	0	68⅓	74	40	35	17	43
Hector Carrasco	4.69	5	4	69	1	0	1	78⅔	90	46	41	38	64
Jeff Fassero	4.78	8	8	38	23	0	0	130	153	72	69	50	97
Pete Schourek	5.11	3	10	21	21	0	0	107⅓	116	67	61	38	63
Tim Wakefield	5.48	6	10	51	17	0	0	159⅓	170	107	97	65	102
Rolando Arrojo	5.63	10	11	32	32	0	0	172⅔	187	118	108	68	124
Ramon Martinez	6.13	10	8	27	27	0	0	127⅔	143	94	87	67	89

Chicago White Sox

BATTING	BA	G	AB	R	H	TB	2B	3B	HR	RBI	SB	BB	SO
Frank Thomas	.328	159	582	115	191	364	44	0	43	143	1	112	94
Magglio Ordonez	.315	153	588	102	185	321	34	3	32	126	18	60	64
Charles Johnson	.304	128	421	76	128	245	24	0	31	91	2	52	106
Herbert Perry	.302	109	411	71	124	185	30	1	12	62	4	24	75
Carlos Lee	.301	152	572	107	172	277	29	2	24	92	13	38	94
Paul Konerko	.298	143	524	84	156	252	31	1	21	97	1	47	72
Ray Durham	.280	151	614	121	172	276	35	9	17	75	25	75	105
Jeff Abbott	.274	80	215	31	59	85	15	1	3	29	2	21	38
Jose Valentin	.273	144	568	107	155	279	37	6	25	92	19	59	106
Harold Baines	.254	96	283	26	72	118	13	0	11	39	0	36	50
Chris Singleton	.254	147	511	83	130	195	22	5	11	62	22	35	85
Greg Norton	.244	71	201	25	49	75	6	1	6	28	1	26	47
Mark Johnson	.225	75	213	29	48	68	11	0	3	23	3	27	40

PITCHING	ERA	W	L	G	GS	CG	SV	INN	H	R	ER	BB	SO
Kelly Wunsch	2.93	6	3	83	0	0	1	61⅓	50	22	22	29	51
Keith Foulke	2.97	3	1	72	0	0	34	88	66	31	29	22	91
Bob Howry	3.17	2	4	65	0	0	7	71	54	26	25	29	60
Bill Simas	3.46	2	3	60	0	0	0	67⅔	69	27	26	22	49
Mike Sirotka	3.79	15	10	32	32	1	0	197	203	101	83	69	128
Jim Parque	4.28	13	6	33	32	0	0	187	208	105	89	71	111
Cal Eldred	4.58	10	2	20	20	2	0	112	103	61	57	59	97
James Baldwin	4.65	14	7	29	28	2	0	178	185	96	92	59	116
Sean Lowe	5.48	4	1	50	5	0	0	70⅔	78	47	43	39	53
Kip Wells	6.02	6	9	20	20	0	0	98⅔	126	76	66	58	71
Jon Garland	6.46	4	8	15	13	0	0	69⅔	82	55	50	40	42
Ken Hill	7.16	5	8	18	17	0	0	81⅔	107	67	65	59	50

Cleveland Indians

BATTING	BA	G	AB	R	H	TB	2B	3B	HR	RBI	SB	BB	SO
Manny Ramirez	.351	118	439	92	154	306	34	2	38	122	1	86	117
David Segui	.334	150	574	93	192	293	42	1	19	103	0	53	84
Travis Fryman	.321	155	574	93	184	296	38	4	22	106	1	73	111
Roberto Alomar	.310	155	610	111	189	290	40	2	19	89	39	64	82
Sandy Alomar	.289	97	356	44	103	144	16	2	7	42	2	16	41
Omar Vizquel	.287	156	613	101	176	230	27	3	7	66	22	87	72
Kenny Lofton	.278	137	543	107	151	229	23	5	15	73	30	79	72
Wil Cordero	.276	127	496	64	137	230	35	5	16	68	1	32	76
Einar Diaz	.272	75	250	29	68	98	14	2	4	25	4	11	29
Jim Thome	.269	158	557	106	150	296	33	1	37	106	1	118	171
Jolbert Cabrera	.251	100	175	27	44	55	3	1	2	15	6	8	15
Russell Branyan	.238	67	193	32	46	105	7	2	16	38	0	22	76

PITCHING	ERA	W	L	G	GS	CG	SV	INN	H	R	ER	BB	SO
Bob Wickman	3.10	3	5	69	0	0	30	72⅔	51	30	34	32	55
Justin Speier	3.29	5	2	47	0	0	0	68⅓	57	27	25	28	69
Paul Shuey	3.39	4	2	57	0	0	0	63⅔	51	25	24	30	69
Steve Karsay	3.76	5	9	72	0	0	20	76⅓	79	33	32	25	66
Bartolo Colon	3.88	15	8	30	30	2	0	188	163	86	81	98	212
Chuck Finley	4.17	16	11	34	34	3	0	218	211	108	101	101	189
Steve Reed	4.34	2	0	57	0	0	0	56	58	30	27	21	39
Dave Burba	4.47	16	6	32	32	0	0	191⅓	199	99	95	91	190
Jason Bere	5.47	12	10	31	31	0	0	169¼	180	107	103	89	142
Steve Woodard	5.85	4	10	40	22	1	0	147⅞	182	105	96	44	100
Jim Brower	6.24	2	3	17	11	0	0	62	80	45	43	31	32
Charles Nagy	8.21	2	7	11	11	0	0	57	71	53	52	21	14

Detroit Tigers

BATTING	BA	G	AB	R	H	TB	2B	3B	HR	RBI	SB	BB	SO
Deivi Cruz	.302	156	583	68	176	262	46	5	10	82	1	13	43
Billy McMillon	.301	46	123	20	37	58	7	1	4	24	1	19	19
Bobby Higginson	.300	154	597	104	179	321	44	4	30	102	15	74	99
Juan Gonzalez	.289	115	461	69	133	233	30	2	22	67	1	32	84
Juan Encarnacion	.289	141	547	75	158	237	25	6	14	72	16	29	90
Hal Morris	.278	99	169	24	47	67	9	1	3	14	0	31	26
Tony Clark	.274	60	208	32	57	110	14	0	13	37	0	24	51
Wendell Magee	.274	91	186	31	51	80	4	2	7	31	1	10	28
Brad Ausmus	.266	150	523	75	139	191	25	3	7	51	11	69	79
Shane Halter	.261	105	238	26	62	87	12	2	3	27	5	14	49
Damion Easley	.259	126	464	76	120	193	27	2	14	58	13	55	79
Dean Palmer	.256	145	524	73	134	247	22	2	29	102	4	66	146
Jose Macias	.254	73	173	25	44	63	3	5	2	24	2	18	24
Robert Fick	.252	66	163	18	41	61	7	2	3	22	2	22	39
Rich Becker	.242	115	285	59	69	107	14	0	8	39	2	67	87

PITCHING	ERA	W	L	G	GS	CG	SV	INN	H	R	ER	BB	SO
Todd Jones	3.52	2	4	67	0	0	42	64	67	28	25	25	67
Danny Patterson	3.97	5	1	58	0	0	0	56⅔	69	26	25	14	29
Steve Sparks	4.07	7	5	20	15	1	1	104	108	55	47	29	53
Doug Brocail	4.09	5	4	49	0	0	0	50⅓	57	25	23	14	41
Jeff Weaver	4.32	11	15	31	30	2	0	200	205	102	96	52	136
Brian Moehler	4.50	12	9	29	29	2	0	178	222	99	89	40	103
Matt Anderson	4.72	3	2	69	0	0	1	74⅓	61	44	39	45	71
Hideo Nomo	4.74	8	12	32	31	1	0	190	191	102	100	89	181
Willie Blair	4.88	10	6	47	17	0	0	156⅔	185	89	85	35	74
C.J. Nitkowski	5.25	4	9	67	11	0	0	109⅔	124	79	64	49	81
Dave Mlicki	5.58	6	11	24	21	0	0	119⅓	143	79	74	44	57

Kansas City Royals

BATTING	BA	G	AB	R	H	TB	2B	3B	HR	RBI	SB	BB	SO
Mike Sweeney	.333	159	618	105	206	323	30	0	29	144	8	71	67
Johnny Damon	.327	159	655	136	214	324	42	10	16	88	46	65	60
Jermaine Dye	.321	157	601	107	193	337	41	2	33	118	0	69	99
Joe Randa	.304	158	612	88	186	268	29	4	15	106	6	36	66
Mark Quinn	.294	135	500	76	147	244	33	2	20	78	5	35	91
Jorge Fabregas	.282	43	142	13	40	53	4	0	3	17	1	8	11
David McCarty	.278	103	270	34	75	129	14	2	12	53	0	22	68
Gregg Zaun	.274	83	234	36	64	96	11	0	7	33	7	43	34
Rey Sanchez	.273	143	509	68	139	164	18	2	1	38	7	28	55
Carlos Febles	.257	100	339	59	87	107	12	1	2	29	17	36	48
Carlos Beltran	.247	98	372	49	92	136	15	4	7	44	13	35	69
Jeff Reboulet	.242	66	182	29	44	51	7	0	0	14	3	23	32
Todd Dunwoody	.208	61	178	12	37	49	9	0	1	23	3	8	42

PITCHING	ERA	W	L	G	GS	CG	SV	INN	H	R	ER	BB	SO
Jose Santiago	3.91	8	6	45	0	0	2	69	70	33	30	26	44
Mac Suzuki	4.34	8	10	32	29	1	0	188⅔	195	100	91	94	135
Blake Stein	4.68	8	5	17	17	1	0	107⅞	98	57	56	57	78
Dan Reichert	4.70	8	10	44	18	1	2	153⅓	157	92	80	91	94
Ricky Bottalico	4.83	9	6	62	0	0	16	72⅔	65	40	39	41	56
Jeff Suppan	4.94	10	9	35	33	3	0	217	240	121	119	84	128
Brian Meadows	5.13	13	10	33	32	2	0	196.1	234	119	112	64	79
Chris Fussell	6.30	5	3	20	9	0	0	70	76	52	49	44	46
Chad Durbin	8.21	2	5	16	16	0	0	72⅓	91	71	66	43	37
Miguel Batista	8.54	2	7	18	9	0	0	65⅓	85	68	62	37	37

Minnesota Twins

BATTING	BA	G	AB	R	H	TB	2B	3B	HR	RBI	SB	BB	SO
Matt Lawton	.305	156	561	84	171	258	44	2	13	88	23	91	63
Corey Koskie	.300	146	474	79	142	209	32	4	9	64	5	77	104
Denny Hocking	.298	134	373	52	111	155	24	4	4	47	7	48	77
Jacque Jones	.284	154	523	66	149	242	26	5	19	76	7	26	111
David Ortiz	.282	130	415	59	117	185	36	1	10	63	1	57	81
Torii Hunter	.280	99	336	44	94	137	14	7	5	44	4	18	68
Ron Coomer	.270	140	544	64	147	226	29	1	16	82	2	36	50
Jay Canizaro	.269	102	346	43	93	137	21	1	7	40	4	24	57
Cristian Guzman	.247	156	631	89	156	245	25	20	8	54	28	46	101
Chad Moeller	.211	48	128	13	27	35	3	1	1	9	1	9	33
Marcus Jensen	.209	52	139	16	29	47	7	1	3	14	0	24	36
Matthew LeCroy	.174	56	167	18	29	54	10	0	5	17	0	17	38

PITCHING	ERA	W	L	G	GS	CG	SV	INN	H	R	ER	BB	SO
LaTroy Hawkins	3.39	2	5	66	0	0	14	87⅓	85	34	33	32	59
Bob Wells	3.65	0	7	76	0	0	10	86⅓	80	39	35	15	76
Travis Miller	3.90	2	3	67	0	0	1	67	83	35	29	32	62
Eddie Guardado	3.94	7	4	70	0	0	9	61⅓	55	27	27	25	52
Brad Radke	4.45	12	16	34	34	4	0	226⅔	261	119	112	51	141
Mark Redman	4.76	12	9	32	24	0	0	151⅓	168	81	80	45	117
Eric Milton	4.86	13	10	33	33	0	0	200	205	123	108	44	160
Joe Mays	5.56	7	15	31	21	2	0	160½	193	105	99	67	102
Johan Santana	6.49	2	3	30	5	0	0	86	102	64	62	54	64
J.C. Romero	7.02	2	7	12	11	0	0	57⅔	72	51	45	30	50
Sean Bergman	9.66	4	5	15	14	0	0	68	111	76	73	33	35

New York Yankees

BATTING	BA	G	AB	R	H	TB	2B	3B	HR	RBI	SB	BB	SO
Derek Jeter	.339	148	593	119	201	285	31	4	15	73	22	68	99
Bernie Williams	.307	141	537	108	165	304	37	6	30	121	13	71	84
Glenallen Hill	.293	104	300	45	88	180	9	1	27	58	0	19	76
Jorge Posada	.287	151	505	92	145	266	35	1	28	86	2	107	151
David Justice	.286	146	524	89	150	306	31	1	41	118	2	77	91
Luis Sojo	.286	95	301	33	86	127	18	1	7	37	2	17	22
Paul O'Neill	.283	142	566	79	160	240	26	0	18	100	14	51	90
Chuck Knoblauch	.283	102	400	75	113	154	22	2	5	26	15	46	45
Shane Spencer	.282	73	248	33	70	114	11	3	9	40	1	19	45
Luis Polonia	.276	117	344	48	95	140	14	5	7	30	12	29	32
Tino Martinez	.258	155	569	69	147	240	37	4	16	91	4	52	74
Jose Canseco	.252	98	329	47	83	146	18	0	15	49	2	64	102
Jose Vizcaino	.251	113	267	32	67	81	10	2	0	14	6	22	43
Scott Brosius	.230	135	470	57	108	176	20	0	16	64	0	45	73
Clay Bellinger	.207	98	184	33	38	68	8	2	6	21	5	17	48

PITCHING	ERA	W	L	G	GS	CG	SV	INN	H	R	ER	BB	SO
Jeff Nelson	2.45	8	4	73	0	0	0	69⅔	44	24	19	45	71
Mariano Rivera	2.85	7	4	66	0	0	36	75⅔	58	26	24	25	58
Roger Clemens	3.70	13	8	32	32	1	0	204⅓	184	96	84	84	188
Mike Stanton	4.10	2	3	69	0	0	0	68	68	32	31	24	75
Ramiro Mendoza	4.25	7	4	14	9	1	0	65⅔	66	32	31	20	30
Andy Pettitte	4.35	19	9	32	32	3	0	204⅔	219	111	99	80	125
Orlando Hernandez	4.51	12	13	29	29	3	0	195⅔	186	104	98	51	141
Denny Neagle	4.52	15	9	34	33	1	0	209	210	109	105	81	146
Dwight Gooden	4.71	6	5	27	14	0	2	105	119	64	55	44	55
Jason Grimsley	5.04	3	2	63	4	0	1	96½	100	58	54	42	53
David Cone	6.91	4	14	30	29	0	0	155	192	124	119	82	120

Oakland Athletics

BATTING	BA	G	AB	R	H	TB	2B	3B	HR	RBI	SB	BB	SO
Jason Giambi	.333	152	510	108	170	330	29	1	43	137	2	137	96
Olmeda Saenz	.313	76	214	40	67	110	12	2	9	33	1	25	40
Adam Piatt	.299	60	157	24	47	76	5	5	5	23	0	23	44
Terrence Long	.288	138	584	104	168	264	34	4	18	80	5	43	77
Ben Grieve	.279	158	594	92	166	289	40	1	27	104	3	73	130
Randy Velarde	.278	122	485	82	135	194	23	0	12	41	9	54	95
Eric Chavez	.277	153	501	89	139	248	23	4	26	86	2	62	94
Miquel Tejada	.275	160	607	105	167	291	32	1	30	115	6	66	102
Frank Menechino	.255	66	145	31	37	66	9	1	6	26	1	20	45
Jeremy Giambi	.254	104	260	42	66	110	10	2	10	50	0	32	61
Ryan Christenson	.248	121	129	31	32	50	2	2	4	18	1	19	33
Ramon Hernandez	.241	143	419	52	101	162	19	0	14	62	1	38	64
Mike Stanley	.238	90	282	33	67	121	12	0	14	46	0	44	65
Matt Stairs	.227	143	476	74	108	197	26	0	21	81	5	78	122

PITCHING	ERA	W	L	G	GS	CG	SV	INN	H	R	ER	BB	SO
Jeff Tam	2.63	3	3	72	0	0	3	85⅔	86	30	25	23	46
Barry Zito	2.72	7	4	14	14	1	0	92⅔	64	30	28	45	78
Jim Mecir	2.96	10	3	63	0	0	5	85	70	31	28	36	70
Jason Isringhausen	3.78	6	4	66	0	0	33	69	67	34	29	32	57
Doug Jones	3.93	4	2	54	0	0	2	73⅓	86	34	32	18	54
Gil Heredia	4.12	15	11	32	32	2	0	198⅔	214	106	91	66	101
Tim Hudson	4.14	20	6	32	32	2	0	202⅓	169	100	93	82	169
Kevin Appier	4.52	15	11	31	31	1	0	195¼	200	109	98	102	129
Mark Mulder	5.44	9	10	27	27	0	0	154	191	106	93	69	88
T.J. Mathews	6.03	2	3	50	0	0	0	59⅔	73	40	40	25	42
Omar Olivares	6.75	4	8	21	16	1	0	108	134	86	81	60	57

American League Team-by-Team Statistical Leaders *(Cont.)*

Seattle Mariners

BATTING	BA	G	AB	R	H	TB	2B	3B	HR	RBI	SB	BB	SO
Edgar Martinez	.324	153	556	100	180	322	31	0	37	145	3	96	95
Alex Rodriguez	.316	148	554	134	175	336	34	2	41	132	15	100	121
Al Martin	.285	135	480	81	137	217	15	10	15	36	10	36	85
John Olerud	.285	159	565	84	161	248	45	0	14	103	0	102	96
Stan Javier	.275	105	342	61	94	137	18	5	5	40	4	42	64
Mike Cameron	.267	155	543	96	145	238	28	4	19	78	24	78	133
Joe Oliver	.265	69	200	33	53	98	13	1	10	35	2	14	38
Carlos Guillen	.257	90	288	45	74	114	15	2	7	42	1	28	53
Jay Buhner	.253	112	364	50	92	190	20	0	26	82	0	59	98
David Bell	.247	133	454	57	112	173	24	2	11	47	2	42	66
Mark McLemore	.245	138	481	72	118	152	23	1	3	46	30	81	78
Dan Wilson	.235	90	268	31	63	90	12	0	5	27	1	22	51
Rickey Henderson	.233	123	420	75	98	128	14	2	4	32	36	88	75
Chris Widger	.233	96	292	32	68	128	17	2	13	35	1	30	63

PITCHING	ERA	W	L	G	GS	CG	SV	INN	H	R	ER	BB	SO
Sasaki Kazuhiro	3.16	2	5	63	0	0	37	62⅔	42	25	22	31	78
Jose Paniagua	3.47	3	0	69	0	0	5	80⅓	68	31	31	38	72
Gil Meche	3.78	4	4	15	15	1	0	85⅔	75	37	36	40	60
Freddy Garcia	3.91	9	5	21	20	0	0	124⅓	112	62	54	64	79
Paul Abbott	4.22	9	7	35	27	0	0	179	164	89	84	80	100
Arthur Rhodes	4.28	5	8	72	0	0	0	69⅓	51	34	33	29	77
Aaron Sele	4.51	17	10	34	34	2	0	211⅔	221	110	106	74	137
Brett Tomko	4.68	7	5	32	8	0	1	92⅓	92	53	48	40	59
John Halama	5.08	14	9	30	30	1	0	166⅔	206	108	94	56	87
Jose Mesa	5.36	4	6	66	0	0	1	80⅔	89	48	48	41	84
Jamie Moyer	5.49	13	10	26	26	0	0	154	173	103	94	53	98

Tampa Bay Devil Rays

BATTING	BA	G	AB	R	H	TB	2B	3B	HR	RBI	SB	BB	SO
Aubrey Huff	.287	39	122	12	35	54	7	0	4	14	0	5	18
Steve Cox	.283	116	318	44	90	144	19	1	11	35	1	46	47
Fred McGriff	.277	158	566	82	157	256	18	0	27	106	2	91	120
Gerald Williams	.274	146	632	87	173	270	30	2	21	89	12	34	103
John Flaherty	.261	109	394	36	103	148	15	0	10	39	0	20	57
Miguel Cairo	.261	119	375	49	98	123	18	2	1	34	28	29	34
Greg Vaughn	.254	127	461	83	117	230	27	1	28	74	8	80	128
Jose Guillen	.253	105	316	40	80	136	16	5	10	41	3	18	65
Randy Winn	.252	51	159	28	40	48	5	0	1	16	6	26	25
Mike DiFelice	.240	60	204	23	49	82	13	1	6	19	0	12	40
Russ Johnson	.239	100	230	32	55	69	8	0	2	20	5	27	40
Bobby Smith	.234	49	175	21	41	67	8	0	6	26	2	14	59
Vinny Castilla	.221	85	331	22	73	102	9	1	6	42	1	14	41
Felix Martinez	.214	106	299	42	64	89	11	4	2	17	9	32	68

PITCHING	ERA	W	L	G	GS	CG	SV	INN	H	R	ER	BB	SO
Roberto Hernandez	3.19	4	7	68	0	0	32	73⅓	76	33	26	23	61
Albie Lopez	4.13	11	13	45	24	4	2	185⅓	199	95	85	70	96
Bryan Rekar	4.41	7	10	30	27	2	0	173⅓	200	92	85	39	95
Doug Creek	4.60	1	3	45	0	0	1	60⅔	49	33	31	39	73
Tanyon Sturtze	4.74	5	2	29	6	0	0	68⅓	72	39	36	29	45
Cory Lidle	5.03	4	6	31	11	0	0	96⅔	114	61	54	29	62
Esteban Yan	6.21	7	8	43	20	0	0	137⅔	158	98	95	42	111
Ryan Rupe	6.92	5	6	18	18	0	0	91	121	75	70	31	61
Dave Eiland	7.24	2	3	17	10	0	0	54⅔	77	46	44	18	17

Texas Rangers

BATTING	BA	G	AB	R	H	TB	2B	3B	HR	RBI	SB	BB	SO
Ivan Rodriguez	.347	91	363	66	126	242	27	4	27	83	5	19	48
Gabe Kapler	.302	116	444	59	134	210	32	1	14	66	8	42	57
Rusty Greer	.297	105	394	65	117	181	34	3	8	65	4	51	61
Luis Alicea	.294	139	540	85	159	218	25	8	6	63	1	59	75
Ruben Mateo	.291	52	206	32	60	92	11	0	7	19	6	10	34
Frank Catalanotto	.291	103	282	55	82	129	13	2	10	42	6	33	36
Rafael Palmeiro	.288	158	565	102	163	315	29	3	39	120	2	103	77
Scott Sheldon	.282	58	124	21	35	58	11	0	4	19	0	10	37
Mike Lamb	.278	138	493	65	137	184	25	2	6	47	0	34	60
Bill Haselman	.275	62	193	23	53	89	18	0	6	26	0	15	36
Chad Curtis	.272	108	335	48	91	142	25	1	8	48	3	37	71
Royce Clayton	.242	148	513	70	124	197	21	5	14	54	11	42	92
Ricky Ledee	.236	137	467	59	110	178	19	5	13	77	13	59	98
Scarborough Green	.234	79	124	21	29	32	1	1	0	9	10	10	26

PITCHING	ERA	W	L	G	GS	CG	SV	INN	H	R	ER	BB	SO
Mike Venafro	3.83	3	1	77	0	0	1	56⅓	64	27	24	21	32
John Wetteland	4.20	6	5	62	0	0	34	60	67	35	28	24	53
Rick Helling	4.48	16	13	35	35	0	0	217	212	122	108	99	146
Kenny Rogers	4.55	13	13	34	34	2	0	227½	257	126	115	78	127
Tim Crabtree	5.15	2	7	68	0	0	2	80½	86	52	46	31	54
Jeff Zimmerman	5.30	4	5	65	0	0	1	69⅔	80	45	41	34	74
Francisco Cordero	5.35	1	2	56	0	0	0	77⅓	87	51	46	48	49
Doug Davis	5.38	7	6	30	13	1	0	98⅔	109	61	59	58	66
Ryan Glynn	5.58	5	7	16	16	0	0	88⅔	107	65	55	41	33
Matt Perisho	7.37	2	7	34	13	0	0	105	136	99	86	67	74
Darren Oliver	7.42	2	9	21	21	0	0	108	151	95	89	42	49

Toronto Blue Jays

BATTING	BA	G	AB	R	H	TB	2B	3B	HR	RBI	SB	BB	SO
Carlos Delgado	.344	162	569	115	196	378	57	1	41	137	0	123	104
Darrin Fletcher	.320	122	416	43	133	214	19	1	20	58	1	20	45
Shannon Stewart	.319	136	583	107	186	302	43	5	21	69	20	37	79
Brad Fullmer	.295	133	482	76	142	269	29	1	32	104	3	30	68
Craig Grebeck	.295	66	241	38	71	99	19	0	3	23	0	25	33
Dave Martinez	.274	132	457	60	125	169	19	5	5	47	7	48	65
Raul Mondesi	.271	96	388	78	105	203	22	2	24	67	22	32	73
Mickey Morandini	.257	126	409	41	105	128	15	4	0	29	6	36	76
Alex Gonzalez	.252	141	527	68	133	213	31	2	15	69	4	43	113
Marty Cordova	.245	62	200	23	49	68	7	0	4	18	3	18	35
Jose Cruz	.242	162	603	91	146	281	32	5	31	76	15	71	129
Homer Bush	.215	76	297	38	64	75	8	0	1	18	9	18	60

PITCHING	ERA	W	L	G	GS	CG	SV	INN	H	R	ER	BB	SO
Billy Koch	2.63	9	3	68	0	0	33	78⅔	78	28	23	18	60
Frank Castillo	3.59	10	5	25	24	0	0	138	112	58	55	56	104
David Wells	4.11	20	8	35	35	9	0	229⅔	266	115	105	31	166
Paul Quantrill	4.52	2	5	68	0	0	1	83⅔	100	45	42	25	47
Esteban Loaiza	4.56	10	13	34	31	1	1	199½	228	112	101	57	137
Mark Guthrie	4.67	3	6	76	0	0	0	71⅓	53	41	27	22	53
Lance Painter	4.73	2	0	42	2	0	0	66⅔	69	37	35	22	53
Steve Trachsel	4.80	8	15	34	34	3	0	200⅔	232	116	107	74	110
Kelvim Escobar	5.35	10	15	43	24	3	2	180	186	118	107	85	142
John Frascatore	5.42	2	4	60	0	0	0	73	87	51	44	33	30
Chris Carpenter	6.26	10	12	34	24	2	0	175¼	204	130	122	83	113
Pedro Burbon	6.48	1	1	59	0	0	1	41⅓	45	37	30	38	29
Roy Halladay	10.64	4	7	19	13	0	0	67⅔	107	87	80	42	44

FOR THE RECORD·Year by Year

The World Series

Results

1903	Boston (A) 5, Pittsburgh (N) 3	1952	New York (A) 4, Brooklyn (N) 3
1904	No series	1953	New York (A) 4, Brooklyn (N) 2
1905	New York (N) 4, Philadelphia (A) 1	1954	New York (N) 4, Cleveland (A) 0
1906	Chicago (A) 4, Chicago (N) 2	1955	Brooklyn (N) 4, New York (A) 3
1907	Chicago (N) 4, Detroit (A) 0; 1 tie	1956	New York (A) 4, Brooklyn (N) 3
1908	Chicago (N) 4, Detroit (A) 1	1957	Milwaukee (N) 4, New York (A) 3
1909	Pittsburgh (N) 4, Detroit (A) 3	1958	New York (A) 4, Milwaukee (N) 3
1910	Philadelphia (A) 4, Chicago (N) 1	1959	Los Angeles (N) 4, Chicago (A) 2
1911	Philadelphia (A) 4, New York (N) 2	1960	Pittsburgh (N) 4, New York (A) 3
1912	Boston (A) 4, New York (N) 3; 1 tie	1961	New York (A) 4, Cincinnati (N) 1
1913	Philadelphia (A) 4, New York (N) 1	1962	New York (A) 4, San Francisco (N) 3
1914	Boston (N) 4, Philadelphia (A) 0	1963	Los Angeles (N) 4, New York (A) 0
1915	Boston (A) 4, Philadelphia (N) 1	1964	St. Louis (N) 4, New York (A) 3
1916	Boston (A) 4, Brooklyn (N) 1	1965	Los Angeles (N) 4, Minnesota (A) 3
1917	Chicago (A) 4, New York (N) 2	1966	Baltimore (A) 4, Los Angeles (N) 0
1918	Boston (A) 4, Chicago (N) 2	1967	St. Louis (N) 4, Boston (A) 3
1919	Cincinnati (N) 5, Chicago (A) 3	1968	Detroit (A) 4, St. Louis (N) 3
1920	Cleveland (A) 5, Brooklyn (N) 2	1969	New York (N) 4, Baltimore (A) 1
1921	New York (N) 5, New York (A) 3	1970	Baltimore (A) 4, Cincinnati (N) 1
1922	New York (N) 4, New York (A) 0; 1 tie	1971	Pittsburgh (N) 4, Baltimore (A) 3
1923	New York (A) 4, New York (N) 2	1972	Oakland (A) 4, Cincinnati (N) 3
1924	Washington (A) 4, New York (N) 3	1973	Oakland (A) 4, New York (N) 3
1925	Pittsburgh (N) 4, Washington (A) 3	1974	Oakland (A) 4, Los Angeles (N) 1
1926	St. Louis (N) 4, New York (A) 3	1975	Cincinnati (N) 4, Boston (A) 3
1927	New York (A) 4, Pittsburgh (N) 0	1976	Cincinnati (N) 4, New York (A) 0
1928	New York (A) 4, St. Louis (N) 0	1977	New York (A) 4, Los Angeles (N) 2
1929	Philadelphia (A) 4, Chicago (N) 1	1978	New York (A) 4, Los Angeles (N) 2
1930	Philadelphia (A) 4, St. Louis (N) 2	1979	Pittsburgh (N) 4, Baltimore (A) 3
1931	St. Louis (N) 4, Philadelphia (A) 3	1980	Philadelphia (N) 4, Kansas City (A) 2
1932	New York (A) 4, Chicago (N) 0	1981	Los Angeles (N) 4, New York (A) 2
1933	New York (N) 4, Washington (A) 1	1982	St. Louis (N) 4, Milwaukee (A) 3
1934	St. Louis (N) 4, Detroit (A) 3	1983	Baltimore (A) 4, Philadelphia (N) 1
1935	Detroit (A) 4, Chicago (N) 2	1984	Detroit (A) 4, San Diego (N) 1
1936	New York (A) 4, New York (N) 2	1985	Kansas City (A) 4, St. Louis (N) 3
1937	New York (A) 4, New York (N) 1	1986	New York (N) 4, Boston (A) 3
1938	New York (A) 4, Chicago (N) 0	1987	Minnesota (A) 4, St. Louis (N) 3
1939	New York (A) 4, Cincinnati (N) 0	1988	Los Angeles (N) 4, Oakland (A) 1
1940	Cincinnati (N) 4, Detroit (A) 3	1989	Oakland (A) 4, San Francisco (N) 0
1941	New York (A) 4, Brooklyn (N) 1	1990	Cincinnati (N) 4, Oakland (A) 0
1942	St. Louis (N) 4, New York (A) 1	1991	Minnesota (A) 4, Atlanta (N) 3
1943	New York (A) 4, St. Louis (N) 1	1992	Toronto (A) 4, Atlanta (N) 2
1944	St. Louis (N) 4, St. Louis (A) 2	1993	Toronto (A) 4, Philadelphia (N) 2
1945	Detroit (A) 4, Chicago (N) 3	1994	Series canceled due to players' strike.
1946	St. Louis (N) 4, Boston (A) 3	1995	Atlanta (N) 4, Cleveland (A) 2
1947	New York (A) 4, Brooklyn (N) 3	1996	New York (A) 4, Atlanta (N) 2
1948	Cleveland (A) 4, Boston (N) 2	1997	Florida (N) 4, Cleveland (A) 3
1949	New York (A) 4, Brooklyn (N) 1	1998	New York (A) 4, San Diego (N) 0
1950	New York (A) 4, Philadelphia (N) 0	1999	New York (A) 4, Atlanta (N) 0
1951	New York (A) 4, New York (N) 2	2000	New York (A) 4 , New York (N) 1

Most Valuable Players

1955	Johnny Podres, Bklyn
1956	Don Larsen, NY (A)
1957	Lew Burdette, Mil
1958	Bob Turley, NY (A)
1959	Larry Sherry, LA
1960	Bobby Richardson, NY (A)
1961	Whitey Ford, NY (A)
1962	Ralph Terry, NY (A)
1963	Sandy Koufax, LA
1964	Bob Gibson, StL
1965	Sandy Koufax, LA
1966	Frank Robinson, Balt
1967	Bob Gibson, StL
1968	Mickey Lolich, Det
1969	Donn Clendenon, NY (N)
1970	Brooks Robinson, Balt
1971	Roberto Clemente, Pitt
1972	Gene Tenace, Oak
1973	Reggie Jackson, Oak
1974	Rollie Fingers, Oak
1975	Pete Rose, Cin
1976	Johnny Bench, Cin
1977	Reggie Jackson, NY (A)
1978	Bucky Dent, NY (A)
1979	Willie Stargell, Pitt
1980	Mike Schmidt, Phil
1981	Ron Cey, Steve Yeager, Pedro Guerrero, LA
1982	Darrell Porter, StL
1983	Rick Dempsey, Balt
1984	Alan Trammell, Det
1985	Bret Saberhagen, KC
1986	Ray Knight, NY (N)
1987	Frank Viola, Minn
1988	Orel Hershiser, LA
1989	Dave Stewart, Oak
1990	Jose Rijo, Cin
1991	Jack Morris, Minn
1992	Pat Borders, Tor
1993	Paul Molitor, Tor
1994	Series canceled due to strike
1995	Tom Glavine, Atl
1996	John Wetteland, NY (A)
1997	Livan Hernandez, Fla
1998	Scott Brosius, NY (A)
1999	Mariano Rivera, NY (A)
2000	Derek Jeter, NY (A)

Career Batting Leaders (Minimum 50 at bats)

GAMES

Yogi Berra	75
Mickey Mantle	65
Elston Howard	54
Hank Bauer	53
Gil McDougald	53
Phil Rizzuto	52
Joe DiMaggio	51
Frankie Frisch	50
Pee Wee Reese	44
Roger Maris	41
Babe Ruth	41

AT BATS

Yogi Berra	259
Mickey Mantle	230
Joe DiMaggio	199
Frankie Frisch	197
Gil McDougald	190
Hank Bauer	188
Phil Rizzuto	183
Elston Howard	171
Pee Wee Reese	169
Roger Maris	152

HITS

Yogi Berra	71
Mickey Mantle	59
Frankie Frisch	58
Joe DiMaggio	54
Pee Wee Reese	46
Hank Bauer	46
Phil Rizzuto	45
Gil McDougald	45
Lou Gehrig	43
Eddie Collins	42
Babe Ruth	42
Elston Howard	42

BATTING AVERAGE

Paul Molitor	.418
Pepper Martin	.418
Lou Brock	.391
Marquis Grissom	.390
George Brett	.373
Thurman Munson	.373
Hank Aaron	.364
Frank Baker	.363
Roberto Clemente	.362
Lou Gehrig	.361

HOME RUNS

Mickey Mantle	18
Babe Ruth	15
Yogi Berra	12
Duke Snider	11
Reggie Jackson	10
Lou Gehrig	10
Frank Robinson	8
Bill Skowron	8
Joe DiMaggio	8
Goose Goslin	7
Hank Bauer	7
Gil McDougald	7

RUNS BATTED IN

Mickey Mantle	40
Yogi Berra	39
Lou Gehrig	35
Babe Ruth	33
Joe DiMaggio	30
Bill Skowron	29
Duke Snider	26
Reggie Jackson	24
Bill Dickey	24
Hank Bauer	24
Gil McDougald	24

RUNS

Mickey Mantle	42
Yogi Berra	41
Babe Ruth	37
Lou Gehrig	30
Joe DiMaggio	27
Roger Maris	26
Elston Howard	25
Gil McDougald	23
Jackie Robinson	22
Gene Woodling	21
Reggie Jackson	21
Duke Snider	21
Phil Rizzuto	21
Hank Bauer	21

STOLEN BASES

Lou Brock	14
Eddie Collins	14
Frank Chance	10
Davey Lopes	10
Phil Rizzuto	10
Honus Wagner	9
Frankie Frisch	9
Johnny Evers	8
Roberto Alomar	7
Joe Tinker	7
Pepper Martin	7
Joe Morgan	7
Rickey Henderson	7

Career Batting Leaders *(Cont.)*

TOTAL BASES

Mickey Mantle	123
Yogi Berra	117
Babe Ruth	96
Lou Gehrig	87
Joe DiMaggio	84
Duke Snider	79
Hank Bauer	75
Reggie Jackson	74
Frankie Frisch	74
Gil McDougald	72

SLUGGING AVERAGE

Reggie Jackson	.755
Babe Ruth	.744
Lou Gehrig	.731
Lenny Dykstra	.700
Al Simmons	.658
Lou Brock	.655
Pepper Martin	.636
Paul Molitor	.636
Hank Greenberg	.624
Charlie Keller	.611

STRIKEOUTS

Mickey Mantle	54
Elston Howard	37
Duke Snider	33
Babe Ruth	30
Gil McDougald	29
Bill Skowron	26
Hank Bauer	25
Reggie Jackson	24
Bob Meusel	24
Frank Robinson	23
George Kelly	23
Tony Kubek	23
Joe DiMaggio	23

Career Pitching Leaders

GAMES

Whitey Ford	22
Rollie Fingers	16
Allie Reynolds	15
Bob Turley	15
Mike Stanton	15
Clay Carroll	14
Mariano Rivera	14
Clem Labine	13
Mark Wohlers	13
Jeff Nelson	13

INNINGS PITCHED

Whitey Ford	146
Christy Mathewson	101⅔
Red Ruffing	85⅔
Chief Bender	85
Waite Hoyt	83⅔
Bob Gibson	81
Art Nehf	79
Allie Reynolds	77
Jim Palmer	65
Catfish Hunter	63

WINS

Whitey Ford	10
Bob Gibson	7
Red Ruffing	7
Allie Reynolds	7
Lefty Gomez	6
Chief Bender	6
Waite Hoyt	6
Jack Coombs	5
Three Finger Brown	5
Herb Pennock	5
Christy Mathewson	5
Vic Raschi	5
Catfish Hunter	5

LOSSES

Whitey Ford	8
Eddie Plank	5
Schoolboy Rowe	5
Joe Bush	5
Rube Marquard	5
Christy Mathewson	5

SAVES

Mariano Rivera	7
Rollie Fingers	6
Allie Reynolds	4
Johnny Murphy	4
John Wetteland	4
Roy Face	3
Herb Pennock	3
Kent Tekulve	3
Firpo Marberry	3
Will McEnaney	3
Todd Worrell	3
Tug McGraw	3

*EARNED RUN AVERAGE

Harry Brecheen	0.83
Babe Ruth	0.87
Sherry Smith	0.89
Sandy Koufax	0.95
Hippo Vaughn	1.00
Monte Pearson	1.01
Christy Mathewson	1.06
Babe Adams	1.29
Eddie Plank	1.32
Rollie Fingers	1.35

SHUTOUTS

Christy Mathewson	4
Three Finger Brown	3
Whitey Ford	3
Bill Hallahan	2
Lew Burdette	2
Bill Dinneen	2
Sandy Koufax	2
Allie Reynolds	2
Art Nehf	2
Bob Gibson	2

COMPLETE GAMES

Christy Mathewson	10
Chief Bender	9
Bob Gibson	8
Red Ruffing	7
Whitey Ford	7
George Mullin	6
Eddie Plank	6
Art Nehf	6
Waite Hoyt	6

STRIKEOUTS

Whitey Ford	94
Bob Gibson	92
Allie Reynolds	62
Sandy Koufax	61
Red Ruffing	61
Chief Bender	59
George Earnshaw	56
John Smoltz	52
Waite Hoyt	49
Christy Mathewson	48

BASES ON BALLS

Whitey Ford	34
Allie Reynolds	32
Art Nehf	32
Jim Palmer	31
Bob Turley	29
Paul Derringer	27
Red Ruffing	27
Don Gullett	26
Burleigh Grimes	26
Vic Raschi	25

Minimum 25 innings pitched.

Alltime Team Rankings (by championships)

Team	W	L	Appearances	Pct.	Most Recent	Last Championship
New York Yankees	26	11	37	.703	2000	2000
Phil/KC/Oakland Athletics	9	5	14	.643	1990	1989
St. Louis Cardinals	9	6	15	.600	1987	1982
Brooklyn/LA Dodgers	6	12	18	.333	1988	1988
Pittsburgh Pirates	5	2	7	.714	1979	1979
Cincinnati Reds	5	4	9	.556	1990	1990
Boston Red Sox	5	4	9	.556	1986	1918
New York/San Francisco Giants	5	11	16	.313	1989	1954
Detroit Tigers	4	5	9	.444	1984	1984
Washington/Minnesota Twins	3	3	6	.500	1991	1991
St. Louis/Baltimore Orioles	3	4	7	.429	1983	1983
Boston/Milwaukee/Atlanta Braves	3	6	9	.333	1999	1995
Toronto Blue Jays	2	0	2	1.000	1993	1993
New York Mets	2	2	4	.500	2000	1986
Chicago White Sox	2	2	4	.500	1959	1917
Cleveland Indians	2	3	5	.400	1997	1948
Chicago Cubs	2	8	10	.200	1945	1908
Florida Marlins	1	0	1	1.000	1997	1997
Kansas City Royals	1	1	2	.500	1985	1985
Philadelphia Phillies	1	4	5	.200	1993	1980
Seattle/Milwaukee Brewers	0	1	1	.000	1982	—
San Diego Padres	0	2	2	.000	1998	—

League Championship Series

National League

1969	New York (E) 3, Atlanta (W) 0
1970	Cincinnati (W) 3, Pittsburgh (E) 0
1971	Pittsburgh (E) 3, San Francisco (W) 1
1972	Cincinnati (W) 3, Pittsburgh (E) 2
1973	New York (E) 3, Cincinnati (W) 2
1974	Los Angeles (W) 3, Pittsburgh (E) 1
1975	Cincinnati (W) 3, Pittsburgh (E) 0
1976	Cincinnati (W) 3, Philadelphia (E) 0
1977	Los Angeles (W) 3, Philadelphia (E) 1
1978	Los Angeles (W) 3, Philadelphia (E) 1
1979	Pittsburgh (E) 3, Cincinnati (W) 0
1980	Philadelphia (E) 3, Houston (W) 2
1981	Los Angeles (W) 3, Montreal (E) 2
1982	St. Louis (E) 3, Atlanta (W) 0
1983	Philadelphia (E) 3, Los Angeles (W) 1
1984	San Diego (W) 3, Chicago (E) 2
1985	St. Louis (E) 4, Los Angeles (W) 2
1986	New York (E) 4, Houston (W) 2
1987	St. Louis (E) 4, San Francisco (W) 3
1988	Los Angeles (W) 4, New York (E) 3
1989	San Francisco (W) 4, Chicago (E) 1
1990	Cincinnati (W) 4, Pittsburgh (E) 2
1991	Atlanta (W) 4, Pittsburgh (E) 3
1992	Atlanta (W) 4, Pitsburgh (E) 3
1993	Philadelphia (E) 4, Atlanta (W) 2
1994	Playoffs canceled due to players' strike.
1995	Atlanta (E) 4, Cincinnati (C) 0
1996	Atlanta (E) 4, St. Louis (C) 3
1997	Florida (wc) 4, Atlanta (E) 2
1998	San Diego (W) 4, Atlanta (E) 2
1999	Atlanta (E) 4, New York (wc) 2
2000	New York (wc) 4, St. Louis (C) 1

American League

1969	Baltimore (E) 3, Minnesota (W) 0
1970	Baltimore (E) 3, Minnesota (W) 0
1971	Baltimore (E) 3, Oakland (W) 0
1972	Oakland (W) 3, Detroit (E) 2
1973	Oakland (W) 3, Baltimore (E) 2
1974	Oakland (W) 3, Baltimore (E) 1
1975	Boston (E) 3, Oakland (W) 0
1976	New York (E) 3, Kansas City (W) 2
1977	New York (E) 3, Kansas City (W) 2
1978	New York (E) 3, Kansas City (W) 1
1979	Baltimore (E) 3, California (W) 1
1980	Kansas City (W) 3, New York (E) 0
1981	New York (E) 3, Oakland (W) 0
1982	Milwaukee (E) 3, California (W) 2
1983	Baltimore (E) 3, Chicago (W) 1
1984	Detroit (E) 3, Kansas City (W) 0
1985	Kansas City (W) 4, Toronto (E) 3
1986	Boston (E) 4, California (W) 3
1987	Minnesota (W) 4, Detroit (E) 1
1988	Oakland (W) 4, Boston (E) 0
1989	Oakland (W) 4, Toronto (E) 1
1990	Oakland (W) 4, Boston (E) 0
1991	Minnesota (W) 4, Toronto (E) 1
1992	Toronto (E) 4, Oakland (W) 2
1993	Toronto (E) 4, Chicago (W) 2
1994	Playoffs canceled due to players' strike.
1995	Cleveland (C) 4, Seattle (W) 2
1996	New York (E) 4, Baltimore (wc) 1
1997	Cleveland (C) 4, Baltimore (E) 2
1998	New York (E) 4, Cleveland (C) 2
1999	New York (E) 4, Boston (wc) 1
2000	New York (E) 4, Seattle (wc) 2

NLCS Most Valuable Player

1977 ....Dusty Baker, LA	1985 ....Ozzie Smith, StL	1993 ....Curt Schilling, Phil
1978 ....Steve Garvey, LA	1986 ....Mike Scott, Hou	1994 ....Playoffs canceled
1979 ....Willie Stargell, Pitt	1987 ....Jeffrey Leonard, SF	1995 ....Mike Devereaux, Atl
1980 ....Manny Trillo, Phil	1988 ....Orel Hershiser, LA	1996 ....Javier Lopez, Atl
1981 ....Burt Hooton, LA	1989 ....Will Clark, SF	1997 ....Livan Hernandez, Fla
1982 ....Darrell Porter, StL	1990 ....R. Myers/R. Dibble, Cin	1998 ....Sterling Hitchcock, SD
1983 ....Gary Matthews, Phil	1991 ....Steve Avery, Atl	1999 ....Eddie Perez, Atl
1984 ....Steve Garvey, SD	1992 ....John Smoltz, Atl	2000 ....Mike Hampton, NY

ALCS Most Valuable Player

1980 ....Frank White, KC	1987 ....Gary Gaetti, Minn	1994 ....Playoffs canceled
1981 ....Graig Nettles, NY	1988 ....Dennis Eckersley, Oak	1995 ....Orel Hershiser, Clev
1982 ....Fred Lynn, Calif	1989 ....Rickey Henderson, Oak	1996 ....Bernie Williams, NY
1983 ....Mike Boddicker, Balt	1990 ....Dave Stewart, Oak	1997 ....Marquis Grissom, Clev
1984 ....Kirk Gibson, Det	1991 ....Kirby Puckett, Minn	1998 ....David Wells, NY
1985 ....George Brett, KC	1992 ....Roberto Alomar, Tor	1999 ....Orlando Hernandez, NY
1986 ....Marty Barrett, Bos	1993 ....Dave Stewart, Tor	2000 ....David Justice, NY

Divisional Playoffs

National League

1995 ....Atlanta (E) 3, Colorado (wc) 1	
	Cincinnati (C) 3, Los Angeles (W) 0
1996 ....St. Louis (C) 3, San Diego (W) 0	
	Atlanta (E) 3, Los Angeles (wc) 0
1997 ....Atlanta (E) 3, Houston (C) 0	
	Florida (wc) 3, San Francisco (W) 0
1998 ....San Diego (W) 3, Houston (C) 1	
	Atlanta (E) 3, Chicago (wc) 0
1999 ....Atlanta (E) 3, Houston (C) 1	
	New York (wc) 3, Arizona (W) 1
2000 ....St. Louis (C) 3, Atlanta (E) 0	
	New York (wc) 3, San Francisco (W) 1

American League

1995 ....Cleveland (C) 3, Boston (E) 0	
	Seattle (W) 3, New York (wc) 2
1996 ....Baltimore (wc) 3, Cleveland (C) 1	
	New York (E) 3, Texas (W) 1
1997 ....Baltimore (E) 3, Seattle (W) 1	
	Cleveland (C) 3, New York (wc) 2
1998 ....New York (E) 3, Texas (W) 0	
	Cleveland (C) 3, Boston (wc) 1
1999 ....New York (E) 3, Texas (W) 1	
	Boston (wc) 3, Cleveland (C) 2
2000 ....New York (E) 3, Oakland (W) 2	
	Seattle (wc) 3, Chicago (C) 0

The All-Star Game

Results

Date	Winner	Score	Site	Date	Winner	Score	Site
7-6-33	American	4–2	Comiskey Park, Chi	7-8-58	American	4–3	Memorial Stadium, Balt
7-10-34	American	9–7	Polo Grounds, NY	7-7-59	National	5–4	Forbes Field, Pitt
7-8-35	American	4–1	Municipal Stadium, Clev	8-3-59	American	5–3	Memorial Coliseum, LA
7-7-36	National	4–3	Braves Field, Bos	7-11-60	National	5–3	Municipal Stadium, KC
7-7-37	American	8–3	Griffith Stadium, Wash	7-13-60	National	6–0	Yankee Stadium, NY
7-6-38	National	4–1	Crosley Field, Cin	7-11-61	National	5–4	Candlestick Park, SF
7-11-39	American	3–1	Yankee Stadium, NY	7-31-61	Tie*	1–1	Fenway Park, Bos
7-10-40	National	4–0	Sportsman's Park, StL	7-10-62	National	3–1	D.C. Stadium, Wash
7-8-41	American	7–5	Briggs Stadium, Det	7-30-62	American	9–4	Wrigley Field, Chi
7-6-42	American	3–1	Polo Grounds, NY	7-9-63	National	5–3	Municipal Stadium, Clev
7-13-43	American	5–3	Shibe Park, Phil	7-7-64	National	7–4	Shea Stadium, NY
7-11-44	National	7–1	Forbes Field, Pitt	7-13-65	National	6–5	Metropolitan Stadium, Minn
1945	No game due to wartime travel restrictions.						
7-9-46	American	12–0	Fenway Park, Bos	7-12-66	National	2–1	Busch Stadium, StL
7-8-47	American	2–1	Wrigley Field, Chi	7-11-67	National	2–1	Anaheim Stadium, Cal
7-13-48	American	5–2	Sportsman's Park, StL	7-9-68	National	1–0	Astrodome, Hou
7-12-49	American	11–7	Ebbets Field, Bklyn	7-23-69	National	9–3	R.F.K. Memorial Stadium, Wash
7-11-50	National	4–3	Comiskey Park, Chi				
7-10-51	National	8–3	Briggs Stadium, Det	7-14-70	National	5–4	Riverfront Stadium, Cin
7-8-52	National	3–2	Shibe Park, Phil	7-13-71	American	6–4	Tiger Stadium, Det
7-14-53	National	5–1	Crosley Field, Cin	7-25-72	National	4–3	Atlanta Stadium, Atl
7-13-54	American	11–9	Municipal Stadium, Clev	7-24-73	National	7–1	Royals Stadium, KC
7-12-55	National	6–5	County Stadium, Mil	7-23-74	National	7–2	Three Rivers Stadium, Pitt
7-10-56	National	7–3	Griffith Stadium, Wash	7-15-75	National	6–3	County Stadium, Mil
7-9-57	American	6–5	Busch Stadium, StL	7-13-76	National	7–1	Veterans Stadium, Phil

*Game called because of rain after nine innings.

Results *(Cont.)*

Date	Winner	Score	Site	Date	Winner	Score	Site
7-19-77	National	7–5	Yankee Stadium, NY	7-10-90	American	2–0	Wrigley Field, Chi
7-11-78	National	7–3	Jack Murphy Stadium, SD	7-9-91	American	4–2	SkyDome, Tor
7-17-79	National	7–6	Kingdome, Sea	7-14-92	American	13–6	Jack Murphy Stadium, SD
7-8-80	National	4–2	Dodger Stadium, LA	7-13-93	American	9–3	Camden Yards, Balt
8-9-81	National	5–4	Municipal Stadium, Clev	7-12-94	National	8–7	Three Rivers Stadium, Pitt
7-13-82	National	4–1	Olympic Stadium, Mtl	7-11-95	National	3–2	The Ballpark in
7-6-83	American	13–3	Comiskey Park, Chi				Arlington, Tex
7-10-84	National	3–1	Candlestick Park, SF	7-9-96	National	6–0	Veterans Stadium, Phil
7-16-85	National	6–1	Metrodome, Minn	7-8-97	American	3–1	Jacobs Field, Clev
7-15-86	American	3–2	Astrodome, Hou	7-7-98	American	13–8	Coors Field, Col
7-14-87	National	2–0	Oakland Coliseum, Oak	7-13-99	American	4–1	Fenway Park, Bos
7-12-88	American	2–1	Riverfront Stadium, Cin	7-11-00	American	6–3	Turner Field, Atl
7-11-89	American	5–3	Anaheim Stadium, Cal				

Most Valuable Players

1962	Maury Wills, LA	NL	1975	Bill Madlock, Chi	NL	1988	Terry Steinbach, Oak	AL
	Leon Wagner, LA	AL		Jon Matlack, NY	NL	1989	Bo Jackson, KC	AL
1963	Willie Mays, SF	NL	1976	George Foster, Cin	NL	1990	Julio Franco, Tex	AL
1964	Johnny Callison, Phil	NL	1977	Don Sutton, LA	NL	1991	Cal Ripken Jr, Balt	AL
1965	Juan Marichal, SF	NL	1978	Steve Garvey, LA	NL	1992	Ken Griffey Jr, Sea	AL
1966	Brooks Robinson, Balt	AL	1979	Dave Parker, Pitt	NL	1993	Kirby Puckett, Minn	AL
1967	Tony Perez, Cin	NL	1980	Ken Griffey, Cin	NL	1994	Fred McGriff, Atl	NL
1968	Willie Mays, SF	NL	1981	Gary Carter, Mtl	NL	1995	Jeff Conine, Fla	NL
1969	Willie McCovey, SF	NL	1982	Dave Concepcion, Cin	NL	1996	Mike Piazza, LA	NL
1970	Carl Yastrzemski, Bos	AL	1983	Fred Lynn, Calif	AL	1997	Sandy Alomar, Clev	AL
1971	Frank Robinson, Balt	AL	1984	Gary Carter, Mtl	NL	1998	Roberto Alomar, Balt	AL
1972	Joe Morgan, Cin	NL	1985	LaMarr Hoyt, SD	NL	1999	Pedro Martinez, Bos	AL
1973	Bobby Bonds, SF	NL	1986	Roger Clemens, Bos	AL	2000	Derek Jeter, NY	AL
1974	Steve Garvey, LA	NL	1987	Tim Raines, Mtl	NL			

The Regular Season

Most Valuable Players

NATIONAL LEAGUE

Year	Name and Team	Position	Noteworthy
1911	Wildfire Schulte, Chi	Outfield	21 HR†, 121 RBI†, .300
1912	*Larry Doyle, NY	Second base	10 HR, 90 RBI, .330
1913	Jake Daubert, Bklyn	First base	52 RBI, .350†
1914	*Johnny Evers, Bos	Second base	FA .976†, .279
1915–23	No selection		
1924	Dazzy Vance, Bklyn	Pitcher	28†–6, 2.16 ERA†, 262 K†
1925	Rogers Hornsby, StL	Second base, Manager	39 HR†, 143 RBI†, .403†
1926	*Bob O'Farrell, StL	Catcher	7 HR, 68 RBI, .293
1927	*Paul Waner, Pitt	Outfield	237 hits†, 131 RBI†, .380†
1928	*Jim Bottomley, StL	First base	31 HR†, 136 RBI†, .325
1929	*Rogers Hornsby, Chi	Second base	39 HR, 149 RBI, 156 runs†, .380
1930	No selection		
1931	*Frankie Frisch, StL	Second base	4 HR, 82 RBI, 28 SB†, .311
1932	Chuck Klein, Phil	Outfield	38 HR†, 137 RBI, 226 hits†, .348
1933	*Carl Hubbell, NY	Pitcher	23†–12, 1.66 ERA†, 10 SO†
1934	*Dizzy Dean, StL	Pitcher	30†–7, 2.66 ERA, 195 K†
1935	*Gabby Hartnett, Chi	Catcher	13 HR, 91 RBI, .344
1936	*Carl Hubbell, NY	Pitcher	26†–6, 2.31 ERA†
1937	Joe Medwick, StL	Outfield	31 HR‡, 154 RBI†, 111 runs†, .374†
1938	Ernie Lombardi, Cin	Catcher	19 HR, 95 RBI, .342†
1939	*Bucky Walters, Cin	Pitcher	27†–11, 2.29 ERA†, 137 K‡
1940	*Frank McCormick, Cin	First base	19 HR, 127 RBI, 191 hits†, .309
1941	*Dolph Camilli, Bklyn	First base	34 HR†, 120 RBI†, .285
1942	*Mort Cooper, StL	Pitcher	22†–7, 1.78 ERA†, 10 SO†
1943	*Stan Musial, StL	Outfield	13 HR, 81 RBI, 220 hits†, .357†
1944	*Marty Marion, StL	Shortstop	FA .972†, 63 RBI

*Played for pennant or, after 1968, division winner. †Led league. ‡Tied for league lead.

Most Valuable Players (Cont.)

NATIONAL LEAGUE (Cont.)

Year	Name and Team	Position	Noteworthy
1945	*Phil Cavarretta, Chi	First base	6 HR, 97 RBI, .355†
1946	*Stan Musial, StL	First base, Outfield	103 RBI, 124 runs†, 228 hits†, .365†
1947	Bob Elliott, Bos	Third base	22 HR, 113 RBI, .317
1948	Stan Musial, StL	Outfield	39 HR, 131 RBI†, .376†
1949	*Jackie Robinson, Bklyn	Second base	16 HR, 124 RBI, 37 SB†, .342†
1950	*Jim Konstanty, Phil	Pitcher	16–7, 22 saves†, 2.66 ERA
1951	Roy Campanella, Bklyn	Catcher	33 HR, 108 RBI, .325
1952	Hank Sauer, Chi	Outfield	37 HR‡, 121 RBI†, .270
1953	*Roy Campanella, Bklyn	Catcher	41 HR, 142 RBI†, .312
1954	*Willie Mays, NY	Outfield	41 HR, 110 RBI, 13 3B†, .345†
1955	*Roy Campanella, Bklyn	Catcher	32 HR, 107 RBI, .318
1956	*Don Newcombe, Bklyn	Pitcher	27†–7, 3.06 ERA
1957	*Hank Aaron, Mil	Outfield	44 HR†, 132 RBI†, .322
1958	Ernie Banks, Chi	Shortstop	47 HR†, 129 RBI†, .313
1959	Ernie Banks, Chi	Shortstop	45 HR, 143 RBI†, .304
1960	*Dick Groat, Pitt	Shortstop	2 HR, 50 RBI, .325†
1961	*Frank Robinson, Cin	Outfield	37 HR, 124 RBI, .323
1962	Maury Wills, LA	Shortstop	104 SB†, 208 hits, .299, GG
1963	*Sandy Koufax, LA	Pitcher	25‡–5, 1.88 ERA†, 306 K†
1964	*Ken Boyer, StL	Third Base	24 HR, 119 RBI†, .295
1965	Willie Mays, SF	Outfield	52 HR†, 112 RBI, .317
1966	Roberto Clemente, Pitt	Outfield	29 HR, 119 RBI, 202 hits, .317, GG
1967	*Orlando Cepeda, StL	First base	25 HR, 111 RBI†, .325
1968	*Bob Gibson, StL	Pitcher	22–9, 1.12 ERA†, 268 K†, 13 SO†, GG
1969	Willie McCovey, SF	First base	45 HR†, 126 RBI†, .320
1970	*Johnny Bench, Cin	Catcher	45 HR†, 148 RBI†, .293, GG
1971	Joe Torre, StL	Third base	24 HR, 137 RBI†, .363†
1972	*Johnny Bench, Cin	Catcher	40 HR†, 125 RBI†, .270, GG
1973	*Pete Rose, Cin	Outfield	5 HR, 64 RBI, .338†, 230 hits†
1974	*Steve Garvey, LA	First base	21 HR, 111 RBI, 200 hits, .312, GG
1975	*Joe Morgan, Cin	Second base	17 HR, 94 RBI, 67 SB, .327, GG
1976	*Joe Morgan, Cin	Second base	27 HR, 111 RBI, 60 SB, .320, GG
1977	George Foster, Cin	Outfield	52 HR†, 149 RBI†, .320
1978	Dave Parker, Pitt	Outfield	30 HR, 117 RBI, .334†, GG
1979	Keith Hernandez, StL	First base	11 HR, 105 RBI, 210 hits, .344†, GG
	*Willie Stargell, Pitt	First base	32 HR, 82 RBI, .281
1980	*Mike Schmidt, Phil	Third base	48 HR†, 121 RBI†, .286, GG
1981	Mike Schmidt, Phil	Third base	31 HR†, 91 RBI†, 78 runs†, .316, GG
1982	*Dale Murphy, Atl	Outfield	36 HR, 109 RBI‡, .281, GG
1983	Dale Murphy, Atl	Outfield	36 HR, 121 RBI†, .302, GG
1984	*Ryne Sandberg, Chi	Second base	19 HR, 84 RBI, 114 runs†, .314, GG
1985	*Willie McGee, StL	Outfield	10 HR, 82 RBI, 18 3B†, .353†, GG
1986	Mike Schmidt, Phil	Third base	37 HR†, 119 RBI†, .290, GG
1987	Andre Dawson, Chi	Outfield	49 HR†, 137 RBI†, .287, GG
1988	*Kirk Gibson, LA	Outfield	25 HR, 76 RBI, 106 runs, .290
1989	*Kevin Mitchell, SF	Outfield	47 HR†, 125 RBI†, .291
1990	*Barry Bonds, Pitt	Outfield	33 HR, 114 RBI, .301
1991	*Terry Pendleton, Atl	Third base	23 HR, 86 RBI, .319†
1992	Barry Bonds, Pitt	Outfield	34 HR, 103 RBI, .311
1993	Barry Bonds, SF	Outfield	46 HR†, 123 RBI†, .336
1994	Jeff Bagwell, Hou	First base	39 HR, 116 RBI†, .368
1995	*Barry Larkin, Cin	Shortstop	15 HR, 66 RBI, 51 SB, .319
1996	*Ken Caminiti, SD	Third base	40 HR, 130 RBI, .326
1997	Larry Walker, Col	Outfield	49 HR†, 130 RBI, .452 OBA†, .366, GG
1998	Sammy Sosa, Chi	Outfield	66 HR, 158 RBI†, 134 runs†, 416 TB†, .308
1999	*Chipper Jones, Atl	Third Base	45 HR, 110 RBI, 116 runs, .319

*Played for pennant or, after 1968, division winner. †Led league. ‡Tied for league lead.

Most Valuable Players (Cont.)
AMERICAN LEAGUE

Year	Name and Team	Position	Noteworthy
1911	Ty Cobb, Det	Outfield	8 HR, 144 RBI†, 24 3B†, .420†
1912	*Tris Speaker, Bos	Outfield	10 HR†, 98 RBI, 53 2B†, .383
1913	Walter Johnson, Wash	Pitcher	36†–7, 1.09 ERA†, 11 SO†, 243 K†
1914	*Eddie Collins, Phil	Second base	2 HR, 85 RBI, 122 runs†, .344
1915-21	No selection		
1922	George Sisler, StL	First base	8 HR, 105 RBI, 246 hits†, .420†
1923	*Babe Ruth, NY	Outfield	41 HR†, 131 RBI, .393
1924	*Walter Johnson, Wash	Pitcher	23†–7, 2.72 ERA†, 158 K†
1925	*Roger Peckinpaugh, Wash	Shortstop	4 HR, 64 RBI, .294
1926	George Burns, Clev	First base	114 RBI, 216 hits†, 64 2B†, .358
1927	*Lou Gehrig, NY	First base	47 HR, 175 RBI†, 52 2B†, .373
1928	Mickey Cochrane, Phil	Catcher	10 HR, 57 RBI, .293
1929	No selection		
1930	No selection		
1931	*Lefty Grove, Phil	Pitcher	31†–4, 2.06 ERA†, 175 K†
1932	Jimmie Foxx, Phil	First base	58 HR†, 169 RBI†, 151 runs†, .364
1933	Jimmie Foxx, Phil	First base	48 HR†, 163 RBI†, .356†
1934	*Mickey Cochrane, Det	Catcher	2 HR, 76 RBI, .320
1935	*Hank Greenberg, Det	First base	36 HR‡, 170 RBI†, 203 hits, .328
1936	*Lou Gehrig, NY	First base	49 HR†, 152 RBI, 167 runs†, .354
1937	Charlie Gehringer, Det	Second base	14 HR, 96 RBI, 133 runs, .371†
1938	Jimmie Foxx, Bos	First base	50 HR, 175 RBI†, .349†
1939	*Joe DiMaggio, NY	Outfield	30 HR, 126 RBI, .381†
1940	*Hank Greenberg, Det	Outfield	41 HR†, 150 RBI†, 50 2B†, .340
1941	*Joe DiMaggio, NY	Outfield	30 HR, 125 RBI†, .357
1942	*Joe Gordon, NY	Second base	18 HR, 103 RBI, .322
1943	*Spud Chandler, NY	Pitcher	20†–4, 1.64 ERA†, 5 SO‡
1944	Hal Newhouser, Det	Pitcher	29†–9, 2.22 ERA†, 187 K†
1945	*Hal Newhouser, Det	Pitcher	25†–9, 1.81 ERA†, 8 SO†, 212 K†
1946	*Ted Williams, Bos	Outfield	38 HR, 123 RBI, 142 runs†, .342
1947	*Joe DiMaggio, NY	Outfield	20 HR, 97 RBI, .315
1948	*Lou Boudreau, Clev	Shortstop	18 HR, 106 RBI, .355
1949	Ted Williams, Bos	Outfield	43 HR†, 159 RBI‡, 150 runs†, .343
1950	*Phil Rizzuto, NY	Shortstop	125 runs, 200 hits, .324
1951	*Yogi Berra, NY	Catcher	27 HR, 88 RBI, .294
1952	Bobby Shantz, Phil	Pitcher	24†–7, 2.48 ERA
1953	Al Rosen, Clev	Third base	43 HR†, 145 RBI†, 115 runs†, .336
1954	Yogi Berra, NY	Catcher	22 HR, 125 RBI, .307
1955	*Yogi Berra, NY	Catcher	27 HR, 108 RBI, .272
1956	*Mickey Mantle, NY	Outfield	52 HR†, 130 RBI†, 132 runs†, .353†
1957	*Mickey Mantle, NY	Outfield	34 HR, 94 RBI, 121 runs†, .365
1958	Jackie Jensen, Bos	Outfield	35 HR, 122 RBI†, .286
1959	*Nellie Fox, Chi	Second base	2 HR, 70 RBI, .306, GG
1960	*Roger Maris, NY	Outfield	39 HR, 112 RBI†, .283, GG
1961	*Roger Maris, NY	Outfield	61 HR†, 142 RBI†, .269
1962	*Mickey Mantle, NY	Outfield	30 HR, 89 RBI, .321, GG
1963	*Elston Howard, NY	Catcher	28 HR, 85 RBI, .287, GG
1964	Brooks Robinson, Balt	Third base	28 HR, 118 RBI†, .317, GG
1965	*Zoilo Versalles, Minn	Shortstop	126 runs†, 45 2B‡, 12 3B‡, GG
1966	*Frank Robinson, Balt	Outfield	49 HR†, 122 RBI†, 122 runs†, .316†
1967	*Carl Yastrzemski, Bos	Outfield	44 HR‡, 121 RBI†, 112 runs†, .326†, GG
1968	*Denny McLain, Det	Pitcher	31†–6, 1.96 ERA, 280 K
1969	*Harmon Killebrew, Minn	Third base, First base	49 HR†, 140 RBI†, .276
1970	*Boog Powell, Balt	First base	35 HR, 114 RBI, .297
1971	*Vida Blue, Oak	Pitcher	24–8, 1.82 ERA†, 8 SO†, 301 K
1972	Dick Allen, Chi	First base	37 HR†, 113 RBI†, .308
1973	*Reggie Jackson, Oak	Outfield	32 HR†, 117 RBI†, 99 runs†, .293
1974	Jeff Burroughs, Tex	Outfield	25 HR, 118 RBI†, .301
1975	*Fred Lynn, Bos	Outfield	21 HR, 105 RBI, 103 runs†, .331, GG
1976	*Thurman Munson, NY	Catcher	17 HR, 105 RBI, .302
1977	Rod Carew, Minn	First base	100 RBI, 128 runs†, 239 hits†, .388†
1978	Jim Rice, Bos	Outfield, DH	46 HR†, 139 RBI†, 213 hits†, .315
1979	*Don Baylor, Calif	Outfield, DH	36 HR, 139 RBI†, 120 runs†, .296
1980	*George Brett, KC	Third base	24 HR, 118 RBI, .390†

Most Valuable Players (Cont.)
AMERICAN LEAGUE (Cont.)

Year	Name and Team	Position	Noteworthy
1981	*Rollie Fingers, Mil	Pitcher	6–3, 28 saves†, 1.04 ERA
1982	*Robin Yount, Mil	Shortstop	29 HR, 114 RBI, 210 hits†, .331, GG
1983	*Cal Ripken, Balt	Shortstop	27 HR, 102 RBI, 121 runs†, 211 hits†, .318
1984	*Willie Hernandez, Det	Pitcher	9–3, 32 saves, 1.92 ERA
1985	Don Mattingly, NY	First base	35 HR, 145 RBI†, 48 2B†, .324, GG
1986	*Roger Clemens, Bos	Pitcher	24†–4, 2.48 ERA†, 238 K
1987	George Bell, Tor	Outfield	47 HR, 134 RBI†, .308
1988	*Jose Canseco, Oak	Outfield	42 HR†, 124 RBI†, 40 SB, .307
1989	Robin Yount, Mil	Outfield	21 HR, 103 RBI, 101 runs, .318
1990	*Rickey Henderson, Oak	Outfield	28 HR, 119 runs†, 65 SB†, .325
1991	Cal Ripken Jr, Balt	Shortstop	34 HR, 114 RBI, .323
1992	Dennis Eckersley, Oak	Pitcher	7–1, 1.91 ERA, 51 saves
1993	Frank Thomas, Chi	First base	41 HR, 128 RBI, .317
1994	Frank Thomas, Chi	First base	38 HR, 101 RBI, .353
1995	*Mo Vaughn, Bos	First base	39 HR, 126 RBI, .300
1996	*Juan Gonzalez, Tex	Outfield	47 HR, 144 RBI, .314
1997	*Ken Griffey Jr, Sea	Outfield	56 HR†, 125 runs†, 393 TB†, 147 RBI†, .304
1998	*Juan Gonzalez, Tex	Outfield	45 HR, 157 RBI†, 50 2B†, .318
1999	*Ivan Rodriguez, Tex	Catcher	35 HR, 113 RBI, 116 runs, .332, GG

*Played for pennant or, after 1968, division winner. †Led league. ‡Tied for league lead.

Notes: 2B=doubles; 3B=triples; FA=fielding average; GG=won Gold Glove, award begun in 1957; K=strikeouts; SO=shutouts; SB=stolen bases; TB=total bases.

Rookies of the Year

NATIONAL LEAGUE		AMERICAN LEAGUE	
1947*	Jackie Robinson, Bklyn (1B)	1949	Roy Sievers, StL (OF)
1948*	Alvin Dark, Bos (SS)	1950	Walt Dropo, Bos (1B)
1949	Don Newcombe, Bklyn (P)	1951	Gil McDougald, NY (3B)
1950	Sam Jethroe, Bos (OF)	1952	Harry Byrd, Phil (P)
1951	Willie Mays, NY (OF)	1953	Harvey Kuenn, Det (SS)
1952	Joe Black, Bklyn (P)	1954	Bob Grim, NY (P)
1953	Junior Gilliam, Bklyn (2B)	1955	Herb Score, Clev (P)
1954	Wally Moon, StL (OF)	1956	Luis Aparicio, Chi (SS)
1955	Bill Virdon, StL (OF)	1957	Tony Kubek, NY (OF, SS)
1956	Frank Robinson, Cin (OF)	1958	Albie Pearson, Wash (OF)
1957	Jack Sanford, Phil (P)	1959	Bob Allison, Wash (OF)
1958	Orlando Cepeda, SF (1B)	1960	Ron Hansen, Balt (SS)
1959	Willie McCovey, SF (1B)	1961	Don Schwall, Bos (P)
1960	Frank Howard, LA (OF)	1962	Tom Tresh, NY (SS)
1961	Billy Williams, Chi (OF)	1963	Gary Peters, Chi (P)
1962	Ken Hubbs, Chi (2B)	1964	Tony Oliva, Minn (OF)
1963	Pete Rose, Cin (2B)	1965	Curt Blefary, Balt (OF)
1964	Dick Allen, Phil (3B)	1966	Tommie Agee, Chi (OF)
1965	Jim Lefebvre, LA (2B)	1967	Rod Carew, Minn (2B)
1966	Tommy Helms, Cin (2B)	1968	Stan Bahnsen, NY (P)
1967	Tom Seaver, NY (P)	1969	Lou Piniella, KC (OF)
1968	Johnny Bench, Cin (C)	1970	Thurman Munson, NY (C)
1969	Ted Sizemore, LA (2B)	1971	Chris Chambliss, Clev (1B)
1970	Carl Morton, Mtl (P)	1972	Carlton Fisk, Bos (C)
1971	Earl Williams, Atl (C)	1973	Al Bumbry, Balt (OF)
1972	Jon Matlack, NY (P)	1974	Mike Hargrove, Tex (1B)
1973	Gary Matthews, SF (OF)	1975	Fred Lynn, Bos (OF)
1974	Bake McBride, StL (OF)	1976	Mark Fidrych, Det (P)
1975	John Montefusco, SF (P)	1977	Eddie Murray, Balt (DH)
1976	Pat Zachry, Cin (P)	1978	Lou Whitaker, Det (2B)
	Butch Metzger, SD (P)	1979	Alfredo Griffin, Tor (SS)
1977	Andre Dawson, Mtl (OF)		John Castino, Minn (3B)
1978	Bob Horner, Atl (3B)	1980	Joe Charboneau, Clev (OF)
1979	Rick Sutcliffe, LA (P)	1981	Dave Righetti, NY (P)
1980	Steve Howe, LA (P)	1982	Cal Ripken, Balt (SS)
1981	Fernando Valenzuela, LA (P)	1983	Ron Kittle, Chi (OF)
1982	Steve Sax, LA (2B)	1984	Alvin Davis, Sea (1B)

*Just one selection for both leagues.

Rookies of the Year *(Cont.)*

NATIONAL LEAGUE *(Cont.)*	AMERICAN LEAGUE *(Cont.)*
1983 ....Darryl Strawberry, NY (OF)	1985 ....Ozzie Guillen, Chi (SS)
1984 ....Dwight Gooden, NY (P)	1986 ....Jose Canseco, Oak (OF)
1985 ....Vince Coleman, StL (OF)	1987 ....Mark McGwire, Oak (1B)
1986 ....Todd Worrell, StL (P)	1988 ....Walt Weiss, Oak (SS)
1987 ....Benito Santiago, SD (C)	1989 ....Gregg Olson, Balt (P)
1988 ....Chris Sabo, Cin (3B)	1990 ....Sandy Alomar Jr, Clev (C)
1989 ....Jerome Walton, Chi (OF)	1991 ....Chuck Knoblauch, Minn (2B)
1990 ....Dave Justice, Atl (OF)	1992 ....Pat Listach, Mil (SS)
1991 ....Jeff Bagwell, Hou (3B)	1993 ....Tim Salmon, Calif (OF)
1992 ....Eric Karros, LA (1B)	1994 ....Bob Hamelin, Minn (DH)
1993 ....Mike Piazza, LA (C)	1995 ....Marty Cordova, Minn (OF)
1994 ....Raul Mondesi, LA (OF)	1996 ....Derek Jeter, NY (SS)
1995 ....Hideo Nomo, LA (P)	1997 ....Nomar Garciaparra, Bos (SS)
1996 ....Todd Hollandsworth, LA (OF)	1998 ....Ben Grieve, Oak (OF)
1997 ....Scott Rolen, Phil (3B)	1999 ....Carlos Beltran, KC (OF)
1998 ....Kerry Wood, Chi (P)	
1999 ....Scott Williamson, Cin (P)	

Cy Young Award

Year		W–L	Sv	ERA	Year		W–L	Sv	ERA
1956	....*Don Newcombe, Bklyn (NL)	27–7	0	3.06	1962	....Don Drysdale, LA (NL)	25–9	1	2.83
1957	....Warren Spahn, Mil (NL)	21–11	3	2.69	1963	....*Sandy Koufax, LA (NL)	25–5	0	1.88
1958	....Bob Turley, NY (AL)	21–7	1	2.97	1964	....Dean Chance, LA (AL)	20–9	4	1.65
1959	....Early Wynn, Chi (AL)	22–10	0	3.17	1965	....Sandy Koufax, LA (NL)	26–8	2	2.04
1960	....Vernon Law, Pitt (NL)	20–9	0	3.08	1966	....Sandy Koufax, LA (NL)	27–9	0	1.73
1961	....Whitey Ford, NY (AL)	25–4	0	3.21					

NATIONAL LEAGUE

Year		W–L	Sv	ERA
1967	.....Mike McCormick, SF	22–10	0	2.85
1968	.....*Bob Gibson, StL	22–9	0	1.12
1969	.....Tom Seaver, NY	25–7	0	2.21
1970	.....Bob Gibson, StL	23–7	0	3.12
1971	.....Ferguson Jenkins, Chi	24–13	0	2.77
1972	.....Steve Carlton, Phil	27–10	0	1.97
1973	.....Tom Seaver, NY	19–10	0	2.08
1974	.....Mike Marshall, LA	15–12	21	2.42
1975	.....Tom Seaver, NY	22–9	0	2.38
1976	.....Randy Jones, SD	22–14	0	2.74
1977	.....Steve Carlton, Phil	23–10	0	2.64
1978	.....Gaylord Perry, SD	21–6	0	2.72
1979	.....Bruce Sutter, Chi	6–6	37	2.23
1980	.....Steve Carlton, Phil	24–9	0	2.34
1981	.....Fernando Valenzuela, LA	13–7	0	2.48
1982	.....Steve Carlton, Phil	23–11	0	3.10
1983	.....John Denny, Phil	19–6	0	2.37
1984	.....†Rick Sutcliffe, Chi	16–1	0	2.69
1985	.....Dwight Gooden, NY	24–4	0	1.53
1986	.....Mike Scott, Hou	18–10	0	2.22
1987	.....Steve Bedrosian, Phil	5–3	40	2.83
1988	.....Orel Hershiser, LA	23–8	1	2.26
1989	.....Mark Davis, SD	4–3	44	1.85
1990	.....Doug Drabek, Pitt	22–6	0	2.76
1991	.....Tom Glavine, Atl	20–11	0	2.55
1992	.....Greg Maddux, Chi	20–11	0	2.18
1993	.....Greg Maddux, Atl	20–10	0	2.36
1994	.....Greg Maddux, Atl	16–6	0	1.56
1995	.....Greg Maddux, Atl	19–2	0	1.63
1996	.....John Smoltz, Atl	24–8	0	2.94
1997	.....Pedro Martinez, Mtl	17–8	0	1.90
1998	.....Tom Glavine, Atl	20–6	0	2.47
1999	.....Randy Johnson, Ariz	17–9	0	2.48

AMERICAN LEAGUE

Year		W–L	Sv	ERA
1967	.....Jim Lonborg, Bos	22–9	0	3.16
1968	.....*Denny McLain, Det	31–6	0	1.96
1969	.....Denny McLain, Det	24–9	0	2.80
	Mike Cuellar, Balt	23–11	0	2.38
1970	.....Jim Perry, Minn	24–12	0	3.03
1971	.....*Vida Blue, Oak	24–8	0	1.82
1972	.....Gaylord Perry, Clev	24–16	1	1.92
1973	.....Jim Palmer, Balt	22–9	1	2.40
1974	.....Catfish Hunter, Oak	25–12	0	2.49
1975	.....Jim Palmer, Balt	23–11	1	2.09
1976	.....Jim Palmer, Balt	22–13	0	2.51
1977	.....Sparky Lyle, NY	13–5	26	2.17
1978	.....Ron Guidry, NY	25–3	0	1.74
1979	.....Mike Flanagan, Balt	23–9	0	3.08
1980	.....Steve Stone, Balt	25–7	0	3.23
1981	.....*Rollie Fingers, Mil	6–3	28	1.04
1982	.....Pete Vuckovich, Mil	18–6	0	3.34
1983	.....LaMarr Hoyt, Chi	24–10	0	3.66
1984	.....*Willie Hernandez, Det	9–3	32	1.92
1985	.....Bret Saberhagen, KC	20–6	0	2.87
1986	.....*Roger Clemens, Bos	24–4	0	2.48
1987	.....Roger Clemens, Bos	20–9	0	2.97
1988	.....Frank Viola, Minn	24–7	0	2.64
1989	.....Bret Saberhagen, KC	23–6	0	2.16
1990	.....Bob Welch, Oak	27–6	0	2.95
1991	.....Roger Clemens, Bos	18–10	0	2.62
1992	.....*Dennis Eckersley, Oak	7–1	51	1.91
1993	.....Jack McDowell, Chi	22–10	0	3.37
1994	.....David Cone, KC	16–4	0	2.94
1995	.....Randy Johnson, Sea	18–2	0	2.48
1996	.....Pat Hentgen, Tor	20–10	0	3.22
1997	.....Roger Clemens, Tor	21–7	0	2.05
1998	.....Roger Clemens, Tor	20–6	0	2.65
1999	.....Pedro Martinez, Bos	23–4	0	1.55

*Pitchers who won the MVP and Cy Young awards in the same season.
†NL games only. Sutcliffe pitched 15 games with Cleveland before being traded to the Cubs.

Career Individual Batting

GAMES

Pete Rose	3562
Carl Yastrzemski	3308
Hank Aaron	3298
Ty Cobb	3034
Stan Musial	3026
Eddie Murray	3026
Willie Mays	2992
Dave Winfield	2973
Rusty Staub	2951
Brooks Robinson	2896
*Cal Ripken Jr.	2873
*Rickey Henderson	2856
Robin Yount	2856
Al Kaline	2834
Eddie Collins	2826
Reggie Jackson	2820
Frank Robinson	2808
*Harold Baines	2798
Tris Speaker	2789
Honus Wagner	2786

AT BATS

Pete Rose	14053
Hank Aaron	12364
Carl Yastrzemski	11988
Ty Cobb	11429
Eddie Murray	11336
*Cal Ripken Jr.	11074
Robin Yount	11008
Dave Winfield	11003
Stan Musial	10972
Willie Mays	10881
Paul Molitor	10835
Brooks Robinson	10654
Honus Wagner	10427
George Brett	10349
Lou Brock	10332
*Rickey Henderson	10331
Luis Aparicio	10230
Tris Speaker	10208
Al Kaline	10116
Rabbit Maranville	10078

HOME RUNS

Hank Aaron	755
Babe Ruth	714
Willie Mays	660
Frank Robinson	586
Harmon Killebrew	573
Reggie Jackson	563
*Mark McGwire	554
Mike Schmidt	548
Mickey Mantle	536
Jimmie Foxx	534
Ted Williams	521
Willie McCovey	521
Eddie Mathews	512
Ernie Banks	512
Mel Ott	511
Eddie Murray	504
*Barry Bonds	494
Lou Gehrig	493
Willie Stargell	475
Stan Musial	475

HITS

Pete Rose	4256
Ty Cobb	4189
Hank Aaron	3771
Stan Musial	3630
Tris Speaker	3515
Honus Wagner	3430
Carl Yastrzemski	3419
Paul Molitor	3319
Eddie Collins	3313
Willie Mays	3283
Eddie Murray	3255
Nap Lajoie	3251
George Brett	3154
Paul Waner	3152
Robin Yount	3142
Dave Winfield	3110
*Tony Gwynn	3108
*Cal Ripken	3070
Rod Carew	3053
Cap Anson	3041

BATTING AVERAGE (5000 AB)

Ty Cobb	.367
Rogers Hornsby	.358
Dan Brouthers	.349
Ed Delahanty	.346
Willie Keeler	.345
Tris Speaker	.345
Ted Williams	.344
Billy Hamilton	.344
Jesse Burkett	.342
Babe Ruth	.342
Harry Heilmann	.342
Bill Terry	.341
George Sisler	.340
Lou Gehrig	.340
Cap Anson	.339
Nap Lajoie	.339
*Tony Gwynn	.338
Sam Thompson	.336
Al Simmons	.334
Paul Waner	.333

RUNS

Ty Cobb	2245
*Rickey Henderson	2178
Babe Ruth	2174
Hank Aaron	2174
Pete Rose	2165
Willie Mays	2062
Stan Musial	1949
Lou Gehrig	1888
Tris Speaker	1881
Mel Ott	1859
Frank Robinson	1829
Eddie Collins	1820
Carl Yastrzemski	1816
Ted Williams	1798
Paul Molitor	1782
Charlie Gehringer	1774
Jimmie Foxx	1751
Honus Wagner	1740
Jesse Burkett	1720
Willie Keeler	1722

DOUBLES

Tris Speaker	793
Pete Rose	746
Stan Musial	725
Ty Cobb	724
George Brett	665
Honus Wagner	651
Nap Lajoie	648
Carl Yastrzemski	646
Hank Aaron	624
Paul Molitor	605
Paul Waner	604
*Cal Ripken Jr	587
Robin Yount	583
Wade Boggs	578
Charlie Gehringer	574
Eddie Murray	560
Harry Heilmann	542
Rogers Hornsby	541
Joe Medwick	540
Dave Winfield	540

TRIPLES

Sam Crawford	312
Ty Cobb	297
Honus Wagner	252
Jake Beckley	244
Roger Connor	233
Tris Speaker	223
Fred Clarke	223
Dan Brouthers	206
Joe Kelley	194
Paul Waner	190
Bid McPhee	189
Eddie Collins	187
Harry Stovey	185
Sam Rice	184
Ed Delahanty	183
Jesse Burkett	182
Edd Roush	182
Ed Konetchy	181
Buck Ewing	178
Rabbit Maranville	177
Stan Musial	177

BASES ON BALLS

Babe Ruth	2062
*Rickey Henderson	2060
Ted Williams	2019
Joe Morgan	1865
Carl Yastrzemski	1845
Mickey Mantle	1735
Mel Ott	1708
Eddie Yost	1614
Darrell Evans	1605
Stan Musial	1599
Pete Rose	1566
Harmon Killebrew	1559
*Barry Bonds	1547
Lou Gehrig	1508
Mike Schmidt	1507
Eddie Collins	1503
Willie Mays	1463
Jimmie Foxx	1452
Eddie Mathews	1444
Frank Robinson	1420

* Active

Career Individual Batting (Cont.)

RUNS BATTED IN

Hank Aaron	2297
Babe Ruth	2213
Lou Gehrig	1995
Stan Musial	1951
Ty Cobb	1937
Jimmie Foxx	1922
Eddie Murray	1917
Willie Mays	1903
Cap Anson	1879
Mel Ott	1860
Carl Yastrzemski	1844
Ted Williams	1839
Dave Winfield	1833
Al Simmons	1827
Frank Robinson	1812
Honus Wagner	1732
Reggie Jackson	1702
Tony Perez	1652
Ernie Banks	1636
*Cal Ripken	1627

STOLEN BASES

*Rickey Henderson	1370
Lou Brock	938
Billy Hamilton	912
Ty Cobb	892
Tim Raines	807
Vince Coleman	752
Eddie Collins	744
Arlie Latham	739
Max Carey	738
Honus Wagner	722
Joe Morgan	689
Willie Wilson	668
Tom Brown	657
Bert Campaneris	649
George Davis	616
Dummy Hoy	594
Otis Nixon	620
Maury Wills	586
George Van Haltren	583
Ozzie Smith	580

TOTAL BASES

Hank Aaron	6856
Stan Musial	6134
Willie Mays	6066
Ty Cobb	5854
Babe Ruth	5793
Pete Rose	5752
Carl Yastrzemski	5539
Eddie Murray	5397
Frank Robinson	5373
Dave Winfield	5221
Tris Speaker	5101
Lou Gehrig	5060
George Brett	5044
Mel Ott	5041
*Cal Ripken Jr	4996
Jimmie Foxx	4956
Ted Williams	4884
Honus Wagner	4862
Paul Molitor	4854
Al Kaline	4852

SLUGGING AVERAGE

Babe Ruth	.690
Ted Williams	.634
Lou Gehrig	.632
Jimmie Foxx	.609
Hank Greenberg	.605
*Mark McGwire	.593
*Mike Piazza	.580
Joe DiMaggio	.579
*Frank Thomas	.579
Rogers Hornsby	.577
*Ken Griffey Jr	.568
*Barry Bonds	.567
*Juan Gonzalez	.566
*Albert Belle	.564
*Larry Walker	.563
Johnny Mize	.562
Stan Musial	.559
Willie Mays	.557
Mickey Mantle	.557
Hank Aaron	.555

PINCH HITS

Manny Mota	150
Smoky Burgess	145
Greg Gross	143
*Lenny Harris	130
Jose Morales	123
Jerry Lynch	116
*John Vander Wal	116
Red Lucas	114
Steve Braun	113
Terry Crowley	108
Denny Walling	108
Gates Brown	107
Mike Lum	103
Jim Dwyer	102
Rusty Staub	100
Larry Biittner	95
Vic Davalillo	95
Gerald Perry	95
Jerry Hairston	94
Dave Philley	93
Joel Youngblood	93

STRIKEOUTS

Reggie Jackson	2597
Willie Stargell	1936
Mike Schmidt	1883
*Jose Canseco	1867
Tony Perez	1867
Dave Kingman	1816
Bobby Bonds	1757
Dale Murphy	1748
*Andres Galarraga	1741
Lou Brock	1730
Mickey Mantle	1710
Harmon Killebrew	1699
Chili Davis	1698
Dwight Evans	1697
Dave Winfield	1686
Gary Gaetti	1599
*Fred McGriff	1592
Lee May	1570
Dick Allen	1556
Willie McCovey	1550

The 30–30 Club (30 HR, 30 SB in single season)

Year		HR	SB	Year		HR	SB
1922	Kenny Williams, StL	39	37	1991	Ron Gant, Atl	32	34
1956	Willie Mays, NYG	36	40	1991	Howard Johnson, NYM	38	30
1957	Willie Mays, NYG	35	38	1992	Barry Bonds, Pitt	34	39
1963	Hank Aaron, Mil	44	31	1993	Sammy Sosa, ChiC	33	36
1969	Bobby Bonds, SF	32	45	1995	Barry Bonds, SF	33	31
1970	Tommy Harper, Mil	31	38	1995	Sammy Sosa, ChiC	36	34
1973	Bobby Bonds, SF	39	43	1996	Barry Bonds, SF	42	40
1975	Bobby Bonds, NYY	32	30	1996	Ellis Burks, Col	40	32
1977	Bobby Bonds, Cal	37	41	1996	Barry Larkin, Cin	33	36
1978	Bobby Bonds, Chi/Tex	31	43	1996	Dante Bichette, Col	31	31
1983	Dale Murphy, Atl	36	30	1997	Larry Walker, Col	49	33
1987	Joe Carter, Clev	32	31	1997	Jeff Bagwell, Hou	43	31
1987	Eric Davis, Cin	37	50	1997	Raul Mondesi, LA	30	32
1987	Darryl Strawberry, NYM	39	36	1997	Barry Bonds, SF	40	37
1987	Howard Johnson, NYM	36	32	1998	Alex Rodriguez, Sea	42	46
1988	Jose Canseco, Oak	42	40	1998	Shawn Green, Tor	35	35
1989	Howard Johnson, NYM	36	41	1999	Jeff Bagwell, Hou	42	30
1990	Ron Gant, Atl	32	33	1999	Raul Mondesi, LA	33	36
1990	Barry Bonds, Pitt	33	52	2000	Preston Wilson, Fla	31	36

Career Individual Pitching

GAMES

*Jesse Orosco	1096
Dennis Eckersley	1071
Hoyt Wilhelm	1070
Kent Tekulve	1050
Lee Smith	1022
Goose Gossage	1002
Lindy McDaniel	987
Rollie Fingers	944
*John Franco	940
Gene Garber	931
Cy Young	906
Sparky Lyle	899
Jim Kaat	898
*Dan Plesac	884
Paul Assenmacher	884
Jeff Reardon	880
Don McMahon	874
Phil Niekro	864
Charlie Hough	858
Roy Face	848

INNINGS PITCHED

Cy Young	7356⅔
Pud Galvin	5941⅓
Walter Johnson	5914⅔
Phil Niekro	5404⅓
Nolan Ryan	5386
Gaylord Perry	5350⅓
Don Sutton	5282⅓
Warren Spahn	5243⅔
Steve Carlton	5217⅓
Grover Alexander	5190
Kid Nichols	5056½
Tim Keefe	5047⅓
Bert Blyleven	4970
Mickey Welch	4802
Tom Seaver	4782⅔
Christy Mathewson	4780⅔
Tommy John	4710⅓
Robin Roberts	4688⅔
Early Wynn	4564
John Clarkson	4536⅓

WINS

Cy Young	511
Walter Johnson	417
Grover Alexander	373
Christy Mathewson	373
Warren Spahn	363
Kid Nichols	361
Pud Galvin	360
Tim Keefe	342
Steve Carlton	329
John Clarkson	328
Eddie Plank	326
Nolan Ryan	324
Don Sutton	324
Phil Niekro	318
Gaylord Perry	314
Tom Seaver	311
Charley Radbourn	309
Mickey Welch	307
Lefty Grove	300
Early Wynn	300

LOSSES

Cy Young	316
Pud Galvin	308
Nolan Ryan	292
Walter Johnson	279
Phil Niekro	274
Gaylord Perry	265
Don Sutton	256
Jack Powell	254
Eppa Rixey	251
Bert Blyleven	250
Robin Roberts	245
Warren Spahn	245
Steve Carlton	244
Early Wynn	244
Jim Kaat	237
Frank Tanana	236
Gus Weyhing	232
Tommy John	231
Bob Friend	230
Ted Lyons	230

WINNING PERCENTAGE

*Pedro Martinez	.691
Dave Foutz	.690
Whitey Ford	.690
Bob Caruthers	.688
Lefty Grove	.680
Vic Raschi	.667
Larry Corcoran	.665
Christy Mathewson	.665
Sam Leever	.660
Sal Maglie	.657
Sandy Koufax	.655
Johnny Allen	.654
*Randy Johnson	.653
Ron Guidry	.651
Lefty Gomez	.649
John Clarkson	.648
Three Finger Brown	.648
*Roger Clemens	.647
*Mike Mussina	.645
Dizzy Dean	.644

SAVES

Lee Smith	478
*John Franco	420
Dennis Eckersley	390
Jeff Reardon	367
Randy Myers	347
Rollie Fingers	341
*John Wetteland	330
*Rick Aguilera	318
Tom Henke	311
Goose Gossage	310
Jeff Montgomery	304
*Doug Jones	303
Bruce Sutter	300
*Trevor Hoffman	271
*Roberto Hernandez	266
*Rod Beck	260
Todd Worrell	256
Dave Righetti	252
Dan Quisenberry	244
Sparky Lyle	238

EARNED RUN AVERAGE

Ed Walsh	1.82
Addie Joss	1.89
Three Finger Brown	2.06
John Ward	2.10
Christy Mathewson	2.13
Rube Waddell	2.16
Walter Johnson	2.17
Orval Overall	2.23
Tommy Bond	2.25
Ed Reulbach	2.28
Will White	2.28
Jim Scott	2.30
Eddie Plank	2.35
Larry Corcoran	2.36
Eddie Cicotte	2.38
Ed Killian	2.38
George McQuillan	2.38
Doc White	2.39
Nap Rucker	2.42
Terry Larkin	2.43
Jim McCormick	2.43
Jeff Tesreau	2.43

SHUTOUTS

Walter Johnson	110
Grover Alexander	90
Christy Mathewson	79
Cy Young	76
Eddie Plank	69
Warren Spahn	63
Nolan Ryan	61
Tom Seaver	61
Bert Blyleven	60
Don Sutton	58
Pud Galvin	57
Ed Walsh	57
Bob Gibson	56
Three Finger Brown	55
Steve Carlton	55
Jim Palmer	53
Gaylord Perry	53
Juan Marichal	52
Rube Waddell	50
Vic Willis	50

COMPLETE GAMES

Cy Young	749
Pud Galvin	639
Tim Keefe	554
Walter Johnson	531
Kid Nichols	531
Mickey Welch	525
Charley Radbourn	489
John Clarkson	485
Tony Mullane	468
Jim McCormick	466
Gus Weyhing	448
Grover Alexander	437
Christy Mathewson	434
Jack Powell	422
Eddie Plank	410
Will White	394
Amos Rusie	392
Vic Willis	388
Warren Spahn	382
Jim Whitney	377

* Active.

Career Individual Pitching (Cont.)

STRIKEOUTS

Nolan Ryan	5714
Steve Carlton	4136
Bert Blyleven	3701
Tom Seaver	3640
Don Sutton	3574
Gaylord Perry	3534
Walter Johnson	3509
*Roger Clemens	3504
Phil Niekro	3342
Ferguson Jenkins	3192
Bob Gibson	3117
*Randy Johnson	3040
Jim Bunning	2855
Mickey Lolich	2832
Cy Young	2803
Frank Tanana	2773
Warren Spahn	2583
Bob Feller	2581
Jerry Koosman	2556
*David Cone	2540

BASES ON BALLS

Nolan Ryan	2795
Steve Carlton	1833
Phil Niekro	1809
Early Wynn	1775
Bob Feller	1764
Bobo Newsom	1732
Amos Rusie	1704
Charlie Hough	1665
Gus Weyhing	1566
Red Ruffing	1541
Bump Hadley	1442
Warren Spahn	1434
Earl Whitehill	1431
Tony Mullane	1408
Sad Sam Jones	1396
Jack Morris	1390
Tom Seaver	1390
Gaylord Perry	1379
Mike Torrez	1371
Walter Johnson	1363

Alltime Winningest Managers

CAREER

	W	L	Pct	Yrs		W	L	Pct	Yrs
Connie Mack	3755	3967	.486	53	*Tony LaRussa	1761	1603	.523	22
John McGraw	2810	1987	.586	33	*Bobby Cox	1671	1312	.560	19
Sparky Anderson	2238	1855	.547	26	Ralph Houk	1627	1539	.514	20
Bucky Harris	2168	2228	.493	29	Fred Clarke	1609	1189	.575	19
Joe McCarthy	2155	1346	.616	24	Dick Williams	1592	1474	.519	21
Walter Alston	2063	1634	.558	23	Tommy Lasorda	1589	1434	.526	20
Leo Durocher	2015	1717	.540	24	Earl Weaver	1506	1080	.582	17
Casey Stengel	1942	1868	.510	25	Clark Griffith	1491	1367	.522	20
Gene Mauch	1907	2044	.483	26	Miller Huggins	1431	1149	.555	17
Bill McKechnie	1904	1737	.523	25	Al Lopez	1412	1012	.583	17

REGULAR SEASON

	W	L	Pct	Yrs		W	L	Pct	Yrs
Connie Mack	3731	3948	.486	53	*Tony LaRussa	1734	1578	.524	22
John McGraw	2784	1959	.587	33	Ralph Houk	1619	1531	.514	20
Sparky Anderson	2194	1834	.545	26	*Bobby Cox	1616	1271	.560	19
Bucky Harris	2157	2218	.493	29	Fred Clarke	1602	1181	.576	19
Joe McCarthy	2125	1333	.615	24	Dick Williams	1571	1451	.520	21
Walter Alston	2040	1613	.558	23	Tommy Lasorda	1558	1404	.526	20
Leo Durocher	2008	1709	.540	24	Clark Griffith	1491	1367	.522	20
Casey Stengel	1905	1842	.508	25	Earl Weaver	1480	1060	.583	17
Gene Mauch	1902	2037	.483	26	Miller Huggins	1413	1134	.555	17
Bill McKechnie	1896	1723	.524	25	Al Lopez	1410	1004	.584	17

WORLD SERIES

	W	L	T	Pct	App	WS		W	L	T	Pct	App	WS
Casey Stengel	37	26	0	.587	10	7	Bucky Harris	11	10	0	.524	3	2
Joe McCarthy	30	13	0	.698	9	7	Billy Southworth	11	11	0	.500	4	2
John McGraw	26	28	2	.482	9	2	Earl Weaver	11	13	0	.458	4	1
Connie Mack	24	19	0	.558	8	5	*Bobby Cox	11	18	0	.379	5	1
Walter Alston	20	20	0	.500	7	4	Whitey Herzog	10	11	0	.476	3	1
Miller Huggins	18	15	1	.544	6	3	Bill Carrigan	8	2	0	.800	2	2
*Joe Torre	16	3	0	.842	4	4	Cito Gaston	8	4	0	.667	2	2
Sparky Anderson	16	12	0	.571	5	3	Danny Murtaugh	8	6	0	.571	2	2
Tommy Lasorda	12	11	0	.522	4	2	*Tom Kelly	8	6	0	.571	2	2
Dick Williams	12	14	0	.462	4	2	Ralph Houk	8	8	0	.500	3	2
Frank Chance	11	9	1	.548	4	2	Bill McKechnie	8	14	0	.364	4	2

* Active.

Individual Batting (Single Season)

HITS

George Sisler, 1920	.257
Lefty O'Doul, 1929	.254
Bill Terry, 1930	.254
Al Simmons, 1925	.253
Rogers Hornsby, 1922	.250
Chuck Klein, 1930	.250
Ty Cobb, 1911	.248
George Sisler, 1922	.246
Heinie Manush, 1928	.241
Babe Herman, 1930	.241

BATTING AVERAGE

Hugh Duffy, 1894	.440
Tip O'Neill, 1887	.435
Ross Barnes, 1876	.429
Nap Lajoie, 1901	.426
Willie Keeler, 1897	.424
Rogers Hornsby, 1924	.424
George Sisler, 1922	.420
Ty Cobb, 1911	.420
Fred Dunlap, 1884	.412
Ed Delahanty, 1899	.410

DOUBLES

Earl Webb, 1931	.67
George Burns, 1926	.64
Joe Medwick, 1936	.64
Hank Greenberg, 1934	.63
Paul Waner, 1932	.62
Charlie Gehringer, 1936	.60
Tris Speaker, 1923	.59
Chuck Klein, 1930	.59
Todd Helton, 2000	.59
Billy Herman, 1936	.57
Billy Herman, 1935	.57
Carlos Delgado, 2000	.57

TOTAL BASES

Babe Ruth, 1921	.457
Rogers Hornsby, 1922	.450
Lou Gehrig, 1927	.447
Chuck Klein, 1930	.445
Jimmie Foxx, 1932	.438
Stan Musial, 1948	.429
Hack Wilson, 1930	.423
Chuck Klein, 1932	.420
Lou Gehrig, 1930	.419
Joe DiMaggio, 1937	.418

TRIPLES

Chief Wilson, 1912	.36
Dave Orr, 1886	.31
Heinie Reitz, 1894	.31
Perry Werden, 1893	.29
Harry Davis, 1897	.28
George Davis, 1893	.27
Sam Thompson, 1894	.27
Jimmy Williams, 1899	.27
John Reilly, 1890	.26
George Treadway, 1894	.26
Joe Jackson, 1912	.26
Sam Crawford, 1914	.26
Kiki Cuyler, 1925	.26

HOME RUNS

Mark McGwire, 1998	.70
Sammy Sosa, 1998	.66
Mark McGwire, 1999	.65
Sammy Sosa, 1999	.63
Roger Maris, 1961	.61
Babe Ruth, 1927	.60
Babe Ruth, 1921	.59
Jimmie Foxx, 1932	.58
Hank Greenberg, 1938	.58
Mark McGwire, 1997	.58

RUNS BATTED IN

Hack Wilson, 1930	.190
Lou Gehrig, 1931	.184
Hank Greenberg, 1937	.183
Lou Gehrig, 1927	.175
Jimmie Foxx, 1938	.175
Lou Gehrig, 1930	.174
Babe Ruth, 1921	.171
Chuck Klein, 1930	.170
Hank Greenberg, 1935	.170
Jimmie Foxx, 1932	.169

STRIKEOUTS

Bobby Bonds, 1970	.189
Bobby Bonds, 1969	.187
Preston Wilson, 2000	.187
Rob Deer, 1987	.186
Pete Incaviglia, 1986	.185
Cecil Fielder, 1990	.182
Mo Vaughn, 2000	.181
Mike Schmidt, 1975	.180
Rob Deer, 1986	.179
Dave Nicholson, 1963	.175
Gorman Thomas, 1979	.175
Jose Canseco, 1986	.175
Rob Deer, 1991	.175
Jay Buhner, 1997	.175

RUNS

Billy Hamilton, 1894	.192
Tom Brown, 1891	.177
Babe Ruth, 1921	.177
Tip O'Neill, 1887	.167
Lou Gehrig, 1936	.167
Billy Hamilton, 1895	.166
Willie Keeler, 1894	.165
Joe Kelley, 1894	.165
Arlie Latham, 1887	.163
Babe Ruth, 1928	.163
Lou Gehrig, 1931	.163

STOLEN BASES

Hugh Nicol, 1887	.138
Rickey Henderson, 1982	.130
Arlie Latham, 1887	.129
Lou Brock, 1974	.118
Charlie Comiskey, 1887	.117
John Ward, 1887	.111
Billy Hamilton, 1889	.111
Billy Hamilton, 1891	.111
Vince Coleman, 1985	.110
Arlie Latham, 1888	.109
Vince Coleman, 1987	.109

BASES ON BALLS

Babe Ruth, 1923	.170
Ted Williams, 1947	.162
Ted Williams, 1949	.162
Mark McGwire, 1998	.162
Ted Williams, 1946	.156
Eddie Yost, 1956	.151
Eddie Joost, 1949	.149
Jeff Bagwell, 1999	.149
Babe Ruth, 1920	.148
Eddie Stanky, 1945	.148
Jimmy Wynn, 1969	.148

SLUGGING AVERAGE

Babe Ruth, 1920	.847
Babe Ruth, 1921	.846
Babe Ruth, 1927	.772
Lou Gehrig, 1927	.765
Babe Ruth, 1923	.764
Rogers Hornsby, 1925	.756
Mark McGwire, 1998	.752
Jeff Bagwell, 1994	.750
Jimmie Foxx, 1932	.749
Babe Ruth, 1924	.739

Individual Pitching (Single Season)

GAMES

Mike Marshall, 1974.............106
Kent Tekulve, 1979...............94
Mike Marshall, 1973..............92
Kent Tekulve, 1978...............91
Wayne Granger, 1969.............90
Mike Marshall, 1979..............90
Kent Tekulve, 1987...............90
Mark Eichhorn, 1987..............89
Wilbur Wood, 1968.................88
Mike Myers, 1997..................88

GAMES STARTED

Will White, 1879....................75
Jim Galvin, 1883...................75
Jim McCormick, 1880.............74
Charley Radbourn, 1884.......73
Guy Hecker, 1884..................73
Jim Galvin, 1884...................72
John Clarkson, 1889..............72
Bill Hutchison, 1892..............71
John Clarkson, 1885..............70
Matt Kilroy, 1887...................69

INNINGS PITCHED

Will White, 1878 ....680.0
Charley Radbourn, 1884....678.2
Guy Hecker, 1884...........670.2
Jim McCormick, 1880.......657.2
Jim Galvin, 1883 ....656.1
Jim Galvin, 1884 ....636.1
Charley Radbourn, 1883...632.1
Bill Hutchison, 1892..........627.0
John Clarkson, 1885.........623.0
Jim Devlin, 1876 ....622.0

WINS

Charley Radbourn, 1884 59
John Clarkson, 1885..............53
Guy Hecker, 1884..................52
John Clarkson, 1889..............49
Charley Radbourn, 1883 48
Charlie Buffinton, 1884 48
Al Spalding, 1876 47
John Ward, 1879 47
Jim Galvin, 1883..................46
Jim Galvin, 1884...................46
Matt Kilroy, 1887...................46

LOSSES

John Coleman, 1883.............48
Will White, 1880 42
Larry McKeon, 1884 41
George Bradley, 1879 40
Jim McCormick, 1879............40
Henry Porter, 1888................37
Kid Carsey, 1891...................37
George Cobb, 1892................37
Stump Weidman, 1886 36
Bill Hutchison, 1892..............36

WINNING PERCENTAGE

Roy Face, 1959.................. .947
Johnny Allen, 1937...............938
Greg Maddux, 1995 .... .905
Randy Johnson, 1995........ .900
Ron Guidry, 1978.................893
Freddie Fitzsimmons, 1940... .889
Lefty Grove, 1931 886
Bob Stanley, 1978 882
Preacher Roe, 1951.............880
Fred Goldsmith, 1880........ .875
Tom Seaver, 1981.............. .875

SAVES

Bobby Thigpen, 1990...........57
Randy Myers, 1993..............53
Trevor Hoffman, 1998...........53
Dennis Eckersley, 1992........51
Rod Beck, 1998....................51
Dennis Eckersley, 1990........48
Rod Beck, 1993....................48
Jeff Shaw, 1998...................48
Lee Smith, 1991...................47
Lee Smith, 1993...................46
Dave Righetti, 1986 46
Bryan Harvey, 1991.............46
Jose Mesa, 1995 46
Tom Gordon, 1998................46

EARNED RUN AVERAGE

Tim Keefe, 1880.................0.86
Dutch Leonard, 1914..........0.96
Three Finger Brown, 1906....1.04
Bob Gibson, 1968...............1.12
Christy Mathewson, 1909 ...1.14
Walter Johnson, 1913.........1.14
Jack Pfiester, 1907 ....1.15
Addie Joss, 1908................1.16
Carl Lundgren, 1907...........1.17
Denny Driscoll, 1882 ....1.21

SHUTOUTS

George Bradley, 1876 16
Grover Alexander, 1916 16
Jack Coombs, 1910..............13
Bob Gibson, 1968.................13
Jim Galvin, 1884 12
Ed Morris, 1886 12
Grover Alexander, 1915 12
Tommy Bond, 1879 11
Charley Radbourn, 1884 11
Dave Foutz, 1886..................11
Christy Mathewson, 1908 11
Ed Walsh, 1908.....................11
Walter Johnson, 1913............11
Sandy Koufax, 1963 11
Dean Chance, 1964...............11

COMPLETE GAMES

Will White, 1879 75
Charley Radbourn, 1884 73
Jim McCormick, 1880.............72
Jim Galvin, 1883....................72
Guy Hecker, 1884..................72
Jim Galvin, 1884...................71
Tim Keefe, 1883....................68
John Clarkson, 1885..............68
John Clarkson, 1889..............68
Bill Hutchison, 1892..............67

STRIKEOUTS

Matt Kilroy, 1886..................513
Toad Ramsey, 1886.............499
Hugh Daily, 1884.................483
Dupee Shaw, 1884 451
Charley Radbourn, 1884 441
Charlie Buffinton, 1884 417
Guy Hecker, 1884................385
Nolan Ryan, 1973................383
Sandy Koufax, 1965 382
Bill Sweeney, 1884 374

BASES ON BALLS

Amos Rusie, 1890................289
Mark Baldwin, 1889..............274
Amos Rusie, 1892................267
Amos Rusie, 1891................262
Mark Baldwin, 1890..............249
Jack Stivetts, 1891...............232
Mark Baldwin, 1891..............227
Phil Knell, 1891....................226
Bob Barr, 1890 219
Amos Rusie 1893................218

Manager of the Year

NATIONAL LEAGUE	AMERICAN LEAGUE
1983 ....Tommy Lasorda, LA	1983 ....Tony La Russa, Chi
1984 ....Jim Frey, Chi	1984 ....Sparky Anderson, Det
1985 ....Whitey Herzog, StL	1985 ....Bobby Cox, Tor
1986 ....Hal Lanier, Hou	1986 ....John McNamara, Bos
1987 ....Buck Rodgers, Mtl	1987 ....Sparky Anderson, Det
1988 ....Tommy Lasorda, LA	1988 ....Tony La Russa, Oak
1989 ....Don Zimmer, Chi	1989 ....Frank Robinson, Balt
1990 ....Jim Leyland, Pitt	1990 ....Jeff Torborg, Chi
1991 ....Bobby Cox, Atl	1991 ....Tom Kelly, Minn
1992 ....Jim Leyland, Pitt	1992 ....Tony La Russa, Oak
1993 ....Dusty Baker, SF	1993 ....Gene Lamont, Chi
1994 ....Felipe Alou, Mtl	1994 ....Buck Showalter, NY
1995 ....Don Baylor, Col	1995 ....Lou Piniella, Sea
1996 ....Bruce Bochy, SD	1996 ....Joe Torre, NY
1997 ....Dusty Baker, SF	Johnny Oates, Tex
1998 ....Larry Dierker, Hou	1997 ....Davey Johnson, Balt
1999 ....Jack McKeon, Cin	1998 ....Joe Torre, NY
	1999 ....Jimy Williams, Bos

Individual Batting (Single Game)

MOST RUNS

7 ....Guy Hecker, Lou Aug 15, 1886

MOST HITS

7 ....Wilbert Robinson, Balt June 10, 1892
Rennie Stennett, Pitt Sept 16, 1975

MOST HOME RUNS

4 ....Bobby Lowe, Bos (N) May 30, 1894
Ed Delahanty, Phil July 13, 1896
Lou Gehrig, NY (A) June 3, 1932
Gil Hodges, Bklyn Aug 31, 1950
Joe Adcock, Mil (N) July 31, 1954
Rocky Colavito, Clev June 10, 1959
Willie Mays, SF April 30, 1961
Bob Horner, Atl July 6, 1986
Mark Whiten, StL Sept 7, 1993

MOST GRAND SLAMS

2 ....Tony Lazzeri, NY (A) May 24, 1936
Jim Tabor, Bos (A) July 4, 1939
Rudy York, Bos (A) July 27, 1946
Jim Gentile, Balt May 9, 1961
Tony Cloninger, Atl July 3, 1966
Jim Northrup, Det June 24, 1968
Frank Robinson, Balt June 26, 1970
Robin Ventura, Chi (A) Sept 4, 1995
Fernando Tatis, StL Apr 23, 1999
N. Garciaparra, Bos May 10, 1999

MOST RBI

12 .....Jim Bottomley, StL Sept 16, 1924
Mark Whiten, StL Sept 7, 1993

Individual Batting (Single Inning)

MOST RUNS

3 ....Tommy Burns, Chi (N) Sept 6, 1883, 7th inning
Ned Williamson, Chi (N) Sept 6, 1883, 7th inning
Sammy White, Bos (A) June 18, 1953, 7th inning

MOST HITS

3 ....Tommy Burns, Chi (N) Sept 6, 1883, 7th inning
Fred Pfeiffer, Chi (N) Sept 6, 1883, 7th inning
Ned Williamson, Chi (N) Sept 6, 1883, 7th inning
Gene Stephens, Bos (A) June 18, 1953, 7th inning

MOST RBI

8.......Fernando Tatis, StL Apr 23, 1999 3rd inning

Note: All single-game hitting records for nine-inning game.

Individual Pitching (Single Game)

	MOST INNINGS PITCHED	
26	Leon Cadore, Bklyn	May 1, 1920, tie 1–1
	Joe Oeschger, Bos (N)	May 1, 1920, tie 1–1

MOST RUNS ALLOWED

24	Al Travers, Det	May 18, 1912

MOST HITS ALLOWED

36	Jack Wadsworth, Lou	Aug 17, 1894

MOST STRIKEOUTS

20	Roger Clemens, Bos (A)	April 29, 1986
20	Roger Clemens, Bos (A)	Sept 18, 1996
20	Kerry Wood, Chi (N)	May 6, 1998

MOST WALKS ALLOWED

16	Bill George, NY (N)	May 30, 1887
	George Van Haltren, Chi (N)	June 27, 1887
	Henry Gruber, Clev	Apr 19, 1890
	Bruno Haas, Phil (A)	June 2, 1915

MOST WILD PITCHES

6	J.R. Richard, Hou	April 10, 1979
	Phil Niekro, Atl	Aug 14, 1979
	Bill Gullickson, Mtl	April 10, 1982

Individual Pitching (Single Inning)

MOST RUNS ALLOWED

13	Lefty O'Doul, Bos (A)	July 7, 1923

MOST WALKS ALLOWED

8	Dolly Gray, Wash	Aug 28, 1909

MOST WILD PITCHES

4	Walter Johnson, Wash	Sept 21, 1914
	Phil Niekro, Atl	Aug 14, 1979

Miscellaneous

LONGEST GAME, BY INNINGS

26	Brooklyn 1, Boston 1	May 1, 1920

LONGEST NINE-INNING GAME, BY TIME

4:22	Baltimore 13, New York 9	Sept 5, 1997
	Milwaukee 14, Chicago (N) 8	May 11, 2000

Baseball Hall of Fame

Players

	Position	Career	Selected		Position	Career	Selected
Hank Aaron	OF	1954–76	1982	Frank Chance	1B	1898–1914	1946
Grover Alexander	P	1911–30	1938	Oscar Charleston*	OF		1976
Cap Anson	1B	1876–97	1939	Jack Chesbro	P	1899–1909	1946
Luis Aparicio	SS	1956–73	1984	Fred Clarke	OF	1894–1915	1945
Luke Appling	SS	1930–50	1964	John Clarkson	P	1882–94	1963
Richie Ashburn	OF	1948–62	1995	Roberto Clemente	OF	1955–72	1973
Earl Averill	OF	1929–41	1975	Ty Cobb	OF	1905–28	1936
Frank Baker	3B	1908–22	1955	Mickey Cochrane	C	1925–37	1947
Dave Bancroft	SS	1915–30	1971	Eddie Collins	2B	1906–30	1939
Ernie Banks	SS-1B	1953–71	1977	Jimmy Collins	3B	1895–1908	1945
Jake Beckley	1B	1888–1907	1971	Earle Combs	OF	1924–35	1970
Cool Papa Bell*	OF		1974	Roger Connor	1B	1880–97	1976
Johnny Bench	C	1967–83	1989	Stan Coveleski	P	1912–28	1969
Chief Bender	P	1903–25	1953	Sam Crawford	OF	1899–1917	1957
Yogi Berra	C	1946–65	1972	Joe Cronin	SS	1926–45	1956
Jim Bottomley	1B	1922–37	1974	Candy Cummings	P	1872–77	1939
Lou Boudreau	SS	1938–52	1970	Kiki Cuyler	OF	1921–38	1968
Roger Bresnahan	C	1897–1915	1945	Ray Dandridge*	3B		1987
George Brett	3B	1973–93	1999	George Davis	SS	1890–1909	1998
Lou Brock	OF	1961–79	1985	Leon Day*	P		1995
Dan Brouthers	1B	1879–1904	1945	Dizzy Dean	P	1930–47	1953
Three Finger Brown	P	1903–16	1949	Ed Delahanty	OF	1888–1903	1945
Jim Bunning	P	1955–1971	1996	Bill Dickey	C	1928–46	1954
Jesse Burkett	OF	1890–1905	1946	Martin Dihigo*	P-OF		1977
Roy Campanella	C	1948–57	1969	Joe DiMaggio	OF	1936–51	1955
Rod Carew	1B-2B	1967–85	1991	Larry Doby	OF	1947–59	1998
Max Carey	OF	1910–29	1961	Bobby Doerr	2B	1937–51	1986
Steve Carlton	P	1965–88	1994	Don Drysdale	P	1956–69	1984
Orlando Cepeda	1B	1958–74	1999	Hugh Duffy	OF	1888–1906	1945

Note: Career dates indicate first and last appearances in the majors.
*Elected on the basis of his career in the Negro leagues.

Players (Cont.)

Name	Position	Career	Selected
Johnny Evers	2B	1902–29	1939
Buck Ewing	C	1880–97	1946
Red Faber	P	1914–33	1964
Bob Feller	P	1936–56	1962
Rick Ferrell	C	1929–47	1984
Rollie Fingers	P	1968–85	1992
Carlton Fisk	C	1969–93	2000
Elmer Flick	OF	1898–1910	1963
Whitey Ford	P	1950–67	1974
Bill Foster*	P		1996
Nellie Fox	2B	1947–65	1997
Jimmie Foxx	1B	1925–45	1951
Frankie Frisch	2B	1919–37	1947
Pud Galvin	P	1879–92	1965
Lou Gehrig	1B	1923–39	1939
Charlie Gehringer	2B	1924–42	1949
Bob Gibson	P	1959–75	1981
Josh Gibson*	C		1972
Lefty Gomez	P	1930–43	1972
Goose Goslin	OF	1921–38	1968
Hank Greenberg	1B	1930–47	1956
Burleigh Grimes	P	1916–34	1964
Lefty Grove	P	1925–41	1947
Chick Hafey	OF	1924–37	1971
Jesse Haines	P	1918–37	1970
Billy Hamilton	OF	1888–1901	1961
Gabby Hartnett	C	1922–41	1955
Harry Heilmann	OF	1914–32	1952
Billy Herman	2B	1931–47	1975
Harry Hooper	OF	1909–25	1971
Rogers Hornsby	2B	1915–37	1942
Waite Hoyt	P	1918–38	1969
Carl Hubbell	P	1928–43	1947
Catfish Hunter	P	1965–79	1987
Monte Irvin	OF	1949–56	1973
Reggie Jackson	OF	1967–87	1993
Travis Jackson	SS	1922–36	1982
Ferguson Jenkins	P	1965–83	1991
Hugh Jennings	SS	1891–1918	1945
Judy Johnson*	3B		1975
Walter Johnson	P	1907–27	1936
Addie Joss	P	1902–10	1978
Al Kaline	OF	1953–74	1980
Tim Keefe	P	1880–93	1964
Willie Keeler	OF	1892–1910	1939
George Kell	3B	1943–57	1983
Joe Kelley	OF	1891–1908	1971
George Kelly	1B	1915–32	1973
King Kelly	C	1878–93	1945
Harmon Killebrew	1B-3B	1954–75	1984
Ralph Kiner	OF	1946–55	1975
Chuck Klein	OF	1928–44	1980
Sandy Koufax	P	1955–66	1972
Nap Lajoie	2B	1896–1916	1937
Tony Lazzeri	2B	1926–39	1991
Bob Lemon	P	1941–58	1976
Buck Leonard*	1B		1977
Fred Lindstrom	3B	1924–36	1976
Pop Lloyd*	SS-1B		1977
Ernie Lombardi	C	1931–47	1986
Ted Lyons	P	1923–46	1955
Mickey Mantle	OF	1951–68	1974
Heinie Manush	OF	1923–39	1964
Rabbit Maranville	SS-2B	1912–35	1954
Juan Marichal	P	1960–75	1983
Rube Marquard	P	1908–25	1971
Eddie Mathews	3B	1952–68	1978
Christy Mathewson	P	1900–16	1936
Willie Mays	OF	1951–73	1979
Tommy McCarthy	OF	1884–96	1946
Willie McCovey	1B	1959–80	1986
Joe McGinnity	P	1899–1908	1946
Bid McPhee	2B	1882–99	2000
Joe Medwick	OF	1932–48	1968
Johnny Mize	1B	1936–53	1981
Joe Morgan	2B	1963–84	1990
Stan Musial	OF-1B	1941–63	1969
Hal Newhouser	P	1939–55	1992
Kid Nichols	P	1890–1906	1949
Phil Niekro	P	1964–87	1997
Jim O'Rourke	OF	1876–1904	1945
Mel Ott	OF	1926–47	1951
Satchel Paige*	P	1948–65	1971
Jim Palmer	P	1965–84	1990
Herb Pennock	P	1912–34	1948
Tony Perez	1B	1964–86	2000
Gaylord Perry	P	1962–83	1991
Eddie Plank	P	1901–17	1946
Charley Radbourn	P	1880–91	1939
Pee Wee Reese	SS	1940–58	1984
Sam Rice	OF	1915–35	1963
Eppa Rixey	P	1912–33	1963
Phil Rizzuto	SS	1941–56	1994
Robin Roberts	P	1948–66	1976
Brooks Robinson	3B	1955–77	1983
Frank Robinson	OF	1956–76	1982
Jackie Robinson	2B	1947–56	1962
Joe (Bullet) Rogan*	P		1998
Edd Roush	OF	1913–31	1962
Red Ruffing	P	1924–47	1967
Amos Rusie	P	1889–1901	1977
Babe Ruth	OF	1914–35	1936
Nolan Ryan	P	1966–93	1999
Ray Schalk	C	1912–29	1955
Mike Schmidt	3B	1972–89	1995
Red Schoendienst	2B	1945–63	1989
Tom Seaver	P	1967–86	1992
Joe Sewell	SS	1920–33	1977
Al Simmons	OF	1924–44	1953
George Sisler	1B	1915–30	1939
Enos Slaughter	OF	1938–59	1985
Duke Snider	OF	1947–64	1980
Warren Spahn	P	1942–65	1973
Al Spalding	P	1871–78	1939
Tris Speaker	OF	1907–28	1937
Willie Stargell	OF-1B	1962–82	1988
Turkey Stearns*	CF		2000
Don Sutton	P	1966–88	1998
Bill Terry	1B	1923–36	1954
Sam Thompson	OF	1885–1906	1974
Joe Tinker	SS	1902–16	1946
Pie Traynor	3B	1920–37	1948
Dazzy Vance	P	1915–35	1955
Arky Vaughan	SS	1932–48	1985
Rube Waddell*	P	1897–1910	1946
Honus Wagner	SS	1897–1917	1936
Bobby Wallace	SS	1894–1918	1953
Ed Walsh	P	1904–17	1946
Lloyd Waner	OF	1927–45	1967
Paul Waner	OF	1926–45	1952
John Ward	2B-P	1878–94	1964
Mickey Welch	P	1880–92	1973

Players (Cont.)

	Position	Career	Selected
Willie Wells*	SS	1924–49	1997
Zach Wheat	OF	1909–27	1959
Hoyt Wilhelm	P	1952–72	1985
Billy Williams	OF	1959–76	1987
Ted Williams	OF	1939–60	1966
Vic Willis	P	1898–1910	1995
Hack Wilson	OF	1923–34	1979
Early Wynn	P	1939–63	1972
Carl Yastrzemski	OF	1961–83	1989
Cy Young	P	1890–1911	1937
Ross Youngs	OF	1917–26	1972
Robin Yount	SS	1974–93	1999

Umpires

	Year Selected
Al Barlick	1989
Nestor Chylak	1999
Jocko Conlan	1974
Tom Connolly	1953
Billy Evans	1973
Cal Hubbard	1976
Bill Klem	1953
Bill McGowan	1992

Pioneers/Executives

	Year Selected
Ed Barrow (manager-executive)	1953
Morgan Bulkeley (executive)	1937
Alexander Cartwright (executive)	1938
Henry Chadwick (writer-executive)	1938
Happy Chandler (commissioner)	1982
Charles Comiskey (manager-executive)	1939
Rube Foster (player-manager-executive)	1981
Ford Frick (commissioner-executive)	1970

Pioneers/Executives (Cont.)

	Year Selected
Warren Giles (executive)	1979
Will Harridge (executive)	1972
William Hulbert (executive)	1995
Ban Johnson (executive)	1937
Kenesaw M. Landis (commissioner)	1944
Larry MacPhail (executive)	1978
Lee MacPhail Jr (executive)	1998
Branch Rickey (manager-executive)	1967
Al Spalding (player-executive)	1939
Bill Veeck (owner)	1991
George Weiss (executive)	1971
George Wright (player-manager)	1937
Harry Wright (player-manager-executive)	1953
Tom Yawkey (executive)	1980

Managers

	Years Managed	Year Selected
Walt Alston	1954–76	1983
Sparky Anderson	1970–94	2000
Leo Durocher	1939–73	1994
Clark Griffith	1901–20	1946
Bucky Harris	1924–56	1975
Ned Hanlon	1899–1907	1996
Miller Huggins	1913–29	1964
Tom Lasorda	1977–96	1997
Al Lopez	1951–69	1977
Connie Mack	1894–1950	1937
Joe McCarthy	1926–50	1957
John McGraw	1899–1932	1937
Bill McKechnie	1915–46	1962
Wilbert Robinson	1902–31	1945
Frank Selee	1890–1905	1999
Casey Stengel	1934–65	1966
Earl Weaver	1968–82, 85–86	1996

Notable Achievements

No-Hit Games, 9 Innings or More

NATIONAL LEAGUE

Date	Pitcher and Game	Date	Pitcher and Game
1876......July 15	George Bradley, StL vs Hart 2–0	1892......Oct 15	Bumpus Jones, Cin vs Pitt 7–1 (first major league game)
1880......June 12	John Richmond, Wor vs Clev 1–0 (perfect game)	1893......Aug 16	Bill Hawke, Balt vs Wash 5–0
June 17	Monte Ward, Prov vs Buff 5–0 (perfect game)	1897......Sept 18	Cy Young, Clev vs Cin 6–0
Aug 19	Larry Corcoran, Chi vs Bos 6–0	1898......Apr 22	Ted Breitenstein, Cin vs Pitt 11–0
Aug 20	Pud Galvin, Buff at Wor 1–0	Apr 22	Jim Hughes, Balt vs Bos 8–0
1882......Sept 20	Larry Corcoran, Chi vs Wor 5–0	July 8	Frank Donahue, Phil vs Bos 5–0
Sept 22	Tim Lovett, Bklyn vs NY 4–0	Aug 21	Walter Thornton, Chi vs Bklyn 2–0
1883......July 25	Hoss Radbourn, Prov at Clev 8–0	1899......May 25	Deacon Phillippe, Lou vs NY 7–0
Sept 13	Hugh Daily, Clev at Phil 1–0	Aug 7	Vic Willis, Bos vs Wash 7–1
1884......June 27	Larry Corcoran, Chi vs Prov 6–0	1900......July 12	Noodles Hahn, Cin vs Phil 4–0
Aug 4	Pud Galvin, Buff at Det 18–0	1901......July 15	Christy Mathewson, NY at StL 5–0
1885......July 27	John Clarkson, Chi at Prov 4–0	1903......Sept 18	Chick Fraser, Phil at Chi 10–0
Aug 29	Charles Ferguson, Phil vs Prov 1–0	1904......June 11	Bob Wicker, Chi at NY 1–0 (hit in 10th; won in 12th)
1891......July 31	Amos Rusie, NY vs Bklyn 6–0	1905......June 13	Christy Mathewson, NY at Chi 1–0
June 22	Tom Lovett, Bklyn vs NY 4–0	1906......May 1	John Lush, Phil at Bklyn 6–0
1892......Aug 6	Jack Stivetts, Bos vs Bklyn 11–0	July 20	Mal Eason, Bklyn at StL 2–0
Aug 22	Alex Sanders, Lou vs Balt 6–2		

No-Hit Games, 9 Innings or More (Cont.)

NATIONAL LEAGUE (Cont.)

Date	Pitcher and Game	Date	Pitcher and Game
1906......Aug 1	Harry McIntire, Bklyn vs Pitt 0–1 (hit in 11th; lost in 13th)	1965......Sept 9	Sandy Koufax, LA vs Chi 1–0 (perfect game)
1907......May 8	Frank Pfeffer, Bos vs Cin 6–0	1967......June 18	Don Wilson, Hou vs Atl 2–0
Sept 20	Nick Maddox, Pitt vs Bklyn 2–1	1968......July 29	George Culver, Cin at Phil 6–1
1908......July 4	George Wiltse, NY vs Phil 1–0 (10 innings)	Sept 17	Gaylord Perry, SF vs StL 1–0
		Sept 18	Ray Washburn, StL at SF 2–0
Sept 5	Nap Rucker, Bklyn vs Bos 6–0	1969......Apr 17	Bill Stoneman, Mtl at Phil 7–0
1909......Apr 15	Leon Ames, NY vs Bklyn 0–3 (hit in 10th; lost in 13th)	Apr 30	Jim Maloney, Cin vs Hou 10–0
		May 1	Don Wilson, Hou at Cin 4–0
1912......Sept 6	Jeff Tesreau, NY at Phil 3–0	Aug 19	Ken Holtzman, Chi vs Atl 3–0
1914......Sept 9	George Davis, Bos vs Phil 7–0	Sept 20	Bob Moose, Pitt at NY 4–0
1915......Apr 15	Rube Marquard, NY vs Bklyn 2–0	1970......June 12	Dock Ellis, Pitt at SD 2–0
Aug 31	Jimmy Lavender, Chi at NY 2–0	July 20	Bill Singer, LA vs Phil 5–0
1916......June 16	Tom Hughes, Bos vs Pitt 2–0	1971......June 3	Ken Holtzman, Chi at Cin 1–0
1917......May 2	Jim Vaughn, Chi vs Cin 0–1 (hit in 10th; lost in 10th)	June 23	Rick Wise, Phil at Cin 4–0
		Aug 14	Bob Gibson, StL at Pitt 11–0
May 2	Fred Toney, Cin at Chi 1–0 (10 innings)	1972......Apr 16	Burt Hooton, Chi vs Phil 4–0
		Sept 2	Milt Pappas, Chi vs SD 8–0
1919......May 11	Hod Eller, Cin vs StL 6–0	Oct 2	Bill Stoneman, Mtl vs NY 7–0
1922......May 7	Jesse Barnes, NY vs Phil 6–0	1973......Aug 5	Phil Niekro, Atl vs SD 9–0
1924......July 17	Jesse Haines, StL vs Bos 5–0	1975......Aug 24	Ed Halicki, SF vs NY 6–0
1925......Sept 13	Dazzy Vance, Bklyn vs Phil 10–1	1976......July 9	Larry Dierker, Hou vs Mtl 6–0
1929......May 8	Carl Hubbell, NY vs Pitt 11–0	Aug 9	John Candelaria, Pitt vs LA 2–0
1934......Sept 21	Paul Dean, StL vs Bklyn 3–0	Sept 29	John Montefusco, SF at Atl 9–0
1938......June 11	Johnny Vander Meer, Cin vs Bos 3–0	1978......Apr 16	Bob Forsch, StL vs Phil 5–0
		June 16	Tom Seaver, Cin vs StL 4–0
June 15	Johnny Vander Meer, Cin at Bklyn 6–0	1979......Apr 7	Ken Forsch, Hou vs Atl 6–0
		1980......June 27	Jerry Reuss, LA at SF 8–0
1940......Apr 30	Tex Carleton, Bklyn at Cin, 3–0	1981......May 10	Charlie Lea, Mtl vs SF 4–0
1941......Aug 30	Lon Warneke, StL at Cin 2–0	Sept 26	Nolan Ryan, Hou vs LA 5–0
1944......Apr 27	Jim Tobin, Bos vs Bklyn 2–0	1983......Sept 26	Bob Forsch, StL vs Mtl 3–0
May 15	Clyde Shoun, Cin vs Bos 1–0	1986......Sept 25	Mike Scott, Hou vs SF 2–0
1946......Apr 23	Ed Head, Bklyn vs Bos 5–0	1988......Sept 16	Tom Browning, Cin vs LA 1–0 (perfect game)
1947......June 18	Ewell Blackwell, Cin vs Bos 6–0		
1948......Sept 9	Rex Barney, Bklyn at NY 2–0	1990 June 29	Fernando Valenzuela, LA vs StL 6–0
1950......Aug 11	Vern Bickford, Bos vs Bklyn 7–0		
1951......May 6	Cliff Chambers, Pitt at Bos 3–0	1990......Aug 15	Terry Mulholland, Phil vs SF 6–0
1952......June 19	Carl Erskine, Bklyn vs Chi 5–0	1991......May 23	Tommy Greene, Phil at Mtl 2–0
1954......June 12	Jim Wilson, Mil vs Phil 2–0	July 26	Mark Gardner, Mtl at LA 0–1 (hit in 10th, lost in 10th)
1955......May 12	Sam Jones, Chi vs Pitt 4–0		
1956......May 12	Carl Erskine, Bklyn vs NY 3–0	July 28	Dennis Martinez, Mtl at LA 2–0 (perfect game)
Sept 25	Sal Maglie, Bklyn vs Phil 5–0		
1959......May 26	Harvey Haddix, Pitt at Mil 0–1 (hit in 13th; lost in 13th)	Sept 11	Kent Mercker (6), Mark Wohlers (2), and Alejandro Pena (1), Atl at SD 1–0
1960......May 15	Don Cardwell, Chi vs StL 4–0		
Aug 18	Lew Burdette, Mil vs Phil 1–0	1992......Aug 17	Kevin Gross, LA vs SF 2–0
Sept 16	Warren Spahn, Mil vs Phil 4–0	1993......Sept 8	Darryl Kile, Hou vs NY 7–1
1961......Apr 28	Warren Spahn, Mil vs SF 1–0	1994......Apr 8	Kent Mercker, Atl vs LA 6–0
1962......June 30	Sandy Koufax, LA vs NY 5–0	1995......June 3	Pedro Martinez, Mtl vs SD 1–0 (perfect through 9, hit in 10th)
1963......May 11	Sandy Koufax, LA vs SF 8–0		
May 17	Don Nottebart, Hou vs Phil 4–1	July 14	Ramon Martinez, LA vs Fla 7–0
June 15	Juan Marichal, SF vs Hou 1–0	1996......May 11	Al Leiter, Fla vs Col 11–0
1964......Apr 23	Ken Johnson, Hou vs Cin 0–1	Sept 17	Hideo Nomo, LA at Col 9–0
June 4	Sandy Koufax, LA at Phil 3–0	1997......June 10	Kevin Brown, Fla vs SF 9–0
June 21	Jim Bunning, Phil at NY 6–0 (perfect game)	July 12	Francisco Cordova (9) and Ricardo Rincon (1), Pitt vs Col 3–0
1965......June 14	Jim Maloney, Cin vs NY 0–1 (hit in 11th; lost in 11th)	1999......June 25	Jose Jimenez, StL at Ariz 1–0
Aug 19	Jim Maloney, Cin at Chi 1–0 (10 innings)		

Note: Includes the games struck from the official record book on September 4, 1991, when baseball's committee on statistical accuracy voted to define no-hitters as games of 9 innings or more that end with a team getting no hits.

No-Hit Games, 9 Innings or More *(Cont.)*

AMERICAN LEAGUE

Date	Pitcher and Game	Date	Pitcher and Game
1901......May 9	Earl Moore, Clev vs Chi 2–4 (hit in 10th; lost in 10th)	1956......July 14	Mel Parnell, Bos vs Chi 4–0
1902......Sept 20	Jimmy Callahan, Chi vs Det 3–0	1966......Oct 8	Don Larsen, NY (A) vs Bklyn (N) 2–0 (World Series) (perfect game)
1904......May 5	Cy Young, Bos vs Phil 3–0 (perfect game)	1957......Aug 20	Bob Keegan, Chi vs Wash 6–0
Aug 17	Jesse Tannehill, Bos at Chi 6–0	1958......July 20	Jim Bunning, Det at Bos 3–0
1905......July 22	Weldon Henley, Phil at StL 6–0	Sept 20	Hoyt Wilhelm, Balt vs NY 1–0
Sept 6	Frank Smith, Chi at Det 15–0	1962......May 5	Bo Belinsky, LA vs Balt 2–0
Sept 27	Bill Dinneen, Bos vs Chi 2–0	June 26	Earl Wilson, Bos vs LA 2–0
1908......June 30	Cy Young, Bos at NY 8–0	Aug 1	Bill Monbouquette, Bos at Chi 1–0
Sept 18	Bob Rhoades, Clev vs Bos 2–1	Aug 26	Jack Kralick, Minn vs KC 1–0
Sept 20	Frank Smith, Chi vs Phil 1–0	1965......Sept 16	Dave Morehead, Bos vs Clev 2–0
1908......Oct 2	Addie Joss, Clev vs Chi 1–0 (perfect game)	1966......June 10	Sonny Siebert, Clev vs Wash 2–0
1910......Apr 20	Addie Joss, Clev at Chi 1–0	1967......Apr 30	Steve Barber (8⅔) and Stu Miller (⅓), Balt vs Det 1–2
May 12	Chief Bender, Phil vs Clev 4–0	Aug 25	Dean Chance, Minn at Clev 2–1
Aug 30	Tom Hughes, NY vs Clev 0–5 (hit in 10th; lost in 11th)	Sept 10	Joel Horlen, Chi vs Det 6–0
1911......July 29	Joe Wood, Bos vs StL 5–0	1968......Apr 27	Tom Phoebus, Balt vs Bos 6–0
Aug 27	Ed Walsh, Chi vs Bos 5–0	May 8	Catfish Hunter, Oak vs Minn 4–0 (perfect game)
1912......July 4	George Mullin, Det vs StL 7–0	1969......Aug 13	Jim Palmer, Balt vs Oak 8–0
Aug 30	Earl Hamilton, StL at Det 5–1	1970......July 3	Clyde Wright, Cal vs Oak 4–0
1914......May 14	Jim Scott, Chi at Wash 0–1 (hit in 10th; lost in 10th)	Sept 21	Vida Blue, Oak vs Minn 6–0
May 31	Joe Benz, Chi vs Clev 6–1	1973......Apr 27	Steve Busby, KC at Det 3–0
1916......June 21	George Foster, Bos vs NY 2–0	May 15	Nolan Ryan, Cal at KC 3–0
Aug 26	Joe Bush, Phil vs Clev 5–0	July 15	Nolan Ryan, Cal at Det 6–0
Aug 30	Dutch Leonard, Bos vs StL 4–0	July 30	Jim Bibby, Tex at Oak 6–0
1917......Apr 14	Ed Cicotte, Chi at StL 11–0	1974......June 19	Steve Busby, KC at Mil 2–0
Apr 24	George Mogridge, NY at Bos 2–1	July 19	Dick Bosman, Clev vs Oak 4–0
May 5	Ernie Koob, StL vs Chi 1–0	Sept 28	Nolan Ryan, Cal vs Minn 4–0
May 6	Bob Groom, StL vs Chi 3–0	1975......June 1	Nolan Ryan, Cal vs Balt 1–0
June 23	Ernie Shore, Bos vs Wash 4–0 (perfect game)	Sept 28	Vida Blue (5), Glenn Abbott and Paul Lindblad (1), Rollie Fingers (2), Oak vs Cal 5–0
1918......June 3	Dutch Leonard, Bos at Det 5–0	1976......July 28	John Odom (5) and Francisco Barrios (4), Chi at Oak 2–1
1919......Sept 10	Ray Caldwell, Clev at NY 3–0	1977......May 14	Jim Colborn, KC vs Tex 6–0
1920......July 1	Walter Johnson, Wash at Bos 1–0	May 30	Dennis Eckersley, Clev vs Cal 1–0
1922......Apr 30	Charlie Robertson, Chi at Det 2–0 (perfect game)	Sept 22	Bert Blyleven, Tex at Cal 6–0
1923......Sept 4	Sam Jones, NY at Phil 2–0	1981......May 15	Len Barker, Clev vs Tor 3–0 (perfect game)
Sept 7	Howard Ehmke, Bos at Phil 4–0	1983......July 4	Dave Righetti, NY vs Bos 4–0
1926......Aug 21	Ted Lyons, Chi at Bos 6–0	Sept 29	Mike Warren, Oak vs Chi 3–0
1931......Apr 29	Wes Ferrell, Clev vs StL 9–0	1984......Apr 7	Jack Morris, Det at Chi 4–0
Aug 8	Bob Burke, Wash vs Bos 5–0	Sept 30	Mike Witt, Cal at Tex 1–0 (perfect game)
1934......Sept 18	Bobo Newsom, StL vs Bos 1–2 (hit in 10th; lost in 10th)	1986......Sept 19	Joe Cowley, Chi at Cal 7–1
1935......Aug 31	Vern Kennedy, Chi vs Clev 5–0	1987......Apr 15	Juan Nieves, Mil at Balt 7–0
1937......June 1	Bill Dietrich, Chi vs StL 8–0	1990......Apr 11	Mark Langston (7), Mike Witt (2), Cal vs Sea 1–0
1938......Aug 27	Mtle Pearson, NY vs Clev 13–0	June 2	Randy Johnson, Sea vs Det 2–0
1940......Apr 16	Bob Feller, Clev at Chi 1–0 (opening day)	June 11	Nolan Ryan, Tex at Oak 5–0
1945......Sept 9	Dick Fowler, Phil vs StL 1–0	June 29	Dave Stewart, Oak at Tor 5–0
1946......Apr 30	Bob Feller, Clev at NY 1–0	1990......July 1	Andy Hawkins, NY at Chi 0–4 (pitched 8 innings of 9–inning game)
1947......July 10	Don Black, Clev vs Phil 3–0	Sept 2	Dave Stieb, Tor at Clev 3–0
Sep 3	Bill McCahan, Phil vs Wash 3–0	1991......May 1	Nolan Ryan, Tex vs Tor 3–0
1948......June 30	Bob Lemon, Clev at Det 2–0	July 13	Bob Milacki (6), Mike Flanagan (1), Mark Williamson (1), and Gregg Olson (1), Balt at Oak 2–0
1951......July 1	Bob Feller, Clev vs Det 2–1	Aug 11	Wilson Alvarez, Chi at Balt 7–0
July 12	Allie Reynolds, NY at Clev 1–0	Aug 26	Bret Saberhagen, KC vs Chi 7–0
Sept 28	Allie Reynolds, NY vs Bos 8–0		
1952......May 15	Virgil Trucks, Det vs Wash 1–0		
Aug 25	Virgil Trucks, Det at NY 1–0		
1953......May 6	Bobo Holloman, StL vs Phil 6–0 (first major league start)		

No-Hit Games, 9 Innings or More *(Cont.)*

AMERICAN LEAGUE *(CONT.)*

Date	Pitcher and Game	Date	Pitcher and Game
1993......Apr 22	Chris Bosio, Sea vs Bos 7–0	1998......May 17	David Wells, NY vs Minn 4–0
Sept 4	Jim Abbott, NY vs Clev 4–0		(perfect game)
1994......Apr 27	Scott Erickson, Minn vs Mil 6–0	1999......July 18	David Cone, NY vs Mtl 6–0
July 28	Kenny Rogers, Texas vs Cal 4–0		(perfect game)
	(perfect game)	Sept 11	Eric Milton, Minn vs Ana 7–0
1996......May 14	Dwight Gooden, NY vs Sea 2–0		

Longest Hitting Streaks

NATIONAL LEAGUE

Player and Team	Year	G
Willie Keeler, Balt	1897	44
Pete Rose, Cin	1978	44
Bill Dahlen, Chi	1894	42
Tommy Holmes, Bos	1945	37
Billy Hamilton, Phil	1894	36
Fred Clarke, Lou	1895	35
Benito Santiago, SD	1987	34
George Davis, NY	1893	33
Rogers Hornsby, StL	1922	32
Ed Delahanty, Phil	1899	31
Willie Davis, LA	1969	31
Rico Carty, Atl	1970	31
Vladimir Guerrero, Mtl	1999	31

AMERICAN LEAGUE

Player and Team	Year	G
Joe DiMaggio, NY	1941	56
George Sisler, StL	1922	41
Ty Cobb, Det	1911	40
Paul Molitor, Mil	1987	39
Ty Cobb, Det	1917	35
Ty Cobb, Det	1912	34
George Sisler, StL	1925	34
John Stone, Det	1930	34
George McQuinn, StL	1938	34
Dom DiMaggio, Bos	1949	34
Hal Chase, NY	1907	33
Heinie Manush, Wash	1933	33
Nap Lajoie, Clev	1906	31
Sam Rice, Wash	1924	31
Ken Landreaux, Minn	1980	31

Triple Crown Hitters

NATIONAL LEAGUE

Player and Team	Year	HR	RBI	BA
Paul Hines, Prov	1878	4	50	.358
Hugh Duffy, Bos	1894	18	145	.438
Heinie Zimmerman*, Chi	1912	14	103	.372
Rogers Hornsby, StL	1922	42	152	.401
	1925	39	143	.403
Chuck Klein, Phil	1933	28	120	.368
Joe Medwick, StL	1937	31	154	.374

*Zimmerman ranked first in RBIs as calculated by Ernie Lanigan, but only third as calculated by Information Concepts Inc.

AMERICAN LEAGUE

Player and Team	Year	HR	RBI	BA
Nap Lajoie, Phil	1901	14	125	.422
Ty Cobb, Det	1909	9	115	.377
Jimmie Foxx, Phil	1933	48	163	.356
Lou Gehrig, NY	1934	49	165	.363
Ted Williams, Bos	1942	36	137	.356
	1947	32	114	.343
Mickey Mantle, NY	1956	52	130	.353
Frank Robinson, Balt	1966	49	122	.316
Carl Yastrzemski, Bos	1967	44	121	.326

THEY SAID IT

Sammy Sosa, Cubs slugger, after being told he'd tied Joe DiMaggio with his 361st career home run: "That's the guy whose girlfriend was Marilyn Monroe?"

Triple Crown Pitchers

NATIONAL LEAGUE						AMERICAN LEAGUE					
Player and Team	Year	W	L	SO	ERA	Player and Team	Year	W	L	SO	ERA
Tommy Bond, Bos	1877	40	17	170	2.11	Cy Young, Bos	1901	33	10	158	1.62
Hoss Radbourn, Prov	1884	60	12	441	1.38	Rube Waddell, Phil	1905	26	11	287	1.48
Tim Keefe, NY	1888	35	12	333	1.74	Walter Johnson, Wash	1913	36	7	303	1.09
John Clarkson, Bos	1889	49	19	284	2.73		1918	23	13	162	1.27
Amos Rusie, NY	1894	36	13	195	2.78		1924	23	7	158	2.72
Christy Mathewson, NY	1905	31	8	206	1.27	Lefty Grove, Phil	1930	28	5	209	2.54
	1908	37	11	259	1.43		1931	31	4	175	2.06
Grover Alexander, Phil	1915	31	10	241	1.22	Lefty Gomez, NY	1934	26	5	158	2.33
	1916	33	12	167	1.55		1937	21	11	194	2.33
	1917	30	13	201	1.86	Hal Newhouser, Det	1945	25	9	212	1.81
Hippo Vaughn, Chi	1918	22	10	148	1.74	Roger Clemens, Tor	1997	21	7	292	2.05
Grover Alexander, Chi	1920	27	14	173	1.91		1998	20	6	271	2.64
Dazzy Vance, Bklyn	1924	28	6	262	2.16	Pedro Martinez, Bos	1999	23	4	313	2.07
Bucky Walters, Cin	1939	27	11	137	2.29						
Sandy Koufax, LA	1963	25	5	306	1.88						
	1965	26	8	382	2.04						
	1966	27	9	317	1.73						
Steve Carlton, Phil	1972	27	10	310	1.97						
Dwight Gooden, NY	1985	24	4	268	1.53						

Consecutive Games Played, 500 or More Games

Cal Ripken Jr	2,632	Frank McCormick	652
Lou Gehrig	2,130	Sandy Alomar Sr	648
Everett Scott	1,307	Eddie Brown	618
Steve Garvey	1,207	Roy McMillan	585
Billy Williams	1,117	George Pinckney	577
Joe Sewell	1,103	Steve Brodie	574
Stan Musial	895	Aaron Ward	565
Eddie Yost	829	Candy LaChance	540
Gus Suhr	822	Buck Freeman	535
Nellie Fox	798	Fred Luderus	533
Pete Rose	745	Clyde Milan	511
Dale Murphy	740	Charlie Gehringer	511
Richie Ashburn	730	Vada Pinson	508
Ernie Banks	717	Tony Cuccinello	504
Earl Averill	673	Charlie Gehringer	504
Pete Rose	678	Omar Moreno	503

Unassisted Triple Plays

Player and Team	Date	Pos	Opp	Opp Batter
Neal Ball, Clev	7-19-09	SS	Bos	Amby McConnell
Bill Wambsganss, Clev	10-10-20	2B	Bklyn	Clarence Mitchell
George Burns, Bos	9-14-23	1B	Clev	Frank Brower
Ernie Padgett, Bos	10-6-23	SS	Phil	Walter Holke
Glenn Wright, Pitt	5-7-25	SS	StL	Jim Bottomley
Jimmy Cooney, Chi	5-30-27	SS	Pitt	Paul Waner
Johnny Neun, Det	5-31-27	1B	Clev	Homer Summa
Ron Hansen, Wash	7-30-68	SS	Clev	Joe Azcue
Mickey Morandini, Phil	9-20-92	2B	Pitt	Jeff King
John Valentin, Bos	7-15-94	SS	Minn	Marc Newfield
Randy Velarde, Oak	5-29-00	2B	NYY	Shane Spencer

Pennant Winners

Year	Team	Manager	W	L	Pct	GA
1900	Brooklyn	Ned Hanlon	82	54	.603	4½
1901	Pittsburgh	Fred Clarke	90	49	.647	7½
1902	Pittsburgh	Fred Clarke	103	36	.741	27½
1903	Pittsburgh	Fred Clarke	91	49	.650	6½
1904	New York	John McGraw	106	47	.693	13
1905	New York	John McGraw	105	48	.686	9
1906	Chicago	Frank Chance	116	36	.763	20
1907	Chicago	Frank Chance	107	45	.704	17
1908	Chicago	Frank Chance	99	55	.643	1
1909	Pittsburgh	Fred Clarke	110	42	.724	6½
1910	Chicago	Frank Chance	104	50	.675	13
1911	New York	John McGraw	99	54	.647	7½
1912	New York	John McGraw	103	48	.682	10
1913	New York	John McGraw	101	51	.664	12½
1914	Boston	George Stallings	94	59	.614	10½
1915	Philadelphia	Pat Moran	90	62	.592	7
1916	Brooklyn	Wilbert Robinson	94	60	.610	2½
1917	New York	John McGraw	98	56	.636	10
1918	Chicago	Fred Mitchell	84	45	.651	10½
1919	Cincinnati	Pat Moran	96	44	.686	9
1920	Brooklyn	Wilbert Robinson	93	61	.604	7
1921	New York	John McGraw	94	59	.614	4
1922	New York	John McGraw	93	61	.604	7
1923	New York	John McGraw	95	58	.621	4½
1924	New York	John McGraw	93	60	.608	1½
1925	Pittsburgh	Bill McKechnie	95	58	.621	8½
1926	St. Louis	Rogers Hornsby	89	65	.578	2
1927	Pittsburgh	Donie Bush	94	60	.610	1½
1928	St. Louis	Bill McKechnie	95	59	.617	2
1929	Chicago	Joe McCarthy	98	54	.645	10½
1930	St. Louis	Gabby Street	92	62	.597	2
1931	St. Louis	Gabby Street	101	53	.656	13
1932	Chicago	Charlie Grimm	90	64	.584	4
1933	New York	Bill Terry	91	61	.599	5
1934	St. Louis	Frankie Frisch	95	58	.621	2
1935	Chicago	Charlie Grimm	100	54	.649	4
1936	New York	Bill Terry	92	62	.597	5
1937	New York	Bill Terry	95	57	.625	3
1938	Chicago	Gabby Hartnett	89	63	.586	2
1939	Cincinnati	Bill McKechnie	97	57	.630	4½
1940	Cincinnati	Bill McKechnie	100	53	.654	12
1941	Brooklyn	Leo Durocher	100	54	.649	2½
1942	St. Louis	Billy Southworth	106	48	.688	2
1943	St. Louis	Billy Southworth	105	49	.682	18
1944	St. Louis	Billy Southworth	105	49	.682	14½
1945	Chicago	Charlie Grimm	98	56	.636	3
1946	St. Louis*	Eddie Dyer	98	58	.628	2
1947	Brooklyn	Burt Shotton	94	60	.610	5
1948	Boston	Billy Southworth	91	62	.595	6½
1949	Brooklyn	Burt Shotton	97	57	.630	1
1950	Philadelphia	Eddie Sawyer	91	63	.591	2
1951	New York†	Leo Durocher	98	59	.624	1
1952	Brooklyn	Chuck Dressen	96	57	.627	4½
1953	Brooklyn	Chuck Dressen	105	49	.682	13
1954	New York	Leo Durocher	97	57	.630	5
1955	Brooklyn	Walt Alston	98	55	.641	13½
1956	Brooklyn	Walt Alston	93	61	.604	1
1957	Milwaukee	Fred Haney	95	59	.617	8
1958	Milwaukee	Fred Haney	92	62	.597	8
1959	Los Angeles‡	Walt Alston	88	68	.564	2
1960	Pittsburgh	Danny Murtaugh	95	59	.617	7
1961	Cincinnati	Fred Hutchinson	93	61	.604	4
1962	San Francisco#	Al Dark	103	62	.624	1
1963	Los Angeles	Walt Alston	99	63	.611	6
1964	St. Louis	Johnny Keane	93	69	.574	1

Pennant Winners (Cont.)

Year	Team	Manager	W	L	Pct	GA
1965	Los Angeles	Walt Alston	97	65	.599	2
1966	Los Angeles	Walt Alston	95	67	.586	1½
1967	St. Louis	Red Schoendienst	101	60	.627	10½
1968	St. Louis	Red Schoendienst	97	65	.599	9
1969	New York (E)††	Gil Hodges	100	62	.617	8
1970	Cincinnati (W)††	Sparky Anderson	102	60	.630	14½
1971	Pittsburgh (E)††	Danny Murtaugh	97	65	.599	7
1972	Cincinnati (W)††	Sparky Anderson	95	59	.617	10½
1973	New York (E)††	Yogi Berra	82	79	.509	1½
1974	Los Angeles (W)††	Walt Alston	102	60	.630	4
1975	Cincinnati (W)††	Sparky Anderson	108	54	.667	20
1976	Cincinnati (W)††	Sparky Anderson	102	60	.630	10
1977	Los Angeles (W)††	Tommy Lasorda	98	64	.605	10
1978	Los Angeles (W)††	Tommy Lasorda	95	67	.586	2½
1979	Pittsburgh (E)††	Chuck Tanner	98	64	.605	2
1980	Philadelphia (E)††	Dallas Green	91	71	.562	1
1981	Los Angeles (W)††	Tommy Lasorda	63	47	.573	**
1982	St. Louis (E)††	Whitey Herzog	92	70	.568	3
1983	Philadelphia (E)††	Pat Corrales/Paul Owens	90	72	.556	6
1984	San Diego (W)††	Dick Williams	92	70	.568	12
1985	St. Louis (E)††	Whitey Herzog	101	61	.623	3
1986	New York (E)††	Dave Johnson	108	54	.667	21½
1987	St. Louis (E)††	Whitey Herzog	95	67	.586	3
1988	Los Angeles (W)††	Tommy Lasorda	94	67	.584	7
1989	San Francisco (W)††	Roger Craig	92	70	.568	3
1990	Cincinnati (W)††	Lou Piniella	91	71	.562	5
1991	Atlanta (W)††	Bobby Cox	94	68	.580	1
1992	Atlanta (W)††	Bobby Cox	98	64	.605	8
1993	Philadelphia (E)††	Jim Fregosi	97	65	.599	3
1994	Season ended Aug. 11 due to players' strike.					
1995	Atlanta (E)††	Bobby Cox	90	54	.625	21
1996	Atlanta (E)††	Bobby Cox	96	66	.593	8
1997	Florida (wc)††	Jim Leyland	92	70	.568	—
1998	San Diego (W)††	Bruce Bochy	98	64	.605	9½
1999	Atlanta Braves (E)††	Bobby Cox	103	59	.636	6½
2000	New York Mets (wc)††	Bobby Valentine	94	68	.580	—

*Defeated Brooklyn, two games to none, in playoff for pennant. †Defeated Brooklyn, two games to one, in playoff for pennant. ‡Defeated Milwaukee, two games to none, in playoff for pennant. #Defeated Los Angeles, two games to one, in playoff for pennant. ††Won Championship Series. **First half 36–21; second half 27–26, in season split by strike; defeated Houston in playoff for Western Division title.

This Tiger is a Pussycat

Someone forgot to tell Tigers closer Todd Jones that baseball is supposed to be a coldhearted business. Jones, 32, who pitched in his first All-Star Game in July, said he would not seek an exorbitant salary or no-trade clause if Detroit offers him a contract extension. What's more, Jones said, as long as he's a Tiger, he'll help groom his likely successor, 23-year-old righthander Matt Anderson. "It's my job, if I move on, to have a seamless transition from me to him," said Jones who had 42 saves in 46 opportunities this season and is signed through next season at $3.65 million per year. "If he doesn't do his job, then I've failed. I want to help the Tigers, and if I can help the Tigers by being traded, that's fine."

Leading Batsmen

Year	Player and Team	BA	Year	Player and Team	BA
1900	Honus Wagner, Pitt	.381	1951	Stan Musial, StL	.355
1901	Jesse Burkett, StL	.382	1952	Stan Musial, StL	.336
1902	Ginger Beaumtl, Pitt	.357	1953	Carl Furillo, Bklyn	.344
1903	Honus Wagner, Pitt	.355	1954	Willie Mays, NY	.345
1904	Honus Wagner, Pitt	.349	1955	Richie Ashburn, Phil	.338
1905	Cy Seymour, Cin	.377	1956	Hank Aaron, Mil	.328
1906	Honus Wagner, Pitt	.339	1957	Stan Musial, StL	.351
1907	Honus Wagner, Pitt	.350	1958	Richie Ashburn, Phil	.350
1908	Honus Wagner, Pitt	.354	1959	Hank Aaron, Mil	.355
1909	Honus Wagner, Pitt	.339	1960	Dick Groat, Pitt	.325
1910	Sherry Magee, Phil	.331	1961	Roberto Clemente, Pitt	.351
1911	Honus Wagner, Pitt	.334	1962	Tommy Davis, LA	.346
1912	Heinie Zimmerman, Chi	.372	1963	Tommy Davis, LA	.326
1913	Jake Daubert, Bklyn	.350	1964	Roberto Clemente, Pitt	.339
1914	Jake Daubert, Bklyn	.329	1965	Roberto Clemente, Pitt	.329
1915	Larry Doyle, NY	.320	1966	Matty Alou, Pitt	.342
1916	Hal Chase, Cin	.339	1967	Roberto Clemente, Pitt	.357
1917	Edd Roush, Cin	.341	1968	Pete Rose, Cin	.335
1918	Zach Wheat, Bklyn	.335	1969	Pete Rose, Cin	.348
1919	Edd Roush, Cin	.321	1970	Rico Carty, Atl	.366
1920	Rogers Hornsby, StL	.370	1971	Joe Torre, StL	.363
1921	Rogers Hornsby, StL	.397	1972	Billy Williams, Chi	.333
1922	Rogers Hornsby, StL	.401	1973	Pete Rose, Cin	.338
1923	Rogers Hornsby, StL	.384	1974	Ralph Garr, Atl	.353
1924	Rogers Hornsby, StL	.424	1975	Bill Madlock, Chi	.354
1925	Rogers Hornsby, StL	.403	1976	Bill Madlock, Chi	.339
1926	Bubbles Hargrave, Cin	.353	1977	Dave Parker, Pitt	.338
1927	Paul Waner, Pitt	.380	1978	Dave Parker, Pitt	.334
1928	Rogers Hornsby, Bos	.387	1979	Keith Hernandez, StL	.344
1929	Lefty O'Doul, Phil	.398	1980	Bill Buckner, Chi	.324
1930	Bill Terry, NY	.401	1981	Bill Madlock, Pitt	.341
1931	Chick Hafey, StL	.349	1982	Al Oliver, Mtl	.331
1932	Lefty O'Doul, Bklyn	.368	1983	Bill Madlock, Pitt	.323
1933	Chuck Klein, Phil	.368	1984	Tony Gwynn, SD	.351
1934	Paul Waner, Pitt	.362	1985	Willie McGee, StL	.353
1935	Arky Vaughan, Pitt	.385	1986	Tim Raines, Mtl	.334
1936	Paul Waner, Pitt	.373	1987	Tony Gwynn, SD	.370
1937	Joe Medwick, StL	.374	1988	Tony Gwynn, SD	.313
1938	Ernie Lombardi, Cin	.342	1989	Tony Gwynn, SD	.336
1939	Johnny Mize, StL	.349	1990	Willie McGee, StL	.335
1940	Debs Garms, Pitt	.355	1991	Terry Pendleton, Atl	.319
1941	Pete Reiser, Bklyn	.343	1992	Gary Sheffield, SD	.330
1942	Ernie Lombardi, Bos	.330	1993	Andres Galarraga, Col	.370
1943	Stan Musial, StL	.357	1994	Tony Gwynn, SD	.394
1944	Dixie Walker, Bklyn	.357	1995	Tony Gwynn, SD	.368
1945	Phil Cavarretta, Chi	.355	1996	Tony Gwynn, SD	.353
1946	Stan Musial, StL	.365	1997	Tony Gwynn, SD	.372
1947	Harry Walker, StL-Phil	.363	1998	Larry Walker, Col	.363
1948	Stan Musial, StL	.376	1999	Larry Walker, Col	.379
1949	Jackie Robinson, Bklyn	.342	2000	Todd Helton, Col	.372
1950	Stan Musial, StL	.346			

Leaders in Runs Scored

Year	Player and Team	Runs	Year	Player and Team	Runs
1900	Roy Thomas, Phil	131	1952	Stan Musial, StL	105
1901	Jesse Burkett, StL	139		Solly Hemus, StL	105
1902	Honus Wagner, Pitt	105	1953	Duke Snider, Bklyn	132
1903	Ginger Beaumont, Pitt	137	1954	Stan Musial, StL	120
1904	George Browne, NY	99		Duke Snider, Bklyn	120
1905	Mike Donlin, NY	124	1955	Duke Snider, Bklyn	126
1906	Honus Wagner, Pitt	103	1956	Frank Robinson, Cin	122
	Frank Chance, Chi	103	1957	Hank Aaron, Mil	118
1907	Spike Shannon, NY	104	1958	Willie Mays, SF	121
1908	Fred Tenney, NY	101	1959	Vada Pinson, Cin	131
1909	Tommy Leach, Pitt	126	1960	Bill Bruton, Mil	112
1910	Sherry Magee, Phil	110	1961	Willie Mays, SF	129
1911	Jimmy Sheckard, Chi	121	1962	Frank Robinson, Cin	134
1912	Bob Bescher, Cin	120	1963	Hank Aaron, Mil	121
1913	Tommy Leach, Chi	99	1964	Dick Allen, Phil	125
	Max Carey, Pitt	99	1965	Tommy Harper, Cin	126
1914	George Burns, NY	100	1966	Felipe Alou, Atl	122
1915	Gavvy Cravath, Phil	89	1967	Hank Aaron, Atl	113
1916	George Burns, NY	105		Lou Brock, StL	113
1917	George Burns, NY	103	1968	Glenn Beckert, Chi	98
1918	Heinie Groh, Cin	88	1969	Bobby Bonds, SF	120
1919	George Burns, NY	86		Pete Rose, Cin	120
1920	George Burns, NY	115	1970	Billy Williams, Chi	137
1921	Rogers Hornsby, StL	131	1971	Lou Brock, StL	126
1922	Rogers Hornsby, StL	141	1972	Joe Morgan, Cin	122
1923	Ross Youngs, NY	121	1973	Bobby Bonds, SF	131
1924	Frankie Frisch, NY	121	1974	Pete Rose, Cin	110
	Rogers Hornsby, StL	121	1975	Pete Rose, Cin	112
1925	Kiki Cuyler, Pitt	144	1976	Pete Rose, Cin	130
1926	Kiki Cuyler, Pitt	113	1977	George Foster, Cin	124
1927	Lloyd Waner, Pitt	133	1978	Ivan DeJesus, Chi	104
	Rogers Hornsby, NY	133	1979	Keith Hernandez, StL	116
1928	Paul Waner, Pitt	142	1980	Keith Hernandez, StL	111
1929	Rogers Hornsby, Chi	156	1981	Mike Schmidt, Phil	78
1930	Chuck Klein, Phil	158	1982	Lonnie Smith, StL	120
1931	Bill Terry, NY	121	1983	Tim Raines, Mtl	133
	Chuck Klein, Phil	121	1984	Ryne Sandberg, Chi	114
1932	Chuck Klein, Phil	152	1985	Dale Murphy, Atl	118
1933	Pepper Martin, StL	122	1986	Von Hayes, Phil	107
1934	Paul Waner, Pitt	122		Tony Gwynn, SD	107
1935	Augie Galan, Chi	133	1987	Tim Raines, Mtl	123
1936	Arky Vaughan, Pitt	122	1988	Brett Butler, SF	109
1937	Joe Medwick, StL	111	1989	Howard Johnson, NY	104
1938	Mel Ott, NY	116		Will Clark, SF	104
1939	Billy Werber, Cin	115		Ryne Sandberg, Chi	104
1940	Arky Vaughan, Pitt	113	1990	Ryne Sandberg, Chi	116
1941	Pete Reiser, Bklyn	117	1991	Brett Butler, LA	112
1942	Mel Ott, NY	118	1992	Barry Bonds, Pitt	109
1943	Arky Vaughan, Bklyn	112	1993	Lenny Dykstra, Phil	143
1944	Bill Nicholson, Chi	116	1994	Jeff Bagwell, Hou	104
1945	Eddie Stanky, Bklyn	128	1995	Craig Biggio, Hou	123
1946	Stan Musial, StL	124	1996	Ellis Burks, Col	142
1947	Johnny Mize, NY	137	1997	Craig Biggio, Hou	146
1948	Stan Musial, StL	135	1998	Sammy Sosa, Chi	134
1949	Pee Wee Reese, Bklyn	132	1999	Jeff Bagwell, Hou	143
1950	Earl Torgeson, Bos	120	2000	Jeff Bagwell, Hou	152
1951	Stan Musial, StL	124			
	Ralph Kiner, Pitt	124			

Leaders in Hits

Year	Player and Team	Hits	Year	Player and Team	Hits
1900	Willie Keeler, Bklyn	208	1953	Richie Ashburn, Phil	205
1901	Jesse Burkett, StL	228	1954	Don Mueller, NY	212
1902	Ginger Beaumont, Pitt	194	1955	Ted Kluszewski, Cin	192
1903	Ginger Beaumont, Pitt	209	1956	Hank Aaron, Mil	200
1904	Ginger Beaumont, Pitt	185	1957	Red Schoendienst, NY-Mil	200
1905	Cy Seymour, Cin	219	1958	Richie Ashburn, Phil	215
1906	Harry Steinfeldt, Chi	176	1959	Hank Aaron, Mil	223
1907	Ginger Beaumont, Bos	187	1960	Willie Mays, SF	190
1908	Honus Wagner, Pitt	201	1961	Vada Pinson, Cin	208
1909	Larry Doyle, NY	172	1962	Tommy Davis, LA	230
1910	Honus Wagner, Pitt	178	1963	Vada Pinson, Cin	204
	Bobby Byrne, Pitt	178	1964	Roberto Clemente, Pitt	211
1911	Doc Miller, Bos	192		Curt Flood, StL	211
1912	Heinie Zimmerman, Chi	207	1965	Pete Rose, Cin	209
1913	Gavvy Cravath, Phil	179	1966	Felipe Alou, Atl	218
1914	Sherry Magee, Phil	171	1967	Roberto Clemente, Pitt	209
1915	Larry Doyle, NY	189	1968	Felipe Alou, Atl	210
1916	Hal Chase, Cin	184		Pete Rose, Cin	210
1917	Heinie Groh, Cin	182	1969	Matty Alou, Pitt	231
1918	Charlie Hollocher, Chi	161	1970	Pete Rose, Cin	205
1919	Ivy Olson, Bklyn	164		Billy Williams, Chi	205
1920	Rogers Hornsby, StL	218	1971	Joe Torre, StL	230
1921	Rogers Hornsby, StL	235	1972	Pete Rose, Cin	198
1922	Rogers Hornsby, StL	250	1973	Pete Rose, Cin	230
1923	Frankie Frisch, NY	223	1974	Ralph Garr, Atl	214
1924	Rogers Hornsby, StL	227	1975	Dave Cash, Phil	213
1925	Jim Bottomley, StL	227	1976	Pete Rose, Cin	215
1926	Eddie Brown, Bos	201	1977	Dave Parker, Pitt	215
1927	Paul Waner, Pitt	237	1978	Steve Garvey, LA	202
1928	Freddy Lindstrom, NY	231	1979	Garry Templeton, StL	211
1929	Lefty O'Doul, Phil	254	1980	Steve Garvey, LA	200
1930	Bill Terry, NY	254	1981	Pete Rose, Phil	140
1931	Lloyd Waner, Pitt	214	1982	Al Oliver, Mtl	204
1932	Chuck Klein, Phil	226	1983	Jose Cruz, Hou	189
1933	Chuck Klein, Phil	223		Andre Dawson, Mtl	189
1934	Paul Waner, Pitt	217	1984	Tony Gwynn, SD	213
1935	Billy Herman, Chi	227	1985	Willie McGee, StL	216
1936	Joe Medwick, StL	223	1986	Tony Gwynn, SD	211
1937	Joe Medwick, StL	237	1987	Tony Gwynn, SD	218
1938	Frank McCormick, Cin	209	1988	Andres Galarraga, Mtl	184
1939	Frank McCormick, Cin	209	1989	Tony Gwynn, SD	203
1940	Stan Hack, Chi	191	1990	Brett Butler, SF	192
	Frank McCormick, Cin	191		Lenny Dykstra, Phil	192
1941	Stan Hack, Chi	186	1991	Terry Pendleton, Atl	187
1942	Enos Slaughter, StL	188	1992	Terry Pendleton, Atl	199
1943	Stan Musial, StL	220		Andy Van Slyke, Pitt	199
1944	Stan Musial, StL	197	1993	Lenny Dykstra, Phil	194
	Phil Cavarretta, Chi	197	1994	Tony Gwynn, SD	165
1945	Tommy Holmes, Bos	224	1995	Dante Bichette, Col	197
1946	Stan Musial, StL	228		Tony Gwynn, SD	197
1947	Tommy Holmes, Bos	191	1996	Lance Johnson, NY	227
1948	Stan Musial, StL	230	1997	Tony Gwynn, SD	220
1949	Stan Musial, StL	207	1998	Dante Bichette, Col	219
1950	Duke Snider, Bklyn	199	1999	Luis Gonzalez, Ariz	206
1951	Richie Ashburn, Phil	221	2000	Todd Helton, Col	216
1952	Stan Musial, StL	194			

Home Run Leaders

Year	Player and Team	HR	Year	Player and Team	HR
1900	Herman Long, Bos	12	1948	Ralph Kiner, Pitt	40
1901	Sam Crawford, Cin	16		Johnny Mize, NY	40
1902	Tommy Leach, Pitt	6	1949	Ralph Kiner, Pitt	54
1903	Jimmy Sheckard, Bklyn	9	1950	Ralph Kiner, Pitt	47
1904	Harry Lumley, Bklyn	9	1951	Ralph Kiner, Pitt	42
1905	Fred Odwell, Cin	9	1952	Ralph Kiner, Pitt	37
1906	Tim Jordan, Bklyn	12		Hank Sauer, Chi	37
1907	Dave Brain, Bos	10	1953	Eddie Mathews, Mil	47
1908	Tim Jordan, Bklyn	12	1954	Ted Kluszewski, Cin	49
1909	Red Murray, NY	7	1955	Willie Mays, NY	51
1910	Fred Beck, Bos	10	1956	Duke Snider, Bklyn	43
	Wildfire Schulte, Chi	10	1957	Hank Aaron, Mil	44
1911	Wildfire Schulte, Chi	21	1958	Ernie Banks, Chi	47
1912	Heinie Zimmerman, Chi	14	1959	Eddie Mathews, Mil	46
1913	Gavvy Cravath, Phil	19	1960	Ernie Banks, Chi	41
1914	Gavvy Cravath, Phil	19	1961	Orlando Cepeda, SF	46
1915	Gavvy Cravath, Phil	24	1962	Willie Mays, SF	49
1916	Dave Robertson, NY	12	1963	Hank Aaron, Mil	44
	Cy Williams, Chi	12		Willie McCovey, SF	44
1917	Dave Robertson, NY	12	1964	Willie Mays, SF	47
	Gavvy Cravath, Phil	12	1965	Willie Mays, SF	52
1918	Gavvy Cravath, Phil	8	1966	Hank Aaron, Atl	44
1919	Gavvy Cravath, Phil	12	1967	Hank Aaron, Atl	39
1920	Cy Williams, Phil	15	1968	Willie McCovey, SF	36
1921	George Kelly, NY	23	1969	Willie McCovey, SF	45
1922	Rogers Hornsby, StL	42	1970	Johnny Bench, Cin	45
1923	Cy Williams, Phil	41	1971	Willie Stargell, Pitt	48
1924	Jack Fournier, Bklyn	27	1972	Johnny Bench, Cin	40
1925	Rogers Hornsby, StL	39	1973	Willie Stargell, Pitt	44
1926	Hack Wilson, Chi	21	1974	Mike Schmidt, Phil	36
1927	Hack Wilson, Chi	30	1975	Mike Schmidt, Phil	38
	Cy Williams, Phil	30	1976	Mike Schmidt, Phil	38
1928	Hack Wilson, Chi	31	1977	George Foster, Cin	52
	Jim Bottomley, StL	31	1978	George Foster, Cin	40
1929	Chuck Klein, Phil	43	1979	Dave Kingman, Chi	48
1930	Hack Wilson, Chi	56	1980	Mike Schmidt, Phil	48
1931	Chuck Klein, Phil	31	1981	Mike Schmidt, Phil	31
1932	Chuck Klein, Phil	38	1982	Dave Kingman, NY	37
	Mel Ott, NY	38	1983	Mike Schmidt, Phil	40
1933	Chuck Klein, Phil	28	1984	Dale Murphy, Atl	36
1934	Ripper Collins, StL	35		Mike Schmidt, Phil	36
	Mel Ott, NY	35	1985	Dale Murphy, Atl	37
1935	Wally Berger, Bos	34	1986	Mike Schmidt, Phil	37
1936	Mel Ott, NY	33	1987	Andre Dawson, Chi	49
1937	Mel Ott, NY	31	1988	Darryl Strawberry, NY	39
	Joe Medwick, StL	31	1989	Kevin Mitchell, SF	47
1938	Mel Ott, NY	36	1990	Ryne Sandberg, Chi	40
1939	Johnny Mize, StL	28	1991	Howard Johnson, NY	38
1940	Johnny Mize, StL	43	1992	Fred McGriff, SD	35
1941	Dolph Camilli, Bklyn	34	1993	Barry Bonds, SF	46
1942	Mel Ott, NY	30	1994	Matt Williams, SF	43
1943	Bill Nicholson, Chi	29	1995	Dante Bichette, Col	40
1944	Bill Nicholson, Chi	33	1996	Andres Galarraga, Col	47
1945	Tommy Holmes, Bos	28	1997	Larry Walker, Col	49
1946	Ralph Kiner, Pitt	23	1998	Mark McGwire, StL	70
1947	Ralph Kiner, Pitt	51	1999	Mark McGwire, StL	65
	Johnny Mize, NY	51	2000	Sammy Sosa, Chi	50

Runs Batted In Leaders

Year	Player and Team	RBI	Year	Player and Team	RBI
1900	Elmer Flick, Phil	110	1951	Monte Irvin, NY	121
1901	Honus Wagner, Pitt	126	1952	Hank Sauer, Chi	121
1902	Honus Wagner, Pitt	91	1953	Roy Campanella, Bklyn	142
1903	Sam Mertes, NY	104	1954	Ted Kluszewski, Cin	141
1904	Bill Dahlen, NY	80	1955	Duke Snider, Bklyn	136
1905	Cy Seymour, Cin	121	1956	Stan Musial, StL	109
1906	Jim Nealon, Pitt	83	1957	Hank Aaron, Mil	132
	Harry Steinfeldt, Chi	83	1958	Ernie Banks, Chi	129
1907	Sherry Magee, Phil	85	1959	Ernie Banks, Chi	143
1908	Honus Wagner, Pitt	109	1960	Hank Aaron, Mil	126
1909	Honus Wagner, Pitt	100	1961	Orlando Cepeda, SF	142
1910	Sherry Magee, Phil	123	1962	Tommy Davis, LA	153
1911	Wildfire Schulte, Chi	121	1963	Hank Aaron, Mil	130
1912	Heinie Zimmerman, Chi	103	1964	Ken Boyer, StL	119
1913	Gavvy Cravath, Phil	128	1965	Deron Johnson, Cin	130
1914	Sherry Magee, Phil	103	1966	Hank Aaron, Atl	127
1915	Gavvy Cravath, Phil	115	1967	Orlando Cepeda, StL	111
1916	Heinie Zimmerman, Chi-NY	83	1968	Willie McCovey, SF	105
1917	Heinie Zimmerman, NY	102	1969	Willie McCovey, SF	126
1918	Sherry Magee, Phil	76	1970	Johnny Bench, Cin	148
1919	Hi Myers, Bklyn	73	1971	Joe Torre, StL	137
1920	George Kelly, NY	94	1972	Johnny Bench, Cin	125
	Rogers Hornsby, StL	94	1973	Willie Stargell, Pitt	119
1921	Rogers Hornsby, StL	126	1974	Johnny Bench, Cin	129
1922	Rogers Hornsby, StL	152	1975	Greg Luzinski, Phil	120
1923	Irish Meusel, NY	125	1976	George Foster, Cin	121
1924	George Kelly, NY	136	1977	George Foster, Cin	149
1925	Rogers Hornsby, StL	143	1978	George Foster, Cin	120
1926	Jim Bottomley, StL	120	1979	Dave Winfield, SD	118
1927	Paul Waner, Pitt	131	1980	Mike Schmidt, Phil	121
1928	Jim Bottomley, StL	136	1981	Mike Schmidt, Phil	91
1929	Hack Wilson, Chi	159	1982	Dale Murphy, Atl	109
1930	Hack Wilson, Chi	190		Al Oliver, Mtl	109
1931	Chuck Klein, Phil	121	1983	Dale Murphy, Atl	121
1932	Don Hurst, Phil	143	1984	Gary Carter, Mtl	106
1933	Chuck Klein, Phil	120		Mike Schmidt, Phil	106
1934	Mel Ott, NY	135	1985	Dave Parker, Cin	125
1935	Wally Berger, Bos	130	1986	Mike Schmidt, Phil	119
1936	Joe Medwick, StL	138	1987	Andre Dawson, Chi	137
1937	Joe Medwick, StL	154	1988	Will Clark, SF	109
1938	Joe Medwick, StL	122	1989	Kevin Mitchell, SF	125
1939	Frank McCormick, Cin	128	1990	Matt Williams, SF	122
1940	Johnny Mize, StL	137	1991	Howard Johnson, NY	117
1941	Dolph Camilli, Bklyn	120	1992	Darren Daulton, Phil	109
1942	Johnny Mize, NY	110	1993	Barry Bonds, SF	123
1943	Bill Nicholson, Chi	128	1994	Jeff Bagwell, Hou	116
1944	Bill Nicholson, Chi	122	1995	Dante Bichette, Col	128
1945	Dixie Walker, Bklyn	124	1996	Andres Galarraga, Col	150
1946	Enos Slaughter, StL	130	1997	Andres Galarraga, Col	140
1947	Johnny Mize, NY	138	1998	Sammy Sosa, Chi	158
1948	Stan Musial, StL	131	1999	Mark McGwire, StL	147
1949	Ralph Kiner, Pitt	127	2000	Todd Helton, Col	147
1950	Del Ennis, Phil	126			

Leading Base Stealers

Year	Player and Team	SB	Year	Player and Team	SB
1900	George Van Haltren, NY	45	1949	Jackie Robinson, Bklyn	37
	Patsy Donovan, StL	45	1950	Sam Jethroe, Bos	35
1901	Honus Wagner, Pitt	48	1951	Sam Jethroe, Bos	35
1902	Honus Wagner, Pitt	43	1952	Pee Wee Reese, Bklyn	30
1903	Jimmy Sheckard, Bklyn	67	1953	Bill Bruton, Mil	26
	Frank Chance, Chi	67	1954	Bill Bruton, Mil	34
1904	Honus Wagner, Pitt	53	1955	Bill Bruton, Mil	35
1905	Billy Maloney, Chi	59	1956	Willie Mays, NY	40
	Art Devlin, NY	59	1957	Willie Mays, NY	38
1906	Frank Chance, Chi	57	1958	Willie Mays, SF	31
1907	Honus Wagner, Pitt	61	1959	Willie Mays, SF	27
1908	Honus Wagner, Pitt	53	1960	Maury Wills, LA	50
1909	Bob Bescher, Cin	54	1961	Maury Wills, LA	35
1910	Bob Bescher, Cin	70	1962	Maury Wills, LA	104
1911	Bob Bescher, Cin	80	1963	Maury Wills, LA	40
1912	Bob Bescher, Cin	67	1964	Maury Wills, LA	53
1913	Max Carey, Pitt	61	1965	Maury Wills, LA	94
1914	George Burns, NY	62	1966	Lou Brock, StL	74
1915	Max Carey, Pitt	36	1967	Lou Brock, StL	52
1916	Max Carey, Pitt	63	1968	Lou Brock, StL	62
1917	Max Carey, Pitt	46	1969	Lou Brock, StL	53
1918	Max Carey, Pitt	58	1970	Bobby Tolan, Cin	57
1919	George Burns, NY	40	1971	Lou Brock, StL	64
1920	Max Carey, Pitt	52	1972	Lou Brock, StL	63
1921	Frankie Frisch, NY	49	1973	Lou Brock, StL	70
1922	Max Carey, Pitt	51	1974	Lou Brock, StL	118
1923	Max Carey, Pitt	51	1975	Davey Lopes, LA	77
1924	Max Carey, Pitt	49	1976	Davey Lopes, LA	63
1925	Max Carey, Pitt	46	1977	Frank Taveras, Pitt	70
1926	Kiki Cuyler, Pitt	35	1978	Omar Moreno, Pitt	71
1927	Frankie Frisch, StL	48	1979	Omar Moreno, Pitt	77
1928	Kiki Cuyler, Chi	37	1980	Ron LeFlore, Mtl	97
1929	Kiki Cuyler, Chi	43	1981	Tim Raines, Mtl	71
1930	Kiki Cuyler, Chi	37	1982	Tim Raines, Mtl	78
1931	Frankie Frisch, StL	28	1983	Tim Raines, Mtl	90
1932	Chuck Klein, Phil	20	1984	Tim Raines, Mtl	75
1933	Pepper Martin, StL	26	1985	Vince Coleman, StL	110
1934	Pepper Martin, StL	23	1986	Vince Coleman, StL	107
1935	Augie Galan, Chi	22	1987	Vince Coleman, StL	109
1936	Pepper Martin, StL	23	1988	Vince Coleman, StL	81
1937	Augie Galan, Chi	23	1989	Vince Coleman, StL	65
1938	Stan Hack, Chi	16	1990	Vince Coleman, StL	77
1939	Stan Hack, Chi	17	1991	Marquis Grissom, Mtl	76
	Lee Handley, Pitt	17	1992	Marquis Grissom, Mtl	78
1940	Lonny Frey, Cin	22	1993	Chuck Carr, Fla	58
1941	Danny Murtaugh, Phil	18	1994	Craig Biggio, Hou	39
1942	Pete Reiser, Bklyn	20	1995	Quilvio Veras, Fla	56
1943	Arky Vaughan, Bklyn	20	1996	Eric Young, Col	53
1944	Johnny Barrett, Pitt	28	1997	Tony Womack, Pitt	60
1945	Red Schoendienst, StL	26	1998	Tony Womack, Pitt	58
1946	Pete Reiser, Bklyn	34	1999	Tony Womack, Ariz	72
1947	Jackie Robinson, Bklyn	29	2000	Luis Castillo, Fla	62
1948	Richie Ashburn, Phil	32			

Leading Pitchers—Winning Percentage

Year	Pitcher and Team	W	L	Pct	Year	Pitcher and Team	W	L	Pct
1900	Jesse Tannehill, Pitt	20	6	.769	1951	Preacher Roe, Bklyn	22	3	.880
1901	Jack Chesbro, Pitt	21	10	.677	1952	Hoyt Wilhelm, NY	15	3	.833
1902	Jack Chesbro, Pitt	28	6	.824	1953	Carl Erskine, Bklyn	20	6	.769
1903	Sam Leever, Pitt	25	7	.781	1954	Johnny Antonelli, NY	21	7	.750
1904	Joe McGinnity, NY	35	8	.814	1955	Don Newcombe, Bklyn	20	5	.800
1905	Sam Leever, Pitt	20	5	.800	1956	Don Newcombe, Bklyn	27	7	.794
1906	Ed Reulbach, Chi	19	4	.826	1957	Bob Buhl, Mil	18	7	.720
1907	Ed Reulbach, Chi	17	4	.810	1958	Warren Spahn, Mil	22	11	.667
1908	Ed Reulbach, Chi	24	7	.774		Lew Burdette, Mil	20	10	.667
1909	Christy Mathewson, NY	25	6	.806	1959	Roy Face, Pitt	18	1	.947
	Howie Camnitz, Pitt	25	6	.806	1960	Ernie Broglio, StL	21	9	.700
1910	King Cole, Chi	20	4	.833	1961	Johnny Podres, LA	18	5	.783
1911	Rube Marquard, NY	24	7	.774	1962	Bob Purkey, Cin	23	5	.821
1912	Claude Hendrix, Pitt	24	9	.727	1963	Ron Perranoski, LA	16	3	.842
1913	Bert Humphries, Chi	16	4	.800	1964	Sandy Koufax, LA	19	5	.792
1914	Bill James, Bos	26	7	.788	1965	Sandy Koufax, LA	26	8	.765
1915	Grover Alexander, Phil	31	10	.756	1966	Juan Marichal, SF	25	6	.806
1916	Tom Hughes, Bos	16	3	.842	1967	Dick Hughes, StL	16	6	.727
1917	Ferdie Schupp, NY	21	7	.750	1968	Steve Blass, Pitt	18	6	.750
1918	Claude Hendrix, Chi	19	7	.731	1969	Tom Seaver, NY	25	7	.781
1919	Dutch Ruether, Cin	19	6	.760	1970	Bob Gibson, StL	23	7	.767
1920	Burleigh Grimes, Bklyn	23	11	.676	1971	Don Gullett, Cin	16	6	.727
1921	Bill Doak, StL	15	6	.714	1972	Gary Nolan, Cin	15	5	.750
1922	Pete Donohue, Cin	18	9	.667	1973	Tommy John, LA	16	7	.696
1923	Dolf Luque, Cin	27	8	.771	1974	Andy Messersmith, LA	20	6	.769
1924	Emil Yde, Pitt	16	3	.842	1975	Don Gullett, Cin	15	4	.789
1925	Bill Sherdel, StL	15	6	.714	1976	Steve Carlton, Phil	20	7	.741
1926	Ray Kremer, Pitt	20	6	.769	1977	John Candelaria, Pitt	20	5	.800
1927	Larry Benton, Bos-NY	17	7	.708	1978	Gaylord Perry, SD	21	6	.778
1928	Larry Benton, NY	25	9	.735	1979	Tom Seaver, Cin	16	6	.727
1929	Charlie Root, Chi	19	6	.760	1980	Jim Bibby, Pitt	19	6	.760
1930	Freddie Fitzsimmons, NY	19	7	.731	1981*	Tom Seaver, Cin	14	2	.875
1931	Paul Derringer, StL	18	8	.692	1982	Phil Niekro, Atl	17	4	.810
1932	Lon Warneke, Chi	22	6	.786	1983	John Denny, Phil	19	6	.760
1933	Ben Cantwell, Bos	20	10	.667	1984	Rick Sutcliffe, Chi	16	1	.941
1934	Dizzy Dean, StL	30	7	.811	1985	Orel Hershiser, LA	19	3	.864
1935	Bill Lee, Chi	20	6	.769	1986	Bob Ojeda, NY	18	5	.783
1936	Carl Hubbell, NY	26	6	.813	1987	Dwight Gooden, NY	15	7	.682
1937	Carl Hubbell, NY	22	8	.733	1988	David Cone, NY	20	3	.870
1938	Bill Lee, Chi	22	9	.710	1989	Mike Bielecki, Chi	18	7	.720
1939	Paul Derringer, Cin	25	7	.781	1990	Doug Drabeck, Pitt	22	6	.786
1940	Freddie Fitzsimmons, Bklyn	16	2	.889	1991	John Smiley, Pitt	20	8	.714
1941	Elmer Riddle, Cin	19	4	.826		Jose Rijo, Cin	15	6	.714
1942	Larry French, Bklyn	15	4	.789	1992	Bob Tewksbury, StL	16	5	.762
1943	Mort Cooper, StL	21	8	.724	1993	Tom Glavine, Atl	22	6	.786
1944	Ted Wilks, StL	17	4	.810	1994	Ken Hill, Mtl	16	5	.762
1945	Harry Brecheen, StL	15	4	.789	1995	Greg Maddux, Atl	19	2	.905
1946	Murray Dickson, StL	15	6	.714	1996	John Smoltz, Atl	24	8	.750
1947	Larry Jansen, NY	21	5	.808	1997	Denny Neagle, Atl	20	5	.800
1948	Harry Brecheen, StL	20	7	.741	1998	John Smoltz, Atl	17	3	.850
1949	Preacher Roe, Bklyn	15	6	.714	1999	Mike Hampton, Hou	22	4	.846
1950	Sal Maglie, NY	18	4	.818	2000	Randy Johnson, Ariz	19	7	.730

*1981 percentages based on 10 or more victories. Note: Percentages based on 15 or more victories in all other years.

Leading Pitchers—Earned Run Average

Year	Player and Team	ERA	Year	Player and Team	ERA
1900	Rube Waddell, Pitt	2.37	1951	Chet Nichols, Bos	2.88
1901	Jesse Tannehill, Pitt	2.18	1952	Hoyt Wilhelm, NY	2.43
1902	Jack Taylor, Chi	1.33	1953	Warren Spahn, Mil	2.10
1903	Sam Leever, Pitt	2.06	1954	Johnny Antonelli, NY	2.29
1904	Joe McGinnity, NY	1.61	1955	Bob Friend, Pitt	2.84
1905	Christy Mathewson, NY	1.27	1956	Lew Burdette, Mil	2.71
1906	Three Finger Brown, Chi	1.04	1957	Johnny Podres, Bklyn	2.66
1907	Jack Pfiester, Chi	1.15	1958	Stu Miller, SF	2.47
1908	Christy Mathewson, NY	1.43	1959	Sam Jones, SF	2.82
1909	Christy Mathewson, NY	1.14	1960	Mike McCormick, SF	2.70
1910	George McQuillan, Phil	1.60	1961	Warren Spahn, Mil	3.01
1911	Christy Mathewson, NY	1.99	1962	Sandy Koufax, LA	2.54
1912	Jeff Tesreau, NY	1.96	1963	Sandy Koufax, LA	1.88
1913	Christy Mathewson, NY	2.06	1964	Sandy Koufax, LA	1.74
1914	Bill Doak, StL	1.72	1965	Sandy Koufax, LA	2.04
1915	Grover Alexander, Phil	1.22	1966	Sandy Koufax, LA	1.73
1916	Grover Alexander, Phil	1.55	1967	Phil Niekro, Atl	1.87
1917	Grover Alexander, Phil	1.83	1968	Bob Gibson, StL	1.12
1918	Hippo Vaughn, Chi	1.74	1969	Juan Marichal, SF	2.10
1919	Grover Alexander, Chi	1.72	1970	Tom Seaver, NY	2.81
1920	Grover Alexander, Chi	1.91	1971	Tom Seaver, NY	1.76
1921	Bill Doak, StL	2.58	1972	Steve Carlton, Phil	1.98
1922	Rosy Ryan, NY	3.00	1973	Tom Seaver, NY	2.08
1923	Dolf Luque, Cin	1.93	1974	Buzz Capra, Atl	2.28
1924	Dazzy Vance, Bklyn	2.16	1975	Randy Jones, SD	2.24
1925	Dolf Luque, Cin	2.63	1976	John Denny, StL	2.52
1926	Ray Kremer, Pitt	2.61	1977	John Candelaria, Pitt	2.34
1927	Ray Kremer, Pitt	2.47	1978	Craig Swan, NY	2.43
1928	Dazzy Vance, Bklyn	2.09	1979	J.R. Richard, Hou	2.71
1929	Bill Walker, NY	3.08	1980	Don Sutton, LA	2.21
1930	Dazzy Vance, Bklyn	2.61	1981	Nolan Ryan, Hou	1.69
1931	Bill Walker, NY	2.26	1982	Steve Rogers, Mtl	2.40
1932	Lon Warneke, Chi	2.37	1983	Atlee Hammaker, SF	2.25
1933	Carl Hubbell, NY	1.66	1984	Alejandro Pena, LA	2.48
1934	Carl Hubbell, NY	2.30	1985	Dwight Gooden, NY	1.53
1935	Cy Blanton, Pitt	2.59	1986	Mike Scott, Hou	2.22
1936	Carl Hubbell, NY	2.31	1987	Nolan Ryan, Hou	2.76
1937	Jim Turner, Bos	2.38	1988	Joe Magrane, StL	2.18
1938	Bill Lee, Chi	2.66	1989	Scott Garrelts, SF	2.28
1939	Bucky Walters, Cin	2.29	1990	Danny Darwin, Hou	2.21
1940	Bucky Walters, Cin	2.48	1991	Dennis Martinez, Mtl	2.39
1941	Elmer Riddle, Cin	2.24	1992	Bill Swift, SF	2.08
1942	Mort Cooper, StL	1.77	1993	Greg Maddux, Atl	2.36
1943	Howie Pollet, StL	1.75	1994	Greg Maddux, Atl	1.56
1944	Ed Heusser, Cin	2.38	1995	Greg Maddux, Atl	1.63
1945	Hank Borowy, Chi	2.14	1996	Kevin Brown, Fla	1.89
1946	Howie Pollet, StL	2.10	1997	Pedro Martinez, Mtl	1.90
1947	Warren Spahn, Bos	2.33	1998	Greg Maddux, Atl	1.98
1948	Harry Brecheen, StL	2.24	1999	Randy Johnson, Ariz	2.48
1949	Dave Koslo, NY	2.50	2000	Kevin Brown, LA	2.58
1950	Jim Hearn, StL-NY	2.49			

Note: Based on 10 complete games through 1950, then 154 innings until National League expanded in 1962, when it became 162 innings. In strike-shortened 1981, one inning per game required.

Leading Pitchers—Strikeouts

Year	Player and Team	SO	Year	Player and Team	SO
1900	Rube Waddell, Pitt	133	1951	Warren Spahn, Bos	164
1901	Noodles Hahn, Cin	233		Don Newcombe, Bklyn	164
1902	Vic Willis, Bos	226	1952	Warren Spahn, Bos	183
1903	Christy Mathewson, NY	267	1953	Robin Roberts, Phil	198
1904	Christy Mathewson, NY	212	1954	Robin Roberts, Phil	185
1905	Christy Mathewson, NY	206	1955	Sam Jones, Chi	198
1906	Fred Beebe, Chi-StL	171	1956	Sam Jones, Chi	176
1907	Christy Mathewson, NY	178	1957	Jack Sanford, Phil	188
1908	Christy Mathewson, NY	259	1958	Sam Jones, StL	225
1909	Orval Overall, Chi	205	1959	Don Drysdale, LA	242
1910	Christy Mathewson, NY	190	1960	Don Drysdale, LA	246
1911	Rube Marquard, NY	237	1961	Sandy Koufax, LA	269
1912	Grover Alexander, Phil	195	1962	Don Drysdale, LA	232
1913	Tom Seaton, Phil	168	1963	Sandy Koufax, LA	306
1914	Grover Alexander, Phil	214	1964	Bob Veale, Pitt	250
1915	Grover Alexander, Phil	241	1965	Sandy Koufax, LA	382
1916	Grover Alexander, Phil	167	1966	Sandy Koufax, LA	317
1917	Grover Alexander, Phil	200	1967	Jim Bunning, Phil	253
1918	Hippo Vaughn, Chi	148	1968	Bob Gibson, StL	268
1919	Hippo Vaughn, Chi	141	1969	Ferguson Jenkins, Chi	273
1920	Grover Alexander, Chi	173	1970	Tom Seaver, NY	283
1921	Burleigh Grimes, Bklyn	136	1971	Tom Seaver, NY	289
1922	Dazzy Vance, Bklyn	134	1972	Steve Carlton, Phil	310
1923	Dazzy Vance, Bklyn	197	1973	Tom Seaver, NY	251
1924	Dazzy Vance, Bklyn	262	1974	Steve Carlton, Phil	240
1925	Dazzy Vance, Bklyn	221	1975	Tom Seaver, NY	243
1926	Dazzy Vance, Bklyn	140	1976	Tom Seaver, NY	235
1927	Dazzy Vance, Bklyn	184	1977	Phil Niekro, Atl	262
1928	Dazzy Vance, Bklyn	200	1978	J.R. Richard, Hou	303
1929	Pat Malone, Chi	166	1979	J.R. Richard, Hou	313
1930	Bill Hallahan, StL	177	1980	Steve Carlton, Phil	286
1931	Bill Hallahan, StL	159	1981	Fernando Valenzuela, LA	180
1932	Dizzy Dean, StL	191	1982	Steve Carlton, Phil	286
1933	Dizzy Dean, StL	199	1983	Steve Carlton, Phil	275
1934	Dizzy Dean, StL	195	1984	Dwight Gooden, NY	276
1935	Dizzy Dean, StL	182	1985	Dwight Gooden, NY	268
1936	Van Lingle Mungo, Bklyn	238	1986	Mike Scott, Hou	306
1937	Carl Hubbell, NY	159	1987	Nolan Ryan, Hou	270
1938	Clay Bryant, Chi	135	1988	Nolan Ryan, Hou	228
1939	Claude Passeau, Phil-Chi	137	1989	Jose DeLeon, StL	201
	Bucky Walters, Cin	137	1990	David Cone, NY	233
1940	Kirby Higbe, Phil	137	1991	David Cone, NY	241
1941	Johnny Vander Meer, Cin	202	1992	John Smoltz, Atl	215
1942	Johnny Vander Meer, Cin	186	1993	Jose Rijo, Cin	227
1943	Johnny Vander Meer, Cin	174	1994	Andy Benes, SD	189
1944	Bill Voiselle, NY	161	1995	Hideo Nomo, LA	236
1945	Preacher Roe, Pitt	148	1996	John Smoltz, Atl	276
1946	Johnny Schmitz, Chi	135	1997	Curt Schilling, Phil	319
1947	Ewell Blackwell, Cin	193	1998	Curt Schilling, Phil	300
1948	Harry Brecheen, StL	149	1999	Randy Johnson, Ariz	364
1949	Warren Spahn, Bos	151	2000	Randy Johnson, Ariz	347
1950	Warren Spahn, Bos	191			

Leading Pitchers—Saves

Year	Player and Team	SV	Year	Player and Team	SV
1947	Hugh Casey, Bklyn	18	1974	Mike Marshall, LA	21
1948	Harry Gumpert, Cin	17	1975	Al Hrabosky, StL	22
1949	Ted Wilks, StL	9		Rawly Eastwick, Cin	22
1950	Jim Konstanty, Phil	22	1976	Rawly Eastwick, Cin	26
1951	Ted Wilks, StL, Pitt	13	1977	Rollie Fingers, SD	35
1952	Al Brazle, StL	16	1978	Rollie Fingers, SD	37
1953	Al Brazle, StL	18	1979	Bruce Sutter, Chi	37
1954	Jim Hughes, Bklyn	24	1980	Bruce Sutter, Chi	28
1955	Jack Meyer, Phil	16	1981	Bruce Sutter, StL	25
1956	Clem Labine, Bklyn	19	1982	Bruce Sutter, StL	36
1957	Clem Labine, Bklyn	17	1983	Lee Smith, Chi	29
1958	Roy Face, Pitt	20	1984	Bruce Sutter, StL	45
1959	Lindy McDaniel, StL	15	1985	Jeff Reardon, Mtl	41
	Don McMahon, Mil	15	1986	Todd Worrell, StL	36
1960	Lindy McDaniel, StL	26	1987	Steve Bedrosian, Phil	40
1961	Stu Miller, SF	17	1988	John Franco, Cin	39
	Roy Face, Pitt	17	1989	Mark Davis, SD	44
1962	Roy Face, Pitt	28	1990	John Franco, NY	33
1963	Lindy McDaniel, Chi	22	1991	Lee Smith, StL	47
1964	Hal Woodeshick, Hou	23	1992	Lee Smith, StL	42
1965	Ted Abernathy, Chi	31	1993	Randy Myers, Chi	53
1966	Phil Regan, LA	21	1994	John Franco, NY	30
1967	Ted Abernathy, Cin	28	1995	Randy Myers, Chi	38
1968	Phil Regan, Chi, LA	25	1996	Jeff Brantley, Cin	44
1969	Fred Gladding, Hou	29		Todd Worrell, LA	44
1970	Wayne Granger, Cin	35	1997	Jeff Shaw, Cin	42
1971	Dave Giusti, Pitt	30	1998	Trevor Hoffman, SD	53
1972	Clay Carroll, Cin	37	1999	Ugueth Urbina, Mtl	41
1973	Mike Marshall, Mtl	13	2000	Antonio Alfonseca, Fla	45

Tear Down Wrigley!

They pour into Wrigley every year, more than two million strong—Kiwanis clubs from the Quad Cities, frat buddies from Lincoln Park, businessmen from loop offices, families from Arlington Heights and Oak Forest, baseball purists and tourists from around the world. The fans pack Wrigley on hot summer days and nights to quaff Old Style, regale one another with Harry Caray stories, check out the action in the stands. At these big, happy outdoor parties, it hardly matters whether the beloved Cubbies win or lose. Which is precisely why Wrigley Field must go.

The Sammy Sosa trade business is the last straw. It tells you all you need to know about why the Cubs will never win a World Series at Wrigley. Sosa, a 60-home-run man, wants to be one of the highest-paid players in the game, wants to know that he's loved. He'll never get that love from the Cubs, for the same reason big-market Chicago didn't do everything in its power to keep Greg Maddux, and the same reason the Cubs never make plays for guys like Kevin Brown or Ken Griffey Jr. The Cubs don't need Sosa, Brown or Griffey. Year after mediocre year Wrigley fills up with fans.

All over baseball, teams looking to change their fortunes are tearing down old parks. Unlike Cincinnati, Milwaukee or Pittsburgh, though, Chicago already generates revenue with an appealing, quirky throwback venue. What the Cubs need is a change of heart, a karmic conversion, a blood sacrifice. Preservationists may shudder at the idea of a wrecking ball smashing Wrigley's famously ivied walls. But what really is preserved at Wrigley other than a nearly century-long tradition of haplessness? Their environs are a national landmark, but the Cubs themselves are a national laughingstock.

It's unrealistic to ask fans simply not to show up; rationalists have been making that plea for years, to no avail. The Wrigley siren is too tempting. Tribune Company, which owns the Cubs, must wean itself from its cash cow. No Cubs fan should be content until ownership puts a decent product on the field, and that will happen only when Wrigley lies in smoldering ruins and the Cubs are playing in a cold, charmless cement home where nobody wants to linger any longer than they have to.

After all, it worked for the White Sox.

—Mark Mravic

Pennant Winners

Year	Team	Manager	W	L	Pct	GA
1901	Chicago	Clark Griffith	83	53	.610	4
1902	Philadelphia	Connie Mack	83	53	.610	5
1903	Boston	Jimmy Collins	91	47	.659	14½
1904	Boston	Jimmy Collins	95	59	.617	1½
1905	Philadelphia	Connie Mack	92	56	.622	2
1906	Chicago	Fielder Jones	93	58	.616	3
1907	Detroit	Hughie Jennings	92	58	.613	1½
1908	Detroit	Hughie Jennings	90	63	.588	½
1909	Detroit	Hughie Jennings	98	54	.645	3½
1910	Philadelphia	Connie Mack	102	48	.680	14½
1911	Philadelphia	Connie Mack	101	50	.669	13½
1912	Boston	Jake Stahl	105	47	.691	14
1913	Philadelphia	Connie Mack	96	57	.627	6½
1914	Philadelphia	Connie Mack	99	53	.651	8½
1915	Boston	Bill Carrigan	101	50	.669	2½
1916	Boston	Bill Carrigan	91	63	.591	2
1917	Chicago	Pants Rowland	100	54	.649	9
1918	Boston	Ed Barrow	75	51	.595	2½
1919	Chicago	Kid Gleason	88	52	.629	3½
1920	Cleveland	Tris Speaker	98	56	.636	2
1921	New York	Miller Huggins	98	55	.641	4½
1922	New York	Miller Huggins	94	60	.610	1
1923	New York	Miller Huggins	98	54	.645	16
1924	Washington	Bucky Harris	92	62	.597	2
1925	Washington	Bucky Harris	96	55	.636	8½
1926	New York	Miller Huggins	91	63	.591	3
1927	New York	Miller Huggins	110	44	.714	19
1928	New York	Miller Huggins	101	53	.656	2½
1929	Philadelphia	Connie Mack	104	46	.693	18
1930	Philadelphia	Connie Mack	102	52	.662	8
1931	Philadelphia	Connie Mack	107	45	.704	13½
1932	New York	Joe McCarthy	107	47	.695	13
1933	Washington	Joe Cronin	99	53	.651	7
1934	Detroit	Mickey Cochrane	101	53	.656	7
1935	Detroit	Mickey Cochrane	93	58	.616	3
1936	New York	Joe McCarthy	102	51	.667	19½
1937	New York	Joe McCarthy	102	52	.662	13
1938	New York	Joe McCarthy	99	53	.651	9½
1939	New York	Joe McCarthy	106	45	.702	17
1940	Detroit	Del Baker	90	64	.584	1
1941	New York	Joe McCarthy	101	53	.656	17
1942	New York	Joe McCarthy	103	51	.669	9
1943	New York	Joe McCarthy	98	56	.636	13½
1944	St. Louis	Luke Sewell	89	65	.578	1
1945	Detroit	Steve O'Neill	88	65	.575	1½
1946	Boston	Joe Cronin	104	50	.675	12
1947	New York	Bucky Harris	97	57	.630	12
1948	Cleveland†	Lou Boudreau	97	58	.626	1
1949	New York	Casey Stengel	97	57	.630	1
1950	New York	Casey Stengel	98	56	.636	3
1951	New York	Casey Stengel	98	56	.636	5
1952	New York	Casey Stengel	95	59	.617	2
1953	New York	Casey Stengel	99	52	.656	8½
1954	Cleveland	Al Lopez	111	43	.721	8
1955	New York	Casey Stengel	96	58	.623	3
1956	New York	Casey Stengel	97	57	.630	9
1957	New York	Casey Stengel	98	56	.636	8
1958	New York	Casey Stengel	92	62	.597	10
1959	Chicago	Al Lopez	94	60	.610	5
1960	New York	Casey Stengel	97	57	.630	8
1961	New York	Ralph Houk	109	53	.673	8
1962	New York	Ralph Houk	96	66	.593	5
1963	New York	Ralph Houk	104	57	.646	10½
1964	New York	Yogi Berra	99	63	.611	1
1965	Minnesota	Sam Mele	102	60	.630	7
1966	Baltimore	Hank Bauer	97	63	.606	9

Pennant Winners *(Cont.)*

Year	Team	Manager	W	L	Pct	GA
1967	Boston	Dick Williams	92	70	.568	1
1968	Detroit	Mayo Smith	103	59	.636	12
1969	Baltimore (E)‡	Earl Weaver	109	53	.673	19
1970	Baltimore (E)‡	Earl Weaver	108	54	.667	15
1971	Baltimore (E)‡	Earl Weaver	101	57	.639	12
1972	Oakland (W)‡	Dick Williams	93	62	.600	5½
1973	Oakland (W)‡	Dick Williams	94	68	.580	6
1974	Oakland (W)‡	Al Dark	90	72	.556	5
1975	Boston (E)‡	Darrell Johnson	95	65	.594	4½
1976	New York (E)‡	Billy Martin	97	62	.610	10½
1977	New York (E)‡	Billy Martin	100	62	.617	2½
1978	New York (E)†‡	Billy Martin, Bob Lemon	100	63	.613	1
1979	Baltimore (E)‡	Earl Weaver	102	57	.642	8
1980	Kansas City (E)‡	Jim Frey	97	65	.599	14
1981	New York (E)‡	Gene Michael, Bob Lemon	59	48	.551	#
1982	Milwaukee (E)‡	Buck Rodgers, Harvey Kuenn	95	67	.586	1
1983	Baltimore (E)‡	Joe Altobelli	98	64	.605	6
1984	Detroit (E)‡	Sparky Anderson	104	58	.642	15
1985	Kansas City (W)‡	Dick Howser	91	71	.562	1
1986	Boston (E)‡	John McNamara	95	66	.590	5½
1987	Minnesota (W)‡	Tom Kelly	85	77	.525	2
1988	Oakland (W)‡	Tony La Russa	104	58	.642	13
1989	Oakland (W)‡	Tony La Russa	99	63	.611	7
1990	Oakland (W)‡	Tony La Russa	103	59	.636	9
1991	Minnesota (W)‡	Tom Kelly	95	67	.586	8
1992	Toronto‡	Cito Gaston	96	66	.593	4
1993	Toronto‡	Cito Gaston	95	67	.586	7
1994	Season ended Aug. 11 due to players' strike					
1995	Cleveland (C)‡	Mike Hargrove	100	44	.694	30
1996	New York (E)‡	Joe Torre	92	70	.568	4
1997	Cleveland (C)‡	Mike Hargrove	86	75	.534	6
1998	New York (E)‡	Joe Torre	114	48	.704	22
1999	New York (E)‡	Joe Torre	98	64	.605	4
2000	New York (E)‡	Joe Torre	87	74	.540	2½

†Defeated Boston in one-game playoff. ‡Won championship series.
#First half 34–22; second 25–26, in season split by strike; defeated Milwaukee in playoff for Eastern Divison title.

Leading Batsmen

Year	Player and Team	BA	Year	Player and Team	BA
1901	Nap Lajoie, Phil	.422	1924	Babe Ruth, NY	.378
1902	Ed Delahanty, Wash	.376	1925	Harry Heilmann, Det	.393
1903	Nap Lajoie, Clev	.355	1926	Heinie Manush, Det	.378
1904	Nap Lajoie, Clev	.381	1927	Harry Heilmann, Det	.398
1905	Elmer Flick, Clev	.306	1928	Goose Goslin, Wash	.379
1906	George Stone, StL	.358	1929	Lew Fonseca, Clev	.369
1907	Ty Cobb, Det	.350	1930	Al Simmons, Phil	.381
1908	Ty Cobb, Det	.324	1931	Al Simmons, Phil	.390
1909	Ty Cobb, Det	.377	1932	Dale Alexander, Det-Bos	.367
1910	Nap Lajoie, Clev*	.383	1933	Jimmie Foxx, Phil	.356
1911	Ty Cobb, Det	.420	1934	Lou Gehrig, NY	.363
1912	Ty Cobb, Det	.410	1935	Buddy Myer, Wash	.349
1913	Ty Cobb, Det	.390	1936	Luke Appling, Chi	.388
1914	Ty Cobb, Det	.368	1937	Charlie Gehringer, Det	.371
1915	Ty Cobb, Det	.369	1938	Jimmie Foxx, Bos	.349
1916	Tris Speaker, Clev	.386	1939	Joe DiMaggio, NY	.381
1917	Ty Cobb, Det	.383	1940	Joe DiMaggio, NY	.352
1918	Ty Cobb, Det	.382	1941	Ted Williams, Bos	.406
1919	Ty Cobb, Det	.384	1942	Ted Williams, Bos	.356
1920	George Sisler, StL	.407	1943	Luke Appling, Chi	.328
1921	Harry Heilmann, Det	.394	1944	Lou Boudreau, Clev	.327
1922	George Sisler, StL	.420	1945	Snuffy Stirnweiss, NY	.309
1923	Harry Heilmann, Det	.403	1946	Mickey Vernon, Wash	.353

*League president Ban Johnson declared Ty Cobb batting champion with a .385 average, beating Lajoie's .384. However, subsequent research has led to the revision of Lajoie's average to .383 and Cobb's to .382.

Leading Batsmen (Cont.)

Year	Player and Team	BA	Year	Player and Team	BA
1947	Ted Williams, Bos	.343	1974	Rod Carew, Minn	.364
1948	Ted Williams, Bos	.369	1975	Rod Carew, Minn	.359
1949	George Kell, Det	.343	1976	George Brett, KC	.333
1950	Billy Goodman, Bos	.354	1977	Rod Carew, Minn	.388
1951	Ferris Fain, Phil	.344	1978	Rod Carew, Minn	.333
1952	Ferris Fain, Phil	.327	1979	Fred Lynn, Bos	.333
1953	Mickey Vernon, Wash	.337	1980	George Brett, KC	.390
1954	Bobby Avila, Clev	.341	1981	Carney Lansford, Bos	.336
1955	Al Kaline, Det	.340	1982	Willie Wilson, KC	.332
1956	Mickey Mantle, NY	.353	1983	Wade Boggs, Bos	.361
1957	Ted Williams, Bos	.388	1984	Don Mattingly, NY	.343
1958	Ted Williams, Bos	.328	1985	Wade Boggs, Bos	.368
1959	Harvey Kuenn, Det	.353	1986	Wade Boggs, Bos	.357
1960	Pete Runnels, Bos	.320	1987	Wade Boggs, Bos	.363
1961	Norm Cash, Det	.361	1988	Wade Boggs, Bos	.366
1962	Pete Runnels, Bos	.326	1989	Kirby Puckett, Minn	.339
1963	Carl Yastrzemski, Bos	.321	1990	George Brett, KC	.329
1964	Tony Oliva, Minn	.323	1991	Julio Franco, Tex	.341
1965	Tony Oliva, Minn	.321	1992	Edgar Martinez, Sea	.343
1966	Frank Robinson, Balt	.316	1993	John Olerud, Tor	.363
1967	Carl Yastrzemski, Bos	.326	1994	Paul O'Neill, NY	.359
1968	Carl Yastrzemski, Bos	.301	1995	Edgar Martinez, Sea	.356
1969	Rod Carew, Minn	.332	1996	Alex Rodriguez, Sea	.358
1970	Alex Johnson, Cal	.329	1997	Frank Thomas, Chi	.347
1971	Tony Oliva, Minn	.337	1998	Bernie Williams, NY	.339
1972	Rod Carew, Minn	.318	1999	Nomar Garciaparra, Bos	.357
1973	Rod Carew, Minn	.350	2000	Nomar Garciaparra, Bos	.372

Leaders in Runs Scored

Year	Player and Team	Runs	Year	Player and Team	Runs
1901	Nap Lajoie, Phil	145	1937	Joe DiMaggio, NY	151
1902	Dave Fultz, Phil	110	1938	Hank Greenberg, Det	144
1903	Patsy Dougherty, Bos	108	1939	Red Rolfe, NY	139
1904	Patsy Dougherty, Bos-NY	113	1940	Ted Williams, Bos	134
1905	Harry Davis, Phil	92	1941	Ted Williams, Bos	135
1906	Elmer Flick, Clev	98	1942	Ted Williams, Bos	141
1907	Sam Crawford, Det	102	1943	George Case, Wash	102
1908	Matty McIntyre, Det	105	1944	Snuffy Stirnweiss, NY	125
1909	Ty Cobb, Det	116	1945	Snuffy Stirnweiss, NY	107
1910	Ty Cobb, Det	106	1946	Ted Williams, Bos	142
1911	Ty Cobb, Det	147	1947	Ted Williams, Bos	125
1912	Eddie Collins, Phil	137	1948	Tommy Henrich, NY	138
1913	Eddie Collins, Phil	125	1949	Ted Williams, Bos	150
1914	Eddie Collins, Phil	122	1950	Dom DiMaggio, Bos	131
1915	Ty Cobb, Det	144	1951	Dom DiMaggio, Bos	113
1916	Ty Cobb, Det	113	1952	Larry Doby, Clev	104
1917	Donie Bush, Det	112	1953	Al Rosen, Clev	115
1918	Ray Chapman, Clev	84	1954	Mickey Mantle, NY	129
1919	Babe Ruth, Bos	103	1955	Al Smith, Clev	123
1920	Babe Ruth, NY	158	1956	Mickey Mantle, NY	132
1921	Babe Ruth, NY	177	1957	Mickey Mantle, NY	121
1922	George Sisler, StL	134	1958	Mickey Mantle, NY	127
1923	Babe Ruth, NY	151	1959	Eddie Yost, Det	115
1924	Babe Ruth, NY	143	1960	Mickey Mantle, NY	119
1925	Johnny Mostil, Chi	135	1961	Mickey Mantle, NY	132
1926	Babe Ruth, NY	139		Roger Maris, NY	132
1927	Babe Ruth, NY	158	1962	Albie Pearson, LA	115
1928	Babe Ruth, NY	163	1963	Bob Allison, Minn	99
1929	Charlie Gehringer, Det	131	1964	Tony Oliva, Minn	109
1930	Al Simmons, Phil	152	1965	Zoilo Versalles, Minn	126
1931	Lou Gehrig, NY	163	1966	Frank Robinson, Balt	122
1932	Jimmie Foxx, Phil	151	1967	Carl Yastrzemski, Bos	112
1933	Lou Gehrig, NY	138	1968	Dick McAuliffe, Det	95
1934	Charlie Gehringer, Det	134	1969	Reggie Jackson, Oak	123
1935	Lou Gehrig, NY	125	1970	Carl Yastrzemski, Bos	125
1936	Lou Gehrig, NY	167	1971	Don Buford, Balt	99

Leaders in Runs Scored *(Cont.)*

Year	Player and Team	Runs	Year	Player and Team	Runs
1972	Bobby Murcer, NY	102	1988	Wade Boggs, Bos	128
1973	Reggie Jackson, Oak	99	1989	Rickey Henderson, NY-Oak	113
1974	Carl Yastrzemski, Bos	93		Wade Boggs, Bos	113
1975	Fred Lynn, Bos	103	1990	Rickey Henderson, Oak	119
1976	Roy White, NY	104	1991	Paul Molitor, Mil	133
1977	Rod Carew, Minn	128	1992	Tony Phillips, Det	114
1978	Ron LeFlore, Det	126	1993	Rafael Palmeiro, Tex	124
1979	Don Baylor, Cal	120	1994	Frank Thomas, Chi	106
1980	Willie Wilson, KC	133	1995	Albert Belle, Clev	121
1981	Rickey Henderson, Oak	89		Edgar Martinez, Sea	121
1982	Paul Molitor, Mil	136	1996	Alex Rodriguez, Sea	141
1983	Cal Ripken, Balt	121	1997	Ken Griffey Jr, Sea	125
1984	Dwight Evans, Bos	121	1998	Derek Jeter, NY	127
1985	Rickey Henderson, NY	146	1999	Roberto Alomar, Clev	138
1986	Rickey Henderson, NY	130	2000	Johnny Damon, KC	136
1987	Paul Molitor, Mil	114			

Leaders in Hits

Year	Player and Team	Hits	Year	Player and Team	Hits
1901	Nap Lajoie, Phil	229	1943	Dick Wakefield, Det	200
1902	Piano Legs Hickman, Bos-Clev	194	1944	Snuffy Stirnweiss, NY	205
1903	Patsy Dougherty, Bos	195	1945	Snuffy Stirnweiss, NY	195
1904	Nap Lajoie, Clev	211	1946	Johnny Pesky, Bos	208
1905	George Stone, StL	187	1947	Johnny Pesky, Bos	207
1906	Nap Lajoie, Clev	214	1948	Bob Dillinger, StL	207
1907	Ty Cobb, Det	212	1949	Dale Mitchell, Clev	203
1908	Ty Cobb, Det	188	1950	George Kell, Det	218
1909	Ty Cobb, Det	216	1951	George Kell, Det	191
1910	Nap Lajoie, Clev	227	1952	Nellie Fox, Chi	192
1911	Ty Cobb, Det	248	1953	Harvey Kuenn, Det	209
1912	Ty Cobb, Det	227	1954	Nellie Fox, Chi	201
1913	Joe Jackson, Clev	197		Harvey Kuenn, Det	201
1914	Tris Speaker, Bos	193	1955	Al Kaline, Det	200
1915	Ty Cobb, Det	208	1956	Harvey Kuenn, Det	196
1916	Tris Speaker, Clev	211	1957	Nellie Fox, Chi	196
1917	Ty Cobb, Det	225	1958	Nellie Fox, Chi	187
1918	George Burns, Phil	178	1959	Harvey Kuenn, Det	198
1919	Ty Cobb, Det	191	1960	Minnie Minoso, Chi	184
	Bobby Veach, Det	191	1961	Norm Cash, Det	193
1920	George Sisler, StL	257	1962	Bobby Richardson, NY	209
1921	Harry Heilmann, Det	237	1963	Carl Yastrzemski, Bos	183
1922	George Sisler, StL	246	1964	Tony Oliva, Minn	217
1923	Charlie Jamieson, Clev	222	1965	Tony Oliva, Minn	185
1924	Sam Rice, Wash	216	1966	Tony Oliva, Minn	191
1925	Al Simmons, Phil	253	1967	Carl Yastrzemski, Bos	189
1926	George Burns, Clev	216	1968	Bert Campaneris, Oak	177
	Sam Rice, Wash	216	1969	Tony Oliva, Minn	197
1927	Earle Combs, NY	231	1970	Tony Oliva, Minn	204
1928	Heinie Manush, StL	241	1971	Cesar Tovar, Minn	204
1929	Dale Alexander, Det	215	1972	Joe Rudi, Oak	181
	Charlie Gehringer, Det	215	1973	Rod Carew, Minn	203
1930	Johnny Hodapp, Clev	225	1974	Rod Carew, Minn	218
1931	Lou Gehrig, NY	211	1975	George Brett, KC	195
1932	Al Simmons, Phil	216	1976	George Brett, KC	215
1933	Heinie Manush, Wash	221	1977	Rod Carew, Minn	239
1934	Charlie Gehringer, Det	214	1978	Jim Rice, Bos	213
1935	Joe Vosmik, Clev	216	1979	George Brett, KC	212
1936	Earl Averill, Clev	232	1980	Willie Wilson, KC	230
1937	Beau Bell, StL	218	1981	Rickey Henderson, Oak	135
1938	Joe Vosmik, Bos	201	1982	Robin Yount, Mil	210
1939	Red Rolfe, NY	213	1983	Cal Ripken, Balt	211
1940	Rip Radcliff, StL	200	1984	Don Mattingly, NY	207
	Barney McCosky, Det	200	1985	Wade Boggs, Bos	240
	Doc Cramer, Bos	200	1986	Don Mattingly, NY	238
1941	Cecil Travis, Wash	218	1987	Kirby Puckett, Minn	207
1942	Johnny Pesky, Bos	205		Kevin Seitzer, KC	207

Leaders in Hits (Cont.)

Year	Player and Team	Hits	Year	Player and Team	Hits
1988	Kirby Puckett, Minn	234	1995	Lance Johnson, Chi	186
1989	Kirby Puckett, Minn	215	1996	Paul Molitor, Minn	225
1990	Rafael Palmeiro, Tex	191	1997	Nomar Garciaparra, Bos	209
1991	Paul Molitor, Mil	216	1998	Alex Rodriguez, Sea	213
1992	Kirby Puckett, Minn	210	1999	Derek Jeter, NY	219
1993	Paul Molitor, Tor	211	2000	Darin Erstad, Ana	240
1994	Kenny Lofton, Clev	160			

Home Run Leaders

Year	Player and Team	HR	Year	Player and Team	HR
1901	Nap Lajoie, Phil	13	1954	Larry Doby, Clev	32
1902	Socks Seybold, Phil	16	1955	Mickey Mantle, NY	37
1903	Buck Freeman, Bos	13	1956	Mickey Mantle, NY	52
1904	Harry Davis, Phil	10	1957	Roy Sievers, Wash	42
1905	Harry Davis, Phil	8	1958	Mickey Mantle, NY	42
1906	Harry Davis, Phil	12	1959	Rocky Colavito, Clev	42
1907	Harry Davis, Phil	8		Harmon Killebrew, Wash	42
1908	Sam Crawford, Det	7	1960	Mickey Mantle, NY	40
1909	Ty Cobb, Det	9	1961	Roger Maris, NY	61
1910	Jake Stahl, Bos	10	1962	Harmon Killebrew, Minn	48
1911	Frank Baker, Phil	9	1963	Harmon Killebrew, Minn	45
1912	Frank Baker, Phil	10	1964	Harmon Killebrew, Minn	49
	Tris Speaker, Bos	10	1965	Tony Conigliaro, Bos	32
1913	Frank Baker, Phil	13	1966	Frank Robinson, Balt	49
1914	Frank Baker, Phil	9	1967	Harmon Killebrew, Minn	44
1915	Braggo Roth, Chi-Clev	7		Carl Yastrzemski, Bos	44
1916	Wally Pipp, NY	12	1968	Frank Howard, Wash	44
1917	Wally Pipp, NY	9	1969	Harmon Killebrew, Minn	49
1918	Babe Ruth, Bos	11	1970	Frank Howard, Wash	44
	Tilly Walker, Phil	11	1971	Bill Melton, Chi	33
1919	Babe Ruth, Bos	29	1972	Dick Allen, Chi	37
1920	Babe Ruth, NY	54	1973	Reggie Jackson, Oak	32
1921	Babe Ruth, NY	59	1974	Dick Allen, Chi	32
1922	Ken Williams, StL	39	1975	Reggie Jackson, Oak	36
1923	Babe Ruth, NY	41		George Scott, Mil	36
1924	Babe Ruth, NY	46	1976	Graig Nettles, NY	32
1925	Bob Meusel, NY	33	1977	Jim Rice, Bos	39
1926	Babe Ruth, NY	47	1978	Jim Rice, Bos	46
1927	Babe Ruth, NY	60	1979	Gorman Thomas, Mil	45
1928	Babe Ruth, NY	54	1980	Reggie Jackson, NY	41
1929	Babe Ruth, NY	46		Ben Oglivie, Mil	41
1930	Babe Ruth, NY	49	1981	Tony Armas, Oak	22
1931	Babe Ruth, NY	46	1981	Dwight Evans, Bos	22
	Lou Gehrig, NY	46		Bobby Grich, Cal	22
1932	Jimmie Foxx, Phil	58		Eddie Murray, Balt	22
1933	Jimmie Foxx, Phil	48	1982	Reggie Jackson, Cal	39
1934	Lou Gehrig, NY	49		Gorman Thomas, Mil	39
1935	Jimmie Foxx, Phil	36	1983	Jim Rice, Bos	39
	Hank Greenberg, Det	36	1984	Tony Armas, Bos	43
1936	Lou Gehrig, NY	49	1985	Darrell Evans, Det	40
1937	Joe DiMaggio, NY	46	1986	Jesse Barfield, Tor	40
1938	Hank Greenberg, Det	58	1987	Mark McGwire, Oak	49
1939	Jimmie Foxx, Bos	35	1988	Jose Canseco, Oak	42
1940	Hank Greenberg, Det	41	1989	Fred McGriff, Tor	36
1941	Ted Williams, Bos	37	1990	Cecil Fielder, Det	51
1942	Ted Williams, Bos	36	1991	Jose Canseco, Oak	44
1943	Rudy York, Det	34		Cecil Fielder, Det	44
1944	Nick Etten, NY	22	1992	Juan Gonzalez, Tex	43
1945	Vern Stephens, StL	24	1993	Juan Gonzalez, Tex	46
1946	Hank Greenberg, Det	44	1994	Ken Griffey Jr., Sea	40
1947	Ted Williams, Bos	32	1995	Albert Belle, Clev	50
1948	Joe DiMaggio, NY	39	1996	Mark McGwire, Oak	52
1949	Ted Williams, Bos	43	1997	Ken Griffey Jr, Sea	56
1950	Al Rosen, Clev	37	1998	Ken Griffey Jr, Sea	56
1951	Gus Zernial, Chi-Phil	33	1999	Ken Griffey Jr, Sea	48
1952	Larry Doby, Clev	32	2000	Troy Glaus, Ana	47
1953	Al Rosen, Clev	43			

Runs Batted In Leaders

Year	Player and Team	RBI	Year	Player and Team	RBI
1907	Ty Cobb, Det	116	1953	Al Rosen, Clev	145
1908	Ty Cobb, Det	108	1954	Larry Doby, Clev	126
1909	Ty Cobb, Det	107	1955	Ray Boone, Det	116
1910	Sam Crawford, Det	120		Jackie Jensen, Bos	116
1911	Ty Cobb, Det	144	1956	Mickey Mantle, NY	130
1912	Frank Baker, Phil	133	1957	Roy Sievers, Wash	114
1913	Frank Baker, Phil	126	1958	Jackie Jensen, Bos	122
1914	Sam Crawford, Det	104	1959	Jackie Jensen, Bos	112
1915	Sam Crawford, Det	112	1960	Roger Maris, NY	112
	Bobby Veach, Det	112	1961	Roger Maris, NY	142
1916	Del Pratt, StL	103	1962	Harmon Killebrew, Minn	126
1917	Bobby Veach, Det	103	1963	Dick Stuart, Bos	118
1918	Bobby Veach, Det	78	1964	Brooks Robinson, Balt	118
1919	Babe Ruth, Bos	114	1965	Rocky Colavito, Clev	108
1920	Babe Ruth, NY	137	1966	Frank Robinson, Balt	122
1921	Babe Ruth, NY	171	1967	Carl Yastrzemski, Bos	121
1922	Ken Williams, StL	155	1968	Ken Harrelson, Bos	109
1923	Babe Ruth, NY	131	1969	Harmon Killebrew, Minn	140
1924	Goose Goslin, Wash	129	1970	Frank Howard, Wash	126
1925	Bob Meusel, NY	138	1971	Harmon Killebrew, Minn	119
1926	Babe Ruth, NY	145	1972	Dick Allen, Chi	113
1927	Lou Gehrig, NY	175	1973	Reggie Jackson, Oak	117
1928	Babe Ruth, NY	142	1974	Jeff Burroughs, Tex	118
	Lou Gehrig, NY	142	1975	George Scott, Mil	109
1929	Al Simmons, Phil	157	1976	Lee May, Balt	109
1930	Lou Gehrig, NY	174	1977	Larry Hisle, Minn	119
1931	Lou Gehrig, NY	184	1978	Jim Rice, Bos	139
1932	Jimmie Foxx, Phil	169	1979	Don Baylor, Cal	139
1933	Jimmie Foxx, Phil	163	1980	Cecil Cooper, Mil	122
1934	Lou Gehrig, NY	165	1981	Eddie Murray, Balt	78
1935	Hank Greenberg, Det	170	1982	Hal McRae, KC	133
1936	Hal Trosky, Clev	162	1983	Cecil Cooper, Mil	126
1937	Hank Greenberg, Det	183		Jim Rice, Bos	126
1938	Jimmie Foxx, Bos	175	1984	Tony Armas, Bos	123
1939	Ted Williams, Bos	145	1985	Don Mattingly, NY	145
1940	Hank Greenberg, Det	150	1986	Joe Carter, Clev	121
1941	Joe DiMaggio, NY	125	1987	George Bell, Tor	134
1942	Ted Williams, Bos	137	1988	Jose Canseco, Oak	124
1943	Rudy York, Det	118	1989	Ruben Sierra, Tex	119
1944	Vern Stephens, StL	109	1990	Cecil Fielder, Det	132
1945	Nick Etten, NY	111	1991	Cecil Fielder, Det	133
1946	Hank Greenberg, Det	127	1992	Cecil Fielder, Det	124
1947	Ted Williams, Bos	114	1993	Albert Belle, Clev	129
1948	Joe DiMaggio, NY	155	1994	Kirby Puckett, Minn	112
1949	Ted Williams, Bos	159	1995	Albert Belle, Clev	126
	Vern Stephens, Bos	159		Mo Vaughn, Bos	126
1950	Walt Dropo, Bos	144	1996	Albert Belle, Clev	148
	Vern Stephens, Bos	144	1997	Ken Griffey Jr, Sea	147
1951	Gus Zernial, Chi-Phil	129	1998	Juan Gonzales, Tex	157
1952	Al Rosen, Clev	105	1999	Manny Ramirez, Clev	165
			2000	Edgar Martinez, Sea	145

Note: Runs Batted In not compiled before 1907; officially adopted in 1920.

Leading Base Stealers

Year	Player and Team	SB	Year	Player and Team	SB
1901	Frank Isbell, Chi	48	1911	Ty Cobb, Det	83
1902	Topsy Hartsel, Phil	54	1912	Clyde Milan, Wash	88
1903	Harry Bay, Clev	46	1913	Clyde Milan, Wash	75
1904	Elmer Flick, Clev	42	1914	Fritz Maisel, NY	74
	Harry Bay, Clev	42	1915	Ty Cobb, Det	96
1905	Danny Hoffman, Phil	46	1916	Ty Cobb, Det	68
1906	Elmer Flick, Clev	39	1917	Ty Cobb, Det	55
	John Anderson, Wash	39	1918	George Sisler, StL	45
1907	Ty Cobb, Det	49	1919	Eddie Collins, Chi	33
1908	Patsy Dougherty, Chi	47	1920	Sam Rice, Wash	63
1909	Ty Cobb, Det	76	1921	George Sisler, StL	35
1910	Eddie Collins, Phil	81	1922	George Sisler, StL	51

Leading Base Stealers *(Cont.)*

Year	Player and Team	SB	Year	Player and Team	SB
1923	Eddie Collins, Chi	49	1962	Luis Aparicio, Chi	31
1924	Eddie Collins, Chi	42	1963	Luis Aparicio, Balt	40
1925	John Mostil, Chi	43	1964	Luis Aparicio, Balt	57
1926	John Mostil, Chi	35	1965	Bert Campaneris, KC	51
1927	George Sisler, StL	27	1966	Bert Campaneris, KC	52
1928	Buddy Myer, Bos	30	1967	Bert Campaneris, KC	55
1929	Charlie Gehringer, Det	27	1968	Bert Campaneris, Oak	62
1930	Marty McManus, Det	23	1969	Tommy Harper, Sea	73
1931	Ben Chapman, NY	61	1970	Bert Campaneris, Oak	42
1932	Ben Chapman, NY	38	1971	Amos Otis, KC	52
1933	Ben Chapman, NY	27	1972	Bert Campaneris, Oak	52
1934	Bill Werber, Bos	40	1973	Tommy Harper, Bos	54
1935	Bill Werber, Bos	29	1974	Bill North, Oak	54
1936	Lyn Lary, StL	37	1975	Mickey Rivers, Cal	70
1937	Bill Werber, Phil	35	1976	Bill North, Oak	75
	Ben Chapman, Wash-Bos	35	1977	Freddie Patek, KC	53
1938	Frank Crosetti, NY	27	1978	Ron LeFlore, Det	68
1939	George Case, Wash	51	1979	Willie Wilson, KC	83
1940	George Case, Wash	35	1980	Rickey Henderson, Oak	100
1941	George Case, Wash	33	1981	Rickey Henderson, Oak	56
1942	George Case, Wash	44	1982	Rickey Henderson, Oak	130
1943	George Case, Wash	61	1983	Rickey Henderson, Oak	108
1944	Snuffy Stirnweiss, NY	55	1984	Rickey Henderson, Oak	66
1945	Snuffy Stirnweiss, NY	33	1985	Rickey Henderson, NY	80
1946	George Case, Clev	28	1986	Rickey Henderson, NY	87
1947	Bob Dillinger, StL	34	1987	Harold Reynolds, Sea	60
1948	Bob Dillinger, StL	28	1988	Rickey Henderson, NY	93
1949	Bob Dillinger, StL	20	1989	Rickey Henderson, NY-Oak	77
1950	Dom DiMaggio, Bos	15	1990	Rickey Henderson, Oak	65
1951	Minnie Minoso, Clev-Chi	31	1991	Rickey Henderson, Oak	58
1952	Minnie Minoso, Chi	22	1992	Kenny Lofton, Clev	66
1953	Minnie Minoso, Chi	25	1993	Kenny Lofton, Clev	70
1954	Jackie Jensen, Bos	22	1994	Kenny Lofton, Clev	60
1955	Jim Rivera, Chi	25	1995	Kenny Lofton, Clev	54
1956	Luis Aparicio, Chi	21	1996	Kenny Lofton, Clev	75
1957	Luis Aparicio, Chi	28	1997	Brian Hunter, Det	74
1958	Luis Aparicio, Chi	29	1998	Rickey Henderson, Oak	66
1959	Luis Aparicio, Chi	56	1999	Brian Hunter, Sea	44
1960	Luis Aparicio, Chi	51	2000	Johnny Damon, KC	46
1961	Luis Aparicio, Chi	53			

Leading Pitchers—Winning Percentage

Year	Pitcher and Team	W	L	Pct	Year	Pitcher and Team	W	L	Pct
1901	Clark Griffith, Chi	24	7	.774	1924	Walter Johnson, Wash	23	7	.767
1902	Bill Bernhard, Phil-Clev	18	5	.783	1925	Stan Coveleski, Wash	20	5	.800
1903	Earl Moore, Clev	22	7	.759	1926	George Uhle, Clev	27	11	.711
1904	Jack Chesbro, NY	41	12	.774	1927	Waite Hoyt, NY	22	7	.759
1905	Jess Tannehill, Bos	22	9	.710	1928	General Crowder, StL	21	5	.808
1906	Eddie Plank, Phil	19	6	.760	1929	Lefty Grove, Phil	20	6	.769
1907	Wild Bill Donovan, Det	25	4	.862	1930	Lefty Grove, Phil	28	5	.848
1908	Ed Walsh, Chi	40	15	.727	1931	Lefty Grove, Phil	31	4	.886
1909	George Mullin, Det	29	8	.784	1932	Johnny Allen, NY	17	4	.810
1910	Chief Bender, Phil	23	5	.821	1933	Lefty Grove, Phil	24	8	.750
1911	Chief Bender, Phil	17	5	.773	1934	Lefty Gomez, NY	26	5	.839
1912	Smoky Joe Wood, Bos	34	5	.872	1935	Eldon Auker, Det	18	7	.720
1913	Walter Johnson, Wash	36	7	.837	1936	Monte Pearson, NY	19	7	.731
1914	Chief Bender, Phil	17	3	.850	1937	Johnny Allen, Clev	15	1	.938
1915	Smoky Joe Wood, Bos	15	5	.750	1938	Red Ruffing, NY	21	7	.750
1916	Eddie Cicotte, Chi	15	7	.682	1939	Lefty Grove, Bos	15	4	.789
1917	Reb Russell, Chi	15	5	.750	1940	Schoolboy Rowe, Det	16	3	.842
1918	Sad Sam Jones, Bos	16	5	.762	1941	Lefty Gomez, NY	15	5	.750
1919	Eddie Cicotte, Chi	29	7	.806	1942	Ernie Bonham, NY	21	5	.808
1920	Jim Bagby, Clev	31	12	.721	1943	Spud Chandler, NY	20	4	.833
1921	Carl Mays, NY	27	9	.750	1944	Tex Hughson, Bos	18	5	.783
1922	Joe Bush, NY	26	7	.788	1945	Hal Newhouser, Det	25	9	.735
1923	Herb Pennock, NY	19	6	.760	1946	Boo Ferriss, Bos	25	6	.806

Leading Pitchers—Winning Percentage (Cont.)

Year	Pitcher and Team	W	L	Pct	Year	Pitcher and Team	W	L	Pct
1947	Allie Reynolds, NY	19	8	.704	1974	Mike Cuellar, Balt	22	10	.688
1948	Jack Kramer, Bos	18	5	.783	1975	Mike Torrez, Balt	20	9	.690
1949	Ellis Kinder, Bos	23	6	.793	1976	Bill Campbell, Minn	17	5	.773
1950	Vic Raschi, NY	21	8	.724	1977	Paul Splittorff, KC	16	6	.727
1951	Bob Feller, Clev	22	8	.733	1978	Ron Guidry, NY	25	3	.893
1952	Bobby Shantz, Phil	24	7	.774	1979	Mike Caldwell, Mil	16	6	.727
1953	Ed Lopat, NY	16	4	.800	1980	Steve Stone, Balt	25	7	.781
1954	Sandy Consuegra, Chi	16	3	.842	1981*	Pete Vuckovich, Mil	14	4	.778
1955	Tommy Byrne, NY	16	5	.762	1982	Pete Vuckovich, Mil	18	6	.750
1956	Whitey Ford, NY	19	6	.760		Jim Palmer, Balt	15	5	.750
1957	Dick Donovan, Chi	16	6	.727	1983	Richard Dotson, Chi	22	7	.759
	Tom Sturdivant, NY	16	6	.727	1984	Doyle Alexander, Tor	17	6	.739
1958	Bob Turley, NY	21	7	.750	1985	Ron Guidry, NY	22	6	.786
1959	Bob Shaw, Chi	18	6	.750	1986	Roger Clemens, Bos	24	4	.857
1960	Jim Perry, Clev	18	10	.643	1987	Roger Clemens, Bos	20	9	.690
1961	Whitey Ford, NY	25	4	.862	1988	Frank Viola, Minn	24	7	.774
1962	Ray Herbert, Chi	20	9	.690	1989	Bret Saberhagen, KC	23	6	.793
1963	Whitey Ford, NY	24	7	.774	1990	Bob Welch, Oak	27	6	.818
1964	Wally Bunker, Balt	19	5	.792	1991	Scott Erickson, Minn	20	8	.714
1965	Mudcat Grant, Minn	21	7	.750	1992	Mike Mussina, Balt	18	5	.783
1966	Sonny Siebert, Clev	16	8	.667	1993	Jimmy Key, NY	18	6	.750
1967	Joel Horlen, Chi	19	7	.731	1994	Jimmy Key, NY	17	4	.810
1968	Denny McLain, Det	31	6	.838	1995	Randy Johnson, Sea	18	2	.900
1969	Jim Palmer, Balt	16	4	.800	1996	Charles Nagy, Clev	17	5	.773
1970	Mike Cuellar, Balt	24	8	.750	1997	Randy Johnson, Sea	20	4	.833
1971	Dave McNally, Balt	21	5	.808	1998	David Wells, NY	18	4	.818
1972	Catfish Hunter, Oak	21	7	.750	1999	Pedro Martinez, Bos	23	4	.852
1973	Catfish Hunter, Oak	21	5	.808	2000	Tim Hudson, Oak	20	6	.769

*1981 percentages based on 10 or more victories. Note: Percentages based on 15 or more victories in all other years.

Leading Pitchers—Earned Run Average

Year	Player and Team	ERA	Year	Player and Team	ERA
1913	Walter Johnson, Wash	1.14	1946	Hal Newhouser, Det	1.94
1914	Dutch Leonard, Bos	1.01	1947	Spud Chandler, NY	2.46
1915	Smoky Joe Wood, Bos	1.49	1948	Gene Bearden, Clev	2.43
1916	Babe Ruth, Bos	1.75	1949	Mel Parnell, Bos	2.78
1917	Eddie Cicotte, Chi	1.53	1950	Early Wynn, Clev	3.20
1918	Walter Johnson, Wash	1.27	1951	Saul Rogovin, Det-Chi	2.78
1919	Walter Johnson, Wash	1.49	1952	Allie Reynolds, NY	2.07
1920	Bob Shawkey, NY	2.46	1953	Ed Lopat, NY	2.43
1921	Red Faber, Chi	2.47	1954	Mike Garcia, Clev	2.64
1922	Red Faber, Chi	2.80	1955	Billy Pierce, Chi	1.97
1923	Stan Coveleski, Clev	2.76	1956	Whitey Ford, NY	2.47
1924	Walter Johnson, Wash	2.72	1957	Bobby Shantz, NY	2.45
1925	Stan Coveleski, Wash	2.84	1958	Whitey Ford, NY	2.01
1926	Lefty Grove, Phil	2.51	1959	Hoyt Wilhelm, Balt	2.19
1927	Wilcy Moore, NY#	2.28	1960	Frank Baumann, Chi	2.68
1928	Garland Braxton, Wash	2.52	1961	Dick Donovan, Wash	2.40
1929	Lefty Grove, Phil	2.81	1962	Hank Aguirre, Det	2.21
1930	Lefty Grove, Phil	2.54	1963	Gary Peters, Chi	2.33
1931	Lefty Grove, Phil	2.06	1964	Dean Chance, LA	1.65
1932	Lefty Grove, Phil	2.84	1965	Sam McDowell, Clev	2.18
1933	Monte Pearson, Clev	2.33	1966	Gary Peters, Chi	1.98
1934	Lefty Gomez, NY	2.33	1967	Joe Horlen, Chi	2.06
1935	Lefty Grove, Bos	2.70	1968	Luis Tiant, Clev	1.60
1936	Lefty Grove, Bos	2.81	1969	Dick Bosman, Wash	2.19
1937	Lefty Gomez, NY	2.33	1970	Diego Segui, Oak	2.56
1938	Lefty Grove, Bos	3.07	1971	Vida Blue, Oak	1.82
1939	Lefty Grove, Bos	2.54	1972	Luis Tiant, Bos	1.91
1940	Bob Feller, Clev†	2.62	1973	Jim Palmer, Balt	2.40
1941	Thornton Lee, Chi	2.37	1974	Catfish Hunter, Oak	2.49
1942	Ted Lyons, Chi	2.10	1975	Jim Palmer, Balt	2.09
1943	Spud Chandler, NY	1.64	1976	Mark Fidrych, Det	2.34
1944	Dizzy Trout, Det	2.12	1977	Frank Tanana, Cal	2.54
1945	Hal Newhouser, Det	1.81	1978	Ron Guidry, NY	1.74

Leading Pitchers—Earned Run Average (Cont.)

Year	Player and Team	ERA	Year	Player and Team	ERA
1979	Ron Guidry, NY	2.78	1990	Roger Clemens, Bos	1.93
1980	Rudy May, NY	2.47	1991	Roger Clemens, Bos	2.62
1981	Steve McCatty, Oak	2.32	1992	Roger Clemens, Bos	2.41
1982	Rick Sutcliffe, Clev	2.96	1993	Kevin Appier, KC	2.56
1983	Rick Honeycutt, Tex	2.42	1994	Steve Ontiveros, Oak	2.65
1984	Mike Boddicker, Balt	2.79	1995	Randy Johnson, Sea	2.48
1985	Dave Stieb, Tor	2.48	1996	Juan Guzman, Tor	2.93
1986	Roger Clemens, Bos	2.48	1997	Roger Clemens, Tor	2.05
1987	Jimmy Key, Tor	2.76	1998	Roger Clemens, Tor	2.64
1988	Allan Anderson, Minn	2.45	1999	Pedro Martinez, Bos	2.07
1989	Bret Saberhagen, KC	2.16	2000	Pedro Martinez, Bos	1.74

Note: Based on 10 complete games through 1950, then, 154 innings until the American League expanded in 1961, when it became 162 innings. In strike-shortened 1981, one inning per game required. Earned runs not tabulated in American League prior to 1913.

#Wilcy Moore pitched only six complete games—he started 12—in 1927 but was recognized as leader because of 213 innings pitched. †Ernie Bonham, New York, had 1.91 ERA and 10 complete games in 1940 but appeared in only 12 games and 99 innings, and Bob Feller was recognized as leader.

Leading Pitchers—Strikeouts

Year	Player and Team	SO	Year	Player and Team	SO
1901	Cy Young, Bos	159	1947	Bob Feller, Clev	196
1902	Rube Waddell, Phil	210	1948	Bob Feller, Clev	164
1903	Rube Waddell, Phil	301	1949	Virgil Trucks, Det	153
1904	Rube Waddell, Phil	349	1950	Bob Lemon, Clev	170
1905	Rube Waddell, Phil	286	1951	Vic Raschi, NY	164
1906	Rube Waddell, Phil	203	1952	Allie Reynolds, NY	160
1907	Rube Waddell, Phil	226	1953	Billy Pierce, Chi	186
1908	Ed Walsh, Chi	269	1954	Bob Turley, Balt	185
1909	Frank Smith, Chi	177	1955	Herb Score, Clev	245
1910	Walter Johnson, Wash	313	1956	Herb Score, Clev	263
1911	Ed Walsh, Chi	255	1957	Early Wynn, Clev	184
1912	Walter Johnson, Wash	303	1958	Early Wynn, Chi	179
1913	Walter Johnson, Wash	243	1959	Jim Bunning, Det	201
1914	Walter Johnson, Wash	225	1960	Jim Bunning, Det	201
1915	Walter Johnson, Wash	203	1961	Camilo Pascual, Minn	221
1916	Walter Johnson, Wash	228	1962	Camilo Pascual, Minn	206
1917	Walter Johnson, Wash	188	1963	Camilo Pascual, Minn	202
1918	Walter Johnson, Wash	162	1964	Al Downing, NY	217
1919	Walter Johnson, Wash	147	1965	Sam McDowell, Clev	325
1920	Stan Coveleski, Clev	133	1966	Sam McDowell, Clev	225
1921	Walter Johnson, Wash	143	1967	Jim Lonborg, Bos	246
1922	Urban Shocker, StL	149	1968	Sam McDowell, Clev	283
1923	Walter Johnson, Wash	130	1969	Sam McDowell, Clev	279
1924	Walter Johnson, Wash	158	1970	Sam McDowell, Clev	304
1925	Lefty Grove, Phil	116	1971	Mickey Lolich, Det	308
1926	Lefty Grove, Phil	194	1972	Nolan Ryan, Cal	329
1927	Lefty Grove, Phil	174	1973	Nolan Ryan, Cal	383
1928	Lefty Grove, Phil	183	1974	Nolan Ryan, Cal	367
1929	Lefty Grove, Phil	170	1975	Frank Tanana, Cal	269
1930	Lefty Grove, Phil	209	1976	Nolan Ryan, Cal	327
1931	Lefty Grove, Phil	175	1977	Nolan Ryan, Cal	341
1932	Red Ruffing, NY	190	1978	Nolan Ryan, Cal	260
1933	Lefty Gomez, NY	163	1979	Nolan Ryan, Cal	223
1934	Lefty Gomez, NY	158	1980	Len Barker, Clev	187
1935	Tommy Bridges, Det	163	1981	Len Barker, Clev	127
1936	Tommy Bridges, Det	175	1982	Floyd Bannister, Sea	209
1937	Lefty Gomez, NY	194	1983	Jack Morris, Det	232
1938	Bob Feller, Clev	240	1984	Mark Langston, Sea	204
1939	Bob Feller, Clev	246	1985	Bert Blyleven, Clev-Minn	206
1940	Bob Feller, Clev	261	1986	Mark Langston, Sea	245
1941	Bob Feller, Clev	260	1987	Mark Langston, Sea	262
1942	Bobo Newsom, Wash		1988	Roger Clemens, Bos	291
	Tex Hughson, Bos	113	1989	Nolan Ryan, Tex	301
1943	Allie Reynolds, Clev	151	1990	Nolan Ryan, Tex	232
1944	Hal Newhouser, Det	187	1991	Roger Clemens, Bos	241
1945	Hal Newhouser, Det	212	1992	Randy Johnson, Sea	241
1946	Bob Feller, Clev	348	1993	Randy Johnson, Sea	308

Leading Pitchers—Strikeouts (Cont.)

Year	Player and Team	SO	Year	Player and Team	SO
1994	Randy Johnson, Sea	204	1998	Roger Clemens, Tor	271
1995	Randy Johnson, Sea	294	1999	Pedro Martinez, Bos	313
1996	Roger Clemens, Bos	257	2000	Pedro Martinez, Bos	284
1997	Roger Clemens, Tor	292			

Leading Pitchers—Saves

Year	Player and Team	SV	Year	Player and Team	SV
1947	Joe Page, NY	17	1974	Terry Forster, Chi	24
1948	Russ Christopher, Clev	17	1975	Goose Gossage, Chi	26
1949	Joe Page, NY	29	1976	Sparky Lyle, NY	23
1950	Mickey Harris, Wash	15	1977	Bill Campbell, Bos	31
1951	Ellis Kinder, Bos	14	1978	Goose Gossage, NY	27
1952	Harry Dorish, Chi	11	1979	Mike Marshall, Minn	32
1953	Ellis Kinder, Bos	27	1980	Dan Quisenberry, KC	33
1954	Johnny Sain, NY	22	1981	Rollie Fingers, Mil	28
1955	Ray Narleski, Clev	19	1982	Dan Quisenberry, KC	35
1956	George Zuverink, Bal	16	1983	Dan Quisenberry, KC	35
1957	Bob Grim, NY	19	1984	Dan Quisenberry, KC	44
1958	Ryne Duren, NY	20	1985	Dan Quisenberry, KC	37
1959	Turk Lown, Chi	15	1986	Dave Righetti, NY	46
1960	Mike Fornieles, Bos	14	1987	Tom Henke, Tor	34
	Johnny Klippstein, Clev	14	1988	Dennis Eckersley, Oak	45
1961	Luis Arroyo, NY	29	1989	Jeff Russell, Tex	38
1962	Dick Radatz, Bos	24	1990	Bobby Thigpen, Chi	57
1963	Stu Miller, Bal	27	1991	Bryan Harvey, Cal	46
1964	Dick Radatz, Bos	29	1992	Dennis Eckersley, Oak	51
1965	Ron Kline, Wash	29	1993	Jeff Montgomery, KC	45
1966	Jack Aker, KC	32		Duane Ward, Tor	45
1967	Minnie Rojas, Cal	27	1994	Lee Smith, Bal	33
1968	Al Worthington, Minn	18	1995	Jose Mesa, Clev	46
1969	Ron Perranoski, Minn	31	1996	John Wetteland, NY	43
1970	Ron Perranoski, Minn	34	1997	Randy Myers, Balt	45
1971	Ken Sanders, Mil	31	1998	Tom Gordon, Bos	46
1972	Sparky Lyle, NY	35	1999	Mariano Rivera, NY	45
1973	John Hiller, Det	38	2000	Todd Jones, Det	42

The Commissioners of Baseball

Kenesaw Mountain Landis — Elected November 12, 1920. Served until his death on November 25, 1944.

Happy Chandler — Elected April 24, 1945. Served until July 15, 1951.

Ford Frick — Elected September 20, 1951. Served until November 16, 1965.

William Eckert — Elected November 17, 1965. Served until December 20, 1968.

Bowie Kuhn — Elected February 8, 1969. Served until September 30, 1984.

Peter Ueberroth — Elected March 3, 1984. Took office October 1, 1984. Served through March 31, 1989.

A. Bartlett Giamatti — Elected September 8, 1988. Took office April 1, 1989. Served until his death on September 1, 1989.

Francis Vincent Jr — Appointed Acting Commissioner September 2, 1989. Elected Commissioner September 13, 1989. Served through September 7, 1992.

Allan H. (Bud) Selig — Elected chairman of the executive council and given the powers of interim commissioner on September 9, 1992. Unanimously elected Commissioner July 9, 1998.

Pro Football

Kurt Warner of the
Super Bowl
champion Rams

Topsy-Turvy

Up was down, down up, in a wide-open season that played like a fairy tale for the Rams and quarterback Kurt Warner

BY DAVID FLEMING

THROUGHOUT THE week leading up to Super Bowl XXXIV the members of the St. Louis Rams' defense talked about how one big tackle, one huge stick, one perfectly timed crunch, especially if it affected the outcome of the big game significantly, could immortalize an otherwise anonymous player. Who better for this role than Rams linebacker Mike Jones, whose very name, in its ordinariness, suggests anonymity?

An eight-year veteran who went undrafted after a career as a running back at the University of Missouri, Jones had been toiling in obscurity on the Rams' defense since 1997. A few years ago he walked into the Boys & Girls Club in Columbia, Miss., and volunteered to hold a free football camp. The club's director stared at Jones for a few minutes and then replied, "Who are you?"

That problem, of course, vanished after Jones became the hero of Super Bowl XXXIV with his game-saving tackle of Tennessee wideout Kevin Dyson at the Rams'

one-yard line. The Tackle, as it has become known (Jones has even tried to copyright the phrase), preserved the Rams' 23–16 win and capped one of the most exciting Super Bowls ever and one of the zaniest, most unsettling seasons in recent memory.

On the Monday following the Super Bowl, Jones flew to New York City and was met by a stretch limo. His first trip to the Big Apple turned out to be quite a doozy. In a two-day whirlwind Jones signed autographs, dined with stars and dignitaries, took in some of the sights with his wife, Leslie, retold the story of the Tackle a thousand times—"The truth is, I could have drilled him, but I'll take it," says Jones—and made appearances on, among others, *Live–With Regis and Kathie Lee*, *Inside the NFL*, CNBC, *Charlie Rose* and ESPN. "It was crazy," he said. "But so was this whole season. The Super Bowl and then the trip to New York was just like a storybook ending to a crazy season."

It is fitting that the man who so heroically ended the season should have the last word on it, too. For Jones's description is apt: The NFL in 1999 was a topsy-turvy, wild ride of a season that turned nobodies into heroes and ended like a dream come true, at least for Jones and his Rams teammates.

And so, for every amazed mention of Rams quarterback Kurt Warner—the hero of the St. Louis fairy tale—there was a somber reference to the retirement of Miami's Dan Marino, a 17-year veteran and holder of most NFL passing records. Somber because Marino's grand career ended without a Super Bowl ring and in most ignominious fashion—after a 62–7 loss to the Jaguars in the second round of the playoffs.

But the shellacking wasn't enough to dim Marino's legacy, which includes 61,361 yards passing (9,886 more than John Elway, who is second on the alltime passing yardage list) and 420 touchdowns (78 more than Fran Tarkenton, No. 2 on the TD list). "Going against him," said Marino's longtime nemesis, defensive end Bruce Smith of Buffalo, "was like playing against DiMaggio every day."

In opposition to the delightful rebirth of the Cleveland Browns, there were the tragic deaths of Chicago Bears Hall of Fame running back Walter Payton, who succumbed to liver disease and cancer in November, and Kansas City Chiefs Pro Bowl linebacker Derrick Thomas, who died in February due to complications from a car accident. Payton remains the alltime leader in career rushing yards, with 16,726, and he holds the single-game rushing record as well, having sprung for 275 yards against the Vikings in 1977.

When Payton died, on Nov. 1, Rams running back Marshall Faulk—who gained an NFL-record 2,429 yards from scrimmage this season—petitioned the league to wear Payton's No. 34 jersey for the remainder of the season. The league turned down his request, which was harsh but appropriate. For there will never be another Walter Payton, the man they called Sweetness. "Walter," said former Bears coach Mike Ditka, "was the greatest player who ever lived."

For every tale of triumph, like the Tennessee Titans' astounding victory—dubbed the Music City Miracle—in the first round

WALTER IOSS JR.

Sadly, Marino's Hall of Fame career ended with a drubbing in Jacksonville.

of the playoffs against Buffalo (more on that later), there were an equal number of tales of tragedy, like the news that two active NFL players, Carolina wideout Rae Carruth and Baltimore linebacker Ray Lewis, had been charged with murder in two separate incidents that highlighted the NFL's escalating problem with off-the-field violence. Murder charges against Lewis were dropped in June 2000; Carruth's case is pending.

For every shocking departure of a star like Detroit running back Barry Sanders, who retired suddenly prior to training camp, there was a head-turning breakout season, like that of Washington runner Stephen Davis, who led the league with 17 rushing touchdowns and an NFC-best 1,405 yards on the ground.

For every sad tale of an injured veteran,

PETER READ MILLER

drastic effect on teams' production, records, confidence and swagger."

As the Rams and the Niners exchanged recent NFL roles, so did the Colts and the Cowboys. Led by young star quarterback Peyton Manning, Indianapolis (13–3) ran away with the tough AFC East, while aging Dallas (8–8) struggled to make the playoffs. Seattle emerged as a playoff team under former Packers coach Mike Holmgren, while Green Bay *sub*merged, missing the playoffs for the first time since '92. The traditionally weak Buccaneers, led by Defensive Player of the Year Warren Sapp, won the NFC Central, while the two-time defending champion Broncos finished last in the AFC West.

Indeed, hampered by injuries and inconsistent play, all four of the previous year's conference finalists (Denver, the New York Jets, Atlanta and Minnesota) did 180s, going a combined 9–22 by midseason. Missing quarterback John Elway (retired) and running back Terrell Davis (injured knee), the 1998 league MVP, Denver opened the season 0–4. One veteran defensive player said, "We're finished," and he was right. The Broncos won only six games all season.

The upside to all of this madness, of course, was that it opened up the league and let in some badly needed fresh faces and new story lines. "I like the game the way it is today," said Tampa Bay director of player personnel Jerry Angelo. "Because I know when I go to the stadium, we're going to see two teams get after each other. What we're getting are games played with more intensity because players know anything can happen."

No one knows that better than Warner, the regular-season and Super Bowl MVP. Five years ago Warner was stocking shelves

like the Jets' Vinny Testaverde (ankle) or the 49ers' Steve Young (concussion), there was the uplifting story of Carolina passer Steve Beuerlein, a career backup who made the Pro Bowl in 1999.

There were rookie sensations (Colts running back Edgerrin James rushed for a league-high 1,553 yards) and rookie flops (1998 Heisman Trophy winner Ricky Williams gained only 885 yards for the Saints). Of the rookie quarterback class of '99, only Tampa's Shaun King, a second-round pick from Tulane, shined, leading the Bucs to the NFC title game. King's more highly touted peers, Tim Couch of Cleveland, Akili Smith of Cincinnati and Donovan McNabb of Philadelphia all struggled.

For every high-scoring win of the previously hapless Rams, there was a lopsided loss of the once proud 49ers, who suffered their first losing season in 16 years. "How much more can this league withstand?" said San Francisco coach Steve Mariucci. "The injuries and retirements have had a

Vermeil, in his words, went from jerk to genius in '99.

RICK BOWMER/AP

at the Hy-Vee supermarket in Cedar Falls, Iowa. After being cut by the Packers in '94, Warner signed on with the Iowa Barnstormers of the Arena Football League. In '96 the parents of his wife, Brenda, were killed in a tornado in Mountain View, Ark. Warner weathered all of the difficulty and battled back to the NFL, joining the Rams as a backup in '98. When starter Trent Green injured his knee in the '99 preseason, Warner stepped in and acted like an NFL veteran—scratch that; an NFL Hall of Famer: He completed 65.1% of his passes, throwing for 4,353 yards and 41 touchdowns.

"He's in a zone, and I've never been around anybody who's this hot," said Rams coach Dick Vermeil.

Thanks in large part to Warner, Vermeil completed a turnaround that was perfectly in sync with the rest of the NFL in '99. One year after a near mutiny by his team, Vermeil was NFL Coach of the Year. St. Louis went 4–12 (0–8 in the NFC West) in '98; in '99 the Rams were 13–3 (8–0 in the NFC West). Halfway through the season Vermeil turned to Warner on the practice field and said, "You know, in seven weeks, you've turned me from a jerk to a genius." Seizing the chance to go out on top, Vermeil, 62, retired after the Rams' Super Bowl win.

As the pressure and the victories mounted in the second half of the season, Warner remained remarkably calm. "How can you be in awe of something that you expect yourself to do?" he said. "Sure, I had my tough times, but you don't sit there and say, 'Wow, I was stocking groceries five years ago, and look at me now.' You don't think about it, and when you do achieve something, you know that luck has nothing to do with it."

Warner's passer rating for the season was 109.2, fifth-best alltime. In the Super Bowl

he completed 24 of 45 passes for two touchdowns and a Super Bowl–record 414 yards.

The first half of the game was as drab as the second half was exciting. Both teams played sloppily, and the Rams built a 16–0 lead. But the Titans, led by running back Eddie George and elusive quarterback Steve McNair, scratched back to tie the game.

With 2:12 to go and the ball on the St. Louis 27, Warner found receiver Isaac Bruce in one-on-one coverage on the right side of the field. Warner released his pass just before Tennessee's massive rookie defensive end, Jevon Kearse, piled into him. The ball was underthrown, but Bruce came back to it, made the catch at the Tennessee 43, sliced to the middle of the field and outraced the Titans' secondary for a 73-yard touchdown. The Rams led 23–16.

The Titans, though, would have one more shot. With 22 seconds on the clock, McNair scrambled behind the line of scrimmage, shedding would-be tacklers like a series of overcoats. Finally, he zipped a pass to Dyson at the Rams' 10. Tennessee took a timeout, and with six seconds remaining in the season, McNair hooked up with Dyson again on a slant route over the middle. Tight end Frank Wycheck had run into the end zone hoping to draw defenders, including Jones, but the ploy didn't work. "It seemed like slow motion," said Jones, describing how he cheated back to the middle to save the day, chopping out

Music City Miracle: Dyson (87) scampered 75 yards for the winning score against Buffalo.

Dyson's legs with his left hand as the receiver made the catch.

Dyson reached out desperately with the ball, but he was one yard short of the goal line. After an incredible run that included three wins over the preseason Super Bowl favorite Jacksonville Jaguars, the nomadic Titans, who left Houston in '96, were fresh out of miracles.

Truth be told, they'd used them all up. In the first round of the playoffs, the Titans trailed the Bills by a point with 16 seconds to play. They lined up to receive what would surely be a game-ending kickoff, and the coaching staff opted for a desperation play: Home Run Throwback. There was one slight problem. Injuries to the Titans' top two kick returners forced Tennessee to turn to Dyson, who had never run the play or, for that matter, returned an NFL kickoff.

Titans coach Jeff Fisher screamed the instructions into Dyson's ear as the receiver ran onto the field. And, somehow, the play went as scripted. Fullback Lorenzo Neal fielded a short kickoff and handed the ball to Wycheck, who shuffled to his right and then turned and fired the ball overhand across the field to Dyson, who was waiting behind a wall of blockers. He took the ball

and scampered 75 yards to win the game 22–16. At first glance Dyson appeared to be upfield from Wycheck, which would have made the tight end's toss an illegal forward pass. But official instant replays showed that the ball was thrown not forward but straight across the field, and the play, the Music City Miracle, stood.

The debate raged on after the game, however, and the NFL's revamped instant-replay system was not without its detractors. In keeping with the season's uncommon vicissitude, opinions about the system fluctuated wildly. Even the ordinarily calm and classy Tampa Bay coach, Tony Dungy, went so far as to say the system stunk. Nonetheless, owners voted to continue using replay in 2000.

Controversy aside, Dyson's runback kept the Titans alive, and it may one day take a place alongside the Catch, the Drive and the Immaculate Reception in NFL lore. In the postgame celebration back at Fisher's house, Hot Chocolate's *You Sexy Thing* blared from the stereo speakers. Fisher's wife, Juli, sang along with the lyrics, shouting, "I believe in miracles!"

"Yeah," said Fisher, "I believe in them too."

The Music City Miracle? The Rams as Super Bowl champs? Kurt Warner? Mike Jones? You had to believe in miracles after the 1999 NFL season.

FOR THE RECORD · 1999-2000

1999 NFL Final Standings

American Football Conference

EASTERN DIVISION

	W	L	T	Pct	Pts	OP
Indianapolis	13	3	0	.813	423	333
†Buffalo	11	5	0	.688	320	229
†Miami	9	7	0	.563	326	336
NY Jets	8	8	0	.500	308	309
New England	8	8	0	.500	299	284

CENTRAL DIVISION

	W	L	T	Pct	Pts	OP
Jacksonville	14	2	0	.875	396	217
†Tennessee	13	3	0	.813	392	324
Baltimore	8	8	0	.500	324	277
Pittsburgh	6	10	0	.375	317	320
Cincinnati	4	12	0	.250	283	460
Cleveland	2	14	0	.125	217	437

WESTERN DIVISION

	W	L	T	Pct	Pts	OP
Seattle	9	7	0	.563	338	298
Kansas City	9	7	0	.563	390	322
San Diego	8	8	0	.500	269	316
Oakland	8	8	0	.500	390	329
Denver	6	10	0	.375	314	318

†Wild-card team.

National Football Conference

EASTERN DIVISION

	W	L	T	Pct	Pts	OP
Washington	10	6	0	.625	443	377
†Dallas	8	8	0	.500	352	276
NY Giants	7	9	0	.438	299	358
Arizona	6	10	0	.375	245	382
Philadelphia	5	11	0	.313	272	357

CENTRAL DIVISION

	W	L	T	Pct	Pts	OP
Tampa Bay	11	5	0	.688	270	235
†Minnesota	10	6	0	.625	399	335
†Detroit	8	8	0	.500	322	323
Green Bay	8	8	0	.500	357	341
Chicago	6	10	0	.375	272	341

WESTERN DIVISION

	W	L	T	Pct	Pts	OP
St. Louis	13	3	0	.813	526	242
Carolina	8	8	0	.500	421	381
Atlanta	5	11	0	.313	285	380
San Francisco	4	12	0	.250	295	453
New Orleans	3	13	0	.188	260	434

1999-2000 NFL Playoffs

AFC FIRST ROUND	AFC DIVISIONAL PLAYOFF	AFC CHAMPIONSHIP	NFC CHAMPIONSHIP	NFC DIVISIONAL PLAYOFF	NFC FIRST ROUND

SUPER BOWL XXXIV
January 30, 2000

Buffalo 16
Tennessee 22

Tennessee 19

Tennessee 33

Indianapolis 16

ST. LOUIS 23
Tennessee 16

Miami 20
Seattle 17

Miami 7

Jacksonville 14

Jacksonville 62

Washington 13

Tampa Bay 6

Tampa Bay 14

St. Louis 11

St. Louis 49

Minnesota 37

Detroit 13
Washington 27

Dallas 10
Minnesota 27

AFC Wild-card Games

Buffalo	0	0	7	9—16
Tennessee	0	12	0	10—22

Miami	3	0	10	7—20
Seattle	7	3	7	0—17

SECOND QUARTER

Tennessee: Safety (Johnson forced out of end zone by Kearse), 11:19.
Tennessee: McNair 1 run (Del Greco kick), 7:55. Drive: 28 yards, 5 plays.
Tennessee: FG Del Greco 40, 0:00. Drive: 56 yards, 11 plays.

THIRD QUARTER

Buffalo: Smith 4 run (Christie kick), 12:28. Drive: 62 yards, 5 plays.

FOURTH QUARTER

Buffalo: Smith 1 run (Two-point attempt failed), 11:08. Drive: 65 yards, 9 plays.
Tennessee: FG Del Greco 36, 1:48. Drive: 27 yards, 10 plays.
Buffalo: FG Christie 41, 0:16. Drive: 38 yards, 6 plays.
Tennessee: Dyson 75 kickoff return (Del Greco kick), 0:03.
A: 66,782; T: 3:19.

FIRST QUARTER

Seattle: Dawkins 9 pass from Kitna (Peterson kick), 6:18. Drive: 47 yards, 8 plays.
Miami: FG Mare 32, 2:05. Drive: 37 yards, 7 plays.

SECOND QUARTER

Seattle: FG Peterson 50, 0:45. Drive: 49 yards, 8 plays.

THIRD QUARTER

Miami: Gadsden 1 pass from Marino (Mare kick), 8:55. Drive: 60 yards, 10 plays.
Seattle: Rogers 85 kickoff return (Peterson kick), 8:37.
Miami: FG Mare 50, 2:22. Drive: 32 yards, 6 plays.

FOURTH QUARTER

Miami: Johnson 2 run (Mare kick), 4:48. Drive: 85 yards, 11 plays.
A: 66,170; T: 2:55.

NFC Wild-card Games

Detroit	0	0	0	13—13
Washington	14	13	0	0—27

Dallas	10	0	0	0—10
Minnesota	3	14	3	7—27

FIRST QUARTER

Washington: Davis 1 run (Conway kick), 9:09. Drive: 69 yards, 9 plays.
Washington: Davis 4 run (Conway kick), 2:28. Drive: 87 yards, 8 plays.

SECOND QUARTER

Washington: FG Conway 33, 13:50. Drive: 24 yards, 4 plays.
Washington: FG Conway 23, 9:50. Drive: 45 yards, 6 plays.
Washington: Connell 30 pass from Johnson (Conway kick), 1:19. Drive: 82 yards, 8 plays.

FOURTH QUARTER

Detroit: Rice 94 blocked field goal return (Two-point conversion failed), 9:23.
Detroit: Rivers 5 pass from Frerotte (Hanson kick), 0:00. Drive 90 yards, 12 plays.
A: 79,411; T: 3:14.

FIRST QUARTER

Dallas: FG Murray 18, 11:09. Drive: 78 yards, 7 plays.
Minnesota: FG Anderson 47, 7:59. Drive: 1 yard, 4 plays.
Dallas: Smith 5 run (Murray kick), 5:00. Drive: 79 yards, 7 plays.

SECOND QUARTER

Minnesota: Smith 26 pass from George (Anderson kick), 5:00. Drive: 23 yards, 4 plays.
Minnesota: Moss 58 pass from George (Anderson kick), 0:28. Drive: 82 yards, 6 plays.

THIRD QUARTER

Minnesota: FG Anderson 38, 3:10. Drive: 60 yards, 10 plays.

FOURTH QUARTER

Minnesota: Carter 5 pass from George (Anderson kick), 12:40. Drive: 67 yards, 7 plays.
A: 64,056; T: 3:03.

AFC Divisional Games

Miami	0	7	0	0 —7
Jacksonville	24	17	14	7—62

FIRST QUARTER

Jacksonville: Smith 8 pass from Brunell (Hollis kick), 10:32. Drive: 73 yards, 9 plays.
Jacksonville: FG Hollis 45, 6:19. Drive: 14 yards, 9 plays.
Jacksonville: Taylor 90 run (Hollis kick), 3:46. Drive: 91 yards, 2 plays.
Jacksonville: Brackens 16 fum return (Hollis kick), 3:21.

SECOND QUARTER

Jacksonville: Taylor 39 pass from Brunell (Hollis kick), 14:48. Drive: 53 yards, 4 plays.
Jacksonville: Stewart 25 run (Hollis kick), 12:05. Drive: 21 yards, 3 plays.
Jacksonville: FG Hollis 28, 1:51. Drive: 20 yards, 5 plays.
Miami: Gadsden 20 pass from Marino (Mare kick), 0:03. Drive: 80 yards, 9 plays.

THIRD QUARTER

Jacksonville: Smith 70 pass from Fiedler (Hollis kick), 12:03. Drive: 78 yards, 3 plays.
Jacksonville: Whitted 38 pass from Fiedler (Hollis kick), 6:19. Drive: 69 yards, 5 plays.

FOURTH QUARTER

Jacksonville: Howard 5 run (Hollis kick), 10:37. Drive 5 yards, 1 play.
A: 75,173; T: 3:23.

Tennessee	0	6	7	6—19
Indianapolis	3	6	0	7—16

FIRST QUARTER

Indianapolis: FG Vanderjagt 40, 7:13. Drive: 42 yards, 9 plays.

SECOND QUARTER

Tennessee: FG Del Greco 49, 14:45. Drive: 46 yards, 7 plays.
Indianapolis: FG Vanderjagt 40, 5:38. Drive: 62 yards, 7 plays.
Tennessee: FG Del Greco 37, 3:15. Drive: 34 yards, 7 plays.
Indianapolis: FG Vanderjagt 34, 0:01. Drive: 66 yards, 12 plays.

THIRD QUARTER

Tennessee: George 68 run (Del Greco kick), 13:19. Drive: 80 yards, 3 plays.

FOURTH QUARTER

Tennessee: FG Del Greco 25, 12:57. Drive: 73 yards, 13 plays.
Tennessee: FG Del Greco 43, 4:19. Drive: 17 yards, 7 plays.
Indianapolis: Manning 15 run (Vanderjagt kick), 1:51. Drive 61 yards, 9 plays.
A: 57,097; T: 3:20.

NFC Divisional Games

Washington	0	3	10	0—13
Tampa Bay	0	0	7	7—14

SECOND QUARTER

Washington: FG Conway 28, 5:37. Drive: 33 yards, 8 plays.

THIRD QUARTER

Washington: Mitchell 100 kickoff return (Conway kick), 14:41.
Washington: FG Conway 48, 8:10. Drive: 6 yards, 4 plays.
Tampa Bay: Alstott 2 run (Gramatica kick), 2:03. Drive: 73 yards, 6 plays.

FOURTH QUARTER

Tampa Bay: Davis 1 pass from King (Gramatica kick), 7:29. Drive: 32 yards, 10 plays.
A: 65,835; T: 3:01.

Minnesota	3	14	0	20—37
St. Louis	14	0	21	14—49

FIRST QUARTER

Minn: FG Anderson 31, 9:23. Drive: 60 yards, 11 plays.
StL: Bruce 77 pass from Warner (Wilkins kick), 9:02. Drive: 77 yards, 1 play.
StL: Faulk 41 pass from Warner (Wilkins kick), 4:19. Drive: 82 yards, 4 plays.

SECOND QUARTER

Minn: Carter 22 pass from George (Anderson kick), 9:53. Drive: 96 yards, 8 plays.
Minn: Hoard 4 run (Anderson kick), 2:40. Drive: 53 yards, 7 plays.

THIRD QUARTER

StL: Horne 95 kickoff return (Wilkins kick), 14:42.
StL: Faulk 1 run (Wilkins kick), 8:28. Drive: 51 yards, 9 plays.
StL: Robinson 13 pass from Warner (Wilkins kick), 0:22. Drive: 61 yards, 8 plays.

FOURTH QUARTER

StL: Tucker 1 pass from Warner (Wilkins kick), 13:36. Drive: 23 yards, 4 plays.
StL: Williams 2 pass from Warner (Wilkins kick), 8:13. Drive: 62 yards, 8 plays.
Minn: Reed 4 pass from George (Hoard run for two-point conversion), 4:56. Drive: 80 yards, 6 plays.
Minn: Moss 44 pass from George (Two-point conversion failed), 3:48. Drive: 63 yards, 5 plays.
Minn: Moss 2 pass from George (Two-point conversion failed), 0:31. Drive: 85 yards, 16 plays.
A: 66,194; T: 3:34.

AFC Championship

Tennessee	7	3	16	7—33
Jacksonville	7	7	0	0—14

FIRST QUARTER

Jacksonville: Brady 7 pass from Brunell (Hollis kick), 11:20. Drive: 62 yards, 5 plays.
Tennessee: Thigpen 9 pass from McNair (Del Greco kick), 5:30. Drive: 51 yards, 9 plays.

SECOND QUARTER

Jacksonville: Stewart 33 run, 4:36 (Hollis kick). Drive: 65 yards, 4 plays.
Tennessee: FG Greco 34, 0:20. Drive: 3 yards, 4 plays.

THIRD QUARTER

Tennessee: McNair 1 run, 9:24. Drive: 76 yards, 6 plays.
Tennessee: Safety (Brunell sacked by Evans and Fisk), 5:13.
Tennessee: Mason 80 kickoff return (Del Greco kick), 4:56 .

FOURTH QUARTER

Tennessee: McNair 1 run (Del Greco kick), 6:59 Drive: 61 yards, 4 plays.
A: 75,206; T: 2:59.

NFC Championship

Tampa Bay	3	0	3	0— 6
St. Louis	3	2	0	6—11

FIRST QUARTER

Tampa Bay: FG Gramatica 25, 12:22. Drive: 13 yards, 6 plays.
St. Louis: FG Wilkins 24, 4:17. Drive: 74 yards, 16 plays.

SECOND QUARTER

St. Louis: Safety (King forced out of end zone, by team).

THIRD QUARTER

Tampa Bay: FG Gramatica 23, 10:28. Drive: 66 yards, 9 plays.

FOURTH QUARTER

St. Louis: Proehl 30 pass from Warner, (two-point conversion failed), 4:44. Drive: 47 yards, 6 plays.
A: 66,496; T: 3:07.

Super Bowl Box Score

St. Louis	3	6	7	7—23
Tennessee	0	0	6	10—16

FIRST QUARTER

St. Louis: FG Wilkins 27, 3:00. Drive: 54 yards, 6 plays. Key plays: Warner 32 pass to Holt to Tennessee 42; Warner 17 pass to Faulk to Tennessee 14. **St. Louis 3–0.**

SECOND QUARTER

St. Louis: FG Wilkins 29, 4:16. Drive: 73 yards, 11 plays. Key plays: Warner 11 pass to Bruce to St. Louis 27; Warner 15 pass to Bruce to Tennessee 45; Warner 13 pass to Holt to Tennessee 32; Warner 15 pass to Holt to Tennessee 16. **St. Louis 6–0.**
St. Louis: FG Wilkins 28, 0:15. Drive: 67 yards, 13 plays. Key plays: Warner 16 pass to Holt on 3rd-and-13 to St. Louis 36; Warner 18 pass to Holt to St. Louis 47; Warner 15 pass to Bruce to Tennessee 38; Warner 17 pass to Hakim to Tennessee 21. **St. Louis 9–0.**

THIRD QUARTER

St. Louis: Holt 9 pass from Warner (Wilkins kick), 7:20. Drive: 68 yards, 8 plays. Key plays: Warner 8 pass to Faulk on 3rd-and-7 to St. Louis 43; Warner 32 pass to Bruce to Tennessee 27; Warner 16 pass to Conwell to Tennessee 10. **St. Louis 16–0.**

THIRD QUARTER *(CONT.)*

Tennessee: George 1 run (two-point conversion failed), 0:14. Drive: 66 yards, 12 plays. Key plays: George 9 yard run to Tenn 48; McNair 5 pass to Wycheck on 3rd-and-3 to St. Louis 40; McNair 7 pass to Wycheck to St. Louis 31; McNair 2 run on 3rd-and-1 to St. Louis 29; McNair 23 run to St. Louis 2. **St. Louis 16–6.**

FOURTH QUARTER

Tennessee: George 2 run (Del Greco kick), 7:21. Drive:79 yards, 13 plays. Key plays: McNair 9 pass to Dyson on 3rd-and-6 to Tennessee 34; McNair 2 run on 4th-and-1 to Tennessee 45; McNair 21 pass to Byrd to St. Louis 24; McNair 21 pass to Harris to St. Louis 3. **St. Louis 16–13.**
Tennessee: FG Del Greco 43, 2:12. Drive: 28 yards, 8 plays. Key plays: McNair 11 run to St. Louis 42; Harris 6 pass from McNair on 3rd-and-2 to St. Louis 28; Byrd recovery of Harris fumble at St. Louis 28. **St. Louis 16, Tennessee 16.**
St. Louis: Bruce 73 pass from Warner, 1:54. Drive:73 yards, 1 play. **St. Louis 23–16.**

Team Statistics

	St. Louis	Tennessee
FIRST DOWNS	23	27
Rushing	1	12
Passing	18	13
Penalty	4	2
THIRD DOWN EFF.	5–12	6–13
FOURTH DOWN EFF	0–1	1–1
TOTAL NET YARDS	436	367
Total plays	59	73
Avg gain	7.4	5.0
NET YARDS RUSHING	29	159
Rushes	13	36
Avg per rush	2.2	4.4
NET YARDS PASSING	407	208
Completed–Att.	24–45	22–36
Yards per pass	8.8	5.6
Sacked–yards lost	1–7	1–6
Had intercepted	0	0
PUNTS–Avg.	2–38.5	3–43.0
TOTAL RETURN YARDS	63	121
Punt returns	2–8	1–(-1)
Kickoff returns	4–55	5–122
Interceptions	0–0	0–0
PENALTIES–Yds.	8–60	7–45
FUMBLES–Lost	2–0	1–0
TIME OF POSSESSION	23:34	36:26

Passing

ST. LOUIS

	Comp	Att	Yds	Int	TD
Warner	24	45	414	0	2

TENNESSEE

	Comp	Att	Yds	Int	TD
McNair	22	36	214	0	0

Rushing

ST. LOUIS

	No.	Yds	Lg	TD
Faulk	10	17	4	0
Holcombe	1	11	11	0
Warner	1	1	1	0
Horan	1	0	0	0

TENNESSEE

	No.	Yds	Lg	TD
George	28	95	13	2
McNair	8	64	23	0

Receiving

ST. LOUIS

	No.	Yds	Lg	TD
Holt	7	109	32	1
Bruce	6	162	73	1
Faulk	5	90	52	0
Hakim	1	17	17	0
Conwell	1	16	16	0
Proehl	1	11	11	0

TENNESSEE

	No.	Yds	Lg	TD
Harris	7	64	21	0
Wycheck	5	35	13	0
Dyson	4	41	16	0
George	2	35	32	0
Byrd	2	21	21	0
Mason	2	18	9	0

Defense

ST. LOUIS

	Tck	Ast	Int	Sack
Jenkins	9	3	0	0
Fletcher	9	2	0	0
Jones	7	2	0	0
McCleon	5	1	0	0
Lyght	4	2	0	0
Collins	2	3	0	0
Carter	3	0	0	1
Farr	3	0	0	0
Wistrom	3	0	0	0
Zgonina	3	0	0	0
Bush	2	0	0	0
Williams	1	1	0	0
Agnew	1	0	0	0
Bly	1	0	0	0

TENNESSEE

	Tck	Ast	Int	Sack
Bishop	4	1	0	0
Dorsett	1	4	0	0
Kearse	4	0	0	0
Sidney	4	0	0	0
Robinson	3	1	0	0
Evans	3	0	0	0
Walker	3	0	0	0
Bowden	2	1	0	0
Fisk	2	0	0	1
Wortham	2	0	0	0
Mitchell	1	1	0	0
Jackson	1	0	0	0
Phenix	1	0	0	0
Rolle	1	0	0	0

1999 Associated Press All-Pro Team

OFFENSE

Marvin Harrison, Indianapolis	Wide Receiver
Cris Carter, Minnesota	Wide Receiver
Tony Gonzalez, Kansas City	Tight End
Tony Boselli, Jacksonville	Tackle
Orlando Pace, St. Louis	Tackle
Larry Allen, Dallas	Guard
Bruce Matthews, Tennessee	Guard
Kevin Mawae, New York Jets	Center
Kurt Warner, St. Louis	Quarterback
Marshall Faulk, St. Louis	Running Back
Edgerrin James, Indianapolis	Running Back
Mike Alstott, Tampa Bay	Fullback

DEFENSE

Jevon Kearse, Tennessee	Defensive End
Kevin Carter, St. Louis	Defensive End
Warren Sapp, Tampa Bay	Tackle
Trevor Pryce, Denver	Tackle
Derrick Brooks, Tampa Bay	Outside Linebacker
Kevin Hardy, Jacksonville	Outside Linebacker
Ray Lewis, Baltimore	Inside Linebacker
Zach Thomas, Miami	Inside Linebacker
Sam Madison, Miami	Cornerback
Charles Woodson, Oakland	Cornerback
John Lynch, Tampa Bay	Safety
Lawyer Milloy, New England	Safety

SPECIALISTS

Olindo Mare, Miami	Kicker
Tom Tupa, NY Jets	Punter
Glyn Milburn, Chicago	Kick Returner

1999 AFC Team-by-Team Results

BALTIMORE RAVENS (8–8)

10	at St. Louis	27
20	PITTSBURGH	23
17	CLEVELAND	10
19	at Atlanta (OT)	13
11	at Tennessee	14
	OPEN DATE	
8	KANSAS CITY	35
10	BUFFALO	13
41	at Cleveland	9
3	at Jacksonville	6
34	at Cincinnati	31
23	JACKSONVILLE	30
41	TENNESSEE	14
31	at Pittsburgh	24
31	NEW ORLEANS	8
22	CINCINNATI	0
3	at New England	20
324		277

BUFFALO BILLS (11–5)

14	at Indianapolis	31
17	NY JETS	3
26	PHILADELPHIA	0
23	at Miami	18
31	PITTSBURGH	24
14	OAKLAND	20
16	at Seattle	26
13	at Baltimore	10
34	at Washington	17
23	MIAMI	3
7	at NY Jets	17
17	NEW ENGLAND	7
	OPEN DATE	
17	NY GIANTS	19
31	at Arizona	21
13	at New England (OT)	10
31	INDIANAPOLIS	6
327		232

CINCINNATI BENGALS (4–12)

35	at Tennessee	36
7	SAN DIEGO	34
3	at Carolina	27
10	ST. LOUIS	38
18	at Cleveland	17
3	PITTSBURGH	17
10	at Indianapolis	31
10	JACKSONVILLE	41
20	at Seattle	37
14	TENNESSEE	24
31	BALTIMORE	34
27	at Pittsburgh	20
44	SAN FRANCISCO	30
44	CLEVELAND	28
	OPEN DATE	
0	at Baltimore	22
7	at Jacksonville	24
283		460

CLEVELAND BROWNS (2–14)

0	PITTSBURGH	43		16	at Pittsburgh	15
9	at Tennessee	26		17	CAROLINA	31
10	at Baltimore	17		21	TENNESSEE	33
7	NEW ENGLAND	19		10	at San Diego	23
17	CINCINNATI	18		28	at Cincinnati	44
7	at Jacksonville	24		14	JACKSONVILLE	24
3	at St. Louis	34		28	INDIANAPOLIS	29
21	at New Orleans	16			OPEN DATE	
9	BALTIMORE	41		217		437

DENVER BRONCOS (6–10)

21	MIAMI	38
10	at Kansas City	26
10	at Tampa Bay	13
13	NY JETS	21
16	at Oakland	13
31	GREEN BAY	10
23	at New England	24
20	MINNESOTA	23
33	at San Diego	17
17	at Seattle	20
27	OAKLAND (OT)	21
	OPEN DATE	
10	KANSAS CITY	16
24	at Jacksonville	27
36	SEATTLE (OT)	30
17	at Detroit	7
6	SAN DIEGO	12
314		**318**

INDIANAPOLIS COLTS (13–3)

31	BUFFALO	14
28	at New England	31
27	at San Diego	19
	OPEN DATE	
31	MIAMI	34
16	at NY Jets	13
31	CINCINNATI	10
34	DALLAS	24
25	KANSAS CITY	17
27	at NY Giants	19
44	at Philadelphia	17
13	NY JETS	6
37	at Miami	34
20	NEW ENGLAND	15
24	WASHINGTON	21
29	at Cleveland	28
6	at Buffalo	31
495		**308**

JACKSONVILLE JAGUARS (14–2)

41	SAN FRANCISCO	3
22	at Carolina	20
19	TENNESSEE	20
17	at Pittsburgh	3
	OPEN DATE	
16	at NY Jets	6
24	CLEVELAND	7
41	at Cincinnati	10
30	at Atlanta	7
6	BALTIMORE	3
41	NEW ORLEANS	23
30	at Baltimore	23
20	PITTSBURGH	6
27	DENVER	24
24	at Cleveland	14
14	at Tennessee	41
24	CINCINNATI	7
424		**206**

KANSAS CITY CHIEFS (9–7)

17	at Chicago	20
26	DENVER	10
31	DETROIT	21
14	at San Diego	21
16	NEW ENGLAND	14
	OPEN DATE	
35	at Baltimore	8
34	SAN DIEGO	0
17	at Indianapolis	25
10	at Tampa Bay	17
19	SEATTLE	31
37	at Oakland	34
16	at Denver	10
31	MINNESOTA	28
35	PITTSBURGH	19
14	at Seattle	23
38	OAKLAND (OT)	41
390		**322**

MIAMI DOLPHINS (9–7)

38	at Denver	21
19	ARIZONA	16
	OPEN DATE	
18	BUFFALO	23
34	at Indianapolis	31
31	at New England	30
16	PHILADELPHIA	13
16	at Oakland	9
17	TENNESSEE	0
3	at Buffalo	23
27	NEW ENGLAND	17
0	at Dallas	20
34	INDIANAPOLIS	37
20	at NY Jets	28
12	SAN DIEGO	9
31	NY JETS	38
10	at Washington	21
326		**336**

NEW ENGLAND PATRIOTS (8–8)

30	at NY Jets	28
31	INDIANAPOLIS	28
16	NY GIANTS	14
19	at Cleveland	7
14	at Kansas City	16
30	MIAMI	31
24	DENVER	23
27	at Arizona	3
	OPEN DATE	
17	NY JETS	24
17	at Miami	27
7	at Buffalo	17
13	DALLAS	6
15	at Indianapolis	20
9	at Philadelphia	24
10	BUFFALO (OT)	13
20	BALTIMORE	3
299		**284**

NEW YORK JETS (8–8)

28	NEW ENGLAND	30
3	at Buffalo	17
20	WASHINGTON	27
21	at Denver	13
6	JACKSONVILLE	16
13	INDIANAPOLIS	16
23	at Oakland	24
	OPEN DATE	
12	ARIZONA	7
24	at New England	17
17	BUFFALO	7
6	at Indianapolis	13
28	at NY Giants	41
28	MIAMI	20
22	at Dallas	21
38	at Miami	31
19	SEATTLE	9
308		**309**

OAKLAND RAIDERS (8–8)

24	at Green Bay	28
22	at Minnesota	17
24	CHICAGO	17
21	at Seattle	22
13	DENVER	16
20	at Buffalo	14
24	NY JETS	23
9	MIAMI	16
	OPEN DATE	
28	SAN DIEGO	9
21	at Denver (OT)	27
34	KANSAS CITY	37
30	SEATTLE	21
14	at Tennessee	21
45	TAMPA BAY	0
20	at San Diego	23
41	at Kansas City (OT)	38
390		**329**

PITTSBURGH STEELERS (6–10)

43	at Cleveland	0
23	at Baltimore	20
10	SEATTLE	29
3	JACKSONVILLE	17
21	at Buffalo	24
17	at Cincinnati	3
13	ATLANTA	9
	OPEN DATE	
27	at San Francisco	6
15	CLEVELAND	16
10	at Tennessee	16
20	CINCINNATI	27
6	at Jacksonville	20
24	BALTIMORE	31
19	at Kansas City	35
30	CAROLINA	20
36	TENNESSEE	47
317		**320**

SAN DIEGO CHARGERS (8-8)

	OPEN DATE	
34	at Cincinnati	7
19	INDIANAPOLIS	27
21	KANSAS CITY	14
20	at Detroit	10
13	at Seattle	10
3	GREEN BAY	31
0	at Kansas City	34
17	DENVER	33
9	at Oakland	28
20	CHICAGO (OT)	23
27	at Minnesota	35
23	CLEVELAND	10
19	at Seattle	16
9	at Miami	12
23	OAKLAND	20
12	at Denver	6
269		316

SEATTLE SEAHAWKS (9-7)

20	DETROIT	28
14	at Chicago	13
29	at Pittsburgh	10
22	OAKLAND	21
	OPEN DATE	
10	at San Diego	13
26	BUFFALO	16
27	at Green Bay	7
37	CINCINNATI	20
20	DENVER	17
31	at Kansas City	19
3	TAMPA BAY	16
21	at Oakland	30
16	SAN DIEGO	19
30	at Denver (OT)	36
23	KANSAS CITY	14
9	at NY Jets	19
338		298

TENNESSEE TITANS (13-3)

36	CINCINNATI	35
26	CLEVELAND	9
20	at Jacksonville	19
22	at San Francisco	24
14	BALTIMORE	11
24	at New Orleans	21
	OPEN DATE	
24	ST LOUIS	21
0	at Miami	17
24	at Cincinnati	14
16	PITTSBURGH	10
33	at Cleveland	21
14	at Baltimore	41
21	OAKLAND	14
30	ATLANTA	17
41	JACKSONVILLE	14
47	at Pittsburgh	36
392		324

1999 NFC Team-by-Team Results

ARIZONA CARDINALS (6-10)

25	at Philadelphia	24
16	at Miami	19
10	SAN FRACISCO	24
7	at Dallas	35
14	NY GIANTS	3
10	WASHINGTON	24
	OPEN DATE	
3	NEW ENGLAND	27
7	at NY Jets	12
23	DETROIT	19
13	DALLAS	9
34	at NY Giants	24
21	PHILADELPHIA	17
3	at Washington	28
21	BUFFALO	31
14	at Atlanta	37
24	at Green Bay	49
245		382

ATLANTA FALCONS (5-11)

14	MINNESOTA	17
7	at Dallas	24
7	at St Louis	35
14	BALTIMORE (OT)	19
20	at New Orleans	17
13	ST. LOUIS	41
9	at Pittsburgh	13
27	CAROLINA	20
7	JACKSONVILLE	30
	OPEN DATE	
10	at Tampa Bay	19
28	at Carolina	34
35	NEW ORLEANS	12
7	at San Francisco	26
17	at Tennessee	30
37	ARIZONA	14
34	SAN FRANCISCO	29
286		380

CAROLINA PANTHERS (8-8)

10	at New Orleans	19
20	JACKSONVILLE	22
27	CINCINNATI	3
36	at Washington	38
	OPEN DATE	
31	at San Francisco	29
9	DETROIT	24
20	at Atlanta	27
33	PHILADELPHIA	7
10	at St. Louis	35
31	at Cleveland	17
34	ATLANTA	28
21	ST. LOUIS	34
33	at Green Bay	31
41	SAN FRANCISCO	24
20	at Pittsburgh	30
45	NEW ORLEANS	13
421		381

CHICAGO BEARS (6-10)

20	KANSAS CITY	17
13	SEATTLE	14
17	at Oakland	24
14	NEW ORLEANS	10
24	at Minnesota	22
16	PHILADELPHIA	20
3	at Tampa Bay	6
22	at Washington	48
14	at Green Bay	13
24	MINNESOTA (OT)	27
23	at San Diego (OT)	20
17	at Detroit	21
19	GREEN BAY	35
	OPEN DATE	
28	DETROIT	10
12	at St. Louis	34
6	TAMPA BAY	20
272		341

DALLAS COWBOYS (8-8)

41	at Washington (OT)	35
24	ATLANTA	7
	OPEN DATE	
35	ARIZONA	7
10	at Philadelphia	13
10	at NY Giants	13
38	WASHINGTON	20
24	at Indianapolis	34
17	at Minnesota	27
27	GREEN BAY	13
9	at Arizona	13
20	MIAMI	0
6	at New England	13
20	PHILADELPHIA	10
21	NY JETS	22
24	at New Orleans	31
26	NY GIANTS	18
352		276

DETROIT LIONS (8-8)

28	at Seattle	20
23	GREEN BAY	15
21	at Kansas City	31
	OPEN DATE	
10	SAN DIEGO	20
25	MINNESOTA	23
24	at Carolina	9
20	TAMPA BAY	3
31	ST. LOUIS	27
19	at Arizona	23
17	at Green Bay	26
21	CHICAGO	17
33	WASHINGTON	17
16	at Tampa Bay	23
10	at Chicago	28
7	DENVER	17
17	at Minnesota	24
322		323

GREEN BAY PACKERS (8–8)

28	OAKLAND	24
15	at Detroit	23
23	MINNESOTA	20
	OPEN DATE	
26	TAMPA BAY	23
10	at Denver	31
31	at San Diego	3
7	SEATTLE	27
13	CHICAGO	14
13	at Dallas	27
26	DETROIT	17
20	at San Francisco	3
35	at Chicago	19
31	CAROLINA	33
20	at Minnesota	24
10	at Tampa Bay	29
49	ARIZONA	24
357		**341**

MINNESOTA VIKINGS (10–6)

17	at Atlanta	14
17	OAKLAND	22
20	at Green Bay	23
21	TAMPA BAY	14
22	CHICAGO	24
23	at Detroit	25
40	SAN FRANCISCO	16
23	at Denver	20
27	DALLAS	17
27	at Chicago (OT)	24
	OPEN DATE	
35	SAN DIEGO	27
17	at Tampa Bay	24
28	at Kansas City	31
24	GREEN BAY	20
34	at NY Giants	17
24	DETROIT	17
399		**335**

NEW ORLEANS SAINTS (3–13)

19	CAROLINA	10
21	at San Francisco	28
	OPEN DATE	
10	at Chicago	14
17	ATLANTA	20
21	TENNESSEE	24
3	at NY Giants	31
16	CLEVELAND	21
16	TAMPA BAY	31
24	SAN FRANCISCO	6
23	at Jacksonville	41
12	at St. Louis	43
12	at Atlanta	35
14	ST. LOUIS	30
8	at Baltimore	31
31	DALLAS	24
13	at Carolina	45
260		**434**

NEW YORK GIANTS (7–9)

17	at Tampa Bay	13
21	WASHINGTON	50
14	at New England	16
16	PHILADELPHIA	15
3	at Arizona	14
13	DALLAS	10
31	NEW ORLEANS	3
23	at Philadelphia (OT)	17
	OPEN DATE	
19	INDIANAPOLIS	27
13	at Washington	23
24	ARIZONA	34
41	NY JETS	28
19	at Buffalo	17
10	at St. Louis	31
17	MINNESOTA	34
18	at Dallas	26
306		**389**

PHILADELPHIA EAGLES (5–11)

24	ARIZONA	25
5	TAMPA BAY	19
0	at Buffalo	26
15	at NY Giants	16
13	DALLAS	10
20	at Chicago	16
13	at Miami	16
17	NY GIANTS (OT)	23
7	at Carolina	33
35	WASHINGTON	28
17	INDIANAPOLIS	44
17	at Washington (OT)	20
17	at Arizona	21
10	at Dallas	20
24	NEW ENGLAND	9
	OPEN DATE	
38	ST. LOUIS	31
272		**357**

ST. LOUIS RAMS (13–3)

27	BALTIMORE	10
	OPEN DATE	
35	ATLANTA	7
38	at Cincinnati	10
42	SAN FRANCISCO	20
41	at Atlanta	13
34	CLEVELAND	3
21	at Tennessee	24
27	at Detroit	31
35	CAROLINA	10
23	at San Francisco	7
43	NEW ORLEANS	12
34	at Carolina	21
30	at New Orleans	14
31	NY GIANTS	10
34	CHICAGO	12
31	at Philadelphia	38
526		**242**

SAN FRANCISCO 49ERS (4–12)

3	at Jacksonville	41
28	NEW ORLEANS	21
24	at Arizona	10
24	TENNESSEE	22
20	at St. Louis	42
29	CAROLINA	31
16	at Minnesota	40
	OPEN DATE	
6	PITTSBURGH	27
6	at New Orleans	24
7	ST. LOUIS	23
3	GREEN BAY	20
30	at Cincinnati	44
26	ATLANTA	7
24	at Carolina	41
20	WASHINGTON (OT)	26
29	at Atlanta	34
295		**453**

TAMPA BAY BUCCANEERS (11–5)

13	NY GIANTS	17
19	at Philadelphia	5
13	DENVER	10
14	at Minnesota	21
23	at Green Bay	26
	OPEN DATE	
6	CHICAGO	3
3	at Detroit	20
31	at New Orleans	16
17	KANSAS CITY	10
19	ATLANTA	10
16	at Seattle	3
24	MINNESOTA	17
23	DETROIT	16
0	at Oakland	45
29	GREEN BAY	10
20	at Chicago	6
270		**235**

WASHINGTON REDSKINS (10–6)

35	DALLAS (OT)	41
50	at NY Giants	21
27	at NY Jets	20
38	CAROLINA	36
	OPEN DATE	
24	at Arizona	10
20	at Dallas	38
48	CHICAGO	22
17	BUFFALO	34
28	at Philadelphia	35
23	NY Giants	13
20	PHILADELPHIA (OT)	17
17	at Detroit	33
28	ARIZONA	3
21	at Indianapolis	24
26	at San Francisco (OT)	20
21	MIAMI	10
443		**377**

1999 NFL Individual Leaders

American Football Conference

Scoring

TOUCHDOWNS	TD	Rush	Rec	Ret	Pts	KICKING	PAT	FG	Lg	Pts
James, Ind	17	13	4	0	102	Vanderjagt, Ind	43/43	34/38	53	145
George, Tenn	13	9	4	0	78	Mare, Mia	27/27	39/46	54	144
Stewart, Jax	13	13	0	0	78	Peterson, Sea	32/32	34/40	51	134
Harrison, Ind	12	0	12	0	72	Hollis, Jax	37/37	31/38	50	130
Gonzalez, Kan	11	0	11	0	66	Stover, Balt	32/32	28/33	50	116
Wheatley, Oak	11	8	3	0	66	Elam, Den	29/29	29/36	55	116
Mayes, Sea	10	0	10	0	60	Carney, SD	22/23	31/36	50	115
Allen, NE	9	8	1	0	54	Stoyanovich, KC	45/45	21/28	51	108
Dudley, Oak	9	0	9	0	54	Christie, Buff	33/33	25/34	52	108
Kirby, Clev	9	6	3	0	54	Hall, NYJ	27/29	27/33	48	108

Passing

	Att	Comp	Pct Comp	Yds	Avg Gain	TD	Pct TD	Int	Pct Int	Lg	Rating Pts
Manning, Ind	533	331	62.1	4135	7.80	26	4.9	15	2.8	t80	90.7
Gannon, Oak	515	304	59.0	3840	7.50	24	4.7	14	2.7	50	86.5
Lucas, NYJ	272	161	59.2	1678	6.20	14	5.1	6	2.2	t56	85.1
Brunell, Jax	441	259	58.7	3060	6.90	14	3.2	9	2.0	62	82.0
Grbac, KC	499	294	58.9	3389	6.80	22	4.4	15	3.0	t86	81.7
Banks, Balt	320	169	52.8	2136	6.70	17	5.3	8	2.5	t76	81.2
McNair, Tenn	331	187	56.5	2179	6.60	12	3.6	8	2.4	t65	78.6
Kitna, Sea	495	270	54.5	3346	6.80	23	4.6	16	3.2	51	77.7
Blake, Cin	389	215	55.3	2670	6.90	16	4.1	12	3.1	t76	77.6
Tomczak, Pitt,	258	139	53.9	1625	6.30	12	4.7	8	3.1	49	75.8

Pass Receiving

RECEPTIONS	No.	Yds	Avg	Lg	TD	YARDS	Yds	No.	Avg	Lg	TD
J. Smith, Jax	116	1636	14.1	62	6	Harrison, Ind	1663	115	14.5	t57	12
Harrison, Ind	115	1663	14.5	t57	12	J. Smith, Jax	1636	116	14.1	62	6
T. Brown, Oak	90	1344	14.9	47	6	T. Brown, Oak	1344	90	14.9	47	6
Johnson, NYJ	89	1170	13.1	65	8	Johnson, NYJ	1170	89	13.1	65	8
R. Smith, Den	79	1020	12.9	71	4	Glenn, NE	1147	69	16.6	67	4
McCardell, Jax	78	891	11.4	49	5	Q. Ismail, Balt	1105	68	16.3	t76	6
Gonzalez, KC	76	849	11.2	t73	11	Martin, Mia	1037	67	15.5	t69	5
McCaffrey, Den	71	1018	14.3	t78	7	Scott, Cinn	1022	68	15.0	t76	7
Glenn, NE	69	1147	16.6	67	4	R. Smith, Den	1020	79	12.9	71	4
Wycheck, Tenn	69	641	9.3	35	2	McCaffrey, Den	1018	71	14.3	t78	7

Rushing

	Att	Yds	Avg	Lg	TD
James, Ind	369	1553	4.2	72	13
Martin, NYJ	367	1464	4.0	50	5
George, Ten	320	1304	4.1	40	9
Watters, Sea	325	1210	3.7	45	5
Dillon, Cin	263	1200	4.6	50	5
Gary, Den	276	1159	4.2	71	7
Bettis, Pitt	299	1091	3.6	35	7
Wheatley, Oak	242	936	3.9	t30	8
J. Stewart, Jax	249	931	3.7	t44	13
T. Allen, NE	254	896	3.5	39	8
Rhett, Balt	236	852	3.6	t52	5

Total Yards from Scrimmage

	Total	Rush	Rec
James, Ind	2139	1553	586
George, Tenn	1762	1304	458
Martin, NYJ	1723	1464	259
Harrison, Ind	1667	4	1663
J. Smith, Jax	1636	0	1636
Watters, Sea	1597	1210	387
Dillon, Cin	1490	1200	290
T. Brown, Oak	1348	4	1344
Gary, Den	1318	1159	159
Bettis, Pitt	1201	1091	110
Johnson, NYJ	1176	6	1170

Interceptions

	No.	Yds	Lg	TD
Hasty, KC	7	98	t56	2
Madison, Mia	7	164	42	1
Woodson, Balt	6	195	t66	2
Beasley, Jax	6	200	t93	2
Coleman, NYJ	6	165	t98	1

Sacks

Kearse, Ten	14.5
Pryce, Den	13.0
Brackens, Jax	12.0
Bartzke, Ind	12.0
McCrary, Balt	11.5
Hardy, Jax	10.5

American Football Conference *(Cont.)*

Punting

	No.	Yds	Avg	Net Avg	TB	In 20	Lg	Blk	Ret	Ret Yds
Rouen, Den	84	3908	46.5	35.6	16	19	65	0	43	600
Miller, Pitt	84	3795	45.2	38.1	10	27	75	0	39	392
Tupa, NYJ	81	3659	45.2	38.2	7	25	69	0	47	427
Bennett, SD	89	3910	43.9	38.7	6	32	60	0	41	343
Gardocki, Clev	106	4645	43.8	34.6	11	20	61	0	68	762

Punt Returns

	No.	Yds	Avg	Lg	TD
Rogers, Sea	22	318	14.5	t94	1
Jacquet, Mia	28	351	12.5	45	0
Vanover, KC	51	627	12.3	t84	2
Barlow, Jax	38	414	10.9	t74	1
T. Brown, NE	38	405	10.7	52	0

Kickoff Returns

	No.	Yds	Avg	Lg	TD
Mack, Cin	51	1382	27.1	t99	1
Marion, Mia	62	1524	24.6	93	0
Stone, NYJ	28	689	24.6	50	0
K. Faulk, NE	39	943	24.2	95	0
Watson, Den	48	1138	23.7	71	0

National Football Conference

Scoring

TOUCHDOWNS	TD	Rush	Rec	Ret	Pts	KICKING	PAT	FG	Lg	Pts
S. Davis, Wash	17	17	0	0	102	Wilkins, StL	64/64	20/28	51	124
Carter, Minn	13	0	13	0	78	Conway, Wash	49/50	22/32	51	115
Smith, Dall	13	11	2	0	78	Longwell, GB	38/38	25/30	50	113
Bruce, StL	12	0	12	0	72	Gramatica, TB	25/25	27/32	53	106
Faulk, StL	12	7	5	0	72	Hanson, Det	28/29	26/32	52	106
Jeffers, Minn	12	0	12	0	72	Anderson, Minn	46/46	19/30	44	103
Moss, Minn	12	0	11	1	72	Kasay, Car	33/33	22/25	52	99
Walls, Car	12	0	12	0	72	Richey, SF	30/31	21/23	52	93
Hoard, Minn	10	10	0	0	60	Brien, NO	20/21	24/29	52	92
Levens, GB	10	9	1	0	60	Cunningham, Car	44/45	15/25	47	89

Passing

	Att	Comp	Pct Comp	Yds	Avg Gain	TD	Pct TD	Int	Pct Int	Lg	Rating Pts
Warner, StL	499	325	65.1	4353	8.70	41	8.2	13	2.6	t75	109.2
Beuerlein, Car	571	343	60.1	4436	7.80	36	6.3	15	2.6	t88	94.6
George, Minn	329	191	58.1	2816	8.60	23	7.0	12	3.6	t80	94.2
B. Johnson, Wash	519	316	60.9	4005	7.70	24	4.6	13	2.5	t65	90.0
Batch, Det	270	151	55.9	1957	7.30	13	4.8	7	2.4	t74	84.1
Frerotte, Det	288	175	60.8	2117	7.40	9	3.1	7	4.2	t77	83.6
Chandler, Atl	307	174	56.7	2339	7.60	16	5.2	11	3.6	t60	83.5
Aikman, Dall	442	263	59.5	2964	6.70	17	3.8	12	2.7	t90	81.1
Matthews, Chi	275	167	60.7	1645	6.00	10	3.6	6	2.2	56	80.6

Pass Receiving

RECEPTIONS	No.	Yds	Avg	Lg	TD	YARDS	Yds	No.	Avg	Lg	TD
Muhammad, Car	96	1253	13.1	t60	8	Moss, Minn	1413	80	17.7	t67	11
Carter, Minn	90	1241	13.8	68	13	Robinson, Chi	1400	84	16.7	t80	9
Engram, Chi	88	947	10.8	56	4	Crowell, Det	1338	81	16.5	t77	7
Faulk, StL	87	1048	12.0	t57	5	Muhammad, Car	1253	96	13.1	t60	8
Robinson, Chi	84	1400	16.7	t80	9	Carter, Minn	1241	90	13.8	68	13
Crowell, Det	81	1338	16.5	t77	7	Westbrook, Wash	1191	65	18.3	t65	9
Mathis, Atl	81	1016	12.5	52	6	Toomer, NYG	1183	79	15.0	t80	6
R. Ismail, Dall	80	1097	13.7	t76	6	Bruce, StL	1165	77	15.1	60	12
Morton, Det	80	1129	14.1	48	5	Connell, Wash	1132	62	18.3	t62	7
Moss, Minn	80	1413	17.7	t67	11	Morton, Det	1129	80	14.1	48	5

National Football Conference *(Cont.)*

Rushing

	Att	Yds	Avg	Lg	TD
Davis, Wash	290	1405	4.8	t76	17
E. Smith, Dall	329	1397	4.2	t63	11
Faulk, StL	253	1381	5.5	58	7
Staley, Phil	325	1273	3.9	29	4
Garner, SF	241	1229	5.1	53	4
Levens, GB	279	1034	3.7	36	9
R. Smith, Minn	221	1015	4.6	t70	2
Alstott, TB	242	949	3.9	30	7
Enis, Chi	287	916	3.2	19	3
R. Williams, NO	253	884	3.5	25	2

Total Yards from Scrimmage

	Total	Rush	Rec
Faulk, StL	2429	1381	1048
Garner, SF	1764	1229	535
Levens, GB	1607	1034	573
Staley, Phil	1567	1273	294
S. Davis	1516	1405	111
E. Smith, Dall	1516	1397	119
Moss, Minn	1456	43	1413
Robinson, Chi	1400	0	1400
Crowell, Det.	1376	38	1338
Enis, Chi	1256	916	340

Interceptions

	No.	Yds	Lg	TD
Abraham, TB	7	115	t55	2
Vincent, Phil	7	91	35	0
Schulters, SF	6	127	t64	1
Lyght, StL	6	112	t57	1

Four others tied with six.

Sacks

K. Carter, StL	17.0
Rice, Ariz	16.5
Porcher, Det	15.0
Sapp, TB	12.5
Greene, Car	12.0
B. Young, SF	11.0

Punting

	No.	Yds	Avg	Net Avg	TB	In 20	Lg	Blk	Ret	Ret Yds
Berger, Minn	61	2769	45.4	38.4	9	18	75	0	28	246
Gowin, Dall	81	3500	43.2	35.1	10	24	64	0	43	459
Royals, TB	90	3882	43.1	37.4	8	23	66	0	49	360
Jett, Det	86	3637	42.3	34.8	12	27	62	0	42	402
Landeta, Phil	107	4524	42.3	35.1	12	21	60	1	59	490
Player, Ariz	94	3948	42.0	36.7	8	18	60	0	53	340

Punt Returns

	No.	Yds	Avg	Lg	TD
Cody, Ariz	32	373	11.7	31	0
Barber, NYG	44	506	11.5	t85	1
Milburn, Chi	30	346	11.5	54	0
Sanders, Dall	30	344	11.5	76	1
Dwight, Atl	20	220	11.0	t70	1

Kickoff Returns

	No.	Yds	Avg	Lg	TD
Horne, StL	30	892	29.7	t101	2
Tucker, Dall	22	613	27.9	79	0
Tate, Minn	25	627	25.1	t76	1
Rossum, Phil	54	1347	24.9	t89	1
Bates, Car	52	1287	24.8	t100	2

1999 NFL Team Leaders

AFC Total Offense

	Total Yds	Yds Rush	Yds Pass	Time of Poss	Avg Pts/Game
Indianapolis	5726	1660	4066	30:45	26.4
Oakland	5693	2084	3609	32:06	24.3
Jacksonville	5586	2091	3495	31:57	24.7
Buffalo	5333	2040	3293	32:12	20.0
Kansas City	5321	2082	3239	30:20	24.3
Tennessee	5296	1811	3485	31:30	24.5
Denver	5283	1864	3419	31:06	19.6
Cincinnati	5277	2051	3226	29:59	17.6
New England	5062	1426	3636	28:49	18.6
Miami	4938	1453	3485	31:34	20.3
Pittsburgh	4874	1991	2883	31:28	19.8
Seattle	4805	1408	3397	27:48	21.1
Baltimore	4778	1754	3024	29:24	20.2
NY Jets	4752	1961	2791	30:45	19.2
San Diego	4589	1246	3343	30:00	16.8
Cleveland	3762	1150	2612	23:38	13.5

AFC Total Defense

	Opp Total Yds	Opp Yds Rush	Opp Yds Pass	Avg PA/Game
Buffalo	4045	1370	2675	14.3
Baltimore	4222	1231	2991	17.3
Jacksonville	4334	1444	2890	13.5
Miami	4404	1476	2928	21.0
Denver	4753	1737	3016	19.8
New England	4808	1795	3013	17.7
Oakland	4880	1559	3321	20.5
Pittsburgh	4884	1958	2926	20.0
San Diego	4905	1321	3584	19.7
Kansas City	5039	1557	3482	20.1
Indianapolis	5221	1715	3506	20.8
Tennessee	5245	1550	3695	20.2
NY Jets	5379	1703	3676	19.3
Seattle	5426	1934	3492	18.6
Cincinnati	5497	1699	3798	28.7
Cleveland	6046	2736	3310	27.3

NFC Total Offense

	Total Yds	Yds Rush	Yds Pass	Time of Poss	Avg Pts/Game
St. Louis	6412	2059	4353	31:50	32.8
Washington	5965	2039	3926	29:33	27.6
Minnesota	5793	1804	3989	29:21	24.9
Carolina	5686	1525	4161	29:23	26.3
Chicago	5523	1387	4136	29:24	17.0
Green Bay	5419	1519	3900	29:13	22.3
San Francisco	5380	2085	3295	30:17	18.4
Dallas	5178	2051	3127	31:51	22.0
NY Giants	5127	1410	3717	30:31	18.6
New Orleans	4983	1690	3293	30:54	16.2
Detroit	4931	1245	3686	29:15	20.1
Atlanta	4542	1196	3346	28:44	17.8
Tampa Bay	4254	1776	2478	32:11	16.8
Arizona	4010	1207	2803	27:09	15.3
Philadelphia	3830	1746	2084	27:03	17.0

NFC Total Defense

	Opp Total Yds	Opp Yds Rush	Opp Yds Pass	Avg PA/Game
Tampa Bay	4280	1407	2873	14.6
St. Louis	4698	1189	3509	15.1
Dallas	4840	1444	3396	17.2
NY Giants	4981	1560	3421	22.3
Atlanta	5223	2062	3161	23.7
Detroit	5291	1531	3760	20.1
Green Bay	5309	1804	3505	21.3
New Orleans	5318	1774	3544	27.1
Arizona	5422	2265	3157	23.8
Philadelphia	5462	2001	3461	22.3
Carolina	5503	1898	3605	23.8
Minnesota	5597	1617	3980	20.9
San Francisco	5687	1619	4068	28.3
Chicago	5704	1882	3822	21.3
Washington	5705	1973	3732	23.5

Takeaways/Giveaways

American Football Conference

	Takeaways Int	Fum	Total	Giveaways Int	Fum	Total	Net Diff
Kansas City	25	20	45	15	9	24	21
Tennessee	16	24	40	13	9	22	18
NY Jets	24	11	35	16	6	22	13
Jacksonville	19	11	30	11	7	18	12
Oakland	20	13	33	14	15	29	4
Pittsburgh	14	14	28	18	7	25	3
Seattle	30	6	36	16	17	33	3
Baltimore	21	10	31	20	11	31	0
Denver	15	11	26	18	10	28	-2
New England	16	15	31	21	12	33	-2
Cincinnati	12	15	27	18	14	32	-5
Indianapolis	10	13	23	17	11	28	-5
Buffalo	12	9	21	16	11	27	-6
Miami	18	10	28	21	13	34	-6
San Diego	15	12	27	24	11	35	-8
Cleveland	8	12	20	15	16	31	-11

National Football Conference

	Takeaways Int	Fum	Total	Giveaways Int	Fum	Total	Net Diff
Washington	24	13	37	14	11	25	12
Dallas	24	9	33	13	10	23	10
Detroit	16	16	32	14	8	22	10
Philadelphia	28	18	46	18	21	39	7
Green Bay	26	15	41	23	13	36	5
St. Louis	29	7	36	15	16	31	5
Chicago	14	19	33	22	15	37	-4
Tampa Bay	21	10	31	16	19	35	-4
Carolina	15	14	29	15	19	34	-5
New Orleans	19	15	34	30	9	39	-5
NY Giants	17	7	24	20	12	32	-8
Minnesota	12	18	30	21	19	40	-10
San Francisco	13	7	20	19	13	32	-12
Arizona	17	10	27	30	10	40	-13
Atlanta	12	6	18	19	16	35	-17

Conference Rankings

American Football Conference

	Offense Total	Rush	Pass	Defense Total	Rush	Pass
Baltimore	13	10	13	2	1	5
Buffalo	4	5	10	1	3	1
Cincinnati	8	4	12	15	9	16
Cleveland	16	16	16	16	16	8
Denver	7	8	7	5	12	7
Indianapolis	1	11	1	11	11	12
Jacksonville	3	1	4	3	4	2
Kansas City	5	3	11	10	7	10
Miami	10	12	5	4	5	4
New England	9	13	2	6	13	6
NY Jets	14	7	15	13	10	14
Oakland	2	2	3	8	8	9
Pittsburgh	11	6	14	7	15	3
San Diego	15	15	9	9	2	13
Seattle	12	14	8	14	14	11
Tennessee	6	9	6	12	6	15

National Football Conference

	Offense Total	Rush	Pass	Defense Total	Rush	Pass
Arizona	14	14	13	9	15	2
Atlanta	12	15	9	5	14	3
Carolina	4	9	2	11	11	10
Chicago	5	12	3	14	10	13
Dallas	8	3	12	3	3	4
Detroit	11	13	8	6	4	12
Green Bay	6	10	6	7	9	7
Minnesota	3	5	4	12	6	14
New Orleans	10	8	11	8	8	9
NY Giants	9	11	7	4	5	5
Philadelphia	15	7	15	10	13	6
St. Louis	1	2	1	2	1	8
San Francisco	7	1	2	13	12	2
Tampa Bay	13	6	14	1	2	1
Washington	2	4	5	15	12	11

1999 AFC Team-by-Team Statistical Leaders

Baltimore Ravens

SCORING	Rush	Rec	Ret	PAT	FG	S	Pts
		TD					
Stover	0	0	0	32/32	28/33	0	116
Rhett	5	2	0	0/0	0/0	0	42
Ismail	0	6	0	0/0	0/0	0	36
Armour	0	4	0	0/0	0/0	0	24

RUSHING	No.	Yds	Avg	Lg	TD
Rhett	236	852	3.6	t52	5
Holmes	89	506	5.7	72	1
Case	36	141	3.9	28	3

PASSING	Att	Comp	Pct Comp	Yds	Avg Gain	TD	Int	Rating Pts
Banks	320	169	52.8	2136	6.68	17	8	81.2
Case	170	77	45.3	988	5.81	3	8	50.3

RECEIVING	No.	Yds	Avg	Lg	TD
Ismail	68	1105	16.3	t76	6
Armour	37	538	14.5	t54	4
Evans	32	235	7.3	27	1
Johnson	29	526	18.1	t76	3
J. Lewis	25	281	11.2	46	2

INTERCEPTIONS: Woodson, 7

PUNTING	No.	Yds	Avg	Net Avg	TB	In 20	Lg	Blk
Richard'n	103	4355	42.3	35.5	10	39	63	1

SACKS: McCrary, 11.5

Buffalo Bills

SCORING	Rush	Rec	Ret	PAT	FG	S	Pts
		TD					
Christie	0	0	0	33/33	25/34	0	108
Moulds	0	7	0	0/0	0/0	0	42
Linton	5	1	0	0/0	0/0	0	38
A. Smith	6	0	0	0/0	0/0	0	36
Riemersma	0	4	0	0/0	0/0	0	24

RUSHING	No.	Yds	Avg	Lg	TD
Linton	205	695	3.4	18	5
A. Smith	165	614	3.7	t52	6
Flutie	88	476	5.4	t24	1
Thomas	36	152	4.2	31	0

PASSING	Att	Comp	Pct Comp	Yds	Avg Gain	TD	Int	Rating Pts
Flutie	478	264	55.2	3171	6.63	19	16	75.1
R. Johnsn	34	25	73.5	298	8.76	2	0	119.5

RECEIVING	No.	Yds	Avg	Lg	TD
Moulds	65	994	15.3	t54	7
Reed	52	536	10.3	30	1
Riemersma	37	496	13.4	38	4
P. Price	31	393	12.7	45	3
K. Williams	31	381	12.3	35	0
Linton	29	228	7.9	28	1

INTERCEPTIONS: Schulz, 3

PUNTING	No.	Yds	Avg	Net Avg	TB	In 20	Lg	Blk
Mohr	73	2840	38.9	33.9	7	20	60	0

SACKS: B. Smith, 7

Cincinnati Bengals

SCORING	Rush	Rec	Ret	PAT	FG	S	Pts
		TD					
Pelfrey	0	0	0	27/27	18/27	0	81
Scott	0	7	0	0/0	0/0	0	42
Pickens	0	6	0	0/0	0/0	0	36
Dillon	5	1	0	0/0	0/0	0	36
Jackson	0	2	0	0/0	0/0	0	14

RUSHING	No.	Yds	Avg	Lg	TD
Dillon	263	1200	4.6	50	5
Blake	63	332	5.3	16	2

PASSING	Att	Comp	Pct Comp	Yds	Avg Gain	TD	Int	Rating Pts
Blake	389	215	55.3	2670	6.86	16	12	77.6
Smith	153	80	52.3	805	5.26	2	6	55.6

RECEIVING	No.	Yds	Avg	Lg	TD
Scott	68	1022	15.0	t76	7
Pickens	57	737	12.9	t75	6
Jackson	31	369	11.9	29	2

INTERCEPTIONS: Heath, 3

PUNTING	No.	Yds	Avg	Net Avg	TB	In 20	Lg	Blk
Brice	60	2475	41.3	32.1	4	12	72	2

SACKS: Bankston, 6

Cleveland Browns

SCORING	Rush	Rec	Ret	PAT	FG	S	Pts
		TD					
Kirby	6	3	0	0/0	0/0	0	54
Dawson	1	0	0	23/24	8/12	0	53
Johnson	0	8	0	0/0	0/0	0	48
Chiaverini	0	4	0	0/0	0/0	0	24
Edwards	2	0	0	0/0	0/0	0	12

RUSHING	No.	Yds	Avg	Lg	TD
Kirby	130	452	3.5	28	6
Abdul-Jabbar	115	350	3.0	21	0
Couch	40	267	6.7	40	1

PASSING	Att	Comp	Pct Comp	Yds	Avg Gain	TD	Int	Rating Pts
Couch	399	223	55.9	2447	6.13	15	13	73.2
Detmer	91	47	51.6	548	6.02	4	2	75.7

RECEIVING	No.	Yds	Avg	Lg	TD
Johnson	66	986	14.9	t64	8
Kirby	58	528	9.1	t78	3
Chiaverini	44	487	11.1	t28	4
Edwards	27	212	7.9	t27	2
I. Smith	24	222	9.3	22	1
Shepherd	23	274	11.9	36	0

INTERCEPTIONS: Pope, 2

PUNTING	No.	Yds	Avg	Net Avg	TB	In 20	Lg	Blk
Gardocki	106	4645	43.8	34.6	11	20	61	0

SACKS: Thierry, 7

Denver Broncos

SCORING	Rush	Rec	Ret	PAT	FG	S	Pts
			TD				
Elam	0	0	0	29/29	29/36	0	116
Gary	7	0	0	0/0	0/0	0	44
McCaffrey	0	7	0	0/0	0/0	0	42
R. Smith	0	4	0	0/0	0/0	0	24
Griese	2	0	0	0/0	0/0	0	12

RUSHING	No.	Yds	Avg	Lg	TD
Gary	276	1159	4.2	71	7
Davis	67	211	3.1	26	2

PASSING	Att	Comp	Pct Comp	Yds	Avg Gain	TD	Int	Rating Pts
Griese	452	261	57.7	3032	6.71	14	14	75.6
C. Miller	81	46	56.8	527	6.51	2	1	79.6

RECEIVING	No.	Yds	Avg	Lg	TD
R. Smith	79	1020	12.9	71	4
McCaffrey	71	1018	14.3	t78	7
Chamberlain	32	488	15.3	88	2
Griffith	26	192	7.4	20	1
Carswell	24	201	8.4	20	2

INTERCEPTIONS: James, 5

PUNTING	No.	Yds	Avg	Net Avg	TB	In 20	Lg	Blk
Rouen	84	3908	46.5	35.6	16	19	65	0

SACKS: Pryce, 13

Indianapolis Colts

SCORING	Rush	Rec	Ret	PAT	FG	S	Pts
			TD				
Vanderjagt	0	0	0	43/43	34/38	0	145
James	13	4	0	0/0	0/0	0	102
Harrison	0	12	0	0/0	0/0	0	74
Wilkins	0	4	3	0/0	0/0	0	42
Pollard	0	4	0	0/0	0/0	0	24

RUSHING	No.	Yds	Avg	Lg	TD
James	369	1553	4.2	72	13
Manning	35	73	2.1	13	2
Elias	13	28	2.2	8	0

PASSING	Att	Comp	Pct Comp	Yds	Avg Gain	TD	Int	Rating Pts
Manning	533	331	62.1	4135	7.76	26	15	90.7

RECEIVING	No.	Yds	Avg	Lg	TD
Harrison	115	1663	14.5	t57	12
James	62	586	9.5	54	4
Wilkins	42	565	13.5	t80	4
Dilger	40	479	12.0	30	2
Pollard	34	374	11.0	33	4

INTERCEPTIONS: Poole, 3

PUNTING	No.	Yds	Avg	Net Avg	TB	In 20	Lg	Blk
Smith	58	2467	42.5	30.6	8	16	61	2

SACKS: Bratzke, 12

Jacksonville Jaguars

SCORING	Rush	Rec	Ret	PAT	FG	S	Pts
			TD				
Hollis	0	0	0	37/37	31/38	0	130
J. Stewart	13	0	0	0/0	0/0	0	78
J. Smith	0	6	0	0/0	0/0	0	38
Taylor	6	0	0	0/0	0/0	0	36

RUSHING	No.	Yds	Avg	Lg	TD
J. Stewart	249	931	3.7	t44	13
Taylor	159	732	4.6	52	6
Brunell	47	208	4.4	15	1

PASSING	Att	Comp	Pct Comp	Yds	Avg Gain	TD	Int	Rating Pts
Brunell	441	259	58.7	3060	6.94	14	9	82.0
Fiedler	94	61	64.9	656	6.98	2	2	83.5

RECEIVING	No.	Yds	Avg	Lg	TD
J. Smith	116	1636	14.1	62	6
McCardell	78	891	11.4	49	5
Brady	32	346	10.8	30	1
J. Stewart	21	108	5.1	19	0
Jones	19	221	11.6	31	4

INTERCEPTIONS: Beasley, 6

PUNTING	No.	Yds	Avg	Net Avg	TB	In 20	Lg	Blk
Barker	78	3260	45.0	36.9	6	32	83	0

SACKS: Brackens, 12

Kansas City Chiefs

SCORING	Rush	Rec	Ret	PAT	FG	S	Pts
			TD				
Stoyanovich	0	0	0	45/45	21/28	0	108
Gonzalez	0	11	0	0/0	0/0	0	66
Bennett	8	0	0	0/0	0/0	0	48
Horn	0	6	0	0/0	0/0	0	36
Morris	0	3	0	0/0	0/0	0	18

RUSHING	No.	Yds	Avg	Lg	TD
Bennett	161	627	3.9	44	8
Morris	120	414	3.5	24	3
Richardson	84	387	4.6	26	1
Shehee	65	238	3.7	18	1

PASSING	Att	Comp	Pct Comp	Yds	Avg Gain	TD	Int	Rating Pts
Grbac	499	294	58.9	3389	6.79	22	15	81.7

RECEIVING	No.	Yds	Avg	Lg	TD
Gonzalez	76	849	11.2	t73	11
Alexander	54	832	15.4	t86	2
Horn	35	586	16.7	t76	6
Lockett	34	426	12.5	t39	2
Richardson	24	141	5.9	29	0

INTERCEPTIONS: Hasty, 7

PUNTING	No.	Yds	Avg	Net Avg	TB	In 20	Lg	Blk
Pope	101	4218	41.8	35.1	10	20	64	2

SACKS: Patton, 7

Miami Dolphins

SCORING	Rush	TD Rec	Ret	PAT	FG	S	Pts
Mare	0	0	0	27/27	39/46	0	144
Gadsden	0	6	0	0/0	0/0	0	36
Pritchett	1	4	0	0/0	0/0	0	30
Martin	0	5	0	0/0	0/0	0	30
Johnson	0	4	0	0/0	0/0	0	24

RUSHING	No.	Yds	Avg	Lg	TD
Johnson	164	558	3.4	34	4
Collins	131	414	3.2	t25	2
Pritchett	47	158	3.4	25	1

PASSING	Att	Comp	Pct Comp	Yds	Avg Gain	TD	Int	Rating Pts
Marino	369	204	55.3	2448	6.63	12	17	67.4
Huard	216	125	57.9	1288	5.96	8	4	79.8

RECEIVING	No.	Yds	Avg	Lg	TD
Martin	67	1037	15.5	t69	5
Gadsden	48	803	16.7	62	6
McDuffie	43	516	12.0	34	2
Pritchett	43	312	7.3	30	4
Konrad	34	251	7.4	25	1
Drayton	32	299	9.3	26	1

INTERCEPTIONS: Madison, 7

PUNTING	No.	Yds	Avg	Net Avg	TB	In 20	Lg	Blk
Hutton	73	2978	40.8	35.1	3	22	63	0

SACKS: Owens, 8.5

New York Jets

SCORING	Rush	TD Rec	Ret	PAT	FG	S	Pts
Hall	0	0	0	27/29	27/33	0	108
K. Johnson	0	8	0	0/0	0/0	0	48
Martin	5	0	0	0/0	0/0	0	30
Anderson	0	3	0	0/0	0/0	0	18
Chrebet	0	3	0	0/0	0/0	0	18

RUSHING	No.	Yds	Avg	Lg	TD
Martin	367	1464	4.0	50	5
Lucas	41	144	3.5	21	1
Parmalee	27	133	4.9	18	0

PASSING	Att	Comp	Pct Comp	Yds	Avg Gain	TD	Int	Rating Pts
Lucas	272	161	59.2	1678	6.17	14	6	85.1
Mirer	176	95	54.0	1062	6.03	5	9	60.4

RECEIVING	No.	Yds	Avg	Lg	TD
K. Johnson	89	1170	13.2	65	8
Chrebet	48	631	13.2	t50	3
Martin	45	259	5.8	34	0
Anderson	29	302	10.4	29	3
Ward	22	325	14.8	t56	3

INTERCEPTIONS: Coleman, 6

PUNTING	No.	Yds	Avg	Net Avg	TB	In 20	Lg	Blk
Tupa	811	3659	45.2	38.2	7	25	69	0

SACKS: Lewis, 5.5

New England Patriots

SCORING	Rush	TD Rec	Ret	PAT	FG	S	Pts
Vinatieri	0	0	0	29/30	26/33	0	107
Allen	8	1	0	0/0	0/0	0	54
Jefferson	0	6	0	0/0	0/0	0	36
Glenn	0	4	0	0/0	0/0	0	24
Faulk	1	1	0	0/0	0/0	0	12

RUSHING	No.	Yds	Avg	Lg	TD
Allen	254	896	3.5	39	8
Faulk	67	227	3.4	43	1
Warren	35	120	3.4	18	0

PASSING	Att	Comp	Pct Comp	Yds	Avg Gain	TD	Int	Rating Pts
Bledsoe	539	305	56.6	3985	7.39	19	21	75.6

RECEIVING	No.	Yds	Avg	Lg	TD
Glenn	69	1147	16.6	67	4
Jefferson	40	698	17.5	t68	6
Brown	36	471	13.1	37	1
Coates	32	370	11.6	27	2
Warren	29	262	9.0	21	1

INTERCEPTIONS: Milloy, 4

PUNTING	No.	Yds	Avg	Net Avg	TB	In 20	Lg	Blk
Johnson	90	3735	41.5	34.6	14	23	58	0

SACKS: McGinest, 9

Oakland Raiders

SCORING	Rush	TD Rec	Ret	PAT	FG	S	Pts
Husted	0	0	0	30/30	20/31	0	90
Wheatley	8	3	0	0/0	0/0	0	66
Dudley	0	9	0	0/0	0/0	0	54
Brown	0	6	0	0/0	0/0	0	36
Crockett	4	1	0	0/0	0/0	0	30
Kaufman	2	1	0	0/0	0/0	0	18

RUSHING	No.	Yds	Avg	Lg	TD
Wheatley	242	936	3.9	t30	8
Kaufman	138	714	5.2	t75	2
Gannon	46	298	6.5	39	2
Crockett	45	91	2.0	7	4

PASSING	Att	Comp	Pct Comp	Yds	Avg Gain	TD	Int	Rating Pts
Gannon	515	304	59.0	3840	7.46	24	14	86.5

RECEIVING	No.	Yds	Avg	Lg	TD
T. Brown	90	1344	14.9	47	6
Ritchie	45	408	9.1	t20	1
Dudley	39	555	14.2	35	9
Jett	39	552	14.2	43	2
Wheatley	21	196	9.3	28	3

INTERCEPTIONS: Three tied with three.

PUNTING	No.	Yds	Avg	Net Avg	TB	In 20	Lg	Blk
Araguz	76	3045	40.1	32.3	4	25	56	1

SACKS: Johnstone, 10

Pittsburgh Steelers

SCORING

	TD						
	Rush	Rec	Ret	PAT	FG	S	Pts
K. Brown	0	0	0	30/31	25/29	0	105
Huntley	0	5	3	0/0	0/0	0	48
Ward	0	7	0	0/0	0/0	0	44
Bettis	7	0	0	0/0	0/0	0	42
Edwards	0	5	0	0/0	0/0	0	30

RUSHING

	No.	Yds	Avg	Lg	TD
Bettis	299	1091	3.6	35	7
Huntley	93	567	6.1	52	5
Stewart	56	258	4.6	21	2
Zereoue	18	48	2.7	8	0

PASSING

	Att	Comp	Pct Comp	Yds	Avg Gain	TD	Int	Rating Pts
Stewart	275	160	58.2	1464	5.32	6	10	64.9
Tomczak	258	139	53.9	1625	6.30	12	8	75.8

RECEIVING

	No.	Yds	Avg	Lg	TD
Edwards	61	714	11.7	41	5
Ward	61	638	10.5	42	7
Hawkins	30	285	9.5	23	0
Shaw	28	387	13.8	49	3
Huntley	27	253	9.4	25	3

INTERCEPTIONS: Shields and Washington, 3

PUNTING

	No.	Yds	Avg	Net Avg	TB	In 20	Lg	Blk
Miller	84	3795	45.2	38.1	10	27	75	0

SACKS: Gildon, 8.5

Seattle Seahawks

SCORING

	TD						
	Rush	Rec	Ret	PAT	FG	S	Pts
Peterson	0	0	0	32/32	34/40	0	134
Mayes	0	10	0	0/0	0/0	0	60
Watters	5	2	0	0/0	0/0	0	42
Dawkins	0	7	0	0/0	0/0	0	42
Pritchard	0	2	0	0/0	0/0	0	12

RUSHING

	No.	Yds	Avg	Lg	TD
Watters	325	1210	3.7	45	5
Green	26	120	4.6	21	0
Kitna	35	56	1.6	10	0

PASSING

	Att	Comp	Pct Comp	Yds	Avg Gain	TD	Int	Rating Pts
Kitna	495	270	54.5	3346	6.76	23	16	77.7

RECEIVING

	No.	Yds	Avg	Lg	TD
Mayes	62	829	13.4	t43	10
Dawkins	58	992	17.1	t45	7
Watters	40	387	9.7	25	2
Fauria	35	376	10.7	25	0

INTERCEPTIONS: Springs, 5

PUNTING

	No.	Yds	Avg	Net Avg	TB	In 20	Lg	Blk
Feagles	84	3425	40.8	35.2	5	34	59	0

SACKS: Daniels, 9

San Diego Chargers

SCORING

	TD						
	Rush	Rec	Ret	PAT	FG	S	Pts
Carney	0	0	0	22/23	31/36	0	115
Means	4	1	0	0/0	0/0	0	30
Stephens	3	1	0	0/0	0/0	0	24
Bynum	0	1	2	0/0	0/0	0	18
Lewis	0	0	2	0/0	0/0	0	12

RUSHING

	No.	Yds	Avg	Lg	TD
Fazande	91	365	4.0	54	2
Bynum	92	287	3.1	25	1
Means	112	277	2.5	15	4

PASSING

	Att	Comp	Pct Comp	Yds	Avg Gain	TD	Int	Rating Pts
Harbaugh	434	249	57.4	2761	6.36	10	14	70.6
Kramer	141	78	55.3	788	5.59	2	10	46.6

RECEIVING

	No.	Yds	Avg	Lg	TD
J. Graham	57	968	17.0	54	2
F. Jones	56	670	12.0	36	2
Fletcher	45	360	8.0	25	0
Ricks	40	429	10.7	50	0
McCrary	37	201	5.4	38	1

INTERCEPTIONS: Lewis and Spencer, 4

PUNTING

	No.	Yds	Avg	Net Avg	TB	In 20	Lg	Blk
Bennett	89	3910	43.9	38.7	6	32	60	0

SACKS: Johnson, 10.5

Tennessee Oilers

SCORING

	TD						
	Rush	Rec	Ret	PAT	FG	S	Pts
Del Greco	0	0	0	43/43	21/25	0	106
E. George	9	4	0	0/0	0/0	0	78
McNair	8	0	0	0/0	0/0	0	48
Thigpen	0	4	0	0/0	0/0	0	24
Dyson	0	4	0	0/0	0/0	0	24

RUSHING

	No.	Yds	Avg	Lg	TD
E. George	320	1304	4.1	40	9
McNair	72	337	4.7	38	8
Thomas	43	164	3.8	22	1

PASSING

	Att	Comp	Pct Comp	Yds	Avg Gain	TD	Int	Rating Pts
McNair	331	187	56.5	2179	6.58	12	8	78.6
O'Donnell	195	116	59.5	1382	7.09	10	5	87.6

RECEIVING

	No.	Yds	Avg	Lg	TD
Wycheck	69	641	9.3	35	2
Dyson	54	658	12.2	t47	4
E. George	47	458	9.7	t54	4
Thigpen	38	648	17.1	35	4
Harris	26	297	11.4	t62	1
Sanders	20	336	16.8	t48	1

INTERCEPTIONS: Rolle, 4

PUNTING

	No.	Yds	Avg	Net Avg	TB	In 20	Lg	Blk
Hentrich	90	3824	42.5	38.1	3	35	78	0

SACKS: Kearse, 14.5

Arizona Cardinals

SCORING

		TD					
	Rush	Rec	Ret	PAT	FG	S	Pts
Jacke	0	0	0	26/26	19/27	0	83
Bates	9	0	0	0/0	0/0	0	54
Moore	0	5	0	0/0	0/0	0	30
Pittman	2	0	0	0/0	0/0	0	12
Plummer	2	0	0	0/0	0/0	0	12
Boston	0	2	0	0/0	0/0	0	12

RUSHING

	No.	Yds	Avg	Lg	TD
Murrell	193	553	2.9	22	0
Pittman	64	289	4.5	t58	2
Bates	72	202	2.8	16	9

PASSING

	Att	Comp	Pct Comp	Yds	Avg Gain	TD	Int	Rating Pts
Plummer	381	201	52.8	2111	5.54	9	24	50.8
Da. Brown	169	84	49.7	944	5.59	2	6	55.9

RECEIVING

	No.	Yds	Avg	Lg	TD
Sanders	79	954	12.1	63	1
Murrell	49	335	6.8	23	0
Boston	40	473	11.8	43	2
Moore	37	621	16.8	71	5
Hardy	30	322	7.4	23	0

INTERCEPTIONS: Lassiter, 2

PUNTING

	No.	Yds	Avg	Net Avg	TB	In 20	Lg	Blk
Player	94	3948	42.0	36.7	8	18	60	0

SACKS: Rice, 16.5

Atlanta Falcons

SCORING

		TD					
	Rush	Rec	Ret	PAT	FG	S	Pts
Andersen	0	0	0	34/34	15/21	0	79
Dwight	1	7	1	0/0	0/0	0	54
Christian	5	2	0	0/0	0/0	0	42
Mathis	0	6	0	0/0	0/0	0	36
German	0	3	0	0/0	0/0	0	18
Oxendine	1	1	0	0/0	0/0	0	12

RUSHING

	No.	Yds	Avg	Lg	TD
Oxendine	141	452	3.2	20	1
Handspard	136	383	2.8	15	1
Christian	38	174	4.6	t33	5

PASSING

	Att	Comp	Pct Comp	Yds	Avg Gain	TD	Int	Rating Pts
Chandler	307	174	56.7	2339	7.62	16	11	83.5
Graziani	118	62	52.5	759	6.43	2	4	64.2

RECEIVING

	No.	Yds	Avg	Lg	TD
Mathis	81	1016	12.5	52	6
Christain	40	354	8.9	36	2
Dwight	32	669	20.9	t60	7
Calloway	22	314	14.3	33	1
Oxendine	17	172	10.1	32	1

INTERCEPTIONS: Buchanan, 4

PUNTING

	No.	Yds	Avg	Net Avg	TB	In 20	Lg	Blk
Stryzinski	80	3163	39.5	37.1	4	27	55	0

SACKS: Smith, 10

Carolina Panthers

SCORING

		TD					
	Rush	Rec	Ret	PAT	FG	S	Pts
Kasay	0	0	0	33/33	22/25	0	99
Walls	0	12	0	0/0	0/0	0	72
Jeffers	0	12	0	0/0	0/0	0	72
Muhammad	0	8	0	0/0	0/0	0	48
Biakabutuka	0	6	0	0/0	0/0	0	36

RUSHING

	No.	Yds	Avg	Lg	TD
Biakabutuka	138	718	5.2	t67	6
Lane	115	475	4.1	t41	1
Beuerlein	27	124	4.6	16	2

PASSING

	Att	Comp	Pct Comp	Yds	Avg Gain	TD	Int	Rating Pts
Beuerlein	571	343	60.1	4436	7.77	36	15	94.6

RECEIVING

	No.	Yds	Avg	Lg	TD
Muhammad	96	1253	13.1	t60	8
Jeffers	63	1082	17.2	t88	12
Walls	63	822	13.0	t37	12
Biakabutuka	23	189	8.2	32	0
Lane	23	163	7.1	23	0
Floyd	21	179	8.5	25	1

INTERCEPTIONS: E. Davis, 5

PUNTING

	No.	Yds	Avg	Net Avg	TB	In 20	Lg	Blk
Walter	65	2562	39.4	36.7	1	18	56	0

SACKS: Greene, 12

Chicago Bears

SCORING

		TD					
	Rush	Rec	Ret	PAT	FG	S	Pts
M. Robinson	0	9	0	0/0	0/0	0	54
Boniol	0	0	0	17/18	11/18	0	50
Enis	3	2	0	0/0	0/0	0	30
Conway	0	4	0	0/0	0/0	0	24
Engram	0	4	0	0/0	0/0	0	24

RUSHING

	No.	Yds	Avg	Lg	TD
Enis	287	916	3.2	19	3
McNown	32	160	5.0	18	0
Allen	32	119	3.7	13	0

PASSING

	Att	Comp	Pct Comp	Yds	Avg Gain	TD	Int	Rating Pts
Matthews	275	167	60.7	1645	5.98	10	6	80.6
McNown	235	127	54.0	1465	6.23	8	10	66.7
Miller	174	110	63.2	1242	7.14	7	6	83.5

RECEIVING

	No.	Yds	Avg	Lg	TD
Engram	88	947	10.8	56	4
M. Robinson	84	1400	16.7	t80	9
Enis	45	340	7.6	28	2
Conway	44	426	9.7	t30	4
Wetnight	38	277	7.3	22	1

INTERCEPTIONS: Hudson, 3

PUNTING

	No.	Yds	Avg	Net Avg	TB	In 20	Lg	Blk
Sauerbrun	85	3478	40.9	35.4	10	20	65	0

SACKS: Simmons, 7

Dallas Cowboys

SCORING	Rush	Rec	Ret	PAT	FG	S	Pts
Cunningham	0	0	0	40/40	29/35	0	127
E. Smith	13	2	0	0/0	0/0	0	90
Warren	4	1	0	0/0	0/0	0	30
Mills	0	4	0	0/0	0/0	0	24
Sanders	0	0	3	0/0	0/0	0	18

RUSHING	No.	Yds	Avg	Lg	TD
E. Smith	319	1332	4.2	32	13
Warren	59	291	4.9	49	4
S. Williams	64	220	3.4	24	1

PASSING	Att	Comp	Pct Comp	Yds	Avg Gain	TD	Int	Rating Pts
Aikman	442	263	59.5	2964	6.71	17	12	81.1

RECEIVING	No.	Yds	Avg	Lg	TD
Ismail	80	1097	13.7	t76	6
LaFleur	35	322	9.2	25	7
Warren	34	224	6.6	24	0
Mills	30	325	10.8	36	0
E. Smith	27	119	4.4	t14	2
Tucker	23	439	19.1	t90	2

INTERCEPTIONS: Coakley, 4

PUNTING	No.	Yds	Avg	Net Avg	TB	In 20	Lg	Blk
Gowin	81	3500	43.2	35.1	10	24	64	0

SACKS: Ellis, 7.5

Green Bay Packers

SCORING	Rush	Rec	Ret	PAT	FG	S	Pts
Longwell	0	0	0	38/38	25/30	0	113
Levens	9	1	0	0/0	0/0	0	60
Freeman	0	6	0	0/0	0/0	0	36
Bradford	0	5	0	0/0	0/0	0	32
Schroeder	0	5	0	0/0	0/0	0	30

RUSHING	No.	Yds	Avg	Lg	TD
Levens	279	1034	3.7	36	9
Parker	36	184	5.1	26	2
Favre	28	142	5.1	20	0
Mitchell	29	117	4.0	15	0

PASSING	Att	Comp	Pct Comp	Yds	Avg Gain	TD	Int	Rating Pts
Favre	595	341	57.3	4091	6.88	22	23	74.7

RECEIVING	No.	Yds	Avg	Lg	TD
Freeman	74	1074	14.5	51	6
Schroeder	74	1051	14.2	51	5
Levens	71	573	8.1	53	1
Bradford	37	637	17.2	t74	5
Henderson	30	203	6.8	22	1

INTERCEPTIONS: M. McKenzie, 6

PUNTING	No.	Yds	Avg	Net Avg	TB	In 20	Lg	Blk
Aguiar	75	2954	39.4	33.9	4	20	64	0

SACKS: K. McKenzie, 8

Detroit Lions

SCORING	Rush	Rec	Ret	PAT	FG	S	Pts
Hanson	0	0	0	28/29	26/32	0	106
Crowell	0	7	0	0/0	0/0	0	44
Morton	0	5	0	0/0	0/0	0	30
Irvin	4	0	0	0/0	0/0	0	24
Sloan	0	4	0	0/0	0/0	0	24

RUSHING	No.	Yds	Avg	Lg	TD
Hill	144	542	3.8	45	2
Rivers	82	295	3.6	37	0
Irvin	36	133	3.7	51	4

PASSING	Att	Comp	Pct Comp	Yds	Avg Gain	TD	Int	Rating Pts
Frerotte	288	175	60.8	2117	7.35	9	7	83.6
Batch	270	151	55.9	1957	7.25	13	7	84.1

RECEIVING	No.	Yds	Avg	Lg	TD
Crowell	81	1338	16.5	t77	7
Morton	80	1129	14.1	48	5
Sloan	47	591	12.6	t74	4
Irvin	25	233	9.3	31	0
Rivers	22	173	7.9	t31	1

INTERCEPTIONS: Rice, 5

PUNTING	No.	Yds	Avg	Net Avg	TB	In 20	Lg	Blk
Jett	86	3637	42.3	34.8	12	27	62	0

SACKS: Porcher, 15

Minnesota Vikings

SCORING	Rush	Rec	Ret	PAT	FG	S	Pts
Anderson	0	0	0	46/46	19/30	0	103
Carter	0	13	0	0/0	0/0	0	78
R. Moss	0	11	1	0/0	0/0	0	72
Hoard	10	0	0	0/0	0/0	0	60
J. Reed	0	2	0	0/0	0/0	0	12
R. Smith	2	0	0	0/0	0/0	0	12

RUSHING	No.	Yds	Avg	Lg	TD
R. Smith	221	1015	4.6	t70	2
Hoard	138	555	4.0	53	10
M. Williams	24	69	2.9	10	1

PASSING	Att	Comp	Pct Comp	Yds	Avg Gain	TD	Int	Rating Pts
George	329	191	58.1	2816	8.56	23	12	94.2
Cunningh'm	200	124	62.0	1475	7.38	8	9	79.1

RECEIVING	No.	Yds	Avg	Lg	TD
Carter	90	1241	13.8	68	13
R. Moss	80	1413	17.7	t67	11
J. Reed	44	643	14.6	50	2
Glover	28	327	11.7	31	1
R. Smith	24	166	6.9	34	0

INTERCEPTIONS: Griffith, 3

PUNTING	No.	Yds	Avg	Net Avg	TB	In 20	Lg	Blk
Berger	61	2769	45.4	38.4	9	18	75	0

SACKS: Randle, 10

New Orleans Saints

SCORING	Rush	TD Rec	Ret	PAT	FG	S	Pts
Brien	0	0	0	20/21	24/29	0	92
Poole	0	6	0	0/0	0/0	0	36
Kennison	0	4	0	0/0	0/0	0	26
Tolliver	3	0	0	0/0	0/0	0	18
Williams	2	0	0	0/0	0/0	0	12
Delhomme	2	0	0	0/0	0/0	0	12

RUSHING	No.	Yds	Avg	Lg	TD
Williams	253	884	3.5	25	2
L. Smith	60	205	3.4	24	0

PASSING	Att	Comp	Pct Comp	Yds	Avg Gain	TD	Int	Rating Pts
Tolliver	268	139	51.9	1916	7.15	7	16	58.9
Hobert	159	85	53.5	970	6.10	6	6	68.9
Delhomme	76	42	55.3	521	6.86	3	5	62.4

RECEIVING	No.	Yds	Avg	Lg	TD
Kennison	61	835	13.7	t90	4
Poole	42	796	19.0	t67	6
Hastings	40	764	14.1	42	1
Williams	28	172	6.1	29	0
Cleeland	26	325	12.5	31	1

INTERCEPTIONS: Ambrose, 6

PUNTING	No.	Yds	Avg	Net Avg	TB	In 20	Lg	Blk
Barnhardt	82	3262	39.8	35.1	5	14	52	0

SACKS: Glover, 8.5

Philadelphia Eagles

SCORING	Rush	TD Rec	Ret	PAT	FG	S	Pts
N. Johnson	0	0	0	25/25	18/25	0	79
Staley	4	2	0	0/0	0/0	0	36
Broughton	0	4	0	0/0	0/0	0	24
Small	0	4	0	0/0	0/0	0	24
Lewis	0	3	0	0/0	0/0	0	18

RUSHING	No.	Yds	Avg	Lg	TD
Staley	325	1273	3.9	29	4
McNabb	47	313	6.7	27	0

PASSING	Att	Comp	Pct Comp	Yds	Avg Gain	TD	Int	Rating Pts
Pederson	227	119	52.4	1276	5.62	7	9	62.9
McNabb	216	106	49.1	948	4.39	8	7	60.1

RECEIVING	No.	Yds	Avg	Lg	TD
Small	49	655	13.4	t84	4
Staley	41	294	7.2	19	2
C. Johnson	34	414	12.2	36	1
Broughton	26	295	11.3	33	4
Brown	18	188	10.4	27	1

INTERCEPTIONS: Vincent, 7

PUNTING	No.	Yds	Avg	Net Avg	TB	In 20	Lg	Blk
Landeta	107	4524	42.3	35.1	12	21	60	1

SACKS: Mamula, 8.5

New York Giants

SCORING	Rush	TD Rec	Ret	PAT	FG	S	Pts
Blanchard	0	0	0	19/19	18/21	0	73
Toomer	0	6	0	0/0	0/0	0	36
Daluiso	0	0	0	9/9	7/9	0	30
Montgomery	3	0	0	0/0	0/0	0	20
Mitchell	0	3	0	0/0	0/0	0	18

RUSHING	No.	Yds	Avg	Lg	TD
Montgomery	115	348	3.0	14	3
Barber	62	258	4.2	30	0
Brown	55	177	3.2	28	0

PASSING	Att	Comp	Pct Comp	Yds	Avg Gain	TD	Int	Rating Pts
K. Collins	332	191	57.5	2316	6.98	8	11	73.3
Graham	271	160	59.0	1697	6.26	9	9	74.6

RECEIVING	No.	Yds	Avg	Lg	TD
Toomer	79	1183	15.0	t80	6
Hilliard	72	996	13.8	46	3
Barber	66	609	9.2	56	2
Mitchell	58	520	9.0	25	1

INTERCEPTIONS: Ellsworth, 6

PUNTING	No.	Yds	Avg	Net Avg	TB	In 20	Lg	Blk
Maynard	89	3651	41.0	35.1	6	31	63	0

SACKS: Armstead, 9

St. Louis Rams

SCORING	Rush	TD Rec	Ret	PAT	FG	S	Pts
Wilkins	0	0	0	64/64	20/28	0	124
Bruce	0	12	0	0/0	0/0	0	74
Faulk	7	5	0	0/0	0/0	0	74
Hakim	0	8	1	0/0	0/0	0	54

RUSHING	No.	Yds	Avg	Lg	TD
Faulk	253	1381	5.5	58	7
Holcombe	78	294	3.8	34	4
Watson	47	179	3.8	21	0
Warner	23	92	4.0	22	1

PASSING	Att	Comp	Pct Comp	Yds	Avg Gain	TD	Int	Rating Pts
Warner	499	325	65.1	4353	8.72	41	13	109.2

RECEIVING	No.	Yds	Avg	Lg	TD
Faulk	87	1048	12.0	t57	5
Bruce	77	1165	15.1	60	12
Holt	52	788	15.2	t63	6
Hakim	36	677	18.8	t75	8

INTERCEPTIONS: Lyght, 6

PUNTING	No.	Yds	Avg	Net Avg	TB	In 20	Lg	Blk
Horan	26	1048	40.3	35.3	4	7	57	0
Tuten	32	1359	42.5	34.9	7	9	70	0

SACKS: Carter, 17

San Francisco 49ers

SCORING

	TD						
	Rush	Rec	Ret	PAT	FG	S	Pts
Richey	0	0	0	30/31	21/23	0	93
Garner	4	2	0	0/0	0/0	0	36
Rice	0	5	0	0/0	0/0	0	30
Beasley	4	0	0	0/0	0/0	0	24
Owens	0	4	0	0/0	0/0	0	24
Stokes	0	0	0	0/0	0/0	0	36

RUSHING

	No.	Yds	Avg	Lg	TD
Garner	241	1229	5.1	53	4
Beasley	58	276	4.8	t44	4
Garcia	46	221	4.8	25	2

PASSING

	Att	Comp	Pct Comp	Yds	Avg Gain	TD	Int	Rating Pts
Garcia	375	225	60.0	2544	6.78	11	11	77.9
Stenstrom	100	54	54.0	536	5.36	0	4	52.8

RECEIVING

	No.	Yds	Avg	Lg	TD
Rice	67	830	12.4	62	5
Owens	60	754	12.6	36	4
Garner	56	535	9.6	53	2
Stokes	34	429	12.6	47	3
Clark	34	347	10.2	24	0
Beasley	32	282	8.8	24	0

INTERCEPTIONS: Schulters, 6

PUNTING

	No.	Yds	Avg	Net Avg	TB	In 20	Lg	Blk
Stanley	69	2737	39.7	30.7	9	20	70	2

SACKS: B. Young, 11

Tampa Bay Buccaneers

SCORING

	TD						
	Rush	Rec	Ret	PAT	FG	S	Pts
Gramatica	0	0	0	25/25	27/32	0	106
Alstott	7	2	0	0/0	0/0	0	54
Moore	0	5	0	0/0	0/0	0	30
Green	0	3	0	0/0	0/0	0	18
Abraham	0	0	2	0/0	0/0	0	12
Dunn	0	2	0	0/0	0/0	0	12

RUSHING

	No.	Yds	Avg	Lg	TD
Alstott	242	949	3.9	30	7
Dunn	195	616	3.2	33	0
Dilfer	35	144	4.1	28	0

PASSING

	Att	Comp	Pct Comp	Yds	Avg Gain	TD	Int	Rating Pts
Dilfer	244	146	59.8	1619	6.64	11	11	75.8
King	146	89	61.0	875	5.99	7	4	82.4

RECEIVING

	No.	Yds	Avg	Lg	TD
Dunn	64	589	9.2	68	2
Green	56	791	14.1	t62	3
Anthony	30	296	9.9	30	1
Alstott	27	239	8.9	24	2
Moore	23	276	12.0	t35	5

INTERCEPTIONS: Abraham, 7

PUNTING

	No.	Yds	Avg	Net Avg	TB	In 20	Lg	Blk
Royals	90	3882	43.1	37.4	8	23	66	0

SACKS: Sapp, 12.5

Washington Redskins

SCORING

	TD						
	Rush	Rec	Ret	PAT	FG	S	Pts
Conway	0	0	0	49/50	22/32	0	115
Davis	17	0	0	0/0	0/0	0	104
Westbrook	0	9	0	0/0	0/0	0	56
Connell	0	7	0	0/0	0/0	0	42

RUSHING

	No.	Yds	Avg	Lg	TD
Davis	290	1405	4.8	t76	17
Hicks	78	257	3.3	24	3
Mitchell	40	220	5.5	16	1

PASSING

	Att	Comp	Pct Comp	Yds	Avg Gain	TD	Int	Rating Pts
Johnson	519	316	60.9	4005	7.72	24	13	90.0

RECEIVING

	No.	Yds	Avg	Lg	TD
Centers	69	544	7.9	t33	3
Westbrook	65	1191	18.3	t65	9
Connell	62	1132	18.3	t62	7
Mitchell	31	305	9.8	36	0
Alexander	29	324	11.2	t27	3

INTERCEPTIONS: Stevens, 6

PUNTING

	No.	Yds	Avg	Net Avg	TB	In 20	Lg	Blk
M. Turk	62	2564	41.4	35.6	10	16	57	0

SACKS: Wilkinson, 8

2000 NFL Draft

First two rounds of the 65th annual NFL Draft held April 15–16 in New York City.

First Round

Team	Selection	Position
1. ....Cleveland	Courtney Brown, Penn State	DE
2. ....Washington	La Varr Arrington, Penn State	LB
3. ....Washington	Chris Samuels, Alabama	OT
4. ....Cincinnati	Peter Warrick, Florida St	WR
5. ....Baltimore	Jamal Lewis, Tennessee	RB
6. ....Philadelphia	Corey Simon, Florida St	DT
7. ....Arizona	Thomas Jones, Virginia	RB
8. ....Pittsburgh	Plaxico Burress, Michigan St	WR
9. ....Chicago	Brian Urlacher, New Mexico	LB
10. ......Baltimore	Travis Taylor, Florida	WR
11. ......NY Giants	Ron Dayne, Wisconsin	RB
12. ......NY Jets	Shaun Ellis, Tennessee	DE
13. ......NY Jets	John Abraham, S Carolina	LB
14. ......Green Bay	Daniel Franks, Miami	TE
15. ......Denver	Deltha O'Neal, California	CB
16. ......San Francisco	Julian Peterson, Michigan St	LB
17. ......Oakland	Sebastian Janikowski, Florida St	K
18. ......NY Jets	Chad Pennington, Marshall	QB
19. ......Seattle	Shaun Alexander, Alabama	RB
20. ......Detroit	Stockar McDougle, Oklahoma	OT
21. ......Kansas City	Sylvester Morris, Jackson St	WR
22. ......Seattle	Chris McIntosh, Wisconsin	OT
23. ......Carolina	Rashard Anderson, Jackson St	CB
24. ......San Francisco	Ahmed Plummer, Ohio St	CB
25. ......Minnesota	Chris Hovan, Boston College	DT
26. ......Buffalo	Erik Flowers, Arizona St	LB
27. ......NY Jets	Anthony Becht, W Virginia	TE
28. ......Indianapolis	Rob Morris, Brigham Young	LB
29. ......Jacksonville	R. Jay Soward, Southern California	WR
30. ......Tennessee	Keith Bulluck, Syracuse	LB
31. ......St. Louis	Trung Canidate, Arizona	RB

Second Round

Team	Selection	Position
32. ......Cleveland	Dennis Northcutt, Arizona	WR
33. ......New Orleans	Darren Howard, Kansas St	DE
34. ......Cincinnati	Mark Roman, Louisiana St	CB
35. ......San Francisco	John Engelberger, Virginia Tech	DE
36. ......Philadelphia	Todd Pinkston, Southern Mississippi	WR
37. ......Atlanta	Travis Claridge, Southern California	OG
38. ......Pittsburgh	Marvel Smith, Arizona St	OT
39. ......Chicago	Mike Brown, Nebraska	S
40. ......Denver	Ian Gold, Michigan	LB
41. ......Arizona	Raynoch Thompson, Tennessee	LB
42. ......NY Giants	Cornelius Griffin, Alabama	DT
43. ......San Diego	Rogers Beckett, Marshall	S
44. ......Green Bay	Chad Clifton, Tennessee	OT
45. ......Denver	Kenoy Kennedy, Arkansas	S
46. ......New England	Adrian Klemm, Hawaii	OT
47. ......Oakland	Jerry Porter, W Virginia	WR
48. ......San Francisco	Jason Webster, Texas A&M	CB
49. ......Dallas	Dwayne Goodrich, Tennessee	CB
50. ......Detroit	Barrett Green, W Virginia	LB
51. ......Tampa Bay	Cosey Coleman, Tennessee	OG
52. ......Seattle	Ike Charlton, Virginia Tech	CB
53. ......Miami	Todd Wade, Ole Miss	OT
54. ......Kansas City	William Bartee, Oklahoma	CB
55. ......Minnesota	Fred Robbins, Wake Forest	DT
56. ......Minnesota	Michael Boireau, Miami	DE
57. ......Carolina	Deon Grant, Tennessee	S
58. ......Buffalo	Travares Tillman, Georgia Tech	S
59. ......Indianapolis	Marcus Washington, Auburn	LB
60. ......Jacksonville	Brad Meester, Northern Iowa	OL
61. ......Philadelphia	Bobby Williams, Arkansas	OG
62. ......St. Louis	Jacoby Shepherd, Oklahoma St	DB

But Check Out His Dropkick

With Steve Young sidelined by a concussion in the fall of 1999, 49ers coach Steve Mariucci considered using punter Chad Stanley as his emergency third quarterback. But after rating Stanley's passing arm, Mariucci quipped, "I wouldn't let him throw a paper on my porch."

Final Standings

	W	L	T	Pct	Pts	OP
Rhein*	7	3	0	.700	279	209
Scotland*	6	4	0	.600	273	165
Barcelona	5	5	0	.500	194	212
Amsterdam	4	6	0	.400	206	243
Frankfurt	4	6	0	.400	206	269
Berlin	4	6	0	.400	189	249

*Clinched World Bowl '99 berth.

2000 World Bowl

June 25, 2000, in Frankfurt

Scottish Claymores	7	3	0	0—10
Rhein Fire	3	3	0	7—13

FIRST QUARTER

Rhein: FG Burgsmuller 21, 9:48.
Scotland: Stecker 36 run (Hart kick), 8:38.

SECOND QUARTER

Scotland: FG Hart 32, 9:03.
Rhein: FG Burgsmuller 23, 4:59.

FOURTH QUARTER

Rhein: Pearson 1 run (Burgsmuller kick), 1:12.
A: 35,860.

NFL Europe Individual Leaders

PASSING

	Att	Comp	Pct Comp	Yds	Avg Gain	TD	Pct TD	Int	Pct Int	Lg	Rating Pts
K. Daft, Scotland	185	111	60.0	1231	6.65	19	10.2	3	1.6	t65	107.3
D. Wuerffel, Rhein	260	161	61.9	2042	7.85	25	9.6	7	2.7	59	107.2
P. Barnes, Frankfurt	250	138	55.2	1954	7.82	18	7.2	10	4.0	t69	88.0
C. Sauter, Barcelona	163	102	62.6	961	5.83	6	3.7	2	1.2	t38	84.8
R. Powlus, Amsterdam	287	156	54.4	1784	6.22	13	4.5	5	1.7	57	81.2

RECEIVING

RECEPTIONS	No.	Yds	Avg	Lg	TD
J. Copeland, Barcelona	74	821	11.1	42	6
M. Bailey, Frankfurt	53	873	16.5	t69	10
L.C. Stevens, Amst.	48	619	12.9	t64	6
T. Floyd, Frankfurt	45	757	16.8	t71	5
J. Ogden, Rhein	44	635	14.4	59	7

YARDS	Yds	No.	Avg	Lg	TD
M. Bailey, Frankfurt	873	53	16.5	t69	10
J. Copeland, Barcelona	821	74	11.1	42	6
D. Dunn, Berlin	794	41	19.9	t75	6
T. Floyd, Frankfurt	757	45	16.8	t71	5
J. Ogden, Rhein	635	44	14.4	59	7

RUSHING

	Att	Yds	Avg	Lg	TD
A. Stecker, Scotland	176	774	4.4	t59	7
P. Pearson, Rhein	102	486	4.8	46	3
B. Shay, Berlin	125	460	3.7	29	3
T. Battle, Barcelona	80	444	5.6	t69	4
J. Haynes, Barcelona	77	341	4.4	27	3

Other Statistical Leaders

Points (TDs)	K. Drake, Rhein	72
Points (Kicking)	R. Hart, Scotland	55
Yards from Scrimmage	A. Stecker, Scotland	1050
Interceptions	B. McElmurry, Scotland/	
	D. Hawthorne, Scotland	4
Sacks	J. Brown, Berlin	10
Punting Avg.	B. Moorman, Berlin	46.4
Punt Return Avg.	D. Gibson, Scotland	14.9
Kickoff Return Avg.	S. Sanford, Scotland	32.3

†Formerly World League of American Football.

1999 Canadian Football League

EASTERN DIVISION

	W	L	T	Pts	Pct	PF	PA
Montreal	12	6	0	24	.666	495	395
Hamilton	11	7	0	22	.611	603	378
Toronto	9	9	0	18	.500	386	373
Winnipeg	6	12	0	12	.333	362	601

WESTERN DIVISION

	W	L	T	Pts	Pct	PF	PA
British Columbia	13	5	0	26	.722	429	373
Calgary	12	6	0	24	.666	503	393
Edmonton	6	12	0	12	.333	459	502
Saskatchewan	3	15	0	6	.166	370	592

Regular Season Statistical Leaders

Points (TDs)	Ronald Williams, Hamilton	90
Points (Kicking)	Paul Osbaldiston, Hamilton	203
Yards (Rushing)	Michael Pringle, Montreal	1656
Yards (Passing)	Kerwin Bell, Winnipeg	4647
Yards (Receiving)	Allen Pitts, Calgary	1449
Receptions	Allen Pitts, Calgary	97

1999 Playoff Results

DIVISION SEMIFINALS

East: HAMILTON 27, Toronto 6
West: CALGARY 30, Edmonton 17

DIVISION FINALS

East: HAMILTON 27, Montreal 26
West: CALGARY 26, British Columbia 24

1999 Grey Cup Championship

Nov. 28, 1999, at Vancouver, British Columbia

Hamilton Tiger-Cats	10	11	4	7—32
Calgary Stampeders	0	0	14	7—21

A: 45,118.

Light Heavyweight

Six weeks into his first NFL season Jevon Kearse was finally disheartened. The Titans' defensive end had stood his ground against linemen who outweighed him by as much as 100 pounds. He was so impressive in Tennessee's first three games that he was named the NFL's Defensive Rookie of the Month for September 1999. Then Kearse was staring at a lumpy white mound in front of him, a defeated look in his eye. He could deal with gargantuan offensive tackles and double teams, but the curdled pile looming ominously before him?

"I'm just not a cottage cheese man," Kearse said, pursing his lips and shaking his head. That setback was minor though, in what was Kearse's toughest test as a pro—maintaining an adequate playing weight. The chiseled 6'4" Kearse was still listed at 265 pounds but dropped almost 20 pounds in October. Strength and rehabilitation coach Steve Watterson, concerned that Kearse's eating habits were no match calorically for the rigors of the NFL, started him on a daily regimen centered not in the weight room but in the dining room of Kearse's suburban Nashville town house. On one night, in an effort to consume roughly 3,500 calories, Kearse—while steering clear of the cottage cheese—attacked most everything else lying on the two catering trays before him, a cornucopia of steak, chicken kabobs, grilled trout, pasta with scallops and shrimp, crab salad, chicken salad, potatoes, garlic bread and a fruit basket. "If I don't put some weight on," he said through a mouthful of chicken, "I'm in trouble."

FOR THE RECORD · Year by Year

The Super Bowl

Results

	Date	Winner (Share)	Loser (Share)	Score	Site (Attendance)
I	1-15-67	Green Bay ($15,000)	Kansas City ($7,500)	35–10	Los Angeles (61,946)
II	1-14-68	Green Bay ($15,000)	Oakland ($7,500)	33–14	Miami (75,546)
III	1-12-69	NY Jets ($15,000)	Baltimore ($7,500)	16–7	Miami (75,389)
IV	1-11-70	Kansas City ($15,000)	Minnesota ($7,500)	23–7	New Orleans (80,562)
V	1-17-71	Baltimore ($15,000)	Dallas ($7,500)	16–13	Miami (79,204)
VI	1-16-72	Dallas ($15,000)	Miami ($7,500)	24–3	New Orleans (81,023)
VII	1-14-73	Miami ($15,000)	Washington ($7,500)	14–7	Los Angeles (90,182)
VIII	1-13-74	Miami ($15,000)	Minnesota ($7,500)	24–7	Houston (71,882)
IX	1-12-75	Pittsburgh ($15,000)	Minnesota ($7,500)	16–6	New Orleans (80,997)
X	1-18-76	Pittsburgh ($15,000)	Dallas ($7,500)	21–17	Miami (80,187)
XI	1-9-77	Oakland ($15,000)	Minnesota ($7,500)	32–14	Pasadena (103,438)
XII	1-15-78	Dallas ($18,000)	Denver ($9,000)	27–10	New Orleans (75,583)
XIII	1-21-79	Pittsburgh ($18,000)	Dallas ($9,000)	35–31	Miami (79,484)
XIV	1-20-80	Pittsburgh ($18,000)	Los Angeles ($9,000)	31–19	Pasadena (103,985)
XV	1-25-81	Oakland ($18,000)	Philadelphia ($9,000)	27–10	New Orleans (76,135)
XVI	1-24-82	San Francisco ($18,000)	Cincinnati ($9,000)	26–21	Pontiac, MI (81,270)
XVII	1-30-83	Washington ($36,000)	Miami ($18,000)	27–17	Pasadena (103,667)
XVIII	1-22-84	LA Raiders ($36,000)	Washington ($18,000)	38–9	Tampa (72,920)
XIX	1-20-85	San Francisco ($36,000)	Miami ($18,000)	38–16	Stanford (84,059)
XX	1-26-86	Chicago ($36,000)	New England ($18,000)	46–10	New Orleans (73,818)
XXI	1-25-87	NY Giants ($36,000)	Denver ($18,000)	39–20	Pasadena (101,063)
XXII	1-31-88	Washington ($36,000)	Denver ($18,000)	42–10	San Diego (73,302)
XXIII	1-22-89	San Francisco ($36,000)	Cincinnati ($18,000)	20–16	Miami (75,129)
XXIV	1-28-90	San Francisco ($36,000)	Denver ($18,000)	55–10	New Orleans (72,919)
XXV	1-27-91	NY Giants ($36,000)	Buffalo ($18,000)	20–19	Tampa (73,813)
XXVI	1-26-92	Washington ($36,000)	Buffalo ($18,000)	37–24	Minneapolis (63,130)
XXVII	1-31-93	Dallas ($36,000)	Buffalo ($18,000)	52–17	Pasadena (98,374)
XXVIII	1-30-94	Dallas ($38,000)	Buffalo ($23,500)	30–13	Atlanta (72,817)
XXIX	1-29-95	San Francisco ($42,000)	San Diego ($26,000)	49–26	Miami (74,107)
XXX	1-28-96	Dallas ($42,000)	Pittsburgh ($27,000)	27–17	Tempe, AZ (76,347)
XXXI	1-26-97	Green Bay ($48,000)	New England ($29,000)	35–21	New Orleans (72,301)
XXXII	1-25-98	Denver ($48,000)	Green Bay ($27,500)	31–24	San Diego (68,912)
XXXIII	1-31-99	Denver ($53,000)	Atlanta ($32,500)	34–19	Miami (74,803)
XXXIV	1-30-00	St. Louis ($58,000)	Tennessee ($33,000)	23–16	Atlanta (72,625)

Most Valuable Players

Super Bowl	Player/ Team	Position	Super Bowl	Player/ Team	Position
I	Bart Starr, GB	QB	XVIII	Marcus Allen, Rai	RB
II	Bart Starr, GB	QB	XIX	Joe Montana, SF	QB
III	Joe Namath, NYJ	QB	XX	Richard Dent, Chi	DE
IV	Len Dawson, KC	QB	XXI	Phil Simms, NYG	QB
V	Chuck Howley, Dall	LB	XXII	Doug Williams, Wash	QB
VI	Roger Staubach, Dall	QB	XXIII	Jerry Rice, SF	WR
VII	Jake Scott, Mia	S	XXIV	Joe Montana, SF	QB
VIII	Larry Csonka, Mia	RB	XXV	Ottis Anderson, NYG	RB
IX	Franco Harris, Pitt	RB	XXVI	Mark Rypien, Wash	QB
X	Lynn Swann, Pitt	WR	XXVII	Troy Aikman, Dall	QB
XI	Fred Biletnikoff, Oak	WR	XXVIII	Emmitt Smith, Dall	RB
XII	Randy White, Dall	DT	XXIX	Steve Young, SF	QB
	Harvey Martin, Dall	DE	XXX	Larry Brown, Dall	DB
XIII	Terry Bradshaw, Pitt	QB	XXXI	Desmond Howard, GB	KR
XIV	Terry Bradshaw, Pitt	QB	XXXII	Terrell Davis, Den	RB
XV	Jim Plunkett, Oak	QB	XXXIII	John Elway, Den	QB
XVI	Joe Montana, SF	QB	XXXIV	Kurt Warner, StL	QB
XVII	John Riggins, Wash	RB			

Composite Standings

	W	L	Pct	Pts	Opp Pts
San Francisco 49ers	5	0	1.000	188	89
New York Giants	2	0	1.000	59	39
Chicago Bears	1	0	1.000	46	10
New York Jets	1	0	1.000	16	7
Pittsburgh Steelers	4	1	.800	120	100
Green Bay Packers	3	1	.750	127	76
Oakland/LA Raiders	3	1	.750	111	66
Dallas Cowboys	5	3	.625	221	132
Washington Redskins	3	2	.600	122	103
Baltimore Colts	1	1	.500	23	29
Kansas City Chiefs	1	1	.500	33	42
Los Angeles/St. Louis Rams	1	1	.500	42	47
Miami Dolphins	2	3	.400	74	103
Denver Broncos	2	4	.333	115	206
Philadelphia Eagles	0	1	.000	10	27
San Diego Chargers	0	1	.000	26	49
Atlanta Falcons	0	1	.000	19	34
Tennesse Titans	0	1	.000	16	23
Cincinnati Bengals	0	2	.000	37	46
New England Patriots	0	2	.000	31	81
Buffalo Bills	0	4	.000	73	139
Minnesota Vikings	0	4	.000	34	95

Career Leaders

Passing

	GP	Att	Comp	Pct Comp	Yds	Avg Gain	TD	Pct TD	Int	Pct Int	Lg	Rating Pts
Joe Montana, SF	4	122	83	68.0	1142	9.36	11	9.0	0	0.0	44	127.8
Jim Plunkett, Rai	2	46	29	63.0	433	9.41	4	8.7	0	0.0	t80	122.8
Terry Bradshaw, Pitt	4	84	49	58.3	932	11.10	9	10.7	4	4.8	t75	112.8
Troy Aikman, Dall	3	80	56	70.0	689	8.61	5	6.3	1	1.3	t56	111.9
Bart Starr, GB	2	47	29	61.7	452	9.62	3	6.4	1	2.1	t62	106.0
Kurt Warner, StL	1	45	24	53.3	414	9.20	2	4.4	0	0.0	t73	99.6
Brett Favre, GB	2	69	39	56.5	502	7.28	5	7.2	1	1.4	t81	97.7
Roger Staubach, Dall	4	98	61	62.2	734	7.49	8	8.2	4	4.1	t45	95.4
Len Dawson, KC	2	44	28	63.6	353	8.02	2	4.5	2	4.5	t46	84.8
Bob Griese, Mia	3	41	26	63.4	295	7.20	1	2.4	2	4.9	t28	72.7

Note: Minimum 40 attempts.

Rushing

	GP	Yds	Att	Avg	Lg	TD
Franco Harris, Pitt	4	354	101	3.5	25	4
Larry Csonka, Mia	3	297	57	5.2	9	2
Emmitt Smith, Dall	3	289	70	4.1	38	5
Terrell Davis, Den	2	259	75	4.1	15	3
John Riggins, Wash	2	230	64	3.6	43	2
Timmy Smith, Wash	1	204	22	9.3	58	2
Thurman Thomas, Buff	4	204	52	3.9	31	4
Roger Craig, SF	3	198	52	3.8	18	2
Marcus Allen, Rai	1	191	20	9.6	t74	2
Tony Dorsett, Dall	2	162	31	5.2	29	1

Receiving

	GP	No.	Yds	Avg	Lg	TD
Jerry Rice, SF	3	28	512	18.3	t44	7
Andre Reed, Buff	4	27	323	11.9	40	0
Roger Craig, SF	3	20	212	10.6	40	2
Thurman Thomas, Buff	4	20	144	7.2	24	0
Jay Novacek, Dall	3	17	178	10.5	23	2
Lynn Swann, Pitt	4	16	364	22.8	t64	3
Michael Irvin, Dall	3	16	256	16.0	25	2
Chuck Foreman, Minn	3	15	139	9.3	26	0
Cliff Branch, Rai	3	14	181	12.9	50	3
Preston Pearson, Balt-Pitt-Dall	5	12	105	8.8	14	0
Don Beebe, Buff-GB	5	12	171	14.3	43	2
Kenneth Davis, Buff	4	12	72	6.0	19	0
Antonio Freeman, GB	2	12	231	19.3	t81	3

Single-Game Leaders

Scoring

	Pts
Roger Craig: XIX, San Francisco vs Miami (1 R, 2 P)	18
Jerry Rice: XXIV, San Francisco vs Denver (3 P); XXIX, SF vs San Diego (3 P)	18
Ricky Watters: XXIX, San Francisco vs San Diego (1 R, 2 P)	18
Terrell Davis: XXXII, Denver vs Green Bay (3 R)	18

Rushing Yards

	Yds
Timmy Smith: XXII, Washington vs Denver	204
Marcus Allen: XVIII, LA Raiders vs Washington	191
John Riggins: XVII, Washington vs Miami	166
Franco Harris: IX, Pittsburgh vs Minnesota	158
Terrell Davis: XXXII, Denver vs Green Bay	157
Larry Csonka: VIII, Miami vs Minnesota	145
Clarence Davis: XI, Oakland vs Minnesota	137
Thurman Thomas: XXV, Buffalo vs NY Giants	135
Emmitt Smith: XXVIII, Dallas vs Buffalo	132
Matt Snell: III, New York Jets vs Baltimore Colts	121

Receptions

	No.
Dan Ross: XVI, Cincinnati vs San Francisco	11
Jerry Rice: XXIII, San Francisco vs Cincinnati	11
Tony Nathan: XIX, Miami vs San Francisco	10
Jerry Rice: XXIX, San Francisco vs San Diego	10
Andre Hastings: XXX, Pittsburgh vs Dallas	10
Ricky Sanders: XXII, Washington vs Denver	9
Antonio Freeman: XXXII, Green Bay vs Denver	9
Six tied with eight.	

Touchdown Passes

	No.
Steve Young: XXIX, San Francisco vs San Diego	6
Joe Montana: XXIV, San Francisco vs Denver	5
Terry Bradshaw: XIII, Pittsburgh vs Dallas	4
Doug Williams: XXII, Washington vs Denver	4
Troy Aikman: XXVII, Dallas vs Buffalo	4
Five tied with three.	

Receiving Yards

	Yds
Jerry Rice: XXIII, San Francisco vs Cincinnati	215
Ricky Sanders: XXII, Washington vs Denver	193
Isaac Bruce: XXXIV, St.Louis vs Tennessee	162
Lynn Swann: X, Pittsburgh vs Dallas	161
Andre Reed: XXVII, Buffalo vs Dallas	152
Rod Smith: XXXIII, Denver vs Atlanta	152
Jerry Rice: XXIX, San Francisco vs San Diego	149
Jerry Rice: XXIV, San Francisco vs Denver	148
Max McGee: I, Green Bay vs Kansas City	138

Passing Yards

	Yds
Kurt Warner: XXXIV, St. Louis vs Tennessee	414
Joe Montana: XXIII, San Francisco vs Cincinnati	357
Doug Williams: XXII, Washington vs Denver	340
John Elway: XXXIII, Denver vs Atlanta	336
Joe Montana: XIX, San Francisco vs Miami	331
Steve Young: XXIX, San Francisco vs San Diego	325
Terry Bradshaw: XIII, Pittsburgh vs Dallas	318
Dan Marino: XIX, Miami vs San Francisco	318
Terry Bradshaw: XIV, Pittsburgh vs LA Rams	309

NFL Playoff History

1933
NFL championship Chicago Bears 23, NY Giants 21

1934
NFL championship NY Giants 30, Chicago Bears 13

1935
NFL championship Detroit 26, NY Giants 7

1936
NFL championship Green Bay 21, Boston 6

1937
NFL championship Washington 28, Chicago Bears 21

1938
NFL championship NY Giants 23, Green Bay 17

1939
NFL championship Green Bay 27, NY Giants 0

1940
NFL championship Chicago Bears 73, Washington 0

1941
W. div. playoff Chicago Bears 33, Green Bay 14
NFL championship Chicago Bears 37, NY Giants 9

1942
NFL championship Washington 14, Chicago Bears 6

1943
E. div. playoff Washington 28, NY Giants 0
NFL championship Chicago Bears 41, Washington 21

1944
NFL championship Green Bay 14, NY Giants 7

1945
NFL championship Cleveland 15, Washington 14

1946
NFL championship Chicago Bears 24, NY Giants 14

1947
E. div. playoff Philadelphia 21, Pittsburgh 0
NFL championship Chi Cardinals 28, Philadelphia 21

1948
NFL championship Philadelphia 7, Chi Cardinals 0

1949
NFL championship Philadelphia 14, Los Angeles 0

1950
Am. Conf. playoff Cleveland 8, NY Giants 3
Nat. Conf. playoff Los Angeles 24, Chicago Bears 14
NFL championship Cleveland 30, Los Angeles 28

1951
NFL championship Los Angeles 24, Cleveland 17

1952

Nat. Conf. playoff	Detroit 31, Los Angeles 21
NFL championship	Detroit 17, Cleveland 7

1953

NFL championship	Detroit 17, Cleveland 16

1954

NFL championship	Cleveland 56, Detroit 10

1955

NFL championship	Cleveland 38, Los Angeles 14

1956

NFL championship	NY Giants 47, Chicago Bears 7

1957

W. Conf. playoff	Detroit 31, San Francisco 27
NFL championship	Detroit 59, Cleveland 14

1958

E. Conf. playoff	NY Giants 10, Cleveland 0
NFL championship	Baltimore 23, NY Giants 17

1959

NFL championship	Baltimore 31, NY Giants 16

1960

NFL championship	Philadelphia 17, Green Bay 13
AFL championship	Houston 24, LA Chargers 16

1961

NFL championship	Green Bay 37, NY Giants 0
AFL championship	Houston 10, San Diego 3

1962

NFL championship	Green Bay 16, NY Giants 7
AFL championship	Dallas Texans 20, Houston 17

1963

NFL championship	Chicago 14, NY Giants 10
AFL E. div. playoff	Boston 26, Buffalo 8
AFL championship	San Diego 51, Boston 10

1964

NFL championship	Cleveland 27, Baltimore 0
AFL championship	Buffalo 20, San Diego 7

1965

NFL W. Conf. playoff	Green Bay 13, Baltimore 10
NFL championship	Green Bay 23, Cleveland 12
AFL championship	Buffalo 23, San Diego 0

1966

NFL championship	Green Bay 34, Dallas 27
AFL championship	Kansas City 31, Buffalo 7

1967

NFL E. Conf. championship	Dallas 52, Cleveland 14
NFL W. Conf. championship	Green Bay 28, Los Angeles 7
NFL championship	Green Bay 21, Dallas 17
AFL championship	Oakland 40, Houston 7

1968

NFL E. Conf. championship	Cleveland 31, Dallas 20
NFL W. Conf. championship	Baltimore 24, Minnesota 14
NFL championship	Baltimore 34, Cleveland 0

1968 (Cont.)

AFL W. div. playoff	Oakland 41, Kansas City 6
AFL championship	NY Jets 27, Oakland 23

1969

NFL E. Conf. championship	Cleveland 38, Dallas 14
NFL W. Conf. championship	Minnesota 23, Los Angeles 20
NFL championship	Minnesota 27, Cleveland 7
AFL div. playoffs	Kansas City 13, NY Jets 6
	Oakland 56, Houston 7
AFL championship	Kansas City 17, Oakland 7

1970

AFC div. playoffs	Baltimore 17, Cincinnati 0
	Oakland 21, Miami 14
AFC championship	Baltimore 27, Oakland 17
NFC div. playoffs	Dallas 5, Detroit 0
	San Francisco 17, Minnesota 14
NFC championship	Dallas 17, San Francisco 10

1971

AFC div. playoffs	Miami 27, Kansas City 24
	Baltimore 20, Cleveland 3
AFC championship	Miami 21, Baltimore 0
NFC div. playoffs	Dallas 20, Minnesota 12
	San Francisco 24, Washington 20
NFC championship	Dallas 14, San Francisco 3

1972

AFC div. playoffs	Pittsburgh 13, Oakland 7
	Miami 20, Cleveland 14
AFC championship	Miami 21, Pittsburgh 17
NFC div. playoffs	Dallas 30, San Francisco 28
	Washington 16, Green Bay 3
NFC championship	Washington 26, Dallas 3

1973

AFC div. playoffs	Oakland 33, Pittsburgh 14
	Miami 34, Cincinnati 16
AFC championship	Miami 27, Oakland 10
NFC div. playoffs	Minnesota 27, Washington 20
	Dallas 27, Los Angeles 16
NFC championship	Minnesota 27, Dallas 10

1974

AFC div. playoffs	Oakland 28, Miami 26
	Pittsburgh 32, Buffalo 14
AFC championship	Pittsburgh 24, Oakland 13
NFC div. playoffs	Minnesota 30, St Louis 14
	Los Angeles 19, Washington 10
NFC championship	Minnesota 14, Los Angeles 10

1975

AFC div. playoffs	Pittsburgh 28, Baltimore 10
	Oakland 31, Cincinnati 28
AFC championship	Pittsburgh 16, Oakland 10
NFC div. playoffs	Los Angeles 35, St Louis 23
	Dallas 17, Minnesota 14
NFC championship	Dallas 37, Los Angeles 7

1976

AFC div. playoffs	Oakland 24, New England 21
	Pittsburgh 40, Baltimore 14
AFC championship	Oakland 24, Pittsburgh 7
NFC div. playoffs	Minnesota 35, Washington 20
	Los Angeles 14, Dallas 12
NFC championship	Minnesota 24, Los Angeles 13

1977

AFC div. playoffs	Denver 34, Pittsburgh 21
	Oakland 37, Baltimore 31
AFC championship	Denver 20, Oakland 17
NFC div. playoffs	Dallas 37, Chicago 7
	Minnesota 14, Los Angeles 7
NFC championship	Dallas 23, Minnesota 6

1978

AFC 1st-rd. playoff	Houston 17, Miami 9
AFC div. playoffs	Houston 31, New England 14
	Pittsburgh 33, Denver 10
AFC championship	Pittsburgh 34, Houston 5
NFC 1st-rd. playoff	Atlanta 14, Philadelphia 13
NFC div. playoffs	Dallas 27, Atlanta 20
	Los Angeles 34, Minnesota 10
NFC championship	Dallas 28, Los Angeles 0

1979

AFC 1st-rd. playoff	Houston 13, Denver 7
AFC div. playoffs	Houston 17, San Diego 14
	Pittsburgh 34, Miami 14
AFC championship	Pittsburgh 27, Houston 13
NFC 1st-rd. playoff	Philadelphia 27, Chicago 17
NFC div. playoffs	Tampa Bay 24, Philadelphia 17
	Los Angeles 21, Dallas 19
NFC championship	Los Angeles 9, Tampa Bay 0

1980

AFC 1st-rd. playoff	Oakland 27, Houston 7
AFC div. playoffs	San Diego 20, Buffalo 14
	Oakland 14, Cleveland 12
AFC championship	Oakland 34, San Diego 27
NFC 1st-rd. playoff	Dallas 34, Los Angeles 13
NFC div. playoffs	Philadelphia 31, Minnesota 16
	Dallas 30, Atlanta 27
NFC championship	Philadelphia 20, Dallas 7

1981

AFC 1st-rd. playoff	Buffalo 31, NY Jets 27
AFC div. playoffs	San Diego 41, Miami 38
	Cincinnati 28, Buffalo 21
AFC championship	Cincinnati 27, San Diego 7
NFC 1st-rd. playoff	NY Giants 27, Philadelphia 21
NFC div. playoffs	Dallas 38, Tampa Bay 0
	San Francisco 38, NY Giants 24
NFC championship	San Francisco 28, Dallas 27

1982

AFC 1st-rd. playoffs	Miami 28, New England 13
	LA Raiders 27, Cleveland 10
	NY Jets 44, Cincinnati 17
	San Diego 31, Pittsburgh 28
AFC div. playoffs	NY Jets 17, LA Raiders 14
	Miami 34, San Diego 13
AFC championship	Miami 14, NY Jets 0
NFC 1st-rd. playoffs	Washington 31, Detroit 7
	Green Bay 41, St Louis 16
	Minnesota 30, Atlanta 24
	Dallas 30, Tampa Bay 17
NFC div. playoffs	Washington 21, Minnesota 7
	Dallas 37, Green Bay 26
NFC championship	Washington 31, Dallas 17

1983

AFC 1st-rd. playoff	Seattle 31, Denver 7
AFC div. playoffs	Seattle 27, Miami 20
	LA Raiders 38, Pittsburgh 10
AFC championship	LA Raiders 30, Seattle 14
NFC 1st-rd. playoff	LA Rams 24, Dallas 17

1983 *(Cont.)*

NFC div. playoffs	San Francisco 24, Detroit 23
	Washington 51, LA Rams 7
NFC championship	Washington 24, San Francisco 21

1984

AFC 1st-rd. playoff	Seattle 13, LA Raiders 7
AFC div. playoffs	Miami 31, Seattle 10
	Pittsburgh 24, Denver 17
AFC championship	Miami 45, Pittsburgh 28
NFC 1st-rd. playoff	NY Giants 16, LA Rams 13
NFC div. playoffs	San Francisco 21, NY Giants 10
	Chicago 23, Washington 19
NFC championship	San Francisco 23, Chicago 0

1985

AFC 1st-rd. playoff	New England 26, NY Jets 14
AFC div. playoffs	Miami 24, Cleveland 21
	New England 27, LA Raiders 20
AFC championship	New England 31, Miami 14
NFC 1st-rd. playoff	NY Giants 17, San Francisco 3
NFC div. playoffs	LA Rams 20, Dallas 0
	Chicago 21, NY Giants 0
NFC championship	Chicago 24, LA Rams 0

1986

AFC 1st-rd. playoff	NY Jets 35, Kansas City 15
AFC div. playoffs	Cleveland 23, NY Jets 20
	Denver 22, New England 17
AFC championship	Denver 23, Cleveland 20
NFC 1st-rd. playoff	Washington 19, LA Rams 7
NFC div playoffs	Washington 27, Chicago 13
	NY Giants 49, San Francisco 3
NFC championship	NY Giants 17, Washington 0

1987

AFC 1st-rd. playoff	Houston 23, Seattle 20
AFC div. playoffs	Cleveland 38, Indianapolis 21
	Denver 34, Houston 10
AFC championship	Denver 38, Cleveland 33
NFC 1st-rd. playoff	Minnesota 44, New Orleans 10
NFC div playoffs	Minnesota 36, San Francisco 24
	Washington 21, Chicago 17
NFC championship	Washington 17, Minnesota 10

1988

AFC 1st-rd. playoff	Houston 24, Cleveland 23
AFC div. playoffs	Cincinnati 21, Seattle 13
	Buffalo 17, Houston 10
AFC championship	Cincinnati 21, Buffalo 10
NFC 1st-rd. playoff	Minnesota 28, LA Rams 17
NFC div. playoffs	Chicago 20, Philadelphia 12
	San Francisco 34, Minnesota 9
NFC championship	San Francisco 28, Chicago 3

1989

AFC 1st-rd. playoff	Pittsburgh 26, Houston 23
AFC div. playoffs	Cleveland 34, Buffalo 30
	Denver 24, Pittsburgh 23
AFC championship	Denver 37, Cleveland 21
NFC 1st-rd. playoff	LA Rams 21, Philadelphia 7
NFC div. playoffs	LA Rams 19, NY Giants 13
	San Francisco 41, Minnesota 13
NFC championship	San Francisco 30, LA Rams 3

1990

AFC 1st-rd. playoffs	Miami 17, Kansas City 16
	Cincinnati 41, Houston 14
AFC div. playoffs	Buffalo 44, Miami 34
	LA Raiders 20, Cincinnati 10
AFC championship	Buffalo 51, LA Raiders 3
NFC 1st-rd. playoffs	Chicago 16, New Orleans 6

1990 *(Cont.)*

NFC 1st-rd playoffs	Washington 20, Philadelphia 6
NFC div. playoffs	NY Giants 31, Chicago 3
	San Francisco 28, Washington 10
NFC championship	NY Giants 15, San Francisco 13

1991

AFC 1st-rd. playoffs	Houston 17, NY Jets 10
	Kansas City 10, LA Raiders 6
AFC div. playoffs	Denver 26, Houston 24
	Buffalo 37, Kansas City 14
AFC championship	Buffalo 10, Denver 7
NFC 1st-rd. playoffs	Atlanta 27, New Orleans 20
	Dallas 17, Chicago 13
NFC div. playoffs	Washington 24, Atlanta 7
	Detroit 38, Dallas 6
NFC championship	Washington 41, Detroit 10

1992

AFC 1st-rd. playoffs	San Diego 17, Kansas City 0
	Buffalo 41, Houston 38 (OT)
AFC div. playoffs	Buffalo 24, Pittsburgh 3
	Miami 31, San Diego 0
AFC championship	Buffalo 29, Miami 10
NFC 1st-rd. playoffs	Washington 24, Minnesota 7
	Philadelphia 36, New Orleans 20
NFC div. playoffs	San Francisco 20, Washington 13
	Dallas 34, Philadelphia 10
NFC championship	Dallas 30, San Francisco 20

1993

AFC 1st-rd. playoffs	LA Raiders 42, Denver 24
	Kansas City 27, Pittsburgh 24 (OT)
AFC div. playoffs	Buffalo 29, LA Raiders 23
	Kansas City 28, Houston 20
AFC championship	Buffalo 30, Kansas City 13
NFC 1st-rd. playoffs	NY Giants 17, Minnesota 10
	Green Bay 28, Detroit 24
NFC div. playoffs	San Francisco 44, NY Giants 3
	Dallas 27, Green Bay 17
NFC championship	Dallas 38, San Francisco 21

1994

AFC 1st-rd. playoffs	Miami 27, Kansas City 17
	Cleveland 20, New England 13
AFC div. playoffs	San Diego 22, Miami 21
	Pittsburgh 29, Cleveland 9
AFC championship	San Diego 17, Pittsburgh 13
NFC 1st-rd. playoffs	Green Bay 16, Detroit 12
	Chicago 35, Minnesota 18
NFC div. playoffs	Dallas 35, Green Bay 9
	San Francisco 44, Chicago 15
NFC championship	San Francisco 38, Dallas 28

1995

AFC 1st-rd. playoffs	Buffalo 37, Miami 22
	Indianapolis 35, San Diego 20
AFC div. playoffs	Pittsburgh 40, Buffalo 21
	Indianapolis 10, Kansas City 7
AFC championship	Pittsburgh 20, Indianapolis 16
NFC 1st-rd. playoffs	Philadelphia 58, Detroit 37
	Green Bay 37, Atlanta 20
NFC div. playoffs	Dallas 30, Philadelphia 11
	Green Bay 27, San Francisco 17
NFC championship	Dallas 38, Green Bay 27

1996

AFC 1st-rd. playoffs	Jacksonville 30, Buffalo 27
	Pittsburgh 42, Indianapolis 14
AFC div. playoffs	Jacksonville 30, Denver 27
	New England 28, Pittsburgh 3
AFC championship	New England 20, Jacksonville 6

1996 *(Cont.)*

NFC 1st-rd. playoffs	Dallas 40, Minnesota 15
	San Francisco 14, Philadelphia 0
NFC div. playoffs	Green Bay 35, San Francisco 14
	Carolina 26, Dallas 17
NFC championship	Green Bay 30, Carolina 13

1997

AFC 1st-rd. playoffs	Denver 42, Jacksonville 17
	New England 17, Miami 3
AFC div. playoffs	Denver 14, Kansas City 0
	Pittsburgh 7, New England 6
AFC championship	Denver 24, Pittsburgh 21
NFC 1st-rd. playoffs	Minnesota 23, NY Giants 22
	Tampa Bay 20, Detroit 10
NFC div. playoffs	Green Bay 21, Tampa Bay 7
	San Francisco 38, Minnesota 22
NFC championship	Green Bay 23, San Francisco 10

1998

AFC 1st-rd. playoffs	Miami 24, Buffalo 17
	Jacksonville 25, New England 10
AFC div. playoffs	Denver 38, Miami 3
	NY Jets 34, Jacksonville 24
AFC championship	Denver 23, NY Jets 10
NFC 1st-rd. playoffs	Arizona 20, Dallas 7
	San Francisco 30, Green Bay 27
NFC div. playoffs	Atlanta 20, San Francisco 18
	Minnesota 41, Arizona 21
NFC championship	Atlanta 30, Minnesota 27 (OT)

1999

AFC 1st-rd. playoffs	Tennessee 22, Buffalo 16
	Miami 20, Seattle 17
AFC div. playoffs	Jacksonville 62, Miami 7
	Tennessee 19, Indianapolis 16
AFC championship	Tennessee 33, Jacksonville 14
NFC 1st-rd. playoffs	Washington 27, Detroit 13
	Minnesota 27, Dallas 10
NFC div. playoffs	Tampa Bay 14, Washington 13
	St Louis 49, Minnesota 37
NFC championship	St Louis 11, Tampa Bay 6

Light My Ire

A bitter rivalry is born: After Akili Smith, the third pick in the 1999 draft, quarterbacked the Bengals to a last-second 18–17 win over No. 1 pick Tim Couch and the Browns, Couch said he was angered by Smith's excessive celebrating on the field. "I'll definitely remember that," Couch said. Countered Smith, who drew Couch's ire by pounding his chest after the winning score, yelling at the Cleveland bench and dancing in front of the Dawg Pound after the game: "I hope he remembers it the rest of his career. There's no doubt in my mind who the better quarterback is. Period."

Career Leaders

Scoring

	Yrs	TD	FG	PAT	Pts
George Blanda	26	9	335	943	2002
†Gary Anderson	18	0	439	631	1948
†Morten Andersen	18	0	416	592	1840
†Norm Johnson	18	0	366	638	1736
Nick Lowery	18	0	383	562	1711
Jan Stenerud	19	0	373	580	1699
†Eddie Murray	18	0	344	532	1564
Pat Leahy	18	0	304	558	1470
†Al Del Greco	16	0	320	506	1466
Jim Turner	16	1	304	521	1439
Matt Bahr	17	0	300	522	1422
Mark Moseley	16	0	300	482	1382
Jim Bakken	17	0	282	534	1380
Fred Cox	15	0	282	519	1365
Lou Groza	17	1	234	641	1349
Jim Breech	14	0	243	517	1246
Chris Bahr	14	0	241	490	1213
Kevin Butler	13	0	265	426	1208
†Pete Stoyanovich	11	0	267	394	1195
Gino Cappelletti	11	42	176	350	1130

Cappelletti's total includes four two-point conversions.

Rushing

	Yrs	Att	Yds	Avg	Lg	TD
Walter Payton	13	3,838	16,726	4.4	76	110
Barry Sanders	10	3,062	15,269	5.0	85	99
†Emmitt Smith	10	3,243	13,963	4.3	75	138
Eric Dickerson	11	2,996	13,259	4.4	85	90
Tony Dorsett	12	2,936	12,739	4.3	99	77
Jim Brown	9	2,359	12,312	5.2	80	106
Marcus Allen	16	3,022	12,243	4.1	61	123
Franco Harris	13	2,949	12,120	4.1	75	91
†Thurman Thomas	12	2,849	11,938	4.1	80	66
John Riggins	14	2,916	11,352	3.9	66	104
O.J. Simpson	11	2,404	11,236	4.7	94	61
Ottis Anderson	14	2,562	10,273	4.0	76	81
Earl Campbell	8	2,187	9,407	4.3	81	74
†Ricky Watters	8	2,272	9,083	4.0	57	70
Jim Taylor	10	1,941	8,597	4.4	84	83
†Jerome Bettis	7	2,106	8,463	4.0	t71	41
Joe Perry	14	1,737	8,378	4.8	78	53
Earnest Byner	14	2,095	8,261	3.9	54	56
Herschel Walker	12	1,954	8,225	4.2	91	61
Roger Craig	11	1,991	8,189	4.1	71	56

Touchdowns

	Yrs	Rush	Pass Rec	Ret	Total TD		Yrs	Rush	Pass Rec	Ret	Total TD
†Jerry Rice	15	10	169	1	180	Franco Harris	13	91	9	0	100
†Emmitt Smith	10	136	11	0	147	Eric Dickerson	11	90	6	0	96
Marcus Allen	16	123	21	1	145	Jim Taylor	10	83	10	0	93
Jim Brown	9	106	20	0	126	Tony Dorsett	12	77	13	1	91
Walter Payton	13	110	15	0	125	Bobby Mitchell	11	18	65	8	91
John Riggins	14	104	12	0	116	Leroy Kelly	10	74	13	3	90
†Cris Carter	13	0	114	1	115	Charley Taylor	13	11	79	0	90
Lenny Moore	12	63	48	2	113	Don Maynard	15	0	88	0	88
Barry Sanders	10	99	10	0	109	Lance Alworth	11	2	85	0	87
Don Hutson	11	3	99	3	105	†Andre Reed	15	1	86	0	87
Steve Largent	14	1	100	0	101	†Thurman Thomas	12	65	22	0	87

Combined Yards Gained

	Yrs	Total	Rush	Rec	Int Ret	Punt Ret	Kickoff Ret	Fum Ret
Walter Payton	13	21,803	16,726	4,538	0	0	539	0
†Jerry Rice	15	19,075	627	18,442	0	0	6	0
Barry Sanders	10	18,308	15,269	2,921	0	0	118	0
Herschel Walker	12	18,168	8,225	4,859	0	0	5,084	0
Marcus Allen	16	17,648	12,243	5,411	0	0	0	-6
†Brian Mitchell	10	16,905	1,751	2,087	0	3,476	9,586	5
†Eric Metcalf	11	16,727	2,385	5,553	0	3,042	5,747	0
†Emmitt Smith	10	16,691	13,963	2,728	0	0	0	0
Tony Dorsett	12	16,326	12,739	3,554	0	0	0	33
†Thurman Thomas	12	16,279	11,938	4,341	0	0	0	0
Henry Ellard	16	15,718	50	13,777	0	1,527	364	0
Jim Brown	9	15,459	12,312	2,499	0	0	648	0
Eric Dickerson	11	15,411	13,259	2,137	0	0	0	15
†Tim Brown	12	15,408	120	10,944	0	3,106	1,235	3
†Irving Fryar	16	15,030	226	12,237	0	2,055	505	7
James Brooks	12	14,910	7,962	3,621	0	565	2,762	0
Franco Harris	13	14,622	12,120	2,287	0	0	233	-18
O.J. Simpson	11	14,368	11,236	2,142	0	0	990	0
James Lofton	16	14,277	246	14,004	0	0	0	27
Bobby Mitchell	11	14,078	2,735	7,954	0	699	2,690	0

† Active player.

Career Leaders *(Cont.)*

Passing
PASSING EFFICIENCY*

	Yrs	Att	Comp	Pct Comp	Yds	Avg Gain	TD	Pct TD	Int	Pct Int	Rating Pts
Steve Young	15	4,149	2,667	64.3	33,124	7.98	232	5.6	107	2.6	96.8
Joe Montana	15	5,391	3,409	63.2	40,551	7.52	273	5.1	139	2.6	92.3
†Brett Favre	9	4,352	2,659	61.1	30,894	7.10	235	5.4	141	3.2	87.1
Dan Marino	17	8,358	4,967	59.4	61,361	7.34	420	5.0	252	3.0	86.4
†Mark Brunell	6	2,160	1,297	60.0	15,572	7.21	86	4.0	52	2.4	85.4
Jim Kelly	11	4,779	2,874	60.1	35,467	7.42	237	5.0	175	3.7	84.4
Roger Staubach	11	2,958	1,685	57.0	22,700	7.67	153	5.2	109	3.7	83.4
Neil Lomax	8	3,153	1,817	57.6	22,771	7.22	136	4.3	90	2.9	82.7
†Troy Aikman	11	4,453	2,742	61.6	31,310	7.03	158	3.5	127	2.9	82.6
Sonny Jurgensen	18	4,262	2,433	57.1	32,224	7.56	255	6.0	189	4.4	82.6
Len Dawson	19	3,741	2,136	57.1	28,711	7.67	239	6.4	183	4.9	82.6
†Neil O'Donnell	10	3,057	1,766	57.8	20,408	6.68	114	3.7	62	2.0	82.0
Ken Anderson	16	4,475	2,654	59.3	32,838	7.34	197	4.4	160	3.6	81.9
Bernie Kosar	12	3,365	1,994	59.3	23,301	6.92	124	3.7	87	2.6	81.8
Danny White	13	2,950	1,761	59.7	21,959	7.44	155	5.3	132	4.5	81.7
Dave Krieg	19	5,311	3,105	58.5	38,147	7.18	261	4.9	199	3.7	81.5
†Randall Cunningham	14	4,075	2,301	56.5	28,557	7.01	198	4.9	128	3.1	81.4
†Chris Chandler	12	2,894	1,668	57.6	20,865	7.21	135	4.7	101	3.5	81.2
†Steve Beuerlein	13	2,615	1,469	56.2	19,002	7.27	120	4.6	84	3.2	81.1
Boomer Esiason	14	5,205	2,969	57.0	37,920	7.29	247	4.7	184	3.5	81.1

*1,500 or more attempts. The passer ratings are based on performance standards established for completion percentage, interception percentage, touchdown percentage and average gain. Passers are allocated points according to how their marks compare with those standards.

YARDS

	Yrs	Att	Comp	Pct Comp	Yds		Yrs	Att	Comp	Pct Comp	Yds
Dan Marino	17	8,358	4,967	59.4	61,361	Jim Everett	12	4,923	2,841	57.7	34,837
John Elway	16	7,250	4,123	56.9	51,475	Jim Hart	19	5,076	2,593	51.1	34,665
†Warren Moon	16	6789	3,973	58.5	49,117	Steve DeBerg	17	4,746	2,924	61.6	34,241
Fran Tarkenton	18	6,467	3,686	57.0	47,003	John Hadl	16	4,687	2,363	50.4	33,503
Dan Fouts	15	5,604	3,297	58.8	43,040	Phil Simms	14	4,647	2,576	55.4	33,462
Joe Montana	15	5,391	3,409	63.2	40,551	Steve Young	15	4,149	2,667	64.3	33,124
Johnny Unitas	18	5,186	2,830	54.6	40,239	Ken Anderson	16	4,475	2,654	59.3	32,838
Dave Krieg	19	5,311	3,105	58.5	38,147	†Vinny Testaverde	13	4,618	2,569	55.7	32,575
Boomer Esiason	14	5,205	2,969	57.0	37,920	Sonny Jurgensen	18	4,262	2,433	57.1	32,224
Jim Kelly	11	4,779	2,874	60.1	35,467	John Brodie	17	4,491	2,469	55.0	31,548

TOUCHDOWNS

	No.		No.		No.
Dan Marino	420	John Hadl	244	†Vinny Testaverde	205
Fran Tarkenton	342	Len Dawson	239	Jim Everett	203
John Elway	300	Jim Kelly	237	Phil Simms	199
Johnny Unitas	290	George Blanda	236	†Randall Cunningham	198
†Warren Moon	290	†Brett Favre	235	Ken Anderson	197
Joe Montana	273	Steve Young	232	Joe Ferguson	196
Dave Krieg	261	John Brodie	214	Bobby Layne	196
Sonny Jurgensen	255	Terry Bradshaw	212	Norm Snead	196
Dan Fouts	254	Y.A. Tittle	212	Steve DeBerg	196
Boomer Esiason	247	Jim Hart	209	Ken Stabler	194

† Active player.

Career Leaders *(Cont.)*

Receiving

RECEPTIONS

	Yrs	No.	Yds	Avg	Lg	TD		Yrs	No.	Yds	Avg	Lg	TD
†Jerry Rice	15	1,206	18,442	15.3	96	169	†Michael Irvin	12	750	11,904	15.9	87	65
†Andre Reed	15	941	13,095	13.9	83	86	†Andre Rison	11	702	9,599	13.7	80	78
Art Monk	16	940	12,721	13.5	79	68	Gary Clark	11	699	10,856	15.5	84	65
†Cris Carter	13	924	11,688	12.6	80	114	Ozzie Newsome	13	662	7,980	12.1	74	47
Steve Largent	14	819	13,089	16.0	74	100	Charley Taylor	13	649	9,110	14.0	88	79
Henry Ellard	16	814	13,777	16.9	81	65	Drew Hill	14	634	9,831	15.5	81	60
†Irving Fryar	16	810	12,237	15.1	80	79	Don Maynard	15	633	11,834	18.7	87	88
†Tim Brown	12	770	10,944	14.2	80	75	Raymond Berry	13	631	9,275	14.7	70	68
James Lofton	16	764	14,004	18.3	80	75	†Rob Moore	10	628	9,368	14.9	71	49
Charlie Joiner	18	750	12,146	16.2	87	65	†Herman Moore	9	626	8,664	13.8	93	59

YARDS

†Jerry Rice	18,442	Charlie Joiner	12,146	Harold Jackson	10,372
James Lofton	14,004	†Michael Irvin	11,904	Lance Alworth	10,266
Henry Ellard	13,777	Don Maynard	11,834	Drew Hill	9,831
†Andre Reed	13,095	†Cris Carter	11,688	†Andre Rison	9,599
Steve Largent	13,089	†Tim Brown	10,944	†Rob Moore	9,368
Art Monk	12,721	Gary Clark	10,856	Raymond Berry	9,275
†Irving Fryar	12,237	Stanley Morgan	10,716		

Sacks

Reggie White	192.5	Chris Doleman	150.5
†Bruce Smith	171.0	Richard Dent	137.5
Kevin Greene	160.0		

Note: Officially compiled since 1982.

Interceptions

	Yrs	No.	Yds	Avg	Lg	TD
Paul Krause	16	81	1185	14.6	81	3
Emlen Tunnell	14	79	1282	16.2	55	4
Dick (Night Train) Lane	14	68	1207	17.8	80	5
Ken Riley	15	65	596	9.2	66	5
Ronnie Lott	14	63	730	11.6	83	5

Punt Returns

	Yrs	No.	Yds	Avg	Lg	TD
George McAfee	8	112	1431	12.8	74	2
Jack Christiansen	8	85	1084	12.8	89	8
Claude Gibson	5	110	1381	12.6	85	3
†Darrien Gordon	6	219	2726	12.4	94	6
†Karl Williams	4	89	1107	12.4	88	2

Note: 75 or more returns.

Punting

	Yrs	No.	Yds	Avg	Lg	Blk
Sammy Baugh	16	338	15,245	45.1	85	9
Tommy Davis	11	511	22,833	44.7	82	2
†Darren Bennett	5	432	19,244	44.5	66	1
Yale Lary	11	503	22,279	44.3	74	4
†Tom Rouen	7	470	20,784	44.2	76	3

Note: 250 or more punts.

Kickoff Returns

	Yrs	No.	Yds	Avg	Lg	TD
Gale Sayers	7	91	2781	30.6	103	6
Lynn Chandnois	7	92	2720	29.6	93	3
Abe Woodson	9	193	5538	28.7	105	5
Claude (Buddy) Young	6	90	2514	27.9	104	2
Travis Williams	5	102	2801	27.5	105	6

Note: 75 or more returns.

† Active player.

Single-Season Leaders

Scoring

POINTS

	Year	TD	PAT	FG	Pts
Paul Hornung, GB	1960	15	41	15	176
Gary Anderson, Minn	1998	0	59	35	164
Mark Moseley, Wash	1983	0	62	33	161
Gino Cappelletti, Bos	1964	7	38	25	155
Emmitt Smith, Dall	1995	25	0	0	150
Chip Lohmiller, Wash	1991	0	56	31	149
Gino Cappelletti, Bos	1961	8	48	17	147
Paul Hornung, GB	1961	10	41	15	146
Jim Turner, NYJ	1968	0	43	34	145
John Kasay, Car	1996	0	34	37	145
Mike Vanderjagt	1999	0	34	38	145
John Riggins, Wash	1983	24	0	0	144
Kevin Butler, Chi	1985	0	51	31	144
Olindo Mare, Mia	1999	0	27	39	144

Note: Cappelletti's 1964 total includes a two-point conversion.

TOUCHDOWNS

	Year	Rush	Rec	Ret	Total
Emmitt Smith, Dall	1995	25	0	0	25
John Riggins, Wash	1983	24	0	0	24
O.J. Simpson, Buff	1975	16	7	0	23
Jerry Rice, SF	1987	1	22	0	23
Terrell Davis, Den	1998	21	2	0	23
Gale Sayers, Chi	1965	14	6	2	22
Emmitt Smith, Dall	1994	21	1	0	22

FIELD GOALS

	Year	Att	No.
Olindo Mare, Mia	1999	46	39
John Kasay, Car	1996	45	37
Cary Blanchard, Ind	1996	40	36
Al Del Greco, Tenn	1998	39	36
Gary Anderson, Minn	1998	35	35
Jeff Jaeger, LA Raiders	1993	44	35
Ali Haji-Sheikh, NYG	1983	42	35

Six tied with 34.

Rushing

YARDS GAINED

	Year	Att	Yds	Avg
Eric Dickerson, LA Rams	1984	379	2105	5.6
Barry Sanders, Det	1997	335	2053	6.1
Terrell Davis, Den	1998	392	2008	5.1
O.J. Simpson, Buff	1973	332	2003	6.0
Earl Campbell, Hou	1980	373	1934	5.2
Jim Brown, Clev	1963	291	1883	6.4
Barry Sanders, Det	1994	331	1883	5.7
Walter Payton, Chi	1977	339	1852	5.5
Jamal Anderson, Atl	1998	410	1846	4.5
Eric Dickerson, LA Rams	1986	404	1821	4.5
O.J. Simpson, Buff	1975	329	1817	5.5
Eric Dickerson, LA Rams	1983	390	1808	4.6

AVERAGE GAIN

	Year	Avg
Beattie Feathers, Chi	1934	8.44
Randall Cunningham, Phil	1990	7.98
Bobby Douglass, Chi	1972	6.87

Minimum 100 attempts.

TOUCHDOWNS

	Year	No.
Emmitt Smith, Dall	1995	25
John Riggins, Wash	1983	24
Emmitt Smith, Dall	1994	21
Joe Morris, NYG	1985	21
Terry Allen, Wash	1996	21
Terrell Davis, Den	1998	21

Passing

YARDS GAINED

	Year	Att	Comp	Pct	Yds
Dan Marino, Mia	1984	564	362	64.2	5084
Dan Fouts, SD	1981	609	360	59.1	4802
Dan Marino, Mia	1986	623	378	60.7	4746
Dan Fouts, SD	1980	589	348	59.1	4715
Warren Moon, Hou	1991	655	404	61.7	4690
Warren Moon, Hou	1990	584	362	62.0	4689
Neil Lomax, StL Cards	1984	560	345	61.6	4614
Drew Bledsoe, NE	1994	691	400	57.9	4555
Lynn Dickey, GB	1983	484	289	59.7	4458
Dan Marino, Mia	1994	615	385	62.6	4453

PASSER RATING

	Year	Rat.
Steve Young, SF	1994	112.8
Joe Montana, SF	1989	112.4
Milt Plum, Clev	1960	110.4
Sammy Baugh, Wash	1945	109.9
Kurt Warner, Rams	1999	109.2

TOUCHDOWNS

	Year	No.
Dan Marino, Mia	1984	48
Dan Marino, Mia	1986	44
Kurt Warner, StL	1999	41
Brett Favre, GB	1995	38

Three tied with 36

Single-Season Leaders (Cont.)
Receiving

RECEPTIONS

	Year	No.	Yds
Herman Moore, Det	1995	123	1686
Cris Carter, Minn	1994	122	1256
Jerry Rice, SF	1995	122	1848
Cris Carter, Minn	1995	122	1371
Isaac Bruce, Rams	1995	119	1781
Jimmy Smith, Jax	1999	116	1636
Marvin Harrison, Ind	1999	115	1663
Sterling Sharpe, GB	1993	112	1274
Jerry Rice, SF	1994	112	1499
Terance Mathis, Atl	1994	111	1342
Michael Irvin, Dall	1995	111	1603

YARDS GAINED

	Year	Yds
Jerry Rice, SF	1995	1848
Isaac Bruce, Rams	1995	1781
Charley Hennigan, Hou	1961	1746
Herman Moore, Det	1995	1686
Marvin Harrison, Ind	1999	1663

TOUCHDOWNS

	Year	No.
Jerry Rice, SF	1987	22
Mark Clayton, Mia	1984	18
Sterling Sharpe, GB	1994	18

Six tied with 17.

All-Purpose Yards

	Year	Run	Rec	Ret	Total
Lionel James, SD	1985	516	1027	992	2535
Terry Metcalf, StL Cards	1975	816	378	1268	2462
Mack Herron, NE	1974	824	474	1146	2444
Gale Sayers, Chi	1966	1231	447	762	2440
Marshall Faulk, Rams	1999	1381	1048	0	2429
Timmy Brown, Phil	1963	841	487	1100	2428
Barry Sanders, Det	1997	2053	305	0	2358
Tim Brown, Rai	1988	50	725	1542	2317
Marcus Allen, Rai	1985	1759	555	-6	2308
Timmy Brown, Phil	1962	545	849	912	2306
Gale Sayers, Chi	1965	867	507	898	2272
Eric Dickerson, Rams	1984	2105	139	15	2259

Interceptions

	Year	No.
Dick (Night Train) Lane, Rams	1952	14
Dan Sandifer, Wash	1948	13
Spec Sanders, NY Yanks	1950	13
Lester Hayes, Oak	1980	13

Nine tied with 12.

Punt Returns

	Year	Avg
Herb Rich, Balt Colts	1950	23.0
Jack Christiansen, Det	1952	21.5
Dick Christy, NY Titans	1961	21.3
Bob Hayes, Dall	1968	20.8

Punting

	Year	No.	Yds	Avg
Sammy Baugh, Wash	1940	35	1799	51.4
Yale Lary, Det	1963	35	1713	48.9
Sammy Baugh, Wash	1941	30	1462	48.7
Yale Lary, Det	1961	52	2516	48.4
Sammy Baugh, Wash	1942	37	1783	48.2

Sacks

	Year	No.
Mark Gastineau, NYJ	1984	22
Reggie White, Phil	1987	21
Chris Doleman, Minn	1989	21
Lawrence Taylor, NYG	1986	20.5

Kickoff Returns

	Year	Avg
Travis Williams, GB	1967	41.1
Gale Sayers, Chi	1967	37.7
Ollie Matson, Chi Cards	1958	35.5
Jim Duncan, Balt Colts	1970	35.4
Lynn Chandnois, Pitt	1952	35.2

Single-Game Leaders
Scoring

POINTS

	Date	Pts
Ernie Nevers, Chi Cards vs Chi	11-28-29	40
Dub Jones, Clev vs Chi	11-25-51	36
Gale Sayers, Chi vs SF	12-12-65	36
Paul Hornung, GB vs Balt Colts	10-8-61	33

On Thanksgiving Day, 1929, Nevers scored all the Cardinals' points on six rushing TDs and four PATs. The Cards defeated Red Grange and the Bears, 40-6. Jones and Sayers each rushed for four touchdowns and scored two more on returns in their teams' victories. Hornung scored four touchdowns and kicked 6 PATs and a field goal in a 45-7 win over the Colts.

FIELD GOALS

	Date	No.
Jim Bakken, StL Cards vs Pitt	9-24-67	7
Rich Karlis, Minn vs Rams	11-5-89	7
Chris Boniol, Dall vs GB	11-18-96	7

Fourteen players tied with 6 FGs each.
Bakken was 7 for 9, Karlis and Boniol 7 for 7.

Single-Game Leaders *(Cont.)*

Scoring *(Cont.)*

TOUCHDOWNS

	Date	No.
Ernie Nevers, Chi Cards vs Chi	11-28-29	6
Dub Jones, Clev vs Chi	11-25-51	6
Gale Sayers, Chi vs SF	12-12-65	6
Bob Shaw, Chi Cards vs Balt Colts	10-2-50	5
Jim Brown, Clev vs Balt Colts	11-1-59	5
Abner Haynes, Dall Texans vs Oak	11-26-61	5
Billy Cannon, Hou vs NY Titans	12-10-61	5
Cookie Gilchrist, Buff vs NYJ	12-8-63	5
Paul Hornung, GB vs Balt Colts	12-12-65	5
Kellen Winslow, SD vs Oak	11-22-81	5
Jerry Rice, SF vs Atl	10-14-90	5
James Stewart, Jax vs Phil	10-12-97	5

Rushing

YARDS GAINED

	Date	Yds
Walter Payton, Chi vs Minn	11-20-77	275
O.J. Simpson, Buff vs Det	11-25-76	273
O.J. Simpson, Buff vs NE	9-16-73	250
Willie Ellison, Rams vs NO	12-5-71	247
Corey Dillon, Cin vs Tenn	12-4-97	246

CARRIES

	Date	No.
Jamie Morris, Wash vs Cin	12-17-88	45
Butch Woolfolk, NYG vs Phil	11-20-83	43
James Wilder, TB vs GB	9-30-84	43
James Wilder, TB vs Pitt	10-30-83	42
Franco Harris, Pitt vs Cin	10-17-76	41
Gerald Riggs, Atl vs Rams	11-17-85	41

TOUCHDOWNS

	Date	No.
Ernie Nevers, Chi Cards vs Chi	11-28-29	6
Jim Brown, Clev vs Balt Colts	11-1-59	5
Cookie Gilchrist, Buff vs NYJ	12-8-63	5
James Stewart, Jax vs Phil	10-12-97	5

Passing

YARDS GAINED

	Date	Yds
N. Van Brocklin, Rams vs NY Yanks	9-28-51	554
Warren Moon, Hou vs KC	12-16-90	527
Boomer Esiason, Ariz vs Wash	11-10-96	522
Dan Marino, Mia vs NYJ	10-23-88	521
Phil Simms, NYG vs Cin	10-13-85	513

COMPLETIONS

	Date	No.
Drew Bledsoe, NE vs Minn	11-13-94	45
Richard Todd, NYJ vs SF	9-21-80	42
Warren Moon, Hou vs Dall	11-10-91	41
Ken Anderson, Cin vs SD	12-20-82	40
Phil Simms, NYG vs Cin	10-13-85	40
Vinny Testaverde, NYJ vs Sea	12-6-98	42

TOUCHDOWNS

	Date	No.
Sid Luckman, Chi vs NYG	11-14-43	7
Adrian Burk, Phil vs Wash	10-17-54	7
George Blanda, Hou vs NY Titans	11-19-61	7
Y. A. Tittle, NYG vs Wash	10-28-62	7
Joe Kapp, Minn vs Balt Colts	9-28-69	7

Receiving

YARDS GAINED

	Date	Yds
Flipper Anderson, Rams vs NO	11-26-89	336
Stephone Paige, KC vs SD	12-22-85	309
Jim Benton, Clev vs Det	11-22-45	303
Cloyce Box, Det vs Balt Colts	12-3-50	302
Jerry Rice, SF vs Minn	12-18-95	289

RECEPTIONS

	Date	No.
Tom Fears, Rams vs GB	12-3-50	18
Clark Gaines, NYJ vs SF	9-21-80	17
Sonny Randle, StL Cards vs NYG	11-4-62	16
Jerry Rice, SF vs Rams	11-20-94	16
Keenan McCardell, Jax vs Rams	10-20-96	16
Rickey Young, Minn vs NE	12-16-79	15
William Andrews, Atl vs Pitt	11-15-81	15
Andre Reed, Buff vs GB	11-20-94	15
Isaac Bruce, Rams vs Mia	12-24-95	15

Single-Game Leaders (Cont.)

Receiving (Cont.)

TOUCHDOWNS

	Date	No.
Bob Shaw, Chi Cards vs Balt Colts	10-2-50	5
Kellen Winslow, SD vs Oak	11-22-81	5
Jerry Rice, SF vs Atl	10-14-90	5

All-Purpose Yards

	Date	Yds
Glyn Milburn, Den vs Sea	12-10-95	404
Billy Cannon, Hou vs NY Titans	12-10-61	373
Tyrone Hughes, NO vs LA Rams	10-23-94	347
Lionel James, SD vs LA Rai	11-10-85	345
Timmy Brown, Phil vs St.L Cards	12-16-62	341

Longest Plays

RUSHING	Opponent	Year	Yds
Tony Dorsett, Dall	Minn	1983	99
Andy Uram, GB	Chi Cards	1939	97
Bob Gage, Pitt	Chi	1949	97
Jim Spitival, Balt Colts	GB	1950	96
Bob Hoernschemeyer, Det	NY Yanks	1950	96
Garrison Hearst, SF	NYJ	1998	96

PASSING	Opponent	Year	Yds
Frank Filchock to Andy Farkas, Wash	Pitt	1939	99
George Izo to Bobby Mitchell, Wash	Clev	1963	99
Karl Sweatan to Pat Studstill, Det	Balt Colts	1966	99
Sonny Jurgensen to Gerry Allen, Wash	Chi	1968	99
Jim Plunkett to Cliff Branch, LA Rai	Wash	1983	99
Ron Jaworski to Mike Quick, Phil	Atl	1985	99
Stan Humphries to Tony Martin, SD	Sea	1994	99
Brett Favre to Robert Brooks, GB	Chi	1995	99

FIELD GOALS	Opponent	Year	Yds
Tom Dempsey, NO	Det	1970	63
Jason Elam, Den	Jax	1998	63
Steve Cox, Clev	Cin	1984	60
Morten Andersen, NO	Chi	1991	60

PUNTS	Opponent	Year	Yds
Steve O'Neal, NYJ	Den	1969	98
Joe Lintzenich, Chi	NYG	1931	94
Shawn McCarthy, NE	Buff	1991	93
Randall Cunningham, Phil	NYG	1989	91

INTERCEPTION RETURNS	Opponent	Year	Yds
Vencie Glenn, SD	Den	1987	103
Louis Oliver, Mia	Buff	1992	103
Six players tied at 102.			

KICKOFF RETURNS	Opponent	Year	Yds
Al Carmichael, GB	Chi	1956	106
Noland Smith, KC	Den	1967	106
Roy Green, StL Cards	Dall	1979	106

PUNT RETURNS	Opponent	Year	Yds
Robert Bailey, LA Rams	NO	1994	103
Gil LeFebvre, Cin	Brooklyn	1933	98
Charlie West, Minn	Wash	1968	98
Dennis Morgan, Dall	StL Cards	1974	98
Terance Mathis, NYJ	Dall	1990	98

You Are What You Eat — Broncos linebacker Bill Romanowski, a noted supplement freak, began testing his urine and stool samples to "see if there's anything else, any other supplement I can take to help myself" get an edge on the field.

Rushing

Year	Player, Team	Att.	Yards	Avg.	TD
1932	Cliff Battles, Bos	148	576	3.9	3
1933	Jim Musick, Bos	173	809	4.7	5
1934	Beattie Feathers, Chi	101	1004	9.9	8
1935	Doug Russell, Chi Cards	140	499	3.6	0
1936	Alphonse Leemans, NY	206	830	4.0	2
1937	Cliff Battles, Wash	216	874	4.0	5
1938	Byron White, Pitt	152	567	3.7	4
1939	Bill Osmanski, Chi	121	699	5.8	7
1940	Byron White, Det	146	514	3.5	5
1941	Clarence Manders, Bklyn	111	486	4.4	5
1942	Bill Dudley, Pitt	162	696	4.3	5
1943	Bill Paschal, NY	147	572	3.9	10
1944	Bill Paschal, NY	196	737	3.8	9
1945	Steve Van Buren, Phil	143	832	5.8	15
1946	Bill Dudley, Pitt	146	604	4.1	3
1947	Steve Van Buren, Phil	217	1008	4.6	13
1948	Steve Van Buren, Phil	201	945	4.7	10
1949	Steve Van Buren, Phil	263	1146	4.4	11
1950	Marion Motley, Clev	140	810	5.8	3
1951	Eddie Price, NY	271	971	3.6	7
1952	Dan Towler, LA	156	894	5.7	10
1953	Joe Perry, SF	192	1018	5.3	10
1954	Joe Perry, SF	173	1049	6.1	8
1955	Alan Ameche, Balt	213	961	4.5	9
1956	Rick Casares, Chi	234	1126	4.8	12
1957	Jim Brown, Clev	202	942	4.7	9
1958	Jim Brown, Clev	257	1527	5.9	17
1959	Jim Brown, Clev	290	1329	4.6	14
1960	Jim Brown, Clev, NFL	215	1257	5.8	9
	Abner Haynes, Dall Texans, AFL	156	875	5.6	9
1961	Jim Brown, Clev, NFL	305	1408	4.6	8
	Billy Cannon, Hou, AFL	200	948	4.7	6
1962	Jim Taylor, GB, NFL	272	1474	5.4	19
	Cookie Gilchrist, Buff, AFL	214	1096	5.1	13
1963	Jim Brown, Clev, NFL	291	1863	6.4	12
	Clem Daniels, Oak, AFL	215	1099	5.1	3
1964	Jim Brown, Clev, NFL	280	1446	5.2	7
	Cookie Gilchrist, Buff, AFL	230	981	4.3	6
1965	Jim Brown, Clev, NFL	289	1544	5.3	17
	Paul Lowe, SD, AFL	222	1121	5.0	7
1966	Jim Nance, Bos, AFL	299	1458	4.9	11
	Gale Sayers, Chi, NFL	229	1231	5.4	8
1967	Jim Nance, Bos, AFL	269	1216	4.5	7
	Leroy Kelly, Clev, NFL	235	1205	5.1	11
1968	Leroy Kelly, Clev, NFL	248	1239	5.0	16
	Paul Robinson, Cin, AFL	238	1023	4.3	8
1969	Gale Sayers, Chi, NFL	236	1032	4.4	8
	Dickie Post, SD, AFL	182	873	4.8	6
1970	Larry Brown, Wash, NFC	237	1125	4.7	5
	Floyd Little, Den, AFC	209	901	4.3	3
1971	Floyd Little, Den, AFC	284	1133	4.0	6
	John Brockington, GB, NFC	216	1105	5.1	4
1972	O.J. Simpson, Buff, AFC	292	1251	4.3	6
	Larry Brown, Wash, NFC	285	1216	4.3	8
1973	O.J. Simpson, Buff, AFC	332	2003	6.0	12
	John Brockington, GB, NFC	265	1144	4.3	3
1974	Otis Armstrong, Den, AFC	263	1407	5.3	9
	Lawrence McCutcheon, LA, NFC	236	1109	4.7	3
1975	O.J. Simpson, Buff, AFC	329	1817	5.5	16
	Jim Otis, StL, NFC	269	1076	4.0	5
1976	O.J. Simpson, Buff, AFC	290	1503	5.2	8
	Walter Payton, Chi, NFC	311	1390	4.5	13
1977	Walter Payton, Chi, NFC	339	1852	5.5	14
	Mark van Eeghen, Oak, AFC	324	1273	3.9	7
1978	Earl Campbell, Hou, AFC	302	1450	4.8	13
	Walter Payton, Chi, NFC	333	1395	4.2	11
1979	Earl Campbell, Hou, AFC	368	1697	4.6	19
	Walter Payton, Chi, NFC	369	1610	4.4	14
1980	Earl Campbell, Hou, AFC	373	1934	5.2	13
	Walter Payton, Chi, NFC	317	1460	4.6	6
1981	George Rogers, NO, NFC	378	1674	4.4	13
	Earl Campbell, Hou, AFC	361	1376	3.8	10
1982	Freeman McNeil, NY Jets, AFC	151	786	5.2	6
	Tony Dorsett, Dall, NFC	177	745	4.2	5
1983	Eric Dickerson, LA Rams, NFC	390	1808	4.6	18
	Curt Warner, Sea, AFC	335	1449	4.3	13
1984	Eric Dickerson, LA Rams, NFC	379	2105	5.6	14
	Earnest Jackson, SD, AFC	296	1179	4.0	8
1985	Marcus Allen, LA Raiders, AFC	380	1759	4.6	11
	Gerald Riggs, Atl, NFC	397	1719	4.3	10
1986	Eric Dickerson, LA Rams, NFC	404	1821	4.5	11
	Curt Warner, Sea, AFC	319	1481	4.6	13
1987	Charles White, LA Rams, NFC	324	1374	4.2	11
	Eric Dickerson, Ind, AFC	223	1011	4.5	5
1988	Eric Dickerson, Ind, AFC	388	1659	4.3	14
	Herschel Walker, Dall, NFC	361	1514	4.2	5
1989	Christian Okoye, KC, AFC	370	1480	4.0	12
	Barry Sanders, Det, NFC	280	1470	5.3	14
1990	Barry Sanders, Det, NFC	255	1304	5.1	13
	Thurman Thomas, Buff, AFC	271	1297	4.8	11
1991	Emmitt Smith, Dall, NFC	365	1563	4.3	12
	Thurman Thomas, Buff, AFC	288	1407	4.9	7

Rushing *(Cont.)*

Year	Player, Team	Att.	Yards	Avg.	TD
1992	Emmitt Smith, Dall, NFC	373	1713	4.6	18
	Barry Foster, Pitt, AFC	390	1690	4.3	11
1993	Emmitt Smith, Dall, NFC	283	1486	5.3	9
	Thurman Thomas, Buff, AFC	355	1315	3.7	6
1994	Barry Sanders, Det, NFC	331	1883	5.7	7
	Chris Warren, Sea, AFC	333	1545	4.6	9
1995	Emmitt Smith, Dall, NFC	377	1773	4.7	25
	Curtis Martin, NE, AFC	368	1487	4.0	14
1996	Barry Sanders, Det, NFC	307	1553	5.1	11
	Terrell Davis, Den, AFC	345	1538	4.5	13
1997	Barry Sanders, Det, NFC	335	2053	6.1	11
	Terrell Davis, Den, AFC	369	1730	4.7	15
1998	Terrell Davis, Den, AFC	392	2008	5.1	21
	Jamal Anderson, Atl, NFC	410	1846	4.5	14
1999	Edgerrin James, Ind, AFC	369	1553	4.2	13
	Stephen Davis, Wash, NFC	290	1405	4.8	17

Passing*

Year	Player, Team	Att.	Comp	Yards	TD	Int
1932	Arnie Herber, GB	101	37	639	9	9
1933	Harry Newman, NY	136	53	973	11	17
1934	Arnie Herber, GB	115	42	799	8	12
1935	Ed Danowski, NY	113	57	794	10	9
1936	Arnie Herber, GB	173	77	1239	11	13
1937	Sammy Baugh, Wash	171	81	1127	8	14
1938	Ed Danowski, NY	129	70	848	7	8
1939	Parker Hall, Clev	208	106	1227	9	13
1940	Sammy Baugh, Wash	177	111	1367	12	10
1941	Cecil Isbell, GB	206	117	1479	15	11
1942	Cecil Isbell, GB	268	146	2021	24	14
1943	Sammy Baugh, Wash	239	133	1754	23	19
1944	Frank Filchock, Wash	147	84	1139	13	9
1945	Sammy Baugh, Wash	182	128	1669	11	4
	Sid Luckman, Chi	217	117	1725	14	10
1946	Bob Waterfield, LA	251	127	1747	18	17
1947	Sammy Baugh, Wash	354	210	2938	25	15
1948	Tommy Thompson, Phil	246	141	1965	25	11
1949	Sammy Baugh, Wash	255	145	1903	18	14
1950	Norm Van Brocklin, LA	233	127	2061	18	14
1951	Bob Waterfield, LA	176	88	1566	13	10
1952	Norm Van Brocklin, LA	205	113	1736	14	17
1953	Otto Graham, Clev	258	167	2722	11	9
1954	Norm Van Brocklin, LA	260	139	2637	13	21
1955	Otto Graham, Clev	185	98	1721	15	8
1956	Ed Brown, Chi	168	96	1667	11	12
1957	Tommy O'Connell, Clev	110	63	1229	9	8
1958	Eddie LeBaron, Wash	145	79	1365	11	10
1959	Charlie Conerly, NY	194	113	1706	14	4
1960	Milt Plum, Clev, NFL	250	151	2297	21	5
	Jack Kemp, LA, AFL	406	211	3018	20	25
1961	George Blanda, Hou, AFL	362	187	3330	36	22
	Milt Plum, Clev, NFL	302	177	2416	18	10
1962	Len Dawson, Dall, AFL	310	189	2759	29	17
	Bart Starr, GB, NFL	285	178	2438	12	9
1963	Y.A. Tittle, NY, NFL	367	221	3145	36	14
	Tobin Rote, SD, AFL	286	170	2510	20	17
1964	Len Dawson, KC, AFL	354	199	2879	30	18
	Bart Starr, GB, NFL	272	163	2144	15	4
1965	Rudy Bukich, Chi, NFL	312	176	2641	20	9
	John Hadl, SD, AFL	348	174	2798	20	21
1966	Bart Starr, GB, NFL	251	156	2257	14	3
	Len Dawson, KC, AFL	284	159	2527	26	10
1967	Sonny Jurgensen, Wash, NFL	508	288	3747	31	16
	Daryle Lamonica, Oakland, AFL	425	220	3228	30	20
1968	Len Dawson, KC, AFL	224	131	2109	17	9
	Earl Morrall, Balt, NFL	317	182	2909	26	17
1969	Sonny Jurgensen, Wash, NFL	442	274	3102	22	15
	Greg Cook, Cin, AFL	197	106	1854	15	11
1970	John Brodie, SF, NFC	378	223	2941	24	10
	Daryle Lamonica, Oak, AFC	356	179	2516	22	15
1971	Roger Staubach, Dall, NFC	211	126	1882	15	4
	Bob Griese, Mia, AFC	263	145	2089	19	9
1972	Norm Snead, NY, NFC	325	196	2307	17	12
	Earl Morrall, Mia, AFC	150	83	1360	11	7
1973	Roger Staubach, Dall, NFC	286	179	2428	23	15
	Ken Stabler, Oak, AFC	260	163	1997	14	10
1974	Ken Anderson, Cin, AFC	328	213	2667	18	10
	Sonny Jurgensen, Wash, NFC	167	107	1185	11	5
1975	Ken Anderson, Cin, AFC	377	228	3169	21	11
	Fran Tarkenton, Minn, NFC	425	273	2994	25	13
1976	Ken Stabler, Oak, AFC	291	194	2737	27	17
	James Harris, LA, NFC	158	91	1460	8	6
1977	Bob Griese, Mia, AFC	307	180	2252	22	13
	Roger Staubach, Dall, NFC	361	210	2620	18	9
1978	Roger Staubach, Dall, NFC	413	231	3190	25	16
	Terry Bradshaw, Pitt, AFC	368	207	2915	28	20
1979	Roger Staubach, Dall, NFC	461	267	3586	27	11
	Dan Fouts, SD, AFC	530	332	4082	24	24
1980	Brian Sipe, Clev, AFC	554	337	4132	30	14
	Ron Jaworski, Phi, NFC	451	257	3529	27	12
1981	Ken Anderson, Cin, AFC	479	300	3754	29	10
	Joe Montana, SF, NFC	488	311	3565	19	12
1982	Ken Anderson, Cin, AFC	309	218	2495	12	9
	Joe Theismann, Wash, NFC	252	161	2033	13	9
1983	Steve Bartkowski, Atl, NFC	432	274	3167	22	5
	Dan Marino, Mia AFC	296	173	2210	20	6
1984	Dan Marino, Mia, AFC	564	362	5084	48	17
	Joe Montana, SF, NFC	432	279	3630	28	10
1985	Ken O'Brien, NY, AFC	488	297	3888	25	8
	Joe Montana, SF, NFC	494	303	3653	27	13

Passing (Cont.)

Year	Player, Team	Att.	Comp	Yards	TD	Int
1986	Tommy Kramer, Minn, NFC	372	208	3000	24	10
	Dan Marino, Mia, AFC	623	378	4746	44	23
1987	Joe Montana, SF, NFC	398	266	3054	31	13
	Bernie Kosar, Clev, AFC	389	241	3033	22	9
1988	Boomer Esiason, Cin, AFC	388	223	3572	28	14
	Wade Wilson, Minn, NFC	332	204	2746	15	9
1989	Joe Montana, SF, NFC	386	271	3521	26	8
	Boomer Esiason, Cin, AFC	455	258	3525	28	11
1990	Jim Kelly, Buffalo, AFC	346	219	2829	24	9
	Phil Simms, NY, NFC	311	184	2284	15	4
1991	Steve Young, SF, NFC	279	180	2517	17	8
	Jim Kelly, Buff, AFC	474	304	3844	33	17
1992	Steve Young, SF, NFC	402	268	3465	25	7
	Warren Moon, Hou, AFC	346	224	2521	18	12
1993	Steve Young, SF, NFC	462	314	4023	29	16
	John Elway, Den, AFC	551	348	4030	25	10
1994	Steve Young, SF, NFC	461	324	3969	35	10
	Dan Marino, Mia, AFC	615	385	4453	30	17
1995	Brett Favre, GB, NFC	570	359	4413	38	13
	Jeff Blake, Cin, AFC	567	326	3822	28	17
1996	Vinny Testaverde, Balt, AFC	549	325	4177	33	19
	Brett Favre, GB, NFC	543	325	3899	39	13
1997	Steve Young, SF, NFC	356	241	3029	19	6
	Mark Brunell, Jax, AFC	435	264	3281	18	7
1998	Randall Cunningham, Minn, NFC	425	259	3704	34	10
	Vinny Testaverde, NYJ, AFC	421	259	3256	29	7
1999	Kurt Warner, StL, NFC	499	325	4353	41	13
	Peyton Manning, Ind, AFC	533	331	4135	26	15

*Since 1973, the annual passing leaders have been determined by a passer rating system that compares individual performances to a fixed performance standard.

Pass Receiving*

Year	Player, Team	No.	Yds	Avg	TD
1932	Ray Flaherty, NY	21	350	16.7	3
1933	John Kelly, Brooklyn	22	246	11.2	3
1934	Joe Carter, Phil	16	238	14.9	4
	Morris Badgro, NY	16	206	12.9	1
1935	Tod Goodwin, NY	26	432	16.6	4
1936	Don Hutson, GB	34	536	15.8	8
1937	Don Hutson, GB	41	552	13.5	7
1938	Gaynell Tinsley, Chi Cards	41	516	12.6	1
1939	Don Hutson, GB	34	846	24.9	6
1940	Don Looney, Phil	58	707	12.2	4
1941	Don Hutson, GB	58	738	12.7	10
1942	Don Hutson, GB	74	1211	16.4	17
1943	Don Hutson, GB	47	776	16.5	11
1944	Don Hutson, GB	58	866	14.9	9
1945	Don Hutson, GB	47	834	17.7	9
1946	Jim Benton, LA	63	981	15.6	6
1947	Jim Keane, Chi	64	910	14.2	10
1948	Tom Fears, LA	51	698	13.7	4
1949	Tom Fears, LA	77	1013	13.2	9
1950	Tom Fears, LA	84	1116	13.3	7
1951	Elroy Hirsch, LA	66	1495	22.7	17
1952	Mac Speedie, Clev	62	911	14.7	5
1953	Pete Pihos, Phil	63	1049	16.7	10
1954	Pete Pihos, Phil	60	872	14.5	10
	Billy Wilson, SF	60	830	13.8	5
1955	Pete Pihos, Phil	62	864	13.9	7
1956	Billy Wilson, SF	60	889	14.8	5
1957	Billy Wilson, SF	52	757	14.6	6
1958	Raymond Berry, Balt	56	794	14.2	9
	Pete Retzlaff, Phil	56	766	13.7	2
1959	Raymond Berry, Balt	66	959	14.5	14
1960	Lionel Taylor, Den, AFL	92	1235	13.4	12
	Raymond Berry, Balt, NFL	74	1298	17.5	10
1961	Lionel Taylor, Den, AFL	100	1176	11.8	4
	Jim Phillips, LA, NFL	78	1092	14.0	5
1962	Lionel Taylor, Den, AFL	77	908	11.8	4
	Bobby Mitchell, Wash, NFL	72	1384	19.2	11
1963	Lionel Taylor, Den, AFL	78	1101	14.1	10
	Bobby Joe Conrad, St. Louis, NFL	73	967	13.2	10
1964	Charley Hennigan, Houston, AFL	101	1546	15.3	8
	Johnny Morris, Chi, NFL	93	1200	12.9	10
1965	Lionel Taylor, Den, AFL	85	1131	13.3	6
	Dave Parks, SF, NFL	80	1344	16.8	12
1966	Lance Alworth, SD, AFL	73	1383	18.9	13
	Charley Taylor, Wash, NFL	72	1119	15.5	12
1967	George Sauer, NY, AFL	75	1189	15.9	6
	Charley Taylor, Wash, NFL	70	990	14.1	9
1968	Clifton McNeil, SF, NFL	71	994	14.0	7
	Lance Alworth, SD, AFL	68	1312	19.3	10
1969	Dan Abramowicz, NO, NFL	73	1015	13.9	7
	Lance Alworth, SD, AFL	64	1003	15.7	4
1970	Dick Gordon, Chi, NFC	71	1026	14.5	13
	Marlin Briscoe, Buff, AFC	57	1036	18.2	8
1971	Fred Biletnikoff, Oak, AFC	61	929	15.2	9
	Bob Tucker, NY, NFC	59	791	13.4	4
1972	Harold Jackson, Phil, NFC	62	1048	16.9	4
	Fred Biletnikoff, Oak, AFC	58	802	13.8	7
1973	Harold Carmichael, Phil, NFC	67	1116	16.7	9
	Fred Willis, Hou, AFC	57	371	6.5	1
1974	Lydell Mitchell, Balt, AFC	72	544	7.6	2
	Charles Young, Phil, NFC	63	696	11.0	3
1975	Chuck Foreman, Minn, NFC	73	691	9.5	9
	Reggie Rucker, Clev, AFC	60	770	12.8	3
	Lydell Mitchell, Balt, AFC	60	544	9.1	4
1976	MacArthur Lane, KC, AFC	66	686	10.4	1
	Drew Pearson, Dall, NFC	58	806	13.9	6

*Most catches.

Pass Receiving *(Cont.)*

Year	Player, Team	No.	Yds	Avg	TD
1977	Lydell Mitchell, Balt, AFC	71	620	8.7	4
	Ahmad Rashad, Minn, NFC	51	681	13.4	2
1978	Rickey Young, Minn, NFC	88	704	8.0	5
	Steve Largent, Sea, AFC	71	1168	16.5	8
1979	Joe Washington, Balt, AFC	82	750	9.1	3
	Ahmad Rashad, Minn, NFC	80	1156	14.5	9
1980	Kellen Winslow, SD, AFC	89	1290	14.5	9
	Earl Cooper, SF, NFC	83	567	6.8	4
1981	Kellen Winslow, SD, AFC	88	1075	12.2	10
	Dwight Clark, SF, NFC	85	1105	13.0	4
1982	Dwight Clark, SF, NFC	60	913	15.2	5
	Kellen Winslow, SD, AFC	54	721	13.4	6
1983	Todd Christensen, LA, AFC	92	1247	13.6	12
	Roy Green, StL, NFC	78	1227	15.7	14
	Charlie Brown, Wash, NFC	78	1225	15.7	8
	Earnest Gray, NY, NFC	78	1139	14.6	5
1984	Art Monk, Wash, NFC	106	1372	12.9	7
	Ozzie Newsome, Clev, AFC	89	1001	11.2	5
1985	Roger Craig, SF, NFC	92	1016	11.0	6
	Lionel James, SD, AFC	86	1027	11.9	6
1986	Todd Christensen, LA Rai, AFC	95	1153	12.1	8
	Jerry Rice, SF, NFC	86	1570	18.3	15
1987	J.T. Smith, StL Card, NFC	91	1117	12.3	8
	Al Toon, NY, AFC	68	976	14.4	5
1988	Al Toon, NY, AFC	93	1067	11.5	5
	Henry Ellard, LA Rams, NFC	86	1414	16.4	10
1989	Sterling Sharpe, GB, NFC	90	1423	15.8	12
	Andre Reed, Buff, AFC	88	1312	14.9	9
1990	Jerry Rice, SF, NFC	100	1502	15.0	13
	Haywood Jeffires, Hou, AFC	74	1048	14.2	8
	Drew Hill, Hou, AFC	74	1019	13.8	5
1991	Haywood Jeffires, Hou, AFC	100	1181	11.8	7
	Michael Irvin, Dall, NFC	93	1523	16.4	8
1992	Sterling Sharpe, GB, NFC	108	1461	13.5	13
	Haywood Jeffires, Hou, AFC	90	913	10.1	9
1993	Sterling Sharpe, GB, NFC	112	1274	11.4	11
	Reggie Langhorne, Ind, AFC	85	1038	12.2	3
1994	Cris Carter, Minn, NFC	122	1256	10.3	7
	Ben Coates, NE, AFC	96	1174	12.2	7
1995	Herman Moore, Det, NFC	123	1686	13.7	14
	Carl Pickens, Cin, AFC	99	1234	12.5	17
1996	Jerry Rice, SF, NFC	108	1254	11.6	8
	Carl Pickens, Cin, AFC	100	1180	11.8	12
1997	Herman Moore, Det, NFC	104	1293	12.4	8
	Tim Brown, Oak, AFC	104	1408	13.5	5
1998	Frank Sanders, Ariz, NFC	89	1145	12.9	3
	O.J. McDuffie, Mia, AFC	90	1050	11.7	7
1999	Mushin Muhammad, Car, NFC	96	1253	13.1	8
	Jimmy Smith, Jax, AFC	116	1636	14.1	6

Young Talks Dirty

"It's kind of sad that we play football indoors," San Francisco quarterback Steve Young said in 1999. "It's like playing golf indoors—it's a joke. When we play indoors I bring some dirt to have the feel of dirt on my hands. It's not superstition; it's actually what I use... I've had to deal with bad dirt, good dirt, clay dirt, soft dirt, silty dirt. It's tough to find good dirt nowadays, to be honest with you. Sometimes I'll bring it, you know? Though there are times I've forgotten it all the way up till we're coming back in for warmups and go, 'I don't have any dirt!' And I'll send a kid out for dirt outside the Superdome—he'll go out there looking for dirt. Yeah, if I find good dirt, I'll keep it with me....If anyone knows where good dirt is, I'd pay for good dirt ... but it's like anything nowadays—everything's kind of processed, and, you know, even dirt seems to be kind of processed now, and you don't get the good stuff like the old days...you know the apocalypse is near when you can't find good dirt."

Scoring

Year	Player, Team	TD	FG	PAT	TP
1932	Earl Clark, Portsmouth	6	3	10	55
1933	Ken Strong, NY	6	5	13	64
	Glenn Presnell, Ports	6	6	10	64
1934	Jack Manders, Chi	3	10	31	79
1935	Earl Clark, Det	6	1	16	55
1936	Earl Clark, Det	7	4	19	73
1937	Jack Manders, Chi	5	18	15	69
1938	Clarke Hinkle, GB	7	3	7	58
1939	Andy Farkas, Wash	11	0	2	68
1940	Don Hutson, GB	7	0	15	57
1941	Don Hutson, GB	12	1	20	95
1942	Don Hutson, GB	17	1	33	138
1943	Don Hutson, GB	12	3	36	117
1944	Don Hutson, GB	9	0	31	85
1945	Steve Van Buren, Phil	18	0	2	110
1946	Ted Fritsch, GB	10	9	13	100
1947	Pat Harder, Chicago Cards	7	7	39	102
1948	Pat Harder, Chicago Cards	6	7	53	110
1949	Pat Harder, Chicago Cards	8	3	45	102
	Gene Roberts, NY	17	0	0	102
1950	Doak Walker, Det	11	8	38	128
1951	Elroy Hirsch, LA	17	0	0	102
1952	Gordy Soltau, SF	7	6	34	94
1953	Gordy Soltau, SF	6	10	48	114
1954	Bobby Walston, Phil	11	4	36	114
1955	Doak Walker, Det	7	9	27	96
1956	Bobby Layne, Det	5	12	33	99
1957	Sam Baker, Wash	1	14	29	77
	Lou Groza, Clev	0	15	32	77
1958	Jim Brown, Clev	18	0	0	108
1959	Paul Hornung, GB	7	7	31	94
1960	Paul Hornung, GB	15	15	41	176
	Gene Mingo, Den, AFL	6	18	33	123
1961	Gino Cappelletti, Bos, AFL	8	17	48	147
	Paul Hornung, GB, NFL	10	15	41	146
1962	Gene Mingo, Den, AFL	4	27	32	137
	Jim Taylor, GB, NFL	19	0	0	114
1963	Gino Cappelletti, Bos, AFL	2	22	35	113
	Don Chandler, NY, NFL	0	18	52	106
1964	Gino Cappelletti, Bos, AFL	7	25	36	155
	Lenny Moore, Balt, NFL	20	0	0	120
1965	Gale Sayers, Chi, NFL	22	0	0	132
	Gino Cappelletti, Bos, AFL	9	17	27	132
1966	Gino Cappelletti, Bos, AFL	6	16	35	119
	Bruce Gossett, LA, NFL	0	28	29	113
1967	Jim Bakken, StL, NFL	0	27	36	117
	George Blanda, Oak, AFL	0	20	56	116
1968	Jim Turner, NY, AFL	0	34	43	145
	Leroy Kelly, Clev, NFL	20	0	0	120
1969	Jim Turner, NY, AFL	0	32	33	129
	Fred Cox, Minn, NFL	0	26	43	121
1970	Fred Cox, Minn, NFC	0	30	35	125
	Jan Stenerud, KC, AFC	0	30	26	116
1971	Garo Yepremian, Mia, AFC	0	28	33	117
	Curt Knight, Wash, NFC	0	29	27	114
1972	Chester Marcol, GB, NFC	0	33	29	128
	Bobby Howfield, NY AFC	0	27	40	121
1973	David Ray, LA, NFC	0	30	40	130
	Roy Gerela, Pitt, AFC	0	29	36	123
1974	Chester Marcol, GB, NFC	0	25	19	94
	Roy Gerela, Pitt, AFC	0	20	33	93
1975	O.J. Simpson, Buff, AFC	23	0	0	138
	Chuck Foreman, Minn, NFC	22	0	0	132
1976	Toni Linhart, Balt, AFC	0	20	49	109
	Mark Moseley, Wash, NFC	0	22	31	97
1977	Errol Mann, Oak, AFC	0	20	39	99
	Walter Payton, Chi, NFC	16	0	0	96
1978	Frank Corral, LA, NFC	0	29	31	118
	Pat Leahy, NY, AFC	0	22	41	107
1979	John Smith, NE, AFC	0	23	46	115
	Mark Moseley, Wash, NFC	0	25	39	114
1980	John Smith, NE, AFC	0	26	51	129
	Ed Murray, Det, NFC	0	27	35	116
1981	Ed Murray, Det, NFC	0	25	46	121
	Rafael Septien, Dall, NFC	0	27	40	121
	Jim Breech, Cin, AFC	0	22	49	115
	Nick Lowery, KC, AFC	0	26	37	115
1982	Marcus Allen, LA, AFC	14	0	0	84
	Wendell Tyler, LA, NFC	13	0	0	78
1983	Mark Moseley, Wash, NFC	0	33	62	161
	Gary Anderson, Pitt, AFC	0	27	38	119
1984	Ray Wersching, SF, NFC	0	25	56	131
	Gary Anderson, Pitt, AFC	0	24	45	117
1985	Kevin Butler, Chi, NFC	0	31	51	144
	Gary Anderson, Pitt, AFC	0	33	40	139
1986	Tony Franklin, NE, AFC	0	32	44	140
	Kevin Butler, Chi, NFC	0	28	36	120
1987	Jerry Rice, SF, NFC	23	0	0	138
	Jim Breech, Cin, AFC	0	24	25	97
1988	Scott Norwood, Buff, AFC	0	32	33	129
	Mike Cofer, SF, NFC	0	27	40	121
1989	Mike Cofer, SF, NFC	0	29	49	136
	David Treadwell, Den, AFC	0	27	39	120
1990	Nick Lowery, KC, AFC	0	34	37	139
	Chip Lohmiller, Wash, NFC	0	30	41	131
1991	Chip Lohmiller, Wash, NFC	0	31	56	149
	Pete Stoyanovich, Mia, AFC	0	31	28	121
1992	Pete Stoyanovich, Mia, AFC	0	30	34	124
	Morten Anderson, NO, NFC	0	29	33	120
	Chip Lohmiller, Wash, NFC	0	30	30	120
1993	Jeff Jaeger, Rai, AFC	0	35	27	132
	Jason Hanson, Det, NFC	0	34	28	130
1994	John Carney, SD, NFC	0	34	33	135
	Fuad Reveiz, Minn, NFC	0	34	30	132
	Emmitt Smith, Dall, NFC	22	0	0	132
1995	Emmitt Smith, Dall, NFC	25	0	0	150
	Norm Johnson, Pitt, AFC	0	34	39	141
1996	John Kasay, Car, NFC	0	37	34	145
	Cary Blanchard, Ind, AFC	0	36	27	135
1997	Richie Cunningham, Dall, NFC	0	34	24	126
	Mike Hollis, Jax, AFC	0	41	31	134
1998	Gary Anderson, Minn, NFC	0	35	59	164
	Steve Christie, Buff, AFC	0	33	41	140
1999	Jeff Wilkins, StL, NFC	0	20	28	124
	Mike Vanderjagt, Ind, AFC	0	34	38	145

Pro Bowl Alltime Results

Date	Result	Date	Result	Date	Result
1-15-39	NY Giants 13, Pro All-Stars 10	1-13-63	NFL East 30, West 20	1-29-79	NFC 13, AFC 7
1-14-40	Green Bay 16, NFL All-Stars 7	1-12-64	NFL West 31, East 17	1-27-80	NFC 37, AFC 27
12-29-40	Chi Bears 28, NFL All-Stars 14	1-19-64	AFL West 27, East 24	2-1-81	NFC 21, AFC 7
1-4-42	Chi Bears 35, NFL All-Stars 24	1-10-65	NFL West 34, East 14	1-31-82	AFC 16, NFC 13
12-27-42	NFL All-Stars 17, Washington 14	1-16-65	AFL West 38, East 14	2-6-83	NFC 20, AFC 19
1-14-51	A Conf 28, N Conf 27	1-15-66	AFL All-Stars 30, Buffalo 19	1-29-84	NFC 45, AFC 3
1-12-52	N Conf 30, A Conf 13	1-15-66	NFL East 36, West 7	1-27-85	AFC 22, NFC 14
1-10-53	N Conf 27, A Conf 7	1-21-67	AFL East 30, West 23	2-2-86	NFC 28, AFC 24
1-17-54	East 20, West 9	1-22-67	NFL East 20, West 10	2-1-87	AFC 10, NFC 6
1-16-55	West 26, East 19	1-21-68	AFL East 25, West 24	2-7-88	AFC 15, NFC 6
1-15-56	East 31, West 30	1-21-68	NFL West 38, East 20	1-29-89	NFC 34, AFC 3
1-13-57	West 19, East 10	1-19-69	AFL West 38, East 25	2-4-90	NFC 27, AFC 21
1-12-58	West 26, East 7	1-19-69	NFL West 10, East 7	2-3-91	AFC 23, NFC 21
1-11-59	East 28, West 21	1-17-70	AFL West 26, East 3	2-2-92	NFC 21, AFC 15
1-17-60	West 38, East 21	1-18-70	NFL West 16, East 13	2-7-93	AFC 23, NFC 20
1-15-61	West 35, East 31	1-24-71	NFC 27, AFC 6	2-6-94	NFC 17, AFC 3
1-7-62	AFL West 47, East 27	1-23-72	AFC 26, NFC 13	2-5-95	AFC 41, NFC 13
1-14-62	NFL West 31, East 30	1-21-73	AFC 33, NFC 28	2-4-96	NFC 20, AFC 13
1-13-63	AFL West 21, East 14	1-20-74	AFC 15, NFC 13	2-2-97	AFC 26, NFC 23
		1-20-75	NFC 17, AFC 10	2-1-98	AFC 29, NFC 24
		1-26-76	NFC 23, AFC 20	2-7-99	AFC 23, NFC 10
		1-17-77	AFC 24, NFC 14	2-6-00	NFC 51, AFC 31
		1-23-78	NFC 14, AFC 13		

Chicago All-Star Game Results

Date	Result (Attendance)	Date	Result (Attendance)
8-31-34	Chi Bears 0, All-Stars 0 (79,432)	8-10-56	Cleveland 26, All-Stars 0 (75,000)
8-29-35	Chi Bears 5, All-Stars 0 (77,450)	8-9-57	NY Giants 22, All-Stars 12 (75,000)
9-3-36	All-Stars 7, Detroit 7 (76,000)	8-15-58	All-Stars 35, Detroit 19 (70,000)
9-1-37	All-Stars 6, Green Bay 0 (84,560)	8-14-59	Baltimore 29, All-Stars 0 (70,000)
8-31-38	All-Stars 28, Washington 16 (74,250)	8-12-60	Baltimore 32, All-Stars 7 (70,000)
8-30-39	NY Giants 9, All-Stars 0 (81,456)	8-4-61	Philadelphia 28, All-Stars 14 (66,000)
8-29-40	Green Bay 45, All-Stars 28 (84,567)	8-3-62	Green Bay 42, All-Stars 20 (65,000)
8-28-41	Chi Bears 37, All-Stars 13 (98,203)	8-2-63	All-Stars 20, Green Bay 17 (65,000)
8-28-42	Chi Bears 21, All-Stars 0 (101,100)	8-7-64	Chicago 28, All-Stars 17 (65,000)
8-25-43	All-Stars 27, Washington 7 (48,471)	8-6-65	Cleveland 24, All-Stars 16 (68,000)
8-30-44	Chi Bears 24, All-Stars 21 (48,769)	8-5-66	Green Bay 38, All-Stars 0 (72,000)
8-30-45	Green Bay 19, All-Stars 7 (92,753)	8-4-67	Green Bay 27, All-Stars 0 (70,934)
8-23-46	All-Stars 16, Los Angeles 0 (97,380)	8-2-68	Green Bay 34, All-Stars 17 (69,917)
8-22-47	All-Stars 16, Chi Bears 0 (105,840)	8-1-69	NY Jets 26, All-Stars 24 (74,208)
8-20-48	Chi Cardinals 28, All-Stars 0 (101,220)	7-31-70	Kansas City 24, All-Stars 3 (69,940)
8-12-49	Philadelphia 38, All-Stars 0 (93,780)	7-30-71	Baltimore 24, All-Stars 17 (52,289)
8-11-50	All-Stars 17, Philadelphia 7 (88,885)	7-28-72	Dallas 20, All-Stars 7 (54,162)
8-17-51	Cleveland 33, All-Stars 0 (92,180)	7-27-73	Miami 14, All-Stars 3 (54,103)
8-15-52	Los Angeles 10, All-Stars 7 (88,316)	1974	No game
8-14-53	Detroit 24, All-Stars 10 (93,818)	8-1-75	Pittsburgh 21, All-Stars 14 (54,103)
8-13-54	Detroit 31, All-Stars 6 (93,470)	7-23-76	Pittsburgh 24, All-Stars 0 (52,895)
8-12-55	All-Stars 30, Cleveland 27 (75,000)		

Getting "Favred"

If their first four games of the 1999 season had ended at the two-minute warning, the Packers would have been 0–4. But at 3–1 Green Bay had hope. His name was Brett Favre. On October 10, for the third time that season, he threw a last-minute, game-winning touchdown pass, this one beating the Buccaneers 26–23. "We got Favred," moaned Tampa Bay quarterback Trent Dilfer.

Alltime Winningest NFL Coaches

Most Career Wins

Coach	Yrs	Teams	Regular Season				Career			
			W	L	T	Pct	W	L	T	Pct
Don Shula	33	Colts, Dolphins	328	156	6	.676	347	173	6	.665
George Halas	40	Bears	318	148	31	.671	324	151	31	.671
Tom Landry	29	Cowboys	250	162	6	.605	270	178	6	.601
Curly Lambeau	33	Packers, Cardinals, Redskins	226	132	22	.624	229	134	22	.623
Chuck Noll	23	Steelers	193	148	1	.566	209	156	1	.572
Chuck Knox	22	Rams, Bills, Seahawks	186	147	1	.558	193	158	1	.550
†Dan Reeves	19	Broncos, Giants, Falcons	167	128	1	.565	177	136	1	.563
Paul Brown	21	Browns, Bengals	166	100	6	.621	170	108	6	.609
Bud Grant	18	Vikings	158	96	5	.620	168	108	5	.607
Marv Levy	17	Chiefs, Bills	143	112	0	.561	154	120	0	.562
Steve Owen	23	Giants	151	100	17	.595	153	108	17	.581
M. Schottenheimer	15	Browns, Chiefs	145	85	1	.630	150	96	1	.607
Bill Parcells	15	Giants, Patriots, Jets	138	100	1	.579	149	106	1	.582
Joe Gibbs	12	Redskins	124	60	0	.674	140	65	0	.683
Hank Stram	17	Chiefs, Saints	131	97	10	.571	136	100	10	.573
Weeb Ewbank	20	Colts, Jets	130	129	7	.502	134	130	7	.507
Mike Ditka	14	Bears, Saints	121	95	0	.560	127	101	0	.557
Sid Gillman	18	Rams, Chargers, Oilers	122	99	7	.550	123	104	7	.541
George Allen	12	Rams, Redskins	116	47	5	.705	118	54	5	.681
†George Seifert	9	49ers, Panthers	106	38	0	.736	116	43	0	.729

†Active coach.

Top Winning Percentages

	W	L	T	Pct		W	L	T	Pct
Vince Lombardi	105	35	6	.740	George Halas	324	151	31	.671
John Madden	112	39	7	.731	Don Shula	347	173	6	.665
†George Seifert	116	43	0	.729	Curly Lambeau	229	134	22	.623
Joe Gibbs	140	65	0	.683	Bill Walsh	102	63	1	.617
George Allen	118	54	5	.681	Paul Brown	170	108	6	.609

Note: Minimum 100 victories.

†Active coach.

Alltime Number-One Draft Choices

Year	Team	Selection	Position
1936	Philadelphia	Jay Berwanger, Chicago	HB
1937	Philadelphia	Sam Francis, Nebraska	FB
1938	Cleveland	Corbett Davis, Indiana	FB
1939	Chicago Cardinals	Ki Aldrich, Texas Christian	C
1940	Chicago Cardinals	George Cafego, Tennessee	HB
1941	Chicago Bears	Tom Harmon, Michigan	HB
1942	Pittsburgh	Bill Dudley, Virginia	HB
1943	Detroit	Frank Sinkwich, Georgia	HB
1944	Boston	Angelo Bertelli, Notre Dame	QB
1945	Chicago Cardinals	Charley Trippi, Georgia	HB
1946	Boston	Frank Dancewicz, Notre Dame	QB
1947	Chicago Bears	Bob Fenimore, Oklahoma A&M	HB
1948	Washington	Harry Gilmer, Alabama	QB
1949	Philadelphia	Chuck Bednarik, Pennsylvania	C
1950	Detroit	Leon Hart, Notre Dame	E
1951	New York Giants	Kyle Rote, Southern Methodist	HB
1952	Los Angeles	Bill Wade, Vanderbilt	QB
1953	San Francisco	Harry Babcock, Georgia	E
1954	Cleveland	Bobby Garrett, Stanford	QB
1955	Baltimore	George Shaw, Oregon	QB
1956	Pittsburgh	Gary Glick, Colorado A&M	DB
1957	Green Bay	Paul Hornung, Notre Dame	HB
1958	Chicago Cardinals	King Hill, Rice	QB
1959	Green Bay	Randy Duncan, Iowa	QB
1960	Los Angeles	Billy Cannon, Louisiana State	RB

Alltime Number-One Draft Choices (Cont.)

Year	Team	Selection	Position
1961	Minnesota	Tommy Mason, Tulane	RB
	Buffalo (AFL)	Ken Rice, Auburn	G
1968	Minnesota	Ron Yary, Southern California	T
1969	Buffalo (AFL)	O.J. Simpson, Southern California	RB
1970	Pittsburgh	Terry Bradshaw, Louisiana Tech	QB
1971	New England	Jim Plunkett, Stanford	QB
1972	Buffalo	Walt Patulski, Notre Dame	DE
1973	Houston	John Matuszak, Tampa	DE
1974	Dallas	Ed Jones, Tennessee State	DE
1975	Atlanta	Steve Bartkowski, California	QB
1976	Tampa Bay	Lee Roy Selmon, Oklahoma	DE
1977	Tampa Bay	Ricky Bell, Southern California	RB
1978	Houston	Earl Campbell, Texas	RB
1979	Buffalo	Tom Cousineau, Ohio State	LB
1980	Detroit	Billy Sims, Oklahoma	RB
1981	New Orleans	George Rogers, South Carolina	RB
1982	New England	Kenneth Sims, Texas	DT
1983	Baltimore	John Elway, Stanford	QB
1984	New England	Irving Fryar, Nebraska	WR
1985	Buffalo	Bruce Smith, Virginia Tech	DE
1986	Tampa Bay	Bo Jackson, Auburn	RB
1987	Tampa Bay	Vinny Testaverde, Miami (FL)	QB
1988	Atlanta	Aundray Bruce, Auburn	LB
1989	Dallas	Troy Aikman, UCLA	QB
1990	Indianapolis	Jeff George, Illinois	QB
1991	Dallas	Russell Maryland, Miami (FL)	DT
1992	Indianapolis	Steve Emtman, Washington	DT
1993	New England	Drew Bledsoe, Washington State	QB
1994	Cincinnati	Dan Wilkinson, Ohio State	DT
1995	Cincinnati	Ki-Jana Carter, Penn State	RB
1996	New York Jets	Keyshawn Johnson, Southern California	WR
1997	St Louis	Orlando Pace, Ohio State	OT
1998	Indianapolis	Peyton Manning, Tennessee	QB
1999	Cleveland	Tim Couch, Kentucky	QB
2000	Cleveland	Courtney Brown, Penn State	DE

From 1947 through 1958, the first selection in the draft was a bonus pick, awarded to the winner of a random draw. That club, in turn, forfeited its last-round draft choice. The winner of the bonus choice was eliminated from future draws. The system was abolished after 1958, by which time all clubs had received a bonus choice.

Members of the Pro Football Hall of Fame

Herb Adderley
Lance Alworth
Doug Atkins
Morris (Red) Badgro
Lem Barney
Cliff Battles
Sammy Baugh
Chuck Bednarik
Bert Bell
Bobby Bell
Raymond Berry
Charles W. Bidwill, Sr.
Fred Biletnikoff
George Blanda
Mel Blount
Terry Bradshaw
Jim Brown
Paul Brown
Roosevelt Brown
Willie Brown
Buck Buchanan
Dick Butkus
Earl Campbell
Tony Canadeo

Joe Carr
Guy Chamberlin
Jack Christiansen
Earl (Dutch) Clark
George Connor
Jimmy Conzelman
Lou Creekmur
Larry Csonka
Al Davis
Willie Davis
Len Dawson
Eric Dickerson
Dan Dierdorf
Mike Ditka
Art Donovan
Tony Dorsett
John (Paddy) Driscoll
Bill Dudley
Albert Glen (Turk) Edwards
Weeb Ewbank
Tom Fears
Jim Finks
Ray Flaherty
Len Ford

Dan Fortmann
Dan Fouts
Frank Gatski
Bill George
Joe Gibbs
Frank Gifford
Sid Gillman
Otto Graham
Harold (Red) Grange
Bud Grant
Joe Greene
Forrest Gregg
Bob Griese
Lou Groza
Joe Guyon
George Halas
Jack Ham
John Hannah
Franco Harris
Mike Haynes
Ed Healey
Mel Hein
Ted Hendricks
Wilbur (Pete) Henry

Arnie Herber
Bill Hewitt
Clarke Hinkle
Elroy (Crazylegs) Hirsch
Paul Hornung
Ken Houston
Cal Hubbard
Sam Huff
Lamar Hunt
Don Hutson
Jimmy Johnson
John Henry Johnson
Charlie Joiner
David (Deacon) Jones
Stan Jones
Henry Jordan
Sonny Jurgensen
Leroy Kelly
Walt Kiesling
Frank (Bruiser) Kinard
Paul Krause
Earl (Curly) Lambeau
Jack Lambert
Tom Landry
Dick (Night Train) Lane
Jim Langer
Willie Lanier
Steve Largent
Yale Lary
Dante Lavelli
Bobby Layne
Alphonse (Tuffy) Leemans
Bob Lilly
Larry Little
Vince Lombardi
Howie Long
Ronnie Lott
Sid Luckman
William Roy (Link) Lyman
Tom Mack
John Mackey
Tim Mara
Wellington Mara
Gino Marchetti

George Preston Marshall
Ollie Matson
Don Maynard
George McAfee
Mike McCormack
Tommy McDonald
Hugh McElhenny
Johnny (Blood) McNally
Mike Michalske
Wayne Millner
Bobby Mitchell
Ron Mix
Joe Montana
Lenny Moore
Marion Motley
Anthony Munoz
George Musso
Bronko Nagurski
Joe Namath
Earle (Greasy) Neale
Ernie Nevers
Ozzie Newsome
Ray Nitschke
Chuck Noll
Leo Nomellini
Merlin Olsen
Jim Otto
Steve Owen
Alan Page
Clarence (Ace) Parker
Jim Parker
Walter Payton
Joe Perry
Pete Pihos
Hugh (Shorty) Ray
Dan Reeves
Mel Renfro
John Riggins
Jim Ringo
Andy Robustelli
Art Rooney
Dan Rooney
Pete Rozelle
Bob St. Clair

Gale Sayers
Joe Schmidt
Tex Schramm
Lee Roy Selmon
Billy Shaw
Art Shell
Don Shula
O.J. Simpson
Mike Singletary
Jackie Smith
Bart Starr
Roger Staubach
Ernie Stautner
Jan Stenerud
Dwight Stephenson
Ken Strong
Joe Stydahar
Fran Tarkenton
Charley Taylor
Jim Taylor
Lawrence Taylor
Jim Thorpe
Y.A. Tittle
George Trafton
Charley Trippi
Emlen Tunnell
Clyde (Bulldog) Turner
Johnny Unitas
Gene Upshaw
Norm Van Brocklin
Steve Van Buren
Doak Walker
Bill Walsh
Paul Warfield
Bob Waterfield
Mike Webster
Arnie Weinmeister
Randy White
Dave Wilcox
Bill Willis
Larry Wilson
Kellen Winslow
Alex Wojciechowicz
Willie Wood

Champions of Other Leagues

Canadian Football League Grey Cup

Year	Results	Site	Attendance
1909	U of Toronto 26, Parkdale 6	Toronto	3,807
1910	U of Toronto 16, Hamilton Tigers 7	Hamilton	12,000
1911	U of Toronto 14, Toronto 7	Toronto	13,687
1912	Hamilton Alerts 11, Toronto 4	Hamilton	5,337
1913	Hamilton Tigers 44, Parkdale 2	Hamilton	2,100
1914	Toronto 14, U of Toronto 2	Toronto	10,500
1915	Hamilton Tigers 13, Toronto RAA 7	Toronto	2,808
1916-19	No game		
1920	U of Toronto 16, Toronto 3	Toronto	10,088
1921	Toronto 23, Edmonton 0	Toronto	9,558
1922	Queen's U 13, Edmonton 1	Kingston	4,700
1923	Queen's U 54, Regina 0	Toronto	8,629
1924	Queen's U 11, Balmy Beach 3	Toronto	5,978
1925	Ottawa Senators 24, Winnipeg 1	Ottawa	6,900
1926	Ottawa Senators 10, Toronto U 7	Toronto	8,276
1927	Balmy Beach 9, Hamilton Tigers 6	Toronto	13,676
1928	Hamilton Tigers 30, Regina 0	Hamilton	4,767
1929	Hamilton Tigers 14, Regina 3	Hamilton	1,906
1930	Balmy Beach 11, Regina 6	Toronto	3,914
1931	Montreal AAA 22, Regina 0	Montreal	5,112
1932	Hamilton Tigers 25, Regina 6	Hamilton	4,806
1933	Toronto 4, Sarnia 3	Sarnia	2,751
1934	Sarnia 20, Regina 12	Toronto	8,900
1935	Winnipeg 18, Hamilton Tigers 12	Hamilton	6,405
1936	Sarnia 26, Ottawa RR 20	Toronto	5,883
1937	Toronto 4, Winnipeg 3	Toronto	11,522
1938	Toronto 30, Winnipeg 7	Toronto	18,778
1939	Winnipeg 8, Ottawa 7	Ottawa	11,738
1940	Ottawa 12, Balmy Beach 5	Ottawa	1,700
1940	Ottawa 8, Balmy Beach 2	Toronto	4,998
1941	Winnipeg 18, Ottawa 16	Toronto	19,065
1942	Toronto RCAF 8, Winnipeg RCAF 5	Toronto	12,455
1943	Hamilton F Wild 23, Winnipeg RCAF 14	Toronto	16,423
1944	Montreal St H-D Navy 7, Hamilton F Wild 6	Hamilton	3,871
1945	Toronto 35, Winnipeg 0	Toronto	18,660
1946	Toronto 28, Winnipeg 6	Toronto	18,960
1947	Toronto 10, Winnipeg 9	Toronto	18,885
1948	Calgary 12, Ottawa 7	Toronto	20,013
1949	Montreal Als 28, Calgary 15	Toronto	20,087
1950	Toronto 13, Winnipeg 0	Toronto	27,101
1951	Ottawa 21, Saskatchewan 14	Toronto	27,341
1952	Toronto 21, Edmonton 11	Toronto	27,391
1953	Hamilton Ticats 12, Winnipeg 6	Toronto	27,313
1954	Edmonton 26, Montreal 25	Toronto	27,321
1955	Edmonton 34, Montreal 19	Vancouver	39,417
1956	Edmonton 50, Montreal 27	Toronto	27,425
1957	Hamilton 32, Winnipeg 7	Toronto	27,051
1958	Winnipeg 35, Hamilton 28	Vancouver	36,567
1959	Winnipeg 21, Hamilton 7	Toronto	33,133
1960	Ottawa 16, Edmonton 6	Vancouver	38,102
1961	Winnipeg 21, Hamilton 14	Toronto	32,651
1962	Winnipeg 28, Hamilton 27	Toronto	32,655
1963	Hamilton 21, British Columbia 10	Vancouver	36,545
1964	British Columbia 34, Hamilton 24	Toronto	32,655
1965	Hamilton 22, Winnipeg 16	Toronto	32,655
1966	Saskatchewan 29, Ottawa 14	Vancouver	36,553
1967	Hamilton 24, Saskatchewan 1	Ottawa	31,358
1968	Ottawa 24, Calgary 21	Toronto	32,655
1969	Ottawa 29, Saskatchewan 11	Montreal	33,172
1970	Montreal 23, Calgary 10	Toronto	32,669
1971	Calgary 14, Toronto 11	Vancouver	34,484
1972	Hamilton 13, Saskatchewan 10	Hamilton	33,993
1973	Ottawa 22, Edmonton 18	Toronto	36,653
1974	Montreal 20, Edmonton 7	Vancouver	34,450
1975	Edmonton 9, Montreal 8	Calgary	32,454

Canadian Football League Grey Cup *(Cont.)*

Year	Results	Site	Attendance
1976	Ottawa 23, Saskatchewan 20	Toronto	53,467
1977	Montreal 41, Edmonton 6	Montreal	68,318
1978	Edmonton 20, Montreal 13	Toronto	54,695
1979	Edmonton 17, Montreal 9	Montreal	65,113
1980	Edmonton 48, Hamilton 10	Toronto	54,661
1981	Edmonton 26, Ottawa 23	Montreal	52,478
1982	Edmonton 32, Toronto 16	Toronto	54,741
1983	Toronto 18, British Columbia 17	Vancouver	59,345
1984	Winnipeg 47, Hamilton 17	Edmonton	60,081
1985	British Columbia 37, Hamilton 24	Montreal	56,723
1986	Hamilton 39, Edmonton 15	Vancouver	59,621
1987	Edmonton 38, Toronto 36	Vancouver	59,478
1988	Winnipeg 22, British Columbia 21	Ottawa	50,604
1989	Saskatchewan 43, Hamilton 40	Toronto	54,088
1990	Winnipeg 50, Edmonton 11	Vancouver	46,968
1991	Toronto 36, Calgary 21	Winnipeg	51,985
1992	Calgary 24, Winnipeg 10	Toronto	45,863
1993	Edmonton 33, Winnipeg 23	Calgary	50,035
1994	British Columbia 26, Baltimore 23	Vancouver	55,097
1995	Baltimore 37, Calgary 20	Regina, Saskatchewan	52,564
1996	Toronto 43, Edmonton 37	Hamilton, Ontario	38,595
1997	Toronto 47, Saskatchewan 23	Edmonton	60,431
1998	Calgary 26, Hamilton 24	Winnipeg	34,157
1999	Hamilton 32, Calgary 21	Vancouver	45,118

In 1909, Earl Grey, the Governor-General of Canada, donated a trophy for the Rugby Football Championship of Canada. The trophy, which subsequently became known as the Grey Cup, was originally open only to teams registered with the Canada Rugby Union. Since 1954, it has been awarded to the winner of the Canadian Football League's championship game.

AMERICAN FOOTBALL LEAGUE I

Year	Champion	Record
1926	Philadelphia Quakers	7-2

AMERICAN FOOTBALL LEAGUE II

Year	Champion	Record
1936	Boston Shamrocks	8-3
1937	LA Bulldogs	8-0

AMERICAN FOOTBALL LEAGUE III

Year	Champion	Record
1940	Columbus Bullies	8-1-1
1941	Columbus Bullies	5-1-2

ALL-AMERICAN FOOTBALL CONFERENCE

Year	Championship Game
1946	Cleveland 14, NY Yankees 9
1947	Cleveland 14, NY Yankees 3
1948	Cleveland 49, Buffalo 7
1949	Cleveland 21, San Francisco 7

WORLD FOOTBALL LEAGUE

Year	World Bowl Championship
1974	Birmingham 22, Florida 21
1975	Disbanded midseason

UNITED STATES FOOTBALL LEAGUE

Year	Championship Game
1983	Michigan 24, Philadelphia 22, at Denver
1984	Philadelphia 23, Arizona 3, at Tampa
1985	Baltimore 28, Oakland 24, at East Rutherford

NFL EUROPE

Year	Champion	Record
1991	London	9-1-0
1992	Sacramento	8-2-0
1995	Frankfurt	6-4-0
1996	Scotland	7-3-0
1997	Barcelona	5-5-0
1998	Rhein	7-3-0
1999	Frankfurt	6-4-0
2000	Rhein	7-3-0

Known as World League of American Football until 1998.

Peter Warrick
of national champion
Florida State

College
Football

Live and Learn

Peter Warrick and national champion Florida State led the way in a season of redemption and hard lessons

BY B.J. SCHECTER

A FEW MONTHS before the Sugar Bowl, the game between Florida State and Virginia Tech that would decide college football's national champion, the Seminoles' Peter Warrick sat in his Tallahassee apartment and cried, thinking he had thrown everything away.

The source of Warrick's tears was both silly and bizarre. In early October he and teammate Laveranues Coles were charged with paying $21.40 for $412.38 worth of clothing at a Dillard's department store. Coles was kicked off the team—he had been in trouble with the law several times before this incident—and Warrick eventually pled no contest to a misdemeanor. That caused him to miss two games and ruined his chances of capturing college football's most prestigious award, which he certainly would have won.

Warrick had paid a heavy price, but now he was getting a second chance, and he was determined to make the most of it. As the minutes dwindled down in the Sugar Bowl

and the Seminoles tried to shake the pesky Hokies, Warrick faced the moment he'd been waiting for, the very reason he had come back for his senior season. He had vowed to make his final collegiate game his most memorable, and to this point he had been the game's biggest star, scoring two spectacular touchdowns. With Florida State clinging to a 39–29 lead late in the fourth quarter, Warrick was ready to deliver the knockout punch.

He entered the huddle, stepped to the center and called his own number. "Y'all want me to finish them?" he asked. A few Seminoles smiled, others nodded, and then Warrick finished the Hokies. He zipped down the left sideline, cut across the middle of the end zone and made a dazzling, 43-yard touchdown catch with a Virginia Tech defender draped over his outstretched arms. The Tech defensive back had committed pass interference, and was whistled for it, but it didn't matter. Warrick would not be denied, whether defenders stayed within the rules or not.

Warrick's second touchdown of the game put the Seminoles ahead 28–7.

Florida State's sensational wide receiver strutted to the sideline, and when he reached the bench it dawned on him that a national championship was far sweeter than the Heisman Trophy he was supposed to have won. As his teammates and coaches mobbed him, he thought about his mistake earlier in the season, and how alone he had felt. Redemption was sweet indeed. But after the last high five, Warrick found himself alone with the team chaplain, Clint Purvis, and lost it. He put his head on Purvis's shoulder and began to cry. As the tears streamed down his cheeks, Warrick told Purvis, "This is the way I wanted it to end. This is why I came back."

Warrick finished the game with 163 receiving yards and three touchdowns, including one on a 59-yard punt return. Florida State won 46–29 to capture its second national championship of

BILL FRAKES

the 1990s. The Seminoles also became the first team ever to go wire-to-wire as the No. 1 team in the nation. The Seminoles went 12–0, giving coach Bobby Bowden the first perfect season of his 34-year career.

For Warrick and Florida State, 1999 was a remarkable turnaround. The previous season had ended so poorly and left such a sour taste that winning the national title was more than a goal, it was a necessity. Florida State had received a gift in making it to last year's Fiesta Bowl thanks to late-season losses by UCLA and Kansas State. But when the Seminoles sized up Tennessee, their opponent in the title game, they saw an opponent they felt they could easily beat (even with-

out starting quarterback Chris Weinke). In the days leading up to the game, Florida State walked around cocky and arrogant. The fact that they could lose never entered the Seminoles' minds.

But Florida State and Warrick played miserably. Warrick finished with one catch for seven yards, and Florida State gained only 253 yards on offense while incurring 12 penalties for 110 yards. The scene in the locker room after the game left an indelible impression on every Seminole who would be returning the following year. "Nobody was yelling or throwing anything," said safety Sean Key. "You could just hear all this crying." Bowden said he had never seen a team

AL TIELEMANS

found out what tremendous character Pete has. I'm glad y'all found out. I wouldn't recommend him doing it the way he did, but I think Pete's shown everybody that he's learned from his mistake."

Warrick wasn't the only one who learned a lot this year in college football. By season's end understudies were playing like experienced upperclassmen and upperclassmen were playing like pros. Virginia Tech's first-year quarterback, Michael Vick, who redshirted in '98, was shaky in the Hokies' first three games, but in their last three he played like an All-America. Against Clemson in a nationally televised Thursday-night game on Sept. 23, Vick nearly cost Virginia Tech the game by throwing three interceptions. But Vick got better and better each week. To bring the young QB along slowly, Virginia Tech coaches limited the number of plays and formations Vick would have to memorize, and they almost never let him throw over the middle. He shook off an early-season ankle injury and then zoomed over the learning curve normally afforded to freshman quarterbacks. He had the speed and agility of a running back and could throw a football 70 yards. In the open field, he was positively unmatched, shedding would-be tacklers with startling ease. The more comfortable he became behind the Hokies' offensive line, the more he dominated.

When the season was over, Vick had passed for 1,840 yards and 12 touchdowns, rushed for 585 yards and eight touchdowns and set an NCAA record for passing efficiency by a freshman (180.4)—and firmly

more devastated by a single game, and the loss was talked about so much early in the season that by year's end he had abandoned it as a motivational ploy.

Bowden thought his team could make it back to the title game, but he didn't expect to have Warrick. Most observers assumed the receiver would enter the NFL draft, but every time Warrick thought about leaving Florida State he remembered the Fiesta Bowl fiasco. He didn't want to go out with such a dreadful performance.

Warrick returned to get his degree and win a national championship and learn a few valuable lessons along the way. "You never learn about a person's character until they are faced with adversity," said Bowden. "If this never happened we never would have established himself as the player of the future. He was so good that he even edged into the Heisman Trophy picture late in the season, finishing third in the voting.

That coveted trophy was won by Wisconsin's burly fullback, Ron Dayne, who also learned from some early-season mistakes—thanks in part to a little wake-up call from the good folks at SPORTS ILLUSTRATED. The 5'10", 260-pound Dayne had long been criticized for being overweight and injury prone, but the big knock on him was that he disappeared when it mattered most. This was the case as Wisconsin struggled to a 2–2 start. Sure, he rushed for more than 600 yards in those four games, but when his team needed him the most Dayne dropped the ball, literally. Against Cincinnati, which had lost to Division I-AA Troy State the previous week, Dayne fumbled on the Cincinnati goal line late in the game, and the Badgers lost 17–12. Against Michigan the following week, Dayne gained zero yards rushing in the second half, and the Wolverines won 21–16.

After the Michigan loss Dayne's Heisman chances faded considerably, and SI listed him as one of the 10 biggest early-season disappointments in college football. Dayne posted the SI list in his locker and looked at it every day. "I'm not going to lie about that," said Dayne. "That really motivated me to go out and play harder." For the remainder of the season he lived up to his nickname, the Great Dayne. He rushed for 214 yards and two touchdowns in a 40–10 victory over powerful Michigan State. He entered Wisconsin's final game of the season, against Iowa, needing 99 yards to break Ricky Williams's Division I-A career rushing record of 6,279 yards, set in '98. Dayne rumbled for 216 yards on 27 carries in the Badgers' 41–3 victory. The performance locked up the Heisman for him. More important, it led the Badgers to a second consecutive berth, and victory, in the Rose Bowl, where Wisconsin knocked off Stanford 17–9.

While the Badgers became past masters of postseason triumph, other teams were learning, or relearning, how to win in '99.

Hawaii entered the season with the longest losing streak (18 games) in Division I-A, and hadn't had a winning season since '92. But with former Atlanta Falcons coach June Jones and a flashy run-and-shoot offense, the Rainbow Warriors executed the greatest turnaround in Division I-A history, going 9–4 and defeating Oregon State 23–17 in the Oahu Bowl. Oregon State also had a new coach, former Seattle Seahawks man Dennis Erickson, and also reacquainted itself with winning. The Beavers finished above .500 (7–5) for the first time since 1970.

In Division III, Swarthmore, that seat of learning outside Philadelphia, finally conquered the nation's longest losing streak, defeating Oberlin 42–6 for its first victory in four years and 29 games. At the other end of the Division III spectrum, Mount Union defeated Otterbein 44–20 on Oct. 16 to win its 48th consecutive game, breaking the all-division NCAA record set by Oklahoma in the 1950s. The Purple Raiders would extend the streak to 54 games before losing to Rowan in the Division III semifinals.

Back at "the Program" in Tallahassee, Bowden proved he knows most of what there is to know about winning by seizing his 300th college coaching victory. The landmark win—only four other major college coaches have reached this milestone—came on Oct. 23 against Clemson, which happens to be coached by Bowden's son Tommy. Washington junior Marcus Tuiasosopo taught his quarterbacking peers a few new tricks, becoming the first major college quarterback to throw for more than 300 yards and rush for more than 200 in a single game, a 35–30 win over Stanford on Oct. 30. Before the season started, Tuiasosopo's coach, Rick Neuheisel, played a dirty trick on his former team, the Colorado Buffaloes, bolting in January for Washington, and a $1 million–a–year salary, to coach the Huskies. Colorado players felt bitter and betrayed, and on Sept. 25 they got a chance to teach Neuheisel a lesson about loyalty when the Buffaloes traveled to Seattle to face the Huskies. But Washington came away with a hard-fought 31–24 victory, and when it was over, the Colorado players lined up

RICHARD MACKSON

Dayne shook off a slow start and rumbled his way to the Heisman.

at midfield to hug their former coach.

The college football community also learned tragic, difficult lessons in '99 about the fleeting nature of life. On Aug. 11, Nancy Bennett, the wife of Kansas State defensive coordinator Phil Bennett, went out for a leisurely jog near the Bennett home in Manhattan, Kans., and was struck by lightning. She went into a coma and died 17 days later. On Nov. 18, 11 Texas A&M students and one alumnus were killed in the collapse of the massive log structure they were building for the annual bonfire before the Texas game. Eight days later A&M pulled off a shocking and courageous 20–16 upset. Said Aggies linebacker Brian Gamble after the game, "Life is a precious thing. One day it's going to slip out from under you, and you're not going to be here."

Gamble's words were a reminder that life's experiences and joys are to be cher-

ished, a lesson certainly not lost on the voluble Bowden. Well known for his good cheer and memorable one-liners, the 70-year-old Bowden has been criticized at times for a perceived lack of intensity. Bowden's wife, Ann, for one, knows the criticism is unfounded. Before the Sugar Bowl she told reporters about the evening in December when she and her husband were watching television and Bobby suddenly turned deadly serious and said, "We should have beaten Tennessee, you know that? We should have beaten those boys."

By the end of the season, though, such thoughts no longer plagued him, and he came across like a lovable teddy bear. During the postgame celebration he was handed a cell phone, and he greeted his caller, President Clinton, saying, "How come you're not working tonight?" The pair chatted like good ol' boys for a spell, and when Bowden hung up he said, "See ya, buddy."

And with that we said goodbye to another college football season.

Final Polls

Associated Press

	Record	Pts	Head Coach	SI Preseason Rank
1. Florida St (70)	12–0	1750	Bobby Bowden	2
2. Virginia Tech	11–1	1647	Frank Beamer	17
3. Nebraska	12–1	1634	Frank Solich	6
4. Wisconsin	10–2	1519	Barry Alvarez	11
5. Michigan	10–2	1406	Lloyd Carr	15
6. Kansas St	11–1	1402	Bill Snyder	23
7. Michigan St	10–2	1357	Nick Saban	33
8. Alabama	10–3	1236	Mike DuBose	16
9. Tennessee	9–3	1168	Phillip Fulmer	4
10. Marshall	13–0	1136	Bob Pruett	24
11. Penn St	10–3	1038	Joe Paterno	1
12. Florida	9–4	941	Steve Spurrier	7
13. Mississippi St	10–2	923	Jackie Sherrill	35
14. Southern Mississippi	9–3	788	Jeff Bower	41
15. Miami (FL)	9–4	678	Butch Davis	13
16. Georgia	8–4	640	Jim Donnan	18
17. Arkansas	8–4	575	Houston Nutt	22
18. Minnesota	8–4	452	Glen Mason	40
19. Oregon	9–3	358	Mike Belotti	34
20. Georgia Tech	8–4	345	George O'Leary	9
21. Texas	9–5	340	Mack Brown	20
22. Mississippi	8–4	281	David Cutcliffe	32
23. Texas A&M	8–4	272	R.C. Slocum	8
24. Illinois	8–4	201	Ron Turner	77
25. Purdue	7–5	198	Joe Tiller	21

Note: As voted by a panel of 70 sportswriters and broadcasters following bowl games (1st-place votes in parentheses).

USA Today/ESPN

	Pts	Prev Rank			Pts	Prev Rank
1. Florida St (59)	1475	1	14. Florida		713	10
2. Nebraska	1390	3	15. Miami (FL)		605	23
3. Virginia Tech	1366	2	16. Georgia		505	24
4. Wisconsin	1283	4	17. Minnesota		395	12
5. Michigan	1189	8	18. Oregon		375	—
6. Kansas St	1188	7	19. Arkansas		357	—
7. Michigan St	1117	9	20. Texas A&M		344	13
8. Alabama	1042	6	21. Georgia Tech		337	15
9. Tennessee	985	5	22. Mississippi		231	—
10. Marshall	956	11	23. Texas		173	18
11. Penn St	840	17	24. Stanford		155	21
12. Mississippi St	810	16	25. Illinois		139	—
13. Southern Mississippi	763	14				

Note: As voted by a panel of 59 Division I–A head coaches; 25 points for 1st, 24 for 2nd, etc. (1st-place votes in parentheses).

Bowls and Playoffs

NCAA Division I-A Bowl Results

Date	Bowl	Result	Payout/Team ($)	Attendance
12-18-99	Las Vegas	Utah 17, Fresno St 16	1.2 million	28,227
12-22-99	Mobile Alabama	TCU 28, E Carolina 14	750,000	34,200
12-25-99	Aloha	Wake Forest 23, Arizona St 3	800,000	40,974
12-25-99	Oahu	Hawaii 23, Oregon St 17	800,000	40,974
12-27-99	Motor City	Marshall 21, BYU 3	750,000	52,449
12-28-99	Alamo	Penn St 24, Texas A&M 0	1.2 million	65,380
12-29-99	Music City	Syracuse 20, Kentucky 13	750,000	59,221
12-29-99	Holiday	Kansas St 24, Washington 20	1.8 million	57,118

NCAA Division I-A Bowl Results *(Cont.)*

Date	Bowl	Result	Payout/Team ($)	Attendance
12-30-99	Humanitarian	Boise St 34, Louisville 31	750,000	29,283
12-30-99	MicronPC.com	Illinois 63, Virginia 21	750,000	31,089
12-30-99	Peach	Mississippi St 17, Clemson 7	1.6 million	73,315
12-31-99	Sun	Oregon 24, Minnesota 20	1.2 million	48,757
12-31-99	Insight.com	Colorado 62, Boston College 28	750,000	35,762
12-31-99	Liberty	Southern Miss 23, Colorado St 17	1.2 million	54,866
12-31-99	Independence	Mississippi 27, Oklahoma 25	1 million	49,873
1-1-00	Cotton	Arkansas 27, Texas 6	2.5 million	72,723
1-1-00	Outback	Georgia 28, Purdue 25 (OT)	1.9 million	54,059
1-1-00	Gator	Miami (FL) 27, Georgia Tech 13	1.4 million	43,416
1-1-00	Citrus	Michigan St 37, Florida 34	3.8 million	62,011
1-1-00	Rose	Wisconsin 17, Stanford 9	12 million	93,731
1-1-00	Orange	Michigan 35, Alabama 34 (OT)	11-13 million	70,461
1-2-00	Fiesta	Nebraska 31, Tennessee 21	11-13 million	71,526
1-4-00	Sugar	Florida St 46, Virginia Tech 29	11-13 million	79,280

NCAA Division I-AA Championship Boxscore

Youngstown St	7	3	7—24	
Georgia Southern	10	28	7	14—59

FIRST QUARTER

GS: FG Chambers 25, 10:20.
YS: Brown 2 run (Griffith kick), 4:51.
GS: Hill 42 run (Chambers kick), 2:51.

SECOND QUARTER

YS: Ryan 3 run (Griffith kick), 14:34.
GS: Peterson 3 run (Chambers kick), 10:25.
GS: Cunningham 57 run (Chambers kick), 9:05.
GS: Peterson 22 run (Chambers kick), 5:27.
GS: Williams 72 punt return (Chambers kick), 2:09.

THIRD QUARTER

YS: FG Griffith 30, 4:47.
GS: Peterson 1 run (Chambers kick), 3:05.

FOURTH QUARTER

GS: Myers 5 run (Chambers kick), 9:57.
GS: Revere 66 run (Chambers kick), 7:27.
YS: Brown 1 run (Griffith kick), 3:48.

	Youngstown St	GA Southern
First downs	17	24
Rushing yardage	44–163	59–638
Passing yardage	175	17
Return yardage	0	120
Passes (comp-att-int)	11-20-1	1-4-0
Punts (no.–avg)	7-36.0	1-25.0
Fumbles (no.–lost)	1–0	1–0
Penalties (no.–yards)	3–11	9–82

Att: 20,052

Small College Championship Summaries

NCAA DIVISION II

First round: Carson-Newman (TN) 40, Arkansas Tech 28; Catawba (NC) 48, Ft. Valley St (GA) 17; UC–Davis 33, Central Oklahoma 17; Northeastern St (OK) 27, Western Washington 24 (ot); Indiana (PA) 27, Slippery Rock (PA) 20 (ot); Millersville (PA) 21, Shepherd (WV) 14; Northern Colorado 34, Pittsburg St (KS) 31; NW Missouri St 20, N Dakota 13 (ot).
Quarterfinals: Carson-Newman 28, Catawba 25; Northeastern St 19, UC–Davis 14; Indiana 26, Millersville 21; NW Missouri St 41, Northern Colorado 35.
Semifinals: Carson-Newman 42, Northeastern St 7; NW Missouri St 20, Indiana 12.

Championship: 12-11-99 Florence, AL

NW Missouri St	7	0	7	30	0	0	8	6—58
Carson-Newman	10	14	6	14	0	0	8	0—52

NCAA DIVISION III

First round: Augustana (IL) 39, St. Norbert (WI) 32; Ohio Northern 56, Hanover (IN) 14; Wittenberg (OH) 42, Alma (MI) 19; Montclair St 37, Buffalo St 34; Rowan (NJ) 29, Rensselaer (NY) 10; Ursinus (PA) 43, Bridgewater St (MA) 38; Pacific Lutheran (WA) 28, Willamette (OR) 24; Central (IA) 38, WI–LaCrosse 17; St. John's (MN) 23, WI-Stevens Point 10; Western Maryland 20, Catholic

(DC) 16; Hardin-Simmons (TX) 28, Washington (MO) 21; Washington & Jefferson (PA) 14, Lycoming (PA) 7.
Second Round: Mt Union (OH) 42, Augustana 33; Ohio Northern 58, Wittenberg 24; Montclair St 32, Western Connecticut St 24; Rowan 55, Ursinus 0; Pacific Lutheran 49, Wartburg (IA) 14; St. John's 10, Central 9; Trinity (TX) 20, Western Maryland 16; Hardin-Simmons 51, Washington & Jefferson 3.
Quarterfinals: Mt Union 56, Ohio Northern 31; Rowan 42, Montclair St 13; Pacific Lutheran 19, St. John's 9; Trinity 40, Hardin-Simmons 33.
Semifinals: Rowan 24, Mt Union 17 (ot); Pacific Lutheran 49, Trinity 28.

Championship: 12-18-99 Salem, VA

Rowan	7	0	6	0—13
Pacific Lutheran	14	13	8	7—42

NAIA CHAMPIONSHIP

12-18-99 Hardin County, TN

Georgetown, KY	7	13	0	6—26
NW Oklahoma	0	0	21	13—34

Awards

Heisman Memorial Trophy

Player, School	Class	Pos	1st	2nd	3rd	Total
Ron Dayne, Wisconsin	Sr	RB	586	121	42	2042
Joe Hamilton, Georgia Tech	Sr	QB	96	285	136	994
Michael Vick, Virginia Tech	Fr	QB	25	72	100	319
Drew Brees, Purdue	Jr	QB	3	89	121	308
Chad Pennington, Marshall	Sr	QB	21	45	94	247
Peter Warrick, Florida St	Sr	WR	14	50	61	203
Shaun Alexander, Alabama	Sr	RB	11	43	52	171
Thomas Jones, Virginia	Sr	RB	10	32	46	140
LaVar Arrington, Penn St	Jr	LB	3	14	17	54
Tim Rattay, Louisiana Tech	Sr	QB	1	5	16	29

Note: Former Heisman winners and the media vote, with ballots allowing for three names (3 points for 1st, 2 for 2nd, 1 for 3rd).

Offensive Players of the Year

Maxwell Award (Player)............................Ron Dayne, Wisconsin, RB
Walter Camp Player of the Year (Back) .....Ron Dayne, Wisconsin, RB
Davey O'Brien Award (QB) ....Joe Hamilton, Georgia Tech, QB
Doak Walker Award (RB) ....Ron Dayne, Wisconsin, RB

Other Awards

Biletnikoff Award (WR) ....Troy Walters, Stanford, WR
Vince Lombardi/Rotary Award (Lineman)...Corey Moore, Virginia Tech, DE
Outland Trophy (Interior lineman) ....Chris Samuels, Alabama, OT
Butkus Award (Linebacker).........................LaVar Arrington, Penn St, LB
Jim Thorpe Award (Defensive back)..........Tyrone Carter, Minnesota, S
Sporting News Player of the Year ....Ron Dayne, Wisconsin, RB
Walter Payton Award (Div I-AA Player) ......Adrian Peterson, Georgia Southern, RB
Harlon Hill Trophy (Div II Player) ....Corte McGuffey, Northern Colorado, QB

Coaches' Awards

Walter Camp Award ....Frank Beamer, Virginia Tech
Eddie Robinson Award (Div I-AA)..............L.C. Cole, Tennessee State
Bobby Dodd Award ....Frank Beamer, Virginia Tech
Bear Bryant Award ....Frank Beamer, Virginia Tech

AFCA COACHES OF THE YEAR

Division I-A ....Frank Beamer, Virginia Tech
Division I-AA..Paul Johnson, Georgia Southern
Division II..Mel Tjeerdsma, NW Missouri St
Division III ....Frosty Westering, Pacific Lutheran

Football Writers Association of America All-America Team

OFFENSE

Peter Warrick, Florida St, Sr ....Wide receiver
Troy Walters, Stanford, Sr ....Wide receiver
James Whalen, Kentucky, Sr ....Tight end
Mike Malano, San Diego St, Sr............OL
Brad Bedell, Colorado, Sr ....OL
Cosey Coleman, Tennessee, Jr ....OL
Chris McIntosh, Wisconsin, Sr ....OL
Chris Samuels, Alabama, Sr ....OL
Joe Hamilton, Georgia Tech, Sr..........Quarterback
Ron Dayne, Wisconsin, Sr...................Running back
Thomas Jones, Virginia, Sr..................Running back
Sebastian Janikowski, Florida St, Jr....Placekicker
Dennis Northcutt, Arizona, Sr..............Kick returner

DEFENSE

Corey Simon, Florida St, Sr ....DL
Courtney Brown, Penn St, Sr...............DL
Corey Moore, Virginia Tech, Sr ....DL
Casey Hampton, Texas, Jr...................DL
LaVar Arrington, Penn St, Jr................Linebacker
Brandon Short, Penn St, Sr ....Linebacker
Mark Simoneau, Kansas St, Sr............Linebacker
Mike Brown, Nebraska, Sr....................Defensive back
Tyrone Carter, Minnesota, Sr ....Defensive back
Deltha O'Neal, California, Sr ....Defensive back
Brian Urlacher, New Mexico, Sr ....Defensive back
Andrew Bayes, E Carolina, Sr ....Punter

Division I-A

ATLANTIC COAST CONFERENCE

	Conference		Full Season		
	W	L	W	L	Pct
Florida St	8	0	12	0	1.000
Georgia Tech	5	3	8	4	.667
Virginia	5	3	7	5	.583
Clemson	5	3	6	6	.500
Wake Forest	3	5	7	5	.583
N Carolina St	3	5	6	6	.500
Duke	3	5	3	8	.273
Maryland	2	6	5	6	.455
N Carolina	2	6	3	8	.273

BIG EAST CONFERENCE

	Conference		Full Season		
	W	L	W	L	Pct
Virginia Tech	7	0	11	1	.917
Miami	6	1	9	4	.692
Boston College	4	3	8	4	.667
Syracuse	3	4	7	5	.583
W Virginia	3	4	4	7	.364
Pittsburgh	2	5	5	6	.455
Temple	2	5	2	9	.182
Rutgers	1	6	1	10	.091

BIG TEN CONFERENCE

	Conference		Full Season		
	W	L	W	L	Pct
Wisconsin	7	1	10	2	.833
Michigan	6	2	10	2	.833
Michigan St	6	2	10	2	.833
Minnesota	5	3	8	4	.667
Penn St	5	3	10	3	.769
Illinois	4	4	8	4	.667
Purdue	4	4	7	5	.583
Ohio St	3	5	6	6	.500
Indiana	3	5	4	7	.364
Northwestern	1	7	3	8	.273
Iowa	0	8	1	10	.091

BIG 12 CONFERENCE

	Conference		Full Season		
	W	L	W	L	Pct
NORTH					
*Nebraska	7	1	12	1	.923
Kansas St	7	1	11	1	.916
Colorado	5	3	7	5	.583
Kansas	3	5	5	7	.417
Iowa St	1	7	4	7	.364
Missouri	1	7	4	7	.364
SOUTH					
*Texas	6	2	9	5	.642
Texas Tech	5	3	6	5	.545
Oklahoma	5	3	7	5	.636
Texas A&M	5	3	8	4	.667
Oklahoma St	3	5	5	6	.455
Baylor	0	8	1	10	.091

*Full season record includes Big 12 Championship Game in which Nebraska defeated Texas 22–6, on Dec. 4.

BIG WEST CONFERENCE

	Conference		Full Season		
	W	L	W	L	Pct
Boise St	5	1	10	3	.769
Idaho	4	2	7	4	.636
N Mexico St	3	3	6	5	.545
Arkansas St	3	3	4	7	.364
Utah St	3	3	4	7	.364
Nevada	2	4	3	8	.273
N Texas	1	5	2	9	.182

Division I-A (Cont.)

CONFERENCE USA

	Conference		Full Season		
	W	L	W	L	Pct
Southern Mississippi	6	0	9	3	.750
E Carolina	4	2	9	3	.750
Louisville	4	2	7	5	.583
Memphis	4	2	5	6	.455
Alabama-Birmingham	4	2	5	6	.455
Houston	3	3	7	4	.636
Tulane	1	5	3	8	.273
Army	1	5	3	8	.273
Cincinnati	0	6	3	8	.273

MID-AMERICAN ATHLETIC CONFERENCE

	Conference		Full Season		
EAST	W	L	W	L	Pct
*Marshall	8	0	13	0	1.000
Miami (OH)	6	2	7	4	.636
Akron	5	3	7	4	.636
Ohio	5	3	5	6	.455
Bowling Green	3	5	5	6	.455
Kent	2	6	2	9	.182
Buffalo	0	8	0	11	.000
WEST					
*Western Michigan	6	2	7	5	.583
Toledo	5	3	6	5	.545
Northern Illinois	5	3	5	6	.455
Eastern Michigan	4	4	4	7	.364
Central Michigan	3	5	4	7	.364
Ball St	0	8	0	11	.000

*Full season record includes MAC Championship Game in which Marshall defeated Western Michigan 34–30, on Dec. 3.

MOUNTAIN WEST CONFERENCE

	Conference		Full Season		
	W	L	W	L	Pct
Colorado St	5	2	8	4	.667
Utah	5	2	9	3	.750
Brigham Young	5	2	8	4	.667
Wyoming	4	3	7	4	.636
New Mexico	3	4	4	7	.364
San Diego St	3	4	5	6	.454
Air Force	2	5	6	5	.545
UNLV	1	6	3	8	.273

PACIFIC 10 CONFERENCE

	Conference		Full Season		
	W	L	W	L	Pct
Stanford	7	1	8	3	.727
Oregon	6	2	8	3	.727
Washington	6	2	7	4	.636
Arizona St	5	3	6	5	.545
Oregon St	4	4	7	4	.636
Arizona	3	5	6	6	.500
Southern California	3	5	6	6	.500
California	3	5	4	7	.364
UCLA	2	6	4	7	.364
Washington St	1	7	3	9	.250

Division I-A *(Cont.)*

SOUTHEASTERN CONFERENCE

EAST	Conference		Full Season		
	W	L	W	L	Pct
*Florida	7	1	9	4	.692
Tennessee	6	2	9	3	.750
Georgia	5	3	8	4	.667
Kentucky	4	4	6	6	.500
Vanderbilt	2	6	5	6	.455
S Carolina	0	8	0	11	.000
WEST					
*Alabama	7	1	10	3	.769
Mississippi St	6	2	10	2	.833
Mississippi	4	4	8	4	.667
Arkansas	4	4	8	4	.667
Auburn	2	6	5	6	.455
Louisiana St	1	7	3	8	.273

*Full season record includes SEC Championship Game in which Alabama defeated Florida 34–7, on Dec. 4.

WESTERN ATHLETIC CONFERENCE

	Conference		Full Season		
	W	L	W	L	Pct
Hawaii	5	2	9	4	.692
Texas Christian	5	2	8	4	.667
Fresno St	5	2	8	5	.615
Rice	4	3	5	6	.455
Southern Methodist	3	3	4	6	.400
Texas–El Paso	3	4	5	7	.417
San Jose St	1	5	3	7	.300
Tulsa	1	6	2	9	.182

INDEPENDENTS

	Full Season		
	W	L	Pct
Louisiana Tech	8	3	.727
Louisiana-Monroe	5	6	.455
Notre Dame	5	7	.417
Navy	5	7	.417
Central Florida	4	7	.364
Middle Tennessee St	3	8	.273
Louisiana-Lafayette	2	9	.182

Division I-AA

ATLANTIC 10

	Conference		Full Season		
	W	L	W	L	Pct
James Madison	7	1	8	4	.667
Massachusetts	7	1	9	4	.692
Villanova	6	2	7	4	.636
Delaware	5	3	7	4	.636
William & Mary	5	3	6	5	.545
Connecticut	3	5	4	7	.364
Maine	3	5	4	7	.364
New Hampshire	3	5	5	6	.455
Richmond	3	5	5	6	.455
Northeastern	1	7	2	9	.182
Rhode Island	1	7	1	10	.091

Division I-AA (Cont.)

BIG SKY CONFERENCE

	Conference		Full Season		
	W	L	W	L	Pct
Montana	7	1	9	3	.750
Portland St	6	2	8	3	.727
Northern Arizona	6	2	8	4	.667
Eastern Washington	6	2	7	4	.636
Cal St–Northridge	4	4	5	6	.455
Cal St–Sacramento	3	5	6	5	.545
Weber St	2	6	3	8	.273
Idaho St	1	7	3	8	.273
Montana St	1	7	3	8	.273

GATEWAY COLLEGIATE ATHLETIC CONFERENCE

	Conference		Full Season		
	W	L	W	L	Pct
Illinois St	6	0	11	3	.786
Youngstown St	5	1	12	3	.800
Northern Iowa	3	3	8	3	.727
Western Illinois	2	4	7	4	.636
SW Missouri St	2	4	5	6	.455
Indiana St	2	4	3	8	.273
Southern Illinois	1	5	5	6	.455

IVY LEAGUE

	Conference		Full Season		
	W	L	W	L	Pct
Brown	6	1	9	1	.900
Yale	6	1	9	1	.900
Cornell	5	2	7	3	.700
Pennsylvania	4	3	5	5	.500
Harvard	3	4	5	5	.500
Dartmouth	2	5	2	8	.200
Columbia	1	6	3	7	.300
Princeton	1	6	3	7	.300

METRO ATLANTIC ATHLETIC CONFERENCE

	Conference		Full Season		
	W	L	W	L	Pct
Fairfield	7	1	9	2	.818
Georgetown	7	1	9	2	.818
Duquesne	6	2	8	3	.727
Marist	5	3	6	5	.545
Iona	4	4	5	5	.500
LaSalle	3	5	4	6	.400
Siena	3	5	3	7	.300
St. Peter's	1	7	1	10	.091
Canisius	0	8	1	10	.091

MID-EASTERN ATHLETIC LEAGUE

	Conference		Full Season		
	W	L	W	L	Pct
N Carolina A&T	8	0	11	2	.846
Florida A&M	7	1	10	4	.714
Hampton	5	3	8	4	.667
Bethune Cookman	4	4	7	4	.636
Howard	4	4	5	6	.455
Delaware St	4	4	4	7	.364
S Carolina St	2	5	4	6	.400
Norfolk St	1	7	2	9	.182
Morgan St	0	7	2	8	.200

Division I-AA *(Cont.)*

NORTHEAST CONFERENCE

	Conference		Full Season		
	W	L	W	L	Pct
Robert Morris	7	0	8	2	.800
Albany	6	1	7	2	.778
Wagner	5	2	5	5	.500
Stony Brook	4	3	5	5	.500
Central Connecticut St	3	4	4	6	.400
Monmouth	2	5	2	8	.200
St. Francis (PA)	1	6	2	9	.182
Sacred Heart	0	7	2	9	.182

OHIO VALLEY CONFERENCE

	Conference		Full Season		
	W	L	W	L	Pct
Tennessee St	7	0	11	1	.917
Murray St	5	2	7	4	.636
Eastern Kentucky	4	3	7	4	.636
Western Kentucky	4	3	6	5	.545
Tennessee Tech	4	3	5	5	.500
SE Missouri	2	5	3	8	.273
Eastern Illinois	2	5	2	10	.167
Tennessee-Martin	0	7	1	10	.091

PATRIOT LEAGUE

	Conference		Full Season		
	W	L	W	L	Pct
Colgate	5	1	10	2	.833
Lehigh	5	1	10	2	.833
Towson	4	2	7	4	.636
Bucknell	3	3	7	4	.636
Holy Cross	2	4	3	8	.273
Lafayette	2	4	4	7	.364
Fordham	0	6	0	11	.000

PIONEER FOOTBALL LEAGUE

	Conference		Full Season		
	W	L	W	L	Pct
Dayton	4	0	6	4	.600
Valparaiso	3	1	9	2	.818
Drake	2	2	7	4	.636
San Diego	1	3	5	5	.500
Butler	0	4	5	5	.500

SOUTHERN CONFERENCE

	Conference		Full Season		
	W	L	W	L	Pct
Georgia Southern	7	1	13	2	.867
Appalachian St	7	1	9	3	.750
Furman	7	1	9	3	.750
Wofford	5	3	6	5	.545
E Tennessee St	4	4	6	5	.545
Chattanooga	3	5	5	6	.455
Western Carolina	2	6	3	8	.273
The Citadel	1	7	2	9	.182
Virginia Military	0	8	1	10	.091

Division I-AA *(Cont.)*

SOUTHLAND FOOTBALL LEAGUE

	Conference		Full Season		
	W	L	W	L	Pct
Troy St	6	1	11	2	.846
Stephen F. Austin	6	1	8	3	.727
McNeese St	5	2	6	5	.545
Sam Houston St	4	3	6	5	.545
Northwestern St	3	4	4	7	.364
SW Texas	2	5	3	8	.273
Jacksonville St	1	6	2	9	.182
Nicholls St	1	6	1	10	.091

SOUTHWESTERN

	Conference		Full Season		
EASTERN	W	L	W	L	Pct
*Jackson St	7	2	9	3	.750
Alabama A&M	4	4	6	5	.545
Mississippi Valley St	3	5	3	8	.273
Alabama St	2	6	2	9	.182
Alcorn St	2	7	3	7	.300
WESTERN					
*Southern	9	0	11	2	.846
Grambling	6	3	7	4	.636
Texas Southern	4	3	6	5	.545
Arkansas–Pine Bluff	5	4	6	5	.545
Prairie View A&M	0	8	2	8	.200

*Full season record includes SWAC Championship Game in which Southern defeated Jackson St 31–30, on Dec. 11.

INDEPENDENTS

	Full Season		
	W	L	Pct
Hofstra	11	2	.846
Elon	9	2	.818
Southern Utah	8	3	.727
Davidson	8	3	.727
Samford	7	4	.636
S Florida	7	4	.636
St. John's (NY)	7	4	.636
Morehead St	5	5	.500
Charleston Southern	4	6	.400
Liberty	4	7	.364
Jacksonville	3	6	.333
Cal Poly–San Luis Obispo	3	8	.273
Austin Peay	3	8	.273
St. Mary's (CA)	2	9	.182

1999 NCAA Individual Leaders

Division I-A

SCORING

	Class	GP	TD	XP	FG	Pts	Pts/Game
Shaun Alexander, Alabama	Sr	11	24	0	0	144	13.09
Travis Prentice, Miami (OH)	Sr	11	21	0	0	126	11.45
Sebastian Janikowski, Florida St	Jr	11	0	47	23	116	10.55
Ron Dayne, Wisconsin	Sr	11	19	0	0	114	10.36
Frank Moreau, Louisville	Sr	10	17	0	0	102	10.20
Ladainian Tomlinson, Texas Christian	Jr	11	18	0	0	108	9.82
Shayne Graham, Virginia Tech	Sr	11	0	56	17	107	9.73
Ken Simonton, Oregon St	So	11	17	4	0	106	9.64
Travis Zachery, Clemson	So	10	16	0	0	96	9.60
Jamie Rheem, Kansas St	Jr	10	0	41	18	95	9.50

FIELD GOALS

	Class	GP	FGA	FG	Pct	FG/Game
Sebastian Janikowski, Florida St	Jr	11	30	23	.767	2.09
Neil Rackers, Illinois	Sr	11	25	20	.800	1.82
Jamie Rheem, Kansas St	Jr	10	21	18	.857	1.80
Jeff Chandler, Florida	Jr	12	24	21	.875	1.75
Travis Forney, Penn St	Sr	12	26	21	.808	1.75
Paul Edinger, Michigan St	Sr	11	22	18	.818	1.64
Scott Westerfield, Mississippi St	Jr	11	24	18	.750	1.64
Owen Pochman, Brigham Young	Jr	11	25	18	.720	1.64
Todd France, Toledo	So	11	26	18	.692	1.64
Travis Dorsche, Purdue	So	11	28	18	.643	1.64

TOTAL OFFENSE

			Rushing		Passing		Total Offense			
	Class	GP	Car	Net	Att	Yds	Yds	Yds/Play	TDR*	Yds/Game
Tim Rattay, Louisiana Tech	Sr	10	46	-112	516	3922	3810	6.78	35	381.00
Joe Hamilton, Georgia Tech	Sr	11	154	738	305	3060	3798	8.27	35	345.27
Drew Brees, Purdue	Jr	11	70	181	494	3531	3712	6.58	25	337.45
David Neill, Nevada	So	11	100	209	423	3402	3611	6.90	25	328.27
Chad Pennington, Marshall	Sr	12	55	105	405	3799	3904	8.49	39	325.33
Chris Redman, Louisville	Sr	11	43	-110	489	3647	3537	6.65	30	321.55
Kevin Feterik, Brigham Young	Sr	11	88	-77	452	3554	3477	6.44	26	316.09
Dan Robinson, Hawaii	Sr	12	60	-91	556	3853	3762	6.11	32	313.50
Josh Heupel, Oklahoma	Jr	11	47	-98	500	3460	3362	6.15	35	305.64
Patrick Ramsey, Tulane	So	11	64	-61	513	3410	3349	5.80	26	304.45

*Touchdowns responsible for are TDs scored and passed for.

RUSHING

	Class	GP	Car	Yds	Avg	TD	Yds/Game
LaDainian Tomlinson, TCU	Jr	11	268	1850	6.9	18	168.18
Ron Dayne, Wisconsin	Sr	11	303	1834	6.1	19	166.73
Thomas Jones, Virginia	Sr	11	334	1798	5.4	16	163.45
Travis Prentice, Miami (OH)	Sr	11	354	1659	4.7	17	150.82
Lamont Jordan, Maryland	Jr	11	266	1632	6.1	16	148.36
Demario Brown, Utah St	Sr	11	279	1536	5.5	14	139.64
Trung Canidate, Arizona	Sr	12	253	1602	6.3	11	133.50
Frank Moreau, Louisville	Sr	10	233	1289	5.5	17	128.90
Darren Davis, Iowa St	Sr	11	287	1388	4.8	14	126.18
Shaun Alexander, Alabama	Sr	11	302	1383	4.6	19	125.73

PASSING EFFICIENCY

	Class	GP	Att	Comp	Pct Comp	Yds	Yds/Att	TD	Int	Rating Pts
Michael Vick, Virginia Tech	So	10	152	90	59.21	1840	12.11	12	5	180.4
Joe Hamilton, Georgia Tech	Sr	11	305	203	66.56	3060	10.03	29	11	175.0
Chad Pennington, Marshall	Sr	12	405	275	67.90	3799	9.38	37	11	171.4
Billy Volek, Fresno St	Sr	12	355	235	66.20	2559	7.21	30	3	152.9
Tim Rattay, Louisiana Tech	Sr	10	516	342	66.28	3922	7.60	35	12	147.9
Jay Stuckey, Texas–El Paso	Sr	12	225	145	64.44	1918	8.52	15	13	146.5
Chris Weinke, Florida St	Jr	11	377	232	61.54	3103	8.23	25	14	145.1
Dan Ellis, Virginia	Jr	10	258	156	60.47	2050	7.95	20	10	145.0
Jeff Kelly, Southern Mississippi	So	11	260	153	58.85	2062	7.93	21	11	143.7
Tim Lester, Western Michigan	Sr	12	470	262	60.00	3639	7.74	34	13	143.4

Note: Minimum 15 attempts per game.

RECEPTIONS PER GAME

	Class	GP	No.	Yds	TD	R/Game
Trevor Insley, Nevada	Sr	11	134	2060	13	12.18
Chris Daniels, Purdue	Sr	11	109	1133	5	9.91
Jajaun Dawson, Tulane	Sr	10	96	1051	8	9.60
Arnold Jackson, Louisville	Sr	11	101	1209	9	9.18
James Whalen, Kentucky	Sr	11	90	1019	10	8.18

Division I-A *(Cont.)*

RECEIVING YARDS PER GAME

	Class	GP	No.	Yds	TD	Yds/Game
Trevor Insley, Nevada	Sr	11	134	2060	13	187.27
Troy Walters, Stanford	Sr	11	74	1456	10	132.36
Dennis Northcutt, Arizona	Sr	12	88	1422	8	118.50
Arnold Jackson, Louisville	Sr	11	101	1209	9	109.91
Drew Haddad, Buffalo	Sr	11	85	1158	6	105.27

ALL-PURPOSE RUNNERS

	Class	GP	Rush	Rec	PR	KOR	Yds	Yds/Game
Trevor Insley, Nevada	Sr	11	5	2060	111	0	2176	197.82
Dennis Northcutt, Arizona	Sr	12	200	1422	436	191	2249	187.42
Thomas Jones, Virginia	Sr	11	1798	239	17	0	2054	186.73
LaDainian Tomlinson, TCU	Jr	11	1850	55	0	69	1974	179.45
Travis Prentice, Miami (OH)	Sr	11	1659	270	0	0	1929	175.36

INTERCEPTIONS

	Class	GP	No.	Int/Game
Deltha O'Neal, California	Sr	11	9	.82
Deon Grant, Tennessee	Jr	11	9	.82
Rodregis Brooks, UAB	Jr	11	9	.82
Erik Olson, Colorado St.	Sr	9	6	.67
Jamar Fletcher, Wisconsin	So	11	7	.64
Mike James, Houston	Sr	11	7	.64

PUNT RETURNS

	Class	No.	Yds	TD	Avg
Dennis Northcutt, Arizona	Sr	23	436	2	18.96
Bobby Newcombe, Nebraska	Jr	16	294	1	18.38
Vinny Sutherland, Purdue	Jr	17	295	2	17.35
Rodregis Brooks, UAB	Jr	19	325	0	17.11
Stevonne Smith, Utah	Jr	29	495	3	17.07

Note: Minimum 1.2 per game.

PUNTING

	Class	No.	Avg
Andrew Bayes, East Carolina	Sr	47	48.06
Brian Schmitz, N Carolina	Sr	74	47.81
Shane Lechler, Texas A&M	Sr	60	46.45
Ray Cheetany, UNLV	Jr	65	45.38
Dan Hadenfeldt, Nebraska	Sr	65	44.98

Note: Minimum of 3.6 per game.

KICKOFF RETURNS

	Class	No.	Yds	TD	Avg
James Williams, Marshall	Sr	15	493	1	32.87
Brandon Daniels, Oklahoma	Sr	16	508	1	31.75
John Stone, Wake Forest	So	13	389	1	29.92
Deltha O'Neal, California	Sr	19	555	1	29.21
Ben Kelly, Colorado	Jr	19	547	2	28.79

Note: Minimum of 1.2 per game.

Division I-A Team Single-Game Highs

RUSHING AND PASSING

Rushing and passing plays: 82—Drew Brees, Purdue, Nov 6 (vs Wisconsin).
Rushing and passing yards: 541—Tim Rattay, Louisiana Tech, Oct 23 (vs UCF).
Rushing plays: 45—Reuben Droughns, Oregon, Oct 23 (vs Arizona); Zain Gilmore, Missouri, Oct 30 (vs Texas Tech).
Net rushing yards: 406—LaDaninian Tomlinson, Texas Christian, Nov 20 (vs UTEP).
Passes attempted: 68—Tim Rattay, Louisiana Tech, Oct 26 (vs Southern Cal).
Passes completed: 46—Tim Rattay, Louisiana Tech, Oct 23 (vs Central Florida).
Passing yards: 561—Tim Rattay, Louisiana Tech, Oct 23 (vs Central Florida).

RECEIVING AND RETURNS

Passes caught: 21—Chris Daniels, Purdue, Oct 16, (vs Michigan St.)
Receiving yards: 301—Chris Daniels, Purdue, Oct 16, (vs Michigan St.)
Punt return yards: 214—Dallas Davis, Colorado St, Oct 2 (vs New Mexico St.)
Kickoff return yards: 229—Brandon Daniels, Oklahoma, Oct 2 (vs Notre Dame).

Division I-AA

SCORING

	Class	GP	TD	XP	FG	Pts	Pts/Game
Adrian Peterson, Georgia Southern	So	11	29	0	0	174	15.82
Ronald Jean, Lehigh	Sr	11	26	0	0	156	14.18
Charles Roberts, Cal St-Sac	Jr	11	22	6	0	138	12.55
Matt Cannon, Southern Utah	Jr	11	23	0	0	138	12.55
David Dinkins, Morehead St.	Jr	10	20	2	0	122	12.20

Division I-AA *(Cont.)*

FIELD GOALS

	Class	GP	FGA	FG	Pct	FG/Game
Brett Sterba, William & Mary	Jr	11	23	18	.783	1.64
David Collett, Tennessee Tech	So	10	24	16	.667	1.60
Jason Feinberg, Pennsylvania	Jr	10	21	15	.714	1.50
Mike Minnoch, Weber St	Jr	10	17	13	.765	1.30
Pete Garces, Idaho St	Sr	10	19	13	.684	1.30
Mike Murawczyk, Yale	Jr	10	19	13	.684	1.30

TOTAL OFFENSE

			Rushing				Passing		Total Offense		
	Class	GP	Car	Gain	Loss	Net	Att	Yds	Yds	Yds/Play	TDR*	Yds/Game
Joe Lee, Towson	Sr	11	31	13	150	-137	577	4168	4031	6.63	22	366.45
Drew Miller, Montana	Jr	10	26	16	162	-146	368	3461	3315	8.41	32	331.50
James Perry, Brown	Sr	10	25	40	112	-72	467	3255	3183	6.47	27	318.30
Chris Sanders, Chattanooga	Jr	11	34	47	95	-48	490	3539	3491	6.66	28	317.36
Ryan Helming, N Iowa	Jr	11	46	121	121	0	403	3469	3469	7.73	34	315.36

*Touchdowns responsible for are TDs scored and passed for.

RUSHING

	Class	GP	Car	Yds	Avg	TD	Yds/Game
Charles Roberts, Cal St–Sacramento	Jr	11	303	2082	6.9	22	189.27
Adrian Peterson, Georgia Southern	So	11	248	1807	7.3	28	164.27
Randall Joseph, Colgate	Jr	9	193	1446	7.5	15	160.67
Corey Holmes, Mississippi Valley St	Jr	11	331	1692	5.1	11	153.82
Curtis Keaton, James Madison	Sr	11	290	1659	5.7	19	150.82

PASSING EFFICIENCY

					Pct					Rating
	Class	GP	Att	Comp	Comp	Yds	Yds/Att	TD	Int	Pts
Drew Miller, Montana	Jr	10	368	240	65.22	3461	9.40	32	8	168.6
Mark Washington, Jackson St	Sr	12	287	147	51.22	2788	9.71	29	10	159.2
Jimmy Blanchard, Portland St	Jr	11	355	212	59.72	3098	8.73	29	3	158.3
Phil Stambaugh, Lehigh	Sr	11	347	236	68.01	2995	8.63	26	13	157.7
JaJuan Seider, Florida A&M	Sr	11	253	150	59.29	2086	8.25	23	2	157.0

Note: Minimum 15 attempts per game.

RECEPTIONS PER GAME

	Class	GP	No.	Yds	TD	R/G
Murle Sango, Villanova	So	11	98	1064	10	8.91
Stephen Campbell, Brown	Jr	10	89	1107	11	8.90
Elijah Thurmon, Howard	Sr	11	84	1366	9	7.74
Jamal White, Towson	So	11	82	1322	8	7.45
Phil Wendler, Princeton	Sr	10	74	822	4	7.40

INTERCEPTIONS

	Class	GP	No.	Yds	TD	Int/G
Ryan Crawford, Davidson	Jr	11	8	63	0	.73
Jim Gallagher, G'town	Sr	11	7	84	1	.64
Dan Mulhern, Delaware	Fr	11	7	65	0	.64
Lance Small, Rhode Island	So	11	7	60	0	.64
Eric Kenesie, Valparaiso	Sr	11	7	35	0	.64

RECEIVING YARDS PER GAME

	Class	GP	No.	Yds	TD	Yds/G
Cornell Craig, S Illinois	Sr	11	77	1419	15	129.0
Elijah Thurmon, Howard	Sr	11	84	1366	9	124.2
Gerald Foster, Duquesne	Sr	11	72	1340	10	121.8
Jamal White, Towson	So	11	82	1322	8	120.2
Stephen Campbell, Brown	Jr	10	89	1107	11	110.7

PUNTING

	Class	No.	Avg
Matthew Peot, Montana St	Jr	48	45.73
Brian Bivens, Murray St	Fr	43	44.79
Ethan Beck, Cal St–Northridge	Jr	41	43.44
Rick Barrow, SW Texas St	Jr	66	42.53
Brian Reilly, Appalachian St	Sr	41	42.41

ALL-PURPOSE RUNNERS

	Class	GP	Rush	Rec	PR	KOR	Yds*	Yds/Game
Rick Sarille, Wagner	Sr	10	1373	226	0	475	2074	207.40
Charles Roberts, Cal St–Sacramento	Jr	11	2082	108	12	0	2202	200.18
Cornell Craig, Southern Illinois	Sr	11	1	1419	190	394	2004	182.18
Ronald Jean, Lehigh	Sr	11	1358	163	0	469	1990	180.91
Adrian Peterson, Georgia Southern	So	11	1807	163	0	0	1970	179.07

*Includes interception return yards.

Division II

SCORING

	Class	GP	TD	XP	FG	Pts	Pts/Game
Kavin Gailliard, American Int'l	Sr	12	34	2	0	206	17.2
Josh Ranek, S Dakota St	So	11	28	2	0	170	15.5
Jamel White, S Dakota	Sr	11	24	0	0	144	13.1
Wesley Cates, California (PA)	So	11	23	0	0	138	12.5
Lamar Gordon, N Dakota St	So	11	22	0	0	132	12.0

FIELD GOALS

	Class	GP	FGA	FG	Pct	FG/Game
Milan Smado, Southeastern Oklahoma	So	11	19	17	89.5	1.55
Aaron Turner, Chadron St	Jr	10	20	15	75.0	1.50
Jeremy Thompson, Harding	Sr	10	21	14	66.7	1.40
Volker Olbrich, Nebraska-Kearney	Sr	10	19	14	73.7	1.40
Jason Williams, Southern Arkansas	Jr	10	26	14	53.8	1.40

TOTAL OFFENSE

	Class	GP	Yds	Yds/Game
Ted Larkin, Bentley	Jr	11	3490	317.3
Matt Kissell, Mercyhurst	Sr	10	3070	307.0
Justin Coleman, Nebraska-Kearney	Jr	10	2966	296.6
Mike Mitros, West Chester	Sr	10	2928	292.8
Corte McGuffey, Northern Colorado	Sr	11	3031	275.5

RUSHING

	Class	GP	Car	Yds	TD	Yds/Game
Kavin Gailliard, American Int'l	Sr	12	320	2635	32	221.1
Josh Ranek, S Dakota St	So	11	329	2055	25	186.8
Wesley Cates, California (PA)	So	11	298	1935	23	175.9
Mo Harris, Ferris St	Sr	10	212	1653	11	165.3
Jamel White, S Dakota	Sr	11	316	1807	19	164.3

PASSING EFFICIENCY

	Class	GP	Att	Comp	Pct Comp	Yds	TD	Int	Rating Pts
Rick Hebert, American Int'l	Sr	12	234	166	70.9	2351	25	4	187.2
Corte McGuffey, Northern Colorado	Sr	11	296	189	63.8	2893	31	11	173.0
Eric Miller, Bloomsburg	Jr	10	270	171	63.3	2571	25	6	169.4
Justin Coleman, Nebraka-Kearney	Jr	10	311	179	57.5	3167	28	7	168.3
Chris Gicking, Shippensburg	Jr	11	294	164	55.7	2832	25	5	161.3

Note: Minimum 15 attempts per game.

RECEPTIONS PER GAME

	Class	GP	No.	Yds	TD	Rec/Game
Mark DeBrito, Bentley	Sr	11	101	1637	19	9.2
Kevin Ingram, West Chester	Sr	9	82	1050	16	9.1
Damon Thompson, Virginia St	Jr	10	90	1517	10	9.0
Sean Scott, Millersville	Jr	8	67	1030	6	8.4
Mike Juhasz, N Dakota	Sr	10	79	895	9	7.9

RECEIVING YARDS PER GAME

	Class	GP	No.	Yds	TD	Yds/Game
Damon Thompson, Virginia St	Jr	10	90	1517	10	151.7
Mark DeBrito, Bentley	Sr	11	101	1637	19	148.8
Sean Scott, Millersville	Jr	8	67	1030	6	128.8
Matt Wilson, Bloomsburg	Sr	11	64	1345	16	122.3
Jamie Ware, Shippensburg	Sr	11	74	1334	10	121.3

Division II (Cont.)

INTERCEPTIONS

	Class	GP	No.	Yds	Int/ Game
Tommie Dawson, Virginia Union	Jr	8	8	79	1.0
Jerico Washington, Clark Atlanta	So	8	6	117	.8
Brent Burnside, MO Western St.	Sr	11	8	117	.7
Craig Neuhaus, NE-Kearney	So	10	7	65	.7
Jon Johnson, Mansfield	Jr	10	7	0	.7

PUNTING

	Class	No.	Avg
Nathan White, Fairmont St	So	43	44.9
Ryan Schneider, Winona St	Sr	38	44.6
Jeff Works, Ouachita Baptist	Sr	55	43.7
Andrew Patton, Harding	Sr	52	43.4
Ryan Corn, Western St	Jr	51	43.0

Note: Minimum 3.6 per game.

Division III

SCORING

	Class	GP	TD	XP	FG	Pts	Pts/Game
R.J. Bowers, Grove City	Jr	10	25	4	0	154	15.4
Scott Pingel, Westminster (MO)	Sr	10	24	4	0	148	14.8
Andrew Notarfrancesco, Catholic	Sr	10	23	0	0	138	13.8
Chuck Moore, Mt Union	Jr	10	22	0	0	132	13.2
Ron Lewis, Montclair St	Sr	8	16	0	0	96	12.0

FIELD GOALS

	Class	GP	FGA	FG	Pct	FG/Game
Ryan Geisler, Cal Lutheran	Jr	9	18	14	77.8	1.56
Haakon Nelson, St. Olaf	Sr	10	20	15	75.0	1.50
Chris Baughman, Wheaton (IL)	Jr	9	13	12	92.3	1.33
Keith Debbaudt, Albion	Jr	9	16	11	68.8	1.22
Roman Natoli, Chicago	So	9	20	11	55.0	1.22

TOTAL OFFENSE

	Class	GP	Yds	Yds/Game
Justin Peery, Westminster (MO)	Sr	10	4419	441.9
Danny Ragsdale, Redlands	Sr	9	3855	428.3
Adam Ryan, Wilmington (OH)	So	10	3478	347.8
Brian Partlow, Randolph-Macon	Sr	10	3400	340.0
Josh Wakefield, Alma	Sr	9	2990	332.2

RUSHING

	Class	GP	Car	Yds	TD	Yds/Game
R.J. Bowers, Grove City	Jr	10	344	2098	25	209.8
Kenneth Sasu, Marietta	Jr	9	332	1770	15	196.7
D'Andra Freeman, Fitchburg St	Sr	10	365	1871	14	187.1
Steve Tardif, Maine Maritime	Sr	9	271	1567	14	174.1
Ben Smith, Buena Vista	Sr	10	254	1583	16	158.3

PASSING EFFICIENCY

	Class	GP	Att	Comp	Pct Comp	Yds	TD	Int	Rating Pts
Gary Smeck, Mt Union	Jr	10	199	131	65.8	2274	30	3	208.6
Matt LeFever, Western Connecticut St	Jr	10	158	95	60.1	1874	25	7	203.1
Danny Ragsdale, Redlands	Sr	9	380	247	65.0	3639	33	7	170.4
Jesse Lowry, Thomas More	Fr	9	159	98	61.6	1540	14	4	167.1
Dan Mauer, Bridgewater (MA)	Sr	10	168	86	51.1	1672	23	12	165.7

Note: Minimum 15 attempts per game.

Division III (Cont.)

RECEPTIONS PER GAME

	Class	GP	No.	Yds	TD	Rec/Game
Scott Pingel, Westminster (MO)	Sr	10	136	1648	24	13.6
Sean Eaton, Randolph-Macon	Sr	10	95	1289	15	9.5
Mike Groll, Defiance	Sr	9	84	1010	11	9.3
Tarrik Wilson, Hanover	Sr	9	83	974	7	9.2
Darryl DeShields, Greenville	Fr	10	92	1515	12	9.2

RECEIVING YARDS PER GAME

	Class	GP	No.	Yds	TD	Yds/Game
Scott Pingel, Westminster (MO)	Sr	10	136	1648	24	164.8
Matt Eisenberg, Juniata	Jr	10	76	1547	19	154.7
Darryl DeShields, Greenville	Fr	10	92	1515	12	151.5
Adam Marino, Mt Union	Jr	10	73	1456	19	145.6
Matt Perceval, Wesleyan (CT)	Sr	8	73	1137	13	142.1

INTERCEPTIONS

	Class	GP	No.	Yds	Int/G
Steven Cella, Trinity (CT)	Jr	8	9	106	1.1
Eric Newsome, Hobart	Jr	8	9	148	1.1
Chris Swartz, RPI	Jr	9	10	118	1.1
Jeremy Presar, Ohio Northern	Jr	10	10	40	1.0
Charles Verdone, Benedictine	Jr	10	10	101	1.0
Antonia Nash, Susquehanna	Fr	10	10	90	1.0
Jason Fosdick, Augustana (IL)	Sr	9	9	165	1.0

PUNTING

	Class	No.	Avg
Steve Vagedes, Ohio Northern	Sr	37	46.2
Phil Barry, St. John's (MN)	Sr	49	44.4
Wilson Hillman, Mississippi College	Jr	61	42.0
Keith Scranton, Brockport St	Sr	69	41.5
Richard Harr, Ferrum	Sr	51	40.9

Note: Minimum 3.6 per game.

1999 NCAA Division I-A Team Leaders

Offense

SCORING

	GP	Pts	Avg
Virginia Tech	11	455	41.4
Georgia Tech	11	448	40.7
Kansas St	11	433	39.4
Louisville	11	412	37.5
Florida St	11	412	37.5
Stanford	11	409	37.2
Marshall	12	442	36.8
Oklahoma	11	405	36.8
Wisconsin	11	392	35.6
Louisiana Tech	11	389	35.4

RUSHING

	GP	Car	Yds	Avg	TD	Yds/Game
Navy	12	680	3506	5.2	30	292.2
Air Force	11	635	3140	4.9	25	285.5
Wisconsin	11	583	3075	5.3	34	279.5
Nebraska	12	633	3191	5.0	37	265.9
Army	11	636	2915	4.6	24	265.0
Ohio	11	624	2883	4.6	26	262.1
Rice	11	655	2835	4.3	22	257.7
Virginia Tech	11	559	2793	5.0	35	253.9
Texas Christian	11	518	2640	5.1	26	240.0
Toledo	11	492	2631	5.3	21	239.2

TOTAL OFFENSE

	GP	Plays	Yds	Avg	TD*	Yds/Game
Georgia Tech	11	822	5603	6.8	58	509.36
Nevada	11	843	5192	6.2	39	472.00
Arizona	12	870	5663	6.5	42	471.92
Louisiana Tech	11	822	5181	6.3	50	471.00
Stanford	11	793	5138	6.5	47	467.09
Louisville	11	851	5136	6.0	46	466.91
Marshall	12	841	5584	6.6	57	465.33
Purdue	11	859	5016	5.8	38	456.00
Virginia Tech	11	758	4970	6.6	49	451.82
Oregon St	11	857	4774	5.6	41	434.00

*Defensive and special teams TDs not included.

Offense (Cont.)

PASSING

	GP	Att	Comp	Yds	Pct Comp	Yds/Att	TD	Int	Yds/Game
Louisiana Tech	11	566	372	4434	65.7	7.8	38	12	403.1
Louisville	11	501	322	3687	64.3	7.4	29	13	335.2
Hawaii	12	577	297	3944	51.5	6.8	28	19	328.7
Purdue	11	508	306	3608	60.2	7.1	23	12	328.0
Tulane	11	556	326	3600	58.6	6.5	25	25	327.3
Nevada	11	457	263	3590	57.5	7.9	20	9	326.4
Marshall	12	427	286	3901	67.0	9.1	37	11	325.1
Brigham Young	11	458	280	3567	61.1	7.8	25	16	324.3
Oklahoma	11	512	319	3539	62.3	6.9	31	15	321.7
Stanford	11	385	219	3448	56.9	9.0	25	12	313.5

Single-Game Highs

Points Scored: 73—New Mexico St, Sept 4 (vs N.M. Highlands).
Net Rushing Yards: 413—Rice, Oct 16 (vs San Jose St).
Passing Yards: 597—Louisiana Tech, Oct 23 (vs Central Florida).
Rushing and Passing Yards: 767—Colorado, Sept 11 (vs San Jose St).
Fewest Rushing and Passing Yards Allowed: 61—Oklahoma St, Sept 4 (vs La.-Lafayette).

Defense

SCORING

	GP	Pts	Avg
Virginia Tech	11	116	10.5
Marshall	12	134	11.2
Nebraska	12	150	12.5
Kansas St	11	144	13.1
Wisconsin	11	145	13.2
Mississippi St	11	149	13.5
Tennessee	11	163	14.8
Southern Miss	11	172	15.6
Minnesota	11	172	15.6
Florida St	11	174	15.8

TOTAL DEFENSE

	GP	Plays	Yds	Avg	Yds/Game
Mississippi St	11	734	2448	3.3	222.5
Kansas St	11	693	2585	3.7	235.0
Virginia Tech	11	732	2720	3.7	247.3
Nebraska	12	815	3022	3.7	251.8
Texas Christian	11	729	3129	4.3	284.5
Texas	13	876	3727	4.3	286.7
Marshall	12	882	3516	4.0	293.0
Southern Miss	11	754	3235	4.3	294.1
Alabama	12	749	3568	4.8	297.3
Oklahoma St	11	683	3273	4.8	297.5

RUSHING

	GP	Car	Yds	Avg	TD	Yds/Game
Mississippi St	11	403	736	1.8	7	66.9
Alabama	12	335	904	2.7	6	75.3
Virginia Tech	11	388	835	2.2	5	75.9
Mississippi	11	369	846	2.3	10	76.9
Michigan St	11	376	847	2.3	7	77.0
Nebraska	12	427	928	2.2	6	77.3
Tennessee	11	364	986	2.7	3	89.6
Southern Miss	11	403	1006	2.5	6	91.5
Florida	12	416	1099	2.6	15	91.6
Florida St	11	387	1087	2.8	6	98.8

TURNOVER MARGIN

		Turnovers Gained		Turnovers Lost			Margin/
	GP	Fum	Int	Total	Fum	Int	Total	Game
Kansas St	11	17	21	38	12	9	21	1.55
Illinois	11	11	14	25	7	5	12	1.18
Southern Cal	12	18	21	39	11	14	25	1.17
Marshall	12	6	24	30	6	11	17	1.08
Wisconsin	11	6	16	22	8	3	11	1.00
Stanford	11	13	17	30	8	12	20	.91
Southern Miss	11	15	15	30	6	14	20	.91
Michigan	11	12	10	22	4	8	12	.91

PASSING EFFICIENCY

	GP	Att	Comp	Yds	Pct Comp	Yds/Att	TD	Pct TD	Int	Pct Int	Rating Pts
Kansas St	11	315	118	1364	37.46	4.33	5	1.59	21	6.67	65.74
Nebraska	12	388	165	2094	42.53	5.40	11	2.84	18	4.64	87.94
Marshall	12	432	226	2308	52.31	5.34	8	1.85	24	5.56	92.19
Mississippi St	11	331	172	1712	51.96	5.17	7	2.11	15	4.53	93.33
Wisconsin	11	351	176	1994	50.14	5.68	8	2.28	16	4.56	96.27
Utah	11	359	179	2113	49.86	5.89	7	1.95	16	4.46	96.82
Virginia Tech	11	344	166	1885	48.26	5.48	10	2.91	10	2.91	98.06
Minnesota	11	340	159	1921	46.76	5.65	9	2.65	8	2.35	98.25
Oregon St	11	355	174	2104	49.01	5.93	8	2.25	13	3.66	98.91
E Carolina	11	389	200	2305	51.41	5.93	10	2.57	17	4.37	100.93

National Champions

Year	Champion	Record	Bowl Game	Head Coach
1883	Yale	8-0-0	No bowl	Ray Tompkins (Captain)
1884	Yale	9-0-0	No bowl	Eugene L. Richards (Captain)
1885	Princeton	9-0-0	No bowl	Charles DeCamp (Captain)
1886	Yale	9-0-1	No bowl	Robert N. Corwin (Captain)
1887	Yale	9-0-0	No bowl	Harry W. Beecher (Captain)
1888	Yale	13-0-0	No bowl	Walter Camp
1889	Princeton	10-0-0	No bowl	Edgar Poe (Captain)
1890	Harvard	11-0-0	No bowl	George A. Stewart/George C. Adams
1891	Yale	13-0-0	No bowl	Walter Camp
1892	Yale	13-0-0	No bowl	Walter Camp
1893	Princeton	11-0-0	No bowl	Tom Trenchard (Captain)
1894	Yale	16-0-0	No bowl	William C. Rhodes
1895	Pennsylvania	14-0-0	No bowl	George Woodruff
1896	Princeton	10-0-1	No bowl	Garrett Cochran
1897	Pennsylvania	15-0-0	No bowl	George Woodruff
1898	Harvard	11-0-0	No bowl	W. Cameron Forbes
1899	Harvard	10-0-1	No bowl	Benjamin H. Dibblee
1900	Yale	12-0-0	No bowl	Malcolm McBride
1901	Michigan	11-0-0	Won Rose	Fielding Yost
1902	Michigan	11-0-0	No bowl	Fielding Yost
1903	Princeton	11-0-0	No bowl	Art Hillebrand
1904	Pennsylvania	12-0-0	No bowl	Carl Williams
1905	Chicago	11-0-0	No bowl	Amos Alonzo Stagg
1906	Princeton	9-0-1	No bowl	Bill Roper
1907	Yale	9-0-1	No bowl	Bill Knox
1908	Pennsylvania	11-0-1	No bowl	Sol Metzger
1909	Yale	10-0-0	No bowl	Howard Jones
1910	Harvard	8-0-1	No bowl	Percy Houghton
1911	Princeton	8-0-2	No bowl	Bill Roper
1912	Harvard	9-0-0	No bowl	Percy Houghton
1913	Harvard	9-0-0	No bowl	Percy Houghton
1914	Army	9-0-0	No bowl	Charley Daly
1915	Cornell	9-0-0	No bowl	Al Sharpe
1916	Pittsburgh	8-0-0	No bowl	Pop Warner
1917	Georgia Tech	9-0-0	No bowl	John Heisman
1918	Pittsburgh	4-1-0	No bowl	Pop Warner
1919	Harvard	9-0-1	Won Rose	Bob Fisher
1920	California	9-0-0	Won Rose	Andy Smith
1921	Cornell	8-0-0	No bowl	Gil Dobie
1922	Cornell	8-0-0	No bowl	Gil Dobie
1923	Illinois	8-0-0	No bowl	Bob Zuppke
1924	Notre Dame	10-0-0	Won Rose	Knute Rockne
1925	Alabama (H)	10-0-0	Won Rose	Wallace Wade
	Dartmouth (D)	8-0-0	No bowl	Jesse Hawley
1926	Alabama (H)	9-0-1	Tied Rose	Wallace Wade
	Stanford (D)(H)	10-0-1	Tied Rose	Pop Warner
1927	Illinois	7-0-1	No bowl	Bob Zuppke
1928	Georgia Tech (H)	10-0-0	Won Rose	Bill Alexander
	Southern Cal (D)	9-0-1	No bowl	Howard Jones
1929	Notre Dame	9-0-0	No bowl	Knute Rockne
1930	Notre Dame	10-0-0	No bowl	Knute Rockne
1931	Southern Cal	10-1-0	Won Rose	Howard Jones
1932	Southern Cal (H)	10-0-0	Won Rose	Howard Jones
	Michigan (D)	8-0-0	No bowl	Harry Kipke
1933	Michigan	7-0-1	No bowl	Harry Kipke
1934	Minnesota	8-0-0	No bowl	Bernie Bierman
1935	Minnesota (H)	8-0-0	No bowl	Bernie Bierman
	Southern Methodist (D)	12-1-0	Lost Rose	Matty Bell
1936	Minnesota	7-1-0	No bowl	Bernie Bierman
1937	Pittsburgh	9-0-1	No bowl	Jock Sutherland
1938	Texas Christian (AP)	11-0-0	Won Sugar	Dutch Meyer
	Notre Dame (D)	8-1-0	No bowl	Elmer Layden
1939	Southern Cal (D)	8-0-2	Won Rose	Howard Jones
	Texas A&M (AP)	11-0-0	Won Sugar	Homer Norton
1940	Minnesota	8-0-0	No bowl	Bernie Bierman
1941	Minnesota	8-0-0	No bowl	Bernie Bierman
1942	Ohio St	9-1-0	No bowl	Paul Brown

Year	Champion	Record	Bowl Game	Head Coach
1943	Notre Dame	9-1-0	No bowl	Frank Leahy
1944	Army	9-0-0	No bowl	Red Blaik
1945	Army	9-0-0	No bowl	Red Blaik
1946	Notre Dame	8-0-1	No bowl	Frank Leahy
1947	Notre Dame	9-0-0	No bowl	Frank Leahy
	Michigan*	10-0-0	Won Rose	Fritz Crisler
1948	Michigan	9-0-0	No bowl	Bennie Oosterbaan
1949	Notre Dame	10-0-0	No bowl	Frank Leahy
1950	Oklahoma	10-1-0	Lost Sugar	Bud Wilkinson
1951	Tennessee	10-1-0	Lost Sugar	Bob Neyland
1952	Michigan St	9-0-0	No bowl	Biggie Munn
1953	Maryland	10-1-0	Lost Orange	Jim Tatum
1954	Ohio St	10-0-0	Won Rose	Woody Hayes
	UCLA (UPI)	9-0-0	No bowl	Red Sanders
1955	Oklahoma	11-0-0	Won Orange	Bud Wilkinson
1956	Oklahoma	10-0-0	No bowl	Bud Wilkinson
1957	Auburn	10-0-0	No bowl	Shug Jordan
	Ohio St (UPI)	9-1-0	Won Rose	Woody Hayes
1958	Louisiana St	11-0-0	Won Sugar	Paul Dietzel
1959	Syracuse	11-0-0	Won Cotton	Ben Schwartzwalder
1960	Minnesota	8-2-0	Lost Rose	Murray Warmath
1961	Alabama	11-0-0	Won Sugar	Bear Bryant
1962	Southern Cal	11-0-0	Won Rose	John McKay
1963	Texas	11-0-0	Won Cotton	Darrell Royal
1964	Alabama	10-1-0	Lost Orange	Bear Bryant
1965	Alabama	9-1-1	Won Orange	Bear Bryant
	Michigan St (UPI)	10-1-0	Lost Rose	Duffy Daugherty
1966	Notre Dame	9-0-1	No bowl	Ara Parseghian
1967	Southern Cal	10-1-0	Won Rose	John McKay
1968	Ohio St	10-0-0	Won Rose	Woody Hayes
1969	Texas	11-0-0	Won Cotton	Darrell Royal
1970	Nebraska	11-0-1	Won Orange	Bob Devaney
	Texas (UPI)	10-1-0	Lost Cotton	Darrell Royal
1971	Nebraska	13-0-0	Won Orange	Bob Devaney
1972	Southern Cal	12-0-0	Won Rose	John McKay
1973	Notre Dame	11-0-0	Won Sugar	Ara Parseghian
	Alabama (UPI)	11-1-0	Lost Sugar	Bear Bryant
1974	Oklahoma	11-0-0	No bowl	Barry Switzer
	Southern Cal (UPI)	10-1-1	Won Rose	John McKay
1975	Oklahoma	11-1-0	Won Orange	Barry Switzer
1976	Pittsburgh	12-0-0	Won Sugar	Johnny Majors
1977	Notre Dame	11-1-0	Won Cotton	Dan Devine
1978	Alabama	11-1-0	Won Sugar	Bear Bryant
	Southern Cal (UPI)	12-1-0	Won Rose	John Robinson
1979	Alabama	12-0-0	Won Sugar	Bear Bryant
1980	Georgia	12-0-0	Won Sugar	Vince Dooley
1981	Clemson	12-0-0	Won Orange	Danny Ford
1982	Penn St	11-1-0	Won Sugar	Joe Paterno
1983	Miami (FL)	11-1-0	Won Orange	Howard Schnellenberger
1984	Brigham Young	13-0-0	Won Holiday	LaVell Edwards
1985	Oklahoma	11-1-0	Won Orange	Barry Switzer
1986	Penn St	12-0-0	Won Fiesta	Joe Paterno
1987	Miami (FL)	12-0-0	Won Orange	Jimmy Johnson
1988	Notre Dame	12-0-0	Won Fiesta	Lou Holtz
1989	Miami (FL)	11-1-0	Won Sugar	Dennis Erickson
1990	Colorado	11-1-1	Won Orange	Bill McCartney
	Georgia Tech (UPI)	11-0-1	Won Citrus	Bobby Ross
1991	Miami (FL)	12-0-0	Won Orange	Dennis Erickson
	Washington (CNN)	12-0-0	Won Rose	Don James
1992	Alabama	13-0-0	Won Sugar	Gene Stallings
1993	Florida St	12-1-0	Won Orange	Bobby Bowden
1994	Nebraska	13-0-0	Won Orange	Tom Osborne
1995	Nebraska	12-0-0	Won Fiesta	Tom Osborne
†1996	Florida	12-1	Won Sugar	Steve Spurrier

National Champions (Cont.)

Year	Champion	Record	Bowl Game	Head Coach
1997	Michigan	12–0	Won Rose	Lloyd Carr
	Nebraska (ESPN)	13–0	Won Orange	Tom Osborne
1998	Tennessee	13–0	Won Fiesta	Phillip Fulmer
1999	Florida St	12–0	Won Sugar	Bobby Bowden

*The AP, which had voted Notre Dame No. 1, took a second vote, giving the national title to Michigan after its 49–0 win over Southern Cal in the Rose Bowl.   Note: Selectors: Helms Athletic Foundation (H) 1883–1935, The Dickinson System (D) 1924–40, The Associated Press (AP) 1936–present, United Press International (UPI) 1958–90, *USA Today*/CNN (CNN) 1991–96, and *USA Today*/ESPN (ESPN) 1997–present. †In 1996 the NCAA introduced overtime to break ties.

Results of Major Bowl Games

Rose Bowl

1-1-02 ....Michigan 49, Stanford 0
1-1-16 ....Washington St 14, Brown 0
1-1-17 ....Oregon 14, Pennsylvania 0
1-1-18 ....Mare Island 19, Camp Lewis 7
1-1-19 ....Great Lakes 17, Mare Island 0
1-1-20 ....Harvard 7, Oregon 6
1-1-21 ....California 28, Ohio St 0
1-2-22 ....Washington & Jefferson 0, California 0
1-1-23 ....Southern Cal 14, Penn St 3
1-1-24 ....Navy 14, Washington 14
1-1-25 ....Notre Dame 27, Stanford 10
1-1-26 ....Alabama 20, Washington 19
1-1-27 ....Alabama 7, Stanford 7
1-2-28 ....Stanford 7, Pittsburgh 6
1-1-29 ....Georgia Tech 8, California 7
1-1-30 ....Southern Cal 47, Pittsburgh 14
1-1-31 ....Alabama 24, Washington St 0
1-1-32 ....Southern Cal 21, Tulane 12
1-2-33 ....Southern Cal 35, Pittsburgh 0
1-1-34 ....Columbia 7, Stanford 0
1-1-35 ....Alabama 29, Stanford 13
1-1-36 ....Stanford 7, Southern Methodist 0
1-1-37 ....Pittsburgh 21, Washington 0
1-1-38 ....California 13, Alabama 0
1-2-39 ....Southern Cal 7, Duke 3
1-1-40 ....Southern Cal 14, Tennessee 0
1-1-41 ....Stanford 21, Nebraska 13
1-1-42 ....Oregon St 20, Duke 16
1-1-43 ....Georgia 9, UCLA 0
1-1-44 ....Southern Cal 29, Washington 0
1-1-45 ....Southern Cal 25, Tennessee 0
1-1-46 ....Alabama 34, Southern Cal 14
1-1-47 ....Illinois 45, UCLA 14
1-1-48 ....Michigan 49, Southern Cal 0
1-1-49 ....Northwestern 20, California 14
1-2-50 ....Ohio St 17, California 14
1-1-51 ....Michigan 14, California 6
1-1-52 ....Illinois 40, Stanford 7
1-1-53 ....Southern Cal 7, Wisconsin 0
1-1-54 ....Michigan St 28, UCLA 20
1-1-55 ....Ohio St 20, Southern Cal 7
1-2-56 ....Michigan St 17, UCLA 14
1-1-57 ....Iowa 35, Oregon St 19
1-1-58 ....Ohio St 10, Oregon 7
1-1-59 ....Iowa 38, California 12
1-1-60 ....Washington 44, Wisconsin 8
1-2-61 ....Washington 17, Minnesota 7
1-1-62 ....Minnesota 21, UCLA 3
1-1-63 ....Southern Cal 42, Wisconsin 37

1-1-64 ....Illinois 17, Washington 7
1-1-65 ....Michigan 34, Oregon St 7
1-1-66 ....UCLA 14, Michigan St 12
1-2-67 ....Purdue 14, Southern Cal 13
1-1-68 ....Southern Cal 14, Indiana 3
1-1-69 ....Ohio St 27, Southern Cal 16
1-1-70 ....Southern Cal 10, Michigan 3
1-1-71 ....Stanford 27, Ohio St 17
1-1-72 ....Stanford 13, Michigan 12
1-1-73 ....Southern Cal 42, Ohio St 17
1-1-74 ....Ohio St 42, Southern Cal 21
1-1-75 ....Southern Cal 18, Ohio St 17
1-1-76 ....UCLA 23, Ohio St 10
1-1-77 ....Southern Cal 14, Michigan 6
1-2-78 ....Washington 27, Michigan 20
1-1-79 ....Southern Cal 17, Michigan 10
1-1-80 ....Southern Cal 17, Ohio St 16
1-1-81 ....Michigan 23, Washington 6
1-1-82 ....Washington 28, Iowa 0
1-1-83 ....UCLA 24, Michigan 14
1-2-84 ....UCLA 45, Illinois 9
1-1-85 ....Southern Cal 20, Ohio St 17
1-1-86 ....UCLA 45, Iowa 28
1-1-87 ....Arizona St 22, Michigan 15
1-1-88 ....Michigan St 20, Southern Cal 17
1-2-89 ....Michigan 22, Southern Cal 14
1-1-90 ....Southern Cal 17, Michigan 10
1-1-91 ....Washington 46, Iowa 34
1-1-92 ....Washington 34, Michigan 14
1-1-93 ....Michigan 38, Washington 31
1-1-94 ....Wisconsin 21, UCLA 16
1-2-95 ....Penn St 38, Oregon 20
1-1-96 ....Southern Cal 41, Northwestern 32
1-1-97 ....Ohio St 20, Arizona St 17
1-1-98 ....Michigan 21, Washington St 16
1-1-99 ....Wisconsin 38, UCLA 31
1-1-00 ....Wisconsin 17, Stanford 9

City: Pasadena. Stadium: Rose Bowl, capacity 96,576.
Playing Sites: Tournament Park (1902, 1916-22), Rose Bowl (1923-41, since 1943), Duke Stadium, Durham, NC (1942).

Orange Bowl

1-1-35 ....Bucknell 26, Miami (FL) 0
1-1-36 ....Catholic 20, Mississippi 19
1-1-37 ....Duquesne 13, Mississippi St 12
1-1-38 ....Auburn 6, Michigan St 0
1-2-39 ....Tennessee 17, Oklahoma 0

Note: The Fiesta, Orange, Rose and Sugar Bowls constitute the Bowl Alliance, formed in 1995. The Alliance holds eight-berths: one each for the champions of the ACC, Big 10, Big 12, Big East, Pac 10 and SEC, and two at-large, reserved for any Division I-A team which is ranked sixth or higher in the BCS standings. Otherwise, any team can qualify for the at-large berth if they have at least nine wins and are ranked in the top 12 of the BCS rankings. Of the eight teams, the two highest-ranked go to the Orange Bowl in 2001, the Rose Bowl in 2002, and the Fiesta Bowl in 2003. Once these four BCS matches have been set conferences may place the remaining qualified teams in the other bowls. Teams that have won at least six games against Division I-A teams qualify.

Orange Bowl *(Cont.)*

1-1-40	Georgia Tech 21, Missouri 7
1-1-41	Mississippi St 14, Georgetown 7
1-1-42	Georgia 40, Texas Christian 26
1-1-43	Alabama 37, Boston College 21
1-1-44	Louisiana St 19, Texas A&M 14
1-1-45	Tulsa 26, Georgia Tech 12
1-1-46	Miami (FL) 13, Holy Cross 6
1-1-47	Rice 8, Tennessee 0
1-1-48	Georgia Tech 20, Kansas 14
1-1-49	Texas 41, Georgia 28
1-2-50	Santa Clara 21, Kentucky 13
1-1-51	Clemson 15, Miami (FL) 14
1-1-52	Georgia Tech 17, Baylor 14
1-1-53	Alabama 61, Syracuse 6
1-1-54	Oklahoma 7, Maryland 0
1-1-55	Duke 34, Nebraska 7
1-2-56	Oklahoma 20, Maryland 6
1-1-57	Colorado 27, Clemson 21
1-1-58	Oklahoma 48, Duke 21
1-1-59	Oklahoma 21, Syracuse 6
1-1-60	Georgia 14, Missouri 0
1-2-61	Missouri 21, Navy 14
1-1-62	Louisiana St 25, Colorado 7
1-1-63	Alabama 17, Oklahoma 0
1-1-64	Nebraska 13, Auburn 7
1-1-65	Texas 21, Alabama 17
1-1-66	Alabama 39, Nebraska 28
1-2-67	Florida 27, Georgia Tech 12
1-1-68	Oklahoma 26, Tennessee 24
1-1-69	Penn St 15, Kansas 14
1-1-70	Penn St 10, Missouri 3
1-1-71	Nebraska 17, Louisiana St 12
1-1-72	Nebraska 38, Alabama 6
1-1-73	Nebraska 40, Notre Dame 6
1-1-74	Penn St 16, Louisiana St 9
1-1-75	Notre Dame 13, Alabama 11
1-1-76	Oklahoma 14, Michigan 6
1-1-77	Ohio St 27, Colorado 10
1-2-78	Arkansas 31, Oklahoma 6
1-1-79	Oklahoma 31, Nebraska 24
1-1-80	Oklahoma 24, Florida St 7
1-1-81	Oklahoma 18, Florida St 17
1-1-82	Clemson 22, Nebraska 15
1-1-83	Nebraska 21, Louisiana St 20
1-2-84	Miami (FL) 31, Nebraska 30
1-1-85	Washington 28, Oklahoma 17
1-1-86	Oklahoma 25, Penn St 10
1-1-87	Oklahoma 42, Arkansas 8
1-1-88	Miami (FL) 20, Oklahoma 14
1-2-89	Miami (FL) 23, Nebraska 3
1-1-90	Notre Dame 21, Colorado 6
1-1-91	Colorado 10, Notre Dame 9
1-1-92	Miami (FL) 22, Nebraska 0
1-1-93	Florida St 27, Nebraska 14
1-1-94	Florida St 18, Nebraska 16
1-1-95	Nebraska 24, Miami (FL) 17
1-1-96	Florida St 31, Notre Dame 26
12-31-96	Nebraska 41, Virginia Tech 21
1-2-98	Nebraska 42, Tennessee 17
1-2-99	Florida 31, Syracuse 10
1-1-00	Michigan 35, Alabama 34 (ot)

City: Miami. Stadium: Pro Player Stadium, capacity 72,000.
Playing Sites: Orange Bowl (1935-96), Pro Player Stadium
(since 1996).

Sugar Bowl

1-1-35	Tulane 20, Temple 14
1-1-36	Texas Christian 3, Louisiana St 2
1-1-37	Santa Clara 21, Louisiana St 14
1-1-38	Santa Clara 6, Louisiana St 0
1-2-39	Texas Christian 15, Carnegie Tech 7
1-1-40	Texas A&M 14, Tulane 13
1-1-41	Boston Col 19, Tennessee 13
1-1-42	Fordham 2, Missouri 0
1-1-43	Tennessee 14, Tulsa 7
1-1-44	Georgia Tech 20, Tulsa 18
1-1-45	Duke 29, Alabama 26
1-1-46	Oklahoma St 33, St Mary's (CA) 13
1-1-47	Georgia 20, N Carolina 10
1-1-48	Texas 27, Alabama 7
1-1-49	Oklahoma 14, N Carolina 6
1-2-50	Oklahoma 35, Louisiana St 0
1-1-51	Kentucky 13, Oklahoma 7
1-1-52	Maryland 28, Tennessee 13
1-1-53	Georgia Tech 24, Mississippi 7
1-1-54	Georgia Tech 42, W Virginia 19
1-1-55	Navy 21, Mississippi 0
1-2-56	Georgia Tech 7, Pittsburgh 0
1-1-57	Baylor 13, Tennessee 7
1-1-58	Mississippi 39, Texas 7
1-1-59	Louisiana St 7, Clemson 0
1-1-60	Mississippi 21, Louisiana St 0
1-2-61	Mississippi 14, Rice 6
1-1-62	Alabama 10, Arkansas 3
1-1-63	Mississippi 17, Arkansas 13
1-1-64	Alabama 12, Mississippi 7
1-1-65	Louisiana St 13, Syracuse 10
1-1-66	Missouri 20, Florida 18
1-2-67	Alabama 34, Nebraska 7
1-1-68	Louisiana St 20, Wyoming 13
1-1-69	Arkansas 16, Georgia 2
1-1-70	Mississippi 27, Arkansas 22
1-1-71	Tennessee 34, Air Force 13
1-1-72	Oklahoma 40, Auburn 22
12-31-72	Oklahoma 14, Penn St 0
12-31-73	Notre Dame 24, Alabama 23
12-31-74	Nebraska 13, Florida 10
12-31-75	Alabama 13, Penn St 6
1-1-77	Pittsburgh 27, Georgia 3
1-2-78	Alabama 35, Ohio St 6
1-1-79	Alabama 14, Penn St 7
1-1-80	Alabama 24, Arkansas 9
1-1-81	Georgia 17, Notre Dame 10
1-1-82	Pittsburgh 24, Georgia 20
1-1-83	Penn St 27, Georgia 23
1-2-84	Auburn 9, Michigan 7
1-1-85	Nebraska 28, Louisiana St 10
1-1-86	Tennessee 35, Miami (FL) 7
1-1-87	Nebraska 30, Louisiana St 15
1-1-88	Syracuse 16, Auburn 16
1-2-89	Florida St 13, Auburn 7
1-1-90	Miami (FL) 33, Alabama 25
1-1-91	Tennessee 23, Virginia 22
1-1-92	Notre Dame 39, Florida 28
1-1-93	Alabama 34, Miami (FL) 13
1-1-94	Florida 41, West Virginia 7
1-2-95	Florida St 23, Florida 17
12-31-95	Virginia Tech 28, Texas 10
1-2-97	Florida 52, Florida St 20
1-1-98	Florida St 31, Ohio St 14

Sugar Bowl (Cont.)

1-1-99 ....Ohio St 24, Texas A&M 14
1-4-00 ....Florida St 46, Virginia Tech 29

City: New Orleans. Stadium: Louisiana Superdome, capacity 71,023.

Playing Sites: Tulane Stadium (1935–74), Louisiana Superdome (since 1975).

Cotton Bowl

1-1-37 ....Texas Christian 16, Marquette 6
1-1-38 ....Rice 28, Colorado 14
1-2-39 ....St. Mary's (CA) 20, Texas Tech 13
1-1-40 ....Clemson 6, Boston Col 3
1-1-41 ....Texas A&M 13, Fordham 12
1-1-42 ....Alabama 29, Texas A&M 21
1-1-43 ....Texas 14, Georgia Tech 7
1-1-44 ....Texas 7, Randolph Field 7
1-1-45 ....Oklahoma St 34, Texas Christian 0
1-1-46 ....Texas 40, Missouri 27
1-1-47 ....Arkansas 0, Louisiana St 0
1-1-48 ....SMU 13, Penn St 13
1-1-49 ....SMU 21, Oregon 13
1-2-50 ....Rice 27, N Carolina 13
1-1-51 ....Tennessee 20, Texas 14
1-1-52 ....Kentucky 20, Texas Christian 7
1-1-53 ....Texas 16, Tennessee 0
1-1-54 ....Rice 28, Alabama 6
1-1-55 ....Georgia Tech 14, Arkansas 6
1-2-56 ....Mississippi 14, Texas Christian 13
1-1-57 ....Texas Christian 28, Syracuse 27
1-1-58 ....Navy 20, Rice 7
1-1-59 ....Texas Christian 0, Air Force 0
1-1-60 ....Syracuse 23, Texas 14
1-2-61 ....Duke 7, Arkansas 6
1-1-62 ....Texas 12, Mississippi 7
1-1-63 ....Louisiana St 13, Texas 0
1-1-64 ....Texas 28, Navy 6
1-1-65 ....Arkansas 10, Nebraska 7
1-1-66 ....Louisiana St 14, Arkansas 7
12-31-66 ....Georgia 24, SMU 9
1-1-68 ....Texas A&M 20, Alabama 16
1-1-69 ....Texas 36, Tennessee 13
1-1-70 ....Texas 21, Notre Dame 17
1-1-71 ....Notre Dame 24, Texas 11
1-1-72 ....Penn St 30, Texas 6
1-1-73 ....Texas 17, Alabama 13
1-1-74 ....Nebraska 19, Texas 3
1-1-75 ....Penn St 41, Baylor 20
1-1-76 ....Arkansas 31, Georgia 10
1-1-77 ....Houston 30, Maryland 21
1-2-78 ....Notre Dame 38, Texas 10
1-1-79 ....Notre Dame 35, Houston 34
1-1-80 ....Houston 17, Nebraska 14
1-1-81 ....Alabama 30, Baylor 2
1-1-82 ....Texas 14, Alabama 12
1-1-83 ....SMU 7, Pittsburgh 3
1-2-84 ....Georgia 10, Texas 9
1-1-85 ....Boston Col 45, Houston 28
1-1-86 ....Texas A&M 36, Auburn 16
1-1-87 ....Ohio St 28, Texas A&M 12
1-1-88 ....Texas A&M 35, Notre Dame 10
1-2-89 ....UCLA 17, Arkansas 3
1-1-90 ....Tennessee 31, Arkansas 27
1-1-91 ....Miami (FL) 46, Texas 3
1-1-92 ....Florida St 10, Texas A&M 2
1-1-93 ....Notre Dame 28, Texas A&M 3
1-1-94 ....Notre Dame 24, Texas A&M 21

Cotton Bowl (Cont.)

1-2-95 ....Southern Cal 55, Texas Tech 14
1-1-96 ....Colorado 38, Oregon 6
1-1-97 ....Brigham Young 19, Kansas St 15
1-1-98 ....UCLA 29, Texas A&M 23
1-1-99 ....Texas 38, Mississippi St 11
1-1-00 ....Arkansas 27, Texas 6

City: Dallas. Stadium: Cotton Bowl, capacity 68,252.

Sun Bowl

1-1-36 ....Hardin-Simmons 14, New Mexico St 14
1-1-37 ....Hardin-Simmons 34, UTEP 6
1-1-38 ....W Virginia 7, Texas Tech 6
1-2-39 ....Utah 26, New Mexico 0
1-1-40 ....Catholic 0, Arizona St 0
1-1-41 ....Case Reserve 26, Arizona St 13
1-1-42 ....Tulsa 6, Texas Tech 0
1-1-43 ....2nd Air Force 13, Hardin-Simmons 7
1-1-44 ....Southwestern (TX) 7, New Mexico 0
1-1-45 ....Southwestern (TX) 35, New Mexico 0
1-1-46 ....New Mexico 34, Denver 24
1-1-47 ....Cincinnati 18, Virginia Tech 6
1-1-48 ....Miami (OH) 13, Texas Tech 12
1-1-49 ....W Virginia 21, UTEP 12
1-2-50 ....UTEP 33, Georgetown 20
1-1-51 ....West Texas St 14, Cincinnati 13
1-1-52 ....Texas Tech 25, Pacific 14
1-1-53 ....Pacific 26, Southern Miss 7
1-1-54 ....UTEP 37, Southern Miss 14
1-1-55 ....UTEP 47, Florida St 20
1-2-56 ....Wyoming 21, Texas Tech 14
1-1-57 ....George Washington 13, UTEP 0
1-1-58 ....Louisville 34, Drake 20
12-31-58 ....Wyoming 14, Hardin-Simmons 6
12-31-59 ....New Mexico St 28, N Texas 8
12-31-60 ....New Mexico St 20, Utah St 13
12-30-61 ....Villanova 17, Wichita St 9
12-31-62 ....W Texas St 15, Ohio 14
12-31-63 ....Oregon 21, SMU 14
12-26-64 ....Georgia 7, Texas Tech 0
12-31-65 ....UTEP 13, Texas Christian 12
12-24-66 ....Wyoming 28, Florida St 20
12-30-67 ....UTEP 14, Mississippi 7
12-28-68 ....Auburn 34, Arizona 10
12-20-69 ....Nebraska 45, Georgia 6
12-19-70 ....Georgia Tech 17, Texas Tech 9
12-18-71 ....Louisiana St 33, Iowa St 15
12-30-72 ....N Carolina 32, Texas Tech 28
12-29-73 ....Missouri 34, Auburn 17
12-28-74 ....Mississippi St 26, N Carolina 24
12-26-75 ....Pittsburgh 33, Kansas 19
1-2-77 ....Texas A&M 37, Florida 14
12-31-77 ....Stanford 24, Louisiana St 14
12-23-78 ....Texas 42, Maryland 0
12-22-79 ....Washington 14, Texas 7
12-27-80 ....Nebraska 31, Mississippi St 17
12-26-81 ....Oklahoma 40, Houston 14
12-25-82 ....N Carolina 26, Texas 10
12-24-83 ....Alabama 28, SMU 7
12-22-84 ....Maryland 28, Tennessee 27
12-28-85 ....Georgia 13, Arizona 13
12-25-86 ....Alabama 28, Washington 6
12-25-87 ....Oklahoma St 35, W Virginia 33
12-24-88 ....Alabama 29, Army 28
12-30-89 ....Pittsburgh 31, Texas A&M 28
12-31-90 ....Michigan St 17, Southern Cal 16
12-31-91 ....UCLA 6, Illinois 3

Sun Bowl *(Cont.)*

12-31-92 ....Baylor 20, Arizona 15
12-24-93 ....Oklahoma 41, Texas Tech 10
12-30-94 ....Texas 35, N Carolina 31
12-29-95 ....Iowa 38, Washington 18
12-31-96 ....Stanford 38, Michigan St 0
12-31-97 ....Arizona St 17, Iowa 7
12-31-98 ....Texas Christian 28, Southern Cal 19
12-31-99 ....Oregon 24, Minnesota 20

City: El Paso. Stadium: Sun Bowl, capacity 51,270.
Name Changes: Sun Bowl (1936–86; 94–), John Hancock
Sun Bowl (1987–88), John Hancock Bowl (1989–93).
Playing Sites: Kidd Field (1936–62), Sun Bowl (since 1963).

Gator Bowl

1-1-46 ....Wake Forest 26, S Carolina 14
1-1-47 ....Oklahoma 34, N Carolina St 13
1-1-48 ....Maryland 20, Georgia 20
1-1-49 ....Clemson 24, Missouri 23
1-2-50 ....Maryland 20, Missouri 7
1-1-51 ....Wyoming 20, Washington & Lee 7
1-1-52 ....Miami (FL) 14, Clemson 0
1-1-53 ....Florida 14, Tulsa 13
1-1-54 ....Texas Tech 35, Auburn 13
12-31-54 ....Auburn 33, Baylor 13
12-31-55 ....Vanderbilt 25, Auburn 13
12-29-56 ....Georgia Tech 21, Pittsburgh 14
12-28-57 ....Tennessee 3, Texas A&M 0
12-27-58 ....Mississippi 7, Florida 3
1-2-60 ....Arkansas 14, Georgia Tech 7
12-31-60 ....Florida 13, Baylor 12
12-30-61 ....Penn St 30, Georgia Tech 15
12-29-62 ....Florida 17, Penn St 7
12-28-63 ....N Carolina 35, Air Force 0
1-2-65 ....Florida St 36, Oklahoma 19
12-31-65 ....Georgia Tech 31, Texas Tech 21
12-31-66 ....Tennessee 18, Syracuse 12
12-30-67 ....Penn St 17, Florida St 17
12-28-68 ....Missouri 35, Alabama 10
12-27-69 ....Florida 14, Tennessee 13
1-2-71 ....Auburn 35, Mississippi 28
12-31-71 ....Georgia 7, N Carolina 3
12-30-72 ....Auburn 24, Colorado 3
12-29-73 ....Texas Tech 28, Tennessee 19
12-30-74 ....Auburn 27, Texas 3
12-29-75 ....Maryland 13, Florida 0
12-27-76 ....Notre Dame 20, Penn St 9
12-30-77 ....Pittsburgh 34, Clemson 3
12-29-78 ....Clemson 17, Ohio St 15
12-28-79 ....N Carolina 17, Michigan 15
12-29-80 ....Pittsburgh 37, S Carolina 9
12-28-81 ....N Carolina 31, Arkansas 27
12-30-82 ....Florida St 31, W Virginia 12
12-30-83 ....Florida 14, Iowa 6
12-28-84 ....Oklahoma St 21, S Carolina 14
12-30-85 ....Florida St 34, Oklahoma St 23
12-27-86 ....Clemson 27, Stanford 21
12-31-87 ....Louisiana St 30, S Carolina 13
1-1-89 ....Georgia 34, Michigan St 27
12-30-89 ....Clemson 27, W Virginia 7
1-1-91 ....Michigan 35, Mississippi 3
12-29-91 ....Oklahoma 48, Virginia 14
12-31-92 ....Florida 27, N Carolina St 10
12-31-93 ....Alabama 24, North Carolina 10
12-30-94 ....Tennessee 45, Virginia Tech 23
1-1-96 ....Syracuse 41, Clemson 0
1-1-97 ....N Carolina 20, W Virginia 13
1-1-98 ....N Carolina 42, Viginia Tech 13

Gator Bowl (Cont.)

1-1-99 ....Georgia Tech 35, Notre Dame 28
1-1-00 ....Miami 27, Georgia Tech 13

City: Jacksonville, FL. Stadium: Alltel Stadium, capacity
76,976.

Florida Citrus Bowl

1-1-47 ....Catawba 31, Maryville (TN) 6
1-1-48 ....Catawba 7, Marshall 0
1-1-49 ....Murray St 21, Sul Ross St 21
1-2-50 ....St Vincent 7, Emory & Henry 6
1-1-51 ....Morris Harvey 35, Emory & Henry 14
1-1-52 ....Stetson 35, Arkansas St 20
1-1-53 ....E Texas St 33, Tennessee Tech 0
1-1-54 ....E Texas St 7, Arkansas St 7
1-1-55 ....NE-Omaha 7, Eastern Kentucky 6
1-2-56 ....Juniata 6, Missouri Valley 6
1-1-57 ....W Texas St 20, Southern Miss 13
1-1-58 ....E Texas St 10, Southern Miss 9
12-27-58 ....E Texas St 26, Missouri Valley 7
1-1-60 ....Middle Tennessee St 21, Presbyterian 12
12-30-60 ....Citadel 27, Tennessee Tech 0
12-29-61 ....Lamar 21, Middle Tennessee St 14
12-22-62 ....Houston 49, Miami (OH) 21
12-28-63 ....Western Kentucky 27, Coast Guard 0
12-12-64 ....E Carolina 14, Massachusetts 13
12-11-65 ....E Carolina 31, Maine 0
12-10-66 ....Morgan St 14, West Chester 6
12-16-67 ....TN-Martin 25, West Chester 8
12-27-68 ....Richmond 49, Ohio 42
12-26-69 ....Toledo 56, Davidson 33
12-28-70 ....Toledo 40, William & Mary 12
12-28-71 ....Toledo 28, Richmond 3
12-29-72 ....Tampa 21, Kent St 18
12-22-73 ....Miami (OH) 16, Florida 7
12-21-74 ....Miami (OH) 21, Georgia 10
12-20-75 ....Miami (OH) 20, S Carolina 7
12-18-76 ....Oklahoma St 49, Brigham Young 21
12-23-77 ....Florida St 40, Texas Tech 17
12-23-78 ....N Carolina St 30, Pittsburgh 17
12-22-79 ....Louisiana St 34, Wake Forest 10
12-20-80 ....Florida 35, Maryland 20
12-19-81 ....Missouri 19, Southern Miss 17
12-18-82 ....Auburn 33, Boston Col 26
12-17-83 ....Tennessee 30, Maryland 23
12-22-84 ....Georgia 17, Florida St 17
12-28-85 ....Ohio St 10, Brigham Young 7
1-1-87 ....Auburn 16, Southern Cal 7
1-1-88 ....Clemson 35, Penn St 10
1-2-89 ....Clemson 13, Oklahoma 6
1-1-90 ....Illinois 31, Virginia 21
1-1-91 ....Georgia Tech 45, Nebraska 21
1-1-92 ....California 37, Clemson 13
1-1-93 ....Georgia 21, Ohio State 14
1-1-94 ....Penn State 31, Tennessee 13
1-2-95 ....Alabama 24, Ohio St 17
1-1-96 ....Tennessee 20, Ohio St 14
1-1-97 ....Tennessee 48, Northwestern 28
1-1-98 ....Florida 21, Penn St 6
1-1-99 ....Michigan 45, Arkansas 31
1-1-00 ....Michigan St 37, Florida 34

City: Orlando, FL. Stadium: Florida Citrus Bowl, capacity 70,000.
Name Change: Tangerine Bowl (1947–82).
Playing Sites: Tangerine Bowl (1947–72, 1974–82);
Florida Field, Gainesville (1973); Orlando Stadium
(1983–85); Florida Citrus Bowl-Orlando (since 1986).
Tangerine Bowl, Orlando Stadium and Florida Citrus
Bowl-Orlando are identical site.

Liberty Bowl

12-19-59..........Penn St 7, Alabama 0
12-17-60..........Penn St 41, Oregon 12
12-16-61..........Syracuse 15, Miami (FL) 14
12-15-62..........Oregon St 6, Villanova 0
12-21-63..........Mississippi St 16, N Carolina St 12
12-19-64..........Utah 32, W Virginia 6
12-18-65..........Mississippi 13, Auburn 7
12-10-66..........Miami (FL) 14, Virginia Tech 7
12-16-67..........N Carolina St 14, Georgia 7
12-14-68..........Mississippi 34, Virginia Tech 17
12-13-69..........Colorado 47, Alabama 33
12-12-70..........Tulane 17, Colorado 3
12-20-71..........Tennessee 14, Arkansas 13
12-18-72..........Georgia Tech 31, Iowa St 30
12-17-73..........N Carolina St 31, Kansas 18
12-16-74..........Tennessee 7, Maryland 3
12-22-75..........Southern Cal 20, Texas A&M 0
12-20-76..........Alabama 36, UCLA 6
12-19-77..........Nebraska 21, N Carolina 17
12-23-78..........Missouri 20, Louisiana St 15
12-22-79..........Penn St 9, Tulane 6
12-27-80..........Purdue 28, Missouri 25
12-30-81..........Ohio St 31, Navy 28
12-29-82..........Alabama 21, Illinois 15
12-29-83..........Notre Dame 19, Boston Col 18
12-27-84..........Auburn 21, Arkansas 15
12-27-85..........Baylor 21, Louisiana St 7
12-29-86..........Tennessee 21, Minnesota 14
12-29-87..........Georgia 20, Arkansas 17
12-28-88..........Indiana 34, S Carolina 10
12-28-89..........Mississippi 42, Air Force 29
12-27-90..........Air Force 23, Ohio St 11
12-29-91..........Air Force 38, Mississippi St 15
12-31-92..........Mississippi 13, Air Force 0
12-28-93..........Louisville 18, Michigan St 7
12-31-94..........Illinois 30, E Carolina 0
12-30-95..........East Carolina 19, Stanford 13
12-27-96..........Syracuse 30, Houston 17
12-31-97..........Southern Miss 41, Pittsburgh 7
12-31-98..........Tulane 41, Brigham Young 27
12-31-99..........Southern Miss 23, Colorado St 17

City: Memphis (since 1965). Stadium: Liberty Bowl
Memorial Stadium, capacity 62,921.
Playing Sites: Philadelphia (Municipal Stadium, 1959–63),
Atlantic City (Convention Center, 1964).

Bluebonnet Bowl

12-19-59..........Clemson 23, Texas Christian 7
12-17-60..........Texas 3, Alabama 1
12-16-61..........Kansas 33, Rice 7
12-22-62..........Missouri 14, Georgia Tech 10
12-21-63..........Baylor 14, LSU 7
12-19-64..........Tulsa 14, Mississippi 7
12-18-65..........Tennessee 27, Tulsa 6
12-17-66..........Texas 19, Mississippi 0
12-23-67..........Colorado 31, Miami (FL) 21
12-31-68..........SMU 28, Oklahoma 27
12-31-69..........Houston 36, Auburn 7
12-31-70..........Alabama 24, Oklahoma 24
12-31-71..........Colorado 29, Houston 17
12-30-72..........Tennessee 24, Louisiana St 17
12-29-73..........Houston 47, Tulane 7
12-23-74..........N Carolina St 31, Houston 31
12-27-75..........Texas 38, Colorado 21
12-31-76..........Nebraska 27, Texas Tech 24
12-31-77..........Southern Cal 47, Texas A&M 28
12-31-78..........Stanford 25, Georgia 22

Bluebonnet Bowl *(Cont.)*

12-31-79..........Purdue 27, Tennessee 22
12-31-80..........N Carolina 16, Texas 7
12-31-81..........Michigan 33, UCLA 14
12-31-82..........Arkansas 28, Florida 24
12-31-83..........Oklahoma St 24, Baylor 14
12-31-84..........W Virginia 31, Texas Christian 14
12-31-85..........Air Force 24, Texas 16
12-31-86..........Baylor 21, Colorado 9
12-31-87..........Texas 32, Pittsburgh 27

City: Houston. Playing sites: Rice Stadium (1959–67;
1985–86), Astrodome (1968–84, 1987).

Name change: Astro-Bluebonnet Bowl (1968–76). Bowl
was discontinued after 1987.

Peach Bowl

12-30-68..........Louisiana St 31, Florida St 27
12-30-69..........W Virginia 14, S Carolina 3
12-30-70..........Arizona St 48, N Carolina 26
12-30-71..........Mississippi 41, Georgia Tech 18
12-29-72..........N Carolina St 49, W Virginia 13
12-28-73..........Georgia 17, Maryland 16
12-28-74..........Vanderbilt 6, Texas Tech 6
12-31-75..........W Virginia 13, N Carolina St 10
12-31-76..........Kentucky 21, N Carolina 0
12-31-77..........N Carolina St 24, Iowa St 14
12-25-78..........Purdue 41, Georgia Tech 21
12-31-79..........Baylor 24, Clemson 18
1-2-81............Miami (FL) 20, Virginia Tech 10
12-31-81..........W Virginia 26, Florida 6
12-31-82..........Iowa 28, Tennessee 22
12-30-83..........Florida St 28, N Carolina 3
12-31-84..........Virginia 27, Purdue 24
12-31-85..........Army 31, Illinois 29
12-31-86..........Virginia Tech 25, N Carolina St 24
1-2-88............Tennessee 27, Indiana 22
12-31-88..........N Carolina St 28, Iowa 23
12-30-89..........Syracuse 19, Georgia 18
12-29-90..........Auburn 27, Indiana 23
1-1-92............E Carolina 37, N Carolina St 34
1-2-93............North Carolina 21, Mississippi St 17
12-31-93..........Clemson 14, Kentucky 13
1-1-95............N Carolina St 28, Mississippi St 24
12-30-95..........Virginia 34, Georgia 23
12-28-96..........Louisiana St 10, Clemson 7
1-2-98............Auburn 21, Clemson 17
12-31-98..........Georgia 35, Virginia 33
12-30-99..........Mississippi St 17, Clemson 7

City: Atlanta. Stadium: Georgia Dome, capacity 71,228.
Playing Sites: Grant Field (1968–70), Atlanta-Fulton
County Stadium (1971–92), Georgia Dome (since 1993).

Fiesta Bowl

12-27-71..........Arizona St 45, Florida St 38
12-23-72..........Arizona St 49, Missouri 35
12-21-73..........Arizona St 28, Pittsburgh 7
12-28-74..........Oklahoma St 16, Brigham Young 6
12-26-75..........Arizona St 17, Nebraska 14
12-25-76..........Oklahoma 41, Wyoming 7
12-25-77..........Penn St 42, Arizona St 30
12-25-78..........Arkansas 10, UCLA 10
12-25-79..........Pittsburgh 16, Arizona 10
12-26-80..........Penn St 31, Ohio St 19
1-1-82............Penn St 26, Southern Cal 10
1-1-83............Arizona St 32, Oklahoma 21
1-2-84............Ohio St 28, Pittsburgh 23
1-1-85............UCLA 39, Miami (FL) 37
1-1-86............Michigan 27, Nebraska 23

Fiesta Bowl *(Cont.)*

1-2-87 ....Penn St 14, Miami (FL) 10
1-1-88 ....Florida St 31, Nebraska 28
1-2-89 ....Notre Dame 34, W Virginia 21
1-1-90 ....Florida St 41, Nebraska 17
1-1-91 ....Louisville 34, Alabama 7
1-1-92 ....Penn St 42, Tennessee 17
1-1-93 ....Syracuse 26, Colorado 22
1-1-94 ....Arizona 29, Miami (FL) 0
1-2-95 ....Colorado 41, Notre Dame 24
1-2-96 ....Nebraska 62, Florida 24
1-1-97 ....Penn St 38, Texas 15
12-31-97 ....Kansas St 35, Syracuse 18
1-4-99 ....Tennessee 23, Florida St 16
1-2-00 ....Nebraska 31, Tennessee 21

City: Tempe, AZ. Stadium: Sun Devil Stadium, capacity 73,259.

Independence Bowl

12-13-76 ....McNeese St 20, Tulsa 16
12-17-77 ....Louisiana Tech 24, Louisville 14
12-16-78 ....E Carolina 35, Louisiana Tech 13
12-15-79 ....Syracuse 31, McNeese St 7
12-13-80 ....Southern Miss 16, McNeese St 14
12-12-81 ....Texas A&M 33, Oklahoma St 16
12-11-82 ....Wisconsin 14, Kansas St 3
12-10-83 ....Air Force 9, Mississippi 3
12-15-84 ....Air Force 23, Virginia Tech 7
12-21-85 ....Minnesota 20, Clemson 13
12-20-86 ....Mississippi 20, Texas Tech 17
12-19-87 ....Washington 24, Tulane 12
12-23-88 ....Southern Miss 38, UTEP 18
12-16-89 ....Oregon 27, Tulsa 16
12-15-90 ....Louisiana Tech 34, Maryland 34
12-29-91 ....Georgia 24, Arkansas 15
12-31-92 ....Wake Forest 39, Oregon 35
12-31-93 ....Virginia Tech 45, Indiana 20
12-28-94 ....Virginia 20, Texas Christian 10
12-29-95 ....Louisiana St 45, Michigan St 26
12-31-96 ....Auburn 32, Army 29
12-28-97 ....Louisiana St 27, Notre Dame 9
12-31-98 ....Mississippi 35, Texas Tech 18
12-31-99 ....Mississippi 27, Oklahoma 25

City: Shreveport, LA. Stadium: Independence Stadium, capacity 50,459.

All-American Bowl

12-22-77 ....Maryland 17, Minnesota 7
12-20-78 ....Texas A&M 28, Iowa St 12
12-29-79 ....Missouri 24, S Carolina 14
12-27-80 ....Arkansas 34, Tulane 15
12-31-81 ....Mississippi St 10, Kansas 0
12-31-82 ....Air Force 36, Vanderbilt 28
12-22-83 ....W Virginia 20, Kentucky 16
12-29-84 ....Kentucky 20, Wisconsin 19
12-31-85 ....Georgia Tech 17, Michigan St 14
12-31-86 ....Florida St 27, Indiana 13
12-22-87 ....Virginia 22, Brigham Young 16
12-29-88 ....Florida 14, Illinois 10
12-28-89 ....Texas A&M 49, Duke 21
12-28-90 ....N Carolina St 31, S Mississippi 27

City: Birmingham, AL. Stadium: Legion Field.
Name Change: Hall of Fame Classic (1977–84). Bowl was discontinued after 1990.

Holiday Bowl

12-22-78 ....Navy 23, Brigham Young 16
12-21-79 ....Indiana 38, Brigham Young 37
12-19-80 ....Brigham Young 46, SMU 45
12-18-81 ....Brigham Young 38, Washington St 36
12-17-82 ....Ohio St 47, Brigham Young 17
12-23-83 ....Brigham Young 21, Missouri 17
12-21-84 ....Brigham Young 24, Michigan 17
12-22-85 ....Arkansas 18, Arizona St 17
12-30-86 ....Iowa 39, San Diego St 38
12-30-87 ....Iowa 20, Wyoming 19
12-30-88 ....Oklahoma St 62, Wyoming 14
12-29-89 ....Penn St 50, Brigham Young 39
12-29-90 ....Texas A&M 65, Brigham Young 14
12-30-91 ....Iowa 13, Brigham Young 13
12-30-92 ....Hawaii 27, Illinois 17
12-30-93 ....Ohio St 28, Brigham Young 21
12-30-94 ....Michigan 24, Colorado St 14
12-29-95 ....Kansas St 54, Colorado St 21
12-30-96 ....Colorado 33, Washington 21
12-29-97 ....Colorado St 35, Missouri 24
12-30-98 ....Arizona 23, Nebraska 20
12-29-99 ....Kansas St 24, Washington 20

City: San Diego. Stadium: Qualcomm Stadium, capacity 70,000.

Las Vegas Bowl

12-19-81 ....Toledo 27, San Jose St 25
12-18-82 ....Fresno St 29, Bowling Green 28
12-17-83 ....Northern Illinois 20, Cal St-Fullerton 13
12-15-84 ....UNLV 30, Toledo 13*
12-14-85 ....Fresno St 51, Bowling Green 7
12-13-86 ....San Jose St 37, Miami (OH) 7
12-12-87 ....Eastern Michigan 30, San Jose St 27
12-10-88 ....Fresno St 35, Western Michigan 30
12-9-89 ....Fresno St 27, Ball St 6
12-8-90 ....San Jose St 48, Central Michigan 24
12-14-91 ....Bowling Green 28, Fresno St 21
12-18-92 ....Bowling Green 35, Nevada 34
12-17-93 ....Utah St 42, Ball St 33
12-15-94 ....UNLV 52, Central Michigan 24
12-14-95 ....Toledo 40, Nevada 37
12-19-96 ....Nevada 18, Ball St 15
12-19-97 ....Oregon 41, Air Force 13
12-19-98 ....N Carolina 20, San Diego St 13
12-18-99 ....Utah 17, Fresno St 16

* Toledo won later by forfeit.

City: Las Vegas (since 1992). Stadium: Sam Boyd Silver Bowl Stadium, capacity 40,000.
Name change: California Bowl (1981–91).
Playing sites: Fresno, CA (Bulldog Stadium, 1981–91), Las Vegas.

Aloha Bowl

12-25-82 ....Washington 21, Maryland 20
12-26-83 ....Penn St 13, Washington 10
12-29-84 ....SMU 27, Notre Dame 20
12-28-85 ....Alabama 24, Southern Cal 3
12-27-86 ....Arizona 30, N Carolina 21
12-25-87 ....UCLA 20, Florida 16
12-25-88 ....Washington St 24, Houston 22
12-25-89 ....Michigan St 33, Hawaii 13
12-25-90 ....Syracuse 28, Arizona 0
12-25-91 ....Georgia Tech 18, Stanford 17
12-25-92 ....Kansas 23, Brigham Young 20
12-25-93 ....Colorado 41, Fresno St 30

Aloha Bowl *(Cont.)*

12-25-94 ....Boston College 12, Kansas St 7
12-25-95 ....Kansas 51, UCLA 30
12-25-96 ....Navy 42, California 38
12-25-97 ....Washington 51, Michigan St 23
12-25-98 ....Colorado 51, Oregon 43
12-25-99 ....Wake Forest 23, Arizona St 3

City: Honolulu. Stadium: Aloha Stadium, capacity 50,000.

Freedom Bowl

12-16-84 ....Iowa 55, Texas 17
12-30-85 ....Washington 20, Colorado 17
12-30-86 ....UCLA 31, Brigham Young 10
12-30-87 ....Arizona St 33, Air Force 28
12-29-88 ....Brigham Young 20, Colorado 17
12-30-89 ....Washington 34, Florida 7
12-29-90 ....Colorado St 32, Oregon 31
12-30-91 ....Tulsa 28, San Diego St 17
12-29-92 ....Fresno St 24, Southern Cal 7
12-30-93 ....Southern Cal 28, Utah 21
12-29-94 ....Utah 16, Arizona 13

City: Anaheim. Stadium: Anaheim Stadium. Bowl was discontinued after 1994.

Outback Bowl

12-23-86 ....Boston College 27, Georgia 24
1-2-88 ....Michigan 28, Alabama 24
1-2-89 ....Syracuse 23, Louisiana St 10
1-1-90 ....Auburn 31, Ohio St 14
1-1-91 ....Clemson 30, Illinois 0
1-1-92 ....Syracuse 24, Ohio St 17
1-1-93 ....Tennessee 38, Boston College 23
1-1-94 ....Michigan 42, N Carolina St 7
1-2-95 ....Wisconsin 34, Duke 20
1-1-96 ....Penn St 43, Auburn 14
1-1-97 ....Alabama 17, Michigan 14
1-1-98 ....Georgia 33, Wisconsin 6
1-1-99 ....Penn St 26, Kentucky 14
1-1-00 ....Georgia 28, Purdue 25

City: Tampa. Stadium: Raymond James Stadium, capacity 65,000.

Name change: Hall of Fame Bowl (1986–95).

Insight.com Bowl

12-31-89 ....Arizona 17, N Carolina St 10
12-31-90 ....California 17, Wyoming 15
12-31-91 ....Indiana 24, Baylor 0
12-29-92 ....Washington St 31, Utah 28
12-29-93 ....Kansas St 52, Wyoming 17
12-29-94 ....Brigham Young 31, Oklahoma 6
12-27-95 ....Texas Tech 55, Air Force 41
12-27-96 ....Wisconsin 38, Utah 10
12-27-97 ....Arizona 20, New Mexico 14
12-26-98 ....Missouri 34, W Virginia 31
12-31-99 ....Colorado 62, Boston College 28

City: Tucson. Stadium: Arizona Stadium, capacity 55,883.
Name change: Copper Bowl 1989–97.

Micron PC Bowl

12-28-90 ....Florida St 24, Penn St 17
12-28-91 ....Alabama 30, Colorado 25
1-1-93 ....Stanford 24, Penn St 3
1-1-94 ....Boston College 31, Virginia 13
1-2-95 ....S Carolina 24, W Virginia 21
12-30-95 ....N Carolina 20, Arkansas 10
12-27-96 ....Miami (FL) 31, Virginia 21
12-29-97 ....Georgia Tech 35, West Virginia 30
12-29-98 ....Miami (FL) 46, N Carolina St 23
12-30-99 ....Illinois 63, Virginia 21

City: Miami. Stadium: Pro Player Stadium, capacity 72,000.
Name Changes: Blockbuster Bowl (1990–93), Carquest Bowl (1994–97).

Alamo Bowl

12-31-93 ....California 37, Iowa 3
12-31-94 ....Washington St 10, Baylor 3
12-28-95 ....Texas A&M 22, Michigan 20
12-29-96 ....Iowa 27, Texas Tech 0
12-30-97 ....Purdue 33, Oklahoma St 20
12-29-98 ....Purdue 37, Kansas St 34
12-28-99 ....Penn St 24, Texas A&M 0

City: San Antonio, TX. Stadium: Alamodome, capacity 65,000.

There's Another Edwards in Town

All his life, Georgia freshman receiver Terrence Edwards had been known as Robert Edwards's little brother. On Sept. 4, 1999, Terrence made a name for himself by catching 10 passes for 196 yards and two touchdowns in Georgia's 38–7 rout of Utah State. Robert, who was a running back for the Bulldogs from 1994 to 1996 and who had just completed a stellar rookie season with the New England Patriots when he suffered a career-ending knee injury while playing flag football in February '99 at the Pro Bowl, was on hand for his little brother's eye-opener. "He was giving me tips as the game was going on," said Terrence, who fell two yards shy of breaking Georgia's single-game record for receiving yards. "I'm blessed to have a big brother. I think that he was injured just so he could be sent here to watch over me."

1936

		Record	Coach
1.	Minnesota	7-1-0	Bernie Bierman
2.	Louisiana St	9-0-1	Bernie Moore
3.	Pittsburgh	7-1-1	Jack Sutherland
4.	Alabama	8-0-1	Frank Thomas
5.	Washington	7-1-1	Jimmy Phelan
6.	Santa Clara	7-1-0	Buck Shaw
7.	Northwestern	7-1-0	Pappy Waldorf
8.	Notre Dame	6-2-1	Elmer Layden
9.	Nebraska	7-2-0	Dana X. Bible
10.	Pennsylvania	7-1-0	Harvey Harman
11.	Duke	9-1-0	Wallace Wade
12.	Yale	7-1-0	Ducky Pond
13.	Dartmouth	7-1-1	Red Blaik
14.	Duquesne	7-2-0	John Smith
15.	Fordham	5-1-2	Jim Crowley
16.	Texas Christian	8-2-2	Dutch Meyer
17.	Tennessee	6-2-2	Bob Neyland
18.	Arkansas	7-3-0	Fred Thomsen
19.	Navy	6-3-0	Tom Hamilton
20.	Marquette	7-1-0	Frank Murray

1937

		Record	Coach
1.	Pittsburgh	9-0-1	Jack Sutherland
2.	California	9-0-1	Stub Allison
3.	Fordham	7-0-1	Jim Crowley
4.	Alabama	9-0-0	Frank Thomas
5.	Minnesota	6-2-0	Bernie Bierman
6.	Villanova	8-0-1	Clipper Smith
7.	Dartmouth	7-0-2	Red Blaik
8.	Louisiana St	9-1-0	Bernie Moore
9.	Notre Dame	6-2-1	Elmer Layden
	Santa Clara	8-0-0	Buck Shaw
11.	Nebraska	6-1-2	Biff Jones
12.	Yale	6-1-1	Ducky Pond
13.	Ohio St	6-2-0	Francis Schmidt
14.	Holy Cross	8-0-2	Eddie Anderson
	Arkansas	6-2-2	Fred Thomsen
16.	Texas Christian	4-2-2	Dutch Meyer
17.	Colorado	8-0-0	Bunnie Oakes
18.	Rice	5-3-2	Jimmy Kitts
19.	N Carolina	7-1-1	Ray Wolf
20.	Duke	7-2-1	Wallace Wade

1938

		Record	Coach
1.	Texas Christian	10-0-0	Dutch Meyer
2.	Tennessee	10-0-0	Bob Neyland
3.	Duke	9-0-0	Wallace Wade
4.	Oklahoma	10-0-0	Tom Stidham
5.	#Notre Dame	8-1-0	Elmer Layden
6.	Carnegie Tech	7-1-0	Bill Kern
7.	Southern Cal	8-2-0	Howard Jones
8.	Pittsburgh	8-2-0	Jack Sutherland
9.	Holy Cross	8-1-0	Eddie Anderson
10.	Minnesota	6-2-0	Bernie Bierman
11.	Texas Tech	10-0-0	Pete Cawthon
12.	Cornell	5-1-1	Carl Snavely
13.	Alabama	7-1-1	Frank Thomas
14.	California	10-1-0	Stub Allison
15.	Fordham	6-1-2	Jim Crowley
16.	Michigan	6-1-1	Fritz Crisler
17.	Northwestern	4-2-2	Pappy Waldorf

1938 (Cont.)

		Record	Coach
18.	Villanova	8-0-1	Clipper Smith
19.	Tulane	7-2-1	Red Dawson
20.	Dartmouth	7-2-0	Red Blaik

#Selected No. 1 by the Dickinson System.

1939

		Record	Coach
1.	Texas A&M	10-0-0	Homer Norton
2.	Tennessee	10-0-0	Bob Neyland
3.	#Southern Cal	7-0-2	Howard Jones
4.	Cornell	8-0-0	Carl Snavely
5.	Tulane	8-0-1	Red Dawson
6.	Missouri	8-1-0	Don Faurot
7.	UCLA	6-0-4	Babe Horrell
8.	Duke	8-1-0	Wallace Wade
9.	Iowa	6-1-1	Eddie Anderson
10.	Duquesne	8-0-1	Buff Donelli
11.	Boston College	9-1-0	Frank Leahy
12.	Clemson	8-1-0	Jess Neely
13.	Notre Dame	7-2-0	Elmer Layden
14.	Santa Clara	5-1-3	Buck Shaw
15.	Ohio St	6-2-0	Francis Schmidt
16.	Georgia Tech	7-2-0	Bill Alexander
17.	Fordham	6-2-0	Jim Crowley
18.	Nebraska	7-1-1	Biff Jones
19.	Oklahoma	6-2-1	Tom Stidham
20.	Michigan	6-2-0	Fritz Crisler

#Selected No. 1 by the Dickinson System.

1940

		Record	Coach
1.	Minnesota	8-0-0	Bernie Bierman
2.	Stanford	9-0-0	C. Shaughnessy
3.	Michigan	7-1-0	Fritz Crisler
4.	Tennessee	10-0-0	Bob Neyland
5.	Boston College	10-0-0	Frank Leahy
6.	Texas A&M	8-1-0	Homer Norton
7.	Nebraska	8-1-0	Biff Jones
8.	Northwestern	6-2-0	Pappy Waldorf
9.	Mississippi St	9-0-1	Allyn McKeen
10.	Washington	7-2-0	Jimmy Phelan
11.	Santa Clara	6-1-1	Buck Shaw
12.	Fordham	7-1-0	Jim Crowley
13.	Georgetown	8-1-0	Jack Hagerty
14.	Pennsylvania	6-1-1	George Munger
15.	Cornell	6-2-0	Carl Snavely
16.	SMU	8-1-1	Matty Bell
17.	Hard.-Simmons	9-0-0	Abe Woodson
18.	Duke	7-2-0	Wallace Wade
19.	Lafayette	9-0-0	Hooks Mylin
20.	—		

Only 19 teams selected.

1941

		Record	Coach
1.	Minnesota	8-0-0	Bernie Bierman
2.	Duke	9-0-0	Wallace Wade
3.	Notre Dame	8-0-0	Frank Leahy
4.	Texas	8-1-1	Dana X. Bible
5.	Michigan	6-1-1	Fritz Crisler
6.	Fordham	7-1-0	Jim Crowley
7.	Missouri	8-1-0	Don Faurot
8.	Duquesne	8-0-0	Buff Donelli
9.	Texas A&M	9-1-0	Homer Norton
10.	Navy	7-1-1	Swede Larson
11.	Northwestern	5-3-0	Pappy Waldorf
12.	Oregon St	7-2-0	Lon Stiner
13.	Ohio St	6-1-1	Paul Brown
14.	Georgia	8-1-1	Wally Butts
15.	Pennsylvania	7-1-1	George Munger
16.	Mississippi St	8-1-1	Allyn McKeen
17.	Mississippi	6-2-1	Harry Mehre
18.	Tennessee	8-2-0	John Barnhill
19.	Washington St	6-4-0	Babe Hollingbery
20.	Alabama	8-2-0	Frank Thomas

1942

		Record	Coach
1.	Ohio St	9-1-0	Paul Brown
2.	Georgia	10-1-0	Wally Butts
3.	Wisconsin	8-1-1	H. Stuhldreher
4.	Tulsa	10-0-0	Henry Frnka
5.	Georgia Tech	9-1-0	Bill Alexander
6.	Notre Dame	7-2-2	Frank Leahy
7.	Tennessee	8-1-1	John Barnhill
8.	Boston College	8-1-0	Denny Myers
9.	Michigan	7-3-0	Fritz Crisler
10.	Alabama	7-3-0	Frank Thomas
11.	Texas	8-2-0	Dana X. Bible
12.	Stanford	6-4-0	Marchie Schwartz
13.	UCLA	7-3-0	Babe Horrell
14.	William & Mary	9-1-1	Carl Voyles
15.	Santa Clara	7-2-0	Buck Shaw
16.	Auburn	6-4-1	Jack Meagher
17.	Washington St	6-2-2	Babe Hollingbery
18.	Mississippi St	8-2-0	Allyn McKeen
19.	Minnesota	5-4-0	George Hauser
	Holy Cross	5-4-1	Ank Scanlon
	Penn St	6-1-1	Bob Higgins

1943

		Record	Coach
1.	Notre Dame	9-1-0	Frank Leahy
2.	Iowa Pre-Flight	9-1-0	Don Faurot
3.	Michigan	8-1-0	Fritz Crisler
4.	Navy	8-1-0	Billick Whelchel
5.	Purdue	9-0-0	Elmer Burnham
6.	Great Lakes	10-2-0	Tony Hinkle
7.	Duke	8-1-0	Eddie Cameron
8.	Del Monte P-F	7-1-0	Bill Kern
9.	Northwestern	6-2-0	Pappy Waldorf
10.	March Field	9-1-0	Paul Schissler
11.	Army	7-2-1	Red Blaik
12.	Washington	4-0-0	Ralph Welch
13.	Georgia Tech	7-3-0	Bill Alexander

1943 *(Cont.)*

		Record	Coach
14.	Texas	7-1-0	Dana X. Bible
15.	Tulsa	6-0-1	Henry Frnka
16.	Dartmouth	6-1-0	Earl Brown
17.	Bainbridge NTS	7-0-0	Joe Maniaci
18.	Colorado College	7-0-0	Hal White
19.	Pacific	7-2-0	Amos A. Stagg
20.	Pennsylvania	6-2-1	George Munger

1944

		Record	Coach
1.	Army	9-0-0	Red Blaik
2.	Ohio St	9-0-0	Carroll Widdoes
3.	Randolph Field	11-0-0	Frank Tritico
4.	Navy	6-3-0	Oscar Hagberg
5.	Bainbridge NTS	9-0-0	Joe Maniaci
6.	Iowa Pre-Flight	10-1-0	Jack Meagher
7.	Southern Cal	7-0-2	Jeff Cravath
8.	Michigan	8-2-0	Fritz Crisler
9.	Notre Dame	8-2-0	Ed McKeever
10.	March Field	7-1-2	Paul Schissler
11.	Duke	5-4-0	Eddie Cameron
12.	Tennessee	8-0-1	John Barnhill
13.	Georgia Tech	8-2-0	Bill Alexander
	Norman P-F	6-0-0	John Gregg
15.	Illinois	5-4-1	Ray Eliot
16.	El Toro Marines	8-1-0	Dick Hanley
17.	Great Lakes	9-2-1	Paul Brown
18.	Fort Pierce	9-0-0	Hamp Pool
19.	St. Mary's P-F	4-4-0	Jules Sikes
20.	2nd Air Force	7-2-1	Bill Reese

1945

		Record	Coach
1.	Army	9-0-0	Red Blaik
2.	Alabama	9-0-0	Frank Thomas
3.	Navy	7-1-1	Oscar Hagberg
4.	Indiana	9-0-1	Bo McMillan
5.	Oklahoma A&M	8-0-0	Jim Lookabaugh
6.	Michigan	7-3-0	Fritz Crisler
7.	St. Mary's (CA)	7-1-0	Jimmy Phelan
8.	Pennsylvania	6-2-0	George Munger
9.	Notre Dame	7-2-1	Hugh Devore
10.	Texas	9-1-0	Dana X. Bible
11.	Southern Cal	7-3-0	Jeff Cravath
12.	Ohio St	7-2-0	Carroll Widdoes
13.	Duke	6-2-0	Eddie Cameron
14.	Tennessee	8-1-0	John Barnhill
15.	Louisiana St	7-2-0	Bernie Moore
16.	Holy Cross	8-1-0	John DeGrosa
17.	Tulsa	8-2-0	Henry Frnka
18.	Georgia	8-2-0	Wally Butts
19.	Wake Forest	4-3-1	Peahead Walker
20.	Columbia	8-1-0	Lou Little

1946

		Record	Coach
1.	Notre Dame	8-0-1	Frank Leahy
2.	Army	9-0-1	Red Blaik
3.	Georgia	10-0-0	Wally Butts
4.	UCLA	10-0-0	B. LaBrucherie

Note: Except where indicated with an asterisk, the polls from 1936 through 1964 were taken before the bowl games and those from 1965 through the present were taken after the bowl games.

1946 *(Cont.)*

		Record	Coach
5.	Illinois	7-2-0	Ray Eliot
6.	Michigan	6-2-1	Fritz Crisler
7.	Tennessee	9-1-0	Bob Neyland
8.	Louisiana St	9-1-0	Bernie Moore
9.	N Carolina	8-1-0	Carl Snavely
10.	Rice	8-2-0	Jess Neely
11.	Georgia Tech	8-2-0	Bobby Dodd
12.	Yale	7-1-1	Howard Odell
13.	Pennsylvania	6-2-0	George Munger
14.	Oklahoma	7-3-0	Jim Tatum
15.	Texas	8-2-0	Dana X. Bible
16.	Arkansas	6-3-1	John Barnhill
17.	Tulsa	9-1-0	J.O. Brothers
18.	N Carolina St	8-2-0	Beattie Feathers
19.	Delaware	9-0-0	Bill Murray
20.	Indiana	6-3-0	Bo McMillan

1947

		Record	Coach
1.	Notre Dame	9-0-0	Frank Leahy
2.	#Michigan	9-0-0	Fritz Crisler
3.	SMU	9-0-1	Matty Bell
4.	Penn St	9-0-0	Bob Higgins
5.	Texas	9-1-0	Blair Cherry
6.	Alabama	8-2-0	Red Drew
7.	Pennsylvania	7-0-1	George Munger
8.	Southern Cal	7-1-1	Jeff Cravath
9.	N Carolina	8-2-0	Carl Snavely
10.	Georgia Tech	9-1-0	Bobby Dodd
11.	Army	5-2-2	Red Blaik
12.	Kansas	8-0-2	George Sauer
13.	Mississippi	8-2-0	Johnny Vaught
14.	William & Mary	9-1-0	Rube McCray
15.	California	9-1-0	Pappy Waldorf
16.	Oklahoma	7-2-1	Bud Wilkinson
17.	N Carolina St	5-3-1	Beattie Feathers
18.	Rice	6-3-1	Jess Neely
19.	Duke	4-3-2	Wallace Wade
20.	Columbia	7-2-0	Lou Little

#The AP, which had voted Notre Dame No. 1 before the bowl games, took a second vote, giving the title to Michigan after its 49-0 win over Southern Cal in the Rose Bowl.

1948

		Record	Coach
1.	Michigan	9-0-0	Bennie Oosterbaan
2.	Notre Dame	9-0-1	Frank Leahy
3.	N Carolina	9-0-1	Carl Snavely
4.	California	10-0-0	Pappy Waldorf
5.	Oklahoma	9-1-0	Bud Wilkinson
6.	Army	8-0-1	Red Blaik
7.	Northwestern	7-2-0	Bob Voigts
8.	Georgia	9-1-0	Wally Butts
9.	Oregon	9-1-0	Jim Aiken
10.	SMU	8-1-1	Matty Bell
11.	Clemson	10-0-0	Frank Howard
12.	Vanderbilt	8-2-1	Red Sanders
13.	Tulane	9-1-0	Henry Frnka
14.	Michigan St	6-2-2	Biggie Munn
15.	Mississippi	8-1-0	Johnny Vaught
16.	Minnesota	7-2-0	Bernie Bierman
17.	William & Mary	6-2-2	Rube McCray
18.	Penn St	7-1-1	Bob Higgins
19.	Cornell	8-1-0	Lefty James
20.	Wake Forest	6-3-0	Peahead Walker

1949

		Record	Coach
1.	Notre Dame	10-0-0	Frank Leahy
2.	Oklahoma	10-0-0	Bud Wilkinson
3.	California	10-0-0	Pappy Waldorf
4.	Army	9-0-0	Red Blaik
5.	Rice	9-1-0	Jess Neely
6.	Ohio St	6-1-2	Wes Fesler
7.	Michigan	6-2-1	Bennie Oosterbaan
8.	Minnesota	7-2-0	Bernie Bierman
9.	Louisiana St	8-2-0	Gaynell Tinsley
10.	Pacific	11-0-0	Larry Siemering
11.	Kentucky	9-2-0	Bear Bryant
12.	Cornell	8-1-0	Lefty James
13.	Villanova	8-1-0	Jim Leonard
14.	Maryland	8-1-0	Jim Tatum
15.	Santa Clara	7-2-1	Len Casanova
16.	N Carolina	7-3-0	Carl Snavely
17.	Tennessee	7-2-1	Bob Neyland
18.	Princeton	6-3-0	Charlie Caldwell
19.	Michigan St	6-3-0	Biggie Munn
20.	Missouri	7-3-0	Don Faurot
	Baylor	8-2-0	Bob Woodruff

1950

		Record	Coach
1.	Oklahoma	10-0-0	Bud Wilkinson
2.	Army	8-1-0	Red Blaik
3.	Texas	9-1-0	Blair Cherry
4.	Tennessee	10-1-0	Bob Neyland
5.	California	9-0-1	Pappy Waldorf
6.	Princeton	9-0-0	Charlie Caldwell
7.	Kentucky	10-1-0	Bear Bryant
8.	Michigan St	8-1-0	Biggie Munn
9.	Michigan	5-3-1	Bennie Oosterhaan
10.	Clemson	8-0-1	Frank Howard
11.	Washington	8-2-0	Howard Odell
12.	Wyoming	9-0-0	Bowden Wyatt
13.	Illinois	7-2-0	Ray Eliot
14.	Ohio St	6-3-0	Wes Fesler
15.	Miami (FL)	9-0-1	Andy Gustafson
16.	Alabama	9-2-0	Red Drew
17.	Nebraska	6-2-1	Bill Glassford
18.	Wash & Lee	8-2-0	George Barclay
19.	Tulsa	9-1-1	J.O. Brothers
20.	Tulane	6-2-1	Henry Frnka

1951

		Record	Coach
1.	Tennessee	10-0-0	Bob Neyland
2.	Michigan St	9-0-0	Biggie Munn
3.	Maryland	9-0-0	Jim Tatum
4.	Illinois	8-0-1	Ray Eliot
5.	Georgia Tech	10-0-1	Bobby Dodd
6.	Princeton	9-0-0	Charlie Caldwell
7.	Stanford	9-1-0	Chuck Taylor
8.	Wisconsin	7-1-1	Ivy Williamson
9.	Baylor	8-1-1	George Sauer
10.	Oklahoma	8-2-0	Bud Wilkinson
11.	Texas Christian	6-4-0	Dutch Meyer
12.	California	8-2-0	Pappy Waldorf
13.	Virginia	8-1-0	Art Guepe
14.	San Francisco	9-0-0	Joe Kuharich
15.	Kentucky	7-4-0	Bear Bryant
16.	Boston Univ	6-4-0	Buff Donelli
17.	UCLA	5-3-1	Red Sanders
18.	Washington St	7-3-0	Forest Evashevski

1951 *(Cont.)*

		Record	Coach
19.	Holy Cross	8-2-0	Eddie Anderson
20.	Clemson	7-2-0	Frank Howard

1952

		Record	Coach
1.	Michigan St	9-0-0	Biggie Munn
2.	Georgia Tech	11-0-0	Bobby Dodd
3.	Notre Dame	7-2-1	Frank Leahy
4.	Oklahoma	8-1-1	Bud Wilkinson
5.	Southern Cal	9-1-0	Jess Hill
6.	UCLA	8-1-0	Red Sanders
7.	Mississippi	8-0-2	Johnny Vaught
8.	Tennessee	8-1-1	Bob Neyland
9.	Alabama	9-2-0	Red Drew
10.	Texas	8-2-0	Ed Price
11.	Wisconsin	6-2-1	Ivy Williamson
12.	Tulsa	8-1-1	J.O. Brothers
13.	Maryland	7-2-0	Jim Tatum
14.	Syracuse	7-2-0	Ben Schwartzwalder
15.	Florida	7-3-0	Bob Woodruff
16.	Duke	8-2-0	Bill Murray
17.	Ohio St	6-3-0	Woody Hayes
18.	Purdue	4-3-2	Stu Holcomb
19.	Princeton	8-1-0	Charlie Caldwell
20.	Kentucky	5-4-2	Bear Bryant

1953

		Record	Coach
1.	Maryland	10-0-0	Jim Tatum
2.	Notre Dame	9-0-1	Frank Leahy
3.	Michigan St	8-1-0	Biggie Munn
4.	Oklahoma	8-1-1	Bud Wilkinson
5.	UCLA	8-1-0	Red Sanders
6.	Rice	8-2-0	Jess Neely
7.	Illinois	7-1-1	Ray Eliot
8.	Georgia Tech	8-2-1	Bobby Dodd
9.	Iowa	5-3-1	Forest Evashevski
10.	West Virginia	8-1-0	Art Lewis
11.	Texas	7-3-0	Ed Price
12.	Texas Tech	10-1-0	DeWitt Weaver
13.	Alabama	6-2-3	Red Drew
14.	Army	7-1-1	Red Blaik
15.	Wisconsin	6-2-1	Ivy Williamson
16.	Kentucky	7-2-1	Bear Bryant
17.	Auburn	7-2-1	Shug Jordan
18.	Duke	7-2-1	Bill Murray
19.	Stanford	6-3-1	Chuck Taylor
20.	Michigan	6-3-0	Bennie Oosterbaan

1954

		Record	Coach
1.	Ohio St	9-0-0	Woody Hayes
2.	#UCLA	9-0-0	Red Sanders
3.	Oklahoma	10-0-0	Bud Wilkinson
4.	Notre Dame	9-1-0	Terry Brennan
5.	Navy	7-2-0	Eddie Erdelatz
6.	Mississippi	9-1-0	Johnny Vaught
7.	Army	7-2-0	Red Blaik
8.	Maryland	7-2-1	Jim Tatum
9.	Wisconsin	7-2-0	Ivy Williamson
10.	Arkansas	8-2-0	Bowden Wyatt
11.	Miami (FL)	8-1-0	Andy Gustafson
12.	West Virginia	8-1-0	Art Lewis
13.	Auburn	7-3-0	Shug Jordan

1954 *(Cont.)*

		Record	Coach
14.	Duke	7-2-1	Bill Murray
15.	Michigan	6-3-0	Bennie Oosterbaan
16.	Virginia Tech	8-0-1	Frank Moseley
17.	Southern Cal	8-3-0	Jess Hill
18.	Baylor	7-3-0	George Sauer
19.	Rice	7-3-0	Jess Neely
20.	Penn St	7-2-0	Rip Engle

#Selected No. 1 by UP.

1955

		Record	Coach
1.	Oklahoma	10-0-0	Bud Wilkinson
2.	Michigan St	8-1-0	Duffy Daugherty
3.	Maryland	10-0-0	Jim Tatum
4.	UCLA	9-1-0	Red Sanders
5.	Ohio St	7-2-0	Woody Hayes
6.	Texas Christian	9-1-0	Abe Martin
7.	Georgia Tech	8-1-1	Bobby Dodd
8.	Auburn	8-1-1	Shug Jordan
9.	Notre Dame	8-2-0	Terry Brennan
10.	Mississippi	9-1-0	Johnny Vaught
11.	Pittsburgh	7-3-0	John Michelosen
12.	Michigan	7-2-0	Bennie Oosterbaan
13.	Southern Cal	6-4-0	Jess Hill
14.	Miami (FL)	6-3-0	Andy Gustafson
15.	Miami (OH)	9-0-0	Ara Parseghian
16.	Stanford	6-3-1	Chuck Taylor
17.	Texas A&M	7-2-1	Bear Bryant
18.	Navy	6-2-1	Eddie Erdelatz
19.	West Virginia	8-2-0	Art Lewis
20.	Army	6-3-0	Red Blaik

1956

		Record	Coach
1.	Oklahoma	10-0-0	Bud Wilkinson
2.	Tennessee	10-0-0	Bowden Wyatt
3.	Iowa	8-1-0	Forest Evashevski
4.	Georgia Tech	9-1-0	Bobby Dodd
5.	Texas A&M	9-0-1	Bear Bryant
6.	Miami (FL)	8-1-1	Andy Gustafson
7.	Michigan	7-2-0	Bennie Oosterbaan
8.	Syracuse	7-1-0	Ben Schwartzwalder
9.	Michigan St	7-2-0	Duffy Daugherty
10.	Oregon St	7-2-1	Tommy Prothro
11.	Baylor	8-2-0	Sam Boyd
12.	Minnesota	6-1-2	Murray Warmath
13.	Pittsburgh	7-2-1	John Michelosen
14.	Texas Christian	7-3-0	Abe Martin
15.	Ohio St	6-3-0	Woody Hayes
16.	Navy	6-1-2	Eddie Erdelatz
17.	Geo Washington	7-1-1	Gene Sherman
18.	Southern Cal	8-2-0	Jess Hill
19.	Clemson	7-1-2	Frank Howard
20.	Colorado	7-2-1	Dallas Ward
	Penn St	6-2-1	Rip Engle

1957

		Record	Coach
1.	Auburn	10-0-0	Shug Jordan
2.	#Ohio St	8-1-0	Woody Hayes
3.	Michigan St	8-1-0	Duffy Daugherty
4.	Oklahoma	9-1-0	Bud Wilkinson
5.	Navy	8-1-1	Eddie Erdelatz
6.	Iowa	7-1-1	Forest Evashevski
7.	Mississippi	8-1-1	Johnny Vaught
8.	Rice	7-3-0	Jess Neely
9.	Texas A&M	8-2-0	Bear Bryant
10.	Notre Dame	7-2-0	Terry Brennan
11.	Texas	6-3-1	Darrell Royal
12.	Arizona St	10-0-0	Dan Devine
13.	Tennessee	7-3-0	Bowden Wyatt
14.	Mississippi St	6-2-1	Wade Walker
15.	N Carolina St	7-1-2	Earle Edwards
16.	Duke	6-2-2	Bill Murray
17.	Florida	6-2-1	Bob Woodruff
18.	Army	7-2-0	Red Blaik
19.	Wisconsin	6-3-0	Milt Brunt
20.	VMI	9-0-1	John McKenna

#Selected No. 1 by UP.

1958

		Record	Coach
1.	Louisiana St	10-0-0	Paul Dietzel
2.	Iowa	7-1-1	Forest Evashevski
3.	Army	8-0-1	Red Blaik
4.	Auburn	9-0-1	Shug Jordan
5.	Oklahoma	9-1-0	Bud Wilkinson
6.	Air Force	9-0-1	Ben Martin
7.	Wisconsin	7-1-1	Milt Bruhn
8.	Ohio St	6-1-2	Woody Hayes
9.	Syracuse	8-1-0	Ben Schwartzwalder
10.	Texas Christian	8-2-0	Abe Martin
11.	Mississippi	8-2-0	Johnny Vaught
12.	Clemson	8-2-0	Frank Howard
13.	Purdue	6-1-2	Jack Mollenkopf
14.	Florida	6-3-1	Bob Woodruff
15.	S Carolina	7-3-0	Warren Giese
16.	California	7-3-0	Pete Elliott
17.	Notre Dame	6-4-0	Terry Brennan
18.	SMU	6-4-0	Bill Meek
19.	Oklahoma St	7-3-0	Cliff Speegle
20.	Rutgers	8-1-0	John Stiegman

1959

		Record	Coach
1.	Syracuse	10-0-0	Ben Schwartzwalder
2.	Mississippi	9-1-0	Johnny Vaught
3.	Louisiana St	9-1-0	Paul Dietzel
4.	Texas	9-1-0	Darrell Royal
5.	Georgia	9-1-0	Wally Butts
6.	Wisconsin	7-2-0	Milt Bruhn
7.	Texas Christian	8-2-0	Abe Martin
8.	Washington	9-1-0	Jim Owens
9.	Arkansas	8-2-0	Frank Broyles
10.	Alabama	7-1-2	Bear Bryant
11.	Clemson	8-2-0	Frank Howard

1959 *(Cont.)*

		Record	Coach
12.	Penn St	8-2-0	Rip Engle
13.	Illinois	5-3-1	Ray Eliot
14.	Southern Cal	8-2-0	Don Clark
15.	Oklahoma	7-3-0	Bud Wilkinson
16.	Wyoming	9-1-0	Bob Devaney
17.	Notre Dame	5-5-0	Joe Kuharich
18.	Missouri	6-4-0	Dan Devine
19.	Florida	5-4-1	Bob Woodruff
20.	Pittsburgh	6-4-0	John Michelosen

1960

		Record	Coach
1.	Minnesota	8-1-0	Murray Warmath
2.	Mississippi	9-0-1	Johnny Vaught
3.	Iowa	8-1-0	Forest Evashevski
4.	Navy	9-1-0	Wayne Hardin
5.	Missouri	9-1-0	Dan Devine
6.	Washington	9-1-0	Jim Owens
7.	Arkansas	8-2-0	Frank Broyles
8.	Ohio St	7-2-0	Woody Hayes
9.	Alabama	8-1-1	Bear Bryant
10.	Duke	7-3-0	Bill Murray
11.	Kansas	7-2-1	Jack Mitchell
12.	Baylor	8-2-0	John Bridgers
13.	Auburn	8-2-0	Shug Jordan
14.	Yale	9-0-0	Jordan Oliver
15.	Michigan St	6-2-1	Duffy Daugherty
16.	Penn St	6-3-0	Rip Engle
17.	New Mexico St	10-0-0	Warren Woodson
18.	Florida	8-2-0	Ray Graves
19.	Syracuse	7-2-0	Ben Schwartzwalder
	Purdue	4-4-1	Jack Mollenkopf

1961

		Record	Coach
1.	Alabama	10-0-0	Bear Bryant
2.	Ohio St	8-0-1	Woody Hayes
3.	Texas	9-1-0	Darrell Royal
4.	Louisiana St	9-1-0	Paul Dietzel
5.	Mississippi	9-1-0	Johnny Vaught
6.	Minnesota	7-2-0	Murray Warmath
7.	Colorado	9-1-0	Sonny Grandelius
8.	Michigan St	7-2-0	Duffy Daugherty
9.	Arkansas	8-2-0	Frank Broyles
10.	Utah St	9-0-1	John Ralston
11.	Missouri	7-2-1	Dan Devine
12.	Purdue	6-3-0	Jack Mollenkopf
13.	Georgia Tech	7-3-0	Bobby Dodd
14.	Syracuse	7-3-0	Ben Schwartzwalder
15.	Rutgers	9-0-0	John Bateman
16.	UCLA	7-3-0	Bill Barnes
17.	Rice	7-3-0	Jess Neely
	Penn St	7-3-0	Rip Engle
	Arizona	8-1-1	Jim LaRue
20.	Duke	7-3-0	Bill Murray

1962

		Record	Coach
1.	Southern Cal	10-0-0	John McKay
2.	Wisconsin	8-1-0	Milt Bruhn
3.	Mississippi	9-0-0	Johnny Vaught
4.	Texas	9-0-1	Darrell Royal
5.	Alabama	9-1-0	Bear Bryant
6.	Arkansas	9-1-0	Frank Broyles
7.	Louisiana St	8-1-1	Charlie McClendon
8.	Oklahoma	8-2-0	Bud Wilkinson
9.	Penn St	9-1-0	Rip Engle
10.	Minnesota	6-2-1	Murray Warmath

11-20: UPI

11.	Georgia Tech	7-2-1	Bobby Dodd
12.	Missouri	7-1-2	Dan Devine
13.	Ohio St	6-3-0	Woody Hayes
14.	Duke	8-2-0	Bill Murray
	Washington	7-1-2	Jim Owens
16.	Northwestern	7-2-0	Ara Parseghian
	Oregon St	8-2-0	Tommy Prothro
18.	Arizona St	7-2-1	Frank Kush
	Miami (FL)	7-3-0	Andy Gustafson
	Illinois	2-7-0	Pete Elliott

1963

		Record	Coach
1.	Texas	10-0-0	Darrell Royal
2.	Navy	9-1-0	Wayne Hardin
3.	Illinois	7-1-1	Pete Elliott
4.	Pittsburgh	9-1-0	John Michelosen
5.	Auburn	9-1-0	Shug Jordan
6.	Nebraska	9-1-0	Bob Devaney
7.	Mississippi	7-0-2	Johnny Vaught
8.	Alabama	8-2-0	Bear Bryant
9.	Oklahoma	8-2-0	Bud Wilkinson
10.	Michigan St	6-2-1	Duffy Daugherty

11-20: UPI

11.	Mississippi St	6-2-2	Paul Davis
12.	Syracuse	8-2-0	Ben Schwartzwalder
13.	Arizona St	8-1-0	Frank Kush
14.	Memphis St	9-0-1	Billy J. Murphy
15.	Washington	6-4-0	Jim Owens
16.	Penn St	7-3-0	Rip Engle
	Southern Cal	7-3-0	John McKay
	Missouri	7-3-0	Dan Devine
19.	N Carolina	8-2-0	Jim Hickey
20.	Baylor	7-3-0	John Bridgers

1964

		Record	Coach
1.	Alabama	10-0-0	Bear Bryant
2.	Arkansas	10-0-0	Frank Broyles
3.	Notre Dame	9-1-0	Ara Parseghian
4.	Michigan	8-1-0	Bump Elliott
5.	Texas	9-1-0	Darrell Royal
6.	Nebraska	9-1-0	Bob Devaney
7.	Louisiana St	7-2-1	Charlie McClendon
8.	Oregon St	8-2-0	Tommy Prothro
9.	Ohio St	7-2-0	Woody Hayes
10.	Southern Cal	7-3-0	John McKay

1964 *(Cont.)*

		Record	Coach

11-20: UPI

11.	Florida St	8-1-1	Bill Peterson
12.	Syracuse	7-3-0	Ben Schwartzwalder
13.	Princeton	9-0-0	Dick Colman
14.	Penn St	6-4-0	Rip Engle
	Utah	8-2-0	Ray Nagel
16.	Illinois	6-3-0	Pete Elliott
	New Mexico	9-2-0	Bill Weeks
18.	Tulsa	8-2-0	Glenn Dobbs
19.	Missouri	6-3-1	Dan Devine
20.	Mississippi	5-4-1	Johnny Vaught
	Michigan St	4-5-1	Duffy Daugherty

1965

		Record	Coach
1.	Alabama	9-1-1	Bear Bryant
2.	#Michigan St	10-1-0	Duffy Daugherty
3.	Arkansas	10-1-0	Frank Broyles
4.	UCLA	8-2-1	Tommy Prothro
5.	Nebraska	10-1-0	Bob Devaney
6.	Missouri	8-2-1	Dan Devine
7.	Tennessee	8-1-2	Doug Dickey
8.	Louisiana St	8-3-0	Charlie McClendon
9.	Notre Dame	7-2-1	Ara Parseghian
10.	Southern Cal	7-2-1	John McKay

11-20: UPI

11.	Texas Tech	8-2-0	J.T. King
12.	Ohio St	7-2-0	Woody Hayes
13.	Florida	7-3-0	Ray Graves
14.	Purdue	7-2-1	Jack Mollenkopf
15.	Georgia	6-4-0	Vince Dooley
16.	Tulsa	8-2-0	Glenn Dobbs
17.	Mississippi	6-4-0	Johnny Vaught
18.	Kentucky	6-4-0	Charlie Bradshaw
19	Syracuse	7-3-0	Ben Schwartzwalder
20.	Colorado	6-2-2	Eddie Crowder

#Selected No. 1 by UPI.

1966*

		Record	Coach
1.	Notre Dame	9-0-1	Ara Parseghian
2.	Michigan St	9-0-1	Duffy Daugherty
3.	Alabama	10-0-0	Bear Bryant
4.	Georgia	9-1-0	Vince Dooley
5.	UCLA	9-1-0	Tommy Prothro
6.	Nebraska	9-1-0	Bob Devaney
7.	Purdue	8-2-0	Jack Mollenkopf
8.	Georgia Tech	9-1-0	Bobby Dodd
9.	Miami (FL)	7-2-1	Charlie Tate
10.	SMU	8-2-0	Hayden Fry

11-20: UPI

11.	Florida	8-2-0	Ray Graves
12.	Mississippi	8-2-0	Johnny Vaught
13.	Arkansas	8-2-0	Frank Broyles
14.	Tennessee	7-3-0	Doug Dickey
15.	Wyoming	9-1-0	Lloyd Eaton
16.	Syracuse	8-2-0	Ben Schwartzwalder
17.	Houston	8-2-0	Bill Yeoman
18.	Southern Cal	7-3-0	John McKay
19.	Oregon St	7-3-0	Dee Andros
20.	Virginia Tech	8-1-1	Jerry Claiborne

Note: Except where indicated with an asterisk, the polls from 1936 through 1964 were taken before the bowl games and those from 1965 through the present were taken after the bowl games. Additionally, the AP ranked only ten teams in its polls from 1962–67; positions 11–20 from those years are from the UPI poll.

1967*

		Record	Coach
1.	Southern Cal	9-1-0	John McKay
2.	Tennessee	9-1-0	Doug Dickey
3.	Oklahoma	9-1-0	Chuck Fairbanks
4.	Indiana	9-1-0	John Pont
5.	Notre Dame	8-2-0	Ara Parseghian
6.	Wyoming	10-0-0	Lloyd Eaton
7.	Oregon St.	7-2-1	Dee Andros
8.	Alabama	8-1-1	Bear Bryant
9.	Purdue	8-2-0	Jack Mollenkopf
10.	Penn St.	8-2-0	Joe Paterno

11-20: UPI†

11.	UCLA	7-2-1	Tommy Prothro
12.	Syracuse	8-2-0	Ben Schwartzwalder
13.	Colorado	8-2-0	Eddie Crowder
14.	Minnesota	8-2-0	Murray Warmath
15.	Florida St.	7-2-1	Bill Peterson
16.	Miami (FL)	7-3-0	Charlie Tate
17.	N Carolina St.	8-2-0	Earle Edwards
18.	Georgia	7-3-0	Vince Dooley
19.	Houston	9-2-0	Bill Yeoman
20.	Arizona St.	8-2-0	Frank Kush

†UPI ranked Penn St 11th and did not rank Alabama, which was on probation.

1968

		Record	Coach
1.	Ohio St	10-0-0	Woody Hayes
2.	Penn St.	11-0-0	Joe Paterno
3.	Texas	9-1-1	Darrell Royal
4.	Southern Cal	9-1-1	John McKay
5.	Notre Dame	7-2-1	Ara Parseghian
6.	Arkansas	10-1-0	Frank Broyles
7.	Kansas	9-2-0	Pepper Rodgers
8.	Georgia	8-1-2	Vince Dooley
9.	Missouri	8-3-0	Dan Devine
10.	Purdue	8-2-0	Jack Mollenkopf
11.	Oklahoma	7-4-0	Chuck Fairbanks
12.	Michigan	8-2-0	Bump Elliott
13.	Tennessee	8-2-1	Doug Dickey
14.	SMU	8-3-0	Hayden Fry
15.	Oregon St.	7-3-0	Dee Andros
16.	Auburn	7-4-0	Shug Jordan
17.	Alabama	8-3-0	Bear Bryant
18.	Houston	6-2-2	Bill Yeoman
19.	Louisiana St	8-3-0	Charlie McClendon
20.	Ohio	10-1-0	Bill Hess

1969

		Record	Coach
1.	Texas	11-0-0	Darrell Royal
2.	Penn St.	11-0-0	Joe Paterno
3.	Southern Cal	10-0-1	John McKay
4.	Ohio St	8-1-0	Woody Hayes
5.	Notre Dame	8-2-1	Ara Parseghian
6.	Missouri	9-2-0	Dan Devine
7.	Arkansas	9-2-0	Frank Broyles
8.	Mississippi	8-3-0	Johnny Vaught
9.	Michigan	8-3-0	Bo Schembechler
10.	Louisiana St	9-1-0	Charlie McClendon

1969 (Cont.)

		Record	Coach
11.	Nebraska	9-2-0	Bob Devaney
12.	Houston	9-2-0	Bill Yeoman
13.	UCLA	8-1-1	Tommy Prothro
14.	Florida	9-1-1	Ray Graves
15.	Tennessee	9-2-0	Doug Dickey
16.	Colorado	8-3-0	Eddie Crowder
17.	West Virginia	10-0-1	Jim Carlen
18.	Purdue	8-2-0	Jack Mollenkopf
19.	Stanford	7-2-1	John Ralston
20.	Auburn	8-3-0	Shug Jordan

1970

		Record	Coach
1.	Nebraska	11-0-1	Bob Devaney
2.	Notre Dame	10-1-0	Ara Parseghian
3.	#Texas	10-1-0	Darrell Royal
4.	Tennessee	11-0-1	Bill Battle
5.	Ohio St	9-1-0	Woody Hayes
6.	Arizona St.	11-0-0	Frank Kush
7.	Louisiana St	9-3-0	Charlie McClendon
8.	Stanford	9-3-0	John Ralston
9.	Michigan	9-1-0	Bo Schembechler
10.	Auburn	9-2-0	Shug Jordan
11.	Arkansas	9-2-0	Frank Broyles
12.	Toledo	12-0-0	Frank Lauterbur
13.	Georgia Tech	9-3-0	Bud Carson
14.	Dartmouth	9-0-0	Bob Blackman
15.	Southern Cal	6-4-1	John McKay
16.	Air Force	9-3-0	Ben Martin
17.	Tulane	8-4-0	Jim Pittman
18.	Penn St.	7-3-0	Joe Paterno
19.	Houston	8-3-0	Bill Yeoman
20.	Oklahoma	7-4-1	Chuck Fairbanks
	Mississippi	7-4-0	Johnny Vaught

#Selected No. 1 by UPI.

1971

		Record	Coach
1.	Nebraska	13-0-0	Bob Devaney
2.	Oklahoma	11-1-0	Chuck Fairbanks
3.	Colorado	10-2-0	Eddie Crowder
4.	Alabama	11-1-0	Bear Bryant
5.	Penn St.	11-1-0	Joe Paterno
6.	Michigan	11-1-0	Bo Schembechler
7.	Georgia	11-1-0	Vince Dooley
8.	Arizona St.	11-1-0	Frank Kush
9.	Tennessee	10-2-0	Bill Battle
10.	Stanford	9-3-0	John Ralston
11.	Louisiana St	9-3-0	Charlie McClendon
12.	Auburn	9-2-0	Shug Jordan
13.	Notre Dame	8-2-0	Ara Parseghian
14.	Toledo	12-0-0	John Murphy
15.	Mississippi	10-2-0	Billy Kinard
16.	Arkansas	8-3-1	Frank Broyles
17.	Houston	9-3-0	Bill Yeoman
18.	Texas	8-3-0	Darrell Royal
19.	Washington	8-3-0	Jim Owens
20.	Southern Cal	6-4-1	John McKay

Note: Except where indicated with an asterisk, the polls from 1936 through 1964 were taken before the bowl games and those from 1965 through the present were taken after the bowl games. Additionally, the AP ranked only ten teams in its polls from 1962–67; positions 11–20 from those years are from the UPI poll.

1972

	Record	Coach
1. Southern Cal	12-0-0	John McKay
2. Oklahoma	11-1-0	Chuck Fairbanks
3. Texas	10-1-0	Darrell Royal
4. Nebraska	9-2-1	Bob Devaney
5. Auburn	10-1-0	Shug Jordan
6. Michigan	10-1-0	Bo Schembechler
7. Alabama	10-2-0	Bear Bryant
8. Tennessee	10-2-0	Bill Battle
9. Ohio St	9-2-0	Woody Hayes
10. Penn St	10-2-0	Joe Paterno
11. Louisiana St	9-2-1	Charlie McClendon
12. N Carolina	11-1-0	Bill Dooley
13. Arizona St	10-2-0	Frank Kush
14. Notre Dame	8-3-0	Ara Parseghian
15. UCLA	8-3-0	Pepper Rodgers
16. Colorado	8-4-0	Eddie Crowder
17. N Carolina St	8-3-1	Lou Holtz
18. Louisville	9-1-0	Lee Corso
19. Washington St	7-4-0	Jim Sweeney
20. Georgia Tech	7-4-1	Bill Fulcher

1973

	Record	Coach
1. Notre Dame	11-0-0	Ara Parseghian
2. Ohio St	10-0-1	Woody Hayes
3. Oklahoma	10-0-1	Barry Switzer
4. #Alabama	11-1-0	Bear Bryant
5. Penn St	12-0-0	Joe Paterno
6. Michigan	10-0-1	Bo Schembechler
7. Nebraska	9-2-1	Tom Osborne
8. Southern Cal	9-2-1	John McKay
9. Arizona St	11-1-0	Frank Kush
Houston	11-1-0	Bill Yeoman
11. Texas Tech	11-1-0	Jim Carlen
12. UCLA	9-2-0	Pepper Rodgers
13. Louisiana St	9-3-0	Charlie McClendon
14. Texas	8-3-0	Darrell Royal
15. Miami (OH)	11-0-0	Bill Mallory
16. N Carolina St	9-3-0	Lou Holtz
17. Missouri	8-4-0	Al Onofrio
18. Kansas	7-4-1	Don Fambrough
19. Tennessee	8-4-0	Bill Battle
20. Maryland	8-4-0	Jerry Claiborne
Tulane	9-3-0	Bennie Ellender

#Selected No. 1 by UPI.

1974

	Record	Coach
1. Oklahoma	11-0-0	Barry Switzer
2. #Southern Cal	10-1-1	John McKay
3. Michigan	10-1-0	Bo Schembechler
4. Ohio St	10-2-0	Woody Hayes
5. Alabama	11-1-0	Bear Bryant
6. Notre Dame	10-2-0	Ara Parseghian
7. Penn St	10-2-0	Joe Paterno
8. Auburn	10-2-0	Shug Jordan
9. Nebraska	9-3-0	Tom Osborne
10. Miami (OH)	10-0-1	Dick Crum
11. N Carolina St	9-2-1	Lou Holtz
12. Michigan St	7-3-1	Denny Stolz

1974 *(Cont.)*

	Record	Coach
13. Maryland	8-4-0	Jerry Claiborne
14. Baylor	8-4-0	Grant Teaff
15. Florida	8-4-0	Doug Dickey
16. Texas A&M	8-3-0	Emory Ballard
17. Mississippi St	9-3-0	Bob Tyler
Texas	8-4-0	Darrell Royal
19. Houston	8-3-1	Bill Yeoman
20. Tennessee	7-3-2	Bill Battle

#Selected No. 1 by UPI.

1975

	Record	Coach
1. Oklahoma	11-1-0	Barry Switzer
2. Arizona St	12-0-0	Frank Kush
3. Alabama	11-1-0	Bear Bryant
4. Ohio St	11-1-0	Woody Hayes
5. UCLA	9-2-1	Dick Vermeil
6. Texas	10-2-0	Darrell Royal
7. Arkansas	10-2-0	Frank Broyles
8. Michigan	8-2-2	Bo Schembechler
9. Nebraska	10-2-0	Tom Osborne
10. Penn St	9-3-0	Joe Paterno
11. Texas A&M	10-2-0	Emory Bellard
12. Miami (OH)	11-1-0	Dick Crum
13. Maryland	9-2-1	Jerry Claiborne
14. California	8-3-0	Mike White
15. Pittsburgh	8-4-0	Johnny Majors
16. Colorado	9-3-0	Bill Mallory
17. Southern Cal	8-4-0	John McKay
18. Arizona	9-2-0	Jim Young
19. Georgia	9-3-0	Vince Dooley
20. West Virginia	9-3-0	Bobby Bowden

1976

	Record	Coach
1. Pittsburgh	12-0-0	Johnny Majors
2. Southern Cal	11-1-0	John Robinson
3. Michigan	10-2-0	Bo Schembechler
4. Houston	10-2-0	Bill Yeoman
5. Oklahoma	9-2-1	Barry Switzer
6. Ohio St	9-2-1	Woody Hayes
7. Texas A&M	10-2-0	Emory Bellard
8. Maryland	11-1-0	Jerry Claiborne
9. Nebraska	9-3-1	Tom Osborne
10. Georgia	10-2-0	Vince Dooley
11. Alabama	9-3-0	Bear Bryant
12. Notre Dame	9-3-0	Dan Devine
13. Texas Tech	10-2-0	Steve Sloan
14. Oklahoma St	9-3-0	Jim Stanley
15. UCLA	9-2-1	Terry Donahue
16. Colorado	8-4-0	Bill Mallory
17. Rutgers	11-0-0	Frank Burns
18. Kentucky	9-3-0	Fran Curci
19. Iowa St	8-3-0	Earle Bruce
20. Mississippi St	9-2-0	Bob Tyler

1977

		Record	Coach
1.	Notre Dame	11-1-0	Dan Devine
2.	Alabama	11-1-0	Bear Bryant
3.	Arkansas	11-1-0	Lou Holtz
4.	Texas	11-1-0	Fred Akers
5.	Penn St	11-1-0	Joe Paterno
6.	Kentucky	10-1-0	Fran Curci
7.	Oklahoma	10-2-0	Barry Switzer
8.	Pittsburgh	9-2-1	Jackie Sherrill
9.	Michigan	10-2-0	Bo Schembechler
10.	Washington	10-2-0	Don James
11.	Ohio St	9-3-0	Woody Hayes
12.	Nebraska	9-3-0	Tom Osborne
13.	Southern Cal	8-4-0	John Robinson
14.	Florida St	10-2-0	Bobby Bowden
15.	Stanford	9-3-0	Bill Walsh
16.	San Diego St	10-1-0	Claude Gilbert
17.	N Carolina	8-3-1	Bill Dooley
18.	Arizona St	9-3-0	Frank Kush
19.	Clemson	8-3-1	Charley Pell
20.	Brigham Young	9-2-0	LaVell Edwards

1978

		Record	Coach
1.	Alabama	11-1-0	Bear Bryant
2.	#Southern Cal	12-1-0	John Robinson
3.	Oklahoma	11-1-0	Barry Switzer
4.	Penn St	11-1-0	Joe Paterno
5.	Michigan	10-2-0	Bo Schembechler
6.	Clemson	11-1-0	Charley Pell
7.	Notre Dame	9-3-0	Dan Devine
8.	Nebraska	9-3-0	Tom Osborne
9.	Texas	9-3-0	Fred Akers
10.	Houston	9-3-0	Bill Yeoman
11.	Arkansas	9-2-1	Lou Holtz
12.	Michigan St	8-3-0	Darryl Rogers
13.	Purdue	9-2-1	Jim Young
14.	UCLA	8-3-1	Terry Donahue
15.	Missouri	8-4-0	Warren Powers
16.	Georgia	9-2-1	Vince Dooley
17.	Stanford	8-4-0	Bill Walsh
18.	N Carolina St	9-3-0	Bo Rein
19.	Texas A&M	8-4-0	Emory Bellard (4–2) Tom Wilson (4–2)
20.	Maryland	9-3-0	Jerry Claiborne

#Selected No. 1 by UPI.

1979

		Record	Coach
1.	Alabama	12-0-0	Bear Bryant
2.	Southern Cal	11-0-1	John Robinson
3.	Oklahoma	11-1-0	Barry Switzer
4.	Ohio St	11-1-0	Earle Bruce
5.	Houston	11-1-0	Bill Yeoman
6.	Florida St	11-1-0	Bobby Bowden
7.	Pittsburgh	11-1-0	Jackie Sherrill
8.	Arkansas	10-2-0	Lou Holtz
9.	Nebraska	10-2-0	Tom Osborne
10.	Purdue	10-2-0	Jim Young
11.	Washington	10-1-0	Don James
12.	Texas	9-3-0	Fred Akers
13.	Brigham Young	11-1-0	LaVell Edwards
14.	Baylor	8-4-0	Grant Teaff
15.	N Carolina	8-3-1	Dick Crum
16.	Auburn	8-3-0	Doug Barfield
17.	Temple	10-2-0	Wayne Hardin

1979 *(Cont.)*

		Record	Coach
18.	Michigan	8-4-0	Bo Schembechler
19.	Indiana	8-4-0	Lee Corso
20.	Penn St	8-4-0	Joe Paterno

1980

		Record	Coach
1.	Georgia	12-0-0	Vince Dooley
2.	Pittsburgh	11-1-0	Jackie Sherrill
3.	Oklahoma	10-2-0	Barry Switzer
4.	Michigan	10-2-0	Bo Schembechler
5.	Florida St	10-2-0	Bobby Bowden
6.	Alabama	10-2-0	Bear Bryant
7.	Nebraska	10-2-0	Tom Osborne
8.	Penn St	10-2-0	Joe Paterno
9.	Notre Dame	9-2-1	Dan Devine
10.	N Carolina	11-1-0	Dick Crum
11.	Southern Cal	8-2-1	John Robinson
12.	Brigham Young	12-1-0	LaVell Edwards
13.	UCLA	9-2-0	Terry Donahue
14.	Baylor	10-2-0	Grant Teaff
15.	Ohio St	9-3-0	Earle Bruce
16.	Washington	9-3-0	Don James
17.	Purdue	9-3-0	Jim Young
18.	Miami (FL)	9-3-0	H. Schnellenberger
19.	Mississippi St	9-3-0	Emory Bellard
20.	SMU	8-4-0	Ron Meyer

1981

		Record	Coach
1.	Clemson	12-0-0	Danny Ford
2.	Texas	10-1-1	Fred Akers
3.	Penn St	10-2-0	Joe Paterno
4.	Pittsburgh	11-1-0	Jackie Sherrill
5.	SMU	10-1-0	Ron Meyer
6.	Georgia	10-2-0	Vince Dooley
7.	Alabama	9-2-1	Bear Bryant
8.	Miami (FL)	9-2-0	H. Schnellenberger
9.	N Carolina	10-2-0	Dick Crum
10.	Washington	10-2-0	Don James
11.	Nebraska	9-3-0	Tom Osborne
12.	Michigan	9-3-0	Bo Schembechler
13.	Brigham Young	11-2-0	LaVell Edwards
14.	Southern Cal	9-3-0	John Robinson
15.	Ohio St	9-3-0	Earle Bruce
16.	Arizona St	9-2-0	Darryl Rogers
17.	West Virginia	9-3-0	Don Nehlen
18.	Iowa	8-4-0	Hayden Fry
19.	Missouri	8-4-0	Warren Powers
20.	Oklahoma	7-4-1	Barry Switzer

1982

		Record	Coach
1.	Penn St	11-1-0	Joe Paterno
2.	SMU	11-0-1	Bobby Collins
3.	Nebraska	12-1-0	Tom Osborne
4.	Georgia	11-1-0	Vince Dooley
5.	UCLA	10-1-1	Terry Donahue
6.	Arizona St	10-2-0	Darryl Rogers
7.	Washington	10-2-0	Don James
8.	Clemson	9-1-1	Danny Ford
9.	Arkansas	9-2-1	Lou Holtz
10.	Pittsburgh	9-3-0	Foge Fazio
11.	Louisiana St	8-3-1	Jerry Stovall
12.	Ohio St	9-3-0	Earle Bruce

1982 *(Cont.)*

		Record	Coach
13.	Florida St	9-3-0	Bobby Bowden
14.	Auburn	9-3-0	Pat Dye
15.	Southern Cal	8-3-0	John Robinson
16.	Oklahoma	8-4-0	Barry Switzer
17.	Texas	9-3-0	Fred Akers
18.	N Carolina	8-4-0	Dick Crum
19.	West Virginia	9-3-0	Don Nehlen
20.	Maryland	8-4-0	Bobby Ross

1983

		Record	Coach
1.	Miami (FL)	11-1-0	H. Schnellenberger
2.	Nebraska	12-1-0	Tom Osborne
3.	Auburn	11-1-0	Pat Dye
4.	Georgia	10-1-1	Vince Dooley
5.	Texas	11-1-0	Fred Akers
6.	Florida	9-2-1	Charlie Pell
7.	Brigham Young	11-1-0	LaVell Edwards
8.	Michigan	9-3-0	Bo Schembechler
9.	Ohio St	9-3-0	Earle Bruce
10.	Illinois	10-2-0	Mike White
11.	Clemson	9-1-1	Danny Ford
12.	SMU	10-2-0	Bobby Collins
13.	Air Force	10-2-0	Ken Hatfield
14.	Iowa	9-3-0	Hayden Fry
15.	Alabama	8-4-0	Ray Perkins
16.	West Virginia	9-3-0	Don Nehlen
17.	UCLA	7-4-1	Terry Donahue
18.	Pittsburgh	8-3-1	Foge Fazio
19.	Boston College	9-3-0	Jack Bicknell
20.	E Carolina	8-3-0	Ed Emory

1984

		Record	Coach
1.	Brigham Young	13-0-0	LaVell Edwards
2.	Washington	11-1-0	Don James
3.	Florida	9-1-1	Chas Pell (0-1-1) Galen Hall (9-0)
4.	Nebraska	10-2-0	Tom Osborne
5.	Boston College	10-2-0	Jack Bicknell
6.	Oklahoma	9-2-1	Barry Switzer
7.	Oklahoma St	10-2-0	Pat Jones
8.	SMU	10-2-0	Bobby Collins
9.	UCLA	9-3-0	Terry Donahue
10.	Southern Cal	10-3-0	Ted Tollner
11.	South Carolina	10-2-0	Joe Morrison
12.	Maryland	9-3-0	Bobby Ross
13.	Ohio St	9-3-0	Earle Bruce
14.	Auburn	9-4-0	Pat Dye
15.	Louisiana St	8-3-1	Bill Arnsparger
16.	Iowa	8-4-1	Hayden Fry
17.	Florida St	7-3-2	Bobby Bowden
18.	Miami (FL)	8-5-0	Jimmy Johnson
19.	Kentucky	9-3-0	Jerry Claiborne
20.	Virginia	8-2-2	George Welsh

1985

		Record	Coach
1.	Oklahoma	11-1-0	Barry Switzer
2.	Michigan	10-1-1	Bo Schembechler
3.	Penn St	11-1-0	Joe Paterno
4.	Tennessee	9-1-2	Johnny Majors
5.	Florida	9-1-1	Galen Hall
6.	Texas A&M	10-2-0	Jackie Sherrill
7.	UCLA	9-2-1	Terry Donahue
8.	Air Force	12-1-0	Fisher DeBerry

1985 *(Cont.)*

		Record	Coach
9.	Miami (FL)	10-2-0	Jimmy Johnson
10.	Iowa	10-2-0	Hayden Fry
11.	Nebraska	9-3-0	Tom Osborne
12.	Arkansas	10-2-0	Ken Hatfield
13.	Alabama	9-2-1	Ray Perkins
14.	Ohio St	9-3-0	Earle Bruce
15.	Florida St	9-3-0	Bobby Bowden
16.	Brigham Young	11-3-0	LaVell Edwards
17.	Baylor	9-3-0	Grant Teaff
18.	Maryland	9-3-0	Bobby Ross
19.	Georgia Tech	9-2-1	Bill Curry
20.	Louisiana St	9-2-1	Bill Arnsparger

1986

		Record	Coach
1.	Penn St	12-0-0	Joe Paterno
2.	Miami (FL)	11-1-0	Jimmy Johnson
3.	Oklahoma	11-1-0	Barry Switzer
4.	Arizona St	10-1-1	John Cooper
5.	Nebraska	10-2-0	Tom Osborne
6.	Auburn	10-2-0	Pat Dye
7.	Ohio St	10-3-0	Earle Bruce
8.	Michigan	11-2-0	Bo Schembechler
9.	Alabama	10-3-0	Ray Perkins
10.	Louisiana St	9-3-0	Bill Arnsparger
11.	Arizona	9-3-0	Larry Smith
12.	Baylor	9-3-0	Grant Teaff
13.	Texas A&M	9-3-0	Jackie Sherrill
14.	UCLA	8-3-1	Terry Donahue
15.	Arkansas	9-3-0	Ken Hatfield
16.	Iowa	9-3-0	Hayden Fry
17.	Clemson	8-2-2	Danny Ford
18.	Washington	8-3-1	Don James
19.	Boston College	9-3-0	Jack Bicknell
20.	Virginia Tech	9-2-1	Bill Dooley

1987

		Record	Coach
1.	Miami (FL)	12-0-0	Jimmy Johnson
2.	Florida St	11-1-0	Bobby Bowden
3.	Oklahoma	11-1-0	Barry Switzer
4.	Syracuse	11-0-1	Dick MacPherson
5.	Louisiana St	10-1-1	Mike Archer
6.	Nebraska	10-2-0	Tom Osborne
7.	Auburn	9-1-2	Pat Dye
8.	Michigan St	9-2-1	George Perles
9.	UCLA	10-2-0	Terry Donahue
10.	Texas A&M	10-2-0	Jackie Sherrill
11.	Oklahoma St	10-2-0	Pat Jones
12.	Clemson	10-2-0	Danny Ford
13.	Georgia	9-3-0	Vince Dooley
14.	Tennessee	10-2-1	Johnny Majors
15.	S Carolina	8-4-0	Joe Morrison
16.	Iowa	10-3-0	Hayden Fry
17.	Notre Dame	8-4-0	Lou Holtz
18.	Southern Cal	8-4-0	Larry Smith
19.	Michigan	8-4-0	Bo Schembechler
20.	Arizona St	7-4-1	John Cooper

1988

		Record	Coach
1.	Notre Dame	12-0-0	Lou Holtz
2.	Miami (FL)	11-1-0	Jimmy Johnson
3.	Florida St	11-1-0	Bobby Bowden
4.	Michigan	9-2-1	Bo Schembechler
5.	West Virginia	11-1-0	Don Nehlen
6.	UCLA	10-2-0	Terry Donahue
7.	Southern Cal	10-2-0	Larry Smith
8.	Auburn	10-2-0	Pat Dye
9.	Clemson	10-2-0	Danny Ford
10.	Nebraska	11-2-0	Tom Osborne
11.	Oklahoma St	10-2-0	Pat Jones
12.	Arkansas	10-2-0	Ken Hatfield
13.	Syracuse	10-2-0	Dick MacPherson
14.	Oklahoma	9-3-0	Barry Switzer
15.	Georgia	9-3-0	Vince Dooley
16.	Washington St	9-3-0	Dennis Erickson
17.	Alabama	9-3-0	Bill Curry
18.	Houston	9-3-0	Jack Pardee
19.	Louisiana St	8-4-0	Mike Archer
20.	Indiana	8-3-1	Bill Mallory

†1989

		Record	Coach
1.	Miami (FL)	11-1-0	Dennis Erickson
2.	Notre Dame	12-1-0	Lou Holtz
3.	Florida St	10-2-0	Bobby Bowden
4.	Colorado	11-1-0	Bill McCartney
5.	Tennessee	11-1-0	Johnny Majors
6.	Auburn	10-2-0	Pat Dye
7.	Michigan	10-2-0	Bo Schembechler
8.	Southern Cal	9-2-1	Larry Smith
9.	Alabama	10-2-0	Bill Curry
10.	Illinois	10-2-0	John Mackovic
11.	Nebraska	10-2-0	Tom Osborne
12.	Clemson	10-2-0	Danny Ford
13.	Arkansas	10-2-0	Ken Hatfield
14.	Houston	9-2-0	Jack Pardee
15.	Penn St	8-3-1	Joe Paterno
16.	Michigan St	8-4-0	George Perles
17.	Pittsburgh	8-3-1	Mike Gottfried
18.	Virginia	10-3-0	George Welsh
19.	Texas Tech	9-3-0	Spike Dykes
20.	Texas A&M	8-4-0	R.C. Slocum
21.	West Virginia	8-3-1	Don Nehlen
22.	Brigham Young	10-3-0	LaVell Edwards
23.	Washington	8-4-0	Don James
24.	Ohio St	8-4-0	John Cooper
25.	Arizona	8-4-0	Dick Tomey

1990

		Record	Coach
1.	Colorado	11-1-1	Bill McCartney
2.	#Georgia Tech	11-0-1	Bobby Ross
3.	Miami (FL)	10-2-0	Dennis Erickson
4.	Florida St	10-2-0	Bobby Bowden
5.	Washington	10-2-0	Don James
6.	Notre Dame	9-3-0	Lou Holtz
7.	Michigan	9-3-0	Gary Moeller
8.	Tennessee	9-2-2	Johnny Majors
9.	Clemson	10-2-0	Ken Hatfield
10.	Houston	10-1-0	John Jenkins
11.	Penn St	9-3-0	Joe Paterno
12.	Texas	10-2-0	David McWilliams

1990 *(Cont.)*

		Record	Coach
13.	Florida	9-2-0	Steve Spurrier
14.	Louisville	10-1-1	H. Schnellenberger
15.	Texas A&M	9-3-1	R.C. Slocum
16.	Michigan St	8-3-1	George Perles
17.	Oklahoma	8-3-0	Gary Gibbs
18.	Iowa	8-4-0	Hayden Fry
19.	Auburn	8-3-1	Pat Dye
20.	Southern Cal	8-4-1	Larry Smith
21.	Mississippi	9-3-0	Billy Brewer
22.	Brigham Young	10-3-0	LaVell Edwards
23.	Virginia	8-4-0	George Wells
24.	Nebraska	9-3-0	Tom Osborne
25.	Illinois	8-4-0	John Mackovic

#Selected No. 1 by UPI.

1991

		Record	Coach
1.	Miami (FL)	12-0-0	Dennis Erickson
2.	#Washington	12-0-0	Don James
3.	Penn St	11-2-0	Joe Paterno
4.	Florida St	11-2-0	Bobby Bowden
5.	Alabama	11-1-0	Gene Stallings
6.	Michigan	10-2-0	Gary Moeller
7.	Florida	10-2-0	Steve Spurrier
8.	California	10-2-0	Bruce Snyder
9.	E Carolina	11-1-0	Bill Lewis
10.	Iowa	10-1-1	Hayden Fry
11.	Syracuse	10-2-0	Paul Pasqualoni
12.	Texas A&M	10-2-0	R.C. Slocum
13.	Notre Dame	10-3-0	Lou Holtz
14.	Tennessee	9-3-0	Johnny Majors
15.	Nebraska	9-2-1	Tom Osborne
16.	Oklahoma	9-3-0	Gary Gibbs
17.	Georgia	9-3-0	Ray Goff
18.	Clemson	9-2-1	Ken Hatfield
19.	UCLA	9-3-0	Terry Donahue
20.	Colorado	8-3-1	Bill McCartney
21.	Tulsa	10-2-0	David Rader
22.	Stanford	8-4-0	Dennis Green
23.	Brigham Young	8-3-2	LaVell Edwards
24.	N Carolina St	9-3-0	Dick Sheridan
25.	Air Force	10-3-0	Fisher DeBerry

#Selected No. 1 by *USA Today*/ CNN.

1992

		Record	Coach
1.	Alabama	13-0-0	Gene Stallings
2.	Florida St	11-1-0	Bobby Bowden
3.	Miami	11-1-0	Dennis Erickson
4.	Notre Dame	10-1-1	Lou Holtz
5.	Michigan	9-0-3	Gary Moeller
6.	Syracuse	10-2-0	Paul Pasqualoni
7.	Texas A&M	12-1-0	R.C. Slocum
8.	Georgia	10-2-0	Ray Goff
9.	Stanford	10-3-0	Bill Walsh
10.	Florida	9-4-0	Steve Spurrier
11.	Washington	9-3-0	Don James
12.	Tennessee	9-3-0	Johnny Majors
13.	Colorado	9-2-1	Bill McCartney
14.	Nebraska	9-3-0	Tom Osborne
15.	Washington St	9-3-0	Mike Price
16.	Mississippi	9-3-0	Billy Brewer
17.	N Carolina St	9-3-1	Dick Sheridan
18.	Ohio St	8-3-1	John Cooper
19.	N Carolina	9-3-0	Mack Brown
20.	Hawaii	11-2-0	Bob Wagner

1992 (Cont.)

		Record	Coach
21.	Boston College	8-3-1	Tom Coughlin
22.	Kansas	8-4-0	Glen Mason
23.	Mississippi St	7-5-0	Jackie Sherrill
24.	Fresno St	9-4-0	Jim Sweeney
25.	Wake Forest	8-4-0	Bill Dooley

1993

		Record	Coach
1.	Florida St	12-1-0	Bobby Bowden
2.	Notre Dame	11-1-0	Lou Holtz
3.	Nebraska	11-1-0	Tom Osborne
4.	Auburn	11-0-0	Terry Bowden
5.	Florida	11-2-0	Steve Spurrier
6.	Wisconsin	10-1-1	Barry Alvarez
7.	West Virginia	11-1-0	Don Nehlen
8.	Penn St	10-2-0	Joe Paterno
9.	Texas A&M	10-2-0	R.C. Slocum
10.	Arizona	10-2-0	Dick Tomey
11.	Ohio St	10-1-1	John Cooper
12.	Tennessee	9-2-1	Phil Fulmer
13.	Boston College	9-3-0	Tom Coughlin
14.	Alabama	9-3-1	Gene Stallings
15.	Miami	9-3-0	Dennis Erickson
16.	Colorado	8-3-1	Bill McCartney
17.	Oklahoma	9-3-0	Gary Gibbs
18.	UCLA	8-4-0	Terry Donahue
19.	N Carolina	10-3-0	Mack Brown
20.	Kansas St	9-2-1	Bill Snyder
21.	Michigan	8-4-0	Gary Moeller
22.	Virginia Tech	9-3-0	Frank Beamer
23.	Clemson	9-3-0	Ken Hatfield
24.	Louisville	9-3-0	H. Schnellenberger
25.	California	9-4-0	Keith Gilbertson

1994

		Record	Coach
1.	Nebraska	13-0-0	Tom Osborne
2.	Penn St	12-0-0	Joe Paterno
3.	Colorado	11-1-0	Bill McCartney
4.	Florida St	10-1-1	Bobby Bowden
5.	Alabama	12-1-0	Gene Stallings
6.	Miami (FL)	10-2-0	Dennis Erickson
7.	Florida	10-2-1	Steve Spurrier
8.	Texas A&M	10-0-1	R.C. Slocum
9.	Auburn	9-1-1	Terry Bowden
10.	Utah	10-2-0	Ron McBride
11.	Oregon	9-4-0	Rich Brooks
12.	Michigan	8-4-0	Gary Moeller
13.	Southern Cal	8-3-1	John Robinson
14.	Ohio St	9-4-0	John Cooper
15.	Virginia	9-3-0	George Welsh
16.	Colorado St	10-2-0	Sonny Lubick
17.	N Carolina St	9-3-0	Mike O'Cain
18.	Brigham Young	10-3-0	LaVell Edwards
19.	Kansas St	9-3-0	Bill Snyder
20.	Arizona	8-4-0	Dick Tomey
21.	Washington St	8-4-0	Mike Price
22.	Tennessee	8-4-0	Phillip Fulmer
23.	Boston College	7-4-1	Dan Henning
24.	Mississippi St	8-4-0	Jackie Sherrill
25.	Texas	8-4-0	John Mackovic

1995

		Record	Coach
1.	Nebraska	12-0-0	Tom Osborne
2.	Florida	12-1-0	Steve Spurrier
3.	Tennessee	11-1-0	Phillip Fulmer
4.	Florida St	10-2-0	Bobby Bowden
5.	Colorado	10-2-0	Rick Neuheisel
6.	Ohio St	11-2-0	John Cooper
7.	Kansas St	10-2-0	Bill Snyder
8.	Northwestern	10-2-0	Gary Barnett
9.	Kansas	10-2-0	Glen Mason
10.	Virginia Tech	10-2-0	Frank Beamer
11.	Notre Dame	9-3-0	Lou Holtz
12.	Southern Cal	9-2-1	John Robinson
13.	Penn St	9-3-0	Joe Paterno
14.	Texas	10-2-1	John Mackovic
15.	Texas A&M	9-3-0	S.C. Slocum
16.	Virginia	9-4-0	George Welsh
17.	Michigan	9-4-0	Lloyd Carr
18.	Oregon	9-3-0	Mike Bellotti
19.	Syracuse	9-3-0	Paul Pasqualoni
20.	Miami (FL)	8-3-0	Butch Davis
21.	Alabama	8-3-0	Gene Stallings
22.	Auburn	8-4-0	Terry Bowden
23.	Texas Tech	9-3-0	Spike Dykes
24.	Toledo	11-0-1	Gary Pinkel
25.	Iowa	8-4-0	Hayden Fry

1996

		Record*	Coach
1.	Florida	12-1	Steve Spurrier
2.	Ohio St	11-1	John Cooper
3.	Florida St	11-1	Bobby Bowden
4.	Arizona St	11-1	Bruce Snyder
5.	Brigham Young	14-1	LaVell Edwards
6.	Nebraska	11-2	Tom Osborne
7.	Penn St	11-2	Joe Paterno
8.	Colorado	10-2	Rick Neuheisel
9.	Tennessee	10-2	Phillip Fulmer
10.	North Carolina	10-2	Mack Brown
11.	Alabama	10-3	Gene Stallings
12.	Louisiana St	10-2	Gerry DiNardo
13.	Virginia Tech	10-2	Frank Beamer
14.	Miami (FL)	9-3	Butch Davis
15.	Northwestern	9-3	Gary Barnett
16.	Washington	9-3	Jim Lambright
17.	Kansas St	9-3	Bill Snyder
18.	Iowa	9-3	Hayden Fry
19.	Notre Dame	8-3	Lou Holtz
20.	Michigan	8-4	Lloyd Carr
21.	Syracuse	9-3	Paul Pasqualoni
22.	Wyoming	10-2	Joe Tiller
23.	Texas	8-5	John Mackovic
24.	Auburn	8-4	Terry Bowden
25.	Army	10-2	Bob Sutton

†In 1989 the Associated Press expanded its final poll to 25 teams.

*In 1996 the NCAA introduced overtime to break ties.

1997

		Record	Coach
1.	Michigan	12–0	Lloyd Carr
2.	Nebraska	13–0	Tom Osborne
3.	Florida St	11–1	Bobby Bowden
4.	Florida	10–2	Steve Spurrier
5.	UCLA	10–2	Bob Toledo
6.	N Carolina	11–1	Mack Brown
7.	Tennessee	11–2	Phillip Fulmer
8.	Kansas St	11–1	Bill Snyder
9.	Washington St	10–2	Mike Price
10.	Georgia	10–2	Jim Donnan
11.	Auburn	10–3	Terry Bowden
12.	Ohio St	10–3	John Cooper
13.	Louisiana St	9–3	Gerry DiNardo
14.	Arizona St	8–3	Bruce Snyder
15.	Purdue	9–3	Joe Tiller
16.	Penn St	9–3	Joe Paterno
17.	Colorado St	11–2	Sonny Lubick
18.	Washington	8–4	Jim Lambright
19.	Southern Mississippi	9–3	Jeff Bower
20.	Texas A&M	9–4	R. C. Slocum
21.	Syracuse	9–4	Paul Pasqualoni
22.	Mississippi	8–4	Tommy Tuberville
23.	Missouri	7–5	Larry Smith
24.	Oklahoma St	8–4	Bob Simmons
25.	Georgia Tech	7–5	George O'Leary

1998

		Record	Coach
1.	Tennessee	13–0	Phillip Fulmer
2.	Ohio St	11–1	John Cooper
3.	Florida St	11–2	Bobby Bowden
4.	Arizona	12–1	Dick Tomey
5.	Florida	10–2	Steve Spurrier
6.	Wisconsin	11–1	Barry Alvarez
7.	Tulane	12–0	Tommy Bowden
8.	UCLA	10–2	Bob Toledo
9.	Georgia Tech	10–2	George O'Leary
10.	Kansas St	11–2	Bill Snyder
11.	Texas A&M	11–3	R.C. Slocum
12.	Michigan	10–3	Lloyd Carr
13.	Air Force	12–1	Fisher DeBerry
14.	Georgia	9–3	Jim Donnan
15.	Texas	9–3	Mack Brown
16.	Arkansas	9–3	Houston Nutt
17.	Penn St	9–3	Joe Paterno
18.	Virginia	9–3	George Welsh
19.	Nebraska	9–4	Frank Solich
20.	Miami (FL)	9–3	Butch Davis
21.	Missouri	8–4	Larry Smith
22.	Notre Dame	9–3	Bob Davie
23.	Virginia Tech	9–3	Frank Beamer
24.	Purdue	9–4	Joe Tiller
25.	Syracuse	8–4	Paul Pasqualoni

1999

		Record	Coach
1.	Florida St	12–0	Bobby Bowden
2.	Virginia Tech	11–1	Frank Beamer
3.	Nebraska	12–1	Frank Solich
4.	Wisconsin	10–2	Barry Alvarez
5.	Michigan	10–2	Lloyd Carr
6.	Kansas St	11–1	Bill Snyder
7.	Michigan St	10–2	Nick Saban
8.	Alabama	10–3	Mike DuBose
9.	Tennessee	9–3	Phillip Fulmer
10.	Marshall	13–0	Bob Pruett
11.	Penn St	10–3	Joe Paterno
12.	Florida	9–4	Steve Spurrier
13.	Mississippi St	10–2	Jackie Sherrill
14.	Southern Miss	9–3	Jeff Bower
15.	Miami (FL)	9–4	Butch Davis
16.	Georgia	8–4	Jim Donnan
17.	Arkansas	8–4	Houston Nutt
18.	Minnesota	8–4	Glen Mason
19.	Oregon	9–3	Mike Bellotti
20.	Georgia Tech	8–4	Goerge O'Leary
21.	Texas	9–5	Mack Brown
22.	Mississippi	8–4	David Cutcliffe
23.	Texas A&M	8–4	R.C. Slocum
24.	Illinois	8–4	Ron Turner
25.	Purdue	7–5	Joe Tiller

YET ANOTHER SIGN THAT THE APOCALYPSE IS UPON US

Among Michigan State's $1.1 million in expenses for the 2000 Citrus Bowl was $2,250 for a Cher lookalike and $2,150 for psychics and spiritualists for a New Year's Eve Party

NCAA Divisional Championships

Division I-AA

Year	Winner	Runner-Up	Score
1978	Florida A&M	Massachusetts	35–28
1979	Eastern Kentucky	Lehigh	30–7
1980	Boise St	Eastern Kentucky	31–29
1981	Idaho St	Eastern Kentucky	34–23
1982	Eastern Kentucky	Delaware	17–14
1983	Southern Illinois	Western Carolina	43–7
1984	Montana St	Louisiana Tech	19–6
1985	Georgia Southern	Furman	44–42
1986	Georgia Southern	Arkansas St	48–21
1987	NE Louisiana	Marshall	43–42
1988	Furman	Georgia Southern	17–12
1989	Georgia Southern	SF Austin St	37–34
1990	Georgia Southern	NV-Reno	36–13
1991	Youngstown St	Marshall	25–17
1992	Marshall	Youngstown St	31–28
1993	Youngstown St	Marshall	17–5
1994	Youngstown St	Boise St	28–14
1995	Montana	Marshall	22–20
1996	Marshall	Montana	49–29
1997	Youngstown St	McNesse St	10–9
1998	Massachusetts	Georgia Southern	55–43
1999	Georgia Southern	Youngstown St	59–24

Division II

Year	Winner	Runner-Up	Score
1973	Louisiana Tech	Western Kentucky	34–0
1974	Central Michigan	Delaware	54–14
1975	Northern Michigan	Western Kentucky	16–14
1976	Montana St	Akron	24–13
1977	Lehigh	Jacksonville St	33–0
1978	Eastern Illinois	Delaware	10–9
1979	Delaware	Youngstown St	38–21
1980	Cal Poly SLO	Eastern Illinois	21–13
1981	SW Texas St	N Dakota St	42–13
1982	SW Texas St	UC-Davis	34–9
1983	N Dakota St	Central St (OH)	41–21
1984	Troy St	N Dakota St	18–17
1985	N Dakota St	N Alabama	35–7
1986	N Dakota St	S Dakota	27–7
1987	Troy St	Portland St	31–17
1988	N Dakota St	Portland St	35–21
1989	Mississippi College	Jacksonville St	3–0
1990	N Dakota St	Indiana (PA)	51–11
1991	Pittsburg St	Jacksonville St	23–6
1992	Jacksonville St	Pittsburg St	17–13
1993	N Alabama	Indiana (PA)	41–34
1994	N Alabama	Texas A&M-Kingsville	16–10
1995	N Alabama	Pittsburg St	27–7
1996	Northern Colorado	Carson-Newman	23–14
1997	Northern Colorado	New Haven	51–0
1998	NW Missouri St	Carson-Newman	24–6
1999	NW Missouri St	Carson-Newman	58–52 (OT)

Division III

Year	Winner	Runner-Up	Score
1973	Wittenberg	Juniata	41–0
1974	Central (IA)	Ithaca	10–8
1975	Wittenberg	Ithaca	28–0
1976	St John's (MN)	Towson St	31–28
1977	Widener	Wabash	39–36
1978	Baldwin-Wallace	Wittenberg	24–10
1979	Ithaca	Wittenberg	14–10
1980	Dayton	Ithaca	63–0
1981	Widener	Dayton	17–10
1982	W Georgia	Augustana (IL)	14–0
1983	Augustana (IL)	Union (NY)	21–17

Division III *(Cont.)*

Year	Winner	Runner-Up	Score
1984	Augustana (IL)	Central (IA)	21–12
1985	Augustana (IL)	Ithaca	20–7
1986	Augustana (IL)	Salisbury St	31–3
1987	Wagner	Dayton	19–3
1988	Ithaca	Central (IA)	39–24
1989	Dayton	Union (NY)	17–7
1990	Allegheny	Lycoming	21–14 (OT)
1991	Ithaca	Dayton	34–20
1992	WI-LaCrosse	Washington & Jefferson	16–12
1993	Mount Union	Rowan	34–24
1994	Albion	Washington & Jefferson	38–15
1995	WI-LaCrosse	Rowan	36–7
1996	Mount Union	Rowan	56–24
1997	Mount Union	Lycoming	61–12
1998	Mount Union	Rowan	44–24
1999	Pacific Lutheran	Rowan	42–13

NAIA Divisional Championships

Division I

Year	Winner	Runner-Up	Score
1956	St Joseph's (IN)/ Montana St		0–0
1957	Pittsburg St (KS)	Hillsdale (MI)	27–26
1958	NE Oklahoma	Northern Arizona	19–13
1959	Texas A&I	Lenoir-Rhyne (NC)	20–7
1960	Lenoir-Rhyne (NC)	Humboldt St (CA)	15–14
1961	Pittsburg St (KS)	Linfield (OR)	12–7
1962	Central St (OK)	Lenoir-Rhyne (NC)	28–13
1963	St John's (MN)	Prairie View (TX)	33–27
1964	Concordia-Moorhead/ Sam Houston		7–7
1965	St John's (MN)	Linfield (OR)	33–0
1966	Waynesburg (PA)	WI-Whitewater	42–21
1967	Fairmont St (WV)	Eastern Washington	28–21
1968	Troy St (MI)	Texas A&I	43–35
1969	Texas A&I	Concordia-Moorhead (MN)	32–7
1970	Texas A&I	Wofford (SC)	48–7
1971	Livingston (AL)	Arkansas Tech	14–12
1972	E Texas St	Carson-Newman (TN)	21–18
1973	Abilene Christian	Elon (NC)	42–14
1974	Texas A&I	Henderson St (AR)	34–23
1975	Texas A&I	Salem (WV)	37–0
1976	Texas A&I	Central Arkansas	26–0
1977	Abilene Christian	SW Oklahoma	24–7
1978	Angelo St (TX)	Elon (NC)	34–14
1979	Texas A&I	Central St (OK)	20–14
1980	Elon (NC)	NE Oklahoma	17–10
1981	Elon (NC)	Pittsburg St	3–0
1982	Central St (OK)	Mesa (CO)	14–11
1983	Carson-Newman (TN)	Mesa (CO)	36–28
1984	Carson-Newman (TN)/ Central Arkansas		19–19
1985	Central Arkansas/ Hillsdale (MI)		10–10
1986	Carson-Newman (TN)	Cameron (OK)	17–0
1987	Cameron (OK)	Carson-Newman (TN)	30–2
1988	Carson-Newman (TN)	Adams St (CO)	56–21
1989	Carson-Newman (TN)	Emporia St (KS)	34–20
1990	Central St (OH)	Mesa St (CO)	38–16
1991	Central Arkansas	Central St (OH)	19–16
1992	Central St (OH)	Gardner-Webb (NC)	19–16
1993	East Central (OK)	Glenville St (WV)	49–35
1994	Northeastern St (OK)	Arkansas-Pine Bluff	13–12
1995	Central St (OH)	Northeastern St (OK)	37–7
1996	SW Oklahoma St	Montana Tech	33–31
1997	Findlay (OH)	Willamette (OR)	14–7
1998	Azusa Pacific	Olivet Nazarene	17–14
1999	Northwestern Oklahoma St	Georgetown (KY)	34–26

Division II

Year	Winner	Runner-Up	Score
1970	Westminster (PA)	Anderson (IN)	21–16
1971	California Lutheran	Westminster (PA)	30–14
1972	Missouri Southern	Northwestern (IA)	21–14
1973	Northwestern (IA)	Glenville St (WV)	10–3
1974	Texas Lutheran	Missouri Valley	42–0
1975	Texas Lutheran	California Lutheran	34–8
1976	Westminster (PA)	Redlands (CA)	20–13
1977	Westminster (PA)	California Lutheran	17–9
1978	Concordia-Moorhead (MN)	Findlay (OH)	7–0
1979	Findlay (OH)	Northwestern (IA)	51–6
1980	Pacific Lutheran	Wilmington (OH)	38–10
1981	Austin Coll./ Conc.-Moorhead (MN)		24–24
1982	Linfield (OR)	William Jewell (MO)	33–15
1983	Northwestern (IA)	Pacific Lutheran	25–21
1984	Linfield (OR)	Northwestern (IA)	33–22
1985	WI-La Crosse	Pacific Lutheran	24–7
1986	Linfield (OR)	Baker (KS)	17–0
1987	Pacific Lutheran	WI-Stevens Point*	16–16
1988	Westminster (PA)	WI-La Crosse	21–14
1989	Westminster (PA)	WI-La Crosse	51–30
1990	Peru St (NE)	Westminster (PA)	17–7
1991	Georgetown (KY)	Pacific Lutheran	28–20
1992	Findlay (OH)	Linfield (OR)	26–13
1993	Pacific Lutheran (WA)	Westminster (PA)	50–20
1994	Westminster (PA)	Pacific Lutheran	27–7
1995	Findlay (OH)/ Central Washington		21–21
1996	Sioux Falls (SD)	Western Washington	47–25

*Forfeited 1987 season due to use of an ineligible player.   †In 1997 the NAIA consolidated its two divisions into one.

Awards

Heisman Memorial Trophy

Awarded to the best college player by the Downtown Athletic Club of New York City. The trophy is named after John W. Heisman, who coached Georgia Tech to the national championship in 1917 and later served as DAC athletic director.

Year	Winner, College, Position	Winner's Season Statistics	Runner-Up, College
1935	Jay Berwanger, Chicago, HB	Rush: 119 Yds: 577 TD: 6	Monk Meyer, Army
1936	Larry Kelley, Yale, E	Rec: 17 Yds: 372 TD: 6	Sam Francis, Nebraska
1937	Clint Frank, Yale, HB	Rush: 157 Yds: 667 TD: 11	Byron White, Colorado
1938	†Davey O'Brien, Texas Christian, QB	Att/Comp: 194/110 Yds: 1733 TD: 19	Marshall Goldberg, Pittsburgh
1939	Nile Kinnick, Iowa, HB	Rush: 106 Yds: 374 TD: 5	Tom Harmon, Michigan
1940	Tom Harmon, Michigan, HB	Rush: 191 Yds: 852 TD: 16	John Kimbrough, Texas A&M
1941	†Bruce Smith, Minnesota, HB	Rush: 98 Yds: 480 TD: 6	Angelo Bertelli, Notre Dame
1942	Frank Sinkwich, Georgia, HB	Att/Comp: 166/84 Yds: 1392 TD: 10	Paul Governali, Columbia
1943	Angelo Bertelli, Notre Dame, QB	Att/Comp: 36/25 Yds: 511 TD: 10	Bob Odell, Pennsylvania
1944	Les Horvath, Ohio State, QB	Rush: 163 Yds: 924 TD: 12	Glenn Davis, Army
1945	*†Doc Blanchard, Army, FB	Rush: 101 Yds: 718 TD: 13	Glenn Davis, Army
1946	Glenn Davis, Army, HB	Rush: 123 Yds: 712 TD: 7	Charley Trippi, Georgia
1947	†John Lujack, Notre Dame, QB	Att/Comp: 109/61 Yds: 777 TD: 9	Bob Chappius, Michigan
1948	*Doak Walker, Southern Methodist, HB	Rush: 108 Yds: 532 TD: 8	Charlie Justice, N Carolina
1949	†Leon Hart, Notre Dame, E	Rec: 19 Yds: 257 TD: 5	Charlie Justice, N Carolina
1950	*Vic Janowicz, Ohio St, HB	Att/Comp: 77/32 Yds: 561 TD: 12	Kyle Rote, Southern Methodist
1951	Dick Kazmaier, Princeton, HB	Rush: 149 Yds: 861 TD: 9	Hank Lauricella, Tennessee
1952	Billy Vessels, Oklahoma, HB	Rush: 167 Yds: 1072 TD: 17	Jack Scarbath, Maryland
1953	John Lattner, Notre Dame, HB	Rush: 134 Yds: 651 TD: 6	Paul Giel, Minnesota
1954	Alan Ameche, Wisconsin, FB	Rush: 146 Yds: 641 TD: 9	Kurt Burris, Oklahoma
1955	Howard Cassady, Ohio St, HB	Rush: 161 Yds: 958 TD: 15	Jim Swink, Texas Christian
1956	Paul Hornung, Notre Dame, QB	Att/Comp: 111/59 Yds: 917 TD: 3	Johnny Majors, Tennessee
1957	John David Crow, Texas A&M, HB	Rush: 129 Yds: 562 TD: 10	Alex Karras, Iowa
1958	Pete Dawkins, Army, HB	Rush: 78 Yds: 428 TD: 6	Randy Duncan, Iowa

Heisman Memorial Trophy (Cont.)

Year	Winner, College, Position	Winner's Season Statistics	Runner-Up, College
1959	...Billy Cannon, Louisiana St, HB	Rush: 139 Yds: 598 TD: 6	Rich Lucas, Penn St
1960	...Joe Bellino, Navy, HB	Rush: 168 Yds: 834 TD: 18	Tom Brown, Minnesota
1961	...Ernie Davis, Syracuse, HB	Rush: 150 Yds: 823 TD: 15	Bob Ferguson, Ohio St
1962	...Terry Baker, Oregon St, QB	Att/Comp: 203/112 Yds: 1738 TD: 15	Jerry Stovall, Louisiana St
1963	...*Roger Staubach, Navy, QB	Att/Comp: 161/107 Yds: 1474 TD: 7	Billy Lothridge, Georgia Tech
1964	...John Huarte, Notre Dame, QB	Att/Comp: 205/114 Yds: 2062 TD: 16	Jerry Rhome, Tulsa
1965	...Mike Garrett, Southern Cal, HB	Rush: 267 Yds: 1440 TD: 16	Howard Twilley, Tulsa
1966	...Steve Spurrier, Florida, QB	Att/Comp: 291/179 Yds: 2012 TD: 16	Bob Griese, Purdue
1967	...Gary Beban, UCLA, QB	Att/Comp: 156/87 Yds: 1359 TD: 8	O.J. Simpson, Southern Cal
1968	...O.J. Simpson, Southern Cal, HB	Rush: 383 Yds: 1880 TD: 23	Leroy Keyes, Purdue
1969	...Steve Owens, Oklahoma, FB	Rush: 358 Yds: 1523 TD: 23	Mike Phipps, Purdue
1970	...Jim Plunkett, Stanford, QB	Att/Comp: 358/191 Yds: 2715 TD: 18	Joe Theismann, Notre Dame
1971	...Pat Sullivan, Auburn, QB	Att/Comp: 281/162 Yds: 2012 TD: 20	Ed Marinaro, Cornell
1972	...Johnny Rodgers, Nebraska, FL	Rec: 55 Yds: 942 TD: 17	Greg Pruitt, Oklahoma
1973	...John Cappelletti, Penn St, HB	Rush: 286 Yds: 1522 TD: 17	John Hicks, Ohio St
1974	...*Archie Griffin, Ohio St, HB	Rush: 256 Yds: 1695 TD: 12	Anthony Davis, Southern Cal
1975	...Archie Griffin, Ohio St, HB	Rush: 262 Yds: 1450 TD: 4	Chuck Muncie, California
1976	...†Tony Dorsett, Pittsburgh, HB	Rush: 370 Yds: 2150 TD: 23	Ricky Bell, Southern Cal
1977	...Earl Campbell, Texas, FB	Rush: 267 Yds: 1744 TD: 19	Terry Miller, Oklahoma St
1978	...*Billy Sims, Oklahoma, HB	Rush: 231 Yds: 1762 TD: 20	Chuck Fusina, Penn St
1979	...Charles White, Southern Cal, HB	Rush: 332 Yds: 1803 TD: 19	Billy Sims, Oklahoma
1980	...George Rogers, S Carolina, HB	Rush: 324 Yds: 1894 TD: 14	Hugh Green, Pittsburgh
1981	...Marcus Allen, Southern Cal, HB	Rush: 433 Yds: 2427 TD: 23	Herschel Walker, Georgia
1982	...*Herschel Walker, Georgia, HB	Rush: 335 Yds: 1752 TD: 17	John Elway, Stanford
1983	...Mike Rozier, Nebraska, HB	Rush: 275 Yds: 2148 TD: 29	Steve Young, Brigham Young
1984	...Doug Flutie, Boston College, QB	Att/Comp: 396/233 Yds: 3454 TD: 27	Keith Byars, Ohio St
1985	...Bo Jackson, Auburn, HB	Rush: 278 Yds: 1786 TD: 17	Chuck Long, Iowa
1986	...Vinny Testaverde, Miami (FL), QB	Att/Comp: 276/175 Yds: 2557 TD: 26	Paul Palmer, Temple
1987	...Tim Brown, Notre Dame, WR	Rec: 39 Yds: 846 TD: 7	Don McPherson, Syracuse
1988	...*Barry Sanders, Oklahoma St, RB	Rush: 344 Yds: 2628 TD: 39	Rodney Peete, Southern Cal
1989	...*Andre Ware, Houston, QB	Att/Comp: 578/365 Yds: 4699 TD: 46	Anthony Thompson, Indiana
1990	...*Ty Detmer, Brigham Young, QB	Att/Comp: 562/361 Yds: 5188 TD: 41	Raghib Ismail, Notre Dame
1991	...*Desmond Howard, Michigan, WR	Rec: 61 Yds: 950 TD: 23	Casey Weldon, Florida St
1992	...Gino Torretta, Miami (FL), QB	Att/Comp: 402/228 Yds: 3060 TD: 19	Marshall Faulk, San Diego St
1993	...†Charlie Ward, Florida St, QB	Att/Comp: 380/264 Yds: 3032 TD: 27	Heath Shuler, Tennessee
1994	...Rashaan Salaam, Colorado, RB	Rush: 298 Yds: 2055 TD: 24	Ki-Jana Carter, Penn St
1995	...Eddie George, Ohio State, RB	Rush: 303 Yds: 1826 TD: 23	Tommie Frazier, Nebraska
1996	...†Danny Wuerffel, Florida, QB	Att/Comp: 360/207 Yds: 3625 TD: 39	Troy Davis, Iowa St
1997	...†Charles Woodson, Michigan, CB/ WR	7 interceptions; Rec: 11 Yds: 231 TD: 4	Peyton Manning, Tennessee
1998	...Ricky Williams, Texas, RB	Rush: 361 Yds: 2124 TD: 28	Michael Bishop, Kansas St
1999	...Ron Dayne, Wisconsin, RB	Rush: 303 Yds: 1834 TD: 19	Joe Hamilton, Georgia Tech

*Juniors (all others seniors).   †Winners who played for national championship teams the same year.

Note: Former Heisman winners and national media cast votes, with ballots allowing for three names (3 points for first, 2 for second and 1 for third).

Maxwell Award

Given to the nation's outstanding college football player by the Maxwell Football Club of Philadelphia.

Year	Player, College, Position	Year	Player, College, Position
1937	Clint Frank, Yale, HB	1969	Mike Reid, Penn St, DT
1938	Davey O'Brien, Texas Christian, QB	1970	Jim Plunkett, Stanford, QB
1939	Nile Kinnick, Iowa, HB	1971	Ed Marinaro, Cornell, RB
1940	Tom Harmon, Michigan, HB	1972	Brad Van Pelt, Michigan St, DB
1941	Bill Dudley, Virginia, HB	1973	John Cappelletti, Penn St, RB
1942	Paul Governali, Columbia, QB	1974	Steve Joachim, Temple, QB
1943	Bob Odell, Pennsylvania, HB	1975	Archie Griffin, Ohio St, RB
1944	Glenn Davis, Army, HB	1976	Tony Dorsett, Pittsburgh, RB
1945	Doc Blanchard, Army, FB	1977	Ross Browner, Notre Dame, DE
1946	Charley Trippi, Georgia, HB	1978	Chuck Fusina, Penn St, QB
1947	Doak Walker, Southern Meth, HB	1979	Charles White, Southern Cal, RB
1948	Chuck Bednarik, Pennsylvania, C	1980	Hugh Green, Pittsburgh, DE
1949	Leon Hart, Notre Dame, E	1980	Hugh Green, Pittsburgh, DE
1950	Reds Bagnell, Pennsylvania, HB	1981	Marcus Allen, Southern Cal, RB
1951	Dick Kazmaier, Princeton, HB	1982	Herschel Walker, Georgia, RB
1952	John Lattner, Notre Dame, HB	1983	Mike Rozier, Nebraska, RB
1953	John Lattner, Notre Dame, HB	1984	Doug Flutie, Boston College, QB
1954	Ron Beagle, Navy, E	1985	Chuck Long, Iowa, QB
1955	Howard Cassady, Ohio St, HB	1986	Vinny Testaverde, Miami (FL), QB
1956	Tommy McDonald, Oklahoma, HB	1987	Don McPherson, Syracuse, QB
1957	Bob Reifsnyder, Navy, T	1988	Barry Sanders, Oklahoma St, RB
1958	Pete Dawkins, Army, HB	1989	Anthony Thompson, Indiana, RB
1959	Rich Lucas, Penn St, QB	1990	Ty Detmer, Brigham Young, QB
1960	Joe Bellino, Navy, HB	1991	Desmond Howard, Michigan, WR
1961	Bob Ferguson, Ohio St, FB	1992	Gino Torretta, Miami (FL), QB
1962	Terry Baker, Oregon St, QB	1993	Charlie Ward, Florida St, QB
1963	Roger Staubach, Navy, QB	1994	Kerry Collins, Penn St, QB
1964	Glenn Ressler, Penn St, C	1995	Eddie George, Ohio St, RB
1965	Tommy Nobis, Texas, LB	1996	Danny Wuerffel, Florida, QB
1966	Jim Lynch, Notre Dame, LB	1997	Peyton Manning, Tennessee, QB
1967	Gary Beban, UCLA, QB	1998	Ricky Williams, Texas, RB
1968	O.J. Simpson, Southern Cal, RB	1999	Ron Dayne, Wisconsin, RB

Davey O'Brien National Quarterback Award

Given to the top quarterback in the nation by the Davey O'Brien Educational and Charitable Trust of Fort Worth. Named for Texas Christian Hall of Fame quarterback Davey O'Brien (1936-38).

Year	Player, College	Year	Player, College
1981	Jim McMahon, Brigham Young	1991	Ty Detmer, Brigham Young
1982	Todd Blackledge, Penn St	1992	Gino Torretta, Miami (FL)
1983	Steve Young, Brigham Young	1993	Charlie Ward, Florida St
1984	Doug Flutie, Boston College	1994	Kerry Collins, Penn St
1985	Chuck Long, Iowa	1995	Danny Wuerffel, Florida
1986	Vinny Testaverde, Miami (FL)	1996	Danny Wuerffel, Florida
1987	Don McPherson, Syracuse	1997	Peyton Manning, Tennessee
1988	Troy Aikman, UCLA	1998	Michael Bishop, Kansas St
1989	Andre Ware, Houston	1999	Joe Hamilton, Georgia Tech
1990	Ty Detmer, Brigham Young		

Note: Originally known as the Davey O'Brien Memorial Trophy, honoring the outstanding football player in the Southwest as follows: 1977—Earl Campbell, Texas, RB; 1978—Billy Sims, Oklahoma, RB; 1979—Mike Singletary, Baylor, LB; 1980—Mike Singletary, Baylor, LB.

Vince Lombardi/Rotary Award

Given to the outstanding college football lineman of the year, the award is sponsored by the Rotary Club of Houston.

Year	Player, College, Position	Year	Player, College, Position
1970	Jim Stillwagon, Ohio St, MG	1985	Tony Casillas, Oklahoma, NG
1971	Walt Patulski, Notre Dame, DE	1986	Cornelius Bennett, Alabama, LB
1972	Rich Glover, Nebraska, MG	1987	Chris Spielman, Ohio St, LB
1973	John Hicks, Ohio St, OT	1988	Tracy Rocker, Auburn, DT
1974	Randy White, Maryland, DT	1989	Percy Snow, Michigan St, LB
1975	Lee Roy Selmon, Oklahoma, DT	1990	Chris Zorich, Notre Dame, NG
1976	Wilson Whitley, Houston, DT	1991	Steve Emtman, Washington, DT
1977	Ross Browner, Notre Dame, DE	1992	Marvin Jones, Florida St, LB
1978	Bruce Clark, Penn St, DT	1993	Aaron Taylor, Notre Dame, OT
1979	Brad Budde, Southern Cal, G	1994	Warren Sapp, Miami (FL), DT
1980	Hugh Green, Pittsburgh, DE	1995	Orlando Pace, Ohio St, OT
1981	Kenneth Sims, Texas, DT	1996	Orlando Pace, Ohio St, OT
1982	Dave Rimington, Nebraska, C	1997	Grant Wistrom, Nebraska, DE
1983	Dean Steinkuhler, Nebraska, G	1998	Dat Nguyen, Texas A&M, LB
1984	Tony Degrate, Texas, DT	1999	Corey Moore, Virginia Tech, DE

Outland Trophy

Given to the outstanding interior lineman, selected by the Football Writers Association of America.

Year	Player, College, Position	Year	Player, College, Position
1946	George Connor, Notre Dame, T	1973	John Hicks, Ohio St, OT
1947	Joe Steffy, Army, G	1974	Randy White, Maryland, DE
1948	Bill Fischer, Notre Dame, G	1975	Lee Roy Selmon, Oklahoma, DT
1949	Ed Bagdon, Michigan St, G	1976	*Ross Browner, Notre Dame, DE
1950	Bob Gain, Kentucky, T	1977	Brad Shearer, Texas, DT
1951	Jim Weatherall, Oklahoma, T	1978	Greg Roberts, Oklahoma, G
1952	Dick Modzelewski, Maryland, T	1979	Jim Ritcher, N Carolina St, C
1953	J.D. Roberts, Oklahoma, G	1980	Mark May, Pittsburgh, OT
1954	Bill Brooks, Arkansas, G	1981	*Dave Rimington, Nebraska, C
1955	Calvin Jones, Iowa, G	1982	Dave Rimington, Nebraska, C
1956	Jim Parker, Ohio St, G	1983	Dean Steinkuhler, Nebraska, G
1957	Alex Karras, Iowa, T	1984	Bruce Smith, Virginia Tech, DT
1958	Zeke Smith, Auburn, G	1985	Mike Ruth, Boston Col, NG
1959	Mike McGee, Duke, T	1986	Jason Buck, Brigham Young, DT
1960	Tom Brown, Minnesota, G	1987	Chad Hennings, Air Force, DT
1961	Merlin Olsen, Utah St, T	1988	Tracy Rocker, Auburn, DT
1962	Bobby Bell, Minnesota, T	1989	Mohammed Elewonibi, Brigham Young, G
1963	Scott Appleton, Texas, T	1990	Russell Maryland, Miami (FL), DT
1964	Steve DeLong, Tennessee, T	1991	*Steve Emtman, Washington, DT
1965	Tommy Nobis, Texas, G	1992	Will Shields, Nebraska, G
1966	Loyd Phillips, Arkansas, T	1993	Rob Waldrop, Arizona, NG
1967	Ron Yary, Southern Cal, T	1994	Zach Wiegert, Nebraska, G
1968	Bill Stanfill, Georgia, T	1995	Jonathan Ogden, UCLA, OT
1969	Mike Reid, Penn St, DT	1996	*Orlando Pace, Ohio St, OT
1970	Jim Stillwagon, Ohio St, MG	1997	Aaron Taylor, Nebraska, G
1971	Larry Jacobson, Nebraska, DT	1998	Kris Farris, UCLA, OL
1972	Rich Glover, Nebraska, MG	1999	Chris Samuels, Alabama, OL

*Juniors (all others seniors).

Butkus Award

Given to the top collegiate linebacker, the award was established by the Downtown Athletic Club of Orlando and named for college Hall of Famer Dick Butkus of Illinois.

Year	Player, College	Year	Player, College
1985	Brian Bosworth, Oklahoma	1993	Trev Alberts, Nebraska
1986	Brian Bosworth, Oklahoma	1994	Dana Howard, Illinois
1987	Paul McGowan, Florida St	1995	Kevin Hardy, Illinois
1988	Derrick Thomas, Alabama	1996	Matt Russell, Colorado
1989	Percy Snow, Michigan St	1997	Andy Katzenmoyer, Ohio St
1990	Alfred Williams, Colorado	1998	Chris Claiborne, Southern Cal
1991	Erick Anderson, Michigan	1999	LaVar Arrington, Penn St
1992	Marvin Jones, Florida St		

Jim Thorpe Award

Given to the best defensive back of the year, the award is presented by the Jim Thorpe Athletic Club of Oklahoma City.

Year	Player, College	Year	Player, College
1986	Thomas Everett, Baylor	1993	Antonio Langham, Alabama
1987	Bennie Blades, Miami (FL)	1994	Chris Hudson, Colorado
	Rickey Dixon, Oklahoma	1995	Greg Myers, Colorado St
1988	Deion Sanders, Florida St	1996	Lawrence Wright, Florida
1989	Mark Carrier, Southern Cal	1997	Charles Woodson, Michigan
1990	Darryl Lewis, Arizona	1998	Antoine Winfield, Ohio St
1991	Terrell Buckley, Florida St	1999	Tyrone Carter, Minnesota
1992	Deon Figures, Colorado		

Walter Payton Player of the Year Award

Given to the top Division I-AA player as voted by Division I-AA sports information directors. Sponsored by Sports Network.

Year	Player, College, Position	Year	Player, College, Position
1987	Kenny Gamble, Colgate, RB	1994	Steve McNair, Alcorn St, QB
1988	Dave Meggett, Towson St, RB	1995	Dave Dickenson, Montana, QB
1989	John Friesz, Idaho, QB	1996	Archie Amerson, Northern Arizona, RB
1990	Walter Dean, Grambling, RB	1997	Brian Finneran, Villanova, WR
1991	Jamie Martin, Weber St, QB	1998	Jerry Azumah, New Hampshire, RB
1992	Michael Payton, Marshall, QB	1999	Adrian Peterson, Georgia Southern, RB
1993	Doug Nussmeier, Idaho, QB		

The Harlon Hill Trophy

Given to the outstanding NCAA Division II college football player, the award is sponsored by
the National Harlon Hill Awards Committee, Florence, AL.

Year	Player, College, Position	Year	Player, College, Position
1986	Jeff Bentrim, N Dakota St, QB	1993	Roger Graham, New Haven, RB
1987	Johnny Bailey, Texas A&I, RB	1994	Chris Hatcher, Valdosta St, QB
1988	Johnny Bailey, Texas A&I, RB	1995	Ronald McKinnon, N Alabama, LB
1989	Johnny Bailey, Texas A&I, RB	1996	Jarrett Anderson, Truman St, RB
1990	Chris Simdorn, N Dakota St, QB	1997	Irvin Sigler, Bloomsburg, RB
1991	Ronnie West, Pittsburg St, WR	1998	Brian Shay, Emporia St, RB
1992	Ronald Moore, Pittsburg St, RB	1999	Corte McGuffey, Northern Colorado, QB

NCAA Division I-A Individual Records

Career

SCORING

Most Points Scored: 468 — Travis Prentice, Miami (OH), 1996–99
Most Points Scored per Game: 12.1 — Marshall Faulk, San Diego St, 1991-93
Most Touchdowns Scored: 78 — Travis Prentice, Miami (OH), 1996–99
Most Touchdowns Scored per Game: 2.0 — Marshall Faulk, San Diego St, 1991-93
Most Touchdowns Scored, Rushing: 73 — Travis Prentice, Miami (OH), 1996–99
Most Touchdowns Scored, Passing: 121 — Ty Detmer, Brigham Young, 1988-91
Most Touchdowns Scored, Receiving: 50 — Troy Edwards, Louisiana Tech, 1996–98
Most Touchdowns Scored, Interception Returns: 5 — Ken Thomas, San Jose St, 1979-82; Jackie Walker, Tennessee, 1969-71
Most Touchdowns Scored, Punt Returns: 7 — Johnny Rodgers, Nebraska, 1970-72; Jack Mitchell, Oklahoma, 1946-48; David Allen, Kansas St, 1997-99
Most Touchdowns Scored, Kickoff Returns: 6 — Anthony Davis, Southern Cal, 1972-74

TOTAL OFFENSE

Most Plays: 1795 — Ty Detmer, Brigham Young, 1988-91
Most Plays per Game: 48.5 — Doug Gaynor, Long Beach St, 1984-85
Most Yards Gained: 14,665 — Ty Detmer, Brigham Young, 1988-91 (15,031 passing, -366 rushing)
Most Yards Gained per Game: 382.4 — Tim Rattay, Louisiana Tech, 1997–99
Most 300+ Yard Games: 33 —Ty Detmer, Brigham Young, 1988-91

RUSHING

Most Rushes: 1,215 — Steve Bartalo, Colorado St, 1983–86 (4813 yds)
Most Rushes per Game: 34.0 — Ed Marinaro, Cornell, 1969–71
Most Yards Gained: 6,397 — Ron Dayne, Wisconsin, 1996–99
Most Yards Gained per Game: 174.6 — Ed Marinaro, Cornell, 1969–71

Most 100+ Yard Games: 33 — Tony Dorsett, Pittsburgh, 1973–76; Archie Griffin, Ohio St, 1972–75
Most 200+ Yard Games: 11 — Marcus Allen, Southern Cal, 1978–81; Ricky Williams, Texas, 1995–98; Ron Dayne, Wisconsin, 1996–99

PASSING

Highest Passing Efficiency Rating: 163.6— Danny Wuerffel, Florida, 1993–96 (1,170 attempts, 708 completions, 42 interceptions, 10,875 yards, 114 touchdown passes)
Most Passes Attempted: 1,530—Ty Detmer, Brigham Young, 1988–91
Most Passes Attempted per Game: 47.0—Tim Rattay, Louisiana Tech, 1997–99
Most Passes Completed: 1,031—Chris Redman, Louisville, 1996–99
Most Passes Completed per Game: 30.8—Tim Rattay, Louisiana Tech, 1997–99
*Highest Completion Percentage: 67.1—Tim Couch, Kentucky, 1996–98
Most Yards Gained: 15,031—Ty Detmer, Brigham Young, 1988–91
Most Yards Gained per Game: 386.2—Tim Rattay, Louisiana Tech, 1997–99
*Minimum 1100 attempts.

RECEIVING

Most Passes Caught: 298—Trevor Insley, Nevada, 1996–99
Most Passes Caught per Game: 10.5 — Emmanuel Hazard, Houston, 1989-90
Most Yards Gained: 5,005—Trevor Insley, Nevada, 1996–99
Most Yards Gained per Game: 140.9 — Alex Van Dyke, Nevada, 1994–95
Highest Average Gain per Reception: 25.7 — Wesley Walker, California, 1973–75

Career *(Cont.)*

ALL-PURPOSE RUNNING

Most Plays: 1347 — Steve Bartalo, Colorado St, 1983-86 (1,215 rushes, 132 receptions)
Most Yards Gained: 7206 — Ricky Williams, Texas, 1995–98 (6,279 rushing, 927 receiving)
Most Yards Gained per Game: 237.8 — Ryan Benjamin, Pacific, 1990–92
Highest Average Gain per Play: 17.4 — Anthony Carter, Michigan, 1979–82

INTERCEPTIONS

Most Passes Intercepted: 29 — Al Brosky, Illinois, 1950–52
Most Passes Intercepted per Game: 1.1 — Al Brosky, Illinois, 1950–52
Most Yards on Interception Returns: 501 — Terrell Buckley, Florida St, 1989–91
Highest Average Gain per Interception: 26.5 — Tom Pridemore, W Virginia, 1975–77

SPECIAL TEAMS

Highest Punt Return Average: 23.6 — Jack Mitchell, Oklahoma, 1946–48
Highest Kickoff Return Average: 36.2 — Forrest Hall, San Francisco, 1946–47
Highest Average Yards per Punt: 46.3 — Todd Sauerbrun, West Virginia, 1991–94

Single Season

SCORING

Most Points Scored: 234 — Barry Sanders, Oklahoma St, 1988
Most Points Scored per Game: 21.3 — Barry Sanders, Oklahoma St, 1988
Most Touchdowns Scored: 39 — Barry Sanders, Oklahoma St, 1988
Most Touchdowns Scored, Rushing: 37 — Barry Sanders, Oklahoma St, 1988
Most Touchdowns Scored, Passing: 54 — David Klingler, Houston, 1990
Most Touchdowns Scored, Receiving: 27 — Troy Edwards, Louisiana Tech, 1998
Most Touchdowns Scored, Interception Returns: 4 — Deltha O'Neal, California, 1999
Most Touchdowns Scored, Punt Returns: 4 — David Allen, Kansas St, 1998; Quinton Spotwood, Syracuse, 1997; Tinker Keck, Cincinnati, 1997; James Henry, Southern Miss, 1987; Golden Richards, Brigham Young, 1971; Cliff Branch, Colorado, 1971
Most Touchdowns Scored, Kickoff Returns: 3 — Leland McElroy, Texas A&M, 1993; Terance Mathis, New Mexico, 1989; Willie Gault, Tennessee, 1980; Anthony Davis, Southern Cal, 1974; Stan Brown, Purdue, 1970; Forrest Hall, San Francisco, 1946

TOTAL OFFENSE

Most Plays: 704 — David Klingler, Houston, 1990
Most Yards Gained: 5,221 — David Klingler, Houston, 1990
Most Yards Gained per Game: 474.6 — David Klingler, Houston, 1990
Most 300+ Yard Games: 12 — Ty Detmer, Brigham Young, 1990

RUSHING

Most Rushes: 403 — Marcus Allen, Southern Cal, 1981
Most Rushes per Game: 39.6 — Ed Marinaro, Cornell, 1971
Most Yards Gained: 2628 — Barry Sanders, Oklahoma St, 1988
Most Yards Gained per Game: 238.9 — Barry Sanders, Oklahoma St, 1988
Most 100+ Yard Games: 11 — By 14 players, most recently Ahman Green, Nebraska, 1997

PASSING

Highest Passing Efficiency Rating: 183.3 — Shaun King, Tulane, 1998 (328 attempts, 223 completions, 6 interceptions, 3232 yards, 36 TD passes)
Most Passes Attempted: 643 — David Klingler, Houston, 1990
Most Passes Attempted per Game: 58.5 — David Klingler, Houston, 1990
Most Passes Completed: 400 — Tim Couch, Kentucky, 1998
Most Passes Completed per Game: 36.4 — Tim Couch, Kentucky, 1998
Highest Completion Percentage: 73.6 — Daunte Culpepper, Central Florida, 1998
Most Yards Gained: (12 games) 5188 — Ty Detmer, Brigham Young, 1990; (11 games) 5140 — David Klingler, Houston, 1990
Most Yards Gained per Game: 467.3 — David Klingler, Houston, 1990

RECEIVING

Most Passes Caught: 142 — Emmanuel Hazard, Houston, 1989
Most Passes Caught per Game: 13.4 — Howard Twilley, Tulsa, 1965
Most Yards Gained: 2060 — Trevor Insley, Nevada, 1999
Most Yards Gained per Game: 187.3 — Trevor Insley, Nevada, 1999
Highest Average Gain per Reception: 27.9 — Elmo Wright, Houston, 1968 (min. 30 receptions)

ALL-PURPOSE RUNNING

Most Plays: 432 — Marcus Allen, Southern Cal, 1981
Most Yards Gained: 3,250 — Barry Sanders, Oklahoma St, 1988
Most Yards Gained per Game: 295.5 — Barry Sanders, Oklahoma St, 1988
Highest Average Gain per Play: 18.5 — Henry Bailey, UNLV, 1992

Single Season *(Cont.)*

INTERCEPTIONS

Most Passes Intercepted: 14 — Al Worley, Washington, 1968
Most Yards on Interception Returns: 302 — Charles Phillips, Southern Cal, 1974
Highest Average Gain per Interception: 50.6 — Norm Thompson, Utah, 1969

SPECIAL TEAMS

Highest Punt Return Average: 25.9 — Bill Blackstock, Tennessee, 1951
Highest Kickoff Return Average: 40.1 — Paul Allen, Brigham Young, 1961
Highest Average Yards per Punt: 50.3 — Chad Kessler, Louisiana St, 1997

Single Game

SCORING

Most Points Scored: 48 — Howard Griffith, Illinois, 1990 (vs Southern Illinois)
Most Field Goals: 7 — Dale Klein, Nebraska, 1985 (vs Missouri); Mike Prindle, Western Michigan, 1984 (vs Marshall)
Most Extra Points (Kick): 13 — Derek Mahoney, Fresno St, 1991 (vs New Mexico); Terry Leiweke, Houston, 1968 (vs Tulsa)
Most Extra Points (2-Pts): 6 — Jim Pilot, New Mexico St, 1961 (vs Hardin-Simmons)

TOTAL OFFENSE

Most Yards Gained: 732 — David Klingler, Houston, 1990 (vs Arizona St)

RUSHING

Most Yards Gained: 406 — LaDainian Tomlinson, Texas Christian, 1999 (vs UTEP)
Most Touchdowns Rushed: 8 — Howard Griffith, Illinois, 1990 (vs Southern Illinois)

PASSING

Most Passes Completed: 55 — Rusty LaRue, Wake Forest, 1995 (vs Duke); Drew Brees, Purdue, 1998 (vs Wisconsin)
Most Yards Gained: 716 — David Klingler, Houston, 1990 (vs Arizona St)
Most Touchdown Passes: 11 — David Klingler, Houston, 1990 [vs Eastern Washington (I-AA)]

RECEIVING

Most Passes Caught: 23 — Randy Gatewood, UNLV, 1994 (vs Idaho)
Most Yards Gained: 405 — Troy Edwards, Louisiana Tech, 1998 (vs Nebraska)
Most Touchdown Catches: 6 — Tim Delaney, San Diego St, 1969 (vs New Mexico St)

NCAA Division I-AA Individual Records

Career

SCORING

Most Points Scored: 418 — Jerry Azumah, New Hampshire, 1995–98
Most Touchdowns Scored: 69 — Jerry Azumah, New Hampshire, 1995–98
Most Touchdowns Scored, Rushing: 60 — Jerry Azumah, New Hampshire, 1995–98
Most Touchdowns Scored, Passing: 139 — Willie Totten, Mississippi Valley, 1982–85
Most Touchdowns Scored, Receiving: 50 — Jerry Rice, Mississippi Valley, 1981–84

RUSHING

Most Rushes: 1,044 — Jerry Azumah, New Hampshire, 1995–98
Most Rushes per Game: 38.2 — Arnold Mickens, Butler, 1994–95
Most Yards Gained: 6,193 — Jerry Azumah, New Hampshire, 1995–98
Most Yards Gained per Game: 151.0 — Jerry Azumah, New Hampshire, 1995–98

PASSING

Highest Passing Efficiency Rating: 170.8 — Shawn Knight, William & Mary, 1991–94
Most Passes Attempted: 1,680 — Steve McNair, Alcorn St, 1991–94
Most Passes Completed: 934 — Jamie Martin, Weber St, 1989–92
Most Passes Completed per Game: 25.1 — Aaron Flowers, Cal St–Northridge, 1996–97
Highest Completion Percentage: 67.3 — Dave Dickenson, Montana, 1992–95
Most Yards Gained: 14,496 — Steve McNair, Alcorn St, 1991–94
Most Yards Gained per Game: 350 — Neil Lomax, Portland St, 1978–80

RECEIVING

Most Passes Caught: 301 — Jerry Rice, Mississippi Valley, 1981–84
Most Yards Gained: 4,693 — Jerry Rice, Mississippi Valley, 1981–84
Most Yards Gained per Game: 114.5 — Jerry Rice, Mississippi Valley, 1981–84
Highest Average Gain per Reception: 24.3 — John Taylor, Delaware St, 1982–85

Single Season

SCORING

Most Points Scored: 174 — Adrian Peterson, Georgia Southern, 1999
Most Touchdowns Scored: 29 — Adrian Peterson, Georgia Southern, 1999
Most Touchdowns Scored, Rushing: 28 — Adrian Peterson, Georgia Southern, 1999
Most Touchdowns Scored, Passing: 56 — Willie Totten, Mississippi Valley, 1984
Most Touchdowns Scored, Receiving: 27 — Jerry Rice, Mississippi Valley, 1984

RUSHING

Most Rushes: 409 — Arnold Mickens, Butler, 1994
Most Rushes per Game: 40.9 — Arnold Mickens, Butler, 1994
Most Yards Gained: 2,260 — Charles Roberts, Cal St–Sacramento, 1998
Most Yards Gained per Game: 225.5 — Arnold Mickens, Butler, 1994

PASSING

Highest Passing Efficiency Rating: 204.6 — Shawn Knight, William & Mary, 1993
Most Passes Attempted: 577 — Joe Lee, Towson, 1999
Most Passes Completed: 324 — Willie Totten, Mississippi Valley, 1984
Most Passes Completed per Game: 32.4 — Willie Totten, Mississippi Valley, 1984
Highest Completion Percentage: 70.6 — Giovanni Carmazzi, Hofstra, 1997
Most Yards Gained: 4,863 — Steve McNair, Alcorn St, 1994
Most Yards Gained per Game: 455.7 — Willie Totten, Mississippi Valley, 1984

RECEIVING

Most Passes Caught: 115 — Brian Forster, Rhode Island, 1985
Most Yards Gained: 1,712 — Eddie Conti, Delaware, 1998
Most Yards Gained per Game: 168.2 — Jerry Rice, Mississippi Valley, 1984
Highest Average Gain per Reception: 28.9 — Mikhael Ricks, Stephen F. Austin, 1997; (min. 35 receptions)

Single Game

SCORING

Most Points Scored: 42 — Jesse Burton, McNeese St, 1998 (vs Southern Utah); Archie Amerson, Northern Arizona, 1996 (vs Weber St)
Most Field Goals: 8 — Goran Lingmerth, Northern Arizona, 1986 (vs Idaho)

RUSHING

Most Yards Gained: 409 — Charles Roberts, Cal St–Northridge, 1999 (vs Idaho St)
Most Touchdowns Rushed: 7 — Archie Amerson, Northern Arizona, 1996 (vs Weber St)

PASSING

Most Passes Completed: 48 — Clayton Millis, Cal St–Northridge, 1995 (vs St Mary's [CA])
Most Yards Gained: 649 — Steve McNair, Alcorn St, 1994 (vs Southern–BR)
Most Touchdown Passes: 9 — Willie Totten, Mississippi Valley, 1984 (vs Kentucky St)

RECEIVING

Most Passes Caught: 24 — Jerry Rice, Mississippi Valley, 1983 (vs Southern–BR)
Most Yards Gained: 370 — Michael Lerch, Princeton, 1991 (vs Brown)
Most Touchdown Catches: 5 — Five players, most recently by Sylvester Morris, Jackson St, 1998 (vs Grambling)

NCAA Division II Individual Records

Career

SCORING

Most Points Scored: 544 — Brian Shay, Emporia St, 1995–98
Most Touchdowns Scored: 88 — Brian Shay, Emporia St, 1995–98
Most Touchdowns Scored, Rushing: 81 — Brian Shay, Emporia St, 1995–98
Most Touchdowns Scored, Passing: 116 — Chris Hatcher, Valdosta St, 1991–94
Most Touchdowns Scored, Receiving: 49 — Bruce Cerone, Yankton/Emporia St, 1965–69

RUSHING

Most Rushes: 1,072 — Bernie Peeters, Luther, 1968–71
Most Rushes per Game: 29.8 — Bernie Peeters, Luther, 1968–71
Most Yards Gained: 6,958 — Brian Shay, Emporia St, 1995–98
Most Yards Gained per Game: 183.4 — Anthony Gray, Western NM, 1997–98

Career *(Cont.)*

PASSING

Highest Passing Efficiency Rating: 167.0 — Wilkie Perez, Glenville St, 1997–98
Most Passes Attempted: 1,719 — Bob McLaughlin, Lock Haven, 1992–95
Most Passes Completed: 1,001 — Chris Hatcher, Valdosta St, 1991–94
Most Passes Completed per Game: 25.7 — Chris Hatcher, Valdosta St, 1991–94
Highest Completion Percentage: 69.6 — Chris Peterson, UC-Davis, 1985–86
Most Yards Gained: 10,878 — Chris Hatcher, Valdosta St, 1991–94
Most Yards Gained per Game: 312.1 — Grady Benton, West Texas A&M, 1994–95

RECEIVING

Most Passes Caught: 262 — Carlos Ferralls, Glenville St, 1994–97
Most Yards Gained: 4,468 — James Roe, Norfolk St, 1992–95
Most Yards Gained per Game: 160.8 — Chris George, Glenville St, 1993–94
Highest Average Gain per Reception: 22.8 — Tyrone Johnson, Western St (CO), 1990–93

Single Season

SCORING

Most Points Scored: 198 — Brian Shay, Emporia St, 1997
Most Touchdowns Scored: 32 — Brian Shay, Emporia St, 1997
Most Touchdowns Scored, Rushing: 29 — Brian Shay, Emporia St, 1997 and 1998; Kavin Gailliard, American Int'l, 1999
Most Touchdowns Scored, Passing: 50 — Chris Hatcher, Valdosta St, 1994
Most Touchdowns Scored, Receiving: 21 — Kevin Ingram, West Chester, 1998; Chris Perry, Adams St, 1995

RUSHING

Most Rushes: 385 — Joe Gough, Wayne St (MI), 1994
Most Rushes per Game: 38.6 — Mark Perkins, Hobart, 1968
Most Yards Gained: 2,455 — Kavin Gailliard, American Int'l, 1999
Most Yards Gained per Game: 223.2 — Kavin Gailliard, American Int'l, 1999

PASSING

Highest Passing Efficiency Rating: 210.1 — Boyd Crawford, College of Idaho, 1953
Most Passes Attempted: 544 — Lance Funderburk, Valdosta St, 1995
Most Passes Completed: 356 — Lance Funderburk, Valdosta St, 1995
Most Passes Completed per Game: 32.4 — Lance Funderburk, Valdosta St, 1995
Highest Completion Percentage: 74.7 — Chris Hatcher, Valdosta St, 1994
Most Yards Gained: 4,189 — Wilkie Perez, Glenville St, 1997
Most Yards Gained per Game: 393.4 — Grady Benton, W Texas A&M, 1994

RECEIVING

Most Passes Caught: 119 — Brad Bailey, W Texas A&M, 1994
Most Yards Gained: 1,876 — Chris George, Glenville St, 1993
Most Yards Gained per Game: 187.6 — Chris George, Glenville St, 1993
Highest Average Gain per Reception: 32.5 — Tyrone Johnson, Western St, 1991 (min. 30 receptions)

Single Game

SCORING

Most Points Scored: 48 — Paul Zaeske, N Park, 1968 (vs N Central); Junior Wolf, Panhandle St, 1958 (vs St Mary [KS])
Most Field Goals: 6 — Steve Huff, Central Missouri St, 1985 (vs SE Missouri St)

RUSHING

Most Yards Gained: 403 — Rob Davidson, Fairmont St, 1998 (vs Concord)
Most Touchdowns Rushed: 8 — Junior Wolf, Panhandle St, 1958 (vs St Mary [KS])

PASSING

Most Passes Completed: 56 — Jarrod DeGeorgia, Wayne St (NE), 1996 (vs Drake)
Most Yards Gained: 642 — Wilkie Perez, Glenville St, 1997, (vs Concord)
Most Touchdowns Passed: 10 — Bruce Swanson, N Park, 1968 (vs N Central)

RECEIVING

Most Passes Caught: 23 — Chris George, Glenville St, 1994 (vs W VA Wesleyan); Barry Wagner, Alabama A&M, 1989 (vs Clark Atlanta)
Most Yards Gained: 401 — Kevin Ingram, West Chester, 1998 (vs Clarion)
Most Touchdown Catches: 8 — Paul Zaeske, N Park, 1968 (vs N Central)

NCAA Division III Individual Records

Career

SCORING

Most Points Scored: 528 — Carey Bender, Coe, 1991–94
Most Touchdowns Scored: 86 — Carey Bender, Coe, 1991–94
Most Touchdowns Scored, Rushing: 76 — Joe Dudek, Plymouth St, 1982–85
Most Touchdowns Scored, Passing: 148 — Justin Peery, Westminster (MO), 1996–99
Most Touchdowns Scored, Receiving: 72 — Scott Pingel, Westminster (MO), 1996–99

RUSHING

Most Rushes: 1,190 — Steve Tardif, Maine Maritime, 1996–99
Most Rushes per Game: 32.7 — Chris Sizemore, Bridgewater (VA), 1972–74
Most Yards Gained: 6,125 — Carey Bender, Coe, 1991–94
Most Yards Gained per Game: 175.1 — Ricky Gales, Simpson, 1988–89

PASSING

Highest Passing Efficiency Rating: 194.2 — Bill Borchert, Mt Union, 1994–97
Most Passes Attempted: 1,696 — Kirk Baumgartner, WI–Stevens Point, 1986–89
Most Passes Completed: 1,012 — Justin Peery, Westminster (MO), 1996–99
Most Passes Completed per Game: 25.9 — Justin Peery, Westminster (MO), 1996–99
Highest Completion Percentage: 66.5 — Bill Borchert, Mt Union (OH) 1994–97
Most Yards Gained: 13,262 — Justin Peery, Westminster (MO), 1996–99
Most Yards Gained per Game: 340.1 — Justin Peery, Westminster (MO), 1996–99

RECEIVING

Most Passes Caught: 436 — Scott Pingel, Westminster (MO), 1996–99
Most Yards Gained: 6,108 — Scott Pingel, Westminster (MO), 1996–99
Most Yards Gained per Game: 156.6 — Scott Pingel, Westminster (MO), 1996–99
Highest Average Gain per Reception: 22.9 — Kirk Aikens, Hartwick, 1995–98

Single Season

SCORING

Most Points Scored: 206 — R. J. Bowers, Grove City, 1998
Most Points Scored per Game: 20.8 — James Regan, Pomona-Pitzer, 1997
Most Touchdowns Scored: 34 — R. J. Bowers, Grove City, 1998
Most Touchdowns Scored, Rushing: 34 — R. J. Bowers, Grove City, 1998
Most Touchdowns Scored, Passing: 54 — Justin Peery, Westminster (MO), 1999
Most Touchdowns Scored, Receiving: 26 — Scott Pingel, Westminster (MO), 1998

RUSHING

Most Rushes: 380 — Mike Birosak, Dickinson, 1989
Most Rushes per Game: 38.0 — Mike Birosak, Dickinson, 1989
Most Yards Gained: 2,385 — Dante Brown, Marietta, 1996

PASSING

Highest Passing Efficiency Rating: 225.0 — Mike Simpson, Eureka, 1994
Most Passes Attempted: 527 — Kirk Baumgartner, WI–Stevens Point, 1988
Most Passes Completed: 329 — Justin Peery, Westminster (MO), 1999
Most Passes Completed per Game: 32.9 — Justin Peery, Westminster (MO), 1999
Highest Completion Percentage: 73.4 — Mike Simpson, Eureka, 1994
Most Yards Gained: 4,501 — Justin Peery, Westminster (MO), 1998
Most Yards Gained per Game: 450.1 — Justin Peery, Westminster (MO), 1998

RECEIVING

Most Passes Caught: 136 — Scott Pingel, Westminster (MO), 1999
Most Yards Gained: 2,157 — Scott Pingel, Westminster, (MO), 1998
Most Yards Gained per Game: 215.7 — Scott Pingel, Westminster, (MO), 1998
Highest Average Gain per Reception: 26.9 — Marty Redlawsk, Concordia (IL), 1985

Single Game

SCORING

Most Field Goals: 6 — Jim Hever, Rhodes, 1984 (vs Millsaps)

PASSING

Most Passes Completed: 50 — Justin Peery, Westminster (MO), 1998 (vs MacMurray); Tim Lynch, Hofstra, 1991 (vs Fordham)
Most Yards Gained: 619 — Justin Peery, Westminster (MO), 1998 (vs MacMurray)
Most Touchdowns Passed: 9 — Joe Zarlinga, Ohio Northern, 1998 (vs Capital)

RUSHING

Most Yards Gained: 441 — Dante Brown, Marietta, 1996 (vs Baldwin-Wallace)
Most Touchdowns Rushed: 8 — Carey Bender, Coe, 1994 (vs Beloit)

RECEIVING

Most Passes Caught: 23 — Sean Munroe, Mass-Boston, 1992 (vs Mass-Maritime)
Most Yards Gained: 397 — Matt Eisenberg, Juniata, 1999 (vs Widener)
Most Touchdown Catches: 7 — Matt Perceval, Wesleyan (Conn), 1998 (vs Middlebury)

Career

Scoring

POINTS (KICKERS)

	Years	Pts
Roman Anderson, Houston	1988–91	423
Carlos Huerta, Miami (FL)	1988–91	397
Jason Elam, Hawaii	1988–92	395
Derek Schmidt, Florida St	1984–87	393
Kris Brown, Nebraska	1995–98	388

POINTS (NON-KICKERS)

	Years	Pts
Travis Prentice, Miami (OH)	1996–99	468
Ricky Williams, Texas	1995–98	452
Anthony Thompson, Indiana	1986–89	394
Ron Dayne, Wisconsin	1996–99	378
Marshall Faulk, San Diego St	1991–93	376

POINTS PER GAME (NON-KICKERS)

	Years	Pts/Game
Marshall Faulk, San Diego St	1991–93	12.1
Ed Marinaro, Cornell	1969–71	11.8
Bill Burnett, Arkansas	1968–70	11.3
Steve Owens, Oklahoma	1967–69	11.2
Eddie Talboom, Wyoming	1948–50	10.8

Total Offense

YARDS GAINED

	Years	Yds
Ty Detmer, Brigham Young	1988–91	14,665
Tim Rattay, Louisiana Tech	1997–99	12,618
Chris Redman, Louisville	1996–99	12,129
Doug Flutie, Boston College	1981–84	11,317
Tim Lester, Western Michigan	1996–99	11,081

YARDS PER GAME

	Years	Yds/Game
Tim Rattay, Louisiana Tech	1997–99	382.4
Chris Vargas, Nevada	1992–93	320.9
Ty Detmer, Brigham Young	1988–91	318.8
Daunte Culpepper, C Florida	1996–98	313.5
Mike Perez, San Jose St	1986–87	309.1

Rushing

YARDS GAINED

	Years	Yds
Ron Dayne, Wisconsin	1996–99	6,397
Ricky Williams, Texas	1995–98	6,279
Tony Dorsett, Pittsburgh	1973–76	6,082
Charles White, Southern Cal	1976–79	5,598
Travis Prentice, Miami (OH)	1996–99	5,596

YARDS PER GAME

	Years	Yds/Game
Ed Marinaro, Cornell	1969–71	174.6
O.J. Simpson, Southern Cal	1967–68	164.4
Herschel Walker, Georgia	1980–82	159.4
LeShon Johnson, N Illinois	1992–93	150.6
Ron Dayne, Wisconsin	1996–99	148.8

TOUCHDOWNS RUSHING

	Years	TD
Travis Prentice, Miami (OH)	1996–99	73
Ricky Williams, Texas	1995–98	72
Anthony Thompson, Indiana	1986–89	64
Ron Dayne, Wisconsin	1996–99	63
Marshall Faulk, San Diego St	1991–93	57

Passing

PASSING EFFICIENCY

	Years	Rating
Danny Wuerffel, Florida	1993–96	163.6
Ty Detmer, Brigham Young	1988–91	162.7
Steve Sarkisian, Brigham Young	1995–96	162.0
Billy Blanton, San Diego St	1993–96	157.1
Jim McMahon, Brigham Young	1977–78, 80–81	156.9

Note: Minimum 500 completions.

YARDS GAINED

	Years	Yds
Ty Detmer, Brigham Young	1988–91	15,031
Tim Rattay, Louisiana Tech	1997–99	12,746
Chris Redman, Louisville	1996–99	12,541
Todd Santos, San Diego St	1984–87	11,425
Tim Lester, Western Michigan	1997–99	11,299

Note: Minimum 500 completions.

COMPLETIONS

	Years	Comp
Chris Redman, Louisville	1996–99	1,031
Tim Rattay, Louisiana Tech	1997–99	1,015
Ty Detmer, Brigham Young	1988–91	958
Todd Santos, San Diego St	1984–87	910
Brian McClure, Bowling Green	1982–85	900

Note: Minimum 500 completions.

TOUCHDOWNS PASSING

	Years	TD
Ty Detmer, Brigham Young	1988–91	121
Tim Rattay, Louisiana Tech	1997–99	115
Danny Wuerffel, Florida	1993–96	114
Chad Pennington, Marshall	1997–99	100
David Klingler, Houston	1988–91	92

Receiving

CATCHES

	Years	No.
Trevor Insley, Nevada	1996–99	298
Geoff Noisy, Nevada	1995–98	295
Troy Edwards, Louisiana Tech	1996–99	280
Aaron Turner, Pacific	1989–92	266
Chad Mackey, Louisiana Tech	1993–96	264

CATCHES PER GAME

	Years	No./Game
Emmanuel Hazard, Houston	1989–90	10.5
Alex Van Dyke, Nevada	1994–95	10.3
Howard Twilley, Tulsa	1963–65	10.0
Jason Phillips, Houston	1987–88	9.4
Troy Edwards, Louisiana Tech	1996–98	8.2
Bryan Reeves, Nevada	1992–93	8.2

YARDS GAINED

	Years	Yds
Trevor Insley, Nevada	1996–99	5,005
Marcus Harris, Wyoming	1993–96	4,518
Ryan Yarborough, Wyoming	1990–93	4,357
Troy Edwards, Louisiana Tech	1996–98	4,352
Aaron Turner, Pacific	1989–92	4,345

TOUCHDOWN CATCHES

	Years	TD
Troy Edwards, Louisiana Tech	1996–98	50
Aaron Turner, Pacific	1989–92	43
Ryan Yarborough, Wyoming	1990–93	42
Marcus Harris, Wyoming	1993–96	38
Clarkston Hines, Duke	1986–89	38

Career (Cont.)

All-Purpose Running

YARDS GAINED	Years	Yds
Ricky Williams, Texas	1996–98	7,206
Napoleon McCallum, Navy	1981–85	7,172
Darrin Nelson, Stanford	1977–78, 80–81	6,885
Kevin Faulk, Louisiana St	1995–98	6,833
Ron Dayne, Wisconsin	1996–99	6,701
Terance Mathis, New Mexico	1985–87, 89	6,691

YARDS PER GAME	Years	Yds/Game
Ryan Benjamin, Pacific	1990–92	237.8
Sheldon Canley, San Jose St	1988–90	205.8
Howard Stevens, Louisville	1971–72	193.7
O.J. Simpson, Southern Cal	1967–68	192.9
Alex Van Dyke, Nevada	1994–95	188.5

THEY SAID IT

Bobby Bowden, Florida State football coach, on his players' legal problems in 1999:
"When it rains, it snows."

Interceptions

PLAYER/SCHOOL	Years	Int
Al Brosky, Illinois	1950–52	29
John Provost, Holy Cross	1972–74	27
Martin Bayless, Bowling Green	1980–83	27
Tom Curtis, Michigan	1967–69	25
Tony Thurman, Boston Col	1981–84	25
Tracy Saul, Texas Tech	1989–92	25

Punting Average

PLAYER/SCHOOL	Years	Avg
Todd Sauerbrun, W Virginia	1991–94	46.3
Reggie Roby, Iowa	1979–82	45.6
Greg Montgomery, Michigan St	1985–87	45.4
Tom Tupa, Ohio St	1984–87	45.2
Barry Helton, Colorado	1984–87	44.9

Note: At least 150 punts.

Punt Return Average

PLAYER/SCHOOL	Years	Avg
Jack Mitchell, Oklahoma	1946–48	23.6
Gene Gibson, Cincinnati	1949–50	20.5
Eddie Macon, Pacific	1949–51	18.9
Jackie Robinson, UCLA	1939–40	18.8
Mike Fuller, Auburn	1972–74	17.7
Bobby Dillon, Texas	1949–51	17.7

Note: At least 1.2 punt returns per game.

Kickoff Return Average

PLAYER/SCHOOL	Years	Avg
Anthony Davis, Southern Cal	1972–74	35.1
Eric Booth, Southern Miss	1994–97	32.4
Overton Curtis, Utah St	1957–58	31.0
Fred Montgomery, New Mexico St	1991–92	30.5
Altie Taylor, Utah St	1966–68	29.3
Stan Brown, Purdue	1968–70	28.8

Note: At least 1.2 kickoff returns per game. Min. 30 returns.

Single Season

Scoring

POINTS	Year	Pts
Barry Sanders, Oklahoma St	1988	234
Troy Edwards, Louisiana Tech	1998	188
Mike Rozier, Nebraska	1983	174
Lydell Mitchell, Penn St	1971	174
Ricky Williams, Texas	1998	168

FIELD GOALS	Year	FG
John Lee, UCLA	1984	29
Paul Woodside, W Virginia	1982	28
Luis Zendejas, Arizona St	1983	28
Fuad Reveiz, Tennessee	1982	27

Four tied with 25.

All-Purpose Running

YARDS GAINED	Year	Yds
Barry Sanders, Oklahoma St	1988	3,250
Ryan Benjamin, Pacific	1991	2,995
Mike Pringle, Fullerton St	1989	2,690
Paul Palmer, Temple	1986	2,633
Ryan Benjamin, Pacific	1992	2,597

All-Purpose Running (Cont.)

YARDS PER GAME	Year	Yds/Game
Barry Sanders, Oklahoma St	1988	295.5
Ryan Benjamin, Pacific	1991	249.6
Byron (Whizzer) White, Colorado	1937	246.3
Mike Pringle, Fullerton St	1989	244.6
Paul Palmer, Temple	1986	239.4

Total Offense

YARDS GAINED	Year	Yds
David Klingler, Houston	1990	5,221
Ty Detmer, Brigham Young	1990	5,022
Tim Rattay, Louisiana Tech	1998	4,840
Andre Ware, Houston	1989	4,661
Jim McMahon, Brigham Young	1980	4,627
Ty Detmer, Brigham Young	1989	4,433

YARDS PER GAME	Year	Yds/Game
David Klingler, Houston	1990	474.6
Andre Ware, Houston	1989	423.7
Ty Detmer, Brigham Young	1990	418.5
Tim Rattay, Louisiana Tech	1998	403.3

Single Season *(Cont.)*

Rushing

YARDS GAINED

	Year	Yds
Barry Sanders, Oklahoma St	1988	2,628
Marcus Allen, Southern Cal	1981	2,342
Troy Davis, Iowa St	1996	2,185
Mike Rozier, Nebraska	1983	2,148
Ricky Williams, Texas	1998	2,124

YARDS PER GAME

	Year	Yds/Game
Barry Sanders, Oklahoma St	1988	238.9
Marcus Allen, Southern Cal	1981	212.9
Ed Marinaro, Cornell	1971	209.0
Troy Davis, Iowa St	1996	198.6
Ricky Williams, Texas	1998	193.1

TOUCHDOWNS RUSHING

	Year	TD
Barry Sanders, Oklahoma St	1988	37
Mike Rozier, Nebraska	1983	29
Ricky Williams, Texas	1998	27

Four tied with 24.

Passing

PASSING EFFICIENCY

	Year	Rating
Shaun King, Tulane	1998	183.3
Michael Vick, Virginia Tech	1999	180.4
Danny Wuerffel, Florida	1995	178.4
Jim McMahon, Brigham Young	1980	176.9
Ty Detmer, Brigham Young	1989	175.6

Passing *(Cont.)*

YARDS GAINED

	Year	Yds
Ty Detmer, Brigham Young	1990	5,188
David Klingler, Houston	1990	5,140
Andre Ware, Houston	1989	4,699
Tim Rattay, Louisiana Tech	1998	4,943
Jim McMahon, Brigham Young	1980	4,571

COMPLETIONS

	Year	Att	Comp
Tim Couch, Kentucky	1998	553	400
Tim Rattay, Louisiana Tech	1998	559	380
David Klingler, Houston	1990	643	374
Andre Ware, Houston	1989	578	365
Tim Couch, Kentucky	1997	547	363

TOUCHDOWNS PASSING

	Year	TD
David Klingler, Houston	1990	54
Jim McMahon, Brigham Young	1980	47
Andre Ware, Houston	1989	46
Tim Rattay, Louisiana Tech	1998	46
Ty Detmer, Brigham Young	1990	41

Receiving

CATCHES

	Year	GP	No.
Emmanuel Hazard, Houston	1989	11	142
Troy Edwards, Louisiana Tech	1998	12	140
Howard Twilley, Tulsa	1965	10	134
Trevor Insley, Nevada	1999	11	134
Alex Van Dyke, Nevada	1995	11	129

CATCHES PER GAME

	Year	No.	No./Game
Howard Twilley, Tulsa	1965	134	13.4
Emmanuel Hazard, Houston	1989	142	12.9
Trevor Insley, Nevada	1999	134	12.2
Troy Edwards, Louisiana Tech	1998	140	11.7
Alex Van Dyke, Nevada	1995	129	11.7

YARDS GAINED

	Year	Yds
Trevor Insley, Nevada	1999	2,060
Troy Edwards, Louisiana Tech	1998	1,996
Alex Van Dyke, Nevada	1995	1,854
Howard Twilley, Tulsa	1965	1,779
Troy Edwards, Louisiana Tech	1997	1,707

TOUCHDOWN CATCHES

	Year	TD
Troy Edwards, Louisiana Tech	1998	27
Randy Moss, Marshall	1997	25
Emmanuel Hazard, Houston	1989	22
Desmond Howard, Michigan	1991	19

Five tied with 18.

Single Game

Scoring

POINTS

	Opponent	Year	Pts
Howard Griffith, Illinois	Southern Illinois	1990	48
Marshall Faulk, San Diego St	Pacific	1991	44
Jim Brown, Syracuse	Colgate	1956	43
Showboat Boykin, Mississippi	Mississippi St	1951	42
Fred Wendt, UTEP*	New Mexico St	1948	42

*UTEP was Texas Mines in 1948.

FIELD GOALS

	Opponent	Year	FG
Dale Klein, Nebraska	Missouri	1985	7
Mike Prindle, Western Michigan	Marshall	1984	7

Note: Klein's distances were 32-22-43-44-29-43-43.
Prindle's distances were 32-44-42-23-48-41-27.

Single Game (Cont.)

Total Offense

YARDS GAINED	Opponent	Year	Yds
David Klingler, Houston ...Arizona St		1990	732
Matt Vogler,			
Texas Christian ....Houston		1990	696
David Klingler, Houston ...Texas Christian		1990	625
Scott Mitchell, Utah..........Air Force		1988	625
Jimmy Klingler, Houston...Rice		1992	612

Passing

YARDS GAINED	Opponent	Year	Yds
David Klingler, Houston ...Arizona St		1990	716
Matt Vogler,			
Texas Christian ....Houston		1990	690
Scott Mitchell, Utah..........Air Force		1988	631
Jeremy Leach,			
New Mexico ....Utah		1989	622
Dave Wilson, Illinois ....Ohio St		1980	621

COMPLETIONS	Opponent	Year	Comp
Drew Brees, Purdue.................Wisconsin		1998	55
Rusty LaRue, Wake Forest.......Duke		1995	55
Rusty LaRue, Wake Forest.......NC St		1995	50
David Klingler, Houston ....SMU		1990	48
Tim Couch, Kentucky...............Arkansas		1998	47

TOUCHDOWNS PASSING	Opponent	Year	TD
David Klingler, Houston...........E. Wash		1990	11

Note: Klingler's TD passes were 5-48-29-7-3-7-40-10-7-8-51.

Rushing

YARDS GAINED	Opponent	Year	Yds
LaDainian Tomlinson ....UTEP		1999	406
Texas Christian			
Tony Sands, Kansas........Missouri		1991	396
Marshall Faulk,			
San Diego St....................Pacific		1991	386
Troy Davis, Iowa St...........Missouri		1996	378
Anthony Thompson,			
Indiana.............................Wisconsin		1989	377

TOUCHDOWNS RUSHING	Opponent	Year	TD
Howard Griffith, Illinois .....Southern Illinois		1990	8

Note: Griffith's TD runs were 5-51-7-41-5-18-5-3.

Receiving

CATCHES	Opponent	Year	No.
Randy Gatewood, UNLV.....Idaho		1994	23
Jay Miller, Brigham Young ..New Mexico		1973	22
Troy Edwards, La. Tech......Nebraska		1998	21
Chris Daniels, Purdue ....Michigan St		1999	21
Rick Eber, Tulsa ....Idaho St		1967	20

YARDS GAINED	Opponent	Year	Yds
Troy Edwards,Louisiana Tech...Nebraska		1998	405
Randy Gatewood, UNLV.........Idaho		1994	363
Chuck Hughes, UTEP*............N Texas St		1965	349
Rick Eber, Tulsa ....Idaho St		1967	322
Harry Wood, Tulsa..................Idaho St		1967	318

*UTEP was Texas Western in 1965.

TOUCHDOWN CATCHES	Opponent	Year	TD
Tim Delaney, San Diego St ....New Mexico St		1969	6

Note: Delaney's TD catches were 2-22-34-31-30-9.

Longest Plays (since 1941)

PASSING	Opponent	Year	Yds
Fred Owens to Jack Ford,			
Portland..................................St Mary's (CA)		1947	99
Bo Burris to Warren			
McVea, Houston ....Washington St		1966	99
Colin Clapton to Eddie			
Jenkins, Holy Cross ....Boston U		1970	99
Terry Peel to Robert Ford,			
Houston..................................Syracuse		1970	99
Terry Peel to Robert Ford,			
Houston..................................San Diego St		1972	99
Cris Collinsworth to Derrick			
Gaffney, Florida ....Rice		1977	99
Scott Ankrom to James			
Maness, Texas Christian.......Rice		1984	99
Gino Toretta to Horace			
Copeland, Miami...................Arkansas		1991	99
John Paci to Thomas Lewis,			
Indiana..................................Penn St		1993	99
Troy DeGar to Wes Caswell,			
Tulsa ....Oklahoma		1996	99
Drew Brees to Vinny Sutherland,			
Purdue ....Northwestern		1999	99

RUSHING	Opponent	Year	Yd
Gale Sayers, Kansas ....Nebraska		1963	99
Max Anderson, Arizona St ....Wyoming		1967	99
Ralph Thompson,			
W Texas St............................Wichita St		1970	99
Kelsey Finch, Tennessee......Florida		1977	99

FIELD GOALS	Opponent	Year	Yds
Steve Little, Arkansas.............Texas		1977	67
Russell Erxleben, Texas.........Rice		1977	67
Joe Williams, Wichita St ....Southern IL		1978	67
Martin Gramatica, Kansas St .Northern IL		1998	65
Tony Franklin, Texas A&M .....Baylor		1976	65
Tony Franklin, Texas A&M .....Baylor		1976	64

PUNTS	Opponent	Year	Yds
Pat Brady, Nevada* ....Loyola (CA)		1950	99
George O'Brien, Wisconsin....Iowa		1952	96
John Hadl, Kansas.................Oklahoma		1959	94
Carl Knox, Texas Christian.....Oklahoma St		1947	94
Preston Johnson, SMU..........Pittsburgh		1940	94

*Nevada was Nevada-Reno in 1950.

DIVISION I-A WINNINGEST TEAMS
Alltime Winning Percentage

	Yrs	W	L	T	Pct	GP	Bowl Record
Notre Dame	111	767	237	42	.753	1,046	13-10-0
Michigan	120	796	259	36	.746	1,091	15-15-0
Alabama	105	734	268	43	.723	1,045	28-19-3
Nebraska	110	743	297	40	.706	1,080	19-19-0
Ohio St	110	716	283	53	.705	1,052	14-17-0
Texas	107	735	299	33	.704	1,067	18-19-2
Oklahoma	105	689	278	53	.701	1,020	20-12-1
Penn St	113	734	305	41	.698	1,080	23-11-2
Tennessee	103	699	288	52	.697	1,039	22-18-0
Southern Cal	107	673	281	54	.694	1,008	25-14-0
Florida St	53	381	183	17	.670	581	17-9-2
Boise St	32	241	127	2	.654	370	1-0-0
Miami (OH)	111	591	327	44	.637	962	5-2-0
Washington	110	606	335	50	.637	991	13-12-1
Georgia	106	633	358	54	.632	1,045	18-14-3
Central Michigan	99	510	292	36	.630	838	0-2-0
Arizona St	87	484	283	24	.627	791	10-7-1
Louisiana St	106	610	356	47	.625	1013	14-16-1
Army	110	617	364	51	.623	1,032	2-2-0
Auburn	107	601	361	47	.619	1,009	14-10-2
Colorado	110	608	368	36	.619	1,012	11-12-0
Miami (FL)	73	461	281	19	.618	761	13-11-0
Florida	93	554	344	40	.612	938	12-14-0
Texas A&M	105	602	381	48	.607	1,031	12-13-0
Syracuse	110	632	406	49	.604	1,087	11-8-1

Note: Includes bowl games.

Alltime Victories

Michigan	796	Georgia	633	Georgia Tech	592
Notre Dame	767	Syracuse	632	Miami (OH)	591
Nebraska	743	Army	617	Pittsburgh	589
Texas	735	Louisiana St	610	Arkansas	588
Alabama	734	Colorado	608	Minnesota	581
Penn St	734	Washington	606	Navy	578
Ohio St	716	Texas A&M	602	Virginia Tech	568
Tennessee	699	Auburn	601	Clemson	562
Oklahoma	689	W Virginia	596	Michigan St	556
Southern Cal	673	N Carolina	594	California	555

NUMBER ONE VS NUMBER TWO

The No. 1 and No. 2 teams, according to the Associated Press Poll, have met 33 times, including 13 bowl games, since the poll's inception in 1936. The No. 1 teams have a 20-11-2 record in these matchups. Notre Dame (4-3-2) has played in nine of the games.

Date	Results	Stadium
10-9-43	No. 1 Notre Dame 35, No. 2 Michigan 12	Michigan (Ann Arbor)
11-20-43	No. 1 Notre Dame 14, No. 2 Iowa Pre-Flight 13	Notre Dame (South Bend)
12-2-44	No. 1 Army 23, No. 2 Navy 7	Municipal (Baltimore)
11-10-45	No. 1 Army 48, No. 2 Notre Dame 0	Yankee (New York
12-1-45	No. 1 Army 32, No. 2 Navy 13	Municipal (Philadelphia)
11-9-46	No. 1 Army 0, No. 2 Notre Dame 0	Yankee (New York)
1-1-63	No. 1 Southern Cal 42, No. 2 Wisconsin 37 (Rose Bowl)	Rose Bowl (Pasadena)
10-12-63	No. 2 Texas 28, No. 1 Oklahoma 7	Cotton Bowl (Dallas)
1-1-64	No. 1 Texas 28, No. 2 Navy 6 (Cotton Bowl)	Cotton Bowl (Dallas)
11-19-66	No. 1 Notre Dame 10, No. 2 Michigan St 10	Spartan (East Lansing)
9-28-68	No. 1 Purdue 37, No. 2 Notre Dame 22	Notre Dame (South Bend)
1-1-69	No. 1 Ohio St 27, No. 2 Southern Cal 16 (Rose Bowl)	Rose Bowl (Pasadena)
12-6-69	No. 1 Texas 15, No. 2 Arkansas 14	Razorback (Fayetteville)
11-25-71	No. 1 Nebraska 35, No. 2 Oklahoma 31	Owen Field (Norman)
1-1-72	No. 1 Nebraska 38, No. 2 Alabama 6 (Orange Bowl)	Orange Bowl (Miami)
1-1-79	No. 2 Alabama 14, No. 1 Penn St 7 (Sugar Bowl)	Sugar Bowl (New Orleans)
9-26-81	No. 1 Southern Cal 28, No. 2 Oklahoma 24	Coliseum (Los Angeles)
1-1-83	No. 2 Penn St 27, No. 1 Georgia 23 (Sugar Bowl)	Sugar Bowl (New Orleans)

NUMBER ONE VS NUMBER TWO *(Cont.)*

Date	Results	Stadium
10-19-85	No. 1 Iowa 12, No. 2 Michigan 10	Kinnick (Iowa City)
9-27-86	No. 2 Miami (FL) 28, No. 1 Oklahoma 16	Orange Bowl (Miami)
1-2-87	No. 2 Penn St 14, No. 1 Miami (FL) 10 (Fiesta Bowl)	Sun Devil (Tempe)
11-21-87	No. 2 Oklahoma 17, No. 1 Nebraska 7	Memorial (Lincoln)
1-1-88	No. 2 Miami (FL) 20, No. 1 Oklahoma 14 (Orange Bowl)	Orange Bowl (Miami)
11-26-88	No. 1 Notre Dame 27, No. 2 Southern Cal 10	Coliseum (Los Angeles)
9-16-89	No. 1 Notre Dame 24, No. 2 Michigan 19	Michigan (Ann Arbor)
11-16-91	No. 2 Miami (FL) 17, No. 1 Florida St 16	Campbell (Tallahassee)
1-1-93	No. 2 Alabama 34, No. 1 Miami (FL) 13 (Sugar Bowl)	Superdome (New Orleans)
11-13-93	No. 2 Notre Dame 31, No. 1 Florida St 24	Notre Dame (South Bend)
1-1-94	No. 1 Florida St 18, No. 2 Nebraska 16 (Orange Bowl)	Orange Bowl (Miami)
1-2-96	No. 1 Nebraska 62, No. 2 Florida 24 (Fiesta Bowl)	Sun Devil (Tempe)
11-30-96	No. 2 Florida St 24, No. 1 Florida 21	Campbell (Tallahassee)
1-4-99	No. 1 Tennessee 23, No. 2 Florida St 16 (Fiesta Bowl)	Sun Devil (Tempe)
1-4-00	No. 1 Florida St 46, No. 2 Virginia Tech 29 (Sugar Bowl)	Superdome (New Orleans)

LONGEST DIVISION I-A WINNING STREAKS

Wins	Team	Yrs	Ended by	Score
47	Oklahoma	1953–57	Notre Dame	7–0
39	Washington	1908–14	Oregon St	0–0
37	Yale	1890–93	Princeton	6–0
37	Yale	1887–89	Princeton	10–0
35	Toledo	1969–71	Tampa	21–0
34	Pennsylvania	1894–96	Lafayette	6–4
31	Oklahoma	1948–50	Kentucky	13–7
31	Pittsburgh	1914–18	Cleveland Naval Reserve	10–9
31	Pennsylvania	1896–98	Harvard	10–0
30	Texas	1968–70	Notre Dame	24–11

LONGEST DIVISION I-A UNBEATEN STREAKS

No.	W	T	Team	Yrs	Ended by	Score
63	59	4	Washington	1907–17	California	27–0
56	55	1	Michigan	1901–05	Chicago	2–0
50	46	4	California	1920–25	Olympic Club	15–0
48	47	1	Oklahoma	1953–57	Notre Dame	7–0
48	47	1	Yale	1885–89	Princeton	10–0
47	42	5	Yale	1879–85	Princeton	6–5
44	42	2	Yale	1894–96	Princeton	24–6
42	39	3	Yale	1904–08	Harvard	4–0
39	37	2	Notre Dame	1946–50	Purdue	28–14
37	36	1	Oklahoma	1972–75	Kansas	23–3
37	37	0	Yale	1890–93	Princeton	6–0
35	35	0	Toledo	1969–71	Tampa	21–0
35	34	1	Minnesota	1903–05	Wisconsin	16–12
34	33	1	Nebraska	1912–16	Kansas	7–3
34	34	0	Pennsylvania	1894–96	Lafayette	6–4
34	32	2	Princeton	1884–87	Harvard	12–0
34	29	5	Princeton	1877–82	Harvard	1–0
33	30	3	Tennessee	1926–30	Alabama	18–6
33	31	2	Georgia Tech	1914–18	Pittsburgh	32–0
33	30	3	Harvard	1911–15	Cornell	10–0
32	31	1	Nebraska	1969–71	UCLA	20–17
32	30	2	Army	1944–47	Columbia	21–20
32	31	1	Harvard	1898–1900	Yale	28–0
31	30	1	Alabama	1991–93	Louisiana St	17–13
31	30	1	Penn St	1967–70	Colorado	41–13
31	30	1	San Diego St	1967–70	Long Beach St	27–11
31	29	2	Georgia Tech	1950–53	Notre Dame	27–14
31	31	0	Oklahoma	1948–50	Kentucky	13–7
31	31	0	Pittsburgh	1919–22	Cleveland Naval	10–9
31	31	0	Pennsylvania	1896–98	Harvard	10–0

Note: Includes bowl games.

LONGEST DIVISION I-A LOSING STREAKS

Losses		Seasons	Ended Against	Score
34	Northwestern	1979–82	Northern Illinois	31–6
28	Virginia	1958–61	William & Mary	21–6
28	Kansas St	1945–48	Arkansas St	37–6
27	New Mexico St	1988–90	Cal St–Fullerton	43–9
27	Eastern Michigan	1980–82	Kent St	9–7

MOST-PLAYED DIVISION I-A RIVALRIES

GP	Opponents (Series Leader Listed First)	Record	First Game	GP	Opponents (Series Leader Listed First)	Record	First Game
109	Minnesota-Wisconsin	57-44-8	1890	100	Army-Navy	48-45-7	1890
108	Missouri-Kansas	50-49-9	1891	97	Utah-Utah St	64-29-4	1892
106	Nebraska-Kansas	82-21-3	1892	97	Clemson-S Carolina	58-35-4	1896
106	Texas-Texas A&M	67-34-5	1894	97	Kansas-Kansas St	61-31-5	1902
104	Miami (OH)-Cincinnati	55-42-7	1888	96	N Carolina-Wake Forest	64-30-2	1888
104	N Carolina-Virginia	55-45-4	1892	96	Michigan-Ohio St	55-35-6	1897
103	Baylor-Texas Christian*	49-47-7	1899	96	Mississippi-Miss St	54-36-6	1901
103	Auburn-Georgia	49-46-8	1892	95	Oklahoma-Kansas	62-27-6	1903
103	Oregon-Oregon St	52-41-10	1894	95	Tennessee-Kentucky	63-23-9	1893
102	Purdue-Indiana	62-34-6	1891	95	Penn St-Pittsburgh	50-41-4	1893
102	Stanford-California	52-39-11	1892		*Have not met since 1996.		

NCAA Coaches' Records

ALLTIME WINNINGEST DIVISION I-A COACHES

Coach (Alma Mater)	Colleges Coached	Yrs	W	L	T	Pct
Knute Rockne (Notre Dame '14)†	Notre Dame 1918–30	13	105	12	5	.881
Frank W. Leahy (Notre Dame '31)†	Boston Col 1939–40; Notre Dame 1941–43, 1946–53	13	107	13	9	.864
George W. Woodruff (Yale 1889)†	Pennsylvania 1892–01; Illinois 1903; Carlisle 1905	12	142	25	2	.846
Barry Switzer (Arkansas '60)	Oklahoma 1973–88	16	157	29	4	.837
Tom Osborne (Hastings '59)†	Nebraska 1973–98	25	255	49	3	.836
Percy D. Haughton (Harvard 1899)†	Cornell 1899–1900; Harvard 1908–16; Columbia 1923–24	13	96	17	6	.832
Bob Neyland (Army '16)†	Tennessee 1926–34, 1936–40, 1946–52	21	173	31	12	.829
Fielding Yost† (W Virginia 1895)†	Ohio Wesleyan 1897; Nebraska 1898; Kansas 1899; Stanford 1900; Michigan 1901–23, 1925–26	29	196	36	12	.828
Bud Wilkinson (Minnesota '37)†	Oklahoma 1947–63	17	145	29	4	.826
Jock Sutherland (Pittsburgh '18)†	Lafayette 1919–23; Pittsburgh 1924–38	20	144	28	14	.812
Bob Devaney (Alma, MI '39)†	Wyoming 1957–61; Nebraska 1962–72	16	136	30	7	.806
Frank W. Thomas (Notre Dame '23)†	Tenn.-Chattanooga 1925–28; Alabama 1931–42, 1944–46	19	141	33	9	.795
Joe Paterno (Brown '50)*	Penn St 1966–present	34	317	83	3	.790
Henry L. Williams (Yale 1891)†	Army 1891; Minnesota 1900–21	23	141	34	12	.786
Gil Dobie (Minnesota '02)†	N Dakota St 1906–07; Washington 1908-16; Navy 1917–19; Cornell 1920–35; Boston College 1936–38	33	180	45	15	.781
Bear Bryant (Alabama '36)†	Maryland 1945, Kentucky 1946–53, Texas A&M 1954–57, Alabama 1958–82	38	323	85	17	.780

*Active coach. †Hall of Fame member.

Note: Minimum 10 years as head coach at Division I institutions; record at four-year colleges only; bowl games included; ties computed as half won, half lost.

ALLTIME WINNINGEST DIVISION I-A COACHES (Cont.)
By Victories

	Yrs	W	L	T	Pct		Yrs	W	L	T	Pct
Paul (Bear) Bryant	38	323	85	17	.780	Bo Schembechler	27	234	65	8	.775
Glenn (Pop) Warner	44	319	106	32	.733	Hayden Fry	37	232	178	10	.564
*Joe Paterno	34	317	83	3	.790	*Lou Holtz	28	216	106	7	.667
Amos Alonzo Stagg	57	314	199	35	.605	Jess Neely	40	207	176	19	.539
*Bobby Bowden	34	304	85	4	.779	Warren Woodson	31	203	95	14	.673
Tom Osborne	25	255	49	3	.836	Vince Dooley	25	201	77	10	.715
*LaVell Edwards	28	251	94	3	.726	Eddie Anderson	39	201	128	15	.606
Woody Hayes	33	238	72	10	.759	*Active coach.					

Most Bowl Victories

	W	L	T		W	L	T
*Joe Paterno	20	9	1	Barry Switzer	8	5	0
*Bobby Bowden	17	5	1	Darrell Royal	8	7	1
Paul (Bear) Bryant	15	12	2	Vince Dooley	8	10	2
Jim Wacker	13	2	0	John Robinson	7	1	0
Tom Osborne	12	13	0	Bob Devaney	7	3	0
Don James	10	5	0	Dan Devine	7	3	0
*Lou Holtz	10	8	2	Earle Bruce	7	5	0
John Vaught	10	8	0	Charlie McClendon	7	6	0
Bobby Dodd	9	4	0	Hayden Fry	7	9	1
Johnny Majors	9	7	0	*LaVell Edwards	7	11	1
Terry Donahue	8	4	1	Pat Dye	7	2	1
*Active coach.				*Jackie Sherrill	7	6	0

WINNINGEST ACTIVE DIVISION I-A COACHES
By Percentage

Coach, College	Yrs	W	L	T	Pct#	Bowls W	L	T
Phillip Fulmer, Tennessee	8	76	14	0	.844	5	3	0
Joe Paterno, Penn St	34	317	83	3	.790	20	9	1
Bobby Bowden, Florida St	34	304	85	4	.779	17	5	1
Steve Spurrier, Florida	13	122	35	2	.774	5	5	0
R. C. Slocum, Texas A&M	11	102	32	2	.757	2	7	0
Dennis Erickson, Oregon St	14	120	44	1	.730	*5	6	0
LaVell Edwards, Brigham Young	28	251	95	3	.723	7	14	1
John Robinson, UNLV	13	107	43	4	.708	7	1	0
Paul Pasqualoni, Syracuse	14	109	48	1	.693	*5	3	0
John Cooper, Ohio St	23	184	80	6	.693	5	8	0

#Bowl games included in overall record. Ties computed as half win, half loss. *Includes record in NCAA and/or NAIA championships.

Note: Minimum five years as Division I-A head coach; record at four-year colleges only.

Like Landlord, Like Tenant

During the summers of 1998 and '99 Stanford quarterback Todd Husak rented the guest house of an alumnus of Stanford who lives near campus. After the Cardinal's 31–13 defeat of Cal on November 20, Husak shared more than an address with former Stanford quarterback Jim Plunkett. They've both guided a team to the Rose Bowl. Husak said that he absorbed a lot from being around Plunkett, an All-America in 1970. "We never sat down and really talked about football," Husak said. "Just being around a guy who has been through so much, seeing how his teammates still act around him, gave me some perspective on how to lead a team. Having a Heisman Trophy around wasn't so bad, either."

WINNINGEST ACTIVE DIVISION I-A COACHES *(Cont.)*
By Victories

Joe Paterno, Penn St	317	John Cooper, Ohio St	184
Bobby Bowden, Florida St	304	George Welsh, Virginia	183
LaVell Edwards, Brigham Young	251	Jackie Sherrill, Mississippi St	164
Lou Holtz, S Carolina	216	Dick Tomey, Arizona	153
Don Nehlen, W Virginia	195	Ken Hatfield, Rice	144

WINNINGEST ACTIVE DIVISION I-AA COACHES
By Percentage

Coach, College	Yrs	W	L	T	Pct*
Mike Kelly, Dayton	19	177	36	1	.829
Al Bagnoli, Pennsylvania	18	143	41	0	.777
Pete Richardson, Southern	12	107	32	1	.768
Larry Blakeney, Troy St	9	82	27	1	.750
Joe Gardi, Hofstra	10	81	29	2	.732
Roy Kidd, Eastern Kentucky	36	293	112	8	.719
Tubby Raymond, Delaware	34	284	111	3	.717
Greg Gattuso, Duquesne	7	53	21	0	.716
Walt Hamelin, Wagner	19	141	56	2	.714
Billy Joe, Florida A&M	26	205	82	4	.711

*Playoff games included.

Note: Minimum five years as a Division I-A and/or Division I-AA head coach; record at four-year colleges only.

By Victories

Roy Kidd, Eastern Kentucky	293	Bill Hayes, N Carolina A&T	175
Tubby Raymond, Delaware	284	Willie Jeffries, S Carolina St	170
Billy Joe, Florida A&M	205	Al Bagnoli, Pennsylvania	143
Ron Randleman, Sam Houston St	184	Walt Hamelin, Wagner	141
Mike Kelly, Dayton	177	Bob Ricca, St. John's (N.Y.)	140

WINNINGEST ACTIVE DIVISION II COACHES
By Percentage

Coach, College	Yrs	W	L	T	Pct*
Chuck Broyles, Pittsburg St	10	103	18	2	.846
Ken Sparks, Carson-Newman	20	197	46	2	.808
Peter Yetten, Bentley	12	84	30	1	.735
Bob Biggs, UC–Davis	7	59	23	1	.717
Gene Nicholson, Westminster (PA)	8	64	25	2	.714
Danny Hale, Bloomsburg	12	92	37	1	.712
Gene Carpenter, Millersville	31	214	86	6	.709
Frank Cignetti, Indiana (PA)	18	149	62	1	.705
Brian Kelly, Grand Valley St	9	70	29	2	.703
Joe Glenn, Northern Colorado	15	118	54	1	.685

*Ties computed as half win, half loss. Playoff games included.

Note: Minimum five years as a college head coach; record at four-year colleges only.

By Victories

Ron Harms, Texas A&M-Kingsville*	219	Claire Boroff, Nebraska-Kearney	169
Gene Carpenter, Millersville	214	Hampton Smith, Albany St. (GA)	159
Ken Sparks, Carson-Newman	197	Dennis Douds, E Stroudsburg	149
Willard Bailey, Virginia Union	183	Frank Cignetti, Indiana (PA)	149
Bud Elliott, Eastern New Mexico	173	Gary Howard, Central Oklahoma	147

*Formerly Texas A&I.

WINNINGEST ACTIVE DIVISION III
By Percentage

Coach, College	Yrs	W	L	T	Pct*
Larry Kehres, Mount Union	14	150	17	3	.891
Dick Farley, Williams	13	88	13	3	.861
Tom Clark, Catholic	6	50	10	1	.828
Tim Coen, Salve Regina	7	54	13	0	.806
K.C. Keeler, Rowan	7	70	17	1	.801
Roger Harring, WI-La Crosse	31	261	75	7	.771
John Gagliardi, St John's (MN)	51	364	107	11	.767
Frosty Westering, Pacific Lutheran	35	277	84	7	.762
Frank Girardi, Lycoming	28	211	66	5	.757
Bob Packard, Baldwin-Wallace	19	144	46	2	.755

*Ties computed as half won, half lost. Playoff games included.

Note: Minimum five years as a college head coach; record at four-year colleges only.

By Victories

John Gagliardi, St John's (MN)	364	Peter Mazzaferro, Bridgewater (MA)	180
Frosty Westering, Pacific Lutheran	277	Don Miller, Trinity (CT)	179
Roger Harring, WI-La Crosse	261	Tom Gilburg, Franklin & Marshall	155
Jim Christopherson, Concordia-M'head	213	Larry Kehres, Mount Union	150
Frank Girardi, Lycoming	211	Bob Packard, Baldwin-Wallace	144

NAIA Coaches' Records

WINNINGEST ACTIVE NAIA COACHES
By Percentage

Coach, College	Yrs	W	L	T	Pct*
Ted Kessinger, Bethany (KS)	24	193	45	1	.808
Hank Biesiot, Dickinson St (ND)	24	171	59	1	.740
Geno DeMarco, Geneva (PA)	7	52	21	0	.712
Carl Poelker, McKendree (IL)	17	114	51	1	.687
Monty Lewis, Southwestern (KS)	7	48	23	0	.676
Bob Young, Sioux Falls (SD)	17	119	60	3	.654
Vic Wallace, Lambuth (TN)	19	130	68	4	.644
Larry Wilcox, Benedictine (KS)	21	137	79	0	.634
Bill Ramseyer, Virginia's College at Wise	28	167	93	4	.633

*Playoff games included.

Note: Minimum five years as a collegiate head coach and includes record against four-year institutions only.

By Victories

Ted Kessinger, Bethany (KS)	193	Kevin Donley, St. Francis (IN)	125
Hank Biesiot, Dickinson St (ND)	171	Bob Young, Sioux Falls (SD)	117
Bill Ramseyer, Virginia's College at Wise	167	Carl Poelker, McKendree (IL)	114
Larry Wilcox, Benedictine (KS)	137	Jim Dennison, Walsh (OH)	113
Vic Wallace, Lambuth (TN)	130	Fran Schwenk, Doane (NE)	90

Shaquille O'Neal (34)
of the NBA champion
Los Angeles Lakers

JOHN W. MCDONOUGH

Pro Basketball

Hollywood Thriller

A season with triumph, tragedy and subplots enough for a Tinseltown epic ended, appropriately, with a title for Los Angeles

BY MARTY BURNS

THE 1999–2000 NBA season had all the ingredients of a good Hollywood movie: triumph (Vince Carter's regular season) and tragedy (Bobby Phills, Malik Sealy); a comeback (Sean Elliott) and a farewell (Charles Barkley); a hero (Kobe Bryant) and a villain (Isaiah Rider).

There was even a surprise ending of sorts (Shaq finally wins the big one!).

So perhaps it was only fitting that when the curtain fell, it would be the team from Tinseltown—the Los Angeles Lakers—that raised the championship trophy. With center Shaquille O'Neal and shooting guard Bryant successfully meshing their considerable talents, and new coach Phil Jackson calling the shots, the Lakers brought Showtime back to L.A. and defeated the Indiana Pacers in six games to win the NBA Finals.

Even the championship series featured story lines right out of a Hollywood screenwriter's imagination. Could O'Neal, the league's MVP, finally win the title that had eluded him his first seven NBA seasons? Or

would Indiana rally behind star shooting guard Reggie Miller (the theatrical string bean from UCLA) and soon-to-be-retiring coach Larry Bird (the longtime Lakers antagonist) and win one for the underdog? Call it *Mission Impossible* meets *Hoosiers*.

With the usual array of celebrities ringing the Staples Center court, the Lakers opened the Finals by easily taking Games 1 and 2. O'Neal led the way, scoring a combined 83 points and grabbing 43 rebounds. Not even Indiana's Hack-a-Shaq defense—based on the assumption that O'Neal, a horrendous free throw shooter, could be contained if he were constantly sent to the line—could slow him down. The Pacers put Shaq on the foul line a Finals-record 39 times in Game 2, but he made 18—just enough to foil the strategy. Miller, for his part, made only one of 16 field goals in a disastrous Game 1 and was held to two points in the fourth quarter of Game 2.

Like so many silver screen underdogs, however, Reggie and the Pacers refused to die. With Bryant unable to play in Game 3 because of a sprained left ankle, Miller and

Bryant soared to a title in his fourth year.

JOHN W. MCDONOUGH

forward Jalen Rose combined for 54 points as the Pacers got back in the series with a 100–91 victory at Conseco Fieldhouse. Though Shaq had another monster night, scoring 33 points and pulling down 13 rebounds, it was clear that he missed the penetration and scoring of his 21-year-old sidekick, Bryant.

Fortunately for the Lakers, Bryant returned for Game 4, and his presence would indeed prove crucial. In a Finals classic, Bryant scored eight of his 28 points in overtime, including two on a balletic reverse tip-in, to propel L.A. to a 120–118 victory and a commanding 3–1 series lead. Even O'Neal, who had 36 points and 21 rebounds before fouling out in overtime, had to admit, "Kobe was the hero tonight."

Though the Pacers bounced back and whipped the Lakers 120–87 in Game 5 to send Bird off a winner in his final home game and force a Game 6 in L.A., there would be no *Hoosiers* finish for Indiana fans. O'Neal (41 points) and Bryant (26 points) combined to lead L.A. to a 116–111 victory and wrap up the 12th championship in franchise history, the first since '88. Afterward O'Neal, who averaged 38.0 points and 16.7 rebounds per game and was the unanimous choice for Finals MVP, broke down in tears with the trophy.

"I've held the emotion for about 11 years—three years in college and eight years in the league," said O'Neal, the sometime actor and rapper whom critics had said lacked the dedication to win a title. "It just came out. It just came out."

While Shaq established himself as the game's dominant player in 1999–2000, it was Carter, the high-flying Raptors forward, who became its most popular. In just his second pro season, the 6'7" Carter received 1,911,973 votes from fans for the All-Star Game, second only to Michael Jordan's '97 tally of 2,451,136. He then catapulted himself into the realm of megastar with an electrifying performance at the

MANNY MILLAN

Slam Dunk Contest, in which he threw down a 360-degree windmill dunk and a jaw-dropping, between-the-legs tomahawk slam.

Vin-stantaneously, Carter became the talk of the NBA. He was besieged with endorsement offers, invited to appear on late-night talk shows, and his agent at the time, Tank Black, estimated that Carter would earn $20 million in off-court income. Though he sometimes bristled at the demands of instant stardom, Carter showed he was more than just flash. He finished the year with better numbers than he had during his 1998–99 Rookie of the Year season and helped lead the Raptors to their first postseason appearance.

As breathtaking as Carter's All-Star performance was, it paled in comparison to what San Antonio Spurs forward Elliott accomplished simply by putting on his uniform. On March 14, Elliott became the first pro athlete ever to play after having a kidney transplant. With 26,708 fans in the Alamodome looking on—including his older brother, Noel, who had donated the kidney—Elliott took the floor as a starter and scored two points in 12 minutes as the Spurs defeated the Atlanta Hawks.

Elliott's successful return (he would go on to average 6.0 points and 2.5 rebounds in 19 games) was one of the feel-good stories of the year in sports and gave the Spurs renewed hope of defending their NBA title. Unfortu-

nately for San Antonio, star forward Tim Duncan suffered torn cartilage in his left knee in a late-season game and was forced to sit out the team's first-round playoff series against the Phoenix Suns. Without their superstar, Elliott and the Spurs were eliminated in four games.

It was that kind of up-and-down season for the Spurs—and the entire NBA. For every personal triumph, such as Elliott's comeback, there was a corresponding heartbreak, such as the deaths of Charlotte Hornets swingman Phills and Minnesota Timberwolves shooting guard Sealy in separate auto accidents. For every happy return, such as Jordan's taking over as president of the

Washington Wizards, there was a sad farewell, such as the retirement of Houston Rockets forward Barkley, who suffered a ruptured knee tendon in a game on Dec. 8 in Philadelphia and returned only to play in his team's final game, on April 19 against the Vancouver Grizzlies, before calling an end to his 16-year Hall of Fame career.

Along the way there were the usual plot twists and colorful characters to spice up an NBA season. In Philly, Sixers guard Allen Iverson continued his war of wills with coach Larry Brown. In New York, the debate raged about whether the Knicks were better with or without their aging franchise center, Patrick Ewing. And in Dallas, Dennis Rodman made a brief comeback, at the behest of new Mavericks owner Mark Cuban, only to wear out his welcome and get waived a few weeks later.

Still, when it came to controversy, no player came up bigger than Hawks shooting guard Rider. Acquired in a trade with the Portland Trail Blazers before the season, the talented but troubled Rider was supposed to find peace with a fresh start in Atlanta under the steady hand of veteran coach Lenny Wilkens, the NBA's alltime winningest coach. Instead Rider continued his pattern of showing up late for practices and games, performed indifferently at times, and generally became a cancer in the locker room.

By March the Hawks had seen enough. With the team well on its way to a 28–54 finish, the worst in Wilkens's 27-year coaching career, Atlanta cut Rider even though it meant the franchise would have to pay him the rest of his $5.4 million annual salary. Rider, looking as carefree as ever in a floppy fishing hat and flip-flops, said at a farewell press conference that he had been made a scapegoat for the team's poor play and vowed to return to the NBA next season.

The Rider episode was an unwelcome p.r. blow for a league still suffering in the aftermath of Jordan's retirement and the '99 lockout. TV ratings stayed flat for the second straight year, and attendance sagged in many cities that didn't have a winning team or a new arena. At the same time, alternative pursuits such as pro wrestling and so-called extreme sports were drawing more eyeballs to TV sets and threatening to cut into the league's younger demographics.

That's not to say, however, that the NBA didn't have reason to be optimistic. Thanks to new rules to crack down on physical play, which were implemented before the season, the game flowed better than it had in years, and scoring increased about six points per game per team. Teams like the surprising Orlando Magic, which despite an austere rebuilding plan somehow finished .500 with dynamic rookie coach Doc Rivers, showed that parity was alive and well. And the NBA's sister league, the WNBA, continued to thrive in its fourth year of existence, drawing average crowds of 8,536 and making stars of players such as Cynthia Cooper, Chamique Holdsclaw and Sheryl Swoopes.

In L.A. the NBA also had that rare jewel that all pro sports leagues crave: a potential dynasty in the nation's second-largest market. Once a collection of talented underachievers with no leadership, the Lakers came together in spectacular fashion under Jackson, reeling off winning streaks of 16, 19, and 11 games to firmly establish themselves as the league's best team. They finished the regular season at 67–15, a whopping eight games ahead of division runner-up Portland, a team with a league-high $74 million payroll.

O'Neal produced his best season ever, leading the league in points per game (29.7) and field goal percentage (57.4), and ranking second in rebounds (13.6). Despite facing double and triple teams on a nightly basis, he was unstoppable. In addition to his Finals MVP award, Shaq took home co-MVP honors at the All-Star Game (with Duncan) and won his first regular-season MVP award, joining Jordan and Willis Reed as the only players ever to sweep all three in the same year.

Clearly the biggest difference for L.A., however, was the calming presence of Jackson, the Zen-preaching former Bulls coach. Lured out of his Montana off-season residence by a five-year, $30 million contract, Jackson immediately began working to

Miller (left) peaked in the 2000 playoffs, and they may have been his last chance.

mend the frayed relationship between the team's two young stars, O'Neal and Bryant. Flashing his six championship rings from his Chicago days, he convinced them that only by playing together could they achieve their ultimate goals.

Jackson's influence also proved vital in the playoffs, when the Lakers repeatedly struggled to close out opponents. Against Portland in the Western Conference finals, L.A. blew a 3–1 series lead and trailed by 15 points in the fourth quarter of Game 7 before rallying furiously to win the game and the series, thus avoiding a colossal embarrassment. Jackson never panicked or took drastic measures, brushing the difficulties off as growing pains for a team still learning how to win a title.

The championship gave Jackson his seventh title—his first without Jordan—in just his first season coaching a team that had been ousted from the playoffs in each of O'Neal and Bryant's three previous seasons together. "I want to thank Phil Jackson, the real coach of the year," Shaq said in the euphoria of the Lakers' victory celebration.

Jackson also brought his own touch of Hollywood to the Lakers. In an effort to get his various messages across to his club, he occasionally spliced clips from movies such as *American History X* and *The Green Mile* into their scouting videos. In fact, as Jackson and the Lakers rejoiced on the Staples Center floor after Game 6 of the Finals, with gold and purple confetti swirling around them, it was clear they had discovered an old Tinseltown formula for success: find two marquee stars, surround them with a good supporting cast, then get the right director to make sure they follow the script.

With the Lakers closest rivals—Miller's Pacers, Robinson's Spurs, Ewing's Knicks and Scottie Pippen's Blazers—aging or breaking up, the question for the rest of the NBA was how many sequels would L.A. be able to produce?

NBA Final Standings

Eastern Conference

ATLANTIC DIVISION

Team	W	L	Pct	GB
Miami	52	30	.634	—
New York	50	32	.610	2
Philadelphia	49	33	.598	3
Orlando	41	41	.500	11
Boston	35	47	.427	17
New Jersey	31	51	.378	21
Washington	29	53	.354	23

CENTRAL DIVISION

Team	W	L	Pct	GB
Indiana	56	26	.683	—
Charlotte	49	33	.598	7
Toronto	45	37	.549	11
Detroit	42	40	.512	14
Milwaukee	42	40	.512	14
Cleveland	32	50	.390	24
Atlanta	28	54	.341	28
Chicago	17	65	.207	39

Western Conference

MIDWEST DIVISION

Team	W	L	Pct	GB
Utah	55	27	.671	—
San Antonio	53	29	.646	2
Minnesota	50	32	.610	5
Dallas	40	42	.488	15
Denver	35	47	.427	20
Houston	34	48	.415	21
Vancouver	22	60	.268	33

PACIFIC DIVISION

Team	W	L	Pct	GB
LA Lakers	67	15	.817	—
Portland	59	23	.720	8
Phoenix	53	29	.646	14
Seattle	45	37	.549	22
Sacramento	44	38	.537	23
Golden State	19	63	.232	48
LA Clippers	15	67	.183	52

2000 NBA Playoffs

EASTERN CONFERENCE — 1st ROUND · SEMIFINALS · FINALS

WESTERN CONFERENCE — FINALS · SEMIFINALS · 1st ROUND

NBA FINALS

Eastern Conference 1st Round: Indiana, Milwaukee, Charlotte, Philadelphia, New York, Toronto, Miami, Detroit

Indiana (3–2)
Philadelphia (3–1)
New York (3–0)
Miami (3–0)
Indiana (4–2)
New York (4–3)
Indiana (4–2)

LA LAKERS (4–2)

LA Lakers (3–2)
LA Lakers (4–1)
Phoenix (3–1)
LA Lakers (4–3)
Portland (3–1)
Portland (4–1)
Utah (3–2)

Western Conference 1st Round: LA Lakers, Sacramento, San Antonio, Phoenix, Portland, Minnesota, Utah, Seattle

2000 NBA Playoff Results

Eastern Conference First Round

April 23	Milwaukee	85	at Indiana	88
April 27	Milwaukee	104	at Indiana	91
April 29	Indiana	109	at Milwaukee	96
May 1	Indiana	87	at Milwaukee	100
May 4	Milwaukee	95	at Indiana	96

Indiana won series 3–2.

April 22	Detroit	85	at Miami	95
April 25	Detroit	82	at Miami	84
April 30	Miami	91	at Detroit	72

Miami won series 3–0.

April 23	Toronto	88	at New York	92
April 26	Toronto	83	at New York	84
April 29	New York	87	at Toronto	80

New York won series 3–0.

April 22	Philadelphia	92	at Charlotte	82
April 24	Philadelphia	98	at Charlotte	108*
April 28	Charlotte	76	at Philadelphia	81
May 1	Charlotte	99	at Philadelphia	105

Philadelphia won series 3–1.

Western Conference First Round

April 23	Sacramento	107	at LA Lakers	117
April 27	Sacramento	89	at LA Lakers	113
April 30	LA Lakers	91	at Sacramento	99
May 2	LA Lakers	88	at Sacramento	101
May 5	Sacramento	86	at LA Lakers	113

LA Lakers won series 3–2.

April 22	Seattle	93	at Utah	104
April 24	Seattle	87	at Utah	101
April 29	Utah	78	at Seattle	89
May 3	Utah	93	at Seattle	104
May 5	Seattle	93	at Utah	96

Utah won series 3–2.

April 23	Minnesota	88	at Portland	91
April 26	Minnesota	82	at Portland	86
April 30	Portland	87	at Minnesota	94
May 2	Portland	85	at Minnesota	77

Portland won series 3–1.

April 22	Phoenix	72	at San Antonio	70
April 25	Phoenix	70	at San Antonio	85
April 29	San Antonio	94	at Phoenix	101
May 2	San Antonio	78	at Phoenix	89

Phoenix won series 3–1.

Eastern Conference Semifinals

May 6	Philadelphia	91	at Indiana	108
May 8	Philadelphia	97	at Indiana	103
May 10	Indiana	97	at Philadelphia	89
May 13	Indiana	90	at Philadelphia	92
May 15	Philadelphia	107	at Indiana	86
May 19	Indiana	106	at Philadelphia	90

Indiana won series 4–2.

May 7	New York	83	at Miami	87
May 9	New York	82	at Miami	76
May 12	Miami	77	at New York	76*
May 14	Miami	83	at New York	91
May 17	New York	81	at Miami	87
May 19	Miami	70	at New York	72
May 21	New York	83	at Miami	82

New York won series 4–3.

Western Conference Semifinals

May 7	Phoenix	77	at LA Lakers	105
May 10	Phoenix	96	at LA Lakers	97
May 12	LA Lakers	105	at Phoenix	99
May 14	LA Lakers	98	at Phoenix	117
May 16	Phoenix	65	at LA Lakers	87

LA Lakers won series 4–1.

May 7	Portland	94	at Utah	75
May 9	Portland	103	at Utah	85
May 11	Utah	84	at Portland	103
May 14	Utah	88	at Portland	85
May 16	Portland	81	at Utah	79

Portland won series 4–1.

Eastern Conference Finals

May 23	New York	88	at Indiana	102
May 25	New York	84	at Indiana	88
May 27	Indiana	95	at New York	98
May 29	Indiana	89	at New York	91
May 31	New York	79	at Indiana	88
June 2	Indiana	93	at New York	80

Indiana won series 4–2.

Western Conference Finals

May 20	Portland	94	at LA Lakers	109
May 22	Portland	106	at LA Lakers	77
May 26	LA Lakers	93	at Portland	91
May 28	LA Lakers	103	at Portland	91
May 30	Portland	96	at LA Lakers	88
June 2	LA Lakers	93	at Portland	103
June 4	Portland	84	at LA Lakers	89

LA Lakers won series 4–3.

Finals

June 7	Indiana	87	at LA Lakers	104
June 9	Indiana	104	at LA Lakers	111
June 11	LA Lakers	91	at Indiana	100
June 14	LA Lakers	120	at Indiana	118*

June 16	LA Lakers	87	at Indiana	120
June 19	Indiana	111	at LA Lakers	116

LA Lakers won series 4–2.

*Overtime game.

NBA Finals Composite Box Score

INDIANA PACERS

Player	GP	Field Goals FGM	Field Goals Pct	3-Pt FG FGM	3-Pt FG FGA	Free Throws FTM	Free Throws Pct	Rebounds Off	Rebounds Total	A	Stl	TO	BS	Avg	Hi
Miller	6	43	41.3	15	40	45	97.8	0	16	22	5	8	2	24.3	35
Rose	6	50	46.7	8	16	30	83.3	2	27	18	5	17	2	23.0	32
Croshere	6	24	54.5	4	10	39	86.7	8	36	5	2	7	6	15.2	24
Smits	6	27	46.6	0	0	6	100.0	8	24	3	3	8	7	10.0	24
Jackson	6	19	41.3	8	20	12	80.0	3	32	46	5	11	0	9.7	18
Davis	6	23	57.5	0	0	6	54.5	19	60	6	2	0	6	8.7	20
Perkins	6	11	37.9	11	23	3	75.0	1	24	6	3	4	0	6.0	10
Best	6	14	46.7	2	4	5	83.3	4	7	13	4	4	1	5.8	14
Bender	2	2	66.7	0	0	3	75.0	0	1	0	1	0	0	3.5	4
McKey	6	3	50.0	1	2	4	66.7	6	19	1	2	5	1	1.8	4
Mullin	3	1	50.0	0	1	2	66.7	0	0	1	1	1	1	1.3	4
Tabak	3	1	50.0	0	0	—	—	1	1	0	0	0	0	0.7	2
Totals	6	218	46.3	49	116	155	85.2	52	247	121	33	65	26	106.7	120

LOS ANGELES LAKERS

Player	GP	Field Goals FGM	Field Goals Pct	3-Pt FG FGM	3-Pt FG FGA	Free Throws FTM	Free Throws Pct	Rebounds Off	Rebounds Total	A	Stl	TO	BS	Avg	Hi
O'Neal	6	96	61.1	0	0	36	38.7	34	100	14	6	13	16	38.0	43
Bryant	5	33	35.2	2	10	10	90.9	6	23	21	5	6	7	15.6	28
Rice	6	22	40.0	12	19	13	65.0	1	15	10	5	9	1	11.5	21
Harper	6	26	46.4	6	15	7	70.0	4	20	29	8	12	1	10.8	21
Horry	6	22	51.2	3	15	8	72.7	8	31	17	5	9	6	9.2	17
Fox	6	11	61.1	5	8	13	86.7	3	10	6	3	4	0	6.7	11
Fisher	6	12	42.9	7	12	5	83.3	2	6	23	5	3	0	6.0	10
Green	6	12	57.1	0	0	6	85.7	9	20	3	1	2	0	5.0	7
Shaw	6	8	21.6	0	12	2	100.0	3	17	17	2	5	0	3.0	6
Knight	4	2	66.7	0	0	1	50.0	2	2	0	0	1	0	1.3	3
Salley	4	2	66.7	0	0	0	—	1	3	0	1	0	0	1.0	4
George	1	0	00.0	0	1	0	50.0	0	1	0	0	1	0	1.0	1
Totals	6	246	48.0	35	92	102	57.0	73	248	140	41	65	31	104.8	120

NBA Finals Box Scores

Game 1

INDIANA 87

INDIANA	Min	FG M-A	FT M-A	Reb O-T	A	PF	S	TO	TP
Davis	28	4-5	1-2	3-8	0	3	1	0	9
Rose	36	5-12	0-0	0-2	4	0	3	12	12
Smits	20	5-12	2-2	0-5	0	6	1	4	12
Jackson	28	6-8	4-5	1-5	7	3	0	0	18
Miller	41	1-16	5-5	0-2	4	1	1	0	7
Croshere	26	6-7	4-7	1-6	0	3	0	3	16
Perkins	21	1-5	2-2	0-2	0	3	1	1	5
Best	19	2-7	0-0	1-2	2	0	2	1	4
McKey	12	0-1	0-0	0-4	0	1	0	1	0
Tabak	3	0-0	0-0	0-0	0	0	0	0	0
Mullin	4	0-0	0-0	0-0	1	0	0	1	0
Bender	2	2-3	0-0	0-0	0	0	0	0	4
Totals	240	32-76	18-23	6-36	16	23	6	14	87

Percentages: FG—.421, FT—.783. 3-pt goals: 5–14, .357 (Rose 2–3, Jackson 2–3, Miller 0–3, Croshere 0–1, Perkins 1–3, McKey 0–1). Team rebounds: 7. Blocked shots: 5 (Smits 2, Croshere, Best, Davis).

LA LAKERS 104

LA LAKERS	Min	FG M-A	FT M-A	Reb O-T	A	PF	S	TO	TP
Green	22	2-6	0-0	1-5	1	1	0	0	4
Rice	27	1-8	1-2	1-3	2	2	2	2	3
O'Neal	44	21-31	1-6	6-19	4	2	0	2	43
Bryant	38	6-13	2-2	0-3	5	4	1	2	14
Harper	21	4-6	3-5	1-1	5	2	0	1	12
Horry	23	3-5	0-0	1-4	2	4	3	1	6
Fox	24	3-4	4-4	0-4	2	1	1	1	11
Fisher	10	2-4	0-0	1-2	2	2	1	5	5
Shaw	4	2-9	0-0	1-5	3	0	0	1	4
Knight	1	1-2	0-0	2-2	0	1	0	0	2
Salley	3	0-0	0-0	0-0	0	0	0	0	0
Totals	240	45-88	11-19	14-48	25	19	9	11	104

Percentages: FG—.511, FT—.579. 3-pt goals: 3–12, .250 (Rice 0–2, Bryant 0–2, Harper 1–2, Fox 1–1, Fisher 1–1, Shaw 0–4). Team rebounds: 9. Blocked shots: 6 (O'Neal 3, Bryant 2, Horry).
A: 18,997. Officials: Crawford, Nies, Durham

Game 2

INDIANA 104

INDIANA	Min	FG M-A	FT M-A	Reb O-T	A	PF	S	TO	TP
Davis	34	4-9	1-1	4-10	1	6	0	0	9
Rose	48	10-23	10-14	1-9	1	3	1	2	30
Smits	16	2-6	0-0	1-2	2	5	0	0	4
Jackson	29	2-9	1-2	0-9	8	4	2	1	7
Miller	36	7-16	6-6	0-2	4	4	0	0	21
Croshere	25	6-15	12-12	4-6	1	4	1	0	24
Perkins	24	2-5	0-0	0-0	1	6	1	0	6
McKey	6	0-1	1-2	2-3	1	2	0	1	1
Best	19	0-3	2-2	0-1	0	1	0	0	2
Tabak	3	0-1	0-0	1-0	0	3	0	0	0
Totals	240	33-88	33-39	13-46	19	38	5	4	104

Percentages: FG—.375, FT—.846. 3-pt goals: 5–20, .250 (Rose 0–1, Jackson 2–7, Miller 1–5, Croshere 0–2, Perkins 2–4, Best 0–1). Team rebounds:13. Blocked shots: 5 (Croshere 2, Davis 2, Rose).

LA LAKERS 111

LA LAKERS	Min	FG M-A	FT M-A	Reb O-T	A	PF	S	TO	TP
Green	15	2-4	0-0	3-4	1	1	0	1	4
Rice	35	7-15	2-2	0-4	3	4	0	1	21
O'Neal	46	11-18	18-39	5-24	4	5	0	2	40
Bryant	9	1-3	0-0	0-1	4	1	0	0	2
Harper	21	8-12	4-5	0-3	6	4	0	3	21
Horry	33	2-6	3-4	1-6	1	5	0	1	7
Fox	15	2-3	2-3	1-2	0	4	1	1	6
Fisher	16	2-4	1-2	0-0	3	1	0	0	6
Shaw	32	1-9	2-2	1-3	7	1	1	0	4
Knight	1	0-0	0-0	0-0	0	0	0	0	0
Salley	1	0-1	0-0	0-0	0	0	1	0	0
Totals	240	36-75	32-57	11-47	29	26	3	9	111

Percentages: FG—.480, FT—.561. 3-pt goals: 7–15, .467 (Rice 5–6, Bryant 0–1, Harper 1–2, Horry 0–2, Fisher 1–1, Shaw 0–3). Team rebounds: 19. Blocked shots: 8 (Horry 4, O'Neal 3, Bryant).
A: 18,997. Officials: Crawford, Salvatore, Rush.

Game 3

LA LAKERS 91

LA LAKERS	Min	FG M-A	FT M-A	Reb O-T	A	PF	S	TO	TP
Green	14	1-2	2-2	0-1	1	3	0	0	4
Rice	27	3-9	0-0	0-1	1	0	1	2	7
O'Neal	47	15-24	3-13	4-13	1	3	2	3	33
Harper	38	6-14	0-0	1-5	2	2	5	5	14
Shaw	31	3-10	0-0	0-5	1	4	1	2	6
Horry	33	5-8	0-0	3-7	6	4	0	3	10
Knight	2	0-0	0-0	0-0	0	2	0	0	0
Fisher	27	3-5	2-2	0-1	10	4	0	1	10
Fox	21	2-4	1-2	0-0	1	5	0	1	7
Totals	240	38-76	8-19	8-33	23	27	9	16	91

Percentages: FG—.500, FT—.421. 3-pt goals: 7–17, .412 (Rice 1–3, Harper 2–3, Shaw 0–3, Horry 0–2, Fisher 2–3, Fox 2–3). Team rebounds: 10. Blocked shots: 4 (O'Neal 2, Rice, Harper).

INDIANA 100

INDIANA	Min	FG M-A	FT M-A	Reb O-T	A	PF	S	TO	TP
Davis	28	1-5	0-0	4-12	1	6	0	0	2
Rose	45	9-18	3-3	0-6	2	2	1	2	21
Smits	19	3-11	0-0	3-6	0	4	1	1	6
Jackson	27	2-5	1-2	0-2	6	1	2	3	6
Miller	46	11-22	9-9	0-2	2	1	0	3	33
Perkins	22	1-4	0-0	0-4	1	2	1	1	3
Croshere	27	4-6	3-4	0-3	0	1	0	0	12
Best	21	5-7	2-2	1-1	2	2	2	1	14
McKey	5	0-0	3-4	1-3	0	1	0	1	3
Totals	240	36-78	21-24	9-39	14	18	8	12	100

Percentages: FG—.462, FT—.875. 3-pt goals: 7–18, .389 (Rose 0–4, Jackson 1–1, Miller 2–7, Perkins 1–3, Croshere 1–1, Best 2–2). Team rebounds: 12. Blocked shots: 3 (Smits 2, Croshere).
A: 18,345. Officials: Garretson, Fryer, Evans.

Game 4

LA LAKERS 120

LA LAKERS	Min	FG M-A	FT M-A	Reb O-T	A	PF	S	TO	TP
Green	16	2-2	1-2	1-3	0	3	0	0	5
Rice	39	3-8	3-3	0-1	1	3	0	3	11
O'Neal	47	13-25	10-17	7-21	1	6	2	3	36
Bryant	47	14-27	0-0	2-4	5	4	1	3	28
Harper	26	2-6	0-0	0-3	2	2	0	0	4
Fox	15	3-5	1-1	1-3	2	5	0	1	8
Horry	37	6-10	5-7	2-6	2	4	2	1	17
Shaw	13	2-4	0-0	1-1	3	0	0	0	4
Fisher	20	3-6	0-0	0-0	4	2	1	1	7
Salley	5	0-0	0-0	0-0	0	2	0	0	0
Totals	265	48-93	20-30	14-42	20	31	6	12	120

Percentages: FG—.576, FT—.667. 3-pt goals: 4–12, .333 (Rice 2–3, Harper 0–2, Fox 1–2, Horry 0–2, Shaw 0–1, Fisher 1–2). Team rebounds: 10. Blocked shots: 4 (Bryant 2, O'Neal 2).

INDIANA 118

INDIANA	Min	FG M-A	FT M-A	Reb O-T	A	PF	S	TO	TP
Davis	29	2-4	0-2	0-8	0	6	1	0	4
Rose	44	5-16	4-4	0-3	5	3	1	3	14
Smits	22	11-14	2-2	1-3	0	4	1	2	24
Jackson	32	2-8	2-2	0-2	7	2	0	1	7
Miller	50	9-19	11-12	0-5	3	1	1	1	35
Croshere	19	3-6	4-4	1-7	3	1	0	1	10
Perkins	22	3-6	1-2	0-4	2	5	0	1	6
McKey	23	2-2	0-0	3-5	0	2	1	1	4
Mullin	3	0-0	0-0	0-0	0	0	0	0	0
Best	21	5-9	0-0	2-2	4	2	0	2	10
Totals	265	42-84	24-28	9-39	22	28	5	12	118

Percentages: FG—.500, FT—.857. 3-pt goals: 10–19, .526 (Jackson 1–3, Miller 6–9, Croshere 0–1, Perkins 3–5, Best 0–1). Team rebounds: 10. Blocked shots: 3 (Smits 2, Miller).
A: 18,345. Officials: Bavetta, Javie, Nunn.

Game 5

LA LAKERS 87

LA LAKERS	Min	FG M–A	FT M–A	Reb O–T	A	PF	S	TO	TP
Green	16	3–4	1–1	1–2	0	2	0	0	7
Rice	30	3–8	4–7	0–0	2	2	1	1	11
O'Neal	42	17–27	1–6	7–11	3	2	2	3	35
Bryant	37	4–20	0–0	1–5	3	5	2	0	8
Harper	25	3–8	0–0	2–5	5	2	1	2	8
Fox	15	0–1	1–1	0–0	0	2	1	0	1
Horry	29	3–8	0–0	0–4	2	5	0	1	7
Shaw	12	0–4	0–0	0–1	2	4	0	2	0
Fisher	22	0–6	2–2	1–2	1	3	2	1	2
Knight	5	1–1	1–2	0–0	0	2	0	1	3
Salley	4	2–2	0–0	1–3	0	2	0	0	4
George	3	0–1	1–2	0–1	0	2	0	1	1
Totals	240	36–90	11–21	13–34	18	33	9	12	87

Percentages: FG—.400, FT—.524. 3-pt goals: 4–19, .211 (Rice 1–2, Bryant 0–1, Harper 2–4, Fox 0–1, Horry 1–6, Shaw 0–1, Fisher 0–3, George 0–1). Team rebounds: 12. Blocked shots: 2 (O'Neal 2).

INDIANA 120

INDIANA	Min	FG M–A	FT M–A	Reb O–T	A	PF	S	TO	TP
Davis	23	4–7	0–0	1–8	1	3	0	0	8
Rose	44	12–18	4–4	0–6	5	4	2	5	32
Smits	14	5–7	2–2	1–2	0	5	0	0	12
Jackson	30	4–9	2–2	2–6	7	0	0	5	10
Miller	39	7–12	7–7	0–4	6	1	1	2	25
Perkins	29	2–7	0–0	1–7	1	3	0	0	6
Croshere	25	1–3	11–12	1–9	3	3	1	2	13
McKey	12	0–0	0–0	0–3	0	1	1	0	0
Best	10	2–2	1–2	0–0	3	1	0	0	5
Tabak	5	1–1	0–0	0–0	0	3	0	0	2
Mullin	4	1–2	0–0	0–0	0	0	1	0	3
Bender	4	0–0	3–4	0–1	0	0	1	0	3
Totals	240	39–68	32–36	6–46	26	24	7	14	120

Percentages: FG—.574, FT—.889. 3-pt goals: 10–20, .500 (Rose 4–5, Jackson 0–2, Miller 4–6, Perkins 2–6, Mullin 0–1). Team rebounds: 5. Blocked shots: 4 (Miller, Rose, Croshere, Mullin).
A: 18,345. Officials: Salvatore, Nies, Crawford.

Game 6

INDIANA 111

INDIANA	Min	FG M–A	FT M–A	Reb O–T	A	PF	S	TO	TP
Davis	35	8–10	4–6	5–14	3	4	0	0	20
Rose	42	9–20	9–11	1–1	3	3	0	2	29
Smits	25	1–8	0–0	2–6	1	5	0	1	2
Jackson	40	3–7	2–2	0–8	11	3	1	1	10
Miller	40	8–19	7–7	0–1	3	1	1	2	25
McKey	14	1–2	0–0	0–1	0	4	0	1	3
Perkins	13	2–2	0–0	0–4	1	1	0	1	6
Croshere	23	4–7	5–6	1–5	0	5	0	1	16
Best	8	0–2	0–0	0–1	2	1	0	0	0
Totals	240	36–77	27–32	9–41	24	27	2	9	111

Percentages: FG—.468, FT—.844. 3-pt goals: 12–25, .480 (Rose 2–3, Jackson 2–4, Miller 2–10, McKey 1–1, Perkins 2–2, Croshere 3–5). Team rebounds: 8. Blocked shots: 6 (Davis 3, Smits, Croshere, McKey).

LA LAKERS 116

LA LAKERS	Min	FG M–A	FT M–A	Reb O–T	A	PF	S	TO	TP
Green	20	2–3	2–2	3–5	0	1	1	1	6
Rice	35	5–7	3–6	0–6	2	3	1	0	16
O'Neal	47	19–32	3–12	5–12	1	2	0	0	41
Bryant	45	8–27	8–9	3–10	4	4	1	1	26
Harper	37	3–10	0–0	0–3	9	2	2	1	6
Horry	27	3–6	0–0	1–4	4	6	0	2	8
Shaw	7	0–1	0–0	0–2	1	2	0	0	0
Fox	14	1–1	4–4	1–1	1	3	0	0	7
Fisher	8	2–3	0–0	0–1	3	1	0	0	6
Totals	240	43–90	20–33	13–44	25	24	5	5	116

Percentages: FG—.478, FT—.606. 3-pt goals: 10–17, .588 (Rice 3–3, Bryant 2–6, Harper 0–2, Horry 2–3, Fox 1–1, Fisher 2–2). Team rebounds: 8. Blocked shots: 7 (O'Neal 4, Bryant 2, Horry).
A: 18,997. Officials: Evans, Crawford, Garretson

NBA Awards

All-NBA Teams

FIRST TEAM	SECOND TEAM	THIRD TEAM
G Gary Payton, Seattle	Allen Iverson, Philadelphia	Eddie Jones, Charlotte
G Jason Kidd, Phoenix	Kobe Bryant, LA Lakers	Stephon Marbury, New Jersey
C Shaquille O'Neal, LA Lakers	Alonzo Mourning, Miami	David Robinson, San Antonio
F Kevin Garnett, Minnesota	Karl Malone, Utah	Chris Webber, Sacramento
F Tim Duncan, San Antonio	Grant Hill, Detroit	Vince Carter, Toronto

NBA All-Defensive Teams

FIRST TEAM	SECOND TEAM
G Gary Payton, Seattle	Jason Kidd, Phoenix
G Kobe Bryant, LA Lakers	Eddie Jones, Charlotte
C Alonzo Mourning, Miami	Shaquille O'Neal, LA Lakers
F Tim Duncan, San Antonio	Scottie Pippen, Portland
F Kevin Garnett, Minnesota	Clifford Robinson, Phoenix

All-Rookie Teams
(Chosen Without Regard to Position)

FIRST TEAM	SECOND TEAM
Elton Brand, Chicago	Shawn Marion, Phoenix
Steve Francis, Houston	Ron Artest, Chicago
Lamar Odom, LA Clippers	James Posey, Denver
Wally Szczerbiak, Minnesota	Jason Terry, Atlanta
Andre Miller, Cleveland	Chucky Atkins, Orlando

NBA Individual Leaders

Scoring

	GP	Pts	Avg
Shaquille O'Neal, LA Lakers	79	2344	29.7
Allen Iverson, Phil	70	1989	28.4
Grant Hill, Det	74	1906	25.8
Vince Carter, Tor	82	2107	25.7
Karl Malone, Utah	82	2095	25.5
Chris Webber, Sac	75	1834	24.5
Gary Payton, Sea	82	1982	24.2
Jerry Stackhouse, Det	82	1939	23.6
Tim Duncan, SA	74	1716	23.2
Kevin Garnett, Minn	81	1857	22.9

Rebounds

	GP	Reb	Avg
Dikembe Mutombo, Atl	82	1157	14.1
Shaquille O'Neal, LA Lakers	79	1078	13.6
Tim Duncan, SA	74	918	12.4
Kevin Garnett, Minn	81	956	11.8
Chris Webber, Sac	75	787	10.5
Shareef Abdur-Rahim, Van	82	825	10.1
Elton Brand, Chi	81	810	10.0
Dale Davis, Ind	74	729	9.9
David Robinson, SA	80	770	9.6
Jerome Williams, Det	82	789	9.6

Assists

	GP	Assists	Avg
Jason Kidd, Phoe	67	678	10.1
Sam Cassell, Mil	81	729	9.0
Nick Van Exel, Den	79	714	9.0
Terrell Brandon, Minn	71	629	8.9
Gary Payton, Sea	82	732	8.9
John Stockton, Utah	82	703	8.6
Stephon Marbury, NJ	74	622	8.4
Mike Bibby, Van	82	665	8.1
Mark Jackson, Ind	81	650	8.0
Eric Snow, Phil	82	624	7.6

Field-Goal Percentage

	FGA	FGM	Pct
Shaquille O'Neal, LA Lakers	1665	956	.574
Dikembe Mutombo, Atl	573	322	.562
Alonzo Mourning, Mia	1184	652	.551
Ruben Patterson, Sea	661	354	.536
Rasheed Wallace, Port	1045	542	.519
David Robinson, SA	1031	528	.512
Wally Szczerbiak, Minn	669	342	.511
Karl Malone, Utah	1476	752	.509
Antonio McDyess, Den	1211	614	.507
Othella Harrington, Van	830	420	.506

Free-Throw Percentage

	FTA	FTM	Pct
Jeff Hornacek, Utah	180	170	.950
Reggie Miller, Ind	406	373	.919
Darrell Armstrong, Orl	247	225	.911
Terrell Brandon, Minn	208	187	.899
Ray Allen, Mil	398	353	.887
Predrag Stojakovic, Sac	153	135	.882
Derek Anderson, LA Clippers	309	271	.877
Jim Jackson, Atl	212	186	.877
Sam Cassell, Mil	445	390	.876
Mitch Richmond, Wash	340	298	.876

Three-Point Field-Goal Percentage

	FGA	FGM	Pct
Hubert Davis, Dall	167	82	.491
Jeff Hornacek, Utah	138	66	.478
Matt Bullard, Hou	177	79	.446
Rodney Rogers, Phoe	262	115	.439
Allan Houston, NY	243	106	.436
Terry Porter, SA	207	90	.435
Lindsey Hunter, Det	389	168	.432
Tracy Murray, Wash	263	113	.430
Jon Barry, Sac	154	66	.429
Wesley Person, Clev	250	106	.424

Steals

	GP	Steals	Avg
Eddie Jones, Char	72	192	2.67
Paul Pierce, Bos	73	152	2.08
Darrell Armstrong, Orl	82	169	2.06
Allen Iverson, Phil	70	144	2.06
Mookie Blaylock, GS	73	146	2.00
Jason Kidd, Phoe	67	134	2.00
Terrell Brandon, Minn	71	134	1.89
Gary Payton, Sea	82	153	1.87
Kendall Gill, NJ	76	139	1.83
John Stockton, Utah	82	143	1.74

Blocked Shots

	GP	BS	Avg
Alonzo Mourning, Mia	79	294	3.72
Dikembe Mutombo, Atl	82	269	3.28
Shaquille O'Neal, LA Lakers	79	239	3.03
Theo Ratliff, Phil	57	171	3.00
Shawn Bradley, Dall	77	190	2.47
David Robinson, SA	80	183	2.29
Tim Duncan, SA	74	165	2.23
Raef LaFrentz, Den	81	180	2.22
Greg Ostertag, Utah	81	172	2.12
Marcus Camby, NY	59	116	1.97

Offense

| Team | Field Goals | | 3-Pt Field Goals | | Free Throws | | Rebounds | | A | Stl | Scoring |
	FGM	Pct	3FGM	Pct	FTM	Pct	Off	Total			Avg
Sacramento	3276	45.0	534	32.2	1521	75.4	1057	3692	1953	787	105.0
Detroit	3044	45.9	439	35.9	1956	78.1	917	3375	1707	665	103.5
Dallas	3195	45.3	519	39.1	1407	80.4	931	3375	1810	592	101.4
Indiana	3047	45.9	583	39.2	1629	81.1	842	3454	1857	559	101.3
Milwaukee	3174	46.5	394	36.9	1558	78.6	1016	3389	1852	671	101.2
LA Lakers	3137	45.9	344	32.9	1649	69.6	1117	3855	1921	613	100.8
Orlando	3169	45.2	294	33.8	1574	73.5	1145	3685	1709	743	100.1
Houston	3001	45.0	581	35.8	1573	73.3	1008	3594	1774	613	99.5
Boston	3054	44.4	417	33.1	1621	74.5	1108	3528	1741	795	99.3
Seattle	3108	44.7	546	33.9	1363	69.5	1042	3525	1878	657	99.1
Denver	3057	44.2	470	33.6	1531	72.4	1073	3663	1911	554	99.0
Phoenix	3093	45.7	458	36.8	1467	75.9	1026	3579	2098	744	98.9
Minnesota	3226	46.7	248	34.6	1379	78.0	1016	3487	2205	622	98.5
Charlotte	2935	44.9	339	33.9	1863	75.8	884	3519	2023	732	98.4
New Jersey	2979	43.3	477	34.7	1601	78.4	1040	3355	1688	720	98.0
Portland	3021	47.0	407	36.1	1542	76.0	965	3526	1925	633	97.5
Toronto	2980	43.3	425	36.3	1583	76.5	1098	3547	1947	666	97.2
Cleveland	2977	44.2	343	37.3	1653	75.0	1010	3509	1941	715	97.0
Washington	3010	45.1	335	37.6	1566	74.3	1064	3502	1771	594	96.6
Utah	2962	46.4	329	38.5	1661	77.3	936	3362	2041	629	96.5
San Antonio	2952	46.2	330	37.4	1652	74.6	927	3593	1819	614	96.2
Golden State	2996	42.0	345	32.3	1497	69.7	1302	3737	1851	731	95.5
Philadelphia	2993	44.2	208	32.3	1577	70.8	1147	3615	1817	791	94.8
Miami	2974	46.0	446	37.1	1345	73.6	921	3540	1931	582	94.4
Atlanta	3000	44.1	258	31.7	1477	74.3	1146	3716	1548	500	94.3
Vancouver	2892	44.9	324	36.1	1594	77.4	1005	3329	1700	608	93.9
New York	2897	45.5	351	37.5	1410	78.1	802	3323	1588	515	92.1
LA Clippers	2877	42.6	429	33.9	1363	74.6	955	3332	1479	578	92.0
Chicago	2565	41.5	340	32.9	1482	70.9	1032	3356	1645	646	84.8

Defense (Opponent's Statistics)

| Team | Field Goals | | 3-Pt Field Goals | | Free Throws | | Rebounds | | Stl | Scoring | |
	FGM	Pct	3FGM	Pct	FTM	Pct	Off	Total		Avg	Diff
San Antonio	2884	42.5	355	34.3	1276	73.9	986	3396	645	90.2	+5.9
New York	2711	42.4	404	33.8	1609	74.7	927	3368	603	90.7	+1.4
Portland	2825	43.1	394	33.0	1422	71.6	978	3198	652	91.0	+6.5
Miami	2782	42.2	408	36.1	1512	74.8	974	3315	621	91.3	+3.1
Utah	2781	44.6	388	35.4	1598	74.6	887	3123	588	92.0	+4.5
LA Lakers	2838	41.6	372	32.6	1518	74.2	1007	3538	627	92.3	+8.5
Philadelphia	2867	43.5	417	35.6	1510	75.5	1065	3566	631	93.4	+1.4
Phoenix	2825	42.4	403	35.2	1630	73.9	1071	3536	733	93.7	+5.2
Chicago	2916	45.6	358	34.1	1533	74.1	1000	3416	853	94.1	-9.3
Charlotte	3048	44.8	410	37.8	1347	74.5	966	3516	604	95.8	+2.6
Minnesota	2924	44.5	380	35.6	1644	75.2	916	3356	591	96.0	+2.5
Indiana	3113	44.6	329	32.7	1374	75.5	1040	3585	610	96.7	+4.6
Toronto	3002	45.4	346	33.9	1631	76.4	961	3513	557	97.3	-0.1
Seattle	3132	45.1	440	34.0	1343	74.8	1084	3695	590	98.1	+1.0
New Jersey	3125	46.4	368	36.3	1503	74.7	1129	3786	568	99.0	-1.0
Orlando	3076	44.5	431	33.8	1567	74.5	1094	3567	724	99.4	+0.7
Vancouver	3136	47.4	361	33.3	1530	76.9	970	3306	725	99.5	-5.6
Atlanta	3211	45.5	373	36.7	1381	76.9	1052	3526	655	99.7	-5.4
Washington	3005	45.9	390	37.1	1790	74.4	962	3380	686	99.9	-3.3
Boston	2960	47.0	359	36.1	1929	75.3	857	3391	638	100.1	-0.8
Houston	3226	45.6	350	35.4	1425	77.9	1027	3478	735	100.3	-0.8
Cleveland	2983	44.3	420	34.2	1851	77.6	1013	3599	659	100.5	-3.5
Milwaukee	3033	45.7	531	39.1	1685	75.2	1037	3405	637	101.0	+0.2
Denver	3129	45.0	399	35.4	1632	75.1	1027	3633	616	101.1	-2.1
Dallas	3225	45.7	429	34.5	1484	74.0	1251	3970	604	101.9	-0.5
Detroit	3119	46.5	458	37.1	1669	74.6	973	3477	652	102.0	+1.5
Sacramento	3269	45.2	396	35.3	1434	75.1	1143	3904	753	102.0	+3.0
LA Clippers	3281	47.7	417	38.7	1512	74.1	1038	3737	621	103.5	-11.5
Golden State	3165	46.7	427	36.7	1755	75.4	1091	3782	690	103.8	-8.3

Atlanta Hawks

Player	GP	Min	Field Goals		3-Pt FG		Free Throws		Rebounds		A	Stl	TO	BS	Avg
			FGM	Pct	FGA	FGM	FTM	Pct	Off	Total					
Rider	60	2084	449	41.9	180	56	204	78.5	63	258	219	41	168	6	19.3
Jackson	79	2767	507	41.1	303	117	186	87.7	101	394	230	57	185	10	16.7
Henderson	82	2775	429	46.1	10	1	224	67.1	265	571	77	81	139	54	13.2
Mutombo	82	2984	322	56.2	0	0	298	70.8	304	1157	105	27	174	269	11.5
Ellis	58	1309	209	45.0	21	3	66	69.5	98	290	59	32	52	25	8.4
Terry	81	1888	209	41.5	157	46	113	80.7	24	166	346	90	156	10	8.1
Coles	80	1924	276	45.5	39	8	85	81.7	30	172	290	58	103	11	8.1
McLeod	44	860	131	39.5	13	2	54	77.1	41	138	52	16	59	5	7.2
Glover	30	446	66	38.6	45	12	51	72.9	15	38	27	15	28	4	6.5
Wright	75	1205	180	49.9	3	1	87	64.4	117	305	21	29	66	40	6.0
Crawford	55	668	91	39.7	27	7	63	77.8	51	99	33	17	37	16	4.6
Bowdler	46	423	49	42.6	1	0	24	63.2	22	85	14	14	21	9	2.7
Barry	16	159	15	45.5	18	7	4	80.0	0	12	33	2	13	0	2.6
Hawks	**82**	**19830**	**3000**	**44.1**	**814**	**258**	**1477**	**74.3**	**1146**	**3716**	**1548**	**500**	**1219**	**461**	**94.3**
Opponents	**82**	**19830**	**3211**	**45.5**	**1015**	**373**	**1381**	**76.9**	**1052**	**3526**	**1886**	**655**	**1001**	**404**	**99.7**

Boston Celtics

Player	GP	Min	Field Goals		3-Pt FG		Free Throws		Rebounds		A	Stl	TO	BS	Avg
			FGM	Pct	FGA	FGM	FTM	Pct	Off	Total					
Walker	82	3003	648	43.0	285	73	311	69.9	199	652	305	117	259	32	20.5
Pierce	73	2583	486	44.2	280	96	359	79.8	83	396	221	152	178	62	19.5
Anderson	82	2593	434	44.0	220	85	196	77.5	55	225	420	139	130	8	14.0
Potapenko	79	1797	307	49.9	1	0	109	68.1	182	499	77	41	145	29	9.2
Fortson	55	856	140	52.8	0	0	139	73.5	141	366	29	20	67	5	7.6
Williams	68	1378	165	42.7	72	25	134	79.3	55	156	93	44	66	16	7.2
Barros	72	1139	196	45.1	144	59	66	86.8	13	99	133	31	66	4	7.2
Griffin	72	1927	175	42.4	57	16	119	75.3	128	372	177	116	93	15	6.7
Battie	82	1505	219	47.7	8	1	102	67.5	152	410	63	47	67	70	6.6
Cheaney	67	1309	120	44.0	54	18	9	42.9	23	138	80	44	46	14	4.0
McCarty	61	879	78	33.9	110	34	39	72.2	33	110	70	24	67	23	3.8
Overton	48	432	61	39.6	28	10	20	95.2	14	33	53	10	20	0	3.2
Ellison	30	269	19	44.2	0	0	15	71.4	29	67	13	10	13	8	1.8
Celtics	**82**	**19730**	**3054**	**44.4**	**1260**	**417**	**1621**	**74.5**	**1108**	**3528**	**1741**	**795**	**1221**	**286**	**99.3**
Opponents	**82**	**19730**	**2960**	**47.0**	**995**	**359**	**1929**	**75.3**	**857**	**3391**	**1798**	**638**	**1395**	**473**	**100.1**

Charlotte Hornets

Player	GP	Min	Field Goals		3-Pt FG		Free Throws		Rebounds		A	Stl	TO	BS	Avg
			FGM	Pct	FGA	FGM	FTM	Pct	Off	Total					
Jones	72	2807	478	42.7	341	128	362	86.4	81	343	305	192	160	49	20.1
Coleman	74	2347	446	45.6	141	51	296	78.5	124	632	175	34	173	130	16.7
Wesley	82	2760	407	42.6	248	88	214	77.8	39	225	463	109	159	11	13.6
Phills	28	825	152	45.4	91	30	47	72.3	17	71	79	41	48	8	13.6
Campbell	78	2538	370	44.6	6	0	247	69.0	168	590	129	56	127	150	12.7
Mason	82	3133	317	48.0	1	0	314	74.6	145	699	367	74	160	29	11.6
Miller	55	961	135	46.1	2	0	153	78.5	113	293	45	23	48	35	7.7
Robinson	67	1112	212	54.9	4	0	47	73.4	54	184	32	48	39	25	7.0
B. Davis	82	1523	182	42.0	111	25	97	63.4	48	165	309	97	140	19	5.9
Brown	63	1096	148	45.1	10	2	36	69.2	35	167	66	20	45	18	5.3
R. Davis	48	570	94	50.3	4	0	39	76.5	29	83	62	30	46	8	4.7
Ellis	42	564	66	41.5	100	37	9	69.2	13	56	14	13	20	0	4.2
Fuller	41	399	51	41.8	0	0	32	60.4	36	110	5	9	27	8	3.3
Recasner	7	28	3	42.9	4	1	0	—	0	4	5	0	0	0	1.0
Hawkins	12	36	3	23.1	5	1	1	50.0	0	7	13	0	3	0	0.7
Hornets	**82**	**19780**	**2935**	**44.9**	**1001**	**339**	**1863**	**75.8**	**884**	**3519**	**2023**	**732**	**1160**	**480**	**98.4**
Opponents	**82**	**19780**	**3048**	**44.8**	**1086**	**410**	**1347**	**74.5**	**966**	**2550**	**1903**	**604**	**1297**	**421**	**95.8**

Chicago Bulls

Player	GP	Min	Field Goals		3-Pt FG		Free Throws		Rebounds		A	Stl	TO	BS	Avg
			FGM	Pct	FGA	FGM	FTM	Pct	Off	Total					
Brand	82	2999	630	48.2	2	0	367	68.5	348	810	155	66	228	132	20.1
Starks	37	1190	203	37.5	171	59	50	84.7	101	181	181	42	67	4	13.9
Artest	72	2238	309	40.7	191	60	188	67.4	62	308	202	119	166	39	12.0
Carr	57	1166	196	39.5	101	32	107	85.6	41	173	84	30	117	15	9.3
Hoiberg	31	845	89	38.7	94	32	69	90.8	7	110	85	40	43	2	9.0
Hawkins	61	1622	159	42.4	141	55	107	89.9	31	175	134	74	100	15	7.9
Armstrong	27	583	83	44.6	29	13	22	88.0	2	47	78	7	40	1	7.4
Brown	59	1625	157	36.1	6	3	62	73.8	23	144	202	61	105	15	6.4
Maloney	51	1175	114	35.8	174	62	37	82.2	10	64	138	32	63	3	6.4
Anstey	73	1007	161	44.2	6	1	116	78.9	90	280	65	29	80	25	6.0
Simpkins	69	1651	111	40.5	1	0	65	54.2	124	372	100	22	128	22	4.2
Ruffin	71	975	58	42.0	0	0	43	48.9	117	250	44	26	59	26	2.2
Bulls	82	19805	2565	41.5	1032	340	1482	70.9	1032	3355	1645	646	1438	383	84.8
Opponents	82	19805	2916	45.6	1049	358	1533	74.1	1000	3416	1902	853	1244	461	94.2

Cleveland Cavaliers

Player	GP	Min	Field Goals		3-Pt FG		Free Throws		Rebounds		A	Stl	TO	BS	Avg
			FGM	Pct	FGA	FGM	FTM	Pct	Off	Total					
Kemp	82	2492	484	41.7	6	2	493	77.6	231	725	138	100	291	96	17.8
Murray	74	2365	460	45.1	139	51	204	76.1	127	423	132	105	184	36	15.9
Sura	73	2216	356	43.7	332	122	175	69.7	50	288	284	91	148	19	13.8
Miller	82	2093	339	44.9	49	10	226	77.4	85	280	476	84	166	17	11.1
Knight	65	1754	230	41.2	10	2	140	76.1	38	193	146	40	157	21	9.3
Person	79	2056	280	42.8	250	106	61	79.2	44	267	146	40	60	19	9.2
Ferry	63	1326	189	49.7	75	33	52	91.2	55	238	67	22	55	24	7.3
DeClercq	82	1831	225	50.8	0	0	94	58.8	156	439	58	63	108	66	6.6
Bryant	75	1712	174	50.3	0	0	76	80.9	126	352	61	31	87	31	5.7
Henderson	61	1107	129	39.6	15	1	69	66.3	34	140	55	39	68	17	5.4
Boykins	26	261	56	48.3	20	8	18	78.3	12	26	48	12	17	1	5.3
Langdon	10	145	15	37.5	20	8	11	100.0	4	15	11	5	6	0	4.9
Reid	34	602	53	41.7	7	1	43	76.8	29	117	18	19	20	5	4.4
Traylor	44	447	58	47.5	4	0	41	60.3	50	115	20	25	27	25	3.6
Stack	25	198	17	33.3	1	0	18	66.7	18	45	5	4	17	11	2.1
Ketner	22	132	13	40.6	0	0	8	66.7	12	34	1	4	10	3	1.5
Cavs	82	19855	2977	44.2	919	343	1653	75.0	1010	3509	1941	715	1382	363	97.0
Opponents	82	19855	2983	44.3	1229	420	1851	77.6	1013	3599	1942	659	1389	500	100.5

Dallas Mavericks

Player	GP	Min	Field Goals		3-Pt FG		Free Throws		Rebounds		A	Stl	TO	BS	Avg
			FGM	Pct	FGA	FGM	FTM	Pct	Off	Total					
Finley	82	3464	748	45.7	247	99	260	82.0	122	518	438	109	196	32	22.6
Nowitzki	82	2938	515	46.1	306	116	289	83.0	102	430	203	63	141	68	17.5
Ceballos	69	2064	447	44.6	134	44	248	84.3	172	462	90	56	125	24	16.6
Trent	11	301	70	49.3	2	0	11	52.4	20	52	22	8	25	3	13.7
Strickland	68	2025	316	43.3	186	73	162	83.1	69	323	211	105	102	13	12.8
Pack	29	665	96	41.7	11	4	63	80.8	7	42	168	31	76	3	8.9
Nash	56	1532	173	47.7	149	60	75	88.2	34	121	272	37	102	3	8.6
Bradley	77	1901	266	47.9	5	1	114	76.5	160	497	60	71	74	190	8.4
Davis	79	1817	217	46.8	167	82	67	87.0	17	134	141	24	70	3	7.4
Buckner	48	923	111	47.6	26	10	43	68.3	56	174	55	38	36	20	5.7
Murdock	40	693	79	38.5	42	16	51	63.8	15	77	108	47	58	5	5.6
Jones	55	612	80	38.5	114	41	32	66.7	12	55	96	18	40	1	4.2
Sundov	14	61	12	38.7	0	0	2	100.0	5	12	2	2	4	2	1.9
Rhodes	1	8	0	—	0	0	0	—	1	1	0	2	2	0	0.0
Mavericks	82	19730	3195	45.3	1326	519	1407	80.4	931	3375	1810	592	1081	416	101.4
Opponents	82	19730	3225	45.7	1244	429	1484	74.0	1251	3970	1901	604	1318	416	102.0

Denver Nuggets

Player	GP	Min	Field Goals		3-Pt FG		Free Throws		Rebounds		A	Stl	TO	BS	Avg
			FGM	Pct	FGA	FGM	FTM	Pct	Off	Total					
McDyess	81	2698	614	50.7	2	0	323	62.6	234	685	159	69	230	139	19.1
Van Exel	79	2950	473	39.0	401	133	196	81.7	34	311	714	68	221	11	16.1
LaFrentz	81	2435	392	44.6	183	60	162	68.6	170	641	97	42	96	180	12.4
Lenard	53	1434	228	40.7	228	89	84	79.2	37	153	136	41	80	15	11.9
Abdul-Wahad	61	1578	274	42.4	23	3	146	75.6	101	291	98	59	106	28	11.4
McCloud	78	2118	266	41.7	283	107	148	81.8	72	285	246	48	134	26	10.1
Clark	81	1850	286	54.2	8	1	121	68.8	162	505	71	45	125	114	8.6
Posey	81	2052	230	42.9	220	82	120	80.0	85	317	146	98	95	33	8.2
Stith	45	691	86	45.5	56	17	64	83.1	23	84	61	18	33	12	5.6
Strickland	58	663	122	54.5	0	0	40	71.4	44	140	22	15	24	18	4.9
Herren	45	597	45	36.3	67	24	27	67.5	12	52	111	15	42	2	3.1
Alexander	29	329	28	28.6	35	9	17	77.3	8	42	58	24	28	2	2.8
Jones	40	330	44	42.3	3	2	14	73.7	41	103	19	3	13	6	2.6
Bowen	52	589	46	39.3	9	1	38	71.7	75	114	20	39	14	13	2.5
Rogers	40	355	35	39.8	1	0	19	46.3	33	80	9	2	10	38	2.2
Nuggets	82	19855	3057	44.2	1397	470	1531	72.4	1073	3663	1911	554	1235	618	99.0
Opponents	82	19855	3129	45.0	1126	399	1632	75.1	1027	2606	2003	616	1179	462	101.1

Detroit Pistons

Player	GP	Min	Field Goals		3-Pt FG		Free Throws		Rebounds		A	Stl	TO	BS	Avg
			FGM	Pct	FGA	FGM	FTM	Pct	Off	Total					
Hill	74	2776	696	48.9	98	34	480	79.5	97	490	385	103	240	43	25.8
Stackhouse	82	3148	619	42.8	288	83	618	81.5	118	315	365	103	311	36	23.6
Hunter	82	2919	378	42.5	389	168	117	76.0	35	250	327	129	145	22	12.7
Laettner	82	2443	379	47.3	24	7	237	81.2	175	553	186	83	186	45	12.2
Williams	82	2102	257	56.4	3	0	175	61.6	277	789	68	95	105	21	8.4
Moore	29	488	87	62.1	0	0	54	79.4	44	112	17	9	23	31	7.9
Mills	82	1842	214	43.9	242	95	25	73.5	50	390	85	38	46	24	6.7
Curry	82	1611	182	48.0	5	1	141	83.9	21	104	87	33	73	5	6.2
Crotty	69	937	106	42.2	80	33	80	86.0	17	75	128	27	54	5	4.7
Buechler	58	657	55	35.3	83	18	2	28.6	30	91	33	25	13	16	2.2
Vaught	43	292	32	36.0	3	0	11	68.8	26	91	11	6	11	4	1.7
Jackson	7	73	1	9.1	1	0	5	62.5	1	11	4	3	7	0	1.0
Montross	51	332	17	30.9	0	0	6	50.0	18	72	7	6	22	9	0.8
Pistons	82	19830	3044	45.9	1223	439	1956	78.1	917	3375	1707	665	1250	273	103.5
Opponents	82	19830	3119	46.5	1234	458	1669	74.6	973	3477	1893	652	1400	396	102.0

Golden State Warriors

Player	GP	Min	Field Goals		3-Pt FG		Free Throws		Rebounds		A	Stl	TO	BS	Avg
			FGM	Pct	FGA	FGM	FTM	Pct	Off	Total					
Jamison	43	1556	356	47.1	7	2	127	61.1	172	359	90	30	113	15	19.6
Mills	20	649	123	42.1	30	8	68	81.0	46	123	47	18	25	4	16.1
Hughes	82	2324	459	40.0	125	29	279	74.0	113	349	205	115	195	28	15.0
Marshall	64	2071	331	39.4	138	49	199	78.0	189	637	167	68	123	68	14.2
Blaylock	73	2459	327	39.1	301	101	67	70.5	55	270	489	146	143	22	11.3
V. Cummings	75	1793	265	40.5	151	49	127	75.1	57	184	247	91	132	13	9.4
T. Cummings	22	398	76	42.9	0	0	32	82.1	45	107	21	13	27	8	8.4
Dampier	21	495	70	40.5	0	0	27	52.9	48	134	19	8	29	15	8.0
Farmer	74	1199	127	40.7	44	8	203	76.6	118	295	74	66	82	16	6.3
Davis	23	464	56	40.9	2	0	31	66.0	31	84	38	25	40	4	6.2
Foyle	76	1654	193	50.8	0	0	34	37.8	174	424	42	26	71	136	5.5
Del Negro	67	1211	153	47.1	24	8	35	89.7	9	107	160	36	48	0	5.2
Jacobson	52	681	108	50.9	24	9	30	73.2	25	71	32	30	33	3	4.9
Curley	28	309	29	42.6	1	0	18	72.0	18	50	14	13	21	4	2.7
Young	25	137	13	33.3	0	0	28	77.8	13	35	5	2	9	1	2.2
Warriors	82	19755	2996	42.0	1069	345	1497	69.7	1300	3738	1851	731	1255	356	95.5
Opponents	82	19755	3165	46.7	1163	427	1755	75.4	1091	3782	2036	690	1338	495	103.8

Houston Rockets

Player	GP	Min	FGM	Pct	FGA	FGM	FTM	Pct	Off	Total	A	Stl	TO	BS	Avg
			Field Goals		3-Pt FG		Free Throws		Rebounds						
Francis	77	2776	497	44.5	310	107	287	78.6	152	409	507	118	306	29	18.0
Mobley	81	2496	437	43.0	292	104	299	84.7	59	288	208	87	186	32	15.8
Anderson	82	2700	368	47.3	225	79	194	76.7	91	384	239	96	194	32	12.3
Williams	76	1859	312	45.8	261	102	101	82.1	69	306	157	49	113	44	10.9
Olajuwon	44	1049	193	45.8	2	0	69	61.6	65	274	61	41	73	70	10.3
Cato	65	1581	216	53.7	4	0	135	64.9	102	389	26	33	71	124	8.7
Thomas	72	1797	212	39.9	122	32	138	66.0	147	437	113	54	112	22	8.3
Rogers	53	1101	170	52.5	14	1	81	59.1	98	275	42	14	63	34	8.0
Norris	30	502	69	43.4	29	12	57	78.1	16	68	94	23	30	1	6.9
Bullard	56	1024	139	40.9	177	79	25	83.3	13	138	63	19	36	13	6.8
Drew	72	1293	158	38.3	163	59	45	84.9	23	103	162	41	66	1	5.8
Massenburg	10	109	16	44.4	0	0	14	87.5	7	27	3	2	9	5	4.6
Miller	35	476	52	53.6	0	0	26	51.0	49	164	16	11	19	10	3.7
Gray	21	124	15	40.5	0	0	19	65.5	11	25	5	5	4	3	2.3
Rockets	82	19830	3001	45.0	1625	581	1573	73.3	1008	3594	1774	613	1358	438	99.5
Opponents	82	19830	3226	45.6	990	350	1425	77.9	1027	3478	1863	735	1126	433	100.3

Indiana Pacers

Player	GP	Min	FGM	Pct	FGA	FGM	FTM	Pct	Off	Total	A	Stl	TO	BS	Avg
			Field Goals		3-Pt FG		Free Throws		Rebounds						
Rose	80	2978	563	47.1	196	77	254	82.7	42	387	320	84	188	49	18.2
Miller	81	2987	466	44.8	404	165	373	91.9	50	239	187	85	129	25	18.1
Smits	79	1852	431	48.4	1	0	156	73.9	94	401	85	20	108	100	12.9
Croshere	81	1885	288	44.1	174	63	196	84.8	135	516	89	44	121	60	10.3
Davis	74	2127	302	50.2	0	0	139	68.5	256	729	64	52	91	94	10.0
Best	82	1691	271	48.3	93	35	156	82.1	16	142	272	76	107	5	8.9
Jackson	81	2190	246	43.2	221	89	79	80.6	63	296	650	76	174	10	8.1
Perkins	81	1620	184	41.7	218	89	80	82.5	64	289	68	31	63	33	6.6
Harrington	50	854	121	45.8	34	8	78	70.3	47	159	38	25	65	9	6.6
Mullin	47	582	80	42.8	110	45	37	90.2	14	76	37	28	28	9	5.1
McKey	32	634	43	39.8	23	10	43	76.8	29	135	35	29	19	13	4.3
Bender	24	130	23	32.9	12	2	16	66.7	4	21	3	1	7	5	2.7
Foster	19	86	13	56.5	12	2	16	68.0	12	32	5	5	2	1	2.3
Tabak	18	114	16	47.1	0	0	5	62.5	16	32	4	3	11	9	2.1
Pacers	82	19730	3047	45.9	1487	583	1629	81.1	842	3454	1857	559	1113	422	101.3
Opponents	82	19730	3113	44.6	1006	329	1374	75.5	1040	3585	1735	610	1126	323	96.7

Los Angeles Clippers

Player	GP	Min	FGM	Pct	FGA	FGM	FTM	Pct	Off	Total	A	Stl	TO	BS	Avg
			Field Goals		3-Pt FG		Free Throws		Rebounds						
Taylor	62	2227	458	46.4	8	1	143	71.1	96	400	101	51	169	48	17.1
Anderson	64	2201	377	43.8	178	55	271	87.7	80	258	220	90	167	11	16.9
Odom	76	2767	449	43.8	164	59	302	71.9	159	595	317	91	258	95	16.6
Nesby	73	2317	364	39.8	281	94	151	79.1	82	275	121	75	102	31	13.3
Olowokandi	80	2493	330	43.7	0	0	123	65.1	194	656	38	35	177	140	9.8
Piatkowski	75	1712	238	41.5	243	93	85	85.0	74	222	81	44	57	13	8.7
McInnis	25	597	80	43.0	21	7	13	76.5	18	72	89	15	27	2	7.2
Skinner	33	775	68	50.7	0	0	43	66.2	63	201	11	16	37	44	5.4
Rooks	71	1001	122	43.1	0	0	65	73.0	82	248	68	29	70	52	4.4
Closs	57	820	96	48.7	3	0	46	59.0	65	179	25	13	34	73	4.2
Jones	56	662	66	32.8	118	39	17	73.9	17	62	94	30	28	5	3.4
Bohannon	13	118	7	53.8	0	0	15	62.5	13	31	5	2	10	6	2.2
Chilcutt	56	601	53	41.7	26	6	8	100.0	46	131	27	15	20	10	2.1
Avent	49	377	29	30.2	0	0	23	71.9	23	74	11	16	24	15	1.7
Clippers	82	19705	2877	42.6	1267	429	1363	74.6	955	3332	1479	578	1265	494	92.0
Opponents	82	19705	3281	47.7	1077	417	1512	74.1	1038	3737	1975	621	1172	377	103.5

Los Angeles Lakers

Player	GP	Min	Field Goals FGM	Pct	3-Pt FG FGA	FGM	Free Throws FTM	Pct	Rebounds Off	Total	A	Stl	TO	BS	Avg
O'Neal	79	3163	956	57.4	1	0	432	52.4	336	1078	299	36	223	239	29.7
Bryant	66	2524	554	46.8	144	46	331	82.1	108	416	323	106	182	62	22.5
Rice	80	2530	421	43.0	229	84	346	87.4	56	327	176	47	114	12	15.9
Harper	80	2042	212	39.9	106	33	100	68.0	96	337	270	85	132	39	7.0
Fox	82	1473	206	41.4	181	59	63	80.8	63	198	138	52	87	26	6.5
Fisher	78	1803	167	34.6	166	52	105	72.4	22	143	216	80	75	3	6.3
Lue	8	146	19	48.7	8	4	6	75.0	2	12	17	3	9	0	6.0
Horry	76	1685	159	43.8	94	29	89	78.8	133	361	118	84	73	80	5.7
Green	82	1929	173	44.7	4	1	66	69.5	160	486	80	53	53	18	5.0
Shaw	74	1249	123	38.2	58	18	41	75.9	45	216	201	35	75	14	4.1
George	49	345	56	38.9	47	16	27	65.9	29	75	12	10	21	4	3.2
Celestand	16	185	15	33.3	9	2	5	83.3	1	11	20	7	16	0	2.3
Knight	63	410	46	39.0	0	0	17	60.7	46	129	23	6	26	23	1.7
Salley	45	303	25	36.2	0	0	21	75.0	20	65	26	8	18	14	1.6
Lakers	**82**	**19805**	**3137**	**45.9**	**1047**	**344**	**1649**	**69.6**	**1117**	**3855**	**1921**	**613**	**1106**	**534**	**100.8**
Opponents	**82**	**19805**	**2838**	**41.6**	**1142**	**372**	**1518**	**74.2**	**1007**	**3538**	**1597**	**627**	**1196**	**345**	**92.3**

Miami Heat

Player	GP	Min	Field Goals FGM	Pct	3-Pt FG FGA	FGM	Free Throws FTM	Pct	Rebounds Off	Total	A	Stl	TO	BS	Avg
Mourning	79	2748	652	55.1	4	0	414	71.1	215	753	123	40	217	294	21.7
Mashburn	76	2828	515	44.5	278	112	186	77.8	64	381	298	79	180	14	17.5
Hardaway	52	1672	246	38.6	256	94	110	82.7	25	150	385	49	119	4	13.4
Gatling	80	1811	365	45.5	70	18	266	71.3	154	502	71	82	169	23	11.9
Brown	80	2302	322	48.0	1	0	120	75.5	216	600	145	65	100	61	9.6
Majerle	69	2308	170	40.3	304	110	56	81.2	27	333	206	89	62	17	7.3
Weatherspoon	78	1615	215	51.3	0	0	135	73.8	128	449	93	51	100	49	7.2
Carter	79	1859	201	39.5	23	3	93	75.0	48	199	378	93	173	5	6.3
Thorpe	51	777	125	51.4	3	0	29	60.4	56	166	33	26	59	9	5.5
Buford	34	386	62	41.1	29	7	16	72.7	10	48	33	26	59	9	4.3
Bowen	69	878	72	37.1	58	27	25	58.1	27	96	34	23	19	15	2.8
James	4	23	5	35.7	0	0	1	33.3	3	4	2	0	3	2	2.8
Causwell	25	185	20	54.1	0	0	26	68.4	11	47	2	2	10	16	2.6
Jamison	12	74	7	35.0	0	0	4	22.2	16	21	4	2	4	1	1.5
Heat	**82**	**19830**	**2974**	**46.0**	**1202**	**446**	**1345**	**73.6**	**921**	**3540**	**1931**	**582**	**1182**	**524**	**94.4**
Opponents	**82**	**19830**	**2782**	**42.2**	**1130**	**408**	**1512**	**74.8**	**974**	**3315**	**1582**	**621**	**1150**	**364**	**91.3**

Milwaukee Bucks

Player	GP	Min	Field Goals FGM	Pct	3-Pt FG FGA	FGM	Free Throws FTM	Pct	Rebounds Off	Total	A	Stl	TO	BS	Avg
Allen	82	3070	642	45.5	407	172	353	88.7	83	359	308	110	183	19	22.1
Robinson	81	2909	690	47.2	237	86	227	80.2	107	485	193	78	223	41	20.9
Cassell	81	2899	545	46.6	90	26	390	87.6	69	301	729	102	267	8	18.6
Caffey	71	2159	323	47.9	2	0	206	59.7	189	482	119	62	170	20	12.0
Thomas	80	2093	347	46.1	182	63	188	77.4	100	332	113	59	129	31	11.8
Williams	68	1488	213	50.0	0	0	94	72.9	177	448	28	40	65	66	7.6
Owens	62	1305	150	41.9	34	11	63	59.4	99	301	97	33	85	21	6.0
Ham	35	792	71	55.5	1	0	35	44.9	85	172	42	29	29	29	5.1
Johnson	80	2129	144	51.6	1	0	95	60.5	233	648	44	81	80	127	4.8
Manning	72	1217	149	44.0	4	1	34	65.4	50	208	73	62	55	29	4.6
Alston	27	361	27	28.4	14	3	3	75.0	5	23	70	12	29	0	2.2
Turkcan	17	90	14	36.8	6	0	5	62.5	13	33	5	3	8	1	1.9
Bucks	**82**	**19855**	**3174**	**46.5**	**1069**	**394**	**1558**	**78.6**	**1016**	**3389**	**1852**	**671**	**1183**	**381**	**101.2**
Opponents	**82**	**19855**	**3033**	**45.7**	**1357**	**531**	**1685**	**75.2**	**1037**	**3405**	**1987**	**637**	**1303**	**340**	**101.0**

Minnesota Timberwolves

Player	GP	Min	Field Goals		3-Pt FG		Free Throws		Rebounds		A	Stl	TO	BS	Avg
			FGM	Pct	FGA	FGM	FTM	Pct	Off	Total					
Garnett	81	3243	759	49.7	81	30	309	76.5	223	956	401	120	268	126	22.9
Brandon	71	2587	486	46.6	132	53	187	89.9	44	238	629	134	184	30	17.1
Szczerbiak	73	2171	342	51.1	78	28	133	82.6	89	272	201	58	83	23	11.6
Sealy	82	2392	371	47.6	35	10	177	81.2	119	352	197	76	110	19	11.3
Smith	78	1975	289	46.4	1	1	195	75.6	186	484	88	45	119	85	9.9
Peeler	82	2073	316	43.6	255	85	87	79.8	58	174	195	62	85	10	9.8
Mitchell	66	1227	168	44.7	23	10	81	88.0	28	138	111	27	44	14	6.5
Nesterovic	82	1723	206	47.6	2	0	59	57.3	135	379	93	21	71	85	5.7
Jackson	73	1034	140	40.5	46	13	76	77.6	50	153	172	48	58	7	5.1
Avery	59	484	56	30.9	63	18	24	66.7	8	40	88	14	42	2	2.6
Hammonds	56	372	42	43.3	0	0	33	58.9	34	101	10	8	21	3	2.1
Garrett	56	604	42	44.4	0	0	18	69.2	41	140	19	8	21	40	2.0
Patterson	5	20	3	75.0	0	0	0	—	1	2	1	1	1	0	1.2
T'wolves	82	19905	3226	46.7	716	248	1379	78.0	1016	3487	2205	622	1107	444	98.5
Opponents	82	19905	2924	44.5	1066	380	1644	2185	916	3356	1737	591	1232	344	96.0

New Jersey Nets

Player	GP	Min	Field Goals		3-Pt FG		Free Throws		Rebounds		A	Stl	TO	BS	Avg
			FGM	Pct	FGA	FGM	FTM	Pct	Off	Total					
Marbury	74	2881	569	43.2	233	66	436	81.3	61	240	622	112	270	15	22.2
Van Horn	80	2782	559	44.5	228	84	333	84.7	200	676	158	64	245	60	19.2
Gill	76	2355	396	41.4	78	20	181	71.0	82	283	210	139	89	41	13.1
Kittles	62	1896	305	43.7	240	96	101	79.5	46	225	142	79	56	19	13.0
Newman	82	1763	278	44.6	190	72	192	83.8	39	154	65	53	89	11	10.0
Harris	77	1510	198	42.8	115	38	79	79.8	53	187	100	65	42	6	6.7
Burrell	74	1336	165	39.4	232	82	39	78.0	65	256	72	67	38	44	6.1
Douglas	20	309	45	50.0	16	5	25	89.3	13	29	34	17	24	0	6.0
Feick	81	2241	181	42.8	3	3	94	70.7	264	755	68	43	59	38	5.7
Perry	60	803	128	43.5	39	11	50	80.6	13	61	139	39	60	1	5.3
Muresan	30	267	41	45.6	0	0	23	60.5	24	68	9	0	16	12	3.5
Eschmeyer	31	373	38	52.8	0	0	15	50.0	40	108	21	8	21	21	2.9
McIlvane	66	1048	64	41.6	0	0	29	51.8	106	230	36	26	38	117	2.4
Nets	82	19830	2979	43.3	1374	477	1601	78.4	1040	3355	1688	720	1051	393	98.0
Opponents	82	19830	3125	46.4	1013	368	1503	74.7	1129	3786	1866	568	1366	469	99.0

New York Knicks

Player	GP	Min	Field Goals		3-Pt FG		Free Throws		Rebounds		A	Stl	TO	BS	Avg
			FGM	Pct	FGA	FGM	FTM	Pct	Off	Total					
Houston	82	3169	614	48.3	243	106	280	83.8	38	271	224	65	186	14	19.7
Sprewell	82	3276	568	43.5	127	44	344	86.6	49	349	332	109	226	22	18.6
Ewing	62	2035	361	46.6	2	0	207	73.1	140	604	58	36	142	84	15.0
Johnson	70	2281	282	43.3	174	58	128	76.6	87	380	175	42	94	7	10.7
Camby	59	1548	226	48.0	2	1	148	67.0	174	461	49	43	72	116	10.2
Thomas	80	1971	270	50.5	3	1	100	78.1	144	505	82	51	105	42	8.0
Ward	72	1986	189	42.3	264	102	48	82.8	22	228	300	95	102	16	7.3
Wallace	60	798	155	46.7	3	0	82	80.4	42	135	22	10	63	14	6.5
Childs	71	1675	146	40.9	104	37	47	79.7	17	147	285	36	105	4	5.3
Lang	19	244	28	43.8	0	0	3	42.9	16	60	3	8	5	6	3.1
Brunson	37	289	29	41.4	13	2	11	61.1	3	27	49	9	31	1	1.9
Dudley	47	459	23	34.3	0	0	9	33.3	63	136	5	7	18	21	1.2
Wingate	7	32	1	11.1	0	0	0	—	1	2	3	1	2	2	0.3
Knicks	82	19830	2897	45.5	937	351	1410	78.1	802	3323	1588	515	1157	349	92.1
Opponents	82	19830	2711	42.4	1197	404	1609	74.7	927	3368	1609	603	1161	354	90.7

Orlando Magic

Player	GP	Min	Field Goals		3-Pt FG		Free Throws		Rebounds		A	Stl	TO	BS	Avg
			FGM	Pct	FGA	FGM	FTM	Pct	Off	Total					
Mercer	68	2377	460	42.6	48	15	213	78.9	64	250	158	75	151	23	16.9
Armstrong	82	2590	484	43.3	403	137	225	91.1	65	270	501	169	248	9	16.2
Amaechi	80	1684	306	43.7	6	1	223	76.6	62	266	95	35	139	37	10.5
Atkins	82	1626	314	42.4	163	57	97	72.9	20	126	306	52	142	3	9.5
Williams	75	1501	263	48.9	5	2	123	74.1	96	250	106	46	109	17	8.7
Billups	13	305	34	33.7	41	7	37	84.1	8	34	39	10	24	2	8.6
Maggette	77	1370	224	47.8	11	2	196	75.1	123	303	61	24	138	26	8.4
Garrity	82	1479	258	44.1	197	79	80	72.1	44	210	58	31	85	19	8.2
Doleac	81	1335	242	45.2	2	1	80	84.2	89	334	63	29	65	34	7.0
Outlaw	82	2326	204	60.2	3	0	82	50.6	202	525	245	113	133	148	6.0
Wallace	81	1959	168	50.3	0	0	54	47.4	211	665	67	72	67	130	4.8
Harpring	4	63	4	23.5	2	2	6	85.7	5	12	8	5	1	1	4.0
Johnson	56	637	62	37.8	11	2	28	71.8	21	51	72	33	32	4	2.8
Strong	20	148	21	43.8	4	1	11	78.6	11	44	4	5	12	2	2.7
Taylor	6	34	5	35.7	1	1	0	—	2	6	1	1	2	1	1.8
Magic	**82**	**19755**	**3169**	**45.2**	**870**	**294**	**1574**	**73.5**	**1145**	**3685**	**1709**	**743**	**1417**	**467**	**100.1**
Opponents	**82**	**19755**	**3076**	**44.5**	**1277**	**431**	**1567**	**74.5**	**1094**	**3567**	**1991**	**724**	**1488**	**475**	**99.4**

Philadelphia 76ers

Player	GP	Min	Field Goals		3-Pt FG		Free Throws		Rebounds		A	Stl	TO	BS	Avg
			FGM	Pct	FGA	FGM	FTM	Pct	Off	Total					
Iverson	70	2853	729	42.1	261	89	442	71.3	71	267	328	144	230	5	28.4
Kukoc	56	1784	297	40.8	168	44	192	72.5	75	273	265	77	146	28	14.8
Hill	68	2155	318	48.5	1	0	179	69.1	220	625	52	64	124	27	12.0
Ratliff	57	1795	247	50.3	0	0	182	77.1	140	435	36	32	108	171	11.9
Geiger	65	1406	260	44.1	4	0	109	77.9	154	387	39	29	91	22	9.7
Lynch	75	2416	297	46.1	36	15	113	61.7	216	582	136	119	120	38	9.6
McKie	82	1952	244	41.1	121	44	121	82.9	47	246	240	108	113	18	8.0
Snow	82	2866	257	43.0	45	11	126	71.2	42	261	624	140	162	8	7.9
MacCulloch	56	528	89	55.3	0	0	28	51.9	48	146	13	11	26	37	3.7
Mohammed	28	190	21	38.9	0	0	12	54.5	16	50	2	4	18	12	1.9
Ollie	40	290	22	44.9	0	0	28	75.7	4	31	46	10	10	0	1.8
Jones	33	138	22	37.9	4	2	11	61.1	16	38	5	6	14	5	1.7
Lang	10	38	6	16.7	0	0	4	80.0	0	5	2	4	2	1	0.6
Bowman	11	20	2	100.0	0	0	1	50.0	0	2	1	1	1	0	0.5
76ers	**82**	**19830**	**2993**	**44.2**	**643**	**208**	**1577**	**70.8**	**1147**	**3615**	**1817**	**791**	**1251**	**386**	**94.8**
Opponents	**82**	**19830**	**2867**	**43.5**	**1172**	**417**	**1510**	**75.5**	**1065**	**3566**	**1828**	**631**	**1444**	**531**	**93.4**

Phoenix Suns

Player	GP	Min	Field Goals		3-Pt FG		Free Throws		Rebounds		A	Stl	TO	BS	Avg
			FGM	Pct	FGA	FGM	FTM	Pct	Off	Total					
Robinson	80	2839	530	46.4	324	120	298	78.2	105	359	224	90	166	61	18.5
Hardaway	60	2253	378	47.4	102	33	226	79.0	91	347	315	94	153	38	16.9
Kidd	67	2616	350	40.9	166	56	203	82.9	96	483	678	134	226	28	14.3
Rogers	82	2286	428	48.6	262	115	159	63.9	138	447	170	94	163	47	13.8
Gugliotta	54	1767	310	48.1	8	1	117	77.5	141	425	124	80	106	31	13.7
Marion	51	1260	222	47.1	22	4	72	84.7	105	332	69	38	51	53	10.2
Day	58	941	130	39.4	165	64	72	66.7	31	129	65	44	50	22	6.8
Johnson	6	113	16	57.1	1	1	7	100.0	0	16	24	2	7	0	6.7
Chapman	53	957	124	38.8	123	41	59	75.6	10	80	62	22	38	1	6.6
Miller	51	1088	137	58.8	0	0	49	67.1	87	261	68	42	74	80	6.3
Longley	72	1417	186	46.6	0	0	80	97	100	323	77	22	136	42	6.3
Livingston	79	1081	155	34.5	55	19	52	83.9	25	130	170	49	92	13	4.8
Bailey	46	449	58	41.4	10	2	45	69.2	26	72	30	13	24	4	3.5
Blount	38	446	44	49.4	2	0	19	57.6	52	113	10	15	28	7	2.8
MacLean	16	143	18	36.7	6	2	4	66.7	6	23	8	2	8	1	2.6
Suns	**82**	**19805**	**3093**	**45.7**	**1246**	**458**	**1467**	**75.9**	**1022**	**3580**	**2098**	**744**	**1331**	**433**	**98.9**
Opponents	**82**	**19805**	**2825**	**42.4**	**1146**	**403**	**1630**	**73.9**	**1071**	**3536**	**1700**	**733**	**1422**	**427**	**93.7**

Portland Trail Blazers

Player	GP	Min	Field Goals		3-Pt FG		Free Throws		Rebounds		A	Stl	TO	BS	Avg
			FGM	Pct	FGA	FGM	FTM	Pct	Off	Total					
Wallace	81	2845	542	51.9	50	8	233	70.4	129	566	142	87	157	107	16.4
Smith	82	2689	420	46.7	241	96	289	85.0	123	313	209	71	117	31	14.9
Stoudamire	78	2372	386	43.2	212	80	122	84.1	61	243	405	77	149	1	12.5
Pippen	82	2749	388	45.1	263	86	160	71.7	114	513	406	117	208	41	12.5
Sabonis	66	1688	302	50.5	19	7	167	84.3	97	513	118	43	97	78	11.8
Wells	66	1162	236	49.2	53	20	129	88	78	182	97	69	97	12	8.8
Schrempf	77	1662	187	43.2	52	21	179	83.3	79	332	197	37	100	17	7.5
B. Grant	63	1322	173	49.1	2	1	112	67.5	121	344	64	32	84	28	7.3
Anthony	82	1548	169	40.6	233	88	88	77.2	17	133	208	59	85	9	6.3
G. Grant	3	24	6	42.9	0	0	0	—	0	3	1	1	2	0	4.0
O'Neal	70	859	108	48.6	1	0	57	58.2	97	229	18	11	47	55	3.9
Augmon	59	692	83	47.4	2	0	37	67.3	42	116	53	27	38	11	3.4
Thomas	7	46	8	44.4	3	0	1	100.0	1	5	6	1	5	0	2.4
Harvey	19	137	17	56.7	0	0	7	58.3	8	33	5	1	12	6	2.2
Kleine	7	31	4	36.4	0	0	3	100.0	0	6	2	1	2	1	1.6
Trail Blazers	82	19780	3021	47.0	1128	407	1542	76.0	966	3526	1925	633	1195	396	97.5
Opponents	82	19780	2825	43.1	1195	394	1422	71.6	978	3198	1705	652	1186	350	91.0

Sacramento Kings

Player	GP	Min	Field Goals		3-Pt FG		Free Throws		Rebounds		A	Stl	TO	BS	Avg
			FGM	Pct	FGA	FGM	FTM	Pct	Off	Total					
Webber	75	2880	748	48.3	95	27	311	75.1	189	787	345	120	218	128	24.5
Williams	81	2760	363	37.3	505	145	128	75.3	22	230	589	117	296	8	12.3
Divac	82	2374	384	50.3	26	7	230	69.1	174	656	244	103	190	103	12.3
Stojakovic	74	1749	321	44.8	267	100	135	88.2	74	276	106	52	88	7	11.9
Anderson	72	2094	306	39.1	397	132	37	48.7	83	339	123	94	95	16	10.8
Williamson	76	1707	311	50.0	0	0	163	76.9	122	290	82	38	110	19	10.3
Barry	62	1281	161	46.5	154	66	107	92.2	38	159	150	75	85	7	8.0
Funderburke	75	1026	184	52.3	2	0	115	70.6	98	234	33	32	40	20	6.4
Delk	46	682	120	43.0	40	9	47	79.7	36	88	55	35	32	5	6.4
Martin	71	893	133	38.0	124	38	98	82.4	7	44	122	28	62	2	5.7
Pollard	76	1336	149	52.7	0	0	114	71.7	168	404	43	55	50	59	5.4
Robertson	1	25	2	33.3	2	0	1	100.0	0	0	0	0	0	0	5.0
Corbin	54	941	88	35.6	44	10	33	84.6	40	165	60	36	29	5	4.1
Wennington	7	57	6	31.6	0	0	2	100.0	5	19	1	2	1	2	2.0
Kings	82	19805	3276	45.0	1656	534	1521	75.4	1056	3691	1953	787	1296	381	105.0
Opponents	82	19805	3269	45.2	1123	396	1434	75.1	1143	3904	1950	753	1437	404	102.0

San Antonio Spurs

Player	GP	Min	Field Goals		3-Pt FG		Free Throws		Rebounds		A	Stl	TO	BS	Avg
			FGM	Pct	FGA	FGM	FTM	Pct	Off	Total					
Duncan	74	2875	628	49.0	11	1	459	76.1	262	918	234	66	242	165	23.2
Robinson	80	2557	528	51.2	2	0	371	72.6	193	770	142	97	164	183	17.8
Johnson	82	2571	402	47.3	9	1	114	73.5	33	158	491	76	140	18	11.2
Porter	68	1613	207	44.7	207	90	137	80.6	24	191	221	50	100	9	9.4
Elie	79	2217	195	42.7	186	74	126	84.6	48	249	193	73	130	9	7.5
Rose	74	1341	176	45.7	3	1	143	72.2	133	335	47	35	99	52	6.7
Jackson	81	1691	186	38.1	306	108	33	64.7	34	181	118	54	66	7	6.3
Daniels	68	1195	163	47.4	66	22	72	71.3	16	86	177	55	58	5	6.2
Elliott	19	391	38	35.8	37	13	25	68.3	6	47	28	12	19	2	6.0
Walker	71	980	137	44.9	0	0	86	68.3	77	272	38	10	64	35	5.1
Dial	8	95	17	37.0	12	3	3	60.0	14	26	5	1	6	1	5.0
Kersey	72	1310	146	41.2	9	0	29	70.7	58	225	69	67	51	47	4.5
Kerr	32	268	32	43.2	31	16	9	81.8	3	19	12	4	7	0	2.8
Spencer	26	149	15	45.5	0	0	20	66.7	15	39	3	6	9	8	1.9
Spurs	82	19855	2952	46.2	882	330	1652	74.6	927	3593	1819	614	1183	551	96.2
Opponents	82	19855	2884	42.5	1036	355	1276	73.9	986	3396	1667	645	1181	429	90.2

Seattle SuperSonics

Player	GP	Min	Field Goals FGM	Pct	3-Pt FG FGA	FGM	Free Throws FTM	Pct	Rebounds Off	Total	A	Stl	TO	BS	Avg
Payton	82	3425	747	44.8	520	177	311	73.5	100	529	732	153	224	18	24.2
Baker	79	2849	514	36.1	8	2	281	68.2	227	605	148	47	213	66	16.6
Barry	80	2726	327	46.3	399	164	127	80.9	50	372	291	103	142	31	11.8
Patterson	81	2097	354	53.6	27	12	222	69.2	218	434	126	94	144	40	11.6
Maxwell	47	989	169	34.5	223	67	108	73.0	15	79	75	38	53	9	10.9
Lewis	82	1575	275	48.6	120	40	84	68.3	127	336	70	62	78	36	8.2
Grant	76	2688	266	44.4	4	0	80	72.1	167	591	188	55	61	60	8.1
Williams	43	517	84	37.3	81	24	33	64.7	12	52	78	18	40	0	5.2
McCoy	58	746	102	57.6	0	0	45	49.5	54	179	24	15	45	46	4.3
Davis	54	701	80	36.4	103	31	26	68.4	15	100	70	38	44	5	4.0
Borrell	17	167	28	44.4	3	0	6	54.5	14	40	10	6	6	3	3.6
Foster	60	718	91	40.6	15	3	18	64.3	16	107	41	10	28	18	3.4
Person	37	340	37	30.1	95	24	4	50.0	6	53	22	5	12	2	2.8
Stepania	30	202	29	36.7	6	0	17	47.2	21	47	3	10	22	11	2.5
Vinson	8	40	5	29.4	7	2	1	50.0	0	1	0	3	4	0	1.6
SuperSonics	**82**	**19780**	**3108**	**44.7**	**1611**	**546**	**1363**	**69.5**	**1042**	**3525**	**1878**	**657**	**1116**	**345**	**99.1**
Opponents	**82**	**19780**	**3132**	**45.1**	**1293**	**440**	**1343**	**74.8**	**1084**	**3695**	**1939**	**590**	**1258**	**433**	**98.1**

Toronto Raptors

Player	GP	Min	Field Goals FGM	Pct	3-Pt FG FGA	FGM	Free Throws FTM	Pct	Rebounds Off	Total	A	Stl	TO	BS	Avg
Carter	82	3126	788	46.5	236	95	436	79.1	150	476	322	110	178	92	25.7
McGrady	79	2462	459	45.1	65	18	277	70.7	188	501	263	90	160	151	15.4
Christie	73	2264	311	40.7	275	99	182	84.3	63	285	321	102	144	43	12.4
Davis	79	2479	313	44.0	0	0	284	76.5	235	696	105	38	121	100	11.5
Willis	79	1679	236	41.5	3	1	131	79.9	201	482	49	36	98	48	7.6
Curry	67	1095	194	42.7	242	95	24	75.0	11	100	89	32	40	9	7.6
Brown	38	673	93	36.0	187	67	11	68.8	9	54	86	24	39	5	6.9
Oakley	80	2431	234	41.8	41	14	66	77.6	117	540	253	102	154	45	6.9
Williams	55	779	114	39.7	55	16	48	73.8	27	85	126	34	47	11	5.3
Bogues	80	1731	157	43.9	51	17	79	90.8	25	135	299	65	59	4	5.1
Workman	36	350	31	34.4	43	14	10	66.7	1	26	61	20	18	0	2.4
Radojevic	3	24	7	28.6	0	0	3	50.0	2	8	1	2	5	1	2.3
Thomas	55	477	49	45.8	1	0	16	39.0	37	75	9	12	14	14	2.1
Marks	5	12	2	33.3	1	0	4	100.0	0	2	0	1	3	1	1.6
Stewart	42	389	20	37.7	0	0	18	56.3	33	94	6	5	17	19	1.4
Raptors	**82**	**19755**	**2980**	**43.3**	**1171**	**425**	**1583**	**76.5**	**1098**	**3547**	**1947**	**666**	**1085**	**544**	**97.2**
Opponents	**82**	**19755**	**3002**	**45.4**	**1021**	**346**	**1631**	**76.4**	**961**	**3513**	**1790**	**557**	**1250**	**434**	**97.3**

Utah Jazz

Player	GP	Min	Field Goals FGM	Pct	3-Pt FG FGA	FGM	Free Throws FTM	Pct	Rebounds Off	Total	A	Stl	TO	BS	Avg
Malone	82	2947	752	50.9	8	2	589	79.7	169	779	304	79	231	71	25.5
Russell	82	2900	408	44.6	268	106	237	75.0	99	427	158	128	101	23	14.1
Stockton	82	2432	363	50.1	121	43	221	86.0	45	215	703	143	179	15	12.1
Eisley	82	2096	282	41.8	163	60	84	82.4	23	170	347	59	132	9	8.6
Gilliam	50	782	133	43.6	1	0	67	77.9	72	209	42	12	55	16	6.7
Polynice	82	1819	203	51.0	2	1	28	31.1	166	453	37	30	70	84	5.3
Ostertag	81	1606	124	46.4	1	0	119	63.6	172	482	18	20	79	172	4.5
Lewis	74	896	111	37.2	63	23	38	73.1	46	113	40	24	46	15	3.8
Vaughn	78	884	109	41.6	34	14	57	75.0	11	65	121	32	77	0	3.7
Padgett	47	432	44	31.4	44	13	19	70.4	24	88	25	14	22	8	2.6
Keefe	62	604	53	40.8	1	0	29	80.6	45	136	34	17	46	13	2.2
Jazz	**82**	**19755**	**2962**	**46.4**	**854**	**329**	**1661**	**77.3**	**936**	**3362**	**2041**	**629**	**1160**	**446**	**96.5**
Opponents	**82**	**19755**	**2781**	**44.6**	**1097**	**388**	**1598**	**74.6**	**887**	**3123**	**1620**	**588**	**1270**	**411**	**92.0**

Vancouver Grizzlies

Player	GP	Min	FGM	Pct	FGA	FGM	FTM	Pct	Off	Total	A	Stl	TO	BS	Avg
			Field Goals		**3-Pt FG**		**Free Throws**		**Rebounds**						
Abdur-Rahim	82	3223	594	46.5	96	29	446	80.9	218	825	271	89	249	87	20.3
Dickerson	82	3103	554	43.6	291	119	269	83.0	78	279	208	116	165	45	18.2
Bibby	82	3155	459	44.5	212	77	195	78.0	73	306	665	132	247	15	14.5
Harrington	82	2677	420	50.6	2	0	236	79.2	196	563	97	36	217	58	13.1
Reeves	69	1773	252	44.8	4	0	107	64.8	126	390	82	33	119	38	8.9
Scott	66	1263	125	37.5	189	71	48	84.2	16	106	69	28	30	9	5.6
Long	42	920	74	44.3	4	0	55	77.5	86	234	43	45	49	10	4.8
Lopez	65	781	111	42.5	18	3	67	61.5	59	124	44	32	53	17	4.5
West	38	581	59	40.7	3	0	34	85.0	18	71	43	12	19	8	4.0
Price	41	424	41	34.5	68	25	34	87.2	8	37	69	17	47	1	3.4
Ekezie	39	351	41	46.6	0	0	43	67.2	34	92	8	9	26	4	3.2
Parks	56	808	72	49.7	1	0	24	64.9	55	183	35	29	28	45	3.0
Palacio	53	394	43	43.9	2	0	22	59.5	17	51	48	20	44	0	2.0
Grizzlies	82	19855	2892	44.9	898	324	1594	77.4	1005	3329	1700	608	1308	346	93.9
Opponents	82	19855	3136	47.4	1083	361	1530	76.9	970	3306	1932	725	1234	519	99.5

Washington Wizards

Player	GP	Min	FGM	Pct	FGA	FGM	FTM	Pct	Off	Total	A	Stl	TO	BS	Avg
			Field Goals		**3-Pt FG**		**Free Throws**		**Rebounds**						
Richmond	74	2397	447	42.6	241	93	298	87.6	37	213	185	110	154	13	17.4
Howard	82	2909	509	45.9	7	0	202	73.5	132	470	247	67	225	21	14.9
Strickland	69	2188	327	42.9	21	1	214	70.2	73	259	519	94	187	18	12.6
Murray	80	1831	290	43.3	263	113	120	85.1	63	271	72	45	84	24	10.2
Hamilton	71	1373	254	42.0	77	28	103	36.4	38	129	108	28	84	6	9.0
Whitney	82	1627	217	41.7	255	96	112	84.8	20	134	313	55	107	5	7.8
A. Williams	81	1545	235	52.2	3	0	146	72.6	159	409	58	41	80	92	7.6
White	80	1537	228	50.7	0	0	113	53.6	202	553	15	31	94	83	7.1
Austin	59	1173	151	42.9	4	1	94	68.6	64	282	74	17	107	38	6.7
Smith	46	1145	108	56.3	1	0	73	72.3	121	331	56	27	45	23	6.3
King	62	1060	139	50.2	0	0	49	74.2	84	250	49	34	41	15	5.3
Booth	11	143	16	34.8	0	0	10	71.4	15	32	7	3	6	14	3.8
Reid	38	498	60	53.6	0	0	24	70.6	31	102	11	24	23	31	3.8
Profit	33	225	21	35.6	17	3	4	40.0	2	26	25	7	19	4	1.5
Wizards	82	19805	3010	45.1	890	335	1566	74.3	1064	3502	1771	593	1267	383	96.6
Opponents	82	19805	3005	45.9	1052	390	1494	74.4	962	3380	1793	686	1225	503	99.9

2000 NBA Draft

The 2000 NBA Draft was held on June 28 in Minneapolis, MN

First Round

1. Kenyon Martin, New Jersey
2. Stromile Swift, Vancouver
3. Darius Miles, LA Clippers
4. Marcus Fizer, Chicago
5. Mike Miller, Orlando
6. DerMarr Johnson, Atlanta
7. Chris Mihm, Chicago (to Cleveland)
8. Jamal Crawford, Cleveland (to Chicago)
9. Joel Przybilla, Houston (to Milwaukee)
10. Keyon Dooling, Orlando (to LA Clippers)
11. Jerome Moiso, Boston
12. Etan Thomas, Dallas
13. Courtney Alexander, Orlando (to Dallas)
14. Mateen Cleaves, Detroit
15. Jason Collier, Milwaukee (to Houston)
16. Hidayet Turkoglu, Sacramento
17. Desmond Mason, Seattle

18. Quentin Richardson, LA Clippers
19. Jamaal Magloire, Charlotte
20. Craig Claxton, Philadelphia
21. Morris Peterson, Toronto
22. Donnell Harvey, New York (to Dallas)
23. DeShawn Stevenson, Utah
24. Dalibor Bagaric, Chicago
25. Iakovos Tsakalidis, Phoenix
26. Mamadou N'diaye, Denver
27. Primoz Brezec, Indiana
28. Erick Barkley, Portland
29. Mark Madsen, LA Lakers

Second Round

30. Marko Jaric, LA Clippers
31. Dan Langhi, Dallas (to Houston)
32. A.J. Guyton, Chicago
33. Jake Voskuhl, Chicago
34. Khalid El-Amin, Chicago
35. Mike Smith, Washington
36. Soumaila Samake, New Jersey

37. Eddie House, Miami
38. Eduardo Najera, Houston (to Dallas)
39. Lavor Postell, New York
40. Hanno Möttölä, Atlanta
41. Chris Carrawell, San Antonio
42. Olumide Oyedeji, Seattle
43. Michael Redd, Milwaukee
44. Brian Cardinal, Detroit
45. Jabari Smith, Sacramento
46. DeAndre Hulett, Toronto
47. Josip Sesar, Seattle (to Boston)
48. Mark Karcher, Philadelphia
49. Jason Hart, Milwaukee
50. Kaniel Dickens, Utah
51. Igor Rakocevic, Minnesota
52. Ernest Brown, Miami
53. Dan McClintock, Denver
54. Cory Hightower, San Antonio
55. Chris Porter, Golden State
56. Jaquay Walls, Indiana
57. Scoonie Penn, Atlanta
58. Pete Mickeal, Dallas

Women's National Basketball Association

Final Standings

EASTERN CONFERENCE

Team	W	L	Pct	GB
†New York	20	12	.625	—
*Cleveland	17	15	.531	3
*Orlando	16	16	.500	4
*Washington	14	18	.438	6
Detroit	14	18	.438	6
Miami	13	19	.406	7
Indiana	9	23	.281	11
Charlotte	8	24	.250	12

WESTERN CONFERENCE

Team	W	L	Pct	GB
†Los Angeles	28	4	.875	—
*Houston	27	5	.844	1
*Sacramento	21	11	.656	7
*Phoenix	20	12	.625	8
Utah	18	14	.563	10
Minnesota	15	17	.469	13
Portland	10	22	.313	18
Seattle	6	26	.188	22

†Clinched conference title.   *Clinched playoff berth

2000 Playoffs

FIRST ROUND

EASTERN CONFERENCE

Aug 12	New York	72	at Washington	63
Aug 14	Washington	57	at New York	78

New York won series 2–0

Aug 11	Cleveland	55	at Orlando	62
Aug 13	Orlando	54	at Cleveland	63
Aug 16	Orlando	43	at Cleveland	72

Cleveland won series 2–1

WESTERN CONFERENCE

Aug 11	Los Angeles	86	at Phoenix	71
Aug 13	Phoenix	76	at Los Angeles	101

Los Angeles won series 2–0

Aug 12	Houston	72	at Sacramento	64
Aug 14	Sacramento	70	at Houston	75

Houston won series 2–0

EASTERN CONFERENCE FINALS

Aug 17	New York	43	at Cleveland	56
Aug 20	Cleveland	45	at New York	51
Aug 21	Cleveland	67	at New York	81

New York won series 2–1

WESTERN CONFERENCE FINALS

Aug. 17	Houston	77	at Los Angeles	56
Aug. 20	Los Angeles	69	at Houston	74

Houston won series 2–0

WNBA CHAMPIONSHIP

Aug. 24	Houston	59	at New York	52
Aug. 26	New York	73	at Houston	79*

Houston won series 2–0

*Overtime game.

Classic Dunk

Upon receiving his league MVP award, scholar-center Shaquille O'Neal showed off his grasp of the Western canon. "From this day on I would like to be known as the Big Aristotle," said O'Neal, "because it was Aristotle that said, 'Excellence is not a singular act but a habit.'" Right on—as long as Shaq calls the rim Sosias when he's at the free throw line. That's the name of the slave in Aristophenes' *Wasps* who cries out, "Oh my god! Whence did this brick fall on me?"

FOR THE RECORD·Year by Year

NBA Champions

Season	Winner	Series	Runner-Up	Winning Coach	Finals MVP
1946–47	Philadelphia	4–1	Chicago	Eddie Gottlieb	—
1947–48	Baltimore	4–2	Philadelphia	Buddy Jeannette	—
1948–49	Minneapolis	4–2	Washington	John Kundla	—
1949–50	Minneapolis	4–2	Syracuse	John Kundla	—
1950–51	Rochester	4–3	New York	Les Harrison	—
1951–52	Minneapolis	4–3	New York	John Kundla	—
1952–53	Minneapolis	4–1	New York	John Kundla	—
1953–54	Minneapolis	4–3	Syracuse	John Kundla	—
1954–55	Syracuse	4–3	Ft Wayne	Al Cervi	—
1955–56	Philadelphia	4–1	Ft Wayne	George Senesky	—
1956–57	Boston	4–3	St Louis	Red Auerbach	—
1957–58	St Louis	4–2	Boston	Alex Hannum	—
1958–59	Boston	4–0	Minneapolis	Red Auerbach	—
1959–60	Boston	4–3	St Louis	Red Auerbach	—
1960–61	Boston	4–1	St Louis	Red Auerbach	—
1961–62	Boston	4–3	LA Lakers	Red Auerbach	—
1962–63	Boston	4–2	LA Lakers	Red Auerbach	—
1963–64	Boston	4–1	San Francisco	Red Auerbach	—
1964–65	Boston	4–1	LA Lakers	Red Auerbach	—
1965–66	Boston	4–3	LA Lakers	Red Auerbach	—
1966–67	Philadelphia	4–2	San Francisco	Alex Hannum	—
1967–68	Boston	4–2	LA Lakers	Bill Russell	—
1968–69	Boston	4–3	LA Lakers	Bill Russell	Jerry West, LA
1969–70	New York	4–3	LA Lakers	Red Holzman	Willis Reed, NY
1970–71	Milwaukee	4–0	Baltimore	Larry Costello	Kareem Abdul-Jabbar, Mil
1971–72	LA Lakers	4–1	New York	Bill Sharman	Wilt Chamberlain, LA
1972–73	New York	4–1	LA Lakers	Red Holzman	Willis Reed, NY
1973–74	Boston	4–3	Milwaukee	Tommy Heinsohn	John Havlicek, Bos
1974–75	Golden State	4–0	Washington	Al Attles	Rick Barry, GS
1975–76	Boston	4–2	Phoenix	Tommy Heinsohn	JoJo White, Bos
1976–77	Portland	4–2	Philadelphia	Jack Ramsay	Bill Walton, Port
1977–78	Washington	4–3	Seattle	Dick Motta	Wes Unseld, Wash
1978–79	Seattle	4–1	Washington	Lenny Wilkens	Dennis Johnson, Sea
1979–80	LA Lakers	4–2	Philadelphia	Paul Westhead	Magic Johnson, LA
1980–81	Boston	4–2	Houston	Bill Fitch	Cedric Maxwell, Bos
1981–82	LA Lakers	4–2	Philadelphia	Pat Riley	Magic Johnson, LA
1982–83	Philadelphia	4–0	LA Lakers	Billy Cunningham	Moses Malone, Phil
1983–84	Boston	4–3	LA Lakers	K.C. Jones	Larry Bird, Bos
1984–85	LA Lakers	4–2	Boston	Pat Riley	Kareem Abdul-Jabbar, LA
1985–86	Boston	4–2	Houston	K.C. Jones	Larry Bird, Bos
1986–87	LA Lakers	4–2	Boston	Pat Riley	Magic Johnson, LA
1987–88	LA Lakers	4–3	Detroit	Pat Riley	James Worthy, LA
1988–89	Detroit	4–0	LA Lakers	Chuck Daly	Joe Dumars, Det
1989–90	Detroit	4–1	Portland	Chuck Daly	Isiah Thomas, Det
1990–91	Chicago	4–1	LA Lakers	Phil Jackson	Michael Jordan, Chi
1991–92	Chicago	4–2	Portland	Phil Jackson	Michael Jordan, Chi
1992–93	Chicago	4–2	Phoenix	Phil Jackson	Michael Jordan, Chi
1993–94	Houston	4–3	New York	Rudy Tomjanovich	Hakeem Olajuwon, Hou
1994–95	Houston	4–0	Orlando	Rudy Tomjanovich	Hakeem Olajuwon, Hou
1995–96	Chicago	4–2	Seattle	Phil Jackson	Michael Jordan, Chi
1996–97	Chicago	4–2	Utah	Phil Jackson	Michael Jordan, Chi
1997–98	Chicago	4–2	Utah	Phil Jackson	Michael Jordan, Chi
1998–99	San Antonio	4–1	New York	Gregg Popovich	Tim Duncan, SA
1999–00	LA Lakers	4–2	Indiana	Phil Jackson	Shaquille O'Neal, LA

Most Valuable Player: Maurice Podoloff Trophy

Season	Player, Team	GP	Field Goals		3-Pt FG		Free Throws		Rebounds		A	Stl	BS	Avg
			FGM	Pct	FGM	Pct	FTM	Pct	Off	Total				
1955–56	Bob Pettit, StL	72	646	42.9	–	–	557	73.6	–	1,164	189	–	–	25.7
1956–57	Bob Cousy, Bos	64	478	37.8	–	–	363	82.1	–	309	478	–	–	20.6
1957–58	Bill Russell, Bos	69	456	44.2	–	–	230	51.9	–	1,564	202	–	–	16.6
1958–59	Bob Pettit, StL	72	719	43.8	–	–	667	75.9	–	1,182	221	–	–	29.2
1959–60	Wilt Chamberlain, Phil	72	1,065	46.1	–	–	577	58.2	–	1,941	168	–	–	37.6
1960–61	Bill Russell, Bos	78	532	42.6	–	–	258	55.0	–	1,868	264	–	–	16.9
1961–62	Bill Russell, Bos	76	575	45.7	–	–	286	59.5	–	1,891	341	–	–	18.9
1962–63	Bill Russell, Bos	78	511	43.2	–	–	287	55.5	–	1,843	348	–	–	16.8
1963–64	Oscar Robertson, Cin	79	840	48.3	–	–	800	85.3	–	783	868	–	–	31.4
1964–65	Bill Russell, Bos	78	429	43.8	–	–	244	57.3	–	1,878	410	–	–	14.1
1965–66	Wilt Chamberlain, Phil	79	1,074	54.0	–	–	501	51.3	–	1,943	414	–	–	33.5
1966–67	Wilt Chamberlain, Phil	81	785	68.3	–	–	386	44.1	–	1,957	630	–	–	24.1
1967–68	Wilt Chamberlain, Phil	82	819	59.5	–	–	354	38.0	–	1,952	702	–	–	24.3
1968–69	Wes Unseld, Balt	82	427	47.6	–	–	277	60.5	–	1,491	213	–	–	13.8
1969–70	Willis Reed, NY	81	702	50.7	–	–	351	75.6	–	1,126	161	–	–	21.7
1970–71	Kareem Abdul-Jabbar, Mil	82	1,063	57.7	–	–	470	69.0	–	1,311	272	–	–	31.7
1971–72	Kareem Abdul-Jabbar, Mil	81	1,159	57.4	–	–	504	68.9	–	1,346	370	–	–	34.8
1972–73	Dave Cowens, Bos	82	740	45.2	–	–	204	77.9	–	1,329	333	–	–	20.5
1973–74	Kareem Abdul-Jabbar, Mil	81	948	53.9	–	–	295	70.2	287	1,178	386	112	283	27.0
1974–75	Bob McAdoo, Buff	82	1,095	51.2	–	–	641	80.5	307	1,155	179	92	174	34.5
1975–76	Kareem Abdul-Jabbar, LA	82	914	52.9	–	–	447	70.3	272	1,383	413	119	338	37.7
1976–77	Kareem Abdul-Jabbar, LA	82	888	57.9	–	–	376	70.1	266	1,090	319	101	261	26.2
1977–78	Bill Walton, Port	58	460	52.2	–	–	177	72.0	118	766	291	60	146	18.9
1978–79	Moses Malone, Hou	82	716	54.0	–	–	599	73.9	587	1,444	147	79	119	24.8
1979–80	Kareem Abdul-Jabbar, LA	82	835	60.4	0	00.0	364	76.5	190	886	371	81	280	24.8
1980–81	Julius Erving, Phil	82	794	52.1	4	22.2	422	78.7	244	657	364	173	147	24.6
1981–82	Moses Malone, Hou	81	945	51.9	0	00.0	630	76.2	558	1,188	142	76	125	31.1
1982–83	Moses Malone, Phil	78	654	50.1	0	00.0	600	76.1	445	1,194	101	89	157	24.5
1983–84	Larry Bird, Bos	79	758	49.2	18	24.7	374	88.8	181	796	520	144	69	24.2
1984–85	Larry Bird, Bos	80	918	52.2	56	42.7	403	88.2	164	842	531	129	98	28.7
1985–86	Larry Bird, Bos	82	796	49.6	82	42.3	441	89.6	190	805	557	166	51	25.8
1986–87	Magic Johnson, LA Lakers	80	683	52.2	8	20.5	535	84.8	122	504	977	138	36	23.9
1987–88	Michael Jordan, Chi	82	1,069	53.5	7	13.2	723	84.1	139	449	485	259	131	35.0
1988–89	Magic Johnson, LA Lakers	77	579	50.9	59	31.4	513	91.1	111	607	988	138	22	22.5
1989–90	Magic Johnson, LA Lakers	79	546	48.0	106	38.4	567	89.0	128	522	907	132	34	22.3
1990–91	Michael Jordan, Chi	82	990	53.9	29	31.2	571	85.1	118	492	453	223	83	31.5
1991–92	Michael Jordan, Chi	80	943	51.9	27	27.0	491	83.2	91	511	489	182	75	30.1
1992–93	Charles Barkley, Phoe	76	716	52.0	67	30.5	445	76.5	237	928	385	119	74	25.6
1993–94	Hakeem Olajuwon, Hou	80	894	52.8	8	42.1	388	71.6	229	955	287	128	297	27.3
1994–95	David Robinson, SA	81	788	53.0	6	30.0	656	77.4	234	877	236	134	262	27.6
1995–96	Michael Jordan, Chi	82	916	49.5	111	42.7	548	83.4	148	543	352	180	42	30.4
1996–97	Karl Malone, Utah	82	864	55.0	0	00.0	521	75.5	193	809	368	113	48	27.4
1997–98	Michael Jordan, Chi	82	881	46.5	30	23.8	565	78.4	130	475	283	141	45	28.7
1998–99	Karl Malone, Utah	49	393	49.3	0	00.0	378	78.8	107	463	201	62	28	23.8
1999–00	Shaquille O'Neal, LA Lakers	79	956	57.4	0	00.0	432	52.4	336	1078	299	36	239	29.7

Coach of the Year: Arnold "Red" Auerbach Trophy

1962–63...Harry Gallatin, StL	1975–76...Bill Fitch, Clev	1988–89...Cotton Fitzsimmons, Phoe
1963–64...Alex Hannum, SF	1976–77...Tom Nissalke, Hou	1989–90...Pat Riley, LA Lakers
1964–65...Red Auerbach, Bos	1977–78...Hubie Brown, Atl	1990–91...Don Chaney, Hou
1965–66...Dolph Schayes, Phil	1978–79...Cotton Fitzsimmons, KC	1991–92...Don Nelson, GS
1966–67...Johnny Kerr, Chi	1979–80...Bill Fitch, Bos	1992–93...Pat Riley, NY
1967–68...Richie Guerin, StL	1980–81...Jack McKinney, Ind	1993–94...Lenny Wilkens, Atl
1968–69...Gene Shue, Balt	1981–82...Gene Shue, Wash	1994–95...Del Harris, LA Lakers
1969–70...Red Holzman, NY	1982–83...Don Nelson, Mil	1995–96...Phil Jackson, Chi
1970–71...Dick Motta, Chi	1983–84...Frank Layden, Utah	1996–97...Pat Riley, Mia
1971–72...Bill Sharman, LA	1984–85...Don Nelson, Mil	1997–98...Larry Bird, Ind
1972–73...Tom Heinsohn, Bos	1985–86...Mike Fratello, Atl	1998–99...Mike Dunleavy, Port
1973–74...Ray Scott, Det	1986–87...Mike Schuler, Port	1999–00...Glenn (Doc) Rivers, Orl
1974–75...Phil Johnson, KC-Oma	1987–88...Doug Moe, Den	

Note: Award named after Auerbach in 1986.

Rookie of the Year: Eddie Gottlieb Trophy

1952–53...Don Meineke, FW
1953–54...Ray Felix, Balt
1954–55...Bob Pettit, Mil
1955–56...Maurice Stokes, Roch
1956–57...Tom Heinsohn, Bos
1957–58...Woody Sauldsberry, Phil
1958–59...Elgin Baylor, Minn
1959–60...Wilt Chamberlain, Phil
1960–61...Oscar Robertson, Cin
1961–62...Walt Bellamy, Chi
1962–63...Terry Dischinger, Chi
1963–64...Jerry Lucas, Cin
1964–65...Willis Reed, NY
1965–66...Rick Barry, SF
1966–67...Dave Bing, Det
1967–68...Earl Monroe, Balt
1968–69...Wes Unseld, Balt

1969–70...K. Abdul-Jabbar, Mil
1970–71...Dave Cowens, Bos
        Geoff Petrie, Port
1971–72...Sidney Wicks, Port
1972–73...Bob McAdoo, Buff
1973–74...Ernie DiGregorio, Buff
1974–75...Keith Wilkes, GS
1975–76...Alvan Adams, Phoe
1976–77...Adrian Dantley, Buff
1977–78...Walter Davis, Phoe
1978–79...Phil Ford, KC
1979–80...Larry Bird, Bos
1980–81...Darrell Griffith, Utah
1981–82...Buck Williams, NJ
1982–83...Terry Cummings, SD
1983–84...Ralph Sampson, Hou
1984–85...Michael Jordan, Chi

1985–86...Patrick Ewing, NY
1986–87...Chuck Person, Ind
1987–88...Mark Jackson, NY
1988–89...Mitch Richmond, GS
1989–90...David Robinson, SA
1990–91...Derrick Coleman, NJ
1991–92...Larry Johnson, Char
1992–93...Shaquille O'Neal, Orl
1993–94...Chris Webber, GS
1994–95...Jason Kidd, Dal
        Grant Hill, Det
1995–96...Damon Stoudamire, Tor
1996–97...Allen Iverson, Phil
1997–98...Tim Duncan, SA
1998–99...Vince Carter, Tor
1999–00..Steve Francis, Hou
        Elton Brand, Chi

Defensive Player of the Year

1982–83...Sidney Moncrief, Mil
1983–84...Sidney Moncrief, Mil
1984–85...Mark Eaton, Utah
1985–86...Alvin Robertson, SA
1986–87...Michael Cooper, Lakers
1987–88...Michael Jordan, Chi

1988–89...Mark Eaton, Utah
1989–90...Dennis Rodman, Det
1990–91...Dennis Rodman, Det
1991–92...David Robinson, SA
1992–93...Hakeem Olajuwon, Hou
1993–94...Hakeem Olajuwon, Hou

1994–95...Dikembe Mutombo, Den
1995–96...Gary Payton, Sea
1996–97...Dikembe Mutombo, Den
1997–98...Dikembe Mutombo, Atl
1998–99...Alonzo Mourning, Mia
1999–00...Alonzo Mourning, Mia

Sixth Man Award

1982–83...Bobby Jones, Phil
1983–84...Kevin McHale, Bos
1984–85...Kevin McHale, Bos
1985–86...Bill Walton, Bos
1986–87...Ricky Pierce, Mil
1987–88...Roy Tarpley, Dall

1988–89...Eddie Johnson, Phoe
1989–90...Ricky Pierce, Mil
1990–91...Detlef Schrempf, Ind
1991–92...Detlef Schrempf, Ind
1992–93...Cliff Robinson, Port
1993–94...Dell Curry, Char

1994–95...Anthony Mason, NY
1995–96...Tony Kukoc, Chi
1996–97...John Starks, NY
1997–98...Danny Manning, Phoe
1998–99...Darrell Armstrong, Orl
1999–00...Rodney Rogers, Phoe

J. Walter Kennedy Citizenship Award

1974–75...Wes Unseld, Wash
1975–76...Slick Watts, Sea
1976–77...Dave Bing, Wash
1977–78...Bob Lanier, Det
1978–79...Calvin Murphy, Hou
1979–80...Austin Carr, Clev
1980–81...Mike Glenn, NY
1981–82...Kent Benson, Det
1982–83...Julius Erving, Phil

1983–84...Frank Layden, Utah
1984–85...Dan Issel, Den
1985–86...Michael Cooper, Lakers
        Rory Sparrow, NY
1986–87...Isiah Thomas, Det
1987–88...Alex English, Den
1988–89...Thurl Bailey, Utah
1989–90...Glenn Rivers, Atl
1990–91...Kevin Johnson, Phoe

1991–92...Magic Johnson, Lakers
1992–93...Terry Porter, Port
1993–94...Joe Dumars, Det
1994–95...Joe O'Toole, Atl
1995–96...Chris Dudley, Port
1996–97...P.J. Brown, Mia
1997–98...Steve Smith, Atl
1998–99...Brian Grant, Port
1999–00...Vlade Divac, Sac

Most Improved Player

1985–86...Alvin Robertson, SA
1986–87...Dale Ellis, Sea
1987–88...Kevin Duckworth, Port
1988–89...Kevin Johnson, Phoe
1989–90...Rony Seikaly, Mia
1990–91...Scott Skiles, Orl

1991–92...Pervis Ellison, Wash
1992–93...Chris Jackson, Den
1993–94...Don MacLean, Wash
1994–95...Dana Barros, Phil
1995–96...Gheorghe Muresan, Wash

1996–97...Isaac Austin, Mia
1997–98...Alan Henderson, Atl
1998–99...Darrell Armstrong, Orl
1999–00...Jalen Rose, Ind

Executive of the Year

1972–73...Joe Axelson, KC-Oma
1973–74...Eddie Donovan, Buff
1974–75...Dick Vertlieb, GS
1975–76...Jerry Colangelo, Phoe
1976–77...Ray Patterson, Hou
1977–78...Angelo Drossos, SA
1978–79...Bob Ferry, Wash
1979–80...Red Auerbach, Bos
1980–81...Jerry Colangelo, Phoe
1981–82...Bob Ferry, Wash

1982–83...Zollie Volchok, Sea
1983–84...Frank Layden, Utah
1984–85...Vince Boryla, Den
1985–86...Stan Kasten, Atl
1986–87...Stan Kasten, Atl
1987–88...Jerry Krause, Chi
1988–89...Jerry Colangelo, Phoe
1989–90...Bob Bass, SA
1990–91...Bucky Buckwalter, Port
1991–92...Wayne Embry, Clev

1992–93...Jerry Colangelo, Phoe
1993–94...Bob Whitsitt, Sea
1994–95...Jerry West, LA Lakers
1995–96...Jerry Krause, Chi
1996–97...Bob Bass, Char
1997–98...Wayne Embry, Clev
1998–99...Geoff Petrie, Sac
1999–00...John Gabriel, Orl

Sponsored by *The Sporting News.*

NBA Alltime Individual Leaders

Scoring

MOST POINTS, CAREER

	Pts	Avg
Kareem Abdul-Jabbar	38,387	24.6
Wilt Chamberlain	31,419	30.1
Karl Malone	31,041	26.0
Michael Jordan	29,277	31.5
Moses Malone	27,409	20.6
Elvin Hayes	27,313	21.0
Oscar Robertson	26,710	25.7
Dominique Wilkins	26,669	24.8
John Havlicek	26,395	20.8
Hakeem Olajuwon	25,822	23.0

MOST POINTS, SEASON

Wilt Chamberlain, Phil	4,029	1961–62
Wilt Chamberlain, SF	3,586	1962–63
Michael Jordan, Chi	3,041	1986–87
Wilt Chamberlain, Phil	3,033	1960–61
Wilt Chamberlain, SF	2,948	1963–64
Michael Jordan, Chi	2,868	1987–88
Bob McAdoo, Buff	2,831	1974–75
Rick Barry, SF	2,775	1966–67
Michael Jordan, Chi	2,753	1989–90
Elgin Baylor, LA	2,719	1962–63

HIGHEST SCORING AVERAGE, CAREER

Michael Jordan	31.5	930 games
Wilt Chamberlain	30.1	1,045 games
Shaquille O'Neal	27.5	534 games
Elgin Baylor	27.4	846 games
Jerry West	27.0	932 games
Bob Pettit	26.4	792 games
George Gervin	26.2	791 games
Karl Malone	26.0	1,192 games
Oscar Robertson	25.7	1,040 games
Dominique Wilkins	24.8	1,074 games

HIGHEST SCORING AVERAGE, SEASON

Wilt Chamberlain, Phil	50.4	1961–62
Wilt Chamberlain, SF	44.8	1962–63
Wilt Chamberlain, Phil	38.4	1960–61
Wilt Chamberlain, Phil	37.6	1959–60
Michael Jordan, Chi	37.1	1986–87
Wilt Chamberlain, SF	36.9	1963–64
Rick Barry, SF	35.6	1966–67
Michael Jordan, Chi	35.0	1987–88
Elgin Baylor, LA	34.8	1960–61

Note: Minimum 70 games.

MOST POINTS, GAME

	Player, Team	Opp	Date
100	Wilt Chamberlain, Phil	NY	3/2/62
78	Wilt Chamberlain, Phil	LA	12/8/61
73	Wilt Chamberlain, Phil	Chi	1/13/62
73	Wilt Chamberlain, SF	NY	11/16/62
73	David Thompson, Den	Det	4/9/78
72	Wilt Chamberlain, SF	LA	11/3/62
71	David Robinson, SA	LAC	4/24/94
71	Elgin Baylor, LA	NY	11/15/60
70	Wilt Chamberlain, SF	Syr	3/10/63
69	Michael Jordan, Chi	Clev	3/28/90

Field-Goal Percentage

Highest FG Percentage, Career: .599—Artis Gilmore
Highest FG Percentage, Season: .727—Wilt Chamberlain, LA Lakers, 1972–73 (426/586)

Free Throws

HIGHEST FREE-THROW PERCENTAGE, CAREER

Mark Price	.904
Rick Barry	.900
Calvin Murphy	.892
Scott Skiles	.889
Larry Bird	.886

Note: Minimum 1200 free throws made.

HIGHEST FREE-THROW PERCENTAGE, SEASON

Calvin Murphy, Hou	.958	1980–81
Mahmoud Abdul-Rauf, Den	.956	1993–94
Jeff Hornacek, Utah	.950	1999–00
Mark Price, Clev	.948	1992–93
Mark Price, Clev	.947	1991–92

MOST FREE THROWS MADE, CAREER

	No.	Yrs	Pct
Moses Malone	8,531	19	.769
Oscar Robertson	7,694	14	.838
Karl Malone	8,100	15	.735
Jerry West	7,160	14	.814
Dolph Schayes	6,979	16	.844

Three-Point Field Goals

Most Three-Point Field-Goals, Career: 1,867—Reggie Miller

Highest Three-Point Field-Goal Percentage, Career: .463—Steve Kerr

Most Three-Point Field Goals, Season: 267—Dennis Scott, Orl, 1995–96

Highest Three-Point Field-Goal Percentage, Season: .524—Steve Kerr, Chi, 1994–95

Most Three-Point Field Goals, Game: 11—Dennis Scott, Orlando vs Atlanta, 4/18/96

Note: First year of shot: 1979–80.

Steals

Most Steals, Career: 2,844—John Stockton

Most Steals, Season: 301—Alvin Robertson, San Antonio, 1985–86

Most Steals, Game: 11—Kendall Gill, New Jersey vs Miami, 4/3/99; Larry Kenon, San Antonio vs Kansas City, 12/26/76

Rebounds

MOST REBOUNDS, CAREER

	No.	Yrs	Avg
Wilt Chamberlain	23,924	14	22.9
Bill Russell	21,620	13	22.5
Kareem Abdul-Jabbar	17,440	20	11.4
Elvin Hayes	16,279	16	12.5
Moses Malone	16,212	19	12.2
Robert Parish	14,715	21	9.1
Nate Thurmond	14,464	14	15.0
Walt Bellamy	14,241	14	13.7
Wes Unseld	13,769	13	14.0
Hakeem Olajuwon	12,951	16	11.6

Rebounds (Cont.)

MOST REBOUNDS, SEASON

Wilt Chamberlain, Phil	2,149	1960–61
Wilt Chamberlain, Phil	2,052	1961–62
Wilt Chamberlain, Phil	1,957	1966–67
Wilt Chamberlain, Phil	1,952	1967–68
Wilt Chamberlain, SF	1,946	1962–63
Wilt Chamberlain, Phil	1,943	1965–66
Wilt Chamberlain, Phil	1,941	1959–60
Bill Russell, Bos	1,930	1963–64
Bill Russell, Bos	1,878	1964–65
Bill Russell, Bos	1,868	1960–61

MOST REBOUNDS, GAME

	Player, Team	Opp	Date
55	Wilt Chamberlain, Phil	Bos	11/24/60
51	Bill Russell, Bos	Syr	2/5/60
49	Bill Russell, Bos	Phil	11/16/57
49	Bill Russell, Bos	Det	3/11/65
45	Wilt Chamberlain, Phil	Syr	2/6/60
45	Wilt Chamberlain, Phil	LA	1/21/61

Assists

MOST ASSISTS, CAREER

John Stockton	13,790
Magic Johnson	10,141
Oscar Robertson	9,887
Isiah Thomas	9,061
Mark Jackson	8,574

Assists (Cont.)

MOST ASSISTS, SEASON

John Stockton, Utah	1,164	1990–91
John Stockton, Utah	1,134	1989–90
John Stockton, Utah	1,128	1987–88
John Stockton, Utah	1,126	1991–92
Isiah Thomas, Det	1,123	1984–85

MOST ASSISTS, GAME: 30—Scott Skiles, Orlando vs Denver, 12/30/90

Blocked Shots

MOST BLOCKED SHOTS, CAREER

Hakeem Olajuwon	3,652
Kareem Abdul-Jabbar	3,189
Mark Eaton	3,064
Patrick Ewing	2,758
Wayne (Tree) Rollins	2,542

MOST BLOCKED SHOTS, SEASON

Mark Eaton, Utah	456	1984–85
Manute Bol, Wash	397	1985–86
Elmore Smith, LA	393	1973–74

MOST BLOCKED SHOTS, GAME: 17—Elmore Smith, LA Lakers vs Portland, 10/28/73

NBA Alltime Playoff Leaders

Scoring

MOST POINTS, CAREER

	Pts	Yrs	Avg
Michael Jordan	5,987	13	33.4
Kareem Abdul-Jabbar	5,762	18	24.3
Jerry West	4,457	13	29.1
Karl Malone	4,203	15	26.6
Larry Bird	3,897	12	23.8
John Havlicek	3,776	13	22.0
Hakeem Olajuwon	3,727	14	27.0
Magic Johnson	3,701	13	19.5
Elgin Baylor	3,623	12	27.0
Wilt Chamberlain	3,607	13	22.5

*HIGHEST SCORING AVERAGE, CAREER

	Avg	Games
Michael Jordan	33.4	179
Jerry West	29.1	153
Shaquille O'Neal	27.7	89
Elgin Baylor	27.0	134
George Gervin	27.0	59
Hakeem Olajuwon	26.6	136
Karl Malone	26.6	158
Bob Pettit	25.5	88
Dominique Wilkins	25.4	55
Rick Barry	24.8	74

*Minimum of 25 games.

Scoring (Cont.)

MOST POINTS, GAME

	Player, Team	Opp	Date
†63	Michael Jordan, Chi	Bos	4/20/86
61	Elgin Baylor, LA	Bos	4/14/62
56	Wilt Chamberlain, Phil	Syr	3/22/62
56	Michael Jordan, Chi	Mia	4/29/92
56	Charles Barkley, Phoe	GS	5/4/94
55	Rick Barry, SF	Phil	4/18/67
55	Michael Jordan, Chi	Clev	5/1/88
55	Michael Jordan, Chi	Phoe	4/16/95
55	Michael Jordan, Chi	Wash	4/27/97

†Double overtime game.

Rebounds

MOST REBOUNDS, CAREER

	No.	Yrs	Avg
Bill Russell	4,104	13	24.9
Wilt Chamberlain	3,913	13	24.5
Kareem Abdul-Jabbar	2,481	18	10.5
Wes Unseld	1,777	12	14.9
Karl Malone	1,769	15	11.1

MOST REBOUNDS, GAME

	Player, Team	Opp	Date
41	Wilt Chamberlain, Phil	Bos	4/5/67
40	Bill Russell, Bos	Phil	3/23/58
40	Bill Russell, Bos	StL	3/29/60
*40	Bill Russell, Bos	LA	4/18/62

Three tied at 39.
*Overtime game.

Assists

MOST ASSISTS, CAREER

	No.	Games
Magic Johnson	2,346	190
John Stockton	1,716	168
Larry Bird	1,062	164
Dennis Johnson	1,006	180
Scottie Pippen	1,011	198

MOST ASSISTS, GAME

Player, Team	Opp	Date
24 .... Magic Johnson, LAL	Pho	5/15/84
24 .... John Stockton, Utah	LAL	5/17/88
23 .... Magic Johnson, LAL	Port	5/3/85
22 .... Doc Rivers, Atl	Bos	5/16/88
Four tied at 21.		

Games played

Kareem Abdul-Jabbar	237
Scottie Pippen	198
Danny Ainge	193
Magic Johnson	190
Robert Parish	184

Appearances

Kareem Abdul-Jabbar	18
Robert Parish	16
John Stockton	16
Dolph Schayes	15
Clyde Drexler	15
Tree Rollins	15
Jerome Kersey	15
Karl Malone	15

NBA Season Leaders

Scoring

Year	Player, Team	Pts		Year	Player, Team	Avg
1946–47	Joe Fulks, Phil	1389		1973–74	Bob McAdoo, Buff	30.6
1947–48	Max Zaslofsky, Chi	1007		1974–75	Bob McAdoo, Buff	34.5
1948–49	George Mikan, Minn	1698		1975–76	Bob McAdoo, Buff	31.1
1949–50	George Mikan, Minn	1865		1976–77	Pete Maravich, NO	31.1
1950–51	George Mikan, Minn	1932		1977–78	George Gervin, SA	27.2
1951–52	Paul Arizin, Phil	1674		1978–79	George Gervin, SA	29.6
1952–53	Neil Johnston, Phil	1564		1979–80	George Gervin, SA	33.1
1953–54	Neil Johnston, Phil	1759		1980–81	Adrian Dantley, Utah	30.7
1954–55	Neil Johnston, Phil	1631		1981–82	George Gervin, SA	32.3
1955–56	Bob Pettit, StL	1849		1982–83	Alex English, Den	28.4
1956–57	Paul Arizin, Phil	1817		1983–84	Adrian Dantley, Utah	30.6
1957–58	George Yardley, Det	2001		1984–85	Bernard King, NY	32.9
1958–59	Bob Pettit, StL	2105		1985–86	Dominique Wilkins, Atl	30.3
1959–60	Wilt Chamberlain, Phil	2707		1986–87	Michael Jordan, Chi	37.1
1960–61	Wilt Chamberlain, Phil	3033		1987–88	Michael Jordan, Chi	35.0
1961–62	Wilt Chamberlain, Phil	4029		1988–89	Michael Jordan, Chi	32.5
1962–63	Wilt Chamberlain, SF	3586		1989–90	Michael Jordan, Chi	33.6
1963–64	Wilt Chamberlain, SF	2948		1990–91	Michael Jordan, Chi	31.5
1964–65	Wilt Chamberlain, SF-Phil	2534		1991–92	Michael Jordan, Chi	30.1
1965–66	Wilt Chamberlain, Phil	2649		1992–93	Michael Jordan, Chi	32.6
1966–67	Rick Barry, SF	2775		1993–94	David Robinson, SA	29.8
1967–68	Dave Bing, Det	2142		1994–95	Shaquille O'Neal, Orl	29.3
1968–69	Elvin Hayes, SD	2327		1995–96	Michael Jordan, Chi	30.4
1969–70	Jerry West, LA	*31.2		1996–97	Michael Jordan, Chi	29.6
1970–71	Kareem Abdul-Jabbar, Mil	31.7		1997–98	Michael Jordan, Chi	28.7
1971–72	Kareem Abdul-Jabbar, Mil	34.8		1998–99	Allen Iverson, Phil	26.8
1972–73	Nate Archibald, KC-Oma	34.0		1999–00	Shaquille O'Neal, LA Lakers	29.7

*Based on per game average since 1969–70.

Rebounding

Year	Player, Team	No.		Year	Player, Team	No.
1950–51	Dolph Schayes, Syr	1080		1961–62	Wilt Chamberlain, Phil	2052
1951–52	Larry Foust, FW	880		1962–63	Wilt Chamberlain, SF	1946
	Mel Hutchins, Mil	880		1963–64	Bill Russell, Bos	1930
1952–53	George Mikan, Minn	1007		1964–65	Bill Russell, Bos	1878
1953–54	Harry Gallatin, NY	1098		1965–66	Wilt Chamberlain, Phil	1943
1954–55	Neil Johnston, Phil	1085		1966–67	Wilt Chamberlain, Phil	1957
1955–56	Bob Pettit, StL	1164		1967–68	Wilt Chamberlain, Phil	1952
1956–57	Maurice Stokes, Roch	1256		1968–69	Wilt Chamberlain, LA	1712
1957–58	Bill Russell, Bos	1564		1969–70	Elvin Hayes, SD	*16.9
1958–59	Bill Russell, Bos	1612		1970–71	Wilt Chamberlain, LA	18.2
1959–60	Wilt Chamberlain, Phil	1941		1971–72	Wilt Chamberlain, LA	19.2
1960–61	Wilt Chamberlain, Phil	2149		1972–73	Wilt Chamberlain, LA	18.6
				1973–74	Elvin Hayes, Capital	18.1

Rebounding *(Cont.)*

1974–75	Wes Unseld, Wash	14.8	1988–89	Hakeem Olajuwon, Hou	13.5
1975–76	Kareem Abdul-Jabbar, LA	16.9	1989–90	Hakeem Olajuwon, Hou	14.0
1976–77	Bill Walton, Port	14.4	1990–91	David Robinson, SA	13.0
1977–78	Len Robinson, NO	15.7	1991–92	Dennis Rodman, Det	18.7
1978–79	Moses Malone, Hou	17.6	1992–93	Dennis Rodman, Det	18.3
1979–80	Swen Nater, SD	15.0	1993–94	Dennis Rodman, SA	17.3
1980–81	Moses Malone, Hou	14.8	1994–95	Dennis Rodman, SA	16.8
1981–82	Moses Malone, Hou	14.7	1995–96	Dennis Rodman, Chi	14.9
1982–83	Moses Malone, Phil	15.3	1996–97	Dennis Rodman, Chi	16.1
1983–84	Moses Malone, Phil	13.4	1997–98	Dennis Rodman, Chi	15.0
1984–85	Moses Malone, Phil	13.1	1998–99	Chris Webber, Sac	13.0
1985–86	Bill Laimbeer, Det	13.1	1999–00	Dikembe Mutombo, Atl	14.1
1986–87	Charles Barkley, Phil	14.6			
1987–88	Michael Cage, LA Clippers	13.0			

*Based on per game average since 1969–70.

Assists

1946–47	Ernie Calverly, Prov	202	1973–74	Ernie DiGregorio, Buff	8.2
1947–48	Howie Dallmar, Phil	120	1974–75	Kevin Porter, Wash	8.0
1948–49	Bob Davies, Roch	321	1975–76	Don Watts, Sea	8.1
1949–50	Dick McGuire, NY	386	1976–77	Don Buse, Ind	8.5
1950–51	Andy Phillip, Phil	414	1977–78	Kevin Porter, NJ-Det	10.2
1951–52	Andy Phillip, Phil	539	1978–79	Kevin Porter, Det	13.4
1952–53	Bob Cousy, Bos	547	1979–80	Micheal Richardson, NY	10.1
1953–54	Bob Cousy, Bos	578	1980–81	Kevin Porter, Wash	9.1
1954–55	Bob Cousy, Bos	557	1981–82	Johnny Moore, SA	9.6
1955–56	Bob Cousy, Bos	642	1982–83	Magic Johnson, LA	10.5
1956–57	Bob Cousy, Bos	478	1983–84	Magic Johnson, LA	13.1
1957–58	Bob Cousy, Bos	463	1984–85	Isiah Thomas, Det	13.9
1958–59	Bob Cousy, Bos	557	1985–86	Magic Johnson, LA Lakers	12.6
1959–60	Bob Cousy, Bos	715	1986–87	Magic Johnson, LA Lakers	12.2
1960–61	Oscar Robertson, Cin	690	1987–88	John Stockton, Utah	13.8
1961–62	Oscar Robertson, Cin	899	1988–89	John Stockton, Utah	13.6
1962–63	Guy Rodgers, SF	825	1989–90	John Stockton, Utah	14.5
1963–64	Oscar Robertson, Cin	868	1990–91	John Stockton, Utah	14.2
1964–65	Oscar Robertson, Cin	861	1991–92	John Stockton, Utah	13.7
1965–66	Oscar Robertson, Cin	847	1992–93	John Stockton, Utah	12.0
1966–67	Guy Rodgers, Chi	908	1993–94	John Stockton, Utah	12.6
1967–68	Wilt Chamberlain, Phil	702	1994–95	John Stockton, Utah	12.3
1968–69	Oscar Robertson, Cin	772	1995–96	John Stockton, Utah	11.2
1969–70	Len Wilkens, Sea	*9.1	1996–97	Mark Jackson, Ind	11.4
1970–71	Norm Van Lier, Cin	10.1	1997–98	Rod Strickland, Wash	10.1
1971–72	Jerry West, LA	9.7	1998–99	Jason Kidd, Phoe	10.8
1972–73	Nate Archibald, KC-Oma	11.4	1999–00	Jason Kidd, Phoe	10.1

*Based on per game average since 1969–70.

Field-Goal Percentage

1946–47	Bob Feerick, Wash	40.1	1965–66	Wilt Chamberlain, Phil	54.0
1947–48	Bob Feerick, Wash	34.0	1966–67	Wilt Chamberlain, Phil	68.3
1948–49	Arnie Risen, Roch	42.3	1967–68	Wilt Chamberlain, Phil	59.5
1949–50	Alex Groza, Ind	47.8	1968–69	Wilt Chamberlain, LA	58.3
1950–51	Alex Groza, Ind	47.0	1969–70	Johnny Green, Cin	55.9
1951–52	Paul Arizin, Phil	44.8	1970–71	Johnny Green, Cin	58.7
1952–53	Neil Johnston, Phil	45.2	1971–72	Wilt Chamberlain, LA	64.9
1953–54	Ed Macauley, Bos	48.6	1972–73	Wilt Chamberlain, LA	72.7
1954–55	Larry Foust, FW	48.7	1973–74	Bob McAdoo, Buff	54.7
1955–56	Neil Johnston, Phil	45.7	1974–75	Don Nelson, Bos	53.9
1956–57	Neil Johnston, Phil	44.7	1975–76	Wes Unseld, Wash	56.1
1957–58	Jack Twyman, Cin	45.2	1976–77	Kareem Abdul-Jabbar, LA	57.9
1958–59	Ken Sears, NY	49.0	1977–78	Bobby Jones, Den	57.8
1959–60	Ken Sears, NY	47.7	1978–79	Cedric Maxwell, Bos	58.4
1960–61	Wilt Chamberlain, Phil	50.9	1979–80	Cedric Maxwell, Bos	60.9
1961–62	Walt Bellamy, Chi	51.9	1980–81	Artis Gilmore, Chi	67.0
1962–63	Wilt Chamberlain, SF	52.8	1981–82	Artis Gilmore, Chi	65.2
1963–64	Jerry Lucas, Cin	52.7	1982–83	Artis Gilmore, SA	62.6
1964–65	Wilt Chamberlain, SF-Phil	51.0	1983–84	Artis Gilmore, SA	63.1

Field-Goal Percentage *(Cont.)*

1984–85	James Donaldson, LA Clippers	63.7
1985–86	Steve Johnson, SA	63.2
1986–87	Kevin McHale, Bos	60.4
1987–88	Kevin McHale, Bos	60.4
1988–89	Dennis Rodman, Det	59.5
1989–90	Mark West, Phoe	62.5
1990–91	Buck Williams, Port	60.2
1991–92	Buck Williams, Port	60.4
1992–93	Cedric Ceballos, Phoe	57.6
1993–94	Shaquille O'Neal, Orl	59.9
1994–95	Chris Gatling, GS	63.3
1995–96	Gheorghe Muresan, Wash	58.4
1996–97	Gheorghe Muresan, Wash	60.4
1997–98	Shaquille O'Neal, LA Lakers	58.4
1998–99	Shaquille O'Neal, LA Lakers	57.6
1999–00	Shaquille O'Neal, LA Lakers	57.4

Free-Throw Percentage

1946–47	Fred Scolari, Wash	81.1
1947–48	Bob Feerick, Wash	78.8
1948–49	Bob Feerick, Wash	85.9
1949–50	Max Zaslofsky, Chi	84.3
1950–51	Joe Fulks, Phil	85.5
1951–52	Bob Wanzer, Roch	90.4
1952–53	Bill Sharman, Bos	85.0
1953–54	Bill Sharman, Bos	84.4
1954–55	Bill Sharman, Bos	89.7
1955–56	Bill Sharman, Bos	86.7
1956–57	Bill Sharman, Bos	90.5
1957–58	Dolph Schayes, Syr	90.4
1958–59	Bill Sharman, Bos	93.2
1959–60	Dolph Schayes, Syr	89.2
1960–61	Bill Sharman, Bos	92.1
1961–62	Dolph Schayes, Syr	89.6
1962–63	Larry Costello, Syr	88.1
1963–64	Oscar Robertson, Cin	85.3
1964–65	Larry Costello, Phil	87.7
1965–66	Larry Siegfried, Bos	88.1
1966–67	Adrian Smith, Cin	90.3
1967–68	Oscar Robertson, Cin	87.3
1968–69	Larry Siegfried, Bos	86.4
1969–70	Flynn Robinson, Mil	89.8
1970–71	Chet Walker, Chi	85.9
1971–72	Jack Marin, Balt	89.4
1972–73	Rick Barry, GS	90.2
1973–74	Ernie DiGregorio, Buff	90.2
1974–75	Rick Barry, GS	90.4
1975–76	Rick Barry, GS	92.3
1976–77	Ernie DiGregorio, Buff	94.5
1977–78	Rick Barry, GS	92.4
1978–79	Rick Barry, Hou	94.7
1979–80	Rick Barry, Hou	93.5
1980–81	Calvin Murphy, Hou	95.8
1981–82	Kyle Macy, Phoe	89.9
1982–83	Calvin Murphy, Hou	92.0
1983–84	Larry Bird, Bos	88.8
1984–85	Kyle Macy, Phoe	90.7
1985–86	Larry Bird, Bos	89.6
1986–87	Larry Bird, Bos	91.0
1987–88	Jack Sikma, Mil	92.2
1988–89	Magic Johnson, LA Lakers	91.1
1989–90	Larry Bird, Bos	93.0
1990–91	Reggie Miller, Ind	91.8
1991–92	Mark Price, Clev	94.7
1992–93	Mark Price, Clev	94.8
1993–94	Mahmoud Abdul-Rauf, Den	95.6
1994–95	Spud Webb, Sac	93.4
1995–96	Mahmoud Abdul-Rauf, Den	93.0
1996–97	Mark Price, GS	90.6
1997–98	Chris Mullin, Ind	93.9
1998–99	Reggie Miller, Ind	91.5
1999–00	Jeff Hornacek, Utah	95.0

Three-Point Field-Goal Percentage

1979–80	Fred Brown, Sea	44.3
1980–81	Brian Taylor, SD	38.3
1981–82	Campy Russell, NY	43.9
1982–83	Mike Dunleavy, SA	34.5
1983–84	Darrell Griffith, Utah	36.1
1984–85	Byron Scott, LA Lakers	43.3
1985–86	Craig Hodges, Mil	45.1
1986–87	Kiki Vandeweghe, Por	48.1
1987–88	Craig Hodges, Mil-Phoe	49.1
1988–89	Jon Sundvold, Mia	52.2
1989–90	Steve Kerr, Clev	50.7
1990–91	Jim Les, Sac	46.1
1991–92	Dana Barros, Sea	44.6
1992–93	B.J. Armstrong, Chi	45.3
1993–94	Tracy Murray, Por	45.9
1994–95	Steve Kerr, Chi	52.4
1995–96	Tim Legler, Wash	52.2
1996–97	Kevin Gamble, Sac	48.2
1997–98	Dale Ellis, Sea	46.0
1998–99	Dell Curry, Char	47.6
1999–00	Hubert Davis, Dall	49.1

Steals

1973–74	Larry Steele, Por	2.68
1974–75	Rick Barry, GS	2.85
1975–76	Don Watts, Sea	3.18
1976–77	Don Buse, Ind	3.47
1977–78	Ron Lee, Phoe	2.74
1978–79	M.L. Carr, Det	2.46
1979–80	Micheal Richardson, NY	3.23
1980–81	Magic Johnson, LA	3.43
1981–82	Magic Johnson, LA	2.67
1982–83	Micheal Richardson, GS-NJ	2.84
1983–84	Rickey Green, Utah	2.65
1984–85	Micheal Richardson, NJ	2.96
1985–86	Alvin Robertson, SA	3.67
1986–87	Alvin Robertson, SA	3.21
1987–88	Michael Jordan, Chi	3.16
1988–89	John Stockton, Utah	3.21
1989–90	Michael Jordan, Chi	2.77
1990–91	Alvin Robertson, Mil	3.04
1991–92	John Stockton, Utah	2.98
1992–93	Michael Jordan, Chi	2.83
1993–94	Nate McMillan, Sea	2.96
1994–95	Scottie Pippen, Chi	2.94
1995–96	Gary Payton, Sea	2.85
1996–97	Mookie Blaylock, Atl	2.72
1997–98	Mookie Blaylock, Atl	2.61
1998–99	Kendall Gill, NJ	2.68
1999–00	Eddie Jones, Char	2.67

Blocked Shots

1973–74	Elmore Smith, LA	4.85
1974–75	Kareem Abdul-Jabbar, Mil	3.26
1975–76	Kareem Abdul-Jabbar, LA	4.12
1976–77	Bill Walton, Port	3.25
1977–78	George Johnson, NJ	3.38
1978–79	Kareem Abdul-Jabbar, LA	3.95
1979–80	Kareem Abdul-Jabbar, LA	3.41
1980–81	George Johnson, SA	3.39
1981–82	George Johnson, SA	3.12
1982–83	Wayne Rollins, Atl	4.29
1983–84	Mark Eaton, Utah	4.28
1984–85	Mark Eaton, Utah	5.56
1985–86	Manute Bol, Wash	4.96
1986–87	Mark Eaton, Utah	4.06
1987–88	Mark Eaton, Utah	3.71
1988–89	Manute Bol, GS	4.31
1989–90	Hakeem Olajuwon, Hou	4.59
1990–91	Hakeem Olajuwon, Hou	3.95
1991–92	David Robinson, SA	4.49
1992–93	Hakeem Olajuwon, Hou	4.17
1993–94	Dikembe Mutombo, Den	4.10
1994–95	Dikembe Mutombo, Den	3.91
1995–96	Dikembe Mutombo, Den	4.49
1996–97	Shawn Bradley, NJ	3.40
1997–98	Marcus Camby, Tor	3.65
1998–99	Alonzo Mourning, Mia	3.91
1999–2000	Alonzo Mourning, Mia	3.72

NBA All-Star Game Results

Year	Result	Site	Winning Coach	Most Valuable Player
1951	East 111, West 94	Boston	Joe Lapchick	Ed Macauley, Bos
1952	East 108, West 91	Boston	Al Cervi	Paul Arizin, Phil
1953	West 79, East 75	Ft Wayne	John Kundla	George Mikan, Minn
1954	East 98, West 93 (OT)	New York	Joe Lapchick	Bob Cousy, Bos
1955	East 100, West 91	New York	Al Cervi	Bill Sharman, Bos
1956	West 108, East 94	Rochester	Charley Eckman	Bob Pettit, StL
1957	East 109, West 97	Boston	Red Auerbach	Bob Cousy, Bos
1958	East 130, West 118	St Louis	Red Auerbach	Bob Pettit, StL
1959	West 124, East 108	Detroit	Ed Macauley	B. Pettit, StL/ E. Baylor, Minn
1960	East 125, West 115	Philadelphia	Red Auerbach	Wilt Chamberlain, Phil
1961	West 153, East 131	Syracuse	Paul Seymour	Oscar Robertson, Cin
1962	West 150, East 130	St Louis	Fred Schaus	Bob Pettit, StL
1963	East 115, West 108	Los Angeles	Red Auerbach	Bill Russell, Bos
1964	East 111, West 107	Boston	Red Auerbach	Oscar Robertson, Cin
1965	East 124, West 123	St Louis	Red Auerbach	Jerry Lucas, Cin
1966	East 137, West 94	Cincinnati	Red Auerbach	Adrian Smith, Cin
1967	West 135, East 120	San Francisco	Fred Schaus	Rick Barry, SF
1968	East 144, West 124	New York	Alex Hannum	Hal Greer, Phil
1969	East 123, West 112	Baltimore	Gene Shue	Oscar Robertson, Cin
1970	East 142, West 135	Philadelphia	Red Holzman	Willis Reed, NY
1971	West 108, East 107	San Diego	Larry Costello	Lenny Wilkens, Sea
1972	West 112, East 110	Los Angeles	Bill Sharman	Jerry West, LA
1973	East 104, West 84	Chicago	Tom Heinsohn	Dave Cowens, Bos
1974	West 134, East 123	Seattle	Larry Costello	Bob Lanier, Det
1975	East 108, West 102	Phoenix	K.C. Jones	Walt Frazier, NY
1976	East 123, West 109	Philadelphia	Tom Heinsohn	Dave Bing, Wash
1977	West 125, East 124	Milwaukee	Larry Brown	Julius Erving, Phil
1978	East 133, West 125	Atlanta	Billy Cunningham	Randy Smith, Buff
1979	West 134, East 129	Detroit	Lenny Wilkens	David Thompson, Den
1980	East 144, West 135 (OT)	Washington	Billy Cunningham	George Gervin, SA
1981	East 123, West 120	Cleveland	Billy Cunningham	Nate Archibald, Bos
1982	East 120, West 118	New Jersey	Bill Fitch	Larry Bird, Bos
1983	East 132, West 123	Los Angeles	Billy Cunningham	Julius Erving, Phil
1984	East 154, West 145 (OT)	Denver	K.C. Jones	Isiah Thomas, Det
1985	West 140, East 129	Indiana	Pat Riley	Ralph Sampson, Hou
1986	East 139, West 132	Dallas	K.C. Jones	Isiah Thomas, Det
1987	West 154, East 149 (OT)	Seattle	Pat Riley	Tom Chambers, Sea
1988	East 138, West 133	Chicago	Mike Fratello	Michael Jordan, Chi
1989	West 143, East 134	Houston	Pat Riley	Karl Malone, Utah
1990	East 130, West 113	Miami	Chuck Daly	Magic Johnson, LA Lakers
1991	East 116, West 114	Charlotte	Chris Ford	Charles Barkley, Phil
1992	West 153, East 113	Orlando	Don Nelson	Magic Johnson, LA Lakers
1993	West 135, East 132	Salt Lake City	Paul Westphal	K. Malone/ J. Stockton ,Utah
1994	East 127, West 118	Minneapolis	Lenny Wilkens	Scottie Pippen, Chi
1995	West 139, East 112	Phoenix	Paul Westphal	Mitch Richmond, Sac
1996	East 129, West 118	San Antonio	Phil Jackson	Michael Jordan, Chi
1997	East 132, West 120	Cleveland	Doug Collins	Glen Rice, Char
1998	East 135, West 114	New York	Larry Bird	Michael Jordan, Chi
1999	Cancelled due to lockout.			
2000	West 137, East 126	Oakland	Phil Jackson	Shaquille O'Neal, Lakers/ Tim Duncan, SA

Members of the Basketball Hall of Fame

Contributors

Senda Abbott (1984)
Forest C. (Phog) Allen (1959)
Clair F. Bee (1967)
Danny Biasone (2000)
Walter A. Brown (1965)
John W. Bunn (1964)
Bob Douglas (1971)
Al Duer (1981)
Wayne Embry (1999)
Clifford Fagan (1983)
Harry A. Fisher (1973)
Larry Fleisher (1991)
Edward Gottlieb (1971)
Luther H. Gulick (1959)
Lester Harrison (1979)
Ferenc Hepp (1980)

Edward J. Hickox (1959)
Paul D. (Tony) Hinkle (1965)
Ned Irish (1964)
R. William Jones (1964)
J. Walter Kennedy (1980)
Emil S. Liston (1974)
John B. McLendon (1978)
Bill Mokray (1965)
Ralph Morgan (1959)
Frank Morgenweck (1962)
James Naismith (1959)
Peter F. Newell (1978)
C.M. Newton (2000)
John J. O'Brien (1961)
Larry O'Brien (1991)
Harold G. Olsen (1959)

Maurice Podoloff (1973)
H. V. Porter (1960)
William A. Reid (1963)
Elmer Ripley (1972)
Lynn W. St. John (1962)
Abe Saperstein (1970)
Arthur A. Schabinger (1961)
Amos Alonzo Stagg (1959)
Boris Stankovic (1991)
Edward Steitz (1983)
Chuck Taylor (1968)
Oswald Tower (1959)
Arthur L. Trester (1961)
Clifford Wells (1971)
Lou Wilke (1982)
Fred Zollner (1999)

Players

Kareem Abdul-Jabbar (1995)
Nate (Tiny) Archibald (1991)
Paul J. Arizin (1977)
Thomas B. Barlow (1980)
Rick Barry (1987)
Elgin Baylor (1976)
John Beckman (1972)
Walt Bellamy (1993)
Sergei Belov (1992)
Dave Bing (1990)
Larry Bird (1998)
Carol Blazejowski (1994)
Bennie Borgmann (1961)
Bill Bradley (1982)
Joseph Brennan (1974)
Al Cervi (1984)
Wilt Chamberlain (1978)
Charles (Tarzan) Cooper (1976)
Kresimir Cosic (1996)
Bob Cousy (1970)
Dave Cowens (1991)
Joan Crawford (1997)
Billy Cunningham (1986)
Denise Curry (1992)
Bob Davies (1969)
Forrest S. DeBernardi (1961)
Dave DeBusschere (1982)
H.G. (Dutch) Dehnert (1968)
Anne Donovan (1995)
Paul Endacott (1971)
Alex English (1997)
Julius Erving (1993)
Harold (Bud) Foster (1964)
Walter (Clyde) Frazier (1987)
Max (Marty) Friedman (1971)
Joe Fulks (1977)
Lauren (Laddie) Gale (1976)
Harry (the Horse) Gallatin (1991)
William Gates (1989)
George Gervin (1996)

Tom Gola (1975)
Gail Goodrich (1996)
Hal Greer (1981)
Robert (Ace) Gruenig (1963)
Clifford O. Hagan (1977)
Victor Hanson (1960)
John Havlicek (1983)
Connie Hawkins (1992)
Elvin Hayes (1990)
Marques Haynes (1998)
Tom Heinsohn (1986)
Nat Holman (1964)
Robert J. Houbregs (1987)
Bailey Howell (1997)
Chuck Hyatt (1959)
Dan Issel (1993)
Harry (Buddy) Jeannette (1994)
William C. Johnson (1976)
D. Neil Johnston (1990)
K.C. Jones (1989)
Sam Jones (1983)
Edward (Moose) Krause (1975)
Bob Kurland (1961)
Bob Lanier (1992)
Joe Lapchick (1966)
Nancy Lieberman-Cline (1996)
Clyde Lovellette (1988)
Jerry Lucas (1979)
Angelo (Hank) Luisetti (1959)
C. Edward Macauley (1960)
Peter P. Maravich (1987)
Slater Martin (1981)
Bob McAdoo (2000)
Branch McCracken (1960)
Jack McCracken (1962)
Bobby McDermott (1988)
Dick McGuire (1993)
Kevin McHale (1999)
Ann Meyers (1993)
George L. Mikan (1959)

Vern Mikkelsen (1995)
Cheryl Miller (1995)
Earl Monroe (1990)
Calvin Murphy (1993)
Charles (Stretch) Murphy (1960)
H. O. (Pat) Page (1962)
Bob Pettit (1970)
Andy Phillip (1961)
Jim Pollard (1977)
Frank Ramsey (1981)
Willis Reed (1981)
Arnie Risen (1998)
Oscar Robertson (1979)
John S. Roosma (1961)
Bill Russell (1974)
John (Honey) Russell (1964)
Adolph Schayes (1972)
Ernest J. Schmidt (1973)
John J. Schommer (1959)
Barney Sedran (1962)
Uljana Semjonova (1993)
Bill Sharman (1975)
Christian Steinmetz (1961)
Lusia Harris Stewart (1992)
Isiah Thomas (2000)
David Thompson (1996)
John A. (Cat) Thompson (1962)
Nate Thurmond (1984)
Jack Twyman (1982)
Wes Unseld (1988)
Robert (Fuzzy) Vandivier (1974)
Edward A. Wachter (1961)
Bill Walton (1993)
Robert F. Wanzer (1987)
Jerry West (1979)
Nera White (1992)
Lenny Wilkens (1989)
John R. Wooden (1960)
George (Bird) Yardley (1996)

Coaches

Harold Anderson (1984)
Red Auerbach (1968)
Sam Barry (1978)
Ernest A. Blood (1960)
Howard G. Cann (1967)
H. Clifford Carlson (1959)

Lou Carnesecca (1992)
Ben Carnevale (1969)
Pete Carril (1997)
Everett Case (1981)
Jody Conradt (1998)
Denny Crum (1994)

Chuck Daly (1994)
Everett S. Dean (1966)
Antonio Diaz-Miguel (1997)
Edgar A. Diddle (1971)
Bruce Drake (1972)
Clarence Gaines (1981)

Note: Year of election in parentheses.

Coaches *(Cont.)*

Jack Gardner (1983)
Amory T. (Slats) Gill (1967)
Aleksandr Gomelsky (1995)
Alex Hannum (1998)
Marv Harshman (1984)
Don Haskins (1997)
Edgar S. Hickey (1978)
Howard A. Hobson (1965)
Red Holzman (1986)
Hank Iba (1968)
Alvin F. (Doggie) Julian (1967)
Frank W. Keaney (1960)
George E. Keogan (1961)
Bob Knight (1991)
John Kundla (1995)

Ward L. Lambert (1960)
Harry Litwack (1975)
Kenneth D. Loeffler (1964)
A.C. (Dutch) Lonborg (1972)
Arad A. McCutchan (1980)
Al McGuire (1992)
Frank McGuire (1976)
Walter E. Meanwell (1959)
Raymond J. Meyer (1978)
Ralph Miller (1988)
Billie Moore (1999)
Aleksandar Nikolic (1998)
Jack Ramsay (1992)
Cesare Rubini (1994)
Adolph F. Rupp (1968)

Leonard D. Sachs (1961)
Everett F. Shelton (1979)
Dean Smith (1982)
Pat Summitt (2000)
Fred R. Taylor (1985)
Bertha Teague (1984)
John Thompson (1999)
Margaret Wade (1984)
Stanley H. Watts (1985)
Lenny Wilkens (1998)
John R. Wooden (1972)
Morgan Wooten (2000)
Phil Woolpert (1992)

Referees

James E. Enright (1978)
George T. Hepbron (1960)
George Hoyt (1961)
Matthew P. Kennedy (1959)
Lloyd Leith (1982)
Zigmund J. Mihalik (1985)

John P. Nucatola (1977)
Ernest C. Quigley (1961)
J. Dallas Shirley (1979)
Earl Strom (1995)
David Tobey (1961)
David H. Walsh (1961)

Teams

Buffalo Germans (1961)
First Team (1959)
Original Celtics (1959)
Renaissance (1963)

ABA Champions

Year	Champion	Series	Loser	Winning Coach
1968	Pittsburgh Pipers	4–3	New Orleans Bucs	Vince Cazetta
1969	Oakland Oaks	4–1	Indiana Pacers	Alex Hannum
1970	Indiana Pacers	4–2	Los Angeles Stars	Bob Leonard
1971	Utah Stars	4–3	Kentucky Colonels	Bill Sharman
1972	Indiana Pacers	4–2	New York Nets	Bob Leonard
1973	Indiana Pacers	4–3	Kentucky Colonels	Bob Leonard
1974	New York Nets	4–1	Utah Stars	Kevin Loughery
1975	Kentucky Colonels	4–1	Indiana Pacers	Hubie Brown
1976	New York Nets	4–2	Denver Nuggets	Kevin Loughery

ABA Postseason Awards

Most Valuable Player

1967–68 ....Connie Hawkins, Pitt
1968–69 ....Mel Daniels, Ind
1969–70 ....Spencer Haywood, Den
1970–71 ....Mel Daniels, Ind
1971–72 ....Artis Gilmore, Ken
1972–73 ....Billy Cunningham, Car
1973–74 ....Julius Erving, NY
1974–75 ....Julius Erving, NY
　　　　　　　　　　George McGinnis, Ind
1975–76 ....Julius Erving, NY

Coach of the Year

1967–68 ....Vince Cazetta, Pitt
1968–69 ....Alex Hannum, Oak
1969–70 ....Bill Sharman, LA
　　　　　　　　　　Joe Belmont, Den
1970–71 ....Al Bianchi, Vir
1971–72 ....Tom Nissalke, Dall
1972–73 ....Larry Brown, Car
1973–74 ....Babe McCarthy, Ken
　　　　　　　　　　Joe Mullaney, Utah
1974–75 ....Larry Brown, Den
1975–76 ....Larry Brown, Den

Rookie of the Year

1967–68 ....Mel Daniels, Minn
1968–69 ....Warren Armstrong, Oak
1969–70 ....Spencer Haywood, Den
1970–71 ....Charlie Scott, Vir
　　　　　　　　　　Dan Issel, Ken
1971–72 ....Artis Gilmore, Ken
1972–73 ....Brian Taylor, NY
1973–74 ....Swen Nater, SA
1974–75 ....Marvin Barnes, StL
1975–76 ....David Thompson, Den

ABA Season Leaders

Scoring

	GP	Pts	Avg
1967–68...Connie Hawkins, Pitt	70	1875	26.8
1968–69...Rick Barry, Oak	35	1190	34.0
1969–70...Spencer Haywood, Den	84	2519	30.0
1970–71...Dan Issel, Ken	83	2480	29.4
1971–72...Charlie Scott, Vir	73	2524	34.6
1972–73...Julius Erving, Vir	71	2268	31.9
1973–74...Julius Erving, NY	84	2299	27.4
1974–75...George McGinnis, Ind	79	2353	29.8
1975–76...Julius Erving, NY	84	2462	29.3

Rebounds

1967–68................Mel Daniels, Minn	15.6
1968–69................Mel Daniels, Ind	16.5
1969–70................Spencer Haywood, Den	19.5
1970–71................Mel Daniels, Ind	18.0
1971–72................Artis Gilmore, Ken	17.8
1972–73................Artis Gilmore, Ken	17.5
1973–74................Artis Gilmore, Ken	18.3
1974–75................Swen Nater, SA	16.4
1975–76................Artis Gilmore, Ken	15.5

Assists

1967–68................Larry Brown, NO	6.5
1968–69................Larry Brown, Oak	7.1
1969–70................Larry Brown, Wash	7.1
1970–71................Bill Melchionni, NY	8.3
1971–72................Bill Melchionni, NY	8.4
1972–73................Bill Melchionni, NY	7.5
1973–74................Al Smith, Den	8.2
1974–75................Mack Calvin, Den	7.7
1975–76................Don Buse, Ind	8.2

Steals

1973–74................Ted McClain, Car	2.98
1974–75................Brian Taylor, NY	2.80
1975–76................Don Buse, Ind	4.12

Blocked Shots

1973–74................Caldwell Jones, SD	4.00
1974–75................Caldwell Jones, SD	3.24
1975–76................Billy Paultz, SA	3.05

World Championship of Basketball

Year	Winner	Runner-Up	Score	Site
1950	Argentina	United States	†	Rio de Janeiro
1954	United States	Brazil	†	Rio de Janeiro
1959	Brazil	United States	†	Santiago, Chile
1963	Brazil	Yugoslavia	†	Rio de Janeiro
1967	Soviet Union	Yugoslavia	†	Montevideo, Uruguay
1970	Yugoslavia	Brazil	†	Ljubljana, Yugoslavia
1974	Soviet Union	Yugoslavia	†	San Juan
1978	Yugoslavia	Soviet Union	82–81 (OT)	Manila
1982	Soviet Union	United States	95–94	Cali, Colombia
1986	United States	Soviet Union	87–85	Madrid
1990	Yugoslavia	Soviet Union	92–75	Buenos Aires
1994*	United States	Russia	137–91	Toronto
1998	Yugoslavia	Russia	64–62	Athens

*U.S. professionals began competing in 1994. In 1998, a labor dispute resulted in a boycott of the World Championship by NBA stars; the U.S. roster was filled by members of the CBA and European professional leagues and college players.
†Result determined by overall record in final round of competition.

THEY SAID IT

Mookie Blaylock, Warriors guard, 32, on whispers that injuries and age are catching up with him: "I don't care. I'm too old for that stuff."

Coach Tom Izzo and
NCAA champion
Michigan State

College
Basketball

Heart And Soul

Michigan State had plenty of the former and helped college basketball recover the latter in a season of self-doubt and scandal

BY B.J. SCHECTER

NEARLY LOST amid the tales of seedy summer coaches and greedy agents, half buried by the steady flow of players leaving school early and almost obscured by the increasingly popular notion that the college game has lost its luster, were a coach and a team that reminded us why we fell in love with NCAA basketball in the first place. When it appeared that the game may have suffered irreparable damage, along came Tom Izzo and Michigan State. Izzo's Spartans proved that the lure of the NBA and the temptations of agents had not drained the college game of all of its top players or its core values, which include the notion that to win a national championship you need wisdom and experience—i.e., upperclassmen—to go along with heart and desire.

Nobody epitomized heart and desire more than Michigan State's senior point guard Mateen Cleaves, who put the NBA on hold and returned to East Lansing for his senior season, only to suffer a broken right foot in preseason practice. He would miss the Spartans' first 13 games, but Cleaves handled the situation remarkably well and without complaint until Michigan State's nationally televised game at North Carolina on Dec 1. At the shootaround the day before the game, Cleaves had to choke back tears as he gazed up at Michael Jordan's jersey in the rafters, and then at his broken foot, wondering if he had made a huge mistake by coming back to school. Frustrated by his injury and what he perceived as the Spartans' lackadaisical attitude during the shootaround, Cleaves unleashed his anger with a fiery speech to his teammates in the locker room before the game, which the Spartans, duly inspired, won 86–76.

And when he rejoined the team in January, Cleaves's determination had redoubled. His game was a little rusty, but his leadership skills were as sharp as ever. When the Spartans weren't playing well, Izzo never had to worry about the team missing his message: Cleaves was always there to drive the point home. Sometimes he even went further. When No. 1–seeded Michigan State trailed Syracuse by 10 points at halftime in the second round of the NCAA tournament, it was Cleaves, not

Cleaves got off the mat to inspire his teammates in the title game against Florida.

Izzo, who delivered a profanity-laced tirade to the team in the locker room. The Spartans rallied to win the game 75–58.

In the Midwest Regional final against second seed Iowa State, Cleaves made two steals, blocked two shots and scored 10 points to propel the Spartans to a hard-fought 75–64 victory and into the Final Four for the second consecutive year. There the Spartans faced their Big Ten rivals, the Wisconsin Badgers, who lived up to their nickname with a harassing defense. The eighth-seeded Badgers had scratched their way past three favored opponents, including No. 1–seed Arizona, to reach the Final Four.

Michigan State had beaten Wisconsin three times during the season, most recently in the semifinals of the Big Ten tournament, but this game was anything but easy. It wasn't easy on the eyes, either. The first half was uglier than a Pop Warner football game, with a score to match, as Michigan State led 19–17 at the break. The early pace played right into the Badgers' claws, but Izzo and Cleaves kept their team composed and the Spartans gradually pulled away, winning 53–41. Michigan State had more rebounds (42) than the Badgers had points. Cleaves was just happy it was over. "Whenever you play Wisconsin it's going to be an ugly game," he said. "I'm just glad I don't have to play them again. Ever."

Florida coach Billy Donovan was probably thinking the same thing about Cleaves after the point guard's performance against his Gators in the national championship game. The youthful Gators were one of the biggest surprises of the season and perhaps gave us a glimpse of where college basketball is headed. Inexperienced but talented, naive but bold, Florida dashed to the championship game with upset victories over top-seeded Duke and third-seed Oklahoma State before knocking off North Carolina, another dark horse team, in the semifinals. Donovan, 34, a former Providence College star and Rick Pitino disciple, marshaled a run-and-gun group that went 12 deep. More important, Donovan's Gators regularly forced turnovers with a swarming, suffocating defense.

Some observers thought Florida might surprise Michigan State, but the Spartans proved early on that they could muzzle the

Gators and their vaunted defense. Cleaves, his backcourt mate Charlie Bell and forward Morris Peterson were flawless, forcing Donovan to abandon the press 16 minutes into the first half. Michigan State led 43–32 at intermission and appeared to be in control, but the young Gators made a run early in the second half. They'd cut the Spartans' lead to six when things almost came crashing down entirely for Michigan State. Attempting a layup, Cleaves got tangled with Florida guard Teddy Dupay. Dupay grabbed Cleaves and inadvertently hooked his right foot around Cleaves's right ankle, sending the Spartan point guard awkwardly to the floor. Cleaves's ankle wrenched grotesquely on impact. His face registering excruciating pain, he looked toward the Michigan State bench and mouthed, "It's broke, it's broke."

Thinking Dupay had deliberately tried to hurt Cleaves, Izzo was livid. He gathered his team together and said, "We're going to war! They took out our leader. Who's going to step up?" The entire team responded. Bell ran the point as smoothly as he had during Cleaves's 13-game absence in the regular season; Peterson took control inside with silky moves to the hoop; and A.J. Granger and Mike Chappell were deadly from three-point range. During the 4 1/2 minutes that Cleaves was out, Michigan State increased its lead.

While his teammates held the fort, Cleaves writhed in agony as trainers worked on his ankle. "I dropped a couple of tears," he said, "but I told the trainer he'd have to amputate my leg to keep me out of this one." Cleaves limped back to the Michigan State bench, about to pull a Willis Reed. He hobbled past Izzo to the scorers' table, and the RCA Dome thundered with the cheers of the Spartan faithful. Cleaves didn't score a point during the final 12 minutes (he finished the game with 18), but he didn't have to. His return was like an adrenaline injection to his teammates, who ran away with the game 89–76.

When the final buzzer sounded, Cleaves hugged everyone from his mother, Frances, to Michigan State legend Magic Johnson, but the impact of the accomplishment had yet to hit him. A few minutes later, leaning on a pair of crutches at midcourt, he watched a video monitor replay highlights of the tournament to the tune of the song "One Shining Moment." When the Spartans appeared onscreen at the end, Cleaves stared, mouth agape, and began to sob. His mother embraced him, and all Cleaves could say was, "Oh, my god, we did it. We actually did it."

There were plenty of shining moments in the early rounds of the NCAA tournament, but few of the perennial stunning upsets. St. Bonaventure and Butler, No. 12 seeds both, *almost* pulled off shockers, but each lost to No. 5 seeds in the first round. The Bonnies had Kentucky on the ropes, forcing two overtimes before losing 85–80. Butler, the host school for the Final Four in Indianapolis, led Florida by one point with 8.1 seconds to play in overtime, but the Gators' Mike Miller broke the underdogs' hearts with a buzzer-beater, and Florida escaped with a 69–68 victory. The Big Dance of 2000 will be remembered as the year Cinderella stayed home. In fact, the Sweet 16 included only one team (Wisconsin) that had not been ranked in the Associated Press Top 25 during the regular season.

An unfortunate subplot to the tournament was the career-threatening injury to Cincinnati star and national player of the year Kenyon Martin. Thanks largely to Martin's dominance, the Bearcats were ranked No. 1 in the nation for most of the season; this was supposed to be their year. Like Cleaves, Martin had spurned the NBA draft to return for his senior season and a shot at a championship. But a few days before the tournament began, Martin's, and Cincinnati's, season crumbled in an instant. The star forward broke his leg in a tangle beneath the basket during a quarterfinal Conference USA tournament game against Saint Louis. The Bearcats lost the game and, a week later, their previously guaranteed status as a No. 1 seed in the NCAAs. Demoted to the second seed in the South Regional, Cincinnati

After a subpar regular season, Guthridge's Tar Heels surprised everyone in the NCAAs.

BOB DONNAN

beat UNC Wilmington in the first round, but lost to Tulsa in round 2. Happily, Martin recovered from his injury, and the New Jersey Nets made him the No. 1 pick in the 2000 NBA draft.

Lacking Cinderella, the 2000 tournament had Wisconsin, marginally more talented and considerably less attractive. The Badgers and their wily coach, Dick Bennett, resembled another team from Wisconsin with a crafty coach—Vince Lombardi's Green Bay Packers. Earthbound, scrappy, the Badgers emphasized defense and ... defense. The five players Wisconsin put on the floor were far inferior to their counterparts from Fresno State, Arizona, LSU and Purdue, yet the Badgers beat every one of them to advance to the Final Four. "If we had to play teams one-on-one we'd lose every time," said Wisconsin junior forward Mark Vershaw.

The Badgers' run demonstrated that college basketball is above all a *team* game, and coaches like Bennett and North Carolina's Bill Guthridge can make a difference if they get all of their players on the same page. That took a while to happen this year in Chapel Hill, but when it did, the Tar Heels provided one of the tournament's most cheering story lines. Before the field was selected, there was talk that North Carolina (18–13) might miss the NCAAs for the first time since 1974. All season hoop-crazed Tar Heel fans were calling for Guthridge's head. After a loss to Wake Forest, one headline screamed: GUT-TER BALL. The Tar Heels lost twice to Wake and were swept by archrival Duke during the regular season. But they put it all together come tournament time, knocking off top-seeded Stanford and tough fourth-seed Tennessee en route to their second Final Four in three seasons under Guthridge. In Indianapolis, center Brendan Haywood pointedly said that any fan wishing to hop back on the Carolina bandwagon should "go root for [North Carolina] State."

If Carolina's regular season was bad, the rest of college basketball's was worse. Several players, including UCLA's JaRon Rush and his brother Kareem, a freshman at Missouri, were suspended for multiple games for illegally accepting money from their AAU summer-league coach. Programs from UNLV to Duke were investigated for possible NCAA violations. And Indiana coach Bob Knight continued his tiresome antics. At the Big Ten Conference media day, much was made of the fact that Knight and former Hoosier star guard Steve Alford, the first-year coach at Iowa, didn't acknowledge one another. Apparently in response to the media, Knight entered the court behind the Iowa bench and shook Alford's hand prior to tip-off of a January meeting between the two teams in Bloomington. He then ripped reporters for making the Knight-Alford relationship an issue. On the eve of the NCAA tournament, CNN/SI aired a report in which former Hoosier Neil Reed accused Knight of choking him during a practice. Knight steadfastly denied the allegations, and a member of the Indiana

MANNY MILLAN

board of trustees went so far as to say that he would "put no stock in" Reed's charges. A few weeks later CNN/SI obtained a copy of a 1997 practice tape showing Knight choking Reed.

Several other damning allegations—that he showed his team a soiled piece of toilet paper, berated a secretary and threatened the Indiana athletic director—later came to light, and it appeared that Knight would be fired. In early May the board of trustees ended their investigation and left the decision to school president Myles Brand. Brand caved in. Instead of removing Knight, he suspended the coach for three games, fined him $30,000 and instituted a zero tolerance policy. Brand said that he had been ready to fire the man known in Bloomington as the General, but that Knight, in an eleventh-hour meeting, convinced the president he could change. "He made a personal pledge to me to change his behavior," said Brand. "And I believe him."

Thankfully, the women's game was devoid of any sordid drama or contro-

versy. The two best teams in the country, Connecticut and Tennessee, met for the title in a rubber match of what has become the best rivalry in women's college basketball. In 10 games against each other, each team had won five times, and in every encounter either a No. 1 ranking, a Final Four berth, an appearance in the championship game or the national title had been at stake. The two teams split during the regular season as UConn won in Knoxville and Tennessee handed the Huskies their first loss in Storrs.

It had been five years to the day since the Huskies won their first championship (over Tennessee, naturally), and Connecticut would mark the anniversary with a performance to remember. There was little doubt that this had been the Huskies' year, and aside from a one-point loss to the Vols, Connecticut had outscored its opponents by an average of 30.6 points per game. But few expected the 71–52 pasting that UConn administered to coach Pat Summitt's team.

Tennessee's troubles began during the morning shootaround when it lost junior guard Kristen (Ace) Clement to a badly sprained ankle. Clement was in so much pain and screaming so loudly that Summitt had to ask her to calm down because she was "scaring the team." The Huskies tied their own championship-game record by forcing 26 turnovers. They blocked 11 shots (a title game–record nine by Kelly Schumacher) and held All-Americas Tamika Catchings and Semeka Randall to a combined 22 points. "No question about it, they were awesome," said Summitt. "They schooled us."

So the 1999–2000 college basketball season will be remembered for the team that schooled its opponents and for the players who decided to stay in school. The men's regular season may have left us shaking our heads, but Michigan State and the UConn women did their best to redeem it.

NCAA Championship Game Box Score

Michigan St 89

MICHIGAN ST	Min	FG M–A	FT M–A	Reb O–T	A	PF	TP
Hutson	23	2–4	2–2	0–1	3	4	6
Peterson	32	7–14	4–6	1–2	5	3	21
Granger	34	7–11	2–2	2–9	1	2	19
Cleaves	33	7–11	1–1	0–2	4	1	18
Bell	33	3–6	2–3	3–8	5	2	9
Richardson	15	4–7	1–2	1–2	0	1	9
Anagonye	11	0–0	0–0	2–3	0	0	0
Chappell	6	2–4	0–0	1–1	0	4	6
Ballinger	6	1–1	0–0	0–0	0	2	2
Thomas	4	0–0	0–0	1–1	1	1	0
Smith	1	0–0	0–0	0–0	0	0	0
Cherry	1	0–0	0–0	0–0	0	0	0
Ishbia	1	0–1	0–0	0–0	0	0	0
Totals	200	33–59	12–16	11–29	19	20	89

Percentages: FG—.559, FT—.750. 3-pt goals: 11–22, .500 (Peterson 3–8, Granger 3–5, Cleaves 3–4, Bell 1–2, Chappell 1–3). Team rebounds: 3. Blocked shots: 1 (Anagonye). Turnovers: 14 (Peterson 3, Anagonye 2, Bell 2, Cleaves 2, Granger 2, Chappell, Hutson, Thomas). Steals: 5 (Bell 2, Chappell, Peterson, Richardson).

Florida 76

FLORIDA	Min	FG M–A	FT M–A	Reb O–T	A	PF	TP
Wright	29	5–8	3–5	4–10	4	4	13
Miller	31	2–5	5–6	1–3	2	0	10
Haslem	28	10–12	7–7	2–2	0	4	27
Dupay	15	0–4	0–0	0–0	1	2	0
Hamilton	14	0–1	0–0	0–0	0	1	0
Nelson	26	4–10	0–0	1–4	3	1	11
Bonner	7	0–3	0–0	1–3	0	1	0
Weaks	22	1–3	0–0	1–1	1	2	3
Harvey	16	3–11	3–4	4–6	0	2	9
Parker	12	1–3	0–0	0–0	2	2	3
Totals	200	26–60	18–22	14–29	13	19	76

Percentages: FG—.433, FT—.818. 3-pt goals: 6–18, .333 (Wright 0–1, Miller 1–2, Dupay 0–2, Hamilton 0–1, Nelson 3–6, Bonner 0–2, Weaks 1–1, Parker 1–3). Team rebounds: 1. Blocked shots: 2 (Haslem, Harvey). Turnovers: 13 (Haslem 3, Nelson 3, Harvey 2, Miller 2, Parker, Weaks, Wright). Steals: 5 (Nelson 2, Weaks 2, Wright).

Halftime: Michigan St 43, Florida 32. A: 43,116.
Officials: Burr, Boudreaux, Hall.

Final AP Top 25

Poll taken before NCAA Tournament.

1. Duke	27–4	
2. Michigan St	26–7	
3. Stanford	26–3	
4. Arizona	26–6	
5. Temple	26–5	
6. Iowa St	29–4	
7. Cincinnati	28–3	
8. Ohio St	22–6	
9. St John's	24–7	
10. Louisiana St	26–5	
11. Tennessee	24–6	
12. Oklahoma	26–6	
13. Florida	24–7	
14. Oklahoma St	24–6	
15. Texas	23–8	
16. Syracuse	24–5	
17. Maryland	24–9	
18. Tulsa	29–4	
19. Kentucky	22–9	
20. Connecticut	24–9	
21. Illinois	21–9	
22. Indiana	20–8	
23. Miami (FL)	21–10	
24. Auburn	23–9	
25. Purdue	21–9	

National Invitation Tournament Scores

First round: Siena 66, Massachusetts 65; Penn St 55, Princeton 41; Kent St 73, Rutgers 62; Villanova 72, Delaware 63; Notre Dame 75, Michigan 65; Xavier 67, Marquette 63; Brigham Young 81, Bowling Green 54; Southern Illinois 94, Colorado 92; N Carolina St 64, Tulane 60; Arizona St 83, New Mexico St 77, SW Missouri St 77, Southern Methodist 64; Mississippi 62, UNC–Charlotte 45; Wake Forest 83, Vanderbilt 68; New Mexico 64, S Florida 58; Georgetown 115, Virginia 111 (3 OT); California 70, Long Beach St 66.
Second round: Penn St 105, Siena 103; Kent St 81, Villanova 67; Notre Dame 76, Xavier 64; Brigham Young 82, Southern Illinois 57; N Carolina St 60, Arizona St 57; Mississippi 70, SW Missouri St 48; Wake Forest 72, New Mexico 65; California 60, Georgetown 49.
Third round: Penn St 81, Kent St 74; Notre Dame 64, Brigham Young 52; N Carolina St 77, Mississippi 54; Wake Forest 76, California 59.
Semifinals: Notre Dame 73, Penn St 52; Wake Forest 62, N Carolina St 59 (OT).
Consolation game: Penn St 74, N Carolina St 72.
Championship: Wake Forest 71, Notre Dame 61.

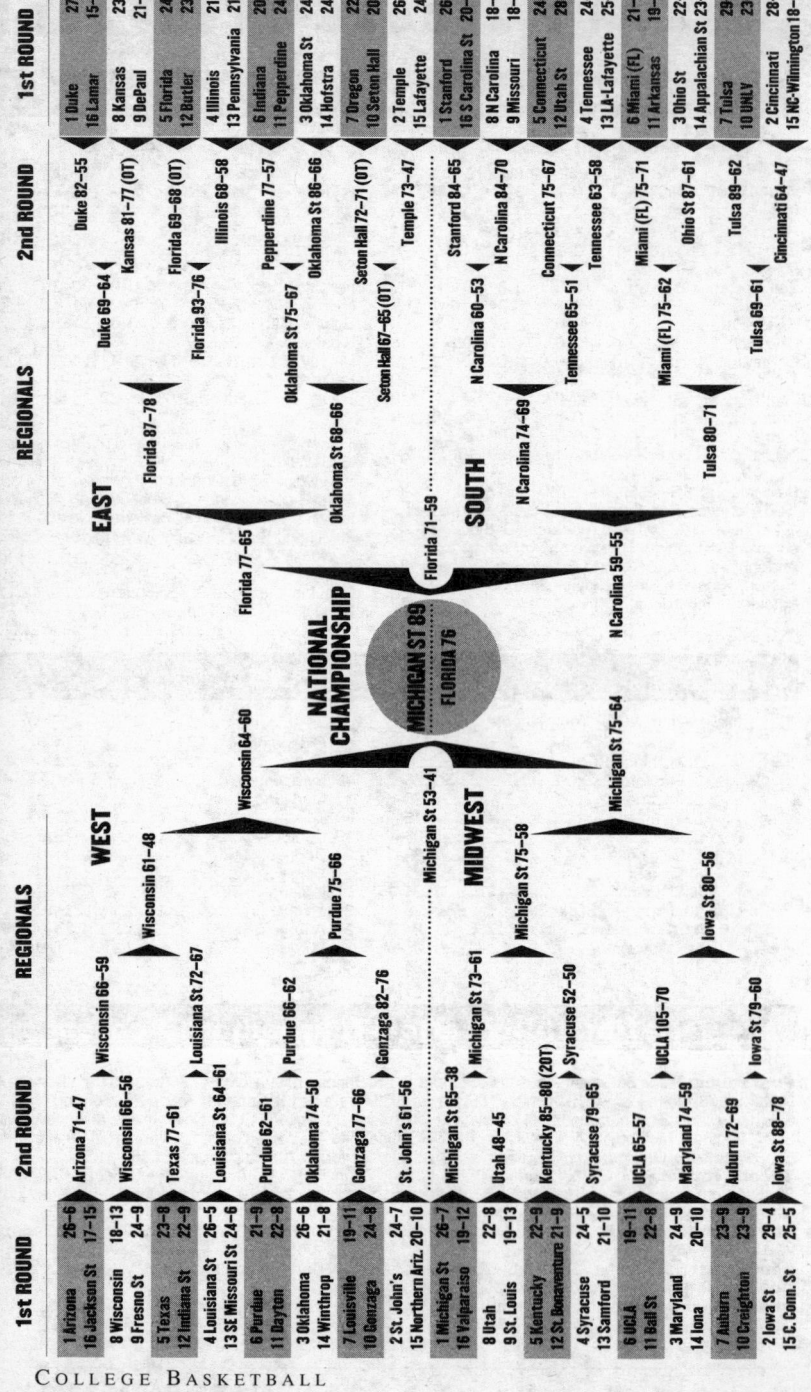

2000 NCAA Basketball Men's Division I Tournament

1st ROUND

1 Duke	27–4
16 Lamar	15–15
8 Kansas	23–9
9 DePaul	21–11
5 Florida	24–7
12 Butler	23–7
4 Illinois	21–9
13 Pennsylvania	21–7
6 Indiana	20–8
11 Pepperdine	24–8
3 Oklahoma St	24–6
14 Hofstra	24–6
7 Oregon	22–7
10 Seton Hall	20–9
2 Temple	26–5
15 Lafayette	24–6
1 Stanford	26–3
16 S Carolina St	20–13
8 N Carolina	18–13
9 Missouri	18–12
5 Connecticut	24–9
12 Utah St	28–5
4 Tennessee	24–6
13 LA-Lafayette	25–8
6 Miami (FL)	21–10
11 Arkansas	19–14
3 Ohio St	22–6
14 Appalachian St	23–8
7 Tulsa	29–4
10 UNLV	23–7
2 Cincinnati	28–3
15 NC-Wilmington	18–12

2nd ROUND

Duke 82–55
Kansas 81–77 (OT)
Florida 69–68 (OT)
Illinois 68–58
Pepperdine 77–57
Oklahoma St 86–66
Seton Hall 72–71 (OT)
Temple 73–47

Stanford 84–65
N Carolina 84–70
Connecticut 75–67
Tennessee 63–58
Miami (FL) 75–71
Ohio St 87–61
Tulsa 89–62
Cincinnati 64–47

REGIONALS

EAST

Duke 69–64
Florida 93–76
Oklahoma St 75–67
Seton Hall 67–65 (OT)

Florida 87–78
Oklahoma St 68–66

Florida 77–65

SOUTH

N Carolina 60–53
Tennessee 65–51
Miami (FL) 75–62
Tulsa 69–61

N Carolina 74–69
Tulsa 80–71

N Carolina 59–55

Florida 71–59

NATIONAL CHAMPIONSHIP

MICHIGAN ST 89
FLORIDA 76

WEST

Wisconsin 64–60

Wisconsin 61–48
Purdue 75–66

Wisconsin 66–59
Purdue 66–62
Gonzaga 82–76

MIDWEST

Michigan St 53–41

Michigan St 75–58
Iowa St 80–56

Michigan St 73–61
Syracuse 52–50
UCLA 105–70
Iowa St 79–60

Michigan St 75–64

2nd ROUND

Arizona 71–47
Wisconsin 66–56
Texas 77–61
Louisiana St 64–61
Purdue 62–61
Oklahoma 74–50
Gonzaga 77–66
St. John's 61–56

Michigan St 65–38
Utah 48–45
Kentucky 85–80 (2OT)
Syracuse 79–65
UCLA 65–57
Maryland 74–59
Auburn 72–69
Iowa St 86–78

1st ROUND

1 Arizona	26–6
16 Jackson St	17–15
8 Wisconsin	18–13
9 Fresno St	24–9
5 Texas	23–8
12 Indiana St	22–9
4 Louisiana St	26–5
13 SE Missouri St	24–6
6 Purdue	21–9
11 Dayton	22–8
3 Oklahoma	26–6
14 Winthrop	21–8
7 Louisville	19–11
10 Gonzaga	24–8
2 St. John's	24–7
15 Northern Ariz.	20–10
1 Michigan St	26–7
16 Valparaiso	19–12
8 Utah	22–8
9 St. Louis	19–13
5 Kentucky	22–9
12 St. Bonaventure	21–9
4 Syracuse	24–5
13 Samford	21–10
6 UCLA	19–11
11 Ball St	22–8
3 Maryland	24–9
14 Iona	20–10
7 Auburn	23–9
10 Creighton	23–9
2 Iowa St	29–4
15 C. Conn. St	25–5

America East

	Conference			All Games		
	W	L	Pct	W	L	Pct
†Hofstra	16	2	.889	24	7	.774
Maine	15	3	.833	24	7	.774
Delaware	14	4	.778	24	8	.750
Vermont	11	7	.611	16	12	.571
Drexel	9	9	.500	13	17	.433
Towson	7	11	.389	11	17	.393
Hartford	6	12	.333	10	19	.345
Boston	5	13	.278	7	22	.241
Northeastern	5	13	.278	7	21	.250
New Hampshire	2	16	.111	3	25	.107

Atlantic Coast

	Conference			All Games		
	W	L	Pct	W	L	Pct
†Duke	15	1	.938	29	5	.853
Maryland	11	5	.688	25	10	.714
N Carolina	9	7	.563	22	13	.629
Virginia	9	7	.563	19	12	.613
Wake Forest	7	9	.438	20	14	.588
N Carolina St	6	10	.375	20	12	.625
Florida St	6	10	.375	12	17	.414
Georgia Tech	5	11	.313	13	17	.433
Clemson	4	12	.250	10	20	.333

Atlantic 10

EAST	Conference			All Games		
	W	L	Pct	W	L	Pct
†Temple	14	2	.875	27	6	.818
St. Bonaventure	11	5	.688	21	10	.677
Massachusetts	9	7	.563	17	16	.515
St. Joseph's	7	9	.438	13	16	.448
Fordham	7	9	.438	14	15	.483
Rhode Island	2	14	.125	5	25	.167
WEST						
Dayton	11	5	.688	22	9	.710
George Washington	9	7	.563	15	15	.500
Xavier	9	7	.563	21	12	.636
Virginia Tech	8	8	.500	16	15	.516
La Salle	5	11	.313	11	17	.393
Duquesne	4	12	.250	9	20	.310

Big East

	Conference			All Games		
	W	L	Pct	W	L	Pct
Syracuse	13	3	.813	26	6	.813
Miami (FL)	13	3	.813	23	11	.676
†St. John's	12	4	.774	25	8	.758
Connecticut	10	6	.625	25	10	.714
Seton Hall	10	6	.625	22	10	.688
Villanova	8	8	.500	20	13	.606
Notre Dame	8	8	.500	22	15	.595
W Virginia	6	10	.375	14	14	.500
Georgetown	6	10	.375	19	15	.559
Rutgers	6	10	.375	15	16	.484
Pittsburgh	5	11	.313	13	15	.464
Providence	4	12	.250	11	19	.367
Boston College	3	13	.188	11	19	.367

Big Sky

	Conference			All Games		
	W	L	Pct	W	L	Pct
Montana	12	4	.750	17	11	.607
Eastern Wash.	12	4	.750	15	12	.556
†Northern Arizona	11	5	.688	20	11	.645
Weber St	10	6	.625	18	10	.643
Cal St-Northridge	10	6	.625	20	10	.667
Portland St	7	9	.438	15	14	.517
Montana St	4	12	.250	12	17	.414
Cal St-Sacramento	3	13	.188	9	18	.333
Idaho St	3	13	.188	8	19	.296

Big South

	Conference			All Games		
	W	L	Pct	W	L	Pct
Radford	12	2	.857	18	10	.643
†Winthrop	11	3	.786	21	8	.724
Elon	7	7	.500	13	15	.464
NC-Asheville	7	7	.500	11	19	.367
Coastal Carolina	7	7	.500	10	18	.357
High Point	5	9	.357	11	17	.393
Liberty	4	10	.286	14	14	.500
Charleston So.	3	11	.214	8	21	.276

Big Ten

	Conference			All Games		
	W	L	Pct	W	L	Pct
Ohio St	13	3	.813	23	7	.767
†Michigan St	13	3	.813	32	7	.821
Purdue	12	4	.750	24	10	.706
Illinois	11	5	.688	21	9	.700
Indiana	10	6	.625	20	9	.689
Wisconsin	8	8	.500	22	14	.611
Iowa	6	10	.375	14	16	.467
Michigan	6	10	.375	15	14	.517
Penn St	5	11	.333	18	17	.514
Minnesota	4	12	.267	12	16	.400
Northwestern	0	16	.000	5	25	.167

Big 12

	Conference			All Games		
	W	L	Pct	W	L	Pct
†Iowa St	14	2	.875	32	5	.865
Texas	13	3	.813	24	9	.727
Oklahoma	12	4	.750	27	7	.794
Oklahoma St	12	4	.750	27	7	.794
Kansas	11	5	.688	24	10	.706
Missouri	10	6	.625	18	13	.581
Colorado	7	9	.438	18	14	.563
Nebraska	4	12	.250	11	19	.367
Baylor	4	12	.250	14	15	.483
Texas A&M	4	12	.250	8	20	.286
Texas Tech	3	13	.188	12	16	.429
Kansas St	2	14	.125	9	19	.321

†Conference tourney winner.
Note: Standings based on regular-season conference play only; overall records include all tournament play.

Big West

EAST	Conference			All Games		
	W	L	Pct	W	L	Pct
†Utah St	16	0	1.000	28	6	.824
New Mexico St	11	5	.688	22	10	.687
Nevada	6	10	.375	9	20	.310
Idaho	6	10	.375	12	17	.414
Boise St	6	10	.375	12	15	.444
N Texas	5	11	.312	7	20	.259
WEST						
Long Beach St	15	1	.938	24	6	.800
UC-Santa Barbara	10	6	.625	14	14	.500
UC-Irvine	7	9	.438	14	14	.500
Pacific	6	10	.375	11	18	.379
Cal Poly	5	11	.312	10	18	.357
Cal St-Fullerton	3	13	.188	8	19	.296

Colonial Athletic

	Conference			All Games		
	W	L	Pct	W	L	Pct
James Madison	12	4	.750	20	9	.690
George Mason	12	4	.750	19	11	.633
Richmond	11	5	.688	18	12	.600
†UNC-Wilmington	8	8	.500	18	13	.581
VA Commonwealth	7	9	.438	14	14	.500
William & Mary	6	10	.375	11	17	.393
Old Dominion	6	10	.375	11	19	.367
American	5	11	.312	11	18	.379
E Carolina	5	11	.312	10	18	.357

Conference USA

AMERICAN	Conference			All Games		
	W	L	Pct	W	L	Pct
Cincinnati	16	0	1.000	29	4	.879
Louisville	10	6	.625	19	12	.613
DePaul	9	7	.563	21	12	.636
Marquette	8	8	.500	15	14	.517
†St. Louis	7	9	.438	19	14	.576
UNC-Charlotte	7	9	.438	17	15	.531
NATIONAL						
Tulane	8	8	.500	20	11	.645
S Florida	8	8	.500	17	14	.548
Southern Miss	7	9	.438	17	12	.586
AL-Birmingham	7	9	.438	14	14	.500
Memphis	7	9	.438	15	16	.484
Houston	2	14	.125	9	22	.290

Ivy League

	Conference			All Games		
	W	L	Pct	W	L	Pct
Pennsylvania	14	0	1.000	21	8	.724
Princeton	11	3	.786	19	11	.633
Columbia	7	7	.500	13	14	.482
Harvard	7	7	.500	12	15	.444
Dartmouth	5	9	.357	9	18	.333
Yale	5	9	.357	7	20	.259
Brown	4	10	.286	8	19	.296
Cornell	3	11	.214	10	17	.370

Metro Atlantic Athletic

	Conference			All Games		
	W	L	Pct	W	L	Pct
Siena	15	3	.833	24	9	.727
†Iona	13	5	.722	20	11	.645
Fairfield	11	7	.611	14	15	.483
Niagara	10	8	.556	17	12	.586
Marist	10	8	.556	14	14	.500
Manhattan	9	9	.500	12	15	.444
Rider	8	10	.444	16	14	.533
Canisius	8	10	.444	10	20	.333
Loyola (MD)	4	14	.222	7	21	.250
St. Peter's	2	16	.111	5	23	.179

Mid-American

EAST	Conference			All Games		
	W	L	Pct	W	L	Pct
Bowling Green	14	4	.778	22	8	.733
Kent	13	5	.722	23	8	.742
Marshall	11	7	.611	21	9	.700
Akron	11	7	.611	17	11	.607
Ohio	11	7	.611	20	13	.606
Miami (OH)	8	10	.444	15	15	.500
Buffalo	3	15	.167	5	23	.179
WEST						
†Ball St	11	7	.611	22	9	.710
Toledo	11	7	.611	18	13	.581
Eastern Michigan	9	9	.500	15	13	.536
Northern Illinois	7	11	.389	13	15	.464
Western Michigan	6	12	.333	10	18	.357
Central Michigan	2	16	.111	6	23	.207

Mid-Continent

	Conference			All Games		
	W	L	Pct	W	L	Pct
Oakland	11	5	.688	13	17	.433
†Valparaiso	10	6	.625	19	13	.594
MO-Kansas City	10	6	.625	16	13	.552
Southern Utah	10	6	.625	16	13	.552
Youngstown St	9	7	.563	12	16	.429
Oral Roberts	8	8	.500	13	17	.433
Chicago St	7	9	.438	10	18	.357
IU/PUI	4	12	.250	7	21	.250
Western Illinois	3	13	.188	8	22	.267

Mid-Eastern Athletic

	Conference			All Games		
	W	L	Pct	W	L	Pct
†S Carolina St	14	5	.737	20	14	.588
Hampton	13	5	.722	17	12	.586
Coppin St	13	5	.722	15	15	.500
Bethune-Cookman	12	6	.667	14	15	.483
Norfolk St	11	7	.611	12	16	.429
N Carolina A&T	11	8	.579	14	15	.483
MD-Eastern Shore	8	10	.444	12	17	.414
Florida A&M	7	11	.389	9	22	.290
Delaware St	5	13	.278	6	22	.214
Morgan St	5	13	.278	5	24	.172
Howard	1	17	.056	1	27	.036

†Conference tourney winner.

Midwestern Collegiate

	Conference			All Games		
	W	L	Pct	W	L	Pct
†Butler	12	2	.857	23	8	.742
Cleveland St	9	5	.643	16	14	.533
Detroit	8	6	.571	20	12	.625
WI-Milwaukee	6	8	.429	15	14	.517
WI-Green Bay	6	8	.429	14	16	.467
Wright St	6	8	.429	11	17	.393
IL-Chicago	5	9	.357	11	20	.355
Loyola (IL)	4	10	.286	14	14	.500

Missouri Valley

	Conference			All Games		
	W	L	Pct	W	L	Pct
Indiana St	14	4	.778	22	10	.688
SW Missouri St	13	5	.722	23	11	.676
Southern Illinois	12	6	.667	20	13	.606
†Creighton	11	7	.611	23	10	.697
Bradley	10	8	.556	14	16	.467
Evansville	9	9	.500	18	12	.600
Northern Iowa	7	11	.389	14	15	.483
Wichita St	5	13	.278	12	17	.414
Illinois St	5	13	.278	10	20	.333
Drake	4	14	.222	11	18	.379

Mountain West

	Conference			All Games		
	W	L	Pct	W	L	Pct
Utah	10	4	.714	23	9	.719
†UNLV	10	4	.714	23	8	.742
New Mexico	9	5	.643	19	14	.576
Colorado St	8	6	.571	18	12	.600
Wyoming	8	6	.571	19	12	.613
Brigham Young	7	7	.500	22	11	.667
Air Force	4	10	.286	8	20	.286
San Diego St	0	14	.000	5	23	.179

Northeast

	Conference			All Games		
	W	L	Pct	W	L	Pct
†Central Conn. St	15	3	.833	25	6	.806
Fairleigh Dickinson	13	5	.722	17	11	.607
Robert Morris	13	5	.722	18	12	.600
Quinnipiac	12	6	.667	18	10	.643
St. Francis (NY)	12	6	.667	18	12	.600
Monmouth	9	9	.500	12	18	.429
MD-Balt. County	7	11	.389	11	18	.379
Mount St. Mary's	7	11	.389	9	20	.310
St. Francis (PA)	7	11	.389	10	18	.357
Wagner	6	12	.333	11	16	.407
Long Island	5	13	.278	8	19	.296
Sacred Heart	2	16	.111	3	25	.107

Ohio Valley

	Conference			All Games		
	W	L	Pct	W	L	Pct
Murray St	14	4	.778	24	7	.774
†SE Missouri	14	4	.778	23	9	.719
Austin Peay	11	7	.611	18	10	.643
Eastern Illinois	11	7	.611	17	12	.586
Tennessee Tech	11	7	.611	16	12	.571
Middle Tennessee	10	8	.555	15	13	.536
Tennessee-Martin	7	11	.389	10	19	.345
Tennessee St	6	12	.333	7	22	.241
Morehead St	4	14	.222	9	18	.333
Eastern Kentucky	2	16	.111	6	21	.222

Pacific 10

	Conference			All Games		
	W	L	Pct	W	L	Pct
Stanford	15	3	.833	27	4	.871
Arizona	15	3	.833	27	7	.794
Oregon	13	5	.722	22	8	.733
UCLA	10	8	.556	21	12	.636
Arizona St	10	8	.556	19	13	.594
Southern Cal	9	9	.500	16	14	.533
California	7	11	.389	18	15	.545
Oregon St	5	13	.278	13	16	.448
Washington	5	13	.278	10	20	.333
Washington St	1	17	.056	6	22	.214

Patriot

	Conference			All Games		
	W	L	Pct	W	L	Pct
†Lafayette	11	1	.917	24	7	.774
Navy	11	1	.917	23	6	.793
Bucknell	8	4	.667	17	11	.607
Colgate	4	8	.333	13	16	.448
Holy Cross	3	9	.250	10	18	.357
Lehigh	3	9	.250	8	21	.276
Army	2	10	.167	5	23	.179

Southeastern

	Conference			All Games		
	W	L	Pct	W	L	Pct
EASTERN						
Tennessee	12	4	.750	26	7	.788
Kentucky	12	4	.750	23	10	.697
Florida	12	4	.750	29	8	.784
Vanderbilt	8	8	.500	19	11	.633
S Carolina	5	11	.313	15	17	.469
Georgia	3	13	.188	10	20	.333
WESTERN						
Louisiana St	12	4	.750	28	6	.824
Auburn	9	7	.563	24	10	.706
†Arkansas	7	9	.438	19	15	.559
Alabama	6	10	.375	13	16	.448
Mississippi St	5	11	.313	14	16	.467
Mississippi	5	11	.313	19	14	.576

†Conference tourney winner.

Southern

	Conference			All Games		
NORTH	W	L	Pct	W	L	Pct
†Appalachian St	13	3	.813	23	9	.719
Davidson	10	6	.625	15	13	.536
UNC-Greensboro	9	7	.563	15	13	.536
E Tennessee St	8	8	.500	14	15	.483
Western Carolina	7	9	.438	14	14	.500
VMI	1	15	.063	6	23	.207
SOUTH						
Coll. of Charleston	13	3	.813	24	6	.800
Georgia Southern	10	6	.625	16	12	.571
Wofford	8	8	.500	14	16	.467
Chattanooga	6	10	.375	10	19	.345
Citadel	5	10	.333	9	20	.310
Furman	5	10	.333	14	18	.438

Southland

	Conference			All Games		
	W	L	Pct	W	L	Pct
Sam Houston St	15	3	.833	22	7	.759
Louisiana-Monroe	13	5	.722	19	9	.679
TX-San Antonio	12	6	.667	15	13	.536
Northwestern St	11	7	.611	17	13	.567
TX-Arlington	11	7	.611	15	12	.556
†Lamar	8	10	.444	15	16	.484
SW Texas	8	10	.444	12	17	.414
Nicholls St	8	10	.444	11	17	.393
Southeastern LA	5	13	.278	10	17	.370
McNeese St	5	13	.278	6	21	.222
Stephen F. Austin	3	15	.167	6	21	.222

Southwestern Athletic

	Conference			All Games		
	W	L	Pct	W	L	Pct
Alcorn St	15	3	.833	19	10	.655
Alabama A&M	14	4	.778	18	10	.643
Southern	14	4	.778	18	11	.621
Texas Southern	10	8	.556	15	14	.517
†Jackson St	10	8	.556	17	16	.515
Alabama St	10	8	.556	13	15	.464
Mississippi Valley	7	11	.389	7	21	.250
Prairie View	5	13	.278	7	21	.250
AR-Pine Bluff	5	13	.278	6	21	.222
Grambling	0	18	.000	1	30	.032

Sun Belt

	Conference			All Games		
	W	L	Pct	W	L	Pct
†Louisiana	13	3	.813	25	9	.735
S Alabama	13	3	.813	20	10	.667
Louisiana Tech	12	4	.750	21	8	.724
Florida International	9	7	.563	16	14	.533
Western Kentucky	8	8	.500	11	18	.379
Arkansas St	7	9	.438	10	18	.357
New Orleans	6	10	.375	11	18	.379
Denver	3	13	.188	6	22	.214
AR-Little Rock	1	15	.063	4	24	.143

Trans America

	Conference			All Games		
	W	L	Pct	W	L	Pct
Troy St	13	5	.722	17	11	.607
Georgia St	13	5	.722	17	12	.586
†Samford	12	6	.667	21	11	.656
Jacksonville St	12	6	.667	17	11	.607
Central Florida	10	8	.556	14	18	.438
Campbell	10	8	.556	12	16	.429
Stetson	8	10	.444	13	15	.464
Mercer	7	11	.389	12	21	.364
Jacksonville	5	13	.278	8	19	.296
Florida Atlantic	0	18	.000	2	28	.070

West Coast

	Conference			All Games		
PACIFIC	W	L	Pct	W	L	Pct
Pepperdine	12	2	.857	25	9	.735
†Gonzaga	11	3	.786	26	9	.743
San Diego	10	4	.714	20	9	.690
Santa Clara	9	5	.643	19	12	.613
San Francisco	7	7	.500	19	9	.679
Portland	4	10	.286	10	18	.357
St. Mary's	3	11	.214	8	20	.286
Loyola Marymount	0	14	.000	2	26	.071

Western Athletic

	Conference			All Games		
	W	L	Pct	W	L	Pct
Tulsa	12	2	.857	32	5	.865
†Fresno St	11	3	.786	24	10	.706
Southern Methodist	9	5	.643	21	9	.700
Texas Christian	8	6	.571	18	14	.563
San Jose St	6	8	.429	15	15	.500
Hawaii	5	9	.357	17	12	.583
Texas-El Paso	4	10	.286	13	15	.464
Rice	1	13	.071	5	22	.185

Independents

	All Games		
	W	L	Pct
Texas A&M-C. C.	13	13	.500
TX-Pan American	12	16	.429
Albany	10	18	.357
Centenary	10	18	.357
Belmont	7	21	.250
Stony Brook	6	23	.207

†Conference tourney winner.

Scoring

			Field Goals			3-Pt FG		Free Throws				
	Class	GP	FGA	FG	Pct	FGA	FG	FTA	FT	Pct	Reb	Pts	Avg
Courtney Alexander, Fresno St	Sr	27	564	252	44.7	175	58	137	107	78.1	128	669	24.8
SirValiant Brown, Geo. Washington	Fr	30	668	222	33.2	277	73	273	221	81.0	100	738	24.6
Ronnie McCollum, Centenary	Jr	28	577	226	39.2	258	92	153	123	80.4	103	667	23.8
Eddie House, Arizona St	Sr	32	623	263	42.2	200	73	164	137	83.5	175	736	23.0
Harold Arceneaux, Weber St	Sr	28	416	213	51.2	103	38	226	180	79.6	207	644	23.0
Rashad Phillips, Detroit	Sr	32	513	226	44.1	252	102	208	181	87.0	96	735	23.0
Demond Stewart, Niagara	Jr	29	515	217	42.1	164	55	244	176	72.1	195	665	22.9
Marcus Fizer, Iowa St	Jr	37	562	327	58.2	42	15	239	175	73.2	285	844	22.8
Craig Claxton, Hofstra	Sr	31	538	253	47.0	134	51	195	149	76.4	168	706	22.8
Troy Murphy, Notre Dame	So	37	557	274	49.2	92	30	323	261	80.8	380	839	22.7
Dan Langhi, Vanderbilt	Sr	30	465	222	47.7	144	58	186	162	87.1	181	664	22.1
Tierre Brown, McNeese St	Jr	27	469	217	46.3	94	30	177	129	72.9	135	593	22.0
Maurice Bell, Louisiana-Monroe	Sr	28	488	235	48.2	1	0	179	142	79.3	193	612	21.9
Chris Davis, N Texas	Fr	27	536	203	37.9	229	77	104	104	69.3	137	587	21.7
Durelle Brown, Manhattan	Jr	27	436	218	50.0	88	28	146	112	76.7	165	576	21.3
Will Solomon, Clemson	So	30	531	213	40.1	248	93	158	108	68.4	123	627	20.9
Damian Woolfolk, Norfolk St	Sr	28	498	205	41.2	120	39	173	136	78.6	118	585	20.9
Mike Pegues, Delaware	Sr	32	484	248	51.2	54	17	201	154	76.6	245	667	20.8
Brandon Wolfram, Texas-El Paso	Jr	28	389	215	55.3	30	12	166	138	83.1	191	580	20.7
Marquise Gainous, Texas Christian	Sr	32	433	215	49.7	35	12	261	220	84.3	265	662	20.7
Brian Merriweather, TX-Pan American	Jr	28	452	192	42.5	275	114	86	74	86.0	81	572	20.4
Aubrey Reese, Murray St	Sr	32	434	200	46.1	153	54	243	199	81.9	171	653	20.4
Jason Perez, Wichita St	Sr	29	459	206	44.9	161	56	152	119	78.3	203	587	20.2
Mike Smith, Louisiana-Monroe	Sr	28	441	187	42.4	222	75	141	113	80.1	264	562	20.1
Isaac Spencer, Murray St	Sr	32	432	240	58.0	49	20	205	138	67.3	261	638	19.9
Tamar Slay, Marshall	So	30	434	216	49.8	215	93	102	72	70.6	132	597	19.9
T.J. Lux, Northern Illinois	Sr	28	427	209	48.9	8	2	189	137	72.5	250	557	19.9
Michael Jackson, MO-Kansas City	So	29	384	226	58.9	1	0	154	121	78.6	164	573	19.8
Monty Mack, Massachusetts	Sr	32	533	221	41.5	266	96	115	94	81.7	110	632	19.8
Demetric Reese, MD-Eastern Shore	Sr	29	422	171	40.5	213	92	200	136	68.0	100	570	19.7

FIELD-GOAL PERCENTAGE

	Class	GP	FGA	FG	Pct
Brendan Haywood, N Carolina	Jr	36	274	191	69.7
John Whorton, Kent	Sr	31	250	159	63.6
Joel Przybilla, Minnesota	So	21	199	122	61.3
Stromile Swift, Louisiana St	So	34	342	208	60.8
Patrick Chambers, AR-Pine Bluff	Sr	27	287	174	60.6
Melvin Ely, Fresno St	Jr	31	297	180	60.6
Roderick Johnson, SE Missouri	Sr	31	270	163	60.4
Etan Thomas, Syracuse	Sr	29	246	148	60.2
Dan McClintock, Northern AZ	Sr	31	318	190	59.7
Oliver Morton, Chattanooga	Jr	28	258	153	59.3

Note: Minimum 5 made per game.

FREE-THROW PERCENTAGE

	Class	GP	FTA	FT	Pct
Clay McKnight, Pacific	Sr	24	78	74	94.9
Troy Bell, Boston College	Fr	27	180	161	89.4
Lee Nosse, Middle Tennessee St	Jr	28	93	83	89.2
Khalid El-Amin, Connecticut	Jr	35	120	107	89.2
Brad Buddenborg, Oakland	So	28	120	107	89.2
Joe Crispin, Penn St	Jr	35	203	181	89.2
Josh Heard, Tennessee Tech	Sr	28	100	89	89.0
Ross Land, Northern Arizona	Sr	31	131	116	88.5
Rimas Kaukenas, Seton Hall	Sr	32	110	97	88.2
B.J. Proffitt, Belmont	So	28	82	72	87.8

Note: Minimum 2.5 made per game.

REBOUNDS

	Class	GP	Reb	Avg
Darren Phillip, Fairfield	Sr	29	405	14.0
Josh Sankes, Holy Cross	Jr	28	334	11.9
Larry Abney, Fresno St	Sr	34	402	11.8
Shaun Stonerook, Ohio	Sr	33	387	11.7
Jarrett Stephens, Penn St	Sr	35	368	10.5
Darren Fenn, Canisius	Jr	30	315	10.5
Chris Mihm, Texas	Sr	33	346	10.5
Darryl Neal, Norfolk St	Jr	27	282	10.4
Troy Murphy, Note Dame	So	37	380	10.3
Matt Williams, Montana	Sr	28	287	10.3

ASSISTS

	Class	GP	A	Avg
Mark Dickel, UNLV	Sr	31	280	9.0
Doug Gottlieb, Oklahoma St	Sr	34	293	8.6
Chico Fletcher, Arkansas St	Sr	28	232	8.3
Brandon Granville, Southern Cal	So	30	248	8.3
Ed Cota, N Carolina	Sr	35	284	8.1
Pepe Sanchez, Temple	Jr	25	201	8.0
Casey Rogers, Western Carolina	So	28	213	7.6
Cornelius Jackson, Marshall	Jr	30	218	7.3
Elliott Prasse-Freeman, Harvard	Fr	27	196	7.3
Eddie Gill, Weber St	Sr	28	195	7.0

*Includes games played in tournaments.

THREE-POINT FIELD-GOAL PERCENTAGE

	Class	GP	FGA	FG	Pct
Jonathan Whitworth, Middle TN	Jr	28	99	50	50.5
Jason Thornton, Central Florida	So	32	190	94	49.5
Aki Palmer, Colorado St	Fr	30	143	70	49.0
Pete Conway, Montana St	Fr	29	90	44	48.9
Stephen Brown, Idaho St	Sr	27	133	65	48.9
Albert Mouring, Connecticut	Jr	35	180	86	47.8
Keith McLeod, Bowling Green	So	30	107	51	47.7
Jason Kapono, UCLA	Fr	33	173	82	47.4
John Sivesind, Colorado St	Jr	30	158	74	46.8
Brett Blizzard, UNC-Wilmington	Fr	31	201	94	46.8

Note: Minimum 1.5 made per game.

THREE-POINT FIELD GOALS MADE PER GAME

	Class	GP	FG	Avg
Brian Merriweather, TX-Pan Am	Jr	28	114	4.1
Josh Heard, Tennessee Tech	Sr	28	112	4.0
Tevis Stukes, Baylor	Sr	29	100	3.4
Adam Fellers, Campbell	So	28	96	3.4
Gordon Scott, Idaho	Jr	28	96	3.4
Matthew Haggerty, Albany	Sr	28	94	3.4
Ryan Hercek, Atlantic	Sr	29	97	3.3
Angel Santana, St. Francis (NY)	Sr	30	100	3.3
Alan Barksdale, AR-Little Rock	Sr	24	80	3.3
Jason Harris, Fordham	Jr	28	93	3.3

BLOCKED SHOTS

	Class	GP	BS	Avg
Ken Johnson, Ohio St	Sr	30	161	5.4
Wojciech Myrda, Louisiana-Monroe	So	28	144	5.1
Loren Woods, Arizona	Jr	26	102	3.9
Joel Przybilla, Minnesota	So	21	81	3.9
Sitapha Savane, Navy	Sr	29	111	3.8
Etan Thomas, Syracuse	Sr	29	107	3.7
Samuel Dalembert, Seton Hall	Fr	30	107	3.6
Kenyon Martin, Cincinnati	Sr	31	107	3.5
Brian Carroll, Loyola (MD)	Jr	27	89	3.3
Nakiea Miller, Iona	Jr	30	98	3.3

STEALS

	Class	GP	S	Avg
Carl Williams, Liberty	Sr	28	107	3.8
Rick Mickens, Central Connecticut	Sr	26	93	3.6
Pepe Sanchez, Temple	Jr	25	85	3.4
Fred House, Southern Utah	Jr	29	98	3.4
Eric Coley, Tulsa	Sr	37	123	3.3
Tim Winn, St. Bonaventure	Sr	31	103	3.3
Craig Claxton, Hofstra	Sr	31	102	3.3
Jarion Childs, American	Sr	29	95	3.3
Jeff Trepagnier, Southern Cal	Jr	29	94	3.2
Eddie Gill, Weber St	Sr	28	90	3.2

Single-Game Highs

POINTS

61 ....Eddie House, Arizona St, Jan 8 (vs California)
51 ....David Webber, Central Michigan, Feb 24 (vs Ball St)
47 ....Damon Stringer, Cleveland St, Jan 29 (vs WI-Milwaukee)

REBOUNDS

35 ....Larry Abney, Fresno St, Feb 17 (vs Southern Methodist)
28 ....David Bluthenthal, Southern Cal, Jan 20 (vs Arizona St)
25 ....Darren Phillip, Fairfield, Jan 5 (vs Marist)

ASSISTS

20 ....Mateen Cleaves, Michigan St, Mar 4 (vs Michigan)
18 ....Mark Dickel, UNLV, Mar 10 (vs Wyoming)
17 ....Ed Cota, N Carolina, Dec 4 (vs UNLV)

THREE-POINT FIELD GOALS

10 ....Spencer Gloser, Princeton, Dec 18 (vs Alabama-Brimingham)
10 ....Jason Harris, Fordham, Dec 21 (vs Quinnipiac)
10 ....Marc Polite, Eastern Illinois, Dec 23 (vs Arkansas St)
10 ....Donta Wade, Providence, Feb 23 (vs Notre Dame)
10 ....Desmond Ferguson, Detroit, Feb 26 (vs WI-Milwaukee)
10 ....Jason Stewart, Miami (OH), Mar 6 (vs Marshall)

STEALS

10 ....Jeff Trepagnier, Southern Cal, Nov 24 (vs Utah St)
10 ....Mike Kelley, Wisconsin, Dec 7 (vs Texas)
10 ....Collis Temple, Louisiana St, Jan 12 (vs Florida)

BLOCKED SHOTS

14 ....Loren Woods, Arizona, Feb 3 (vs Oregon)
12 ....Darrick Davenport, Texas Christian, Nov 20 (vs AK-Fairbanks)
11 ....Wojciech Myrda, Louisiana-Monroe, Dec 30 (vs Nicholls St)
11 ....Samuel Dalembert, Seton Hall, Jan 18 (vs St. John's (NY))
11 ....Ken Johnson, Ohio St, Jan 22 (vs St. John's (NY))
11 ....Derrick Davenport, Texas Christian, Mar 3 (vs Rice)

SCORING OFFENSE

	GP	W	L	Pts	Avg		GP	W	L	Pts	Avg
Duke	34	29	5	2992	88.0	Fresno St	34	24	10	2799	82.3
Texas Christian	32	18	14	2813	87.9	UNLV	31	23	8	2548	82.2
Siena	33	24	9	2862	86.7	Virginia	31	19	12	2526	81.5
Florida	37	29	8	3102	83.8	Marshall	30	21	9	2442	81.4
Wyoming	31	19	12	2567	82.8	Tennessee Tech	28	16	12	2279	81.4

SCORING DEFENSE

	GP	W	L	Pts	Avg		GP	W	L	Pts	Avg
Princeton	30	19	11	1637	54.6	WI-Green Bay	30	14	16	1735	57.8
Temple	33	27	6	1808	54.8	College of Charleston	30	24	6	1759	58.6
Butler	31	23	8	1728	55.7	Michigan St	39	32	7	2299	58.9
Wisconsin	36	22	14	2007	55.8	Stanford	31	27	4	1850	59.7
UNC-Wilmington	31	18	13	1781	57.5	San Jose St	30	15	15	1792	59.7

SCORING MARGIN

	Off	Def	Mar		Off	Def	Mar
Stanford	78.9	59.7	19.3	Florida	83.8	68.9	15.0
Tulsa	80.4	62.9	17.5	Oklahoma St	77.1	62.3	14.8
Duke	88.0	71.3	16.7	Temple	68.5	54.8	13.7
Cincinnati	77.6	61.5	16.1	Iowa St	78.3	65.1	13.2
Michigan St	74.1	58.9	15.1	Louisiana St	75.8	62.7	13.1

FIELD-GOAL PERCENTAGE

	FGA	FG	Pct		FGA	FG	Pct
Samford	1649	825	50.0	MO-Kansas City	1566	765	48.9
Long Beach St	1784	884	49.6	Maine	1744	851	48.8
Austin Peay	1618	797	49.3	Louisiana St	1880	915	48.7
Bowling Green	1578	777	49.2	Appalachian St	1882	915	48.6
N Carolina	2066	1014	49.1	Iowa St	2140	1038	48.5

FIELD-GOAL PERCENTAGE DEFENSE

	FGA	FG	Pct		FGA	FG	Pct
Stanford	1893	667	35.2	Bucknell	1500	571	38.1
Temple	1747	633	36.2	Louisiana St	2046	781	38.2
Princeton	1558	577	37.0	College of Charleston	1676	640	38.2
Ohio St	1730	654	37.8	Cincinnati	1941	743	38.3
SE Missouri St	1765	670	38.0	Central Connecticut St	1835	703	38.3

FREE-THROW PERCENTAGE

	FTA	FT	Pct		FTA	FT	Pct
Montana St	609	481	79.0	Delaware	693	522	75.3
Tennessee Tech	693	532	76.8	UNC-Asheville	701	528	75.3
Texas Christian	812	621	76.5	Maine	549	413	75.2
Akron	767	585	76.3	Weber St	718	540	75.2
Morehead St	515	390	75.7	Northern Arizona	622	467	75.1

THREE-POINT FIELD GOALS MADE PER GAME

	GP	FG	Avg		GP	FG	Avg
Tennessee Tech	28	279	10.0	Troy St	28	253	9.0
Samford	32	313	9.8	Oakland	30	271	9.0
Belmont	28	273	9.8	WI-Milwaukee	29	256	8.8
Missouri	31	291	9.4	Creighton	33	289	8.8
TX-Arlington	27	247	9.1	Arkansas	34	292	8.6

THREE-POINT FIELD-GOAL PERCENTAGE

	GP	FGA	FG	Pct		GP	FGA	FG	Pct
Colorado St	30	579	255	44.0	Morehead St	27	560	224	40.0
Creighton	33	694	289	41.6	Stanford	31	613	245	40.0
Coastal Carolina	28	551	224	40.7	Ball St	31	538	215	40.0
Troy St	28	625	253	40.5	Montana	28	493	197	40.0
Eastern Illinois	29	512	206	40.2	Central Florida	32	586	233	39.8

Note: Minimum 3.0 made per game.

NCAA Women's Championship Game Box Score

Connecticut 71

Connecticut	Min	FG M-A	FT M-A	Reb O-T	A	PF	TP
Abrosimova	28	5–9	3–4	1–5	2	2	14
Cash	18	4–8	1–2	1–3	0	4	9
Schumacher	20	3–4	0–0	2–6	0	2	6
Bird	35	2–8	0–0	1–3	4	1	4
Ralph	28	7–8	1–2	1–3	7	3	15
Williams	14	3–4	0–0	2–2	2	4	6
Jones	22	5–14	2–3	4–8	2	1	12
Johnson	23	1–3	1–2	0–1	3	2	3
Hansmeyer	5	0–1	0–2	0–0	1	1	0
Sauer	3	1–1	0–0	0–1	0	0	2
Czel	2	0–0	0–0	0–0	0	0	0
Rigby	2	0–1	0–0	0–0	0	0	0
Totals	200	31–61	8–15	12–32	21	20	71

Percentages: FG—.508, FT—.533. 3-pt goals: 1–9, .111 (Abrosimova 1–3, Bird 0–3, Johnson 0–2, Hansmeyer 0–1). Team rebounds: 2. Blocked shots: 11 (Schumacher 9, Ralph, Jones). Turnovers: 14 (Abrosimova 5, Williams 3, Cash, Czel, Hansmeyer, Johnson, Ralph, Schumacher). Steals: 12 (Ralph 6, Cash 2, Abrosimova, Johnson, Schumacher, Williams).

Tennessee 52

Tennessee	Min	FG M-A	FT M-A	Reb O-T	A	PF	TP
Randall	35	1–11	4–6	4–8	2	1	6
Catchings	36	4–6	5–10	2–4	1	4	16
Snow	26	2–9	1–2	4–4	0	4	5
Elzy	19	3–5	2–2	2–5	0	2	8
Lawson	35	3–13	0–0	0–6	3	2	6
McDivitt	21	1–2	2–2	0–0	0	2	5
Jackson	12	2–4	0–0	2–7	0	0	4
Pillow	11	0–1	2–2	1–2	0	1	2
Butts	5	0–0	0–0	0–0	0	1	0
Totals	200	16–51	16–24	15–36	6	17	52

Percentages: FG—.314, FT—.667. 3-pt goals: 4–7, .571 (Catchings 3–3, Lawson 0–2, McDivitt 1–2). Team rebounds: 3. Blocked shots: 3 (Snow 2, Jackson). Turnovers: 25 (Catchings 6, Elzy 6, Randall 6, Jackson 2, Lawson, McDivitt, Pillow, Snow). Steals: 7 (Catchings 2, Lawson 2, Jackson, Randall, Snow).

Halftime: Connecticut 32, Tennessee 19.
A: 20,060. Officials: Bell, Demayo, Bomengen.

Better Late Than Never

West Virginia guard Tim Lyles overcame numerous traveling violations before starring in the Mountaineers' 69–64 defeat of Georgetown on Jan. 26. He had returned to his hometown of Baltimore to attend a friend's funeral and was supposed to fly back to West Virginia on the afternoon of Jan. 25. His flight was canceled because of a snowstorm, however, so the Mountaineers' basketball office checked to see if Lyles could get a seat on the Hoyas' charter plane that was going to fly to West Virginia out of Dulles International the next morning. But that plane was full so he booked a reservation on a flight out of Baltimore the day of the game, at 12:05 p.m. That, too, was canceled.

He then headed to Washington to catch a flight that would land in Charleston, W.Va., at 3:30. That plane did leave, but Lyles wasn't on it. He had arrived at the gate five minutes late after the car service he had taken got lost.

Finally he got a flight from D.C.'s National Airport to Pittsburgh, where he connected to another flight that was due to arrive in Charleston at 6:27, 38 minutes before tip-off. His connecting flight was delayed, however, and didn't land until 8:13. He changed into his uniform during the eight-minute ride to Charleston's Civic Center Coliseum and arrived with 11:41 left to play and West Virginia trailing by seven. Coach Gale Catlett put Lyles, a 5'11" freshman, in the game moments later, whereupon he scored nine points down the stretch to help the Mountaineers win.

2000 NCAA Basketball Women's Division I Tournament

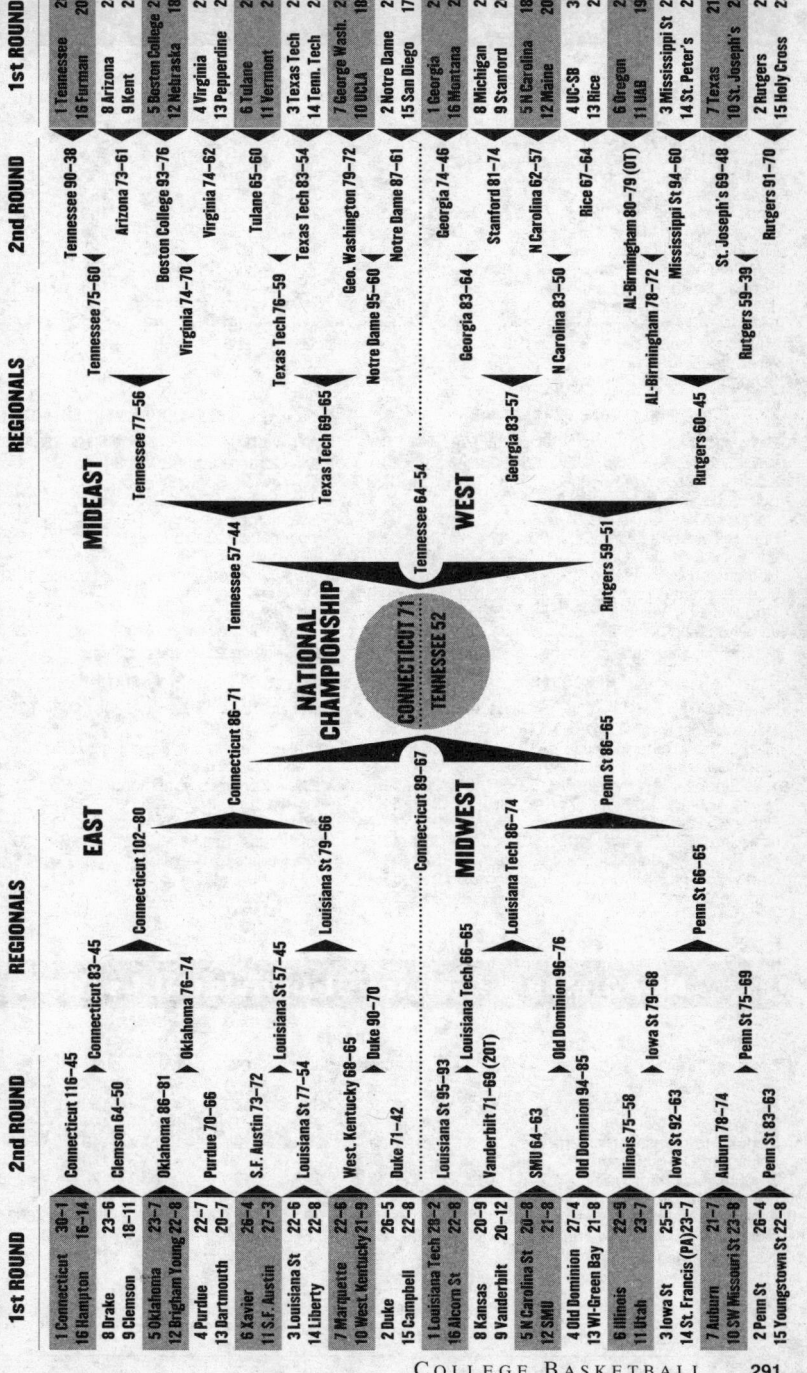

1st ROUND		2nd ROUND	REGIONALS	REGIONALS	2nd ROUND	1st ROUND	

EAST

1 Connecticut 30–1
16 Hampton 16–14
Connecticut 116–45
Connecticut 83–45
8 Drake 23–6
9 Clemson 18–11
Clemson 64–50
Connecticut 102–80
5 Oklahoma 23–7
12 Brigham Young 22–8
Oklahoma 86–81
Oklahoma 76–74
4 Purdue 22–7
13 Dartmouth 20–7
Purdue 70–66
Connecticut 86–71
6 Xavier 26–4
11 S.F. Austin 27–3
S.F. Austin 73–72
Louisiana St 57–45
3 Louisiana St 22–6
14 Liberty 22–8
Louisiana St 77–54
Louisiana St 79–66
7 Marquette 22–6
10 West. Kentucky 21–9
West. Kentucky 68–65
Duke 90–70
2 Duke 26–5
15 Campbell 22–8
Duke 71–42

MIDEAST

1 Tennessee 28–3
16 Furman 20–10
Tennessee 90–38
Tennessee 75–60
8 Arizona 24–6
9 Kent 25–5
Arizona 73–61
Tennessee 77–56
5 Boston College 25–8
12 Nebraska 18–12
Boston College 93–76
Virginia 74–70
4 Virginia 23–8
13 Pepperdine 21–9
Virginia 74–62
Tennessee 57–44
6 Tulane 26–4
11 Vermont 25–5
Tulane 65–60
Texas Tech 83–54
3 Texas Tech 25–4
14 Tenn. Tech 24–8
Texas Tech 76–59
Texas Tech 69–65
7 George Wash. 25–5
10 UCLA 18–10
Geo. Washington 79–72
Notre Dame 87–61
2 Notre Dame 25–4
15 San Diego 17–12
Notre Dame 95–60

NATIONAL CHAMPIONSHIP

CONNECTICUT 71
TENNESSEE 52

Tennessee 64–54

WEST

1 Georgia 29–3
16 Montana 22–7
Georgia 74–46
Georgia 83–64
8 Michigan 22–7
9 Stanford 20–8
Stanford 81–74
Georgia 83–57
5 N Carolina 18–12
12 Maine 20–10
N Carolina 62–57
Georgia 64–54
4 UC-SB 30–3
13 Rice 21–9
Rice 67–64
6 Oregon 23–7
11 UAB 19–12
Al-Birmingham 80–79 (OT)
Al-Birmingham 78–72
3 Mississippi St 23–7
14 St. Peter's 23–7
Mississippi St 94–60
Rutgers 60–45
7 Texas 21–12
10 St. Joseph's 24–5
St. Joseph's 69–48
Rutgers 59–39
2 Rutgers 22–7
15 Holy Cross 23–6
Rutgers 91–70

MIDWEST

Connecticut 89–67
Rutgers 59–51

1 Louisiana Tech 29–2
16 Alcorn St 22–8
Louisiana Tech 95–93
Louisiana Tech 66–65
8 Kansas 20–9
9 Vanderbilt 20–12
Vanderbilt 71–69 (2OT)
Louisiana Tech 86–74
5 N Carolina 20–8
12 SMU 21–8
SMU 64–63
Old Dominion 96–76
4 Old Dominion 27–4
13 Wi-Green Bay 21–8
Old Dominion 94–85
Penn St 86–65
6 Illinois 22–9
11 Utah 23–7
Illinois 75–58
Iowa St 79–68
3 Iowa St 25–5
14 St. Francis (PA) 23–7
Iowa St 92–63
Penn St 66–65
7 Auburn 21–7
10 SW Missouri St 23–8
Auburn 78–74
Penn St 75–69
2 Penn St 26–4
15 Youngstown St 22–8
Penn St 83–63

COLLEGE BASKETBALL   291

NCAA Women's Division I Individual Leaders

SCORING

Player and Team	Class	GP	TFG	3FG	FT	Pts	Avg
Jackie Stiles, SW Missouri St	Jr	32	297	58	238	890	27.8
Diana Caramanico, Pennsylvania	Jr	28	268	4	154	694	24.8
Jess Zinobile, St. Francis	Sr	31	251	22	200	724	23.4
Madinah Slaise, Cincinnati	Sr	30	214	44	182	654	21.8
Grace Daley, Tulane	Sr	32	227	53	185	692	21.6
Linda Frohlich, UNLV	So	28	229	37	109	604	21.6
Jamie Cassidy, Maine	Sr	31	235	10	188	668	21.5
Edwina Brown, Texas	Sr	34	274	2	172	722	21.2
Jennifer Crow, Oklahoma St	Sr	30	192	74	175	633	21.1
Rhonda Smith, Long Beach St	Sr	32	270	0	135	675	21.1
Julie Szabo, Stony Brook	Fr	28	172	76	169	589	21.0
LaToya Thomas, Mississippi	Fr	32	260	10	142	672	21.0
Phylesha Whaley, Oklahoma	Sr	33	265	39	117	686	20.8
Alli Nieman, Idaho	Sr	28	220	18	118	576	20.6
Shauna Geronzin, Canisius	So	29	208	27	152	595	20.5

FIELD-GOAL PERCENTAGE

Player and Team	Class	GP	FGA	FG	Pct
Angie Welle, Iowa St	So	33	286	185	64.7
Karalyn Church, Vermont	Sr	31	401	258	64.3
Becky Cummings, Michigan St	Jr	31	272	169	62.1
DeTrina White, Louisiana St	So	32	264	163	61.7
Ruth Riley, Notre Dame	Jr	32	314	193	61.5
Lucienne Berthieu, ODU	Jr	26	275	167	60.7
Hamchetou Maiga, ODU	Jr	34	336	201	59.8
Carla Bennett, Drake	Fr	30	292	174	59.6
Tere Williams, Virginia Tech	Jr	27	262	156	59.5
Janell Burse, Tulane	Jr	32	392	233	59.4

Note: Minimum 5 made per game.

FREE-THROW PERCENTAGE

Player and Team	Class	GP	FTA	FT	Pct
Paula Corder-King, SE MO St	Sr	27	74	69	93.2
T. Raniewicz, St. Bonaventure	Fr	29	115	102	88.7
D-dra Rucker, SMU	Jr	31	130	115	88.5
Alissa Murphy, Boston College	Sr	35	160	141	88.1
Jennifer Crow, Oklahoma St	Sr	30	199	175	87.9
Kelli Werling, IU/PUI	Sr	27	115	101	87.8
Karen Culbertson, Iona	Jr	28	139	122	87.8
Jill Morton, Louisville	Sr	27	128	112	87.5
Kylie Galloway, Hawaii	Jr	29	118	103	87.3
C. Von Wald, WI-Milwaukee	So	27	133	115	86.5

Note: Minimum 2.5 made per game.

REBOUNDS

Player and Team	Class	GP	Reb	Avg
Malveata Johnson, N Carolina A&T	Jr	27	363	13.4
Elise James, Robert Morris	Sr	28	367	13.1
Diana Caramanico, Pennsylvania	Jr	28	334	11.9
Jess Zinobile, St. Francis (PA)	Sr	31	366	11.8
Mercy Aghedo, St. Peter's	Sr	30	352	11.7
Deanna Jackson, AL-Birmingham	So	33	385	11.7
Nekesha Jewell, Grambling	Jr	30	350	11.7
Gail Strumpf, Fairfield	Jr	33	378	11.5
Linda Frohlich, UNLV	So	28	319	11.4
Andrea Gardner, Howard	So	28	316	11.3

ASSISTS

Player and Team	Class	GP	A	Avg
Helen Darling, Penn St	Sr	35	274	7.8
Angela Zampella, St. Joseph's	Sr	31	241	7.8
Sharin Milner, Troy St	Fr	27	206	7.6
Michele Koclanes, Richmond	So	27	204	7.6
Rochelle Luckett, VCU	So	30	214	7.1
Clarissa Tomlinson, Stanford	Sr	29	201	6.9
Shala Crook, Ball St	So	29	197	6.8
Tricia Brenitsky, Canisius	So	29	197	6.8
Amy Vachon, Maine	Sr	31	209	6.7
Lindsay Logan, Fresno St	Fr	29	192	6.6

NCAA Men's Division II Individual Leaders

SCORING

Player and Team	Class	GP	TFG	3FG	FT	Pts	Avg
David Evans, BYU-Hawaii	Sr	28	300	48	134	782	27.9
Ajamu Gaines, Charleston (WV)	Sr	32	318	96	160	892	27.9
Bryan Moore, Assumption	Sr	27	217	49	161	644	23.9
Markus Hallgrimson, Montana St	Sr	26	204	160	49	617	23.7
Kweemada King, Chadron St	Sr	26	200	74	138	612	23.5
Otis Frazier, Chadron St	Sr	27	198	54	176	626	23.2
Brandon Hughes, Newberry	Sr	27	229	34	128	620	23.0
Antwon Morgan, LeMoyne-Owen	Sr	29	214	74	160	662	22.8
John Flynn, Grand Valley St	So	28	230	34	145	639	22.8
Randy Dickerson, Missouri Western	Sr	24	190	9	157	546	22.8

NCAA Men's Division II Individual Leaders (Cont.)

REBOUNDS

Player and Team	Class	GP	Reb	Avg
Howard Jackson, Lincoln Memorial...Jr		24	321	13.4
Earl Ike, Montevallo...Sr		24	301	12.5
Brent Swain, Mercyhurst...Jr		24	288	12.0
Lonnie Benjamin, Tuskegee...Sr		25	297	11.9
Lachlan Teasdale, St. Edward's...Jr		27	319	11.8
Latif McMorrin, NJIT...Sr		27	298	11.0
Eric Henderson, Wayne St...Sr		32	352	11.0
Rafi Stevens, W Georgia...Jr		27	297	11.0
Damon Reed, St. Rose...Sr		30	327	10.9
Anthony Rollins, St. Andrews...Sr		30	325	10.8

ASSISTS

Player and Team	Class	GP	A	Avg
Todd Chappell, Texas Wesleyan...Jr		27	263	9.7
Javar Cheatham, Gannon...So		28	242	8.6
Mike McShane, Montana-Billings...Sr		26	214	8.2
Adam Kaufman, Edinboro...Jr		26	211	8.1
Nate Tibbetts, S Dakota...Jr		28	216	7.7
B. Manning, TAMU-Commerce...Sr		26	194	7.5
Ken Johnson, Southern Arkansas...Sr		28	206	7.4
Terrence Baxter, Pfeiffer...Jr		31	227	7.3
Eddin Santiago, MO Southern St...So		32	232	7.3
Joe Smith, AL-Huntsville...Jr		29	209	7.2

FIELD-GOAL PERCENTAGE

Player and Team	Class	GP	FGA	FG	Pct
Shaun Bass, Drury...Sr		28	237	156	65.8
Kelvin Wylie, Gardner-Webb...Sr		30	248	162	65.3
Terence Herbert, MO-St. Louis...Sr		23	181	118	65.2
Randy Dickerson, MO-Western...Sr		24	292	190	65.1
Terrell Davis, Cal Poly-Pomona...Sr		27	234	148	63.2
Ewan Auguste, Washburn...Jr		30	324	202	62.3
Peter Praznovsky, Tarleton St...Sr		20	169	105	62.1
Osiris Ricardo, MO Southern St..Sr		33	277	171	61.7
Willie Robinson, WI-Parkside...Sr		26	258	158	61.2
Mike Palm, Western Wash. ...Fr		27	227	138	60.8

Note: Minimum 5 made per game.

FREE-THROW PERCENTAGE

Player and Team	Class	GP	FTA	FT	Pct
Jason Kreider, Michigan Tech...Sr		31	91	84	92.3
Michael Jones, Pittsburg St...Sr		29	84	76	90.5
Calvin Mackey, Montevallo...Jr		26	93	84	90.3
Ty Moss, SIU-Edwardsville...So		22	93	84	90.3
Ryan Skogstad, Seattle Pacific...Sr		32	92	83	90.2
Brad Burdick, St. Edwards...So		27	106	93	87.7
T.J. Trimboli, Southern Conn....Sr		29	130	114	87.7
M. Kinnebrew, UC-CO Springs...Jr		26	80	70	87.5
Jerry Barlow, Presbyterian...Fr		22	80	70	87.5
Nate Strong, Montana-Billings...So		25	119	104	87.4

Note: Minimum 2.5 made per game.

NCAA Women's Division II Individual Leaders

SCORING

Player and Team	Class	GP	TFG	3FG	FT	Pts	Avg
Angie Hupfer, St. Joe's (IN)...Sr		26	245	22	147	659	25.3
Marin Hightower, Edinboro...Sr		26	241	4	127	613	23.6
Becky Gonzalez, NM Highlands...So		22	189	34	97	509	23.1
Sasha Leverentz, Northern Michigan...Sr		31	280	45	98	703	22.7
Darcy Stracke, Nebraska-Omaha...Sr		27	219	25	148	611	22.6
Denise Shelton, Mars Hill...So		28	216	14	166	612	21.9
Jamie Scheppman, Ouachita...Sr		28	194	43	177	608	21.7
Theresa Carroll, Philadelphia Textile...Sr		31	252	1	166	671	21.6
Misi Clark, SIU-Edwardsville...Jr		27	185	36	171	577	21.4
Jackie Bucher, Abilene Christian...Sr		27	229	1	118	577	21.4

REBOUNDS

Player and Team	Class	GP	Reb	Avg
Tracy Sprolden, Valdosta St...Jr		26	382	14.7
Shannon Donnelly, Cal St-Stanislaus...Fr		29	371	12.8
Taquina Billups, Queens (NC)...Sr		27	337	12.5
Anastacia Sands, St. Augustine...Sr		27	334	12.4
Erica Harris, Montevallo...So		24	286	11.9
Erica Cash, Salem-Teikyo...Sr		27	313	11.6
Stacy Knapp, Merrimack...So		29	332	11.4
Segeeta Bland, W Florida...Sr		27	309	11.4
TeNay Garrett, Midwestern St...Sr		26	293	11.3
Tierney Pugh, Limestone...So		24	269	11.2

ASSISTS

Player and Team	Class	GP	A	Avg
Adrianne Harlow, W Liberty...Jr		30	240	8.0
Jennifer Perine, Emporia St...Sr		32	247	7.7
Sabrina Stout, Glenville St...Jr		29	207	7.1
Mesach Rhoades, Regis...Jr		29	205	7.1
Brandy Agee, Salem-Teikyo...Jr		26	175	6.7
Marie Schlegel, E Stroudsburg...Sr		26	166	6.4
Rae Keith, Kentucky Wesleyan...Sr		26	166	6.4
Jami Cornwell, S Carolina-Aiken...Fr		25	157	6.3
Maya Grady, Lenoir-Rhyne...Fr		27	167	6.2
Jennifer Sylvester, S Dakota...Sr		27	163	6.0

NCAA Women's Division II Individual Leaders (Cont.)

FIELD-GOAL PERCENTAGE

Player and Team	Class	GP	FGA	FG	Pct
Jackie Bucher, Abilene Christian...Sr		27	330	229	69.4
Staci Elder, W Alabama ....Sr		26	271	177	65.3
Kelly Easton, W Liberty St........Sr		29	287	183	63.8
Temeshia Dawkins, Wingate .....Jr		25	257	162	63.0
Brianne Homyak, Kutztown ....Sr		27	257	158	61.5
Angie Harris, Arkansas Tech ....Jr		31	321	195	60.7
Becky Siembak, Slippery Rock ...Fr		30	334	200	59.9
Denise Sump, NW Missouri St...Sr		26	298	177	59.4
Chervara Smith, Tampa ....Sr		24	225	133	59.1
Angela Thornton, Gardner-Webb...Jr		26	249	147	59.0

Note: Minimum 5 made per game.

FREE-THROW PERCENTAGE

Player and Team	Class	GP	FTA	FT	Pct
Shanna Renken, Cal St-Dom Hills...Sr		25	77	70	90.9
Regina McCoy, Anderson........Sr		26	94	85	90.4
Betsy Foy, Georgia C&SU........So		27	151	134	88.7
Kelly Flint, Lock Haven.............Jr		26	95	84	88.4
April Longo, Bloomsburg ....Jr		24	69	61	88.4
Stacy Mattioli, Assumption........Sr		26	85	75	88.2
Jill Razor, Rollins ....Jr		32	204	179	87.7
Jamie Scheppmann, Ouachita .Sr		28	202	177	87.6
Jamie Holderman,					
IU/PU-Ft. Wayne...................Jr		29	151	132	87.4
Karen Wusinich, Philadelphia...Sr		31	214	185	86.4

Note: Minimum 2.5 made per game.

NCAA Men's Division III Individual Leaders

SCORING

Player and Team	Class	GP	TFG	3FG	FT	Pts	Avg
Willie Chandler, Misericordia................................Fr		27	249	92	114	704	26.1
Greg Hardin, Hunter ....Sr		21	209	39	85	542	25.8
Josh Estelle, Wabash ....Sr		27	207	105	166	685	25.4
Brant Bailey, WI-Stevens ....Sr		30	252	0	219	723	24.1
Rob Pisanelli, Hobart ....Sr		25	208	56	126	598	23.9
Elliott Broadnax, Colorado ....Sr		21	189	8	108	494	23.5
Jaron Warner, Clarke ....Sr		23	188	58	106	540	23.5
Chris Coates, Keene St ....Jr		20	174	45	76	469	23.5
Corey Dickerson, King's (PA) ....Jr		24	195	43	126	559	23.3
Josh Metzer, WI-Lutheran......................................Jr		25	215	32	118	580	23.2

REBOUNDS

Player and Team	Class	GP	Reb	Avg
Jeff Gibbs, Otterbein.....................So		23	307	13.3
Greg Hardin, Hunter ....Sr		21	273	13.0
Dana Griffin, Worcester Tech ....Sr		19	231	12.2
Patrick Glover, Johnson St.............So		23	264	11.5
Antoine Sinclair, Chris Newport .....Jr		28	321	11.5
Robert Jones, New Paltz St............Jr		24	267	11.1
Manny Benjamin, Williams ....Jr		24	266	11.1
Corey Grace, Thomas More...........Jr		23	251	10.9
Juahmal Sturgeon, William Penn....Jr		25	271	10.8
Earl Thomas, Polytechnic (NY)........Jr		22	238	10.8

FIELD-GOAL PERCENTAGE

Player and Team	Class	GP	FGA	FG	Pct
Jack Jirak, Hampden-Sydney...Sr		28	220	147	66.8
Jared Rivers, ME-Farmington ...Sr		21	257	165	64.2
Neil Edwards, York (NY) ....Sr		26	260	165	63.5
Ted Davis, Shenandoah...........Jr		25	237	150	63.3
Demarkus Byrd, Methodist.......Jr		23	211	133	63.0
Kareem McKinnon, Alfred........Jr		24	205	129	62.9
John Ellenwood, Wooster ....Sr		29	241	150	62.2
Rory Neal, Trinity......................Sr		21	224	139	62.1
Maurice Davis, Rowan..............Sr		26	317	196	61.8
Jon Wallenfelsz, WI-Eau Claire...Sr		30	359	221	61.6

Note: Minimum 5 made per game.

ASSISTS

Player and Team	Class	GP	A	Avg
Daniel Martinez, McMurry...............Sr		29	229	7.9
Tim Kelly, Pacific Lutheran ....Sr		24	179	7.5
Matt Lucero, Austin ....Jr		24	175	7.3
Brian Nigro, Mt. St. Vincent...........Sr		24	173	7.2
Jimmy Driggs, Hamilton.................Jr		27	187	6.9
Tom Roeder, St. Joseph's (NY)......So		25	173	6.9
Eric Saucier, Clarkson...................Jr		26	176	6.8
Cody Skarning, Grinnell ....Jr		21	138	6.6
Michael Pinto, Stevens Tech..........So		25	164	6.6
Matt LaPointe, Bates.....................Fr		24	157	6.5

FREE-THROW PERCENTAGE

Player and Team	Class	GP	FTA	FT	Pct
Korey Coon, IL Wesleyan ....Sr		25	163	157	96.3
Al Callejas, Scranton ....Jr		28	78	71	91.0
Jason Luisi, Suffolk ....So		25	75	68	90.7
Brent Cahill, Marietta ....Sr		25	115	104	90.4
Ryan Knupple, Elmhurst............Jr		25	72	65	90.3
Travis Daugherty, Anderson .....Jr		24	110	99	90.0
Rob Strcula, Waynesburg.........So		20	60	54	90.0
Patrick Russell, Macalester.......So		24	79	71	89.9
Chris McGuire, Capital..............Jr		25	95	85	89.5
Pat Britton, Ithaca ....Sr		28	164	146	89.0

Note: Minimum 2.5 made per game.

SCORING

Player and Team	Class	GP	TFG	3FG	FT	Pts	Avg
Tara Carleton, Randolph-Macon	Sr	24	207	32	142	588	24.5
Laura Cargill, CCNY	Fr	25	189	86	120	584	23.4
Ronda Jo Miller, Gallaudet	Sr	26	225	3	137	590	22.7
Holly Patterson, Johnson St	Sr	25	222	31	89	564	22.6
Keri Canning, Mount Union	Jr	24	207	31	79	524	21.8
Jayme Anderson, WI-Eau Claire	Jr	29	248	2	132	630	21.7
Amanda St. Louis, Medgar Evers	Fr	26	224	3	108	559	21.5
Jill Dewane, Lakeland	So	26	205	40	102	552	21.2
Joanne Polakoski, King's (PA)	Sr	30	251	1	129	632	21.1
Marissa Garrity, Clark	Sr	30	249	41	82	621	20.7

REBOUNDS

Player and Team	Class	GP	Reb	Avg
Heather Stewart, New Rochelle	Sr	23	395	17.2
Lachelle Waller, Chowan	Jr	23	363	15.8
Julia Salas, Cal Tech	Fr	15	232	15.5
Jen Olson, Benedictine (IL)	So	24	351	14.6
Melisa Buchanan, Ferrum	Sr	24	339	14.1
Brandy Trice, Wentworth Inst.	Jr	23	317	13.8
Joy Silver, Rutgers-Camden	Fr	18	248	13.8
Heather Kile, Swarthmore	So	25	343	13.7
Miracle Wright, Agnes Scott	Fr	19	258	13.6
Tiffany Corey, Johnson St	So	25	335	13.4

FIELD-GOAL PERCENTAGE

Player and Team	Class	GP	FGA	FG	Pct
Jen Bulkeley, Sewanee	Sr	25	240	160	66.7
Laura Wendorff, St. Benedict	Sr	24	271	178	65.7
Jessica Justice, Mt Holyoke	Fr	25	259	158	61.0
Shannon Rexrode, Frostburg St.	Sr	26	318	193	60.7
Teri Antolick, Allentown	Fr	28	273	163	59.7
Michelle Stover, Simpson	So	28	311	185	59.5
Gretchen MacColl, Trinity	Sr	27	249	148	59.4
Jamie Luchtel, Upper Iowa	Jr	25	223	131	58.7
Katy Sturtz, Ohio Wesleyan	So	25	278	163	58.6
Ekaterina Markova, Rosemont	Fr	25	298	173	58.1

Note: Minimum 5 made per game.

ASSISTS

Player and Team	Class	GP	A	Avg
Alisa DiBonaventura, Delaware Valley	Jr	24	205	8.5
Tara Galiardo, Staten Island	Sr	27	178	6.6
Wendy Coleman, Albertus Magnus	Sr	22	144	6.5
Leslie Livingstone, Misericordia	Sr	23	141	6.1
Carrie Nestor, Penn St-Behren	Sr	27	165	6.1
Carrie McConnell, Roanoke	Sr	29	177	6.1
Emily Clark, Baldwin Wallace	So	30	182	6.1
Kara Grishkat, Otterbein	Jr	25	148	5.9
Crystal Gadsden, Kean	Fr	24	142	5.9
Kelli Young, Juniata	So	25	143	5.7

FREE-THROW PERCENTAGE

Player and Team	Class	GP	FTA	FT	Pct
Missy Pederson, St. Thomas	So	30	93	82	88.2
Jennifer Pelletier, Plymouth St	Fr	29	91	79	86.8
Alison Grubbs, Lake Forest	Jr	24	125	108	86.4
Heather Dana, Redlands	Jr	25	94	81	86.2
Helen Dinan, Regis	So	24	94	81	86.2
Mary Deitemeyer, Concordia	Fr	25	115	99	86.1
Kelly Smith, Emory & Henry	So	27	164	141	86.0
Melissa Smock, Salem St	Jr	26	84	72	85.7
Jill Dewane, Lakeland	So	26	119	102	85.7
Carrie Kulp, Gettysburg	Sr	23	70	60	85.7

Note: Minimum 2.5 made per game.

Billy Goat

Thank goodness CBS college basketball analyst Billy Packer never became a paramedic. With 54 seconds remaining in the first overtime of March's Stanford–UCLA game, the Bruins, trailing by three, missed a field goal attempt, and center Jason Collins of the top-ranked Cardinal rebounded the ball, prompting Packer to say, "Ball game."

"Already?" responded his incredulous broadcast partner, Jim Nantz.

"Yup," said Packer. Whereupon the Bruins proved him wrong, winning 94–93 in what was the best college game of this fledgling decade.

Packer, who has 21 years of experience calling college games, should have known better than to pronounce the patient dead while a pulse remained. He also should have known

better a week earlier at the Duke–St. John's game, when he made derogatory remarks toward two female Duke students at Cameron Indoor Stadium.

Junior Sarah Bradley and Jen Feinberg were just doing their job checking press credentials. When Packer entered the arena without displaying a media pass, Feinberg asked him for identification. He responded rudely and then said, "Since when do we let women control who gets into a men's basketball game? Why don't you go find a women's game to let people into?" At week's end, according to CBS, Packer was planning to contact Bradley and Feinberg to discuss the incident.

Let's hope that this was Packer's one swineing moment.

NCAA Men's Division I Championship Results

NCAA Final Four Results

Year	Winner	Score	Runner-up	Third Place	Fourth Place	Winning Coach
1939	Oregon	46–33	Ohio St	*Oklahoma	*Villanova	Howard Hobson
1940	Indiana	60–42	Kansas	*Duquesne	*Southern Cal	Branch McCracken
1941	Wisconsin	39–34	Washington St	*Pittsburgh	*Arkansas	Harold Foster
1942	Stanford	53–38	Dartmouth	*Colorado	*Kentucky	Everett Dean
1943	Wyoming	46–34	Georgetown	*Texas	*DePaul	Everett Shelton
1944	Utah	42–40 (OT)	Dartmouth	*Iowa St	*Ohio St	Vadal Peterson
1945	Oklahoma St	49–45	NYU	*Arkansas	*Ohio St	Hank Iba
1946	Oklahoma St	43–40	N Carolina	Ohio St	California	Hank Iba
1947	Holy Cross	58–47	Oklahoma	Texas	CCNY	Alvin Julian
1948	Kentucky	58–42	Baylor	Holy Cross	Kansas St	Adolph Rupp
1949	Kentucky	46–36	Oklahoma St	Illinois	Oregon St	Adolph Rupp
1950	CCNY	71–68	Bradley	N Carolina St	Baylor	Nat Holman
1951	Kentucky	68–58	Kansas St	Illinois	Oklahoma St	Adolph Rupp
1952	Kansas	80–63	St. John's (NY)	Illinois	Santa Clara	Forrest Allen
1953	Indiana	69–68	Kansas	Washington	Louisiana St	Branch McCracken
1954	La Salle	92–76	Bradley	Penn St	Southern Cal	Kenneth Loeffler
1955	San Francisco	77–63	La Salle	Colorado	Iowa	Phil Woolpert
1956	San Francisco	83–71	Iowa	Temple	Southern Meth	Phil Woolpert
1957	N Carolina	54–53 (3OT)	Kansas	San Francisco	Michigan St	Frank McGuire
1958	Kentucky	84–72	Seattle	Temple	Kansas St	Adolph Rupp
1959	California	71–70	W Virginia	Cincinnati	Louisville	Pete Newell
1960	Ohio St	75–55	California	Cincinnati	NYU	Fred Taylor
1961	Cincinnati	70–65 (OT)	Ohio St	Vacated‡	Utah	Edwin Jucker
1962	Cincinnati	71–59	Ohio St	Wake Forest	UCLA	Edwin Jucker
1963	Loyola (IL)	60–58 (OT)	Cincinnati	Duke	Oregon St	George Ireland
1964	UCLA	98–83	Duke	Michigan	Kansas St	John Wooden
1965	UCLA	91–80	Michigan	Princeton	Wichita St	John Wooden
1966	UTEP	72–65	Kentucky	Duke	Utah	Don Haskins
1967	UCLA	79–64	Dayton	Houston	N Carolina	John Wooden
1968	UCLA	78–55	N Carolina	Ohio St	Houston	John Wooden
1969	UCLA	92–72	Purdue	Drake	N Carolina	John Wooden
1970	UCLA	80–69	Jacksonville	New Mexico St	St. Bonaventure	John Wooden
1971	UCLA	68–62	Vacated‡	Vacated‡	Kansas	John Wooden
1972	UCLA	81–76	Florida St	N Carolina	Louisville	John Wooden
1973	UCLA	87–66	Memphis St	Indiana	Providence	John Wooden
1974	N Carolina St	76–64	Marquette	UCLA	Kansas	Norm Sloan
1975	UCLA	92–85	Kentucky	Louisville	Syracuse	John Wooden
1976	Indiana	86–68	Michigan	UCLA	Rutgers	Bob Knight
1977	Marquette	67–59	N Carolina	UNLV	NC-Charlotte	Al McGuire
1978	Kentucky	94–88	Duke	Arkansas	Notre Dame	Joe Hall
1979	Michigan St	75–64	Indiana St	DePaul	Penn	Jud Heathcote
1980	Louisville	59–54	Vacated‡	Purdue	Iowa	Denny Crum
1981	Indiana	63–50	N Carolina	Virginia	Louisiana St	Bob Knight
1982	N Carolina	63–62	Georgetown	*Houston	*Louisville	Dean Smith
1983	N Carolina St	54–52	Houston	*Georgia	*Louisville	Jim Valvano
1984	Georgetown	84–75	Houston	*Kentucky	*Virginia	John Thompson
1985	Villanova	66–64	Georgetown	St. John's (NY)	Vacated‡	Rollie Massimino
1986	Louisville	72–69	Duke	*Kansas	*Louisiana St	Denny Crum
1987	Indiana	74–73	Syracuse	*UNLV	*Providence	Bob Knight
1988	Kansas	83–79	Oklahoma	*Arizona	*Duke	Larry Brown
1989	Michigan	80–79 (OT)	Seton Hall	*Duke	*Illinois	Steve Fisher
1990	UNLV	103–73	Duke	*Arkansas	*Georgia Tech	Jerry Tarkanian
1991	Duke	72–65	Kansas	*UNLV	*N Carolina	Mike Krzyzewski
1992	Duke	71–51	Michigan	*Cincinnati	*Indiana	Mike Krzyzewski
1993	N Carolina	77–71	Michigan	*Kansas	*Kentucky	Dean Smith
1994	Arkansas	76–72	Duke	*Arizona	*Florida	Nolan Richardson
1995	UCLA	89–78	Arkansas	*N Carolina	*Oklahoma St	Jim Harrick
1996	Kentucky	76–67	Syracuse	Vacated‡	Mississippi St	Rick Pitino
1997	Arizona	84–79 (OT)	Kentucky	*Minnesota	*N Carolina	Lute Olson
1998	Kentucky	78–69	Utah	*Stanford	*N Carolina	Tubby Smith
1999	Connecticut	77–74	Duke	*Michigan St	*Ohio St	Jim Calhoun
2000	Michigan St	89–76	Florida	*Wisconsin	*N Carolina	Tom Izzo

*Tied for third place. ‡Student-athletes representing St. Joseph's (PA) in 1961, Villanova in 1971, Western Kentucky in 1971, UCLA in 1980, Memphis State in 1985 and Massachusetts in 1996 were declared ineligible subsequent to the tournament. Under NCAA rules, the teams' and ineligible student-athletes' records were deleted, and the teams' places in the standings were vacated.

NCAA Final Four MVPs

Year	Winner, School	GP	Field Goals		3-Pt FG		Free Throws		Reb	A	Stl	BS	Avg
			FGM	Pct	FGA	FGM	FTM	Pct					
1939	....None selected												
1940	....Marv Huffman, Indiana	2	7	—	—	—	4	—	—	—	—	—	9.0
1941	....John Kotz, Wisconsin	2	8	—	—	—	6	—	—	—	—	—	11.0
1942	....Howard Dallmar, Stanford	2	8	—	—	—	4	66.7	—	—	—	—	10.0
1943	....Ken Sailors, Wyoming	2	10	—	—	—	8	72.7	—	—	—	—	14.0
1944	...Arnie Ferrin, Utah	2	11	—	—	—	6	—	—	—	—	—	14.0
1945	....Bob Kurland, Oklahoma St	2	16	—	—	—	5	—	—	—	—	—	18.5
1946	....Bob Kurland, Oklahoma St	2	21	—	—	—	10	66.7	—	—	—	—	26.0
1947	...George Kaftan, Holy Cross	2	18	—	—	—	12	70.6	—	—	—	—	24.0
1948	...Alex Groza, Kentucky	2	16	—	—	—	5	—	—	—	—	—	18.5
1949	...Alex Groza, Kentucky	2	19	—	—	—	14	—	—	—	—	—	26.0
1950	....Irwin Dambrot, CCNY	2	12	42.9	—	—	4	50.0	—	—	—	—	14.0
1951	....None selected												
1952	....Clyde Lovellette, Kansas	2	24	—	—	—	18	—	—	—	—	—	33.0
1953	....*B.H. Horn, Kansas	2	17	—	—	—	17	—	—	—	—	—	25.5
1954	....Tom Gola, La Salle	2	12	—	—	—	14	—	—	—	—	—	19.0
1955	....Bill Russell, San Francisco	2	19	—	—	—	9	—	—	—	—	—	23.5
1956	....*Hal Lear, Temple	2	32	—	—	—	16	—	—	—	—	—	40.0
1957	....*Wilt Chamberlain, Kansas	2	18	51.4	—	—	19	70.4	25	—	—	—	32.5
1958	....*Elgin Baylor, Seattle	2	18	34.0	—	—	12	75.0	41	—	—	—	24.0
1959	....*Jerry West, West Virginia	2	22	66.7	—	—	22	68.8	25	—	—	—	33.0
1960	....Jerry Lucas, Ohio State	2	16	66.7	—	—	3	100.0	23	—	—	—	17.5
1961	....*Jerry Lucas, Ohio State	2	20	71.4	—	—	16	94.1	25	—	—	—	28.0
1962	....Paul Hogue, Cincinnati	2	23	63.9	—	—	12	63.2	38	—	—	—	29.0
1963	....Art Heyman, Duke	2	18	41.0	—	—	15	68.2	19	—	—	—	25.5
1964	....Walt Hazzard, UCLA	2	11	55.0	—	—	8	66.7	10	—	—	—	15.0
1965	....*Bill Bradley, Princeton	2	34	63.0	—	—	19	95.0	24	—	—	—	43.5
1966	....*Jerry Chambers, Utah	2	25	53.2	—	—	20	83.3	35	—	—	—	35.0
1967	....Lew Alcindor, UCLA	2	14	60.9	—	—	11	45.8	38	—	—	—	19.5
1968	....Lew Alcindor, UCLA	2	22	62.9	—	—	9	90.0	34	—	—	—	26.5
1969	....Lew Alcindor, UCLA	2	23	67.7	—	—	16	64.0	41	—	—	—	31.0
1970	....Sidney Wicks, UCLA	2	15	71.4	—	—	9	60.0	34	—	—	—	19.5
1971	....*†Howard Porter, Villanova	2	20	48.8	—	—	7	77.8	24	—	—	—	23.5
1972	....Bill Walton, UCLA	2	20	69.0	—	—	17	73.9	41	—	—	—	28.5
1973	....Bill Walton, UCLA	2	28	82.4	—	—	2	40.0	30	—	—	—	29.0
1974	....David Thompson, NC State	2	19	51.4	—	—	11	78.6	17	—	—	—	24.5
1975	....Richard Washington, UCLA	2	23	54.8	—	—	8	72.7	20	—	—	—	27.0
1976	....Kent Benson, Indiana	2	17	50.0	—	—	7	63.6	18	—	—	—	20.5
1977	....Butch Lee, Marquette	2	11	34.4	—	—	8	100.0	6	2	1	1	15.0
1978	....Jack Givens, Kentucky	2	28	65.1	—	—	8	66.7	17	4	1	3	32.0
1979	....Earvin Johnson, Michigan St	2	17	68.0	—	—	19	86.4	17	3	0	2	26.5
1980	....Darrell Griffith, Louisville	2	23	62.2	—	—	11	68.8	7	15	0	2	28.5
1981	....Isiah Thomas, Indiana	2	14	56.0	—	—	9	81.8	4	9	3	4	18.5
1982	....James Worthy, N Carolina	2	20	74.1	—	—	2	28.6	8	9	0	4	21.0
1983	....*Akeem Olajuwon, Houston	2	16	55.2	—	—	9	64.3	40	3	2	5	20.5
1984	....Patrick Ewing, Georgetown	2	8	57.1	—	—	2	100.0	18	1	1	15	9.0
1985	....Ed Pinckney, Villanova	2	8	57.1	—	—	12	75.0	15	6	3	0	14.0
1986	....Pervis Ellison, Louisville	2	15	60.0	—	—	6	75.0	24	2	3	1	18.0
1987	....Keith Smart, Indiana	2	14	63.6	1	0	7	77.8	7	7	0	2	17.5
1988	....Danny Manning, Kansas	2	25	55.6	1	0	6	66.7	17	4	8	9	28.0
1989	....Glen Rice, Michigan	2	24	49.0	16	7	4	100.0	16	1	0	3	29.5
1990	....Anderson Hunt, UNLV	2	19	61.3	16	9	2	50.0	4	9	1	1	24.5
1991	....Christian Laettner, Duke	2	12	54.5	1	1	21	91.3	17	2	1	2	23.0
1992	....Bobby Hurley, Duke	2	10	41.7	12	7	8	80.0	3	11	0	3	17.5
1993	....Donald Williams, N Carolina	2	15	65.2	14	10	10	100.0	4	2	2	0	25.0
1994	....Corliss Williamson, Arkansas	2	21	50.0	0	0	10	71.4	21	8	4	3	26.0
1995	....Ed O'Bannon, UCLA	2	16	45.7	8	3	10	76.9	25	3	7	1	22.5
1996	....Tony Delk, Kentucky	2	15	41.7	16	8	6	54.6	9	2	3	2	22.0
1997	....Miles Simon, Arizona	2	17	45.9	10	3	17	77.3	8	6	0	1	27.0
1998	....Jeff Sheppard, Kentucky	2	16	55.2	10	4	7	77.8	10	7	4	0	21.5
1999	....Richard Hamilton, Connecticut	2	20	51.3	7	3	8	72.7	12	4	2	1	25.5
2000	....Mateen Cleaves, Michigan St	2	8	44.4	4	3	10	83.3	6	5	2	0	14.5

*Not a member of the championship-winning team.   †Record later vacated.

Best NCAA Tournament Single-Game Scoring Performances

Player and Team	Year	Round	FG	3FG	FT	TP
Austin Carr, Notre Dame vs Ohio	1970	1st	25	—	11	61
Bill Bradley, Princeton vs Wichita St.	1965	C*	22	—	14	58
Oscar Robertson, Cincinnati vs Arkansas	1958	C	21	—	14	56
Austin Carr, Notre Dame vs Kentucky	1970	2nd	22	—	8	52
Austin Carr, Notre Dame vs Texas Christian	1971	1st	20	—	12	52
David Robinson, Navy vs Michigan	1987	1st	22	0	6	50
Elvin Hayes, Houston vs Loyola (IL)	1968	1st	20	—	9	49
Hal Lear, Temple vs SMU	1956	C*	17	—	14	48
Austin Carr, Notre Dame vs Houston	1971	C	17	—	13	47
Dave Corzine, DePaul vs Louisville	1978	2nd	18	—	10	46

C=regional third place; C*=third-place game.

NIT Championship Results

Year	Winner	Score	Runner-up	Year	Winner	Score	Runner-up
1938	Temple	60–36	Colorado	1970	Marquette	65–53	St. John's (NY)
1939	Long Island U	44–32	Loyola (IL)	1971	N Carolina	84–66	Georgia Tech
1940	Colorado	51–40	Duquesne	1972	Maryland	100–69	Niagara
1941	Long Island U	56–42	Ohio U	1973	Virginia Tech	92–91 (OT)	Notre Dame
1942	W Virginia	47–45	W Kentucky	1974	Purdue	97–81	Utah
1943	St. John's (NY)	48–27	Toledo	1975	Princeton	80–69	Providence
1944	St. John's (NY)	47–39	DePaul	1976	Kentucky	71–67	NC-Charlotte
1945	DePaul	71–54	Bowling Green	1977	St. Bonaventure	94–91	Houston
1946	Kentucky	46–45	Rhode Island	1978	Texas	101–93	N Carolina St
1947	Utah	49–45	Kentucky	1979	Indiana	53–52	Purdue
1948	St. Louis	65–52	NYU	1980	Virginia	58–55	Minnesota
1949	San Francisco	48–47	Loyola (IL)	1981	Tulsa	86–84 (OT)	Syracuse
1950	CCNY	69–61	Bradley	1982	Bradley	67–58	Purdue
1951	BYU	62–43	Dayton	1983	Fresno St	69–60	DePaul
1952	La Salle	75–64	Dayton	1984	Michigan	83–63	Notre Dame
1953	Seton Hall	58–46	St. John's (NY)	1985	UCLA	65–62	Indiana
1954	Holy Cross	71–62	Duquesne	1986	Ohio St	73–63	Wyoming
1955	Duquesne	70–58	Dayton	1987	Southern Miss	84–80	La Salle
1956	Louisville	93–80	Dayton	1988	Connecticut	72–67	Ohio St
1957	Bradley	84–83	Memphis St	1989	St. John's (NY)	73–65	St. Louis
1958	Xavier (OH)	78–74 (OT)	Dayton	1990	Vanderbilt	74–72	St. Louis
1959	St. John's (NY)	76–71 (OT)	Bradley	1991	Stanford	78–72	Oklahoma
1960	Bradley	88–72	Providence	1992	Virginia	81–76	Notre Dame
1961	Providence	62–59	St. Louis	1993	Minnesota	62–61	Georgetown
1962	Dayton	73–67	St. John's (NY)	1994	Villanova	80–73	Vanderbilt
1963	Providence	81–66	Canisius	1995	Virginia Tech	65–64 (OT)	Marquette
1964	Bradley	86–54	New Mexico	1996	Nebraska	60–56	St. Joseph's
1965	St. John's (NY)	55–51	Villanova	1997	Michigan	82–73	Florida St
1966	BYU	97–84	NYU	1998	Minnesota	79–72	Penn St
1967	Southern Illinois	71–56	Marquette	1999	California	61–60	Clemson
1968	Dayton	61–48	Kansas	2000	Wake Forest	71–61	Notre Dame
1969	Temple	89–76	Boston College				

NCAA Men's Division I Season Leaders

Scoring Average

Year	Player and Team	Ht	Class	GP	FG	3FG	FT	Pts	Avg
1948	Murray Wier, Iowa	5-9	Sr	19	152	—	95	399	21.0
1949	Tony Lavelli, Yale	6-3	Sr	30	228	—	215	671	22.4
1950	Paul Arizin, Villanova	6-3	Sr	29	260	—	215	735	25.3
1951	Bill Mlkvy, Temple	6-4	Sr	25	303	—	125	731	29.2
1952	Clyde Lovellette, Kansas	6-9	Sr	28	315	—	165	795	28.4
1953	Frank Selvy, Furman	6-3	Jr	25	272	—	194	738	29.5
1954	Frank Selvy, Furman	6-3	Sr	29	427	—	355	1209	41.7
1955	Darrell Floyd, Furman	6-1	Jr	25	344	—	209	897	35.9
1956	Darrell Floyd, Furman	6-1	Sr	28	339	—	268	946	33.8
1957	Grady Wallace, S Carolina	6-4	Sr	29	336	—	234	906	31.2
1958	Oscar Robertson, Cincinnati	6-5	So	28	352	—	280	984	35.1
1959	Oscar Robertson, Cincinnati	6-5	Jr	30	331	—	316	978	32.6
1960	Oscar Robertson, Cincinnati	6-5	Sr	30	369	—	273	1011	33.7
1961	Frank Burgess, Gonzaga	6-1	Sr	26	304	—	234	842	32.4
1962	Billy McGill, Utah	6-9	Sr	26	394	—	221	1009	38.8
1963	Nick Werkman, Seton Hall	6-3	Jr	22	221	—	208	650	29.5
1964	Howard Komives, Bowling Green	6-1	Sr	23	292	—	260	844	36.7
1965	Rick Barry, Miami (FL)	6-7	Sr	26	340	—	293	973	37.4

Scoring Average (Cont.)

Year	Player and Team	Ht	Class	GP	FG	3FG	FT	Pts	Avg
1966	....Dave Schellhase, Purdue	6-4	Sr	24	284	—	213	781	32.5
1967	....Jim Walker, Providence	6-3	Sr	28	323	—	205	851	30.4
1968	....Pete Maravich, Louisiana St	6-5	So	26	432	—	274	1138	43.8
1969	....Pete Maravich, Louisiana St	6-5	Jr	26	433	—	282	1148	44.2
1970	....Pete Maravich, Louisiana St	6-5	Sr	31	522	—	337	1381	44.5
1971	....Johnny Neumann, Mississippi	6-6	So	23	366	—	191	923	40.1
1972	....Dwight Lamar, Southwestern Louisiana	6-1	Jr	29	429	—	196	1054	36.3
1973	....William Averitt, Pepperdine	6-1	Sr	25	352	—	144	848	33.9
1974	....Larry Fogle, Canisius	6-5	So	25	326	—	183	835	33.4
1975	....Bob McCurdy, Richmond	6-7	Sr	26	321	—	213	855	32.9
1976	....Marshall Rodgers, TX-Pan American	6-2	Sr	25	361	—	197	919	36.8
1977	....Freeman Williams, Portland St	6-4	Jr	26	417	—	176	1010	38.8
1978	....Freeman Williams, Portland St	6-4	Sr	27	410	—	149	969	35.9
1979	....Lawrence Butler, Idaho St	6-3	Sr	27	310	—	192	812	30.1
1980	....Tony Murphy, Southern-BR	6-3	Sr	29	377	—	178	932	32.1
1981	....Zam Fredrick, S Carolina	6-2	Sr	27	300	—	181	781	28.9
1982	....Harry Kelly, Texas Southern	6-7	Jr	29	336	—	190	862	29.7
1983	....Harry Kelly, Texas Southern	6-7	Sr	29	333	—	169	835	28.8
1984	....Joe Jakubick, Akron	6-5	Sr	27	304	—	206	814	30.1
1985	....Xavier McDaniel, Wichita St	6-8	Sr	31	351	—	142	844	27.2
1986	....Terrance Bailey, Wagner	6-2	Jr	29	321	—	212	854	29.4
1987	....Kevin Houston, Army	5-11	Sr	29	311	63	268	953	32.9
1988	....Hersey Hawkins, Bradley	6-3	Sr	31	377	87	284	1125	36.3
1989	....Hank Gathers, Loyola Marymount	6-7	Jr	31	419	0	177	1015	32.7
1990	....Bo Kimble, Loyola Marymount	6-5	Sr	32	404	92	231	1131	35.3
1991	....Kevin Bradshaw, U.S. Int'l	6-6	Sr	28	358	60	278	1054	37.6
1992	....Brett Roberts, Morehead St	6-8	Sr	29	278	66	193	815	28.1
1993	....Greg Guy, TX-Pan American	6-1	Jr	19	189	67	111	556	29.3
1994	....Glenn Robinson, Purdue	6-8	Jr	34	368	79	215	1030	30.3
1995	....Kurt Thomas, Texas Christian	6-9	Sr	27	288	3	202	781	28.9
1996	....Kevin Granger, Texas Southern	6-3	Sr	24	194	30	230	648	27.0
1997	....Charles Jones, LIU-Brooklyn	6-3	Jr	30	338	109	118	903	30.1
1998	....Charles Jones, LIU-Brooklyn	6-3	Sr	30	326	116	101	869	29.0
1999	....Alvin Young, Niagara	6-3	Sr	29	253	65	157	728	25.1
2000	....Courtney Alexander, Fresno St	6-6	Sr	27	252	58	107	669	24.8

Rebounds

Year	Player and Team	Ht	Class	GP	Reb	Avg
1951	...............Ernie Beck, Pennsylvania	6-4	So	27	556	20.6
1952	...............Bill Hannon, Army	6-3	So	17	355	20.9
1953	...............Ed Conlin, Fordham	6-5	So	26	612	23.5
1954	...............Art Quimby, Connecticut	6-5	Jr	26	588	22.6
1955	...............Charlie Slack, Marshall	6-5	Jr	21	538	25.6
1956	...............Joe Holup, George Washington	6-6	Sr	26	604	†.256
1957	...............Elgin Baylor, Seattle	6-6	Jr	25	508	†.235
1958	...............Alex Ellis, Niagara	6-5	Sr	25	536	†.262
1959	...............Leroy Wright, Pacific	6-8	Jr	26	652	†.238
1960	...............Leroy Wright, Pacific	6-8	Sr	17	380	†.234
1961	...............Jerry Lucas, Ohio St	6-8	Jr	27	470	†.198
1962	...............Jerry Lucas, Ohio St	6-8	Sr	28	499	†.211
1963	...............Paul Silas, Creighton	6-7	Sr	27	557	20.6
1964	...............Bob Pelkington, Xavier (OH)	6-7	Sr	26	567	21.8
1965	...............Toby Kimball, Connecticut	6-8	Sr	23	483	21.0
1966	...............Jim Ware, Oklahoma City	6-8	Sr	29	607	20.9
1967	...............Dick Cunningham, Murray St	6-10	Jr	22	479	21.8
1968	...............Neal Walk, Florida	6-10	Jr	25	494	19.8
1969	...............Spencer Haywood, Detroit	6-8	So	22	472	21.5
1970	...............Artis Gilmore, Jacksonville	7-2	Jr	28	621	22.2
1971	...............Artis Gilmore, Jacksonville	7-2	Sr	26	603	23.2
1972	...............Kermit Washington, American	6-8	Jr	23	455	19.8
1973	...............Kermit Washington, American	6-8	Sr	22	439	20.0
1974	...............Marvin Barnes, Providence	6-9	Sr	32	597	18.7
1975	...............John Irving, Hofstra	6-9	So	21	323	15.4
1976	...............Sam Pellom, Buffalo	6-8	So	26	420	16.2
1977	...............Glenn Mosley, Seton Hall	6-8	Sr	29	473	16.3
1978	...............Ken Williams, N Texas St	6-7	Sr	28	411	14.7
1979	...............Monti Davis, Tennessee St	6-7	Jr	26	421	16.2
1980	...............Larry Smith, Alcorn St	6-8	Sr	26	392	15.1
1981	...............Darryl Watson, Miss Valley	6-7	Sr	27	379	14.0
1982	...............LaSalle Thompson, Texas	6-10	Jr	27	365	13.5
1983	...............Xavier McDaniel, Wichita St	6-7	So	28	403	14.4
1984	...............Akeem Olajuwon, Houston	7-0	Jr	37	500	13.5

Rebounds (Cont.)

Year	Player and Team	Ht	Class	GP	Reb	Avg
1985	Xavier McDaniel, Wichita St	6-8	Sr	31	460	14.8
1986	David Robinson, Navy	6-11	Jr	35	455	13.0
1987	Jerome Lane, Pittsburgh	6-6	So	33	444	13.5
1988	Kenny Miller, Loyola (IL)	6-9	Fr	29	395	13.6
1989	Hank Gathers, Loyola (CA)	6-7	Jr	31	426	13.7
1990	Anthony Bonner, St. Louis	6-8	Sr	33	456	13.8
1991	Shaquille O'Neal, Louisiana St	7-1	So	28	411	14.7
1992	Popeye Jones, Murray St	6-8	Sr	30	431	14.4
1993	Warren Kidd, Middle Tenn St	6-9	Sr	26	386	14.8
1994	Jerome Lambert, Baylor	6-8	Jr	24	355	14.8
1995	Kurt Thomas, Texas Christian	6-9	Sr	27	393	14.6
1996	Marcus Mann, Mississippi Valley	6-8	Sr	29	394	13.6
1997	Tim Duncan, Wake Forest	6-11	Sr	31	457	14.7
1998	Ryan Perryman, Dayton	6-7	Sr	33	412	12.5
1999	Ian McGinnis, Dartmouth	6-8	So	26	317	12.2
2000	Darren Phillips, Fairfield	6-7	Sr	29	405	14.0

†From 1956–1962, title was based on highest individual recoveries out of total by both teams in all games.

Assists

Year	Player and Team	Class	GP	A	Avg
1984	Craig Lathen, IL-Chicago	Jr	29	274	9.45
1985	Rob Weingard, Hofstra	Sr	24	228	9.50
1986	Mark Jackson, St. John's (NY)	Jr	36	328	9.11
1987	Avery Johnson, Southern-BR	Jr	31	333	10.74
1988	Avery Johnson, Southern-BR	Sr	30	399	13.30
1989	Glenn Williams, Holy Cross	Sr	28	278	9.93
1990	Todd Lehmann, Drexel	Sr	28	260	9.29
1991	Chris Corchiani, N Carolina St	Sr	31	299	9.65
1992	Van Usher, Tennessee Tech	Sr	29	254	8.76
1993	Sam Crawford, New Mex St	Sr	34	310	9.12
1994	Jason Kidd, California	So	30	272	9.06
1995	Nelson Haggerty, Baylor	Sr	28	284	10.10
1996	Raimonds Miglinieks, UC-Irvine	Sr	27	230	8.52
1997	Kenny Mitchell, Dartmouth	Sr	26	203	7.81
1998	Ahlon Lewis, Arizona St	Sr	32	294	9.19
1999	Doug Gottlieb, Oklahoma St	Jr	34	299	8.79
2000	Mark Dickel, UNLV	Sr	31	280	9.03

Blocked Shots

Year	Player and Team	Class	GP	BS	Avg
1986	David Robinson, Navy	Jr	35	207	5.91
1987	David Robinson, Navy	Sr	32	144	4.50
1988	Rodney Blake, St. Joseph's (PA)	Sr	29	116	4.00
1989	Alonzo Mourning, Georgetown	Fr	34	169	4.97
1990	Kenny Green, Rhode Island	Sr	26	124	4.77
1991	Shawn Bradley, Brigham Young	Fr	34	177	5.21
1992	Shaquille O'Neal, Louisiana St	Jr	30	157	5.23
1993	Theo Ratliff, Wyoming	Jr	28	124	4.43
1994	Grady Livingston, Howard	Jr	26	115	4.42
1995	Keith Closs, Central Conn St	Fr	26	139	5.35
1996	Keith Closs, Central Conn St	So	28	178	6.36
1997	Adonal Foyle, Colgate	Jr	28	180	6.43
1998	Jerome James, Florida A&M	Sr	27	125	4.63
1999	Tarvis Williams, Hampton	Jr	27	135	5.00
2000	Ken Johnson, Ohio St	Sr	30	161	5.37

Steals

Year	Player and Team	Class	GP	S	Avg
1986	Darron Brittman, Chicago St	Sr	28	139	4.96
1987	Tony Fairley, Charleston Sou	Sr	28	114	4.07
1988	Aldwin Ware, Florida A&M	Sr	29	142	4.90
1989	Kenny Robertson, Cleveland St	Jr	28	111	3.96
1990	Ronn McMahon, E Washington	Sr	29	130	4.48
1991	Van Usher, Tennessee Tech	Jr	28	104	3.71
1992	Victor Snipes, NE Illinois	So	25	86	3.44
1993	Jason Kidd, California	Fr	29	110	3.80
1994	Shawn Griggs, SW Louisiana	Sr	30	120	4.00
1995	Roderick Anderson, Texas	Sr	30	101	3.37
1996	Pointer Williams, McNeese St	Sr	27	118	4.37
1997	Joel Hoover, MD-Eastern Shore	Fr	28	90	3.21
1998	Bonzi Wells, Ball St	Sr	29	103	3.55
1999	Shawnta Rogers, George Wash	Sr	29	103	3.55
2000	Carl Williams, Liberty	Sr	28	107	3.82

Single Game Records

SCORING HIGHS VS NON-DIVISION I OPPONENT

Pts	Player and Team vs Opponent	Date
72	Kevin Bradshaw, U.S. Int'l vs Loyola Marymount	1-5-91
69	Pete Maravich, Louisiana St vs Alabama	2-7-70
68	Calvin Murphy, Niagara vs Syracuse	12-7-68
66	Jay Handlan, Washington & Lee vs Furman	2-17-51
66	Pete Maravich, Louisiana St vs Tulane	2-10-69
66	Anthony Roberts, Oral Roberts vs N Carolina A&T	2-19-77
65	Anthony Roberts, Oral Roberts vs Oregon	3-9-77
65	Scott Haffner, Evansville vs Dayton	2-18-89
64	Pete Maravich, Louisiana St vs Kentucky	2-21-70
63	Johnny Neumann, Mississippi vs Louisiana St	1-30-71
63	Hersey Hawkins, Bradley vs Detroit	2-22-88

SCORING HIGHS VS NON-DIVISION I OPPONENT

Pts	Player and Team vs Opponent	Date
100	Frank Selvy, Furman vs Newberry	2-13-54
85	Paul Arizin, Villanova vs Philadelphia NAMC	2-12-49
81	Freeman Williams, Portland St vs Rocky Mountain	2-3-78
73	Bill Mlkvy, Temple vs Wilkes	3-3-51
71	Freeman Williams, Portland St vs Southern Oregon	2-9-77

REBOUNDING HIGHS BEFORE 1973

Reb	Player and Team vs Opponent	Date
51	Bill Chambers, William & Mary vs Virginia	2-14-53
43	Charlie Slack, Marshall vs Morris Harvey	1-12-54
42	Tom Heinsohn, Holy Cross vs Boston College	3-1-55
40	Art Quimby, Connecticut vs Boston U	1-11-55
39	Maurice Stokes, St. Francis (PA) vs John Carroll	1-28-55
39	Dave DeBusschere, Detroit vs Central Michigan	1-30-60
39	Keith Swagerty, Pacific vs UC-Santa Barbara	3-5-65

REBOUNDING HIGHS SINCE 1973*

Reb	Player and Team vs Opponent	Date
35	Larry Abney, Fresno St vs Southern Methodist	2-17-00
34	David Vaughn, Oral Roberts vs Brandeis	1-8-73
32	Jervaughn Scales, Southern-BR vs Grambling	2-7-94
32	Durand Macklin, Louisiana St vs Tulane	11-26-76
31	Jim Bradley, Northern Illinois vs WI-Milwaukee	2-19-73
31	Calvin Natt, NE Louisiana vs Georgia Southern	12-29-76

ASSISTS

A	Player and Team vs Opponent	Date
22	Tony Fairley, Baptist vs Armstrong St	2-9-87
22	Avery Johnson, Southern-BR vs Texas Southern	1-25-88
22	Sherman Douglas, Syracuse vs Providence	1-28-89
21	Mark Wade, UNLV vs Navy	12-29-86
21	Kelvin Scarborough, New Mexico vs Hawaii	2-13-87
21	Anthony Manuel, Bradley vs UC-Irvine	12-19-87
21	Avery Johnson, Southern-BR vs Alabama St	1-16-88

STEALS

S	Player and Team vs Opponent	Date
13	Mookie Blaylock, Oklahoma vs Centenary	12-12-87
13	Mookie Blaylock, Oklahoma vs Loyola Marymount	12-17-88
12	Kenny Robertson, Cleveland St vs Wagner	12-3-88
12	Terry Evans, Oklahoma vs Florida A&M	1-27-93
12	Richard Duncan, Middle Tenn St vs Eastern Kentucky	2-20-99

Single Game Records *(Cont.)*

BLOCKED SHOTS

BS	Player and Team vs Opponent	Date
14	David Robinson, Navy vs NC-Wilmington	1-4-86
14	Shawn Bradley, Brigham Young vs Eastern Kentucky	12-7-90
14	Roy Rogers, Alabama vs Georgia	2-10-96
14	Loren Woods, Arizona vs Oregon	2-3-00
13	Kevin Roberson, Vermont vs New Hampshire	1-9-92
13	Jim McIlvaine, Marquette vs Northeastern (IL)	12-9-92
13	Keith Closs, Central Conn. St vs St. Francis (PA)	12-21-94

Single Season Records

POINTS

Player and Team	Year	GP	FG	3FG	FT	Pts
Pete Maravich, Louisiana St	1970	31	522	—	337	1381
Elvin Hayes, Houston	1968	33	519	—	176	1214
Frank Selvy, Furman	1954	29	427	—	355	1209
Pete Maravich, Louisiana St	1969	26	433	—	282	1148
Pete Maravich, Louisiana St	1968	26	432	—	274	1138
Bo Kimble, Loyola Marymount	1990	32	404	92	231	1131
Hersey Hawkins, Bradley	1988	31	377	87	284	1125
Austin Carr, Notre Dame	1970	29	444	—	218	1106
Austin Carr, Notre Dame	1971	29	430	—	241	1101
Otis Birdsong, Houston	1977	36	452	—	186	1090

SCORING AVERAGE

Player and Team	Year	GP	FG	3FG	FT	Pts
Pete Maravich, Louisiana St	1970	31	522	337	1381	44.5
Pete Maravich, Louisiana St	1969	26	433	282	1148	44.2
Pete Maravich, Louisiana St	1968	26	432	274	1138	43.8
Frank Selvy, Furman	1954	29	427	355	1209	41.7
Johnny Neumann, Mississippi	1971	23	366	191	923	40.1
Freeman Williams, Portland St	1977	26	417	176	1010	38.8
Billy McGill, Utah	1962	26	394	221	1009	38.8
Calvin Murphy, Niagara	1968	24	337	242	916	38.2
Austin Carr, Notre Dame	1970	29	444	218	1106	38.1
Austin Carr, Notre Dame	1971	29	430	241	1101	38.0

REBOUNDS

Player and Team	Year	GP	Reb	Player and Team	Year	GP	Reb
Walt Dukes, Seton Hall	1953	33	734	Artis Gilmore, Jacksonville	1970	28	621
Leroy Wright, Pacific	1959	26	652	Tom Gola, La Salle	1955	31	618
Tom Gola, La Salle	1954	30	652	Ed Conlin, Fordham	1953	26	612
Charlie Tyra, Louisville	1956	29	645	Art Quimby, Connecticut	1955	25	611
Paul Silas, Creighton	1964	29	631	Bill Russell, San Francisco	1956	29	609
Elvin Hayes, Houston	1968	33	624	Jim Ware, Oklahoma City	1966	29	607

REBOUND AVERAGE BEFORE 1973

Player and Team	Year	GP	Reb	Avg
Charlie Slack, Marshall	1955	21	538	25.6
Leroy Wright, Pacific	1959	26	652	25.1
Art Quimby, Connecticut	1955	25	611	24.4
Charlie Slack, Marshall	1956	22	520	23.6
Ed Conlin, Fordham	1953	26	612	23.5

REBOUND AVERAGE SINCE 1973*

Player and Team	Year	GP	Reb	Avg
Kermit Washington, American	1973	22	439	20.0
Marvin Barnes, Providence	1973	30	571	19.0
Marvin Barnes, Providence	1974	32	597	18.7
Pete Padgett, NV-Reno	1973	26	462	17.8
Jim Bradley, Northern Illinois	1973	24	426	17.8

*Freshmen became eligible for varsity play in 1973.

Single Season Records *(Cont.)*

ASSISTS

Player and Team	Year	GP	A
Mark Wade, UNLV	1987	38	406
Avery Johnson, Southern-BR	1988	30	399
Anthony Manuel, Bradley	1988	31	373
Avery Johnson, Southern-BR	1987	31	333
Mark Jackson, St. John's (NY)	1986	32	328
Sherman Douglas, Syracuse	1989	38	326
Sam Crawford, New Mex. St	1993	34	310
Greg Anthony, UNLV	1991	35	310
Reid Gettys, Houston	1984	37	309
Carl Golston, Loyola (IL)	1985	33	305

ASSIST AVERAGE

Player and Team	Year	GP	A	Avg
Avery Johnson, Southern-BR	1988	30	399	13.3
Anthony Manuel, Bradley	1988	31	373	12.0
Avery Johnson, Southern-BR	1987	31	333	10.7
Mark Wade, UNLV	1987	38	406	10.7
Nelson Haggerty, Baylor	1995	28	284	10.1
Glenn Williams, Holy Cross	1989	28	278	9.9
Chris Corchiani, N Carolina St	1991	31	299	9.6
Tony Fairley, Charleston So.*	1987	28	270	9.6
Tyrone Bogues, Wake Forest	1987	29	276	9.5
Ron Weingard, Hofstra	1985	24	228	9.5
Craig Neal, Georgia Tech	1988	32	303	9.5

*Formerly Baptist.

FIELD-GOAL PERCENTAGE

Player and Team	Year	GP	FG	FGA	Pct
Steve Johnson, Oregon St	1981	28	235	315	74.6
Dwayne Davis, Florida	1989	33	179	248	72.2
Keith Walker, Utica	1985	27	154	216	71.3
Steve Johnson, Oregon St	1980	30	211	297	71.0
Oliver Miller, Arkansas	1991	38	254	361	70.4
Alan Williams, Princeton	1987	25	163	232	70.3
Mark McNamara, California	1982	27	231	329	70.2
Warren Kidd, Middle Tennessee St	1991	30	173	247	70.0
Pete Freeman, Akron	1991	28	175	250	70.0
Joe Senser, West Chester	1977	25	130	186	69.9

Based on qualifiers for annual championship.

FREE-THROW PERCENTAGE

Player and Team	Year	GP	FT	FTA	Pct
Craig Collins, Penn St	1985	27	94	98	95.9
Rod Foster, UCLA	1982	27	95	100	95.0
Clay McKnight, Pacific	2000	24	74	78	94.9
Danny Basile, Marist	1994	27	84	89	94.4
Carlos Gibson, Marshall	1978	28	84	89	94.4
Jim Barton, Dartmouth	1986	26	65	69	94.2
Jack Moore, Nebraska	1982	27	123	131	93.9
Dandrea Evans, Troy St	1994	27	72	77	93.5
Rob Robbins, New Mexico	1990	34	101	108	93.5
Tommy Boyer, Arkansas	1962	23	125	134	93.3

Based on qualifiers for annual championship.

THREE-POINT FIELD-GOAL PERCENTAGE

Player and Team	Year	GP	3FG	3FGA	Pct
Glenn Tropf, Holy Cross	1988	29	52	82	63.4
Sean Wightman, Western Michigan	1992	30	48	76	63.2
Keith Jennings, E Tennessee St	1991	33	84	142	59.2
Dave Calloway, Monmouth (NJ)	1989	28	48	82	58.5
Steve Kerr, Arizona	1988	38	114	199	57.3
Reginald Jones, Prairie View	1987	28	64	112	57.1
Jim Cantamessa, Siena	1998	29	66	117	56.4
Joel Tribelhorn, Colorado St	1989	33	76	135	56.3
Mike Joseph, Bucknell	1988	28	65	116	56.0
Brian Jackson, Evansville	1995	27	53	95	55.8

Based on qualifiers for annual championship.

Single Season Records *(Cont.)*

STEALS

Player and Team	Year	GP	S
Mookie Blaylock, Oklahoma	1988	39	150
Aldwin Ware, Florida A&M	1988	29	142
Darron Brittman, Chicago St	1986	28	139
Nadav Henefeld, Connecticut	1990	37	138
Mookie Blaylock, Oklahoma	1989	35	131

BLOCKED SHOTS

Player and Team	Year	GP	BS
David Robinson, Navy	1986	35	207
Adonal Foyle, Colgate	1997	28	180
Keith Closs, Central Conn St	1996	28	178
Shawn Bradley, BYU	1991	34	177
Alonzo Mourning, Georgetown	1989	34	169

STEAL AVERAGE

Player and Team	Year	GP	S	Avg
Darron Brittman, Chicago St	1986	28	139	4.96
Aldwin Ware, Florida A&M	1988	29	142	4.90
Ronn McMahon, E Washington	1990	29	130	4.48
Pointer Williams, McNeese St	1996	27	118	4.37
Jim Paguaga, St Francis (NY)	1986	28	120	4.29

BLOCKED-SHOT AVERAGE

Player and Team	Year	GP	BS	Avg
Adonal Foyle, Colgate	1997	28	180	6.43
Keith Closs, Central Conn St	1996	28	178	6.36
David Robinson, Navy	1986	35	207	5.91
Adonal Foyle, Colgate	1996	29	165	5.69
Ken Johnson, Ohio St	2000	30	161	5.37

Career Records

POINTS

Player and Team	Ht	Final Year	GP	FG	3FG*	FT	Pts
Pete Maravich, Louisiana St	6-5	1970	83	1387	—	893	3667
Freeman Williams, Portland St	6-4	1978	106	1369	—	511	3249
Lionel Simmons, La Salle	6-7	1990	131	1244	56	673	3217
Alphonso Ford, Mississippi Valley	6-2	1993	109	1121	333	590	3165
Harry Kelly, Texas Southern	6-7	1983	110	1234	—	598	3066
Hersey Hawkins, Bradley	6-3	1988	125	1100	118	690	3008
Oscar Robertson, Cincinnati	6-5	1960	88	1052	—	869	2973
Danny Manning, Kansas	6-10	1988	147	1216	10	509	2951
Alfredrick Hughes, Loyola (IL)	6-5	1985	120	1226	—	462	2914
Elvin Hayes, Houston	6-8	1968	93	1215	—	454	2884
Larry Bird, Indiana St	6-9	1979	94	1154	—	542	2850
Otis Birdsong, Houston	6-4	1977	116	1176	—	480	2832
Kevin Bradshaw, Bethune-Cookman, U.S. Int'l	6-6	1991	111	1027	132	618	2804
Allan Houston, Tennessee	6-6	1993	128	902	346	651	2801
Hank Gathers, Southern Cal, Loyola Marymount	6-7	1990	117	1127	0	469	2723
Reggie Lewis, Northeastern	6-7	1987	122	1043	30 (1)	592	2708
Daren Queenan, Lehigh	6-5	1988	118	1024	29	626	2703
Byron Larkin, Xavier (OH)	6-3	1988	121	1022	51	601	2696
David Robinson, Navy	7-1	1987	127	1032	1	604	2669
Wayman Tisdale, Oklahoma	6-9	1985	104	1077	—	507	2661

*Listed is the number of three-pointers scored since it became the national rule in 1987; the number in the parentheses is number scored prior to 1987—these counted as three points in the game but counted as two-pointers in the national rankings. The three-pointers in the parentheses are not included in total points.

SCORING AVERAGE

Player and Team	Final Year	GP	FG	FT	Pts	Avg
Pete Maravich, Louisiana St	1968	83	1387	893	3667	44.2
Austin Carr, Notre Dame	1971	74	1017	526	2560	34.6
Oscar Robertson, Cincinnati	1960	88	1052	869	2973	33.8
Calvin Murphy, Niagara	1970	77	947	654	2548	33.1
Dwight Lamar, Southwestern Louisiana	1973	57	768	326	1862	32.7
Frank Selvy, Furman	1954	78	922	694	2538	32.5
Rick Mount, Purdue	1970	72	910	503	2323	32.3
Darrell Floyd, Furman	1956	71	868	545	2281	32.1
Nick Werkman, Seton Hall	1964	71	812	649	2273	32.0
Willie Humes, Idaho St	1971	48	565	380	1510	31.5
William Averitt, Pepperdine	1973	49	615	311	1541	31.4
Elgin Baylor, Coll. of Idaho, Seattle	1958	80	956	588	2500	31.3
Elvin Hayes, Houston	1968	93	1215	454	2884	31.0
Freeman Williams, Portland St	1978	106	1369	511	3249	30.7
Larry Bird, Indiana St	1979	94	1154	542	2850	30.3

Career Records (Cont.)

REBOUNDS BEFORE 1973

Player and Team	Final Year	GP	Reb
Tom Gola, La Salle	1955	118	2201
Joe Holup, George Washington	1956	104	2030
Charlie Slack, Marshall	1956	88	1916
Ed Conlin, Fordham	1955	102	1884
Dickie Hemric, Wake Forest	1955	104	1802

REBOUNDS SINCE 1973*

Player and Team	Final Year	GP	Reb
Tim Duncan, Wake Forest	1997	128	1570
Derrick Coleman, Syracuse	1990	143	1537
Malik Rose, Drexel	1996	120	1514
Ralph Sampson, Virginia	1983	132	1511
Pete Padgett, NV-Reno	1976	104	1464

ASSISTS

Player and Team	Final Year	GP	A
Bobby Hurley, Duke	1993	140	1076
Chris Corchiani, N Carolina St	1991	124	1038
Ed Cota, N Carolina	2000	138	1030
Keith Jennings, E Tennessee St	1991	127	983
Sherman Douglas, Syracuse	1989	138	960

FIELD-GOAL PERCENTAGE

Player and Team	Final Year	FG	FGA	Pct
Ricky Nedd, Appalachian St	1994	412	597	69.0
Stephen Scheffler, Purdue	1990	408	596	68.5
Steve Johnson, Oregon St	1981	828	1222	67.8
Murray Brown, Florida St	1980	566	847	66.8
Lee Campbell, SW Missouri St	1990	411	618	66.5

Note: Minimum 400 field goals.

FREE-THROW PERCENTAGE

Player and Team	Final Year	FT	FTA	Pct
Greg Starrick, Kentucky; Southern Illinois	1972	341	375	90.9
Jack Moore, Nebraska	1982	446	495	90.1
Steve Henson, Kansas St	1990	361	401	90.0
Steve Alford, Indiana	1987	535	596	89.8
Bob Lloyd, Rutgers	1967	543	605	89.8

Note: Minimum 300 free throws.

*Freshmen became eligible for varsity play in 1973.

Sit Down and Cheer

During Stanford's NCAA tournament games in Birmingham, Cardinal yell leader Joe Cavanaugh sat near one corner of the court—except when an opposing player went to shoot a free throw. Then Cavanaugh would wheel himself under the basket to scream and try to distract the shooter.

Cavanaugh, a junior who uses a wheelchair, believes he is a cheerleading pioneer. "I never saw anybody in a chair do it," Cavanaugh says, "so I thought, I'll see if I can be the first." He and the other yell leaders work with the Stanford band, whose notoriously questionable taste led at least one opponent to believe Cavanaugh was pulling a prank. When the Cardinal visited UCLA in February, a media relations worker for the Bruins, who were buffeted last year by a handicapped-parking scandal involving athletes, couldn't believe Cavanaugh had the gall to show up at Pauley Pavilion in a wheelchair. "Why do you guys keep harping on the scandal?" he was asked.

Cavanaugh played tailback and safety at Regis Jesuit High in Aurora, Colo. In the summer of '95, before his junior year, he contracted Epstein-Barr syndrome. The virus brought on transverse myelitis, an inflammation of the spinal cord that cost him the use of his legs. Cavanaugh saw yell leading as the next best thing to playing. After Stanford's first-round win, fellow yell leader Mark Ganek jumped clear over Cavanaugh to dunk.

Career Records (Cont.)

THREE-POINT FIELD GOALS MADE

Player and Team	Final Year	GP	3FG
Curtis Staples, Virginia	1998	122	413
Keith Veney, Lamar; Marshall	1997	111	409
Doug Day, Radford	1993	117	401
Ronnie Schmitz, MO-Kansas City	1993	112	378
Mark Alberts, Akron	1993	103	375

THREE-POINT FIELD-GOAL PERCENTAGE

Player and Team	Final Year	3FG	3FGA	Pct
Tony Bennett, WI-Green Bay	1992	290	584	49.7
Keith Jennings, E Tennessee St	1991	223	452	49.3
Kirk Manns, Michigan St	1990	212	446	47.5
Tim Locum, Wisconsin	1991	227	481	47.2
David Olson, Eastern Illinois	1992	262	562	46.6

Note: Minimum 200 3-point field goals.

STEALS

Player and Team	Final Year	GP	S
Eric Murdock, Providence	1991	117	376
Pepe Sanchez, Temple	2000	116	365
Bonzi Wells, Ball St	1998	116	347
Gerald Walker, San Francisco	1996	111	344
Johnny Rhodes, Maryland	1996	122	344

BLOCKED SHOTS

Player and Team	Final Year	GP	BS
Adonal Foyle, Colgate	1997	87	492
Tim Duncan, Wake Forest	1997	128	481
Alonzo Mourning, Georgetown	1992	120	453
Lorenzo Coleman, Tennessee Tech	1997	113	437
Calvin Booth, Penn St	1999	114	428

NCAA Men's Division I Team Leaders

Division I Team Alltime Wins

Team	First Year	Yrs	W	L	T
Kentucky	1903	97	1771	548	1
N Carolina	1911	90	1755	622	0
Kansas	1899	102	1712	734	0
Duke	1906	95	1614	760	0
St. John's (NY)	1908	93	1607	723	0
Temple	1895	104	1547	830	0
Syracuse	1901	99	1524	710	0
Pennsylvania	1897	100	1496	846	2
Oregon St	1902	99	1482	1015	0
Indiana	1901	100	1473	787	0
UCLA	1920	81	1466	633	0
Notre Dame	1898	95	1463	807	1
Purdue	1897	102	1428	781	0
Utah	1909	92	1427	746	0
Princeton	1901	100	1427	862	0

Note: Minimum of 25 years in Division I.

Division I Alltime Winning Percentage

Team	First Year	Yrs	W	L	T	Pct
Kentucky	1903	97	1771	548	1	.764
N Carolina	1911	90	1755	622	0	.738
UNLV	1959	42	870	328	0	.726
Kansas	1899	102	1712	734	0	.700
UCLA	1920	81	1466	633	0	.698
St. John's (NY)	1908	93	1607	723	0	.690
Syracuse	1901	99	1524	710	0	.682
Duke	1906	95	1614	760	0	.680
Western Kentucky	1915	81	1390	703	0	.664
Arkansas	1924	77	1334	697	0	.657
Utah	1909	92	1427	746	0	.657
Indiana	1901	100	1473	787	0	.652
Louisville	1912	86	1375	739	0	.650
Temple	1895	104	1547	830	0	.651
DePaul	1924	77	1221	666	0	.647

Note: Minimum of 25 years in Division I.

NCAA Men's Division I Winning Streaks

Longest—Full Season

Team	Games	Years	Ended by
UCLA	88	1971–74	Notre Dame (71–70)
San Francisco	60	1955–57	Illinois (62–33)
UCLA	47	1966–68	Houston (71–69)
UNLV	45	1990–91	Duke (79–77)
Texas	44	1913–17	Rice (24–18)
Seton Hall	43	1939–41	LIU-Brooklyn (49–26)
LIU-Brooklyn	43	1935–37	Stanford (45–31)
UCLA	41	1968–69	Southern Cal (46–44)
Marquette	39	1970–71	Ohio St (60–59)
Cincinnati	37	1962–63	Wichita St (65–64)
N Carolina	37	1957–58	W Virginia (75–64)

Longest—Regular Season

Team	Games	Years	Ended by
UCLA	76	1971–74	Notre Dame (71–70)
Indiana	57	1975–77	Toledo (59–57)
Marquette	56	1970–72	Detroit (70–49)
Kentucky	54	1952–55	Georgia Tech (59–58)
San Francisco	51	1955–57	Illinois (62–33)
Pennsylvania	48	1970–72	Temple (57–52)
Ohio State	47	1960–62	Wisconsin (86–67)
Texas	44	1913–17	Rice (24–18)
UCLA	43	1966–68	Houston (71–69)
LIU-Brooklyn	43	1935–37	Stanford (45–31)
Seton Hall	42	1939–41	LIU-Brooklyn (49–26)

Longest—Home Court

Team	Games	Years
Kentucky	129	1943–55
St. Bonaventure	99	1948–61
UCLA	98	1970–76
Cincinnati	86	1957–64
Marquette	81	1967–73
Arizona	81	1945–51

Team	Games	Years
Lamar	80	1978–84
Long Beach St	75	1968–74
UNLV	72	1974–78
Arizona	71	1987–92
Cincinnati	68	1972–78
Western Kentucky	67	1949–55

NCAA Men's Division I Winningest Coaches

Active Coaches

WINS

Coach and Team	W
James Phelan, Mt. St. Mary's (MD)	809
Bob Knight, Indiana	763
Lefty Driesell, Georgia St	733
Jerry Tarkanian, Fresno St	733
Lou Henson, New Mexico St	726
Denny Crum, Louisville	663
Eddie Sutton, Oklahoma St	659
John Chaney, Temple	632
Lute Olson, Arizona	613
Jim Calhoun, Connecticut	577

Note: Minimum 5 years as a Division I head coach; includes record at 4-year colleges only.

WINNING PERCENTAGE

Coach and Team	Yrs	W	L	Pct
Jerry Tarkanian, Fresno St	29	733	180	.803
John Kresse, Coll. of Charleston	21	517	127	.803
Roy Williams, Kansas	12	329	82	.800
Jim Boeheim, Syracuse	24	575	199	.743
Rick Majerus, Utah	16	360	125	.742
Bob Huggins, Cincinnati	19	444	158	.738
John Chaney, Temple	28	632	225	.737
Lute Olson, Arizona	27	613	226	.731
Bob Knight, Indiana	35	763	290	.725
Nolan Richardson, Arkansas	20	475	181	.724

Note: Minimum 5 years as a Division I head coach; includes record at 4-year colleges only.

Alltime Winningest Men's Division I Coaches

WINS

Coach (Team)	W
Dean Smith (N Carolina)	879
Adolph Rupp (Kentucky)	876
Jim Phelan (Mt. St. Mary's)	809
Hank Iba (NW Missouri St, Colorado, Oklahoma St)	767
Bob Knight (Army, Indiana)	763
Ed Diddle (Western Kentucky)	759
Phog Allen (Baker, Kansas, Haskell, Central Missouri St, Kansas)	746
Jerry Tarkanian (Long Beach St, UNLV, Fresno St)	733
Lefty Driesell (Davidson, Maryland, James Madison, Georgia St)	733
Norm Stewart (Northern Iowa, Missouri)	731
Lou Henson (Hardin-Simmons, New Mexico St, Illinois)	726
Ray Meyer (DePaul)	724
Don Haskins (UTEP)	719
John Wooden (Indiana St, UCLA)	664
Denny Crum (Louisville)	663
Eddie Sutton (Creighton, Arkansas, Kentucky, Oklahoma St)	659

Note: Minimum 10 head coaching seasons in Division I.

Alltime Winningest Men's Division I Coaches *(Cont.)*
WINNING PERCENTAGE

Coach (Team, Years)	Yrs	W	L	Pct
Clair Bee (Rider 29–31, LIU-Brooklyn 32–45, 46–51)	21	412	87	.826
Adolph Rupp (Kentucky 31–72)	41	876	190	.822
John Wooden (Indiana St 47–48, UCLA 49–75)	29	664	162	.804
Jerry Tarkanian (Long Beach St 69–73, UNLV 74–92, Fresno St 95–)	29	733	180	.803
Roy Williams (Kansas 89–)	12	329	82	.800
Dean Smith (N Carolina 62–97)	36	879	254	.776
Harry Fisher (Columbia 07–16, Army 22–23, 25)	13	147	44	.770
Frank Keaney (Rhode Island 21–48)	27	387	117	.768
George Keogan (St. Louis 16, Allegheny 19, Valparaiso 20–21, Notre Dame 24–43)	24	385	117	.767
Jack Ramsay (St. Joseph's [PA] 56–66)	11	231	71	.765
Vic Bubas (Duke 60–69)	10	213	67	.761
Charles (Chick) Davies (Duquesne 25–43, 47–48)	21	314	106	.748
Ray Mears (Wittenberg 57–62, Tennessee 63–77)	21	399	135	.747
Jim Boeheim (Syracuse 77–)	24	575	199	.743
Rick Majerus (Marquette 84–86, Ball St 88–89, Utah 90–)	16	360	125	.742
Al McGuire (Belmont Abbey 58–64, Marquette 65–77)	20	405	143	.739
Rick Pitino (Boston 79–83, Providence 86–87, Kentucky 90–97)	15	352	124	.739
Phog Allen (Baker 06–08, Kansas 08–09, Haskell 09, Cent MO St 13–19, Kansas 20–56)	48	746	264	.739
Everett Case (N Carolina St 47–64)	18	376	133	.739
Bob Huggins (Walsh 81–83, Akron 85–89, Cincinnati 90–)	19	444	158	.738

Note: Minimum 10 head coaching seasons in Division I.

NCAA Women's Division I Championship Results

Year	Winner	Score	Runner-up	Winning Coach
1982	Louisiana Tech	76–62	Cheyney	Sonja Hogg
1983	Southern Cal	69–67	Louisiana Tech	Linda Sharp
1984	Southern Cal	72–61	Tennessee	Linda Sharp
1985	Old Dominion	70–65	Georgia	Marianne Stanley
1986	Texas	97–81	Southern Cal	Jody Conradt
1987	Tennessee	67–44	Louisiana Tech	Pat Summitt
1988	Louisiana Tech	56–54	Auburn	Leon Barmore
1989	Tennessee	76–60	Auburn	Pat Summitt
1990	Stanford	88–81	Auburn	Tara VanDerveer
1991	Tennessee	70–67 (OT)	Virginia	Pat Summitt
1992	Stanford	78–62	Western Kentucky	Tara VanDerveer
1993	Texas Tech	84–82	Ohio State	Marsha Sharp
1994	N Carolina	60–59	Louisiana Tech	Sylvia Hatchell
1995	Connecticut	70–64	Tennessee	Geno Auriemma
1996	Tennessee	83–65	Georgia	Pat Summitt
1997	Tennessee	68–59	Old Dominion	Pat Summitt
1998	Tennessee	93–75	Louisiana Tech	Pat Summitt
1999	Purdue	62–45	Duke	Carolyn Peck
2000	Connecticut	71–52	Tennessee	Geno Auriemma

NCAA Women's Division I Alltime Individual Leaders

Single-Game Records

SCORING HIGHS

Pts	Player and Team vs Opponent	Year
60	Cindy Brown, Long Beach St vs San Jose St	1987
58	Kim Perrot, SW Louisiana vs SE Louisiana	1990
58	Lorri Bauman, Drake vs SW Missouri St	1984
56	Jackie Stiles, SW Missouri St vs Evansville	2000
55	Patricia Hoskins, Mississippi Valley vs Southern-BR	1989
55	Patricia Hoskins, Mississippi Valley vs Alabama St	1989
54	Anjinea Hopson, Grambling vs Jackson St	1994
54	Mary Lowry, Baylor vs Texas	1994
54	Wanda Ford, Drake vs SW Missouri St	1986

Three tied with 53.

Single-Game Records *(Cont.)*

REBOUNDS

Reb	Player and Team vs Opponent	Year
40	Deborah Temple, Delta St vs AL-Birmingham	1983
37	Rosina Pearson, Bethune-Cookman vs Florida Memorial	1985
33	Maureen Formico, Pepperdine vs Loyola (CA)	1985
31	Darlene Beale, Howard vs S Carolina St	1987
30	Cindy Bonforte, Wagner vs Queens (NY)	1983
30	Kayone Hankins, New Orleans vs. Nicholls St	1994
30	Wanda Ford, Drake vs Eastern Illinois	1985
29	Gail Norris, Alabama St vs Texas Southern	1992
29	Joy Kellogg, Oklahoma City vs Oklahoma Christian	1984
29	Joy Kellogg, Oklahoma City vs UTEP	1984

ASSISTS

A	Player and Team vs Opponent	Year
23	Michelle Burden, Kent St vs Ball St	1991
22	Shawn Monday, Tennessee Tech vs Morehead St	1988
22	Veronica Pettry, Loyola (IL) vs Detroit	1989
22	Tine Freil, Pacific vs Wichita St	1991
21	Tine Freil, Pacific vs Fresno St	1992
21	Amy Bauer, Wisconsin vs Detroit	1989
21	Neacole Hall, Alabama St vs Southern-BR	1989

Five tied with 20.

Single Season Records

POINTS

Player and Team	Year	GP	FG	3FG	FT	Pts
Cindy Brown, Long Beach St	1987	35	362	—	250	974
Genia Miller, Cal St-Fullerton	1991	33	376	0	217	969
Sheryl Swoopes, Texas Tech	1993	34	356	32	211	955
Andrea Congreaves, Mercer	1992	28	353	77	142	925
Wanda Ford, Drake	1986	30	390	—	139	919
Chamique Holdsclaw, Tennessee	1998	39	370	9	166	915
Barbara Kennedy, Clemson	1982	31	392	—	124	908
Patricia Hoskins, Mississippi Valley	1989	27	345	13	205	908
LaTaunya Pollard, Long Beach St	1983	31	376	—	155	907
Tina Hutchinson, San Diego St	1984	30	383	—	132	898

SEASON SCORING AVERAGE

Player and Team	Year	GP	FG	3FG	FT	Pts	Avg
Patricia Hoskins, Mississippi Valley	1989	27	345	13	205	908	33.6
Andrea Congreaves, Mercer	1992	28	353	77	142	925	33.0
Deborah Temple, Delta St	1984	28	373	—	127	873	31.2
Andrea Congreaves, Mercer	1993	26	302	51	150	805	31.0
Wanda Ford, Drake	1986	30	390	—	139	919	30.6
Anucha Browne, Northwestern	1985	28	341	—	173	855	30.5
LeChandra LeDay, Grambling	1988	28	334	36	146	850	30.4
Kim Perrot, Southwestern Louisiana	1990	28	308	95	128	839	30.0
Tina Hutchinson, San Diego St	1984	30	383	—	132	898	29.9
Jan Jensen, Drake	1991	30	358	6	166	888	29.6
Genia Miller, Cal St-Fullerton	1991	33	376	0	217	969	29.4
Barbara Kennedy, Clemson	1982	31	392	—	124	908	29.3
LaTaunya Pollard, Long Beach St	1983	31	376	—	155	907	29.3
Lisa McMullen, Alabama St	1991	28	285	126	119	815	29.1
Tresa Spaulding, BYU	1987	28	347	—	116	810	28.9
Hope Linthicum, Central Conn. St	1987	23	282	—	101	665	28.9

Season Records *(Cont.)*

REBOUNDS

Player and Team	Year	GP	Reb	Player and Team	Year	GP	Reb
Wanda Ford, Drake	1985	30	534	Rosina Pearson, Beth.-Cookman	1985	26	480
Wanda Ford, Drake	1986	30	506	Patricia Hoskins, Miss Valley	1987	28	476
Anne Donovan, Old Dominion	1983	35	504	Cheryl Miller, Southern Cal	1985	30	474
Darlene Jones, Miss Valley	1983	31	487	Darlene Beale, Howard	1987	29	459
Melanie Simpson, Okla. City	1982	37	481	Olivia Bradley, W Virginia	1985	30	458

REBOUND AVERAGE

Player and Team	Year	GP	Reb	Avg
Rosina Pearson, Bethune-Cookman	1985	26	480	18.5
Wanda Ford, Drake	1985	30	534	17.8
Katie Beck, E Tennessee St	1988	25	441	17.6
DeShawne Blocker, E Tennessee St	1994	26	450	17.3
Patricia Hoskins, Mississippi Valley	1987	28	476	17.0
Wanda Ford, Drake	1986	30	506	16.9
Patricia Hoskins, Mississippi Valley	1989	27	440	16.3
Joy Kellogg, Oklahoma City	1984	23	373	16.2
Deborah Mitchell, Mississippi Coll.	1983	28	447	16.0

FIELD-GOAL PERCENTAGE

Player and Team	Year	GP	FG	FGA	Pct
Myndee Larsen, Southern Utah	1998	28	249	344	72.4
Deneka Knowles, Southeastern La.	1996	26	199	276	72.1
Barbara Farris, Tulane	1998	27	151	210	71.9
Renay Adams, Tennessee Tech	1991	30	185	258	71.7
Regina Days, Georgia Southern	1986	27	234	332	70.5
Kim Wood, WI-Green Bay	1994	27	188	271	69.4
Kelly Lyons, Old Dominion	1990	31	308	444	69.4
Alisha Hill, Howard	1995	28	194	281	69.0
Ruth Riley, Notre Dame	1999	31	198	290	68.3
Trina Roberts, Georgia Southern	1982	31	189	277	68.2
Lidiya Varbanova, Boise St	1991	22	128	188	68.1

Based on qualifiers for annual championship.

FREE-THROW PERCENTAGE

Player and Team	Year	GP	FT	FTA	Pct
Ginny Doyle, Richmond	1992	29	96	101	95.0
Paula Corder, SE Missouri St	1999	28	111	118	94.1
Linda Cyborski, Delaware	1991	29	74	79	93.7
Paula Corder-King, SE Missouri St	2000	27	69	74	93.2
Jennifer Howard, N Carolina St	1994	27	118	127	92.9
Keely Feeman, Cincinnati	1986	30	76	82	92.7
Amy Slowikowski, Kent St	1989	27	112	121	92.6
Lea Ann Parsley, Marshall	1990	28	96	104	92.3
Chris Starr, NV-Reno	1986	25	119	129	92.2

Based on qualifiers for annual championship.

Career Records
POINTS

Player and Team	Yrs	GP	Pts
Patricia Hoskins, Mississippi Valley	1985–89	110	3122
Lorri Bauman, Drake	1981–84	120	3115
Chamique Holdsclaw, Tennessee	1995–99	148	3025
Cheryl Miller, Southern Cal	1983–86	128	3018
Cindy Blodgett, Maine	1994–98	118	3005
Valorie Whiteside, Appalachian St	1984–88	116	2944
Joyce Walker, Louisiana St	1981–84	117	2906
Sandra Hodge, New Orleans	1981–84	107	2860
Andrea Congreaves, Mercer	1989–93	108	2796
Karen Pelphrey, Marshall	1983–86	114	2746

SCORING AVERAGE

Player and Team	Yrs	GP	FG	3FG	FT	Pts	Avg
Patricia Hoskins, Mississippi Valley	1985–89	110	1196	24	706	3122	28.4
Sandra Hodge, New Orleans	1981–84	107	1194	—	472	2860	26.7
Lorri Bauman, Drake	1981–84	120	1104	—	907	3115	26.0
Andrea Congreaves, Mercer	1989–93	108	1107	153	429	2796	25.9
Cindy Blodgett, Maine	1994–98	118	1055	219	676	3005	25.5
Valorie Whiteside, Appalachian St	1984–88	116	1153	0	638	2944	25.4
Joyce Walker, Louisiana St	1981–84	117	1259	—	388	2906	24.8
Jackie Stiles, SW Missouri St	1997-	94	795	156	585	2331	24.8
Tarcha Hollis, Grambling	1988–91	85	904	3	247	2058	24.2
Korie Hlede, Duquesne	1994–98	109	1045	162	379	2631	24.1
Karen Pelphrey, Marshall	1983–86	114	1175	—	396	2746	24.1

NCAA Men's Division II Championship Results

Year	Winner	Score	Runner-up	Third Place	Fourth Place
1957	Wheaton (IL)	89–65	Kentucky Wesleyan	Mount St Mary's (MD)	Cal St-Los Angeles
1958	S Dakota	75–53	St. Michael's	Evansville	Wheaton (IL)
1959	Evansville	83–67	SW Missouri St	N Carolina A&T	Cal St-Los Angeles
1960	Evansville	90–69	Chapman	Kentucky Wesleyan	Cornell College
1961	Wittenberg	42–38	SE Missouri St	S Dakota St	Mount St Mary's (MD)
1962	Mount St Mary's (MD)	58–57 (OT)	Cal St-Sacramento	Southern Illinois	Nebraska Wesleyan
1963	S Dakota St	44–42	Wittenberg	Oglethorpe	Southern Illinois
1964	Evansville	72–59	Akron	N Carolina A&T	Northern Iowa
1965	Evansville	85–82 (OT)	Southern Illinois	N Dakota	St Michael's
1966	Kentucky Wesleyan	54–51	Southern Illinois	Akron	N Dakota
1967	Winston-Salem	77–74	SW Missouri St	Kentucky Wesleyan	Illinois St
1968	Kentucky Wesleyan	63–52	Indiana St	Trinity (TX)	Ashland
1969	Kentucky Wesleyan	75–71	SW Missouri St	†Vacated	Ashland
1970	Philadelphia Textile	76–65	Tennessee St	UC-Riverside	Buffalo St
1971	Evansville	97–82	Old Dominion	†Vacated	Kentucky Wesleyan
1972	Roanoke	84–72	Akron	Tennessee St	Eastern Mich
1973	Kentucky Wesleyan	78–76 (OT)	Tennessee St	Assumption	Brockport St
1974	Morgan St	67–52	SW Missouri St	Assumption	New Orleans
1975	Old Dominion	76–74	New Orleans	Assumption	TN-Chattanooga
1976	Puget Sound	83–74	TN-Chattanooga	Eastern Illinois	Old Dominion
1977	TN-Chattanooga	71–62	Randolph-Macon	N Alabama	Sacred Heart
1978	Cheyney	47–40	WI-Green Bay	Eastern Illinois	Central Florida
1979	N Alabama	64–50	WI-Green Bay	Cheyney	Bridgeport
1980	Virginia Union	80–74	New York Tech	Florida Southern	N Alabama
1981	Florida Southern	73–68	Mount St Mary's (MD)	Cal Poly-SLO	WI-Green Bay
1982	District of Columbia	73–63	Florida Southern	Kentucky Wesleyan	Cal St-Bakersfield
1983	Wright St	92–73	District of Columbia	*Cal St-Bakersfield	*Morningside
1984	Central Missouri St	81–77	St. Augustine's	*Kentucky Wesleyan	*N Alabama
1985	Jacksonville St	74–73	S Dakota St	*Kentucky Wesleyan	*Mount St. Mary's (MD)
1986	Sacred Heart	93–87	SE Missouri St	*Cheyney	*Florida Southern
1987	Kentucky Wesleyan	92–74	Gannon	*Delta St	*Eastern Montana
1988	Lowell	75–72	AK-Anchorage	Florida Southern	Troy St

*Indicates tied for third. †Student-athletes representing American International in 1969 and Southwestern Louisiana in 1971 were declared ineligible subsequent to the tournament. Under NCAA rules, the teams' and ineligible student-athletes' records were deleted, and the teams' places in the final standings were vacated.

Year	Winner	Score	Runner-up	Third Place	Fourth Place
1989	N Carolina Central	73–46	SE Missouri St	UC-Riverside	Jacksonville St
1990	Kentucky Wesleyan	93–79	Cal St-Bakersfield	N Dakota	Morehouse
1991	N Alabama	79–72	Bridgeport (CT)	*Cal St-Bakersfield	*Virginia Union
1992	Virginia Union	100–75	Bridgeport (CT)	*Cal St-Bakersfield	*California (PA)
1993	Cal St-Bakersfield	85–72	Troy St (AL)	*New Hampshire Coll	*Wayne St (MI)
1994	Cal St-Bakersfield	92–86	Southern Indiana	*New Hampshire Coll	*Washburn
1995	Southern Indiana	71–63	UC-Riverside	*Norfolk St	*Indiana (PA)
1996	Fort Hays St	70–63	Northern Kentucky	*California (PA)	*Virginia Union
1997	Cal St-Bakersfield	57–56	Northern Kentucky	*Lynn	*Salem-Teikyo
1998	UC-Davis	83–77	Kentucky Wesleyan	*St. Rose	*Virginia Union
1999	Kentucky Wesleyan	75–60	Metropolitan St	*Truman St	*Florida Southern
2000	Metropolitan St	97–79	Kentucky Wesleyan	*Missouri Southern	*Seattle Pacific

NCAA Men's Division II Alltime Individual Leaders

SINGLE-GAME SCORING HIGHS

Pts	Player and Team vs Opponent	Date
113	Bevo Francis, Rio Grande vs Hillsdale	1954
84	Bevo Francis, Rio Grande vs Alliance	1954
82	Bevo Francis, Rio Grande vs Bluffton	1954
80	Paul Crissman, Southern Cal Col vs Pacific Christian	1966
77	William English, Winston-Salem vs Fayetteville St	1968

Single Season Records
SCORING AVERAGE

Player and Team	Year	GP	FG	FT	Pts	Avg
Bevo Francis, Rio Grande	1954	27	444	367	1255	46.5
Earl Glass, Mississippi Industrial	1963	19	322	171	815	42.9
Earl Monroe, Winston-Salem	1967	32	509	311	1329	41.5
John Rinka, Kenyon	1970	23	354	234	942	41.0
Willie Shaw, Lane	1964	18	303	121	727	40.4

REBOUND AVERAGE

Player and Team	Year	GP	Reb	Avg
Tom Hart, Middlebury	1956	21	620	29.5
Tom Hart, Middlebury	1955	22	649	29.5
Frank Stronczek, American Int'l	1966	26	717	27.6
R.C. Owens, College of Idaho	1954	25	677	27.1
Maurice Stokes, St Francis (PA)	1954	26	689	26.5

ASSISTS

Player and Team	Year	GP	A
Steve Ray, Bridgeport	1989	32	400
Steve Ray, Bridgeport	1990	33	385
Tony Smith, Pfeiffer	1992	35	349
Jim Ferrer, Bentley	1989	31	309
Rob Paternostro, New Hamp. Coll	1995	33	309

ASSIST AVERAGE

Player and Team	Year	GP	A	Avg
Steve Ray, Bridgeport	1989	32	400	12.5
Steve Ray, Bridgeport	1990	33	385	11.7
Demetri Beekman, Assumption	1993	23	264	11.5
Ernest Jenkins, NM Highlands	1995	27	291	10.8
Brian Gregory, Oakland	1989	28	300	10.7

FIELD-GOAL PERCENTAGE

Player and Team	Year	Pct
Todd Linder, Tampa	1987	75.2
Maurice Stafford, N Alabama	1984	75.0
Matthew Cornegay, Tuskegee	1982	74.8
Brian Moten, W Georgia	1992	73.4
Ed Phillips, Alabama A&M	1968	73.3

FREE-THROW PERCENTAGE

Player and Team	Year	Pct
Paul Cluxton, Northern Kentucky	1997	100.0
Tomas Rimkus, Pace	1997	95.6
Billy Newton, Morgan St	1976	94.4
Kent Andrews, McNeese St	1968	94.4
Mike Sanders, Northern Colorado	1987	94.3

Career Records
POINTS

Player and Team	Yrs	Pts
Travis Grant, Kentucky St	1969–72	4045
Bob Hopkins, Grambling	1953–56	3759
Tony Smith, Pfeiffer	1989–92	3350
Earnest Lee, Clark Atlanta	1984–87	3298
Joe Miller, Alderson-Broaddus	1954–57	3294

Career Records (Cont.)

CAREER SCORING AVERAGE

Player and Team	Yrs	GP	Pts	Avg
Travis Grant, Kentucky St	1969–72	121	4045	33.4
John Rinka, Kenyon	1967–70	99	3251	32.8
Florindo Vieira, Quinnipiac	1954–57	69	2263	32.8
Willie Shaw, Lane	1961–64	76	2379	31.3
Mike Davis, Virginia Union	1966–69	89	2758	31.0

REBOUND AVERAGE

Player and Team	Yrs	GP	Reb	Avg
Tom Hart, Middlebury	1953, 55–56	63	1738	27.6
Maurice Stokes, St. Francis (PA)	1953–55	72	1812	25.2
Frank Stronczek, American Int'l	1965–67	62	1549	25.0
Bill Thieben, Hofstra	1954–56	76	1837	24.2
Hank Brown, Lowell Tech	1965–67	49	1129	23.0

ASSISTS

Player and Team	Yrs	A
Demetri Beekman, Assumption	1990–93	1044
Rob Paternostro, New Hamp. Coll.	1992–95	919
Gallagher Driscoll, St. Rose	1989–92	878
Tony Smith, Pfeiffer	1989–92	828
Jamie Stevens, Montana St-Billings	1996–99	805

ASSIST AVERAGE

Player and Team	Yrs	GP	A	Avg
Steve Ray, Bridgeport	1989–90	65	785	12.1
Demetri Beekman, Assumption	1990–93	119	1044	8.8
Ernest Jenkins, NM Highlands	1992–95	84	699	8.3
Mark Benson, Texas A&I	1989–91	86	674	7.8
Pat Madden, Jacksonville St	1989–91	88	688	7.8

Note: Minimum 550 Assists.

FIELD-GOAL PERCENTAGE

Player and Team	Yrs	Pct
Todd Linder, Tampa	1984–87	70.8
Tom Schurfranz, Bellarmine	1989–92	70.2
Chad Scott, California (PA)	1991–94	70.0
Ed Phillips, Alabama, A&M	1968–71	68.9
Ulysses Hackett, SC-Spartanburg	1990–92	67.9

Note: Minimum 400 FGM.

FREE-THROW PERCENTAGE

Player and Team	Yrs	Pct
Paul Cluxton, Northern Kentucky	1994–97	93.5
Kent Andrews, McNeese St	1967–69	91.6
Jon Hagen, Mankato St	1963–65	90.0
Dave Reynolds, Davis & Elkins	1986–89	89.3
Michael Shue, Lock Haven	1994–97	88.5

Note: Minimum 250 FTM.

NCAA Men's Division III Championship Results

Year	Winner	Score	Runner-up	Third Place	Fourth Place
1975	LeMoyne-Owen	57–54	Glassboro St	Augustana (IL)	Brockport St
1976	Scranton	60–57	Wittenberg	Augustana (IL)	Plattsburgh St
1977	Wittenberg	79–66	Oneonta St	Scranton	Hamline
1978	North Park	69–57	Widener	Albion	Stony Brook
1979	North Park	66–62	Potsdam St	Franklin & Marshall	Centre
1980	North Park	83–76	Upsala	Wittenberg	Longwood
1981	Potsdam St	67–65 (OT)	Augustana (IL)	Ursinus	Otterbein
1982	Wabash	83–62	Potsdam St	Brooklyn	Cal St-Stanislaus
1983	Scranton	64–63	Wittenberg	Roanoke	WI-Whitewater
1984	WI-Whitewater	103–86	Clark (MA)	DePauw	Upsala
1985	North Park	72–71	Potsdam St	Nebraska Wesleyan	Widener
1986	Potsdam St	76–73	LeMoyne-Owen	Nebraska Wesleyan	Jersey City St
1987	North Park	106–100	Clark (MA)	Wittenberg	Stockton St
1988	Ohio Wesleyan	92–70	Scranton	Nebraska Wesleyan	Hartwick
1989	WI-Whitewater	94–86	Trenton St	Southern Maine	Centre
1990	Rochester	43–42	DePauw	Washington (MD)	Calvin
1991	WI-Platteville	81–74	Franklin & Marshall	Otterbein	Ramapo (NJ)
1992	Calvin	62–49	Rochester	WI-Platteville	Jersey City St
1993	Ohio Northern	71–68	Augustana	Mass-Dartmouth	Rowan
1994	Lebanon Valley Coll	66–59 (OT)	New York University	Wittenberg	St Thomas (MN)
1995	WI-Platteville	69–55	Manchester	Rowan	Trinity (CT)
1996	Rowan	100–93	Hope (MI)	Illinois Wesleyan	Franklin & Marshall
1997	Illinois Wesleyan	89–86	Nebraska Wesleyan	Williams	Alvernia
1998	WI-Platteville	69–56	Hope (MI)	Williams	Wilkes
1999	WI-Platteville	76–75 (2 OT)	Hampden-Sydney	William Paterson	Connecticut Coll.
2000	Calvin	79–74	WI-Eau Claire	Salem St	Franklin & Marshall

SINGLE-GAME SCORING HIGHS

Pts	Player and Team vs Opponent	Year
77	Jeff Clement, Grinnell vs Illinois College	1998
69	Steve Diekmann, Grinnell vs Simpson	1995
63	Joe DeRoche, Thomas vs St. Joseph's (ME)	1988
62	Shannon Lilly, Bishop vs Southwest Assembly of God	1983
61	Steve Honderd, Calvin vs Kalamazoo	1993
61	Dana Wilson, Husson vs Ricker	1974

Single Season Records

SCORING AVERAGE

Player and Team	Year	GP	FG	FT	Pts	Avg
Steve Diekmann, Grinnell	1995	20	223	162	745	37.3
Rickey Sutton, Lyndon St	1976	14	207	93	507	36.2
Shannon Lilly, Bishop	1983	26	345	218	908	34.9
Dana Wilson, Husson	1974	20	288	122	698	34.9
Rickey Sutton, Lyndon St	1977	16	223	112	558	34.9

REBOUND AVERAGE

Player and Team	Year	GP	Reb	Avg
Joe Manley, Bowie St	1976	29	579	20.0
Fred Petty, New Hampshire College	1974	22	436	19.8
Larry Williams, Pratt	1977	24	457	19.0
Charles Greer, Thomas	1977	17	318	18.7
Larry Parker, Plattsburgh St	1975	23	430	18.7

ASSISTS

Player and Team	Year	GP	A
Robert James, Kean	1989	29	391
Ricky Spicer, WI-Whitewater	1989	31	295
Joe Marcotte, New Jersey Tech	1995	30	292
Andre Bolton, Chris. Newport	1996	30	289
Ron Torgalski, Hamilton	1989	26	275

ASSIST AVERAGE

Player and Team	Year	GP	A	Avg
Robert James, Kean	1989	29	391	13.5
Albert Kirchner, Mt. St. Vincent	1990	24	267	11.1
Ron Torgalski, Hamilton	1989	26	275	10.6
Louis Adams, Rust	1989	22	227	10.3
Eric Johnson, Coe	1991	24	238	9.9

FIELD-GOAL PERCENTAGE

Player and Team	Year	Pct
Travis Weiss, St. John's (MN)	1994	76.6
Pete Metzelaars, Wabash	1982	75.3
Tony Rychlec, Mass. Maritime	1981	74.9
Tony Rychlec, Mass. Maritime	1982	73.1
Russ Newnan, Menlo	1991	73.0

FREE-THROW PERCENTAGE

Player and Team	Year	Pct
Korey Coon, IL Wesleyan	2000	96.3
Chanse Young, Manchester	1998	95.6
Andy Enfield, Johns Hopkins	1991	95.3
Chris Carideo, Widener	1992	95.2
Yudi Teichman, Yeshiva	1989	95.2

Career Records

POINTS

Player and Team	Yrs	Pts
Andre Foreman, Salisbury St	1989–92	2940
Lamont Strothers, Chris. Newport	1988–91	2709
Matt Hancock, Colby	1987–90	2678
Scott Fitch, Geneseo St	1990–94	2634
Greg Grant, Trenton St	1987–89	2611

CAREER SCORING AVERAGE

Player and Team	Yrs	GP	Avg
Dwain Govan, Bishop	1974–75	55	32.8
Dave Russell, Shepherd	1974–75	60	30.6
Rickey Sutton, Lyndon St	1976–79	80	29.7
John Atkins, Knoxville	1976–78	70	28.7
Steve Peknik, Windham	1974–77	76	27.6

REBOUND AVERAGE

Player and Team	Yrs	GP	Reb	Avg
Larry Parker, Plattsburgh St	1975–78	85	1482	17.4
Charles Greer, Thomas	1975–77	58	926	16.0
Willie Parr, LeMoyne-Owen	1974–76	76	1182	15.6
Michael Smith, Hamilton	1989–92	107	1632	15.2
Dave Kufeld, Yeshiva	1977–80	81	1222	15.1
E. Owens, Hampden-Sydney	1977–80	77	1160	15.1

ASSIST AVERAGE

Player and Team	Yrs	Avg
Phil Dixon, Shenandoah	1993–96	8.6
Steve Artis, Chris. Newport	1990–93	8.1
David Genovese, Mt. St. Vincent	1992–95	7.5
Kevin Root, Eureka	1989–91	7.1
Dennis Jacobi, Bowdoin	1989–92	7.1

Hockey

Scott Stevens of the
Stanley Cup champion
New Jersey Devils.

Devils' Triumph

A heartstopping postseason and a thrilling Cup run by New Jersey overshadowed some fiendish behavior on and off the ice

BY DAVID FLEMING

HE WAS THREE MILES away, sitting in a hospital bed at the Baylor University Medical Center in downtown Dallas, but there were subtle reminders everywhere of New Jersey winger Petr Sykora after the Devils won the Stanley Cup across town in Reunion Arena. Devils coach Larry Robinson donned Sykora's jersey when it was his turn to hoist Lord Stanley's trophy. During the locker room celebration a cell phone passed from player to player so teammates could chat with Sykora as they sipped champagne and then beer from the Cup. And later, winger Patrick Elias walked through a cloud of cigar smoke inside the Devils' locker room wearing his injured teammate's jersey backward so that Sykora's name was facing front.

Sykora had been knocked off balance by Stars defenseman Sylvain Coté and then leveled by Derian Hatcher, who sent him sprawling to the ice, where he lay flat and motionless for several minutes. Sykora, the Devils' leading goal scorer in the playoffs, was eventually strapped to a board and taken to the hospital. Fortunately, his CAT scan was normal, but he was kept in the hospital overnight anyway. "I'll take the Cup to him in the hospital myself, if I have to," said Devils winger Jason Arnott.

While Arnott may not have transported the trophy to the hospital, he certainly delivered the Cup to the Devils. With 8:20 left in the second overtime of Game 6, the 25-year-old winger flicked the puck from the top of the Dallas crease over Stars' goalie Ed Belfour and into the top of the net for the Cup-winner. The goal was especially sweet for Arnott, who had been knocked out of Game 4 by Hatcher (the Body Snatcher), who dealt him a blow to the head so vicious it broke Arnott's six-tooth bridge. But afterward the only player on Arnott's mind was Sykora. "We said we have to do this for our boy [Sykora]," said Arnott. "So there's no question that goal was for him."

Of course, the goal made a lot of other people pretty happy, too. In addition to securing the Devils and their faithful their second championship in six years, Arnott's

DAVID E. KLUTHO

championship winner provided an ideal send-off for New Jersey owner John McMullen, who, with much public handwringing, was in the process of selling the Devils for $175 million to George Steinbrenner's YankeeNets. (McMullen bought the Devils in 1982 for a measly $10 million.) The triumph also vindicated general manager Lou Lamoriello, who made the gutsy and controversial decision to dump Devils coach Robbie Ftorek with eight games remaining in the regular season—a move that infused the sluggish club with new life. "We did it the hard way," said goalie Martin Brodeur. "It's so nice to win with all that adversity."

Believe it Arnott, the Cup-winning goal also made the Devils only the sixth team in NHL history to win three road games in the Stanley Cup finals. As impressive as that distinction is, it pales in comparison to the record tied by the NHL's true road warriors of 1999–2000, the St. Louis Blues, who won 10 straight regular-season road games to equal the mark set by the 1983–84 Buffalo Sabres. The Blues' road rage was powered by defenseman Chris Pronger, who won the regular-season MVP award, the Hart Trophy.

Arnott scored eight goals in the playoffs, including the Cup-winner in double OT.

The St. Louis captain emerged as the league's best player in 1998–99, when he averaged a league-high 30:24 of ice time and racked up a +40 plus-minus rating. Pronger became the first defenseman since Bobby Orr in 1972 to win both the Hart Trophy and the Norris Trophy as the NHL's best defenseman. "He's the most dominant player in the league," said Flyers wing Rick Tocchet. "He shuts everybody down." Well, maybe not everybody. Although the Blues led the league with 114 points during the regular season, they were bumped off in the playoffs by No. 8 seed San Jose.

The Devils were nearly rubbed out of the playoffs themselves, by Philadelphia in the Eastern Conference finals. New Jersey rallied from a three-games-to-one deficit in that series, a feat unmatched that deep in the playoffs during the last 33 years. The first champions of the 21st century, the Devils were both a throwback to old-time hockey (tough defense, heart-on-the-sleeve loyalty to their fallen teammate) and a

Pronger (left) was named league MVP, while Lindros (center) struggled in Philly.

promising vision of the NHL's future (taut, quality hockey contested by increasingly diverse players, such as the Devils' Rookie of the Year forward, Scott Gomez, the league's first Hispanic player.)

The undisputed leader of this unique and selfless bunch was captain Scott Stevens, a hard-charging defenseman. The Conn Smythe Trophy winner as the playoff MVP, Stevens played the entire postseason with a stinging pinched nerve in his neck. Yet he rose to the occasion whenever it mattered most. He helped the Devils survive a savage first period against the Stars

in the decisive Game 6 of the Finals, and in Game 7 against the Flyers in the previous round, Stevens played so well that some observers called his performance one of the greatest playoff games ever by an NHL defenseman.

In the first period the 6'1", 215-pound Stevens pulverized Philly forward Keith Primeau. He also blocked five shots. But to his great dismay, Stevens will forever be known as the guy who delivered the hit that knocked Flyers center Eric Lindros out of Game 7 and perhaps out of the NHL for good with his sixth concussion. Stevens stuck Lindros with a clean hit as the Philadelphia center carried the puck into the Devils' zone with his head down. "I've never seen a player so physically dominating," said Devils center Bobby Holik. "Teams were like, 'Oh, hey, let's not go this way, there's Scott Stevens.'"

Another player the Devils' opponents tried to bypass, but couldn't, was Brodeur. The New Jersey netminder was nearly flawless in Game 6 as he held up his end of a tremendous goaltending duel with Belfour, his Dallas counterpart. Belfour had a nightmare in the Cup opener, giving up six goals on only 18 shots in the Stars' 7–3 loss, a debacle he promptly blamed on a dose of cold medicine that had made him sluggish. Whatever the cause of his poor start, Belfour recovered beautifully. In Games 5 and 6, the Stars and the Devils combined for 165 shots in three hours, 14 minutes and 41 seconds of play. Only four goals were put past Belfour and Brodeur in that span, and they combined for a gold-plated save percentage of .976.

In Game 4 of the Eastern Conference semifinals, the Penguins and the Flyers staged a similarly tense and high-quality duel as they battled for seven hours and most of five overtimes. The third-longest game in NHL history (2:32:01), it was settled by Primeau, who wristed in the game-winner with 7:59 left in OT No. 5, the eighth period of hockey the teams had played that night. The Flyers were too exhausted to celebrate, as were most of the 5,000 die-hard fans who had stayed until 2:35 a.m. to see the 2–1 win. Said Pittsburgh superstar Jaromir Jagr, "You don't even know you're playing hockey. You're skating, but you can't even think."

Mind-altering action on the ice has long been Jagr's specialty. The dazzling right-winger scored 42 goals and led the league with 96 points in 1999–2000. His peers voted him the league's most outstanding player, and he lost out to Pronger for the Hart Trophy by one vote. Florida forward Pavel Bure, who led the league with 58 goals, tied Jagr for second in the Hart voting. Fully recovered from an ACL injury he suffered a year ago, Bure became just the second European player to score a hat trick in the NHL All-Star Game. In a 13-game span during December, Bure scored 12 goals and passed off for 10 assists, prompting teammate Scott Mellanby to say, "What he brings to the team is, obviously, the entire offense."

There was a time not too long ago when Bruins defenseman Ray Bourque seemed to be both the entire offense *and* the entire defense in Boston. That's stretching a point, certainly, but Bourque was the only marquee name on the Bruins' roster for much of the '80s and '90s, and his title hopes were fading. In March the Bruins gracefully complied with his wish to go to a contender to pursue his Stanley Cup dream. Alas, Bourque and his new team, Colorado, were eliminated by Dallas in Game 7 of the Western Conference finals.

The classy move by Boston to let Bourque go, the scintillating play of the league's stars and the heart-stopping post-season were welcome antidotes to a year plagued by ugly incidents and bad news on and off the ice. In Montreal the league lost an icon and one of its alltime greats when Hall of Famer Maurice (the Rocket) Richard died at the age of 78 in May. The Rocket's 50 goals in 50 games in the 1944–45 season are an NHL landmark. He led the league in goals five times and led his hometown Canadiens to eight Stanley Cups.

The Montreal family had already experienced hardship in 2000. On Jan. 20, Canadiens forward Trent McCleary nearly died from a fractured larynx after diving headfirst to block a slap shot. McCleary, who underwent emergency medical treatment on the ice to restore his breathing, spent the rest of the season recuperating from his injury. The Habs struggled in the standings as well, going 35-38-9 and missing the playoffs. It was the first time since 1944 that Montreal had gone seven seasons without winning the Cup.

In Ottawa, in what has become one of the sporting world's ugliest contract squabbles, Senators forward Alexei Yashin sat out the entire season (his third holdout in his six-year career), refusing to honor the fifth year of the $13.5 million contract he signed in 1995. In an unprecedented move, disgruntled fans in Ottawa tried in vain to sue

Bourque's 21-year quest for the Cup took him to Colorado but remained unfulfilled.

Flyers went on to a 2–0 win and a 3–0 lead in the series. Fans placards at Game 4 said it all: HOLY NET, BETTMAN, NO GOAL. "Embarrassing is what it is," said Sabres right wing Dixon Ward.

Embarrassing might be the kindest word to describe the actions of Bruins defenseman Marty McSorley. In the closing minutes of a Boston-Vancouver game in February, McSorley skated up behind the Canucks'

Yashin for not playing. An arbitrator later ruled that Yashin would remain under contract to the Senators for one more year.

In Philadelphia, the Flyers minted their title as Team Controversy. Even though the team had stripped him of his captaincy, Lindros made a courageous but perhaps ill-advised return to the ice after a two-month layoff following his fourth and fifth concussions. By comparison to coach Roger Neilson, Lindros got off easy. When Neilson wanted to return to the bench after undergoing cancer treatment, the team replied with a curt no thanks and left Craig Ramsay in charge. Neither Neilson nor Lindros felt much Brotherly Love in Philly.

In Buffalo, where fans still bemoan Dallas forward Brett Hull's controversial 1999 Cup–winning goal, the Sabres were once again victims of questionable officiating. No Goal II, as Buffalo fans now refer to it, came in Game 2 of the Eastern Conference quarterfinals. Philly wing John LeClair unleashed a shot that replays clearly showed went through the twine on the outside of the right post. But NHL replay officials, who did not catch the error until several minutes later, after play had resumed, allowed the play to stand. The

Donald Brashear, and in an attempt to entice Brashear into a brawl, whacked him in the temple with his stick. Brashear fell backward and hit his head on the ice. He suffered a severe concussion that left him bleeding and twitching on the ice. The entire scene was caught on videotape and replayed ad nauseam as the sports world's ugliest incident in 1999–2000. A 17-year veteran, McSorley was immediately suspended for the remaining 23 games of the season (the harshest penalty ever handed down by the NHL for an on-ice infraction) and was later tried on criminal charges by prosecutors in British Columbia.

Thankfully, though, no amount of bad news could overshadow what the Devils accomplished in the postseason. As they left Reunion Arena hours after Game 6, Stevens and defenseman Scott Niedermayer paused for a quiet moment near a loading dock. There, sitting on a dolly by itself in the still Dallas night, was the Stanley Cup. Niedermayer and Stevens walked over and gave the trophy one final rub before it was wheeled off and shipped to its first house call. Sitting up in his hospital bed well after doctors had told him to get some sleep, Petr Sykora waited for the Cup to arrive.

NHL Final Standings

Eastern Conference

NORTHEAST DIVISION

	GP	W	L	T	RT	GF	GA	Pts
Toronto	82	45	30	7	3	246	222	100
Ottawa	82	41	30	11	2	244	210	95
Buffalo	82	35	36	11	4	213	204	85
Montreal	82	35	38	9	4	196	194	83
Boston	82	24	39	19	6	210	248	73

ATLANTIC DIVISION

	GP	W	L	T	RT	GF	GA	Pts
Philadelphia	82	45	25	12	3	237	179	105
New Jersey	82	45	29	8	5	251	203	103
Pittsburgh	82	37	37	8	6	241	236	88
NY Rangers	82	29	41	12	3	218	246	73
NY Islanders	82	24	49	9	1	194	275	58

SOUTHEAST DIVISION

	GP	W	L	T	RT	GF	GA	Pts
Washington	82	44	26	12	2	227	194	102
Florida	82	43	33	6	6	244	209	98
Carolina	82	37	35	10	0	217	216	84
Tampa Bay	82	19	54	9	7	204	310	54
Atlanta	82	14	61	7	4	170	313	39

Western Conference

CENTRAL DIVISION

	GP	W	L	T	RT	GF	GA	Pts
St. Louis	82	51	20	11	1	248	165	114
Detroit	82	48	24	10	2	278	210	108
Chicago	82	33	39	10	2	242	245	78
Nashville	82	28	47	7	7	199	240	70

PACIFIC DIVISION

	GP	W	L	T	RT	GF	GA	Pts
Dallas	82	43	29	10	6	211	184	102
Los Angeles	82	39	31	12	4	245	228	94
Phoenix	82	39	35	8	4	232	228	90
San Jose	82	35	37	10	7	225	214	87
Anaheim	82	34	36	12	3	217	227	83

NORTHWEST DIVISION

	GP	W	L	T	RT	GF	GA	Pts
Colorado	82	42	29	11	1	233	201	96
Edmonton	82	32	34	16	8	226	212	88
Vancouver	82	30	37	15	8	227	237	83
Calgary	82	31	41	10	5	211	256	77

RT=regulation ties—games lost in overtime; worth 1 pt.

2000 Stanley Cup Playoffs

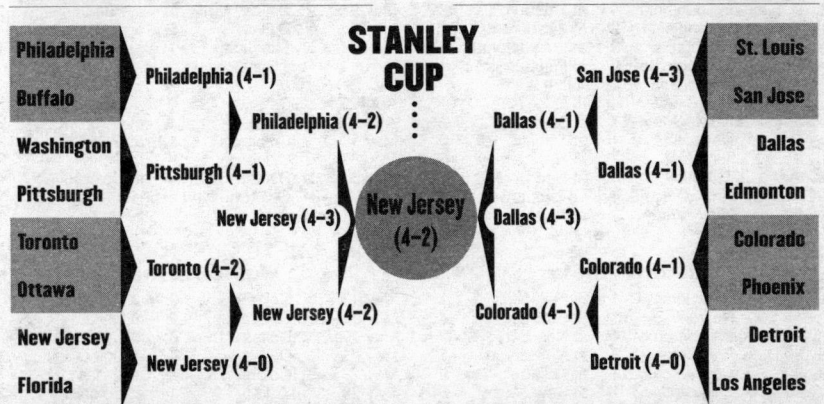

EASTERN CONFERENCE

QUARTERFINALS · SEMIFINALS · CONFERENCE FINAL

WESTERN CONFERENCE

CONFERENCE FINAL · SEMIFINALS · QUARTERFINALS

STANLEY CUP

New Jersey (4–2)

Philadelphia · Buffalo · Washington · Pittsburgh · Toronto · Ottawa · New Jersey · Florida

Philadelphia (4–1)
Philadelphia (4–2)
Pittsburgh (4–1)
New Jersey (4–3)
Toronto (4–2)
New Jersey (4–2)
New Jersey (4–0)

San Jose (4–3) · St. Louis · San Jose
Dallas (4–1) · Dallas
Dallas (4–1) · Edmonton
Dallas (4–3) · Colorado
Colorado (4–1) · Phoenix
Colorado (4–1) · Detroit
Detroit (4–0) · Los Angeles

Stanley Cup Playoff Results

Conference Quarterfinals

EASTERN CONFERENCE

April 13	Buffalo	2	at Philadelphi	3
April 14	Buffalo	1	at Philadelphia	2
April 16	Philadelphia	1	at Buffalo	0
April 18	Philadelphia	2	at Buffalo	3*
April 20	Buffalo	2	at Philadelphia	5

Philadelphia won series 4–1.

Conference Quarterfinals (Cont.)

EASTERN CONFERENCE (Cont.)

April 13	Pittsburgh	7	at Washington	0			
April 14	Pittsburgh	2	at Washington	1*			
April 16	Washington	3	at Pittsburgh	4			
April 18	Washington	3	at Pittsburgh	2			
April 20	Pittsburgh	2	at Washington	1			

Pittsburgh won series 4–1.

April 12	Ottawa	0	at Toronto	2
April 15	Ottawa	2	at Toronto	5
April 17	Toronto	3	at Ottawa	4
April 19	Toronto	1	at Ottawa	2
April 22	Ottawa	1	at Toronto	2*
April 24	Toronto	4	at Ottawa	2

Toronto won series 4–2.

April 13	Florida	3	at New Jersey	4
April 16	Florida	1	at New Jersey	2
April 18	New Jersey	2	at Florida	1

April 20	New Jersey	4	at Florida	1

New Jersey won series 4–0.

WESTERN CONFERENCE

April 12	San Jose	3	at St. Louis	5
April 15	San Jose	4	at St. Louis	2
April 17	St. Louis	1	at San Jose	2
April 19	St. Louis	2	at San Jose	3
April 21	San Jose	3	at St. Louis	5
April 23	St. Louis	6	at San Jose	2
April 25	San Jose	3	at St. Louis	1

San Jose won series 4–3.

April 13	Phoenix	3	at Colorado	6
April 15	Phoenix	1	at Colorado	3
April 17	Colorado	4	at Phoenix	2
April 19	Colorado	2	at Phoenix	3
April 21	Phoenix	1	at Colorado	2

Colorado won series 4–1.

April 12	Edmonton	1	at Dallas	2
April 13	Edmonton	0	at Dalas	3
April 16	Dallas	2	at Edmonton	5
April 18	Dallas	4	at Edmonton	3
April 21	Edmonton	2	at Dallas	3

Dallas won series 4–1.

April 13	Los Angeles	0	at Detroit	2
April 15	Los Angeles	5	at Detroit	8
April 17	Detroit	2	at Los Angeles	1
April 19	Detroit	3	at Los Angeles	0

Detroit won series 4–0.

Conference Semifinals

EASTERN CONFERENCE

April 27	Pittsburgh	2	at Philadelphia	0
April 29	Pittsburgh	4	at Philadelphia	1
May 2	Philadelphia	4	at Pittsburgh	3*
May 4	Philadelphia	2	at Pittsburgh	1**
May 7	Pittsburgh	3	at Philadelphia	6
May 9	Philadelphia	2	at Pittsburgh	1

Philadelphia won series 4–2.

WESTERN CONFERENCE

April 28	San Jose	0	at Dallas	4
April 30	San Jose	0	at Dallas	1
May 2	Dallas	1	at San Jose	2
May 5	Dallas	5	at San Jose	4
May 7	San Jose	1	at Dallas	4

Dallas won series 4–1.

April 27	New Jersey	1	at Toronto	2
April 29	New Jersey	1	at Toronto	0
May 1	Toronto	1	at New Jersey	5
May 3	Toronto	3	at New Jersey	2
May 6	New Jersey	4	at Toronto	3
May 8	New Jersey	3	at Toronto	0

New Jersey won series 4–2.

April 27	Detroit	0	at Colorado	2
April 29	Detroit	1	at Colorado	3
May 1	Colorado	1	at Detroit	3
May 3	Colorado	3	at Detroit	2*
May 5	Detroit	2	at Colorado	4

Colorado won series 4–1.

Eastern Finals

May 14	New Jersey	4	at Philadelphia	1
May 16	New Jersey	2	at Philadelphia	4
May 18	Philadelphia	4	at New Jersey	2
May 20	Philadelphia	3	at New Jersey	1
May 22	New Jersey	4	at Philadelphia	2
May 24	Philadelphia	1	at New Jersey	2
May 26	New Jersey	2	at Philadelphia	1

New Jersey won series 4–3.

Western Finals

May 13	Colorado	2	at Dallas	0
May 15	Colorado	2	at Dallas	3
May 19	Dallas	0	at Colorado	2
May 21	Dallas	4	at Colorado	1
May 23	Colorado	2	at Dallas	3*
May 25	Dallas	1	at Colorado	2
May 27	Colorado	2	at Dallas	3

Dallas won series 4–3.

Stanley Cup Finals

May 30	Dallas	3	at New Jersey	7
June 1	Dallas	2	at New Jersey	1
June 3	New Jersey	2	at Dallas	1
June 5	New Jersey	3	at Dallas	1

June 8	Dallas	1	at New Jersey	0#
June 10	New Jersey	2	at Dallas	1†

New Jersey won series 4–2.

*Overtime game. †Double overtime game. # Triple overtime game **Quintuple overtime game.

Stanley Cup Championship Box Scores

Game 1

```
Dallas..............1    0    2—3
New Jersey......1    3    3—7
```

FIRST PERIOD

Scoring: 1, NJ, Arnott 5 (Sykora, Elias), 7:22. 2, Dallas, Sydor 1 (Lehtinen, Keane), 13:13. Penalties: None.

SECOND PERIOD

Scoring: 3, NJ, Daneyko 1 (Brylin, Madden), 2:52. 4, NJ, Sykora 7 (Elias, Arnott), 10:28. 5, NJ, Stevens 3 (Pandolfo, Rafalski), 16:04. Penalties: Hatcher, Dall (slashing), 18:20.

THIRD PERIOD

Scoring: 6, NJ, Brylin 2 (McKay), 2:21. 7, NJ, Sykora 8 (Arnott, Elias), 3:02. 8, NJ, Arnott 6 (power play)

THIRD PERIOD *(CONT.)*

(Holik, Sykora), 5:12. 9, Dall, Sim 1 (Carbonneau), 7:43. 10, Dall, Muller 2 (Carbonneau), 7:43. Penalties: Thornton, Dall (roughing), 3:35; Manson, Dall (slashing), 12:05; Manson, Dall (elbowing), 19:55.

Shots on goal: Dallas—5-7-6—18. NJ—7-9-10—26. Power-play opportunities: Dall 0 of 0, NJ 1 of 4. Goalies: Dall, Belfour (18 shots, 12 saves), Fernandez (8 shots, 7 saves), NJ Brodeur (18 shots, 15 saves). A: 19,040.

Referees: Koharski, McCreary. Linesmen: Scapinello, Sharrers.

Game 2

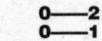

```
Dallas..............1    0    1—2
New Jersey......1    0    0—1
```

FIRST PERIOD

Scoring: 1, Dall, Hull 10 (Modano, Matvichuk), 4:25. 2, NJ, Mogilny 4 (Gomez, Stevens), 12:42. Penalties: Lemieux, NJ (holding), 8:20; Sloan, Dall (roughing), 10:56; Rafalski, NJ (roughing), 10:56; Matvichuk, Dall (roughing), 13:52; Holik, NJ (roughing), 13:52; Matvichuk, Dall (roughing), 18:27.

SECOND PERIOD

Scoring: None. Penalties: None.

THIRD PERIOD

Scoring: 3, Dall, Hull 11 (Lehtinen, Modano), 15:44. Penalties: Sim, Dall (hooking), 10:48.

Shots on goal: Dall—3-7-7—17. NJ—9-8-11—28. Power-play opportunities: Dall 0-of-1; NJ 0-of-2. Goalies: Dall, Belfour (28 shots, 27 saves), NJ, Brodeur (17 shots, 15 saves). A: 19,040. Referees: Fraser, Marouelli. Linesmen: Broseker, Schachte.

Game 3

```
New Jersey......1    1    0—2
Dallas..............1    0    0—1
```

FIRST PERIOD

Scoring:1, Dall, Cote 2 (power play) (unassisted), 13:08. 2, NJ, Arnott 7 (Rafalski, White), 18:06. Penalties: Nemchinov, NJ (slashing), 12:46; Malakhov, NJ (interference), 13:51; Lemieux, NJ (cross checking), 15:02.

SECOND PERIOD

Scoring: 3, NJ, Sykora 9 (power play) (Arnott, Rafalski), 12:27. Penalties: Hull, Dall (interference), 8:09; Cote, Dall (elbowing), 11:03.

THIRD PERIOD

Scoring: None. Penalties: Brodeur, NJ served by Arnott (Delay of game), 15:45.

Shots on goal: NJ—10-16-5—31. Dall—7-9-7—23. Power-play opportunities: NJ 1-of-2; Dall 1-of-4. Goalies: NJ, Brodeur (23 shots, 22 saves), Dall, Belfour (31 shots, 30 saves). A: 17,001. Referees: Gregson, Koharski. Linesmen: Scapinello, Sharrers.

Game 4

```
New Jersey......0    0    3—3
Dallas..............0    1    0—1
```

FIRST PERIOD

Scoring: None. Penalties: Morrow, Dall (tripping), 14:38; Manson, Dall (slashing), 17:27; Niedermayer, NJ (holding), 19:34.

SECOND PERIOD

Scoring: 1, Dall, Nieuwendyk 7 (power play) (Sydor, Hull), 18:02. Penalties: Sykora, NJ (hooking), 5:45; Keane, Dall (boarding), 8:45; McKay, NJ (hooking), 11:59; Malakhov, NJ (cross checking), 16:38.

THIRD PERIOD

Scoring: 2, NJ, Brylin 3 (Mogilny, Malakhov), 2:27. 3, NJ, Madden 3 (shorthanded) (Nemchinov, Daneyko), 4:51. 4, NJ, Rafalski 2 (Elias), 6:08. Penalties: White, NJ (interference), 3:17; Sim, Dall (slashing), 11:43.

Shots on goal: NJ—8-8-15—31. Dall—6-7-4—17. Power-play opportunities: NJ 0-of-4; Dall 1-of-5. Goalies: NJ, Brodeur (17 shots, 16 saves), Dall, Belfour (31 shots, 28 saves). A: 17,001. Referees: Fraser, McCreary. Linesmen: Broseker, Schachte.

Game 5

Dallas	0	0	0	0	0	1—1
New Jersey	0	0	0	0	0	0—0

FIRST PERIOD
Scoring: None. Penalties: Hatcher, Dall (hooking), 11:01; Holik, NJ (interference), 11:43.

SECOND PERIOD
Scoring: None. Penalties: Sykora, NJ (high sticking), 17:01.

THIRD PERIOD
Scoring: None. Penalties: Morrow, Dall (tripping), 13:45.

THIRD OVERTIME
Scoring: 1, Dall, Modano 10 (Hull, Lehtinen), 6:21.

Shots on goal: Dall—11-6-5-5-12-2—41. NJ—7-11-9-10-8-3—48. Power-play opportunities: Dall 0-of-2; NJ 0-of-3. Goalies: Dall, Belfour (48 shots, 48 saves); NJ, Brodeur (41 shots, 40 saves). A: 19,040.
Referees: Marouelli, Koharski. Linesmen: Scapinello, Sharrers.

Game 6

New Jersey	0	1	0	0	1—2
Dallas	0	1	0	0	0—1

FIRST PERIOD
Scoring: None. Penalties: Daneyko, NJ (slashing), 4:46; Sim, Dall (elbowing), 6:54; Daneyko, NJ (high sticking), 13:45.

SECOND PERIOD
Scoring: 1, NJ, Niedermayer 5 (shorthanded) (Lemieux, Pandolfo), 5:18. 2, Dall, Keane 2 (Thornton, Modano), 6:27. Penalties: Rafalski, NJ (holding), 3:30; Stevens, NJ (roughing), 13:48; Hatcher, Dall (roughing), 13:48; White, NJ (roughing), 19:21; Thornton, Dall (roughing), 19:21.

THIRD PERIOD
Scoring: None.

SECOND OVERTIME
Scoring: 3, NJ, Arnott 8 (Elias, Stevens), 8:20.

Shots on goal: NJ—11-13-7-11-3—45. Dall—7-9-13-1-1—31. Power-play opportunities: NJ 0-of-1; Dall 0-for-4. Goalies: NJ, Brodeur (31 shots, 30 saves); Dall, Belfour (45 shots, 43 saves). A: 17,001.
Referees: Gregson, McCreary. Linesmen: Broseker, Schachte.

Individual Playoff Leaders

Scoring

POINTS

Player and Team	GP	G	A	Pts	+/–	PM
Brett Hull, Dall	23	11	13	24	3	4
Mike Modano, Dall	23	10	13	23	3	10
Jason Arnott, NJ	23	8	12	20	7	18
Patrik Elias, NJ	23	7	13	20	9	9
Mark Recchi, Phil	18	6	12	18	3	6
Petr Sykora, NJ	23	9	8	17	8	10
Jaromir Jagr, Pitt	11	8	8	16	5	6
Peter Forsberg, Col	16	8	15	9	12	
Adam Deadmarsh, Col	17	4	11	15	7	21
Chris Drury, Col	17	4	10	14	7	4
John LeClair, Phil	18	6	7	13	3	6
Keith Primeau, Phil	18	2	11	13	-4	13
Jan Hrdina, Pitt	9	4	8	12	9	2
Martin Straka, Pitt	11	3	9	12	5	10
Eric Desjardins, Phil	18	2	10	12	1	2
Rick Tocchet, Phil	18	5	6	11	-2	49
Scott Stevens, NJ	23	3	8	11	9	6
Owen Nolan, SJ	10	8	2	10	-2	6
Joe Nieuwendyk, Dall	23	7	3	10	-2	18
Daymond Langkow, Phil	16	5	5	10	2	23
Simon Gagne, Phil	17	5	5	10	0	2
Sandis Ozolinsh, Col	17	5	5	10	1	20
Jochen Hecht, StL	7	4	6	1-	1	2
Scott Gomez, NJ	23	4	6	10	1	4

GOALS

Player and Team	GP	G
Brett Hull, Dall	23	11
Mike Modano, Dall	23	10
Petr Sykora, NJ	23	9
Owen Nolan, SJ	10	8
Jaromir Jagr, Pitt	11	8
Jason Arnott, NJ	23	8
Peter Forsberg, Col	16	7

GAME-WINNING GOALS

Player and Team	GP	GW
Jaromir Jagr, Pitt	11	4
Peter Forsberg, Col	16	4
Brett Hull, Dall	23	4

Owen Nolan, SJ	10	3
Petr Sykora, NJ	23	3
Ten tied with two.		

POWER PLAY GOALS

Player and Team	GP	PP
Mike Modano, Dall	23	4
John LeClair, Phil	18	4
Seven tied with three.		

SHORT-HANDED GOALS

Player and Team	GP	SH
Scott Niedermayer	22	2
Owen Nolan, SJ	10	2
Ten tied with one.		

ASSISTS

Player and Team	GP	A
Patrik Elias, NJ	23	13
Brett Hull, Dall	23	13
Mike Modano, Dall	23	13
Mark Recchi, Phil	18	12
Jason Arnott, NJ	23	12

PLUS/MINUS

Player and Team	GP	+/–
Jan Hrdina, Pitt	9	9
Peter Forsberg, Col	16	9
Patrik Elias, NJ	23	9
Scott Stevens, NJ	23	9
Colin White, NJ	23	9
Three tied with eight.		

Goaltending (Minimum 420 minutes)

GOALS AGAINST AVERAGE					SAVE PERCENTAGE							
Player and Team	GP	Mins	GA	Avg	Player and Team	GP	Mins	GA	SA	Pct	W	L
Martin Brodeur, NJ	23	1450	39	1.61	Ron Tugnutt, Pitt	11	746	22	376	.945	6	5
Ron Tugnutt, Pitt	11	746	22	1.77	Curtis Joseph, Tor	12	729	25	344	.932	6	6
Patrick Roy, Col	17	1039	31	1.79	Ed Belfour, Dall	23	1443	45	606	.931	14	9
Ed Belfour, Dall	23	1443	45	1.87	Patrick Roy, Col	17	1039	31	400	.928	11	6
Chris Osgood, Det	9	547	18	1.97	Martin Brodeur, NJ	23	1450	39	498	.927	16	7

NHL Awards

Award	Player and Team	Award	Player and Team
Hart Trophy (MVP)	Chris Pronger, StL	Selke Trophy (top defensive forward)	Steve Yzerman, Det
Calder Trophy (top rookie)	Scott Gomez, NJ	Jennings Trophy (goaltender on club allowing fewest goals)	Roman Turek, StL
Vezina Trophy (top goaltender)	Olaf Kolzig, Wash		
Norris Trophy (top defenseman)	Chris Pronger, StL	Conn Smythe Trophy (playoff MVP)	Scott Stevens, NJ
Lady Byng Trophy (for gentlemanly play)	Pavol Demitra, StL		
Adams Award (top coach)	Joel Quenneville, StL		

NHL Individual Leaders

Scoring

POINTS

Player and Team	GP	G	A	Pts	+/–	PM	Player and Team	GP	G	A	Pts	+/–	PM
Jaromir Jagr, Pitt	63	42	54	96	25	50	Brendan Shanahan, Det	78	41	37	78	24	105
Pavel Bure, Fla	74	58	36	94	25	16	Jeremy Roenick, Phoe	75	34	44	78	11	102
Mark Recchi, Phil	82	28	63	91	20	50	John LeClair, Phil	82	40	37	77	8	36
Paul Kariya, Ana	74	42	44	86	22	24	Valeri Bure, Cal	82	35	40	75	-7	50
Teemu Selanne, Ana	79	33	52	85	6	12	Luc Robitaille, LA	71	36	38	74	11	68
Tony Amonte, Chi	82	43	41	84	10	48	Mats Sundin, Tor	73	32	41	73	16	46
Owen Nolan, SJ	78	44	40	84	-1	110	Ron Francis, Car	78	23	50	73	10	18
Joe Sakic, Col	60	28	53	81	30	28	Nicklas Lidstrom, Det	81	20	53	73	19	18
Mike Modano, Dall	77	38	43	81	0	48	Doug Weight, Edm	77	21	51	72	6	54
Steve Yzerman, Det	78	35	44	79	28	34	Milan Hejduk, Col	82	36	36	72	14	16

GOALS

Player and Team	GP	G
Pavel Bure, Fla	74	58
Owen Nolan, SJ	78	44
Tony Amonte, Chi	82	43
Paul Kariya, Ana	74	42
Jaromir Jagr, Pitt	63	42

GAME-WINNING GOALS

Player and Team	GP	GW
Pavel Bure, Fla	74	14
Jeremy Roenick, Phoe	75	12
Four tied with nine.		

ASSISTS

Player and Team	GP	A
Mark Recchi, Phil	82	63
Adam Oates, Wash	82	56
Jaromir Jagr, Pitt	63	54
Nicklas Lidstrom, Det	81	53
Viktor Kizlov, Fla	80	53
Joe Sakic, Col	60	53

POWER PLAY GOALS

Player and Team	GP	PP
Owen Nolan, SJ	78	18
Mariusz Czerkawski, NYI	79	16
Steve Yzerman, Det	78	15
Six tied with 13.		

SHORT-HANDED GOALS

Player and Team	GP	SHG
John Madden, NJ	74	6
Tony Amonte, Chi	82	5
Seven tied with four.		

PLUS/MINUS

Player and Team	GP	+/–
Chris Pronger, StL	79	52
Chris Chelios, Det	81	48
Scott Stevens, NJ	78	30
Joe Sakic, Col	60	30
Pierre Turgeon, StL	52	30

Goaltending (Minimum 25 games)

GOALS AGAINST AVERAGE					SAVE PERCENTAGE							
Player and Team	GP	Mins	GA	Avg	Player and Team	GP	GA	SA	Pct	W	L	T
Brian Boucher, Phil	35	2038	65	1.91	Ed Belfour, Dall	62	127	1444	.919	32	21	7
Roman Turek, StL	67	3960	129	1.95	Jose Theodore, Mon	30	58	659	.919	12	13	2
Jose Theodore, Mon	30	1665	58	2.10	Dominik Hasek, Buff	35	76	861	.919	15	11	6
Ed Belfour, Dall	62	3620	127	2.10	Mike Vernon, Fla	34	83	937	.919	18	13	2
John Vanbiesbrouck, Phil	50	2950	108	2.20	Brian Boucher, Phil	35	65	725	.918	20	10	3
Dominik Hasek, Buff	35	2066	76	2.21	Olaf Kolzig, Wash	73	163	1794	.917	41	20	11
Olaf Kolzig, Wash	73	4371	163	2.24	Curtis Joseph, Tor	63	158	1696	.915	36	20	7

Goaltending (Cont.)

WINS

Player and Team	GP	Mins	W	L	T
Martin Brodeur, NJ	72	4312	43	20	8
Roman Turek, StL	67	3960	42	15	9
Olaf Kolzig, Wash	73	4371	41	20	11
Curtis Joseph, Tor	63	3801	36	20	7
Arturs Irbe, Car	75	4345	34	28	9
Ed Belfour, Dall	62	3620	32	21	7
Patrick Roy, Col	63	3704	32	21	8

SHUTOUTS

Player and Team	GP	Mins	SO	W	L	T
Roman Turek, StL	67	3960	7	42	15	9
Martin Brodeur, NJ	72	4312	6	43	20	8
Chris Osgood, Det	53	3148	6	30	14	8
Olaf Kolzig, Wash	73	4371	5	41	20	11
Arturs Irbe, Car	75	4345	5	34	28	9
Martin Biron, Buff	41	2229	5	19	18	2
Fred Brathwaite, Cal	61	3448	5	25	25	7

NHL Team-by-Team Statistical Leaders

Anaheim Mighty Ducks

SCORING

Player	GP	G	A	Pts	+/–	PM
Paul Kariya, L	74	42	44	86	22	24
Teemu Selanne, R	79	79	33	52	6	12
Steve Rucchin, C	71	19	38	57	9	16
Oleg Tverdovsky, D	82	15	36	51	5	30
Matt Cullen, C	80	13	26	39	5	24
Fredrik Olausson, D	70	15	19	34	-13	28
Ted Donato, R	81	11	19	30	-3	26
Marty Mcinnis, L	62	10	18	28	-4	26
Kip Miller, C	30	6	17	23	1	4
*Ladislav Kohn, L	77	5	16	21	-17	27
Mike Leclerc, R	69	8	11	19	-15	70
Jeff Nielsen, L	79	8	10	18	4	14
Antti Aalto, C	63	7	11	18	-13	26
Pavle Trnka, D	57	2	15	17	12	34
Tony Hrkac, C	60	4	7	11	-2	8
Ruslan Salei, D	71	5	5	10	3	94
Niklas Havelid, D	50	2	7	9	0	20
Kevin Haller, D	67	3	5	8	-8	61
Jim McKenzie, R	31	3	3	6	-4	48
Pascal Trepanier, D	37	0	4	4	2	54
Stu Grimson, R	50	1	2	3	0	116

GOALTENDING

Player	GP	Mins	Avg	W	L	T	SO
Guy Hebert	68	3975	2.50	28	31	9	4
Dominic Roussel	20	988	3.15	6	5	3	1
Team total	82	4963	2.63	34	36	12	5

*Rookie.

Boston Bruins

SCORING

Player	GP	G	A	Pts	+/–	PM
Joe Thornton, C	81	23	37	60	-5	82
Anson Carter, C	59	22	25	47	8	14
Sergei Samsonov, R	77	19	26	45	-6	4
Ray Bourque, D	65	10	28	38	-11	20
Dave Andreychuk, R	63	19	14	33	-11	20
Darren Van Impe, D	79	5	23	28	-19	73
Jason Allison, L	37	10	18	28	5	20
P.J. Axelsson, L	81	10	16	26	1	24
Steve Heinze, L	75	12	13	25	-8	36
Rob DiMaio, L	50	5	16	21	-1	42
*Andre Savage, C	43	7	13	20	-8	10
Kyle McLaren, D	71	8	11	19	-4	67
Mikko Eloranta, R	50	6	12	18	-10	36
Don Sweeney, D	81	1	13	14	-14	48
Joe Murphy, R	26	7	7	14	-7	41
Cameron Mann, L	32	8	4	12	-6	13
Shawn Bates, C	44	5	7	12	-17	14
Hal Gill, D	81	3	9	12	0	51
*Eric Nickulas, L	20	5	6	11	-1	12
Brian Rolston, R	16	5	4	9	-4	6
*Antti Laaksonen, R	27	6	3	9	3	2
Mattias Timander, D	60	0	8	8	-11	22
Brandon Smith, D	22	2	4	6	-4	10
Marty McSorley, D	27	2	3	5	2	62

GOALTENDING

Player	GP	Mins	Avg	W	L	T	SO
Byron Dafoe	41	2306	2.96	13	16	10	3
Rob Tallas	27	1363	3.16	4	13	4	0
John Grahame	24	1344	2.45	7	10	5	2
Team total	82	5013	2.88	24	39	19	5

Atlanta Thrashers

SCORING

Player	GP	G	A	Pts	+/–	PM
Andrew Brunette, R	81	23	27	50	-32	30
Ray Ferraro, C	81	19	25	44	-33	88
Nelson Emerson, L	58	14	19	33	-24	47
Yannick Tremblay, D	75	10	21	31	-42	22
Dean Sylvester, L	52	16	10	26	-14	24
*Patrik Stefan, C	72	5	20	25	-20	30
Mike Stapleton, C	62	10	12	22	-29	30
*Petr Buzek, D	63	5	14	19	-22	41
Darryl Shannon, D	49	5	13	18	-14	65
Kelly Buchberger, R	68	5	12	17	-34	139
Johan Garpenlov, R	52	2	14	16	-30	31
Hnat Domenichelli, C	27	6	9	15	-21	4
*Andreas Karlsson, C	51	5	9	14	-17	14

SCORING (CONT.)

Player	GP	G	A	Pts	+/–	PM
Steve Guolla, C	20	4	9	13	-13	4
Shean Donovan, L	33	4	7	11	-13	18
Denny Lambert, R	73	5	6	11	-17	219
Gord Murphy, D	58	1	10	11	-28	38
Donald Audette, L	14	7	4	11	-4	12
Chris Tamer, D	69	2	8	10	-32	91

GOALTENDING

Player	GP	Mins	Avg	W	L	T	SO
*Norm Maracle	32	1618	3.48	4	19	2	1
Damian Rhodes	28	1561	3.88	5	19	3	1
*Scott Fankhouser	16	919	3.19	2	11	2	0
*Scott Langkow	15	765	4.31	3	11	0	0
Team total	82	4,902	3.70	14	60	7	2

*Rookie.

Buffalo Sabres

SCORING

Player	GP	G	A	Pts	+/-	PM
Miroslav Satan, L	81	33	34	67	16	32
Curtis Brown, C	74	22	29	51	19	42
Stu Barnes, C	82	20	25	45	-3	16
Mike Peca, C	73	20	21	41	6	67
Vaclav Varada, L	76	10	27	37	12	62
*Maxim Afinogenov, L	65	16	18	34	-4	41
Michal Grosek, R	61	11	23	34	12	35
Jason Wooley, D	74	8	25	33	14	52
Geoff Sanderson, R	67	13	13	26	4	22
Brian Holzinger, C	59	7	17	24	4	30
Dixon Ward, R	71	11	9	20	1	41
Vladimir Tsyplakov, R	34	6	13	19	17	10
Doug Gilmour, C	11	3	14	17	3	12
Jay McKee, D	78	5	12	17	5	50
Erik Rasmussen, C	67	8	6	14	1	43
Alexei Zhitnik, D	74	2	11	13	-6	95
James Patrick, D	66	5	8	13	8	22
Wayne Primeau, C	41	5	7	12	-8	38
Richard Smehlik, D	64	2	9	11	13	50
Chris Gratton, C	14	1	7	8	1	15
*Brian Campbell, D	12	1	4	5	-2	4
Rob Ray, R	69	1	3	4	0	158

GOALTENDING

Player	GP	Mins	Avg	W	L	T	SO
*Martin Biron	41	2228	2.42	19	18	2	5
Dominik Hasek	35	2066	2.20	15	11	6	3
Dwayne Roloson	14	677	2.83	1	7	3	0
Team total	82	4971	2.38	35	36	11	8

Calgary Flames

SCORING

Player	GP	G	A	Pts	+/-	PM
Valeri Bure, L	82	35	40	75	-7	50
Jarome Iginla, L	77	29	34	63	0	26
Phil Housely, D	78	11	44	55	-12	24
Marc Savard, C	78	22	31	53	-2	56
Derek Morris, D	78	9	29	38	2	80
Andrei Nazarov, L	76	10	22	32	3	78
Jeff Shantz, C	74	13	18	31	-13	30
Jason Wiemer, R	64	11	11	22	-10	120
Clarke Wilm, C	78	10	12	22	-6	67
Cory Stillman, C	37	12	9	21	-9	12
Bill Lindsay, R	80	8	12	20	-7	86
*Martin St. Louis, C	56	3	15	18	-5	22
Hnat Domenichelli, C	32	5	9	14	0	12
Rene Corbet, R	48	4	10	14	-7	60
*Robyn Regehr, D	57	5	7	12	-2	46
Sergei Krivokrasov, L	12	1	10	11	2	4
Andreas Johansson, R	28	3	7	10	-3	14
Bobby Dollas, D	49	3	7	10	4	28
Tommy Albelin, D	41	4	6	10	-3	12
Darryl Shannon, D	27	1	8	9	-13	22
Cale Hulse, D	47	1	6	7	-11	47
*Jeff Cowan, R	13	4	1	5	2	16
Marc Bureau, C	9	1	3	4	-3	2
Steve Smith, D	20	0	4	4	-13	42
*Sergei Varlamov, L	7	3	0	3	0	0
Steve Begin, R	13	1	1	2	-3	18
Travis Brigley, R	17	0	2	2	-6	4

GOALTENDING

Player	GP	Mins	Avg	W	L	T	SO
Fred Brathwaite	61	3447	2.75	25	25	7	5
Grant Fuhr	23	1206	3.83	5	13	2	0
J.S. Giguere	7	330	2.72	1	3	1	0
Team total	82	4983	3.01	31	41	10	5

Carolina Hurricanes

SCORING

Player	GP	G	A	Pts	+/-	PM
Ron Francis, C	78	23	50	73	10	18
Jeff O'Neill, C	80	25	38	63	-9	72
Gary Roberts, R	69	23	30	53	-10	62
Sami Kapanen, L	76	24	24	48	10	12
Sean Hill, D	62	13	31	44	3	59
Robert Kron, R	81	13	27	40	-4	8
Paul Coffey, D	69	11	29	40	-6	40
Andrei Kovalenko, L	76	15	24	39	-13	38
Bates Battaglia, R	77	16	18	34	20	39
Martin Gelinas, R	81	14	16	30	-10	40
Paul Ranheim, R	79	9	13	22	-14	6
Glen Wesley, D	78	7	15	22	-4	38
Marek Malik, D	57	4	10	14	13	63
Rod Brind'Amour, C	33	4	10	14	-12	22
*Tommy Westlund, L	81	4	8	12	-10	19

SCORING (CONT.)

Player	GP	G	A	Pts	+/-	PM
Steve Halko, D	58	0	8	8	0	25
Jeff Daniels, R	69	3	4	7	-8	10
Kent Manderville, C	56	1	4	5	-8	12
David Karpa, D	27	1	4	5	9	52
Nolan Pratt, D	64	3	1	4	-22	90
*David Tanabe, D	31	4	0	4	-4	14
*Byron Ritchie, C	26	0	2	2	-10	17
Curtis Leschyshyn, D	53	0	2	2	-19	31
Arturs, Irbe, G	75	0	1	1	0	14

GOALTENDING

Player	GP	Mins	Avg	W	L	T	SO
Arturs Irbe	75	4346	2.41	34	28	9	5
Eric Fichaud	9	489	2.94	3	5	1	1
Mark Fitzpatrick	3	107	4.48	0	2	0	0
Team total	82	4942	2.51	37	35	10	6

*Rookie.

Chicago Blackhawks
SCORING

Player	GP	G	A	Pts	+/-	PM
Tony Amonte, L	82	43	41	84	10	48
Steve Sullivan, C	73	22	42	64	20	52
Alexei Zhamnov, C	71	23	37	60	7	61
Doug Gilmour, C	63	22	34	56	-12	51
Michael Nylander, C	66	23	28	51	9	26
Boris Mironov, D	58	9	28	37	-3	72
Eric Daze, L	59	23	13	36	-16	28
Dean McAmmond, R	76	14	18	32	11	72
Anders Eriksson, D	73	3	25	28	4	20
Bryan McCabe, D	79	6	19	25	-8	139
Sylvain Cote, D	45	6	18	24	-4	14
Josef Marha, C	81	10	12	22	-10	18
J.P. Dumont, L	47	10	8	18	-6	18
Bob Probert, R	69	4	11	15	10	114
Blair Atcheynum, L	47	5	7	12	-8	6
Kevin Dean, D	27	2	8	10	9	12
Brad Brown, D	57	0	9	9	-1	134
Doug Zmolek, D	43	2	7	9	6	60
Jean-Yves Leroux, R	54	3	5	8	-10	43
Dave Manson, D	37	0	7	7	2	40
Michal Grosek, R	14	2	4	6	-1	12

GOALTENDING

Player	GP	Mins	Avg	W	L	T	SO
Jocelyn Thibault	60	3437	2.75	25	26	7	3
Steve Passmore	24	1388	2.72	7	12	3	1
*Marc Lamothe	2	116	5.17	1	1	0	0
Team total	82	4941	2.80	33	39	10	4

Colorado Avalanche
SCORING

Player	GP	G	A	Pts	+/-	PM
Joe Sakic, C	60	28	53	81	30	28
Milan Hejduk, L	82	36	36	72	14	16
Chris Drury, C	82	20	47	67	8	42
Sandis Ozolinsh, D	82	16	36	52	17	46
Peter Forsberg, C	49	14	37	51	9	52
*Alex Tanguay, C	76	17	34	51	6	22
Adam Deadmarsh, L	71	18	27	45	-10	106
Stephane Yelle, C	79	8	14	22	9	28
Shjon Podein, R	75	11	8	19	12	29
Brian Rolston, R	50	8	10	18	-6	12
Dave Reid, R	65	11	7	18	12	29
Adam Foote, D	59	5	13	18	5	98
*Martin Skoula, D	80	3	13	16	5	20
Ray Bourque, D	14	8	6	14	9	6
Jon Klemm, D	73	5	7	12	26	34
Chris Dingman, R	68	8	3	11	-2	132
Greg DeVries, D	69	2	7	9	-7	73
Eric Messier, D	61	3	6	9	0	24
Claude Lemieux, L	13	3	6	9	0	4
Aaron Miller, D	53	1	7	8	3	36
*Dan Hinote, L	27	1	3	4	0	10
Alexei Gusarov, D	34	2	2	4	-8	10
Jeff Odgers, L	62	1	2	3	-7	162

GOALTENDING

Player	GP	Mins	Avg	W	L	T	SO
Patrick Roy	63	3704	2.28	32	21	8	2
*Marc Denis	23	1203	2.54	9	8	3	3
Rick Tabaracci	2	60	2.00	1	0	0	0
Team total	82	4967	2.34	42	29	11	5

Dallas Stars
SCORING

Player	GP	G	A	Pts	+/-	PM
Mike Modano, C	77	38	43	81	0	48
Brett Hull, L	79	24	35	59	-21	43
Sergei Zubov, D	77	9	33	42	-2	18
Jamie Langenbrunner, L	65	18	21	39	16	68
Darryl Sydor, D	74	8	26	34	6	32
Joe Nieuwendyk, C	48	15	19	34	-1	26
Mike Keane, L	81	13	21	34	9	41
*Brenden Morrow, R	64	14	19	33	8	81
Richard Matvichuk, D	70	4	21	25	7	42
Derian Hatcher, D	57	2	22	24	6	68
Kirk Muller, C	47	7	15	22	-3	24
*Blake Sloan, L	67	4	13	17	11	50
Guy Carbonneau, C	69	10	6	16	10	36
Aaron Gavey, C	41	7	6	13	0	44
*Roman Lyashenko, C	58	6	6	12	-2	10
Sylvain Cote, D	28	2	8	10	6	14
Scott Thornton, C	30	6	3	9	-5	38
Jere Lehtinen, R	17	3	5	8	1	0
Jamie Pushor, D	62	0	8	8	0	53
Grant Marshall, L	45	2	6	8	-5	38

GOALTENDING

Player	GP	Mins	Avg	W	L	T	SO
Ed Belfour	62	3620	2.10	32	21	7	4
*Manny Fernandez	24	1352	2.13	11	8	3	1
Team total	82	4972	2.11	43	29	10	5

Detroit Red Wings
SCORING

Player	GP	G	A	Pts	+/-	PM
Steve Yzerman, C	78	35	44	79	28	34
Brendan Shanahan, R	78	41	37	78	24	105
Nicklas Lidstrom, D	81	20	53	73	19	18
Sergei Fedorov, C	68	27	35	62	8	22
Pat Verbeek, L	68	22	26	48	22	95
Igor Larianov, C	79	9	38	47	13	28
Martin Lapointe, L	82	16	25	41	17	121
Steve Duchesne, D	79	10	31	41	12	42
Larry Murphy, D	81	10	30	40	4	146
Slava Kozlov, R	72	18	18	36	11	28
Tomas Holmstrom, R	72	13	22	35	4	43
Chris Chelios, D	81	3	31	34	48	103
Doug Brown, L	51	10	8	18	8	12
Mathieu Dandenault, D	81	6	12	18	-12	20
Stacy Roest, C	49	7	9	16	-1	12
Kirk Maltby, L	41	6	8	14	1	24
Darren McCarty, L	24	6	6	12	1	48
Kris Draper, C	51	5	7	12	3	28
*Jiri Fischer, D	52	0	8	8	1	45
*Yuri Butsayev, C	57	5	3	8	-6	12
Brent Gilchrist, R	24	4	2	6	1	24
*Darryl Laplante, C	30	0	6	6	-2	10

GOALTENDING

Player	GP	Mins	Avg	W	L	T	S
Chris Osgood	53	3147	2.40	30	14	8	6
Ken Wregget	29	1578	2.66	14	10	2	0
Manny Legace	4	239	2.76	4	0	0	0
Team total	82	4964	2.50	48	24	10	6

* Rookie.

Edmonton Oilers

SCORING

Player	GP	G	A	Pts	+/–	PM
Doug Weight, C	77	21	51	72	6	54
Ryan Smyth, R	82	28	26	54	-2	58
Alexander Selivanov, L	67	27	20	47	2	46
Bill Guerin, L	70	24	22	46	4	123
Roman Hamrlik, D	80	8	37	45	1	68
Todd Marchant, C	82	17	23	40	7	70
Tom Poti, D	76	9	26	35	8	65
Janne Niinimaa, D	81	8	25	33	14	89
Mike Grier, L	65	9	22	31	9	68
Boyd Devereaux, C	76	8	19	27	7	20
Ethan Moreau, L	73	17	10	27	8	62
Jim Dowd, C	69	5	18	23	10	45
Pat Falloon, L	33	5	13	18	6	4
Josef Beranek, C	58	9	8	17	-6	39
Georges Laraque, L	76	8	8	16	5	123
Rem Murray, C	44	9	5	14	-2	8
Jason Smith, D	80	3	11	14	16	60
Sean Brown, D	72	4	8	12	1	192
Chad Kilger, C	40	3	2	5	-6	18
Christian Laflamme, D	50	0	5	5	-4	32
Dan Cleary, R	17	3	2	5	-1	8
German Titov, R	7	0	4	4	2	4
Bert Robertsson, D	52	0	4	4	-3	34
*Paul Comrie, C	15	1	2	3	-2	4
Igor Ulanov, D	14	0	3	3	-3	10

GOALTENDING

Player	GP	Mins	Avg	W	L	T	SO
Tommy Salo	70	4164	2.33	27	28	13	2
Bill Ranford	16	785	3.59	4	6	3	0
*Mike Minard	1	60	3.00	1	0	0	0
Team total	82	5009	2.53	32	34	16	2

Florida Panthers

SCORING

Player	GP	G	A	Pts	+/–	PM
Pavel Bure, L	74	58	36	94	25	16
Ray Whitney, R	81	29	42	71	16	35
Viktor Kozlov, C	80	17	53	70	24	16
Robert Svehla, D	82	9	40	49	23	64
Scott Mellanby, L	77	18	28	46	14	126
Mark Parrish, L	81	26	18	44	1	39
Jaroslav Spacek, D	82	10	26	36	7	53
Rob Niedermayer, C	81	10	23	33	-5	46
Bret Hedican, D	76	6	19	25	4	68
Oleg Kvasha, L	78	5	20	25	3	34
Mike Wilson, D	60	4	16	20	10	35
Ray Sheppard, L	47	10	10	20	-4	4
Radek Dvorak, L	35	7	10	17	5	6
Ryan Johnson, C	66	4	12	16	1	14
Cam Stewart, R	65	9	7	16	-2	30
Paul Laus, D	77	3	8	11	-1	172
Len Barrie, C	14	4	6	10	4	6
Peter Worrell, R	48	3	6	9	-7	169
Mike Sillinger, C	13	4	4	8	-1	16
Lance Pitlick, D	62	3	5	8	7	44
Todd Simpson, D	82	1	6	7	5	202
*Filip Kuba, D	13	1	5	6	-3	2
Mike Vernon, G	34	0	3	3	0	2
Alex Hicks, R	8	1	2	3	3	4

GOALTENDING

Player	GP	Mins	Avg	W	L	T	SO
Mike Vernon	34	2019	2.46	18	13	2	1
Trevor Kidd	28	1573	2.63	14	11	2	1
Mikhail Shtalenkov	15	882	2.31	8	4	2	0
Sean Burke	7	418	2.58	2	5	0	0
Rich Shulmistra	1	60	1.00	1	0	0	0
Team total	82	4952	2.48	43	33	6	2

Los Angeles Kings

SCORING

Player	GP	G	A	Pts	+/–	PM
Luc Robitaille, R	71	36	38	74	11	68
Zigmund Palffy, L	64	27	39	66	18	32
Glen Murray, L	78	29	33	62	13	60
Jozef Stumpel, C	57	17	41	58	23	10
Rob Blake, D	77	18	39	57	10	112
Bryan Smolinski, C	79	20	36	56	2	48
Donald Audette, L	49	12	20	32	6	45
Garry Galley, D	70	9	21	30	9	52
Jason Blake, C	64	5	18	23	4	26
Craig Johnson, R	76	9	14	23	-10	28
Ian Laperriere, C	79	9	13	22	-14	185
Marko Tuomainen, L	63	9	8	17	-12	80
Aki Berg, D	70	3	13	16	-1	45
*Jere Karalahti, D	48	6	10	16	3	18
Sean O'Donnell, D	80	2	12	14	4	114
Mattias Norstrom, D	82	1	13	14	22	66
Vladimir Tsyplakov, R	29	6	7	13	6	4

Player	GP	G	A	Pts	+/–	PM
Len Barrie, C	46	5	8	13	5	56
*Brad Chartrand, L	50	6	6	12	4	17
Bob Corkum, L	45	5	6	11	0	14
Dan Bylsma, R	64	3	6	9	-2	55
Frantisek Kaberle, D	37	0	9	9	3	4
Jaroslav Modry, D	26	5	4	9	-2	18
Steve McKenna, R	46	0	5	5	3	125
Kelly Buchberger, R	13	2	1	3	-2	13
Nelson Emerson, L	5	1	1	2	1	0

GOALTENDING

Player	GP	Mins	Avg	W	L	T	SO
Stephane Fiset	47	2592	2.75	20	15	7	1
Jamie Storr	42	2206	2.52	18	15	5	1
Marcel Cousineau	5	170	2.11	1	1	0	0
Team total	82	4968	2.63	39	31	12	2

* Rookie.

Montreal Canadiens

SCORING

Player	GP	G	A	Pts	+/–	PM
Martin Rucinsky, R	80	25	24	49	1	70
Dainius Zubrus, L	73	14	28	42	-1	54
Sergei Zholtok, C	68	26	12	38	2	28
Patrice Brisebois, D	54	10	25	35	-1	18
Trevor Linden, C	50	13	17	30	-3	34
Eric Weinrich, D	77	4	25	29	4	39
Brian Savage, L	38	17	12	29	-4	19
Benoit Brunet, R	50	14	15	29	3	13
Shayne Corson, R	70	8	20	28	-2	115
Oleg Petrov, L	44	2	24	26	10	8
Turner Stevenson, L	64	8	13	21	-1	61
Saku Koivu, C	24	3	18	21	7	14
Karl Dykhuis, D	67	7	12	19	-3	40
Craig Darby, C	76	7	10	17	-14	14
Craig Rivet, D	61	3	14	17	11	76
*Francis Bouillon, D	74	3	13	16	-7	38
Patrick Poulin, C	82	10	5	15	-15	17
Jesse Belanger, C	16	3	6	9	2	2
Jim Cummins, L	47	3	5	8	-5	92
Scott Lachance, D	57	0	6	6	-4	22
*Arron Asham, L	33	4	2	6	-7	24

GOALTENDING

Player	GP	Mins	Avg	W	L	T	SO
Jeff Hackett	56	3300	2.40	23	25	7	3
Jose Theodore	30	1655	2.10	12	13	2	5
Team total	82	4955	2.30	35	38	9	8

Nashville Predators

SCORING

Player	GP	G	A	Pts	+/–	PM
Cliff Ronning, C	82	26	36	62	-13	34
Patric Kjelberg, R	82	23	23	46	-11	14
Greg Johnson, C	82	11	33	44	-15	40
Kimmo Timonen, D	51	8	25	33	-5	26
Vitali Yachmenev, L	68	16	16	32	5	12
Drake Berehowsky, D	79	12	20	32	-4	87
Scott Walker, L	69	7	21	28	-16	90
Ville Peltonen, R	79	6	22	28	-1	22
*David Legwand, C	71	13	15	28	-6	30
Sergei Krivokrasov, L	63	9	17	26	-7	40
Robert Valicevic, C	80	14	11	25	-11	21
*Randy Robitaille, C	69	11	14	25	-13	10
Sebastien Bordeleau, C	60	10	13	23	-12	30
Tom Fitzgerald, L	82	13	9	22	-18	66
Craig Millar, D	57	3	11	14	-6	28
Bill Houlder, D	57	2	12	14	-6	24
*Karlis Skrastins, D	59	5	6	11	-7	20
Mark Mowers, L	41	4	5	9	0	10
Bob Boughner, D	62	2	4	6	-13	97
*Richard Lintner, D	33	1	5	6	-6	22
Dan Keczmer, D	24	0	5	5	-2	28
Joel Bouchard, D	52	1	4	5	-11	23

GOALTENDING

Player	GP	Mins	Avg	W	L	T	SO
Mike Dunham	52	3077	2.84	19	27	6	0
Tomas Vokoun	33	1878	2.77	9	20	1	1
Team total	82	4955	2.82	28	47	7	1

New Jersey Devils

SCORING

Player	GP	G	A	Pts	+/–	PM
Patrik Elias, R	72	35	37	72	16	58
*Scott Gomez, C	82	19	51	70	14	78
Petr Sykora, L	79	25	43	68	24	26
Jason Arnott, L	76	22	34	56	22	51
Bobby Holik, C	79	23	23	46	7	106
Randy McKay, L	67	16	23	39	8	80
Scott Niedermayer, D	71	7	31	38	-3	86
Claude Lemieux, L	70	17	21	38	-3	86
*Brian Rafalski, D	75	5	27	32	21	28
Scott Stevens, D	78	8	21	29	30	103
Sergei Nemchinov, C	53	10	16	26	1	18
Brendan Morrison, C	44	5	21	26	8	8
*John Madden, R	74	16	9	25	7	6
Sergei Brylin, C	64	9	11	20	0	20
Lyle Odelein, D	57	1	15	16	-10	104
Krzysztof Oliwa, L	69	6	10	16	-2	184
Jay Pandolfo, R	71	7	8	15	0	4
Sheldon Souray, D	52	0	8	8	-6	70
Vadim Sharifijanov, L	20	3	4	7	-6	8
Alexander Mogilny, L	12	3	3	6	-4	4
Denis Pederson, C	35	3	3	6	-7	16
Ken Daneyko, D	78	0	6	6	13	98

GOALTENDING

Player	GP	Mins	Avg	W	L	T	SO
Martin Brodeur	72	4311	2.24	43	20	8	6
Chris Terreri	12	648	3.42	2	9	0	0
Team total	82	4959	2.39	45	29	8	7

New York Islanders

SCORING

Player	GP	G	A	Pts	+/–	PM
Mariusz Czerkawski, L	79	35	35	70	-16	34
Brad Isbister, R	64	22	20	42	-18	100
*Tim Connolly, C	81	14	20	34	-25	44
Claude Lapointe, C	76	15	16	31	-22	60
Jorgen Jonsson, R	68	11	17	28	-6	16
Dave Scratchard, C	44	12	14	26	0	93
Josh Green, R	49	12	14	26	-7	41
Kenny Jonsson, D	65	1	24	25	-15	32
Olli Jokinen, C	82	11	10	21	0	80
Jamie Rivers, D	75	1	16	17	-4	84
Jamie Heward, D	54	6	11	17	-9	26
Mats Lindgren, C	43	9	7	16	0	24
Gino Odjick, L	46	5	10	15	-7	90
Mike Watt, R	45	5	6	11	-8	17
*Dmitri Nabokov, R	26	4	7	11	-8	16
Zdeno Chara, D	65	2	9	11	-27	57
Niklas Andersson, R	17	3	7	10	-3	8
Eric Cairns, D	67	2	7	9	-5	196
*Mathieu Biron, D	60	4	4	8	-13	38
Steve Webb, R	65	1	3	4	-4	103
Ted Drury, C	55	2	1	3	-8	31

GOALTENDING

Player	GP	Mins	Avg	W	L	T	SO
Kevin Weekes	36	2025	3.40	10	20	4	1
Roberto Luongo	24	1292	3.25	7	14	1	1
Felix Potvin	22	1273	3.20	5	14	3	1
Team total	82	4963	3.21	24	49	9	3

New York Rangers
SCORING

Player	GP	G	A	Pts	+/–	PM
Petr Nedved, C	76	24	44	68	2	40
Theo Fleury, L	80	15	49	64	-4	68
*Mike York, C	82	26	24	50	-17	18
John MacLean, L	77	18	24	42	-2	52
*Jan Hlavac, R	67	19	23	42	3	16
Adam Graves, R	77	23	17	40	-15	14
Radek Dvorak, L	46	11	22	33	0	10
Valeri Kamensky, R	58	13	19	32	-13	24
Mathieu Schneider, D	80	10	20	30	-6	78
Brian Leetch, D	50	7	19	26	-16	20
Alexandre Daigle, L	58	8	18	26	-5	23
Kevin Hatcher, D	74	4	19	23	-10	38
*Kim Johnsson, D	76	6	15	21	-13	46
Tim Taylor, C	76	9	11	20	-4	72
Stephane Quintal, D	75	2	14	16	-10	77
Michael Knuble, L	59	9	5	14	-5	18
Eric Lacroix, R	70	4	8	12	-12	24
Sylvain Lefebvre, D	82	2	10	12	-13	43
Kevin Stevens, R	38	3	5	8	-7	43
Todd Harvey, L	31	3	3	6	-9	62
Rich Pilon, D	45	0	4	4	0	36
Rob DiMaio, L	12	1	3	4	-8	8
Johan Witehall, R	9	1	1	2	0	2

GOALTENDING

Player	GP	Mins	Avg	W	L	T	SO
Mike Richter	61	3621	2.86	22	31	8	0
Kirk McLean	22	1205	2.88	7	8	4	0
Team total	82	4972	2.88	29	41	12	0

Philadelphia Flyers
SCORING

Player	GP	G	A	Pts	+/–	PM
Mark Recchi, L	82	28	63	91	20	50
John LeClair, R	82	40	37	77	8	36
Eric Lindros, C	55	27	32	59	11	83
Eric Desjardins, D	81	14	41	55	20	32
Daymond Langkow, C	82	18	32	50	1	56
*Simon Gagne, C	80	20	28	48	11	22
Valeri Zelepukin, R	77	11	21	32	-3	55
Mikael Renberg, L	62	8	21	29	-1	30
Keith Jones, L	57	9	16	25	8	82
Daniel McGillis, D	68	4	14	18	16	55
Keith Primeau, C	23	7	10	17	10	31
Chris Therien, D	80	4	9	13	11	66
Jody Hull, L	67	10	3	13	8	4
Craig Berube, R	77	4	8	12	3	162
Sandy McCarthy, L	58	6	5	11	-5	111
Rod Brind'Amour, C	12	5	3	8	-1	4
*Andy Delmore, D	27	2	5	7	-1	8
Luke Richardson, D	74	2	5	7	14	140
Adam Burt, D	67	1	6	7	-2	45
Mikael Andersson, R	36	2	3	5	-2	0
Marc Bureau, C	54	2	2	4	-1	10
Ulf Samuelsson, D	49	1	2	3	8	58

GOALTENDING

Player	GP	Mins	Avg	W	L	T	SO
J. Vanbiesbrouck	50	2949	2.19	25	15	9	3
*Brian Boucher	35	2037	1.91	20	10	3	4
Team total	82	4986	2.08	45	25	12	7

Ottawa Senators
SCORING

Player	GP	G	A	Pts	+/–	PM
Radek Bonk, C	80	23	37	60	-2	53
Daniel Alfredsson, L	57	21	38	59	11	28
Marian Hossa, R	78	29	27	56	5	32
Vaclav Prospal, C	79	22	33	55	-2	40
Shawn McEachern, R	69	29	22	51	2	24
Joe Juneau, C	65	13	24	37	3	22
Wade Redden, D	81	10	26	36	-1	49
Andreas Dackell, L	82	10	25	35	5	18
Jason York, D	79	8	22	30	-3	60
Magnus Arvedson, R	47	15	13	28	4	36
Shaun Van Allen, C	75	9	19	28	20	37
Patrick Traverse, D	66	6	17	23	17	21
Rob Zamuner, R	57	9	12	21	-6	32
Chris Phillips, D	65	5	14	19	12	39
Igor Kravchuk, D	64	6	12	18	-5	20
Sami Salo, D	37	6	8	14	6	2
Janne Laukkanen, D	60	1	11	12	14	55
Kevin Dineen, L	67	4	8	12	2	57
*Mike Fisher, C	32	4	5	9	-6	15
*Andre Roy, R	73	4	3	7	3	145
Colin Forbes, R	45	2	5	7	-1	12

GOALTENDING

Player	GP	Mins	Avg	W	L	T	SO
Ron Tugnutt	44	2434	2.53	18	12	8	4
Patrick Lalime	38	2037	2.32	19	14	3	3
Tom Barrasso	7	418	3.15	3	4	0	0
Team total	82	5062	2.45	41	30	11	7

Phoenix Coyotes
SCORING

Player	GP	G	A	Pts	+/–	PM
Jeremy Roenick, C	75	34	44	78	11	102
Shane Doan, L	81	26	25	51	6	66
Greg Adams, R	69	19	27	46	-1	14
Travis Green, C	78	25	21	46	-4	45
Dallas Drake, L	79	15	30	45	11	62
Keith Tkachuk, R	50	22	21	43	7	82
Teppo Numminen, D	79	8	34	42	21	16
Jyrki Lumme, D	74	8	32	40	9	44
*Trevor Letowski, C	82	19	20	39	2	20
Rick Tocchet, L	64	12	17	29	-5	67
Juha Ylonen, C	76	6	23	29	-6	12
Mika Alatalo, R	82	10	17	27	-3	36
Keith Carney, D	82	4	20	24	11	87
Mike Sullivan, C	79	5	10	15	-4	10
Benoit Hogue, R	27	3	10	13	-1	10
Stanislav Neckar, D	66	2	8	10	1	36
Deron Quint, D	50	3	7	10	0	22
J.J. Daigneault, D	53	1	6	7	-17	22
Louie DeBrusk, R	61	4	3	7	1	78

GOALTENDING

Player	GP	Mins	Avg	W	L	T	SO
Sean Burke	35	2074	2.54	17	14	3	3
Bob Essensa	30	1573	2.78	13	10	3	1
Mikhail Shtalenkov	15	904	2.38	7	6	2	2
*Robert Esche	8	408	3.38	2	5	0	0
Team total	82	4959	2.66	39	35	8	6

* Rookie.

Pittsburgh Penguins

SCORING

Player	GP	G	A	Pts	+/-	PM
Jaromir Jagr, L	63	42	54	96	25	50
Alexei Kovalev, L	82	26	40	66	-3	94
Robert Lang, C	78	23	42	65	-9	14
Martin Straka, C	71	20	39	59	24	26
Jan Hrdina, C	70	13	33	46	13	43
German Titov, R	63	17	25	42	-3	34
Aleksey Morozov, L	68	12	19	31	12	14
Jiri Slegr, D	74	11	20	31	20	82
Matthew Barnaby, R	64	12	12	24	3	197
Rob Brown, L	50	10	13	23	-13	10
Tyler Wright, C	50	12	10	22	4	45
*Michal Rozsival, D	75	4	17	21	11	48
Kip Miller, C	44	4	15	19	-1	10
Darius Kasparaitis, D	73	3	12	15	-12	146
Hans Jonsson, D	68	3	11	14	-5	12
Pat Falloon, L	30	4	9	13	-2	10
Ian Moran, D	73	4	8	12	-10	28
Brad Werenka, D	61	3	8	11	15	69
Josef Beranek, C	13	4	4	8	-6	18
Peter Popovic, D	54	1	5	6	-8	30
Steve Leach, L	56	2	3	5	-11	24

GOALTENDING

Player	GP	Mins	Avg	W	L	T	SO
*J.S. Aubin	51	2788	2.58	23	21	3	2
Peter Skudra	20	922	3.12	5	7	3	1
Tom Barrasso	18	869	3.17	5	7	2	1
Ron Tugnutt	18	374	2.40	4	2	0	0
Team total	82	4953	2.77	37	37	8	4

St. Louis Blues

SCORING

Player	GP	G	A	Pts	+/-	PM
Pavol Demitra, L	71	28	47	75	34	8
Pierre Turgeon, C	52	26	40	66	30	8
Chris Pronger, D	79	14	48	62	52	92
Michal Handzus, C	81	25	28	53	19	44
Lubos Bartecko, R	67	16	23	39	25	51
Scott Young, L	75	24	15	39	12	18
Al MacInnis, D	61	11	28	39	20	34
Mike Eastwood, C	79	19	15	34	5	32
*Jochen Hecht, L	63	13	21	34	20	28
Craig Conroy, C	79	12	15	27	5	36
Todd Reirden, D	56	4	21	25	18	32
Stephane Richer, L	36	8	17	25	7	14
*Marty Reasoner, C	32	10	14	24	9	20
Scott Pellerin, R	80	8	15	23	8	48
Jamal Mayers, L	79	7	10	17	0	90
Terry Yake, L	26	4	9	13	2	22
*Tyson Nash, R	66	4	9	13	6	150
Jeff Finley, D	74	2	8	10	26	38
Dave Ellett, D	52	2	8	10	-4	12
Derek King, R	19	2	7	9	0	6
Marc Bergevin, D	81	1	8	9	27	75
Ricard Persson, D	41	0	8	8	-2	38
*Ladislav Nagy, L	11	2	4	6	2	2
Bob Bassen, C	27	1	3	4	-3	26
Geoff Courtnall, R	6	2	2	4	3	6
Chris McAlpine, D	21	1	1	2	1	14

GOALTENDING

Player	GP	Mins	Avg	W	L	T	SO
Roman Turek	67	3960	1.95	42	15	9	7
Jamie McLennan	19	1008	1.96	9	5	2	2
Team total	82	4968	1.95	51	20	11	9

San Jose Sharks

SCORING

Player	GP	G	A	Pts	+/-	PM		Player	GP	G	A	Pts	+/-	PM
Owen Nolan, L	78	44	40	84	-1	110		Ronnie Stern, L	67	4	5	9	-9	151
Vincent Damphousse, C	82	21	49	70	4	58		Dave Lowry, R	32	1	4	5	1	18
Jeff Friesen, R	82	26	35	61	-2	47		Bryan Marchmant, D	49	0	4	4	3	72
Mike Ricci, C	82	20	24	44	14	60		*Scott Hannan, D	30	1	2	3	7	10
Patrick Marleau, C	81	17	23	40	-9	36		Andy Sutton, D	40	1	1	2	-5	80
Niklas Sundstrom, R	79	12	25	37	9	22		Murray Craven, C	19	0	2	2	-2	4
*Brad Stuart, D	82	10	26	36	3	32		Steve Shields, G	67	0	1	1	0	29
Alexander Korolyuk, R	57	14	21	35	4	35		Bob Rouse, D	26	0	1	1	-3	19
Gary Suter, D	76	6	28	34	7	52		Brantt Myhres, L	13	0	1	1	0	97
Marco Sturm, R	74	12	15	27	4	22		Mike Vernon, G	15	0	0	0	0	0
Stephane Matteau, L	69	12	12	24	-3	61								
Jeff Norton, D	62	0	20	20	-2	49								
Marcus Ragnarsson, D	63	3	13	16	13	38								
Mike Rathje, D	66	2	14	16	-2	31		**GOALTENDING**						
Tony Granato, R	48	6	7	13	2	39		Player	GP	Mins	Avg	W	L	T	SO
Todd Harvey, L	40	8	4	12	-2	78		Steve Shields	67	3796	2.56	27	30	8	4
Ron Sutter, C	78	5	6	11	-3	34		Mike Vernon	15	772	2.48	6	5	1	0

Additional San Jose goaltending:

Player	GP	Mins	Avg	W	L	T	SO
Steve Shields	67	3796	2.56	27	30	8	4
Mike Vernon	15	772	2.48	6	5	1	0
*Evgeni Nabokov	11	414	2.17	2	2	1	1
Team total	82	4982	2.51	35	37	10	5

* Rookie.

Tampa Bay Lightning

SCORING

Player	GP	G	A	Pts	+/−	PM
Vincent Lecavalier, C	80	25	42	67	-25	43
Fredrik Modin, R	80	22	26	48	-26	18
Mike Sillinger, L	67	19	25	44	-29	86
Chris Gratton, C	58	14	27	41	-24	121
Darcy Tucker, R	50	14	20	34	-15	108
Stan Drulia, L	68	11	22	33	-18	24
Pavel Kubina, D	69	8	18	26	-19	93
Petr Svoboda, D	70	2	23	25	-11	170
Todd Warriner, C	55	11	13	24	-14	34
Mike Johnson, L	28	10	12	22	-2	4
*Paul Mara, D	54	7	11	18	-27	73
Robert Petrovicky, R	43	7	10	17	2	14
Steve Guolla, C	46	6	10	16	2	11
Dan Kesa, C	50	4	10	14	-11	21
Steve Martins, C	57	5	7	12	-12	37
Stepahne Richer, L	20	7	5	12	2	4
Andrei Zyuzin, D	34	2	9	11	-11	33
Jaroslav Svejkovsky, R	29	5	5	10	-7	28
Bruce Gardiner, L	41	3	6	9	-21	37
*Ben Clymer, D	60	2	6	8	-26	87
Brian Holzinger, C	14	3	3	6	-7	21
Andreas Johansson, R	12	2	3	5	1	8
Wayne Primeau, C	17	2	3	5	-4	25
Sergey Gusev, D	28	2	3	5	-9	6
Nils Ekman, L	28	2	2	4	-8	36

GOALTENDING

Player	GP	Mins	Avg	W	L	T	SO
Dan Cloutier	52	2492	3.49	9	30	3	0
Kevin Hodson	24	768	3.67	2	7	4	0
Rich Parent	14	697	3.70	2	7	1	0
*Zac Bierk	12	508	3.66	4	4	1	0
Darren Puppa	5	248	4.59	1	2	0	0
*Dieter Kochan	5	238	4.28	1	4	0	0
Team total	82	4951	3.65	19	54	9	0

Toronto Maple Leafs

SCORING

Player	GP	G	A	Pts	+/−	PM
Mats Sundin, C	73	32	41	73	16	46
Steve Thomas, L	81	26	37	63	1	68
Jonas Hoglund, R	82	29	27	56	-2	10
Igor Korolev, L	80	20	26	46	12	22
Yanic Perreault, C	58	18	27	45	3	22
Tomas Kaberle, D	82	7	33	40	3	24
Sergei Berezin, R	61	26	13	39	8	2
Bryan Berard, D	64	3	27	30	11	42
Dmitri Khristich, R	53	12	18	30	8	24
Nik Antropov, C	66	12	18	30	14	41
Dimitri Yushkevich, D	77	3	24	27	2	55
Mike Johnson, L	52	11	14	25	8	23
Garry Valk, L	73	10	14	24	-2	44
Darcy Tucker, R	27	7	10	17	3	55
A. Karpovtsev, D	69	3	14	17	9	54
Cory Cross, D	71	4	11	15	13	64
Tie Domi, L	70	5	9	14	-5	198
Kevyn Adams, C	52	5	8	13	-7	39
Alyn McCauley, C	45	5	5	10	-6	10
Danny Markov, D	59	0	10	10	13	28
Kris King, R	39	2	4	6	4	55
Todd Warriner, C	18	3	1	4	6	2
Wendel Clark, R	20	2	2	4	-3	21
Chris McAllister, D	36	0	3	3	-4	68

GOALTENDING

Player	GP	Mins	Avg	W	L	T	SO
Curtis Joseph	63	3801	2.49	36	20	7	4
Glenn Healy	20	1163	3.04	9	10	0	2
Team total	82	4964	2.62	45	30	7	6

Vancouver Canucks

SCORING

Player	GP	G	A	Pts	+/−	PM
Markus Naslund, R	82	27	38	65	-5	64
Andrew Cassels, C	79	17	45	62	8	16
Mark Messier, C	66	17	37	54	-15	30
Todd Bertuzzi, L	80	25	25	50	-2	126
Alexander Mogilny, L	47	21	17	38	7	16
*Peter Schaefer, R	71	16	15	31	0	20
Ed Jovanovski, D	75	5	21	26	-3	54
Adrian Aucoin, D	57	10	14	24	7	30
Greg Hawgood, D	79	5	17	22	5	26
Mattias Ohlund, D	42	4	16	20	6	24
Trent Klatt, L	47	10	10	20	-8	26
*Steve Kariya, R	45	8	11	19	9	22
Harry York, C	54	4	13	17	-4	20
*Harold Druken, C	33	7	9	16	14	10
Brad May, R	59	9	7	16	-2	90
Donald Brashear, R	60	11	2	13	-9	136
Bill Muckalt, L	33	4	8	12	6	17
Murray Baron, D	81	2	10	12	8	67
Matt Cooke, R	51	5	7	12	3	39
Chris Joseph, D	38	2	9	11	-4	6
*Artem Chubarov, C	49	1	8	9	-4	10
Brendan Morrison, C	12	2	7	9	4	10
Darby Hendrickson, C	40	5	4	9	-3	14
Josh Holden, C	6	1	5	6	2	2
*Brent Sopel, D	18	2	4	6	9	12

GOALTENDING

Player	GP	Mins	Avg	W	L	T	SO
Felix Potvin	34	1966	2.59	12	13	7	0
Garth Snow	32	1712	2.66	10	15	3	0
Kevin Weekes	20	986	2.86	6	7	4	1
Corey Schwab	6	268	3.58	2	1	1	0
Team total	82	5001	2.74	30	37	15	1

* Rookie.

Washington Capitals

SCORING

Player	GP	G	A	Pts	+/–	PM
Adam Oates, C	82	15	56	71	13	14
Sergei Gonchar, D	73	18	36	54	27	52
Chris Simon, R	75	29	20	49	11	146
Steve Konowalchuk, R	82	16	27	43	19	80
Peter Bondra, L	62	21	17	38	5	30
Ulf Dahlen, L	75	15	23	38	11	8
Richard Zednik, R	69	19	16	35	6	54
Calle Johansson, D	82	7	25	32	13	24
Jan Bulis, C	56	9	22	31	7	30
*Jeff Halpern, C	79	18	11	29	21	39
Andrei Nikolishin, C	76	11	14	25	6	28
Joe Sacco, R	79	7	16	23	7	50
Dmitri Mironov, D	73	3	19	22	6	28
Ken Klee, D	80	7	13	20	8	79
*Glen Metropolit, C	30	6	13	19	5	4
James Black, R	49	8	9	17	-1	6
Joe Murphy, L	29	5	8	13	8	53

Player	GP	G	A	Pts	+/–	PM
Terry Yake, L	35	6	5	11	2	12
Brendan Witt, D	77	1	7	8	5	114
Joe Reekie, D	59	0	7	7	21	50
Jim McKenzie, R	30	1	2	3	0	16
Jaroslav Svejkovsky, R	23	1	2	3	-7	2
Jeff Toms, R	20	1	2	3	-1	4
Rob Zettler, D	12	0	2	2	-1	19
*Alex Tezikov, D	23	1	1	2	-2	2

GOALTENDING

Player	GP	Mins	Avg	W	L	T	SO
Olaf Kolzig	73	4370	2.23	41	20	11	5
Craig Billington	13	611	2.74	3	6	1	2
Team total	82	4981	2.30	44	26	12	7

* Rookie.

2000 NHL Draft

First Round

The opening round of the 2000 NHL draft was held on June 24 in Calgary.

	Team	Selection	Position
1.	NY Islanders	Rick DiPietro	G
2.	Atlanta	Dany Heatley	L
3.	Minnesota	Marian Gaborik	L
4.	Columbus	Rostislav Klesla	D
5.	NY Islanders	Raffi Torres	L
6.	Nashville	Scott Hartnell	C
7.	Boston	Lars Jonsson	D
8.	Tampa Bay	Nikita Alxeev	R
9.	Calgary	Brent Krahn	G
10.	Chicago	Mikhail Yakubov	C
11.	Chicago	Pavel Vorobiev	R
12.	Anaheim	Alexei Smirnov	L
13.	Montreal	Ron Hainsey	D
14.	Colorado	Vaclav Nedorost	C
15.	Buffalo	Artem Kriukov	C
16.	Montreal	Marcel Hossa	C
17.	Edmonton	Alexei Mikhnov	L
18.	Pittsburgh	Brooks Orpik	D
19.	Phoenix	Krys Kolanos	C
20.	Los Angeles	Alexander Frolov	L
21.	Ottawa	Anton Volchenkov	D
22.	New Jersey	David Hale	D
23.	Vancouver	Nathan Smith	C
24.	Toronto	Brad Boyes	C
25.	Dallas	Steve Ott	L
26.	Washington	Brian Sutherby	C
27.	Boston	Martin Samuelsson	L
28.	Philadelphia	Justin Williams	R
29.	Detroit	Niklas Kronvall	D
30.	St. Louis	Jeff Taffe	C

The More Refs, The Merrier

One thing you probably didn't notice during the 2000 conference finals was the refereeing—and that's a good thing. Several players in the Flyers-Devils series praised the refs for consistently "letting us play," while out West the Stars and Avalanche were also satisfied with the officiating. (Dallas, in fact, didn't gripe even after being assessed eight straight penalties in Game 3.)

This was remarkable, partly because 10 refs appeared in each series and no two worked together twice in a series. When the two-referee system was phased in the previous year, some NHL executives advocated using one or two set pairs of referees to govern each playoff series, feeling such a setup would lead to more consistency. The league's collective bargaining agreement with the officials, however, mandates that they use a total of 10 refs in the conference finals. "The system has worked as well as I could have imagined," said Bryan Lewis, the NHL's head of officiating. "We're able to keep people fresh."

Apparently 20 eyes are better than four for another reason. "Say you had only two guys for the series and you got them angry early on," said Devils coach Larry Robinson. "Then you'd be stuck with them."

The Stanley Cup

Awarded annually to the team that wins the NHL's best-of-seven final-round playoffs. The Stanley Cup is the oldest trophy competed for by professional athletes in North America. It was donated in 1893 by Frederick Arthur, Lord Stanley of Preston.

Results

WINNERS PRIOR TO FORMATION OF NHL IN 1917

1892–93.....Montreal A.A.A.	1900–01.....Winnipeg Victorias	1907–08.....Montreal Wanderers
1893–94.....Montreal A.A.A.	1901–02.....Winnipeg Victorias (Jan)	1908–09.....Ottawa Senators
1894–95.....Montreal Victorias	1901–02.....Montreal A.A.A. (Mar)	1909–10.....Montreal Wanderers
1895–96.....Winnipeg Victorias (Feb)	1902–03.....Montreal A.A.A. (Feb)	1910–11.....Ottawa Senators
1895–96.....Montreal Victorias (Dec)	1902–03.....Ottawa Silver Seven (Mar)	1911–12.....Quebec Bulldogs
1896–97.....Montreal Victorias	1903–04.....Ottawa Silver Seven	1912–13.....Quebec Bulldogs
1897–98.....Montreal Victorias	1904–05.....Ottawa Silver Seven	1913–14.....Toronto Blueshirts
1898–99.....Montreal Victorias (Feb)	1905–06.....Ottawa Silver Seven (Feb)	1914–15.....Vancouver Millionaires
1898–99.....Montreal Shamrocks (Mar)	1905–06.....Montreal Wanderers (Mar)	1915–16.....Montreal Canadiens
1899–1900..Montreal Shamrocks	1906–07.....Kenora Thistles (Jan)	1916–17.....Seattle Metropolitans
	1906–07.....Montreal Wanderers (Mar)	

NHL WINNERS AND FINALISTS

Season	Champion	Finalist	GP in Final
1917–18	Toronto Arenas	Vancouver Millionaires	5
1918–19	No decision*	No decision*	5
1919–20	Ottawa Senators	Seattle Metropolitans	5
1920–21	Ottawa Senators	Vancouver Millionaires	5
1921–22	Toronto St. Pats	Vancouver Millionaires	5
1922–23	Ottawa Senators	Vancouver Maroons, Edmonton Eskimos	2, 4
1923–24	Montreal Canadiens	Vancouver Maroons, Calgary Tigers	2, 2
1924–25	Victoria Cougars	Montreal Canadiens	4
1925–26	Montreal Maroons	Victoria Cougars	4
1926–27	Ottawa Senators	Boston Bruins	4
1927–28	New York Rangers	Montreal Maroons	5
1928–29	Boston Bruins	New York Rangers	2
1929–30	Montreal Canadiens	Boston Bruins	2
1930–31	Montreal Canadiens	Chicago Blackhawks	5
1931–32	Toronto Maple Leafs	New York Rangers	3
1932–33	New York Rangers	Toronto Maple Leafs	4
1933–34	Chicago Blackhawks	Detroit Red Wings	4
1934–35	Montreal Maroons	Toronto Maple Leafs	3
1935–36	Detroit Red Wings	Toronto Maple Leafs	4
1936–37	Detroit Red Wings	New York Rangers	5
1937–38	Chicago Blackhawks	Toronto Maple Leafs	4
1938–39	Boston Bruins	Toronto Maple Leafs	5
1939–40	New York Rangers	Toronto Maple Leafs	6
1940–41	Boston Bruins	Detroit Red Wings	4
1941–42	Toronto Maple Leafs	Detroit Red Wings	7
1942–43	Detroit Red Wings	Boston Bruins	4
1943–44	Montreal Canadiens	Chicago Blackhawks	4
1944–45	Toronto Maple Leafs	Detroit Red Wings	7
1945–46	Montreal Canadiens	Boston Bruins	5
1946–47	Toronto Maple Leafs	Montreal Canadiens	6
1947–48	Toronto Maple Leafs	Detroit Red Wings	4
1948–49	Toronto Maple Leafs	Detroit Red Wings	4
1949–50	Detroit Red Wings	New York Rangers	7
1950–51	Toronto Maple Leafs	Montreal Canadiens	5
1951–52	Detroit Red Wings	Montreal Canadiens	4
1952–53	Montreal Canadiens	Boston Bruins	5
1953–54	Detroit Red Wings	Montreal Canadiens	7
1954–55	Detroit Red Wings	Montreal Canadiens	7
1955–56	Montreal Canadiens	Detroit Red Wings	5
1956–57	Montreal Canadiens	Boston Bruins	5
1957–58	Montreal Canadiens	Boston Bruins	6
1958–59	Montreal Canadiens	Toronto Maple Leafs	5
1959–60	Montreal Canadiens	Toronto Maple Leafs	4
1960–61	Chicago Blackhawks	Detroit Red Wings	6

NHL WINNERS AND FINALISTS (Cont.)

Season	Champion	Finalist	GP in Final
1961–62	Toronto Maple Leafs	Chicago Blackhawks	6
1962–63	Toronto Maple Leafs	Detroit Red Wings	5
1963–64	Toronto Maple Leafs	Detroit Red Wings	7
1964–65	Montreal Canadiens	Chicago Blackhawks	7
1965–66	Montreal Canadiens	Detroit Red Wings	6
1966–67	Toronto Maple Leafs	Montreal Canadiens	6
1967–68	Montreal Canadiens	St. Louis Blues	4
1968–69	Montreal Canadiens	St. Louis Blues	4
1969–70	Boston Bruins	St. Louis Blues	4
1970–71	Montreal Canadiens	Chicago Blackhawks	7
1971–72	Boston Bruins	New York Rangers	6
1972–73	Montreal Canadiens	Chicago Blackhawks	6
1973–74	Philadelphia Flyers	Boston Bruins	6
1974–75	Philadelphia Flyers	Buffalo Sabres	6
1975–76	Montreal Canadiens	Philadelphia Flyers	4
1976–77	Montreal Canadiens	Boston Bruins	4
1977–78	Montreal Canadiens	Boston Bruins	6
1978–79	Montreal Canadiens	New York Rangers	5
1979–80	New York Islanders	Philadelphia Flyers	6
1980–81	New York Islanders	Minnesota North Stars	5
1981–82	New York Islanders	Vancouver Canucks	4
1982–83	New York Islanders	Edmonton Oilers	4
1983–84	Edmonton Oilers	New York Islanders	5
1984–85	Edmonton Oilers	Philadelphia Flyers	5
1985–86	Montreal Canadiens	Calgary Flames	6
1986–87	Edmonton Oilers	Philadelphia Flyers	7
1987–88	Edmonton Oilers	Boston Bruins	4
1988–89	Calgary Flames	Montreal Canadiens	6
1989–90	Edmonton Oilers	Boston Bruins	5
1990–91	Pittsburgh Penguins	Minnesota North Stars	6
1991–92	Pittsburgh Penguins	Chicago Blackhawks	4
1992–93	Montreal Canadiens	Los Angeles Kings	5
1993–94	New York Rangers	Vancouver Canucks	7
1994–95	New Jersey Devils	Detroit Red Wings	4
1995–96	Colorado Avalanche	Florida Panthers	4
1996–97	Detroit Red Wings	Philadelphia Flyers	4
1997–98	Detroit Red Wings	Washington Capitals	4
1998–99	Dallas Stars	Buffalo Sabres	6
1999–00	New Jersey Devils	Dallas Stars	6

*In 1919 the Montreal Canadiens traveled to meet Seattle, the PCHL champions. After 5 games had been played—the teams were tied at 2 wins and 1 tie—the series was called off by the local Department of Health because of the influenza epidemic and the death of Canadian defenseman Joe Hall from influenza.

Conn Smythe Trophy

Awarded to the Most Valuable Player of the Stanley Cup playoffs, as selected by the Professional Hockey Writers Association. The trophy is named after the former coach, general manager, president and owner of the Toronto Maple Leafs.

1965	Jean Beliveau, Mtl	1984	Mark Messier, Edm
1966	Roger Crozier, Det	1985	Wayne Gretzky, Edm
1967	Dave Keon, Tor	1986	Patrick Roy, Mtl
1968	Glenn Hall, StL	1987	Ron Hextall, Phil
1969	Serge Savard, Mtl	1988	Wayne Gretzky, Edm
1970	Bobby Orr, Bos	1989	Al MacInnis, Cgy
1971	Ken Dryden, Mtl	1990	Bill Ranford, Edm
1972	Bobby Orr, Bos	1991	Mario Lemieux, Pitt
1973	Yvan Cournoyer, Mtl	1992	Mario Lemieux, Pitt
1974	Bernie Parent, Phil	1993	Patrick Roy, Mtl
1975	Bernie Parent, Phil	1994	Brian Leetch, NYR
1976	Reggie Leach, Phil	1995	Claude Lemieux, NJ
1977	Guy Lafleur, Mtl	1996	Joe Sakic, Col
1978	Larry Robinson, Mtl	1997	Mike Vernon, Det
1979	Bob Gainey, Mtl	1998	Steve Yzerman, Det
1980	Bryan Trottier, NYI	1999	Joe Nieuwendyk, Dall
1981	Butch Goring, NYI	2000	Scott Stevens, NJ
1982	Mike Bossy, NYI		
1983	Bill Smith, NYI		

Alltime Stanley Cup Playoff Leaders

Points

	Yrs	GP	G	A	Pts		Yrs	GP	G	A	Pts
Wayne Gretzky, four teams	17	208	122	260	382	Denis Potvin, NYI	14	185	56	108	164
*Mark Messier, Edm, NYR	17	236	109	186	295	Mike Bossy, NYI	10	129	85	75	160
Jari Kurri, four teams	15	200	106	127	233	Gordie Howe, Det, Hart	20	157	68	92	160
Glenn Anderson, four teams	15	225	93	121	214	Bobby Smith, Minn, Mtl	13	184	64	96	160
*Paul Coffey, six teams	16	198	59	137	196	*Brett Hull, Cal, StL, Dall	15	153	88	71	159
Bryan Trottier, NYI, Pitt	17	221	71	113	184	*Claude Lemieux, Mtl, NJ, Col	15	221	80	77	157
Jean Beliveau, Mtl	17	162	79	97	176	Mario Lemieux, Pitt	7	89	70	85	155
Denis Savard, Chi, Mtl	16	169	66	109	175	*Steve Yzerman, Det	15	154	61	91	152
*Doug Gilmour, five teams	15	157	54	118	172	*Larry Murphy, six teams	19	209	37	114	151
*Ray Bourque, Bos, Col	20	193	37	133	170	Stan Mikita, Chi	18	155	59	91	150

*Active player.

Goals

	Yrs	GP	G
Wayne Gretzky, four teams	17	208	122
*Mark Messier, Edm, NYR	17	236	109
Jari Kurri, five teams	15	200	106
Glenn Anderson, four teams	15	225	93
*Brett Hull, Cgy, StL, Dall	15	153	88
Mike Bossy, NYI	10	129	85
Maurice Richard, Mtl	15	133	82
*Claude Lemieux, Mtl, NJ, Col	15	221	80
Jean Beliveau, Mtl	17	162	79
Dino Ciccarelli, five teams	14	141	73

*Active player.

Assists

	Yrs	GP	A
Wayne Gretzky, four teams	17	208	260
*Mark Messier, Edm, NYR	17	236	186
*Paul Coffey, six teams	16	198	137
*Ray Bourque, Bos, Col	20	193	133
Jari Kurri, five teams	15	196	127
Glenn Anderson, four teams	15	225	121
*Doug Gilmour, five teams	15	152	118
Larry Robinson, Mtl, LA	20	227	116
*Larry Murphy, six teams	19	209	114
Bryan Trottier, NYI, Pitt	17	221	113

*Active player.

Goaltending

WINS	W	L	Pct
*Patrick Roy, Mtl, Col	127	75	.628
*Grant Fuhr, five teams	92	50	.648
Billy Smith, LA, NYI	88	36	.710
Ken Dryden, Mtl	80	32	.714
*Mike Vernon, four teams	77	60	.562
*Ed Belfour, Chi, SJ, Dall	75	51	.595
Jacques Plante, five teams	71	37	.657
Andy Moog, four teams	68	57	.544
*Tom Barrasso, Buff, Pitt, Ott	59	50	.596
Turk Broda, Tor	58	42	.580

*Active player.

SHUTOUTS	GP	W	SO
Clint Benedict, Ott, Mtl M	48	25	15
*Patrick Roy, Mtl, Col	194	121	15
Jacques Plante, five teams	112	71	14
Ed Belfour, Chi, SJ, Dall	131	75	14
Turk Broda, Tor	101	58	13

GOALS AGAINST AVG	Avg
George Hainsworth, Mtl, Tor	1.93
Turk Broda, Tor	1.98
*Chris Osgood, Det	2.02
Jacques Plante, five teams	2.17
*John Vanbiesbrouck, NYR, Fla, Phil	2.18

Note: At least 50 games played.

Alltime Stanley Cup Standings

TEAM	W	L	Pct	TEAM	W	L	Pct
Montreal	381	249	.605	Colorado**	86	76	.530
Boston	236	252	.484	New Jersey†	73	60	.548
Detroit	233	215	.520	Calgary*	69	87	.442
Toronto	225	244	.479	Washington	65	77	.457
Chicago	187	214	.467	Los Angeles	55	91	.376
NY Rangers	183	195	.484	Vancouver††	54	70	.435
Philadelphia	158	139	.531	Phoenix††	27	59	.313
Edmonton	131	82	.615	Carolina§	20	35	.364
NY Islanders	128	90	.587	San Jose	20	29	.408
Dallas#	126	121	.510	Florida	13	18	.419
St. Louis	120	146	.451	Ottawa	10	18	.357
Pittsburgh	100	90	.526	Anaheim	4	11	.267
Buffalo	92	104	.469	Tampa Bay	2	4	.333

*Atlanta Flames 1972–80. †Colorado Rockies 1976–82. #Minnesota North Stars 1967–93. **Quebec Nordiques 1979–95. ††Winnipeg Jets 1979–96. §Hartford Whalers 1979–97. Note: Teams ranked by playoff victories.

Stanley Cup Coaching Records

Coach	Team	Yrs	Series	W	L	Games	W	L	T	Cups	Pct
			Series				**Games**				
Glen Sather	Edm	10	27	21	6	*126	89	37	0	4	.706
Toe Blake	Mtl	13	23	18	5	119	82	37	0	8	.689
†Scott Bowman	Five teams	26	63	45	18	323	205	119	0	8	.634
Hap Day	Tor	9	14	10	4	80	49	31	0	5	.613
Jacques Lemaire	Mtl, NJ	6	15	10	5	83	49	34	0	1	.590
Al Arbour	StL, NYI	16	42	30	12	209	123	86	0	4	.589
Mike Keenan	five teams	11	28	18	10	160	91	69	0	1	.569
Fred Shero	Phil, NYR	8	21	15	6	108	61	47	0	2	.565
Jacques Demers	Que, StL, Det, Mtl	9	19	11	8	104	57	47	0	1	.548
Bob Johnson	Cgy, Pitt	6	14	9	5	76	41	35	0	1	.539

*Does not include suspended game, May 24, 1988. †Active coach.
Note: Coaches ranked by winning percentage. Minimum: 65 games.

The 10 Longest Overtime Games

Date	Result	OT	Scorer	Series	Series Winner
3-24-36	Det 1 vs Mtl M 0	116:30	Mud Bruneteau	SF	Det
4-3-33	Tor 1 vs Bos 0	104:46	Ken Doraty	SF	Tor
5-4-00	Phil 2 vs Pitt 1	92:01	Keith Primeau	CSF	Phil
4-24-96	Pitt 3 vs Wash 2	79:15	Petr Nedved	CQF	Pitt
3-23-43	Tor 3 vs Det 2	70:18	Jack McLean	SF	Det
3-28-30	Mtl 2 vs NYR 1	68:52	Gus Rivers	SF	Mtl
4-18-87	NYI 3 vs Wash 2	68:47	Pat LaFontaine	DSF	NYI
4-27-94	Buff 1 vs NJ 0	65:43	Dave Hannan	CQF	NJ
3-27-51	Mtl 3 vs Det 2	61:09	Maurice Richard	SF	Mtl
3-27-38	NYA 3 vs NYR 2	60:40	Lorne Carr	QF	NYA

NHL Awards

Hart Memorial Trophy

Awarded annually "to the player adjudged to be the most valuable to his team." The original trophy was donated by Dr. David A. Hart, father of Cecil Hart, former manager-coach of the Montreal Canadiens. In the decade of the 1980s Wayne Gretzky won the award nine of 10 times.

Year	Winner	Key Statistics	Runner-Up
1924	Frank Nighbor, Ott	10 goals, 3 assists in 20 games	Sprague Cleghorn, Mtl
1925	Billy Burch, Ham	20 goals, 4 assists in 27 games	Howie Morenz, Mtl
1926	Nels Stewart, Mtl M	42 points in 36 games	Sprague Cleghorn, Mtl
1927	Herb Gardiner, Mtl	12 points in 44 games as defenseman	Bill Cook, NYR
1928	Howie Morenz, Mtl	33 goals, 18 assists	Roy Worters, Pitt
1929	Roy Worters, NYA	1.21 goals against, 13 shutouts	Ace Bailey, Tor
1930	Nels Stewart, Mtl M	39 goals, 16 assists	Lionel Hitchman, Bos
1931	Howie Morenz, Mtl	28 goals, 23 assists	Eddie Shore, Bos
1932	Howie Morenz, Mtl	24 goals, 25 assists	Ching Johnson, NYR
1933	Eddie Shore, Bos	27 assists in 48 games as defenseman	Bill Cook, NYR
1934	Aurel Joliat, Mtl	27 points	Lionel Conacher, Chi
1935	Eddie Shore, Bos	26 assists in 48 games as defenseman	Charlie Conacher, Tor
1936	Eddie Shore, Bos	16 assists in 46 games as defenseman	Hooley Smith, Mtl M
1937	Babe Siebert, Mtl	28 points	Lionel Conacher, Mtl M
1938	Eddie Shore, Bos	17 points in 47 games as defenseman	Paul Thompson, Chi
1939	Toe Blake, Mtl	led NHL in points (47)	Syl Apps, Tor
1940	Ebbie Goodfellow, Det	28 points	Syl Apps, Tor
1941	Bill Cowley, Bos	led NHL in assists (45) and points (62)	Dit Clapper, Bos
1942	Tom Anderson, Bos	41 points	Syl Apps, Tor
1943	Bill Cowley, Bos	led NHL in assists (45)	Doug Bentley, Chi
1944	Babe Pratt, Tor	57 points in 50 games	Bill Cowley, Bos
1945	Elmer Lach, Mtl	led NHL in assists (54) and points (80)	Maurice Richard, Mtl
1946	Max Bentley, Chi	61 points in 47 games	Gaye Stewart, Tor
1947	Maurice Richard, Mtl	led NHL in goals (45); 26 assists	Milt Schmidt, Bos
1948	Buddy O'Connor, NYR	60 points in 60 games	Frank Brimsek, Bos
1949	Sid Abel, Det	28 goals, 26 assists	Bill Durnan, Mtl

Hart Memorial Trophy *(Cont.)*

Year	Winner	Key Statistics	Runner-Up
1950	Charlie Rayner, NYR	6 shutouts	Ted Kennedy, Tor
1951	Milt Schmidt, Bos	61 points in 62 games	Maurice Richard, Mtl
1952	Gordie Howe, Det	led NHL in goals (47) and points (86)	Elmer Lach, Mtl
1953	Gordie Howe, Det	led NHL in goals (49) and points (95)	Al Rollins, Chi
1954	Al Rollins, Chi	5 shutouts	Red Kelly, Det
1955	Ted Kennedy, Tor	52 points	Harry Lumley, Tor
1956	Jean Beliveau, Mtl	led NHL in goals (47) and points (88)	Tod Sloan, Tor
1957	Gordie Howe, Det	led NHL in goals (44) and points (89)	Jean Beliveau, Mtl
1959	Andy Bathgate, NYR	74 points in 70 games	Gordie Howe, Det
1960	Gordie Howe, Det	45 assists, 73 points	Bobby Hull, Chi
1961	Bernie Geoffrion, Mtl	50 goals, 95 points	Johnny Bower, Tor
1962	Jacques Plante, Mtl	42 wins, 2.37 goals against avg.	Doug Harvey, NYR
1963	Gordie Howe, Det	47 assists, 73 points	Stan Mikita, Chi
1964	Jean Beliveau, Mtl	50 assists, 78 points	Bobby Hull, Chi
1965	Bobby Hull, Chi	39 goals, 32 assists	Norm Ullman, Det
1966	Bobby Hull, Chi	led NHL in goals (54) and points (97)	Jean Beliveau, Mtl
1967	Stan Mikita, Chi	led NHL in goals (62) and points (97)	Ed Giacomin, NYR
1968	Stan Mikita, Chi	40 goals, 47 assists	Jean Beliveau, Mtl
1969	Phil Esposito, Bos	led NHL in assists (77) and points (126)	Jean Beliveau, Mtl
1970	Bobby Orr, Bos	led NHL in assists (87) and points (120)	Tony Esposito, Chi
1971	Bobby Orr, Bos	102 assists, 139 points	Tony Esposito, Chi
1972	Bobby Orr, Bos	80 assists, 117 points	Ken Dryden, Mtl
1973	Bobby Clarke, Phil	67 assists, 104 points	Phil Esposito, Bos
1974	Phil Esposito, Bos	led NHL in goals (68) and points (145)	Bernie Parent, Phil
1975	Bobby Clarke, Phil	89 assists, 116 points	Rogatien Vachon, LA
1976	Bobby Clarke, Phil	89 assists, 119 points	Denis Potvin, NYI
1977	Guy Lafleur, Mtl	led NHL in assists (80) and points (136)	Bobby Clarke, Phil
1978	Guy Lafleur, Mtl	led NHL in goals (60) and points (132)	Bryan Trottier, NYI
1979	Bryan Trottier, NYI	led NHL in assists (87) and points (134)	Guy Lafleur, Mtl
1980	Wayne Gretzky, Edm	51 goals, 86 assists	Marcel Dionne, LA
1981	Wayne Gretzky, Edm	led NHL in assists (109) and points (164)	Mike Liut, StL
1982	Wayne Gretzky, Edm	NHL-record 92 goals and 212 points	Bryan Trottier, NYI
1983	Wayne Gretzky, Edm	led NHL in goals (71) and points (196)	Pete Peeters, Bos
1984	Wayne Gretzky, Edm	led NHL in goals (87) and points (205)	Rod Langway, Wash
1985	Wayne Gretzky, Edm	led NHL in goals (73) and points (208)	Dale Hawerchuk, Winn
1986	Wayne Gretzky, Edm	NHL-record 163 assists and 215 points	Mario Lemieux, Pitt
1987	Wayne Gretzky, Edm	led NHL in assists (121) and points (183)	Ray Bourque, Bos
1988	Mario Lemieux, Pitt	led NHL in goals (70) and points (168)	Grant Fuhr, Edm
1989	Wayne Gretzky, LA	114 assists, 168 points	Mario Lemieux, Pitt
1990	Mark Messier, Edm	84 assists, 129 points ·	Ray Bourque, Bos
1991	Brett Hull, StL	led NHL in goals (86); 131 points	Wayne Gretzky, LA
1992	Mark Messier, NYR	72 assists, 107 points	Patrick Roy, Mtl
1993	Mario Lemieux, Pitt	69 goals, 91 assists in 60 games	Doug Gilmour, Tor
1994	Sergei Fedorov, Det	56 goals, 64 assists	Dominik Hasek, Buff
1995	Eric Lindros, Phil	29 goals, 41 assists in 46 games	Jaromir Jagr, Pitt
1996	Mario Lemieux, Pitt	led NHL in goals (69) and points (161)	Mark Messier, NYR
1997	Dominik Hasek, Buff	5 shutouts, 2.27 goals against	Paul Kariya, Ana
1998	Dominik Hasek, Buff	13 shutouts, 2.09 goals against	Jaromir Jagr, Pitt
1999	Jaromir Jagr, Pitt	44 goals, 127 points	Alexei Yashin, Ott
2000	Chris Pronger, StL	62 points, +52 plus/minus rating	Jaromir Jagr, Pitt

Can't Live Without It

Play at the World Junior Championships in Sweden in January 2000 may have put the kibosh on one of the more drastic ideas for changing the NHL game. As the league has tinkered with the rules in recent years to boost scoring, some observers have suggested that it imitate the NCAA and eliminate the red line. Because a pass that crosses the center line and either blue line usually results in an offsides call, the theory goes that abolishing the red line would enable the NHL's swift skaters to take advantage of long passes and generate more scoring chances.

For the second straight year the World Juniors was played without the red line, and once again the result was plodding, defensive hockey. Defenders were so wary of surrendering a bomb that they routinely retreated to their own zone instead of forechecking. Near the end of the tournament Tommy Tomth, the head of the Swedish junior program, called hockey without the center line "a disgrace." All of which should mean that, no matter how badly the NHL wants to increase scoring, the red line is here to stay.

Art Ross Trophy

Awarded annually "to the player who leads the league in scoring points at the end of the regular season." The trophy was presented to the NHL in 1947 by Arthur Howie Ross, former manager-coach of the Boston Bruins. The tie-breakers, in order, are as follows: (1) player with most goals, (2) player with fewer games played, (3) player scoring first goal of the season. Bobby Orr is the only defenseman in NHL history to win this trophy, and he won it twice (1970 and 1975).

Year	Winner	Pts	Year	Winner	Pts
1919	Newsy Lalonde, Mtl	44	1959	Dickie Moore, Mtl	96
1920	Joe Malone, Que	30	1960	Bobby Hull, Chi	81
1921	Newsy Lalonde, Mtl	48	1961	Bernie Geoffrion, Mtl	95
1922	Punch Broadbent, Ott	41	1962	Bobby Hull, Chi	84
1923	Babe Dye, Tor	46	1963	Gordie Howe, Det	86
1924	Cy Denneny, Ott	37	1964	Stan Mikita, Chi	89
1925	Babe Dye, Tor	23	1965	Stan Mikita, Chi	87
1926	Nels Stewart, Mtl M	44	1966	Bobby Hull, Chi	97
1927	Bill Cook, NYR	42	1967	Stan Mikita, Chi	97
1928	Howie Morenz, Mtl	37	1968	Stan Mikita, Chi	87
1929	Ace Bailey, Tor	51	1969	Phil Esposito, Bos	126
1930	Cooney Weiland, Bos	32	1970	Bobby Orr, Bos	120
1931	Howie Morenz, Mtl	73	1971	Phil Esposito, Bos	152
1932	Harvey Jackson, Tor	51	1972	Phil Esposito, Bos	133
1933	Bill Cook, NYR	53	1973	Phil Esposito, Bos	130
1934	Charlie Conacher, Tor	50	1974	Phil Esposito, Bos	145
1935	Charlie Conacher, Tor	57	1975	Bobby Orr, Bos	135
1936	Sweeney Schriner, NYA	45	1976	Guy Lafleur, Mtl	125
1937	Sweeney Schriner, NYA	46	1977	Guy Lafleur, Mtl	136
1938	Gordie Drillon, Tor	52	1978	Guy Lafleur, Mtl	132
1939	Toe Blake, Mtl	47	1979	Bryan Trottier, NYI	134
1940	Milt Schmidt, Bos	52	1980	Marcel Dionne, LA	137
1941	Bill Cowley, Bos	62	1981	Wayne Gretzky, Edm	164
1942	Bryan Hextall, NYR	56	1982	Wayne Gretzky, Edm	212
1943	Doug Bentley, Chi	73	1983	Wayne Gretzky, Edm	196
1944	Herb Cain, Bos	82	1984	Wayne Gretzky, Edm	205
1945	Elmer Lach, Mtl	80	1985	Wayne Gretzky, Edm	208
1946	Max Bentley, Chi	61	1986	Wayne Gretzky, Edm	215
1947	*Max Bentley, Chi	72	1987	Wayne Gretzky, Edm	183
1948	Elmer Lach, Mtl	61	1988	Mario Lemieux, Pitt	168
1949	Roy Conacher, Chi	68	1989	Mario Lemieux, Pitt	199
1950	Ted Lindsay, Det	78	1990	Wayne Gretzky, LA	142
1951	Gordie Howe, Det	86	1991	Wayne Gretzky, LA	163
1952	Gordie Howe, Det	86	1992	Mario Lemieux, Pitt	131
1953	Gordie Howe, Det	95	1993	Mario Lemieux, Pitt	160
1954	Gordie Howe, Det	81	1994	Wayne Gretzky, LA	130
1955	Bernie Geoffrion, Mtl	75	1995	Jaromir Jagr, Pitt	70
1956	Jean Beliveau, Mtl	88	1996	Mario Lemieux, Pitt	161
1957	Gordie Howe, Det	89	1997	Mario Lemieux, Pitt	122
1958	Dickie Moore, Mtl	84	1998	Jaromir Jagr, Pitt	102
			1999	Jaromir Jagr, Pitt	127
			2000	Jaromir Jagr, Pitt	96

Note: Listing includes scoring leaders prior to inception of Art Ross Trophy in 1947–48.

THEY SAID IT

Bob Ceparano, Islanders fan, after being invited to a pancake breakfast with prospective team owners Charles Wang and Sanjay Kumar: "They're billionaires, and they're taking us to IHOP?"

Lady Byng Memorial Trophy

Awarded annually "to the player adjudged to have exhibited the best type of sportsmanship and gentlemanly conduct combined with a high standard of playing ability." Lady Byng, who first presented the trophy in 1925, was the wife of Canada's Governor-General. She donated a second trophy in 1936 after the first was given permanently to Frank Boucher of the New York Rangers, who won it seven times in eight seasons. Stan Mikita, one of the league's most penalized players during his early years in the NHL, won the trophy twice late in his career (1967 and 1968).

1925..........Frank Nighbor, Ott	1964..........Ken Wharram, Chi
1926..........Frank Nighbor, Ott	1965..........Bobby Hull, Chi
1927..........Billy Burch, NYA	1966..........Alex Delvecchio, Det
1928..........Frank Boucher, NYR	1967..........Stan Mikita, Chi
1929..........Frank Boucher, NYR	1968..........Stan Mikita, Chi
1930..........Frank Boucher, NYR	1969..........Alex Delvecchio, Det
1931..........Frank Boucher, NYR	1970..........Phil Goyette, StL
1932..........Joe Primeau, Tor	1971..........John Bucyk, Bos
1933..........Frank Boucher, NYR	1972..........Jean Ratelle, NYR
1934..........Frank Boucher, NYR	1973..........Gilbert Perreault, Buff
1935..........Frank Boucher, NYR	1974..........John Bucyk, Bos
1936..........Doc Romnes, Chi	1975..........Marcel Dionne, Det
1937..........Marty Barry, Det	1976..........Jean Ratelle, NYR-Bos
1938..........Gordie Drillon, Tor	1977..........Marcel Dionne, LA
1939..........Clint Smith, NYR	1978..........Butch Goring, LA
1940..........Bobby Bauer, Bos	1979..........Bob MacMillan, Atl
1941..........Bobby Bauer, Bos	1980..........Wayne Gretzky, Edm
1942..........Syl Apps, Tor	1981..........Rick Kehoe, Pitt
1943..........Max Bentley, Chi	1982..........Rick Middleton, Bos
1944..........Clint Smith, Chi	1983..........Mike Bossy, NYI
1945..........Billy Mosienko, Chi	1984..........Mike Bossy, NYI
1946..........Toe Blake, Mtl	1985..........Jari Kurri, Edm
1947..........Bobby Bauer, Bos	1986..........Mike Bossy, NYI
1948..........Buddy O'Connor, NYR	1987..........Joe Mullen, Cgy
1949..........Bill Quackenbush, Det	1988..........Mats Naslund, Mtl
1950..........Edgar Laprade, NYR	1989..........Joe Mullen, Cgy
1951..........Red Kelly, Det	1990..........Brett Hull, StL
1952..........Sid Smith, Tor	1991..........Wayne Gretzky, LA
1953..........Red Kelly, Det	1992..........Wayne Gretzky, LA
1954..........Red Kelly, Det	1993..........Pierre Turgeon, NYI
1955..........Sid Smith, Tor	1994..........Wayne Gretzky, LA
1956..........Earl Reibel, Det	1995..........Ron Francis, Pitt
1957..........Andy Hebenton, NYR	1996..........Paul Kariya, Ana
1958..........Camille Henry, NYR	1997..........Paul Kariya, Ana
1959..........Alex Delvecchio, Det	1998..........Ron Francis, Pitt
1960..........Don McKenney, Bos	1999..........Wayne Gretzky, NYR
1961..........Red Kelly, Tor	2000..........Pavol Demitra, StL
1962..........Dave Keon, Tor	
1963..........Dave Keon, Tor	

Awarded annually "to the defense player

Heroic Figurines

Todd McFarlane, creator of the hit comic book *Spawn*, knows from cult classics, which explains the centerpieces of his latest line of McFarlane Toys, hauntingly lifelike, 6½" action figures of hockey stars. Why honor *Slapshot's* Hanson brothers, hockey filmdom's most celebrated thug trio? "As Canadian males, three things are entrenched in our psyche," says McFarlane, also a part-owner of the Oilers. "Hockey, the Hanson Brothers and the MacKenzie Brothers." Yes, *Strange Brew's* Bob and Doug are available too—sticks and skates are not included.

James Norris Memorial Trophy

who demonstrates throughout the season the greatest all-around ability in the position." James Norris was the former owner-president of the Detroit Red Wings. Bobby Orr holds the record for most consecutive times winning the award (eight, 1968–1975).

1954 ....Red Kelly, Det	1970 ....Bobby Orr, Bos	1986 ....Paul Coffey, Edm
1955 ....Doug Harvey, Mtl	1971 ....Bobby Orr, Bos	1987 ....Ray Bourque, Bos
1956 ....Doug Harvey, Mtl	1972 ....Bobby Orr, Bos	1988 ....Ray Bourque, Bos
1957 ....Doug Harvey, Mtl	1973 ....Bobby Orr, Bos	1989 ....Chris Chelios, Mtl
1958 ....Doug Harvey, Mtl	1974 ....Bobby Orr, Bos	1990 ....Ray Bourque, Bos
1959 ....Tom Johnson, Mtl	1975 ....Bobby Orr, Bos	1991 ....Ray Bourque, Bos
1960 ....Doug Harvey, Mtl	1976 ....Denis Potvin, NYI	1992 ....Brian Leetch, NYR
1961 ....Doug Harvey, Mtl	1977 ....Larry Robinson, Mtl	1993 ....Chris Chelios, Chi
1962 ....Doug Harvey, NYR	1978 ....Denis Potvin, NYI	1994 ....Ray Bourque, Bos
1963 ....Pierre Pilote, Chi	1979 ....Denis Potvin, NYI	1995 ....Paul Coffey, Det
1964 ....Pierre Pilote, Chi	1980 ....Larry Robinson, Mtl	1996 ....Chris Chelios, Chi
1965 ....Pierre Pilote, Chi	1981 ....Randy Carlyle, Pitt	1997 ....Brian Leetch, NYR
1966 ....Jacques Laperriere, Mtl	1982 ....Doug Wilson, Chi	1998 ....Rob Blake, LA
1967 ....Harry Howell, NYR	1983 ....Rod Langway, Wash	1999 ....Al MacInnis, StL
1968 ....Bobby Orr, Bos	1984 ....Rod Langway, Wash	2000 ....Chris Pronger, StL
1969 ....Bobby Orr, Bos	1985 ....Paul Coffey, Edm	

Calder Memorial Trophy

Awarded annually "to the player selected as the most proficient in his first year of competition in the National Hockey League." Frank Calder was a former NHL president. Sergei Makarov, who won the award in 1989–90, was the oldest recipient of the trophy, at 31. Players are no longer eligible for the award if they are 26 or older as of September 15th of the season in question.

1933 ....Carl Voss, Det	1956 ....Glenn Hall, Det	1979 ....Bobby Smith, Minn
1934 ....Russ Blinko, Mtl M	1957 ....Larry Regan, Bos	1980 ....Ray Bourque, Bos
1935 ....Dave Schriner, NYA	1958 ....Frank Mahovlich, Tor	1981 ....Peter Stastny, Que
1936 ....Mike Karakas, Chi	1959 ....Ralph Backstrom, Mtl	1982 ....Dale Hawerchuk, Winn
1937 ....Syl Apps, Tor	1960 ....Bill Hay, Chi	1983 ....Steve Larmer, Chi
1938 ....Cully Dahlstrom, Chi	1961 ....Dave Keon, Tor	1984 ....Tom Barrasso, Buff
1939 ....Frank Brimsek, Bos	1962 ....Bobby Rousseau, Mtl	1985 ....Mario Lemieux, Pitt
1940 ....Kilby MacDonald, NYR	1963 ....Kent Douglas, Tor	1986 ....Gary Suter, Cgy
1941 ....Johnny Quilty, Mtl	1964 ....Jacques Laperriere, Mtl	1987 ....Luc Robitaille, LA
1942 ....Grant Warwick, NYR	1965 ....Roger Crozier, Det	1988 ....Joe Nieuwendyk, Cgy
1943 ....Gaye Stewart, Tor	1966 ....Brit Selby, Tor	1989 ....Brian Leetch, NYR
1944 ....Gus Bodnar, Tor	1967 ....Bobby Orr, Bos	1990 ....Sergei Makarov, Cgy
1945 ....Frank McCool, Tor	1968 ....Derek Sanderson, Bos	1991 ....Ed Belfour, Chi
1946 ....Edgar Laprade, NYR	1969 ....Danny Grant, Minn	1992 ....Pavel Bure, Van
1947 ....Howie Meeker, Tor	1970 ....Tony Esposito, Chi	1993 ....Teemu Selanne, Winn
1948 ....Jim McFadden, Det	1971 ....Gilbert Perreault, Buff	1994 ....Martin Brodeur, NJ
1949 ....Pentti Lund, NYR	1972 ....Ken Dryden, Mtl	1995 ....Peter Forsberg, Que
1950 ....Jack Gelineau, Bos	1973 ....Steve Vickers, NYR	1996 ....Daniel Alfredsson, Ott
1951 ....Terry Sawchuk, Det	1974 ....Denis Potvin, NYI	1997 ....Bryan Berard, NYI
1952 ....Bernie Geoffrion, Mtl	1975 ....Eric Vail, Atl	1998 ....Sergei Samsonov, Bos
1953 ....Gump Worsley, NYR	1976 ....Bryan Trottier, NYI	1999 ....Chris Drury, Col
1954 ....Camille Henry, NYR	1977 ....Willi Plett, Atl	2000 ....Scott Gomez, NJ
1955 ....Ed Litzenberger, Chi	1978 ....Mike Bossy, NYI	

Vezina Trophy

Awarded annually "to the goalkeeper adjudged to be the best at his position." The trophy is named after Georges Vezina, an outstanding goalie for the Montreal Canadiens who collapsed during a game on November 28, 1925, and died four months later of tuberculosis. The general managers of the NHL teams vote on the award.

1927 ....George Hainsworth, Mtl	1956 ....Jacques Plante, Mtl	1978 ....Ken Dryden, Mtl
1928 ....George Hainsworth, Mtl	1957 ....Jacques Plante, Mtl	Michel Larocque, Mtl
1929 ....George Hainsworth, Mtl	1958 ....Jacques Plante, Mtl	1979 ....Ken Dryden, Mtl
1930 ....Tiny Thompson, Bos	1959 ....Jacques Plante, Mtl	Michel Larocque, Mtl
1931 ....Roy Worters, NYA	1960 ....Jacques Plante, Mtl	1980 ....Bob Sauve, Buff
1932 ....Charlie Gardiner, Chi	1961 ....Johnny Bower, Tor	Don Edwards, Buff
1933 ....Tiny Thompson, Bos	1962 ....Jacques Plante, Mtl	1981 ....Richard Sevigny, Mtl
1934 ....Charlie Gardiner, Chi	1963 ....Glenn Hall, Chi	Denis Herron, Mtl
1935 ....Lorne Chabot, Chi	1964 ....Charlie Hodge, Mtl	Michel Larocque, Mtl
1936 ....Tiny Thompson, Bos	1965 ....Terry Sawchuk, Tor	1982 ....Billy Smith, NYI
1937 ....Normie Smith, Det	Johnny Bower, Tor	1983 ....Pete Peeters, Bos
1938 ....Tiny Thompson, Bos	1966 ....Gump Worsley, Mtl	1984 ....Tom Barrasso, Buff
1939 ....Frank Brimsek, Bos	Charlie Hodge, Mtl	1985 ....Pelle Lindbergh, Phil
1940 ....Dave Kerr, NYR	1967 ....Glenn Hall, Chi	1986 ....John Vanbiesbrouck,
1941 ....Turk Broda, Tor	Rogie Vachon, Mtl	NYR
1942 ....Frank Brimsek, Bos	1969 ....Jacques Plante, StL	1987 ....Ron Hextall, Phil
1943 ....Johnny Mowers, Det	Glenn Hall, StL	1988 ....Grant Fuhr, Edm
1944 ....Bill Durnan, Mtl	1970 ....Tony Esposito, Chi	1989 ....Patrick Roy, Mtl
1945 ....Bill Durnan, Mtl	1971 ....Ed Giacomin, NYR	1990 ....Patrick Roy, Mtl
1946 ....Bill Durnan, Mtl	Gilles Villemure, NYR	1991 ....Ed Belfour, Chi
1947 ....Bill Durnan, Mtl	1972 ....Tony Esposito, Chi	1992 ....Patrick Roy, Mtl
1948 ....Turk Broda, Tor	Gary Smith, Chi	1993 ....Ed Belfour, Chi
1949 ....Bill Durnan, Mtl	1973 ....Ken Dryden, Mtl	1994 ....Dominik Hasek, Buff
1950 ....Bill Durnan, Mtl	1974 ....Bernie Parent, Phil	1995 ....Dominik Hasek, Buff
1951 ....Al Rollins, Tor	Tony Esposito, Chi	1996 ....Jim Carey, Wash
1952 ....Terry Sawchuk, Det	1975 ....Bernie Parent, Phil	1997 ....Dominik Hasek, Buff
1953 ....Terry Sawchuk, Det	1976 ....Ken Dryden, Mtl	1998 ....Dominik Hasek, Buff
1954 ....Harry Lumley, Tor	1977 ....Ken Dryden, Mtl	1999 ....Dominik Hasek, Buff
1955 ....Terry Sawchuk, Det	Michel Larocque, Mtl	2000 ....Olaf Kolzig, Wash

Selke Trophy

Awarded annually "to the forward who best excels in the defensive aspects of the game." The trophy is named after Frank J. Selke, the architect of the Montreal Canadians dynasty that won five consecutive Stanley Cups in the late '50s. The winner is selected by a vote of the Professional Hockey Writers Association

1978........Bob Gainey, Mtl	1986........Troy Murray, Chi	1994........Sergei Fedorov, Det
1979........Bob Gainey, Mtl	1987........Dave Poulin, Phil	1995........Ron Francis, Pitt
1980........Bob Gainey, Mtl	1988........Guy Carbonneau, Mtl	1996........Sergei Fedorov, Det
1981........Bob Gainey, Mtl	1989........Guy Carbonneau, Mtl	1997........Michael Peca, Buff
1982........Steve Kasper, Bos	1990........Rick Meagher, StL	1998........Jere Lehtinen, Dall
1983........Bobby Clarke, Phil	1991........Dirk Graham, Chi	1999........Jere Lehtinen, Dall
1984........Doug Jarvis, Wash	1992........Guy Carbonneau, Mtl	2000........Steve Yzerman, Det
1985........Craig Ramsay, Buff	1993........Doug Gilmour, Tor	1974 .....Fred Shero, Phil

Revenge is Sweet

In 1990 goalie Arturs Irbe bolted the Soviet team to protest the U.S.S.R.'s invasion of Latvia, his homeland. Latvia was on the verge of declaring independence from the Soviet Union, and Irbe and his family traced their nationalistic pride to when his grandfather fought for the Latvian Legion against the Soviets in World War II. Now Irbe is the Hurricanes' starting netminder, and he and his wife, Ilze, and their two children return to Latvia each off-season. So it came as no surprise that Irbe agreed to play for his native country in the World Championships in St. Petersburg, Russia. The shocker occurred when Irbe led lightly regarded Latvia past powerful Russia in a second-round game that helped lead to Russia's elimination from the tournament. (Latvia had advanced to the quarterfinals.) Irbe made 37 saves, including several big stops in the third period to preserve the lead. "I have lived 33 years in my life," Irbe said afterward, "and I basically lived for this one game."

Adams Award

Awarded annually "to the NHL coach adjudged to have contributed the most to his team's success." The trophy is named in honor of Jack Adams, longtime coach and general manager of the Detroit Red Wings. The winner is selected by a vote of the National Hockey League Broadcasters' Association.

1975 .....Bob Pulford, LA	1984 .....Bryan Murray, Wash	1993 .....Pat Burns, Tor
1976 .....Don Cherry, Bos	1985 .....Mike Keenan, Phil	1994 .....Jacques Lemaire, NJ
1977 .....Scott Bowman, Mtl	1986 .....Glen Sather, Edm	1995 .....Marc Crawford, Que
1978 .....Bobby Kromm, Det	1987 .....Jacques Demers, Det	1996 ....Scotty Bowman, Det
1979 .....Al Arbour, NYI	1988 .....Jacques Demers, Det	1997 .....Ted Nolan, Buff
1980 .....Pat Quinn, Phil	1989 ....Pat Burns, Mtl	1998 ....Pat Burns, Bos
1981 .....Red Berenson, StL	1990 .....Bob Murdoch, Winn	1999 ....Jacques Martin, Ott
1982 .....Tom Watt, Winn	1991 .....Brian Sutter, StL	2000 .....Joel Quenneville, StL
1983 ....Orval Tessier, Chi	1992 .....Pat Quinn, Van	

Career Records

Alltime Point Leaders

	Player	Yrs	GP	G	A	Pts	Pts/game
1.	Wayne Gretzky, Edm, LA, StL, NYR	20	1487	894	1963	2857	1.921
2.	Gordie Howe, Det, Hart	26	1767	801	1049	1850	1.047
3.	Marcel Dionne, Det, LA, NYR	18	1348	731	1040	1771	1.314
4.	*Mark Messier, Edm, NYR, Van	21	1479	627	1087	1714	1.158
5.	Phil Esposito, Chi, Bos, NYR	18	1282	717	873	1590	1.240
6.	*Steve Yzerman, Det	17	1256	627	935	1562	1.243
7.	*Ron Francis, Hart, Pitt, Car	19	1407	472	1087	1559	1.108
8.	*Paul Coffey, eight teams	20	1391	396	1131	1527	1.097
9.	*Ray Bourque, Bos, Col	21	1532	403	1117	1520	.992
10.	Mario Lemieux, Pitt	12	745	613	881	1494	2.005
11.	Stan Mikita, Chi	22	1394	541	926	1467	1.052
12.	Bryan Trottier, NYI, Pitt	18	1279	524	901	1425	1.114
13.	Dale Hawerchuk, Winn, Buff, StL, Phil	16	1188	518	891	1409	1.186
14.	Jari Kurri, Edm, LA, NYR, Ana, Col	17	1251	601	797	1397	1.118
15.	John Bucyk, Det, Bos	23	1540	556	813	1369	.889

*Active in 1999–00.

Alltime Goal-Scoring Leaders

	Player	Yrs	GP	G	G/game
1.	Wayne Gretzky, Edm, LA, StL, NYR	20	1487	894	.601
2.	Gordie Howe, Det, Hart	26	1767	801	.453
3.	Marcel Dionne, Det, LA, NYR	18	1348	731	.542
4.	Phil Esposito, Chi, Bos, NYR	18	1282	717	.559
5.	Mike Gartner, Wash, Minn, NYR, Tor, Phoe	19	1432	708	.494
6.	*Mark Messier, Edm, NYR, Van	21	1479	627	.423
7.	*Steve Yzerman, Det	17	1256	627	.499
8.	Mario Lemieux, Pitt	12	745	613	.823
9.	Bobby Hull, Chi, Winn, Hart	16	1063	610	.574
10.	*Brett Hull, Cal, StL, Dall	15	940	610	.648

*Active in 1999–00.

Alltime Assist Leaders

	Player	Yrs	GP	A	A/game
1.	Wayne Gretzky, Edm, LA, StL, NYR	20	1487	1963	1.320
2.	*Paul Coffey, eight teams	20	1391	1131	.813
3.	*Ray Bourque, Bos, Col	21	1532	1117	.729
4.	*Mark Messier, Edm, NYR, Van	21	1479	1087	.734
5.	*Ron Francis, Hart, Pitt, Car	19	1407	1087	.772
6.	Gordie Howe, Det, Hart	26	1767	1049	.594
7.	Marcel Dionne, Det, LA, NYR	18	1348	1040	.771
8.	*Steve Yzerman, Det	17	1256	935	.744
9.	Stan Mikita, Chi	22	1394	926	.664
10.	*Larry Murphy, six teams	20	1558	910	.584

*Active player.

Alltime Penalty Minutes Leaders

	Player	Yrs	GP	PIM	Min/game
1.	Dave Williams, Tor, Van, Det, LA, Hart	14	962	3966	4.12
2.	Dale Hunter, Que, Wash, Col	19	1407	3565	2.53
3.	*Marty McSorley, six teams	17	961	3381	3.52
4.	Tim Hunter, Calg, Que, Van, SJ	16	815	3146	3.86
5.	Chris Nilan, Mtl, NYR, Bos	13	688	3043	4.42
6.	*Bob Probert, Det, Chi	14	795	3021	3.80
7.	*Rick Tocchet, Phil, Pitt, LA, Bos, Wash, Phoe	16	1054	2838	2.69
8.	*Craig Berube, Phil, Tor, Cgy, Wash	14	873	2813	3.22
9.	*Pat Verbeek, NJ, Hart, NYR, Dall, Det	18	1293	2760	2.13
10.	*Rob Ray, Buff	11	714	2687	3.76

*Active player.

The Cat on The Hat

Chinese ideograms, known in the U.S. by the Japanese word kanji, have become the tattoos of choice among rappers and their fans, and now puckheads are sporting the symbols as well. After the NHL unveiled a line of baseball caps emblazoned with the kanji corresponding to each team's nickname, it made sense that Predators general manger Dave Poile and his Penguins counterpart, Craig Patrick, donned their respective kanji caps for the announcement that Nashville and Pittsburgh would play two regular-season games in Japan in October 2000.

Poile, however, won't be wearing that same cap in Tokyo. Shortly after the announcement, one of the Predators' minority owners, Terry London, showed the cap to his Japanese daughter-in-law, who pointed out that the kanji on it would be translated as "pussycat." That's a far less intimidating creature than the snarling, fanged feline on Nashville's logo would seem to suggest, and lest the Predators get heckled for being a bunch of ...well, you know, the NHL stopped production on the new Nashville caps and will issue new ones with the kanji for tiger.

Goaltending Records

ALLTIME WIN LEADERS

Goaltender	W	L	T	Pct
Terry Sawchuk, five teams	447	330	173	.562
*Patrick Roy, Mtl, Col	444	264	103	.611
Jacques Plante, five teams	434	246	147	.614
Tony Esposito, Mtl, Chi	423	306	152	.566
Glenn Hall, Det, Chi, StL	407	327	163	.545
*Grant Fuhr, six teams	403	295	114	.567
Andy Moog, Edm, Bos, Dall, Mtl	372	209	88	.622
*Mike Vernon, Cgy, Det, SJ, Fla	371	241	86	.593
*John Vanbiesbrouck, NYR, Fla, Phil	358	318	114	.525
Rogie Vachon, Mtl, LA, Det, Bos	355	291	127	.541

*Active player.

ACTIVE GOALTENDING LEADERS

Goaltender	W	L	T	Pct
Chris Osgood, Det	196	91	42	.660
Martin Brodeur, NJ	244	125	65	.637
Patrick Roy, Mtl, Col	444	264	103	.611
Ed Belfour, Chi, SJ, Dall	308	195	82	.597
Mike Vernon, Cgy, Det, SJ, Fla	371	241	86	.593
Dominik Hasek, Chi, Buff	210	151	68	.569
Tom Barrasso, Buff, Pitt, Ott	353	259	81	.568
Grant Fuhr, six teams	403	295	114	.567
Curtis Joseph, StL, Edm, Tor	284	216	68	560
Mike Richter, NYR	252	205	65	.545

Note: Ranked by winning percentage; minimum 250 games played.

ALLTIME SHUTOUT LEADERS

Goaltender	Team	Yrs	GP	SO
Terry Sawchuk	Det, Bos, Tor, LA, NYR	21	971	103
George Hainsworth	Mtl, Tor	11	465	94
Glenn Hall	Det, Chi, StL	18	906	84
Jacques Plante	Mtl, NYR, StL, Tor, Bos	18	837	82
Tiny Thompson	Bos, Det	12	553	81
Alex Connell	Ott, Det, NYA, Mtl M	12	417	81
Tony Esposito	Mtl, Chi	16	886	76
Lorne Chabot	NYR, Tor, Mtl, Chi, Mtl M, NYA	11	411	73
Harry Lumley	Det, NYR, Chi, Tor, Bos	16	804	71
Roy Worters	Pitt Pir, NYA, *Mtl	12	484	66

*Played 1 game for Canadiens in 1929–30, not a shutout.

ALLTIME GOALS AGAINST AVERAGE LEADERS (PRE-1950)

Goaltender	Team	Yrs	GP	GA	GAA
George Hainsworth	Mtl, Tor	11	465	937	1.91
Alex Connell	Ott, Det, NYA, Mtl M	12	417	830	1.91
Chuck Gardiner	Chi	7	316	664	2.02
Lorne Chabot	NYR, Tor, Mtl, Chi, Mtl M, NYA	11	411	861	2.04
Tiny Thompson	Bos, Det	12	553	1183	2.08

ALLTIME GOALS AGAINST AVERAGE LEADERS (POST-1950)

Goaltender	Team	Yrs	GP	GA	GAA
Ken Dryden	Mtl	8	397	870	2.24
*Dominik Hasek	Chi, Buff	10	449	977	2.35
*Martin Brodeur	NJ	8	447	950	2.36
*Chris Osgood	Det	7	337	773	2.37
Jacques Plante	Mtl, NYR, StL, Tor, Bos	18	837	1965	2.38

*Active player

Note: Minimum 250 games played. Goals against average equals goals against per 60 minutes played.

Coaching Records

Coach	Team	Seasons	W	L	T	Pct
*Scott Bowman	five teams	1967–87, 91–	1148	539	295	.654
Toe Blake	Mtl	1955–68	500	255	159	.634
Glen Sather	Edm	1979–89, 93–94	464	268	110	.616
Fred Shero	Phil, NYR	1971–81	390	225	119	.612
Mike Keenan	five teams	1984–1999	506	360	115	.574
Emile Francis	NYR, StL	1965–77, 81–83	388	273	117	.574
Billy Reay	Tor, Chi	1957–59, 63–77	542	385	175	.571
*Terry Murray	Wash, Phil, Fla	1989–	354	265	82	.563
Bryan Murray	Wash, Det, Fla	1981–98	484	368	123	.559
*Pat Burns	Mtl, Tor, Bos	1988–	409	310	128	.558

Note: Minimum 600 regular-season games. Ranked by percentage.

Single-Season Records

Goals

Player	Season	GP	G	Player	Season	GP	G
Wayne Gretzky, Edm	1981–82	80	92	Wayne Gretzky, Edm	1982–83	80	71
Wayne Gretzky, Edm	1983–84	74	87	Brett Hull, StL	1991–92	73	70
Brett Hull, StL	1990–91	78	86	Mario Lemieux, Pitt	1987–88	77	70
Mario Lemieux, Pitt	1988–89	76	85	Bernie Nicholls, LA	1988–89	79	70
Alexander Mogilny, Buff	1992–93	77	76	Mario Lemieux, Pitt	1992–93	60	69
Phil Esposito, Bos	1970–71	78	76	Mario Lemieux, Pitt	1995–96	70	69
Teemu Selanne, Winn	1992–93	84	76	Mike Bossy, NYI	1978–79	80	69
Wayne Gretzky, Edm	1984–85	80	73	Phil Esposito, Bos	1973–74	78	68
Brett Hull, StL	1989–90	80	72	Jari Kurri, Edm	1985–86	78	68
Jari Kurri, Edm	1984–85	73	71	Mike Bossy, NYI	1980–81	79	68

Assists

Player	Season	GP	A	Player	Season	GP	A
Wayne Gretzky, Edm	1985–86	80	163	Wayne Gretzky, LA	1989–90	73	102
Wayne Gretzky, Edm	1984–85	80	135	Bobby Orr, Bos	1970–71	78	102
Wayne Gretzky, Edm	1982–83	80	125	Mario Lemieux, Pitt	1987–88	77	98
Wayne Gretzky, LA	1990–91	78	122	Adam Oates, LA	1992–93	84	97
Wayne Gretzky, Edm	1986–87	79	121	Doug Gilmour, Tor	1992–93	83	95
Wayne Gretzky, Edm	1981–82	80	120	Pat LaFontaine, Buff	1992–93	84	95
Wayne Gretzky, Edm	1983–84	74	118	Mario Lemieux, Pitt	1985–86	79	93
Mario Lemieux, Pitt	1988–89	76	114	Peter Stastny, Que	1981–82	80	93
Wayne Gretzky, LA	1988–89	78	114	Wayne Gretzky, LA	1993–94	81	92
Wayne Gretzky, Edm	1987–88	64	109	Mario Lemieux, Pitt	1995–96	70	92
Wayne Gretzky, Edm	1980–81	80	109	Ron Francis, Pitt	1995–96	77	92

Points

Player	Season	G	A	Pts	Player	Season	G	A	Pts
Wayne Gretzky, Edm	1985–86	52	163	215	Wayne Gretzky, LA	1990–91	41	122	163
Wayne Gretzky, Edm	1981–82	92	120	212	Mario Lemieux, Pitt	1995–96	69	92	161
Wayne Gretzky, Edm	1984–85	73	135	208	Mario Lemieux, Pitt	1992–93	69	91	160
Wayne Gretzky, Edm	1983–84	87	118	205	Steve Yzerman, Det	1988–89	65	90	155
Mario Lemieux, Pitt	1988–89	85	114	199	Phil Esposito, Bos	1970–71	76	76	152
Wayne Gretzky, Edm	1982–83	71	125	196	Bernie Nicholls, LA	1988–89	70	80	150
Wayne Gretzky, Edm	1986–87	62	121	183	Wayne Gretzky, Edm	1987–88	40	109	149
Mario Lemieux, Pitt	1987–88	70	98	168	Pat LaFontaine, Buff	1992–93	53	95	148
Wayne Gretzky, LA	1988–89	54	114	168	Mike Bossy, NYI	1981–82	64	83	147
Wayne Gretzky, Edm	1980–81	55	109	164	Phil Esposito, Bos	1973–74	68	77	145

Points per Game

Player	Season	GP	Pts	Avg	Player	Season	GP	Pts	Avg
Wayne Gretzky, Edm	1983–84	74	205	2.77	Mario Lemieux, Pitt	1987–88	77	168	2.18
Wayne Gretzky, Edm	1985–86	80	215	2.69	Wayne Gretzky, LA	1988–89	78	168	2.15
Mario Lemieux, Pitt	1992–93	60	160	2.67	Wayne Gretzky, LA	1990–91	78	163	2.09
Wayne Gretzky, Edm	1981–82	80	212	2.65	Mario Lemieux, Pitt	1989–90	59	123	2.08
Mario Lemieux, Pitt	1988–89	76	199	2.62	Wayne Gretzky, Edm	1980–81	80	164	2.05
Wayne Gretzky, Edm	1984–85	80	208	2.60	Mario Lemieux, Pitt	1991–92	64	131	2.05
Wayne Gretzky, Edm	1982–83	80	196	2.45	Bill Cowley, Bos	1943–44	36	71	1.97
Wayne Gretzky, Edm	1987–88	64	149	2.33	Phil Esposito, Bos	1970–71	78	152	1.95
Wayne Gretzky, Edm	1986–87	79	183	2.32	Wayne Gretzky, LA	1989–90	73	142	1.95
Mario Lemieux, Pitt	1995–96	70	161	2.30	Steve Yzerman, Det	1988–89	80	155	1.94

Note: Minimum 50 points in one season.

Goals per Game

Player	Season	GP	G	Avg
Joe Malone, Mtl	1917–18	20	44	2.20
Cy Denneny, Ott	1917–18	22	36	1.64
Newsy Lalonde, Mtl	1917–18	14	23	1.64
Joe Malone, Que	1919–20	24	39	1.63
Newsy Lalonde, Mtl	1919–20	23	36	1.57
Joe Malone, Ham	1920–21	20	30	1.50
Babe Dye, Ham-Tor	1920–21	24	35	1.46
Cy Denneny, Ott	1920–21	24	34	1.42
Reg Noble, Tor	1917–18	20	28	1.40
Newsy Lalonde, Mtl	1920–21	24	33	1.38

Note: Minimum 20 goals in one season.

Assists per Game

Player	Season	GP	A	Avg
Wayne Gretzky, Edm	1985–86	80	163	2.04
Wayne Gretzky, Edm	1987–88	64	109	1.70
Wayne Gretzky, Edm	1984–85	80	135	1.69
Wayne Gretzky, Edm	1983–84	74	118	1.59
Wayne Gretzky, Edm	1982–83	80	125	1.56
Wayne Gretzky, LA	1990–91	78	122	1.56
Wayne Gretzky, Edm	1986–87	79	121	1.53
Mario Lemieux, Pitt	1992–93	60	91	1.52
Wayne Gretzky, Edm	1981–82	80	120	1.50
Mario Lemieux, Pitt	1988–89	76	114	1.50

Note: Minimum 35 assists in one season.

Shutout Leaders

	Season	SO	Length of Schedule
George Hainsworth, Mtl	1928–29	22	44
Alex Connell, Ott	1925–26	15	36
Alex Connell, Ott	1927–28	15	44
Hal Winkler, Bos	1927–28	15	44
Tony Esposito, Chi	1969–70	15	76
George Hainsworth, Mtl	1926–27	14	44
Clint Benedict, Mtl M	1926–27	13	44
Alex Connell, Ott	1926–27	13	44
George Hainsworth, Mtl	1927–28	13	44
John Roach, NYR	1928–29	13	44
Roy Worters, NYA	1928–29	13	44
Harry Lumley, Tor	1953–54	13	70
Dominik Hasek, Buff	1997–98	13	82
Tiny Thompson, Bos	1928–29	12	44
Lorne Chabot, Tor	1928–29	12	44
Chuck Gardiner, Chi	1930–31	12	44
Terry Sawchuk, Det	1951–52	12	70
Terry Sawchuk, Det	1953–54	12	70
Terry Sawchuk, Det	1954–55	12	70
Glenn Hall, Det	1955–56	12	70
Bernie Parent, Phil	1973–74	12	78
Bernie Parent, Phil	1974–75	12	80

	Season	SO	Length of Schedule
Lorne Chabot, NYR	1927–28	11	44
Harry Holmes, Det	1927–28	11	44
Clint Benedict, Mtl M	1928–29	11	44
Joe Miller, Pitt Pirates	1928–29	11	44
Tiny Thompson, Bos	1932–33	11	48
Terry Sawchuk, Det	1950–51	11	70
Lorne Chabot, NYR	1926–27	10	44
Roy Worters, Pitt Pirates	1927–28	10	44
Clarence Dolson, Det	1928–29	10	44
John Roach, Det	1932–33	10	48
Chuck Gardiner, Chi	1933–34	10	48
Tiny Thompson, Bos	1935–36	10	48
Frank Brimsek, Bos	1938–39	10	48
Bill Durnan, Mtl	1948–49	10	60
Gerry McNeil, Mtl	1952–53	10	70
Harry Lumley, Tor	1952–53	10	70
Tony Esposito, Chi	1973–74	10	78
Ken Dryden, Mtl	1976–77	10	80
Martin Brodeur, NJ	1996–97	10	82
Martin Brodeur, NJ	1997–98	10	82
Byron Dafoe, Bos	1998–99	10	82

Wins

	Season	Record
Bernie Parent, Phil	1973–74	47-13-12
Bernie Parent, Phil	1974–75	44-14-9
Terry Sawchuk, Det	1950–51	44-13-13
Terry Sawchuk, Det	1951–52	44-14-12
Tom Barasso, Pitt	1992–93	43-14-5
Ed Belfour, Chi	1990–91	43-19-7
Martin Brodeur, NJ	1997–98	43-17-8
Martin Brodeur, NJ	1999–00	43-20-8
Jacques Plante, Mtl	1955–56	42-12-10
Jacques Plante, Mtl	1961–62	42-14-14
Ken Dryden, Mtl	1975–76	42-10-8
Mike Richter, NYR	1993–94	42-12-6
Roman Turek, StL	1999–00	42-15-9

Goals Against Average

(PRE-1950)

	Season	GP	GAA
George Hainsworth, Mtl	1928–29	44	0.92
George Hainsworth, Mtl	1927–28	44	1.05
Alex Connell, Ott	1925–26	36	1.12
Tiny Thompson, Bos	1928–29	44	1.18
Roy Worters, NYA	1928–29	38	1.21

(POST-1950)

	Season	GP	GAA
Al Rollins, Tor	1950–51	40	1.7744
Tony Esposito, Chi	1971–72	48	1.7698
Ron Tugnutt, Ott	1998–99	43	1.7943
Jacques Plante, Mtl	1955–56	64	1.8594
Harry Lumley, Tor	1953–54	69	1.8551
Dominik Hasek, Buff	1998–99	64	1.8706
Martin Brodeur, NJ	1996–97	67	1.8759
Ed Belfour, Dall	1997–98	61	1.8766

Single-Game Records

Goals

	Date	G
Joe Malone, Que vs Tor	1-31-20	7
Newsy Lalonde, Mtl vs Tor	1-10-20	6
Joe Malone, Que vs Ott	3-10-20	6
Corb Denneny, Tor vs Ham	1-26-21	6
Cy Denneny, Ott vs Ham	3-7-21	6
Syd Howe, Det vs NYR	2-3-44	6
Red Berenson, StL vs Phil	11-7-68	6
Darryl Sittler, Tor vs Bos	2-7-76	6

Assists

	Date	A
Billy Taylor, Det vs Chi	3-16-47	7
Wayne Gretzky, Edm vs Wash	2-15-80	7
Wayne Gretzky, Edm vs Chi	12-11-85	7
Wayne Gretzky, Edm vs Que	2-14-86	7

Note: 19 tied with 6.

Points

	Date	G	A	Pts
Darryl Sittler, Tor vs Bos	2-7-76	6	4	10
Maurice Richard, Mtl vs Det	12-28-44	5	3	8
Bert Olmstead, Mtl vs Chi	1-9-54	4	4	8
Tom Bladon, Phil vs Clev	12-11-77	4	4	8
Bryan Trottier, NYI vs NYR	12-23-78	5	3	8
Peter Stastny, Que vs Wash	2-22-81	4	4	8
Anton Stastny, Que vs Wash	2-22-81	3	5	8
Wayne Gretzky, Edm vs NJ	11-19-83	3	5	8
Wayne Gretzky, Edm vs Minn	1-4-84	4	4	8
Paul Coffey, Edm vs Det	3-14-86	2	6	8
Mario Lemieux, Pitt vs StL	10-15-88	2	6	8
Bernie Nicholls, LA vs Tor	12-1-88	2	6	8
Mario Lemieux, Pitt vs NJ	12-31-88	5	3	8

NHL Season Leaders

Points

Season	Player and Club	Pts	Season	Player and Club	Pts
1917–18	Joe Malone, Mtl	44	1952–53	Gordie Howe, Det	95
1918–19	Newsy Lalonde, Mtl	30	1953–54	Gordie Howe, Det	81
1919–20	Joe Malone, Que	48	1954–55	Bernie Geoffrion, Mtl	75
1920–21	Newsy Lalonde, Mtl	41	1955–56	Jean Beliveau, Mtl	88
1921–22	Punch Broadbent, Ott	46	1956–57	Gordie Howe, Det	89
1922–23	Babe Dye, Tor	37	1957–58	Dickie Moore, Mtl	84
1923–24	Cy Denneny, Ott	23	1958–59	Dickie Moore, Mtl	96
1924–25	Babe Dye, Tor	44	1959–60	Bobby Hull, Chi	81
1925–26	Nels Stewart, Mtl M	42	1960–61	Bernie Geoffrion, Mtl	95
1926–27	Bill Cook, NY	37	1961–62	Andy Bathgate, NY	84
1927–28	Howie Morenz, Mtl	51		Bobby Hull, Chi	84
1928–29	Ace Bailey, Tor	32	1962–63	Gordie Howe, Det	86
1929–30	Cooney Weiland, Bos	73	1963–64	Stan Mikita, Chi	89
1930–31	Howie Morenz, Mtl	51	1964–65	Stan Mikita, Chi	87
1931–32	Harvey Jackson, Tor	53	1965–66	Bobby Hull, Chi	97
1932–33	Bill Cook, NY	50	1966–67	Stan Mikita, Chi	97
1933–34	Charlie Conacher, Tor	52	1967–68	Stan Mikita, Chi	87
1934–35	Charlie Conacher, Tor	57	1968–69	Phil Esposito, Bos	126
1935–36	Sweeney Schriner, NYA	45	1969–70	Bobby Orr, Bos	120
1936–37	Sweeney Schriner, NYA	46	1970–71	Phil Esposito, Bos	152
1937–38	Gord Drillon, Tor	52	1971–72	Phil Esposito, Bos	133
1938–39	Hector Blake, Mtl	47	1972–73	Phil Esposito, Bos	130
1939–40	Milt Schmidt, Bos	52	1973–74	Phil Esposito, Bos	145
1940–41	Bill Cowley, Bos	62	1974–75	Bobby Orr, Bos	135
1941–42	Bryan Hextall, NY	54	1975–76	Guy Lafleur, Mtl	125
1942–43	Doug Bentley, Chi	73	1976–77	Guy Lafleur, Mtl	136
1943–44	Herb Cain, Bos	82	1977–78	Guy Lafleur, Mtl	132
1944–45	Elmer Lach, Mtl	80	1978–79	Bryan Trottier, NYI	134
1945–46	Max Bentley, Chi	61	1979–80	Marcel Dionne, LA	137
1946–47	Max Bentley, Chi	72		Wayne Gretzky, Edm	137
1947–48	Elmer Lach, Mtl	61	1980–81	Wayne Gretzky, Edm	164
1948–49	Roy Conacher, Chi	68	1981–82	Wayne Gretzky, Edm	212
1949–50	Ted Lindsay, Det	78	1982–83	Wayne Gretzky, Edm	196
1950–51	Gordie Howe, Det	86	1983–84	Wayne Gretzky, Edm	205
1951–52	Gordie Howe, Det	86	1984–85	Wayne Gretzky, Edm	208

Points (Cont.)

Season	Player and Club	Pts	Season	Player and Club	Pts
1985–86	Wayne Gretzky, Edm	215	1993–94	Wayne Gretzky, LA	130
1986–87	Wayne Gretzky, Edm	183	1994–95	Jaromir Jagr, Pitt	70
1987–88	Mario Lemieux, Pitt	168	1995–96	Mario Lemieux, Pitt	161
1988–89	Mario Lemieux, Pitt	199	1996–97	Mario Lemieux, Pitt	122
1989–90	Wayne Gretzky, LA	142	1997–98	Jaromir Jagr, Pitt	102
1990–91	Wayne Gretzky, LA	163	1998–99	Jaromir Jagr, Pitt	127
1991–92	Mario Lemieux, Pitt	131	1999–00	Jaromir Jagr, Pitt	96
1992–93	Mario Lemieux, Pitt	160			

Goals

Season	Player and Club	G	Season	Player and Club	G
1917–18	Joe Malone, Mtl	44	1959–60	Bobby Hull, Chi	39
1918–19	Odie Cleghorn, Mtl	23		Bronco Horvath, Bos	39
1919–20	Joe Malone, Que	39	1960–61	Bernie Geoffrion, Mtl	50
1920–21	Babe Dye, Ham-Tor	35	1961–62	Bobby Hull, Chi	50
1921–22	Punch Broadbent, Ott	32	1962–63	Gordie Howe, Det	38
1922–23	Babe Dye, Tor	26	1963–64	Bobby Hull, Chi	43
1923–24	Cy Denneny, Ott	22	1964–65	Norm Ullman, Det	42
1924–25	Babe Dye, Tor	38	1965–66	Bobby Hull, Chi	54
1925–26	Nels Stewart, Mtl	34	1966–67	Bobby Hull, Chi	52
1926–27	Bill Cook, NY	33	1967–68	Bobby Hull, Chi	44
1927–28	Howie Morenz, Mtl	33	1968–69	Bobby Hull, Chi	58
1928–29	Ace Bailey, Tor	22	1969–70	Phil Esposito, Bos	43
1929–30	Cooney Weiland, Bos	43	1970–71	Phil Esposito, Bos	76
1930–31	Bill Cook, NY	30	1971–72	Phil Esposito, Bos	66
1931–32	Charlie Conacher, Tor	34	1972–73	Phil Esposito, Bos	55
	Bill Cook, NY	34	1973–74	Phil Esposito, Bos	68
1932–33	Bill Cook, NY	28	1974–75	Phil Esposito, Bos	61
1933–34	Charlie Conacher, Tor	32	1975–76	Guy Lafleur, Mtl	56
1934–35	Charlie Conacher, Tor	36	1976–77	Steve Shutt, Mtl	60
1935–36	Charlie Conacher, Tor	23	1977–78	Guy Lafleur, Mtl	60
	Bill Thoms, Tor	23	1978–79	Mike Bossy, NYI	69
1936–37	Larry Aurie, Det	23	1979–80	Charlie Simmer, LA	56
	Nels Stewart, Bos-NYA	23		Blaine Stoughton, Hart	56
1937–38	Gord Drill, Tor	26	1980–81	Mike Bossy, NYI	68
1938–39	Roy Conacher, Bos	26	1981–82	Wayne Gretzky, Edm	92
1939–40	Bryan Hextall, NY	24	1982–83	Wayne Gretzky, Edm	71
1940–41	Bryan Hextall, NY	26	1983–84	Wayne Gretzky, Edm	87
1941–42	Lynn Patrick, NY	32	1984–85	Wayne Gretzky, Edm	73
1942–43	Doug Bentley, Chi	43	1985–86	Jari Kurri, Edm	68
1943–44	Doug Bentley, Chi	38	1986–87	Wayne Gretzky, Edm	62
1944–45	Maurice Richard, Mtl	50	1987–88	Mario Lemieux, Pitt	70
1945–46	Gaye Stewart, Tor	37	1988–89	Mario Lemieux, Pitt	85
1946–47	Maurice Richard, Mtl	50	1989–90	Brett Hull, StL	72
1947–48	Ted Lindsay, Det	33	1990–91	Brett Hull, StL	78
1948–49	Sid Abel, Det	28	1991–92	Brett Hull, StL	70
1949–50	Maurice Richard, Mtl	43	1992–93	Alexander Mogilny, Buff	76
1950–51	Gordie Howe, Det	43		Teemu Selanne, Winn	76
1951–52	Gordie Howe, Det	47	1993–94	Pavel Bure, Van	60
1952–53	Gordie Howe, Det	49	1994–95	Peter Bondra, Wash	34
1953–54	Maurice Richard, Mtl	37	1995–96	Mario Lemieux, Pitt	69
1954–55	Bernie Geoffrion, Mtl	38	1996–97	Keith Tkachuk, Phoe	52
	Maurice Richard, Mtl	38	1997–98	Teemu Selanne, Ana	52
1955–56	Jean Beliveau, Mtl	47		Peter Bondra, Wash	52
1957–58	Dickie Moore, Mtl	36	1998–99	Teemu Selanne, Ana	47
1956–57	Gordie Howe, Det	44	1999–00	Pavel Bure, Fla	58
1958–59	Jean Beliveau, Mtl	45			

Assists

Season	Player and Club	A		Season	Player and Club	A
1917–18	statistic not kept			1961–62	Andy Bathgate, NY	56
1918–19	Newsy Lalonde, Mtl	9		1962–63	Henri Richard, Mtl	50
1919–20	Corbett Denneny, Tor	12		1963–64	Andy Bathgate, NY-Tor	58
1920–21	Louis Berlinquette, Mtl	9		1964–65	Stan Mikita, Chi	59
1921–22	Punch Broadbench, Ott	14		1965–66	Stan Mikita, Chi	48
1922–23	Babe Dye, Tor	11			Bobby Rousseau, Mtl	48
1923–24	Billy Boucher, Mtl	6			Jean Beliveau, Mtl	48
1924–25	Cy Denneny, Ott	15		1966–67	Stan Mikita, Chi	62
1925–26	Cy Denneny, Ott	12		1967–68	Phil Esposito, Bos	49
1926–27	Dick Irvin, Chi	18		1968–69	Phil Esposito, Bos	77
1927–28	Howie Morenz, Mtl	18		1969–70	Bobby Orr, Bos	87
1928–29	Frank Boucher, NY	16		1970–71	Bobby Orr, Bos	102
1929–30	Frank Boucher, NY	36		1971–72	Bobby Orr, Bos	80
1930–31	Joe Primeau, Tor	36		1972–73	Phil Esposito, Bos	75
1931–32	Joe Primeau, Tor	37		1973–74	Bobby Orr, Bos	89
1932–33	Frank Boucher, NY	28		1974–75	Bobby Clarke, Phil	89
1933–34	Joe Primeau, Tor	32			Bobby Orr, Bos	89
1934–35	Art Chapman, NYA	28		1975–76	Bobby Clarke, Phil	89
1935–36	Art Chapman, NYA	28		1976–77	Guy Lafleur, Mtl	80
1936–37	Syl Apps, Tor	29		1977–78	Bryan Trottier, NYI	77
1937–38	Syl Apps, Tor	29		1978–79	Bryan Trottier, NYI	87
1938–39	Bill Cowley, Bos	34		1979–80	Wayne Gretzky, Edm	86
1939–40	Milt Schmidt, Bos	30		1980–81	Wayne Gretzky, Edm	109
1940–41	Bill Cowley, Bos	45		1981–82	Wayne Gretzky, Edm	120
1941–42	Phil Watson, NY	37		1982–83	Wayne Gretzky, Edm	125
1942–43	Bill Cowley, Bos	45		1983–84	Wayne Gretzky, Edm	118
1943–44	Clint Smith, Chi	49		1984–85	Wayne Gretzky, Edm	135
1944–45	Elmer Lach, Mtl	54		1985–86	Wayne Gretzky, Edm	163
1945–46	Elmer Lach, Mtl	34		1986–87	Wayne Gretzky, Edm	121
1946–47	Billy Taylor, Det	46		1987–88	Wayne Gretzky, Edm	109
1947–48	Doug Bentley, Chi	37		1988–89	Wayne Gretzky, LA	114
1948–49	Doug Bentley, Chi	43			Mario Lemieux, Pitt	114
1949–50	Ted Lindsay, Det	55		1989–90	Wayne Gretzky, LA	102
1950–51	Gordie Howe, Det	43		1990–91	Wayne Gretzky, LA	122
	Ted Kennedy, Tor	43		1991–92	Wayne Gretzky, LA	90
1951–52	Elmer Lach, Mtl	50		1992–93	Adam Oates, Bos	97
1952–53	Gordie Howe, Det	46		1993–94	Wayne Gretzky, LA	92
1953–54	Gordie Howe, Det	48		1994–95	Ron Francis, Pitt	48
1954–55	Bert Olmstead, Mtl	48		1995–96	Mario Lemieux, Pitt	92
1955–56	Bert Olmstead, Mtl	56			Ron Francis, Pitt	92
1956–57	Ted Lindsay, Det	55		1996–97	Mario Lemieux, Pitt	72
1957–58	Henri Richard, Mtl	52		1997–98	Jaromir Jagr, Pitt	67
1958–59	Dickie Moore, Mtl	55			Wayne Gretzky, NYR	67
1959–60	Bobby Hull, Chi	42		1998–99	Jaromir Jagr, Pitt	83
1960–61	Jean Beliveau, Mtl	58		1999–00	Mark Recchi, Phil	63

Rash Judgements

Ever since he was scratched from the Predators' lineup on November 11, 1999, Nashville defenseman Jan Vopat had been itching to return to the ice. Trouble is, itching is what got him scratched in the first place. It appeared that after playing hockey his whole life, Vopat had become allergic to something in his uniform and pads.

The condition developed late in the 1998–99 season, when Vopat broke out in a rash that covered most of his body. Team doctors were baffled, and Vopat visited specialists in several cities to no avail. Finally, a Louisville dermatologist diagnosed the ailment as a reaction to a combination of soaps and detergent. Vopat was treated with an ointment and cleared to practice, but the condition returned within two weeks. Even worse, Vopat irritated the rash every time he broke out in a sweat. As a result he had been inactive since mid-November 1999. "He can't sweat," said Predators coach Barry Trotz. "What can we do?"

Though he remained on the injured reserve, Vopat finally returned to practice with liners sewn to the inside of his pads and uniform. "At this point all I can do is laugh about it," said Vopat, a 26-year-old Czech who had played in only six games during the 1999–00 season after having five goals and six assists in 55 games the previous year. "If I don't, I will just make myself crazy."

—Mark Beech

Goals Against Average

Season	Goaltender and Club	GP	Min	GA	SO	Avg
1917–18	Georges Vezina, Mtl	21	1282	84	1	3.93
1918–19	Clint Benedict, Ott	18	1113	53	2	2.86
1919–20	Clint Benedict, Ott	24	1444	64	5	2.66
1920–21	Clint Benedict, Ott	24	1457	75	2	3.09
1921–22	Clint Benedict, Ott	24	1508	84	2	3.34
1922–23	Clint Benedict, Ott	24	1478	54	4	2.19
1923–24	Georges Vezina, Mtl	24	1459	48	3	1.97
1924–25	Georges Vezina, Mtl	30	1860	56	5	1.81
1925–26	Alex Connell, Ott	36	2251	42	15	1.12
1926–27	Clint Benedict, Mtl M	43	2748	65	13	1.42
1927–28	George Hainsworth, Mtl	44	2730	48	13	1.05
1928–29	George Hainsworth, Mtl	44	2800	43	22	0.92
1929–30	Tiny Thompson, Bos	44	2680	98	3	2.19
1930–31	Roy Worters, NYA	44	2760	74	8	1.61
1931–32	Chuck Gardiner, Chi	48	2989	92	4	1.85
1932–33	Tiny Thompson, Bos	48	3000	88	11	1.76
1933–34	Wilf Cude, Det-Mtl	30	1920	47	5	1.47
1934–35	Lorne Chabot, Chi	48	2940	88	8	1.80
1935–36	Tiny Thompson, Bos	48	2930	82	10	1.68
1936–37	Normie Smith, Det	48	2980	102	6	2.05
1937–38	Tiny Thompson, Bos	48	2970	89	7	1.80
1938–39	Frank Brimsek, Bos	43	2610	68	10	1.56
1939–40	Dave Kerr, NYR	48	3000	77	8	1.54
1940–41	Turk Broda, Tor	48	2970	99	5	2.00
1941–42	Frank Brimsek, Bos	47	2930	115	3	2.35
1942–43	Johnny Mowers, Det	50	3010	124	6	2.47
1943–44	Bill Durnan, Mtl	50	3000	109	2	2.18
1944–45	Bill Durnan, Mtl	50	3000	121	1	2.42
1945–46	Bill Durnan, Mtl	40	2400	104	4	2.60
1946–47	Bill Durnan, Mtl	60	3600	138	4	2.30
1947–48	Turk Broda, Tor	60	3600	143	5	2.38
1948–49	Bill Durnan, Mtl	60	3600	126	10	2.10
1949–50	Bill Durnan, Mtl	64	3840	141	8	2.20
1950–51	Al Rollins, Tor	40	2367	70	5	1.77
1951–52	Terry Sawchuk, Det	70	4200	133	12	1.90
1952–53	Terry Sawchuk, Det	63	3780	120	9	1.90
1953–54	Harry Lumley, Tor	69	4140	128	13	1.86
1954–55	Harry Lumley, Tor	69	4140	134	8	1.94
	Terry Sawchuk, Det	68	4060	132	12	1.94
1955–56	Jacques Plante, Mtl	64	3840	119	7	1.86
1956–57	Jacques Plante, Mtl	61	3660	123	9	2.02
1957–58	Jacques Plante, Mtl	57	3386	119	9	2.11
1958–59	Jacques Plante, Mtl	67	4000	144	9	2.16
1959–60	Jacques Plante, Mtl	69	4140	175	3	2.54
1960–61	Johnny Bower, Tor	58	3480	145	2	2.50
1961–62	Jacques Plante, Mtl	70	4200	166	4	2.37
1962–63	Jacques Plante, Mtl	56	3320	138	5	2.49
1963–64	Johnny Bower, Tor	51	3009	106	5	2.11
1964–65	Johnny Bower, Tor	34	2040	81	3	2.38
1965–66	Johnny Bower, Tor	35	1998	75	3	2.25
1966–67	Glenn Hall, Chi	32	1664	66	2	2.38
1967–68	Gump Worsley, Mtl	40	2213	73	6	1.98
1968–69	Jacques Plante, StL	37	2139	70	5	1.96
1969–70	Ernie Wakely, StL	30	1651	58	4	2.11
1970–71	Jacques Plante, Tor	40	2329	73	4	1.88
1971–72	Tony Esposito, Chi	48	2780	82	9	1.77
1972–73	Ken Dryden, Mtl	54	3165	119	6	2.26
1973–74	Bernie Parent, Phil	73	4314	136	12	1.89
1974–75	Bernie Parent, Phil	68	4041	137	12	2.03
1975–76	Ken Dryden, Mtl	62	3580	121	8	2.03
1976–77	Michael Larocque, Mtl	26	1525	53	4	2.09
1977–78	Ken Dryden, Mtl	52	3071	105	5	2.05
1978–79	Ken Dryden, Mtl	47	2814	108	5	2.30
1979–80	Bob Sauve, Buff	32	1880	74	4	2.36
1980–81	Richard Sevigny, Mtl	33	1777	71	2	2.40

Goals Against Average *(Cont.)*

Season	Goaltender and Club	GP	Min	GA	SO	Avg
1981–82	Denis Herron, Mtl	27	1547	68	3	2.64
1982–83	Pete Peeters, Bos	62	3611	142	8	2.36
1983–84	Pat Riggin, Wash	41	2299	102	4	2.66
1984–85	Tom Barrasso, Buff	54	3248	144	5	2.66
1985–86	Bob Froese, Phil	51	2728	116	5	2.55
1986–87	Brian Hayward, Mtl	37	2178	102	1	2.81
1987–88	Pete Peeters, Wash	35	1896	88	2	2.78
1988–89	Patrick Roy, Mtl	48	2744	113	4	2.47
1989–90	Patrick Roy, Mtl	54	3173	134	3	2.53
	Mike Liut, Hart-Wash	37	2161	91	4	2.53
1990–91	Ed Belfour, Chi	74	4127	170	4	2.47
1991–92	Patrick Roy, Mtl	67	3935	155	5	2.36
1992–93	*Felix Potvin, Tor	48	2781	116	2	2.50
1993–94	Dominik Hasek, Buff	58	3358	109	7	1.95
1994–95	Dominik Hasek, Buff	41	2416	85	5	2.11
1995–96	Ron Hextall, Phil	53	3102	112	4	2.17
	Chris Osgood, Det	50	2933	106	5	2.17
1996–97	Martin Brodeur, NJ	67	3838	120	10	1.88
1997–98	Ed Belfour, Dall	61	3581	112	9	1.88
1998–99	Ron Tugnutt, Ott	43	2508	75	3	1.79
1999–00	Brian Boucher, Phil	35	2038	65	4	1.91

*Rookie.

Penalty Minutes

Season	Player and Club	GP	PIM	Season	Player and Club	GP	PIM
1918–19	Joe Hall, Mtl	17	85	1959–60	Carl Brewer, Tor	67	150
1919–20	Cully Wilson, Tor	23	79	1960–61	Pierre Pilote, Chi	70	165
1920–21	Bert Corbeau, Mtl	24	86	1961–62	Lou Fontinato, Mtl	54	167
1921–22	Sprague Cleghorn, Mtl	24	63	1962–63	Howie Young, Det	64	273
1922–23	Billy Boucher, Mtl	24	52	1963–64	Vic Hadfield, NYR	69	151
1923–24	Bert Corbeau, Tor	24	55	1964–65	Carl Brewer, Tor	70	177
1924–25	Billy Boucher, Mtl	30	92	1965–66	Reggie Fleming, Bos-NYR	69	166
1925–26	Bert Corbeau, Tor	36	121	1966–67	John Ferguson, Mtl	67	177
1926–27	Nels Stewart, Mtl M	44	133	1967–68	Barclay Plager, StL	49	153
1927–28	Eddie Shore, Bos	44	165	1968–69	Forbes Kennedy, Phil-Tor	77	219
1928–29	Red Dutton, Mtl M	44	139	1969–70	Keith Magnuson, Chi	76	213
1929–30	Joe Lamb, Ott	44	119	1970–71	Keith Magnuson, Chi	76	291
1930–31	Harvey Rockburn, Det	42	118	1971–72	Brian Watson, Pitt	75	212
1931–32	Red Dutton, NYA	47	107	1972–73	Dave Schultz, Phil	76	259
1932–33	Red Horner, Tor	48	144	1973–74	Dave Schultz, Phil	73	348
1933–34	Red Horner, Tor	42	126	1974–75	Dave Schultz, Phil	76	472
1934–35	Red Horner, Tor	46	125	1975–76	Steve Durbano, Pitt-KC	69	370
1935–36	Red Horner, Tor	43	167	1976–77	Dave Williams, Tor	77	338
1936–37	Red Horner, Tor	48	124	1977–78	Dave Schultz, LA-Pitt	74	405
1937–38	Red Horner, Tor	47	82	1978–79	Dave Williams, Tor	77	298
1938–39	Red Horner, Tor	48	85	1979–80	Jimmy Mann, Winn	72	287
1939–40	Red Horner, Tor	30	87	1980–81	Dave Williams, Van	77	343
1940–41	Jimmy Orlando, Det	48	99	1981–82	Paul Baxter, Pitt	76	409
1941–42	Jimmy Orlando, Det	48	81	1982–83	Randy Holt, Wash	70	275
1942–43	Jimmy Orlando, Det	40	89	1983–84	Chris Nilan, Mtl	76	338
1943–44	Mike McMahon, Mtl	42	98	1984–85	Chris Nilan, Mtl	77	358
1944–45	Pat Egan, Bos	48	86	1985–86	Joey Kocur, Det	59	377
1945–46	Jack Stewart, Det	47	73	1986–87	Tim Hunter, Cgy	73	361
1946–47	Gus Mortson, Tor	60	133	1987–88	Bob Probert, Det	74	398
1947–48	Bill Barilko, Tor	57	147	1988–89	Tim Hunter, Cgy	75	375
1948–49	Bill Ezinicki, Tor	52	145	1989–90	Basil McRae, Minn	66	351
1949–50	Bill Ezinicki, Tor	67	144	1990–91	Bob Ray, Buff	66	350
1950–51	Gus Mortson, Tor	60	142	1991–92	Mike Peluso, Chi	63	408
1951–52	Gus Kyle, Bos	69	127	1992–93	Marty McSorley, LA	81	399
1952–53	Maurice Richard, Mtl	70	112	1993–94	Tie Domi, Winn	81	347
1953–54	Gus Mortson, Chi	68	132	1994–95	Enrico Ciccone, TB	41	225
1954–55	Fern Flaman, Bos	70	150	1995–96	Matthew Barnaby, Buff	73	335
1955–56	Lou Fontinato, NYR	70	202	1996–97	Gino Odjick, Van	70	371
1956–57	Gus Mortson, Chi	70	147	1997–98	Donald Brashear, Van	77	372
1957–58	Lou Fontinato, NYR	70	152	1998–99	Rob Ray, Buff	76	261
1958–59	Ted Lindsay, Chi	70	184	1999–00	Denny Lambert, Atl	73	219

NHL All-Star Game

First played in 1947, this game was scheduled before the start of the regular season and used to match the defending Stanley Cup Champions against a squad made up of the league All-stars from other teams. In 1966 the games were moved to mid-season, although there was no game that year. The format changed to a conference versus conference showdown in 1969.

Results

Year	Site	Score	MVP	Attendance
1947	Toronto	All-Stars 4, Toronto 3	None named	14,169
1948	Chicago	All-Stars 3, Toronto 1	None named	12,794
1949	Toronto	All-Stars 3, Toronto 1	None named	13,541
1950	Detroit	Detroit 7, All-Stars 1	None named	9,166
1951	Toronto	1st team 2, 2nd team 2	None named	11,469
1952	Detroit	1st team 1, 2nd team 1	None named	10,680
1953	Montreal	All-Stars 3, Montreal 1	None named	14,153
1954	Detroit	All-Stars 2, Detroit 2	None named	10,689
1955	Detroit	Detroit 3, All-Stars 1	None named	10,111
1956	Montreal	All-Stars 1, Montreal 1	None named	13,095
1957	Montreal	All-Stars 5, Montreal 3	None named	13,003
1958	Montreal	Montreal 6, All-Stars 3	None named	13,989
1959	Montreal	Montreal 6, All-Stars 1	None named	13,818
1960	Montreal	All-Stars 2, Montreal 1	None named	13,949
1961	Chicago	All-Stars 3, Chicago 1	None named	14,534
1962	Toronto	Toronto 4, All-Stars 1	Eddie Shack, Tor	14,236
1963	Toronto	All-Stars 3, Toronto 3	Frank Mahovlich, Tor	14,034
1964	Toronto	All-Stars 3, Toronto 2	Jean Beliveau, Mtl	14,232
1965	Montreal	All-Stars 5, Montreal 2	Gordie Howe, Det	13,529
1967	Montreal	Montreal 3, All-Stars 0	Henri Richard, Mtl	14,284
1968	Toronto	Toronto 4, All-Stars 3	Bruce Gamble, Tor	15,753
1969	Montreal	East 3, West 3	Frank Mahovlich, Det	16,260
1970	St Louis	East 4, West 1	Bobby Hull, Chi	16,587
1971	Boston	West 2, East 1	Bobby Hull, Chi	14,790
1972	Minnesota	East 3, West 2	Bobby Orr, Bos	15,423
1973	NY Rangers	East 5, West 4	Greg Polis, Pitt	16,986
1974	Chicago	West 6, East 4	Garry Unger, StL	16,426
1975	Montreal	Wales 7, Campbell 1	Syl Apps Jr, Pitt	16,080
1976	Philadelphia	Wales 7, Campbell 5	Pete Mahovlich, Mtl	16,436
1977	Vancouver	Wales 4, Campbell 3	Rick Martin, Buff	15,607
1978	Buffalo	Wales 3, Campbell 2 (OT)	Billy Smith, NYI	16,433
1980	Detroit	Wales 6, Campbell 3	Reg Leach, Phil	21,002
1981	Los Angeles	Campbell 4, Wales 1	Mike Liut, StL	15,761
1982	Washington	Wales 4, Campbell 2	Mike Bossy, NYI	18,130
1983	NY Islanders	Campbell 9, Wales 3	Wayne Gretzky, Edm	15,230
1984	NJ Devils	Wales 7, Campbell 6	Don Maloney, NYR	18,939
1985	Calgary	Wales 6, Campbell 4	Mario Lemieux, Pitt	16,825
1986	Hartford	Wales 4, Campbell 3 (OT)	Grant Fuhr, Edm	15,100
1988	St Louis	Wales 6, Campbell 5 (OT)	Mario Lemieux, Pitt	17,878
1989	Edmonton	Campbell 9, Wales 5	Wayne Gretzky, LA	17,503
1990	Pittsburgh	Wales 12, Campbell 7	Mario Lemieux, Pitt	16,236
1991	Chicago	Campbell 11, Wales 5	Vince Damphousse, Tor	18,472
1992	Philadelphia	Campbell 10, Wales 6	Brett Hull, StL	17,380
1993	Montreal	Wales 16, Campbell 6	Mike Gartner, NYR	17,137
1994	NY Rangers	East 9, West 8	Mike Richter, NYR	18,200
1996	Boston	East 5, West 4	Ray Bourque, Bos	17,565
1997	San Jose	East 11, West 7	Mark Recchi, Mtl	17,565
1998	Vancouver	North America 8, World 7	Teemu Selanne, Ana (World)	18,422
1999	Tampa Bay	North America 8, World 6	Wayne Gretzky, NYR (N America)	19,758
2000	Toronto	World 9, North America 4	Pavel Bure, Fla (World)	19,300

Note: The Challenge Cup, a series between the NHL All-Stars and the Soviet Union, was played instead of the All-Star Game in 1979. Eight years later, Rendez-Vous '87, a two-game series matching the Soviet Union and the NHL All-Stars, replaced the All-Star Game. The 1995 NHL All-Star game was cancelled due to a labor dispute. The 1998 NHL All-Star game, billed as a preview to the 1998 Winter Olympics in Nagano, Japan, matched North Amercian–born All-Stars and All-Stars born elsewhere.

Hockey Hall of Fame

Located in Toronto, the Hockey Hall of Fame was officially opened on August 26, 1961. The current chairman is William C. Hay. There are, at present, 306 members of the Hockey Hall of Fame—209 players, 84 "builders," and 14 on-ice officials. (One member, Alan Eagleson, resigned from the Hall 3-25-98.) To be eligible, player and referee/linesman candidates should have been out of the game for three years, but the Hall's Board of Directors can make exceptions.

Players

Sid Abel (1969)
Jack Adams (1959)
Charles (Syl) Apps (1961)
George Armstrong (1975)
Irvine (Ace) Bailey (1975)
Donald H. (Dan) Bain (1945)
Hobey Baker (1945)
Bill Barber (1990)
Marty Barry (1965)
Andy Bathgate (1978)
Bobby Bauer (1996)
Jean Beliveau (1972)
Clint Benedict (1965)
Douglas Bentley (1964)
Max Bentley (1966)
Hector (Toe) Blake (1966)
Leo Boivin (1986)
Dickie Boon (1952)
Mike Bossy (1991)
Emile (Butch) Bouchard (1966)
Frank Boucher (1958)
George (Buck) Boucher (1960)
Johnny Bower (1976)
Russell Bowie (1945)
Frank Brimsek (1966)
Harry L. (Punch) Broadbent (1962)
Walter (Turk) Broda (1967)
John Bucyk (1981)
Billy Burch (1974)
Harry Cameron (1962)
Gerry Cheevers (1985)
Francis (King) Clancy (1958)
Aubrey (Dit) Clapper (1947)
Bobby Clarke (1987)
Sprague Cleghorn (1958)
Neil Colville (1967)
Charlie Conacher (1961)
Lionel Conacher (1994)
Roy Conacher (1998)
Alex Connell (1958)
Bill Cook (1952)
Fred (Bun) Cook (1995)
Arthur Coulter (1974)
Yvan Cournoyer (1982)
Bill Cowley (1968)
Samuel (Rusty) Crawford (1962)
Jack Darragh (1962)
Allan M. (Scotty) Davidson (1950)
Clarence (Hap) Day (1961)
Alex Delvecchio (1977)
Cy Denneny (1959)
Marcel Dionne (1992)
Gordie Drillon (1975)
Charles Drinkwater (1950)

Ken Dryden (1983)
Woody Dumart (1992)
Thomas Dunderdale (1974)
Bill Durnan (1964)
Mervyn A. (Red) Dutton (1958)
Cecil (Babe) Dye (1970)
Phil Esposito (1984)
Tony Esposito (1988)
Arthur F. Farrell (1965)
Ferdinand (Fern) Flaman (1990)
Frank Foyston (1958)
Frank Frederickson (1958)
Bill Gadsby (1970)
Bob Gainey (1992)
Chuck Gardiner (1945)
Herb Gardiner (1958)
Jimmy Gardner (1962)
Bernie (Boom Boom) Geoffrion (1972)
Eddie Gerard (1945)
Ed Giacomin (1987)
Rod Gilbert (1982)
Hamilton (Billy) Gilmour (1962)
Frank (Moose) Goheen (1952)
Ebenezer R. (Ebbie) Goodfellow (1963)
Michel Goulet (1998)
Mike Grant (1950)
Wilfred (Shorty) Green (1962)
Wayne Gretzky (1999)
Si Griffis (1950)
George Hainsworth (1961)
Glenn Hall (1975)
Joe Hall (1961)
Doug Harvey (1973)
George Hay (1958)
William (Riley) Hern (1962)
Bryan Hextall (1969)
Harry (Hap) Holmes (1972)
Tom Hooper (1962)
George (Red) Horner (1965)
Miles (Tim) Horton (1977)
Gordie Howe (1972)
Syd Howe (1965)
Harry Howell (1979)
Bobby Hull (1983)
John (Bouse) Hutton (1962)
Harry M. Hyland (1962)
James (Dick) Irvin (1958)
Harvey (Busher) Jackson (1971)
Ernest (Moose) Johnson (1952)
Ivan (Ching) Johnson (1958)
Tom Johnson (1970)
Aurel Joliat (1947)
Gordon (Duke) Keats (1958)

Leonard (Red) Kelly (1969)
Ted (Teeder) Kennedy (1966)
Dave Keon (1986)
Elmer Lach (1966)
Guy Lafleur (1988)
Edouard (Newsy) Lalonde (1950)
Jacques Laperriere (1987)
Guy LaPointe (1993)
Edgar Laprade (1993)
Reed Larson (1996)
Jean (Jack) Laviolette (1962)
Hugh Lehman (1958)
Jacques Lemaire (1984)
Mario Lemieux (1997)
Percy LeSueur (1961)
Herbert A. Lewis (1989)
Ted Lindsay (1966)
Harry Lumley (1980)
Lanny McDonald (1992)
Frank McGee (1945)
Billy McGimsie (1962)
George McNamara (195)
Duncan (Mickey) MacK (
Frank Mahovlich (1981)
Joe Malone (1950)
Sylvio Mantha (1960)
Jack Marshall (1965)
Fred G. (Steamer) Maxwell (1962)
Stan Mikita (1983)
Dicky Moore (1974)
Patrick (Paddy) Moran (1958)
Howie Morenz (1945)
Billy Mosienko (1965)
Joe Mullen (2000)
Frank Nighbor (1947)
Reg Noble (1962)
Herbert (Buddy) O'Connor (1988)
Harry Oliver (1967)
Bert Olmstead (1985)
Bobby Orr (1979)
Bernie Parent (1984)
Brad Park (1988)
Lester Patrick (1947)
Lynn Patrick (1980)
Gilbert Perreault (1990)
Tommy Phillips (1945)
Pierre Pilote (1975)
Didier (Pit) Pitre (1962)
Jacques Plante (1978)
Denis Potvin (1991)
Walter (Babe) Pratt (1966)
Joe Primeau (1963)
Marcel Pronovost (1978)
Bob Pulford (1991)

Players *(Cont.)*

Harvey Pulford (1945)
Hubert (Bill) Quackenbush (1976)
Frank Rankin (1961)
Jean Ratelle (1985)
Claude (Chuck) Rayner (1973)
Kenneth Reardon (1966)
Henri Richard (1979)
Maurice (Rocket) Richard (1961)
George Richardson (1950)
Gordon Roberts (1971)
Larry Robinson (1995)
Art Ross (1945)
Blair Russel (1965)
Ernest Russell (1965)
Jack Ruttan (1962)
Borje Salming (1996)
Denis Savard (2000)
Serge Savard (1986)
Terry Sawchuk (1971)
Fred Scanlan (1965)
Milt Schmidt (1961)
Dave (Sweeney) Schriner (1962)
Earl Seibert (1963)
Oliver Seibert (1961)
Eddie Shore (1947)
Steve Shutt (1993)
Albert C. (Babe) Siebert (1964)
Harold (Bullet Joe) Simpson (1962)
Daryl Sittler (1989)
Alfred E. Smith (1962)
Billy Smith (1993)
Clint Smith (1991)
Reginald (Hooley) Smith (1972)
Thomas Smith (1973)
Allan Stanley (1981)
Russell (Barney) Stanley (1962)
Peter Stastny (1998)
John (Black Jack) Stewart (1964)
Nels Stewart (1962)
Bruce Stuart (1961)
Hod Stuart (1945)
Frederic (Cyclone) (O.B.E.)
    Taylor (1947)
Cecil R. (Tiny) Thompson
    (1959)
Vladislav Tretiak (1989)
Harry J. Trihey (1950)
Bryan Trottier (1997)
Norm Ullman (1982)
Georges Vezina (1945)
Jack Walker (1960)
Marty Walsh (1962)
Harry Watson (1994)
Harry E. Watson (1962)
Ralph (Cooney) Weiland (1971)
Harry Westwick (1962)
Fred Whitcroft (1962)
Gordon (Phat) Wilson (1962)
Lorne (Gump) Worsley (1980)
Roy Worters (1969)

Builders

Charles Adams (1960)
Weston W. Adams (1972)
Thomas (Frank) Ahearn (1962)
John (Bunny) Ahearne (1977)
Montagu Allan (C.V.O.) (1945)
Keith Allen (1992)
Al Arbour (1996)
Harold Ballard (1977)
David Bauer (1989)
John Bickell (1978)
Scott Bowman (1991)
George V. Brown (1961)
Walter A. Brown (1962)
Frank Buckland (1975)
Walter L. Bush (2000)
Jack Butterfield (1980)
Frank Calder (1947)
Angus D. Campbell (1964)
Clarence Campbell (1966)
Joe Cattarinich (1977)
Bob Cole (1996)
Joseph (Leo) Dandurand (1963)
Francis Dilio (1964)
George S. Dudley (1958)
James A. Dunn (1968)
Robert Alan Eagleson (1989–98*)
Sergio Gambucci (1996)
Emile Francis (1982)
Jack Gibson (1976)
Tommy Gorman (1963)
Frank Griffiths (1993)
William Hanley (1986)
Charles Hay (1974)
James C. Hendy (1968)
Foster Hewitt (1965)
William Hewitt (1947)
Fred J. Hume (1962)
George (Punch) Imlach (1984)
Tommy Ivan (1974)
William M. Jennings (1975)
Bob Johnson (1992)
Gordon W. Juckes (1979)
John Kilpatrick (1960)
Seymour Knox III (1993)
George Leader (1969)
Robert LeBel (1970)
Thomas F. Lockhart (1965)
Paul Loicq (1961)
Frederic McLaughlin (1963)
John Mariucci (1985)
Frank Mathers (1992)
John (Jake) Milford (1984)
Hartland Molson (1973)
Scotty Morrison (1999)
Mngr. Athol (Pere) Murray (1998)
Francis Nelson (1947)
Bruce A. Norris (1969)
James Norris, Sr. (1958)
James D. Norris (1962)
William M. Northey (1947)

Builders *(Cont.)*

John O'Brien (1962)
Brian O'Neill (1994)
Fred Page (1993)
Craig Patrick (1996)
Frank Patrick (1958)
Allan W. Pickard (1958)
Rudy Pilous (1985)
Norman (Bud) Poile (1990)
Samuel Pollock (1978)
Donat Raymond (1958)
John Robertson (1947)
Claude C. Robinson (1947)
Philip D. Ross (1976)
Gunther Sabetzki (1995)
Glen Sather (1997)
Frank J. Selke (1960)
Harry Sinden (1983)
Frank D. Smith (1962)
Conn Smythe (1958)
Edward M. Snider (1988)
Lord Stanley of Preston
    (G.C.B.) (1945)
James T. Sutherland (1947)
Anatoli V. Tarasov (1974)
Bill Torrey (1995)
Lloyd Turner (1958)
William Tutt (1978)
Carl Potter Voss (1974)
Fred C. Waghorn (1961)
Arthur Wirtz (1971)
Bill Wirtz (1976)
John A. Ziegler, Jr. (1987)

Referees/Linesmen

Neil Armstrong (1991)
John Ashley (1981)
William L. Chadwick (1964)
John D'Amico (1993)
Chaucer Elliott (1961)
George Hayes (1988)
Robert W. Hewitson (1963)
Fred J. (Mickey) Ion (1961)
Matt Pavelich (1987)
Mike Rodden (1962)
J. Cooper Smeaton (1961)
Roy (Red) Storey (1967)
Frank Udvari (1973)
Andy van Hellemond (1999)

Note: Year of election to the Hall of Fame is in parentheses after the member's name.
*Eagleson resigned from Hall March 25, 1998.

Tennis

Wimbledon and
U.S. Open champion
Venus Williams

Sister Act

With exciting rivalries, superb play and the irrepressible Williams sisters, the women's tour stole the spotlight in 2000

BY B.J. SCHECTER

THE GAME of tennis is changing—players are getting stronger, faster, their games more powerful—and no where is the shift more profound than in the women's game. No longer taking a backseat to the men, the women are producing what is arguably a more exciting brand of tennis. They're more pleasing to watch (and we're not talking about Anna Kournikova); they play the game with an intensity and vigor absent from most of the men's games; and they've generated rivalries that produce epic matches.

Richard Williams, the outspoken and outlandish father of stars Venus and Serena, was right about at least one thing: His daughters are responsible for redefining the women's game. After taking six months off, Venus finished the year as the best player in women's tennis, winning Wimbledon, the U.S. Open and an Olympic gold medal. Her power, quickness and astonishing range proved more than most of her opponents could handle, but Venus's ascent almost never happened.

She began 2000 battling tendinitis in both her wrists. The nagging soreness wouldn't relent and finally forced her out of the Australian Open in January, whereupon she disappeared from the game. At the Ericsson Open in March, her father said that he had advised Venus to retire. While Venus never followed that advice, she acknowledged that during the first part of the year she stayed at her home in Palm Beach Gardens, Fla., and hardly practiced. "It was great," she said. "Serena and my mom would be gone on the tour, and me and Daddy were on the couch watching *Zorro* at midnight. I'd fall asleep and wake up disoriented, and my dad would put me into bed. I'd been there so long, it was strange finally leaving home. No more *Zorro*."

Venus rejoined the tour in time for the French Open, where she advanced to the quarterfinals, losing to Arantxa Sánchez Vicario. Venus came to Wimbledon with no grass-court preparation but nonetheless used the fabled venue as the launchpad for a 32-match winning streak that would stretch

into September and encompass two Grand Slam titles and a gold medal in Sydney. One of her Wimbledon victims was her sister, Serena. Though the sisters downplayed the possible matchup, the press couldn't help looking ahead to the enticing prospect of the semifinals, where, if they kept winning, Venus and Serena were slated to meet. After Venus disposed of Martina Hingis in the quarters, it happened, marking the first time sisters had ever met in the semis of a Grand Slam.

Serena was in better form at the time, having lost only 13 games in her previous five matches, but she completely fell apart against her older sister on Centre Court. Leading 4–2 in the second set (she'd lost the first), Serena dropped 10 straight points to allow Venus to regain control of the match. Some observers made the insulting suggestion that the Williams sisters were fixing the outcome. They weren't. After Venus beat her sister, she was somber and consoled Serena at the net. "Let's get out of here," Venus told Serena. "It was terrible," Venus would say later. "Serena believed she was going to win Wimbledon. We both believed [we were going to win]. For either one of us to lose was terrible."

For nearly a year Venus had stewed over the fact that her younger sister had won a Slam (the 1999 U.S. Open) before she did. And in the final, with her first major title there for the taking, Venus was nervous and erratic. But so was defending champion Lindsay Davenport. In a match plagued by double faults and unforced errors, the elder Williams sister seized her opportunity. After championship point in her 6–3, 7–6 victory, the crowd erupted and Venus jumped up and down in jubilation. Her father held up handmade signs (one of which said IT'S VENUS'S PARTY AND NO ONE WAS INVITED) and later stepped out on top of the NBC broadcast booth and did some celebrating of his own. "We thought the roof was coming down," said commentator Chris Evert.

With her remarkable performance in the U.S. Open two months later, Venus brought the curtain, if not the roof, down on a spectacular season. Though she didn't quite have her "A" game in the early rounds, she showed a will to win that must have intimidated her opponents; they knew that whether or not she was on her game, Venus wasn't going down without a fight.

The draw was such that if the Williams sisters were to meet, it would be in the final, and it seemed like that was all people talked about, including the players. "Everyone was expecting an all-Williams final," said Davenport. "Martina and I had a little talk and didn't want that to happen." Davenport made sure it didn't, and her comments, which she made after she defeated Serena 6–4, 6–2 in the quarterfinals, sparked a few days' worth of controversy.

But, clearly, it's only a matter of time before the Williamses meet in a Grand Slam final. In the '99 U.S. Open, they were a match away from doing so, but Hingis beat Venus in a semifinal slugfest. This year Hingis and Venus met again in the semis, and another heavyweight bout unfolded, a 4–6, 6–3, 7–5 thriller that was easily the match of the year. Hingis had Williams on the ropes for much of the match but couldn't put her away. After they split the first two sets, Hingis led 5–3 in the third. She had just won an astounding 29-stroke rally to go ahead 15–30 and was two points away from the final. Richard Williams, unable to stand the pressure bearing down on his daughter, left the stadium. The next point, a 21-stroke gem, turned on a lob by Venus. Instead of slamming home a winner, Hingis overcautiously returned a gettable ball, and Williams ripped a backhand past her to even the game at 30. Williams won that game and the next three to seal the victory.

She won the final in similar fashion. Two points away from going up 5–1 in the first set, Davenport dumped an easy volley and hit a routine backhand into the net. Williams came back to win that game and took control of the match for a 6–4, 7–5 victory. Her triumph meant that a Williams had won three of the last four Grand Slams. "Straight out of Compton! And Watts too!" Richard Williams yelled to the crowd after Venus's win.

The more buttoned-down Pete Sampras didn't have to shout to be noticed in 2000. With his victory at Wimbledon, he surpassed Roy Emerson as the player with the most career Grand Slams (13). He had missed chances to break the record at both the Australian Open, where he lost to Andre Agassi in the semifinals, and at the French, where he made his usual early exit, losing in the second round. Setting the record at hallowed Wimbledon, where he had won six times, would be special for Sampras, but it almost didn't happen.

Following his first-round match at the All England club, Sampras experienced a flareup of tendinitis in his left shin. The pain was severe enough to keep him out of practice until the day before the final. An extra smattering of rain delays aided Sampras's recovery, but he later admitted that had it been any other tournament he probably would have withdrawn.

Somehow, though, Sampras battled his way to the final. True, he never faced a player ranked higher than No. 12, but it was nevertheless a gritty performance. As was his play against Patrick Rafter in the final, the start of which was delayed by more than an hour due to rain. During the match there were two more rain delays lasting a combined two hours. Sampras kept his focus through it all, and, leading two sets to one and up 5–2 in the fourth set, he realized it was his moment and began to cry. "It all hit me that I was going to win, and it hit me hard," Sampras said later. "It was going to happen: the moment I've dreamed about."

The moment arrived at 8:56 p.m., London time, when Sampras put away championship point. As he approached the net his eyes began to well up. He made his way to the grandstand, where he embraced his parents, who were there to witness their son in a Grand Slam final for the first time since the 1992 U.S. Open. He turned to his fiancée, Bridget Wilson, to whom he proposed before coming to Wimbledon, and Tom Gullikson, the twin brother of his deceased coach Tim, and lost it. "You get older, and other things are more important than tennis," Sampras said. "It is important to me that they were here, that they were part of it, because those are the memories you'll have when you're done."

It was perhaps appropriate that Sampras should look to the future after his record 13th Grand Slam title, because in the next Grand Slam final, the U.S. Open, he came face to face with it in the person of Marat Safin, a 6' 4", 20-year-old Russian with a booming serve and teen-idol good looks. Safin blanked Sampras 6–4, 6–3, 6–3. "It reminded me of when I was 19 and steamrolled over Andre," said Sampras, alluding to his win over Agassi in the '90 Open final. And look what *he* went on to accomplish.

FOR THE RECORD · 1999 – 2000

2000 Grand Slam Champions

Australian Open

Men's Singles

	Winner	Finalist	Score
Quarterfinals	Andre Agassi (1) ....Hicham Arazi		6–4, 6–4, 6–2
	Yevgeny Kafelnikov (2) ....Younes El Aynaoui		6–0, 6–3, 7–6 (7–4)
	Pete Sampras (3) ....Chris Woodruff		7–5, 6–3, 6–3
	Magnus Norman (12)..............Nicolas Kiefer (4)		3–6, 6–3, 6–1, 7–6 (7–4)
Semifinals	Andre Agassi ....Pete Sampras		6–4, 3–6, 6–7 (0–7), 7–6 (7–5), 6–1
	Yevgeny Kafelnikov.................Magnus Norman		6–1, 6–2, 6–4
Final	Andre Agassi ....Yevgeny Kafelnikov		3–6, 6–3, 6–2, 6–4

Women's Singles

	Winner	Finalist	Score
Quarterfinals	Martina Hingis (1)...................Arantxa Sánchez Vicario (13)		6–1, 6–1
	Lindsay Davenport (2) ....Julie Halard-Decugis (9)		6–1, 6–2
	Jennifer Capriati....................Ai Sugiyama		6–0, 6–2
	Conchita Martinez (10)............Elena Likhovtseva (16)		6–3, 4–6, 9–7
Semifinals	Martina Hingis ....Conchita Martinez		6–3, 6–2
	Lindsay Davenport.................Jennifer Capriati		6–2, 7–6 (7–4)
Final	Lindsay Davenport.................Martina Hingis		6–1, 7–5

Doubles

	Winner	Finalist	Score
Men's Final	Ellis Ferreira/ Rick Leach (5)	Wayne Black/ Andrew Kratzmann (8)	6–4, 3–6, 6–3, 3–6, 18–16
Women's Final	Lisa Raymond/ Rennae Stubbs (1)	Mary Pierce/ Martina Hingis (3)	6–4, 5–7, 6–4
Mixed Final	Jared Palmer/ Rennae Stubbs (3)	Todd Woodbridge/ Arantxa Sánchez Vicario (4)	7–5, 7–6 (7–3)

French Open

Men's Singles

	Winner	Finalist	Score
Quarterfinals	Magnus Norman (3) ....Marat Safin (12)		6–4, 6–3, 4–6, 7–5
	Gustavo Kuerten (5)................Yevgeny Kafelnikov (4)		6–3, 3–6, 4–6, 6–4, 6–2
	Juan Carlos Ferrero (16).........Alex Corretja (10)		6–4, 6–4, 6–2
	Franco Squillari ....Albert Costa		6–4, 6–4, 2–6, 6–4
Semifinals	Magnus Norman ....Franco Squillari		6–1, 6–4, 6–3
	Gustavo Kuerten ....Juan Carlos Ferrero		7–5, 4–6, 2–6, 6–4, 6–3
Final	Gustavo Kuerten ....Magnus Norman		6–2, 6–3, 2–6, 7–6 (8–6)

Women's Singles

	Winner	Finalist	Score
Quarterfinals	Martina Hingis (1)...................Chanda Rubin		6–1, 6–3
	Mary Pierce (6).......................Monica Seles (3)		6–4, 3–6, 6–4
	Arantxa Sánchez Vicario (8) ...Venus Williams (4)		6–0, 1–6, 6–2
	Conchita Martinez (5).............Marta Marrero		7–6 (7–5), 6–1
Semifinals	Mary Pierce ....Martina Hingis		6–4, 5–7, 6–2
	Conchita Martinez ....Arantxa Sánchez Vicario		6–1, 6–2
Final	Mary Pierce ....Conchita Martinez		6–2, 7–5

Note: Seedings in parentheses.

French Open *(Cont.)*
Doubles

	Winner	Finalist	Score
Men's Final	Todd Woodbridge/ Mark Woodforde (2)	Paul Haarhuis/ Sandon Stolle (3)	7–6 (9–7), 6–4
Women's Final	Martina Hingis/ Mary Pierce (3)	V. Ruano-Pascual/ Paola Suarez (10)	6–2, 6–4
Mixed Final	Mariaan De Swardt/ David Adams (12)	Rennae Stubbs/ Todd Woodbridge (1)	6–3, 3–6, 6–3

Wimbledon
Men's Singles

	Winner	Finalist	Score
Quarterfinals	Pete Sampras (1)	Jan-Michael Gambill	6–4, 6–7 (4–7), 6–4, 6–4
	Andre Agassi (2)	Mark Philippoussis (10)	7–6 (7–4), 6–3, 6–4
	Patrick Rafter (12)	Alexander Popp	6–3, 6–2, 7–6 (7–1)
	Vladimir Voltchkov	Byron Black	7–6 (7–2), 7–6 (7–2), 6–4
Semifinals	Pete Sampras	Vladimir Voltchkov	7–6 (7–4), 6–2, 6–4
	Patrick Rafter	Andre Agassi	7–5, 4–6, 7–5, 4–6, 6–3
Final	Pete Sampras	Patrick Rafter	6–7 (10–12), 7–6 (7–5), 6–4, 6–2

Women's Singles

	Winner	Finalist	Score
Quarterfinals	Venus Williams (5)	Martina Hingis (1)	6–3, 4–6, 6–4
	Lindsay Davenport (2)	Monica Seles (6)	6–7 (4–7), 6–4, 6–0
	Serena Williams (8)	Lisa Raymond	6–2, 6–0
	Jelena Dokic	Magui Serna	6–3, 6–2
Semifinals	Lindsay Davenport	Jelena Dokic	6–4, 6–2
	Venus Williams	Serena Williams	6–2, 7–6 (7–3)
Final	Venus Williams	Lindsay Davenport	6–3, 7–6 (7–3)

Doubles

	Winner	Finalist	Score
Men's Final	Todd Woodbridge/ Mark Woodforde(1)	Paul Haarhuis/ Sandon Stolle (2)	6–3, 6–4, 6–1
Women's Final	Serena Williams/ Venus Williams (8)	Julie Halard-Decugis/ Ai Sugiyama (4)	6–3, 6–2
Mixed Final	Donald Johnson/ Kimberly Po (8)	Lleyton Hewitt/ Kim Clijsters	6–4, 7–6 (7–3)

U.S. Open
Men's Singles

	Winner	Finalist	Score
Quarterfinals	Pete Sampras (4)	Richard Krajicek	4–6, 7–6 (8–6), 6–4, 6–2
	Lleyton Hewitt (9)	Arnaud Clement	6–2, 6–4, 6–3
	Marat Safin (6)	Nicolas Kiefer (14)	7–5, 4–6, 7–6 (7–5), 6–3
	Todd Martin	Thomas Johansson	6–4, 6–4, 3–6, 7–5
Semifinals	Pete Sampras	Lleyton Hewitt	7–6 (9–7), 6–4, 7–6 (7–5)
	Marat Safin	Todd Martin	6–3, 7–6 (7–4), 7–6 (7–1)
Final	Marat Safin	Pete Sampras	6–4, 6–3, 6–3

Note: Seedings in parentheses.

U.S. Open *(Cont.)*
Women's Singles

	Winner	Finalist	Score
Quarterfinals	Martina Hingis (1)	Monica Seles (6)	6–0, 7–5
	Venus Williams (3)	Nathalie Tauziat (8)	6–4, 1–6, 6–1
	Lindsay Davenport (2)	Serena Williams (5)	6–4, 6–2
	Elena Dementieva	Anke Huber (10)	6–1, 3–6, 6–3
Semifinals	Lindsay Davenport	Elena Dementieva	6–2, 7–6 (7–5)
	Venus Williams	Martina Hingis	4–6, 6–3, 7–5
Final	Venus Williams	Lindsay Davenport	6–4, 7–5

Doubles

	Winner	Finalist	Score
Men's Final	Lleyton Hewitt/ Max Mirnyi	Ellis Ferreira/ Rick Leach (4)	6–4, 5–7, 7–6 (7–5)
Women's Final	Julie Halard-Decugis/ Ai Sugiyama (2)	Cara Black/ Elena Likhovtseva (10)	6–0, 1–6, 6–1
Mixed Final	Arantxa Sánchez Vicario/ Jared Palmer (2)	Anna Kournikova/ Max Mirnyi (4)	6–4, 6–3

Major Tournament Results

Men's Tour (late 1999)

Date	Tournament	Site	Winner	Finalist	Score
Oct 4–10	Swiss Indoors	Basel, Switzerland	Karol Kucera	Tim Henman	6–4, 7–6 (12–10), 4–6, 4–6, 7–6 (7–2)
Oct 4–10	Heineken Open	Shanghai	Magnus Norman	Marcelo Rios	2–6, 6–3, 7–5
Oct 11–17	CA Tennis Trophy	Vienna	Greg Rusedski	Nicolas Kiefer	6–7 (5–7), 2–6, 6–3 7–5, 6–4
Oct 11–17	Heineken Open	Singapore	Marcelo Rios	Mikael Tillstrom	6–2, 7–6 (7–5)
Oct 18–24	Grand Prix of Tennis	Lyon, France	Nicolas Lapentti	Lleyton Hewitt	6–3, 6–2
Oct 25–31	Eurocard Open	Stuttgart, Germany	Thomas Enqvist	Richard Krajicek	6–1, 6–4, 5–7, 7–5
Nov 1–7	Paris Open	Paris	Andre Agassi	Marat Safin	7–6 (7–1), 6–2, 4–6 6–4
Nov 8–14	Stockholm Open	Stockholm	Thomas Enqvist	M. Gustafsson	6–3, 6–4, 6–2
Nov 8–14	Kremlin Cup	Moscow	Y. Kafelnikov	Byron Black	7–6 (7–2), 6–4
Nov 23–29	ATP Tour Championship	Hannover, Germany	Pete Sampras	Andre Agassi	6–1, 7–5, 6–4

Men's Tour (Through September 10, 2000)

Date	Tournament	Site	Winner	Finalist	Score
Jan 3–9	Qatar Open	Doha, Qatar	Fabrice Santoro	Rainer Schuttler	3–6, 6–3, 6–2
Jan 17–30	Australian Open	Melbourne	Andre Agassi	Yevgeny Kafelnikov	3–6, 6–3, 6–2, 6–4
Feb 7–13	Marseille Open	Marseille, France	Marc Rosset	Roger Federer	2–6, 6–3, 7–6 (7–5)
Feb 7–13	Dubai Open	Dubai, UAE	Nicolas Kiefer	Juan-Carlos Ferrero	7–5, 4–6, 6–3
Feb 14–20	ABN/Amro Tournament	Rotterdam, Amsterdam	Cedric Pioline	Tim Henman	6–7 (3–7), 6–4, 7–6 (7–4)
Feb 14–20	Kroger St. Jude	Memphis	Magnus Larsson	Byron Black	6–2, 1–6, 6–3
Feb 21–27	AXA Cup	London	Marc Rosset	Yevgeny Kafelnikov	6–4, 6–4
Mar 13–19	Champions Cup	Indian Wells, California	Alex Corretja	Thomas Enqvist	6–4, 6–4, 6–3
Mar 23–Apr 2	Ericcson Open	Miami	Pete Sampras	Gustavo Kuerten	6–1, 6–7 (2–7), 7–6 (7–5), 7–6 (10–8)
Apr 10–16	Estoril Open	Estoril, Portugal	Carlos Moya	Francisco Clavet	6–3, 6–2
Apr 17–23	Monte Carlo Open	Monte Carlo	Cedric Pioline	Dominik Hrbaty	6–4, 7–6 (7–3), 7–6 (8–6)
Apr 24–30	Open Seat Godo	Barcelona	Marat Safin	Juan Carlos Ferrero	6–3, 6–3, 6–4

Men's Tour (Through September 10, 2000) *(Cont.)*

Date	Tournament	Site	Winner	Finalist	Score
May 1–7	BMW Open	Munich	Franco Squillari	Tommy Haas	6–4, 6–4
May 8–14	Italian Open	Rome	Magnus Norman	Gustavo Kuerten	6–3, 4–6, 6–4, 6–4
May15–21	German Open	Hamburg	Gustavo Kuerten	Marat Safin	6–4, 5–7, 6–4, 5–7 7–6 (7–3)
May 29–Jun 11	French Open	Paris	Gustavo Kuerten	Magnus Norman	6–2, 6–3, 2–6, 7–6 (8–6)
June 12–18	Gerry Weber Open	Halle, Germany	David Prinosil	Richard Krajicek	6–3, 6–2
June 19–25	Heineken Trophy	'S-Hertogenbosch Netherlands	Patrick Rafter	Nicolas Escude	6–1, 6–3
June 26–July 9	Wimbledon	Wimbledon	Pete Sampras	Patrick Rafter	6–7 (10–12), 7–6 (7–5), 6–4, 6–2
July 10–16	Gstaad Open	Gstaad, Switzerland	Alex Corretja	Mariano Puerta	6–1, 6–3
July 17–23	Mercedes Cup	Stuttgart, Germany	Franco Squillari	Gaston Gaudio	6–2, 3–6, 4–6, 6–4, 6–2
July 24–30	Generali Open	Kitzbuhel, Austria	Alex Corretja	Emilio Alvarez	6–3, 6–1, 3–0 retired
Jul 31–Aug 6	Canadian Open	Toronto	Marat Safin	Harel Levy	6–2, 6–3
Aug 7–13	ATP Championship	Cincinnati	Thomas Enqvist	Tim Henman	7–6 (7–5), 6–4
Aug 14–20	RCA Championships	Indianapolis	Gustavo Kuerten	Marat Safin	3–6, 7–6 (7–2), 7–6 (7–2)
Aug 14–20	Legg Mason Classic	Wash., D.C.	Alex Corretja	Andre Agassi	6–2, 6–3
Aug 28–Sep 10	U.S. Open	New York City	Marat Safin	Pete Sampras	6–4, 6–3, 6–3

Women's Tour (Late 1999)

Date	Tournament	Site	Winner	Finalist	Score
Oct 11–17	Swisscom Challenge	Zurich	Venus Williams	Martina Hingis	6–3, 6–4
Oct 18–24	Ladies Kremlin Cup	Moscow	Nathalie Tauziat	Barbara Schett	2–6, 6–4, 6–1
Nov 1–7	Sparkassen Cup	Leipzig, Germany	Nathalie Tauziat	K. Hrdlickova	6–1, 6–3
Nov 8–14	Advanta Champ'ships	Philadelphia	L. Davenport	Martina Hingis	6–3, 6–4
Nov 15–21	Chase Champ'ships	New York	L. Davenport	Martina Hingis	6–4, 6–2

Women's Tour (Through September 10, 2000)

Date	Tournament	Site	Winner	Finalist	Score
Jan 10–16	Sydney International	Sydney	A. Mauresmo	L. Davenport	6–1, 7–5
Jan 17–30	Australian Open	Melbourne	L. Davenport	Martina Hingis	6–1, 7–5
Jan 31–Feb 6	Pan Pacific Open	Tokyo	Martina Hingis	Sandrine Testud	6–3, 7–5
Feb 7–13	Open Gaz de France	Paris	Nathalie Tauziat	Serena Williams	7–5, 6–2
Feb 14–20	Faber Grand Prix	Hannover, Germany	Serena Williams	D. Chladkova	6–1, 6–1
Mar 10–18	Tennis Masters Series	Indian Wells, California	L. Davenport	Martina Hingis	4–6, 6–4, 6–0
Mar 23–Apr 2	Ericsson Open	Miami	Martina Hingis	L. Davenport	6–3, 6–2
Apr 10–16	Bausch & Lomb Championships	Amelia Island, Florida	Monica Seles	Conchita Martinez	6–2, 6–3
Apr 17–23	Family Circle Cup	Hilton Head, S Carolina	Mary Pierce	A. Sánchez Vicario	6–1, 6–0
May 1–7	Betty Barclay Cup	Hamburg	Martina Hingis	A. Sánchez Vicario	6–3, 6–3
May 8–14	German Open	Berlin	C. Martinez	Amanda Coetzer	6–1, 6–2
May 15–21	Tennis Masters Series	Rome	Monica Seles	A. Mauresmo	6–2, 7–6 (7–4)
May 22–27	Int'l de Strasbourg	Strasbourg, France	Silvija Talaja	Rita Kuti Kis	7–5, 4–6, 6–3
May 29–Jun 11	French Open	Paris	Mary Pierce	Conchita Martinez	6–2, 7–5
June 19–25	Direct Line Champ'ships	Eastbourne, England	Julie Halard-Decugis	Dominique Van Roost	7–6 (7–4), 6–4
June 26–July 9	Wimbledon	Wimbledon	Venus Williams	L. Davenport	6–3, 7–6 (7–3)
July 24–30	Bank of the West	Stanford	Venus Williams	L. Davenport	6–1, 6–4
July 31–Aug 6	Acura Classic	San Diego	Venus Williams	Monica Seles	6–0, 6–7 (3–7) 6–3
Aug 7–13	Estyle.com Classic	Los Angeles	Serena Williams	L. Davenport	4–6, 6–4, 7–6 (7–1)

Women's Tour (Through September 10, 2000) *(Cont.)*

Date	Tournament	Site	Winner	Finalist	Score
Aug 14–20	du Maurier Open	Montreal	Martina Hingis	Serena Williams	0–6, 6–3, 3–0 ret.
Aug 21–27	Pilot Pen Int'l	New Haven,CT	Venus Williams	Monica Seles	6–2, 6–4
Aug 28–Sep 10	U.S. Open	New York City	Venus Williams	L. Davenport	6–4, 7–5

1999 Singles Leaders

Men

Rank	Player	Tournament Wins	Match Record	Earnings ($)
1.	Andre Agassi	5	63–14	4,269,265
2.	Yevgeny Kafelnikov	3	61–32	2,360,498
3.	Pete Sampras	5	40–8	2,816,406
4.	Thomas Enqvist	3	48–28	1,729,056
5.	Gustavo Kuerten	2	50–25	1,762,269
6.	Nicolas Kiefer	3	54–25	1,232,268
7.	Todd Martin	1	42–40	1,185,394
8.	Nicolas Lapentti	2	58–24	1,234,278
9.	Marcelo Rios	3	47–18	1,794,244
10.	Richard Krajicek	2	43–21	1,348,977
11.	Tommy Haas	1	47–26	1,447,308
12.	Tim Henman	0	44–29	1,537,594
13.	Cedric Pioline	1	43–32	723,428
14.	Greg Rusedski	2	48–26	2,122,535
15.	Magnus Norman	5	44–22	609,035
16.	Patrick Rafter	1	38–16	1,254,574
17.	Karol Kucera	1	43–22	870,957
18.	Albert Costa	3	40–22	620,629
19.	Mark Philippoussis	2	35–17	1,019,856
20.	Vincent Spadea	0	33–27	605,609

Note: Compiled by the ATP Tour.

Women

Rank	Player	Tournament Wins	Match Record	Earnings ($)
1.	Martina Hingis	7	71–13	3,291,780
2.	Lindsay Davenport	7	59–10	2,734,205
3.	Venus Williams	6	58–12	2,316,005
4.	Serena Williams	5	40–7	2,605,102
5.	Mary Pierce	1	45–20	996,442
6.	Monica Seles	1	36–12	822,218
7.	Nathalie Tauziat	2	37–23	864,507
8.	Barbara Schett	0	46–24	725,685
9.	Julie Halard-Decugis	2	47–20	514,070
10.	Amelie Mauresmo	1	31–15	582,468
11.	Amanda Coetzer	0	37–25	486,120
12.	Anna Kournikova	0	35–19	748,424
13.	Sandrine Testud	0	36–25	488,496
14.	Dominique Van Roost	0	37–25	450,401
15.	Conchita Martinez	1	38–22	486,392
16.	Anke Huber	0	31–26	411,487
17.	Arantxa Sánchez Vicario	1	24–18	807,921
18.	Elena Likhovtseva	0	34–29	525,307
19.	Amy Frazier	1	31–19	257,686
20.	Ruxandra Dragomir	0	30–22	309,222

Note: Compiled by the Women's Tennis Association (WTA).

THEY SAID IT

*Anna Kournikova, tennis vixen,
when asked about her love life
during a press conference to promote
the undergarments she endorses:
"I'm not here to talk about
my personal life. I'm here to talk
about bras."*

1999 Davis Cup World Group Final

Australia def. France 3–2, Dec. 3–5 in Nice, France
 Mark Philippoussis (AUS) def. Sebastian Grosjean (FRA), 6–4, 6–2, 6–4
 Cedric Pioline (FRA) def. Lleyton Hewitt (AUS), 7–6, 7–6, 7–5
 Mark Woodforde and Todd Woodbridge (AUS) def. Olivier Delaitre and Fabrice Santoro (FRA) 2–6, 7–5, 6–2, 6–2
 Mark Phlippoussis (AUS) def. Cedric Pioline (FRA) 6–3, 5–7, 6–1, 6–2
 Sebastian Grojean (FRA) def. Lleyton Hewitt (AUS) 6–4, 6–3

2000 Davis Cup World Group Tournament

FIRST ROUND

United States def. Zimbabwe, 3–2
Czech Republic def. Great Britain, 4–1
Australia def. Switzerland, 3–2
Spain def. Italy, 4–1
Russia def. Belgium, 4–1
Slovakia def. Austria, 3–2
Brazil def. France, 4–1
Germany def. Netherlands, 4–1

QUARTERFINAL ROUND

United States def. Czech Republic, 3–2
Australia def. Germany, 3–2
Spain def. Russia, 4–1
Brazil def. Slovakia, 3–2

SEMIFINALS

Spain def. United States, 5–0
 Juan Carlos Ferrero (SPA) def. Vincent Spadea (USA), 4–6, 6–1, 6–4
 Juan Balcells (SPA) def. Jan-Michael Gambill (USA), 1–6, 7–6 (7–2), 6–4
 Alex Corretja and Juan Balcells (SPA) def. Todd Martin and Chris Woodruff (USA), 7–6 (8–6), 2–6, 6–3, 6–7 (5–7), 6–3
 Albert Costa (SPA) def. Todd Martin (USA), 6–4, 6–4, 6–4
 Alex Corretja (SPA) def. Jan-Michael Gambill (USA), 1–6, 6–3, 6–4, 6–4

Australia def. Brazil, 5–0
 Lleyton Hewitt (AUS) def. André Sá (BRA), 6–4, 6–1
 Patrick Rafter (AUS) def. Fernando Meligeni (BRA), 6–4, 6–3
 Sandon Stolle and Mark Woodforde (AUS) def. Gustavo Kuerten and Jaime Oncins (BRA), 6–7 (3–7), 6–4, 3–6, 6–3, 6–4
 Patrick Rafter (AUS) def. Gustavo Kuerten (BRA), 6–3, 6–2, 6–3
 Lleyton Hewitt (AUS) def. Fernando Meligeni (BRA), 6–4, 6–2, 6–3

FINAL: Spain versus Australia to be held Dec. 8–10, 2000, in Barcelona.

2000 Federation Cup World Group Tournament

FIRST ROUND†

GROUP A			GROUP B			GROUP C		
Country	W	L	Country	W	L	Country	W	L
Spain*	3	0	Czech Rep.*	3	0	Belgium*	3	0
Germany	2	1	Switzerland	2	1	France	2	1
Italy	1	2	Austria	1	2	Russia	1	2
Croatia	0	3	Slovakia	0	3	Australia	0	3

*Advanced to semifinal round.

Note: As defending champion, the United States received a bye to the semifinals.

†Semifinals and finals to be held Nov. 24–26, 2000, in Las Vegas.

Grand Slam Tournaments

MEN
Australian Championships

Year	Winner	Finalist	Score
1905	Rodney Heath	A. H. Curtis	4–6, 6–3, 6–4, 6–4
1906	Tony Wilding	H. A. Parker	6–0, 6–4, 6–4
1907	Horace M. Rice	H. A. Parker	6–3, 6–4, 6–4
1908	Fred Alexander	A. W. Dunlop	3–6, 3–6, 6–0, 6–2, 6–3
1909	Tony Wilding	E. F. Parker	6–1, 7–5, 6–2
1910	Rodney Heath	Horace M. Rice	6–4, 6–3, 6–2
1911	Norman Brookes	Horace M. Rice	6–1, 6–2, 6–3
1912	J. Cecil Parke	A. E. Beamish	3–6, 6–3, 1–6, 6–1, 7–5
1913	E. F. Parker	H. A. Parker	2–6, 6–1, 6–2, 6–3
1914	Pat O'Hara Wood	G. L. Patterson	6–4, 6–3, 5–7, 6–1
1915	Francis G. Lowe	Horace M. Rice	4–6, 6–1, 6–1, 6–4
1916–18	No tournament		
1919	A. R. F. Kingscote	E. O. Pockley	6–4, 6–0, 6–3
1920	Pat O'Hara Wood	Ron Thomas	6–3, 4–6, 6–8, 8–1, 6–3
1921	Rhys H. Gemmell	A. Hedeman	7–5, 6–1, 6–4
1922	Pat O'Hara Wood	Gerald Patterson	6–0, 3–6, 3–6, 6–3, 6–2
1923	Pat O'Hara Wood	C. B. St John	6–1, 6–1, 6–3
1924	James Anderson	R. E. Schlesinger	6–3, 6–4, 3–6, 5–7, 6–3
1925	James Anderson	Gerald Patterson	11–9, 2–6, 6–2, 6–3
1926	John Hawkes	J. Willard	6–1, 6–3, 6–1
1927	Gerald Patterson	John Hawkes	3–6, 6–4, 3–6, 18–16, 6–3
1928	Jean Borotra	R. O. Cummings	6–4, 6–1, 4–6, 5–7, 6–3
1929	John C. Gregory	R. E. Schlesinger	6–2, 6–2, 5–7, 7–5
1930	Gar Moon	Harry C. Hopman	6–3, 6–1, 6–3
1931	Jack Crawford	Harry C. Hopman	6–4, 6–2, 2–6, 6–1
1932	Jack Crawford	Harry C. Hopman	4–6, 6–3, 3–6, 6–3, 6–1
1933	Jack Crawford	Keith Gledhill	2–6, 7–5, 6–3, 6–2
1934	Fred Perry	Jack Crawford	6–3, 7–5, 6–1
1935	Jack Crawford	Fred Perry	2–6, 6–4, 6–4, 6–4
1936	Adrian Quist	Jack Crawford	6–2, 6–3, 4–6, 3–6, 9–7
1937	Vivian B. McGrath	John Bromwich	6–3, 1–6, 6–0, 2–6, 6–1
1938	Don Budge	John Bromwich	6–4, 6–2, 6–1
1939	John Bromwich	Adrian Quist	6–4, 6–1, 6–3
1940	Adrian Quist	Jack Crawford	6–3, 6–1, 6–2
1941–45	No tournament		
1946	John Bromwich	Dinny Pails	5–7, 6–3, 7–5, 3–6, 6–2
1947	Dinny Pails	John Bromwich	4–6, 6–4, 3–6, 7–5, 8–6
1948	Adrian Quist	John Bromwich	6–4, 3–6, 6–3, 2–6, 6–3
1949	Frank Sedgman	Ken McGregor	6–3, 6–3, 6–2
1950	Frank Sedgman	Ken McGregor	6–3, 6–4, 4–6, 6–1
1951	Richard Savitt	Ken McGregor	6–3, 2–6, 6–3, 6–1
1952	Ken McGregor	Frank Sedgman	7–5, 12–10, 2–6, 6–2
1953	Ken Rosewall	Mervyn Rose	6–0, 6–3, 6–4
1954	Mervyn Rose	Rex Hartwig	6–2, 0–6, 6–4, 6–2
1955	Ken Rosewall	Lew Hoad	9–7, 6–4, 6–4
1956	Lew Hoad	Ken Rosewall	6–4, 3–6, 6–4, 7–5
1957	Ashley Cooper	Neale Fraser	6–3, 9–11, 6–4, 6–2
1958	Ashley Cooper	Mal Anderson	7–5, 6–3, 6–4
1959	Alex Olmedo	Neale Fraser	6–1, 6–2, 3–6, 6–3
1960	Rod Laver	Neale Fraser	5–7, 3–6, 6–3, 8–6, 8–6
1961	Roy Emerson	Rod Laver	1–6, 6–3, 7–5, 6–4
1962	Rod Laver	Roy Emerson	8–6, 0–6, 6–4, 6–4
1963	Roy Emerson	Ken Fletcher	6–3, 6–3, 6–1
1964	Roy Emerson	Fred Stolle	6–3, 6–4, 6–2
1965	Roy Emerson	Fred Stolle	7–9, 2–6, 6–4, 7–5, 6–1
1966	Roy Emerson	Arthur Ashe	6–4, 6–8, 6–2, 6–3
1967	Roy Emerson	Arthur Ashe	6–4, 6–1, 6–1
1968	Bill Bowrey	Juan Gisbert	7–5, 2–6, 9–7, 6–4
1969*	Rod Laver	Andres Gimeno	6–3, 6–4, 7–5

*Became Open (amateur and professional) in 1969.

MEN *(Cont.)*

Australian Championships *(Cont.)*

Year	Winner	Finalist	Score
1970	Arthur Ashe	Dick Crealy	6–4, 9–7, 6–2
1971	Ken Rosewall	Arthur Ashe	6–1, 7–5, 6–3
1972	Ken Rosewall	Mal Anderson	7–6, 6–3, 7–5
1973	John Newcombe	Onny Parun	6–3, 6–7, 7–5, 6–1
1974	Jimmy Connors	Phil Dent	7–6, 6–4, 4–6, 6–3
1975	John Newcombe	Jimmy Connors	7–5, 3–6, 6–4, 7–5
1976	Mark Edmondson	John Newcombe	6–7, 6–3, 7–6, 6–1
1977 (Jan)	Roscoe Tanner	Guillermo Vilas	6–3, 6–3, 6–3
1977 (Dec)	Vitas Gerulaitis	John Lloyd	6–3, 7–6, 5–7, 3–6, 6–2
1978	Guillermo Vilas	John Marks	6–4, 6–4, 3–6, 6–3
1979	Guillermo Vilas	John Sadri	7–6, 6–3, 6–2
1980	Brian Teacher	Kim Warwick	7–5, 7–6, 6–3
1981	Johan Kriek	Steve Denton	6–2, 7–6, 6–7, 6–4
1982	Johan Kriek	Steve Denton	6–3, 6–3, 6–2
1983	Mats Wilander	Ivan Lendl	6–1, 6–4, 6–4
1984	Mats Wilander	Kevin Curren	6–7, 6–4, 7–6, 6–2
1985 (Dec)	Stefan Edberg	Mats Wilander	6–4, 6–3, 6–3
1987 (Jan)	Stefan Edberg	Pat Cash	6–3, 6–4, 3–6, 5–7, 6–3
1988	Mats Wilander	Pat Cash	6–3, 6–7, 3–6, 6–1, 8–6
1989	Ivan Lendl	Miloslav Mecir	6–2, 6–2, 6–2
1990	Ivan Lendl	Stefan Edberg	4–6, 7–6, 5–2, ret.
1991	Boris Becker	Ivan Lendl	1–6, 6–4, 6–4, 6–4
1992	Jim Courier	Stefan Edberg	6–3, 3–6, 6–4, 6–2
1993	Jim Courier	Stefan Edberg	6–2, 6–1, 2–6, 7–5
1994	Pete Sampras	Todd Martin	7–6, 6–4, 6–4
1995	Andre Agassi	Pete Sampras	4–6, 6–1, 7–6, 6–4
1996	Boris Becker	Michael Chang	6–2, 6–4, 2–6, 6–2
1997	Pete Sampras	Carlos Moya	6–2, 6–3, 6–3
1998	Petr Korda	Marcelo Ríos	6–2, 6–2, 6–2
1999	Yevgeny Kafelnikov	Thomas Enqvist	4–6, 6–0, 6–3, 7–6
2000	Andre Agassi	Yevgeny Kafelnikov	3–6, 6–3, 6–2, 6–4

French Championships

Year	Winner	Finalist	Score
1925†	Rene Lacoste	Jean Borotra	7–5, 6–1, 6–4
1926	Henri Cochet	Rene Lacoste	6–2, 6–4, 6–3
1927	Rene Lacoste	Bill Tilden	6–4, 4–6, 5–7, 6–3, 11–9
1928	Henri Cochet	Rene Lacoste	5–7, 6–3, 6–1, 6–3
1929	Rene Lacoste	Jean Borotra	6–3, 2–6, 6–0, 2–6, 8–6
1930	Henri Cochet	Bill Tilden	3–6, 8–6, 6–3, 6–1
1931	Jean Borotra	Claude Boussus	2–6, 6–4, 7–5, 6–4
1932	Henri Cochet	Giorgio de Stefani	6–0, 6–4, 4–6, 6–3
1933	Jack Crawford	Henri Cochet	8–6, 6–1, 6–3
1934	Gottfried von Cramm	Jack Crawford	6–4, 7–9, 3–6, 7–5, 6–3
1935	Fred Perry	Gottfried von Cramm	6–3, 3–6, 6–1, 6–3
1936	Gottfried von Cramm	Fred Perry	6–0, 2–6, 6–2, 2–6, 6–0
1937	Henner Henkel	Henry Austin	6–1, 6–4, 6–3
1938	Don Budge	Roderick Menzel	6–3, 6–2, 6–4
1939	Don McNeill	Bobby Riggs	7–5, 6–0, 6–3
1940	No tournament		
1941‡	Bernard Destremau	n/a	n/a
1942‡	Bernard Destremau	n/a	n/a
1943‡	Yvon Petra	n/a	n/a
1944‡	Yvon Petra	n/a	n/a
1945‡	Yvon Petra	Bernard Destremau	7–5, 6–4, 6–2
1946	Marcel Bernard	Jaroslav Drobny	3–6, 2–6, 6–1, 6–4, 6–3
1947	Joseph Asboth	Eric Sturgess	8–6, 7–5, 6–4
1948	Frank Parker	Jaroslav Drobny	6–4, 7–5, 5–7, 8–6
1949	Frank Parker	Budge Patty	6–3, 1–6, 6–1, 6–4
1950	Budge Patty	Jaroslav Drobny	6–1, 6–2, 3–6, 5–7, 7–5
1951	Jaroslav Drobny	Eric Sturgess	6–3, 6–3, 6–3
1952	Jaroslav Drobny	Frank Sedgman	6–2, 6–0, 3–6, 6–4
1953	Ken Rosewall	Vic Seixas	6–3, 6–4, 1–6, 6–2

MEN *(Cont.)*
French Championships *(Cont.)*

Year	Winner	Finalist	Score
1954	Tony Trabert	Arthur Larsen	6–4, 7–5, 6–1
1955	Tony Trabert	Sven Davidson	2–6, 6–1, 6–4, 6–2
1956	Lew Hoad	Sven Davidson	6–4, 8–6, 6–3
1957	Sven Davidson	Herbie Flam	6–3, 6–4, 6–4
1958	Mervyn Rose	Luis Ayala	6–3, 6–4, 6–4
1959	Nicola Pietrangeli	Ian Vermaak	3–6, 6–3, 6–4, 6–1
1960	Nicola Pietrangeli	Luis Ayala	3–6, 6–3, 6–4, 4–6, 6–3
1961	Manuel Santana	Nicola Pietrangeli	4–6, 6–1, 3–6, 6–0, 6–2
1962	Rod Laver	Roy Emerson	3–6, 2–6, 6–3, 9–7, 6–2
1963	Roy Emerson	Pierre Darmon	3–6, 6–1, 6–4, 6–4
1964	Manuel Santana	Nicola Pietrangeli	6–3, 6–1, 4–6, 7–5
1965	Fred Stolle	Tony Roche	3–6, 6–0, 6–2, 6–3
1966	Tony Roche	Istvan Gulyas	6–1, 6–4, 7–5
1967	Roy Emerson	Tony Roche	6–1, 6–4, 2–6, 6–2
1968*	Ken Rosewall	Rod Laver	6–3, 6–1, 2–6, 6–2
1969	Rod Laver	Ken Rosewall	6–4, 6–3, 6–4
1970	Jan Kodes	Zeljko Franulovic	6–2, 6–4, 6–0
1971	Jan Kodes	Ilie Nastase	8–6, 6–2, 2–6, 7–5
1972	Andres Gimeno	Patrick Proisy	4–6, 6–3, 6–1, 6–1
1973	Ilie Nastase	Nikki Pilic	6–3, 6–3, 6–0
1974	Bjorn Borg	Manuel Orantes	6–7, 6–0, 6–1, 6–1
1975	Bjorn Borg	Guillermo Vilas	6–2, 6–3, 6–4
1976	Adriano Panatta	Harold Solomon	6–1, 6–4, 4–6, 7–6
1977	Guillermo Vilas	Brian Gottfried	6–0, 6–3, 6–0
1978	Bjorn Borg	Guillermo Vilas	6–1, 6–1, 6–3
1979	Bjorn Borg	Victor Pecci	6–3, 6–1, 6–7, 6–4
1980	Bjorn Borg	Vitas Gerulaitis	6–4, 6–1, 6–2
1981	Bjorn Borg	Ivan Lendl	6–1, 4–6, 6–2, 3–6, 6–1
1982	Mats Wilander	Guillermo Vilas	1–6, 7–6, 6–0, 6–4
1983	Yannick Noah	Mats Wilander	6–2, 7–5, 7–6
1984	Ivan Lendl	John McEnroe	3–6, 2–6, 6–4, 7–5, 7–5
1985	Mats Wilander	Ivan Lendl	3–6, 6–4, 6–2, 6–2
1986	Ivan Lendl	Mikael Pernfors	6–3, 6–2, 6–4
1987	Ivan Lendl	Mats Wilander	7–5, 6–2, 3–6, 7–6
1988	Mats Wilander	Henri Leconte	7–5, 6–2, 6–1
1989	Michael Chang	Stefan Edberg	6–1, 3–6, 4–6, 6–4, 6–2
1990	Andres Gomez	Andre Agassi	6–3, 2–6, 6–4, 6–4
1991	Jim Courier	Andre Agassi	3–6, 6–4, 2–6, 6–1, 6–4
1992	Jim Courier	Petr Korda	7–5, 6–2, 6–1
1993	Sergi Bruguera	Jim Courier	6–4, 2–6, 6–2, 3–6, 6–3
1994	Sergi Bruguera	Alberto Berasategui	6–3, 7–5, 2–6, 6–1
1995	Thomas Muster	Michael Chang	7–5, 6–2, 6–4
1996	Yevgeny Kafelnikov	Michael Stich	7–6, 7–5, 7–6
1997	Gustavo Kuerten	Sergi Bruguera	6–3, 6–4, 6–2
1998	Carlos Moya	Alex Corretja	6–3, 7–5, 6–3
1999	Andre Agassi	Andrei Medvedev	1–6, 2–6, 6–4, 6–3, 6–4
2000	Gustavo Kuerten	Magnus Norman	6–2, 6–3, 2–6, 7–6

*Became Open (amateur and professional) in 1968 but closed to contract professionals in 1972.

†1925 was the first year that entries were accepted from all countries.

‡From 1941 to 1945 the event was called Tournoi de France and was closed to all foreigners.

Wimbledon Championships

Year	Winner	Finalist	Score
1877	Spencer W. Gore	William C. Marshall	6–1, 6–2, 6–4
1878	P. Frank Hadow	Spencer W. Gore	7–5, 6–1, 9–7
1879	John T. Hartley	V. St Leger Gould	6–2, 6–4, 6–2
1880	John T. Hartley	Herbert F. Lawford	6–0, 6–2, 2–6, 6–3
1881	William Renshaw	John T. Hartley	6–0, 6–2, 6–1
1882	William Renshaw	Ernest Renshaw	6–1, 2–6, 4–6, 6–2, 6–2
1883	William Renshaw	Ernest Renshaw	2–6, 6–3, 6–3, 4–6, 6–3
1884	William Renshaw	Herbert F. Lawford	6–0, 6–4, 9–7
1885	William Renshaw	Herbert F. Lawford	7–5, 6–2, 4–6, 7–5

MEN *(Cont.)*

Wimbledon Championship *(Cont.)*

Year	Winner	Finalist	Score
1886	William Renshaw	Herbert F. Lawford	6–0, 5–7, 6–3, 6–4
1887	Herbert F. Lawford	Ernest Renshaw	1–6, 6–3, 3–6, 6–4, 6–4
1888	Ernest Renshaw	Herbert F. Lawford	6–3, 7–5, 6–0
1889	William Renshaw	Ernest Renshaw	6–4, 6–1, 3–6, 6–0
1890	William J. Hamilton	William Renshaw	6–8, 6–2, 3–6, 6–1, 6–1
1891	Wilfred Baddeley	Joshua Pim	6–4, 1–6, 7–5, 6–0
1892	Wilfred Baddeley	Joshua Pim	4–6, 6–3, 6–3, 6–2
1893	Joshua Pim	Wilfred Baddeley	3–6, 6–1, 6–3, 6–2
1894	Joshua Pim	Wilfred Baddeley	10–8, 6–2, 8–6
1895	Wilfred Baddeley	Wilberforce V. Eaves	4–6, 2–6, 8–6, 6–2, 6–3
1896	Harold S. Mahoney	Wilfred Baddeley	6–2, 6–8, 5–7, 8–6, 6–3
1897	Reggie F. Doherty	Harold S. Mahoney	6–4, 6–4, 6–3
1898	Reggie F. Doherty	H. Laurie Doherty	6–3, 6–3, 2–6, 5–7, 6–1
1899	Reggie F. Doherty	Arthur W. Gore	1–6, 4–6, 6–2, 6–3, 6–3
1900	Reggie F. Doherty	Sidney H. Smith	6–8, 6–3, 6–1, 6–2
1901	Arthur W. Gore	Reggie F. Doherty	4–6, 7–5, 6–4, 6–4
1902	H. Laurie Doherty	Arthur W. Gore	6–4, 6–3, 3–6, 6–0
1903	H. Laurie Doherty	Frank L. Riseley	7–5, 6–3, 6–0
1904	H. Laurie Doherty	Frank L. Riseley	6–1, 7–5, 8–6
1905	H. Laurie Doherty	Norman E. Brookes	8–6, 6–2, 6–4
1906	H. Laurie Doherty	Frank L. Riseley	6–4, 4–6, 6–2, 6–3
1907	Norman E. Brookes	Arthur W. Gore	6–4, 6–2, 6–2
1908	Arthur W. Gore	H. Roper Barrett	6–3, 6–2, 4–6, 3–6, 6–4
1909	Arthur W. Gore	M. J. G. Ritchie	6–8, 1–6, 6–2, 6–2, 6–2
1910	Anthony F. Wilding	Arthur W. Gore	6–4, 7–5, 4–6, 6–2
1911	Anthony F. Wilding	H. Roper Barrett	6–4, 4–6, 2–6, 6–2 ret
1912	Anthony F. Wilding	Arthur W. Gore	6–4, 6–4, 4–6, 6–4
1913	Anthony F. Wilding	Maurice E. McLoughlin	8–6, 6–3, 10–8
1914	Norman E. Brookes	Anthony F. Wilding	6–4, 6–4, 7–5
1915–18	No tournament		
1919	Gerald L. Patterson	Norman E. Brookes	6–3, 7–5, 6–2
1920	Bill Tilden	Gerald L. Patterson	2–6, 6–3, 6–2, 6–4
1921	Bill Tilden	Brian I. C. Norton	4–6, 2–6, 6–1, 6–0, 7–5
1922	Gerald L. Patterson	Randolph Lycett	6–3, 6–4, 6–2
1923	Bill Johnston	Francis T. Hunter	6–0, 6–3, 6–1
1924	Jean Borotra	Rene Lacoste	6–1, 3–6, 6–1, 3–6, 6–4
1925	Rene Lacoste	Jean Borotra	6–3, 6–3, 4–6, 8–6
1926	Jean Borotra	Howard Kinsey	8–6, 6–1, 6–3
1927	Henri Cochet	Jean Borotra	4–6, 4–6, 6–3, 6–4, 7–5
1928	Rene Lacoste	Henri Cochet	6–1, 4–6, 6–4, 6–2
1929	Henri Cochet	Jean Borotra	6–4, 6–3, 6–4
1930	Bill Tilden	Wilmer Allison	6–3, 9–7, 6–4
1931	Sidney B. Wood Jr	Francis X. Shields	walkover
1932	Ellsworth Vines	Henry Austin	6–4, 6–2, 6–0
1933	Jack Crawford	Ellsworth Vines	4–6, 11–9, 6–2, 2–6, 6–4
1934	Fred Perry	Jack Crawford	6–3, 6–0, 7–5
1935	Fred Perry	Gottfried von Cramm	6–2, 6–4, 6–4
1936	Fred Perry	Gottfried von Cramm	6–1, 6–1, 6–0
1937	Don Budge	Gottfried von Cramm	6–3, 6–4, 6–2
1938	Don Budge	Henry Austin	6–1, 6–0, 6–3
1939	Bobby Riggs	Elwood Cooke	2–6, 8–6, 3–6, 6–3, 6–2
1940–45	No tournament		
1946	Yvon Petra	Geoff E. Brown	6–2, 6–4, 7–9, 5–7, 6–4
1947	Jack Kramer	Tom P. Brown	6–1, 6–3, 6–2
1948	Bob Falkenburg	John Bromwich	7–5, 0–6, 6–2, 3–6, 7–5
1949	Ted Schroeder	Jaroslav Drobny	3–6, 6–0, 6–3, 4–6, 6–4
1950	Budge Patty	Frank Sedgman	6–1, 8–10, 6–2, 6–3
1951	Dick Savitt	Ken McGregor	6–4, 6–4, 6–4
1952	Frank Sedgman	Jaroslav Drobny	4–6, 6–3, 6–2, 6–3
1953	Vic Seixas	Kurt Nielsen	9–7, 6–3, 6–4
1954	Jaroslav Drobny	Ken Rosewall	13–11, 4–6, 6–2, 9–7
1955	Tony Trabert	Kurt Nielsen	6–3, 7–5, 6–1
1956	Lew Hoad	Ken Rosewall	6–2, 4–6, 7–5, 6–4
1957	Lew Hoad	Ashley Cooper	6–2, 6–1, 6–2

MEN *(Cont.)*
Wimbledon Championships *(Cont.)*

Year	Winner	Finalist	Score
1958	Ashley Cooper	Neale Fraser	3–6, 6–3, 6–4, 13–11
1959	Alex Olmedo	Rod Laver	6–4, 6–3, 6–4
1960	Neale Fraser	Rod Laver	6–4, 3–6, 9–7, 7–5
1961	Rod Laver	Chuck McKinley	6–3, 6–1, 6–4
1962	Rod Laver	Martin Mulligan	6–2, 6–2, 6–1
1963	Chuck McKinley	Fred Stolle	9–7, 6–1, 6–4
1964	Roy Emerson	Fred Stolle	6–4, 12–10, 4–6, 6–3
1965	Roy Emerson	Fred Stolle	6–2, 6–4, 6–4
1966	Manuel Santana	Dennis Ralston	6–4, 11–9, 6–4
1967	John Newcombe	Wilhelm Bungert	6–3, 6–1, 6–1
1968*	Rod Laver	Tony Roche	6–3, 6–4, 6–2
1969	Rod Laver	John Newcombe	6–4, 5–7, 6–4, 6–4
1970	John Newcombe	Ken Rosewall	5–7, 6–3, 6–2, 3–6, 6–1
1971	John Newcombe	Stan Smith	6–3, 5–7, 2–6, 6–4, 6–4
1972	Stan Smith	Ilie Nastase	4–6, 6–3, 6–3, 4–6, 7–5
1973	Jan Kodes	Alex Metreveli	6–1, 9–8, 6–3
1974	Jimmy Connors	Ken Rosewall	6–1, 6–1, 6–4
1975	Arthur Ashe	Jimmy Connors	6–1, 6–1, 5–7, 6–4
1976	Bjorn Borg	Ilie Nastase	6–4, 6–2, 9–7
1977	Bjorn Borg	Jimmy Connors	3–6, 6–2, 6–1, 5–7, 6–4
1978	Bjorn Borg	Jimmy Connors	6–2, 6–2, 6–3
1979	Bjorn Borg	Roscoe Tanner	6–7, 6–1, 3–6, 6–3, 6–4
1980	Bjorn Borg	John McEnroe	1–6, 7–5, 6–3, 6–7, 8–6
1981	John McEnroe	Bjorn Borg	4–6, 7–6, 7–6, 6–4
1982	Jimmy Connors	John McEnroe	3–6, 6–3, 6–7, 7–6, 6–4
1983	John McEnroe	Chris Lewis	6–2, 6–2, 6–2
1984	John McEnroe	Jimmy Connors	6–1, 6–1, 6–2
1985	Boris Becker	Kevin Curren	6–3, 6–7, 7–6, 6–4
1986	Boris Becker	Ivan Lendl	6–4, 6–3, 7–5
1987	Pat Cash	Ivan Lendl	7–6, 6–2, 7–5
1988	Stefan Edberg	Boris Becker	4–6, 7–6, 6–4, 6–2
1989	Boris Becker	Stefan Edberg	6–0, 7–6, 6–4
1990	Stefan Edberg	Boris Becker	6–2, 6–2, 3–6, 3–6, 6–4
1991	Michael Stich	Boris Becker	6–4, 7–6, 6–4
1992	Andre Agassi	Goran Ivanisevic	6–7, 6–4, 6–4, 1–6, 6–4
1993	Pete Sampras	Jim Courier	7–6, 7–6, 3–6, 6–3
1994	Pete Sampras	Goran Ivanisevic	7–6, 7–6, 6–0
1995	Pete Sampras	Boris Becker	6–7, 6–2, 6–4, 6–2
1996	Richard Krajicek	MaliVai Washington	6–3, 6–4, 6–3
1997	Pete Sampras	Cedric Pioline	6–4, 6–2, 6–4
1998	Pete Sampras	Goran Ivanisevic	6–7, 7–6, 6–4, 3–6, 6–2
1999	Pete Sampras	Andre Agassi	6–3, 6–4, 7–5
2000	Pete Sampras	Patrick Rafter	6–7, 7–6, 6–4, 6–2

*Became Open (amateur and professional) in 1968 but closed to contract professionals in 1972

Note: Prior to 1922 the tournament was run on a challenge-round system. The previous year's winner "stood out"of an All Comers event, which produced a challenger to play him for the title.

United States Championships

Year	Winner	Finalist	Score
1881	Richard D. Sears	W.E. Glyn	6–0, 6–3, 6–2
1882	Richard D. Sears	C.M. Clark	6–1, 6–4, 6–0
1883	Richard D. Sears	James Dwight	6–2, 6–0, 9–7
1884	Richard D. Sears	H.A. Taylor	6–0, 1–6, 6–0, 6–2
1885	Richard D. Sears	G.M. Brinley	6–3, 4–6, 6–0, 6–3
1886	Richard D. Sears	R.L. Beeckman	4–6, 6–1, 6–3, 6–4
1887	Richard D. Sears	H.W. Slocum Jr	6–1, 6–3, 6–2
1888‡	H. W. Slocum Jr	H.A. Taylor	6–4, 6–1, 6–0
1889	H. W. Slocum Jr	Q.A. Shaw	6–3, 6–1, 4–6, 6–2
1890	Oliver S. Campbell	H.W. Slocum Jr	6–2, 4–6, 6–3, 6–1
1891	Oliver S. Campbell	Clarence Hobart	2–6, 7–5, 7–9, 6–1, 6–2
1892	Oliver S. Campbell	Frederick H. Hovey	7–5, 3–6, 6–3, 7–5
1893‡	Robert D. Wrenn	Frederick H. Hovey	6–4, 3–6, 6–4, 6–4
1894	Robert D. Wrenn	M.F. Goodbody	6–8, 6–1, 6–4, 6–4
1895	Frederick H. Hovey	Robert D. Wrenn	6–3, 6–2, 6–4

MEN *(Cont.)*

United States Championships *(Cont.)*

Year	Winner	Finalist	Score
1896	Robert D. Wrenn	Frederick H. Hovey	7–5, 3–6, 6–0, 1–6, 6–1
1897	Robert D. Wrenn	Wilberforce V. Eaves	4–6, 8–6, 6–3, 2–6, 6–2
1898‡	Malcolm D. Whitman	Dwight F. Davis	3–6, 6–2, 6–2, 6–1
1899	Malcolm D. Whitman	J. Parmly Paret	6–1, 6–2, 3–6, 7–5
1900	Malcolm D. Whitman	William A. Larned	6–4, 1–6, 6–2, 6–2
1901‡	William A. Larned	Beals C. Wright	6–2, 6–8, 6–4, 6–4
1902	William A. Larned	Reggie F. Doherty	4–6, 6–2, 6–4, 8–6
1903	H. Laurie Doherty	William A. Larned	6–0, 6–3, 10–8
1904‡	Holcombe Ward	William J. Clothier	10–8, 6–4, 9–7
1905	Beals C. Wright	Holcombe Ward	6–2, 6–1, 11–9
1906	William J. Clothier	Beals C. Wright	6–3, 6–0, 6–4
1907‡	William A. Larned	Robert LeRoy	6–2, 6–2, 6–4
1908	William A. Larned	Beals C. Wright	6–1, 6–2, 8–6
1909	William A. Larned	William J. Clothier	6–1, 6–2, 5–7, 1–6, 6–1
1910	William A. Larned	Thomas C. Bundy	6–1, 5–7, 6–0, 6–8, 6–1
1911	William A. Larned	Maurice E. McLoughlin	6–4, 6–4, 6–2
1912†	Maurice E. McLoughlin	Bill Johnson	3–6, 2–6, 6–2, 6–4, 6–2
1913	Maurice E. McLoughlin	Richard N. Williams	6–4, 5–7, 6–3, 6–1
1914	Richard N. Williams	Maurice E. McLoughlin	6–3, 8–6, 10–8
1915	Bill Johnston	Maurice E. McLoughlin	1–6, 6–0, 7–5, 10–8
1916	Richard N. Williams	Bill Johnston	4–6, 6–4, 0–6, 6–2, 6–4
1917#	R.L. Murray	N. W. Niles	5–7, 8–6, 6–3, 6–3
1918	R.L. Murray	Bill Tilden	6–3, 6–1, 7–5
1919	Bill Johnston	Bill Tilden	6–4, 6–4, 6–3
1920	Bill Tilden	Bill Johnston	6–1, 1–6, 7–5, 5–7, 6–3
1921	Bill Tilden	Wallace F. Johnson	6–1, 6–3, 6–1
1922	Bill Tilden	Bill Johnston	4–6, 3–6, 6–2, 6–3, 6–4
1923	Bill Tilden	Bill Johnston	6–4, 6–1, 6–4
1924	Bill Tilden	Bill Johnston	6–1, 9–7, 6–2
1925	Bill Tilden	Bill Johnston	4–6, 11–9, 6–3, 4–6, 6–3
1926	Rene Lacoste	Jean Borotra	6–4, 6–0, 6–4
1927	Rene Lacoste	Bill Tilden	11–9, 6–3, 11–9
1928	Henri Cochet	Francis T. Hunter	4–6, 6–4, 3–6, 7–5, 6–3
1929	Bill Tilden	Francis T. Hunter	3–6, 6–3, 4–6, 6–2, 6–4
1930	John H. Doeg	Francis X. Shields	10–8, 1–6, 6–4, 16–14
1931	Ellsworth Vines	George M. Lott Jr	7–9, 6–3, 9–7, 7–5
1932	Ellsworth Vines	Henri Cochet	6–4, 6–4, 6–4
1933	Fred Perry	Jack Crawford	6–3, 11–9, 4–6, 6–0, 6–1
1934	Fred Perry	Wilmer L. Allison	6–4, 6–3, 1–6, 8–6
1935	Wilmer L. Allison	Sidney B. Wood Jr	6–2, 6–2, 6–3
1936	Fred Perry	Don Budge	2–6, 6–2, 8–6, 1–6, 10–8
1937	Don Budge	Gottfried von Cramm	6–1, 7–9, 6–1, 3–6, 6–1
1938	Don Budge	Gene Mako	6–3, 6–8, 6–2, 6–1
1939	Bobby Riggs	Welby Van Horn	6–4, 6–2, 6–4
1940	Don McNeill	Bobby Riggs	4–6, 6–8, 6–3, 6–3, 7–5
1941	Bobby Riggs	Francis Kovacs II	5–7, 6–1, 6–3, 6–3
1942	Ted Schroeder	Frank Parker	8–6, 7–5, 3–6, 4–6, 6–2
1943	Joseph R. Hunt	Jack Kramer	6–3, 6–8, 10–8, 6–0
1944	Frank Parker	William F. Talbert	6–4, 3–6, 6–3, 6–3
1945	Frank Parker	William F. Talbert	14–12, 6–1, 6–2
1946	Jack Kramer	Tom P. Brown	9–7, 6–3, 6–0
1947	Jack Kramer	Frank Parker	4–6, 2–6, 6–1, 6–0, 6–3
1948	Pancho Gonzales	Eric W. Sturgess	6–2, 6–3, 14–12
1949	Pancho Gonzales	Ted Schroeder	16–18, 2–6, 6–1, 6–2, 6–4
1950	Arthur Larsen	Herbie Flam	6–3, 4–6, 5–7, 6–4, 6–3
1951	Frank Sedgman	Vic Seixas	6–4, 6–1, 6–1
1952	Frank Sedgman	Gardnar Mulloy	6–1, 6–2, 6–3
1953	Tony Trabert	Vic Seixas	6–3, 6–2, 6–3
1954	Vic Seixas	Rex Hartwig	3–6, 6–2, 6–4, 6–4
1955	Tony Trabert	Ken Rosewall	9–7, 6–3, 6–3
1956	Ken Rosewall	Lew Hoad	4–6, 6–2, 6–3, 6–3
1957	Mal Anderson	Ashley J. Cooper	10–8, 7–5, 6–4
1958	Ashley J. Cooper	Mal Anderson	6–2, 3–6, 4–6, 10–8, 8–6

MEN *(Cont.)*
United States Championships *(Cont.)*

Year	Winner	Finalist	Score
1959	Neale Fraser	Alex Olmedo	6–3, 5–7, 6–2, 6–4
1960	Neale Fraser	Rod Laver	6–4, 6–4, 9–7
1961	Roy Emerson	Rod Laver	7–5, 6–3, 6–2
1962	Rod Laver	Roy Emerson	6–2, 6–4, 5–7, 6–4
1963	Rafael Osuna	Frank Froehling III	7–5, 6–4, 6–2
1964	Roy Emerson	Fred Stolle	6–4, 6–2, 6–4
1965	Manuel Santana	Cliff Drysdale	6–2, 7–9, 7–5, 6–1
1966	Fred Stolle	John Newcombe	4–6, 12–10, 6–3, 6–4
1967	John Newcombe	Clark Graebner	6–4, 6–4, 8–6
1968*	Arthur Ashe	Tom Okker	14–12, 5–7, 6–3, 3–6, 6–3
1968**	Arthur Ashe	Bob Lutz	4–6, 6–3, 8–10, 6–0, 6–4
1969	Rod Laver	Tony Roche	7–9, 6–1, 6–3, 6–2
1969**	Stan Smith	Bob Lutz	9–7, 6–3, 6–1
1970	Ken Rosewall	Tony Roche	2–6, 6–4, 7–6, 6–3
1971	Stan Smith	Jan Kodes	3–6, 6–3, 6–2, 7–6
1972	Ilie Nastase	Arthur Ashe	3–6, 6–3, 6–7, 6–4, 6–3
1973	John Newcombe	Jan Kodes	6–4, 1–6, 4–6, 6–2, 6–3
1974	Jimmy Connors	Ken Rosewall	6–1, 6–0, 6–1
1975	Manuel Orantes	Jimmy Connors	6–4, 6–3, 6–3
1976	Jimmy Connors	Bjorn Borg	6–4, 3–6, 7–6, 6–4
1977	Guillermo Vilas	Jimmy Connors	2–6, 6–3, 7–6, 6–0
1978	Jimmy Connors	Bjorn Borg	6–4, 6–2, 6–2
1979	John McEnroe	Vitas Gerulaitis	7–5, 6–3, 6–3
1980	John McEnroe	Bjorn Borg	7–6, 6–1, 6–7, 5–7, 6–4
1981	John McEnroe	Bjorn Borg	4–6, 6–2, 6–4, 6–3
1982	Jimmy Connors	Ivan Lendl	6–3, 6–2, 4–6, 6–4
1983	Jimmy Connors	Ivan Lendl	6–3, 6–7, 7–5, 6–0
1984	John McEnroe	Ivan Lendl	6–3, 6–4, 6–1
1985	Ivan Lendl	John McEnroe	7–6, 6–3, 6–4
1986	Ivan Lendl	Miloslav Mecir	6–4, 6–2, 6–0
1987	Ivan Lendl	Mats Wilander	6–7, 6–0, 7–6, 6–4
1988	Mats Wilander	Ivan Lendl	6–4, 4–6, 6–3, 5–7, 6–4
1989	Boris Becker	Ivan Lendl	7–6, 1–6, 6–3, 7–6
1990	Pete Sampras	Andre Agassi	6–4, 6–3, 6–2
1991	Stefan Edberg	Jim Courier	6–2, 6–4, 6–0
1992	Stefan Edberg	Pete Sampras	3–6, 6–4, 7–6, 6–2
1993	Pete Sampras	Cedric Pioline	6–4, 6–4, 6–3
1994	Andre Agassi	Michael Stich	6–1, 7–6, 7–5
1995	Pete Sampras	Andre Agassi	6–4, 6–3, 4–6, 7–5
1996	Pete Sampras	Michael Chang	6–1, 6–4, 7–6
1997	Patrick Rafter	Greg Rusedski	6–3, 6–2, 4–6, 7–5
1998	Patrick Rafter	Mark Philippoussis	6–3, 3–6, 6–2, 6–0
1999	Andre Agassi	Todd Martin	6–4, 6–7, 6–7, 6–3, 6–2
2000	Marat Safin	Pete Sampras	6–4, 6–3, 6–3

‡No challenge round played.*Became Open (amateur and professional) in 1968.†Challenge round abolished; #National Patriotic Tournament.**Amateur event held.

WOMEN
Australian Championships

Year	Winner	Finalist	Score
1922	Margaret Molesworth	Esna Boyd	6–3, 10–8
1923	Margaret Molesworth	Esna Boyd	6–1, 7–5
1924	Sylvia Lance	Esna Boyd	6–3, 3–6, 6–4
1925	Daphne Akhurst	Esna Boyd	1–6, 8–6, 6–4
1926	Daphne Akhurst	Esna Boyd	6–1, 6–3
1927	Esna Boyd	Sylvia Harper	5–7, 6–1, 6–2
1928	Daphne Akhurst	Esna Boyd	7–5, 6–2
1929	Daphne Akhurst	Louise Bickerton	6–1, 5–7, 6–2
1930	Daphne Akhurst	Sylvia Harper	10–8, 2–6, 7–5
1931	Coral Buttsworth	Margorie Crawford	1–6, 6–3, 6–4
1932	Coral Buttsworth	Kathrine Le Messurier	9–7, 6–4
1933	Joan Hartigan	Coral Buttsworth	6–4, 6–3

WOMEN *(Cont.)*

Australian Championships *(Cont.)*

Year	Winner	Finalist	Score
1934	Joan Hartigan	Margaret Molesworth	6–1, 6–4
1935	Dorothy Round	Nancye Wynne Bolton	1–6, 6–1, 6–3
1936	Joan Hartigan	Nancye Wynne Bolton	6–4, 6–4
1937	Nancye Wynne Bolton	Emily Westacott	6–3, 5–7, 6–4
1938	Dorothy Bundy	D. Stevenson	6–3, 6–2
1939	Emily Westacott	Nell Hopman	6–1, 6–2
1940	Nancye Wynne Bolton	Thelma Coyne	5–7, 6–4, 6–0
1941–45	No tournament		
1946	Nancye Wynne Bolton	Joyce Fitch	6–4, 6–4
1947	Nancye Wynne Bolton	Nell Hopman	6–3, 6–2
1948	Nancye Wynne Bolton	Marie Toomey	6–3, 6–1
1949	Doris Hart	Nancye Wynne Bolton	6–3, 6–4
1950	Louise Brough	Doris Hart	6–4, 3–6, 6–4
1951	Nancye Wynne Bolton	Thelma Long	6–1, 7–5
1952	Thelma Long	H. Angwin	6–2, 6–3
1953	Maureen Connolly	Julia Sampson	6–3, 6–2
1954	Thelma Long	J. Staley	6–3, 6–4
1955	Beryl Penrose	Thelma Long	6–4, 6–3
1956	Mary Carter	Thelma Long	3–6, 6–2, 9–7
1957	Shirley Fry	Althea Gibson	6–3, 6–4
1958	Angela Mortimer	Lorraine Coghlan	6–3, 6–4
1959	Mary Carter-Reitano	Renee Schuurman	6–2, 6–3
1960	Margaret Smith	Jan Lehane	7–5, 6–2
1961	Margaret Smith	Jan Lehane	6–1, 6–4
1962	Margaret Smith	Jan Lehane	6–0, 6–2
1963	Margaret Smith	Jan Lehane	6–2, 6–2
1964	Margaret Smith	Lesley Turner	6–3, 6–2
1965	Margaret Smith	Maria Bueno	5–7, 6–4, 5–2 ret.
1966	Margaret Smith	Nancy Richey	Default
1967	Nancy Richey	Lesley Turner	6–1, 6–4
1968	Billie Jean King	Margaret Smith	6–1, 6–2
1969*	Margaret Smith Court	Billie Jean King	6–4, 6–1
1970	Margaret Smith Court	Kerry Melville Reid	6–3, 6–1
1971	Margaret Smith Court	Evonne Goolagong	2–6, 7–6, 7–5
1972	Virginia Wade	Evonne Goolagong	6–4, 6–4
1973	Margaret Smith Court	Evonne Goolagong	6–4, 7–5
1974	Evonne Goolagong	Chris Evert	7–6, 4–6, 6–0
1975	Evonne Goolagong	Martina Navratilova	6–3, 6–2
1976	Evonne Goolagong Cawley	Renata Tomanova	6–2, 6–2
1977 (Jan)	Kerry Melville Reid	Dianne Balestrat	7–5, 6–2
1977 (Dec)	Evonne Goolagong Cawley	Helen Gourlay	6–3, 6–0
1978	Chris O'Neil	Betsy Nagelsen	6–3, 7–6
1979	Barbara Jordan	Sharon Walsh	6–3, 6–3
1980	Hana Mandlikova	Wendy Turnbull	6–0, 7–5
1981	Martina Navratilova	Chris Evert Lloyd	6–7, 6–4, 7–5
1982	Chris Evert Lloyd	Martina Navratilova	6–3, 2–6, 6–3
1983	Martina Navratilova	Kathy Jordan	6–2, 7–6
1984	Chris Evert Lloyd	Helena Sukova	6–7, 6–1, 6–3
1985 (Dec)	Martina Navratilova	Chris Evert Lloyd	6–2, 4–6, 6–2
1987 (Jan)	Hana Mandlikova	Martina Navratilova	7–5, 7–6
1988	Steffi Graf	Chris Evert	6–1, 7–6
1989	Steffi Graf	Helena Sukova	6–4, 6–4
1990	Steffi Graf	Mary Joe Fernandez	6–3, 6–4
1991	Monica Seles	Jana Novotna	5–7, 6–3, 6–1
1992	Monica Seles	Mary Joe Fernandez	6–2, 6–3
1993	Monica Seles	Steffi Graf	4–6, 6–3, 6–2
1994	Steffi Graf	Arantxa Sánchez Vicario	6–0, 6–2
1995	Mary Pierce	Arantxa Sánchez Vicario	6–3, 6–2
1996	Monica Seles	Anke Huber	6–4, 6–1
1997	Martina Hingis	Mary Pierce	6–2, 6–2
1998	Martina Hingis	Conchita Martinez	6–3, 6–3
1999	Martina Hingis	Amelie Mauresmo	6–2, 6–3
2000	Lindsay Davenport	Martina Hingis	6–1, 7–5

*Became Open (amateur and professional) in 1969.

WOMEN *(Cont.)*
French Championships

Year	Winner	Finalist	Score
1925†	Suzanne Lenglen	Kathleen McKane	6–1, 6–2
1926	Suzanne Lenglen	Mary K. Browne	6–1, 6–0
1927	Kea Bouman	Irene Peacock	6–2, 6–4
1928	Helen Wills	Eileen Bennett	6–1, 6–2
1929	Helen Wills	Simone Mathieu	6–3, 6–4
1930	Helen Wills Moody	Helen Jacobs	6–2, 6–1
1931	Cilly Aussem	Betty Nuthall	8–6, 6–1
1932	Helen Wills Moody	Simone Mathieu	7–5, 6–1
1933	Margaret Scriven	Simone Mathieu	6–2, 4–6, 6–4
1934	Margaret Scriven	Helen Jacobs	7–5, 4–6, 6–1
1935	Hilde Sperling	Simone Mathieu	6–2, 6–1
1936	Hilde Sperling	Simone Mathieu	6–3, 6–4
1937	Hilde Sperling	Simone Mathieu	6–2, 6–4
1938	Simone Mathieu	Nelly Landry	6–0, 6–3
1939	Simone Mathieu	Jadwiga Jedrzejowska	6–3, 8–6
1940–45	No tournament		
1946	Margaret Osborne	Pauline Betz	1–6, 8–6, 7–5
1947	Patricia Todd	Doris Hart	6–3, 3–6, 6–4
1948	Nelly Landry	Shirley Fry	6–2, 0–6, 6–0
1949	Margaret Osborne duPont	Nelly Adamson	7–5, 6–2
1950	Doris Hart	Patricia Todd	6–4, 4–6, 6–2
1951	Shirley Fry	Doris Hart	6–3, 3–6, 6–3
1952	Doris Hart	Shirley Fry	6–4, 6–4
1953	Maureen Connolly	Doris Hart	6–2, 6–4
1954	Maureen Connolly	Ginette Bucaille	6–4, 6–1
1955	Angela Mortimer	Dorothy Knode	2–6, 7–5, 10–8
1956	Althea Gibson	Angela Mortimer	6–0, 12–10
1957	Shirley Bloomer	Dorothy Knode	6–1, 6–3
1958	Zsuzsi Kormoczi	Shirley Bloomer	6–4, 1–6, 6–2
1959	Christine Truman	Zsuzsi Kormoczi	6–4, 7–5
1960	Darlene Hard	Yola Ramirez	6–3, 6–4
1961	Ann Haydon	Yola Ramirez	6–2, 6–1
1962	Margaret Smith	Lesley Turner	6–3, 3–6, 7–5
1963	Lesley Turner	Ann Haydon Jones	2–6, 6–3, 7–5
1964	Margaret Smith	Maria Bueno	5–7, 6–1, 6–2
1965	Lesley Turner	Margaret Smith	6–3, 6–4
1966	Ann Jones	Nancy Richey	6–3, 6–1
1967	Francoise Durr	Lesley Turner	4–6, 6–3, 6–4
1968*	Nancy Richey	Ann Jones	5–7, 6–4, 6–1
1969	Margaret Smith Court	Ann Jones	6–1, 4–6, 6–3
1970	Margaret Smith Court	Helga Niessen	6–2, 6–4
1971	Evonne Goolagong	Helen Gourlay	6–3, 7–5
1972	Billie Jean King	Evonne Goolagong	6–3, 6–3
1973	Margaret Smith Court	Chris Evert	6–7, 7–6, 6–4
1974	Chris Evert	Olga Morozova	6–1, 6–2
1975	Chris Evert	Martina Navratilova	2–6, 6–2, 6–1
1976	Sue Barker	Renata Tomanova	6–2, 0–6, 6–2
1977	Mima Jausovec	Florenza Mihai	6–2, 6–7, 6–1
1978	Virginia Ruzici	Mima Jausovec	6–2, 6–2
1979	Chris Evert Lloyd	Wendy Turnbull	6–2, 6–0
1980	Chris Evert Lloyd	Virginia Ruzici	6–0, 6–3
1981	Hana Mandlikova	Sylvia Hanika	6–2, 6–4
1982	Martina Navratilova	Andrea Jaeger	7–6, 6–1
1983	Chris Evert Lloyd	Mima Jausovec	6–1, 6–2
1984	Martina Navratilova	Chris Evert Lloyd	6–3, 6–1
1985	Chris Evert Lloyd	Martina Navratilova	6–3, 6–7, 7–5
1986	Chris Evert Lloyd	Martina Navratilova	2–6, 6–3, 6–3
1987	Steffi Graf	Martina Navratilova	6–4, 4–6, 8–6
1988	Steffi Graf	Natalia Zvereva	6–0, 6–0
1989	Arantxa Sánchez Vicario	Steffi Graf	7–6, 3–6, 7–5
1990	Monica Seles	Steffi Graf	7–6, 6–4
1991	Monica Seles	Arantxa Sánchez Vicario	6–3, 6–4
1992	Monica Seles	Steffi Graf	6–2, 3–6, 10–8

WOMEN (Cont.)
French Championships (Cont.)

Year	Winner	Finalist	Score
1993	Steffi Graf	Mary Joe Fernandez	4–6, 6–2, 6–4
1994	Arantxa Sánchez Vicario	Mary Pierce	6–4, 6–4
1995	Steffi Graf	Arantxa Sánchez Vicario	7–5, 4–6, 6–0
1996	Steffi Graf	Arantxa Sánchez Vicario	6–3, 6–7 (4–7), 10–8
1997	Iva Majoli	Martina Hingis	6–4, 6–2
1998	Arantxa Sánchez Vicario	Monica Seles	7–6 (7–5), 0–6, 6–2
1999	Steffi Graf	Martina Hingis	4–6, 7–5, 6–2
2000	Mary Pierce	Conchita Martinez	6–2, 7–5

†1925 was the first year that entries were accepted from all countries.

*Became Open (amateur and professional) in 1968 but closed to contract professionals in 1972.

Wimbledon Championships

Year	Winner	Finalist	Score
1884	Maud Watson	Lilian Watson	6–8, 6–3, 6–3
1885	Maud Watson	Blanche Bingley	6–1, 7–5
1886	Blanche Bingley	Maud Watson	6–3, 6–3
1887	Charlotte Dod	Blanche Bingley	6–2, 6–0
1888	Charlotte Dod	Blanche Bingley Hillyard	6–3, 6–3
1889	Blanche Bingley Hillyard	n/a	n/a
1890	Lena Rice	n/a	n/a
1891	Charlotte Dod	n/a	n/a
1892	Charlotte Dod	Blanche Bingley Hillyard	6–1, 6–1
1893	Charlotte Dod	Blanche Bingley Hillyard	6–8, 6–1, 6–4
1894	Blanche Bingley Hillyard	n/a	n/a
1895	Charlotte Cooper	n/a	
1896	Charlotte Cooper	Mrs. W. H. Pickering	6–2, 6–3
1897	Blanche Bingley Hillyard	Charlotte Cooper	5–7, 7–5, 6–2
1898	Charlotte Cooper	n/a	n/a
1899	Blanche Bingley Hillyard	Charlotte Cooper	6–2, 6–3
1900	Blanche Bingley Hillyard	Charlotte Cooper	4–6, 6–4, 6–4
1901	Charlotte Cooper Sterry	Blanche Bingley Hillyard	6–2, 6–2
1902	Muriel Robb	Charlotte Cooper Sterry	7–5, 6–1
1903	Dorothea Douglass	n/a	n/a
1904	Dorothea Douglass	Charlotte Cooper Sterry	6–0, 6–3
1905	May Sutton	Dorothea Douglass	6–3, 6–4
1906	Dorothea Douglass	May Sutton	6–3, 9–7
1907	May Sutton	Dorothea Douglass Lambert Chambers	6–1, 6–4
1908	Charlotte Cooper Sterry	n/a	n/a
1909	Dora Boothby	n/a	n/a
1910	Dorothea Douglass Lambert Chambers	Dora Boothby	6–2, 6–2
1911	Dorothea Douglass Lambert Chambers	Dora Boothby	6–0, 6–0
1912	Ethel Larcombe	n/a	n/a
1913	Dorothea Douglass Lambert Chambers		
1914	Dorothea Douglass Lambert Chambers	Ethel Larcombe	7–5, 6–4
1915–18	No tournament		
1919	Suzanne Lenglen	Dorothea Douglass Lambert Chambers	10–8, 4–6, 9–7
1920	Suzanne Lenglen	Dorothea Douglass Lambert Chambers	6–3, 6–0
1921	Suzanne Lenglen	Elizabeth Ryan	6–2, 6–0
1922	Suzanne Lenglen	Molla Mallory	6–2, 6–0
1923	Suzanne Lenglen	Kathleen McKane	6–2, 6–2
1924	Kathleen McKane	Helen Wills	4–6, 6–4, 6–2
1925	Suzanne Lenglen	Joan Fry	6–2, 6–0
1926	Kathleen McKane Godfree	Lili de Alvarez	6–2, 4–6, 6–3
1927	Helen Wills	Lili de Alvarez	6–2, 6–4
1928	Helen Wills	Lili de Alvarez	6–2, 6–3
1929	Helen Wills	Helen Jacobs	6–1, 6–2

WOMEN *(Cont.)*
Wimbledon Championships *(Cont.)*

Year	Winner	Finalist	Score
1930	Helen Wills Moody	Elizabeth Ryan	6–2, 6–2
1931	Cilly Aussem	Hilde Kranwinkel	7–5, 7–5
1932	Helen Wills Moody	Helen Jacobs	6–3, 6–1
1933	Helen Wills Moody	Dorothy Round	6–4, 6–8, 6–3
1934	Dorothy Round	Helen Jacobs	6–2, 5–7, 6–3
1935	Helen Wills Moody	Helen Jacobs	6–3, 3–6, 7–5
1936	Helen Jacobs	Hilde Kranwinkel Sperling	6–2, 4–6, 7–5
1937	Dorothy Round	Jadwiga Jedrzejowska	6–2, 2–6, 7–5
1938	Helen Wills Moody	Helen Jacobs	6–4, 6–0
1939	Alice Marble	Kay Stammers	6–2, 6–0
1940–45	No tournament		
1946	Pauline Betz	Louise Brough	6–2, 6–4
1947	Margaret Osborne	Doris Hart	6–2, 6–4
1948	Louise Brough	Doris Hart	6–3, 8–6
1949	Louise Brough	Margaret Osborne duPont	10–8, 1–6, 10–8
1950	Louise Brough	Margaret Osborne duPont	6–1, 3–6, 6–1
1951	Doris Hart	Shirley Fry	6–1, 6–0
1952	Maureen Connolly	Louise Brough	6–4, 6–3
1953	Maureen Connolly	Doris Hart	8–6, 7–5
1954	Maureen Connolly	Louise Brough	6–2, 7–5
1955	Louise Brough	Beverly Fleitz	7–5, 8–6
1956	Shirley Fry	Angela Buxton	6–3, 6–1
1957	Althea Gibson	Darlene Hard	6–3, 6–2
1958	Althea Gibson	Angela Mortimer	8–6, 6–2
1959	Maria Bueno	Darlene Hard	6–4, 6–3
1960	Maria Bueno	Sandra Reynolds	8–6, 6–0
1961	Angela Mortimer	Christine Truman	4–6, 6–4, 7–5
1962	Karen Hantze Susman	Vera Sukova	6–4, 6–4
1963	Margaret Smith	Billie Jean Moffitt	6–3, 6–4
1964	Maria Bueno	Margaret Smith	6–4, 7–9, 6–3
1965	Margaret Smith	Maria Bueno	6–4, 7–5
1966	Billie Jean King	Maria Bueno	6–3, 3–6, 6–1
1967	Billie Jean King	Ann Haydon Jones	6–3, 6–4
1968*	Billie Jean King	Judy Tegart	9–7, 7–5
1969	Ann Haydon Jones	Billie Jean King	3–6, 6–3, 6–2
1970	Margaret Smith Court	Billie Jean King	14–12, 11–9
1971	Evonne Goolagong	Margaret Smith Court	6–4, 6–1
1972	Billie Jean King	Evonne Goolagong	6–3, 6–3
1973	Billie Jean King	Chris Evert	6–0, 7–5
1974	Chris Evert	Olga Morozova	6–0, 6–4
1975	Billie Jean King	Evonne Goolagong Cawley	6–0, 6–1
1976	Chris Evert	Evonne Goolagong Cawley	6–3, 4–6, 8–6
1977	Virginia Wade	Betty Stove	4–6, 6–3, 6–1
1978	Martina Navratilova	Chris Evert	2–6, 6–4, 7–5
1979	Martina Navratilova	Chris Evert Lloyd	6–4, 6–4
1980	Evonne Goolagong Cawley	Chris Evert Lloyd	6–1, 7–6
1981	Chris Evert Lloyd	Hana Mandlikova	6–2, 6–2
1982	Martina Navratilova	Chris Evert Lloyd	6–1, 3–6, 6–2
1983	Martina Navratilova	Andrea Jaeger	6–0, 6–3
1984	Martina Navratilova	Chris Evert Lloyd	7–6, 6–2
1985	Martina Navratilova	Chris Evert Lloyd	4–6, 6–3, 6–2
1986	Martina Navratilova	Hana Mandlikova	7–6, 6–3
1987	Martina Navratilova	Steffi Graf	7–5, 6–3
1988	Steffi Graf	Martina Navratilova	5–7, 6–2, 6–1
1989	Steffi Graf	Martina Navratilova	6–2, 6–7, 6–1
1990	Martina Navratilova	Zina Garrison	6–4, 6–1
1991	Steffi Graf	Gabriela Sabatini	6–4, 3–6, 8–6
1992	Steffi Graf	Monica Seles	6–2, 6–1
1993	Steffi Graf	Jana Novotna	7–6, 1–6, 6–4
1994	Conchita Martinez	Martina Navratilova	6–4, 3–6, 6–3
1995	Steffi Graf	Arantxa Sánchez Vicario	4–6, 6–1, 7–5
1996	Steffi Graf	Arantxa Sánchez Vicario	6–3, 7–5
1997	Martina Hingis	Jana Novotna	2–6, 6–3, 6–3

WOMEN (Cont.)

Wimbledon Championships (Cont.)

Year	Winner	Finalist	Score
1998	Jana Novotna	Nathalie Tauziat	6–4, 7–6
1999	Lindsay Davenport	Steffi Graf	6–4, 7–5
2000	Venus Williams	Lindsay Davenport	6–3, 7–6

*Became Open (amateur and professional) in 1968 but closed to contract professionals in 1972.

Note: Prior to 1922 the tournament was run on a challenge-round system. The previous year's winner "stood out" of an All-Comers event, which produced a challenger to play her for the title.

United States Championships

Year	Winner	Finalist	Score
1887	Ellen Hansell	Laura Knight	6–1, 6–0
1888	Bertha L. Townsend	Ellen Hansell	6–3, 6–5
1889	Bertha L. Townsend	Louise Voorhes	7–5, 6–2
1890	Ellen C. Roosevelt	Bertha L. Townsend	6–2, 6–2
1891	Mabel Cahill	Ellen C. Roosevelt	6–4, 6–1, 4–6, 6–3
1892	Mabel Cahill	Elisabeth Moore	5–7, 6–3, 6–4, 4–6, 6–2
1893	Aline Terry	Alice Schultze	6–1, 6–3
1894	Helen Hellwig	Aline Terry	7–5, 3–6, 6–0, 3–6, 6–3
1895	Juliette Atkinson	Helen Hellwig	6–4, 6–2, 6–1
1896	Elisabeth Moore	Juliette Atkinson	6–4, 4–6, 6–2, 6–2
1897	Juliette Atkinson	Elisabeth Moore	6–3, 6–3, 4–6, 3–6, 6–3
1898	Juliette Atkinson	Marion Jones	6–3, 5–7, 6–4, 2–6, 7–5
1899	Marion Jones	Maud Banks	6–1, 6–1, 7–5
1900	Myrtle McAteer	Edith Parker	6–2, 6–2, 6–0
1901	Elisabeth Moore	Myrtle McAteer	6–4, 3–6, 7–5, 2–6, 6–2
1902**	Marion Jones	Elisabeth Moore	6–1, 1–0, ret.
1903	Elisabeth Moore	Marion Jones	7–5, 8–6
1904	May Sutton	Elisabeth Moore	6–1, 6–2
1905	Elisabeth Moore	Helen Homans	6–4, 5–7, 6–1
1906	Helen Homans	Maud Barger-Wallach	6–4, 6–3
1907	Evelyn Sears	Carrie Neely	6–3, 6–2
1908	Maud Barger–Wallach	Evelyn Sears	6–3, 1–6, 6–3
1909	Hazel Hotchkiss	Maud Barger–Wallach	6–0, 6–1
1910	Hazel Hotchkiss	Louise Hammond	6–4, 6–2
1911	Hazel Hotchkiss	Florence Sutton	8–10, 6–1, 9–7
1912†	Mary K. Browne	Eleanora Sears	6–4, 6–2
1913	Mary K. Browne	Dorothy Green	6–2, 7–5
1914	Mary K. Browne	Marie Wagner	6–2, 1–6, 6–1
1915	Molla Bjurstedt	Hazel Hotchkiss Wightman	4–6, 6–2, 6–0
1916	Molla Bjurstedt	Louise Hammond Raymond	6–0, 6–1
1917‡	Molla Bjurstedt	Marion Vanderhoef	4–6, 6–0, 6–2
1918	Molla Bjurstedt	Eleanor Goss	6–4, 6–3
1919	Hazel Hotchkiss Wightman	Marion Zinderstein	6–1, 6–2
1920	Molla Bjurstedt Mallory	Marion Zinderstein	6–3, 6–1
1921	Molla Bjurstedt Mallory	Mary K. Browne	4–6, 6–4, 6–2
1922	Molla Bjurstedt Mallory	Helen Wills	6–3, 6–1
1923	Helen Wills	Molla Bjurstedt Mallory	6–2, 6–1
1924	Helen Wills	Molla Bjurstedt Mallory	6–1, 6–3
1925	Helen Wills	Kathleen McKane	3–6, 6–0, 6–2
1926	Molla Bjurstedt Mallory	Elizabeth Ryan	4–6, 6–4, 9–7
1927	Helen Wills	Betty Nuthall	6–1, 6–4
1928	Helen Wills	Helen Jacobs	6–2, 6–1
1929	Helen Wills	Phoebe Holcroft Watson	6–4, 6–2
1930	Betty Nuthall	Anna McCune Harper	6–1, 6–4
1931	Helen Wills Moody	Eileen Whitingstall	6–4, 6–1
1932	Helen Jacobs	Carolin Babcock	6–2, 6–2
1933	Helen Jacobs	Helen Wills Moody	8–6, 3–6, 3–0, ret.
1934	Helen Jacobs	Sarah Palfrey	6–1, 6–4
1935	Helen Jacobs	Sarah Palfrey Fabyan	6–2, 6–4
1936	Alice Marble	Helen Jacobs	4–6, 6–3, 6–2
1937	Anita Lizana	Jadwiga Jedrzejowska	6–4, 6–2
1938	Alice Marble	Nancye Wynne	6–0, 6–3
1939	Alice Marble	Helen Jacobs	6–0, 8–10, 6–4
1940	Alice Marble	Helen Jacobs	6–2, 6–3
1941	Sarah Palfrey Cooke	Pauline Betz	7–5, 6–2

WOMEN *(Cont.)*

United States Championships *(Cont.)*

Year	Winner	Finalist	Score
1942	Pauline Betz	Louise Brough	4–6, 6–1, 6–4
1943	Pauline Betz	Louise Brough	6–3, 5–7, 6–3
1944	Pauline Betz	Margaret Osborne	6–3, 8–6
1945	Sarah Palfrey Cooke	Pauline Betz	3–6, 8–6, 6–4
1946	Pauline Betz	Patricia Canning	11–9, 6–3
1947	Louise Brough	Margaret Osborne	8–6, 4–6, 6–1
1948	Margaret Osborne duPont	Louise Brough	4–6, 6–4, 15–13
1949	Margaret Osborne duPont	Doris Hart	6–4, 6–1
1950	Margaret Osborne duPont	Doris Hart	6–4, 6–3
1951	Maureen Connolly	Shirley Fry	6–3, 1–6, 6–4
1952	Maureen Connolly	Doris Hart	6–3, 7–5
1953	Maureen Connolly	Doris Hart	6–2, 6–4
1954	Doris Hart	Louise Brough	6–8, 6–1, 8–6
1955	Doris Hart	Patricia Ward	6–4, 6–2
1956	Shirley Fry	Althea Gibson	6–3, 6–4
1957	Althea Gibson	Louise Brough	6–3, 6–2
1958	Althea Gibson	Darlene Hard	3–6, 6–1, 6–2
1959	Maria Bueno	Christine Truman	6–1, 6–4
1960	Darlene Hard	Maria Bueno	6–4, 10–12, 6–4
1961	Darlene Hard	Ann Haydon	6–3, 6–4
1962	Margaret Smith	Darlene Hard	9–7, 6–4
1963	Maria Bueno	Margaret Smith	7–5, 6–4
1964	Maria Bueno	Carole Graebner	6–1, 6–0
1965	Margaret Smith	Billie Jean Moffitt	8–6, 7–5
1966	Maria Bueno	Nancy Richey	6–3, 6–1
1967	Billie Jean King	Ann Haydon Jones	11–9, 6–4
1968*	Virginia Wade	Billie Jean King	6–4, 6–4
1968#	Margaret Smith Court	Maria Bueno	6–2, 6–2
1969	Margaret Smith Court	Nancy Richey	6–2, 6–2
1969#	Margaret Smith Court	Virginia Wade	4–6, 6–3, 6–0
1970	Margaret Smith Court	Rosie Casals	6–2, 2–6, 6–1
1971	Billie Jean King	Rosie Casals	6–4, 7–6
1972	Billie Jean King	Kerry Melville	6–3, 7–5
1973	Margaret Smith Court	Evonne Goolagong	7–6, 5–7, 6–2
1974	Billie Jean King	Evonne Goolagong	3–6, 6–3, 7–5
1975	Chris Evert	Evonne Goolagong Cawley	5–7, 6–4, 6–2
1976	Chris Evert	Evonne Goolagong Cawley	6–3, 6–0
1977	Chris Evert	Wendy Turnbull	7–6, 6–2
1978	Chris Evert	Pam Shriver	7–6, 6–4
1979	Tracy Austin	Chris Evert Lloyd	6–4, 6–3
1980	Chris Evert Lloyd	Hana Mandlikova	5–7, 6–1, 6–1
1981	Tracy Austin	Martina Navratilova	1–6, 7–6, 7–6
1982	Chris Evert Lloyd	Hana Mandlikova	6–3, 6–1
1983	Martina Navratilova	Chris Evert Lloyd	6–1, 6–3
1984	Martina Navratilova	Chris Evert Lloyd	4–6, 6–4, 6–4
1985	Hana Mandlikova	Martina Navratilova	7–6, 1–6, 7–6
1986	Martina Navratilova	Helena Sukova	6–3, 6–2
1987	Martina Navratilova	Steffi Graf	7–6, 6–1
1988	Steffi Graf	Gabriela Sabatini	6–3, 3–6, 6–1
1989	Steffi Graf	Martina Navratilova	3–6, 6–4, 6–2
1990	Gabriela Sabatini	Steffi Graf	6–2, 7–6
1991	Monica Seles	Martina Narvatilova	7–6, 6–1
1992	Monica Seles	Arantxa Sánchez Vicario	6–3, 6–2
1993	Steffi Graf	Helena Sukova	6–3, 6–3
1994	Arantxa Sánchez Vicario	Steffi Graf	1–6, 7–6, 6–4
1995	Steffi Graf	Monica Seles	7–6, 0–6, 6–3
1996	Steffi Graf	Monica Seles	7–5, 7–4
1997	Martina Hingis	Venus Williams	6–0, 6–4
1998	Lindsay Davenport	Martina Hingis	6–3, 7–5
1999	Serena Williams	Martina Hingis	6–3, 7–6
2000	Venus Williams	Lindsay Davenport	6–4, 7–5

**Five-set final abolished; †Challenge round abolished.

*Became Open (amateur and professional) in 1968.

‡National Patriotic Tournament; #Amateur event held.

Grand Slams

Singles
Don Budge, 1938
Maureen Connolly, 1953
Rod Laver, 1962, 1969
Margaret Smith Court, 1970
Steffi Graf, 1988

Doubles
Frank Sedgman and Ken McGregor, 1951
Martina Navratilova and Pam Shriver, 1984
Maria Bueno and two partners: Christine Truman
(Australian), Darlene Hard (French, Wimbledon
and U.S. Championships), 1960
Martina Hingis and two partners: Mirjana Lucic
(Australian), Jana Novotna (French, Wimbledon
and U.S. Championships), 1998

Mixed Doubles
Margaret Smith and Ken Fletcher, 1963
Owen Davidson and two partners: Lesley Turner
(Australian), Billie Jean King (French, Wimbledon
and U.S. Championships), 1967

Alltime Grand Slam Champions

MEN

Player	Aus. S-D-M	French S-D-M	Wim. S-D-M	U.S. S-D-M	Total
Roy Emerson	6-3-0	2-6-0	2-3-0	2-4-0	28
John Newcombe	2-5-0	0-3-0	3-6-0	2-3-1	25
Frank Sedgman	2-2-2	0-2-2	1-3-2	2-2-2	22
Bill Tilden	†	0-0-1	3-1-0	7-5-4	21
Rod Laver	3-4-0	2-1-1	4-1-2	2-0-0	20
John Bromwich	2-8-1	0-0-0	0-2-2	0-3-1	19
Jean Borotra	1-1-1	1-5-2	2-3-1	0-0-1	18
Fred Stolle	0-3-1	1-2-0	0-2-3	1-3-2	18
Ken Rosewall	4-3-0	2-2-0	0-2-0	2-2-1	18
Neale Fraser	0-3-1	0-3-0	1-2-0	2-3-3	18
Adrian Quist	3-10-0	0-1-0	0-2-0	0-1-0	17
John McEnroe	0-0-0	0-0-1	3-4-0	4-5-0	17
Jack Crawford	4-4-3	1-1-1	1-1-1	0-0-0	17
*Mark Woodforde	0-2-2	0-1-1	0-6-1	0-3-1	17

†Did not compete.

WOMEN

Player	Aus. S-D-M	French S-D-M	Wim. S-D-M	U.S. S-D-M	Total
Margaret Smith Court	11-8-2	5-4-4	3-2-5	5-5-8	62
Martina Navratilova	3-8-0	2-7-2	9-7-3	4-9-2	56
Billie Jean King	1-0-1	1-1-2	6-10-4	4-5-4	39
Doris Hart	1-1-2	2-5-3	1-4-5	2-4-5	35
Helen Wills Moody	†	4-2-0	8-3-1	7-4-2	31
Louise Brough	1-1-0	0-3-0	4-5-4	1-8-3	30**
Margaret Osborne duPont	†	2-3-0	1-5-1	3-8-6	29**
Elizabeth Ryan	†	0-4-0	0-12-7	0-1-2	26
Steffi Graf	4-0-0	6-0-0	7-1-0	5-0-0	23
Pam Shriver	0-7-0	0-4-1	0-5-0	0-5-0	22
Chris Evert	2-0-0	7-2-0	3-1-0	6-0-0	21
Darlene Hard	†	1-3-2	0-4-3	2-6-0	21
Suzanne Lenglen	†	2-2-2#	6-6-3	0-0-0	21
Nancye Wynne Bolton	6-10-4	0-0-0	0-0-0	0-0-0	20
Maria Bueno	0-1-0	0-1-1	3-5-0	4-4-0	19
Thelma Coyne Long	2-12-4	0-0-1	0-0-0	0-0-0	19

*Active player. †Did not compete.
#Suzanne Lenglen also won four singles titles at the French Championships before 1925, when competition was first
opened to entries from all nations.
**From 1940–45, with competition in the U.S. Championships thinned due to wartime constraints, Louise Brough Clapp
also won four doubles titles (1942–45) and one mixed doubles title (1942); and Margaret Osborne duPont won five
doubles titles (1941–45) and three mixed doubles titles (1943–45).

Alltime Grand Slam Singles Champions

MEN

Player	Aus.	French	Wim.	U.S.	Total
*Pete Sampras	2	0	7	4	13
Roy Emerson	6	2	2	2	12
Bjorn Borg	0	6	5	0	11
Rod Laver	3	2	4	2	11
Bill Tilden	†	0	3	7	10
Jimmy Connors	1	0	2	5	8
Ivan Lendl	2	3	0	3	8
Fred Perry	1	1	3	3	8
Ken Rosewall	4	2	0	2	8
Henri Cochet	†	4	2	1	7
Rene Lacoste	†	3	2	2	7
Bill Larned	†	†	0	7	7
John McEnroe	0	0	3	4	7
John Newcombe	2	0	3	2	7
Willie Renshaw	†	†	7	†	7
Dick Sears	†	†	0	7	7

*Active player. †Did not compete.

WOMEN

Player	Aus.	French	Wim.	U.S.	Total
Margaret Smith Court	11	5	3	5	24
Steffi Graf	4	6	7	5	22
Helen Wills Moody	†	4	8	7	19
Chris Evert	2	7	3	6	18
Martina Navratilova	3	2	9	4	18
Billie Jean King	1	1	6	4	12
Maureen Connolly	1	2	3	3	9
*Monica Seles	4	3	0	2	9
Suzanne Lenglen	†	2#	6	0	8
Molla Bjurstedt Mallory	†	†	0	8	8
Maria Bueno	0	0	3	4	7
Evonne Goolagong	4	1	2	0	7
Dorothea D.L. Chambers	†	†	7	0	7
Nancye Wynne Bolton	6	0	0	0	6
Louise Brough	1	0	4	1	6
Margaret Osborne duPont	†	2	1	3	6
Doris Hart	1	2	1	2	6
Blanche Bingley Hillyard	†	†	6	†	6

*Active player. †Did not compete.
#Suzanne Lenglen also won four singles titles at the French Championships before 1925, when competition was first opened to entries from all nations.

Unhappy	Pete Sampras was displeased with the ATP tour's 2000 ad campaign touting young players such as Tommy Haas and Juan Carlos Ferrero, who are pictured in ads and posters that read NEW BALLS PLEASE. "Those guys are the future of the game," Sampras said, "but they [the ATP] probably could have come up with a better slogan."

Davis Cup

Started in 1900 as the International Lawn Tennis Challenge Trophy by America's Dwight Davis, the runner-up in the 1898 U.S. Championships. A Davis Cup meeting between two countries is known as a tie and is a three-day event consisting of two singles matches, followed by one doubles match and then two more singles matches. The United States boasts the greatest number of wins (31), followed by Australia (20).

Year	Winner	Finalist	Site	Score
1900	United States	Great Britain	Boston	3–0
1901	No tournament			
1902	United States	Great Britain	New York	3–2
1903	Great Britain	United States	Boston	4–1
1904	Great Britain	Belgium	Wimbledon	5–0
1905	Great Britain	United States	Wimbledon	5–0
1906	Great Britain	United States	Wimbledon	5–0
1907	Australasia	Great Britain	Wimbledon	3–2
1908	Australasia	United States	Melbourne	3–2
1909	Australasia	United States	Sydney	5–0
1910	No tournament			
1911	Australasia	United States	Christchurch, NZ	5–0
1912	Great Britain	Australasia	Melbourne	3–2
1913	United States	Great Britain	Wimbledon	3–2
1914	Australasia	United States	New York	3–2
1915–18	No tournament			
1919	Australasia	Great Britain	Sydney	4–1
1920	United States	Australasia	Auckland, NZ	5–0
1921	United States	Japan	New York	5–0
1922	United States	Australasia	New York	4–1
1923	United States	Australasia	New York	4–1
1924	United States	Australia	Philadelphia	5–0
1925	United States	France	Philadelphia	5–0
1926	United States	France	Philadelphia	4–1
1927	France	United States	Philadelphia	3–2
1928	France	United States	Paris	4–1
1929	France	United States	Paris	3–2
1930	France	United States	Paris	4–1
1931	France	Great Britain	Paris	3–2
1932	France	United States	Paris	3–2
1933	Great Britain	France	Paris	3–2
1934	Great Britain	United States	Wimbledon	4–1
1935	Great Britain	United States	Wimbledon	5–0
1936	Great Britain	Australia	Wimbledon	3–2
1937	United States	Great Britain	Wimbledon	4–1
1938	United States	Australia	Philadelphia	3–2
1939	Australia	United States	Philadelphia	3–2
1940–45	No tournament			
1946	United States	Australia	Melbourne	5–0
1947	United States	Australia	New York	4–1
1948	United States	Australia	New York	5–0
1949	United States	Australia	New York	4–1
1950	Australia	United States	New York	4–1
1951	Australia	United States	Sydney	3–2
1952	Australia	United States	Adelaide	4–1
1953	Australia	United States	Melbourne	3–2
1954	United States	Australia	Sydney	3–2
1955	Australia	United States	New York	5–0
1956	Australia	United States	Adelaide	5–0
1957	Australia	United States	Melbourne	3–2
1958	United States	Australia	Brisbane	3–2
1959	Australia	United States	New York	3–2
1960	Australia	Italy	Sydney	4–1
1961	Australia	Italy	Melbourne	5–0
1962	Australia	Mexico	Brisbane	5–0
1963	United States	Australia	Adelaide	3–2
1964	Australia	United States	Cleveland	3–2
1965	Australia	Spain	Sydney	4–1
1966	Australia	India	Melbourne	4–1
1967	Australia	Spain	Brisbane	4–1
1968	United States	Australia	Adelaide	4–1

Davis Cup *(Cont.)*

Year	Winner	Finalist	Site	Score
1969	United States	Romania	Cleveland	5–0
1970	United States	W Germany	Cleveland	5–0
1971	United States	Romania	Charlotte, NC	3–2
1972	United States	Romania	Bucharest	3–2
1973	Australia	United States	Cleveland	5–0
1974	South Africa	India	*	walkover
1975	Sweden	Czechoslovakia	Stockholm	3–2
1976	Italy	Chile	Santiago	4–1
1977	Australia	Italy	Sydney	3–1
1978	United States	Great Britain	Palm Springs	4–1
1979	United States	Italy	San Francisco	5–0
1980	Czechoslovakia	Italy	Prague	4–1
1981	United States	Argentina	Cincinnati	3–1
1982	United States	France	Grenoble, France	4–1
1983	Australia	Sweden	Melbourne	3–2
1984	Sweden	United States	Göteborg, Sweden	4–1
1985	Sweden	W Germany	Munich	3–2
1986	Australia	Sweden	Melbourne	3–2
1987	Sweden	India	Göteborg, Sweden	5–0
1988	West Germany	Sweden	Göteborg, Sweden	4–1
1989	West Germany	Sweden	Stuttgart	3–2
1990	United States	Australia	St. Petersburg	3–2
1991	France	United States	Lyon	3–1
1992	United States	Switzerland	Fort Worth, TX	3–1
1993	Germany	Australia	Dusseldorf	4–1
1994	Sweden	Russia	Moscow	4–1
1995	United States	Russia	Moscow	3–2
1996	France	Sweden	Malmö, Sweden	3–2
1997	Sweden	United States	Göteborg, Sweden	5–0
1998	Sweden	Italy	Milan	4–1
1999	Australia	France	Nice, France	3–2

*India refused to play the final in protest over South Africa's governmental policy of apartheid.
Note: Prior to 1972 the challenge-round system was in effect, with the previous year's winner "standing out" of the competition until the finals. A straight 16-nation tournament has been held since 1981.

Federation Cup

The Federation Cup was started in 1963 by the International Lawn Tennis Federation (now the ITF). Until 1991 all entrants gathered at one site at one time for a tournament that was concluded within one week. Since 1995 the Fed Cup, as it is now called, has been contested in three rounds by a World Group of eight nations. A meeting between two countries now consists of five matches: four singles and one doubles. The United States has the most wins (15), followed by Australia (7).

Year	Winner	Finalist	Site	Score
1963	United States	Australia	London	2–1
1964	Australia	United States	Philadelphia	2–1
1965	Australia	United States	Melbourne	2–1
1966	United States	W Germany	Turin	3–0
1967	United States	Great Britain	W Berlin	2–0
1968	Australia	Netherlands	Paris	3–0
1969	United States	Australia	Athens	2–1
1970	Australia	Great Britain	Freiburg	3–0
1971	Australia	Great Britain	Perth	3–0
1972	South Africa	Great Britain	Johannesburg	2–1
1973	Australia	South Africa	Bad Homburg	3–0
1974	Australia	United States	Naples	2–1
1975	Czechoslovakia	Australia	Aix-en-Provence	3–0
1976	United States	Australia	Philadelphia	2–1
1977	United States	Australia	Eastbourne, G.B.	2–1
1978	United States	Australia	Melbourne	2–1
1979	United States	Australia	Madrid	3–0
1980	United States	Australia	W Berlin	3–0
1981	United States	Great Britain	Nagoya	3–0
1982	United States	W Germany	Santa Clara, CA	3–0
1983	Czechoslovakia	W Germany	Zurich	2–1
1984	Czechoslovakia	Australia	Sao Paulo	2–1
1985	Czechoslovakia	United States	Tokyo	2–1

Federation Cup (Cont.)

Year	Winner	Finalist	Site	Score
1986	United States	Czechoslovakia	Prague	3–0
1987	W Germany	United States	Vancouver	2–1
1988	Czechoslovakia	USSR	Melbourne	2–1
1989	United States	Spain	Tokyo	3–0
1990	United States	USSR	Atlanta	2–1
1991	Spain	United States	Nottingham	2–1
1992	Germany	Spain	Frankfurt	2–1
1993	Spain	Australia	Frankfurt	3–0
1994	Spain	United States	Frankfurt	3–0
1995	Spain	United States	Valencia, Spain	3–2
1996	United States	Spain	Atlantic City	5–0
1997	France	Netherlands	Hertogenbosch, Neth.	4–1
1998	Spain	Switzerland	Geneva	3–2
1999	United States	Russia	Palo Alto, California	4–1

Rankings

ATP Computer Year-End Top 10
MEN

1973
1 ....Ilie Nastase
2 ....John Newcombe
3 ....Jimmy Connors
4 ....Tom Okker
5 ....Stan Smith
6 ....Ken Rosewall
7 ....Manuel Orantes
8 ....Rod Laver
9 ....Jan Kodes
10 ..Arthur Ashe

1974
1 ....Jimmy Connors
2 ....John Newcombe
3 ....Bjorn Borg
4 ....Rod Laver
5 ....Guillermo Vilas
6 ....Tom Okker
7 ....Arthur Ashe
8 ....Ken Rosewall
9 ....Stan Smith
10 ..Ilie Nastase

1975
1 ....Jimmy Connors
2 ....Guillermo Vilas
3 ....Bjorn Borg
4 ....Arthur Ashe
5 ....Manuel Orantes
6 ....Ken Rosewall
7 ....Ilie Nastase
8 ....John Alexander
9 ....Roscoe Tanner
10 ..Rod Laver

1976
1 ....Jimmy Connors
2 ....Bjorn Borg
3 ....Ilie Nastase
4 ....Manuel Orantes
5 ....Raul Ramirez
6 ....Guillermo Vilas
7 ....Adriano Panatta
8 ....Harold Solomon
9 ....Eddie Dibbs
10 ..Brian Gottfried

1977
1 ....Jimmy Connors
2 ....Guillermo Vilas
3 ....Bjorn Borg
4 ....Vitas Gerulaitis
5 ....Brian Gottfried
6 ....Eddie Dibbs
7 ....Manuel Orantes
8 ....Raul Ramirez
9 ....Ilie Nastase
10 ..Dick Stockton

1978
1 ....Jimmy Connors
2 ....Bjorn Borg
3 ....Guillermo Vilas
4 ....John McEnroe
5 ....Vitas Gerulaitis
6 ....Eddie Dibbs
7 ....Brian Gottfried
8 ....Raul Ramirez
9 ....Harold Solomon
10 ..Corrado Barazzutti

1979
1 ....Bjorn Borg
2 ....Jimmy Connors
3 ....John McEnroe
4 ....Vitas Gerulaitis
5 ....Roscoe Tanner
6 ....Guillermo Vilas
7 ....Arthur Ashe
8 ....Harold Solomon
9 ....Jose Higueras
10 ..Eddie Dibbs

1980
1 ....Bjorn Borg
2 ....John McEnroe
3 ....Jimmy Connors
4 ....Gene Mayer
5 ....Guillermo Vilas
6 ....Ivan Lendl
7 ....Harold Solomon
8 ....Jose–Luis Clerc
9 ....Vitas Gerulaitis
10 ..Eliot Teltscher

1981
1 ....John McEnroe
2 ....Ivan Lendl
3 ....Jimmy Connors
4 ....Bjorn Borg
5 ....Jose–Luis Clerc
6 ....Guillermo Vilas
7 ....Gene Mayer
8 ....Eliot Teltscher
9 ....Vitas Gerulaitis
10 ..Peter McNamara

ATP Computer Year-End Top 10
MEN *(CONT.)*

1982
1 ....John McEnroe
2 ....Jimmy Connors
3 ....Ivan Lendl
4 ....Guillermo Vilas
5 ....Vitas Gerulaitis
6 ....Jose–Luis Clerc
7 ....Mats Wilander
8 ....Gene Mayer
9 ....Yannick Noah
10 ..Peter McNamara

1983
1 ....John McEnroe
2 ....Ivan Lendl
3 ....Jimmy Connors
4 ....Mats Wilander
5 ....Yannick Noah
6 ....Jimmy Arias
7 ....Jose Higueras
8 ....Jose–Luis Clerc
9 ....Kevin Curren
10 ..Gene Mayer

1984
1 ....John McEnroe
2 ....Jimmy Connors
3 ....Ivan Lendl
4 ....Mats Wilander
5 ....Andres Gomez
6 ....Anders Jarryd
7 ....Henrik Sundstrom
8 ....Pat Cash
9 ....Eliot Teltscher
10 ..Yannick Noah

1985
1 ....Ivan Lendl
2 ....John McEnroe
3 ....Mats Wilander
4 ....Jimmy Connors
5 ....Stefan Edberg
6 ....Boris Becker
7 ....Yannick Noah
8 ....Anders Jarryd
9 ....Miloslav Mecir
10 ..Kevin Curren

1986
1 ....Ivan Lendl
2 ....Boris Becker
3 ....Mats Wilander
4 ....Yannick Noah
5 ....Stefan Edberg
6 ....Henri Leconte
7 ....Joakim Nystrom
8 ....Jimmy Connors
9 ....Miloslav Mecir
10 ..Andres Gomez

1987
1 ....Ivan Lendl
2 ....Stefan Edberg
3 ....Mats Wilander
4 ....Jimmy Connors
5 ....Boris Becker
6 ....Miloslav Mecir
7 ....Pat Cash
8 ....Yannick Noah
9 ....Tim Mayotte
10 ..John McEnroe

1988
1 ....Mats Wilander
2 ....Ivan Lendl
3 ....Andre Agassi
4 ....Boris Becker
5 ....Stefan Edberg
6 ....Kent Carlsson
7 ....Jimmy Connors
8 ....Jakob Hlasek
9 ....Henri Leconte
10 ..Tim Mayotte

1989
1 ....Ivan Lendl
2 ....Boris Becker
3 ....Stefan Edberg
4 ....John McEnroe
5 ....Michael Chang
6 ....Brad Gilbert
7 ....Andre Agassi
8 ....Aaron Krickstein
9 ....Alberto Mancini
10 ..Jay Berger

1990
1 ....Stefan Edberg
2 ....Boris Becker
3 ....Ivan Lendl
4 ....Andre Agassi
5 ....Pete Sampras
6 ....Andres Gomez
7 ....Thomas Muster
8 ....Emilio Sanchez
9 ....Goran Ivanisevic
10 ..Brad Gilbert

1991
1 ....Stefan Edberg
2 ....Jim Courier
3 ....Boris Becker
4 ....Michael Stich
5 ....Ivan Lendl
6 ....Pete Sampras
7 ....Guy Forget
8 ....Karel Novacek
9 ....Petr Korda
10 ..Andre Agassi

1992
1 ....Jim Courier
2 ....Stefan Edberg
3 ....Pete Sampras
4 ....Goran Ivanisevic
5 ....Boris Becker
6 ....Michael Chang
7 ....Petr Korda
8 ....Ivan Lendl
9 ....Andre Agassi
10 ..Richard Krajicek

1993
1 ....Pete Sampras
2 ....Michael Stich
3 ....Jim Courier
4 ....Sergi Bruguera
5 ....Stefan Edberg
6 ....Andrei Medvedev
7 ....Goran Ivanisevic
8 ....Michael Chang
9 ....Thomas Muster
10 ..Cedric Pioline

1994
1 ....Pete Sampras
2 ....Andre Agassi
3 ....Boris Becker
4 ....Sergi Bruguera
5 ....Goran Ivanisevic
6 ....Michael Chang
7 ....Stefan Edberg
8 ....Alberto Berasategui
9 ....Michael Stich
10 ..Todd Martin

1995
1 ....Pete Sampras
2 ....Andre Agassi
3 ....Thomas Muster
4 ....Boris Becker
5 ....Michael Chang
6 ....Yevgeny Kafelnikov
7 ....Thomas Enqvist
8 ....Jim Courier
9 ....Wayne Ferreira
10 ..Goran Ivanisevic

1996
1 ....Pete Sampras
2 ....Michael Chang
3 ....Yevgeny Kafelnikov
4 ....Goran Ivanisevic
5 ....Thomas Muster
6 ....Boris Becker
7 ....Richard Krajicek
8 ....Andre Agassi
9 ....Thomas Enqvist
10 ..Wayne Ferreira

ATP Computer Year-End Top 10
MEN (CONT.)

1997
1 ....Pete Sampras
2 ....Patrick Rafter
3 ...Michael Chang
4 ...Jonas Bjorkman
5 ....Yevgeny Kafelnikov
6 ...Greg Rusedski
7 ...Carlos Moya
8 ....Sergei Bruguera
9 ...Thomas Muster
10...Marcelo Ríos

1998
1 ....Pete Sampras
2 ....Marcelo Rios
3 ...Alex Corretja
4 ....Patrick Rafter
5 ....Carlos Moya
6 ....Andre Agassi
7 ....Tim Henman
8 ....Karol Kucera
9 ..Greg Rusedski
10...Richard Krajicek

1999
1 ....Andre Agassi
2 ....Yevgeny Kafelnikov
3 ....Pete Sampras
4 ....Thomas Enqvist
5 ....Gustavo Kuerten
6 ...Nicolas Kiefer
7 ....Todd Martin
8 ...Nicolas Lapentti
9 ....Marcelo Rios
10 ..Richard Krajicek

WTA Computer Year-End Top 10
WOMEN

1973
1 ....Margaret Smith
  Court
2 ....Billie Jean King
3 ...Evonne Goolagong
4 ...Chris Evert
5 ...Rosie Casals
6 ...Virginia Wade
7 ...Kerry Reid
8 ...Nancy Gunter
9 ...Julie Heldman
10...Helga Masthoff

1974
1 ....Billie Jean King
2 ...Evonne Goolagong
3 ...Chris Evert
4 ...Virginia Wade
5 ...Julie Heldman
6 ...Rosie Casals
7 ...Kerry Reid
8 ...Olga Morozova
9 ...Lesley Hunt
10...Francoise Durr

1975
1 ....Chris Evert
2 ....Billie Jean King
3 ....Evonne Goolagong
  Cawley
4 ...Martina Navratilova
5 ...Virginia Wade
6 ...Margaret Smith
  Court
7 ....Olga Morozova
8 ...Nancy Gunter
9 ....Francoise Durr
10...Rosie Casals

1976
1 ....Chris Evert
2 ....Evonne Goolagong
  Cawley
3 ...Virginia Wade
4 ...Martina Navratilova
5 ...Sue Barker
6 ...Betty Stove
7 ...Dianne Balestrat
8 ...Mima Jausovec
9 ...Rosie Casals
10...Francoise Durr

1977
1 ....Chris Evert
2 ....Billie Jean King
3 ...Martina Navratilova
4 ...Virginia Wade
5 ...Sue Barker
6 ...Rosie Casals
7 ...Betty Stove
8 ...Dianne Balestrat
9 ...Wendy Turnbull
10...Kerry Reid

1978
1 ....Martina Navratilova
2 ...Chris Evert
3 ...Evonne Goolagong
  Cawley
4 ...Virginia Wade
5 ...Billie Jean King
6 ...Tracy Austin
7 ...Wendy Turnbull
8 ...Kerry Reid
9 ...Betty Stove
10...Dianne Balestrat

1979
1 ....Martina Navratilova
2 ...Chris Evert Lloyd
3 ...Tracy Austin
4 ....Evonne Goolagong
  Cawley
5 ...Billie Jean King
6 ...Dianne Balestrat
7 ...Wendy Turnbull
8 ...Virginia Wade
9 ...Kerry Reid
10...Sue Barker

1980
1 ....Chris Evert Lloyd
2 ...Tracy Austin
3 ...Martina Navratilova
4 ...Hana Mandlikova
5 ...Evonne Goolagong
  Cawley
6 ...Billie Jean King
7 ...Andrea Jaeger
8 ...Wendy Turnbull
9 ...Pam Shriver
10...Greer Stevens

1981
1 ....Chris Evert Lloyd
2 ...Tracy Austin
3 ...Martina Navratilova
4 ...Andrea Jaeger
5 ...Hana Mandlikova
6 ...Sylvia Hanika
7 ...Pam Shriver
8 ...Wendy Turnbull
9 ...Bettina Bunge
10...Barbara Potter

1982
1 ...Martina Navratilova
2 ...Chris Evert Lloyd
3 ...Andrea Jaeger
4 ...Tracy Austin
5 ...Wendy Turnbull
6 ...Pam Shriver
7 ...Hana Mandlikova
8 ...Barbara Potter
9 ...Bettina Bunge
10...Sylvia Hanika

1983
1 ....Martina Navratilova
2 ...Chris Evert Lloyd
3 ...Andrea Jaeger
4 ...Pam Shriver
5 ...Sylvia Hanika
6 ...Jo Durie
7 ...Bettina Bunge
8 ...Wendy Turnbull
9 ...Tracy Austin
10...Zina Garrison

1984
1 ...Martina Navratilova
2 ...Chris Evert Lloyd
3 ...Hana Mandlikova
4 ...Pam Shriver
5 ...Wendy Turnbull
6 ...Manuela Maleeva
7 ...Helena Sukova
8 ....Claudia Kohde-
  Kilsch
9 ....Zina Garrison
10...Kathy Jordan

WTA Computer Year-End Top 10 (Cont.)

WOMEN (CONT.)

1985
1 ....Martina Navratilova
2 ....Chris Evert Lloyd
3 ....Hana Mandlikova
4 ....Pam Shriver
5 ....Claudia Kohde-
Kilsch
6 ....Steffi Graf
7 ....Manuela Maleeva
8 ....Zina Garrison
9 ....Helena Sukova
10...Bonnie Gadusek

1986
1 ....Martina Navratilova
2 ....Chris Evert Lloyd
3 ....Pam Shriver
4 ....Hana Mandlikova
5 ....Helena Sukova
6 ....Pam Shriver
7 ....Claudia Kohde-
Kilsch
8 ....Manuela Maleeva
9 ....Kathy Rinaldi
10...Gabriela Sabatini

1987
1 ....Steffi Graf
2 ....Martina Navratilova
3 ....Chris Evert
4 ....Pam Shriver
5 ....Hana Mandlikova
6 ....Gabriela Sabatini
7 ....Helena Sukova
8 ....Manuela Maleeva
9 ....Zina Garrison
10...Claudia Kohde-
Kilsch

1988
1 ....Steffi Graf
2 ....Martina Navratilova
3 ....Chris Evert
4 ....Gabriela Sabatini
5 ....Pam Shriver
6 ....Manuela Maleeva-
Fragniere
7 ....Natalia Zvereva
8 ....Helena Sukova
9 ....Zina Garrison
10...Barbara Potter

1989
1 ....Steffi Graf
2 ....Martina Navratilova
3 ....Gabriela Sabatini
4 ....Zina Garrison
5 ....Arantxa Sánchez
Vicario
6 ....Monica Seles
7 ....Conchita Martinez
8 ....Helena Sukova
9 ....Manuela Maleeva-
Fragniere
10...*Chris Evert

1990
1 ....Steffi Graf
2 ....Monica Seles
3 ....Martina Navratilova
4 ....Mary Joe Fernandez
5 ....Gabriela Sabatini
6 ....Katerina Maleeva
7 ....Arantxa Sánchez
Vicario
8 ....Jennifer Capriati
9 ....Manuela Maleeva-
Fragniere
10...Zina Garrison

1991
1 ....Monica Seles
2 ....Steffi Graf
3 ....Gabriela Sabatini
4 ....Martina Navratilova
5 ....Arantxa Sánchez
Vicario
6 ....Jennifer Capriati
7 ....Jana Novotna
8 ....Mary Joe Fernandez
9 ....Conchita Martinez
10 ..Manuela Maleeva-
Fragniere

1992
1 ....Monica Seles
2 ....Steffi Graf
3 ....Gabriela Sabatini
4 ....Arantxa Sánchez
Vicario
5 ....Martina Navratilova
6 ....Mary Joe Fernandez
7 ....Jennifer Capriati
8 ....Conchita Martinez
9 ....Manuela Maleeva-
Fragniere
10 ..Jana Novotna

1993
1 ....Steffi Graf
2 ....Arantxa Sánchez
Vicario
3 ....Martina Navratilova
4 ....Conchita Martinez
5 ....Gabriela Sabatini
6 ....Jana Novotna
7 ....Mary Joe Fernandez
8 ....Monica Seles
9 ....Jennifer Capriati
10 ..Anke Huber

1994
1 ....Steffi Graf
2 ....Arantxa Sánchez
Vicario
3 ....Conchita Martinez
4 ....Jana Novotna
5 ....Mary Pierce
6 ....Lindsay Davenport
7 ....Gabriela Sabatini
8 ....Martina Navratilova
9 ....Kimiko Date
10 ..Natasha Zvereva

1995
1 ....Steffi Graf (co-No. 1)
1 ....Monica Seles
(co-No. 1)
2 ....Conchita Martinez
3 ....Arantxa Sánchez
Vicario
4 ....Kimiko Date
5 ....Mary Pierce
6 ....Magdalena Maleeva
7 ....Gabriela Sabatini
8 ....Mary Joe Fernandez
9 ....Iva Majoli
10 ..Anke Huber

1996
1 ....Steffi Graf
2 ....Monica Seles
3 ....Jana Novotna
4 ....Lindsay Davenport
5 ....Martina Hingis
6 ....Stephanie de Ville
7 ....Tamarine
Tanasugarn
8 ....Anke Huber
9 ....Conchita Martinez
10 ..Julie Halard-
Decugis

1997
1 ....Martina Hingis
2 ....Jana Novotna
3 ....Lindsay Davenport
4 ....Amanda Coetzer
5 ....Monica Seles
6 ....Iva Majoli
7 ....Mary Pierce
8 ....Irina Spirlea
9 ....Arantxa Sánchez Vicario
10...Mary Joe Fernandez

1998
1 ....Lindsay Davenport
2 ....Martina Hingis
3 ....Jana Novotna
4 ....Arantxa Sánchez Vicario
5 ....Venus Williams
6 ....Monica Seles
7 ....Mary Pierce
8 ....Conchita Martinez
9 ....Steffi Graf
10...Nathalie Tauziat

1999
1 ....Martina Hingis
2 ....Lindsay Davenport
3 ....Venus Williams
4 ....Serena Williams
5 ....Mary Pierce
6 ....Monica Seles
7 ....Nathalie Tauziat
8 ....Barbara Schett
9 ....Julie Halard-Decugis
10 ..Amelie Mauresmo

*When Chris Evert announced her retirement at the 1989 United States Open, she was ranked fourth in the world. That was her last official series tournament.

Prize Money

Top 25 Men's Career Prize Money Leaders

Note: From arrival of Open tennis in 1968 through October 2, 2000.

	Earnings ($)
Pete Sampras	40,733,159
Boris Becker	25,079,186
Ivan Lendl	21,262,417
Stefan Edberg	20,630,941
Andre Agassi	20,244,074
Michael Chang	18,510,306
Goran Ivanisevic	18,389,750
Yevgeny Kafelnikov	15,630,656
Jim Courier	14,033,132
Michael Stich	12,590,152
John McEnroe	12,539,622
Thomas Muster	12,224,410
Sergi Bruguera	11,406,296
Petr Korda	10,447,665
Richard Krajicek	9,762,111
Patrick Rafter	9,297,819
Jimmy Connors	8,641,040
Marcelo Rios	8,388,813
Mark Woodforde	8,322,151
Mats Wilander	7,976,256
Alex Corretja	7,721,397
Todd Woodbridge	7,715,042
Wayne Ferreira	7,651,002
Thomas Enqvist	7,373,238
Jonas Bjorkman	7,309,440

Top 25 Women's Career Prize Money Leaders

Note: From arrival of Open tennis in 1968 through October 1, 2000.

	Earnings ($)
Steffi Graf	21,895,277
Martina Navratilova	20,394,149
Arantxa Sánchez Vicario	15,624,202
Martina Hingis	13,611,750
Monica Seles	12,597,708
Lindsay Davenport	11,485,378
Jana Novotna	11,249,134
Conchita Martinez	9,209,063
Chris Evert	8,896,195
Gabriela Sabatini	8,785,850
Natasha Zvereva	7,714,430
Venus Williams	6,613,227
Helena Sukova	6,391,245
Mary Pierce	6,169,661
Pam Shriver	5,460,566
Nathalie Tauziat	5,449,992
Mary Joe Fernandez	5,252,571
Gigi Fernandez	4,681,906
Zina Garrison Jackson	4,590,816
Anke Huber	4,251,770
Amanda Coetzer	4,106,478
Larisa Neiland	4,083,936
Serena Williams	3,808,061
Iva Majoli	3,569,988
Lori McNeil	3,474,115

Making a Habit of Losing

As Andre Agassi knows, tennis can be a game of dramatic highs and lows. But the abyss into which Vince Spadea has plunged is virtually unfathomable. After having finished 1999 with a career-best No. 20 ranking—and an 8-3 record against players ranked in the top 10—the 25-year-old Spadea went into free fall. His 7-5, 7-5, 6-4 first-round loss at the 2000 French Open to 13th seed Tim Henman was his 19th straight defeat, one shy of the ATP tour record, set in 1986 and '87 by Gar Donnelly. "Obviously I'm a better player than where I stand now," said Spadea. "This thing is a long haul and I'm not going to let it get to me."

Spadea was beset by injuries in 2000, and he had to default a match in Portugal because of food poisoning. Most of his problems, though, are above the neck. The notoriously temperamental Spadea is quick to blow a gasket when he falls behind early in a match. Formerly coached by his demanding father and namesake, young Vince retained ex-Wimbledon champ Pat Cash to help extricate him from his slump.

Spadea's ranking plummeted in 2000. Heading into the French Open, he was 129th. Winless since the fall of 1999, Spadea was in danger of falling so far so fast that he'd have to qualify to reach the main draw in most big events. He tried to end his ignominious streak at Queens Club, a Wimbledon tune-up in London, but his chances did not look good, given that none of his 33 victories in 1999 was on grass. And indeed, Spadea was bounced from the Queens Club in the first round. But a ray of hope cut through the clouds at Wimbledon as Spadea ended his losing 22-match losing streak with a grueling five-set win over 14th seed Greg Rusedski in the first round.

Open Era Overall Wins

Men's Career Leaders—Singles Titles Won

The top tournament-winning men from the institution of Open tennis in 1968 through October 1, 2000.

	W		W
Jimmy Connors	109	Thomas Muster	44
Ivan Lendl	94	Stefan Edberg	41
John McEnroe	77	Stan Smith	39
Pete Sampras	63	Michael Chang	34
Bjorn Borg	62	Arthur Ashe	33
Guillermo Vilas	62	Mats Wilander	33
Ilie Nastase	57	John Newcombe	32
Boris Becker	49	Manuel Orantes	32
Rod Laver	47	Ken Rosewall	32
Andre Agassi	45	Tom Okker	31

Women's Career Leaders—Singles Titles Won

The top tournament-winning women from the institution of Open tennis in 1968 through October 1, 2000.

	W		W
Martina Navratilova	167	Tracy Austin	29
Chris Evert	157	Lindsay Davenport	28
Steffi Graf	108	Hana Mandlikova	27
Evonne Goolagong Cawley	88	Gabriela Sabatini	27
Margaret Smith Court	79	Arantxa Sánchez Vicario	27
Billie Jean King	67	Nancy Richey	25
Virginia Wade	55	Jana Novotna	24
Monica Seles	47	Kerry Melville Reid	22
Conchita Martinez	32	Sue Barker	21
Martina Hingis	30	Pam Shriver	21

Annual ATP/WTA Champions

Men—ATP Tour World Championship

Year	Player	Year	Player
1970	Stan Smith	1986 (Jan)	Ivan Lendl
1971	Ilie Nastase	1986 (Dec)	Ivan Lendl
1972	Ilie Nastase	1987	Ivan Lendl
1973	Ilie Nastase	1988	Boris Becker
1974	Guillermo Vilas	1989	Stefan Edberg
1975	Ilie Nastase	1990	Andre Agassi
1976	Manuel Orantes	1991	Pete Sampras
1977	Not held	1992	Boris Becker
1978	Jimmy Connors	1993	Michael Stich
1979	John McEnroe	1994	Pete Sampras
1980	Bjorn Borg	1995	Boris Becker
1981	Bjorn Borg	1996	Pete Sampras
1982	Ivan Lendl	1997	Pete Sampras
1983	Ivan Lendl	1998	Alex Corretja
1984	John McEnroe	1999	Pete Sampras
1985	John McEnroe		

Note: Event held twice in 1986. *Since 1984 the final has been best-of-five sets.

Women—WTA Tour Championship

Year	Player	Year	Player
1972	Chris Evert	1986 (Nov)	Martina Navratilova
1973	Chris Evert	1987	Steffi Graf
1974	Evonne Goolagong	1988	Gabriela Sabatini
1975	Chris Evert	1989	Steffi Graf
1976	Evonne Goolagong Cawley	1990	Monica Seles
1977	Chris Evert	1991	Monica Seles
1978	Martina Navratilova	1992	Monica Seles
1979	Martina Navratilova	1993	Steffi Graf
1980	Tracy Austin	1994	Gabriela Sabatini
1981	Martina Navratilova	1995	Steffi Graf
1982	Sylvia Hanika	1996	Steffi Graf
1983	Martina Navratilova	1997	Jana Novotna
1984*	Martina Navratilova	1998	Martina Hingis
1985	Martina Navratilova	1999	Lindsay Davenport
1986 (Mar)	Martina Navratilova		

Davis Slays Goliath

It was a Faustian bargain. When USTA officials named John McEnroe as Davis Cup captain in fall 1999, they knew they'd be getting his unfettered opinions and lapses in decorum. But he was also supposed to do what his predecessor, Tom Gullikson, could not: coax/menace/humiliate the top American players into participating in the century-old international competition. On the night of his appointment, McEnroe, providing television commentary for the U.S. Open, mischievously phoned Pete Sampras at home and, live on the air, prodded him about playing.

Yet, after Spain's doubles team of Alex Corretja and Juan Balcells finished off Todd Martin and Chris Woodruff in five sets in July 2000, giving host Spain a 3–0 lead on way to a 5–0 sweep at the Davis Cup semifinal, McEnroe was left commiserating with a U.S. team that had been strictly jayvee. McEnroe had been as obstreperous as ever. He arrived wearing only a bathrobe for a meeting with Spanish team captain Javier Duarte and a Davis Cup judge and dismissed the heavily favored Spaniards as "chokers." But Sampras and Andre Agassi—who lobbied vigorously last year for McEnroe to be captain—had begged off Davis Cup duty with suspiciously convenient excuses: Sampras blamed sore shins from Wimbledon; Agassi cited a back injury from an auto accident (one he never reported to police). "I'm disappointed and hurt," said McEnroe. "I believed that my presence would be a way of uniting the team, but I have come up against players who promise to play and then a couple of days later say no."

It's unlikely McEnroe will hear many yesses in the near future. The demands of the Davis Cup schedule—four weekends of best-of-five-set matches each year—are high, especially considering that Sampras and Agassi are in their sunset years and need to ration their energy. The USTA has attempted to throw money at the problem by paying players $100,000 per weekend. But as Sampras has noted, "American fans simply don't care enough" about the Davis Cup to make it worth his while.

All of which raises an obvious question: How long before the captain jumps ship? McEnroe, perhaps the most unflinchingly loyal Davis Cupper in U.S. history, has a three-year contract, but it's hard to imagine his continuing to oversee such a halfhearted endeavor. "This hasn't worked out the way I planned," he concedes. "But I still believe Davis Cup is an event worth fighting for." Rest assured that somewhere Tom Gullikson is chuckling.

—L. Jon Wertheim

Pauline Betz Addie (1965)
George T. Adee (1964)
Fred B. Alexander (1961)
Wilmer L. Allison (1963)
Manuel Alonso (1977)
Malcolm Anderson (2000)
Arthur Ashe (1985)
Juliette Atkinson (1974)
H.W. Bunny Austin (1997)
Tracy Austin (1992)
Lawrence A. Baker Sr. (1975)
Maud Barger–Wallach (1958)
Angela Mortimer Barrett (1993)
Karl Behr (1969)
Bjorn Borg (1987)
Jean Borotra (1976)
Lesley Turner Bowrey (1997)
Maureen Connolly Brinker(1968)
John Bromwich (1984)
Norman Everard Brookes (1977)
Mary K. Browne (1957)
Jacques Brugnon (1976)
J. Donald Budge (1964)
Maria E. Bueno (1978)
May Sutton Bundy (1956)
Mabel E. Cahill (1976)
Rosie Casals (1996)
Oliver S. Campbell (1955)
Malcolm Chace (1961)
Dorothea Douglass
    Chambers (1981)
Philippe Chatrier (1992)
Louise Brough Clapp (1967)
Clarence Clark (1983)
Joseph S. Clark (1955)
William J. Clothier (1956)
Henri Cochet (1976)
Arthur W. (Bud) Collins Jr. (1994)
Jimmy Connors (1998)
Ashley Cooper (1991)
Margaret Smith Court (1979)
Gottfried von Cramm (1977)
Jack Crawford (1979)
Joseph F. Cullman III (1990)
Allison Danzig (1968)
Sarah Palfrey Danzig (1963)
Herman David (1998)
Dwight F. Davis (1956)
Charlotte Dod (1983)
John H. Doeg (1962)
Lawrence Doherty (1980)
Reginald Doherty (1980)
Jaroslav Drobny (1983)
Margaret Osborne duPont
    (1967)

James Dwight (1955)
Roy Emerson (1982)
Pierre Etchebaster (1978)
Chris Evert (1995)
Robert Falkenburg (1974)
Neale Fraser (1984)
Shirley Fry-Irvin (1970)
Charles S. Garland (1969)
Althea Gibson (1971)
Kathleen McKane Godfree
    (1978)
Richard A. Gonzales (1968)
Evonne Goolagong Cawley
    (1988)
Bryan M. Grant Jr. (1972)
David Gray (1985)
Clarence Griffin (1970)
King Gustaf V of Sweden
    (1980)
Harold H. Hackett (1961)
Ellen Forde Hansell (1965)
Darlene R. Hard (1973)
Doris J. Hart (1969)
Gladys M. Heldman (1979)
W.E. (Slew) Hester Jr. (1981)
Bob Hewitt (1992)
Lew Hoad (1980)
Harry Hopman (1978)
Fred Hovey (1974)
Joseph R. Hunt (1966)
Lamar Hunt (1993)
Francis T. Hunter (1961)
Helen Hull Jacobs (1962)
William Johnston (1958)
Ann Haydon Jones (1985)
Perry Jones (1970)
Robert Kelleher (2000)
Billie Jean King (1987)
Jan Kodes (1990)
John A. Kramer (1968)
Rene Lacoste (1976)
Al Laney (1979)
William A. Larned (1956)
Arthur D. Larsen (1969)
Rod G. Laver (1981)
Suzanne Lenglen (1978)
Dorothy Round Little (1986)
George M. Lott Jr. (1964)
Gene Mako (1973)
Molla Bjurstedt Mallory (1958)
Hana Mandlikova (1994)
Alice Marble (1964)
Alastair B. Martin (1973)
Dan Maskell (1996)
William McChesney Martin (1982)

John McEnroe (1999)
Ken McGregor (1999)
Chuck McKinley (1986)
Maurice McLoughlin (1957)
Frew McMillan (1992)
W. Donald McNeill (1965)
Elisabeth H. Moore (1971)
Gardnar Mulloy (1972)
R. Lindley Murray (1958)
Julian S. Myrick (1963)
Ilie Nastase (1991)
Martina Navratilova (2000)
John D. Newcombe (1986)
Arthur C. Nielsen Sr (1971)
Alex Olmedo (1987)
Rafael Osuna (1979)
Mary Ewing Outerbridge (1981)
Frank A. Parker (1966)
Gerald Patterson (1989)
Budge Patty (1977)
Theodore R. Pell (1966)
Fred Perry (1975)
Tom Pettitt (1982)
Nicola Pietrangeli (1986)
Adrian Quist (1984)
Dennis Ralston (1987)
Ernest Renshaw (1983)
William Renshaw (1983)
Vincent Richards (1961)
Bobby Riggs (1967)
Helen Wills Moody Roark
    (1959)
Anthony D. Roche (1986)
Ellen C. Roosevelt (1975)
Ken Rosewall (1980)
Elizabeth Ryan (1972)
Manuel Santana (1984)
Richard Savitt (1976)
Frederick R. Schroeder (1966)
Eleonora Sears (1968)
Richard D. Sears (1955)
Frank Sedgman (1979)
Pancho Segura (1984)
Vic Seixas Jr. (1971)
Francis X. Shields (1964)
Betty Nuthall Shoemaker (1977)
Henry W. Slocum Jr. (1955)
Stan Smith (1987)
Fred Stolle (1985)
William F. Talbert (1967)
Bill Tilden (1959)
Lance Tingay (1982)
Ted Tinling (1986)
Bertha Townsend Toulmin
    (1974)

Tony Trabert (1970)
James H. Van Alen (1965)
John Van Ryn (1963)
Guillermo Vilas (1991)
Ellsworth Vines (1962)
Virginia Wade (1989)
Marie Wagner (1969)
Holcombe Ward (1956)
Watson Washburn (1965)

Malcolm D. Whitman (1955)
Hazel Hotchkiss Wightman (1957)
Anthony Wilding (1978)
Richard Norris Williams II (1957)
Major Walter Clopton Wingfield (1997)
Sidney B. Wood (1964)

Robert D. Wrenn (1955)
Beals C. Wright (1956)

Note: Years in parentheses are dates of induction.

Trouble at Home

It was no small feat for Byron Black to reach the fourth round of Wimbledon for the first time in his nine-year professional career. His play in July 2000 was all the more remarkable given that issues far weightier than tennis had been on his mind. As Black and his brother, Wayne, and sister, Cara, were playing their early-round matches at the All England Club, their native country, Zimbabwe, was awash in political turmoil.

In a highly contested election marked by intimidation, the assassination of an opposition candidate and more than 20 other deaths, the party of President Robert Mugabe narrowly retained control of Zimbabwe on June 27. Mugabe advocates, among other controversial policies, the redistribution of land—often through violent occupation—from white farm owners to members of the nation's black majority. Byron Black and his siblings, who are white, were raised on a 22-acre avocado farm outside the capital city, Harare, and have white friends whose property has been seized by armed squatters. "We're trying to follow the situation as best we can, but I'm also trying not to let it interfere with my tennis," Black said. "It sounds like things have calmed down in the past few days."

Away from their country playing tennis during the election, none of the Blacks could cast a vote. Since they are prominent members of the racial minority in Zimbabwe—and were treated as national heroes during Zimbabwe's near upset of the U.S. in Davis Cup play last February—they are reluctant to take much of a political stand. That Mugabe's wife, Grace, is a leading patron of Zimbabwean tennis further complicates their position. "I will say this: It's good that there's some competition, that there's now a party to keep the ruling party in check," said Byron. "Before this there was never any real opposition."

All three Blacks intend to settle in Zimbabwe when their playing careers end. Byron, who's ranked 52nd in the world but has been as high as 22, owns a flat in London, but he and his wife, Fiona, recently built a house near his parents' farm. Both brothers will have a better sense of the political climate when they return home.

"You obviously play tennis for yourself," says Byron, "but I'd like to think that in some small way playing well at Wimbledon and playing Davis Cup is helping with unity at home, giving the people of Zimbabwe something positive to take their minds off the day-to-day."

—L. Jon Wertheim

Golf

The incomparable
Tiger Woods

ROBERT BECK

Burning Bright

Every golf story in 2000—and there were some notable ones—took a backseat to the history-making Tiger Woods

BY MARTY BURNS

AS A YOUNG boy Tiger Woods dreamed of one day dominating pro golf the way his hero Jack Nicklaus did. At age 10 Tiger even taped a list of the Golden Bear's records to the headboard of his bed, a reminder of his goals each night before he lay down to sleep.

Funny how innocent the dreams of children can be. For in 2000 the grown-up Woods outdistanced the competition on the PGA tour by a wider margin than he could have ever imagined, eclipsing the glorious feats of Nicklaus and anybody else who ever played the game. In fact, were he not so good at avoiding bunkers, one might even say Woods turned the sport into his own personal sandbox.

In just his fourth full pro season Woods won the U.S. Open, the British Open and the PGA Championship to join Ben Hogan ('53) as the only players in history to win three majors in a single year. Along the way he became, at age 24, the youngest player to complete the career Grand Slam, the record holder for low score in all four majors and

arguably the world's most recognizable sports figure. His spectacular season drew immense galleries and TV ratings, landed him on the cover of *Time* and earned him a record $100 million endorsement deal with Nike. No other story in golf—the tributes to the late Payne Stewart, Vijay Singh's impressive win at the Masters or Karrie Webb's ascendancy as the dominant woman player (see sidebar)—came close.

It wasn't only that Woods won so often in 2000, it was also the thoroughly convincing way in which he won. In his three major victories he made the game look as easy as he did bouncing that golf ball on the blade of his wedge in his well-known TV commercial.

Consider:

• He won the U.S. Open (at Pebble Beach) by 15 strokes, shattering the record for a major championship set by Old Tom Morris in the 1862 British Open. He also became the first player to win a U.S. Open in double digits below par (12 under).

• He became the youngest golfer to achieve the career Grand Slam (Nicklaus was 26

consecutive PGA Tour victory, the longest such streak in 52 years.

Though an opening-round 75 cost him any shot at adding a second Masters green jacket to his collection this year (he still rallied to finish fifth, six strokes behind Singh), Woods bounced back in historic fashion at the U.S. Open. In perhaps the most dominating four-round performance ever, Woods never three-putted en route to a 65-69-71-67. His stone-cold determination to win was so fierce he skipped a ceremony the day before the tournament honoring the late Stewart, the '99 Open champ who had died eight months earlier in a plane crash. "I felt going [to the ceremony] would be more of a deterrent for me during the tournament, because I don't want to be thinking about it," said Woods, who played a practice round instead.

His steely focus carried over to the British Open, where he put on a sizzling display of power and precision to card rounds of 67-66-67-69 without benefit of a single eagle. His consistency was mind-boggling. Despite thick rough and 112 bunkers on the Old Course, he never once hit the ball into the sand.

In a dramatic finale to his astounding summer, Woods outdueled Bob May in a three-hole playoff to become the first repeat PGA champion since Denny Shute in 1937. Unlike his U.S. and British Open victories, however, Woods had to sweat this one out. The unheralded May, whose only career victory had come on the European tour, matched Tiger shot for shot, birdie for birdie. "Probably one of the greatest duels I've ever had in my life," said Woods, who merely birdied the last two holes of regulation to force the tie and then won the playoff with a 20-foot birdie putt on the 16th hole and a shot out of a greenside bunker to within two feet of the cup on the 18th.

It was breathtaking shots like those, which Woods made seem almost routine in 2000,

when he accomplished the feat in 1966) with an eight-stroke victory in the British Open. His 19-under-par 269 at St. Andrews set a record for lowest score in relation to par at a major.

• His triumph at the PGA Championship, at Valhalla, was his second straight PGA title and his fourth major in five tries. His 18-under 270 was the lowest score in relation to par in PGA history and left him with the distinction of holding the scoring record in all four major championships.

Through September Woods had won nine of the 17 PGA Tour events he entered in 2000, earning a record $8.3 million in prize money and leaving everyone else to play for second place. Indeed, Ernie Els endured five runner-up finishes, four to Woods, in a season that otherwise might have merited the player of the year award. "[Tiger's] the best who ever played," veteran pro Mark Calcavecchia said after the British Open, summing up the feelings of most of his fellow Tour pros. "And he's 24."

The Year of the Tiger began in Hawaii at the Mercedes Championships, the season's first event, when he finished eagle-birdie-birdie and defeated Els in a playoff. A month later he rallied from seven shots down with seven holes to play to win the Pebble Beach National Pro-Am. It was Woods's sixth that captured the public's fascination and elevated Tiger to an early entry in golf's pantheon. Like Michael Jordan did in basketball, Woods offered even casual fans a chance to see something they had never seen before. Even Woods's boyhood idol, Nicklaus, who likely played in his final British and U.S. Opens in 2000, was amazed. "I kept saying, 'I can't understand why we don't have anybody else playing that well,'" said Nicklaus. "I am more understanding now. He's that much better."

Indeed, Tiger had turned the game into mere child's play.

Tigress of the LPGA

She's the LPGA's answer to Tiger Woods. Like Woods, Australian sensation Karrie Webb, 25, won her tour's rookie of the year award in '96 and its player of the year award in '99. Like Woods, she has a wide and powerful swing and has been known to spend long hours on the practice tees. And like Woods, she lives in Florida during the off-season.

Aussie rules: Webb dominated the LPGA.

But what really makes Webb Tiger-like is the way she dominated her sport in 2000. With six victories and nine Top 10 finishes through September, including triumphs at two majors (the Nabisco and the Women's U.S. Open), Webb stamped her name on the women's tour like no player in years. "She's the best in the world right now," said tour player Cristie Kerr after finishing second to Webb at the Open. "I'd really like to see her go against Tiger, head-to-head. I'd love to see who would win."

In any other year Webb's performance would have been big news. Instead, thanks to Tiger, it went largely unnoticed. On the same day Woods won the British Open, Webb notched her second major of the season—and third of her career—with a Tiger-esque five-stroke victory at the Women's Open in suburban Chicago. The win put her on pace to break her own record of $1.6 million in prize winnings and earned her enough points to automatically qualify for the LPGA Hall of Fame, but it was overshadowed by Tiger's historic day.

"I don't think I would enjoy being the face of the LPGA," Webb said, shrugging off the lack of attention. "As long as I keep golf my Number 1 priority, I'll be the happiest person going."

Unlike Tiger, Webb had to deal with a close pursuer in 2000. Sweden's Annika Sorenstam won five tour events through September, including one in a playoff over Webb. Still, there was no dispute that the year belonged to the blonde-haired Australian with the reserved manner and the single-minded focus. "To be compared to Tiger and what he's doing is a compliment," Webb said. "He's unbelievable."

In 2000, so was Webb. Even if few outside the LPGA noticed.

Men's Majors

The Masters
Augusta National GC (par 72; 6,985 yds); Augusta, GA, April 6–9

Player	Score	Earnings ($)
Vijay Singh	72-67-70-69—278	828,000
Ernie Els	72-67-74-68—281	496,800
David Duval	73-65-74-70—282	266,800
Loren Roberts	73-69-71-69—282	266,800
Tiger Woods	75-72-68-69—284	184,000
Tom Lehman	69-72-75-69—285	165,600
Phil Mickelson	71-68-76-71—286	143,367
Davis Love III	75-72-68-71—286	143,367
Carlos Franco	79-68-70-69—286	143,367
Hal Sutton	72-75-71-69—287	124,200
Nick Price	74-69-73-72—288	105,800
Fred Couples	76-72-70-70—288	105,800
Greg Norman	80-68-70-70—288	105,800
Dennis Paulson	68-76-73-72—289	80,500
John Huston	77-69-72-71—289	80,500
Jim Furyk	73-74-71-71—289	80,500
Chris Perry	73-75-72-69—289	80,500
Jeff Sluman	73-69-77-71—290	69,000
Steve Stricker	70-73-75-73—291	53,820
Bob Estes	72-71-77-71—291	53,820
Padraig Harrington	76-69-75-71—291	53,820
Glen Day	79-67-74-71—291	53,820
Jean Van de Velde	76-70-75-70—291	53,820
Colin Montgomerie	76-69-77-69—291	53,820

U.S. Open
Pebble Beach Golf Links Course (par 71; 6,828 yds); Pebble Beach, CA, June 15–18

Player	Score	Earnings ($)
Tiger Woods	65-69-71-67—272	800,000
Miguel Angel Jiménez	66-74-76-71—287	391,150
Ernie Els	74-73-68-72—287	391,150
John Huston	67-75-76-70—288	212,779
Lee Westwood	71-71-76-71—289	162,526
Padraig Harrington	73-71-72-73—289	162,526
Nick Faldo	69-74-76-71—290	137,203
Loren Roberts	68-78-73-72—291	112,766
David Duval	75-71-74-71—291	112,766
Stewart Cink	77-72-72-70—291	112,766
Vijay Singh	70-73-80-68—291	112,766
Paul Azinger	71-73-79-69—292	86,223
Retief Goosen	77-72-72-71—292	86,223
Michael Campbell	71-77-71-73—292	86,223
José María Olazábal	70-71-76-75—292	86,223
Fred Couples	70-75-75-73—293	65,214
Phil Mickelson	71-73-73-76—293	65,214
Mike Weir	76-72-76-69—293	65,214
Scott Hoch	73-76-75-69—293	65,214
Justin Leonard	73-73-75-72—293	65,214
David Toms	73-76-72-72—293	65,214

British Open
Old Course (par 72; 7,115 yds); St. Andrews, Scotland, July 20–23

Player	Score	Earnings ($)
Tiger Woods	67-66-67-69—269	759,150
Thomas Bjorn	69-69-68-71—277	371,984
Ernie Els	66-72-70-69—277	371,984
Tom Lehman	68-70-70-70—278	197,379
David Toms	69-67-71-71—278	197,379
Fred Couples	70-68-72-69—279	151,830
Paul Azinger	69-72-72-67—280	100,587
Pierre Fulke	69-72-70-69—280	100,587
Loren Roberts	69-68-70-73—280	100,587
Darren Clarke	70-69-68-73—280	100,587
David Duval	70-70-66-75—281	56,346
Mark McNulty	69-72-70-70—281	56,346
Davis Love III	74-66-74-67—281	56,346
Vijay Singh	70-70-73-68—281	56,346
Stuart Appleby	73-70-68-70—281	56,346
Bob May	72-72-66-71—281	56,346
Bernhard Langer	74-70-66-71—281	56,346
Phil Mickelson	72-66-71-72—281	56,346
Dennis Paulson	68-71-69-73—281	56,346
Notah Begay	69-73-69-71—282	38,717
Padraig Harrington	68-72-70-72—282	38,717
Steve Pate	73-70-71-68—282	38,717
Paul McGinley	69-72-71-70—282	38,717
Bob Estes	72-69-70-71—282	38,717
Steve Flesch	67-70-71-74—282	38,717

PGA Championship
Valhalla GC (par 72; 7,167 yds), Louisville, August 17–20

Player	Score	Earnings ($)
Tiger Woods†	66-67-70-67—270	900,000
Bob May	72-66-66-66—270	540,000
Thomas Bjorn	72-68-67-68—275	340,000
Jose Maria Olazabal	76-68-63-69—276	198,667
Stuart Appleby	70-69-68-69—276	198,667
Greg Chalmers	71-69-66-70—276	198,667
Franklin Langham	72-71-65-69—277	157,000
Notah Begay	72-66-70-70—278	145,000
Scott Dunlap	66-68-70-75—279	112,500
Davis Love III	68-69-72-70—279	112,500
Phil Mickelson	70-70-69-70—279	112,500
Fred Funk	69-68-74-68—279	112,500
Darren Clarke	68-72-72-67—279	112,500
Michael Clark II	73-70-67-70—280	77,500
Chris DiMarco	73-70-69-68—280	77,500
Lee Westwood	72-72-69-67—280	77,500
Stewart Cink	72-71-70-67—280	77,500
Tom Kite	70-72-69-70—281	56,200
Robert Allenby	73-71-68-69—281	56,200
Angel Cabrera	72-71-71-67—281	56,200
J.P. Hayes	69-68-68-76—281	56,200
Lee Janzen	76-70-70-65—281	56,200

† Won three-hole playoff.

Men's Tour Results

Late 1999 PGA Tour Events

Tournament	Final Round	Winner	Score/ Under Par	Earnings ($)
National Car Rental Classic	Oct 24	Tiger Woods	271/–17	450,000
The Tour Championship	Oct 31	Tiger Woods	269/–15	900,000
Southern Farm Bureau Classic#	Nov 1	Brian Henninger	202/–14	360,000
World Golf Championships**	Nov 7	Tiger Woods	278/–6	1,000,000
Shark Shootout**	Nov 14	Fred Couples/David Duval	184/–32	175,000 each
JC Penney Classic**	Dec 6	Laura Davies/John Daly*	260/–24	220,000 each
Diners Club Matches**	Dec 12	Fred Couples/Mark Calcavecchia	1 up	200,000 each

2000 PGA Tour Events

Tournament	Final Round	Winner	Score/ Under Par	Earnings ($)
Mercedes Championships	Jan 9	Tiger Woods	276/–16	522,000
Sony Open	Jan 16	Paul Azinger	261/–19	522,000
Bob Hope Classic	Jan 23	Jesper Parnevik	331/–27	540,000
Phoenix Open	Jan 30	Tom Lehman	270/–14	576,000
Pebble Beach National Pro-Am	Feb 7	Tiger Woods	273/–15	720,000
Buick Invitational	Feb 13	Phil Mickelson	270/–18	540,000
Nissan Open	Feb 20	Kirk Triplett	272/–12	558,000
Tucson Open	Feb 27	Jim Carter	269/–19	540,000
Match Play Championship	Feb 27	Darren Clarke	4 & 3	1,000,000
Doral-Ryder Open	Mar 5	Jim Furyk	265/–23	540,000
Honda Classic	Mar 12	Dudley Hart	269/–19	522,000
Bay Hill Invitational	Mar 19	Tiger Woods	270/–18	540,000
The Players Championship	Mar 27	Hal Sutton	278/–10	1,080,000
BellSouth Classic#	Apr 2	Phil Mickelson*	205/–11	504,000
The Masters	Apr 9	Vijay Singh	278/–10	828,000
MCI Classic	Apr 16	Stewart Cink	270/–14	540,000
Greater Greensboro Classic	Apr 23	Hal Sutton	274/–14	540,000
Houston Open	Apr 30	Robert Allenby*	275/–13	504,000
Compaq Classic	May 7	Carlos Franco*	270/–18	612,000
Byron Nelson Classic	May 14	Jesper Parnevik*	269/–11	720,000
The Colonial	May 21	Phil Mickelson	268/–12	594,000
The Memorial	May 28	Tiger Woods	269/–19	558,000
Kemper Open	June 4	Tom Scherrer	271/–13	540,000
Buick Classic	June 11	Dennis Paulson*	276/–8	540,000
U.S. Open	June 18	Tiger Woods	272/–12	800,000
St. Jude Classic	June 25	Notah Begay	271/–13	540,000
Greater Hartford Open	July 2	Notah Begay	260/–20	504,000
Western Open	July 9	Robert Allenby*	274/–14	540,000
Greater Milwaukee Open	July 16	Loren Roberts	260/–24	450,000
British Open	July 23	Tiger Woods	269/–19	759,150
B.C. Open	July 23	Brad Faxon	270/–18	360,000
John Deere Classic	July 31	Michael Clark*	265/–19	468,000
Qwest International	Aug 6	Ernie Els	487‡	630,000
Buick Open	Aug 13	Rocco Mediate*	268/–20	486,000
PGA Championship	Aug 20	Tiger Woods*	270/–18	900,000
World Golf Championships/ NEC Invit.	Aug 27	Tiger Woods	259/–21	1,000,000
Reno-Tahoe Open	Aug 27	Scott Verplank*	275/–13	540,000
Air Canada Championship	Sep 3	Rory Sabbatini	268/–16	540,000
Canadian Open	Sep 10	Tiger Woods	266/–22	594,000
SEI Pennsylvania Classic	Sep 17	Chris DiMarco	270/–14	576,000
Texas Open	Sept 24	Justin Leonard	261/–19	468,000
Buick Challenge	Oct 1	David Duval	269/–19	414,000
Michelob Championship	Oct 8	David Toms*	271/–19	540,000
Invensys Classic	Oct 15	Billy Andrade	332/–28	765,000

* Won sudden-death playoff. †Won on the second extra hole of match play. # Tournament shortened by rain. ‡ Revised Stableford scoring.
** Not an official event.

Nabisco Championship

Mission Hills CC; Rancho Mirage, CA
(par 72; 6,520 yds) March 23–26

Player	Score	Earnings ($)
Karrie Webb	67-70-67-70—274	187,500
Dottie Pepper	68-72-72-72—284	116,366
Meg Mallon	75-70-73-67—285	84,916
Cathy Johnston-Forbes	74-71-71-70—286	59,755
Michele Redman	73-73-69-71—286	59,755
Helen Dobson	73-74-72-68—287	40,570
Chris Johnson	73-68-73-73—287	40,570
Rosie Jones	74-71-74-69—288	31,135
Kim Saiki	72-77-68-71—288	31,135
Jenny Lidback	75-72-74-68—289	24,170
Wendy Doolan	73-73-69-74—289	24,170
Pat Hurst	72-72-70-75—289	24,170
A.S. Wongluekiet*	75-71-68-75—289	—
Kristi Albers	77-71-72-70—290	20,845
Se Ri Pak	73-71-77-70—291	18,957
Janice Moodie	74-72-70-75—291	18,957

LPGA Championship

DuPont Country Club; Wilmington, DE
(par 71; 6,408 yds) June 22–25

Player	Score	Earnings ($)
†Juli Inkster	72-69-65-75—281	210,000
Stefania Croce	72-67-74-68—281	130,330
Se Ri Pak	73-69-69-71—282	76,319
Nancy Scranton	72-70-67-73—282	76,319
Wendy Ward	69-69-68-76—282	76,319
Heather Bowie	74-70-70-69—283	42,503
Laura Davies	70-66-75-72—283	42,503
Jane Crafter	72-69-69-73—283	42,503
Akiko Fukushima	71-72-71-70—284	29,839
Karrie Webb	72-70-69-73—284	29,839
Jan Stephenson	70-69-69-76—284	29,839
Kelly Robbins	72-72-73-68—285	21,885
Amy Fruhwirth	74-71-70-70—285	21,885
Leta Lindley	71-73-71-70—285	21,885
Annika Sorenstam	70-73-70-72—285	21,885
Mi Hyun Kim	70-73-70-72—285	21,885
Dawn Coe-Jones	71-73-72-70—286	16,602
Meg Mallon	72-73-69-72—286	16,602
Jane Geddes	66-74-73-73—286	16,602
Pat Hurst	71-70-71-74—286	16,602
Wendy Doolan	69-71-71-75—286	16,602

†Won on second playoff hole.

U.S. Women's Open

Merit Club; Libertyville, IL
(par 72; 6,540 yds) July 20–23

Player	Score	Earnings ($)
Karrie Webb	69-72-68-73—282	500,000
Cristie Kerr	72-71-74-70—287	240,228
Meg Mallon	68-72-73-74—287	240,228
Rosie Jones	73-71-72-72—288	120,119
Mi Hyun Kim	74-72-70-72—288	120,119
Grace Park	74-72-73-70—289	90,458
Kelli Kuehne	71-74-73-71—289	90,458
Beth Daniel	71-74-72-73—290	79,345
Annika Sorenstam	73-75-73-70—291	67,369
Kelly Robbins	74-73-71-73—291	67,369
Laura Davies	73-71-72-75—291	67,369
Jennifer Rosales	75-75-69-73—292	55,355
Pat Hurst	73-72-72-75—292	55,355
Dorothy Delasin	76-68-72-76—292	55,355
Se Ri Pak	74-75-75-69—293	47,846
Kellee Booth	70-78-75-70—293	47,846
Janice Moodie	73-77-75-69—294	40,586
Kathryn Marshall	72-72-77-73—294	40,586
Shani Waugh	69-75-73-77—294	40,586
Lorie Kane	71-74-72-77—294	40,586

du Maurier Classic

Royal Ottawa GC; Aylmer, Quebec
(par 72; 6,403 yds) August 10–13

Player	Score	Earnings ($)
Meg Mallon	73-68-72-69—282	180,000
Rosie Jones	74-70-71-68—283	111,711
Annika Sorenstam	69-69-72-74—284	81,519
Diana D'Alessio	67-73-73-72—285	63,404
Juli Inkster	72-68-74-72—286	46,797
Lorie Kane	72-67-71-76—286	46,797
Becky Iverson	74-74-71-70—289	30,192
Karrie Webb	71-72-76-70—289	30,192
Se Ri Pak	69-76-72-72—289	30,192
Laura Philo	71-69-77-72—289	30,192
Kim Williams	71-75-72-72—290	22,986
Carin Koch	72-73-74-72—291	21,174
Jane Crafter	74-71-75-72—292	18,758
Mhairi McKay	70-73-75-74—292	18,758
Kristi Albers	69-74-75-74—292	18,758
Rachel Hetherington	72-73-73-75—293	16,041
Trish Johnson	72-72-70-79—293	16,041
Leslie Spalding	71-76-75-72—294	13,928
Dana Dormann	72-73-77-72—294	13,928
Kelli Kuehne	72-73-76-73—294	13,928
Brandie Burton	78-70-72-74—294	13,928
Leigh Ann Mills	70-75-74-75—294	13,928

* Amateur.

Late 1999 LPGA Tour Events

Tournament	Final Round	Winner	Score/Under Par	Earnings ($)
Mizuno Classic	Nov 7	Maria Hjorth	201/–15	120,000
LPGA Tour Championship	Nov 14	Se Ri Pak*	276/–12	215,000
JC Penney Classic**	Dec 5	Laura Davies/John Daly	260/–24	220,000 each
Diners Club Matches**	Dec 12	Julie Inkster/Dottie Pepper	4 & 3	100,000 each

2000 LPGA Tour Events

Tournament	Final Round	Winner	Score/Under Par	Earnings ($)
LPGA Office Depot	Jan 16	Karrie Webb	281/–7	112,500
Naples LPGA Memorial	Jan 23	Nancy Scranton*	275/–13	127,500
Los Angeles Women's Championship	Feb 13	Laura Davies	211/–5	112,500
Hawaiian Ladies Open	Feb 19	Betsy King	204/–12	97,500
Australian Ladies Masters	Feb 27	Karrie Webb	274/–14	112,500
Takefuji Classic	Mar 4	Karrie Webb*	207/–9	120,000
Welch's/Circle K Championship	Mar 12	Annika Sorenstam*	269/–19	105,000
Standard Register PING	Mar 19	Charlotta Sorenstam	276/–12	127,500
Nabisco Championship	Mar 26	Karrie Webb	274/–15	187,500
Longs Drugs Challenge	Apr 16	Juli Inkster	275/–13	105,000
Chick-fil-A Championship	Apr 30	Sophie Gustafson	206/–10	135,000
Philips Invitational	May 7	Laura Davies	275/–5	127,500
Electrolux Championship	May 14	Pat Hurst	275/–13	120,000
Firstar LPGA Classic	May 21	Annika Sorenstam	197/–19	97,500
Corning Classic	May 28	Betsy King*	276/–12	120,000
Kathy Ireland Greens.com	June 4	Grace Park	274/–14	112,500
Rochester International	June 11	Meg Mallon	280/–8	150,000
Evian Masters	June 17	Annika Sorenstam*	276/–12	270,000
LPGA Championship	June 25	Juli Inkster*	281/–3	210,000
ShopRite Classic	July 2	Janice Moodie	203/–10	165,000
Jamie Farr Kroger Classic	July 9	Annika Sorenstam*	274/–10	150,000
Big Apple Classic	July 16	Annika Sorenstam	206/–7	135,000
U.S. Women's Open	July 23	Karrie Webb	282/–6	500,000
Giant Eagle LPGA Classic	July 30	Dorothy Delasin*	205/–11	150,000
Michelob Light Classic	Aug 6	Lorie Kane	205/–11	120,000
du Maurier Classic	Aug 13	Meg Mallon	282/–6	180,000
Women's British Open	Aug 20	Sophie Gustafson	282/–10	178,800
Oldsmobile Classic	Aug 27	Karrie Webb	265/–13	112,500
Rail Classic	Sep 3	Laurel Kean	198/–18	135,000
Betsy King Classic	Sep 10	Michele Redman	202/–14	120,000
Safeway LPGA Championship	Sept 24	Mi Hyun Kim*	215/–1	120,000
New Albany Golf Classic	Oct 1	Lorie Kane*	277/–11	150,000
Samsung World Championship	Oct 15	Juli Inkster	274/–14	152,000

* Won sudden-death playoff. #Shortened due to rain. **Not an official event.

Will the USGA Fight Back?

In case you hadn't noticed, the last three USGA Opens produced record scores. Juli Inkster began the cycle at the '99 Women's Open at Old Waverly in West Point, Miss., where her 16-under-par 272 was 6 strokes more under par than any previous winning performance in the championship's history. Tiger Woods's 12-under 272 at Pebble Beach in 2000 was four strokes more under par than any previous winner's. Finally, Hale Irwin's 17-under 267 at Saucon Valley in July 2000 broke the Senior Open records for total score and for number of strokes under par by three.

Has the USGA, which usually favors a winning score right around par, gone soft? No, says Tim Moraghan, director of agronomy for the USGA championships. In the case of the Women's and Senior Opens, the primary reason for the low score was heavy rain on the eve of the tournaments. "There was no wind at either event, and the players were throwing darts in there," he says. "We got it just right at Pebble Beach, because the next best score to Tiger's was three over. Also, as amazing as Tiger was, he got some breaks with the weather."

Moraghan says that because "ultimately rain is the one thing we can't control," he would like to see the USGA cover the greens with portable tents at future Opens. "But as far as how we set up the courses, we don't have any regrets", he says. As for the immediate future, ... the 2001 U.S. Open at Southern Hills in Tulsa and the next Senior Open, at Salem Country Club in Peabody, Mass.— Moraghan says the USGA will stick to its game plan.

Late 1999 Senior Tour Events

Tournament	Final Round	Winner	Score/ Under Par	Earnings ($)
EMC Kaanapali Classic	Oct 24	Bruce Fleisher	199/–17	150,000
Pacific Bell Senior Classic	Oct 31	Joe Inman	199/–14	180,000
Senior Tour Championship	Nov 7	Gary McCord	276/–12	347,000
Senior Match Play Challenge**	Nov 14	Larry Nelson	3 & 2	240,000
Diners Club Matches	Dec 12	Tom Watson/Jack Nicklaus	1-up	200,000 each

2000 Senior Tour Events

Tournament	Final Round	Winner	Score/ Under Par	Earnings ($)
MasterCard Championship	Jan 24	George Archer	207/–9	199,000
Royal Caribbean Classic	Feb 6	Bruce Fleisher	+30‡	165,000
ACE Group Classic	Feb 13	Lanny Wadkins*	202/–14	180,000
GTE Classic	Feb 20	Bruce Fleisher	200/–13	195,000
LiquidGolf.com Invitational	Feb 27	Tom Wargo*	202/–14	180,000
Toshiba Classic#	Mar 5	Allen Doyle	136/–6	195,000
Audi Senior Classic	Mar 12	Hubert Green	197/–19	225,000
Legends of Golf**	Mar 19	Jim Colbert/Andy North	191/–26	161,000 each
Emerald Coast Classic	Mar 26	Gil Morgan	197/–13	187,500
The Tradition	April 2	Tom Kite*	280/–8	240,000
PGA Seniors Championship	April 17	Doug Tewell	201/–15	324,000
Las Vegas Senior Classic	April 23	Larry Nelson	197/–19	210,000
Bruno's Memorial Classic	April 30	John Jacobs*	203/–13	195,000
Home Depot Invitational	May 7	Bruce Fleisher*	203/–13	195,000
Nationwide Championship	May 14	Hale Irwin	207/–9	217,500
TD Waterhouse Championship	May 21	Dana Quigley	198/–18	195,000
Boone Valley Classic	May 28	Larry Nelson	200/–16	225,000
BellSouth Senior Classic	June 4	Hale Irwin	198/–18	225,000
SBC Senior Open	June 11	Tom Kite	207/–9	210,000
SBC Championship	June 18	Doug Tewell	202/–14	165,000
Cadillac NFL Golf Classic	June 25	Lee Trevino	202/–14	165,000
U.S. Senior Open	July 2	Hale Irwin	267/–17	400,000
State Farm Classic	July 9	Leonard Thompson*	205/–11	202,500
Senior Players Championship	July 16	Ray Floyd	273/–15	345,000
Instinet Classic	July 23	Gil Morgan	199/–17	210,000
Long Island Classic	July 30	Bruce Fleisher	198/–18	225,000
Burnet Senior Classic	Aug 6	Ed Dougherty	197/–19	240,000
Canada Senior Open	Aug 13	Tom Jenkins	274/–14	217,500
Utah Showdown	Aug 20	Doug Tewell	199/–17	217,500
FleetBoston Classic	Aug 27	Larry Nelson	203/–13	195,000
Foremost Insurance Championship	Sep 3	Larry Nelson	198/–18	165,000
Comfort Classic#	Sep 10	Gil Morgan	131/–13	187,500
Kroger Senior Classic	Sep 17	Hubert Green	200/–10	210,000
Bank One Senior Championship	Sep 24	Larry Nelson	203/–13	210,000
Vantage Championship	Oct 1	Larry Nelson*	198/–12	225,000
The Transamerica	Oct 8	Jim Thorpe	198/–18	165,000
Gold Rush Classic	Oct 15	Jim Thorpe	195/–21	165,000

*Won sudden-death playoff. #Shortened due to rain. **Not an official event. ‡ Revised Stableford scoring.

U.S. Amateur Results

Tournament	Final Round	Winner	Score	Runner-Up
Women's Amateur Public Links	July 9	Catherine Cartwright	3 & 1	R. Gulyanamitta
Men's Amateur Public Links	July 15	D.J. Trahan	37 holes	Ben Dickerson
Girls' Junior Amateur	Aug 5	Lisa Ferrero	3 & 1	Ina Kim
Boys' Junior Amateur	Aug 5	Matthew Rosenfeld	3 & 2	Ryan Moore
Women's Amateur	Aug 12	Marcy Newton	8 & 7	Laura Myerscough
Men's Amateur	Aug 28	Jeff Quinney	39 holes	James Driscoll
Men's Mid-Amateur	Sept 14	Greg Puga	3 & 1	Wayne Raath
Senior Women	Sept 23	Carol Semple Thompson	5 & 4	Toni Wiesner
Senior Men	Sep 29	Bill Shean Jr	2 & 1	Dick Van Leuvan
Women's Mid-Amateur	Oct 8	Ellen Port	3 & 2	Anna Schultz

International Results

Tournament	Final Round	Winner	Score	Runner-Up
Curtis Cup	June 25	United States	10–8	GB/Ireland
Solheim Cup	Oct 8	Europe	14½ – 11½	United States

PGA Tour Final 1999 Money Leaders

Name	Events	Best Finish	Scoring Average*	Money ($)
Tiger Woods	21	1 (8)	68.43	6,616,585
David Duval	21	1 (4)	69.17	3,641,906
Davis Love III	23	2 (4)	69.37	2,475,328
Vijay Singh	29	1 (1)	69.83	2,283,233
Chris Perry	31	2 (2)	70.00	2,145,707
Hal Sutton	25	1 (1)	69.66	2,127,578
Payne Stewart	20	1 (2)	69.98	2,077,950
Justin Leonard	28	2 (2)	69.59	2,020,991
Jeff Maggert	23	1 (1)	70.15	2,016,469
David Toms	32	1 (2)	70.54	1,959,672

*Adjusted for average score of field in each tournament entered.

LPGA Tour Final 1999 Money Leaders

Name	Events	Best Finish	Scoring Average	Money ($)
Karrie Webb	25	1 (6)	69.43	1,591,959
Juli Inkster	24	1 (5)	70.04	1,337,253
Se Ri Pak	27	1 (4)	70.77	956,926
Annika Sorenstam	22	1 (2)	70.40	863,816
Lorie Kane	30	2 (3)	70.62	757,844
Meg Mallon	25	1 (2)	70.71	679,929
Sherri Steinhauer	30	1 (2)	71.20	663,356
Mi Hyun Kim	30	1 (2)	70.66	584,246
Rosie Jones	24	1 (1)	70.99	583,796
Dottie Pepper	21	1 (2)	70.32	577,875

Senior Tour Final 1999 Money Leaders

Name	Events	Best Finish	Scoring Average	Money ($)
Bruce Fleisher	32	1 (7)	69.19	2,515,705
Hale Irwin	26	1 (5)	69.58	2,025,232
Allen Doyle	31	1 (4)	70.02	1,911,640
Larry Nelson	28	1 (2)	70.25	1,513,524
Gil Morgan	27	1 (2)	69.69	1,493,282
Dana Quigley	38	2 (2)	70.39	1,327,658
Tom Jenkins	29	1 (1)	69.90	1,167,176
Bruce Summerhays	36	2 (1)	70.57	1,118,377
Vicente Fernandez	28	1 (1)	70.25	1,108,245
José María Canizares	33	2 (1)	70.22	1,087,284

Going for The Golf

Shane Hamman can hit the ball a ton, which isn't surprising considering that he can lift half a ton. What *is* surprising is how Hamman, a 28-year-old Olympic weightlifter who set the world record (1,008 pounds) in the superheavyweight division, is able to swing a golf club around a body that's as wide as a phone booth. "I'm really flexible," says Hamman, whose tale of the tape reads as follows: height, 5'9"; weight, 360 pounds; chest, 62"; biceps, 22"; thighs, 35". "As part of my training I stretch so many times a day I never let myself get tight." He is so supple he can do a standing backflip and dunk a basketball.

On the course Hamman turns fast enough to pound out 350-yard drives but also battles a nasty slice. Thanks to a deft short game, he has whittled his handicap to 14. "A hundred twenty yards and in with my pitching wedge is my money shot," says Hamman, who has played golf for seven years.

After graduating from Mustang (Okla.) High in 1990, Hamman stocked watermelons at his father's produce business for eight years. At about the same time he tried powerlifting, teaching himself techniques for the squat, bench press and deadlift by reading magazines. "In my first competition, when I was 18, I broke all the teenage world records," he says. But after watching the 1996 Games on TV, Hamman switched to Olympic-style weightlifting (the snatch and the clean and jerk). "I saw how professional they were," says Hamman, "and how much media there was."

Although no one had ever successfully switched from power- to Olympic lifting, Hamman won the national superheavyweight crown his first time out, in 1997, and has retained his title every year since. Ranked ninth in the world, Hamman was considered a dark horse for a medal in Sydney [he finished tenth]. "Weightlifting is my sport," he says, "but golf is my favorite sport."

Despite the dichotomy between golf and weightlifting, Hamman finds similarities between the swing and the snatch: "Lifting the bar from the ground over your head in one move is not about muscling it up. It's all about technique, timing and body position. When you do it right, it feels as if there is no weight on the bar at all, just like when you hit it pure in golf, and it feels as if you didn't even swing."

—Scott Gummer

Men's Golf

THE MAJOR TOURNAMENTS
The Masters

Year	Winner	Score	Runner-Up
1934	Horton Smith	284	Craig Wood
1935	Gene Sarazen* (144)	282	Craig Wood (149)
	(only 36-hole playoff)		
1936	Horton Smith	285	Harry Cooper
1937	Byron Nelson	283	Ralph Guldahl
1938	Henry Picard	285	Ralph Guldahl
			Harry Cooper
1939	Ralph Guldahl	279	Sam Snead
1940	Jimmy Demaret	280	Lloyd Mangrum
1941	Craig Wood	280	Byron Nelson
1942	Byron Nelson* (69)	280	Ben Hogan (70)
1943–45	No tournament		
1946	Herman Keiser	282	Ben Hogan
1947	Jimmy Demaret	281	Byron Nelson
			Frank Stranahan
1948	Claude Harmon	279	Cary Middlecoff
1949	Sam Snead	282	Johnny Bulla
			Lloyd Mangrum
1950	Jimmy Demaret	283	Jim Ferrier
1951	Ben Hogan	280	Skee Riegel
1952	Sam Snead	286	Jack Burke Jr
1953	Ben Hogan	274	Ed Oliver Jr
1954	Sam Snead* (70)	289	Ben Hogan (71)
1955	Cary Middlecoff	279	Ben Hogan
1956	Jack Burke Jr	289	Ken Venturi
1957	Doug Ford	282	Sam Snead
1958	Arnold Palmer	284	Doug Ford
			Fred Hawkins
1959	Art Wall Jr	284	Cary Middlecoff
1960	Arnold Palmer	282	Ken Venturi
1961	Gary Player	280	Charles R. Coe
			Arnold Palmer
1962	Arnold Palmer* (68)	280	Gary Player (71)
			D. Finsterwald (77)
1963	Jack Nicklaus	286	Tony Lema
1964	Arnold Palmer	276	Dave Marr
			Jack Nicklaus
1965	Jack Nicklaus	271	Arnold Palmer
			Gary Player
1966	Jack Nicklaus* (70)	288	Tommy Jacobs (72)
			Gay Brewer Jr (78)
1967	Gay Brewer Jr	280	Bobby Nichols
1968	Bob Goalby	277	Roberto DeVicenzo
1969	George Archer	281	Billy Casper
			George Knudson
			Tom Weiskopf
1970	Billy Casper* (69)	279	Gene Littler (74)
1971	Charles Coody	279	Johnny Miller
			Jack Nicklaus
1972	Jack Nicklaus	286	Bruce Crampton
			Bobby Mitchell
			Tom Weiskopf
1973	Tommy Aaron	283	J.C. Snead
1974	Gary Player	278	Tom Weiskopf
			Dave Stockton
1975	Jack Nicklaus	276	Johnny Miller
			Tom Weiskopf
1976	Ray Floyd	271	Ben Crenshaw
1977	Tom Watson	276	Jack Nicklaus
1978	Gary Player	277	Hubert Green
			Rod Funseth
			Tom Watson
1979	Fuzzy Zoeller* (4–3)†	280	Ed Sneed (4–4)
			Tom Watson (4–4)
1980	Seve Ballesteros	275	Gibby Gilbert
			Jack Newton
1981	Tom Watson	280	Johnny Miller
			Jack Nicklaus
1982	Craig Stadler* (4)	284	Dan Pohl (5)
1983	Seve Ballesteros	280	Ben Crenshaw
			Tom Kite
1984	Ben Crenshaw	277	Tom Watson
1985	Bernhard Langer	282	Curtis Strange
			Seve Ballesteros
			Ray Floyd
1986	Jack Nicklaus	279	Greg Norman
			Tom Kite
1987	Larry Mize* (4–3)	285	Seve Ballesteros (5)
			Greg Norman (4–4)
1988	Sandy Lyle	281	Mark Calcavecchia
1989	Nick Faldo* (5–3)	283	Scott Hoch (5–4)
1990	Nick Faldo* (4–4)	278	Ray Floyd (4–x)
1991	Ian Woosnam	277	José María Olazábal
1992	Fred Couples	275	Ray Floyd
1993	Bernhard Langer	277	Chip Beck
1994	José María Olazábal	279	Tom Lehman
1995	Ben Crenshaw	274	Davis Love III
1996	Nick Faldo	276	Greg Norman
1997	Tiger Woods	270	Tom Kite
1998	Mark O'Meara	279	David Duval
			Fred Couples
1999	José María Olazábal	280	Davis Love III
2000	Vijay Singh	278	Ernie Els

*Winner in playoff. Playoff scores are in parentheses. †Playoff cut from 18 holes to sudden death.
Note: Played at Augusta National Golf Club, Augusta, GA.

United States Open Championship

Year	Winner	Score	Runner-Up	Site
1895	Horace Rawlins	†173	Willie Dunn	Newport GC, Newport, RI
1896	James Foulis	†152	Horace Rawlins	Shinnecock Hills GC, Southampton, NY
1897	Joe Lloyd	†162	Willie Anderson	Chicago GC, Wheaton, IL
1898	Fred Herd	328	Alex Smith	Myopia Hunt Club, Hamilton, MA
1899	Willie Smith	315	George Low	Baltimore CC, Baltimore
			Val Fitzjohn	
			W.H. Way	
1900	Harry Vardon	313	John H. Taylor	Chicago GC, Wheaton, IL
1901	Willie Anderson* (85)	331	Alex Smith (86)	Myopia Hunt Club, Hamilton, MA
1902	Laurie Auchterlonie	307	Stewart Gardner	Garden City GC, Garden City, NY
1903	Willie Anderson* (82)	307	David Brown (84)	Baltusrol GC, Springfield, NJ
1904	Willie Anderson	303	Gil Nicholls	Glen View Club, Golf, IL
1905	Willie Anderson	314	Alex Smith	Myopia Hunt Club, Hamilton, MA
1906	Alex Smith	295	Willie Smith	Onwentsia Club, Lake Forest, IL
1907	Alex Ross	302	Gil Nicholls	Philadelphia Cricket Club, Chestnut Hill, PA
1908	Fred McLeod* (77)	322	Willie Smith (83)	Myopia Hunt Club, Hamilton, MA
1909	George Sargent	290	Tom McNamara	Englewood GC, Englewood, NJ
1910	Alex Smith* (71)	298	John McDermott (75)	Philadelphia Cricket Club, Chestnut Hill, PA
			Macdonald Smith (77)	
1911	John McDermott* (80)	307	Mike Brady (82)	Chicago GC, Wheaton, IL
			George Simpson (85)	
1912	John McDermott	294	Tom McNamara	CC of Buffalo, Buffalo
1913	Francis Ouimet* (72)	304	Harry Vardon (77)	The Country Club, Brookline, MA
			Edward Ray (78)	
1914	Walter Hagen	290	Chick Evans	Midlothian CC, Blue Island, IL
1915	Jerry Travers	297	Tom McNamara	Baltusrol GC, Springfield, NJ
1916	Chick Evans	286	Jock Hutchison	Minikahda Club, Minneapolis
1917–18	No tournament			
1919	Walter Hagen* (77)	301	Mike Brady (78)	Brae Burn CC, West Newton, MA
1920	Edward Ray	295	Harry Vardon	Inverness CC, Toledo
			Jack Burke	
			Leo Diegel	
			Jock Hutchison	
1921	Jim Barnes	289	Walter Hagen	Columbia CC, Chevy Chase, MD
			Fred McLeod	
1922	Gene Sarazen	288	John L. Black	Skokie CC, Glencoe, IL
			Bobby Jones	
1923	Bobby Jones* (76)	296	Bobby Cruickshank (78)	Inwood CC, Inwood, NY
1924	Cyril Walker	297	Bobby Jones	Oakland Hills CC, Birmingham, MI
1925	W. MacFarlane* (75–72)	291	Bobby Jones (75–73)	Worcester CC, Worcester, MA
1926	Bobby Jones	293	Joe Turnesa	Scioto CC, Columbus, OH
1927	Tommy Armour* (76)	301	Harry Cooper (79)	Oakmont CC, Oakmont, PA
1928	Johnny Farrell* (143)	294	Bobby Jones (144)	Olympia Fields CC, Matteson, IL
1929	Bobby Jones* (141)	294	Al Espinosa (164)	Winged Foot GC, Mamaroneck, NY
1930	Bobby Jones	287	Macdonald Smith	Interlachen CC, Hopkins, MN
1931	Billy Burke* (149–148)	292	George Von Elm	Inverness Club, Toledo
			(149–149)	
1932	Gene Sarazen	286	Phil Perkins	Fresh Meadows CC, Flushing, NY
			Bobby Cruickshank	
1933	Johnny Goodman	287	Ralph Guldahl	North Shore CC, Glenview, IL
1934	Olin Dutra	293	Gene Sarazen	Merion Cricket Club, Ardmore, PA
1935	Sam Parks Jr.	299	Jimmy Thompson	Oakmont CC, Oakmont, PA
1936	Tony Manero	282	Harry Cooper	Baltusrol GC (Upper Course), Springfield, NJ
1937	Ralph Guldahl	281	Sam Snead	Oakland Hills CC, Birmingham, MI
1938	Ralph Guldahl	284	Dick Metz	Cherry Hills CC, Denver
1939	Byron Nelson* (68–70)	284	Craig Wood (68–73)	Philadelphia CC, Philadelphia
			Denny Shute (76)	
1940	Lawson Little* (70)	287	Gene Sarazen (73)	Canterbury GC, Cleveland
1941	Craig Wood	284	Denny Shute	Colonial Club, Fort Worth
1942–45	No tournament			
1946	Lloyd Mangrum* (72–72)	284	Vic Ghezzi (72–73)	Canterbury GC, Cleveland
			Byron Nelson (72–73)	

United States Open Championship (Cont.)

Year	Winner	Score	Runner-Up	Site
1947	Lew Worsham* (69)	282	Sam Snead (70)	St. Louis CC, Clayton, MO
1948	Ben Hogan	276	Jimmy Demaret	Riviera CC, Los Angeles
1949	Cary Middlecoff	286	Sam Snead	Medinah CC, Medinah, IL
			Clayton Heafner	
1950	Ben Hogan* (69)	287	Lloyd Mangrum (73)	Merion GC, Ardmore, PA
			George Fazio (75)	
1951	Ben Hogan	287	Clayton Heafner	Oakland Hills CC, Birmingham, MI
1952	Julius Boros	281	Ed Oliver	Northwood CC, Dallas
1953	Ben Hogan	283	Sam Snead	Oakmont CC, Oakmont, PA
1954	Ed Furgol	284	Gene Littler	Baltusrol GC (Lower Course), Springfield, NJ
1955	Jack Fleck* (69)	287	Ben Hogan (72)	Olympic Club (Lake Course), San Francisco
1956	Cary Middlecoff	281	Ben Hogan	Oak Hill CC, Rochester, NY
			Julius Boros	
1957	Dick Mayer* (72)	282	Cary Middlecoff (79)	Inverness Club, Toledo
1958	Tommy Bolt	283	Gary Player	Southern Hills CC, Tulsa
1959	Billy Casper	282	Bob Rosburg	Winged Foot GC, Mamaroneck, NY
1960	Arnold Palmer	280	Jack Nicklaus	Cherry Hills CC, Denver
1961	Gene Littler	281	Bob Goalby	Oakland Hills CC, Birmingham, MI
			Doug Sanders	
1962	Jack Nicklaus* (71)	283	Arnold Palmer (74)	Oakmont CC, Oakmont, PA
1963	Julius Boros* (70)	293	Jacky Cupit (73)	The Country Club, Brookline, MA
			Arnold Palmer (76)	
1964	Ken Venturi	278	Tommy Jacobs	Congressional CC, Bethesda, MD
1965	Gary Player* (71)	282	Kel Nagle (74)	Bellerive CC, St. Louis
1966	Billy Casper* (69)	278	Arnold Palmer (73)	Olympic Club (Lake Course), San Francisco
1967	Jack Nicklaus	275	Arnold Palmer	Baltusrol GC (Lower Course), Springfield, NJ
1968	Lee Trevino	275	Jack Nicklaus	Oak Hill CC, Rochester, NY
1969	Orville Moody	281	Deane Beman	Champions GC (Cypress Creek Course),
			Al Geiberger	Houston
			Bob Rosburg	
1970	Tony Jacklin	281	Dave Hill	Hazeltine GC, Chaska, MN
1971	Lee Trevino* (68)	280	Jack Nicklaus (71)	Merion GC (East Course), Ardmore, PA
1972	Jack Nicklaus	290	Bruce Crampton	Pebble Beach GL, Pebble Beach, CA
1973	Johnny Miller	279	John Schlee	Oakmont CC, Oakmont, PA
1974	Hale Irwin	287	Forrest Fezler	Winged Foot GC, Mamaroneck, NY
1975	Lou Graham* (71)	287	John Mahaffey (73)	Medinah GC, Medinah, IL
1976	Jerry Pate	277	Tom Weiskopf	Atlanta Athletic Club, Duluth, GA
			Al Geiberger	
1977	Hubert Green	278	Lou Graham	Southern Hills CC, Tulsa
1978	Andy North	285	Dave Stockton	Cherry Hills CC, Denver
			J.C. Snead	
1979	Hale Irwin	284	Gary Player	Inverness Club, Toledo
			Jerry Pate	
1980	Jack Nicklaus	272	Isao Aoki	Baltusrol GC (Lower Course), Springfield, NJ
1981	David Graham	273	George Burns	Merion GC, Ardmore, PA
			Bill Rogers	
1982	Tom Watson	282	Jack Nicklaus	Pebble Beach GL, Pebble Beach, CA
1983	Larry Nelson	280	Tom Watson	Oakmont CC, Oakmont, PA
1984	Fuzzy Zoeller* (67)	276	Greg Norman (75)	Winged Foot GC, Mamaroneck, NY
1985	Andy North	279	Dave Barr	Oakland Hills CC, Birmingham, MI
			T.C. Chen	
			Denis Watson	
1986	Ray Floyd	279	Lanny Wadkins	Shinnecock Hills GC, Southampton, NY
			Chip Beck	
1987	Scott Simpson	277	Tom Watson	Olympic Club (Lake Course), San Francisco
1988	Curtis Strange* (71)	278	Nick Faldo (75)	The Country Club, Brookline, MA
1989	Curtis Strange	278	Chip Beck	Oak Hill CC, Rochester, NY
			Mark McCumber	
			Ian Woosnam	
1990	Hale Irwin* (74) (3)	280	Mike Donald (74) (4)	Medinah CC, Medinah, IL
1991	Payne Stewart (75)	282	Scott Simpson (77)	Hazeltine GC, Chaska, MN
1992	Tom Kite	285	Jeff Sluman	Pebble Beach GL, Pebble Beach, CA
1993	Lee Janzen	272	Payne Stewart	Baltusrol GC, Springfield, NJ

U.S. Open (Cont.)

Year	Winner	Score	Runner-Up	Site
1994	Ernie Els*	279	Loren Roberts	Oakmont CC, Oakmont, PA
			Colin Montgomerie	
1995	Corey Pavin	280	Greg Norman	Shinnecock Hills GC, Southampton, NY
1996	Steve Jones	278	Davis Love III	Oakland Hills CC, Birmingham, MI
			Tom Lehman	
1997	Ernie Els	276	Colin Montgomerie	Congressional CC, Bethesda, MD
1998	Lee Janzen	280	Payne Stewart	The Olympic Club, San Francisco, CA
1999	Payne Stewart	279	Phil Mickelson	Pinehurst Resort and CC, Pinehurst, NC
2000	Tiger Woods	272	Miguel Angel Jiménez	Pebble Beach GL, Pebble Beach, CA
			Ernie Els	

*Winner in playoff. Playoff scores are in parentheses. The 1990 playoff went to one hole of sudden death after an 18-hole playoff. In the 1994 playoff, Montgomerie was eliminated after 18 playoff holes, and Els beat Roberts on the 20th.
†Before 1898, 36 holes. From 1898 on, 72 holes.

British Open

Year	Winner	Score	Runner-Up	Site
1860†	Willie Park	174	Tom Morris Sr	Prestwick, Scotland
1861‡	Tom Morris Sr	163	Willie Park	Prestwick, Scotland
1862	Tom Morris Sr	163	Willie Park	Prestwick, Scotland
1863	Willie Park	168	Tom Morris Sr	Prestwick, Scotland
1864	Tom Morris, Sr	160	Andrew Strath	Prestwick, Scotland
1865	Andrew Strath	162	Willie Park	Prestwick, Scotland
1866	Willie Park	169	David Park	Prestwick, Scotland
1867	Tom Morris Sr	170	Willie Park	Prestwick, Scotland
1868	Tom Morris Jr	154	Tom Morris Sr	Prestwick, Scotland
1869	Tom Morris Jr	157	Tom Morris Sr	Prestwick, Scotland
1870	Tom Morris Jr	149	David Strath	Prestwick, Scotland
			Bob Kirk	
1871	No tournament			
1872	Tom Morris Jr	166	David Strath	Prestwick, Scotland
1873	Tom Kidd	179	Jamie Anderson	St. Andrews, Scotland
1874	Mungo Park	159	No record	Musselburgh, Scotland
1875	Willie Park	166	Bob Martin	Prestwick, Scotland
1876	Bob Martin#	176	David Strath	St. Andrews, Scotland
1877	Jamie Anderson	160	Bob Pringle	Musselburgh, Scotland
1878	Jamie Anderson	157	Robert Kirk	Prestwick, Scotland
1879	Jamie Anderson	169	Andrew Kirkaldy	St. Andrews, Scotland
			James Allan	
1880	Robert Ferguson	162	No record	Musselburgh, Scotland
1881	Robert Ferguson	170	Jamie Anderson	Prestwick, Scotland
1882	Robert Ferguson	171	Willie Fernie	St. Andrews, Scotland
1883	Willie Fernie*	159	Robert Ferguson	Musselburgh, Scotland
1884	Jack Simpson	160	Douglas Rolland	Prestwick, Scotland
			Willie Fernie	
1885	Bob Martin	171	Archie Simpson	St. Andrews, Scotland
1886	David Brown	157	Willie Campbell	Musselburgh, Scotland
1887	Willie Park Jr	161	Bob Martin	Prestwick, Scotland
1888	Jack Burns	171	Bernard Sayers	St. Andrews, Scotland
			David Anderson	
1889	Willie Park Jr* (158)	155	Andrew Kirkaldy (163)	Musselburgh, Scotland
1890	John Ball	164	Willie Fernie	Prestwick, Scotland
1891	Hugh Kirkaldy	166	Andrew Kirkaldy	St. Andrews, Scotland
			Willie Fernie	
1892	Harold Hilton	**305	John Ball	Muirfield, Scotland
			Hugh Kirkaldy	
1893	William Auchterlonie	322	John E. Laidlay	Prestwick, Scotland
1894	John H. Taylor	326	Douglas Rolland	Royal St. George's, England
1895	John H. Taylor	322	Alexander Herd	St. Andrews, Scotland
1896	Harry Vardon* (157)	316	John H. Taylor (161)	Muirfield, Scotland
1897	Harold Hilton	314	James Braid	Hoylake, England
1898	Harry Vardon	307	Willie Park Jr	Prestwick, Scotland
1899	Harry Vardon	310	Jack White	Royal St. George's, England
1900	John H. Taylor	309	Harry Vardon	St. Andrews, Scotland
1901	James Braid	309	Harry Vardon	Muirfield, Scotland
1902	Alexander Herd	307	Harry Vardon	Hoylake, England

British Open (Cont.)

Year	Winner	Score	Runner-Up	Site
1903	Harry Vardon	300	Tom Vardon	Prestwick, Scotland
1904	Jack White	296	John H. Taylor	Royal St. George's, England
1905	James Braid	318	John H. Taylor	St. Andrews, Scotland
			Rolland Jones	
1906	James Braid	300	John H. Taylor	Muirfield, Scotland
1907	Arnaud Massy	312	John H. Taylor	Hoylake, England
1908	James Braid	291	Tom Ball	Prestwick, Scotland
1909	John H. Taylor	295	James Braid	Deal, England
			Tom Ball	
1910	James Braid	299	Alexander Herd	St. Andrews, Scotland
1911	Harry Vardon	303	Arnaud Massy	Royal St. George's, England
1912	Ted Ray	295	Harry Vardon	Muirfield, Scotland
1913	John H. Taylor	304	Ted Ray	Hoylake, England
1914	Harry Vardon	306	John H. Taylor	Prestwick, Scotland
1915–19	No tournament			
1920	George Duncan	303	Alexander Herd	Deal, England
1921	Jock Hutchison* (150)	296	Roger Wethered (159)	St. Andrews, Scotland
1922	Walter Hagen	300	George Duncan	Royal St. George's, England
			Jim Barnes	
1923	Arthur G. Havers	295	Walter Hagen	Troon, Scotland
1924	Walter Hagen	301	Ernest Whitcombe	Hoylake, England
1925	Jim Barnes	300	Archie Compston	Prestwick, Scotland
			Ted Ray	
1926	Bobby Jones	291	Al Watrous	Royal Lytham & St. Anne's, England
1927	Bobby Jones	285	Aubrey Boomer	St. Andrews, Scotland
1928	Walter Hagen	292	Gene Sarazen	Royal St. George's, England
1929	Walter Hagen	292	Johnny Farrell	Muirfield, Scotland
1930	Bobby Jones	291	Macdonald Smith	Hoylake, England
			Leo Diegel	
1931	Tommy Armour	296	Jose Jurado	Carnoustie, Scotland
1932	Gene Sarazen	283	Macdonald Smith	Prince's, England
1933	Denny Shute* (149)	292	Craig Wood (154)	St. Andrews, Scotland
1934	Henry Cotton	283	Sidney F. Brews	Royal St. George's, England
1935	Alfred Perry	283	Alfred Padgham	Muirfield, Scotland
1936	Alfred Padgham	287	James Adams	Hoylake, England
1937	Henry Cotton	290	Reginald A. Whitcombe	Carnoustie, Scotland
1938	Reginald A. Whitcombe	295	James Adams	Royal St. George's, England
1939	Richard Burton	290	Johnny Bulla	St. Andrews, Scotland
1940–45	No tournament			
1946	Sam Snead	290	Bobby Locke	St. Andrews, Scotland
			Johnny Bulla	
1947	Fred Daly	293	Reginald W. Horne	Hoylake, England
			Frank Stranahan	
1948	Henry Cotton	294	Fred Daly	Muirfield, Scotland
1949	Bobby Locke* (135)	283	Harry Bradshaw (147)	Royal St. George's, England
1950	Bobby Locke	279	Roberto DeVicenzo	Troon, Scotland
1951	Max Faulkner	285	Tony Cerda	Portrush, Ireland
1952	Bobby Locke	287	Peter Thomson	Royal Lytham & St. Anne's, England
1953	Ben Hogan	282	Frank Stranahan	Carnoustie, Scotland
			Dai Rees	
			Peter Thomson	
			Tony Cerda	
1954	Peter Thomson	283	Sidney S. Scott	Royal Birkdale, England
			Dai Rees	
			Bobby Locke	
1955	Peter Thomson	281	John Fallon	St. Andrews, Scotland
1956	Peter Thomson	286	Flory Van Donck	Hoylake, England
1957	Bobby Locke	279	Peter Thomson	St. Andrews, Scotland
1958	Peter Thomson* (139)	278	Dave Thomas (143)	Royal Lytham & St. Anne's, England
1959	Gary Player	284	Flory Van Donck	Muirfield, Scotland
1960	Kel Nagle	278	Arnold Palmer	St. Andrews, Scotland

British Open (Cont.)

Year	Winner	Score	Runner-Up	Site
1961	Arnold Palmer	284	Dai Rees	Royal Birkdale, England
1962	Arnold Palmer	276	Kel Nagle	Troon, Scotland
1963	Bob Charles* (140)	277	Phil Rodgers (148)	Royal Lytham & St. Anne's, England
1964	Tony Lema	279	Jack Nicklaus	St. Andrews, Scotland
1965	Peter Thomson	285	Brian Huggett Christy O'Connor	Southport, England
1966	Jack Nicklaus	282	Doug Sanders Dave Thomas	Muirfield, Scotland
1967	Robert DeVicenzo	278	Jack Nicklaus	Hoylake, England
1968	Gary Player	289	Jack Nicklaus Bob Charles	Carnoustie, Scotland
1969	Tony Jacklin	280	Bob Charles	Royal Lytham & St. Anne's, England
1970	Jack Nicklaus* (72)	283	Doug Sanders (73)	St. Andrews, Scotland
1971	Lee Trevino	278	Lu Liang Huan	Royal Birkdale, England
1972	Lee Trevino	278	Jack Nicklaus	Muirfield, Scotland
1973	Tom Weiskopf	276	Johnny Miller	Troon, Scotland
1974	Gary Player	282	Peter Oosterhuis	Royal Lytham & St. Anne's, England
1975	Tom Watson* (71)	279	Jack Newton (72)	Carnoustie, Scotland
1976	Johnny Miller	279	Jack Nicklaus Seve Ballesteros	Royal Birkdale, England
1977	Tom Watson	268	Jack Nicklaus	Turnberry, Scotland
1978	Jack Nicklaus	281	Ben Crenshaw Tom Kite Ray Floyd Simon Owen	St. Andrews, Scotland
1979	Seve Ballesteros	283	Ben Crenshaw Jack Nicklaus	Royal Lytham & St. Anne's, England
1980	Tom Watson	271	Lee Trevino	Muirfield, Scotland
1981	Bill Rogers	276	Bernhard Langer	Royal St. George's, England
1982	Tom Watson	284	Nick Price Peter Oosterhuis	Troon, Scotland
1983	Tom Watson	275	Andy Bean	Royal Birkdale, England
1984	Seve Ballesteros	276	Tom Watson Bernhard Langer	St. Andrews, Scotland
1985	Sandy Lyle	282	Payne Stewart	Royal St. George's, England
1986	Greg Norman	280	Gordon Brand	Turnberry, Scotland
1987	Nick Faldo	279	Paul Azinger Rodger Davis	Muirfield, Scotland
1988	Seve Ballesteros	273	Nick Price	Royal Lytham & St. Anne's, England
1989††	Mark Calcavecchia* (4-3-3-3)	275	Wayne Grady (4-4-4-4) Greg Norman (3-3-4-x)	Troon, Scotland
1990	Nick Faldo	270	Payne Stewart Mark McNulty	St. Andrews, Scotland
1991	Ian Baker-Finch	272	Mike Harwood	Royal Birkdale, England
1992	Nick Faldo	272	John Cook	Muirfield, Scotland
1993	Greg Norman	267	Nick Faldo	Royal St. George's, England
1994	Nick Price	268	Jesper Parnevik	Turnberry, Scotland
1995	John Daly* (4-3-4-4)	282	C. Rocca (5-4-7-3)	St. Andrews, Scotland
1996	Tom Lehman	271	Mark McCumber Ernie Els	Royal Lytham & St. Anne's, England
1997	Justin Leonard	272	Jesper Parnevik Darren Clarke	Troon, Scotland
1998	Mark O'Meara* (4-4-5-4)	280	Brian Watts (5-4-5-5)	Southport, England
1999	Paul Lawrie* (5-4-3-3)	290	Jean Van de Velde (6-4-3-5) Justin Leonard (5-4-4-5)	Carnoustie GC, Carnoustie, Scotland
2000	Tiger Woods	269	Thomas Bjorn Ernie Els	St. Andrews, Scotland

*Winner in playoff. Playoff scores are in parentheses. †The first event was open only to professional golfers.
‡The second annual open was open to amateurs and pros. #Tied, but refused playoff.
**Championship extended from 36 to 72 holes. ††Playoff cut from 18 holes to 4 holes.

PGA Championship

Year	Winner	Score	Runner-Up	Site
1916	Jim Barnes	1 up	Jock Hutchison	Siwanoy CC, Bronxville, NY
1917–18	No tournament			
1919	Jim Barnes	6 & 5	Fred McLeod	Engineers CC, Roslyn, NY
1920	Jock Hutchison	1 up	J. Douglas Edgar	Flossmoor CC, Flossmoor, IL
1921	Walter Hagen	3 & 2	Jim Barnes	Inwood CC, Far Rockaway, NY
1922	Gene Sarazen	4 & 3	Emmet French	Oakmont CC, Oakmont, PA
1923	Gene Sarazen	1 up	Walter Hagen	Pelham CC, Pelham, NY
		38 holes		
1924	Walter Hagen	2 up	Jim Barnes	French Lick CC, French Lick, IN
1925	Walter Hagen	6 & 5	William Mehlhorn	Olympia Fields CC, Olympia Fields, IL
1926	Walter Hagen	5 & 3	Leo Diegel	Salisbury GC, Westbury, NY
1927	Walter Hagen	1 up	Joe Turnesa	Cedar Crest CC, Dallas
1928	Leo Diegel	6 & 5	Al Espinosa	Five Farms CC, Baltimore
1929	Leo Diegel	6 & 4	Johnny Farrell	Hillcrest CC, Los Angeles
1930	Tommy Armour	1 up	Gene Sarazen	Fresh Meadow CC, Flushing, NY
1931	Tom Creavy	2 & 1	Denny Shute	Wannamoisett CC, Rumford, RI
1932	Olin Dutra	4 & 3	Frank Walsh	Keller GC, St. Paul
1933	Gene Sarazen	5 & 4	Willie Goggin	Blue Mound CC, Milwaukee
1934	Paul Runyan	1 up	Craig Wood	Park CC, Williamsville, NY
1935	Johnny Revolta	5 & 4	Tommy Armour	Twin Hills CC, Oklahoma City
		38 holes		
1936	Denny Shute	3 & 2	Jimmy Thomson	Pinehurst CC, Pinehurst, NC
1937	Denny Shute	1 up	Harold McSpaden	Pittsburgh FC, Aspinwall, PA
		37 holes		
1938	Paul Runyan	8 & 7	Sam Snead	Shawnee CC, Shawnee-on-Delaware, PA
1939	Henry Picard	1 up	Byron Nelson	Pomonok CC, Flushing, NY
		37 holes		
1940	Byron Nelson	1 up	Sam Snead	Hershey CC, Hershey, PA
1941	Vic Ghezzi	1 up	Byron Nelson	Cherry Hills CC, Denver
		38 holes		
1942	Sam Snead	2 & 1	Jim Turnesa	Seaview CC, Atlantic City
1943	No tournament			
1944	Bob Hamilton	1 up	Byron Nelson	Manito G & CC, Spokane, WA
1945	Byron Nelson	4 & 3	Sam Byrd	Morraine CC, Dayton
1946	Ben Hogan	6 & 4	Ed Oliver	Portland GC, Portland, OR
1947	Jim Ferrier	2 & 1	Chick Harbert	Plum Hollow CC, Detroit
1948	Ben Hogan	7 & 6	Mike Turnesa	Norwood Hills CC, St. Louis
1949	Sam Snead	3 & 2	Johnny Palmer	Hermitage CC, Richmond
1950	Chandler Harper	4 & 3	Henry Williams Jr	Scioto CC, Columbus, OH
1951	Sam Snead	7 & 6	Walter Burkemo	Oakmont CC, Oakmont, PA
1952	Jim Turnesa	1 up	Chick Harbert	Big Spring CC, Louisville
1953	Walter Burkemo	2 & 1	Felice Torza	Birmingham CC, Birmingham, MI
1954	Chick Harbert	4 & 3	Walter Burkemo	Keller GC, St. Paul
1955	Doug Ford	4 & 3	Cary Middlecoff	Meadowbrook CC, Detroit
1956	Jack Burke	3 & 2	Ted Kroll	Blue Hill CC, Boston
1957	Lionel Hebert	2 & 1	Dow Finsterwald	Miami Valley CC, Dayton
1958	Dow Finsterwald	276	Billy Casper	Llanerch CC, Havertown, PA
1959	Bob Rosburg	277	Jerry Barber	Minneapolis GC, St. Louis Park, MN
			Doug Sanders	
1960	Jay Hebert	281	Jim Ferrier	Firestone CC, Akron
1961	Jerry Barber* (67)	277	Don January (68)	Olympia Fields CC, Olympia Fields, IL
1962	Gary Player	278	Bob Goalby	Aronimink GC, Newton Square, PA
1963	Jack Nicklaus	279	Dave Ragan Jr	Dallas Athletic Club, Dallas
1964	Bobby Nichols	271	Jack Nicklaus	Columbus CC, Columbus, OH
			Arnold Palmer	
1965	Dave Marr	280	Billy Casper	Laurel Valley CC, Ligonier, PA
			Jack Nicklaus	
1966	Al Geiberger	280	Dudley Wysong	Firestone CC, Akron
1967	Don January* (69)	281	Don Massengale (71)	Columbine CC, Littleton, CO
1968	Julius Boros	281	Bob Charles	Pecan Valley CC, San Antonio
			Arnold Palmer	
1969	Ray Floyd	276	Gary Player	NCR CC, Dayton
1970	Dave Stockton	279	Arnold Palmer	Southern Hills CC, Tulsa
			Bob Murphy	

PGA Championship (Cont.)

Year	Winner	Score	Runner-Up	Site
1971	Jack Nicklaus	281	Billy Casper	PGA Nat'l GC, Palm Beach Gardens, FL
1972	Gary Player	281	Tommy Aaron	Oakland Hills CC, Birmingham, MI
			Jim Jamieson	
1973	Jack Nicklaus	277	Bruce Crampton	Canterbury GC, Cleveland
1974	Lee Trevino	276	Jack Nicklaus	Tanglewood GC, Winston-Salem, NC
1975	Jack Nicklaus	276	Bruce Crampton	Firestone CC, Akron
1976	Dave Stockton	281	Ray Floyd	Congressional CC, Bethesda, MD
			Don January	
1977†	Lanny Wadkins* (4-4-4)	282	Gene Littler (4-4-5)	Pebble Beach GL, Pebble Beach, CA
1978	John Mahaffey* (4–3)	276	Jerry Pate (4–4)	Oakmont CC, Oakmont, PA
			Tom Watson (4–5)	
1979	David Graham* (4-4-2)	272	Ben Crenshaw (4-4-4)	Oakland Hills CC, Birmingham, MI
1980	Jack Nicklaus	274	Andy Bean	Oak Hill CC, Rochester, NY
1981	Larry Nelson	273	Fuzzy Zoeller	Atlanta Athletic Club, Duluth, GA
1982	Raymond Floyd	272	Lanny Wadkins	Southern Hills CC, Tulsa
1983	Hal Sutton	274	Jack Nicklaus	Riviera CC, Pacific Palisades, CA
1984	Lee Trevino	273	Gary Player	Shoal Creek, Birmingham, AL
			Lanny Wadkins	
1985	Hubert Green	278	Lee Trevino	Cherry Hills CC, Denver
1986	Bob Tway	276	Greg Norman	Inverness CC, Toledo
1987	Larry Nelson* (4)	287	Lanny Wadkins (5)	PGA Natl GC, Palm Beach Gardens, FL
1988	Jeff Sluman	272	Paul Azinger	Oak Tree GC, Edmond, OK
1989	Payne Stewart	276	Mike Reid	Kemper Lakes GC, Hawthorn Woods, IL
1990	Wayne Grady	282	Fred Couples	Shoal Creek, Birmingham, AL
1991	John Daly	276	Bruce Lietzke	Crooked Stick GC, Carmel, IN
1992	Nick Price	278	Jim Gallagher Jr	Bellerive CC, St. Louis
1993	Paul Azinger* (4–4)	272	Greg Norman (4–5)	Inverness CC, Toledo
1994	Nick Price	269	Corey Pavin	Southern Hills CC, Tulsa
1995	Steve Elkington* (3)	267	Colin Montgomerie (4)	Riviera CC, Pacific Palisades, CA
1996	Mark Brooks* (3)	277	Kenny Perry (x)	Valhalla GC, Louisville
1997	Davis Love III	269	Justin Leonard	Winged Foot GC, Mamaroneck, NY
1998	Vijay Singh	271	Steve Stricker	Sahalee CC, Redmond, WA
1999	Tiger Woods	277	Sergio Garcia	Medinah CC, Medinah, IL
2000	Tiger Woods* (3-4-5)	270	Bob May (4-4-x)	Valhalla GC, Louisville

*Winner in playoff. Playoff scores are in parentheses. †Playoff changed from 18 holes to sudden death.

Alltime Major Championship Winners

	Masters	U.S. Open	British Open	PGA Champ.	U.S. Amateur	British Amateur	Total
†Jack Nicklaus	6	4	3	5	2	0	20
Bobby Jones	0	4	3	0	5	1	13
Walter Hagen	0	2	4	5	0	0	11
Ben Hogan	2	4	1	2	0	0	9
†Gary Player	3	1	3	2	0	0	9
John Ball	0	0	1	0	0	8	9
†Arnold Palmer	4	1	2	0	1	0	8
†Tom Watson	2	1	5	0	0	0	8
Harold Hilton	0	0	2	0	1	4	7
Gene Sarazen	1	2	1	3	0	0	7
Sam Snead	3	0	1	3	0	0	7
Harry Vardon	0	1	6	0	0	0	7

*Active PGA player. †Active Senior PGA player.

Alltime Multiple Professional Major Winners

MASTERS		U.S. OPEN (Cont.)		BRITISH OPEN (Cont.)		PGA CHAMPIONSHIP	
Jack Nicklaus	6	Hale Irwin	3	Tom Watson	5	Walter Hagen	5
Arnold Palmer	4	Julius Boros	2	Walter Hagen	4	Jack Nicklaus	5
Jimmy Demaret	3	Billy Casper	2	Bobby Locke	4	Gene Sarazen	3
Nick Faldo	3	Ernie Els	2	Tom Morris Sr	4	Sam Snead	3
Gary Player	3	Ralph Guldahl	2	Tom Morris Jr	4	Jim Barnes	2
Sam Snead	3	Walter Hagen	2	Willie Park	4	Leo Diegel	2
Seve Ballesteros	2	Lee Janzen	2	Jamie Anderson	3	Raymond Floyd	2
Ben Crenshaw	2	John McDermott	2	Seve Ballesteros	3	Ben Hogan	2
Ben Hogan	2	Cary Middlecoff	2	Henry Cotton	3	Byron Nelson	2
Bernhard Langer	2	Andy North	2	Nick Faldo	3	Larry Nelson	2
Byron Nelson	2	Gene Sarazen	2	Robert Ferguson	3	Gary Player	2
José María Olazábal	2	Alex Smith	2	Bobby Jones	3	Paul Runyan	2
Horton Smith	2	Payne Stewart	2	Jack Nicklaus	3	Denny Shute	2
Tom Watson	2	Curtis Strange	2	Gary Player	3	Dave Stockton	2
		Lee Trevino	2	Harold Hilton	2	Lee Trevino	2
U.S. OPEN				Bob Martin	2	Tiger Woods	2
				Greg Norman	2		
Willie Anderson	4	**BRITISH OPEN**		Arnold Palmer	2		
Ben Hogan	4			Willie Park Jr	2		
Bobby Jones	4	Harry Vardon	6	Lee Trevino	2		
Jack Nicklaus	4	James Braid	5				
		J.H. Taylor	5				
		Peter Thomson	5				

THE PGA TOUR

Most Career Wins

	Wins		Wins		Wins
Sam Snead	81	Billy Casper	51	Tom Watson	34
Jack Nicklaus	70	Walter Hagen	40	Horton Smith	32
Ben Hogan	63	Cary Middlecoff	40	Harry Cooper	31
Arnold Palmer	60	Gene Sarazen	38	Jimmy Demaret	31
Byron Nelson	52	Lloyd Mangrum	36	Leo Diegel	30

Season Money Leaders

Year	Player	Earnings ($)	Year	Player	Earnings ($)	Year	Player	Earnings ($)
1934	Paul Runyan	6,767.00	1956	Ted Kroll	72,835.83	1978	Tom Watson	362,428.93
1935	Johnny Revolta	9,543.00	1957	Dick Mayer	65,835.00	1979	Tom Watson	462,636.00
1936	Horton Smith	7,682.00	1958	Arnold Palmer	42,607.50	1980	Tom Watson	530,808.33
1937	Harry Cooper	14,138.69	1959	Art Wall	53,167.60	1981	Tom Kite	375,698.84
1938	Sam Snead	19,534.49	1960	Arnold Palmer	75,262.85	1982	Craig Stadler	446,462.00
1939	Henry Picard	10,303.00	1961	Gary Player	64,540.45	1983	Hal Sutton	426,668.00
1940	Ben Hogan	10,655.00	1962	Arnold Palmer	81,448.33	1984	Tom Watson	476,260.00
1941	Ben Hogan	18,358.00	1963	Arnold Palmer	128,230.00	1985	Curtis Strange	542,321.00
1942	Ben Hogan	13,143.00	1964	Jack Nicklaus	113,284.50	1986	Greg Norman	653,296.00
1943	No statistics compiled		1965	Jack Nicklaus	140,752.14	1987	Curtis Strange	925,941.00
1944	Byron Nelson*	37,967.69	1966	Billy Casper	121,944.92	1988	Curtis Strange	1,147,644.00
1945	Byron Nelson*	63,335.66	1967	Jack Nicklaus	188,998.08	1989	Tom Kite	1,395,278.00
1946	Ben Hogan	42,556.16	1968	Billy Casper	205,168.67	1990	Greg Norman	1,165,477.00
1947	Jimmy Demaret	27,936.83	1969	Frank Beard	164,707.11	1991	Corey Pavin	979,430.00
1948	Ben Hogan	32,112.00	1970	Lee Trevino	157,037.63	1992	Fred Couples	1,344,188.00
1949	Sam Snead	31,593.83	1971	Jack Nicklaus	244,490.50	1993	Nick Price	1,478,557.00
1950	Sam Snead	35,758.83	1972	Jack Nicklaus	320,542.26	1994	Nick Price	1,499,927.00
1951	Lloyd Mangrum	26,088.83	1973	Jack Nicklaus	308,362.10	1995	Greg Norman	1,654,959.00
1952	Julius Boros	37,032.97	1974	Johnny Miller	353,021.59	1996	Tom Lehman	1,780,159.00
1953	Lew Worsham	34,002.00	1975	Jack Nicklaus	298,149.17	1997	Tiger Woods	2,066,833.00
1954	Bob Toski	65,819.81	1976	Jack Nicklaus	266,438.57	1998	David Duval	2,591,031.00
1955	Julius Boros	63,121.55	1977	Tom Watson	310,653.16	1999	Tiger Woods	6,616,585.00

* War bonds. Note: Total money listed from 1968 through 1974. Official money listed from 1975 on.

Career Money Leaders*

	Earnings ($)			Earnings ($)			Earnings ($)
1.	Tiger Woods 19,601,950		18.	Ernie Els...................9,418,512		35.	Ben Crenshaw 7,083,396
2.	Davis Love III 14,619,961		19.	Loren Roberts 9,199,413		36.	David Frost 6,981,405
3.	Greg Norman........13,087,832		20.	Corey Pavin 9,077,769		37.	Fred Funk.................6,941,347
4.	Nick Price 12,771,503		21.	Jim Furyk 8,953,859		38.	Jesper Parnevik 6,646,762
5.	Phil Mickelson.......12,534,115		22.	Justin Leonard 8,944,857		39.	Andrew Magee 6,598,634
6.	David Duval 12,330,792		23.	Jeff Sluman 8,685,833		40.	Billy Mayfair 6,540,879
7.	Fred Couples 12,254,484		24.	Jeff Maggert 8,485,614		41.	Bruce Lietzke..........6,465,954
8.	Hal Sutton 12,077,000		25.	Steve Elkington 8,343,073		42.	Larry Mize................6,414,397
9.	Payne Stewart 11,737,008		26.	John Cook...............8,340,099		43.	Lanny Wadkins 6,355,681
10.	Scott Hoch 11,605,057		27.	Craig Stadler...........8,306,811		44.	Mark Brooks............6,255,578
11.	Mark O'Meara 11,586,578		28.	John Huston............8,245,277		45.	Chip Beck 6,199,550
12.	Mark Calcavecchia 11,184,440		29.	Lee Janzen 8,001,633		46.	Chris Perry 6,029,013
13.	Tom Kite................10,654,707		30.	Jay Haas.................7,857,693		47.	Hale Irwin................5,952,866
14.	Vijay Singh 10,497,157		31.	Brad Faxon 7,626,867		48.	Bill Glasson.............5,924,725
15.	Tom Lehman 10,082,736		32.	Curtis Strange 7,435,112		49.	Scott Simpson 5,838,933
16.	Paul Azinger 9,975,501		33.	Bob Tway.................7,187,390		50.	Kirk Triplett..............5,831,888
17.	Tom Watson.............9,583,681		34.	Steve Pate...............7,115,809			

*Through 10/15/00.

Year by Year Statistical Leaders

SCORING AVERAGE

1980	Lee Trevino	69.73
1981	Tom Kite	69.80
1982	Tom Kite	70.21
1983	Raymond Floyd	70.61
1984	Calvin Peete	70.56
1985	Don Pooley	70.36
1986	Scott Hoch	70.08
1987	David Frost	70.09
1988	Greg Norman	69.38
1989	Payne Stewart	69.485†
1990	Greg Norman	69.10
1991	Fred Couples	69.59
1992	Fred Couples	69.38
1993	Greg Norman	68.90
1994	Greg Norman	68.81
1995	Greg Norman	69.06
1996	Tom Lehman	69.32
1997	Nick Price	68.98
1998	David Duval	69.13
1999	Tiger Woods	68.43

Note: Scoring average per round, with adjustments made at each round for the field's course scoring average.

DRIVING DISTANCE

		Yds
1980	Dan Pohl	274.3
1981	Dan Pohl	280.1
1982	Bill Calfee	275.3
1983	John McComish	277.4
1984	Bill Glasson	276.5
1985	Andy Bean	278.2
1986	Davis Love III	285.7
1987	John McComish	283.9
1988	Steve Thomas	284.6
1989	Ed Humenik	280.9
1990	Tom Purtzer	279.6
1991	John Daly	288.9

DRIVING DISTANCE (Cont.)

1992	John Daly	283.4
1993	John Daly	288.9
1994	Davis Love III	283.8
1995	John Daly	289.0
1996	John Daly	288.8
1997	John Daly	302.0
1998	John Daly	299.4
1999	John Daly	305.6

Note: Average computed by charting distance of two tee shots on a predetermined par-four or par-five hole (one on front nine, one on back nine).

DRIVING ACCURACY

1980	Mike Reid	79.5
1981	Calvin Peete	81.9
1982	Calvin Peete	84.6
1983	Calvin Peete	81.3
1984	Calvin Peete	77.5
1985	Calvin Peete	80.6
1986	Calvin Peete	81.7
1987	Calvin Peete	83.0
1988	Calvin Peete	82.5
1989	Calvin Peete	82.6
1990	Calvin Peete	83.7
1991	Hale Irwin	78.3
1992	Doug Tewell	82.3
1993	Doug Tewell	82.5
1994	David Edwards	81.6
1995	Fred Funk	81.3
1996	Fred Funk	78.7
1997	Allen Doyle	80.8
1998	Bruce Fleisher	81.4
1999	Fred Funk	80.2

Note: Percentage of fairways hit on number of par-four and par-five holes played; par-three holes excluded.

GREENS IN REGULATION

1980	Jack Nicklaus	72.1
1981	Calvin Peete	73.1
1982	Calvin Peete	72.4
1983	Calvin Peete	71.4
1984	Andy Bean	72.1
1985	John Mahaffey	71.9
1986	John Mahaffey	72.0
1987	Gil Morgan	73.3
1988	John Adams	73.9
1989	Bruce Lietzke	72.6
1990	Doug Tewell	70.9
1991	Bruce Lietzke	73.3
1992	Tim Simpson	74.0
1993	Fuzzy Zoeller	73.6
1994	Bill Glasson	73.0
1995	Lenny Clements	72.3
1996	Fred Couples	71.8
	Mark O'Meara	71.8
1997	Tom Lehman	72.7
1998	Hal Sutton	71.3
1999	Tiger Woods	71.4

Note: Average of greens reached in regulation out of total holes played; hole is considered hit in regulation if any part of the ball rests on the putting surface in two shots less than the hole's par—a par-5 hit in two shots is one green in regulation.

PUTTING

1980	Jerry Pate	28.81
1981	Alan Tapie	28.70
1982	Ben Crenshaw	28.65
1983	Morris Hatalsky	27.96
1984	Gary McCord	28.57
1985	Craig Stadler	28.627†
1986	Greg Norman	1.736
1987	Ben Crenshaw	1.743
1988	Don Pooley	1.729

† Number had to be carried to extra decimal place to determine winner.

Year by Year Statistical Leaders *(Cont.)*

PUTTING *(Cont.)*

1989	Steve Jones	1.734	1993	David Frost	1.739	1997	Don Pooley	1.718
1990	Larry Rinker	1.7467†	1994	Loren Roberts	1.737	1998	Rick Fehr	1.722
1991	Jay Don Blake	1.7326†	1995	Jim Furyk	1.708	1999	Brad Faxon	1.723
1992	Mark O'Meara	1.731	1996	Brad Faxon	1.709			

Note: Average number of putts taken on greens reached in regulation; prior to 1986, based on average number of putts per 18 holes.

ALL-AROUND

1987	Dan Pohl	170	1992	Fred Couples	256	1997	Bill Glasson	282
1988	Payne Stewart	170	1993	Gil Morgan	252	1998	John Huston	151
1989	Paul Azinger	250	1994	Bob Estes	227	1999	Tiger Woods	120
1990	Paul Azinger	162	1995	Justin Leonard	323			
1991	Scott Hoch	283	1996	Fred Couples	214			

Note: Sum of the places of standing from the other seven statistical categories; the player with the number closest to zero leads.

SAND SAVES

1980	Bob Eastwood	65.4	1987	Paul Azinger	63.2	1994	Corey Pavin	65.4
1981	Tom Watson	60.1	1988	Greg Powers	63.5	1995	Billy Mayfair	68.6
1982	Isao Aoki	60.2	1989	Mike Sullivan	66.0	1996	Gary Rusnak	64.0
1983	Isao Aoki	62.3	1990	Paul Azinger	67.2	1997	Bob Estes	70.3
1984	Peter Oosterhuis	64.7	1991	Ben Crenshaw	64.9	1998	Keith Fergus	71.0
1985	Tom Purtzer	60.8	1992	Mitch Adcock	66.9	1999	Jeff Sluman	67.3
1986	Paul Azinger	63.8	1993	Ken Green	64.4			

Note: Percentage of up-and-down efforts from greenside sand traps only—fairway bunkers excluded.

PAR BREAKERS

1980	Tom Watson	.213	1984	Craig Stadler	.220	1988	Ken Green	.236
1981	Bruce Lietzke	.225	1985	Craig Stadler	.218	1989	Greg Norman	.224
1982	Tom Kite	.2154†	1986	Greg Norman	.248	1990	Greg Norman	.219
1983	Tom Watson	.211	1987	Mark Calcavecchia	.221			

Note: Average based on total birdies and eagles scored out of total holes played. Discontinued as an official category after 1990.

EAGLES

1980	Dave Eichelberger	16	1986	Joey Sindelar	16	1993	Davis Love III	15
1981	Bruce Lietzke	12	1987	Phil Blackmar	20	1994	Davis Love III	18
1982	Tom Weiskopf	10	1988	Ken Green	21	1995	Kelly Gibson	16
	J.C. Snead	10	1989	Lon Hinkle	14	1996	Tom Watson	97.2
	Andy Bean	10		Duffy Waldorf	14	1997	Tiger Woods	104.1
1983	Chip Beck	15	1990	Paul Azinger	14	1998	Davis Love III	83.3
1984	Gary Hallberg	15	1991	Andy Bean	15	1999	Vijay Singh	104.8
1985	Larry Rinker	14	1992	Dan Forsman	18			

Note: Total of eagles scored 1980–1995. Since 1996 winner determined by number of holes played per eagle.

BIRDIES

1980	Andy Bean	388	1987	Dan Forsman	409	1994	Brad Bryant	397
1981	Vance Heafner	388	1988	Dan Forsman	465	1995	Steve Lowery	410
1982	Andy Bean	392	1989	Ted Schulz	415	1996	Fred Couples	4.20
1983	Hal Sutton	399	1990	Mike Donald	401	1997	Tiger Woods	4.25
1984	Mark O'Meara	419	1991	Scott Hoch	446	1998	David Duval	4.29
1985	Joey Sindelar	411	1992	Jeff Sluman	417	1999	Tiger Woods	4.46
1986	Joey Sindelar	415	1993	John Huston	426			

Note: Total of birdies scored 1980–95. Since 1996, winner determined by average number of birdies per round.

PGA Player of the Year Award

1948	Ben Hogan	1966	Billy Casper	1984	Tom Watson
1949	Sam Snead	1967	Jack Nicklaus	1985	Lanny Wadkins
1950	Ben Hogan	1968	Not awarded	1986	Bob Tway
1951	Ben Hogan	1969	Orville Moody	1987	Paul Azinger
1952	Julius Boros	1970	Billy Casper	1988	Curtis Strange
1953	Ben Hogan	1971	Lee Trevino	1989	Tom Kite
1954	Ed Furgol	1972	Jack Nicklaus	1990	Wayne Levi
1955	Doug Ford	1973	Jack Nicklaus	1991	Fred Couples
1956	Jack Burke	1974	Johnny Miller	1992	Fred Couples
1957	Dick Mayer	1975	Jack Nicklaus	1993	Nick Price
1958	Dow Finsterwald	1976	Jack Nicklaus	1994	Nick Price
1959	Art Wall	1977	Tom Watson	1995	Greg Norman
1960	Arnold Palmer	1978	Tom Watson	1996	Tom Lehman
1961	Jerry Barber	1979	Tom Watson	1997	Tiger Woods
1962	Arnold Palmer	1980	Tom Watson	1998	David Duval
1963	Julius Boros	1981	Bill Rogers	1999	Tiger Woods
1964	Ken Venturi	1982	Tom Watson		
1965	Dave Marr	1983	Hal Sutton		

Vardon Trophy: Scoring Average

Year	Winner	Avg	Year	Winner	Avg	Year	Winner	Avg
1937	Harry Cooper	*500	1961	Arnold Palmer	69.85	1981	Tom Kite	69.80
1938	Sam Snead	520	1962	Arnold Palmer	70.27	1982	Tom Kite	70.21
1939	Byron Nelson	473	1963	Billy Casper	70.58	1983	Raymond Floyd	70.61
1940	Ben Hogan	423	1964	Arnold Palmer	70.01	1984	Calvin Peete	70.56
1941	Ben Hogan	494	1965	Billy Casper	70.85	1985	Don Pooley	70.36
1942–46	No award		1966	Billy Casper	70.27	1986	Scott Hoch	70.08
1947	Jimmy Demaret	69.90	1967	Arnold Palmer	70.18	1987	Don Pohl	70.25
1948	Ben Hogan	69.30	1968	Billy Casper	69.82	1988	Chip Beck	69.46
1949	Sam Snead	69.37	1969	Dave Hill	70.34	1989	Greg Norman	69.49
1950	Sam Snead	69.23	1970	Lee Trevino	70.64	1990	Greg Norman	69.10
1951	Lloyd Mangrum	70.05	1971	Lee Trevino	70.27	1991	Fred Couples	69.59
1952	Jack Burke	70.54	1972	Lee Trevino	70.89	1992	Fred Couples	69.38
1953	Lloyd Mangrum	70.22	1973	Bruce Crampton	70.57	1993	Nick Price	69.11
1954	E.J. Harrison	70.41	1974	Lee Trevino	70.53	1994	Greg Norman	68.81
1955	Sam Snead	69.86	1975	Bruce Crampton	70.51	1995	Steve Elkington	69.62
1956	Cary Middlecoff	70.35	1976	Don January	70.56	1996	Tom Lehman	69.32
1957	Dow Finsterwald	70.30	1977	Tom Watson	70.32	1997	Nick Price	68.98
1958	Bob Rosburg	70.11	1978	Tom Watson	70.16	1998	David Duval	69.13
1959	Art Wall	70.35	1979	Tom Watson	70.27	1999	Tiger Woods	68.43
1960	Billy Casper	69.95	1980	Lee Trevino	69.73			

*Point system used, 1937–41.
Note: As of 1988, based on minimum of 60 rounds per year. Adjusted for average score of field in tournaments entered.

Alltime PGA Tour Records*

Scoring

90 HOLES

325—(67-67-64-65-62) by Tom Kite, at four courses, Indian Hills, CA, in winning the 1993 Bob Hope Classic (35 under par).

72 HOLES

257—(60-68-64-65) by Mike Souchak, at Brackenridge Park GC, San Antonio, to win 1955 Texas Open (27 under par).

260—(63-65-66-66) by John Huston, at Waialae CC, Honolulu, at the 1998 Hawaiian Open (28 under par).

54 HOLES, OPENING ROUNDS

189—(64-62-63) by John Cook, at the TPC at Southwind, Memphis, en route to winning the 1996 St. Jude Classic.

54 HOLES, CONSECUTIVE ROUNDS

189—(63-63-63) by Chandler Harper in the last three rounds to win the 1954 Texas Open at Brackenridge Park GC, San Antonio.

189—(64-62-63) by John Cook, at the TPC at Southwind, Memphis, in the first three rounds of the 1996 St. Jude Classic.

Alltime PGA Tour Records (Cont.)*

Scoring (Cont.)

36 HOLES, OPENING ROUNDS

125—(64–61) by Tiger Woods, in the 2000 World Golf Championships/ NEC Invitational, which he won, at Firestone CC, Akron.

36 HOLES, CONSECUTIVE ROUNDS

125—(64–61) by Gay Brewer in the middle rounds of the 1967 Pensacola Open, which he won, at Pensacola CC, Pensacola, FL.

125—(63–62) by Ron Streck in the last two rounds to win the 1978 Texas Open at Oak Hills CC, San Antonio.

125—(62–63) by Blaine McCallister in the middle two rounds of the 1988 Hardee's Golf Classic, which he won at Oakwood CC, Coal Valley, IL.

125—(62–63) by John Cook, in the middle two rounds of the 1996 St. Jude Classic, which he won at the TPC at Southwind, Memphis.

125—(62–63) by John Cook, in the fourth and fifth rounds in winning the 1997 Bob Hope Chrysler Classic at Indian Wells CC, Indian Hills, CA.

125—(64–61) by Tiger Woods, in the first two rounds of the 2000 World Golf Championship/ NEC Invitational, which he won at Firestone CC, Akron.

18 HOLES

59—by Al Geiberger, at Colonial Country Club, Memphis, in second round in winning the 1977 Memphis Classic.

59—by Chip Beck, at Sunrise Golf Club, Las Vegas, in third round of the 1991 Las Vegas Invitational.

59—by David Duval on the Palmer Course at PGA West, La Quinta, CA, in the fifth round of the 1999 Bob Hope Chrysler Classic.

9 HOLES

27—by Mike Souchak, at Brackenridge Park GC, San Antonio, on par-35 second nine of first round in the 1955 Texas Open.

27—by Andy North at En-Joie GC, Endicott, NY, on par-34 second nine of first round in the 1975 BC Open.

MOST CONSECUTIVE ROUNDS UNDER 70

19—Byron Nelson in 1945.

MOST BIRDIES IN A ROW

8—Bob Goalby at Pasadena GC, St. Petersburg, FL, during fourth round in winning the 1961 St Petersburg Open.

8—Fuzzy Zoeller, at Oakwood CC, Coal Valley, IL, during first round of 1976 Quad Cities Open.

8—Dewey Arnette, at Warwick Hills GC, Grand Blanc, MI, during first round of the 1987 Buick Open.

8—Edward Fryatt, at the Blue Course of the Doral Resort and Spa, Miami, during second round of the 2000 Doral-Ryder Open.

MOST BIRDIES IN A ROW TO WIN

5—Jack Nicklaus to win 1978 Jackie Gleason Inverrary Classic (last 5 holes).

Wins

MOST CONSECUTIVE YEARS WINNING AT LEAST ONE TOURNAMENT

17—Jack Nicklaus, 1962–78.

17—Arnold Palmer, 1955–71.

16—Billy Casper, 1956–71.

MOST CONSECUTIVE WINS

11—Byron Nelson, from Miami Four Ball, March 8–11, 1945, through Canadian Open, August 2–4, 1945.

MOST WINS IN A SINGLE EVENT

8—Sam Snead, Greater Greensboro Open, 1938, 1946, 1949, 1950, 1955, 1956, 1960, and 1965.

MOST CONSECUTIVE WINS IN A SINGLE EVENT

4—Walter Hagen, PGA Championships, 1924–27.

4—Gene Sarazen, Miami Open, 1926, (schedule change) 1928–30.

MOST WINS IN A CALENDAR YEAR

18—Byron Nelson, 1945

MOST YEARS BETWEEN WINS

15 yrs, 5 mos—Butch Baird, 1961–76.

MOST YEARS FROM FIRST WIN TO LAST

28 yrs, 11 mos, 20 days—Raymond Floyd, 1963–92.

YOUNGEST WINNERS

19 yrs, 10 mos—John McDermott, 1911 U.S. Open.

OLDEST WINNER

52 yrs, 10 mos—Sam Snead, 1965 Greater Greensboro Open.

WIDEST WINNING MARGIN: STROKES

16—Bobby Locke, 1948 Chicago Victory National Championship.

Putting

FEWEST PUTTS, ONE ROUND

18—Andy North, at Kingsmill GC, in second round of 1990 Anheuser Busch Golf Classic.

18—Kenny Knox, at Harbour Town GL, in first round of 1989 MCI Heritage Classic.

18—Mike McGee, at Colonial CC, in first round of 1987 Federal Express St. Jude Classic.

18—Sam Trahan, at Whitemarsh Valley CC, in final round of 1979 IVB Philadelphia Golf Classic.

18—Jim McGovern, at TPC at Southwind, in second round of 1992 Federal Express St. Jude Classic.

FEWEST PUTTS, FOUR ROUNDS

93—Kenny Knox, in 1989 MCI Heritage Classic at Harbour Town GL.

*Through 10/15/00.

THE MAJOR TOURNAMENTS
LPGA Championship

Year	Winner	Score	Runner-Up	Site
1955	Beverly Hanson† (4 & 3)	220	Louise Suggs	Orchard Ridge CC, Ft Wayne, IN
1956	Marlene Hagge*	291	Patty Berg	Forest Lake CC, Detroit
1957	Louise Suggs	285	Wiffi Smith	Churchill Valley CC, Pittsburgh
1958	Mickey Wright	288	Fay Crocker	Churchill Valley CC, Pittsburgh
1959	Betsy Rawls	288	Patty Berg	Sheraton Hotel CC, French Lick, IN
1960	Mickey Wright	292	Louise Suggs	Sheraton Hotel CC, French Lick, IN
1961	Mickey Wright	287	Louise Suggs	Stardust CC, Las Vegas
1962	Judy Kimball	282	Shirley Spork	Stardust CC, Las Vegas
1963	Mickey Wright	294	Mary Lena Faulk Mary Mills Louise Suggs	Stardust CC, Las Vegas
1964	Mary Mills	278	Mickey Wright	Stardust CC, Las Vegas
1965	Sandra Haynie	279	Clifford A. Creed	Stardust CC, Las Vegas
1966	Gloria Ehret	282	Mickey Wright	Stardust CC, Las Vegas
1967	Kathy Whitworth	284	Shirley Englehorn	Pleasant Valley CC, Sutton, MA
1968	Sandra Post* (68)	294	Kathy Whitworth (75)	Pleasant Valley CC, Sutton, MA
1969	Betsy Rawls	293	Susie Berning Carol Mann	Concord GC, Kiameshia Lake, NY
1970	Shirley Englehorn* (74)	285	Kathy Whitworth (78)	Pleasant Valley CC, Sutton, MA
1971	Kathy Whitworth	288	Kathy Ahern	Pleasant Valley CC, Sutton, MA
1972	Kathy Ahern	293	Jane Blalock	Pleasant Valley CC, Sutton, MA
1973	Mary Mills	288	Betty Burfeindt	Pleasant Valley CC, Sutton, MA
1974	Sandra Haynie	288	JoAnne Carner	Pleasant Valley CC, Sutton, MA
1975	Kathy Whitworth	288	Sandra Haynie	Pine Ridge GC, Baltimore
1976	Betty Burfeindt	287	Judy Rankin	Pine Ridge GC, Baltimore
1977	Chako Higuchi	279	Pat Bradley Sandra Post Judy Rankin	Bay Tree Golf Plantation, N Myrtle Beach, SC
1978	Nancy Lopez	275	Amy Alcott	Jack Nicklaus GC, Kings Island, OH
1979	Donna Caponi	279	Jerilyn Britz	Jack Nicklaus GC, Kings Island, OH
1980	Sally Little	285	Jane Blalock	Jack Nicklaus GC, Kings Island, OH
1981	Donna Caponi	280	Jerilyn Britz Pat Meyers	Jack Nicklaus GC, Kings Island, OH
1982	Jan Stephenson	279	JoAnne Carner	Jack Nicklaus GC, Kings Island, OH
1983	Patty Sheehan	279	Sandra Haynie	Jack Nicklaus GC, Kings Island, OH
1984	Patty Sheehan	272	Beth Daniel Pat Bradley	Jack Nicklaus GC, Kings Island, OH
1985	Nancy Lopez	273	Alice Miller	Jack Nicklaus GC, Kings Island, OH
1986	Pat Bradley	277	Patty Sheehan	Jack Nicklaus GC, Kings Island, OH
1987	Jane Geddes	275	Betsy King	Jack Nicklaus GC, Kings Island, OH
1988	Sherri Turner	281	Amy Alcott	Jack Nicklaus GC, Kings Island, OH
1989	Nancy Lopez	274	Ayako Okamoto	Jack Nicklaus GC, Kings Island, OH
1990	Beth Daniel	280	Rosie Jones	Bethesda CC, Bethesda, MD
1991	Meg Mallon	274	Pat Bradley Ayako Okamoto	Bethesda CC, Bethesda, MD
1992	Betsy King	267	Karen Noble	Bethesda CC, Bethesda, MD
1993	Patty Sheehan	275	Lauri Merten	Bethesda CC, Bethesda, MD
1994	Laura Davies	279	Alice Ritzman	DuPont CC, Wilmington, DE
1995	Kelly Robbins	274	Laura Davies	DuPont CC, Wilmington, DE
1996	Laura Davies	213†	Julie Piers	DuPont CC, Wilmington, DE
1997	Chris Johnson*	281	Leta Lindley	DuPont CC, Wilmington, DE
1998	Se Ri Pak	273	Donna Andrews	DuPont CC, Wilmington, DE
1999	Juli Inkster	268	Liselotte Neumann	DuPont CC, Wilmington, DE
2000	Juli Inkster*	281	Stefania Croce	DuPont CC, Wilmington, DE

*Won in playoff. Playoff scores are in parentheses. 1956 and 1997 were sudden death; 1968 and 1970 were 18-hole playoffs. †Won match-play final. #Shortened due to rain.

U.S. Women's Open

Year	Winner	Score	Runner-Up	Site
1946	Patty Berg	5 & 4	Betty Jameson	Spokane CC, Spokane, WA
1947	Betty Jameson	295	Sally Sessions	Starmount Forest CC, Greensboro, NC
			Polly Riley	
1948	Babe Zaharias	300	Betty Hicks	Atlantic City CC, Northfield, NJ
1949	Louise Suggs	291	Babe Zaharias	Prince George's G & CC, Landover, MD
1950	Babe Zaharias	291	Betsy Rawls	Rolling Hills CC, Wichita, KS
1951	Betsy Rawls	293	Louise Suggs	Druid Hills GC, Atlanta
1952	Louise Suggs	284	Marlene Bauer	Bala GC, Philadelphia
			Betty Jameson	
1953	Betsy Rawls* (71)	302	Jackie Pung (77)	CC of Rochester, Rochester, NY
1954	Babe Zaharias	291	Betty Hicks	Salem CC, Peabody, MA
1955	Fay Crocker	299	Mary Lena Faulk	Wichita CC, Wichita, KS
			Louise Suggs	
1956	Kathy Cornelius* (75)	302	Barbara McIntire (82)	Northland CC, Duluth, MN
1957	Betsy Rawls	299	Patty Berg	Winged Foot GC, Mamaroneck, NY
1958	Mickey Wright	290	Louise Suggs	Forest Lake CC, Detroit
1959	Mickey Wright	287	Louise Suggs	Churchill Valley CC, Pittsburgh
1960	Betsy Rawls	292	Joyce Ziske	Worcester CC, Worcester, MA
1961	Mickey Wright	293	Betsy Rawls	Baltusrol GC (Lower Course), Springfield, NJ
1962	Murle Breer	301	Jo Ann Prentice	Dunes GC, Myrtle Beach, SC
			Ruth Jessen	
1963	Mary Mills	289	Sandra Haynie	Kenwood CC, Cincinnati
			Louise Suggs	
1964	Mickey Wright* (70)	290	Ruth Jessen (72)	San Diego CC, Chula Vista, CA
1965	Carol Mann	290	Kathy Cornelius	Atlantic City CC, Northfield, NJ
1966	Sandra Spuzich	297	Carol Mann	Hazeltine Natl GC, Chaska, MN
1967	Catherine LaCoste	294	Susie Berning	Hot Springs GC (Cascades Course),
			Beth Stone	Hot Springs, VA
1968	Susie Berning	289	Mickey Wright	Moslem Springs GC, Fleetwood, PA
1969	Donna Caponi	294	Peggy Wilson	Scenic Hills CC, Pensacola, FL
1970	Donna Caponi	287	Sandra Haynie	Muskogee CC, Muskogee, OK
			Sandra Spuzich	
1971	JoAnne Carner	288	Kathy Whitworth	Kahkwa CC, Erie, PA
1972	Susie Berning	299	Kathy Ahern	Winged Foot GC, Mamaroneck, NY
			Pam Barnett	
			Judy Rankin	
1973	Susie Berning	290	Gloria Ehret	CC of Rochester, Rochester, NY
			Shelley Hamlin	
1974	Sandra Haynie	295	Carol Mann	La Grange CC, La Grange, IL
			Beth Stone	
1975	Sandra Palmer	295	JoAnne Carner	Atlantic City CC, Northfield, NJ
			Sandra Post	
			Nancy Lopez	
1976	JoAnne Carner* (76)	292	Sandra Palmer (78)	Rolling Green CC, Springfield, PA
1977	Hollis Stacy	292	Nancy Lopez	Hazeltine Natl GC, Chaska, MN
1978	Hollis Stacy	289	JoAnne Carner	CC of Indianapolis, Indianapolis
			Sally Little	
1979	Jerilyn Britz	284	Debbie Massey	Brooklawn CC, Fairfield, CT
			Sandra Palmer	
1980	Amy Alcott	280	Hollis Stacy	Richland CC, Nashville
1981	Pat Bradley	279	Beth Daniel	La Grange CC, La Grange, IL
1982	Janet Anderson	283	Beth Daniel	Del Paso CC, Sacramento
			Sandra Haynie	
			Donna White	
			JoAnne Carner	
1983	Jan Stephenson	290	JoAnne Carner	Cedar Ridge CC, Tulsa
			Patty Sheehan	
1984	Hollis Stacy	290	Rosie Jones	Salem CC, Peabody, MA
1985	Kathy Baker	280	Judy Dickinson	Baltusrol GC (Upper Course), Springfield, NJ
1986	Jane Geddes* (71)	287	Sally Little (73)	NCR GC, Dayton
1987	Laura Davies* (71)	285	Ayako Okamoto (73)	Plainfield CC, Plainfield, NJ
			JoAnne Carner (74)	
1988	Liselotte Neumann	277	Patty Sheehan	Baltimore CC, Baltimore
1989	Betsy King	278	Nancy Lopez	Indianwood G & CC, Lake Orion, MI
1990	Betsy King	284	Patty Sheehan	Atlanta Athletic Club, Duluth, GA
1991	Meg Mallon	283	Pat Bradley	Colonial Club, Fort Worth

U.S. Women's Open *(Cont.)*

Year	Winner	Score	Runner-Up	Site
1992	Patty Sheehan* (72)	280	Juli Inkster	Oakmont CC, Oakmont, PA
1993	Lauri Merten	280	Donna Andrew	Crooked Stick, Carmel, IN
			Helen Alfredsson	
1994	Patty Sheehan	277	Tammie Green	Indianwood G & CC, Lake Orion, MI
1995	Annika Sorenstam	278	Meg Mallon	The Broadmoor GC, Colorado Springs, CO
1996	Annika Sorenstam	272	Kris Tschetter	Pine Needles GC, Southern Pines, NC
1997	Alison Nicholas	274	Nancy Lopez	Pumpkin Ridge CC, North Plains, OR
1998	Se Ri Pak†	290	Jenny Chuasiriporn	Blackwolf Run Golf Resort, Kohler, WI
1999	Juli Inkster	272	Sherri Turner	Old Waverly GC, West Point, MS
2000	Karrie Webb	282	Cristie Kerr	Merit GC, Libertyville, IL
			Meg Mallon	

* Winner in playoff; 18-hole playoff scores are in parentheses. † Winner on second hole of sudden death after 18-hole playoff ended in a tie.

Nabisco Championship

Year	Winner	Score	Runner-Up	Year	Winner	Score	Runner-Up
1972	Jane Blalock	213	Carol Mann	1987	Betsy King*	283	Patty Sheehan
			Judy Rankin	1988	Amy Alcott	274	Colleen Walker
1973	Mickey Wright	284	Joyce Kazmierski	1989	Juli Inkster	279	Tammie Green
1974	Jo Ann Prentice*	289	Jane Blalock				JoAnne Carner
			Sandra Haynie	1990	Betsy King	283	Kathy Postlewait
1975	Sandra Palmer	283	Kathy McMullen				Shirley Furlong
1976	Judy Rankin	285	Betty Burfeindt	1991	Amy Alcott	273	Dottie Mochrie
1977	Kathy Whitworth	289	JoAnne Carner	1992	Dottie Mochrie*	279	Juli Inkster
			Sally Little	1993	Helen Alfredsson	284	Amy Benz
1978	Sandra Post*	283	Penny Pulz				Tina Barrett
1979	Sandra Post	276	Nancy Lopez				Betsy King
1980	Donna Caponi	275	Amy Alcott	1994	Donna Andrews	276	Laura Davies
1981	Nancy Lopez	277	Carolyn Hill	1995	Nanci Bowen	285	Susie Redman
1982	Sally Little	278	Hollis Stacy	1996	Patti Sheehan	281	Kelly Robbins
			Sandra Haynie				Meg Mallon
1983	Amy Alcott	282	Beth Daniel				Annika Sörenstam
			Kathy Whitworth	1997	Betsy King	276	Kris Tschetter
1984	Juli Inkster*	280	Pat Bradley	1998	Pat Hurst	281	Helen Dobson
1985	Alice Miller	275	Jan Stephenson	1999	Dottie Pepper	269	Meg Mallon
1986	Pat Bradley	280	Val Skinner	2000	Karrie Webb	274	Dottie Pepper

*Winner in sudden-death playoff. Note: Designated fourth major in 1983; played at Mission Hills CC, Rancho Mirage, CA.

du Maurier Classic

Year	Winner	Score	Runner-Up	Site
1973	Jocelyne Bourassa*	214	Sandra Haynie	Montreal GC, Montreal
			Judy Rankin	
1974	Carole Jo Callison	208	JoAnne Carner	Candiac GC, Montreal
1975	JoAnne Carner*	214	Carol Mann	St. George's CC, Toronto
1976	Donna Caponi*	212	Judy Rankin	Cedar Brae G & CC, Toronto
1977	Judy Rankin	214	Pat Meyers	Lachute G & CC, Montreal
			Sandra Palmer	
1978	JoAnne Carner	278	Hollis Stacy	St. George's CC, Toronto
1979	Amy Alcott	285	Nancy Lopez	Richelieu Valley CC, Montreal
1980	Pat Bradley	277	JoAnne Carner	St. George's CC, Toronto
1981	Jan Stephenson	278	Nancy Lopez	Summerlea CC, Dorion, Quebec
			Pat Bradley	
1982	Sandra Haynie	280	Beth Daniel	St. George's CC, Toronto
1983	Hollis Stacy	277	JoAnne Carner	Beaconsfield GC, Montreal
			Alice Miller	
1984	Juli Inkster	279	Ayako Okamoto	St. George's G & CC, Toronto
1985	Pat Bradley	278	Jane Geddes	Beaconsfield CC, Montreal
1986	Pat Bradley*	276	Ayako Okamoto	Board of Trade CC, Toronto
1987	Jody Rosenthal	272	Ayako Okamoto	Islesmere GC, Laval, Quebec
1988	Sally Little	279	Laura Davies	Vancouver GC, Coquitlam, British Columbia
1989	Tammie Green	279	Pat Bradley	Beaconsfield GC, Montreal
			Betsy King	
1990	Cathy Johnston	276	Patty Sheehan	Westmount G & CC, Kitchener, Ontario

du Maurier Classic (Cont.)

Year	Winner	Score	Runner-Up	Site
1991	Nancy Scranton	279	Debbie Massey	Vancouver GC, Coquitlam, British Columbia
1992	Sherri Steinhauer	277	Judy Dickinson	St. Charles CC, Winnipeg, Manitoba
1993	Brandie Burton	277	Betsy King	London Hunt and CC, London, Ontario
1994	Martha Nause	279	Michelle McGann	Ottawa Hunt and GC, Ottawa, Ont.
1995	Jenny Lidback	280	Liselotte Neumann	Beaconsfield GC, Pointe-Claire, Quebec
1996	Laura Davies	277	Nancy Lopez	Edmonton CC, Edmonton, Alberta
			Karrie Webb	
1997	Colleen Walker	278	Liselotte Neumann	Glen Abbey GC, Oakville, Ontario
1998	Brandie Burton	270	Annika Sorenstam	Essex G & CC, Windsor, Ontario
1999	Karrie Webb	277	Laura Davies	Priddis Greens G & CC, Calgary, Alberta
2000	Meg Mallon	282	Rosie Jones	Royal Ottawa GC, Aylmer, Quebec

*Winner in sudden-death playoff. Note: Designated third major in 1979.

Alltime Major Championship Winners

	LPGA	U.S. Open	Dinah Shore	du Maurier	#Titleholders	†Western	U.S. Am	British Am	Total
Patty Berg	0	1	0	0	7	7	1	0	16
Mickey Wright	4	4	0	0	2	3	0	0	13
Louise Suggs	1	2	0	0	4	4	1	1	13
Babe Zaharias	0	3	0	0	3	4	1	1	12
*Juli Inkster	2	1	2	1	0	0	3	0	9
Betsy Rawls	2	4	0	0	0	2	0	0	8
*JoAnne Carner	0	2	0	0	0	0	5	0	7
Kathy Whitworth	3	0	0	0	2	1	0	0	6
Pat Bradley	1	1	1	3	0	0	0	0	6
*Patty Sheehan	3	2	1	0	0	0	0	0	6
Glenna Vare	0	0	0	0	0	0	6	0	6
*Betsy King	1	2	3	0	0	0	0	0	6

*Active LPGA player.
#Major from 1937–1972. †Major from 1937–1967.

Alltime Multiple Professional Major Winners

LPGA
Mickey Wright	4
Nancy Lopez	3
Patty Sheehan	3
Kathy Whitworth	3
Donna Caponi	2
Sandra Haynie	2
Mary Mills	2
Betsy Rawls	2
Laura Davies	2
Juli Inkster	2

U.S. OPEN
Betsy Rawls	4
Mickey Wright	4

U.S. OPEN (Cont.)
Susie Maxwell Berning	3
Hollis Stacy	3
Babe Zaharias	3
JoAnne Carner	2
Donna Caponi	2
Betsy King	2
Patty Sheehan	2
Louise Suggs	2
Annika Sorenstam	2

NABISCO/DINAH SHORE
Amy Alcott	3
Betsy King	3
Juli Inkster	2

DU MAURIER
Pat Bradley	3
Brandie Burton	2
JoAnne Carner	2

TITLEHOLDERS
Patty Berg	7
Louise Suggs	4
Babe Zaharias	3
Dorothy Kirby	2
Marilynn Smith	2
Kathy Whitworth	2
Mickey Wright	2

WESTERN OPEN
Patty Berg	7
Louise Suggs	4
Babe Zaharias	4
Mickey Wright	3
June Beebe	2
Opal Hill	2
Betty Jameson	2
Betsy Rawls	2

THE LPGA TOUR

Most Career Wins†

	Wins		Wins		Wins
Kathy Whitworth	88	*JoAnne Carner	42	Pat Bradley	31
Mickey Wright	82	Sandra Haynie	42	Babe Zaharias	31
Patty Berg	57	Carol Mann	38	Amy Alcott	29
Betsy Rawls	55	*Patty Sheehan	35	Jane Blalock	29
Louise Suggs	50	*Betsy King	33	Judy Rankin	26
*Nancy Lopez	48	*Beth Daniel	32		

*Active LPGA player. †Through 10/15/00.

Season Money Leaders

	Earnings ($)		Earnings ($)		Earnings ($)
1950...Babe Zaharias	14,800	1967...Kathy Whitworth	32,937	1984...Betsy King	266,771
1951...Babe Zaharias	15,087	1968...Kathy Whitworth	48,379	1985...Nancy Lopez	416,472
1952...Betsy Rawls	14,505	1969...Carol Mann	49,152	1986...Pat Bradley	492,021
1953...Louise Suggs	19,816	1970...Kathy Whitworth	30,235	1987...Ayako Okamoto	466,034
1954...Patty Berg	16,011	1971...Kathy Whitworth	41,181	1988...Sherri Turner	350,851
1955...Patty Berg	16,492	1972...Kathy Whitworth	65,063	1989...Betsy King	654,132
1956...Marlene Hagge	20,235	1973...Kathy Whitworth	82,864	1990...Beth Daniel	863,578
1957...Patty Berg	16,272	1974...JoAnne Carner	87,094	1991...Pat Bradley	763,118
1958...Beverly Hanson	12,639	1975...Sandra Palmer	76,374	1992...Dottie Mochrie	693,335
1959...Betsy Rawls	26,774	1976...Judy Rankin	150,734	1993...Betsy King	595,992
1960...Louise Suggs	16,892	1977...Judy Rankin	122,890	1994...Laura Davies	687,201
1961...Mickey Wright	22,236	1978...Nancy Lopez	189,814	1995...Annika Sorenstam	666,533
1962...Mickey Wright	21,641	1979...Nancy Lopez	197,489	1996...Karrie Webb	1,002,000
1963...Mickey Wright	31,269	1980...Beth Daniel	231,000	1997...Annika Sorenstam	1,236,789
1964...Mickey Wright	29,800	1981...Beth Daniel	206,998	1998...Annika Sorenstam	1,092,748
1965...Kathy Whitworth	28,658	1982...JoAnne Carner	310,400	1999...Karrie Webb	1,591,959
1966...Kathy Whitworth	33,517	1983...JoAnne Carner	291,404		

Career Money Leaders†

	Earnings ($)		Earnings ($)		Earnings ($)
1. Betsy King	6,811,179	11. Laura Davies	5,171,376	21. Jan Stephenson	2,987,515
2. Annika Sorenstam	6,129,096	12. Rosie Jones	4,859,205	22. JoAnne Carner	2,936,726
3. Juli Inkster	6,034,775	13. Liselotte Neumann	4,015,002	23. Michelle McGann	2,897,108
4. Karrie Webb	6,029,095	14. Kelly Robbins	3,933,828	24. Colleen Walker	2,747,279
5. Beth Daniel	5,978,379	15. Jane Geddes	3,705,450	25. Ayako Okamoto	2,746,254
6. Pat Bradley	5,734,628	16. Sherri Steinhauer	3,595,746	26. Donna Andrews	2,733,195
7. Dottie Pepper	5,591,631	17. Tammie Green	3,380,028	27. Dawn Coe-Jones	2,610,035
8. Patty Sheehan	5,500,983	18. Amy Alcott	3,368,340	28. D. Ammaccapane	2,598,762
9. Meg Mallon	5,434,736	19. Chris Johnson	3,360,592	29. Hollis Stacy	2,580,041
10. Nancy Lopez	5,292,646	20. Brandie Burton	3,136,669	30. Helen Alfredsson	2,490,831

†Through 10/15/00.

LPGA Player of the Year

1966	Kathy Whitworth	1978	Nancy Lopez	1990	Beth Daniel
1967	Kathy Whitworth	1979	Nancy Lopez	1991	Pat Bradley
1968	Kathy Whitworth	1980	Beth Daniel	1992	Dottie Mochrie
1969	Kathy Whitworth	1981	JoAnne Carner	1993	Betsy King
1970	Sandra Haynie	1982	JoAnne Carner	1994	Beth Daniel
1971	Kathy Whitworth	1983	Patty Sheehan	1995	Annika Sörenstam
1972	Kathy Whitworth	1984	Betsy King	1996	Laura Davies
1973	Kathy Whitworth	1985	Nancy Lopez	1997	Annika Sörenstam
1974	JoAnne Carner	1986	Pat Bradley	1998	Annika Sörenstam
1975	Sandra Palmer	1987	Ayako Okamoto	1999	Karrie Webb
1976	Judy Rankin	1988	Nancy Lopez		
1977	Judy Rankin	1989	Betsy King		

Vare Trophy: Best Scoring Average

		Avg			Avg			Avg
1953	Patty Berg	75.00	1969	Kathy Whitworth	72.38	1985	Nancy Lopez	70.73
1954	Babe Zaharias	75.48	1970	Kathy Whitworth	72.26	1986	Pat Bradley	71.10
1955	Patty Berg	74.47	1971	Kathy Whitworth	72.88	1987	Betsy King	71.14
1956	Patty Berg	74.57	1972	Kathy Whitworth	72.38	1988	Colleen Walker	71.26
1957	Louise Suggs	74.64	1973	Judy Rankin	73.08	1989	Beth Daniel	70.38
1958	Beverly Hanson	74.92	1974	JoAnne Carner	72.87	1990	Beth Daniel	70.54
1959	Betsy Rawls	74.03	1975	JoAnne Carner	72.40	1991	Pat Bradley	70.76
1960	Mickey Wright	73.25	1976	Judy Rankin	72.25	1992	Dottie Mochrie	70.80
1961	Mickey Wright	73.55	1977	Judy Rankin	72.16	1993	Nancy Lopez	70.83
1962	Mickey Wright	73.67	1978	Nancy Lopez	71.76	1994	Beth Daniel	70.90
1963	Mickey Wright	72.81	1979	Nancy Lopez	71.20	1995	Annika Sorenstam	71.00
1964	Mickey Wright	72.46	1980	Amy Alcott	71.51	1996	Annika Sorenstam	70.47
1965	Kathy Whitworth	72.61	1981	JoAnne Carner	71.75	1997	Karrie Webb	70.00
1966	Kathy Whitworth	72.60	1982	JoAnne Carner	71.49	1998	Annika Sorenstam	69.99
1967	Kathy Whitworth	72.74	1983	JoAnne Carner	71.41	1999	Karrie Webb	69.43
1968	Carol Mann	72.04	1984	Patty Sheehan	71.40			

Alltime LPGA Tour Records†

Scoring

72 HOLES

261—(71-61-63-66) by Se Ri Pak to win at the Highland Meadows CC, Sylvania, OH, in the 1998 Jamie Farr Kroger Classic (23 under par).

54 HOLES

193—(66-61-66) by Karrie Webb to lead at the Walnut Hills CC, East Lansing, MI, in the 2000 Oldsmobile Classic (23 under par).

36 HOLES

127—(66-61) by Karrie Webb to lead at the Walnut Hills CC, East Lansing MI, in the 2000 Oldsmobile Classic (17 under par).

18 HOLES

61—by Se Ri Pak at Highland Meadows CC, Sylvania, OH, in the second round in winning 1998 Jamie Farr Kroger Classic (10 under par)

61—by Annika Sorenstam at Hermitage Golf Course, Old Hickory, TN, in the first round in leading the 1999 Sara Lee Classic (11 under par).

61—by Karrie Webb at the Walnut CC, East Lansing, MI, in the second round in leading the 2000 Oldsmobile Classic (11 under par).

9 HOLES

28—by Mary Beth Zimmerman at Rail GC, 1984 Rail Charity Golf Classic, Springfield, IL (par 36). Zimmerman shot 64.

28—by Pat Bradley at Green Gables CC, Denver, 1984 Columbia Savings Classic (par 35). Bradley shot 65.

28—by Muffin Spencer-Devlin at Knollwood CC, Elmsford, NY, in winning the 1985 MasterCard International Pro-Am (par 35). Spencer-Devlin shot 64.

†Through 10/15/00.

Scoring (Cont.)

9 HOLES (CONT.)

28—by Peggy Kirsch at Squaw Creek CC, Vienna, OH, in the 1991 Phar-Mor (par 35).

28—by Renee Heiken at Highland Meadows CC, Sylvania, OH, in the 1996 Jamie Farr Kroger Classic (par 34).

MOST CONSECUTIVE ROUNDS UNDER 70

9—Beth Daniel, in 1990.

MOST BIRDIES IN A ROW

9—Beth Daniel at Onion Creek Club in Austin, TX, in the second round of the 1999 Philips Invitational. Daniel shot 62 (8 under par).

Wins

MOST CONSECUTIVE WINS IN SCHEDULED EVENTS

4—Mickey Wright, in 1962.

4—Mickey Wright, in 1963.

4—Kathy Whitworth, in 1969.

MOST CONSECUTIVE WINS IN ENTERED TOURNAMENTS

5—Nancy Lopez, in 1987.

MOST WINS IN A CALENDAR YEAR

13—Mickey Wright, in 1963.

WIDEST WINNING MARGIN, STROKES

14—Louise Suggs, 1949 U.S. Women's Open.

14—Cindy Mackey, 1986 MasterCard Int'l Pro-Am.

U.S. Senior Open

Year	Winner	Score	Runner-Up	Site
1980	Roberto DeVicenzo	285	William C. Campbell	Winged Foot GC, Mamaroneck, NY
1981	Arnold Palmer* (70)	289	Bob Stone (74)	Oakland Hills CC, Birmingham, MI
			Billy Casper (77)	
1982	Miller Barber	282	Gene Littler	Portland GC, Portland, OR
			Dan Sikes, Jr	
1983	Billy Casper* (75) (3)	288	Rod Funseth (75) (4)	Hazeltine GC, Chaska, MN
1984	Miller Barber	286	Arnold Palmer	Oak Hill CC, Rochester, NY
1985	Miller Barber	285	Roberto DeVicenzo	Edgewood Tahoe GC, Stateline, NV
1986	Dale Douglass	279	Gary Player	Scioto CC, Columbus, OH
1987	Gary Player	270	Doug Sanders	Brooklawn CC, Fairfield, CT
1988	Gary Player* (68)	288	Bob Charles (70)	Medinah CC, Medinah, IL
1989	Orville Moody	279	Frank Beard	Laurel Valley GC, Ligonier, PA
1990	Lee Trevino	275	Jack Nicklaus	Ridgewood CC, Paramus, NJ
1991	Jack Nicklaus (65)	282	Chi Chi Rodriguez (69)	Oakland Hills CC, Birmingham, MI
1992	Larry Laoretti	275	Jim Colbert	Saucon Valley CC, Bethlehem, PA
1993	Jack Nicklaus	278	Tom Weiskopf	Cherry Hills CC, Englewood, CO
1994	Simon Hobday	274	Jim Albus	Pinehurst Resort & CC, Pinehurst, NC
1995	Tom Weiskopf	275	Jack Nicklaus	Congressional CC, Bethesda, MD
1996	Dave Stockton	277	Hale Irwin	Canterbury GC, Beachwood, OH
1997	Graham Marsh	280	Hale Irwin	Olympia Fields CC, Olympia Fields, IL
1998	Hale Irwin	285	Vicente Fernandez	Riviera CC, Pacific Palisades, CA
1999	Dave Eichelberger	281	Ed Dougherty	Des Moines G & CC, Des Moines, IA
2000	Hale Irwin	267	Bruce Fleisher	Saucon Valley CC, Bethlehem, PA

*Winner in playoff. Playoff scores are in parentheses. The 1983 playoff went to one hole of sudden death after an 18-hole playoff.

SENIOR TOUR
Season Money Leaders

	Earnings ($)		Earnings ($)		Earnings ($)
1980...Don January	44,100	1987...Chi Chi Rodriguez	509,145	1994...Dave Stockton	1,402,519
1981...Miller Barber	83,136	1988...Bob Charles	533,929	1995...Jim Colbert	1,444,386
1982...Miller Barber	106,890	1989...Bob Charles	725,887	1996...Jim Colbert	1,627,890
1983...Don January	237,571	1990...Lee Trevino	1,190,518	1997...Hale Irwin	2,449,420
1984...Don January	328,597	1991...Mike Hill	1,065,657	1998...Hale Irwin	2,861,945
1985...Peter Thomson	386,724	1992...Lee Trevino	1,027,002	1999...Bruce Fleisher	2,515,705
1986...Bruce Crampton	454,299	1993...Dave Stockton	1,175,944		

Career Money Leaders†

	Earnings ($)		Earnings ($)		Earnings ($)
1. Hale Irwin	11,570,733	11. Iaso Aoki	6,881,214	21. Jim Albus	5,322,449
2. Jim Colbert	9,573,003	12. Chi Chi Rodriguez	6,518,534	22. Al Geiberger	5,131,636
3. Lee Trevino	9,197,496	13. Dale Douglass	6,272,217	23. Bruce Summerhays	5,029,068
4. Dave Stockton	8,590,120	14. Bob Murphy	6,251,679	24. Bruce Fleisher	4,837,311
5. Bob Charles	8,281,477	15. Jay Sigel	5,871,743	25. Bruce Crampton	4,652,684
6. Gil Morgan	7,776,606	16. Larry Nelson	5,795,261	26. Dana Quigley	4,606,136
7. George Archer	7,717,543	17. J.C. Snead	5,783,824	27. Rocky Thompson	4,276,836
8. Ray Floyd	7,626,594	18. Graham Marsh	5,748,034	28. Kermit Zarley	4,250,961
9. Jim Dent	7,508,626	19. Tom Wargo	5,530,513	29. John Bland	4,233,246
10. Mike Hill	7,023,822	20. Gary Player	5,345,927	30. Vincente Fernandez	4,120,796

Most Career Wins†

	Wins		Wins
Lee Trevino	29	Gary Player	19
Hale Irwin	28	Jim Colbert	19
Miller Barber	24	George Archer	19
Bob Charles	23	Mike Hill	18
Don January	22	Gil Morgan	18
Chi Chi Rodriguez	22	Dave Stockton	14
Bruce Crampton	20	Ray Floyd	14

†Through 10/15/00.

MAJOR MEN'S AMATEUR CHAMPIONSHIPS
U.S. Amateur

Year	Winner	Score	Runner-Up	Site
1895	Charles B. Macdonald	12 & 11	Charles E. Sands	Newport GC, Newport, RI
1896	H.J. Whigham	8 & 7	J.G Thorp	Shinnecock Hills GC, Southampton, NY
1897	H.J. Whigham	8 & 6	W. Rossiter Betts	Chicago GC, Wheaton, IL
1898	Findlay S. Douglas	5 & 3	Walter B. Smith	Morris County GC, Morristown, NJ
1899	H.M. Harriman	3 & 2	Findlay S. Douglas	Onwentsia Club, Lake Forest, IL
1900	Walter Travis	2 up	Findlay S. Douglas	Garden City GC, Garden City, NY
1901	Walter Travis	5 & 4	Walter E. Egan	CC of Atlantic City, NJ
1902	Louis N. James	4 & 2	Eben M. Byers	Glen View Club, Golf, IL
1903	Walter Travis	5 & 4	Eben M. Byers	Nassau CC, Glen Cove, NY
1904	H. Chandler Egan	8 & 6	Fred Herreshoff	Baltusrol GC, Springfield, NJ
1905	H. Chandler Egan	6 & 5	D.E. Sawyer	Chicago GC, Wheaton, IL
1906	Eben M. Byers	2 up	George S. Lyon	Englewood GC, Englewood, NJ
1907	Jerry Travers	6 & 5	Archibald Graham	Euclid Club, Cleveland, OH
1908	Jerry Travers	8 & 7	Max H. Behr	Garden City GC, Garden City, NY
1909	Robert A. Gardner	4 & 3	H. Chandler Egan	Chicago GC, Wheaton, IL
1910	William C. Fownes Jr	4 & 3	Warren K. Wood	The Country Club, Brookline, MA
1911	Harold Hilton	1 up	Fred Herreshoff	The Apawamis Club, Rye, NY
1912	Jerry Travers	7 & 6	Charles Evans Jr	Chicago GC, Wheaton, IL
1913	Jerry Travers	5 & 4	John G. Anderson	Garden City GC, Garden City, NY
1914	Francis Ouimet	6 & 5	Jerry Travers	Ekwanok CC, Manchester, VT
1915	Robert A. Gardner	5 & 4	John G. Anderson	CC of Detroit, Grosse Pt. Farms, MI
1916	Chick Evans	4 & 3	Robert A. Gardner	Merion Cricket Club, Haverford, PA
1917–18	No tournament			
1919	S. Davidson Herron	5 & 4	Bobby Jones	Oakmont CC, Oakmont, PA
1920	Chick Evans	7 & 6	Francis Ouimet	Engineers' CC, Roslyn, NY
1921	Jesse P. Guilford	7 & 6	Robert A. Gardner	St. Louis CC, Clayton, MO
1922	Jess W. Sweetser	3 & 2	Chick Evans	The Country Club, Brookline, MA
1923	Max R. Marston	1 up	Jess W. Sweetser	Flossmoor CC, Flossmoor, IL
1924	Bobby Jones	9 & 8	George Von Elm	Merion Cricket Club, Ardmore, PA
1925	Bobby Jones	8 & 7	Watts Gunn	Oakmont CC, Oakmont, PA
1926	George Von Elm	2 & 1	Bobby Jones	Baltusrol GC, Springfield, NJ
1927	Bobby Jones	8 & 7	Chick Evans	Minikahda Club, Minneapolis
1928	Bobby Jones	10 & 9	T. Phillip Perkins	Brae Burn CC, West Newton, MA
1929	Harrison R. Johnston	4 & 3	Dr. O.F. Willing	Del Monte G & CC, Pebble Beach, CA
1930	Bobby Jones	8 & 7	Eugene V. Homans	Merion Cricket Club, Ardmore, PA
1931	Francis Ouimet	6 & 5	Jack Westland	Beverly CC, Chicago, IL
1932	C. Ross Somerville	2 & 1	John Goodman	Baltimore CC, Timonium, MD
1933	George T. Dunlap Jr	6 & 5	Max R. Marston	Kenwood CC, Cincinnati, OH
1934	Lawson Little	8 & 7	David Goldman	The Country Club, Brookline, MA
1935	Lawson Little	4 & 2	Walter Emery	The Country Club, Cleveland, OH
1936	John W. Fischer	1 up	Jack McLean	Garden City GC, Garden City, NY
1937	John Goodman	2 up	Raymond E. Billows	Alderwood CC, Portland, OR
1938	William P. Turnesa	8 & 7	B. Patrick Abbott	Oakmont CC, Oakmont, PA
1939	Marvin H. Ward	7 & 5	Raymond E. Billows	North Shore CC, Glenview, IL
1940	Richard D. Chapman	11 & 9	W. McCullough Jr	Winged Foot GC, Mamaroneck, NY
1941	Marvin H. Ward	4 & 3	B. Patrick Abbott	Omaha Field Club, Omaha, NE
1942–45	No tournament			
1946	Ted Bishop	1 up	Smiley L. Quick	Baltusrol GC, Springfield, NJ
1947	Skee Riegel	2 & 1	John W. Dawson	Del Monte G & CC, Pebble Beach, CA
1948	William P. Turnesa	2 & 1	Raymond E. Billows	Memphis CC, Memphis, TN
1949	Charles R. Coe	11 & 10	Rufus King	Oak Hill CC, Rochester, NY
1950	Sam Urzetta	1 up	Frank Stranahan	Minneapolis GC, Minneapolis, MN
1951	Billy Maxwell	4 & 3	Joseph F. Gagliardi	Saucon Valley CC, Bethlehem, PA
1952	Jack Westland	3 & 2	Al Mengert	Seattle GC, Seattle, WA
1953	Gene Littler	1 up	Dale Morey	Oklahoma City G & CC, Oklahoma City
1954	Arnold Palmer	1 up	Robert Sweeny	CC of Detroit, Grosse Pt. Farms, MI
1955	E. Harvie Ward Jr	9 & 8	William Hyndman III	CC of Virginia, Richmond, VA
1956	E. Harvie Ward Jr	5 & 4	Charles Kocsis	Knollwood Club, Lake Forest, IL
1957	Hillman Robbins Jr	5 & 4	Dr. Frank M. Taylor	The Country Club, Brookline, MA
1958	Charles R. Coe	5 & 4	Tommy Aaron	Olympic Club, San Francisco, CA
1959	Jack Nicklaus	1 up	Charles R. Coe	Broadmoor GC, Colorado Springs, CO
1960	Deane Beman	6 & 4	Robert W. Gardner	St. Louis CC, Clayton, MO
1961	Jack Nicklaus	8 & 6	H. Dudley Wysong	Pebble Beach GL, Pebble Beach, CA

U.S. Amateur (Cont.)

Year	Winner	Score	Runner-Up	Site
1962	Labron E. Harris Jr	1 up	Downing Gray	Pinehurst CC, Pinehurst, NC
1963	Deane Beman	2 & 1	Richard H. Sikes	Wakonda Club, Des Moines, IA
1964	William C. Campbell	1 up	Edgar M. Tutwiler	Canterbury GC, Cleveland, OH
1965	Robert J. Murphy Jr	291	Robert B. Dickson	Southern Hills, CC, Tulsa
1966	Gary Cowan	285–75	Deane Beman	Merion GC, Ardmore, PA
1967	Robert B. Dickson	285	Marvin Giles III	Broadmoor GC, Colorado Springs
1968	Bruce Fleisher	284	Marvin Giles III	Scioto CC, Columbus, OH
1969	Steven N. Melnyk	286	Marvin Giles III	Oakmont CC, Oakmont, PA
1970	Lanny Wadkins	279	Tom Kite	Waverley CC, Portland, OR
1971	Gary Cowan	280	Eddie Pearce	Wilmington CC, Wilmington DE
1972	Marvin Giles III	285	two tied	Charlotte CC, Charlotte, NC
1973	Craig Stadler	6 & 5	David Strawn	Inverness Club, Toledo
1974	Jerry Pate	2 & 1	John P. Grace	Ridgewood CC, Ridgewood, NJ
1975	Fred Ridley	2 up	Keith Fergus	CC of Virginia, Richmond
1976	Bill Sander	8 & 6	C. Parker Moore Jr	Bel Air CC, Los Angeles
1977	John Fought	9 & 8	Doug Fischesser	Aronimink GC, Newton Square, PA
1978	John Cook	5 & 4	Scott Hoch	Plainfield CC, Plainfield, NJ
1979	Mark O'Meara	8 & 7	John Cook	Canterbury GC, Cleveland
1980	Hal Sutton	9 & 8	Bob Lewis	CC of North Carolina, Pinehurst, NC
1981	Nathaniel Crosby	1 up	Brian Lindley	Olympic Club, San Francisco
1982	Jay Sigel	8 & 7	David Tolley	The Country Club, Brookline, MA
1983	Jay Sigel	8 & 7	Chris Perry	North Shore CC, Glenview, IL
1984	Scott Verplank	4 & 3	Sam Randolph	Oak Tree GC, Edmond, OK
1985	Sam Randolph	1 up	Peter Persons	Montclair GC, West Orange, NJ
1986	Buddy Alexander	5 & 3	Chris Kite	Shoal Creek, Shoal Creek, AL
1987	Bill Mayfair	4 & 3	Eric Rebmann	Jupiter Hills Club, Jupiter, FL
1988	Eric Meeks	7 & 6	Danny Yates	Va. Hot Springs G & CC, VA
1989	Chris Patton	3 & 1	Danny Green	Merion GC, Ardmore, PA
1990	Phil Mickelson	5 & 4	Manny Zerman	Cherry Hills CC, Englewood, CO
1991	Mitch Voges	7 & 6	Manny Zerman	The Honors Course, Ooltewah, TN
1992	Justin Leonard	8 & 7	Tom Scherrer	Muirfield Village GC, Dublin, OH
1993	John Harris	5 & 3	Danny Ellis	Champions GC, Houston
1994	Tiger Woods	2 up	Trip Kuehne	TPC-Sawgrass, Ponte Vedre, FL
1995	Tiger Woods	2 up	Buddy Marucci	Newport Country Club, Newport, RI
1996	Tiger Woods	38 holes	Steve Scott	Pumpkin Ridge GC, Cornelius, OR
1997	Matthew Kuchar	2 & 1	Joel Kribel	Cog Hill G & CC, Lemont, IL
1998	Hank Kuehne	2 & 1	Tom McKnight	Oak Hill CC, Rochester, NY
1999	David Gossett	9 & 8	Sung Yoon Kim	Pebble Beach GL, Pebble Beach, CA
2000	Jeff Quinney	39 holes	James Driscoll	Baltusrol GC, Upper Springfield, NJ

Note: All stroke play from 1965 to 1972.

U.S. Junior Amateur

1948...Dean Lind	1962...Jim Wiechers	1976...Madden Hatcher III	1990...Mathew Todd
1949...Gay Brewer	1963...Gregg McHatton	1977...Willie Wood Jr.	1991...Tiger Woods
1950...Mason Rudolph	1964...Johnny Miller	1978...Don Hurter	1992...Tiger Woods
1951...Tommy Jacobs	1965...James Masserio	1979...Jack Larkin	1993...Tiger Woods
1952...Don Bisplinghoff	1966...Gary Sanders	1980...Eric Johnson	1994...Terry Noe
1953...Rex Baxter	1967...John Crooks	1981...Scott Erickson	1995...D. Scott Hailes
1954...Foster Bradley	1968...Eddie Pearce	1982...Rich Marik	1996...Shane McMenamy
1955...William Dunn	1969...Aly Trompas	1983...Tim Straub	1997...Jason Allred
1956...Harlan Stevenson	1970...Gary Koch	1984...Doug Martin	1998...James Oh
1957...Larry Beck	1971...Mike Brannan	1985...Charles Rymer	1999...Hunter Mahan
1958...Buddy Baker	1972...Bob Byman	1986...Brian Montgomery	2000...Matthew Rosenfeld
1959...Larry Lee	1973...Jack Renner	1987...Brett Quigley	
1960...Bill Tindall	1974...David Nevatt	1988...Jason Widener	
1961...Charles McDowell	1975...Brett Mullin	1989...David Duval	

Note: Event is for amateur golfers younger than 18 years of age.

Mid-Amateur Championship

1981...Jim Holtgrieve	1986...Bill Loeffler	1991...Jim Stuart	1996...John Miller
1982...William Hoffer	1987...Jay Sigel	1992...Danny Yates	1997...Ken Bakst
1983...Jay Sigel	1988...David Eger	1993...Jeff Thomas	1998...John Miller
1984...Mike Podolak	1989...James Taylor	1994...Tim Jackson	1999...Danny Green
1985...Jay Sigel	1990...Jim Stuart	1995...Jerry Courville Jr	2000...Greg Puga

Note: Event is for amateur golfers at least 25 years of age.

British Amateur

Year	Winner
1887	H. G. Hutchinson
1888	John Ball
1889	J.E. Laidlay
1890	John Ball
1891	J.E. Laidlay
1892	John Ball
1893	Peter Anderson
1894	John Ball
1895	L.M.B. Melville
1896	F.G. Tait
1897	A.J.T. Allan
1898	F.G. Tait
1899	John Ball
1900	H.H. Hilton
1901	H.H. Hilton
1902	C. Hutchings
1903	R. Maxwell
1904	W.J. Travis
1905	A.G. Barry
1906	James Robb
1907	John Ball
1908	E.A. Lassen
1909	R. Maxwell
1910	John Ball
1911	H.H. Hilton
1912	John Ball
1913	H.H. Hilton
1914	J.L.C. Jenkins
1915–19	not held
1920	C.J.H. Tolley
1921	W.I. Hunter
1922	E.W.E. Holderness
1923	R.H. Wethered
1924	E.W.E. Holderness
1925	R. Harris
1926	Jess Sweetser
1927	Dr. W. Tweddell
1928	T.P. Perkins
1929	C.J.H. Tolley
1930	Robert T. Jones Jr
1931	E. Martin Smith
1932	J. DeForest
1933	M. Scott
1934	W. Lawson Little
1935	W. Lawson Little
1936	H. Thomson
1937	R. Sweeney Jr
1938	C.R. Yates
1939	A.T. Kyle
1940–45	not held
1946	J. Bruen
1947	Willie D. Turnesa
1948	Frank R. Stranahan
1949	S.M. McReady
1950	Frank R. Stranahan
1951	Richard D. Chapman
1952	E.H. Ward
1953	J.B. Carr
1954	D.W. Bachli
1955	J.W. Conrad
1956	J.C. Beharrel
1957	R. Reid Jack
1958	J.B. Carr
1959	Deane Beman
1960	J.B. Carr
1961	M. Bonallack
1962	R. Davies
1963	M. Lunt
1964	C. Clark
1965	M. Bonallack
1966	C.R. Cole
1967	R. Dickson
1968	M. Bonallack
1969	M. Bonallack
1970	M. Bonallack
1971	Steve Melnyk
1972	Trevor Homer
1973	R. Siderowf
1974	Trevor Homer
1975	M. Giles
1976	R. Siderowf
1977	P. McEvoy
1978	P. McEvoy
1979	J. Sigel
1980	D. Evans
1981	P. Ploujoux
1982	M. Thompson
1983	A. Parkin
1984	J.M. Olazabal
1985	G. McGimpsey
1986	D. Curry
1987	P. Mayo
1988	C. Hardin
1989	S. Dodd
1990	R. Muntz
1991	G. Wolstenholme
1992	S. Dundas
1993	I. Pyman
1994	L. James
1995	G. Sherry
1996	W. Bladon
1997	C. Watson
1998	Sergio Garcia
1999	Graeme Storm
2000	Christian Reimbold

Amateur Public Links

Year	Winner
1922	Edmund R. Held
1923	Richard J. Walsh
1924	Joseph Coble
1925	Raymond J. McAuliffe
1926	Lester Bolstad
1927	Carl F. Kauffmann
1928	Carl F. Kauffmann
1929	Carl F. Kauffmann
1930	Robert E. Wingate
1931	Charles Ferrera
1932	R.L. Miller
1933	Charles Ferrera
1934	David A. Mitchell
1935	Frank Strafaci
1936	B. Patrick Abbott
1937	Bruce N. McCormick
1938	Al Leach
1939	Andrew Szwedko
1940	Robert C. Clark
1941	William M. Welch Jr
1942–45	not held
1946	Smiley L. Quick
1947	Wilfred Crossley
1948	Michael R. Ferentz
1949	Kenneth J. Towns
1950	Stanley Bielat
1951	Dave Stanley
1952	Omer L. Bogan
1953	Ted Richards Jr
1954	Gene Andrews
1955	Sam D. Kocsis
1956	James H. Buxbaum
1957	Don Essig III
1958	Daniel D. Sikes Jr
1959	William A. Wright
1960	Verne Callison
1961	Richard H. Sikes
1962	Richard H. Sikes
1963	Robert Lunn
1964	William McDonald
1965	Arne Dokka
1966	Lamont Kaser
1967	Verne Callison
1968	Gene Towry
1969	John M. Jackson Jr
1970	Robert Risch
1971	Fred Haney
1972	Bob Allard
1973	Stan Stopa
1974	Charles Barenaba
1975	Randy Barenaba
1976	Eddie Mudd
1977	Jerry Vidovic
1978	Dean Prince
1979	Dennis Walsh
1980	Jodie Mudd
1981	Jodie Mudd
1982	Billy Tuten
1983	Billy Tuten
1984	Bill Malley
1985	Jim Sorenson
1986	Bill Mayfair
1987	Kevin Johnson
1988	Ralph Howe III
1989	Tim Hobby
1990	Michael Combs
1991	David Berganio Jr
1992	Warren Schulte
1993	David Berganio Jr
1994	Guy Yamamoto
1995	Chris Wollmann
1996	Tim Hogarth
1997	Tim Clark
1998	Trevor Immelman
1999	Hunter Haas

U.S. Senior Golf

1955 ....J. Wood Platt	1971 ....Tom Draper	1987 ....John Richardson
1956 ....Frederick J. Wright	1972 ....Lewis W. Oehmig	1988 ....Clarence Moore
1957 ....J. Clark Espie	1973 ....William Hyndman III	1989 ....Bo Williams
1958 ....Thomas C. Robbins	1974 ....Dale Morey	1990 ....Jackie Cummings
1959 ....J. Clark Espie	1975 ....William F. Colm	1991 ....Bill Bosshard
1960 ....Michael Cestone	1976 ....Lewis W. Oehmig	1992 ....Clarence Moore
1961 ....Dexter H. Daniels	1977 ....Dale Morey	1993 ....Joe Ungvary
1962 ....Merrill L. Carlsmith	1978 ..........K.K. Compton	1994 ....O. Gordon Brewer
1963 ....Merrill L. Carlsmith	1979 ....William C. Campbell	1995 ....James Stahl Jr
1964 ....William D. Higgins	1980 ....William C. Campbell	1996 ....O. Gordon Brewer
1965 ....Robert B. Kiersky	1981 ....Ed Updegraff	1997 ....Cliff Cunningham
1966 ....Dexter H. Daniels	1982 ....Alton Duhon	1998 ....Bill Shean Jr
1967 ....Ray Palmer	1983 ....William Hyndman III	1999 ....Bill Ploeger
1968 ....Curtis Person Sr	1984 ....Bob Rawlins	2000 ....Bill Shean Jr
1969 ....Curtis Person Sr	1985 ....Lewis W. Oehmig	
1970 ....Gene Andrews	1986 ....Bo Williams	

Note: Event is for amateur golfers at least 55 years of age.

MAJOR WOMEN'S AMATEUR CHAMPIONSHIPS

U.S. Women's Amateur

Year	Winner	Score	Runner-Up	Site
1895 ....Mrs. Charles S. Brown		132	Nellie Sargent	Meadow Brook Club, Hempstead, NY
1896 ....Beatrix Hoyt		2 & 1	Mrs. Arthur Turnure	Morris Couty GC, Morristown, NJ
1897 ....Beatrix Hoyt		5 & 4	Nellie Sargent	Essex County Club, Manchester, MA
1898 ....Beatrix Hoyt		5 &3	Maude Wetmore	Ardsley Club, Ardsley-on-Hudson, NY
1899 ....Ruth Underhill		2 & 1	Margaret Fox	Philadelphia CC, Philadelphia, PA
1900 ....Frances C. Griscom		6 & 5	Margaret Curtis	Shinnecock Hills GC, Shinnecock Hills, NY
1901 ....Genevieve Hecker		5 &3	Lucy Herron	Baltusrol GC, Springfield, NJ
1902 ....Genevieve Hecker		4 & 3	Louisa A. Wells	The Country Club, Brookline, MA
1903 ....Bessie Anthony		7 & 6	J. Anna Carpenter	Chicago GC, Wheaton, IL
1904 ....Georgianna M. Bishop		5 &3	Mrs. E.F. Sanford	Merion Cricket Club, Haverford, PA
1905 ....Pauline Mackay		1 up	Margaret Curtis	Morris County GC, Convent, NJ
1906 ....Harriot S. Curtis		2 & 1	Mary B. Adams	Brae Burn CC, West Newton, MA
1907 ....Margaret Curtis		7 & 6	Harriot S. Curtis	Midlothian CC, Blue Island, IL
1908 ....Katherine C. Harley		6 & 5	Mrs. T.H. Polhemus	Chevy Chase Club, Chevy Chase, MD
1909 ....Dorothy I. Campbell		3 & 2	Nonna Barlow	Merion Cricket Club, Haverford, PA
1910 ....Dorothy I. Campbell		2 & 1	Mrs. G.M. Martin	Homewood CC, Flossmoor, IL
1911 ....Margaret Curtis		5 & 3	Lillian B. Hyde	Baltusrol GC, Springfield, NJ
1912 ....Margaret Curtis		3 & 2	Nonna Barlow	Essex County Club, Manchester, MA
1913 ....Gladys Ravenscroft		2 up	Marion Hollins	Wilmington CC, Wilmington, DE
1914 ....Katherine Harley		1 up	Elaine V. Rosenthal	Nassau CC, Glen Cove, NY
1915 ....Florence Vanderbeck		3 & 2	Margaret Gavin	Onwentsia Club, Lake Forest, IL
1916 ....Alexa Stirling		2 & 1	Mildred Caverly	Belmont Springs CC, Waverley, MA
1917–18 .....No tournament				
1919 ....Alexa Stirling		6 & 5	Margaret Gavin	Shawnee CC, Shawnee-on-Delaware, PA
1920 ....Alexa Stirling		5 & 4	Dorothy Campbell	Mayfield CC, Cleveland
1921 ....Marion Hollins		5 & 4	Alexa Stirling	Hollywood GC, Deal, NJ
1922 ....Glenna Collett		5 & 4	Margaret Gavin	Greenbriar GC, White Sulphur Springs, WV
1923 ....Edith Cummings		3 & 2	Alexa Stirling	Westchester-Biltmore CC, Rye, NY
1924 ....Dorothy Campbell		7 & 6	Mary K. Browne	Rhode Island CC, Nyatt, RI
1925 ....Glenna Collett		9 & 8	Alexa Stirling	St. Louis CC, Clayton, MO
1926 ....Helen Stetson		3 & 1	Elizabeth Goss	Merion Cricket Club, Ardmore, PA
1927 ....Miiriam Burns Horn		5 & 4	Maureen Orcutt	Cherry Valley Club, Garden City, NY
1928 ....Glenna Collett		13 & 12	Virginia Van Wie	Va. Hot Springs G & TC, Hot Springs, VA
1929 ....Glenna Collett		4 & 3	Leona Pressler	Oakland Hills CC, Birmingham, MI
1930 ....Glenna Collett		6 & 5	Virginia Van Wie	Los Angeles CC, Beverly Hills, CA
1931 ....Helen Hicks		2 & 1	Glenna Collet Vare	CC of Buffalo, Williamsville, NY
1932 ....Virginia Van Wie		10 & 8	Glenna Collet Vare	Salem CC, Peabody, MA
1933 ....Virginia Van Wie		4 & 3	Helen Hicks	Exmoor CC, Highland Park, IL
1934 ....Virginia Van Wie		2 & 1	Dorothy Traung	Whitemarsh Valley CC, Chestnut Hill, PA
1935 ....Glenna Collett Vare		3 & 2	Patty Berg	Interlachen CC, Hopkins, MN
1936 ....Pamela Barton		4 & 3	Maureen Orcutt	Canoe Brook CC, Summit, NJ
1937 ....Estelle Lawson		7 & 6	Patty Berg	Memphis CC, Memphis, TN
1938 ....Patty Berg		6 & 5	Estelle Lawson	Westmoreland CC, Wilmette, IL

U.S. Women's Amateur (Cont.)

Year	Winner	Score	Runner-Up	Site
1939	Betty Jameson	3 & 2	Dorothy Kirby	Wee Burn Club, Darien, CT
1940	Betty Jameson	6 & 5	Jane S. Cothran	Del Monte G & CC, Pebble Beach, CA
1941	Elizabeth Hicks	5 & 3	Helen Sigel	The Country Club, Brookline, MA
1942–45	No tournament			
1946	Babe Zaharias	11 & 9	Clara Sherman	Southern Hills CC, Tulsa
1947	Louise Suggs	2 up	Dorothy Kirby	Franklin Hills CC, Franklin, MI
1948	Grace S. Lenczyk	4 & 3	Helen Sigel	Del Monte G & CC, Pebble Beach, CA
1949	Dorothy Porter	3 & 2	Dorothy Kielty	Merion GC, Ardmore, PA
1950	Beverly Hanson	6 & 4	Mae Murray	Atlanta AC, Atlanta
1951	Dorothy Kirby	2 & 1	Claire Doran	Town & CC, St. Paul
1952	Jacqueline Pung	2 & 1	Shirley McFedters	Waverley CC, Portland, OR
1953	Mary Lena Faulk	3 & 2	Polly Riley	Rhode Island CC, West Barrington, RI
1954	Barbara Romack	4 & 2	Mickey Wright	Allegheny CC, Sewickley, PA
1955	Patricia A. Lesser	7 & 6	Jane Nelson	Myers Park CC, Charlotte
1956	Marlene Stewart	2 & 1	JoAnne Gunderson	Meridian Hills CC, Indianapolis
1957	JoAnne Gunderson	8 & 6	Ann Casey Johnstone	Del Paso CC, SacramentoA
1958	Anne Quast	3 & 2	Barbara Romack	Wee Burn CC, Darien, CT
1959	Barbara McIntire	4 & 3	Joanne Goodwin	Congressional CC, Washington, D.C.
1960	JoAnne Gunderson	6 & 5	Jean Ashley	Tulsa CC, Tulsa
1961	Anne Quast Decker	14 & 13	Phyllis Preuss	Tacoma G & CC, Tacoma, WA
1962	JoAnne Gunderson	9 & 8	Anne Baker	CC of Rochester, Rochester, NY
1963	Anne Quast Decker	2 & 1	Peggy Conley	Taconic GC, Williamstown, MA
1964	Barbara McIntire	3 & 2	JoAnne Gunderson	Prairie Dunes CC, Hutchinson, KS
1965	Jean Ashley	5 & 4	Anne Quast Decker	Lakewood CC, Denver
1966	JoAnne Gunderson	1 up	Marlene Stewart Streit	Sewickley Heights GC, Sewickley, PA
1967	Mary Lou Dill	5 & 4	Jean Ashley	Annandale GC, Pasadena
1968	JoAnne Gunderson Carner	5 & 4	Anne Quast Decker	Birmingham CC, Birmingham, MI
1969	Catherine Lacoste	3 & 2	Shelley Hamling	Las Colinas CC, Irving, TX
1970	Martha Wilkinson	3 & 2	Cynthia Hall	Wee Burn CC, Darien, CT
1971	Laura Baugh	1 up	Beth Barry	Atlanta CC, Atlanta
1972	Mary Budke	5 & 4	Cynthia Hill	St. Louis CC, St. Louis
1973	Carol Semple	1 up	Anne Quast Decker	Montclair GC, Montclair, NJ
1974	Cynthia Hill	5 & 4	Carol Semple	Broadmoor GC, Seattle
1975	Beth Daniel	3 & 2	Donna Horton	Brae Burn CC, West Newton, MA
1976	Donna Horton	2 & 1	Marianne Bretton	Del Paso CC, Sacramento
1977	Beth Daniel	3 & 1	Cathy Sherk	Cincinnati CC, Cincinnati
1978	Cathy Sherk	4 & 3	Judith Oliver	Sunnybrook GC, Plymouth Meeting, PA
1979	Carolyn Hill	7 & 6	Patty Sheehan	Memphis CC, Memphis
1980	Juli Inkster	2 up	Patti Rizzo	Prairie Dunes CC, Hutchinson, KS
1981	Juli Inkster	1 up	Lindy Goggin	Waverley CC, Portland, OR
1982	Juli Inkster	4 & 3	Cathy Hanlon	Broadmoor GC, Colorado Springs, CO
1983	Joanne Pacillo	2 & 1	Sally Quinlan	Canoe Brook CC, Summit, NJ
1984	Deb Richard	1 up	Kimberly Williams	Broadmoor GC, Seattle
1985	Michiko Hattori	5 & 4	Cheryl Stacy	Fox Chapel CC, Pittsburgh
1986	Kay Cockerill	9 & 7	Kathleen McCarthy	Pasatiempo GC, Santa Cruz, CA
1987	Kay Cockerill	3 & 2	Tracy Kerdyk	Rhode Island CC, Barrington, RI
1988	Pearl Sinn	6 & 5	Karen Noble	Minikahda Club, Minneapolis
1989	Vicki Goetze	4 & 3	Brandie Burton	Pinehurst CC (No. 2), Pinehurst, NC
1990	Pat Hurst	37 holes	Stephanie Davis	Canoe Brook CC, Summit, NJ
1991	Amy Fruhwirth	5 & 4	Heidi Voorhees	Prairie Dunes CC, Hutchinson, KN
1992	Vicki Goetz	1 up	Annika Sorensteam	Kemper Lakes GC, Hawthorne Hills, IL
1993	Jill McGill	1 up	Sarah Ingram	San Diego CC, Chula Vista, CA
1994	Wendy Ward	2 & 1	Jill McGill	The Homestead, Hot Springs, WV
1995	Kelli Kuehne	4 & 3	Anne-Marie Knight	The Country Club, Brookline, MA
1996	Kelli Kuehne	2 & 1	Marisa Baena	Firethorn GC, Lincoln, NE
1997	Silvia Cavalleri	5 & 4	Robin Burke	Brae Burn CC, West Newton, MA
1998	Grace Park	7 & 6	Jenny Chuasiriporn	Barton Hills CC, Ann Arbor, MI
1999	Dorothy Delasin	4 & 3	Jimin Kang	Biltmore Forest CC, Asheville, NC
2000	Marcy Newton	8 & 7	Laura Myerscough	Waverley CC, Portland, OR

U.S. Girls' Junior Amateur

1949 ....Marlene Bauer	1967 ....Elizabeth Story	1985 ....Dana Lofland
1950 ....Patricia Lesser	1968 ....Peggy Harmon	1986 ....Pat Hurst
1951 ....Arlene Brooks	1969 ....Hollis Stacy	1987 ....Michelle McGann
1952 ....Mickey Wright	1970 ....Hollis Stacy	1988 ....Jamille Jose
1953 ....Millie Meyerson	1971 ....Hollis Stacy	1989 ....Brandie Burton
1954 ....Margaret Smith	1972 ....Nancy Lopez	1990 ....Sandrine Mendiburu
1955 ....Carole Jo Kabler	1973 ....Amy Alcott	1991 ....Emilee Klein
1956 ....JoAnne Gunderson	1974 ....Nancy Lopez	1992 ....Jamie Koizumi
1957 ....Judy Eller	1975 ....Dayna Benson	1993 ....Kellee Booth
1958 ....Judy Eller	1976 ....Pilar Dorado	1962 ....Maureen Orcutt
1959 ....Judy Rand	1977 ....Althea Tome	1963 ....Sis Choate
1960 ....Carol Sorenson	1978 ....Lori Castillo	1994 ....Kelli Kuehne
1961 ....Mary Lowell	1979 ....Penny Hammel	1995 ....Marcy Newton
1962 ....Mary Lou Daniel	1980 ....Laurie Rinker	1996 ....Dorothy Delasin
1963 ....Janis Ferraris	1981 ....Kay Cornelius	1997 ....Beth Bauer
1964 ....Peggy Conley	1982 ....Heather Farr	1998 ....Leigh Anne Hardin
1965 ....Gail Sykes	1983 ....Kim Saiki	1999 ....Aree Wongluekiet
1966 ....Claudia Mayhew	1984 ....Cathy Mockett	2000 ....Lisa Ferrero

Women's British Amateur

1893 ....Lady Margaret Scott	1928 ....Miss N. Le Blan	1964 ....C. Sorenson
1894 ....Lady Margaret Scott	1929 ....Miss J. Wethered	1965 ....B. Varangot
1895 ....Lady Margaret Scott	1930 ....Miss D. Fishwick	1966 ....E. Chadwick
1896 ....Miss Pascoe	1931 ....Miss E. Wilson	1967 ....E. Chadwick
1897 ....Miss E.C. Orr	1932 ....Miss E. Wilson	1968 ....B. Varangot
1898 ....Miss L. Thomson	1933 ....Miss E. Wilson	1975 ....C. Lacoste
1899 ....Miss M. Hezlet	1934 ....Mrs. A.M. Holm	1976 ....D. Oxley
1900 ....Miss Adair	1935 ....Miss W. Morgan	1977 ....A. Uzielli
1901 ....Miss Graham	1936 ....Miss P. Barton	1978 ....E. Kennedy
1902 ....Miss M. Hezlet	1937 ....Miss J. Anderson	1979 ....M. Madill
1903 ....Miss Adair	1938 ....Mrs. A.M. Holm	1980 ....A. Quast
1904 ....Miss L. Dod	1939 ....Miss P. Barton	1981 ..............I.C. Robertson
1905 ....Miss B. Thompson	1940–45 ....not held	1982 ....K. Douglas
1906 ....Mrs. Kennon	1946 ..............G.W. Hetherington	1983 ....J. Thornhill
1907 ....Miss M. Hezlet	1947 ....B. Zaharias	1984 ....J. Rosenthal
1908 ....Miss M. Titterton	1948 ....L. Suggs	1985 ....L. Beman
1909 ....Miss D. Campbell	1949 ....F. Stephens	1986 ....M. McGuire
1910 ....Miss Grant Suttie	1950 ....Vicomtesse de Saint	1987 ....J. Collingham
1911 ....Miss D. Campbell	..............Sauveur	1988 ....J. Furby
1912 ....Miss G. Ravenscroft	1951 ..............P.J. MacCann	1989 ....H. Dobson
1913 ....Miss M. Dodd	1952 ....M. Paterson	1990 ....J. Hall
1914 ....Miss C. Leitch	1953 ....M. Stewart	1991 ....V. Michaud
1915–19 ....not held	1954 ....F. Stephens	1992 ....P. Pedersen
1920 ....Miss C. Leitch	1955 ....J. Valentine	1993 ....Catriona Lambert
1921 ....Miss C. Leitch	1956 ....M. Smith	1994 ....Emma Duggleby
1922 ....Miss J. Wethered	1957 ....P. Garvey	1995 ....Julie Hall
1923 ....Miss D. Chambers	1958 ....J. Valentine	1996 ....Kelli Kuehne
1924 ....Miss J. Wethered	1959 ....E. Price	1997 ....Alison Rose
1925 ....Miss J. Wethered	1960 ....B. McIntyre	1998 ....K. Rostron
1926 ....Miss C. Leitch	1961 ....M. Spearman	1999 ....Marine Monnet
1927 ....Miss Thion de la	1962 ....M. Spearman	2000 ....Rebecca Hudson
..............Chaume	1963 ....B. Varangot	

Women's Amateur Public Links

1977 ....Kelly Fuiks	..............Ammaccapane	1994 ....Jill McGill
1978 ....Kelly Fuiks	1986 ....Cindy Schreyer	1995 ....Jo Jo Robertson
1979 ....Lori Castillo	1987 ....Tracy Kerdyk	1996 ....Heather Graff
1980 ....Lori Castillo	1988 ....Pearl Sinn	1997 ....Jo Jo Robertson
1981 ....Mary Enright	1989 ....Pearl Sinn	1998 ....Amy Spooner
1982 ....Nancy Taylor	1990 ....Cathy Mockett	1999 ....Jody Niemann
1983 ....Kelli Antolock	1991 ....Tracy Hanson	2000 ....Catherine Cartwright
1984 ....Heather Farr	1992 ....Amy Fruhwirth	
1985 ....Danielle	1993 ....Connie Masterson	

U.S. Senior Women's Amateur

1964 ....Loma Smith	1977 ....Dorothy Porter	1990 ....Anne Sander
1965 ....Loma Smith	1978 ....Alice Dye	1991 ....Phyllis Preuss
1966 ....Maureen Orcutt	1979 ....Alice Dye	1992 ....Rosemary Thompson
1967 ....Marge Mason	1980 ....Dorothy Porter	1993 ....Anne Sander
1968 ....Carolyn Cudone	1981 ....Dorothy Porter	1994 ....Marlene Streit
1969 ....Carolyn Cudone	1982 ....Edean Ihlanfeldt	1995 ....Jean Smith
1970 ....Carolyn Cudone	1983 ....Dorothy Porter	1996 ....Gayle Borthwick
1971 ....Carolyn Cudone	1984 ....Constance Guthrie	1997 ....Nancy Fitzgerald
1972 ....Carolyn Cudone	1985 ....Marlene Streit	1998 ....Gayle Borthwick
1973 ....Gwen Hibbs	1986 ....Connie Guthrie	1999..........C. Semple Thompson
1974 ....Justine Cushing	1987 ....Anne Sander	2000 ....C. Semple Thompson
1975 ....Alberta Bower	1988 ....Lois Hodge	
1976 ....Cecile H. Maclaurin	1989 ....Anne Sander	

Women's Mid-Amateur Championship

1987 ....Cindy Scholefield	1992 ....M. Mamey-McInerney	1997 ....C. Semple Thompson
1988 ....Martha Lang	1993 ....Sarah Ingram	1998 ....Virginia Derby Grimes
1989 ....Robin Weiss	1994 ....Sarah Ingram	1999 ....Alissa Herron
1990 ....C. Semple Thompson	1995 ....Ellen Port	2000 ....Ellen Port
1991 ....Sarah LeBrun Ingram	1996 ....Ellen Port	

International Golf

Ryder Cup Matches

Year	Results	Site
1927	United States 9½, Great Britain 2½	Worcester CC, Worcester, MA
1929	Great Britain 7, United States 5	Moortown GC, Leeds, England
1931	United States 9, Great Britain 3	Scioto CC, Columbus, OH
1933	Great Britain 6½, United States 5½	Southport and Ainsdale Courses, Southport, England
1935	United States 9, Great Britain 3	Ridgewood CC, Ridgewood, NJ
1937	United States 8, Great Britain 4	Southport and Ainsdale Courses, Southport, England
1939–1945	No tournament	
1947	United States 11, Great Britain 1	Portland GC, Portland, OR
1949	United States 7, Great Britain 5	Ganton GC, Scarborough, England
1951	United States 9½, Great Britain 2½	Pinehurst CC, Pinehurst, NC
1953	United States 6½, Great Britain 5½	Wentworth Club, Surrey, England
1955	United States 8, Great Britain 4	Thunderbird Ranch & CC, Palm Springs, CA
1957	Great Britain 7½, United States 4½	Lindrick GC, Yorkshire, England
1959	United States 8½, Great Britain 3½	Eldorado CC, Palm Desert, CA
1961	United States 14½, Great Britain 9½	Royal Lytham & St. Anne's GC, St Anne's-on-the-Sea, England
1963	United States 23, Great Britain 9	East Lake CC, Atlanta
1965	United States 19½, Great Britain 12½	Royal Birkdale GC, Southport, England
1967	United States 23½, Great Britain 8½	Champions GC, Houston
1969	United States 16, Great Britain 16	Royal Birkdale GC, Southport, England
1971	United States 18½, Great Britain 13½	Old Warson CC, St. Louis
1973	United States 19, Great Britain 13	Hon Co of Edinburgh Golfers, Muirfield, Scotland
1975	United States 21, Great Britain 11	Laurel Valley GC, Ligonier, PA
1977	United States 12½, Great Britain 7½	Royal Lytham & St. Anne's GC, St. Anne's-on-the-Sea, England
1979	United States 17, Europe 11	Greenbrier, White Sulphur Springs, WV
1981	United States 18½, Europe 9½	Walton Heath GC, Surrey, England
1983	United States 14½, Europe 13½	PGA National GC, Palm Beach Gardens, FL
1985	Europe 16½, United States 11½	Belfry GC, Sutton Coldfield, England
1987	Europe 15, United States 13	Muirfield GC, Dublin, OH
1989	Europe 14, United States 14	Belfry GC, Sutton Coldfield, England
1991	United States 14½, Europe 13½	Ocean Course, Kiawah Island, SC
1993	United States 15, Europe 13	Belfry GC, Sutton Coldfield, England
1995	Europe 14½, United States 13½	Oak Hill CC, Rochester, NY
1997	Europe 14½, United States 13½	Valderrama GC, Sotogrande, Spain
1999	United States 14½, Europe 13½	The Country Club, Brookline, MA

Team matches held every odd year between U.S. professionals and those of Great Britain/Europe (since 1979—prior to that it was U.S. vs G.B.). Team members selected on basis of finishes in PGA and European tour events.

Walker Cup Matches

Year	Results	Site
1922	United States 8, Great Britain 4	Nat'l Golf Links of America, Southampton, NY
1923	United States 6, Great Britain 5	St. Andrews, Scotland
1924	United States 9, Great Britain 3	Garden City GC, Garden City, NY
1926	United States 6, Great Britain 5	St. Andrews, Scotland
1928	United States 11, Great Britain 1	Chicago GC, Wheaton, IL
1930	United States 10, Great Britain 2	Royal St. George GC, Sandwich, England
1932	United States 8, Great Britain 1	The Country Club, Brookline, MA
1934	United States 9, Great Britain 2	St. Andrews, Scotland
1936	United States 9, Great Britain 0	Pine Valley GC, Clementon, NJ
1938	Great Britain 7, United States 4	St. Andrews, Scotland
1940–46	No tournament	
1947	United States 8, Great Britain 4	St. Andrews, Scotland
1949	United States 10, Great Britain 2	Winged Foot GC, Mamaroneck, NY
1951	United States 6, Great Britain 3	Birkdale GC, Southport, England
1953	United States 9, Great Britain 3	The Kittansett Club, Marion, MA
1955	United States 10, Great Britain 2	St. Andrews, Scotland
1957	United States 8, Great Britain 3	Minikahda Club, Minneapolis
1959	United States 9, Great Britain 3	Muirfield, Scotland
1961	United States 11, Great Britain 1	Seattle GC, Seattle
1963	United States 12, Great Britain 8	Ailsa Course, Turnberry, Scotland
1965	Great Britain 11, United States 11	Baltimore CC, Five Farms, Baltimore, MD
1967	United States 13, Great Britain 7	Royal St. George's GC, Sandwich, England
1969	United States 10, Great Britain 8	Milwaukee CC, Milwaukee, WI
1971	Great Britain 13, United States 11	St. Andrews, Scotland
1973	United States 14, Great Britain 10	The Country Club, Brookline, MA
1975	United States 15½, Great Britain 8½	St. Andrews, Scotland
1977	United States 16, Great Britain 8	Shinnecock Hills GC, Southampton, NY
1979	United States 15½, Great Britain 8½	Muirfield, Scotland
1981	United States 15, Great Britain 9	Cypress Point Club, Pebble Beach, CA
1983	United States 13½, Great Britain 10½	Royal Liverpool GC, Hoylake, England
1985	United States 13, Great Britain 11	Pine Valley GC, Pine Valley, NJ
1987	United States 16½, Great Britain 7½	Sunningdale GC, Berkshire, England
1989	Great Britain 12½, United States 11½	Peachtree Golf Club, Atlanta
1991	United States 14, Great Britain 10	Portmarnock GC, Dublin, Ireland
1993	United States 19, Great Britain 5	Interlachen CC, Edina, MN
1995	Great Britain/Ireland 14, United States 10	Royal Porthcawl, Porthcawl, Wales
1997	United States 18, Great Britain/Ireland 6	Quaker Ridge GC, Scarsdale, NY
1999	Great Britain/Ireland 15, United States 9	Nairn GC, Nairn, Scotland

Men's amateur team competition every other year between United States and Great Britain/Ireland. U.S. team members selected by USGA.

Solheim Cup Matches

Year	Results	Site
1990	United States 11½, Europe 4½	Lake Nona GC, Orlando, FL
1992	Europe 11½, United States 6½	Dalmahoy Hotel GC, Edinburgh
1994	United States 13, Europe 7	The Greenbriar, White Sulpher Springs, WV
1996	United States 17, Europe 11	Marriot St Pierre Hotel & CC, Chepstow, Wales
1998	United States 16, Europe 12	Muirfield Village GC, Dublin, OH
2000	Europe 14½, United States, 11½	Loch Lomond GC, Luss, Scotand

Team matches held every other year between U.S. professionals and those of Europe. Team members selected on basis of finishes in LPGA and European tour events.

Curtis Cup Matches

Year	Results	Site
1932	United States 5½, British Isles 3½	Wentworth GC, Wentworth, England
1934	United States 6½, British Isles 2½	Chevy Chase Club, Chevy Chase, MD
1936	United States 4½, British Isles 4½	King's Course, Gleneagles, Scotland
1938	United States 5½, British Isles 3½	Essex CC, Manchester, MA
1940–46	No tournament	
1948	United States 6½, British Isles 2½	Birkdale GC, Southport, England
1950	United States 7½, British Isles 1½	CC of Buffalo, Williamsville, NY
1952	British Isles 5, United States 4	Muirfield, Scotland
1954	United States 6, British Isles 3	Merion GC, Ardmore, PA
1956	British Isles 5, United States 4	Prince's GC, Sandwich Bay, England

Curtis Cup Matches *(Cont.)*

Year	Results	Site
1958	British Isles 4½, United States 4½	Brae Burn CC, West Newton, Mass.
1960	United States 6½, British Isles 2½	Lindrick GC, Worksop, England
1962	United States 8, British Isles 1	Broadmoor CG, Colorado Springs,CO
1964	United States 10½, British Isles 7½	Royal Porthcawl GC, Porthcawl, South Wales
1966	United States 13, British Isles 5	Va. Hot Springs G & TC, Hot Springs, VA
1968	United States 10½, British Isles 7½	Royal County Down GC, Newcastle, N. Ire.
1970	United States 11½, British Isles 6½	Brae Burn CC, West Newton, MA
1972	United States 10, British Isles 8	Western Gailes, Ayrshire, Scotland
1974	United States 13, British Isles 5	San Francisco GC, San Francisco, CA
1976	United States 11½, British Isles 6½	Royal Lytham & St. Anne's GC, England
1978	United States 12, British Isles 6	Apawamis Club, Rye, NY
1980	United States 13, British Isles 5	St. Pierre G & CC, Chepstow, Wales
1982	United States 14½, British Isles 3½	Denver CC, Denver
1984	United States 9½, British Isles 8½	Muirfield, Scotland
1986	British Isles 13, United States 5	Prairie Dunes CC, Hutchinson, KS
1988	British Isles 11, United States 7	Royal St. George's GC, Sandwich, England
1990	United States 14, British Isles 4	Somerset Hills CC, Bernardsville, NJ
1992	Great Britain/Ireland 10, United States 8	Royal Liverpool GC, Hoylake, England
1994	Great Britain/Ireland 9, United States 9	The Honors Course, Ooltewah, TN
1996	Great Britain/Ireland 11½, United States 6½	Killarney Golf & Fishing Club, Killarney, Ireland
1998	United States 10, Great Britain/Ireland 8	The Minikahda Club, Minneapolis
2000	United States 10, Great Britain/Ireland 8	Ganton GC, North Yorkshire, England

Women's amateur team competition every other year between the United States and Great Britain/Ireland. U.S. team members selected by USGA.

The Greatest Show on Earth

It's a strange job, traipsing about, typing sports. You forget how to tingle. Your Amaze-o-Meter gets stuck on empty. A comeback to win the Supe Bowl? *Yawn, scribble.* A 9.9 to win the gold? *Scribble, yawn.* Almost 220 mph on that last lap? *Yawn, yawn.*

Then along comes Tiger Woods, and a job becomes a privilege. I would pogo from Bangor to Birmingham to see Woods play. I would wear spike heels, a see-through muumuu and Ru Paul's curlers if it were the only way through the gate. I ought to buy my dad a box of cigars for having me the year that he did.

We're lucky. All of us. We're alive when the single most dominating athlete in 70 years is at his jaw-dropping best. Bathe in it. Wallow in it. Savor it. Take notes. Get video. Save newspapers. Your grandkids will want details.

Michael Jordan? This guy is better. Jordan had teammates. Woods is out there by himself. Jordan beat guys one-on-one, one-on-two. Woods won the unforgettable 2000 PGA Championship at Valhalla one-on-149. What's more, Woods never got cheap calls from refs.

Woods is pureeing everybody, everywhere, every way—from miles ahead and from two behind, as he was at the PGA with 12 holes to play. How many guys are good enough to win a major playing off cart paths on the last two holes? He thumps great players, and he survives the guy pulling gold monkeys out of his ear. Staring into the biggest upset since Colts-Jets, he snuffed out a toy pit bull named Bob May with a mile of must-make putts. All he did was birdie eight of 13 holes, including the first playoff hole. You can't Buster Douglas Tiger Woods. He stuffs every Cinderella back into the pumpkin.

Woods is the most amazing performer I've ever seen, and I've seen Ali, Gretzky, Jordan, Montana and Nicklaus. What Woods is doing is so hard it's like climbing Everest in flip flops. Performing heart transplants in oven mitts. The four major championships have been played 344 times, and Woods now holds or shares the scoring record in all four of them? That's *sick.*

...You're sick of hearing about Tiger Woods. You're going to hear more. He has more than twice as much jing as the next guy on the PGA Tour money list. He has more than triple the points of the next guy on the U.S. Ryder Cup list. He has more than twice as many points as the next guy in the World Golf Ranking. Ali was great, but was he twice as great as Joe Frazier?

The grumps in the press tent keep trying to find a buzzkill in all this. *Hey, Nicklaus had to beat Gary Player and Tom Watson.* Hey, if Woods didn't exist, wouldn't Ernie Els be Player by now? Might not David Duval have a chance to be Watson? Brilliant careers are going around stuck on Woods's golf spikes.

What do you have to shoot to win around here? Stuart Appleby was asked at the PGA.

"Tiger Woods," he said.

Go see this kid while you're breathing. Three straight majors? Not done in 47 years. Four of the last five majors? Not done, ever. Now he's leaning on the doorbell of something nobody thought would ever be done: the Grand Slam. Oh, yes, it is. If Woods wins the 2001 Masters, that *is* the Grand Slam. It's not the continuous Slam or the asterisk slam, just the Grand Slam. He says so. I say so. Hell, sportswriters invented it; sportswriters make the rules. And don't give me Bobby Jones. Beating three guys named Nigel and two sheep at the British Amateur doesn't even compute.

Woods and Jack Nicklaus were walking down the first fairway at the 2000 PGA, their ears ringing from the roars, "Man it's loud." Nicklaus said to Woods. "Thank God, I'm done playing. Now you get to deal with this the rest of your career."

As well he should.

—Rick Reilly

Total Player Rankings

Introduction

As 2000 ends, many panels of experts are offering their lists of the century's greatest athletes. In the following 15 pages, the editors at Total Sports offer something slightly different. Instead of rating the top athletes based on personal opinion, they have applied analytical methods to provide an objective ranking of players in a variety of sports. The goal is a fair comparison of athletes from different eras. Some of these methods are more scientific or rigorous than others. Some have been around for many years, while others are relatively new. These rankings may spur more debate than they settle, but the editors will be content if they have shed light on some great, undeservedly obscure athletes.

Statistical research and ratings were provided by: Bob Bellotti, Bob Carroll, Dan Diamond, Sean Lahman, Mike Meserole, Pete Palmer, Greg Spira and John Thorn.

Auto Racing

Stock Car Racing

Sanctioned by NASCAR since 1947. Ranking based on performance points system which awards points for top-six finishes.

	Driver	Career	Points	Wins	Championships
1	Richard Petty	1958–1992	3490	200	7
2	David Pearson	1960–1986	1865	105	3
3	Bobby Allison	1961–1988	1848	85	1
4	Darrell Waltrip*	1972–	1593	84	3
5	Dale Earnhardt*	1975–	1559	75	7
6	Cale Yarborough	1957–1988	1500	83	3
7	Lee Petty	1949–1964	1220	54	3
8	Buck Baker	1949–1976	1205	46	2
9	Ned Jarrett	1953–1966	1007	50	2
10	Rusty Wallace*	1980–	979	53	1
11	Mark Martin*	1981–	906	32	0
12	Buddy Baker	1959–1984	878	19	0
13	Benny Parsons	1964–1988	838	21	1
14	Bill Elliott*	1976–	833	40	1
15	Jeff Gordon*	1992–	790	52	3
16	Terry Labonte*	1978–	788	21	2
17	Junior Johnson	1953–1966	781	50	0
18	Herb Thomas	1949–1962	772	48	2
19	Bobby Isaac	1961–1976	757	37	1
20	Jim Paschal	1949–1972	721	25	0

*Active in 2000. Includes races through 10-2-00.

Indy Car Racing

Sanctioned by the AAA from 1909–1954, USAC 1955–1978, CART 1979–1999. Ranking based on 5 points for winning the annual PPG Cup championship, 2 points for each race won, an additional 3 points for each win in the Indianapolis 500.

	Driver	Career	Points	Wins	Championships	Indy 500 Wins
1	A.J. Foyt	1957–1992	181	67	7	4
2	Mario Andretti	1964–1994	127	52	4	1
3	Al Unser	1964–1993	105	39	3	4
4	Bobby Unser	1962–1981	89	35	2	3
5T	Michael Andretti*	1983–	85	41	1	0
5T	Rick Mears	1976–1992	85	29	3	4
7	Al Unser Jr	1982–1999	78	31	2	2
8	Tommy Milton	1917–1925	69	23	2	2
9T	Ralph DePalma	1908–1936	68	24	2	1
9T	Johnny Rutherford	1962–1989	68	27	1	3
9T	Rodger Ward	1951–1966	68	26	2	2
12	Bobby Rahal	1982–1998	66	24	3	1
13	Jimmy Bryan	1953–1958	63	19	3	1
14	Earl Cooper	1912–1926	62	20	3	0
15	Gordon Johncock	1964–1992	61	25	1	2
16	Jimmy Murphy	1920–1924	58	19	2	1
17T	Emerson Fittipaldi	1984–1996	55	22	1	2
17T	Louie Meyer	1924–1939	55	12	3	3
19	Tony Bettenhausen	1946–1961	54	22	0	0
20	Ralph Mulford	1910–1919	51	17	0	0

*Active in 2000. Includes races through 10-2-00.

Auto Racing (Cont.)

Grand Prix Racing

Sanctioned by Formula One from 1950–1999. Ranking based on performance points system which awards points for top-six finishes.

	Driver	Career	Points	Wins	Championships	Country
1	Alain Prost	1980–1993	798.5	51	4	France
2	Michael Schumacher*	1991–	658	42	2	Germany
3	Ayrton Senna	1984–1994	614	41	3	Brazil
4	Nelson Piquet	1978–1991	485.5	23	3	Brazil
5	Nigel Mansell	1980–1995	482	31	1	England
6	Niki Lauda	1971–1985	420.5	25	3	Austria
7	Gerhard Berger	1984–1997	385	10	0	Austria
8	Mika Hakkinen*	1991–	374	18	2	Finland
9T	Damon Hill	1992–1999	360	22	1	England
9T	Jackie Stewart	1965–1973	360	27	3	Scotland
11	Carlos Reutemann	1972–1982	310	12	0	Argentina
12	Graham Hill	1958–1975	289	14	0	England
13	David Coulthard*	1994–	284	9	3	England
14T	Emerson Fittipaldi	1970–1980	281	14	2	Brazil
14T	Riccardo Patrese	1977–1993	281	6	0	Italy
16	Juan Manuel Fangio	1950–1958	277.64	24	5	Argentina
17	Jim Clark	1960–1968	274	25	2	Scotland
18	Jack Brabham	1955–1970	261	14	3	Australia
19	Jody Scheckter	1972–1980	255	10	1	South Africa
20	Denny Hulme	1965–1974	248	8	1	New Zealand

*Active in 2000. Includes races through 10-2-00.

Baseball

Total Player Ratings (TPR) are an estimate of the number of wins a player contributed based on batting, pitching, fielding and baserunning. Players who played primarily in the 19th century are excluded.

Top Players By Position

	Pitcher	TPR	Won	Lost	E.R.A.
1	Walter Johnson	90.1	417	279	2.17
2	Cy Young	79.8	511	316	2.63
3	Grover Alexander	64.9	373	208	2.56
4	Christy Mathewson	62.8	373	188	2.13
5	Lefty Grove	61.2	300	141	3.06
6	Kid Nichols	60.9	361	208	2.95
7	Greg Maddux*	59.6	240	135	2.83
8	Roger Clemens*	53.9	260	142	3.07
9	Tom Seaver	48.2	311	205	2.86
10	Warren Spahn	47.0	363	245	3.09
11	Bob Gibson	44.0	251	174	2.91
12	Ed Walsh	43.3	195	126	1.82
13	Hal Newhouser	40.8	207	150	3.06
14	Hoyt Wilhelm	39.7	143	122	2.52
15	Carl Hubbell	39.2	253	154	2.98
16	Whitey Ford	37.2	236	106	2.75
17	Bob Lemon	36.9	207	128	3.23
18	Ted Lyons	36.7	260	230	3.67
19	Carl Mays	36.2	208	126	2.92
20	Jim Palmer	35.5	268	152	2.86
21	Phil Niekro	35.4	318	274	3.35
22	Three Finger Brown	34.8	239	130	2.06
23	Dizzy Trout	34.5	170	161	3.23
24	Gaylord Perry	34.4	314	265	3.11
25	Don Drysdale	34.0	209	166	2.95
26	Steve Carlton	33.2	329	244	3.22
27	Kevin Brown*	32.7	170	114	3.21
28	Wes Ferrell	32.4	193	128	4.04
29	John Franco*	32.0	82	74	2.68
30	Pedro Martinez*	31.5	125	56	2.68

*Active in 2000. Totals include 2000 regular season.

Pitcher		TPR	Won	Lost	E.R.A.
31	Fergie Jenkins	30.9	284	226	3.34
32T	Bert Blyleven	30.8	287	250	3.31
32T	Tom Glavine*	30.8	208	125	3.39
34	Randy Johnson*	30.6	179	95	3.19
35	Rich Gossage	29.5	124	107	3.01
36	Clark Griffith	29.0	237	146	3.31
37	Juan Marichal	28.9	243	142	2.89
38	Tommy Bridges	28.7	194	138	3.57
39	Bob Feller	28.5	266	162	3.25
40	Bret Saberhagen	27.8	166	115	3.33
41	Stan Coveleski	27.5	215	142	2.89
42	Dave Stieb	27.1	176	137	3.44
43T	Red Faber	27.0	254	213	3.15
43T	Eddie Plank	27.0	326	194	2.35
43T	Dazzy Vance	27.0	197	140	3.24
46	Red Ruffing	26.8	273	225	3.80
47	Dennis Eckersley	26.7	197	171	3.50
48	Bucky Walters	26.4	198	160	3.30
49	Dolf Luque	26.3	194	179	3.24
50	Eddie Rommel	26.0	171	119	3.54

Catcher		TPR	Avg.	HR	RBI
1	Gabby Hartnett	40.1	.297	236	1179
2	Mike Piazza*	36.5	.328	278	881
3	Yogi Berra	36.2	.285	358	1430
4	Bill Dickey	35.4	.313	202	1209
5	Mickey Cochrane	31.4	.320	119	832
6	Gary Carter	29.6	.262	324	1225
7	Johnny Bench	24.3	.267	389	1376
8	Carlton Fisk	24.0	.269	376	1330
9	Roy Campanella	21.6	.276	242	856
10	Roger Bresnahan	19.8	.279	26	530

1st Base		TPR	Avg.	HR	RBI
1	Lou Gehrig	65.7	.340	493	1995
2	Jimmie Foxx	54.3	.325	534	1922
3	Jeff Bagwell*	47.0	.305	310	1093
4	Frank Thomas*	42.1	.321	344	1183
5	Mark McGwire*	37.5	.267	554	1350
6	Willie McCovey	36.5	.270	521	1555
7	Johnny Mize	36.2	.312	359	1337
8	Dick Allen	35.3	.292	351	1119
9	Keith Hernandez	34.4	.296	162	1071
10	Eddie Murray	34.1	.287	504	1917

2nd Base		TPR	Avg.	HR	RBI
1	Nap Lajoie	94.1	.338	82	1599
2	Rogers Hornsby	81.2	.358	301	1584
3	Eddie Collins	69.8	.333	47	1300
4	Joe Morgan	56.3	.271	268	1133
5	Charlie Gehringer	44.4	.320	184	1427
6	Bobby Grich	44.0	.266	224	864
7T	Bobby Doerr	39.0	.288	223	1247
7T	Frankie Frisch	39.0	.316	105	1244
9	Craig Biggio*	37.6	.291	160	741
10	Roberto Alomar*	37.1	.304	170	918

3rd Base		TPR	Avg.	HR	RBI
1	Mike Schmidt	78.4	.267	548	1595
2	Eddie Mathews	51.6	.271	512	1453
3	Wade Boggs	43.3	.328	118	1014
4	Ron Santo	39.5	.277	342	1331
5	George Brett	39.0	.305	317	1595
6	Darrell Evans	34.7	.248	414	1354
7	Frank Baker	33.8	.307	96	987
8T	Heinie Groh	27.2	.292	26	566
8T	Stan Hack	27.2	.301	57	642
10T	Jimmy Collins	23.1	.294	65	983
10T	Matt Williams*	23.1	.269	346	1097

*Active in 2000. Totals include 2000 regular season.

Baseball (Cont.)

	Shortstop	TPR	Avg.	HR	RBI
1.	Honus Wagner	81.1	.327	101	1732
2.	Barry Larkin*	47.5	.300	179	834
3.	Robin Yount	43.1	.285	251	1406
4.	Ozzie Smith	43.0	.262	28	793
5.	Lou Boudreau	41.3	.295	68	789
6.	Luke Appling	40.7	.310	45	1116
7.	Cal Ripken*	40.6	.277	417	1627
8.	Joe Cronin	39.4	.301	170	1424
9.	Arky Vaughan	39.2	.318	96	926
10.	Dave Bancroft	35.2	.279	32	591

	Left Field	TPR	Avg.	HR	RBI
1.	Barry Bonds*	89.5	.289	494	1405
2.	Ted Williams	85.7	.344	521	1839
3.	Rickey Henderson*	80.3	.282	282	1052
4.	Stan Musial	70.5	.331	475	1951
5.	Tim Raines*	51.8	.295	168	964
6.	Carl Yastrzemski	45.5	.285	452	1844
7.	Joe Jackson	37.5	.356	54	785
8.	Bob Johnson	35.6	.296	288	1283
9.	Albert Belle*	35.5	.295	381	1239
10.	Willie Stargell	32.8	.282	475	1540

	Center Field	TPR	Avg.	HR	RBI
1.	Willie Mays	92.2	.302	660	1903
2.	Ty Cobb	91.1	.366	117	1937
3.	Tris Speaker	86.5	.345	117	1529
4.	Mickey Mantle	76.1	.298	536	1509
5.	Ken Griffey Jr*	47.6	.296	438	1270
6.	Joe DiMaggio	46.9	.325	361	1537
7.	Richie Ashburn	30.2	.308	29	586
8.	Kirby Puckett	29.1	.318	207	1085
9.	Cesar Cedeno	28.3	.285	199	976
10.	Bernie Williams*	26.1	.304	181	802

	Right Field	TPR	Avg.	HR	RBI
1.	Babe Ruth	124.8	.342	714	2213
2.	Hank Aaron	89.8	.305	755	2297
3.	Frank Robinson	69.0	.294	586	1812
4.	Mel Ott	62.7	.304	511	1860
5.	Tony Gwynn*	48.5	.338	131	1121
6.	Al Kaline	44.6	.297	399	1583
7.	Roberto Clemente	42.9	.317	240	1305
8.	Reggie Jackson	42.8	.262	563	1702
9.	Dave Winfield	38.6	.283	465	1833
10.	Paul Waner	36.1	.333	113	1309

*Active in 2000. Totals include 2000 regular season.

Basketball

Points Created (PC) evaluates overall performance. It adds the good things a player did (points, rebounds, assists, steals and blocked shots) and subtracts the bad things (missed field goals and free throws, turnovers and personal fouls). With Points Created, a player's statistics are pared down to a single number—the points a player "creates" through his overall play.

Based on the NBA's average points scored per possession, the system assigns a value to each statistical category. Because the average points per possession changes from year to year and decade to decade—for example, NBA teams averaged 74.6 points per 100 possessions in 1963–64 and 88.9 points in 1998–99—Points Created is a viable way to compare players from different eras.

Ppg = Points per game; Rpg = Rebounds per game; Apg = Assists per game; PC/min = Points Created per minute.

	Overall Players	Ppg	Rpg	Apg	PC/min
1.	Wilt Chamberlain	30.1	22.9	4.4	.880
2.	Magic Johnson	19.5	7.2	11.2	.794
3.	Michael Jordan	31.5	6.3	5.4	.786
4.	Kareem Abdul-Jabbar	24.6	11.2	3.6	.782
5.	Bob Pettit	26.4	16.2	3.0	.781

*Active in 1999–2000. †Includes player's ABA statistics. Minimum 500 regular-season games.

Overall Players		Ppg	Rpg	Apg	PC/min
6	Oscar Robertson	25.7	7.5	9.5	.777
7	David Robinson*	23.7	11.3	2.8	.767
8	Shaquille O'Neal*	27.5	12.4	2.7	.766
9	Larry Bird	24.3	10.0	6.3	.765
10	Elgin Baylor	27.4	13.5	4.3	.745
11T	Hakeem Olajuwon*	23.1	11.6	2.6	.733
11T	Charles Barkley*	22.1	11.7	3.9	.733
13	Jerry West	27.0	5.8	6.7	.722
14	Karl Malone*	26.0	10.6	3.4	.716
15	Julius Erving†	24.2	8.5	4.2	.703
16	Paul Arizin	22.8	8.6	2.3	.693
17	Bob Lanier	20.1	10.1	3.1	.690
18	George Mikan	23.1	13.4	2.8	.687
19	Artis Gilmore†	18.8	12.3	1.4	.682
20T	Bill Russell	15.1	22.5	4.3	.681
20T	Dolph Schayes	18.5	12.1	3.1	.681
22	Moses Malone	20.6	12.2	1.4	.673
23	Jerry Lucas	17.0	15.6	3.3	.671
24	Bob McAdoo	22.1	9.4	2.3	.668
25	Dan Issel†	22.6	9.1	2.4	.667
26	Patrick Ewing*	22.8	10.4	2.0	.656
27	Billy Cunningham†	21.1	10.4	4.3	.664
28	George McGinnis†	20.2	11.0	3.7	.663
29	Walt Bellamy	20.1	13.7	2.4	.658
30	John Stockton*	13.3	2.7	11.0	.657
31	Mel Daniels	18.7	15.1	1.8	.654
32T	Rick Barry†	24.8	6.7	4.9	.653
32T	Bob Cousy	5.2	7.5	18.4	.653
34	Cliff Hagan†	17.7	6.6	3.2	.634
35T	Alvan Adams	14.1	7.0	4.1	.633
35T	Kevin Johnson	18.0	3.3	9.2	.633
37	Bailey Howell	18.7	9.9	2.0	.632
38	George Gervin†	26.2	4.6	2.8	.629
39T	Clyde Drexler	20.4	6.1	5.6	.626
39T	Alonzo Mourning*	21.1	10.1	1.5	.626
41	Willis Reed	18.7	12.9	1.8	.625
42	Larry Nance	17.1	8.0	2.6	.623
43T	Alex English	21.5	5.5	3.6	.622
43T	Swen Nater†	12.2	10.8	2.0	.622
45	Robert Parish	14.5	9.1	1.4	.620
46	Kevin McHale	17.9	7.3	1.7	.618
47	Dave Cowens	17.6	13.6	3.8	.615
48	Connie Hawkins†	18.3	8.8	3.8	.614
49	Adrian Dantley	24.3	5.7	3.0	.611
50	Tom Boerwinkle	7.2	9.0	3.2	.608

Forwards		Ppg	Rpg	Apg	PC/min
1	Bob Pettit	26.4	16.2	3.0	.781
2	Larry Bird	24.3	10.0	6.3	.765
3	Elgin Baylor	27.4	13.5	4.3	.745
4	Charles Barkley*	22.1	11.7	3.9	.735
5	Karl Malone*	26.0	10.6	3.4	.716
6	Julius Erving†	24.2	8.5	4.2	.703
7	Paul Arizin	22.8	8.6	2.3	.693
8	Dolph Schayes	18.5	12.1	3.1	.681
9	Jerry Lucas	17.0	15.6	3.3	.671
10	Billy Cunningham†	21.1	10.4	4.3	.664
11	George McGinnis†	20.2	11.0	3.7	.663
12	Mel Daniels	18.7	15.1	1.8	.654
13	Rick Barry†	24.8	6.7	4.9	.653
14	Cliff Hagan†	17.7	6.6	3.2	.634
15	Bailey Howell	18.7	9.9	2.0	.632
16	Willis Reed	18.7	12.9	1.8	.625
17	Larry Nance	17.1	8.0	2.6	.623
18	Alex English	21.5	5.5	3.6	.622
19	Kevin McHale	17.9	7.3	1.7	.618
20	Connie Hawkins†	18.3	8.8	3.8	.614

*Active in 1999–2000. †Includes player's ABA statistics. Minimum 500 regular-season games.

Basketball (Cont.)

	Centers	Ppg	Rpg	Apg	PC/min
1	Wilt Chamberlain	30.1	22.9	4.4	.880
2	Kareem Abdul-Jabbar	24.6	11.2	3.6	.782
3	David Robinson*	23.7	11.3	2.8	.767
4	Shaquille O'Neal*	27.5	12.4	2.7	.766
5	Hakeem Olajuwon*	23.1	11.6	2.6	.733
6	Bob Lanier	20.1	10.1	3.1	.690
7	George Mikan	23.1	13.4	2.8	.687
8	Artis Gilmore†	18.8	12.3	1.4	.682
9	Bill Russell	15.1	22.5	4.3	.681
10	Moses Malone	20.6	12.2	1.4	.673
11	Bob McAdoo	22.1	9.4	2.3	.668
12	Dan Issel†	22.6	9.1	2.4	.667
13	Walt Bellamy	20.1	13.7	2.4	.658
14	Patrick Ewing*	22.8	10.4	2.0	.656
15	Alvan Adams	14.1	7.0	4.1	.633
16	Alonzo Mourning*	21.1	10.1	1.5	.626
17	Swen Nater†	12.2	10.8	2.0	.622
18	Robert Parish	14.5	9.1	1.4	.620
19	Dave Cowens	17.6	13.6	3.8	.615
20	Tom Boerwinkle	7.2	9.0	3.2	.608

	Guards	Ppg	Rpg	Apg	PC/min
1	Magic Johnson	19.5	7.2	11.2	.794
2	Michael Jordan	31.5	6.3	5.4	.786
3	Oscar Robertson	25.7	7.5	9.5	.777
4	Jerry West	27.0	5.8	6.7	.722
5	John Stockton*	13.3	2.7	11.0	.657
6	Bob Cousy	5.2	7.5	18.4	.653
7	Kevin Johnson	18.0	3.3	9.2	.633
8	George Gervin†	26.2	4.6	2.8	.629
9	Clyde Drexler	20.4	6.1	5.6	.626
10T	Walt Frazier	18.9	5.9	6.1	.590
10T	Paul Westphal	15.6	1.9	4.4	.590
12	Fat Lever	13.9	6.0	6.2	.581
13	Walter Davis	18.9	3.0	3.8	.579
14	Sam Jones	17.7	4.9	2.5	.577
15	Pete Maravich	24.2	4.2	5.4	.569
16	Richie Guerin	17.3	5.0	5.0	.565
17	Ray Williams	15.5	3.6	5.8	.560
18	Tim Hardaway*	19.0	3.5	8.9	.554
19T	Isiah Thomas	19.2	3.6	9.3	.552
19T	Lenny Wilkens	16.5	4.7	6.7	.552

*Active in 1999–2000. †Includes player's ABA statistics. Minimum 500 regular-season games.

Boxing

Points awarded to lineal champions as follows: Years held title multiplied by weighted record in title fights (plus one point for a win, plus a half point for a draw, minus one point for a loss). Does not include 19th-century fighters or records in non-title fights.

	Heavyweights	Years	W	L	D	Points
1	Joe Louis	11.690	26	1	0	303.94
2	Larry Holmes	7.285	21	2	0	145.70
3	Muhammad Ali	7.247	22	3	0	144.94
4	Jim Jeffries	5.926	8	1	0	47.41
5	Joe Frazier	4.888	10	2	0	43.99
6	Jack Dempsey	7.222	6	2	0	36.11
7	Jack Johnson	6.301	5	1	1	34.66
8	Tommy Burns	2.838	11	1	0	31.22
9	Rocky Marciano	3.595	7	0	0	28.76
10	George Foreman	4.819	7	3	0	24.10

	Light Heavyweights	Years	W	L	D	Points
1.	Bob Foster	6.321	15	0	0	101.14
2.	Archie Moore	9.164	9	0	0	91.64
3.	Gus Lesnevich	7.159	6	1	0	42.95
4.	John Henry Lewis	3.668	5	0	0	22.01
5.	Michael Spinks	2.518	5	0	0	15.11

	Middleweights	Years	W	L	D	Points
1.	Carlos Monzon	6.732	14	0	0	100.98
2.	Marvin Hagler	6.526	13	1	1	88.10
3.	Tommy Ryan	6.932	3	0	0	27.73
4.	Mickey Walker	4.545	4	0	0	22.73
5.	Sugar Ray Robinson	5.018	8	5	0	20.01

	Welterweights	Years	W	L	D	Points
1.	Jose Napoles	6.137	15	2	0	85.92
2.	Henry Armstrong	2.351	21	2	0	47.01
3.	Emile Griffith	4.649	10	2	0	41.84
4.	Pernell Whitaker	4.107	8	1	1	34.91
5.	Jack Britton	4.805	6	2	0	24.03

	Lightweights	Years	W	L	D	Points
1.	Roberto Duran	6.608	13	0	0	92.52
2.	Benny Leonard	7.644	9	0	0	76.44
3.	Joe Brown	5.663	12	1	0	67.96
4.	Joe Gans	4.318	16	3	0	60.45
5.	Carlos Ortiz	5.605	11	2	0	56.05

	Featherweights	Years	W	L	D	Points
1.	Abe Attell	6.005	12	1	3	81.07
2.	Willie Pep	7.523	11	2	0	75.23
3.	Johnny Kilbane	11.285	6	2	3	73.35
4.	Sandy Saddler	6.668	5	1	0	33.34
5.	Vicente Saldivar	3.649	10	2	0	32.84

	Bantamweights	Years	W	L	D	Points
1.	Manuel Ortiz	7.482	21	2	0	149.64
2.	Panama Al Brown	5.959	12	1	0	71.51
3.	Eder Jofre	4.712	8	2	0	32.99
4.	Jeff Chandler	3.400	9	1	0	32.30
5.	Johnny Coulon	4.266	5	1	0	21.33

	Flyweights	Years	W	L	D	Points
1.	Miguel Canto Solis	5.693	15	1	1	88.24
2.	Yuri Arbachakov	5.395	10	1	0	53.95
3.	Sot Chitalda	5.504	11	3	1	52.29
4.	Pascual Perez	5.395	10	2	0	48.55
5.	Jimmy Wilde	7.348	5	1	0	36.74

Includes fights through 10-2-00.

Football

Two-Way Players (1920–49)

Players ranked based on years as All-Pro through 1999, with points given as follows:
C: Eight points for Consensus All-Pro from all teams selected; 1st: Five points for first-team All-Pro for any major all-pro team or Pro Bowl; 2nd: Three points for Second team All-Pro for any major all-pro team.

	Ends	C	1st	2nd	Total		Tackles	C	1st	2nd	Total
1.	Don Hutson	7	2	2	72	1.	Albert Wistert	5	2	1	53
2.	Lavie Dilweg	5	2	1	53	2T.	Turk Edwards	4	3	1	50
3.	Bill Hewitt	4	2	0	42	2T.	Bruiser Kinard	4	3	1	50
4T.	Guy Chamberlin	3	1	0	29	4.	Ed Healey	4	3	0	47
4T.	Ray Flaherty	2	2	1	29	5.	Cal Hubbard	5	1	0	45
4T.	Red Badgro	3	1	0	29						

Two-Way Players (1920–49) *(Cont.)*

Guards	C	1st	2nd	Total
1...... Danny Fortmann	6	1	1	56
2...... Mike Michalske	6	1	0	53
3...... Riley Matheson	4	2	2	48
4...... Ox Emerson	4	2	0	42
5...... Ray Bray	3	2	0	34

Backs	C	1st	2nd	Total
1...... Paddy Driscoll	7	1	1	64
2...... Dutch Clark	6	0	0	48
3...... Clarke Hinkle	3	4	3	41
4T.... Ernie Nevers	5	0	0	40
4T.... Ken Strong	4	1	1	40

Centers	C	1st	2nd	Total
1...... Mel Hein	7	1	4	73
2...... Bulldog Turner	7	2	1	69
3...... George Trafton	3	2	1	37
4...... Nate Barrager	2	0	3	25

One-Way Players (1950–99)

Quarterbacks	C	1st	2nd	Total
1...... Otto Graham	9	1	0	77
2...... Johnny Unitas	5	6	0	70
3T.... Sammy Baugh	5	3	2	61
3T.... Fran Tarkenton	2	9	0	61
5...... Dan Marino*	3	6	0	54
6...... Sid Luckman	5	1	2	51
7...... John Elway	1	8	0	48
8T.... Jack Kemp	2	6	0	46
8T.... Joe Montana	2	6	0	46
10.... Warren Moon*	0	9	0	45

Offensive Tackles	C	1st	2nd	Total
1...... Anthony Munoz	9	2	0	82
2...... Rosey Brown	8	2	1	77
3...... Ron Mix	9	0	0	72
4...... Jim Tyrer	7	3	0	71
5...... Forrest Gregg	6	4	0	68
6...... Lou Groza	5	4	2	66
7...... Lou Creekmur	6	3	0	63
8...... Ron Yary	7	1	0	61
9...... Bob Brown	6	1	1	56
10.... Art Shell	6	1	0	53

Running Backs	C	1st	2nd	Total
1...... Jim Brown	8	1	0	69
2...... Barry Sanders	6	4	0	68
3...... Walter Payton	7	2	0	66
4...... Lenny Moore	5	3	0	65
5...... Ollie Matson	4	4	0	52
6...... Franco Harris	2	7	0	51
7...... Steve Van Buren	5	1	1	48
8T.... Frank Gifford	4	3	0	47
8T.... Emmitt Smith*	4	3	0	47
9T.... O. J. Simpson	5	1	0	45
9T.... Eric Dickerson	5	1	0	45

Offensive Guards	C	1st	2nd	Total
1...... John Hannah	9	1	1	80
2...... Bruce Matthews*	7	4	0	76
3...... Tom Mack	7	3	0	71
4...... Jim Parker	7	2	0	66
5...... Gene Upshaw	5	5	0	65
6...... Randall McDaniel*	6	4	0	58
7...... Larry Little	5	2	1	53
8T.... Billy Shaw	4	4	0	52
8T.... Steve Wisniewski*	4	4	0	52
10T.. Ed Budde	2	7	0	51
10T.. Joe DeLamielleure	6	0	1	51
10T.. Mike Munchak	2	7	0	51

Receivers	C	1st	2nd	Total
1...... Jerry Rice*	8	4	0	84
2...... Paul Warfield	6	2	0	58
3...... Lance Alworth	7	0	0	56
4...... Pete Pihos	5	2	2	52
5T.... James Lofton	2	6	0	46
5T.... Charley Taylor	3	5	1	46
7T.... Steve Largent	1	5	4	45
7T.... Mac Speedie	5	1	0	45
9T.... Fred Biletnikoff	2	4	1	39
9T.... Dante Lavelli	3	3	2	39

Centers	C	1st	2nd	Total
1...... Jim Otto	12	1	0	101
2...... Jim Ringo	6	4	1	71
3...... Mike Webster	5	5	1	68
4...... Mick Tinglehoff	7	0	0	56
5...... Dermonti Dawson*	5	2	0	50
6...... Jim Langer	5	1	0	45
7...... Dwight Stephenson	5	0	0	40
8...... Ray Wietecha	1	6	0	38
9T.... Tom Banks	4	1	0	37
9T.... Frank Gatski	4	1	0	37
9T.... Jay Hilgenberg	2	5	0	37

Tight Ends	C	1st	2nd	Total
1...... Shannon Sharpe*	4	3	0	47
2T.... Fred Arbanas	3	3	0	39
2T.... Keith Jackson	3	3	0	39
4...... Mike Ditka	3	2	1	37
5T.... Kellen Winslow	3	2	0	34
5T.... John Mackey	3	2	0	34
7...... Ozzie Newsome	1	3	3	32
8T.... Todd Christensen	2	3	0	31
8T.... Ben Coates*	2	3	0	31
10.... Steve Jordan	0	6	0	30

Defensive Ends	C	1st	2nd	Total
1...... Reggie White	9	4	0	92
2...... Gino Marchetti	7	4	0	76
3...... Bruce Smith*	6	5	0	73
4...... Carl Eller	6	2	1	61
5...... Andy Robustelli	3	6	2	60
6T.... Jack Youngblood	6	2	0	58
6T.... Deacon Jones	6	2	0	58
8T.... Doug Atkins	2	7	0	51
8T.... Claude Humphrey	4	2	3	51
10.... Howie Long	3	5	0	49

*Active in 1999.

One-Way Players (1950–99) (Cont.)

Defensive Tackles	C	1st	2nd	Total		Defensive Backs	C	1st	2nd	Total
1...... Merlin Olsen	7	7	0	91		1...... Ken Houston	6	6	0	78
2...... Joe Greene	9	2	0	82		2...... Paul Krause	6	3	1	66
3...... Alan Page	7	4	0	76		3T.... Willie Wood	5	5	0	65
4T.... Bob Lilly	8	1	0	69		3T.... Emlen Tunnell	5	5	0	65
4T.... Randy White	8	1	0	69		3T.... Ronnie Lott	5	5	0	65
6...... Leo Nomellini	5	4	2	66		6...... Johnny Robinson	6	3	0	63
7...... Bill Willis	5	3	0	55		7...... Deion Sanders*	5	4	0	60
8T.... George Connor	6	1	0	51		8...... Larry Wilson	6	2	0	58
8T.... Alex Karras	4	2	3	51		9...... Dick (Night Train) Lane	4	5	0	57
10.... Buck Buchanan	4	3	1	50		10.... Mel Renfro	2	8	0	56
						11.... Yale Lary	3	6	0	54
Linebackers	C	1st	2nd	Total		12T.. Willie Brown	6	1	0	53
1...... Lawrence Taylor	8	2	0	74		12T.. Roger Wehrli	6	1	0	53
2...... Ted Hendricks	6	5	0	73		14.... Dave Grayson	4	3	1	50
3...... Joe Schmidt	7	3	0	71		15.... Herb Adderley	3	5	0	49
4...... Chuck Bednarik	7	2	1	69		16T.. Cornell Green	4	3	0	47
5T.... Bill George	7	2	0	66		16T.. Rod Woodson*	4	3	0	47
5T.... Jack Lambert	7	2	0	66		18T.. Lemar Parrish	2	6	0	46
5T.... Mike Singletary	7	2	0	66		18T.. Steve Atwater*	2	6	0	46
8...... Jack Ham	7	1	1	64		20.... Jack Christiansen	5	1	0	45
9...... Nick Buoniconti	6	3	0	63						
10.... Bobby Bell	7	1	0	61						
11.... Dick Butkus	6	2	0	58						
12.... Larry Grantham	3	4	1	57						
13.... Junior Seau*	5	3	0	55						
14T.. Chuck Howley	4	4	0	52						
14T.. Willie Lanier	4	4	0	52						
16.... Maxie Baughan	2	7	0	51						
17.... Robert Brazile	5	2	0	50						
18.... Andy Russell	3	4	1	48						
18T.. Bill Bergey	5	1	1	48						
20.... Mike Stratton	4	3	0	47						

*Active in 1999.

Golf

Men

Based on PGA results from 1916–2000. Excludes events on the PGA Senior Tour. Point system based on three points for each tour win, two points for each second place, one point for each third place and 10 bonus points for each major championship.

	Golfer	1st	2nd	3rd	Majors	Pts	Turned Pro
1..................	Jack Nicklaus	70	59	35	18	543	1961
2..................	Sam Snead	81	63	54	7	493	1934
3..................	Ben Hogan	63	46	30	9	401	1931
4..................	Arnold Palmer	60	42	29	7	363	1954
5..................	Byron Nelson	52	36	34	5	346	1932
6..................	Walter Hagen	40	23	19	11	295	1912
7..................	Billy Casper	51	36	24	3	279	1954
8..................	Gene Sarazen	37	30	31	7	272	1920
9..................	Tom Watson*	34	31	23	8	267	1971
10....	Gary Player	21	33	22	9	241	1953
11T..............	Cary Middlecoff	39	30	23	3	230	1947
11T..............	Lee Trevino	27	34	21	6	230	1960
13..............	Jimmmy Demaret	31	34	29	3	220	1927
14..............	Lloyd Mangrum	36	28	43	1	217	1929
15..............	Horton Smith	30	37	24	2	208	1926
16..............	Harry Cooper	30	37	26	0	190	1923
17..............	Gene Littler	29	34	20	1	185	1954
18..............	Leo Diegel	29	23	16	2	169	1916
19..............	Paul Runyan	28	20	24	2	168	1930

*Active in 2000. Results updated through 10-2-00.

Golf (Cont.)

Men (Cont.)

	Golfer	1st	2nd	3rd	Majors	Pts	Turned Pro
20	Ray Floyd	22	24	13	4	167	1961
21	Hale Irwin	20	25	24	3	164	1968
22	Johnny Farrell	22	26	35	1	163	1922
23	Tommy Armour	24	23	12	3	160	1924
24	Craig Wood	21	28	20	2	159	1920
25T	Tom Kite	19	29	22	1	147	1972
25T	Greg Norman*	18	31	11	2	147	1976

Women

Based on LPGA results from 1950–1999. Women's rankings based on three points for each tour win, one point for each second place finish, and three bonus points for each victory in a major championship.

	Golfer	1st	2nd	Majors	Pts
1	Kathy Whitworth	96	99	7	408
2	Mickey Wright	87	52	14	355
3	Betsy Rawls	56	43	8	235
4	Louise Suggs	49	49	11	229
5	Nancy Lopez*	51	57	4	222
6	Joanne Carner*	48	61	4	217
7	Sandra Haynie	43	63	4	204
8	Patty Berg	36	42	15	195
9	Pat Bradley*	35	57	6	180
10	Patty Sheehan*	36	35	6	161
11	Beth Daniel*	36	47	1	158
12	*Betsy King	35	33	6	156
13	Carol Mann	38	33	2	153
14T	Amy Alcott*	30	26	5	131
14T	Donna Caponi	28	29	6	131
14T	Judy Rankin	28	41	2	131
17	Jane Blalock	31	32	1	128
18	Babe Didrikson Zaharias	27	11	10	122
19	Juli Inkster*	27	18	6	117
20	Marlene Bauer Hagge	25	37	1	115
21	Sandra Palmer	26	26	3	113
22	Annika Sorenstam*	25	21	2	102
23T	Hollis Stacy*	20	27	4	99
23T	Laura Davies*	21	24	4	99
23T	Marilynn Smith	23	24	2	99

*Active in 2000. Results updated through 10-2-00.

Hockey

NHL Players ranked by adjusted points, a method for normalizing statistics across different eras.

	Player	Adjusted Points	Adj. Goals	Adj. Assists	First Season	Last Season
1	Wayne Gretzky	2259	779	1480	1979–80	1998–99
2	Gordie Howe	2109	988	1121	1946–47	1979–80
3	Phil Esposito	1444	708	736	1963–64	1980–81
4	Mark Messier*	1419	572	847	1979–80	—
5	Stan Mikita	1411	577	834	1958–59	1979–80
6	Marcel Dionne	1387	627	760	1971–72	1988–89
7	Alex Delvecchio	1363	538	825	1950–51	1973–74
8	Jean Beliveau	1337	615	722	1950–51	1970–71
9	John Bucyk	1335	595	740	1955–56	1977–78
10	Steve Yzerman*	1324	583	741	1983–84	—
11	Ron Francis*	1311	442	869	1981–82	—
12	Norm Ullman	1254	554	700	1955–56	1974–75
13	Bobby Hull	1234	699	535	1957–58	1979–80
14	Ray Bourque*	1229	368	861	1979–80	—
15	Paul Coffey*	1214	351	863	1980–81	—
16	Mario Lemieux	1198	544	654	1984–85	1996–97
17	Maurice Richard	1174	677	497	1942–43	1959–60
18T	Jean Ratelle	1127	484	643	1960–61	1980–81
18T	Howie Morenz	1127	508	619	1923–24	1936–37
20	Frank Mahovlich	1123	593	530	1956–57	1973–74

*Active during 1999–2000 season.

	Player	Adjusted Points	Adj. Goals	Adj. Assists	First Season	Last Season
21	Jari Kurri	1106	519	587	1980–81	1997–98
22	Dale Hawerchuk	1100	449	651	1981–82	1996–97
23	Doug Gilmour*	1096	395	701	1983–84	—
24	Nels Stewart	1090	594	496	1925–26	1939–40
25	Bryan Trottier	1089	443	646	1975–76	1993–94
26	Mike Gartner	1086	623	463	1979–80	1997–98
27	Aurel Joliat	1085	499	586	1922–23	1937–38
28	Guy Lafleur	1079	491	588	1971–72	1990–91
29	Henri Richard	1076	413	663	1955–56	1974–75
30	Andy Bathgate	1062	421	641	1952–53	1970–71
31	Gilbert Perreault	1051	448	603	1970–71	1986–87
32	Ted Lindsay	1046	485	561	1944–45	1964–65
33	Denis Savard	1040	412	628	1980–81	1996–97
34	Adam Oates*	1032	295	737	1985–86	—
35	Frank Boucher	1020	286	734	1921–22	1943–44
36	Luc Robitaille*	1019	538	481	1986–87	—
37	Brett Hull*	1011	602	409	1985–86	—
38	Dave Andreychuk*	1002	518	484	1982–83	—
39	Dino Ciccarelli	995	545	450	1980–81	1998–99
40	Bernie Nicholls	992	431	561	1981–82	1998–99
41	Bobby Clarke	973	325	648	1969–70	1983–84
42	Joe Sakic*	970	408	562	1988–89	—
43	Larry Murphy*	969	265	704	1980–81	—
44	Hooley Smith	966	362	604	1924–25	1940–41
45	Rod Gilbert	957	419	538	1960–61	1977–78
46	Bernie Geoffrion	951	493	458	1950–51	1967–68
47T	Red Kelly	949	349	600	1947–48	1966–67
47T	Pierre Turgeon*	949	421	528	1987–88	—
49	Dave Keon	940	419	521	1960–61	1981–82
50	Phil Housley*	934	287	647	1982–83	—
51	Jaromir Jagr*	931	420	511	1990–91	—
52	Peter Stastny	928	375	553	1980–81	1994–95
53	Al MacInnis*	915	287	628	1981–82	—
54	Dean Prentice	914	453	461	1952–53	1973–74
55	Darryl Sittler	896	422	474	1970–71	1984–85
56T	Michel Goulet	882	457	425	1979–80	1993–94
56T	Vincent Damphousse*	882	357	525	1986–87	—
58	Pat Verbeek*	880	474	406	1982–83	—
59	Glenn Anderson	864	427	437	1980–81	1995–96
60	Joe Mullen	861	443	418	1979–80	1996–97
61	Mike Bossy	859	475	384	1977–78	1986–87
62	Theoren Fleury*	858	404	454	1988–89	—
63	Mark Recchi*	856	366	490	1988–89	—
64T	Pat LaFontaine	843	425	418	1983–84	1997–98
64T	Bernie Federko	843	307	536	1976–77	1989–90
66	Brian Bellows	836	435	401	1982–83	1998–99
67	Bobby Orr	818	268	550	1966–67	1978–79
68	Brendan Shanahan*	815	443	372	1987–88	—
69	Dave Taylor	810	361	449	1977–78	1993–94
70	Steve Larmer	807	388	419	1980–81	1994–95
71	Dit Clapper	805	382	423	1927–28	1946–47
72T	Denis Potvin	803	265	538	1973–74	1987–88
72T	Dale Hunter	803	286	517	1980–81	1998–99
74	Busher Jackson	801	392	409	1929–30	1943–44
75	Bill Cook	800	427	373	1926–27	1936–37
76	Yvan Cournoyer	799	431	368	1963–64	1978–79
77	Rick Tocchet*	797	411	386	1984–85	—
78	Jeremy Roenick*	792	375	417	1988–89	—
79	Lanny McDonald	787	424	363	1973–74	1988–89
80	Cy Denneny	786	401	385	1917–18	1928–29
81	Joe Nieuwendyk*	785	436	349	1986–87	—
82	George Armstrong	782	356	426	1949–50	1970–71
83	Milt Schmidt	781	316	465	1936–37	1954–55
84	Syd Howe	777	347	430	1929–30	1945–46
85	Bobby Smith	774	297	477	1978–79	1992–93
86	Brian Propp	761	354	407	1979–80	1993–94
87	Rick Middleton	755	373	382	1974–75	1987–88

*Active during 1999–2000 season.

Player	Adjusted Points	Adj. Goals	Adj. Assists	First Season	Last Season
88..........Kirk Muller*	754	318	436	1984–85	—
89..........Mike Modano*	750	356	394	1988–89	—
90..........Mats Sundin*	746	348	398	1990–91	—
91..........Elmer Lach	745	256	489	1940–41	1953–54
92..........Tomas Sandstrom	743	377	367	1984–85	1998–99
93..........Doug Mohns	740	290	450	1953–54	1974–75
94..........Jacques Lemaire	737	356	381	1967–68	1978–79
95..........Pit Martin	736	326	410	1961–62	1978–79
96..........John MacLean*	735	395	340	1983–84	—
97..........Steve Thomas*	731	363	368	1984–85	—
98T.........Charlie Conacher	728	396	332	1929–30	1940–41
98T.........Ken Hodge	728	328	400	1964–65	1977–78
100T.......Reg Noble	726	262	464	1917–18	1932–33
100T.......Bill Cowley	726	255	471	1934–35	1946–47

Goaltender†	Points	Games	Wins	Losses	Ties	Shutouts
1.............Terry Sawchuk	1169	971	447	330	172	103
2.............Jacques Plante	1097	837	435	247	145	82
3.............Tony Esposito	1073	886	423	306	151	76
4.............Glenn Hall	1061	906	407	326	163	84
5.............Patrick Roy*	1039	841	444	264	103	48
6.............Grant Fuhr*	945	868	403	295	114	25
7.............Rogie Vachon	888	795	355	291	127	51
8.............Harry Lumley	874	803	330	329	143	71
9.............John Vanbiesbrouck*	868	829	358	318	114	38
10...........Gump Worsley	863	861	335	352	150	43
11...........Andy Moog	860	713	372	209	88	28
12...........Mike Vernon*	851	722	371	241	86	23
13...........Tom Barrasso*	822	733	353	259	81	35
14...........Turk Broda	767	629	302	224	101	62
15...........Ed Belfour*	747	612	308	195	82	49
16...........Billy Smith	737	680	305	233	105	22
17...........Ed Giacomin	729	610	289	208	97	54
18...........Tiny Thompson	724	553	284	194	75	81
19...........Bernie Parent	717	608	271	198	121	55
20...........Dan Bouchard	712	655	286	232	113	27
21...........Gilles Meloche	691	788	270	351	131	20
22...........Mike Liut	685	663	293	271	74	25
23...........Ron Hextall	684	608	296	214	69	23
24...........Curtis Joseph*	662	587	284	216	68	26
25...........George Hainsworth	660	465	246	145	74	94
26...........Kelly Hrudey	647	677	271	265	88	17
27...........Ken Dryden	636	397	258	57	74	46
28...........Don Beaupre	628	667	268	277	75	17
29...........Johnny Bower	627	552	250	195	90	37
30...........Frank Brimsek	624	514	252	182	80	40
31...........Martin Brodeur*	595	447	244	125	65	42
32...........Mike Richter*	591	553	252	205	65	22
33...........Eddie Johnston	580	592	234	257	80	32
34...........Bill Ranford*	571	647	240	279	76	15
35...........Glenn (Chico) Resch	570	571	231	224	82	26
36...........Kirk McLean*	567	589	237	252	71	22
37T.........Pete Peeters	564	489	246	155	51	21
37T.........John Roach	564	492	219	204	68	58
39...........Gerry Cheevers	560	418	230	102	74	26
40...........Reggie Lemelin	547	507	236	162	63	12
41...........Lorne Chabot	537	411	201	148	62	73
42...........Greg Millen	536	604	215	284	89	17
43...........Alex Connell	534	417	193	156	67	81
44...........Dominik Hasek*	533	449	210	150	68	45
45...........Davey Kerr	532	427	203	148	75	51
46...........Sean Burke	531	571	218	252	73	22
47T.........Roger Crozier	512	518	206	197	70	30
47T.........Bill Durnan	512	383	208	112	62	34
47T.........Ken Wregget*	512	575	225	248	53	9
50...........Don Edwards	506	459	208	155	74	16

†NHL goaltenders ranked by points, two points per win, one per tie, and one per shutout.

*Active during 1999–2000 season.

Olympics

Athletes are ranked by comparing the ratio of their Olympic scores to the world record (WR) for that event at the time. For track events, only times recorded in the medal rounds are included. Includes Summer Olympic Games from 1900–2000. All measurements of height and distance are given in feet and inches.

Men

100 Meters

	Athlete	Country	Olympics	Time	WR	Ratio
1	Bob Hayes	United States	Tokyo 1964	10.0	10.0	1.000
2	Jim Hines	United States	Mexico City 1968	9.95	9.90	.995
3	Carl Lewis	United States	Los Angeles 1984	9.99	9.93	.994
4	Maurice Greene	United States	Sydney 2000	9.87	9.79	.992
5	Carl Lewis	United States	Seoul 1988	9.92	9.83	.991

Note: Canadian Ben Johnson ran 9.79 in 1988, breaking the world record of 9.83, a ratio of 1.004. His medal was withdrawn by the IOC when he failed the post-race drug test.

1,500 Meters

	Athlete	Country	Olympics	Time	WR	Ratio
1	Charles Bennett	Great Britain	Paris 1900	4:06.2	4:10.4	1.017
2	Henri Deloge	France	Paris 1900	4:06.6	4:10.4	1.015
3	John Bray	United States	Paris 1900	4:07.2	4:10.4	1.013
4	John Lovelock	New Zealand	Berlin 1936	3:47.8	3:48.8	1.004
5	Jim Lightbody	United States	St. Louis 1904	4:05.4	4:06.2	1.003

5,000 Meters

	Athlete	Country	Olympics	Time	WR	Ratio
1	J. Kolehmainen	Finland	Stockholm 1912	14:36.6	15:01.2	1.028
2	Jean Bouin	France	Stockholm 1912	14:36.7	15:01.2	1.028
3	Vladimir Kuts	Soviet Union	Melbourne 1956	13:39.6	13:36.8	.997
4	Paavo Nurmi	Finland	Paris 1924	14:31.2	14:28.2	.997
5	Ville Ritola	Finland	Paris 1924	14:31.4	14:28.2.	996

Long Jump

	Athlete	Country	Olympics	Dist.	WR	Ratio
1	Bob Beamon	United States	Mexico City 1968	29-2½	27-4¾	1.066
2	Albert Gutterson	United States	Stockholm 1912	24-11¼	24-11¾	.999
3	Jesse Owens	United States	Berlin 1936	26-5½	26-8¼	.991
4	Ralph Boston	United States	Rome 1960	26-7¾	26-11¼	.989
5	Bo Roberson	United States	Rome 1960	26-7¼	26-11¼	.988

High Jump

	Athlete	Country	Olympics	Ht	WR	Ratio
1	Gerd Wessig	East Germany	Moscow 1980	7-8¾	7-8½	1.004
2	Charles Dumas	United States	Melbourne 1956	6-11½	7-0½	.986
3	Hennady Avdeyenko	Soviet Union	Seoul 1988	7-9¾	7-11½	.983
4	Dietmar Mogenburg	West Germany	Los Angeles 1984	7-8½	7-10	.983
5	Jacek Wszola	Poland	Moscow 1980	7-7	7-8½	.983

Pole Vault

	Athlete	Country	Olympics	Ht.	WR	Ratio
1	Frank Foss	United States	Antwerp 1920	13-5	13-2¼	1.017
2	W. Kozakiewicz	Poland	Moscow 1980	18-11½	18-11	1.002
3	Bob Seagren	United States	Mexico City 1968	17-8½	17-9	.998
4	Claus Schiprowski	West Germany	Mexico City 1968	17-8½	17-9	.998
5	Wolfgang Nordwig	East Germany	Mexico City 1968	17-8½	17-9	.998

Decathlon

	Athlete	Country	Olympics	Score	WR	Ratio
1	Jim Thorpe	United States	Stockholm 1912	8412	7414	1.135
2	Hugo Wieslander	Sweden	Stockholm 1912	7724	7414	1.042
3	Harold Osborn	United States	Paris 1924	7711	7482	1.031
4	James Bausch	United States	Los Angeles 1932	8462	8255	1.025
5	Bruce Jenner	United States	Montreal 1976	8618	8538	1.009

Women

100 Meters

	Athlete	Country	Olympics	Time	WR	Ratio
1	Wilma Rudolph	United States	Rome 1960	11.0	11.3	1.027
2	Helen Stephens	United States	Berlin 1936	11.5	11.6	1.009
3	Wyomia Tyus	United States	Mexico City 1968	11.08	11.1	1.002
4	Renate Stecher	East Germany	Munich 1972	11.07	11.08	1.001
5	Dorothy Hyman	Great Britain	Rome 1960	11.3	11.3	1.000

High Jump

	Athlete	Country	Olympics	Ht.	WR	Ratio
1	Jean Shiley	United States	Los Angeles 1932	5-5¼	5-3¾	1.023
2	Babe Didrikson	United States	Los Angeles 1932	5-5¼	5-3¾	1.023
3	Mildred McDaniel	United States	Melbourne 1956	5-9¼	5-8¾	1.006
4	Ulrike Meyfarth	West Germany	Munich 1972	6-3½	6-3½	1.000
5	Iolanda Balas	Romania	Tokyo 1964	6-2¾	6-3¼	.995

Long Jump

	Athlete	Country	Olympics	Dist.	WR	Ratio
1	Mary Rand	Great Britain	Tokyo 1964	22-2¼	21-11¾	1.009
2	Viorica Viscopoleanu	Romania	Mexico City 1968	22-4½	22-2¼	1.009
3	Elzbieta Krzesinska	Poland	Melbourne 1956	20-10	20-10	1.000
4	Yvette Williams	New Zealand	Helsinki 1952	20-5¾	20-6¼	.998
5	Tatiana Kolpakova	Soviet Union	Moscow 1980	23-2	23-3¾	.996

Javelin

	Athlete	Country	Olympics	Dist.	WR	Ratio
1	Trine Hattestad	Norway	Sydney 2000	226-1	227-11	.992
2	Mihaela Penes	Romania	Tokyo 1964	198-7	201-4¼	.986
3	Ruth Fuchs	East Germany	Munich 1972	209-7	213-5½	.982
4	Maria Colon	Cuba	Moscow 1980	224-5	229-10	.976
5	Mirella Maniani-Tzelili	Greece	Sydney 2000	221-6	227-11	.972

Shot Put

	Athlete	Country	Olympics	Dist.	WR	Ratio
1	Margitta Gummel	East Germany	Mexico City 1968	64-4	61-11	1.039
2	Nadezhda Chizhova	Soviet Union	Munich 1972	69-0	67-8¼	1.019
3	Galina Zybina	Soviet Union	Helsinki 1952	50-1¾	49-10	1.006
4	Ilona Slupianek	East Germany	Moscow 1980	73-6¼	73-8	.998
5	Marita Lange	East Germany	Mexico City 1968	61-7½	61-11	.995

Tennis

Men

Rankings based on five points for each win in a Grand Slam singles event, and two points for finishing as runner-up. Includes all Grand Slam singles events from 1900–1999.

		Won	2nd	Pts	Career
1.	Pete Sampras*	13	3	71	1988–
2.	Rod Laver	11	6	67	1959–1979
3.	Roy Emerson	12	3	66	1959–1983
4.	Bjorn Borg	11	5	65	1972–1993
5.	Ivan Lendl	8	11	62	1978–1994
6.	Bill Tilden	10	5	60	1920–1930
7.	Ken Rosewall	8	8	56	1953–1980
8.	Jimmy Connors	8	7	54	1970–1996
9.	Fred Perry	8	2	44	1931–1936
10T.	John McEnroe	7	4	43	1977–1994
10T.	Mats Wilander	7	4	43	1980–1996
12.	Jack Crawford	6	6	42	1928–1937
13T.	Henri Cochet	7	3	41	1922–1933
13T.	John Newcombe	7	3	41	1963–1981
13T.	Rene Lacoste	7	3	41	1923–1928
16T.	Andre Agassi*	6	5	40	1985–
16T.	Stefan Edberg	6	5	40	1982–1996
18.	Bill Larned	7	2	39	1902–1912
19.	Boris Becker	6	4	38	1983–1999
20T.	Jean Borotra	4	6	32	1922–1932
20T.	Don Budge	6	1	32	1935–1953
20T.	Laurence Doherty	6	1	32	1900–1906
20T.	Tony Wilding	6	1	32	1904–1914
24.	Frank Sedgman	5	3	31	1949–1974
25.	Arthur Ashe	4	4	28	1963–1979

Women

		Won	2nd	Pts	Career
1.	Margaret Smith Court	24	5	130	1960–1975
2.	Steffi Graf	21	9	123	1982–2000
3.	Chris Evert	18	16	122	1971–1989
4.	Martina Navratilova	18	14	118	1973–1994
5.	Helen Wills Moody	19	3	101	1919–1938
6.	Billie Jean King	12	4	68	1963–1983
7.	Evonne Goolagong Cawley	7	11	57	1969–1985
8.	Monica Seles*	9	4	53	1988–
9.	Doris Hart	6	11	52	1942–1955
10T.	Helen Jacobs	5	11	47	1928–1940
10T.	Maria Bueno	7	6	47	1965–1977
12.	Louise Brough	6	8	46	1941–1957
13.	Maureen Connolly	9	0	45	1949–1954
14.	Suzanne Lenglen	8	0	40	1919–1926
15.	Margaret Osborne duPont	6	4	38	1941–1962
16.	Arantxa Sánchez Vicario*	4	8	36	1986–
17.	Martina Hingis*	5	5	35	1994–
18.	Pauline Betz	5	3	31	1939–1947
19.	Althea Gibson	5	2	29	1950–1968
20T.	Hana Mandlikova	4	4	28	1978–1990
20T.	Shirley Fry	4	4	28	1941–1957
22T.	Dorothea Chambers	4	3	26	1903–1925
22T.	Molla Mallory	4	3	26	1915–1929
24T.	Alice Marble	5	0	25	1933–1941
24T.	Daphne Akhurst	5	0	25	1925–1931

*Active in 2000. Includes all events through 2000 U.S. Open.

PAGE 433 PHOTO CREDITS (Clockwise from upper left): Manny Millan (Erving); Dick Garrett/ *Columbus Citizen* (Nicklaus); Fred Kaplan (Aaron); Andy Hayt (Gretzky); Corbis-Bettman (Didrikson).

Boxing

IBF and WBC
heavyweight champion
Lennox Lewis

Cleanup Project

Several fighters helped restore a measure of class to boxing, a sport long polluted by controversy and scandal

BY MARTY BURNS

THIS WAS the year boxing cleaned up its act. O.K., not really. After all, Mike Tyson and Don King were still around. But there was something refreshing—if not spectacular—about what happened to the sweet science in 2000. Gentlemen fighters like Lennox Lewis, Roy Jones Jr. and Shane Mosley dominated the headlines, restoring a modicum of respectability to a sport racked by scandal in 1999.

Not that the bouts in the first year of the new millennium were particularly good, the scoring more fair or the characters more honest. No, boxing laid the sleaze of '99 to rest simply because the big stories of 2000, for the most part, occurred inside the ropes: Lewis put a stranglehold on the heavyweight division; Jones showed that he's still the best pure fighter around; Mosley staked his claim as the sport's next standard-bearer. After all the questionable fight rulings, lawsuits and investigations of '99, these developments were a welcome relief.

Leading the way was Lewis, the well-spoken British giant who had dethroned Evander Holyfield in November '99 as the consensus heavyweight champion. Most observers believe Lewis won his first meeting with Holyfield, in March '99, but that bout ended in a dubious draw. There was nothing doubtful about the return match, though, and after he followed it up with back-to-back knockouts of Michael Grant and Frans Botha, the velvety-voiced, dreadlocked, chess-playing Lewis had proved that he was boxing's reigning big man. His destruction of Botha on July 15 in London Arena was especially impressive. Fighting on home soil for the first time since his loss to Oliver McCall in '94, the 6'5", 250-pound Lewis bludgeoned the stolid South African with a sharp four-punch combo that left Botha reeling drunkenly on the ropes late in the second round. Referee Larry O'Connell stepped in and ended the bout, giving Lewis (37-1-1) his second straight second-round triumph. (He had KO'd the 6'7" Grant on April 29.)

After stopping Botha, Lewis wasted no time proclaiming himself the top heavyweight in the world and trying to clear the

In the year's best fight, Mosley (right) defeated De La Hoya in Los Angeles.

stage for a showdown with Tyson. "Tell Mike Tyson to either put up or shut up," Lewis said, referring to controversial comments that Iron Mike had made days before the Lewis-Botha bout. Having just vanquished a tomato can named Lou Savarese, Tyson claimed that he could dominate Lewis in the ring and announced his intention to "eat [Lewis's] children." Lewis, who has no children, held up his right hand after the Botha fight and said, "I'll show him what he can eat."

Unfortunately, as much as boxing fans wanted to see it, a Tyson-Lewis megabout would have to wait until 2001 at the earliest. Disputes over TV rights would have to be settled first, and both fighters would have to beat challengers in previously scheduled bouts. For Lewis that meant a date with hard-hitting David Tua (37–1 with 32 KO's), the No. 1–ranked contender, in November.

While Lewis controlled boxing's marquee division in 2000, Jones left no doubt

as to who was the best fighter, pound for pound. Now a light heavyweight (he has won titles at middleweight and super middleweight), Jones ran his record to 42–1 with decisive victories over David Telesco in January and Richard Hall in May. Against Hall, a 6'3" Jamaican, Jones gave away some $4\frac{1}{2}$ inches in height, but it didn't matter. Wiggling and high-stepping, he toyed with Hall, doling out a steady beating until the referee stopped the lopsided bout in the 11th round.

Jones was so dominating in 2000 that he even toyed with the idea of moving up two classes to fight Lewis. Although he quickly dismissed the notion—Lewis outweighed him by about 60 pounds—Jones clearly was getting frustrated with the lack of competition. The good news was that an intriguing prospect, WBO champ Dariusz Michalczewski (42–0), was quickly gaining respect throughout the division. Jones and Michalczewski seemed to be on a collision course for 2001, a prospect that could only help boxing.

With Jones and Lewis struggling to find

quality opponents, it was left largely to the little guys to give boxing a pulse in 2000. This was where Mosley came in, providing fight fans with a compelling new champion. Nicknamed Sugar for his sweet disposition outside the ring as well as his artistry inside it, the 5' 9" Mosley (35–0) won the WBC welterweight title with a 12-round split decision over Oscar De La Hoya in June.

The fight featured everything a boxing fan could want. Mosley, 28, was the dimpled, well-mannered kid from Pomona, Calif., who played the saxophone on the side and had worked his way up the welterweight ladder. De La Hoya, 27, was the pinup-handsome former Olympic gold medalist from East L.A. who had won world titles in four weight divisions. De La Hoya was the most popular nonheavyweight in the world; Mosley was a likable star on the rise. It was the bout of the year, and it didn't disappoint.

Before a sellout crowd of 20,744 at L.A.'s Staples Center, the two engaged in a ferocious, free-swinging battle. Mosley proved too quick and elusive for the hard-punching De La Hoya. Neither fighter scored a knockdown, and both had their moments of advantage, but Mosley took control of the bout in a memorable 12th round that featured unrestrained, desperate punching by both boxers. "De La Hoya is a great champion," Mosley said. "But I was the better man tonight."

The triumph catapulted Mosley to the top shelf of boxing's hierarchy and may have signaled an end to De La Hoya's reign as the sport's golden boy. With two losses in his last three fights, De La Hoya (32–2) said afterward that he was considering retirement even though a November rematch with Mosley had already been arranged.

Stirring though it was, the Mosley–De La Hoya masterpiece couldn't mask all of boxing's warts. In April, IBF founder Robert W. Lee stood trial in federal court on charges that he took bribes from promoters to fix matches and sanction fights. Although Lee was acquitted on 27 of 33 counts, testimony during the trial revealed what many observers had long suspected: The sport is awash in payoffs and shady dealings. After-

ward top promoters such as King and Bob Arum came under government scrutiny, and the IBF was placed under the control of a court-appointed monitor.

Then there was Tyson, who found new ways to embarrass himself and his sport. His sucker punch of Orlin Norris after the first-round bell in an October '99 bout earned him a "no contest" decision and a ban from the Nevada boxing commission. His next fight, a brutal second-round KO of one Julius Francis in Manchester, England, was preceded by protests from women's groups over the British government's decision to allow Tyson, a convicted rapist, to enter the country.

Finally, in June, Tyson knocked out Savarese in 38 seconds in Glasgow and then pushed the referee to the canvas in an effort to get at his fallen opponent. Then came his now infamous comments about eating Lewis's children. In August the British boxing commission found Tyson guilty of misconduct for his actions in the ring and fined him $187,500. Still, no one banned Tyson (48–3) from future fights, and he was slated to face Andrew Golota later in the year, probably in Hong Kong.

Lewis may not have had any children, but the fight game, especially the women's side, consumed the progeny of boxing champions as never before. Six daughters of famous pugilists experimented with the sport in 2000: Laila Ali (daughter of Muhammed Ali); Freeda George Foreman (George Foreman); Jacquelyn Frazier-Lyde (Joe Frazier); Maria Johansson (Ingemar Johansson); Irichelle Duran (Roberto Duran); and J'Marie Moore (Archie Moore). Each was skilled enough to keep from getting eaten alive in the ring, but only the 22-year-old Ali (7–0) appeared to have much of a future in boxing.

While waiting for a true hero (or heroine?) to excite the masses as the fathers of Laila, Freeda and Co., had once done, the sport was much rejuvenated from the previous year. In Lewis, Jones and Mosley, boxing had three skilled fighters who helped return the focus to events inside the ring. It might not sound like much, but it was a start.

FOR THE RECORD·1999–2000

Current Champions

Division	Weight Limit	WBC Champion	WBA Champion	IBF Champion
Heavyweight	None	Lennox Lewis	Evander Holyfield	Lennox Lewis
Cruiserweight	190	Juan Carlos Gomez	Fabrice Tiozzo	Vassily Jirov
Light heavyweight	175	Roy Jones Jr	Roy Jones Jr	Roy Jones Jr
Super middleweight	168	Glenn Catley	Bruno Girard	Sven Ottke
Middleweight	160	Keith Holmes	William Joppy Jr	Bernard Hopkins
Junior middleweight	154	Javier Castillejo	Felix Trinidad	Fernando Vargas
Welterweight	147	Shane Mosley	James Page	VACANT
Junior welterweight	140	Kostya Tszyu	Sharmba Mitchell	Zab Judah
Lightweight	135	Jose Luis Castillo	Takanori Hatakeyama	Paul Spadafora
Junior lightweight	130	Floyd Mayweather	Joel Casamayor	Diego Corrales
Featherweight	126	Guty Espadas	Freddy Norwood	Paul Ingle
Junior featherweight	122	Erik Morales	Clarence Adams	Benedict Ledwaba
Bantamweight	118	Veerapol Sahaprom	Paulie Ayala	Tim Austin
Junior bantamweight	115	Cho In-Joo	Hideki Todaka	Felix Machado
Flyweight	112	Malcolm Tunacao	Eric Morel	Irene Pacheco
Junior flyweight	108	Choi Yo-Sam	Beibis Mendoza	Ricardo Lopez
Strawweight	105	Jose Antonio Aguirre	Joma Gamboa	Zolani Petelo

Note: WBC = World Boxing Council; WBA = World Boxing Association; IBF = International Boxing Federation

Championship and Major Fights of 1999 and 2000

Abbreviations: WBC=World Boxing Council; WBA= World Boxing Association; IBF=International Boxing Federation; KO=knockout; TKO=technical knockout; Dec=decision; Split=split decision; Disq=disqualification.

Heavyweight

Date	Winner	Loser	Result	Title	Site
Nov 13	Lennox Lewis	Evander Holyfield	Dec 12	IBF/WBA/WBC	Las Vegas
Apr 29	Lennox Lewis	Michael Grant	KO 2	IBF/WBA/WBC	New York
July 15	Lennox Lewis	Frans Botha	TKO 2	IBF/WBC	London
Aug 12	Evander Holyfield	John Ruiz	Dec 12	WBA	Las Vegas

Cruiserweight

Date	Winner	Loser	Result	Title	Site
Nov 13	Fabrice Tiozzo	Ken Murphy	TKO 8	WBA	Las Vegas
Dec 11	Juan Carlos Gomez	Napoleon Tagoe	KO 9	WBC	Hamburg, Germany
Feb 12	Vassiliy Jirov	Saul Montana	KO 9	IBF	Boise, ID
Mar 11	Juan Carlos Gomez	Mohamed Siluvangi	TKO 2	WBC	Luebeck, Germany
Apr 8	Fabrice Tiozzo	Valery Vikhor	KO 6	WBA	Paris
May 6	Juan Carlos Gomez	Imamu Mayfield	KO 3	WBC	Neuss, Germany

Light Heavyweight

Date	Winner	Loser	Result	Title	Site
Jan 15	Roy Jones	David Telesco	Dec 12	IBF/WBA/WBC	New York
May 13	Roy Jones	Richard Hall	TKO 11	IBF/WBA/WBC	Indianapolis, IN

Super Middleweight

Date	Winner	Loser	Result	Title	Site
Oct 23	Markus Beyer	Richie Woodhall	Dec 12	WBC	London
Nov 27	Sven Ottke	Glen Johnson	Dec 12	IBF	Dusseldorf, Germany
Dec 11	Byron Mitchell	Bruno Girard	Draw	WBA	Tunica, MS
Jan 29	Markus Beyer	Leif Keiski	KO 7	WBC	Riesa, Germany
Mar 11	Sven Ottke	Lloyd Bryan	Dec 12	IBF	Magdeburg, Germany
Apr 8	Bruno Girard	Byron Mitchell	Dec 12	WBA	Paris
May 6	Glenn Catley	Markus Beyer	TKO 12	WBC	Frankfurt
June 3	Sven Ottke	Tocker Pudwill	Dec 12	IBF	Karlsruhe, Germany

Middleweight

Date	Winner	Loser	Result	Title	Site
Dec 12	Bernard Hopkins	Antwun Echols	Dec 12	IBF	Miami
Apr 29	Keith Holmes	Robert McCracken	TKO 11	WBC	London
May 13	Bernard Hopkins	Syd Vanderpool	Dec 12	IBF	Indianapolis, IN
May 20	William Joppy	Rito Ruvalcaba	TKO 1	WBA	Tunica, MS

Junior Middleweight (Super Welterweight)

Date	Winner	Loser	Result	Title	Site
Dec 4	Fernando Vargas	Ronald Wright	Dec 12	IBF	Lincoln City, OR
Dec 17	Javier Castillejo	Mik Rask	TKO 7	WBC	Leganes, Spain
Mar 3	Felix Trinidad	David Reid	Dec 12	WBA	Las Vegas
Apr 15	Fernando Vargas	Ike Quartey	Dec 12	IBF	Las Vegas
July 21	Javier Castillejo	Tony Marshall	Dec 12	WBC	Leganes, Spain
July 22	Felix Trinidad	Mamadou Thiam	TKO 3	WBA	Miami

Welterweight

Date	Winner	Loser	Result	Title	Site
June 17	Shane Mosley	Oscar De La Hoya	Dec 12	WBC	Los Angeles

Junior Welterweight (Super Lightweight)

Date	Winner	Loser	Result	Title	Site
Nov 13	Sharmba Mitchell	Elio Ortiz	Dec 12	WBA	Las Vegas
Feb 12	Zab Judah	Jan Bergman	KO 4	IBF	Uncasville, CT
Feb 12	Kostya Tszyu	Ahmed Santos	KO 8	WBC	Uncasville, CT
June 24	Zab Judah	Junior Witter	Dec 12	IBF	Glasgow, Scotland
July 29	Kostya Tszyu	Julio Cesar Chavez	TKO 6	WBC	Phoenix, AZ
Aug 5	Zab Judah	Terronn Millett	TKO 4	IBF	Uncasville, CT

Lightweight

Date	Winner	Loser	Result	Title	Site
Nov 13	Gilbert Serrano	Stefano Zoff	TKO 10	WBA	Las Vegas
Nov 29	Steve Johnston	Billy Schwer	Dec 12	WBC	London
Dec 17	Paul Spadafora	Renato Cornett	TKO 11	IBF	Pittsburgh, PA
Mar 3	Paul Spadafora	Victoriano Sosa	Dec 12	IBF	Verona, NY
Mar 12	Gilbert Serrano	Hiroyuki Sakamoto	TKO 5	WBA	Tokyo
Mar 17	Steve Johnston	Julio Alvarez	TKO 2	WBC	Denver, CO
May 6	Paul Spadafora	Mike Griffith	Dec 10	IBF	Pittsburgh, PA
June 11	Takanori Hatakeyama	Gilbert Serrano	TKO 8	WBA	Tokyo
June 17	Jose Luis Castillo	Steve Johnston	Dec 12	WBC	Bell Gardens, CA

ONE MORE SIGN THAT THE APOCALYPSE IS UPON US

Oscar De La Hoya's rematch with Shane Mosley, which had been tentatively scheduled for October 2000, was pushed back because De La Hoya was too busy that month promoting his first CD.

Junior Lightweight (Super Featherweight)

Date	Winner	Loser	Result	Title	Site
Oct 23	Diego Corrales	Roberto Garcia	KO 7	IBF	Las Vegas
Oct 31	Jong Kwon Baek	Lakva Sim	Dec 12	WBA	Pusan, S Korea
Nov 20	Joel Casamayor	David Santos	Dec 12	interim WBA	Miami
Dec 4	Diego Corrales	John Brown	Dec 12	IBF	Lincoln City, OR
Jan 30	Jong Kwon Baek	Choi Kyu Chul	Draw	WBA	Pohang, S Korea
Mar 18	Floyd Mayweather	Goyo Vargas	Dec 12	WBC	Las Vegas
Mar 18	Diego Corrales	Derrick Gainer	TKO 3	IBF	Las Vegas
May 21	Joel Casamayor	Jong Kwon Baek	TKO 5	WBA	Kansas City, MO

Featherweight

Date	Winner	Loser	Result	Title	Site
Oct 22	Naseem Hamed	Cesar Soto	Dec 12	WBC	Detroit
Nov 13	Paul Ingle	Manuel Medina	Dec 12	IBF	London
Jan 30	Freddy Norwood	Takashi Koshimoto	KO 9	WBA	Fukuoka, Japan
Apr 14	Guty Espadas	Luisito Espinoza	Dec 11	WBC	Merida, Mexico
Apr 29	Paul Ingle	Junior Jones	TKO 11	IBF	New York
May 25	Freddy Norwood	Pablo Chacon	Dec 12	WBA	Mendoza, Argentina
June 23	Guty Espadas	W. Sakmuangklang	Dec 12	WBC	Merida, Mexico

Junior Featherweight (Super Bantamweight)

Date	Winner	Loser	Result	Title	Site
Sept 25	Benedict Ledwaba	Edison Valencia	TKO 4	IBF	Temecula, CA
Oct 9	Antonio Cermeno	Yober Ortega	Dec 12	interim WBA	Caracus, Venezuela
Oct 22	Erik Morales	Wayne McCullough	Dec 12	WBC	Detroit
Nov 21	Nestor Garza	Kozo Ishii	TKO 12	WBA	Nagoya, Japan
Feb 19	Erik Morales	Marco Antonio Barrera	Dec 12	WBC	Las Vegas
Mar 4	Clarence Adams	Nestor Garza	Dec 12	WBA	Las Vegas
Apr 7	Benedict Ledwaba	Ernesto Grey	TKO 8	IBF	Bristol, England
Aug 5	Clarence Adams	Andres Fernandez	TKO 6	WBA	Madison, WI

Bantamweight

Date	Winner	Loser	Result	Title	Site
Oct 23	Paulie Ayala	Saohin Srithai-Condo	Dec 12	WBA	Ft. Worth, TX
Dec 18	Tim Austin	Bernardo Menoza	TKO 1	IBF	Tunica, MS
Mar 4	Paulie Ayala	Johnni Bredahl	Dec 12	WBA	Las Vegas
Mar 11	Veerapol Sahaprom	Adan Vargas	Dec 12	WBC	Aranyaprathet, Thailand
June 25	Veerapol Sahaprom	Toshiaki Nishioka	Dec 12	WBC	Takasago, Japan
Aug 11	Tim Austin	Arthur Johnson	Dec 12	IBF	Las Vegas

Junior Bantamweight (Super Flyweight)

Date	Winner	Loser	Result	Title	Site
Nov 7	Hideki Todaka	Akihiko Nago	Dec 12	WBA	Tokyo
Nov 19	Mark Johnson	Raul Juarez	No contest	IBF	Washington, D.C.
Jan 2	Cho In-Joo	Gerry Penalosa	Dec 12	WBC	Seoul, S Korea
Apr 23	Hideki Todaka	Yokthai Sith Oar	TKO 11	WBA	Nagoya, Japan
May 14	Cho In-Joo	Julio Cesar Avila	Dec 12	WBC	Seoul, S Korea
May 20	Julio Gamboa	Felix Machado	Draw	IBF	Tunica, MS
July 22	Felix Machado	Julio Gamboa	Dec 12	IBF	Miami

Flyweight

Date	Winner	Loser	Result	Title	Site
Oct 16	Irene Pacheco	Ferid Ben Jeddou	KO 4	IBF	Barranquilla, Colombia
Jan 14	Irene Pacheco	Pedro Pena	TKO 11	IBF	El Paso, TX
Feb 25	Medgoen Singsurat	Masaki Kawabata	Dec 12	WBC	Samut Sakorn, Thailand
Apr 8	S. Pisnurachan	Gilberto Gonzalez	TKO 5	WBA	Kalasin, Thailand
May 19	Malcolm Tunacao	Medgoen Singsurat	TKO 7	WBC	Udonthani, Thailand
Aug 5	Eric Morel	S. Pisnurachan	Dec 12	WBA	Madison, WI
Aug 20	Malcolm Tunacao	Celes Kobayashi	Draw	WBC	Tokyo

Junior Flyweight

Date	Winner	Loser	Result	Title	Site
Oct 2	Ricardo Lopez	Will Grigsby	Dec 12	IBF	Las Vegas
Oct 17	Choi Yo-Sam	Saman Sorjaturong	Dec 12	WBC	Seoul, S Korea
Feb 4	Phichitchor Siriwat	Yang Sang-ik	Dec 12	WBA	Bangkok, Thailand
June 17	Choi Yo-Sam	Chart Kiatpetch	KO 5	WBC	Seoul, S Korea
Aug 12	Beibis Mendoza	Rosendo Alvarez	DQ 7	WBA	Las Vegas

Strawweight (Mini Flyweight)

Date	Winner	Loser	Result	Title	Site
Oct 9	Noel Arambulet	Joma Gamboa	Dec 12	WBA	Caracas, Venezuela
Dec 3	Zolani Petelo	Juanito Rubillar	Dec 12	IBF	Peterborough, England
Dec 4	Joma Gamboa	Satoru Abe	TKO 6	interim WBA	Nagoya, Japan
Feb 11	Jose Antonio Aguirre	Wandee Charoen	Dec 12	WBC	Samut Sakorn, Thailand
Mar 4	Noel Arambulet	Jose Garcia	Dec 12	WBA	Coro, Venezuela
Apr 9	Joma Gamboa	Atsushi Sai	Dec 12	interim WBA	Hachinohe, Japan
June 2	Zolani Petelo	Mickey Cantwell	TKO 8	IBF	Kent, England
July 7	Jose Antonio Aguirre	Jose Luis Zepeda	TKO 5	WBC	Villahermosa, Mexico
Aug 20	Joma Gamboa	Noel Arambulet	Dec 12	WBA	Tokyo

"Iron Mike!"

In July, Jesse Ventura, the wrestler turned governor of Minnesota, sold the musical rights to his life story to Broadway producer Pierre Cossette (*The Will Rogers Follies*), who plans to create an extravaganza called *The Body Ventura*. But Ventura's not the only athlete whose life will soon be set to show tunes, for we've just completed the closing numbers to another new Broadway musical. (Sung roughly to the tune of "Be Our Guest," from *Beauty and the Beast*.)

Yikes!/Iron Mike's/Feeling ravenous
  toward tykes
All those years/He ate ears/But the boxer's switching gears
He finds toddler/Apple cobbler/To be
  easy on the gobbler
(Call the media salacious/But he's
  pedia-voracious).

The appeal?/It's like veal/Or maybe baby
  seal
(Snickers satisfies your hunger/But Iron
  Mike wants something younger)
Told the Scots:/"Serve me tots!/Not old
  men with liver spots"...
Just like that/Turned young brats/Into
  bräts! (slower, with leg kicks)
Wife's a doctor/Never socked her/But
  his ex-wife said he clocked her—
Robin Givens/Has forgiven/Him
  posthaste
Still she'd like to ask one question/
  About acid indigestion...
Does a child/Leave a mild/Aftertaaaste?

(curtain)

—Steve Rushin

FOR THE RECORD·Year by Year

World Champions

Sanctioning bodies: the National Boxing Association (NBA), the New York State Athletic Commission (NY), the World Boxing Association (WBA), the World Boxing Council (WBC), and the International Boxing Federation (IBF).

Heavyweights
(Weight: Unlimited)

Champion	Reign	Champion	Reign	Champion	Reign
John L. Sullivan	1885–92	Muhammad Ali	1964–70	Mike Tyson* WBC	1986–87
James J. Corbett	1892–97	Ernie Terrell* WBA	1965–67	James Bonecrusher	
Bob Fitzsimmons	1897–99	Joe Frazier* NY	1968–70	Smith* WBA	1986–87
James J. Jeffries	1899–1905†	Jimmy Ellis* WBA	1968–70	Tony Tucker* IBF	1987
Marvin Hart	1905–06	Joe Frazier	1970–73	Mike Tyson	1987–90
Tommy Burns	1906–08	George Foreman	1973–74	Buster Douglas	1990
Jack Johnson	1908–15	Muhammad Ali	1974–78	Evander Holyfield	1990–92
Jess Willard	1915–19	Leon Spinks	1978	Lennox Lewis* WBC	1993–95
Jack Dempsey	1919–26	Ken Norton* WBC	1978	Riddick Bowe	1992–93
Gene Tunney	1926–28	Larry Holmes* WBC	1978–80	Evander Holyfield	1993–94
Max Schmeling	1930–32	Muhammad Ali	1978–79†	Michael Moorer	1994
Jack Sharkey	1932–33	John Tate* WBA	1979–80	George Foreman	1994–95
Primo Carnera	1933–34	Mike Weaver* WBA	1980–82	Oliver McCall* WBC	1995
Max Baer	1934–35	Larry Holmes	1980–85	Frank Bruno* WBC	1995–96
James J. Braddock	1935–37	Michael Dokes* WBA	1982–83	Bruce Seldon* WBA	1995–96
Joe Louis	1937–49†	Gerrie Coetzee* WBA	1983–84	Mike Tyson WBA	1996
Ezzard Charles	1949–51	Tim Witherspoon* WBC	1984	Michael Moorer* IBF	1996–97
Jersey Joe Walcott	1951–52	Pinklon Thomas* WBC	1984–86	Lennox Lewis* WBC	1997–
Rocky Marciano	1952–56†	Greg Page* WBA	1984–85	E. Holyfield WBA, IBF	1996–99
Ingemar Johansson	1959–60	Michael Spinks	1985–87	Lennox Lewis	1999–
Floyd Patterson	1960–62	Tim Witherspoon* WBA	1986	E. Holyfield* WBA	2000–
Sonny Liston	1962–64	Trevor Berbick* WBC	1986		

Cruiserweights
(Weight Limit: 190 pounds)

Champion	Reign	Champion	Reign	Champion	Reign
Marvin Camel* WBC	1980	Ricky Parkey* IBF	1986–87	Alfred Cole* IBF	1992–96
Carlos De Leon* WBC	1980–82	E. Holyfield* WBA/IBF	1987–88	Orlin Norris* WBA	1993–95
Ossie Ocasio* WBA	1982–84	Evander Holyfield	1988†	Nate Miller* WBA	1995–97
S.T. Gordon* WBC	1982–83	Toufik Belbouli* WBA	1989	Marcelo	
Carlos De Leon* WBC	1983–85	Robert Daniels* WBA	1989–91	Dominguez* WBC	1996–98
Marvin Camel* IBF	1983–84	Carlos De Leon* WBC	1989–90	A. Washington* IBF	1996–97
Lee Roy Murphy* IBF	1984–86	Glenn McCrory* IBF	1989–90	Uriah Grant* IBF	1997
Piet Crous* WBA	1984–85	Jeff Lampkin* IBF	1990	Imamu Mayfield* IBF	1997–98
Alfonso Ratliff* WBC	1985	M. Duran* WBC	1990–91	Fabrice Tiozzo* WBA	1997–
Dwight Braxton* WBA	1985–86	Bobby Czyz* WBA	1991–92†	J.C. Gomez* WBC	1998–
Bernard Benton* WBC	1985–86	Anaclet Wamba* WBC	1991–95	Arthur Williams* IBF	1998–99
Carlos De Leon* WBC	1986–88	James Pritchard* IBF	1991	Vassiliy Jirov* IBF	1999–
Evander Holyfield* WBA	1986–88	James Warring* IBF	1991–92		

Note: Division called Junior Heavyweight by the WBA.

Light Heavyweights
(Weight Limit: 175 pounds)

Champion	Reign	Champion	Reign	Champion	Reign
Jack Root	1903	Maxie Rosenbloom	1930–34	Willie Pastrano	1963–65
George Gardner	1903	George Nichols* NBA	1932	Jose Torres	1965–66
Bob Fitzsimmons	1903–05	Bob Godwin* NBA	1933	Dick Tiger	1966–68
Philadelphia Jack		Bob Olin	1934–35	Bob Foster	1968–74†
O'Brien	1905–12†	John Henry Lewis	1935–38	Vicente Rondon* WBA	1971–72
Jack Dillon	1914–16	Melio Bettina	1939	John Conteh* WBC	1974–77
Battling Levinsky	1916–20	Billy Conn	1939–40†	Victor Galindez* WBA	1974–78
Georges Carpentier	1920–22	Anton Christoforidis	1941	Miguel A. Cuello* WBC	1977–78
Battling Siki	1922–23	Gus Lesnevich	1941–48	Mate Parlov* WBC	1978
Mike McTigue	1923–25	Freddie Mills	1948–50	Mike Rossman* WBA	1978–79
Paul Berlenbach	1925–26	Joey Maxim	1950–52	Marvin Johnson* WBC	1978–79
Jack Delaney	1926–27†	Archie Moore	1952–62†	Matthew Saad	
Jimmy Slattery* NBA	1927	Harold Johnson* NBA	1961	Muhammad* WBC	1979–81
Tommy Loughran	1927–29	Harold Johnson	1962–63	Marvin Johnson* WBA	1979–80

*Champion not generally recognized. †Champion retired or relinquished title.

BOXING   457

Light Heavyweights *(Cont.)*

Champion	Reign	Champion	Reign	Champion	Reign
Eddie Mustapha Muhammad* WBA	1980–81	Leslie Stewart* WBA	1987	Iran Barkley* WBA	1992
Michael Spinks* WBA	1981–83	Virgil Hill* WBA	1987–91	Virgil Hill* WBA	1992–97
D. Muhammad		Pr Charles Williams* IBF	1987–93	Henry Maske* IBF	1993–96
Qawi* WBC	1981–83	Thomas Hearns* WBC	1987†	Mike McCallum* WBC	1994–95
Michael Spinks	1983–85†	Donny Lalonde* WBC	1987–88	Fabrice Tiozzo* WBC	1995–96
J. B. Williamson* WBC	1985–86	Sugar Ray Leonard* WBC	1988	Roy Jones Jr WBC/WBA	1997–
Slobodan Kacar* IBF	1985–86	Dennis Andries* WBC	1989	William Guthrie* IBF	1997–98
Marvin Johnson* WBA	1986–87	Jeff Harding* WBC	1989–90	Reggie Johnson* IBF	1998–99
Dennis Andries* WBC	1986–87	Dennis Andries* WBC	1990–91	Roy Jones Jr	1999–
Bobby Czyz* IBF	1986–87	Thomas Hearns* WBA	1991–92		
		Jeff Harding* WBC	1991–94		

Super Middleweights
(Weight Limit: 168 pounds)

Champion	Reign	Champion	Reign	Champion	Reign
Murray Sutherland* IBF	1984	Victor Cordova* WBA	1991	V. Nardiello* WBC	1996
Chong-Pal Park* IBF	1984–87	Darrin Van Horn* IBF	1991–92	Robin Reid* WBC	1996–97
Chong-Pal Park* WBA	1987–88	Iran Barkley *IBF	1992	Charles Brewer* IBF	1997–98
G. Rocchigiani* IBF	1988–89	Nigel Benn* WBC	1992–96	Thulane Malinga* WBC	1997–98
F. Obelmejias* WBA	1988–89	James Toney* IBF	1992–94	Richie Woodhall* WBC	1998–99
Sugar Ray Leonard* WBC	1988–90†	Michael Nunn* WBA	1992–94	Sven Ottke* IBF	1998–
In-Chul Baek* WBA	1989–90	Steve Little* WBA	1994	Byron Mitchell* WBA	1999–00
Lindell Holmes* IBF	1990–91	Frank Liles* WBA	1994–99	Markus Beyer* WBC	1999–00
C. Tiozzo* WBA	1990–91	Roy Jones Jr* IBF	1994–96	Bruno Girard* WBA	2000–
Mauro Galvano* WBC	1990–92	Thulane Malinga* WBC	1996	Glenn Catley* WBC	2000–

Middleweights
(Weight Limit: 160 pounds)

Champion	Reign	Champion	Reign	Champion	Reign
Jack Dempsey	1884–91	Marcel Cerdan	1948–49	Alan Minter	1980
Bob Fitzsimmons	1891–97	Jake La Motta	1949–51	Marvin Hagler	1980–87
Kid McCoy	1897–98	Sugar Ray Robinson	1951	Sugar Ray Leonard	1987†
Tommy Ryan	1898–1907	Randy Turpin	1951	Frank Tate* IBF	1987–88
Stanley Ketchel	1908	Sugar Ray Robinson	1951–52	Sumbu Kalambay* WBA	1987–89
Billy Papke	1908	Bobo Olson	1953–55	Thomas Hearns* WBC	1987–88
Stanley Ketchel	1908–10	Sugar Ray Robinson	1955–57	Iran Barkley* WBC	1988–89
Frank Klaus	1913	Gene Fullmer	1957	Michael Nunn* IBF	1988–91
George Chip	1913–14	Sugar Ray Robinson	1957	Roberto Duran* WBC	1989–90†
Al McCoy	1914–17	Carmen Basilio	1957–58	Mike McCallum* WBA	1989–91
Mike O'Dowd	1917–20	Sugar Ray Robinson	1958–60	Julian Jackson* WBC	1990–93
Johnny Wilson	1920–23	Gene Fullmer* NBA	1959–62	James Toney* IBF	1991–93†
Harry Greb	1923–26	Paul Pender	1960–61	Reggie Johnson* WBA	1992–94
Tiger Flowers	1926	Terry Downes	1961–62	Roy Jones Jr* IBF	1993–95†
Mickey Walker	1926–31†	Paul Pender	1962–63	G. McClellan* WBC	1993–95†
Gorilla Jones	1931–32	Dick Tiger* WBA	1962–63	Jorge Castro* WBA	1994–95
Marcel Thil	1932–37	Dick Tiger	1963	Shinji Takehara* WBA	1995–96
Fred Apostoli	1937–39	Joey Giardello	1963–65	Jullian Jackson*WBC	1995
Al Hostak* NBA	1938	Dick Tiger	1965–66	Quincy Taylor* WBC	1995–96
Solly Krieger* NBA	1938–39	Emile Griffith	1966–67	Bernard Hopkins* IBF	1995–
Al Hostak* NBA	1939–40	Nino Benvenuti	1967	Keith Holmes* WBC	1996–98
Ceferino Garcia	1939–40	Emile Griffith	1967–68	William Joppy Jr* WBA	1996–97
Ken Overlin	1940–41	Nino Benvenuti	1968–70	J.C. Green* WBA	1997
Tony Zale* NBA	1940–41	Carlos Monzon	1970–77†	William Joppy Jr.* WBA	1998–
Billy Soose	1941	Rodrigo Valdez* WBC	1974–76	Hassine Cherifi* WBC	1998–99
Tony Zale	1941–47	Rodrigo Valdez	1977–78	Keith Holmes* WBC	1999–
Rocky Graziano	1947–48	Hugo Corro	1978–79		
Tony Zale	1948	Vito Antuofermo	1979–80		

Junior Middleweights
(Weight Limit: 154 pounds)

Champion	Reign	Champion	Reign	Champion	Reign
Emile Griffith (EBU)	1962–63	Nino Benvenuti	1965–66	Carmelo Bossi	1970–71
Dennis Moyer	1962–63	Ki-Soo Kim	1966–68	Koichi Wajima	1971–74
Ralph Dupas	1963	Sandro Mazzinghi	1968	Oscar Albarado	1974–75
Sandro Mazzinghi	1963–65	Freddie Little	1969–70	Koichi Wajima	1975

*Champion not generally recognized. †Champion retired or relinquished title.

Junior Middleweights *(Cont.)*

Champion	Reign	Champion	Reign	Champion	Reign
Miguel de Oliveira* WBC	1975–76	Mark Medal* IBF	1984	Vinny Pazienza* WBA	1991–92
Jae-Do Yuh	1975–76	Thomas Hearns	1984–86†	Julio C. Vasquez* WBA	1992–95
Elisha Obed* WBC	1975–76	Mike McCallum* WBA	1984–87†	Simon Brown* WBC	1993–94
Koichi Wajima	1976	Carlos Santos* IBF	1984–86	Terry Norris *WBC	1994–97
Jose Duran	1976	Buster Drayton* IBF	1986–87	Vincent Pettway* IBF	1994–95
Eckhard Dagge* WBC	1976–77	Duane Thomas* WBC	1986–87	Paul Vaden* IBF	1995
Miguel Angel Castellini	1976–77	Matthew Hilton* IBF	1987–88	Carl Daniels* WBA	1995
Eddie Gazo	1977–78	Lupe Aquino* WBC	1987	Terry Norris WBC	1995–97
Rocky Mattioli* WBC	1977–79	Gianfranco Rosi* WBC	1987–88	Terry Norris IBF	1995–96†
Masashi Kudo	1978–79	Julian Jackson* WBA	1987–90	L. Boudouani* WBA	1996–99
Maurice Hope* WBC	1979–81	Donald Curry* WBC	1988–89	Raul Marquez* IBF	1997
Ayub Kalule	1979–81	Robert Hines* IBF	1988–89	Keith Mullings* WBC	1997–99
Wilfred Benitez* WBC	1981–82	Darrin Van Horn* IBF	1989	Yori Boy Campas* IBF	1997–98
Sugar Ray Leonard	1981–82†	Rene Jacquot* WBC	1989	Fernando Vargas* IBF	1998–
Tadashi Mihara* WBA	1981–82	John Mugabi* WBC	1989–90	F. Javier Castillejo* WBC	1999–
Davey Moore* WBA	1982–83	Gianfranco Rosi* IBF	1989–94	David Reid* WBA	1999–00
Thomas Hearns* WBC	1982–84	Terry Norris* WBC	1990–93	Felix Trinidad* WBA	2000–
Roberto Duran* WBA	1983–84	Gilbert Dele* WBA	1991		

Note: Division called Super Welterweight by the WBC.

Welterweights
(Weight Limit: 147 pounds)

Champion	Reign	Champion	Reign	Champion	Reign
Paddy Duffy	1888–90	Jimmy McLarnin	1933–34	Pipino Cuevas* WBA	1976–80
Mysterious Billy Smith	1892–94	Barney Ross	1934	Wilfredo Benitez	1979
Tommy Ryan	1894–98	Jimmy McLarnin	1934–35	Sugar Ray Leonard	1979–80
Mysterious Billy Smith	1898–1900	Barney Ross	1935–38	Roberto Duran	1980
Rube Ferns	1900	Henry Armstrong	1938–40	Thomas Hearns* WBA	1980–81
Matty Matthews	1900–01	Fritzie Zivic	1940–41	Sugar Ray Leonard	1980–82†
Rube Ferns	1901	Red Cochrane	1941–46	Donald Curry* WBA	1983–85
Joe Walcott	1901–04	Marty Servo	1946	Milton McCrory* WBC	1983–85
The Dixie Kid	1904–05	Sugar Ray Robinson	1946–51†	Donald Curry	1985–86
Honey Mellody	1906–07	Johnny Bratton	1951	Lloyd Honeyghan	1986–87
Twin Sullivan	1907–08	Kid Gavilan	1951–54	Jorge Vaca WBC	1987–88
Jimmy Gardner	1908	Johnny Saxton	1954–55	Lloyd Honeyghan WBC	1988–89
Jimmy Clabby	1910–11	Tony DeMarco	1955	Mark Breland* WBA	1987
Waldemar Holberg	1914	Carmen Basilio	1955–56	Marlon Starling* WBA	1987–88
Tom McCormick	1914	Johnny Saxton	1956	Tomas Molinares* WBA	1988–89
Matt Wells	1914–15	Carmen Basilio	1956–57	Simon Brown* IBF	1988–91
Mike Glover	1915	Virgil Akins	1958	Mark Breland* WBA	1989–90
Jack Britton	1915	Don Jordan	1958–60	Marlon Starling* WBC	1989–90
Ted "Kid" Lewis	1915–16	Kid Paret	1960–61	Aaron Davis* WBA	1990–91
Jack Britton	1916–17	Emile Griffith	1961	Maurice Blocker* WBC	1990–91
Ted "Kid" Lewis	1917–19	Kid Paret	1961–62	Meldrick Taylor* WBA	1991–92
Jack Britton	1919–22	Emile Griffith	1962–63	Simon Brown* WBC	1991
Mickey Walker	1922–26	Luis Rodriguez	1963	Buddy McGirt* WBC	1991–93
Pete Latzo	1926–27	Emile Griffith	1963–66	Felix Trinidad* IBF	1993–
Joe Dundee	1927–29	Curtis Cokes	1966–69	Pernell Whitaker WBC	1993–97
Jackie Fields	1929–30	Jose Napoles	1969–70	Crisanto Espana* WBA	1992–94
Young Jack Thompson	1930	Billy Backus	1970–71	Ike Quartey* WBA	1994–97†
Tommy Freeman	1930–31	Jose Napoles	1971–75	Oscar De La Hoya* WBC	1997–99
Young Jack Thompson	1931	Hedgemon Lewis* NY	1972–73	James Page* WBA	1998–
Lou Brouillard	1931–32	Angel Espada* WBA	1975–76	Felix Trinidad IBF, WBC	1999–00†
Jackie Fields	1932–33	John H. Stracey	1975–76	Shane Mosley* WBC	2000–
Young Corbett III	1933	Carlos Palomino	1976–79		

Junior Welterweights
(Weight Limit: 140 pounds)

Champion	Reign	Champion	Reign	Champion	Reign
Pinkey Mitchell	1922–25	Sammy Fuller*	1932–33	Duilio Loi	1960–62
Red Herring	1925	Battling Shaw	1933	Eddie Perkins	1962
Mushy Callahan	1926–30	Tony Canzoneri	1933	Duilio Loi	1962–63
Jack (Kid) Berg	1930–31	Barney Ross	1933–35	Roberto Cruz* WBA	1963
Tony Canzoneri	1931–32	Tippy Larkin	1946	Eddie Perkins	1963–65
Johnny Jadick	1932–33	Carlos Ortiz	1959–60	Carlos Hernandez	1965–66

Junior Welterweights *(Cont.)*

Champion	Reign	Champion	Reign	Champion	Reign
Sandro Lopopolo	1966–67	Bill Costello* WBC	1984–85	Rafael Pineda* IBF	1991–92
Paul Fujii	1967–68	Gene Hatcher* WBA	1984–85	Akinobu Hiranaka* WBA	1992
Nicolino Loche	1968–72	Ubaldo Sacco* WBA	1985–86	Pernell Whitaker*† IBF	1992–93
Pedro Adigue* WBC	1968–70	Lonnie Smith* WBC	1985–86	Charles Murray* IBF	1993–94
Bruno Arcari* WBC	1970–74	Patrizio Oliva* WBA	1986–87	Jake Rodriguez* IBF	1994–95
Alfonso Frazer	1972	Gary Hinton* IBF	1986	Juan Coggi* WBA	1993–94
Antonio Cervantes	1972–76	Rene Arredondo* WBC	1986	Frankie Randall* WBC	1994
Perico Fernandez* WBC	1974–75	Tsuyoshi Hamada* WBC	1986–87	Frankie Randall* WBA	1994–96
S. Muangsurin* WBC	1975–76	Joe Louis Manley* IBF	1986–87	Juan Coggi* WBA	1996
Wilfred Benitez	1976–79†	Terry Marsh* IBF	1987	Julio César Chávez WBC	1994–96
M. Velasquez* WBC	1976	Juan Coggi* WBA	1987–90	Kostya Tszyu* IBF	1995–97
S. Muangsurin* WBC	1976–78	Rene Arredondo* WBC	1987	Frankie Randall* WBA	1996–97
A. Cervantes* WBA	1977–80	R. Mayweather* WBC	1987–89	Oscar De La Hoya WBC	1996–97†
Sang-Hyun Kim* WBC	1978–80	James McGirt* IBF	1988	Khalid Rahilou* WBA	1997–98
Saoul Mamby* WBC	1980–82	Meldrick Taylor* IBF	1988–90	Vincent Phillips* IBF	1997–99
Aaron Pryor* WBA	1980–83	Julio César Chávez WBC	1989–94	Sharmba Mitchell* WBA	1998–
Leroy Haley* WBC	1982–83	Julio César Chávez* IBF	1990–91	Kostya Tszyu* WBC	1998–
Aaron Pryor* IBF	1983–85	Loreto Garza* WBA	1990–91	Terronn Millett* IBF	1999–00
Bruce Curry* WBC	1983–84	Juan Coggi* WBA	1991	Zab Judah* IBF	2000–
Johnny Bumphus* WBA	1984	Edwin Rosario* WBA	1991–92		

Lightweights
(Weight Limit: 135 pounds)

Champion	Reign	Champion	Reign	Champion	Reign
Jack McAuliffe	1886–94	James Carter	1952–54	Edwin Rosario* WBA	1986–87
Kid Lavigne	1896–99	Paddy DeMarco	1954	Julio César Chávez* WBA	1987–88
Frank Erne	1899–1902	James Carter	1954–55	Jose Luis Ramirez* WBC	1987–88
Joe Gans	1902–04	Wallace Smith	1955–56	Julio César Chávez	1988–89
Jimmy Britt	1904–05	Joe Brown	1956–62	Vinny Pazienza* IBF	1987–88
Battling Nelson	1905–06	Carlos Ortiz	1962–65	Greg Haugen* IBF	1988–89
Joe Gans	1906–08	Ismael Laguna	1965	P. Whitaker* WBC, IBF	1989–90
Battling Nelson	1908–10	Carlos Ortiz	1965–68	Edwin Rosario* WBA	1989–90
Ad Wolgast	1910–12	Carlos Teo Cruz	1968–69	Juan Nazario* WBA	1990
Willie Ritchie	1912–14	Mando Ramos	1969–70	P. Whitaker* WBA, WBC	1990–92
Freddie Welsh	1915–17	Ismael Laguna	1970	Pernell Whitaker* IBF	1991–92
Benny Leonard	1917–25†	Ken Buchanan	1970–72	Julio César Chávez* IBF	1990–91
Jimmy Goodrich	1925	Roberto Duran	1972–79†	Edwin Rosario* WBA	1991–92
Rocky Kansas	1925–26	Chango Carmona* WBC	1972	Julio César Chávez* WBC	1990–92
Sammy Mandell	1926–30	Rodolfo Gonzalez* WBC	1972–74	Miguel Gonzalez* WBC	1992–95
Al Singer	1930	Ishimatsu Suzuki* WBC	1974–76	Joey Gamache* WBA	1992–93
Tony Canzoneri	1930–33	Estaban DeJesus* WBC	1976–78	Dingaan Thobela* WBA	1993
Barney Ross	1933–35†	Jim Watt* WBC	1979–81	Fred Pendleton* IBF	1993–94
Tony Canzoneri	1935–36	Ernesto Espana* WBA	1979–80	Orzubek Nazarov* WBA	1993–98
Lou Ambers	1936–38	Hilmer Kenty* WBA	1980–81	Rafael Ruelas* IBF	1994–95
Henry Armstrong	1938–39	Sean O'Grady* WBA	1981	Phillip Holiday* IBF	1995–97
Lou Ambers	1939–40	Claude Noel* WBA	1981	Jean B. Mendy* WBC	1996–97
Sammy Angott* NBA	1940–41	Alexis Arguello* WBC	1981–82	Steve Johnston* WBC	1997–98
Lew Jenkins	1940–41	Arturo Frias* WBA	1981–82	Shane Mosley* IBF	1997–99†
Sammy Angott	1941–42†	Ray Mancini* WBA	1982–84	Jean B. Mendy* WBC	1998–99
Beau Jack* NY	1942–43	Alexis Arguello	1982–83	Cesar Bazan* WBC	1998–99
Bob Montgomery* NY	1943	Edwin Rosario* WBC	1983–84	Steve Johnston* WBC	1999–00
Sammy Angott* NBA	1943–44	Choo Choo Brown* IBF	1984	Julien Lorcy* WBA	1999
Beau Jack* NY	1943–44	L. Bramble* WBA	1984–86	Stefano Zoff* WBA	1999
Bob Montgomery* NY	1944–47	Jose Luis Ramirez* WBC	1984–85	Paul Spadafora* IBF	1999–
Juan Zurita* NBA	1944–45	Harry Arroyo* IBF	1984–85	Gilbert Serrano* WBA	1999–00
Ike Williams	1947–51	Jimmy Paul* IBF	1985–86	T. Hatakeyama* WBA	2000–
James Carter	1951–52	Hector Camacho* WBC	1985–86	Jose Luis Castillo* WBC	2000–
Lauro Salas	1952	Greg Haugen* IBF	1986–87		

*Champion not generally recognized. †Champion retired or relinquished title.

Junior Lightweights
(Weight Limit: 130 pounds)

Champion	Reign
Johnny Dundee	1921–23
Jack Bernstein	1923
Johnny Dundee	1923–24
Steve (Kid) Sullivan	1924–25
Mike Ballerino	1925
Tod Morgan	1925–29
Benny Bass	1929–31
Kid Chocolate	1931–33
Frankie Klick	1933–34
Sandy Saddler	1949–50
Harold Gomes	1959–60
Gabriel (Flash) Elorde	1960–67
Yoshiaki Numata	1967
Hiroshi Kobayashi	1967–71
Rene Barrientos* WBC	1969–70
Yoshiaki Numata* WBC	1970–71
Alfredo Marcano	1971–72
R. Arredondo* WBC	1971–74
Ben Villaflor	1972–73
Kuniaki Shibata	1973
Ben Villaflor	1973–76
Kuniaki Shibata* WBC	1974–75

Champion	Reign
Alfredo Escalera* WBC	1975–78
Samuel Serrano	1976–80
Alexis Arguello* WBC	1978–80
Yasutsune Uehara	1980–81
Rafael Limon* WBC	1980–81
C. Boza-Edwards* WBC	1981
Samuel Serrano	1981–83
R. Navarrete* WBC	1981–82
Rafael Limon* WBC	1982
Bobby Chacon* WBC	1982–83
Roger Mayweather	1983–84
Hector Camacho* WBC	1983–84
Rocky Lockridge	1984–85
Hwan-Kil Yuh* IBF	1984–85
Julio César Chávez* WBC	1984–87
Lester Ellis* IBF	1985
Wilfredo Gomez	1985–86
Barry Michael* IBF	1985–87
Alfredo Layne* WBA	1986
Brian Mitchell* WBA	1986–91
Rocky Lockridge* IBF	1987–88
Azumah Nelson* WBC	1988–94

Champion	Reign
Tony Lopez* IBF	1988–89
Juan Molina* IBF	1989–90
Tony Lopez* IBF	1990–91
Joey Gamache WBA	1991
Brian Mitchell* IBF	1991
Genaro Hernandez* WBA	1991–95
James Leija* WBC	1994
Juan Molina* IBF	1991–95
Gabriel Ruelas* WBC	1994–95
Eddie Hopson* IBF	1995
Tracy Patterson* IBF	1995
Azumah Nelson* WBC	1995–97
Choi Yong-Soo* WBA	1995–98
Arturo Gatti* IBF	1995–98†
Genaro Hernandez* WBC	1997–98
Roberto Garcia* IBF	1998–99
Floyd Mayweather* WBC	1998–
T. Hatakeyama* WBA	1998–99
Lakva Sim* WBA	1999
Diego Corrales* IBF	1999–
Jong Kwon Baek* WBA	1999–00
Joel Casamayor* WBA	2000–

Featherweights
(Weight Limit: 126 pounds)

Champion	Reign
Torpedo Billy Murphy	1890
Young Griffo	1890–92
George Dixon	1892–97
Solly Smith	1897–98
Dave Sullivan	1898
George Dixon	1898–1900
Terry McGovern	1900–01
Young Corbett II	1901–04
Jimmy Britt	1904
Tommy Sullivan	1904–05
Abe Attell	1906–12
Johnny Kilbane	1912–23
Eugene Criqui	1923
Johnny Dundee	1923–24
"Kid" Kaplan	1925–26
Benny Bass	1927–28
Tony Canzoneri	1928
Andre Routis	1928–29
Battling Battalino	1929–32
Tommy Paul* NBA	1932–33
Kid Chocolate* NY	1932–33
Freddie Miller* NBA	1933–36
Mike Beloise* NY	1936–37
Petey Sarron* NBA	1936–37
Maurice Holtzer	1937–38
Henry Armstrong	1937–38
Joey Archibald* NY	1938–39
Leo Rodak* NBA	1938–39
Joey Archibald	1939–40
Petey Scalzo* NBA	1940–41
Harry Jeffra	1940–41
Joey Archibald	1941
Richie Lamos* NBA	1941
Chalky Wright	1941–42

Champion	Reign
Jackie Wilson* NBA	1941–43
Willie Pep	1942–48
Jackie Callura* NBA	1943
Phil Terranova* NBA	1943–44
Sal Bartolo* NBA	1944–46
Sandy Saddler	1948–49
Willie Pep	1949–50
Sandy Saddler	1950–57†
Kid Bassey	1957–59
Davey Moore	1959–63
Sugar Ramos	1963–64
Vicente Saldivar	1964–67†
Paul Rojas* WBA	1968
Jose Legra* WBC	1968–69
Shozo Saijyo* WBA	1968–71
J. Famechon* WBC	1969–70
Vicente Saldivar WBC	1970
Kuniaki Shibata WBC	1970–72
Antonio Gomez WBC	1971–72
C. Sanchez WBC	1972
Ernesto Marcel* WBA	1972–74
Jose Legra WBC	1972–73
Eder Jofre WBC	1973–74
Ruben Olivares* WBA	1974
Bobby Chacon* WBC	1974–75
Alexis Arguello WBA	1974–76
Ruben Olivares* WBC	1975
Poison Kotey* WBC	1975–76
Danny Lopez WBC	1976–80
Rafael Ortega* WBA	1977
Cecilio Lastra* WBA	1977–78
Eusebio Pedroza* WBA	1978–85
S. Sanchez WBC	1980–82
Juan LaPorte* WBC	1982–84

Champion	Reign
Wilfredo Gomez* WBC	1984
Min-Keun Oh* IBF	1984–85
Azumah Nelson* WBC	1984–88
Barry McGuigan* WBA	1985–86
Ki Young Chung* IBF	1985–86
Steve Cruz* WBA	1986–87
Antonio Rivera* IBF	1986–88
A. Esparragoza* WBA	1987–91
Calvin Grove* IBF	1988
Jorge Paez* IBF	1988–91
Jeff Fenech* WBC	1988–90†
Marcos Villasana* WBC	1990–91
Paul Hodkinson* WBC	1991–93
Troy Dorsey* IBF	1991
Manuel Medina* IBF	1991–93
Yung Kyun Park* WBA	1991–93
Gregorio Vargas* WBC	1993
Tom Johnson* IBF	1993–97†
Eloy Rojas* WBA	1993–96
Kevin Kelley* WBC	1993–95
A. Gonzalez* WBC	1995
Manuel Medina* WBC	1995–95
Luisito Espinosa* WBC	1995–99
Wilfredo Vazquez* WBA	1996–98†
Hector Lizarraga* IBF	1997–98
Freddy Norwood* WBA	1998
Manuel Medina* IBF	1998–99
Antonio Cermeno* WBA	1998–99
Cesar Soto* WBC	1999
Freddy Norwood* WBA	1999–
Naseem Hamed* WBC	1999†
Paul Ingle* IBF	1999–
Guty Espadas* WBC	2000–

Junior Featherweights
(Weight Limit: 122 pounds)

Champion	Reign
Jack (Kid) Wolfe*	1922–23
Carl Duane*	1923–24
Rigoberto Riasco* WBC	1976
Royal Kobayashi* WBC	1976
Dong-Kyun Yum* WBC	1976–77
Wilfredo Gomez* WBC	1977–83
Soo-Hwan Hong* WBA	1977–78
Ricardo Cardona* WBA	1978–80
Leo Randolph* WBA	1980
Sergio Palma* WBA	1980–82
Leonardo Cruz* WBA	1982–84
Jaime Garza* WBC	1983
Bobby Berna* IBF	1983–84
Loris Stecca* WBA	1984
Seung-Il Suh* IBF	1984–85
Victor Callejas* WBA	1984–86
Juan (Kid) Meza* WBC	1984–85

Champion	Reign
Ji-Won Kim* IBF	1985–86
Lupe Pintor* WBC	1985–86
Samart Payakaroon* WBC	1986–87
Seung-Hoon Lee* IBF	1987–88
Louie Espinoza* WBA	1987
Jeff Fenech* WBC	1987
Julio Gervacio* WBA	1987–88
Daniel Zaragoza* WBC	1988–90
Jose Sanabria* IBF	1988–89
Bernardo Pinango* WBA	1988
Juan Jose Estrada* WBA	1988–89
Fabrice Benichou* IBF	1989–90
Jesus Salud* WBA	1989–90
Welcome Ncita* IBF	1990–92
Paul Banke* WBC	1990

Champion	Reign
Luis Mendoza* WBA	1990–91
Rual Perez* WBA	1992
Pedro Decima* WBC	1990–91
K. Hatanaka* WBC	1991
Daniel Zaragoza* WBC	1991–92
Tracy Patterson* WBC	1992–94
Kennedy McKinney* IBF	1993–94
Wilfredo Vasquez* WBA	1992–95
Vuyani Bungu* IBF	1994–99†
H. Acero Sanchez* WBC	1994–95
Antonio Cermeno* WBA	1995–98†
Daniel Zaragoza* WBC	1995–97
Erik Morales* WBC	1997–
Enrique Sanchez* WBA	1998
Nestor Garza* WBA	1998–00
Benedict Ledwaba* IBF	1999–
Clarence Adams* WBA	2000–

Bantamweights
(Weight Limit: 118 pounds)

Champion	Reign
Spider Kelly	1887
Hughey Boyle	1887–88
Spider Kelly	1889
Chappie Moran	1889–90
George Dixon	1890–91
Pedlar Palmer*	1895–99
Terry McGovern	1899–1900
Harry Harris	1901–02
Harry Forbes	1902–03
Frankie Neil	1903–04
Joe Bowker	1904–05
Jimmy Walsh	1905–06
Owen Moran	1907–08
Monte Attell*	1909–10
Frankie Conley	1910–11
Johnny Coulon	1911–14
Kid Williams	1914–17
Kewpie Ertle*	1915
Pete Herman	1917–20
Joe Lynch	1920–21
Pete Herman	1921
Johnny Buff	1921–22
Joe Lynch	1922–24
Abe Goldstein	1924
Cannonball Martin	1924–25
Phil Rosenberg	1925–27
Bud Taylor NBA	1927–28
Bushy Graham* NY	1928–29
Panama Al Brown	1929–35
Sixto Escobar* NBA	1934–35
Baltazar Sangchilli	1935–36
Lou Salica* NBA	1935
Sixto Escobar* NBA	1935–36
Tony Marino	1936
Sixto Escobar	1936–37
Harry Jeffra	1937–38†
Sixto Escobar	1938–39

Champion	Reign
Georgie Pace NBA	1939–40
Lou Salica	1940–42
Manuel Ortiz	1942–47
Harold Dade	1947
Manuel Ortiz	1947–50
Vic Toweel	1950–52
Jimmy Carruthers	1952–54†
Robert Cohen	1954–56
Paul Macias* NBA	1955–57
Mario D'Agata	1956–57
Alphonse Halimi	1957–59
Joe Becerra	1959–60†
Eder Jofre	1961–65
Fighting Harada	1965–68
Lionel Rose	1968–69
Ruben Olivares	1969–70
Chucho Castillo	1970–71
Ruben Olivares	1971–72
Rafael Herrera	1972
Enrique Pinder	1972–73
Romeo Anaya	1973
Rafael Herrera* WBC	1973–74
Soo-Hwan Hong	1974–75
Rodolfo Martinez* WBC	1974–76
Alfonso Zamora	1975–77
Carlos Zarate* WBC	1976–79
Jorge Lujan	1977–80
Lupe Pintor* WBC	1979–83
Julian Solis	1980
Jeff Chandler	1980–84
Albert Davila* WBC	1983–85
Richard Sandoval	1984–86
Satoshi Shingaki* IBF	1984–85
Jeff Fenech* IBF	1985
Daniel Zaragoza* WBC	1985
Miguel Lora* WBC	1985–88
Gaby Canizales	1986

Champion	Reign
Bernardo Pinango	1986–87
W. Vasquez* WBA	1987–88
Kevin Seabrooks* IBF	1987–88
Kaokor Galaxy* WBA	1988
Moon Sung-Kil* WBA	1988–89
Kaokor Galaxy* WBA	1989
Raul Perez* WBC	1988–91
O. Canizales* IBF	1988–95
Luisito Espinosa* WBA	1989–91
Israel Contreras* WBA	1991–92
Eddie Cook* WBA	1992–93
Greg Richardson* WBC	1991
J. Tatsuyoshi, WBC	1991–92
Victor Rabanales* WBC	1992–93
Jung-Il Byun* WBC	1993
Jorge Julio WBA	1993
Yasuei Yakushiji* WBC	1993–95
Junior Jones* WBA	1994
John M. Johnson* WBA	1994
D. Chuvatana* WBA	1994–95
V. Sahaprom* WBA	1995–96
W. McCullough* WBC	1995–96
Harold Mestre* IBF	1995
Mbulelo Botile* IBF	1995–97
Nana Yaw Konadu* WBA	1996–98
S. Singmanassak* WBC	1996–97
Tim Austin* IBF	1997–
J. Tatsuyoshi* WBC	1997–98
Johnny Tapia* WBA	1998–99
V. Sahaprom* WBC	1998–
Paulie Ayala* WBA	1999–

*Champion not generally recognized. †Champion retired or relinquished title.

Junior Bantamweights
(Weight Limit: 115 pounds)

Champion	Reign
Rafael Orono* WBC	1980–81
Chul-Ho Kim* WBC	1981–82
Gustavo Ballas* WBA	1981
Rafael Pedroza* WBA	1981–82
Jiro Watanabe* WBA	1982–84
Rafael Orono* WBC	1982–83
Payao Poontarat* WBC	1983–84
Joo-Do Chun* IBF	1983–85
Jiro Watanabe	1984–86
Kaosai Galaxy* WBA	1984
Ellyas Pical* IBF	1985–86
Cesar Polanco* IBF	1986
Gilberto Roman* WBC	1986–87
Ellyas Pical* IBF	1986

Champion	Reign
Santos Laciar* WBC	1987
Tae-Il Chang* IBF	1987
Sugar Rojas* WBC	1987–88
Ellyas Pical* IBF	1987–89
Giberto Roman* WBC	1988–89
Juan Polo Perez* IBF	1989–90
Nana Konadu* WBC	1989–90
Sung-Kil Moon* WBC	1990–93
Robert Quiroga* IBF	1990–93
Julio Borboa* IBF	1993–94
Katsuya Onizuka* WBA	1993–94
Lee Hyung-Chul* WBA	1994–95
Jose Luis Bueno* WBC	1993–94
Hiroshi Kawashima*WBC	1994–97

Champion	Reign
Harold Grey* IBF	1994–95
Alimi Goitia* WBA	1995–96
Yokthai Sith-Oar* WBA	1996–97
Carlos Salazar* IBF	1995–96
Harold Grey* IBF	1996
Danny Romero* IBF	1996–97
Gerry Penalosa* WBC	1997–98
Johnny Tapia* IBF	1997–99†
Satoshi Iida* WBA	1997–98
Cho In-Joo* WBC	1998–
Jesus Rojas* WBA	1998–99
Mark Johnson* IBF	1999–00
Hideki Todaka* WBA	1999–
Felix Machado* IBF	2000–

Flyweights
(Weight Limit: 112 pounds)

Champion	Reign
Sid Smith	1913
Bill Ladbury	1913–14
Percy Jones	1914
Joe Symonds	1914–16
Jimmy Wilde	1916–23
Pancho Villa	1923–25
Fidel LaBarba	1925–27†
Frenchy Belanger NBA	1927–28
Izzy Schwartz NY	1927–29
Frankie Genaro NBA	1928–29
Spider Pladner NBA	1929
Frankie Genaro NBA	1929–31
Midget Wolgast* NY	1930–35
Young Perez NBA	1931–32
Jackie Brown NBA	1932–35
Benny Lynch	1935–38
Small Montana* NY	1935–37
Peter Kane	1938–43
Little Dado* NY	1938–40
Jackie Paterson	1943–48
Rinty Monaghan	1948–50
Terry Allen	1950
Dado Marino	1950–52
Yoshio Shirai	1953–54
Pascual Perez	1954–60
Pone Kingpetch	1960–62
Masahiko Harada	1962–63
Pone Kingpetch	1963
Hiroyuki Ebihara	1963–64
Pone Kingpetch	1964–65
Salvatore Burrini	1965–66
H. Accavallo* WBA	1966–68
Walter McGowan	1966
Chartchai Chionoi	1966–69
Efren Torres	1969–70
Hiroyuki Ebihara* WBA	1969

Champion	Reign
B. Villacampo* WBA	1969–70
Chartchai Chionoi	1970
B. Chartvanchai* WBA	1970
Masao Ohba* WBA	1970–73
Erbito Salavarria	1970–73
B. Gonzalez* WBA	1972
V. Borkorsor* WBC	1972–73
Venice Borkorsor	1973
Chartchai Chionoi* WBA	1973–74
B. Gonzalez* WBA	1973–74
Shoji Oguma* WBC	1974–75
S. Hanagata* WBA	1974–75
Miguel Canto* WBC	1975–79
Erbito Salavarria* WBA	1975–76
Alfonso Lopez* WBA	1976
G. Espadas* WBA	1976–78
B. Gonzalez* WBA	1978–79
Chan-Hee Park* WBC	1979–80
Luis Ibarra* WBA	1979–80
Tae-Shik Kim* WBA	1980
Shoji Oguma* WBC	1980–81
Peter Mathebula* WBA	1980–81
Santos Laciar* WBA	1981
Antonio Avelar* WBC	1981–82
Luis Ibarra* WBA	1981
Juan Herrera* WBA	1981–82
P. Cardona* WBC	1982
Santos Laciar* WBA	1982–85
Freddie Castillo* WBC	1982
E. Mercedes* WBC	1982–83
Charlie Magri* WBC	1983
Frank Cedeno* WBC	1983–84
Soon-Chun Kwon* IBF	1983–85
Koji Kobayashi* WBC	1984
Gabriel Bernal* WBC	1984
Sot Chitalada* WBC	1984–88

Champion	Reign
Hilario Zapate* WBA	1985–87
Chong-Kwan	
Chung* IBF	1985–86
Bi-Won Chung* IBF	1986
Hi-Sup Shin* IBF	1986–87
Dodie Penalosa* IBF	1987
Fidel Bassa* WBA	1987–89
Choi-Chang Ho* IBF	1987–88
Rolando Bohol* IBF	1988
Yong-Kang Kim* WBC	1988–89
Duke McKenzie* IBF	1988–89
Sot Chitalada* WBC	1989–91
Dave McAuley* IBF	1989–92
Jesus Rojas* WBA	1989–90
Yul-Woo Lee* WBA	1990
L. Tamakuma* WBA	1990–91
M. Kittikasem* WBC	1991–92
Yuri Arbachakov* WBC	1992–97
Yong Kang Kim* WBA	1991–92
Rodolfo Blanco* IBF	1992–93
P. Sithbangprachan* IBF	1993–95
David Griman* WBA	1992–94
S.S. Ploenchit* WBA	1994–96
Francisco Tejedor* IBF	1995
Danny Romero* IBF	1995–96
Mark Johnson* IBF	1996–99†
Jose Bonilla* WBA	1996–98
Chatchai Sasakul* WBC	1997–98
Hugo Soto* WBA	1998–99
Manny Pacquiao* WBC	1998–99
Leo Gamez* WBA	1999
Irene Pacheco* IBF	1999–
S. Pisnurachan* WBA	1999–00
M. Sinsurat* WBC	1999–00
Malcolm Tunacao* WBC	2000–
Eric Morel* WBA	2000–

Junior Flyweights
(Weight Limit: 108 pounds)

Champion	Reign
Franco Udella* WBC	1975
Jaime Rios* WBA	1975–76
Luis Estaba* WBC	1975–78
Juan Guzman* WBA	1976
Yoko Gushiken* WBA	1976–81
Freddy Castillo* WBC	1978
Netrnoi Vorasingh* WBC	1978
Sung-Jun Kim* WBC	1978–80
Shigeo Nakajima* WBC	1980
Hilario Zapata* WBC	1980–82
Pedro Flores* WBA	1981
Hwan-Jin Kim* WBA	1981
Katsuo Tokashiki* WBA	1981–83
Amado Urzua* WBC	1982
Tadashi Tomori* WBC	1982
Hilario Zapata* WBC	1982–83
Jung-Koo Chang* WBC	1983–88

Champion	Reign
Lupe Madera* WBA	1983–84
Dodie Penalosa* IBF	1983–86
Francisco Quiroz* WBA	1984–85
Joey Olivo* WBA	1985
Myung-Woo Yuh* WBA	1985–91
Jum-Hwan Choi* IBF	1986–88
Tacy Macalos* IBF	1988–89
German Torres* WBC	1988–89
Yul-Woo Lee* WBC	1989
Muangchai Kittikasem* IBF	1989–90
Humberto Gonzalez* WBC	1989–90
Michael Carbajal* IBF	1990–94
R. Pascua* WBC	1990
M. C. Castro* WBC	1991
H. Gonzalez* WBC	1991–93

Champion	Reign
Hirokia Ioka* WBA	1991–92
Michael Carbajal, WBC	1993–94
Myung-Woo Yuh* WBA	1993
Leo Gamez* WBA	1993–95
H. Gonzalez* WBC, IBF	1994–95
Choi Hi-Yong* WBA	1995–96
S. Sor Jaturong* WBC, IBF	1995–96
Carlos Murillo* WBA	1996
Keiji Yamaguchi* WBA	1996
Michael Carbajal* IBF	1996–97
S. Sor Jaturong* WBC	1995–99
Phichitchor Siriwat* WBA	1996–00
Mauricio Pastrana* IBF	1997–98†
Will Grigsby* IBF	1998–99
Ricardo Lopez* IBF	1999–
Choi Yo-Sam* WBC	1999–
Beibis Mendoza* WBA	2000–

Strawweights
(Weight Limit: 105 pounds)

Champion	Reign
Kyung-Yun Lee* IBF	1987
Hiroki Ioka* WBC	1987–88
Leo Gamez* WBA	1988–89
S. Sithnaruepol* IBF	1988–89
N. Kiatwanchai* WBC	1988–89
Bong-Jun Kim* WBA	1989–91
Nico Thomas* IBF	1989
Eric Chavez* IBF	1989–90
Jum-Hwan Choi* WBC	1989–90
Hideyuki Ohaski* WBC	1990

Champion	Reign
F. Lookmingkwan* IBF	1990–92
Ricardo Lopez* WBC	1990–98
Hi-Yong Choi* WBA	1991–92
Manny Melchor* IBF	1992
Hideyuki Ohashi* WBA	1992–93
R.S. Voraphin* IBF	1992–96
Chana Porpaoin* WBA	1993–95
Rosendo Alvarez* WBA	1995–98
R. Sor Vorapin* IBF	1996–97
Zolani Petelo* IBF	1997–

Champion	Reign
W. Chor Charoen* WBC	1998–00
Ricardo Lopez WBA, WBC	1998–99†
Songkram Popaoin* WBA	1999
Noel Arambulet* WBA	1999–00
J. Antonio Aguirre* WBC	2000–
Joma Gamboa* WBA	2000–

*Champion not generally recognized. †Champion retired or relinquished title.

Alltime Career Leaders

Total Bouts

Name	Years Active	Bouts	Name	Years Active	Bouts
Len Wickwar	1928–47	463	Maxie Rosenbloom	1923–39	299
Jack Britton	1905–30	350	Harry Greb	1913–26	298
Johnny Dundee	1910–32	333	Young Stribling	1921–33	286
Billy Bird	1920–48	318	Battling Levinsky	1910–29	282
George Marsden	1928–46	311	Ted (Kid) Lewis	1909–29	279

Note: Based on records in *The Ring Record Book* and *Boxing Encyclopedia.*

Most Knockouts

Name	Years Active	KOs	Name	Years Active	KOs
Archie Moore	1936–63	130	Sandy Saddler	1944–56	103
Young Stribling	1921–33	126	Sam Langford	1902–26	102
Billy Bird	1920–48	125	Henry Armstrong	1931–45	100
George Odwell	1930–45	114	Jimmy Wilde	1911–23	98
Sugar Ray Robinson	1940–65	110	Len Wickwar	1928–47	93

Note: Based on records in *The Ring Record Book* and *Boxing Encyclopedia.*

Date	Winner	Wgt	Loser	Wgt	Result	Site
Sept 7, 1892	James J. Corbett*	178	John L. Sullivan	212	KO 21	New Orleans
Jan 25, 1894	James J. Corbett	184	Charley Mitchell	158	KO 3	Jacksonville, FL
Mar 17, 1897	Bob Fitzsimmons*	167	James J. Corbett	183	KO 14	Carson City, NV
June 9, 1899	James J. Jeffries*	206	Bob Fitzsimmons	167	KO 11	Coney Island, NY
Nov 3, 1899	James J. Jeffries	215	Tom Sharkey	183	Ref 25	Coney Island, NY
Apr 6, 1900	James J. Jeffries	n/a	Jack Finnegan	n/a	KO 1	Detroit
May 11, 1900	James J. Jeffries	218	James J. Corbett	188	KO 23	Coney Island, NY
Nov 15, 1901	James J. Jeffries	211	Gus Ruhlin	194	TKO 6	San Francisco
July 25, 1902	James J. Jeffries	219	Bob Fitzsimmons	172	KO 8	San Francisco
Aug 14, 1903	James J. Jeffries	220	James J. Corbett	190	KO 10	San Francisco
Aug 25, 1904	James J. Jeffries	219	Jack Munroe	186	TKO 2	San Francisco
July 3, 1905	Marvin Hart*	190	Jack Root	171	KO 12	Reno
Feb 23, 1906	Tommy Burns*	180	Marvin Hart	188	Ref 20	Los Angeles
Oct 2, 1906	Tommy Burns	n/a	Jim Flynn	n/a	KO 15	Los Angeles
Nov 28, 1906	Tommy Burns	172	Jack O'Brien	163½	Draw 20	Los Angeles
May 8, 1907	Tommy Burns	180	Jack O'Brien	167	Ref 20	Los Angeles
Jul 4, 1907	Tommy Burns	181	Bill Squires	180	KO 1	Colma, CA
Dec 2, 1907	Tommy Burns	177	Gunner Moir	204	KO 10	London
Feb 10, 1908	Tommy Burns	n/a	Jack Palmer	n/a	KO 4	London
Mar 17, 1908	Tommy Burns	n/a	Jem Roche	n/a	KO 1	Dublin
Apr 18, 1908	Tommy Burns	n/a	Jewey Smith	n/a	KO 5	Paris
June 13, 1908	Tommy Burns	184	Bill Squires	183	KO 8	Paris
Aug 24, 1908	Tommy Burns	181	Bill Squires	184	KO 13	Sydney
Sept 2, 1908	Tommy Burns	183	Bill Lang	187	KO 6	Melbourne
Dec 26, 1908	Jack Johnson*	192	Tommy Burns	168	TKO 14	Sydney
Mar 10, 1909	Jack Johnson	n/a	Victor McLaglen	n/a	ND 6	Vancouver
May 19, 1909	Jack Johnson	205	Jack O'Brien	161	ND 6	Philadelphia
June 30, 1909	Jack Johnson	207	Tony Ross	214	ND 6	Pittsburgh
Sept 9, 1909	Jack Johnson	209	Al Kaufman	191	ND 10	San Francisco
Oct 16, 1909	Jack Johnson	205½	Stanley Ketchel	170¼	KO 12	Colma, CA
July 4, 1910	Jack Johnson	208	James J. Jeffries	227	KO 15	Reno
July 4, 1912	Jack Johnson	195½	Jim Flynn	175	TKO 9	Las Vegas
Dec 19, 1913	Jack Johnson	n/a	Jim Johnson	n/a	Draw 10	Paris
June 27, 1914	Jack Johnson	221	Frank Moran	203	Ref 20	Paris
Apr 5, 1915	Jess Willard*	230	Jack Johnson	205½	KO 26	Havana
Mar 25, 1916	Jess Willard	225	Frank Moran	203	ND 10	New York City
July 4, 1919	Jack Dempsey*	187	Jess Willard	245	TKO 4	Toledo, OH
Sept 6, 1920	Jack Dempsey	185	Billy Miske	187	KO 3	Benton Harbor, MI
Dec 14, 1920	Jack Dempsey	188¼	Bill Brennan	197	KO 12	New York City
July 2, 1921	Jack Dempsey	188	Georges Carpentier	172	KO 4	Jersey City
July 4, 1923	Jack Dempsey	188	Tommy Givvons	175½	Ref 15	Shelby, MT
Sept 14, 1923	Jack Dempsey	192½	Luis Firpo	216½	KO 2	New York City
Sept 23, 1926	Gene Tunney*	189½	Jack Dempsey	190	UD 10	Philadelphia
Sept 22, 1927	Gene Tunney	189½	Jack Dempsey	192½	UD 10	Chicago
July 26, 1928	Gene Tunney	192	Tom Heeney	203½	TKO 11	New York City
June 12, 1930	Max Schmeling*	188	Jack Sharkey	197	DQ 4	New York City
July 3, 1931	Max Schmeling	189	Young Stribling	186½	TKO 15	Cleveland
June 21, 1932	Jack Sharkey*	205	Max Schmeling	188	Split 15	Long Island City
June 29, 1933	Primo Carnera*	260½	Jack Sharkey	201	KO 6	Long Island City
Oct 22, 1933	Primo Carnera	259½	Paulino Uzcudun	229¼	UD 15	Rome
Mar 1, 1934	Primo Carnera	270	Tommy Loughran	184	UD 15	Miami
June 14, 1934	Max Baer*	209½	Primo Carnera	263¼	TKO 11	Long Island City
June 13, 1935	James J. Braddock*	193¾	Max Baer	209½	UD 15	Long Island City
June 22, 1937	Joe Louis	197¼	James J. Braddock	197	KO 8	Chicago
Aug 30, 1937	Joe Louis	197	Tommy Farr	204¼	UD 15	New York City
Feb 23, 1938	Joe Louis	200	Nathan Mann	193½	KO 3	New York City
Apr 1, 1938	Joe Louis	202½	Harry Thomas	196	KO 5	Chicago
June 22, 1938	Joe Louis	198¼	Max Schmeling	193	KO 1	New York City
Jan 25, 1939	Joe Louis	200¼	John Henry Lewis	180¾	KO 1	New York City
Apr 17, 1939	Joe Louis	201¼	Jack Roper	204¾	KO 1	Los Angeles
June 28, 1939	Joe Louis	200¾	Tony Galento	233¾	TKO 4	New York City
Sept 20, 1939	Joe Louis	200	Bob Pastor	183	KO 11	Detroit
Feb 9, 1940	Joe Louis	203	Arturo Godoy	202	Split 15	New York City
Mar 29, 1940	Joe Louis	201½	Johnny Paychek	187½	KO 2	New York City
June 20, 1940	Joe Louis	199	Arturo Godoy	201¼	TKO 8	New York City
Dec 16, 1940	Joe Louis	202¼	Al McCoy	180¾	TKO 6	Boston
Jan 31, 1941	Joe Louis	202½	Red Burman	188	KO 5	New York City

World Heavyweight Championship Fights *(Cont.)*

Date	Winner	Wgt	Loser	Wgt	Result	Site
Feb 17, 1941	Joe Louis	203½	Gus Dorazio	193½	KO 2	Philadelphia
Mar 21, 1941	Joe Louis	202	Abe Simon	254½	TKO 13	Detroit
Apr 8, 1941	Joe Louis	203½	Tony Musto	199½	TKO 9	St Louis
May 23, 1941	Joe Louis	201½	Buddy Baer	237½	DQ 7	Washington, DC
June 18, 1941	Joe Louis	199½	Billy Conn	174	KO 13	New York City
Sept 29, 1941	Joe Louis	202¼	Lou Nova	202½	TKO 6	New York City
Jan 9, 1942	Joe Louis	206¾	Buddy Baer	250	KO 1	New York City
Mar 27, 1942	Joe Louis	207½	Abe Simon	255½	KO 6	New York City
June 9, 1946	Joe Louis	207	Billy Conn	187	KO 8	New York City
Sept 18, 1946	Joe Louis	211	Tami Mauriello	198½	KO 1	New York City
Dec 5, 1947	Joe Louis	211½	Jersey Joe Walcott	194½	Split 15	New York City
June 25, 1948	Joe Louis	213½	Jersey Joe Walcott	194¾	KO 11	New York City
June 22, 1949	Ezzard Charles*	181¾	Jersey Joe Walcott	195½	UD 15	Chicago
Aug 10, 1949	Ezzard Charles	180	Gus Lesnevich	182	TKO 8	New York City
Oct 14, 1949	Ezzard Charles	182	Pat Valentino	188½	KO 8	San Francisco
Aug 15, 1950	Ezzard Charles	183¼	Freddie Beshore	184½	TKO 14	Buffalo
Sept 27, 1950	Ezzard Charles	184½	Joe Louis	218	UD 15	New York City
Dec 5, 1950	Ezzard Charles	185	Nick Barone	178½	KO 11	Cincinnati
Jan 12, 1951	Ezzard Charles	185	Lee Oma	193	TKO 10	New York City
Mar 7, 1951	Ezzard Charles	186	Jersey Joe Walcott	193	UD 15	Detroit
May 30, 1951	Ezzard Charles	182	Joey Maxim	181½	UD 15	Chicago
July 18, 1951	Jersey Joe Walcott*	194	Ezzard Charles	182	KO 7	Pittsburgh
June 5, 1952	Jersey Joe Walcott	196	Ezzard Charles	191½	UD 15	Philadelphia
Sept 23, 1952	Rocky Marciano*	184	Jersey Joe Walcott	196	KO 13	Philadelphia
May 15, 1953	Rocky Marciano	184½	Jersey Joe Walcott	197¾	KO 1	Chicago
Sept 24, 1953	Rocky Marciano	185	Roland LaStarza	184¾	TKO 11	New York City
June 17, 1954	Rocky Marciano	187½	Ezzard Charles	185½	UD 15	New York City
Sept 17, 1954	Rocky Marciano	187	Ezzard Charles	192½	KO 8	New York City
May 16, 1955	Rocky Marciano	189	Don Cockell	205	TKO 9	San Francisco
Sept 21, 1955	Rocky Marciano	188¼	Archie Moore	188	KO 9	New York City
Nov 30, 1956	Floyd Patterson*	182¼	Archie Moore	187¾	KO 5	Chicago
July 29, 1957	Floyd Patterson	184	Tommy Jackson	192½	TKO 10	New York City
Aug 22, 1957	Floyd Patterson	187¼	Pete Rademacher	202	KO 6	Seattle
Aug 18, 1958	Floyd Patterson	184½	Roy Harris	194	TKO 13	Los Angeles
May 1, 1959	Floyd Patterson	182½	Brian London	206	KO 11	Indianapolis
June 26, 1959	Ingemar Johansson*	196	Floyd Patterson	182	TKO 3	New York City
June 20, 1960	Floyd Patterson*	190	Ingemar Johansson	194¾	KO 5	New York City
Mar 13, 1961	Floyd Patterson	194¾	Ingemar Johansson	206½	KO 6	Miami Beach
Dec 4, 1961	Floyd Patterson	188½	Tom McNeeley	197	KO 4	Toronto
Sept 25, 1962	Sonny Liston*	214	Floyd Patterson	189	KO 1	Chicago
July 22, 1963	Sonny Liston	215	Floyd Patterson	194½	KO 1	Las Vegas
Feb 25, 1964	Cassius Clay	210½	Sonny Liston	218	TKO 7	Miami Beach
Mar 5, 1965	Ernie Terrell WBA*	199	Eddie Machen	192	UD 15	Chicago
May 25, 1965	Muhammad Ali	206	Sonny Liston	215¼	KO 1	Lewiston, ME
Nov 1, 1965	Ernie Terrell WBA*	206	George Chuvalo	209	UD 15	Toronto
Nov 22, 1965	Muhammad Ali	210	Floyd Patterson	196¾	TKO 12	Las Vegas
Mar 29, 1966	Muhammad Ali	214½	George Chuvalo	216	UD 15	Toronto
May 21, 1966	Muhammad Ali	201½	Henry Cooper	188	TKO 6	London
June 28, 1966	Ernie Terrell WBA*	209½	Doug Jones	187½	UD 15	Houston
Aug 6, 1966	Muhammad Ali	209½	Brian London	201½	KO 3	London
Sept 10, 1966	Muhammad Ali	203½	Karl Mildenberger	194¼	TKO 12	Frankfurt
Nov 14, 1966	Muhammad Ali	212¾	Cleveland Williams	210½	TKO 3	Houston
Feb 6, 1967	Muhammad Ali	212¼	Ernie Terrell WBA	212½	UD 15	Houston
Mar 22, 1967	Muhammad Ali	211½	Zora Folley	202½	KO 7	New York City
Mar 4, 1968	Joe Frazier*	204½	Buster Mathis	243½	TKO 11	New York City
Apr 27, 1968	Jimmy Ellis*	197	Jerry Quarry	195	Maj 15	Oakland
June 24, 1968	Joe Frazier NY*	203½	Manuel Ramos	208	TKO 2	New York City
Aug 14, 1968	Jimmy Ellis WBA*	198	Floyd Patterson	188	Ref 15	Stockholm
Dec 10, 1968	Joe Frazier NY*	203	Oscar Bonavena	207	UD 15	Philadelphia
Apr 22, 1969	Joe Frazier NY*	204½	Dave Zyglewicz	190½	KO 1	Houston
June 23, 1969	Joe Frazier NY*	203½	Jerry Quarry	198½	TKO 8	New York City
Feb 16, 1970	Joe Frazier NY*	205	Jimmy Ellis WBA	201	TKO 5	New York City
Nov 18, 1970	Joe Frazier*	209	Bob Foster	188	KO 2	Detroit
Mar 8, 1971	Joe Frazier*	205½	Muhammad Ali	215	UD 15	New York City
Jan 15, 1972	Joe Frazier	215½	Terry Daniels	195	TKO 4	New Orleans
May 26, 1972	Joe Frazier	217½	Ron Stander	218	TKO 5	Omaha
Jan 22, 1973	George Foreman*	217½	Joe Frazier	214	TKO 2	Kingston, Jam.

World Heavyweight Championship Fights *(Cont.)*

Date	Winner	Wgt	Loser	Wgt	Result	Site
Sept 1, 1973	George Foreman	219½	Jose Roman	196½	KO 1	Tokyo
Mar 26, 1974	George Foreman	224¼	Ken Norton	212¼	TKO 2	Caracas
Oct 30, 1974	Muhammad Ali*	216½	George Foreman	220	KO 8	Kinshasa, Zaire
Mar 24, 1975	Muhammad Ali	223½	Chuck Wepner	225	TKO 15	Cleveland
May 16, 1975	Muhammad Ali	224½	Ron Lyle	219	TKO 11	Las Vegas
July 1, 1975	Muhammad Ali	224½	Joe Bugner	230	UD 15	Kuala Lumpur, Malay.
Oct 1, 1975	Muhammad Ali	224½	Joe Frazier	215	TKO 15	Manila
Feb 20, 1976	Muhammad Ali	226	Jean Pierre Coopman	206	KO 5	San Juan
Apr 30, 1976	Muhammad Ali	230	Jimmy Young	209	UD 15	Landover, MD
May 24, 1976	Muhammad Ali	230	Richard Dunn	206½	TKO 5	Munich
Sept 28, 1976	Muhammad Ali	221	Ken Norton	217½	UD 15	New York City
May 16, 1977	Muhammad Ali	221¼	Alfredo Evangelista	209¼	UD 15	Landover, MD
Sept 29, 1977	Muhammad Ali	225	Earnie Shavers	211¼	UD 15	New York City
Feb 15, 1978	Leon Spinks*	197¼	Muhammad Ali	224¼	Split 15	Las Vegas
June 9, 1978	Larry Holmes*	209	Ken Norton WBC	220	Split 15	Las Vegas
Sept 15, 1978	Muhammad Ali*	221	Leon Spinks	201	UD 15	New Orleans
Nov 10, 1978	Larry Holmes WBC*	214	Alfredo Evangelista	208¼	KO 7	Las Vegas
Mar 23, 1979	Larry Holmes WBC*	214	Osvaldo Ocasio	207	TKO 7	Las Vegas
June 22, 1979	Larry Holmes WBC*	215	Mike Weaver	202	TKO 12	New York City
Sept 28, 1979	Larry Holmes WBC*	210	Earnie Shavers	211	TKO 11	Las Vegas
Oct 20, 1979	John Tate*	240	Gerrie Coetzee	222	UD 15	Pretoria
Feb 3, 1980	Larry Holmes WBC*	213½	Lorenzo Zanon	215	TKO 6	Las Vegas
Mar 31, 1980	Mike Weaver*	232	John Tate WBA	232	KO 15	Knoxville
Mar 31, 1980	Larry Holmes WBC*	211	Leroy Jones	254½	TKO 8	Las Vegas
July 7, 1980	Larry Holmes WBC*	214¼	Scott LeDoux	226	TKO 7	Minneapolis
Oct 2, 1980	Larry Holmes WBC*	211¼	Muhammad Ali	217½	TKO 11	Las Vegas
Oct 25, 1980	Mike Weaver WBA*	210	Gerrie Coetzee	226½	KO 13	Sun City, S.A.
Apr 11, 1981	Larry Holmes	215	Trevor Berbick	215½	UD 15	Las Vegas
June 12, 1981	Larry Holmes	212¼	Leon Spinks	200¼	TKO 3	Detroit
Oct 3, 1981	Mike Weaver WBA*	215	James Quick Tillis	209	UD 15	Rosemont, IL
Nov 6, 1981	Larry Holmes	213¼	Renaldo Snipes	215¾	TKO 11	Pittsburgh
June 11, 1982	Larry Holmes	212½	Gerry Cooney	225½	TKO 13	Las Vegas
Nov 26, 1982	Larry Holmes	217½	Tex Cobb	234¼	UD 15	Houston
Dec 10, 1982	Michael Dokes*	216	Mike Weaver WBA	209¾	TKO 1	Las Vegas
Mar 27, 1983	Larry Holmes	221	Lucien Rodriguez	209	UD 12	Scranton, PA
May 20, 1983	Michael Dokes WBA*	223	Mike Weaver	218½	Draw 15	Las Vegas
May 20, 1983	Larry Holmes	213	Tim Witherspoon	219½	Split 12	Las Vegas
Sept 10, 1983	Larry Holmes	223	Scott Frank	211¼	TKO 5	Atlantic City
Sept 23, 1983	Gerrie Coetzee*	215	Michael Dokes WBA	217	KO 10	Richfield, OH
Nov 25, 1983	Larry Holmes	219	Marvis Frazier	200	TKO 1	Las Vegas
Mar 9, 1984	Tim Witherspoon	220¼	Greg Page	239½	Maj 12	Las Vegas
Aug 31, 1984	Pinklon Thomas*	216	Tim Witherspoon WBC	217	Maj 12	Las Vegas
Nov 9, 1984	Larry Holmes IBF	221½	James Smith	227	TKO 12	Las Vegas
Dec 1, 1984	Greg Page*	236½	Gerrie Coetzee WBA	218	KO 8	Sun City, S.A.
Mar 15, 1985	Larry Holmes	223½	David Bey	233¼	TKO 10	Las Vegas
Apr 29, 1985	Tony Tubbs*	229	Greg Page WBA	239½	UD 15	Buffalo
May 20, 1985	Larry Holmes	224¼	Carl Williams	215	UD 15	Las Vegas
June 15, 1985	Pinklon Thomas*	220¼	Mike Weaver	221¼	KO 8	Las Vegas
Sept 21, 1985	Michael Spinks*	200	Larry Holmes IBF	221½	UD 15	Las Vegas
Jan 17, 1986	Tim Witherspoon	227	Tony Tubbs WBA	229	Maj 15	Atlanta
Mar 22, 1986	Trevor Berbick*	218½	Pinklon Thomas WBC	222¾	UD 15	Las Vegas
Apr 19, 1986	Michael Spinks	205	Larry Holmes	223	Split 15	Las Vegas
July 19, 1986	Tim Witherspoon*	234¾	Frank Bruno	228	TKO 11	Wembley, Eng.
Sept 6, 1986	Michael Spinks	201	Steffen Tangstad	214¾	TKO 4	Las Vegas
Nov 22, 1986	Mike Tyson*	221¼	Trevor Berbick WBC	218½	TKO 2	Las Vegas
Dec 12, 1986	James Smith*	228½	Tim Witherspoon WBA	233½	TKO 1	New York City
Mar 7, 1987	Mike Tyson WBC*	219	James Smith WBA	233	UD 12	Las Vegas
May 30, 1987	Mike Tyson*	218¾	Pinklon Thomas	217¾	TKO 6	Las Vegas
May 30, 1987	Tony Tucker	222¼	Buster Douglas	227¼	TKO 10	Las Vegas
June 15, 1987	Michael Spinks	208¾	Gerry Cooney	238	TKO 5	Atlantic City
Aug 1, 1987	Mike Tyson*	221	Tony Tucker IBF	221	UD 12	Las Vegas
Oct 16, 1987	Mike Tyson*	216	Tyrell Biggs	228¾	TKO 7	Atlantic City
Jan 22, 1988	Mike Tyson*	215¾	Larry Holmes	225¾	TKO 4	Atlantic City
Mar 20, 1988	Mike Tyson*	216¼	Tony Tubbs	238¼	KO 2	Tokyo
June 27, 1988	Mike Tyson*	218¼	Michael Spinks	212¼	KO 1	Atlantic City
Feb 25, 1989	Mike Tyson	218	Frank Bruno	228	TKO 5	Las Vegas
July 21, 1989	Mike Tyson	219¼	Carl Williams	218	TKO 1	Atlantic City

Date	Winner	Wgt	Loser	Wgt	Result	Site
Feb 10, 1990	Buster Douglas	231½	Mike Tyson	220½	KO 10	Tokyo
Oct 25, 1990	Evander Holyfield	208	Buster Douglas	246	KO 3	Las Vegas
Apr 19, 1991	Evander Holyfield	212	George Foreman	257	UD 12	Atlantic City
Nov 23, 1991	Evander Holyfield	210	Bert Cooper	215	TKO 7	Atlanta
June 19, 1992	Evander Holyfield	210	Larry Holmes	233	UD 12	Las Vegas
Nov 13, 1992	Riddick Bowe	235	Evander Holyfield	205	UD 12	Las Vegas
Feb 6, 1993	Riddick Bowe	243	Michael Dokes	244	KO 1	New York City
May 8, 1993	Lennox Lewis*	235	Tony Tucker	235	UD 12	Las Vegas
May 22, 1993	Riddick Bowe	244	Jesse Ferguson	224	KO 2	Washington, DC
Oct 2, 1993	Lennox Lewis*	229	Frank Bruno	233	KO 7	London
Nov 6, 1993	Evander Holyfield	217	Riddick Bowe	246	Split 12	Las Vegas
Apr 22, 1994	Michael Moorer	214	Evander Holyfield	214	Split 12	Las Vegas
May 6, 1994	Lennox Lewis*	235	Phil Jackson	218	TKO 8	Atlantic City
Nov 6, 1994	George Foreman	250	Michael Moorer	222	KO 10	Las Vegas
Mar 11, 1995	Riddick Bowe*	241	Herbie Hide	214	KO 6	Las Vegas
Apr 8, 1995	Oliver McCall*	231	Larry Holmes	236	UD 12	Las Vegas
Apr 8, 1995	Bruce Seldon*	236	Tony Tucker	243	TKO 7	Las Vegas
Apr 22, 1995	George Foreman	256	Axel Schulz	221	Split 12	Las Vegas
Jun 17, 1995	Riddick Bowe*	243	Jorge Luis Gonzalez	237	KO 6	Las Vegas
Aug 19, 1995	Bruce Seldon*	234	Joe Hipp	233	TKO 10	Las Vegas
Sept 2, 1995	Frank Bruno*	247¾	Oliver McCall	234¾	UD 12	London
Dec 9, 1995	Frans Botha*	237	Axel Shulz	223	Split 12	Stuttgart
Mar 16, 1996	Mike Tyson*	220	Frank Bruno	247	TKO 3	Las Vegas
June 22, 1996	Michael Moorer*	222¼	Axel Shulz	222¾	Split 12	Dortmund, Ger.
Sept 7, 1996	Mike Tyson	219	Bruce Seldon	229	TKO 1	Las Vegas
Nov 9, 1996	Evander Holyfied	215	Mike Tyson	222	TKO 11	Las Vegas
Feb 7, 1997	Lennox Lewis*	251	Oliver McCall	237	TKO 5	Las Vegas
June 28, 1997	Evander Holyfied	218	Mike Tyson	218	DQ 4	Las Vegas
Oct 4, 1997	Lennox Lewis*	244	Andrew Golota	244	TKO 1	Atlantic City
Nov 8, 1997	Evander Holyfied	214	Michael Moorer	223	TKO 8	Las Vegas
Mar 28, 1998	Lennox Lewis*	243	Shannon Briggs	228	TKO 5	Atlantic City
Mar 13, 1999	Evander Holyfield	215	Lennox Lewis	246	Draw 12	New York City
Nov 13, 1999	Lennox Lewis	242	Evander Holyfield	217	UD 12	Las Vegas
Apr 29, 2000	Lennox Lewis	247	Michael Grant	250	KO 2	New York
July 15, 2000	Lennox Lewis	250	Frans Botha	236	TKO 2	London
Aug 12, 2000	Evander Holyfield*	221	John Ruiz	224	UD 12	Las Vegas

*Champion not generally recognized. KO=knockout; TKO=technical knockout; UD=unanimous decision; Split=split decision; Ref=referee's decision; DQ=disqualification; ND=no decision.

Ring Magazine Fighter and Fight of the Year

Year	Fighter	Year	Fighter	Year	Fighter
1928	Gene Tunney	1935	Barney Ross	1940	Billy Conn
1929	Tommy Loughran	1936	Joe Louis	1941	Joe Louis
1930	Max Schmeling	1937	Henry Armstrong	1942	Ray Robinson
1932	Jack Sharkey	1938	Joe Louis	1943	Fred Apostoli
1934	T. Canzoneri/B. Ross	1939	Joe Louis	1944	Beau Jack

Note: No award in 1933; no fight of the year named until 1945

Year	Fighter	Fight	Winner	Site
1945	Willie Pep	Rocky Graziano–Freddie Cochrane	Rocky Graziano	New York City
1946	Tony Zale	Tony Zale–Rocky Graziano	Tony Zale	New York City
1947	Gus Lesnevich	Rocky Graziano–Tony Zale	Rocky Graziano	Chicago
1948	Ike Williams	Marcel Cerdan–Tony Zale	Marcel Cerdan	Jersey City
1949	Ezzard Charles	Willie Pep–Sandy Saddler	Willie Pep	New York City
1950	Ezzard Charles	Jake LaMotta–Laurent Dauthuille	Jake LaMotta	Detroit
1951	Ray Robinson	Jersey Joe Walcott–Ezzard Charles	Jersey Joe Walcott	Pittsburgh
1952	Rocky Marciano	Rocky Marciano–Jersey Joe Walcott	Rocky Marciano	Philadelphia
1953	Carl Olson	Rocky Marciano–Roland LaStarza	Rocky Marciano	New York City
1954	Rocky Marciano	Rocky Marciano–Ezzard Charles	Rocky Marciano	New York City
1955	Rocky Marciano	Carmen Basilio–Tony DeMarco	Carmen Basilio	Boston
1956	Floyd Patterson	Carmen Basilio–Johnny Saxton	Carmen Basilio	Syracuse
1957	Carmen Basilio	Carmen Basilio–Ray Robinson	Carmen Basilio	New York City
1958	Ingemar Johansson	Ray Robinson–Carmen Basilio	Ray Robinson	Chicago
1959	Ingemar Johansson	Gene Fullmer–Carmen Basilio	Gene Fullmer	San Francisco
1960	Floyd Patterson	Floyd Patterson–Ingemar Johansson	Floyd Patterson	New York City
1961	Joe Brown	Joe Brown–Dave Charnley	Joe Brown	London
1962	Dick Tiger	Joey Giardello–Henry Hank	Joey Giardello	Philadelphia
1963	Cassius Clay	Cassius Clay–Doug Jones	Cassius Clay	New York City
1964	Emile Griffith	Cassius Clay–Sonny Liston	Cassius Clay	Miami Beach
1965	Dick Tiger	Floyd Patterson–George Chuvalo	Floyd Patterson	New York City
1966	No award	Jose Torres–Eddie Cotton	Jose Torres	Las Vegas
1967	Joe Frazier	Nino Benvenuti–Emile Griffith	Nino Benvenuti	New York City
1968	Nino Benvenuti	Dick Tiger–Frank DePaula	Dick Tiger	New York City
1969	Jose Napoles	Joe Frazier–Jerry Quarry	Joe Frazier	New York City
1970	Joe Frazier	Carlos Monzon–Nino Benvenuti	Carlos Monzon	Rome
1971	Joe Frazier	Joe Frazier–Muhammad Ali	Joe Frazier	New York City
1972	Muhammad Ali Carlos Monzon	Bob Foster–Chris Finnegan	Bob Foster	London
1973	George Foreman	George Foreman–Joe Frazier	George Foreman	Kingston, Jam.
1974	Muhammad Ali	Muhammad Ali–George Foreman	Muhammad Ali	Kinshasa, Zaire
1975	Muhammad Ali	Muhammad Ali–Joe Frazier	Muhammad Ali	Manila
1976	George Foreman	George Foreman–Ron Lyle	George Foreman	Las Vegas
1977	Carlos Zarate	Joe Young–George Foreman	Joe Young	San Juan
1978	Muhammad Ali	Leon Spinks–Muhammad Ali	Leon Spinks	Las Vegas
1979	Ray Leonard	Danny Lopez–Mike Ayala	Danny Lopez	San Antonio
1980	Thomas Hearns	Saad Muhammad–Yaqui Lopez	Saad Muhammad	McAfee, NJ
1981	Ray Leonard Salvador Sanchez	Ray Leonard–Tommy Hearns	Ray Leonard	Las Vegas
1982	Larry Holmes	Bobby Chacon–Rafael Limon	Bobby Chacon	Sacramento
1983	Marvin Hagler	Bobby Chacon–Cornelius Boza-Edwards	Bobby Chacon	Las Vegas
1984	Thomas Hearns	Jose Luis Ramirez–Edwin Rosario	Jose Luis Ramirez	San Juan
1985	Donald Curry Marvin Hagler	Marvin Hagler–Tommy Hearns	Marvin Hagler	Las Vegas
1986	Mike Tyson	Stevie Cruz–Barry McGuigan	Stevie Cruz	Las Vegas
1987	Evander Holyfield	Ray Leonard–Marvin Hagler	Ray Leonard	Las Vegas
1988	Mike Tyson	Tony Lopez–Rocky Lockridge	Tony Lopez	Inglewood, CA
1989	Pernell Whitaker	Roberto Duran–Iran Barkley	Roberto Duran	Atlantic City
1990	Julio César Chávez	Julio César Chávez–Meldrick Taylor	Julio César Chávez	Las Vegas
1991	James Toney	Robert Quiroga–Kid Akeem Anifowoshe	Robert Quiroga	San Antonio
1992	Riddick Bowe	Riddick Bowe–Evander Holyfield	Riddick Bowe	Las Vegas
1993	Michael Carbajal	Michael Carbajal–Humberto Gonzalez	Michael Carbajal	Las Vegas
1994	Roy Jones	Jorge Castro–John David Jackson	Jorge Castro	Monterrey, Mex.
1995	Oscar De La Hoya	Saman Sor Jaturong–Chiquita Gonzalez	Saman Sor Jaturong	Inglewood, CA
1996	Evander Holyfield	Evander Holyfield–Mike Tyson	Evander Holyfield	Las Vegas
1997	Evander Holyfield	Arturo Gatti–Gabriel Ruelas	Arturo Gatti	Atlantic City
1998	Floyd Mayweather	Ivan Robinson–Arturo Gatti	Ivan Robinson	Atlantic City
1999	Paulie Ayala	Paulie Ayala–Johnny Tapia	Paulie Ayala	Las Vegas

LIGHT FLYWEIGHT
1984 ....Paul Gonzales

FLYWEIGHT
1904 ....George Finnegan
1920 ....Frank Di Gennara
1024 ....Fidel LaBarba
1952 ....Nathan Brooks
1976 ....Leo Randolph
1984 ....Steve McCrory

BANTAMWEIGHT
1904 ....Oliver Kirk
1988 ....Kennedy McKinney

FEATHERWEIGHT
1904 ....Oliver Kirk
1924 ....John Fields
1984 ....Meldrick Taylor

LIGHTWEIGHT
1904 ....Harry Spanger
1920 ....Samuel Mosberg
1968 ....Ronald W. Harris
1976 ....Howard Davis
1984 ....Pernell Whitaker
1992 ....Oscar De La Hoya

LIGHT WELTERWEIGHT
1952 ....Charles Adkins
1972 ....Ray Seales
1976 ....Ray Leonard
1984 ....Jerry Page

WELTERWEIGHT
1904 ....Albert Young
1932 ....Edward Flynn
1984 ....Mark Breland

LIGHT MIDDLEWEIGHT
1960 ....Wilbert McClure
1984 ....Frank Tate
1996 ....David Reid

MIDDLEWEIGHT
1904 ....Charles Mayer
1932 ....Carmen Bath
1952 ....Floyd Patterson
1960 ....Edward Crook
1976 ....Michael Spinks

LIGHT HEAVYWEIGHT
1920 ....Eddie Eagan
1952 ....Norvel Lee
1956 ....James Boyd
1960 ....Cassius Clay
1976 ....Leon Spinks
1988 ....Andrew Maynard

HEAVYWEIGHT
1984 ....Henry Tillman
1988 ....Ray Mercer

SUPER HEAVYWEIGHT
1904 ....Samuel Berger
1952 ....H. Edward Sanders
1956 ....T. Peter
               Rademacher
1964 ....Joe Frazier
1968 ....George Foreman
1984 ....Tyrell Biggs

Live From New York!

This is not your grandfather's boxing show. Unless, of course, your grandfather happens to be a hip-hopping, cigar-smoking, lingerie-model-ogling, break-dancing aficionado who likes his boxing all heavyweight and a massage at his ringside seats. If that's your grandpa, he's going to love Heavyweight Explosion, the monthly nothing-but-big-boys (and occasional big girls) fight card held at New York City's venerable Hammerstein Ballroom. The brainchild of 51-year-old rock impresario turned boxing promoter Cedric Kushner, the series made its debut in January and has been rocking a mostly packed house on the last Thursday of each month since. Call it TKO meets MTV.

"It's been eight years since anyone has staged regular live fight cards in New York," says Kushner, a rotund South African with a bushy mustache. "It seemed it was time to try something a little different. I envision this as a monthly party in an intimate setting."

Intimate it is. With two steeply tiered wooden balconies, overhanging "luxury" boxes and chandeliers, the 94-year-old Hammerstein has the air of a small European opera house gone to seed. Throw in 1,500 fans (who pay from $125 for ringside seats to $25 for a perch in the upper balcony), and it

feels more like a high-concept frat party than a fight night. Party favors include free cigars and massages in a downstairs VIP room for the high rollers—who get to hobnob with the likes of Rocky actor Burt Young, ubiquitous sports sketcher LeRoy Neiman and a Baldwin brother. There's usually a go-go dancer or two gyrating on a platform above the crowd, and a break-dance troupe takes over the ring between bouts. One evening you could stop by a table for a free copy of Gallery magazine and have it autographed by that month's "Girl Next Door." Another month the table was, er, manned by lingerie models. Oh, yeah, there's also the boxing.

The fighters are paid from $600 for an undercard match to $20,000 for a main event. While the skill level is less than championship caliber, the action is usually spirited and well received. "The ambience is terrific," said Lou DiBella, HBO's senior vice president of programming, from a ringside seat. "These events do more to build up boxing than any number of pay-per-view bouts. This is what live boxing is all about."

Just ask Grandpa—if you can tear him out of the massage chair.

—Rich O'Brien

Horse Racing

BILL FRAKES

Fast Starter

Horse racing bolted the gate in 2000, only to falter and leave its potential unfulfilled

BY MARTY BURNS

THE SPORT of kings certainly enjoyed some regal flourishes in 2000: Fusaichi Pegasus won the Kentucky Derby in spectacular fashion; Lemon Drop Kid made a run for Horse of the Year; and Laffit Pincay Jr. rode into history as the sport's alltime winningest jockey. But when it came to the big prize—the Triple Crown—horse racing once more pulled up lame. This time, it wasn't even close.

Unlike in each of the past three years, when Silver Charm ('97), Real Quiet ('98) and Charismatic ('99) went into the Belmont with a chance to make history, the drama in 2000 short-circuited during the second leg, the Preakness. Only fans of Affirmed, the last horse to win the sport's most coveted prize, in '78, could have been happy about it.

Making the letdown all the harder to swallow was that Fusaichi Pegasus had been an honest-to-goodness contender. An offspring of Mr. Prospector and the Danzig mare Angel Fever, the handsome black colt was touted as a potential superhorse since the day in July '98 when Japanese businessman Fusao Sekiguchi purchased him for $4 million at the Keeneland yearling sale. Even the colt's name (a combination of his owner's first name and the Japanese word *ichi*, which means the number one) seemed to augur something special; it definitely caught the public's fancy.

So did Pegasus's pre-Derby performances, which included a comfortable victory over a strong field at the Wood Memorial in April. As the first Saturday in May approached, Fusaichi Pegasus was easily the most-hyped Derby contender. And with 153,204 enthralled racing fans watching the 126th Run for the Roses, he lived up to the hype. At the eighth pole Pegasus snatched the lead from More Than Ready and bounded away to win by $1\frac{1}{2}$ lengths over Aptitude. His victory made him the first favorite to win the Derby since Spectacular Bid in '79, and his winning time of 2:01.12 was the sixth-fastest in the race's history. "He exploded," jockey Kent Desormeaux said. "I was awestruck. I felt like I could fly."

The triumph was sweet vindication for the flamboyant Sekiguchi—a venture capitalist who showed up at the winner's circle with four kimono-clad geishas—and Neil Drysdale, the colt's 52-year-old British-

SKIP DICKSTEIN

The '99 Belmont winner, Lemon Drop Kid, aimed for Horse of the Year in 2000.

born trainer. Drysdale had never started a horse in the Derby (in '92 he scratched A.P. Indy on the day of the race because of a bruise to the horse's hoof), and his debut could not possibly have gone better. Fusaichi Pegasus quickly became the consensus favorite to win the Triple Crown. Hoping to make history, Drysdale did everything he could to keep Pegasus on an even keel going into the Preakness two weeks later. He maintained the horse's unorthodox training regimen—light walks and jogs rather than speed workouts—and, to avoid the stress of relocation, kept him in Kentucky for 10 days after the Derby. When they finally arrived in Baltimore three days before the race, Drysdale stabled his charge in a cinder block shed far from the traditional Preakness barn and the curious media horde.

Alas, Drysdale couldn't control the weather. On a soupy, muddy track soaked by two days of cold rains, a golden chestnut named Red Bullet—who had skipped the Kentucky Derby—took an early lead and held off Pegasus down the stretch to win by nearly four lengths. To the chagrin of many in the crowd of 98,304, the arrival of a 12th Triple Crown champion had been delayed at least another year. "We started slippin' and slidin'," a disappointed Desormeaux said. "It was [too] greasy out there."

Team Pegasus would experience further disappointment several weeks later when the colt suffered a minor hoof injury that kept him out of the Belmont. With Red Bullet also sitting out the race—to save energy for a fall push to the Breeders' Cup—the field for the third leg of the series was surprisingly thin, and it showed. In the second slowest Belmont in 30 years, Commendable, a 19–1 long shot who had finished out of the money in his previous six starts, held off Aptitude for an uninspiring victory.

With his shot at the Triple Crown gone, the next goal for Fusaichi Pegasus was to win Horse of the Year. To earn that honor, however, he would have to contend with Lemon Drop Kid, the '99 Belmont winner, who was enjoying a dazzling season as a 4-year-old. With three straight victories (the Suburban Handicap, the Brooklyn Handicap and the Whitney Handicap) heading into the Sept. 16 Woodward, the Kid was threatening to dominate racing and fill the void left by Cigar and Skip Away. Considering his lackluster races early in his career, Lemon Drop Kid's ascendancy was astounding. After winning the Belmont and, later in the season, the Travers, he hit his stride in 2000 when trainer Scotty Schulhofer put blinkers on him to improve his focus. The colt's three subsequent triumphs, especially the Whitney, in which he left such contenders as Behrens, Cat Thief, Running Stag and Golden Missile in the dust, set the racing world buzzing. "He's the best horse I've ever trained," said Schulhofer, who has trained four champions in his Hall of Fame career.

Also in the Horse of the Year running was international thoroughbred Dubai Millennium. Owned by Sheikh Mohammed bin Rashid al Maktoum, the Crown Prince of

MAX NASHAP

Pincay from jockeys all over the country. Making the occasion all the sweeter for Pincay was that the victory came aboard a horse trained by Richard Mandella, a longtime friend who had stuck by Pincay through his trying battles with weight over the years.

Indeed, few riders have waged the battle of the bulge that Pincay has. The son of a jockey, who got his start working as an unpaid hotwalker and groom at age 15, Pincay flashed instant potential two years later, winning his first race on just his second career mount. But he would struggle mightily to maintain his weight over the next 35 years. He considered quitting several times, but his love for racing kept him in the sport. "I just love racing horses," said Pincay. He still sticks to a strict 850-calorie-per-day diet at age 52. "That's all I want to do for as long as I can."

As Pincay approached 9,000 wins, another figure in the sport longed for just one trip to the winner's circle. Zippy Chippy, a 9-year-old gelding with an 0–87 record, made headlines of the wrong kind in August when he lost a 40-yard race against a human before a minor league baseball game in Rochester, N.Y. Known for having trouble getting out of the gate, Zippy stood motionless for several seconds as the man (a minor league baseball player) got off to a big lead. By the time Zippy's motor kicked in, it was too late once again.

The 2000 Triple Crown series was just the opposite: a great start followed by a precipitous letdown. But while his efforts to make history got stuck in the mud, Fusaichi Pegasus didn't come away empty-handed. In June an Irish-based thoroughbred empire known as Coolmore Stud paid an estimated $70 million for the breeding rights to the muscular colt, the most money ever spent on an animal. For Team Pegasus, at least, 2000 was not without consolation.

Duabi, Dubai Millennium steamrollered the competition at the $6 million Dubai World Cup and won nine of 10 starts. Sadly, the sensational horse broke his right hind leg in a workout in August, leaving Fusaichi Pegasus and Lemon Drop Kid to battle it out in the Breeders' Cup Classic in November.

Next to the spirited competition for Horse of the Year, the best story of the season was jockey Pincay's entry into the record books. On Dec. 10, 1999, Pincay surpassed Bill Shoemaker as the world's winningest rider. He rode Irish Nip to victory in the sixth race at Hollywood Park for career win No. 8,834, one more than Shoemaker. In the winner's circle afterward, Pincay's fellow jockeys hoisted him onto their shoulders and carried him around, spraying him with champagne. Then they presented him with a new white Porsche, compliments of California racetracks. Shoemaker, who has been confined to a wheelchair since a '91 car accident, was on hand to witness Pincay break his 29-year-old record.

There was also a moving video tribute to

The Triple Crown

126th Kentucky Derby

May 6, 2000. Grade I, 3-year-olds; 8th race, Churchill Downs, Louisville. All 126 lbs. Distance: 1¼ miles. Stakes value: $1,338,500; Winner: $1,038,500; Second: $170,000; Third: $85,000; Fourth: $45,000. Track: Fast. Off: 5:29 p.m. Winner: Fusaichi Pegasus (B. c, Mr Prospector by Raise a Native—Angel Fever by Danzig); Times: 0:22.47, 0:45.99, 1:09.99, 1:35.74, 2:01.12. Won: Driving. Breeder: Arthur B. Hancock III and Stonerside Ltd.

Horse	Finish-PP	Margin	Jockey/Owner
Fusaichi Pegasus	1–15	1½	Kent Desormeaux/Fusao Sekiguchi
Aptitude	2–2	4	Alex Solis/Juddmonte Farms
Impeachment	3–14	½	Craig Perret/Dogwood Stable
More Than Ready	4–9	neck	John Velazquez/James Scatuorchio
Wheelaway	5–3	3	Richard Migliore/Caesar Kimmel and Philip Solondz
China Visit	6–11	head	Frankie Dettori/Godolphin Racing Inc.
Curule	7–11	4½	Marlon St. Julien/Godolphin Racing Inc.
Captain Steve	8–7	¾	Robbie Albarado/Michael Pegram
War Chant	9–8	3¾	Jerry Bailey/Marjorie and Irving Cowan
Deputy Warlock	10–6	½	Mark Guidry/Select Stable
Trippi	11–6	1	Jorge Chavez/Dogwood Stable
Exchange Rate	12–16	—	Calvin Borel/Padua Stables
Anees	13–1	2¾	Corey Nakatani/The Thoroughbred Corp.
The Deputy	14–10	¾	Chris McCarron/Team Valor and Gary Barber
High Yield	15–17	neck	Pat Day/Beverly and Robert Lewis, M. Tabor, J. Magnier
Hal's Hope	16–4	1¾	Roger Velez/Rose Family Stables
Commendable	17–12	3½	Edgar Prado/Beverly and Robert Lewis
Ronton	18–19	—	Brice Blanc/Jaltipan LLC
Graeme Hall	19–13	—	Shane Sellers/Laura and Eugene Melnyk

125th Preakness Stakes

May 20, 2000. Grade I, 3-year-olds; 10th race, Pimlico Race Course, Baltimore. All 126 lbs. Distance: 1³⁄₁₆ miles; Stakes value: $1,000,000; Winner: $650,000; Second: $200,000; Third: $100,000; Fourth: $50,000. Track: Good. Off: 5:28 p.m. Winner: Red Bullet (B. c, Unbridled by Fappiano—Cargo by Caro); Times: 0:23.30, 0:46.62, 1:11.21, 1:37.06, 1:56.04. Won: Driving. Breeder: Frank Stronach.

Horse	Finish-PP	Margin	Jockey/Owner
Red Bullet	1–4	3¾	Jerry Bailey/Stronach Stable
Fusaichi Pegasus	2–7	head	Kent Desormeaux/Fusao Sekiguchi
Impeachment	3–3	neck	Craig Perret/Dogwood Stable
Captain Steve	4–6	3¼	Robbie Albarado/Michael Pegram
Snuck In	5–2	1	Cash Asmussen/Ackerley Brothers Farm
Hugh Hefner	6–1	½	Victor Espinoza/King Edward Racing Stable
High Yield	7–5	30	Pat Day/Beverly and Robert Lewis, M. Tabor, J. Magnier
Hal's Hope	8–8	—	Roger Velez/Rose Family Stables
Valhol	9–12	1	Edgar Prado/James Jackson

132nd Belmont Stakes

June 10, 2000. Grade I, 3-year-olds; 9th race, Belmont Park, Elmont, NY. All 126 lbs. Distance: 1½ miles. Stakes purse: $1,000,000; Winner: $600,000; Second: $200,000; Third: $110,000; Fourth: $50,000; Fifth: $30,000. Track: Good. Off: 5:28 p.m. Winner: Commendable (B. c, Gone West by Mr. Prospector—Bought Twice by In Reality); Times: 0:24.12, 49.29, 1:14.39, 139.11, 2:05.13, 2:31.19. Won: Driving. Breeder: Edward J. Kelly and Michael M. Kelly.

Horse	Finish-PP	Margin	Jockey/Owner
Commendable	1–3	1½	Pat Day/Beverly and Robert Lewis
Aptitude	2–5	1	Alex Solis/Juddmonte Farms Inc.
Unshaded	3–4	6	Shane Sellers/James Tafel
Wheelaway	4–9	3¼	Richard Migliore/Caesar Kimmel and Philip Solondz
Impeachment	5–8	6¾	Craig Perret/Dogwood Stable
Appearing Now	6–1	2¼	Mike Luzzi/John Valentino
Postponed	7–2	1¼	Edgar Prado/Jeanne Vance
Hugh Hefner	8–10	1	Jorge Chavez/King Edward Racing Stable
Tahkodha Hills	9–11	neck	Eibar Coa/Centaur Farms Inc.
Globalize	10–6	—	Mike Smith/G. Todaro, H. Litt and J. Hollendorfer
Curule	11–7	—	Jerry Bailey/Godolphin Racing Inc.

Major Stakes Races

Late 1999

Date	Race	Track	Distance	Winner	Jockey/Trainer	Purse ($)
Sept 18	Woodward Stakes	Belmont Park	1⅛ miles	River Keen	Chris Antley/ Bob Baffert	500,000
Sept 19	Atto Mile Stakes	Woodbine	1 mile	Quiet Resolve	Robert Landry/ M. Froslad	1,050,000
Sept 25	Kentucky Cup Classic Handicap	Turfway Park	1⅛ miles	Da Devil	Calvin Borel/ F. Kaelin	500,000
Oct 2	Super Derby	Louisiana Downs	1¼ miles	Ecton Park	Alex Solis/ E. Walden	500,000
Oct 2	Yellow Ribbon Stakes	Santa Anita Park	1¼ miles	Spanish Fern	Chris McCarron/ R. Frankel	500,000
Oct 2	Indiana Derby	Hoosier Park	1¹⁄₁₆ miles	Forty One Carats	Jorge Chavez/ D. Fawkes	313,500
Oct 3	Flower Bowl Invitational Handicap	Belmont Park	1¼ miles	Soaring Softly	Jerry Bailey/ J. Toner	500,000
Oct 9	Queen Elizabeth II Challenge Cup	Keeneland	1⅛ miles	Perfect Sting	Pat Day/ J. Omeno	500,000
Oct 9	Turf Classic Invitational	Belmont Park	1½ miles	Val's Prince	Jorge Chavez/ J. Bond	600,000
Oct 9	Hawthorne Gold Cup	Hawthorne	1¼ miles	Supreme Sound	Randall Meier/ M. Dickinson	300,000
Oct 10	The Jockey Club Gold Cup	Belmont Park	1¼ miles	River Keen	Chris Antley/ Bob Baffert	1,000,000
Oct 10	Frizette Stakes	Belmont Park	1¹⁄₁₆ miles	Surfside	Pat Day/ D. Wayne Lukas	400,000
Oct 10	Beldame Stakes	Belmont Park	1⅛ miles	Beautiful Pleasure	Jorge Chavez/ J. Ward	500,000
Oct 10	Lane's End Breeders Futurity	Keeneland	1¹⁄₁₆ miles	Captain Steve	Garrett Gomez/ Bob Baffert	442,000
Oct 15	Meadowlands Cup Handicap	Meadowlands	1⅛ miles	Pleasant Breeze	Jorge Chavez/ J. Bond	500,000
Oct 16	Spinster Stakes	Keeneland	1⅛ miles	Keeper Hill	Kent Desormeaux/ R. Frankel	555,500
Oct 16	Goodwood Breeders Cup Handicap	Santa Anita	1⅛ miles	Budroyale	Garrett Gomez/ T. West	498,000
Oct 17	Alcibiades Stakes	Keeneland	1¹⁄₁₆ miles	Scratch Pad	Willie Martinez/ J. Waursch	442,400
Oct 17	Canadian International Stakes	Woodbine	1½ miles	Thornfield	R. Dos Ramos/ P. England	1,500,000
Oct 17	E.P. Taylor Stakes	Woodbine	1¼ miles	Insight	Mike Smith/ J. Hammond	500,000
Oct 29	Pegasus Handicap	Meadowlands	1⅛ miles	Forty One Carats	Jorge Chavez/ D. Fawkes	400,000
Nov 6	Breeders' Cup Classic	Gulfstream Park	1¼ miles	Cat Thief	Pat Day/ D. Wayne Lukas	4,000,000
Nov 6	Breeders' Cup Turf	Gulfstream Park	1½ miles	Daylami	Frankie Dettori/ S. bin Suroor	1,832,000
Nov 6	Breeders' Cup Sprint	Gulfstream Park	6 furlongs	Artax	Jorge Chavez/ L. Albertrani	1,000,000
Nov 6	Breeders' Cup Mile	Gulfstream Park	1 mile	Silic	Corey Nakatani/ J. Canani	1,000,000
Nov 6	Breeders' Cup Juvenile Fillies	Gulfstream Park	1¹⁄₁₆ miles	Cash Run	Jerry Bailey/ D. Wayne Lukas	1,000,000
Nov 6	Breeders' Cup Distaff	Gulfstream Park	1⅛ miles	Beautiful Pleasure	Jorge Chavez/ J. Ward	2,000,000
Nov 6	Breeders' Cup Juvenile	Gulfstream Park	1¹⁄₁₆ miles	Anees	Gary Stevens/ A. Hassinger	1,000,000
Nov 26	Clark Handicap	Churchill Downs	1⅛ miles	Littlebit-lively	Calvin Borel/ B. Barnett	458,800
Nov 27	Cigar Mile Handicap	Aqueduct	1 mile	Affirmed Success	Jorge Chavez/ R. Schosberg	350,000
Nov 27	Citation Handicap	Hollywood Park	1¹⁄₁₆ miles	Brave Act	Alex Solis/ R. McAnally	500,000
Nov 29	Matriarch Stakes	Hollywood Park	1⅛ miles	Happyan-unoit	Brice Blanc/ R. Frankel	500,000
Nov 29	Hollywood Derby	Hollywood Park	1⅛ miles	Super Quercus	Alex Solis/ R. Frankel	500,000

2000 (Through September 9)

Date	Race	Track	Distance	Winner	Jockey/Trainer	Purse ($)
Jan 15	San Fernando B.C. Stakes	Santa Anita	1 1/16 miles	Saint's Honor	Kent Desormeaux/ C. Dollase	317,000
Feb 26	Gulfstream Park Handicap	Gulfstream Park	1 1/4 miles	Behrens	Jorge Chavez/ J. Bond	350,000
Mar 4	Santa Anita Handicap	Santa Anita Park	1 1/4 miles	General Challenge	Corey Nakatani/ B. Baffert	1,000,000
Mar 5	Santa Margarita Handicap	Santa Anita Park	1 1/8 miles	Riboletta	Corey Nakatani/ E. Inda	300,000
Mar 6	New Orleans Handicap	Fair Grounds	1 1/8 miles	Allen's Oop	Willie Martinez/ D. Keen	500,000
Mar 11	Florida Derby	Gulfstream Park	1 1/8 miles	Hal's Hope	Roger Velez/ H. Rose	750,000
Mar 11	Fair Grounds Oaks	Fair Grounds	1 1/16 miles	Shawnee Country	Donnie Meche/ D. Wayne Lukas	350,000
Mar 12	Louisiana Derby	Fair Grounds	1 1/16 miles	Mighty	Shane Sellers/ F. Brothers	750,000
Mar 12	Santa Anita Oaks	Santa Anita Park	1 1/16 miles	Surfside	Pat Day/ D. Wayne Lukas	300,000
Mar 25	Turfway Spiral Stakes	Turfway Park	1 1/8 miles	Globalize	Frank Torres/ J. Hollendorfer	600,000
Mar 25	Dubai World Cup	Nad Al Sheba	1 1/4 miles	Dubai Millennium	Frankie Dettori/ S. bin Suroor	6,000,000
Apr 8	Santa Anita Derby	Santa Anita Park	1 1/8 miles	The Deputy	Chris McCarron/ J. Sahadi	1,000,000
Apr 8	Oaklawn Handicap	Oaklawn Park	1 1/8 miles	K One King	Calvin Borel/ A. Gothard	600,000
Apr 8	Ashland Stakes	Keeneland	1 1/16 miles	Rings A Chime	Shane Sellers/ L. Arterburn	550,000
Apr 9	Apple Blossom Handicap	Oaklawn Park	1 1/16 miles	Heritage of Gold	Shane Sellers/ T. Amoss	500,000
Apr 15	Arkansas Derby	Oaklawn Park	1 1/8 miles	Graeme Hall	Robbie Albarado/ T. Plelcher	500,000
Apr 15	Bluegrass Stakes	Keeneland	1 1/8 miles	High Yield	Pat Day/ D. Wayne Lukas	750,000
Apr 15	Wood Memorial Stakes	Aqueduct	1 1/8 miles	Fusaichi Pegasus	Kent Desormeaux/ N. Drysdale	750,000
Apr 22	San Juan Capistrano Invitational	Santa Anita	1 1/4 miles	Sunshine Street	Jerry Bailey/ N. Drysdale	400,000
May 6	Kentucky Derby	Churchill Downs	1 1/4 miles	Fusaichi Pegasus	Kent Desormeaux/ N. Drysdale	1,000,000
May 13	Illinois Derby	Sportsman's Park	1 1/8 miles	Performing Magic	Shane Sellers/ A. Hossinger	500,000
May 20	Preakness Stakes	Pimlico	1 3/16 miles	Red Bullet	Jerry Bailey/ J. Orseno	1,000,000
May 29	Metropolitan Handicap	Belmont Park	1 mile	Yankee Victor	Herbery Castillo/ C. Morales	750,000
May 29	Lone Star Park Handicap	Lone Star Park	1 1/16 miles	Luftikus	David Flores/ V. Cenn	300,000
May 29	Charles Whittingham Handicap	Hollywood Park	1 1/4 miles	White Heart	Kent Desormeaux/ N. Drysdale	300,000
June 3	Massachusetts Handicap	Suffolk Downs	1 1/8 miles	Running Stag	John Velazquez/ P. Mitchell	600,000
June 3	Fleur De Lis Handicap	Churchill Downs	1 1/8 miles	Heritage of Gold	Shane Sellers/ T. Amoss	324,600
June 10	Belmont Stakes	Belmont Park	1 1/2 miles	Commendable	Pat Day/ D. Wayne Lukas	1,000,000
June 11	Stephen Foster Handicap	Churchill Downs	1 1/8 miles	Golden Missile	Kent Desormeaux/ J. Orseno	810,000
June 18	Shoemaker Breeders' Cup Mile	Hollywood Park	1 mile	Silic	Corey Nakatani/ J. Canani	488,000
June 25	Vanity Handicap	Hollywood Park	1 1/8 miles	Riboletta	Chris McCarron/ E. Inda	300,000
June 25	Queen's Plate	Woodbine	1 1/4 miles	Scatter The Gold	T. Kabel/ M. Frostad	1,000,000
July 2	Irish Derby	The Curragh	1 1/2 miles	Sinndar	Johnny Murtagh/ J. Oxx	*959,108

2000 (Through September 9) (Cont.)

Date	Race	Track	Distance	Winner	Jockey/Trainer	Purse ($)
July 4	Suburban Handicap	Belmont Park	1¼ miles	Lemon Drop Kid	Edgar Prado/ F. Schulhofer	500,000
July 9	Hollywood Gold Cup	Hollywood Park	1¼ miles	Early Pioneer	Victor Espinoza/ V. Cenn	1,000,000
July 15	Princess Rooney Handicap	Calder	6 furlongs	Hurricane Bertie	Pat Day/ B. Flin	400,000
July 23	Swaps Stakes	Hollywood Park	1⅛ miles	Captain Steve	Corey Nakatani/ Bob Baffert	500,000
July 23	Sunset Handicap	Hollywood Park	1½ miles	Bienamado	Chris McCarron/ P. Gonzalez	250,000
July 23	Delaware Handicap	Delaware Park	1¼ miles	Lu Ravi	Pat Day/ C. Bowman	600,900
Aug 6	Whitney Handicap	Saratoga	1⅛ miles	Lemon Drop Kid	Edgar Prado/ F. Schulhofer	750,000
Aug 8	Haskell Invitational	Monmouth Park	1⅛ miles	Menifee	Pat Day/ E. Walden	1,000,000
Aug 19	Arlington Million	Arlington	1¼ miles	Chester House	Jerry Bailey/ R. Frankel	2,000,000
Aug 25	Personal Ensign Handicap	Saratoga	1¼ miles	Beautiful Pleasure	Jorge Chavez/ J. Ward	400,000
Aug 26	Travers Stakes	Saratoga	1¼ miles	Unshaded	Shane Sellers/ C. Nafzger	1,000,000
Aug 26	Pacific Classic	Del Mar	1¼ miles	Skimming	Garrett Gomez/ B. Frankel	1,000,000
Sept 4	Diana Handicap	Saratoga	1⅛ miles	Perfect Sting	Jerry Bailey/ J. Orseno	500,000
Sept 9	Man O' War	Belmont Park	1⅜ miles	Fantastic Light	Jerry Bailey/ S. bin Suroor	500,000

*Irish pounds

1999 Statistical Leaders

Horses

Horse	Starts	1st	2nd	3rd	Purses ($)	Horse	Starts	1st	2nd	3rd	Purses ($)
Almutawkel	4	1	1	1	3,290,000	Behrens	9	4	4	0	1,735,000
Cat Thief	13	2	3	5	3,020,500	Beautiful Pleasure	7	4	2	0	1,716,404
Daylami	2	1	0	0	2,190,000	Silverbulletday	11	8	1	0	1,707,640
Charismatic	10	4	2	1	2,007,404	Menifee	9	3	4	1	1,695,400
Budroyale	11	4	5	1	1,735,640	General Challenge	11	6	2	0	1,658,100

Jockeys

Jockey	Mounts	1st	2nd	3rd	Purses ($)	Win Pct	$ Pct*
Pat Day	1265	254	209	209	18,092,845	.20	.53
Jerry Bailey	984	244	167	135	17,650,705	.25	.55
Jorge Chavez	1595	319	216	209	17,013,337	.20	.47
Shane Sellers	1279	245	213	151	13,065,825	.19	.48
Alex Solis	1119	200	190	179	12,884,862	.18	.51
David Flores	1197	208	178	155	11,938,125	.17	.45
John Velazquez	1432	259	216	214	11,148,255	.18	.48
Robby Albarado	1421	249	250	186	10,793,785	.18	.48
Edgar Prado	1902	402	307	276	10,581,436	.21	.52
Corey Nakatani	829	159	133	137	10,110,510	.19	.52

*Percentage in the Money (1st, 2nd, and 3rd).

Trainers

Trainer	Starts	1st	2nd	3rd	Purses ($)	Win Pct	$ Pct*
Bob Baffert	735	169	130	95	16,934,607	.23	.54
D. Wayne Lukas	739	126	95	86	12,068,460	.17	.42
W. Elliot Walden	436	105	52	49	7,752,758	.24	.47
Robert J. Frankel	299	58	45	50	7,044,738	.19	.51
Richard Mandella	391	67	58	63	6,934,363	.17	.48
William I. Mott	521	107	77	65	6,337,634	.21	.48
Saeed bin Suroor	29	4	4	2	6,333,200	.14	.34
John Kimmel	419	92	78	50	5,411,582	.22	.53
Jerry Hollendorfer	952	224	148	133	5,326,901	.24	.53
Todd Pletcher	673	110	106	85	4,985,810	.16	.45

*Percentage in the Money (1st, 2nd, and 3rd).

Owners

Owner	Starts	1st	2nd	3rd	Purses ($)
Stronach Stable	576	124	96	67	6,221,147
John Franks	798	130	107	102	5,735,827
Golden Eagle Farm	411	87	65	57	5,629,474
Michael Pegram	205	57	26	25	5,122,905
Overbrook Farm	230	45	33	33	5,052,194
The Thoroughbred Corporation	272	56	51	32	4,598,903
Robert and Beverly Lewis	166	30	22	20	3,738,761
Robert and Bea Roberts	471	80	84	68	3,308,423
Sheik Hamdan bin Rashid al Maktoum	3	2	0	0	3,300,000
Paraneck Stable	275	32	43	36	2,968,796

HARNESS RACING

Major Stakes Races

Late 1999

Date	Race	Location	Winner	Driver/Trainer	Purse ($)
Oct 15	Three Diamonds Pace Filly Pace	Garden State Park	Art's Virtue	John D. Campbell/ James A. Campbell	394,100
Oct 29	BC Two-year-old Colt/Gelding Trot	Mohawk Raceway	Master Lavec	Daniel Daley/ Daniel Daley	662,529
Oct 29	BC Two-year-old Filly Pace	Mohawk Raceway	Eternal Camnation	Eric Ledford/ Jeffrey Miller	637,833
Oct 29	BC Two-year-old Colt/Gelding Pace	Mohawk Raceway	Tyberwood	Richard Silverman/ Gary Machiz	823,347
Oct 29	BC Two-year-old Filly Trot	Mohawk Raceway	Dream of Joy	James Meittinis/ Per Eriksson	652,092
Oct 29	BC Three-year-old Colt/Gelding Trot	Mohawk Raceway	CR Renegade	Rodney Allen/ Carl Allen	588,000
Oct 29	BC Three-year-old Filly Trot	Mohawk Raceway	Oolong	Ronald Pierce/ Per Henriksen	588,000
Oct 29	BC Three-year-old Filly Pace	Mohawk Raceway	Odies Fame	David Wall/ Harold Wellwood	764,400
Oct 29	BC Three-year-old Colt/Gelding Pace	Mohawk Raceway	Grinfromeartoear	Chris Chrisoforou/ Brett Pelling	588,000
Nov 20	Governor's Cup	Garden State Park	Tyberwood	Richard Silverman/ Gary Machiz	572,400

2000 (Through September 21)

Date	Race	Location	Winner	Driver/Trainer	Purse ($)
June 3	New Jersey Classic	Meadowlands	Riverboat King	Jim Morrill Jr Steve Elliott	500,000
June 24	North America Cup	Woodbine	Gallo Blue Chip	Daniel Dubel/ Mark Ford	1,000,000

Major Stakes Races *(Cont.)*

2000 (Through September 21) *(Cont.)*

Date	Race	Location	Winner	Driver/Trainer	Purse ($)
July 14	Beacon Course Trot	Meadowlands	Dreamaster	Dave Magee/ Dirk Simpson	380,000
July 15	Meadowlands Pace	Meadowlands	Gallo Blue Chip	Daniel Dube/ Mark Ford	1,150,000
July 29	BC Three and up Open Trot	Meadowlands	Magician	David Miller/ Earl Cruise	1,000,000
July 29	BC Three and up Mare Pace	Meadowlands	Ron's Girl	Michel Lachance/ Mike Bishop	332,500
July 29	BC Three and up Open Pace	Meadowlands	Western Ideal	Michel Lachance/ Brett Pelling	440,000
Aug 3	P. Haughton Memorial	Meadowlands	Yankee Mustang	Berndt Lindstedt/ Jan Johnson	460,400
Aug 4	Sweetheart Pace	Meadowlands	Hawaiian Jenna	George Brennan/ Duane Stoliker	433,800
Aug 4	Woodrow Wilson	Meadowlands	Whitefish Falls	Catello Manzi/ Mervin Burke	703,000
Aug 5	Hambletonian	Meadowlands	Yankee Paco	Trevor Ritchie/ Doug McIntosh	1,000,000
Aug 5	Hambletonian Oaks	Meadowlands	Marita's Victory	Berndt Lindstedt/ Jan Johnson	500,000
Sept 21	Little Brown Jug	Delaware, OH	Astreos	Chris Christoforou/ Brett Pelling	547,972

Major Races

The Hambletonian

Raced at The Meadowlands, East Rutherford, NJ, on August 5, 2000.

Horse	Driver	PP	¼	½	¾	Stretch-Margin	Finish-Margin
Yankee Paco	T.J. Ritchie	7	6°	3°	2°	1–Head	1–¾
Credit Winner	J.M. Meittinis	1	5	8°	9°	7–4¼	2–¾
Armbro Trick	R.W. Schnittker	4	7	9°	7°	5–3	3–1½
Fast Photo	C.R. Manzi	10	8°	5°	4°	4–1¾	4–1¾
Dreamaster	D.R. Magee	3	2°	4°	5	6–3¼	5–2½
Legendary Lover K	D.S. Minor	8	4°	1	1	2–Head	6–2¾
Uhadadream	D. Dube	5	1°°	2°	3°	3–1¼	7–4
Monte Hall	R.D. Pierce	9	9	7	6	8–5¼	8–5
Pine Drop	J.D. Campbell	2	3	6	8	x9x–15¼	x9x–34
Berndt Hanover	M. Lachance						

Times: 0:27.0, 0:55.2, 1:25.0, 1:53.2; Fast.

The Little Brown Jug

Raced at the Delaware County Fairgrounds, in Delaware, OH, on September 21, 2000.

Horse	Driver	PP	¼	½	¾	Stretch–Margin	Finish–Margin
Astreos	Chris Christoforou	3	1	1	1	1–H	1–1
Gallo Blue Chip	Daniel Dube	4	2	2	3	3–1Q	2–1
George Scooter	R.D. Pierce	1	3	3	2	2–H	3–1T
Profita	Michel Lachance	2	4	4	4	4–1 H	4–2 T

Time: 0:28.0, 0:58.4, 1:27.3, 1:55.3; Fast

Note: The 2000 Little Brown Jug was decided by a race-off.

1999 Statistical Leaders

1999 Leading Moneywinners by Age, Sex and Gait

Division	Horse	Starts	1st	2nd	3rd	Earnings ($)
2-Year-Old Pacing Colts	Tyberwood	13	7	4	2	871,876
2-Year-Old Pacing Fillies	Eternal Camnation	13	12	1	0	660,894
3-Year-Old Pacing Colts	Blissful Hall	23	15	3	4	1,326,819
3-Year-Old Pacing Fillies	Odies Fame	21	8	5	2	799,511
Aged Pacing Horses	Red Bow Tie	16	9	2	1	818,250
Aged Pacing Mares	Art's Secret	40	20	5	7	454,580
2-Year-Old Trotting Colts	Master Lavec	12	10	0	0	533,781
2-Year-Old Trotting Fillies	Dream of Joy	10	3	2	2	826,601
3-Year-Old Trotting Colts	Self Possessed	14	9	2	0	1,065,220
3-Year-Old Trotting Fillies	Oolong	21	7	2	5	704,580
Aged Trotting Horses	Supergrit	8	4	1	2	705,570
Aged Trotting Mares	Moni Maker*	21	14	4	2	1,494,972

* Statistics include foreign start information.

Drivers

Driver	Earnings ($)	Driver	Earnings ($)
Luc Ouelette	10,841,495	Ron Pierce	6,155,563
John Campbell	10,318,997	Randy Waples	5,110,233
Michel Lachance	9,304,941	Jack Moiseyev	4,997,614
Chris Christoforou	6,669,192	Eric Ledford	4,836,738
David Miller	6,272,912	Steve Condren	4,280,509

Derby Spotlight Saps Contender

Perhaps only Fusaichi Pegasus went into this year's Triple Crown campaign under the weight of more lofty expectations than Jenine Sahadi, the trainer of The Deputy. Sahadi went to Churchill Downs bidding to become the first woman to train a Kentucky Derby winner, and her diminutive bay colt, who had romped to victory in the Santa Anita Derby on April 8, was widely regarded as one of the most talented contenders in the race. But after The Deputy finished 14th, more than 23 lengths behind Pegasus, Sahadi had no satisfactory answer for the only question anyone was asking: What happened?

Sahadi, 37, who was beset by a constant flood of well-wishers and media types for the better part of a month at Churchill, believes that the spectacle leading up to and including the Derby might have been too much for her horse to handle. "The whole experience took a lot out of him," she said. "We were both going a little bit nuts."

For a month after the Derby, The Deputy holed up in Sahadi's stable at Santa Anita. She fed him peppermints and walked him twice a day. She also postponed any decisions about the colt's future. "I'm not convinced he's ready to get back out to the grind," said Sahadi.

—Mark Beech

FOR THE RECORD · Year by Year

THOROUGHBRED RACING

Kentucky Derby

Run at Churchill Downs, Louisville, KY, on the first Saturday in May.

Year	Winner (Margin)	Jockey	Second	Third	Time
1875	Aristides (1)	Oliver Lewis	Volcano	Verdigris	2:37¾
1876	Vagrant (2)	Bobby Swim	Creedmoor	Harry Hill	2:38¼
1877	Baden-Baden (2)	William Walker	Leonard	King William	2:38
1878	Day Star (2)	Jimmie Carter	Himyar	Leveler	2:37¼
1879	Lord Murphy (1)	Charlie Shauer	Falsetto	Strathmore	2:37
1880	Fonso (1)	George Lewis	Kimball	Bancroft	2:37½
1881	Hindoo (4)	Jimmy McLaughin	Lelex	Alfambra	2:40
1882	Apollo (½)	Babe Hurd	Runnymede	Bengal	2:40¼
1883	Leonatus (3)	Billy Donohue	Drake Carter	Lord Raglan	2:43
1884	Buchanan (2)	Isaac Murphy	Loftin	Audrain	2:40¼
1885	Joe Cotton (Neck)	Erskine Henderson	Bersan	Ten Booker	2:37¼
1886	Ben Ali (½)	Paul Duffy	Blue Wing	Free Knight	2:36½
1887	Montrose (2)	Isaac Lewis	Jim Gore	Jacobin	2:39¼
1888	MacBeth II (1)	George Covington	Gallifet	White	2:38¼
1889	Spokane (Nose)	Thomas Kiley	Proctor Knott	Once Again	2:34½
1890	Riley (2)	Isaac Murphy	Bill Letcher	Robespierre	2:45
1891	Kingman (1)	Isaac Murphy	Balgowan	High Tariff	2:52¼
1892	Azra (Nose)	Alonzo Clayton	Huron	Phil Dwyer	2:41½
1893	Lookout (5)	Eddie Kunze	Plutus	Boundless	2:39¼
1894	Chant (2)	Frank Goodale	Pearl Song	Sigurd	2:41
1895	Halma (3)	Soup Perkins	Basso	Laureate	2:37½
1896	Ben Brush (Nose)	Willie Simms	Ben Eder	Semper Ego	2:07¼
1897	Typhoon II (Head)	Buttons Garner	Ornament	Dr. Catlett	2:12½
1898	Plaudit (Neck)	Willie Simms	Lieber Karl	Isabey	2:09
1899	Manuel (2)	Fred Taral	Corsini	Mazo	2:12
1900	Lieut. Gibson (4)	Jimmy Boland	Florizar	Thrive	2:06¼
1901	His Eminence (2)	Jimmy Winkfield	Sannazarro	Driscoll	2:07¾
1902	Alan-a-Dale (Nose)	Jimmy Winkfield	Inventor	The Rival	2:08¾
1903	Judge Himes (¾)	Hal Booker	Early	Bourbon	2:09
1904	Elwood (½)	Frankie Prior	Ed Tierney	Brancas	2:08½
1905	Agile (3)	Jack Martin	Ram's Horn	Layson	2:10¾
1906	Sir Huon (2)	Roscoe Troxler	Lady Navarre	James Reddick	2:08⅕
1907	Pink Star (2)	Andy Minder	Zal	Ovelando	2:12⅗
1908	Stone Street (1)	Arthur Pickens	Sir Cleges	Dunvegan	2:15⅕
1909	Wintergreen (4)	Vincent Powers	Miami	Dr. Barkley	2:08⅕
1910	Donau (½)	Fred Herbert	Joe Morris	Fighting Bob	2:06⅖
1911	Meridian (¾)	George Archibald	Governor Gray	Colston	2:05
1912	Worth (Neck)	Carroll H. Schilling	Duval	Flamma	2:09⅖
1913	Donerail (½)	Roscoe Goose	Ten Point	Gowell	2:04⅘
1914	Old Rosebud (8)	John McCabe	Hodge	Bronzewing	2:03⅖
1915	Regret (2)	Joe Notter	Pebbles	Sharpshooter	2:05⅖
1916	George Smith (Neck)	Johnny Loftus	Star Hawk	Franklin	2:04
1917	Omar Khayyam (2)	Charles Borel	Ticket	Midway	2:04⅗
1918	Exterminator (1)	William Knapp	Escoba	Viva America	2:10⅘
1919	Sir Barton (5)	Johnny Loftus	Billy Kelly	Under Fire	2:09⅘
1920	Paul Jones (Head)	Ted Rice	Upset	On Watch	2:09
1921	Behave Yourself (Head)	Charles Thompson	Black Servant	Prudery	2:04⅕
1922	Morvich (½)	Albert Johnson	Bet Mosie	John Finn	2:04⅗
1923	Zev (1½)	Earl Sande	Martingale	Vigil	2:05⅖
1924	Black Gold (½)	John Mooney	Chilhowee	Beau Butler	2:05⅕
1925	Flying Ebony (1½)	Earl Sande	Captain Hal	Son of John	2:07⅗
1926	Bubbling Over (5)	Albert Johnson	Bagenbaggage	Rock Man	2:03⅗
1927	Whiskery (Head)	Linus McAtee	Osmond	Jock	2:06
1928	Reigh Count (3)	Chick Lang	Misstep	Toro	2:10⅖
1929	Clyde Van Dusen (2)	Linus McAtee	Naishapur	Panchio	2:10⅘
1930	Gallant Fox (2)	Earl Sande	Gallant Knight	Ned O.	2:07⅗
1931	Twenty Grand (4)	Charles Kurtsinger	Sweep All	Mate	2:01⅘
1932	Burgoo King (5)	Eugene James	Economic	Stepenfetchit	2:05⅕
1933	Brokers Tip (Nose)	Don Meade	Head Play	Charley O.	2:06⅘
1934	Cavalcade (2½)	Mack Garner	Discovery	Agrarian	2:04
1935	Omaha (1½)	Willie Saunders	Roman Soldier	Whiskolo	2:05
1936	Bold Venture (Head)	Ira Hanford	Brevity	Indian Broom	2:03⅗

Kentucky Derby *(Cont.)*

Year	Winner (Margin)	Jockey	Second	Third	Time
1937	War Admiral (1¾)	Charles Kurtsinger	Pompoon	Reaping Reward	2:03⅕
1938	Lawrin (1)	Eddie Arcaro	Dauber	Can't Wait	2:04⅘
1939	Johnstown (8)	James Stout	Challedon	Heather Broom	2:03⅗
1940	Gallahadion (1½)	Carroll Bierman	Bimelech	Dit	2:05
1941	Whirlaway (8)	Eddie Arcaro	Staretor	Market Wise	2:01⅖
1942	Shut Out (2½)	Wayne Wright	Alsab	Valdina Orphan	2:04⅖
1943	Count Fleet (3)	John Longden	Blue Swords	Slide Rule	2:04
1944	Pensive (4½)	Conn McCreary	Broadcloth	Stir Up	2:04⅕
1945	Hoop Jr. (6)	Eddie Arcaro	Pot o' Luck	Darby Dieppe	2:07
1946	Assault (8)	Warren Mehrtens	Spy Song	Hampden	2:06⅗
1947	Jet Pilot (Head)	Eric Guerin	Phalanx	Faultless	2:06⅘
1948	Citation (3½)	Eddie Arcaro	Coaltown	My Request	2:05⅖
1949	Ponder (3)	Steve Brooks	Capot	Palestinian	2:04⅕
1950	Middleground (1¼)	William Boland	Hill Prince	Mr. Trouble	2:01⅗
1951	Count Turf (4)	Conn McCreary	Royal Mustang	Ruhe	2:02⅗
1952	Hill Gail (2)	Eddie Arcaro	Sub Fleet	Blue Man	2:01⅗
1953	Dark Star (Head)	Hank Moreno	Native Dancer	Invigorator	2:02
1954	Determine (1½)	Ray York	Hasty Road	Hasseyampa	2:03
1955	Swaps (1½)	Bill Shoemaker	Nashua	Summer Tan	2:01⅘
1956	Needles (¾)	Dave Erb	Fabius	Come On Red	2:03⅖
1957	Iron Liege (Nose)	Bill Hartack	Gallant Man	Round Table	2:02⅕
1958	Tim Tam (½)	Ismael Valenzuela	Lincoln Road	Noureddin	2:05
1959	Tomy Lee (Nose)	Bill Shoemaker	Sword Dancer	First Landing	2:02⅕
1960	Venetian Way (3½)	Bill Hartack	Bally Ache	Victoria Park	2:02⅖
1961	Carry Back (¾)	John Sellers	Crozier	Bass Clef	2:04
1962	Decidedly (2¼)	Bill Hartack	Roman Line	Ridan	2:00⅖
1963	Chateaugay (1¼)	Braulio Baeza	Never Bend	Candy Spots	2:01⅘
1964	Northern Dancer (Neck)	Bill Hartack	Hill Rise	The Scoundrel	2:00
1965	Lucky Debonair (Neck)	Bill Shoemaker	Dapper Dan	Tom Rolfe	2:01⅕
1966	Kauai King (½)	Don Brumfield	Advocator	Blue Skyer	2:02
1967	Proud Clarion (1)	Bobby Ussery	Barbs Delight	Damascus	2:00⅗
1968	Forward Pass (Disq.)	Ismael Valenzuela	Francie's Hat	T.V. Commercial	2:02⅕
1969	Majestic Prince (Neck)	Bill Hartack	Arts and Letters	Dike	2:01⅘
1970	Dust Commander (5)	Mike Manganello	My Dad George	High Echelon	2:03⅖
1971	Canonero II (3¾)	Gustavo Avila	Jim French	Bold Reason	2:03⅕
1972	Riva Ridge (3¼)	Ron Turcotte	No Le Hace	Hold Your Peace	2:01⅘
1973	Secretariat (2½)	Ron Turcotte	Sham	Our Native	1:59⅖
1974	Cannonade (2¼)	Angel Cordero Jr.	Hudson County	Agitate	2:04
1975	Foolish Pleasure (1¾)	Jacinto Vasquez	Avatar	Diabolo	2:02
1976	Bold Forbes (1)	Angel Cordero Jr.	Honest Pleasure	Elocutionist	2:01⅗
1977	Seattle Slew (1¾)	Jean Cruguet	Run Dusty Run	Sanhedrin	2:02⅕
1978	Affirmed (1¼)	Steve Cauthen	Alydar	Believe It	2:01⅕
1979	Spectacular Bid (2¾)	Ronald J. Franklin	General Assembly	Golden Act	2:02⅖
1980	Genuine Risk (1)	Jacinto Vasquez	Rumbo	Jaklin Klugman	2:02
1981	Pleasant Colony (¾)	Jorge Velasquez	Woodchopper	Partez	2:02
1982	Gato Del Sol (2½)	Eddie Delahoussaye	Laser Light	Reinvested	2:02⅕
1983	Sunny's Halo (2)	Eddie Delahoussaye	Desert Wine	Caveat	2:02⅕
1984	Swale (3¼)	Laffit Pincay Jr.	Coax Me Chad	At the Threshold	2:02⅖
1985	Spend A Buck (5)	Angel Cordero Jr.	Stephan's Odyssey	Chief's Crown	2:00⅕
1986	Ferdinand (2¼)	Bill Shoemaker	Bold Arrangement	Broad Brush	2:02⅘
1987	Alysheba (¾)	Chris McCarron	Bet Twice	Avies Copy	2:03⅖
1988	Winning Colors (Neck)	Gary Stevens	Forty Niner	Risen Star	2:02⅕
1989	Sunday Silence (2½)	Pat Valenzuela	Easy Goer	Awe Inspiring	2:05
1990	Unbridled (3½)	Craig Perret	Summer Squall	Pleasant Tap	2:02
1991	Strike the Gold (1¾)	Chris Antley	Best Pal	Mane Minister	2:03
1992	Lil E. Tee (1)	Pat Day	Casual Lies	Dance Floor	2:03
1993	Sea Hero (2½)	Jerry Bailey	Prairie Bayou	Wild Gale	2:02⅖
1994	Go for Gin (2½)	Chris McCarron	Strodes Creek	Blumin Affair	2:03⅗
1995	Thunder Gulch (2¼)	Gary Stevens	Tejano Run	Timber Country	2:01⅕
1996	Grindstone (Nose)	Jerry Bailey	Cavonnier	Prince of Thieves	2:01
1997	Silver Charm (Head)	Gary Stevens	Captain Bodgit	Free House	2:02⅖
1998	Real Quiet (½)	Kent Desormeaux	Victory Gallop	Indian Charlie	2:02⅒
1999	Charismatic (Neck)	Chris Antley	Menifee	Cat Thief	2:03⅕
2000	Fusaichi Pegasus (1½)	Kent Desormeaux	Aptitude	Impeachment	2:01.12

Note: Distance: 1½ miles (1875–95), 1¼ miles (1896–present).

Preakness

Run at Pimlico Race Course, Baltimore, Md., two weeks after the Kentucky Derby.

Year	Winner (Margin)	Jockey	Second	Third	Time
1873	Survivor (10)	G. Barbee	John Boulger	Artist	2:43
1874	Culpepper (¾)	W. Donohue	King Amadeus	Scratch	2:56½
1875	Tom Ochiltree (2)	L. Hughes	Viator	Bay Final	2:43½
1876	Shirley (4)	G. Barbee	Rappahannock	Algerine	2:44¾
1877	Cloverbrook (4)	C. Holloway	Bombast	Lucifer	2:45½
1878	Duke of Magenta (6)	C. Holloway	Bayard	Albert	2:41¾
1879	Harold (3)	L. Hughes	Jericho	Rochester	2:40½
1880	Grenada (¾)	L. Hughes	Oden	Emily F.	2:40½
1881	Saunterer (½)	T. Costello	Compensation	Baltic	2:40½
1882	Vanguard (Neck)	T. Costello	Heck	Col Watson	2:44½
1883*	Jacobus (4)	G. Barbee	Parnell		2:42½
1884*	Knight of Ellerslie (2)	S. Fisher	Welcher		2:39½
1885	Tecumseh (2)	Jim McLaughlin	Wickham	John C.	2:49
1886	The Bard (3)	S. Fisher	Eurus	Elkwood	2:45
1887	Dunboyne (1)	W. Donohue	Mahoney	Raymond	2:39½
1888	Refund (3)	F. Littlefield	Judge Murray	Glendale	2:49
1889*	Buddhist (8)	W. Anderson	Japhet	*	2:17½
1890*	Montague (3)	W. Martin	Philosophy	Barrister	2:36¾
1894	Assignee (3)	Fred Taral	Potentate	Ed Kearney	1:49¼
1895	Belmar (1)	Fred Taral	April Fool	Sue Kittie	1:50½
1896	Margrave (1)	H. Griffin	Hamilton II	Intermission	1:51
1897	Paul Kauvar (1½)	C. Thorpe	Elkins	On Deck	1:51¼
1898	Sly Fox (2)	C. W. Simms	The Huguenot	Nuto	1:49⅗
1899	Half Time (1)	R. Clawson	Filigrane	Lackland	1:47
1900	Hindus (Head)	H. Spencer	Sarmation	Ten Candles	1:48⅖
1901	The Parader (2)	F. Landry	Sadie S.	Dr. Barlow	1:47⅕
1902	Old England (Nose)	L. Jackson	Major Daingerfield	Namtor	1:45⅘
1903	Flocarline (½)	W. Gannon	Mackey Dwyer	Rightful	1:44⅘
1904	Bryn Mawr (1)	E. Hildebrand	Wotan	Dolly Spanker	1:44⅕
1905	Cairngorm (Head)	W. Davis	Kiamesha	Coy Maid	1:45⅘
1906	Whimsical (4)	Walter Miller	Content	Larabie	1:45
1907	Don Enrique (1)	G. Mountain	Ethon	Zambesi	1:45⅖
1908	Royal Tourist (4)	E. Dugan	Live Wire	Robert Cooper	1:46⅖
1909	Effendi (1)	Willie Doyle	Fashion Plate	Hilltop	1:39⅘
1910	Layminster (½)	R. Estep	Dalhousie	Sager	1:40⅗
1911	Watervale (1)	E. Dugan	Zeus	The Nigger	1:51
1912	Colonel Holloway (5)	C. Turner	Bwana Tumbo	Tipsand	1:56⅗
1913	Buskin (Neck)	J. Butwell	Kleburne	Barnegat	1:53⅖
1914	Holiday (¾)	A. Schuttinger	Brave Cunarder	Defendum	1:53⅘
1915	Rhine Maiden (1½)	Douglas Hoffman	Half Rock	Runes	1:58
1916	Damrosch (1½)	Linus McAtee	Greenwood	Achievement	1:54⅘
1917	Kalitan (2)	E. Haynes	Al M. Dick	Kentucky Boy	1:54⅖
1918*	War Cloud (¾)	Johnny Loftus	Sunny Slope	Lanius	1:53⅗
1918*	Jack Hare, Jr (2)	C. Peak	The Porter	Kate Bright	1:53⅖
1919	Sir Barton (4)	Johnny Loftus	Eternal	Sweep On	1:53
1920	Man o' War (1½)	Clarence Kummer	Upset	Wildair	1:51⅗
1921	Broomspun (¾)	F. Coltiletti	Polly Ann	Jeg	1:54⅕
1922	Pillory (Head)	L. Morris	Hea	June Grass	1:51⅗
1923	Vigil (1¼)	B. Marinelli	General Thatcher	Rialto	1:53⅗
1924	Nellie Morse (1½)	J. Merimee	Transmute	Mad Play	1:57⅕
1925	Coventry (4)	Clarence Kummer	Backbone	Almadel	1:59
1926	Display (Head)	J. Maiben	Blondin	Mars	1:59⅘
1927	Bostonian (½)	A. Abel	Sir Harry	Whiskery	2:01⅗
1928	Victorian (Nose)	Sonny Workman	Toro	Solace	2:00⅕
1929	Dr. Freeland (1)	Louis Schaefer	Minotaur	African	2:01⅗
1930	Gallant Fox (¾)	Earl Sande	Crack Brigade	Snowflake	2:00⅗
1931	Mate (1½)	G. Ellis	Twenty Grand	Ladder	1:59
1932	Burgoo King (Head)	E. James	Tick On	Boatswain	1:59⅘
1933	Head Play (4)	Charles Kurtsinger	Ladysman	Utopian	2:02
1934	High Quest (Nose)	R. Jones	Cavalcade	Discovery	1:58⅕
1935	Omaha (6)	Willie Saunders	Firethorn	Psychic Bid	1:58⅖
1936	Bold Venture (Nose)	George Woolf	Granville	Jean Bart	1:59
1937	War Admiral (Head)	Charles Kurtsinger	Pompoon	Flying Scot	1:58⅖
1938	Dauber (7)	M. Peters	Cravat	Menow	1:59⅘
1939	Challedon (1¼)	George Seabo	Gilded Knight	Volitant	1:59⅘
1940	Bimelech (3)	F. A. Smith	Mioland	Gallahadion	1:58⅗

Preakness (Cont.)

Year	Winner (Margin)	Jockey	Second	Third	Time
1941	Whirlaway (5½)	Eddie Arcaro	King Cole	Our Boots	1:58⅘
1942	Alsab (1)	B. James	Requested Sun Again	(dead heat for second)	1:57
1943	Count Fleet (8)	Johnny Longden	Blue Swords	Vincentive	1:57⅖
1944	Pensive (¾)	Conn McCreary	Platter	Stir Up	1:59⅕
1945	Polynesian (2½)	W. D. Wright	Hoop Jr.	Darby Dieppe	1:58⅘
1946	Assault (Neck)	Warren Mehrtens	Lord Boswell	Hampden	2:01⅖
1947	Faultless (1¼)	Doug Dodson	On Trust	Phalanx	1:59
1948	Citation (5½)	Eddie Arcaro	Vulcan's Forge	Boyard	2:02⅖
1949	Capot (Head)	Ted Atkinson	Palestinian	Noble Impulse	1:56
1950	Hill Prince (5)	Eddie Arcaro	Middleground	Dooley	1:59⅕
1951	Bold (7)	Eddie Arcaro	Counterpoint	Alerted	1:56⅖
1952	Blue Man (3½)	Conn McCreary	Jampol	One Count	1:57⅖
1953	Native Dancer (Neck)	Eric Guerin	Jamie K.	Royal Bay Gem	1:57⅘
1954	Hasty Road (Neck)	Johnny Adams	Correlation	Hasseyampa	1:57⅖
1955	Nashua (1)	Eddie Arcaro	Saratoga	Traffic Judge	1:54⅗
1956	Fabius (¾)	Bill Hartack	Needles	No Regrets	1:58⅖
1957	Bold Ruler (2)	Eddie Arcaro	Iron Liege	Inside Tract	1:56⅕
1958	Tim Tam (1½)	I. Valenzuela	Lincoln Road	Gone Fishin'	1:57⅕
1959	Royal Orbit (4)	William Harmatz	Sword Dancer	Dunce	1:57
1960	Bally Ache (4)	Bobby Ussery	Victoria Park	Celtic Ash	1:57⅗
1961	Carry Back (¾)	Johnny Sellers	Globemaster	Crozier	1:57⅗
1962	Greek Money (Nose)	John Rotz	Ridan	Roman Line	1:56⅕
1963	Candy Spots (3½)	Bill Shoemaker	Chateaugay	Never Bend	1:56⅕
1964	Northern Dancer (2¼)	Bill Hartack	The Scoundrel	Hill Rise	1:56⅘
1965	Tom Rolfe (Neck)	Ron Turcotte	Dapper Dan	Hail to All	1:56⅕
1966	Kauai King (1¾)	Don Brumfield	Stupendous	Amberoid	1:55⅖
1967	Damascus (2¼)	Bill Shoemaker	In Reality	Proud Clarion	1:55⅕
1968	Forward Pass (6)	I. Valenzuela	Out of the Way	Nodouble	1:56⅘
1969	Majestic Prince (Head)	Bill Hartack	Arts and Letters	Jay Ray	1:55⅗
1970	Personality (Neck)	Eddie Belmonte	My Dad George	Silent Screen	1:56⅕
1971	Canonero II (1½)	Gustavo Avila	Eastern Fleet	Jim French	1:54
1972	Bee Bee Bee (1¼)	Eldon Nelson	No Le Hace	Key to the Mint	1:55⅗
1973	Secretariat (2½)	Ron Turcotte	Sham	Our Native	1:54⅖
1974	Little Current (7)	Miguel Rivera	Neapolitan Way	Cannonade	1:54⅗
1975	Master Derby (1)	Darrel McHargue	Foolish Pleasure	Diabolo	1:56⅖
1976	Elocutionist (3)	John Lively	Play the Red	Bold Forbes	1:55
1977	Seattle Slew (1½)	Jean Cruguet	Iron Constitution	Run Dusty Run	1:54⅖
1978	Affirmed (Neck)	Steve Cauthen	Alydar	Believe It	1:54⅖
1979	Spectacular Bid (5½)	Ron Franklin	Golden Act	Screen King	1:54⅕
1980	Codex (4¾)	Angel Cordero Jr.	Genuine Risk	Colonel Moran	1:54⅕
1981	Pleasant Colony (1)	Jorge Velasquez	Bold Ego	Paristo	1:54⅗
1982	Aloma's Ruler (½)	Jack Kaenel	Linkage	Cut Away	1:55⅖
1983	Deputed Testamony (2¾)	Donald Miller Jr.	Desert Wine	High Honors	1:55⅖
1984	Gate Dancer (1½)	Angel Cordero Jr.	Play On	Fight Over	1:53⅗
1985	Tank's Prospect (Head)	Pat Day	Chief's Crown	Eternal Prince	1:53⅖
1986	Snow Chief (4)	Alex Solis	Ferdinand	Broad Brush	1:54⅘
1987	Alysheba (½)	Chris McCarron	Bet Twice	Cryptoclearance	1:55⅘
1988	Risen Star (1¼)	E. Delahoussaye	Brian's Time	Winning Colors	1:56⅕
1989	Sunday Silence (Nose)	Pat Valenzuela	Easy Goer	Rock Point	1:53⅘
1990	Summer Squall (2¼)	Pat Day	Unbridled	Mister Frisky	1:53⅗
1991	Hansel (Head)	Jerry Bailey	Corporate Report	Mane Minister	1:54
1992	Pine Bluff (¾)	Chris McCarron	Alydeed	Casual Lies	1:55⅗
1993	Prairie Bayou (½)	Mike Smith	Cherokee Run	El Bakan	1:56⅗
1994	Tabasco Cat (¾)	Pat Day	Go For Gin	Concern	1:56⅖
1995	Timber Country (½)	Pat Day	Oliver's Twist	Thunder Gulch	1:54⅖
1996	Louis Quatorze (3¼)	Pat Day	Skip Away	Editor's Note	1:53⅖
1997	Silver Charm (Head)	Gary Stevens	Free House	Captain Bodgit	1:54⅖
1998	Real Quiet (2¼)	Kent Desormeaux	Victory Gallop	Classic Cat	1:54⅗
1999	Charismatic (1½)	Chris Antley	Menifee	Badge	1:55⅕
2000	Red Bullet (3¾)	Jerry Bailey	Fusaichi Pegasus	Impeachment	1:56.04

*Preakness was a two-horse race in 1883, '84 and '89. It was not run 1891–1893; and in 1918, it was run in two divisions.

Note: Distance: 1½ miles (1873–88), 1¼ miles (1889), 1½ miles (1890), 1 1/16 miles (1894–1900), 1 mile and 70 yards (1901–1907), 1 1/16 miles (1908), 1 mile (1909–10), 1⅛ miles (1911–24), 1 3/16 miles (1925–present).

Belmont

Run at Belmont Park, Elmont, NY, three weeks after the Preakness Stakes. Held previously at two locations in the Bronx (NY): Jerome Park (1867–1889) and Morris Park (1890–1904).

Year	Winner (Margin)	Jockey	Second	Third	Time
1867	Ruthless (Head)	J. Gilpatrick	De Courcy	Rivoli	3:05
1868	General Duke (2)	R. Swim	Northumberland	Fannie Ludlow	3:02
1869	Fenian (Unknown)	C. Miller	Glenelg	Invercauld	3:04¼
1870	Kingfisher (½)	E. Brown	Foster	Midday	2:59½
1871	Harry Bassett (3)	W. Miller	Stockwood	By-the-Sea	2:56
1872	Joe Daniels (¾)	James Rowe	Meteor	Shylock	2:58¼
1873	Springbok (4)	James Rowe	Count d'Orsay	Strachino	3:01¾
1874	Saxon (Neck)	G. Barbee	Grinstead	Aaron Pennington	2:39½
1875	Calvin (2)	R. Swim	Aristides	Milner	2:40¼
1876	Algerine (Head)	W. Donahue	Fiddlestick	Barricade	2:40½
1877	Cloverbrook (1)	C. Holloway	Loiterer	Baden-Baden	2:46
1878	Duke of Magenta (2)	L. Hughes	Bramble	Sparta	2:43½
1879	Spendthrift (5)	S. Evans	Monitor	Jericho	2:42¾
1880	Grenada (½)	L. Hughes	Ferncliffe	Turenne	2:47
1881	Saunterer (Neck)	T. Costello	Eole	Baltic	2:47
1882	Forester (5)	James McLaughlin	Babcock	Wyoming	2:43
1883	George Kinney (2)	James McLaughlin	Trombone	Renegade	2:42½
1884	Panique (½)	James McLaughlin	Knight of Ellerslie	Himalaya	2:42
1885	Tyrant (3½)	Paul Duffy	St. Augustine	Tecumseh	2:43
1886	Inspector B (1)	James McLaughlin	The Bard	Linden	2:41
1887*	Hanover (28-32)	James McLaughlin	Oneko		2:43½
1888*	Sir Dixon (12)	James McLaughlin	Prince Royal		2:40¼
1889	Eric (Head)	W. Hayward	Diable	Zephyrus	2:47
1890	Burlington (1)	S. Barnes	Devotee	Padishah	2:07¾
1891	Foxford (Neck)	E. Garrison	Montana	Laurestan	2:08¾
1892*	Patron (Unknown)	W. Hayward	Shellbark		2:17
1893	Comanche (Head)	Willie Simms	Dr. Rice	Rainbow	1:53¼
1894	Henry of Navarre (2-4)	Willie Simms	Prig	Assignee	1:56½
1895	Belmar (Head)	Fred Taral	Counter Tenor	Nanki Pooh	2:11½
1896	Hastings (Neck)	H. Griffin	Handspring	Hamilton II	2:24½
1897	Scottish Chieftain (1)	J. Scherrer	On Deck	Octagon	2:23¼
1898	Bowling Brook (8)	P. Littlefield	Previous	Hamburg	2:32
1899	Jean Bereaud (Head)	R. R. Clawson	Half Time	Glengar	2:23
1900	Ildrim (Head)	N. Turner	Petrucio	Missionary	2:21½
1901	Commando (½)	H. Spencer	The Parader	All Green	2:21
1902	Masterman (2)	John Bullmann	Ranald	King Hanover	2:22½
1903	Africander (2)	John Bullmann	Whorler	Red Knight	2:23⅕
1904	Delhi (3½)	George Odom	Graziallo	Rapid Water	2:06⅗
1905	Tanya (1/2)	E. Hildebrand	Blandy	Hot Shot	2:08
1906	Burgomaster (4)	L. Lyne	The Quail	Accountant	2:20
1907	Peter Pan (1)	G. Mountain	Superman	Frank Gill	Unknown
1908	Colin (Head)	Joe Notter	Fair Play	King James	Unknown
1909	Joe Madden (8)	E. Dugan	Wise Mason	Donald MacDonald	2:21⅗
1910*	Sweep (6)	J. Butwell	Duke of Ormonde		2:22
1913	Prince Eugene (½)	Roscoe Troxler	Rock View	Flying Fairy	2:18
1914	Luke McLuke (8)	M. Buxton	Gainer	Charlestonian	2:20
1915	The Finn (4)	G. Byrne	Half Rock	Pebbles	2:18⅖
1916	Friar Rock (3)	E. Haynes	Spur	Churchill	2:22
1917	Hourless (10)	J. Butwell	Skeptic	Wonderful	2:17⅘
1918	Johren (2)	Frank Robinson	War Cloud	Cum Sah	2:20⅖
1919	Sir Barton (5)	Johnny Loftus	Sweep On	Natural Bridge	2:17⅖
1920*	Man o' War (20)	Clarence Kummer	Donnacona		2:14⅕
1921	Grey Lag (3)	Earl Sande	Sporting Blood	Leonardo II	2:16⅘
1922	Pillory (2)	C. H. Miller	Snob II	Hea	2:18⅘
1923	Zev (1½)	Earl Sande	Chickvale	Rialto	2:19
1924	Mad Play (2)	Earl Sande	Mr. Mutt	Modest	2:18⅘
1925	American Flag (8)	Albert Johnson	Dangerous	Swope	2:16⅘
1926	Crusader (1)	Albert Johnson	Espino	Haste	2:32⅕
1927	Chance Shot (1½)	Earl Sande	Bois de Rose	Flambino	2:32⅖
1928	Vito (3)	Clarence Kummer	Genie	Diavolo	2:33⅕
1929	Blue Larkspur (¾)	Mack Garner	African	Jack High	2:32⅘
1930	Gallant Fox (3)	Earl Sande	Whichone	Questionnaire	2:31⅗

Belmont (Cont.)

Year	Winner (Margin)	Jockey	Second	Third	Time
1931	Twenty Grand (10)	Charles Kurtsinger	Sun Meadow	Jamestown	2:29 3/5
1932	Faireno (1½)	T. Malley	Osculator	Flag Pole	2:32 4/5
1933	Hurryoff (1½)	Mack Garner	Nimbus	Union	2:32 3/5
1934	Peace Chance (6)	W. D. Wright	High Quest	Good Goods	2:29 1/5
1935	Omaha (1½)	Willie Saunders	Firethorn	Rosemont	2:30 3/5
1936	Granville (Nose)	James Stout	Mr. Bones	Hollyrood	2:30
1937	War Admiral (3)	Charles Kurtsinger	Sceneshifter	Vamoose	2:28 3/5
1938	Pasteurized (Neck)	James Stout	Dauber	Cravat	2:29 2/5
1939	Johnstown (5)	James Stout	Belay	Gilded Knight	2:29 3/5
1940	Bimelech (¾)	F. A. Smith	Your Chance	Andy K	2:29 3/5
1941	Whirlaway (2½)	Eddie Arcaro	Robert Morris	Yankee Chance	2:31
1942	Shut Out (2)	Eddie Arcaro	Alsab	Lochinvar	2:29 1/5
1943	Count Fleet (25)	Johnny Longden	Fairy Manhurst	Deseronto	2:28 1/5
1944	Bounding Home (½)	G. L. Smith	Pensive	Bull Dandy	2:32 1/5
1945	Pavot (5)	Eddie Arcaro	Wildlife	Jeep	2:30 1/5
1946	Assault (3)	Warren Mehrtens	Natchez	Cable	2:30 4/5
1947	Phalanx (5)	R. Donoso	Tide Rips	Tailspin	2:29 2/5
1948	Citation (8)	Eddie Arcaro	Better Self	Escadru	2:28 1/5
1949	Capot (½)	Ted Atkinson	Ponder	Palestinian	2:30 1/5
1950	Middleground (1)	William Boland	Lights Up	Mr. Trouble	2:28 3/5
1951	Counterpoint (4)	D. Gorman	Battlefield	Battle Morn	2:29
1952	One Count (2½)	Eddie Arcaro	Blue Man	Armageddon	2:30 1/5
1953	Native Dancer (Neck)	Eric Guerin	Jamie K.	Royal Bay Gem	2:38 3/5
1954	High Gun (Neck)	Eric Guerin	Fisherman	Limelight	2:30 4/5
1955	Nashua (9)	Eddie Arcaro	Blazing Count	Portersville	2:29
1956	Needles (Neck)	David Erb	Career Boy	Fabius	2:29 4/5
1957	Gallant Man (8)	Bill Shoemaker	Inside Tract	Bold Ruler	2:26 3/5
1958	Cavan (6)	Pete Anderson	Tim Tam	Flamingo	2:30 1/5
1959	Sword Dancer (¾)	Bill Shoemaker	Bagdad	Royal Orbit	2:28 2/5
1960	Celtic Ash (5½)	Bill Hartack	Venetian Way	Disperse	2:29 3/5
1961	Sherluck (2¼)	Braulio Baeza	Globemaster	Guadalcanal	2:29 1/5
1962	Jaipur (Nose)	Bill Shoemaker	Admiral's Voyage	Crimson Satan	2:28 4/5
1963	Chateaugay (2½)	Braulio Baeza	Candy Spots	Choker	2:30 1/5
1964	Quadrangle (2)	Manuel Ycaza	Roman Brother	Northern Dancer	2:28 2/5
1965	Hail to All (Neck)	John Sellers	Tom Rolfe	First Family	2:28 2/5
1966	Amberold (2½)	William Boland	Buffle	Advocator	2:29 3/5
1967	Damascus (2½)	Bill Shoemaker	Cool Reception	Gentleman James	2:28 4/5
1968	Stage Door Johnny (1¼)	Hellodoro Gustines	Forward Pass	Call Me Prince	2:27 1/5
1969	Arts and Letters (5½)	Braulio Baeza	Majestic Prince	Dike	2:28 4/5
1970	High Echelon (¾)	John L. Rotz	Needles N Pins	Naskra	2:34
1971	Pass Catcher (¾)	Walter Blum	Jim French	Bold Reason	2:30 2/5
1972	Riva Ridge (7)	Ron Turcotte	Ruritania	Cloudy Dawn	2:28
1973	Secretariat (31)	Ron Turcotte	Twice a Prince	My Gallant	2:24
1974	Little Current (7)	Miguel A. Rivera	Jolly Johu	Cannonade	2:29 1/5
1975	Avatar (Neck)	Bill Shoemaker	Foolish Pleasure	Master Derby	2:28 1/5
1976	Bold Forbes (Neck)	Angel Cordero Jr.	McKenzie Bridge	Great Contractor	2:29
1977	Seattle Slew (4)	Jean Cruguet	Run Dusty Run	Sanhedrin	2:29 3/5
1978	Affirmed (Head)	Steve Cauthen	Alydar	Darby Creek Road	2:26 4/5
1979	Coastal (3¼)	Ruben Hernandez	Golden Act	Spectacular Bid	2:28 3/5
1980	Temperence Hill (2)	Eddie Maple	Genuine Risk	Rockhill Native	2:29 4/5
1981	Summing (Neck)	George Martens	Highland Blade	Pleasant Colony	2:29
1982	Conquistador Cielo (14½)	Laffit Pincay, Jr.	Gato Del Sol	Illuminate	2:28 1/5
1983	Caveat (3½)	Laffit Pincay Jr.	Slew o'Gold	Barberstown	2:27 4/5
1984	Swale (4)	Laffit Pincay Jr.	Pine Circle	Morning Bob	2:27 1/5
1985	Creme Fraiche (½)	Eddie Maple	Stephan's Odyssey	Chief's Crown	2:27
1986	Danzig Connection (1¼)	Chris McCarron	Johns Treasure	Ferdinand	2:29 4/5
1987	Bet Twice (14)	Craig Perret	Cryptoclearance	Gulch	2:28 1/5
1988	Risen Star (14¾)	Eddie Delahoussaye	Kingpost	Brian's Time	2:26 2/5
1989	Easy Goer (8)	Pat Day	Sunday Silence	Le Voyageur	2:26
1990	Go and Go (8¼)	Michael Kinane	Thirty Six Red	Baron de Vaux	2:27 1/5
1991	Hansel (Head)	Jerry Bailey	Strike the Gold	Mane Minister	2:28
1992	A.P. Indy (¾)	Eddie Delahoussaye	My Memoirs	Pine Bluff	2:26
1993	Colonial Affair (2¼)	Julie Krone	Kissin Kris	Wild Gale	2:29 4/5
1994	Tabasco Cat (2)	Pat Day	Go For Gin	Strodes Creek	2:26 4/5

Belmont (Cont.)

Year	Winner (Margin)	Jockey	Second	Third	Time
1995	Thunder Gulch (2)	Gary Stevens	Star Standard	Citadeed	2:32
1996	Editor's Note (1)	Rene Douglas	Skip Away	My Flag	2:28⅜
1997	Touch Gold (¾)	Chris McCarron	Silver Charm	Free House	2:28⅜
1998	Victory Gallop (Nose)	Gary Stevens	Real Quiet	Thomas Jo	2:28⅜
1999	Lemon Drop Kid (Head)	Jose Santos	Vision and Verse	Charismatic	2:27⅞
2000	Commendable (1½)	Pat Day	Aptitude	Unshaded	2:31.19

*Belmont was a two-horse race in 1887, '88, '92, 1910 and '20; and was not held in 1911–1912.
Note: Distance: 1 mile 5 furlongs (1867–89), 1¼ miles (1890–1905), 1⅜ miles (1906–25), 1½ miles (1926–present).

Triple Crown Winners

Year	Horse	Jockey	Owner	Trainer
1919	Sir Barton	John Loftus	J. K. L. Ross	H. G. Bedwell
1930	Gallant Fox	Earle Sande	Belair Stud	James Fitzsimmons
1935	Omaha	William Saunders	Belair Stud	James Fitzsimmons
1937	War Admiral	Charles Kurtsinger	Samuel D. Riddle	George Conway
1941	Whirlaway	Eddie Arcaro	Calumet Farm	Ben Jones
1943	Count Fleet	John Longden	Mrs J. D. Hertz	Don Cameron
1946	Assault	Warren Mehrtens	King Ranch	Max Hirsch
1948	Citation	Eddie Arcaro	Calumet Farm	Jimmy Jones
1973	Secretariat	Ron Turcotte	Meadow Stable	Lucien Laurin
1977	Seattle Slew	Jean Cruguet	Karen L. Taylor	William H. Turner Jr.
1978	Affirmed	Steve Cauthen	Harbor View Farm	Laz Barrera

Awards

Horse of the Year

Year	Horse	Owner	Trainer	Breeder
1936	Granville	Belair Stud	James Fitzsimmons	Belair Stud
1937	War Admiral	Samuel D. Riddle	George Conway	Mrs. Samuel D. Riddle
1938	Seabiscuit	Charles S. Howard	Tom Smith	Wheatley Stable
1939	Challedon	William L. Brann	Louis J. Schaefer	Branncastle Farm
1940	Challedon	William L. Brann	Louis J. Schaefer	Branncastle Farm
1941	Whirlaway	Calumet Farm	Ben Jones	Calumet Farm
1942	Whirlaway	Calumet Farm	Ben Jones	Calumet Farm
1943	Count Fleet	Mrs. John D. Hertz	Don Cameron	Mrs. John D. Hertz
1944	Twilight Tear	Calumet Farm	Ben Jones	Calumet Farm
1945	Busher	Louis B. Mayer	George Odom	Idle Hour Stock Farm
1946	Assault	King Ranch	Max Hirsch	King Ranch
1947	Armed	Calumet Farm	Jimmy Jones	Calumet Farm
1948	Citation	Calumet Farm	Jimmy Jones	Calumet Farm
1949	Capot	Greentree Stable	John M. Gaver Sr.	Greentree Stable
1950	Hill Prince	C.T. Chenery	Casey Hayes	C.T. Chenery
1951	Counterpoint	C.V. Whitney	Syl Veitch	C.V. Whitney
1952	One Count	Mrs. W. M. Jeffords	O. White	W M. Jeffords
1953	Tom Fool	Greentree Stable	John M. Gaver Sr.	D.A. Headley
1954	Native Dancer	A.G. Vanderbilt	Bill Winfrey	A.G. Vanderbilt
1955	Nashua	Belair Stud	James Fitzsimmons	Belair Stud
1956	Swaps	Ellsworth-Galbreath	Mesh Tenney	R. Ellsworth
1957	Bold Ruler	Wheatley Stable	James Fitzsimmons	Wheatley Stable
1958	Round Table	Kerr Stables	Willy Molter	Claiborne Farm
1959	Sword Dancer	Brookmeade Stable	Elliott Burch	Brookmeade Stable
1960	Kelso	Bohemia Stable	C. Hanford	Mrs. R.C. duPont
1961	Kelso	Bohemia Stable	C. Hanford	Mrs. R.C. duPont
1962	Kelso	Bohemia Stable	C. Hanford	Mrs. R.C. duPont
1963	Kelso	Bohemia Stable	C. Hanford	Mrs. R.C. duPont
1964	Kelso	Bohemia Stable	C. Hanford	Mrs. R.C. duPont
1965	Roman Brother	Harbor View Stable	Burley Parke	Ocala Stud
1966	Buckpasser	Ogden Phipps	Eddie Neloy	Ogden Phipps
1967	Damascus	Mrs. E. W. Bancroft	Frank Y. Whiteley Jr.	Mrs. E. W. Bancroft
1968	Dr. Fager	Tartan Stable	John A. Nerud	Tartan Farms
1969	Arts and Letters	Rokeby Stable	Elliott Burch	Paul Mellon
1970	Fort Marcy	Rokeby Stable	Elliott Burch	Paul Mellon

Horse of the Year (Cont.)

Year	Horse	Owner	Trainer	Breeder
1971	Ack Ack	E.E. Fogelson	Charlie Whittingham	H.F. Guggenheim
1972	Secretariat	Meadow Stable	Lucien Laurin	Meadow Stud
1973	Secretariat	Meadow Stable	Lucien Laurin	Meadow Stud
1974	Forego	Lazy F Ranch	Sherrill W. Ward	Lazy F Ranch
1975	Forego	Lazy F Ranch	Sherrill W. Ward	Lazy F Ranch
1976	Forego	Lazy F Ranch	Frank Y. Whiteley Jr.	Lazy F Ranch
1977	Seattle Slew	Karen L. Taylor	Billy Turner Jr.	B.S. Castleman
1978	Affirmed	Harbor View Farm	Laz Barrera	Harbor View Farm
1979	Affirmed	Harbor View Farm	Laz Barrera	Harbor View Farm
1980	Spectacular Bid	Hawksworth Farm	Bud Delp	Mmes. Gilmore and Jason
1981	John Henry	Dotsam Stable	Ron McAnally and Lefty Nickerson	Golden Chance Farm
1982	Conquistador Cielo	H. de Kwiatkowski	Woody Stephens	L.E. Landoli
1983	All Along	Daniel Wildenstein	P.L. Biancone	Dayton
1984	John Henry	Dotsam Stable	Ron McAnally	Golden Chance Farm
1985	Spend a Buck	Hunter Farm	Cam Gambolati	Irish Hill & R.W. Harper
1986	Lady's Secret	Mr. & Mrs. Eugene Klein	D. Wayne Lukas	R.H. Spreen
1987	Ferdinand	Mrs. H.B. Keck	Charlie Whittingham	H.B. Keck
1988	Alysheba	D. & P. Scharbauer	Jack Van Berg	Preston Madden
1989	Sunday Silence	Gaillard, Hancock, & Whittingham	Charlie Whittingham	Oak Cliff Thoroughbreds
1990	Criminal Type	Calumet Farm	D. Wayne Lukas	Calumet Farm
1991	Black Tie Affair	Jeffrey Sullivan	Ernie Poulos	Stephen D. Peskoff
1992	A.P. Indy	Tomonori Tsurumaki	Neil Drysdale	W.S. Farish & W.S. Kilroy
1993	Kotashaan	La Presle Farm	Richard Mandella	La Presle Farm
1994	Holy Bull	Jimmy Croll	Jimmy Croll	Pelican Stable
1995	Cigar	Allen E. Paulson	William Mott	Allen E. Paulson
1996	Cigar	Allen E. Paulson	William Mott	Allen E. Paulson
1997	Favorite Trick	Joseph LaCombe	William Mott	Mr. & Mrs. M.L. Wood
1998	Skip Away	Carolyn Hine	Hubert Hine	Anna Marie Barnhart
1999	Charismatic	Robert & Beverly Lewis	D. Wayne Lukas	William Farish/Partners

Note: From 1936 to 1970, the *Daily Racing Form* annually selected a "Horse of the Year." In 1971 the *Daily Racing Form*, with the Thoroughbred Racing Association and the National Turf Writers Association, jointly created the Eclipse Awards.

Eclipse Award Winners

	2-YEAR-OLD COLT	2-YEAR-OLD FILLY	3-YEAR-OLD COLT
1971	Riva Ridge	Numbered Account	Canonero II
1972	Secretariat	La Prevoyante	Key to the Mint
1973	Protagonist	Talking Picture	Secretariat
1974	Foolish Pleasure	Ruffian	Little Current
1975	Honest Pleasure	Dearly Precious	Wajima
1976	Seattle Slew	Sensational	Bold Forbes
1977	Affirmed	Lakeville Miss	Seattle Slew
1978	Spectacular Bid	Candy Eclair, It's in the Air	Affirmed
1979	Rockhill Native	Smart Angle	Spectacular Bid
1980	Lord Avie	Heavenly Cause	Temperence Hill
1981	Deputy Minister	Before Dawn	Pleasant Colony
1982	Roving Boy	Landaluce	Conquistador Cielo
1983	Devil's Bag	Althea	Slew o' Gold
1984	Chief's Crown	Outstandingly	Swale
1985	Tasso	Family Style	Spend A Buck
1986	Capote	Brave Raj	Snow Chief
1987	Forty Niner	Epitome	Alysheba
1988	Easy Goer	Open Mind	Risen Star
1989	Rhythm	Go for Wand	Sunday Silence
1990	Fly So Free	Meadow Star	Unbridled
1991	Arazi	Pleasant Stage	Hansel
1992	Gilded Time	Eliza	A.P. Indy
1993	Dehere	Phone Chatter	Prairie Bayou
1994	Timber Country	Flanders	Holy Bull
1995	Maria's Mon	Golden Attraction	Thunder Gulch
1996	Boston Harbor	Storm Song	Skip Away
1997	Favorite Trick	Countess Diana	Silver Charm
1998	Answer Lively	Silverbullettday	Real Quiet
1999	Anees	Chilukki	Charismatic

Eclipse Award Winners (Cont.)

3-YEAR-OLD FILLY

1971 ....Turkish Trousers
1972 ....Susan's Girl
1973 ....Desert Vixen
1974 ....Chris Evert
1975 ....Ruffian
1976 ....Revidere
1977 ....Our Mims
1978 ....Tempest Queen
1979 ....Davona Dale
1980 ....Genuine Risk
1981 ....Wayward Lass
1982 ....Christmas Past
1983 ....Heartlight No. One
1984 ....Life's Magic
1985 ....Mom's Command
1986 ....Tiffany Lass
1987 ....Sacahuista
1988 ....Winning Colors
1989 ....Open Mind
1990 ....Go for Wand
1991 ....Dance Smartly
1992 ....Saratoga Dew
1993 ....Hollywood Wildcat
1994 ....Heavenly Prize
1995 ....Serena's Song
1996 ....Yank's Music
1997 ....Ajina
1998 ....Banshee Breeze
1999 ....Silverbulletday

OLDER COLT, HORSE OR GELDING

1971 ....Ack Ack (5)
1972 ....Autobiography (4)
1973 ....Riva Ridge (4)
1974 ....Forego (4)
1975 ....Forego (5)
1976 ....Forego (6)
1977 ....Forego (7)
1978 ....Seattle Slew (4)
1979 ....Affirmed (4)
1980 ....Spectacular Bid (4)
1981 ....John Henry (6)
1982 ....Lemhi Gold (4)
1983 ....Bates Motel (4)
1984 ....Slew o'Gold (4)
1985 ....Vanlandingham (4)
1986 ....Turkoman (4)
1987 ....Ferdinand (4)
1988 ....Alysheba (4)
1989 ....Blushing John (4)
1990 ....Criminal Type (5)
1991 ....Black Tie Affair (5)
1992 ....Pleasant Tap (5)
1993 ....Bertrando (4)
1994 ....The Wicked North (5)
1995 ....Cigar (5)
1996 ....Cigar (6)
1997 ....Skip Away (4)
1998 ....Skip Away (5)
1999 ....Victory Gallop (4)

OLDER FILLY OR MARE

1971 ....Shuvee (5)
1972 ....Typecast (6)
1973 ....Susan's Girl (4)
1974 ....Desert Vixen (4)
1975 ....Susan's Girl (6)
1976 ....Proud Delta (4)
1977 ....Cascapedia (4)
1978 ....Late Bloomer (4)
1979 ....Waya (5)

OLDER FILLY OR MARE (Cont.)

1980 ....Glorious Song (4)
1981 ....Relaxing (5)
1982 ....Track Robbery (6)
1983 ....Ambassador of Luck (4)
1984 ....Princess Rooney (4)
1985 ....Life's Magic (4)
1986 ....Lady's Secret (4)
1987 ....North Sider (5)
1988 ....Personal Ensign (4)
1989 ....Bayakoa (5)
1990 ....Bayakoa (6)
1991 ....Queena (5)
1992 ....Paseana (5)
1993 ....Paseana (6)
1994 ....Sky Beauty (4)
1995 ....Inside Information (4)
1996 ....Jewel Princess (4)
1997 ....Hidden Lake (4)
1998 ....Escena (5)
1999 ....Beautiful Pleasure (4)

CHAMPION TURF HORSE

1971 .....Run the Gantlet (3)
1972 .....Cougar II (6)
1973 .....Secretariat (3)
1974 .....Dahlia (4)
1975 .....Snow Knight (3)
1976 .....Youth (3)
1977 .....Johnny D (3)
1978 .....Mac Diarmida (3)

CHAMPION MALE TURF HORSE

1979 .....Bowl Game (5)
1980 .....John Henry (5)
1981 .....John Henry (6)
1982 .....Perrault (5)
1983 .....John Henry (8)
1984 .....John Henry (9)
1985 .....Cozzene (4)
1986 .....Manila (3)
1987 .....Theatrical (5)
1988 .....Sunshine Forever (3)
1989 .....Steinlen (6)
1990 .....Itsallgreektome (3)
1991 .....Tight Spot (4)
1992 .....Sky Classic (5)
1993 .....Kotashaan (5)
1994 .....Paradise Creek (5)
1995 .....Northern Spur (4)
1996 .....Singspiel (4)
1997 .....Chief Bearhart (4)
1998 .....Buck's Boy (5)
1999 .....Daylami (5)

CHAMPION FEMALE TURF HORSE

1979 .....Trillion (5)
1980 .....Just a Game II (4)
1981 .....De La Rose (3)
1982 .....April Run (4)
1983 .....All Along (4)
1984 .....Royal Heroine (4)
1985 .....Pebbles (4)
1986 .....Estrapade (6)
1987 .....Miesque (3)
1988 .....Miesque (4)
1989 .....Brown Bess (7)
1990 .....Laugh and Be Merry (5)
1991 .....Miss Alleged (4)
1992 .....Flawlessly (4)
1993 .....Flawlessly (5)

CHAMPION FEMALE TURF HORSE (Cont.)

1994 .....Hatoof (5)
1995 .....Possibly Perfect (5)
1996 .....Wandesta (5)
1997 .....Ryafan (3)
1998 .....Fiji (4)
1999 .....Soaring Softly (4)

STEEPLECHASE OR HURDLE HORSE

1971 .....Shadow Brook (7)
1972 .....Soothsayer (5)
1973 .....Athenian Idol (5)
1974 .....Gran Kan (8)
1975 .....Life's Illusion (4)
1976 .....Straight & True (6)
1977 .....Cafe Prince (7)
1978 .....Cafe Prince (8)
1979 .....Martie's Anger (4)
1980 .....Zaccio (4)
1981 .....Zaccio (5)
1982 .....Zaccio (6)
1983 .....Flatterer (4)
1984 .....Flatterer (5)
1985 .....Flatterer (6)
1986 .....Flatterer (7)
1987 .....Inlander (6)
1988 .....Jimmy Lorenzo (6)
1989 .....Highland Bud (4)
1990 .....Morley Street (7)
1991 .....Morley Street (8)
1992 .....Lonesome Glory (4)
1993 .....Lonesome Glory (5)
1994 .....Warm Spell (6)
1995 .....Lonesome Glory (7)
1996 .....Corregio (5)
1997 .....Lonesome Glory (9)
1998 .....Flat Top (5)
1999 .....Lonesome Glory (11)

SPRINTER

1971 .....Ack Ack (5)
1972 .....Chou Croute (4)
1973 .....Shecky Greene (3)
1974 .....Forego (4)
1975 .....Gallant Bob (3)
1976 .....My Juliet (4)
1977 .....What a Summer (4)
1978 .....Dr. Patches (4)
           J.O. Tobin (4)
1979 .....Star de Naskra (4)
1980 .....Plugged Nickel (3)
1981 .....Guilty Conscience (5)
1982 .....Gold Beauty (3)
1983 .....Chinook Pass (4)
1984 .....Eillo (4)
1985 .....Precisionist (4)
1986 .....Smile (4)
1987 .....Groovy (4)
1988 .....Gulch (4)
1989 .....Safely Kept (3)
1990 .....Housebuster (3)
1991 .....Housebuster (4)
1992 .....Rubiano (5)
1993 .....Cardmania (7)
1994 .....Cherokee Run (4)
1995 .....Not Surprising (5)
1996 .....Lit de Justice (6)
1997 .....Smoke Glacken (3)
1998 .....Reraise (4)
1999 .....Artax (4)

Eclipse Award Winners (Cont.)

OUTSTANDING OWNER

1971.....Mr. & Mrs. E. E. Fogleson
1974.....Dan Lasater
1975.....Dan Lasater
1976.....Dan Lasater
1977.....Maxwell Gluck
1978.....Harbor View Farm
1979.....Harbor View Farm
1980.....Mr. & Mrs. Bertram
1981.....Dotsam Stable
1982.....Viola Sommer
1983.....John Franks
1984.....John Franks
1985.....Mr. & Mrs. Eugene Klein
1986.....Mr. & Mrs. Eugene Klein
1987.....Mr. & Mrs. Eugene Klein
1988.....Ogden Phipps
1989.....Ogden Phipps
1990.....Frances Genter
1991.....Sam-Son Farm
1992.....Juddmonte Farms
1993.....John Franks
1994.....John Franks
1995.....Allen E. Paulson
1996.....Allen E. Paulson
1997.....Carolyn Hine
1998.....Frank Stronach
1999.....Frank Stronach

OUTSTANDING TRAINER

1971.....Charlie Whittingham
1972.....Lucien Laurin
1973.....H. Allen Jerkens
1974.....Sherrill Ward
1975.....Steve DiMauro
1976.....Lazaro Barrera
1977.....Lazaro Barrera
1978.....Lazaro Barrera
1979.....Lazaro Barrera
1980.....Bud Delp
1981.....Ron McAnally
1982.....Charlie Whittingham
1983.....Woody Stephens
1984.....Jack Van Berg
1985.....D. Wayne Lukas
1986.....D. Wayne Lukas
1987.....D. Wayne Lukas
1988.....Claude R. McGaughey III
1989.....Charlie Whittingham
1990.....Carl Nafzger
1991.....Ron McAnally
1992.....Ron McAnally
1993.....Bobby Frankel
1994.....D. Wayne Lukas
1995.....William Mott
1996.....William Mott
1997.....Bob Baffert
1998.....Bob Baffert
1999.....Bob Baffert

OUTSTANDING JOCKEY

1971.....Laffit Pincay Jr.
1972.....Braulio Baeza

OUTSTANDING JOCKEY (Cont.)

1973.....Laffit Pincay Jr
1974.....Laffit Pincay Jr
1975.....Braulio Baeza
1976.....Sandy Hawley
1977.....Steve Cauthen
1978.....Darrel McHargue
1979.....Laffit Pincay Jr.
1980.....Chris McCarron
1981.....Bill Shoemaker
1982.....Angel Cordero Jr
1983.....Angel Cordero Jr
1984.....Pat Day
1985.....Laffit Pincay Jr
1986.....Pat Day
1987.....Pat Day
1988.....Jose Santos
1989.....Kent Desormeaux
1990.....Craig Perret
1991.....Pat Day
1992.....Kent Desormeaux
1993.....Mike Smith
1994.....Mike Smith
1995.....Jerry Bailey
1996.....Jerry Bailey
1997.....Jerry Bailey
1998.....Gary Stevens
1999.....Jorge Chavez

OUTSTANDING APPRENTICE JOCKEY

1971.....Gene St. Leon
1972.....Thomas Wallis
1973.....Steve Valdez
1974.....Chris McCarron
1975.....Jimmy Edwards
1976.....George Martens
1977.....Steve Cauthen
1978.....Ron Franklin
1979.....Cash Asmussen
1980.....Frank Lovato Jr.
1981.....Richard Migliore
1982.....Alberto Delgado
1983.....Declan Murphy
1984.....Wesley Ward
1985.....Art Madrid Jr.
1986.....Allen Stacy
1987.....Kent Desormeaux
1988.....Steve Capanas
1989.....Michael Luzzi
1990.....Mark Johnston
1991.....Mickey Walls
1992.....Jesus A. Bracho
1993.....Juan Umana
1994.....Dale Beckner
1995.....Ramon Perez
1996.....Neil Pozansky
1997.....Phil Teator
          Roberto Rosado
1998.....Shaun Bridgmohan
1999.....Ariel Smith

OUTSTANDING BREEDER

1974.....John W. Galbreath
1975.....Fred W. Hooper
1976.....Nelson Bunker Hunt
1977.....Edward Plunket Taylor
1978.....Harbor View Farm
1979.....Claiborne Farm
1980.....Mrs. Henry D. Paxson
1981.....Golden Chance Farm
1982.....Fred W. Hooper
1983.....Edward Plunket Taylor
1984.....Claiborne Farm
1985.....Nelson Bunker Hunt
1986.....Paul Mellon
1987.....Nelson Bunker Hunt
1988.....Ogden Phipps
1989.....North Ridge Farm
1990.....Calumet Farm
1991.....John and Betty Mabee
1992.....William S. Farish III
1993.....Allen Paulson
1994.....William T. Young
1995.....Juddmonte Farms
1996.....Fansworth Farms
1997.....Golden Eagle Farm
1998.....John and Betty Mabee
1999.....William Farish/Partners

AWARD OF MERIT

1976.....Jack J. Dreyfus
1977.....Steve Cauthen
1978.....Ogden Phipps
1979.....Frank E. Kilroe
1980.....John D. Schapiro
1981.....Bill Shoemaker
1984.....John Gaines
1985.....Keene Daingerfield
1986.....Herman Cohen
1987.....J. B. Faulconer
1988.....John Forsythe
1989.....Michael P. Sandler
1991.....Fred W. Hooper
1994.....Alfred G. Vanderbilt
1996.....Allen E. Paulson

SPECIAL AWARD

1971.....Robert J. Kleberg
1974.....Charles Hatton
1976.....Bill Shoemaker
1980.....John T. Landry
          Pierre E. Bellocq (Peb)
1984.....C. V. Whitney
1985.....Arlington Park
1987.....Anheuser-Busch
1988.....Edward J. DeBartolo Sr.
1989.....Richard Duchossois
1994.....John Longden
          Edward Arcaro
1998.....Oak Tree Racing
          Association

Note: Special Award and Award of Merit, for long-term and/or outstanding service to the industry, not presented annually.

Breeders' Cup

Location: Hollywood Park (CA) 1984, '87, '97; Aqueduct Racetrack (NY) 1985; Santa Anita Park (CA) 1986, '93; Churchill Downs (KY) 1988, '91, '98; Gulfstream Park (FL) 1989, '92, '99; Belmont Park (NY) 1990, '95; Woodbine (Toronto) 1996.

Juveniles

Year	Winner (Margin)	Jockey	Second	Third	Time
1984	Chief's Crown (¾)	Don MacBeth	Tank's Prospect	Spend a Buck	1:36⅕
1985	Tasso (Nose)	Laffit Pincay Jr.	Storm Cat	Scat Dancer	1:36⅕
1986	Capote (1¼)	Laffit Pincay Jr.	Qualify	Alysheba	1:43⅘
1987	Success Express (1¾)	Jose Santos	Regal Classic	Tejano	1:35⅕
1988	Is It True (1¼)	Laffit Pincay Jr.	Easy Goer	Tagel	1:46⅗
1989	Rhythm (2)	Craig Perret	Grand Canyon	Slavic	1:43⅗
1990	Fly So Free (3)	Jose Santos	Take Me Out	Lost Mountain	1:43⅖
1991	Arazi (4¾)	Pat Valenzuela	Bertrando	Snappy Landing	1:44⅗
1992	Gilded Time (¾)	Chris McCarron	It'sali'lknownfact	River Special	1:43⅖
1993	Brocco (5)	Gary Stevens	Blumin Affair	Tabasco Cat	1:42⅘
1994	Timber Country (½)	Pat Day	Eltish	Tejano Run	1:44⅖
1995	Unbridled's Song (Neck)	Mike Smith	Hennessy	Editor's Note	1:41⅗
1996	Boston Harbor (Neck)	Jerry Bailey	Acceptable	Ordway	1:43⅖
1997	Favorite Trick (5½)	Pat Day	Dawson's Legacy	Nationalore	1:41⅗
1998	Answer Lively (Head)	Jerry Bailey	Aly's Alley	Cat Thief	1:44
1999	Anees (2½)	Gary Stevens	Chief Seattle	High Yield	1:42.29

Note: One mile (1984–85, '87), 1¹⁄₁₆ miles (1986 and since 1988).

Juvenile Fillies

Year	Winner (Margin)	Jockey	Second	Third	Time
1984	Outstandingly*	Walter Guerra	Dusty Heart	Fine Spirit	1:37⅘
1985	Twilight Ridge (1)	Jorge Velasquez	Family Style	Steal a Kiss	1:35⅘
1986	Brave Raj (5½)	Pat Valenzuela	Tappiano	Saros Brig	1:43⅕
1987	Epitome (Nose)	Pat Day	Jeanne Jones	Dream Team	1:36⅖
1988	Open Mind (1¾)	Angel Cordero Jr.	Darby Shuffle	Lea Lucinda	1:46⅗
1989	Go for Wand (2¾)	Randy Romero	Sweet Roberta	Stella Madrid	1:44⅕
1990	Meadow Star (5)	Jose Santos	Private Treasure	Dance Smartly	1:44
1991	Pleasant Stage (Neck)	Eddie Delahoussaye	La Spia	Cadillac Women	1:46⅖
1992	Eliza (1½)	Pat Valenzuela	Educated Risk	Boots 'n Jackie	1:42⅘
1993	Phone Chatter (Head)	Laffit Pincay	Sardula	Heavenly Prize	1:43
1994	Flanders (Head)	Pat Day	Serena's Song	Stormy Blues	1:45⅕
1995	My Flag (½)	Jerry Bailey	Cara Rafaela	Golden Attraction	1:42⅖
1996	Storm Song (4½)	Craig Perret	Love That Jazz	Critical Factor	1:43⅗
1997	Countess Diana (8½)	Shane Sellers	Career Collection	Primaly	1:42⅕
1998	Silverbulletday (½)	Gary Stevens	Excellent Meeting	Three Ring	1:43⅗
1999	Cash Run (1¼)	Jerry Bailey	Chilukki	Surfside	1:43.31

*In 1984, winner Fran's Valentine was disqualified for interference in the stretch and placed 10th.
Note: One mile (1984–85, '87), 1¹⁄₁₆ miles (1986 and since 1988).

Sprint

Year	Winner (Margin)	Jockey	Second	Third	Time
1984	Eillo (Nose)	Craig Perret	Commemorate	Fighting Fit	1:10⅕
1985	Precisionist (¾)	Chris McCarron	Smile	Mt. Livermore	1:08⅖
1986	Smile (1¼)	Jacinto Vasquez	Pine Tree Lane	Bedside Promise	1:08⅖
1987	Very Subtle (4)	Pat Valenzuela	Groovy	Exclusive Enough	1:08⅘
1988	Gulch (¾)	Angel Cordero Jr	Play the King	Afleet	1:10⅖
1989	Dancing Spree (Neck)	Angel Cordero Jr	Safely Kept	Dispersal	1:09
1990	Safely Kept (Neck)	Craig Perret	Dayjur	Black Tie Affair	1:09⅗
1991	Sheikh Albadou (Neck)	Pat Eddery	Pleasant Tap	Robyn Dancer	1:09⅕
1992	Thirty Slews (Neck)	Eddie Delahoussaye	Meafara	Rubiano	1:08⅕
1993	Cardmania (Neck)	Eddie Delahoussaye	Meafara	Gilded Time	1:08⅗
1994	Cherokee Run (Head)	Mike Smith	Soviet Problem	Cardmania	1:09⅖
1995	Desert Stormer (Neck)	Kent Desormeaux	Mr. Greeley	Lit de Justice	1:09
1996	Lit de Justice (1¼)	Corey Nakatani	Paying Dues	Honour and Glory	1:08⅗
1997	Elmhurst (½)	Corey Nakatani	Hesabull	Bet on Sunshine	1:08
1998	Reraise (2)	Corey Nakatani	Grand Slam	Kona Gold	1:09
1999	Artax (½)	Jorge Chavez	Kona Gold	Big Jag	1:07.89

Note: Six furlongs (since 1984).

Breeders' Cup *(Cont.)*

Mile

Year	Winner (Margin)	Jockey	Second	Third	Time
1984	Royal Heroine (1½)	Fernando Toro	Star Choice	Cozzene	1:32⅗
1985	Cozzene (2¼)	Walter Guerra	Al Mamoon*	Shadeed	1:35
1986	Last Tycoon (Head)	Yves St-Martin	Palace Music	Fred Astaire	1:35⅕
1987	Miesque (3½)	Freddie Head	Show Dancer	Sonic Lady	1:32⅘
1988	Miesque (4)	Freddie Head	Steinlen	Simply Majestic	1:38⅗
1989	Steinlen (¾)	Jose Santos	Sabona	Most Welcome	1:37⅕
1990	Royal Academy (Neck)	Lester Piggott	Itsallgreektome	Priolo	1:35⅕
1991	Opening Verse (2¼)	Pat Valenzuela	Val de Bois	Star of Cozzene	1:37⅖
1992	Lure (3)	Mike Smith	Paradise Creek	Brief Truce	1:32⅘
1993	Lure (2¼)	Mike Smith	Ski Paradise	Fourstars Allstar	1:33⅖
1994	Barathea (Head)	Frankie Dettori	Johann Quatz	Unfinished Symph	1:34⅖
1995	Ridgewood Pearl (2)	John Murtagh	Fastness	Sayyedati	1:43⅗
1996	Da Hoss (1½)	Gary Stevens	Spinning World	Same Old Wish	1:35⅘
1997	Spinning World (2)	Cash Asmussen	Geri	Decorated Hero	1:32⅘
1998	Da Hoss (Head)	John Velazquez	Hawksley Hill	Labeeb	1:35⅕
1999	Silic (Neck)	Corey Nakatani	Tuzla	Docksider	1:34.26

*2nd place finisher Palace Music was disqualified for interference and placed 9th.

Distaff

Year	Winner (Margin)	Jockey	Second	Third	Time
1984	Princess Rooney (7)	Eddie Delahoussaye	Life's Magic	Adored	2:02⅖
1985	Life's Magic (6¼)	Angel Cordero Jr.	Lady's Secret	Dontstop Themusic	2:02
1986	Lady's Secret (2½)	Pat Day	Fran's Valentine	Outstandingly	2:01⅕
1987	Sacahuista (2¼)	Randy Romero	Clabber Girl	Oueee Bebe	2:02⅘
1988	Personal Ensign (Nose)	Randy Romero	Winning Colors	Goodbye Halo	1:52
1989	Bayakoa (1½)	Laffit Pincay Jr.	Gorgeous	Open Mind	1:47⅖
1990	Bayakoa (6¾)	Laffit Pincay Jr.	Colonial Waters	Valay Maid	1:49⅕
1991	Dance Smarty (½)	Pat Day	Versailles Treaty	Brought to Mind	1:50⅘
1992	Paseana (4)	Chris McCarron	Versailles Treaty	Magical Maiden	1:48
1993	Hollywood Wildcat (Nose)	Eddie Delahoussaye	Paseana	Re Toss	1:48⅕
1994	One Dreamer (Neck)	Gary Stevens	Heavenly Prize	Miss Dominique	1:50⅗
1995	Inside Information (13½)	Mike Smith	Heavenly Prize	Lakeway	1:46
1996	Jewel Princess (1½)	Corey Nakatani	Serena's Song	Different	1:48⅖
1997	Ajina (2)	Mike Smith	Sharp Cat	Escena	1:47⅕
1998	Escena (Nose)	Gary Stevens	Banshee Breeze	Keeper Hill	1:49⅘
1999	Beautiful Pleasure (¾)	Jorge Chavez	Banshee Breeze	Heritage of Gold	1:47.56

Note: 1¼ miles (1984–87), 1⅛ miles (since 1988).

Turf

Year	Winner (Margin)	Jockey	Second	Third	Time
1984	Lashkari (Neck)	Yves St. Martin	All Along	Raami	2:25⅕
1985	Pebbles (Neck)	Pat Eddery	Strawberry Rd II	Mourjane	2:27
1986	Manila (Neck)	Jose Santos	Theatrical	Estrapade	2:25⅖
1987	Theatrical (½)	Pat Day	Trempolino	Village Star II	2:24⅖
1988	Great Communicator (½)	Ray Sibille	Sunshine Forever	Indian Skimmer	2:35⅕
1989	Prized (Head)	Eddie Delahoussaye	Sierra Roberta	Star Lift	2:28
1990	In the Wings (½)	Gary Stevens	With Approval	El Senor	2:29⅗
1991	Miss Alleged (2)	Eric Legrix	Itsallgreektome	Quest for Fame	2:30⅘
1992	Fraise (Nose)	Pat Valenzuela	Sky Classic	Quest For Fame	2:24
1993	Kotashaan (½)	Kent Desormeaux	Bien Bien	Luazar	2:25
1994	Tikkanen (1½)	Mike Smith	Hatoof	Paradise Creek	2:26⅖
1995	Northern Spur (Neck)	Chris McCarron	Freedom Cry	Carnegie	2:42
1996	Pilsudski (1¼)	Walter Swinburn	Singspiel	Swain	2:30⅕
1997	Chief Bearhart (¾)	Jose Santos	Borgia	Flag Down	2:23⅘
1998	Buck's Boy (1¼)	Shane Sellers	Yagli	Dushyantor	2:28⅗
1999	Daylami (2½)	Frankie Dettori	Royal Anthem	Buck's Boy	2:24.73

Note: 1½ miles.

Breeders' Cup *(Cont.)*

Classic

Year	Winner (Margin)	Jockey	Second	Third	Time
1984	Wild Again (Head)	Pat Day	Slew o' Gold*	Gate Dancer	2:03⅖
1985	Proud Truth (Head)	Jorge Velasquez	Gate Dancer	Turkoman	2:00⅘
1986	Skywalker (1¼)	Laffit Pincay Jr.	Turkoman	Precisionist	2:00⅖
1987	Ferdinand (Nose)	Bill Shoemaker	Alysheba	Judge Angelucci	2:01⅖
1988	Alysheba (Nose)	Chris McCarron	Seeking the Gold	Waquoit	2:04⅘
1989	Sunday Silence (½)	Chris McCarron	Easy Goer	Blushing John	2:00⅕
1990	Unbridled (1)	Pat Day	Ibn Bey	Thirty Six Red	2:02⅕
1991	Black Tie Affair (1¼)	Jerry Bailey	Twilight Agenda	Unbridled	2:02⅘
1992	A.P. Indy (2)	Eddie Delahoussaye	Pleasant Tap	Jolypha	2:00⅕
1993	Arcangues (2)	Jerry Bailey	Bertrando	Kissin Kris	2:00⅘
1994	Concern (Neck)	Jerry Bailey	Tabasco Cat	Dramatic Gold	2:02⅖
1995	Cigar (2½)	Jerry Bailey	L'Carriere	Unaccounted For	1:59⅖
1996	Alphabet Soup (Nose)	Chris McCarron	Louis Quatorze	Cigar	2:01
1997	Skip Away (6)	Mike Smith	Deputy Commander	Dowty	1:59⅕
1998	Awesome Again (¾)	Pat Day	Silver Charm	Swain	2:02
1999	Cat Thief (1¼)	Pat Day	Budroyale	Golden Missile	1:59.52

*2nd place finisher Gate Dancer was disqualified for interference and placed 3rd.

Note: 1¼ miles.

England's Triple Crown Winners

England's Triple Crown consists of the Two Thousand Guineas, held at Newmarket; the Epsom Derby, held at Epsom Downs; and the St. Leger Stakes, held at Doncaster.

Year	Horse	Owner	Year	Horse	Owner
1853	West Australian	Mr. Bowes	1900	Diamond Jubilee	Prince of Wales
1865	Gladiateur	F. DeLagrange	1903	*Rock Sand	J. Miller
1866	Lord Lyon	R. Sutton	1915	Pommern	S. Joel
1886	*Ormonde	Duke of Westminster	1917	Gay Crusader	Mr. Fairie
1891	Common	†F. Johnstone	1918	Gainsborough	Lady James Douglas
1893	Isinglass	H. McCalmont	1935	*Bahram	Aga Khan
1897	Galtee More	J. Gubbins	1970	‡Nijinsky II	C. W. Engelhard
1899	Flying Fox	Duke of Westminster			

*Imported into United States. †Raced in name of Lord Alington in Two Thousand Guineas. ‡Canadian-bred.

Catching Up With Spectacular Bid

It is a sad fact of horse racing that the best runners don't always make the best sires, that a champion's legend can be diminished by the quality of his genes. So it is with Spectacular Bid, a modestly bred colt who became one of the best racehorses of all time but who has been a spectacular flop at stud. From 1978 to '80 he won 13 Grade I stakes. In the last 20 years, however, his progeny have won just one, and his stud fee has fallen from a lofty $150,000 in '84 to only $3,500 in 2000. "He's still a legitimate stallion," insists veterinarian Jonathan Davis, the Bid's syndicate manager at Miller Farm in Unadilla, N.Y. "He just hasn't cloned himself."

—Mark Beech

Horse—Money Won

Year	Horse	Age	Starts	1st	2nd	3rd	Winnings ($)
1919	Sir Barton	3	13	8	3	2	88,250
1920	Man o' War	3	11	11	0	0	166,140
1921	Morvich	2	11	11	0	0	115,234
1922	Pillory	3	7	4	1	1	95,654
1923	Zev	3	14	12	1	0	272,008
1924	Sarzen	3	12	8	1	1	95,640
1925	Pompey	2	10	7	2	0	121,630
1926	Crusader	3	15	9	4	0	166,033
1927	Anita Peabody	2	7	6	0	1	111,905
1928	High Strung	2	6	5	0	0	153,590
1929	Blue Larkspur	3	6	4	1	0	153,450
1930	Gallant Fox	3	10	9	1	0	308,275
1931	Gallant Flight	2	7	7	0	0	219,000
1932	Gusto	3	16	4	3	2	145,940
1933	Singing Wood	2	9	3	2	2	88,050
1934	Cavalcade	3	7	6	1	0	111,235
1935	Omaha	3	9	6	1	2	142,255
1936	Granville	3	11	7	3	0	110,295
1937	Seabiscuit	4	15	11	2	2	168,580
1938	Stagehand	3	15	8	2	3	189,710
1939	Challedon	3	15	9	2	3	184,535
1940	Bimelech	3	7	4	2	1	110,005
1941	Whirlaway	3	20	13	5	2	272,386
1942	Shut Out	3	12	8	2	0	238,872
1943	Count Fleet	3	6	6	0	0	174,055
1944	Pavot	2	8	8	0	0	179,040
1945	Busher	3	13	10	2	1	273,735
1946	Assault	3	15	8	2	3	424,195
1947	Armed	6	17	11	4	1	376,325
1948	Citation	3	20	19	1	0	709,470
1949	Ponder	3	21	9	5	2	321,825
1950	Noor	5	12	7	4	1	346,940
1951	Counterpoint	3	15	7	2	1	250,525
1952	Crafty Admiral	4	16	9	4	1	277,225
1953	Native Dancer	3	10	9	1	0	513,425
1954	Determine	3	15	10	3	2	328,700
1955	Nashua	3	12	10	1	1	752,550
1956	Needles	3	8	4	2	0	440,850
1957	Round Table	3	22	15	1	3	600,383
1958	Round Table	4	20	14	4	0	662,780
1959	Sword Dancer	3	13	8	4	0	537,004
1960	Bally Ache	3	15	10	3	1	445,045
1961	Carry Back	3	16	9	1	3	565,349
1962	Never Bend	2	10	7	1	2	402,969
1963	Candy Spots	3	12	7	2	1	604,481
1964	Gun Bow	4	16	8	4	2	580,100
1965	Buckpasser	2	11	9	1	0	568,096
1966	Buckpasser	3	14	13	1	0	669,078
1967	Damascus	3	16	12	3	1	817,941
1968	Forward Pass	3	13	7	2	0	546,674
1969	Arts and Letters	3	14	8	5	1	555,604
1970	Personality	3	18	8	2	1	444,049
1971	Riva Ridge	2	9	7	0	0	503,263
1972	Droll Role	4	19	7	3	4	471,633
1973	Secretariat	3	12	9	2	1	860,404
1974	Chris Evert	3	8	5	1	2	551,063
1975	Foolish Pleasure	3	11	5	4	1	716,278
1976	Forego	6	8	6	1	1	401,701
1977	Seattle Slew	3	7	6	0	1	641,370
1978	Affirmed	3	11	8	2	0	901,541
1979	Spectacular Bid	3	12	10	1	1	1,279,334
1980	Temperence Hill	3	17	8	3	1	1,130,452
1981	John Henry	6	10	8	0	0	1,798,030
1982	Perrault	5	8	4	1	2	1,197,400
1983	All Along	4	7	4	1	1	2,138,963
1984	Slew o'Gold	4	6	5	1	0	2,627,944

Horse—Money Won *(Cont.)*

Year	Horse	Age	Starts	1st	2nd	3rd	Winnings ($)
1985	Spend A Buck	3	7	5	1	1	3,552,704
1986	Snow Chief	3	9	6	1	1	1,875,200
1987	Alysheba	3	10	3	3	1	2,511,156
1988	Alysheba	4	9	7	1	0	3,808,600
1989	Sunday Silence	3	9	7	2	0	4,578,454
1990	Unbridled	3	11	4	3	2	3,718,149
1991	Dance Smartly	3	8	8	0	0	2,876,821
1992	A.P. Indy	3	7	5	0	1	2,622,560
1993	Kotashaan	3	10	6	3	0	2,619,014
1994	Paradise Creek	5	11	8	2	1	2,610,187
1995	Cigar	5	10	10	0	0	4,819,800
1996	Cigar	6	8	5	2	1	4,910,000
1997	Skip Away	4	11	4	5	2	4,089,000
1998	Silver Charm	4	9	6	2	0	4,696,506
1999	Almutawakel	4	4	1	1	1	3,290,000

Trainer—Money Won

Year	Trainer	Wins	Winnings ($)	Year	Trainer	Wins	Winnings ($)
1908	James Rowe, Sr.	50	284,335	1955	Sunny Jim Fitzsimmons	66	1,270,055
1909	Sam Hildreth	73	123,942	1956	Willie Molter	142	1,227,402
1910	Sam Hildreth	84	148,010	1957	Jimmy Jones	70	1,150,910
1911	Sam Hildreth	67	49,418	1958	Willie Molter	69	1,116,544
1912	John F. Schorr	63	58,110	1959	Willie Molter	71	847,290
1913	James Rowe, Sr.	18	45,936	1960	Hirsch Jacobs	97	748,349
1914	R. C. Benson	45	59,315	1961	Jimmy Jones	62	759,856
1915	James Rowe, Sr.	19	75,596	1962	Mesh Tenney	58	1,099,474
1916	Sam Hildreth	39	70,950	1963	Mesh Tenney	40	860,703
1917	Sam Hildreth	23	61,698	1964	Bill Winfrey	61	1,350,534
1918	H. Guy Bedwell	53	80,296	1965	Hirsch Jacobs	91	1,331,628
1919	H. Guy Bedwell	63	208,728	1966	Eddie Neloy	93	2,456,250
1920	L. Feustal	22	186,087	1967	Eddie Neloy	72	1,776,089
1921	Sam Hildreth	85	262,768	1968	Eddie Neloy	52	1,233,101
1922	Sam Hildreth	74	247,014	1969	Elliott Burch	26	1,067,936
1923	Sam Hildreth	75	392,124	1970	Charlie Whittingham	82	1,302,354
1924	Sam Hildreth	77	255,608	1971	Charlie Whittingham	77	1,737,115
1925	G. R. Tompkins	30	199,245	1972	Charlie Whittingham	79	1,734,020
1926	Scott P. Harlan	21	205,681	1973	Charlie Whittingham	85	1,865,385
1927	W. H. Bringloe	63	216,563	1974	Pancho Martin	166	2,408,419
1928	John F. Schorr	65	258,425	1975	Charlie Whittingham	93	2,437,244
1929	James Rowe, Jr.	25	314,881	1976	Jack Van Berg	496	2,976,196
1930	Sunny Jim Fitzsimmons	47	397,355	1977	Laz Barrera	127	2,715,848
1931	Big Jim Healey	33	297,300	1978	Laz Barrera	100	3,307,164
1932	Sunny Jim Fitzsimmons	68	266,650	1979	Laz Barrera	98	3,608,517
1933	Humming Bob Smith	53	135,720	1980	Laz Barrera	99	2,969,151
1934	Humming Bob Smith	43	249,938	1981	Charlie Whittingham	74	3,993,300
1935	Bud Stotler	87	303,005	1982	Charlie Whittingham	63	4,587,457
1936	Sunny Jim Fitzsimmons	42	193,415	1983	D. Wayne Lukas	78	4,267,261
1937	Robert McGarvey	46	209,925	1984	D. Wayne Lukas	131	5,835,921
1938	Earl Sande	15	226,495	1985	D. Wayne Lukas	218	11,155,188
1939	Sunny Jim Fitzsimmons	45	266,205	1986	D. Wayne Lukas	259	12,345,180
1940	Silent Tom Smith	14	269,200	1987	D. Wayne Lukas	343	17,502,110
1941	Plain Ben Jones	70	475,318	1988	D. Wayne Lukas	318	17,842,358
1942	John M. Gaver Sr.	48	406,547	1989	D. Wayne Lukas	305	16,103,998
1943	Plain Ben Jones	73	267,915	1990	D. Wayne Lukas	267	14,508,871
1944	Plain Ben Jones	60	601,660	1991	D. Wayne Lukas	289	15,942,223
1945	Silent Tom Smith	52	510,655	1992	D. Wayne Lukas	230	9,806,436
1946	Hirsch Jacobs	99	560,077	1993	Robert Frankel	79	8,883,252
1947	Jimmy Jones	85	1,334,805	1994	D. Wayne Lukas	147	9,247,457
1948	Jimmy Jones	81	1,118,670	1995	D. Wayne Lukas	194	12,842,865
1949	Jimmy Jones	76	978,587	1996	D. Wayne Lukas	192	15,966,344
1950	Preston Burch	96	637,754	1997	D. Wayne Lukas	175	10,338,957
1951	John M. Gaver Sr.	42	616,392	1998	Bob Baffert	139	15,000,870
1952	Plain Ben Jones	29	662,137	1999	Bob Baffert	169	16,934,607
1953	Harry Trotsek	54	1,028,873				
1954	Willie Molter	136	1,107,860				

Jockey—Money Won

Year	Jockey	Mts	1st	2nd	3rd	Pct	Winnings ($)
1919	John Loftus	177	65	36	24	.37	252,707
1920	Clarence Kummer	353	87	79	48	.25	292,376
1921	Earl Sande	340	112	69	59	.33	263,043
1922	Albert Johnson	297	43	57	40	.14	345,054
1923	Earl Sande	430	122	89	79	.28	569,394
1924	Ivan Parke	844	205	175	121	.24	290,395
1925	Laverne Fator	315	81	54	44	.26	305,775
1926	Laverne Fator	511	143	90	86	.28	361,435
1927	Earl Sande	179	49	33	19	.27	277,877
1928	Pony McAtee	235	55	43	25	.23	301,295
1929	Mack Garner	274	57	39	33	.21	314,975
1930	Sonny Workman	571	152	88	79	.27	420,438
1931	Charles Kurtsinger	519	93	82	79	.18	392,095
1932	Sonny Workman	378	87	48	55	.23	385,070
1933	Robert Jones	471	63	57	70	.13	226,285
1934	Wayne D. Wright	919	174	154	114	.19	287,185
1935	Silvio Coucci	749	141	125	103	.19	319,760
1936	Wayne D. Wright	670	100	102	73	.15	264,000
1937	Charles Kurtsinger	765	120	94	106	.16	384,202
1938	Nick Wall	658	97	94	82	.15	385,161
1939	Basil James	904	191	165	105	.21	353,333
1940	Eddie Arcaro	783	132	143	112	.17	343,661
1941	Don Meade	1,164	210	185	158	.18	398,627
1942	Eddie Arcaro	687	123	97	89	.18	481,949
1943	John Longden	871	173	140	121	.20	573,276
1944	Ted Atkinson	1,539	287	231	213	.19	899,101
1945	John Longden	778	180	112	100	.23	981,977
1946	Ted Atkinson	1,377	233	213	173	.17	1,036,825
1947	Douglas Dodson	646	141	100	75	.22	1,429,949
1948	Eddie Arcaro	726	188	108	98	.26	1,686,230
1949	Steve Brooks	906	209	172	110	.23	1,316,817
1950	Eddie Arcaro	888	195	153	144	.22	1,410,160
1951	Bill Shoemaker	1,161	257	197	161	.22	1,329,890
1952	Eddie Arcaro	807	188	122	109	.23	1,859,591
1953	Bill Shoemaker	1,683	485	302	210	.29	1,784,187
1954	Bill Shoemaker	1,251	380	221	142	.30	1,876,760
1955	Eddie Arcaro	820	158	126	108	.19	1,864,796
1956	Bill Hartack	1,387	347	252	184	.25	2,343,955
1957	Bill Hartack	1,238	341	208	178	.28	3,060,501
1958	Bill Shoemaker	1,133	300	185	137	.26	2,961,693
1959	Bill Shoemaker	1,285	347	230	159	.27	2,843,133
1960	Bill Shoemaker	1,227	274	196	158	.22	2,123,961
1961	Bill Shoemaker	1,256	304	186	175	.24	2,690,819
1962	Bill Shoemaker	1,126	311	156	128	.28	2,916,844
1963	Bill Shoemaker	1,203	271	193	137	.22	2,526,925
1964	Bill Shoemaker	1,056	246	147	133	.23	2,649,553
1965	Braulio Baeza	1,245	270	200	201	.22	2,582,702
1966	Braulio Baeza	1,341	298	222	190	.22	2,951,022
1967	Braulio Baeza	1,064	256	184	127	.24	3,088,888
1968	Braulio Baeza	1,089	201	184	145	.18	2,835,108
1969	Jorge Velasquez	1,442	258	230	204	.18	2,542,315
1970	Laffit Pincay Jr.	1,328	269	208	187	.20	2,626,526
1971	Laffit Pincay Jr.	1,627	380	288	214	.23	3,784,377
1972	Laffit Pincay Jr.	1,388	289	215	205	.21	3,225,827
1973	Laffit Pincay Jr.	1,444	350	254	209	.24	4,093,492
1974	Laffit Pincay Jr.	1,278	341	227	180	.27	4,251,060
1975	Braulio Baeza	1,190	196	208	180	.16	3,674,398
1976	Angel Cordero Jr.	1,534	274	273	235	.18	4,709,500
1977	Steve Cauthen	2,075	487	345	304	.23	6,151,750
1978	Darrel McHargue	1,762	375	294	263	.21	6,188,353
1979	Laffit Pincay Jr.	1,708	420	302	261	.25	8,183,535
1980	Chris McCarron	1,964	405	318	282	.20	7,666,100
1981	Chris McCarron	1,494	326	251	207	.22	8,397,604
1982	Angel Cordero Jr.	1,838	397	338	227	.22	9,702,520
1983	Angel Cordero Jr.	1,792	362	296	237	.20	10,116,807
1984	Chris McCarron	1,565	356	276	218	.23	12,038,213
1985	Laffit Pincay Jr.	1,409	289	246	183	.21	13,415,049

Jockey—Money Won (Cont.)

Year	Jockey	Mts	1st	2nd	3rd	Pct	Winnings ($)
1986...........Jose Santos		1,636	329	237	222	.20	11,329,297
1987...........Jose Santos		1,639	305	268	208	.19	12,407,355
1988...........Jose Santos		1,867	370	287	265	.20	14,877,298
1989...........Jose Santos		1,459	285	238	220	.20	13,847,003
1990...........Gary Stevens		1,504	283	245	202	.19	13,881,198
1991...........Chris McCarron		1,440	265	228	206	.18	14,441,083
1992...........Kent Desormeaux		1,568	361	260	208	.23	14,193,006
1993...........Mike Smith		1,510	343	235	214	.23	14,008,148
1994...........Mike Smith		1,484	317	250	196	.21	15,979,820
1995...........Jerry Bailey		1,265	287	193	144	.23	16,308,230
1996...........Jerry Bailey		1,187	298	189	165	.25	19,465,376
1997...........Jerry Bailey		1,143	272	186	178	.26	18,260,553
1998...........Gary Stevens		869	178	145	122	.20	19,358,840
1999...........Pat Day		1,265	254	209	209	.20	18,092,845

Jockey—Races Won

Year	Jockey	Mts	1st	2nd	3rd	Pct
1895...........J. Perkins		762	192	177	129	.25
1896...........J. Scherrer		1,093	271	227	172	.24
1897...........H. Martin		803	173	152	116	.21
1898...........T. Burns		973	277	213	149	.28
1899...........T. Burns		1,064	273	173	266	.26
1900...........C. Mitchell		874	195	140	139	.23
1901...........W. O'Connor		1,047	253	221	192	.24
1902...........J. Ranch		1,069	276	205	181	.26
1903...........G.C. Fuller		918	229	152	122	.25
1904...........E. Hildebrand		1,169	297	230	171	.25
1905...........D. Nicol		861	221	143	136	.26
1906...........W. Miller		1,384	388	300	199	.28
1907...........W. Miller		1,194	334	226	170	.28
1908...........V. Powers		1,260	324	204	185	.26
1909...........V. Powers		704	173	121	114	.25
1910...........G. Garner		947	200	188	153	.20
1911...........T. Koerner		813	162	133	112	.20
1912...........P. Hill		967	168	141	129	.17
1913...........M. Buxton		887	146	131	136	.16
1914...........J. McTaggart		787	157	132	106	.20
1915...........M. Garner		775	151	118	90	.19
1916...........F. Robinson		791	178	131	124	.23
1917...........W. Crump		803	151	140	101	.19
1918...........F. Robinson		864	185	140	108	.21
1919...........C. Robinson		896	190	140	126	.21
1920...........J. Butwell		721	152	129	139	.21
1921...........C. Lang		696	135	110	105	.19
1922...........M. Fator		859	188	153	116	.22
1923...........I. Parke		718	173	105	95	.24
1924...........I. Parke		844	205	175	121	.24
1925...........A. Mortensen		987	187	145	138	.19
1926...........R. Jones		1,172	190	163	152	.16
1927...........L. Hardy		1,130	207	192	151	.18
1928...........J. Inzelone		1,052	155	152	135	.15
1929...........M. Knight		871	149	132	133	.17
1930...........H.R. Riley		861	177	145	123	.21
1931...........H. Roble		1,174	173	173	155	.15
1932...........J. Gilbert		1,050	212	144	160	.20
1933...........J. Westrope		1,224	301	235	166	.25
1934...........M. Peters		1,045	221	179	147	.21
1935...........C. Stevenson		1,099	206	169	146	.19
1936...........B. James		1,106	245	195	161	.22
1937...........J. Adams		1,265	260	186	177	.21
1938...........J. Longden		1,150	236	168	171	.21
1939...........D. Meade		1,284	255	221	180	.20
1940...........E. Dew		1,377	287	201	180	.21
1941...........D. Meade		1,164	210	185	158	.18
1942...........J. Adams		1,120	245	185	150	.22
1943...........J. Adams		1,069	228	159	171	.21

Jockey—Races Won (Cont.)

Year	Jockey	Mts	1st	2nd	3rd	Pct
1944	T. Atkinson	1,539	287	231	213	.19
1945	J.D. Jessop	1,085	290	182	168	.27
1946	T. Atkinson	1,377	233	213	173	.17
1947	J. Longden	1,327	316	250	195	.24
1948	J. Longden	1,197	319	233	161	.27
1949	G. Glisson	1,347	270	217	181	.20
1950	W. Shoemaker	1,640	388	266	230	.24
1951	C. Burr	1,319	310	232	192	.24
1952	A. DeSpirito	1,482	390	247	212	.26
1953	W. Shoemaker	1,683	485	302	210	.29
1954	W. Shoemaker	1,251	380	221	142	.30
1955	W. Hartack	1,702	417	298	215	.25
1956	W. Hartack	1,387	347	252	184	.25
1957	W. Hartack	1,238	341	208	178	.28
1958	W. Shoemaker	1,133	300	185	137	.26
1959	W. Shoemaker	1,285	347	230	159	.27
1960	W. Hartack	1,402	307	247	190	.22
1961	J. Sellers	1,394	328	212	227	.24
1962	R. Ferraro	1,755	352	252	226	.20
1963	W. Blum	1,704	360	286	215	.21
1964	W. Blum	1,577	324	274	170	.21
1965	J. Davidson	1,582	319	228	190	.20
1966	A. Gomez	996	318	173	142	.32
1967	J. Velasquez	1,939	438	315	270	.23
1968	A. Cordero Jr.	1,662	345	278	219	.21
1969	L. Snyder	1,645	352	290	243	.21
1970	S. Hawley	1,908	452	313	265	.24
1971	L Pincay Jr.	1,627	380	288	214	.23
1972	S. Hawley	1,381	367	269	200	.27
1973	S. Hawley	1,925	515	336	292	.27
1974	C.J. McCarron	2,199	546	392	297	.25
1975	C.J. McCarron	2,194	458	389	305	.21
1976	S. Hawley	1,637	413	245	201	.25
1977	S. Cauthen	2,075	487	345	304	.23
1978	E. Delahoussaye	1,666	384	285	238	.23
1979	D. Gall	2,146	479	396	326	.22
1980	C.J. McCarron	1,964	405	318	282	.20
1981	D. Gall	1,917	376	305	297	.20
1982	Pat Day	1,870	399	326	255	.21
1983	Pat Day	1,725	454	321	251	.26
1984	Pat Day	1,694	399	296	259	.24
1985	C.W. Antley	2,335	469	371	288	.20
1986	Pat Day	1,417	429	246	202	.30
1987	Kent Desormeaux	2,207	450	370	294	.28
1988	Kent Desormeaux	1,897	474	295	276	.25
1989	Kent Desormeaux	2,312	598	385	309	.25
1990	Pat Day	1,421	364	265	222	.26
1991	Pat Day	1,405	430	256	213	.31
1992	Russell Baze	1,691	433	296	237	.25
1993	Russell Baze	1,579	410	297	225	.26
1994	Russell Baze	1,588	415	301	266	.26
1995	Russell Baze	1,531	445	310	232	.29
1996	Russell Baze	1,482	415	297	200	.28
1997	Edgar S. Prado	2,037	533	384	308	.26
1998	Edgar S. Prado	1,969	470	377	285	.23
1999	Edgar S. Prado	1,902	402	307	276	.21

Leading Jockeys—Career Records

Jockey	Years Riding	Mts	1st	2nd	3rd	Win Pct	Winnings ($)
Laffit Pincay Jr.	35	45,488	8,979	7,339	6,266	.197	213,103,177
Bill Shoemaker (1990)	42	40,350	8,833	6,136	4,987	.219	123,375,524
Pat Day	28	35,726	7,805	6,063	5,097	.218	236,390,728
Dave Gall (1999)	41	41,775	7,396	6,525	6,131	.177	24,547,584
Russell Baze	27	34,084	7,080	5,583	4,813	.208	101,432,051
Angel Cordero (1992)	31	38,646	7,057	6,136	5,359	.183	164,561,227
Chris McCarron	26	33,176	6,928	5,501	4,532	.209	240,973,258
Jorge Velasquez (1998)	35	40,852	6,795	6,178	5,755	.166	125,544,379
Sandy Hawley (1998)	31	31,455	6,449	4,825	4,159	.205	88,681,292
Larry Snyder (1994)	35	35,681	6,388	5,030	3,440	.179	47,207,289
Carl Gambardella (1994)	39	39,018	6,349	5,953	5,353	.163	29,389,041
Eddie Delahoussaye	31	37,698	6,161	5,451	5,342	.163	179,708,129
Earlie Fires	36	42,228	6,133	5,214	5,029	.145	76,773,945
John Longden (1966)	40	32,413	6,032	4,914	4,273	.186	24,665,800
Jacinto Vasquez (1998)	38	37,390	5,231	4,721	4,513	.140	80,764,853
Ron Ardoin	28	30,624	5,012	4,134	3,597	.164	55,019,480
Jerry Bailey	27	26,826	4,876	3,819	3,356	.182	194,492,461
Rodolfo Baez (1999)	26	28,609	4,875	4,291	4,103	.170	30,039,543
Eddie Arcaro (1961)	31	24,092	4,779	3,807	3,302	.198	30,039,543
Rick Wilson	29	33,045	4,612	3,963	3,225	.140	67,437,068
Don Brumfield (1989)	37	33,223	4,573	4,076	3,758	.138	43,567,861
Gary Stevens (1999)	26	25,443	4,511	4,024	3,652	.177	187,176,371
Steve Brooks (1975)	34	30,330	4,451	4,219	3,658	.147	18,239,817
Eddie Maple (1998)	31	33,974	4,398	4,516	4,335	.129	105,338,573

Note: Records go through September 10,1999, and include available statistics for races ridden in foreign countries. Figures in parentheses after jockey's name indicate last year in which he rode.

Leading jockeys courtesy of *National Thoroughbred Racing Association*.

An Early End to A Stellar Career

After all he had been through—the months of throbbing pain in his knees—jockey Gary Stevens finally conceded in early 2000 that degenerative arthritis would prematurely end his surpassing career. "It's hard when you've done something for 21 years and suddenly you can't do it anymore," Stevens said. "I'm only 37, and it was just taken away. It's bone on bone now, a lot of poppin' and grindin' goin' on. And a lot of depression."

Only three years earlier, in 1997, Stevens had it all—the smarts and style reminiscent of the old master Eddie Aracaro, the movie-star smile and good looks and a reputation as the finest money rider in North America, if not the world. That was the year that Stevens, just voted into racing's Hall of Fame, won his third Kentucky Derby, on Silver Charm. But it was also the year doctors performed the first of three surgeries on his right knee. Though in increasing pain while crouching on horses, he did not yield a centimeter in the hottest winds of combat. In '98 he won the Dubai World Cup on Silver Charm as well as The Belmont on Victory Gallop, and that fall he won his fifth and sixth Breeders' Cup races.

In the summer of 1999, hoping that riding full time on soft grass might prolong his career, Stevens moved to England. But the torturous, undulating courses—not to mention the damp, chilly weather—exacerbated his miseries. That notwithstanding, Stevens made his mark in Europe, winning 12 graded stakes, and had himself a royal ball. In the walking ring at Ascot in June 1999, as Stevens was waiting to board a mount named Blueprint, the horse's owner instructed him to lie fourth until the final straight. "Wait until about a furlong out to make your move," Queen Elizabeth II told him.

Recalled Stevens, "I just did what the Queen told me and won it. What a racing memory."

There were far fewer in his future than anyone might have imagined. He hobbled to the Breeders' Cup on November 6, 1999, at Gulfstream Park. "That morning my knee was so swollen I couldn't bend it," he says. Still he rode Anees to a 2½-length win in the Cup Juvenile, his last major victory. On Dec. 26 at Santa Anita, following his third knee operation, Stevens tried to come back, but the pain was too much.

HORSES

Ack Ack (1986, 1966)
Affectionately (1989, 1960)
Affirmed (1980, 1975)
All Along (1990, 1979)
Alsab (1976, 1939)
Alydar (1989, 1975)
Alysheba (1993, 1984)
American Eclipse (1970, 1814)
A.P. Indy (2000, 1989)
Armed (1963, 1941)
Artful (1956, 1902)
Arts and Letters (1994, 1966)
Assault (1964, 1943)
Battleship (1969, 1927)
Bayakoa (1998, 1984)
Bed o' Roses (1976, 1947)
Beldame (1956, 1901)
Ben Brush (1955, 1893)
Bewitch (1977, 1945)
Bimelech (1990, 1937)
Black Gold (1989, 1921)
Black Helen (1991, 1932)
Blue Larkspur (1957, 1926)
Bold 'n Determined (1997, 1977)
Bold Ruler (1973, 1954)
Bon Nouvel (1976, 1960)
Boston (1955, 1833)
Broomstick (1956, 1901)
Buckpasser (1970, 1963)
Busher (1964, 1942)
Bushranger (1967, 1930)
Cafe Prince (1985, 1970)
Carry Back (1975, 1958)
Cavalcade (1993, 1931)
Challedon (1977, 1936)
Chris Evert (1988, 1971)
Cicada (1967, 1959)
Citation (1959, 1945)
Coaltown (1983, 1945)
Colin (1956, 1905)
Commando (1956, 1898)
Count Fleet (1961, 1940)
Crusader (1995, 1923)
Dahlia (1981, 1970)
Damascus (1974, 1964)
Dark Mirage (1974, 1965)
Davona Dale (1985, 1976)
Desert Vixen (1979, 1970)
Devil Diver (1980, 1939)
Discovery (1969, 1931)
Domino (1955, 1891)
Dr. Fager (1971, 1964)
Easy Goer (1997, 1986)
Eight Thirty (1994, 1936)

Elkridge (1966, 1938)
Emperor of Norfolk (1988, 1885)
Equipoise (1957, 1928)
Exceller (1999, 1973)
Exterminator (1957, 1915)
Fairmount (1985, 1921)
Fair Play (1956, 1905)
Fashion (1980, 1837)
Firenze (1981, 1884)
Flatterer (1994, 1979)
Foolish Pleasure (1995, 1972)
Forego (1979, 1970)
Fort Marcy (1998, 1964)
Gallant Bloom (1977, 1966)
Gallant Fox (1957, 1927)
Gallant Man (1987, 1954)
Gallorette (1962, 1942)
Gamely (1980, 1964)
Genuine Risk (1986, 1977)
Go For Wand (1996, 1987)
Good and Plenty (1956, 1900)
Grandville (1997, 1933)
Grey Lag (1957, 1918)
Gun Bow (1999, 1960)
Hamburg (1986, 1895)
Hanover (1955, 1884)
Henry of Navarre (1985, 1891)
Hill Prince (1991, 1947)
Hindoo (1955, 1878)
Imp (1965, 1894)
Jay Trump (1971, 1957)
John Henry (1990, 1975)
Johnstown (1992, 1936)
Jolly Roger (1965, 1922)
Kelso (1967, 1957)
Kentucky (1983, 1861)
Kingston (1955, 1884)
Lady's Secret (1992, 1982)
La Prevoyante (1995, 1970)
L'Escargot (1977, 1963)
Lexington (1955, 1850)
Longfellow (1971, 1867)
Luke Blackburn (1956, 1877)
Majestic Prince (1988, 1966)
Man o' War (1957, 1917)
Miesque (1999, 1984)
Miss Woodford (1967, 1880)
Myrtlewood (1979, 1932)
Nashua (1965, 1952)
Native Dancer (1963, 1950)
Native Diver (1978, 1959)
Needles (2000, 1953)
Neji (1966, 1950)
Northern Dancer (1976, 1961)

Oedipus (1978, 1946)
Old Rosebud (1968, 1911)
Omaha (1965, 1932)
Pan Zareta (1972, 1910)
Parole (1984, 1873)
Personal Ensign (1993, 1984)
Peter Pan (1956, 1904)
Princess Doreen (1982, 1921)
Princess Rooney (1991, 1980)
Real Delight (1987, 1949)
Regret (1957, 1912)
Reigh Count (1978, 1923)
Riva Ridge (1998, 1969)
Roamer (1981, 1911)
Roseben (1956, 1901)
Round Table (1972, 1954)
Ruffian (1976, 1972)
Ruthless (1975, 1864)
Salvator (1955, 1886)
Sarazen (1957, 1921)
Seabiscuit (1958, 1933)
Searching (1978, 1952)
Seattle Slew (1981, 1974)
Secretariat (1974, 1970)
Shuvee (1975, 1966)
Silver Spoon (1978, 1956)
Sir Archy (1955, 1805)
Sir Barton (1957, 1916)
Slew o' Gold (1992, 1980)
Spectacular Bid (1982, 1976)
Stymie (1975, 1941)
Sun Beau (1996, 1925)
Sunday Silence (1996, 1986)
Susan's Girl (1976, 1969)
Swaps (1966, 1952)
Sword Dancer (1977, 1956)
Sysonby (1956, 1902)
Ta Wee (1994, 1967)
Ten Broeck (1982, 1872)
Tim Tam (1985, 1955)
Tom Fool (1960, 1949)
Top Flight (1966, 1929)
Tosmah (1984, 1961)
Twenty Grand (1957, 1928)
Twilight Tear (1963, 1941)
Two Lea (1982, 1946)
War Admiral (1958, 1934)
Whirlaway (1959, 1938)
Whisk Broom II (1979, 1907)
Winning Colors (2000, 1985)
Zaccio (1990, 1976)
Zev (1983, 1920)

Note: Years of election and foaling in parentheses.

HARNESS RACING

Major Races

Hambletonian

Year	Winner	Driver	Year	Winner	Driver
1926	Guy McKinney	Nat Ray	1964	Ayres	J. Simpson Sr.
1927	Iosola's Worthy	Marvin Childs	1965	Egyptian Candor	Del Cameron
1928	Spenser	W. H. Leese	1966	Kerry Way	Frank Ervin
1929	Walter Dear	Walter Cox	1967	Speedy Streak	Del Cameron
1930	Hanover's Bertha	Tom Berry	1968	Nevele Pride	Stanley Dancer
1931	Calumet Butler	R. D. McMahon	1969	Lindy's Pride	H. Beissinger
1932	The Marchioness	William Caton	1970	Timothy T.	J. Simpson Jr.
1933	Mary Reynolds	Ben White	1971	Speedy Crown	H. Beissinger
1934	Lord Jim	Doc Parshall	1972	Super Bowl	Stanley Dancer
1935	Greyhound	Sep Palin	1973	Flirth	Ralph Baldwin
1936	Rosalind	Ben White	1974	Christopher T.	Bill Haughton
1937	Shirley Hanover	Henry Thomas	1975	Bonefish	Stanley Dancer
1938	McLin Hanover	Henry Thomas	1976	Steve Lobell	Bill Haughton
1939	Peter Astra	Doc Parshall	1977	Green Speed	Bill Haughton
1940	Spencer Scott	Fred Egan	1978	Speedy Somolli	H. Beissinger
1941	Bill Gallon	Lee Smith	1979	Legend Hanover	George Sholty
1942	The Ambassador	Ben White	1980	Burgomeister	Bill Haughton
1943	Volo Song	Ben White	1981	Shiaway St. Pat	Ray Remmen
1944	Yankee Maid	Henry Thomas	1982	Speed Bowl	Tom Haughton
1945	Titan Hanover	H. Pownall Sr.	1983	Duenna	Stanley Dancer
1946	Chestertown	Thomas Berry	1984	Historic Freight	Ben Webster
1947	Hoot Mon	Sep Palin	1985	Prakas	Bill O'Donnell
1948	Demon Hanover	Harrison Hoyt	1986	Nuclear Kosmos	Ulf Thoresen
1949	Miss Tilly	Fred Egan	1987	Mack Lobell	John Campbell
1950	Lusty Song	Del Miller	1988	Armbro Goal	John Campbell
1951	Mainliner	Guy Crippen	1989	Park Ave. Joe/Probe*	R. Waples/B. Fahy
1952	Sharp Note	Bion Shively	1990	Harmonious	John Campbell
1953	Helicopter	Harry Harvey	1991	Giant Victory	Jack Moiseyev
1954	Newport Dream	Del Cameron	1992	Alf Palema	Mickey McNichol
1955	Scott Frost	Joe O'Brien	1993	American Winner	Ron Pierce
1956	The Intruder	Ned Bower	1994	Victory Dream	Michel Lachance
1957	Hickory Smoke	J. Simpson Sr.	1995	Tagliabue	John Campbell
1958	Emily's Pride	Flave Nipe	1996	Continentalvictory	Michel Lachance
1959	Diller Hanover	Frank Ervin	1997	Malabar Man	Mal Burroughs
1960	Blaze Hanover	Joe O'Brien	1998	Muscles Yankee	John Campbell
1961	Harlan Dean	James Arthur	1999	Self Possessed	Michel Lachance
1962	A. C.'s Viking	Sanders Russell	2000	Yankee Paco	T.J. Ritchie
1963	Speedy Scot	Ralph Baldwin			

*Park Avenue Joe and Probe dead-heated for win. Park Avenue finished first in the summary 2-1-1 to Probe's 1-9-1 finish.
Note: Run at 1 mile since 1947.

Little Brown Jug

Year	Winner	Driver	Year	Winner	Driver
1946	Ensign Hanover	Wayne Smart	1967	Best of All	James Hackett
1947	Forbes Chief	Del Cameron	1968	Rum Customer	Bill Haughton
1948	Knight Dream	Frank Safford	1969	Laverne Hanover	Bill Haughton
1949	Good Time	Frank Ervin	1970	Most Happy Fella	Stanley Dancer
1950	Dudley Hanover	Del Miller	1971	Nansemond	Herve Filion
1951	Tar Heel	Del Cameron	1972	Strike Out	Keith Waples
1952	Meadow Rice	Wayne Smart	1973	Melvin's Woe	Joe O'Brien
1953	Keystoner	Frank Ervin	1974	Armbro Omaha	Bill Haughton
1954	Adios Harry	Morris MacDonald	1975	Seatrain	Ben Webster
1955	Quick Chief	Bill Haughton	1976	Keystone Ore	Stanley Dancer
1956	Noble Adios	John Simpson Sr.	1977	Governor Skipper	John Chapman
1957	Torpid	John Simpso Sr.	1978	Happy Escort	William Popfinger
1958	Shadow Wave	Joe O'Brien	1979	Hot Hitter	Herve Filion
1959	Adios Butler	Clint Hodgins	1980	Niatross	Clint Galbraith
1960	Bullet Hanover	John Simpson Sr.	1981	Fan Hanover	Glen Garnsey
1961	Henry T. Adios	Stanley Dancer	1982	Merger	John Campbell
1962	Lehigh Hanover	Stanley Dancer	1983	Ralph Hanover	Ron Waples
1963	Overtrick	John Patterson	1984	Colt Fortysix	Chris Boring
1964	Vicar Hanover	Bill Haughton	1985	Nihilator	Bill O'Donnell
1965	Bret Hanover	Frank Ervin	1986	Barberry Spur	Bill O'Donnell
1966	Romeo Hanover	George Sholty	1987	Jaguar Spur	Dick Stillings

Little Brown Jug (Cont.)

Year	Winner	Driver	Year	Winner	Driver
1988	B. J. Scoot	Michel Lachance	1995	Nick's Fantasy	John Campbell
1989	Goalie Jeff	Michel Lachance	1996	Armbro Operative	Jack Moiseyev
1990	Beach Towel	Ray Remmen	1997	Western Dreamer	Michel Lachance
1991	Precious Bunny	Jack Moiseye	1998	Shady Character	Ron Pierce
1992	Fake Left	Ron Waples	1999	Blissful Hall	Ron Pierce
1993	Life Sign	John Campbell	2000	Astreos	Chris Christoforou
1994	Magical Mike	Michel Lachance			

Breeders' Crown

1984

Div	Winner	Driver
2PC	Dragon's Lair	Jeff Mallet
2PF	Amneris	John Campbell
3PC	Troublemaker	Bill O'Donnell
3PF	Naughty But Nice	Tommy Haughton
2TC	Workaholic	Berndt Lindstedt
2TF	Conifer	George Sholty
3TC	Baltic Speed	Jan Nordin
3TF	Fancy Crown	Bill O'Donnell

1985

Div	Winner	Driver
2PC	Robust Hanover	John Campbell
2PF	Caressable	Herve Filion
3PC	Nihilator	Bill O'Donnell
3PF	Stienam	Buddy Gilmour
2TC	Express Ride	John Campbell
2TF	JEF's Spice	Mickey McNichol
3TC	Prakas	John Campbell
3TF	Armbro Devona	Bill O'Donnell
AP	Division Street	Michel Lachance
AT	Sandy Bowl	John Campbell

1986

Div	Winner	Driver
2PC	Sunset Warrior	Bill Gale
2PF	Halcyon	Ray Remmen
3PC	Masquerade	Richard Silverman
3PF	Glow Softly	Ron Waples
2TC	Mack Lobell	John Campbell
2TF	Super Flora	Ron Waples
3TC	Sugarcane Hanover	Ron Waples
3TF	JEF's Spice	Bill O'Donnell
APM	Samshu Bluegrass	Michel Lachance
ATM	Grades Singing	Herve Filion
APH	Forrest Skipper	Lucien Fontaine
ATH	Nearly Perfect	Mickey McNichol

1987

Div	Winner	Driver
2PC	Camtastic	Bill O'Donnell
2PF	Leah Almahurst	Bill Fahy
3PC	Call For Rain	Clint Galbraith
3PF	Pacific	Tom Harmer
2TC	Defiant One	Howard Beissinger
2TF	Nan's Catch	Berndt Lindstedt
3TC	Mack Lobell	John Campbell
3TF	Armbro Fling	George Sholty
APM	Follow My Star	John Campbell
ATM	Grades Singing	Olle Goop
APH	Armbro Emerson	Walter Whelan
ATH	Sugarcane Hanover	Ron Waples

1988

Div	Winner	Driver
2PC	Kentucky Spur	Dick Stillings
2PF	Central Park West	John Campbell
3PC	Camtastic	Bill O'Donnell
3PF	Sweet Reflection	Bill O'Donnell
2TC	Valley Victory	Bill O'Donnell
2TF	Peace Corps	John Campbell
3TC	Firm Tribute	Mark O'Mara
3TF	Nalda Hanover	Mickey McNichol
APM	Anniecrombie	Dave Magee
ATM	Armbro Flori	Larry Walker
APH	Call For Rain	Clint Galbraith
ATH	Mack Lobell	John Campbell

1989

Div	Winner	Driver
2PC	Till We Meet Again	Mickey McNichol
2PF	Town Pro	Doug Brown
3PC	Goalie Jeff	Michel Lachance
3PF	Cheery Hello	John Campbell
2TC	Royal Troubador	Carl Allen
2TF	Delphi's Lobell	Ron Waples
3TC	Esquire Spur	Dick Stillings
3TF	Pace Corps	John Campbell
APM	Armbro Feather	John Kopas
ATM	Grades Singing	Olle Goop
APH	Matt's Scooter	Michel Lachance
ATH	Delray Lobell	John Campbell

1990

Div	Winner	Driver
2PC	Artsplace	John Campbell
2PF	Miss Easy	John Campbell
3PC	Beach Towel	Ray Remmen
3PF	Town Pro	Doug Brown
2TC	Crysta's Best	Dick Richardson Jr.
2TF	Jean Bi	Jan Nordin
3TC	Embassy Lobell	Michel Lachance
3TF	Me Maggie	Berndt Lindstedt
APM	Caesar's Jackpot	Bill Fahy
ATM	Peace Corps	Stig Johansson
APH	Bay's Fella	Paul MacDonell
ATH	No Sex Please	Ron Waples

Note: 2=Two-year-old; T=Trotter; C=Colt; 3=Three-year-old; P=Pacer; F=Filly; A=Aged; H=Horse; M=Mare.

Breeders' Crown *(Cont.)*

1991

Div	Winner	Driver
2PC	Digger Almahurst	Doug Brown
2PF	Hazleton Kay	John Campbell
3PC	Three Wizzards	Bill Gale
3PF	Miss Easy	John Campbell
2TC	King Conch	Bill Gale
2TF	Armbro Keepsake	John Campbell
3TC	Giant Victory	Ron Pierce
3TF	Twelve Speed	Ron Waples
APM	Delinquent Account	Bill O'Donnell
ATM	Me Maggie	Berndt Lindstedt
APH	Camluck	Michel Lachance
ATH	Billyjojimbob	Paul MacDonell

1992

Div	Winner	Driver
2PC	Village Jiffy	Ron Waples
2PF	Immortality	John Campbell
3PC	Kingsbridge	Roger Mayotte
3PF	So Fresh	John Campbell
2TC	Giant Chill	John Patterson Jr.
2TF	Winky's Goal	Cat Manzi
3TC	Baltic Striker	Michel Lachance
3TF	Imperfection	Michel Lachance
APM	Shady Daisy	Ron Pierce
ATM	Peace Corps	Torbjorn Jansson
APH	Artsplace	John Campbell
ATH	No Sex Please	Ron Waples

1993

Div	Winner	Driver
2PC	Expensive Scooter	Jack Moiseyev
2PF	Electric Scooter	Mike Lachance
3PC	Life Sign	John Campbell
3PF	Immortality	John Campbell
2TC	Westgate Crown	John Campbell
2TF	Gleam	Jimmy Takter
3TC	Pine Chip	John Campbell
3TF	Expressway Hanover	Per Henriksen
APM	Swing Back	Kelly Sheppard
ATM	Lifetime Dream	Paul MacDonell
APH	Staying Together	Bill O'Donnell
ATH	Earl	Chris Christoforou Jr.

1994

Div	Winner	Driver
2PC	Jenna's Beach Boy	Bill Fahy
2PF	Yankee Cashmere	Peter Wrenn
3PC	Magical Mike	Michel Lachance
3PF	Hardie Hanover	Tim Twaddle
2TC	Eager Seelster	Teddy Jacobs
2TF	Lookout Victory	John Patterson
3TC	Incredible Abe	Italo Tamborrino
3TF	Imageofa Clear Day	Bill O'Donnell
APM	Shady Daisy	Michel Lachance
ATM	Armbro Keepsake	Stig Johansson
APH	Village Jiffy	Paul MacDonell
ATH	Pine Chip	John Campbell

1995

Div	Winner	Driver
2PC	John Street North	Jack Moiseyev
2PF	Paige Nicole Q	John Campbell
3PC	Jenna's Beach Boy	Bill Fahy
3PF	Headline Hanover	Doug Brown
2TC	Armbro Officer	Steve Condren
2TF	Continentalvictory	Michel Lachance
3TC	Abundance	Bill O'Donnell
3TF	Lookout Victory	Sonny Patterson
APM	Ellamony	Mike Saftic
ATM	CR Kay Suzie	Rod Allen
APH	That'll Be Me	Roger Mayotte
ATH	Panifesto	Luc Ouellette

1996

Div	Winner	Driver
2PC	His Mattjesty	Doug Brown
2PF	Before Sunrise	Steve Condren
3PC	Armbro Operative	Michel Lachance
3PF	Mystical Maddy	Michel Lachance
2TC	Malabar Man	Mal Burroughs
2TF	Armbro Prowess	Jimmy Takter
3TC	Running Sea	Wally Hennessey
3TF	Personal Banner	Peter Wrenn
APM	She's A Great Lady	John Campbell
APH	Jenna's Beach Boy	Bill Fahy
AT	CR Kay Suzie	Rod Allen

1997

Div	Winner	Driver
2PC	Artiscape	Michel Lachance
2PF	Take Flight	Luc Ouellette
3PC	Village Jasper	Paul McDonnell
3PF	Stienam's Place	Jack Moiseyev
2TC	Catch As Catch Can	Wally Hennessey
2TF	My Dolly	Wally Hennessey
3TC	Malabar Man	Malvern Burroughs
3TF	No Nonsense Woman	Jim Doherty
APM	Jay's Table	John Campbell
APH	Red Bow Tie	Luc Ouellette
AT	Moni Maker	Wally Hennessey

1998

Div	Winner	Driver
2PC	Badlands Hanover	Ron Pierce
2PF	Juliet's Fate	George Brennan
3PC	Artiscape	Michel Lachance
3PF	Galleria	George Brennan
2TC	CR Commando	Carl Allen
2TF	Musical Victory	Luc Ouellette
3TC	Muscles Yankee	John Campbell
3TF	Lassie's Goal	Mark O'Mara
APM	Shore By Five	Daniel Dube
APH	Red Bow Tie	Luc Ouellette
AT	Supergrit	Ron Pierce

Note: 2=Two-year-old; T=Trotter; C=Colt; 3=Three-year-old; P=Pacer; F=Filly; A=Aged; H=Horse; M=Mare.

Breeders' Crown (Cont.)

1999

Div	Winner	Driver
2PC	Tyberwood	Richard Silverman
2PF	Eternal Camnation	Eric Ledford
3PC	Grinfromeartoear	Chris Christoforou
3PF	Odies Fame	David Wall
2TC	Master Lavec	Daniel Daley
2TF	Dream of Joy	James Meittinis

1999 (Cont.)

Div	Winner	Driver
3TC	CR Renegade	Rodney Allen
3TF	Oolong	Ronald Pierce
APM	Shore By Five	Daniel Dube
APH	Red Bow Tie	Luc Ouellette
AT	Supergrit	Ronald Pierce

Triple Crown Winners

Trotting

Trotting's Triple Crown consists of the Hambletonian (first run in 1926), the Kentucky Futurity (first run in 1893) and the Yonkers Trot (known as the Yonkers Futurity when it began in 1955).

Year	Horse	Owner	Breeder	Trainer & Driver
1955	Scott Frost	S.A. Camp Farms	Est of W.N. Reynolds	Joe O'Brien
1963	Speedy Scot	Castleton Farms	Castleton Farms	Ralph Baldwin
1964	Ayres	Charlotte Sheppard	Charlotte Sheppard	John Simpson Sr
1968	Nevele Pride	Nevele Acres & Lou Resnick	Mr & Mrs E.C. Quin	Stanley Dancer
1969	Lindy's Pride	Lindy Farm	Hanover Shoe Farms	Howard Beissinger
1972	Super Bowl	Rachel Dancer & Rose Hild Breeding Farm	Stoner Creek Stud	Stanley Dancer

Pacing

Pacing's Triple Crown consists of the Cane Pace (called the Cane Futurity when it began in 1955), the Little Brown Jug (first run in 1946) and the Messenger Stakes (first run in 1956).

Year	Horse	Owner	Breeder	Trainer/Driver
1959	Adios Butler	Paige West & Angelo Pellillo	R.C. Carpenter	Paige West/Clint Hodgins
1965	Bret Hanover	Richard Downing	Hanover Shoe Farms	Frank Ervin
1966	Romeo Hanover	Lucky Star Stables & Morton Finder	Hanover Shoe Farms	Jerry Silverman/ William Meyer (Cane) & George Sholty (Jug & Messenger)
1968	Rum Customer	Kennilworth Farms & L. C. Mancuso	Mr. & Mrs. R.C. Larkin	Bill Haughton
1970	Most Happy Fella	Egyptian Acres Stable	Stoner Creek Stud	Stanley Dancer
1980	Niatross	Niagara Acres, C. Galbraith & Niatross Stables	Niagara Acres	Clint Galbraith
1983	Ralph Hanover	Waples Stable, Pointsetta Stable, Grant's Direct Stable & P. J. Baugh	Hanover Shoe Farms	Stew Firlotte/Ron Waples
1997	Western Dreamer	Daniel and Matthew Daly and Patrick Daly Jr.	Kentuckiana Farms	Bill Robinson/Michel Lachance
1999	Blissful Hall	Daniel Plouffe	Walnut Hall Limited	Ben Wallace/Ron Pierce

Awards

Horse of the Year

Year	Horse	Gait	Owner
1947	Victory Song	T	Castleton Farm
1948	Rodney	T	R.H. Johnston
1949	Good Time	P	William Cane
1950	Proximity	T	Ralph and Gordon Verhurst
1951	Pronto Don	T	Hayes Fair Acres Stable
1952	Good Time	P	William Cane
1953	Hi Lo's Forbes	P	Mr. and Mrs. Earl Wagner
1954	Stenographer	T	Max Hempt
1955	Scott Frost	T	S.A. Camp Farms
1956	Scott Frost	T	S.A. Camp Farms
1957	Torpid	P	Sherwood Farm
1958	Emily's Pride	T	Walnut Hall and Castleton Farms
1959	Bye Bye Byrd	P	Mr. and Mrs. Rex Larkin
1960	Adios Butler	P	Adios Butler Syndicate
1961	Adios Butler	P	Adios Butler Syndicate
1962	Su Mac Lad	T	I.W. Berkemeyer
1963	Speedy Scot	T	Castleton Farm
1964	Bret Hanover	P	Richard Downing
1965	Bret Hanover	P	Richard Downing
1966	Bret Hanover	P	Richard Downing
1967	Nevele Pride	T	Nevele Acres

Horse of the Year (Cont.)

Year	Horse	Gait	Owner
1968	Nevele Pride	T	Nevele Acres, Louis Resnick
1969	Nevele Pride	T	Nevele Acres, Louis Resnick
1970	Fresh Yankee	T	Duncan MacDonald
1971	Albatross	P	Albatross Stable
1972	Albatross	P	Amicable Stable
1973	Sir Dalrae	P	A La Carte Racing Stable
1974	Delmonica Hanover	T	Delvin Miller, W. Arnold Hanger
1975	Savoir	T	Allwood Stable
1976	Keystone Ore	P	Mr. and Mrs. Stanley Dancer, Rose Hild Farms, Robert Jones
1977	Green Speed	T	Beverly Lloyds
1978	Abercrombie	P	Shirley Mitchell, L. Keith Bulen
1979	Niatross	P	Niagara Acres, Clint Galbraith
1980	Niatross	P	Niatross Syndicate, Niagara Acres, Clint Galbraith
1981	Fan Hanover	P	Dr. J. Glen Brown
1982	Cam Fella	P	Norm Clements, Norm Faulkner
1983	Cam Fella	P	JEF's Standardbred, Norm Clements, Norm Faulkner
1984	Fancy Crown	T	Fancy Crown Stable
1985	Nihilator	P	Wall Street-Nihilator Syndicate
1986	Forrest	P	Forrest L. Bartlett
1987	Mack Lobell	T	One More Time Stable and Fair Wind Farm
1988	Mack Lobell	T	John Erik Magnusson
1989	Matt's Scooter	P	Gordon and Illa Rumpel, Charles Jurasvinski
1990	Beach Towel	P	Uptown Stables
1991	Precious Bunny	P	R. Peter Heffering
1992	Artsplace	P	George Segal
1993	Staying Together	P	Robert Hamather
1994	Cam's Card Shark	P	Jeffrey S. Snyder
1995	CR Kay Suzie	T	Carl & Rod Allen Stable, Inc.
1996	Continental-victory	T	Continentalvictory Stables
1997	Malabar Man	T	Malvern Burroughs
1998	Moni Maker	T	Moni Maker Stable
1999	Moni Maker	T	Moni Maker Stable

Note: Balloting is conducted by the U.S Trotting Association for the U.S. Harness Writers Association.

Leading Drivers—Money Won

Year	Driver	Winnings ($)	Year	Driver	Winnings ($)
1946	Thomas Berry	121,933	1973	Herve Filion	2,233,303
1947	H.C. Fitzpatrick	133,675	1974	Herve Filion	3,474,315
1948	Ralph Baldwin	153,222	1975	Carmine Abbatiello	2,275,093
1949	Clint Hodgins	184,108	1976	Herve Filion	2,278,634
1950	Del Miller	306,813	1977	Herve Filion	2,551,058
1951	John Simpson Sr.	333,316	1978	Carmine Abbatiello	3,344,457
1952	Bill Haughton	311,728	1979	John Campbell	3,308,984
1953	Bill Haughton	374,527	1980	John Campbell	3,732,306
1954	Bill Haughton	415,577	1981	Bill O'Donnell	4,065,608
1955	Bill Haughton	599,455	1982	Bill O'Donnell	5,755,067
1956	Bill Haughton	572,945	1983	John Campbell	6,104,082
1957	Bill Haughton	586,950	1984	Bill O'Donnell	9,059,184
1958	Bill Haughton	816,659	1985	Bill O'Donnell	10,207,372
1959	Bill Haughton	771,435	1986	John Campbell	9,515,055
1960	Del Miller	567,282	1987	John Campbell	10,186,495
1961	Stanley Dancer	674,723	1988	John Campbell	11,148,565
1962	Stanley Dancer	760,343	1989	John Campbell	9,738,450
1963	Bill Haughton	790,086	1990	John Campbell	11,620,878
1964	Stanley Dancer	1,051,538	1991	Jack Moiseyev	9,568,468
1965	Bill Haughton	889,943	1992	John Campbell	8,202,108
1966	Stanley Dancer	1,218,403	1993	John Campbell	9,926,482
1967	Bill Haughton	1,305,773	1994	John Campbell	9,834,139
1968	Bill Haughton	1,654,463	1995	John Campbell	9,469,797
1969	Del Insko	1,635,463	1996	Michel Lachance	8,408,231
1970	Herve Filion	1,647,837	1997	Michel Lachance	9,215,388
1971	Herve Filion	1,915,945	1998	John Campbell	10,768,771
1972	Herve Filion	2,473,265	1999	Luc Ouellette	10,841,495

Motor Sports

Daytona 500 winner
Dale Jarrett

Fast and Steady

Consistency was at least as valued as speed in 2000, a season of wide-open, exciting points races

BY MARK BECHTEL

DALE JARRETT won the 1999 Winston Cup despite finishing 37th in the season's first race, the Daytona 500. When he showed up at Daytona in February 2000, he seemed convinced not to put himself in a hole again—and he wasn't the only driver to come out blazing in the 21st century.

At Speed Weeks, the season-opening series of races in Daytona, Jarrett blew away all comers with wins in the Bud Shootout qualifier, the Bud Shootout and the granddaddy of them all, the Daytona 500. And he won all three without breaking a sweat. In fact, he won the 500 even though his car suffered fairly significant body damage the evening before the race, when it collided with Bill Elliott's car during practice. Three fabricators were flown in from North Carolina to fix the damage the morning before the race, and the biggest challenge Jarrett's team faced was getting the paint on the front left panel to dry before the race started. A blow-dryer finished the task.

His car properly styled, Jarrett won the race with a late pass of upstart Johnny Benson, but all week the racing at Daytona had been nearly devoid of excitement. Passing was rare, and the soothingly sonorous tone of the engines, combined with the lack of decisive action, led Larry McReynolds, Ken Schrader's crew chief, to suggest that the infield grandstand be replaced by cots. Dale Earnhardt said it was the worst racing he had seen at Daytona and testily declared that "[late NASCAR founder] Mr. Bill France Sr. probably rolled over in his grave if he saw that deal."

The triumph may not have been pretty, but Jarrett wasn't complaining. The ease of his victory, combined with his incredible display of consistency in winning the '99 title, gave every appearance that it was going to be a long season for the rest of NASCAR's drivers. But, led by Bobby Labonte, they would gradually reel Jarrett back to the pack.

In its early stages the Formula One season also looked like a runaway. Michael Schumacher won the first three races, while two-time defending champion Mika Hakki-

GEORGE TIEDEMANN

left a hole in its schedule over Memorial Day, allowing its teams to compete in the Indy 500. Only Ganassi had the inclination—and the money—to cross over and run his teams at the Brickyard, and Montoya won the race easily.

Apart from that dominating victory, though, 2000 was an unspectacular season for Montoya. He led more laps than any other driver—by far—but mechanical failures and wrecks hounded him all year, and he was never a factor in the points race. In the fall, as expected, Williams announced he was bringing Montoya back to the F/1 circuit in 2001.

While that was unfolding, a host of other drivers gave CART fans one of the best points races in recent years. Gil de Ferran, who won a makeup race at Nazareth on the eve of the Indy 500 to give owner Roger Penske his 100th career win (and first in three years), took the lead with a second place finish at Laguna Seca in September. But as the season wound down, de Ferran had several close pursuers, including Michael Andretti of the U.S. and Brazil's Roberto Moreno, who broke a 12-year winless drought in July.

nen failed to finish the first two races and trailed the German 30–6 after three. Ferrari, behind strong performances from Schumacher and teammate Rubens Barrichello, had what looked to be an equally strong grip on the constructors title, which it hadn't won in 21 years. Hakkinen and David Coulthard, who drive for Ferrari's chief rival, McLaren, failed to score a point until the third race of the season.

With a rout brewing, it looked as if the F/1 story of the year would be the courtship of Juan Montoya. The defending CART champ, who was a test driver for F/1 owner Frank Williams before CART's Chip Ganassi hired him in 1999, had long been rumored to be heading back to Williams. After he won the CART championship in '99, the only thing Montoya hadn't accomplished on this side of the pond in open-wheel racing was to win the Indianapolis 500. For the first time since the CART-IRL schism of 1996, CART

The NASCAR points race, despite Jarrett's dominating performance in the season-opening event, became a barn burner as well. Taking a page out of Jarrett's '99 book (Jarrett scored 24 Top 5 finishes in '99 but won only four races), Labonte showed the steadiness of a surgeon all summer. During a remarkable 11-race stretch he finished out of the top six only three times, but won one only event. "We've lost by margins you could fit in a measuring cup," said Labonte. "Those are hard to swallow. But we know the key is getting Top 5 finishes, and if you have a bad day, don't let it be as bad as it could be."

At Pocono, for instance, Labonte's car was handling poorly at the start, and the situation quickly degenerated when his exhaust pipe cracked. Since the pipe is under the driver's seat, Labonte's backside got toasted for the better part of three hours. "I'll need some ice for my ass when this thing is done," he said. "It is burning up."

The mishaps could have hindered his championship hopes, but Labonte held on and finished 13th. At Bristol in August his leg cramped up so severely that his team put Dave Blaney on standby as a potential relief driver. To make matters worse, Labonte got into two scrapes with Mike Skinner. But he finished the race, in 15th place. By avoiding disastrous finishes, Labonte held on to his lead as the campaign wound down, despite the best efforts of veterans like Earnhardt, Jarrett and Rusty Wallace, all of whom kept the pressure on Labonte.

But we shouldn't suggest that youth wasn't served as well in NASCAR's 2000 season. At Texas Motor Speedway in April, Dale Earnhardt Jr. won the first race of his career in his 12th start—the second-quickest win in the modern era. Following the race his dad hurried out of his car (which finished seventh) and into Victory Lane.

"He told me he loved me, and then he said he just wanted to make sure I took the time to enjoy this and realize what we accomplished today," Junior said. "That was pretty cool on his part to be thinking about that at that particular time. This was a product of his work. He's proud of his son, but he's also proud that he built this team and the team won the race." As if dear old dad needed another reason to smile, Junior added, "He's the car owner, too, so I guess he gets a cut of the check."

Most impressive was the way Junior pulled off the victory. All afternoon he found himself repeating the same pattern: He would pull away from the pack, a caution would come out, his crew would hustle to get him out of the pits first, then the green would fall and the whole cycle would start again. Crew chief Tony Eury Sr. gave Junior a dominant car, one so good that the rookie was tempted to overdo it. "It's hard to keep him slowed down when the car's good," Eury said. "He wants to show it. We just keep him toned down all the time. He's like a wild horse."

Junior showed the win was no fluke when he became the season's first repeat winner a month later at Richmond. Two weeks after that he won the Winston Open, and his fellow rookie Matt Kenseth won the next race on the schedule, the grueling Coca-Cola 600.

But not all news connected to the youngsters was good. Adam Petty, who became the first fourth-generation Winston Cup driver when he finished 40th at Texas in April, was killed on May 12 after crashing during practice for a Busch race at New Hampshire International Speedway.

When the Winston Cup circuit came to New Hampshire in July, 30-year-old Kenny Irwin died after hitting the wall mere feet from where Petty's car had crashed. Both accidents were blamed on stuck throttles, and the similarities between the two wrecks raised eyebrows and then concerns. Eventually NASCAR mandated that cars be outfitted with engine-kill switches on the steering wheel near the driver's thumb, and when drivers returned to New Hampshire in the fall, their cars were equipped with restrictor plates to slow them down.

F/1 also had its share of tragedy. During the Italian GP at Monza, Ferrari's home course, a Lap 1 wreck scattered debris, killing a race worker. Race winner Michael Schumacher was so overcome with grief he could barely speak on the podium afterward.

Though it came under tragic circumstances, the win put Schumacher squarely back into the season points race, which he had controlled so commandingly early in the season. Following his quick start, though, Schumacher suffered a string of four DNF's in five races and allowed Hakkinen, who launched a streak of six straight Top 2 showings, to pass him. (McLaren also crept past Ferrari in the constructors standings.) As the F/1 teams prepared for the United States Grand Prix, in Indianapolis, Hakkinen held a two-point lead over Schumacher, proving that, at least in 2000, a good start wasn't everything.

Indy Racing League

Indianapolis 500

Results of the 84th running of the Indianapolis 500 and fourth race of the 2000 Indy Racing League season. Held Sunday May 28, 2000, at the 2.5-mile Indianapolis Motor Speedway in Indianapolis.
Distance, 500 miles; starters, 33; time of race, 2 hours, 58 minutes, 59.431 seconds; average speed, 167.607 mph; margin of victory, 7.184 seconds; caution flags, 7 for 39 laps; lead changes, 6 among 4 drivers.

TOP 10 FINISHERS

Pos.	Driver (start pos.)	Chassis-Engine	Qual. Speed	Laps	Status
1	Juan Montoya (2)	G Force-Aurora	223.372	200	Running
2	Buddy Lazier (16)	Dallara-Aurora	220.482	200	Running
3	Eliseo Salazar (3)	G Force-Aurora	223.231	200	Running
4	Jeff Ward (6)	G Force-Aurora	222.639	200	Running
5	Eddie Cheever Jr (10)	Dallara-Infiniti	221.270	200	Running
6	Robby Gordon (4)	Dallara-Aurora	222.885	200	Running
7	Jimmy Vasser (7)	G Force-Aurora	221.976	199	Running
8	Stephan Gregoire (20)	G Force-Aurora	219.970	199	Running
9	Scott Goodyear (13)	Dallara-Aurora	220.629	199	Running
10	Scott Sharp (5)	Dallara-Aurora	222.810	198	Running

2000 Indy Racing League Results

Date	Race	Winner (start pos.)	Chassis-Engine	Avg Speed
Jan 29	Delphi Indy 200	Robbie Buhl (22)	G Force-Aurora	102.292
Mar 19	MCI WorldCom Indy 200	Buddy Lazier (26)	Riley & Scott-Aurora	111.957
Apr 22	Vegas Indy 300	Al Unser Jr (21)	G Force-Aurora	136.691
May 28	Indy 500	Juan Montoya (2)	G Force-Aurora	167.607
June 10	Casino Magic 500	Scott Sharp (12)	Dallara-Aurora	169.182
June 18	Radisson Indy 200	Eddie Cheever Jr (10)	Dallara-Infiniti	135.230
July 15	Midas 500 Classic	Greg Ray (1)	Dallara-Aurora	153.403
Aug 27	Belterra Resort Indy 300	Buddy Lazier (7)	Dallara-Aurora	164.601

Note: Distances are in miles unless followed by K (kilometers).

1999 Final Championship Standings

Driver	Starts	Highest Finish	Pts
Greg Ray	10	1	293
Kenny Brack	10	1	256
Mark Dismore	10	1	240
Davey Hamilton	10	2	237
Sam Schmidt	10	1	233

Championship Auto Racing Teams

Michigan 500

Results of the 5th running of the Michigan 500 (formerly the U.S. 500) and 11th race of the 2000 CART Series. Held Sunday, July 23, 2000, at the 2-mile Michigan International Speedway in Brooklyn, MI.
Distance, 500 miles; starters, 24; time of race, 2:48:49.790; average speed, 177.694 mph; margin of victory, .040 seconds; caution flags, five for 38 laps; lead changes, 52 among 10 drivers.

TOP 10 FINISHERS

Pos	Driver (start pos.)	Car	Qual. Speed	Laps	Status
1	Juan Montoya (7)	Lola-Toyota	232.536	250	Running
2	Michael Andretti (2)	Lola-Ford Cosworth	234.627	250	Running
3	Dario Franchitti (4)	Reynard-Honda Turbo V8	233.176	250	Running
4	Patrick Carpentier (9)	Reynard-Ford Cosworth	231.989	250	Running
5	Helio Castroneves (13)	Reynard-Honda Turbo V8	230.762	250	Running
6	Adrian Fernandez (12)	Reynard-Ford Cosworth	231.169	250	Running
7	Paul Tracy (1)	Reynard-Honda Turbo V8	234.949	250	Running
8	Oriol Servia (15)	Reynard-Toyota	229.511	249	Running
9	Max Papis (11)	Reynard-Ford Cosworth	231.310	247	Mechanical
10	Memo Gidley (21)	Reynard-Toyota	224.628	247	Running

2000 CART Championship Series Results (Through September 18)

Date	Event	Winner (start pos.)	Car	Avg Speed
Mar 26	Grand Prix of Miami	Max Papis (13)	Reynard-Ford	164.788
Apr 16	Grand Prix of Long Beach	Paul Tracy (17)	Reynard-Honda	82.626
Apr 30	Rio 200	Adrian Fernandez (16)	Reynard-Ford	124.256
May 14	Motegi 500	Michael Andretti (8)	Lola-Ford	157.154
May 27	Nazareth Grand Prix	Gil de Ferran (5)	Reynard-Honda	101.219
June 4	Milwaukee 225	Juan Montoya (1)	Lola-Toyota	166.258
June 18	Grand Prix of Detroit	Helio Castroneves (3)	Reynard-Honda	97.401
June 25	Portland 200	Gil de Ferran (2)	Reynard-Honda	109.564
July 2	Grand Prix of Cleveland	Roberto Moreno (1)	Reynard-Ford	112.619
July 16	Toronto Indy	Michael Andretti (3)	Lola-Ford	98.348
July 23	Michigan 500	Juan Montoya (7)	Lola-Toyota	177.694
July 30	Chicago Grand Prix	Cristiano da Matta (5)	Reynard-Toyota	114.432
Aug 13	Mid-Ohio 200	Helio Castroneves (2)	Reynard-Honda	106.558
Aug 20	Road America 220	Paul Tracy (7)	Reynard-Honda	136.457
Sept 3	Vancouver Indy	Paul Tracy (2)	Reynard-Honda	85.034
Sept 10	Monterey 300	Helio Castroneves (1)	Reynard-Honda	104.949
Sept 17	Motorola 300	Juan Montoya (1)	Lola-Toyota	155.519

1999 Championship Standings

Driver	Starts	Wins	Pts
Juan Montoya	20	7	212
Dario Franchitti	20	3	212
Paul Tracy	19	2	161
Michael Andretti	20	1	151
Max Papis	19	0	150
Adrian Fernandez	16	2	140
Christian Fittipaldi	15	1	121
Gil de Ferran	20	1	108
Jimmy Vasser	20	0	104
Greg Moore	20	1	97

National Association for Stock Car Auto Racing

Daytona 500

Results of the 42nd Daytona 500, the opening round of the 2000 Winston Cup series. Held Sunday, February 20, at the 2.5-mile high-banked Daytona International Speedway.

Distance, 500 miles; starters, 43; time of race, 3:12:43; average speed, 155.669 mph; margin of victory, under caution; caution flags, 6 for 24 laps; lead changes, 9 among 7 drivers.

TOP 10 FINISHERS

Pos	Driver (start pos.)	Car	Laps	Winnings ($)
1	Dale Jarrett (1)	Ford	200	2,277,975
2	Jeff Burton (14)	Ford	200	840,825
3	Bill Elliott (3)	Ford	200	528,475
4	Rusty Wallace (5)	Ford	200	420,775
5	Mark Martin (9)	Ford	200	326,175
6	Bobby Labonte (13)	Pontiac	200	228,275
7	Terry Labonte (25)	Chevrolet	200	198,625
8	Ward Burton (6)	Pontiac	200	166,775
9	Ken Schrader (23)	Pontiac	200	143,975
10	Matt Kenseth (24)	Ford	200	182,875

Late 1999 Winston Cup Series Results

Date	Track/Distance	Winner (start pos.)	Car	Avg Speed	Winnings ($)
Oct 3	Martinsville 500*	Jeff Gordon (5)	Chevrolet	72.624	110,090
Oct 10	Charlotte 500	Jeff Gordon (22)	Chevrolet	160.306	140,350
Oct 17	Talladega 500	Dale Earnhardt (27)	Chevrolet	166.632	120,290
Oct 24	N Carolina 400	Jeff Burton (6)	Ford	131.103	104,715
Nov 7	Phoenix 500 K	Tony Stewart (11)	Pontiac	118.132	168,485
Nov 14	Miami 400	Tony Stewart (7)	Pontiac	140.335	278,265
Nov 21	Atlanta 500	Bobby Labonte (37)	Pontiac	137.942	174,300

Note: Distances are in miles unless followed by * (laps) or K (kilometers).

2000 Winston Cup Series Results (through September 25)

Date	Track/Distance	Winner (start pos.)	Car	Avg Speed	Winnings ($)
Feb 20	Daytona 500	Dale Jarrett (1)	Ford	155.669	2,277,975
Feb 27	N Carolina 400	Bobby Labonte (3)	Pontiac	127.875	131,385
Mar 5	Las Vegas 400	Jeff Burton (11)	Ford	119.982	358,925
Mar 12	Atlanta 500	Dale Earnhardt (35)	Chevrolet	131.759	123,100
Mar 19	Darlington 400	Ward Burton (3)	Pontiac	128.076	132,725
Mar 26	Bristol 500*	Rusty Wallace (6)	Ford	88.018	87,585
Apr 2	Texas 500	Dale Earnhardt Jr (4)	Chevrolet	131.152	374,675
Apr 9	Martinsville 500*	Mark Martin (21)	Ford	71.161	104,650
Apr 16	Talladega 500	Jeff Gordon (36)	Chevrolet	161.157	159,755
Apr 30	California 500	Jeremy Mayfield (24)	Ford	149.378	125,925
May 6	Richmond 400*	Dale Earnhardt Jr (5)	Chevrolet	99.374	118,850
May 20	Charlotte 70*	Dale Earnhardt Jr (5)	Chevrolet	167.035	516,410
May 28	Charlotte 600	Matt Kenseth (21)	Ford	142.640	200,950
June 4	Dover Downs 400	Tony Stewart (16)	Pontiac	109.514	152,830
June 11	Michigan 400	Tony Stewart (28)	Pontiac	143.926	123,800
June 19	Pocono 500	Jeremy Mayfield (22)	Ford	139.741	121,020
June 25	Sears Point 350 K	Jeff Gordon (5)	Chevrolet	78.782	143,025
July 1	Daytona 400	Jeff Burton (9)	Ford	148.576	152,450
July 9	New Hampshire 300	Tony Stewart (6)	Pontiac	103.145	164,800
July 23	Pocono 500	Rusty Wallace (2)	Ford	130.662	125,745
Aug 5	Indianapolis 400	Bobby Labonte (3)	Pontiac	155.912	831,225
Aug 14	Watkins Glen 90*	Steve Park (18)	Chevrolet	91.336	124,870
Aug 20	Michigan 400	Rusty Wallace (10)	Ford	132.597	110,460
Aug 27	Bristol 500*	Rusty Wallace (1)	Ford	85.394	107.540
Sept 3	Darlington 500	Bobby Labonte (37)	Pontiac	108.275	198.180
Sept 9	Richmond 400*	Jeff Gordon (13)	Chevrolet	99.871	130,220
Sept 17	New Hampshire 300*	Jeff Burton (2)	Ford	102.003	195,800
Sept 24	Dover Downs 400	Tony Stewart (27)	Pontiac	115.191	158,535

Note: Distances are in miles unless followed by * (laps) or K (kilometers).

1999 Winston Cup Final Standings

Driver	Car	Starts	Wins	Pts
Dale Jarrett	Ford	34	4	5262
Bobby Labonte	Pontiac	34	5	5061
Mark Martin	Ford	34	2	4943
Tony Stewart	Pontiac	34	3	4774
Jeff Burton	Ford	34	6	4733
Jeff Gordon	Chevrolet	34	7	4620
Dale Earnhardt	Chevrolet	34	3	4492
Rusty Wallace	Ford	34	1	4155
Ward Burton	Pontiac	34	0	4062
Mike Skinner	Chevrolet	34	0	4003

1999 Winston Cup Driver Winnings

Driver	Winnings ($)
Jeff Gordon	5,281,361
Jeff Burton	5,211,301
Dale Jarrett	3,608,829
Bobby Labonte	3,550,341
Mark Martin	2,783,296
Dale Earnhardt	2,712,089
Tony Stewart	2,615,226
Terry Labonte	2,303,146
Mike Skinner	2,222,321
Rusty Wallace	2,167,429

Formula One Grand Prix Racing

2000 Formula One Results (Through September 25)

Date	Grand Prix	Winner	Car	Time
Mar 12	Australia	Michael Schumacher	Ferrari	1:34:01.987
Mar 26	Brazil	Michael Schumacher	Ferrari	1:31:35.271
Apr 9	San Marino	Michael Schumacher	Ferrari	1:31.39.776
Apr 23	Great Britain	David Coulthard	McLaren-Mercedes	1:28.50.108
May 7	Spain	Mika Hakkinen	McLaren-Mercedes	1:33:55.390
May 21	European	Michael Schumacher	Ferrari	1:42:00.307
June 4	Monaco	David Coulthard	McLaren-Mercedes	1:49:28.213
June 18	Canada	Michael Schumacher	Ferrari	1:41:12.313
July 2	France	David Coulthard	McLaren-Mercedes	1:38:05.538
July 16	Austria	Mika Hakkinen	McLaren-Mercedes	1:28:15.818
July 30	Germany	Rubens Barrichello	Ferrari	1:25:34.418
Aug 13	Hungary	Mika Hakkinen	McLaren-Mercedes	1:45:33.869
Aug 27	Belgium	Mika Hakkinen	McLaren-Mercedes	1:28:14.494
Sept 10	Italy	Michael Schumacher	Ferrari	1:27:31.638
Sept 24	United States	Michael Schumacher	Ferrari	1:36:30.883

1999 World Championship Final Standings

Drivers compete in Grand Prix races for the title of World Driving Champion. Below are the top 10 drivers from the 1999 season. Points are awarded for places 1–6 as follows: 10-6-4-3-2-1.

Driver, Country	Starts	Wins	Car	Pts
Mika Hakkinen, Finland	16	5	McLaren-Mercedes	76
Eddie Irvine, Great Britain	16	4	Ferrari	74
Heinz-Harald Frentzen, Germany	16	2	Jordan-Mugan Honda	54
David Coulthard, Great Britain	16	2	McLaren-Mercedes	48
Michael Schumacher, Germany	10	2	Ferrari	44
Ralf Schumacher, Germany	16	0	Williams	35
Rubens Barrichello, Brazil	16	0	Stewart-Ford	21
Johnny Herbert, Great Britain	16	1	Stewart-Ford	15
Giancarlo Fisichella, Italy	16	0	Benetton-Playlife	13
Mika Salo, Finland	10	0	Ferrari, BAR Honda	10

Professional Sports Car Racing, Inc.

The 24 Hours of Daytona

Held at the Daytona International Speedway on February 5–6, the 24 Hours of Daytona serves as the opening round of Grand American Road Racing Association's season.

Place	Drivers	Car (Class)	Distance
1	Olivier Beretta, Karl Wendlinger, Dominique Dupuy	Dodge Viper (GTO)	723 laps (107.207 mph)
2	Justin Bell, Ron Fellows, Chris Kneifel	Chevrolet Corvette (GTO)	723 laps
3	David Donahue, Jean Philippe Belloc, Ni Amorim	Dodge Viper (GTO)	719 laps
4	James Weaver, Max Papis, Elliott Forbes-Robinson, Rob Dyson	Ford R&S MKIII (SR)	717 laps
5	Tommy Archer, Marc Duez, Vincent Vosse	Dodge Viper (GTO)	691 laps

2000 American Le Mans Series—Prototype Class (Through September 18)

Date	Race	Winners	Car
Mar 18	12 Hours at Sebring	Frank Biela, Tom Kristensen, Emanuele Pirro	Audi
Apr 1	Grand Prix of Charlotte	J.J. Lehto, Jörg Müller	BMW
May 13	USA Challenge	J.J. Lehto, Jörg Müller	BMW
July 9	Nurburg 1000 K	Jan Magnussen, David Brabham	Panoz LMP
July 23	Grand Prix of Sonoma	Allan McNish, Rinaldo Capello	Audi
Aug 6	Grand Prix at Mosport	Allan McNish, Rinaldo Capello	Audi
Sept 2	Grand Prix of Texas	Emanuele Pirro, Frank Biela	Audi
Sept 10	Grand Prix of Portland	Rinaldo Capello, Allan McNish	Audi

2000 American Le Mans Series—GTS Class (Through September 18)

Date	Race	Winners	Car
Mar 18	12 Hours at Sebring	Olivier Beretta, Karl Wendlinger, Dominique Dupuy	Dodge Viper
Apr 1	Grand Prix of Charlotte	Karl Wendlinger, Olivier Beretta	Dodge Viper
May 13	USA Challenge	Olivier Beretta, Karl Wendlinger	Dodge Viper
July 9	Nurburg 1000 K	Olivier Beretta, Karl Wendlinger, Marc Duez	Dodge Viper
July 23	Grand Prix of Sonoma	David Donohue, Tommy Archer	Dodge Viper
Aug 6	Grand Prix at Mosport	Olivier Beretta, Karl Wendlinger	Dodge Viper
Sept 2	Grand Prix of Texas	Ron Fellows, Andy Pilgrim, Justin Bell	Corvette
Sept 10	Grand Prix of Portland	Olivier Beretta, Karl Wendlinger	Dodge Viper

2000 American Le Mans Series—GT Class (Through September 18)

Date	Race	Winners	Car
Mar 18	12 Hours at Sebring	Dirk Müller, Lucas Luhr	Porsche 911
Apr 1	Grand Prix of Charlotte	Bob Wollek, Sascha Maassen	Porsche 911
May 13	USA Challenge	Bob Wollek, Sascha Maassen	Porsche 911
July 9	Nurburg 1000 K	Dirk Müller, Lucas Luhr	Porsche 911
July 23	Grand Prix of Sonoma	Dirk Müller, Lucas Luhr	Porsche 911
Aug 6	Grand Prix at Mosport	Randy Pobst, Bruno Lambert	Porsche 911
Sept 2	Grand Prix of Texas	Randy Pobst, Bruno Lambert	Porsche 911
Sept 10	Grand Prix of Portland	Sascha Maassen, Bob Wollek	Porsche 911

1999 American Le Mans Series Championship Final Standings

PROTOTYPE CLASS	Pts	GTS CLASS	Pts	GT CLASS	Pts
Elliott Forbes-Robinson	141	Olivier Beretta	151	Cort Wagner	168
Eric Bernard	135	Karl Wendlinger	137	Brian Cunningham	146
David Brabham	135	Martin Snow	129	Johannes van Overbeek	144
J.J.Lehto	123	David Donohue	117	Dirk Müller	141
Steve Soper	122	Kelly Collins	116	Darryl Havens	121
Jan Magnussen	121	Tommy Archer	107	Mike Fitzgerald	117
Johnny O'Connell	120	Ron Johnson	105	Hans Stuck	114
Butch Leitzinger	110	Terry Borcheller	105	Mark Simo	109
Bill Auberlen	95	Ron Fellows	98	Randy Pobst	101
James Weaver	84	Franz Konrad	82	Joel Reiser	96

24 Hours of Le Mans

Held at Le Mans, France, on June 17–18, 2000, the 24 Hours of Le Mans is the most prestigious international event in endurance racing.

Place	Drivers	Car	Laps
1	Frank Biela, Tom Kristensen, Emanuele Pirro	Audi R8	368 (3,111.8 mi)
2	Laurent Aiello, Allan McNish, Stephane Ortelli	Audi R8	367
3	Michele Alboreto, Christian Abt, Rinaldo Capello	Audi R8	365
4	Sebastien Bourdais, Olivier Grouillard, Emmanuel Clerico	Courage C52	344
5	Hiroki Kato, Johnny O'Connell, Pierre-Henri Raphanel	Panoz Spyder LMP	342
6	Toshio Suzuki, Masahiko Kageyama, Masami Kageyama	Panoz Spyder LMP	340
7	Olivier Beretta, Karl Wendlinger, Dominique Dupuy	Dodge Viper	333
8	Keiichi Tsuchiya, Masahiko Kondo, Akira Iida	Panoz Spyder LMP	330
9	David Donohue, Ni Amorim, Anthony Belthoise	Dodge Viper	328
10	Andy Pilgrim, Kelly Collins, Franck Freon	Corvette	327

National Hot Rod Association

2000 Results (Through September 18)
TOP FUEL

Date	Race, Site	Winner	Time	Speed
Feb 3–6	Winternationals, Pomona, CA	Gary Scelzi	4.613	317.79
Feb 24–27	Arizona Nationals, Phoenix	Tony Schumacher	5.095	289.57
Mar 16–19	Mac Tools Gatornationals, Gainesville, FL	Doug Kalitta	4.614	313.58
Apr 6–9	Las Vegas Nationals	Kenny Bernstein	4.907	282.78
Apr 13–16	O'Reilly Nationals, Houston	Larry Dixon	4.665	316.90
Apr 27–30	Virginia Nationals, Richmond	Larry Dixon	4.674	314.53
May 4–7	Southern Nationals, Atlanta	Gary Scelzi	4.629	310.70
May 25–28	Castrol Nationals, Dallas	Gary Scelzi	4.614	316.67
June 1–4	Fram Route 66 Nationals, Chicago	Gary Scelzi	4.642	314.53
June 15–18	Pontiac Nationals, Columbus, OH	Tony Schumacher	4.648	316.15
June 22–24	Sears Nationals, Madison, IL	Gary Scelzi	5.892	284.99
July 7–9	Winston Showdown, Bristol, CT	Cory McClenathan	4.852	291.32
July 13–16	Mile-High Nationals, Denver	Joe Amato	4.837	300.53
July 28–30	Northwest Nationals, Seattle	Gary Scelzi	4.711	303.98
Aug 4–6	Autolite Nationals, Sonoma, CA	Doug Kalitta	5.247	274.33
Aug 17–20	NHRA Nationals, Brainerd, MN	Tony Schumacher	4.585	318.69
Aug 30–Sept 4	U.S. Nationals, Indianapolis	Tony Schumacher	4.644	316.90
Sept 8–9	Matco Supernationals, Englishtown, NJ	Doug Kalitta	4.637	313.29
Sept 14–17	Keystone Nationals, Reading, PA	Joe Amato	4.626	310.27

FUNNY CAR

Date	Race, Site	Winner	Time	Speed
Feb 3–6	Winternationals, Pomona, CA	Jerry Toliver	4.970	309.06
Feb 24–27	Arizona Nationals, Phoenix	John Force	4.993	313.88
Mar 16–19	Mac Tools Gatornationals, Gainesville, FL	Jerry Toliver	5.071	296.50
Apr 6–9	Las Vegas Nationals	Jim Eppler	4.983	302.21
Apr 13–16	O'Reilly Nationals, Houston	Bob Gilbertson	5.067	304.25

2000 Results (Through September 18) *(Cont.)*
FUNNY CAR *(CONT.)*

Date	Race, Site	Winner	Time	Speed
Apr 27–30	Virginia Nationals, Richmond	John Force	5.913	236.01
May 4–7	Southern Nationals, Atlanta	John Force	4.929	289.14
May 25–28	Castrol Nationals, Dallas	John Force	4.919	313.26
June 1–4	Fram Route 66 Nationals, Chicago	John Force	4.842	318.08
June 15–18	Pontiac Nationals, Columbus, OH	Tony Pedregon	4.893	316.08
June 22–24	Sears Nationals, Madison, IL	Jerry Toliver	6.771	186.69
July 7–9	Winston Showdown, Bristol, CT	Frank Manzo	5.869	250.69
July 13–16	Mile-High Nationals, Denver	Whit Bazemore	4.990	301.20
July 28–30	Northwest Nationals, Seattle	John Force	4.973	299.60
Aug 4–6	Autolite Nationals, Sonoma, CA	John Force	9.055	101.81
Aug 17–20	NHRA Nationals, Brainerd, MN	John Force	4.935	309.34
Aug 30–Sept 4	U.S. Nationals, Indianapolis	Jim Epler	5.017	285.41
Sept 8–9	Matco Supernationals, Englishtown, NJ	Cruz Pedregon	5.543	124.18
Sept 14–17	Keystone Nationals, Reading, PA	Bruce Sarver	4.993	303.03

PRO STOCK

Date	Race, Site	Winner	Time	Speed
Feb 3–6	Winternationals, Pomona, CA	Jeg Coughlin	6.894	199.17
Feb 24–27	Arizona Nationals, Phoenix	Jeg Coughlin	6.961	198.44
Mar 16–19	Mac Tools Gatornationals, Gainesville, FL	Warren Johnson	6.900	199.35
Apr 6–9	Las Vegas Nationals	Jeg Coughlin	7.072	195.56
Apr 13–16	O'Reilly Nationals, Houston	Jeg Coughlin	6.905	199.29
Apr 27–30	Virginia Nationals, Richmond	Jeg Coughlin	6.891	199.73
May 4–7	Southern Nationals, Atlanta	Jeg Coughlin	6.957	198.12
May 25–28	Castrol Nationals, Dallas	V. Gaines	7.041	196.93
June 1–4	Fram Route 66 Nationals, Chicago	Ron Krisher	8.888	199.43
June 15–18	Pontiac Nationals, Columbus, OH	Mark Pawuk	6.980	197.33
June 22–24	Sears Nationals, Madison, IL	Ron Krisher	6.900	198.44
July 7–9	Winston Showdown, Bristol, CT	Troy Coughlin	7.086	194.10
July 13–16	Mile-High Nationals, Denver	Kurt Johnson	7.358	188.04
July 28–30	Northwest Nationals, Seattle	Richie Stevens	7.018	195.70
Aug 4–6	Autolite Nationals, Sonoma, CA	Kurt Johnson	6.974	198.61
Aug 17–20	NHRA Nationals, Brainerd, MN	Kurt Johnson	6.986	196.59
Aug 30–Sept 4	U.S. Nationals, Indianapolis	Jeg Coughlin	6.968	196.96
Sept 8–9	Matco Supernationals, Englishtown, NJ	Jeg Coughlin	6.943	198.41
Sept 14–17	Keystone Nationals, Reading, PA	Kurt Johnson	6.885	200.14

1999 Standings

TOP FUEL

Driver	Wins	Pts
Tony Schumacher	1	1,488
Gary Scelzi	3	1,380
Joe Amato	5	1,345
Mike Dunn	4	1,327
Doug Kalitta	1	1,306
Kenny Bernstein	0	1,260
Doug Herbert	4	1,259
Larry Dixon	2	1,210
Cory McClenathan	2	1,149
Bob Vandergriff	0	1,131

FUNNY CAR

Driver	Wins	Pts
John Force	11	2,071
Tony Pedregon	3	1,604
Whit Bazemore	1	1,413
Frank Pedregon	1	1,028
Dean Skuza	0	977
Jim Epler	0	960
Del Worsham	1	928
Jerry Toliver	1	923
Ron Capps	0	891
Tommy Johnson Jr	2	881

PRO STOCK

Driver	Wins	Pts
Warren Johnson	9	1,802
Jeg Coughlin	5	1,458
Kurt Johnson	3	1,434
Jim Yates	2	1,288
Richie Stevens	1	1,141
Troy Coughlin	0	1,046
Mike Edwards	2	1,029
Mark Pawuk	0	1,004
Allen Johnson	1	916
Greg Anderson	0	795

Indianapolis 500

First held in 1911, the Indianapolis 500—200 laps of the 2.5-mile Indianapolis Motor Speedway Track (called the Brickyard in honor of its original pavement)—grew to become the most famous auto race in the world. Though the Memorial Day weekend event lost participants and prestige in the mid-1990s due to feuding in the world of U.S. open-wheel racing, it annually attracts crowds of over 100,000.

Year	Winner (start pos.)	Car	Avg Speed	Pole Winner	Speed
1911	Ray Harroun (28)	Marmon Wasp	74.590	Lewis Strang	Awarded pole
1912	Joe Dawson (7)	National	78.720	Gil Anderson	Drew pole
1913	Jules Goux (7)	Peugeot	75.930	Caleb Bragg	Drew pole
1914	Rene Thomas (15)	Delage	82.470	Jean Chassagne	Drew pole
1915	Ralph DePalma (2)	Mercedes	89.840	Howard Wilcox	98.90
1916	Dario Resta (4)	Peugeot	84.000	John Aitken	96.69
1917–18	No race				
1919	Howard Wilcox (2)	Peugeot	88.050	Rene Thomas	104.78
1920	Gaston Chevrolet (6)	Monroe	88.620	Ralph DePalma	99.15
1921	Tommy Milton (20)	Frontenac	89.620	Ralph DePalma	100.75
1922	Jimmy Murphy (1)	Murphy Special	94.480	Jimmy Murphy	100.50
1923	Tommy Milton (1)	H.C.S. Special	90.950	Tommy Milton	108.17
1924	L.L. Corum Joe Boyer (21)	Duesenberg Special	98.230	Jimmy Murphy	108.037
1925	Peter DePaolo (2)	Duesenberg Special	101.130	Leon Duray	113.196
1926	Frank Lockhart (20)	Miller Special	95.904	Earl Cooper	111.735
1927	George Souders (22)	Duesenberg	97.545	Frank Lockhart	120.100
1928	Louis Meyer (13)	Miller Special	99.482	Leon Duray	122.391
1929	Ray Keech (6)	Simplex Piston Ring Special	97.585	Cliff Woodbury	120.599
1930	Billy Arnold (1)	Miller Hartz Special	100.448	Billy Arnold	113.268
1931	Louis Schneider (13)	Bowes Seal-Fast Special	96.629	Russ Snowberger	112.796
1932	Fred Frame (27)	Miller Hartz Special	104.144	Lou Moore	117.363
1933	Louis Meyer (6)	Tydol Special	104.162	Bill Cummings	118.524
1934	Bill Cummings (10)	Boyle Products Special	104.863	Kelly Petillo	119.329
1935	Kelly Petillo (22)	Gilmore Speedway Special	106.240	Rex Mays	120.736
1936	Louis Meyer (28)	Ring-Free Special	109.069	Rex Mays	119.664
1937	Wilbur Shaw (2)	Shaw-Gilmore Special	113.580	Bill Cummings	123.343
1938	Floyd Roberts (1)	Burd Piston Ring Special	117.200	Floyd Roberts	125.681
1939	Wilbur Shaw (3)	Boyle Special	115.035	Jimmy Snyder	130.138
1940	Wilbur Shaw (2)	Boyle Special	114.277	Rex Mays	127.850
1941	Floyd Davis Mauri Rose (17)	Noc-Out Hose Clamp Special	115.117	Mauri Rose	128.691
1942–45	No race				
1946	George Robson (15)	Thorne Engineering Special	114.820	Cliff Bergere	126.471
1947	Mauri Rose (3)	Blue Crown Spark Plug Special	116.338	Ted Horn	126.564
1948	Mauri Rose (3)	Blue Crown Spark Plug Special	119.814	Rex Mays	130.577
1949	Bill Holland (4)	Blue Crown Spark Plug Special	121.327	Duke Nalon	132.939
1950	Johnnie Parsons (5)	Wynn's Friction Proofing	124.002	Walt Faulkner	134.343
1951	Lee Wallard (2)	Belanger Special	126.244	Duke Nalon	136.498
1952	Troy Ruttman (7)	Agajanian Special	128.922	Fred Agabashian	138.010
1953	Bill Vukovich (1)	Fuel Injection Special	128.740	Bill Vukovich	138.392
1954	Bill Vukovich (19)	Fuel Injection Special	130.840	Jack McGrath	141.033
1955	Bob Sweikert (14)	John Zink Special	128.209	Jerry Hoyt	140.045
1956	Pat Flaherty (1)	John Zink Special	128.490	Pat Flaherty	145.596
1957	Sam Hanks (13)	Belond Exhaust Special	135.601	Pat O'Connor	143.948
1958	Jim Bryan (7)	Belond AP Parts Special	133.791	Dick Rathmann	145.974
1959	Rodger Ward (6)	Leader Card 500 Roadster	135.857	Johnny Thomson	145.908
1960	Jim Rathmann (2)	Ken-Paul Special	138.767	Eddie Sachs	146.592
1961	A.J. Foyt (7)	Bowes Seal-Fast Special	139.130	Eddie Sachs	147.481
1962	Rodger Ward (2)	Leader Card 500 Roadster	140.293	Parnelli Jones	150.370
1963	Parnelli Jones (1)	Agajanian-Willard Special	143.137	Parnelli Jones	151.153
1964	A.J. Foyt (5)	Sheraton-Thompson Special	147.350	Jim Clark	158.828
1965	Jim Clark (2)	Lotus Ford	150.686	A.J. Foyt	161.233
1966	Graham Hill (15)	American Red Ball Special	144.317	Mario Andretti	165.899
1967	A.J. Foyt (4)	Sheraton-Thompson Special	151.207	Mario Andretti	168.982
1968	Bobby Unser (3)	Rislone Special	152.882	Joe Leonard	171.559
1969	Mario Andretti (2)	STP Oil Treatment Special	156.867	A.J. Foyt	170.568
1970	Al Unser (1)	Johnny Lightning 500 Special	155.749	Al Unser	170.221
1971	Al Unser (5)	Johnny Lightning Special	157.735	Peter Revson	178.696
1972	Mark Donohue (3)	Sunoco McLaren	162.962	Bobby Unser	195.940
1973	Gordon Johncock (11)	STP Double Oil Filters	159.036	Johnny Rutherford	198.413
1974	Johnny Rutherford (25)	McLaren	158.589	A.J. Foyt	191.632

Year	Winner (start pos.)	Car	Avg speed	Pole Winner	Speed
1975	Bobby Unser (3)	Jorgensen Eagle	149.213	A.J. Foyt	193.976
1976	Johnny Rutherford (1)	Hy-Gain McLaren/Goodyear	148.725	Johnny Rutherford	188.957
1977	A.J. Foyt (4)	Gilmore Racing Team	161.331	Tom Sneva	198.884
1978	Al Unser (5)	FNCTC Chaparral Lola	161.361	Tom Sneva	202.156
1979	Rick Mears (1)	The Gould Charge	158.899	Rick Mears	193.736
1980	Johnny Rutherford (1)	Pennzoil Chaparral	142.862	Johnny Rutherford	192.256
1981	Bobby Unser (1)	Norton Spirit Penske PC-9B	139.084	Bobby Unser	200.546
1982	Gordon Johncock (5)	STP Oil Treatment	162.026	Rick Mears	207.004
1983	Tom Sneva (4)	Texaco Star	162.117	Teo Fabi	207.395
1984	Rick Mears (3)	Pennzoil Z-7	163.612	Tom Sneva	210.029
1985	Danny Sullivan (8)	Miller American Special	152.982	Pancho Carter	212.583
1986	Bobby Rahal (4)	Budweiser/Truesports/March	170.722	Rick Mears	216.828
1987	Al Unser (20)	Cummins Holset Turbo	162.175	Mario Andretti	215.390
1988	Rick Mears (1)	Penske-Chevrolet	144.809	Rick Mears	219.198
1989	Emerson Fittipaldi (3)	Penske-Chevrolet	167.581	Rick Mears	223.885
1990	Arie Luyendyk (3)	Domino's Pizza Chevrolet	185.981*	Emerson Fittipaldi	225.301
1991	Rick Mears (1)	Penske-Chevrolet	176.457	Rick Mears	224.113
1992	Al Unser Jr (12)	G92-Chevrolet	134.477	Roberto Guerrero	232.482
1993	Emerson Fittipaldi (9)	Penske-Chevrolet	157.207	Arie Luyendyk	223.967
1994	Al Unser Jr (1)	Penske-Mercedes	160.872	Al Unser Jr	228.011
1995	Jacques Villeneuve (5)	Reynard-Ford	153.616	Scott Brayton	231.616
1996	Buddy Lazier (5)	Reynard-Ford	147.956	Tony Stewart	233.100†
1997	Arie Luyendyk (1)	G Force Aurora	145.827	Arie Luyendyk	231.468
1998	Eddie Cheever (17)	Dallara Aurora	145.155	Billy Boat	223.503
1999	Kenny Brack (8)	Dallara Aurora	153.176	Arie Luyendyk	225.179
2000	Juan Montoya (2)	G Force Aurora	167.607	Greg Ray	223.471

*Track record, winning time. †Track record, qualifying time.

Indianapolis 500 Rookie of the Year Award

1952 ....Art Cross	1969 ....Mark Donohue*	1985 ....Arie Luyendyk*
1953 ....Jimmy Daywalt	1970 ....Donnie Allison	1986 ....Randy Lanier
1954 ....Larry Crockett	1971 ....Denny Zimmerman	1987 ....Fabrizio Barbazza
1955 ....Al Herman	1972 ....Mike Hiss	1988 ....Billy Vukovich III
1956 ....Bob Veith	1973 ....Graham McRae	1989 ....Bernard Jourdain
1957 ....Don Edmunds	1974 ....Pancho Carter	Scott Pruett
1958 ....George Amick	1975 ....Bill Puterbaugh	1990 ....Eddie Cheever*
1959 ....Bobby Grim	1976 ....Vern Schuppan	1991 ....Jeff Andretti
1960 ....Jim Hurtubise	1977 ....Jerry Sneva	1992 ....Lyn St. James
1961 ....Parnelli Jones*	1978 ....Rick Mears*	1993 ....Nigel Mansell
Bobby Marshman	Larry Rice	1994 ....Jacques Villeneuve*
1962 ....Jimmy McElreath	1979 ....Howdy Holmes	1995 ....Gil de Ferran
1963 ....Jim Clark*	1980 ....Tim Richmond	1996 ....Tony Stewart
1964 ....Johnny White	1981 ....Josele Garza	1997 ....Jeff Ward
1965 ....Mario Andretti*	1982 ....Jim Hickman	1998 ....Steve Knapp
1966 ....Jackie Stewart	1983 ....Teo Fabi	1999 ....Robby McGehee
1967 ....Denis Hulme	1984 ....Michael Andretti	2000 ....Juan Montoya*
1968 ....Billy Vukovich	Roberto Guerrero	*Future winner of Indy 500.

Championship Auto Racing Teams

CART Championship Series Champions

From 1909 to 1955, this championship was awarded by the American Automobile Association (AAA), and from 1956 to 1979 by the United States Auto Club (USAC). Since 1979, Championship Auto Racing Teams (CART) has conducted the championship. Known as PPG CART World Series until 1998.

1909 ....George Robertson	1920 ....Tommy Milton	1931 ....Louis Schneider
1910 ....Ray Harroun	1921 ....Tommy Milton	1932 ....Bob Carey
1911 ....Ralph Mulford	1922 ....Jimmy Murphy	1933 ....Louis Meyer
1912 ....Ralph DePalma	1923 ....Eddie Hearne	1934 ....Bill Cummings
1913 ....Earl Cooper	1924 ....Jimmy Murphy	1935 ....Kelly Petillo
1914 ....Ralph DePalma	1925 ....Peter DePaolo	1936 ....Mauri Rose
1915 ....Earl Cooper	1926 ....Harry Hartz	1937 ....Wilbur Shaw
1916 ....Dario Resta	1927 ....Peter DePaolo	1938 ....Floyd Roberts
1917 ....Earl Cooper	1928 ....Louis Meyer	1939 ....Wilbur Shaw
1918 ....Ralph Mulford	1929 ....Louis Meyer	1940 ....Rex Mays
1919 ....Howard Wilcox	1930 ....Billy Arnold	1941 ....Rex Mays

PPG CART World Series Champions *(Cont.)*

1942–45 ......No racing	1964 ............A.J. Foyt	1982 ....Rick Mears
1946 ....Ted Horn	1965 ....Mario Andretti	1983 ....Al Unser
1947 ....Ted Horn	1966 ....Mario Andretti	1984 ....Mario Andretti
1948 ....Ted Horn	1967 ............A.J. Foyt	1985 ....Al Unser
1949 ....Johnnie Parsons	1968 ....Bobby Unser	1986 ....Bobby Rahal
1950 ....Henry Banks	1969 ....Mario Andretti	1987 ....Bobby Rahal
1951 ....Tony Bettenhausen	1970 ....Al Unser	1988 ....Danny Sullivan
1952 ....Chuck Stevenson	1971 ....Joe Leonard	1989 ....Emerson Fittipaldi
1953 ....Sam Hanks	1972 ....Joe Leonard	1990 ....Al Unser Jr
1954 ....Jimmy Bryan	1973 ....Roger McCluskey	1991 ....Michael Andretti
1955 ....Bob Sweikert	1974 ....Bobby Unser	1992 ....Bobby Rahal
1956 ....Jimmy Bryan	1975 ............A.J. Foyt	1993 ....Nigel Mansell
1957 ....Jimmy Bryan	1976 ....Gordon Johncock	1994 ....Al Unser Jr
1958 ....Tony Bettenhausen	1977 ....Tom Sneva	1995 ....Jacques Villeneuve
1959 ....Rodger Ward	1978 ....Tom Sneva	1996 ....Jimmy Vasser
1960 ............A.J. Foyt	1979 ............A.J. Foyt	1997 ....Alex Zanardi
1961 ............A.J. Foyt	1979 ....Rick Mears	1998 ....Alex Zanardi
1962 ....Rodger Ward	1980 ....Johnny Rutherford	1999 ....Juan Montoya
1963 ............A.J. Foyt	1981 ....Rick Mears	

Alltime CART Leaders

WINS		WINNINGS ($)		POLE POSITIONS	
A.J. Foyt	67	Al Unser Jr	18,828,406	Mario Andretti	67
Mario Andretti	52	Bobby Rahal	16,344,008	A.J. Foyt	53
*Michael Andretti	40	*Michael Andretti	16,686,369	Bobby Unser	49
Al Unser	39	Emerson Fittipaldi	14,293,625	Rick Mears	40
Bobby Unser	35	Mario Andretti	11,552,154	*Michael Andretti	32
Al Unser Jr	31	Rick Mears	11,050,807	Al Unser	27
Rick Mears	29	*Jimmy Vasser	9,519,994	Johnny Rutherford	23
Johnny Rutherford	27	Danny Sullivan	8,884,126	Gordon Johncock	20
Rodger Ward	26	Arie Luyendyk	7,732,188	Rex Mays	19
Gordon Johncock	25	Raul Boesel	6,971,887	Danny Sullivan	19
Bobby Rahal	24	*Paul Tracy	7,814,270	Bobby Rahal	18
Ralph DePalma	24	Al Unser	6,740,843	Emerson Fittipaldi	17
Tommy Milton	23	Alex Zanardi	5,733,750	Tony Bettenhausen	14
Tony Bettenhausen	22	Scott Pruett	5,440,144	Don Branson	14
Emerson Fittipaldi	22	Adrian Fernandez	5,284,265	Tom Sneva	14
Earl Cooper	20	A.J. Foyt	5,357,589	*Paul Tracy	13
Jimmy Bryan	19	Teo Fabi	5,045,881	*Juan Montoya	13
Jimmy Murphy	19	Scott Brayton	4,807,274	Parnelli Jones	12
*Paul Tracy	18	Scott Goodyear	4,579,451	Rodger Ward	11
Danny Sullivan	17	Roberto Guerrero	4,275,163	Danny Ongais	11

*Active driver. Note: Leaders through September 19, 2000.

National Association for Stock Car Auto Racing

Stock Car Racing's Major Events

Winston offers a $1 million bonus to any driver to win three of NASCAR's top four events in the same season. These races are the richest (Daytona 500), the fastest (Talladega 500), the longest (World 600 at Charlotte) and the oldest (Southern 500 at Darlington). These events form the backbone of NASCAR racing. Only four drivers, Lee Roy Yarbrough (1969), David Pearson (1976), Bill Elliott (1985) and Jeff Gordon (1997) have scored the three-track hat trick.

Daytona 500

Year	Winner	Car	Avg Speed	Pole Winner	Speed
1959	Lee Petty	Oldsmobile	135.520	Cotton Owens	143.198
1960	Junior Johnson	Chevrolet	124.740	Fireball Roberts	151.556
1961	Marvin Panch	Pontiac	149.601	Fireball Roberts	155.709
1962	Fireball Roberts	Pontiac	152.529	Fireball Roberts	156.995
1963	Tiny Lund	Ford	151.566	Johnny Rutherford	165.183
1964	Richard Petty	Plymouth	154.345	Paul Goldsmith	174.910
1965	Fred Lorenzen	Ford	141.539	Darel Dieringer	171.151
1966	Richard Petty	Plymouth	160.627	Richard Petty	175.165
1967	Mario Andretti	Ford	149.926	Curtis Turner	180.831
1968	Cale Yarborough	Mercury	143.251	Cale Yarborough	189.222
1969	Lee Roy Yarbrough	Ford	157.950	David Pearson	190.029

Daytona 500 *(Cont.)*

Year	Winner	Car	Avg Speed	Pole Winner	Speed
1970	Pete Hamilton	Plymouth	149.601	Cale Yarborough	194.015
1971	Richard Petty	Plymouth	144.462	A.J. Foyt	182.744
1972	A.J. Foyt	Mercury	161.550	Bobby Isaac	186.632
1973	Richard Petty	Dodge	157.205	Buddy Baker	185.662
1974	Richard Petty	Dodge	140.894	David Pearson	185.017
1975	Benny Parsons	Chevrolet	153.649	Donnie Allison	185.827
1976	David Pearson	Mercury	152.181	A.J. Foyt	185.943
1977	Cale Yarborough	Chevrolet	153.218	Donnie Allison	188.048
1978	Bobby Allison	Ford	159.730	Cale Yarborough	187.536
1979	Richard Petty	Oldsmobile	143.977	Buddy Baker	196.049
1980	Buddy Baker	Oldsmobile	177.602*	A.J. Foyt	195.020
1981	Richard Petty	Buick	169.651	Bobby Allison	194.624
1982	Bobby Allison	Buick	153.991	Benny Parsons	196.317
1983	Cale Yarborough	Pontiac	155.979	Ricky Rudd	198.864
1984	Cale Yarborough	Chevrolet	150.994	Cale Yarborough	201.848
1985	Bill Elliott	Ford	172.265	Bill Elliott	205.114
1986	Geoff Bodine	Chevrolet	148.124	Bill Elliott	205.039
1987	Bill Elliott	Ford	176.263	Bill Elliott	210.364†
1988	Bobby Allison	Buick	137.531	Ken Schrader	193.823
1989	Darrell Waltrip	Chevrolet	148.466	Ken Schrader	196.996
1990	Derrike Cope	Chevrolet	165.761	Ken Schrader	196.515
1991	Ernie Irvan	Chevrolet	148.148	Davey Allison	195.955
1992	Davey Allison	Ford	160.256	Sterling Marlin	192.213
1993	Dale Jarrett	Chevrolet	154.972	Kyle Petty	189.426
1994	Sterling Marlin	Chevrolet	156.931	Loy Allen Jr	190.158
1995	Sterling Marlin	Chevrolet	141.710	Dale Jarrett	193.498
1996	Dale Jarrett	Ford	154.308	Dale Earnhardt	189.510
1997	Jeff Gordon	Chevrolet	148.295	Mike Skinner	189.813
1998	Dale Earnhardt	Chevrolet	172.712	Bobby Labonte	192.415
1999	Jeff Gordon	Chevrolet	161.551	Jeff Gordon	195.067
2000	Dale Jarrett	Ford	155.669	Dale Jarrett	191.091

*Track record, winning time. †Track record, qualifying time. Note: The Daytona 500, held annually in February, now opens the NASCAR season with 200 laps around the high-banked Daytona International Speedway.

World 600

Year	Winner	Car	Avg Speed	Pole Winner
1960	Joe Lee Johnson	Chevrolet	107.752	J.L. Johnson
1961	David Pearson	Pontiac	111.634	Richard Petty
1962	Nelson Stacy	Ford	125.552	Fireball Roberts
1963	Fred Lorenzen	Ford	132.418	Junior Johnson
1964	Jim Paschal	Plymouth	125.772	Junior Johnson
1965	Fred Lorenzen	Ford	121.772	Fred Lorenzon
1966	Marvin Panch	Plymouth	135.042	Paul Goldsmith
1967	Jim Paschal	Plymouth	135.832	Cale Yarborough
1968	Buddy Baker	Dodge	104.207	Donnie Allison
1969	Lee Yarbrough	Mercury	134.631	Donnie Allison
1970	Donnie Allison	Ford	129.680	Bobby Isaac
1971	Bobby Allison	Mercury	140.442	Charlie Glotzbach
1972	Buddy Baker	Dodge	142.255	Bobby Allison
1973	Buddy Baker	Dodge	134.890	Buddy Baker
1974	David Pearson	Mercury	135.720	David Pearson
1975	Richard Petty	Dodge	145.327	David Pearson
1976	David Pearson	Mercury	137.352	David Pearson
1977	Richard Petty	Dodge	137.636	David Pearson
1978	Darrell Waltrip	Chevrolet	138.355	David Pearson
1979	Darrell Waltrip	Chevrolet	136.674	Neil Bonnet
1980	Benny Parsons	Chevrolet	119.265	Cale Yarborough
1981	Bobby Allison	Buick	129.326	Neil Bonnett
1982	Neil Bonnett	Ford	130.508	David Pearson
1983	Neil Bonnett	Chevrolet	140.406	Buddy Baker
1984	Bobby Allison	Buick	129.233	Harry Gant
1985	Darrell Waltrip	Chevrolet	141.807	Bill Elliott
1986	Dale Earnhardt	Chevrolet	140.406	Geoff Bodine
1987	Kyle Petty	Ford	131.483	Bill Elliott
1988	Darrell Waltrip	Chevrolet	124.460	Davey Allison
1989	Darrell Waltrip	Chevrolet	144.077	Alan Kulwicki
1990	Rusty Wallace	Pontiac	137.650	Ken Schrader
1991	Davey Allison	Ford	138.951	Mark Martin

World 600 (Cont.)

Year	Winner	Car	Avg Speed	Pole Winner
1992	Dale Earnhardt	Chevrolet	132.980	Bill Elliott
1993	Dale Earnhardt	Chevrolet	145.504	Ken Schrader
1994	Jeff Gordon	Chevrolet	139.445	Jeff Gordon
1995	Bobby Labonte	Chevrolet	151.952	Jeff Gordon
1996	Dale Jarrett	Ford	147.581	Jeff Gordon
1997	Jeff Gordon	Chevrolet	136.745	Jeff Gordon
1998	Jeff Gordon	Chevrolet	136.424	Jeff Gordon
1999	Jeff Burton	Ford	151.367	Bobby Labonte
2000	Matt Kenseth	Ford	142.640	Dale Earnhardt Jr

Note: Held at the 1.5-mile high-banked Lowe's Motor Speedway in Charlotte on Memorial Day weekend.

Talladega 500

Year	Winner	Car	Avg Speed	Pole Winner	Speed
1969	Richard Brickhouse	Dodge	153.778	Charlie Glotzbach	199.466
1970	Pete Hamilton	Plymouth	158.517	Bobby Isaac	186.834
1971	Bobby Allison	Mercury	145.945	Davey Allison	187.323
1972	James Hylton	Mercury	148.728	Bobby Isaac	190.677
1973	Dick Brooks	Plymouth	145.454	Bobby Allison	187.064
1974	Richard Petty	Dodge	148.637	David Pearson	184.926
1975	Buddy Baker	Ford	130.892	Dave Marcis	191.340
1976	Dave Marcis	Dodge	157.547	Dave Marcis	190.651
1977	Davey Allison	Chevrolet	162.524	Benny Parsons	192.682
1978	Lennie Pond	Oldsmobile	174.700	Cale Yarborough	192.917
1979	Darrell Waltrip	Oldsmobile	161.229	Neil Bonnet	193.600
1980	Neil Bonnett	Mercury	166.894	Buddy Baker	198.545
1981	Ron Bouchard	Buick	156.737	Harry Gant	195.897
1982	Darrell Waltrip	Buick	168.157	Geoff Bodine	199.400
1983	Dale Earnhardt	Ford	170.611	Cale Yarborough	201.744
1984	Dale Earnhardt	Chevrolet	155.485	Cale Yarborough	202.474
1985	Cale Yarborough	Ford	148.772	Bill Elliott	207.578
1986	Bobby Hillin	Buick	151.552	Bill Elliott	209.005
1987	Bill Elliott	Ford	171.293	Bill Elliott	203.827
1988	Ken Schrader	Chevrolet	154.505	Darrell Waltrip	196.274
1989	Terry Labonte	Ford	157.354	Mark Martin	194.800
1990	Dale Earnhardt	Chevrolet	174.430	Dale Earnhardt	192.513
1991	Harry Gant	Oldsmobile	165.620	Sterling Marlin	192.085
1992	Ernie Irvan	Chevrolet	176.309	Sterling Marlin	190.586
1993	Dale Earnhardt	Chevrolet	153.858	Bill Elliott	192.397
1994	Jimmy Spencer	Ford	163.217	Dale Earnhardt	193.470
1995	Sterling Marlin	Chevrolet	173.188	Sterling Marlin	194.212
1996	Jeff Gordon	Chevrolet	133.387	Jeremy Mayfield	192.370
1997	Mark Martin	Ford	188.345	John Andretti	193.627
1998	Bobby Labonte	Pontiac	163.439	Bobby Labonte	195.728
1999	Dale Earnhardt	Chevrolet	163.395	Ken Schrader	197.765
2000	Jeff Gordon	Chevrolet	161.157	Jeremy Mayfield	186.969

Note: Held every spring at the 2.66-mile Talladega Superspeedway.

Southern 500

Year	Winner	Car	Avg Speed	Pole Winner
1950	Johnny Mantz	Plymouth	76.260	Wally Campbell
1951	Herb Thomas	Hudson	76.900	Marshall Teague
1952	Fonty Flock	Oldsmobile	74.510	Dick Rathman
1953	Buck Baker	Oldsmobile	92.780	Fonty Flock
1954	Herb Thomas	Hudson	94.930	Buck Baker
1955	Herb Thomas	Chevrolet	92.281	Tim Flock
1956	Curtis Turner	Ford	95.067	Buck Baker
1957	Speedy Thompson	Chevrolet	100.100	Paul Goldsmith
1958	Fireball Roberts	Chevrolet	102.590	Fireball Roberts
1959	Jim Reed	Chevrolet	111.836	Fireball Roberts
1960	Buck Baker	Pontiac	105.901	Cotton Owens
1961	Nelson Stacy	Ford	117.880	Fireball Roberts
1962	Larry Frank	Ford	117.965	Fireball Roberts
1963	Fireball Roberts	Ford	129.784	Fireball Roberts
1964	Buck Baker	Dodge	117.757	Richard Petty
1965	Ned Jarrett	Ford	115.924	Junior Johnson
1966	Darel Dieringer	Mercury	114.830	Lee Yarborough

Southern 500 (Cont.)

Year	Winner	Car	Avg Speed	Pole Winner
1967	Richard Petty	Plymouth	131.933	David Pearson
1968	Cale Yarborough	Mercury	126.132	Charlie Glotzbach
1969	Lee Roy Yarbrough	Ford	105.612	Cale Yarborough
1970	Buddy Baker	Dodge	128.817	David Pearson
1971	Bobby Allison	Mercury	131.398	Bobby Allison
1972	Bobby Allison	Chevrolet	128.124	David Pearson
1973	Cale Yarborough	Chevrolet	134.033	David Pearson
1974	Cale Yarborough	Chevrolet	111.075	Richard Petty
1975	Bobby Allison	Matador	116.825	David Pearson
1976	David Pearson	Mercury	120.534	David Pearson
1977	David Pearson	Mercury	106.797	Darrell Waltrip
1978	Cale Yarborough	Oldsmobile	116.828	David Pearson
1979	David Pearson	Chevrolet	126.259	Bobby Allison
1980	Terry Labonte	Chevrolet	115.210	Darrell Waltrip
1981	Neil Bonnett	Ford	126.410	Harry Gant
1982	Cale Yarborough	Buick	126.703	David Pearson
1983	Bobby Allison	Buick	123.343	Neil Bonnett
1984	Harry Gant	Chevrolet	128.270	Harry Gant
1985	Bill Elliott	Ford	121.254	Bill Elliott
1986	Tim Richmond	Chevrolet	121.068	Tim Richmond
1987	Dale Earnhardt	Chevrolet	115.520	Davey Allison
1988	Bill Elliott	Ford	128.297	Bill Elliott
1989	Dale Earnhardt	Chevrolet	135.462	Alan Kulwicki
1990	Dale Earnhardt	Chevrolet	123.141	Dale Earnhardt
1991	Harry Gant	Oldsmobile	133.508	Davey Allison
1992	Darrell Waltrip	Chevrolet	129.114	Sterling Marlin
1993	Mark Martin	Ford	137.932	Ken Schrader
1994	Bill Elliott	Ford	127.915	Geoff Bodine
1995	Jeff Gordon	Chevrolet	121.231	John Andretti
1996	Jeff Gordon	Chevrolet	135.757	Dale Jarrett
1997	Jeff Gordon	Chevrolet	121.149	Bobby Labonte
1998	Jeff Gordon	Chevrolet	139.031	Dale Jarrett
1999	Jeff Burton	Ford	100.816	Kenny Irwin
2000	Bobby Labonte	Pontiac	108.275	Jeremy Mayfield

Note: Held at the 1.366-mile Darlingtor. (SC) Raceway on Labor Day weekend.

Winston Cup NASCAR Champions

Year	Driver	Car	Wins	Poles	Winnings ($)
1949	Red Byron	Oldsmobile	2	0	5,800
1950	Bill Rexford	Oldsmobile	1	0	6,175
1951	Herb Thomas	Hudson	7	4	18,200
1952	Tim Flock	Hudson	8	4	20,210
1953	Herb Thomas	Hudson	11	10	27,300
1954	Lee Petty	Dodge	7	3	26,706
1955	Tim Flock	Chrysler	18	19	33,750
1956	Buck Baker	Chrysler	14	12	29,790
1957	Buck Baker	Chevrolet	10	5	24,712
1958	Lee Petty	Oldsmobile	7	4	20,600
1959	Lee Petty	Plymouth	10	2	45,570
1960	Rex White	Chevrolet	6	3	45,260
1961	Ned Jarrett	Chevrolet	1	4	27,285
1962	Joe Weatherly	Pontiac	9	6	56,110
1963	Joe Weatherly	Mercury	3	6	58,110
1964	Richard Petty	Plymouth	9	8	98,810
1965	Ned Jarrett	Ford	13	9	77,966
1966	David Pearson	Dodge	14	7	59,205
1967	Richard Petty	Plymouth	27	18	130,275
1968	David Pearson	Ford	16	12	118,824
1969	David Pearson	Ford	11	14	183,700
1970	Bobby Isaac	Dodge	11	13	121,470
1971	Richard Petty	Plymouth	21	9	309,225
1972	Richard Petty	Plymouth	8	3	227,015
1973	Benny Parsons	Chevrolet	1	0	114,345
1974	Richard Petty	Dodge	10	7	299,175
1975	Richard Petty	Dodge	13	3	378,865
1976	Cale Yarborough	Chevrolet	9	2	387,173
1977	Cale Yarborough	Chevrolet	9	3	477,499

Winston Cup NASCAR Champions (Cont.)

Year	Driver	Car	Wins	Poles	Winnings ($)
1978	Cale Yarborough	Oldsmobile	10	8	530,751
1979	Richard Petty	Chevrolet	5	1	531,292
1980	Dale Earnhardt	Chevrolet	5	0	588,926
1981	Darrell Waltrip	Buick	12	11	693,342
1982	Darrell Waltrip	Buick	12	7	873,118
1983	Bobby Allison	Buick	6	0	828,355
1984	Terry Labonte	Chevrolet	2	2	713,010
1985	Darrell Waltrip	Chevrolet	3	4	1,318,735
1986	Dale Earnhardt	Chevrolet	5	1	1,783,880
1987	Dale Earnhardt	Chevrolet	11	1	2,099,243
1988	Bill Elliott	Ford	6	6	1,574,639
1989	Rusty Wallace	Pontiac	6	4	2,247,950
1990	Dale Earnhardt	Chevrolet	9	4	3,083,056
1991	Dale Earnhardt	Chevrolet	4	0	2,396,685
1992	Alan Kulwicki	Ford	2	6	2,322,561
1993	Dale Earnhardt	Chevrolet	6	2	3,353,789
1994	Dale Earnhardt	Chevrolet	4	2	3,400,733
1995	Jeff Gordon	Chevrolet	7	8	4,347,343
1996	Terry Labonte	Chevrolet	2	4	4,030,648
1997	Jeff Gordon	Chevrolet	10	1	4,201,227
1998	Jeff Gordon	Chevrolet	13	7	6,175,867
1999	Dale Jarrett	Ford	4	0	3,590,829

Alltime NASCAR Leaders

WINS

Richard Petty	200
David Pearson	105
Bobby Allison	84
*Darrell Waltrip	84
Cale Yarborough	83
*Dale Earnhardt	75
Lee Petty	55
*Rusty Wallace	53
*Jeff Gordon	52
Ned Jarrett	50
Junior Johnson	50
Herb Thomas	48
Buck Baker	46
*Bill Elliott	40
Tim Flock	40

WINNINGS ($)

*Dale Earnhardt	37,587,624
*Jeff Gordon	28,883,275
*Rusty Wallace	22,714,389
*Bill Elliott	22,583,340
*Mark Martin	22,476,943
*Terry Labonte	22,143,418
*Dale Jarrett	21,443,476
*Darrell Waltrip	18,941,149
*Ricky Rudd	18,319,026
*Bobby Labonte	15,186,998
*Jeff Burton	15,028,300
*Ken Schrader	14,742,426
*Geoff Bodine	14,620,331
*Sterling Marlin	14,331,698
*Kyle Petty	12,239,978

POLE POSITIONS

Richard Petty	126
David Pearson	113
Cale Yarborough	70
*Darrell Waltrip	59
Bobby Allison	57
Bobby Isaac	51
*Bill Elliott	50
Junior Johnson	47
Buck Baker	44
Buddy Baker	40
*Mark Martin	39
Tim Flock	39
Herb Thomas	39
*Geoff Bodine	37

*Active drivers. Note: NASCAR leaders through September 15, 2000.

Formula One Grand Prix Racing

World Driving Champions

Year	Winner	Car	Year	Winner	Car
1950	Guiseppe Farina, Italy	Alfa Romeo	1961	Phil Hill, United States	Ferrari
1951	Juan-Manuel Fangio, Argentina	Alfa Romeo	1962	Graham Hill, England	BRM
			1963	Jim Clark, Scotland	Lotus-Climax
1952	Alberto Ascari, Italy	Ferrari	1964	John Surtees, England	Ferrari
1953	Alberto Ascari, Italy	Ferrari	1965	Jim Clark, Scotland	Lotus-Climax
1954	Juan-Manuel Fangio, Argentina	Maserati/ Mercedes	1966	Jack Brabham, Australia	Brabham-Climax
			1967	Denis Hulme, New Zealand	Brabham-Repco
1955	Juan-Manuel Fangio, Argentina	Mercedes	1968	Graham Hill, England	Lotus-Ford
			1969	Jackie Stewart, Scotland	Matra-Ford
1956	Juan-Manuel Fangio, Argentina	Ferrari	1970	Jochen Rindt, Austria*	Lotus-Ford
			1971	Jackie Stewart, Scotland	Tyrell-Ford
1957	Juan-Manuel Fangio, Argentina	Maserati	1972	Emerson Fittipaldi, Brazil	Lotus-Ford
			1973	Jackie Stewart, Scotland	Tyrell-Ford
1958	Mike Hawthorne, England	Ferrari	1974	Emerson Fittipaldi, Brazil	McLaren-Ford
1959	Jack Brabham, Australia	Cooper-Climax	1975	Niki Lauda, Austria	Ferrari
1960	Jack Brabham, Australia	Cooper-Climax			

World Driving Champions *(Cont.)*

Year	Winner	Car	Year	Winner	Car
1976	James Hunt, England	McLaren-Ford	1988	Ayrton Senna, Brazil	McLaren-Honda
1977	Niki Lauda, Austria	Ferrari	1989	Alain Prost, France	McLaren-Honda
1978	Mario Andretti, U.S.	Lotus-Ford	1990	Ayrton Senna, Brazil	McLaren-Honda
1979	Jody Scheckter, S Africa	Ferrari	1991	Ayrton Senna, Brazil	McLaren-Honda
1980	Alan Jones, Australia	Williams-Ford	1992	Nigel Mansell, Gr. Britain	Williams-Renault
1981	Nelson Piquet, Brazil	Brabham-Ford	1993	Alain Prost, France	Williams-Renault
1982	Keke Rosberg, Finland	Williams-Ford	1994	Michael Schumacher, Ger	Benetton-Ford
1983	Nelson Piquet, Brazil	Brabham-BMW	1995	Michael Schumacher, Ger	Benetton-Renault
1984	Niki Lauda, Austria	McLaren-Porsche	1996	Damon Hill, Great Britain	Williams-Renault
1985	Alain Prost, France	McLaren-Porsche	1997	Jacques Villeneuve, Canada	Williams-Renault
1986	Alain Prost, France	McLaren-Porsche	1998	Mika Hakkinen, Finland	McLaren-Mercedes
1987	Nelson Piquet, Brazil	Williams-Honda	1999	Mika Hakkinen, Finland	McLaren-Mercedes

Alltime Grand Prix Winners

Driver	Wins	Driver	Wins
Alain Prost, France	51	Jim Clark, Great Britain	25
*Michael Schumacher, Germany	42	Niki Lauda, Austria	25
Ayrton Senna, Brazil	41	Juan Manuel Fangio, Argentina	24
Nigel Mansell, Great Britain	31	Nelson Piquet, Brazil	23
Jackie Stewart, Great Britain	27	Damon Hill, Great Britain	22

*Active driver. Note: Grand Prix winners through September 25, 2000.

Alltime Grand Prix Pole Winners

Driver	Poles	Driver	Poles
Ayrton Senna, Brazil	65	Juan Manuel Fangio, Argentina	29
Alain Prost, France	33	*Mika Hakkinen, Finland	26
Jim Clark, Great Britain	33	Niki Lauda, Austria	24
Nigel Mansell, Great Britain	32	Nelson Piquet, Brazil	24
*Michael Schumacher, Germany	30	Damon Hill, Great Britain	20

*Active driver. Note: Pole winners through September 25, 2000.

Professional Sports Car Racing, Inc.

The 24 Hours of Daytona

Year	Winner	Car	Avg Speed	Distance
1962	Dan Gurney	Lotus 19-Class SP11	104.101 mph	3 hrs (312.42 mi)
1963	Pedro Rodriguez	Ferrari-Class 12	102.074 mph	3 hrs (308.61 mi)
1964	Pedro Rodriguez/Phil Hill	Ferrari 250 LM	98.230 mph	2,000 km
1965	Ken Miles/Lloyd Ruby	Ford	99.944 mph	2,000 km
1966	Ken Miles/Lloyd Ruby	Ford Mark II	108.020 mph	24 hrs (2,570.63 mi)
1967	Lorenzo Bandini/Chris Amon	Ferrari 330 P4	105.688 mph	24 hrs (2,537.46 mi)
1968	Vic Elford/Jochen Neerpasch	Porsche 907	106.697 mph	24 hrs (2,565.69 mi)
1969	Mark Donohue/Chuck Parsons	Chevy Lola	99.268 mph	24 hrs (2,383.75 mi)
1970	Pedro Rodriguez/Leo Kinnunen	Porsche 917	114.866 mph	24 hrs (2,758.44 mi)
1971	Pedro Rodriguez/Jackie Oliver	Porsche 917K	109.203 mph	24 hrs (2,621.28 mi)
1972*	Mario Andretti/Jacky Ickx	Ferrari 312/P	122.573 mph	6 hrs (738.24 mi)
1973	Peter Gregg/Hurley Haywood	Porsche Carrera	106.225 mph	24 hrs (2,552.7 mi)
1974	(No race)			
1975	Peter Gregg/Hurley Haywood	Porsche Carrera	108.531 mph	24 hrs (2,606.04 mi)
1976†	Peter Gregg/Brian Redman/ John Fitzpatrick	BMW CSL	104.040 mph	24 hrs (2,092.8 mi)
1977	John Graves/Hurley Haywood/ Dave Helmick	Porsche Carrera	108.801 mph	24 hrs (2,615 mi)
1978	Rolf Stommelen/ Antoine Hezemans/Peter Gregg	Porsche Turbo	108.743 mph	24 hrs (2,611.2 mi)
1979	Ted Field/Danny Ongais/ Hurley Haywood	Porsche Turbo	109.249 mph	24 hrs (2,626.56 mi)
1980	Volkert Meri/Rolf Stommelen/ Reinhold Joest	Porsche Turbo	114.303 mph	24 hrs

The 24 Hours of Daytona *(Cont.)*

Year	Winner	Car	Avg Speed	Distance
1981	Bob Garretson/Bobby Rahal/ Brian Redman	Porsche Turbo	113.153 mph	24 hrs
1982	John Paul Jr/John Paul Sr/ Rolf Stommelen	Porsche Turbo	114.794 mph	24 hrs
1983	Preston Henn/Bob Wollek/ Claude Ballot-Lena/A. J. Foyt	Porsche Turbo	98.781 mph	24 hrs
1984	Sarel van der Merwe/ Graham Duxbury/Tony Martin	Porsche March	103.119 mph	24 hrs (2,476.8 mi)
1985	A. J. Foyt/Bob Wollek/ Al Unser/Thierry Boutsen	Porsche 962	104.162 mph	24 hrs (2,502.68 mi)
1986	Al Holbert/Derek Bell/Al Unser Jr	Porsche 962	105.484 mph	24 hrs (2,534.72 mi)
1987	Chip Robinson/Derek Bell/ Al Holbert/Al Unser Jr	Porsche 962	111.599 mph	24 hrs (2,680.68 mi)
1988	Martin Brundle/John Nielsen/ Raul Boesel	Jaguar XJR-9	107.943 mph	24 hrs (2,591.68 mi)
1989	John Andretti/Derek Bell/ Bob Wollek	Porsche 962	92.009 mph	24 hrs (2,210.76 mi)
1990	Davy Jones/ Jan Lammers/ Andy Wallace	Jaguar XJR-12	112.857 mph	24 hrs (2,709.16 mi)
1991	Hurley Haywood/ John Winter/ Frank Jelinski/ Henri Pescarolo/ Bob Wollek	Porsche 962C	106.633 mph	24 hrs (2,559.64 mi)
1992	Massahiro Hasemi/ Kazuoyshi Hoshino/ Toshio Suzuki/ Anders Olofsson	Nissan R91CP	112.987 mph	24 hrs (2,712.72 mi)
1993	P.J. Jones/Mark Dismore/ Rocky Moran	Toyota Eagle MK III	103.537 mph	24 hrs (2,484.88 mi)
1994	Paul Gentilozzi/ Scott Pruett/ Butch Leitzinger/ Steve Millen	Nissan 300 ZX	104.80 mph	24 hrs (2,693.67 mi)
1995	Jurgen Lassig/ Christophe Buochut/ Giovanni Lavaggi/ Marco Werner	Porsche Spyder K8	102.28 mph	690 laps (2,456.4 mi)
1996	Wayne Taylor/ Scott Sharp/ Jim Pace	Oldsmobile Mark III	103.32 mph	697 laps (2,481.32 mi)
1997	Elliot Forbes/John Schneider/ Rob Dyson/John Paul Jr/ Butch Leitzinger/James Weaver/ Andy Wallace	Ford R & S MK III	102.292 mph	690 laps (2,456.4 mi)
1998	Arie Luyendyk/Didier Theys/ Mauro Baldi	Ferrari 333 SP	105.565 mph	711 laps (2,531.16 mi)
1999	Elliott Forbes-Robinson/Butch Leitzinger/ Andy Wallace	Ford R & S MK III	104.9 mph	708 laps (2,520.48 mi)
2000	Olivier Beretta/Karl Wendlinger/ Dominique Dupuy	Dodge Viper	107.207 mph	723 laps (2,573.88 m)

*Race shortened due to fuel crisis. †Course lengthened from 3.81 miles to 3.84 miles.

World SportsCar Champions*

Year	Winner	Car	Year	Winner	Car
1978	Peter Gregg	Porsche 935	1989	Geoff Brabham	Nissan GTP
1979	Peter Gregg	Porsche 935	1990	Geoff Brabham	Nissan GTP
1980	John Fitzpatrick	Porsche 935	1991	Geoff Brabham	Nissan NPT
1981	Brian Redman	Chevy Lola	1992	Juan Fangio II	Toyota EGL MKIII
1982	John Paul Jr	Chevy Lola	1993	Juan Fangio II	Toyota EGL MKIII
1983	Al Holbert	Chevy March	1994	Wayne Taylor	Mazda Kudzu
1984	Randy Lanier	Chevy March	1995	Fermin Velez	Ferrari 333 SP
1985	Al Holbert	Porsche 962	1996	Wayne Taylor	Mazda Kudzu
1986	Al Holbert	Porsche 962	1997	Butch Leitzinger	Ford R&S MKIII
1987	Chip Robinson	Porsche 962	1998	Butch Leitzinger	Ford R&S MKIII
1988	Geoff Brabham	Nissan GTP			

*1978–93 champions raced in the GT series, which in 1994 was replaced by the World SportsCar series. Beginning in 1999, racing was reclassified according to the American Le Mans Series. The Series is comprised of two different types of race cars divided into two categories and five separate classes. The Prototype category features open-cockpit prototype World Sports Cars (WSC) and Le Mans Prototypes (LMP), as well as Grand Touring Prototype (GTP) class cars. The Grand Touring category features the Grand Touring S (GTS) class cars, formerly known as GT2, and Grand Touring (GT) cars, formerly known as GT3. Both classes feature purpose-built race cars with an emphasis on spectator car identification.

Alltime SportsCar Leaders

PROTOTYPE WINS (WSC/GTP ERA: 1994–2000)

James Weaver	14
Butch Leitzinger	13
Wayne Taylor	8
Gianpiero Moretti	7
J.J. Lehto	6
Fermin Velez	5
John Paul Jr	5
Eric van de Poele	5
Andy Wallace	5
Jeremy Dale	4

GTS AND GT WINS (IMSA GT: 1971–1993)

Al Holbert	49
Peter Gregg	41
Hurley Haywood	31
Geoff Brabham	26
Parker Johnstone	25
Jim Downing	23
Irv Hoerr	23
Jack Baldwin	22
Don Devendorf	22
Bob Earl	22
Tommy Riggins	22

Note: Leaders through September 22, 2000.

24 Hours of Le Mans

Year	Winning Drivers	Car
1923	André Lagache/René Léonard	Chenard & Walker
1924	John Duff/Francis Clement	Bentley
1925	Gérard de Courcelles/André Rossignol	La Lorraine
1926	Robert Bloch/André Rossignol	La Lorraine
1927	J. Dudley Benjafield/Sammy Davis	Bentley
1928	Woolf Barnato/Bernard Rubin	Bentley
1929	Woolf Barnato/Sir Henry Birkin	Bentley Speed 6
1930	Woolf Barnato/Glen Kidston	Bentley Speed 6
1931	Earl Howe/Sir Henry Birkin	Alfa Romeo 8C-2300 sc
1932	Raymond Sommer/Luigi Chinetti	Alfa Romeo 8C-2300 sc
1933	Raymond Sommer/Tazio Nuvolari	Alfa Romeo 8C-2300 sc
1934	Luigi Chinetti/Philippe Etancelin	Alfa Romeo 8C-2300 sc
1935	John Hindmarsh/Louis Fontés	Lagonda M45R
1936	Race cancelled	
1937	Jean-Pierre Wimille/Robert Benoist	Bugatti 57G sc
1938	Eugene Chaboud/Jean Tremoulet	Delahaye 135M
1939	Jean-Pierre Wimille/Pierre Veyron	Bugatti 57G sc
1940–48	Races cancelled	
1949	Luigi Chinetti/Lord Selsdon	Ferrari 166MM
1950	Louis Rosier/Jean-Louis Rosier	Talbot-Lago
1951	Peter Walker/Peter Whitehead	Jaguar C
1952	Hermann Lang/Fritz Reiss	Mercedes-Benz 300 SL
1953	Tony Rolt/Duncan Hamilton	Jaguar C
1954	Froilan Gonzales/Maurice Trintignant	Ferrari 375
1955	Mike Hawthorn/Ivor Bueb	Jaguar D
1956	Ron Flockhart/Ninian Sanderson	Jaguar D
1957	Ron Flockhart/Ivor Buab	Jaguar D
1958	Olivier Gendebien/Phil Hill	Ferrari 250 TR58
1959	Carroll Shelby/Roy Salvadori	Aston Martin DBR1
1960	Olivier Gendebien/Paul Fräre	Ferrari 250 TR59/60
1961	Olivier Gendebien/Phil Hill	Ferrari 250 TR61
1962	Olivier Gendebien/Phil Hill	Ferrari 250P
1963	Lodovico Scarfiotti/Lorenzo Bandini	Ferrari 250P
1964	Jean Guichel/Nino Vaccarella	Ferrari 275P
1965	Jochen Rindt/Masten Gregory	Ferrari 250LM
1966	Chris Amon/Bruce McLaren	Ford Mk2
1967	Dan Gurney/A. J. Foyt	Ford Mk4
1968	Pedro Rodriguez/Lucien Bianchi	Ford GT40
1969	Jacky Ickx/Jackie Oliver	Ford GT40
1970	Hans Herrmann/Richard Attwood	Porsche 917
1971	Helmut Marko/Gijs van Lennep	Porsche 917
1972	Henri Pescarolo/Graham Hill	Matra-Simca MS670
1973	Henri Pescarolo/Gérard Larrousse	Matra-Simca MS670B

Year	Winning Drivers	Car
1974	Henri Pescarolo/Gérard Larrousse	Matra-Simca MS670B
1975	Jacky Ickx/Derek Bell	Mirage-Ford MB
1976	Jacky Ickx/Gijs van Lennep	Porsche 936
1977	Jacky Ickx/Jurgen Barth/Hurley Haywood	Porsche 936
1978	Jean-Pierre Jaussaud/Didier Pironi	Renault-Alpine A442
1979	Klaus Ludwig/Bill Whittington/Don Whittington	Porsche 935
1980	Jean-Pierre Jaussaud/Jean Rondeau	Rondeau-Ford M379B
1981	Jacky Ickx/Derek Bell	Porsche 936-81
1982	Jacky Ickx/Derek Bell	Porsche 956
1983	Vern Schuppan/Hurley Haywood/Al Holbert	Porsche 956-83
1984	Klaus Ludwig/Henri Pescarolo	Porsche 956B
1985	Klaus Ludwig/Paolo Barilla/John Winter	Porsche 956B
1986	Derek Bell/Hans-Joachim Stuck/Al Holbert	Porsche 962C
1987	Derek Bell/Hans-Joachim Stuck/Al Holbert	Porsche 962C
1988	Jan Lammers/Johnny Dumfries/Andy Wallace	Jaguar XJR9LM
1989	Jochen Mass/Manuel Reuter/Stanley Dickens	Sauber-Mercedes C9-88
1990	John Nielsen/Price Cobb/Martin Brundle	TWR Jaguar XJR-12
1991	Volker Weidler/Johnny Herbert/Bertrand Gachof	Mazda 787B
1992	Derek Warwick/Yannick Dalmas/Mark Blundell	Peugeot 905B
1993	Geoff Brabham/Christophe Bouchut/Eric Helary	Peugeot 905
1994	Yannick Dalmas/Hurley Haywood/Mauro Baldi	Porsche 962
1995	Yannick Dalmas/J.J. Lehto/Masanori Sekiya	McLaren BMW
1996	Manuel Reuter/Davy Jones/Alexander Wurz	TWR Porsche
1997	Michele Alboreto/Stefan Johansson/Tom Kristensen	TWR Porsche
1998	Alan McNish/Laurent Aiello/Stephane Ortelli	Porsche GT One
1999	Yannick Dalmas/Joachim Winkelhock/Pierluigi Martini	BMW V12 LMR
2000	Frank Biela/Tom Kristensen/Emanuele Pirro	Audi R8

Friendly Intruder

MEMORANDUM
To: Sylvester Stallone
From: SI's Inside Motor Sports

Sly,

Read in *Variety* that you are developing a movie about open-wheel racing. Now, we're not saying you don't know what's in Hollywood, but we seem to recall a certain film called *Stop! Or My Mom Will Shoot*. So allow us to offer a little advice: Your movie is going to need the requisite dashing, brash young driver who will be great if he can only harness his raw, natural ability. (See *Days of Thunder* and its $82.7 million domestic gross.) So read up on Juan Montoya, the defending CART champ who ran away with the Indianapolis 500 in his first try on Sunday.

Face it, the kid's straight out of central casting. He''s handsome, young (24) and cheeky. He got his job in much the same way Willie Mays Hayes got his in Major League ($49.8 million U.S. gross): CART team owner Chip Ganassi was in Barcelona watching Alex Zanardi practice with his new Formula One team in September '98 when a dashing young Colombian tooling around the track in a test session caught his eye. Everyone knew Ganassi needed a driver to replace Zanardi, a two-time CART champ, so the owner had grown accustomed to having his backside kissed on a regular basis. "When you own a championship team, you've got these athletes falling all over you," says Ganassi. "Juan didn't give a damn who I was."

Now here's the great part, Sly. When our lead character goes into the most important race of his life and people are wondering if a guy who doesn't seem to know that cars have brake pedals can win the Big One, he pulls it off and it actually is believable. Montoya's performance in May 2000, on a tricky track at a distance he had never won at, was dominant. (The longest of his seven CART wins was 225 miles.) From the moment the green flag fell, Montoya raced as if his life depended on winning. Starting second, he caught pole sitter and IRL champion Greg Ray on Lap 27 and by Lap 50 had amassed a lead of at least 20 seconds on the third-place car. At 200 mph, that means Montoya led 31 of the other 32 cars by a mile.

The only thing missing was drama. With 21 laps to go Montoya blew by teammate Jimmy Vasser, who had taken the lead by skipping a chance to pit under caution, and won by a cozy 7.2 seconds over 1996 Indy 500 champion Buddy Lazier. All that came a day after Montoya and Vasser ran in the CART race in Nazareth, Pa., finishing fourth and seventh, respectively.

So come on, Sly. We just want to see this story done right. Oh, and we wouldn't mind an executive producer credit.

—Mark Bechtel

Top Fuel
ELAPSED TIME

Time (Sec.)	Driver	Date	Site
9.00	Jack Chrisman	Feb 18, 1961	Pomona, CA
8.97	Jack Chrisman	May 20, 1961	Empona, VA
7.96	Bobby Vodnick	May 16, 1964	Bayview, MD
6.97	Don Johnson	May 7, 1967	Carlsbad, CA
5.97	Mike Snively	Nov 17, 1972	Ontario, CA
5.78	Don Garlits	Nov 18, 1973	Ontario, CA
5.698	Gary Beck	Oct 10, 1975	Ontario, CA
5.573	Gary Beck	Oct 18, 1981	Irvine, CA
5.484	Gary Beck	Sept 6, 1982	Clermont, IN
5.391	Gary Beck	Oct 1, 1983	Fremont, CA
5.280	Darrell Gwynn	Sept 25, 1986	Ennis, TX
5.176	Darrell Gwynn	April 4, 1987	Ennis, TX
5.090	Joe Amato	Oct 1, 1987	Ennis, TX
4.990	Eddie Hill	April 9, 1988	Ennis, TX
4.881	Gary Ormsby	Sept 28, 1990	Topeka, KS
4.799	Cory McClenathan	Sept 19, 1992	Mohnton, PA
4.762	Cory McClenathan	Oct 3, 1993	Topeka, KS
4.690	Michael Brotherton	May 20, 1994	Englishtown, NJ
4.595	Joe Amato	July 5, 1996	Topeka, KS
4.539	Joe Amato	Mar 21, 1998	Baytown, TX
4.525	Gary Scelzi	Oct 23, 1998	Ennis, TX
4.503	Mike Dunn	Feb 5, 1999	Pomona, CA
4.486	Larry Dixon	Apr 9, 1999	Houston
4.480	Gary Scelzi	Oct 31, 1999	Houston

SPEED

MPH	Driver	Date	Site
180.36	Connie Kalitta	Sept 3, 1962	Indianapolis
190.26	Don Garlits	Sept 21, 1963	East Haddam, CT
201.34	Don Garlits	Aug 1, 1964	Great Meadows, NJ
211.26	Donny Milani	May 15, 1965	Sacramento, CA
223.32	Don Cook	Apr 24, 1965	Fremont, CA
230.17	James Warren	Apr 10, 1967	Fresno, CA
243.24	Don Garlits	March 18, 1973	Gainesville, FL
250.69	Don Garlits	Oct 11, 1975	Ontario, CA
260.11	Joe Amato	March 18, 1984	Gainesville, FL
272.56	Don Garlits	March 23, 1986	Gainesville, FL
282.13	Joe Amato	Sept 5, 1987	Clermont, IN
291.54	Connie Kalitta	Feb 11, 1989	Pomona, CA
301.70	Kenny Bernstein	March 20, 1992	Gainesville, FL
311.86	Kenny Bernstein	Oct 30, 1994	Pomona, CA
319.82	Joe Amato	Mar 21, 1998	Baytown, TX
323.50	Joe Amato	May 17, 1998	Englishtown, NJ
326.44	Gary Scelzi	Nov 2, 1998	Houston
326.91	Tony Schumacher	Oct 22, 1999	Dallas

The Boss is Going Drag

For about what it cost him to claim a brawny over-the-hill slugger off waivers, George Steinbrenner bought himself one of the fastest cars in the world. At the NHRA nationals in September, the Yankees' owner announced that he would become the primary sponsor of the top-fuel dragster driven by Mike Dunn next year. The Steinbrenner family and businessman Darrell Gwynn will co-own the car, which is, of course, navy blue with pinstripes.

The three-year sponsorship deal will cost Steinbrenner $3.3 million annually, which is significantly cheaper than the $10 million to $15 million required to sponsor a Winston Cup car, and there's a chance Steinbrenner

will get real bang for his buck. Next year the NHRA will heavily promote its 50th anniversary.

The Boss is also getting something he treasures more than a bargain: a chance to win a title. Dunn and Gwynn finished fourth in the 1999 top-fuel points race, but their sponsor pulled out, leaving them without a car in 2000. Along with Steinbrenner's backing, which should give them the resources to compete for a title, come expectations. "George gave Billy Martin five chances," says Gwynn, who will oversee the team's day-to-day operations. "I hope he gives us that many too."

—Mark Bechtel

Funny Car

ELAPSED TIME

Time (Sec.)	Driver	Date	Site
6.92	Leroy Goldstein	Sept 3, 1970	Clermont, IN
5.987	Don Prudhomme	Oct 12, 1975	Ontario, CA
5.868	Raymond Beadle	July 16, 1981	Englishtown, NJ
5.799	Tom Anderson	Sept 3, 1982	Clermont, IN
5.637	Don Prudhomme	Sept 4, 1982	Clermont, IN
5.588	Rick Johnson	Feb 3, 1985	Pomona, CA
5.425	Kenny Bernstein	Sept 26, 1986	Ennis, TX
5.397	Kenny Bernstein	April 5, 1987	Ennis, TX
5.255	Ed McCulloch	April 17, 1988	Ennis, TX
5.193	Don Prudhomme	March 2, 1989	Baytown, TX
5.077	Cruz Pedregon	Sept 20, 1992	Mohnton, PA
4.987	Chuck Etcholis	Oct 2, 1993	Topeka, KS
4.819	Cruz Pedregon	Mar 21, 1998	Baytown, TX
4.807	Cruz Pedregon	Nov 1, 1998	Houston
4.788	John Force	Apr 11, 1999	Houston

SPEED

MPH	Driver	Date	Site
200.44	Gene Snow	August, 1968	Houston
250.00	Don Prudhomme	May 23, 1982	Baton Rouge, LA
260.11	Kenny Bernstein	March 18, 1984	Gainesville, FL
271.41	Kenny Bernstein	Aug 30, 1986	Indianapolis
280.72	Mike Dunn	Oct 2, 1987	Ennis, TX
290.13	Jim White	Oct 11, 1991	Ennis, TX
291.82	Jim White	Oct 25, 1991	Pomona, CA
300.40	Jim Epler	Oct 3, 1993	Topeka, KS
303.64	John Force	Sept 2, 1995	Indianapolis
308.74	John Force	Sept 28, 1997	Topeka, KS
317.46	John Force	Mar 21, 1998	Baytown, TX
323.89	John Force	May 17, 1998	Englishtown, NJ
324.05	John Force	Mar 19, 1999	Gainesville, FL

Pro Stock

ELAPSED TIME

Time (Sec.)	Driver	Date	Site
7.778	Lee Shepherd	March 12, 1982	Gainesville, FL
7.655	Lee Shepherd	Oct 1, 1982	Fremont, CA
7.557	Bob Glidden	Feb 2, 1985	Pomona, CA
7.497	Bob Glidden	Sep 13, 1985	Maple Grove, PA
7.377	Bob Glidden	Aug 28, 1986	Clermont, IN
7.294	Frank Sanchez	Oct 7, 1988	Baytown, TX
7.184	Darrell Alderman	Oct 12, 1990	Ennis, TX
7.099	Scott Geoffrion	Sept 19, 1992	Mohnton, PA
6.988	Kurt Johnson	May 20, 1994	Englishtown, NJ
6.873	Warren Johnson	Mar 14, 1998	Gainesville, FL
6.867	Warren Johnson	Oct 23, 1998	Ennis, TX
6.866	Warren Johnson	Mar 19, 1999	Gainesville, FL
6.843	Warren Johnson	Apr 30, 1999	Dinwiddie, VA
6.840	Kurt Johnson	May 1, 1999	Dinwiddie, VA
6.822	Warren Johnson	Oct 23, 1999	Dallas

Pro Stock *(Cont.)*

SPEED

MPH	Driver	Date	Site
181.08	Warren Johnson	Oct 1, 1982	Fremont, CA
190.07	Warren Johnson	Aug 29, 1986	Clermont, IN
191.32	Bob Glidden	Sep 4, 1987	Clermont, IN
192.18	Warren Johnson	Oct 13, 1990	Ennis, TX
193.21	Bob Glidden	July 28, 1991	Sonoma, CA
194.51	Warren Johnson	July 31, 1992	Sonoma, CA
195.99	Warren Johnson	May 21, 1993	Englishtown, NJ
196.24	Warren Johnson	Mar 19, 1993	Gainesville, FL
197.15	Warren Johnson	Apr 23, 1994	Commerce, GA
199.15	Warren Johnson	Mar 10, 1995	Baytown, TX
201.20	Warren Johnson	Mar 14, 1998	Gainesville, FL
201.34	Warren Johnson	Oct 23, 1998	Ennis, TX
201.37	Warren Johnson	Mar 19, 1999	Gainesville, FL
202.24	Warren Johnson	Apr 30,1999	Dinwiddie, VA
202.33	Warren Johnson	Oct 23, 1999	Dallas
202.36	Warren Johnson	Oct 31, 1999	Houston

Alltime Drag Racing Leaders

NHRA CAREER WINS

*John Force	89
Bob Glidden	85
*Warren Johnson	80
*Kenny Bernstein	53
*Joe Amato	52
Don Prudhomme	49
*David Schultz	44
Don Garlits	35
John Myers	33
*Darrell Alderman	27

BEST WON-LOST RECORD (WINNING PCT.)

*Matt Hines	185–40 (.822)
John Myers	268–69 (.795)
*Jeg Coughlin	134–41 (.766)
*David Schultz	349–109 (.762)
*Angelle Seeling	140–45 (.757)
*John Force	680–230 (.747)
*Bob Panella Jr	79–28 (.738)
*Gary Scelzi	173–64 (.730)
*Warren Johnson	712–268 (.727)
*Darrell Alderman	220–97 (.694)

*Active driver. Note: Leaders through September 20, 2000.

Up in Smoke

For the du Maurier Classic, the LPGA major that was extinguished in August 2000 as a result of Canadian legislation banning cigarette companies from sponsoring sports events, the loss of Big Tobacco is a big headache. The LPGA has not found a sponsor to replace the Imperial Tobacco Co. and the roughly $5.5 million needed to fund the event for 2001. Given prevailing attitudes in the U.S. and Canada toward tobacco advertising, the du Maurier's fate could await a number of other sporting events.

Although cigarette sponsorships have been on the decline in the U.S. for years—Virginia Slims, for instance, dropped title sponsorship of the WTA tour more than a decade ago—the 1998 tobacco settlement, which limits tobacco companies to one brand-name sports sponsorship annually, has forced the issue for the few remaining tobacco-dependent sports. Take auto racing. In 1995 R.J. Reynolds' Winston brand sponsored five major racing properties. Now Winston will be permitted to lend its name only to one (most likely the Winston Cup) after the current contracts run out. The loss of tobacco money left the grassroots driver development program formerly known as Winston Racing without a sponsor, forcing NASCAR to foot the entire bill for the 2000 season.

Surprisingly, the tobacco cutbacks have been a boon for some folks in auto racing. With fewer events to sponsor, RJR doubled Winston Cup's season-ending prize money this year, from $5 million to $10 million. As tobacco is weeded out of the racing game, tech firms, dot.coms and other "nontraditional" sponsors such as FedEx have been filling the void. The five-year-old Indy Racing Northern Lights Series does not have a single tobacco-sponsored team or event. The wave of new sponsors is so strong in high-profile motor sports that even if future rulings kill off the granddaddy of automotive smokefests, the Winston Cup, NASCAR isn't worried. "We don't want to look like we're not grateful for Winston's involvement," says John Griffin, NASCAR's managing director of worldwide communications, "but let's just say we have a savvy marketing team and a game plan that would go into effect pretty quickly."

While racing may be able to cope with tobacco withdrawal, lower-profile sports aren't faring as well.... As such events scramble to find multiple smaller sponsors to replace lost money, some athletes have been left to ponder a cruel irony: Eliminating cigarettes can be hazardous to the health of your sport.

Bowling

PWBA Bowler of the Decade Wendy Macpherson

Wonder Wendy

While a pair of hometown rivals battled on the men's tour, Wendy Macpherson made history on the women's

BY HANK HERSCH

CLERMONT, FLA., is five square miles nestled among cool, clear lakes, citrus groves and rolling hills. A half-hour west of Orlando and Disney World, it's a hotbed of fishing and boating and golf. Two of the most famous of Clermont's 6,910 residents relish those pursuits, often engaging in all three in a single day. Mostly, though, they throw themselves into a sport more closely associated with the Rust Belt, sharing in its ups and downs and preparing for those days when they can compete on television for a hefty paycheck and bragging rights.

Clermont residents Jason Couch, the son of an Orlando bowling center owner, and Norm Duke, the son of a bowling center owner in Mount Pleasant, Texas, provided much of the fireworks on the PBA tour in 1999–2000. Though neither of them was named Bowler of the Year (that honor went to Parker Bohn III) or Bowler of the Decade (Walter Ray Williams Jr.), each won one major title and finished second in another. "On the lanes it seems like com-

plete and total war every time we are out there," Duke said. "It's an ongoing soap opera."

An especially spicy installment came in November at the '99 Brunswick World Tournament of Champions in Overland Park, Kans., with Couch in the starring role. In the event's last frame he needed two strikes and seven pins to defeat Chris Barnes. As the 30-year-old Couch approached those final shots, he didn't think of the $100,000 first prize at stake but of the chance to win a title he had dreamed of since he was four. Not that that thought made it easier. "I still don't know how I got that last shot off my hand," Couch said. He did, though. It was his third strike in the frame.

In February 2000, in Toledo, Clermont's finest got a chance to play out their neighborhood rivalry: Couch—an analytical left-hander who trains at a special bowling center in Sebring, Fla., to take advantage of the most sophisticated equipment—versus Duke, the '94 Player of the Year and a savvy righthander whose versatility allows

Couch in the Clutch: Three strikes in the 10th frame brought Couch the T of C title.

him to adjust to any lane conditions on the fly. They went head-to-head twice in the final round of match play at the PBA national championship, and Couch prevailed both times. They met again the next day, in the playoff finals, on TV, the title at stake. Said Couch, "The friendship goes out the window when we are playing for money and trying to feed our families."

Duke's brood—one of whom shares a birthday with one of Couch's kids— ate a little better that week. Their dad won 214–198 and pocketed a $23,000 check. "I know I wouldn't like to beat Jason three times," Duke said. "I lost the last two matches against him, but this is the one that counts."

Though Couch would get even one month later in the finals of the Southern Region Open, Duke's victory in Toledo, along with his 1994 triumph at the Tournament of Champions, gave him two thirds of bowling's Triple Crown. At the U.S. Open in Phoenix, Duke quickly took aim at joining Billy Hardwick, Mike Aulby and Pete Weber as the only winners of all three top majors. But to defeat Robert Smith in the finals, he had a task almost as daunting as Couch's at the T of C: He needed a strike in the 10th frame. Smith, seeking his first tour win, buried his face in a towel and waited for the crowd to react to Duke's first throw. He left the 8-pin standing. "There was a lot at stake for me today," a disappointed Duke said afterward. "That probably played a big role in my last shot."

Wendy Macpherson would know about that sort of pressure in a major, and she didn't have to travel far from her Henderson, Nev., home to find it. She entered the finals of the 1999 Sam's Town Invitational in Las Vegas with a) a $14,000 first prize, b) a third career Bowler of the Year trophy and c) a shot at Bowler of the Decade on the line. In the seventh frame of her nip-and-tuck match against Marianne DiRupo, the 31-year-old Macpherson had to stop her approach, fearful she was going to trip. "I was having trouble putting one foot in front of the other," she said.

But in the 10th frame Macpherson recovered to deliver two strikes and a seven count. DiRupo left a 6-7-10 split, and Macpherson prevailed 209–195. Said the Bowler of the Year and the Bowler of the 1990s, "What a great way to end the decade. My first win of the '90s was here, and now I've won again in the last tournament of the century."

The Majors

MEN

1999 Brunswick World Tournament of Champions

CHAMPIONSHIP ROUND

Bowler	Games	Total	Earnings ($)
Jason Couch	2	427	100,000
Chris Barnes	1	193	32,000
Roger Bowker	2	434	23,000
Brian Himmler	2	441	16,000
David Ozio	1	221	12,000

Playoff Results: Himmler def. Ozio, 236–221; Bowker def. Himmler, 232–205; Couch def. Bowker, 230–202; Couch def. Barnes, 197–193.

Held at Incred-A-Bowl, Overland Park, KS, November 10–17, 1999.

2000 PBA National Championship

CHAMPIONSHIP ROUND

Bowler	Games	Total	Earnings ($)
Norm Duke	2	492	23,000
Jason Couch	1	198	12,000
Jess Stayrook	1	201	8,000
Dale Traber	3	683	6,000
Chris Barnes	1	246	5,500
Justin Hromek	1	213	5,000
Eric Forkel	1	204	4,500
Roger Bowker	1	202	4,000

Playoff Results: Traber def. Forkel and Bowker, 227–204–202; Traber def. Barnes and Hromek, 258–246–213; Duke def. Stayrook and Traber, 278–201–198; Duke def. Couch, 214–198.

Held at Southwyck Lanes, Toledo, OH, February 12–19, 2000.

Bayer/Brunswick Touring Players Championship

CHAMPIONSHIP ROUND

Bowler	Games	Total	Earnings ($)
Dennis Horan	4	924	40,000
Pete Weber	1	189	21,000
Ryan Shafer	1	198	12,000
Eric Forkel	1	199	9,000
Patrick Healey Jr.	1	189	7,000
Danny Wiseman	1	176	6,000
Bryon Smith	1	145	5,500
Jeff Lizzi	1	215	5,000

Playoff Results: Horan def. Lizzi and Smith, 237–215–145; Horan def. Healey and Wiseman, 226–189–176; Horan def. Forkel and Shafer, 200–199–198; Horan def. Weber, 266–189.

Held at Stonehedge Family Fun Center, Akron, OH, February 20–27, 2000.

2000 ABC Masters

CHAMPIONSHIP ROUND

Bowler	Games	Total	Earnings ($)
Mika Koivuniemi	2	482	35,000
Pete Weber	1	235	19,000
Paul Fleming	2	514	13,000
Jason Duran	2	452	9,000
Chris Barnes	1	222	7,000

MEN *(Cont.)*

2000 ABC Masters (Cont.)

Playoff Results: Duran def. Barnes, 257–222; Fleming def. Duran, 278–195; Koivuniemi def. Fleming, 246–236; Koivuniemi def. Weber, 236–235.

Held at Albuquerque Convention Center, Albuquerque, NM, June 10–17, 2000.

2000 United States Open

Bowler	Games	CHAMPIONSHIP ROUND Total	Earnings ($)
Robert Smith	1	202	35,000
Norm Duke	2	480	20,000
Jeff Lizzi	1	224	15,000
Paul Fleming	1	214	10,000

Playoff Results: Duke def. Lizzi and Fleming, 279–224–214; Smith def. Duke, 202–201.

Held at Arizona Veterans Memorial Coliseum, Phoenix, AZ, July 8–15, 2000

WOMEN

1999 AMF Gold Cup

Bowler	Games	CHAMPIONSHIP ROUND Total	Earnings ($)
Dana Miller-Mackie	1	236	35,000
Cara Honeychurch	3	778	19,000
Cathy Dorin	1	222	14,000
Aleta Sill	1	238	11,000
Wendy Macpherson	1	213	8,400

Playoff Results: Honeychurch def. Sill and Macpherson, 300–238–213; Honeychurch def. Dorin, 256–222; Miller-Mackie def. Honeychurch, 236–222.

Held at AMF Hanover Lanes, Richmond, VA, October 5–9, 1999.

1999 Sam's Town Invitational

Bowler	Games	CHAMPIONSHIP ROUND Total	Earnings ($)
Wendy Macpherson	1	209	14,000
Marianne DiRupo	3	637	7,700
Cheryl Daniels	1	213	5,200
Jody Ellis	1	195	4,400
Kim Canady	1	168	3,800

Playoff Results: DiRupo def. Ellis and Canady, 216–195–168; DiRupo def. Daniels, 216–213; Macpherson def. DiRupo, 209–195.

Held at Sam's Town Bowling Center, Las Vegas, October 30–November 6, 1999.

2000 WIBC Queens

Bowler	Games	CHAMPIONSHIP ROUND Total	Earnings ($)
Wendy Macpherson	1	227	23,000
Marianne DiRupo	2	438	13,000
Kim Terrell	2	447	9,000
Leanne Barrette	1	228	6,500
Sharon Aronson	1	140	5,000

Playoff Results: Terrell def. Barrette and Aronson, 234–228–140; DiRupo def. Terrell, 236–213; Macpherson def. DiRupo, 227–202.

Held at National Bowling Stadium, Reno, NV, May 22–28, 2000.

WOMEN *(Cont.)*

2000 United States Open

CHAMPIONSHIP ROUND

Bowler	Games	Total	Earnings ($)
Tennelle Grijalva	2	452	35,000
Kelly Kulick	1	155	20,000
Carol Gianotti-Block	1	196	15,000
Liz Johnson	1	203	10,000

Playoff Results: Grijalva def. Johnson and Gianotti, 213–203–196; Grijalva def. Kulick, 239–155.

Held at Arizona Veterans Memorial Coliseum, Phoenix, NV, July 9–15, 2000.

PBA Tour Results

1999 Fall Tour

Date	Event	Winner	Earnings ($)	Runner-Up
Sept 16–19	Oronamin C Japan Cup	Parker Bohn III	50,000	Norm Duke
Oct 2–6	ACDelco Challenge	Mark Mosayebi	31,000	Jason Couch
Oct 8–12	Brunswick ProSource Open	Rick Lawrence	19,000	Parker Bohn III
Oct 16–20	Track/Dexter Open	Parker Bohn III	20,000	W.R. Williams Jr
Oct 23–27	Greater Detroit Open	Dave Wodka	15,000	Steve Hoskins
Oct 30–Nov 3	Bay City Classic	Jason Couch	15,000	Tim Criss
Nov 6–10	Indianapolis Open	Randy Pedersen	15,000	Eric Forkel
Nov 13–17	Brunswick World Tournament of Champions	Jason Couch	100,000	Chris Barnes
Dec 6–8	Sand's Regency National Resident Pro Championship	Mike Scroggins	6,000	Tony Franklin

2000 Winter Tour

Date	Event	Winner	Earnings ($)	Runner-Up
Jan 16–21	Orleans Casino Open	Ryan Shafer	25,000	Mike Aulby
Jan 25–29	Brunswick ProSource Don Carter Classic	Norm Duke	20,000	Steve Jaros
Feb 1–5	Chattanooga Open	Parker Bohn III	20,000	John May
Feb 8–12	Parker Bohn III Empire State Open	Pete Weber	15,000	Brian Himmler
Feb 13–19	PBA National Championship	Norm Duke	23,000	Jason Couch
Feb 21–27	Bayer/Brunswick TPC	Dennis Horan	40,000	Pete Weber

2000 Summer Tour

Date	Event	Winner	Earnings ($)	Runner-Up
June 11–17	ABC Masters	Mika Koivuniemi	35,000	Pete Weber
June 27–July 1	Wichita Open	Ryan Shafer	15,000	Bob Learn Jr
July 4–8	MSN Open	Norm Duke	20,000	Chris Barnes
July 8–15	U.S. Open	Robert Smith	35,000	Norm Duke

1999–2000 Senior Tour

Date	Event	Winner	Earnings ($)	Runner-Up
Sept 25–29	Naples Senior Open	Johnny Petraglia	9,000	Chuck Pierce
Oct 3–9	The Villages Senior Tournament of Champions	Dave Soutar	10,000	John Hricsina
Oct 16–22	PBA Senior National Championship	Steve Neff	20,000	Bob Glass
Jan 4–9	ABC Senior Masters	Dave Soutar	18,000	Donald Breihan
Jan 11–15	National Bowling Stadium National Senior Doubles	Pete Couture / Dave Husted	30,000	Bob Glass / Robert Smith
Mar 25–31	Villages Senior World Championship	Roger Workman	20,000	Gene Stus
May 13–18	Central Pennsylvania Senior Open	Bob Glass	8,000	Pete Couture
May 27–June 1	Seattle Senior Open	Butch Soper	8,000	Norb Wetzel
June 4–8	Northwest Senior Classic	Al Sanford	9,000	Norb Wetzel
June 8–23	Orleans Casino Senior Open	Dave Davis	18,000	Dick Baker
July 2–6	Northern California Senior Classic	Lauri Karppala	8,500	Larry Laub

†PWBA Tour Results

1999 Fall Tour

Date	Event	Winner	Earnings ($)	Runner-Up
Sept 24–30	Visionary Bowling Products Classic	Carolyn Dorin-Ballard	14,400	Marianne DiRupo
Oct 8–14	Three Rivers Open	Cathy Dorin	11,500	Michelle Feldman
Oct 15–21	Brunswick Women's World Open	Cara Honeychurch	14,400	Tiff Stanbrough
Nov 7–14	Sam's Town Invitational	Wendy Macpherson	14,000	Marianne DiRupo

2000 Spring/Summer Tour

Date	Event	Winner	Earnings ($)	Runner-Up
Apr 17–20	Las Cruces New Mexico Open	Kim Adler	11,000	Paulina Aalto
Apr 23–28	Bowl for Blindness Classic	Carolyn Dorin-Ballard	11,000	Michelle Feldman
May 1–8	Greater San Diego Open	Carolyn Dorin-Ballard	11,000	Michelle Feldman
May 7–11	Track Doubles	Jeanne Naccarato	21,000	C. Gianotti-Block
		Robbin Mossontte		Maxine Nable
May 14–18	Bowl the Rogue Open	Michelle Feldman	11,000	Kim Adler
May 22–26	WIBC Queens	Wendy Macpherson	23,000	Marianne DiRupo
May 29–June 2	Omaha Open	Michelle Feldman	11,000	Lynda Barnes
June 5–8	St. Clair Classic	Kim Adler	11,600	W. Macpherson
June 11–15	Greater Terre Haute Open	Carol Gianotti-Block	11,500	Kim Adler
July 8–15	U.S. Open	Tennelle Grijalva	35,000	Kelly Kulick
July 23–27	Southern Virginia Open	Wendy Macpherson	11,000	C. Dorin-Ballard
July 29–Aug 2	Lady Ebonite Classic	Michelle Feldman	14,400	Leanne Barrette
Aug 5–9	Greater Atlanta Open	Aleta Sill	11,000	Tish Johnson

†Known as LBPT until 1998.

1999 Tour Leaders

PBA

MONEY LEADERS				AVERAGE		
Name	Titles	Tournaments	Earnings ($)	Name	Games	Average
Parker Bohn III	5	24	232,595	Parker Bohn III	844	228.04
Jason Couch	2	23	220,990	Jason Couch	931	225.18
Chris Barnes	2	26	123,965	Norm Duke	851	224.81
Norm Duke	0	23	92,930	Walter Ray Williams Jr	769	224.47
Bob Learn Jr	1	23	92,498	Ryan Shafer	867	224.26

Seniors

MONEY LEADERS				AVERAGE		
Name	Titles	Tournaments	Earnings ($)	Name	Games	Average
Dave Soutar	1	14	137,190	Robert Glass	368	225.45
Dale Eagle	4	14	79,465	Dale Eagle	600	225.28
Steve Neff	2	11	40,150	Mike Pullin	401	225.15
John Petraglia	2	7	34,320	Steve Neff	439	225.15
Roger Workman	1	12	33,505	Dave Soutar	607	224.98

PWBA

MONEY LEADERS				AVERAGE		
Name	Titles	Tournaments	Earnings ($)	Name	Games	Average
Wendy Macpherson	2	18	86,265	Wendy Macpherson	740	218.85
Kim Adler	2	18	83,495	Carolyn Dorin-Ballard	682	216.56
Leanne Barrette	2	18	78,835	Leanne Barrette	660	215.03
Carolyn Dorin-Ballard	2	18	71,015	Kim Canady	658	214.56
Dana Miller-Mackie	1	16	63,580	Anne Marie Duggan	641	214.10

Men's Majors

BPAA United States Open

Year	Winner	Score	Runner-Up	Site
1942	John Crimmins	265.09–262.33	Joe Norris	Chicago
1943	Connie Schwoegler	not available	Frank Benkovic	Chicago
1944	Ned Day	315.21–298.21	Paul Krumske	Chicago
1945	Buddy Bomar	304.46–296.16	Joe Wilman	Chicago
1946	Joe Wilman	310.27–305.37	Therman Gibson	Chicago
1947	Andy Varipapa	314.16–308.04	Allie Brandt	Chicago
1948	Andy Varipapa	309.23–309.06	Joe Wilman	Chicago
1949	Connie Schwoegler	312.31–307.27	Andy Varipapa	Chicago
1950	Junie McMahon	318.37–307.17	Ralph Smith	Chicago
1951	Dick Hoover	305.29–304.07	Lee Jouglard	Chicago
1952	Junie McMahon	309.29–305.41	Bill Lillard	Chicago
1953	Don Carter	304.17–297.36	Ed Lubanski	Chicago
1954	Don Carter	308.02–307.25	Bill Lillard	Chicago
1955	Steve Nagy	307.17–303.34	Ed Lubanski	Chicago
1956	Bill Lillard	304.30–304.22	Joe Wilman	Chicago
1957	Don Carter	308.49–305.45	Dick Weber	Chicago
1958	Don Carter	311.03–308.09	Buzz Fazio	Minneapolis
1959	Billy Welu	311.48–310.26	Ray Bluth	Buffalo
1960	Harry Smith	312.24–308.12	Bob Chase	Omaha
1961	Bill Tucker	318.49–309.11	Dick Weber	San Bernardino, CA
1962	Dick Weber	299.34–297.38	Roy Lown	Miami Beach
1963	Dick Weber	642–591	Billy Welu	Kansas City, MO
1964	Bob Strampe	714–616	Tommy Tuttle	Dallas
1965	Dick Weber	608–586	Jim St. John	Philadelphia
1966	Dick Weber	684–681	Nelson Burton Jr.	Lansing, MI
1967	Les Schissler	613–610	Pete Tountas	St. Ann, MO
1968	Jim Stefanich	12,401–12,104	Billy Hardwick	Garden City, NY
1969	Billy Hardwick	12,585–11,463	Dick Weber	Miami
1970	Bobby Cooper	12,936–12,307	Billy Hardwick	Northbrook, IL
1971	Mike Limongello	397 (2 games)	Teata Semiz	St. Paul, MN
1972	Don Johnson	233 (1 game)	George Pappas	New York City
1973	Mike McGrath	712 (3 games)	Earl Anthony	New York City
1974	Larry Laub	749 (3 games)	Dave Davis	New York City
1975	Steve Neff	279 (1 game)	Paul Colwell	Grand Prairie, TX
1976	Paul Moser	226 (1 game)	Jim Frazier	Grand Prairie, TX
1977	Johnny Petraglia	279 (1 game)	Bill Spigner	Greensboro, NC
1978	Nelson Burton Jr.	873 (4 games)	Jeff Mattingly	Greensboro, NC
1979	Joe Berardi	445 (2 games)	Earl Anthony	Windsor Locks, CT
1980	Steve Martin	930 (4 games)	Earl Anthony	Windsor Locks, CT
1981	Marshall Holman	684 (3 games)	Mark Roth	Houston
1982	Dave Husted	1011 (4 games)	Gil Sliker	Houston
1983	Gary Dickinson	214 (1 game)	Steve Neff	Oak Lawn, IL
1984	Mark Roth	244 (1 game)	Guppy Troup	Oak Hill, IL
1985	Marshall Holman	233 (1 game)	Wayne Webb	Venice, FL
1986	Steve Cook	467 (2 games)	Frank Ellenburg	Venice, FL
1987	Del Ballard Jr.	525 (2 games)	Pete Weber	Tacoma, WA
1988	Pete Weber	929 (4 games)	Marshall Holman	Atlantic City, NJ
1989	Mike Aulby	429 (2 games)	Jim Pencak	Edmond, OK
1990	Ron Palombi Jr.	269 (1 game)	Amleto Monacelli	Indianapolis
1991	Pete Weber	956 (4 games)	Mark Thayer	Indianapolis
1992	Robert Lawrence	667 (3 games)	Scott Devers	Canandaigua, NY
1993	Del Ballard Jr.	505 (2 games)	Walter Ray Williams Jr.	Canandaigua, NY
1994	Justin Hromek	267 (1 game)	Parker Bohn III	Troy, MI
1995	Dave Husted	266 (1 game)	Paul Koehler	Troy, MI
1996	Dave Husted	730 (3 games)	George Brooks	Indianapolis, IN
1997	No event—tournament rescheduled to April, beginning in 1998.			
1998	Walter Ray Williams Jr.	466 (2 games)	Tim Criss	Fairfield, CT
1999	Bob Learn Jr.	231 (1 game)	Jason Couch	Uncasville, CT
2000	Robert Smith	202 (1 game)	Norm Duke	Phoenix, AZ

Note: From 1942 to 1970, the tournament was called the BPAA All-Star. Peterson scoring was used from 1942 through 1962. Under this system, the winner of an individual match game gets one point, plus one point for each 50 pins knocked down. From 1963 through 1967, a three-game championship was held between the two top qualifiers. From 1968 through 1970 total pinfall determined the winner. From 1971 to the present, five qualifiers compete for the championship.

Touring Players Championship

Year	Winner	Score	Runner-Up	Site
1996	Mike Aulby	268 (1 game)	Parker Bohn III	Harmarville, PA
1997	Steve Hoskins	932 (4 games)	Danny Wiseman	Harmarville, PA
1998	Dennis Horan	481 (2 games)	Parker Bohn III	Akron, OH
1999	Steve Hoskins	503 (2 games)	Parker Bohn III	Akron, OH
2000	Dennis Horan	924 (4 games)	Pete Weber	Akron, OH

PBA National Championship

Year	Winner	Score	Runner-Up	Site
1960	Don Carter	6512 (30 games)	Ronnie Gaudern	Memphis
1961	Dave Soutar	5792 (27 games)	Morrie Oppenheim	Cleveland
1962	Carmen Salvino	5369 (25 games)	Don Carter	Philadelphia
1963	Billy Hardwick	13,541 (61 games)	Ray Bluth	Long Island, NY
1964	Bob Strampe	13,979 (61 games)	Ray Bluth	Long Island, NY
1965	Dave Davis	13,895 (61 games)	Jerry McCoy	Detroit
1966	Wayne Zahn	14,006 (61 games)	Nelson Burton Jr.	Long Island, NY
1967	Dave Davis	421 (2 games)	Pete Tountas	New York City
1968	Wayne Zahn	14,182 (60 games)	Nelson Burton Jr.	New York City
1969	Mike McGrath	13,670 (60 games)	Bill Allen	Garden City, NY
1970	Mike McGrath	660 (3 games)	Dave Davis	Garden City, NY
1971	Mike Limongello	911 (4 games)	Dave Davis	Paramus, NJ
1972	Johnny Guenther	12,986 (56 games)	Dick Ritger	Rochester, NY
1973	Earl Anthony	212 (1 game)	Sam Flanagan	Oklahoma City
1974	Earl Anthony	218 (1 game)	Mark Roth	Downey, CA
1975	Earl Anthony	245 (1 game)	Jim Frazier	Downey, CA
1976	Paul Colwell	191 (1 game)	Dave Davis	Seattle
1977	Tommy Hudson	206 (1 game)	Jay Robinson	Seattle
1978	Warren Nelson	453 (2 games)	Joseph Groskind	Reno
1979	Mike Aulby	727 (3 games)	Earl Anthony	Las Vegas
1980	Johnny Petraglia	235 (1 game)	Gary Dickinson	Sterling Heights, MI
1981	Earl Anthony	242 (1 game)	Ernie Schlegel	Toledo, OH
1982	Earl Anthony	233 (1 game)	Charlie Tapp	Toledo, OH
1983	Earl Anthony	210 (1 game)	Mike Durbin	Toledo, OH
1984	Bob Chamberlain	961 (4 games)	Dan Eberl	Toledo, OH
1985	Mike Aulby	476 (2 games)	Steve Cook	Toledo, OH
1986	Tom Crites	190 (1 game)	Mike Aulby	Toledo, OH
1987	Randy Pedersen	759 (3 games)	Amleto Monacelli	Toledo, OH
1988	Brian Voss	246 (1 game)	Todd Thompson	Toledo, OH
1989	Pete Weber	221 (1 game)	Dave Ferraro	Toledo, OH
1990	Jim Pencak	900 (4 games)	Chris Warren	Toledo, OH
1991	Mike Miller	450 (2 games)	Norm Duke	Toledo, OH
1992	Eric Forkel	833 (4 games)	Bob Vespi	Toledo, OH
1993	Ron Palombi Jr.	237 (1 game)	Eugene McCune	Toledo, OH
1994	David Traber	196 (1 game)	Dale Traber	Toledo, OH
1995	Scott Alexander	246 (1 game)	Wayne Webb	Toledo, OH
1996	Butch Soper	442 (2 games)	Walter Ray Williams Jr.	Toledo, OH
1997	Rick Steelsmith	888 (4 games)	Brian Voss	Toledo, OH
1998	Pete Weber	277 (1 game)	David Ozio	Toledo, OH
1999	Tim Criss	238 (1 game)	Dave Arnold	Toledo, OH
2000	Norm Duke	492 (2 games)	Jason Couch	Toledo, OH

Note: Totals from 1963–66, 1968–69 and 1972 include bonus pins.

Tournament of Champions

Year	Winner	Score	Runner-Up	Site
1965	Billy Hardwick	484 (2 games)	Dick Weber	Akron, OH
1966	Wayne Zahn	595 (3 games)	Dick Weber	Akron, OH
1967	Jim Stefanich	227 (1 game)	Don Johnson	Akron, OH
1968	Dave Davis	213 (1 game)	Don Johnson	Akron, OH
1969	Jim Godman	266 (1 game)	Jim Stefanich	Akron, OH
1970	Don Johnson	299 (1 game)	Dick Ritger	Akron, OH
1971	Johnny Petraglia	245 (1 game)	Don Johnson	Akron, OH
1972	Mike Durbin	775 (3 games)	Tim Harahan	Akron, OH
1973	Jim Godman	451 (2 games)	Barry Asher	Akron, OH
1974	Earl Anthony	679 (3 games)	Johnny Petraglia	Akron, OH
1975	Dave Davis	448 (2 games)	Barry Asher	Akron, OH
1976	Marshall Holman	441 (2 games)	Billy Hardwick	Akron, OH
1977	Mike Berlin	434 (2 games)	Mike Durbin	Akron, OH
1978	Earl Anthony	237 (1 game)	Teata Semiz	Akron, OH
1979	George Pappas	224 (1 game)	Dick Ritger	Akron, OH
1980	Wayne Webb	750 (3 games)	Gary Dickinson	Akron, OH

Tournament of Champions (Cont.)

Year	Winner	Score	Runner-Up	Site
1981	Steve Cook	287 (1 game)	Pete Couture	Akron, OH
1982	Mike Durbin	448 (2 games)	Steve Cook	Akron, OH
1983	Joe Berardi	865 (4 games)	Henry Gonzalez	Akron, OH
1984	Mike Durbin	950 (4 games)	Mike Aulby	Akron, OH
1985	Mark Williams	616 (3 games)	Bob Handley	Akron, OH
1986	Marshall Holman	233 (1 game)	Mark Baker	Akron, OH
1987	Pete Weber	928 (4 games)	Jim Murtishaw	Akron, OH
1988	Mark Williams	237 (1 game)	Tony Westlake	Fairlawn, OH
1989	Del Ballard Jr.	490 (2 games)	Walter Ray Williams Jr.	Fairlawn, OH
1990	Dave Ferraro	226 (1 game)	Tony Westlake	Fairlawn, OH
1991	David Ozio	476 (2 games)	Amleto Monacelli	Fairlawn, OH
1992	Marc McDowell	471 (2 games)	Don Genalo	Fairlawn, OH
1993	George Branham III	227 (1 game)	Parker Bohn III	Fairlawn, OH
1994	Norm Duke	422 (2 games)	Eric Forkel	Fairlawn, OH
1995	Mike Aulby	502 (2 games)	Bob Spaulding	Lake Zurich, IL
1996	Dave D'Entremont	971 (4 games)	Dave Arnold	Lake Zurich, IL
1997	John Gant	446 (2 games)	Mike Aulby	Reno, NV
1998	Bryan Goebel	245 (1 game)	Steve Hoskins	Overland Park, KS
1999	Jason Couch	427 (2 games)	Chris Barnes	Overland Park, KS

ABC Masters Tournament

Year	Winner	Scoring Avg	Runner-Up	Site
1951	Lee Jouglard	201.8	Joe Wilman	St. Paul, MN
1952	Willard Taylor	200.32	Andy Varipapa	Milwaukee
1953	Rudy Habetler	200.13	Ed Brosius	Chicago
1954	Eugene Elkins	205.19	W. Taylor	Seattle
1955	Buzz Fazio	204.13	Joe Kristof	Ft. Wayne, IN
1956	Dick Hoover	209.9	Ray Bluth	Rochester, NY
1957	Dick Hoover	216.39	Bill Lillard	Ft. Worth, TX
1958	Tom Hennessy	209.15	Lou Frantz	Syracuse, NY
1959	Ray Bluth	214.26	Billy Golembiewski	St. Louis, MO
1960	Billy Golembiewski	206.13	Steve Nagy	Toledo, OH
1961	Don Carter	211.18	Dick Hoover	Detroit
1962	Billy Golembiewski	223.12	Ron Winger	Des Moines, IA
1963	Harry Smith	219.3	Bobby Meadows	Buffalo
1964	Billy Welu	227	Harry Smith	Oakland, CA
1965	Billy Welu	202.12	Don Ellis	St. Paul, MN
1966	Bob Strampe	219.80	Al Thompson	Rochester, NY
1967	Lou Scalia	216.9	Bill Johnson	Miami Beach
1968	Pete Tountas	220.15	Buzz Fazio	Cincinnati
1969	Jim Chestney	223.2	Barry Asher	Madison, WI
1970	Don Glover	215.10	Bob Strampe	Knoxville, TN
1971	Jim Godman	229.8	Don Johnson	Detroit
1972	Bill Beach	220.27	Jim Godman	Long Beach, CA
1973	Dave Soutar	218.61	Dick Ritger	Syracuse, NY
1974	Paul Colwell	234.17	Steve Neff	Indianapolis
1975	Eddie Ressler	213.51	Sam Flanagan	Dayton, OH
1976	Nelson Burton Jr.	220.79	Steve Carson	Oklahoma City
1977	Earl Anthony	218.21	Jim Godman	Reno
1978	Frank Ellenburg	200.61	Earl Anthony	St. Louis
1979	Doug Myers	202.9	Bill Spigner	Tampa, FL
1980	Neil Burton	206.69	Mark Roth	Louisville
1981	Randy Lightfoot	218.3	Skip Tucker	Memphis
1982	Joe Berardi	207.12	Ted Hannahs	Baltimore
1983	Mike Lastowski	212.65	Pete Weber	Niagara Falls, NY
1984	Earl Anthony	212.5	Gil Sliker	Reno
1985	Steve Wunderlich	210.4	Tommy Kress	Tulsa, OK
1986	Mark Fahy	206.5	Del Ballard Jr.	Las Vegas
1987	Rick Steelsmith	210.7	Brad Snell	Niagara Falls, NY
1988	Del Ballard Jr.	219.1	Keith Smith	Jacksonville, FL
1989	Mike Aulby	218.5	Mike Edwards	Wichita
1990	Chris Warren	231.6	David Ozio	Reno
1991	Doug Kent	226.8	George Branham III	Toledo, OH
1992	Ken Johnson	230.0	Dave D'Entremont	Corpus Christi, TX
1993	Norm Duke	245.68	Patrick Allen	Tulsa, OK
1994	Steve Fehr	213.09	Steve Anderson	Greenacres, FL
1995	Mike Aulby	230.7	Mark Williams	Reno
1996	Ernie Schlegel	221.2	Mike Aulby	Salt Lake City
1997	Jason Queen	225.5	Eric Forkel	Huntsville, AL
1998	Mike Aulby	224.0	Parker Bohn III	Reno, NV

ABC Masters Tournament (Cont.)

Year	Winner	Scoring Avg	Runner-Up	Site
1999	Brian Boghosian	246.0	Parker Bohn III	Syracuse. NY
2000	Mika Koivuniemi	241.0	Pete Weber	Albuquerque, NM

Women's Majors

BPAA United States Open

Year	Winner	Score	Runner-Up	Site
1949	Marion Ladewig	113.26–104.26	Catherine Burling	Chicago
1950	Marion Ladewig	151.46–146.06	Stephanie Balogh	Chicago
1951	Marion Ladewig	159.17–148.03	Sylvia Wene	Chicago
1952	Marion Ladewig	154.39–142.05	Shirley Garms	Chicago
1953	Not held			
1954	Marion Ladewig	148.29–143.01	Sylvia Wene	Chicago
1955	Sylvia Wene	142.30–141.11	Sylvia Fanta	Chicago
1955	Anita Cantaline	144.40–144.13	Doris Porter	Chicago
1956	Marion Ladewig	150.16–145.41	Marge Merrick	Chicago
1957	Not held			
1958	Merle Matthews	145.09–143.14	Marion Ladewig	Minneapolis
1959	Marion Ladewig	149.33–143.00	Donna Zimmerman	Buffalo
1960	Sylvia Wene	144.14–143.26	Marion Ladewig	Omaha
1961	Phyllis Notaro	144.13–143.12	Hope Riccilli	San Bernardino, CA
1962	Shirley Garms	138.44–135.49	Joy Abel	Miami Beach
1963	Marion Ladewig	586–578	Bobbie Shaler	Kansas City, MO
1964	LaVerne Carter	683–609	Evelyn Teal	Dallas
1965	Ann Slattery	597–550	Sandy Hooper	Philadelphia
1966	Joy Abel	593–538	Bette Rockwell	Lansing, MI
1967	Gloria Bouvia	578–516	Shirley Garms	St. Ann, MO
1968	Dotty Fothergill	9,000–8,187	Doris Coburn	Garden City, NY
1969	Dotty Fothergill	8,284–8,258	Kayoka Suda	Miami
1970	Mary Baker	8,730–8,465	Judy Cook	Northbrook, IL
1971	Paula Carter	5,660–5,650	June Llewellyn	Kansas City, MO
1972	Lorrie Nichols	5,272–5,189	Mary Baker	Denver
1973	Millie Martorella	5,553–5,294	Patty Costello	Garden City, NY
1974	Patty Costello	219–216	Betty Morris	Irving, TX
1975	Paula Carter	6,500–6,352	Lorrie Nichols	Toledo, OH
1976	Patty Costello	11,341–11,281	Betty Morris	Tulsa, OK
1977	Betty Morris	10,511–10,358	Virginia Norton	Milwaukee
1978	Donna Adamek	236–202	Vesma Grinfelds	Miami
1979	Diana Silva	11,775–11,718	Bev Ortner	Phoenix
1980	Pat Costello	223–199	Shinobu Saitoh	Rockford, IL
1981	Donna Adamek	201–190	Nikki Gianulias	Rockford, IL
1982	Shinobu Saitoh	12,184–12,028	Robin Romeo	Hendersonville, TN
1983	Dana Miller-Mackie	247–200	Aleta Sill	St. Louis
1984	Karen Ellingsworth	236–217	Lorrie Nichols	St. Louis
1985	Pat Mercatani	214–178	Nikki Gianulias	Topeka, KS
1986	Wendy Macpherson	265–179	Lisa Wagner	Topeka, KS
1987	Carol Norman	206–179	Cindy Coburn	Mentor, OH
1988	Lisa Wagner	226–218	Lorrie Nichols	Winston-Salem, NC
1989	Robin Romeo	187–163	Michelle Mullen	Addison, IL
1990	Dana Miller-Mackie	190–189	Tish Johnson	Dearborn Heights, MI
1991	Anne Marie Duggan	196–185	Leanne Barrette	Fountain Valley, CA
1992	Tish Johnson	216–213	Aleta Sill	Fountain Valley, CA
1993	Dede Davidson	213–194	Dana Miller-Mackie	Garland, TX
1994	Aleta Sill	229–170	Anne Marie Duggan	Wichita
1995	Cheryl Daniels	235–180	Tish Johnson	Blaine, MN
1996	Liz Johnson	265–236	Marianne DiRupo	Indianapolis, IN
1997	No event—tournament rescheduled to April, beginning in 1998.			
1998	Aleta Sill	276–151	Tammy Turner	Milford, CT
1999	Kim Adler	213–195	Lynda Barnes	Uncasville, CT
2000	Tennelle Grijalva	239–155	Kelly Kulick	Phoenix, AZ

Note: From 1942 to 1970, tournament was called the BPAA All-Star. Peterson scoring used from 1949–1962. Under this system, the winner of an individual match game gets one point, plus one point for each 50 pins. From 1963–1967, a three-game championship was held between the two top qualifiers. From 1968–1973, 1975–77, 1979 and 1982, total pinfall determined the winner. In the other years, five qualifiers competed in a playoff for the championship, with the final listed above.

AMF Gold Cup

Year	Winner	Score	Runner-Up	Site
1997	Aleta Sill	221–179	C. Gianotti-Block	Richmond, VA
1998	Dana Miller-Mackie	278–170	Dede Davidson	Richmond, VA
1999	Dana Miller-Mackie	236–222	Cara Honeychurch	Richmond, VA

WIBC Queens

Year	Winner	Score	Runner-Up	Site
1961	Janet Harman	794–776	Eula Touchette	Fort Wayne, IN
1962	Dorothy Wilkinson	799–794	Marion Ladewig	Phoenix
1963	Irene Monterosso	852–803	Georgette DeRosa	Memphis
1964	D. D. Jacobson	740–682	Shirley Garms	Minneapolis
1965	Betty Kuczynski	772–739	LaVerne Carter	Portland, OR
1966	Judy Lee	771–742	Nancy Peterson	New Orleans
1967	Millie Ignizio	840–809	Phyllis Massey	Rochester, NY
1968	Phyllis Massey	884–853	Marian Spencer	San Antonio
1969	Ann Feigel	832–765	Millie Ignizio	San Diego
1970	Millie Ignizio	807–797	Joan Holm	Tulsa, OK
1971	Millie Ignizio	809–778	Katherine Brown	Atlanta
1972	Dotty Fothergill	890–841	Maureen Harris	Kansas City, MO
1973	Dotty Fothergill	804–791	Judy Soutar	Las Vegas
1974	Judy Soutar	939–705	Betty Morris	Houston
1975	Cindy Powell	758–674	Patty Costello	Indianapolis
1976	Pam Buckner	214–178	Shirley Sjostrom	Denver
1977	Dana Stewart	175–167	Vesma Grinfelds	Milwaukee
1978	Loa Boxberger	197–176	Cora Fiebig	Miami
1979	Donna Adamek	216–181	Shinobu Saitoh	Tucson, AZ
1980	Donna Adamek	213–165	Cheryl Robinson	Seattle
1981	Katsuko Sugimoto	166–158	Virginia Norton	Baltimore
1982	Katsuko Sugimoto	160–137	Nikki Gianulias	St. Louis
1983	Aleta Sill	214–188	Dana Miller-Mackie	Las Vegas
1984	Kazue Inahashi	248–222	Aleta Sill	Niagara Falls, NY
1985	Aleta Sill	279–192	Linda Graham	Toledo, OH
1986	Cora Fiebig	223–177	Barbara Thorberg	Orange County, CA
1987	Cathy Almeida	850–817	Lorrie Nichols	Hartford, CT
1988	Wendy Macpherson	213–199	Leanne Barrette	Reno/Carson City, NV
1989	Carol Gianotti	207–177	Sandra Jo Shiery	Bismarck-Mandan, ND
1990	Patty Ann	207–173	Vesma Grinfelds	Tampa, FL
1991	Dede Davidson	231–159	Jeanne Maiden	Cedar Rapids, IA
1992	Cindy Coburn-Carroll	184–170	Dana Miller-Mackie	Lansing, MI
1993	Jan Schmidt	201–163	Pat Costello	Baton Rouge, LA
1994	Anne Marie Duggan	224–177	Wendy Macpherson-Papanos	Salt Lake City
1995	Sandra Postma	226–187	Carolyn Dorin	Tucson, AZ
1996	Lisa Wagner	231–226	Tammy Turner	Buffalo, NY
1997	S.J. Shiery-Odom	209–185	Audry Allen	Reno, NV
1998	Lynda Norry	213–157	Karen Stroud	Davenport, IA
1999	Leanne Barrette	256–174	Dede Davidson	Indianapolis, IN
2000	Wendy Macpherson	227–202	Marianne DiRupo	Reno, NV

Sam's Town Invitational

Year	Winner	Score	Runner-Up	Site
1984	Aleta Sill	238 (1 game)	Cheryl Daniels	Las Vegas
1985	Patty Costello	236 (1 game)	Robin Romeo	Las Vegas
1986	Aleta Sill	238 (1 game)	Dina Wheeler	Las Vegas
1987	Debbie Bennett	880 (4 games)	Lorrie Nichols	Las Vegas
1988	Donna Adamek	634 (3 games)	Robin Romeo	Las Vegas
1989	Tish Johnson	210 (1 game)	Dede Davidson	Las Vegas
1990	Wendy Macpherson	900 (4 games)	Jeanne Maiden	Las Vegas
1991	Lorrie Nichols	469 (2 games)	Dana Miller-Mackie	Las Vegas
1992	Tish Johnson	279 (1 game)	Robin Romeo	Las Vegas
1993	Robin Romeo	194 (1 game)	Tammy Turner	Las Vegas
1994	Tish Johnson	178 (1 game)	Carol Gianotti	Las Vegas
1995	Michelle Mullen	202 (1 game)	Cheryl Daniels	Las Vegas
1996	C. Gianotti-Block	892 (4 games)	Leanne Barrette	Las Vegas
1997	Kim Adler	953 (4 games)	Wendy Macpherson	Las Vegas
1998	Julie Gardner	961 (4 games)	Dede Davidson	Las Vegas
1999	Wendy Macpherson	209 (1 game)	Marianne DiRupo	Las Vegas

PWBA Championships

1960...Marion Ladewig	1966...Joy Abel	1972...Patty Costello	1978...Toni Gillard
1961...Shirley Garms	1967...Betty Mivalez	1973...Betty Morris	1979...Cindy Coburn
1962...Stephanie Balogh	1968...Dotty Fothergill	1974...Pat Costello	1980...Donna Adamek
1963...Janet Harman	1969...Dotty Fothergill	1975...Pam Buckner	
1964...Betty Kuczynski	1970...Bobbe North	1976...Patty Costello	
1965...Helen Duval	1971...Patty Costello	1977...Vesma Grinfelds	

Men's Awards

BWAA Bowler of the Year

1942	Johnny Crimmins	1971	Don Johnson
1943	Ned Day	1972	Don Johnson
1944	Ned Day	1973	Don McCune
1945	Buddy Bomar	1974	Earl Anthony
1946	Joe Wilman	1975	Earl Anthony
1947	Buddy Bomar	1976	Earl Anthony
1948	Andy Varipapa	1977	Mark Roth
1949	Connie Schwoegler	1978	Mark Roth
1950	Junie McMahon	1979	Mark Roth
1951	Lee Jouglard	1980	Wayne Webb
1952	Steve Nagy	1981	Earl Anthony
1953	Don Carter	1982	Earl Anthony
1954	Don Carter	1983	Earl Anthony
1955	Steve Nagy	1984	Mark Roth
1956	Bill Lillard	1985	Mike Aulby
1957	Don Carter	1986	Walter Ray Williams Jr.
1958	Don Carter	1987	Marshall Holman
1959	Ed Lubanski	1988	Brian Voss
1960	Don Carter	1989	Mike Aulby
1961	Dick Weber		Amleto Monacelli*
1962	Don Carter	1990	Amleto Monacelli
1963	Dick Weber	1991	David Ozio
	Billy Hardwick*	1992	Dave Ferraro
1964	Billy Hardwick	1993	Walter Ray Williams Jr.
	Bob Strampe*	1994	Norm Duke
1965	Dick Weber	1995	Mike Aulby
1966	Wayne Zahn	1996	Walter Ray Williams Jr.
1967	Dave Davis	1997	Walter Ray Williams Jr.
1968	Jim Stefanich	1998	Walter Ray Williams Jr.
1969	Billy Hardwick	1999	Parker Bohn III
1970	Nelson Burton Jr.		

*PBA Bowler of the Year. The PBA began selecting a player of the year in 1963. Its selection has been the same as the BWAA's in all but three years.

Spare Me All These Strikes

Oh, for crying out loud! This has got to stop. The numbers are soaring out of control. The big moment is now cheaper than Tonya Harding. All these tricked-up houses are making a mockery of this great old game.

Not baseball, you seamhead! Bowling! Do you realize that during the 1998–99 bowling season 34,470 perfect games were rolled? Thirty-four thousand. Thirty years earlier there were 905. That's an increase of, well, that's just a very-hard-to-figure-out increase....

Used to be, you rolled a perfect game and the American Bowling Congress sent you a gold diamond ring. The owner of the alley roped off the lane. Your name appeared on a plaque. ...Your picture was in the newspaper.

For the rest of your life Dolores brought your cheeseburger first.

Now you roll a 300, and the guy behind the counter barely looks up. Your buddies shrug and ask what time next week. The ABC still sends you a ring, but it's made of Siladium, a kind of stainless steel. Your name goes up on a chalkboard, but it's gone by morning. Hell, you're lucky to get a picture of the scoreboard before they clear it.

"In the old days," says 92-year-old Joe Norris of San Diego, who threw a 300 at age 86, "if somebody threw a 300, we'd all sit around the lounge and he'd buy everybody drinks. Now there're too many. We'd all be alcoholics!"

Perfection sure isn't what it used to be....

—Rick Reilly

Women's Awards

BWAA Bowler of the Year

1948.........................Val Mikiel	1976.........................Patty Costello
1949.........................Val Mikiel	1977.........................Betty Morris
1950.........................Marion Ladewig	1978.........................Donna Adamek
1951.........................Marion Ladewig	1979.........................Donna Adamek
1952.........................Marion Ladewig	1980.........................Donna Adamek
1953.........................Marion Ladewig	1981.........................Donna Adamek
1954.........................Marion Ladewig	1982.........................Nikki Gianulias
1955.........................Marion Ladewig	1983.........................Lisa Wagner
1956.........................Sylvia Martin	1984.........................Aleta Sill
1957.........................Anita Cantaline	1985.........................Aleta Sill
1958.........................Marion Ladewig	.............................Patty Costello*
1959.........................Marion Ladewig	1986.........................Lisa Wagner
1960.........................Sylvia Martin	.............................Jeanne Madden*
1961.........................Shirley Garms	1987.........................Betty Morris
1962.........................Shirley Garms	1988.........................Lisa Wagner
1963.........................Marion Ladewig	1989.........................Robin Romeo
1964.........................LaVerne Carter	1990.........................Tish Johnson
1965.........................Betty Kuczynski	.............................Leanne Barrette*
1966.........................Joy Abel	1991.........................Leanne Barrette
1967.........................Millie Martorella	1992.........................Tish Johnson
1968.........................Dotty Fothergill	1993.........................Lisa Wagner
1969.........................Dotty Fothergill	1994.........................Anne Marie
1970.........................Mary Baker	.............................Duggan
1971.........................Paula Sperber Carter	1995.........................Tish Johnson
1972.........................Patty Costello	1996.........................Wendy Macpherson
1973.........................Judy Soutar	1997.........................Wendy Macpherson
1974.........................Betty Morris	1998.........................Carol Gianotti-Block
1975.........................Judy Soutar	1999.........................Wendy Macpherson

*PWBA Bowler of the Year. The PWBA began selecting a player of the year in 1983. Its selection has been the same as the BWAA's in all but three years.

Career Leaders

Earnings

MEN

Walter Ray Williams Jr. $2,428,488
Pete Weber $2,216,348
Mike Aulby $1,990,315
Parker Bohn III $1,871,296
Amleto Monacelli $1,762,208

WOMEN

Aleta Sill $1,043,322
Wendy Macpherson......................$963,195
Tish Johnson $944,635
Lisa Wagner.................................$838,408
Anne Marie Duggan.......................$836,271

Titles

MEN

Earl Anthony...41
Mark Roth...34
Walter Ray Williams Jr...............................30
Don Johnson..26
Dick Weber 26
Mike Aulby 26

WOMEN

Aleta Sill 33
Lisa Wagner..30
Patty Costello 25
Tish Johnson 23
Leanne Barrette 21

Note: Men's leaders through July 17, 2000; women's through August 9, 2000.

Soccer

Power Struggles

While France reaffirmed its dominance in Europe, the mighty were overthrown in Major League Soccer

BY B.J. SCHECTER

SAY THIS for the French: They certainly have a flair for the dramatic. Two years after winning the 1998 World Cup, Les Bleus established themselves as one of the best teams of all time by winning the European championship. It was the first time a team had followed a World Cup triumph with a European title, and the French did it in style, rallying to beat Italy in overtime in an electrifying final. *C'est magnifique!*

The French won the World Cup in '98 without a true goal scorer, and some critics wrote off the title as an aberration, more a product of home field advantage (the Cup was held in France) than dazzling soccer. But in Euro 2000, France had goal scorers to spare: Thierry Henry, only 20 years old during the World Cup, had blossomed into a world-class striker for English club Arsenal, and he was joined by Paris St. Germain star Nicholas Anelka, Christophe Dugarry (Bordeaux), David Trezeguet (Juventus) and Sylvain Wiltord (Arsenal). All of which meant that each time out, France kept three deadly, first-rate finishers on its *bench*.

Despite the added firepower up top, France, as it had in '98, still revolved around crafty midfielder Zinedine Zidane, the 1998 FIFA World Player of the Year. "When we don't know what to do," said defender Bixente Lizarazu, "we just give it to Zizou, and he works something out." With Zidane pulling the strings, France was the class of the tournament, playing imaginative, stylish and, above all, attacking soccer. The dream final would have been France versus the Netherlands, another team with the players and the panache to emphasize offense in such a pressure-packed tournament. But because the Dutch missed five penalty kicks in the semifinals (two of them in regulation time!), what we got was France versus Italy, which defeated the Netherlands in a shootout following a scoreless draw. Not that France-Italy was without its own appeal, to be sure. The Italians are masters of the defensive, counterattacking game and would provide a perfect foil for France's flair for offense. Indeed, for the majority of the final the Azzurri had the upper hand.

The Italians scored in the 56th minute

BILL KOSTROUN/AP

when Marco Delvecchio redirected a beautiful cross from Gianluca Pessotto into the top of the net. Striker Alessandro Del Piero had two golden chances to increase Italy's lead, but he shot wide in the 59th minute and right into the arms of French keeper Fabien Barthez in the 85th. Still, Italy led 1–0 heading into the final minute of stoppage time, and with victory imminent its subs rose from the bench and saluted their fans behind them.

The celebration, it turned out, was premature. With fewer than 20 seconds remaining, Les Bleus got a miracle as second-half substitute Wiltord, in traffic and from a tough angle, punched in the tying goal to send the game into overtime, in which a golden goal would settle the championship. "Everybody thought we were dead," said Henry. "With the French team, it's never over."

Deflated by the last-gasp equalizer, Italy went down to defeat 13 minutes into extra time. Trezeguet, another substitute, took a feed from Robert Pires, who'd made a nice move to get free on the left, and one-timed it into the top of the net. France's thrilling 2–1 victory provided a fitting close to one of the most exciting and highest scoring (85 goals in 31 games) European championships in history. It also carved out a special place in history for Les Bleus, one shared by multiple World Cup winners Brazil, Germany and Italy. "We're even stronger than we were at the World Cup," said Zidane. "We've had two years to mature, and we have several talented strikers now."

Said dejected Italy coach Dino Zoff, "When you feel victory is in your hands and it slips away, it takes a lot of your spirit. But it was a great effort. I'm really sorry, but this is soccer." Del Piero, who missed those two

chances to increase the Azzurri's lead, said, "Regret is to say too little. I feel guilty." Only seconds from victory, Italy was left to lament what might have been.

In the United States, Major League Soccer made several giant strides toward what could be a bright domestic future for the sport. Led by new commissioner Don Garber, the league lured some well-known players into its ranks and significantly improved its level of play. In May, MLS paid a record $4 million transfer fee for speedy striker Luis (el Matador) Hernandez, Mexico's leading scorer in the '98 World Cup. Hernandez joined Bulgaria's legendary Hristo Stoitchkov (Chicago) and former superstar Lothar Matthäus of Germany (New York/New Jersey) in the ranks of MLS's quality foreign signings. The league also proved it could develop domestic talent as the U.S. Olympic team, stocked with young MLS stars, made history by advancing to the semifinals in Sydney. No previous U.S. team had made it out of the first round in the Olympics.

The 2000 regular season was a topsy-turvy version of the previous year. Defending champs D.C. United went from first to worst, missing the playoffs for the first time in the league's five-year history, while 1999's cellar dwellers, the New York/New Jersey MetroStars and the Kansas City Wizards, made the opposite journey, winning division titles a year after finishing dead last.

With midfielder Tab Ramos back in form after an ACL injury, and with help from the improvised dispersal draft, which MLS held as part of the deal that brought Hernandez to the Galaxy, the MetroStars played some of the most exciting soccer in the league. While L.A. got Hernandez from the Mexican league, the MetroStars got Clint Mathis and midfielder Roy Myers from L.A. Mathis, a promising U.S. striker, came via the dispersal draft, and Myers, of Costa Rica, came in a trade because L.A. needed to unload one foreign player so that the addition of Hernandez would not put them over the limit of four per team. Confused yet? Well, then look at it this way: The league knew it could ill afford to have a doormat in the soccer-savvy, media-saturated New York area, and now it no longer does.

Indeed, the MetroStars were good enough to survive the distraction caused by the aging Matthäus, who was a disruptive influence almost from the moment the league acquired him, loudly complaining about front-office changes and the quality of the Metros' play. He finally meshed with the team in the stretch run, after it had established its winning ways in his absence. (He missed a month of the season to play for Germany in Euro 2000.) But even with the legendary Matthäus in its back line, the Metros forte was offense. Forwards Adolfo Valencia and Mathis each scored 16 goals, and Mathis set an MLS record against Dallas on Aug. 26 when he exploded for five goals.

Kansas City displayed a different kind of mastery in August, turning in a remarkable nine shutouts in 12 games. A significant reason behind the Wizards' defensive dominance was former national team goalkeeper Tony Meola, who routinely made spectacular saves and finished the regular season with a league-leading 16 shutouts.

Chicago won the league's toughest division, the Central, with arguably the league's most talented roster. In addition to Stoitchkov, the Fire had Polish international Peter Nowak, and U.S. national teamers Chris Armas, Ante Razov and Josh Wolff at its disposal. Thanks to the dynamic duo of midfielder Carlos Valderrama and striker Mamadou Diallo, who led the league in scoring with 26 goals in 28 games, Tampa Bay finished a close second to the Fire. But the Mutiny crumbled at crunch time, getting swept out of the first round by Los Angeles. The MetroStars swept Dallas in their first-round meeting while New England extended Chicago to three games, only to be blown out 6–0 in the finale.

Kansas City crept through the playoffs at a steady pace, edging sub-.500 Colorado in three games in the first round, and needing more than that to edge Los Angeles in the semis: After tying the series at four points apiece with a 1–0 win in Game 3, the Wizards won it with a goal in the 20-minute, sudden-death mini-game that decided the series. Kansas City's bruising Danish striker Miklos Molnar scored both goals. That was the Wizards' formula all season long: Get an early goal from Molnar and then protect the slim lead with staunch defense and superb goalkeeping. Not particularly sexy, perhaps, but very effective: The Wizards got an 11th-minute goal from Molnar in the championship game against Chicago—which edged the MetroStars in a hardfought, physical semifinal—and made it stand up for a 1–0 victory and the MLS title. Meola, who made several huge saves, including point-blank stops on Dema Kovalenko and Wolff, was a no-brainer choice for MVP of the game. He might not have room on his mantle for the award, though, as he'll have to squeeze it in next to his Goalkeeper of the Year, Comeback Player of the Year and regular-season MVP trophies.

FOR THE RECORD·1999-2000

2000 European Championship

Group Standings

GROUP A

Country	GP	W	L	T	GF	GA	Pts
*Portugal	3	3	0	0	7	2	9
*Romania	3	1	1	1	4	4	4
England	3	1	2	0	5	6	3
Germany	3	0	2	1	1	5	1

GROUP C

Country	GP	W	L	T	GF	GA	Pts
*Spain	3	2	1	0	6	5	6
*Yugoslavia	3	1	1	1	7	7	4
Norway	3	1	1	1	1	1	4
Slovenia	3	0	1	2	4	5	2

GROUP B

Country	GP	W	L	T	GF	GA	Pts
*Italy	3	3	0	0	6	2	9
*Turkey	3	1	1	1	3	2	4
Belgium	3	1	2	0	2	5	3
Sweden	3	0	2	1	2	4	1

GROUP D

Country	GP	W	L	T	GF	GA	Pts
*Netherlands	3	3	0	0	7	2	9
*France	3	2	1	0	7	4	6
Czech Rep.	3	0	2	1	1	6	3
Denmark	3	0	2	1	0	8	0

*Advanced to second round.

Note: In group play, teams are awarded three points for a victory, one for a tie. The top two in each group advance to the quarterfinals.

Group Play Scores

GROUP A

Germany 1, Romania 1
Portugal 3, England 2
Portugal 1, Romania 0
England 1, Germany 0
Romania 3, England 2
Portugal 3, Germany 0

GROUP B

Belgium 2, Sweden 1
Italy 2, Turkey 1
Italy 2, Belgium 0
Sweden 0, Turkey 0
Turkey 2, Belgium 0
Italy 2, Sweden 1

GROUP C

Norway 1, Spain 0
Yugoslavia 3, Slovenia 3
Spain 2, Slovenia 1
Yugoslavia 1, Norway 0
Slovenia 0, Norway 0
Spain 4, Yugoslavia 3

GROUP D

France 3, Denmark 0
Neth. 1, Czech Rep. 0
France 2, Czech Rep. 1
Neth. 3, Denmark 0
Czech Rep. 2, Den. 0
Netherlands 3, France 2

Euro 2000—Quarterfinals

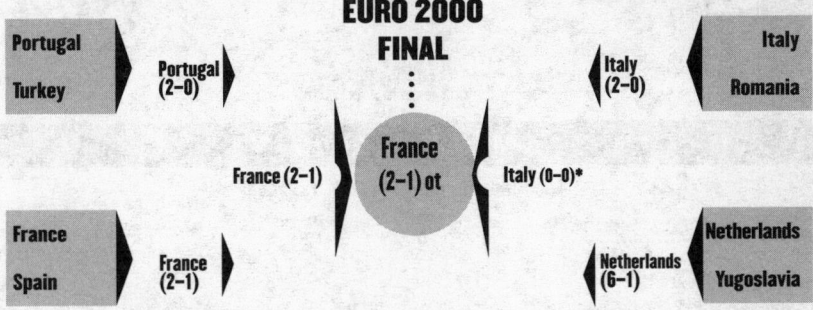

Portugal / Turkey — Portugal (2–0)

France / Spain — France (2–1)

France (2–1) → EURO 2000 FINAL — France (2–1) ot ← Italy (0–0)*

Italy / Romania — Italy (2–0)

Netherlands / Yugoslavia — Netherlands (6–1)

* Italy won penalty-kick shootout 3–1 over the Netherlands in the semifinals.

Major League Soccer

2000 Final Standings

EASTERN DIVISION

Team	Won	Lost	Tied	Pts
NY/NJ (3)	17	12	3	54
New England (7)	13	13	6	45
Miami	12	15	5	41
D.C.	8	18	6	30

CENTRAL DIVISION

Team	Won	Lost	Tied	Pts
Chicago (2)	17	9	6	57
Tampa Bay (4)	16	12	4	52
Dallas (6)	14	14	4	46
Columbus	11	16	5	38

WESTERN DIVISION

Team	Won	Lost	Tied	Pts
Kansas City (1)	16	7	9	57
Los Angeles (5)	14	10	8	50
Colorado (8)	13	15	4	43
San Jose	7	17	8	29

Note: Three points for a win. One point for a tie. Number in parentheses is playoff seed.

SCORING LEADERS

Player, Team	GP	G	A	Pts
Mamadou Diallo, TB	28	26	4	56
Clint Mathis, NY/NJ	29	16	14	46
Ante Razov, Chicago	24	18	6	42
Diego Serna, Miami	31	16	10	42
Adolfo Valencia, NY/NJ	31	16	9	41

GOALS LEADERS

Player, Team	GP	G
Mamadou Diallo, Tampa Bay	28	26
Ante Razov, Chicago	24	18
Adolfo Valencia, NY/NJ	31	16
Clint Mathis, NY/NJ	29	16
Diego Serna, Miami	31	16

ASSISTS LEADERS

Player, Team	GP	A
Carlos Valderrama, Tampa Bay	32	26
Steve Ralston, Tampa Bay	30	17
Martin Machon, Miami	24	16
Preki, Kansas City	31	15
Peter Nowak, Chicago	28	14
Clint Mathis, NY/NJ	29	14

GOALS-AGAINST-AVERAGE LEADERS

Player, Team	GAA
Tony Meola, Kansas City	0.92
Kevin Hartman, Los Angeles	1.00
Zach Thornton, Chicago	1.28
Joe Cannon, San Jose	1.49
Scott Garlick, Tampa Bay	1.53

2000 PLAYOFFS

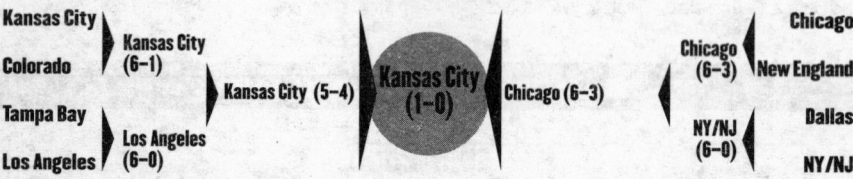

Note: Except for the final, which was a single game, scores in parentheses are points earned (three for a win, one for a tie) in a three-game series, the winner being the first team to accumulate five points.

MLS Cup 2000

WASHINGTON, D.C., OCTOBER 15, 2000

Chicago	0	0	—0
Kansas City	1	0	—1

Goals: Molnar (Klein) 11.

Chicago—Thornton, Brown, Bocanegra, Bonseu, Nowak (Kubik 83), Gutierrez (Beasley 70), Armas, Marsch (Wolff 59), Kovalenko, Stoitchkov, Razov.

Kansas City—Meola, Klein (Gomez 89), Garcia, Vermes, Prideaux, Preki (Okafor 74), McKeon, Zavagnin, Henderson, Johnston, Molnar.
Att: 39,159.

International Competition

1999–2000 U.S. Men's National Team Results

Date	Opponent	Site	Result	U.S. Goals
Nov. 17, 1999	Morocco	Marrakech	1–2 L	Wynalda
Jan. 16, 2000	Iran	Los Angeles	1–1 T	Armas
Jan 29	Chile	Coquimbo, Chile	2–1 W	Lewis, Jones
Feb 12	Haiti*	Miami	3–0 W	Kirovski, Wynalda, Jones
Feb 16	Peru*	Miami	1–0 W	Jones
Feb 19	Colombia*	Miami	2–2 T•	McBride, Armas
March 12	Tunisia	Birmingham, AL	1–1 T	Olsen
April 26	Russia	Moscow	2–0 L	—
June 3	South Africa#	Washington, D.C.	4–0 W	Jones (2), Reyna, Stewart
June 6	Ireland#	Foxboro, MA	1–1 T	Razov
June 11	Mexico#	East Rutherford, NJ	3–0 W	McBride, Hejduk, Razov
July 16	Guatemala†	Mazatanengo, Guat.	1–1 T	Razov
July 23	Costa Rica†	San Jose, Costa Rica	1–2 L	Stewart
Aug 16	Barbados†	Foxboro, MA	7–0 W	Pope, McBride, Moore (2), O'Brien Ramos, Stewart
Sept 3	Guatemala†	Washington, D.C.	1–0 W	McBride
Oct 11	Costa Rica†	Columbus, OH	0–0 T	—

*CONCACAF Gold Cup. # U.S. Cup 2000. †Qualifying for 2002 World Cup. • Colombia won penalty-kick shootout.
Record in full internationals from Nov 17, 1999, through Oct 11, 2000: 7-3-6.

1999–2000 U.S. Women's National Team Results

Date	Opponent	Site	Result	U.S. Goals
Sept. 26, 1999	Brazil	Denver	6–0 W	Milbrett (2), MacMillan (2), Parlow, Fotopoulos
Oct. 3	S Korea	Columbus, OH	5–0 W	Parlow, Hamm, Milbrett, Fotopoulos (2)
Oct. 7	Finland	Kansas City, MO	6–0 W	Milbrett, Fawcett, Whalen, Lilly (2), o.g.
Oct 10	Brazil	Louisville, KY	4–2 W	Hamm (2), Lilly (2)
Jan. 7, 2000	Czech Republic*	Melbourne	8–1 W	Mascaro (2), Kester (2), Bush, Serlenga, Welsh, Zepeda
Jan 10	Sweden*	Melbourne	0–0 T	—
Jan 13	Australia*	Adelaide, Australia	3–1 W	Kester, Slaton, Wagner
Feb 6	Norway	Ft. Lauderdale, FL	2–3 L	Hamm, Lilly
Feb 9	Norway	Ft. Lauderdale, FL	1–2 L	Welsh
March 12	Portugal	Silves, Portugal	7–0 W	Parlow (3), MacMillan, Fawcett, Venturini, Foudy
March 14	Denmark	Faro, Portugal	2–1 W	Fair, MacMillan
March 16	Sweden	Lagos, Portugal	1–0 W	Hamm
March 18	Norway	Loulé, Portugal	1–0 W	Chastain
April 5	Iceland	Davidson, NC	8–0 W	Welsh (3), Wagner, Pearce (2), Hamm, Lilly
April 8	Iceland	Charlotte, NC	0–0 T	—
May 5	Mexico	Portland, OR	8–0 W	MacMillan (2), Lilly, Serlenga, Milbrett, Hamm, Fair, Welsh
May 7	Canada	Portland, OR	4–0 W	Foudy, Parlow, Milbrett, Welsh
May 31	China	Canberra, Australia	0–1 L	—
June 2	Canada	Sydney, Australia	9–1 W	Milbrett (3), MacMillan, Parlow (3), Fair (2)
June 4	New Zealand	Sydney, Australia	5–0 W	Welsh (2), Parlow (3)
June 8	Japan	Newcastle, Australia	4–1 W	Parlow, MacMillan, Chastain, Wagner
June 11	Australia	Newcastle, Australia	1–0 W	MacMillan
June 23	Trinidad & Tobago	Hershey, PA	11–0 W	Parlow (3), Fair (2), Milbrett, Hamm (2), MacMillan, Whalen (2)
June 25	Costa Rica	Louisville, KY	8–0 W	Serlenga (3), Welsh (2), MacMillan, Bush, Whalen
June 27	Brazil	Foxboro, MA	0–0 T	—
July 1	Canada	Louisville, KY	4–1 W	MacMillan (2), Milbrett, Hamm
July 3	Brazil	Foxboro, MA	1–0 W	Milbrett
July 7	Italy	Central Islip, NY	4–1 W	Wagner, Whalen, Bush, Putz
July 16	Norway	Osnabrück, Germany	1–0 W	Milbrett
July 19	China	Göttingen, Germany	1–1 T	Hamm
July 22	Germany	Braunschweig, Germany	1–0 W	Foudy
July 27	Norway	Tromsø, Norway	1–1 T	Serlenga
July 30	Norway	Oslo, Norway	1–2 L	Parlow
Aug 13	Russia	Annapolis, MD	7–1 W	Milbrett (2), Foudy, Hamm, Parlow (2), Akers
Aug 15	Russia	College Park, MD	1–1 T	Fawcett
Aug 20	Canada	Kansas City, MO	1–1 T	Lilly
Sept 1	Brazil	San Jose, CA	4–0 W	Foudy, Fawcett, Hamm (2)

Record from Sept 26, 1999, through Sept 1, 2000: 26-4-7.

International Club Competition

Intercontinental Cup

Competition between winners of European Cup and Libertadores Cup.

TOKYO: NOV 30, 1999

Manchester Utd (Eng).....1   0—1
Palmeiras (Brazil) 0   0—0

Goals: Keane (35).

Att: 60,000.

Manchester United: Bosnich, G. Neville, Irwin, Stam, Silvestre, Keane, Butt, Beckham, Scholes (Sheringham 75), Giggs, Solskjaer, (Yorke 46).
Palmeiras: Marcos, Baiano, Arce, Junior, R. Junior, Sampaio, Zinho, Galeano (Evair 54), Asprilla (Oseas 56), Alex, Nunes (Euller 77).

UEFA Cup

Competition between teams other than league champions and cup-winners from UEFA.

COPENHAGEN: MAY 17, 2000

Galatasaray* (Turkey) 0   0 0   0—0
Arsenal (England) 0   0 0   0—0

Goals: None. ***Galatasaray won 4–1 on penalties.**

Att: 38,000.

Galatasaray: Taffarel, Penbe, Capone, Popesecu, Bulent, K. Suat (Ahmet 95), Hagi, Davala, Okan (Hakan 84), Erdem (Hasan 95), Sukur.
Arsenal: Seaman, Dixon, Silvinho, Keown, Adams, Vieira, Petit, Overmars (Suker 115), Parlour, Bergkamp (Kanu 75), Henry.

European Cup

League champions of the countries belonging to UEFA (Union of European Football Associations).

PARIS: MAY 24, 2000

Real Madrid (Spain) 1   2—3
Valencia (Spain) 0   0—0

Goals: Morientes (39), McManaman (67), Raul (75).

Att: 73,000.

Real Madrid: Casillas, Salgado, Carlos, Helguera (Sanchis 81), Campo, Karanka, Redondo, McManaman, Raul, Anelka (Hierro 85), Morientes, Savio.
Valencia: Canizares, Pellegrino, Bjorklund, Camarasa, Djukic, Mendieta, Farinos, Angulo, Gerard, Lopez, Oscar.

Libertadores Cup

Competition between champion clubs and runners-up of 10 South American National Associations.

(2ND LEG) SAO PAULO: JUNE 21, 2000

Boca Juniors* (Argentina) .0   0—0
Palmeiras (Brazil) 0   0—0

Goals: None. **(*Aggregate: 2–2; Boca Juniors won 4–2 on penalties.)**

Att: 32,000.

Boca Juniors: Cordoba, Ibarra, Bermudez, Samuel, Arruabarrena, Battaglia, Traverso, Basualdo, Riquelme, Barros, Schelotto, Palermo.
Palmeiras: Marcos, Rogerio, Argel, Roque Junior, Junior, Galeano, Cesar Sampaio, Alex, Euller, Pena (Basilio 16), Ramos, (Asprilla 36).

Smart, and Tough as Nails

Welsh factory worker Tony Smart collapsed at a Manchester United soccer match in the spring of 2000. Ten days before the game, it turned out, Smart, 38, was at work when a power tool fell from a great height onto his head. For a week and a half this had no effect on the happy-go-lucky Smart—until he blacked out while supporting his beloved Red Devils.

As it happens, the power tool that had conked him on the coconut was a nail gun, and it had fired a three-inch nail into his brain. "I do not remember anything about the match," said the delightfully named Smart, on his way to a full recovery after surgeons removed the nail from his noggin, presumably with a claw hammer. Smart's breathtaking X-ray quickly became an icon of sorts in British newspapers and medical journals.

—Steve Rushin

Country	League Champion	League Scoring Leader, Club	Cup Winner
Albania	SK Tirana	Arbëri, Tomori	SK Tirana
Andorra	Constelacio Esportiva	n/a	Constelacio Esportiva
Armenia	Shirak Gyumri*	Sarikian, Tsement*	Tsement Ararat*
Austria	Tirol Innsbruck	Vastic, Sturm Graz	Grazer AK
Azerbaijan	FK Shamkir*	Kvaratskhelia, FK Shamkir*	Kapaz Ganca*
Belarus	BATE Barysau*	Stripeikis, Slavia*	Belshina Bobruysk*
Belgium	Anderlecht	Aarst, Ghent	Anderlecht
		Brogno, Westerlo	
Bosnia	Brotnjo Citluk	Zdjelar, Sloboda	Kozara Gradiska
Bulgaria	Levski Sofia	Todorov, Litex Lovetch	Levski Sofia
Croatia	Dinamo Zagreb	Sokota, Dinamo Zagreb	Hajduk Split
Cyprus	Anorthosis	n/a	Omonia Nicosia
Czech Republic	Sparta Prague	n/a	Slovan Liberec
Denmark	Herfølge BK	n/a	Viborg FF
England	Manchester United	Phillips, Sunderland	Chelsea
Estonia	Levadia Maardu*	Krim, Levadia Maardu*	Levadia Maardu*
Faroe Islands	Kĺ Klaksvík*	Borg, B36 Torshavn*	Kĺ Klaksvík*
Finland	Haka Valkeakoski*	Papovits, Haka Valkeakoski*	Jokerit Helsinki*
France	Monaco	Anderson, Lyon	FC Nantes
Georgia	Torpedo Kutaisi*	Ionanidze, Torpedo Kutaisi*	Lokomotiv Tblisi*
Germany	Bayern Munich	Max, 1860 Munich	Bayern Munich
Greece	Olympiakos	n/a	AEK
Hungary	Dunaferr FC	Tokoli, Dunaferr FC	MTK
Iceland	KR Reykjavik*	Johannesson, IBV*	KR Reykjavik*
Ireland	Shelbourne	Morley, Cork City	Shelbourne
Israel	Hapoel Tel-Aviv	Tubi, Maccabi Petah-Tikva	Hapoel Tel-Aviv
Italy	Lazio	Shevchenko, AC Milan	Lazio
Latvia	Skonto Riga*	Dobrecovs, Metalurgs Liepaja*	FK Riga*
Lithuania	Zalgiris Kaunas*	Vasiliauskas, Zalgiris Vilnius*	Kareda Siauliai*
Luxembourg	Grevenmacher	n/a	Jeunesse d'Esch
Macedonia	Sloga Skopje	Beqiri, Sloga Skopje	Sloga Skopje
Malta	Birkirkara	n/a	Sliema Wanderers
Moldova	Zimbru Chisinau	Rogaciov, Serif Tiraspol	Constructorul Chisinau
Netherlands	PSV Eindhoven	van Nistelrooy, PSV Eindhoven	Roda JC
Northern Ireland	Linfield	n/a	Linfield
Norway	Rosenborg*	n/a	Rosenborg*
Poland	Polonia Warsaw	Kompala, Gornik	Polonia Warsaw
Portugal	Sporting Lisbon	Jardel, FC Porto	FC Porto
Romania	Dinamo Bucharest	Savu, National Bucharest	Dinamo Bucharest
Russia	Spartak Moscow*	Demetradze, Alania*	Zenit St. Petersburg*
San Marino	Folgore*	n/a	Cosmos*
Scotland	Glasgow Rangers	Viduka, Glasgow Celtic	Glasgow Celtic
Slovakia	Inter Bratislava	n/a	Inter Bratislava
Slovenia	Maribor Branik	Bozgo, Maribor Branik	SCT Olimpija
Spain	Deportiva Coruna	Ballesta, Racing Santander	Espanyol
Sweden	Helsingborg*	Allbäck, Orgryte*	AIK*
Switzerland	St. Gallen	n/a	FC Zurich
Turkey	Galatasaray	Aykut, Samsunspor K	Galatasaray
Ukraine	Dinamo Kiev	Shatskikh, Dinamo Kiev	Dinamo Kiev
Wales	Llansantffraid	n/a	Bangor City
Yugoslavia	Crvena Belgrade	Kezman, Partizan Belgrade	Crvena Belgrade

Note: Results are from 2000 unless followed by *.

The World Cup

Results

Year	Champion	Score	Runner-Up	Winning Coach
1930	Uruguay	4–2	Argentina	Alberto Supicci
1934	Italy	2–1	Czechoslovakia	Vittorio Pozzo
1938	Italy	4–2	Hungary	Vittorio Pozzo
1950	Uruguay	2–1	Brazil	Juan Lopez
1954	W Germany	3–2	Hungary	Sepp Herberger
1958	Brazil	5–2	Sweden	Vicente Feola
1962	Brazil	3–1	Czechoslovakia	Aymore Moreira
1966	England	4–2	West Germany	Alf Ramsey
1970	Brazil	4–1	Italy	Mario Zagalo
1974	W Germany	2–1	Netherlands	Helmut Schoen
1978	Argentina	3–1	Netherlands	César Menotti
1982	Italy	3–1	W Germany	Enzo Bearzot
1986	Argentina	3–2	W Germany	Carlos Bilardo
1990	W Germany	1–0	Argentina	Franz Beckenbauer
1994	Brazil	0–0 (3–2)	Italy	Carlos Alberto Parreira
1998	France	3–0	Brazil	Aime Jacquet

Alltime World Cup Participation

Of the 62 nations that have taken part in the World Cup Finals, only Brazil has competed in each of the 16 tournaments held to date. West Germany or an undivided Germany (1934, '38, '94 and '98) has played in 15 World Cups.

	Matches	W	T	L	Goals For	Goals Against		Matches	W	T	L	Goals For	Goals Against
Brazil	80	53	14	13	173	78	Bulgaria	25	3	8	14	22	49
*Germany	78	45	17	16	162	103	Costa Rica	4	2	0	2	4	6
Italy	66	38	16	12	105	62	Algeria	6	2	1	3	6	10
Argentina	57	29	10	18	100	68	East Germany	6	2	2	2	5	5
France	41	21	6	14	86	58	Saudi Arabia	7	2	1	4	7	13
England	45	20	13	12	62	42	Norway	8	2	3	3	7	8
Yugoslavia	37	17	6	14	60	46	Morocco	10	2	4	4	10	13
†Russia	34	16	6	12	60	40	Wales	5	1	3	1	4	4
Spain	40	16	10	14	61	48	Republic of Ireland	9	1	5	3	4	7
Uruguay	37	15	8	14	61	52	Tunisia	6	1	2	3	4	6
Hungary	32	15	3	14	87	57	N Korea	4	1	1	2	5	9
Netherlands	31	14	9	8	55	34	Cuba	3	1	1	1	5	12
Poland	25	13	5	7	39	29	Turkey	3	1	0	2	10	11
Sweden	37	13	7	17	62	60	Israel	3	1	0	2	1	3
Austria	29	12	4	13	42	48	Jamaica	3	1	0	2	3	9
Czechoslovakia	30	11	5	14	44	45	Iran	6	1	1	4	4	12
Belgium	32	9	7	16	40	56	Honduras	3	0	2	1	2	3
Romania	21	8	5	8	30	32	Egypt	4	0	2	2	3	6
Mexico	37	8	10	19	39	75	Kuwait	3	0	1	2	2	6
Chile	25	7	6	12	31	40	Australia	3	0	1	2	0	5
Portugal	9	6	0	3	19	12	S Korea	14	0	4	10	11	43
Switzerland	22	6	3	13	33	51	Dutch East Indies	1	0	0	1	0	6
Denmark	9	5	1	3	19	13	Iraq	3	0	0	3	1	4
Croatia	6	4	0	2	9	4	Canada	3	0	0	3	0	5
Nigeria	8	4	0	4	13	13	United Arab Emirates	3	0	0	3	2	11
Peru	15	4	3	8	19	31	New Zealand	3	0	0	3	2	12
Paraguay	15	4	6	5	19	27	Haiti	3	0	0	3	2	14
United States	17	4	1	12	18	38	Zaire	3	0	0	3	0	14
Scotland	23	4	7	12	25	41	Bolivia	6	0	1	5	1	20
Northern Ireland	13	3	5	5	13	23	El Salvador	6	0	0	6	1	22
Colombia	13	3	2	8	14	23	Japan	3	0	0	3	1	4
Cameroon	14	3	6	5	14	25	Greece	3	0	0	3	0	8

*Includes West Germany 1950–90. †Includes USSR 1930–1990.
Note: Matches decided by penalty kicks are shown as drawn games.

World Cup Final Box Scores

URUGUAY 1930

Uruguay 1	3 —4
Argentina 2	0 —2

FIRST HALF

Scoring: 1, Uruguay, Dorado (12); 2, Argentina, Peucelle (20); 3, Argentina, Stabile (37).

SECOND HALF

Scoring: 4, Uruguay, Cea (57); 5, Uruguay, Iriarte (68); 6, Uruguay, Castro (89).

Argentina: Botosso, Della Toree, Paternoster, J. Evaristo, Monti, Suarez, Peucelle, Varallo, Stabile, Ferreira, M. Evaristo.

Uruguay: Ballesteros, Nasazzi, Mascheroni, Andrade, Fernandez, Gestido, Dorado, Scarone, Castro, Cea, Iriarte.

Referee: Langenus (Belgium).

FRANCE 1938

Italy 3	1 —4
Hungary 1	1 —2

FIRST HALF

Scoring: 1, Italy, Colaussi (5); 2, Hungary, Titkos (7); 3, Italy, Piola (16); 4, Italy, Piola (35).

SECOND HALF

Scoring: 5, Hungary, Sarosi (70); 6, Italy, Colaussi (82).

Italy: Olivieri, Foni, Rava, Serantoni, Andreolo, Locatelli, Biavati, Meazza, Piola, Ferrari, Colaussi.

Hungary: Szabo; Polger, Biro, Szalay, Szucs, Lazar, Sas, Vincze, Sarosi, Zsengeller, Titkos.

Referee: Capdeville (France).

SWITZERLAND 1954

W Germany 2	1 —3
Hungary 2	0 —2

FIRST HALF

Scoring: 1, Hungary, Puskas (6); 2, Hungary, Czibor (8); 3, W Germ., Morlock (10); 4, W Germ., Rahn (18).

SECOND HALF

Scoring: 5, W Germany, Rahn (84).

W Germany: Turek; Posipal, Kohlmeyer, Eckel, Liebrich, Mai, Rahn, Morlock, Walter, O., Walter, F., Schaefer.

Hungary: Grosics; Buzansky, Lantos, Bozsik, Lorant, Zakarias, Czibor, Kocsis, Hidegkuti, Puskas, Toth.

Referee: Ling (England).

ITALY 1934

Italy 0	1	1—2
Czechoslovakia ..0	1	0—1

SECOND HALF

Scoring: 1, Czech., Puc (70); 2, Italy, Orsi (80).

OVERTIME

Scoring: 3, Italy, Schiavio (95).

Italy: Combi, Monzeglio, Allemandi, Ferraris Monti, Monti, Bertolini, Guaita, Meazza, Schiavio, Ferrari, Orsi.

Czechoslovakia: Planicka, Zenisek, Ctyroky, Kostalek, Cambal, Cambal, Krcil, Junek, Svoboda, Sobotka, Nejedly, Puc.

Referee: Eklind (Sweden).

BRAZIL 1950

Uruguay 0	2 —2
Brazil 0	1 —1

SECOND HALF

Scoring: 1, Brazil, Friaca (47); 2, Uruguay, Schiaffino (66); 3, Uruguay, Ghiggia (79).

Uruguay: Maspoli, Gonzales, Tejera, Gambretta, Varela, Andrade, Ghiggia, Perez, Miguez, Schiffiano, Moran.

Brazil: Barbosa, Augusto, Juvenal, Bauer, Banilo, Bigode, Friaca, Zizinho, Ademir, Jair, Chico.

Referee: Reader (England).

SWEDEN 1958

Brazil 2	3 —5
Sweden 1	1 —2

FIRST HALF

Scoring: 1, Sweden, Liedholm (3); 2, Brazil, Vava (9); 3, Brazil, Vava (32).

SECOND HALF

Scoring: 4, Brazil, Pelé (55); 5, Brazil, Zagalo (68); 6, Sweden Simonsson (80); 7, Brazil, Pelé (90).

Brazil: Glymar, D. Santos, N. Santos, Zito, Bellini, Orlando, Garrincha, Didi, Vava, Pelé, Zagalo.

Sweden: Svensson, Bergmark, Axbom, Boerjesson, Gustavsson, Parling, Hamrin, Gren, Simonsson, Liedholm, Skoglund.

Referee: Guigue (France).

CHILE 1962

Brazil 1	2 —3
Czechoslovakia 1	0 —1

FIRST HALF

Scoring: 1, Czech., Masopust (15); 2, Brazil, Amarildo (17).

SECOND HALF

Scoring: 3, Brazil, Zito (68); 4, Brazil, Vava (77).

Brazil: Glymar, D. Santos, N. Santos, Zito, Mauro, Zozimo, Garrincha, Didi, Vava, Amarildo, Zagalo.

Czechoslovakia: Schroiff, Tichy, Novak, Pluskal, Popluhar, Masopust, Pospichal, Scherer, Kvasnak, Kadraba, Jelinek.

Referee: Latychev (USSR).

World Cup Final Box Scores (Cont.)

ENGLAND 1966

England	1	1	2——4
W Germany	1	1	0——2

FIRST HALF

Scoring: 1, W Germany, Haller (12); 2, England, Hurst (18).

SECOND HALF

Scoring: 3, England, Peters (78); 4, W. Germany, Weber (90).

OVERTIME

Scoring: 5, England, Hurst (101); 6, England, Hurst (120).

England: Banks, Cohen, Wilson, Stiles, Charlton, J., Moore, Ball, Hurst, Hunt, Charlton, R., Peters.

W Germany: Tilkowski, Hottges, Schmellinger, Beckenbauer, Schulz, Weber, Held, Haller, Seeler, Overath, Emmerich.

Referee: Dienst (Switzerland).

W GERMANY 1974

W Germany	2	0——2
Netherlands	1	0——1

FIRST HALF

Scoring: 1, Netherlands, Neeskens, PK (1); 2, W. Germany, Breitner, PK (26); 3, W Germany, Müller (44).

W Germany: Maier, Vogts, Beckenbauer, Schwarzenbeck, Breitner, Hoeness, Bonhof, Overath, Grabowski, Müller, Holzenbein.

Netherlands: Jongbled, Suurbier, Rijsbergen (de Jong), Haan, Krol, Jansen, Neeskens, van Hanagem, Cruyff, Rensenbrink (van der Kerkhof).

Referee: Taylor (England).

ITALY 1982

Italy	0	3——3
W Germany	0	1——1

SECOND HALF

Scoring: 1, Italy, Rossi (57); 2, Italy, Tardelli (68); 3, Italy, Altobelli (81); 4, W Germany, Breitner (83).

Italy: Zoff, Bergomi, Scirea, Collovati, Cabrini, Oriali, Gentile, Tardelli, Conti, Rossi, Graziani (Altobelli, Causio).

W Germany: Schumacher, Kaltz, Stielike, Foerster, K., Foerster, B., Dremmler (Hrubesch), Breitner, Briegel, Rummenigge (Müller), Fishcher (Littbarski).

Referee: Coelho (Brazil).

MEXICO 1986 (CONT.)

Argentina: Pumpido, Brown, Cuciuffo, Ruggeri, Olarticoecha, Bastista, Giusti, Burruchaga (Trobbiani 90), Enrique, Maradona, Valdona.

W Germany: Schumacher, Jakobs, Forster, Eder, Brehme, Matthaus, Berthold, Magath (Hoeness 62), Briegel, Rummenigge, Allofs (Voller 46).

Referee: Filho (Brazil).

MEXICO 1970

Brazil	1	3——4
Italy	1	0——1

FIRST HALF

Scoring: 1, Brazil, Pelé (18); 2, Italy, Boninsegna (32).

SECOND HALF

Scoring: 3, Brazil, Gerson (65); 4, Brazil, Jairzinho (70); 5, Brazil, Alberto (86).

Brazil: Feliz, Alberto, Brito, Wilson, Piazza, Everaldo, Clodoaldo, Gerson, Jairzinho, Tostao, Pelé, Rivelino.

Italy: Albertosi, Burgnich, Cera, Rosato, Facchetti, Bertini (Juliano), Mazzola, De Sisti, Domenghini, Boninsegna (Rivera), Riva.

Referee: Glockner (E. Germany).

ARGENTINA 1978

Argentina	1	0	2——3
Netherlands	0	1	0——1

FIRST HALF

Scoring: 1, Argentina, Kempes (38).

SECOND HALF

Scoring: 2, Netherlands, Nanninga (81).

OVERTIME

Scoring: 3, Arg., Kempes (104); 4, Arg., Bertoni (114).

Argentina: Fillol, Olguin, Galvan, Passarella, Tarantini, Ardiles (Larrosa), Gallego, Kempes, Bertoni, Luque, Ortiz (Houseman).

Netherlands: Jongbloed, Jansen (Suurbier), Krol, Brandts, Poortvliet, Neeskens, Haan, W. van der Kerkhoff, R. van der Kerkhoff, Rep (Nanninga), Rensenbrink.

Referee: Gonella (Italy).

MEXICO 1986

Argentina	1	2——3
W Germany	0	2——2

FIRST HALF

Scoring: 1, Argentina, Brown (22).

SECOND HALF

Scoring: 2, Arg., Valdano (55); 3, W Germ., Rummenigge (73); 4, W Germ., Voller (81); 5, Arg., Burruchaga (83).

ITALY 1990

W Germany	0	1——1
Argentina	0	0——0

SECOND HALF

Scoring: 1, W Germany, Brehme, PK (84).

W Germany: Illgner, Brehme, Kohler, Augenthaler, Buchwald, Berthold (Reuter), Littbarski, Haessler, Mattaeus, Voeller, Klinsmann.

Argentina: Goychoechea, Lorenzo, Serrizuela, Sensini, Ruggeri (Monzon), Simon, Basualdo, Burruchag (Calderon), Maradona, Troglio, Dezottir.

Referee: Coelho (Brazil).

World Cup Final Box Scores *(Cont.)*

UNITED STATES 1994			
Italy	0	0	0—0
Brazil	0	0	0—0

Scoring: None. Shootout goals: Italy—2: Albertini, Evani; Brazil—3: Romario, Branco, Dunga.

Italy: Pagliuca, Benarrivo, Maldini, Baresi, Mussi (Apolloni 35), Albertini, D. Baggio (Evani 95), Berti, Donadoni, Baggio, Massaro.

Brazil: Taffarel, Jorginho (Cafu 21), Branco, Aldair, Santos, Silva, Dunga, Zinho (Viola 106), Mazinho, Bebeto, Romario.

Referee: Sandor Puhl (Hungary).

FRANCE 1998		
Brazil	0	0—0
France	2	1—3

FIRST HALF
Scoring: 1, France, Zidane (27); 2, France, Zidane (45).

SECOND HALF
Scoring: 3, France, Petit (90).

Brazil: Taffarel, Cafu, Aldair, Baiano, Carlos, Sampaio (Edmundo 74), Dunga, Rivaldo, Leonardo, (Denilson 46), Bebeto, Ronaldo.

France: Barthez, Lizarazu, Desailly, Thuram, Leboeuf, Djorkaeff (Vieira 75) Deschamps, Zidane, Petit, Karembeu (Boghossian 57), Guivarc'h (Dugarry 66).

Referee: Belqola (Morocco).

Alltime Leaders

GOALS

Player, Nation	Tournaments	Goals	Player, Nation	Tournaments	Goals
Gerd Müller, W Germany	1970, '74	14	Ademir, Brazil	1950	9
Just Fontaine, France	1958	13	Eusebio, Portugal	1966	9
Pelé, Brazil	1958, '62, '66, '70	12	Jairzinho, Brazil	1970, '74	9
Sandor Kocsis, Hungary	1954	11	Paolo Rossi, Italy	1982, '86	9
Teofilo Cubillas, Peru	1970, '78	10	Karl-Heinz Rummenigge,		
Gregorz Lato, Poland	1974, '78, '82	10	W Germany	1978, '82, '86	9
Helmut Rahn, W Germany	1954, '58	10	Uwe Seeler, W Germany	1958, '62, '66, '70	9
Gary Lineker, England	1986, '90	10	Vava, Brazil	1958, '62	9

LEADING SCORER, CUP BY CUP

Year	Player, Nation	Goals	Year	Player, Nation	Goals
1930	Guillermo Stabile, Argentina	8	1966	Eusebio Ferreira, Portugal	9
1934	Oldrich Nejedly, Czechoslovakia	5	1970	Gerd Müller, W Germany	10
1938	Leonidas da Silva, Brazil	8	1974	Gregorz Lato, Poland	7
1950	Ademir de Menezes, Brazil	9	1978	Mario Kempes, Argentina	6
1954	Sandor Kocsis, Hungary	11	1982	Paolo Rossi, Italy	6
1958	Just Fontaine, France	13	1986	Gary Lineker, England	6
1962	Florian Albert, Hungary	4	1990	Salvatore Schillaci, Italy	6
	Valentin Ivanov, USSR		1994	Hristo Stoichkov, Bulgaria	6
	Garrincha, Brazil			Oleg Salenko, Russia	
	Drazan Jerkovic, Yugoslavia		1998	Davor Suker, Croatia	6
	Leonel Sanchez, Chile				
	Vava, Brazil				

Most Goals, Individual, One Game

Goals	Player, Nation	Score	Date
5	Oleg Salenko, Russia	Russia–Cameroon, 6–1	6-28-94
4	Leonidas, Brazil	Brazil–Poland, 6–5	6-5-38
4	Ernest Willimowski, Poland	Brazil–Poland, 6–5	6-5-38
4	Gustav Wetterstrïm, Sweden	Sweden–Cuba, 8–0	6-12-38
4	Juan Alberto Schiaffino, Uruguay	Uruguay–Bolivia, 8–0	7-2-50
4	Ademir, Brazil	Brazil–Sweden, 7–1	7-9-50
4	Sandor Kocsis, Hungary	Hungary–W Germany, 8–3	6-20-54
4	Just Fontaine, France	France–W Germany, 6–3	6-28-58
4	Eusebio, Portugal	Portugal–N Korea, 5–3	7-23-66
4	Emilio Butragueño, Spain	Spain–Denmark, 5–1	6-18-86

Note: 30 players have scored 31 World Cup hat tricks. Gerd Müller of West Germany is the only man to have two World Cup hat tricks, both in 1970. The last hat tricks were 6-21-98, Gabriel Batistuta (Arg) vs. Jamaica; 6-23-90, Tomas Skuhravy (Czech) vs. Costa Rica; and 6-17-90, Michel (Spain) vs. South Korea.

Attendance and Goal Scoring, Year by Year

Year	Site	No. of Games	Goals	Goals/Game	Attendance	Avg Att
1930	Uruguay	18	70	3.89	434,500	24,139
1934	Italy	17	70	4.12	395,000	23,235
1938	France	18	84	4.67	483,000	26,833
1950	Brazil	22	88	4.00	1,337,000	60,773
1954	Switzerland	26	140	5.38	943,000	36,269
1958	Sweden	35	126	3.60	868,000	24,800
1962	Chile	32	89	2.78	776,000	24,250
1966	England	32	89	2.78	1,614,677	50,459
1970	Mexico	32	95	2.97	1,673,975	52,312
1974	W Germany	38	97	2.55	1,774,022	46,685
1978	Argentina	38	102	2.68	1,610,215	42,374
1982	Spain	52	146	2.80	1,856,277	35,698
1986	Mexico	52	132	2.54	2,441,731	46,956
1990	Italy	52	115	2.21	2,514,443	48,354
1994	United States	52	140	2.69	3,567,415	68,604
1998	France	64	171	2.67	2,775,400	43,366
Totals		580	1754	3.02	25,064,655	43,215

The United States in the World Cup

URUGUAY 1930: FINAL COMPETITION

Date	Opponent	Result	Scoring
7-13-30	Belgium	3–0 W	US: McGhee 2, Patenaude
7-17-30	Paraguay	3–0 W	US: Patenaude 2, Florie
7-26-30	Argentina	1–6 L	Arg: Monti 2, Scopelli 2, Stabile 2 US: Brown.

ITALY 1934: FINAL COMPETITION

Date	Opponent	Result	Scoring
5-27-34	Italy	1–7 L	US: Donelli ITA: Schiavio 3, Orsi 2, Meazza, Ferrari

BRAZIL 1950: FINAL COMPETITION

Date	Opponent	Result	Scoring
6-25-50	Spain	1–3 L	US: Pariani Spain: Igoa, Basora, Zarra
6-29-50	England	1–0 W	US: Gaetjens.
7-2-50	Chile	2–5 L	US: Wallace, Maca Chile: Robledo, Cremaschi 3, Prieto

ITALY 1990: FINAL COMPETITION

Date	Opponent	Result	Scoring
6-10-90	Czechoslovakia	1–5 L	US: Caligiuri Czech: Skuhravy 2, Hasek, Bilek, Luhovy
6-14-90	Italy	0–1 L	Italy: Giannini
6-19-90	Austria	1–2 L	US: Murray Austria: Rodax, Ogris

UNITED STATES 1994: FINAL COMPETITION

Date	Opponent	Result	Scoring
6-18-94	Switzerland	1–1 T	US: Wynalda Sui: Bregy
6-22-94	Colombia	2–1 W	US: Escobar (own goal), Stewart Colombia: Valencia
6-26-94	Romania	1–0 L	Romania: Petrescu
7-4-94	Brazil	1–0 L	Brazil: Bebeto

FRANCE 1998: FINAL COMPETITION

Date	Opponent	Result	Scoring
6-15-98	Germany	2–0 L	Ger: Möller, Klinsmann
6-21-98	Iran	2–1 L	US: McBride Iran: Estili, Mahdavikia
6-25-98	Yugoslavia	1–0 L	Yugoslavia: Komljenovic

International Competition

European Championship

Official name: the European Football Championship. Held every four years since 1960.

Year	Champion	Score	Runner-up	Year	Champion	Score	Runner-up
1960	USSR	2–1	Yugoslavia	1980	W Germany	2–1	Belgium
1964	Spain	2–1	USSR	1984	France	2–0	Spain
1968	Italy	2–0	Yugoslavia	1988	Holland	2–0	USSR
1972	W Germany	3–0	USSR	1992	Denmark	2–0	Germany
1976	Czechoslovakia*	2–2	W Germany	1996	Germany†	2–1	Czech Republic
				2000	France†	2–1	Italy

*Won on penalty kicks. †Won in sudden-death overtime.

Under-20 World Championship

Year	Host	Champion	Runner-Up
1977	Tunisia	USSR	Mexico
1979	Japan	Argentina	USSR
1981	Australia	W. Germany	Qatar
1983	Mexico	Brazil	Argentina
1985	USSR	Brazil	Spain
1987	Chile	Yugoslavia	W. Germany
1989	Saudi Arabia	Portugal	Nigeria
1991	Portugal	Portugal	Brazil
1993	Australia	Brazil	Ghana
1995	Qatar	Argentina	Brazil
1997	Malaysia	Argentina	Uruguay
1999	Nigeria	Spain	Japan

Under-17 World Championship

Year	Champion
1985	Nigeria
1987	USSR
1989	Saudi Arabia
1991	Ghana
1993	Nigeria

Under-17 *(Cont.)*

Year	Champion
1995	Ghana
1997	Brazil
1999	Brazil

Pan American Games

Year	Champion
1951	Argentina
1955	Argentina
1959	Argentina
1963	Brazil
1967	Mexico
1971	Argentina
1975	Brazil/Mexico (tie)
1979	Brazil
1983	Uruguay
1987	Brazil
1991	United States
1995	Argentina
1999	Mexico

South American Championship (Copa America)

Year	Champion	Host	Year	Champion	Host
1916	Uruguay	Argentina	1949	Brazil	Brazil
1917	Uruguay	Uruguay	1953	Paraguay	Peru
1919	Brazil	Brazil	1955	Argentina	Chile
1920	Uruguay	Chile	1956	Uruguay	Uruguay
1921	Argentina	Argentina	1957	Argentina	Peru
1922	Brazil	Brazil	1958	Argentina	Argentina
1923	Uruguay	Uruguay	1959	Uruguay	Ecuador
1924	Uruguay	Uruguay	1963	Bolivia	Bolivia
1925	Argentina	Argentina	1967	Uruguay	Uruguay
1926	Uruguay	Chile	1975	Peru	Various sites
1927	Argentina	Peru	1979	Paraguay	Various sites
1929	Argentina	Argentina	1983	Uruguay	Various sites
1935	Uruguay	Peru	1987	Uruguay	Argentina
1937	Argentina	Argentina	1989	Brazil	Brazil
1939	Peru	Peru	1990	Brazil	Argentina
1941	Argentina	Chile	1991	Argentina	Chile
1942	Uruguay	Uruguay	1993	Argentina	Ecuador
1945	Argentina	Chile	1995	Uruguay	Uruguay
1946	Argentina	Argentina	1997	Brazil	Bolivia
1947	Argentina	Ecuador	1999	Brazil	Paraguay

Awards

European Footballer of the Year

Year	Player	Club	Year	Player	Club
1956	Stanley Matthews	Blackpool	1974	Johan Cruyff	Barcelona
1957	Alfredo Di Stefano	Real Madrid	1975	Oleg Blokhin	Dynamo Kiev
1958	Raymond Kopa	Real Madrid	1976	Franz Beckenbauer	Bayern Munich
1959	Alfredo Di Stefano	Real Madrid	1977	Allan Simonsen	Borussia M'gladbach
1960	Luis Suarez	Barcelona	1978	Kevin Keegan	SV Hamburg
1961	Omar Sivori	Juventus	1979	Kevin Keegan	SV Hamburg
1962	Josef Masopust	Dukla Prague	1980	Karl-Heinz Rummenigge	Bayern Munich
1963	Lev Yashin	Moscow Dynamo	1981	Karl-Heinz Rummenigge	Bayern Munich
1964	Denis Law	Manchester United	1982	Paolo Rossi	Juventus
1965	Eusebio	Benfica	1983	Michel Platini	Juventus
1966	Bobby Charlton	Manchester United	1984	Michel Platini	Juventus
1967	Florian Albert	Ferencvaros	1985	Michel Platini	Juventus
1968	George Best	Manchester United	1986	Igor Belanov	Dynamo Kiev
1969	Gianni Rivera	AC Milan	1987	Ruud Gullit	AC Milan
1970	Gerd Mueller	Bayern Munich	1988	Marco Van Basten	AC Milan
1971	Johan Cruyff	Ajax	1989	Marco Van Basten	AC Milan
1972	Franz Beckenbauer	Bayern Munich	1990	Lothar Matthaeus	Inter Milan
1973	Johan Cruyff	Barcelona	1991	Jean-Pierre Papin	Olympique Marseille

European Footballer of the Year (Cont.)

Year	Player	Club	Year	Player	Club
1992	Marco Van Basten	AC Milan	1996	Matthias Sammer	Borussia Dortmund
1993	Roberto Baggio	Juventus	1997	Ronaldo	Inter Milan
1994	Hristo Stoichkov	Barcelona	1998	Zinedine Zidane	Juventus
1995	George Weah	AC Milan	1999	Rivaldo	Barcelona

African Footballer of the Year

Year	Player	Club	Year	Player	Club
1970	Salif Keita	St. Etienne	1985	Mohamed Timoumi	Royal Armed Forces
1971	Ibrahim Sunday	Asante Kotoko	1986	Badou Ezaki	Real Mallorca
1972	Chérif Soueymane	Hafia	1987	Rabah Madjer	FC Porto
1973	Tshimen Bwanga	TP Mazembe	1988	Kalusha Bwalya	Cercle Bruges
1974	Paul Moukila	CARA Brazzaville	1989	George Weah	Monaco
1975	Ahmed Faras	Mohammedia	1990	Roger Milla	St. Denis
1976	Roger Milla	Canon Yaounde	1991	Abedi Pele Ayew	Marseille
1977	Tarak Dhiab	Esperance	1992	Abedi Pele Ayew	Marseille
1978	Karim Abdul Razak	Asante Kotoko	1993	Rashidi Yekini	FC Zurich
1979	Thomas Nkono	Canon Yaounde	1994	George Weah	Paris St. Germain
1980	Jean Manga Onguene	Canon Yaounde	1995	George Weah	AC Milan
1981	Lakhdar Belloumi	GCR Mascara	1996	Nwankwo Kanu	Inter Milan
1982	Thomas Nkono	Espanol	1997	Victor Ikpeba	Monaco
1983	Mahmoud Al-Khatib	Al Ahli	1998	Mustapha Hadji	Deportivo Coruna
1984	Theophile Abega	Toulouse	1999	Nwankwo Kanu	Arsenal

South American Player of the Year

Year	Player	Club	Year	Player	Club
1971	Tostao	Cruzeiro	1986	Antonio Alzamendi	River Plate
1972	Teofilo Cubillas	Alianza Lima	1987	Carlos Valderrama	Deportivo Cali
1973	Pelé	Santos	1988	Ruben Paz	Racing Buenos Aires
1974	Elias Figueroa	Internacional	1989	Bebeto	Vasco da Gama
1975	Elias Figueroa	Internacional	1990	Raul Amarilla	Olimpia
1976	Elias Figueroa	Internacional	1991	Oscar Ruggeri	Velez Sarsfield
1977	Zico	Flamengo	1992	Rai	São Paulo
1978	Mario Kempes	Valencia	1993	Carlos Valderrama	Junior Barranquilla
1979	Diego Maradona	Argentinos Juniors	1994	Cafu	São Paulo
1980	Diego Maradona	Boca Juniors	1995	Enzo Francescoli	River Plate
1981	Zico	Flamengo	1996	Jose-Luis Chilavert	Velez Sarsfield
1982	Zico	Flamengo	1997	Marcelo Salas	River Plate
1983	Socrates	Corinthians	1998	Martin Palermo	Boca Juniors
1984	Enzo Francescoli	River Plate	1999	Javier Saviola	River Plate
1985	Julio Cesar Romero	Fluminense			

International Club Competition

Intercontinental Cup

Competition between winners of European Cup and Libertadores Cup.

1960...Real Madrid, Spain	1974...Atletico de Madrid, Spain	1988...Nacional, Uruguay
1961...Penarol, Uruguay	1975...No tournament	1989...Milan, Italy
1962...Santos, Brazil	1976...Bayern Munich	1990...Milan, Italy
1963...Santos, Brazil	1977...Boca Juniors, Argentina	1991...Red Star Belgrade, Yugos.
1964...Inter, Italy	1978...No tournament	1992...São Paulo, Brazil
1965...Inter, Italy	1979...Olimpia, Paraguay	1993...São Paulo, Brazil
1966...Penarol, Uruguay	1980...Nacional, Uruguay	1994...Velez Sarsfield, Argentina
1967...Racing Club, Argentina	1981...Flamengo, Brazil	1995...Ajax Amsterdam, Netherlands
1968...Estudiantes, Argentina	1982...Penarol, Uruguay	1996...Juventus, Italy
1969...Milan, Italy	1983...Gremio, Brazil	1997...Borussia Dortmund, Ger.
1970...Feyenoord, Netherlands	1984...Independiente, Argentina	1998...Real Madrid, Spain
1971...Nacional, Uruguay	1985...Juventus, Italy	1999 ...Manchester United, England
1972...Ajax Amsterdam, Netherlands	1986...River Plate, Argentina	
1973...Independiente, Argentina	1987...Porto, Portugal	

Note: Until 1968 a best-of-three-games format decided the winner. After that a two-game/total-goal format was used until Toyota became the sponsor in 1980, moved the game to Tokyo and switched the format to a one-game championship. The European Cup runner-up substituted for the winner in 1971, 1973, 1974, and 1979.

European Cup

1956...Real Madrid, Spain
1957...Real Madrid, Spain
1958...Real Madrid, Spain
1959...Real Madrid, Spain
1960...Real Madrid, Spain
1961...Benfica, Portugal
1962...Benfica, Portugal
1963...AC Milan, Italy
1964...Inter-Milan, Italy
1965...Inter-Milan, Italy
1966...Real Madrid, Spain
1967...Celtic, Scotland
1968...Manchester United, England
1969...AC Milan, Italy
1970...Feyenoord, Netherlands
1971...Ajax Amsterdam, Netherlands
1972...Ajax Amsterdam, Netherlands

1973...Ajax Amsterdam, Netherlands
1974...Bayern Munich, W Germany
1975...Bayern Munich, W Germany
1976...Bayern Munich, W Germany
1977...Liverpool, England
1978...Liverpool, England
1979...Nottingham Forest, England
1980...Nottingham Forest, England
1981...Liverpool, England
1982...Aston Villa, England
1983...SV Hamburg, W Germany
1984...Liverpool, England
1985...Juventus, Italy

1986...Steaua Bucharest, Romania
1987...Porto, Portugal
1988...PSV Eindhoven, Netherlands
1989...AC Milan, Italy
1990...AC Milan, Italy
1991....Red Star Belgrade, Yugoslav.
1992...Barcelona, Spain
1993...Olympique Marseille, France
1994...AC Milan, Italy
1995...Ajax Amsterdam, Netherlands
1996...Juventus, Italy
1997...Borussia Dortmund, Ger.
1998...Real Madrid, Spain
1999...Manchester United, England
2000...Real Madrid, Spain

Note: On four occasions the European Cup winner has refused to play in the Intercontinental Cup and has been replaced by the runner-up: Panathinaikos (Greece) in 1971, Juventus (Italy) in 1973, Atletico Madrid (Spain) in 1974, and Malmo (Sweden) in 1979.

Libertadores Cup

Competition between champion clubs and runners-up of 10 South American National Associations.

1960...Penarol, Uruguay
1961...Penarol, Uruguay
1962...Santos, Brazil
1963...Santos, Brazil
1964...Independiente, Argentina
1965...Independiente, Argentina
1966...Penarol, Uruguay
1967...Racing Club, Argentina
1968...Estudiantes, Argentina
1969...Estudiantes, Argentina
1970...Estudiantes, Argentina
1971...Nacional, Uruguay
1972...Independiente, Argentina
1973...Independiente, Argentina
1974...Independiente, Argentina

1975...Independiente, Argentina
1976...Cruzeiro, Brazil
1977...Boca Juniors, Argentina
1978...Boca Juniors, Argentina
1979...Olimpia, Paraguay
1980...Nacional, Uruguay
1981...Flamengo, Brazil
1982...Penarol, Uruguay
1983...Gremio, Brazil
1984...Independiente, Argentina
1985...Argentinos Juniors, Arg
1986...River Plate, Argentina
1987...Penarol, Uruguay
1988...Nacional, Uruguay
1989...Atletico Nacional, Colombia

1990...Olimpia, Paraguay
1991...Colo Colo, Chile
1992...São Paulo, Brazil
1993...São Paulo, Brazil
1994...Velez Sarsfield, Argentina
1995...Gremio, Brazil
1996...River Plate, Argentina
1997...Cruzeiro, Brazil
1998...Vasco da Gama, Brazil
1999...Palmeiras, Brazil
2000...Boca Juniors, Argentina

UEFA Cup

Competition between teams other than league champions and cup winners from the Union of European Football Associations.

1958...Barcelona, Spain
1959...No tournament
1960...Barcelona, Spain
1961...AS Roma, Italy
1962...Valencia, Spain
1963...Valencia, Spain
1964...Real Zaragoza, Spain
1965...Ferencvaros, Hungary
1966...Barcelona, Spain
1967...Dynamo Zagreb, Yugoslav.
1968...Leeds United, England
1969...Newcastle United, England
1970...Arsenal, England
1971...Leeds United, England
1972...Tottenham Hotspur, England
1973...Liverpool, England

1974...Feyenoord, Netherlands
1975...Borussia Monchengladbach, W Germany
1976...Liverpool, England
1977...Juventus, Italy
1978...PSV Eindhoven, Netherl.
1979...Borussia Monchengladbach, W Germany
1980...Eintracht Frankfurt, W Germany
1981...Ipswich Town, England
1982...IFK Gothenburg, Sweden
1983...Anderlecht, Belgium
1984...Tottenham Hotspur, England
1985...Real Madrid, Spain
1986...Real Madrid, Spain

1987...IFK Gothenburg, Sweden
1988...Bayer Leverkusen, W Germany
1989...Naples, Italy
1990...Juventus, Italy
1991...Inter-Milan, Italy
1992...Torino, Italy
1993...Juventus, Italy
1994...Internazionale, Italy
1995...Parma, Italy
1996...Bayern Munich, Germany
1997...Schalke 04, Germany
1998...Inter Milan, Italy
1999...Parma, Italy
2000...Galatasaray, Turkey

Club Competition *(Cont.)*

European Cup-Winners' Cup

Competition between cup winners of countries belonging to UEFA.

1961...AC Fiorentina, Italy	1974...Magdeburg, E Germany	1988...Mechelen, Belgium
1962...Atletico Madrid, Spain	1975...Dynamo Kiev, USSR	1989...Barcelona, Spain
1963...Tottenham Hotspur, England	1976...Anderlecht, Belgium	1990...Sampdoria, Italy
1964...Sporting Lisbon, Portugal	1977...SV Hamburg, W. Germ.	1991...Manchester United, England
1965...West Ham United, England	1978...Anderlecht, Belgium	1992...Werder Bremen, Germany
1966...Borussia Dortmund, W Germany	1979...Barcelona, Spain	1993...Parma, Italy
	1980...Valencia, Spain	1994...Arsenal, England
1967...Bayern Munich, W. Germ.	1981...Dynamo Tbilisi, USSR	1995...Real Zaragoza, Spain
1968...AC Milan, Italy	1982...Barcelona, Spain	1996...Paris St. Germain, France
1969...Slovan Bratislava, Czech.	1983...Aberdeen, Scotland	1997...Barcelona, Spain
1970...Manchester City, England	1984...Juventus, Italy	1998...Chelsea, England
1971...Chelsea, England	1985...Everton, England	1999...Lazio, Italy
1972...Glasgow Rangers, Scotland	1986...Dynamo Kiev, USSR	
1973...AC Milan, Italy	1987...Ajax Amsterdam, Netherlands	

Note: the Cup-Winners Cup was discontinued after 1999.

Major League Soccer

Results

Year	Champion	Score	Runner-up	Regular Season MVP
1996	D.C. United	3–2	Los Angeles	Carlos Valderrama, TB
1997	D.C. United	2–1	Colorado	Preki, Kansas City
1998	Chicago	2–0	D.C. United	Marco Etcheverry, D.C.
1999	D.C. United	2–0	Los Angeles	Jason Kreis, Dallas
2000	Kansas City	1–0	Chicago	Tony Meola, Kansas City

D.C.'s D Gets an F

Nobody denies that D.C. United has the best collection of defenders in MLS, including two players (Jeff Agoos and Carlos Llamosa) who excelled on the American back line during the U.S. Cup in June 2000, and another (Eddie Pope) who rejoined the national team for World Cup qualifying in July after recovering from surgery on his left knee in April. So why was United's defense so horrid in 2000, allowing a league-high 63 goals, while the team limped to a 8-18-6 record, second-worst in MLS?

"It's a fallacy that because you have good defenders, you're going to allow fewer goals," Agoos says. "It certainly helps, but you have to defend well as a team, and we haven't done that. A lot of our goals have come against set pieces and on freaky plays like own goals and penalty kicks."

He's right, to an extent. D.C. led MLS in own goals (four) was second in penalty-kick goals allowed (six), and gave up a remarkable number of goals on set pieces, including all three in a 3–1 loss to the New England Revolution on May 13. Those numbers suggest a lack of discipline across the board, but it can't be denied that the D.C. D had an off year in 2000. Agoos was perhaps its best performer, but Carey Talley dropped off from his '99 season, which had earned him a call-up to the national team, and Llamosa and Pope struggled with injuries and poor form all season.

United had problems elsewhere—Marco Etcheverry, the team's linchpin in midfield, had a subpar year; and newcomer Chris Albright did not fill the cleats of departed striker Roy Lassiter, who had to be shipped to Miami for salary-cap reasons after scoring 18 goals in '99—but the decline of its previously stalwart defense was a prominent reason the three-time champion missed the playoffs for the first time in MLS's five-year history.

A-League

Year	Champion	Score	Runner-Up	Regular Season MVP
1991	San Francisco	1–3, 2–0 (1–0 on PKs)	Albany	Jean Harbor, Maryland
1992	Colorado	1–0	Tampa Bay	Taifour Diane, Colorado
1993	Colorado	3–1 (OT)	Los Angeles	Taifour Diane, Colorado
1994	Montreal	1–0	Colorado	Paulinho, Los Angeles
1995	Seattle	1–2 (SO), 3–0, 2–1 (SO)	Atlanta	Peter Hattrup, Seattle
1996	Seattle	2–0	Rochester	Wolde Harris, Colorado
1997	Milwaukee	2–1 (SO)	Carolina	Doug Miller, Rochester
1998	Rochester	3–1	Minnesota	Mark Baena, Seattle
1999	Minnesota	2–1	Rochester	John Swallen, Minnesota
2000	Rochester	3–1	Minnesota	Vitalis (Digital) Takawira, Milwaukee

U.S. Open Cup

Open to all amateur and professional teams in the United States, the annual U.S. Open Cup is the oldest cup competition in the country and among the oldest in the world. The tournament is a single-elimination event running concurrent to the MLS season. The winner advances to the CONCACAF Cup, a tournament of the top club teams from North and Central America.

Year	Champion
1914	Brooklyn Field Club (NYC)
1915	Bethlehem Steel FC (PA)
1916	Bethlehem Steel FC (PA)
1917	Fall River Rovers (MA)
1918	Bethlehem Steel FC (PA)
1919	Bethlehem Steel FC (PA)
1920	Ben Miller FC (St. Louis)
1921	Robbins Dry Dock FC (Brooklyn)
1922	Scullin Steel FC (St. Louis)
1923	Paterson FC (NJ)
1924	Fall River FC (MA)
1925	Shawsheen FC (Andover, MA)
1926	Bethlehem Steel FC (PA)
1927	Fall River FC (MA)
1928	New York National FC (NYC)
1929	Hakoah All Star SC (NYC)
1930	Fall River FC (MA)
1931	Fall River FC (MA)
1932	New Bedford FC (MA)
1933	Stix, Baer and Fuller FC (St. Louis)
1934	Stix, Baer and Fuller FC (St. Louis)
1935	Central Breweries FC (Chicago)
1936	German-Americans (Philadelphia)
1937	New York American FC (NYC)
1938	Sparta A and BA (Chicago)
1939	St. Mary's Celtic SC (Brooklyn)
1940	—
1941	Pawtucket FC (RI)
1942	Gallatin SC (PA)
1943	Brooklyn Hispano SC (NYC)
1944	Brooklyn Hispano SC (NYC)
1945	Brookhattan FC (NYC)
1946	Chicago Viking FC (IL)
1947	Ponta Delgada SC (Fall River, MA)
1948	Simpkins-Ford SC (St. Louis)
1949	Morgan SC (PA)
1950	Simpkins-Ford SC (St. Louis)
1951	German Hungarian SC (NYC)
1952	Harmarville SC (PA)
1953	Falcons SC (Chicago)
1954	New York Americans (NYC)
1955	Eintracht Sport Club (NYC)
1956	Harmarville SC (PA)
1957	Kutis SC (St. Louis)
1958	Los Angeles Kickers (CA)
1959	McIlvaine Canvasbacks (Los Angeles)
1960	Ukrainian Nationals (Philadelphia)
1961	Ukrainian Nationals (Philadelphia)
1962	New York Hungaria (NYC)
1963	Ukrainian Nationals (Philadelphia)
1964	Los Angeles Kickers (CA)
1965	New York Hungaria (NYC)
1966	Ukrainian Nationals (Philadelphia)
1967	Greek American AA (NYC)
1968	Greek American AA (NYC)
1969	Greek American AA (NYC)
1970	Elizabeth SC (Union, NJ)
1971	Hota SC (NYC)
1972	Elizabeth SC (Union, NJ)
1973	Maccabee SC (Los Angeles)
1974	Greek American AA (NYC)
1975	Maccabee SC (Los Angeles)
1976	San Francisco AC (CA)
1977	Maccabee SC (Los Angeles)
1978	Maccabee SC (Los Angeles)
1979	Brooklyn Dodgers SC (NYC)
1980	NY Pancyprian-Freedoms (NYC)
1981	Maccabee SC (Los Angeles)
1982	NY Pancyprian-Freedoms (NYC)
1983	NY Pancyprian-Freedoms (NYC)
1984	AO Krete (NYC)
1985	Greek American AC (San Francisco)
1986	Kutis SC (St. Louis)
1987	Club Espana (Washington, D.C.)
1988	Busch SC (St. Louis)
1989	HRC Kickers (St. Petersburg, FL)
1990	AAC Eagles (Chicago)
1991	Brooklyn Italians SC (East NY)
1992	San Jose Oaks (CA)
1993	Club Deportivo Mexico (San Francisco)
1994	Greek American AC (San Francisco)
1995	Richmond Kickers (VA)
1996	D.C. United (MLS)
1997	Dallas Burn (MLS)
1998	Chicago Fire (MLS)
1999	Rochester Rhinos (A-League)

North American Soccer League

Formed in 1968 by the merger of the National Professional Soccer League and the USA League, both of which had begun operations a year earlier. The NPSL's lone champion was the Oakland Clippers. The USA League, which brought entire teams in from Europe, was won in 1967 by the L.A. Wolves, who were the English League's Wolverhampton Wanderers.

Year	Champion	Score	Runner-Up	Regular Season MVP
1968	Atlanta	0–0, 3–0	San Diego	John Kowalik, Chi
1969	Kansas City	No game	Atlanta	Cirilio Fernandez, KC
1970	Rochester	3–0,1–3	Washington	Carlos Metidieri, Roch
1971	Dallas	1–2, 4–1, 2–0	Atlanta	Carlos Metidieri, Roch
1972	NY	2–1	St. Louis	Randy Horton, NY
1973	Philadelphia	2–0	Dallas	Warren Archibald, Mia
1974	Los Angeles	4–3*	Miami	Peter Silvester, Balt
1975	Tampa Bay	2–0	Portland	Steve David, Mia
1976	Toronto	3–0	Minnesota	Pelé, NY
1977	NY	2–1	Seattle	Franz Beckenbauer, NY
1978	NY	3–1	Tampa Bay	Mike Flanagan, NE
1979	Vancouver	2–1	Tampa Bay	Johan Cruyff, LA
1980	NY	3–0	Ft. Lauderdale	Roger Davies, Sea
1981	Chicago	1–0*	NY	Giorgio Chinaglia, NY
1982	NY	1–0	Seattle	Peter Ward, Sea
1983	Tulsa	2–0	Toronto	Roberto Cabanas, NY
1984	Chicago	2–1, 3–2	Toronto	Steve Zungul, SJ

*Shootout.

Championship Format: 1968 and 1970: Two games/total goals. 1971 and 1984: Best-of-three series. 1972–1983: One-game championship. Title in 1969 went to the regular-season champion.

Statistical Leaders

SCORING

Year	Player/Team	Pts	Year	Player/Team	Pts
1968	John Kowalik, Chi	69	1977	Steven David, LA	58
1969	Kaiser Motaung, Atl	36	1978	Giorgio Chinaglia, NY	79
1970	Kirk Apostolidis, Dall	35	1979	Oscar Fabbiani, Tampa Bay	58
1971	Carlos Metidieri, Roch	46	1980	Giorgio Chinaglia, NY	77
1972	Randy Horton, NY	22	1981	Giorgio Chinaglia, NY	74
1973	Kyle Rote, Dall	30	1982	Giorgio Chinaglia, NY	55
1974	Paul Child, San Jose	36	1983	Roberto Cabanas, NY	66
1975	Steven David, Miami	52	1984	Slavisa Zungul, Golden Bay	50
1976	Giorgio Chinaglia, NY	49			

No Dutch Treat

As the Dutch blitzed through their first four opponents at Euro 2000 by a combined score of 13–3 (inlcuding a 3–2 defeat of France's B team), all of Holland turned into a tangerine dream. One farmer in Arnhem dressed 11 of his cows in orange and outfitted one heifer in dark goggles, a la Dutch midfielder Edgar Davids. Even the Sky High hash bar got into the act, installing a big-screen television, tacking up a poster of the Dutch team alongside one of Bob Marley and offering contraband Euro 2000 T-shirts emblazoned witht the slogan of a joint-paper company: DRAAIT ORANJE NET ZO LEKKER? (Will Holland Roll So Well?).

Then the Dutch dream went up in smoke. After slamming Yugoslavia 6–1 in the quarters, Holland choked in a scoreless semifinal against Italy on June 29, failing to convert two penalty kicks in regular time and botching three more in the tiebreaking shootout. Within minutes of Italy's victory, Frank Rijkaard, a memeber of Holland's 1988 European Championship team, resigned as coach. "I failed," he said, "and I have to take the consequences."

NCAA Sports

DAMIAN STROHMEYER

NCAA baseball champions LSU

Dynasty Reruns

Three of college sports' most venerable programs produced the champions in soccer, hockey and baseball

BY DAVID FLEMING

IN PROFESSIONAL sports, which have free agency and the salary cap, dynasties are getting harder and harder—if not impossible—to establish. But college sports programs, which are limited in establishing dominance only by graduation and recruiting luck, have continued to produce dynasties matching those of old, like UCLA's legendary basketball teams under John Wooden or the halcyon days of Notre Dame and Army football. Most of the crushingly dominant dynasties—Kenyon swimming, Iowa wrestling, North Carolina women's soccer—occur at lower levels or in so-called minor sports, but the 1999–2000 champions in men's soccer, hockey and baseball proved that dynasties are alive and well at all levels of college competition.

MEN'S SOCCER
Most dynasties have two common elements: proof-in-the-pudding stats that reflect their dominance, and one or two transcendent players who take the team, and sometimes the sport, to a new level.

During the past three seasons Indiana's soccer team has had both.

From 1997 to '99 the Hoosiers won an NCAA-record 67 games while losing only six. In December '99, after surviving a four-overtime thriller against UCLA in the NCAA semifinals (the Hoosiers won 3–2), IU beat Santa Clara 1–0 to claim its second straight NCAA title. The key player in both victories was junior sweeper Nick Garcia, who demonstrated that you can be the most valuable player on the field without scoring a single goal.

With five seconds left in the second overtime against UCLA, Garcia cleared a sure Bruins game-winner off the goal line with a lunging stab of his left foot. Two days later, in the final, Garcia topped those defensive heroics. Indiana took a 1–0 lead in the 30th minute when senior midfielder Yuri Lavrinenko, the NCAA Final Four MVP, worked a give-and-go near the top of the box with senior striker Aleksey Korol. Taking the return pass on the left side, 15 yards from goal, Lavrinenko calmly slotted the

After leading IU to a second straight title, Garcia, a junior, left school for Major League Soccer.

ball inside the far post. Indiana was clinging to that 1–0 lead with 20 minutes to play when Santa Clara striker Anthony Chimienti ripped a shot from point-blank range that beat Hoosier keeper T.J. Hannig. Before the ball crossed the line to tie the game, though, Garcia flung his body toward the back of the Hoosiers' net and somehow nodded it up, off the crossbar and out of danger.

Garcia's momentum carried him into the goal's netting, and as he extricated himself, the Broncos had to be feeling a bit tangled up themselves: *What would it take to dethrone these Hoosiers?* Whatever it was, Santa Clara didn't have it, as Indiana held on for the win, and Garcia's play perfectly punctuated the Hoosiers' dominant three-year run.

"You come across special groups when you've been at it as long as I have," said IU coach Jerry Yeagley, who has spent 27 years in Bloomington and won five NCAA titles. "And this was a special group over the last three years."

MEN'S ICE HOCKEY

The fin de siècle North Dakota hockey team was a special bunch, as well, when you consider the Fighting Sioux's tradition of stocking their roster with Bunyanesque bruisers, a style of player that brought five NCAA hockey titles to Fargo from 1959 to '87. But coach Dean Blais sought a new direction in the '90s, recruiting smaller, swifter players. In 1997, the Sioux won their program's sixth NCAA crown, as 5'7", 140-pound David Hoogsteen scored two goals in the title-clinching 6–4 win over Boston University.

In 1999–2000, half the Sioux's 20 players were shorter than six feet, including Hobey Baker Award finalist Jeff Panzer, a forward who stood 5'9". But the diminutive Fighting Sioux once again stood tall, especially 5'7" junior goalie Karl Goehring, who returned from a concussion he sustained in March to mind the Sioux net for the national semifinal against Maine. Before his injury Goehring had set school records for wins (62) and conference shutouts (10), and he picked up right where he had left off, turning aside 30 shots in the Sioux's 2–0 win. It was the first shutout by a Sioux goalie in the NCAA tournament—and the list of North Dakota goaltenders includes Ed Belfour, Jon Casey and Darren Johnson.

"Six weeks ago I don't think we had a championship team," said Blais. "We had lost sight of the WCHA championship. But it kind of worked in reverse for us. Instead of getting bummed out, our guys went to work and made themselves better." But they weren't done yet. Trailing Boston College 2–1 with 17:17 left to play in the final, the Sioux got the tying goal from senior wing Lee Goren, who converted a feed from Ryan Bayda. With 5:38 remaining, center Jason Ulmer slapped in a rebound of a Goren shot to beat Eagles goaltender Scott Clemmensen for the game-winner. Goren, who was named the tournament's most outstanding player (and who, at 6'3", may be the only Sioux who can use the top shelf of his locker), scored an empty-netter to wrap up the game and give the storied North Dakota hockey program its seventh NCAA title and second in four years.

The Sioux experienced a slight hiccup in celebrating the renewal of their dynasty, though. After the game they were stranded inside the Providence Civic Center for several hours because the pilot who was supposed to fly them back to Fargo became ill and a replacement had to be flown in. No matter. North Dakota players worked with volunteers to set up a makeshift party room deep inside the bowels of the arena, where the team, coaching staff and supporters celebrated the victory. The low overhead clearance in the depths of the arena didn't bother the Sioux a bit.

BASEBALL

The office of LSU baseball coach Skip Bertman is known among his players as Plaquemine because during Bertman's 17 years at the school the walls of the room have become so crowded with College Baseball Coach of the Year certificates, All-America awards and NCAA championship plaques that you can barely see them.

And now Bertman needs to find just a little more room, for the Tigers' memorable 2000 NCAA title, the school's fifth championship in 10 years (the others came in 1991, '93, '96 and '97). It's a good thing he's retiring at the end of 2001.

"What Skip has accomplished in the 1990s, I didn't think was possible," said Stanford coach Mark Marquess. "It's truly amazing." Marquess got a firsthand look at how amazing the Tigers could be. In the final game of the College World Series, LSU stormed back from a 5–2 deficit in the bottom of the eighth to beat the Cardinal 6–5. But impossible finishes have become a trademark of the LSU dynasty. The Tigers won the '96 title over Miami with a breathtaking two-out, two-run homer in the bottom of the ninth by second baseman Warren Morris. Another LSU hallmark has been a brawny brand of baseball; Bertman likes to call it Gorillaball in honor of his '97 title team, which set the NCAA record with 188 homers.

But there was no Gorillaball in evidence in Baton Rouge as the Tigers sought title No. 5. For starters, it was the glove, and not the bat, of outfielder Ray Wright, that saved the Tigers in the third inning of the title game. Wright leaped nearly four feet over the rightfield fence to rob Stanford of a two-run home run and what would have been an almost insurmountable lead. And at the plate all season the Tigers opted not for Gorillaball but Turtleball: an homage to their new hitting coach, Henry (Turtle) Thomas, who preached brains over brawn in the batter's box. The new approach helped the Tigers rack up a 52–17 overall record, including a perfect 13–0 postseason run, while setting a school record for hits (864) and batting average (.340).

No one took to Turtleball like senior catcher Brad Cresse, who led LSU with a .388 average and led the nation with 30 homers and 106 RBIs. But Cresse slumped in the series, and when he came to bat in the ninth inning against Stanford, with the score tied 5–5, he brought a 1-for-10 slump (with six strikeouts) with him. There were runners on first and second, and Cresse promptly fell behind 0 and 1 to Cardinal ace Justin Wayne, the fifth pick in the 2000 major league baseball draft. Then, remembering the advice of his father, former Los Angeles Dodgers' bullpen coach Mark Cresse, and the basic tenet of Turtleball—patience—Cresse hung in on a slider and drilled it to leftfield to bring in the winning run.

In what has become something of an annual ritual in Omaha, a sea of fans clad in purple and gold Mardi Gras beads poured out onto the field of Rosenblatt Stadium to celebrate another Tiger title. "Of all the national championships," said Bertman, "this is the best one."

Now, if only he had room for the plaque.

FOR THE RECORD·1999–2000

NCAA Team Champions

Fall 1999

Cross-Country

MEN

	Champion	Runner-Up
Division I:	Arkansas	Wisconsin
Division II:	Western St (CO)	Adams St (CO)
Division III:	N Central	Keene St

WOMEN

Division I:	Brigham Young	Arkansas
Division II:	Adams St (CO)	Western St (CO)
Division III:	Calvin	Middlebury

Field Hockey

WOMEN

	Champion	Runner-Up
Division I:	Maryland	Michigan
Division II	Bloomsburg	Bentley
Division III:	College of New Jersey	Amherst

Football

MEN

	Champion	Runner-Up
Division I-AA:	Georgia Southern	Youngstown St
Division II:	NW Missouri St	Carson-Newman
Division III:	Pacific Lutheran	Rowan

Soccer

MEN

	Champion	Runner-Up
Division I:	Indiana	Santa Clara
Division II:	Southern Connecticut St	Fort Lewis (CO)
Division III:	St. Lawrence (NY)	Wheaton (IL)

WOMEN

Division I:	N Carolina	Notre Dame
Division II:	Franklin Pierce (NH)	Cal Poly Pomona
Division III:	UC-San Diego	Macalester

Volleyball

WOMEN

	Champion	Runner-Up
Division I:	Penn St	Stanford
Division II:	BYU-Hawaii	Tampa
Division III:	Central (IA)	Trinity

Water Polo

MEN

Champion	Runner-Up
UCLA	Stanford

Winter 1999–2000
Basketball

MEN

	Champion	Runner-Up
Division I:	Michigan St	Florida
Division II:	Metropolitan St	Kentucky Wesleyan
Division III:	Calvin	WI-Eau Clair

WOMEN

	Champion	Runner-Up
Division I:	Connecticut	Tennessee
Division II:	Northern Kentucky	N Dakota St
Division III:	Washington (MO)	Southern Maine

Fencing

Champion	Runner-Up
Penn St	Notre Dame

Gymnastics

MEN

Champion	Runner-Up
Penn St	Michigan

WOMEN

UCLA	Utah

Ice Hockey

MEN

	Champion	Runner-Up
Division I:	N Dakota	Boston College
Division III:	Norwich	St. Thomas

Rifle

Champion	Runner-Up
AK-Fairbanks	Xavier

Skiing

Champion	Runner-Up
Denver	Colorado

Swimming and Diving

MEN

	Champion	Runner-Up
Division I:	Texas	Auburn
Division II:	Drury	Cal St-Bakersfield
Division III:	Kenyon	Denison

WOMEN

	Champion	Runner-Up
Division I:	Georgia	Stanford
Division II:	Cal St-Bakersfield	Drury
Division III:	Kenyon	Denison

Wrestling

MEN

	Champion	Runner-Up
Division I:	Iowa	Iowa St
Division II:	N Dakota St	Central Oklahoma
Division III:	Augsburg	Wartburg

Winter 1999–2000 (Cont.)
Indoor Track and Field

MEN

	Champion	Runner-Up
Division I:	Arkansas	Stanford
Division II:	Abilene Christian	St. Augustine's
Division III:	Lincoln (PA)	N Central

WOMEN

	Champion	Runner-Up
Division I:	UCLA	S Carolina
Division II:	Abilene Christian	N Dakota St
Division III:	Wheaton (MA)	Lincoln (PA)

Spring 2000
Baseball

	Champion	Runner-Up
Division I:	Louisiana St	Stanford
Division II:	Southeastern Oklahoma St	Fort Hays St
Division III:	Montclair St	St. Thomas (MN)

Golf

MEN

	Champion	Runner-Up
Division I:	Oklahoma St	Georgia Tech
Division II:	Florida Southern	Grand Canyon
		Cal St-Bakersfield
Division III:	Greensboro	Methodist (NC)

WOMEN

	Champion	Runner-Up
Division I:	Arizona	Stanford
Divisions II:	Florida Southern	Rollins (FL)

Lacrosse

MEN

	Champion	Runner-Up
Division I:	Syracuse	Princeton
Division II:	Limestone	LIU-C.W. Post
Division III:	Middlebury	Salisbury St

WOMEN

	Champion	Runner-Up
Divisions I and II:	Maryland	Princeton
Division III:	College of New Jersey	Williams

Rowing

WOMEN

Champion	Runner-Up
Brown	Washington

Softball

	Champion	Runner-Up
Division I:	Oklahoma	UCLA
Division II:	N Dakota St	Kennesaw St
Division III:	St. Mary's	Chapman (CA)

Tennis

MEN

	Champion	Runner-Up
Division I:	Stanford	Virginia Commonwealth
Division II:	Lander	Hawaii Pacific
Division III:	Trinity	Gustavus Adolphus

NCAA Team Champions (Cont.)

Spring 2000 (Cont.)
Tennis (Cont.)
WOMEN

	Champion	Runner-Up
Division I:	Georgia	Stanford
Division II:	BYU-Hawaii	Lynn
Division III:	Trinity	UC-San Diego

Outdoor Track and Field
MEN

	Champion	Runner-Up
Division I:	Stanford	Arkansas
Division II:	Abilene Christian	St. Augustine's
Division III:	Lincoln (PA), N Central	Central (IA)

WOMEN

Division I:	Louisiana St	Southern Cal
Division II:	St. Augustine's	Abilene Christian
Division III:	Lincoln (PA)	Christopher Newport

Volleyball
MEN

Champion	Runner-Up
UCLA	Ohio St

NCAA Division I Individual Champions

Fall 1999
Cross Country
MEN

Champion	Runner-Up
David Kimani, S Alabama	Michael Power, Arkansas

WOMEN

Champion	Runner-Up
Erica Palmer, Wisconsin	Amy Yoder, Arkansas

Winter 1999–2000
Fencing
MEN

	Champion	Runner-Up
Sabre	Gabor Szelle, Notre Dame	Jakub Krochmalski, Wayne St
Foil	Felix Reichling, Stanford	Ozren Debic, Notre Dame
Épée	Daniel Landgren, Penn St	Alex Roytblat, St. John's

WOMEN

Sabre	Caroline Purcell, MIT	Kim Treiber, N Carolina
Foil	Eva Petschnigg, Princeton	Monique DeBruin, Stanford
Épée	Jessica Burke, Penn St	Emese Takcs, St. John's

Gymnastics
MEN

	Champion	Runner-Up
All-around	Jamie Natalie, Ohio St	Guard Young, Brigham Young
Vault	Guard Young, Brigham Young	Andrew Hampy, California
Parallel bars	Kris Zimmerman, Michigan; Justin Toman, Michigan	
Horizontal bar	Michael Ashe, California	T. Romagnoli, Illinois
Floor exercise	Jamie Natalie, Ohio St	Codey Casey, Cal-Santa Barbara
Pommel horse	Brandon Stefaniak, Penn St; Don Jackson, Iowa	
Rings	Cortney Bramwell, Brigham Young	Scott Vetere, Michigan

Winter 1999–2000 *(Cont.)*
Gymnastics *(Cont.)*
WOMEN

	Champion	Runner-Up
All-around	Mohini Bhardwaj, UCLA; Heather Brink, Nebraska	
Balance beam	Lena Degteva, UCLA	Mohini Bhardwaj, UCLA
Uneven bars	Mohini Bhardwaj, UCLA	Heather Brink, Nebraska
Floor exercise	Suzanne Sears, Georgia	Denise Jones, Utah
Vault	Heather Brink, Nebraska	Andree Pickens, Alabama

Skiing
MEN

	Champion	Runner-Up
Slalom	Andy Leroy, Colorado	Jernej Bukovec, Utah
Giant slalom	Matthew Knittle, Vermont	Brandon Dyksterhouse, Vermont
10-kilometer freestyle	Pietro Broggini, Denver	Jorn Frohs, Denver
20-kilometer classical	Pietro Broggini, Denver	Wolf Wallendorf, Denver

WOMEN

	Champion	Runner-Up
Slalom	Cecilie Larsen, Denver	Gusty Swift, Dartmouth
Giant slalom	Aimee-Noel Hartley, Colorado	Linda Wikstrom, Colorado
5-kilometer freestyle	Katerina Hanusova, Colorado	Britta Wienand, Denver
15-kilometer classical	Kristina Strandberg, New Mexico	Britta Wienand, Denver

Wrestling

	Champion	Runner-Up
125 lb	Jeremy Hunter, Penn St	Steve Garland, Virginia
133 lb	Eric Jouergens, Iowa	Cody Sanderson, Iowa St
141 lb	Carl Perry, Illinois	Michael Lightner, Oklahoma
149 lb	Tony Davis, Northern Iowa	Adam Tirapelle, Illinois
157 lb	Brett Matter, Penn	Larry Quisel, Boise St
165 lb	Don Pritzlaff, Wisconsin	Joe Heskett, Iowa St
174 lb	Byron Tucker, Oklahoma	Josh Koscheck, Edinboro
184 lb	Cael Sanderson, Ohio St	Vertus Jones, W Virginia
197 lb	Brad Vering, Nebraska	Zach Thompson, Iowa St
285 lb	Brock Lesner, Minnesota	Wes Hand, Iowa

Swimming and Diving
MEN

	Champion	Time	Runner-Up	Time
50 m freestyle	Anthony Ervin, California	21.21#*	Roland Schoeman, Arizona	21.22
100 m freestyle	Anthony Ervin, California	47.36	Roland Schoeman, Arizona	47.51
200 m freestyle	Ryk Neethling, Arizona	1:43.90	Adam Messner, Stanford	1:45.01
400 m freestyle	Ryk Neethling, Arizona	3:40.47	Erik Vendt, Southern Cal	3:42.81
1500 m freestyle	Erik Vendt, Southern Cal	14:31.02*	Chris Thompson, Michigan	14:35.95
100 m backstroke	Matt Ulrickson, Texas	52.05	Riley Janes, Texas A&M	52.18
200 m backstroke	Matthew Cole, Florida	1:53.68	Leonardo Costa, Southern Cal	1:54.79
100 m breaststroke	Edward Moses, Virginia	57.66#*	David Denniston, Auburn	58.68
200 m breaststroke	Edward Moses, Virginia	2:06.40#*	David Denniston, Auburn	2:09.46
100 m butterfly	Adam Pine, Nebraska	51.23	Nate Dusing, Texas	52.00*
200 m butterfly	Adam Messner, Stanford	1:55.79	Zsolt Gaspar, S Carolina	1:55.88
200 m IM	Atilla Czene, Arizona St	1:54.65#	Nate Dusing, Texas	1:56.84
400 m IM	Tim Siciliano, Michigan	4:06.02*	Erik Vendt, Southern Cal	4:09.35

	Champion	Pts	Runner-Up	Pts
1-meter diving	Troy Dumais, Texas	605.20	Shannon Roy, Tennessee	570.95
3-meter diving	Troy Dumais, Texas	662.65	Stefan Ahrens, Miami (FL)	624.05
Platform	Tyce Routson, Miami (FL)	596.10	Troy Dumais, Texas	588.80

*American record. #World record.

Winter 1999–2000 *(Cont.)*
Swimming and Diving *(Cont.)*

WOMEN

	Champion	Time	Runner-Up	Time
50 m freestyle	Courtney Shealy, Georgia	24.80	Courtney Allen, Northwestern	24.87
100 m freestyle	Courtney Shealy, Georgia	53.99	Keiko Price, UCLA	54.68
200 m freestyle	Maritza Correia, Georgia	1:57.33	Sarah Tolar, Arizona	1:57.59
400 m freestyle	Christina Teuscher, Columbia	4:04.09	Jessica Foschi, Stanford	4:06.17
1500 m freestyle	Cara Lane, Virginia	16:03.59	Trina Jackson, Arizona	16:14.50
100 m backstroke	Courtney Shealy, Georgia	58.66	Haley Cope, California	59.17
200 m backstroke	Beth Botsford, Arizona	2:06.70*	Shelly Ripple, Stanford	2:08.01
100 m breaststroke	Kristy Kowal, Georgia	1:05.74*	Amy Balcerzak, Northwestern	1:06.79
200 m breaststroke	Kristy Kowal, Georgia	2:22.05*	Amanda Beard, Arizona	2:22.84
100 m butterfly	Limin Liu, Nevada	57.97	Misty Hyman, Stanford	58.60
200 m butterfly	Limin Liu, Nevada	2:06.04	Misty Hyman, Stanford	2:06.55
200 m IM	Kristy Kowal, Georgia	2:10.69	Elli Overton, California	2:10.74
400 m IM	Christina Teuscher, Columbia	4:33.81	Corrie Murphy, Southern Cal	4:37.77

	Champion	Pts	Runner-Up	Pts
1-meter diving	Jamie Watkins, Louisiana St	439.70	Jenny Keim, Miami (FL)	434.00
3-meter diving	Ashley Culpepper, Louisiana St	538.25	Sara Reiling, Indiana	525.10
Platform	Jenny Keim, Miami (FL)	538.80	Lizzy Flynt, Tennessee	472.95

*American record.

Indoor Track and Field

MEN

	Champion	Mark	Runner-Up	Mark
60-meter dash	Terrence Trammell, S Carolina	6.54	Kim Collins, Texas Christian	6.61
60-meter hurdles	Terrence Trammell, S Carolina	7.55	Aubrey Herring, Indiana St	7.64
200-meter dash	Shawn Crawford, Clemson	20.26**	John Capel, Florida	20.26
400-meter dash	Brandon Couts, Baylor	45.79	Andrew Pierce, Ohio St	45.99
800-meter run	Jess Strutzel, UCLA	1:46.57	Derrick Peterson, Missouri	1:46.85
Mile run	Gabriel Jennings, Stanford	3:59.46	Michael Stember, Stanford	4:00.75
3,000-meter run	David Kimani, S Alabama	7:52.64	Tim Broe, Alabama	7:57.30
5,000-meter run	David Kimani, S Alabama	13:52.58	Brent Hauser, Stanford	13:54.27
High jump	Mark Boswell, Texas	7 ft 7¾ in	Kenny Evans, Arkansas	7 ft 7 in
Pole vault	Russ Buller, Louisiana St	18 ft 8¼ in	Toby Stevenson, Stanford	18 ft 4½ in
Long jump	Melvin Lister, Arkansas	26 ft 8½ in	Dwight Phillips, Arizona St	26 ft 7¼ in
Triple jump	Melvin Lister, Arkansas	54 ft 7½ in	Jason Ward, Arkansas	54 ft 6 in
Shot put	Janus Robberts, SMU	65 ft 1¼ in	Joachim Olsen, Idaho	64 ft 8¾ in
35-pound wt throw	Libor Charfreitag, SMU	78 ft 3¾ in*	Xavier Tison, SMU	71 ft 11½ in

WOMEN

	Champion	Mark	Runner-Up	Mark
60-meter dash	Tonya Carter, Florida St	7.21	Peta-Gaye Dowdie, LSU	7.29
60-meter hurdles	Vonette Dixon, Auburn	7.94	Joyce Bates, LSU	7.99
200-meter dash	Mikele Barber, S Carolina	23.06	Debbie Dunn, Norfolk St	23.22
400-meter dash	Aliann Pompey, Manhattan	52.21	Mikele Pompey, S Carolina	52.50
800-meter run	Chantee Earl, Pittsburgh	2:02.19	Svetlana Badrankova, UTEP	2:03.19
Mile run	Carman Douma, Villanova	4:39.91	Autumn Fogg, Georgetown	4:42.72
3,000-meter run	Carrie Tollefson, Villanova	9:13.68	Amy Mortimer, Kansas St	9:16.59
5,000-meter run	Amy Yoder, Arkansas	15:46.89	Carrie Tollefson, Villanova	15:46.89
High jump	Dora Gyorffy, Harvard	6 ft 4¼ in	Carri Long, Purdue	6 ft 1½ in
Pole vault	Tracy O'Hara, UCLA	14 ft 6 in*	Erin Anderson, Kansas St	13 ft 5¼ in
Long jump	Keyon Soley, UCLA	21 ft 4¾ in	Monique Freeman, LSU	21 ft 4¾ in
Triple jump	Keisha Spencer, Louisiana St	46 ft 1½ in	Shelly-Ann Gallimor, Auburn	43 ft 11¼ in
Shot put	Seilala Sua, UCLA	56 ft 8 in	Cheree Hicks, Syracuse	55 ft 7 in
20-pound wt throw	Florence Ezeh, SMU	69 ft 11½ in	Seilala Sua, UCLA	69 ft

*Meet record. **American record.

Rifle

	Champion	Pts	Runner-Up	Pts
Smallbore	Nicole Allaire, Nebraska	1183	Matthew Emmons, AK-Fairbanks	1183
Air rifle	Kelly Mansfield, AK-Fairbanks	398	Emily Caruso, Norwich	396

Spring 2000
Golf
MEN

Champion	Score	Runner-Up	Score
Charles Howell, Oklahoma St	265	Chris Morris, Houston	273

WOMEN

Champion	Score	Runner-Up	Score
Jenna Daniels, Arizona	287	Julia Kraschinski, Arizona	290

Outdoor Track and Field
MEN

	Champion	Mark	Runner-Up	Mark
100-meter dash	Bernard Williams, Florida	10.03	Coby Miller, Auburn	10.14
200-meter dash	Shawn Crawford, Clemson	20.09	Coby Miller, Auburn	20.12
400-meter dash	Avard Moncur, Auburn	44.72	Geno White, Florida	45.02
800-meter run	Patrick Nduwimana, Arizona	1:45.08	Derrick Peterson, Missouri	1:45.18
1,500-meter run	Gabe Jennings, Stanford	3:37.76	Michael Stember, Stanford	3:39.53
3,000-met. steeple	Tim Broe, Alabama	8:39.03	Ian Connor, Ohio St	8:41.16
5,000-meter run	Brad Hauser, Stanford	13:48.80	Matt Lane, William & Mary	13:49.92
10,000-meter run	Brad Hauser, Stanford	30:38.57	Jason Balkman, Stanford	30:38.92
110-meter hurdles	Terrence Trammell, S Carolina	13.43	Aubrey Herring, Indiana St	13.49
400-meter hurdles	Felix Sanchez, Southern Cal	48.41	Bayano Kamani, Baylor	48.43
High jump	Mark Boswell, Texas	7 ft 7 in	David Furman, Florida	7 ft 4½ in
Pole vault	Russ Buller, Louisiana St	18 ft 4½ in	Toby Stevenson, Stanford	18 ft 4½ in
Long jump	Savante Stringfellow, Mississippi	26 ft 9¾ in	Dwight Phillips, Arizona St	26 ft 7¾ in
Triple jump	Melvin Lister, Arkansas	55 ft 7¾ in	Chris Hercules, Texas	54 ft 3¾ in
Shot put	Joachim Olsen, Idaho	66 ft 5¾ in	Janus Robberts, SMU	66 ft 3 in
Discus throw	Gabor Mate, Auburn	215 ft 8 in	Jason Gervais, Wyoming	206 ft 1 in
Hammer throw	Libor Charfreitag, SMU	253 ft 4 in	Andras Haklits, Georgia	250 ft 3 in
Javelin throw	Esko Mikkola, Arizona	238 ft 3 in	Brian Kollar, Virginia	234 ft 4 in
Decathlon	Bevan Hart, California	8002 pts	Claston Bernard, Louisiana St	7806 pts

WOMEN

	Champion	Mark	Runner-Up	Mark
100-meter dash	Angela Williams, Southern Cal	11.12	Peta-Gaye Dowdie, Louisiana St	11.23
200-meter dash	Peta-Gaye Dowdie, Louisiana St	22.51	Kinshasa Davis, Southern Cal	22.79
400-meter dash	Mikele Barber, S Carolina	51.14	Demetria Washington, S Carolina	51.82
800-meter run	Tytti Reho, Southern Methodist	2:01.43	Chantee Earl, Pittsburgh	2:02.54
1,500-meter run	Susan Taylor, Brigham Young	4:13.03	Carmen Douma, Villanova	4:16.09
3,000-meter run	Kara Wheeler, Colorado	9:02.15	Korene Hinds, Kansas St	9:10.10
5,000-meter run	Kara Wheeler, Colorado	15:54.30	Amy Yoder, Arkansas	16:05.70
10,000-meter run	Tara Rohatinsky, Brigham Young	33:49.24	Marty Hernandez, Brigham Young	33:50.45
100-meter hurdles	Joyce Bates, Louisiana St	12.85	Jenny Adams, Houston	12.91
400-meter hurdles	Natasha Danvers, Southern Cal	55.26	Tanya Jarrett, Texas	55.67
High jump	Erin Aldrich, Texas	6 ft 2¾ in	Dora Gyorffy, Harvard	6 ft 1½ in
Pole vault	Tracy O'Hara, UCLA	14 ft 5¼ in*	Erin Anderson, Kansas St	13 ft 9¼ in
Long jump	Jenny Adams, Houston	21 ft 5½ in	Nolle Graham, Seton Hall	21 ft 5¼ in
Triple jump	Keisha Spencer, LSU	45 ft 10 in	Brandi Prieto, Cal St-Northridge	44 ft 3¼ in
Shot put	Seilala Sua, UCLA	56 ft 11½ in	Cheree Hicks, Syracuse	55 ft 4¾ in
Discus throw	Seilala Sua, UCLA	200 ft 9 in	Cheree Hicks, Syracuse	187 ft
Hammer throw	Florence Ezeh, SMU	211 ft 10 in*	Melissa Price, Nebraska	210 ft 9 in
Javelin throw	Angelika Tsiolakoudi, UTEP	197 ft 8 in*	Emily Carlsten, Florida	181 ft 1 in
Heptathlon	Christi Smith, Akron	5797 pts	G.G. Miller, Arkansas	5777 pts

*Meet record.

Tennis
MEN

	Champion	Score	Runner-Up
Singles	Alex Kim, Stanford	6–1, 6–1	Carlos Drada, Kentucky
Doubles	Cary Franklin & Graydon Oliver, Illinois	6–4, 6–2	Ryan Moore & Nick Rainey, Southern Cal

WOMEN

	Champion	Score	Runner-Up
Singles	Laura Granville, Stanford	6–0, 6–4	Marissa Irvin, Stanford
Doubles	Amy Jensen & Claire Curran, California	4–6, 6–1, 7–5	Marissa Catlin & Lori Grey, Georgia

FOR THE RECORD·Year by Year

CHAMPIONSHIP RESULTS

Baseball

DIVISION I

Year	Champion	Coach	Score	Runner-Up	Most Outstanding Player
1947	California*	Clint Evans	8–7	Yale	No award
1948	Southern Cal	Sam Barry	9–2	Yale	No award
1949	Texas*	Bibb Falk	10–3	Wake Forest	Charles Teague, Wake Forest, 2B
1950	Texas	Bibb Falk	3–0	Washington St	Ray VanCleef, Rutgers, CF
1951	Oklahoma*	Jack Baer	3–2	Tennnessee	Sidney Hatfield, Tennessee, P-1B
1952	Holy Cross	Jack Barry	8–4	Missouri	James O'Neill, Holy Cross, P
1953	Michigan	Ray Fisher	7–5	Texas	J.L. Smith, Texas, P
1954	Missouri	John (Hi) Simmons	4–1	Rollins	Tom Yewcic, Michigan St, C
1955	Wake Forest	Taylor Sanford	7–6	Western Michigan	Tom Borland, Oklahoma St, P
1956	Minnesota	Dick Siebert	12–1	Arizona	Jerry Thomas, Minnesota, P
1957	California*	George Wolfman	1–0	Penn St	Cal Emery, Penn St, P-1B
1958	Southern Cal	Rod Dedeaux	8–7†	Missouri	Bill Thom, Southern Cal, P
1959	Oklahoma St	Toby Greene	5–3	Arizona	Jim Dobson, Oklahoma St, 3B
1960	Minnesota	Dick Siebert	2–1‡	Southern Cal	John Erickson, Minnesota, 2B
1961	Southern Cal*	Rod Dedeaux	1–0	Oklahoma St	Littleton Fowler, Oklahoma St, P
1962	Michigan	Don Lund	5–4	Santa Clara	Bob Garibaldi, Santa Clara, P
1963	Southern Cal	Rod Dedeaux	5–2	Arizona	Bud Hollowell, Southern Cal, C
1964	Minnesota	Dick Siebert	5–1	Missouri	Joe Ferris, Maine, P
1965	Arizona St	Bobby Winkles	2–1#	Ohio St	Sal Bando, Arizona St, 3B
1966	Ohio St	Marty Karow	8–2	Oklahoma St	Steve Arlin, Ohio St, P
1967	Arizona St	Bobby Winkles	11–2	Houston	Ron Davini, Arizona St, C
1968	Southern Cal*	Rod Dedeaux	4–3	Southern Illinois	Bill Seinsoth, Southern Cal, 1B
1969	Arizona St	Bobby Winkles	10–1	Tulsa	John Dolinsek, Arizona St, LF
1970	Southern Cal	Rod Dedeaux	2–1	Florida St	Gene Ammann, Florida St, P
1971	Southern Cal	Rod Dedeaux	7–2	Southern Illinois	Jerry Tabb, Tulsa, 1B
1972	Southern Cal	Rod Dedeaux	1–0	Arizona St	Russ McQueen, Southern Cal, P
1973	Southern Cal*	Rod Dedeaux	4–3	Arizona St	Dave Winfield, Minnesota, P-OF
1974	Southern Cal	Rod Dedeaux	7–3	Miami (FL)	George Milke, Southern Cal, P
1975	Texas	Cliff Gustafson	5–1	S Carolina	Mickey Reichenbach, Texas, 1B
1976	Arizona	Jerry Kindall	7–1	Eastern Michigan	Steve Powers, Arizona, P-DH
1977	Arizona St	Jim Brock	2–1	S Carolina	Bob Horner, Arizona St, 3B
1978	Southern Cal*	Rod Dedeaux	10–3	Arizona St	Rod Boxberger, Southern Cal, P
1979	Cal St-Fullerton	Augie Garrido	2–1	Arkansas	Tony Hudson, Cal St-Fullerton, P
1980	Arizona	Jerry Kindall	5–3	Hawaii	Terry Francona, Arizona, LF
1981	Arizona St	Jim Brock	7–4	Oklahoma St	Stan Holmes, Arizona St, LF
1982	Miami (FL)*	Ron Fraser	9–3	Wichita St	Dan Smith, Miami (FL), P
1983	Texas*	Cliff Gustafson	4–3	Alabama	Calvin Schiraldi, Texas, P
1984	Cal St-Fullerton	Augie Garrido	3–1	Texas	John Fishel, Cal St-Fullerton, LF
1985	Miami (FL)	Ron Fraser	10–6	Texas	Greg Ellena, Miami (FL), DH
1986	Arizona	Jerry Kindall	10–2	Florida St	Mike Senne, Arizona, LF
1987	Stanford	Mark Marquess	9–5	Oklahoma St	Paul Carey, Stanford, RF
1988	Stanford	Mark Marquess	9–4	Arizona St	Lee Plemel, Stanford, P
1989	Wichita St	Gene Stephenson	5–3	Texas	Greg Brummett, Wichita St, P
1990	Georgia	Steve Webber	2–1	Oklahoma St	Mike Rebhan, Georgia, P
1991	Louisiana St	Skip Bertman	6–3	Wichita St	Gary Hymel, Louisiana St, C
1992	Pepperdine	Andy Lopez	3–2	Cal St-Fullerton	Phil Nevin, Cal St-Fullerton, 3B
1993	Louisiana St	Skip Bertman	8–0	Wichita St	Todd Walker, Louisiana St, 2B
1994	Oklahoma	Larry Cochell	13–5	Georgia Tech	Chip Glass, Oklahoma, CF
1995	Cal St-Fullerton*	Augie Garrido	11–5	Southern Cal	Mark Kotsay, Cal St-Fullerton, CF-P
1996	Louisiana St	Skip Bertman	9–8	Miami (FL)	Pat Burrell, Miami (FL), 3B
1997	Louisiana St*	Skip Bertman	13–6	Alabama	Brandon Larson, Louisiana St, SS
1998	Southern Cal	Mike Gillespie	21–14	Arizona St	Wes Rachels, Southern Cal, 2B
1999	Miami (FL)	Jim Morris	6–5	Florida St	Marshall McDougall, FSU 3B/2B
2000	Louisiana St*	Skip Bertman	6–5	Stanford	Trey Hodges, Louisiana St, P

*Undefeated teams in College World Series play. †12 innings. ‡10 innings. #15 innings.

DIVISION II

Year	Champion	Year	Champion	Year	Champion
1968	Chapman*	1973	UC-Irvine*	1978	Florida Southern
1969	Illinois St*	1974	UC-Irvine	1979	Valdosta St
1970	Cal St-Northridge	1975	Florida Southern	1980	Cal Poly-Pomona*
1971	Florida Southern	1976	Cal Poly-Pomona	1981	Florida Southern*
1972	Florida Southern	1977	UC-Riverside	1982	UC-Riverside*

Baseball (Cont.)

DIVISION II (Cont.)

Year	Champion	Year	Champion	Year	Champion
1983	Cal Poly-Pomona*	1989	Cal Poly-SLO	1995	Florida Southern*
1984	Cal St-Northridge	1990	Jacksonville St	1996	Kennesaw St*
1985	Florida Southern*	1991	Jacksonville St	1997	Cal St-Chico*
1986	Troy St	1992	Tampa*	1998	Tampa*
1987	Troy St*	1993	Tampa	1999	Cal St-Chico
1988	Florida Southern*	1994	Central Missouri St	2000	SE Oklahoma St

DIVISION III

Year	Champion	Year	Champion	Year	Champion
1976	Cal St-Stanislaus	1985	WI-Oshkosh	1994	WI-Oshkosh
1977	Cal St-Stanislaus	1986	Marietta	1995	La Verne
1978	Glassboro St	1987	Montclair St	1996	William Paterson
1979	Glassboro St	1988	Ithaca	1997	Southern Maine
1980	Ithaca	1989	NC Wesleyan	1998	Eastern Connecticut St
1981	Marietta	1990	Eastern Connecticut St	1999	N Carolina Wesleyan
1982	Eastern Connecticut St	1991	Southern Maine	2000	Montclair St
1983	Marietta	1992	William Paterson		
1984	Ramapo	1993	Montclair St		

*Undefeated teams in final series.

Cross-Country

Men

DIVISION I

Year	Champion	Coach	Pts	Runner-Up	Pts	Individual Champion	Time
1938	Indiana	Earle Hayes	51	Notre Dame	61	Greg Rice, Notre Dame	20:12.9
1939	Michigan St	Lauren Brown	54	Wisconsin	57	Walter Mehl, Wisconsin	20:30.9
1940	Indiana	Earle Hayes	65	Eastern Michigan	68	Gilbert Dodds, Ashland	20:30.2
1941	Rhode Island	Fred Tootell	83	Penn St	110	Fred Wilt, Indiana	20:30.1
1942	Indiana	Earle Hayes	57			Oliver Hunter, Notre Dame	20:18.0
	Penn St	Charles Werner	57				
1943	No meet						
1944	Drake	Bill Easton	25	Notre Dame	64	Fred Feiler, Drake	21:04.2
1945	Drake	Bill Easton	50	Notre Dame	65	Fred Feiler, Drake	21:14.2
1946	Drake	Bill Easton	42	NYU	98	Quentin Brelsford, Ohio Wesleyan	20:22.9
1947	Penn St	Charles Werner	60	Syracuse	72	Jack Milne, N Carolina	20:41.1
1948	Michigan St	Karl Schlademan	41	Wisconsin	69	Robert Black, Rhode Island	19:52.3
1949	Michigan St	Karl Schlademan	59	Syracuse	81	Robert Black, Rhode Island	20:25.7
1950	Penn St	Charles Werner	53	Michigan St	55	Herb Semper Jr, Kansas	20:31.7
1951	Syracuse	Robert Grieve	80	Kansas	118	Herb Semper Jr, Kansas	20:09.5
1952	Michigan St	Karl Schlademan	65	Indiana	68	Charles Capozzoli, Georgetown	19:36.7
1953	Kansas	Bill Easton	70	Indiana	82	Wes Santee, Kansas	19:43.5
1954	Oklahoma St	Ralph Higgins	61	Syracuse	118	Allen Frame, Kansas	19:54.2
1955	Michigan St	Karl Schlademan	46	Kansas	68	Charles Jones, Iowa	19:57.4
1956	Michigan St	Karl Schlademan	28	Kansas	88	Walter McNew, Texas	19:55.7
1957	Notre Dame	Alex Wilson	121	Michigan St	127	Max Truex, Southern Cal	19:12.3
1958	Michigan St	Francis Dittrich	79	Western Michigan	104	Crawford Kennedy, Michigan State	20:07.1
1959	Michigan St	Francis Dittrich	44	Houston	120	Al Lawrence, Houston	20:35.7
1960	Houston	John Morriss	54	Michigan St	80	Al Lawrence, Houston	19:28.2
1961	Oregon St	Sam Bell	68	San Jose St	82	Dale Story, Oregon St	19:46.6
1962	San Jose St	Dean Miller	58	Villanova	69	Tom O'Hara, Loyola (IL)	19:20.3
1963	San Jose St	Dean Miller	53	Oregon	68	Victor Zwolak, Villanova	19:35.0
1964	W Michigan	George Dales	86	Oregon	116	Elmore Banton, Ohio	20:07.5
1965	W Michigan	George Dales	81	Northwestern	114	John Lawson, Kansas	29:24.0
1966	Villanova	James Elliott	79	Kansas St	155	Gerry Lindgren, Washington St	29:01.4
1967	Villanova	James Elliott	91	Air Force	96	Gerry Lindgren, Washington St	30:45.6
1968	Villanova	James Elliott	78	Stanford	100	Michael Ryan, Air Force	29:16.8
1969	UTEP	Wayne Vandenburg	74	Villanova	88	Gerry Lindgren, Wash St	28:59.2
1970	Villanova	James Elliott	85	Oregon	86	Steve Prefontaine, Oregon	28:00.2

Men (Cont.)

DIVISION I (Cont.)

Year	Champion	Coach	Pts	Runner-Up	Pts	Individual Champion	Time
1971	Oregon	Bill Dellinger	83	Washington St	122	Steve Prefontaine, Oregon	29:14.0
1972	Tennessee	Stan Huntsman	134	E Tennessee St	148	Neil Cusack, E Tenn St	28:23.0
1973	Oregon	Bill Dellinger	89	UTEP	157	Steve Prefontaine, Oregon	28:14.0
1974	Oregon	Bill Dellinger	77	Western Kentucky	110	Nick Rose, W Kentucky	29:22.0
1975	UTEP	Ted Banks	88	Washington St	92	Craig Virgin, Illinois	28:23.3
1976	UTEP	Ted Banks	62	Oregon	117	Henry Rono, Washington St	28:06.6
1977	Oregon	Bill Dellinger	100	UTEP	105	Henry Rono, Washington St	28:33.5
1978	UTEP	Ted Banks	56	Oregon	72	Alberto Salazar, Oregon	29:29.7
1979	UTEP	Ted Banks	86	Oregon	93	Henry Rono, Washington St	28:19.6
1980	UTEP	Ted Banks	58	Arkansas	152	Suleiman Nyambui, UTEP	29:04.0
1981	UTEP	Ted Banks	17	Providence	109	Mathews Motshwarateu,UTEP	28:45.6
1982	Wisconsin	Dan McClimon	59	Providence	138	Mark Scrutton, Colorado	30:12.6
1983	Vacated			Wisconsin	164	Zakarie Barie, UTEP	29:20.0
1984	Arkansas	John McDonnell	101	Arizona	111	Ed Eyestone, Brigham Young	29:28.8
1985	Wisconsin	Martin Smith	67	Arkansas	104	Timothy Hacker, Wisconsin	29:17.88
1986	Arkansas	John McDonnell	69	Dartmouth	141	Aaron Ramirez, Arizona	30:27.53
1987	Arkansas	John McDonnell	87	Dartmouth	119	Joe Falcon, Arkansas	29:14.97
1988	Wisconsin	Martin Smith	105	Northern Arizona	160	Robert Kennedy, Indiana	29:20.0
1989	Iowa St	Bill Bergan	54	Oregon	72	John Nuttall, Iowa St	29:30.55
1990	Arkansas	John McDonnell	68	Iowa St	96	Jonah Koech, Iowa St	29:05.0
1991	Arkansas	John McDonnell	52	Iowa St	114	Sean Dollman, Western Ky	30:17.1
1992	Arkansas	John McDonnell	46	Wisconsin	87	Bob Kennedy, Indiana	30:15.3
1993	Arkansas	John McDonnell	31	Brigham Young	153	Josephat Kapkory, Wash St	29:32.4
1994	Iowa St	Bill Bergan	65	Colorado	88	Martin Keino, Arizona	30:08.7
1995	Arkansas	John McDonnell	100	Northern Arizona	142	Godfrey Siamusiye, Arkansas	30:09
1996	Stanford	Vin Lananna	46	Arkansas	74	Godfrey Siamusiye, Arkansas	29:49
1997	Stanford	Vin Lananna	53	Arkansas	56	Mebrahtom Keflezighi, UCLA	28:54
1998	Arkansas	John McDonnell	97	Stanford	114	Adam Goucher, Colorado	29:26
1999	Arkansas	John McDonnell	58	Wisconsin	185	David Kimani, S Alabama	30:06.60

DIVISION II

Year	Champion	Year	Champion	Year	Champion
1958	Northern Illinois	1972	N Dakota St	1986	Edinboro
1959	S Dakota St	1973	S Dakota St	1987	Edinboro
1960	Central St (OH)	1974	SW Missouri St	1988	Edinboro/ Mankato St
1961	Southern Illinois	1975	UC-Irvine	1989	S Dakota St
1962	Central St (OH)	1976	UC-Irvine	1990	Edinboro
1963	Emporia St	1977	Eastern Illinois	1991	MA-Lowell
1964	Kentucky St	1978	Cal Poly-SLO	1992	Adams St
1965	San Diego St	1979	Cal Poly-SLO	1993	Adams St
1966	San Diego St	1980	Humboldt St	1994	Adams St
1967	San Diego St	1981	Millersville	1995	Western St
1968	Eastern Illinois	1982	Eastern Washington	1996	S Dakota St
1969	Eastern Illinois	1983	Cal Poly-Pomona	1997	S Dakota
1970	Eastern Michigan	1984	SE Missouri St	1998	Adams St
1971	Cal St-Fullerton	1985	S Dakota St	1999	Western St

DIVISION III

Year	Champion	Year	Champion	Year	Champion
1973	Ashland	1982	N Central	1991	Rochester
1974	Mount Union	1983	Brandeis	1992	N Central
1975	North Central	1984	St. Thomas (MN)	1993	N Central
1976	North Central	1985	Luther	1994	Williams
1977	Occidental	1986	St. Thomas (MN)	1995	Williams
1978	N Central	1987	N Central	1996	WI-La Crosse
1979	N Central	1988	WI-Oshkosh	1997	N Central
1980	Carleton	1989	WI-Oshkosh	1998	N Central
1981	N Central	1990	WI-Oshkosh	1999	N Central

Women

DIVISION I

Year	Champion	Coach	Pts	Runner-Up	Pts	Individual Champion	Time
1981	Virginia	John Vasvary	36	Oregon	83	Betty Springs, N Carolina St	16:19.0
1982	Virginia	Martin Smith	48	Stanford	91	Lesley Welch, Virginia	16:39.7
1983	Oregon	Tom Heinonen	95	Stanford	98	Betty Springs, N Carolina St	16:30.7
1984	Wisconsin	Peter Tegen	63	Stanford	89	Cathy Branta, Wisconsin	16:15.6

Women *(Cont.)*
DIVISION I *(Cont.)*

Year	Champion	Coach	Pts	Runner-Up	Pts	Individual Champion	Time
1985	Wisconsin	Peter Tegen	58	Iowa St	98	Suzie Tuffey, N Carolina St	16:22.5
1986	Texas	Terry Crawford	62	Wisconsin	64	Angela Chalmers, N Arizona	16:55.49
1987	Oregon	Tom Heinonen	97	N Carolina St	99	Kimberly Betz, Indiana	16:10.85
1988	Kentucky	Don Weber	75	Oregon	128	Michelle Dekkers, Indiana	16:30.0
1989	Villanova	Marty Stern	99	Kentucky	168	Vicki Huber, Villanova	15:59.86
1990	Villanova	Marty Stern	82	Providence	172	Sonia O'Sullivan, Villanova	16:06.0
1991	Villanova	Marty Stern	85	Arkansas	168	Sonia O'Sullivan, Villanova	16:30.3
1992	Villanova	Marty Stern	123	Arkansas	130	Carole Zajac, Villanova	17:01.9
1993	Villanova	Marty Stern	66	Arkansas	71	Carole Zajac, Villanova	16:40.3
1994	Villanova	John Marshall	75	Michigan	108	Jennifer Rhines, Villanova	16:31.2
1995	Providence	Ray Treacy	88	Colorado	123	Kathy Butler, Wisconsin	16:51
1996	Stanford	Beth Alford-Sullivan	101	Villanova	106	Amy Skieresz, Arizona	17:04
1997	BYU	Patrick Shane	100	Stanford	102	Carrie Tollefson, Villanova	16:58
1998	Villanova	Marcus O'Sullivan	106	BYU	110	Katie McGregor, Michigan	16:47.21
1999	BYU	Patrick Shane	72	Arkansas	125	Erica Palmer, Wisconsin	16:39.50

DIVISION II

Year	Champion	Year	Champion	Year	Champion
1981	S Dakota St	1988	Cal Poly-SLO	1995	Adams St
1982	Cal Poly-SLO	1989	Cal Poly-SLO	1996	Adams St
1983	Cal Poly-SLO	1990	Cal Poly-SLO	1997	Adams St
1984	Cal Poly-SLO	1991	Cal Poly-SLO	1998	Adams St
1985	Cal Poly-SLO	1992	Adams St	1999	Adams St
1986	Cal Poly-SLO	1993	Adams St		
1987	Cal Poly-SLO	1994	Adams St		

DIVISION III

Year	Champion	Year	Champion	Year	Champion
1981	Central (IA)	1988	WI-Oshkosh	1996	WI-Oshkosh
1982	St. Thomas (MN)	1989	Cortland St	1997	Cortland St
1983	WI-La Crosse	1990	Cortland St	1998	Calvin
1984	St. Thomas (MN)	1991	WI-Oshkosh	1999	Calvin
1985	Franklin & Marshall	1992	Cortland St		
1986	St. Thomas (MN)	1993	Cortland St		
1987	St. Thomas (MN)	1994	Cortland St		
	WI-Oshkosh	1995	Cortland St		

Fencing

Men's and Women's Combined
TEAM CHAMPIONS

Year	Champion	Coach	Pts	Runner-Up	Pts
1990	Penn St	Emmanuil Kaidanov	36	Columbia-Barnard	35
1991	Penn St	Emmanuil Kaidanov	4700	Columbia-Barnard	4200
1992	Columbia-Barnard	George Kolombatovich / Aladar Kogler	4150	Penn St	3646
1993	Columbia-Barnard	George Kolombatovich / Aladar Kogler	4525	Penn St	4500
1994	Notre Dame	Michael DeCicco	4350	Penn St	4075
1995	Penn St	Emmanuil Kaidanov	440	St. John's (NY)	413
1996	Penn St	Emmanuil Kaidanov	1500	Notre Dame	1190
1997	Penn St	Emmanuil Kaidanov	1530	Notre Dame	1470
1998	Penn St	Emmanuil Kaidanov	149	Notre Dame	147
1999	Penn St	Emmanuil Kaidanov	171	Notre Dame	139
2000	Penn St	Emmanuil Kaidanov	175	Notre Dame	171

Men
TEAM CHAMPIONS

Year	Champion	Coach	Pts	Runner-Up	Pts
1941	Northwestern	Henry Zettleman	28½	Illinois	27
1942	Ohio St	Frank Riebel	34	St. John's (NY)	33½
1943–46	No tournament				
1947	NYU	Martinez Castello	72	Chicago	50½
1948	CCNY	James Montague	30	Navy	28
1949	Army/ Rutgers	S. Velarde/D. Cetrulo	63		

Men (Cont.)

TEAM CHAMPIONS (Cont.)

Year	Champion	Coach	Pts	Runner-Up	Pts
1950	Navy	Joseph Fiems	67½	NYU/ Rutgers	66½
1951	Columbia	Servando Velarde	69	Pennsylvania	64
1952	Columbia	Servando Velarde	71	NYU	69
1953	Pennsylvania	Lajos Csiszar	94	Navy	86
1954	Columbia	Irving DeKoff	61		
	NYU	Hugo Castello	61		
1955	Columbia	Irving DeKoff	62	Cornell	57
1956	Illinois	Maxwell Garret	90	Columbia	88
1957	NYU	Hugo Castello	65	Columbia	64
1958	Illinois	Maxwell Garret	47	Columbia	43
1959	Navy	Andre Deladrier	72	NYU	65
1960	NYU	Hugo Castello	65	Navy	57
1961	NYU	Hugo Castello	79	Princeton	68
1962	Navy	Andre Deladrier	76	NYU	74
1963	Columbia	Irving DeKoff	55	Navy	50
1964	Princeton	Stan Sieja	81	NYU	79
1965	Columbia	Irving DeKoff	76	NYU	74
1966	NYU	Hugo Castello	5–0	Army	5–2
1967	NYU	Hugo Castello	72	Pennsylvania	64
1968	Columbia	Louis Bankuti	92	NYU	87
1969	Pennsylvania	Lajos Csiszar	54	Harvard	43
1970	NYU	Hugo Castello	71	Columbia	63
1971	NYU/ Columbia	Hugo Castello/ Louis Bankuti	68		
1972	Detroit	Richard Perry	73	NYU	70
1973	NYU	Hugo Castello	76	Pennsylvania	71
1974	NYU	Hugo Castello	92	Wayne St (MI)	87
1975	Wayne St (MI)	Istvan Danosi	89	Cornell	83
1976	NYU	Herbert Cohen	79	Wayne St (MI)	77
1977	Notre Dame	Michael DeCicco	114*	NYU	114
1978	Notre Dame	Michael DeCicco	121	Pennsylvania	110
1979	Wayne St (MI)	Istvan Danosi	119	Notre Dame	108
1980	Wayne St (MI)	Istvan Danosi	111	Pennsylvania/ MIT	106
1981	Pennsylvania	Dave Micahnik	113	Wayne St (MI)	111
1982	Wayne St (MI)	Istvan Danosi	85	Clemson	77
1983	Wayne St (MI)	Aladar Kogler	86	Notre Dame	80
1984	Wayne St (MI)	Gil Pezza	69	Penn St	50
1985	Wayne St (MI)	Gil Pezza	141	Notre Dame	140
1986	Notre Dame	Michael DeCicco	151	Columbia	141
1987	Columbia	George Kolombatovich	86	Pennsylvania	78
1988	Columbia	George Kolombatovich	90	Notre Dame	83
		Aladar Kogler			
1989	Columbia	George Kolombatovich	88	Penn St	85
		Aladar Kogler			

*Tie broken by a fence-off. Note: Beginning in 1990, men's and women's combined teams competed for the national championship.

INDIVIDUAL CHAMPIONS

Foil	Sabre	Épée
1941 ....Edward McNamara, Northwestern	William Meyer, Dartmouth	G.H. Boland, Illinois
1942 ....Byron Kreiger, Wayne St (MI)	Andre Deladrier, St. John's (NY)	Ben Burtt, Ohio St
1943–46 No tournament		
1947 ....Abraham Balk, NYU	Oscar Parsons, Temple	Abraham Balk, NYU
1948 ....Albert Axelrod, CCNY	James Day, Navy	William Bryan, Navy
1949 ....Ralph Tedeschi, Rutgers	Alex Treves, Rutgers	Richard C. Bowman, Army
1950 ....Robert Nielsen, Columbia	Alex Treves, Rutgers	Thomas Stuart, Navy
1951 ....Robert Nielsen, Columbia	Chamberless Johnston, Princeton	Daniel Chafetz, Columbia
1952 ....Harold Goldsmith, CCNY	Frank Zimolzak, Navy	James Wallner, NYU
1953 ....Ed Nober, Brooklyn	Robert Parmacek, Pennsylvania	Jack Tori, Pennsylvania
1954 ....Robert Goldman, Pennsylvania	Steve Sobel, Columbia	Henry Kolowrat, Princeton
1955 ....Herman Velasco, Illinois	Barry Pariser, Columbia	Donald Tadrawski, Notre Dame
1956 ....Ralph DeMarco, Columbia	Gerald Kaufman, Columbia	Kinmont Hoitsma, Princeton
1957 ....Bruce Davis, Wayne St (MI)	Bernie Balaban, NYU	James Margolis, Columbia
1958 ....Bruce Davis, Wayne St (MI)	Art Schankin, Illinois	Roland Wommack, Navy

Men (Cont.)

INDIVIDUAL CHAMPIONS (Cont.)

Foil	Sabre	Épée
1959....Joe Paletta, Navy	Al Morales, Navy	Roland Wommack, Navy
1960....Gene Glazer, NYU	Mike Desaro, NYU	Gil Eisner, NYU
1961....Herbert Cohen, NYU	Israel Colon, NYU	Jerry Halpern, NYU
1962....Herbert Cohen, NYU	Barton Nisonson, Columbia	Thane Hawkins, Navy
1963....Jay Lustig, Columbia	Bela Szentivanyi, Wayne St (MI)	Larry Crum, Navy
1964....Bill Hicks, Princeton	Craig Bell, Illinois	Paul Pesthy, Rutgers
1965....Joe Nalven, Columbia	Howard Goodman, NYU	Paul Pesthy, Rutgers
1966....Al Davis, NYU	Paul Apostol, NYU	Bernhardt Hermann, Iowa
1967....Mike Gaylor, NYU	Todd Makler, Pennsylvania	George Masin, NYU
1968....Gerard Esponda, San Francisco	Todd Makler, Pennsylvania	Don Sieja, Cornell
1969....Anthony Kestler, Columbia	Norman Braslow, Penn	James Wetzler, Pennsylvania
1970....Walter Krause, NYU	Bruce Soriano, Columbia	John Nadas, Case Reserve
1971....Tyrone Simmons, Detroit	Bruce Soriano, Columbia	George Szunyogh, NYU
1972....Tyrone Simmons, Detroit	Bruce Soriano, Columbia	Ernesto Fernandez, Penn
1973....Brooke Makler, Pennsylvania	Peter Westbrock, NYU	Risto Hurme, NYU
1974....Greg Benko, Wayne St (MI)	Steve Danosi, Wayne St (MI)	Risto Hurme, NYU
1975....Greg Benko, Wayne St (MI)	Yuri Rabinovich, Wayne St (MI)	Risto Hurme, NYU
1976....Greg Benko, Wayne St (MI)	Brian Smith, Columbia	Randy Eggleton, Pennsylvania
1977....Pat Gerard, Notre Dame	Mike Sullivan, Notre Dame	Hans Wieselgren, NYU
1978....Ernest Simon, Wayne St (MI)	Mike Sullivan, Notre Dame	Bjorne Vaggo, Notre Dame
1979....Andrew Bonk, Notre Dame	Yuri Rabinovich, Wayne St (MI)	Carlos Songini, Cleveland St
1980....Ernest Simon, Wayne St (MI)	Paul Friedberg, Pennsylvania	Gil Pezza, Wayne St (MI)
1981....Ernest Simon, Wayne St (MI)	Paul Friedberg, Pennsylvania	Gil Pezza, Wayne St (MI)
1982....Alexander Flom, George Mason	Neil Hick, Wayne St (MI)	Peter Schifrin, San Jose St
1983....Demetrios Valsamis, NYU	John Friedberg, N Carolina	Ola Harstrom, Notre Dame
1984....Charles Higgs-Coulthard, Notre Dame	Michael Lofton, NYU	Ettore Bianchi, Wayne St (MI)
1985....Stephan Chauvel, Wayne St (MI)	Michael Lofton, NYU	Ettore Bianchi, Wayne St (MI)
1986....Adam Feldman, Penn St	Michael Lofton, NYU	Chris O'Loughlin, Pennsylvania
1987....William Mindel, Columbia	Michael Lofton, NYU	James O'Neill, Harvard
1988....Marc Kent, Columbia	Robert Cottingham, Columbia	Jon Normile, Columbia
1989....Edward Mufel, Penn St	Peter Cox, Penn St	Jon Normile, Columbia
1990....Nick Bravin, Stanford	David Mandell, Columbia	Jubba Beshin, Notre Dame
1991....Ben Atkins, Columbia	Vitali Nazlimov, Penn St	Marc Oshima, Columbia
1992....Nick Bravin, Stanford	Tom Strzalkowski, Penn St	Harald Bauder, Wayne St
1993....Nick Bravin, Stanford	Tom Strzalkowski, Penn St	Ben Atkins, Columbia
1994....Kwame van Leeuwen, Harvard	Tom Strzalkowski, Penn St	Harald Winkman, Princeton
1995....Sean McClain, Stanford	Paul Palestis, NYU	Mike Gattner, Lawrence
1996....Thorstein Becker, Wayne St (MI)	Maxim Pekarev, Princeton	Jeremy Kahn, Duke
1997....Cliff Bayer, Pennsylvania	Keith Smart, St. John's (NY)	Alden Clarke, Stanford
1998....Ayo Griffin, Yale	Luke LaValle, Notre Dame	George Hentea, St. John's (NY)
1999....Felix Reichling, Stanford	Keeth Smart, St. John's (NY)	Alex Roytblat St. John's (NY)
2000....Felix Reichling, Stanford	Gabor Szelle, Notre Dame	Daniel Landgren, Penn St

Women

TEAM CHAMPIONS

Year	Champion	Coach	Rec	Runner-Up	Rec
1982	Wayne St (MI)	Istvan Danosi	7–0	San Jose St	6–1
1983	Penn St	Beth Alphin	5–0	Wayne St (MI)	3–2
1984	Yale	Henry Harutunian	3–0	Penn St	2–1
1985	Yale	Henry Harutunian	3–0	Pennsylvania	2–1
1986	Pennsylvania	David Micahnik	3–0	Notre Dame	2–1
1987	Notre Dame	Yves Auriol	3–0	Temple	2–1
1988	Wayne St (MI)	Gil Pezza	3–0	Notre Dame	2–1
1989	Wayne St (MI)	Gil Pezza	3–0	Columbia-Barnard	2–1

Note: Beginning in 1990, men's and women's combined teams competed for the national championship.

INDIVIDUAL CHAMPIONS

Foil	Foil (Cont.)	Sabre
1982....Joy Ellingson, San Jose St	1992....Olga Cheryak, Penn St	2000....Caroline Purcell, MIT
1983....Jana Angelakis, Penn St	1993....Olga Kalinovskaya, Penn St	
1984....Mary Jane O'Neill, Penn	1994....Olga Kalinovskaya, Penn St	Épée
1985....C. Bilodeaux, Columbia-Barn.	1995....Olga Kalinovskaya, Penn St	1995....Tina Loven, St. John's (NY)
1986....M. Sullivan, Notre Dame	1996....Olga Kalinovskaya, Penn St	1996....N. Dygert, St. John's (NY)
1987....C. Bilodeaux, Columbia-Barn.	1997....Yelena Kalkina, Ohio St	1997....Magda Krol, Notre Dame
1988....M. Sullivan, Notre Dame	1998....F. Zimmermann, Stanford	1998....Charlotte Walker, Penn St
1989....Yasemin Topcu, Wayne St	1999....Monique DeBruin, Stanford	1999....F. Zimmermann, Stanford
1990....Tzu Moy, Columbia-Barn.	2000....Eva Petschnigg, Princeton	2000....Jessica Burke, Penn St
1991....Heidi Piper, Notre Dame		

Field Hockey

DIVISION I

Year	Champion	Coach	Score	Runner-Up
1981	Connecticut	Diane Wright	4–1	Massachusetts
1982	Old Dominion	Beth Anders	3–2	Connecticut
1983	Old Dominion	Beth Anders	3–1 (3 OT)	Connecticut
1984	Old Dominion	Beth Anders	5–1	Iowa
1985	Connecticut	Diane Wright	3–2	Old Dominion
1986	Iowa	Judith Davidson	2–1 (2 OT)	New Hampshire
1987	Maryland	Sue Tyler	2–1 (OT)	N Carolina
1988	Old Dominion	Beth Anders	2–1	Iowa
1989	N Carolina	Karen Shelton	2–1 (3 OT)*	Old Dominion
1990	Old Dominion	Beth Anders	5–0	N Carolina
1991	Old Dominion	Beth Anders	2–0	N Carolina
1992	Old Dominion	Beth Anders	4–0	Iowa
1993	Maryland	Missy Meharg	2–1 (3 OT)*	N Carolina
1994	James Madison	Christy Morgan	2–1 (3 OT)*	N Carolina
1995	N Carolina	Karen Shelton-Scroggs	5–1	Maryland
1996	N Carolina	Karen Shelton-Scroggs	3–0	Princeton
1997	N Carolina	Karen Shelton	3–2	Old Dominion
1998	Old Dominion	Beth Anders	3–2	Princeton
1999	Maryland	Missy Meharg	2–1	Michigan

*Penalty strokes.

DIVISION II (DISCONTINUED, THEN RENEWED)

Year	Champion	Coach	Score	Runner-Up
1981	Pfeiffer	Ellen Briggs	5–3	Bentley
1982	Lock Haven	Sharon E. Taylor	4–1	Bloomsburg
1983	Bloomsburg	Jan Hutchinson	1–0	Lock Haven
1992	Lock Haven	Sharon E. Taylor	3–1	Bloomsburg
1993	Bloomsburg	Jan Hutchinson	2–1 (2 OT)	Lock Haven
1994	Lock Haven	Sharon E. Taylor	2–1	Bloomsburg
1995	Lock Haven	Sharon E. Taylor	1–0	Bloomsburg
1996	Bloomsburg	Jan Hutchinson	1–0	Lock Haven
1997	Bloomsburg	Jan Hutchinson	2–0	Kutztown
1998	Bloomsburg	Jan Hutchinson	4–3 (OT)	Lock Haven
1999	Bloomsburg	Jan Hutchinson	2–0	Bentley

DIVISION III

Year	Champion	Year	Champion	Year	Champion
1981	Trenton St	1988	Trenton St	1995	Trenton St
1982	Ithaca	1989	Lock Haven	1996	College of New Jersey*
1983	Trenton St	1990	Trenton St	1997	William Smith
1984	Bloomsburg	1991	Trenton St	1998	Middlebury
1985	Trenton St	1992	William Smith	1999	College of New Jersey*
1986	Salisbury St	1993	Cortland St		*Formerly Trenton St.
1987	Bloomsburg	1994	Cortland St		

Golf

Men

DIVISION I

Results, 1897–1938

Year	Champion	Site	Individual Champion
1897	Yale	Ardsley Casino	Louis Bayard Jr, Princeton
1898	Harvard (spring)		John Reid Jr, Yale
1898	Yale (fall)		James Curtis, Harvard
1899	Harvard		Percy Pyne, Princeton
1900	No tournament		
1901	Harvard	Atlantic City	H. Lindsley, Harvard
1902	Yale (spring)	Garden City	Charles Hitchcock Jr, Yale
1902	Harvard (fall)	Morris County	Chandler Egan, Harvard
1903	Harvard	Garden City	F.O. Reinhart, Princeton
1904	Harvard	Myopia	A.L. White, Harvard
1905	Yale	Garden City	Robert Abbott, Yale
1906	Yale	Garden City	W.E. Clow Jr, Yale
1907	Yale	Nassau	Ellis Knowles, Yale
1908	Yale	Brae Burn	H.H. Wilder, Harvard
1909	Yale	Apawamis	Albert Seckel, Princeton
1910	Yale	Essex County	Robert Hunter, Yale

Men (Cont.)

DIVISION I (Cont.)

Results, 1897–1938 (Cont.)

Year	Champion	Site	Individual Champion
1911	Yale	Baltusrol	George Stanley, Yale
1912	Yale	Ekwanok	F.C. Davison, Harvard
1913	Yale	Huntingdon Valley	Nathaniel Wheeler, Yale
1914	Princeton	Garden City	Edward Allis, Harvard
1915	Yale	Greenwich	Francis Blossom, Yale
1916	Princeton	Oakmont	J.W. Hubbell, Harvard
1917–18	No tournament		
1919	Princeton	Merion	A.L. Walker Jr, Columbia
1920	Princeton	Nassau	Jess Sweetster, Yale
1921	Dartmouth	Greenwich	Simpson Dean, Princeton
1922	Princeton	Garden City	Pollack Boyd, Dartmouth
1923	Princeton	Siwanoy	Dexter Cummings, Yale
1924	Yale	Greenwich	Dexter Cummings, Yale
1925	Yale	Montclair	Fred Lamprecht, Tulane
1926	Yale	Merion	Fred Lamprecht, Tulane
1927	Princeton	Garden City	Watts Gunn, Georgia Tech
1928	Princeton	Apawamis	Maurice McCarthy, Georgetown
1929	Princeton	Hollywood	Tom Aycock, Yale
1930	Princeton	Oakmont	G.T. Dunlap Jr, Princeton
1931	Yale	Olympia Fields	G.T. Dunlap Jr, Princeton
1932	Yale	Hot Springs	J.W. Fischer, Michigan
1933	Yale	Buffalo	Walter Emery, Oklahoma
1934	Michigan	Cleveland	Charles Yates, Georgia Tech
1935	Michigan	Congressional	Ed White, Texas
1936	Yale	North Shore	Charles Kocsis, Michigan
1937	Princeton	Oakmont	Fred Haas Jr, Louisiana St
1938	Stanford	Louisville	John Burke, Georgetown

Results, 1939–1999

Year	Champion	Coach	Score	Runner-Up	Score	Host or Site	Individual Champion
1939	Stanford	Eddie Twiggs	612	Northwestern	614	Wakonda	Vincent D'Antoni, Tulane
				Princeton	614		
1940	Princeton	Walter Bourne	601			Ekwanok	Dixon Brooke, Virginia
	Louisiana St	Mike Donahue	601				
1941	Stanford	Eddie Twiggs	580	Louisiana St	599	Ohio St	Earl Stewart, Louisiana St
1942	Louisiana St	Mike Donahue	590			Notre Dame	Frank Tatum Jr, Stanford
	Stanford	Eddie Twiggs	590				
1943	Yale	William Neale Jr	614	Michigan	618	Olympia Fields	Wallace Ulrich, Carleton
1944	Notre Dame	George Holderith	311	Minnesota	312	Inverness	Louis Lick, Minnesota
1945	Ohio St	Robert Kepler	602	Northwestern	621	Ohio St	John Lorms, Ohio St
1946	Stanford	Eddie Twiggs	619	Michigan	624	Princeton	George Hamer, Georgia
1947	Louisiana St	T. P. Heard	606	Duke	614	Michigan	Dave Barclay, Michigan
1948	San Jose St	Wilbur Hubbard	579	Louisiana St	588	Stanford	Bob Harris, San Jose St
1949	N Texas	Fred Cobb	590	Purdue	600	Iowa St	Harvie Ward, N Carolina
				Texas	600		
1950	N Texas	Fred Cobb	573	Purdue	577	New Mexico	Fred Wampler, Purdue
1951	N Texas	Fred Cobb	588	Ohio St	589	Ohio St	Tom Nieporte, Ohio St
1952	N Texas	Fred Cobb	587	Michigan	593	Purdue	Jim Vickers, Oklahoma
1953	Stanford	Charles Finger	578	N Carolina	580	Broadmoor	Earl Moeller, Oklahoma St
1954	SMU	Graham Ross	572	N Texas	573	Houston, Rice	Hillman Robbins, Memphis St

Men (Cont.)

DIVISION I (Cont.)

Results, 1939–1999 (Cont.)

Year	Champion	Coach	Score	Runner-Up	Score	Host or Site	Individual Champion
1955	Louisiana St	Mike Barbato	574	N Texas	583	Tennessee	Joe Campbell, Purdue
1956	Houston	Dave Williams	601	N Texas	602	Ohio St	Rick Jones, Ohio St
				Purdue	602		
1957	Houston	Dave Williams	602	Stanford	603	Broadmoor	Rex Baxter Jr, Houston
1958	Houston	Dave Williams	570	Oklahoma St	582	Williams	Phil Rodgers, Houston
1959	Houston	Dave Williams	561	Purdue	571	Oregon	Dick Crawford, Houston
1960	Houston	Dave Williams	603	Purdue	607	Broadmoor	Dick Crawford, Houston
				Oklahoma St	607		
1961	Purdue	Sam Voinoff	584	Arizona St	595	Lafayette	Jack Nicklaus, Ohio St
1962	Houston	Dave Williams	588	Oklahoma St	598	Duke	Kermit Zarley, Houston
1963	Oklahoma St	Labron Harris	581	Houston	582	Wichita St	R. H. Sikes, Ark
1964	Houston	Dave Williams	580	Oklahoma St	587	Broadmoor	Terry Small, San Jose St
1965	Houston	Dave Williams	577	Cal St-LA	587	Tennessee	Marty Fleckman, Houston
1966	Houston	Dave Williams	582	San Jose St	586	Stanford	Bob Murphy, Florida
1967	Houston	Dave Williams	585	Florida	588	Shawnee, PA	Hale Irwin, Colorado
1968	Florida	Buster Bishop	1154	Houston	1156	New Mexico St	Grier Jones, Oklahoma St
1969	Houston	Dave Williams	1223	Wake Forest	1232	Broadmoor	Bob Clark, Cal St-LA
1970	Houston	Dave Williams	1172	Wake Forest	1182	Ohio St	John Mahaffey, Houston
1971	Texas	George Hannon	1144	Houston	1151	Arizona	Ben Crenshaw, Texas
1972	Texas	George Hannon	1146	Houston	1159	Cape Coral	Ben Crenshaw, Texas
							Tom Kite, Texas
1973	Florida	Buster Bishop	1149	Oklahoma St	1159	Oklahoma St	Ben Crenshaw, Texas
1974	Wake Forest	Jess Haddock	1158	Florida	1160	San Diego St	Curtis Strange, Wake Forest
1975	Wake Forest	Jess Haddock	1156	Oklahoma St	1189	Ohio St	Jay Haas, Wake Forest
1976	Oklahoma St	Mike Holder	1166	Brigham Young	1173	New Mexico	Scott Simpson, Southern Cal
1977	Houston	Dave Williams	1197	Oklahoma St	1205	Colgate	Scott Simpson, Southern Cal
1978	Oklahoma St	Mike Holder	1140	Georgia	1157	Oregon	David Edwards, Oklahoma St
1979	Ohio St	James Brown	1189	Oklahoma St	1191	Wake Forest	Gary Hallberg, Wake Forest
1980	Oklahoma St	Mike Holder	1173	Brigham Young	1177	Ohio St	Jay Don Blake, Utah St
1981	Brigham Young	Karl Tucker	1161	Oral Roberts	1163	Stanford	Ron Commans, Southern Cal
1982	Houston	Dave Williams	1141	Oklahoma St	1151	Pinehurst	Billy Ray Brown, Houston
1983	Oklahoma St	Mike Holder	1161	Texas	1168	Fresno St	Jim Carter, Arizona St
1984	Houston	Dave Williams	1145	Oklahoma St	1146	Houston	John Inman, N Carolina
1985	Houston	Dave Williams	1172	Oklahoma St	1175	Florida	Clark Burroughs, Ohio St
1986	Wake Forest	Jess Haddock	1156	Oklahoma St	1160	Wake Forest	Scott Verplank, Oklahoma St
1987	Oklahoma St	Mike Holder	1160	Wake Forest	1176	Ohio St	Brian Watts, Oklahoma St

Men (Cont.)

DIVISION I (Cont.)

Results, 1939–1999 (Cont.)

Year	Champion	Coach	Score	Runner-Up	Score	Host or Site	Individual Champion
1988	....UCLA	Eddie Merrins	1176	UTEP	1179	Southern Cal	E.J. Pfister,
				Oklahoma	1179		Oklahoma St
				Oklahoma St	1179		
1989	....Oklahoma	Gregg Grost	1139	Texas	1158	Oklahoma	Phil Mickelson,
						Oklahoma St	Arizona St
1990	....Arizona St	Steve Loy	1155	Florida	1157	Florida	Phil Mickelson,
							Arizona St
1991	....Oklahoma St	Mike Holder	1161	N Carolina	1168	San Jose St	Warren Schutte,
							UNLV
1992	....Arizona	Rick LaRose	1129	Arizona St	1136	New Mexico	Phil Mickelson,
							Arizona St
1993	....Florida	Buddy Alexander	1145	Georgia Tech	1146	Kentucky	Todd Demsey,
							Arizona St
1994	....Stanford	Wally Goodwin	1129	Texas	1133	McKinney, TX	Justin Leonard,
							Texas
1995	....Oklahoma St*	Mike Holder	1156	Stanford	1156	Ohio St	Chip Spratlin,
							Auburn
1996	....Arizona St	Randy Lein	1186	UNLV	1189	TN-Chattanooga	Tiger Woods,
							Stanford
1997	....Pepperdine	John Geiberger	1148	Wake Forest	1151	Evanston, Ill.	Charles Warren,
							Clemson
1998	....UNLV	Dwaine Knight	1118	Clemson	1121	Albuquerque	James McLean,
							Minnesota
1999	....Georgia	Chris Haack	1180	Oklahoma St	1183	Chaska, MN	Donald Luke,
							Northwestern
2000	....Oklahoma St*	Mike Holder	1116	Georgia Tech	1116	Opelika, AL	Charles Howell,
							Oklahoma St

*Won sudden death playoff. Notes: Match play, 1897–1964; par-70 tournaments held in 1969, 1973 and 1989; par-71 tournaments held in 1968, 1981 and 1988; all other championships par-72 tournaments. Scores are based on 4 rounds instead of 2 after 1967.

DIVISION II

Year	Champion	Year	Champion	Year	Champion
1963	........SW Missouri St	1976	........Troy St	1989	........Columbus St
1964	........Southern Illinois	1977	........Troy St	1990	........Florida Southern
1965	........Middle Tennessee St	1978	........Columbus St	1991	........Florida Southern
1966	........Cal St-Chico	1979	........UC-Davis	1992	........Columbus St
1967	........Lamar	1980	........Columbus St	1993	........Abilene Christian
1968	........Lamar	1981	........Florida Southern	1994	........Columbus St
1969	........Cal St-Northridge	1982	........Florida Southern	1995	........Florida Southern
1970	........Rollins	1983	........SW Texas St	1996	........Florida Southern
1971	........New Orleans	1984	........Troy St	1997	........Columbus St
1972	........New Orleans	1985	........Florida Southern	1998	........Florida Southern
1973	........Cal St-Northridge	1986	........Florida Southern	1999	........Florida Southern
1974	........Cal St-Northridge	1987	........Tampa	2000	........Florida Southern
1975	........UC-Irvine	1988	........Tampa		

Note: Par-71 tournaments held in 1967, 1970, 1976-78, 1985 and 1988; par-70 tournament held in 1996; and all other championships par-72 tournaments.

DIVISION III

Year	Champion	Year	Champion	Year	Champion
1975	........Wooster	1984	........Cal St-Stanislaus	1993	........UC-San Diego
1976	........Cal St-Stanislaus	1985	........Cal St-Stanislaus	1994	........Methodist (NC)
1977	........Cal St-Stanislaus	1986	........Cal St-Stanislaus	1995	........Methodist (NC)
1978	........Cal St-Stanislaus	1987	........Cal St-Stanislaus	1996	........Methodist (NC)
1979	........Cal St-Stanislaus	1988	........Cal St-Stanislaus	1997	........Methodist (NC)
1980	........Cal St-Stanislaus	1989	........Cal St-Stanislaus	1998	........Methodist (NC)
1981	........Cal St-Stanislaus	1990	........Methodist (NC)	1999	........Methodist (NC)
1982	........Rampano	1991	........Methodist (NC)	2000	........Greensboro
1983	........Allegheny	1992	........Methodist (NC)		

Note: All championships par-72 except for 1986 and 1988, which were par-71; fourth round of 1975 championships canceled as a result of bad weather, first round of 1988 championships canceled as a result of rain.

Golf (Cont.)

Women
DIVISION I

Year	Champion	Coach	Score	Runner-Up	Score	Individual Champion
1982	Tulsa	Dale McNamara	1191	Texas Christian	1227	Kathy Baker, Tulsa
1983	Texas Christian	Fred Warren	1193	Tulsa	1196	Penny Hammel, Miami (FL)
1984	Miami (FL)	Lela Cannon	1214	Arizona St	1221	Cindy Schreyer, Georgia
1985	Florida	Mimi Ryan	1218	Tulsa	1233	Danielle Ammaccapane, Arizona St
1986	Florida	Mimi Ryan	1180	Miami (FL)	1188	Page Dunlap, Florida
1987	San Jose St	Mark Gale	1187	Furman	1188	Caroline Keggi, New Mexico
1988	Tulsa	Dale McNamara	1175	Georgia	1182	Melissa McNamara, Tulsa
				Arizona	1182	
1989	San Jose St	Mark Gale	1208	Tulsa	1209	Pat Hurst, San Jose St
1990	Arizona St	Linda Vollstedt	1206	UCLA	1222	Susan Slaughter, Arizona
1991	UCLA*	Jackie Steinmann	1197	San Jose St	1197	Annika Sorenstam, Arizona
1992	San Jose St	Mark Gale	1171	Arizona	1175	Vicki Goetze, Georgia
1993	Arizona St	Linda Vollstedt	1187	Texas	1189	Charlotta Sorenstam, Texas
1994	Arizona St	Linda Vollstedt	1189	Southern Cal	1205	Emilee Klein, Arizona St
1995	Arizona St	Linda Vollstedt	1155	San Jose St	1181	Kristel Mourgue d'Algue, Arizona St
1996	Arizona*	Rick LaRose	1240	San Jose St	1240	Marisa Baena, Arizona
1997	Arizona St	Linda Vollstedt	1178	San Jose St	1180	Heather Bowie, Texas
1998	Arizona St	Linda Vollstedt	1155	Florida	1173	Jennifer Rosales, USC
1999	Duke	Dan Brooks	895	Arizona St/Georgia	903	Grace Park, Arizona St
2000	Arizona	Todd McCorkle	1175	Stanford	1196	Jenna Daniels, Arizona

*Won sudden death playoff. Note: Par-74 tournaments held in 1983 and 1988; par-72 tournament held in 1990 and 2000; all other championships par-73 tournaments.

DIVISIONS II AND III

Year	Champion	Year	Champion
1996	Methodist (NC)	1998	Methodist (NC)
1997	Lynn	1999	Methodist (NC)

DIVISIONS II

Year	Champion
2000	Florida Southern

DIVISION III

Year	Champion
2000	Methodist (NC)

Gymnastics

Men
TEAM CHAMPIONS

Year	Champion	Coach	Pts	Runner-Up	Pts
1938	Chicago	Dan Hoffer	22	Illinois	18
1939	Illinois	Hartley Price	21	Army	17
1940	Illinois	Hartley Price	20	Navy	17
1941	Illinois	Hartley Price	68.5	Minnesota	52.5
1942	Illinois	Hartley Price	39	Penn St	30
1943–47	No tournament				
1948	Penn St	Gene Wettstone	55	Temple	34.5
1949	Temple	Max Younger	28	Minnesota	18
1950	Illinois	Charley Pond	26	Temple	25
1951	Florida St	Hartley Price	26	Illinois	23.5
				Southern Cal	23.5
1952	Florida St	Hartley Price	89.5	Southern Cal	75
1953	Penn St	Gene Wettstone	91.5	Illinois	68
1954	Penn St	Gene Wettstone	137	Illinois	68
1955	Illinois	Charley Pond	82	Penn St	69
1956	Illinois	Charley Pond	123.5	Penn St	67.5
1957	Penn St	Gene Wettstone	88.5	Illinois	80
1958	Michigan St	George Szypula	79		
	Illinois	Charley Pond	79		
1959	Penn St	Gene Wettstone	152	Illinois	87.5
1960	Penn St	Gene Wettstone	112.5	Southern Cal	65.5
1961	Penn St	Gene Wettstone	88.5	Southern Illinois	80.5
1962	Southern Cal	Jack Beckner	95.5	Southern Illinois	75
1963	Michigan	Newton Loken	129	Southern Illinois	73

Men (Cont.)
TEAM CHAMPIONS (Cont.)

Year	Champion	Coach	Pts	Runner-Up	Pts
1964	Southern Illinois	Bill Meade	84.5	Southern Cal	69.5
1965	Penn St	Gene Wettstone	68.5	Washington	51.5
1966	Southern Illinois	Bill Meade	187.200	California	185.100
1967	Southern Illinois	Bill Meade	189.550	Michigan	187.400
1968	California	Hal Frey	188.250	Southern Illinois	188.150
1969	Iowa	Mike Jacobson	161.175	Penn St	160.450
	Michigan*	Newton Loken		Colorado St	
1970	Michigan	Newton Loken	164.150	Iowa St	164.050
				New Mexico St	
1971	Iowa St	Ed Gagnier	319.075	Southern Illinois	316.650
1972	Southern Illinois	Bill Meade	315.925	Iowa St	312.325
1973	Iowa St	Ed Gagnier	325.150	Penn St	323.025
1974	Iowa St	Ed Gagnier	326.100	Arizona St	322.050
1975	California	Hal Frey	437.325	Louisiana St	433.700
1976	Penn St	Gene Wettstone	432.075	Louisiana St	425.125
1977	Indiana St	Roger Counsil	434.475		
	Oklahoma	Paul Ziert	434.475		
1978	Oklahoma	Paul Ziert	439.350	Arizona St	437.075
1979	Nebraska	Francis Allen	448.275	Oklahoma	446.625
1980	Nebraska	Francis Allen	563.300	Iowa St	557.650
1981	Nebraska	Francis Allen	284.600	Oklahoma	281.950
1982	Nebraska	Francis Allen	285.500	UCLA	281.050
1983	Nebraska	Francis Allen	287.800	UCLA	283.900
1984	UCLA	Art Shurlock	287.300	Penn St	281.250
1985	Ohio St	Michael Willson	285.350	Nebraska	284.550
1986	Arizona St	Don Robinson	283.900	Nebraska	283.600
1987	UCLA	Art Shurlock	285.300	Nebraska	284.750
1988	Nebraska	Francis Allen	288.150	Illinois	287.150
1989	Illinois	Yoshi Hayasaki	283.400	Nebraska	282.300
1990	Nebraska	Francis Allen	287.400	Minnesota	287.300
1991	Oklahoma	Greg Buwick	288.025	Penn St	285.500
1992	Stanford	Sadao Hamada	289.575	Nebraska	288.950
1993	Stanford	Sadao Hamada	276.500	Nebraska	275.500
1994	Nebraska	Francis Allen	288.250	Stanford	285.925
1995	Stanford	Sadao Hamada	232.400	Nebraska	231.525
1996	Ohio St	Peter Kormann	232.150	California	231.775
1997	California	Barry Weiner	233.825	Oklahoma	232.725
1998	Caliornia	Barry Weiner	231.200	Iowa	229.675
1999	Michigan	Kurt Golder	232.550	Ohio St	230.850
2000	Penn St	Randy Jepson	231.975	Michigan	231.850

*Trampoline.

ALL-AROUND

1938.....Joe Giallombardo, Illinois
1939.....Joe Giallombardo, Illinois
1940.....Joe Giallombardo, Illinois
Paul Fina, Illinois
1941.....Courtney Shanken, Chicago
1942.....Newt Loken, Minnesota
1948.....Ray Sorenson, Penn St
1949.....Joe Kotys, Kent
1950.....Joe Kotys, Kent
1951.....Bill Roetzheim, Florida St
1952.....Jack Beckner, Southern Cal
1953.....Jean Cronstedt, Penn St
1954.....Jean Cronstedt, Penn St
1955.....Karl Schwenzfeier, Penn St
1956.....Don Tonry, Illinois
1957.....Armando Vega, Penn St
1958.....Abie Grossfeld, Illinois
1959.....Armando Vega, Penn St
1960.....Jay Werner, Penn St
1961.....Gregor Weiss, Penn St
1962.....Robert Lynn, Southern Cal

INDIVIDUAL CHAMPIONS

1963.....Gil Larose, Michigan
1964.....Ron Barak, Southern Cal
1965.....Mike Jacobson, Penn St
1966.....Steve Cohen, Penn St
1967.....Steve Cohen, Penn St
1968.....Makoto Sakamoto, USC
1969.....Mauno Nissinen, Wash
1970.....Yoshi Hayasaki, Wash
1971.....Yoshi Hayasaki, Wash
1972.....Steve Hug, Stanford
1973.....Steve Hug, Stanford
Marshall Avener, Penn St
1974.....Steve Hug, Stanford
1975.....Wayne Young, BYU
1976.....Peter Kormann, Southern
Conn St
1977.....Kurt Thomas, Indiana St
1978.....Bart Conner, Oklahoma
1979.....Kurt Thomas, Indiana St
1980.....Jim Hartung, Nebraska
1981.....Jim Hartung, Nebraska
1982.....Peter Vidmar, UCLA

1983.....Peter Vidmar, UCLA
1984.....Mitch Gaylord, UCLA
1985.....Wes Suter, Nebraska
1986.....Jon Louis, Stanford
1987.....Tom Schlesinger, Nebraska
1988.....Vacated†
1989.....Patrick Kirsey, Nebraska
1990.....Mike Racanelli, Ohio St
1991.....John Roethlisberger, Minn
1992.....John Roethlisberger, Minn
1993.....John Roethlisberger, Minn
1994.....Dennis Harrison, Nebraska
1995.....Richard Grace, Nebraska
1996.....Blaine Wilson, Ohio St
1997.....Blaine Wilson, Ohio St
1998.....Travis Romagnoli, Illinois
1999.....Justin Hardabura, Nebraska
2000.....Jamie Natalie, Ohio St

Men (Cont.)
INDIVIDUAL CHAMPIONS (Cont.)

HORIZONTAL BAR

1938.....Bob Sears, Army
1939.....Adam Walters, Temple
1940.....Norm Boardman, Temple
1941.....Newt Loken, Minnesota
1942.....Norm Boardman, Temple
1948.....Joe Calvetti, Illinois
1949.....Bob Stout, Temple
1950.....Joe Kotys, Kent
1951.....Bill Roetzheim, Florida St
1952.....Charles Simms, USC
1953.....Hal Lewis, Navy
1954.....Jean Cronstedt, Penn St
1955.....Carlton Rintz, Michigan St
1956.....Ronnie Amster, Florida St
1957.....Abie Grossfeld, Illinois
1958.....Abie Grossfeld, Illinois
1959.....Stanley Tarshis, Mich St
1960.....Stanley Tarshis, Mich St
1961.....Bruno Klaus, Southern Ill
1962.....Robert Lynn, USC
1963.....Gil Larose, Michigan
1964.....Ron Barak, USC
1965.....Jim Curzi, Michigan St
          Mike Jacobsen, Penn St
1966.....Rusty Rock, Cal St-
          Northridge
1967.....Rich Grigsby, Cal St-
          Northridge
1968.....Makoto Sakamoto, USC
1969.....Bob Manna, New Mexico
1970.....Yoshi Hayasaki, Wash
1971.....Brent Simmons, Iowa St
1972.....Tom Lindner, Souhern Ill
1973.....Jon Aitken, New Mexico
1974.....Rick Banley, Indiana St
1975.....Rich Larsen, Iowa St
1976.....Tom Beach, California
1977.....John Hart, UCLA
1978.....Mel Cooley, Washington
1979.....Kurt Thomas, Indiana St
1980.....Philip Cahoy, Nebraska
1981.....Philip Cahoy, Nebraska
1982.....Peter Vidmar, UCLA
1983.....Scott Johnson, Nebraska
1984.....Charles Lakes, Illinois
1985.....Dan Hayden, Arizona St
          Wes Suter, Nebraska
1986.....Dan Hayden, Arizona St
1987.....David Moriel, UCLA
1988.....Vacated†
1989.....Vacated†
1990.....Chris Waller, UCLA
1991.....Luis Lopez, New Mexico
1992.....Jair Lynch, Stanford
1993.....Steve McCain, UCLA
1994.....Jim Foody, UCLA
1995.....Rick Kieffer, Nebraska
1996.....Carl Imhauser, Temple
1997.....Marshall Nelson,Nebraska
1998.....Todd Bishop, Oklahoma
1999.....Todd Bishop, Oklahoma
2000.....Michael Ashe, California

PARALLEL BARS

1938.....Erwin Beyer, Chicago
1939.....Bob Sears, Army
1940.....Bob Hanning, Minnesota
1941.....Caton Cobb, Illinois
1942.....Hal Zimmerman, Penn St
1948.....Ray Sorenson, Penn St
1949.....Joe Kotys, Kent
          Mel Stout, Michigan St
1950.....Joe Kotys, Kent
1951.....Jack Beckner, USC
1952.....Jack Beckner, USC
1953.....Jean Cronstedt, Penn St
1954.....Jean Cronstedt, Penn St
1955.....Carlton Rintz, Michigan St
1956.....Armando Vega, Penn St
1957.....Armando Vega, Penn St
1958.....Tad Muzyczko, Mich St
1959.....Armando Vega, Penn St
1960.....Robert Lynn, Southern Cal
1961.....Fred Tijerina, Southern Ill
          Jeff Cardinalli, Springfield
1962.....Robert Lynn, Southern Cal
1963.....Arno Lascari, Michigan
1964.....Ron Barak, Southern Cal
1965.....Jim Curzi, Michigan St
1966.....Jim Curzi, Michigan St
1967.....Makoto Sakamoto, USC
1968.....Makoto Sakamoto, USC
1969.....Ron Rapper, Michigan
1970.....Ron Rapper, Michigan
1971.....Brent Simmons, Iowa St
          Tom Dunn, Penn St
1972.....Dennis Mazur, Iowa St
1973.....Steve Hug, Stanford
1974.....Steve Hug, Stanford
1975.....Yoichi Tomita, Long
          Beach St
1976.....Gene Whelan, Penn St
1977.....Kurt Thomas, Indiana St
1978.....John Corritore, Michigan
1979.....Kurt Thomas, Indiana St
1980.....Philip Cahoy, Nebraska
1981.....Philip Cahoy, Nebraska
          Peter Vidmar, UCLA
          Jim Hartung, Nebraska
1982.....Jim Hartung, Nebraska
1983.....Scott Johnson, Nebraska
1984.....Tim Daggett, UCLA
1985.....Dan Hayden, Arizona St
          Noah Riskin, Ohio St
          Seth Riskin, Ohio St
1986.....Dan Hayden, Arizona St
1987.....Kevin Davis, Nebraska
          Tom Schlesinger, Nebraska
1988.....Kevin Davis, Nebraska
1989.....Vacated†
1990.....Patrick Kirksey, Nebraska
1991.....Scott Keswick, UCLA
          John Roethlisberger, Minn
1992.....Dom Minicucci, Temple
1993.....Jair Lynch, Stanford
1994.....Richard Grace, Nebraska
1995.....Richard Grace, Nebraska
1996.....Jamie Ellis, Stanford
          Blaine Wilson, Ohio St
1997.....Marshall Nelson, Nebraska

1998.....Marshall Nelson, Nebraska
1999.....Justin Toman, Michigan
2000.....Kris Zimmerman, Michigan
          Justin Toman, Michigan

VAULT

1938.....Erwin Beyer, Chicago
1939.....Marv Forman, Illinois
1940.....Earl Shanken, Chicago
1941.....Earl Shanken, Chicago
1942.....Earl Shanken, Chicago
1948.....Jim Peterson, Minnesota
1962.....Bruno Klaus, Southern Ill
1963.....Gil Larose, Michigan
1964.....Sidney Oglesby, Syracuse
1965.....Dan Millman, California
1966.....Frank Schmitz, S Illinois
1967.....Paul Mayer, S Illinois
1968.....Bruce Colter, Cal St-Los
          Angeles
1969.....Dan Bowles, California
          Jack McCarthy, Illinois
1970.....Doug Boger, Arizona
1971.....Pat Mahoney, Cal St-
          Northridge
1972.....Gary Morava, Southern Ill
1973.....John Crosby, S Conn St
1974.....Greg Goodhue, Oklahoma
1975.....Tom Beach, California
1976.....Sam Shaw, Cal St-
          Fullerton
1977.....Steve Wejmar, Wash
1978.....Ron Galimore, Louisiana St
1979.....Leslie Moore, Oklahoma
1980.....Ron Galimore, Iowa St
1981.....Ron Galimore, Iowa St
1982.....Randall Wickstrom, Cal
          Steve Elliott, Nebraska
1983.....Chris Riegel, Nebraska
          Mark Oates, Oklahoma
1984.....Chris Riegel, Nebraska
1985.....Derrick Cornelius,
          Cortland St
1986.....Chad Fox, New Mexico
1987.....Chad Fox, New Mexico
1988.....Chad Fox, New Mexico
1989.....Chad Fox, New Mexico
1990.....Brad Hayashi, UCLA
1991.....Adam Carton, Penn St
1992.....Jason Hebert, Syracuse
1993.....Steve Wiegel, N Mexico
1994.....Steve McCain, UCLA
1995.....Ian Bachrach, Stanford
1996.....Jay Thornton, Iowa
1997.....Blaine Wilson, Ohio St
1998.....Travis Romagnoli, Illinois
1999.....Guard Young, BYU
2000.....Guard Young, BYU

POMMEL HORSE

1938.....Erwin Beyer, Chicago
1939.....Erwin Beyer, Chicago
1940......Harry Koehnemann, Illinois
1941.....Caton Cobb, Illinois
1942.....Caton Cobb, Illinois
1948.....Steve Greene, Penn St

Men (Cont.)

INDIVIDUAL CHAMPIONS (Cont.)

1949.....Joe Berenato, Temple
1950.....Gene Rabbitt, Syracuse
1951.....Joe Kotys, Kent
1952.....Frank Bare, Illinois
1953.....Carlton Rintz, Michigan St
1954.....Robert Lawrence, Penn St
1955.....Carlton Rintz, Michigan St
1956.....James Brown, Cal St-
Los Angeles
1957.....John Davis, Illinois
1958.....Bill Buck, Iowa
1959.....Art Shurlock, California
1960.....James Fairchild, California
1961.....James Fairchild, California
1962.....Mike Aufrecht, Illinois
1963.....Russ Mills, Yale
1964.....Russ Mills, Yale
1965.....Bob Elsinger, Springfield
1966.....Gary Hoskins, Cal St-
Los Angeles
1967.....Keith McCanless, Iowa
1968.....Jack Ryan, Colorado
1969.....Keith McCanless, Iowa
1970.....Russ Hoffman, Iowa St
John Russo, Wisconsin
1971.....Russ Hoffman, Iowa St
1972.....Russ Hoffman, Iowa St
1973.....Ed Slezak, Indiana St
1974.....Ted Marcy, Stanford
1975.....Ted Marcy, Stanford
1976.....Ted Marcy, Stanford
1977.....Chuck Walter, New Mexico
1978.....Mike Burke, Northern Ill
1979.....Mike Burke, Northern Ill
1980.....David Stoldt, Illinois
1981.....Mark Bergman, California
Steve Jennings, New Mexico
1982.....Peter Vidmar, UCLA
Steve Jennings, New Mexico
1983.....Doug Kieso, Northern Ill
1984.....Tim Daggett, UCLA
1985.....Tony Pineda, UCLA
1986.....Curtis Holdsworth, UCLA
1987.....Li Xiao Ping, Cal St-
Fullerton
1988.....Vacated†
Mark Sohn, Penn St
1989.....Mark Sohn, Penn St
Chris Waller, UCLA
1990.....Mark Sohn, Penn St
1991.....Mark Sohn, Penn St
1992.....Che Bowers, Nebraska
1993.....John Roethlisberger, Minn
1994.....Jason Bertram, California
1995.....Drew Durbin, Ohio St
1996.....Drew Durbin, Ohio St

1997.....Drew Durbin, Ohio St
1998.....Josh Birckelbaw, California
1999.....Brandon Stefaniak, Penn St
2000.....Brandon Stefaniak, Penn St
Don Jackson, Iowa

FLOOR EXERCISE

1941.....Lou Fina, Illinois
1953.....Bob Sullivan, Illinois
1954.....Jean Cronstedt, Penn St
1955.....Don Faber, UCLA
1956.....Jamile Ashmore, Florida St
1957.....Norman Marks, Cal St-
Los Angeles
1958.....Abie Grossfeld, Illinois
1959.....Don Tonry, Illinois
1960.....Ray Hadley, Illinois
1961.....Robert Lynn, Southern Cal
1962.....Robert Lynn, Southern Cal
1963.....Tom Seward, Penn St
Mike Henderson, Michigan
1964.....Rusty Mitchell, S Illinois
1965.....Frank Schmitz, S Illinois
1966.....Frank Schmitz, S Illinois
1967.....Dave Jacobs, Michigan
1968.....Toby Towson, Michigan St
1969.....Toby Towson, Michigan St
1970.....Tom Proulx, Colorado St
1971.....Stormy Eaton, New Mexico
1972.....Odessa Lovin, Oklahoma
1973.....Odessa Lovin, Oklahoma
1974.....Doug Fitzjarrell, Iowa St
1975.....Kent Brown, Arizona St
1976.....Bob Robbins, Colorado St
1977.....Ron Galimore, Louisiana St
1978.....Curt Austin, Iowa St
1979.....Mike Wilson, Oklahoma
Bart Conner, Oklahoma
1980.....Steve Elliott, Nebraska
1981.....James Yuhashi, Oregon
1982.....Steve Elliott, Nebraska
1983.....Scott Johnson, Nebraska
David Branch, Arizona St
Donnie Hinton, Arizona St
1984.....Kevin Ekburg, Northern Ill
1985.....Wes Suter, Nebraska
1986.....Jerry Burrell, Arizona St
Brian Ginsberg, UCLA
1987.....Chad Fox, New Mexico
1988.....Chris Wyatt, Temple
1989.....Jody Newman, Arizona St
1990.....Mike Racanelli, Ohio St
1991.....Brad Hayashi, UCLA
1992.....Brian Winkler, Michigan
1993.....Richard Grace, Nebraska

1994.....Mark Booth, Stanford
1995.....Jay Thornton, Iowa
1996.....Ian Bachrach, Stanford
1997.....Jeremy Killen, Oklahoma
1998.....Darin Gerlach, Temple
1999.....Jason Hardabura, Nebraska
2000.......Jamie Natalie, Ohio St

RINGS

1959.....Armando Vega, Penn St
1960.....Sam Garcia, Southern Cal
1961.....Fred Orlofsky, Southern Ill
1962.....Dale Cooper, Michigan St
1963.....Dale Cooper, Michigan St
1964.....Chris Evans, Arizona St
1965.....Glenn Gailis, Iowa
1966.....Ed Gunny, Michigan St
1967.....Josh Robison, California
1968.....Pat Arnold, Arizona
1969.....Paul Vexler, Penn St
Ward Maythaler, Iowa St
1970.....Dave Seal, Indiana St
1971.....Charles Ropiequet, S Illinois
1972.....Dave Seal, Indiana St
1973.....Bob Mahorney, Indiana St
1974.....Keith Heaver, Iowa St
1975.....Keith Heaver, Iowa St
1976.....Doug Wood, Iowa St
1977.....Doug Wood, Iowa St
1978.....Scott McEldowney, Oregon
1979.....Kirk Mango, Northern Ill
1980.....Jim Hartung, Nebraska
1981.....Jim Hartung, Nebraska
1982.....Jim Hartung, Nebraska
1983.....Alex Schwartz, UCLA
1984.....Tim Daggett, UCLA
1985.....Mark Diab, Iowa St
1986.....Mark Diab, Iowa St
1987.....Paul O'Neill, Hou. Baptist
1988.....Paul O'Neill, New Mexico
1989.....Vacated†
Paul O'Neill, New Mexico
1990.....Wayne Cowden, Penn St
1991.....Adam Carton, Penn St
1992.....Scott Keswick, UCLA
1993.....Chris LaMorte, N Mexico
1994.....Chris LaMorte, N Mexico
1995.....Dave Frank, Temple
1996.....Scott McCall, Will. & Mary
Blaine Wilson, Ohio St
1997.....Blaine Wilson, Ohio St
1998.....Dan Fink, Oklahoma
1999.....Cortney Bramwell, BYU
2000.....Cortney Bramwell, BYU

† Championships won by Miguel Rubio (All Around, 1988; Horizontal Bar, 1988-89) and Alfonso Rodriguez (Pommel Horse, 1988; Rings, 1989; Parallel Bars, 1989) were vacated by action of the NCAA Committee on Infractions.

Men (Cont.)

DIVISION II (DISCONTINUED)

Year	Champion	Coach	Pts	Runner-Up	Pts
1968	Cal St-Northridge	Bill Vincent	179.400	Springfield	178.050
1969	Cal St-Northridge	Bill Vincent	151.800	Southern Connecticut St	145.075
1970	Northwestern Louisiana	Armando Vega	160.250	Southern Connecticut St	159.300
1971	Cal St-Fullerton	Dick Wolfe	158.150	Springfield	156.987
1972	Cal St-Fullerton	Dick Wolfe	160.550	Southern Connecticut St	153.050
1973	Southern Connecticut St	Abe Grossfeld	160.750	Cal St-Northridge	158.700
1974	Cal St-Fullerton	Dick Wolfe	309.800	Southern Connecticut St	309.400
1975	Southern Connecticut St	Abe Grossfeld	411.650	IL-Chicago	398.800
1976	Southern Connecticut St	Abe Grossfeld	419.200	IL-Chicago	388.850
1977	Springfield	Frank Wolcott	395.950	Cal St-Northridge	381.250
1978	IL-Chicago	C. Johnson/A. Gentile	406.850	Cal St-Northridge	400.400
1979	IL-Chicago	Clarence Johnson	418.550	WI-Oshkosh	385.650
1980	WI-Oshkosh	Ken Allen	260.550	Cal St-Chico	256.050
1981	WI-Oshkosh	Ken Allen	209.500	Springfield	201.550
1982	WI-Oshkosh	Ken Allen	216.050	E Stroudsburg	211.200
1983	East Stroudsburg	Bruno Klaus	258.650	WI-Oshkosh	257.850
1984	East Stroudsburg	Bruno Klaus	270.800	Cortland St	246.350

Women

TEAM CHAMPIONS

Year	Champion	Coach	Pts	Runner-Up	Pts
1982	Utah	Greg Marsden	148.60	Cal St-Fullerton	144.10
1983	Utah	Greg Marsden	184.65	Arizona St	183.30
1984	Utah	Greg Marsden	186.05	UCLA	185.55
1985	Utah	Greg Marsden	188.35	Arizona St	186.60
1986	Utah	Greg Marsden	186.95	Arizona St	186.70
1987	Georgia	Suzanne Yoculan	187.90	Utah	187.55
1988	Alabama	Sarah Patterson	190.05	Utah	189.50
1989	Georgia	Suzanne Yoculan	192.65	UCLA	192.60
1990	Utah	Greg Marsden	194.900	Alabama	194.575
1991	Alabama	Sarah Patterson	195.125	Utah	194.375
1992	Utah	Greg Marsden	195.650	Georgia	194.600
1993	Georgia	Suzanne Yoculan	198.000	Alabama	196.825
1994	Utah	Greg Marsden	196.400	Alabama	196.350
1995	Utah	Greg Marsden	196.650	Alabama	196.425
				Michigan	196.425
1996	Alabama	Sarah Patterson	198.025	UCLA	197.475
1997	UCLA	Valorie Kondos	197.150	Arizona St	196.850
1998	Georgia	Suzanne Yoculan	197.725	Florida	196.350
1999	Georgia	Suzanne Yoculan	196.850	Michigan	196.55
2000	UCLA	Valorie Kondos	197.300	Utah	196.875

INDIVIDUAL CHAMPIONS

ALL-AROUND

1982 .....Sue Stednitz, Utah
1983 .....Megan McCunniff, Utah
1984 ......Megan McCunniff-Marsden, Utah
1985 ....Penney Hauschild, Alabama
1986 ....Penney Hauschild, Alabama
Jackie Brummer, Arizona St
1987 .....Kelly Garrison-Steves, Oklahoma
1988 .....Kelly Garrison-Steves, Oklahoma
1989 .....Corrinne Wright, Georgia
1990 .....Dee Dee Foster, Alabama
1991 .....Hope Spivey, Georgia
1992 .....Missy Marlowe, Utah
1993 .....Jenny Hansen, Kentucky
1994 .....Jenny Hansen, Kentucky
1995 .....Jenny Hansen, Kentucky
1996 .....Meredith Willard, Alabama
1997 .....Kim Arnold, Georgia
1998 .....Kim Arnold, Georgia

1999 .....Theresa Kulikowski, Utah
2000 .....Mohini Bhardwaj, UCLA
Heather Brink, Nebraska

VAULT

19782...Elaine Alfano, Utah
1983 .....Elaine Alfano, Utah
1984 .....Megan Marsden, Utah
1985 .....Elaine Alfano, Utah
1986 .....Kim Neal, Arizona St
Pam Loree, Penn St
1987 .....Yumi Mordre, Washington
1988 .....Jill Andrews, UCLA
1989 .....Kim Hamilton, UCLA
1990 .....Michele Bryant, Nebraska
1991 .....Anna Basaldva, Arizona
1992 .....Tammy Marshall, Mass.
Heather Stepp, Georgia
Kristein Kenoyer, Utah
1993 .....Heather Stepp, Georgia
1994 .....Jenny Hansen, Kentucky
1995 .....Jenny Hansen, Kentucky

1996 .....Leah Brown, Georgia
1997 .....Susan Hines, Florida
1998 .....Susan Hines, Florida
1999 .....Heidi Moneymaker, UCLA
2000 .....Heather Brink, Nebraska

BALANCE BEAM

1982 .....Sue Stednitz, Utah
1983 .....Julie Goewey, Cal St-Fullerton
1984 .....Heidi Anderson, Oregon St
1985 .....Lisa Zeis, Arizona St
1986 .....Jackie Brummer, Arizona St
1987 .....Yumi Mordre, Washington
1988 .....Kelly Garrison-Steves, Oklahoma
1989 .....Jill Andrews, UCLA
Joy Selig, Oregon St
1990 .....Joy Selig, Oregon St
1991 .....Missy Marlowe, Utah
1992 .....Missy Marlowe, Utah

Women (Cont.)

BALANCE BEAM (Cont.)

1992   Dana Dobransky, Alabama
1993 ....Dana Dobransky, Alabama
1994 .....Jenny Hansen, Kentucky
1995 .....Jenny Hansen, Kentucky
1996 .....Summer Reid, UUtah
1997 .....Summer Reid, Utah
        Elizabeth Reid, Arizona St
1998 .....Larissa Fontaine, Stanford
        Susan Hines, Florida
1999 .....Theresa Kulikowski, Utah
2000 .....Lena Degteva, UCLA

FLOOR EXERCISE

1982 .....Mary Ayotte-Law,
        Oregon St
1983 .....Kim Neal, Arizona St
1984 .....Maria Anz, Florida
1985 .....Lisa Mitzel, Utah
1986 .....Lisa Zeis, Arizona St
        Penney Hauschild,
        Alabama
1987 .....Kim Hamilton, UCLA
1988 .....Kim Hamilton, UCLA
1989 .....Corrinne Wright, Georgia

INDIVIDUAL CHAMPIONS (Cont.)

Kim Hamilton, UCLA
1990 .....Joy Selig, Oregon St
1991 .....Hope Spivey, Georgia
1992 .....Missy Marlowe, Utah
1993 .....Heather Stepp, Georgia
        Tammy Marshall, Mass.
        Amy Durham, Oregon St
1994 .....Hope Spivey-Sheeley, UGA
1995 .....Jenny Hansen, Kentucky
        Stella Umeh, UCLA
        Leslie Angeles, Georgia
1996 .....Heidi Hornbeek, Arizona
        Kim Kelly, Alabama
1997 .....Leah Brown, Georgia
1998 .....Kim Arnold, Georgia
        Jenni Beathard, Georgia
        Betsy Hamm, Florida
1999 .....Marny Oestreng, BGSU
2000 .....Suzanne Sears, Georgia

UNEVEN BARS

1982 .....Lisa Shirk, Pittsburgh
1983 .....Jeri Cameron, Arizona St
1984 .....Jackie Brummer,
        Arizona St

1985 ......Penney Hauschild, Alabama
1986 .....Lucy Wener, Georgia
1987 .....Lucy Wener, Georgia
1988 .....Kelly Garrison-Steves,
        Oklahoma
1989 .....Lucy Wener, Georgia
1990 .....Marie Roethlisberger,
        Minnesota
1991 .....Kelly Macy, Georgia
1992 .....Missy Marlowe, Utah
1993 .....Agina Simpkins, Georgia
        Beth Wymer, Michigan
1994 .....Sandy Woolsey, Utah
        Beth Wymer, Michigan
        Lori Strong, Georgia
1995 .....Beth Wymer, Michigan
1996 .....Stephanie Woods, Alabama
1997 .....Jenni Beathard, Georgia
1998 .....Karin Lichey, Georgia
        Stella Umeh, UCLA
1999 .....Angie Leionard, Utah
2000 .....Mohini Bhardwaj, UCLA

DIVISION II (DISCONTINUED)

Year	Champion	Coach	Pts	Runner-Up	Pts
1982	Cal St-Northridge	Donna Stuart	138.10	Jacksonville St	134.05
1983	Denver	Dan Garcia	174.80	Cal St-Northridge	174.35
1984	Jacksonville St	Robert Dillard	173.40	SE Missouri St	171.45
1985	Jacksonville St	Robert Dillard	176.85	SE Missouri St	173.95
1986	Seattle Pacific	Laurel Tindall	175.80	Jacksonville St	175.15

Ice Hockey

DIVISION I

Year	Champion	Coach	Score	Runner-Up	Most Outstanding Player
1948	Michigan	Vic Heyliger	8–4	Dartmouth	Joe Riley, Dartmouth, F
1949	Boston Coll.	John Kelley	4–3	Dartmouth	Dick Desmond, Dartmouth, G
1950	Colorado Coll.	Cheddy Thompson	13–4	Boston U	Ralph Bevins, Boston U, G
1951	Michigan	Vic Heyliger	7–1	Brown	Ed Whiston, Brown, G
1952	Michigan	Vic Heyliger	4–1	Colorado Coll.	Kenneth Kinsley, Colorado Coll., G
1953	Michigan	Vic Heyliger	7–3	Minnesota	John Matchefts, Michigan, F
1954	Rensselaer	Ned Harkness	5–4 (OT)	Minnesota	Abbie Moore, Rensselaer, F
1955	Michigan	Vic Heyliger	5–3	Colorado Coll.	Philip Hilton, Colorado Coll., D
1956	Michigan	Vic Heyliger	7–5	Michigan Tech	Lorne Howes, Michigan, G
1957	Colorado Coll.	Thomas Bedecki	13–6	Michigan	Bob McCusker, Colorado Coll., F
1958	Denver	Murray Armstrong	6–2	N Dakota	Murray Massier, Denver, F
1959	N Dakota	Bob May	4–3 (OT)	Michigan St	Reg Morelli, N Dakota, F
1960	Denver	Murray Armstrong	5–3	Michigan Tech	Bob Marquis, Boston U, F
1961	Denver	Murray Armstrong	12–2	St. Lawrence	Barry Urbanski, Boston U, G
1962	Michigan Tech	John MacInnes	7–1	Clarkson	Louis Angotti, Michigan Tech, F
1963	N Dakota	Barney Thorndycraft	6–5	Denver	Al McLean, N Dakota, F
1964	Michigan	Allen Renfrew	6–3	Denver	Bob Gray, Michigan, G
1965	Michigan Tech	John MacInnes	8–2	Boston Coll.	Gary Milroy, Michigan Tech, F
1966	Michigan St	Amo Bessone	6–1	Clarkson	Gaye Cooley, Michigan St, G
1967	Cornell	Ned Harkness	4–1	Boston U	Walt Stanowski, Cornell, D
1968	Denver	Murray Armstrong	4–0	N Dakota	Gerry Powers, Denver, G
1969	Denver	Murray Armstrong	4–3	Cornell	Keith Magnuson, Denver, D
1970	Cornell	Ned Harkness	6–4	Clarkson	Daniel Lodboa, Cornell, D
1971	Boston U	Jack Kelley	4–2	Minnesota	Dan Brady, Boston U, G
1972	Boston U	Jack Kelley	4–0	Cornell	Tim Regan, Boston U, G
1973	Wisconsin	Bob Johnson	4–2	Vacated	Dean Talafous, Wisconsin, F
1974	Minnesota	Herb Brooks	4–2	Michigan Tech	Brad Shelstad, Minnesota, G
1975	Michigan Tech	John MacInnes	6–1	Minnesota	Jim Warden, Michigan Tech, G
1976	Minnesota	Herb Brooks	6–4	Michigan Tech	Tom Vanelli, Minnesota, F

DIVISION I (CONT.)

Year	Champion	Coach	Score	Runner-Up	Most Outstanding Player
1977	Wisconsin	Bob Johnson	6–5 (OT)	Michigan	Julian Baretta, Wisconsin, G
1978	Boston U	Jack Parker	5–3	Boston Coll.	Jack O'Callahan, Boston U, D
1979	Minnesota	Herb Brooks	4–3	N Dakota	Steve Janaszak, Minnesota, G
1980	N Dakota	John Gasparini	5–2	Northern Michigan	Doug Smail, N Dakota, F
1981	Wisconsin	Bob Johnson	6–3	Minnesota	Marc Behrend, Wisconsin, G
1982	N Dakota	John Gasparini	5–2	Wisconsin	Phil Sykes, N Dakota, F
1983	Wisconsin	Jeff Sauer	6–2	Harvard	Marc Behrend, Wisconsin, G
1984	Bowling Green	Jerry York	5–4 (OT)	MN-Duluth	Gary Kruzich, Bowling Green, G
1985	Rensselaer	Mike Addesa	2–1	Providence	Chris Terreri, Providence, G
1986	Michigan St	Ron Mason	6–5	Harvard	Mike Donnelly, Michigan St, F
1987	N Dakota	John Gasparini	5–3	Michigan St	Tony Hrkac, N Dakota, F
1988	Lake Superior St	Frank Anzalone	4–3 (OT)	St. Lawrence	Bruce Hoffort, Lake Superior St, G
1989	Harvard	Bill Cleary	4–3 (OT)	Minnesota	Ted Donato, Harvard, F
1990	Wisconsin	Jeff Sauer	7–3	Colgate	Chris Tancill, Wisconsin, F
1991	N Michigan	Rick Comley	8–7 (3OT)	Boston U	Scott Beattie, N Michigan, F
1992	Lake Superior St	Jeff Jackson	4–2	Wisconsin	Paul Constantin, Lake Superior St, F
1993	Maine	Shawn Walsh	5–4	Lake Superior St	Jim Montgomery, Maine, F
1994	Lake Superior St	Jeff Jackson	9–1	Boston U	Sean Tallaire, Lake Superior St, F
1995	Boston U	Jack Parker	6–2	Maine	Chris O'Sullivan, Boston U, F
1996	Michigan	Red Berenson	3–2 (OT)	Colorado Coll.	Brendan Morrison, Michigan, F
1997	N Dakota	Dean Blais	6–4	Boston U	Matt Henderson, N Dakota, F
1998	Michigan	Red Berenson	3–2 (OT)	Boston Coll.	Marty Turco, Michigan, G
1999	Maine	Shawn Walsh	3–2 (OT)	New Hampshire	Alfie Michaud, Maine, G
2000	N Dakota	Dean Blais	4–2	Boston Coll.	Lee Goren, N Dakota, F

DIVISION II (DISCONTINUED)

Year	Champion	Coach	Score	Runner-Up
1978	Merrimack	Thom Lawler	12–2	Lake Forest
1979	Lowell	Bill Riley Jr	6–4	Mankato St
1980	Mankato St	Don Brose	5–2	Elmira
1981	Lowell	Bill Riley Jr	5–4	Plattsburgh St
1982	Lowell	Bill Riley Jr	6–1	Plattsburgh St
1983	RIT	Brian Mason	4–2	Bemidji St
1984	Bemidji St	R.H. (Bob) Peters	14–4*	Merrimack
1993	Bemidji St	R.H. (Bob) Peters	15–6*	Mercyhurst
1994	Bemidji St	R.H. (Bob) Peters	7–6*	AL-Huntsville
1995	Bemidji St	R.H. (Bob) Peters	11–6*	Mercyhurst
1996	AL-Huntsville	Doug Ross	10–1*	Bemidji St
1997	Bemidji St	R.H. (Bob) Peters	7–4*	AL-Huntsville
1998	AL-Huntsville	Doug Ross	11–4*	Bemidji St
1999	St. Michael's (VT)	Lou DiMasi	12–9*	New Hamp. Coll.

*Two-game, total-goal series.

DIVISION III

Year	Champion	Coach	Score	Runner-Up
1984	Babson	Bob Riley	8–0	Union (NY)
1985	Rochester Inst	Bruce Delventhal	5–1	Bemidji St
1986	Bemidji St	R.H. (Bob) Peters	8–5	Vacated
1987	Vacated			Oswego St
1988	WI-River Falls	Rick Kozuback	7–1, 3–5, 3–0	Elmira
1989	WI-Stevens Point	Mark Mazzoleni	3–3, 3–2	RIT
1990	WI-Stevens Point	Mark Mazzoleni	10–1, 3–6, 1–0	Plattsburgh St
1991	WI-Stevens Point	Mark Mazzoleni	6–2	Mankato St
1992	Plattsburgh St	Bob Emery	7–3	WI-Stevens Point
1993	WI-Stevens Point	Joe Baldarotta	4–3	WI-River Falls
1994	WI-River Falls	Dean Talafous	6–4	WI-Superior
1995	Middlebury	Bill Beaney	1–0	Fredonia St
1996	Middlebury	Bill Beaney	3–2	RIT
1997	Middlebury	Bill Beaney	3–2	WI-Superior
1998	Middlebury	Bill Beaney	2–1	WI-Stevens Point
1999	Middlebury	Bill Beaney	5–0	WI-Superior
2000	Norwich	Michael McShane	2–1	St. Thomas

Men
DIVISION I

Year	Champion	Coach	Score	Runner-Up
1971	Cornell	Richie Moran	12–6	Maryland
1972	Virginia	Glenn Thiel	13–12	Johns Hopkins
1973	Maryland	Bud Beardmore	10–9 (2 OT)	Johns Hopkins
1974	Johns Hopkins	Bob Scott	17–12	Maryland
1975	Maryland	Bud Beardmore	20–13	Navy
1976	Cornell	Richie Moran	16–13 (OT)	Maryland
1977	Cornell	Richie Moran	16–8	Johns Hopkins
1978	Johns Hopkins	Henry Ciccarone	13–8	Cornell
1979	Johns Hopkins	Henry Ciccarone	15–9	Maryland
1980	Johns Hopkins	Henry Ciccarone	9–8 (2 OT)	Virginia
1981	N Carolina	Willie Scroggs	14–13	Johns Hopkins
1982	N Carolina	Willie Scroggs	7–5	Johns Hopkins
1983	Syracuse	Roy Simmons Jr	17–16	Johns Hopkins
1984	Johns Hopkins	Don Zimmerman	13–10	Syracuse
1985	Johns Hopkins	Don Zimmerman	11–4	Syracuse
1986	N Carolina	Willie Scroggs	10–9 (OT)	Virginia
1987	Johns Hopkins	Don Zimmerman	11–10	Cornell
1988	Syracuse	Roy Simmons Jr	13–8	Cornell
1989	Syracuse	Roy Simmons Jr	13–12	Johns Hopkins
1990	Syracuse	Roy Simmons Jr	21–9	Loyola (MD)
1991	N Carolina	Dave Klarmann	18–13	Towson St
1992	Princeton	Bill Tierney	10–9	Syracuse
1993	Syracuse	Roy Simmons Jr	13–12	N Carolina
1994	Princeton	Bill Tierney	9–8 (OT)	Virginia
1995	Syracuse	Roy Simmons Jr	13–9	Maryland
1996	Princeton	Bill Tierney	13–12 (OT)	Virginia
1997	Princeton	Bill Tierney	19–7	Maryland
1998	Princeton	Bill Tierney	15–5	Maryland
1999	Virginia	Dom Starsia	12–10	Syracuse
2000	Syracuse	John Desko	13–7	Princeton

DIVISION II *(DISCONTINUED, THEN RENEWED)*

Year	Champion	Coach	Score	Runner-Up
1974	Towson St	Carl Runk	18–17 (OT)	Hobart
1975	Cortland St	Chuck Winters	12–11	Hobart
1976	Hobart	Jerry Schmidt	18–9	Adelphi
1977	Hobart	Jerry Schmidt	23–13	Washington (MD)
1978	Roanoke	Paul Griffin	14–13	Hobart
1979	Adelphi	Paul Doherty	17–12	MD-Baltimore County
1980	MD-Baltimore County	Dick Watts	23–14	Adelphi
1981	Adelphi	Paul Doherty	17–14	Loyola (MD)
1993	Adelphi	Kevin Sheehan	11–7	LIU-C.W. Post
1994	Springfield	Keith Bugbee	15–12	New York Tech
1995	Adelphi	Sandy Kapatos	12–10	Springfield
1996	LIU-C.W. Post	Tom Postel	15–10	Adelphi
1997	New York Tech	Jack Kaley	18–11	Adelphi
1998	Adelphi	Sandy Kapatos	18–6	LIU-C.W. Post
1999	Adelphi	Sandy Kapatos	11–8	LIU-C.W. Post
2000	Limestone	Mike Cerino	10–9	LIU-C.W. Post

DIVISION III

Year	Champion	Coach	Score	Runner-Up
1980	Hobart	Dave Urick	11–8	Cortland St
1981	Hobart	Dave Urick	10–8	Cortland St
1982	Hobart	Dave Urick	9–8 (OT)	Washington (MD)
1983	Hobart	Dave Urick	13–9	Roanoke
1984	Hobart	Dave Urick	12–5	Washington (MD)
1985	Hobart	Dave Urick	15–8	Washington (MD)
1986	Hobart	Dave Urick	13–10	Washington (MD)
1987	Hobart	Dave Urick	9–5	Ohio Wesleyan
1988	Hobart	Dave Urick	18–9	Ohio Wesleyan
1989	Hobart	Dave Urick	11–8	Ohio Wesleyan
1990	Hobart	B.J. O'Hara	18–6	Washington (MD)
1991	Hobart	B.J. O'Hara	12–11	Salisbury St
1992	Nazareth (NY)	Scott Nelson	13–12	Hobart

DIVISION III *(Cont.)*

Year	Champion	Coach	Score	Runner-Up
1993	Hobart	B.J. O'Hara	16–10	Ohio Wesleyan
1994	Salisbury St	Jim Berkman	15–9	Hobart
1995	Salisbury St	Jim Berkman	22–13	Nazareth
1996	Nazareth	Scott Nelson	11–10 (OT)	Washington (MD)
1997	Nazareth	Scott Nelson	15–14 (OT)	Washington (MD)
1998	Washington (MD)	John Haus	16–10	Nazareth
1999	Salisbury St	Jim Berkman	13–6	Middlebury
2000	Middlebury	Erin Quinn	16–12	Salisbury St

Women

DIVISIONS I AND II

Year	Champion	Coach	Score	Runner-Up
1982	Massachusetts	Pamela Hixon	9–6	Trenton St
1983	Delaware	Janet Smith	10–7	Temple
1984	Temple	Tina Sloan Green	6–4	Maryland
1985	New Hampshire	Marisa Didio	6–5	Maryland
1986	Maryland	Sue Tyler	11–10	Penn St
1987	Penn St	Susan Scheetz	7–6	Temple
1988	Temple	Tina Sloan Green	15–7	Penn St
1989	Penn St	Susan Scheetz	7–6	Harvard
1990	Harvard	Carole Kleinfelder	8–7	Maryland
1991	Virginia	Jane Miller	8–6	Maryland
1992	Maryland	Cindy Timchal	11–10	Harvard
1993	Virginia	Jane Miller	8–6 (OT)	Princeton
1994	Princeton	Chris Sailer	10–7	Virginia
1995	Maryland	Cindy Timchal	13–5	Princeton
1996	Maryland	Cindy Timchal	10–5	Virginia
1997	Maryland	Cindy Timchal	8–7	Loyola (MD)
1998	Maryland	Cindy Timchal	11–5	Virginia
1999	Maryland	Cindy Timchal	16–6	Virginia
2000	Maryland	Cindy Timchal	16–8	Princeton

DIVISION III

Year	Champion	Score	Runner-Up	Year	Champion	Score	Runner-Up
1985	Trenton St	7–4	Ursinus	1993	Trenton St	10–9	William Smith
1986	Ursinus	12–10	Trenton St	1994	Trenton St	29–11	William Smith
1987	Trenton St	8–7 (OT)	Ursinus	1995	Trenton St	14–13	William Smith
1988	Trenton St	14–11	William Smith	1996	Trenton St	15–8	Middlebury
1989	Ursinus	8–6	Trenton St	1997	Middlebury	14–9	College of NJ*
1990	Ursinus	7–6	St. Lawrence	1998	Coll. of NJ*	14–9	Williams
1991	Trenton St	7–6	Ursinus	1999	Middlebury	10–9	Amherst
1992	Trenton St	5–3	William Smith	2000	Coll. of NJ*	14–8	Williams

*Formerly Trenton St.

Rifle

Men's and Women's Combined

Year	Champion	Coach	Score	Runner-Up	Score	Individual Champions Air Rifle	Individual Champions Smallbore
1980	Tennessee Tech	James Newkirk	6201	W Virginia	6150	Rod Fitz-Randolph, Tennessee Tech	Rod Fitz-Randolph, Tennessee Tech
1981	Tennessee Tech	James Newkirk	6139	W Virginia	6136	John Rost, W Virginia	Kurt Fitz-Randolph, Tennessee Tech
1982	Tennessee Tech	James Newkirk	6138	W Virginia	6136	John Rost, W Virginia	Kurt Fitz-Randolph, Tennessee Tech
1983	W Virginia	Edward Etzel	6166	Tennessee Tech	6148	Ray Slonena, Tennessee Tech	David Johnson, W Virginia
1984	W Virginia	Edward Etzel	6206	E Tennessee St	6142	Pat Spurgin, Murray St	Bob Broughton, W Virginia
1985	Murray St	Elvis Green	6150	W Virginia	6149	Christian Heller, W Virginia	Pat Spurgin, Murray St
1986	W Virginia	Edward Etzel	6229	Murray St	6163	Marianne Wallace, Murray St	Mike Anti, W Virginia

Rifle (Cont.)

Year	Champion	Coach	Score	Runner-Up	Score	Individual Champions Air Rifle	Smallbore
1987 ...Murray St	Elvis Green	6205	W Virginia	6203	Rob Harbison, TN-Martin	Web Wright, W Virginia
1988 ...W Virginia	Greg Perrine	6192	Murray St	6183	Deena Wigger, Murray St	Web Wright, W Virginia
1989 ...W Virginia	Edward Etzel	6234	S Florida	6180	Michelle Scarborough, S Florida	Deb Sinclair, AK-Fairbanks
1990 ...W Virginia	Marsha Beasley	6205	Navy	6101	Gary Hardy, W Virginia	M. Scarborough, S Florida
1991 ...W Virginia	Marsha Beasley	6171	AK-Fairbanks	6110	Ann Pfiffner, W Virginia	Soma Dutta, UTEP
1992 ...W Virginia	Marsha Beasley	6214	AK-Fairbanks	6166	Ann Pfiffner, W Virginia	Tim Manges, W Virginia
1993 ...W Virginia	Marsha Beasley	6179	AK-Fairbanks	6169	Trevor Gathman, W Virginia	Eric Uptagrafft, W Virginia
1994 ...AK-Fairbanks	Randy Pitney	6194	W Virginia	6187	Nancy Napolski, Kentucky	Cory Brunetti, AK-Fairbanks
1995 ...W Virginia	Marsha Beasley	6241	Air Force	6187	Benji Belden, Murray St	Oleg Selezner, AK-Fairbanks
1996 ...W Virginia	Marsha Beasley	6179	Air Force	6168	Trevor Gathman, W Virginia	Joe Johnson, Navy
1997 ...W Virginia	Marsha Beasley	6223	Kentucky	6175	Marra Hastings, Murray St	Marcos Scrivner, W Virginia
1998 ...W Virginia	Marsha Beasley	6214	AK-Fairbanks	6175	Emily Caruso, Norwich	Karen Juzinuk, Xavier
1999 ...AK-Fairbanks	Randy Pitney	6276	Navy	6168	Kelly Mansfield, AK-Fairbanks	Kelly Mansfield, AK-Fairbanks
2000....AK-Fairbanks	Randy Pitney	6285	Xavier	6156	Kelly Mansfield, AK-Fairbanks	Nicole Allaire, Nebraska

Skiing

Men's and Women's Combined

Year	Champion	Coach	Pts	Runner-Up	Pts	Host or Site
1954 .....Denver	Willy Schaeffler	384.0	Seattle	349.6	NV-Reno
1955 .....Denver	Willy Schaeffler	567.05	Dartmouth	558.935	Norwich
1956 .....Denver	Willy Schaeffler	582.01	Dartmouth	541.77	Winter Park
1957 .....Denver	Willy Schaeffler	577.95	Colorado	545.29	Ogden Snow Basin
1958 .....Dartmouth	Al Merrill	561.2	Denver	550.6	Dartmouth
1959 .....Colorado	Bob Beattie	549.4	Denver	543.6	Winter Park
1960 .....Colorado	Bob Beattie	571.4	Denver	568.6	Bridger Bowl
1961 .....Denver	Willy Schaeffler	376.19	Middlebury	366.94	Middlebury
1962 .....Denver	Willy Schaeffler	390.08	Colorado	374.30	Squaw Valley
1963 .....Denver	Willy Schaeffler	384.6	Colorado	381.6	Solitude
1964 .....Denver	Willy Schaeffler	370.2	Dartmouth	368.8	Franconia Notch
1965 .....Denver	Willy Schaeffler	380.5	Utah	378.4	Crystal Mountain
1966 .....Denver	Willy Schaeffler	381.02	Western Colorado	365.92	Crested Butte
1967 .....Denver	Willy Schaeffler	376.7	Wyoming	375.9	Sugarloaf Mountain
1968 .....Wyoming	John Cress	383.9	Denver	376.2	Mount Werner
1969 .....Denver	Willy Schaeffler	388.6	Dartmouth	372.0	Mount Werner
1970 .....Denver	Willy Schaeffler	386.6	Dartmouth	378.8	Cannon Mountain
1971 .....Denver	Peder Pytte	394.7	Colorado	373.1	Terry Peak
1972 .....Colorado	Bill Marolt	385.3	Denver	380.1	Winter Park
1973 .....Colorado	Bill Marolt	381.89	Wyoming	377.83	Middlebury
1974 .....Colorado	Bill Marolt	176	Wyoming	162	Jackson Hole
1975 .....Colorado	Bill Marolt	183	Vermont	115	Fort Lewis
1976 .....Colorado	Bill Marolt	112			Bates
Dartmouth	Jim Page	112			
1977 .....Colorado	Bill Marolt	179	Wyoming	154.5	Winter Park
1978 .....Colorado	Bill Marolt	152.5	Wyoming	121.5	Cannon Mountain
1979 .....Colorado	Tim Hinderman	153	Utah	130	Steamboat Springs
1980 .....Vermont	Chip LaCasse	171	Utah	151	Lake Placid and Stowe
1981 .....Utah	Pat Miller	183	Vermont	172	Park City
1982 .....Colorado	Tim Hinderman	461	Vermont	436.5	Lake Placid
1983 .....Utah	Pat Miller	696	Vermont	650	Bozeman
1984 .....Utah	Pat Miller	750.5	Vermont	684	New Hampshire

Skiing (Cont.)

Year	Champion	Coach	Pts	Runner-Up	Pts	Host or Site
1985	Wyoming	Tim Ameel	764	Utah	744	Bozeman
1986	Utah	Pat Miller	612	Vermont	602	Vermont
1987	Utah	Pat Miller	710	Vermont	627	Anchorage
1988	Utah	Pat Miller	651	Vermont	614	Middlebury
1989	Vermont	Chip LaCasse	672	Utah	668	Jackson Hole
1990	Vermont	Chip LaCasse	671	Utah	571	Vermont
1991	Colorado	Richard Rokos	713	Vermont	682	Park City, UT
1992	Vermont	Chip LaCasse	693.5	New Mexico	642.5	New Hampshire
1993	Utah	Pat Miller	783	Vermont	700.5	Steamboat Springs
1994	Vermont	Chip LaCasse	688	Utah	667	Sugarloaf, ME
1995	Colorado	Richard Rokos	720.5	Utah	711	New Hampshire
1996	Utah	Pat Miller	719	Denver	635.5	Montana St
1997	Utah	Pat Miller	686	Vermont	646.5	Vermont
1998	Colorado	Richard Rokos	654	Utah	651.5	Montana St
1999	Colorado	Richard Rokos	650	Denver	636	Bates College
2000	Denver	Kurt Smitz	720	Colorado	621	Park City, UT

Soccer

Men

DIVISION I

Year	Champion	Coach	Score	Runner-Up
1959	St. Louis	Bob Guelker	5–2	Bridgeport
1960	St. Louis	Bob Guelker	3–2	Maryland
1961	West Chester	Mel Lorback	2–0	St. Louis
1962	St. Louis	Bob Guelker	4–3	Maryland
1963	St. Louis	Bob Guelker	3–0	Navy
1964	Navy	F.H. Warner	1–0	Michigan St
1965	St. Louis	Bob Guelker	1–0	Michigan St
1966	San Francisco	Steve Negoesco	5–2	LIU-Brooklyn
1967	Michigan St	Gene Kenney	0–0	Game called
	St. Louis	Harry Keough		due to inclement weather
1968	Maryland	Doyle Royal	2–2 (2 OT)	
	Michigan St	Gene Kenney		
1969	St. Louis	Harry Keough	4–0	San Francisco
1970	St. Louis	Harry Keough	1–0	UCLA
1971	Vacated		3–2	St. Louis
1972	St. Louis	Harry Keough	4–2	UCLA
1973	St. Louis	Harry Keough	2–1 (OT)	UCLA
1974	Howard	Lincoln Phillips	2–1 (4 OT)	St. Louis
1975	San Francisco	Steve Negoesco	4–0	SIU-Edwardsville
1976	San Francisco	Steve Negoesco	1–0	Indiana
1977	Hartwick	Jim Lennox	2–1	San Francisco
1978	Vacated		2–0	Indiana
1979	SIU-Edwardsville	Bob Guelker	3–2	Clemson
1980	San Francisco	Steve Negoesco	4–3 (OT)	Indiana
1981	Connecticut	Joe Morrone	2–1 (OT)	Alabama A&M
1982	Indiana	Jerry Yeagley	2–1 (8 OT)	Duke
1983	Indiana	Jerry Yeagley	1–0 (2 OT)	Columbia
1984	Clemson	I.M. Ibrahim	2–1	Indiana
1985	UCLA	Sigi Schmid	1–0 (8 OT)	American
1986	Duke	John Rennie	1–0	Akron
1987	Clemson	I.M. Ibrahim	2–0	San Diego St
1988	Indiana	Jerry Yeagley	1–0	Howard
1989	Santa Clara	Steve Sampson	1–1 (2 OT)	
	Virginia	Bruce Arena		
1990	UCLA	Sigi Schmid	1–0 (OT)	Rutgers
1991	Virginia	Bruce Arena	0–0*	Santa Clara
1992	Virginia	Bruce Arena	2–0	San Diego
1993	Virginia	Bruce Arena	2–0	S Carolina
1994	Virginia	Bruce Arena	1–0	Indiana
1995	Wisconsin	Jim Launder	2–0	Duke
1996	St. John's (NY)	Dave Masur	4–1	Florida International
1997	UCLA	Sigi Schmid	2–1	Virginia
1998	Indiana	Jerry Yeagley	3–1	Stanford
1999	Indiana	Jerry Yeagley	1–0	Santa Clara

*Under a rule passed in 1991, the NCAA determined that when a score is tied after regulation and overtime, and the championship is determined by penalty kicks, the official score will be 0–0.

Men (Cont.)

DIVISION II

Year	Champion
1972	SIU-Edwardsville
1973	MO-St. Louis
1974	Adelphi
1975	Baltimore
1976	Loyola (MD)
1977	Alabama A&M
1978	Seattle Pacific
1979	Alabama A&M
1980	Lock Haven
1981	Tampa

Year	Champion
1982	Florida Int'l
1983	Seattle Pacific
1984	Florida Int'l
1985	Seattle Pacific
1986	Seattle Pacific
1987	Southern Connecticut St
1988	Florida Tech
1989	New Hampshire Col
1990	Southern Connecticut St
1991	Florida Tech

Year	Champion
1992	Southern Connecticut St
1993	Seattle Pacific
1994	Tampa
1995	Southern Connecticut St
1996	Grand Canyon
1997	Cal St-Bakersfield
1998	Southern Connecticut St
1999	Southern Connecticut St

DIVISION III

Year	Champion
1974	Brockport St
1975	Babson
1976	Brandeis
1977	Lock Haven
1978	Lock Haven
1979	Babson
1980	Babson
1981	Glassboro St
1982	NC-Greensboro

Year	Champion
1983	NC-Greensboro
1984	Wheaton (IL)
1985	NC-Greensboro
1986	NC-Greensboro
1987	NC-Greensboro
1988	UC-San Diego
1989	Elizabethtown
1990	Glassboro St
1991	UC-San Diego

Year	Champion
1992	Kean
1993	UC-San Diego
1994	Bethany (WV)
1995	Williams
1996	College of New Jersey
1997	Wheaton (IL)
1998	Ohio Wesleyan
1999	St. Lawrence

Women

DIVISION I

Year	Champion	Coach	Score	Runner-Up
1982	N Carolina	Anson Dorrance	2–0	Central Florida
1983	N Carolina	Anson Dorrance	4–0	George Mason
1984	N Carolina	Anson Dorrance	2–0	Connecticut
1985	George Mason	Hank Leung	2–0	North Carolina
1986	N Carolina	Anson Dorrance	2–0	Colorado Col
1987	N Carolina	Anson Dorrance	1–0	Massachusetts
1988	N Carolina	Anson Dorrance	4–1	North Carolina St
1989	N Carolina	Anson Dorrance	2–0	Colorado Col
1990	N Carolina	Anson Dorrance	6–0	Connecticut
1991	N Carolina	Anson Dorrance	3–1	Wisconsin
1992	N Carolina	Anson Dorrance	9–1	Duke
1993	N Carolina	Anson Dorrance	6–0	George Mason
1994	N Carolina	Anson Dorrance	5–0	Notre Dame
1995	Notre Dame	Chris Petrucelli	1–0	Portland
1996	N Carolina	Anson Dorrance	1–0	Notre Dame
1997	N Carolina	Anson Dorrance	2–0	Connecticut
1998	Florida	Becky Burleigh	1–0	N Carolina
1999	N Carolina	Anson Dorrance	2–0	Notre Dame

DIVISION II

Year	Champion
1988	Cal St-Hayward
1989	Barry
1990	Sonoma St
1991	Cal St-Dominguez Hills
1992	Barry
1993	Barry
1994	Franklin Pierce
1995	Franklin Pierce
1996	Franklin Pierce
1997	Franklin Pierce
1998	Lynn
1999	Franklin Pierce

DIVISION III

Year	Champion
1986	Rochester
1987	Rochester
1988	William Smith
1989	UC-San Diego
1990	Ithaca
1991	Ithaca
1992	Cortland St
1993	Trenton St
1994	Trenton St
1995	UC-San Diego
1996	UC-San Diego
1997	UC-San Diego
1998	Macalester
1999	UC-San Diego

Softball

DIVISION I

Year	Champion	Coach	Score	Runner-Up
1982	UCLA*	Sharron Backus	2–0†	Fresno St
1983	Texas A&M	Bob Brock	2–0‡	Cal St-Fullerton
1984	UCLA	Sharron Backus	1–0#	Texas A&M
1985	UCLA	Sharron Backus	2–1**	Nebraska
1986	Cal St-Fullerton*	Judi Garman	3–0	Texas A&M
1987	Texas A&M	Bob Brock	4–1	UCLA
1988	UCLA	Sharron Backus	3–0	Fresno St
1989	UCLA*	Sharron Backus	1–0	Fresno St
1990	UCLA	Sharron Backus	2–0	Fresno St
1991	Arizona	Mike Candrea	5–1	UCLA
1992	UCLA*	Sharron Backus	2–0	Arizona
1993	Arizona	Mike Candrea	1–0	UCLA
1994	Arizona	Mike Candrea	4–0	Cal St-Northridge
1995	Vacated	—		Arizona
1996	Arizona*	Mike Candrea	6–4	Washington
1997	Arizona	Mike Candrea	10–2***	UCLA
1998	Fresno St	Margie Wright	1–0	Arizona
1999	UCLA	Sue Enquist	3–2	Washington
2000	Oklahoma	Patty Gasso	3–1	UCLA

*Undefeated teams in final series. †Eight innings. ‡12 innings. #13 innings. **Nine innings. ***Five innings.

DIVISION II

Year	Champion	Year	Champion	Year	Champion
1982	Sam Houston St	1989	Cal St-Bakersfield	1996	Kennesaw St
1983	Cal St-Northridge	1990	Cal St-Bakersfield	1997	California (PA)*
1984	Cal St-Northridge	1991	Augustana (SD)	1998	California (PA)
1985	Cal St-Northridge	1992	Missouri Southern	1999	Humboldt St
1986	SF Austin St	1993	Florida Southern	2000	N Dakota St
1987	Cal St-Northridge	1994	Merrimack		
1988	Cal St-Bakersfield	1995	Kennesaw St		

DIVISION III

Year	Champion	Year	Champion	Year	Champion
1982	Sam Houston St	1988	Central (IA)	1995	Chapman
1982	Eastern Connecticut St*	1989	Trenton St*	1996	Trenton St*
1983	Trenton St	1990	Eastern Connecticut St	1997	Simpson*
1984	Buena Vista*	1991	Central (IA)	1998	WI-Stevens Point
1985	Eastern Connecticut St	1992	Trenton St	1999	Simpson (IA)
1986	Eastern Connecticut St	1993	Central (IA)	2000	St. Mary's
1987	Trenton St*	1994	Trenton St		

*Undefeated teams in final series.

Swimming and Diving

Men

DIVISION I

Year	Champion	Coach	Pts	Runner-Up	Pts
1937	Michigan	Matt Mann	75	Ohio St	39
1938	Michigan	Matt Mann	46	Ohio St	45
1939	Michigan	Matt Mann	65	Ohio St	58
1940	Michigan	Matt Mann	45	Yale	42
1941	Michigan	Matt Mann	61	Yale	58
1942	Yale	Robert J. H. Kiphuth	71	Michigan	39
1943	Ohio St	Mike Peppe	81	Michigan	47
1944	Yale	Robert J. H. Kiphuth	39	Michigan	38
1945	Ohio St	Mike Peppe	56	Michigan	48
1946	Ohio St	Mike Peppe	61	Michigan	37
1947	Ohio St	MIke Peppe	66	Michigan	39
1948	Michigan	Matt Mann	44	Ohio St	41
1949	Ohio St	Mike Peppe	49	Iowa	35
1950	Ohio St	Mike Peppe	64	Yale	43
1951	Yale	Robert J. H. Kiphuth	81	Michigan St	60
1952	Ohio St	Mike Peppe	94	Yale	81
1953	Yale	Robert J. H. Kiphuth	96½	Ohio St	73½

Men (Cont.)

DIVISION I (Cont.)

Year	Champion	Coach	Pts	Runner-Up	Pts
1954	Ohio St	Mike Peppe	94	Michigan	67
1955	Ohio St	Mike Peppe	90	Yale	51
				Michigan	51
1956	Ohio St	Mike Peppe	68	Yale	54
1957	Michigan	Gus Stager	69	Yale	61
1958	Michigan	Gus Stager	72	Yale	63
1959	Michigan	Gus Stager	137½	Ohio St	44
1960	Southern Cal	Peter Daland	87	Michigan	73
1961	Michigan	Gus Stager	85	Southern Cal	62
1962	Ohio St	Mike Peppe	92	Southern Cal	46
1963	Southern Cal	Peter Daland	81	Yale	77
1964	Southern Cal	Peter Daland	96	Indiana	91
1965	Southern Cal	Peter Daland	285	Indiana	278½
1966	Southern Cal	Peter Daland	302	Indiana	286
1967	Stanford	Jim Gaughran	275	Southern Cal	260
1968	Indiana	James Counsilman	346	Yale	253
1969	Indiana	James Counsilman	427	Southern Cal	306
1970	Indiana	James Counsilman	332	Southern Cal	235
1971	Indiana	James Counsilman	351	Southern Cal	260
1972	Indiana	James Counsilman	390	Southern Cal	371
1973	Indiana	James Counsilman	358	Tennessee	294
1974	Southern Cal	Peter Daland	339	Indiana	338
1975	Southern Cal	Peter Daland	344	Indiana	274
1976	Southern Cal	Peter Daland	398	Tennessee	237
1977	Southern Cal	Peter Daland	385	Alabama	204
1978	Tennessee	Ray Bussard	307	Auburn	185
1979	California	Nort Thornton	287	Southern Cal	227
1980	California	Nort Thornton	234	Texas	220
1981	Texas	Eddie Reese	259	UCLA	189
1982	UCLA	Ron Ballatore	219	Texas	210
1983	Florida	Randy Reese	238	Southern Meth	227
1984	Florida	Randy Reese	287½	Texas	277
1985	Stanford	Skip Kenney	403½	Florida	302
1986	Stanford	Skip Kenney	404	California	335
1987	Stanford	Skip Kenney	374	Southern Cal	296
1988	Texas	Eddie Reese	424	Southern Cal	369½
1989	Texas	Eddie Reese	475	Stanford	396
1990	Texas	Eddie Reese	506	Southern Cal	423
1991	Texas	Eddie Reese	476	Stanford	420
1992	Stanford	Skip Kenney	632	Texas	356
1993	Stanford	Skip Kenney	520½	Michigan	396
1994	Stanford	Skip Kenney	566½	Texas	445
1995	Michigan	Jon Urbanchek	561	Stanford	475
1996	Texas	Eddie Reese	479	Auburn	443½
1997	Auburn	David Marsh	496½	Stanford	340
1998	Stanford	Skip Kenney	594	Auburn	394½
1999	Auburn	David Marsh	467½	Stanford	414½
2000	Texas	Eddie Reese	538	Auburn	385

DIVISION II

Year	Champion	Year	Champion	Year	Champion
1963	SW Missouri St	1976	Cal St-Chico	1989	Cal St-Bakersfield
1964	Bucknell	1977	Cal St-Northridge	1990	Cal St-Bakersfield
1965	San Diego St	1978	Cal St-Northridge	1991	Cal St-Bakersfield
1966	San Diego St	1979	Cal St-Northridge	1992	Cal St-Bakersfield
1967	UC-Santa Barbara	1980	Oakland (MI)	1993	Cal St-Bakersfield
1968	Long Beach St	1981	Cal St-Northridge	1994	Oakland (MI)
1969	UC-Irvine	1982	Cal St-Northridge	1995	Oakland (MI)
1970	UC-Irvine	1983	Cal St-Northridge	1996	Oakland (MI)
1971	UC-Irvine	1984	Cal St-Northridge	1997	Oakland (MI)
1972	Eastern Michigan	1985	Cal St-Northridge	1998	Cal St-Bakersfield
1973	Cal St-Chico	1986	Cal St-Bakersfield	1999	Drury
1974	Cal St-Chico	1987	Cal St-Bakersfield	2000	Cal St-Bakersfield
1975	Cal St-Northridge	1988	Cal St-Bakersfield		

DIVISION III

Year	Champion	Year	Champion	Year	Champion
1975	Cal St-Chico	1984	Kenyon	1993	Kenyon
1976	St. Lawrence	1985	Kenyon	1994	Kenyon
1977	Johns Hopkins	1986	Kenyon	1995	Kenyon
1978	Johns Hopkins	1987	Kenyon	1996	Kenyon
1979	Johns Hopkins	1988	Kenyon	1997	Kenyon
1980	Kenyon	1989	Kenyon	1998	Kenyon
1981	Kenyon	1990	Kenyon	1999	Kenyon
1982	Kenyon	1991	Kenyon	2000	Kenyon
1983	Kenyon	1992	Kenyon		

Women

DIVISION I

Year	Champion	Coach	Pts	Runner-Up	Pts
1982	Florida	Randy Reese	505	Stanford	383
1983	Stanford	George Haines	418½	Florida	389½
1984	Texas	Richard Quick	392	Stanford	324
1985	Texas	Richard Quick	643	Florida	400
1986	Texas	Richard Quick	633	Florida	586
1987	Texas	Richard Quick	648½	Stanford	631½
1988	Texas	Richard Quick	661	Florida	542½
1989	Stanford	Richard Quick	610½	Texas	547
1990	Texas	Mark Schubert	632	Stanford	622½
1991	Texas	Mark Schubert	746	Stanford	653
1992	Stanford	Richard Quick	735½	Texas	651
1993	Stanford	Richard Quick	649½	Florida	421
1994	Stanford	Richard Quick	512	Texas	421
1995	Stanford	Richard Quick	497½	Michigan	478½
1996	Stanford	Richard Quick	478	SMU	397
1997	Southern Cal	Mark Schubert	406	Stanford	395
1998	Stanford	Richard Quick	422	Arizona	378
1999	Georgia	Jack Bauerle	504½	Stanford	441
2000	Georgia	Jack Bauerle	490½	Arizona	472

DIVISION II

Year	Champion	Year	Champion	Year	Champion
1982	Cal St-Northridge	1989	Cal St-Northridge	1996	Air Force
1983	Clarion	1990	Oakland (MI)	1997	Drury
1984	Clarion	1991	Oakland (MI)	1998	Drury
1985	S Florida	1992	Oakland (MI)	1999	Drury
1986	Clarion	1993	Oakland (MI)	2000	Drury
1987	Cal St-Northridge	1994	Oakland (MI)		
1988	Cal St-Northridge	1995	Air Force		

DIVISION III

Year	Champion	Year	Champion	Year	Champion
1982	Williams	1989	Kenyon	1996	Kenyon
1983	Williams	1990	Kenyon	1997	Kenyon
1984	Kenyon	1991	Kenyon	1998	Kenyon
1985	Kenyon	1992	Kenyon	1999	Kenyon
1986	Kenyon	1993	Kenyon	2000	Kenyon
1987	Kenyon	1994	Kenyon		
1988	Kenyon	1995	Kenyon		

Tennis

Men

INDIVIDUAL CHAMPIONS 1883–1945

Year	Champion	Year	Champion
1883	Joseph Clark, Harvard (spring)	1914	George Church, Princeton
1883	Howard Taylor, Harvard (fall)	1915	Richard Williams II, Harvard
1884	W.P. Knapp, Yale	1916	G. Colket Caner, Harvard
1885	W.P. Knapp, Yale	1917–18	No tournament
1886	G.M. Brinley, Trinity (CT)	1919	Charles Garland, Yale
1887	P.S. Sears, Harvard	1920	Lascelles Banks, Yale
1888	P.S. Sears, Harvard	1921	Philip Neer, Stanford
1889	R.P. Huntington Jr, Yale	1922	Lucien Williams, Yale
1890	Fred Hovey, Harvard	1923	Carl Fischer, Philadelphia Osteo
1891	Fred Hovey, Harvard	1924	Wallace Scott, Washington
1892	William Larned, Cornell	1925	Edward Chandler, California
1893	Malcolm Chace, Brown	1926	Edward Chandler, California
1894	Malcolm Chace, Yale	1927	Wilmer Allison, Texas
1895	Malcolm Chace, Yale	1928	Julius Seligson, Lehigh
1896	Malcolm Whitman, Harvard	1929	Berkeley Bell, Texas
1897	S.G. Thompson, Princeton	1930	Clifford Sutter, Tulane
1898	Leo Ware, Harvard	1931	Keith Gledhill, Stanford
1899	Dwight Davis, Harvard	1932	Clifford Sutter, Tulane
1900	Raymond Little, Princeton	1933	Jack Tidball, UCLA
1901	Fred Alexander, Princeton	1934	Gene Mako, Southern Cal
1902	William Clothier, Harvard	1935	Wilbur Hess, Rice
1903	E.B. Dewhurst, Pennsylvania	1936	Ernest Sutter, Tulane
1904	Robert LeRoy, Columbia	1937	Ernest Sutter, Tulane
1905	E.B. Dewhurst, Pennsylvania	1938	Frank Guernsey, Rice
1906	Robert LeRoy, Columbia	1939	Frank Guernsey, Rice
1907	G. Peabody Gardner Jr, Harvard	1940	Donald McNeil, Kenyon
1908	Nat Niles, Harvard	1941	Joseph Hunt, Navy
1909	Wallace Johnson, Pennsylvania	1942	Frederick Schroeder Jr, Stanford
1910	R.A. Holden Jr, Yale	1943	Pancho Segura, Miami (FL)
1911	E.H. Whitney, Harvard	1944	Pancho Segura, Miami (FL)
1912	George Church, Princeton	1945	Pancho Segura, Miami (FL)
1913	Richard Williams II, Harvard		

DIVISION I

Year	Champion	Coach	Pts	Runner-Up	Pts	Individual Champion
1946	Southern Cal	William Moyle	9	William & Mary	6	Robert Falkenburg, Southern Cal
1947	William & Mary	Sharvey G. Umbeck	10	Rice	4	Gardner Larned, William & Mary
1948	William & Mary	Sharvey G. Umbeck	6	San Francisco	5	Harry Likas, San Francisco
1949	San Francisco	Norman Brooks	7	Rollins/Tulane/ Washington	4	Jack Tuero, Tulane
1950	UCLA	William Ackerman	11	California	5	Herbert Flam, UCLA
				Southern Cal	5	
1951	Southern Cal	Louis Wheeler	9	Cincinnati	7	Tony Trabert, Cincinnati
1952	UCLA	J.D. Morgan	11	California	5	Hugh Stewart, Southern Cal
				Southern Cal	5	
1953	UCLA	J.D. Morgan	11	California	6	Hamilton Richardson, Tulane
1954	UCLA	J.D. Morgan	15	Southern Cal	10	Hamilton Richardson, Tulane
1955	Southern Cal	George Toley	12	Texas	7	Jose Aguero, Tulane
1956	UCLA	J.D. Morgan	15	Southern Cal	14	Alejandro Olmedo, Southern Cal
1957	Michigan	William Murphy	10	Tulane	9	Barry MacKay, Michigan
1958	Southern Cal	George Toley	13	Stanford	9	Alejandro Olmedo, Southern Cal
1959	Notre Dame	Thomas Fallon	8			Whitney Reed, San Jose St
	Tulane	Emmet Pare	8			
1960	UCLA	J.D. Morgan	18	Southern Cal	8	Larry Nagler, UCLA
1961	UCLA	J.D. Morgan	17	Southern Cal	16	Allen Fox, UCLA
1962	Southern Cal	George Toley	22	UCLA	12	Rafael Osuna, Southern Cal
1963	Southern Cal	George Toley	27	UCLA	19	Dennis Ralston, Southern Cal
1964	Southern Cal	George Toley	26	UCLA	25	Dennis Ralston, Southern Cal
1965	UCLA	J.D. Morgan	31	Miami (FL)	13	Arthur Ashe, UCLA
1966	Southern Cal	George Toley	27	UCLA	23	Charles Pasarell, UCLA
1967	Southern Cal	George Toley	28	UCLA	23	Bob Lutz, Southern Cal
1968	Southern Cal	George Toley	31	Rice	23	Stan Smith, Southern Cal
1969	Southern Cal	George Toley	35	UCLA	23	Joaquin Loyo-Mayo, Southern Cal
1970	UCLA	Glenn Bassett	26	Trinity (TX)	22	Jeff Borowiak, UCLA
				Rice	22	

Men (Cont.)
DIVISION I (Cont.)

Year	Champion	Coach		Runner-Up		Individual Champion
1971	UCLA	Glenn Bassett	35	Trinity (TX)	27	Jimmy Connors, UCLA
1972	Trinity (TX)	Clarence Mabry	36	Stanford	30	Dick Stockton, Trinity (TX)
1973	Stanford	Dick Gould	33	Southern Cal	28	Alex Mayer, Stanford
1974	Stanford	Dick Gould	30	Southern Cal	25	John Whitlinger, Stanford
1975	UCLA	Glenn Bassett	27	Miami (FL)	20	Bill Martin, UCLA
1976	Southern Cal	George Toley	21			Bill Scanlon, Trinity (TX)
	UCLA	Glenn Bassett	21			
1977	Stanford	Dick Gould		Trinity (TX)		Matt Mitchell, Stanford
1978	Stanford	Dick Gould		UCLA		John McEnroe, Stanford
1979	UCLA	Glenn Bassett		Trinity (TX)		Kevin Curren, Texas
1980	Stanford	Dick Gould		California		Robert Van't Hof, Southern Cal
1981	Stanford	Dick Gould		UCLA		Tim Mayotte, Stanford
1982	UCLA	Glenn Bassett		Pepperdine		Mike Leach, Michigan
1983	Stanford	Dick Gould		SMU		Greg Holmes, Utah
1984	UCLA	Glenn Bassett		Stanford		Mikael Pernfors, Georgia
1985	Georgia	Dan Magill		UCLA		Mikael Pernfors, Georgia
1986	Stanford	Dick Gould		Pepperdine		Dan Goldie, Stanford
1987	Georgia	Dan Magill		UCLA		Andrew Burrow, Miami (FL)
1988	Stanford	Dick Gould		Louisiana St		Robby Weiss, Pepperdine
1989	Stanford	Dick Gould		Georgia		Donni Leaycraft, Louisiana St
1990	Stanford	Dick Gould		Tennessee		Steve Bryan, Texas
1991	Southern Cal	Dick Leach		Georgia		Jared Palmer, Stanford
1992	Stanford	Dick Gould		Notre Dame		Alex O'Brien, Stanford
1993	Southern Cal	Dick Leach		Georgia		Chris Woodruff, Tennessee
1994	Southern Cal	Dick Leach		Stanford		Mark Merklein, Florida
1995	Stanford	Dick Gould		Mississippi		Sargis Sargsian, Arizona St
1996	Stanford	Dick Gould		UCLA		Cecil Mamiit, Southern Cal
1997	Stanford	Dick Gould		Georgia		Luke Smith, UNLV
1998	Stanford	Dick Gould		Georgia		Bob Bryan, Stanford
1999	Georgia	Manuel Diaz		UCLA		Jeff Morrison, Florida
2000	Stanford	Dick Gould		Va.-Commonwealth		Alex Kim, Stanford

Note: Prior to 1977, individual wins counted in the team's total points. In 1977, a dual-match single-elimination team championship was initiated, eliminating the point system.

DIVISION II

Year	Champion	Year	Champion	Year	Champion
1963	Cal St-LA	1976	Hampton	1989	Hampton
1964	Cal St-LA/S Illinois	1977	UC-Irvine	1990	Cal Poly-SLO
1965	Cal St-LA	1978	SIU-Edwardsville	1991	Rollins
1966	Rollins	1979	SIU-Edwardsville	1992	UC-Davis
1967	Long Beach St	1980	SIU-Edwardsville	1993	Lander
1968	Fresno St	1981	SIU-Edwardsville	1994	Lander
1969	Cal St-Northridge	1982	SIU-Edwardsville	1995	Lander
1970	UC-Irvine	1983	SIU-Edwardsville	1996	Lander
1971	UC-Irvine	1984	SIU-Edwardsville	1997	Lander
1972	UC-Irvine/ Rollins	1985	Chapman	1998	Lander
1973	UC-Irvine	1986	Cal Poly-SLO	1999	Lander
1974	San Diego	1987	Chapman	2000	Lander
1975	UC-Irvine/San Diego	1988	Chapman		

DIVISION III

Year	Champion	Year	Champion	Year	Champion
1976	Kalamazoo	1984	Redlands	1993	Kalamazoo
1977	Swarthmore	1985	Swarthmore	1994	Washington (MD)
1978	Kalamazoo	1986	Kalamazoo	1995	UC-Santa Cruz
1979	Redlands	1987	Kalamazoo	1996	UC-Santa Cruz
1980	Gustavus Adolphus	1988	Washington & Lee	1997	Washington (MD)
1981	Claremont-M-S	1989	UC-Santa Cruz	1998	UC-Santa Cruz
	Swarthmore	1990	Swarthmore	1999	Williams
1982	Gustavus Adolphus	1991	Kalamazoo	2000	Trinity
1983	Redlands	1992	Kalamazoo		

Women
DIVISION I

Year	Champion	Coach	Runner-Up	Individual Champion
1982	Stanford	Frank Brennan	UCLA	Alycia Moulton, Stanford
1983	Southern Cal	Dave Borelli	Trinity (TX)	Beth Herr, Southern Cal
1984	Stanford	Frank Brennan	Southern Cal	Lisa Spain, Georgia
1985	Southern Cal	Dave Borelli	Miami (FL)	Linda Gates, Stanford
1986	Stanford	Frank Brennan	Southern Cal	Patty Fendick, Stanford
1987	Stanford	Frank Brennan	Georgia	Patty Fendick, Stanford
1988	Stanford	Frank Brennan	Florida	Shaun Stafford, Florida
1989	Stanford	Frank Brennan	UCLA	Sandra Birch, Stanford
1990	Stanford	Frank Brennan	Florida	Debbie Graham, Stanford
1991	Stanford	Frank Brennan	UCLA	Sandra Birch, Stanford
1992	Florida	Andy Brandi	Texas	Lisa Raymond, Florida
1993	Texas	Jeff Moore	Stanford	Lisa Raymond, Florida
1994	Georgia	Jeff Wallace	Stanford	Angela Lettiere, Georgia
1995	Texas	Jeff Moore	Florida	Keri Phebus, UCLA
1996	Florida	Andy Brandi	Stanford	Jill Craybas, Florida
1997	Stanford	Frank Brennan	Florida	Lilia Osterloh, Stanford
1998	Florida	Andy Brandi	Duke	Vanessa Webb, Duke
1999	Stanford	Frank Brennan	Florida	Zuzana Lesenarova, UC-SD
2000	Georgia	Jeff Wallace	Stanford	Laura Granville, Stanford

DIVISION II

Year	Champion	Year	Champion	Year	Champion
1982	Cal St-Northridge	1989	SIU-Edwardsville	1996	Armstrong St
1983	TN-Chattanooga	1990	UC-Davis	1997	Lynn
1984	TN-Chattanooga	1991	Cal Poly-Pomona	1998	Lynn
1985	TN-Chattanooga	1992	Cal Poly-Pomona	1999	BYU-Hawaii
1986	SIU-Edwardsville	1993	UC-Davis	2000	BYU-Hawaii
1987	SIU-Edwardsville	1994	N Florida		
1988	SIU-Edwardsville	1995	Armstrong St		

DIVISION III

Year	Champion	Year	Champion	Year	Champion
1982	Occidental	1989	UC-San Diego	1996	Emory
1983	Principia	1990	Gustavus Adolphus	1997	Kenyon
1984	Davidson	1991	Mary Washington	1998	Kenyon
1985	UC-San Diego	1992	Pomona-Pitzer	1999	Amherst
1986	Trenton St	1993	Kenyon	2000	Trinity
1987	UC-San Diego	1994	UC-San Diego		
1988	Mary Washington	1995	Kenyon		

Indoor Track and Field

Men
DIVISION I

Year	Champion	Coach	Pts	Runner-Up	Pts
1965	Missouri	Tom Botts	14	Oklahoma St	12
1966	Kansas	Bob Timmons	14	Southern Cal	13
1967	Southern Cal	Vern Wolfe	26	Oklahoma	17
1968	Villanova	Jim Elliott	35	Southern Cal	25
1969	Kansas	Bob Timmons	41½	Villanova	33
1970	Kansas	Bob Timmons	27½	Villanova	26
1971	Villanova	Jim Elliott	22	UTEP	19¼
1972	Southern Cal	Vern Wolfe	19	Bowling Green/ Mich St	18
1973	Manhattan	Fred Dwyer	18	Kansas/Kent St/UTEP	12
1974	UTEP	Ted Banks	19	Colorado	18
1975	UTEP	Ted Banks	36	Kansas	17½
1976	UTEP	Ted Banks	23	Villanova	15
1977	Washington St	John Chaplin	25½	UTEP	25
1978	UTEP	Ted Banks	44	Auburn	38
1979	Villanova	Jim Elliott	52	UTEP	51
1980	UTEP	Ted Banks	76	Villanova	42
1981	UTEP	Ted Banks	76	SMU	51

Men *(Cont.)*
DIVISION I *(Cont.)*

Year	Champion	Coach	Pts	Runner-Up	Pts
1982	UTEP	John Wedel	67	Arkansas	30
1983	SMU	Ted McLaughlin	43	Villanova	32
1984	Arkansas	John McDonnell	38	Washington St	28
1985	Arkansas	John McDonnell	70	Tennessee	29
1986	Arkansas	John McDonnell	49	Villanova	22
1987	Arkansas	John McDonnell	39	SMU	31
1988	Arkansas	John McDonnell	34	Illinois	29
1989	Arkansas	John McDonnell	34	Florida	31
1990	Arkansas	John McDonnell	44	Texas A&M	36
1991	Arkansas	John McDonnell	34	Georgetown	27
1992	Arkansas	John McDonnell	53	Clemson	46
1993	Arkansas	John McDonnell	66	Clemson	30
1994	Arkansas	John McDonnell	83	UTEP	45
1995	Arkansas	John McDonnell	59	GMU/Tennessee	26
1996	George Mason	John Cook	39	Nebraska	31½
1997	Arkansas	John McDonnell	59	Auburn	27
1998	Arkansas	John McDonnell	56	Stanford	36½
1999	Arkansas	John McDonnell	65	Stanford	42½
2000	Arkansas	John McDonnell	69½	Stanford	52

DIVISION II

Year	Champion	Year	Champion	Year	Champion
1985	SE Missouri St	1991	St. Augustine's	1997	Abilene Christian
1986	not held	1992	St. Augustine's	1998	Abilene Christian
1987	St. Augustine's	1993	Abilene Christian	1999	Abilene Christian
1988	Abil. Christian/ St. August.	1994	Abilene Christian	2000	Abilene Christian
1989	St. Augustine's	1995	St. Augustine's		
1990	St. Augustine's	1996	Abilene Christian		

DIVISION III

Year	Champion	Year	Champion	Year	Champion
1985	St. Thomas (MN)	1991	WI-La Crosse	1997	WI-La Crosse
1986	Frostburg St	1992	WI-La Crosse	1998	Lincoln (PA)
1987	WI-La Crosse	1993	WI-La Crosse	1999	Lincoln (PA)
1988	WI-La Crosse	1994	WI-La Crosse	2000	Lincoln (PA)
1989	N Central	1995	Lincoln (PA)		
1990	Lincoln (PA)	1996	Lincoln (PA)		

Women
DIVISION I

Year	Champion	Coach	Pts	Runner-Up	Pts
1983	Nebraska	Gary Pepin	47	Tennessee	44
1984	Nebraska	Gary Pepin	59	Tennessee	48
1985	Florida St	Gary Winckler	34	Texas	32
1986	Texas	Terry Crawford	31	Southern Cal	26
1987	Louisiana St	Loren Seagrave	49	Tennessee	30
1988	Texas	Terry Crawford	71	Villanova	52
1989	Louisiana St	Pat Henry	61	Villanova	34
1990	Texas	Terry Crawford	50	Wisconsin	26
1991	Louisiana St	Pat Henry	48	Texas	39
1992	Florida	Bev Kearney	50	Stanford	26
1993	Louisiana St	Pat Henry	49	Wisconsin	44
1994	Louisiana St	Pat Henry	48	Alabama	29
1995	Louisiana St	Pat Henry	40	UCLA	37
1996	Louisiana St	Pat Henry	52	Georgia	34
1997	Louisiana St	Pat Henry	49	Texas/ Wisconsin	39
1998	Texas	Bev Kearney	60	Louisiana St	30
1999	Texas	Bev Kearney	61	Louisiana St	57
2000	UCLA	Jeanette Bolden	51	S Carolina	41

Women (Cont.)

DIVISION II

Year	Champion	Year	Champion	Year	Champion
1985	St. Augustine's	1991	Abilene Christian	1997	Abilene Christian
1986	not held	1992	Alabama A&M	1998	Abilene Christian
1987	St. Augustine's	1993	Abilene Christian	1999	Abilene Christian
1988	Abilene Christian	1994	Abilene Christian	2000	Abilene Christian
1989	Abilene Christian	1995	Abilene Christian		
1990	Abilene Christian	1996	Abilene Christian		

DIVISION III

Year	Champion	Year	Champion	Year	Champion
1985	MA-Boston	1991	Cortland St	1997	Christopher Newport
1986	MA-Boston	1992	Christopher Newport	1998	Christopher Newport
1987	MA-Boston	1993	Lincoln (PA)	1999	Wheaton (MA)
1988	Christopher Newport	1994	WI-Oshkosh	2000	Wheaton (MA)
1989	Christopher Newport	1995	WI-Oshkosh		
1990	Christopher Newport	1996	WI-Oshkosh		

Outdoor Track and Field

Men

DIVISION I

Year	Champion	Coach	Pts	Runner-Up	Pts
1921	Illinois	Harry Gill	20†	Notre Dame	16†
1922	California	Walter Christie	28†	Penn St	19†
1923	Michigan	Stephen Farrell	29†	Mississippi St	16
1924	No meet				
1925	Stanford*	R. L. Templeton	31†		
1926	Southern Cal*	Dean Cromwell	27†		
1927	Illinois*	Harry Gill	35†		
1928	Stanford	R. L. Templeton	72	Ohio St	31
1929	Ohio St	Frank Castleman	50	Washington	42
1930	Southern Cal	Dean Cromwell	55†	Washington	40
1931	Southern Cal	Dean Cromwell	77†	Ohio St	31†
1932	Indiana	Billy Hayes	56	Ohio St	49†
1933	Louisiana St	Bernie Moore	58	Southern Cal	54
1934	Stanford	R. L. Templeton	63	Southern Cal	54†
1935	Southern Cal	Dean Cromwell	74†	Ohio St	40†
1936	Southern Cal	Dean Cromwell	103†	Ohio St	73
1937	Southern Cal	Dean Cromwell	62	Stanford	50
1938	Southern Cal	Dean Cromwell	67†	Stanford	38
1939	Southern Cal	Dean Cromwell	86	Stanford	44†
1940	Southern Cal	Dean Cromwell	47	Stanford	28†
1941	Southern Cal	Dean Cromwell	81†	Indiana	50
1942	Southern Cal	Dean Cromwell	85†	Ohio St	44†
1943	Southern Cal	Dean Cromwell	46	California	39
1944	Illinois	Leo Johnson	79	Notre Dame	43
1945	Navy	E.J. Thomson	62	Illinois	48†
1946	Illinois	Leo Johnson	78	Southern Cal	42†
1947	Illinois	Leo Johnson	59†	Southern Cal	34†
1948	Minnesota	James Kelly	46	Southern Cal	41†
1949	Southern Cal	Jess Hill	55†	UCLA	31
1950	Southern Cal	Jess Hill	49†	Stanford	28
1951	Southern Cal	Jess Mortenson	56	Cornell	40
1952	Southern Cal	Jess Mortenson	66†	San Jose St	24†
1953	Southern Cal	Jess Mortenson	80	Illinois	41
1954	Southern Cal	Jess Mortenson	66†	Illinois	31†
1955	Southern Cal	Jess Mortenson	42	UCLA	34
1956	UCLA	Elvin Drake	55†	Kansas	51
1957	Villanova	James Elliott	47	California	32
1958	Southern Cal	Jess Mortenson	48†	Kansas	40†
1959	Kansas	Bill Easton	73	San Jose St	48
1960	Kansas	Bill Easton	50	Southern Cal	37

Men (Cont.)

DIVISION I (Cont.)

Year	Champion	Coach	Pts	Runner-Up	Pts
1961	Southern Cal	Jess Mortenson	65	Oregon	47
1962	Oregon	William Bowerman	85	Villanova	40†
1963	Southern Cal	Vern Wolfe	61	Stanford	42
1964	Oregon	William Bowerman	70	San Jose St	40
1965	Oregon	William Bowerman	32		
	Southern Cal	Vern Wolfe	32		
1966	UCLA	Jim Bush	81	Brigham Young	33
1967	Southern Cal	Vern Wolfe	86	Oregon	40
1968	Southern Cal	Vern Wolfe	58	Washington St	57
1969	San Jose St	Bud Winter	48	Kansas	45
1970	Brigham Young	Clarence Robison	35		
	Kansas	Bob Timmons	35		
	Oregon	William Bowerman	35		
1971	UCLA	Jim Bush	52	Southern Cal	41
1972	UCLA	Jim Bush	82	Southern Cal	49
1973	UCLA	Jim Bush	56	Oregon	31
1974	Tennessee	Stan Huntsman	60	UCLA	56
1975	UTEP	Ted Banks	55	UCLA	42
1976	Southern Cal	Vern Wolfe	64	UTEP	44
1977	Arizona St	Senon Castillo	64	UTEP	50
1978	UCLA/UTEP	Jim Bush/Ted Banks	50		
1979	UTEP	Ted Banks	64	Villanova	48
1980	UTEP	Ted Banks	69	UCLA	46
1981	UTEP	Ted Banks	70	SMU	57
1982	UTEP	John Wedel	105	Tennessee	94
1983	SMU	Ted McLaughlin	104	Tennessee	102
1984	Oregon	Bill Dellinger	113	Washington St	94½
1985	Arkansas	John McDonnell	61	Washington St	46
1986	SMU	Ted McLaughlin	53	Washington St	52
1987	UCLA	Bob Larsen	81	Texas	28
1988	UCLA	Bob Larsen	82	Texas	41
1989	Louisiana St	Pat Henry	53	Texas A&M	51
1990	Louisiana St	Pat Henry	44	Arkansas	36
1991	Tennessee	Doug Brown	51	Washington St	42
1992	Arkansas	John McDonnell	60	Tennessee	46½
1993	Arkansas	John McDonnell	69	LSU/Ohio St	45
1994	Arkansas	John McDonnell	83	UTEP	45
1995	Arkansas	John McDonnell	61½	UCLA	55
1996	Arkansas	John McDonnell	55	George Mason	40
1997	Arkansas	John McDonnell	55	Texas	42½
1998	Arkansas	John McDonnell	58½	Stanford	51
1999	Arkansas	John McDonnell	59	Stanford	52
2000	Stanford	Vin Lananna	72	Arkansas	59

*Unofficial championship. †Fraction of a point.

DIVISION II

Year	Champion	Year	Champion	Year	Champion
1963	MD-Eastern Shore	1976	UC-Irvine	1990	St. Augustine's
1964	Fresno St	1977	Cal St-Hayward	1991	St. Augustine's
1965	San Diego St	1978	Cal St-LA	1992	St. Augustine's
1966	San Diego St	1979	Cal Poly-SLO	1993	St. Augustine's
1967	Long Beach St	1980	Cal Poly-SLO	1994	St. Augustine's
1968	Cal Poly-SLO	1981	Cal Poly-SLO	1995	St. Augustine's
1969	Cal Poly-SLO	1982	Abilene Christian	1996	Abilene Christian
1970	Cal Poly-SLO	1983	Abilene Christian	1997	Abilene Christian
1971	Kentucky St	1984	Abilene Christian	1998	St. Augustine's
1972	Eastern Michigan	1985	Abilene Christian	1999	Abilene Christian
1973	Norfolk St	1986	Abilene Christian	2000	Abilene Christian
1974	Eastern Illinois	1987	Abilene Christian		
	Norfolk St	1988	Abilene Christian		
1975	Cal St-Northridge	1989	St. Augustine's		

Men *(Cont.)*

DIVISION III

Year	Champion	Year	Champion	Year	Champion
1974	Ashland	1983	Glassboro St	1992	WI-La Crosse
1975	Southern-N Orleans	1984	Glassboro St	1993	WI-La Crosse
1976	Southern-N Orleans	1985	Lincoln (PA)	1994	N Central
1977	Southern-N Orleans	1986	Frostburg St	1995	Lincoln (PA)
1978	Occidental	1987	Frostburg St	1996	Lincoln (PA)
1979	Slippery Rock	1988	WI-La Crosse	1997	WI-La Crosse
1980	Glassboro St	1989	N Central	1998	N Central
1981	Glassboro St	1990	Lincoln (PA)	1999	Lincoln (PA)
1982	Glassboro St	1991	WI-La Crosse	2000	Nebraska Wesleyan

Women

DIVISION I

Year	Champion	Coach	Pts	Runner-Up	Pts
1982	UCLA	Scott Chisam	153	Tennessee	126
1983	UCLA	Scott Chisam	116½	Florida St	108
1984	Florida St	Gary Winckler	145	Tennessee	124
1985	Oregon	Tom Heinonen	52	Florida St/LSU	46
1986	Texas	Terry Crawford	65	Alabama	55
1987	Louisiana St	Loren Seagrave	62	Alabama	53
1988	Louisiana St	Loren Seagrave	61	UCLA	58
1989	Louisiana St	Pat Henry	86	UCLA	47
1990	Louisiana St	Pat Henry	53	UCLA	46
1991	Louisiana St	Pat Henry	78	Texas	67
1992	Louisiana St	Pat Henry	87	Florida	81
1993	Louisiana St	Pat Henry	93	Wisconsin	44
1994	Louisiana St	Pat Henry	86	Texas	43
1995	Louisiana St	Pat Henry	69	UCLA	58
1996	Louisiana St	Pat Henry	81	Texas	52
1997	Louisiana St	Pat Henry	63	Texas	62
1998	Texas	Bev Kearney	60	UCLA	55
1999	Texas	Bev Kearney	62	UCLA	60
2000	Louisiana St	Pat Henry	59	Southern Cal	56

DIVISION II

Year	Champion	Year	Champion	Year	Champion
1982	Cal Poly-SLO	1989	Cal Poly-SLO	1996	Abilene Christian
1983	Cal Poly-SLO	1990	Cal Poly-SLO	1997	St. Augustine
1984	Cal Poly-SLO	1991	Cal Poly-SLO	1998	Abilene Christian
1985	Abilene Christian	1992	Alabama A&M	1999	Abilene Christian
1986	Abilene Christian	1993	Alabama A&M	2000	St. Augustine
1987	Abilene Christian	1994	Alabama A&M		
1988	Abilene Christian	1995	Abilene Christian		

DIVISION III

Year	Champion	Year	Champion	Year	Champion
1982	Central (IA)	1989	Chris. Newport	1996	WI-Oshkosh
1983	WI-La Crosse	1990	WI-Oshkosh	1997	WI-Oshkosh
1984	WI-La Crosse	1991	WI-Oshkosh	1998	Chris. Newport
1985	Cortland St	1992	Chris. Newport	1999	Lincoln (PA)
1986	MA-Boston	1993	Lincoln (PA)	2000	Lincoln (PA)
1987	Chris. Newport	1994	Chris. Newport		
1988	Chris. Newport	1995	WI-Oshkosh		

Volleyball

Men

Year	Champion	Coach	Score	Runner-Up	Most Outstanding Player
1970	UCLA	Al Scates	3-0	Long Beach St	Dane Holtzman, UCLA
1971	UCLA	Al Scates	3-0	UC-Santa Barbara	Kirk Kilgore, UCLA
					Tim Bonynge, UC-Santa Barbara
1972	UCLA	Al Scates	3-2	San Diego St	Dick Irvin, UCLA

Men (Cont.)

Year	Champion	Coach	Score	Runner-Up	Most Outstanding Player
1973	San Diego St	Jack Henn	3–1	Long Beach St	Duncan McFarland, San Diego St
1974	UCLA	Al Scates	3–2	UC-Santa Barbara	Bob Leonard, UCLA
1975	UCLA	Al Scates	3–1	UC-Santa Barbara	John Bekins, UCLA
1976	UCLA	Al Scates	3–0	Pepperdine	Joe Mika, UCLA
1977	Southern Cal	Ernie Hix	3–1	Ohio St	Celso Kalache, Southern Cal
1978	Pepperdine	Marv Dunphy	3–2	UCLA	Mike Blanchard, Pepperdine
1979	UCLA	Al Scates	3–1	Southern Cal	Sinjin Smith, UCLA
1980	Southern Cal	Ernie Hix	3–1	UCLA	Dusty Dvorak, Southern Cal
1981	UCLA	Al Scates	3–2	Southern Cal	Karch Kiraly, UCLA
1982	UCLA	Al Scates	3–0	Penn St	Karch Kiraly, UCLA
1983	UCLA	Al Scates	3–0	Pepperdine	Ricci Luyties, UCLA
1984	UCLA	Al Scates	3–1	Pepperdine	Ricci Luyties, UCLA
1985	Pepperdine	Marv Dunphy	3–1	Southern Cal	Bob Ctvrtlik, Pepperdine
1986	Pepperdine	Rod Wilde	3–2	Southern Cal	Steve Friedman, Pepperdine
1987	UCLA	Al Scates	3–0	Southern Cal	Ozzie Volstad, UCLA
1988	Southern Cal	Bob Yoder	3–2	UC-Santa Barbara	Jen-Kai Liu, Southern Cal
1989	UCLA	Al Scates	3–1	Stanford	Matt Sonnichsen, UCLA
1990	Southern Cal	Jim McLaughlin	3–1	Long Beach St	Bryan Ivie, Southern Cal
1991	Long Beach St	Ray Ratelle	3–1	Southern Cal	Brent Hilliard, Long Beach St
1992	Pepperdine	Marv Dunphy	3–0	Stanford	Alon Grinberg, Pepperdine
1993	UCLA	Al Scates	3–0	Cal St-Northridge	Mike Sealy/Jeff Nygaard, UCLA
1994	Penn St	Tom Peterson	3–2	UCLA	Ramon Hernandez, Penn St
1995	UCLA	Al Scates	3–0	Penn St	Jeff Nygaard, UCLA
1996	UCLA	Al Scates	3–2	Hawaii	Yuval Katz, Hawaii
1997	Stanford	Ruben Nieves	3–2	UCLA	Mike Lambert, Stanford
1998	UCLA	Al Scates	3–2	Pepperdine	George Roumain, Pepperdine
1999	Brigham Young	Carl McGown	3–0	Long Beach St	Ossie Antonetti, Brigham Young
2000	UCLA	Al Scates	3–0	Ohio St	Brandon Taliaferro, UCLA

Women

DIVISION I

Year	Champion	Coach	Score	Runner-Up
1981	Southern Cal	Chuck Erbe	3–2	UCLA
1982	Hawaii	Dave Shoji	3–2	Southern Cal
1983	Hawaii	Dave Shoji	3–0	UCLA
1984	UCLA	Andy Banachowski	3–2	Stanford
1985	Pacific	John Dunning	3–1	Stanford
1986	Pacific	John Dunning	3–0	Nebraska
1987	Hawaii	Dave Shoji	3–1	Stanford
1988	Texas	Mick Haley	3–0	Hawaii
1989	Long Beach St	Brian Gimmillaro	3–0	Nebraska
1990	UCLA	Andy Banachowski	3–0	Pacific
1991	UCLA	Andy Banachowski	3–2	Long Beach St
1992	Stanford	Don Shaw	3–1	UCLA
1993	Long Beach St	Brian Gimmillaro	3–1	Penn St
1994	Stanford	Don Shaw	3–1	UCLA
1995	Nebraska	Terry Pettit	3–1	Texas
1996	Stanford	Don Shaw	3–0	Hawaii
1997	Stanford	Don Shaw	3–2	Penn St
1998	Long Beach St	Brian Gimmillaro	3–2	Penn St
1999	Penn St	Russ Rose	3–0	Stanford

DIVISION II

Year	Champion	Year	Champion	Year	Champion
1981	Cal St-Sacramento	1988	Portland St	1995	Barry
1982	UC-Riverside	1989	Cal St-Bakersfield	1996	Nebraska-Omaha
1983	Cal St-Northridge	1990	West Texas A&M	1997	West Texas A&M
1984	Portland St	1991	West Texas A&M	1998	Hawaii Pacific
1985	Portland St	1992	Portland St	1999	BYU-Hawaii
1986	UC-Riverside	1993	Northern Michigan		
1987	Cal St-Northridge	1994	Northern Michigan		

DIVISION III

Year	Champion	Year	Champion	Year	Champion	Year	Champion
1981	UC-San Diego	1986	UC-San Diego	1991	Washington (MO)	1996	Washington (MO)
1982	La Verne	1987	UC-San Diego	1992	Washington (MO)	1997	UC-San Diego
1983	Elmhurst	1988	UC-San Diego	1993	Washington (MO)	1998	Central (IA)
1984	UC-San Diego	1989	Washington (MO)	1994	Washington (MO)	1999	Central (IA)
1985	Elmhurst	1990	UC-San Diego	1995	Washington (MO)		

Water Polo

Year	Champion	Coach	Score	Runner-Up
1969	UCLA	Bob Horn	5–2	California
1970	UC-Irvine	Ed Newland	7–6 (3 OT)	UCLA
1971	UCLA	Bob Horn	5–3	San Jose St
1972	UCLA	Bob Horn	10–5	UC-Irvine
1973	California	Pete Cutino	8–4	UC-Irvine
1974	California	Pete Cutino	7–6	UC-Irvine
1975	California	Pete Cutino	9–8	UC-Irvine
1976	Stanford	Art Lambert	13–12	UCLA
1977	California	Pete Cutino	8–6	UC-Irvine
1978	Stanford	Dante Dettamanti	7–6 (3 OT)	California
1979	UC-Santa Barbara	Pete Snyder	11–3	UCLA
1980	Stanford	Dante Dettamanti	8–6	California
1981	Stanford	Dante Dettamanti	17–6	Long Beach St
1982	UC-Irvine	Ed Newland	7–4	Stanford
1983	California	Pete Cutino	10–7	Southern Cal
1984	California	Pete Cutino	9–8	Stanford
1985	Stanford	Dante Dettamanti	12–11 (2 OT)	UC-Irvine
1986	Stanford	Dante Dettamanti	9–6	California
1987	California	Pete Cutino	9–8 (OT)	Southern Cal
1988	California	Pete Cutino	14–11	UCLA
1989	UC-Irvine	Ed Newland	9–8	California
1990	California	Steve Heaston	8–7	Stanford
1991	California	Steve Heaston	7–6	UCLA
1992	California	Steve Heaston	12–11	Stanford
1993	Stanford	Dante Dettamanti	11–9	Southern Cal
1994	Stanford	Dante Dettamanti	14–10	Southern Cal
1995	UCLA	Guy Baker	10–8	California
1996	UCLA	Guy Baker	8–7	Southern Cal
1997	Pepperdine	Terry Schroeder	8–7 (OT)	Southern Cal
1998	Southern Cal	John Williams	9–8 (2 OT)	Stanford
1999	UCLA	Guy Baker	6–5	Stanford

Wrestling

DIVISION I

Year	Champion	Coach	Pts	Runner-Up	Pts	Most Outstanding Wrestler
1928	Oklahoma St*	E.C. Gallagher				
1929	Oklahoma St	E.C. Gallagher	26	Michigan	18	
1930	Oklahoma St*	E.C. Gallagher	27	Illinois	14	
1931	Oklahoma St*	E.C. Gallagher		Michigan		
1932	Indiana*	W.H. Thom		Oklahoma St		Edwin Belshaw, Indiana
1933	Oklahoma St*	E.C. Gallagher				Allan Kelley, Oklahoma St
	Iowa St*	Hugo Otopalik				Pat Johnson, Harvard
1934	Oklahoma St	E.C. Gallagher	29	Indiana	19	Ben Bishop, Lehigh
1935	Oklahoma St	E.C. Gallagher	36	Oklahoma	18	Ross Flood, Oklahoma St
1936	Oklahoma	Paul Keen	14	Central St (OK)	10	Wayne Martin, Oklahoma
				Oklahoma St	10	
1937	Oklahoma St	E.C. Gallagher	31	Oklahoma	13	Stanley Henson, Oklahoma St
1938	Oklahoma St	E.C. Gallagher	19	Illinois	15	Joe McDaniels, Oklahoma St
1939	Oklahoma St	E.C. Gallagher	33	Lehigh	12	Dale Hanson, Minnesota
1940	Oklahoma St	E.C. Gallagher	24	Indiana	14	Don Nichols, Michigan
1941	Oklahoma St	Art Griffith	37	Michigan St	26	Al Whitehurst, Oklahoma St
1942	Oklahoma St	Art Griffith	31	Michigan St	26	David Arndt, Oklahoma St
1943–45	No tournament					
1946	Oklahoma St	Art Griffith	25	Northern Iowa	24	Gerald Leeman, Northern Iowa
1947	Cornell	Paul Scott	32	Northern Iowa	19	William Koll, Northern Iowa
1948	Oklahoma St	Art Griffith	33	Michigan St	28	William Koll, Northern Iowa
1949	Oklahoma St	Art Griffith	32	Northern Iowa	27	Charles Hetrick, Oklahoma St
1950	Northern Iowa	David McCuskey	30	Purdue	16	Anthony Gizoni, Waynesburg
1951	Oklahoma	Port Robertson	24	Oklahoma St	23	Walter Romanowski, Cornell
1952	Oklahoma	Port Robertson	22	Northern Iowa	21	Tommy Evans, Oklahoma
1953	Penn St	Charles Speidel	21	Oklahoma	15	Frank Bettucci, Cornell
1954	Oklahoma St	Art Griffith	32	Pittsburgh	17	Tommy Evans, Oklahoma
1955	Oklahoma St	Art Griffith	40	Penn St	31	Edward Eichelberger, Lehigh
1956	Oklahoma St	Art Griffith	65	Oklahoma	62	Dan Hodge, Oklahoma
1957	Oklahoma	Port Robertson	73	Pittsburgh	66	Dan Hodge, Oklahoma
1958	Oklahoma St	Myron Roderick	77	Iowa St	62	Dick Delgado, Oklahoma
1959	Oklahoma St	Myron Roderick	73	Iowa St	51	Ron Gray, Iowa St
1960	Oklahoma	Thomas Evans	59	Iowa St	40	Dave Auble, Cornell

Wrestling (Cont.)

DIVISION I (Cont.)

Year	Champion	Coach	Pts	Runner-Up	Pts	Most Outstanding Wrestler
1961	Oklahoma St	Myron Roderick	82	Oklahoma	63	E. Gray Simons, Lock Haven
1962	Oklahoma St	Myron Roderick	82	Oklahoma	45	E. Gray Simons, Lock Haven
1963	Oklahoma	Thomas Evans	48	Iowa St	45	Mickey Martin, Oklahoma
1964	Oklahoma St	Myron Roderick	87	Oklahoma	58	Dean Lahr, Colorado
1965	Iowa St	Harold Nichols	87	Oklahoma St	86	Yojiro Uetake, Oklahoma St
1966	Oklahoma St	Myron Roderick	79	Iowa St	70	Yojiro Uetake, Oklahoma St
1967	Michigan St	Grady Peninger	74	Michigan	63	Rich Sanders, Portland St
1968	Oklahoma St	Myron Roderick	81	Iowa St	78	Dwayne Keller, Oklahoma St
1969	Iowa St	Harold Nichols	104	Oklahoma	69	Dan Gable, Iowa St
1970	Iowa St	Harold Nichols	99	Michigan St	84	Larry Owings, Washington
1971	Oklahoma St	Tommy Chesbro	94	Iowa St	66	Darrell Keller, Oklahoma St
1972	Iowa St	Harold Nichols	103	Michigan St	72½	Wade Schalles, Clarion
1973	Iowa St	Harold Nichols	85	Oregon St	72½	Greg Strobel, Oregon St
1974	Oklahoma	Stan Abel	69½	Michigan	67	Floyd Hitchcock, Bloomsburg
1975	Iowa	Gary Kurdelmeier	102	Oklahoma	77	Mike Frick, Lehigh
1976	Iowa	Gary Kurdelmeier	123½	Iowa St	85¾	Chuch Yagla, Iowa
1977	Iowa St	Harold Nichols	95½	Oklahoma St	88¾	Nick Gallo, Hofstra
1978	Iowa	Dan Gable	94½	Iowa St	94	Mark Churella, Michigan
1979	Iowa	Dan Gable	122½	Iowa St	88	Bruce Kinseth, Iowa
1980	Iowa	Dan Gable	110¾	Oklahoma St	87	Howard Harris, Oregon St
1981	Iowa	Dan Gable	129¾	Oklahoma	100¼	Gene Mills, Syracuse
1982	Iowa	Dan Gable	131¾	Iowa St	111	Mark Schultz, Oklahoma
1983	Iowa	Dan Gable	155	Oklahoma St	102	Mike Sheets, Oklahoma St
1984	Iowa	Dan Gable	123¾	Oklahoma St	98	Jim Zalesky, Iowa
1985	Iowa	Dan Gable	145¼	Oklahoma	98½	Barry Davis, Iowa
1986	Iowa	Dan Gable	158	Oklahoma	84¼	Marty Kistler, Iowa
1987	Iowa St	Jim Gibbons	133	Iowa	108	John Smith, Oklahoma St
1988	Arizona St	Bobby Douglas	93	Iowa	85½	Scott Turner, N Carolina St
1989	Oklahoma St	Joe Seay	91¼	Arizona St	70½	Tim Krieger, Iowa St
1990	Oklahoma St	Joe Seay	117¾	Arizona St	104¾	Chris Barnes, Oklahoma St
1991	Iowa	Dan Gable	157	Oklahoma St	108¾	Jeff Prescott, Penn St
1992	Iowa	Dan Gable	149	Oklahoma St	100½	Tom Brands, Iowa
1993	Iowa	Dan Gable	123¾	Penn St	87½	Terry Steiner, Iowa
1994	Oklahoma St	John Smith	94¾	Iowa	76½	Pat Smith, Oklahoma St
1995	Iowa	Dan Gable	134	Oregon St	77½	T.J. Jaworsky, N Carolina
1996	Iowa	Dan Gable	122½	Iowa St	78½	Les Gutches, Oregon St
1997	Iowa	Dan Gable	170	Oklahoma St	113½	Lincoln McIlravy, Iowa
1998	Iowa	Jim Zalesky	115	Minnesota	102	Joe Williams, Iowa
1999	Iowa	Jim Zalesky	100½	Minnesota	98½	Cael Sanderson, Iowa St
2000	Iowa	Jim Zalesky	116	Iowa St	109½	Cael Sanderson, Iowa St

*Unofficial champions.

DIVISION II

Year	Champion
1963	Western St (CO)
1964	Western St (CO)
1965	Mankato St
1966	Cal Poly-SLO
1967	Portland St
1968	Cal Poly-SLO
1969	Cal Poly-SLO
1970	Cal Poly-SLO
1971	Cal Poly-SLO
1972	Cal Poly-SLO
1973	Cal Poly-SLO
1974	Cal Poly-SLO
1975	Northern Iowa
1976	Cal St-Bakersfield
1977	Cal St-Bakersfield
1978	Northern Iowa
1979	Cal St-Bakersfield
1980	Cal St-Bakersfield
1981	Cal St-Bakersfield
1982	Cal St-Bakersfield
1983	Cal St-Bakersfield
1984	SIU-Edwardsville
1985	SIU-Edwardsville
1986	SIU-Edwardsville
1987	Cal St-Bakersfield
1988	N Dakota St
1989	Portland St
1990	Portland St
1991	NE-Omaha
1992	Central Oklahoma
1993	Central Oklahoma
1994	Central Oklahoma
1995	Central Oklahoma
1996	Pittsburgh-Johnstown
1997	San Francisco St
1998	N Dakota St
1999	Pittsburgh-Johnstown
2000	N Dakota St

DIVISION III

Year	Champion
1974	Wilkes
1975	John Carroll
1976	Montclair St
1977	Brockport St
1978	Buffalo
1979	Trenton St
1980	Brockport St
1981	Trenton St
1982	Brockport St
1983	Brockport St
1984	Trenton St
1985	Trenton St
1986	Montclair St
1987	Trenton St
1988	St. Lawrence
1989	Ithaca
1990	Ithaca
1991	Augsburg
1992	Brockport
1993	Augsburg
1994	Ithaca
1995	Augsburg
1996	Wartburg
1997	Augsburg
1998	Augsburg
1999	Wartburg
2000	Augsburg

INDIVIDUAL CHAMPIONSHIP RECORDS

Swimming

Men

Event	Time	Record Holder	Date
50-yard freestyle	19.14	David Fox, N Carolina St	3-25-93
100-yard freestyle	41.80	Matt Biondi, California	4-4-87
200-yard freestyle	1:33.03	Matt Biondi, California	4-3-87
500-yard freestyle	4:08.75	Tom Dolan, Michigan	3-23-95
1650-yard freestyle	14:29.31	Tom Dolan, Michigan	3-25-95
100-yard backstroke	45.25	Neil Walker, Texas	3-28-97
200-yard backstroke	1:40.64	Jeff Rouse, Stanford	3-28-92
100-yard breaststroke	52.32	Jeremy Linn, Tennessee	3-28-97
200-yard breaststroke	1:53.77	Mike Barrowman, Michigan	3-24-90
100-yard butterfly	45.59	Lars Frolander, Southern Methodist	3-28-98
200-yard butterfly	1:41.78	Melvin Stewart, Tennessee	3-30-91
200-yard individual medley	1:43.52	Greg Burgess, Florida	3-25-93
400-yard individual medley	3:38.18	Tom Dolan, Michigan	3-24-95

Women

Event	Time	Record Holder	Date
50-yard freestyle	21.77	Amy Van Dyken, Colorado St	3-18-94
100-yard freestyle	47.61	Jenny Thompson, Stanford	3-21-92
200-yard freestyle	1:43.08	Martina Moravcova, SMU	3-28-97
500-yard freestyle	4:34.39	Janet Evans, Stanford	3-15-90
1650-yard freestyle	15:39.14	Janet Evans, Stanford	3-17-90
100-yard backstroke	52.36	Marylyn Chiang, California	3-19-99
200-yard backstroke	1:52.98	Whitney Hedgepeth, Texas	3-21-87
100-yard breaststroke	59.71	Beata Kaszuba, Arizona St	3-17-95
200-yard breaststroke	2:09.71	Beata Kaszuba, Arizona St	3-18-95
100-yard butterfly	51.34	Misty Hyman, Stanford	3-21-98
200-yard butterfly	1:53.36	Limin Liu, Nevada	3-20-99
200-yard individual medley	1:55.54	Summer Sanders, Stanford	3-19-92
400-yard individual medley	4:02.28	Summer Sanders, Stanford	3-20-92

Note: Records through 1999. In 2000, the NCAA changed length of championship races from yards to meters.

Indoor Track and Field

Men

Event	Mark	Record Holder	Date
55-meter dash	6.00	Lee McRae, Pittsburgh	3-14-86
55-meter hurdles	7.07	Allen Johnson, N Carolina	3-13-92
200-meter dash	20.26	Shawn Crawford, Clemson	3-10-00
400-meter dash	45.69	Roxbert Martin, Oklahoma	3-8-97
800-meter run	1:45.80	Einars Tupuritis, Wichita St	3-9-96
Mile run	3:55.33	Kevin Sullivan, Michigan	3-11-95
3,000-meter run	7:46.03	Adam Goucher, Colorado	3-14-98
5,000-meter run	13:37.94	Jonah Koech, Iowa St	3-9-90
High jump	7 ft 9¼ in	Hollis Conway, SW Louisiana	3-11-89
Pole vault	19 ft 2¼ in	Jacob Davis, Texas	3-6-99
Long jump	27 ft 10 in	Carl Lewis, Houston	3-13-81
Triple jump	56 ft 9½ in	Keith Connor, SMU	3-13-81
Shot put	69 ft 8½ in	Michael Carter, SMU	3-13-81
		Soren Tallhem, Brigham Young	3-9-85
35-pound weight throw	78 ft 3¾ in	Libor Charfreitag, SMU	3-11-00

Indoor Track and Field (Cont.)

Women

Event	Mark	Record Holder	Date
55-meter dash	6.56	Gwen Torrence, Georgia	3-14-87
55-meter hurdles	7.41	Michelle Freeman	3-13-92
		Angie Vaughn, Texas	3-14-98
200-meter dash	22.90	Holly Hyche, Indiana St	3-11-94
400-meter dash	51.05	Maicel Malone, Arizona St	3-9-91
800-meter run	2:01.77	Hazel Clark, Florida	3-5-99
Mile run	4:30.63	Suzy Favor, Wisconsin	3-11-89
3,000-meter run	8:54.98	Stephanie Herbst, Wisconsin	3-15-86
5,000-meter run	15:39.75	Amy Skieresz, Arizona	3-7-97
High jump	6 ft 5½ in	Amy Acuff, UCLA	3-11-95
Pole vault	14 ft 6 in	Tracy O'Hara, UCLA	3-10-00
Long jump	22 ft 1 in	Daphne Saunders, Louisiana St	3-12-94
Triple jump	46 ft 9 in	Suzette Lee, Louisiana St	3-8-97
Shot put	60 ft 5¼ in	Teri Tunks, SMU	3-14-98
20-point weight throw	71 ft 8¾ in	Dawn Ellerbe, S Carolina	3-7-97

Outdoor Track and Field

Men

Event	Mark	Record Holder	Date
100-meter dash	9.92	Ato Bolden, UCLA	6-1-96
200-meter dash	19.87	Lorenzo Daniel, Mississippi St	6-3-88
		John Capel, Florida	6-5-99
400-meter dash	44.00	Quincy Watts, Southern Cal	6-6-92
800-meter run	1:44.70	Mark Everett, Florida	6-1-90
1,500-meter run	3:35.30	Sydney Maree, Villanova	6-6-81
3,000-meter steeplechase	8:12.39	Henry Rono, Washington St	6-1-78
5,000-meter run	13:20.63	Sydney Maree, Villanova	6-2-79
10,000-meter run	28:01.30	Suleiman Nyambui, UTEP	6-1-79
110-meter high hurdles	13.22	Greg Foster, UCLA	6-2-78
400-meter intermediate hurdles	47.85	Kevin Young, UCLA	6-3-88
High jump	7 ft 9¾ in	Hollis Conway, SW Louisiana	6-3-89
Pole vault	19 ft 1 in	Lawrence Johnson, Tennessee	5-29-96
Long jump	28 ft	Erick Walder, Arkansas	6-3-93
Triple jump	57 ft 7¾ in	Keith Connor, SMU	6-5-82
Shot put	72 ft 2¼ in	John Godina, UCLA	6-3-95
Discus throw	220 ft	Kamy Keshmiri, Nevada	6-5-92
Hammer throw	265 ft 3 in	Balazs Kiss, Southern Cal	5-31-96
Javelin throw	268 ft 7 in	Esko Mikkola, Arizona	6-3-98
Decathlon	8279 pts	Tito Steiner, Brigham Young	6-2/3-81

Women

Event	Mark	Record Holder	Date
100-meter dash	10.78	Dawn Sowell, Louisiana St	6-3-89
200-meter dash	22.04	Dawn Sowell, Louisiana St	6-2-89
400-meter dash	50.18	Pauline Davis, Alabama	6-3-89
800-meter run	1:59.11	Suzy Favor, Wisconsin	6-1-90
1,500-meter run	4:08.26	Suzy Favor, Wisconsin	6-2-90
3,000-meter run	8:47.35	Vicki Huber, Villanova	6-3-88
5,000-meter run	15:37.77	Amy Skieresz, Arizona	6-5-98
10,000-meter run	32:28.57	Sylvia Mosqueda, Cal St-Los Angeles	6-1-88
100-meter hurdles	12.70	Tananjalyn Stanley, Louisiana St	6-3-89
400-meter hurdles	54.54	Ryan Tolbert, Vanderbilt	6-6-97
High jump	6 ft 5 in	Amy Acuff, UCLA	6-3-95
Pole vault	14 ft 5¼ in	Tracy O'Hara, UCLA	6-2-00
Long jump	22 ft 9¼ in	Sheila Echols, Louisiana St	6-5-87
Triple jump	46 ft ¾ in	Sheila Hudson, California	6-2-90
Shot put	61 ft 2¼ in	Tressa Thompson, Nebraska	6-4-98
Discus throw	210 ft 10 in	Seilala Sua, UCLA	6-6-99
Hammer throw	211 ft 10 in	Florence Ezah, SMU	5-31-00
Javelin throw	206 ft 9 in	Karin Smith, Cal Poly-SLO	6-4-82
Heptathlon	6527 pts	Diane Guthrie-Gresham, George Mason	6-2/3-95

Olympics

Up-and-Down Under

Despite a sparkling city, genial hosts and spectacular athletes, the Sydney Games were not without their problems

BY HANK HERSCH

HE WAS LITTLE more than a 6'2", 289-pound obstacle for flashlit cameras and binocular-covered eyes at the opening ceremonies of the 2000 Summer Olympics. The 110,000 people at Stadium Australia had come to glimpse greatness, and as the U.S. contingent paraded around the track, the spectators' enhanced vision zoomed from track star Marion Jones to cyclist Lance Armstrong to Dream Team swingman Vince Carter.

Obstructing their view was a huge and obscure figure (crew cut, chubby cheeks, doughy frame) from a distant and obscure locale (a 250-acre dairy farm in Afton, Wyo.), who would be competing in an ancient and obscure sport (Greco-Roman wrestling). But those who gathered in Sydney on Sept. 15 might have paid more attention to Rulon Gardner had they known that in 12 days he would face one of the most intimidating and dominant competitors in the 104-year history of the modern Games.

That legendary athlete was one of the primary objects of many fans' star searches, and he was not difficult to spot. The menacing, mysterious and massive Alexander Karelin carried the flag for Russia, and his credentials as a front man were impossible to dispute. He was 33, had won three Olympic gold medals and was undefeated in international matches during the past 14 years. Steeled by life in frigid Siberia, the chiseled, 6'4", 290-pound Karelin was capable of picking up his superheavyweight opponents, hoisting them over his shoulder and driving them headfirst into the mat. That maneuver, the reverse lift, inspired enough fear of lifelong injury that some of Karelin's opponents would allow themselves to be pinned rather than suffer it.

"You consider this ancient sport and this monumental man who's had a perfect career," said retired U.S. wrestler Jeff Blatnick, who lost to Karelin in 1987, "and the only thing you can say is that he's what Hercules was to the ancient Greeks."

Gardner had tangled with Karelin in 1997, only four years after the American

BOB MARTIN

switched from freestyle wrestling to Greco-Roman. En route to a (literally) crushing 5–0 loss, Gardner was reverse-lifted three times. "I landed so hard," he said, "that the backs of my heels almost came around and touched my head."

So it was that Henry Kissinger, at the behest of IOC president Juan Antonio Samaranch, was on hand at the Sydney Convention Exhibition Centre as Samaranch presented the gold medal after the superheavyweight finals. Not even such skilled diplomats as Samaranch and Kissinger could disguise the motivation behind their choice of venue: Karelin, a member of the Russian parliament, was aiming for his unprecedented fourth Greco-Roman gold; Gardner, a former Nebraska Cornhusker, had as his most distinguished finish a fifth in the 1997 world championships. Early in the second period Gardner took a 1–0 lead when Karelin made the mistake of breaking a hold. No matter. Surely the great Karelin would find a way to snatch the victory.

Growing up, Gardner rose between 4 a.m.

Gardner stunned three-time Olympic champ Karelin, who had not been beaten in 14 years.

and 5 a.m. to heave bales of hay, lug 50-pound irrigation pipes and move stubborn half-ton cows. He had, for all his puffiness, a resolve to match Karelin's: Like the cows on his family's farm, he was not easily budged. No matter what Karelin tried, Gardner held firm, and the score remained 1–0. As the final seconds ticked away, the huge Russian lowered his head in resignation, defeated at last in what could well be his final match.

No, the binoculars at Stadium Australia, no matter how acute, had no way of appreciating Gardner and what he might accomplish. Nor could they have seen a dire threat to American basketball hegemony in the Lithuanian men's team, a group that, in the semifinals, was only a missed three-pointer away from dropping the Dreamers, who went on to win gold. Nor could they have perceived in Norwegian substitute Dagny Mellgran a doubly-gilded performance: Mellgran scored a golden goal in sudden-death overtime of the gold medal match to

SIMON BRUTY

Thorpe's anchor leg in the men's 400 free relay has already entered Olympic legend.

defeat the reigning world and Olympic champion U.S. women's soccer team.

Indeed, there were dozens of athletes who emerged from the anonymity of the opening ceremonies to greatness by the Games' close. Ben Sheets was a 22-year-old righthanded pitcher toiling for the Milwaukee Brewers' Triple-A affiliate before the Olympics. After the Games, he was a hero who had shut out mighty Cuba 4–0 to deliver the Americans the baseball gold medal. Konstadinos Kederis, 27, was mostly unknown outside of Greece before Sydney 2000. After becoming the first Greek man in 104 years—104!—to win a gold medal in track, he is a possible torchbearer for the 2004 Games in Athens. Kederis came out of nowhere to blitz the 200-meter field and win in 20.09.

Australia's 400-meter-runner Cathy Freeman was well known before the Games, and she won the gold in her event, but few could have predicted that the host Aussies would reap a glittering medal count of 58. For a nation of 18 million, that total far exceeded the per capita output of the U.S. (97), Russia (88) and China (59).

Starting with 17-year-old Aussie swimmer Ian Thorpe's brilliant anchor leg to edge the United States for gold in the men's 4 x 100 freestyle relay (an event in which the Americans had never been beaten at the Olympics or the worlds), the 2000 Olympics were rife with astounding performances. Unfortunately they were also marred by astounding mismanagement and, in some cases, outright scandal.

The women's all-around gymnastics finals were irrevocably tainted when officials set the vault too low at the start of that event. The favorite in the all-around, Svetlana Khorkina of Russia, attempted a difficult $1\frac{1}{2}$ forward twist with a half turn on the vault. She landed on her knees, receiving a 9.343 that destroyed any hope of a medal. But shortly after her attempt it was discovered that the vault had been set at the wrong height: five centimeters low. The athletes who had taken their turns before the height was readjusted were given a chance to try again, but Khorkina was too unnerved to bother. After winning a gold in the uneven parallel bars three days later she said, "It will help me to forget that day, which will remain very, very far from me, somewhere perhaps near the North Pole."

Which, judging by the U.S. TV ratings, might as well have been where the 2000 Games were held. Because Sydney is 15

616 OLYMPICS

time zones ahead of the West Coast and 18 ahead of the East, no events of significance took place in U.S. prime time. NBC, which paid $705 million for the rights to the Olympics, decided to show nothing live, and its nightly five-hour package was heavily edited and larded with features. Bad reviews of the predigested coverage only drove ratings further down. NBC Sports president Dick Ebersol had promised a 16.1 rating, but the Games fell well short (8.9). Despite being the most-watched program almost every night for two weeks, the Games were perceived as a flop on the tube. Witness a headline in the satirical paper *The Onion*, IOC: MANY VIEWERS MAY BE USING OLYMPICS-ENHANCING DRUGS.

Drugs—performance-enhancing ones— were the source of the Sydney Games' greatest controversy. Romanian gymnast Andreea Raducan was stripped of the all-around gold medal because a banned ingredient, which she insisted came from her team-doctor–prescribed cold medicine, showed up in her blood. Four other athletes lost medals for more egregious abuses, such as nandrolone, stanozlol and furosemide. A Romanian hammer thrower was escorted off the track as she was about to compete. And 41 would-be Olympians—27 of them from China, which has hopes of hosting the 2008 Games—were caught cheating before they could reach Sydney.

Worse, though, was the shadow that the suspicion of drug use cast over exceptional performances. Even the great Jones was not immune. When it leaked out that her husband, shot-putter C.J. Hunter, had tested positive four times over the summer, some wondered if she was using as well. Jones won a remarkable three golds and two bronzes in Sydney despite the distractions caused by the revelations about her husband, and—as she has throughout her career—tested negative.

The news concerning Hunter, who did not compete because of a knee injury, led to accusations from the IOC that USA Track & Field was covering up doping among its athletes, with 15 positive tests undisclosed. "The Sydney Games," wrote the national newspaper, *The Australian*, "are in danger of being remembered as the Drugs Olympics."

But in the end, the misdeeds and mismeasurements of a few, no matter how flagrant, could not indelibly tarnish the 2000 Games, particularly for those who saw them untaped and unedited in sparkling Sydney. Watching athletes compete under the enormous pressure of the world's gaze makes for a grand spectacle, and no moment packed as much drama as the final of the women's 400-meter run. The home crowd had come to see the favorite, Freeman— Our Cathy—a world champion of Aboriginal descent who had lit the Olympic flame at the opening ceremonies. "There has been no single occasion," wrote *The Sydney Morning Herald*, "when more has been expected of an Australian sportsperson."

With a nation beseeching her, Freeman charged to the finish in 49.11 seconds, outpacing three women who ran personal bests. Michael Johnson, her male counterpart from the U.S., would also live up to his status as a favorite, cruising to an unprecedented second straight 400 title, in 43.84.

For the American women's softball team, the journey was not so easy. The defending champions came to Sydney with a 110-game winning streak, but in round-robin play they hit their first ever three-game losing skid. Ace righthander Lisa Fernandez felt especially snakebitten, fanning 25 batters in 12 2/3 innings against Australia, only to surrender a decisive two-run homer. Following that bitter defeat the players gathered in the shower, in uniform, for a "voodoo cleansing," Fernandez said. "We scrubbed off the evil spirit that was on us." It must have worked: Fernandez blanked the Aussies for 10 innings in the semifinal, then three-hit Japan for a 2–1 victory in the gold medal game.

Such clutch performances had come to be expected of some Olympians, like men's gymnast Alexei Nemov of Russia, 24, who won not only the all-around gold but also four medals on the individual apparatus, boosting his career total to 12. Under the steady hand of five-time Olympic point guard Teresa Edwards—and with the superb inside play of Lisa Leslie—the U.S. women's basketball team went 6–0, flooring the

Toeing the line: Wilkinson made an impressive return from injury to claim gold.

Aussies 76–54 for the gold medal. Cuba's Felix Savon dominated the heavyweight boxing division for his third straight Games, equaling his countryman Teofilo Stevenson's legacy of excellence. And after deciding to retire in 1996 and soon thereafter discovering he had diabetes, 38-year-old Steven Redgrave of Britain won the coxless fours rowing gold medal for the fifth gold of his unsurpassed career.

Each of those competitors deserved the full NBC up-close-and-personal treatment, with the jump cuts and the soft-focus. Perhaps none of them, though, had quite as good a story line as Laura Wilkinson, a 22-year-old platform diver from The Woodlands, Texas. Six months before the Games, Wilkinson broke three toes on her right foot. Still, she practiced her push-offs, standing in her cast on the platform for six hours a day. She entered the final day of the platform competition in fifth place, 60 points behind the leader. On her fourth dive, an inward 2½ somersault that put extreme pressure on her newly healed bones, Wilkinson tried to banish her fears of hitting her head on the tower by thinking of Hilary Grivich, a teammate who had died in a car crash two years earlier. Wilkinson nailed the dive and then watched the competition unravel around her. With a perfectly executed reverse 2½ somersault with a half twist, she won the gold medal on her final dive. The victory made Wilkinson the first American woman since Lesley Bush in 1964 to win gold in the platform.

And then, of course, there was Gardner, who after his upset of Karelin was feted in Sydney and toasted across the U.S. Gardner would turn out to be the perfect symbol for an upside-down summer Down Under, because in the closing ceremonies he was front-and-center in everyone's view, and no one sought to look past him for a brighter star. He was carrying the American flag, and everyone knew who he was.

MANNY MILLAN

2000 Summer Games

TRACK AND FIELD
Men

100 METERS
1. ..Maurice Green, United States — 9.87
2. ..Ato Boldon, Trinidad and Tobago — 9.99
3. ..Obadele Thomoson, Barbados — 10.04

200 METERS
1. ..Konstadinos Kederis, Greece — 20.09
2. ..Darren Campbell, Great Britain — 20.14
3. ..Ato Boldon, Trinidad and Tobago — 20.20

400 METERS
1. ..Michael Johnson, United States — 43.84
2. ..Alvin Harrison, United States — 44.40
3. ..Gregory Haughton, Jamaica — 44.70

800 METERS
1. ..Nils Schumann, Germany — 1:45.08
2. ..Wilson Kipketer, Denmark — 1:45.14
3. ..Aissa Djabir Said-Guerni, Algeria — 1:45.16

1,500 METERS
1. ..Noah Ngeny, Kenya — 3:32.07 OR
2. ..Hicham El Guerrouj, Morocco — 3:32.32
3. ..Bernard Lagat, Kenya — 3:32.44

5,000 METERS
1. ..Millon Wolde, Ethiopia — 13:35.49
2. ..Ali Saidi-Sief, Algeria — 13:36.20
3. ..Brahim Lahlafi, Morocco — 13:36.47

10,000 METERS
1. ..Haile Gebrselassie, Ethiopia — 27:18.20
2. ..Paul Tergat, Kenya — 27:18.29
3. ..Assefa Mezgebu, Ethiopia — 27:19.75

MARATHON
1. ..Geznghe Abera, Ethiopia — 2:10:11
2. ..Eric Wainaina, Kenya — 2:10:31
3. ..Tesfaye Tola, Ethiopia — 2:11:10

110-METER HURDLES
1. ..Anier Garcia, Cuba — 13.00
2. ..Terrence Trammell, United States — 13.16
3. ..Mark Crear, United States — 13.22

400-METER HURDLES
1. ..Angelo Taylor, United States — 47.50
2. ..Hadi Souan Somalyi, Saudi Arabia — 47.53
3. ..Llewelyn Herbert, South Africa — 47.81

3000-METER STEEPLECHASE
1. ..Reuben Kosgei, Kenya — 8:21.43
2. ..Wilson Boit Kipketer, Kenya — 8:21.77
3. ..Ali Ezzine, Morocco — 8:22.15

4 X 100 METER RELAY
1. ...United States: (Jon Drummond, Bernard Williams III, Brian Lewis, Maurice Greene) — .37.61
2. ..Brazil — 37.90
3. ..Cuba — 38.04

4 X 400 METER RELAY
1. ...United States: (Alvin Harrison, Antonio Pettigrew, Calvin Harrison, Michael Johnson) — 2:56.35
2. ..Nigeria — 2:58.68
3. ..Jamaica — 2:58.78

20-KILOMETER WALK
1. ..Robert Korzeniowski, Poland — 1:18:59
2. ..Noe Hernandez, Mexico — 1:19:03
3. ..Vladimir Andreyev. Russia — 1:19:27

50-KILOMETER WALK
1. ..Robert Korzeniowski, Poland — 3:42:22
2. ..Aigars Fadejevs, Latvia — 3:43:40
3. ..Joel Sanchez, Mexico — 3:44:36

HIGH JUMP
1. ..Sergey Kliugin, Russia — 7 ft 8¼ in
2. ..Javier Sotomayor, Cuba — 7 ft 7¼ in
3. ..Abderrahmane Hammad, Algeria — 7 ft 7¼ in

POLE VAULT
1. ..Nick Hysong, United States — 19 ft 4¼ in
2. ..Lawrence Johnson, United States — 19 ft 4¼ in
3. ..Maksim Tarasov, Russia — 19 ft 4¼ in

LONG JUMP
1. ..Ivan Pedroso, Cuba — 28 ft ¾ in
2. ..Jai Taurima, Australia — 27 ft 10¼ in
3. ..Roman Schurenko, Ukraine — 27 ft 3¼ in

TRIPLE JUMP
1. ..Jonathan Edwards, Great Britain — 58 ft 1¼ in
2. ..Yoel Garcia, Cuba — 57 ft 3¾ in
3. ..Denis Kapustin, Russia — 57 ft 3½ in

SHOT PUT
1. ..Arsi Harju, Finland — 69 ft 10¼ in
2. ..Adam Nelson, United States — 69 ft 7 in
3. ..John Godina, United States — 69 ft 6¾ in

DISCUS THROW
1. ..Virgilijus Alekna, Lithuania — 227 ft 4 in
2. ..Lars Riedel, Germany — 224 ft 9 in
3. ..Frantz Kruger, South Africa — 223 ft 8 in

HAMMER THROW
1. ..Szymon Ziolkowski, Poland — 262 ft 6 in
2. ..Nicola Vizzoni, Italy — 261 ft 3 in
3. ..Igor Astapkovich, Belarus — 259 ft 8½ in

JAVELIN
1. ..Jan Zelezny, Czech Republic — 295 ft 9½ in
2. ..Steve Backley, Great Britain — 294 ft 9½ in
3. ..Sergey Makarov, Russia — 290 ft 10½ in

DECATHLON — Pts
1. ..Erki Nool, Estonia — 8641
2. ..Roman Seberle, Czech Republic — 8606
3. ..Chris Huffins, United States — 8595

Note: OR=Olympic record. WR=world record. EOR=equals Olympic record. EWR=equals world record.

TRACK AND FIELD (Cont.)
Women

100 METERS
1. ..Marion Jones, United States — 10.75
2. ..Ekaterini Thanou, Greece — 11.12
3. ..Tanya Lawrence, Jamaica — 11.18

200 METERS
1. ..Marion Jones, United States — 21.84
2. ..P. Davis-Thompson, Bahamas — 22.27
3. ..Susanthika Jayasinghe, Sri Lanka — 22.28

400 METERS
1. ..Cathy Freeman, Australia — 49.11
2. ..Lorraine Graham, Jamaica — 49.58
3. ..Katharine Merry, Great Britain — 49.72

800 METERS
1. ..Maria Mutola, Mozambique — 1:56.15
2. ..Stephanie Graf, Austria — 1:56.64
3. ..Kelly Holmes, Great Britain — 1:56.80

1,500 METERS
1. ..Nouria Merah-Benida, Algeria — 4:05.10
2. ..Violeta Szekely, Romania — 4:05.15
3. ..Gabriela Szabo, Romania — 4:05.27

5,000 METERS
1. ..Gabriela Szabo, Romania — 14:40.79 OR
2. ..Sonia O'Sullivan, Ireland — 14:41.02
3. ..Gete Wami, Ethiopia — 14:42.23

10,000 METERS
1. ..Derartu Tulu, Ethiopia — 30:17.49 OR
2. ..Gete Wami, Ethiopia — 30:22.48
3. ..Fernanda Ribeiro, Portugal — 30:22.88

MARATHON
1. ..Naoko Takahashi, Japan — 2:23:14 OR
2 ...Lidia Simon, Romania — 2:23:22
3. ..Joyce Chepchumba, Kenya — 2:24:45

100-METER HURDLES
1. ..Irina Shishigina, Kazakhstan — 12.65
2. ..Glory Alozie, Nigeria — 12.68
3. ..Melissa Morrison, United States — 12.76

400-METER HURDLES
1. ..Irina Privalova, Russia — 53.02
2. ..Deon Hemmings, Jamaica — 53.45
3. ..Nouza Bidouane, Morocco — 53.57

4 X 100 METER RELAY
1. ..Bahamas (S. Fynes, C. Sturrup, P. Davis-Thompson, D. Ferguson) — 41.95
2. ..Jamaica — 42.13
3. ..United States — 42.20

4 X 400 METER RELAY
1. ..United States (Jearl Miles-Clark, Monique Hennagan, Marion Jones, La Tasha Colander-Richardson) — 3:22.62
2. ..Jamaica — 3:23.25
3. ..Russia — 3:23.46

20-KILOMETER WALK
1. ..Wang Liping, China — 1:29.05
2. ..Kiersti Plaetzer, Norway — 1:29.33
3. ..Maria Vasco, Spain — 1:30.23

HIGH JUMP
1. ..Yelena Yelesina, Russia — 6 ft 7 in
2. ..Hestrie Cloete, S Africa — 6 ft 7 in
3. ..Kajsa Bergqvist, Sweden — 6 ft 7 in

POLE VAULT
1. ..Stacy Dragila, United States — 15 ft 1 in OR
2. ..Tatiana Grigorieva, Australia — 14 ft 11 in
3. ..Vala Flosadottir, Iceland — 14 ft 9 in

LONG JUMP
1. ..Heike Drechsler, Germany — 22 ft 11¼ in
2. ..Fiona May, Italy — 22 ft 8½ in
3. ..Marion Jones, United States — 22 ft 8½ in

TRIPLE JUMP
1. ..Tereza Marinova, Bulgaria — 49 ft 10½ in
2. ..Tatyana Lebedeva, Russia — 49 ft 2½ in
3. ..Olena Hovorova, Ukraine — 49 ft 1 in

SHOT PUT
1. ...Yanina Korolchik, Belarus — 67 ft 5½ in
2. ..Laris Peleshenko, Russia — 65 ft 4¼ in
3. ..Astrid Kumbernuss, Germany — 64 ft 4½ in

DISCUS THROW
1. ..Ellina Zvereva, Belarus — 224 ft 5 in
2. ..Anastasia Kelesidou, Greece — 215 ft 7 in
3. ..Irina Yatchenko, Belarus — 213 ft 11 in

JAVELIN
1. ..Trine Hattestad, Norway — 226 ft ½ in OR
2. ..Mirella Maniani-Tzelili, Greece — 221 ft 5½ in
3. ..Osleidys Menendez, Cuba — 217 ft 1 in

HEPTATHLON
	Pts
1. ..Denise Lewis, Great Britain	6584
2. ..Yelena Prokhorova, Russia	6531
3. ..Natalya Sazanovich, Belarus	6527

HAMMER THROW
1. ..Kamila Skolimowska, Russia — 233 ft 5 in OR
2. ..Olga Kuzenkova, Russia — 228 ft 11 in
3. ..Kirsten Muenchow, Germany — 227 ft 3 in

INDIVIDUAL ARCHERY

Men
1. ....Simon Fairweather, Australia
2. ....Victor Wuderle, United States
3. ....Wietse van Alten, Netherlands

Women
1. ....Yun Mi-Jin, S Korea
2. ....Kim Nam-Soon, S Korea
3. ....Kim Soo-Nyuong, S Korea

TEAM ARCHERY

Men
1. ....S Korea
2. ....Italy
3. ....United States

Women
1. ....S Korea
2. ....Ukraine
3. ....Germany

Note: OR=Olympic record. WR=world record. EOR=equals Olympic record. EWR=equals world record.

BADMINTON

Men

SINGLES
1. ..Ji Xinpeng, China
2. ..Henra wan, Indonesia
3. ..Xia Xuanze, China

DOUBLES
1. ..Tony Gunawan/ Candra Wijaya, Indonesia
2. ..Lee Dong-soo/ Yoo Yong-sung, S Korea
3. ...Ha Tae-kwan/ Kim Dong-moon, S Korea

Women

SINGLES
1. ..Gong Zhichao, China
2. ..Camilla Martin, Denmark
3. ..Ye Zhaoying, China

DOUBLES
1. ....Ge Fei/ Gu Jun, China
2. ..Huang Nanyan/ Yang Wei, China
3. ..Gao Ling/ Qin Yiyuan, China

MIXED DOUBLES
1. ....Zhang Jun/ Gao Ling, China
2. ....Tri Kushanjanto/ Minarti Timur, Indonesia
3. ....Simon Archer/ Joanne Goode, Great Britain

BASEBALL

1. ....United States
2. ....Cuba
3. ....S Korea

BASKETBALL

Men

Final: United States 85, France 75
Lithuania (3rd)
United States: Shareef Abdur-Rahim, Ray Allen, Vin Baker, Vince Carter, Kevin Garnett, Tim Hardaway, Allan Houston, Jason Kidd, Antonio McDyess, Alonzo Mourning, Gary Payton, Steve Smith

Women

Final: United States 76, Australia 54
Brazil (3rd)
United States: Ruthie Bolton-Holifield, Teresa Edwards, Yolanda Griffith, Chamique Holdsclaw, Lisa Leslie, Nikki McCray, Delisha Milton, Katie Smith Dawn Staley, Sheryl Swoopes, Natalie Williams, Kara Wolters

BOXING

LIGHT FLYWEIGHT (106 LB)
1. ....Brahim Asloum, France
2. ....Rafael Lozano Munoz, Spain
3. ....Un Chol Kim, N Korea
3. ....Maikro Romero Esquirol, Cuba

FLYWEIGHT (112 LB)
1. ....Wijan Ponlid, Thailand
2. ....Bulat Jumadilov, Kazakhstan
3. ....Jerome Thomas, France
3. ....Vladimir Sidorenko, Ukraine

BANTAMWEIGHT (119 LB)
1. ....Guillermo Ortiz, Cuba
2. ....Raimkoul Malakhbekov, Russia
3. ....Serguey Daniltchenko, Ukraine
3. ....Clarence Vinson, United States

FEATHERWEIGHT (125 LB)
1. ....Bekzat Sattarkhanov, Kazakhstan
2. ....Ricardo Juarez, United States
3. ....Tahar Tamsamani, Morocco
3. ....Kamil Dzamalutdinov, Russia

LIGHTWEIGHT (132 LB)
1. ....Mario Kindelan, Cuba
2. ....Andriy Kotelnyk, Ukraine
3. ....Cristian Benitez, Mexico
3. ....Alexandr Maletin, Russia

LIGHT WELTERWEIGHT (139 LB)
1. ....Mahamadkadyz Abdullaev, Uzbekistan
2. ....Ricardo Williams, United States
3. ....Diogenes Luna Martinez, Cuba
3. ....Mohamed Allalou, Algeria

WELTERWEIGHT (147 LB)
1. ....Oleg Saitov, Russia
2. ....Sergey Dotsenko, Ukraine
3. ....Vitalii Grusac, Moldova
3. ....Dorel Simion, Romania

LIGHT MIDDLEWEIGHT (156 LB)
1. ....Yermakhan Ibraimov, Kazakhstan
2. ....Marin Simion, Romania
3. ....Pornchai Thongburan, Thailand
3. ....Jermain Taylor, United States

MIDDLEWEIGHT (165 LB)
1. ....Jorge Gutierrez, Cuba
2. ....Gaidarbek Gaidarbekov, Russia
3. ....Vugar Alekperov, Azerbaijan
3. ....Zsolt Erdei, Hungary

LIGHT HEAVYWEIGHT (178 LB)
1. ....Alexander Lebziak, Russia
2. ....Rudolf Kraj, Czech Republic
3. ....Andri Fedtchouk, Ukraine
3. ....Sergei Mikhailov, Uzbekistan

HEAVYWEIGHT (201 LB)
1. ....Félix Sávon, Cuba
2. ....Sultanahmed Ibzagimov, Russia
3. ....Sebastian Kober, Germany
3. ....Vladimir Tchantouria, Georgia

SUPERHEAVYWEIGHT (201+ LB)
1. ....Audley Harrison, Great Britain
2. ....Mukhtarkhan Dildabkov, Kazakhstan
3. ....Rustam Saidov, Uzbekistan
3. ....Paolo Vidoz, Italy

CANOE/KAYAK

Men

C-1 FLATWATER 500 METERS
1. ...Gyorgy Kolonics, Hungary — 2:24.813
2. ...Maxim Opalev, Russia — 2:25.809
3. ...Andreas Dittmer, Germany — 2:27.591

C-1 FLATWATER 1,000 METERS
1. ...Andreas Dittmer, Germany — 3:54.379
2. ...Ledys Frank Balceiro, Cuba — 3:56.071
3. ...Steve Giles, Canada — 3:56.437

C-2 FLATWATER 500 METERS
1. ...F. Novak/ I. Pulai, Hungary — 1:51.284
2. ...D. Jedraszko/ P. Baraszkiewicz, Poland — 1:51.536
3. ...F. Popescu/ M. Pricop, Romania — 1:54.260

C-2 FLATWATER 1,000 METERS
1. ...F. Popescu/ M. Pricop, Romania — 3:37.355
2. ...I. Rojas/ L. Pereira, Cuba — 3:38.753
3. ...L. Kober/ S. Utess, Germany — 3:41.129

C-1 WHITEWATER SLALOM
		Pts
1.	...Tony Estanguet, France	231.87
2.	...Michal Martikan, Slovakia	233.76
3.	...Juraj Mincik, Slovakia	234.22

C-2 WHITEWATER SLALOM
		Pts
1.	...Pavel/ Peter Hochschorner, Slovakia	237.74
2.	...K. Kolomanski/ M. Staniszewski, Poland	243.81
3.	...M. Jiras/ T. Mader, Czech Republic	249.45

K-1 FLATWATER 500 METERS
1. ...Knut Holmann, Norway — 1:57.847
2. ...Petar Merkov, Bulgaria — 1:58.393
3. ...Michael Kolganov, Israel — 1:59.563

K-1 FLATWATER 1,000 METERS
1. ...Knut Holmann, Norway — 3:33.260
2. ...Petar Merkov, Bulgaria — 3:34.640
3. ...Tim Brabants, Great Britain — 3:35.057

Men (Cont.)

K-2 FLATWATER 500 METERS
1. ...Z. Kammerer/ B. Storcz, Hungary — 1:47.055
2. ...D. Collins/ A. Trim, Australia — 1:47.895
3. ...R. Rauhe/ T. Wieskoetter, Germany — 1:48.771

K-2 FLATWATER 1,000 METERS
1. ...B. Bonomi/ A. Rossi, Italy — 3:14.461
2. ...M. Oscarsson/ H. Nilsson, Sweden — 3:16.075
3. ...K. Bartfai/ K. Vereb, Hungary — 3:16.357

K-4 FLATWATER 1,000 METERS
1. ...Hungary — 2:55.188
2. ...Germany — 2:55.704
3. ...Poland — 2:57.192

K-1 WHITEWATER SLALOM
		Pts
1.	...Thomas Schmidt, Germany	217.25
2.	...Paul Ratcliffe, Great Britain	223.71
3.	...Pierpaolo Ferrazzi, Italy	225.03

Women

K-1 FLATWATER 500 METERS
1. ...Josefa Idem Geurrini, Italy — 2:13.848
2. ...Caroline Brunet, Canada — 2:14.646
3. ...Katrin Borchert, Australia — 2:15.138

K-2 FLATWATER 500 METERS
1. ...B. Fischer/ K. Wagner, Germany — 1:56.996
2. ...K. Kovacs/ S. Szabo, Hungary — 1:58.580
3. ...A. Pastuszka/ B. Sokoloska, Poland — 1:58.784

K-4 FLATWATER 500 METERS
1. ...Germany — 1:34.532
2. ...Hungary — 1:34.946
3. ...Romania — 1:37.010

K-1 WHITEWATER SLALOM
		Pts
1.	...Stepanka Hilgertova, Czech Republic	247.04
2.	...Brigitte Guibal, France	251.88
3.	...Anne-Lise Bardet, France	254.77

CYCLING

Men

ROAD RACE
1. ..Jan Ullrich, Germany — 5:29:17.001
2. ..Alexander Vinokourov, Kazakhstan — 5:29:17.002
3. ..Andreas Kloeden, Germany — 5:29:29.003

INDIVIDUAL TIME TRIAL
1. ..Vyachslev Ekimov, Russia — 57:40.420
2. ..Jan Ullrich, Germany — 57:48.333
3. ..Lance Armstrong, United States — 58:14.267

1KM TIME TRIAL
1. ..Jason Queally, Great Britain — 101.609
2. ..Stefan Nimke, Germany — 102.487
3. ..Shane Kelly, Australia — 102.818

4,000 METER INDIVIDUAL PURSUIT
1. ..Robert Bartko, Germany — 4:18.515 OR
2. ..Jens Lehmann, Germany — 4:23.824
3. ..Bradley McGee, Australia — 4:19.250

4,000 METER TEAM PURSUIT
1. ..Germany (Robert Bartko, Guido Fulst, Daniel Becke, Jens Lehmann) — 3:59.710WR
2. ..Russia — 4:04.520
3. ..Great Britain — 4:01.979

Men (Cont.)

SPRINT
1. ..Marty Nothstein, United States — 10.874
2. ..Florian Rousseau, France — 11.066
3. ..Jens Fiedler, Germany — 10.732

40 KM POINTS RACE
1. ..Juan Llaneras, Spain — 14
2. ..Milton Wynant, Uruguay — 18
3. ..Alexey Markov, Russia — 16

KIERIN
1. ..Florian Rousseau, France — 11.020
2. ..Gary Neiwand, Australia
3. ..Jens Fiedler, Germany

MADISON
1. ..B. Aiken/ S. McGrory, Australia — 26
2. ..E. DeWilde/ M. Gilmore, Belgium — 22
3. ..S. Martinello/ M. Villa, Italy — 15

OLYMPIC SPRINT
1. ..France — 44.233
2. ..Great Britain — 44.680
3. ..Australia — 45.161

CYCLING *(Cont.)*

Women

24 KM POINTS RACE

1. ..Antonella Bellutti, Italy — 19
2. ..Leontien Zijlaard, Netherlands — 16
3. ..Olga Slioussareva, Russia — 15

INDIVIDUAL TIME TRIAL

1. ..Leontien Zijlaard, Netherlands — 42:00.781
2. ..Mari Holden, United States — 42:37.372
3. ..Jeannie Longo-Ciprelli, France — 42:52:547

3,000 METER INDIVIDUAL PURSUIT

1. ..Leontien Zijlaard, Netherlands — 3:33:360
2. ..Marion Clignet, France — 3:38:751
3. ..Yvonne McGregor, Great Britain — 3:38:850

SPRINT

1. ..Felicia Ballanger, France — 12.553
2. ..Oxana Grichina, Russia — 13.112
3. ..Irina Yanovych, Ukraine — 12.310

ROAD RACE

1. ..Leontien Zijlaard, Netherlands — 3:6:31.001
2. ..Hanka Kupfernagel, Germany — 3:6:31.002
3. ..Diana Ziliute, Lithuania — 3:6:31.003

500 M TIME TRIAL

1. ..Felicia Ballanger, France — 34.140
2. ..Michelle Ferris, Australia — 34.696
3. ..Jiang Cuihua, China — 34.768

DIVING

Men
SPRINGBOARD

		Pts
1.	Xiong Ni, China	708.72
2.	Fernando Platas, Mexico	708.42
3.	Dmitri Sautin, Russia	703.20

PLATFORM

		Pts
1.	Tian Liang, China	724.53
2.	Hu Jia, China	713.55
3.	Dmitry Sautin, Russia	679.26

Women
SPRINGBOARD

		Pts
1.	Fu Mingxia, China	609.42
2.	Guo Jingjing, China	597.81
3.	Doerte Linder, Germany	574.35

PLATFORM

		Pts
1.	Laura Wilkinson, United States	543.75
2.	Li Na, China	542.01
3.	Anne Montminy, Canada	540.15

EQUESTRIAN

3-DAY TEAM

1. ......Australia (Phillip Dutton, Andrew Hoy, Stuart Tinney, Matt Ryan) — 146.8
2. ......Great Britain — 161.0
3. ......United States — 175.8

3-DAY INDIVIDUAL

1. ......David O'Connor, United States — 34.00
2. ......Andrew Hoy, Australia — 39.80
3. ......Mark Todd, New Zealand — 42.00

TEAM DRESSAGE

1. ......Germany (Isabell Werth, Nadine Capellmann, Ulla Salzgeber, Alexandra Simons de Ridder) — 5632
2. ......Netherlands — 5579
3. ......United States — 5166

INDIVIDUAL DRESSAGE

1. ......Anky van Grunsven, Netherlands — 239.18
2. ......Isabell Werth, Germany — 234.19
3. ......Ulla Salzberger, Germany — 230.57

TEAM JUMPING

1. ......Germany (Ludger Beerbaum, Lars Nieberg, Marcus Ehning, Otto Becker) — 7.00
2. ......Switzerland — 8.00
3. ......Brazil — 12.00

INDIVIDUAL JUMPING

1. ......Jeroen Dubbeldam, Netherlands — 4.00
2. ......Albert Voorn, Netherlands — 4.00
3. ......Khaled Al Eid, Saudi Arabia — 4.00

FENCING

Men

FOIL

1. ....Kim Young Ho, S Korea
2. ....Ralf Bissdorf, Germany
3. ....Dmitri Chevtchenko, Russia

SABRE

1. ....Mihai Claudiu Covaliu, Romania
2. ....Mathieu Gourdain, France
3. ....Wiradech Kothny, Germany

ÉPÉE

1. ....Pavel Kolobkov, Russia
2. ....Hugues Obry, France
3. ....Lee Sang Ki, S Korea

TEAM FOIL

1. ....France
2. ....China
3. ....Italy

TEAM SABRE

1. ....Russia
2. ....France
3. ....Germany

TEAM ÉPÉE

1. ....Italy
2. ....France
3. ....Cuba

FENCING *(Cont.)*

Women

FOIL
1. ....Valentina Vezzali, Italy
2. ....Rita Koenig, Germany
3. ....Giovanna Trillini, Italy

TEAM FOIL
1. ....Italy
2. ....Poland
3. ....Germany

ÉPÉE
1. ....Timea Nagy, Hungary
2. ....Gianna Habluetzel-Buerki, Switzerland
3. ....Laura Flessel-Colovic, France

TEAM ÉPÉE
1. ....Russia
2. ....Switzerland
3. ....China

FIELD HOCKEY

Men
1. ....Netherlands
2. ....S Korea
3. ....Australia

Women
1. ....Australia
2. ....Argentina
3. ....Netherlands

GYMNASTICS

Men

ALL-AROUND
		Pts
1.	Alexei Nemov, Russia	58.474
2.	Wei Yang, China	58.361
3.	O. Beresh, Ukraine	58.212

HORIZONTAL BAR
		Pts
1.	Alexei Nemov, Russia	9.787
2.	Benjamin Varonian, France	9.787
3.	Joo-hyung Lee, S Korea	9.775

PARALLEL BARS
		Pts
1.	Xiaopeng Li, China	9.825
2.	Joo-hyung Lee, S Korea	9.812
3.	Alexei Nemov, Russia	9.800

VAULT
		Pts
1.	Gervasio Deferr, Spain	9.712
2.	Alexei Bondarenko, Russia	9.587
3.	Leszsk Blanik, Poland	9.475

POMMEL HORSE
		Pts
1.	Marius Urzica, Romania	9.862
2.	Eric Poujade, France	9.825
3.	Alexei Nemov, Russia	9.800

RINGS
		Pts
1.	Szilveszter Csollany, Hungary	9.850
2.	Dimosthenis Tampakos, Kasakhstan	9.762
3.	Iordan Iovtchev, Bulgaria	9.737

FLOOR EXERCISE
		Pts
1.	Igors Vihrovs, Latvia	9.812
2.	Alexei Nemov, Russia	9.800
3.	Iordan Iovtchev, Bulgaria	9.787

TEAM COMBINED EXERCISES
		Pts
1.	China	231.919
2.	Ukraine	230.306
3.	Russia	230.019

Women

ALL-AROUND
		Pts
1.	Simona Amanar, Romania	38.642
2.	Maria Olaru, Romania	38.581
3.	Xuan Li, China	38.418

VAULT
		Pts
1.	Yelena Zamolodtchikova, Russia	9.731
2.	Andreea Raducan, Romania	9.693
3.	Yekaterina Lobazniouk, Russia	9.674

UNEVEN BARS
		Pts
1.	Svetlana Khorkina, Russia	9.862
2.	Ling Jie, China	9.837
2.	Yang Yun, China	9.787

BALANCE BEAM
		Pts
1.	Li Xuan, China	9.825
2.	Yekaterina Lobazniouk, Russia	9.787
3.	Yelena Prodounova, Russia	9.775

FLOOR EXERCISE
		Pts
1.	Yelena Zamolodtchikova, Russia	9.850
2.	Svetlana Khorkina, Russia	9.812
3.	Simona Amanar, Romania	9.712

TEAM COMBINED EXERCISES
		Pts
1.	Romania	154.608
2.	Russia	154.403
3.	China	154.008

RHYTHMIC ALL-AROUND
		Pts
1.	Yulia Barsukova, Russia	39.632
2.	Yulia Raskina, Belarus	39.548
3.	Alina Kabaeva, Russia	39.466

RHYTHMIC TEAM COMBINED EXERCISES
		Pts
1.	Russia	39.500
2.	Belarus	39.500
3.	Greece	39.283

JUDO

Men

EXTRA-LIGHTWEIGHT
1. ....Tadahiro Nomura, Japan
2. ....Jung Bu-Kyung, S Korea
3. ....Manolo Poulot, Cuba
3. ....Aidyn Smagulov, Kirghyzstan

HALF-LIGHTWEIGHT
1. ....Huseyin Ozkan, Turkey
2. ....Larbi Benboudaoud, France
3. ....Giorgi Vazagashvili, Georgia
3. ....Girolamo Giovinazzo, Italy

LIGHTWEIGHT
1. ....Giuseppe Maddaloni, Italy
2. ....Tiago Camilo, Brazil
3. ....Anatoly Laryukov, Belarus
3. ....Vselvolods Zelonijs, Latvia

HALF-MIDDLEWEIGHT
1. ....Makoto Takimoto, Japan
2. ....Cho In Chul, S Korea
3. ....Nuno Delgado, Portugal
3. ....Aleksei Budolin, Estonia

MIDDLEWEIGHT
1. ....Mark Huizinga, Netherlands
2. ....Carlos Honorato, Brazil
3. ....Frederic Demontfaucon, France
3. ....Ruslan Mashurenko, Ukraine

HALF-HEAVYWEIGHT
1. ....Kosei Inoue, Japan
2. ....Nicolas Gill, Canda
3. ....Iouri Stepkine, Russial
3. ....Stéphane Traineau, France

HEAVYWEIGHT
1. ....David Douillet, France
2. ....Shinichi Shinohara, Japan
3. ....Indrek Pertelson, Estonia
3. ....Tamerlan Tmenov, Russia

Women

EXTRA-LIGHTWEIGHT
1. ....Ryoko Tamura, Japan
2. ....Lioubov Brouletova, Russia
3. ....Anna-Maria Gradante, Germany
3. ....Ann Simons, Belgium

HALF-LIGHTWEIGHT
1. ....Legna Verdecia, Cuba
2. ....Noriko Narazaki, Japan
3. ....Kye Sun Hi, N Korea
3. ....Liu Yuxiang, China

LIGHTWEIGHT
1. ....Isabel Fernández, Spain
2. ....Driulis González, Cuba
3. ....Kie Kusakabe, Japan
3. ....Maria Pekli, Australia

HALF-MIDDLEWEIGHT
1. ....Severine Vandenhende, France
2. ....Li Shufang, China
3. ....Gella Vandecaveye, Belgium
3. ....Jung Sung Sook, S Korea

MIDDLEWEIGHT
1. ....Sibelis Veranes, Cuba
2. ....Kate Howey, Great Britain
3. ....Cho Min Sun, S Korea
3. ....Ylenia Scapin, Italy

HALF-HEAVYWEIGHT
1. ....Lin Tang, China
2. ....Celine LeBrun, France
3. ....Simona Marcela Richter, Romania
3. ....Emanuela Pierantozzi, Italy

HEAVYWEIGHT
1. ....Hua Yuan, China
2. ....Daima Mayelis Beltran, Cuba
3. ....Kim Seon-Young, S Korea
3. ....Mayumi Yamashita, Japan

MOUNTAIN BIKING

Men
1. ......Miguel Martinez, France	2:09:02
2. ......Filip Meirhaeghe, Belgium	2:10.05
3. ......Christoph Sauser, Switzerland	2:11:21

Women
1. ......Paola Pezzo, Italy	1:49:24
2. ......Barbara Blatter, Switzerland	1:49.51
3. ......Margarita Fullana, Spain	1:49.57

MODERN PENTATHLON

Men
1. ......Dmitry Svatlovsky, Russia
2. ......Gabor Balogh, Hungary
3. ......Pavel Dovgal, Belarus

Women
1. ......Stephanie Cook, Great Britain
2. ......Emily deRiel, United States
3. ......Kate Allenby, Great Britain

ROWING

Men

SINGLE SCULLS
1. ..Rob Waddell, New Zealand	6:48.90
2. ..Xeno Mueller, Switzerland	6:50.55
3. ..Marcel Hacker, Germany	6:50.83

DOUBLE SCULLS
1. ..I. Cop & L. Spik, Slovenia	6:16.63
2. ..F. Beeken & O Tufte, Norway	6:17.98
3. ..G. Calabrese & N. Sartori, Italy	6:20.49

LIGHTWEIGHT DOUBLE SCULLS
1. ..T. Kucharski & R. Sycz, Poland	6:21.75
2. ..E. Liunii & L. Pettinari, Italy	6:23.57
3. ..T. Chappelle & P. Touron, France	6:24.85

QUADRUPLE SCULLS
1. ..Italy	5:45.56
2. ..Netherlands	5:47.91
3. ..Germany	5:48.64

ROWING (Cont.)

Men (Cont.)

COXLESS PAIR

1. ..M. Andrieux/ J. Rolland, France	6:32.97
2. ..S. Bea/ T. Murphy, United States	6:33.80
3. ..J. Tomkins/ M. Long, Australia	6:34.26

LIGHTWEIGHT COXLESS FOUR

1. ..France	6:01.68
2. ..Australia	6:02.09
3. ..Denmark	6:03.51

COXLESS FOUR

1. ..Great Britain	5:56.24
2. ..Italy	5:56.62
3. ..Australia	5:57.61

EIGHT-OARS

1. ..Great Britain	5:33.08
2. ..Australia	5:33.88
3. ..Croatia	5:34.85

Women

SINGLE SCULLS

1. ..Ekaterina Karsten, Belarus	7:28.14
2. ..Rumyana Neykova, Bulgaria	7:28.15
3. ..K. Rutschow-Stomporowski, Germany	7:28.99

QUADRUPLE SCULLS

1. ..Germany	6:19.58
2. ..Great Britain	6:21.64
3. ..Russia	6:21.65

DOUBLE SCULLS

1. ..K. Boron/ J. Thieme, Germany	6:55.44
2. ..P. Van Dishoeck/ E. Van Nes, Netherlands	7:00.36
3. ..B. Sakickiene/ K. Poplavskaya, Lithuania	7:01.71

COXLESS PAIR

1. ..G. Damian/ D. Ignat, Romania	7:11.00
2. ..R. Taylor/ K. Slatter, Australia	7:12.56
3. ..K. Kraft/ M. Ryan, United States	7:13.00

LIGHTWEIGHT DOUBLE SCULLS

1. ..C. Burcica/ A. Alupei, Romania	7:02.64
2. ..V. Viehoff/ C. Blaserg, Germany	7:02.95
3. ..C. Collins/ S. Garner, United States	7:06.37

EIGHT-OARS

1. ..Romania	6:06.44
2. ..Netherlands	6:09.39
3. ..Canada	6:11.58

SHOOTING

Men

RAPID-FIRE PISTOL

	Pts
1......Serguei Alifirenko, Russia	687.6
2......Michel Ansermet, Switzerland	686.1
3......Iulian Raicen, Romania	684.6

SMALL-BORE RIFLE, PRONE

	Pts
1......Jonas Edman, Swedem	701.3
2......Torben Grimmel, Denmark	700.4
3......Sergei Martynov, Belarus	700.3

FREE PISTOL

	Pts
1......Tanyu Kiriakov, Bulgaria	666.0
2......Igor Basinski, Belarus	663.3
3......Martin Tenk, Czech Republic	662.5

AIR RIFLE

	Pts
1......Yalin Cai, China	tk
2......Artem Khadjibekov, Russia	tk
3......Evgueni Aleinikov, Russia	tk

AIR PISTOL

	Pts
1......Franck Dumoulin, France	688.9
2......Yifu Wang, China	686.9
3......Igor Basinsky, Belarus	682.7

TRAP

	Pts
1......Michael Diamond, Australia	122.0
2......Ian Peel, Great Britain	118.0
3......David Kostelecky, Czech Republic	116.o

RUNNING TARGET

	Pts
1......Ling Yang, China	681.1
2......Oleg Moldovan, Moldova	681.0
3......Zhiyuan Niu, China	677.4

DOUBLE TRAP

	Pts
1......Richard Faulds, Great Britain	187.0
2......Russell Mark, Australia	187.0
3......Fehaid Al Deehani, Kuwait	186.0

SMALL-BORE RIFLE, THREE-POSITION

	Pts
1......Rajmond Debevec,Slovenia	1275.1
2......Juha Hirvi, Finland	1270.5
3......Harald Stenvaag, Norway	1268.6

SKEET

	Pts
1......Mykola Milchen, Ukraine	150.0
2......Petr Malek, Czech Republic	148.0
3......James Graves, United States	147.0

Women

SPORT PISTOL

	Pts
1......Maria Grozdeva, Bulgaria	690.3
2......Luna Tao, China	689.8
3......Lolita Evglevskaya, Belarus	686.0

AIR PISTOL

	Pts
1......Luna Tao, China	488.2
2......Jasna Sekaric, Yugoslavia	486.5
3......Annemarie Forder, Australia	484.0

SHOOTING (Cont.)

Women (Cont.)

SMALL-BORE RIFLE, THREE-POSITION

	Pts
1......Renata Mauer-Rozanska, Poland	684.6
2......Tatiana Goldobina, Russia	680.9
3......Maria Feklistova, Russia	679.9

AIR RIFLE

	Pts
1......Nancy Johnson, United States	.497.7
2......Kang Cho-Hyan, S Korea	497.5
3......Jing Gao, China	497.2

DOUBLE TRAP

	Pts
1......Pia Hansen, United States	148.0
2......Deborah Gelisio, Italy	144.0
3......Kimberly Rhode, United States	139.0

TRAP

	Pts
1......Daina Gudzineviciute, Lithuania	93.0
2......Delphine Racinet, France	92.0
3......E Gao, China	90.0

SKEET

	Pts
1......Zemfira Meftakhetdinova, Azerbaijan	98.0
2......Svetlana Demina, Russia	95.0
3......Diana Igaly, Hungary	93.0

SOCCER

Men

1. ....Cameroon
2. ....Spain
3. ....Chile

Women

1. ....Norway
2. ....United States
3. ....Germany

SOFTBALL

1...............................United States
2...............................Japan
3...............................Australia

SWIMMING

Men

50-METER FREESTYLE

1. ..Gary Hall Jr, United States	21.98
1. ..Anthony Ervin, United States	21.98
3. ..Pieter van den Hoogenband, ...Netherlands	22.03

100-METER FREESTYLE

1. ..Pieter van den Hoogenband, ...Netherlands	48.30
2. ..Alexander Popov, Russia	48.69
3. ..Gary Hall Jr, United States	48.73

200-METER FREESTYLE

1. ..Pieter van den Hoogenband, ...Netherlands	1:45.35 EWR
2. ..Ian Thorpe, Australia	1:45.83
3. ..Massimiliano Rosolino, Italy	1:46.65

400-METER FREESTYLE

1. ..Ian Thorpe, Australia	3:40.59 WR
2. ..Massimiliano Rosolino, Italy	3:43.50
3. ..Klete Keller, United States	3:47.00

1,500-METER FREESTYLE

1. ..Grant Hackett, Australia	14:48.33
2. ..Kieren Perkins Australia	14:53.59
3. ..Chris Thompson, United States	14:56.81

100-METER BACKSTROKE

1. ..Lenny Krayzelburg, United States	53.72 OR
2. ..Matthew Welsh, Australia	54.07
3. ..Stev Theloke, Germany	54.82

200-METER BACKSTROKE

1. ..Lenny Krayzelburg, United States	1:56.76 OR
2. ..Aaron Piersol, United States	1:57.35
3. ..Matthew Welsh, Australia	1:59.59

100-METER BREASTSTROKE

1. ..Domenico Fioravanti, Italy	1:00.46 OR
2. ..Ed Moses, United States	1:00.73
3. ..Roman Sloudnov, Russia	1:00.91

200-METER BREASTSTROKE

1. ..Domenico Fioravanti, Italy	2:10.87
2. ..Terence Parkin, S Africa	2:12.50
3. ..Davide Rummolo, Italy	2:12.73

100-METER BUTTERFLY

1. ..Lars Froelander, Sweden	52.00
2. ..Michael Klim, Australia	52.18
3. ..Geoff Huegill, Australia	52.22

200-METER BUTTERFLY

1. ..Tom Malchow, United States	1:55.35 OR
2. ..Denys Sylant'yev, Ukraine	1:55.76
3. ..Justin Norris, Australia	1:56.17

200-METER INDIVIDUAL MEDLEY

1. ..Massimiliano Rosolino, Italy	1:58.98 OR
2. ..Tom Dolan, United States	1:59.77
3. ..Tom Wilkens, United States	2:00.87

400-METER INDIVIDUAL MEDLEY

1. ..Tom Dolan, United States	4:11.76 WR
2. ..Eric Vendt, United States	4:14.23
3. ..Curtis Myden, Canada	4:15.33

4 X 100 METER MEDLEY RELAY

1. ..United States (Lenny Krayzelburg, Ed Moses, Ian Crocker, Gary Hall Jr)	3:34.84 WR
2. ..Australia	3:35.27
3. ..Germany	3:35.88

4 X 100 METER FREESTYLE RELAY

1. ..Australia (Ian Thorpe, Michael Klim, Ashley Callus, Chris Fydler)	3:13.67 WR
2. ..United States	3:13.86
3. ..Brazil	3:17.40

4 X 200 METER FREESTYLE RELAY

1. ..Australia (Ian Thorpe, Michael Klim, William Kirby, Todd Pearson)	7:07.05 WR
2. ..United States	7:12.64
3. ..Netherlands	7:12.70

Note: OR=Olympic record. WR=world record. EOR=equals Olympic record. EWR=equals world record.

SWIMMING (Cont.)

Women

50-METER FREESTYLE
1. ..Inge de Bruijn, Netherlands   24.32
2. ..Therese Alshammar, Sweden   24.51
3. ..Dara Torres, United States   24.63

100-METER FREESTYLE
1. ..Inge de Bruijn, Netherlands   53.83
2. ..Therese Alshammar, Sweden   54.33
3. ..Dara Torres, United States   54.43

200-METER FREESTYLE
1. ..Susie O'Neill, Australia   1:58.24
2. ..Martina Moravcova, Slovakia   1:58.32
3. ..Claudia Poll Ahrens, Costa Rica   1:58.81

400-METER FREESTYLE
1. ..Brooke Bennett, United States   4:05.80
2. ..Diana Munz, United States   4:07.07
3. ..Claudia Poll Ahrens, Costa Rica   4:07.83

800-METER FREESTYLE
1. ..Brooke Bennett, United States   8:19.67 OR
2. ..Yana Klochkova, Ukraine   8:22.66
3. ..Kaitlin Sandeno, United States   8:24.29

100-METER BACKSTROKE
1. ..Diana Iuliana Mocanu, Romania   1:00.21 OR.
2. ..Mai Nakamura, Japan   1:00.55
3. ..Nina Zhivanevskaya, Spain   1:00.89

200-METER BACKSTROKE
1. ..Diana Iuliana Mocanu, Romania   2:08.16
2. ..Roxana Maracineanu, France   2:10.25
3. ..Miki Nakao, Japan   2:11.05

100-METER BREASTSTROKE
1. ..Megan Quann, United States   1:07.05
2. ..Leisel Jones, Australia   1:07.49
3. ..Penny Heyns, South Africa   1:07.55

200-METER BREASTSTROKE
1. ..Agnes Kovacs, Hungary   2:24.35
2. ..Kristy Kowal, United States   2:24.56
3. ..Amanda Beard, United States   2:25.35

100-METER BUTTERFLY
1. ..Inge de Bruijn, Netherlands   56.61 WR
2. ..Martina Moravcova, Slovakia   57.97
3. ..Dara Torres, United States   58.20

200-METER BUTTERFLY
1. ..Misty Hyman, United States   2:05.88 OR
2. ..Susie O'Neill, Australia   2:06.58
3. ..Petria Thomas, Australia   2:07.12

200-METER INDIVIDUAL MEDLEY
1. ..Yana Klochkova, Ukraine   2:10.68 OR
2. ..Beatrice Nicoleta Caslaru, Romania 2:12.57
3. ..Cristina Teuscher, United States   2:13.32

400-METER INDIVIDUAL MEDLEY
1. ..Yana Klochkova, Ukraine   4:33.59 WR
2. ..Yasuko Tajima, Japan   4:35.90
3. ..Beatrice Nicoleta Caslaru, Romania 4:37.18

4 X 100 METER MEDLEY RELAY
1. ..United States: BJ Bedford,   3:58.30 WR
Megan Quann, Jenny Thompson,
Dara Torres
2. ..Australia   4:01.59
3. ..Japan   4:04.16

4 X 100 METER FREESTYLE RELAY
1. ..United States: Jenny Thompson,   3:36.61 WR
Courtney Shealy, Dara Torres,
Amy Van Dyken
2. ..Netherlands   3:39.83
3. ..Sweden   3:40.30

4 X 200 METER FREESTYLE RELAY
1. ..United States (Samantha Arsenault,   7:57.80 OR
Diana Munz, Lindsay Benko,
Jenny Thompson)
2. ..Australia   7:58.52
3. ..Germany   7:58.64

Note: OR=Olympic record. WR=world record. EOR=equals Olympic record. EWR=equals world record.

SYNCHRONIZED SWIMMING

DUET
1. ..Russia   99.580
2. ..Japan   98.650
3. ..France   97.437

TEAM
1. ..Russia   99.146
2. ..Japan   98.860
3. ..Canada   97.357

SYNCHRONIZED DIVING

Men

3M SPRINGBOARD
Pts
1. ....Xiang Ni/ Xiao Hailang, China   365.58
2. ....D. Sautin/ A. Dobroskoki, Russia   329.97
3. ....D. Pullan/ R. Newbery, Australia   322.86

10M PLATFORM
Pts
1. ....I. Loukachine/ D. Sautin, Russia   365.04
2. ....Tian Liang/ Hu Jia, China   358.74
3. ....J.Hempel/ H. Meyer, Germany   338.88

Women

3M SPRINGBOARD
Pts
1. ....V. Ilina/ I. Pakhalina, Russia   332.64
2. ....Guo Jing Jing/ Fu Mingxia, China   321.60
3. ....G. Sorokina/ O. Zhupina, Ukraine   290.34

10M PLATFORM
Pts
1. ....Li Na/ Sang Zue, China   345.12
2. ....A. Montminy/ E.Heymanns,   312.02
............Canada
3. ....L. Tourky/ R. Gilmore, Australia   301.50

TABLE TENNIS

Men

SINGLES
1. ....Kong Linghui, China
2. ....Jan-Ove Wablner, Sweden
3. ....Liu Guoliang, China

DOUBLES
1. ....Wang Liqin/ Yan Sen, China
2. ....Kong Linghu/ Liu Guoliang, China
3. ....Patrick Chila/ J.P. Gatien, France

Women

SINGLES
1. ....Wang Nan, China
2. ....Li Ju, China
3. ....Chen Jing, Taiwan

DOUBLES
1. ....Li Ju/ Wang Nan, China
2. ....Sun Jin/ Yang Yin, China
3. ....Kim Moo Kyo/ Ji-Hye Ryu, S Korea

TAEKWONDO

Men

FLYWEIGHT
1. ....Michail Mouroutsos, Greece
2. ....Gabriel Esparza, Spain
3. ....Chi-Hsiung Huang, China

FEATHERWEIGHT
1. ....Steven Lopez, United States
2. ....Sin Joon Sik, South Korea
3. ....Hadi Saeibonehkohal, Iran

WELTERWEIGHT
1. ....Angel Valodia Matos Fuentes, Cuba
2. ....Faissal Ebnoutalib, Germany
3. ....Victor Estrada Garibay, Mexico

HEAVYWEIGHT
1. ....Kyong-Hun Kim, South Korea
2. ....Daniel Trenton, Australia
3. ....Pascal Gentil, France

Women

FLYWEIGHT
1. ....Lauren Burns, Australia
2. ....Urbia Melendez Rodriguez, Cuba
3. ....Ju Chi Shu, China

FEATHERWEIGHT
1. ....Jung Jae Eun, S Korea
2. ....Hieu Ngan Tran, Vietnam
3. ....Hamide Bikcin, Turkey

WELTERWEIGHT
1. ....Sun-Hee Lee, South Korea
2. ....Trude Gunderson, Denmark
3. ....Yoriko Okamoto, Japan

HEAVYWEIGHT
1. ....Chen Zhong, China
2. ....Natalia Ivanova, Russia
3. ....Dominique Bosshart, Canada

TEAM HANDBALL

Men
1. ....Russia
2. ....Sweden
3. ....Spain

Women
1. ....Denmark
2. ....Hungary
3. ....Norway

TENNIS

Men

SINGLES
1. ....Yevgeni Kafelnikov, Russia
2. ....Tommy Haas, Germany
3. ....Arnaud Di Pasquale, France

DOUBLES
1. ....Daniel Nestor/ Sebastien Lareau, Canada
2. ....Todd Woodbridge/ Mark Woodforde, Australia
3. ....Alex Corretja/ Albert Costa, Spain

Women

SINGLES
1. ....Venus Williams, United States
2. ....Elena Dementieva, Russia
3. ....Monica Seles, United States

DOUBLES
1. ....V. Williams/ S. Williams, United States
2. ....Kristie Boogert/ Miriam Oremans, Netherlands
3. ....Dominique van Roost/ Els Callens, Belgium

TRAMPOLINE

Men
1. ....Alexandre Mosalenko, Russia   41.70
2. ....Ji Wallace, Australia   39.30
3. ....Mathieu Turgeon, Canada   39.10

Women
1. ....Irina Karavaeva, Russia   38.90
2. ....Oxana Tsyhuleva, Ukraine   37.70
3. ....Karen Cockburn, Canada   37.40

TRIATHLON

Men
1. ....Simon Whitfield, Canada   1:48.24.02
2. ....Stefan Vucovic, Germany   1:48.37.58
3. ....Jan Rehula, Czech Rep.   1:48.46,64

Women
1. ....Brigitte McMahon, Switz.   2:00.40.52:
2. ....Michellie Jones, Australia   2:00.42.55
3. ....Magali Messmer, Switz.   2:01.08.83

VOLLEYBALL

Men
1. Yugoslavia
2. Russia
3. Italy

Women
1. Cuba
2. Russia
3. Brazil

BEACH VOLLEYBALL

Men
1. Dain Blanton/ E. Fonoimoana, United States
2. Ze Marco Melo/ Ricardo Santos, Brazil
3. Joerg Ahmann/ Axel Hager, Germany

Women
1. Kerri Pottharst/ Natalie Cook, Australia
2. Shelda Bede/ Adriana Behar, Brazil
3. Adriana Samuel/ Sandra Pires, Brazil

WATER POLO

Men
1. Hungary
2. Russia
3. Yugoslavia

Women
1. Australia
2. United States
3. Russia

WEIGHTLIFTING

Men

123 POUNDS
1. Halil Mutlu, Turkey — 671 lb WR
2. Wu Wenxiong, China — 631 lb
3. Zhang Xiangxiang, China — 631 lb

137 POUNDS
1. Nikolay Pechaliv, Croatia — 715 lb OR
2. Leonidas Sabanis, Greece — 697 lb
3. Gennady Oleshchuk, Belarus — 697 lb

152 POUNDS
1. Galabin Boevski, Bulgaria — 785 lb OR
2. Georgi Markov, Bulgaria — 774 lb
3. Sergei Lavrenov, Belarus — 680 lb

170 POUNDS
1. Zhan Xugang, China — 807 lb
2. Viktor Mitrou, Greece — 807 lb
3. Arsen Melikyan, Armenia — 803 lb

187 POUNDS
1. Pyrros Dimas, Greece — 858 lb
2. Marc Huster, Germany — 858 lb
3. George Asanidze, Georgia — 858 lb

207 POUNDS
1. Akakios Kakiasvilis, Greece — 891 lb
2. Szymon Kolecki, Poland — 891 lb
3. Alexei Petrov. Russia — 884 lb

231 POUNDS
1. Hossein Tavakoli, Iran — 935 lb
2. Alan Tsagaev, Bulgaria — 928 lb
3. Said Asaad, Qatar — 924 lb

231+ POUNDS
1. Hossein Rezazadeh, Iran — 1,045 lbWR
2. Ronny Weller, Germany — 1,025 lb
3. Andrei Chermerkin, Russia — 1,017 lb

Women

106 POUNDS
1. Tara Nott, United States — 407 lb
2. Raema Rumbewas, Indonesia — 407 lb
3. Sri Indriyani, Indonesia — 400 lb

117 POUNDS
1. Yang Xia, China — 495 lb WR
2. Li Feng ying, Taipei — 466 lb
3. Winarni Slamet, Indonesia — 444 lb

128 POUNDS
1. Soraya Mendivil, Mexico — 488 lb
2. Ri Song Hui, North Korea — 484 lb
3. Khassaraporn Suta, Thailand — 462 lb

139 POUNDS
1. Xiaomin Chen, China — 532 lb
2. Valentina Popova, Russia — 517 lb
3. Ioanna Chatziioannou, Greece — 488 lb

152 POUNDS
1. Lin Weining, Chinat — 532 lb
2. Erzsebet Markus, Hungary — 532 lb
3. Karnam Malleswari. Indonesia — 528 lb

165 POUNDS
1. Maria Isabel Urrutia, Colombia — 539 lb
2. Ruth Ogbeifo, Nigeria — 539 lb
3. Kuo Yi Hang, Taipei — 539 lb

165 + POUNDS
1. Ding Meiyuan, China — 660 lb WR
2. Agata Wrobel, Poland — 649 lb OR
3. Cheryl Haworth, United States — 594 lb

FREESTYLE WRESTLING

119 POUNDS
1. ....Namig Abdullayev, Azerbaijan
2. ....Samuel Henson, United States
3. ....Amiran Karntanov, Greece

127.75 POUNDS
1. ....Alireza Dabir, Iran
2. ....Yevgen Buslovych, Ukraine
3. ....Terry Brands, United States

138.75 POUNDS
1. ....Mourad Oumakhanov, Russia
2. ....Serafim Barzakov, Bulgaria
3. ....Jang Jae Sung, S Korea

152 POUNDS
1. ....Daniel Igali, Canada
2. ....Arsen Gitinov, Russia
3. ....Lincoln McIlvray, United States

167.5 POUNDS
1. ....Alexander Leipold, Germany
2. ....Brandon Slay, United States
3. ....Moon Eui Jae, S Korea

187.25 POUNDS
1. ....Adam Saitiev, Russia
2. ....Yoel Romero, Cuba
3. ....Mogamed Ibragimov, Macedonia

213.75 POUNDS
1. ....Sagid Mourtasaliyev, Russia
2. ....Islam Bairamukov, Kazakhstan
3. ....Eldar Kurtanidze, Georgia

286 POUNDS
1. ....David Moussoulbes, Russia
2. ....Artur Taymazov, Uzbekistan
3. ....Alexis Rodriguez, Cuba

GRECO-ROMAN WRESTLING

119 POUNDS
1. ....Kwon Ho Sim, S Korea
2. ....Lazaro Rivas, Cuba
3. ....Young Gyun Kang, N Korea

127.75 POUNDS
1. ....Armen Nazarian, Bulgaria
2. ....Kim In Sub, S Korea
3. ....Zertian Sheng, China

138.75 POUNDS
1. ....Varteres Samourgachev, Russia
2. ....Juan Luis Maren, Cuba
3. ....Akaki Chachua, Georgia

152 POUNDS
1. ....Filiberto Azcuy, Cuba
2. ....Katsushiko Nagata, Japan
3. ....Alexei Glouchkov, Russia

167.5 POUNDS
1. ....Mourat Kardanov, Russia
2. ....Matt James Lindland, United States
3. ....M. Yli-Hannuksela, Finland

187.25 POUNDS
1. ....Hamza Yerlikaya, Turkey
2. ....Sandor Istvan Bardosi, Hungary
3. ....Mukhran Vakhtangadze, Georgia

213.75 POUNDS
1. ....Mikael Ljundberg, Sweden
2. ....Davyd Saldadze, Ukraine
3. ....Garrett Lowney, United States

286 POUNDS
1. ....Rulon Gardner, United States
2. ....Alexander Karelin, Russia
3. ....Dmitry Debelka, Belarus

YACHTING

MEN'S 470
1. ....Australia
2. ....United States
3. ....Argentina

MEN'S FINN
1. ....Iain Percy, Great Britain
2. ....Luca Devoti, Italy
3. ....Fredrik Loof, Sweden

MEN'S BOARD
1. ....Christoph Sieber, Austria
2. ....Carlos Espinosa, Argentina
3. ....Aaron McIntosh, New Zealand

WOMEN'S 470
1. ....Australia
2. ....United States
3. ....Ukraine

WOMEN'S EUROPE
1. ....Shirley Robertson, Great Britain
2. ....Margriet Matthysse, Netherlands
3. ....Serena Amato, Argentina

WOMEN'S BOARD
1. ....Alessandra Sensini, Italy
2. ....Amelie Lux, Germany
3. ....Barbara Kendall, New Zealand

SOLING
1. ....Denmark
2. ....Germany
3. ....Norway

STAR
1. ....M. Reynolds/ M. Liljedahl, United
....................States
2. ....M. Covell/ I. Walker, Great Britain
3. ....T. Grael/ M. Ferreira, Brazil

TORNADO
1. ....H. Steinacher/ R.Hagara, Austria
2. ....J. Forbes/ D. Bundock, Australia
3. ....R. Gaebler/ R. Schwall, Germany

LASER
1. ....Ben Ainslie, Great Britain
2. ....Robert Scheidt, Brazil
3. ....Michael Blackburn, Australia

49ER
1. ....T. Johnson/ J. Jarvi, Finland
2. ....I. Barker/ S. Hicksocks, Great Britain
3. ....J. McKee/ C. Mckee, United States

BIATHLON

Men
10 KILOMETERS

1.	..Ole Einar Bjorndalen, Norway	27:16.2
2.	..Frode Andresen, Norway	28:17.8
3.	..Ville Raikkonen, FInland	28:21.7

20 KILOMETERS

1.	..Halvard Hanevold, Norway	56:16.4
2.	..Pier Alberto Carrara, Italy	56:21.9
3.	..Aleksei Aidarov, Belarus	56:45.5

4 X 7.5 KILOMETER RELAY

1.	Germany	1:19:43.3
2.	Norway	1:20:03.4
3.	Russia	1:20:19.4

Women
7.5 KILOMETERS

1.	..Galina Koukleva, Russia	23:08.0
2.	..Ursula Disl, Germany	23:08.7
3.	..Katrin Apel, Germany	23:32.4

15 KILOMETERS

1.	..Ekaterina Dofovska, Bulgaria	54:52.0
2.	..Elena Petrova, Ukraine	55:09.8
3.	..Ursula Disl, Germany	55:17.9

3 X 7.5 KILOMETER RELAY

1.	Germany	1:40:13.6
2.	Russia	1:40:25.2
3.	Norway	1:40:37.3

BOBSLED

2-MAN BOB

1.	..Pierre Lueders/ Dave MacEachern, Canada	3:37.24
1.	..Guenther Huber/ Antonio Tartaglia, Italy	3:37.24
3.	..Christoph Langen/ Markus Zimmerman, Germany	3:37.89

4-MAN BOB

1.	Germany II	2:39.41
2.	Switzerland I	2:40.01
3.	Britain I	2:40.06
3.	France I	2:40.06

CURLING

Men

1.	Switzerland
2.	Canada
3.	Norway

Women

1.	Canada
2.	Denmark
3.	Sweden

ICE HOCKEY

Men

1.	Czech Republic
2.	Russia
3.	Finland

Women

1.	United States
2.	Canada
3.	Finland

LUGE

Men
SINGLES

1.	..Georg Hackl, Germany	3:18.44
2.	..Armin Zoeggeler, Italy	3:18.94
3.	.Jens Mueller, Germany	3:19.09

DOUBLES

1.	..Stefan Krausse/ Jan Behrendt, Germany	1:41.105
1.	..Chris Thorpe/ Gordy Sheer, United States	1:41.127
3.	..Mark Grimmette/ Brian Martin, United States	1:41.217

Women
SINGLES

1.	..Silke Kraushaar, Germany	3:23.779
2.	..Barbara Niedernhuber, Germany	3:23.781
3.	..Angelika Neuner, Austria	3:24.253

FIGURE SKATING

Men

1.	Ilia Kulik, Russia
2.	Elvis Stojko, Canada
3.	Philippe Candeloro, France

Women

1.	Tara Lipinski, United States
2.	Michelle Kwan, United States
3.	Lu Chen, China

Pairs

1.	..Oksana Kazakova/ Artur Dmitriev, Russia
2.	..Elena Berezhnaya/ Anton Sikharulidze, Russia
3.	..Mandy Wötzel/ Ingo Steuer, Germany

Ice Dancing

1.	..Pasha Grishuk/ Evgeny Platov, Russia
2.	..Anjelika Krylova/ Oleg Ovsyannikov, Russia
3.	..Marina Anissina/ Gwendal Peizerat, France

SPEED SKATING

Men

500 METERS
1. ...Hiroyasu Shimizu, Japan — 1:11.35*
2. ...Jeremy Wotherspoon, Canada — 1:11.84
3. ...Kevin Overland, Canada — 1:11.86

1000 METERS
1. ...Ids Postma, Netherlands — 1:10.64 OR
2. ...Jan Bos, Netherlands — 1:10.71
3. ...Hiroyasu Shimizu, Japan — 1:11.00

1500 METERS
1. ...Aadne Sondral, Norway — 1:47.87 WR
2. ...Ids Postma, Netherlands — 1:48.13
3. ...Rintje Ritsma, Netherlands — 1:48.52

5000 METERS
1. ...Gianni Romme, Netherlands — 6:22.20 WR
2. ...Rintje Ritsma, Netherlands — 6:28.24
3. ...Bart Veldkamp, Belgium — 6:28.31

10,000 METERS
1. ...Gianni Romme, Netherlands — 13:15.33 WR
2. ...Bob de Jong, Netherlands — 13:25.76
3. ...Rintje Ritsma, Netherlands — 13:28.19

500 METERS SHORT TRACK
1. ...Takafumi Nishitani, Japan — 42.862
2. ...An Yulong, China — 43.022
3. ...Hitoshi Uematsu, Japan — 43.713

1000 METERS SHORT TRACK
1. ...Kim Dong Sung, South Korea — 1:32.375
2. ...Li Jiajun, China — 1:32.428
3. ...Eric Bedard, Canada — 1:32.661

5000-METER SHORT TRACK RELAY
1. ...Canada — 7:06.075
2. ...South Korea — 7:06.776
3. ...China — 7:11.559

Women

500 METERS
1. ...Catriona LeMay Doan, Canada — 1:16.60*
2. ...Susan Auch, Canada — 1:16.93
3. ...Tomoni Okazaki, Japan — 1:17.10

1,000 METERS
1. ...Marianne Timmer, Netherlands — 1:16.51 OR
2. ...Chris Witty, United States — 1:16.79
3. ...Catriona LeMay Doan, Canada — 1:17.37

1,500 METERS
1. ...Marianne Timmer, Netherlands — 1:57.58 WR
2. ...Gunda Niemann-Stirnemann, Ger. — 1:58.66
3. ...Chris Witty, United States — 1:58.97

3,000 METERS
1. ...Gunda Niemann-Stirnemann, Ger. — 4:07.29 OR
2. ...Claudia Pechstein, Germany — 4:08.47
3. ...Anna Friesinger, Germany — 4:09.44

5,000 METERS
1. ...Claudia Pechstein, Germany — 6:59.61 WR
2. ...Gunda Niemann-Stirnemann, Ger. — 6:59.65
3. ...Lyudmila Prokasheva, Kazakhstan — 7:11.14

500 METERS SHORT TRACK
1. ...Annie Perreault, Canada — 46.568
2. ...Yang Yang, China — 46.627
3. ...Chun Lee Kyung, S Korea — 46.335

1,000 METERS SHORT TRACK
1. ...Chun Lee Kyung, S Korea — 1:42.776
2. ...Yang Yang, China — 1:43.343
3. ...Hye Kyung Won, S Korea — 1:43.361

3,000-METER SHORT TRACK RELAY
1. ...S Korea — 4:16.260
2. ...China — 4:16.383
3. ...Canada — 4:21.205

Note: OR=Olympic Record. WR=World Record. EOR=Equals Olympic Record. EWR=Equals World Record. WB=World Best.
* Final standings based on the combined time of two 500-meter runs. Shimizu set an Olympic record with his second-run time of 35.59 seconds, and LeMay Doan set an Olympic record with her second-run time of 38.21 seconds.

ALPINE SKIING

Men

DOWNHILL
1. ...Jean-Luc Crétier, France — 1:50.11
2. ...Lasse Kjus, Norway — 1:50.51
3. ...Hannes Trinkl, Austria — 1:50.63

SLALOM
1. ...Hans-Petter Buraas, Norway — 1:49.31
2. ...Ole Christian Furuseth, Norway — 1:50.64
3. ...Thomas Sykora, Austria — 1:50.68

GIANT SLALOM
1. ...Hermann Maier, Austria — 2:38.51
2. ...Stefan Eberharter, Austria — 2:39.36
3. ...Michael von Grünigen, Switzerland — 2:39.69

SUPER GIANT SLALOM
1. ...Hermann Maier, Austria — 1:34.82
2. ...Didier Cucher, Switzerland — 1:35.43
3. ...Hans Knauss, Austria — 1:35.43

COMBINED
1. ...Mario Reiter, Austria — 3:08.06
2. ...Lasse Kjus, Norway — 3:08.65
3. ...Christian Mayer, Austria — 3:10.11

Women

DOWNHILL
1. ...Katja Seizinger, Germany — 1:28.89
2. ...Pernilla Wiberg, Sweden — 1:29.18
3. ...Florence Masnada, France — 1:29.37

SLALOM
1. ...Hilde Gerg, Germany — 1:32.40
2. ...Deborah Compagnoni, Italy — 1:32.46
3. ...Zali Steggall, Australia — 1:32.67

GIANT SLALOM
1. ...Deborah Compagnoni, Italy — 2:50.59
2. ...Alexandra Meissnitzer, Austria — 2:52.39
3. ...Katja Seizinger, Germany — 2:52.61

SUPER GIANT SLALOM
1. ...Picabo Street, United States — 1:18.02
2. ...Michaela Dorfmeister, Austria — 1:18.03
3. ...Alexandra Meissnitzer, Austria — 1:18.09

COMBINED
1. ...Katja Seizinger, Germany — 2:40.74
2. ...Martina Ertl, Germany — 2:40.92
3. ...Hilde Gerg, Germany — 2:41.50

FREESTYLE SKIING

Men

MOGULS | Pts
1. ..Jonny Moseley, United States | 26.93
2. ..Janne Lahtela, Finland | 26.00
3. ..Sami Mustonen, Finland | 25.76

AERIALS | Pts
1. ..Eric Bergoust, United States | 255.64
2. ..Sebastien Foucras, France | 248.79
3. ..Dmitri Dashchinsky, Belarus | 240.79

Women

MOGULS | Pts
1. ..Tae Satoya, Japan | 25.06
2. ..Tatjana Mittermayer, Germany | 24.62
3. ..Kari Traa, Norway | 24.09

AERIALS | Pts
1. ..Nikki Stone, United States | 193.00
2. ..Nannan Xu, China | 186.97
3. ..Colette Brand, Switzerland | 171.83

NORDIC SKIING

Men

10 KILOMETERS CLASSICAL STYLE
1. ..Bjørn Dæhlie, Norway | 27:24.5
2. ..Markus Gandler, Austria | 27:32.5
3. ..Mika Myllylae, Finland | 27:40.1

15 KILOMETERS PURSUIT FREESTYLE
1. ..Thomas Alsgaard, Norway | 1:07:01.7
2. ..Bjørn Dæhlie, Norway | 1:07:02.8
3. ..Vladimir Smirnov, Kazakhstan | 1:07:31.5

30 KILOMETERS CLASSICAL STYLE
1. ..Mika Myllylae, Finland | 1:33:55.8
2. ..Erling Jevne, Norway | 1:35:27.1
3. ..Silvio Fauner, Italy | 1:36:08.5

50 KILOMETERS FREESTYLE
1. ..Bjørn Dæhlie, Norway | 2:05:08.2
2. ..Niklas Jonsson, Sweden | 2:05:16.3
3. ..Christian Hoffmann, Austria | 2:06:01.8

4 X 10 KILOMETER RELAY MIXED STYLE
1. ....Norway | 1:40:55.7
2. ....Italy | 1:40:55.9
3. ....Finland | 1:42:15.5

90-METER HILL SKI JUMPING | Pts
1. ..Jani Soininen, Finland | 234.5
2. ..Kazuyoshi Funaki, Japan | 233.5
3. ..Andreas Widhoelzl, Austria | 232.5

120-METER HILL SKI JUMPING | Pts
1. ..Kazuyoshi Funaki, Japan | 272.3
2. ..Jani Soininen, Finland | 260.8
3. ..Masahiko Harada, Japan | 258.3

120-METER HILL TEAM SKI JUMPING | Pts
1. ....Japan | 933.0
2. ....Germany | 897.4
3. ....Austria | 881.5

INDIVIDUAL COMBINED | Time behind
1. ..Bjarte Engen Vik, Norway | —
2. ..Samppa Lajunen, Finland | 27.5
3. ..Valery Stoljarov, Russia | 28.2

TEAM COMBINED | Time behind
1. ....Norway | —
2. ....Finland | 1:18.9
3. ....France | 1:41.9

Women

5 KILOMETERS CLASSICAL STYLE
1. ..Larissa Lazhutina, Russia | 17:37.9
2. ..Katerina Neumannova, Czech Rep | 17:42.7
3. ..Bente Martinsen, Norway | 17:49.4

10 KILOMETERS PURSUIT FREESTYLE
1. ..Larissa Lazhutina, Russia | 46:06.9
2. ..Olga Danilova, Russia | 46:13.4
3. ..Katerina Neumannova, Czech Rep | 46:14.2

15 KILOMETERS CLASSICAL STYLE
1. ..Olga Danilova, Russia | 46:55.04
2. ..Larissa Lazhutina, Russia | 47:01.00
3. ..Anita Moen-Guidon, Norway | 47:52.06

30 KILOMETERS FREESTYLE
1. ..Julija Tchepalova, Russia | 1:22:01.5
2. ..Stefania Belmondo, Italy | 1:22:11.7
3. ..Larissa Lazhutina, Russia | 1:23:15.7

4 X 5 KILOMETER RELAY MIXED STYLE
1. ....Russia | 55:13.5
2. ....Norway | 55:38.0
3. ....Italy | 56:53.3

SNOWBOARDING

Men

GIANT SLALOM
1. ..Ross Rebagliati, Canada | 2:03.96
2. ..Thomas Prugger, Italy | 2:03.98
3. ..Ueli Kestenholz, Switzerland | 2:04.08

HALF-PIPE | Pts
1. ..Gian Simmen, Switzerland | 85.2
2. ..Daniel Franck, Norway | 82.4
3. ..Ross Powers, United States | 82.1

Women

GIANT SLALOM
1. ..Karine Ruby, France | 2:17.34
2. ..Heidi Renoth, Germany | 2:19.17
3. ..Brigitte Koeck, Austria | 2:19.42

HALF-PIPE | Pts
1. ..Nicola Thost, Germany | 74.6
2. ..Stine Brun Kjeldaas, Norway | 74.2
3. ..Shannon Dunn, United States | 72.8

FOR THE RECORD·Year by Year

Olympic Games Locations and Dates

Summer

	Year	Site	Dates	Competitors Men	Women	Nations	Most Medals	US Medals
I	1896	Athens, Greece	Apr 6–15	311	0	13	Greece (10-19-18—47)	11-6-2—19 (2nd)
II	1900	Paris, France	May 20–Oct 28	1319	11	22	France (29-41-32—102)	20-14-19—53 (2nd)
III	1904	St Louis, United States	July 1–Nov 23	681	6	12	United States (80-86-72—238)	
—	1906	Athens, Greece	Apr 22–May 28	77	7	20	France (15-9-16—40)	12-6-5—23 (4th)
IV	1908	London, Great Britain	Apr 27–Oct 31	1999	36	23	Britain (56-50-39—145)	23-12-12—47 (2nd)
V	1912	Stockholm, Sweden	May 5–July 22	2490	57	28	Sweden (24-24-17—65)	23-19-19—61 (2nd)
VI	1916	Berlin, Germany	Canceled because of war					
VII	1920	Antwerp, Belgium	Apr 20–Sep 12	2543	64	29	United States (41-27-28—96)	
VIII	1924	Paris, France	May 4–July 27	2956	136	44	United States (45-27-27—99)	
IX	1928	Amsterdam, Netherlands	May 17–Aug 12	2724	290	46	United States (22-18-16—56)	
X	1932	Los Angeles, United States	July 30–Aug 14	1281	127	37	United States (41-32-31—104)	
XI	1936	Berlin, Germany	Aug 1–16	3738	328	49	Germany (33-26-30—89)	24-20-12—56 (2nd)
XII	1940	Tokyo, Japan	Canceled because of war					
XIII	1944	London, Great Britain	Canceled because of war					
XIV	1948	London, Great Britain	July 29–Aug 14	3714	385	59	United States (38-27-19—84)	
XV	1952	Helsinki, Finland	July 19–Aug 3	4407	518	69	United States (40-19-17—76)	
XVI	1956	Melbourne, Australia*	Nov 22–Dec 8	2958	384	67	USSR (37-29-32—98)	32-25-17—74 (2nd)
XVII	1960	Rome, Italy	Aug 25–Sep 11	4738	610	83	USSR (43-29-31—103)	34-21-16—71 (2nd)
XVIII	1964	Tokyo, Japan	Oct 10–24	4457	683	93	United States (36-26-28—90)	
XIX	1968	Mexico City, Mexico	Oct 12–27	4750	781	112	United States (45-28-34—107)	
XX	1972	Munich, West Germany	Aug 26–Sep 10	5848	1299	122	USSR (50-27-22—99)	33-31-30—94 (2nd)
XXI	1976	Montreal, Canada	July 17–Aug 1	4834	1251	92†	USSR (49-41-35—125)	34-35-25—94 (3rd)
XXII	1980	Moscow, USSR	July 19–Aug 3	4265	1088	81‡	USSR (80-69-46—195)	Did not compete
XXIII	1984	Los Angeles, United States	July 28–Aug 12	5458	1620	141#	United States (83-61-30—174)	
XXIV	1988	Seoul, South Korea	Sep 17–Oct 2	7105	2476	160	USSR (55-31-46—132)	36-31-27—94 (3rd)
XXV	1992	Barcelona, Spain	July 25–Aug. 9	7555	3008	172	Unified Team (45-38-29—112)	37-34-37—108 (2nd)
XXVI	1996	Atlanta, United States	July 19–Aug 4	6984	3766	197	United States (44-32-25—101)	
XXVII	2000	Sydney, Australia	Sept 15–Oct 1	6862	4254	199	United States (39-25-33—97)	

*The equestrian events were held in Stockholm, Sweden, June 10–17, 1956.

†This figure includes Cameroon, Egypt, Morocco, and Tunisia, countries that boycotted the 1976 Olympics after some of their athletes had already competed.

‡The U.S. was among 65 countries that did not participate in the 1980 Summer Games in Moscow.

#The USSR, East Germany, and 14 other countries did not participate in the 1984 Summer Games in Los Angeles.

Winter

	Year	Site	Dates	Men	Women	Nations	Most Medals	US Medals
					Competitors			
I	1924	Chamonix, France	Jan 25–Feb 4	281	13	16	Norway (4-7-6—17)	1-2-1—4 (3rd)
II	1928	St Moritz, Switzerland	Feb 11–19	366	27	25	Norway (6-4-5—15)	2-2-2—6 (2nd)
III	1932	Lake Placid, United States	Feb 4–13	277	30	17	United States (6-4-2—12)	
IV	1936	Garmisch-Partenkirchen, Germany	Feb 6–16	680	76	28	Norway (7-5-3—15)	1-0-3—4 (T-5th)
—	1940	Garmisch-Partenkirchen, Germany	Canceled because of war					
—	1944	Cortina d'Ampezzo, Italy	Canceled because of war					
V	1948	St Moritz, Switzerland	Jan 30–Feb 8	636	77	28	Norway (4-3-3—10) Sweden (4-3-3—10) Switzerland (3-4-3—10)	3-4-2—9 (4th)
VI	1952	Oslo, Norway	Feb 14–25	624	108	30	Norway (7-3-6—16)	4-6-1—11 (2nd)
VII	1956	Cortina d'Ampezzo, Italy	Jan 26–Feb 5	687	132	32	USSR (7-3-6—16)	2-3-2—7 (T-4th)
VIII	1960	Squaw Valley, United States	Feb 18–28	502	146	30	USSR (7-5-9—21)	3-4-3—10 (2nd)
IX	1964	Innsbruck, Austria	Jan 29–Feb 9	758	175	36	USSR (11-8-6—25)	1-2-3—6 (7th)
X	1968	Grenoble, France	Feb 6–18	1063	230	37	Norway (6-6-2—14)	1-5-1—7 (T-7th)
XI	1972	Sapporo, Japan	Feb 3–13	927	218	35	USSR (8-5-3—16)	3-2-3—8 (6th)
XII	1976	Innsbruck, Austria	Feb 4–15	1013	248	37	USSR (13-6-8—27)	3-3-4—10 (T-3rd)
XIII	1980	Lake Placid, United States	Feb 13–24	1012	271	37	East Germany (9-7-7—23)	6-4-2—12 (3rd)
XIV	1984	Sarajevo, Yugoslavia	Feb 8–19	1127	283	49	USSR (6-10-9—25)	4-4-0—8 (T-5th)
XV	1988	Calgary, Canada	Feb 13–28	1270	364	57	USSR (11-9-9—29)	2-1-3—6 (T-8th)
XVI	1992	Albertville, France	Feb 8–23	1313	488	65	Germany (10-10-6—26)	5-4-2—11 (6th)
XVII	1994	Lillehammer, Norway	Feb 12–27	1302	542	67	Norway (10-11-5—26)	6-5-2—13 (T-5th)
XVIII	1998	Nagano, Japan	Feb 7–22	2302 (total)		72	Germany (12-9-8—29)	6-3-4—13 (6th)

Alltime Olympic Medal Winners

Summer

NATIONS

Nation	Gold	Silver	Bronze	Total	Nation	Gold	Silver	Bronze	Total
United States	871	659	586	2116	Finland	101	81	114	296
Soviet Union (1952–88)	395	319	296	1010	Japan	97	97	102	296
Great Britain	180	233	225	638	Romania	74	83	108	265
France	188	193	217	598	Poland	56	72	113	241
Italy	179	143	157	479	Canada	51	81	98	230
Sweden	136	156	177	469	China	80	79	64	223
East Germany (1956–88)	159	150	136	445	The Netherlands	61	67	85	213
Hungary	150	135	158	443	Bulgaria	48	82	65	195
Germany (1896–1936, 1992–)	138	138	160	436	Switzerland	47	75	61	183
					Denmark	40	63	58	161
Australia	102	110	138	350	Russia	59	53	47	159
West Germany (1952–88)	77	104	120	301	Czechoslovakia (1924–92)	49	49	44	142

Summer *(Cont.)*

INDIVIDUALS — OVERALL

Men

Athlete, Nation	Sport	G	S	B	Tot
Nikolai Andrianov, USSR	Gym	7	5	3	15
Boris Shakhlin, USSR	Gym	7	4	2	13
Edoardo Mangiarotti, Italy	Fen	6	5	2	13
Takashi Ono, Japan	Gym	5	4	4	13
Paavo Nurmi, Finland	Track	9	3	0	12
Sawao Kato, Japan	Gym	8	3	1	12
Alexei Nemov, Russia	Gym	4	2	6	12
Mark Spitz, United States	Swim	9	1	1	11
Matt Biondi, United States	Swim	8	2	1	11
Viktor Chukarin, USSR	Gym	7	3	*1	11
Carl Osburn, United States	Shoot	5	4	2	11
Ray Ewry, United States	Track	10	0	0	10
Carl Lewis, United States	Track	9	1	0	10
Aladár Gerevich, Hungary	Fen	7	1	2	10
Akinori Nakayama, Japan	Gym	6	2	2	10
Vitaly Scherbo, UT/Belarus	Gym	6	0	4	10
Aleksandr Dityatin, USSR	Gym	3	6	1	10

Women

Athlete, Nation	Sport	G	S	B	Tot
Larissa Latynina, USSR	Gym	9	5	4	18
Vera Cáslavská, Czech	Gym	7	4	0	11
Agnes Keleti, Hungary	Gym	5	3	2	10
Polina Astaknova, USSR	Gym	5	2	3	10
Nadia Comaneci, Romania	Gym	5	3	1	9
Jenny Thompson, United States	Swim	7	1	1	9
Lyudmila Tourischeva, USSR	Gym	4	3	2	9
Kornelia Ender, E Germany	Swim	4	4	0	8
Dawn Fraser, Australia	Swim	4	4	0	8
Shirley Babashoff, United States	Swim	2	6	0	8
Sofia Muratova, USSR	Gym	2	2	4	8
Dara Torres, United States	Swim	4	0	4	8

Eight tied with seven.

INDIVIDUALS — GOLD

Men

Ray Ewry, United States 10
Paavo Nurmi, Finland 9
Carl Lewis, United States 9
Mark Spitz, United States 9

Sawao Kato, Japan 8
Matt Biondi, United States 8
Nikolai Andrianov, USSR 7
Boris Shakhlin, USSR 7

Viktor Chukarin, USSR................7
Aladár Gerevich, Hungary..........7

Women

Larissa Latynina, USSR 9
Jenny Thompson, United States ..8
Vera Cáslavská, Czech 7
Kristin Otto, E Germany..............6
Agnes Keleti, Hungary 5
Nadia Comaneci, Romania 5

Polina Astaknova, USSR 5
Krisztina Egerszegi, Hun 5
Kornelia Ender, E Germany 4
Dawn Fraser, Australia 4
Lyudmila Tourischeva, USSR 4
Evelyn Ashford, United States ...4

Janet Evans, United States........4
Fanny Blankers-Koen, Neth 4
Betty Cuthbert, Australia............4
Pat McCormick, United States ...4
Bärbel Eckert Wöckel, E Ger 4
Amy Van Dyken, United States ..4

Winter

NATIONS

Nation	Gold	Silver	Bronze	Total	Nation	Gold	Silver	Bronze	Total
Norway	83	85	68	236	East Germany (1956–88)	39	36	35	110
Soviet Union (1956–88)	78	57	59	194	Sweden	36	26	34	96
United States	59	58	40	157	Switzerland	29	31	31	91
Austria	39	53	53	145	Germany (1928–36, '92–)	34	29	25	88
Finland	37	49	48	134	Canada	24	25	29	78

INDIVIDUALS — OVERALL

Men

Athlete, Nation	Sport	G	S	B	Tot
Bjørn Dæhlie, Norway	N Ski	8	4	0	12
Sixten Jernberg, Sweden	N Ski	4	3	2	9
A. Clas Thunberg, Finland	S Skat	5	1	1	7
Ivar Ballangrud, Norway	S Skat	4	2	1	7
Veikko Hakulinen, Finland	N Ski	3	3	1	7
Eero Mäntyranta, Finland	N Ski	3	2	2	7
Bogdan Musiol, E Ger/Ger	Bob	1	5	1	7

Women

Athlete, Nation	Sport	G	S	B	Tot
Raisa Smetanina, USSR/UT	N Ski	4	5	1	10
Lyubov Egorova, UT/Russia	N Ski	6	3	0	9
Galina Kulakova, USSR	N Ski	4	2	2	8
Karin (Enke) Kania, E Germany	S Skat	3	4	1	8
Gunda Niemann Stimemann, Ger	S Skat	3	4	1	8
Larissa Lazutina, UT/Russia	N Ski	5	1	1	7
Marja-Liisa Kirvesniemi, Fin	N Ski	3	0	4	7
Andrea Ehrig, E Germany	S Skat	1	5	1	7

INDIVIDUALS — GOLD

Men

Bjørn Dæhlie, Nor 8
A. Clas Thunberg, Fin...5
Eric Heiden, U.S. 5
Sixten Jernberg, Swe...4
Evgeny Grishin, USSR..4
J. Olav Koss, Norway...4

Matti Nykänen, Fin......4
A. Tikhonov, USSR......4
N. Zimyatov, USSR 4
Ivar Ballangrud, Nor ...4
Gunde Svan, Swe 4
T. Wassberg, Swe.......4

Women

Lyubov Egorova,
UT/Russia 6
L. Skoblikova, USSR ...6
Larissa Lazutina,
UT/Russia 5
Bonnie Blair, U.S.........5

Raisa Smetanina,
USSR/UT....................4
G. Kulakova, USSR.....4
Chun Lee Kyung, Kor...4

TRACK AND FIELD
Men

100 METERS

Year	Champion	Time
1896	Thomas Burke, United States	12.0
1900	Frank Jarvis, United States	11.0
1904	Archie Hahn, United States	11.0
1906	Archie Hahn, United States	11.2
1908	Reginald Walker, South Africa	10.8 OR
1912	Ralph Craig, United States	10.8
1920	Charles Paddock, United States	10.8
1924	Harold Abrahams, Great Britain	10.6 OR
1928	Percy Williams, Canada	10.8
1932	Eddie Tolan, United States	10.3 OR
1936	Jesse Owens, United States	10.3
1948	Harrison Dillard, United States	10.3
1952	Lindy Remigino, United States	10.4
1956	Bobby Morrow, United States	10.5
1960	Armin Hary, West Germany	10.2 OR
1964	Bob Hayes, United States	10.0 EWR
1968	Jim Hines, United States	9.95 WR
1972	Valery Borzov, USSR	10.14
1976	Hasely Crawford, Trinidad	10.06
1980	Allan Wells, Great Britain	10.25
1984	Carl Lewis, United States	9.99
1988	Carl Lewis, United States*	9.92 WR
1992	Linford Christie, Great Britain	9.96
1996	Donovan Bailey, Canada	9.84 WR
2000	Maurice Greene, United States	9.87

*Ben Johnson, Canada, disqualified.

200 METERS

Year	Champion	Time
1900	John Walter Tewksbury, United States	22.2
1904	Archie Hahn, United States	21.6 OR
1906	Not held	
1908	Robert Kerr, Canada	22.6
1912	Ralph Craig, United States	21.7
1920	Allen Woodring, United States	22.0
1924	Jackson Scholz, United States	21.6
1928	Percy Williams, Canada	21.8
1932	Eddie Tolan, United States	21.2 OR
1936	Jesse Owens, United States	20.7 OR
1948	Mel Patton, United States	21.1
1952	Andrew Stanfield, United States	20.7
1956	Bobby Morrow, United States	20.6 OR
1960	Livio Berruti, Italy	20.5 EWR
1964	Henry Carr, United States	20.3 OR
1968	Tommie Smith, United States	19.83 WR
1972	Valery Borzov, USSR	20.00
1976	Donald Quarrie, Jamaica	20.23
1980	Pietro Mennea, Italy	20.19
1984	Carl Lewis, United States	19.80 OR
1988	Joe DeLoach, United States	19.75 OR
1992	Mike Marsh, United States	20.01
1996	Michael Johnson, United States	19.32 WR
2000	Konstadinos Kederis, Greece	20.09

400 METERS

Year	Champion	Time
1896	Thomas Burke, United States	54.2
1900	Maxey Long, United States	49.4 OR
1904	Harry Hillman, United States	49.2 OR
1906	Paul Pilgrim, United States	53.2
1908	Wyndham Halswelle, Great Britain	50.0
1912	Charles Reidpath, United States	48.2 OR
1920	Bevil Rudd, South Africa	49.6
1924	Eric Liddell, Great Britain	47.6 OR
1928	Ray Barbuti, United States	47.8
1932	William Carr, United States	46.2 WR
1936	Archie Williams, United States	46.5
1948	Arthur Wint, Jamaica	46.2

400 METERS (CONT.)

Year	Champion	Time
1952	George Rhoden, Jamaica	45.9
1956	Charles Jenkins, United States	46.7
1960	Otis Davis, United States	44.9 WR
1964	Michael Larrabee, United States	45.1
1968	Lee Evans, United States	43.86 WR
1972	Vincent Matthews, United States	44.66
1976	Alberto Juantorena, Cuba	44.26
1980	Viktor Markin, USSR	44.60
1984	Alonzo Babers, United States	44.27
1988	Steve Lewis, United States	43.87
1992	Quincy Watts, United States	43.50 OR
1996	Michael Johnson, United States	43.49 OR
2000	Michael Johnson, United States	43.84

800 METERS

Year	Champion	Time
1896	Edwin Flack, Australia	2:11
1900	Alfred Tysoe, Great Britain	2:01.2
1904	James Lightbody, United States	1:56 OR
1906	Paul Pilgrim, United States	2:01.5
1908	Mel Sheppard, United States	1:52.8 WR
1912	James Meredith, United States	1:51.9 WR
1920	Albert Hill, Great Britain	1:53.4
1924	Douglas Lowe, Great Britain	1:52.4
1928	Douglas Lowe, Great Britain	1:51.8 OR
1932	Thomas Hampson, Great Britain	1:49.8 WR
1936	John Woodruff, United States	1:52.9
1948	Mal Whitfield, United States	1:49.2 OR
1952	Mal Whitfield, United States	1:49.2 EOR
1956	Thomas Courtney, United States	1:47.7 OR
1960	Peter Snell, New Zealand	1:46.3 OR
1964	Peter Snell, New Zealand	1:45.1 OR
1968	Ralph Doubell, Australia	1:44.3 EWR
1972	Dave Wottle, United States	1:45.9
1976	Alberto Juantorena, Cuba	1:43.50 WR
1980	Steve Ovett, Great Britain	1:45.40
1984	Joaquim Cruz, Brazil	1:43.00 OR
1988	Paul Ereng, Kenya	1:43.45
1992	William Tanui, Kenya	1:43.66
1996	Vebjoern Rodal, Norway	1:42.58 OR
2000	Nils Schumann, Germany	1:45.08

1500 METERS

Year	Champion	Time
1896	Edwin Flack, Australia	4:33.2
1900	Charles Bennett, Great Britain	4:06.2 WR
1904	James Lightbody, United States	4:05.4 WR
1906	James Lightbody, United States	4:12.0
1908	Mel Sheppard, United States	4:03.4 OR
1912	Arnold Jackson, Great Britain	3:56.8 OR
1920	Albert Hill, Great Britain	4:01.8
1924	Paavo Nurmi, Finland	3:53.6 OR
1928	Harry Larva, Finland	3:53.2 OR
1932	Luigi Beccali, Italy	3:51.2 OR
1936	Jack Lovelock, New Zealand	3:47.8 WR
1948	Henri Eriksson, Sweden	3:49.8
1952	Josef Barthel, Luxemburg	3:45.1 OR
1956	Ron Delany, Ireland	3:41.2 OR
1960	Herb Elliott, Australia	3:35.6 WR
1964	Peter Snell, New Zealand	3:38.1
1968	Kipchoge Keino, Kenya	3:34.9 OR
1972	Pekkha Vasala, Finland	3:36.3
1976	John Walker, New Zealand	3:39.17
1980	Sebastian Coe, Great Britain	3:38.4
1984	Sebastian Coe, Great Britain	3:32.53 OR
1988	Peter Rono, Kenya	3:35.96
1992	Fermin Cacho, Spain	3:40.12
1996	Noureddine Morceli, Algeria	3:35.78
2000	Noah Ngeni, Kenya	3:32.07 OR

Note: OR=Olympic Record. WR=World Record. EOR=Equals Olympic Record. EWR=Equals World Record. WB=World Best.

TRACK AND FIELD *(Cont.)*

Men *(Cont.)*

5000 METERS

1912	Hannes Kolehmainen, Finland	14:36.6 WR
1920	Joseph Guillemot, France	14:55.6
1924	Paavo Nurmi, Finland	14:31.2 OR
1928	Villie Ritola, Finland	14:38
1932	Lauri Lehtinen, Finland	14:30 OR
1936	Gunnar Höckert, Finland	14:22.2 OR
1948	Gaston Reiff, Belgium	14:17.6 OR
1952	Emil Zatopek, Czechoslovakia	14:06.6 OR
1956	Vladimir Kuts, USSR	13:39.6 OR
1960	Murray Halberg, New Zealand	13:43.4
1964	Bob Schul, United States	13:48.8
1968	Mohamed Gammoudi, Tunisia	14:05.0
1972	Lasse Viren, Finland	13:26.4 OR
1976	Lasse Viren, Finland	13:24.76
1980	Miruts Yifter, Ethiopia	13:21.0
1984	Said Aouita, Morocco	13:05.59 OR
1988	John Ngugi, Kenya	13:11.70
1992	Dieter Baumann, Germany	13:12.52
1996	Venuste Niyongabo, Burundi	13:07.96
2000	Millon Wolde, Ethiopia	13:35.49

10,000 METERS

1912	Hannes Kolehmainen, Finland	31:20.8
1920	Paavo Nurmi, Finland	31:45.8
1924	Vilho (Ville) Ritola, Finland	30:23.2 WR
1928	Paavo Nurmi, Finland	30:18.8 OR
1932	Janusz Kusocinski, Poland	30:11.4 OR
1936	Ilmari Salminen, Finland	30:15.4
1948	Emil Zatopek, Czechoslovakia	29:59.6 OR
1952	Emil Zatopek, Czechoslovakia	29:17.0 OR
1956	Vladimir Kuts, USSR	28:45.6 OR
1960	Pyotr Bolotnikov, USSR	28:32.2 OR
1964	Billy Mills, United States	28:24.4 OR
1968	Naftali Temu, Kenya	29:27.4
1972	Lasse Viren, Finland	27:38.4 WR
1976	Lasse Viren, Finland	27:40.38
1980	Miruts Yifter, Ethiopia	27:42.7
1984	Alberto Cova, Italy	27:47.54
1988	Brahim Boutaib, Morocco	27:21.46 OR
1992	Khalid Skah, Morocco	27:46.70
1996	Haile Gebrselassie, Ethiopia	27:07.34 OR
2000	Haile Gebrselassie, Ethiopia	27:18.20

MARATHON

1896	Spiridon Louis, Greece	2:58:50
1900	Michel Theato, France	2:59:45
1904	Thomas Hicks, United States	3:28:53
1906	William Sherring, Canada	2:51:23.6
1908	John Hayes, United States	2:55:18.4 OR
1912	Kenneth McArthur, South Africa	2:36:54.8
1920	Hannes Kolehmainen, Finland	2:32:35.8 WB
1924	Albin Stenroos, Finland	2:41:22.6
1928	Boughera El Ouafi, France	2:32:57
1932	Juan Zabala, Argentina	2:31:36 OR
1936	Kijung Son, Japan (Korea)	2:29:19.2 OR
1948	Delfo Cabrera, Argentina	2:34:51.6
1952	Emil Zatopek, Czechoslovakia	2:23:03.2 OR
1956	Alain Mimoun O'Kacha, France	2:25:00.0
1960	Abebe Bikila, Ethiopia	2:15:16.2 WB
1964	Abebe Bikila, Ethiopia	2:12:11.2 WB
1968	Mamo Wolde, Ethiopia	2:20:26.4
1972	Frank Shorter, United States	2:12:19.8
1976	Waldemar Cierpinski, E. Germ.	2:09:55 OR
1980	Waldemar Cierpinski, E. Germ.	2:11:03.0
1984	Carlos Lopes, Portugal	2:09:21.0 OR
1988	Gelindo Bordin, Italy	2:10:32
1992	Hwang Young-Cho, S Korea	2:13:23
1996	Josia Thugwane, South Africa	2:12:36
2000	Gezahgne Abera, Ethiopia	2:10:11

110-METER HURDLES

1896	Thomas Curtis, United States	17.6
1900	Alvin Kraenzlein, United States	15.4 OR
1904	Frederick Schule, United States	16.0
1906	Robert Leavitt, United States	16.2
1908	Forrest Smithson, United States	15.0 WR
1912	Frederick Kelly, United States	15.1
1920	Earl Thomson, Canada	14.8 WR
1924	Daniel Kinsey, United States	15.0
1928	Sydney Atkinson, South Africa	14.8
1932	George Saling, United States	14.6
1936	Forrest Towns, United States	14.2
1948	William Porter, United States	13.9 OR
1952	Harrison Dillard, United States	13.7 OR
1956	Lee Calhoun, United States	13.5 OR
1960	Lee Calhoun, United States	13.8
1964	Hayes Jones, United States	13.6
1968	Willie Davenport, United States	13.3 OR
1972	Rod Milburn, United States	13.24 EWR
1976	Guy Drut, France	13.30
1980	Thomas Munkelt, East Germany	13.39
1984	Roger Kingdom, United States	13.20 OR
1988	Roger Kingdom, United States	12.98 OR
1992	Mark McKoy, Canada	13.12
1996	Allen Johnson, United States	12.95 OR
2000	Anier Garcia, Cuba	13.00

400-METER HURDLES

1900	John Walter Tewksbury, U.S.	57.6
1904	Harry Hillman, United States	53.0
1906	Not held	
1908	Charles Bacon, United States	55.0 WR
1912	Not held	
1920	Frank Loomis, United States	54.0 WR
1924	F. Morgan Taylor, United States	52.6
1928	David Burghley, Great Britain	53.4 OR
1932	Robert Tisdall, Ireland	51.7
1936	Glenn Hardin, United States	52.4
1948	Roy Cochran, United States	51.1 OR
1952	Charles Moore, United States	50.8 OR
1956	Glenn Davis, United States	50.1 EOR
1960	Glenn Davis, United States	49.3 EOR
1964	Rex Cawley, United States	49.6
1968	Dave Hemery, Great Britain	48.12 WR
1972	John Akii-Bua, Uganda	47.82 WR
1976	Edwin Moses, United States	47.64 WR
1980	Volker Beck, East Germany	48.70
1984	Edwin Moses, United States	47.75
1988	Andre Phillips, United States	47.19 OR
1992	Kevin Young, United States	46.78 WR
1996	Derrick Adkins, United States	47.54
2000	Angelo Taylor, United States	47.50

3000-METER STEEPLECHASE

1920	Percy Hodge, Great Britain	10:00.4 OR
1924	Vilho (Ville) Ritola, Finland	9:33.6 OR
1928	Toivo Loukola, Finland	9:21.8 WR
1932	Volmari Iso-Hollo, Finland	10:33.4*
1936	Volmari Iso-Hollo, Finland	9:03.8 WR
1948	Thore Sjöstrand, Sweden	9:04.6
1952	Horace Ashenfelter, U.S.	8:45.4 WR
1956	Chris Brasher, Great Britain	8:41.2 OR
1960	Zdzislaw Krzyszkowiak, Poland	8:34.2 OR
1964	Gaston Roelants, Belgium	8:30.8 OR
1968	Amos Biwott, Kenya	8:51
1972	Kipchoge Keino, Kenya	8:23.6 OR
1976	Anders Gärderud, Sweden	8:08.2 WR
1980	Bronislaw Malinowski, Poland	8:09.7
1984	Julius Korir, Kenya	8:11.8
1988	Julius Kariuki, Kenya	8:05.51 OR
1992	Matthew Birir, Kenya	8:08.84
1996	Joseph Keter, Kenya	8:07.12

TRACK AND FIELD (Cont.)

Men (Cont.)

3,000-METER STEEPLECHASE (CONT.)

2000	....Reuben Kosgei, Kenya	8:21.43

*About 3,450 meters; extra lap by error.

4 X 100-METER RELAY

1912	.................Great Britain	42.4 OR
1920	.................United States	42.2 WR
1924	.................United States	41.0 EWR
1928	.................United States	41.0 EWR
1932	.................United States	40.0 EWR
1936	.................United States	39.8 WR
1948	.................United States	40.6
1952	.................United States	40.1
1956	.................United States	39.5 WR
1960	.................West Germany	39.5 EWR
1964	.................United States	39.0 WR
1968	.................United States	38.2 WR
1972	.................United States	38.19 EWR
1976	.................United States	38.33
1980	.................USSR	38.26
1984	.................United States	37.83 WR
1988	.................USSR	38.19
1992	.................United States	37.40 WR
1996	.................Canada	37.69
2000	.................United States	37.61

4 X 400-METER RELAY

1908	.................United States	3:29.4
1912	.................United States	3:16.6 WR
1920	.................Great Britain	3:22.2
1924	.................United States	3:16.0 WR
1928	.................United States	3:14.2 WR
1932	.................United States	3:08.2 WR
1936	.................Great Britain	3:09.0
1948	.................United States	3:10.4 WR
1952	.................Jamaica	3:03.9 WR
1956	.................United States	3:04.8
1960	.................United States	3:02.2 WR
1964	.................United States	3:00.7 WR
1968	.................United States	2:56.16 WR
1972	.................Kenya	2:59.8
1976	.................United States	2:58.65
1980	.................USSR	3:01.1
1984	.................United States	2:57.91
1988	.................United States	2:56.16 EWR
1992	.................United States	2:55.74 WR
1996	.................United States	2:55.99
2000	.................United States	2:56.35

20-KILOMETER WALK

1956	....Leonid Spirin, USSR	1:31:27.4
1960	....Vladimir Golubnichiy, USSR	1:33:07.2
1964	....Kenneth Mathews, Great Britain	1:29:34.0 OR
1968	....Vladimir Golubnichiy, USSR	1:33:58.4
1972	....Peter Frenkel, E Germany	1:26:42.4 OR
1976	....Daniel Bautista, Mexico	1:24:40.6 OR
1980	....Maurizio Damilano, Italy	1:23:35.5 OR
1984	....Ernesto Canto, Mexico	1:23:13.0 OR
1988	....Jozef Pribilinec, Czechoslovakia	1:19:57.0 OR
1992	....Daniel Plaza, Spain	1:21:45.0
1996	....Jefferson Pérez, Ecuador	1:20:07
2000	....Robert Korzeniowski, Poland	1:18:59 OR

50-KILOMETER WALK

1932	....Thomas Green, Great Britain	4:50:10
1936	....Harold Whitlock, Great Britain	4:30:41.4 OR
1948	....John Ljunggren, Sweden	4:41:52
1952	....Giuseppe Dordoni, Italy	4:28:07.8 OR
1956	....Norman Read, New Zealand	4:30:42.8
1960	....Donald Thompson, Great Britain	4:25:30 OR
1964	....Abdon Parnich, Italy	4:11:12.4 OR

50-KILOMETER WALK (CONT.)

1968	....Christoph Höhne, E Germany	4:20:13.6
1972	....Bernd Kannenberg, W Germany	3:56:11.6 OR
1980	....Hartwig Gauder, E Germany	3:49:24.0 OR
1984	....Raul Gonzalez, Mexico	3:47:26.0 OR
1988	....Viacheslav Ivanenko, USSR	3:38:29.0 OR
1992	....Andrey Perlov, Unified Team	3:50:13
1996	....Robert Korzeniowski, Poland	3:43:30
2000	....Robert Korzeniowski, Poland	3:42:22 OR

HIGH JUMP

1896	...Ellery Clark, United States	5 ft 11¼ in
1900	...Irving Baxter, United States	6 ft 2¾ in OR
1904	...Samuel Jones, United States	5 ft 11 in
1906	...Cornelius Leahy, Great Britain/Ireland	5 ft 10 in
1908	...Harry Porter, United States	6 ft 3 in OR
1912	...Alma Richards, United States	6 ft 4 in OR
1920	...Richmond Landon, United States	6 ft 4 in OR
1924	...Harold Osborn, United States	6 ft 6 in OR
1928	...Robert W. King, United States	6 ft 4½ in
1932	...Duncan McNaughton, Canada	6 ft 5½ in
1936	...Cornelius Johnson, United States	6 ft 8 in OR
1948	...John L. Winter, Australia	6 ft 6 in
1952	...Walter Davis, United States	6 ft 8½ in OR
1956	...Charles Dumas, United States	6 ft 11½ in OR
1960	...Robert Shavlakadze, USSR	7 ft 1 in OR
1964	...Valery Brumel, USSR	7 ft 1¾ in OR
1968	...Dick Fosbury, United States	7 ft 4¼ in OR
1972	...Yuri Tarmak, USSR	7 ft 3¾ in
1976	...Jacek Wszola, Poland	7 ft 4½ in OR
1980	...Gerd Wessig, E Germany	7 ft 8¾ in WR
1984	...Dietmar Mögenburg, W Germany	7 ft 8½ in
1988	...Gennadiy Avdeyenko, USSR	7 ft 9¾ in OR
1992	...Javier Sotomayor, Cuba	7 ft 8 in.
1996	...Charles Austin, United States	7 ft 10 in OR
2000	...Sergey Kliugin, Russia	7 ft 8¼ in

POLE VAULT

1896	...William Hoyt, United States	10 ft 10 in
1900	...Irving Baxter, United States	10 ft 10 in
1904	...Charles Dvorak, United States	11 ft 5¾ in
1906	...Fernand Gonder, France	11 ft 5¾ in
1908	...Alfred Gilbert, United States	12 ft 2 in OR
	Edward Cooke Jr, United States	
1912	...Harry Babcock, United States	12 ft 11½ in OR
1920	...Frank Foss, United States	13 ft 5 in WR
1924	...Lee Barnes, United States	12 ft 11½ in
1928	...Sabin Carr, United States	13 ft 9¼ in OR
1932	...William Miller, United States	14 ft 1¾ in OR
1936	...Earle Meadows, United States	14 ft 3¼ in OR
1948	...Guinn Smith, United States	14 ft 1¼ in
1952	...Robert Richards, United States	14 ft 11 in OR
1956	...Robert Richards, United States	14 ft 11½ in OR
1960	...Don Bragg, United States	15 ft 5 in OR
1964	...Fred Hansen, United States	16 ft 8¾ in OR
1968	...Bob Seagren, United States	17 ft 8½ in OR
1972	...Wolfgang Nordwig, E Germany	18 ft ½ in OR
1976	...Tadeusz Slusarski, Poland	18 ft ½ in OR
1980	...Wladyslaw Kozakiewicz, Poland	18 ft 11½ in WR
1984	...Pierre Quinon, France	18 ft 10¼ in
1988	...Sergei Bubka, USSR	19 ft 4¼ in OR
1992	...Maksim Tarasov, Unified Team	19 ft ¼ in
1996	...Jean Galfione, France	19 ft 5 ¼ in OR
2000	...Nick Hysong, United States	19 ft 4¼ in

Note: OR=Olympic Record. WR=World Record. EOR=Equals Olympic Record. EWR=Equals World Record. WB=World Best.

Summer Games Champions *(Cont.)*

TRACK AND FIELD *(Cont.)*

Men *(Cont.)*

LONG JUMP

1896	Ellery Clark, United States	20 ft 10 in
1900	Alvin Kraenzlein, United States	23 ft 6¾ in OR
1904	Meyer Prinstein, United States	24 ft 1 in OR
1906	Meyer Prinstein, United States	23 ft 7½ in
1908	Frank Irons, United States	24 ft 6½ in OR
1912	Albert Gutterson, United States	24 ft 11¼ in OR
1920	William Peterssen, Sweden	23 ft 5½ in
1924	DeHart Hubbard, United States	24 ft 5 in
1928	Edward B. Hamm, United States	25 ft 4½ in OR
1932	Edward Gordon, United States	25 ft ¾ in
1936	Jesse Owens, United States	26 ft 5½ in OR
1948	William Steele, United States	25 ft 8 in
1952	Jerome Biffle, United States	24 ft 10 in
1956	Gregory Bell, United States	25 ft 8¼ in
1960	Ralph Boston, United States	26 ft 7¾ in OR
1964	Lynn Davies, Great Britain	26 ft 5¾ in
1968	Bob Beamon, United States	29 ft 2½ in WR
1972	Randy Williams, United States	27 ft ½ in
1976	Arnie Robinson, United States	27 ft 4¾ in
1980	Lutz Dombrowski, E. Germany	28 ft ¼ in
1984	Carl Lewis, United States	28 ft ¼ in
1988	Carl Lewis, United States	28 ft 7½ in
1992	Carl Lewis, United States	28 ft 5½ in
1996	Carl Lewis, United States	27 ft 10¾ in
2000	Ivan Pedrosa, Cuba	28 ft ¾ in

TRIPLE JUMP

1896	James Connolly, United States	44 ft 11¾ in
1900	Meyer Prinstein, United States	47 ft 5¾ in OR
1904	Meyer Prinstein, United States	47 ft 1 in
1906	Peter O'Connor, Great Britain/Ireland	46 ft 2¼ in
1908	Timothy Ahearne, Great Britain/Ireland	48 ft 11¼ in OR
1912	Gustaf Lindblom, Sweden	48 ft 5¼ in
1920	Vilho Tuulos, Finland	47 ft 7 in
1924	Anthony Winter, Australia	50 ft 11¼ in WR
1928	Mikio Oda, Japan	49 ft 11 in
1932	Chuhei Nambu, Japan	51 ft 7 in WR
1936	Naoto Tajima, Japan	52 ft 6 in WR
1948	Arne Ahman, Sweden	50 ft 6¼ in
1952	Adhemar da Silva, Brazil	53 ft 2¾ in WR
1956	Adhemar da Silva, Brazil	53 ft 7¾ in OR
1960	Jozef Schmidt, Poland	55 ft 2 in
1964	Jozef Schmidt, Poland	55 ft 3½ in OR
1968	Viktor Saneyev, USSR	57 ft ¾ in WR
1972	Viktor Saneyev, USSR	56 ft 11¾ in
1976	Viktor Saneyev, USSR	56 ft 8¾ in
1980	Jaak Uudmae, USSR	56 ft 11¼ in
1984	Al Joyner, United States	56 ft 7½ in
1988	Khristo Markov, Bulgaria	57 ft 9½ in OR
1992	Mike Conley, United States	59 ft 7½ in (w)
1996	Kenny Harrison, United States	59 ft 4¼ in OR
2000	Jonathon Edwards, G. Britain	58 ft 1¼ in

SHOT PUT

1896	Robert Garrett, United States	36 ft 9¾ in
1900	Richard Sheldon, United States	46 ft 3¼ in OR
1904	Ralph Rose, United States	48 ft 7 in WR
1906	Martin Sheridan, United States	40 ft 5¼ in
1908	Ralph Rose, United States	46 ft 7½ in
1912	Pat McDonald, United States	50 ft 4 in OR
1920	Ville Porhola, Finland	48 ft 7¼ in
1924	Clarence Houser, United States	49 ft 2¼ in
1928	John Kuck, United States	52 ft ¾ in WR
1932	Leo Sexton, United States	52 ft 6 in OR

SHOT PUT *(CONT.)*

1936	Hans Woellke, Germany	53 ft 1¾ in OR
1948	Wilbur Thompson, United States	56 ft 2 in OR
1952	Parry O'Brien, United States	57 ft ½ in OR
1956	Parry O'Brien, United States	60 ft 11¼ in OR
1960	William Nieder, United States	64 ft 6¾ in OR
1964	Dallas Long, United States	66 ft 8½ in OR
1968	Randy Matson, United States	67 ft 4¾ in
1972	Wladyslaw Komar, Poland	69 ft 6 in OR
1976	Udo Beyer, E Germany	69 ft ¾ in
1980	Vladimir Kiselyov, USSR	70 ft ½ in OR
1984	Alessandro Andrei, Italy	69 ft 9 in
1988	Ulf Timmermann, E Germany	73 ft 8¾ in OR
1992	Mike Stulce, United States	71 ft 2½ in
1996	Randy Barnes, United States	70 ft 11 in
2000	Arsi Harju, Finland	69 ft 10¼ in

DISCUS THROW

1896	Robert Garrett, United States	95 ft 7½ in
1900	Rudolf Bauer, Hungary	118 ft 3 in OR
1904	Martin Sheridan, United States	128 ft 10½ in OR
1906	Martin Sheridan, United States	136 ft
1908	Martin Sheridan, United States	134 ft 2 in OR
1912	Armas Taipele, Finland	148 ft 3 in OR
1920	Elmer Niklander, Finland	146 ft 7 in
1924	Clarence Houser, United States	151 ft 4 in OR
1928	Clarence Houser, United States	155 ft 3 in OR
1932	John Anderson, United States	162 ft 4 in OR
1936	Ken Carpenter, United States	165 ft 7 in OR
1948	Adolfo Consolini, Italy	173 ft 2 in OR
1952	Sim Iness, United States	180 ft 6 in OR
1956	Al Oerter, United States	184 ft 11 in OR
1960	Al Oerter, United States	194 ft 2 in OR
1964	Al Oerter, United States	200 ft 1 in OR
1968	Al Oerter, United States	212 ft 6 in OR
1972	Ludvik Danek, Czechoslovakia	211 ft 3 in
1976	Mac Wilkins, United States	221 ft 5 in OR
1980	Viktor Rashchupkin, USSR	218 ft 8 in
1984	Rolf Dannenberg, W Germany	218 ft 6 in
1988	Jürgen Schult, E Germany	225 ft 9 in OR
1992	Romas Ubartas, Lithuania	213 ft 8 in
1996	Lars Riedel, Germany	227 ft 8 in OR
2000	Virgilijus Alekna, Lithuania	227 ft 4 in

HAMMER THROW

1900	John Flanagan, United States	163 ft 1 in
1904	John Flanagan, United States	168 ft 1 in OR
1906	Not held	
1908	John Flanagan, United States	170 ft 4 in OR
1912	Matt McGrath, United States	179 ft 7 in OR
1920	Pat Ryan, United States	173 ft 5 in
1924	Fred Tootell, United States	174 ft 10 in
1928	Patrick O'Callaghan, Ireland	168 ft 7 in
1932	Patrick O'Callaghan, Ireland	176 ft 11 in
1936	Karl Hein, Germany	185 ft 4 in OR
1948	Imre Nemeth, Hungary	183 ft 11 in
1952	Jozsef Csermak, Hungary	197 ft 11 in WR
1956	Harold Connolly, United States	207 ft 3 in OR
1960	Vasily Rudenkov, USSR	220 ft 2 in OR
1964	Romuald Klim, USSR	228 ft 10 in OR
1968	Gyula Zsivotsky, Hungary	240 ft 8 in OR
1972	Anatoli Bondarchuk, USSR	247 ft 8 in OR
1976	Yuri Sedykh, USSR	254 ft 4 in OR
1980	Yuri Sedykh, USSR	268 ft 4 in WR
1984	Juha Tiainen, Finland	256 ft 2 in
1988	Sergei Litvinov, USSR	278 ft 2 in OR

TRACK AND FIELD (Cont.)
Men (Cont.)

HAMMER THROW (CONT.)

1992	Andrey Abduvaliyev, Unified Team	270 ft 9 in
1996	Balazs Kiss, Hungary	266 ft 6 in
2000	Szymon Ziolkowski, Poland	262 ft 6 in

JAVELIN

1908	Erik Lemming, Sweden	179 ft 10 in
1912	Erik Lemming, Sweden	198 ft 11 in WR
1920	Jonni Myyrä, Finland	215 ft 10 in OR
1924	Jonni Myyrä, Finland	206 ft 6 in
1928	Eric Lundkvist, Sweden	218 ft 6 in OR
1932	Matti Jarvinen, Finland	238 ft 6 in OR
1936	Gerhard Stöck, Germany	235 ft 8 in
1948	Kai Rautavaara, Finland	228 ft 10½ in
1952	Cy Young, United States	242 ft 1 in OR
1956	Egil Danielson, Norway	281 ft 2¾ in WR
1960	Viktor Tsibulenko, USSR	277 ft 8 in
1964	Pauli Nevala, Finland	271 ft 2 in
1968	Janis Lusis, USSR	295 ft 7 in OR
1972	Klaus Wolfermann, W Germany	296 ft 10 in OR
1976	Miklos Nemeth, Hungary	310 ft 4 in WR
1980	Dainis Kuta, USSR	299 ft 2¾ in
1984	Arto Härkönen, Finland	284 ft 8 in
1988	Tapio Korjus, Finland	276 ft 6 in
1992	Jan Zelezny, Czechoslovakia	294 ft 2 in OR
1996	Jan Zelezny, Czech Republic	289 ft 3 in
2000	Jan Zelezny, Czech Republic	295 ft 9½ in OR

DECATHLON

		Pts
1904	Thomas Kiely, Ireland	6036
1912	Jim Thorpe, United States*	8412 WR
1920	Helge Lövland, Norway	6803
1924	Harold Osborn, United States	7711 WR
1928	Paavo Yrjölä, Finland	8053.29 WR
1932	James Bausch, United States	8462 WR
1936	Glenn Morris, United States	7900 WR
1948	Robert Mathias, United States	7139
1952	Robert Mathias, United States	7887 WR
1956	Milton Campbell, United States	7937 OR
1960	Rafer Johnson, United States	8392 OR
1964	Willi Holdorf, W Germany	7887
1968	Bill Toomey, United States	8193 OR
1972	Nikolai Avilov, USSR	8454 WR
1976	Bruce Jenner, United States	8617 WR
1980	Daley Thompson, Great Britain	8495
1984	Daley Thompson, Great Britain	8798 EWR
1988	Christian Schenk, E Germany	8488
1992	Robert Zmelik, Czechoslovakia	8611
1996	Dan O'Brien, United States	8824 OR
2000	Erki Nool, Estonia	8641

*In 1913, Thorpe was disqualified for having played professional baseball in 1910. His record was restored in 1982.

Women

100 METERS

1928	Elizabeth Robinson, United States	12.2 EWR
1932	Stella Walsh, Poland	11.9 EWR
1936	Helen Stephens, United States	11.5
1948	Francina Blankers-Koen, Netherlands	11.9
1952	Marjorie Jackson, Australia	11.5 EWR
1956	Betty Cuthbert, Australia	11.5 EWR
1960	Wilma Rudolph, United States	11.0
1964	Wyomia Tyus, United States	11.4
1968	Wyomia Tyus, United States	11.0 WR
1972	Renate Stecher, E Germany	11.07
1976	Annegret Richter, W Germany	11.08
1980	Lyudmila Kondratyeva, USSR	11.06
1984	Evelyn Ashford, United States	10.97 OR
1988	Florence Griffith Joyner, United States	10.54 WR
1992	Gail Devers, United States	10.82
1996	Gail Devers, United States	10.94
2000	Marion Jones, United States	10.75

200 METERS

1948	Francina Blankers-Koen, Netherlands	24.4
1952	Marjorie Jackson, Australia	23.7
1956	Betty Cuthbert, Australia	23.4 EOR
1960	Wilma Rudolph, United States	24.0
1964	Edith McGuire, United States	23.0 OR
1968	Irena Szewinska, Poland	22.5 WR
1972	Renate Stecher, E Germany	22.40 EWR
1976	Bärbel Eckert, E Germany	22.37 OR
1980	Bärbel Wöckel (Eckert), E Germ.	22.03 OR
1984	Valerie Brisco-Hooks, U.S.	21.81 OR

200 METERS (CONT.)

1988	Florence Griffith Joyner, U.S.	21.34 WR
1992	Gwen Torrence, United States	21.81
1996	Marie-José Pérec, France	22.12
2000	Marion Jones, United States	21.84

400 METERS

1964	Betty Cuthbert, Australia	52.0 OR
1968	Colette Besson, France	52.0 EOR
1972	Monika Zehrt, E Germany	51.08 OR
1976	Irena Szewinska, Poland	49.29 WR
1980	Marita Koch, E Germany	48.88 OR
1984	Valerie Brisco-Hooks, United States	48.83 OR
1988	Olga Bryzgina, USSR	48.65 OR
1992	Marie-José Pérec, France	48.83
1996	Marie-José Pérec, France	48.25 OR
2000	Cathy Freeman, Australia	49.11

800 METERS

1928	Lina Radke, Germany	2:16.8 WR
1932	Not held 1932–1956	
1960	Lyudmila Shevtsova, USSR	2:04.3 EWR
1964	Ann Packer, Great Britain	2:01.1 OR
1968	Madeline Manning, United States	2:00.9 OR
1972	Hildegard Falck, W Germany	1:58.55 OR
1976	Tatyana Kazankina, USSR	1:54.94 WR
1980	Nadezhda Olizarenko, USSR	1:53.42 WR
1984	Doina Melinte, Romania	1:57.6
1988	Sigrun Wodars, E Germany	1:56.10
1992	Ellen Van Langen, Netherlands	1:55.54
1996	Svetlana Masterkova, Russia	1:57.73
2000	Maria Mutola, Mozambique	1:56.15

Note: OR=Olympic Record. WR=World Record. EOR=Equals Olympic Record. EWR=Equals World Record. WB=World Best.

TRACK AND FIELD (Cont.)
Women (Cont.)

1500 METERS

Year	Champion	Time
1972	Lyudmila Bragina, USSR	4:01.4 WR
1976	Tatyana Kazankina, USSR	4:05.48
1980	Tatyana Kazankina, USSR	3:56.6 OR
1984	Gabriella Dorio, Italy	4:03.25
1988	Paula Ivan, Romania	3:53.96 OR
1992	Hassiba Boulmerka, Algeria	3:55.30
1996	Svetlana Masterkova, Russia	4:00.83
2000	Nouria Merah-Benida, Algeria	4:05.10

3000 METERS

Year	Champion	Time
1984	Maricica Puica, Romania	8:35.96 OR
1988	Tatyana Samolenko, USSR	8:26.53 OR
1992	Elena Romanova, Unified Team	8:46.04

5000 METERS

Year	Champion	Time
1996	Wang Junxia, China	14:57.88
2000	Gabriela Szabo, Romania	14:40.79 OR

10,000 METERS

Year	Champion	Time
1988	Olga Bondarenko, USSR	31:05.21 OR
1992	Derartu Tulu, Ethiopia	31:06.02
1996	Fernanda Ribeiro, Portugal	31:01.63 OR
2000	Derartu Tulu, Ethiopia	30:17.49 OR

MARATHON

Year	Champion	Time
1984	Joan Benoit, United States	2:24:52 OR
1988	Rosa Mota, Portugal	2:25:40
1992	Valentin Yegorova, Unified Team	2:32:41
1996	Fatuma Roba, Ethiopia	2:26:05
2000	Naoko Takahashi, Japan	2:23.14 OR

80-METER HURDLES

Year	Champion	Time
1932	Babe Didrikson, United States	11.7 WR
1936	Trebisonda Valla, Italy	11.7
1948	Francina Blankers-Koen, Netherlands	11.2 OR
1952	Shirley Strickland, Australia	10.9 WR
1956	Shirley Strickland, Australia	10.7 OR
1960	Irina Press, USSR	10.8
1964	Karin Balzer, E Germany	10.5
1968	Maureen Caird, Australia	10.3 OR

100-METER HURDLES

Year	Champion	Time
1972	Annelie Ehrhardt, E Germany	12.59 WR
1976	Johanna Schaller, E Germany	12.77
1980	Vera Komisova, USSR	12.56 OR
1984	Benita Fitzgerald-Brown, United States	12.84
1988	Yordanka Donkova, Bulgaria	12.38 OR
1992	Paraskevi Patoulidou, Greece	12.64
1996	Lyudmila Engqvist, Sweden	12.58
2000	Olga Shishigina, Kazakhstan	12.65

400-METER HURDLES

Year	Champion	Time
1984	Nawal el Moutawakel, Morocco	54.61 OR
1988	Debra Flintoff-King, Australia	53.17 OR
1992	Sally Gunnell, Great Britain	53.23
1996	Deon Hemmings, Jamaica	52.82 OR
2000	Irina Privalova, Russia	53.02

4 X 100-METER RELAY

Year	Champion	Time
1928	Canada	48.4 WR
1932	United States	46.9 WR
1936	United States	46.9
1948	Netherlands	47.5
1952	United States	45.9 WR
1956	Australia	44.5 WR

4 X 100-METER RELAY (CONT.)

Year	Champion	Time
1960	United States	44.5
1964	Poland	43.6
1968	United States	42.8 WR
1972	W Germany	42.81 EWR
1976	E Germany	42.55 OR
1980	E Germany	41.60 WR
1984	United States	41.65
1988	United States	41.98
1992	United States	42.11
1996	United States	41.95
2000	Bahamas	41.95

4 X 400-METER RELAY

Year	Champion	Time
1972	E Germany	3:23 WR
1976	E Germany	3:19.23 WR
1980	USSR	3:20.02
1984	United States	3:18.29 OR
1988	USSR	3:15.18 WR
1992	Unified Team	3:20.20
1996	United States	3:20.91
2000	United States	3:22.62

10-KILOMETER WALK

Year	Champion	Time
1992	Chen Yueling, China	44:32
1996	Elena Nikolayeva, Russia	41:49 OR

20-KILOMETER WALK

Year	Champion	Time
2000	Liping Wang, China	1:29.05

HIGH JUMP

Year	Champion	Mark
1928	Ethel Catherwood, Canada	5 ft 2½ in
1932	Jean Shiley, United States	5 ft 5¼ in WR
1936	Ibolya Csak, Hungary	5 ft 3 in
1948	Alice Coachman, United States	5 ft 6 in OR
1952	Esther Brand, South Africa	5 ft 5¾ in
1956	Mildred L. McDaniel, U.S.	5 ft 9¼ in WR
1960	Iolanda Balas, Romania	6 ft ¾ in OR
1964	Iolanda Balas, Romania	6 ft 2¾ in OR
1968	Miloslava Reskova, Czech.	5 ft 11½ in
1972	Ulrike Meyfarth, W. Germany	6 ft 3½ in EWR
1976	Rosemarie Ackermann, E. Germ	6 ft 4 in OR
1980	Sara Simeoni, Italy	6 ft 5½ in OR
1984	Ulrike Meyfarth, W Germany	6 ft 7½ in OR
1988	Louise Ritter, United States	6 ft 8 in OR
1992	Heike Henkel, Germany	6 ft 7½ in
1996	Stefka Kostadinova, Bulgaria	6 ft 8¾ in OR
2000	Yelena Yelesina, Russia	6 ft 7 in

LONG JUMP

Year	Champion	Mark
1948	Olga Gyarmati, Hungary	18 ft 8¼ in
1952	Yvette Williams, New Zealand	20 ft 5¾ in OR
1956	Elzbieta Krzeskinska, Poland	20 ft 10 in EWR
1960	Vyera Krepkina, USSR	20 ft 10¾ in OR
1964	Mary Rand, Great Britain	22 ft 2¼ in WR
1968	Viorica Viscopoleanu, Romania	22 ft 4½ in WR
1972	Heidemarie Rosendahl, W Germany	22 ft 3 in
1976	Angela Voigt, E Germany	22 ft ¾ in
1980	Tatyana Kolpakova, USSR	23 ft 2 in OR
1984	Anisoara Stanciu, Romania	22 ft 10 in
1988	Jackie Joyner-Kersee, United States	24 ft 3½ in OR
1992	Heike Drechsler, Germany	23 ft 5¼ in
1996	Chioma Ajunwa, Nigeria	23 ft 4½ in
2000	Heike Drechsler, Germany	22 ft 11¼ in

Note: OR=Olympic Record; WR=World Record; EOR=Equals Olympic Record; EWR=Equals World Record; WB=World Best.

TRACK AND FIELD (Cont.)
Women (Cont.)

TRIPLE JUMP
1996	Inessa Kravets, Ukraine	50 ft 3½ in
2000	Tereza Marinova, Bulgaria	49 ft 10½ in

SHOT PUT
1948	Micheline Ostermeyer, France	45 ft 1½ in
1952	Galina Zybina, USSR	50 ft 1¾ in WR
1956	Tamara Tyshkevich, USSR	54 ft 5 in OR
1960	Tamara Press, USSR	56 ft 10 in OR
1964	Tamara Press, USSR	59 ft 6¼ in OR
1968	Margitta Gummel, E. Germany	64 ft 4 in WR
1972	Nadezhda Chizhova, USSR	69 ft WR
1976	Ivanka Hristova, Bulgaria	69 ft 5¼ in OR
1980	Ilona Slupianek, E Germany	73 ft 6¼ in
1984	Claudia Losch, W. Germany	67 ft 2¼ in
1988	Natalya Lisovskaya, USSR	72 ft 11¾ in
1992	Svetlana Kriveleva, Unified Team	69 ft 1¼ in
1996	Astrid Kumbernuss, Germany	67 ft 5½ in
2000	Yanina Korolchik, Belarus	67 ft 5½ in

DISCUS THROW
1928	Helena Konopacka, Poland	129 ft 11¾ in WR
1932	Lillian Copeland, United States	133 ft 2 in OR
1936	Gisela Mauermayer, Germany	156 ft 3 in OR
1948	Micheline Ostermeyer, France	137 ft 6 in
1952	Nina Romaschkova, USSR	168 ft 8 in OR
1956	Olga Fikotova, Czechoslovakia	176 ft 1 in OR
1960	Nina Ponomaryeva, USSR	180 ft 9 in OR
1964	Tamara Press, USSR	187 ft 10 in OR
1968	Lia Manoliu, Romania	191 ft 2 in OR
1972	Faina Melnik, USSR	218 ft 7 in OR
1976	Evelin Schlaak, E Germany	226 ft 4 in OR
1980	Evelin Jahl (Schlaak), E. Germ	229 ft 6 in OR
1984	Ria Stalman, Netherlands	214 ft 5 in
1988	Martina Hellmann, E. Germany	237 ft 2 in OR
1992	Maritza Martén, Cuba	229 ft 10 in
1996	Ilke Wyludda, Germany	228 ft 6 in
2000	Ellina Zvereva, Belarus	224 ft 5 in

HAMMER THROW
2000	Kamila Skolimowska, Russia	233 ft 5 in OR

JAVELIN THROW
1932	Babe Didrikson, United States	143 ft 4 in OR
1936	Tilly Fleischer, Germany	148 ft 3 in OR
1948	Herma Bauma, Austria	149 ft 6 in
1952	Dana Zatopkova, Czechoslovakia	165 ft 7 in
1956	Inese Jaunzeme, USSR	176 ft 8 in
1960	Elvira Ozolina, USSR	183 ft 8 in OR
1964	Mihaela Penes, Romania	198 ft 7 in
1968	Angela Nemeth, Hungary	198 ft
1972	Ruth Fuchs, E Germany	209 ft 7 in OR
1976	Ruth Fuchs, E Germany	216 ft 4 in OR
1980	Maria Colon, Cuba	224 ft 5 in OR
1984	Tessa Sanderson, Great Britain	228 ft 2 in OR
1988	Petra Felke, E Germany	245 ft OR
1992	Silke Renk, Germany	224 ft 2 in
1996	Heli Rantanen, Finland	222 ft 11 in
2000	Trine Hattestad, Norway	226 ft ½ in OR

PENTATHLON
		Pts
1964	Irina Press, USSR	5246 WR
1968	Ingrid Becker, W Germany	5098
1972	Mary Peters, Great Britain	4801 WR*
1976	Siegrun Siegl, E Germany	4745
1980	Nadezhda Tkachenko, USSR	5083 WR

HEPTATHLON
		Pts
1984	Glynis Nunn, Australia	6390 OR
1988	Jackie Joyner-Kersee, U.S.	7291 WR
1992	Jackie Joyner-Kersee, U.S.	7044
1996	Ghada Shouaa, Syria	6780
2000	Denise Lewis, Great Britain	6584

BASKETBALL
Men

1936
Final: United States 19, Canada 8
United States: Ralph Bishop, Joe Fortenberry, Carl Knowles, Jack Ragland, Carl Shy, William Wheatley, Francis Johnson, Samuel Balter, John Gibbons, Frank Lubin, Arthur Mollner, Donald Piper, Duane Swanson, Willard Schmidt

1948
Final: United States 65, France 21
United States: Cliff Barker, Don Barksdale, Ralph Beard, Lewis Beck, Vince Boryla, Gordon Carpenter, Alex Groza, Wallace Jones, Bob Kurland, Ray Lumpp, Robert Pitts, Jesse Renick, Bob Robinson, Ken Rollins

1952
Final: United States 36, USSR 25
United States: Charles Hoag, Bill Hougland, Melvin Dean Kelley, Bob Kenney, Clyde Lovellette, Marcus Freiberger, Victor Wayne Glasgow, Frank McCabe, Daniel Pippen, Howard Williams, Ronald Bontemps, Bob Kurland, William Lienhard, John Keller

1956
Final: United States 89, USSR 55
United States: Carl Cain, Bill Hougland, K. C. Jones, Bill Russell, James Walsh, William Evans, Burdette Haldorson, Ron Tomsic, Dick Boushka, Gilbert Ford, Bob Jeangerard, Charles Darling

1960
Final: United States 90, Brazil 63
United States: Jay Arnette, Walt Bellamy, Bob Boozer, Terry Dischinger, Jerry Lucas, Oscar Robertson, Adrian Smith, Burdette Haldorson, Darrall Imhoff, Allen Kelley, Lester Lane, Jerry West

1964
Final: United States 73, USSR 59
United States: Jim Barnes, Bill Bradley, Larry Brown, Joe Caldwell, Mel Counts, Richard Davies, Walt Hazzard, Lucius Jackson, John McCaffrey, Jeff Mullins, Jerry Shipp, George Wilson

1968
Final: United States 65, Yugoslavia 50
United States: John Clawson, Ken Spain, Jo-Jo White, Michael Barrett, Spencer Haywood, Charles Scott, William Hosket, Calvin Fowler, Michael Silliman, Glynn Saulters, James King, Donald Dee

1972
Final: USSR 51, United States 50
United States: Kenneth Davis, Doug Collins, Thomas Henderson, Mike Bantom, Bobby Jones, Dwight Jones, James Forbes, James Brewer, Tom Burleson, Tom McMillen, Kevin Joyce, Ed Ratleff

BASKETBALL *(Cont.)*

Men *(Cont.)*

1976
Final: United States 95, Yugoslavia 74
United States: Phil Ford, Steve Sheppard, Adrian Dantley, Walter Davis, Quinn Buckner, Ernie Grunfield, Kenny Carr, Scott May, Michel Armstrong, Tom La Garde, Phil Hubbard, Mitch Kupchak

1980
Final: Yugoslavia 86, Italy 77
U.S. participated in boycott.

1984
Final: United States 96, Spain 65
United States: Steve Alford, Leon Wood, Patrick Ewing, Vern Fleming, Alvin Robertson, Michael Jordan, Joe Kleine, Jon Koncak, Wayman Tisdale, Chris Mullin, Sam Perkins, Jeff Turner

1988
Final: USSR 76, Yugoslavia 63
United States (3rd): Mitch Richmond, Charles E. Smith IV, Vernell Coles, Hersey Hawkins, Jeff Grayer, Charles D. Smith, Willie Anderson, Stacey Augmon, Dan Majerle, Danny Manning, J. R. Reid, David Robinson

1992
Final: United States 117, Croatia 85
United States: David Robinson, Christian Laettner, Patrick Ewing, Larry Bird, Scottie Pippen, Michael Jordan, Clyde Drexler, Karl Malone, John Stockton, Chris Mullin, Charles Barkley, Earvin Johnson

1996
Final: United States 95, Yugoslavia 69
United States: Charles Barkley, Anfernee Hardaway, Grant Hill, Karl Malone, Reggie Miller, Hakeem Olajuwon, Shaquille O'Neal, Scottie Pippen, Mitch Richmond, John Stockton, David Robinson, Gary Payton

2000
Final: United States 85, France 75
United States: Shareef Abdur-Rahim, Ray Allen, Vin Baker, Vince Carter, Kevin Garnett, Tim Hardaway, Allan Houston, Jason Kidd, Antonio McDyess, Alonzo Mourning, Gary Payton, Steve Smith.

Women

1976
Gold, USSR; Silver, United States*
United States: Cindy Brogdon, Susan Rojcewicz, Ann Meyers, Lusia Harris, Nancy Dunkle, Charlotte Lewis, Nancy Lieberman, Gail Marquis, Patricia Roberts, Mary Anne O'Connor, Patricia Head, Julienne Simpson

*In 1976 the women played a round-robin tournament, with the gold medal going to the team with the best record. The USSR won with a 5-0 record, and the USA, with a 3-2 record, was given the silver by virtue of a 95-79 victory over Bulgaria, which was also 3-2.

1980
Final: USSR 104, Bulgaria 73
U.S. participated in boycott.

1984
Final: United States 85, Korea 55
United States: Teresa Edwards, Lea Henry, Lynette Woodard, Anne Donovan, Cathy Boswell, Cheryl Miller, Janice Lawrence, Cindy Noble, Kim Mulkey, Denise Curry, Pamela McGee, Carol Menken-Schaudt

1988
Final: United States 77, Yugoslavia 70
United States: Teresa Edwards, Mary Ethridge, Cynthia Brown, Anne Donovan, Teresa Weatherspoon, Bridgette Gordon, Victoria Bullett, Andrea Lloyd, Katrina McClain, Jennifer Gillom, Cynthia Cooper, Suzanne McConnell

1992
Final: Unified Team 76, China 66
United States (3rd): Teresa Edwards, Teresa Weatherspoon, Victoria Bullett, Katrina McClain, Cynthia Cooper, Suzanne McConnell, Daedra Charles, Clarissa Davis, Tammy Jackson, Vickie Orr, Carolyn Jones, Medina Dixon

1996
Final: United States 111, Brazil 87
United States: Jennifer Azzi, Ruthie Bolton, Teresa Edwards, Lisa Leslie, Rebecca Lobo, Katrina McClain, Nikki McCray, Carla McGhee, Dawn Staley, Katy Steding, Sheryl Swoopes, Venus Lacey

2000
Final: United States 76, Australia 54
United States: Ruthie Bolton-Holifield, Teresa Edwards, Yolanda Griffith, Chamique Holdsclaw, Lisa Leslie, Nikki McCray, Delisha Milton, Katie Smith, Dawn Staley, Sheryl Swoopes, Natalie Williams, Kara Wolters.

BOXING

LIGHT FLYWEIGHT (106 LB)

1968 ....Francisco Rodriguez, Venezuela
1972 ....Gyorgy Gedo, Hungary
1976 ....Jorge Hernandez, Cuba
1980 ....Shamil Sabyrov, USSR
1984 ....Paul Gonzalez, United States

LIGHT FLYWEIGHT *(CONT.)*

1988 ....Ivailo Hristov, Bulgaria
1992 ....Rogelio Marcelo, Cuba
1996 ....Daniel Petrov, Bulgaria
2000 ....Brahim Asloum, France

BOXING (Cont.)

FLYWEIGHT (112 LB)
1904 ....George Finnegan, United States
1906-1912 ......Not held
1920 ....Frank Di Gennara, United States
1924 ....Fidel LaBarba, United States
1928 ....Antal Kocsis, Hungary
1932 ....Istvan Enekes, Hungary
1936 ....Willi Kaiser, Germany
1948 ....Pascual Perez, Argentina
1952 ....Nathan Brooks, United States
1956 ....Terence Spinks, Great Britain
1960 ....Gyula Torok, Hungary
1964 ....Fernando Atzori, Italy
1968 ....Ricardo Delgado, Mexico
1972 ....Georgi Kostadinov, Bulgaria
1976 ....Leo Randolph, United States
1980 ....Peter Lessov, Bulgaria
1984 ....Steve McCrory, United States
1988 ....Kim Kwang Sun, South Korea
1992 ....Su Choi Chol, North Korea
1996 ....Maikro Romero, Cuba
2000 ....Wijan Ponlid, Thailand

BANTAMWEIGHT (119 LB)
1904 ....Oliver Kirk, United States
1906 ....Not held
1908 ....A. Henry Thomas, Great Britain
1912 ....Not held
1920 ....Clarence Walker, South Africa
1924 ....William Smith, South Africa
1928 ....Vittorio Tamagnini, Italy
1932 ....Horace Gwynne, Canada
1936 ....Ulderico Sergo, Italy
1948 ....Tibor Csik, Hungary
1952 ....Pentti Hamalainen, Finland
1956 ....Wolfgang Behrendt, E Germany
1960 ....Oleg Grigoryev, USSR
1964 ....Takao Sakurai, Japan
1968 ....Valery Sokolov, USSR
1972 ....Orlando Martinez, Cuba
1976 ....Yong Jo Gu, North Korea
1980 ....Juan Hernandez, Cuba
1984 ....Maurizio Stecca, Italy
1988 ....Kennedy McKinney, United States
1992 ....Joel Casamayor, Cuba
1996 ....István Kovács, Hungary
2000 ....Guillermo Ortiz, Cuba

FEATHERWEIGHT (125 LB)
1904 ....Oliver Kirk, United States
1906 ....Not held
1908 ....Richard Gunn, Great Britain
1912 ....Not held
1920 ....Paul Fritsch, France
1924 ....John Fields, United States
1928 ....Lambertus van Klaveren, Netherlands
1932 ....Carmelo Robledo, Argentina
1936 ....Oscar Casanovas, Argentina
1948 ....Ernesto Formenti, Italy
1952 ....Jan Zachara, Czechoslovakia
1956 ....Vladimir Safronov, USSR
1960 ....Francesco Musso, Italy
1964 ....Stanislav Stephashkin, USSR
1968 ....Antonio Roldan, Mexico
1972 ....Boris Kousnetsov, USSR
1976 ....Angel Herrera, Cuba
1980 ....Rudi Fink, E Germany
1984 ....Meldrick Taylor, United States
1988 ....Giovanni Parisi, Italy
1992 ....Andreas Tews, Germany
1996 ....Somluck Kamsing, Thailand
2000 ....Bekzat Sattarkhanox, Kazakhstan

LIGHTWEIGHT (132 LB)
1904 ....Harry Spanger, United States
1906 ....Not held
1908 ....Frederick Grace, Great Britain
1912 ....Not held
1920 ....Samuel Mosberg, United States
1924 ....Hans Nielsen, Denmark
1928 ....Carlo Orlandi, Italy
1932 ....Lawrence Stevens, South Africa
1936 ....Imre Harangi, Hungary
1948 ....Gerald Dreyer, South Africa
1952 ....Aureliano Bolognesi, Italy
1956 ....Richard McTaggart, Great Britain
1960 ....Kazimierz Pazdzior, Poland
1964 ....Jozef Grudzien, Poland
1968 ....Ronald Harris, United States
1972 ....Jan Szczepanski, Poland
1976 ....Howard Davis, United States
1980 ....Angel Herrera, Cuba
1984 ....Pernell Whitaker, United States
1988 ....Andreas Zuelow, E Germany
1992 ....Oscar De La Hoya, United States
1996 ....Hocine Soltani, Algeria
2000 ....Mario Kindelan, Cuba

LIGHT WELTERWEIGHT (139 LB)
1952 ....Charles Adkins, United States
1956 ....Vladimir Yengibaryan, USSR
1960 ....Bohumil Nemecek, Czechoslovakia
1964 ....Jerzy Kulej, Poland
1968 ....Jerzy Kulej, Poland
1972 ....Ray Seales, United States
1976 ....Ray Leonard, United States
1980 ....Patrizio Oliva, Italy
1984 ....Jerry Page, United States
1988 ....Viatcheslav Janovski, USSR
1992 ....Hector Vinent, Cuba
1996 ....Hector Vinent, Cuba
2000 ....Mahamadkadyz Abdullaev, Uzbekistan

WELTERWEIGHT (147 LB)
1904 ....Albert Young, United States
1906-1912 ......Not held
1920 ....Albert Schneider, Canada
1924 ....Jean Delarge, Belgium
1928 ....Edward Morgan, New Zealand
1932 ....Edward Flynn, United States
1936 ....Sten Suvio, Finland
1948 ....Julius Torma, Czechoslovakia
1952 ....Zygmunt Chychla, Poland
1956 ....Nicolae Linca, Romania
1960 ....Giovanni Benvenuti, Italy
1964 ....Marian Kasprzyk, Poland
1968 ....Manfred Wolke, E Germany
1972 ....Emilio Correa, Cuba
1976 ....Jochen Bachfeld, E Germany
1980 ....Andres Aldama, Cuba
1984 ....Mark Breland, United States
1988 ....Robert Wangila, Kenya
1992 ....Michael Carruth, Ireland
1996 ....Oleg Saitov, Russia
2000 ....Oleg Saitov, Russia

LIGHT MIDDLEWEIGHT (156 LB)
1952 ....Laszlo Papp, Hungary
1956 ....Laszlo Papp, Hungary
1960 ....Wilbert McClure, United States
1964 ....Boris Lagutin, USSR
1968 ....Boris Lagutin, USSR
1972 ....Dieter Kottysch, W Germany
1976 ....Jerzy Rybicki, Poland
1980 ....Armando Martinez, Cuba
1984 ....Frank Tate, United States

BOXING (Cont.)

LIGHT MIDDLEWEIGHT (CONT.)
1988 ....Park Si-Hun, South Korea
1992 ....Juan Lemus, Cuba
1996 ....David Reid, United States
2000 ....Yermakhan Ibraimov, Kazahkstan

MIDDLEWEIGHT (165 LB)
1904 ....Charles Mayer, United States
1908 ....John Douglas, Great Britain
1912 ....Not held
1920 ....Harry Mallin, Great Britain
1924 ....Harry Mallin, Great Britain
1928 ....Piero Toscani, Italy
1932 ....Carmen Barth, United States
1936 ....Jean Despeaux, France
1948 ....Laszlo Papp, Hungary
1952 ....Floyd Patterson, United States
1956 ....Gennady Schatkov, USSR
1960 ....Edward Crook, United States
1964 ....Valery Popenchenko, USSR
1968 ....Christopher Finnegan, Great Britain
1972 ....Vyacheslav Lemechev, USSR
1976 ....Michael Spinks, United States
1980 ....Jose Gomez, Cuba
1984 ....Shin Joon Sup, South Korea
1988 ....Henry Maske, E Germany
1992 ....Ariel Hernandez, Cuba
1996 ....Ariel Hernandez, Cuba
2000 ....Jorge Gutierrez, Cuba

LIGHT HEAVYWEIGHT (178 LB)
1920 ....Edward Eagan, United States
1924 ....Harry Mitchell, Great Britain
1928 ....Victor Avendano, Argentina
1932 ....David Carstens, South Africa
1936 ....Roger Michelot, France
1948 ....George Hunter, South Africa
1952 ....Norvel Lee, United States
1956 ....James Boyd, United States
1960 ....Cassius Clay, United States
1964 ....Cosimo Pinto, Italy
1968 ....Dan Poznyak, USSR
1972 ....Mate Parlov, Yugoslavia
1976 ....Leon Spinks, United States

LIGHT HEAVYWEIGHT (CONT.)
1980 ....Slobodan Kacer, Yugoslavia
1984 ....Anton Josipovic, Yugoslavia
1988 ....Andrew Maynard, United States
1992 ....Torsten May, Germany
1996 ....Vassili Jirov, Kazakhstan
2000 ....Alexander Lebziak, Russia

HEAVYWEIGHT (OVER 201 LB)
1904 ....Samuel Berger, United States
1906 ....Not held
1908 ....Albert Oldham, Great Britain
1912 ....Not held
1920 ....Ronald Rawson, Great Britain
1924 ....Otto von Porat, Norway
1928 ....Arturo Rodriguez Jurado, Argentina
1932 ....Santiago Lovell, Argentina
1936 ....Herbert Runge, Germany
1948 ....Rafael Inglesias, Argentina
1952 ....H. Edward Sanders, United States
1956 ....T. Peter Rademacher, United States
1960 ....Franco De Piccoli, Italy
1964 ....Joe Frazier, United States
1968 ....George Foreman, United States
1972 ....Teofilo Stevenson, Cuba
1976 ....Teofilo Stevenson, Cuba
1980 ....Teofilo Stevenson, Cuba

HEAVYWEIGHT (201* LB)
1984 ....Henry Tillman, United States
1988 ....Ray Mercer, United States
1992 ....Félix Sávon, Cuba
1996 ....Félix Sávon, Cuba
2000 ....Félix Sávon, Cuba

SUPER HEAVYWEIGHT (UNLIMITED)
1984 ....Tyrell Biggs, United States
1988 ....Lennox Lewis, Canada
1992 ....Roberto Balado, Cuba
1996 ....Vladimir Klitchko, Ukraine
2000 ....Audley Harrison, Great Britain

*Until 1984 the heavyweight division was unlimited. With the addition of the super heavyweight division, a limit of 201 pounds was imposed.

SWIMMING

Men

50-METER FREESTYLE
1904 ....Zoltan Halmay, Hungary (50 yds)   28.0
1988 ....Matt Biondi, United States   22.14 WR
1992 ....Aleksandr Popov, Unified Team   22.30
1996 ....Aleksandr Popov, Russia   22.13
2000 ....Anthony Ervin, United States   21.98
      Gary Hall Jr, United States   21.98

100-METER FREESTLYE
1896 ....Alfred Hajos, Hungary   1:22.2 OR
1904 ....Zoltan Halmay, Hungary (100 yds)   1:02.8
1906 ....Charles Daniels, United States   1:13.4
1908 ....Charles Daniels, United States   1:05.6 WR
1912 ....Duke Kahanamoku, United States   1:03.4
1920 ....Duke Kahanamoku, United States   1:00.4 WR
1924 ....John Weissmuller, United States   59.0 OR
1928 ....John Weissmuller, United States   58.6 OR
1932 ....Yasuji Miyazaki, Japan   58.2

100-METER FREESTLYE (CONT.)
1936 ....Ferenc Csik, Hungary   57.6
1948 ....Wally Ris, United States   57.3 OR
1952 ....Clarke Scholes, United States   57.4
1956 ....Jon Henricks, Australia   55.4 OR
1960 ....John Devitt, Australia   55.2 OR
1964 ....Don Schollander, United States   53.4 OR
1968 ....Mike Wenden, Australia   52.2 WR
1972 ....Mark Spitz, United States   51.22 WR
1976 ....Jim Montgomery, United States   49.99 WR
1980 ....Jörg Woithe, East Germany   50.40
1984 ....Rowdy Gaines, United States   49.80 OR
1988 ....Matt Biondi, United States   48.63 OR
1992 ....Aleksandr Popov, Unified Team   49.02
1996 ....Aleksandr Popov, Russia   48.74
2000 ....P. van den Hoogenband, Neth.   48.30

Note: OR=Olympic Record. WR=World Record. EOR=Equals Olympic Record. EWR=Equals World Record. WB=World Best.

SWIMMING (Cont.)
Men (Cont.)

200-METER FREESTYLE

1900	Frederick Lane, Australia	2:25.2 OR
1904	Charles Daniels, United States	2:44.2
1906	Not held 1906–1964	
1968	Michael Wenden, Australia	1:55.2 OR
1972	Mark Spitz, United States	1:52.78 WR
1976	Bruce Furniss, United States	1:50.29 WR
1980	Sergei Kopliakov, USSR	1:49.81 OR
1984	Michael Gross, W Germany	1:47.44 WR
1988	Duncan Armstrong, Australia	1:47.25 WR
1992	Evgueni Sadovyi, Unified Team	1:46.70 OR
1996	Danyon Loader, New Zealand	1:47.63
2000	Pieter van den Hoogenband, Netherlands	1:45.35EWR

400-METER FREESTYLE

1896	Paul Neumann, Austria (500 yds)	8:12.6
1904	Charles Daniels, U.S. (440 yds)	6:16.2
1906	Otto Scheff, Austria (440 yds)	6:23.8
1908	Henry Taylor, Great Britain	5:36.8
1912	George Hodgson, Canada	5:24.4
1920	Norman Ross, United States	5:26.8
1924	John Weissmuller, United States	5:04.2 OR
1928	Albert Zorilla, Argentina	5:01.6 OR
1932	Buster Crabbe, United States	4:48.4 OR
1936	Jack Medica, United States	4:44.5 OR
1948	William Smith, United States	4:41.0 OR
1952	Jean Boiteux, France	4:30.7 OR
1956	Murray Rose, Australia	4:27.3 OR
1960	Murray Rose, Australia	4:18.3 OR
1964	Don Schollander, United States	4:12.2 WR
1968	Mike Burton, United States	4:09.0 OR
1972	Brad Cooper, Australia	4:00.27 OR
1976	Brian Goodell, United States	3:51.93 WR
1980	Vladimir Salnikov, USSR	3:51.31 OR
1984	George DiCarlo, United States	3:51.23 OR
1988	Uwe Dassler, E Germany	3:46.95 WR
1992	Evgueni Sadovyi, Unified Team	3:45.00 WR
1996	Danyon Loader, New Zealand	3:47.97
2000	Ian Thorpe, Australia	3:40.59 WR

1500-METER FREESTYLE

1908	Henry Taylor, Great Britain	22:48.4 WR
1912	George Hodgson, Canada	22:00.0 WR
1920	Norman Ross, United States	22:23.2
1924	Andrew Charlton, Australia	20:06.6 WR
1928	Arne Borg, Sweden	19:51.8 OR
1932	Kusuo Kitamura, Japan	19:12.4 OR
1936	Noboru Terada, Japan	19:13.7
1948	James McLane, United States	19:18.5
1952	Ford Konno, United States	18:30.3 OR
1956	Murray Rose, Australia	17:58.9
1960	John Konrads, Australia	17:19.6 OR
1964	Robert Windle, Australia	17:01.7 OR
1968	Mike Burton, United States	16:38.9 OR
1972	Mike Burton, United States	15:52.58 OR
1976	Brian Goodell, United States	15:02.40 WR
1980	Vladimir Salnikov, USSR	14:58.27 WR
1984	Michael O'Brien, United States	15:05.20
1988	Vladimir Salnikov, USSR	15:00.40
1992	Kieren Perkins, Australia	14:43.48 WR
1996	Kieren Perkins, Australia	14:56.40
2000	Grant Hackett, Australia	14:48.33

100-METER BACKSTROKE

1904	Walter Brack, Germany (100 yds)	1:16.8
1908	Arno Bieberstein, Germany	1:24.6 WR
1912	Harry Hebner, United States	1:21.2

100-METER BACKSTROKE (CONT.)

1920	Warren Kealoha, United States	1:15.2
1924	Warren Kealoha, United States	1:13.2 OR
1928	George Kojac, United States	1:08.2 WR
1932	Masaji Kiyokawa, Japan	1:08.6
1936	Adolph Kiefer, United States	1:05.9 OR
1948	Allen Stack, United States	1:06.4
1952	Yoshi Oyakawa, United States	1:05.4 OR
1956	David Thiele, Australia	1:02.2 OR
1960	David Thiele, Australia	1:01.9 OR
1964	Not held	
1968	Roland Matthes, E Germany	58.7 OR
1972	Roland Matthes, E Germany	56.58 OR
1976	John Naber, United States	55.49 WR
1980	Bengt Baron, Sweden	56.33
1984	Rick Carey, United States	55.79
1988	Daichi Suzuki, Japan	55.05
1992	Mark Tewksbury, Canada	53.98 WR
1996	Jeff Rouse, United States	54.10
2000	Lenny Krayzelburg, United States	53.72 OR

200-METER BACKSTROKE

1900	Ernst Hoppenberg, Germany	2:47.0
1904	Not held 1904-1960	
1964	Jed Graef, United States	2:10.3 WR
1968	Roland Matthes, E Germany	2:09.6 OR
1972	Roland Matthes, E Germany	2:02.82 EWR
1976	John Naber, United States	1:59.19 WR
1980	Sandor Wladar, Hungary	2:01.93
1984	Rick Carey, United States	2:00.23
1988	Igor Polianski, USSR	1:59.37
1992	Martin Lopez-Zubero, Spain	1:58.47 OR
1996	Brad Bridgewater, United States	1:58.54
2000	Lenny Krayzelburg, United States	1:56.76 OR

100-METER BREASTSTROKE

1968	Don McKenzie, United States	1:07.7 OR
1972	Nobutaka Taguchi, Japan	1:04.94 WR
1976	John Hencken, United States	1:03.11 WR
1980	Duncan Goodhew, Great Britain	1:03.44
1984	Steve Lundquist, United States	1:01.65 WR
1988	Adrian Moorhouse, Great Britain	1:02.04
1992	Nelson Diebel, United States	1:01.50 OR
1996	Fred DeBurghgraeve, Belgium	1:00.65
2000	Domenico Fioravanti, Italy	1:00.46 OR

200-METER BREASTSTROKE

1908	Frederick Holman, Great Britain	3:09.2 WR
1912	Walter Bathe, Germany	3:01.8 OR
1920	Haken Malmroth, Sweden	3:04.4
1924	Robert Skelton, United States	2:56.6
1928	Yoshiyuki Tsuruta, Japan	2:48.8 OR
1932	Yoshiyuki Tsuruta, Japan	2:45.4
1936	Tetsuo Hamuro, Japan	2:41.5 OR
1948	Joseph Verdeur, United States	2:39.3 OR
1952	John Davies, Australia	2:34.4 OR
1956	Masura Furukawa, Japan	2:34.7 OR
1960	William Mulliken, United States	2:37.4
1964	Ian O'Brien, Australia	2:27.8 WR
1968	Felipe Munoz, Mexico	2:28.7
1972	John Hencken, United States	2:21.55 WR
1976	David Wilkie, Great Britain	2:15.11 WR
1980	Robertas Zhulpa, USSR	2:15.85
1984	Victor Davis, Canada	2:13.34 WR
1988	Jozsef Szabo, Hungary	2:13.52
1992	Mike Barrowman, United States	2:10.16 WR
1996	Norbert Rózsa, Hungary	2:12.57
2000	Domenico Fioravanti, Italy	2:10.87

Note: OR=Olympic Record. WR=World Record. EOR=Equals Olympic Record. EWR=Equals World Record. WB=World Best.

SWIMMING *(Cont.)*

Men *(Cont.)*

100-METER BUTTERFLY

1968	Doug Russell, United States	55.9 OR
1972	Mark Spitz, United States	54.27 WR
1976	Matt Vogel, United States	54.35
1980	Pär Arvidsson, Sweden	54.92
1984	Michael Gross, W Germany	53.08 WR
1988	Anthony Nesty, Suriname	53.00 OR
1992	Pablo Morales, United States	53.32
1996	Denis Pankratov, Russia	52.27 WR
2000	Lars Froelander, Sweden	52.00

200-METER BUTTERFLY

1956	William Yorzyk, United States	2:19.3 OR
1960	Michael Troy, United States	2:12.8 WR
1964	Kevin Berry, Australia	2:06.6 WR
1968	Carl Robie, United States	2:08.7
1972	Mark Spitz, United States	2:00.70 WR
1976	Mike Bruner, United States	1:59.23 WR
1980	Sergei Fesenko, USSR	1:59.76
1984	Jon Sieben, Australia	1:57.04 WR
1988	Michael Gross, W Germany	1:56.94 WR
1992	Melvin Stewart, United States	1:56.26 OR
1996	Denis Pankratov, Russia	1:56.51
2000	Tom Malchow, United States	1:55.35 OR

200-METER INDIVIDUAL MEDLEY

1968	Charles Hickcox, United States	2:12.0 OR
1972	Gunnar Larsson, Sweden	2:07.17 WR
1984	Alex Baumann, Canada	2:01.42 WR
1988	Tamas Darnyi, Hungary	2:00.17 WR
1992	Tamas Darnyi, Hungary	2:00.76
1996	Attila Czene, Hungary	1:59.91 OR
2000	Massimiliano Rosolino, Italy	1:58.98 OR

400-METER INDIVIDUAL MEDLEY

1964	Richard Roth, United States	4:45.4 WR
1968	Charles Hickcox, United States	4:48.4
1972	Gunnar Larsson, Sweden	4:31.98 OR
1976	Rod Strachan, United States	4:23.68 WR
1980	Aleksandr Sidorenko, USSR	4:22.89 OR
1984	Alex Baumann, Canada	4:17.41 WR
1988	Tamas Darnyi, Hungary	4:14.75 WR
1992	Tamas Darnyi, Hungary	4:14.23 OR
1996	Tom Dolan United States	4:14.90
2000	Tom Dolan, United States	4:11.76 WR

4 X 100-METER MEDLEY RELAY

1960	United States	4:05.4 WR
1964	United States	3:58.4 WR
1968	United States	3:54.9 WR
1972	United States	3:48.16 WR
1976	United States	3:42.22 WR
1980	Australia	3:45.70
1984	United States	3:39.30 WR
1988	United States	3:36.93 WR
1992	United States	3:36.93 EWR
1996	United States	3:34.84 WR
2000	United States	3:33.73 WR

4 X 100-METER FREESTYLE RELAY

1964	United States	3:32.2 WR
1968	United States	3:31.7 WR
1972	United States	3:26.42 WR
1976-1980	Not held	
1984	United States	3:19.03 WR
1988	United States	3:16.53 WR
1992	United States	3:16.74
1996	United States	3:15.41 OR
2000	Australia	3:13.67 WR

4 X 200-METER FREESTYLE RELAY

1906	Hungary (1000 m)	16:52.4
1908	Great Britain	10:55.6
1912	Australia/New Zealand	10:11.6 WR
1920	United States	10:04.4 WR
1924	United States	9:53.4 WR
1928	United States	9:36.2 WR
1932	Japan	8:58.4 WR
1936	Japan	8:51.5 WR
1948	United States	8:46.0 WR
1952	United States	8:31.1 OR
1956	Australia	8:23.6 WR
1960	United States	8:10.2 WR
1964	United States	7:52.1 WR
1968	United States	7:52.33
1972	United States	7:35.78 WR
1976	United States	7:23.22 WR
1980	USSR	7:23.50
1984	United States	7:15.69 WR
1988	United States	7:12.51 WR
1992	Unified Team	7:11.95 WR
1996	United States	7:14.84
2000	Australia	7:07.05 WR

Women

50-METER FREESTYLE

1988	Kristin Otto, East Germany	25.49 OR
1992	Yang Wenyi, China	24.79 WR
1996	Amy Van Dyken, United States	24.87
2000	Inge de Bruijn, Netherlands	24.32 WR

100-METER FREESTYLE

1912	Fanny Durack, Australia	1:22.2
1920	Ethelda Bleibtrey, United States	1:13.6 WR
1924	Ethel Lackie, United States	1:12.4
1928	Albina Osipowich, United States	1:11.0 OR
1932	Helene Madison, United States	1:06.8 OR
1936	Hendrika Mastenbroek, Netherlands	1:05.9 OR
1948	Greta Andersen, Denmark	1:06.3
1952	Katalin Szöke, Hungary	1:06.8
1956	Dawn Fraser, Australia	1:02.0 WR
1960	Dawn Fraser, Australia	1:01.2 OR
1964	Dawn Fraser, Australia	59.5 OR

100-METER FREESTYLE *(CONT.)*

1968	Jan Henne, United States	1:00.0
1972	Sandra Neilson, United States	58.59 OR
1976	Kornelia Ender, East Germany	55.65 WR
1980	Barbara Krause, East Germany	54.79 WR
1984	Carrie Steinseifer, United States	55.92
	Nancy Hogshead, United States	55.92
1988	Kristin Otto, East Germany	54.93
1992	Zhuang Yong, China	54.64 OR
1996	Le Jingyi, China	54.50 OR
2000	Inge de Bruijn, Netherlands	53.83 OR

200-METER FREESTYLE

1968	Debbie Meyer, United States	2:10.5 OR
1972	Shane Gould, Australia	2:03.56 WR
1976	Kornelia Ender, East Germany	1:59.26 WR
1980	Barbara Krause, East Germany	1:58.33 OR
1984	Mary Wayte, United States	1:59.23
1988	Heike Friedrich, East Germany	1:57.65 OR

Note: OR=Olympic Record. WR=World Record. EOR=Equals Olympic Record. EWR=Equals World Record. WB=World Best.

SWIMMING *(Cont.)*
Women *(Cont.)*

200-METER FREESTYLE *(CONT.)*

1992	Nicole Haislett, United States	1:57.90
1996	Claudia Poll, Costa Rica	1:58.16
2000	Susie O'Neill, Australia	1:58.24

400-METER FREESTYLE

1924	Martha Norelius, United States	6:02.2 OR
1928	Martha Norelius, United States	5:42.8 WR
1932	Helene Madison, United States	5:28.5 WR
1936	Hendrika Mastenbroek, Netherlands	5:26.4 OR
1948	Ann Curtis, United States	5:17.8 OR
1952	Valeria Gyenge, Hungary	5:12.1 OR
1956	Lorraine Crapp, Australia	4:54.6 OR
1960	Chris von Saltza, United States	4:50.6 OR
1964	Virginia Duenkel, United States	4:43.3 OR
1968	Debbie Meyer, United States	4:31.8 OR
1972	Shane Gould, Australia	4:19.44 WR
1976	Petra Thümer, E Germany	4:09.89 WR
1980	Ines Diers, E Germany	4:08.76 WR
1984	Tiffany Cohen, United States	4:07.10 OR
1988	Janet Evans, United States	4:03.85 WR
1992	Dagmar Hase, Germany	4:07.18
1996	Michelle Smith, Ireland	4:07.25
2000	Brooke Bennett, United States	4:05.80

800-METER FREESTYLE

1968	Debbie Meyer, United States	9:24.0 OR
1972	Keena Rothhammer, United States	8:53.68 WR
1976	Petra Thümer, E Germany	8:37.14 WR
1980	Michelle Ford, Australia	8:28.90 OR
1984	Tiffany Cohen, United States	8:24.95 OR
1988	Janet Evans, United States	8:20.20 OR
1992	Janet Evans, United States	8:25.52
1996	Brooke Bennett, United States	8:27.89
2000	Brooke Bennett, United States	8:19.67 OR

100-METER BACKSTROKE

1924	Sybil Bauer, United States	1:23.2 OR
1928	Marie Braun, Netherlands	1:22.0
1932	Eleanor Holm, United States	1:19.4
1936	Dina Senff, Netherlands	1:18.9
1948	Karen Harup, Denmark	1:14.4 OR
1952	Joan Harrison, South Africa	1:14.3
1956	Judy Grinham, Great Britain	1:12.9 OR
1960	Lynn Burke, United States	1:09.3 OR
1964	Cathy Ferguson, United States	1:07.7 WR
1968	Kaye Hall, United States	1:06.2 WR
1972	Melissa Belote, United States	1:05.78 OR
1976	Ulrike Richter, E Germany	1:01.83 OR
1980	Rica Reinisch, E Germany	1:00.86 WR
1984	Theresa Andrews, United States	1:02.55
1988	Kristin Otto, E Germany	1:00.89
1992	Krisztina Egerszegi, Hungary	1:00.68 OR
1996	Beth Botsford, United States	1:01.19
2000	Diana Iuliana Mocanu, Romania	1:00.21 OR

200-METER BACKSTROKE

1968	Pokey Watson, United States	2:24.8 OR
1972	Melissa Belote, United States	2:19.19 WR
1976	Ulrike Richter, E Germany	2:13.43 OR
1980	Rica Reinisch, E Germany	2:11.77 WR
1984	Jolanda De Rover, Netherlands	2:12.38
1988	Krisztina Egerszegi, Hungary	2:09.29 OR
1992	Krisztina Egerszegi, Hungary	2:07.06 OR
1996	Krisztina Egerszegi, Hungary	2:07.83
2000	Diana Iuliana Mocanu, Romania	2:08.16

100-METER BREASTSTROKE

1968	Djurdjica Bjedov, Yugoslavia	1:15.8 OR
1972	Catherine Carr, United States	1:13.58 WR
1976	Hannelore Anke, E Germany	1:11.16
1980	Ute Geweniger, E Germany	1:10.22
1984	Petra Van Staveren, Netherlands	1:09.88 OR
1988	Tania Dangalakova, Bulgaria	1:07.95 OR
1992	Elena Roudkovskaia, Unified Team	1:08.00
1996	Penelope Heyns, South Africa	1:07.73
2000	Megan Quann, United States	1:07.05

200-METER BREASTSTROKE

1924	Lucy Morton, Great Britain	3:33.2 OR
1928	Hilde Schrader, Germany	3:12.6
1932	Clare Dennis, Australia	3:06.3 OR
1936	Hideko Maehata, Japan	3:03.6
1948	Petronella Van Vliet, Netherlands	2:57.2
1952	Eva Szekely, Hungary	2:51.7 OR
1956	Ursula Happe, W Germany	2:53.1 OR
1960	Anita Lonsbrough, Great Britain	2:49.5 WR
1964	Galina Prozumenshikova, USSR	2:46.4 OR
1968	Sharon Wichman, United States	2:44.4 OR
1972	Beverly Whitfield, Australia	2:41.71 OR
1976	Marina Koshevaia, USSR	2:33.35 WR
1980	Lina Kaciusyte, USSR	2:29.54 OR
1984	Anne Ottenbrite, Canada	2:30.38
1988	Silke Hoerner, E Germany	2:26.71 WR
1992	Kyoko Iwasaki, Japan	2:26.65 OR
1996	Penelope Heyns, South Africa	2:25.41 OR
2000	Agnes Kovacs, Hungary	2:24.35 OR

100-METER BUTTERFLY

1956	Shelley Mann, United States	1:11.0 OR
1960	Carolyn Schuler, United States	1:09.5 OR
1964	Sharon Stouder, United States	1:04.7 WR
1968	Lynn McClements, Australia	1:05.5
1972	Mayumi Aoki, Japan	1:03.34 WR
1976	Kornelia Ender, E Germany	1:00.13 EWR
1980	Caren Metschuck, E Germany	1:00.42
1984	Mary T. Meagher, United States	59.26
1988	Kristin Otto, E Germany	59.00 OR
1992	Qian Hong, China	58.62 OR
1996	Amy Van Dyken, United States	59.13
2000	Inge de Bruijn, Netherlands	56.61 WR

200-METER BUTTERFLY

1968	Ada Kok, Netherlands	2:24.7 OR
1972	Karen Moe, United States	2:15.57 WR
1976	Andrea Pollack, E Germany	2:11.41 OR
1980	Ines Geissler, E Germany	2:10.44 OR
1984	Mary T. Meagher, United States	2:06.90 OR
1988	Kathleen Nord, E Germany	2:09.51
1992	Summer Sanders, United States	2:08.67
1996	Susan O'Neill, Australia	2:07.76
2000	Misty Hyman, United States	2:05.88 OR

200-METER INDIVIDUAL MEDLEY

1968	Claudia Kolb, United States	2:24.7 OR
1972	Shane Gould, Australia	2:23.07 WR
1976	Not held 1976-1980	
1984	Tracy Caulkins, United States	2:12.64 OR
1988	Daniela Hunger, E Germany	2:12.59 OR
1992	Lin Li, China	2:11.65 WR
1996	Michelle Smith, Ireland	2:13.93
2000	Yana Klochkova, Ukraine	2:10.68 OR

Note: OR=Olympic Record. WR=World Record. EOR=Equals Olympic Record. EWR=Equals World Record. WB=World Best.

SWIMMING *(Cont.)*

Women *(Cont.)*

400-METER INDIVIDUAL MEDLEY

1964	Donna de Varona, United States	5:18.7 OR
1968	Claudia Kolb, United States	5:08.5 OR
1972	Gail Neall, Australia	5:02.97 WR
1976	Ulrike Tauber, E Germany	4:42.77 WR
1980	Petra Schneider, E Germany	4:36.29 WR
1984	Tracy Caulkins, United States	4:39.24
1988	Janet Evans, United States	4:37.76
1992	Krisztina Egerszegi, Hungary	4:36.54
1996	Michelle Smith, Ireland	4:39.18
2000	Yana Klochkova, Ukraine	4:33.59 WR

4 X 100-METER MEDLEY RELAY

1960	United States	4:41.1 WR
1964	United States	4:33.9 WR
1968	United States	4:28.3 OR
1972	United States	4:20.75 WR
1976	E Germany	4:07.95 WR
1980	E Germany	4:06.67 WR
1984	United States	4:08.34
1988	E Germany	4:03.74 OR
1992	United States	4:02.54 WR
1996	United States	4:02.88
2000	United States	3:58.30 WR

4 X 100-METER FREESTYLE RELAY

1912	Great Britain	5:52.8 WR
1920	United States	5:11.6 WR
1924	United States	4:58.8 WR
1928	United States	4:47.6 WR
1932	United States	4:38.0 WR
1936	Netherlands	4:36.0 OR
1948	United States	4:29.2 OR
1952	Hungary	4:24.4 WR
1956	Australia	4:17.1 WR
1960	United States	4:08.9 WR
1964	United States	4:03.8 WR
1968	United States	4:02.5 OR
1972	United States	3:55.19 WR
1976	United States	3:44.82 WR
1980	E Germany	3:42.71 WR
1984	United States	3:43.43
1988	E Germany	3:40.63 OR
1992	United States	3:39.46 WR
1996	United States	3:39.29 OR
2000	United States	3:36.61 WR

4 X 200-METER FREESTYLE RELAY

1996	United States	7:59.87
2000	United States	7:57.80 OR

DIVING

Men

SPRINGBOARD

		Pts
1908	Albert Zürner, Germany	85.5
1912	Paul Günther, Germany	79.23
1920	Louis Kuehn, United States	675.40
1924	Albert White, United States	97.46
1928	Pete DesJardins, United States	185.04
1932	Michael Galitzen, United States	161.38
1936	Richard Degener, United States	163.57
1948	Bruce Harlan, United States	163.64
1952	David Browning, United States	205.29
1956	Robert Clotworthy, United States	159.56
1960	Gary Tobian, United States	170.00
1964	Kenneth Sitzberger, United States	159.90
1968	Bernie Wrightson, United States	170.15
1972	Vladimir Vasin, USSR	594.09
1976	Phil Boggs, United States	619.05
1980	Aleksandr Portnov, USSR	905.02
1984	Greg Louganis, United States	754.41
1988	Greg Louganis, United States	730.80
1992	Mark Lenzi, United States	676.53
1996	Xiong Ni, China	701.46
2000	Xiong Ni, China	708.72

PLATFORM

		Pts
1904	George Sheldon, United States	12.66
1906	Gottlob Walz, Germany	156.0
1908	Hjalmar Johansson, Sweden	83.75
1912	Erik Adlerz, Sweden	73.94
1920	Clarence Pinkston, United States	100.67
1924	Albert White, United States	97.46
1928	Pete DesJardins, United States	98.74
1932	Harold Smith, United States	124.80
1936	Marshall Wayne, United States	113.58
1948	Sammy Lee, United States	130.05
1952	Sammy Lee, United States	156.28
1956	Joaquin Capilla, Mexico	152.44
1960	Robert Webster, United States	165.56
1964	Robert Webster, United States	148.58
1968	Klaus Dibiasi, Italy	164.18
1972	Klaus Dibiasi, Italy	504.12
1976	Klaus Dibiasi, Italy	600.51
1980	Falk Hoffmann, E Germany	835.65
1984	Greg Louganis, United States	710.91
1988	Greg Louganis, United States	638.61
1992	Sun Shuwei, China	677.31
1996	Dmitri Sautin, Russia	692.34
2000	Tian Liang, China	724.53

Women

SPRINGBOARD

		Pts
1920	Aileen Riggin, United States	539.90
1924	Elizabeth Becker, United States	474.50
1928	Helen Meany, United States	78.62
1932	Georgia Coleman, United States	87.52
1936	Marjorie Gestring, United States	89.27
1948	Victoria Draves, United States	108.74

SPRINGBOARD *(CONT.)*

		Pts
1952	Patricia McCormick, United States	147.30
1956	Patricia McCormick, United States	142.36
1960	Ingrid Krämer, E Germany	155.81
1964	Ingrid Engel Krämer, E. Germany	145.00
1968	Sue Gossick, United States	150.77
1972	Micki King, United States	450.03

DIVING (Cont.)
Women (Cont.)

SPRINGBOARD (CONT.)

		Pts
1976	Jennifer Chandler, United States	506.19
1980	Irina Kalinina, USSR	725.91
1984	Sylvie Bernier, Canada	530.70
1988	Gao Min, China	580.23
1992	Gao Min, China	572.40
1996	Fu Mingxia, China	547.68
2000	Fu Mingxia, China	609.42

PLATFORM

		Pts
1912	Greta Johansson, Sweden	39.90
1920	Stefani Fryland-Clausen, Denmark	34.60
1924	Caroline Smith, United States	33.20
1928	Elizabeth B. Pinkston, United States	31.60
1932	Dorothy Poynton, United States	40.26
1936	Dorothy Poynton Hill, United States	33.93

PLATFORM (CONT.)

		Pts
1948	Victoria Draves, United States	68.87
1952	Patricia McCormick, United States	79.37
1956	Patricia McCormick, United States	84.85
1960	Ingrid Krämer, E Germany	91.28
1964	Lesley Bush, United States	99.80
1968	Milena Duchkova, Czechoslovakia	109.59
1972	Ulrika Knape, Sweden	390.00
1976	Elena Vaytsekhovskaya, USSR	406.59
1980	Martina Jäschke, E Germany	596.25
1984	Zhou Jihong, China	435.51
1988	Xu Yanmei, China	445.20
1992	Mingxia Fu, China	461.43
1996	Mingxia Fu, China	521.58
2000	Laura Wilkinson, United States	543.75

GYMNASTICS
Men

ALL-AROUND

		Pts
1900	Gustave Sandras, France	302
1904	Julius Lenhart, Austria	69.80
1906	Pierre Paysse, France	97
1908	Alberto Braglia, Italy	317.0
1912	Alberto Braglia, Italy	135.0
1920	Giorgio Zampori, Italy	88.35
1924	Leon Stukelj, Yugoslavia	110.340
1928	Georges Miez, Switzerland	247.500
1932	Romeo Neri, Italy	140.625
1936	Alfred Schwarzmann, Germany	113.100
1948	Veikko Huhtanen, Finland	229.70
1952	Viktor Chukarin, USSR	115.70
1956	Viktor Chukarin, USSR	114.25
1960	Boris Shakhlin, USSR	115.95
1964	Yukio Endo, Japan	115.95
1968	Sawao Kato, Japan	115.90
1972	Sawao Kato, Japan	114.65
1976	Nikolai Andrianov, USSR	116.65
1980	Aleksandr Dityatin, USSR	118.65
1984	Koji Gushiken, Japan	118.70
1988	Vladimir Artemov, USSR	119.125
1992	Vitaly Scherbo, Unified Team	59.025
1996	Li Xiaoshuang, China	58.423
2000	Alexei Nemov, Russia	58.474

HORIZONTAL BAR

		Pts
1896	Hermann Weingärtner, Germany	—
1904	Anton Heida, United States	40
1924	Leon Stukelj, Yugoslavia	19.73
1928	Georges Miez, Switzerland	19.17
1932	Dallas Bixler, United States	18.33
1936	Aleksanteri Saarvala, Finland	19.367
1948	Josef Stalder, Switzerland	19.85
1952	Jack Günthard, Switzerland	19.55
1956	Takashi Ono, Japan	19.60
1960	Takashi Ono, Japan	19.60
1964	Boris Shakhlin, USSR	19.625
1968	Akinori Nakayama, Japan	19.55
1972	Mitsuo Tsukahara, Japan	19.725
1976	Mitsuo Tsukahara, Japan	19.675
1980	Stoyan Deltchev, Bulgaria	19.825
1984	Shinji Morisue, Japan	20.00
1988	Vladimir Artemov, USSR	19.90
1992	Trent Dimas, United States	9.875
1996	Andreas Wecker, Germany	9.850
2000	Alexei Nemov, Russia	9.787

PARALLEL BARS

		Pts
1896	Alfred Flatow, Germany	—
1904	George Eyser, United States	44
1924	August Güttinger, Switzerland	21.63
1928	Ladislav Vacha, Czechoslovakia	18.83
1932	Romeo Neri, Italy	18.97
1936	Konrad Frey, Germany	19.067
1948	Michael Reusch, Switzerland	19.75
1952	Hans Eugster, Switzerland	19.65
1956	Viktor Chukarin, USSR	19.20
1960	Boris Shakhlin, USSR	19.40
1964	Yukio Endo, Japan	19.675
1968	Akinori Nakayama, Japan	19.475
1972	Sawao Kato, Japan	19.475
1976	Sawao Kato, Japan	19.675
1980	Aleksandr Tkachyov, USSR	19.775
1984	Bart Conner, United States	19.95
1988	Vladimir Artemov, USSR	19.925
1992	Vitaly Scherbo, Unified Team	9.900
1996	Rustan Sharipov, Ukraine	9.837
2000	Xiaopeng Li, China	9.825

VAULT

		Pts
1896	Karl Schumann, Germany	—
1904	George Eyser, United States	36
1924	Frank Kriz, United States	9.98
1928	Eugen Mack, Switzerland	9.58
1932	Savino Guglielmetti, Italy	18.03
1936	Alfred Schwarzmann, Germany	19.20
1948	Paavo Aaltonen, Finland	19.55
1952	Viktor Chukarin, USSR	19.20
1956	Helmut Bantz, Germany	18.85
1960	Takashi Ono, Japan	19.35
1964	Haruhiro Yamashita, Japan	19.60
1968	Mikhail Voronin, USSR	19.00
1972	Klaus Köste, East Germany	18.85
1976	Nikolai Andrianov, USSR	19.45
1980	Nikolai Andrianov, USSR	19.825
1984	Lou Yun, China	19.95
1988	Lou Yun, China	19.875
1992	Vitaly Scherbo, Unified Team	9.856
1996	Alexei Nemov, Russia	9.787
2000	Gervasio Deferr, Spain	9.712

GYMNASTICS (Cont.)
Men (Cont.)

POMMEL HORSE

		Pts
1896	Louis Zutter, Switzerland	—
1900	Not held	
1904	Anton Heida, United States	42
1908	Not held 1908–1920	
1924	Josef Wilhelm, Switzerland	21.23
1928	Hermann Hänggi, Switzerland	19.75
1932	Istvan Pelle, Hungary	19.07
1936	Konrad Frey, Germany	19.333
1948	Paavo Aaltonen, Finland	19.35
1952	Viktor Chukarin, USSR	19.50
1956	Boris Shakhlin, USSR	19.25
1960	Eugen Ekman, Finland	19.375
1964	Miroslav Cerar, Yugoslavia	19.525
1968	Miroslav Cerar, Yugoslavia	19.325
1972	Viktor Klimenko, USSR	19.125
1976	Zoltan Magyar, Hungary	19.70
1980	Zoltan Magyar, Hungary	19.925
1984	Li Ning, China	19.95
1988	Dmitri Bilozerchev, USSR	19.95
1992	Vitaly Scherbo, Unified Team	9.925
1996	Donghua Li, Switzerland	9.875
2000	Marius Urzica, Romania	9.862

RINGS

		Pts
1896	Ioannis Mitropoulos, Greece	—
1900	Not held	
1904	Hermann Glass, United States	45
1908	Not held 1908–1920	
1924	Francesco Martino, Italy	21.553
1928	Leon Stukelj, Yugoslavia	19.25
1932	George Gulack, United States	18.97
1936	Alois Hudec, Czechoslovakia	19.433
1948	Karl Frei, Switzerland	19.80
1952	Grant Shaginyan, USSR	19.75
1956	Albert Azaryan, USSR	19.35
1960	Albert Azaryan, USSR	19.725
1964	Takuji Haytta, Japan	19.475
1968	Akinori Nakayama, Japan	19.45
1972	Akinori Nakayama, Japan	19.35
1976	Nikolai Andrianov, USSR	19.65
1980	Aleksandr Dityatin, USSR	19.875
1984	Koji Gushiken, Japan	19.85
1988	Holger Behrendt, E Germany	19.925
1992	Vitaly Scherbo, Unified Team	9.937
1996	Yuri Chechi, Italy	9.887
2000	Szilveszter Csollany, Hungary	9.862

FLOOR EXERCISE

		Pts
1932	Istvan Pelle, Hungary	9.60
1936	Georges Miez, Switzerland	18.666
1948	Ferenc Pataki, Hungary	19.35
1952	K. William Thoresson, Sweden	19.25
1956	Valentin Muratov, USSR	19.20
1960	Nobuyuki Aihara, Japan	19.45
1964	Franco Menichelli, Italy	19.45
1968	Sawao Kato, Japan	19.475
1972	Nikolai Andrianov, USSR	19.175
1976	Nikolai Andrianov, USSR	19.45
1980	Roland Brückner, E Germany	19.75
1984	Li Ning, China	19.925
1988	Sergei Kharkov, USSR	19.925
1992	Li Xiaoshuang, China	9.925
1996	Ioannis Melissanidis, Greece	9.850
2000	Igors Vihrovs, Latvia	9.812

TEAM COMBINED EXERCISES

		Pts
1904	Turngemeinde Philadelphia	374.43
1906	Norway	19.00
1908	Sweden	438
1912	Italy	265.75
1920	Italy	359.855
1924	Italy	839.058
1928	Switzerland	1718.625
1932	Italy	541.850
1936	Germany	657.430
1948	Finland	1358.30
1952	USSR	574.40
1956	USSR	568.25
1960	Japan	575.20
1964	Japan	577.95
1968	Japan	575.90
1972	Japan	571.25
1976	Japan	576.85
1980	USSR	598.60
1984	United States	591.40
1988	USSR	593.35
1992	Unified Team	585.45
1996	Russia	576.778
2000	China	231.919

Women

ALL-AROUND

		Pts
1952	Maria Gorokhovskaya, USSR	76.78
1956	Larissa Latynina, USSR	74.933
1960	Larissa Latynina, USSR	77.031
1964	Vera Caslavska, Czechoslovakia	77.564
1968	Vera Caslavska, Czechoslovakia	78.25
1972	Lyudmila Tousischeva, USSR	77.025
1976	Nadia Comaneci, Romania	79.275
1980	Yelena Davydova, USSR	79.15
1984	Mary Lou Retton, United States	79.175
1988	Yelena Shushunova, USSR	79.662
1992	Tatiana Gutsu, Unified Team	39.737
1996	Lilia Podkopayeva, Ukraine	39.255
2000	Simona Amanar, Romania	38.642

VAULT

		Pts
1952	Yekaterina Kalinchuk, USSR	19.20
1956	Larissa Latynina, USSR	18.833
1960	Margarita Nikolayeva, USSR	19.316
1964	Vera Caslavska, Czechoslovakia	19.483
1968	Vera Caslavska, Czechoslovakia	19.775
1972	Karin Janz, E Germany	19.525
1976	Nelli Kim, USSR	19.80
1980	Natalya Shaposhnikova, USSR	19.725
1984	Ecaterina Szabo, Romania	19.875
1988	Svetlana Boginskaya, USSR	19.905
1992	Henrietta Onodi, Hungary	9.925
	Lavinia Milosovici, Romania	9.925
1996	Simona Amanar, Romania	9.825
2000	Yelena Zamolodtchikova, Russia	9.731

GYMNASTICS *(Cont.)*
Women *(Cont.)*

UNEVEN BARS

		Pts
1952	Margit Korondi, Hungary	19.40
1956	Agnes Keleti, Hungary	18.966
1960	Polina Astakhova, USSR	19.616
1964	Polina Astakhova, USSR	19.332
1968	Vera Caslavska, Czechoslovakia	19.65
1972	Karin Janz, E Germany	19.675
1976	Nadia Comaneci, Romania	20.00
1980	Maxi Gnauck, E Germany	19.875
1984	Ma Yanhong, China	19.95
1988	Daniela Silivas, Romania	20.00
1992	Lu Li, China	10.00
1996	Svetlana Khorkina, Russia	9.850
2000	Svetlana Khorkina, Russia	9.862

BALANCE BEAM

		Pts
1952	Nina Bocharova, USSR	19.22
1956	Agnes Keleti, Hungary	18.80
1960	Eva Bosakova, Czechoslovakia	19.283
1964	Vera Caslavska, Czechoslovakia	19.449
1968	Natalya Kuchinskaya, USSR	19.65
1972	Olga Korbut, USSR	19.40
1976	Nadia Comaneci, Romania	19.95
1980	Nadia Comaneci, Romania	19.80
1984	Simona Pauca, Romania	19.80
1988	Daniela Silivas, Romania	19.924
1992	Tatiana Lisenko, Unified Team	9.975
1996	Shannon Miller, United States	9.862
2000	Xuan Li, China	9.825

FLOOR EXERCISE

		Pts
1952	Agnes Keleti, Hungary	19.36
1956	Agnes Keleti, Hungary	18.733
1960	Larissa Latynina, USSR	19.583
1964	Larissa Latynina, USSR	19.599
1968	Vera Caslavska, Czechoslovakia	19.675
1972	Olga Korbut, USSR	19.575
1976	Nelli Kim, USSR	19.85
1980	Nadia Comaneci, Romania	19.875

FLOOR EXERCISE *(Cont.)*

		Pts
1984	Ecaterina Szabo, Romania	19.975
1988	Daniela Silivas, Romania	19.937
1992	Lavinia Milosovici, Romania	10.00
1996	Lilia Podkopayeva, Ukraine	9.887
2000	Yelena Zamolodtchikova, Russia	9.850

TEAM COMBINED EXERCISES

		Pts
1928	The Netherlands	316.75
1932	Not held	
1936	Germany	506.50
1948	Czechoslovakia	445.45
1952	USSR	527.03
1956	USSR	444.800
1960	USSR	382.320
1964	USSR	280.890
1968	USSR	382.85
1972	USSR	380.50
1976	USSR	466.00
1980	USSR	394.90
1984	Romania	392.02
1988	USSR	395.475
1992	Unified Team	395.666
1996	United States	389.225
2000	Romania	154.608

RHYTHMIC ALL-AROUND

		Pts
1984	Lori Fung, Canada	57.95
1988	Marina Lobach, USSR	60.00
1992	A. Timoshenko, Unified Team	59.037
1996	E. Serebrianskaya, Ukraine	39.683
2000	Yulia Barsukova, Russia	39.632

RHYTHMIC TEAM COMBINED EXERCISES

		Pts
1996	Spain	38.933
2000	Russia	39.500

SOCCER

Men

1900	Great Britain	1928	Uruguay	1964	Hungary	1988	Soviet Union
1904	Canada	1936	Italy	1968	Hungary	1992	Spain
1908	Great Britain	1948	Sweden	1972	Poland	1996	Nigeria
1912	Great Britain	1952	Hungary	1976	East Germany	2000	Cameroon
1920	Belgium	1956	Soviet Union	1980	Czechoslovakia		
1924	Uruguay	1960	Yugoslavia	1984	France		

Women

1996	United States
2000	Norway

BIATHLON
Men

10 KILOMETERS

1980	Frank Ullrich, East Germany	32:10.69
1984	Eirik Kvalfoss, Norway	30:53.8
1988	Frank-Peter Rötsch, W Germany	25:08.1
1992	Mark Kirchner, Germany	26:02.3
1994	Sergei Tchepikov, Russia	28:07.0
1998	Ole Einar Bjorndalen, Norway	27:16.2

20 KILOMETERS

1960	Klas Lestander, Sweden	1:33:21.6
1964	Vladimir Melyanin, Soviet Union	1:20:26.8
1968	Magnar Solberg, Norway	1:13:45.9
1972	Magnar Solberg, Norway	1:15:55.5
1976	Nikolay Kruglov, Soviet Union	1:14:12.26
1980	Anatoliy Alyabiev, Soviet Union	1:08:16.31
1984	Peter Angerer, W Germany	1:11:52.7

20 KILOMETERS (Cont.)

1988	Frank-Peter Rötsch, W Germany	56:33.3
1992	Evgueni Redkine, Unified Team	57:34.4
1994	Sergei Tarasov, Russia	57:25.3
1998	Halvard Hanevold, Norway	56:16.4

4 X 7.5-KILOMETER RELAY

1968	Soviet Union	2:13:02.4
1972	Soviet Union	1:51:44.92
1976	Soviet Union	1:57:55.64
1980	Soviet Union	1:34:03.27
1984	Soviet Union	1:38:51.7
1988	Soviet Union	1:22:30.0
1992	Germany	1:24:43.5
1994	Germany	1:30:22.1
1998	Germany	1:19:43.3

Women

7.5 KILOMETERS

1992	Antissa Restzova, Unified Team	24:29.2
1994	Myriam Bedard, Canada	26:08.8
1998	Galina Koukleva, Russia	23:08.0

15 KILOMETERS

1992	Antje Misersky, Germany	51:47.2
1994	Myriam Bedard, Canada	52:06.6
1998	Ekaterina Dofovska, Bulgaria	54:52.0

3 X 7.5-KILOMETER RELAY

1992	France	1:15:55.6
1994	Russia	1:47:19.5
1998	Germany	1:40:13.6

BOBSLED

4-MAN BOB

1924	Switzerland (Eduard Scherrer)	5:45.54
1928	United States	3:20.50
	(William Fiske) (5-man)	
1932	United States (William Fiske)	7:53.68
1936	Switzerland (Pierre Musy)	5:19.85
1948	United States (Francis Tyler)	5:20.10
1952	Germany (Andreas Ostler)	5:07.84
1956	Switzerland (Franz Kapus)	5:10.44
1960	Not held	
1964	Canada (Victor Emery)	4:14.46
1968	Italy (Eugenio Monti) (2 runs)	2:17.39
1972	Switzerland (Jean Wicki)	4:43.07
1976	E Germany (Meinhard Nehmer)	3:40.43
1980	E Germany (Meinhard Nehmer)	3:59.92
1984	E Germany (Wolfgang Hoppe)	3:20.22
1988	Switzerland (Ekkehard Fasser)	3:47.51
1992	Austria (Ingo Appelt)	3:53.90
1994	Germany (Harold Czudaj)	3:27.78
1998	Germany (Christoph Langen)	2:39.41

Note: Driver in parentheses.

2-MAN BOB

1932	United States (Hubert Stevens)	8:14.74
1936	United States (Ivan Brown)	5:29.29
1948	Switzerland (Felix Endrich)	5:29.20
1952	Germany (Andreas Ostler)	5:24.54
1956	Italy (Lamberto Dalla Costa)	5:30.14
1960	Not held	
1964	Great Britain (Anthony Nash)	4:21.90
1968	Italy (Eugenio Monti)	4:41.54
1972	W Germany	4:57.07
	(Wolfgang Zimmerer)	
1976	E Germany (Meinhard Nehmer)	3:44.42
1980	Switzerland (Erich Schärer)	4:09.36
1984	E Germany (Wolfgang Hoppe)	3:25.56
1988	USSR (Janis Kipours)	3:53.48
1992	Switzerland (Gustav Weder)	4:03.26
1994	Switzerland (Gustav Weder)	3:30.81
1998	Canada (Pierre Lueders)	3:37.24
	Italy (Guenther Huber)	3:37.24

Note: Driver in parentheses.

CURLING

Men

1998 .....Switzerland, Canada, Norway
Note: Gold, silver, and bronze medals.

Women

1998 .....Canada, Denmark, Sweden
Note: Gold, silver, and bronze medals.

ICE HOCKEY

Men

1920* ....Canada, United States, Czechoslovakia	1972 .....USSR, United States, Czechoslovakia
1924 .....Canada, United States, Great Britain	1976 .....USSR, Czechoslovakia, W Germany
1928 .....Canada, Sweden, Switzerland	1980 .....United States, USSR, Sweden
1932 .....Canada, United States, Germany	1984 .....USSR, Czechoslovakia, Sweden
1936 .....Great Britain, Canada, United States	1988 .....USSR, Finland, Sweden
1948 .....Canada, Czechoslovakia, Switzerland	1992 .....Unified Team, Canada, Czechoslovakia
1952 .....Canada, United States, Sweden	1994 .....Sweden, Canada, Finland
1956 .....USSR, United States, Canada	1998 .....Czech Republic, Russia, Finland
1960 .....United States, Canada, USSR	*Competition held at summer games in Antwerp.
1964 .....USSR, Sweden, Czechoslovakia	Note: Gold, silver, and bronze medals.
1968 .....USSR, Czechoslovakia, Canada	

Women

1998 .....United States, Canada, Finland

Note: Gold, silver, and bronze medals.

LUGE

Men

SINGLES			DOUBLES		
1964 .....Thomas Köhler, East Germany	3:26.77		1964 ....Austria	1:41.62	
1968 .....Manfred Schmid, Austria	2:52.48		1968 ....East Germany	1:35.85	
1972 .....Wolfgang Scheidel, W Germany	3:27.58		1972 ....East Germany	1:28.35	
1976 .....Detlef Guenther, West Germany	3:27.688		1976 ....East Germany	1:25.604	
1980 .....Bernhard Glass, West Germany	2:54.796		1980 ....East Germany	1:19.331	
1984 .....Paul Hildgartner, Italy	3:04.258		1984 ....West Germany	1:23.620	
1988 .....Jens Müller, West Germany	3:05.548		1988 ....East Germany	1:31.940	
1992 .....Georg Hackl, Germany	3:02.363		1992 ....Germany	1:32.053	
1994 .....Georg Hackl, Germany	3:21.571		1994 ....Italy	1:36.720	
1998 .....Georg Hackl, Germany	3:18.44		1998 ....Germany	1:41.105	

Women

SINGLES			SINGLES (Cont.)		
1964 .....Ortrun Enderlein, Germany	3:24.67		1984 .....Steffi Martin, East Germany	2:46.570	
1968 .....Erica Lechner, Italy	2:28.66		1988 .....Steffi Walter (Martin) E Germany	3:03.973	
1972 .....Anna-Maria Müller, East Germany	2:59.18		1992 .....Doris Neuner, Austria	3:06.696	
1976 .....Margit Schumann, East Germany	2:50.621		1994 .....Gerda Weissensteiner, Italy	3:15.517	
1980 .....Vera Zozulya, USSR	2:36.537		1998 .....Silke Kraushaar, Germany	3:23.779	

ONE MORE SIGN THAT THE APOCALYPSE IS UPON US

*Chilean tennis star Marcelo Rios refused to carry his country's flag
in the opening ceremonies at the 2000 Summer Games because his mother and
sister weren't given tickets to the show.*

FIGURE SKATING

Men

1908*	Ulrich Salchow, Sweden
1920†	Gillis Grafström, Sweden
1924	Gillis Grafström, Sweden
1928	Gillis Grafström, Sweden
1932	Karl Schäfer, Austria
1936	Karl Schäfer, Austria
1948	Dick Button, United States
1952	Dick Button, United States
1956	Hayes Alan Jenkins, United States
1960	David Jenkins, United States
1964	Manfred Schnelldorfer, W Germany
1968	Wolfgang Schwarz, Austria
1972	Ondrej Nepela, Czechoslovakia
1976	John Curry, Great Britain
1980	Robin Cousins, Great Britain
1984	Scott Hamilton, United States
1988	Brian Boitano, United States
1992	Victor Petrenko, Unified Team
1994	Alexei Urmanov, Russia
1998	Ilia Kulik, Russia

*Competition held at summer games in London.
†Competition held at summer games in Antwerp.

Women

1908*	Madge Syers, Great Britain
1920†	Magda Julin, Sweden
1924	Herma Szabo-Planck, Austria
1928	Sonja Henie, Norway
1932	Sonja Henie, Norway
1936	Sonja Henie, Norway
1948	Barbara Ann Scott, Canada
1952	Jeanette Altwegg, Great Britain
1956	Tenley Albright, United States
1960	Carol Heiss, United States
1964	Sjoukje Dijkstra, Netherlands
1968	Peggy Fleming, United States
1972	Beatrix Schuba, Austria
1976	Dorothy Hamill, United States
1980	Anett Pötzsch, E Germany
1984	Katarina Witt, E Germany
1988	Katarina Witt, E Germany
1992	Kristi Yamaguchi, United States
1994	Oksana Baiul, Ukraine
1998	Tara Lipinski, United States

Mixed

PAIRS

1908*	Anna Hübler & Heinrich Burger, Germany
1920†	Ludovika & Walter Jakobsson, Finland
1924	Helene Engelmann & Alfred Berger, Austria
1928	Andree Joly & Pierre Brunet, France
1932	Andree Brunet (Joly) & Pierre Brunet, France
1936	Maxi Herber & Ernst Baier, Germany
1948	Micheline Lannoy & Pierre Baugniet, Belgium
1952	Ria Falk and Paul Falk, W Germany
1956	Elisabeth Schwartz & Kurt Oppelt, Austria
1960	Barbara Wagner & Robert Paul, Canada
1964	Lyudmila Beloussova & Oleg Protopopov, USSR
1968	Lyudmila Beloussova & Oleg Protopopov, USSR
1972	Irina Rodnina & Alexei Ulanov, USSR
1976	Irina Rodnina & Aleksandr Zaitzev, USSR
1980	Irina Rodnina & Aleksandr Zaitzev, USSR
1984	Elena Valova & Oleg Vasiliev, USSR
1988	Ekaterina Gordeeva & Sergei Grinkov, USSR
1992	Natalia Michkouteniok & Artour Dmitriev, Unified Team

PAIRS (Cont.)

1994	Ekaterina Gordeeva & Sergei Grinkov, Russia
1998	Oksana Kazakova & Artur Dmitriev, Russia

DANCE

1976	Lyudmila Pakhomova & Aleksandr Gorshkov, USSR
1980	Natalia Linichuk & Gennadi Karponosov, USSR
1984	Jayne Torvill & Christopher Dean, Great Britain
1988	Natalia Bestemianova & Andrei Bukin, USSR
1992	Marina Klimova & Sergei Ponomarenko, Unified Team
1994	Oksana Grishuk and Evgeny Platov, Russia
1998	Pasha Grishuk and Evgeny Platov, Russia

*Competition held at summer games in London.
†Competition held at summer games in Antwerp.

Koss, Still the Boss

To follow Johann Olav Koss around the 2000 Olympics in Sydney for a day was to reawaken to the fact that not all superstar athletes are greedy boors. An IOC member, four-time speed skating gold medalist and SI's 1994 Sportsman of the Year, Koss, 31, runs the philanthropic group Olympic Aid. He receives no salary, living instead off his diminishing savings, the fruits of his speed skating career. "He's an Olympic champion, a humanitarian and a good-looking Norwegian," said U.S. long jump great and Olympic Aid colleague Mike Powell. "How are you going to beat that?"

In his role with Olympic Aid, which establishes grassroots athletic programs for refugee children around the world, Koss had made several trips to Eritrea, trying, as he puts it, "to bring the ideals of sport" to youngsters displaced by the recent border war with Ethiopia. Koss also guided Eritrean sports officials through the Olympic qualifying process. "Our participation is our gold medal," says Abraha Ghermazion Habtezion, president of Eritrea's Olympic committee, which sent its first three athletes to the Games. "We owe much to Johann."
—Jack McCallum

SPEED SKATING

Men

500 METERS

1924	Charles Jewtraw, United States	44.0
1928	Clas Thunberg, Finland	43.4 OR
	Bernt Evensen, Norway	43.4 OR
1932	John Shea, United States	43.4 EOR
1936	Ivar Ballangrud, Norway	43.4 EOR
1948	Finn Helgesen, Norway	43.1 OR
1952	Kenneth Henry, United States	43.2
1956	Yevgeny Grishin, USSR	40.2 EWR
1960	Yevgeny Grishin, USSR	40.2 EWR
1964	Terry McDermott, United States	40.1 OR
1968	Erhard Keller, W Germany	40.3
1972	Erhard Keller, W Germany	39.44 OR
1976	Yevgeny Kulikov, USSR	39.17 OR
1980	Eric Heiden, United States	38.03 OR
1984	Sergei Fokichev, USSR	38.19
1988	Uwe-Jens Mey, E Germany	36.45 WR
1992	Uwe-Jens Mey, E Germany	37.14
1994	Aleksandr Golubev, Russia	36.33
1998	Hiroyasu Shimizu, Japan (second run)	35.59 OR

1000 METERS

1976	Peter Mueller, United States	1:19.32
1980	Eric Heiden, United States	1:15.18 OR
1984	Gaetan Boucher, Canada	1:15.80
1988	Nikolai Gulyaev, USSR	1:13.03 OR
1992	Olaf Zinke, Germany	1:14.85
1994	Dan Jansen, United States	1:12.43 WR
1998	Ids Postma, Netherlands	1:10.64 OR

1500 METERS

1924	Clas Thunberg, Finland	2:20.8
1928	Clas Thunberg, Finland	2:21.1
1932	John Shea, United States	2:57.5
1936	Charles Mathisen, Norway	2:19.2 OR
1948	Sverre Farstad, Norway	2:17.6 OR
1952	Hjalmar Andersen, Norway	2:20.4
1956	Yevgeny Grishin, USSR	2:08.6 WR
	Yuri Mikhailov, USSR	2:08.6 WR
1960	Roald Aas, Norway	2:10.4
	Yevgeny Grishin, USSR	2:10.4
1964	Ants Anston, USSR	2:10.3
1968	Cornelis Verkerk, Netherlands	2:03.4 OR
1972	Ard Schenk, Netherlands	2:02.96 OR
1976	Jan Egil Storholt, Norway	1:59.38 OR
1980	Eric Heiden, United States	1:55.44 OR
1984	Gaetan Boucher, Canada	1:58.36

1500 METERS (Cont.)

1988	Andre Hoffmann, E Germany	1:52.06 WR
1992	Johann Olav Koss, Norway	1:54.81
1994	Johann Olav Koss, Norway	1:51.29 WR
1998	Aadne Sondral, Norway	1:47.87 WR

5000 METERS

1924	Clas Thunberg, Finland	8:39.0
1928	Ivar Ballangrud, Norway	8:50.5
1932	Irving Jaffee, United States	9:40.8
1936	Ivar Ballangrud, Norway	8:19.6 OR
1948	Reidar Liaklev, Norway	8:29.4
1952	Hjalmar Andersen, Norway	8:10.6 OR
1956	Boris Shilkov, USSR	7:48.7 OR
1960	Viktor Kosichkin, USSR	7:51.3
1964	Knut Johannesen, Norway	7:38.4 OR
1968	Fred Anton Maier, Norway	7:22.4 WR
1972	Ard Schenk, Netherlands	7:23.61
1976	Sten Stensen, Norway	7:24.48
1980	Eric Heiden, United States	7:02.29 OR
1984	Sven Tomas Gustafson, Sweden	7:12.28
1988	Tomas Gustafson, Sweden	6:44.63 WR
1992	Geir Karlstad, Norway	6:59.97
1994	Johann Olav Koss, Norway	6:34.96 WR
1998	Gianni Romme, Netherlands	6:22.20 WR

10,000 METERS

1924	Julius Skutnabb, Finland	18:04.8
1928	Not held, thawing of ice	
1932	Irving Jaffee, United States	19:13.6
1936	Ivar Ballangrud, Norway	17:24.3 OR
1948	Ake Seyffarth, Sweden	17:26.3
1952	Hjalmar Andersen, Norway	16:45.8 OR
1956	Sigvard Ericsson, Sweden	16:35.9 OR
1960	Knut Johannesen, Norway	15:46.6 WR
1964	Jonny Nilsson, Sweden	15:50.1
1968	Johnny Höglin, Sweden	15:23.6 OR
1972	Ard Schenk, Netherlands	15:01.35 OR
1976	Piet Kleine, Netherlands	14:50.59 OR
1980	Eric Heiden, United States	14:28.13 WR
1984	Igor Malkov, USSR	14:39.90
1988	Tomas Gustafson, Sweden	13:48.20 WR
1992	Bart Veldkamp, Netherlands	14:12.12
1994	Johann Olav Koss, Norway	13:30.55 WR
1998	Gianni Romme, Netherlands	13:15.33 WR

Women

500 METERS

1960	Helga Haase, E Germany	45.9
1964	Lydia Skoblikova, USSR	45.0 OR
1968	Lyudmila Titova, USSR	46.1
1972	Anne Henning, United States	43.33 OR
1976	Sheila Young, United States	42.76 OR
1980	Karin Enke, E Germany	41.78 OR
1984	Christa Rothenburger, E Germany	41.02 OR

500 METERS (Cont.)

1988	Bonnie Blair, United States	39.10 WR
1992	Bonnie Blair, United States	40.33
1994	Bonnie Blair, United States	39.25
1998	Catriona LeMay Doan, Canada (second run)	38.21 OR

Note: OR=Olympic Record; WR=World Record; EOR=Equals Olympic Record; EWR=Equals World Record; WB=World Best.

SPEED SKATING (Cont.)
Women (Cont.)

1000 METERS
1960	Klara Guseva, USSR	1:34.1
1964	Lydia Skoblikova, USSR	1:33.2 OR
1968	Carolina Geijssen, Netherlands	1:32.6 OR
1972	Monika Pflug, W Germany	1:31.40 OR
1976	Tatiana Averina, USSR	1:28.43 OR
1980	Natalya Petruseva, USSR	1:24.10 OR
1984	Karin Enke, E Germany	1:21.61 OR
1988	Christa Rothenburger, E Germany	1:17.65 WR
1992	Bonnie Blair, United States	1:21.90
1994	Bonnie Blair, United States	1:18.74
1998	Marianne Timmer, Netherlands	1:16.51 OR

1500 METERS
1960	Lydia Skoblikova, USSR	2:25.2 WR
1964	Lydia Skoblikova, USSR	2:22.6 OR
1968	Kaija Mustonen, Finland	2:22.4 OR
1972	Dianne Holum, United States	2:20.85 OR
1976	Galina Stepanskaya, USSR	2:16.58 OR
1980	Anne Borckink, Netherlands	2:10.95 OR
1984	Karin Enke, E Germany	2:03.42 WR
1988	Yvonne van Gennip, Netherlands	2:00.68 OR
1992	Jacqueline Boerner, Germany	2:05.87

1500 METERS (Cont.)
1994	Emese Hunyady, Austria	2:02.19
1998	Marianne Timmer, Netherlands	1:57.58 WR

3000 METERS
1960	Lydia Skoblikova, USSR	5:14.3
1964	Lydia Skoblikova, USSR	5:14.9
1968	Johanna Schut, Netherlands	4:56.2 OR
1972	Christina Baas-Kaiser, Netherlands	4:52.14 OR
1976	Tatiana Averina, USSR	4:45.19 OR
1980	Bjorg Eva Jensen, Norway	4:32.13 OR
1984	Andrea Schöne, E Germany	4:24.79 OR
1988	Yvonne van Gennip, Netherlands	4:11.94 WR
1992	Gunda Niemann, Germany	4:19.90
1994	Svetlana Bazhanova, Russia	4:17.43
1998	Gunda Niemann-Stirnemann, Germany	4:07.29 OR

5000 METERS
1988	Yvonne van Gennip, Netherlands	7:14.13 WR
1992	Gunda Niemann, Germany	7:31.57
1994	Claudia Pechstein, Germany	7:14.37
1998	Claudia Pechstein, Germany	6:59.61 WR

SHORT TRACK SPEED SKATING

Men

500 METERS
1994	Chae Ji-Hoon, South Korea	43.54
1998	Takafumi Nishitani, Japan	42.862

1000 METERS
1992	Kim Ki-Hoon, South Korea	1:30.76
1994	Kim Ki-Hoon, South Korea	1:34.57
1998	Kim Dong Sung, South Korea	1:32.375

5000-METER RELAY
1992	Korea	7:14.02
1994	Italy	7:11.74
1998	Canada	7:06.075

Women

500 METERS
1992	Cathy Turner, United States	47.04
1994	Cathy Turner, United States	45.98
1998	Annie Perreault, Canada	46.568

1000 METERS
1994	Chun Lee Kyung, South Korea	1:36.87
1998	Chun Lee Kyung, South Korea	1:42.776

3000-METER RELAY
1992	Canada	4:36.62
1994	South Korea	4:26.64
1998	South Korea	4:16.260

ALPINE SKIING
Men

DOWNHILL
1948	Henri Oreiller, France	2:55.0
1952	Zeno Colo, Italy	2:30.8
1956	Anton Sailer, Austria	2:52.2
1960	Jean Vuarnet, France	2:06.0
1964	Egon Zimmermann, Austria	2:18.16
1968	Jean-Claude Killy, France	1:59.85
1972	Bernhard Russi, Switzerland	1:51.43
1976	Franz Klammer, Austria	1:45.73
1980	Leonhard Stock, Austria	1:45.50
1984	Bill Johnson, United States	1:45.59
1988	Pirmin Zurbriggen, Switzerland	1:59.63
1992	Patrick Ortlieb, Austria	1:50.37
1994	Tommy Moe, United States	1:45.75
1998	Jean-Luc Crétier, France	1:50.11

SLALOM
1948	Edi Reinalter, Switzerland	2:10.3
1952	Othmar Schneider, Austria	2:00.0
1956	Anton Sailer, Austria	3:14.7
1960	Ernst Hinterseer, Austria	2:08.9
1964	Josef Stiegler, Austria	2:11.13
1968	Jean-Claude Killy, France	1:39.73
1972	Francisco Fernandez Ochoa, Spain	1:49.27
1976	Piero Gros, Italy	2:03.29
1980	Ingemar Stenmark, Sweden	1:44.26
1984	Phil Mahre, United States	1:39.41
1988	Alberto Tomba, Italy	1:39.47
1992	Finn Christian Jagge, Norway	1:44.39
1994	Thomas Stangassinger, Austria	2:02.02
1998	Hans-Petter Buraas, Norway	1:49.31

ALPINE SKIING
Men *(Cont.)*

GIANT SLALOM

1952	Stein Eriksen, Norway	2:25.0
1956	Anton Sailer, Austria	3:00.1
1960	Roger Staub, Switzerland	1:48.3
1964	Francois Bonlieu, France	1:46.71
1968	Jean-Claude Killy, France	3:29.28
1972	Gustav Thöni, Italy	3:09.62
1976	Heini Hemmi, Switzerland	3:26.97
1980	Ingemar Stenmark, Sweden	2:40.74
1984	Max Julen, Switzerland	2:41.18
1988	Alberto Tomba, Italy	2:06.37
1992	Alberto Tomba, Italy	2:06.98
1994	Markus Wasmeier, Germany	2:52.46
1998	Hermann Maier, Austria	2:38.51

SUPER GIANT SLALOM

1988	Franck Piccard, France	1:39.66
1992	Kjetil Andre Aamodt, Norway	1:13.04
1994	Markus Wasmeier, Germany	1:32.53
1998	Hermann Maier, Austria	1:34.82

COMBINED*

		Pts
1936	Franz Pfnür, Germany	99.25
1948	Henri Oreiller, France	3.27
1988	Hubert Strolz, Austria	36.55
1992	Josef Polig, Italy	14.58
1994	Lasse Kjus, Norway	3:17.53
1998	Mario Reiter, Austria	3:08.06

Women

DOWNHILL

1948	Hedy Schlunegger, Switzerland	2:28.3
1952	Trude Jochum-Beiser, Austria	1:47.1
1956	Madeleine Berthod, Switzerland	1:40.7
1960	Heidi Biebl, W Germany	1:37.6
1964	Christl Haas, Austria	1:55.39
1968	Olga Pall, Austria	1:40.87
1972	Marie-Theres Nadig, Switzerland	1:36.68
1976	Rosi Mittermaier, W Germany	1:46.16
1980	Annemarie Moser-Pröll, Austria	1:37.52
1984	Michela Figini, Switzerland	1:13.36
1988	Marina Kiehl, W Germany	1:25.86
1992	Kerrin Lee-Gartner, Canada	1:52.55
1994	Katja Seizinger, Germany	1:35.93
1998	Katja Seizinger, Germany	1:28.89

SLALOM

1948	Gretchen Fraser, United States	1:57.2
1952	Andrea Mead Lawrence, United States	2:10.6
1956	Renee Colliard, Switzerland	1:52.3
1960	Anne Heggtveigt, Canada	1:49.6
1964	Christine Goitschel, France	1:29.86
1968	Marielle Goitschel, France	1:25.86
1972	Barbara Cochran, United States	1:31.24
1976	Rosi Mittermaier, W Germany	1:30.54
1980	Hanni Wenzel, Liechtenstein	1:25.09
1984	Paoletta Magoni, Italy	1:36.47
1988	Vreni Schneider, Switzerland	1:36.69
1992	Petra Kronberger, Austria	1:32.68
1994	Vreni Schneider, Switzerland	1:56.01
1998	Hilde Gerg, Germany	1:32.40

GIANT SLALOM

1952	Andrea Mead Lawrence, U.S.	2:06.8
1956	Ossi Reichert, W Germany	1:56.5
1960	Yvonne Rüegg, Switzerland	1:39.9
1964	Marielle Goitschel, France	1:52.24
1968	Nancy Greene, Canada	1:51.97
1972	Marie-Theres Nadig, Switzerland	1:29.90
1976	Kathy Kreiner, Canada	1:29.13
1980	Hanni Wenzel, Liechtenstein (2 runs)	2:41.66
1984	Debbie Armstrong, United States	2:20.98
1988	Vreni Schneider, Switzerland	2:06.49
1992	Pernilla Wiberg, Sweden	2:12.74
1994	Deborah Compagnoni, Italy	2:30.97
1998	Deborah Compagnoni, Italy	2:50.59

SUPER GIANT SLALOM

1988	Sigrid Wolf, Austria	1:19.03
1992	Deborah Compagnoni, Italy	1:21.22
1994	Diann Roffe-Steinrotter, U.S.	1:22.15
1998	Picabo Street, United States	1:18.02

COMBINED*

		Pts
1988	Anita Wachter, Austria	29.25
1992	Petra Kronberger, Austria	2.55
1994	Pernilla Wiberg, Sweden	3:05.16
1998	Katja Seizinger, Germany	2:40.74

*Beginning in 1994, scoring was based on time.

FREESTYLE SKIING

Men
MOGULS

		Pts
1992	Edgar Grospiron, France	25.81
1994	Jean-Luc Brassard, Canada	27.24
1998	Jonny Moseley, United States	26.93

AERIALS

		Pts
1994	Andreas Schoenbaechler, Switz	234.67
1998	Eric Bergoust, United States	255.64

Women
MOGULS

		Pts
1992	Donna Weinbrecht, United States	23.69
1994	Stine Lise Hattestad, Norway	25.97
1998	Tae Satoya, Japan	25.06

AERIALS

		Pts
1994	Lina Cherjazova, Uzbekistan	166.84
1998	Nikki Stone, United States	193.00

NORDIC SKIING
Men

10 KILOMETERS CLASSICAL STYLE

1992	Vegard Ulvang, Norway	27:36.0
1994	Bjørn Dæhlie, Norway	24:20.1
1998	Bjørn Dæhlie, Norway	27:24.5

15 KILOMETERS CLASSICAL STYLE

1924	Thorlief Haug, Norway	1:14:31.0*
1928	Johan Gröttumsbraaten, Norway	1:37:01.0†
1932	Sven Utterström, Sweden	1:23:07.0‡
1936	Erik-August Larsson, Sweden	1:14:38.0*
1948	Martin Lundström, Sweden	1:13:50.0*
1952	Hallgeir Brenden, Norway	1:01:34.0*
1956	Hallgeir Brenden, Norway	49:39.0
1960	Haakon Brusveen, Norway	51:55.5
1964	Eero Mantyränta, Finland	50:54.1
1968	Harald Grönningen, Norway	47:54.2
1972	Sven-Ake Lundback, Sweden	45:28.24
1976	Nikolay Bajukov, Unified Team	43:58.47
1980	Thomas Wassberg, Sweden	41:57.63
1984	Gunde Swan, Sweden	41:25.6
1988	Michael Deviatyarov, USSR	41:18.9

*Distance was 18 km; †Distance was 19.7 km;
‡Distance was 18.2 km.

15 KILOMETERS PURSUIT FREESTYLE

1992	Bjørn Dæhlie, Norway	1:05:37.9
1994	Bjørn Dæhlie, Norway	1:00:08.8
1998	Thomas Alsgaard, Norway	1:07:01.7

30 KILOMETERS CLASSICAL STYLE

1956	Veikko Hakulinen, Finland	1:44:06.0
1960	Sixten Jernberg, Sweden	1:51:03.9
1964	Eero Mantyränta, Finland	1:30:50.7
1968	Franco Nones, Italy	1:35:39.2
1972	Viaceslav Vedenine, USSR	1:36:31.2
1976	Sergei Savelyev, USSR	1:30:29.38
1980	Nikolai Simyatov, USSR	1:27:02.80
1984	Nikolai Simyatov, USSR	1:28:56.3
1988	Alexey Prokororov, USSR	1:24:26.3
1992	Vegard Ulvang, Norway	1:22:27.8
1994	Thomas Alsgaard, Norway	1:12:26.4
1998	Mika Myllylae, Finland	1:33:55.8

50 KILOMETERS FREESTYLE

1924	Thorleif Haug, Norway	3:44:32.0
1928	Per Erik Hedlund, Sweden	4:52:03.0
1932	Veli Saarinen, Finland	4:28:00.0
1936	Elis Wiklund, Sweden	3:30:11.0
1948	Nils Karlsson, Sweden	3:47:48.0
1952	Veikko Hakulinen, Finland	3:33:33.0
1956	Sixten Jernberg, Sweden	2:50:27.0
1960	Kalevi Hämäläinen, Finland	2:59:06.3
1964	Sixten Jernberg, Sweden	2:43:52.6
1968	Olle Ellefsaeter, Norway	2:28:45.8
1972	Paal Tyldrum, Norway	2:43:14.75
1976	Ivar Formo, Norway	2:37:30.50
1980	Nikolai Simyatov, USSR	2:27:24.60
1984	Thomas Wassberg, Sweden	2:15:55.8
1988	Gunde Svan, Sweden	2:04:30.9
1992	Bjørn Dæhlie, Norway	2:03:41.5
1994	Vladimir Smirnov, Kazakhstan	2:07:20.3
1998	Bjørn Dæhlie, Norway	2:05:08.2

4 X 10 KILOMETER RELAY MIXED STYLE

1936	Finland	2:41:33.0
1948	Sweden	2:32:80.0
1952	Finland	2:20:16.0
1956	USSR	2:15:30.0
1960	Finland	2:18:45.6
1964	Sweden	2:18:34.6
1968	Norway	2:08:33.5
1972	USSR	2:04:47.94
1976	Finland	2:07:59.72
1980	USSR	1:57:03.46
1984	Sweden	1:55:06.3
1988	Sweden	1:43:58.6
1992	Norway	1:39:26.0
1994	Italy	1:41:15.0
1998	Norway	1:40:55.7

SKI JUMPING (NORMAL HILL)

		Pts
1964	Veikko Kankkonen, Finland	229.90
1968	Jiri Raska, Czechoslovakia	216.5
1972	Yukio Kasaya, Japan	244.2
1976	Hans-Georg Aschenbach, E Germany	252.0
1980	Toni Innauer, Austria	266.3
1984	Jens Weissflog, E Germany	215.2
1988	Matti Nykänen, Finland	229.1
1992	Ernst Vettori, Austria	222.8
1994	Espen Bredesen, Norway	282.0
1998	Jani Soininen, Finland	234.5

SKI JUMPING (LARGE HILL)

		Pts
1924	Jacob Tullin Thams, Norway	18.960
1928	Alf Andersen, Norway	19.208
1932	Birger Ruud, Norway	228.1
1936	Birger Ruud, Norway	232.0
1948	Petter Hugsted, Norway	228.1
1952	Arnfinn Bergmann, Norway	226.0
1956	Antti Hyvärinen, Finland	227.0
1960	Helmut Recknagel, E Germany	227.2
1964	Toralf Engan, Norway	230.70
1968	Vladimir Beloussov, USSR	231.3
1972	Wojciech Fortuna, Poland	219.9
1976	Karl Schnabl, Austria	234.8
1980	Jouko Tormanen, Finland	271.0
1984	Matti Nykänen, Finland	231.2
1988	Matti Nykänen, Finland	224.0
1992	Toni Nieminen, Finland	239.5
1994	Jens Weissflog, Germany	274.5
1998	Kazuyoshi Funaki, Japan	272.3

TEAM SKI JUMPING

		Pts
1988	Finland	634.4
1992	Finland	644.4
1994	Germany	970.1
1998	Japan	933.0

NORDIC SKIING (Cont.)
Men (Cont.)

NORDIC COMBINED

		Pts
1924	Thorleif Haug, Norway	18.906*
1928	Johan Gröttumsbraaten, Norway	17.833*
1932	Johan Gröttumsbraaten, Norway	446.0
1936	Oddbjörn Hagen, Norway	430.30
1948	Heikki Hasu, Finland	448.80
1952	Simon Slattvik, Norway	451.621
1956	Sverre Stenersen, Norway	455.0
1960	Georg Thoma, W Germany	457.952
1964	Tormod Knutsen, Norway	469.28
1968	Frantz Keller, W Germany	449.04
1972	Ulrich Wehling, E Germany	413.34
1976	Ulrich Wehling, E Germany	423.39

NORDIC COMBINED (Cont.)

		Pts
1980	Ulrich Wehling, E Germany	432.20
1984	Tom Sandberg, Norway	422.595
1988	Hippolyt Kempf, Switzerland	432.230
1992	Fabrice Guy, France	426.47
1994	Fred B. Lundberg, Norway	457.970
1998	Bjarte Engen Vik, Norway	41:21.1†

TEAM NORDIC COMBINED

1988	W Germany
1992	Japan
1994	Japan
1998	Norway

* Different scoring system; 1924–1952 distance was 18 km; 1952–present, 15 km.

† Times in the cross country race were not converted into points. According to the Gundersen Method, used since 1988, starting times in the race are staggered in proportion to points earned in the ski jumping segment of the event.

Women

5 KILOMETERS CLASSICAL STYLE

1964	Klaudia Boyarskikh, USSR	17:50.5
1968	Toini Gustafsson, Sweden	16:45.2
1972	Galina Kulakova, USSR	17:00.50
1976	Helena Takalo, Finland	15:48.69
1980	Raisa Smetanina, USSR	15:06.92
1984	Marja-Liisa Hamalainen, Finland	17:04.0
1988	Marjo Matikainen, Finland	15:04.0
1992	Marjut Lukkarinen, Finland	14:13.8
1994	Lyubova Egorova, Russia	14:08.8
1998	Larissa Lazhutina, Russia	17:37.9

10 KILOMETERS CLASSICAL STYLE

1952	Lydia Widemen, Finland	41:40.0
1956	Lyubov Kosyryeva, USSR	38:11.0
1960	Maria Gusakova, USSR	39:46.6
1964	Klaudia Boyarskikh, USSR	40:24.3
1968	Toini Gustafsson, Sweden	36:46.5
1972	Galina Kulakova, USSR	34:17.8
1976	Raisa Smetanina, USSR	30:13.41
1980	Barbara Petzold, East Germany	30:31.54
1984	Marja-Lissa Hamalainen, Finland	31:44.2
1988	Vida Ventsene, USSR	30:08.3

10 KILOMETERS PURSUIT FREESTYLE

1992	Lyubov Egorova, Unified Team	40:07.7
1994	Lyubov Egorova, Russia	41:38.1
1998	Larissa Lazhutina, Russia	46:06.9

15 KILOMETERS CLASSICAL STYLE

1992	Lyubov Egorova, Unified Team	42:20.8
1994	Manuela Di Centa, Italy	39:44.5
1998	Olga Danilova, Russia	46:55.04

20 KILOMETERS FREESTYLE

1984	Marja-Liisa Hamalainen, Finland	1:01:45.0
1988	Tamara Tikhonova, USSR	55:53.6

30 KILOMETERS FREESTYLE

1992	Stefania Belmondo, Italy	1:22:30.1
1994	Manuela Di Centa, Italy	1:25:41.6
1998	Julija Tchepalova, Russia	1:22:01.5

4 X 5-KILOMETER RELAY MIXED STYLE

1956	Finland	1:9:01.0
1960	Sweden	1:4:21.4
1964	USSR	59:20.0
1968	Norway	57:30.0
1972	USSR	48:46.15
1976	USSR	1:07:49.75
1980	East Germany	1:02:11.10
1984	Norway	1:06:49.7
1988	USSR	59:51.1
1992	Unified Team	59:34.8
1994	Russia	57:12.5
1998	Russia	55:13.5

SNOWBOARDING

Men

GIANT SLALOM

1998	Ross Rebagliati, Canada	2:03.96

HALF-PIPE

		Pts
1998	Gian Simmen, Switzerland	85.2

Women

GIANT SLALOM

1998	Karine Ruby, France	2:17.34

HALF-PIPE

		Pts
1998	Nicola Thost, Germany	74.6

PETER READ MILLER

Track & Field

Starpower

Though she fell short in her quest for five gold medals, Marion Jones stole the show in Sydney

BY MERRELL NODEN

THERE IS nothing like the Olympics for inspiring grand ambitions. Every four years track and field athletes are swept away by waves of optimism, and everything seems possible. So it was with the first Olympics of the new millennium: As the season built toward its climax in late September, when the Games were held in Sydney, a handful of athletes nursed dreams of truly Olympic proportions. While in the end those dreams were dashed by the blunt realities of flesh, blood and drugs, their pursuit made for an exciting, if bittersweet year in track and field.

From the start two men stood out. Michael Johnson, plagued by hamstring problems since winning an unprecedented 200/400 double at the Atlanta Games, was hoping to duplicate that historic feat at age 33. Standing in Johnson's way in the 200 was Maurice Greene, the antic 100-meter world-record holder and 1999 world champ in both the 100 and the 200. Their reckoning loomed as the most exciting rivalry in years.

But the athlete with the most ambitious goal of all was Marion Jones. After dabbling in basketball for three years—leading track fans to conclude glumly that the sport had lost its greatest female talent—Jones returned to the track in 1997 and announced that she would try to win five gold medals in Sydney, more than any woman had ever even

attempted to win in track at a single Olympics. As talented as Jones is, this was by no means a sure thing, as Carl Lewis's four-gold-medal quest in 1984 had seemed to be. In her dress rehearsal at the 1999 worlds, Jones pulled up lame in the 200 and came away with only one gold, in the 100.

At the trials, held July 14–23 in Sacramento, Jones kept her grand scheme alive by winning both the sprints and the long jump, but the much ballyhooed showdown between Johnson and Greene came to an unexpected denouement. Not only did young John Capel, on sabbatical from the Florida football team, beat them both in a semifinal heat, but in the final both Johnson and Greene pulled up lame, leaving Capel to edge veteran Floyd Heard. The injuries shelved Johnson and Greene for weeks, though they returned to fitness well before the Olympics.

Still, there was a cloud over the 2000 Games from the start, with more open talk of drugs than at any previous Olympics. The IOC announced that for the first time it would be testing for EPO, the drug that boosts the blood's oxygen carrying capabilities, then weakened the threat by ruling that an athlete's urine and blood would both have to test positive to constitute a failed test.

Cynics wondered aloud if the testing, imperfect though it was expected to be, explained the rash of late withdrawals and

Gebrselassie closed with an all-out sprint to edge Tergat in a stirring 10,000.

SIMON BRUTY

later the fact that for the first time not a single track and field world record fell at the Olympics. Among the first to pull out was the hulking C.J. Hunter, world champion in the shot put but better known as Marion Jones's husband. Citing a slow recovery from knee surgery, Hunter watched from the stands in Sydney.

Greene and Jones won their 100s convincingly. Greene clocked a routine—for him—9.87, while Jones more than lived up to the hype, running 10.75 to beat a depleted women's field by .37 seconds, the greatest margin of victory in that race since 1952. But the daunting task to which she'd set herself became even more difficult when, less than 48 hours after the 100 final, a report surfaced that Hunter had tested positive for the steroid nandrolone at not one but four meets during the summer of 2000. Jones sat by her man at a press conference in which he claimed he must have ingested the stuff through a nutritional supplement.

The news was a shame—if not exactly a shock—because Sydney's beauty and the Australians' enthusiasm made these in every other way a great Olympics. Among the highlights were Ethiopia's tiny Haile Gebreselassie's furious sprint to beat his old rival Paul Tergat of Kenya in the 10,000 by inches. Australia's own Cathy Freeman, who lit the torch at the opening ceremonies, won the 400. Stacy Dragila of the U.S. took the inaugural gold medal in women's pole vault (15' 1"), while Nick Hysong became the first U.S. men's vaulter to win Olympic gold since Bob Seagren in 1968. Johnson won the men's 400, as expected, but another favorite, 1,500-meter

world-record holder Hicham El Guerrouj of Morocco, lost for the first time since 1997, finishing second to Kenya's Noah Ngeny. Indeed, every men's medal from the 1,500 to the marathon was won by an African, with Ethiopians winning the women's 10,000 and the men's 5,000, 10,000 and marathon.

Still, there was no mistaking who was the overall star of these Games. Jones made it clear she would say nothing about her husband's case until her own labors were complete, and she stuck to that, smiling and winning applause from the crowd every time she stepped on the track. With the Hunter news still stinging, Jones won the 200 easily, in 21.84. Next up was her toughest test, the long jump. She registered a foul estimated at 24', but Jones was so inconsistent it was a wonder she jumped as far as 22' 8½,", which got her the bronze. Her quest for five gold medals had failed, but she took it well, to say the least: Jones led the crowd in clapping for Heike Drechsler of Germany, the winner of the event.

Jones won another bronze with her anchor of the U.S. 4 x 100 team, which was hampered by horrific baton passing and the absence of both Inger Miller and Gail Devers. Our final fleeting glimpse of Jones at Sydney came in the 4 x 400, in which she blew the race open with a 49.57 third leg to claim a third gold.

Later Jones allowed that she was a little disappointed to have had to "settle for" three golds and two bronzes, even though that was a record total. Still, her greatest feat may have been to have triumphed over the suspicions swirling around her husband. He still has questions to answer, but the lingering memory of Sydney will be Marion Jones, her speed, her smile, her good sportsmanship.

FOR THE RECORD·1999–2000

U.S. Olympic Trials

Sacramento, CA, July 14–23, 2000

Men

100 METERS
1. ....Maurice Greene, Nike — 10.01
2. ....Curtis Johnson, HSI — 10.07
3. ....Jon Drummond, Nike — 10.07

200 METERS
1. ....John Capel, adidas — 19.85
2. ....Floyd Heard, Santa Monica TC — 19.88
3. ....Coby Miller, Nike — 19.96

400 METERS
1. ....Michael Johnson, Nike — 43.68
2. ....Alvin Harrison, Nike — 44.63
3. ....Antonio Pettigrew, adidas — 44.66

800 METERS
1. ....Mark Everett — 1:45.67
2. ....Rich Kenah, Asics — 1:46.05
3. ....Bryan Woodward, Reebok — 1:46.09

1,500 METERS
1. ....Gabe Jennings, Stanford — 3:35.90
2. ....Jason Pyrah, Nike — 3:36.70
3. ....Michael Stember, Stanford — 3:37.04

3,000 M STEEPLECHASE
1. ....Pascal Dobert, Nike — 8:15.77
2. ....Mark Croghan, adidas — 8:16.20
3. ....Tony Cosey, adidas — 8:21.41

5,000 METERS
1. ....Adam Goucher, Fila — 13:27.06
2. ....Brad Hauser, Nike — 13:27.31
3. ....Nick Rogers, Nike — 13:29.48

10,000 METERS
1. ....Mebrahtom Keflezighi, Nike — 28:03.32
2. ....Alan Culpepper, adidas — 28:03.35
3. ....Abdihakim Adbi, Nike — 28:19.03

110-METER HURDLES
1. ....Allen Johnson, Nike — 12.97
2. ....Mark Crear, God Speed TC — 13.11
3. ....Terrence Trammell, S Carolina — 13.19

400-METER HURDLES
1. ....Angelo Taylor, Nike — 47.62
2. ....Eric Thomas, Nike — 48.22
3. ....James Carter, Maryland Elite — 48.46

20-KILOMETER WALK
1. ....Tim Seaman, NYAC — 1:25:41
2. ....Kevin Eastler, USAF — 1:26:38
3. ....Andrew Hermann, Multnomah AC — 1:28:06

HIGH JUMP
1. ....Charles Austin, Nike — 7 ft 7¼ in
2. ....Kenny Evans, Arkansas — 7 ft 5¼ in
3. ....Nathan Leeper, Nike — 7 ft 5¼ in

POLE VAULT
1. ....Lawrence Johnson, adidas — 19 ft 1½ in
2. ....Nick Hysong, Nike — 18 ft 9½ in
3. ....Pat Manson, US West — 18 ft 5½ in

LONG JUMP
1. ....Melvin Lister, Nike — 28 ft 3¾ in
2. ....Dwight Phillips, Nike — 26 ft 8½ in
3. ....Walter Davis, Barton CC — 26 ft 7¼ in

TRIPLE JUMP
1. ....Robert Howard, Reebok — 55 ft 9 in
2. ....LaMark Carter, Nike — 55 ft 7¾ in
3. ....Walter Davis, Barton CC — 55 ft 3 in

SHOT PUT
1. ....Adam Nelson, Nike — 72 ft 7 in
2. ............C.J. Hunter, Nike — 71 ft 9 in
3. ....Andy Bloom, Nike — 69 ft 10¾ in

DISCUSS THROW
1. ....Adam Setliff, Nike — 209 ft 10 in
2. ....John Godina, Reebok — 208 ft 8 in
3. ....Anthony Washington, Qwest — 207 ft 10 in

HAMMER THROW
1. ....Lance Deal, NYAC — 258 ft 9 in
2. ....Kevin McMahon, Reebok — 240 ft 6 in
3. ....Jud Logan, M-F Athletics — 233 ft

JAVELIN THROW
1. ....Breaux Greer, NYAC — 266 ft
2. ....Tomas Pukstys, adidas — 260 ft 4 in
3. ....Todd Riech, Nike — 252 ft 5 in

DECATHLON
1. ....Tom Pappas, adidas — 8467 pts
2. ....Chris Huffins, Oakley Int'l — 8285 pts
3. ....Kip Janvrin — 8057 pts

MARATHON*
1. ....Rod Dehaven — 2:15:30
2. ....Peter Delacerda — 2:16:18
3. ....Mark Coogan — 2:17:04

* Held May 7, 2000 in Pittsburgh, PA

Women

100 METERS
1. ....Marion Jones, Nike — 10.88
2. ....Inger Miller, Nike — 11.05
3. ....Chryste Gaines, adidas — 11.13

200 METERS
1. ....Marion Jones, Nike — 21.94
2. ....Inger Miller, Nike — 22.09
3. ....Nanceen Perry, Mizuno/In Pursuit — 22.38

400 METERS
1. ....Latasha Colander-Richard, Nike — 49.87
2. ....Jearl Miles-Clark, Reebok — 50.23
3. ....Michelle Collins, Nike — 50.29

800 METERS
1. ....Hazel Clark, Nike — 1:58.97
2. ....Jearl Miles-Clark, Reebok — 1:59.12
3. ....Joetta Clark-Diggs, Nike — 1:59.49

1,500 METERS
1. ....Regina Jacobs, Nike — 4:01.01
2. ....Suzy Favor-Hamilton, Nike — 4:01.81
3. ....Marla Runyan, Asics — 4:06.44

3,000 M STEEPLECHASE
1. ....Elizabeth Jackson, BYU — 9:57.20 AR
2. ....Lisa Nye, Nike — 10:00.63
3. ....Kara Ormond, BYU — 10:03.09

5,000 METERS
1. ....Regina Jacobs, Nike — 14:45.35 AR
2. ....Deena Drossin, Reebok — 15:11.55
3. ....Elva Dryer, Nike — 15:12.07

10,000 METERS
1. ....Deena Drossin, Reebok — 31:51.05
2. ....Jen Rhines, adidas — 31:58.34
3. ....Libbie Hickman, Nike — 31:58.68

20 KILOMETER WALK
1. ....Michelle Rohl — 1:32:39
2. ....Yueling Chen — 1:33:40
3. ....Debbi Lawrence, Nike — 1:33:48

100-METER HURDLES
1. ....Gail Devers, Nike — 12.33 AR
2. ....Melissa Morrison, Reebok — 12.63
3. ....Sharon Jewell, adidas — 12.69

400-METER HURDLES
1. ....Sandra Glover, Nike — 53.33
2. ....Kim Batten — 54.70
3. ....Tonja Buford-Bailey, Nike — 54.80

HIGH JUMP
1. ....Karol Damon — 6 ft 4 in
2. ....Erin Aldrich, Texas-Austin — 6 ft 4 in
3. ....Amy Acuff, New Balance — 6 ft 2¾ in

POLE VAULT
1. ....Stacy Dragila, Reebok — 15 ft 2¼ in WR
2. ....Kellie Suttle, Nike — 14 ft 6¼ in
3. ....Melissa Mueller, Nike — 14 ft 2½ in

LONG JUMP
1. ....Marion Jones, Nike — 23 ft ½ in
2. ....Dawn Burrell, U.S. Army — 22 ft 10½ in w
3. ....Shana Williams, Nike — 22 ft 6½ in w

TRIPLE JUMP
1. ....Nicole Gamble, Nike — 45 ft 9¾ in
2. ....Sheila Hudson — 45 ft 8½ in
3. ....Tiombe Hurd, Nike — 45 ft 7¾ in

SHOT PUT
1. ....Connie Price-Smith, Nike — 61 ft 1½ in
2. ....Jesseca Cross, NYAC — 58 ft 2½ in
3. ....Dawn Dumble, Reebok — 57 ft 1 in

DISCUS THROW
1. ....Seilala Sue, Reebok — 216 ft 2 in
2. ....Suzy Powell, Asics — 211 ft 10 in
3. ....Kristin Kuehl, MF Athletics — 202 ft 7 in

HAMMER THROW
1. ....Dawn Ellerbe, NYAC — 227 ft
2. ....Amy Palmer, NYAC — 217 ft 7 in
3. ....Jesseca Cross, NYAC — 217 ft 2 in

JAVELIN
1. ....Lynda Blutreich, Nike — 191 ft 2 in
2. ....Kim Kreiner — 187 ft 2 in
3. ....Emily Carlsten, Florida — 186 ft 11 in

HEPTATHLON
1. ....DeDee Nathan, Indiana Invaders — 6343 pts
2. ....Shelia Burrell, Nike — 6339 pts
3. ....Kelly Blair-LaBounty, Nike — 6180 pts

MARATHON*
1. ....Christine Clark — 2:33:31
2. ....Kristy Johnston — 2:35:36
3. ....Anne Marie Lauck — 2:36:05

w: wind-aided.

* Held February 26, 2000 in Columbia, SC.   AR=American record.

Atlanta, Georgia, March 3–4, 2000

Men

60 METERS

1. ....Jon Drummond, Nike 6.46
2. ....Tim Harden, Nike 6.48
3. ....Gregory Saddler, Nike 6.54

200 METERS

1. ....Chris Chandler, Nebraska 20.84
2. ....Brian Lewis, Reebok 20.86
3. ....Kevin Braunskill 20.97

400 METERS

1. ....James Davis, Goldwin Int'l 45.54
2. ....Ronnie Williams 45.81
3. ....Deon Minor, Nike 46.01

800 METERS

1. ....Bryan Woodward, Reebok Enclave 1:48.69
2. ....Khadevis Robinson, Santa Monica 1:48.83
3. ....Johnny Gray, Santa Monica 1:49.10

MILE

1. ....Jason Pyrah 3:57.83
2. ....Jason Lunn, Nike Farm Team 3:58.50
3. ....Richie Boulet, New Balance 3:58.83

3,000 METERS

1. ....Ray Appenheimer, Nike Farm Team 7:56.22
2. ....Michael Ryan, U.S. Navy 7:57.11
3. ....Scott Strand, New Balance 7:59.73

5,000 METER WALK

1. ....Tim Seaman, NYAC 19:32.11
2. ....Curt Clausen, NYAC 19:53.98
3. ....Al Heppner, NYAC 21:13.66

60-METER HURDLES

1. ....Terrence Trammell, S Carolina 7.57
2. ....Dominique Arnold, Nike 7.57
3. ....Chris Phillips 7.65

4 X 400 METER RELAY

1. ....Bronx Int'l 3:09.64
2. ....Clemson 3:09.75
3. ....Houston 3:10.84

HIGH JUMP

1. ....Matt Hemingway, U.S. West .... 7 ft 9¾ in
2. ....Charles Austin .... 7 ft 5¼ in
3. ....Jeremy Fischer .... 7 ft 5¼ in

POLE VAULT

1. ....Lawrence Johnson, adidas ...... 19 ft ¾ in
2. ....Tye Harvey, Bell Athletic ...... 18 ft 8¾ in
3. ....Jeff Hartwig, Nike .... 18 ft 8¾ in

LONG JUMP

1. ....Savante Stringfellow, Mississippi 26 ft ¾ in
2. ....Jamorya Funderburk .... 25 ft 8¾ in
3. ....Erick Walder, adidas .... 25 ft 8¾ in

TRIPLE JUMP

1. ....LaVar Anderson .... 55 ft 5½ in
2. ....Leonard Cobb .... 54 ft 8¾ in
3. ....Lamark Carter, Nike .... 54 ft 8 in

SHOT PUT

1. ....Andrew Bloom, Nike .... 70 ft 10½ in
2. ....Kevin Toth, Nike .... 65 ft
3. ....Brad Mears, M-F Athletic ...... 64 ft 6½ in

35-POUND WEIGHT THROW

1. ....Lance Deal, NYAC .... 78 ft 4½ in
2. ....Mark McGehearty, NYAC .... 75 ft 8¾ in
3. ....Kevin Mannon .... 72 ft 9¼ in

HEPTATHLON

1. ....Tom Pappas, adidas .... 5933 pts
2. ....Phil McMullen, Asics .... 5828 pts
3. ....Chad Smith .... 5756 pts

Women

60 METERS

1.	Carlette Guidry, adidas	7.12
2.	Passion Richardson, Nike	7.20
3.	Torri Edwards, Nike	7.21

200 METERS

1.	Nanceen Perry, Mizuno TC	22.65
2.	Carlette Guidry, adidas	22.90
3.	LaTasha Jenkins, Nike	23.28

400 METERS

1.	Suziann Reid, adidas	52.50
2.	Kim Graham, adidas	52.74
3.	Shanelle Porter, U.S. West	52.79

800 METERS

1.	Hazel Clark, Nike	2:03.40
2.	Michelle Ave, Asics	2:05.57
3.	Miesha Marzell, Fila	2:05.58

MILE

1.	Regina Jacobs, NYAC	4:25.92
2.	Collette Liss, IN Invaders	4:33.28
3.	Mary Jane Harrelson	4:34.75

3,000 METERS

1.	Marla Runyan, Asics	9:01.29
2.	Cheri Kenah, adidas	9:01.66
3.	Amy Rudolph, Reebok	9:03.14

3,000 METER WALK

1.	Michelle Rohl, Moving Com	12:51.17
2.	Jill Zenner, Miami Valley	13:09.92
3.	Debbi Lawrence	13:26.06

60-METER HURDLES

1.	Melissa Morrison, Reebok	7.86
2.	Sharon Jewell, adidas	7.96
3.	Miesha McKelvy	8.07

4 X 400 METER RELAY

1.	Nebraska	3:35.49
2.	Georgia	3:39.21
3.	N Carolina	3:40.68

HIGH JUMP

1.	Tisha Waller, Nike	6 ft 5 in
2.	Angela Spangler, Asics	6 ft 2¾ in
3.	Gwen Wentland, Nike	6 ft 2¾ in

WR= world record.

POLE VAULT

1.	Stacy Dragila, Reebok	15 ft 1¾ in WR
2.	Melissa Mueller, Nike	14 ft 6 in
3.	Mary Sauer	14 ft 2 in

LONG JUMP

1.	Adrien Sayer, Nike	21 ft 5½ in
2.	Shana Williams, adidas	21 ft
3.	Antoinette Wilks, S Carolina	20 ft 2½ in

TRIPLE JUMP

1.	Tiombe Hurd, Nike	46 ft 1½ in
2.	Stacey Bowers	44 ft 6 in
3.	Vanitta Kinard	44 ft ¾ in

SHOT PUT

1.	Connie Price-Smith, Nike	61 ft 4¼ in
2.	Tressa Thompson, Nike	60 ft 1 in
3.	Jesseca Cross, NYAC	58 ft 7¼ in

20-POUND WEIGHT THROW

1.	Dawn Ellerbe, NYAC	77 ft 5¼ in
2.	Jesseca Cross, NYAC	69 ft 8¼ in
3.	Seilala Sue, UCLA	65 ft 11½ in

IAAF World Cross-Country Championships

Vilamoura, Portugal, March 18–19, 2000

MEN (12,000 METERS; 7.5 MILES)
1. ....Mohammed Mourhit, Belgium — 35:00
2. ....Assefa Mezgebu, Ethiopia — 35:01
3. ....Paul Tergat, Kenya — 35:02

WOMEN (8,000 METERS; 5 MILES)
1. ....Derartu Tulu, Ethiopia — 25:42
2. ....Gete Wami, Ethiopia — 25:48
3. ....Susan Chepkemei, Kenya — 25:50

Major Marathons

Chicago: October 24, 1999

MEN
1. ....Khalid Khannouchi, Morocco — 2:05:42 WR
2. ....Moses Tanui, Kenya — 2:06:16
3. ....Ondoro Osoro, Kenya — 2:08:00

WOMEN
1. ....Joyce Chepchumba, Kenya — 2:25:59
2. ....Margareth Okayo, Kenya — 2:26:00
3. ....Elana Meyer, S Africa — 2:27:17

New York City: November 7, 1999

MEN
1. ....Joseph Chebet, Kenya — 2:09:14
2. ....Domingos Castro, Portugal — 2:09:20
3. ....Shem Kororia, Kenya — 2:09:32

WOMEN
1. ....Adriana Fernandez, Mexico — 2:25:06
2. ....Catherine Ndereba, Kenya — 2:27:34
3. ....Katrin Dorre-Heinig, Germany — 2:28:41

Tokyo: November 21, 1999

WOMEN ONLY
1. ....Eri Yamaguchi, Japan — 2:22:12
2. ....Fatuma Roba, Ethiopia — 2:27:05
3. ....Valentina Yegolova, Russia — 2:28:08

Rome: January 1, 2000

MEN
1. ....Josephat Kiprono, Kenya — 2:08:27
2. ....Giacomo Leone, Italy — 2:08:41
3. ....Francesco Ingargiola, Italy — 2:08:49

WOMEN
1. ....Tegla Loroupe, Kenya — 2:32:04
2. ....Gadissie Edatto, Ethiopia — 2:32:11
3. ....Helen Kimutai, Kenya — 2:33:47

Tokyo: February 13, 2000

MEN ONLY
1. ....Japhet Kosgei, Kenya — 2:07:15
2. ....Lee Bong-joo, S Korea — 2:07:20
3. ....Alberto Juzdado, Spain — 2:08:08

Paris: April 9, 2000

MEN
1. ....Mohamed Ouaadi, France — 2:08:49
2. ....Sammy Otieno, Kenya — 2:09:10
3. ....Abdelah Behar, France — 2:09:13

WOMEN
1. ....Merleen Renders, Belgium — 2:23:43
2. ....Alina Tecuta, Romania — 2:28:18
3. ....Irina Timofeyeva, Russia — 2:30:01

Rotterdam: April 16, 2000

MEN
1. ....Kenneth Cheruiyot, Kenya — 2:08:22
2. ....Francisco Javier Cortes, Spain — 2:08:30
3. ....Vanderlei Lima, Brazil — 2:08:34

WOMEN
1. ....Ana Isabel Alonso, Spain — 2:30:21
2. ....Mineko Yamanouchi, Japan — 2:31:30
3. ....Sue Reinsford, Great Britain — 2:33:41

London: April 16, 2000

MEN
1. ....Antonio Pinto, Portugal — 2:06:36
2. ....Abdelkader El Mouaziz, Morocco — 2:07:33
3. ....Khalid Khannouchi, Morocco — 2:08:36

WOMEN
1. ....Tegla Loroupe, Kenya — 2:24:33
2. ....Lidia Simon, Romania — 2:24:46
3. ....Joyce Chepchumba, Kenya — 2:24:57

Boston: April 17, 2000

MEN
1. ....Elijah Lagat, Kenya — 2:09:47
2. ....Gezahenge Abera, Ethiopia — 2:09:47
3. ....Moses Tanui, Kenya — 2:09:50

WOMEN
1. ....Catherine Ndereba, Kenya — 2:26:11
2. ....Irina Bogacheva, Kyrgyzstan — 2:26:27
3. ....Fatuma Roba, Ethiopia — 2:26:27

WR=world record.

TRACK AND FIELD

World Records

As of October 5, 2000. World outdoor records are recognized by the International Amateur Athletics Federation (IAAF).

Men

Event	Mark	Record Holder	Date	Site
100 meters	9.79	Maurice Greene, United States	6-16-99	Athens
200 meters	19.32	Michael Johnson, United States	8-1-96	Atlanta
400 meters	43.18	Michael Johnson, United States	8-26-99	Seville
800 meters	1:41.11	Wilson Kipketer, Denmark	8-24-97	Cologne
1,000 meters	2:11.96	Noah Ngeny, Kenya	9-5-99	Rieti, Italy
1,500 meters	3:26.00	Hicham El Guerrouj, Morocco	7-14-98	Rome
Mile	3:43.13	Hicham El Guerrouj, Morocco	7-7-99	Rome
2,000 meters	4:44.79	Hicham El Guerrouj, Morocco	9-7-99	Berlin
3,000 meters	7:20.67	Daniel Komen, Kenya	9-1-96	Rieti, Italy
Steeplechase	7:55.72	Bernard Bermasai, Kenya	8-24-97	Cologne
5,000 meters	12:39.36	Haile Gebrselassie, Ethiopia	6-13-98	Helsinki
10,000 meters	26:22.75	Haile Gebrselassie, Ethiopia	6-1-98	Hengelo, Netherlands
20,000 meters	56:55.6	Arturo Barrios, Mexico	3-30-91	La Flâche, France
Hour	21,101 meters	Arturo Barrios, Mexico	3-30-91	La Flâche, France
25,000 meters	1:13:55.8	Toshihiko Seko, Japan	3-22-81	Christchurch, New Zealand
30,000 meters	1:29:18.8	Toshihiko Seko, Japan	3-22-81	Christchurch, New Zealand
Marathon	2:05:42	Khalid Khannouchi, Morocco	10-24-99	Chicago
110-meter hurdles	12.91	Colin Jackson, Great Britain	8-20-93	Stuttgart, Germany
400-meter hurdles	46.78	Kevin Young, United States	8-6-92	Barcelona
20-kilometer walk	1:17:25.6	Bernardo Segura, Mexico	5-7-94	Bergen, Norway
30-kilometer walk	2:01:44.1	Maurizio Damilano, Italy	10-3-92	Cuneo, Italy
50-kilometer walk	3:40:57.9	Thierry Toutain, France	9-29-96	Héricourt, France
4x100-meter relay	37.40	United States (Mike Marsh, Leroy Burrell, Dennis Mitchell, Carl Lewis)	8-8-92	Barcelona
		United States (Jon Drummond, Andre Cason, Dennis Mitchell, Leroy Burrell)	8-21-93	Stuttgart, Germany
4x200-meter relay	1:18.68	Santa Monica TC (Mike Marsh, Leroy Burrell, Floyd Heard, Carl Lewis)	4-17-94	Walnut, CA
4x400-meter relay	2:54.20	United States (Jerome Young, Antonio Pettigrew, Tyree Washington, Michael Johnson)	7-22-98	New York City
4x800-meter relay	7:03.89	Great Britain (Peter Elliott, Garry Cook, Steve Cram, Sebastian Coe)	8-30-82	London
4x1,500-meter relay	14:38.8	West Germany (Thomas Wessinghage, Harald Hudak, Michael Lederer, Karl Fleschen)	8-17-77	Cologne
High jump	8 ft ½ in	Javier Sotomayor, Cuba	7-27-93	Salamanca, Spain
Pole vault	20 ft 1¾ in	Sergei Bubka, Ukraine	7-31-94	Sestriere, Italy
Long jump	29 ft 4½ in	Mike Powell, United States	8-30-91	Tokyo
Triple jump	60 ft ¼ in	Jonathan Edwards, Great Britain	8-7-95	Göteborg, Sweden
Shot put	75 ft 10¼ in	Randy Barnes, United States	5-20-90	Westwood, CA
Discus throw	243 ft 0 in	Jürgen Schult, East Germany	6-6-86	Neubrandenburg, Germany
Hammer throw	284 ft 7 in	Yuri Syedikh, USSR	8-30-86	Stuttgart, Germany
Javelin throw	323 ft 1 in	Jan Zelezny, Czech Republic	5-25-96	Jena, Germany
Decathlon	8994 pts	Tomás Dvorák, Czech Republic	7-3/4-99	Prague

Note: The decathlon consists of 10 events: the 100 meters, long jump, shot put, high jump and 400 meters on the first day; the 110-meter hurdles, discus, pole vault, javelin and 1500 meters on the second.

World Records (Cont.)

Women

Event	Mark	Record Holder	Date	Site
100 meters	10.49	Florence Griffith Joyner, United States	7-16-88	Indianapolis
200 meters	21.34	Florence Griffith Joyner, United States	9-29-88	Seoul
400 meters	47.60	Marita Koch, East Germany	10-6-85	Canberra, Australia
800 meters	1:53.28	Jarmila Kratochvílová, Czechoslovakia	7-26-83	Munich
1,000 meters	2:28.98	Svetlana Masterkova, Russia	8-23-96	Brussels
1,500 meters	3:50.46	Qu Yunxia, China	9-11-93	Beijing
Mile	4:12.56	Svetlana Masterkova, Russia	8-14-96	Zurich
2,000 meters	5:25.36	Sonia O'Sullivan, Ireland	7-8-94	Edinburgh
3,000 meters	8:06.11	Wang Junxia, China	9-13-93	Beijing
Steeplechase	9:40.20	Cristina Iloc-Casandra, Romania	8-30-00	Reims, France
5,000 meters	14:28.09	Jiang Bo, China	10-23-97	Shanghai
10,000 meters	29:31.78	Wang Junxia, China	9-8-93	Beijing
Hour	18,340 meters	Tegla Loroupe, Kenya	8-8-98	Borgholzhausen, Germany
20,000 meters	1:06:48.8	Izumi Maki, Japan	9-19-93	Amagasaki, Japan
25,000 meters	1:29:29.2	Karolina Szabó, Hungary	4-22-88	Budapest
30,000 meters	1:47:05.6	Karolina Szabó, Hungary	4-22-88	Budapest
Marathon	2:20:43	Tegla Loroupe, Kenya	9-26-99	Berlin
100-meter hurdles	12.21	Yordanka Donkova, Bulgaria	8-20-88	Stara Zagora, Bulgaria
400-meter hurdles	52.61	Kim Batten, United States	8-11-95	Göteborg, Sweden
5-kilometer walk	20:13.26	Kerry Saxby, Australia	2-25-96	Hobart, Australia
10-kilometer walk	41:04	Yelena Nikolayeva, Russia	4-20-96	Sochi, Russia
4x100-meter relay	41.37	East Germany (Silke Gladisch, Sabine Reiger, Ingrid Auerswald, Marlies Göhr)	10-6-85	Canberra, Australia
4x200-meter relay	1:27.46	United States (LaTasha Jenkins, LaTasha Colander-Richardson, Nanceen Perry, Marion Jones)	4-29-00	Philadelphia
4x400-meter relay	3:15.17	USSR (Tatyana Ledovskaya, Olga Nazarova, Maria Pinigina, Olga Bryzgina)	10-1-88	Seoul
4x800-meter relay	7:50.17	USSR (Nadezhda Olizarenko, Lyubov Gurina, Lyudmila Borisova, Irina Podyalovskaya)	8-5-84	Moscow
High jump	6 ft 10¼ in	Stefka Kostadinova, Bulgaria	8-30-87	Rome
Pole vault	15 ft 2¼ in	Stacy Dragila, United States	7-23-00	Sacramento, CA
Long jump	24 ft 8¼ in	Galina Chistyakova, USSR	6-11-88	Leningrad
Triple jump	50 ft 10¼ in	Inessa Kravets, Ukraine	8-10-95	Göteborg, Sweden
Shot put	74 ft 3 in	Natalya Lisovskaya, USSR	6-7-87	Moscow
Discus throw	252 ft	Gabriele Reinsch, East Germany	7-9-88	Neubrandenburg, Germany
Hammer throw	247 ft 3 in	Mihaela Melinte, Romania	8-29-99	Rüdlingen, Switzerland
Javelin throw	228 ft 1¼ in	Trine Solberg-Hattestad, Norway	7-28-00	Oslo
Heptathlon	7291 pts	Jackie Joyner-Kersee, United States	9-23/24-88	Seoul

Note: The heptathlon consists of 7 events: the 100-meter hurdles, high jump, shot put and 200 meters on the first day; the long jump, javelin and 800 meters on the second.

American Records

As of September 5, 2000. American outdoor records are recognized by USA Track and Field (USATF). WR=world record. EWR=equals world record.

Men

Event	Mark	Record Holder	Date	Site
100 meters	9.79 WR	Maurice Greene	6-16-99	Athens
200 meters	19.32 WR	Michael Johnson	8-1-96	Atlanta
400 meters	43.18 WR	Michael Johnson	8-26-99	Seville
800 meters	1:42.60	Johnny Gray	8-28-85	Koblenz, Germany
1,000 meters	2:13.9	Rick Wohlhuter	7-30-74	Oslo
1,500 meters	3:29.77	Sydney Maree	8-25-85	Cologne
Mile	3:47.69	Steve Scott	7-7-82	Oslo
2,000 meters	4:52.44	Jim Spivey	9-15-87	Lausanne
3,000 meters	7:30.84	Bob Kennedy	8-8-98	Monte Carlo
Steeplechase	8:09.17	Henry Marsh	8-28-85	Koblenz, Germany
5,000 meters	12:58.21	Bob Kennedy	8-14-96	Zurich
10,000 meters	27:20.56	Mark Nenow	9-5-86	Brussels
20,000 meters	58:25.0	Bill Rodgers	8-9-77	Boston
Hour	20,547 meters	Bill Rodgers	8-9-77	Boston
25,000 meters	1:14:11.8	Bill Rodgers	2-21-79	Saratoga, CA
30,000 meters	1:31:49	Bill Rodgers	2-21-79	Saratoga, CA
Marathon	2:09:32	David Morris	10-24-99	Chicago
110-meter hurdles	12.92	Roger Kingdom	8-16-89	Zurich
		Allen Johnson	6-23-96	Atlanta
		Allen Johnson	8-23-96	Brussels
400-meter hurdles	46.78 WR	Kevin Young	8-6-92	Barcelona
20-kilometer walk	1:23:40	Tim Seaman	8-14-00	La Jolla, CA
30-kilometer walk	2:14:31	Allen James	10-31-93	Atlanta
50-kilometer walk	3:59:41.1	Herman Nelson	6-9-96	Seattle
4x100-meter relay	37.40 WR	United States (Mike Marsh, Leroy Burrell, Dennis Mitchell, Carl Lewis)	8-8-92	Barcelona
		United States (Jon Drummond, Andre Cason, Dennis Mitchell, Leroy Burrell)	8-21-93	Stuttgart, Germany
4x200-meter relay	1:18.68 WR	Santa Monica Track Club (Mike Marsh, Leroy Burrell, Floyd Heard, Carl Lewis)	4-17-94	Walnut, CA
4x400-meter relay	2:54.20 WR	United States (Jerome Young, Antonio Pettigrew, Tyree Washington, Michael Johnson)	7-22-98	New York City
4x800-meter relay	7:06.5	Santa Monica Track Club (James Robinson, David Mack, Earl Jones, Johnny Gray)	4-26-86	Walnut, CA
4x1,500-meter relay	14:46.3	National Team (Dan Aldredge, Andy Clifford, Todd Harbour, Tom Duits)	6-24-79	Bourges, France
High jump	7 ft 10½ in	Charles Austin	8-17-91	Zurich
Pole vault	19 ft 9¼ in	Jeff Hartwig	6-14-00	Jonesboro, AR
Long jump	29 ft 4½ in WR	Mike Powell	8-30-91	Tokyo
Triple jump	59 ft 4¼ in	Kenny Harrison	7-27-96	Atlanta
Shot put	75 ft 10¼ in WR	Randy Barnes	5-20-90	Westwood, CA
Discus throw	237 ft 4 in	Ben Plucknett	7-7-81	Stockholm
Hammer throw	270 ft 9 in	Lance Deal	9-7-96	Milan
Javelin throw	285 ft 10 in	Tom Pukstys	5-25-97	Jena, Germany
Decathlon	8891 pts	Dan O'Brien	9-4/5-92	Talence, France

Women

Event	Mark	Record Holder	Date	Site
100 meters	10.49 WR	Florence Griffith Joyner	7-16-88	Indianapolis
200 meters	21.34 WR	Florence Griffith Joyner	9-29-88	Seoul
400 meters	48.83	Valerie Brisco-Hooks	8-6-84	Los Angeles
800 meters	1:56.40	Jearl Miles-Clark	8-11-99	Zurich
1,500 meters	3:57.12	Mary Slaney	7-26-83	Stockholm
Mile	4:16.71	Mary Slaney	8-21-85	Zurich
2,000 meters	5:32.7	Mary Slaney	8-3-84	Eugene, OR
3,000 meters	8:25.83	Mary Slaney	9-7-85	Rome
Steeplechase	9:57.20	Elizabeth Jackson	7-17-00	Sacramento, CA
5,000 meters	14:45.35	Regina Jacobs	7-21-00	Sacramento, CA
10,000 meters	31:19.89	Lynn Jennings	8-7-92	Barcelona
Marathon	2:21:21	Joan Samuelson	10-20-85	Chicago
100-meter hurdles	12.33	Gail Devers	7-23-00	Sacramento, CA
400-meter hurdles	52.61 WR	Kim Batten	8-11-95	Göteborg, Sweden
5,000-meter walk	20:56.88	Michelle Rohl	4-27-96	Philadelphia
10,000-meter walk	44:41.87	Michelle Rohl	7-26-94	St. Petersburg
4x100-meter relay	41.47	National Team (Chryste Gaines, Marion Jones, Inger Miller, Gail Devers)	8-9-97	Athens
4x200-meter relay	1:27.46 WR	USA Blue (LaTasha Jenkins, LaTasha Colander, Nanceen Perry, Marion Jones)	4-29-00	Philadelphia
4x400-meter relay	3:15.51	United States (Denean Howard, Diane Dixon, Valerie Brisco, Florence Griffith Joyner)	10-1-88	Seoul
4x800-meter relay	8:17.09	Athletics West (Sue Addison, Lee Arbogast, Mary Decker, Chris Mullen)	4-24-83	Walnut, CA
High jump	6 ft 8 in	Louise Ritter	7-9-88	Austin
		Louise Ritter	9-30-88	Seoul
Pole vault	15 ft 2¼ in WR	Stacy Dragila	7-23-00	Sacramento, CA
Long jump	24 ft 7 in	Jackie Joyner-Kersee	5-22-94	New York City
			7-31-94	Sestriere, Italy
Triple jump	47 ft 3½ in	Sheila Hudson	7-8-96	Stockholm
Shot put	66 ft 2½ in	Ramona Pagel	6-25-88	San Diego
Discus throw	216 ft 10 in	Carol Cady	5-31-86	San Jose
Hammer throw	231 ft 2 in	Dawn Ellerbee	4-29-00	Philadelphia
Javelin throw	192 ft 3 in	Lynda Blutreich	7-1-00	New Haven, CT
Heptathlon	7291 pts WR	Jackie Joyner-Kersee	9-23/24-88	Seoul

World and American Indoor Records

As of September 5, 2000. American indoor records are recognized by USA Track and Field. World Indoor records are recognized by the International Amateur Athletics Federation (IAAF).

Men

Event	Mark	Record Holder	Date	Site
50 meters	5.56	Donovan Bailey, Canada (W)	2-9-96	Reno
	5.56	Maurice Greene (A)	2-13-99	Los Angeles
55 meters*	5.99	Obadele Thompson, Barbados (W)	2-22-97	Colorado Springs
	6.00	Lee McRae (A)	3-14-86	Oklahoma City
60 meters	6.39	Maurice Greene (W, A)	3-1-98	Madrid
200 meters	19.92	Frankie Fredericks, Namibia (W)	2-18-96	Liévin, France
	20.26	Shawn Crawford (A)	3-11-00	Fayetteville, AR
400 meters	44.63	Michael Johnson (W, A)	3-4-95	Atlanta
800 meters	1:42.67	Wilson Kipketer, Denmark (W)	3-9-97	Paris
	1:45.00	Johnny Gray (A)	3-8-92	Sindelfingen, Germany
1,000 meters	2:14.96	Wilson Kipketer, Denmark (W)	2-20-00	Birmingham, England
	2:18.19	Ocky Clark (A)	2-12-89	Stuttgart, Germany
1,500 meters	3:31.17	Hicham El Guerrouj, Morocco (W)	2-02-97	Stuttgart, Germany
	3:38.12	Jeff Atkinson (A)	3-5-89	Budapest

Men (Cont.)

Event	Mark	Record Holder	Date	Site
Mile	3:48.45	Hicham El Guerrouj, Morocco (W)	2-12-97	Ghent, Belgium
	3:51.8	Steve Scott (A)	2-20-81	San Diego
3,000 meters	7:24.90	Daniel Komen, Kenya (W)	2-6-98	Budapest
	7:39.94	Steve Scott (A)	2-10-89	East Rutherford, NJ
5,000 meters	12:50.38	Haile Gebrselassie, Ethiopia (W)	2-14-99	Birmingham, England
	13:20.55	Doug Padilla (A)	2-12-82	New York City
50-meter hurdles	6.25	Mark McKoy, Canada (W)	3-5-86	Kobe, Japan
	6.35	Greg Foster (A)	1-27-85	Rosemont, Illinois
	6.35	Greg Foster (A)	1-31-87	Ottawa, Ontario
55-meter hurdles*	6.89	Renaldo Nehemiah (A)	1-20-79	New York City
60-meter hurdles	7.30	Colin Jackson, Great Britain (W)	3-6-94	Sindelfingen, Germany
	7.36	Greg Foster (A)	1-16-87	Los Angeles
5,000-meter walk	18:07.08	Mikhail Shchennikov, Russia (W)	2-14-95	Moscow
	19:18.40	Tim Lewis (A)	3-7-87	Indianapolis
4x200-meter relay	1:22.11	Great Britain (W) (Linford Christie, Darren Braithwaite, Ade Mafe, John Regis)	3-3-91	Glasgow
	1:22.71	National Team (A) (Thomas Jefferson, Raymond Pierre, Antonio McKay Kevin Little)	3-3-91	Glasgow
4x400-meter relay	3:02.83	National Team (W, A) (Andre Morris, Dameon Johnson, Deon Minor, Milt Campbell)	3-7-99	Maebashi, Japan
4x800-meter relay	7:13.94	Global Athletics & Marketing (W) (Rich Kenah, Joel Woody, Karl Paranya, David Krummenacker)	2-6-00	Boston
	7:14.78	Reebok Enclave (A) (Elliot Gaskins, Kevin Murphy, Mike Schroer, Bryan Woodward)	2-6-00	Boston
High jump	7 ft 11½ in	Javier Sotomayor, Cuba (W)	3-4-89	Budapest
	7 ft 10½ in	Hollis Conway (A)	3-10-91	Seville
Pole vault	20 ft 2 in	Sergei Bubka, Ukraine (W)	2-21-93	Donetsk, Ukraine
	19 ft 6¼ in	Jeff Hartwig (A)	3-6-99	Maebashi, Japan
Long jump	28 ft 10¼ in	Carl Lewis (W, A)	1-27-84	New York City
Triple jump	58 ft 6 in	Alicier Urrutia, Cuba (W)	3-1-97	Sindelfingen, Germany
	58 ft 3¼ in	Mike Conley (A)	2-27-87	New York City
Shot put	74 ft 4¼ in	Randy Barnes (W, A)	1-20-89	Los Angeles
Weight throw	84 ft 10¼ in	Lance Deal (W, A)	3-4-95	Atlanta
Pentathlon	4478 pts	Steve Fritz, (W, A)	1-14-95	Lawrence, KS
Heptathlon	6476 pts	Dan O'Brien (W, A)	3-13/14-93	Toronto

*No recognized world record.

Political Ironman

Quick, name a governor who's tougher than Jesse Ventura. Can't do it? Then you haven't seen New Mexico's Gary Johnson hauling his honorable butt through an Ironman triathlon, that test of sinew and sanity that goes like this: swim 2.4 miles, race a bike 112 miles, then run a marathon.

"Your results are measurable and your goal is clear-cut. That's what I like about Ironman," says Johnson, 46, a Republican who endured his first triathlon 19 years ago. Last Saturday he finished 582nd among 1,470 competitors in the Ironman Triathlon World Championship at Kailua-Kona, Hawaii. Luc Van Lierde of Belgium won in eight hours, 17 minutes and 17 seconds, about two hours ahead of Johnson, but at 10:39:16—a personal best—the gov was more than six hours faster than the stragglers in the event, for which more than 50,000 triathletes tried to qualify.

Johnson, who rises to train at 4:30 a.m. seven days a week, has cycled across his state, climbed Mount McKinley and run 25 miles in Army boots with a 35-pound pack on his back. "I tell people, Find out what makes your life work, whether it's knitting, music or art, and get as much of it as possible," he says. "In my case it's fitness."

Why try so hard? For one thing, it's less maddening than hammering out deals with the political crowd. "All you got out here is pain," Johnson says with a grimace that doubles as a grin.

Women

Event	Mark	Record Holder	Date	Site
50 meters	5.96	Irina Privolova, Russia (W)	2-9-95	Madrid
	6.02	Gail Devers (A)	2-21-99	Liévin, France
55 meters*	6.54	Evelyn Ashford (A)	2-26-82	New York
		Jeanette Bolden	2-21-86	Inglewood, CA
60 meters	6.92	Irina Privalova, Russia (W)	2-11-93	Madrid
	6.92	Irina Privalova, Russia (W)	2-9-95	Madrid
	6.95	Gail Devers (A)	3-12-93	Toronto
	6.95	Marion Jones (A)	3-7-98	Maebashi, Japan
200 meters	21.87	Merlene Ottey, Jamaica (W)	2-13-93	Liévin, France
	22.33	Gwen Torrence (A)	3-2-96	Atlanta
400 meters	49.59	Jarmila Kratochvilová, Czech (W)	3-7-82	Milan
	50.64	Diane Dixon (A)	3-10-91	Seville
800 meters	1:56.4	Christine Wachtel, E Germany (W)	2-13-88	Vienna
	1:58.9	Mary Slaney (A)	2-22-80	San Diego
	1:58.92	Suzy Hamilton (A)	3-7-99	Boston
1,000 meters	2:30.94	Maria Mutola, Mozambique (W)	2-25-99	Stockholm
	2:35.29	Regina Jacobs (A)	2-6-00	Boston
1,500 meters	4:00.27	Doina Melinte, Romania (W)	2-9-90	East Rutherford, NJ
	4:00.80	Mary Slaney (A)	2-8-80	New York City
Mile	4:17.14	Doina Melinte, Romania (W)	2-9-90	East Rutherford, NJ
	4:20.5	Mary Slaney (A)	2-19-82	San Diego
3,000 meters	8:33.82	Elly van Hulst, Netherlands (W)	3-4-89	Budapest
	8:39.14	Regina Jacobs (A)	3-7-99	Maebashi, Japan
5,000 meters	14:47.35	Gabriela Szabo, Romania (W)	2-13-99	Dortmund, Germany
	15:22.64	Lynn Jennings (A)	1-7-90	Hanover, NH
50-meter hurdles	6.58	Cornelia Oschkenat, E Germany (W)	2-20-88	Berlin
	6.67	Jackie Joyner-Kersee (A)	2-10-95	Reno
55-meter hurdles*	7.30	Tiffany Lott (A)	2-20-97	Air Force Academy, CO
60-meter hurdles	7.69	Lyudmila Narozhilenko, Russia (W)	2-4-90	Chelyabinsk, Russia
	7.81	Jackie Joyner-Kersee (A)	2-5-89	Fairfax, VA
3,000-meter walk	11:40.33	Claudia Iovan, Romania (W)	1-30-99	Bucharest
	12:20.79	Debbi Lawrence (A)	3-12-93	Toronto
4x200-meter relay	1:32.55	SC Eintracht Hamm, W Gemany (W) (Helga Arendt, Silke-Beate Knoll, Mechthild Kluth, Gisela Kinzel)	2-20-88	Dortmund, W Germany
	1:33.24	National Team (A) (Flirtisha Harris, Chryste Gaines, Terri Dendy, Michele Collins)	2-12-94	Glasgow
4x400-meter relay	3:24.25	Russia (W) (Tatyanna Chebykina, Svetlana Goncharenko, Olga Kotlyarova, Natalya Nazarova)	3-7-99	Maebashi, Japan
	3:27.59	National Team (A) (Michelle Collins, Monique Hennagan, Zundra Feagin-Alexander, Shanelle Porter)	3-7-99	Maebashi, Japan
4x800-meter relay	8:18.71	Russia (W) (Natalya Zaytseva, Olga Kuvnetsova, Yelena Afanasyeva, Yekaterina Podkopayeva)	2-4-94	Moscow
	8:25.50	Villanova (A) (Gina Procaccio, Debbie Grant, Michelle DiMuro, Celeste Halliday)	2-7-87	Gainesville, FL
High jump	6 ft 9½ in	Heike Henkel, Germany (W)	2-8-92	Karlsruhe, Germany
	6 ft 7 in	Tisha Walker (A)	2-28-98	Atlanta
Pole vault	15 ft 1¾ in	Stacy Dragila (W, A)	3-3-00	Atlanta
Long jump	24 ft 2¼ in	Heike Drechsler, E Germany (W)	2-13-88	Vienna
	23 ft 4¾ in	Jackie Joyner-Kersee (A)	3-5-94	Atlanta
Triple jump	49 ft 9 in	Ashia Hansen, Great Britain (W)	2-28-95	Valencia, Spain
	46 ft 8¼ in	Sheila Hudson-Strudwick (A)	3-4-95	Atlanta
Shot put	73 ft 10 in	Helena Fibingerová, Czech. (W)	2-19-77	Jablonec, Czech.
	65 ft ¾ in	Ramona Pagel (A)	2-20-87	Inglewood, CA
Weight throw*	77 ft 5 in	Dawn Ellerbe (W, A)	3-4-00	Atlanta
Pentathlon	4991 pts	Irina Byelova, CIS (W)	2-14/15-92	Berlin
	4753	DeDee Nathan (A)	3-4/5-99	Maebashi, Japan

*No recognized world record.

World Track and Field Championships

Historically, the Olympics have served as the outdoor world championships for track and field. In 1983 the International Amateur Athletic Federation (IAAF) instituted a separate world championship meet, to be held every 4 years between the Olympics. The first was held in Helsinki in 1983, the second in Rome in 1987, the third in Tokyo in 1991, the fourth in Stuttgart, Germany, in 1993, the fifth in Göteborg, Sweden, in 1995, the sixth in Athens in 1997, and the seventh in Seville in 1999. In 1993 the IAAF began to hold the meet on a biennial basis.

Men

100 METERS

1983	Carl Lewis, United States	10.07
1987*	Carl Lewis, United States	9.93 WR
1991	Carl Lewis, United States	9.86 WR
1993	Linford Christie, Great Britain	9.87
1995	Donovan Bailey, Canada	9.97
1997	Maurice Greene, United States	9.86
1999	Maurice Greene, United States	9.80

200 METERS

1983	Calvin Smith, United States	20.14
1987	Calvin Smith, United States	20.16
1991	Michael Johnson, United States	20.01
1993	Frank Fredericks, Namibia	19.85
1995	Michael Johnson, United States	19.79
1997	Ato Boldon, Trinidad and Tobago	20.04
1999	Maurice Greene, United States	19.90

400 METERS

1983	Bert Cameron, Jamaica	45.05
1987	Thomas Schoenlebe, E Germany	44.33
1991	Antonio Pettigrew, United States	44.57
1993	Michael Johnson, United States	43.65
1995	Michael Johnson, United States	43.39
1997	Michael Johnson, United States	44.12
1999	Michael Johnson, United States	43.18WR

800 METERS

1983	Willi Wulbeck, W Germany	1:43.65
1987	Billy Konchellah, Kenya	1:43.06
1991	Billy Konchellah, Kenya	1:43.99
1993	Paul Ruto, Kenya	1:44.71
1995	Wilson Kipketer, Denmark	1:45.08
1997	Wilson Kipketer, Denmark	1:43.38
1999	Wilson Kipketer, Denmark	1:43.30

1,500 METERS

1983	Steve Cram, Great Britain	3:41.59
1987	Abdi Bile, Somalia	3:36.80
1991	Noureddine Morceli, Algeria	3:32.84
1993	Noureddine Morceli, Algeria	3:34.24
1995	Noureddine Morceli, Algeria	3:33.73
1997	Hicham El Guerrouj, Morocco	3:35.83
1999	Hicham El Guerrouj, Morocco	3:27.65

STEEPLECHASE

1983	Patriz Ilg, W Germany	8:15.06
1987	Francesco Panetta, Italy	8:08.57
1991	Moses Kiptanui, Kenya	8:12.59
1993	Moses Kiptanui, Kenya	8:06.36
1995	Moses Kiptanui, Kenya	8:04.16
1997	Wilson Boit Kipketer, Kenya	8:05.84
1999	Christopher Koskei, Kenya	8:11.76

5,000 METERS

1983	Eamonn Coghlan, Ireland	13:28.53
1987	Said Aouita, Morocco	13:26.44
1991	Yobes Ondieki, Kenya	13:14.45
1993	Ismael Kirui, Kenya	13:02.75
1995	Ismael Kirui, Kenya	13:16.77
1997	Daniel Komen, Kenya	13:07.38
1999	Salah Hissou, Morocco	12:58.13

10,000 METERS

1983	Alberto Cova, Italy	28:01.04
1987	Paul Kipkoech, Kenya	27:38.63
1991	Moses Tanui, Kenya	27:38.74
1993	Haile Gebrselassie, Ethiopia	27:46.02
1995	Haile Gebrselassie, Ethiopia	27:12.95
1997	Haile Gebrselassie, Ethiopia	27:24.58
1999	Haile Gebrselassie, Ethiopia	27:57.27

MARATHON

1983	Rob de Castella, Australia	2:10:03
1987	Douglas Wakiihuri, Kenya	2:11:48
1991	Hiromi Taniguchi, Japan	2:14:57
1993	Mark Plaatjes, United States	2:13:57
1995	Martín Fiz, Spain	2:11:41
1997	Abel Anton, Spain	2:13:16
1999	Abel Anton, Spain	2:13:36

110-METER HURDLES

1983	Greg Foster, United States	13.42
1987	Greg Foster, United States	13.21
1991	Greg Foster, United States	13.06
1993	Colin Jackson, Great Britain	12.91 WR
1995	Allen Johnson, United States	13.00
1997	Allen Johnson, United States	12.93
1999	Colin Jackson, Great Britain	13.04

400-METER HURDLES

1983	Edwin Moses, United States	47.50
1987	Edwin Moses, United States	47.46
1991	Samuel Matete, Zambia	47.64
1993	Kevin Young, United States	47.18
1995	Derrick Adkins, United States	47.98
1997	Stéphane Diagana, France	47.70
1999	Fabrizio Mori, Italy	47.72

20-KILOMETER WALK

1983	Ernesto Canto, Mexico	1:20:49
1987	Maurizio Damilano, Italy	1:20:45
1991	Maurizio Damilano, Italy	1:19:37
1993	Valentin Massana, Spain	1:22:31
1995	Michele Didoni, Italy	1:19:59
1997	Daniel Garcia, Mexico	1:21:43
1999	Ilya Markov, Russia	1:23:34

50-KILOMETER WALK

1983	Ronald Weigel, E Germany	3:43:08
1987	Hartwig Gauder, E Germany	3:40:53
1991	Aleksandr Potashov, USSR	3:53:09
1993	Jesus Angel Garcia, Spain	3:41:41
1995	Valentin Kononen, Finland	3:43:42
1997	Robert Korzeniowski, Poland	3:44:46
1999	German Skurygin, Russia	3:44:23

4 X 100 METER RELAY

1983	United States (Emmit King, Willie Gault, Calvin Smith, Carl Lewis)	37.86
1987	United States (Lee McRae, Lee McNeil, Harvey Glance, Carl Lewis)	37.90

WR=World record.   *Ben Johnson, Canada, disqualified.

Men *(Cont.)*

4 X 100 METER RELAY *(CONT.)*

1991..............United States (Andre Cason 37.50 WR
Leroy Burrell, Dennis Mitchell
Carl Lewis)
1993..............United States (Jon Drummond, 37.48
Andre Cason, Dennis Mitchell,
Leroy Burrell)
1995..............Canada (Robert Esmie, 38.31
Glenroy Gilbert, Bruny Surin,
Donovan Bailey)
1997..............Canada (Robert Esmie, 37.86
Glenroy Gilbert, Bruny Surin,
Donovan Bailey)
1999..............United States (Jon Drummond, 37.59
Tim Montgomery, Brian Lewis,
Maurice Greene)

4 X 400 METER RELAY

1983..............USSR (Sergei Lovachev, 3:00.79
Alecksandr Troschilo,
Nikolay Chernyetski, Viktor Markin)
1987..............United States (Danny Everett 2:57.29
Rod Haley, Antonio McKay,
Butch Reynolds)
1991..............Great Britain (Roger Black 2:57.53
Derek Redmond, John Regis,
Kriss Akabusi)
1993..............United States (Andrew 2:54.29 WR
Valmon, Quincy Watts, Butch
Reynolds, Michael Johnson)
1995..............United States (Marlon Ramsey, 2:57.32
Derek Mills, Butch Reynolds,
Michael Johnson)
1997..............United States (Jerome Young, 2:56.47
Antonio Pettigrew, Chris Jones,
Tyree Washington)
1999..............United States (Jerome Davis, 2:56.45
Antonio Pettigrew, Angelo
Taylor, Michael Johnson)

HIGH JUMP

1983..............Gennadi Avdeyenko, USSR 7 ft 7¼ in
1987..............Patrik Sjoberg, Sweden 7 ft 9¾ in
1991..............Charles Austin, United States 7 ft 9¾ in
1993..............Javier Sotomayor, Cuba 7 ft 10½ in
1995..............Troy Kemp, Bahamas 7 ft 9¼ in
1997..............Javier Sotomayor, Cuba 7 ft 9¼ in
1999..............Vyacheslav Voronin, Russia 7 ft 9¼ in

POLE VAULT

1983..............Sergei Bubka, USSR 18 ft 8¼ in
1987..............Sergei Bubka, USSR 19 ft 2¼ in
1991..............Sergei Bubka, USSR 19 ft 6¼ in
1993..............Sergei Bubka, Ukraine 19 ft 8¼ in
1995..............Sergei Bubka, Ukraine 19 ft 5 in
1997..............Sergei Bubka, Ukraine 19 ft 8½ in
1999..............Maksim Tarasov, Russia 19 ft 9 in

LONG JUMP

1983..............Carl Lewis, United States 28 ft ¾ in
1987..............Carl Lewis, United States 28 ft 5¼ in
1991..............Mike Powell, U.S. 29 ft 4½ in WR
1993..............Mike Powell, United States 28 ft 2¼ in
1995..............Ivan Pedroso, Cuba 28 ft 6½ in
1997..............Ivan Pedroso, Cuba 27 ft 7½ in
1999..............Ivan Pedroso, Cuba 28 ft 1 in

TRIPLE JUMP

1983..............Zdzislaw Hoffmann, Poland 57 ft 2 in
1987..............Khristo Markov, Bulgaria 58 ft 9 ½ in
1991..............Kenny Harrison, United States 58 ft 4 in
1993..............Mike Conley, United States 58 ft 7¼ in
1995..............Jonathan Edwards, G.B. 60 ft ¼ in WR
1997..............Yoelvis Quesada, Cuba 58 ft 6¾ in
1999..............Charle Michael Friedek, Ger 57 ft 8½ in

SHOT PUT

1983..............Edward Sarul, Poland 70 ft 2¼ in
1987..............Werner Günthör, Switz 72 ft 11¼ in
1991..............Werner Günthör, Switz 71 ft 1¼ in
1993..............Werner Günthör, Switz 72 ft 1 in
1995 ....John Godina, United States 70 ft 5¼ in
1997..............John Godina, United States 70 ft 4¼ in
1999..............C.J. Hunter, United States 71 ft 6 in

DISCUS THROW

1983 ....Imrich Bugar, Czechoslovakia 222 ft 2 in
1987 ....Juergen Schult, E Germany 225 ft 6 in
1991 ....Lars Riedel, Germany 217 ft 2 in
1993 ....Lars Riedel, Germany 222 ft 2 in
1995 ....Lars Riedel, Germany 225 ft 7 in
1997 ....Lars Riedel, Germany 224 ft 10 in
1999 ....Anthony Washington, U.S. 226 ft 8 in

HAMMER THROW

1983 ....Sergei Litvinov, USSR 271 ft 3 in
1987..............Sergei Litvinov, USSR 272 ft 6 in
1991..............Yuriy Sedykh, USSR 268 ft
1993..............Andrey Abduvaliyev, Tajikistan 267 ft 10 in
1995..............Andrey Abduvaliyev, Tajikistan 267 ft 7 in
1997..............Heinz Weis, Germany 268 ft 4 in
1999..............Karsten Kobs, Germany 263 ft 3 in

JAVELIN

1983 ....Detlef Michel, E Germany 293 ft 7 in
1987 ....Seppo Räty, Finland 274 ft 1 in
1991..............Kimmo Kinnunen, Finland 297 ft 11 in
1993 ....Jan Zelezny, Czech Republic 282 ft 1 in
1995..............Jan Zelezny, Czech Republic 293 ft 11 in
1997..............Marius Corbett, South Africa 290 ft 0 in
1999..............Aki Parviainen, Finland 293 ft 8 in

DECATHLON

1983 ....Daley Thompson, G Britain 8666 pts
1987..............Torsten Voss, E Germany 8680 pts
1991..............Dan O'Brien, United States 8812 pts
1993..............Dan O'Brien, United States 8817 pts
1995..............Dan O'Brien, United States 8695 pts
1997..............Tomás Dvorák, Czech Rep. 8837 pts
1999..............Tomás Dvorák, Czech Rep. 8744 pts

WR=World record.

Women

100 METERS

1983	Marlies Gohr, E Germany	10.97
1987	Silke Gladisch, E Germany	10.90
1991	Katrin Krabbe, Germany	10.99
1993	Gail Devers, United States	10.82
1995	Gwen Torrence, United States	10.85
1997	Marion Jones, United States	10.83
1999	Marion Jones, United States	10.70

200 METERS

1983	Marita Koch, E Germany	22.13
1987	Silke Gladisch, E Germany	21.74
1991	Katrin Krabbe, Germany	22.09
1993	Merlene Ottey, Jamaica	21.98
1995	Merlene Ottey, Jamaica	22.12
1997	Zhanna Pintusevich, Ukraine	22.32
1999	Inger Miller, United States	21.77

400 METERS

1983	Jarmila Kratochvilova, Czech.	47.99
1987	Olga Bryzgina, USSR	49.38
1991	Marie-José Pérec, France	49.13
1993	Jearl Miles, United States	49.82
1995	Marie-José Pérec, France	49.28
1997	Cathy Freeman, Australia	49.77
1999	Cathy Freeman, Australia	49.67

800 METERS

1983	Jarmila Kratochvilova, Czech.	1:54.68
1987	Sigrun Wodars, E Germany	1:55.26
1991	Lilia Nurutdinova, USSR	1:57.50
1993	Maria Mutola, Mozambique	1:55.43
1995	Ana Quirot, Cuba	1:56.11
1997	Ana Quirot, Cuba	1:57.14
1999	Ludmila Formanová, Czech Rep.	1:56.68

1,500 METERS

1983	Mary Slaney, United States	4:00.90
1987	Tatyana Samolenko, USSR	3:58.56
1991	Hassiba Boulmerka, Algeria	4:02.21
1993	Dong Liu, China	4:00.50
1995	Hassiba Boulmerka, Algeria	4:02.42
1997	Carla Sacramento, Portugal	4:04.24
1999	Svetlana Masterkova, Russia	3:59.53

3,000 METERS

1983	Mary Slaney, United States	8:34.62
1987	Tatyana Samolenko, USSR	8:38.73
1991	Tatyana Dorovskikh, USSR	8:35.82
1993	Qu Yunxia, China	8:28.71

5,000 METERS

1995	Sonia O'Sullivan, Ireland	14:46.47
1997	Gabriela Szabo, Romania	14:57.68
1999	Gabriela Szabo, Romania	14:41.82

10,000 METERS

1987	Ingrid Kristiansen, Norway	31:05.85
1991	Liz McColgan, Great Britain	31:14.31
1993	Wang Junxia, China	30:49:30
1995	Fernanda Ribeiro, Portugal	31:04.99
1997	Sally Barsosio, Kenya	31:32.92
1999	Gete Wami, Ethiopia	30:24.56

MARATHON

1983	Grete Waitz, Norway	2:28:09
1987	Rosa Mota, Portugal	2:25:17
1991	Wanda Panfil, Poland	2:29:53
1993	Junko Asari, Japan	2:30:03

*400 meters short.

MARATHON (CONT.)

1995	Manuela Machado, Portugal	2:25:39*
1997	Hiromi Suzuki, Japan	2:29.48
1999	Jong Song-Ok, N Korea	2:26:59

100-METER HURDLES

1983	Bettine Jahn, E Germany	12.35
1987	Ginka Zagorcheva, Bulgaria	12.34
1991	Lyudmila Narozhilenko, USSR	12.59
1993	Gail Devers, United States	12.46
1995	Gail Devers, United States	12.68
1997	Ludmila Engquist, Sweden	12.50
1999	Gail Devers, United States	12.37

400-METER HURDLES

1983	Yekaterina Fesenko, USSR	54.14
1987	Sabine Busch, E Germany	53.62
1991	Tatyana Ledovskaya, USSR	53.11
1993	Sally Gunnell, Great Britain	52.74 WR
1995	Kim Batten, United States	52.61
1997	Nezha Bidouane, Morocco	52.97
1999	Daimi Pernia, Cuba	52.89

10-KILOMETER WALK

1987	Irina Strakhova, USSR	44:12
1991	Alina Ivanova, USSR	42:57
1993	Sari Essayah, Finland	42:59
1995	Irina Stankina, Russia	42:13
1997	Annarita Sidoti, Italy	42:56

20-KILOMETER WALK

1999	Hongyu Liu, China	1:30:50

4 X 100 METER RELAY

1983	E Germany (Silke Gladisch, Marita Koch, Ingrid Auerswald, Marlies Gohr)	41.76
1987	United States (Alice Brown, Diane Williams, Florence Griffith, Pam Marshall)	41.58
1991	Jamaica (Dalia Duhaney, Juliet Cuthbert, Beverley McDonald, Merlene Ottey)	41.94
1993	Russia (Olga Bogoslovskaya, Galina Malchugina, Natalya Voronova, Irina Privalova)	41.49
1995	United States (Celena Mondie-Milner, Carlette Guidry, Chryste Gaines, Gwen Torrence)	42.12
1997	United States (Chryste Gaines, Marion Jones, Inger Miller, Gail Devers)	41.47
1999	Bahamas (Sevatheda Fynes, Chandra Sturrup, Pauline Davis-Thompson, Debbie Ferguson)	41.92

4 X 400 METER RELAY

1983	E Germany (Kerstin Walther, Sabine Busch, Marita Koch, Dagmar Rubsam)	3:19.73
1987	E Germany (Dagmar Neubauer, Kirsten Emmelmann, Petra Müller, Sabine Busch)	3:18.63
1991	USSR (Tatyana Ledovskaya, Lyudmila Dzhigalova, Olga Nazarova, Olga Bryzgina)	3:18.43
1993	United States (Gwen Torrence, Maicel Malone, Natasha Kaiser-Brown, Jearl Miles)	3:16.71

Women *(Cont.)*

4 X 400 METER RELAY *(CONT.)*

1995	United States (Kim Graham, Rochelle Stevens, Camara Jones, Jearl Miles)	3:22.39
1997	Germany (Anke Feller, Uta Rohlander, Anja Rucker, Grit Breuer)	3:20.92
1999	Russia (Tatyana Chebykina, Svetlana Goncharenko, Olga Kotylarova, Natalya Nazarova)	3:21.98

HIGH JUMP

1983	Tamara Bykova, USSR	6 ft 7 in
1987	Stefka Kostadinova, Bulgaria	6 ft 10¼ in
1991	Heike Henkel, Germany	6 ft 8¾ in
1993	Ioamnet Quintero, Cuba	6 ft 6¼ in
1995	Stefka Kostadinova, Bulgaria	6 ft 7 in
1997	Hanne Haugland, Norway	6 ft 6¼ in
1999	Inga Babakova, Ukraine	6 ft 6¼ in

POLE VAULT

1999	Stacy Dragila, U.S.	15 ft 1 in EWR

LONG JUMP

1983	Heike Daute, E Germany	23 ft 10¼ in
1987	Jackie Joyner-Kersee, U.S.	24 ft 1¾ in
1991	Jackie Joyner-Kersee, U.S.	24 ft ¼ in
1993	Heike Drechsler, Germany	23 ft 4 in
1995	Fiona May, Italy	22 ft 10¾ in w
1997	Lyudmila Galkina, Russia	23 ft 1¾ in
1999	Niurka Montalvo, Spain	23 ft 2 in

TRIPLE JUMP

1993	Ana Biryukova, Russia	49 ft 6 ¼ in WR
1995	Inessa Kravets, Ukraine	50 ft 10¼ in WR
1997	S. Kasparkova, Czech Rep.	49 ft 10½ in
1999	Paraskevi Tsiamita, Greece	48 ft 10 in

WR=World record. EWR=equals world record.

SHOT PUT

1983	Helena Fibingerova, Czech.	69 ft ¾ in
1987	Natalya Lisovskaya, USSR	69 ft 8¼ in
1991	Zhihong Huang, China	68 ft 4¼ in
1993	Zhihong Huang, China	67 ft 6 in
1995	Astrid Kumbernuss, Germany	69 ft 7½ in
1997	Astrid Kumbernuss, Germany	67 ft 11½ in
1999	Astrid Kumbernuss, Germany	65 ft 1½ in

HAMMER THROW

1999	Mihaela Melinte, Romania	246 ft 9 in

DISCUS THROW

1983	Martina Opitz, E Germany	226 ft 2 in
1987	Martina Hellmann, E Germany	235 ft
1991	Tsvetanka Khristova, Bulgaria	233 ft
1993	Olga Burova, Russia	221 ft 1 in
1995	Ellina Zvereva, Belarus	225 ft 2 in
1997	Beatrice Faumuina, New Zeal.	219 ft 3 in
1999	Franka Dietzsch, Germany	223 ft 7 in

JAVELIN

1983	Tiina Lillak, Finland	232 ft 4 in
1987	Fatima Whitbread, G.B.	251 ft 5 in
1991	Demei Xu, China	225 ft 8 in
1993	Trine Hattestad, Finland	227 ft
1995	Natalya Shikolenko, Belarus	221 ft 8 in
1997	Trine Hattestad, Norway	225 ft 8 in
1999	Mirela Manjani-Tzelili, Greece	220 ft 1 in

HEPTATHLON

1983	Ramona Neubert, E Germany	6714 pts
1987	Jackie Joyner-Kersee, U.S.	7128 pts
1991	Sabine Braun, Germany	6672 pts
1993	Jackie Joyner-Kersee, U.S.	6837 pts
1995	Ghada Shouaa, Syria	6651 pts
1997	Sabine Braun, Germany	6739 pts
1999	Eunice Barber, France	6861 pts

Track and Field News Athlete of the Year

Each year (since 1959 for men and since 1974 for women) Track & Field News has chosen the outstanding athlete in the sport.

Men

Year	Athlete	Event	Year	Athlete	Event
1959	Martin Lauer, W Germany	110H/Decath	1980	Edwin Moses, United States	400H
1960	Rafer Johnson, United States	Decathlon	1981	Sebastian Coe, Great Britain	800/1,500
1961	Ralph Boston, United States	Long jump	1982	Carl Lewis, United States	100/200/LJ
1962	Peter Snell, New Zealand	800/1,500	1983	Carl Lewis, United States	100/200/LJ
1963	C. K. Yang, Taiwan	Decath/PV	1984	Carl Lewis, United States	100/200/LJ
1964	Peter Snell, New Zealand	800/1,500	1985	Said Aouita, Morocco	1,500/5000
1965	Ron Clarke, Australia	5K/10K	1986	Yuri Syedikh, USSR	Hammer
1966	Jim Ryun, United States	800/1,500	1987	Ben Johnson, Canada	100
1967	Jim Ryun, United States	1,500	1988	Sergei Bubka, USSR	Pole vault
1968	Bob Beamon, United States	Long jump	1989	Roger Kingdom, United States	110H
1969	Bill Toomey, United States	Decathlon	1990	Michael Johnson, United States	200/400
1970	Randy Matson, United States	Shot put	1991	Sergei Bubka, CIS	Pole vault
1971	Rod Milburn, United States	110H	1992	Kevin Young, United States	400H
1972	Lasse Viren, Finland	5K/10K	1993	Noureddine Morceli, Algeria	1,500/mile/3K
1973	Ben Jipcho, Kenya	1,500/5K/ST	1994	Noureddine Morceli, Algeria	1,500/mile/3K
1974	Rick Wohlhuter, United States	800/1,500	1995	Haile Gebrselassie, Ethiopia	5K/10K
1975	John Walker, New Zealand	800/1,500	1996	Michael Johnson, United States	200/400
1976	Alberto Juantorena, Cuba	400/800	1997	Wilson Kipketer, Denmark	800
1977	Alberto Juantorena, Cuba	400/800	1998	Haile Gebrselassie, Ethiopia	5K/10K
1978	Henry Rono, Kenya	5K/10K/ST	1999	Hicham El Guerrouj, Morocco	1,500/Mile
1979	Sebastian Coe, Great Britain	800/1,500			

Women

Year	Athlete	Event	Year	Athlete	Event
1974	Irena Szewinska, Poland	100/200/400	1987	Jackie Joyner-Kersee, U.S	100H/LJ/Hept
1975	Faina Melnik, USSR	Shot/Discus	1988	Florence Griffith Joyner, U.S.	100/200
1976	Tatyana Kazankina, USSR	800/1,500	1989	Ana Quirot, Cuba	400/800
1977	R. Ackermann, E Germany	High jump	1990	Merlene Ottey, Jamaica	100/200
1978	Marita Koch, E Germany	100/200/400	1991	Heike Henkel, Germany	High jump
1979	Marita Koch, E Germany	100/200/400	1992	Heike Drechsler, Germany	Long Jump
1980	Ilona Briesenick, E Germany	Shot put	1993	Wang Junxia, China	1.5K/3K/10K
1981	Evelyn Ashford, United States	100/200	1994	Jackie Joyner-Kersee, U.S.	100H/LJ/Hept
1982	Marita Koch, E Germany	100/200/400	1995	Sonia O'Sullivan, Ireland	1,500/3K/5K
1983	J. Kratochvilova, Czechoslovakia	200/400/800	1996	Svetlana Masterkova, Russia	800/1,500
1984	Evelyn Ashford, United States	100	1997	Marion Jones, United States	100/200/LJ
1985	Marita Koch, E Germany	100/200/400	1998	Marion Jones, United States	100/200/LJ
1986	Jackie Joyner-Kersee, U.S.	LJ/Hept	1999	Gabriela Szabo, Romania	1,500/5,000

Marathon World Record Progression

Men

Record Holder	Time	Date	Site
John Hayes, United States	2:55:18.4	7-24-08	Shepherd's Bush, London
Robert Fowler, United States	2:52:45.4	1-1-09	Yonkers, NY
James Clark, United States	2:46:52.6	2-12-09	New York City
Albert Raines, United States	2:46:04.6	5-8-09	New York City
Frederick Barrett, Great Britain	2:42:31	5-26-09	Shepherd's Bush, London
Harry Green, Great Britain	2:38:16.2	5-12-13	Shepherd's Bush, London
Alexis Ahlgren, Sweden	2:36:06.6	5-31-13	Shepherd's Bush, London
Johannes Kolehmainen, Finland	2:32:35.8	8-22-20	Antwerp, Belgium
Albert Michelsen, United States	2:29:01.8	10-12-25	Port Chester, NY
Fusashige Suzuki, Japan	2:27:49	3-31-35	Tokyo
Yasuo Ikenaka, Japan	2:26:44	4-3-35	Tokyo
Kitei Son, Japan	2:26:42	11-3-35	Tokyo
Yun Bok Suh, Korea	2:25:39	4-19-47	Boston
James Peters, Great Britain	2:20:42.2	6-14-52	Chiswick, England
James Peters, Great Britain	2:18:40.2	6-13-53	Chiswick, England
James Peters, Great Britain	2:18:34.8	10-4-53	Turku, Finland
James Peters, Great Britain	2:17:39.4	6-26-54	Chiswick, England
Sergei Popov, USSR	2:15:17	8-24-58	Stockholm
Abebe Bikila, Ethiopia	2:15:16.2	9-10-60	Rome
Toru Terasawa, Japan	2:15:15.8	2-17-63	Beppu, Japan
Leonard Edelen, United States	2:14:28	6-15-63	Chiswick, England
Basil Heatley, Great Britain	2:13:55	6-13-64	Chiswick, England
Abebe Bikila, Ethiopia	2:12:11.2	6-21-64	Tokyo
Morio Shigematsu, Japan	2:12:00	6-12-65	Chiswick, England
Derek Clayton, Australia	2:09:36.4	12-3-67	Fukuoka, Japan
Derek Clayton, Australia	2:08:33.6	5-30-69	Antwerp, Belgium
Rob de Castella, Australia	2:08:18	12-6-81	Fukuoka, Japan
Steve Jones, Great Britain	2:08:05	10-21-84	Chicago
Carlos Lopes, Portugal	2:07:12	4-20-85	Rotterdam, Netherlands
Belayneh Dinsamo, Ethiopia	2:06:50	4-17-88	Rotterdam, Netherlands
Ronaldo Da Costa, Brazil	2:06:05	9-20-98	Berlin, Germany
Khalid Khannouchi, Morocco	2:05:42	10-24-99	Chicago

Women

Record Holder	Time	Date	Site
Dale Greig, Great Britain	3:27:45	5-23-64	Ryde, England
Mildred Simpson, New Zealand	3:19:33	7-21-64	Auckland, New Zealand
Maureen Wilton, Canada	3:15:22	5-6-67	Toronto
Anni Pede-Erdkamp, W Germany	3:07:26	9-16-67	Waldniel, W Germany
Caroline Walker, United States	3:02:53	2-28-70	Seaside, OR
Elizabeth Bonner, United States	3:01:42	5-9-71	Philadelphia
Adrienne Beames, Australia	2:46:30	8-31-71	Werribee, Australia
Chantal Langlace, France	2:46:24	10-27-74	Neuf Brisach, France
Jacqueline Hansen, United States	2:43:54.5	12-1-74	Culver City, CA
Liane Winter, W Germany	2:42:24	4-21-75	Boston

Women (Cont.)

Record Holder	Time	Date	Site
Christa Vahlensieck, W Germany	2:40:15.8	5-3-75	Dülmen, W Germany
Jacqueline Hansen, United States	2:38:19	10-12-75	Eugene, OR
Chantal Langlace, France	2:35:15.4	5-1-77	Oyarzun, France
Christa Vahlensieck, W Germany	2:34:47.5	9-10-77	Berlin, W Germany
Grete Waitz, Norway	2:32:29.9	10-22-78	New York City
Grete Waitz, Norway	2:27:32.6	10-21-79	New York City
Grete Waitz, Norway	2:25:41.3	10-26-80	New York City
Grete Waitz, Norway	2:25:29	4-17-83	London
Joan Benoit Samuelson, United States	2:22:43	4-18-83	Boston
Ingrid Kristiansen, Norway	2:21:06	4-21-85	London
Tegla Loroupe, Kenya	2:20:47	4-19-98	Rotterdam, Netherlands
Tegla Loroupe, Kenya	2:20:43	9-26-99	Berlin

Boston Marathon

The Boston Marathon began in 1897 as a local Patriot's Day event. Run every year but 1918 since then, it has grown into one of the world's premier marathons.

Men

Year	Winner	Time	Year	Winner	Time
1897	John J. McDermott, United States	2:55:10	1945	John A. Kelley, United States	2:30:40
1898	Ronald J. McDonald, United States	2:42:00	1946	Stylianos Kyriakides, Greece	2:29:27
1899	Lawrence J. Brignolia, United States	2:54:38	1947	Yun Bok Suh, Korea	2:25:39
1900	James J. Caffrey, Canada	2:39:44	1948	Gerard Cote, Canada	2:31:02
1901	James J. Caffrey, Canada	2:29:23	1949	Karl Gosta Leandersson, Sweden	2:31:50
1902	Sammy Mellor, United States	2:43:12	1950	Kee Yong Ham, Korea	2:32:39
1903	John C. Lorden, United States	2:41:29	1951	Shigeki Tanaka, Japan	2:27:45
1904	Michael Spring, United States	2:38:04	1952	Doroteo Flores, Guatemala	2:31:53
1905	Fred Lorz, United States	2:38:25	1953	Keizo Yamada, Japan	2:18:51
1906	Timothy Ford, United States	2:45:45	1954	Veikko Karvonen, Finland	2:20:39
1907	Tom Longboat, Canada	2:24:24	1955	Hideo Hamamura, Japan	2:18:22
1908	Thomas Morrissey, United States	2:25:43	1956	Antti Viskari, Finland	2:14:14
1909	Henri Renaud, United States	2:53:36	1957	John J. Kelley, United States	2:20:05
1910	Fred Cameron, Canada	2:28:52	1958	Franjo Mihalic, Yugoslavia	2:25:54
1911	Clarence H. DeMar, United States	2:21:39	1959	Eino Oksanen, Finland	2:22:42
1912	Mike Ryan, United States	2:21:18	1960	Paavo Kotila, Finland	2:20:54
1913	Fritz Carlson, United States	2:25:14	1961	Eino Oksanen, Finland	2:23:39
1914	James Duffy, Canada	2:25:01	1962	Eino Oksanen, Finland	2:23:48
1915	Edouard Fabre, Canada	2:31:41	1963	Aurele Vandendriessche, Belgium	2:18:58
1916	Arthur Roth, United States	2:27:16	1964	Aurele Vandendriessche, Belgium	2:19:59
1917	Bill Kennedy, United States	2:28:37	1965	Morio Shigematsu, Japan	2:16:33
1918	No race		1966	Kenji Kimihara, Japan	2:17:11
1919	Carl Linder, United States	2:29:13	1967	David McKenzie, New Zealand	2:15:45
1920	Peter Trivoulidas, Greece	2:29:31	1968	Amby Burfoot, United States	2:22:17
1921	Frank Zuna, United States	2:18:57	1969	Yoshiaki Unetani, Japan	2:13:49
1922	Clarence H. DeMar, United States	2:18:10	1970	Ron Hill, England	2:10:30
1923	Clarence H. DeMar, United States	2:23:37	1971	Alvaro Mejia, Colombia	2:18:45
1924	Clarence H. DeMar, United States	2:29:40	1972	Olavi Suomalainen, Finland	2:15:39
1925	Chuck Mellor, United States	2:33:00	1973	Jon Anderson, United States	2:16:03
1926	John C. Miles, Canada	2:25:40	1974	Neil Cusack, Ireland	2:13:39
1927	Clarence H. DeMar, United States	2:40:22	1975	Bill Rodgers, United States	2:09:55
1928	Clarence H. DeMar, United States	2:37:07	1976	Jack Fultz, United States	2:20:19
1929	John C. Miles, Canada	2:33:08	1977	Jerome Drayton, Canada	2:14:46
1930	Clarence H. DeMar, United States	2:34:48	1978	Bill Rodgers, United States	2:10:13
1931	James (Hinky) Henigan, United States	2:46:45	1979	Bill Rodgers, United States	2:09:27
1932	Paul de Bruyn, Germany	2:33:36	1980	Bill Rodgers, United States	2:12:11
1933	Leslie Pawson, United States	2:31:01	1981	Toshihiko Seko, Japan	2:09:26
1934	Dave Komonen, Canada	2:32:53	1982	Alberto Salazar, United States	2:08:52
1935	John A. Kelley, United States	2:32:07	1983	Gregory A. Meyer, United States	2:09:00
1936	Ellison M. (Tarzan) Brown, United States	2:33:40	1984	Geoff Smith, England	2:10:34
1937	Walter Young, Canada	2:33:20	1985	Geoff Smith, England	2:14:05
1938	Leslie Pawson, United States	2:35:34	1986	Rob de Castella, Australia	2:07:51
1939	Ellison M. (Tarzan) Brown, United States	2:28:51	1987	Toshihiko Seko, Japan	2:11:50
1940	Gerard Cote, Canada	2:28:28	1988	Ibrahim Hussein, Kenya	2:08:43
1941	Leslie Pawson, United States	2:30:38	1989	Abebe Mekonnen, Ethiopia	2:09:06
1942	Bernard Joseph Smith, United States	2:26:51	1990	Gelindo Bordin, Italy	2:08:19
1943	Gerard Cote, Canada	2:28:25	1991	Ibrahim Hussein, Kenya	2:11:06
1944	Gerard Cote, Canada	2:31:50	1992	Ibrahim Hussein, Kenya	2:08:14

Year	Winner	Time	Year	Winner	Time
1993...Cosmas N'Deti, Kenya		2:09:33	1979...Joan Benoit, United States		2:35:15
1994...Cosmas N'Deti, Kenya		2:07:15	1980...Jacqueline Gareau, Canada		2:34:28
1995...Cosmas N'Deti, Kenya		2:09:22	1981...Allison Roe, New Zealand		2:26:46
1996...Moses Tanui, Kenya		2:09:16	1982...Charlotte Teske, W Germany		2:29:33
1997...Lameck Aguta, Kenya		2:10:34	1983...Joan Benoit, United States		2:22:43
1998...Moses Tanui, Kenya		2:07:34	1984...Lorraine Moller, New Zealand		2:29:28
1999...Joseph Chebet, Kenya		2:09:52	1985....Lisa Larsen Weidenbach, United States		2:34:06
2000...Elijah Lagat, Kenya		2:09:47	1986...Ingrid Kristiansen, Norway		2:24:55
			1987...Rosa Mota, Portugal		2:25:21

Women

Year	Winner	Time	Year	Winner	Time
			1988...Rosa Mota, Portugal		2:24:30
1966...Roberta Gibb, United States		3:21:40*	1989...Ingrid Kristiansen, Norway		2:24:33
1967...Roberta Gibb, United States		3:27:17*	1990...Rosa Mota, Portugal		2:25:24
1968...Roberta Gibb, United States		3:30:00*	1991...Wanda Panfil, Poland		2:24:18
1969...Sara Mae Berman, United States		3:22:46*	1992...Olga Markova, Russia		2:23:43
1970...Sara Mae Berman, United States		3:05:07*	1993...Olga Markova, Russia		2:25:27
1971...Sara Mae Berman, United States		3:08:30*	1994...Uta Pippig, Germany		2:21:45
1972...Nina Kuscsik, United States		3:10:36	1995...Uta Pippig, Germany		2:25:11
1973...Jacqueline A. Hansen, United States		3:05:59	1996...Uta Pippig, Germany		2:27:12
1974...Miki Gorman, United States		2:47:11	1997...Fatuma Roba, Ethiopia		2:26:23
1975...Liane Winter, W Germany		2:42:24	1998...Fatuma Roba, Ethiopia		2:23:21
1976...Kim Merritt, United States		2:47:10	1999...Fatuma Roba, Ethiopia		2:23:25
1977...Miki Gorman, United States		2:48:33	2000...Catherine Ndereba, Kenya		2:26:11
1978...Gayle Barron, United States		2:44:52	*Unofficial.		

Note: Over the years the Boston course has varied in length. The distances have been 24 miles, 1232 yards (1897–1923); 26 miles, 209 yards (1924–1926); 26 miles 385 yards (1927–1952); and 25 miles, 958 yards (1953–1956). Since 1957, the course has been certified to be the standard marathon distance of 26 miles, 385 yards.

New York City Marathon

From 1970 through 1975 the New York City Marathon was a small local race run in the city's Central Park. In 1976 it was moved to the streets of New York's five boroughs.

Men

Year	Winner	Time	Year	Winner	Time
1970...Gary Muhrcke, United States		2:31:38	1985...Orlando Pizzolato, Italy		2:11:34
1971...Norman Higgins, United States		2:22:54	1986...Gianni Poli, Italy		2:11:06
1972...Sheldon Karlin, United States		2:27:52	1987...Ibrahim Hussein, Kenya		2:11:01
1973...Tom Fleming, United States		2:21:54	1988...Steve Jones, Great Britain		2:08:20
1974...Norbert Sander, United States		2:26:30	1989...Juma Ikangaa, Tanzania		2:08:01
1975...Tom Fleming, United States		2:19:27	1990...Douglas Wakiihuri, Kenya		2:12:39
1976...Bill Rodgers, United States		2:10:10	1991...Salvador Garcia, Mexico		2:09:28
1977...Bill Rodgers, United States		2:11:28	1992...Willie Mtolo, S Africa		2:09:29
1978...Bill Rodgers, United States		2:12:12	1993...Andres Espinosa, Mexico		2:10:04
1979...Bill Rodgers, United States		2:11:42	1994...German Silva, Mexico		2:11:21
1980...Alberto Salazar, United States		2:09:41	1995...German Silva, Mexico		2:11:00
1981...Alberto Salazar, United States		2:08:13	1996...Giacomo Leone, Italy		2:09:54
1982...Alberto Salazar, United States		2:09:29	1997...John Kagwe, Kenya		2:08:12
1983...Rod Dixon, New Zealand		2:08:59	1998...John Kagwe, Kenya		2:08:45
1984...Orlando Pizzolato, Italy		2:14:53	1999...Joseph Chebet, Kenya		2:09:14

Women

Year	Winner	Time	Year	Winner	Time
1970...No finisher			1985...Grete Waitz, Norway		2:28:34
1971...Beth Bonner, United States		2:55:22	1986...Grete Waitz, Norway		2:28:06
1972...Nina Kuscsik, United States		3:08:41	1987...Priscilla Welch, Great Britain		2:30:17
1973...Nina Kuscsik, United States		2:57:07	1988...Grete Waitz, Norway		2:28:07
1974...Katherine Switzer, United States		3:07:29	1989...Ingrid Kristiansen, Norway		2:25:30
1975...Kim Merritt, United States		2:46:14	1990...Wanda Panfiil, Poland		2:30:45
1976...Miki Gorman, United States		2:39:11	1991...Liz McColgan, Scotland		2:27:23
1977...Miki Gorman, United States		2:43:10	1992...Lisa Ondieki, Australia		2:24:40
1978...Grete Waitz, Norway		2:32:30	1993...Uta Pippig, Germany		2:26:24
1979...Grete Waitz, Norway		2:27:33	1994...Tegla Loroupe, Kenya		2:27:37
1980...Grete Waitz, Norway		2:25:41	1995...Tegla Loroupe, Kenya		2:28:06
1981...Allison Roe, New Zealand		2:25:29	1996...Anuta Catuna, Romania		2:28:18
1982...Grete Waitz, Norway		2:27:14	1997....Franziska Rochat-Moser, Switzerland		2:28:43
1983...Grete Waitz, Norway		2:27:00	1998...Franca Fiacconi, Italy		2:25:17
1984...Grete Waitz, Norway		2:29:30	1999...Adriana Fernandez, Mexico		2:25:06

World Cross-Country Championships

Conducted by the International Amateur Athletic Federation (IAAF), this meet annually brings together the best runners in the world at every distance from the mile to the marathon to compete in the same cross-country race.

Men

Year	Winner	Winning Team	Year	Winner	Winning Team
1973	Pekka Paivarinta, Finland	Belgium	1988	John Ngugi, Kenya	Kenya
1974	Eric DeBeck, Belgium	Belgium	1989	John Ngugi, Kenya	Kenya
1975	Ian Stewart, Scotland	New Zealand	1990	Khalid Skah, Morocco	Kenya
1976	Carlos Lopes, Portugal	England	1991	Khalid Skah, Morocco	Kenya
1977	Leon Schots, Belgium	Belgium	1992	John Ngugi, Kenya	Kenya
1978	John Treacy, Ireland	France	1993	William Sigei, Kenya	Kenya
1979	John Treacy, Ireland	England	1994	William Sigei, Kenya	Kenya
1980	Craig Virgin, United States	England	1995	Paul Tergat, Kenya	Kenya
1981	Craig Virgin, United States	Ethiopia	1996	Paul Tergat, Kenya	Kenya
1982	Mohammed Kedir, Ethiopia	Ethiopia	1997	Paul Tergat, Kenya	Kenya
1983	Bekele Debele, Ethiopia	Ethiopia	1998	Paul Tergat, Kenya	Kenya
1984	Carlos Lopes, Portugal	Ethiopia	1999	Paul Tergat, Kenya	Kenya
1985	Carlos Lopes, Portugal	Ethiopia	2000	Mohammed Mourit, Belgium	Kenya
1987	John Ngugi, Kenya	Kenya			

Women

Year	Winner	Winning Team	Year	Winner	Winning Team
1973	Paola Cacchi, Italy	England	1987	Annette Sergent, France	United States
1974	Paola Cacchi, Italy	England	1988	Ingrid Kristiansen, Norway	USSR
1975	Julie Brown, United States	United States	1989	Annette Sergent, France	USSR
1976	Carmen Valero, Spain	USSR	1990	Lynn Jennings, United States	USSR
1977	Carmen Valero, Spain	USSR	1991	Lynn Jennings, United States	Kenya
1978	Grete Waitz, Norway	Romania	1992	Lynn Jennings, United States	Kenya
1979	Grete Waitz, Norway	United States	1993	Albertina Dias, Portugal	Kenya
1980	Grete Waitz, Norway	USSR	1994	Helen Chepngeno, Kenya	Portugal
1981	Grete Waitz, Norway	USSR	1995	Derartu Tulu, Ethiopia	Kenya
1982	Maricica Puica, Romania	USSR	1996	Gete Wami, Ethiopia	Kenya
1983	Grete Waitz, Norway	United States	1997	Derartu Tulu, Ethiopia	Ethiopia
1984	Maricica Puica, Romania	United States	1998	Sonia O'Sullivan, Ireland	Kenya
1985	Zola Budd, England	United States	1999	Gete Wami, Ethiopia	Ethiopia
1986	Zola Budd, England	England	2000	Derartu Tulu, Ethiopia	Ethiopia

Notable Achievements

Longest Winning Streaks

MEN

Event	Name and Nationality	Streak	Years
100 meters	Bob Hayes, United States	49	1962–64
200 meters	Manfred Gemar, Germany	41	1956–60
400 meters	Michael Johnson, United States	58	1989–97
800 meters	Mal Whitfield, United States	40	1951–54
1,500 meters	Hicham El Guerrouj, Morocco	23	1996–00
1,500 meters/mile	Steve Ovett, Great Britain	45	1977–80
Mile	Herb Elliott, Australia	35	1957–60
Steeplechase	Gaston Roelants, Belgium	45	1961–66
5,000 meters	Emil Zátopek, Czechoslovakia	48	1949–52
10,000 meters	Emil Zátopek, Czechoslovakia	38	1948–54
Marathon	Frank Shorter, United States	6	1971–73
110-meter hurdles	Jack Davis, United States	44	1952–55
400-meter hurdles	Edwin Moses, United States	107	1977–87
High jump	Ernie Shelton, United States	46	1953–55
Pole vault	Bob Richards, United States	50	1950–52
Long jump	Carl Lewis, United States	65	1981–91
Triple jump	Adhemar da Silva, Brazil	60	1950–56
Shot put	Parry O'Brien, United States	116	1952–56
Discus throw	Ricky Bruch, Sweden	54	1972–73
Hammer throw	Imre Nemeth, Hungary	73	1946–50
Javelin throw	Janis Lusis, USSR	41	1967–70
Decathlon	Bob Mathias, United States	11	1948–56

Longest Winning Streaks (Cont.)

WOMEN

Event	Name and Nationality	Streak	Years
100 meters	Merlene Ottey, Jamaica	56	1987–91
200 meters	Irena Szewinska, Poland	38	1973–75
400 meters	Irena Szewinska, Poland	36	1973–78
800 meters	Ana Fidelia Quirot, Cuba	36	1987–90
1,500 meters	Paula Ivan, Romania	15	1988–91
1,500 meters/mile	Paula Ivan, Romania	19	1988–90
3,000 meters	Mary Slaney, United States	10	1982–84
10,000 meters	Ingrid Kristiansen, Norway	5	1985–87
Marathon	Katrin Dörre, E Germany	10	1982–86
100-meter hurdles	Annelie Ernhardt, E Germany	44	1972–75
400-meter hurdles	Ann-Louise Skoglund, Sweden	18	1981–83
High jump	Iolanda Balas, Romania	140	1956–67
Long jump	Tatyana Shchelkanova, USSR	19	1964–66
Shot put	Nadezhda Chizhova, USSR	57	1969–73
Discus throw	Gisela Mauermeyer, Germany	65	1935–42
Javelin throw	Ruth Fuchs, E Germany	30	1972–73
Multi	Heide Rosendahl, W Germany	15	1969–72

Most Consecutive Years Ranked No. 1 in the World

MEN

No.	Name and Nationality	Event	Years
11	Sergei Bubka, Ukraine	Pole vault	1984–94
9	Viktor Saneyev, USSR	Triple jump	1968–76
8	Bob Richards, United States	Pole vault	1949–56
8	Ralph Boston, United States	Long jump	1960–67

WOMEN

No.	Name and Nationality	Event	Years
9	Iolanda Balas, Romania	High jump	1958–66
8	Ruth Fuchs, E Germany	Javelin	1972–79
7	Faina Melnick, USSR	Discus throw	1971–77

Major Barrier Breakers

MEN

Event	Mark	Name and Nationality	Date	Site
sub 10-second 100 meters	9.95	Jim Hines, United States	Oct. 14, 1968	Mexico City
sub 20-second 200 meters	19.83	Tommie Smith, United States	Oct. 16, 1968	Mexico City
sub 45-second 400 meters	44.9	Otis Davis, United States	Sept. 6, 1960	Rome
sub 1:45 800 meters	1:44.3	Peter Snell, New Zealand	Feb. 3, 1962	Christchurch, New Zealand
sub four minute mile	3:59.4	Roger Bannister, Great Britain	May 6, 1954	Oxford
sub 3:50 mile	3:49.4	John Walker, New Zealand	Aug. 12, 1975	Göteborg, Sweden
sub 13-minute 5,000 meters	12:58.39	Said Aouita, Morocco	July 22, 1986	Rome
sub 27:00 10,000 meters	26:58.38	Yobes Ondieki, Kenya	July 10, 1993	Oslo
sub 13-second 110-meter hurdles	12.93	Renaldo Nehemiah, United States	Aug. 19, 1981	Zurich
sub 50-second 400-meter hurdles	49.5	Glenn Davis, United States	June 29, 1956	Los Angeles
7' high jump	7' ⅝"	Charles Dumas, United States	June 29, 1956	Los Angeles
8' high jump	8'	Javier Sotomayor, Cuba	July 29, 1989	San Juan
60' triple jump	60' ¼"	Jonathan Edwards, Great Britain	Aug. 7, 1995	Göteborg, Sweden
20' pole vault	20'	Sergei Bubka, USSR	March 15, 1991	San Sebastian, Spain
70' shot put	70' 7¼"	Randy Matson, United States	May 5, 1965	College Station, Texas
200' discus throw	200' 5"	Al Oerter, United States	May 18, 1962	Los Angeles
300' (new) javelin	300' 1"	Steve Backley, Great Britain	Jan. 25, 1992	Auckland, New Zealand

Major Barrier Breakers *(Cont.)*

WOMEN

Event	Mark	Name and Nationality	Date	Site
sub 11-second 100 meters	10.88	Marlies Oelsner, E Germany	July 1, 1977	Dresden
sub 22-second 200 meters	21.71	Marita Koch, E Germany	June 10, 1979	Karl Marx-stadt
sub 50-second 400 meters	49.9	Irena Szewinska, Poland	June 22, 1974	Warsaw
sub 2:00 800 meters	1:59.1	Shin Geum Dan, N Korea	Nov. 12, 1963	Djakarta
sub 4:00 1,500 meters	3:56.0	Tatyana Kazankina, USSR	June 28, 1976	Podolsk, USSR
sub 4:20 mile	4:17.55	Mary Decker, United States	Feb. 16, 1980	Houston
sub 15:00 5,000 meters	14:58.89	Ingrid Kristiansen, Norway	June 28, 1984	Oslo
sub 30:00 10,000 meters	29:31.78	Wang Junxia, China	Sept. 8, 1993	Beijing
sub 2:30 marathon	2:27:33	Grete Waitz, Norway	Oct. 21, 1979	New York City
sub 13-second 100-meter hurdles	12.9	Karin Balzer, E Germany	Sept. 5, 1969	Berlin
6' high jump	6'	Iolanda Balas, Romania	Oct. 18, 1958	Budapest
15' pole vault	15 ½'	Emma George, Australia	March 14, 1998	Melbourne
70' shot put	70' 4½''	Nadyezhda Chizhova, USSR	Sept. 29, 1973	Varna, Bulgaria
200' discus throw	201'	Liesel Westermann, W Germany	Nov. 5, 1967	Sao Paulo
200' javelin throw	201' 4''	Elvira Ozolina, USSR	Aug. 27, 1964	Kiev
first 7,000-point heptathlon	7,148	Jackie Joyner-Kersee, U.S.	July 6–7, 1986	Moscow

Olympic Accomplishments

Oldest Olympic gold medalist—Patrick (Babe) McDonald, United States, 42 years, 26 days, 56-pound weight throw, 1920.
Oldest Olympic medalist—Tebbs Lloyd Johnson, Great Britain, 48 years, 115 days, 1948 (bronze), 50K walk.
Youngest Olympic gold medalist—Barbara Jones, United States, 15 years 123 days, 1952, 4 x 100 relay.
Youngest gold medalist in individual event—Ulrike Meyfarth, W Germany, 16 years, 123 days, 1972, high jump.

World Record Accomplishments*

Most world records equaled or set in a day—6, Jesse Owens, United States, 5-25-35, (9.4 100 yards; 26' 8¼'' long jump; 20.3 200 meters and 220 yards; and 22.6 220-yard hurdles and 200-meter hurdles.
Most records in a year—10, Gunder Hägg, Sweden, 1941–42, 1,500 to 5,000 meters.
Most records in a career—35, Sergei Bubka, 1983–94, pole vault indoors and out.
Longest span of record setting—11 years, 20 days, Irena Szewinska, Poland, 1965–76, 200 meters.
Youngest person to set a set world record—Carolina Gisolf, Holland, 15 years, 5 days, 1928, high jump , 5' 3⅜''.
Youngest man to set a world record—John Thomas, United States, 17 years, 355 days, 1959, high jump, 7' 1¼''.
Oldest person to set world record—Carlos Lopes, Portugal, 38 years, 59 days, marathon, 2:07:12.
Greatest percentage improvement—6.59, Bob Beamon, United States, 1968, long jump.
Longest lasting record—long jump, 26' 8¼'', Jesse Owens, United States, 25 years, 79 days (1935–60).
Highest clearance over head, men—23¼'', Franklin Jacobs, United States (5' 8''), 1978.
Highest clearance over head, woman—12¾'', Yolanda Henry, United States (5' 6''), 1990.

*Marks sanctioned by the IAAF.

Swimming

HEINZ KLUETMEIER

Sydney's Rock Opera

A rowdy, record-smashing affair, the 2000 Olympic swimming competition could have been scored by the Who

BY MARK BECHTEL

IF THE 2000 Olympic swimming meet had an official band, it would be the Who. Before the torch was even lit in Sydney, American sprinter Gary Hall Jr. cranked up the decibel level by writing in an Internet diary that when it came to the host country's swim team, the U.S. would "smash them like guitars," a la Pete Townshend. Indeed, the entire Who catalog could be applied to the Sydney swimming competition:

The Relay. It didn't take long for the Aussies to get a shot at Hall. On the first night of the eight-day event, the Americans looked to continue their dominance of the 400-meter freestyle relay. The U.S. team had never been beaten in the Olympics or in the world championships—never—and they swam well once again in Sydney, breaking their own world record in front of 17,500 Australian fanatics. There was only one problem: Their hosts also came in under the old U.S. record, and they did so .19 of a second ahead of the Americans. The victory came on the strength of an absolutely stunning anchor leg by 17-year-old national hero

Ian Thorpe, who had already set a world record in winning the 400 free that night. The Thorpedo entered the pool slightly ahead of U.S. anchor Hall, who promptly steamed in front and took a half-body-length lead at the wall. Heading for home, though, Thorpe turned it on. Over the final 20 meters, he looked like he was riding a Hovercraft. Hall had no chance. Thorpe touched out the toothy—and mouthy—American, and the Aussies celebrated on the pool deck by strumming air guitars.

But Hall—who took the ribbing with a smile—and the U.S. would get revenge. Hall shared the gold in the 50 free with fellow Yank Anthony Ervin and anchored the world-record-setting 400 medley relay team. The U.S. women swept all three relays and got gold medal swims from Megan Quann (100 breaststroke), Misty Hyman (200 butterfly) and Brooke Bennett (800 free). The Americans left Sydney with 33 medals, 14 of them gold; Australia won 17 (five gold).

My Generation. The grandes dames of U.S. swimming, Jenny Thompson and Dara Torres, finished in a dead heat for the bronze

With three golds and three world records, de Bruijn outshined even Thorpe at Sydney.

medal in the 100-meter freestyle. "All I can say [is] 'irony,'" said Torres of touching the wall at the same time as her teammate and archrival. Thompson won three gold medals on relay teams, giving her eight in her career—all from relays.

That her former training partner Torres was in the Olympics at all was amazing enough. Torres won her first gold medal in Los Angeles in 1984 and took a second in Barcelona eight years later as part of a relay team that also featured Thompson. Then Torres quit swimming and embarked on a career as a broadcaster and a model (she appeared in the 1994 SI swimsuit issue). But in 1999, at age 33, Torres got an itch to swim again. She whipped herself into shape with an intensive, micromanaged regimen (her stretching routine alone called for five people to help contort her body every which way), and made the U.S. team after a seven-year layoff. In Sydney she won three individual bronze medals and a gold in the 400 free relay. And she was old enough to be the mother of some of her teammates, including one, 15-year-old Michael Phelps, who took to greeting her with a hearty, "Hi, Mom."

The Hawker. Prior to 2000 Inge de Bruijn was a pretty good Dutch swimmer. In the new year, though, the 27-year-old went on a tear. She broke eight records before arriving in Sydney, prompting talk that her recent surge was the result of drugs. Amy Van Dyken of the U.S., the defending Olympic champ in the 50 free, came to Sydney, the last competition of her career, with the attitude that if anyone else besides her won the 50 it would be a personal affront. Van Dyken occupied the lane next to de Bruijn in the semis and, in an attempt at intimidation, hawked up a loogie and spit into her rival's lane. De Bruijn wasn't moved. She touched the wall in a world-record time of 24.13 seconds, prompting Van Dyken to mutter, "If I was a man I could swim like that, too," as she walked off the pool deck. De Bruijn took the final in 24.32, while Van Dyken faded to fourth.

Slip Kid. De Bruijn wasn't the only Dutch swimmer making news. Pieter van den Hoogenband, a.k.a. Hoogie (not loogie), proved to be something of a giant killer. He dethroned Alexander Popov of Russia, who was trying to become the first man to win three consecutive 100 free gold medals, and before that, he shocked Thorpe, the heavy favorite in the 200 free. Hoogie pulled away from the Thorpedo down the stretch. "It was so eerie," said van den Hoogenband. "Just 25 meters, and I didn't see him creeping up on me. I thought, Man, he's not going to touch me."

"You don't always get it your own way," said a dejected Thorpe. (He apparently prefers the Stones to the Who.) But Thorpe had nothing to be ashamed of. He won three golds and a silver in his first Olympics, and his already legendary anchor leg was one of the highlights of Sydney 2000. "He was born to swim," said Massomiliano Rosolino of Italy. "He can still get better. He's really, really strong."

In other words, despite a slip-up in the 200, the kid is alright.

FOR THE RECORD·1999-2000

1999-2000 Major Competitions

Men

U.S. OPEN
San Antonio, TX December 2-4 1999

50 free	Sabir Muhammad, United States	22.32
100 free	Pieter van den Hoogenband, Neth	49.18
200 free	Pieter van den Hoogenband, Neth	1:48.30
400 free	Grant Hackett, Australia	3:49.50
1500 free	Grant Hackett, Australia	15:02.83
100 back	Lenny Krayzelburg, United States	50.75†
200 back	Lenny Krayzelburg, United States	1:57.74†
100 breast	Morgan Knabe, Canada	1:02.60
200 breast	Morgan Knabe, Canada	2:16.11
100 fly	Michael Klim, Australia	52.90†
200 fly	Tom Malchow, United States	1:57.16†
200 IM	Marcel Wouda, Netherlands	2:01.31†
400 IM	Grant McGregor, Australia	4:19.52†
400 m relay	Australian Institute of Sport	3:43.04†
400 f relay	Australian Institute of Sport	3:21.93
800 f relay	Australian Institute of Sport	7:23.73

FINA DIVING WORLD CUP
Sydney, Australia January 25-29, 2000

1-m spgbd	Wang Tianling, China	417.60
3-m spgbd	Dmitry Sautin, Russia	708.72
Platform	Tian Lang, China	679.41
3-m sync	Xiong/Xiao, China	353.70
10-m sync	Tian/Huang, China	353.34

FINA SHORT COURSE WORLD CHAMPIONSHIPS
Athens, Greece March 16-19, 2000

50 free	Mark Foster, Great Britain	21.58
100 free	Lars Frolander, Sweden	46.80
200 free	Bela Szabados, Hungary	1:45.27
400 free	Chad Carvin, United States	3:41.13
1500 free	Joerg Hoffman, Germany	14:47.57
50 back	Neil Walker, United States	23.99
100 back	Neil Walker, United States	50.75* WR
200 back	Gordon Kozulj, Croatia	1:53.31†
50 breast	Mark Warnecke, Germany	27.22
100 breast	Roman Sloudnov, Russia	58.57
200 breast	Roman Sloudnov, Russia	2:07.59 WR
50 fly	Mark Foster, Great Britain	23.30
100 fly	Lars Frolander, Sweden	50.44 WR
200 fly	James Hickman, Great Britain	1:53.57
100 IM	Neil Walker, United States	52.79* WR
200 IM	Jani Sievinen, Finland	1:56.27
400 IM	Jani Sievinen, Finland	4:09.54
400 m relay	United States	3:30.03*
400 f relay	Sweden	3:09.57 WR
800 f relay	United States	7:01.33* WR

U.S. NATIONAL CHAMPIONSHIPS
Federal Way, WA, March 28-April 1, 2000

50 free	Neil Walker, United States	22.10
100 free	Neil Walker, United States	49.02
200 free	Josh Davis, United States	1:47.94
400 free	Tom Dolan, United States	3:49.59
800 free	Tom Dolan, United States	7:56.65
1500 free	Graeme Smith, Great Britain	15:10.35
100 back	Neil Walker, United States	54.58
200 back	Aaron Peirsol, United States	1:57.03
100 breast	Ed Moses, United States	1:01.43

*American record. †Meet record. WR World record.

U.S. NATIONAL CHAMPIONSHIPS *(CONT.)*

200 breast	Ed Moses, United States	2:13.86
100 fly	Zsolt Gaspar, Hungary	53.93
200 fly	Stephen Parry, Great Britain	1:56.34
200 IM	Tom Wilkens, United States	2:00.67
400 IM	Tom Wilkens, United States	4:13.84
400 m relay	Irvine Novaquatics	3:43.51
400 f relay	Baywatch Hawaii A	3:23.58
800 f relay	Curl-Burke	7:32.43

U.S. OLYMPIC TRIALS—DIVING
Seattle, WA June 20-25, 2000

3-m spgbd	Mark Ruiz	1130.67
Platform	Mark Ruiz	1154.97

U.S. OLYMPIC TRIALS
Indianapolis, IN August 9-16, 2000

50 free	Gary Hall, Jr.	21.76*
100 free	Neil Walker	48.71
200 free	Josh Davis	1:47.26*
400 free	Klete Keller	3:47.18*
1500 free	Erik Vendt	14:59.11*
100 back	Lenny Krayzelburg	53.67
200 back	Lenny Krayzelburg	1:57.31
100 breast	Ed Moses	1:00.44*
200 breast	Kyle Salyards	2:13.21
100 fly	Ian Crocker	52.78
200 fly	Tom Malchow	1:56.87
200 IM	Tom Dolan	2:00.81
400 IM	Tom Dolan	4:13.72

Women

U.S. OPEN
San Antonio TX December 2–4 1999

50 free	Dara Torres, United States	25.29†
100 free	Jenny Thompson, United States	55.02†
200 free	Martina Moravcova, Slovakia	1:59.54
400 free	Brooke Bennett, United States	4:11.10
800 free	Sachiko Yamada, Japan	8:32.83
100 back	B.J. Bedford, United States	1:02.46
200 back	Kelly Stefanyshyn, Canada	2:13.32
100 breast	Megan Quann, United States	1:07.94*
200 breast	Rebecca Brown, Australia	2:30.13
100 fly	Jenny Thompson, United States	58.36†
200 fly	Susan O'Neill, Australia	2:07.20†
200 IM	Martina Moravcova, Slovakia	2:15.22
400 IM	Cristina Teuscher, United States	4:45.16
400 m relay	Queensland Acad. of Sport	4:10.51
400 f relay	Queensland Acad. of Sport	3:48.07
800 f relay	Queensland Acad. of Sport	8:09.42†

FINA DIVING WORLD CUP
Sydney, Australia, January 25–29,2000

1-m spgbd	Irina Lashko, Russia	287.76
3-m spgbd	Fu Mingxia, China	571.05
Platform	Li Nia, China	552.72
3-m sync	Ilyina/Pakhalina, Russia	320.55
10-m sync	Li/Sing, China	309.24

FINA SHORT COURSE WORLD CHAMPIONSHIPS
Athens, Greece March 16–19, 2000

50 free	Therese Alshammar, Sweden	23.59 WR
100 free	Therese Alshammar, Sweden	52.17 WR
200 free	Yu Yang, China	1:56.06
400 free	Lindsay Benko, United States	4:02.44*
800 free	Hua Chen, China	8:17.03†
50 back	Antje Buschschulte, Germany	27.90
100 back	Sarah Voelker, Germany	58.66
200 back	Antje Buschschulte, Germany	2:07.29
50 breast	Sarah Poewe, South Africa	30.66†
100 breast	Sarah Poewe, South Africa	1:06.21
200 breast	Rebecca Brown, Australia	2:23.41
50 fly	Jenny Thompson, United States	26.13†
100 fly	Jenny Thompson, United States	57.67
200 fly	Mette Jacobsen, Denmark	2:08.10
100 IM	Martina Moravcova, Slovakia	59.71
200 IM	Yana Klochkova, Ukraine	2:08.97
400 IM	Yana Klochkova, Ukraine	4:32.45
400 m relay	Sweden	3:59.53
400 f relay	Sweden	3:35.54
800 f relay	Great Britain	7:49.11 WR

U.S. NATIONAL CHAMPIONSHIPS
Federal Way, WA, March 28–April 1, 2000

50 free	Dara Torres, United States	25.09
100 free	Dara Torres, United States	54.98
200 free	Martina Moravcova, Slovakia	1:59.28
400 free	Diana Munz, United States	4:08.56
800 free	Diana Munz, United States	8:29.11
1500 free	Diana Munz, United States	16:03.30
100 back	Lea Maurer, United States	1:01.47
200 back	Jamie Reid, United States	2:12.00
100 breast	Megan Quann, United States	1:07.54*
200 breast	Kristy Kowal, United States	2:25.74
100 fly	Martina Moravcova, Slovakia	58.41
200 fly	Margaretha Peddar, Gr Britain	2:10.57
200 IM	Martina Moravcova, Slovakia	2:14.44

U.S. NATIONAL CHAMPIONSHIPS (CONT.)

400 IM	Kaitlin Sandeno, United States	4:42.74
400 m relay	Dallas Mustangs A	4:11.99
400 f relay	Southern Methodist A	3:51.69
800 f relay	Bolles School Sharks A	8:20.24

U.S. OLYMPIC TRIALS
Indianapolis, IN August 9–16,2000

50 free	Dara Torres	24.90*
100 free	Jenny Thompson	54.07*
200 free	Lindsay Benko	2:00.45
400 free	Diana Munz	4:08.71
800 free	Brooke Bennett	8:23.92
100 back	B.J. Bedford	101.85
200 back	Amanda Atkins	2:12.97
100 breast	Megan Quann	1:07.26*
200 breast	Kristy Kowal	2:24.75*
100 fly	Jenny Thompson	57.78
200 fly	Misty Hyman	2:09.27
200 IM	Cristina Teuscher	2:13.36
400 IM	Kaitlin Sandeno	4:42.81

U.S OLYMPIC TRIALS—DIVING
Seattle, WA June 20–25,2000

Platform	Laura Wilkinson	869.79
3m spgbd	Jenny Keim	860.31

*American record. †Meet record. WR World record.

World and American Records Set in Late 1999 or 2000

Men

Event	Mark	Record Holder	Date	Site
50 free	21.64	Alexander Popov, Russia (W)	6-16-00	Moscow
	21.76	Gary Hall Jr, United States (A)	8-15-00	Indianapolis
100 free	47.84	Pieter van den Hoogenband, Netherlands (W)	9-19-00	Sydney
200 free	1:45.35	Pieter van den Hoogenband, Netherlands (W)	9-18-00	Sydney
	1:46.73	Josh Davis, United States (A)	9-18-00	Sydney
400 free	3:40.59	Ian Thorpe, Australia (W)	9-16-00	Sydney
	3:47.00	Klete Keller, United States (A)	9-16-00	Sydney
1500 free	14:56.81	Chris Thompson, United States (A)	9-23-00	Sydney
100 breast	1:00.36	Roman Sloudnov, Russia (W)	6-15-00	Moscow
	1:00.44	Ed Moses, United States (A)	8-10-00	Indianapolis
100 fly	51.81	Michael Klim, Australia (W)	12-12-99	Canberra, Australia
200 fly	1:55.18	Tom Malchow (W, A)	6-17-00	Charlotte, NC
200 individual medley	1:59.77	Tom Dolan, United States (A)	9-21-00	Sydney
400 individual medley	4:11.76	Tom Dolan, United States (W,A)	9-17-00	Sydney
4x100 freestyle relay	3:13.67	Australia (W): (Ian Thorpe, Michael Klim, Ashley Callus, Chris Fydler)	9-16-00	Sydney
	3:13.86	United States (A): (Anthony Ervin, Neil Walker, Jason Lezak, Gary Hall Jr)	9-16-00	Sydney
4x200 freestyle relay	7:07.05	Australia (W): (Ian Thorpe, Michael Klim, Bill Kirby, Todd Pearson)	9-19-00	Sydney

Women

Event	Mark	Record Holder	Date	Site
50 free	24.13	Inge de Bruijn, Netherlands (W)	9-22-00	Sydney
	24.63	Dara Torres (A)	9-23-00	Sydney
100 free	53.77	Inge de Bruijn, Netherlands (W)	9-20-00	Sydney
	54.07	Jenny Thompson (A)	8-14-00	Indianapolis
50 breast	31.54	Megan Quann (A)	6-10-00	Federal Way, WA
100 breast	1:07.05	Megan Quann (A)	9-18-00	Sydney
200 breast	2:24.56	Kristy Kowal (A)	9-21-00	Sydney
100 fly	56.61	Inge de Bruijn, Netherlands (W)	9-17-00	Sydney
	57.58	Dara Torres, United States (A)	8-9-00	Indianapolis
200 fly	2:05.81	Susan O'Neill, Australia (W)	5-17-00	Sydney
	2:05.88	Misty Hyman, United States (A)	9-20-00	Sydney
400 individual medley	4:33.59	Yana Klochkova, Ukraine (W)	9-16-00	Sydney
4x100 freestyle relay	3:36.61	United States (W, A) (Jenny Thompson, Courtney Shealy, Dara Torres, Amy van Dyken)	9-16-00	Sydney
4x200 freestyle relay	7:57.80	United States (A): (Samantha Arsenault, Diana Munz, Linday Benko, Jenny Thompson)	9-20-00	Sydney
4x100 medley relay	3:58.30	United States (W, A): (B.J. Bedford, Megan Quann, Jenny Thompson, Dara Torres)	9-23-00	Sydney

W= world record. A= American record.

FOR THE RECORD·Year by Year

World and American Records

MEN

Freestyle

Event	Time	Record Holder	Date	Site
50 meters	21.64	Alexander Popov, Russia (W)	6-16-00	Moscow
	21.76	Gary Hall Jr (A)	8-15-00	Indianapolis
100 meters	47.84	Pieter van den Hoogenband (W) Netherlands	9-19-00	Sydney
	48.42	Matt Biondi (A)	8-8-88	Austin
200 meters	1:45.35	Pieter van den Hoogenband (W) Netherlands	9-18-00	Sydney
	1:46.73	Josh Davis (A)	9-18-00	Sydney
400 meters	3:40.59	Ian Thorpe, Australia (W)	9-16-00	Sydney
	3:47.00	Klete Keller (A)	9-16-00	Sydney
800 meters	7:46.00	Kieran Perkins, Australia (W)	8-24-94	Vancouver, B.C.
	7:52.45	Sean Killion (A)	7-27-87	Clovis, CA
1500 meters	14:41.66	Kieran Perkins, Australia (W)	8-24-94	Vancouver, B.C.
	14.56.81	Chris Thompson (A)	9-23-00	Sydney

Backstroke

Event	Time	Record Holder	Date	Site
50 meters	24.99	Lenny Krayzelburg (W,A)	8-28-99	Sydney
100 meters	53.60	Lenny Krayzelburg (W,A)	8-24-99	Sydney
200 meters	1:55.87	Lenny Krayzelburg (W,A)	8-27-99	Sydney

Breaststroke

Event	Time	Record Holder	Date	Site
100 meters	1:00.36	Roman Sloudnov, Russia (W)	6-15-00	Moscow
	1:00.44	Ed Moses (A)	8-10-00	Indianapolis
200 meters	2:10.16	Mike Barrowman (W,A)	7-29-92	Barcelona

Butterfly

Event	Time	Record Holder	Date	Site
100 meters	51.81	Michael Klim, Australia (W)	12-12-99	Canberra, Australia
	52.76	Neil Walker (A)	8-12-97	Fukuoka, Japan
200 meters	1:55.18	Tom Malchow (W,A)	6-17-00	Charlotte, NC

Individual Medley

Event	Time	Record Holder	Date	Site
200 meters	1:59.36	Jani Sievinen, Finland (W)	9-11-94	Rome
	1:59.77	Tom Dolan (A)	9-21-00	Sydney
400 meters	4:11.76	Tom Dolan (W,A)	9-17-00	Sydney

Relays

Event	Time	Record Holder	Date	Site
400 meter medley	3:33.73	United States (W,A) (Lenny Krayzelburg, Ed Moses, Ian Crocker, Gary Hall Jr)	9-23-00	Sydney
400 meter freestyle	3:13.67	Australia (W) (Ian Thorpe, Michael Klim, Ashley Callus, Chris Fydler)	9-16-00	Sydney
	3:13.86	United States (A) (Anthony Ervin, Neil Walker, Jason Lezak, Gary Hall Jr	9-16-95	Sydney
800 meter freestyle	7:07.05	Australia (W) (Ian Thorpe, Michael Klim, Bill Kirby, Todd Pearson)	9-19-00	Sydney
	7:12.51	United States (A) (Troy Dalbey, Matt Cetlinski, Doug Gjertsen, Matt Biondi	9-21-88	Seoul

Note: Records through Sept. 23, 2000.

WOMEN

Freestyle

Event	Time	Record Holder	Date	Site
50 meters	24.13	Inge de Bruijn, Netherlands (W)	9-22-00	Sydney
	24.63	Dana Torres (A)	9-23-00	Sydney
100 meters	53.77	Inge de Bruijn, Netherlands (W)	9-20-00	Sydney
	54.07	Jenny Thompson (A)	8-14-00	Indianapolis
200 meters	1:56.78	Franziska van Almsick, Germany (W)	9-5-94	Rome
	1:57.90	Nicole Haislett (A)	7-27-90	Barcelona
400 meters	4:03.85	Janet Evans (W, A)	9-22-88	Seoul
800 meters	8:16.22	Janet Evans (W, A)	8-20-89	Tokyo
1500 meters	15:52.10	Janet Evans (W, A)	3-26-88	Orlando, FL

Backstroke

Event	Time	Record Holder	Date	Site
50 meters	28.78	Sandra Volker, Germany (W)	6-12-99	Monte Carlo
	29.01	Natalie Coughlin (A)	8-06-98	Concord, CA
100 meters	1:00.16	Cihong He, China (W)	9-10-94	Rome
	1:00.77	Lea Maurer (A)	1-14-98	Perth, Australia
200 meters	2:06.62	Krisztina Egerszegi, Hungary (W)	8-26-91	Athens, Greece
	2:08.60	Betsy Mitchell (A)	6-27-86	Orlando, FL

Breaststroke

Event	Time	Record Holder	Date	Site
50 meters	30.83	Penelope Heyns, South Africa (W)	8-28-99	Sydney
	31.54	Megan Quann (A)	6-10-00	Federal Way, WA
100 meters	1:06.52	Penelope Heyns, South Africa (W)	8-23-99	Sydney
	1:07.05	Megan Quann (A)	9-18-00	Sydney
200 meters	2:23.64	Penelope Heyns, South Africa (W)	8-27-99	Sydney
	2:24.56	Kristy Kowal (A)	9-21-00	Sydney

Butterfly

Event	Time	Record Holder	Date	Site
50 meters	25.64	Inge de Bruijn, Netherlands (W)	5-27-00	Sheffield, England
	26.55	Amy Van Dyken (A)	5-17-96	Phoenix
100 meters	56.61	Inge de Bruijn, Netherlands (W)	9-17-00	Sydney
	57.58	Dara Torres (A)	8-9-00	Indianapolis
200 meters	2:05.81	Susan O'Neill (W)	5-17-00	Sydney
	2:05.88	Misty Hyman (A)	9-20-00	Sydney

Individual Medley

Event	Time	Record Holder	Date	Site
200 meters	2:09.72	Yanyan Wu, China (W)	10-17-97	Shanghai
	2:11.91	Summer Sanders (A)	7-30-92	Barcelona
400 meters	4:33.59	Yana Klochkova, Ukraine (W)	9-16-00	Sydney
	4:37.58	Summer Sanders (A)	7-26-92	Barcelona

Relays

Event	Time	Record Holder	Date	Site
400 meter medley	3:58.30	United States (W, A) (BJ Bedford, Megan Quann, Jenny Thompson Dana Torres)	9-23-00	Sydney
400 meter freestyle	3:36.61	United States (W, A) (Jenny Thompson, Courtney Shealy, Dara Torres, Amy Van Dyken)	9-16-00	Sydney
800 meter freestyle	7:55.47	East Germany (W) (Manuela Stellmach, Astrid Strauss, Anke Mohring, Heike Friedrich)	8-18-87	Strasbourg, France
	7:57.80	United States (A) (Samantha Arsenault, Diana Munz, Lindsay Benko, Jenny Thompson)	9-20-00	Sydney

Venues: Belgrade, Sept 4–9, 1973; Cali, Colombia, July 18–27, 1975; West Berlin, Aug 20–28, 1978; Guayaquil, Equador, Aug 1–7, 1982; Madrid, Aug 17–22, 1986; Perth, Australia, Jan 7–13, 1991; Rome, Sept 1–11, 1994; Perth, Australia, Jan 8–18, 1998.

MEN

50-meter Freestyle

1986	Tom Jager, United States	22.49‡
1991	Tom Jager, United States	22.16‡
1994	Aleksandr Popov, Russia	22.17
1998	Bill Pilczuk, United States	22.29

100-meter Freestyle

1973	Jim Montgomery, United States	51.70
1975	Andy Coan, United States	51.25
1978	David McCagg, United States	50.24
1982	Jorg Woithe, East Germany	50.18
1986	Matt Biondi, United States	48.94
1991	Matt Biondi, United States	49.18
1994	Aleksandr Popov, Russia	49.12
1998	Aleksandr Popov, Russia	48.93‡

200-meter Freestyle

1973	Jim Montgomery, United States	1:53.02
1975	Tim Shaw, United States	1:52.04‡
1978	Billy Forrester, United States	1:51.02‡
1982	Michael Gross, West Germany	1:49.84
1986	Michael Gross, West Germany	1:47.92
1991	Giorgio Lamberti, Italy	1:47.27‡
1994	Antti Kasvio, Finland	1:47.32
1998	Michael Klim, Australia	1:47.41

400-meter Freestyle

1973	Rick DeMont, United States	3:58.18‡
1975	Tim Shaw, United States	3:54.88‡
1978	Vladimir Salnikov, USSR	3:51.94‡
1982	Vladimir Salnikov, USSR	3:51.30‡
1986	Rainer Henkel, West Germany	3:50.05
1991	Joerg Hoffman, Germany	3:48.04‡
1994	Kieran Perkins, Australia	3:43.80*
1998	Ian Thorpe, Australia	3:46.29

1500-meter Freestyle

1973	Stephen Holland, Australia	15:31.85
1975	Tim Shaw, United States	15:28.92‡
1978	Vladimir Salnikov, USSR	15:03.99‡
1982	Vladimir Salnikov, USSR	15:01.77‡
1986	Rainer Henkel, West Germany	15:05.31
1991	Joerg Hoffman, Germany	14:50.36*
1994	Kieran Perkins, Australia	14:50.52
1998	Grant Hackett, Australia	14:51.70

100-meter Backstroke

1973	Roland Matthes, East Germany	57.47
1975	Roland Matthes, East Germany	58.15
1978	Bob Jackson, United States	56.36‡
1982	Dirk Richter, East Germany	55.95
1986	Igor Polianski, USSR	55.58‡
1991	Jeff Rouse, United States	55.23‡
1994	Martin Lopez Zubero, Spain	55.17‡
1998	Lenny Krayzelburg, United States	55.00‡

200-meter Backstroke

1973	Roland Matthes, East Germany	2:01.87‡
1975	Zoltan Varraszto, Hungary	2:05.05
1978	Jesse Vassallo, United States	2:02.16
1982	Rick Carey, United States	2:00.82‡
1986	Igor Polianski, USSR	1:58.78‡
1991	Martin Zubero, Spain	1:59.52
1994	Vladimir Selkov, Russia	1:57.42‡
1998	Lenny Krayzelburg, United States	1:58.84

100-meter Breaststroke

1973	John Hencken, United States	1:04.02‡
1975	David Wilkie, Great Britain	1:04.26‡
1978	Walter Kusch, West Germany	1:03.56‡
1982	Steve Lundquist, United States	1:02.75‡
1986	Victor Davis, Canada	1:02.71
1991	Norbert Rozsa, Hungary	1:01.45*
1994	Norbert Rozsa, Hungary	1:01.24‡
1998	Frederik Deburghgraeve, Belgium	1:01.34

200-meter Breaststroke

1973	David Wilkie, Great Britain	2:19.28‡
1975	David Wilkie, Great Britain	2:18.23‡
1978	Nick Nevid, United States	2:18.37
1982	Victor Davis, Canada	2:14.77*
1986	Jozsef Szabo, Hungary	2:14.27‡
1991	Mike Barrowman, United States	2:11.23*
1994	Norbert Rozsa, Hungary	2:12.81
1998	Kurt Grote, United States	2:13.40

100-meter Butterfly

1973	Bruce Robertson, Canada	55.69
1975	Greg Jagenburg, United States	55.63
1978	Joe Bottom, United States	54.30
1982	Matt Gribble, United States	53.88‡
1986	Pablo Morales, United States	53.54‡
1991	Anthony Nesty, Suriname	53.29‡
1994	Rafal Szukala, Poland	53.51
1998	Michael Klim, Australia	52.25‡

200-meter Butterfly

1973	Robin Backhaus, United States	2:03.32
1975	Bill Forrester, United States	2:01.95‡
1978	Mike Bruner, United States	1:59.38‡
1982	Michael Gross, East Germany	1:58.85‡
1986	Michael Gross, East Germany	1:56.53‡
1991	Melvin Stewart, United States	1:55.69*
1994	Denis Pankratov, Russia	1:56.54
1998	Denys Sylantyev, Ukraine	1:56.61

200-meter Individual Medley

1973	Gunnar Larsson, Sweden	2:08.36
1975	Andras Hargitay, Hungary	2:07.72
1978	Graham Smith, Canada	2:03.65*
1982	Aleksandr Sidorenko, USSR	2:03.30‡
1986	Tamás Darnyi, Hungary	2:01.57‡
1991	Tamás Darnyi, Hungary	1:59.36*
1994	Jani Sievin, Finland	1:58.16*
1998	Marcel Wouda, Netherlands	2:01.18

400-meter Individual Medley

1973	Andras Hargitay, Hungary	4:31.11
1975	Andras Hargitay, Hungary	4:32.57
1978	Jesse Vassallo, United States	4:20.05*
1982	Ricardo Prado, Brazil	4:19.78*
1986	Tamás Darnyi, Hungary	4:18.98‡
1991	Tamás Darnyi, Hungary	4:12.36*
1994	Tom Dolan, United States	4:12.30*
1998	Tom Dolan, United States	4:14.95

* World record. ‡Meet record.

MEN (Cont.)

400-meter Medley Relay

1973.....United States (Mike Stamm,   3:49.49
John Hencken, Joe Bottom,
Jim Montgomery)
1975.....United States (John Murphy,   3:49.00
Rick Colella, Greg Jagenburg,
Andy Coan)
1978.....United States (Robert Jackson,   3:44.63
Nick Nevid, Joe Bottom,
David McCagg)
1982.....United States (Rick Carey,   3:40.84*
Steve Lundquist, Matt Gribble,
Rowdy Gaines)
1986.....United States (Dan Veatch,   3:41.25
David Lundberg, Pablo Morales,
Matt Biondi)
1991.....United States (Jeff Rouse,   3:39.66‡
Eric Wunderlich, Mark Henderson
Matt Biondi)
1994.....United States (Jeff Rouse, Eric   3:37.74‡
Wunderlich, Mark Henderson,
Gary Hall)
1998.....Australia (Matt Welsh, Phil Rogers,   3:37.98
Robin Backhaus, Rick Klatt,
Jim Montgomery)

400-meter Freestyle Relay

1973.....United States (Mel Nash,   3:27.18
Joe Bottom, Jim Montgomery,
John Murphy)
1975.....United States (Bruce Furniss,   3:24.85
Jim Montgomery, Andy Coan,
John Murphy)
1978.....United States (Jack Babashoff,   3:19.74
Rowdy Gaines, Jim Montgomery,
David McCagg)
1982.....United States (Chris Cavanaugh,   3:19.26*
Robin Leamy, David McCagg,
Rowdy Gaines)
1986.....United States (Tom Jager,   3:19.89
Mike Heath, Paul Wallace,
Matt Biondi)
1991.....United States (Tom Jager,   3:17.15‡
Brent Lang, Doug Gjertsen,
Matt Biondi)
1994.....United States (Jon Olsen,   3:16.90‡
Josh Davis, Ugur Taner, Gary Hall)
1998.....United States (Bryan Jones,   3:16.69†
Jon Olsen, Bradley Schumacher,
Gary Wayne Jr.)

800-meter Freestyle Relay

1973.....United States (Kurt Krumpholz,   7:33.22*
Robin Backhaus, Rick Klatt,
Jim Montgomery)
1975.....West Germany (Klaus Steinbach,   7:39.44
Werner Lampe, Hans Joachim
Geisler, Peter Nocke)
1978.....United States (Bruce Furniss,   7:20.82
Billy Forrester, Bobby Hackett,
Rowdy Gaines)
1982.....United States (Rich Saeger,   7:21.09
Jeff Float, Kyle Miller,
Rowdy Gaines)

1986.....East Germany (Lars Hinneburg,   7:15.91‡
Thomas Flemming, Dirk Richter,
Sven Lodziewski)
1991.....Germany (Peter Sitt,   7:13.50‡
Steffan Zesner, Stefan Pfeiffer,
Michael Gross)
1994.....Sweden (Christer Waller,   7:17.34
Tommy Werner, Lars Frolander,
Anders Holmertz)
1998.....Australia (Daniel Kowalski,   7:12.48†
Grant Hackett, Ian Thorpe,
Anthony Rogis)

WOMEN

50-meter Freestyle

1986	Tamara Costache, Romania	25.28*
1991	Zhuang Yong, China	25.47
1994	Le Jingyi, China	24.51*
1998	Amy Van Dyken, United States	25.15

100-meter Freestyle

1973	Kornelia Ender, East Germany	57.54
1975	Kornelia Ender, East Germany	56.50
1978	Barbara Krause, East Germany	55.68‡
1982	Birgit Meineke, East Germany	55.79
1986	Kristin Otto, East Germany	55.05‡
1991	Nicole Haislett, United States	55.17
1994	Le Jingyi, China	54.01*
1998	Jenny Thompson, United States	54.95

200-meter Freestyle

1973	Keena Rothhammer, United States	2:04.99
1975	Shirley Babashoff, United States	2:02.50
1978	Cynthia Woodhead, United States	1:58.53*
1982	Annemarie Verstappen, Netherlands	1:59.53‡
1986	Heike Friedrich, East Germany	1:58.26‡
1991	Hayley Lewis, Australia	2:00.48
1994	Franziska Van Almsick, Germany	1:56.78*
1998	Claudia Poll, Costa Rica	1:58.90

400-meter Freestyle

1973	Heather Greenwood, United States	4:20.28
1975	Shirley Babashoff, United States	4:22.70
1978	Tracey Wickham, Australia	4:06.28*
1982	Carmela Schmidt, East Germany	4:08.98
1986	Heike Friedrich, East Germany	4:07.45
1991	Janet Evans, United States	4:08.63
1994	Yang Aihua, China	4:09.64
1998	Chen Yan, China	4:06.72

* World record; ‡Meet record.

WOMEN (Cont.)

800-meter Freestyle

1973	Novella Calligaris, Italy	8:52.97
1975	Jenny Turrall, Australia	8:44.75‡
1978	Tracey Wickham, Australia	8:24.94‡
1982	Kim Linehan, United States	8:27.48
1986	Astrid Strauss, East Germany	8:28.24
1991	Janet Evans, United States	8:24.05‡
1994	Janet Evans, United States	8:29.85
1998	Brooke Bennett, United States	8.28.71

100-meter Backstroke

1973	Ulrike Richter, East Germany	1:05.42
1975	Ulrike Richter, East Germany	1:03.30‡
1978	Linda Jezek, United States	1:02.55‡
1982	Kristin Otto, East Germany	1:01.30‡
1986	Betsy Mitchell, United States	1:01.74
1991	Krisztina Egerszegi, Hungary	1:01.78
1994	He Cihong, China	1:00.57
1998	Lea Maurer, United States	1:01.16

200-meter Backstroke

1973	Melissa Belote, United States	2:20.52
1975	Birgit Treiber, East Germany	2:15.46*
1978	Linda Jezek, United States	2:11.93*
1982	Cornelia Sirch, East Germany	2:09.91*
1986	Cornelia Sirch, East Germany	2:11.37
1991	Krisztina Egerszegi, Hungary	2:09.15‡
1994	He Cihong, China	2:07.40
1998	Roxanna Maracineanu, France	2:11.26

100-meter Breaststroke

1973	Renate Vogel, East Germany	1:13.74
1975	Hannalore Anke, East Germany	1:12.72
1978	Julia Bogdanova, USSR	1:10.31*
1982	Ute Geweniger, East Germany	1:09.14‡
1986	Sylvia Gerasch, East Germany	1:08.11*
1991	Linley Frame, Australia	1:08.81
1994	Samantha Riley, Australia	1:07.96*
1998	Kristy Kowal, United States	1:08.42

200-meter Breaststroke

1973	Renate Vogel, East Germany	2:40.01
1975	Hannalore Anke, East Germany	2:37.25‡
1978	Lina Kachushite, USSR	2:31.42*
1982	Svetlana Varganova, USSR	2:28.82‡
1986	Silke Hoerner, East Germany	2:27.40*
1991	Elena Volkova, USSR	2:29.53
1994	Samantha Riley, Australia	2:26.87‡
1998	Agnes Kovacs, Hungary	2:25.45†

100-meter Butterfly

1973	Kornelia Ender, East Germany	1:02.53
1975	Kornelia Ender, East Germany	1:01.24*
1978	Joan Pennington, United States	1:00.20‡
1982	Mary T. Meagher, United States	59.41‡
1986	Kornelia Gressler, East Germany	59.51
1991	Qian Hong, China	59.68
1994	Liu Limin, China	58.98‡
1998	Jenny Thompson, United States	58.46†

200-meter Butterfly

1973	Rosemarie Kother, East Germany	2:13.76‡
1975	Rosemarie Kother, East Germany	2:15.92
1978	Tracy Caulkins, United States	2:09.87*
1982	Ines Geissler, East Germany	2:08.66‡
1986	Mary T. Meagher, United States	2:08.41‡
1991	Summer Sanders, United States	2:09.24
1994	Liu Limin, China	2:07.25‡
1998	Susie O'Neill, Australia	2:07.93†

200-meter Individual Medley

1973	Andrea Huebner, East Germany	2:20.51
1975	Kathy Heddy, United States	2:19.80
1978	Tracy Caulkins, United States	2:14.07*
1982	Petra Schneider, East Germany	2:11.79
1986	Kristin Otto, East Germany	2:15.56
1991	Li Lin, China	2:13.40
1994	Lu Bin, China	2:12.34‡
1998	Wu Yanyan, China	2:10.88

400-meter Individual Medley

1973	Gudrun Wegner, East Germany	4:57.71
1975	Ulrike Tauber, East Germany	4:52.76‡
1978	Tracy Caulkins, United States	4:40.83*
1982	Petra Schneider, East Germany	4:36.10*
1986	Kathleen Nord, East Germany	4:43.75
1991	Lin Li, China	4:41.45
1994	Dai Guohong, China	4:39.14
1998	Chen Yan, China	4:36.66

400-meter Medley Relay

1973	East Germany (Ulrike Richter, Renate Vogel, Rosemarie Kother, Kornelia Ender)	4:16.84
1975	East Germany (Ulrike Richter, Hannelore Anke, Rosemarie Kother, Kornelia Ender)	4:14.74
1978	United States (Linda Jezek, Tracy Caulkins, Joan Pennington, Cynthia Woodhead)	4:08.21‡
1982	East Germany (Kristin Otto, Ute Gewinger, Ines Geissler, Birgit Meineke)	4:05.8*
1986	East Germany (Kathrin Zimmermann, Sylvia Gerasch, Kornelia Gressler, Kristin Otto)	4:04.82
1991	United States (Janie Wagstaff, Tracey McFarlane, Crissy Ahmann-Leighton, Nicole Haislett)	4:06.51
1994	China (He Cihong, Dai Guohong, Liu Limin, Lu Bin)	4:01.67*
1998	United States (Kristy Kowal, Lea Maurer, Jenny Thompson, Amy Van Dyken)	4:01.93

400-meter Freestyle Relay

1973	East Germany (Kornelia Ender, Andrea Eife, Andrea Huebner, Sylvia Eichner)	3:52.45
1975	East Germany (Kornelia Ender, Barbara Krause, Claudia Hempel, Ute Bruckner)	3:49.37
1978	United States (Tracy Caulkins, Stephanie Elkins, Joan Pennington, Cynthia Woodhead)	3:43.43*

WOMEN (Cont.)

400-meter Freestyle Relay (Cont.)

1982	East Germany (Birgit Meineke, Susanne Link, Kristin Otto, Caren Metschuk)	3:43.97
1986	East Germany (Kristin Otto, Manuela Stellmach, Sabine Schulze, Heike Friedrich)	3:40.57*
1991	United States (Nicole Haislett, Julie Cooper, Whitney Hedgepeth, Jenny Thompson)	3:43.26
1994	China (Le Jingyi, Ying Shan, Le Ying, Lu Bin)	3:37.91*
1998	United States (Catherine Fox, Lindsey Farella, Melanie Valerio, B.J. Bedford)	3:42.11

800-meter Freestyle Relay

1986	East Germany (Manuela Stellmach, Astrid Strauss, Nadja Bergknecht, Heike Friedrich)	7:59.33*
1991	Germany (Kerstin Kielgass, Manuela Stellmach, Dagmar Hase, Stephanie Ortwig)	8:02.56
1994	China (Le Ying, Yang Alhua, Zhou Guabin, Lu Bin)	7:57.96
1998	Germany (Silvia Szalai, Antje Buschschulte, Janina Goetz, Franziska Van Almsick)	8:02.56

* World record; ‡Meet record.

World Diving Championships

MEN

1-meter Springboard

		Pts
1991	Edwin Jongejans, Netherlands	588.51
1994	Evan Stewart, Zimbabwe	382.14
1998	Yu Zhuocheng, China	417.54

3-meter Springboard

		Pts
1973	Phil Boggs, United States	618.57
1975	Phil Boggs, United States	597.12
1978	Phil Boggs, United States	913.95
1982	Greg Louganis, United States	752.67
1986	Greg Louganis, United States	750.06
1991	Kent Ferguson, United States	650.25
1994	Wu Zhuocheng, China	655.44
1998	Dmitry Sautin, Russia	746.79

Platform

		Pts
1973	Klaus Dibiasi, Italy	559.53
1975	Klaus Dibiasi, Italy	547.98
1978	Greg Louganis, United States	844.11
1982	Greg Louganis, United States	634.26
1986	Greg Louganis, United States	668.58
1991	Sun Shuwei, China	626.79
1994	Dmitry Sautin, Russia	634.71
1998	Dmitry Sautin, Russia	750.90

3-meter Synchronized

		Pts
1998	China (Sun Shuwei, Tian Liang)	313.50

10-meter Synchronized

		Pts
1998	China (Xu Hao, Yu Zhuocheng)	326.34

WOMEN

1-meter Springboard

		Pts
1991	Gao Min, China	478.26
1994	Chen Lixia, China	279.30
1998	Irina Lashko, Russia	296.07

3-meter Springboard

		Pts
1973	Christa Koehler, East Germany	442.17
1975	Irina Kalinina, USSR	489.81
1978	Irina Kalinina, USSR	691.43
1982	Megan Neyer, United States	501.03
1986	Gao Min, China	582.90
1991	Gao Min, China	539.01
1994	Tan Shuping, China	548.49
1998	Yulia Pakhalina, Russia	544.62

Platform

		Pts
1973	Ulrike Knape, Sweden	406.77
1975	Janet Ely, United States	403.89
1978	Irina Kalinina, USSR	412.71
1982	Wendy Wyland, United States	438.79
1986	Chen Lin, China	449.67
1991	Fu Mingxia, China	426.51
1994	Fu Mingxia, China	434.04
1998	Olena Zhupyna, Ukraine	550.41

3-meter Synchronized

		Pts
1998	Russia (Irina Lashko, Yulia Pakhalina)	282.30

10-meter Synchronized

		Pts
1998	Ukraine (Olena Zhupyna, Svetlana Serbina)	278.28

Men

50-METER FREESTYLE

1988	Matt Biondi	22.14*
2000	Gary Hall Jr. and Anthony Ervin	21.98

100-METER FREESTLYE

1906	Charles Daniels	1:13.4
1908	Charles Daniels	1:05.6*
1912	Duke Kahanamoku	1:03.4
1920	Duke Kahanamoku	1:00.4
1924	John Weissmuller	59.0‡
1928	John Weissmuller	58.6‡
1948	Wally Ris	57.3‡
1952	Clarke Scholes	57.4
1964	Don Schollander	53.4‡
1972	Mark Spitz	51.22*
1976	Jim Montgomery	49.99*
1984	Rowdy Gaines	49.80‡
1988	Matt Biondi	48.63‡

200-METER FREESTYLE

1904	Charles Daniels	2:44.2
1906	Not held 1906–1964	
1972	Mark Spitz	1:52.78*
1976	Bruce Furniss	1:50.29*

400-METER FREESTYLE

1904	Charles Daniels (440 yds)	6:16.2
1920	Norman Ross	5:26.8
1924	John Weissmuller	5:04.2‡
1932	Buster Crabbe	4:48.4‡
1936	Jack Medica	4:44.5‡
1948	William Smith	4:41.0‡
1964	Don Schollander	4:12.2*
1968	Mike Burton	4:09.0‡
1976	Brian Goodell	3:51.93*
1984	George DiCarlo	3:51.23‡

1500-METER FREESTYLE

1920	Norman Ross	22:23.2
1948	James McLane	19:18.5
1952	Ford Konno	18:30.3‡
1968	Mike Burton	16:38.9‡
1972	Mike Burton	15:52.58‡
1976	Brian Goodell	15:02.40*
1984	Michael O'Brien	15:05.20

100-METER BACKSTROKE

1912	Harry Hebner	1:21.2
1920	Warren Kealoha	1:15.2
1924	Warren Kealoha	1:13.2‡
1928	George Kojac	1:08.2*
1936	Adolph Kiefer	1:05.9‡
1948	Allen Stack	1:06.4
1952	Yoshi Oyakawa	1:05.4‡
1976	John Naber	55.49*
1984	Rick Carey	55.79
1996	Jeff Rouse	54.10
2000	Lenny Krayzelburg	53.60‡

200-METER BACKSTROKE

1964	Jed Graef	2:10.3*
1976	John Naber	1:59.19*
1984	Rick Carey	2:00.23
1996	Brad Bridgewater	1:58.54
2000	Lenny Krayzelburg	1:56.76‡

100-METER BREASTSTROKE

1968	Donald McKenzie	1:07.7‡
1976	John Hencken	1:03.11*
1984	Steve Lundquist	1:01.65 *
1992	Nelson Diebel	1:01.50‡

200-METER BREASTSTROKE

1924	Robert Skelton	2:56.6
1948	Joseph Verdeur	2:39.3‡
1960	William Mulliken	2:37.4
1972	John Hencken	2:21.55
1992	Mike Barrowman	2:10.16*

100-METER BUTTERFLY

1968	Douglas Russell	55.9‡
1972	Mark Spitz	54.27*
1976	Matt Vogel	54.35
1992	Pablo Morales	53.32

200-METER BUTTERFLY

1956	William Yorzyk	2:19.3‡
1960	Michael Troy	2:12.8*
1968	Carl Robie	2:08.7
1972	Mark Spitz	2:00.70*
1976	Mike Bruner	1:59.23*
1992	Melvin Stewart	1:56.26
2000	Tom Malchow	1:55.35‡

200-METER INDIVIDUAL MEDLEY

1968	Charles Hickcox	2:12.0‡

400-METER INDIVIDUAL MEDLEY

1964	Richard Roth	4:45.4*
1968	Charles Hickcox	4:48.4
1976	Rod Strachan	4:23.68*
1996	Tom Dolan	4:.14.90
2000	Tom Dolan	4:11.76‡

3-METER SPRINGBOARD DIVING

1920	Louis Kuehn	675.4 points
1924	Albert White	696.4
1928	Pete Desjardins	185.04
1932	Michael Galitzen	161.38
1936	Richard Degener	163.57
1948	Bruce Harlan	163.64
1952	David Browning	205.29
1956	Robert Clotworthy	159.56
1960	Gary Tobian	170.00
1964	Kenneth Sitzberger	159.90
1968	Bernard Wrightson	170.15
1976	Philip Boggs	619.05
1984	Greg Louganis	754.41
1988	Greg Louganis	730.80

PLATFORM DIVING

1904	George Sheldon	12.66 points
1920	Clarence Pinkston	100.67
1924	Albert White	97.46
1928	Pete Desjardins	98.74
1932	Harold Smith	124.80
1936	Marshall Wayne	113.58
1948	Sammy Lee	130.05
1952	Sammy Lee	156.28
1960	Robert Webster	165.56
1964	Robert Webster	148.58
1984	Greg Louganis	576.99
1988	Greg Louganis	638.61

* World record. ‡ Meet (Olympic) record.

Women

50-METER FREESTYLE

1996	Amy Van Dyken	24.87

100-METER FREESTLYE

1920	Ethelda Bleibtrey	1:13.6*
1924	Ethel Lackie	1:12.4
1928	Albina Osipowich	1:11.0‡
1932	Helene Madison	1:06.8‡
1968	Jan Henne	1:00.0
1972	Sandra Neilson	58.59‡
1984	Carrie Steinseifer	55.92
	Nancy Hogshead	55.92

200-METER FREESTYLE

1968	Debbie Meyer	2:10.5‡
1984	Mary Wayte	1:59.23
1992	Nicole Haislett	1:57.90

400-METER FREESTYLE

1924	Martha Norelius	6:02.2‡
1928	Martha Norelius	5:42.8*
1932	Helene Madison	5:28.5*
1948	Ann Curtis	5:17.8‡
1960	Chris von Saltza	4:50.6
1964	Virginia Duenkel	4:43.3‡
1968	Debbie Meyer	4:31.8‡
1984	Tiffany Cohen	4:07.10‡
1988	Janet Evans	4:03.85*

800-METER FREESTYLE

1968	Debbie Meyer	9:24.0‡
1972	Keena Rothhammer	8:53.86*
1984	Tiffany Cohen	8:24.95‡
1988	Janet Evans	8:20.20‡
1992	Janet Evans	8:25.52
1996	Brooke Bennett	8:27.89
2000	Brooke Bennett	8:19.67

100-METER BACKSTROKE

1924	Sybil Bauer	1:23.2‡
1932	Eleanor Holm	1:19.4
1960	Lynn Burke	1:09.3‡
1964	Cathy Ferguson	1:07.7*
1968	Kaye Hall	1:06.2*
1972	Melissa Belote	1:05.78‡
1984	Theresa Andrews	1:02.55
1996	Beth Botsford	1:01.19

200-METER BACKSTROKE

1968	Pokey Watson	2:24.8‡
1972	Melissa Belote	2:19.19*

100-METER BREASTSTROKE

1972	Catherine Carr	1:13.58*
2000	Megan Quann	1:07.05

200-METER BREASTSTROKE

1968	Sharon Wichman	2:44.4‡

100-METER BUTTERFLY

1956	Shelley Mann	1:11.0‡
1960	Carolyn Schuler	1:09.5‡
1964	Sharon Stouder	1:04.7*
1984	Mary T. Meagher	59.26
1996	Amy Van Dyken	59.13

200-METER BUTTERFLY

1972	Karen Moe	2:15.57*
1984	Mary T. Meagher	2:06.90‡
1992	Summer Sanders	2:08.67
2000	Misty Hyman	2:05.88‡

200-METER INDIVIDUAL MEDLEY

1968	Sharon Wichman	2:44.4‡
1984	Tracy Caulkins	2:12.64‡

400-METER INDIVIDUAL MEDLEY

1964	Donna De Varona	5:18.7‡
1968	Claudia Kolb	5:08.5‡
1984	Tracy Caulkins	4:39.24
1988	Janet Evans	4:37.76

3-METER SPRINGBOARD DIVING

1920	Aileen Riggin	539.9 points
1924	Elizabeth Becker	474.5
1928	Helen Meany	78.62
1932	Georgia Coleman	87.52
1936	Marjorie Gestring	89.27
1948	Victoria Draves	108.74
1952	Patricia McCormick	147.30
1956	Patricia McCormick	142.36
1968	Sue Gossick	150.77
1972	Micki King	450.03
1976	Jennifer Chandler	506.19

PLATFORM DIVING

1924	Caroline Smith	33.2 points
1928	Elizabeth Becker Pinkston	31.6
1932	Dorothy Poynton	40.26
1936	Dorothy Poynton Hill	33.93
1948	Victoria Draves	68.87
1952	Patricia McCormick	79.37
1956	Patricia McCormick	84.85
1964	Lesley Bush	99.80
2000	Laura Wilkinson	543.75

* World record; ‡ Meet (Olympic) record.

Notable Achievements

Barrier Breakers

MEN

Event	Barrier	Athlete and Nation	Time	Date
100 Freestyle	1:00	Johnny Weissmuller, United States	58.6	7-9-22
100 Freestyle	:50	James Montgomery, United States	49.99	7-25-76
200 Freestyle	2:00	Don Schollander, United States	1:58.8	7-27-63
200 Freestyle	1:50	Sergei Kopliakov, USSR	1:49.83	4-7-79
400 Freestyle	4:00	Rick DeMont, United States	3:58.18	9-6-73
400 Freestyle	3:50	Vladimir Salnikov, USSR	3:49.57	3-12-82
800 Freestyle	8:00	Vladimir Salnikov, USSR	7:56.49	3-23-79
1500 Freestyle	15:00	Vladimir Salnikov, USSR	14:58.27	7-22-80
100 Backstroke	1:00	Thompson Mann, United States	59.6	10-16-64
200 Backstroke	2:00	John Naber, United States	1:59.19	7-24-76
200 Breaststroke	2:30	Chester Jastremski, United States	2:29.6	8-19-61
100 Butterfly	1:00	Lance Larson, United States	59.0	6-29-60
200 Butterfly	2:00	Roger Pyttel, East Germany	1:59.63	6-3-76

WOMEN

Event	Barrier	Athlete and Nation	Time	Date
100 Freestyle	1:00	Dawn Fraser, Australia	59.9	10-27-62
200 Freestyle	2:00	Kornelia Ender, East Germany	1:59.78	6-2-76
400 Freestyle	4:30	Debbie Meyer, United States	4:29.0	8-18-67
800 Freestyle	10:00	Jane Cederqvist, Sweden	9:55.6	8-17-60
800 Freestyle	9:00	Ann Simmons, United States	8:59.4	9-10-71
1500 Freestyle	20:00	Ilsa Konrads, Australia	19:25.7	1-14-60
	16:00	Janet Evans, United States	15:52.10	3-26-88
200 Backstroke	2:30	Satoko Tanaka, Japan	2:29.6	2-10-63
100 Butterfly	1:00	Christiane Knacke, East Germany	59.78	8-28-77
400 Individual Medley	5:00	Gudrun Wegner, East Germany	4:57.51	9-6-73

Olympic Achievements

MOST INDIVIDUAL GOLDS IN SINGLE OLYMPICS

MEN

No.	Athlete and Nation	Olympic Year	Events
4	Mark Spitz, United States	1972	100, 200 Free; 100, 200 Fly

WOMEN

No.	Athlete and Nation	Olympic Year	Events
4	Kristin Otto, East Germany	1988	50, 100 Free; 100 Back; 100 Fly
3	Debbie Meyer, United States	1968	200, 400, 800 Free
3	Shane Gould, Australia	1972	200, 400 Free; 200 IM
3	Kornelia Ender, East Germany	1976	100, 200 Free; 100 Fly
3	Janet Evans, United States	1988	400, 800 Free; 400 IM
3	Krisztina Egerszegi, Hungary	1992	100, 200 Back; 400 IM
3	Michelle Smith, Ireland	1996	400 Free; 200, 400 IM
3	Inge de Bruijn, Netherlands	2000	50, 100 Free; 100 Fly

Olympic Achievements (Cont.)

MOST INDIVIDUAL OLYMPIC GOLD MEDALS, CAREER

MEN

No.	Athlete and Nation	Olympic Years and Events
4	Charles Meldrum Daniels, United States	1904 (220, 440 Free); 1906 (100 Free); 1908 (100 Free)
4	Roland Matthes, East Germany	1968 (100, 200 Back); 1972 (100, 200 Back)
4	Mark Spitz, United States	1972 (100, 200 Free; 100, 200 Fly)

WOMEN

No.	Athlete and Nation	Olympic Years and Events
4	Kristin Otto, East Germany	1988 (50 Free; 100 Free, Back and Fly)
4	Janet Evans, United States	1988 (400, 800 Free; 400 IM); 1992 (800 Free)
4	Krisztina Egerszegi, Hungary	1992 (100, 200 Back; 400 IM); 1996 (200 Back)

Most Olympic Gold Medals in a Single Olympics, Men—7, Mark Spitz, United States, 1972: 100, 200 Free; 100, 200 Fly; 4 x 100, 4 x 200 Free Relays; 4 x 100 Medley Relay.

Most Olympic Gold Medals in a Single Olympics, Women—6, Kristin Otto, East Germany, 1988: 50, 100 Free; 100 Back; 100 Fly; 4 x 100 Free Relay; 4 x 100 Medley Relay.

Most Olympic Medals in a Career, Men—11, Matt Biondi, United States: 1984 (one gold), '88 (five gold, one silver, one bronze); '92 (two gold, one silver); 11, Mark Spitz, United States: 1968 (two gold, one silver, one bronze), '72 (seven gold).

Most Olympic Medals in a Career, Women—10, Jenny Thompson, United States: 1992 (two gold, one silver), 1996 (three gold), 2000 (three gold, one bronze); 8, Dawn Fraser, Australia: 1956 (two gold, one silver), '60 (one gold, two silver), '64 (one gold, one silver); 8, Kornelia Ender, East Germany: 1972 (three silver), '76 (four gold, one silver); 8, Shirley Babashoff, United States: 1972 (one gold, two silver); '76 (one gold, four silver).

Winner, Same Event, Three Consecutive Olympics—Dawn Fraser, Australia, 100 Freestyle, 1956, '60, '64; Krisztina Egerszegi, Hungary, 200 Back, 1988, '92, '96.

Youngest Person to Win an Olympic Diving Gold—Marjorie Gestring, United States, 1936, 13 years, 9 months, springboard diving.

World Record Achievements

Youngest Person to Win an Olympic Swimming Gold—Krisztina Egerszegi, Hungary, 1988, 14 years, one month, 200 backstroke.

Most World Records, Career, Women—42, Ragnhild Hveger, Denmark, 1936–42.

Most World Records, Career, Men—32, Arne Borg, Sweden, 1921–29.

Most Freestyle Records Held Concurrently—5, Helene Madison, United States, 1931–33; 5, Shane Gould, Australia, 1972.

Most Consecutive Lowerings of a Record—10, Kornelia Ender, East Germany, 100 Freestyle, 7-13-73 to 7-19-76.

Longest Duration of World Record—19 years, 359 days, 1:04.6 in 100 Free, Willy den Ouden, Netherlands.

ALLESSANDRO TROVATI/AP

**Slalom specialist
Kristina Koznick of the
United States**

Skiing

My Oh Maier!

Austria's Hermann Maier continued his dominance with four World Cup titles

BY MARK BECHTEL

SKIING IS NOT a sport that lends itself to nice, round numbers. Races are timed to the thousandth of a second, and points in the season standings are handed out under a dizzying formula that yields head-scratching results. So let us appreciate Hermann Maier's achievement for its simplicity as well as its symmetry. The Herminator became the first skier to amass 2,000 points in a World Cup season. He hit the mark on the nose when he won the season's final Super G event, in Bormio, Italy, by a whopping 1.91 seconds. Maier had vowed to save his energy for the giant slalom, which was run the next day in Bormio, but, much to the delight of the hundreds of fans who attended the race with 2,000 painted on their faces, he achieved the nifty symmetry of 2,000 in 2000 with his win in the Super G.

Outright domination was the norm for Maier and his Austrian countrymen and women this season. With the defending overall champ, Lasse Kjus of Norway, shelved for most of the year by injuries, Maier clinched the championship with a week to spare. His points total doubled that of every other skier except for runner-up Kjetil-André Aamodt of Norway. Maier also became the third man to win four championships in a season by adding the downhill, Super G and Giant Slalom titles to his overall crown. Austrian men claimed the top *five* places in the Super G standings and Austrian women won season titles in three of five disciplines.

The only discipline Maier didn't win was the slalom, which was taken by Aamodt. But even as he wrapped up his slalom title by finishing sixth in Bormio despite suffering back pains so severe he could barely walk, Aamodt was upstaged by one of his countrymen, Finn Christian Jagge. The 1992 Olympic slalom gold medalist with the first name that belies his nation of origin, Jagge announced his retirement, then made his final run down the hill dressed in a tuxedo.

Jagge's black-tie attire notwithstanding,

Hermination: Maier won everything but the slalom.

CARL YARBROUGH

Maier was easily the classiest skier on the mountain. His quadruple triumph put him in the elite company of Pirmin Zubriggen and Jean-Claude Killy as the only men to win four titles in a single season. "I didn't know about that," Maier said after learning of the distinction. "But now that I do, it's cool."

Among the many Austrians doing cool things this season, Renate Götschl also stood out. Götschl, who lives on her family's farm in the village of Obdach, won the women's overall championship, outdistancing Michaela Dorfmeister, of—surprise—Austria. Götschl burst on the scene in 1993, winning the slalom in Hajfell, Norway (one of the Olympic test events), in her first World Cup appearance, but she failed to medal in both the '94 and '98 Games, and had a particularly heartbreaking Super G run in Nagano, where a late error cost her a medal. This year, though, Götschl won the season Super G title and finished within five points of taking the downhill as well, giving her the overall crown by a wide margin. "I can't really believe I did it. This overall makes up for losing the downhill title," she said, understating the case slightly.

While the Austrians dominated, the Americans put up their best showing in years. Daron Rahlves and Kristina Koznick each won a pair of races, giving the U.S. reason to hope that when the Olympics come to Salt Lake City in 2002 a skiing medal won't be out of the question.

Koznick, a 24-year-old Minnesotan who sometimes bleaches her hair white, won the last two slalom races of the year. The wins came after a subpar early season in which she struggled while searching for the right set of skis. "I had many problems getting adjusted to my new equipment," she said. "I had to start everything from scratch."

Rahlves, a Californian who has been known to bleach *his* hair, won back-to-back downhills in Kvitfjell, Norway, in March, the first wins of his career. Rahlves stands just 5'9" and weighs 180 pounds, which is light for a downhiller. But after two dislocated hips in seven years, he now works out religiously. The new regimen has added endurance and power to his modest frame. "Now I know what's inside of me," Rahlves said after his victories. "When I ski my best, it can be the best in the world. That's what I found out in Norway."

Rahlves might have been the best on two occasions, but he didn't cause anyone to forget about Maier. Near season's end the Austrian talked about what the future held for him. "Next year I want to win one race at St. Anton during the world championships and then the Olympic downhill in 2002," Maier said. "It's the last major title I'm missing."

His more immediate plans were a lot simpler. "I want to have a safe week in Italy," he said, heading into the year's final races, "and then have a great party, which will last for weeks. I think I deserve it."

FOR THE RECORD · 1999 – 2000

World Cup Alpine Racing Season Results

Men

Date	Event	Site	Winner
10-31-99	Giant Slalom	Tignes, France	Hermann Maier, Austria
11-23-99	Slalom	Beaver Creek, Colorado	Didier Plaschy, Switzerland
11-24-99	Giant Slalom	Beaver Creek, Colorado	Hermann Maier, Austria
11-27-99	Downhill	Vail, Colorado	Hermann Maier, Austria
11-28-99	Super G	Vail, Colorado	Hermann Maier, Austria
12-4-99	Downhill	Lake Louise, Alberta	Hannes Trinkl, Austria
12-5-99	Super G	Lake Louise, Alberta	Hermann Maier, Austria
12-13-99	Slalom	Madonna di Campiglio, Italy	Finn Christian Jagge, Norway
12-17-99	Downhill	Val Gardena, Italy	Kristian Ghedina, Italy
12-18-99	Giant Slalom	Alta Badia, Italy	Joel Chenal, France
12-18-99	Downhill	Val Gardena, Italy	Andreas Schifferer, Austria
12-21-99	Slalom	Kranjska Gora, Slovenia	Didier Plaschy, Switzerland
12-22-99	Giant Slalom	Saalbach-Hinterglemm, Austria	Christian Mayer, Austria
1-8-00	Downhill	Chamonix, France	Hermann Maier, Austria
1-9-00	Slalom	Chamonix, France	Angelo Weiss, Italy
1-15-00	Downhill	Wengen, Switzerland	Josef Strobl, Austria
1-15-00	Slalom	Wengen, Switzerland	Kjetil Andre Aamodt, Norway
1-21-00	Super G	Kitzbühel, Austria	Hermann Maier, Austria
1-22-00	Downhill	Kitzbühel, Austria	Fritz Strobl, Austria
1-23-00	Slalom	Kitzbühel, Austria	Mario Matt, Austria
1-29-00	Downhill	Garmisch-Partenkirchen, Germany	Hermann Maier, Austria
2-5-00	Giant Slalom	Todtnau, Germany	Hermann Maier, Austria
2-6-00	Slalom	Todtnau, Germany	Rainer Schoenfelder, Austria
2-12-00	Super G	St. Anton, Austria	Josef Strobl, Austria
2-13-00	Super G	St. Anton, Austria	Werner Franz/Fritz Strobl, Austria
2-19-00	Slalom	Adelboden, Switzerland	Matjaz Vrhovnik, Slovenia
2-26-00	Giant Slalom	Yongpyong, S Korea	Benjamin Raich, Austria
2-26-00	Slalom	Yongpyong, S Korea	Mitja Kunc, Slovenia
3-3-00	Downhill	Kvitfjell, Norway	Daron Rahlves, United States
3-4-00	Downhill	Kvitfjell, Norway	Daron Rahlves, United States
3-4-00	Super G	Kvitfjell, Norway	Kristian Ghedina, Italy
3-8-00	Giant Slalom	Kranjska Gora, Slovenia	Christian Mayer, Austria
3-9-00	Slalom	Schladming, Austria	Mario Matt, Austria
3-11-00	Giant Slalom	Hinterstoder, Austria	Christian Mayer, Austria
3-15-00	Downhill	Bormio, Italy	Hannes Trinkl, Austria
3-17-00	Super G	Bormio, Italy	Hermann Maier, Austria
3-18-00	Giant Slalom	Bormio, Italy	Benjamin Raich, Austria
3-19-00	Slalom	Bormio, Italy	Ole Christian Furuseth, Norway

Women

Date	Event	Site	Winner
10-30-99	Giant Slalom	Tignes, France	Sonja Nef, Switzerland
11-17-99	Giant Slalom	Copper Mountain, Colorado	Regine Cavagnoud, France
11-20-99	Slalom	Copper Mountain, Colorado	Christel Saioni, France
11-27-99	Downhill	Lake Louise, Alberta	Isolde Kostner, Italy
11-28-99	Super G	Lake Louise, Alberta	Mojca Suhadolc, Slovenia
12-4-99	Giant Slalom	Serre Chevalier, France	Michaela Dorfmeister, Austria
12-5-99	Slalom	Serre Chevalier, France	Janica Kostelic, Croatia
12-8-99	Super G	Val d'Isere, France	Isolde Kostner, Italy
12-9-00	Giant Slalom	Val d'Isere, France	Michaela Dorfmeister, Austria
12-12-99	Slalom	Sestriere, Italy	Janica Kostelic, Croatia
12-17-99	Downhill	St. Moritz, Switzerland	Isolde Kostner, Italy
12-17-99	Super G	St. Moritz, Switzerland	Karen Putzer, Italy
12-17-99	Downhill	St. Moritz, Switzerland	Pernilla Wiberg, Sweden
12-28-99	Giant Slalom	Lienz, Austria	Anita Wachter, Austria
12-28-99	Slalom	Lienz, Austria	Sabine Egger, Austria
1-5-00	Giant Slalom	Maribor, Slovenia	Michaela Dorfmeister, Austria
1-6-00	Slalom	Maribor, Slovenia	Trine Bakke, Norway
1-8-00	Giant Slalom	Berchtesgaden, Germany	Michaela Dorfmeister, Austria
1-9-00	Slalom	Berchtesgaden, Germany	Spela Pretnar, Slovenia
1-15-00	Downhill	Altenmark-Zauch., Austria	Corinne Rey Bellet, Switzerland
1-15-00	Super G	Altenmark-Zauch., Austria	Renate Götschl, Austria
1-21-00	Downhill	Cortina d'Ampezzo, Italy	Regine Cavagnoud, France
1-23-00	Giant Slalom	Cortina d'Ampezzo, Italy	Anna Ottosson, Sweden
2-10-00	Downhill	Santa Caterina, Italy	Isolde Kostner, Italy
2-11-00	Super G	Santa Caterina, Italy	Michaela Dorfmeister, Austria
2-12-00	Slalom	Santa Caterina, Italy	Spela Pretnar, Slovenia

Women (Cont.)

Date	Event	Site	Winner
2-17-00	Giant Slalom	Are, Sweden	Sonja Nef, Switzerland
2-17-00	Downhill	Are, Sweden	Renate Götschl, Austria
2-17-00	Slalom	Are, Sweden	Spela Pretnar, Slovenia
2-26-00	Super G	Innsbruck, Austria	Melanie Turgeon, Canada
2-26-00	Downhill	Innsbruck, Austria	Renate Götschl, Austria
2-26-00	Super G	Innsbruck, Austria	Renate Götschl, Austria
3-4-00	Downhill	Lenzerheide, Switzerland	Corinne Imlig, Switzerland
3-10-00	Slalom	Sestriere, Italy	Kristina Koznick, United States
3-12-00	Giant Slalom	Sestriere, Italy	Sonja Nef, Switzerland
3-15-00	Slalom	Bormio, Itlay	Kristina Koznick, United States
3-16-00	Super G	Bormio, Italy	Renate Götschl, Austria
3-16-00	Downhill	Bormio, Italy	Regine Cavagnoud, France
3-18-00	Giant Slalom	Bormio, Italy	Brigitte Obermoser, Austria

World Cup Alpine Racing Final Standings

Men

OVERALL
	Pts
Hermann Maier, Austria	2000
Kjetil André Aamodt, Norway	1440
Josef Stroble, Austria	994
Kristian Ghedina, Italy	958
Andreas Schifferer, Austria	905
Stephan Eberharter, Austria	904
Fritz Strobl, Austria	889
Christian Mayer, Austria	802
Benjamin Raich, Austria	788
Franz Werner, Austria	762

DOWNHILL
	Pts
Hermann Maier, Austria	800
Kristian Ghedina, Italy	677
Josef Strobl, Austria	533
Hannes Trinkl, Austria	507
Stephan Eberharter, Austria	454
Fritz Strobl, Austria	453
Andreas Schifferer, Austria	354
Franz Werner, Austria	317
Ed Podivinsky, Canada	298
Daron Rahlves, United States	273

SLALOM
	Pts
Kjetil André Aamodt, Norway	598
O. Furuseth, Norway	544
Matjaz Vrhovnik, Slovenia	538
Mario Matt, Austria	384
Thomas Stangassinger, Austria	369
Benjamin Raich, Austria	368
Rainer Schoenfelder, Austria	307
Didier Plaschy, Switzerland	281
Hans-Petter Buraas, Norway	261
Jure Kosir, Slovenia	238

GIANT SLALOM
	Pts
Hermann Maier, Austria	520
Christian Mayer, Austria	517
Michael von Grünigen, Switz.	466
Benjamin Raich, Austria	420
Joel Chenal, France	349
Marco Buechel, Liechtenstein	290
Fredrik Nyberg, Sweden	279
Mitja Kunc, Slovenia	275
Kjetil André Aamodt, Norway	259
Heinz Schilchegger, Austria	233

SUPER G
	Pts
Hermann Maier, Austria	540
Franz Werner, Austria	371
Fritz Strobl, Austria	354
Josef Strobl, Austria	305
Andreas Schifferer, Austria	294
Fredrik Nyberg, Sweden	272
Stephan Eberharter, Austria	246
Kristian Ghedina, Italy	216
Didier Cuche, Switzerland	214
Daron Rahlves, United States	183

Women

OVERALL
	Pts
Renate Götschl, Austria	1631
Michaela Dorfmeister, Austria	1306
Regine Cavagnoud, France	1036
Isolde Kostner, Italy	878
Brigitte Obermoser, Austria	806
Sonja Nef, Switzerland	789
Spela Pretnar, Slovenia	714
Anja Paerson, Sweden	704
Martina Ertl, Germany	701
Tanja Schneider, Austria	695

DOWNHILL
	Pts
Regina Haeusl, Germany	529
Renate Götschl, Austria	524
Isolde Kostner, Italy	484
Corinne Rey Bellet, Switz.	435
Regine Cavagnoud, France	417
Tanja Schneider, Austria	303
Michaela Dorfmeister, Austria	290
Martina Ertl, Germany	243
Melanie Turgeon, Canada	240
Stefanie Schuster, Austria	232

SLALOM
	Pts
Spela Pretnar, Slovenia	645
Christel Saioni, France	626
Anja Paerson, Sweden	499
Trine Bakke, Norway	434
Kristina Koznick, United States	428
Sabine Egger, Austria	417
Vanessa Vidal, France	305
Karin Koellerer, Austria	279
Natasa Bokal, Slovenia	260
Janica Kostelic, Croatia	250

GIANT SLALOM
	Pts
Michaela Dorfmeister, Austria	684
Sonja Nef, Switzerland	602
Anita Wachter, Austria	470
Anna Ottosson, Sweden	402
Allison Forsyth, Canada	373
Karen Putzer, Italy	371
Birgit Heeb, Liechtenstein	340
Brigitte Obermoser, Austria	313
Christiane Mitterwallner, Austria	271
Renate Götschl, Austria	266

SUPER G
	Pts
Renate Götschl, Austria	554
Melanie Turgeon, Canada	343
Mojca Suhadolc, Slovenia	341
Regine Cavagnoud, France	330
Isolde Kostner, Italy	300
Tanja Schneider, Austria	296
Michaela Dorfmeister, Austria	287
Brigitte Obermoser, Austria	268
Melanie Suchet, France	195
Hilde Gerg, Germany	178

FOR THE RECORD · Year by Year

Event Descriptions

Downhill: A speed event entailing a single run on a course with a minimum vertical drop of 500 meters (800 for Men's World Cup) and very few control gates.
Slalom: A technical event in which times for runs on two courses are totaled to determine the winner. Skiers must make many quick, short turns through a combination of gates (55-75 gates for men, 40-60 for women) over a short course (140-220–meter vertical drop for men, 120-180 for women).
Combined: An event in which scores from designated slalom and downhill races are combined to determine finish order.

Giant Slalom: A faster technical event with fewer, more broadly spaced gates than in the slalom. Times for runs on two courses with vertical drops of 250-400 meters for men and 250-300 meters for women are combined to determine the winner.
Super Giant Slalom: A speed event that is a cross between the downhill and the giant slalom.
Parallel Slalom: A technical event that combines slalom and giant slalom turns.

FIS World Championships

Sites

1931 ....Mürren, Switzerland	1936 ....Innsbruck, Austria
1932 ....Cortina d'Ampezzo, Italy	1937 ....Chamonix, France
1933 ....Innsbruck, Austria	1938 ....Engelberg, Switzerland
1934 ....St Moritz, Switzerland	1939 ....Zakopane, Poland
1935 ....Mürren, Switzerland	

Men

DOWNHILL

1931 ....Walter Prager, Switzerland
1932 ....Gustav Lantschner, Austria
1933 ....Walter Prager, Switzerland
1934 ....David Zogg, Switzerland
1935 ....Franz Zingerle, Austria
1936 ....Rudolf Rominger, Switzerland
1937 ....Émile Allais, France
1938 ....James Couttet, France
1939 ....Hans Lantschner, Germany

SLALOM

1931 ....David Zogg, Switzerland
1932 ....Friedrich Dauber, Germany
1933 ....Anton Seelos, Austria
1934 ....Franz Pfnür, Germany
1935 ....Anton Seelos, Austria
1936 ....Rudi Matt, Austria
1937 ....Émile Allais, France
1938 ....Rudolf Rominger, Switzerland
1939 ....Rudolf Rominger, Switzerland

Women

DOWNHILL

1931 ....Esme Mackinnon, Great Britain
1932 ....Paola Wiesinger, Italy
1933 ....Inge Wersin-Lantschner, Austria
1934 ....Anni Rüegg, Switzerland
1935 ....Christel Cranz, Germany
1936 ....Evie Pinching, Great Britain
1937 ....Christel Cranz, Germany
1938 ....Lisa Resch, Germany
1939 ....Christel Cranz, Germany

SLALOM

1931 ....Esme Mackinnon, Great Britain
1932 ....Rösli Streiff, Switzerland
1933 ....Inge Wersin-Lantschner, Austria
1934 ....Christel Cranz, Germany
1935 ....Anni Rüegg, Switzerland
1936 ....Gerda Paumgarten, Austria
1937 ....Christel Cranz, Germany
1938 ....Christel Cranz, Germany
1939 ....Christel Cranz, Germany

FIS World Alpine Ski Championships

Sites

1950 ....Aspen, Colorado	1982 ....Schladming, Austria
1954 ....Are, Sweden	1985 ....Bormio, Italy
1958 ....Badgastein, Austria	1987 ....Crans-Montana, Switzerland
1962 ....Chamonix, France	1989 ....Vail, Colorado
1966 ....Portillo, Chile	1991 ....Saalbach-Hinterglemm, Austria
1970 ....Val Gardena, Italy	1993 ....Morioka-Shizukuishi, Japan
1974 ....St Moritz, Switzerland	1996 ....Sierra Nevada, Spain
1978 ....Garmisch-Partenkirchen, West Germany	1997 ....Sestriere, Italy
	1999 ....Vail, Colorado

Men

DOWNHILL

1950.............Zeno Colo, Italy
1954.............Christian Pravda, Austria
1958.............Toni Sailer, Austria
1962.............Karl Schranz, Austria
1966.............Jean-Claude Killy, France
1970.............Bernard Russi, Switzerland
1974.............David Zwilling, Austria
1978.............Josef Walcher, Austria
1982.............Harti Weirather, Austria

1985.............Pirmin Zurbriggen, Switzerland
1987.............Peter Müller, Switzerland
1989.............Hansjörg Tauscher, West Germany
1991.............Franz Heinzer, Switzerland
1993.............Urs Lehmann, Switzerland
1996.............Patrick Ortlieb, Austria
1997.............Bruno Kernen, Switzerland
1999.............Hermann Maier, Austria

SLALOM

1950.............Georges Schneider, Switzerland
1954.............Stein Eriksen, Norway
1958.............Josl Rieder, Austria
1962.............Charles Bozon, France
1966.............Carlo Senoner, Italy
1970.............Jean-Noël Augert, France
1974.............Gustavo Thoeni, Italy
1978.............Ingemar Stenmark, Sweden
1982.............Ingemar Stenmark, Sweden

1985.............Jonas Nilsson, Sweden
1987.............Frank Wörndl, West Germany
1989.............Rudolf Nierlich, Austria
1991.............Marc Girardelli, Luxembourg
1993.............Kjetil André Aamodt, Norway
1996.............Alberto Tomba, Italy
1997.............Tom Stiansen, Norway
1999.............Lasse Kjus, Norway

GIANT SLALOM

1950.............Zeno Colo, Italy
1954.............Stein Eriksen, Norway
1958.............Toni Sailer, Austria
1962.............Egon Zimmermann, Austria
1966.............Guy Périllat, France
1970.............Karl Schranz, Austria
1974.............Gustavo Thoeni, Italy
1978.............Ingemar Stenmark, Sweden
1982.............Steve Mahre, United States

1985.............Markus Wasmaier, West Germany
1987.............Pirmin Zurbriggen, Switzerland
1989.............Rudolf Nierlich, Austria
1991.............Rudolf Nierlich, Austria
1993.............Kjetil André Aamodt, Norway
1996.............Alberto Tomba, Italy
1997.............Michael von Grünigen, Switzerland
1999.............Marco Büchel, Liechtenstein

COMBINED

1982.............Michel Vion, France
1985.............Pirmin Zurbriggen, Switzerland
1987.............Marc Girardelli, Luxembourg
1989.............Marc Girardelli, Luxembourg
1991.............Stefan Eberharter, Austria

1993.............Lasse Kjus, Norway
1996.............Marc Girardelli, Luxembourg
1997.............Kjetil André Aamodt, Norway
1999.............Not contested

SUPER G

1987.............Pirmin Zurbriggen, Switzerland
1989.............Martin Hangl, Switzerland
1991.............Stefan Eberharter, Austria
1993.............Cancelled due to weather

1996.............Atle Skaardal, Norway
1997.............Atle Skaardal, Norway
1999.............Hermann Maier, Austria
                  Lasse Kjus, Norway

Women

DOWNHILL

1950.............Trude Beiser-Jochum, Austria
1954.............Ida Schopfer, Switzerland
1958.............Lucile Wheeler, Canada
1962.............Christl Haas, Austria
1966.............Erika Schinegger, Austria
1970.............Annerösli Zryd, Switzerland
1974.............Annemarie Moser-Pröll, Austria
1978.............Annemarie Moser-Pröll, Austria
1982.............Gerry Sorensen, Canada

1985.............Michela Figini, Switzerland
1987.............Maria Walliser, Switzerland
1989.............Maria Walliser, Switzerland
1991.............Petra Kronberger, Austria
1993.............Kate Pace, Canada
1996.............Picabo Street, United States
1997.............Hilary Lindh, United States
1999.............Renate Götschl, Austria

Women *(Cont.)*

SLALOM

1950............Dagmar Rom, Austria	1985............Perrine Pelen, France
1954............Trude Klecker, Austria	1987............Erika Hess, Switzerland
1958............Inger Bjornbakken, Norway	1989............Mateja Svet, Yugoslavia
1962............Marianne Jahn, Austria	1991............Vreni Schneider, Switzerland
1966............Annie Famose, France	1993............Karin Buder, Austria
1970............Ingrid Lafforgue, France	1996............Pernilla Wiberg, Sweden
1974............Hanni Wenzel, Liechtenstein	1997............Deborah Compagnoni, Italy
1978............Lea Sölkner, Austria	1999............Trine Bakke, Norway
1982............Erika Hess, Switzerland	

GIANT SLALOM

1950............Dagmar Rom, Austria	1985 ....Diann Roffe, United States
1954............Lucienne Schmith-Couttet, France	1987 ....Vreni Schneider, Switzerland
1958............Lucile Wheeler, Canada	1989 ....Vreni Schneider, Switzerland
1962............Marianne Jahn, Austria	1991 ....Pernilla Wiberg, Sweden
1966............Marielle Goitschel, France	1993 ....Carole Merle, France
1970............Betsy Clifford, Canada	1996 ....Deborah Compagnoni, Italy
1974............Fabienne Serrat, France	1997 ....Deborah Compagnoni, Italy
1978............Maria Epple, West Germany	1999 ....Anita Wachter, Austria
1982............Erika Hess, Switzerland	

COMBINED

1982 ....Erika Hess, Switzerland	1993 ....Miriam Vogt, Germany
1985 ....Erika Hess, Switzerland	1996 ....Pernilla Wiberg, Sweden
1987 ....Erika Hess, Switzerland	1997 ....Renate Götschl, Austria
1989 ....Tamara McKinney, United States	1999 ....Not contested
1991 ....Chantal Bournissen, Switzerland	

SUPER G

1987 ....Maria Walliser, Switzerland	1996 ....Isolde Kostner, Italy
1989 ....Ulrike Maier, Austria	1997 ....Isolde Kostner, Italy
1991 ....Ulrike Maier, Austria	1999 ....Alexandra Meissnitzer, Austria
1993 ....Katja Seizinger, Germany	

Note: The 1995 FIS World Alpine Ski Championships were postponed to 1996 due to lack of snow.

The Kick of Kitzbühel

Hermann Maier of Austria may have been a world and Olympic champion with the coolest nickname in skiing and a gaudy 352-point lead in skiing in late January 2000, but the Herminator still hadn't won his sport's most prestigious race. He placed fourth in the Hahnenkamm downhill in Kitzbühel, Austria on Jan. 22, a day after winning the Super G there. At the downhill finish, a dejected Maier said, "I thought at one point I should get off my skis and push."

Austrians won three of four events and took eight of the top 10 downhill places in the Hahnenkamm, or "rooster's comb," named for the distinctive red cliffs above the 900-year-old Tyrolean village. The Hahnenkamm's southern hill, the Streif, is Mecca to ski racers, many of whom have found religion on its plunging turns. The downhillers face a drop of 860 meters at speeds of up to 100 mph. They usually pass sections called the Mousetrap—the race started below it in 2000 because of fog—and Steep Wall even before they enter the narrow flats and icy jumps that threaten disaster. In 1989 Brian Stemmle of Canada wound up on life support after a fall at Steep Wall snapped his pelvis.

Asked after Bill Johnson's downhill victory at the '84 Olympics if the American had joined the downhill elite, Austria's Franz Klammer, the '76 Olympic champ and a four-time Hahnenkamm winner, looked out at Sarajevo's tame course and said, "This is for children. He has to win a downhill at Kitzbühel."

Notwithstanding his preeminence in the sport, so does Maier.

World Cup Season Title Holders

Men

OVERALL

1967	Jean-Claude Killy, France
1968	Jean-Claude Killy, France
1969	Karl Schranz, Austria
1970	Karl Schranz, Austria
1971	Gustavo Thoeni, Italy
1972	Gustavo Thoeni, Italy
1973	Gustavo Thoeni, Italy
1974	Piero Gros, Italy
1975	Gustavo Thoeni, Italy
1976	Ingemar Stenmark, Sweden
1977	Ingemar Stenmark, Sweden
1978	Ingemar Stenmark, Sweden
1979	Peter Lüscher, Switzerland
1980	Andreas Wenzel, Liechtenstein
1981	Phil Mahre, United States
1982	Phil Mahre, United States
1983	Phil Mahre, United States
1984	Pirmin Zurbriggen, Switzerland
1985	Marc Girardelli, Luxembourg
1986	Marc Girardelli, Luxembourg
1987	Pirmin Zurbriggen, Switzerland
1988	Pirmin Zurbriggen, Switzerland
1989	Marc Girardelli, Luxembourg
1990	Pirmin Zurbriggen, Switzerland
1991	Marc Girardelli, Luxembourg
1992	Paul Accola, Switzerland
1993	Marc Girardelli, Luxembourg
1994	Kjetil André Aamodt, Norway
1995	Alberto Tomba, Italy
1996	Lasse Kjus, Norway
1997	Luc Alphand, France
1998	Hermann Maier, Austria
1999	Lasse Kjus, Norway
2000	Hermann Maier, Austria

DOWNHILL

1967	Jean-Claude Killy, France
1968	Gerhard Nenning, Austria
1969	Karl Schranz, Austria
1970	Karl Schranz, Austria
	Karl Cordin, Austria
1971	Bernhard Russi, Switzerland
1972	Bernhard Russi, Switzerland
1973	Roland Collumbin, Switzerland
1974	Roland Collumbin, Switzerland
1975	Franz Klammer, Austria
1976	Franz Klammer, Austria
1977	Franz Klammer, Austria
1978	Franz Klammer, Austria
1979	Peter Müller, Switzerland
1980	Peter Müller, Switzerland
1981	Harti Weirather, Austria
1982	Steve Podborski, Canada
	Peter Müller, Switzerland
1983	Franz Klammer, Austria
1984	Urs Raber, Switzerland
1985	Helmut Höflehner, Austria
1986	Peter Wirnsberger, Austria
1987	Pirmin Zurbriggen, Switzerland
1988	Pirmin Zurbriggen, Switzerland
1989	Marc Girardelli, Luxembourg
1990	Helmut Höflehner, Austria
1991	Franz Heinzer, Switzerland
1992	Franz Heinzer, Switzerland
1993	Franz Heinzer, Switzerland
1994	Marc Girardelli, Luxembourg
1995	Luc Alphand, France
1996	Luc Alphand, France
1997	Luc Alphand, France
1998	Andreas Schifferer, Austria
1999	Lasse Kjus, Norway
2000	Hermann Maier, Austria

SLALOM

1967	Jean-Claude Killy, France
1968	Domeng Giovanoli, Switzerland
1969	Jean-Noël Augert, France
1970	Patrick Russel, France
	Alain Penz, France
1971	Jean-Noël Augert, France
1972	Jean-Noël Augert, France
1973	Gustavo Thoeni, Italy
1974	Gustavo Thoeni, Italy
1975	Ingemar Stenmark, Sweden
1976	Ingemar Stenmark, Sweden
1977	Ingemar Stenmark, Sweden
1978	Ingemar Stenmark, Sweden
1979	Ingemar Stenmark, Sweden
1980	Ingemar Stenmark, Sweden
1981	Ingemar Stenmark, Sweden
1982	Phil Mahre, United States
1983	Ingemar Stenmark, Sweden
1984	Marc Girardelli, Luxembourg
1985	Marc Girardelli, Luxembourg
1986	Rok Petrovic, Yugoslavia
1987	Bojan Krizaj, Yugoslavia
1988	Alberto Tomba, Italy
1989	Armin Bittner, West Germany
1990	Armin Bittner, West Germany
1991	Marc Girardelli, Luxembourg
1992	Alberto Tomba, Italy
1993	Tomas Fogdof, Sweden
1994	Alberto Tomba, Italy
1995	Alberto Tomba, Italy
1996	Sebastien Amiez, France
1997	Thomas Sykora, Austria
1998	Thomas Sykora, Austria
1999	Thomas Stangassinger, Austria
2000	Kjetil André Aamodt, Norway

Men (Cont.)

GIANT SLALOM

1967	Jean-Claude Killy, France
1968	Jean-Claude Killy, France
1969	Karl Schranz, Austria
1970	Gustavo Thoeni, Italy
1971	Patrick Russel, France
1972	Gustavo Thoeni, Italy
1973	Hans Hinterseer, Austria
1974	Piero Gros, Italy
1975	Ingemar Stenmark, Sweden
1976	Ingemar Stenmark, Sweden
1977	Heini Hemmi, Switzerland
	Ingemar Stenmark, Sweden
1978	Ingemar Stenmark, Sweden
1979	Ingemar Stenmark, Sweden
1980	Ingemar Stenmark, Sweden
1981	Ingemar Stenmark, Sweden
1982	Phil Mahre, United States
1983	Phil Mahre, United States
1984	Ingemar Stenmark, Sweden
	Pirmin Zurbriggen, Switzerland
1985	Marc Girardelli, Luxembourg
1986	Joël Gaspoz, Switzerland
1987	Joël Gaspoz, Switzerland
	Pirmin Zurbriggen, Switzerland
1988	Alberto Tomba, Italy
1989	Pirmin Zurbriggen, Switzerland
1990	Ole-Cristian Furuseth, Norway
	Günther Mader, Austria
1991	Alberto Tomba, Italy
1992	Alberto Tomba, Italy
1993	Kjetil André Aamodt, Norway
1994	Christian Mayer, Austria
1995	Alberto Tomba, Italy
1996	Michael von Grünigen, Switzerland
1997	Michael von Grünigen, Switzerland
1998	Hermann Maier, Austria
1999	Michael von Grünigen, Switzerland
2000	Hermann Maier, Austria

SUPER G

1986	Markus Wasmeier, West Germany
1987	Pirmin Zurbriggen, Switzerland
1988	Pirmin Zurbriggen, Switzerland
1989	Pirmin Zurbriggen, Switzerland
1990	Pirmin Zurbriggen, Switzerland
1991	Franz Heinzer, Switzerland
1992	Paul Accola, Switzerland
1993	Kjetil André Aamodt, Norway
1994	Jan Einar Thorsen, Norway
1995	Peter Runggaldier, Italy
1996	Atle Skaardal, Norway
1997	Luc Alphand, France
1998	Hermann Maier, Austria
1999	Hermann Maier, Austria
2000	Hermann Maier, Austria

COMBINED

1979	Andreas Wenzel, Liechtenstein
1980	Andreas Wenzel, Liechtenstein
1981	Phil Mahre, United States
1982	Phil Mahre, United States
1983	Phil Mahre, United States
1984	Andreas Wenzel, Liechtenstein
1985	Andreas Wenzel, Liechtenstein
1986	Markus Wasmeier, West Germany
1987	Pirmin Zurbriggen, Switzerland
1988	Hubert Strolz, Austria
1989	Marc Girardelli, Luxembourg
1990	Pirmin Zurbriggen, Switzerland
1991	Marc Girardelli, Luxembourg
1992	Paul Accola, Switzerland
1993	Marc Girardelli, Luxembourg
1994	Kjetil André Aamodt, Norway
1995	Marc Girardelli, Luxembourg
1996	Günther Mader, Austria
1997	Kjetil André Aamodt, Norway
1998	Werner Franz, Austria
1999	Kjetil André Aamodt, Norway
2000	Kjetil André Aamodt, Norway
	Lasse Kjus, Norway

Women

OVERALL

1967	Nancy Greene, Canada
1968	Nancy Greene, Canada
1969	Gertrud Gabl, Austria
1970	Michèle Jacot, France
1971	Annemarie Pröll, Austria
1972	Annemarie Pröll, Austria
1973	Annemarie Pröll, Austria
1974	Annemarie Moser-Pröll, Austria
1975	Annemarie Moser-Pröll, Austria
1976	Rosi Mitermaier, West Germany
1977	Lise-Marie Morerod, Switzerland
1978	Hanni Wenzel, Liechtenstein
1979	Annemarie Moser-Pröll, Austria
1980	Hanni Wenzel, Liechtenstein
1981	Marie-Thérèse Nadig, Switzerland
1982	Erika Hess, Switzerland
1983	Tamara McKinney, United States
1984	Erika Hess, Switzerland
1985	Michela Figini, Switzerland
1986	Maria Walliser, Switzerland
1987	Maria Walliser, Switzerland
1988	Michela Figini, Switzerland
1989	Vreni Schneider, Switzerland
1990	Petra Kronberger, Austria
1991	Petra Kronberger, Austria
1992	Petra Kronberger, Austria
1993	Anita Wachter, Austria
1994	Vreni Schneider, Switzerland
1995	Vreni Schneider, Switzerland
1996	Katja Seizinger, Germany
1997	Pernilla Wiberg, Sweden
1998	Katja Seizinger, Germany
1999	Alexandra Meissnitzer, Austria
2000	Renate Götschl, Austria

Women (Cont.)

DOWNHILL

1967	Marielle Goitschel, France	1984	Maria Walliser, Switzerland
1968	Isabelle Mir, France & Olga Pall, Austria	1985	Michela Figini, Switzerland
1969	Wiltrud Drexel, Austria	1986	Maria Walliser, Switzerland
1970	Isabelle Mir, France	1987	Michela Figini, Switzerland
1971	Annemarie Pröll, Austria	1988	Michela Figini, Switzerland
1972	Annemarie Pröll, Austria	1989	Michela Figini, Switzerland
1973	Annemarie Pröll, Austria	1990	Katrin Gutensohn-Knopf, Germany
1974	Annemarie Moser-Pröll, Austria	1991	Chantal Bournissen, Switzerland
1975	Annemarie Moser-Pröll, Austria	1992	Katja Seizinger, Germany
1976	Brigitte Totschnig, Austria	1993	Katja Seizinger, Germany
1977	Brigitte Totschnig-Habersatter, Austria	1994	Katja Seizinger, Germany
1978	Annemarie Moser-Pröll, Austria	1995	Picabo Street, United States
1979	Annemarie Moser-Pröll, Austria	1996	Picabo Street, United States
1980	Marie-Thérèse Nadig, Switzerland	1997	Renate Götschl, Austria
1981	Marie-Thérèse Nadig, Switzerland	1998	Katja Seizinger, Germany
1982	Marie-Cecile Gros-Gaudenier, France	1999	Renate Götschl, Austria
1983	Doris De Agostini, Switzerland	2000	Regina Haeusl, Germany

SLALOM

1967	Marielle Goitschel, France	1985	Erika Hess, Switzerland
1968	Marielle Goitschel, France	1986	Roswitha Steiner, Austria
1969	Gertrud Gabl, Austria		Erika Hess, Switzerland
1970	Ingrid Lafforgue, France	1987	Corrine Schmidhauser, Switzerland
1971	Britt Lafforgue, France	1988	Roswitha Steiner, Austria
1972	Britt Lafforgue, France	1989	Vreni Schneider, Switzerland
1973	Patricia Emonet, France	1990	Vreni Schneider, Switzerland
1974	Christa Zechmeister, West Germany	1991	Petra Kronberger, Austria
1975	Lise-Marie Morerod, Switzerland	1992	Vreni Schneider, Switzerland
1976	Rosi Mittermaier, West Germany	1993	Vreni Schneider, Switzerland
1977	Lise-Marie Morerod, Switzerland	1994	Vreni Schneider, Switzerland
1978	Hanni Wenzel, Liechtenstein	1995	Vreni Schneider, Switzerland
1979	Regina Sackl, Austria	1996	Elfi Eder, Austria
1980	Perrine Pelen, France	1997	Pernilla Wiberg, Sweden
1981	Erika Hess, Switzerland	1998	Ylva Nowen, Sweden
1982	Erika Hess, Switzerland	1999	Sabine Egger, Austria
1983	Erika Hess, Switzerland	2000	Spela Pretnar, Slovenia
1984	Tamara McKinney, United States		

GIANT SLALOM

1967	Nancy Greene, Canada	1985	Maria Keihl, West Germany
1968	Nancy Greene, Canada		Michela Figini, Switzerland
1969	Marilyn Cochran, United States	1986	Vreni Schneider, Switzerland
1970	Michèle Jacot, France	1987	Vreni Schneider, Switzerland
	Françoise Macchi, France		Maria Walliser, Switzerland
1971	Annemarie Pröll, Austria	1988	Mateja Svet, Yugoslavia
1972	Annemarie Pröll, Austria	1989	Vreni Schneider, Switzerland
1973	Monika Kaserer, Austria	1990	Anita Wachter, Austria
1974	Hanni Wenzel, Liechtenstein	1991	Vreni Schneider, Switzerland
1975	Annemarie Moser-Pröll, Austria	1992	Carole Merle, France
1976	Lise-Marie Morerod, Switzerland	1993	Carole Merle, France
1977	Lise-Marie Morerod, Switzerland	1994	Anita Wachter, Austria
1978	Lise-Marie Morerod, Switzerland	1995	Vreni Schneider, Switzerland
1979	Christa Kinshofer, West Germany	1996	Martina Ertl, Germany
1980	Hanni Wenzel, Liechtenstein	1997	Deborah Compagnoni, Italy
1981	Marie-Thérèse Nadig, Switzerland	1998	Martina Ertl, Germany
1982	Irene Epple, West Germany	1999	Alexandra Meissnitzer, Austria
1983	Tamara McKinney, United States	2000	Michaela Dorfmeister, Austria
1984	Erika Hess, Switzerland		

SUPER G

1986	Maria Kiehl, West Germany	1991	Carole Merle, France
1987	Maria Walliser, Switzerland	1992	Carole Merle, France
1988	Michela Figini, Switzerland	1993	Katja Seizinger, Germany
1989	Carole Merle, France	1994	Katja Seizinger, Germany
1990	Carole Merle, France	1995	Katja Seizinger, Germany

Women (Cont.)

SUPER G (CONT.)

1996 ....Katja Seizinger, Germany	1999 ....Alexandra Meissnitzer, Austria
1997 ....Hilde Gerg, Germany	2000 ....Renate Götschl, Austria
1998 ....Katja Seizinger, Germany	

COMBINED

1979 ....Annemarie Moser-Pröll, Austria	1990 ....Anita Wachter, Austria
Hanni Wenzel, Liechtenstein	1991 ....Sabine Ginther, Austria
1980 ....Hanni Wenzel, Liechtenstein	1992 ....Sabine Ginther, Austria
1981 ....Marie-Thérèse Nadig, Switzerland	1993 ....Anita Wachter, Austria
1982 ....Irene Epple, West Germany	1994 ....Pernilla Wiberg, Sweden
1983 ....Hanni Wenzel, Liechtenstein	1995 ....Pernilla Wiberg, Sweden
1984 ....Erika Hess, Switzerland	1996 ....Anita Wachter, Austria
1985 ....Brigitte Oertli, Switzerland	1997 ....Pernilla Wiberg, Sweden
1986 ....Maria Walliser, Switzerland	1998 ....Hilde Gerg, Germany
1987 ....Brigitte Oertli, Switzerland	1999 ....Hilde Gerg, Germany
1988 ....Brigitte Oertli, Switzerland	2000 ....Renate Götschl, Austria
1989 ....Brigitte Oertli, Switzerland	

World Cup Career Victories

Men

DOWNHILL

25............................Franz Klammer, Austria	
19............................Peter Müller, Switzerland	
15............................Franz Heinzer, Switzerland	

SLALOM

40............................Ingemar Stenmark, Sweden	
35............................Alberto Tomba, Italy	
16............................Marc Girardelli, Luxembourg	

GIANT SLALOM

46............................Ingemar Stenmark, Sweden	
16............................*Michael von Grünigen, Switz	
15............................Alberto Tomba, Italy	

SUPER G

13............................*Hermann Maier, Austria	
10............................Pirmin Zurbriggen, Switzerland	
7..............................Marc Girardelli, Luxembourg	

COMBINED

11............................Phil Mahre, United States	
Pirmin Zurbriggen, Switzerland	
Marc Girardelli, Luxembourg	

Women

DOWNHILL

36............................Annemarie Moser-Pröll, Austria	
17............................Michela Figini, Switzerland	
16............................Katja Seizinger, Germany	

SLALOM

33............................Vreni Schneider, Switzerland	
21............................Erika Hess, Switzerland	
15............................Perrine Pelen, France	

GIANT SLALOM

21............................Vreni Schneider, Switzerland	
16............................Annemarie Moser-Pröll, Austria	
14............................Anita Wachter, Austria	
Lise-Marie Morerod, Switzerland	

SUPER G

16............................Katja Seizinger, Germany	
12............................Carole Merle, France	
4..............................Alexandra Meissnitzer, Austria	

COMBINED

8..............................Hanni Wenzel, Lichtenstein	
7..............................Annemarie Moser-Pröll, Austria	
Brigitte Oertli, Switzerland	

*still active

U.S. Olympic Gold Medalists

Men

Year	Winner	Event
1980 ....Phil Mahre		Combined
1984 ....Bill Johnson		Downhill
1984 ....Phil Mahre		Slalom
1994 ....Tommy Moe		Downhill

Women

Year	Winner	Event
1948 ....Gretchen Fraser		Slalom
1952 ....Andrea Mead Lawrence		Slalom
1952 ....Andrea Mead Lawrence		Giant Slalom
1972 ....Barbara Ann Cochran		Slalom
1984 ....Debbie Armstrong		Giant Slalom
1994 ....Diann Roffe-Steinrotter		Super G
1998 ....Picabo Street		Super G

Figure Skating

PAUL CHIASSON

World champion
Michelle Kwan of
the United States

Skating on Thin Ice

Michelle Kwan of the U.S. and Aleksei Yagudin of Russia won world titles, but just barely

BY MERRELL NODEN

IT MAY BE a new millennium, but figure skating's old battle lines were drawn once more: Youth stalked age, grace and expressiveness tussled with pure athleticism, and the rewards of risk were weighed against the safety of familiar routines.

When all the musical flourishes and hugs had stopped and all the tears had dried, this season looked very much like the last, with Michelle Kwan of the U.S. and Aleksei Yagudin of Russia defending world titles. In a year that was short on brilliance, those two prevailed not so much because they skated beautifully as because their younger, more dazzling rivals made just enough mistakes to permit the judges to vote for the veterans. With the Salt Lake City Olympics less than two years away, Kwan and Yagudin, despite their victories, did little to establish themselves as clear favorites.

At the U.S. figure skating championships in Cleveland in February, Kwan and Michael Weiss both won, but the fireworks were provided by the runners-up. Skating before a hometown crowd, 19-year-old Timothy Goebel became the first U.S. skater to land a quadruple jump at the nationals. In fact, he landed three of them, two Salchows and a toe loop, executing them with such ease and confidence that his coach, Carol Heiss Jenkins, said Goebel might one day land a quintuple.

Alas, between the spectacular leaps, Goebel's skating was slow and dull. Still, three of the nine judges placed him ahead of Weiss, whose goal seemed to be to survive rather than thrill the crowd. The 23-year-old father of two from Fairfax, Va., was sidelined for most of the autumn by a stress fracture in his left ankle, which may explain why he didn't execute the quadruple toe loop he'd landed during the qualifying round at the worlds in 1999. His workmanlike performance was good enough to win, but Weiss will need to take more risks if he is to have any hope of winning in Salt Lake City.

Kwan's pursuer was Sasha Cohen, a 15-year-old from Laguna Niguel, Calif., who stands just 4'9" and looks 12, but skates with the poise and power of a dancer. "We call her the china doll, but don't be fooled," said Cohen's coach, John Nicks. "I've seen her take many hard falls, but I've never, ever

Yagudin won in Nice not so much for what he did as for what Plushchenko failed to do.

seen her cry." Competing as a senior for the first time, Cohen mesmerized the crowd, landing five triple jumps flawlessly. Her only mistake was a fall on a triple toe loop, which seemed to give the edge to Kwan.

In the run-up to the world championships this spring, in Nice, France, there was news both sordid and sad. Former Olympian Tonya Harding was arrested in February for an attack on her live-in boyfriend, Darren Silver, in which she threw a hubcap at him and punched him repeatedly. As Silver put it, Harding was "hooking me like [she was] Mike Tyson." Harding's attorney denied that his client had an alcohol problem, instead blaming the attack on a mixture of alcohol, painkillers and the antidepressant Zoloft. A judge sentenced her to three nights in jail and ordered her not to drink for two years.

Also in February, Rudy Galindo, the 1996 U.S. champion, developed pneumonia, which tests showed was due to the AIDS virus. HIV had already killed his brother George and two of his coaches, Jim Hulick and Rick Inglesi. Doctors told Galindo that by following a drug regimen and taking care of himself he can live a normal life for years, as basketball star Magic Johnson has.

Off-ice news attended the first day of the worlds, as well. Elena Berezhnaya of Russia, who along with partner Anton Sikharulidze won the 1999 world pairs title, tested positive for a banned stimulant. Berezhnaya said she had taken the substance for bronchitis, but she and Sikharulidze withdrew from the championships, and their teammates Maria Petrova and Aleksei Tikhonov won the event.

Yagudin arrived in Nice as two-time defending champ, but he'd lost to countryman Yevgeny Plushchenko at the European championships in February. All nine judges had chosen Plushchenko, who landed a quad and eight triples to Yagudin's six triples.

None of the men performed particularly well in Nice. Elvis Stojko fell on his opening quad; Yagudin started well, landing a quadruple toe–triple toe, but fell on his final triple Lutz. He grimaced, crossed himself

LIONEL CIRONNEAU/AP

and saluted the crowd before exiting, knowing that Plushchenko had yet to skate.

But the 18-year-old Plushchenko, with the title within reach, inexplicably decided to improvise, changing many of his jumps and making several mistakes. "He missed two quads, then I left," said Yagudin. "I understood I'd won." More accurately, he escaped.

In the women's competition, the 19-year-old Kwan showed her toughness. Both her short and long programs were the most ambitious she'd ever skated, and the risks paid off. She was the only skater to hit a triple-triple combination in the freestyle competition, and it was that, more than her vaunted style, that separated her from the field. Irina Slutskaya of Russia took the silver, and the defending champion, Maria Butyrskaya, also from Russia, finished third after two-footing her triple-triple attempt.

With the possible exception of Kwan, though, no skater emerged from the worlds as the favorite for the 2002 Games. Everything is up in the air. But as Kwan could tell you, that's nothing new in this sport of teenage veterans.

FOR THE RECORD 2000

World Champions

Nice, March 26–April 2

Women

1........Michelle Kwan, United States
2........Irina Slutskaya, Russia
3........Maria Butyrskaya, Russia

Men

1.........Aleksei Yagudin, Russia
2.........Elvis Stojko, Canada
3.........Michael Weiss, United States

Pairs

1........Maria Petrova and Aleksei Tikhonov, Russia
2........Shen Xue and Zhao Hongbo, China
3........Sarah Abitol and Stephane Bernadis, France

Dance

1.........Marina Anissina and Gwendal Peizer, France
2.........Barbara Fusar-Poli and Maurizio Margaglio, Italy
3.........Margarita Drobiazko and Povilas Vanagas, Lithuania

World Figure Skating Championships Medal Table

Country	Gold	Silver	Bronze	Total
Russia	2	1	1	4
United States	1	0	1	2
France	1	0	1	2
China	0	1	0	1
Canada	0	1	0	1
Italy	0	1	0	1
Lithuania	0	0	1	1

Champions of the United States

Cleveland, February 6–13

Women

1......................Michelle Kwan, Los Angeles FSC.
2......................Sasha Cohen, Orange County FSC
3......................Sarah Hughes, SC of New York

Men

1......................Michael Weiss, Washington FSC
2......................Timothy Goebel, Winterhurst FSC
3......................Matthew Savoie, Illinois Valley FSC

Pairs

1......................Kyoko Ina and John Zimmerman,
SC of New York/Birmingham FSC
2......................Tiffany Scott and Philip Dulebohn,
Colonial FSC and Univeristy of Del FSC
3......................Larisa Spielberg and Craig Joeright,
Detroit SC

Dance

1......................Naomi Lang and Peter Tchernyshev,
Detroit SC
2......................Jamie Silverstein and Justin Pekarek,
Colonial FSC and Univeristy of Del
3......................Deborah Koegel and Oleg Fediukov,
Ice Works SC

No. 2 with a Bullet

Sasha Cohen moves her 4' 9", 79-pound body about the ice as if she were a prima ballerina: assured, composed, impossibly flexible and elegant. Yes, at 15, elegant. Her hands, her spins, her spirals, her posture, her positions in the air are flawless, often breathtaking. Competing as a senior for the first time [at the 2000 U.S. Nationals in Cleveland], Cohen proved her mettle in the freestyle program, when, unfazed by the pressure of leading, she landed five triple jumps and mesmerized the 15,036 spectators.

Skating Terminology*

Basic Skating Terms

Edges: The two sides of the skating blade, on either side of the grooved center. There is an inside edge, on the inner side of the leg; and an outside edge, on the outer side of the leg.

Free Foot, Hip, Knee, Side, Etc.: The foot a skater is not skating on at any one time is the free foot; everything on that side of the body is then called "free." (See also "skating foot.")

Free Skating (Freestyle): A 4- or 5-minute competition program of free-skating components, choreographed to music, with no set elements. Skating moves include jumps, spins, steps and other linking movements.

Skating Foot, Hip, Knee, Side, Etc.: Opposite of the free foot, hip, knee, side, etc. The foot a skater is skating on at any one time is the skating foot; everything on that side of the body is then called "skating."

Toe Picks (Toe Rakes): The teeth at the front of the skate blade, used primarily for certain jumps and spins.

Trace, Tracing: The line left on the ice by the skater's blade.

Jumps

Waltz: A beginner's jump, involving half a revolution in the air, taken from a forward outside edge and landed on the back outside edge of the other foot.

Toe Loop: A one-revolution jump taken off from and landed on the same back outside edge. This jump is similar to the loop jump except that the skater kicks the toe pick of the free leg into the ice upon takeoff, providing added power.

Toe Walley: A jump similar to the toe loop, except that the takeoff is from the inside edge.

Flip: A jump taken off with the toe pick of the free leg from a back inside edge and landed on a back outside edge, with one in-air revolution.

Lutz: A toe jump similar to the flip, taken off with the toe pick of the free leg from a backward outside edge. The skater enters the jump skating in one direction, and concludes the jump skating in the opposite direction. Usually performed in the corners of the rink. Named after inventor Alois Lutz, who first completed the jump in Vienna, 1918.

Salchow: A one-, two- or three-revolution jump. The skater takes off from the back inside edge of one foot and lands backwards on the outside edge of the right foot, the opposite foot from which the skater took off. Named for its originator and first Olympic champion (1908), Sweden's Ulrich Salchow.

Axel: A combination of the waltz and loop jumps, including one-and-a-half revolutions. The only jump begun from a forward outside edge, the axel is landed on the back outside edge of the opposite foot. Named for its inventor, Norway's Axel Paulsen.

Spins

Spin: The rotation of the body in one place on the ice. Various spins are the back, fast or scratch, sit, camel, butterfly and layback.

Camel Spin: A spin with the skater in an arabesque position (the free leg at right angles to the leg on the ice).

Flying Camel Spin: A jump spin ending in the camel-spin position.

Flying Sit Spin: A jump spin in which the skater leaps off the ice, assumes a sitting position at the peak of the jump, lands and spins in a similar sitting position.

Pair Movements/Techniques

Death Spiral: One of the most dramatic moves in figure skating. The man, acting as the center of a circle, holds tightly to the hand of his partner and pulls her around him. The woman, gliding on one foot, achieves a position almost horizontal to the ice.

Lifts: The most spectacular moves in pairs skating. They involve any maneuver in which the man lifts the woman off the ice. The man often holds his partner above his head with one hand.

Throws: The man lifts the woman into the air and throws her away from him. She spins in the air and lands on one foot.

Twist: The man throws the woman into the air. She spins in the air (either a double- or triple-twist), and he catches her at the landing.

*Compiled by the United States Figure Skating Association.

World Champions

Women

1906	Madge Sayers-Cave, Great Britain
1907	Madge Sayers-Cave, Great Britain
1908	Lily Kronberger, Hungary
1909	Lily Kronberger, Hungary
1910	Lily Kronberger, Hungary
1911	Lily Kronberger, Hungary
1912	Opika von Meray Horvath, Hungary
1913	Opika von Meray Horvath, Hungary
1914	Opika von Meray Horvath, Hungary
1915–21	No competition
1922	Herma Plank-Szabo, Austria
1923	Herma Plank-Szabo, Austria
1924	Herma Plank-Szabo, Austria
1925	Herma Jaross-Szabo, Austria
1926	Herma Jaross-Szabo, Austria
1927	Sonja Henie, Norway
1928	Sonja Henie, Norway
1929	Sonja Henie, Norway
1930	Sonja Henie, Norway
1931	Sonja Henie, Norway
1932	Sonja Henie, Norway
1933	Sonja Henie, Norway
1934	Sonja Henie, Norway
1935	Sonja Henie, Norway
1936	Sonja Henie, Norway
1937	Cecilia Colledge, Great Britain
1938	Megan Taylor, Great Britain
1939	Megan Taylor, Great Britain
1940–46	No competition
1947	Barbara Ann Scott, Canada
1948	Barbara Ann Scott, Canada
1949	Alena Vrzanova, Czechoslovakia
1950	Alena Vrzanova, Czechoslovakia
1951	Jeannette Altwegg, Great Britain
1952	Jacqueline duBief, France
1953	Tenley Albright, United States
1954	Gundi Busch, West Germany
1955	Tenley Albright, United States
1956	Carol Heiss, United States
1957	Carol Heiss, United States

Women (Cont.)

1958	Carol Heiss, United States
1959	Carol Heiss, United States
1960	Carol Heiss, United States
1961	No competition
1962	Sjoukje Dijkstra, Netherlands
1963	Sjoukje Dijkstra, Netherlands
1964	Sjoukje Dijkstra, Netherlands
1965	Petra Burka, Canada
1966	Peggy Fleming, United States
1967	Peggy Fleming, United States
1968	Peggy Fleming, United States
1969	Gabriele Seyfert, East Germany
1970	Gabriele Seyfert, East Germany
1971	Beatrix Schuba, Austria
1972	Beatrix Schuba, Austria
1973	Karen Magnussen, Canada
1974	Christine Errath, East Germany
1975	Dianne DeLeeuw, Netherlands
1976	Dorothy Hamill, United States
1977	Linda Fratianne, United States
1978	Annett Poetzsch, East Germany
1979	Linda Fratianne, United States
1980	Annett Poetzsch, East Germany
1981	Denise Biellmann, Switzerland
1982	Elaine Zayak, United States
1983	Rosalynn Sumners, United States
1984	Katarina Witt, East Germany
1985	Katarina Witt, East Germany
1986	Debi Thomas, United States
1987	Katarina Witt, East Germany
1988	Katarina Witt, East Germany
1989	Midori Ito, Japan
1990	Jill Trenary, United States
1991	Kristi Yamaguchi, United States
1992	Kristi Yamaguchi, United States
1993	Oksana Baiul, Ukraine
1994	Yuka Sato, Japan
1995	Chen Lu, China
1996	Michelle Kwan, United States
1997	Tara Lipinski, United States
1998	Michelle Kwan, United States
1999	Maria Butyrskaya, Russia
2000	Michelle Kwan, United States

Men

1896	Gilbert Fuchs, Germany
1897	Gustav Hugel, Austria
1898	Henning Grenander, Sweden
1899	Gustav Hugel, Austria
1900	Gustav Hugel, Austria
1901	Ulrich Salchow, Sweden
1902	Ulrich Salchow, Sweden
1903	Ulrich Salchow, Sweden
1904	Ulrich Salchow, Sweden
1905	Ulrich Salchow, Sweden
1906	Gilbert Fuchs, Germany
1907	Ulrich Salchow, Sweden
1908	Ulrich Salchow, Sweden
1909	Ulrich Salchow, Sweden
1910	Ulrich Salchow, Sweden
1911	Ulrich Salchow, Sweden
1912	Fritz Kachler, Austria
1913	Fritz Kachler, Austria
1914	Gosta Sandhal, Sweden
1915-21	No competition
1922	Gillis Grafstrom, Sweden
1923	Fritz Kachler, Austria
1924	Gillis Grafstrom, Sweden
1925	Willy Bockl, Austria
1926	Willy Bockl, Austria
1927	Willy Bockl, Austria
1928	Willy Bockl, Austria
1929	Gillis Grafstrom, Sweden
1930	Karl Schafer, Austria
1931	Karl Schafer, Austria
1932	Karl Schafer, Austria
1933	Karl Schafer, Austria
1934	Karl Schafer, Austria
1935	Karl Schafer, Austria
1936	Karl Schafer, Austria
1937	Felix Kaspar, Austria
1938	Felix Kaspar, Austria
1939	Graham Sharp, Great Britain
1940-46	No competition
1947	Hans Gerschwiler, Switzerland
1948	Dick Button, United States
1949	Dick Button, United States
1950	Dick Button, United States
1951	Dick Button, United States
1952	Dick Button, United States
1953	Hayes Alan Jenkins, United States
1954	Hayes Alan Jenkins, United States
1955	Hayes Alan Jenkins, United States
1956	Hayes Alan Jenkins, United States
1957	David W. Jenkins, United States
1958	David W. Jenkins, United States
1959	David W. Jenkins, United States
1960	Alan Giletti, France
1961	No competition
1962	Donald Jackson, Canada
1963	Donald McPherson, Canada
1964	Manfred Schneldorfer, W Germany
1965	Alain Calmat, France
1966	Emmerich Danzer, Austria
1967	Emmerich Danzer, Austria
1968	Emmerich Danzer, Austria
1969	Tim Wood, United States
1970	Tim Wood, United States
1971	Andrej Nepela, Czechoslovakia
1972	Andrej Nepela, Czechoslovakia
1973	Andrej Nepela, Czechoslovakia
1974	Jan Hoffmann, East Germany
1975	Sergei Volkov, USSR
1976	John Curry, Great Britain
1977	Vladimir Kovalev, USSR
1978	Charles Tickner, United States
1979	Vladimir Kovalev, USSR
1980	Jan Hoffmann, East Germany
1981	Scott Hamilton, United States
1982	Scott Hamilton, United States
1983	Scott Hamilton, United States
1984	Scott Hamilton, United States
1985	Aleksandr Fadeev, USSR
1986	Brian Boitano, United States
1987	Brian Orser, Canada
1988	Brian Boitano, United States
1989	Kurt Browning, Canada
1990	Kurt Browning, Canada
1991	Kurt Browning, Canada
1992	Viktor Petrenko, CIS
1993	Kurt Browning, Canada

Men (Cont.)

1994...................Elvis Stojko, Canada
1995...................Elvis Stojko, Canada
1996...................Todd Eldredge, United States
1997...................Elvis Stojko, Canada

1998...................Aleksei Yagudin, Russia
1999...................Aleksei Yagudin, Russia
2000...................Aleksei Yagudin, Russia

Pairs

1908 ....Anna Hubler, Heinrich Burger, Germany
1909 ....Phyllis Johnson, James H. Johnson, Great Britain
1910 ....Anna Hubler, Heinrich Burger, Germany
1911 ....Ludowika Eilers, Walter Jakobsson, Germany/Finland
1912 ....Phyllis Johnson, James H. Johnson, Great Britain
1913 ....Helene Engelmann, Karl Majstrik, Germany
1914 ....Ludowika Jakobsson-Eilers, Walter Jakobsson-Eilers, Finland
1915-21 ......No competition
1922 ....Helene Engelmann, Alfred Berger, Germany
1923 ....Ludowika Jakobsson-Eilers, Walter Jakobsson-Eilers, Finland
1924 ....Helene Engelmann, Alfred Berger, Germany
1925 ....Herma Jaross-Szabo, Ludwig Wrede, Austria
1926 ....Andree Joly, Pierre Brunet, France
1927 ....Herma Jaross-Szabo, Ludwig Wrede, Austria
1928 ....Andree Joly, Pierre Brunet, France
1929 ....Lilly Scholz, Otto Kaiser, Austria
1930 ....Andree Brunet-Joly, Pierre Brunet-Joly, France
1931 ....Emilie Rotter, Laszlo Szollas, Hungary
1932 ....Andree Brunet-Joly, Pierre Brunet-Joly, France
1933 ....Emilie Rotter, Laszlo Szollas, Hungary
1934 ....Emilie Rotter, Laszlo Szollas, Hungary
1935 ....Emilie Rotter, Laszlo Szollas, Hungary
1936 ....Maxi Herber, Ernst Bajer, Germany
1937 ....Maxi Herber, Ernst Bajer, Germany
1938 ....Maxi Herber, Ernst Bajer, Germany
1939 ....Maxi Herber, Ernst Bajer, Germany
1940-46 ......No competition
1947 ....Micheline Lannoy, Pierre Baugniet, Belgium
1948 ....Micheline Lannoy, Pierre Baugniet, Belgium
1949 ....Andrea Kekessy, Ede Kiraly, Hungary
1950 ....Karol Kennedy, Peter Kennedy, United States
1951 ....Ria Baran, Paul Falk, West Germany
1952 ....Ria Baran Falk, Paul Falk, W Germany
1953 ....Jennifer Nicks, John Nicks, Great Britain
1954 ....Frances Dafoe, Norris Bowden, Canada
1955 ....Frances Dafoe, Norris Bowden, Canada
1956 ....Sissy Schwarz, Kurt Oppelt, Austria
1957 ....Barbara Wagner, Robert Paul, Canada
1958 ....Barbara Wagner, Robert Paul, Canada
1959 ....Barbara Wagner, Robert Paul, Canada
1960 ....Barbara Wagner, Robert Paul, Canada
1961 ....No competition
1962 ....Maria Jelinek, Otto Jelinek, Canada

1963 ....Marika Kilius, Hans-Jurgen Baumler, West Germany
1964 ....Marika Kilius, Hans-Jurgen Baumler, West Germany
1965 ....Ljudmila Protopopov, Oleg Protopopov, USSR
1966 ....Ljudmila Protopopov, Oleg Protopopov, USSR
1967 ....Ljudmila Protopopov, Oleg Protopopov, USSR
1968 ....Ljudmila Protopopov, Oleg Protopopov, USSR
1969 ....Irina Rodnina, Alexsei Ulanov, USSR
1970 ....Irina Rodnina, Alexsei Ulanov, USSR
1971 ....Irina Rodnina, Sergei Ulanov, USSR
1972 ....Irina Rodnina, Sergei Ulanov, USSR
1973 ....Irina Rodnina, Aleksandr Zaitsev, USSR
1974 ....Irina Rodnina, Aleksandr Zaitsev, USSR
1975 ....Irina Rodnina, Aleksandr Zaitsev, USSR
1976 ....Irina Rodnina, Aleksandr Zaitsev, USSR
1977 ....Irina Rodnina, Aleksandr Zaitsev, USSR
1978 ....Irina Rodnina, Aleksandr Zaitsev, USSR
1979 ....Tai Babilonia, Randy Gardner, United States
1980 ....Maria Cherkasova, Sergei Shakhrai, USSR
1981 ....Irina Vorobieva, Igor Lisovsky, USSR
1982 ....Sabine Baess, Tassilio Thierbach, East Germany
1983 ....Elena Valova, Oleg Vasiliev, USSR
1984 ....Barbara Underhill, Paul Martini, Canada
1985 ....Elena Valova, Oleg Vasiliev, USSR
1986 ....Ekaterina Gordeeva, Sergei Grinkov, USSR
1987 ....Ekaterina Gordeeva, Sergei Grinkov, USSR
1988 ....Elena Valova, Oleg Vasiliev, USSR
1989 ....Ekaterina Gordeeva, Sergei Grinkov, USSR
1990 ....Ekaterina Gordeeva, Sergei Grinkov, USSR
1991 ....Natalia Mishkutienok, Artur Dmitriev, USSR
1992 ....Natalia Mishkutienok, Artur Dmitriev, CIS
1993 ....Isabelle Brasseur, Lloyd Eisler, Canada
1994 ....Evgenia Shishkova, Vadim Naumov, Russia
1995 ....Radka Kovarikova, Rene Novotny, Czech Republic
1996 ....Marina Eltsova, Andrey Buskhov, Russia
1997 ....Mandy Wötzel, Ingo Steuer, Germany
1998 ....Jenni Meno, Todd Sand, United States
1999 ....Elena Berezhnaya, Anton Sikharulidze, Russia
2000 ....Maria Petrova and Aleksei Tikhonov, Russia

Dance

1950	Lois Waring, Michael McGean, United States
1951	Jean Westwood, Lawrence Demmy, Great Britain
1952	Jean Westwood, Lawrence Demmy, Great Britain
1953	Jean Westwood, Lawrence Demmy, Great Britain
1954	Jean Westwood, Lawrence Demmy, Great Britain
1955	Jean Westwood, Lawrence Demmy, Great Britain
1956	Pamela Wieght, Paul Thomas, Great Britain
1957	June Markham, Courtney Jones, Great Britain
1958	June Markham, Courtney Jones, Great Britain
1959	Doreen D. Denny, Courtney Jones, Great Britain
1960	Doreen D. Denny, Courtney Jones, Great Britain
1961	No competition
1962	Eva Romanova, Pavel Roman, Czechoslovakia
1963	Eva Romanova, Pavel Roman, Czechoslovakia
1964	Eva Romanova, Pavel Roman, Czechoslovakia
1965	Eva Romanova, Pavel Roman, Czechoslovakia
1966	Diane Towler, Bernard Ford, Great Britain
1967	Diane Towler, Bernard Ford, Great Britain
1968	Diane Towler, Bernard Ford, Great Britain
1969	Diane Towler, Bernard Ford, Great Britain
1970	Ljudmila Pakhomova, Aleksandr Gorshkov, USSR
1971	Ljudmila Pakhomova, Aleksandr Gorshkov, USSR
1972	Ljudmila Pakhomova, Aleksandr Gorshkov, USSR
1973	Ljudmila Pakhomova, Aleksandr Gorshkov, USSR
1974	Ljudmila Pakhomova, Aleksandr Gorshkov, USSR
1975	Irina Moiseeva, Andreij Minenkov, USSR
1976	Ljudmila Pakhomova, Aleksandr Gorshkov, USSR
1977	Irina Moiseeva, Andreij Minenkov, USSR
1978	Natalia Linichuk, Gennadi Karponosov, USSR
1979	Natalia Linichuk, Gennadi Karponosov, USSR
1980	Krisztina Regoeczy, Andras Sallai, Hungary
1981	Jayne Torvill, Christopher Dean, Great Britain
1982	Jayne Torvill, Christopher Dean, Great Britain
1983	Jayne Torvill, Christopher Dean, Great Britain
1984	Jayne Torvill, Christopher Dean, Great Britain
1985	Natalia Bestemianova, Andrei Bukin, USSR
1986	Natalia Bestemianova, Andrei Bukin, USSR
1987	Natalia Bestemianova, Andrei Bukin, USSR
1988	Natalia Bestemianova, Andrei Bukin, USSR
1989	Marina Klimova, Sergei Ponomarenko, USSR
1990	Marina Klimova, Sergei Ponomarenko, USSR
1991	Isabelle Duchesnay, Paul Duchesnay, France
1992	Marina Klimova, Sergei Ponomarenko, CIS
1993	Renee Roca, Gorsha Sur, United States
1994	Oksana Grishuk, Evgeny Platov, Russia
1995	Oksana Grishuk, Evgeny Platov, Russia
1996	Oksana Grishuk, Evgeny Platov, Russia
1997	Oksana Grishuk, Evgeny Platov, Russia
1998	Anjelika Krylova and Oleg Ovsyannikov, Russia
1999	Anjelika Krylova and Oleg Ovsyannikov, Russia
2000	Marina Anissina and Gwendal Peizerat, France

Champions of the United States

The championships held in 1914, 1918, 1920 and 1921 under the auspices of the International Skating Union of America were open to Canadians, although they were considered to be United States championships. Beginning in 1922, the championships have been held under the auspices of the United States Figure Skating Association.

Women

1914	Theresa Weld, SC of Boston
1915–17	No competition
1918	Rosemary S. Beresford, New York SC
1919	No competition
1920	Theresa Weld, SC of Boston
1921	Theresa Weld Blanchard, SC of Boston
1922	Theresa Weld Blanchard, SC of Boston
1923	Theresa Weld Blanchard, SC of Boston
1924	Theresa Weld Blanchard, SC of Boston
1925	Beatrix Loughran, New York SC
1926	Beatrix Loughran, New York SC
1927	Beatrix Loughran, New York SC
1928	Maribel Y. Vinson, SC of Boston
1929	Maribel Y. Vinson, SC of Boston
1930	Maribel Y. Vinson, SC of Boston
1931	Maribel Y. Vinson, SC of Boston
1932	Maribel Y. Vinson, SC of Boston
1933	Maribel Y. Vinson, SC of Boston
1934	Suzanne Davis, SC of Boston
1935	Maribel Y. Vinson, SC of Boston
1936	Maribel Y. Vinson, SC of Boston
1937	Maribel Y. Vinson, SC of Boston
1938	Joan Tozzer, SC of Boston
1939	Joan Tozzer, SC of Boston
1940	Joan Tozzer, SC of Boston
1941	Jane Vaughn, Philadelphia SC & HS
1942	Jane Vaughn Sullivan, Philadelphia SC & HS
1943	Gretchen Van Zandt Merrill, SC of Boston
1944	Gretchen Van Zandt Merrill, SC of Boston

Women (Cont.)

1945	Gretchen Van Zandt Merrill, SC of Boston
1946	Gretchen Van Zandt Merrill, SC of Boston
1947	Gretchen Van Zandt Merrill, SC of Boston
1948	Gretchen Van Zandt Merrill, SC of Boston
1949	Yvonne Claire Sherman, SC of New York
1950	Yvonne Claire Sherman, SC of New York
1951	Sonya Klopfer, Junior SC of New York
1952	Tenley E. Albright, SC of Boston
1953	Tenley E. Albright, SC of Boston
1954	Tenley E. Albright, SC of Boston
1955	Tenley E. Albright, SC of Boston
1956	Tenley E. Albright, SC of Boston
1957	Carol E. Heiss, SC of New York
1958	Carol E. Heiss, SC of New York
1959	Carol E. Heiss, SC of New York
1960	Carol E. Heiss, SC of New York
1961	Laurence R. Owen, SC of Boston
1962	Barbara Roles Pursley, Arctic Blades FSC
1963	Lorraine G. Hanlon, SC of Boston
1964	Peggy Fleming, Arctic Blades FSC
1965	Peggy Fleming, Arctic Blades FSC
1966	Peggy Fleming, City of Colorado Springs
1967	Peggy Fleming, Broadmoor SC
1968	Peggy Fleming, Broadmoor SC
1969	Janet Lynn, Wagon Wheel FSC
1970	Janet Lynn, Wagon Wheel FSC
1971	Janet Lynn, Wagon Wheel FSC
1972	Janet Lynn, Wagon Wheel FSC
1973	Janet Lynn, Wagon Wheel FSC
1974	Dorothy Hamill, SC of New York
1975	Dorothy Hamill, SC of New York
1976	Dorothy Hamill, SC of New York
1977	Linda Fratianne, Los Angeles FSC
1978	Linda Fratianne, Los Angeles FSC
1979	Linda Fratianne, Los Angeles FSC
1980	Linda Fratianne, Los Angeles FSC
1981	Elaine Zayak, SC of New York
1982	Rosalynn Sumners, Seattle SC
1983	Rosalynn Sumners, Seattle SC
1984	Rosalynn Sumners, Seattle SC
1985	Tiffany Chin, San Diego FSC
1986	Debi Thomas, Los Angeles FSC
1987	Jill Trenary, Broadmoor SC
1988	Debi Thomas, Los Angeles FSC
1989	Jill Trenary, Broadmoor SC
1990	Jill Trenary, Broadmoor SC
1991	Tonya Harding, Carousel FSC
1992	Kristi Yamaguchi, St Moritz ISC
1993	Nancy Kerrigan, Colonial FSC
1994	Tonya Harding, Portland FSC
1995	Nicole Bobek, Los Angeles FSC
1996	Michelle Kwan, Los Angeles FSC
1997	Tara Lipinski, Detroit SC
1998	Michelle Kwan, Los Angeles FSC
1999	Michelle Kwan, Los Angeles FSC
2000	Michelle Kwan, Los Angeles FSC

Men

1914	Norman M. Scott, WC of Montreal
1915–17	No competition
1918	Nathaniel W. Niles, SC of Boston
1919	No competition
1920	Sherwin C. Badger, SC of Boston
1921	Sherwin C. Badger, SC of Boston
1922	Sherwin C. Badger, SC of Boston
1923	Sherwin C. Badger, SC of Boston
1924	Sherwin C. Badger, SC of Boston
1925	Nathaniel W. Niles, SC of Boston
1926	Chris I. Christenson, Twin City FSC
1927	Nathaniel W. Niles, SC of Boston
1928	Roger F. Turner, SC of Boston
1929	Roger F. Turner, SC of Boston
1930	Roger F. Turner, SC of Boston
1931	Roger F. Turner, SC of Boston
1932	Roger F. Turner, SC of Boston
1933	Roger F. Turner, SC of Boston
1934	Roger F. Turner, SC of Boston
1935	Robin H. Lee, SC of New York
1936	Robin H. Lee, SC of New York
1937	Robin H. Lee, SC of New York
1938	Robin H. Lee, Chicago FSC
1939	Robin H. Lee, St Paul FSC
1940	Eugene Turner, Los Angeles FSC
1941	Eugene Turner, Los Angeles FSC
1942	Robert Specht, Chicago FSC
1943	Arthur R. Vaughn, Jr, Philadelphia SC & HS
1944-45	No competition
1946	Dick Button, Philadelphia SC & HS
1947	Dick Button, Philadelphia SC & HS
1948	Dick Button, Philadelphia SC & HS
1949	Dick Button, Philadelphia SC & HS
1950	Dick Button, SC of Boston
1951	Dick Button, SC of Boston
1952	Dick Button, SC of Boston
1953	Hayes Alan Jenkins, Cleveland SC
1954	Hayes Alan Jenkins, Broadmoor SC
1955	Hayes Alan Jenkins, Broadmoor SC
1956	Hayes Alan Jenkins, Broadmoor SC
1957	David Jenkins, Broadmoor SC
1958	David Jenkins, Broadmoor SC
1959	David Jenkins, Broadmoor SC
1960	David Jenkins, Broadmoor SC
1961	Bradley R. Lord, SC of Boston
1962	Monty Hoyt, Broadmoor SC
1963	Thomas Litz, Hershey FSC
1964	Scott Ethan Allen, SC of New York
1965	Gary C. Visconti, Detroit SC
1966	Scott Ethan Allen, SC of New York
1967	Gary C. Visconti, Detroit SC
1968	Tim Wood, Detroit SC
1969	Tim Wood, Detroit SC
1970	Tim Wood, City of Colorado Springs
1971	John Misha Petkevich, Great Falls FSC
1972	Kenneth Shelley, Arctic Blades FSC
1973	Gordon McKellen, Jr, SC of Lake Placid
1974	Gordon McKellen, Jr, SC of Lake Placid
1975	Gordon McKellen, Jr, SC of Lake Placid
1976	Terry Kubicka, Arctic Blades FSC
1977	Charles Tickner, Denver FSC
1978	Charles Tickner, Denver FSC
1979	Charles Tickner, Denver FSC
1980	Charles Tickner, Denver FSC
1981	Scott Hamilton, Philadelphia SC & HS
1982	Scott Hamilton, Philadelphia SC & HS
1983	Scott Hamilton, Philadelphia SC & HS
1984	Scott Hamilton, Philadelphia SC & HS
1985	Brian Boitano, Peninsula FSC
1986	Brian Boitano, Peninsula FSC
1987	Brian Boitano, Peninsula FSC

Men *(Cont.)*

1988 ....Brian Boitano, Peninsula FSC
1989 ....Christopher Bowman, Los Angeles FSC
1990 ....Todd Eldredge, Los Angeles FSC
1991 ....Todd Eldredge, Los Angeles FSC
1992 ....Christopher Bowman, Los Angeles FSC
1993 ....Scott Davis, Broadmoor SC
1994 ....Scott Davis, Broadmoor SC

1995 ....Todd Eldredge, Detroit SC
1996 ....Rudy Galindo, St Moritz ISC
1997 ....Todd Eldredge, Detroit SC
1998 ....Todd Eldredge, Detroit SC
1999 ....Michael Weiss, Washington FSC
2000 ....Michael Weiss, Washington FSC

Pairs

1914 ......Jeanne Chevalier, Norman M. Scott,
WC of Montreal
1915-17..No competition
1918 ......Theresa Weld, Nathaniel W. Niles,
SC of Boston
1919 .....No competition
1920 ......Theresa Weld, Nathaniel W. Niles,
SC of Boston
1921 ......Theresa Weld Blanchard, Nathaniel W.
Niles, SC of Boston
1922 ......Theresa Weld Blanchard, Nathaniel W.
Niles, SC of Boston
1923 ......Theresa Weld Blanchard, Nathaniel W.
Niles, SC of Boston
1924 ......Theresa Weld Blanchard, Nathaniel W.
Niles, SC of Boston
1925 ......Theresa Weld Blanchard, Nathaniel W.
Niles, SC of Boston
1926 ......Theresa Weld Blanchard, Nathaniel W.
Niles, SC of Boston
1927 ......Theresa Weld Blanchard, Nathaniel W.
Niles, SC of Boston
1928 ......Maribel Y. Vinson, Thornton L. Coolidge,
SC of Boston
1929 ......Maribel Y. Vinson, Thornton L. Coolidge,
SC of Boston
1930 ......Beatrix Loughran, Sherwin C. Badger,
SC of New York
1931 ......Beatrix Loughran, Sherwin C. Badger,
SC of New York
1932 ......Beatrix Loughran, Sherwin C. Badger,
SC of New York
1933 ......Maribel Y. Vinson, George E. B. Hill,
SC of Boston
1934 ......Grace E. Madden, James L. Madden,
SC of Boston
1935 ......Maribel Y. Vinson, George E. B. Hill,
SC of Boston
1936 ......Maribel Y. Vinson, George E. B. Hill,
SC of Boston
1937 ......Maribel Y. Vinson, George E. B. Hill,
SC of Boston
1938 ......Joan Tozzer, M. Bernard Fox, SC of Boston
1939 ......Joan Tozzer, M. Bernard Fox, SC of Boston
1940 ......Joan Tozzer, M. Bernard Fox, SC of Boston
1941 ......Donna Atwood, Eugene Turner, Mercury
FSC/Los Angeles FSC
1942 ......Doris Schubach, Walter Noffke,
Springfield Ice Birds
1943 ......Doris Schubach, Walter Noffke,
Springfield Ice Birds
1944 ......Doris Schubach, Walter Noffke,
Springfield Ice Birds
1945 ......Donna Jeanne Pospisil, Jean-Pierre Brunet,
SC of New York
1946 ......Donna Jeanne Pospisil, Jean-Pierre Brunet,
SC of New York

1947 ......Yvonne Claire Sherman, Robert J.
Swenning, SC of New York
1948 ......Karol Kennedy, Peter Kennedy, Seattle SC
1949 ......Karol Kennedy, Peter Kennedy, Seattle SC
1950 ......Karol Kennedy, Peter Kennedy,
Broadmoor SC
1951 ......Karol Kennedy, Peter Kennedy,
Broadmoor SC
1952 ......Karol Kennedy, Peter Kennedy,
Broadmoor SC
1953 ......Carole Ann Ormaca, Robin Greiner,
SC of Fresno
1954 ......Carole Ann Ormaca, Robin Greiner,
SC of Fresno
1955 ......Carole Ann Ormaca, Robin Greiner,
St Moritz ISC
1956 ......Carole Ann Ormaca, Robin Greiner,
St Moritz ISC
1957 ......Nancy Rouillard Ludington, Ronald
Ludington, Commonwealth FSC/
SC of Boston
1958 ......Nancy Rouillard Ludington, Ronald
Ludington, Commonwealth FSC/
SC of Boston
1959 ......Nancy Rouillard Ludington, Ronald
Ludington, Commonwealth FSC
1960 ......Nancy Rouillard Ludington, Ronald
Ludington, Commonwealth FSC
1961 ......Maribel Y. Owen, Dudley S. Richards,
SC of Boston
1962 ......Dorothyann Nelson, Pieter Kollen,
Village of Lake Placid
1963 ......Judianne Fotheringill, Jerry J. Fotheringill,
Broadmoor SC
1964 ......Judianne Fotheringill, Jerry J. Fotheringill,
Broadmoor SC
1965 ......Vivian Joseph, Ronald Joseph,
Chicago FSC
1966 ......Cynthia Kauffman, Ronald Kauffman,
Seattle SC
1967 ......Cynthia Kauffman, Ronald Kauffman,
Seattle SC
1968 ......Cynthia Kauffman, Ronald Kauffman,
Seattle SC
1969 ......Cynthia Kauffman, Ronald Kauffman,
Seattle SC
1970 ......Jo Jo Starbuck, Kenneth Shelley,
Arctic Blades FSC
1971 ......Jo Jo Starbuck, Kenneth Shelley,
Arctic Blades FSC
1972 ......Jo Jo Starbuck, Kenneth Shelley,
Arctic Blades FSC
1973 ......Melissa Militano, Mark Militano,
SC of New York
1974 ......Melissa Militano, Johnny Johns,
SC of New York/Detroit SC
1975 ......Melissa Militano, Johnny Johns, SC of NY/Detroit SC

Pairs *(Cont.)*

1976 ......Tai Babilonia, Randy Gardner,
Los Angeles FSC
1977 ...:...Tai Babilonia, Randy Gardner, LA FSC
1978 ......Tai Babilonia, Randy Gardner,
Los Angeles FSC/Santa Monica FSC
1979 ......Tai Babilonia, Randy Gardner,
Los Angeles FSC/Santa Monica FSC
1980 ......Tai Babilonia, Randy Gardner,
Los Angeles FSC/Santa Monica FSC
1981 ......Caitlin Carruthers, Peter Carruthers,
SC of Wilmington
1982 ......Caitlin Carruthers, Peter Carruthers,
SC of Wilmington
1983 ......Caitlin Carruthers, Peter Carruthers,
SC of Wilmington
1984 ......Caitlin Carruthers, Peter Carruthers,
SC of Wilmington
1985 ......Jill Watson, Peter Oppegard,
Los Angeles FSC
1986 ......Gillian Wachsman, Todd Waggoner,
SC of Wilmington
1987 ......Jill Watson, Peter Oppegard, Los Angeles FSC

1988 ......Jill Watson, Peter Oppegard,
Los Angeles FSC
1989 ......Kristi Yamaguchi, Rudy Galindo, St Mortiz ISC
1990 ......Kristi Yamaguchi, Rudy Galindo, St Mortiz ISC
1991 ......Natasha Kuchiki, Todd Sand,
Los Angeles FSC
1992 ......Calla Urbanski, Rocky Marval,
U of Delaware FSC/SC of New York
1993 ......Calla Urbanski, Rocky Marval,
U of Delaware FSC/SC of New York
1994 ......Jenni Meno, Todd Sand,
Winterhurst FSC/Los Angeles FSC
1995 ......Jenni Meno, Todd Sand,
Winterhurst FSC/Los Angeles FSC
1996 ......Jenni Meno, Todd Sand,
Winterhurst FSC/Los Angeles FSC
1997 ......Kyoko Ina, Jason Dungjen, SC of New York
1998 ......Kyoko Ina, Jason Dungjen, SC of New York
1999 ......Danielle Hartsell, Steve Hartsell, Detroit SC
2000 ......Kyoko Ina and John Zimmerman,
SC of New York/Birmingham FSC

Dance

1914 ......Waltz: Theresa Weld, Nathaniel W. Niles,
SC of Boston
1915–19..No competition
1920 ......Waltz: Theresa Weld, Nathaniel W. Niles,
SC of Boston
Fourteenstep: Gertrude Cheever Porter,
Irving Brokaw, New York SC
1921 ......Waltz and Fourteenstep: Theresa Weld
Blanchard, Nathaniel W. Niles, SC of Boston
1922 ......Waltz: Beatrix Loughran, Edward M.
Howland, New York SC/SC of Boston
Fourteenstep: Theresa Weld Blanchard,
Nathaniel W. Niles, SC of Boston
1923 ......Waltz: Mr. & Mrs. Henry W. Howe,
New York SC
Fourteenstep: Sydney Goode, James B.
Greene, New York SC
1924 ......Waltz: Rosaline Dunn, Frederick Gabel,
New York SC
Fourteenstep: Sydney Goode, James B.
Greene, New York SC
1925 ......Waltz and Fourteenstep: Virginia Slattery,
Ferrier T. Martin, New York SC
1926 ......Waltz: Rosaline Dunn, Joseph K. Savage,
New York SC
Fourteenstep: Sydney Goode, James B.
Greene, New York SC
1927 ......Waltz and Fourteenstep: Rosaline Dunn,
Joseph K. Savage, New York SC
1928 ......Waltz: Rosaline Dunn, Joseph K. Savage,
New York SC
Fourteenstep: Ada Bauman Kelly, George T.
Braakman, New York SC
1929 ......Waltz and Original Dance combined:
Edith C. Secord, Joseph K. Savage,
SC of New York
1930 ......Waltz: Edith C. Secord, Joseph K. Savage,
SC of New York
Original: Clara Rotch Frothingham, George
E. B. Hill, SC of Boston
1931 ......Waltz: Edith C. Secord, Ferrier T. Martin,
SC of New York

1931 ......Original: Theresa Weld Blanchard, Nathaniel
W. Niles, SC of Boston
1932 ......Waltz: Edith C. Secord, Joseph K. Savage,
SC of New York
Original: Clara Rotch Frothingham, George
E. B. Hill, SC of Boston
1933 ......Waltz: Ilse Twaroschk, Frederick F.
Fleishmann, Brooklyn FSC
Original: Suzanne Davis, Frederick
Goodridge, SC of Boston
1934 ......Waltz: Nettie C. Prantel, Roy Hunt, SC of
New York
Original: Suzanne Davis, Frederick
Goodridge, SC of Boston
1935 ......Waltz: Nettie C. Prantel, Roy Hunt,
SC of New York
1936 ......Marjorie Parker, Joseph K. Savage,
SC of New York
1937 ......Nettie C. Prantel, Harold Hartshorne,
SC of New York
1938 ......Nettie C. Prantel, Harold Hartshorne,
SC of New York
1939 ......Sandy Macdonald, Harold Hartshorne,
SC of New York
1940 ......Sandy Macdonald, Harold Hartshorne,
SC of New York
1941 ......Sandy Macdonald, Harold Hartshorne, SCNY
1942 ......Edith B. Whetstone, Alfred N. Richards, Jr,
Philadelphia SC & HS
1943 ......Marcella May, James Lochead, Jr, Skate & Ski Club
1944 ......Marcella May, James Lochead, Jr, Skate & Ski Club
1945 ......Kathe Mehl Williams, Robert J. Swenning,
SC of New York
1946 ......Anne Davies, Carleton C. Hoffner, Jr,
Washington FSC
1947 ......Lois Waring, Walter H. Bainbridge, Jr,
Baltimore FSC/Washigton FSC
1948 ......Lois Waring, Walter H. Bainbridge, Jr,
Baltimore FSC/Washington FSC
1949 ......Lois Waring, Walter H. Bainbridge, Jr,
Baltimore FSC/Washington FSC
1950 ......Lois Waring, Michael McGean, Baltimore FSC

Dance *(Cont.)*

1951 ......Carmel Bodel, Edward L. Bodel,
St Moritz ISC
1952 ......Lois Waring, Michael McGean,
Baltimore FSC
1953 ......Carol Ann Peters, Daniel C. Ryan,
Washington FSC
1954 ......Carmel Bodel, Edward L. Bodel, St Moritz ISC
1955 ......Carmel Bodel, Edward L. Bodel,
St Moritz ISC
1956 ......Joan Zamboni, Roland Junso,
Arctic Blades FSC
1957 ......Sharon McKenzie, Bert Wright,
Los Angeles FSC
1958 ......Andree Anderson, Donald Jacoby, Buffalo SC
1959 ......Andree Anderson Jacoby, Donald Jacoby,
Buffalo SC
1960 ......Margie Ackles, Charles W. Phillips, Jr,
Los Angeles FSC/Arctic Blades FSC
1961 ......Diane C. Sherbloom, Larry Pierce,
Los Angeles FSC/WC of Indianapolis
1962 ......Yvonne N. Littlefield, Peter F. Betts,
Arctic Blades FSC/ Paramount, CA
1963 ......Sally Schantz, Stanley Urban,
SC of Boston/Buffalo SC
1964 ......Darlene Streich, Charles D. Fetter, Jr,
WC of Indianapolis
1965 ......Kristin Fortune, Dennis Sveum,
Los Angeles FSC
1966 ......Kristin Fortune, Dennis Sveum, Los Angeles FSC
1967 ......Lorna Dyer, John Carrell, Broadmoor SC
1968 ......Judy Schwomeyer, James Sladky,
WC of Indianapolis/Genesee FSC
1969 ......Judy Schwomeyer, James Sladky,
WC of Indianapolis/Genesee FSC
1970 ......Judy Schwomeyer, James Sladky,
WC of Indianapolis/Genesee FSC
1971 ......Judy Schwomeyer, James Sladky,
WC of Indianapolis/Genesee FSC
1972 ......Judy Schwomeyer, James Sladky,
WC of Indianapolis/Genesee FSC
1973 ......Mary Karen Campbell, Johnny Johns,
Lansing SC/Detroit SC
1974 ......Colleen O'Connor, Jim Millns, Broadmoor
SC/ City of Colorado Springs
1975 ......Colleen O'Connor, Jim Millns, Broadmoor SC

1976 ......Colleen O'Connor, Jim Millns,
Broadmoor SC
1977 ......Judy Genovesi, Kent Weigle,
SC of Hartford/Charter Oak FSC
1978 ......Stacey Smith, John Summers,
SC of Wilmington
1979 ......Stacey Smith, John Summers,
SC of Wilmington
1980 ......Stacey Smith, John Summers,
SC of Wilmington
1981 ......Judy Blumberg, Michael Seibert,
Broadmoor SC/ISC of Indianapolis
1982 ......Judy Blumberg, Michael Seibert,
Broadmoor SC/ISC of Indianapolis
1983 ......Judy Blumberg, Michael Seibert,
Pittsburgh FSC
1984 ......Judy Blumberg, Michael Seibert,
Pittsburgh FSC
1985 ......Judy Blumberg, Michael Seibert,
Pittsburgh FSC
1986 ......Renee Roca, Donald Adair,
Genesee FSC/Academy FSC
1987 ......Suzanne Semanick, Scott Gregory,
U of Delaware SC
1988 ......Suzanne Semanick, Scott Gregory,
U of Delaware SC
1989 ......Susan Wynne, Joseph Druar,
Broadmoor SC/Seattle SC
1990 ......Susan Wynne, Joseph Druar,
Broadmoor SC/Seattle SC
1991 ......Elizabeth Punsalan, Jerod Swallow,
Broadmoor SC
1992 ......April Sargent, Russ Witherby,
Ogdensburg FSC/U of Delaware FSC
1993 ......Renee Roca, Gorsha Sur, Broadmoor SC
1994 ......Elizabeth Punsalan, Jerod Swallow,
Broadmoor SC/Detroit SC
1995 ......Renee Roca, Gorsha Sur, Broadmoor SC
1996 ......Elizabeth Punsalan, Jerod Swallow, Detroit SC
1997 ......Elizabeth Punsalan, Jerod Swallow, Detroit SC
1998 ......Elizabeth Punsalan, Jerod Swallow, Detroit SC
1999 ......Naomi Lang, Peter Tchernyshev, Detroit SC
2000 ....Naomi Lang, Peter Tchernyshev, Detroit SC

U.S. Olympic Gold Medalists

Women

1956	Tenley Albright
1960	Carol Heiss
1968	Peggy Fleming
1976	Dorothy Hamill
1992	Kristi Yamaguchi
1998	Tara Lipinski

Men

1948	Richard Button
1952	Richard Button
1956	Hayes Alan Jenkins
1960	David W. Jenkins
1984	Scott Hamilton
1988	Brian Boitano

Special Achievements

Women successfully landing a triple axel in competition:
Midori Ito, Japan, 1988 free-skating competition at Aichi, Japan.
Tonya Harding, United States, 1991 U.S. Figure Skating Championship.
Men successfully landing three quadruple jumps in competition:
Timothy Goebel, United States, 1999 Skate America, Colorado Springs (two Salchows and one toe loop).

Miscellaneous Sports

Tour de France
winner Lance
Armstrong

No Doubt

With an astonishing display of endurance and power, Lance Armstrong won a second Tour and silenced the skeptics

BY DAVID FLEMING

HOLDING AN insurmountable lead, Lance Armstrong turned the final stage of the Tour de France into a leisurely bike ride. After leaving the Eiffel Tower he joked with other riders and donned a long-haired wig. As he rode past the Louvre he took pictures of the crowds, and as he sped down the Champs-Élysées and around the Arc de Triomphe he toasted the flag-waving Americans with champagne.

Stage 21, in essence, was a celebration of Armstrong the cyclist. A Tour de Lance, if you will. His second consecutive Tour victory, this time by a convincing six minutes and two seconds over runner-up Jan Ullrich of Germany, quashed the whispers that Armstrong's first victory was a fluke and elevated him to his current status as the greatest racer in the world. "A total vindication," said Armstrong. "This is sweet."

The finish line, however, was a celebration of something even more poignant and transcendent. It was a tribute to Armstrong the cancer survivor. Here, he hugged his wife, Kristin, and fought back tears as he held up his nine-month-old son, Luke, who was wearing a yellow jersey, just like his pop.

Luke was born three months after Armstrong's 1999 Tour victory. "This one's even more special than last year," said the proud papa. "Partly because of this little guy." Looking on near the finish line was Austin mayor Kirk Watson, also a cancer survivor (Armstrong lives in Austin), and Dr. Craig Nichols, the oncologist Armstrong says saved his life. "Lance is truly a role model of strength and determination for all of us to follow," said Watson.

After bursting onto the pro cycling scene with youthful bravado following the Barcelona Olympics, Armstrong won the 1993 world championships and a couple of Tour de France stages. He seemed to be on the verge of stardom. Then, in October of 1996 he was diagnosed with testicular cancer. He had been feeling pain but had written it off as part of the normal aches associated with his rigorous training. The delay had allowed the cancer to spread to his brain and lungs. With a 40% to 50% chance of survival, Armstrong underwent surgery to have a testicle removed and the tumors in his brain excised. Then came massive doses of chemotherapy in four separate five-day sessions.

"My message now is: There is hope," said Armstrong. "Cancer isn't a death sentence. Survivors can go on, and they are better than they were before."

That was certainly the case with Armstrong. He not only survived, he also came out of his battle with cancer a better, more mature man and, unexpectedly, a much improved racer. He won back-to-back Tours and, in September 2000, grabbed a bronze medal in the time trial at the Olympic Games in Sydney. In addition to these triumphs on his bike, Armstrong has helped raise millions of dollars to promote cancer awareness and research. For that he was nominated for the Congressional Gold Medal.

Armstrong acknowledges that while his victories as a rider are extraordinary, they pale in comparison to his legacy as a role model for cancer patients. Still, the ordeal had some surprisingly beneficial consequences for his cycling. "Cancer was probably the best thing that ever happened to me," he said. "The biggest part and the most important part was the mental side of it. The way I approach the sport now, the way I approach the bike now, my training, my diet, the races. Psychologically it was a good thing for me to be so scared and so fearful and then to be given another chance."

The cancer not only toughened Armstrong mentally, it also helped pare down his frame by 20 pounds, which gave him a more slender, racing-friendly form. "Once I got back into racing in 1998, I could always draw strength from the fact that, no matter how hard things might look at a given moment, they could never be as hard as when I was back in Austin in a hospital bed with my hair falling out," he said. "I knew if I could beat cancer, I could get over any mountain."

Even the Pyrenees and the Alps. Indeed, it was an extraordinary charge early in the mountain stages of the race—an effort that French rider Richard Virenque, a climbing specialist, compared to a plane taking off—that propelled Armstrong to his second yellow jersey. A week

Armstrong said the presence of nine-month-old Luke made this victory all the sweeter.

later Armstrong held off challenges from Virenque, Ullrich and Marco Pantani of Italy before cruising down the Champs-Élysées in front of thousands of his cheering countrymen.

In 1999 some cycling fans had questioned Armstrong's victory for two reasons. First, the skeptics—or perhaps the cynics in this case—believed that such a speedy and triumphant recovery from cancer was not possible without the use of performance-enhancing drugs. The '98 Tour had been marred by a drug scandal that bounced seven teams from the race, and in the cynics' view, Armstrong was the drug story in '99. But the American passed every drug test and stared down every suspicious question from the press. The second reason some fans were skeptical of Armstrong's '99 victory was the absence of several top riders, including Virenque and Pantani, in that race.

He laid those doubts conclusively to rest in 2000. The Tour field was stocked with the sport's best, and Armstrong drove them into the ground. "He was the strongest man, and he met our every attack. He earned this victory," said Ullrich, who won the '97 Tour. "Armstrong is a worthy champion."

Indeed, Armstrong is something even more special—and rare—in today's sports world. He's also a worthy hero.

Archery

National Men's Champions

1879...Will H. Thompson	1909...George Bryant	1941...Larry Hughes	1975...Darrell Pace
1880...L.L. Pedinghaus	1910...Henry Richardson	1946...Wayne Thompson	1976...Darrell Pace
1881...F.H. Walworth	1911...Dr. Robert Elmer	1947...Jack Wilson	1977...Rick McKinney
1882...D.H. Nash	1912...George Bryant	1948...Larry Hughes	1978...Darrell Pace
1883...Col. Robert Williams	1913...George Bryant	1949...Russ Reynolds	1979...Rick McKinney
1884...Col. Robert Williams	1914...Dr. Robert Elmer	1950...Stan Overby	1980...Rick McKinney
1885...Col. Robert Williams	1915...Dr. Robert Elmer	1951...Russ Reynolds	1981...Rick McKinney
1886...W.A. Clark	1916...Dr. Robert Elmer	1952...Robert Larson	1982...Rick McKinney
1887...W.A. Clark	1919...Dr. Robert Elmer	1953...Bill Glackin	1983...Rick McKinney
1888...Lewis Maxson	1920...Dr. Robert Elmer	1954...Robert Rhode	1984...Darrell Pace
1889...Lewis Maxson	1921...James Jiles	1955...Joe Fries	1985...Rick McKinney
1890...Lewis Maxson	1922...Dr. Robert Elmer	1956...Joe Fries	1986...Rick McKinney
1891...Lewis Maxson	1923...Bill Palmer	1957...Joe Fries	1987...Rick McKinney
1892...Lewis Maxson	1924...James Jiles	1958...Robert Bitner	1988...Jay Barrs
1893...Lewis Maxson	1925...Dr. Paul Crouch	1959...Wilbert Vetrovsky	1989...Ed Eliason
1894...Lewis Maxson	1926...Stanley Spencer	1960...Robert Kadlec	1990...Ed Eliason
1895...W.B. Robinson	1927...Dr. Paul Crouch	1961...Clayton Sherman	1991...Ed Eliason
1896...Lewis Maxson	1928...Bill Palmer	1962...Charles Sandlin	1992...Alan Rasor
1897...W.A. Clark	1929...Dr. E.K. Roberts	1963...Dave Keaggy Jr.	1993...Jay Barrs
1898...Lewis Maxson	1930...Russ Hoogerhyde	1964...Dave Keaggy Jr.	1994...Jay Barrs
1899...M.C. Howell	1931...Russ Hoogerhyde	1965...George Slinzer	1995...Justin Huish
1900...A.R. Clark	1932...Russ Hoogerhyde	1966...Hardy Ward	1996...Richard (Butch)
1901...Will H. Thompson	1933...Ralph Miller	1967...Ray Rogers	Johnson
1902...Will H. Thompson	1934...Russ Hoogerhyde	1968...Hardy Ward	1997...Richard (Butch)
1903...Will H. Thompson	1935...Gilman Keasey	1969...Ray Rogers	Johnson
1904...George Bryant	1936...Gilman Keasey	1970...Joe Thornton	1998...Victor Wunderle
1905...George Bryant	1937...Russ Hoogerhyde	1971...John Williams	1999...Victor Wunderle
1906...Henry Richardson	1938...Pat Chambers	1972...Kevin Erlandson	2000...Richard (Butch)
1907...Henry Richardson	1939...Pat Chambers	1973...Darrell Pace	Johnson
1908...Will H. Thompson	1940...Russ Hoogerhyde	1974...Darrell Pace	

National Women's Champions

1879...Mrs. S. Brown	1909...Harriet Case	1939...Belvia Carter	1972...Ruth Rowe
1880...Mrs. T. Davies	1910...J.V. Sullivan	1940...Ann Weber	1973...Doreen Wilber
1881...Mrs. A.H. Gibbes	1911...Mrs. J.S. Taylor	1941...Ree Dillinger	1974...Doreen Wilber
1882...Mrs. A.H. Gibbes	1912...Mrs. Witwer	1946...Ann Weber	1975...Irene Lorensen
1883...Mrs. M.C. Howell	Tayler	1947...Ann Weber	1976...Luann Ryon
1884...Mrs. H. Hall	1913...Mrs. P. Fletcher	1948...Jean Lee	1977...Luann Ryon
1885...Mrs. M.C. Howell	1914...Mrs. B.P. Gray	1949...Jean Lee	1978...Luann Ryon
1886...Mrs. M.C. Howell	1915...Cynthia Wesson	1950...Jean Lee	1979...Lynette Johnson
1887...Mrs. A.M. Phillips	1916...Cynthia Wesson	1951...Jean Lee	1980...Judi Adams
1888...Mrs. A.M. Phillips	1919...Dorothy Smith	1952...Ann Weber	1981...Debra Metzger
1889...Mrs. A.M. Phillips	1920...Cynthia Wesson	1953...Ann Weber	1982...Luann Ryon
1890...Mrs. M.C. Howell	1921...Mrs. L.C. Smith	1954...Luarette Young	1983...Nancy Myrick
1891...Mrs. M.C. Howell	1922...Dorothy Smith	1955...Ann Clark	1984...Ruth Rowe
1892...Mrs. M.C. Howell	1923...Norma Pierce	1956...Carole Meinhart	1985...Terri Pesho
1893...Mrs. M.C. Howell	1924...Dorothy Smith	1957...Carole Meinhart	1986...Debra Ochs
1894...Mrs. Albert Kern	1925...Dorothy Smith	1958...Carole Meinhart	1987...Terry Quinn
1895...Mrs. M.C. Howell	1926...Dorothy Smith	1959...Carole Meinhart	1988...Debra Ochs
1896...Mrs. M.C. Howell	1927...Mrs. R. Johnson	1960...Ann Clark	1989...Debra Ochs
1897...Mrs. J.S. Baker	1928...Beatrice	1961...Victoria Cook	1990...Denise Parker
1898...Mrs. M.C. Howell	Hodgson	1962...Nancy	1991...Denise Parker
1899...Mrs. M.C. Howell	1929...Audrey Grubbs	Vonderheide	1992...Sherry Block
1900...Mrs. M.C. Howell	1930...Audrey Grubbs	1963...Nancy	1993...Denise Parker
1901...Mrs. C.E.	1931...Dorothy	Vonderheide	1994...Judy Adams
Woodruff	Cummings	1964...Victoria Cook	1995...Jessica Carlson
1902...Mrs. M.C. Howell	1932...Ilda Hanchette	1965...Nancy Pfeiffer	1996...Janet Dykman
1903...Mrs. M.C. Howell	1933...Madelaine Taylor	1966...Helen Thornton	1997...Janet Dykman
1904...Mrs. M.C. Howell	1934...Desales Mudd	1967...Ardelle Mills	1998...Janet Dykman
1905...Mrs. M.C. Howell	1935...Ruth Hodgert	1968...Victoria Cook	1999...Denise Parker
1906...Mrs. E.C. Cook	1936...Gladys Hammer	1969...Doreen Wilber	2000...Karen Scavatto
1907...Mrs. M.C. Howell	1937...Gladys Hammer	1970...Nancy Myrick	
1908...Harriet Case	1938...Jean Tenney	1971...Doreen Wilber	

Chess

World Champions

FIDE

1866–94	Wilhelm Steinitz, Austria
1894–1921	Emanuel Lasker, Germany
1921–27	Jose Capablanca, Cuba
1927–35	Alexander Alekhine, France
1935–37	Max Euwe, Holland
1937–47	Alexander Alekhine, France
1948–57	Mikhail Botvinnik, USSR
1957–58	Vassily Smyslov, USSR
1958–59	Mikhail Botvinnik, USSR
1960–61	Mikhail Tal, USSR
1961–63	Mikhail Botvinnik, USSR

FIDE (Cont.)

1963–69	Tigran Petrosian, USSR
1969–72	Boris Spassky, USSR
1972–75	Bobby Fischer, United States
1975–85	Anatoly Karpov, USSR
1985–93	*Garry Kasparov, USSR
1994–98	Anatoly Karpov, Russia
1999–	Alexander Khalifman, Russia

*Kasparov stripped of title by FIDE in 1993; title vacant until '94.

Professional Chess Association

1993–	Garry Kasparov

United States Champions

1857–71	Paul Morphy
1871–76	George Mackenzie
1876–80	James Mason
1880–89	George Mackenzie
1889–90	Samuel Lipschutz
1890	Jackson Showalter
1890–91	Max Judd
1891–92	Jackson Showalter
1892–94	Samuel Lipschutz
1894	Jackson Showalter
1894–95	Albert Hodges
1895–97	Jackson Showalter
1897–1906	Harry Pillsbury
1906–09	Vacant
1909–36	Frank Marshall
1936–44	Samuel Reshevsky
1944–46	Arnold Denker
1946–48	Samuel Reshevsky
1948–51	Herman Steiner
1951–54	Larry Evans
1954–57	Arthur Bisguier

1957–61	Bobby Fischer
1961–62	Larry Evans
1962–68	Bobby Fischer
1968–69	Larry Evans
1969–72	Samuel Reshevsky
1972–73	Robert Byrne
1973–74	Lubomir Kavale / John Grefe
1974–77	Walter Browne
1978–80	Lubomir Kavalek
1980–81	Larry Evans / Larry Christiansen / Walter Browne
1981–83	Walter Browne / Yasser Seirawan
1983	Roman Dzindzichashvili
1983	Larry Christiansen / Walter Browne
1984–85	Lev Alburt
1986	Yasser Seirawan

1987	Joel Benjamin / Nick DeFirmian
1988	Michael Wilder
1989	Roman Dzindzichashvili / Stuart Rachels / Yasser Seirawan
1990	Lev Alburt
1991	Gata Kamski
1992	Patrick Wolff
1993	Alex Yermolinsky / A. Shabalov
1994	Boris Gulko
1995	Patrick Wolff / Nick DeFirmian / Alexander Ivanov
1996	Alex Yermolinsky
1997	Alex Yermolinsky
1998	Alex Yermolinsky
1999	Boris Gulko

Curling

World Men's Champions

Year	Country, Skip	Year	Country, Skip	Year	Country, Skip
1972	Canada, Crest Melesnuk	1982	Canada, Al Hackner	1992	Switzerland, Markus Eggler
1973	Sweden, Kjell Oscarius	1983	Canada, Ed Werenich	1993	Canada, Russ Howard
1974	U.S., Bud Somerville	1984	Norway, Eigil Ramsfjell	1994	Canada, Rick Folk
1975	Switzerland, Otto Danieli	1985	Canada, Al Hackner	1995	Canada, Kerry Burtnyk
1976	U.S., Bruce Roberts	1986	Canada, Ed Luckowich	1996	Canada, Jeff Stoughton
1977	Sweden, Ragnar Kamp	1987	Canada, Russ Howard	1997	Sweden, Peter Lindholm
1978	U.S., Bob Nichols	1988	Norway, Eigil Ramsfjell	1998	Canada, Wayne Middaugh
1979	Norway, Kristian Soerum	1989	Canada, Pat Ryan	1999	Scotland, Hammy McMillan
1980	Canada, Rich Folk	1990	Canada, Ed Werenich	2000	Canada, Greg McAulay
1981	Switzerland, Jurg Tanner	1991	Scotland, David Smith		

World Women's Champions

Year	Country, Skip	Year	Country, Skip	Year	Country, Skip
1979	Switzerland, Gaby Casanova	1985	Canada, Linda Moore	1993	Canada, Sandra Peterson
1980	Canada, Marj Mitchell	1986	Canada, Marilyn Darte	1994	Canada, Sandra Peterson
1981	Sweden, Elisabeth Hogstrom	1987	Canada, Pat Sanders	1995	Sweden, Elisabet Gustafson
1982	Denmark, Marianne Jorgenson	1988	Germany, Andrea Schopp	1996	Canada, Marilyn Bodogh
1983	Switzerland, Erika Mueller	1989	Canada, Heather Houston	1997	Canada, Sandra Schmirler
1984	Canada, Connie Lallberte	1990	Norway, Dordi Nordby	1998	Sweden, Elisabet Gustafson
		1991	Norway, Dordi Nordby	1999	Sweden, Elisabet Gustafson
		1992	Sweden, Elisabet Johanssen	2000	Canada, Kelley Law

U.S. Men's Champions

Year	Site	Winning Club	Skip
1957	Chicago, IL	Hibbing, MN	Harold Lauber
1958	Milwaukee, WI	Detroit, MI	Douglas Fisk
1959	Green Bay, WI	Hibbing, MN	Fran Kleffman
1960	Chicago, IL	Grafton, ND	Orvil Gilleshammer
1961	Grand Forks, ND	Seattle, WA	Frank Crealock
1962	Detroit, MI	Hibbing, MN	Fran Kleffman
1963	Duluth, MN	Detroit, MI	Mike Slyziuk
1964	Utica, NY	Duluth, MN	Robert Magle Jr.
1965	Seattle, WA	Superior, WI	Bud Somerville
1966	Hibbing, MN	Fargo, ND	Joe Zbacnik
1967	Winchester, MA	Seattle, WA	Bruce Roberts
1968	Madison, WI	Superior, WI	Bud Somerville
1969	Grand Forks, ND	Superior, WI	Bud Somerville
1970	Ardsley, NY	Grafton, ND	Art Tallackson
1971	Duluth, MN	Edmore, ND	Dale Dalziel
1972	Wilmette, IL	Grafton, ND	Robert Labonte
1973	Colorado Springs, CO	Winchester, MA	Charles Reeves
1974	Schenectady, NY	Superior, WI	Bud Somerville
1975	Detroit, MI	Seattle, WA	Ed Risling
1976	Wausau, WI	Hibbing, MN	Bruce Roberts
1977	Northbrook, IL	Hibbing, MN	Bruce Roberts
1978	Utica, NY	Superior, WI	Bob Nichols
1979	Superior, WI	Bemidji, MN	Scott Baird
1980	Bemidji, MN	Hibbing, MN	Paul Pustovar
1981	Fairbanks, AK	Superior, WI	Bob Nichols
1982	Brookline, MA	Madison, WI	Steve Brown
1983	Colorado Springs, CO	Colorado Springs, CO	Don Cooper
1984	Hibbing, MN	Hibbing, MN	Bruce Roberts
1985	Mequon, WI	Wilmette, IL	Tim Wright
1986	Seattle, WA	Madison, WI	Steve Brown
1987	Lake Placid, NY	Seattle, WA	Jim Vukich
1988	St. Paul, MN	Seattle, WA	Doug Jones
1989	Detroit, MI	Seattle, WA	Jim Vukich
1990	Superior, WI	Seattle, WA	Doug Jones
1991	Utica, NY	Madison, WI	Steve Brown
1992	Grafton, ND	Seattle, WA	Doug Jones
1993	St. Paul, MN	Bemidji, MN	Scott Baird
1994	Duluth, MN	Bemidji, MN	Scott Baird
1995	Appleton, WI	Superior, WI	Tim Somerville
1996	Bemidji, MN	Superior, WI	Tim Somerville
1997	Seattle,WA	Langdon, ND	Craig Disher
1998	Bismarck, SD	Stevens Pt., WI	Paul Pustovar
1999	Duluth, MN	Superior, WI	Tim Somerville
2000	Ogden, UT	Wisconsin3	Craig Brown

U.S. Women's Champions

Year	Site	Winning Club	Skip
1977	Wilmette, IL	Hastings, NY	Margaret Smith
1978	Duluth, MN	Wausau, WI	Sandy Robarge
1979	Winchester, MA	Seattle, WA	Nancy Langley
1980	Seattle, WA	Seattle, WA	Sharon Kozal
1981	Kettle Moraine, WI	Seattle, WA	Nancy Langley
1982	Bowling Green, OH	Oak Park, IL	Ruth Schwenker
1983	Grafton, ND	Seattle, WA	Nancy Langley
1984	Wauwatosa, WI	Duluth, MN	Amy Hatten
1985	Hershey, PA	Fairbanks, AK	Bev Birklid
1986	Chicago, IL	St Paul, MN	Gerri Tilden
1987	St Paul, MN	Seattle, WA	Sharon Good
1988	Darien, CT	Seattle, WA	Nancy Langley
1989	Detroit, MI	Rolla, ND	Jan Lagasse
1990	Superior, WI	Denver, CO	Bev Behnke
1991	Utica, NY	Houston, TX	Maymar Gemmell
1992	Grafton, ND	Madison, WI	Lisa Schoeneberg
1993	St Paul, MN	Denver, CO	Bev Behnke
1994	Duluth, MN	Denver, CO	Bev Behnke
1995	Appleton, WI	Madison, WI	Lisa Schoeneberg
1996	Bemidji, MN	Madison, WI	Lisa Schoeneberg

U.S. Women's Champions *(Cont.)*

Year	Site	Winning Club	Skip
1997	Seattle, WA	Arlington, WI	Patti Lank
1998	Bismarck, SD	Wilmette, IL	Kari Erickson
1999	Duluth, MN	Madison, WI	Patti Lank
2000	Ogden, UT	Nebraska	Amy Wright

Cycling

Professional Road Race World Champions

1927 ....Alfred Binda, Italy
1928 ....George Ronsse, Belgium
1929 ....George Ronsse, Belgium
1930 ....Alfred Binda, Italy
1931 ....Learco Guerra, Italy
1932 ....Alfred Binda, Italy
1933 ....George Speicher, France
1934 ....Karel Kaers, Belgium
1935 ....Jean Aerts, Belgium
1936 ....Antonio Magne, France
1937 ....Elio Meulenberg, Belgium
1938 ....Marcel Kint, Belgium
No competition 1939–45
1946 ....Hans Knecht, Switzerland
1947 ....Theo. Middelkamp, Holland
1948 ....Alberic Schotte, Belgium
1949 ....Henri Van Steenbergen, Belgium
1950 ....Alberic Schotte, Belgium
1951 ....Ferdinand Kubler, Switzerland
1952 ....Heinz Mueller, Germany
1953 ....Fausto Coppi, Italy
1954 ....Louison Bobet, France
1955 ....Stan Ockers, Belgium
1956 ....Rik Van Steenbergen, Belgium

1957 ....Rik Van Steenbergen, Belgium
1958 ....Ercole Baldini, Italy
1959 ....Andre Darrigade, France
1960 ....Rik van Looy, Belgium
1961 ....Rik van Looy, Belgium
1962 ....Jean Stablenski, France
1963 ....Bennoni Beheyt, Belgium
1964 ....Jan Janssen, Holland
1965 ....Tommy Simpson, England
1966 ....Rudi Altig, West Germany
1967 ....Eddy Merckx, Belgium
1968 ....Vittorio Adorni, Italy
1969 ....Harm Ottenbros, Netherlands
1970 ....J.P. Monseré, Belgium
1971 ....Eddy Merckx, Belgium
1972 ....Marino Basso, Italy
1973 ....Felice Gimondi, Italy
1974 ....Eddy Merckx, Belgium
1975 ....Hennie Kuiper, Holland
1976 ....Freddy Maertens, Belgium
1977 ....Francesco Moser, Italy
1978 ....Gerri Knetemann, Holland
1979 ....Jan Raas, Holland

1980 ....Bernard Hinault, France
1981 ....Freddy Maertens, Belgium
1982 ....Giuseppe Saronni, Italy
1983 ....Greg LeMond, United States
1984 ....Claude Criquielion, Belgium
1985 ....Joop Zoetemelk, Holland
1986 ....Moreno Argentin, Italy
1987 ....Stephen Roche, Ireland
1988 ....Maurizio Fondriest, Italy
1989 ....Greg LeMond, United States
1990 ....Rudy Dhaenene, Belgium
1991 ....Gianni Bugno, Italy
1992 ....Gianni Bugno, Italy
1993 ....Lance Armstrong, United States
1994 ....Luc LeBlanc, France
1995 ....Abraham Olano, Spain
1996 ....Johan Museeuw, Belgium
1997 ....Laurent Brochard, France
1998 ....Oskar Camenzind, Switz
1999 ....Oscar Gomez Freire, Spain

Tour DuPont Winners

Year	Winner	Time
1989	Dag Otto Lauritzen, Norway	33 hrs, 28 min, 48 sec
1990	Raul Alcala, Mexico	45 hrs, 20 min, 9 sec
1991	Erik Breukink, Holland	48 hrs, 56 min, 53 sec
1992	Greg LeMond, United States	44 hrs, 27 min, 43 sec
1993	Raul Alcala, Mexico	46 hrs, 42 min, 52 sec
1994	Viatcheslav Ekimov, Russia	47 hrs, 14 min, 29 sec
1995	Lance Armstrong, United States	46 hrs, 31 min, 16 sec
1996	Lance Armstrong, United States	48 hrs, 20 min, 5 sec

Note: Race not held since 1996.

Tour de France Winners

Year	Winner	Time
1903	Maurice Garin, France	94 hrs, 33 min
1904	Henry Cornet, France	96 hrs, 5 min, 56 sec
1905	Louis Trousselier, France	110 hrs, 26 min, 58 sec
1906	Rene Pottier, France	Not available
1907	Lucien Petit-Breton, France	158 hrs, 54 min, 5 sec
1908	Lucien Petit-Breton, France	Not available
1909	Francois Faber, Luxembourg	157 hrs, 1 min, 22 sec
1910	Octave Lapize, France	162 hrs, 41 min, 30 sec
1911	Gustave Garrigou, France	195 hrs, 37 min
1912	Odile Defraye, Belgium	190 hrs, 30 min, 28 sec
1913	Philippe Thys, Belgium	197 hrs, 54 min
1914	Philippe Thys, Belgium	200 hrs, 28 min, 48 sec
1915–18	No race	
1919	Firmin Lambot, Belgium	231 hrs, 7 min, 15 sec
1920	Philippe Thys, Belgium	228 hrs, 36 min, 13 sec
1921	Leon Scieur, Belgium	221 hrs, 50 min, 26 sec

Tour de France Winners (Cont.)

Year	Winner	Time
1922	Firmin Lambot, Belgium	222 hrs, 8 min, 6 sec
1923	Henri Pelissier, France	222 hrs, 15 min, 30 sec
1924	Ottavio Bottechia, Italy	226 hrs, 18 min, 21 sec
1925	Ottavio Bottechia, Italy	219 hrs, 10 min, 18 sec
1926	Lucien Buysse, Belgium	238 hrs, 44 min, 25 sec
1927	Nicolas Frantz, Luxembourg	198 hrs, 16 min, 42 sec
1928	Nicolas Frantz, Luxembourg	192 hrs, 48 min, 58 sec
1929	Maurice Dewaele, Belgium	186 hrs, 39 min, 16 sec
1930	Andre Leducq, France	172 hrs, 12 min, 16 sec
1931	Antonin Magne, France	177 hrs, 10 min, 3 sec
1932	Andre Leducq, France	154 hrs, 12 min, 49 sec
1933	Georges Speicher, France	147 hrs, 51 min, 37 sec
1934	Antonin Magne, France	147 hrs, 13 min, 58 sec
1935	Romain Maes, Belgium	141 hrs, 32 min
1936	Sylvere Maes, Belgium	142 hrs, 47 min, 32 sec
1937	Roger Lapebie, France	138 hrs, 58 min, 31 sec
1938	Gino Bartali, Italy	148 hrs, 29 min, 12 sec
1939	Sylvere Maes, Belgium	132 hrs, 3 min, 17 sec
1940–46	No race	
1947	Jean Robic, France	148 hrs, 11 min, 25 sec
1948	Gino Bartali, Italy	147 hrs, 10 min, 36 sec
1949	Fausto Coppi, Italy	149 hrs, 40 min, 49 sec
1950	Ferdi Kubler, Switzerland	145 hrs, 36 min, 56 sec
1951	Hugo Koblet, Switzerland	142 hrs, 20 min, 14 sec
1952	Fausto Coppi, Italy	151 hrs, 57 min, 20 sec
1953	Louison Bobet, France	129 hrs, 23 min, 25 sec
1954	Louison Bobet, France	140 hrs, 6 min, 5 sec
1955	Louison Bobet, France	130 hrs, 29 min, 26 sec
1956	Roger Walkowiak, France	124 hrs, 1 min, 16 sec
1957	Jacques Anquetil, France	129 hrs, 46 min, 11 sec
1958	Charly Gaul, Luxembourg	116 hrs, 59 min, 5 sec
1959	Federico Bahamontes, Spain	123 hrs, 46 min, 45 sec
1960	Gastone Nencini, Italy	112 hrs, 8 min, 42 sec
1961	Jacques Anquetil, France	122 hrs, 1 min, 33 sec
1962	Jacques Anquetil, France	114 hrs, 31 min, 54 sec
1963	Jacques Anquetil, France	113 hrs, 30 min, 5 sec
1964	Jacques Anquetil, France	127 hrs, 9 min, 44 sec
1965	Felice Gimondi, Italy	116 hrs, 42 min, 6 sec
1966	Lucien Aimar, France	117 hrs, 34 min, 21 sec
1967	Roger Pingeon, France	136 hrs, 53 min, 50 sec
1968	Jan Janssen, Netherlands	133 hrs, 49 min, 32 sec
1969	Eddy Merckx, Belgium	116 hrs, 16 min, 2 sec
1970	Eddy Merckx, Belgium	119 hrs, 31 min, 49 sec
1971	Eddy Merckx, Belgium	96 hrs, 45 min, 14 sec
1972	Eddy Merckx, Belgium	108 hrs, 17 min, 18 sec
1973	Luis Ocana, Spain	122 hrs, 25 min, 34 sec
1974	Eddy Merckx, Belgium	116 hrs, 16 min, 58 sec
1975	Bernard Thevenet, France	114 hrs, 35 min, 31 sec
1976	Lucien Van Impe, Belgium	116 hrs, 22 min, 23 sec
1977	Bernard Thevenet, France	115 hrs, 38 min, 30 sec
1978	Bernard Hinault, France	108 hrs, 18 min
1979	Bernard Hinault, France	103 hrs, 6 min, 50 sec
1980	Joop Zoetemelk, Netherlands	109 hrs, 19 min, 14 sec
1981	Bernard Hinault, France	96 hrs, 19 min, 38 sec
1982	Bernard Hinault, France	92 hrs, 8 min, 46 sec
1983	Laurent Fignon, France	105 hrs, 7 min, 52 sec
1984	Laurent Fignon, France	112 hrs, 3 min, 40 sec
1985	Bernard Hinault, France	113 hrs, 24 min, 23 sec
1986	Greg LeMond, United States	110 hrs, 35 min, 19 sec
1987	Stephen Roche, Ireland	115 hrs, 27 min, 42 sec
1988	Pedro Delgado, Spain	84 hrs, 27 min, 53 sec
1989	Greg LeMond, United States	87 hrs, 38 min, 35 sec
1990	Greg LeMond, United States	90 hrs, 43 min, 20 sec
1991	Miguel Induráin, Spain	101 hrs, 1 min, 20 sec
1992	Miguel Induráin, Spain	100 hrs, 49 min, 30 sec

Tour de France Winners *(Cont.)*

Year	Winner	Time
1993	Miguel Induráin, Spain	95 hrs, 57 min, 9 sec
1994	Miguel Induráin, Spain	103 hrs, 38 min, 38 sec
1995	Miguel Induráin, Spain	92 hrs, 44 min, 59 sec
1996	Bjarne Riis, Denmark	95 hrs, 57 min, 16 sec
1997	Jan Ullrich, Germany	100 hrs, 30 min, 35 sec
1998	Marco Pantani, Italy	92 hrs, 49 min, 46 sec
1999	Lance Armstrong, United States	91 hrs, 32 min, 16 sec
2000	Lance Armstrong, United States	92 hrs, 33 min, 8 sec

Sled Dog Racing

Iditarod

Year	Winner	Time	Year	Winner	Time
1973	Dick Wilmarth	20 days, 00:49:41	1987	Susan Butcher	11 days, 02:05:13
1974	Carl Huntington	20 days, 15:02:07	1988	Susan Butcher	11 days, 11:41:40
1975	Emmitt Peters	14 days, 14:43:45	1989	Joe Runyan	11 days, 05:24:34
1976	Gerald Riley	18 days, 22:58:17	1990	Susan Butcher	11 days, 01:53:23
1977	Rick Swenson	16 days, 16:27:13	1991	Rick Swenson	12 days, 16:34:39
1978	Dick Mackey	14 days, 18:52:24	1992	Martin Buser	10 days, 19:17:15
1979	Rick Swenson	15 days, 10:37:47	1993	Jeff King	10 days, 15:38:15
1980	Joe May	14 days, 07:11:51	1994	Martin Buser	10 days, 13:02:39
1981	Rick Swenson	12 days, 08:45:02	1995	Doug Swingley	9 days, 02:42:19
1982	Rick Swenson	16 days, 04:40:10	1996	Jeff King	9 days, 05:43:13
1983	Dick Mackey	12 days, 14:10:44	1997	Martin Buser	9 days, 08:30:45
1984	Dean Osmar	12 days, 15:07:33	1998	Jeff King	9 days, 05:52:26
1985	Libby Riddles	18 days, 00:20:17	1999	Doug Swingley	9 days, 14:31:19
1986	Susan Butcher	11 days, 15:06:00	2000	Doug Swingley	9 days, 00:58:06

Fishing

Saltwater Fishing Records

Species	Weight	Where Caught	Date	Angler
Albacore	88 lb 2 oz	Gran Canaria, Canary Islands	Nov 19, 1977	Siegfried Dickemann
Amberjack, greater	155 lb 12 oz	Bermuda	Aug 16, 1992	Larry Trott
Amberjack, Pacific	104 lb	Baja California, Mexico	July 4, 1984	Richard Cresswell
Angler	126 lb 12 oz	Sagnefiorden Hoyanger, Nor	July 4, 1996	Gunnar Thorsteinsen
Barracuda, great	85 lb	Christmas Island, Kiribati	April 11, 1992	John W. Helfrich
Barracuda, Mexican	21 lb	Phantom Isle, Costa Rica	Mar 27, 1987	E. Greg Kent
Barracuda, pickhandle	25 lb 5 oz	Scottburgh, Natal, South Africa	July 3, 1996	Demetrios Stamatis
Bass, barred sand	13 lb 3 oz	Huntington Beach, California	Aug 29, 1988	Robert Halal
Bass, black sea	10 lb 4 oz	Virginia Beach, Virginia	Jan 1, 2000	Allan P. Paschall
Bass, European	20 lb 14 oz	Cap d'Agde, France	Sept. 8, 1999	Robert Mari
Bass, giant sea	563 lb 8 oz	Anacapa Island, California	Aug 20, 1968	James D. McAdam Jr.
Bass, striped	78 lb 8 oz	Atlantic City, New Jersey	Sep 21, 1982	Albert R. McReynolds
Bluefish	31 lb 12 oz	Hatteras Inlet, North Carolina	Jan 30, 1972	James M. Hussey
Bonefish	19 lb	Zululand, South Africa	May 26, 1962	Brian W. Batchelor
Bonito, Atlantic	18 lb 4 oz	Faial Island, Azores	July 8, 1953	D.G. Higgs
Bonito, Pacific	21 lb 3 oz	Malibu, California	July 30, 1978	Gino M. Picciolo
Cabezon	23 lb	Juan De Fuca Strait, Washington	Aug 4, 1990	Wesley Hunter
Cobia	135 lb 9 oz	Shark Bay, Australia	July 9, 1985	Peter W. Goulding
Cod, Atlantic	98 lb 12 oz	Isle of Shoals, New Hampshire	June 8, 1969	Alphonse Bielevich
Cod, Pacific	35 lb	Unalaska Bay, Alaska	June 16, 1999	Jim Johnson
Conger	133 lb 4 oz	South Devon, England	June 5, 1995	Vic Evans
Dolphinfish	88 lb	Highbourne Cay, Bahamas	May 5, 1998	Richard D. Evans
Drum, black	113 lb 1 oz	Lewes, Delaware	Sep 15, 1975	Gerald M. Townsend
Drum, red	94 lb 2 oz	Avon, North Carolina	Nov 7, 1984	David Deuel
Eel, American	9 lb 4 oz	Cape May, New Jersey	Nov 9, 1995	Jeff Pennick
Eel, marbled	36 lb 1 oz	Durban, South Africa	June 10, 1984	Ferdie van Nooten
Flounder, southern	20 lb 9 oz	Nassau Sound, Florida	Dec 23, 1983	Larenza W. Mungin
Flounder, summer	22 lb 7 oz	Montauk, New York	Sep 15, 1975	Charles Nappi
Grouper, warsaw	436 lb 12 oz	Destin, Florida	Dec 22, 1985	Steve Haeusler
Halibut, Atlantic	355 lb 6 oz	Valevag, Norway	Oct 20, 1997	Odd Arve Gunderstad

Saltwater Fishing Records *(Cont.)*

Species	Weight	Where Caught	Date	Angler
Halibut, California	58 lb 9 oz	Santa Rosa Island, California	June 26, 1999	Roger W. Borrell
Halibut, Pacific	459 lb	Dutch Harbor, Alaska	June 11, 1996	Jack Tragis
Jack, crevalle	57 lb 14 oz	Southwest Pass, Louisiana	Aug 15, 1997	Leon Richard
Jack, horse-eye	29 lb 8 oz	Ascencion Island, S Atlantic Ocean	May 28, 1993	Mike Hanson
Jack, Pacific crevalle	39 lb	Playa Zancudo, Costa Rica	Mar 3, 1997	Ingrid Callaghan
Jewfish	680 lb	Fernandina Beach, Florida	May 20, 1961	Lynn Joyner
Kawakawa	29 lb	Isla Clarion, Mexico	Dec 17, 1986	Ronald Nakamura
Lingcod	69 lb 3 oz	Waterfall Resort, Alaska	Aug 18, 1999	Rizwan Sheikh
Mackerel, cero	17 lb 2 oz	Islamorada, Florida	Apr 5, 1986	G. Michael Mills
Mackerel, king	93 lb	San Juan, Puerto Rico	Apr 18, 1999	Steve Perez Graulau
Mackerel, narrowbarred	99 lb	Natal, South Africa	Mar 14, 1982	Michael J. Wilkinson
Mackerel, Spanish	13 lb	Ocracoke Inlet, North Carolina	Nov 4, 1987	Robert Cranton
Marlin, Atlantic blue	1,402 lb 2 oz	Vitoria, Brazil	Feb 29, 1992	Paulo R.A. Amorim
Marlin, black	1,560 lb	Cabo Blanco, Peru	Aug 4, 1953	A.C. Glassell Jr.
Marlin, Pacific blue	1,376 lb	Kaaiwi Point, Hawaii	May 31, 1982	J.W. de Beaubien
Marlin, striped	494 lb	Tutukaka, New Zealand	Jan 16, 1986	Bill Boniface
Marlin, white	181 lb 14 oz	Vitoria, Brazil	Dec 8, 1979	Evandro Luiz Caser
Permit	56 lb 2 oz	Fort Lauderdale, Florida	June 30, 1997	Thomas Sebestyen
Pollock	50 lb	Salstraumen, Norway	Nov 30, 1995	Thor Magnus-Lekang
Pompano, African	50 lb 8 oz	Daytona Beach, Florida	Apr 21, 1990	Tom Sargent
Roosterfish	114 lb	La Paz, Mexico	June 1, 1960	Abe Sackheim
Runner, blue	11 lb 2 oz	Dauphin Island, Alaska	June 28, 1997	Stacey M. Moiren
Runner, rainbow	37 lb 9 oz	Isla Clarion, Mexico	Nov 21, 1991	Tom Pfleger
Sailfish, Atlantic	141 lb 1 oz	Luanda, Angola	Feb 19, 1994	Alfredo de Sousa Neves
Sailfish, Pacific	221 lb	Santa Cruz Island, Ecuador	Feb 12, 1947	C.W. Stewart
Seabass, white	83 lb 12 oz	San Felipe, Mexico	Mar 31, 1953	L.C. Baumgardner
Seatrout, spotted	17 lb 7 oz	Ft. Pierce, Florida	May 11, 1995	Craig F. Carson
Shark, bigeye thresher	802 lb	Tutukaka, New Zealand	Feb 8, 1981	Dianne North
Shark, blue	454 lb	Martha's Vineyard, Massachusetts	July 19, 1996	Pete Bergin
Shark, grter hammrhd	991 lb	Sarasota, Florida	May 30, 1982	Allen Ogle
Shark, Greenland	1,708 lb 9 oz	Trondheimsfjord, Norway	Oct 18, 1987	Terje Nordtvedt
Shark, porbeagle	507 lb	Caithness, Scotland	Mar 9, 1993	Christopher Bennet
Shark, shortfin mako	1115 lb	Black River, Mauritius	Nov 16, 1988	Patrick Guillanton
Shark, tiger	1,780 lb	Cherry Grove, South Carolina	June 14, 1964	Walter Maxwell
Shark, tope	72 lb 12 oz	Parengarenga Harbor, N.Z.	Dec 19, 1986	Melanie B. Feldman
Shark, white	2,664 lb	Ceduna, Australia	Apr 21, 1959	Alfred Dean
Skipjack, black	26 lb	Baja California, Mexico	Oct 23, 1991	Clifford K. Hamaishi
Snapper, cubera	121 lb 8 oz	Cameron, Louisiana	July 5, 1982	Mike Hebert
Snook, common	53 lb 10 oz	Parismina Ranch, Costa Rica	Oct 18, 1978	Gilbert Ponzi
Spearfish, Mediterr.	90 lb 13 oz	Madeira Island, Portugal	June 2, 1980	Joseph Larkin
Spearfish, Atlantic	127 lb 13 oz	Puerto Rico, Gran Canaria, Spain	May 20, 1999	Paul Cashmore
Spearfish, shortbill	74 lb 8 oz	Bay of Islands, New Zealand	Mar 16, 1999	Leonie Kai Patterson
Swordfish	1,182 lb	Iquique, Chile	May 7, 1953	L. Marron
Tarpon	283 lb 4 oz	Sherbro Island, Sierra Leone	Apr 16, 1991	Yvon Victor Sebag
Tautog	25 lb	Ocean City, New Jersey	Jan 20, 1998	Anthony Monica
Tilapia, Mozambique	2 lb 8 oz	Delray Beach, Florida	Nov 10, 1997	Nick Cardella
Trevally, bigeye	31 lb 8 oz	Poivre Island, Seychelles	Apr 23, 1997	Les Sampson
Trevally, giant	145 lb 8 oz	Maui, Hawaii	Mar 28, 1991	Russell Mori
Tuna, Atlantic bigeye	392 lb 6 oz	Puerto Rico, Gran Caneria, Spain	July 25, 1996	Dieter Vogel
Tuna, blackfin	45 lb 8 oz	Key West, Florida	May 4, 1996	Sam J. Burnett
Tuna, bluefin	1496 lb	Aulds Cove, Nova Scotia	Oct 26, 1979	Ken Fraser
Tuna, longtail	79 lb 2 oz	Montague Island, New South Wales, Australia	Apr 12, 1982	Tim Simpson
Tuna, Pacific bigeye	435 lb	Cabo Blanco, Peru	Apr 17, 1957	Russel Lee
Tuna, skipjack	45 lb 4 oz	Baja California, Mexico	Nov 16, 1996	Brian Evans
Tuna, southern bluefin	348 lb 5 oz	Whakatane, New Zealand	Jan 16, 1981	Rex Wood
Tuna, yellowfin	388 lb 12 oz	San Benedicto Is, Mexico	Apr 1, 1977	Curt Wiesenhutter
Tunny, little	35 lb 2 oz	Cape de Garde, Algeria	Dec 14, 1988	Jean Yves Chatard
Wahoo	158 lb 8 oz	Loreto, Baja California, Mexico	June 10, 1996	Keith Winter
Weakfish	19 lb 2 oz	Jones Beach Inlet, New York	Oct 11, 1984	Dennis Rooney
		Delaware Bay, Delaware	May 20, 1989	William E. Thomas
Yellowtail, California	80 lb 11 oz	Alijos Rocks, Baja Calif., Mexico	Nov 12, 1998	Brian Buddell
Yellowtail, southern	114 lb 10 oz	Tauranga, New Zealand	Feb 5, 1984	Mike Godfrey

Freshwater Fishing Records

Species	Weight	Where Caught	Date	Angler
Barramundi	83 lb 7 oz	Lake Tinaroo, N Queensl'd, Aus.	Sept 23, 1999	David Powell
Bass, largemouth	22 lb 4 oz	Montgomery Lake, Georgia	June 2, 1932	George W. Perry
Bass, rock	3 lb	York River, Ontario	Aug 1, 1974	Peter Gulgin
Bass, shoal	8 lb 12 oz	Apalatchicola River, Florida	Jan 28, 1995	Carl W. Davis
Bass, smallmouth	10 lb 14 oz	Dale Hollow, Tennessee	April 24, 1969	John T. Gorman
Bass, Suwannee	3 lb 14 oz	Suwannee River, Florida	Mar 2, 1985	Ronnie Everett
Bass, white	6 lb 13 oz	Orange, Virginia	July 31, 1989	Ronald Sprouse
Bass, whiterock	27 lb 5 oz	Greers Ferry Lake, Arkansas	Apr 24, 1997	Jerald Shaum
Bass, yellow	2 lb 9 oz	Waverly, Tennessee	Feb 27, 1998	John Chappell
Bluegill	4 lb 12 oz	Ketona Lake, Alabama	Apr 9, 1950	T.S. Hudson
Bowfin	21 lb 8 oz	Florence, South Carolina	Jan 29, 1980	Robert Harmon
Buffalo, bigmouth	70 lb 5 oz	Bastrop, Louisiana	Apr 21, 1980	Delbert Sisk
Buffalo, black	63 lb 6 oz	Mississippi River, Iowa	Aug 14, 1999	Jim Winter
Buffalo, smallmouth	82 lb 3 oz	Athens Lake, Georgia	June 6, 1993	Randy Collins
Bullhead, brown	6 lb 1 oz	Waterford, New York	Apr 26, 1998	Bobby Triplett
Bullhead, yellow	4 lb 4 oz	Mormon Lake, Arizona	May 11, 1984	Emily Williams
Burbot	18 lb 11 oz	Angenmanalren, Sweden	Oct 22, 1996	Margit Agren
Carp	75 lb 11 oz	Lac de St Cassien, France	May 21, 1987	Leo van der Gugten
Catfish, blue	111 lb	Tennesee River, Alabama	July 5, 1996	William P. McKinley
Catfish, channel	58 lb	Santee-Cooper Reservoir, SC	July 7, 1964	W.B. Whaley
Catfish, flathead	123 lb 9 oz	Elk City Reservoir, Indep., KS	May 14, 1998	Ken Paulie
Catfish, white	18 lb 14 oz	Inverness, Florida	Sep 21, 1991	Jim Miller
Char, Arctic	32 lb 9 oz	Tree River, Canada	July 30, 1981	Jeffrey Ward
Crappie, white	5 lb 3 oz	Enid Dam, Mississippi	July 31, 1957	Fred L. Bright
Dolly Varden	19 lb 4 oz	Unnamed River, Alaska	Sep 4, 1998	Gary D. Ordway
Dorado	51 lb 5 oz	Corrientes, Argentina	Sep 27, 1984	Armando Giudice
Drum, freshwater	54 lb 8 oz	Nickajack Lake, Tennessee	Apr 20, 1972	Benny E. Hull
Gar, alligator	279 lb	Rio Grande River, Texas	Dec 2, 1951	Bill Valverde
Gar, Florida	15 lb 14 oz	Flagler Beach, Florida	Oct 3, 1999	Randy M. Carmian
Gar, longnose	50 lb 5 oz	Trinity River, Texas	July 30, 1954	Townsend Miller
Gar, shortnose	5 lb 12 oz	Rend Lake, Illinois	July 16, 1995	Donna K. Willmert
Gar, spotted	9 lb 12 oz	Lake Mexia, Texas	Apr 7, 1994	Rick Rivard
Grayling, Arctic	5 lb 15 oz	Katseyedie River, Northwest Territories	Aug 16, 1967	Jeanne P. Branson
Inconnu	53 lb	Pah River, Alaska	Aug 20, 1986	Lawrence Hudnall
Kokanee	9 lb 6 oz	Okanagan Lake, Vernon, BC	June 18, 1988	Norm Kuhn
Muskellunge	67 lb 8 oz	Hayward, Wisconsin	July 24, 1949	Cal Johnson
Muskellunge, tiger	51 lb 3 oz	Lac Vieux-Desert, WI, MI	July 16, 1919	John Knobla
Peacock, speckled	27 lb	Rio Negro, Brazil	Dec 4, 1994	Gerald (Doc) Lawson
Perch, Nile	213 lb	Lake Nasser, Egypt	Dec 18, 1997	Adrian Brayshaw
Perch, white	4 lb 12 oz	Messalonskee Lake, Maine	June 4, 1949	Mrs. Earl Small
Perch, yellow	4 lb 3 oz	Bordentown, New Jersey	May 1865	C.C. Abbot
Pickerel, chain	9 lb 6 oz	Homerville, Georgia	Feb 17, 1961	Baxley McQuaig Jr.
Pike, northern	55 lb 1 oz	Lake of Grefeern, West Germany	Oct 16, 1986	Lothar Louis
Redhorse, greater	9 lb 3 oz	Salmon River, Pulaski, New York	May 11, 1985	Jason Wilson
Redhorse, silver	11 lb 7 oz	Plum Creek, Wisconsin	May 29, 1985	Neal Long
Salmon, Atlantic	79 lb 2 oz	Tana River, Norway	1928	Henrik Henriksen
Salmon, chinook	97 lb 4 oz	Kenai River, Alaska	May 17, 1985	Les Anderson
Salmon, chum	35 lb	Edye Pass, Canada	July 11, 1995	Todd A. Johansson
Salmon, coho	33 lb 4 oz	Pulaski, New York	Sep 27, 1989	Jerry Lifton
Salmon, pink	13 lb 1 oz	Ontario, Canada	Sep 23, 1992	Ray Higaki
Salmon, sockeye	15 lb 3 oz	Kenai River, Alaska	Aug 9, 1987	Stan Roach
Sauger	8 lb 12 oz	Lake Sakakawea, North Dakota	Oct 6, 1971	Mike Fischer
Shad, American	11 lb 4 oz	Connecticut River, Massachusetts	May 19, 1986	Bob Thibodo
Sturgeon, white	468 lb	Benicia, California	July 9, 1983	Joey Pallotta III
Sunfish, green	2 lb 2 oz	Stockton Lake, Missouri	June 18, 1971	Paul M. Dilley
Sunfish, redbreast	1 lb 12 oz	Suwannee River, Florida	May 29, 1984	Alvin Buchanan
Sunfish, redear	5 lb 7 oz	Diverson Canal, Georgia	Nov 6, 1998	Amos M. Gay
Tigerfish, giant	97 lb	Zaire River, Kinshasa, Zaire	July 9, 1988	Raymond Houtmans
Trout, Apache	5 lb 3 oz	Apache Reservation, Arizona	May 29, 1991	John Baldwin
Trout, brook	14 lb 8 oz	Nipigon River, Ontario	July 1916	W.J. Cook
Trout, brown	40 lb 4 oz	Heber Springs, Arkansas	May 9, 1992	Howard L. Collins
Trout, bull	32 lb	Lake Pond Oreille, Idaho	Oct 27, 1949	N.L. Higgins
Trout, cutthroat	41 lb	Pyramid Lake, Nevada	Dec 1925	John Skimmerhorn
Trout, golden	11 lb	Cook's Lake, Wyoming	Aug 5, 1948	Charles S. Reed

Freshwater Fishing Records (Cont.)

Species	Weight	Where Caught	Date	Angler
Trout, lake	72 lb	Great Bear Lake, Northwest Territories	Aug 19, 1995	Lloyd Bull
Trout, rainbow	42 lb 2 oz	Bell Island, Alaska	June 22, 1970	David Robert White
Trout, tiger	20 lb 13 oz	Lake Michigan, Wisconsin	Aug 12, 1978	Pete M. Friedland
Walleye	25 lb	Old Hickory Lake, Tennessee	Aug 2, 1960	Mabry Harper
Warmouth	2 lb 7 oz	Yellow River, Holt, Florida	Oct 19, 1985	Tony D. Dempsey
Whitefish, lake	14 lb 6 oz	Meaford, Ontario	May 21, 1984	Dennis Laycock
Whitefish, mountain	5 lb 8 oz	Elbow River, Calgary, Alberta,	Aug, 1, 1995	Randy G. Woo
Whitefish, broad	9 lb	Tozitna River, Alaska	July 17, 1989	Al Mathews
Whitefish, round	6 lb	Putahow River, Manitoba	June 14, 1984	Allan J. Ristori
Zander	25 lb 2 oz	Trosa, Sweden	June 12, 1986	Harry Lee Tennison

Greyhound Racing

Annual Greyhound Race of Champions Winners*

Year	Winner (Sex)	Affiliation/Owner	Year	Winner	Affiliation/Owner
1982	DD's Jackie (F)	Wonderland Park/ R.H.Walters Jr.	1988	BB's Old Yellow (M)	Supplemental (Southland)/ Margie Bonita Hyers
1983	Comin' Attraction (F)	Rocky Mt Greyhound Park/ Bob Riggin	1989	Osh Kosh Juliet (F)	Tampa Greyhound Track/ William F. Pollard
1984	Fallon (F)	Tampa Greyhound Track/ E.J. Alderson	1990	Daring Don (M)	Interstate Kennel Club/ Perry Padrta
1985	Lady Delight (F)	Lincoln Greyhound Park/ Julian A. Gay	1991	Mo Kick (M)	Flagler Greyhound Track/ Eric M. Kennon
1986	Ben G Speedboat (M)	Multnomah Kennel Club/ Louis Bennett	1992	Dicky Vallie (M)	Dairyland Greyhound Track/ George Benjamin
1987	ET's Pesky (F)	Supplemental (Flagler)/ Emil Tanis	1993	Mega Morris (M)	Jacksonville Kennel Club/ Ferrell's Kennel

* The Greyhound Race of Champions has not been held since 1993.

Gymnastics

World Champions
MEN
All-Around

Year	Champion and Nation	Year	Champion and Nation	Year	Champion and Nation
1903	Joseph Martinez, France	1938	Jan Gajdos, Czechoslovakia	1983	Dimitri Bilozertchev, USSR
1905	Marcel Lalue, France	1950	Walter Lehmann, Switzerland	1985	Yuri Korolev, USSR
1907	Joseph Czada, Czechoslovakia	1954	Valentin Mouratov, USSR Victor Chukarin, USSR	1987	Dimitri Bilozertchev, USSR
1909	Marcos Torres, France	1958	Boris Shaklin, USSR	1989	Igor Korobchinsky, USSR
1911	Ferdinand Steiner, Czechoslovakia	1962	Yuri Titov, USSR	1991	Grigori Misutin, CIS
1913	Marcos Torres, France	1966	Mikhail Voronin, USSR	1993	Vitaly Scherbo, Belarus
1922	Peter Sumi, Yugoslavia F. Pechacek, Czechoslovakia	1970	Eizo Kenmotsu, Japan	1994	Ivan Ivankov, Belarus
1926	Peter Sumi, Yugoslavia	1974	Shigeru Kasamatsu, Japan	1995	Li Xiaoshuang, China
1930	Josip Primozic, Yugoslavia	1978	Nikolai Andrianov, USSR	1997	Ivan Ivankov, Belarus
1934	Eugene Mack, Switzerland	1979	Alexander Ditiatin, USSR	1999	Nicolae Krukov, Russia
		1981	Yuri Korolev, USSR		

Pommel Horse

Year	Champion and Nation	Year	Champion and Nation	Year	Champion and Nation
1930	Josip Primozic, Yugoslavia	1958	Boris Shaklin, USSR	1978	Zoltan Magyar, Hungary
1934	Eugene Mack, Switzerland	1962	Miroslav Cerar, Yugoslavia	1979	Zoltan Magyar, Hungary
1938	Michael Reusch, Switzerland	1966	Miroslav Cerar, Yugoslavia	1981	Michael Mikolai, East Germany
1950	Josef Stalder, Switzerland	1970	Miroslav Cerar, Yugoslavia		Li Xiaoping, China
1954	Grant Chaguinjan, USSR	1974	Zoltan Magyar, Hungary		

World Champions (Cont.)

MEN (Cont.)

Pommel Horse (Cont.)

Year	Champion and Nation
1983	Dmitri Bilozertchev, USSR
1985	Valentin Moguilny, USSR
1987	Zsolt Borkai, Hungary
	Dmitri Bilozertchev, USSR
1989	Valentin Moguilny, USSR

Year	Champion and Nation
1991	Valeri Belenki, USSR
1992	Pae Gil Su, North Korea
	Vitaly Scherbo, CIS
	Li Jing, China
1993	Pae Gil Su, North Korea

Year	Champion and Nation
1994	Marius Urzica, Romania
1995	Li Donghua, Switzerland
1996	Pae Gil Su, North Korea
1997	Valeri Belenki, Germany
1999	Alexei Nemov, Russia

Floor Exercise

Year	Champion and Nation
1930	Josip Primozic, Yugoslavia
1934	Georges Miesz, Switzerland
1938	Jan Gajdos, Czechoslovakia
1950	Josef Stalder, Switzerland
1954	Valentin Mouratov, USSR
	Masao Takemoto, Japan
1958	Masao Takemoto, Japan
1962	Nobuyuki Aihara, Japan
	Yukio Endo, Japan
1966	Akinori Nakayama, Japan

Year	Champion and Nation
1970	Akinori Nakayama, Japan
1974	Shigeru Kasamatsu, Japan
1978	Kurt Thomas, United States
1979	Kurt Thomas, United States
	Roland Brucker, GDR
1981	Yuri Korolev, USSR
	Li Yuejui, Chi
1983	Tong Fei, China
1985	Tong Fei, China
1987	Lou Yun, China

Year	Champion and Nation
1989	Igor Korobchinsky, USSR
1991	Igor Korobchinsky, USSR
1993	Grigori Misutin, Ukraine
1994	Vitaly Scherbo, Belarus
1995	Vitaly Scherbo, Belarus
1996	Vitaly Scherbo, Belarus
1997	Alexei Nemov, Russia
1999	Alexei Nemov, Russia

Rings

Year	Champion and Nation
1930	Emanuel Loffler, Czechoslovakia
1934	Alois Hudec, Czechoslovakia
1938	Alois Hudec, Czechoslovakia
1950	Walter Lehmann, Switzerland
1954	Albert Azarian, USSR
1958	Albert Azarian, USSR
1962	Yuri Titov, USSR
1966	Mikhail Voronin, USSR

Year	Champion and Nation
1970	Akinori Nakayama, Japan
1974	N. Andrianov, USSR
	D. Grecu, Rom.
1978	Nikolai Andrianov, USSR
1979	Alexander Ditiatin, USSR
1981	Alexander Ditiatin, USSR
1983	Dimitri Bilozertchev, USSR
1985	Li Ning, China
	Yuri Korolev, USSR
1987	Yuri Korolev, USSR

Year	Champion and Nation
1989	Andreas Aguilar, West Germany
1991	Grigory Misutin, USSR
1992	Vitaly Scherbo, CIS
1993	Yuri Chechi, Italy
1994	Yuri Chechi, Italy
1995	Yuri Chechi, Italy
1996	Yuri Chechi, Italy
1997	Yuri Chechi, Italy
1999	Zhen Dong, China

Parallel Bars

Year	Champion and Nation
1930	Josip Primozic, Yugoslavia
1934	Eugene Mack, Switzerland
1938	Michael Reusch, Switzerland
1950	Hans Eugster, Switzerland
1954	Victor Chukarin, USSR
1958	Boris Shaklin, USSR
1962	Miroslav Cerar, Yugoslavia
1966	Sergei Diamidov, USSR
1970	Akinori Nakayama, Japan
1974	Eizo Kenmotsu, Japan
1978	Eizo Kenmotsu, Japan

Year	Champion and Nation
1979	Bart Conner, United States
1981	Koji Gushiken, Japan
	Alexandr Ditiatin, USSR
1983	Vladimir Artemov, USSR
	Lou Yun, China
1985	Sylvio Kroll, East Germany
	Valentin Moguilny, USSR
1987	Vladimir Artemov, USSR
1989	Li Jing, China
	Vladimir Artemov, USSR
1991	Li Jing, China

Year	Champion and Nation
1992	Li Jin, China
	Alexei Voropaev, CIS
1993	Vitaly Scherbo, Belarus
1994	Huang Liping, China
1995	Vitaly Scherbo, Belarus
1996	Rustam Sharipov, Ukraine
1997	Zhang Jinjing, China
1999	Joo-Hyung Lee, S Korea

High Bar

Year	Champion and Nation
1930	Istvan Pelle, Hungary
1934	Ernst Winter, Germany
1938	Michael Reusch, Switzerland
1950	Paavo Aaltonen, Finland
1954	Valentin Mouratov, USSR
1958	Boris Shaklin, USSR
1962	Takashi Ono, Japan
1966	Akinori Nakayama, Japan
1970	Eizo Kenmotsu, Japan
1974	Eberhard Gienger, West Germany

Year	Champion and Nation
1978	Shigeru Kasamatsu, Japan
1979	Kurt Thomas, United States
1981	Alexander Takchev, USSR
1983	Dimitri Bilozertchev, USSR
1985	Tong Fei, China
1987	Dimitri Bilozertchev, USSR
1989	Li Chunyang, China
1991	Li Chunyang, China
	R. Buechner, Germ
1992	Grigori Misutin, CIS
1993	Sergei Kharkov, Russia

Year	Champion and Nation
1994	Vitaly Scherbo, Belarus
1995	Andreas Wecker, Germany
1996	Jesús Carballo, Spain
1997	Jani Tanskanen, Finland
1999	Jesus Carballo, Spain

World Champions *(Cont.)*
MEN *(Cont.)*

Vault

Year	Champion and Nation
1934	Eugene Mack, Switzerland
1938	Eugene Mack, Switzerland
1950	Ernst Gebendinger, Switzerland
1954	Leo Sotornik, Czechoslovakia
1958	Yuri Titov, USSR
1962	Premysel Krbec, Czechoslovakia
1966	Haruhiro Yamashita, Japan
1970	Mitsuo Tsukahara, Japan
1974	Shigeru Kasamatsu, Japan
1978	Junichi Shimizu, Japan
1979	Alexander Ditiatin, USSR
1981	Ralf-Peter Hemmann, East Germany
1983	Arthur Akopian, USSR
1985	Yuri Korolev, USSR
1987	Lou Yun, China; Sylvio Kroll, East Germany
1989	Joreg Behrend, East Germany
1991	Yoo Ok Youl, South Korea
1992	Yoo Ok Youl, South Korea
1993	Vitaly Scherbo, Belarus
1994	Vitaly Scherbo, Belarus
1995	G. Misutin, Ukraine; A. Nemov, Russia
1996	Alexei Nemov, Russia
1997	Sergei Fedorchenko, Kazakhstan
1999	Xiaopeng Li, China

WOMEN

All-Around

Year	Champion and Nation
1934	Vlasta Dekanova, Czechoslovakia
1938	Vlasta Dekanova, Czechoslovakia
1950	Helena Rakoczy, Poland
1954	Galina Roudiko, USSR
1958	Larissa Latynina, USSR
1962	Larissa Latynina, USSR
1966	Vera Caslavska, Czechoslovakia
1970	Ludmilla Tourischeva, USSR
1974	Ludmilla Tourischeva, USSR
1978	Elena Mukhina, USSR
1979	Nelli Kim, USSR
1981	Olga Bicherova, USSR
1983	Natalia Yurchenko, USSR
1985	Elena Shoushounova, USSR; Oksana Omeliantchik, USSR
1987	Aurelia Dobre, Romania
1989	Svetlana Bouguinskaia, USSR
1991	Kim Zmeskal, United States
1993	Shannon Miller, United States
1994	Shannon Miller, United States
1995	Lilia Podkopayeva, Ukraine
1997	Svetlana Khorkina, Russia
1999	Maria Olaru, Romania

Floor Exercise

Year	Champion and Nation
1950	Helena Rakoczy, Poland
1954	Tamara Manina, USSR
1958	Eva Bosakava, Czechoslovakia
1962	Larissa Latynina, USSR
1966	Natalia Kuchinskaya, USSR
1970	Ludmilla Tourischeva, USSR
1974	Ludmilla Tourischeva, USSR
1978	Nelli Kim, USSR; Elena Mukhina, USSR
1979	Emilia Eberle, Romania
1981	Natalia Ilenko, USSR
1983	Ecaterina Szabo, Romania
1985	Oksana Omeliantchik, USSR
1987	Elena Shoushounova, USSR; Daniela Silivas, Romania
1989	Svetlana Bouguinskaia, USSR; Daniela Silivas, Romania
1991	Cristina Bontas, Romania; Oksana Tchusovitina, USSR
1992	Kim Zmeskal, United States
1993	Shannon Miller, United States
1994	Dina Kochetkova, Russia
1995	Gina Gogean, Romania
1996	Gina Gogean, Romania
1997	Gina Gogean, Romania
1999	Andreea Raducan, Romania

Uneven Bars

Year	Champion and Nation
1950	Gertchen Kolar, Austria; Anna Pettersson, Sweden
1954	Agnes Keleti, Hungary
1958	Larissa Latynina, USSR
1962	Irina Pervuschina, USSR
1966	Natalia Kuchinskaya, USSR
1970	Karin Janz, East Germany
1974	Annelore Zinke, East Germany
1978	Marcia Frederick, United States
1979	Ma Yanhong, China; Maxi Gnauck, East Germany
1981	Maxi Gnauck, East Germany
1983	Maxi Gnauck, East Germany
1985	Gabriele Fahrnich, East Germany
1987	Daniela Silivas, Romania; Doerte Thuemmler, East Germany
1989	Fan Di, China; Daniela Silivas, Romania
1991	Gwang Suk Kim, North Korea
1992	Lavinia Milosivici, Romania
1993	Shannon Miller, United States
1994	Luo Li, China
1995	Svetlana Khorkina, Russia
1996	Svetlana Khorkina, Russia
1997	Svetlana Khorkina, Russia
1999	Svetlana Khorkina, Russia

World Champions (Cont.)
WOMEN (Cont.)

Balance Beam

Year	Champion and Nation
1950	Helena Rakoczy, Poland
1954	Keiko Tanaka, Japan
1958	Larissa Latynina, USSR
1962	Eva Bosakova, Czechoslovakia
1966	Natalia Kuchinskaya, USSR
1970	Erika Zuchold, East Germany
1974	Ludmilla Tourischeva, USSR

Year	Champion and Nation
1978	Nadia Comaneci, Romania
1979	Vera Cerna, Czechoslovakia
1981	Maxi Gnauck, East Germany
1983	Olga Mostepanova, USSR
1985	Daniela Silivas, Romania
1987	Aurelia Dobre, Romania
1989	Daniela Silivas, Romania
1991	Svetlana Boguinskaia, USSR

Year	Champion and Nation
1992	Kim Zmeskal, United States
1993	Lavinia Milosovici, Romania
1994	Shannon Miller, United States
1995	Mo Huilan, China
1996	Dina Kochetkova, Russia
1997	Gina Gogean, Romania
1999	Elena Zamolodchikova, Russia

Vault

Year	Champion and Nation
1950	Helena Rakoczy, Poland
1954	T. Manina, USSR / Anna Pettersson, Sweden
1958	Larissa Latynina, USSR
1962	Vera Caslavska, Czechoslovakia
1966	Vera Caslavska, Czechoslovakia
1970	Erika Zuchold, East Germany

Year	Champion and Nation
1974	Olga Korbut, USSR
1978	Nelli Kim, USSR
1979	Dumitrita Turner, Romania
1981	Maxi Gnauck, East Germany
1983	Boriana Stoyanova, Bulgaria
1985	Elena Shoushounova, USSR
1987	Elena Shoushounova, USSR
1989	Olesia Durnik, USSR
1991	Lavinia Milosovici, Romania

Year	Champion and Nation
1992	Henrietta Onodi, Hungary
1993	Elena Piskun, Belarus
1994	Gina Gogean, Romania
1995	L. Podkopayeva, Ukraine / Simona Amanar, Rom.
1996	Gina Gogean, Romania
1997	Simona Amanar, Romania
1999	Jie Ling, China

National Champions
MEN
All-Around

Year	Champion
1963	Art Shurlock
1964	Rusty Mitchell
1965	Rusty Mitchell
1966	Rusty Mitchell
1967	Katsuzoki Kanzaki
1968	Yoshi Hayasaki
1969	Steve Hug
1970	Makoto Sakamoto / Mas Watanabe
1971	Yoshi Takei
1972	Yoshi Takei
1973	Marshall Avener
1974	John Crosby
1975	Tom Beach / Bart Conner

Year	Champion
1976	Kurt Thomas
1977	Kurt Thomas
1978	Kurt Thomas
1979	Bart Conner
1980	Peter Vidmar
1981	Jim Hartung
1982	Peter Vidmar
1983	Mitch Gaylord
1984	Mitch Gaylord
1985	Brian Babcock
1986	Tim Daggett
1987	Scott Johnson
1988	Dan Hayden
1989	Tim Ryan
1990	John Roethlisberger

Year	Champion
1991	Chris Waller
1992	John Roethlisberger
1993	John Roethlisberger
1994	Scott Keswick
1995	John Roethlisberger
1996	Blaine Wilson
1997	Blaine Wilson
1998	Blaine Wilson
1999	Blaine Wilson
2000	Blaine Wilson

Floor Exercise

Year	Champion
1963	Tom Seward
1964	Rusty Mitchell
1965	Rusty Mitchell
1966	Dan Millman
1967	Katsuzoki Kanzaki / Ron Aure
1968	Katsuzoki Kanzaki
1969	Steve Hug / Dave Thor
1970	Makoto Sakamoto
1971	John Crosby
1972	Yoshi Takei
1973	John Crosby
1974	John Crosby

Year	Champion
1975	Peter Korman
1977	Ron Galimore
1978	Kurt Thomas
1979	Ron Galimore
1980	Ron Galimore
1981	Jim Hartung
1982	Jim Hartung
1983	Mitch Gaylord
1984	Peter Vidmar
1985	Mark Oates
1986	Robert Sundstrom
1987	John Sweeney
1988	Mark Oates / Charles Lakes

Year	Champion
1989	Mike Racanelli
1990	Bob Stelter
1991	Mike Racanelli
1992	Gregg Curtis
1993	Kerry Huston
1994	Jeremy Killen
1995	Daniel Stover
1996	Jay Thornton
1997	Jason Gatson
1998	Jason Gatson
1999	Jason Gatson
2000	Blaine Wilson

National Champions (Cont.)
MEN (Cont.)

Pommel Horse

Year	Champion	Year	Champion	Year	Champion
1963	Larry Spiegel	1977	Gene Whelan	1990	Patrick Kirksey
1964	Sam Bailie	1978	Jim Hartung	1991	Chris Waller
1965	Jack Ryan	1979	Bart Conner	1992	Chris Waller
1966	Jack Ryan	1980	Jim Hartung	1993	Chris Waller
1967	Paul Mayer/Dave Doty	1981	Jim Hartung	1994	Mihai Begiu
1968	Katsuoki Kanzaki	1982	Jim Hartung	1995	Mark Sohn
1969	Dave Thor	1983	Bart Conner	1996	Josh Stein
1970	Mas Watanabe	1984	Tim Daggett	1997	John Roethlisberger
1971	Leonard Caling	1985	Phil Cahoy	1998	John Roethlisberger
1972	Sadao Hamada	1986	Phil Cahoy	1999	John Roethlisberger
1973	Marshall Avener	1987	Tim Daggett	2000	John Roethlisberger
1974	Marshall Avener	1988	Kevin Davis		
1975	Bart Conner	1989	Kevin Davis		

Rings

Year	Champion	Year	Champion	Year	Champion
1963	Art Shurlock	1975	Tom Beach	1989	Scott Keswick
1964	Glen Gailis	1977	Kurt Thomas	1990	Scott Keswick
1965	Glen Gailis	1978	Mike Silverstein	1991	Scott Keswick
1966	Glen Gailis	1979	Bart Conner	1992	Tim Ryan
1967	Fred Dennis	1980	Jim Hartung	1993	John Roethlisberger
	Don Hatch	1981	Jim Hartung	1994	Scott Keswick
1968	Yoshi Hayasaki	1982	Jim Hartung	1995	Paul O'Neill
1969	Fred Dennis		Peter Vidmar	1996	Kip Simons
	Bob Emery	1983	Mitch Gaylord	1997	Blaine Wilson
1970	Makoto Sakamoto	1984	Jim Hartung	1998	Jeff Johnson
1971	Yoshi Takei	1985	Dan Hayden	1999	Blaine Wilson
1972	Yoshi Takei	1986	Dan Hayden	2000	Blaine Wilson
1973	Jim Ivicek	1987	Scott Johnson		
1974	Tom Weeder	1988	Dan Hayden		

Vault

Year	Champion	Year	Champion	Year	Champion
1963	Art Shurlock	1975	Tom Beach	1988	John Sweeney/Bill Paul
1964	Gary Hery	1977	Ron Galimore	1989	Bill Roth
1965	Brent Williams	1978	Jim Hartung	1990	Lance Ringnald
1966	Dan Millman	1979	Ron Galimore	1991	Scott Keswick
1967	Jack Kenan	1980	Ron Galimore	1992	Trent Dimas
	Sid Jensen	1981	Ron Galimore	1993	Bill Roth
1968	Rich Scorza	1982	Jim Hartung/Jim Mikus	1994	Keith Wiley
1969	Dave Butzman	1983	Chris Reigel	1995	David St. Pierre
1970	Makoto Sakamoto	1984	Chris Reigel	1996	Blaine Wilson
1971	Gary Morava	1985	Scott Johnson	1997	Blaine Wilson
1972	Mike Kelley		Mark Oates	1998	Brent Klaus
1973	Gary Morava	1986	Scott Wilbanks	1999	Guard Young
1974	John Crosby	1987	John Sweeney	2000	Blaine Wilson

Parallel Bars

Year	Champion	Year	Champion	Year	Champion
1963	Tom Seward	1977	Kurt Thomas	1988	D. Hayden/K. Davis
1964	Rusty Mitchell	1978	Bart Conner	1989	Conrad Voorsanger
1965	Glen Gailis	1979	Bart Conner	1990	Trent Dimas
1966	Ray Hadley	1980	Phil Cahoy	1991	Scott Keswick
1967	Katsuzoki Kanzaki		Larry Gerard	1992	Jair Lynch
	Tom Goldsborough	1981	Bart Conner	1993	Chainey Umphrey
1968	Yoshi Hayasaki	1982	Peter Vidmar	1994	Steve McCain
1969	Steve Hug	1983	Mitch Gaylord	1995	John Roethlisberger
1970	Makoto Sakamoto	1984	Peter Vidmar	1996	Jair Lynch
1971	Brent Simmons		Mitch Gaylord	1997	Blaine Wilson
1972	Yoshi Takei		Tim Daggett	1998	Blaine Wilson
1973	Marshall Avener	1985	Tim Daggett	1999	Jason Gatson
1974	Jim Ivicek	1986	Tim Daggett	2000	Trent Wells
1975	Bart Conner	1987	Scott Johnson		

National Champions (Cont.)

MEN (Cont.)

High Bars

Year	Champion	Year	Champion	Year	Champion
1963	Art Shurlock	1977	Kurt Thomas	1990	Trent Dimas
1964	Glen Gailis	1978	Kurt Thomas		Lance Ringnald
1965	Rusty Mitchell	1979	Yoichi Tomita	1991	Lance Ringnald
1966	Katsuzoki Kanzaki	1980	Jim Hartung	1992	Jair Lynch
1967	Katsuzoki Kanzaki	1981	Bart Conner	1993	Steve McCain
	Jerry Fontana	1982	Mitch Gaylord	1994	Scott Keswick
1968	Yoshi Hayasaki	1983	Mario McCutcheon	1995	John Roethlisberger
1969	Rich Grisby	1984	Peter Vidmar	1996	Bill Roth
1970	Makoto Sakamoto		Tim Daggett	1997	Douglas Stibel
1971	Yoshi Takei		Mitch Gaylord	1998	Jason Gatson
1972	Tom Lindner	1985	Dan Hayden	1999	Jamie Natalie
1973	John Crosby	1986	D. Hayden/D. Moriel	2000	Trent Wells
1974	Brent Simmons	1987	David Moriel		Jamie Natalie
1975	Tom Beach	1988	Dan Hayden		
		1989	Tim Ryan		

WOMEN

All-Around

Year	Champion	Year	Champion	Year	Champion
1963	Donna Schanezer	1975	Tammy Manville	1989	Brandy Johnson
1965	Gail Daley	1976	Denise Cheshire	1990	Kim Zmeskal
1966	Donna Schanezer	1977	Donna Turnbow	1991	Kim Zmeskal
1968	Linda Scott	1978	Kathy Johnson	1992	Kim Zmeskal
1969	Joyce Tanac	1979	Leslie Pyfer	1993	Shannon Miller
	Schroeder	1980	Julianne McNamara	1994	Dominique Dawes
1970	Cathy Rigby McCoy	1981	Tracee Talavera	1995	Dominique Moceanu
1971	Joan Moore Gnat	1982	Tracee Talavera	1996	Shannon Miller
	Linda Metheny	1983	Dianne Durham	1997	Vanessa Adler
	Mulvihill	1984	Mary Lou Retton		Kristy Powell
1972	Joan Moore Gnat	1985	Sabrina Mar	1998	Kristen Maloney
	Cathy Rigby McCoy	1986	Jennifer Sey	1999	Kristen Maloney
1973	Joan Moore Gnat	1987	Kristie Phillips	2000	Elise Ray
1974	Joan Moore Gnat	1988	Phoebe Mills		

Vault

Year	Champion	Year	Champion	Year	Champion
1963	Donna Schanezer	1975	Kolleen Casey	1988	Rhonda Faehn
1965	Gail Daley	1976	Debbie Wilcox	1989	Brandy Johnson
1966	Donna Schanezer	1977	Lisa Cawthron	1990	Brandy Johnson
1968	Terry Spencer	1978	Rhonda Schwandt	1991	Kerri Strug
1969	Joyce Tanac		Sharon Shapiro	1992	Kerri Strug
	Schroeder	1979	Christa Canary	1993	Dominique Dawes
	Cleo Carver	1980	J. McNamara/B. Kline	1994	Dominique Dawes
1970	Cathy Rigby McCoy	1981	Kim Neal	1995	Shannon Miller
1971	Joan Moore Gnat	1982	Yumi Mordre	1996	Dominique Dawes
	Adele Gleaves	1983	Dianne Durham	1997	Vanessa Atler
1972	Cindy Eastwood	1984	Mary Lou Retton	1998	Dominique Moceanu
1973	Roxanne Pierce	1985	Yolanda Mavity	1999	Vanessa Atler
	Mancha	1986	Joyce Wilborn	2000	Kristen Maloney
1974	Dianne Dunbar	1987	Rhonda Faehn		

Uneven Bars

Year	Champion	Year	Champion	Year	Champion
1963	Donna Schanezer	1970	Roxanne Pierce	1976	Leslie Wolfsberger
1965	Irene Haworth		Mancha	1977	Donna Turnbow
1966	Donna Schanezer	1971	Joan Moore Gnat	1978	Marcia Frederick
1968	Linda Scott	1972	Cathy Rigby McCoy	1979	Marcia Frederick
1969	Joyce Tanac	1973	Roxanne Pierce	1980	Marcia Frederick
	Schroeder		Mancha	1981	Julianne McNamara
	Lisa Nelson	1974	Diane Dunbar	1982	Marie Roethlisberger
		1975	Leslie Wolfsberger	1983	Julianne McNamara

National Champions (Cont.)
WOMEN (Cont.)
Uneven Bars (Cont.)

Year	Champion	Year	Champion	Year	Champion
1984	Julianne McNamara	1990	Sandy Woolsey	1996	Dominique Dawes
1985	Sabrina Mar	1991	Elisabeth Crandall	1997	Kristy Powell
1986	Marie Roethlisberger	1992	Dominique Dawes	1998	Elise Ray
1987	Melissa Marlowe	1993	Shannon Miller	1999	Jamie Dantzscher
1988	Chelle Stack	1994	Dominique Dawes		Jennie Thompson
1989	Chelle Stack	1995	Dominique Dawes	2000	Elise Ray

Balance Beam

Year	Champion	Year	Champion	Year	Champion
1963	Leissa Krol	1977	Donna Turnbow	1991	Shannon Miller
1965	Gail Daley	1978	Christa Canary	1992	Kerri Strug
1966	Irene Haworth	1979	Heidi Anderson		Kim Zmeskal
	Linda Scott	1980	Kelly Garrison-Steves	1993	Dominique Dawes
1968	Linda Scott	1981	Tracee Talavera	1994	Dominique Dawes
1969	Lonna Woodward	1982	Julianne McNamara	1995	Doni Thompson
1970	Joyce Tanac	1983	Dianne Durham		Monica Flammer
	Schroeder	1984	Pam Bileck	1996	Dominique Dawes
1971	Linda Metheny		Tracee Talavera	1997	Kendall Beck
	Mulvihill	1986	Angie Denkins	1998	Dominique Moceanu
1972	Kim Chace	1987	Kristie Phillips	1999	Vanessa Atler
1973	Nancy Thies Marshall	1985	Kelly Garrison-Steves	2000	Alyssa Beckerman
1974	Joan Moore Gnat	1988	Kelly Garrison-Steves		Amy Chow
1975	Kyle Gayner	1989	Brandy Johnson		
1976	Carrie Englert	1990	Betty Okino		

Floor Exercise

Year	Champion	Year	Champion	Year	Champion
1963	Donna Schanezer	1977	Kathy Johnson	1990	Brandy Johnson
1965	Gail Daley	1978	Kathy Johnson	1991	Kim Zmeskal
1966	Donna Schanezer	1979	Heidi Anderson		Dominique Dawes
1968	Linda Scott	1980	Beth Kline	1992	Kim Zmeskal
1970	Cathy Rigby McCoy	1981	Michelle Goodwin	1993	Shannon Miller
1971	Joan Moore Gnat	1982	Amy Koopman	1994	Dominique Dawes
	Linda Metheny	1983	Dianne Durham	1995	Dominique Dawes
	Mulvihill	1984	Mary Lou Retton	1996	Dominique Dawes
1972	Joan Moore Gnat	1985	Sabrina Mar	1997	Lindsay Wing
1973	Joan Moore Gnat	1986	Yolanda Mavity	1998	Vanessa Atler
1974	Joan Moore Gnat	1987	Kristie Phillips	1999	Elise Ray
1975	Kathy Howard	1988	Phoebe Mills	2000	Kristen Maloney
1976	Carrie Englert	1989	Brandy Johnson		

Handball

National Four-Wall Champions
MEN

Year	Champion	Year	Champion	Year	Champion	Year	Champion
1919	Bill Ranft	1933	Sam Atcheson	1947	Gus Lewis	1961	John Sloan
1920	Max Gold	1934	Sam Atcheson	1948	Gus Lewis	1962	Oscar Obert
1921	Carl Haedge	1935	Joe Platak	1949	Vic Hershkowitz	1963	Oscar Obert
1922	Art Shinners	1936	Joe Platak	1950	Ken Schneider	1964	Jimmy Jacobs
1923	Joe Murray	1937	Joe Platak	1951	Walter Plakan	1965	Jimmy Jacobs
1924	Maynard Laswe	1938	Joe Platak	1952	Vic Hershkowitz	1966	Paul Haber
1925	Maynard Laswe	1939	Joe Platak	1953	Bob Brady	1967	Paul Haber
1926	Maynard Laswe	1940	Joe Platak	1954	Vic Hershkowitz	1968	Stuffy Singer
1927	George Nelson	1941	Joe Platak	1955	Jimmy Jacobs	1969	Paul Haber
1928	Joe Griffin	1942	Jack Clemente	1956	Jimmy Jacobs	1970	Paul Haber
1929	Al Banuet	1943	Joe Platak	1957	Jimmy Jacobs	1971	Paul Haber
1930	Al Banuet	1944	Frank Coyle	1958	John Sloan	1972	Fred Lewis
1931	Al Banuet	1945	Joe Platak	1959	John Sloan	1973	Terry Muck
1932	Angelo Trutio	1946	Angelo Trutio	1960	Jimmy Jacobs	1974	Fred Lewis

National Four-Wall Champions (Cont.)

MEN (Cont.)

1975.....Fred Lewis	1982.....Naty Alvarado	1989.....Poncho Monreal	1996.....David Chapman
1976.....Fred Lewis	1983.....Naty Alvarado	1990.....Naty Alvarado	1997.....Octavio Silveyra
1977.....Naty Alvarado	1984.....Naty Alvarado	1991.....John Bike	1998.....David Chapman
1978.....Fred Lewis	1985.....Naty Alvarado	1992.....Octavio Silveyra	1999.....David Chapman
1979.....Naty Alvarado	1986.....Naty Alvarado	1993.....David Chapman	2000.....David Chapman
1980.....Naty Alvarado	1987.....Naty Alvarado	1994.....Octavio Silveyra	
1981.....Fred Lewis	1988.....Naty Alvarado	1995.....David Chapman	

WOMEN

1980.....Rosemary Bellini	1986.....Peanut Motal	1992.....Lisa Fraser	1998.....Lisa Fraser
1981.....Rosemary Bellini	1987.....Rosemary Bellini	1993.....Anna Engele	1999.....Anna Christoff
1982.....Rosemary Bellini	1988.....Rosemary Bellini	1994.....Anna Engele	2000.....Priscilla
1983.....Diane Harmon	1989.....Anna Engele	1995.....Anna Engele	Shumate
1984.....Rosemary Bellini	1990.....Anna Engele	1996.....Anna Engele	
1985.....Peanut Motal	1991.....Anna Engele	1997.....Lisa Fraser	

National Three-Wall Champions

MEN

1950.....Vic Hershkowitz	1963.....Marty Decatur	1976.....Lou Russo	1989.....John Bike
1951.....Vic Hershkowitz	1964.....Marty Decatur	1977.....Fred Lewis	1990.....Vince Munoz
1952.....Vic Hershkowitz	1965.....Carl Obert	1978.....Fred Lewis	1991.....John Bike
1953.....Vic Herskkowitz	1966.....Marty Decatur	1979.....Naty Alvarado	1992.....John Bike
1954.....Vic Hershkowitz	1967.....Carl Obert	1980.....Lou Russo	1993.....Eric Klarman
1955.....Vic Hershkowitz	1968.....Marty Decatur	1981.....Naty Alvarado	1994.....David Chapman
1956.....Vic Hershkowitz	1969.....Marty Decatur	1982.....Naty Alvarado	1995.....David Chapman
1957.....Vic Hershkowitz	1970.....Steve August	1983.....Naty Alvarado	1996.....Vince Munoz
1958.....Vic Hershkowitz	1971.....Lou Russo	1984.....Naty Alvarado	1997.....Vince Munoz
1959.....Jimmy Jacobs	1972.....Lou Russo	1985.....Vern Roberts	1998.....Vince Munoz
1960.....Jimmy Jacobs	1973.....Paul Haber	1986.....Vern Roberts	1999.....Vince Munoz
1961.....Jimmy Jacobs	1974.....Fred Lewis	1987.....Vern Roberts	2000.....Vince Munoz
1962.....Oscar Obert	1975.....Lou Russo	1988.....Jon Kendler	

WOMEN

1981.....Allison Roberts	1986.....Rosemary Bellini	1991.....Rosemary Bellini	1996.....Anna Engele
1982.....Allison Roberts	1987.....Rosemary Bellini	1992.....Anna Engele	1997.....Allison Roberts
1983.....Allison Roberts	1988.....Rosemary Bellini	1993.....Anna Engele	1998.....Anna Christoff
1984.....Rosemary Bellini	1989.....Rosemary Bellini	1994.....Anna Engele	1999.....Allison Roberts
1985.....Rosemary Bellini	1990.....Rosemary Bellini	1995.....Allison Roberts	2000......Priscilla Shumate

World Four-Wall Champions

1984...................Merv Deckert, Canada	1994...................David Chapman, United States
1986...................Vern Roberts, United States	1997...................John Bike Jr., United States
1988...................Naty Alvarado, United States	
1991...................Pancho Monreal, United States	

Lacrosse

United States Club Lacrosse Association Champions

1960......Mt Washington Club	1974......Long Island Athletic Club	1988......Maryland Lacrosse Club
1961......Baltimore Lacrosse Club	1975......Mt Washington Club	1989......LI-Hofstra Lacrosse Club
1962......Mt Washington Club	1976......Mt Washington Club	1990......Mt Washington Club
1963......University Club	1977......Mt Washington Club	1991......Mt Washington Club
1964......Mt Washington Club	1978......Long Island Athletic Club	1992......Maryland Lacrosse Club
1965......Mt Washington Club	1979......Maryland Lacrosse Club	1993......Mt Washington Club
1966......Mt Washington Club	1980......Long Island Athletic Club	1994......LI-Hofstra Lacrosse Club
1967......Mt Washington Club	1981......Long Island Athletic Club	1995......Mt Washington Club
1968......Long Island Athletic Club	1982......Maryland Lacrosse Club	1996......LI-Hofstra Lacrosse Club
1969......Long Island Athletic Club	1983......Maryland Lacrosse Club	1997......LI-Hofstra Lacrosse Club
1970......Long Island Athletic Club	1984......Maryland Lacrosse Club	1998......LI-Hofstra Lacrosse Club
1971......Long Island Athletic Club	1985......LI-Hofstra Lacrosse Club	1999......New York Athletic Club
1972......Carling	1986......LI-Hofstra Lacrosse Club	2000......Team Toyota (Baltimore)
1973......Long Island Athletic Club	1987......LI-Hofstra Lacrosse Club	

Little League Baseball

Little League World Series Champions

Year	Champion	Runner-Up	Score	Year	Champion	Runner-Up	Score
1947	Williamsport, PA	Lock Haven, PA	16–7	1974	Kao-Hsuing, Taiwan	El Cajun, CA	7–2
1948	Lock Haven, PA	St. Petersburg, FL	6–5	1975	Lakewood, NJ	Tampa, FL	4–3
1949	Hammonton, NJ	Pensacola, FL	5–0	1976	Tokyo, Japan	Campbell, CA	10–3
1950	Houston, TX	Bridgeport, CT	2–1	1977	Kao-Hsuing, Taiwan	El Cajun, CA	7–2
1951	Stamford, CT	Austin, TX	3–0	1978	Pin-Tung, Taiwan	Danville, CA	11–1
1952	Norwalk, CT	Monongahela, PA	4–3	1979	Hsien, Taiwan	Campbell, CA	2–1
1953	Birmingham, AL	Schenectady, NY	1–0	1980	Hua Lian, Taiwan	Tampa, FL	4–3
1954	Schenectady, NY	Colton, CA	7–5	1981	Tai-Chung, Taiwan	Tampa, FL	4–2
1955	Morrisville, PA	Merchantville, NJ	4–3	1982	Kirkland, WA	Hsien, Taiwan	6–0
1956	Roswell, NM	Merchantville, NJ	3–1	1983	Marietta, GA	Barahona, D.Rep.	3–1
1957	Monterrey, Mex.	LaMesa, CA	4–0	1984	Seoul, S. Korea	Altamonte Sgs, FL	6–2
1958	Monterrey, Mex.	Kankakee, IL	10–1	1985	Seoul, S. Korea	Mexicali, Mex.	7–1
1959	Hamtramck, MI	Auburn, CA	12–0	1986	Tainan Park, Taiwan	Tucson, AZ	12–0
1960	Levittown, PA	Ft. Worth, TX	5–0	1987	Hua Lian, Taiwan	Irvine, CA	21–1
1961	El Cajon, CA	El Campo, TX	4–2	1988	Tai-Chung, Taiwan	Pearl City, HI	10–0
1962	San Jose, CA	Kankakee, IL	3–0	1989	Trumbull, CT	Kaohsiung, Taiwan	5–2
1963	Granada Hills, CA	Stratford, CT	2–1	1990	Taipei, Taiwan	Shippensburg, PA	9–0
1964	Staten Island, NY	Monterrey, Mex.	4–0	1991	Tai-Chung, Taiwan	San Ramon Vly, CA	11–0
1965	Windsor Locks, CT	Stoney Creek, Can.	3–1	1992*	Long Beach, CA	Zamboanga, Phil.	6–0
1966	Houston, TX	W. New York, NJ	8–2	1993	Long Beach, CA	David Chiriqui, Pan.	3–2
1967	West Tokyo, Japan	Chicago, IL	4–1	1994	Maracaibo, Venez.	Northridge, CA	4–3
1968	Osaka, Japan	Richmond, VA	1–0	1995	Tainan, Taiwan	Sprint, TX	17–3
1969	Taipei, Taiwan	Santa Clara, CA	5–0	1996	Kao-Hsuing, Taiwan	Cranston, RI	13–3
1970	Wayne, NJ	Campbell, CA	2–0	1997	Guadalupe, Mex.	Mission Viejo, CA	5–4
1971	Tainan, Taiwan	Gary, IN	12–3	1998	Toms River, NJ	Kashima, Japan	12–9
1972	Taipei, Taiwan	Hammond, IN	6–0	1999	Osaka, Japan	Phenix City, AL	5–0
1973	Tainan City, Taiwan	Tucson, AZ	12–0	2000	Maracaibo, Venez.	Bellaire, TX	3–2

*Long Beach declared a 6–0 winner after the international tournament committee determined that Zamboanga City had used players that were not within its city limits.

Motor Boat Racing

American Power Boat Association Gold Cup Champions

Year	Boat	Driver	Avg MPH	Year	Boat	Driver	Avg MPH
1904	Standard (June)	Carl Riotte	23.160	1928	No race		
1904	Vingt-et-Un II (Sep)	W. Sharpe Kilmer	24.900	1929	Imp	Richard Hoyt	48.662
1905	Chip I	J. Wainwright	15.000	1930	Hotsy Totsy	Vic Kliesrath	52.673
1906	Chip II	J. Wainwright	25.000	1931	Hotsy Totsy	Vic Kliesrath	53.602
1907	Chip II	J. Wainwright	23.903	1932	Delphine IV	Bill Horn	57.775
1908	Dixie II	E. J. Schroeder	29.938	1933	El Lagarto	George Reis	56.260
1909	Dixie II	E. J. Schroeder	29.590	1934	El Lagarto	George Reis	55.000
1910	Dixie III	F. K. Burnham	32.473	1935	El Lagarto	George Reis	55.056
1911	MIT II	J. H. Hayden	37.000	1936	Impshi	Kaye Don	45.735
1912	P.D.Q. II	A. G. Miles	39.462	1937	Notre Dame	Clell Perry	63.675
1913	Ankle Deep	Cas Mankowski	42.779	1938	Alagi	Theo Rossi	64.340
1914	Baby Speed Demon II	Jim Blackton & Bob Edgren	48.458	1939	My Sin	Z. G. Simmons, Jr	66.133
1915	Miss Detroit	Johnny Milot & Jack Beebe	37.656	1940	Hotsy Totsy III	Sidney Allen	48.295
				1941	My Sin	Z. G. Simmons, Jr	52.509
1916	Miss Minneapolis	Bernard Smith	48.860	1942–45	No race		—
1917	Miss Detroit II	Gar Wood	54.410	1946	Tempo VI	Guy Lombardo	68.132
1918	Miss Detroit II	Gar Wood	51.619	1947	Miss Peps V	Danny Foster	57.000
1919	Miss Detroit III	Gar Wood	42.748	1948	Miss Great Lakes	Danny Foster	46.845
1920	Miss America I	Gar Wood	62.022	1949	My Sweetie	Bill Cantrell	73.612
1921	Miss America I	Gar Wood	52.825	1950	Slo-Mo-Shun IV	Ted Jones	78.216
1922	Packard Chriscraft	J. G. Vincent	40.253	1951	Slo-Mo-Shun V	Lou Fageol	90.871
1923	Packard Chriscraft	Caleb Bragg	43.867	1952	Slo-Mo-Shun IV	Stan Dollar	79.923
1924	Baby Bootlegger	Caleb Bragg	45.302	1953	Slo-Mo-Shun IV	Joe Taggart & Lou Fageol	99.108
1925	Baby Bootlegger	Caleb Bragg	47.240				
1926	Greenwich Folly	George Townsend	47.984	1954	Slo-Mo-Shun IV	Joe Taggart & Lou Fageol	92.613
				1955	Gale V	Lee Schoenith	99.552
1927	Greenwich Folly	George Townsend	47.662	1956	Miss Thriftaway	Bill Muncey	96.552
				1957	Miss Thriftaway	Bill Muncey	101.787

American Power Boat Association Gold Cup Champions (Cont.)

Year	Boat	Driver	Avg MPH	Year	Boat	Driver	Avg MPH
1958	Hawaii Kai III	Jack Regas	103.000	1980	Miss Budweiser	Dean Chenoweth	106.932
1959	Maverick	Bill Stead	104.481				
1960	—	No race	—	1981	Miss Budweiser	Dean Chenoweth	116.932
1961	Miss Century 21	Bill Muncey	99.678				
1962	Miss Century 21	Bill Muncey	100.710	1982	Atlas Van Lines	Chip Hanauer	120.050
1963	Miss Bardahl	Ron Musson	105.124	1983	Atlas Van Lines	Chip Hanauer	118.507
1964	Miss Bardahl	Ron Musson	103.433	1984	Atlas Van Lines	Chip Hanauer	130.175
1965	Miss Bardahl	Ron Musson	103.132	1985	Miller American	Chip Hanauer	120.643
1966	Tahoe Miss	Mira Slovak	93.019	1986	Miller American	Chip Hanauer	116.523
1967	Miss Bardahl	Bill Shumacher	101.484	1987	Miller American	Chip Hanauer	127.620
1968	Miss Bardahl	Bill Shumacher	108.173	1988	Miss Circus Circus	Chip Hanauer & Jim Prevost	123.756
1969	Miss Budweiser	Bill Sterett	98.504				
1970	Miss Budweiser	Dean Chenoweth	99.562	1989	Miss Budweiser	Tom D'Eath	131.209
				1990	Miss Budweiser	Tom D'Eath	143.176
1971	Miss Madison	Jim McCormick	98.043	1991	Winston Eagle	Mark Tate	137.771
1972	Atlas Van Lines	Bill Muncey	104.277	1992	Miss Budweiser	Chip Hanauer	136.282
1973	Miss Budweiser	Dean Chenoweth	99.043	1993	Miss Budweiser	Chip Hanauer	141.195
				1994	Smokin' Joe Camel	Mark Tate	145.260
1974	Pay 'n Pak	George Henley	104.428	1995	Miss Budweiser	Chip Hanauer	149.160
1975	Pay 'n Pak	George Henley	108.921	1996	PICO American Dream	Dave Villwock	149.328
1976	Miss U.S.	Tom D'Eath	100.412	1997	Miss Budweiser	Dave Villwock	129.366
1977	Atlas Van Lines	Bill Muncey	111.822	1998	Miss Budweiser	Dave Villwock	140.309
1978	Atlas Van Lines	Bill Muncey	111.412	1999	Miss PICO	Chip Hanauer	152.591
1979	Atlas Van Lines	Bill Muncey	100.765	2000	Miss Budweiser	Dave Villwock	162.850

Unlimited Hydroplane Racing Association Annual Champion Drivers

Year	Driver	Boat	Wins	Year	Driver	Boat	Wins
1947	Danny Foster	Miss Peps V	6	1974	George Henley	Pay 'n Pak	7
1948	Dan Arena	Such Crust	2	1975	Billy Schumacher	Weisfield's	2
1949	Bill Cantrell	My Sweetie	7	1976	Bill Muncey	Atlas Van Lines	5
1950	Dan Foster	Such Crust/DaphneX	2	1977	Mickey Remund	Miss Budweiser	3
1951	Chuck Thompson	Miss Pepsi	5	1978	Bill Muncey	Atlas Van Lines	6
1952	Chuck Thompson	Miss Pepsi	3	1979	Bill Muncey	Atlas Van Lines	7
1953	Lee Schoenith	Gale II	1	1980	Dean Chenoweth	Miss Budweiser	5
1954	Lee Schoenith	Gale V	4	1981	Dean Chenoweth	Miss Budweiser	6
1955	Lee Schoenith	Gale V/Wha Hoppen	1	1982	Chip Hanauer	Atlas Van Lines	5
1956	Russ Schleeh	Shanty I	3	1983	Chip Hanauer	Atlas Van Lines	3
1957	Jack Regas	Hawaii Kai III	5	1984	Jim Kropfeld	Miss Budweiser	6
1958	Mira Slovak	Bardah/Miss Buren	3	1985	Chip Hanauer	Miller American	5
1959	Bill Stead	Maverick	5	1986	Jim Kropfeld	Miss Budweiser	3
1960	Bill Muncey	Miss Thriftway	4	1987	Jim Kropfeld	Miss Budweiser	5
1961	Bill Muncey	Miss Century 21	4	1988	Tom D'Eath	Miss Budweiser	4
1962	Bill Muncey	Miss Century 21	5	1989	Chip Hanauer	Miss Circus Circus	3
1963	Bill Cantrell	Gale V	0	1990	Chip Hanauer	Miss Circus Circus	6
1964	Ron Musson	Miss Bardahl	4	1991	Mark Tate	Winston/Oberto	3
1965	Ron Musson	Miss Bardahl	4	1992	Chip Hanauer	Miss Budweiser	7
1966	Mira Slovak	Tahoe Miss	4	1993	Chip Hanauer	Miss Budweiser	7
1967	Bill Schumacher	Miss Bardahl	6	1994	Mark Tate	Smokin' Joe Camel	2
1968	Bill Schumacher	Miss Bardahl	4	1995	Mark Tate	Smokin' Joe Camel	4
1969	Bill Sterett, Sr	Miss Budweiser	4	1996	Dave Villwock	PICO American Dream	6
1970	Dean Chenoweth	Miss Budweiser	4	1997	Mark Tate	Close Call	1
1971	Dean Chenoweth	Miss Budweiser	2	1998	Dave Villwock	Miss Budweiser	8
1972	Bill Muncey	Atlas Van Lines	6	1999	Dave Villwock	Miss Budweiser	8
1973	Mickey Remund	Pay 'n Pak	4	2000	Dave Villwock	Miss Budweiser	6

Unlimited Hydroplane Racing Association Annual Champion Boats

Year	Boat	Owner	Wins	Year	Boat	Owner	Wins
1970	Miss Budweiser	Little-Friedkin	4	1986	Miss Budweiser	Bernie Little	3
1971	Miss Budweiser	Little-Friedkin	2	1987	Miss Budweiser	Bernie Little	5
1972	Atlas Van Lines	Joe Schoenith	6	1988	Miss Budweiser	Bernie Little	4
1973	Pay 'n Pak	Dave Heerensperger	4	1989	Miss Budweiser	Bernie Little	4
1974	Pay 'n Pak	Dave Heerensperger	7	1990	Circus Circus	Bill Bennett	6
1975	Pay 'n Pak	Dave Heerensperger	5	1991	Miss Budweiser	Bernie Little	4
1976	Atlas Van Lines	Bill Muncey	5	1992	Miss Budweiser	Bernie Little	7
1977	Miss Budweiser	Bernie Little	3	1993	Miss Budweiser	Bernie Little	7
1978	Atlas Van Lines	Bill Muncey	6	1994	Miss Budweiser	Bernie Little	4
1979	Atlas Van Lines	Bill Muncey	7	1995	Miss Budweiser	Bernie Little	5
1980	Miss Budweiser	Bernie Little	5	1996	PICO Amer. Dream	Fred Leland	6
1981	Miss Budweiser	Bernie Little	6	1997	Miss Budweiser	Bernie Little	5
1982	Atlas Van Lines	Fran Muncey	5	1998	Miss Budweiser	Bernie Little	8
1983	Atlas Van Lines	Muncey-Lucero	3	1999	Miss Budweiser	Bernie Little	8
1984	Miss Budweiser	Bernie Little	6	2000	Miss Budweiser	Bernie Little	6
1985	Miller American	Muncey-Lucero	5				

Polo

United States Open Polo Champions

1904 ......Wanderers	1933 ......Aurora	1960 ......Oak Brook–	1980 ......Southern Hills
1905–09..Not contested	1934 ......Templeton	C.C.C.	1981 ......Rolex A & K
1910 ......Ranelagh	1935 ......Greentree	1961 ......Milwaukee	1982 ......Retama
1911 ......Not contested	1936 ......Greentree	1962 ......Santa Barbara	1983 ......Ft. Lauderdale
1912 ......Cooperstown	1937 ......Old Westbury	1963 ......Tulsa	1984 ......Retama
1913 ......Cooperstown	1938 ......Old Westbury	1964 ......Concar Oak	1985 ......Carter Ranch
1914 ......Meadow Brook	1939 ......Bostwick Field	Brook	1986 ......Retama II
Magpies	1940 ......Aknusti	1965 ......Oak Brook–	1987 ......Aloha
1915 ......Not contested	1941 ......Gulf Stream	Santa Barbara	1988 ......Les Diables
1916 ......Meadow Brook	1942–45...Not contested	1966 ......Tulsa	Bleus
1917–18..Not contested	1946 ......Mexico	1967 ......Bunntyco–	1989 ......Les Diables
1919 ......Meadow Brook	1947 ......Old Westbury	Oak Brook	Bleus
1920 ......Meadow Brook	1948 ......Hurricanes	1968 ......Midland	1990 ......Les Diables
1921 ......Great Neck	1949 ......Hurricanes	1969 ......Tulsa Greenhill	Bleus
1922 ......Argentine	1950 ......Bostwick	1970 ......Tulsa Greenhill	1991 ......Grant's Farm
1923 ......Meadow Brook	1951 ......Milwaukee	1971 ......Oak Brook	Manor
1924 ......Midwick	1952 ......Beverly Hills	1972 ......Milwaukee	1992 ......Hanalei Bay
1925 ......Orange County	1953 ......Meadow Brook	1973 ......Oak Brook	1993 ......Gehache
1926 ......Hurricanes	1954 ......C.C.C.–	1974 ......Milwaukee	1994 ......Aspen
1927 ......Sands Point	Meadow Brook	1975 ......Milwaukee	1995 ......Outback
1928 ......Meadow Brook	1955 ......C.C.C.	1976 ......Willow Bend	1996 ......Outback
1929 ......Hurricanes	1956 ......Brandywine	1977 ......Retama	1997 ......Isla Carroll
1930 ......Hurricanes	1957 ......Detroit	1978 ......Abercrombie &	1998 ......Esque
1931 ......Santa Paula	1958 ......Dallas	Kent	1999 ......Outback
1932 ......Templeton	1959 ......Circle F	1979 ......Retama	2000 ......Outback

Top-Ranked Players

The United States Polo Association ranks its registered players from minus 2 to plus 10 goals, with 10-Goal players being the game's best. At present, the USPA recognizes twelve 10-Goal and five 9-Goal players:

10-GOAL	9-GOAL
Mariano Aguerre (Greenwich)	Javier Novillo Astrada (Palm Beach)
Michael Azzaro (San Antonio)	Miguel Novillo Astrada (Palm Beach)
Adolfo Cambiaso (Palm Beach)	Lucas Criado (Palm Beach)
Bartolome Castagnolo (Palm Beach)	Hector Galindo (Palm Beach)
Guillermo Gracida, Jr (Palm Beach)	Carlos Gracida (Palm Beach)
Bautista Heguy (Palm Beach)	
Gonzalo Heguy (Palm Beach)	
Ignacio Heguy (Palm Beach)	
Eduardo Heguy (Palm Beach)	
Marcos Heguy (Palm Beach	
Sebastian Merlos (Aiken)	
Juan Ignacio Merlos (Aiken)	

Rodeo

Professional Rodeo Cowboys Association World Champions

All-Around

1929....Earl Thode	1949....Jim Shoulders	1967....Larry Mahan	1985....Lewis Feild
1930....Clay Carr	1950....Bill Linderman	1968....Larry Mahan	1986....Lewis Feild
1931....John Schneider	1951....Casey Tibbs	1969....Larry Mahan	1987....Lewis Feild
1932....Donald Nesbit	1952....Harry Tompkins	1970....Larry Mahan	1988....Dave Appleton
1933....Clay Carr	1953....Bill Linderman	1971....Phil Lyne	1989....Ty Murray
1934....Leonard Ward	1954....Buck Rutherford	1972....Phil Lyne	1990....Ty Murray
1935....Everett Bowman	1955....Casey Tibbs	1973....Larry Mahan	1991....Ty Murray
1936....John Bowman	1956....Jim Shoulders	1974....Tom Ferguson	1992....Ty Murray
1937....Everett Bowman	1957....Jim Shoulders	1975....Tom Ferguson	1993....Ty Murray
1938....Burel Mulkey	1958....Jim Shoulders	1976....Tom Ferguson	1994....Ty Murray
1939....Paul Carney	1959....Jim Shoulders	1977....Tom Ferguson	1995....Joe Beaver
1940....Fritz Truan	1960....Harry Tompkins	1978....Tom Ferguson	1996....Joe Beaver
1941....Homer Pettigrew	1961....Benny Reynolds	1979....Tom Ferguson	1997....Dan Mortensen
1942....Gerald Roberts	1962....Tom Nesmith	1980....Paul Tierney	1998....Ty Murray
1943....Louis Brooks	1963....Dean Oliver	1981....Jimmie Cooper	1999....Fred Whitfield
1944....Louis Brooks	1964....Dean Oliver	1982....Chris Lybbert	
1947....Todd Whatley	1965....Dean Oliver	1983....Roy Cooper	
1948....Gerald Roberts	1966....Larry Mahan	1984....Dee Picket	

Saddle Bronc Riding

1929....Earl Thode	1948....Gene Pruett	1965....Shawn Davis	1982....Monty Henson
1930....Clay Carr	1949....Casey Tibbs	1966....Marty Wood	1983....B. Gjermundson
1931....Earl Thode	1950....Bill Linderman	1967....Shawn Davis	1984....B. Gjermundson
1932....Peter Knight	1951....Casey Tibbs	1968....Shawn Davis	1985....B. Gjermundson
1933....Peter Knight	1952....Casey Tibbs	1969....Bill Smith	1986....Bud Munroe
1934....Leonard Ward	1953....Casey Tibbs	1970....Dennis Reiners	1987....Clint Johnson
1935....Peter Knight	1954....Casey Tibbs	1971....Bill Smith	1988....Clint Johnson
1936....Peter Knight	1955....DebCopenhaver	1972....Mel Hyland	1989....Clint Johnson
1937....Burel Mulkey	1956....DebCopenhaver	1973....Bill Smith	1990....Robert Etbauer
1938....Burel Mulkey	1957....Alvin Nelson	1974....John McBeth	1991....Robert Etbauer
1939....Fritz Truan	1958....Marty Wood	1975....Monty Henson	1992....Billy Etbauer
1940....Fritz Truan	1959....Casey Tibbs	1976....Monty Henson	1993....Dan Mortensen
1941....Doff Aber	1960....Enoch Walker	1977....Bobby Berger	1994....Dan Mortensen
1942....Doff Aber	1961....Winston Bruce	1978....Joe Marvel	1995....Dan Mortensen
1943....Louis Brooks	1962....Kenny McLean	1979....Bobby Berger	1996....Billy Etbauer
1944....Louis Brooks	1963....Guy Weeks	1980....Clint Johnson	1997....Dan Mortensen
1947....Carl Olson	1964....Marty Wood	1981...B. Gjermundson	1998....Dan Mortensen
			1999....Billy Etbauer

Bareback Riding

1932....Smoky Snyder	1951....Casey Tibbs	1968....Clyde Vamvoras	1985....Lewis Feild
1933....Nate Waldrum	1952....Harry Tompkins	1969....Gary Tucker	1986....Lewis Feild
1934....Leonard Ward	1953....Eddy Akridge	1970....Paul Mayo	1987....Bruce Ford
1935....Frank Schneider	1954....Eddy Akridge	1971....Joe Alexander	1988....Marvin Garrett
1936....Smoky Snyder	1955....Eddy Akridge	1972....Joe Alexander	1989....Marvin Garrett
1937....Paul Carney	1956....Jim Shoulders	1973....Joe Alexander	1990....Chuck Logue
1938....Pete Grubb	1957....Jim Shoulders	1974....Joe Alexander	1991....Clint Corey
1939....Paul Carney	1958....Jim Shoulders	1975....Joe Alexander	1992....Wayne Herman
1940....Carl Dossey	1959....Jack Buschbom	1976....Joe Alexander	1993....Deb Greenough
1941....George Mills	1960....Jack Buschbom	1977....Joe Alexander	1994....Marvin Garrett
1942....Louis Brooks	1961....Eddy Akridge	1978....Bruce Ford	1995....Marvin Garrett
1943....Bill Linderman	1962....Ralph Buell	1979....Bruce Ford	1996....Mark Garrett
1944....Louis Brooks	1963....John Hawkins	1980....Bruce Ford	1997....Eric Mouton
1947....Larry Finley	1964....Jim Houston	1981....J.C. Trujillo	1998....Mark Gomes
1948....Sonny Tureman	1965....Jim Houston	1982....Bruce Ford	1999....Lan LaJeunesse
1949....Jack Buschbom	1966....Paul Mayo	1983....Bruce Ford	
1950....Jim Shoulders	1967....Clyde Vamvoras	1984....Larry Peabody	

Bull Riding

1929....John Schneider	1933....Frank Schneider	1939....Dick Griffith	1947....Wag Blessing
1930....John Schneider	1934....Frank Schneider	1940....Dick Griffith	1948....Harry Tompkins
1931....Smokey Snyder	1935....Smokey Snyder	1941....Dick Griffith	1949....Harry Tompkins
1932....John Schneider	1936....Smokey Snyder	1942....Dick Griffith	1950....Harry Tompkins
1932....Smokey Snyder	1937....Smokey Snyder	1943....Ken Roberts	1951....Jim Shoulders
John Schneider	1938....Kid Fletcher	1944....Ken Roberts	1952....Harry Tompkins

Professional Rodeo Cowboys Association World Champions (Cont.)

Bull Riding (Cont.)

1953....Todd Whatley	1965....Larry Mahan	1977....Don Gay	1989....Tuff Hedeman
1954....Jim Shoulders	1966....Ronnie Rossen	1978....Don Gay	1990....Jim Sharp
1955....Jim Shoulders	1967....Larry Mahan	1979....Don Gay	1991....Tuff Hedeman
1956....Jim Shoulders	1968....George Paul	1980....Don Gay	1992....Cody Custer
1957....Jim Shoulders	1969....Doug Brown	1981....Don Gay	1993....Ty Murray
1958....Jim Shoulders	1970....Gary Leffew	1982....Charles Sampson	1994....Daryl Mills
1959....Jim Shoulders	1971....Bill Nelson	1983....Cody Snyder	1995....Jerome Davis
1960....Harry Tompkins	1972....John Quintana	1984....Don Gay	1996....Terry West
1961....Ronnie Rossen	1973....Bobby Steiner	1985....Ted Nuce	1997....Scott Mendes
1962....Freckles Brown	1974....Don Gay	1986....Tuff Hedeman	1998....Ty Murray
1963....Bill Kornell	1975....Don Gay	1987....Lane Frost	1999....Mike White
1964....Bob Wegner	1976....Don Gay	1988....Jim Sharp	

Calf Roping

1929....Everett Bowman	1949....Troy Fort	1967....Glen Franklin	1985....Joe Beaver
1930....Jake McClure	1950....Toots Mansfield	1968....Glen Franklin	1986....Chris Lybbert
1931....Herb Meyers	1951....Don McLaughlin	1969....Dean Oliver	1987....Joe Beaver
1932.....Richard Merchant	1952....Don McLaughlin	1970....Junior Garrison	1988....Joe Beaver
1933....Bill McFarlane	1953....Don McLaughlin	1971....Phil Lyne	1989....Rabe Rabon
1934....Irby Mundy	1954....Don McLaughlin	1972....Phil Lyne	1990....Troy Pruitt
1935....Everett Bowman	1955....Dean Oliver	1973....Ernie Taylor	1991....Fred Whitfield
1936....Clyde Burk	1956....Ray Wharton	1974....Tom Ferguson	1992....Joe Beaver
1937....Everett Bowman	1957....Don McLaughlin	1975....Jeff Copenhaver	1993....Joe Beaver
1938....Burel Mulkey	1958....Dean Oliver	1976....Roy Cooper	1994....Herbert Theriot
1939....Toots Mansfield	1959....Jim Bob Altizer	1977....Roy Cooper	1995....Fred Whitfield
1940....Toots Mansfield	1960....Dean Oliver	1978....Roy Cooper	1996....Fred Whitfield
1941....Toots Mansfield	1961....Dean Oliver	1979....Paul Tierney	1997....Cody Ohl
1942....Clyde Burk	1962....Dean Oliver	1980....Roy Cooper	1998....Cody Ohl
1943....Toots Mansfield	1963....Dean Oliver	1981....Roy Cooper	1999....Fred Whitfield
1944....Clyde Burk	1964....Dean Oliver	1982....Roy Cooper	
1947....Troy Fort	1965....Glen Franklin	1983....Roy Cooper	
1948....Toots Mansfield	1966....Junior Garrison	1984....Roy Cooper	

Steer Wrestling

1929....Gene Ross	1949....Bill McGuire	1967....Roy Duvall	1985....Ote Berry
1930....Everett Bowman	1950....Bill Linderman	1968....Jack Roddy	1986....Steve Duhon
1931....Gene Ross	1951....Dub Phillips	1969....Roy Duvall	1987....Steve Duhon
1932....Hugh Bennett	1952....Harley May	1970....John W. Jones	1988....John W. Jones
1933....Everett Bowman	1953....Ross Dollarhide	1971....Billy Hale	1989....John W. Jones
1934....Shorty Ricker	1954....James Bynum	1972....Roy Duvall	1990....Ote Berry
1935....Everett Bowman	1955....Benny Combs	1973....Bob Marshall	1991....Ote Berry
1936....Jack Kerschner	1956....Harley May	1974....Tommy Puryear	1992....Mark Roy
1937....Gene Ross	1957....Clark McEntire	1975....F. Shepperson	1993....Steve Duhon
1938....Everett Bowman	1958....James Bynum	1976....Tom Ferguson	1994....Blaine Pederson
1939....Harry Hart	1959....Harry Charters	1977....Larry Ferguson	1995....Ote Berry
1940....Homer Pettigrew	1960....Bob A. Robinson	1978....Byron Walker	1996....Chad Bedell
1941....Hub Whiteman	1961....Jim Bynum	1979....Stan Williamson	1997....Brad Gleason
1942....Homer Pettigrew	1962....Tom Nesmith	1980....Butch Myers	1998....Mike Smith
1943....Homer Pettigrew	1963....Jim Bynum	1981....Byron Walker	1999....Mickey Gee
1944....Homer Pettigrew	1964....C.R. Boucher	1982....Stan Williamson	
1947....Todd Whatley	1965....Harley May	1983....Joel Edmondson	
1948....Homer Pettigrew	1966....Jack Roddy	1984....John W. Jones	

Team Roping

1929....Charles Maggini	1942....Verne Castro	1955....Vern Castro	1968....Art Arnold
1930....Norman Cowan	Vic Castro	1956....Dale Smith	1969....Jerold Camarillo
1931....Arthur Beloat	1943....Mark Hull	1957....Dale Smith	1970....John Miller
1932....Ace Gardner	Leonard Block	1958....Ted Ashworth	1971....John Miller
1933....Roy Adams	1944....Murphy Chaney	1959....Jim Rodriguez Jr.	1972....Leo Camarillo
1934....Andy Jauregui	1947....Jim Brister	1960....Jim Rodriguez Jr.	1973....Leo Camarillo
1935....Lawrence Conltk	1948....Joe Glenn	1961....Al Hooper	1974....H.P. Evetts
1936....John Rhodes	1949....Ed Yanez	1962....Jim Rodriguez Jr.	1975....Leo Camarillo
1937....Asbury Schell	1950....Buck Sorrels	1963....Les Hirdes	1976....Leo Camarillo
1938....John Rhodes	1951....Olan Sims	1964....Bill Hamilton	1977....Jerold Camarillo
1939....Asbury Schell	1952....Asbury Schell	1965....Jim Rodriguez Jr.	1978....Doyle Gellerman
1940....Pete Grubb	1953....Ben Johnson	1966....Ken Luman	1979....Allen Bach
1941....Jim Hudson	1954....Eddie Schell	1967....Joe Glenn	1980....Tee Woolman

Team Roping (Cont.)

1981....Walt Woodard	1988....Jake Barnes	Clay O. Cooper
1982....Tee Woolman	1989....Jake Barnes	1995....Bobby Hurley
1983...Leo Camarillo	1990....Allen Bach	Allen Bach
1984....Dee Pickett	1991....Bob Harris	1996....Steve Purcella
1985....Jake Barnes	1992....Clay O. Cooper	Steve Northcott
1986....Clay O. Cooper	1993....Bobby Hurley	1997....Speed Williams
1987....Clay O. Cooper	1994....Jake Barnes	Rich Skelton

1998....Speed Williams	
Rich Skelton	
1999....Speed Williams	
Rich Skelton	

Steer Roping

1929....Charles Maggini	1947....Ike Rude	1965....Sonney Wright	1983....Roy Cooper
1930....Clay Carr	1948....Everett Shaw	1966....Sonny Davis	1984....Guy Allen
1931....Andy Jauregui	1949....Shoat Webster	1967....Jim Bob Altizer	1985....Jim Davis
1932....George Weir	1950....Shoat Webster	1968....Sonny Davis	1986....Jim Davis
1933....John Bowman	1951....Everett Shaw	1969....Walter Arnold	1987....Shaun Burchett
1934....John McEntire	1952....Buddy Neal	1970....Don McLaughlin	1988....Shaun Burchett
1935....Richard Merchant	1953....Ike Rude	1971....Olin Young	1989....Guy Allen
1936....John Bowman	1954....Shoat Webster	1972....Allen Keller	1990....Phil Lyne
1937....Everett Bowman	1955....Shoat Webster	1973....Roy Thompson	1991....Guy Allen
1938....Hugh Bennett	1956....Jim Snively	1974....Olin Young	1992....Guy Allen
1939....Dick Truitt	1957....Clark McEntire	1975....Roy Thompson	1993....Guy Allen
1940....Clay Carr	1958....Clark McEntire	1976....Marvin Cantrell	1994....Guy Allen
1941....Ike Rude	1959....Everett Shaw	1977....Buddy Cockrell	1995....Guy Allen
1942....King Merrit	1960....Don McLaughlin	1978....Sonny Worrell	1996....Guy Allen
1943....Tom Rhodes	1961....Clark McEntire	1979....Gary Good	1997....Guy Allen
1944....Tom Rhodes	1962....Everett Shaw	1980....Guy Allen	1998....Guy Allen
1945....Everett Shaw	1963....Don McLaughlin	1981....Arnold Felts	1999....Guy Allen
1946....Everett Shaw	1964....Sonny Davis	1982....Guy Allen	

Note: In 1945–46 champions were crowned only in Steer Roping.

Rowing

National Collegiate Rowing Champions

MEN'S EIGHT

1985 ....Harvard	1991 ....Pennsylvania	1997 ....Washington
1986 ....Wisconsin	1992 ....Harvard	1998 ....Princeton
1987 ....Harvard	1993 ....Brown	1999 ....California
1988 ....Harvard	1994 ....Brown	2000 ....California
1989 ....Harvard	1995 ....Brown	
1990 ....Wisconsin	1996 ....Princeton	

WOMEN'S EIGHT

1979 ....Yale	1987 ....Washington	1995 ....Princeton
1980 ....California	1988 ....Washington	1996 ....Brown
1981 ....Washington	1989 ....Cornell	1997 ....Washington
1982 ....Washington	1990 ....Princeton	1998 ....Washington
1983 ....Washington	1991 ....Boston University	1999 ....Brown
1984 ....Washington	1992 ....Boston University	2000 ....Brown
1985 ....Washington	1993 ....Princeton	
1986 ....Wisconsin	1994 ....Princeton	

Rugby*

National Men's Club Championship

Year	Winner	Runner-Up	Year	Winner	Runner-Up
1979 ....Old Blues (CA)	St Louis Falcons	1990 ....Denver Barbos	Old Blues (CA)		
1980 ....Old Blues (CA)	St. Louis Falcons	1991 ....Old Mission Beach AC	Washington		
1981 ....Old Blues (CA)	Old Blue (NY)	1992 ....Old Blues (CA)	Mystic River (MA)		
1982 ....Old Blues (CA)	Denver Barbos	1993 ....Old Mission Beach AC	Milwaukee		
1983 ....Old Blues (CA)	Dallas Harlequins	1994 ....Old Mission Beach AC	Life College (GA)		
1984 ....Dallas Harlequins	Los Angeles	1995........Potomac Athletic Club	Old Mission Beach		
1985 ....Milwaukee	Denver Barbos	1996 ....Old Mission Beach AC	Old Blues (CA)		
1986 ....Old Blues (CA)	Old Blue (NY)	1997 ....Gentlemen of Aspen	Old Blue (NY)		
1987 ....Old Blues (CA)	Pittsburgh	1998 ....Gentlemen of Aspen	Old Blue (NY)		
1988 ....Old Mission Beach AC	Milwaukee	1999 ....Gentlemen of Aspen	Golden Gate (CA)		
1989 ....Old Mission Beach AC	Philly/Whitemarsh	2000 ....Gentlemen of Aspen	Hayward Griffins		

Rugby* (Cont.)

National Men's Collegiate Championship

Year	Winner	Runner-Up	Year	Winner	Runner-Up
1980	California	Air Force	1991	California	Army
1981	California	Harvard	1992	California	Army
1982	California	Life College	1993	California	Air Force
1983	California	Air Force	1994	California	Navy
1984	Harvard	Colorado	1995	California	Air Force
1985	California	Maryland	1996	California	Penn St
1986	California	Dartmouth	1997	California	Penn St
1987	San Diego State	Air Force	1998	California	Stanford
1988	California	Dartmouth	1999	California	Penn St
1989	Air Force	Long Beach	2000	California	Wyoming
1990	Air Force	Army			

World Cup Championship

Year	Winner	Runner-Up	Year	Winner	Runner-Up
1987	New Zealand	France	1995	South Africa	New Zealand
1991	Australia	England	1999	Australia	France

*Results are for rugby union competition only.

Sailing

America's Cup Champions

SCHOONERS AND J-CLASS BOATS

Year	Winner	Skipper	Series	Loser	Skipper
1851	America	Richard Brown			
1870	Magic	Andrew Comstock	1–0	Cambria, Great Britain	J. Tannock
1871	Columbia (2–1)	Nelson Comstock	4–1	Livonia, Great Britain	J. R. Woods
	Sappho (2–0)	Sam Greenwood			
1876	Madeleine	Josephus Williams	2–0	Countess of Dufferin, Canada	J. E. Ellsworth
1881	Mischief	Nathanael Clock	2–0	Atalanta, Canada	Alexander Cuthbert
1885	Puritan	Aubrey Crocker	2–0	Genesta, Great Britain	John Carter
1886	Mayflower	Martin Stone	2–0	Galatea, Great Britain	Dan Bradford
1887	Volunteer	Henry Haff	2–0	Thistle, Great Britain	John Barr
1893	Vigilant	William Hansen	3–0	Valkyrie II, Great Britain	William Granfield
1895	Defender	Henry Haff	3–0	Valkyrie III, Great Britain	William Granfield
1899	Columbia	Charles Barr	3–0	Shamrock I, Great Britain	Archie Hogarth
1901	Columbia	Charles Barr	3–0	Shamrock II, Great Britain	E. A. Sycamore
1903	Reliance	Charles Barr	3–0	Shamrock III, Great Britain	Bob Wringe
1920	Resolute	Charles F. Adams	3–2	Shamrock IV, Great Britain	William Burton
1930	Enterprise	Harold Vanderbilt	4–0	Shamrock V, Great Britain	Ned Heard
1934	Rainbow	Harold Vanderbilt	4–2	Endeavour, Great Britain	T. O. M. Sopwith
1937	Ranger	Harold Vanderbilt	4–0	Endeavour II, Great Britain	T. O. M. Sopwith

12-METER BOATS

Year	Winner	Skipper	Series	Loser	Skipper
1958	Columbia	Briggs Cunningham	4–0	Sceptre, Great Britain	Graham Mann
1962	Weatherly	Bus Mosbacher	4–1	Gretel, Australia	Jock Sturrock
1964	Constellation	Bob Bavier & Eric Ridder	4–0	Sovereign, Australia	Peter Scott
1967	Intrepid	Bus Mosbacher	4–0	Dame Pattie, Australia	Jock Sturrock
1970	Intrepid	Bill Ficker	4–1	Gretel II, Australia	Jim Hardy
1974	Courageous	Ted Hood	4–0	Southern Cross, Australia	John Cuneo
1977	Courageous	Ted Turner	4–0	Australia	Noel Robins
1980	Freedom	Dennis Conner	4–1	Australia	Jim Hardy
1983	Australia II	John Bertrand	4–3	Liberty, United States	Dennis Conner
1987	Stars & Stripes	Dennis Conner	4–0	Kookaburra III, Australia	Iain Murray

60-FOOT CATAMARAN VS 133-FOOT MONOHULL

Year	Winner	Skipper	Series	Loser	Skipper
1988	Stars & Stripes	Dennis Conner	2–0	New Zealand	David Barnes

75-FOOT MONOHULL (IACC)

Year	Winner	Skipper	Series	Loser	Skipper
1992	America[3]	Bill Koch	4–1	Il Moro di Venezia, Italy	Paul Cayard
1995	Black Magic I	Russell Coutts	5–0	Young America, United States	Dennis Conner
2000	New Zealand	Russell Coutts	5–0	Luna Rossa, Italy	Francesco de Angelis

Note: Winning entries have been from the United States every year but three: In 1983 an Australian vessel won, and in 1995 and 2000 a vessel from New Zealand won.

Men

50M FREE RIFLE PRONE
1947 .....O. Sannes, Norway
1949 .....A.C. Jackson,
United States
1952 .....A.C. Jackson,
United States
1954 .....G. Boa, Canada
1958 .....M. Nordquist
1962 .....K. Wenk, W Germany
1966 .....D. Boyd, United States
1970 .....M. Fiess, S. Africa
1974 .....K. Bulan, Czech.
1978 .....A. Allan, Great Britain
1982 .....V. Danilschenko, USSR
1986 .....S. Bereczky, Hungary
1990 .....V. Bochkarev, USSR
1994 .....Venjie Li, China
1998 .....Thomas Tamas, U.S.
1999 .....Thomas Tamas, U.S.

AIR RIFLE
1966 .....G. Kümmet, W Germany
1970 .....G. Kusterman, W Germ.
1974 .....E. Pedzisz, Poland
1978 .....O. Schlipf, W. Germany
1979 .....K. Hillenbrand
1981 .....F. Bessy, France
1982 .....F. Rettkowski, E Germ.
1983 .....P. Heberle, France
1985 .....P. Heberle, France
1986 .....H. Riederer, W Germany
1987 .....K. Ivanov, USSR
1989 .....J. P. Amet, France
1990 .....H. Riederer, W Germany
1994 .....Boris Polak, Israel
1998 .....Artem Khadjibekov, Russia
1999 .....Jozef Gonci, Slovakia

THREE POSITION RIFLE
1966 .....M. Thompson,
United States
1970 .....M. Thompson Murdock,
United States
1974 .....A. Pelova, Bulgaria
1978 .....W. Oliver, United States
1982 .....M. Helbig, E Germany
1986 .....V. Letcheva, Bulgaria
1990 .....V. Letcheva, Bulgaria
1994 .....A. Maloukhina, Russia
1998 .....Sonja Pfeilschifter, Germany
1999 .....Sonja Pfeilschifter, Germany

AIR RIFLE
1970 .....V. Cherkasque, USSR
1974 .....T. Ratkinova, USSR
1978 .....W. Oliver, United States
1979 .....K. Monez, United States
1981 .....S. Romaristova, USSR
1982 .....S. Lang, W Germany
1983 .....M. Helbig, E Germany
1985 .....E. Forian, Hungary
1986 .....V. Letcheva, Bulgaria
1987 .....V. Letcheva, Bulgaria
1989 .....V. Letcheva, Bulgaria
1990 .....E. Joc, Hungary

MEN'S TRAP
1929 .....De Lumniczer, Hungary
1930 .....M. Arie, United States
1931 .....Kiszkurno, Poland
1933 .....De Lumniczer, Hungary
1934 .....A. Montagh, Hungary
1935 .....R. Sack, W Germany
1936 .....Kiszkurno, Poland
1937 .....K. Huber, Finland
1938 .....I. Strassburger, Hungary
1939 .....De Lumniczer, Hungary
1947 .....H. Liljedahl, Sweden
1949 .....F. Rocchi, Argentina
1950 .....C. Sala, Italy
1952 .....P.J. Grossi, Argentina
1954 .....C. Merlo, Italy
1958 .....F. Eisenlauer, United States
1959 .....H. Badravi, Egypt
1961 .....E. Mattarelli, Italy
1962 .....W. Zimenko, USSR
1965 .....J.E. Lire, Chile
1966 .....K. Jones, United States
1967 .....G. Rennard, Belgium
1969 .....E. Mattarelli, Italy
1970 .....M. Carrega, France
1971 .....M. Carrega, France
1973 .....A. Andrushkin, USSR
1974 .....M. Carrega, France
1975 .....J. Primrose, Canada
1977 .....E. Azkue, Spain
1978 .....E. Vallduvi, Spain
1979 .....M. Carrega, France
1981 .....A. Asanov, USSR
1982 .....L. Giovonnetti, Italy
1983 .....J. Primrose, Canada
1985 .....M. Bednarik,
Czechoslovakia

Women

AIR RIFLE (Cont.)
1994 .....Sonja Pfeilschifter, Germany
1998 .....Sonja Pfeilschifter, Germany
1999 .....Sonja Pfeilschifter, Germany

SPORT PISTOL
1966 .....N. Rasskazova, USSR
1970 .....N. Stoljarova, USSR
1974 .....N. Stoljarova, USSR
1978 .....K. Dyer, United States
1982 .....P. Balogh, Hungary
1986 .....M. Dobrantcheva, USSR
1990 .....M. Logvinenko, USSR
1994 .....Soon Hee Boo, S Korea
1998 .....Yieqing Cai, China
1999 .....Soon Hee Boo, S Korea

AIR PISTOL
1970 .....S. Carroll, United States
1974 .....Z. Simonian, USSR
1978 .....K. Hansson, Sweden
1979 .....R. Fox, United States
1981 .....N. Kalinina, USSR
1982 .....M. Dobrantcheva, USSR
1983 .....K. Bodin, Sweden
1985 .....M. Dobrantcheva, USSR
1986 .....A. Völker, E Germany

MEN'S TRAP (Cont.)
1986 .....M. Benarik, Czech.
1987 .....D. Monakov, USSR
1989 .....M. Venturini, Italy
1990 .....J. Damne, E Germany
1994 .....Dmitriy Monakov, Ukraine
1995 .....Giovanni Pellielo, Italy
1998 .....Giovanni Pellielo, Italy
1999 .....Joao Rebelo, Portugal

THREE POSITION RIFLE
1929 .....O. Ericsson, Sweden
1930 .....Petersen, Denmark
1931 .....Amundson, Norway
1933 .....De Lisle, France
1935 .....,Leskinnen, Finland
1937 .....Mazoyer, France
1939 .....Steigelmann, Germany
1947 .....I. H. Erben, Sweden
1949 .....P. Janhonen, Finland
1952 .....Kongshaug, Norway
1954 .....A. Bugdanov, USSR
1958 .....Itkis, USSR
1962 .....G. Anderson,
United States
1966 .....G. Anderson,
United States
1970 .....Parkhimovitch, USSR
1974 .....L. Wigger, United States
1978 .....E. Svensson, Sweden
1982 .....K. Ivanov, USSR
1986 .....P. Heinz, W Germany
1990 .....E. C. Lee, S Korea
1994 .....P. Kurka, Czech Republic
1998 ......Jozef Gonci, Slovakia
1999 ......Jozef Gonci, Slovakia

AIR PISTOL (Cont.)
1987 .....J. Brajkovic, Yugoslavia
1989 .....N. Salukvadse, USSR
1990 .....Jasna Sekaric, Yugoslavia
1994 .....Jasna Sekaric, IOP
1998 .....Dorisuren Munkhbayar,
Mongolia
1999 .....Nino Salukvadze,
Georgia

Softball

Men

MAJOR FAST PITCH

1933..........J. L. Gill Boosters, Chicago	1967..........Sealmasters, Aurora, IL
1934..........Ke-Nash-A, Kenosha, WI	1968..........Clearwater (FL) Bombers
1935..........Crimson Coaches, Toledo, OH	1969..........Raybestos Cardinals, Stratford, CT
1936..........Kodak Park, Rochester, NY	1970..........Raybestos Cardinals, Stratford, CT
1937..........Briggs Body Team, Detroit	1971..........Welty Way, Cedar Rapids, IA
1938..........The Pohlers, Cincinnati	1972..........Raybestos Cardinals, Stratford, CT
1939..........Carr's Boosters, Covington, KY	1973..........Clearwater (FL) Bombers
1940..........Kodak Park, Rochester, NY	1974..........Gianella Bros, Santa Rosa, CA
1941..........Bendix Brakes, South Bend, IN	1975..........Rising Sun Hotel, Reading, PA
1942..........Deep Rock Oilers, Tulsa	1976..........Raybestos Cardinals, Stratford, CT
1943..........Hammer Air Field, Fresno	1977..........Billard Barbell, Reading, PA
1944..........Hammer Air Field, Fresno	1978..........Billard Barbell, Reading, PA
1945..........Zollner Pistons, Fort Wayne, IN	1979..........McArdle Pontiac/Cadillac, Midland, MI
1946..........Zollner Pistons, Fort Wayne, IN	1980..........Peterbilt Western, Seattle
1947..........Zollner Pistons, Fort Wayne, IN	1981..........Archer Daniels Midland, Decatur, IL
1948..........Briggs Beautyware, Detroit	1982..........Peterbilt Western, Seattle
1949..........Tip Top Tailors, Toronto	1983..........Franklin Cardinals, Stratford, CT
1950..........Clearwater (FL) Bombers	1984..........California Kings, Merced, CA
1951..........Dow Chemical, Midland, MI	1985..........Pay'n Pak, Seattle
1952..........Briggs Beautyware, Detroit	1986..........Pay'n Pak, Seattle
1953..........Briggs Beautyware, Detroit	1987..........Pay'n Pak, Seattle
1954..........Clearwater (FL) Bombers	1988..........TransAire, Elkhart, IN
1955..........Raybestos Cardinals, Stratford, CT	1989..........Penn Corp, Sioux City, IA
1956..........Clearwater (FL) Bombers	1990..........Penn Corp, Sioux City, IA
1957..........Clearwater (FL) Bombers	1991..........Guanella Brothers, Rohnert Park, CA
1958..........Raybestos Cardinals, Stratford, CT	1992..........Natl Health Care Disc, Sioux City, IA
1959..........Sealmasters, Aurora, IL	1993..........Natl Health Care Disc, Sioux City, IA
1960..........Clearwater (FL) Bombers	1994..........Decatur Pride, Decatur, IL
1961..........Sealmasters, Aurora, IL	1995..........Decatur Pride, Decatur, IL
1962..........Clearwater (FL) Bombers	1996..........Green Bay All-Car, Green Bay, WI
1963..........Clearwater (FL) Bombers	1997..........Green Bay All-Car, Green Bay, WI
1964..........Burch Tool, Detroit	1998..........Meierhoffer-Fleeman, St. Joseph, MO
1965..........Sealmasters, Aurora, IL	1999..........Decatur Pride, Decatur, IL
1966..........Clearwater (FL) Bombers	2000..........Meierhoffer, St. Joseph, MO

SUPER SLOW PITCH

1981..........Howard's/Western Steer, Denver, NC	1991..........Sunbelt/Worth, Centerville, GA
1982..........Jerry's Catering, Miami, Fla.	1992..........Ritch's Superior, Windsor Locks, CT
1983..........Howard's/Western Steer, Denver, NC	1993..........Ritch's Superior, Windsor Locks, CT
1984..........Howard's/Western Steer, Denver, NC	1994..........Bell Corp, Tampa, FL
1985..........Steele's Sports, Grafton, OH	1995..........Lighthouse/Worth, Stone Mt., GA
1986..........Steele's Sports, Grafton, OH	1996..........Ritch's Superior, Windsor Locks, CT
1987..........Steele's Sports, Grafton, OH	1997..........Ritch's Superior, Windsor Locks, CT
1988..........Starpath, Monticello, KY	1998..........Lighthouse/Worth, Stone Mt., GA
1989..........Ritch's Salvage, Harrisburg, NC	1999..........Team Easton, Wilmington, NC
1990..........Steele's Silver Bullets, Grafton, OH	2000..........Team TPS, Louisville, KY

MAJOR SLOW PITCH

1953..........Shields Construction, Newport, KY	1970..........Little Caesar's, Southgate, MI
1954..........Waldneck's Tavern, Cincinnati	1971..........Pile Drivers, Virginia Beach, VA
1955..........Lang Pet Shop, Covington, KY	1972..........Jiffy Club, Louisville, KY
1956..........Gatliff Auto Sales, Newport, KY	1973..........Howard's Furniture, Denver, NC
1957..........Gatliff Auto Sales, Newport, KY	1974..........Howard's Furniture, Denver, NC
1958..........East Side Sports, Detroit	1975..........Pyramid Cafe, Lakewood, OH
1959..........Yorkshire Restaurant, Newport, KY	1976..........Warren Motors, Jacksonville, FL
1960..........Hamilton Tailoring, Cincinnati	1977..........Nelson Painting, Oklahoma City
1961..........Hamilton Tailoring, Cincinnati	1978..........Campbell Carpets, Concord, CA
1962..........Skip Hogan A.C., Pittsburgh	1979..........Nelco Mfg Co, Oklahoma City
1963..........Gatliff Auto Sales, Newport, KY	1980..........Campbell Carpets, Concord, CA
1964..........Skip Hogan A.C., Pittsburgh	1981..........Elite Coating, Gordon, CA
1965..........Skip Hogan A.C., Pittsburgh	1982..........Triangle Sports, Minneapolis
1966..........Michael's Lounge, Detroit	1983..........No. 1 Electric & Heating, Gastonia, NC
1967..........Jim's Sport Shop, Pittsburgh	1984..........Lilly Air Systems, Chicago
1968..........County Sports, Levittown, NY	1985..........Blanton's, Fayetteville, NC
1969..........Copper Hearth, Milwaukee	1986..........Non-Ferrous Metals, Cleveland

Men *(Cont.)*

MAJOR SLOW PITCH *(Cont.)*

1987..........Starpath, Monticello, KY	1994..........Riverside RAM/Taylor Bros., Louisville, KY
1988..........Bell Corp/FAF, Tampa, FL	1995..........Riverside/RAM/Taylor/TPS, Louisville, KY
1989..........Ritch's Salvage, Harrisburg, NC	1996..........Bell 2/Robert's/Easton, Orlando, FL
1990..........New Construction, Shelbyville, IN	1997..........Long Haul/TPS, Albertville, MN
1991..........Riverside Paving, Louisville, KY	1998..........Chase Mortgage/Easton, Wilmington, NC
1992..........Vernon's, Jacksonville, FL	1999..........Gasoline Heaven/Worth, Commack, NY
1993..........Back Porch/Destin Roofing, Destin, FL	2000..........Long Haul/TPS, Albertville, MN

Women

MAJOR FAST PITCH

1933..........Great Northerns, Chicago	1967..........Raybestos Brakettes, Stratford, CT
1934..........Hart Motors, Chicago	1968..........Raybestos Brakettes, Stratford, CT
1935..........Bloomer Girls, Cleveland	1969..........Orange (CA) Lionettes
1936..........Nat'l Screw & Mfg, Cleveland	1970..........Orange (CA) Lionettes
1937..........Nat'l Screw & Mfg, Cleveland	1971..........Raybestos Brakettes, Stratford, CT
1938..........J. J. Krieg's, Alameda, CA	1972..........Raybestos Brakettes, Stratford, CT
1939..........J. J. Krieg's, Alameda, CA	1973..........Raybestos Brakettes, Stratford, CT
1940..........Arizona Ramblers, Phoenix	1974..........Raybestos Brakettes, Stratford, CT
1941..........Higgins Midgets, Tulsa	1975..........Raybestos Brakettes, Stratford, CT
1942..........Jax Maids, New Orleans	1976..........Raybestos Brakettes, Stratford, CT
1943..........Jax Maids, New Orleans	1977..........Raybestos Brakettes, Stratford, CT
1944..........Lind & Pomeroy, Portland, OR	1978..........Raybestos Brakettes, Stratford, CT
1945..........Jax Maids, New Orleans	1979..........Sun City (AZ) Saints
1946..........Jax Maids, New Orleans	1980..........Raybestos Brakettes, Stratford, CT
1947..........Jax Maids, New Orleans	1981..........Orlando (FL) Rebels
1948..........Arizona Ramblers, Phoenix	1982..........Raybestos Brakettes, Stratford, CT
1949..........Arizona Ramblers, Phoenix	1983..........Raybestos Brakettes, Stratford, CT
1950..........Orange (CA) Lionettes	1984..........Los Angeles Diamonds
1951..........Orange (CA) Lionettes	1985..........Hi-Ho Brakettes, Stratford, CT
1952..........Orange (CA) Lionettes	1986..........Southern California Invasion, Los Angeles
1953..........Betsy Ross Rockets, Fresno	1987..........Orange County Majestics, Anaheim, CA
1954..........Leach Motor Rockets, Fresno	1988..........Hi-Ho Brakettes, Stratford, CT
1955..........Orange (CA) Lionettes	1989..........Whittier (CA) Raiders
1956..........Orange (CA) Lionettes	1990..........Raybestos Brakettes, Stratford, CT
1957..........Hacienda Rockets, Fresno	1991..........Raybestos Brakettes, Stratford, CT
1958..........Raybestos Brakettes, Stratford, CT	1992..........Raybestos Brakettes, Stratford, CT
1959..........Raybestos Brakettes, Stratford, CT	1993..........Redding Rebels, Redding, CA
1960..........Raybestos Brakettes, Stratford, CT	1994..........Redding Rebels, Redding, CA
1961..........Gold Sox, Whittier, CA	1995..........Redding Rebels, Redding, CA
1962..........Orange (CA) Lionettes	1996..........California Commotion, Woodland Hills, CA
1963..........Raybestos Brakettes, Stratford, CT	1997..........California Commotion, Woodland Hills, CA
1964..........Erv Lind Florists, Portland, OR	1998..........California Commotion, Woodland Hills, CA
1965..........Orange (CA) Lionettes	1999..........California Commotion, Woodland Hills, CA
1966..........Raybestos Brakettes, Stratford, CT	2000..........Phoenix Storm, Phoenix

MAJOR SLOW PITCH

1959..........Pearl Laundry, Richmond, VA	1980..........Howard's Rubi-Otts, Graham, NC
1960..........Carolina Rockets, High Pt, NC	1981..........Tifton (GA) Tomboys
1961..........Dairy Cottage, Covington, KY	1982..........Richmond (VA) Stompers
1962..........Dana Gardens, Cincinnati	1983..........Spooks, Anoka, MN
1963..........Dana Gardens, Cincinnati	1984..........Spooks, Anoka, MN
1964..........Dana Gardens, Cincinnati	1985..........Key Ford Mustangs, Pensacola, FL
1965..........Art's Acres, Omaha	1986..........Sur-Way Tomboys, Tifton, GA
1966..........Dana Gardens, Cincinnati	1987..........Key Ford Mustangs, Pensacola, FL
1967..........Ridge Maintenance, Cleveland	1988..........Spooks, Anoka, MN
1968..........Escue Pontiac, Cincinnati	1989..........Canaan's Illusions, Houston
1969..........Converse Dots, Hialeah, FL	1990..........Spooks, Anoka, MN
1970..........Rutenschruder Floral, Cincinnati	1991..........Kannan's Illusions, San Antonio, TX
1971..........Gators, Ft Lauderdale, FL	1992..........Universal Plastics, Cookeville, TN
1972..........Riverside Ford, Cincinnati	1993..........Universal Plastics, Cookeville, TN
1973..........Sweeney Chevrolet, Cincinnati	1994..........Universal Plastics, Cookeville, TN
1974..........Marks Brothers Dots, Miami	1995..........Armed Forces, Sacramento, CA
1975..........Marks Brothers Dots, Miami	1996..........Spooks, Anoka, MN
1976..........Sorrento's Pizza, Cincinnati	1997..........Taylor's Major Slow Pitch, Glendale, MD
1977..........Fox Valley Lassies, St Charles, IL	1998..........Lakerettes, Conneaut Lake, PA
1978..........Bob Hoffman's Dots, Miami	1999..........Lakerettes, Conneaut Lake, PA
1979..........Bob Hoffman's Dots, Miami	2000..........Premier Motor Sports, Pittsboro, NC

Speed Skating

All-Around World Champions

MEN

1891 .....Joseph F. Donoghue, U.S.	1934 .....Bernt Evensen, Norway	1971 .....Ard Schenk, Netherlands
1893 .....Jaap Eden, Netherlands	1935 .....Michael Staksrud, Nor.	1972 .....Ard Schenk, Netherlands
1895 .....Jaap Eden, Netherlands	1936 .....Ivar Ballangrud, Norway	1973 .....Göran Claeson, Sweden
1896 .....Jaap Eden, Netherlands	1937 .....Michael Staksrud, Nor.	1974 .....Sten Stensen, Norway
1897 .....Jack K. McCulloch, Can.	1938 .....Ivar Ballangrud, Norway	1975 .....Harm Kuipers, Netherlands
1898 .....Peder Ostlund, Norway	1939 .....Birger Wasenius, Finland	1976 .....Piet Kleine, Neth.
1899 .....Peder Ostlund, Norway	1947 .....Lassi Parkkinen, Finland	1977 .....Eric Heiden, U.S.
1900 .....Edvard Engelsaas, Nor.	1948 .....Odd Lundberg, Norway	1978 .....Eric Heiden, U.S.
1901 .....Franz F. Wathan, Finland	1949 .....Kornel Pajor, Hungary	1979 .....Eric Heiden, U.S.
1904 .....Sigurd Mathisen, Norway	1950 .....Hjalmar Andersen, Nor.	1980 .....Hilbert van der Duin, Neth.
1905 .....C. Coen de Koning, Neth.	1951 .....Hjalmar Andersen, Nor.	1981 .....Amund Sjobrand, Norway
1908 .....Oscar Mathisen, Norway	1952 .....Hjalmar Andersen, Nor.	1982 .....Hilbert van der Duin, Neth.
1909 .....Oscar Mathisen, Norway	1953 .....Oleg Goncharenko, USSR	1983 .....Rolf Falk-Larssen, Nor.
1910 .....Nikolai Strunnikov, Russia	1954 .....Boris Shilkov, USSR	1984 .....Oleg Bozhev, USSR
1911 .....Nikolai Strunnikov, Russia	1955 .....Sigvard Ericsson, Swe.	1985 .....Hein Vergeer, Neth.
1912 .....Oscar Mathisen, Norway	1956 .....Oleg Goncharenko, USSR	1986 .....Hein Vergeer, Neth.
1913 .....Oscar Mathisen, Norway	1957 .....Knut Johannesen, Nor.	1987 .....Nikolai Guliaev, USSR
1914 .....Oscar Mathisen, Norway	1958 .....Oleg Goncharenko, USSR	1988 .....Eric Flaim, U.S.
1922 .....Harald Strom, Norway	1959 .....Juhani Järvinen, Finland	1989 .....Leo Visser, Netherlands
1923 .....Klas Thunberg, Finland	1960 .....Boris Stenin, USSR	1990 .....Johann Olav Koss, Nor.
1924 .....Roald Larsen, Norway	1961 .....Henk van der Grift, Neth.	1991 .....Johann Olav Koss, Nor.
1925 .....Klas Thunberg, Finland	1962 .....Viktor Kosichkin, USSR	1992 .....Roberto Sighel, Italy
1926 .....Ivar Ballangrud, Norway	1963 .....Jonny Nilsson, Sweden	1993 .....Falko Zandstra, Neth.
1927 .....Bernt Evensen, Norway	1964 .....Knut Johannesen, Nor.	1994 .....Johann Olav Koss, Nor.
1928 .....Klas Thunberg, Finland	1965 .....Per Ivar Moe, Norway	1995 .....Rintje Ritsma, Netherlands
1929 .....Klas Thunberg, Finland	1966 .....Kees Verkerk, Neth.	1996 .....Rintje Ritsma, Netherlands
1930 .....Michael Staksrud, Nor.	1967 .....Kees Verkerk, Neth.	1997 .....Ids Postma, Netherlands
1931 .....Klas Thunberg, Finland	1968 .....Fred Anton Maier, Nor.	1998 .....Ids Postma, Netherlands
1932 .....Ivar Ballangrud, Norway	1969 .....Dag Fornaes, Norway	1999 .....Rintje Ritsma, Netherlands
1933 .....Hans Engnestangen, Nor.	1970 .....Ard Schenk, Netherlands	2000 ....Gianni Romme, Netherlands

WOMEN

1936 .....Kit Klein, U.S.	1963 .....Lidia Skoblikova, USSR	1983 .....Andrea Schöne, GDR
1937 .....Laila Schou Nilsen, Nor.	1964 .....Lidia Skoblikova, USSR	1984 .....Karin Enke-Busch, GDR
1938 .....Laila Schou Nilsen, Nor.	1965 .....Inga Artamonova, USSR	1985 .....Andrea Schöne, GDR
1939 .....Verné Lesche, Finland	1966 .....Valentina Stenina, USSR	1986 .....Karin Kania-Enke, GDR
1947 .....Verné Lesche, Finland	1967 .....Stien Kaiser, Neth.	1987 .....Karin Kania, GDR
1948 .....Maria Isakova, USSR	1968 .....Stien Kaiser, Neth.	1988 .....Karin Kania, GDR
1949 .....Maria Isakova, USSR	1969 .....Lasma Kauniste, USSR	1989 .....Constanze Moser, GDR
1950 .....Maria Isakova, USSR	1970 .....Atje Keulen-Deelstra, Neth.	1990 .....Jacqueline Börner, GDR
1951 .....Eevi Huttunen, Finland	1971 .....Nina Statkevich, USSR	1991 .....Gunda Kleemann, Ger.
1952 .....Lidia Selikhova, USSR	1972 .....Atje Keulen-Deelstra, Neth.	1992 .....Gunda Niemann-Kleemann, Germany
1953 ....Khalida Shchegoleeva, USSR	1973 .....Atje Keulen-Deelstra, Neth.	
1954 .....Lidia Selikhova, USSR	1974 .....Atje Keulen-Deelstra, Neth.	1993 .....Gunda Niemann, Germany
1955 .....Rimma Zhukova, USSR	1975 .....Karin Kessow, GDR	1994 .....Emese Hunyady, Austria
1956 .....Sofia Kondakova, USSR	1976 .....Sylvia Burka, Canada	1995 .....Gunda Niemann, Germany
1957 .....Inga Artamonova, USSR	1977 .....Vera Bryndzej, USSR	1996 .....Gunda Niemann, Germany
1958 .....Inga Artamonova, USSR	1978 .....Tatiana Averina, USSR	1997 .....Gunda Niemann, Germany
1959 .....Tamara Rylova, USSR	1979 .....Beth Heiden, U.S.	1997 .....Gunda Niemann, Germany
1960 .....Valentina Stenina, USSR	1980 .....Natalia Petruseva, USSR	1998 .....Gunda Niemann, Germany
1961 .....Valentina Stenina, USSR	1981 .....Natalia Petruseva, USSR	1999 .....Gunda Niemann, Germany
1962 .....Inga Artamonova, USSR	1982 .....Karin Busch, GDR	2000 ....Claudia Pechstein, Ger.

Squash

National Men's Champions

HARD BALL		HARD BALL (Cont.)		HARD BALL (Cont.)	
Year	Champion	Year	Champion	Year	Champion
1907 ....John A. Miskey		1913 ....Morton L. Newhall		1920 ....Charles C. Peabody	
1908 ....John A. Miskey		1914 ....Constantine Hutchins		1921 ....Stanley W. Pearson	
1909 ....William L. Freeland		1915 ....Stanley W. Pearson		1922 ....Stanley W. Pearson	
1910 ....John A. Miskey		1916 ....Stanley W. Pearson		1923 ....Stanley W. Pearson	
1911 ....Francis S. White		1917 ....Stanley W. Pearson		1924 ....Gerald Roberts	
1912 ....Constantine Hutchins		1918–19 ......No tournament		1925 ....W. Palmer Dixon	

National Men's Champions (Cont.)

HARD BALL (Cont.)

Year	Champion
1926	W. Palmer Dixon
1927	Myles Baker
1928	Herbert N. Rawlins Jr.
1929	J. Lawrence Pool
1930	Herbert N. Rawlins Jr.
1931	J. Lawrence Pool
1932	Beckman H. Pool
1933	Beckman H. Pool
1934	Neil J. Sullivan II
1935	Donald Strachan
1936	Germain G. Glidden
1937	Germain G. Glidden
1938	Germain G. Glidden
1939	Donald Strachan
1940	A. Willing Patterson
1941	Charles M. P. Britton
1942	Charles M. P. Britton
1943–45	No tournament
1946	Charles M. P. Britton
1947	Charles M. P. Britton
1948	Stanley W. Pearson Jr.
1949	H. Hunter Lott Jr.
1950	Edward J. Hahn
1951	Edward J. Hahn
1952	Harry B. Conlon
1953	Ernest Howard
1954	G. Diehl Mateer Jr.
1955	Henri R. Salaun
1956	G. Diehl Mateer Jr.
1957	Henri R. Salaun
1958	Henri R. Salaun
1959	Benjamin H. Heckscher

HARD BALL (Cont.)

Year	Champion
1960	G. Diehl Mateer Jr.
1961	Henri R. Salaun
1962	Samuel P. Howe III
1963	Benjamin H. Heckscher
1964	Ralph E. Howe
1965	Stephen T. Vehslage
1966	Victor Niederhoffer
1967	Samuel P. Howe III
1968	Colin Adair
1969	Anil Nayar
1970	Anil Nayar
1971	Colin Adair
1972	Victor Niederhoffer
1973	Victor Niederhoffer
1974	Victor Niederhoffer
1975	Victor Niederhoffer
1976	Peter Briggs
1977	Thomas E. Page
1978	Michael Desaulniers
1979	Mario Sanchez
1980	Michael Desaulniers
1981	Mark Alger
1982	John Nimick
1983	Kenton Jernigan
1984	Kenton Jernigan
1987	Frank J. Stanley IV
1988	Scott Dulmage
1989	Rodolfo Rodriquez
1990	Hector Barragan
1991	Hector Barragan
1992	Hector Barragan

HARD BALL (Cont.)

Year	Champion
1985	Kenton Jernigan
1986	Hugh LaBossier
1993	Hector Barragan
1994	Hector Barragan
1995	W. Keen Butcher
1996	W. Keen Butcher
1997	Rob Hill
1998	Rob Hill
1999	Rob Hill
2000	Thomas Harrity

SOFT BALL

Year	Champion
1983	Kenton Jernigan
1984	Kenton Jernigan
1985	Kenton Jernigan
1986	Darius Pandole
1987	Richard Hashim
1988	John Phelan
1989	Will Carlin
1990	Syed Jafry
1991	Hector Barragan
1992	Phil Yarrow
1993	Phil Yarrow
1994	Roberto Rosales
1995	A. Martin Clark
1996	Mohsen Mir
1997	A. Martin Clark
1998	A. Martin Clark
1999	David McNeely
2000	A. Martin Clark

National Women's Champions

HARD BALL

Year	Champion
1928	Eleanora Sears
1929	Margaret Howe
1930	Hazel Wightman
1931	Ruth Banks
1932	Margaret Howe
1933	Susan Noel
1934	Margaret Howe
1935	Margot Lumb
1936	Anne Page
1937	Anne Page
1938	Cecile Bowes
1939	Anne Page
1940	Cecile Bowes
1941	Cecile Bowes
1942–46	No tournament
1947	Anne Page Homer
1948	Cecile Bowes
1949	Janet Morgan
1950	Betty Howe
1951	Jane Austin
1952	Margaret Howe
1953	Margaret Howe
1954	Lois Dilks
1955	Janet Morgan
1956	Betty Howe Constable
1957	Betty Howe Constable
1958	Betty Howe Constable
1959	Betty Howe Constable
1960	Margaret Varner
1961	Margaret Varner

HARD BALL (Cont.)

Year	Champion
1962	Margaret Varner
1963	Margaret Varner
1964	Ann Wetzel
1965	Joyce Davenport
1966	Betty Meade
1967	Betty Meade
1968	Betty Meade
1969	Joyce Davenport
1970	Nina Moyer
1971	Carol Thesieres
1972	Nina Moyer
1973	Gretchen Spruance
1974	Gretchen Spruance
1975	Ginny Akabane
1976	Gretchen Spruance
1977	Gretchen Spruance
1978	Gretchen Spruance
1979	Heather McKay
1980	Barbara Maltby
1981	Barbara Maltby
1982	Alicia McConnell
1983	Alicia McConnell
1984	Alicia McConnell
1985	Alicia McConnell
1986	Alicia McConnell
1987	Alicia McConnell
1988	Alicia McConnell
1986	Alicia McConnell
1987	Alicia McConnell

HARD BALL (Cont.)

Year	Champion
1988	Alicia McConnell
1989	Demer Holleran
1990	Demer Holleran
1991	Demer Holleran
1992	Demer Holleran
1993	Demer Holleran
1994	Demer Holleran

Note: Tournament not held since 1994.

SOFT BALL

Year	Champion
1983	Alicia McConnell
1984	Julie Harris
1985	Sue Clinch
1986	Julie Harris
1987	Diana Staley
1988	Sara Luther
1989	Nancy Gengler
1990	Joyce Maycock
1991	Ellie Pierce
1992	Demer Holleran
1993	Demer Holleran
1994	Demer Holleran
1995	Ellie Pierce
1996	Demer Holleran
1997	Demer Holleran
1998	Latasha Khan
1999	Demer Holleran
2000	Latasha Khan

Triathlon

Ironman Championship

MEN			WOMEN		
Date	Winner	Time	Date	Winner	Time
1978	Gordon Haller	11:46	1978	No finishers	
1979	Tom Warren	11:15:56	1979	Lyn Lemaire	12:55
1980	Dave Scott	9:24:33	1980	Robin Beck	11:21:24
1981	John Howard	9:38:29	1981	Linda Sweeney	12:00:32
1982	Scott Tinley	9:19:41	1982	Kathleen McCartney	11:09:40
1982	Dave Scott	9:08:23	1982	Julie Leach	10:54:08
1983	Dave Scott	9:05:57	1983	Sylviane Puntous	10:43:36
1984	Dave Scott	8:54:20	1984	Sylviane Puntous	10:25:13
1985	Scott Tinley	8:50:54	1985	Joanne Ernst	10:25:22
1986	Dave Scott	8:28:37	1986	Paula Newby-Fraser	9:49:14
1987	Dave Scott	8:34:13	1987	Erin Baker	9:35:25
1988	Scott Molina	8:31:00	1988	Paula Newby-Fraser	9:01:01
1989	Mark Allen	8:09:15	1989	Paula Newby-Fraser	9:00:56
1990	Mark Allen	8:28:17	1990	Erin Baker	9:13:42
1991	Mark Allen	8:18:32	1991	Paula Newby-Fraser	9:07:52
1992	Mark Allen	8:09:09	1992	Paula Newby-Fraser	8:55:29
1993	Mark Allen	8:07:46	1993	Paula Newby-Fraser	8:58:23
1994	Greg Welch	8:20:27	1994	Paula Newby-Fraser	9:20:14
1995	Mark Allen	8:20:34	1995	Karen Smyers	9:16:46
1996	Luc Van Lierde	8:04:08	1996	Paula Newby-Fraser	9:06:49
1997	Thomas Hellriegel	8:33:01	1997	Heather Fuhr	9:31:43
1998	Peter Reid	8:24:20	1998	Natascha Badmann	9:24:16
1999	Luc Van Lierde	8:17:17	1999	Lori Bowden	9:13:02

Note:The Ironman Championship was contested twice in 1982.

Sites: Waikiki Beach (1978–79); Ala Moana Park (1980); Kailua-Kona (since 1981).

Advanced Metallurgy

In four days Maracaibo went from El Ridículo to lo sublime. El Ridículo is the name of the only bat Venezuela's infield-dirt-poor team brought to this year's Little League World Series in Williamsport, Pa. "El Ridículo is dented and scuffed and made of the same lightweight aluminum used in fences," said team manager Eduvino Quevedo, "but it was all we could afford. Without it, we would never have played for the title."

El Ridículo had accounted for 72 runs over 10 games in Venezuela's national tournament and another 41 runs during the six-game Latin American regionals. But on Aug. 21, following Maracaibo's 3–0 triumph over European champ Dhahran, Saudi Arabia (didn't any of the organizers take geography?) in Williamsport, Little League sponsors laid some heavier metal on the Venezuelans.

Only a few of Quevedo's players brandished El Ridículo in the pivotal 5–4 round-robin victory over Toronto on Aug. 22. And nobody swung it during a 5–4 upset of Tokyo in the International Pool final. "We've retired El Ridículo," Quevedo said before facing U.S. Champ Bellaire, Texas, in the finale. "It will have to watch us from the bat bag...."

In the International Final Maracaibo made Tokyo—representing defending champion Japan—eat crow off Lamade Stadium's turf. Because his boys had routed the Venezuelans 10–0 in the round-robin opener, Tokyo manager Masami Ohmae bypassed unhittable ace Leo Nakayama for the eminently hittable Kazuma Yamada. The second stringer lasted 1²/₃ innings, long enough for Maracaibo to score five runs, all it needed....

Bellaire manager Terry McConn was

equally dismissive of Maracaibo. "We came here to win the U.S. title, which we did," he said after his teamed pasted Davenport, Iowa, 8–0 on Aug. 24. "To us the game with Venezuela is just an exhibition." McConn may have forgotten his boys were playing in the Little League *World* Series.

Quevedo never did. Noting that Bellaire hitters had been feasting on fastballs, he started his best curveballer, a righthander named Rubén Mavárez. "Curves are very dangerous for cars and women," said Quevedo. "Also hitters." Mavárez ... grips the ball with his thumbnail which makes it plunge like an Internet stock.

McConn countered with Alex Atherton, whose own corkscrewy curve seemed to start around Philadelphia...and swerve toward Williamsport. "They were las curvas de Jennifer Lopez," cracked Quevedo. "They drove my kids crazy."

They made Bellaire catcher Terrence McConn a little nutty, too. With the bases loaded and two out in the first inning, Atherton wild-pitched in two runs. Two innings later Mavárez doubled, and then Bellaire rightfielder Andy Zizinia misplayed Manuel Castellano's fly ball like, well, a Little Leaguer. The error brought home the deciding run in Maracaibo's 3–2 victory.

...Mavárez ended the game by striking out Hunter Johnson on his La Recta Celestial, his Celestial Fastball.... "I feel good to be 12 and a champion," said Mavárez. "Next year I can't play Little League. It's a shame to have to grow old."

—Franz Lidz

Volleyball

World Champions

MEN

Year	Winner	Runner-up	Site
1949	Soviet Union	Czechoslovakia	Prague
1952	Soviet Union	Czechoslovakia	Moscow
1956	Czechoslovakia	Soviet Union	Paris
1960	Soviet Union	Czechoslovakia	Rio de Janeiro
1962	Soviet Union	Czechoslovakia	Moscow
1966	Czechoslovakia	Romania	Prague
1970	East Germany	Bulgaria	Sofia, Bulgaria
1974	Poland	Soviet Union	Mexico City
1978	Soviet Union	Italy	Rome
1982	Soviet Union	Brazil	Buenos Aires
1986	United States	Soviet Union	Paris
1990	Italy	Cuba	Rio de Janeiro
1994	Italy	Netherlands	Athens
1998	Italy	Yugoslavia	Tokyo

WOMEN

Year	Winner	Runner-up	Site
1952	Soviet Union	Poland	Moscow
1956	Soviet Union	Romania	Paris
1960	Soviet Union	Japan	Rio de Janeiro
1962	Japan	Soviet Union	Moscow
1966	Japan	United States	Prague
1970	Soviet Union	Japan	Sofia, Bulgaria
1974	Japan	Soviet Union	Mexico City
1978	Cuba	Japan	Rome
1982	China	Peru	Lima, Peru
1986	China	Cuba	Prague
1990	Soviet Union	China	Beijing
1994	Cuba	Brazil	Sao Paulo, Brazil
1998	Cuba	China	Osaka, Japan

Going Postal

Question: Why does the U.S. Postal Service sponsor a cycling team?

Answer: Sure, having Lance Armstrong as your human billboard is great, but if you're a federal agency looking for an endorsement deal—which is odd to begin with—why pick a sport that's far more popular outside the U.S.? "Marketing," explains team coordinator Bob McKenna. "We do it because a surprisingly large number of companies have interests in cycling: Visa, Yahoo!, Nike. We use the team to develop relationships with these and other sponsors." (Unlike most other government entities, the Postal Service has corporate competitors, such as FedEx.) Still, do you really want people picturing bicycles as they get ready to overnight their packages? "The cycling team is a metaphor for the postal service as a whole: Training, planning, teamwork and effort add up to a win," says McKenna. Besides, he adds of the sponsorship, which runs in the low seven figures, "our budget's tight. We can afford cycling. NASCAR's too rich for our blood."

U.S. Men's Open Champions—Gold Division

Year	Champion	Year	Champion
1928	Germantown, PA YMCA	1965	Westside JCC, CA
1929	Hyde Park YMCA, IL	1966	Sand & Sea Club, CA
1930	Hyde Park YMCA, IL	1967	Fresno, CA VBC
1931	San Antonio, TX YMCA	1968	Westside JCC, Los Angeles, CA
1932	San Antonio, TX YMCA	1969	Los Angeles, CA YMCA
1933	Houston, TX YMCA	1970	Chart House, San Diego
1934	Houston, TX YMCA	1971	Santa Monica, CA YMCA
1935	Houston, TX YMCA	1972	Chart House, San Diego
1936	Houston, TX YMCA	1973	Chuck's Steak, Los Angeles
1937	Duncan YMCA, IL	1974	UC Santa Barbara, CA
1938	Houston, TX YMCA	1975	Chart House, San Diego
1939	Houston, TX YMCA	1976	Malibu, Los Angeles
1940	Los Angeles AC, CA	1977	Chuck's, Santa Barbara
1941	North Ave. YMCA, IL	1978	Chuck's, Los Angeles
1942	North Ave. YMCA, IL	1979	Nautilus, Long Beach CA
1943–44	No championships	1980	Olympic Club, San Francisco
1945	North Ave. YMCA, IL	1981	Nautilus, Long Beach CA
1946	Pasadena, CA YMCA	1982	Chuck's, Los Angeles
1947	North Ave. YMCA, IL	1983	Nautilus Pacifica, CA
1948	Hollywood, CA YMCA	1984	Nautilus Pacifica, CA
1949	Downtown YMCA, CA	1985	Molten/SSI Torrance, CA
1950	Long Beach, CA YMCA	1986	Molten, Torrance, CA
1951	Hollywood, CA YMCA	1987	Molten, Torrance, CA
1952	Hollywood, CA YMCA	1988	Molten, Torrance, CA
1953	Hollywood, CA YMCA	1989	Not held
1954	Stockton, CA YMCA	1990	Nike, Carson, CA
1955	Stockton, CA YMCA	1991	Offshore, Woodland Hills, CA
1956	Hollywood, CA YMCA Stars	1992	Creole Six Pack, Elmhurst, NY
1957	Hollywood, CA YMCA Stars	1993	Asics, Huntington Beach, CA
1958	Hollywood, CA YMCA Stars	1994	Asics/Paul Mitchell, Hunt. Beach, CA
1959	Hollywood, CA YMCA Stars	1995	Shakter, Belagarad, Ukraine
1960	Westside JCC, CA	1996	POL-AM-VBC, Brooklyn, NY
1961	Hollywood, CA YMCA	1997	Canuck Stuff VBC, Calgary
1962	Hollywood, CA YMCA	1998	T-Town, Tulsa, OK
1963	Hollywood, CA YMCA	1999	LAAC, Los Angeles
1964	Hollywood, CA YMCA Stars	2000	Paul Mitchell, Huntington Beach, CA

U.S. Women's Open Champions—Gold Division

Year	Champion	Year	Champion
1949	Eagles, Houston	1976	Pasadena, TX
1950	Voit #1, Santa Monica, CA	1977	Spoilers, Hermosa, CA
1951	Eagles, Houston	1978	Nick's, Los Angeles
1952	Voit #1, Santa Monica, CA	1979	Mavericks, Los Angeles
1953	Voit #1, Los Angeles	1980	NAVA, Fountain Valley, CA
1954	Houstonettes, Houston, TX	1981	Utah State, Logan, UT
1955	Mariners, Santa Monica, CA	1982	Monarchs, Hilo, HI
1956	Mariners, Santa Monica, CA	1983	Syntex, Stockton, CA
1957	Mariners, Santa Monica, CA	1984	Chrysler, Palo Alto, CA
1958	Mariners, Santa Monica, CA	1985	Merrill Lynch, AZ
1959	Mariners, Santa Monica, CA	1986	Merrill Lynch, AZ
1960	Mariners, Santa Monica, CA	1987	Chrysler, Pleasanton, CA
1961	Breakers, Long Beach, CA	1988	Chrysler, Hayward, CA
1962	Shamrocks, Long Beach, CA	1989	Plymouth, Hayward, CA
1963	Shamrocks, Long Beach, CA	1990	Plymouth, Hayward, CA
1964	Shamrocks, Long Beach, CA	1991	Fitness, Champaign, IL
1965	Shamrocks, Long Beach, CA	1992	Nick's Kronies, Chicago
1966	Renegades, Los Angeles	1993	Nick's Fishmarket, Chicago
1967	Shamrocks, Long Beach, CA	1994	Nick's Fishmarket, Chicago
1968	Shamrocks, Long Beach, CA	1995	Kittleman/Branfield's/Nick's, Chi.
1969	Shamrocks, Long Beach, CA	1996	Pure Texas Nuts, Austin, TX
1970	Shamrocks, Long Beach, CA	1997	Kittleman/Branfield's/Nick's, Chi.
1971	Renegades, Los Angeles	1998	The Exterminators, Barrington, IL
1972	E Pluribus Unum, Houston	1999	Dominican Dream Team, Santo Domingo, D.R.
1973	E Pluribus Unum, Houston		
1974	Renegades, Los Angeles	2000	Dominican Dream Team, Santo Domingo, D.R.
1975	Adidas, Norwalk, CA		

United States National Champions

1983

FREESTYLE

105.5	Rich Salamone
114.5	Joe Gonzales
125.5	Joe Corso
136.5	Rich Dellagatta*
149.5	Bill Hugent
163	Lee Kemp
180.5	Chris Campbell
198	Pete Bush

FREESTYLE *(Cont.)*

220	Greg Gibson
Hvy	Bruce Baumgartner
Team	Sunkist Kids

GRECO-ROMAN

105.5	T. J. Jones
114.5	Mark Fuller
125.5	Rob Hermann

GRECO-ROMAN *(Cont.)*

136.5	Dan Mello
149.5	Jim Martinez
163	James Andre
180.5	Steve Goss
198	Steve Fraser*
220	Dennis Koslowski
Hvy	No champion
Team	Minn. Wrestling Club

1984

FREESTYLE

105.5	Rich Salamone
114.5	Charlie Heard
125.5	Joe Corso
136.5	Rich Dellagatta*
149.5	Andre Metzger
163	Dave Schultz*
180.5	Mark Schultz
198	Steve Fraser

FREESTYLE *(Cont.)*

220	Harold Smith
Hvy	Bruce Baumgartner
Team	Sunkist Kids

GRECO-ROMAN

105.5	T. J. Jones
114.5	Mark Fuller
136.5	Dan Mello

GRECO-ROMAN *(Cont.)*

149.5	Jim Martinez*
163	John Matthews
180.5	Tom Press
198	Mike Houck
220	No champion
Hvy	No champion
Team	Adirondack 3-Style, WA

1985

FREESTYLE

105.5	Tim Vanni
114.5	Jim Martin
125.5	Charlie Heard
136.5	Darryl Burley
149.5	Bill Nugent*
163	Kenny Monday
180.5	Mike Sheets
198	Mark Schultz

FREESTYLE *(Cont.)*

220	Greg Gibson
286	Bruce Baumgartner
Team	Sunkist Kids

GRECO-ROMAN

105.5	T. J. Jones
114.5	Mark Fuller
125.5	Eric Seward*

GRECO-ROMAN *(Cont.)*

136.5	Buddy Lee
149.5	Jim Martinez
163	David Butler
180.5	Chris Catallo
198	Mike Houck
220	Greg Gibson
286	Dennis Koslowski
Team	U.S. Marine Corps

1986

FREESTYLE

105.5	Rich Salamone
114.5	Joe Gonzales
125.5	Kevin Darkus
136.5	John Smith
149.5	Andre Metzger*
163	Dave Schultz
180.5	Mark Schultz
198	Jim Scherr
220	Dan Severn

FREESTYLE *(Cont.)*

286	Bruce Baumgartner
Team	Sunkist Kids (Div. I)
	Hawkeye Wrestling
	Club (Div. II)

GRECO-ROMAN

105.5	Eric Wetzel
114.5	Shawn Sheldon
125.5	Anthony Amado

GRECO-ROMAN *(Cont.)*

136.5	Frank Famiano
149.5	Jim Martinez
163	David Butler*
180.5	Darryl Gholar
198	Derrick Waldroup
220	Dennis Koslowski
286	Duane Koslowski
Team	U.S. Marine Corps (Div. I)
	U.S. Navy (Div. II)

1987

FREESTYLE

105.5	Takashi Irie
114.5	Mitsuru Sato
125.5	Barry Davis
136.5	Takumi Adachi
149.5	Andre Metzger
163	Dave Schultz*
180.5	Mark Schultz
198	Jim Scherr
220	Bill Scherr

FREESTYLE *(Cont.)*

286	Bruce Baumgartner
Team	Sunkist Kids (Div. I)
	Team Foxcatcher (Div. II)

GRECO-ROMAN

105.5	Eric Wetzel
114.5	Shawn Sheldon
125.5	Eric Seward
136.5	Frank Famiano

GRECO-ROMAN *(Cont.)*

149.5	Jim Martinez
163	David Butler
180.5	Chris Catallo
198	Derrick Waldroup*
220	Dennis Koslowski
286	Duane Koslowski
Team	U.S. Marine Corp (Div. I)
	U.S. Army (Div. II)

United States National Champions *(Cont.)*

1988

FREESTYLE		FREESTYLE *(Cont.)*		GRECO-ROMAN *(Cont.)*	
105.5	Tim Vanni	286	Bruce Baumgartner	149.5	Craig Pollard
114.5	Joe Gonzales	Team	Sunkist Kids (Div. I)	163	Tony Thomas
125.5	Kevin Darkus		Team Foxcatcher (Div. II)	180.5	Darryl Gholar
136.5	John Smith*			198	Mike Carolan
149.5	Nate Carr	**GRECO-ROMAN**		220	Dennis Koslowski
163	Kenny Monday	105.5	T. J. Jones	286	Duane Koslowski
180.5	Dave Schultz	114.5	Shawn Sheldon	Team	U.S. Marine Corps (Div. I)
198	Melvin Douglas III	125.5	Gogi Parseghian*		Sunkist Kids (Div. II)
220	Bill Scherr	136.5	Dalen Wasmund		

1989

FREESTYLE		FREESTYLE *(Cont.)*		GRECO-ROMAN *(Cont.)*	
105.5	Tim Vanni	286	Bruce Baumgartner	149.5	Andy Seras*
114.5	Zeke Jones	Team	Sunkist Kids (Div. I)	163	David Butler
125.5	Brad Penrith		Team Foxcatcher (Div. II)	180.5	John Morgan
136.5	John Smith	**GRECO-ROMAN**		198	Michial Foy
149.5	Nate Carr	105.5	Lew Dorrance	220	Steve Lawson
163	Rob Koll	114.5	Mark Fuller	286	Craig Pittman
180.5	Rico Chiapparelli	125.5	Gogi Parseghian	Team	U.S. Marine Corps (Div. I)
198	Jim Scherr*	136.5	Isaac Anderson		Jets USA (Div. II)
220	Bill Scherr				

1990

FREESTYLE		FREESTYLE *(Cont.)*		GRECO-ROMAN *(Cont.)*	
105.5	Rob Eiter	286	Bruce Baumgartner	149.5	Andy Seras
114.5	Zeke Jones	Team	Sunkist Kids (Div. I)	163	David Butler
125.5	Joe Melchiore		Team Foxcatcher (Div. II)	180.5	Derrick Waldroup
136.5	John Smith	**GRECO-ROMAN**		198	Randy Couture*
149.5	Nate Carr	105.5	Lew Dorrance	220	Chris Tironi
163	Rob Koll	114.5	Sam Henson	286	Matt Ghaffari
180.5	Royce Alger	125.5	Mark Pustelnik	Team	Jets USA (Div. I)
198	Chris Campbell*	136.5	Isaac Anderson		California Jets (Div. II)
220	Bill Scherr				

1991

FREESTYLE		FREESTYLE *(Cont.)*		GRECO-ROMAN *(Cont.)*	
105.5	Tim Vanni	286	Bruce Baumgartner	149.5	Andy Seras
114.5	Zeke Jones	Team	Sunkist Kids (Div. I)	163	Gordy Morgan
125.5	Brad Penrith		Jets USA (Div. II)	180.5	John Morgan*
136.5	John Smith*	**GRECO-ROMAN**		198	Michial Foy
149.5	Townsend Saunders	105.5	Eric Wetzel	220	Dennis Koslowski
163	Kenny Monday	114.5	Shawn Sheldon	286	Craig Pittman
180.5	Kevin Jackson	125.5	Frank Famiano	Team	Jets USA (Div. I)
198	Chris Campbell	136.5	Buddy Lee		Sunkist Kids (Div. II)
220	Mark Coleman				

1992

FREESTYLE		FREESTYLE *(Cont.)*		GRECO-ROMAN *(Cont.)*	
105.5	Rob Eiter	286	Bruce Baumgartner	149.5	Rodney Smith
114.5	Jack Griffin	Team	Sunkist Kids (Div. I)	163	Travis West
125.5	Kendall Cross*		Team Foxcatcher (Div. II)	180.5	John Morgan
136.5	John Fisher	**GRECO-ROMAN**		198	Michial Foy
149.5	Matt Demaray	105.5	Eric Wetzel	220	Dennis Koslowski
163	Greg Elinsky	114.5	Mark Fuller	286	Matt Ghaffari
180.5	Royce Alger	125.5	Dennis Hall	Team	NY Athletic Club (Div. I)
198	Dan Chaid	136.5	Buddy Lee*		Sunkist Kids (Div. II)
220	Bill Scherr				

*Outstanding wrestler.

United States National Champions *(Cont.)*

1993

FREESTYLE

105.5	Rob Eiter
114.5	Zeke Jones
125.5	Brad Penrith
136.5	Tom Brands
149.5	Matt Demaray
163	Dave Schultz*
180.5	Kevin Jackson
198	Melvin Douglas
220	Kirk Trost

FREESTYLE *(Cont.)*

286	Bruce Baumgartner
Team	Sunkist Kids (Div. I)
	Team Foxcatcher (Div. II)

GRECO-ROMAN

105.5	Eric Wetzel
114.5	Shawn Sheldon
125.5	Dennis Hall*
136.5	Shon Lewis

GRECO-ROMAN *(Cont.)*

149.5	Andy Seras
163	Gordy Morgan
180.5	Dan Henderson
198	Randy Couture
220	James Johnson
286	Matt Ghaffari
Team	NY Athletic Club (Div. I)
	Sunkist Kids (Div. II)

1994

FREESTYLE

105.5	Tim Vanni
114.5	Zeke Jones
125.5	Terry Brands
136.5	Tom Brands
149.5	Matt Demaray
163	Dave Schultz
180.5	Royce Alger
198	Melvin Douglas
220	Mark Kerr

FREESTYLE *(Cont.)*

286	Bruce Baumgartner*
Team	Sunkist Kids (Div. I)
	Team Foxcatcher (Div. II)

GRECO-ROMAN

105.5	Isaac Ramaswamy
114.5	Shawn Sheldon
125.5	Dennis Hall
136.5	Shon Lewis

GRECO-ROMAN *(Cont.)*

149.5	Andy Seras*
163	Gordy Morgan
180.5	Dan Henderson
198	Derrick Waldroup

GRECO-ROMAN *(Cont.)*

220	James Johnson
286	Matt Ghaffari
Team	Armed Forces (Div. I)
	NY Athletic Club (Div. II)

1995

FREESTYLE

105.5	Rob Eiter
114.5	Lou Rosselli
125.5	Kendall Cross*
136.5	Tom Brands
149.5	Matt Demaray
163	Dave Schultz
180.5	Kevin Jackson
198	Melvin Douglas
220	Kurt Angle

FREESTYLE *(Cont.)*

286	Bruce Baumgartner
Team	Sunkist Kids (Div. I)
	Team Foxcatcher (Div. II)

GRECO-ROMAN

105.5	Isaac Ramaswamy
114.5	Shawn Sheldon
125.5	Dennis Hall*
136.5	Van Fronhofer

GRECO-ROMAN *(Cont.)*

149.5	Heath Sims
163	Matt Lindland
180.5	Marty Morgan
198	Michial Foy
220	James Johnson
286	Rulon Gardner
Team	Armed Forces (Div. I)
	Sunkist Kids (Div. II)

1996

FREESTYLE

105.5	Rob Eiter
114.5	Lou Rosselli
125.5	Kendall Cross
136.5	Tom Brands
149.5	Townsend Saunders
163	Kenny Monday
180.5	Les Gutches*
198	Melvin Douglas
220	Kurt Angle

FREESTYLE *(Cont.)*

286	Bruce Baumgartner
Team	Sunkist Kids (Div. I)
	NY Athletic Club (Div. II)

GRECO-ROMAN

105.5	Mujaahid Maynard
114.5	Shawn Sheldon
125.5	Dennis Hall*
136.5	Shon Lewis

GRECO-ROMAN *(Cont.)*

149.5	Rodney Smith
163	Keith Sieracki
180.5	Marty Morgan
198	Michial Foy
220	John Oostendrop
286	Matt Ghaffari
Team	Armed Forces (Div. I)
	Sunkist Kids (Div. II)

1997

FREESTYLE

110	Kanamti Soloman
119	Zeke Jones
127.75	Terry Brands
138.75	Carl Kolat
152	Lincoln McIlravy*
167.5	Dan St. John
187.25	Les Gutches
213.75	Melvin Douglas

FREESTYLE *(Cont.)*

275.5	Tom Erikson
Team	Sunkist Kids (Div. I)
	NY Athletic Club (Div. II)

GRECO-ROMAN

110	Mark Yanagihara
119	Broderick Lee
127.75	Dennis Hall

GRECO-ROMAN *(Cont.)*

138.75	Kevin Bracken
152	Chris Saba
167.5	Miguel Spencer
187.25	Dan Henderson
213.75	Randy Couture*
275.5	Rulon Gardner
Team	Armed Forces (Div. I)
	NY Athletic Club (Div. II)

*Outstanding wrestler.

United States National Champions (Cont.)

1998

FREESTYLE

119	Sam Henson
127.75	Tony Purler
138.75	Shawn Charles
152	Lincoln McIlravy
167.5	Steve Marianetti
187.25	Les Gutches*
213.75	Melvin Douglas

FREESTYLE (Cont.)

286	Tolly Thompson
Team	Sunkist Kids (Div. I)
	NY Athletic Club (Div. II)

GRECO-ROMAN

119	Shawn Sheldon
127.75	Dennis Hall
138.75	Shon Lewis

GRECO-ROMAN (Cont.)

152	Chris Saba
167.5	Matt Lindland
187.25	Dan Niebuhr*
213.75	Jason Klohs
286	Matt Ghaffari
Team	Armed Forces (Div. I)
	Sunkist Kids (Div. II)

1999

FREESTYLE

119	Lou Rosselli
127.75	Terry Brands
138.75	Cary Kolat
152	Lincoln McIlravy
167.5	Joe Williams
187.25	Les Gutches
213.75	Dominic Black

FREESTYLE (Cont.)

286	Stephen Neal*
Team	Sunkist Kids (Div. I)
	NY Athletic Club (Div. II)

GRECO-ROMAN

119	Steven Mays
127.75	Dennis Hall
138.75	Glen Nieradka

GRECO-ROMAN (Cont.)

152	David Zuniga
167.5	Matt Lindland
187.25	Quincey Clark
213.75	Randy Couture
286	Dremiel Byers*
Team	Minnesota Storm (Div. I)
	Sunkist Kids (Div. II)

2000

FREESTYLE

119	Sammie Henson
127.75	Keyy Boumans
138.75	Cary Kolat
152	Lincoln McIlravy
167.5	Brandon Slay*
187.25	Les Gutches
213.75	Melvin Douglas

FREESTYLE (Cont.)

286	Kerry McCoy
Team	Sunkist Kids (Div. I)
	NY Athletic Club (Div. II)

GRECO-ROMAN

119	Brandon Paulson
127.75	Dennis Hall
138.75	Kevin Bracken

GRECO-ROMAN (Cont.)

152	Heath Sims
167.5	Matt Lindland
187.25	Quincey Clark*
213.75	Jason Gleasman
286	Rulon Gardner
Team	Armed Forces (Div. I)
	Sunkist Kids (Div. II)

*Outstanding wrestler.

Boy Trouble

At the Senior League Softball World Series for kids age 14 to 16 in Kalamazoo, Mich., an Inverness, Fla., team relinquished its chance at the title by forfeiting to a team from Eloy, Ariz., because the Arizona team included five boys. (Boys have been eligible to play Little League softball since 1996.) Inverness catcher Whitney Gelin, 15, shared her thoughts with SI's Tim Crothers, her brother-in-law.

"It didn't bother us when we got to the World Series and heard that one of the teams had five boys. Then we saw the guys, and they were bigger than some of our dads. Our coaches were worried that one of the boys would knock someone's teeth out with a line drive, so they decided not to let us play them. Some of my teammates cried when they heard we were forfeiting. I was just mad: I wanted to beat those boys. My sister Courtenay and I were so disappointed that instead of going to the field with our team to forfeit, we went to the mall to buy outfits for the awards banquet.

On Saturday the Philippine team forfeited the championship game to Arizona and we beat Kentucky in the third-place game. It was sad not to play for the title, but when we flew home we were treated like champions, with a police escort and even TV interviews. I'm looking on the positive side. We proved we're the best *girls'* team in America, and we got to miss the first week of school."

The Sports Market

WALTER IOOSS JR

Ken Griffey Jr. of the
Cincinnati Reds

The New Breed

With bracingly fresh ideas, several maverick personalities led sports business into the uncertain digital age

BY HANK HERSCH

TAKE A MOMENT and consider: Had Mark Cuban been on the island, who on *Survivor* could have outlasted him? This is, after all, the 41-year-old self-described high school geek who sold his Internet start-up to Yahoo! for $5.7 billion; who bought the Dallas Mavericks for $280 million in January and within weeks not only signed flamboyant forward Dennis Rodman but also lodged him in the guest house of his 24,000-square-foot Dallas home; who in trying to make his team attractive to prospective players upgraded the locker room towels to virtual velour; and who has both delighted and enraged his new colleagues with his chutzpah. As Cuban puts it, "I got no problem being the first owner to be thrown out of a game."

No, even *Survivor*'s survivor, the Machiavellian Richard Hatch, would have been hard-pressed to throw out the conniving Cuban. Now consider: This may be the most encouraging sign the NBA and other major sports can find at the dawn of the

21st century. For as the entertainment spectrum grows more crowded by the microsecond, with cutting-edge new leagues and ultragraphic video games and proliferating dot-com diversions, it is going to take guile like Cuban's for the staples of big-time sports to hold on to their market shares. "In the NBA there's the feeling the industry's going strong, there's nothing to fear," Cuban says. "Like Wang had nothing to fear, like Seagate had nothing to fear." Wang and Seagate are computer companies that got overwhelmed by the Internet wave.

Indeed, the feeling that the NBA—or any other major league—has nothing to fear is hardly supported by the facts. The year 2000 unveiled a far-from-contented fan base, one distracted by new media, disgruntled by work stoppages and disgusted by the cost of attending games. Ticket prices in the four major sports increased an average of 80% in the 1990s, with the average cost for a family of four to go to a game

The Mavericks' maverick: Cuban reinvigorated perennial doormat Dallas.

nation—and desperation—at work in major sports programming. While *MNF* remained the No. 3 program in prime time in 1999, it suffered the lowest ratings share in its 30-year history. In March, ABC lured one of the show's architects, Don Ohlmeyer, out of retirement to right the ship. It was Ohlmeyer's job to make compelling a game that no longer compelled even him: As head of NBC Sports in the late '70s he preferred playing golf to watching his own NFL offerings on Sunday afternoon.

The TV landscape Ohlmeyer re-encountered was starkly different from what he left in 1983. The mammoth $17.6 billion, eight-year NFL-rights package purchased by ABC, CBS, Fox and ESPN intensified the need to drive up football TV ratings. The competition on Monday nights included *Raw Is War*, a Vince McMahon–choreographed wrestlethon that drew 47% more males aged 12 to 24 than *MNF* in '99. Ohlmeyer fired all the staff save play-by-play man Al Michaels, persuaded the league to mount cameras on the referees and launched a rumor-laden search to fill Esiason's spot in the booth. For a while the buzz had conservative rabble-rouser Rush Limbaugh joining Michaels on Monday nights. Ohlmeyer finally settled on a three-man broadcast team consisting of Michaels, former NFL quarterback Dan Fouts and the oddball choice of Dennis

and have a few snacks reaching $254.48—roughly two weeks worth of groceries. Fans choosing to save their dough and eat in front of the tube had a new array of viewing choices that should have been even more terrifying to the big leagues: Reality-based shows of *Survivor*'s ilk were all the rage. They mimicked the drama of a game, drew almost Super Bowl–sized audiences and paid their top competitor less than a backup nosetackle's salary.

One only had to look to the selection of Boomer Esiason's successor in the *Monday Night Football* TV booth to see the imagi-

Miller, an acerbic comedian who specializes in obscure references and had never broadcast a game.

Miller may not save *Monday Night Football*, but his arrival at least created a stir. And with McMahon joining forces with NBC to start a hype-happy and no doubt demographically appealing league, the eight-team XFL, in 2001, the established NFL will have to fight to keep its edge. Ohlmeyer is likely to find a kindred spirit in Cuban-like owner Daniel Snyder, yet another billionaire, who after buying the Washington Redskins for $800 million wanted to stop producing his team's $50,000 media guide because it would be constantly out of date. "I'm always going to encourage people around here to think about making things better," Snyder says. "I'm not, 'This is the way things are because this is the way they've been done for 30 years.' That's not how you run a business."

Baseball, which received a jolt from its record-breaking 1998 season, started 2000 with promising news. In February the Seattle Mariners swung a buzz-making deal, sending free-agent-to-be Ken Griffey Jr. to the Cincinnati Reds, who signed the superstar centerfielder to a nine-year, $116.5 million contract that was far below his market value. Griffey wanted to play in his hometown. (He grew up in Cincy while his father, Ken Griffey Sr., starred for the Reds.) Unless you were a Mariners fan, the 30-year-old Griffey's desire to sign with his hometown, small-market team was a heartwarming story. Unfortunately, the summer provided few further instances of small-market teams making big waves, a problem delineated in the report released by a blue-ribbon panel in July that quantified the dispiriting disparity between the haves and the have-nots.

Two years in the making, the 87-page report noted that teams with payrolls in the top 50% won all the playoff games in the last five years, that nine of the 10 teams in the World Series had payrolls in the top 25% and that only the New York Yankees, Cleveland Indians and Colorado Rockies were profitable from 1995 to '99. Despite growth in baseball's attendance and revenue over that span, the panel concluded, "What makes its current economic structure untenable in the long run is that year after year too many clubs know in spring training that they have no realistic prospect of reaching postseason play."

The logical solutions—starting with a salary cap and revenue sharing—seemed as unlikely as Griffey's returning to Seattle. Under baseball's current rules, owners seeking to implement these solutions can be blocked by a mere minority of a quarter of the owners. Leading that small faction would be the owners' most obstreperous member, Yankees boss George Steinbrenner, whose lucrative local TV contract enabled him to dole out more than $100 million in salaries in 2000, five times more than the Montreal Expos, who have no TV deal, could afford to pay. Further, baseball would face monumental difficulties in selling change to the players' union, which is merely batting 1.000 in opposing checks on the escalating salaries of its members.

With its bargaining agreement in place until 2004, the NHL at least could relax and look forward. Viewership of the 2000 Stanley Cup finals was up significantly, and expansion for 2001–02 added the Columbus Bluejackets and the Minnesota Wild (who proved just how deep into the nickname stockpile teams now have to burrow). Wayne Gretzky was poised to buy a piece of the Phoenix Coyotes, joining fellow former superstar Mario Lemieux of the Pittsburgh Penguins in the owners' ranks. One of their colleagues, freewheeling Internet mogul Ted Leonsis, had nearly tripled the Washington Capitals' season-ticket sales entering his second year and produced a Web site that became the standard for the league. "Whatever we incur in ticket sales and sponsorships will go right back to the team in payroll," Leonsis says. "I'm not in this to make money; I'm in this to win."

Suffering from the Michael-left-me-and-I-got-a-lockout-hangover blues, the NBA struggled in 1999–2000, with regular-

ABC hoped the acerbic, erudite Miller would revitalize *Monday Night Football*.

season TV ratings plunging 21% from the previous year. Even its attempts to cross over (WNBA attendance was down 11%) and to cross borders (Toronto forward Vince Carter had a breakout year, but only 39,000 Canadian viewers tuned in to a Friday-night playoff doubleheader, 152,000 less than watched a repeat of a two-month-old dog show) were disappointing. Interest in the NBA may have reached its zenith this year with the return of Michael Jordan, and he didn't even play a minute. In a move engineered by, yes, Leonsis, who is also a minority owner of the Washington Wizards, Jordan became the team's direc-

tor of basketball operations and a 10% stakeholder.

But while Jordan's team remained in a rut, Cuban's surged. Even with the disruptive Rodman dragging them to a 3–9 skid, the once listless Mavericks went 31–19 over their last 50 games to finish 40–42 and just miss the playoffs. As Cuban maneuvered in the off-season he spoke of charting referees' tendencies, digitizing game film for coaches and installing broadband for high-speed Internet access to every seat in a new arena. "The more somebody else does something, the less likely I am to do it," Cuban says. "No idea is off-limits."

Nor should any be. Not when survival is at stake.

Major League Baseball

Address: 245 Park Avenue
      New York, NY 10167
Telephone: (212) 931-7800
Commissioner: Bud Selig
Chief Operating Officer: Paul Beeston
Executive Director, Public Relations: Richard Levin
www.majorleague baseball.com

Major League Baseball Players Association

Address: 12 East 49th Street, 24th Floor
      New York, NY 10017
Telephone: (212) 826-0808
Executive Director: Donald Fehr
Director of Communications: Greg Bouris
Director of Licensing: Judy Heeter
www.bigleaguers.com

Anaheim Angels

Address: P.O. Box 2000
      Anaheim, CA 92803
Telephone: (714) 940-2000
Stadium (Capacity): Edison International Field of
Anaheim (45,050)
Owner: Walt Disney Company
General Manager: Bill Stoneman
Manager: Mike Scioscia
Vice President of Communications: Tim Mead
www.angelsbaseball.com

Arizona Diamondbacks

Address: 401 East Jefferson Street
      Phoenix, AZ 85001
Telephone: (602) 462-6500
Stadium (Capacity): Bank One Ballpark (49,033)
Managing General Partner: Jerry Colangelo
General Manager: Joe Garagiola Jr.
Manager: Buck Showalter
Director of Public Relations: Mike Swanson
www.azdiamondbacks.com

Atlanta Braves

Address: P.O. Box 4064
      Atlanta, GA 30302
Telephone: (404) 522-7630
Stadium (Capacity): Turner Field (50,062)
Owner: Ted Turner
Executive VP & General Manager: John Schuerholz
Manager: Bobby Cox
Director of Public Relations: Jim Schultz
www.atlantabraves.com

Baltimore Orioles

Address: Oriole Park at Camden Yards
      333 W Camden Street
      Baltimore, MD 21201
Telephone: (410) 685-9800
Stadium (Capacity): Camden Yards (48,876)
Managing Partner and Owner: Peter G. Angelos
Vice Chairman/CEO: Joseph Foss
Manager: Mike Hargrove
Director of Public Relations: Bill Stetka
www.theorioles.com

Boston Red Sox

Address: 4 Yawkey Way
      Fenway Park
      Boston, MA 02215
Telephone: (617) 267-9440
Stadium (Capacity): Fenway Park (33,871)
CEO: John Harrington
Executive VP and GM: Daniel F. Duquette
Manager: Jimy Williams
Vice President, Public Affairs: Dick Bresciani
www.theredsox.com

Chicago Cubs

Address: Wrigley Field
      1060 West Addison
      Chicago, IL 60613
Telephone: (773) 404-2827
Stadium (Capacity): Wrigley Field (39,056)
President and CEO: Andrew B. MacPhail
Executive VP of Business Operations: Mark McGuire
Manager: Don Baylor
Director of Media Relations: Sharon Panozzo
www.cubs.com

Chicago White Sox

Address: Comiskey Park
      333 West 35th Street
      Chicago, IL 60616
Telephone: (312) 674-1000
Stadium (Capacity): Comiskey Park (44,321)
Chairman: Jerry Reinsdorf
General Manager: Ron Schueler
Manager: Jerry Manuel
Director of Publc Relations: Scott Reifert
www.whitesox.com

Cincinnati Reds

Address: 100 Cinergy Field
      Cincinnati, OH 45202
Telephone: (513) 421-4510
Stadium (Capacity): Cinergy Field (52,953)
CEO/General Partner: Carl Lindner
General Manager: James G. Bowden
Managing Executive: John L. Allen
Manager: Jack McKeon
Director of Media Relations: Rob Butcher
www.cincinnatireds.com

Cleveland Indians

Address: Jacobs Field
      2401 Ontario Street
      Cleveland, OH 44115-4003
Telephone: (216) 420-4200
Stadium (Capacity): Jacobs Field (43,368)
President and CEO: Lawrence J. Dolan
Executive VP and General Manager: John Hart
Manager: Charlie Manuel
Vice President, Public Relations: Bob DiBiasio
www.indians.com

Colorado Rockies

Address: 2001 Blake Street
      Denver, CO 80205
Telephone: (303) 292-0200
Stadium (Capacity): Coors Field (50,381)
Chairman, President and CEO: Jerry D. McMorris
Executive VP of Business Operations: Keli McGregor
General Manager and Executive VP: Dan O'Dowd
Manager: Buddy Bell
Senior Director of Public Relations: Jay Alves
www.coloradorockies.com

Detroit Tigers

Address: Comerica Park
      2100 Woodward Avenue
      Detroit, MI 48201
Telephone: (313) 962-4000
Stadium (Capacity): Comerica Park (40,000)
Owner: Mike Ilitch
Chief Executive Officer and President: John McHale
Manager: Phil Garner
Director of Marketing/Communications: Tyler Barnes
www.detroittigers.com

Florida Marlins

Address: 2267 Dan Marino Boulevard
Miami, FL 33056
Telephone: (305) 626-7400
Stadium (Capacity): Pro Player Stadium (36,331)
Chairman: John W. Henry
President and General Manager: Dave Dombrowski
Manager: John Boles
VP of Communications/Broadcasting: Ron Colangelo
www.floridamarlins.com

Houston Astros

Address: P.O. Box 288
Houston, TX 77001
Telephone: (713) 259-8000
Stadium (Capacity): Enron Field (40,900)
Chairman: Drayton McLane
General Manager: Gerry Hunsicker
Manager: Larry Dierker
Director of Media Relations: Warren Miller
www.astros.com

Kansas City Royals

Address: P.O. Box 419969
Kansas City, MO 64141
Telephone: (816) 921-8000
Stadium (Capacity): Kauffman Stadium (40,793)
Owner and Chairman of the Board: David D. Glass
General Manager: Allard Baird
Manager: Tony Muser
Vice President, Communications: Mike Levy
www.kcroyals.com

Los Angeles Dodgers

Address: 1000 Elysian Park Avenue
Los Angeles, CA 90012-1199
Telephone: (323) 224-1500
Stadium (Capacity): Dodger Stadium (56,000)
Managing Partner, Chairman and CEO: Robert Daly
President and COO: Bob Graziano
General Manager: Kevin Malone
Manager: Davey Johnson
Director Media Relations/Publicity: Julio Sarmiento
www.dodgers.com

Milwaukee Brewers

Address: P.O. Box 3099
Milwaukee, WI 53201-3099
Telephone: (414) 933-4114
Stadium (Capacity): Milwaukee County Stadium (53,192)
President and CEO: Wendy Selig-Prieb
Senior VP and GM: Dean Taylor
Manager: Davey Lopes
Media Relations: Jon Greenberg
www.milwaukeebrewers.com

Minnesota Twins

Address: 34 Kirby Puckett Place
Minneapolis, MN 55415
Telephone: (612) 375-1366
Stadium (Capacity): Hubert H. Humphrey
Metrodome (48,678)
Owner: Carl Pohlad
General Manager: Terry Ryan
Manager: Tom Kelly
Manager of Media Relations: Sean Harlin
www.twinsbaseball.com

Montreal Expos

Address: P.O. Box 500
Station M
Montreal
Quebec, Canada H1V 3P2
Telephone: (514) 253-3434

Montreal Expos *(Cont.)*

Stadium (Capacity): Olympic Stadium (46,500)
Chairman and CEO: Jeffrey H. Loria
Vice President and General Manager: Jim Beattie
Manager: Felipe Alou
Director, Media Relations: Peter Loyello
www.montrealexpos.com

New York Mets

Address: Shea Stadium
123-01 Roosevelt Ave.
Flushing, NY 11368
Telephone: (718) 507-6387
Stadium (Capacity): Shea Stadium (56,521)
Chairman: Nelson Doubleday
President and Chief Executive Officer: Fred Wilpon
Senior VP and General Manager: Steve Phillips
Manager: Bobby Valentine
Director of Media Relations: Jay Horwitz
www.mets.com

New York Yankees

Address: Yankee Stadium
Bronx, NY 10451
Telephone: (718) 293-4300
Stadium (Capacity): Yankee Stadium (57,746)
Principal Owner: George Steinbrenner
Chief Operating Officer: Lonn Trost
VP/General Manager: Brian Cashman
Manager: Joe Torre
Director of Media Relations: Rick Cerone
www.yankees.com

Oakland Athletics

Address: 7677 Oakport St., 2nd floor
Oakland, CA 94621
Telephone: (510) 638-4900
Stadium (Capacity): Network Associates Coliseum
(43,662)
Owners: Steve Schott and Ken Hofmann
President: Michael Crowley
General Manager: Billy Beane
Manager: Art Howe
Baseball Information Manager: Mike Selleck
www.oaklandathletics.com

Philadelphia Phillies

Address: P.O. Box 7575
Philadelphia, PA 19101-7575
Telephone: (215) 463-6000
Stadium (Capacity): Veterans Stadium (62,418)
Chairman: Bill Giles
President: David T. Montgomery
General Manager: Ed Wade
Manager: Terry Francona
Vice President, Public Relations: Larry Shenk
www.phillies.com

Pittsburgh Pirates

Address: P.O. Box 7000
Pittsburgh, PA 15212
Telephone: (412) 323-5000
Stadium (Capacity): Three Rivers Stadium (47,687)
CEO and Managing General Partner: Kevin McClatchy
General Manager: Cam Bonifay
Manager: Gene Lamont
Director of Media Relations: Jim Trdinich
www.pirateball.com

St. Louis Cardinals

Address: Busch Stadium
250 Stadium Plaza
St. Louis, MO 63102
Telephone: (314) 421-3060
Stadium (Capacity): Busch Stadium (49,779)
President and CEO: Mark Lamping

St. Louis Cardinals (Cont.)
General Manager: Walt Jocketty
Manager: Tony LaRussa
Director of Media Relations: Brian Bartow
www.stlcardinals.com

San Diego Padres
Address: P.O. Box 122000
San Diego, CA 92112
Telephone: (619) 283-4494
Stadium (Capacity): Qualcomm Stadium (66,307)
Chairman: John Moores
General Manager: Kevin Towers
Manager: Bruce Bochy
Director of Media Relations: Glenn Geffner
www.padres.com

San Francisco Giants
Address: 24 Willie Mays Plaza
San Francisco, CA 94107
Telephone: (415) 468-3700
Stadium (Capacity): Pacific Bell Park (40,930)
President/Managing General Partner: Peter Magowan
General Manager: Brian Sabean
Manager: Dusty Baker
Vice President, Communications: Bob Rose
www.sfgiants.com

Seattle Mariners
Address: P.O. Box 4100
Seattle, WA 98104
Telephone: (206) 346-4000
Stadium (Capacity): SAFECO Field (47,155)
Chairman and CEO: Howard Lincoln
General Manager: Pat Gillick
Manager: Lou Piniella
Director of Baseball Information: Tim Hevly
www.mariners.org

Tampa Bay Devil Rays
Address: One Tropicana Drive
St. Petersburg, FL 33705
Telephone: (727) 825-3137
Stadium (Capacity): Tropicana Field (44,397)
Managing General Partner/CEO: Vincent J. Naimoli
Senior VP and General Manager: Chuck Lamar
Manager: Larry Rothschild
Vice President, Public Relations: Rick Vaughn
www.devilray.com

Texas Rangers
Address: P.O. Box 90111
Arlington, TX 76004
Telephone: (817) 273-5222
Stadium (Capacity): The Ballpark in Arlington (49,166)
Owner: Thomas O. Hicks
General Manager: Doug Melvin
Manager: Johnny Oates
Senior VP, Media Relations: John Blake
www.texasrangers.com

Toronto Blue Jays
Address: SkyDome
1 Blue Jays Way, Suite 3200
Toronto, Ontario, Canada M5V 1J1
Telephone: (416) 341-1000
Stadium (Capacity): SkyDome (45,100)
Senior Chairman: Sam Pollock
President of Baseball Operations/GM: Gord Ash
Manager: Jim Fregosi
Vice President, Media Relations: Howard Starkman
www.bluejays.ca

Pro Football Directory

National Football League
Address: 280 Park Avenue
New York, NY 10017
Telephone: (212) 450-2000
Commissioner: Paul Tagliabue
www.nfl.com

NFL Players Association
Address: 2021 L Street, N.W.
Washington, D.C. 20036
Telephone: (202) 463-2200
Executive Director: Gene Upshaw
Director of Communications: Carl Francis
www.nflpa.org

Arizona Cardinals
Address: P.O. Box 888
Phoenix, AZ 85001
Telephone: (602) 379-0101
Stadium (Capacity): Sun Devil Stadium (73,377)
President and Owner: Bill Bidwill
General Manager: Bob Ferguson
Head Coach: Vince Tobin
Director of Public Relations: Paul Jensen
www.azcardinals.com

Atlanta Falcons
Address: 4400 Falcon Park Way
Flowery Branch, GA 30542
Telephone: (770) 965-3115
Stadium (Capacity): Georgia Dome (71,228)
President: Taylor W. Smith

Atlanta Falcons (Cont.)
VP of Football Operations: Ron Hill
Coach: Dan Reeves
Publicity Director: Aaron Salkin
www.atlantafalcons.com

Baltimore Ravens
Address: 11001 Owings Mills Blvd.
Owings Mills, MD 21117
Telephone: (410) 654-6200
Stadium (Capacity): PSINet Stadium (69,084)
Owner/CEO: Art Modell
President/COO: David Modell
Coach: Brian Billick
VP of Public Relations: Kevin Byrne
www.ravenszone.net

Buffalo Bills
Address: One Bills Drive
Orchard Park, NY 14127
Telephone: (716) 648-1800
Stadium (Capacity): Ralph Wilson Stadium (73,840)
President: Ralph C. Wilson Jr.
Executive VP and General Manager: John Butler
Coach: Wade Phillips
Vice President of Communications: Scott Berchtold
www.buffalobills.com

Carolina Panthers
Address: Ericsson Stadium
              800 South Mint St.
              Charlotte, NC 28202
Telephone: (704) 358-7000
Stadium (Capacity): Ericsson Stadium (73,250)
Founder and Owner: Jerry Richardson
President: Mark Richardson
Coach: George Seifert
Director of Communications: Charlie Dayton
www.panthers.com

Chicago Bears
Address: 1000 Football Drive
              Lake Forest, IL 60045
Telephone: (847) 295-6600
Stadium (Capacity): Soldier Field (66,944)
President: Michael McCaskey
Coach: Dick Jauron
Director of Public Relations: Scott Hagel
www.chicagobears.com

Cincinnati Bengals
Address: One Paul Brown Stadium
              Cincinnati, OH 45202
Telephone: (513) 621-3550
Stadium (Capacity): Cinergy Field (65,600)
President: Mike Brown
Executive Vice President: Katherine Blackburn
Coach: Bruce Coslet
Director of Public Relations: Jack Brennan
www.bengals.com

Dallas Cowboys
Address: One Cowboys Parkway
              Irving, TX 75063
Telephone: (972) 556-9900
Stadium (Capacity): Texas Stadium (65,675)
Owner, President and General Manager: Jerry Jones
Coach: Dave Campo
Public Relations Director: Rich Dalrymple
www.dallascowboys.com

Denver Broncos
Address: 13655 Broncos Parkway
              Englewood, CO 80112
Telephone: (303) 649-9000
Stadium (Capacity): Mile High Stadium (76,098)
President and Chief Executive Officer: Pat Bowlen
General Manager: Neal Dahlen
Coach: Mike Shanahan
Director of Media Relations: Jim Saccomano
www.denverbroncos.com

Detroit Lions
Address: 1200 Featherstone Road
              Pontiac, MI 48342
Telephone: (248) 335-4131
Stadium (Capacity): Pontiac Silverdome (80,311)
Chairman and President: William Clay Ford
Executive Vice President and CEO: Chuck Schmidt
Coach: Bobby Ross
Director of Media Relations: Steve Reaven
www.detroitlions.com

Green Bay Packers
Address: 1265 Lombardi Avenue
              Green Bay, WI 54304
Telephone: (920) 496-5700
Stadium (Capacity): Lambeau Field (60,890)
President: Bob Harlan
General Manager: Ron Wolf
Coach: Mike Sherman
Public Relations Director: Lee Remmel
www.packers.com

Indianapolis Colts
Address: P.O. Box 535000
              Indianapolis, IN 46253
Telephone: (317) 297-2658
Stadium (Capacity): RCA Dome (56,127)
Owner and Chief Executive Officer: Jim Irsay
President: Bill Polian
Vice Chairman and COO: Michael Schernoff
Coach: Jim Mora
Vice President of Public Relations: Craig Kelley
www.colts.com

Jacksonville Jaguars
Address: One Alltel Stadium Place
              Jacksonville, FL 32202
Telephone: (904) 633-6000
Stadium (Capacity): Alltel Stadium (73,000)
Owner: J. Wayne Weaver
Vice President and CFO: Bill Prescott
Senior VP of Football Operations: Michael Huyghue
Coach: Tom Coughlin
Executive Director of Communications: Dan Edwards
www.jaguars.com

Kansas City Chiefs
Address: One Arrowhead Drive
              Kansas City, MO 64129
Telephone: (816) 920-9300
Stadium (Capacity): Arrowhead Stadium (79,451)
Founder: Lamar Hunt
CEO, President and General Manager: Carl Peterson
Coach: Gunther Cunningham
Public Relations Director: Bob Moore
www.kcchiefs.com

Miami Dolphins
Address: 7500 S.W. 30th Street
              Davie, FL 33314
Telephone: (954) 452-7000
Stadium (Capacity): Pro Player Stadium (75,540)
Chairman of the Board/Owner: H. Wayne Huizenga
President and COO: Eddie J. Jones
VP of Player Personnel: Rick Spielman
Head Coach: Dave Wannstedt
VP Media Relations: Harvey Greene
www.miamidolphins.com

Minnesota Vikings
Address: 9520 Viking Drive
              Eden Prairie, MN 55344
Telephone: (612) 828-6500
Stadium (Capacity): HHH Metrodome (64,121)
Owner: Red McCombs
President: Gary Woods
Coach: Dennis Green
Public Relations Director: Bob Hagan
www.vikings.com

New England Patriots
Address: Foxboro Stadium
              60 Washington St.
              Foxboro, MA 02035
Telephone: (508) 543-8200
Stadium (Capacity): Foxboro Stadium (60,292)
Owner and Chairman: Robert K. Kraft
Vice Chairman: Jonathan Kraft
Senior VP and COO: Andy Wasynczuk
Coach: Bill Belichick
VP of Player Development and Community Relations:
  Donald Lowery
www.patriots.com

New Orleans Saints
Address: 5800 Airline Highway
             Metairie, LA 70003
Telephone: (504) 733-0255
Stadium (Capacity): Louisiana Superdome (70,054)
Owner: Tom Benson
GM of Football Operations: Randy Mueller
Head Coach: Jim Haslett
Director of Media Relations: Greg Bensel
www.neworleanssaints.com

New York Giants
Address: Giants Stadium
             East Rutherford, NJ 07073
Telephone: (201) 935-8111
Stadium (Capacity): Giants Stadium (79,469)
President and co-CEO: Wellington T. Mara
Chairman and co-CEO: Preston Robert Tisch
Senior VP and General Manager: Ernie Accorsi
Coach: Jim Fassel
Vice President of Communications: Pat Hanlon
www.giants.com

New York Jets
Address: 1000 Fulton Avenue
             Hempstead, NY 11550
Telephone: (516) 560-8100
Stadium (Capacity): Giants Stadium (79,469)
Owner: Robert Wood Johnson IV
Director of Player Personnel: Dick Haley
Coach: Al Groh
Director of Public Relations: Frank Ramos
www.newyorkjets.com

Oakland Raiders
Address: 1220 Harbor Bay Parkway
             Alameda, CA 94502
Telephone: (510) 864-5000
Stadium (Capacity): Oakland-Alameda County
Coliseum (62,500)
President of the General Partner: Al Davis
Coach: Jon Gruden
Executive Assistant: Al LoCasale
Director of Public Relations: Mike Taylor

Philadelphia Eagles
Address: Veterans Stadium
             3501 South Broad Street
             Philadelphia, PA 19148
Telephone: (215) 463-2500
Stadium (Capacity): Veterans Stadium (65,352)
President and CEO: Jeffrey Lurie
Executive Vice President and COO: Joe Banner
Director of Football Operations: Tom Modrak
Coach: Andy Reid
Football Media Services Coordinator: Derek Boyko
www.philadelphiaeagles.com

Pittsburgh Steelers
Address: 3400 South Water Street
             Pittsburgh, PA 15203
Telephone: (412) 432-7800
Stadium (Capacity): Three Rivers Stadium (59,600)
President: Dan Rooney
Director of Football Operations: Kevin Colbert
Coach: Bill Cowher
Director of Communications: Ron Wahl
www.steelers.com

St. Louis Rams
Address: One Rams Way
             St. Louis, MO 63045
Telephone: (314) 982-7267
Stadium (Capacity): Trans World Dome (66,000)
Owner and Chairman: Georgia Frontiere
Vice Chairman and Owner: Stan Kroenke

St. Louis Rams *(Cont.)*
President: John Shaw
Coach: Mike Martz
Director of Public Relations: Rick Smith
www.stlouisrams.com

San Francisco 49ers
Address: 4949 Centennial Boulevard
             Santa Clara, CA 95054
Telephone: (408) 562-4949
Stadium (Capacity): 3Com Park (70,207)
Owner: Denise DeBartolo-York
President: Peter Harris
Vice President: John York
VP/General Manager: Bill Walsh
Coach: Steve Mariucci
Public Relations Director: Kirk Reynolds
www.sf49ers.com

Tampa Bay Buccaneers
Address: One Buccaneer Place
             Tampa, FL 33607
Telephone: (813) 870-2700
Stadium (Capacity): Raymond James Stadium (66,321)
Owner: Malcolm Glazer
General Manager: Rich McKay
Coach: Tony Dungy
Director of Communications: Reggie Roberts
www.buccaneers.com

Washington Redskins
Address: 21300 Redskins Park Drive
             Ashburn, VA 20147
Telephone: (703) 478-8900
Stadium (Capacity): Fedex Field (85,407)
Owner: Daniel M. Snyder
Director of Player Personnel: Vinny Cerrato
Coach: Norv Turner
Vice President of Public Relations: John Maroon
www.redskins.com

San Diego Chargers
Address: Qualcomm Stadium
             4020 Murphy Canyon Road
             San Diego, CA 92123
Telephone: (858) 874-4500
Stadium (Capacity): Qualcomm Stadium (71,400)
Chairman: Alex G. Spanos
President/Vice Chairman: Dean A. Spanos
VP of Football Operations: Ed McGuire
Coach: Mike Riley
Director of Public Relations: Bill Johnston
www.chargers.com

Seattle Seahawks
Address: 11220 N.E. 53rd Street
             Kirkland, WA 98033
Telephone: (425) 827-9777
Stadium (Capacity): Husky Stadium (68,589)
Owner: Paul Allen
President: Bob Whitsitt
Coach/GM: Mike Holmgren
VP of Administration and Communications: Gary Wright
Director of Public Relations: Dave Pearson
www.seahawks.com

Tennessee Titans
Address: 460 Great Circle Road
             Nashville, TN 37228
Telephone: 615-565-4000
Stadium (Capacity): Adelphia Coliseum (68,498)
President: Jeff Diamond
General Manager: Floyd Reese
Coach: Jeff Fisher
Director of Media Relations: Robbie Bohren
www.titansonline.com

Other Leagues

Canadian Football League
Address: 110 Eglinton Avenue West, 5th floor
    Toronto, Ontario M4R1A3, Canada
Telephone: (416) 322-9650
Commissioner: John Tory
President/Chief Operating Officer: Jeff Giles
Director of Communications: Jim Neish
www.cfl.ca

NFL EUROPE
Address: 280 Park Avenue
    New York, NY 10017
Telephone: (212) 450-2000
President: Bill Peterson (London)
Chief Operating Officer: Dan Margoshes (London)
Director of Communications: David Tossel
www.nfleurope.com

Pro Basketball Directory

National Basketball Association

National Basketball Association
Address: 645 Fifth Avenue
    New York, NY 10022
Telephone: (212) 826-7000
Commissioner: David Stern
Deputy Commissioner: Russell Granik
Sr. VP of Communications: Brian McIntyre
www.nba.com

National Basketball Association Players Association
Address: 1700 Broadway
    Suite 1400
    New York, NY 10019
Telephone: (212) 655-0880
Executive Director: William Hunter
www.nbapa.com

Atlanta Hawks
Address: One CNN Center, South Tower
    Suite 405
    Atlanta, GA 30303
Telephone: (404) 827-3800
Arena (Capacity): Philips Arena (19,445)
Owner: Ted Turner
President: Stan Kasten
VP and General Manager: Pete Babcock
Coach: Lon Kruger
VP of Communications: Arthur Triche
www.hawks.com

Boston Celtics
Address: 151 Merrimac Street
    Boston, MA 02114
Telephone: (617) 523-6050
Arena (Capacity): FleetCenter (18,624)
Owner and Chairman of the Board: Paul Gaston
President and Head Coach: Rick Pitino
General Manager: Chris Wallace
Director of Media Relations: R. Jeffrey Twiss
www.celtics.com

Charlotte Hornets
Address: 100 Hive Drive
    Charlotte, NC 28217
Telephone: (704) 357-0252
Arena (Capacity): Charlotte Coliseum (23,799)
Owners: George Shinn and Ray Wooldridge
Coach: Paul Silas
VP of Public Relations: Harold Kaufman
www.hornets.com

Chicago Bulls
Address: 1901 W. Madison Street
    Chicago, IL 60612
Telephone: (312) 455-4000
Arena (Capacity): United Center (21,711)

Chicago Bulls *(Cont.)*
Chairman: Jerry Reinsdorf
GM and VP of Basketball Operations: Jerry Krause
Coach: Tim Floyd
Senior Director of Media Services: Tim Hallam
www.bulls.com

Cleveland Cavaliers
Address: One Center Court
    Cleveland, OH 44115
Telephone: (216) 420-2000
Arena (Capacity): Gund Arena (20,562)
Chairman: Gordon Gund
Senior VP and GM: Jim Paxson
Coach: Randy Wittman
Sr. Director of Communications/PR: Bob Price
www.cavs.com

Dallas Mavericks
Address: Reunion Arena
    777 Sports Street
    Dallas, TX 75207
Telephone: (214) 748-1808
Arena (Capacity): Reunion Arena (18,187)
Owner: Mark Cuban
General Manager and Head Coach: Don Nelson
Director of Player Personnel: Donn Nelson
Sr. VP of Marketing/Communications: Matt Fitzgerald
www.dallasmavericks.com

Denver Nuggets
Address: Pepsi Center
    1000 Chopper Circle
    Denver, CO 80204
Telephone: (303) 405-1100
Arena (Capacity): Pepsi Center (19,099)
Owner: E. Stanley Kroenke
President/Coach: Dan Issel
Media Relations Director: Tommy Sheppard
www.nuggets.com

Detroit Pistons
Address: The Palace of Auburn Hills
    Two Championship Drive
    Auburn Hills, MI 48326
Telephone: (248) 377-0100
Arena (Capacity): The Palace of Auburn Hills (22,076)
Owner: William M. Davidson
President of Basketball Operations: Joe Dumars
Coach: George Irvine
VP of Public Relations: Matt Dobek
www.palacenet.com

National Basketball Association (Cont.)

Golden State Warriors
Address: 1011 Broadway
            Oakland, CA 94607-4019
Telephone: (510) 986-2200
Arena (Capacity): The Arena in Oakland
  (19,596)
Owner and CEO: Christopher Cohan
General Manager: Garry St. Jean
Coach: Dave Cowens
Director of Public Relations: Raymond Ridder
www.gs-warriors.com

Houston Rockets
Address: Two Greenway Plaza, Suite 400
            Houston, TX 77046
Telephone: (713) 627-3865
Arena (Capacity): Compaq Center (16,285)
Owner: Leslie Alexander
Chief Operating Officer: George Postolos
Executive VP of Basketball Affairs: Carroll Dawson
Coach: Rudy Tomjanovich
Director of Team Communications: Tim Frank
www.rockets.com

Indiana Pacers
Address: 125 S. Pennsylvania Street
            Indianapolis, IN 46204
Telephone: (317) 917-2500
Arena (Capacity): Conseco Fieldhouse (18,345)
Owners: Melvin Simon and Herbert Simon
President: Donnie Walsh
General Manager: David Kahn
Head Coach: Isiah Thomas
Media Relations Director: David Benner
www.pacers.com

Los Angeles Clippers
Address: The Staples Center
            1111 S. Figueroa Street - St. 1100
            Los Angeles, CA 90015
Telephone: (213) 742-7500
Arena (Capacity): The Staples Center (18,964)
Owner: Donald T. Sterling
Vice President of Basketball Operations: Elgin Baylor
Coach: Alvin Gentry
Vice President of Communications: Joe Safety
www.clippers.com

Los Angeles Lakers
Address: 555 North Nash Street
            El Segundo, CA 90245
Telephone: (310) 426-6000
Arena (Capacity): The Staples Center (19,282)
Owner: Dr. Jerry Buss
General Manager: Mitch Kupchak
Coach: Phil Jackson
Director of Public Relations: John Black
www.lakers.com

Miami Heat
Address: American Airlines Arena
            601 Biscayne Boulevard
            Miami, FL 33132
Telephone: (305) 577-4328
Arena (Capacity): American Airlines Arena (19,600)
Managing General Partner: Micky Arison
Executive Emeritus: Pauline Winick
President and Coach: Pat Riley
President/GM of Basketball Operations: Randy Pfund
Director of Sports Media Relations: Tim Donovan
www.heat.com

Milwaukee Bucks
Address: The Bradley Center
            1001 N. Fourth Street
            Milwaukee, WI 53203
Telephone: (414) 227-0500
Arena (Capacity): The Bradley Center (18,717)
Owner: Herb Kohl
General Manager: Ernie Grunfeld
Coach: George Karl
Public Relations Director: Cheri Hanson
www.bucks.com

Minnesota Timberwolves
Address: 600 First Avenue North
            Minneapolis, MN 55403
Telephone: (612) 673-1600
Arena (Capacity): Target Center (19,006)
Owner: Glen Taylor
VP of Basketball Operations: Kevin McHale
General Manager and Coach: Phil (Flip) Saunders
Manager of PR and Communications: Kent Wipf
www.timberwolves.com

New Jersey Nets
Address: Nets Champion Center
            390 Murray Hill Parkway
            East Rutherford, NJ 07073
Telephone: (201) 935-8888
Arena (Capacity): Continental Airlines Arena (20,049)
Principal Owner: Lewis Katz
President: Rod Thorn
General Manager: John Nash
Coach: Byron Scott
Director of Public Relations: John Mertz
www.njnets.com

New York Knickerbockers
Address: Madison Square Garden
            Two Pennsylvania Plaza
            New York, NY 10121
Telephone: (212) 465-5867
Arena (Capacity): Madison Square Garden (19,763)
Owner: ITT/Sheraton and Cablevision
Governor/CEO of MSG: David W. Checketts
Executive VP and General Manager: Scott Layden
Coach: Jeff Van Gundy
Vice President of Public Relations: Lori Hamamoto
www.nyknicks.com

Orlando Magic
Address: P.O. Box 76
            Orlando, FL 32802
Telephone: (407) 916-2400
Arena (Capacity): TD Waterhouse Centre (17,248)
Owner: Rich DeVos
Senior Executive Vice President: Pat Williams
General Manager: John Gabriel
Coach: Glenn "Doc" Rivers
Director of Communications: Joel Glass
www.orlandomagic.com

National Basketball Association (Cont.)

Philadelphia 76ers
Address: First Union Center
            3601 South Broad Street
            Philadelphia, PA 19148
Telephone: (215) 339-7600
Arena (Capacity): First Union Center (20,444)
Owner and President: Pat Croce
Head Coach and Vice President of Basketball
  Operations: Larry Brown
General Manager: Billy King
Director of Media Relations: Karen Frascona
www.sixers.com

Phoenix Suns
Address: P.O. Box 1369
            Phoenix, AZ 85001
Telephone: (602) 379-7900
Arena (Capacity): America West Arena (19,023)
Owner, CEO and Managing General Partner: Jerry
Colangelo
President: Bryan Colangelo
Coach: Scott Skiles
VP of Basketball Communications: Julie Fie
www.suns.com

Portland Trail Blazers
Address: One Center Court
            Suite 200
            Portland, OR 97227
Telephone: (503) 234-9291
Arena (Capacity): Rose Garden Arena (19,980)
Chairman of the Board: Paul Allen
President and General Manager: Bob Whitsitt
Coach: Mike Dunleavy
Director of Sports Communications: Sue Carpenter
www.blazers.com

Sacramento Kings
Address: One Sports Parkway
            Sacramento, CA 95834
Telephone: (916) 928-0000
Arena (Capacity): ARCO Arena (17,317)
Owners: Joe and Gavin Maloof
Vice President of Basketball Operations: Geoff Petrie
Coach: Rick Adelman
Director of Media Relations: Troy Hanson
www.kings.com

San Antonio Spurs
Address: Alamodome
            100 Montana
            San Antonio, TX 78203
Telephone: (210) 554-7787
Arena (Capacity): Alamodome (34,215)
Chairman: Peter Holt
Head Coach and General Manager: Gregg Popovich
Director of Media Services: Tom James
www.spurs.com

Seattle SuperSonics
Address: 351 Elliott Avenue West
            Suite 500
            Seattle, WA 98119
Telephone: (206) 281-5847
Arena (Capacity): KeyArena (17,072)
Owner: Barry Ackerley
President and General Manager: Wally Walker
Coach: Paul Westphal
Director of Media Relations: Marc Moquin
www.supersonics.com

Toronto Raptors
Address: 40 Bay Street, Suite 400
            Toronto, Ontario, Canada M5J 2X2
Telephone: (416) 815-5600
Arena (Capacity): Air Canada Centre (19,800)
Owner: Maple Leaf Sports and Entertainment, Ltd.
VP and General Manager: Glen Grunwald
Coach: Lenny Wilkens
Manager of Media Relations: Jim Labumbard
www.raptors.com

Utah Jazz
Address: 301 West So. Temple
            Salt Lake City, UT 84101
Telephone: (801) 575-7800
Arena (Capacity): Delta Center (19,911)
Owner: Larry H. Miller
President: Larry Haslam
VP of Basketball Operations: Kevin O'Connor
Coach: Jerry Sloan
Director of Media Relations: Kim Turner
www.utahjazz.com

Vancouver Grizzlies
Address: 770 Pacific Boulevard
            Vancouver, B.C., Canada V6B 5E7
Telephone: (604) 899-4666
Arena (Capacity): General Motors Place (19,193)
Owner: Michael E. Heisley
President: Dick Versace
General Manager: Billy Knight
Coach: Sidney Lowe
Director of Media Relations: Debbie Butt
www.grizzlies.com

Washington Wizards
Address: 601 F Street NW
            Washington D.C. 20004
Telephone: (202) 661-5000
Arena (Capacity): MCI Center (20,674)
Owner: Abe Pollin
General Manager and Vice President: Wes Unseld
President of Basketball Operations: Michael Jordan
Coach: Leonard Hamilton
Director of Public Relations: Maureen Lewis
www.nba.com/wizards

Women's National Basketball Association

Women's National Basketball Association
Address: 645 Fifth Avenue
             New York, NY 10022
Telephone: (212) 688-9622
President: Valerie B. Ackerman
Director of Communications: Mark Pray
www.wnba.com

Charlotte Sting
Address: 3308 Oak Lake Boulevard
             Suite B
             Charlotte, NC 28208
Telephone: (704) 357-0252
Arena (Capacity): Charlotte Coliseum (8,333)
Executive Vice President: Sam Russo
Coach: T.R. Dunn
Vice President of Public Relations: Harold Kaufman
www.charlottesting.com

Cleveland Rockers
Address: Gund Arena
             One Center Court
             Cleveland, OH 44115
Telephone: (216) 420-2000
Arena (Capacity): Gund Arena (20,500)
Chairman: Gordon Gund
President, CEO and COO: James C. Boland
Coach: Dan Hughes
Director of Media Relations: Lori Montgomery
www.clevelandrockers.com

Detroit Shock
Address: 2 Championship Drive
             Auburn Hills, MI 48326
Telephone: (248) 377-0100
Arena (Capacity): The Palace of Auburn Hills (19,000)
Managing Partner: William Davidson
President: Tom Wilson
General Manager/ Coach: Nancy Lieberman-Cline
Director of Media Relations: Dennis Sampier
www.detroitshock.com

Houston Comets
Address: Two Greenway Plaza, Suite 400
             Houston, TX 77046-3865
Telephone: (713) 627-9622
Arena (Capacity): The Compaq Center (16,000)
President: Leslie L. Alexander
Coach and General Manager: Van Chancellor
Interim Manager, Media Services: Bob Schranz
www.houstoncomets.com

Indiana Fever
Address: 125 S. Pennsylvania Street
             Indianapolis, IN 46284
Telephone: (317) 917-2500
Arena (Capacity): Conseco Field House (18,345)
President: Donnie Walsh
Chief Operating Officer: Kelly Kraus Koupf
Coach: Nell Fortner
Director of Media Relations: Tom Savage
www.wnba.com/fever

Los Angeles Sparks
Address: Great Western Forum
             3900 W. Manchester Boulevard
             Inglewood, CA 90306
Telephone: (310) 330-2434
Arena (Capacity): Great Western Forum (17,005)
Chairman: Dr. Jerry Buss
President and GM: Virginia (Penny) Toller

Los Angeles Sparks (Cont.)
Coach: Michael Cooper
Media Relations Director: Krystal Shipp
www.lasparks.com

Minnesota Lynx
Address: Target Center
             600 First Avenue North
             Minneapolis, MN 55403
Telephone: (612) 673-8400
Arena (Capacity): Target Center (19,006)
Chief Operating Officer: Roger Griffith
General Manager/Coach: Brian Agler
Public Relations Manager: Lisa Helgeson
www.wnba.com/lynx

New York Liberty
Address: Two Penn Plaza
             New York, NY 10121
Telephone: (212) 465-5867
Arena (Capacity): Madison Square Garden (19,763)
GM and Vice President: Carol Blazejowski
Coach: Richie Adubato
Director, Public Relations: Jeff Schwartzenberg
www.nyliberty.com

Orlando Miracle
Address: Two Magic Place
             8701 Maitland Summit Boulevard
             Orlando, FL 32810
Telephone: (407) 916-2400
Arena (Capacity): TD Waterhouse Centre (17,306)
Chairman: Rich DeVos
President: Bob Van der Weide
General Manager/ Coach: Carolyn Peck
Director of Media Relations: Katherine Wu
www.orlandomiracle.com

Miami Sol
Address: American Airlines Arena
             601 Biscayne Blvd.
             Miami, FL 33132
Telephone: (305) 577-4328
Arena (Capacity): American Airlines Arena (10,412)
President, Basketball Operations: Randy Pfund
General Manager/ Coach: Ron Rothstein
Media Relations Manager: Amanda Ludwig
www.miami-sol.com

Phoenix Mercury
Address: 201 East Jefferson Street
             Phoenix, AZ 85004
Telephone: (602) 514-8333
Arena (Capacity): America West Arena (17,623)
Owner, Phoenix Arena Sports: Jerry Colangelo
Chief Executive Officer: Bryan Colangelo
General Manager/ Coach: Cheryl Miller
Media Relations Director: Neda Kia
www.phoenixmercury.com

Portland Fire
Address: One Center Court
             Suite 150
             Portland, OR 97227
Telephone: (503) 235-9291
Arena (Capacity): The Rose Garden (19,980)
Chairman: Paul Allen
Vice President of Business Operations: Sandi Bittles
General Manager/ Coach: Linda Hargrove
Director of Communications: Jill Wiggins
www.firebasketball.com

Women's National Basketball Association *(Cont.)*

Sacramento Monarchs
Address: One Sports Parkway
Sacramento, CA 95834
Telephone: (916) 455-4647
Arena (Capacity): ARCO Arena (17,317)
Managing General Partner: Jim Thomas
President: John Thomas
General Manager: Jerry Reynolds
Coach: Sonny Allen
Director, Media Relations: Andrea Lepore
www.sacramentomonarchs.com

Seattle Storm
Address: Elliott Avenue West
Suite 500
Seattle, WA 98119
Telephone: (206) 281-5800
Arena (Capacity): Key Arena (12,000)
Owners: Barry & Ginger Ackerley
President of Sports & Entertainment: John Dresel
General Manager/ Coach: Lin Dunn
Director, Media Relations: TBD
www.wnba.com/storm

Utah Starzz
Address: 301 W. South Temple
Salt Lake City, UT 84101
Telephone: (801) 325-7827
Arena (Capacity): Delta Center (8,916)
Owner: Larry H. Miller
President: Dennis Haslam
Coach: Fred Williams
Media Relations Manager: Tami Scott
www.utahstarzz.com

Washington Mystics
Address: MCI Center
601 F Street, NW
Washington, DC 20004
Telephone: (202) 661-5000
Arena (Capacity): MCI Center (19,093)
Chairman: Abe Pollin
President: TBD
Coach: TBD
Director, Public Relations: Julie Demeo
www.washingtonmystics.com

Other Leagues

Continental Basketball Association
Address: Two Arizona Center
400 North 5th Street, Suite 1425
Phoenix, AZ 85004
Telephone: (602) 254-6677
President and Chief Marketing Officer: Don Welsh
Senior VP of Basketball Operations: Wade Morehead
www.cbahoops.com

Hockey Directory

National Hockey League
Address: 1251 Avenue of the Americas
47th floor
New York, NY 10020-1198
Telephone: (212) 789-2000
Commissioner: Gary Bettman
President of NHL Enterprises: Richie Woodworth
Executive VP and Dir. of Hockey Operations: Colin Campbell
VP of Media Relations: Frank Brown
www.nhl.com

National Hockey League Players Association
Address: 777 Bay Street, Suite 2400
Toronto, Ontario, Canada M5G 2C8
Telephone: (416) 313-2300
Executive Director: Bob Goodenow
www.nhlpa.com

Mighty Ducks of Anaheim
Address: Arrowhead Pond of Anaheim
2695 Katella Avenue
Anaheim, CA 92806
Telephone: (714) 940-2900
Arena (Capacity): Arrowhead Pond of Anaheim (17,174)
Chairman and Governor: Tony Tavares
President and General Manager: Pierre Gauthier
Coach: Craig Hartsburg
Manager of Communications: Alex Gilchrist
www.mightyducks.com

Atlanta Thrashers
Address: 1 CNN Center
P.O. Box 15538
Atlanta, GA 30348
Telephone: (404) 827-5300
Arena (Capacity): Philips Arena (18,500)
Owner: Time Warner
President and Governor: Stan Kasten
VP and General Manager: Don Waddell
Coach: Curt Fraser
Director of Public Relations: Tom Hughes
www.atlantathrashers.com

Boston Bruins
Address: One FleetCenter, Suite 250
Boston, MA 02114-1303
Telephone: (617) 624-1900
Arena (Capacity): FleetCenter (17,565)
Owner and Governor: Jeremy M. Jacobs
Alternative Governor, President and General
Manager: Harry Sinden
Coach: Pat Burns
Director of Media Relations: Heidi Holland
www.bostonbruins.com

Buffalo Sabres
Address: HSBC Arena
One Seymour H. Knox III Plaza
Buffalo, NY 14203
Telephone: (716) 855-4100
Arena (Capacity): HSBC Arena (18,690)

Buffalo Sabres (Cont.)
Chairman of the Board: John J. Rigas
CEO: Tim J. Rigas
General Manager: Darcy Regier
Coach: Lindy Ruff
VP of Communications: Michael Gilbert
www.sabres.com

Calgary Flames
Address: Pengrowth Saddledome
555 Saddledome Rise, SE
Calgary, Alberta T2G 2W1
Telephone: (403) 777-2177
Arena (Capacity): Pengrowth Saddledome (17,139)
Owners: Grant A. Bartlett, Harley N. Hotchkiss, N.
Murray Edwards, Ronald V. Joyce, Alvin G. Libin,
Allan P. Markin, J.R. "Bud" McCaig, Byron J.
Seaman, Daryl K. Seaman
President and CEO: Ron Bremner
VP/General Manager: Craig Button
Coach: Don Hay
Director of Communications: Peter Hanlon
www.calgaryflames.com

Carolina Hurricanes
Address: 1400 Edwards Mill Road
Raleigh, NC 27607
Telephone: (919) 467-7825
Arena (Capacity): Entertainment and Sports Arena
(18,711)
Owner: Peter Karmanos
CEO and General Manager: Jim Rutherford
VP/Assistant General Manager: Jason Karmanos
Coach: Paul Maurice
Director of Public Relations: Jerry Peters
www.carolinahurricanes.com

Chicago Blackhawks
Address: United Center
1901 W. Madison Street
Chicago, IL 60612
Telephone: (312) 455-7000
Arena (Capacity): United Center (20,500)
President: William W. Wirtz
Senior Vice President and GM: Robert Pulford
Manager of Hockey Operations: Mike Smith
Coach: Alpo Suhonen
Public Relations Director: Jim DeMaria
www.chicagoblackhawks.com

Colorado Avalanche
Address: Pepsi Center
1000 Chopper Circle
Denver, CO 80204
Telephone: (303) 405-1100
Arena (Capacity): Pepsi Center (18,007)
Owner: E. Stanley Kroenke
President and General Manager: Pierre Lacroix
Coach: Bob Hartley
VP of Communications and Team Services:
Jean Martineau
www.coloradoavalanche.com

Columbus Blue Jackets
Address: 200 West Nationwide Boulevard
Columbus, OH 43215
Telephone: (614) 246-4625
Arena (Capacity): Nationwide Arena (18,524)
Owner: John H. McConnell
President and General Manager: Doug MacLean
Coach: Dave King
Director of Communications: Todd Sharrock
www.bluejackets.com

Dallas Stars
Address: 211 Cowboys Parkway
Irving, TX 75063
Telephone: (972) 831-2401
Arena (Capacity): Reunion Arena (17,001)
Owner: Thomas O. Hicks
General Manager: Bob Gainey
Coach: Ken Hitchcock
Director of Media Relations: Larry Kelly
www.dallasstars.com

Detroit Red Wings
Address: Joe Louis Arena
600 Civic Center Drive
Detroit, MI 48226
Telephone: (313) 396-7544
Arena (Capacity): Joe Louis Arena (19,983)
Senior Vice President: Jim Devellano
Head Coach: Scott Bowman
General Manager: Ken Holland
Director of Media Relations: John Hahn
www.detroitredwings.com

Edmonton Oilers
Address: 11230 110th Street
Edmonton, Alberta T5G 3H7
Telephone: (780) 414-4000
Arena (Capacity): Skyreach Centre (17,100)
Owner: Edmonton Investors Group
Governor: Cal Nichols
President and Alt. Governor: Patrick LaForge
Coach: Craig MacTavish
VP of Public Relations, Hockey: Bill Tuele
www.edmontonoilers.com

Florida Panthers
Address: 1 Panther Parkway
Sunrise, FL 33323
Telephone: (954) 835-7000
Arena (Capacity): National Car Rental Center
(19,250)
Owner: H. Wayne Huizenga
General Manager: Bryan Murray
Coach: Terry Murray
Director of Broadcasting and Communications: Mike
Hanson
www.flpanthers.com

Los Angeles Kings
Address: The Staples Center
1111 South Figueroa Street
Los Angeles, CA 90037
Telephone: (213) 742-7100
Arena (Capacity): The Staples Center (18,118)
President: Tim Leiweke
General Manager: Dave Taylor
Coach: Andy Murray
Director of Media Relations: Mike Altieri
www.lakings.com

Minnesota Wild
Address: 317 Washington Street
St. Paul, MN, 55102
Telephone: (651) 602-6000
Arena (Capacity): Excel Energy Center (18,600)
Chairman: Bob Naegele Jr.
General Manager: Doug Risebrough
Coach: Jacques Lemaire
VP of Communications/Broadcasting: Bill Robertson
www.wild.com

Montreal Canadiens
Address: Molson Centre
            1260 de la Gauchetiere West
            Montreal, Quebec H3B 5E8
Telephone: (514) 932-2582
Arena (Capacity): Molson Centre (21,273)
President and Governor: Pierre Boivin
General Manager: Regean Houle
Coach: Alain Vigneault
Director of Communications: Donald Beauchamp
www.canadiens.com

New Jersey Devils
Address: Continental Airlines Arena, PO Box 504
            East Rutherford, NJ 07073
Telephone: (201) 935-6050
Arena (Capacity): Continental Airlines Arena (19,040)
Owner: Puck Holdings
CEO, President and GM: Lou Lamoriello
Coach: Larry Robinson
Director of Public Relations: Kevin Dessart
www.newjerseydevils.com

New York Islanders
Address: Nassau Veterans Memorial Coliseum
            Uniondale, NY 11553
Telephone: (516) 794-4100
Arena (Capacity): Nassau Coliseum (16,297)
Owners: Charles Wong and Sanjay Kumar
Co-Chairman and Alt. Governor: Edward Milstein
General Manager: Mike Milbury
Coach: Butch Goring
VP of Communications: Chris Botta
www.newyorkislanders.com

New York Rangers
Address: Madison Square Garden
            2 Pennsylvania Plaza
            New York, NY 10121
Telephone: (212) 465-6000
Arena (Capacity): Madison Square Garden (18,200)
Owner: Cablevision
President and General Manager: Glen Sather
Coach: Ron Low
VP of Public Relations: John Rosasco
www.newyorkrangers.com

Ottawa Senators
Address: The Corel Centre
            1000 Palladium Drive
            Kanata, Ontario K2V 1A5
Telephone: (613) 599-0250
Arena (Capacity): The Corel Centre (18,500)
Founder: Bruce M. Firestone
Chairman and Governor: Rod Bryden
President and Chief Executive Officer: Roy Mlakar
General Manager: Marshall Johnston
Coach: Jacques Martin
Director of Media Relations: Steve Keogh
www.ottawasenators.com

Philadelphia Flyers
Address: First Union Center
            3601 South Broad Street
            Philadelphia, PA 19148
Telephone: (215) 465-4500
Arena (Capacity): First Union Center (19,541)
Majority Owner: Comcast Spectacor
Chairman: Ed Snider
President and General Manager: Bob Clarke
Coach: Craig Ramsay
Director of Public Relations: Zack Hill
www.philadelphiaflyers.com

Phoenix Coyotes
Address: ALLTEL Ice Den
            9375 East Belle Road
            Scottsdale, AZ 85260
Telephone: (480) 473-5600
Arena (Capacity): America West Arena (16,210)
Chief Executive Officer and Governor: Richard Burke
Owner, CEO and Governor: Richard Burke
GM and Alternate Governor: Bobby Smith
Coach: Bob Francis
VP of Media and Player Relations: Richard Nairn
www.phoenixcoyotes.com

Pittsburgh Penguins
Address: Mellon Arena
            66 Mario Lemieux Place
            Pittsburgh, PA 15219
Telephone: (412) 642-1300
Arena (Capacity): Mellon Arena (16,958)
Owner: Mario Lemieux (Lemieux Ownership Group)
General Manager: Craig Patrick
Coach: Ivan Hlinka
Director of Media Relations: Steve Bovino
www.pittsburghpenguins.com

St. Louis Blues
Address: Savvis Center
            1401 Clark Avenue
            St. Louis, MO 63103
Telephone: (314) 622-2500
Arena (Capacity): Savvis Center (19,260)
President and Chief Executive Officer: Mark Sauer
Coach: Joel Quenneville
Senior VP and General Manager: Larry Pleau
Director of Public Relations: Jeff Trammel
www.stlouisblues.com

San Jose Sharks
Address: San Jose Arena
            525 West Santa Clara Street
            San Jose, CA 95113
Telephone: (408) 287-7070
Arena (Capacity): San Jose Arena (17,496)
Owners: George and Gordon Gund
Executive VP and General Manager: Dean Lombardi
Coach: Darryl Sutter
Director of Media Relations: Ken Arnold
www.sjsharks.com

Tampa Bay Lightning
Address: 401 Channelside Drive
            Tampa, FL 33602
Telephone: (813) 229-2658
Arena (Capacity): Ice Palace (19,758)
Owner: Palace Sports & Entertainment/Bill Davidson
and David Hermelin
President, CEO and Governor: Ron Campbell
Senior VP & General Manager: Rick Dudley
Coach: Steve Ludzik
VP of Public Relations: Bill Wickett
www.icepalace.com

Toronto Maple Leafs
Address: Air Canada Centre
            40 Bay Street - St. 400
            Toronto, Ontario M5J 2X2
Telephone: (416) 815-5500
Arena (Capacity): Air Canada Centre (18,819)
Chairman of the Board: Steve A. Stavro
President: Ken Dryden
Coach/GM: Pat Quinn
Director of Media Relations: Pat Park
www.torontomapleleafs.com

Vancouver Canucks
Address: General Motors Place
800 Griffiths Way
Vancouver, B.C. V6B 6G1
Telephone: (604) 899-4600
Arena (Capacity): General Motors Place (18,422)
Chairman and Governor: John E. McCaw Jr.
Deputy Chairman, Orca Bay Sports and
  Entertainment: Stanley McCammon
Chief Operating Officer: David Cobb
President and GM: Brian Burke
Coach: Marc Crawford
Manager of Media Relations: Chris Brumwell
Media Relations Coordinator: T.C. Carling
www.canucks.com

Washington Capitals
Address: 401 Ninth Street, NW
Suite 750
Washington, DC 20004
Telephone: (202) 266-2200
Arena (Capacity): MCI Center (18,672)
Owners: Ted Leonsis, John Ledecky, Raul Fernandez
and Michael Jordan
Owner and President: Richard M. Patrick
VP and General Manager: George McPhee
Coach: Ron Wilson
Senior VP of Business Operations: Declan J. Bolger
www.washingtoncaps.com

College Sports Directory

**NATIONAL COLLEGIATE ATHLETIC
ASSOCIATION (NCAA)**
Address: P.O. Box 6222
Indianapolis, IN 46206-6222
Telephone: (317) 917-6222
President: Cedric Dempsey
Director of Public Relations: Wallace I. Renfro
www.ncaa.org

ATLANTIC COAST CONFERENCE
Address: P.O. Drawer ACC
Greensboro, NC 27417-6724
Telephone: (336) 854-8787
Commissioner: John Swofford
Asst. Com. of Media Relations: Brian Morrison
www.theacc.com

Clemson University
Address: P.O. Box 632
Clemson, SC 29633
Nickname: Tigers
Telephone: (864) 656-2114
Football Stadium (Capacity): Clemson Memorial
  Stadium (81,474)
Basketball Arena (Capacity): Littlejohn Coliseum (11,020)
President: James F. Barker
Athletic Director: Bobby Robinson
Football Coach: Tommy Bowden
Basketball Coach: Larry Shyatt
Sports Information Director: Tim Bourret
www.clemsontigers.com

Duke University
Address: P.O. Box 90557
Durham, NC 27708
Nickname: Blue Devils
Telephone: (919) 684-2633
Football Stadium (Capacity): Wallace Wade Stadium
  (33,941)
Basketball Arena (Capacity): Cameron Indoor
  Stadium (9,314)
President: Nan Keohane
Athletic Director: Joe Alleva
Football Coach: Carl Franks
Men's Basketball Coach: Mike Krzyzewski
Women's Basketball Coach: Gail Goestenkors
Sports Information Director: Jon Jackson
www.goduke.com

Florida State University
Address: P.O. Box 2195
Tallahassee, FL 32316
Nickname: Seminoles

Florida State University (Cont.)
Telephone: (850) 644-1403
Football Stadium (Capacity): Doak S. Campbell
  Stadium (80,000)
Basketball Arena (Capacity): Leon County Civic
  Center (12,200)
President: Sandy D'Alemberte
Athletic Director: Dave Hart
Football Coach: Bobby Bowden
Basketball Coach: Steve Robinson
Sports Information Director: Rob Wilson
www.seminoles.com

Georgia Tech
Address: 150 Bobby Dodd Way
Atlanta, GA 30332
Nickname: Yellow Jackets
Telephone: (404) 894-5445
Football Stadium (Capacity): Bobby Dodd
  Stadium at Grant Field (46,000)
Basketball Arena (Capacity): Alexander Memorial
  Coliseum at McDonald's Center (10,000)
President: G. Wayne Clough
Athletic Director: David Braine
Football Coach: George O'Leary
Basketball Coach: Paul Hewitt
Director of Communications: Mike Stamus
www.ramblinwreck.com

University of Maryland
Address: P.O. Box 295
College Park, MD 20741-0295
Nickname: Terrapins
Telephone: (301) 314-7064
Football Stadium (Capacity): Byrd Stadium (48,055)
Basketball Arena (Capacity): Cole Fieldhouse
  (14,500)
President: Dr. C.D. Mote, Jr.
Athletic Director: Deborah A. Yow
Football Coach: Ron Vanderlinden
Basketball Coach: Gary Williams
Sports Information Director: David Haglund
www.umterps.com

University of North Carolina
Address: P.O. Box 2126
Chapel Hill, NC 27515
Nickname: Tar Heels
Telephone: (919) 962-2123
Football Stadium (Capacity): Kenan Memorial
  Stadium (60,000)
Basketball Arena (Capacity): Dean E. Smith Center
  (21,572)

University of North Carolina *(Cont.)*

Chancellor: Dr. James Moeser
Athletic Director: Dick Baddour
Football Coach: Carl Torbush
Men's Basketball Coach: Matt Doherty
Women's Basketball Coach: Sylvia Hatchell
Sports Information Director: Steve Kirschner
www.tarheelblue.com

North Carolina State University

Address: Box 8501
             Raleigh, NC 27695
Nickname: Wolfpack
Telephone: (919) 515-2102
Football Stadium (Capacity): Carter-Finley Stadium
  (51,500)
Basketball Arena (Capacity): Entertainment and
  Sports Arena (20,000)
Chancellor: Dr. Marye Anne Fox
Athletic Director: TBA
Football Coach: Chuck Amato
Basketball Coach: Herb Sendex
Asst. Media Relations Director: Bruce Winkworth
www.athletics.ncsu.edu

University of Virginia

Address: P.O. Box 3785
             Charlottesville, VA 22903
Nickname: Cavaliers
Telephone: (804) 982-5500
Football Stadium (Capacity): Carl Smith Center,
  Home of David A. Harrison III Field at Scott Stadium
  (61,500)
Basketball Arena (Capacity): University Hall (8,457)
President: John Casteen III
Athletic Director: Terry Holland
Football Coach: George Welsh
Men's Basketball Coach: Pete Gillen
Women's Basketball Coach: Debbie Ryan
Sports Information Director: Rich Murray
www.virginiasports.com

Wake Forest University

Address: P.O. Box 7426
             Winston-Salem, NC 27109
Nickname: Demon Deacons
Telephone: (336) 758-5640
Football Stadium (Capacity): Groves Stadium (31,500)
Basketball Arena (Capacity): Lawrence Joel Veterans
  Memorial Coliseum (14,407)
President: Dr. Thomas K. Hearn Jr.
Athletic Director: Ron Wellman
Football Coach: Jim Caldwell
Basketball Coach: Dave Odom
Media Relations Director: Dean Buchan
www.wakeforestsports.com

BIG EAST CONFERENCE

Address: 222 Richmond St, 1st fl.
             Providence, RI 02903
Telephone: (401) 272-9108
Commissioner: Michael A. Tranghese
Associate Commissioner for PR: John Paquette
www.bigeast.com

Boston College

Address: Conte Forum 321
             Chestnut Hill, MA 02467
Nickname: Eagles
Telephone: (617) 552-3004
Football Stadium (Capacity): Alumni Stadium (44,500)
Basketball Arena (Capacity): Silvio O. Conte Forum (8,606)
President: Rev. William P. Leahy, S.J.

Boston College *(Cont.)*

Athletic Director: Gene DeFilippo
Football Coach: Tom O'Brien
Basketball Coach: Al Skinner
Sports Information Director: Michael Enright
www.bceagles.com

University of Connecticut

Address: 2095 Hillside Road
             Storrs, CT 06269-3078
Nickname: Huskies
Telephone: (860) 486-3531
Football Stadium (Capacity): Memorial Stadium (16,200)
Basketball Arena (Capacity): Harry A. Gampel
  Pavilion (10,027)
President: Philip E. Austin
Athletic Director: Lew Perkins
Football Coach: Randy Edsall
Men's Basketball Coach: Jim Calhoun
Women's Basketball Coach: Geno Auriemma
Sports Information Director: Tim Tolokan
www.uconnhuskies.com
Note: Division I-A football.

Georgetown University

Address: McDonough Arena
             Box 571124
             Washington, DC 20057-1124
Nickname: Hoyas
Telephone: (202) 687-2492
Football Stadium (Capacity): Kehoe Field (2,400)
Basketball Arena (Capacity): MCI Center (26,000)
President: Rev. Leo J. O'Donovan S.J.
Athletic Director Emeritus: Francis X. Rienzo
Sr Associate Dir. of Athletics/COO: Dennis Kanach
Athletic Director: Joseph Lang
Football Coach: Robert Benson
Basketball Coach: Craig Esherick
Sports Information Director: Mike Tuberosa, (Men's
  basketball) Bill Shapland
www.guhoyas.com
Note: Division I-AA football.

University of Miami

Address: 5821 San Amaro Drive
             Coral Gables, FL 33146
Nickname: Hurricanes
Telephone: (305) 284-3244
Football Stadium (Capacity): Orange Bowl (72,319)
Basketball Arena (Capacity): Miami Arena (15,388)
President: Edward T. Foote II
Athletic Director: Paul Dee
Football Coach: Butch Davis
Basketball Coach: Perry Clarke
Sports Information Director: Doug Walker
www.hurricanesports.com

University of Pittsburgh

Address: Dept. of Athletics
             P.O. Box 7436
             Pittsburgh, PA 15213-0436
Nickname: Panthers
Telephone: (412) 648-8240
Football Stadium (Capacity): Three Rivers Stadium (59,600)
Basketball Arena (Capacity): Fitzgerald Field House
  (6,798), Pittsburgh Civic Arena (17,159)
Chancellor: Mark A. Nordenberg
Athletic Director: Steven Pederson
Football Coach: Walt Harris
Basketball Coach: Ben Howland
Sports Information Director: E.J. Borghetti
www.pittsburghpanthers.com

Providence College
Address: 549 River Avenue
             Providence, RI 02918
Nickname: Friars
Telephone: (401) 865-2272
Basketball Arena (Capacity): Providence Civic
 Center (13,410)
President: Rev. Philip A. Smith, O.P.
Assistant VP for Athletics: John Marinatto
Basketball Coach: Tim Welsh
Sports Information Director: TBA
www.friars.fansonly.com
Note: No football program.

Rutgers University
Address: 83 Rockefeller Road
             Piscataway, NJ 08854-7005
Nickname: Scarlet Knights
Telephone: (732) 445-8053
Football Stadium (Capacity): Rutgers Stadium (42,000)
Basketball Arena (Capacity): Louis Brown Athletic
 Center (8,500)
President: Dr. Francis L. Lawrence
Athletic Director: Bob Mulcahy III
Football Coach: Terry Shea
Men's Basketball Coach: Kevin Bannon
Women's Basketball Coach: C. Vivian Stringer
Sports Information Director: John Wooding
scarletknights.com [no www.]

St. John's University
Address: 8000 Utopia Parkway
             Jamaica, NY 11439
Nickname: Red Storm
Telephone: (718) 990-6367
Football Stadium (Capacity): DaSilva Mem. Field (3,000)
Basketball Arena (Capacity): Alumni Hall (6,008),
 Madison Square Garden (19,876)
President: Rev. Donald J. Harrington, C.M.
Athletic Director: Edward J. Manetta Jr.
Football Coach: Bob Ricca
Basketball Coach: Mike Jarvis
Sports Information Director: Dominic Scianna
www.redstormsports.com
Note: Division I-AA football.

Seton Hall University
Address: 400 South Orange Avenue
             South Orange, NJ 07079
Nickname: Pirates
Telephone: (973) 761-9493
Basketball Arena (Capacity): Walsh Gymnasium
 (2,600), Continental Airlines Arena (20,029)
President: Monsignor Robert T. Sheeran
Athletic Director: Jeff Fogelson
Basketball Coach: Tommy Amaker
Sports Information Director: Marie Wozniak
www.athletics.shu.edu
Note: No football program.

Syracuse University
Address: Manley Field House
             Syracuse, NY 13244-5020
Nickname: Orangemen
Telephone: (315) 443-2608
Football Stadium (Capacity): Carrier Dome (49,550)
Basketball Arena (Capacity): Carrier Dome (33,000)
Chancellor: Dr. Kenneth Shaw
Athletic Director: Jake Crouthamel
Football Coach: Paul Pasqualoni
Basketball Coach: Jim Boeheim
Sports Information Director: Sue Cornelius Edson
www.athletics.syr.edu

Temple University
Address: Vivacqua Hall, 4th Floor
             1700 North Broad Street
             Philadelphia, PA 19122-0842
Nickname: Owls
Telephone: (215) 204-7445
Football Stadium (Capacity): Veterans Stadium (66,592)
Basketball Arena (Capacity): Apollo of Temple (10,224)
President: Dr. David Adamany
Athletic Director: Dave O'Brien
Football Coach: Bobby Wallace
Basketball Coach: John Chaney
Sports Information Director: Brian Kirschner
www.owlsports.com
Note: Plays football in Big East, basketball in Atlantic 10
Conference.

Villanova University
Address: 800 Lancaster Avenue
             Villanova, PA 19085
Nickname: Wildcats
Telephone: (610) 519-4110
Football Stadium (Capacity): Villanova Stadium (12,000)
Basketball Arena (Capacity): The Pavilion (6,500),
 First Union Spectrum (18,060), First Union Center
 (22,000)
President: Rev. Edmund Dobbin, O.S.A.
Athletic Director: Vince Nicastro
Football Coach: Andy Talley
Basketball Coach: Steve Lappas
Sports Information Director: Dean Kenefick
www.villanova.com
Note: Division I-AA football.

Virginia Tech
Address: Jamerson Athletic Center
             Blacksburg, VA 24061
Nickname: Hokies
Telephone: (540) 231-6726
Football Stadium (Capacity): Lane Stadium/Worsham
 Field (51,907)
Basketball Arena (Capacity): Cassell Coliseum
 (10,052)
President: Charles Steger
Athletic Director: Jim Weaver
Football Coach: Frank Beamer
Basketball Coach: Ricky Stokes
Sports Information Director: Dave Smith
www.hokiesports.com

West Virginia University
Address: P.O. Box 0877
             Morgantown, WV 26507-0877
Nickname: Mountaineers
Telephone: (304) 293-2821
Football Stadium (Capacity): Mountaineer Field (63,500)
Basketball Arena (Capacity): WVU Coliseum (14,000)
President: David Hardesty
Athletic Director: Ed Pastilong
Football Coach: Don Nehlen
Basketball Coach: Gale Catlett
Sports Information Director: Shelley Poe
www.wvu.edu/~sports

BIG TEN CONFERENCE
Address: 1500 West Higgins Road
             Park Ridge, IL 60068
Telephone: (847) 696-1010
Commissioner: James E. Delany
Associate Commissioner: Mark Rudner
www.bigten.org

University of Illinois
Address: 1700 S 4th Street
             Champaign, IL 61820
Nickname: Fighting Illini
Telephone: (217) 333-1391
Football Stadium (Capacity): Memorial Stadium (70,904)
Basketball Arena (Capacity): Assembly Hall (16,450)
President: James Stukel
Athletic Director: Ronald Guenther
Football Coach: Ron Turner
Men's Basketball Coach: Bill Self
Sports Information Director: Kent Brown
www.fightingillini.com

Indiana University
Address: Assembly Hall
             1001 E. 17th Street
             Bloomington, IN 47408-1590
Nickname: Hoosiers
Telephone: (812) 855-2421
Football Stadium (Capacity): Memorial Stadium (52,354)
Basketball Arena (Capacity): Assembly Hall (17,357)
President: Myles Brand
Athletic Director: Clarence Doninger
Football Coach: Cam Cameron
Basketball Coach: Bob Knight
Sports Information Director: Jeff Fanter
www.athletics.indiana.edu

University of Iowa
Address: 157 Carver-Hawkeye Arena
             Iowa City, IA 52242
Nickname: Hawkeyes
Telephone: (319) 335-9411
Football Stadium (Capacity): Kinnick Stadium (70,397)
Basketball Arena (Capacity): Carver-Hawkeye (15,500)
President: Mary Sue Coleman
Athletic Director: Robert Bowlsby
Football Coach: Kirk Ferentz
Men's Basketball Coach: Steve Alford
Women's Basketball Coach: Lisa Bluder
Sports Information Director: Phil Haddy (Men's),
    Matt Weitzel, Tony Wirt (Women's Asst. Directors)
www.hawkeyesports.com

University of Michigan
Address: 1000 S. State Street
             Ann Arbor, MI 48109
Nickname: Wolverines
Telephone: (734) 763-4423
Football Stadium (Capacity): Michigan
    Stadium (107,501)
Basketball Arena (Capacity): Crisler Arena (13,562)
President: Lee Bollinger
Athletic Director: William C. Martin
Football Coach: Lloyd Carr
Basketball Coach: Brian Ellerbe
Sports Information Director: Bruce Madej
www.mgoblue.com

Michigan State University
Address: 401 Olds Hall
             East Lansing, MI 48824
Nickname: Spartans
Telephone: (517) 355-2271
Football Stadium (Capacity): Spartan Stadium (72,027)
Basketball Arena (Capacity): Jack Breslin Student
    Events Center (14,659)
President: M. Peter McPherson
Athletic Director: Clarence Underwood
Football Coach: Bobby Williams
Basketball Coach: Tom Izzo
Sports Information Director: John Lewandowski
www.msuspartans.com

University of Minnesota
Address: 208 Bierman Athletic Building
             516 15th Ave SE
             Minneapolis, MN 55455
Nickname: Golden Gophers
Telephone: (612) 625-4090
Football Stadium (Capacity): Hubert H. Humphrey
    Metrodome (64,172)
Basketball Arena (Capacity): Williams Arena (14,625)
President: Mark Yudof
Athletic Director: Tom Moe
Football Coach: Glen Mason
Basketball Coach: Dan Monson
Sports Information Director: Bill Crumley
www.gophersports.com

Northwestern University
Address: 1501 Central Street
             Evanston, IL 60208
Nickname: Wildcats
Telephone: (847) 491-7503
Football Stadium (Capacity): Ryan Field (47,130)
Basketball Arena (Capacity): Welsh-Ryan Arena (8,117)
President: Henry S. Bienen
Athletic Director: Rick Taylor
Football Coach: Randy Walker
Basketball Coach: Kevin O'Neill
Director of Media Services: Brad Hurlbut
www.nusports.com

Ohio State University
Address: 410 Woody Hayes Drive
             St. John Arena, Room 124
             Columbus, OH 43210
Nickname: Buckeyes
Telephone: (614) 292-6861
Football Stadium (Capacity): Ohio Stadium (91,470)
Basketball Arena (Capacity): Jerome Schottenstein
Center (19,000)
President: William Kirwin
Athletic Director: Andy Geiger
Football Coach: John Cooper
Basketball Coach: Jim O'Brien
Sports Information Director: Steve Snapp
www.ohiostatebuckeyes.com

Penn State University
Address: 101D Bryce Jordan Center
             University Park, PA 16802
Nickname: Nittany Lions
Telephone: (814) 865-1757
Football Stadium (Capacity): Beaver Stadium (93,967)
Basketball Arena (Capacity): Bryce Jordan Center
    (15,000)
President: Dr. Graham Spanier
Athletic Director: Tim Curley
Football Coach: Joe Paterno
Men's Basketball Coach: Jerry Dunn
Women's Basketball Coach: Rene Portland
Sports Information Director: Jeff Nelson
www.goPSUsports.com

Purdue University
Address: Mackey Arena, Room 15
             West Lafayette, IN 47907
Nickname: Boilermakers
Telephone: (765) 494-3200
Football Stadium (Capacity): Ross-Ade Stadium
    (67,331)
Basketball Arena (Capacity): Mackey Arena (14,123)
President: Martin C. Jishke

Purdue University *(Cont.)*
Athletic Director: Morgan Burke
Football Coach: Joe Tiller
Basketball Coach: Gene Keady
Sports Information Director: Tom Schott
www.purdue.edu/sports

University of Wisconsin
Address: 1440 Monroe Street
             Madison, WI 53711
Nickname: Badgers
Telephone: (608) 262-1811
Football Stadium (Capacity): Camp Randall
  Stadium (76,129)
Basketball Arena (Capacity): Kohl Center (17,142)
Chancellor: David Ward
Athletic Director: Pat Richter
Football Coach: Barry Alvarez
Basketball Coach: Dick Bennett
Sports Information Director: Steve Malchow
www.wisc.edu/ath/front.html

BIG 12 CONFERENCE
Address: 2201 Stemmons Freeway, 28th floor
             Dallas, TX 75207
Telephone: (214) 742-1212
Commissioner: Kevin Weiberg
Director of Media Relations: Bo Carter
www.big12sports.com

Baylor University
Address: 150 Bear Run
             Waco, TX 76711
Nickname: Bears
Telephone: (254) 710-1234
Football Stadium (Capacity): Floyd Casey
  Stadium (50,000)
Basketball Arena (Capacity): Ferrell Center (10,078)
President: Robert Sloan
Athletic Director: Tom Stanton
Football Coach: Kevin Steele
Basketball Coach: Dave Bliss
Sports Information Director: Scott Stricklin
www.baylorsportsnet.com

University of Colorado
Address: Campus Box 357
             Boulder, CO 80309
Nickname: Buffaloes
Telephone: (303) 492-5626
Football Stadium (Capacity): Folsom Field (51,808)
Basketball Arena (Capacity): Coors Event
  Center (11,198)
President: John Buechner
Athletic Director: Dick Tharpe
Football Coach: Gary Barnett
Men's Basketball Coach: Ricardo Patton
Women's Basketball Coach: Ceal Barry
Sports Information Director: David Plati
www.baylorsportsnet.com

Iowa State University
Address: 1800 S. Fourth Street
             Jacobson Building
             Ames, IA 50011
Nickname: Cyclones
Telephone: (515) 294-3372
Football Stadium (Capacity): Jack Trice Stadium
  (43,000)
Basketball Arena (Capacity): James H. Hilton
  Coliseum (14,092)

Iowa State University *(Cont.)*
Interim President: Dr. Richard Seagrave
Interim Athletic Director: J. Elaine Hieber
Football Coach: Dan McCarney
Men's Basketball Coach: Larry Eustachy
Women's Basketball Coach: Bill Fennelly
www.cyclones.com

University of Kansas
Address: Allen Field House, Room 104
             Lawrence, KS 66045
Nickname: Jayhawks
Telephone: (785) 864-3417
Football Stadium (Capacity): Memorial
  Stadium (50,250)
Basketball Arena (Capacity): Allen Field
  House (16,300)
Chancellor: Robert Hemenway
Athletic Director: Dr. Bob Fredrick
Football Coach: Terry Allen
Men's Basketball Coach: Roy Williams
Women's Basketball Coach: Marian Washington .
Sports Information Director: Doug Vance
www.kuathletics.com

Kansas State University
Address: 1800 College Ave., Suite 144
             Manhattan, KS 66502
Nickname: Wildcats
Telephone: (785) 532-6735
Football Stadium (Capacity): KSU Stadium-Wagner
  Field (50,000)
Basketball Arena (Capacity): Bramlage Coliseum
  (13,500)
President: Dr. Jon Wefald
Athletic Director: Max Urick
Football Coach: Bill Snyder
Basketball Coach: John Wooldridge
Sports Information Director: Doug Dull
www.kstatesports.com

University of Missouri
Address: P.O. Box 677
             Columbia, MO 65205
Nickname: Tigers
Telephone: (573) 882-3241
Football Stadium (Capacity): Faurot Field/Memorial
  Stadium (62,000)
Basketball Arena (Capacity): Hearnes Center (13,300)
Chancellor: Dr. Richard Wallace
Athletic Director: Michael F. Alden
Football Coach: Larry Smith
Basketball Coach: Quin Snyder
Interim Sports Information Director: Chad Moller
www.mutigers.com

University of Nebraska
Address: 116 South Stadium
             Lincoln, NE 68588
Nickname: Cornhuskers
Telephone: (402) 472-2263
Football Stadium (Capacity): Memorial
  Stadium (72,700)
Basketball Arena (Capacity): Bob Devaney Sports
  Center (13,500)
President: L. Dennis Smith
Athletic Director: Bill Byrne
Football Coach: Frank Solich
Basketball Coach: Barry Collier
Sports Information Director: Chris Anderson
www.huskers.com

University of Oklahoma
Address: 180 W. Brooks, Room 235
             Norman, OK 73019
Nickname: Sooners
Telephone: (405) 325-8231
Football Stadium (Capacity): Memorial Stadium/Owen
Field (75,004)
Basketball Arena (Capacity): Lloyd Noble
Center (11,100)
President: David Boren
Athletic Director: Joe Castiglione
Football Coach: Bob Stoops
Men's Basketball Coach: Kelvin Sampson
Women's Basketball Coach: Sherri Coale
Sports Media Relations Director: Mike Prusinski
www.soonersports.com

Oklahoma State University
Address: 424 Squires Street
             Stillwater, OK 74078
Nickname: Cowboys
Telephone: (405) 707-7830
Football Stadium (Capacity): Lewis Field (50,614)
Basketball Arena (Capacity): Gallagher-Iba
Arena (6,381)
President: Dr. James Halligan
Athletic Director: Terry Don Phillips
Football Coach: Bob Simmons
Basketball Coach: Eddie Sutton
Sports Information Director: Steve Buzzard
www.okstate.edu

University of Texas
Address: P.O. Box 7399
             Austin, TX 78713
Nickname: Longhorns
Telephone: (512) 471-7437
Football Stadium (Capacity): Darrell K. Royal/Texas
Memorial Stadium (80,216)
Basketball Arena (Capacity): Erwin Special Events
Center (16,231)
Chancellor: Larry Faulkner
Athletic Director (M): DeLoss Dodds
Athletic Director (W): Jody Conradt
Football Coach: Mack Brown
Basketball Coach: Rick Barnes
Sports Information Director: (M) John Bianco, (W)
Jody Conradt
www.texassports.com

Texas A&M University
Address: John Koldus Building, Room 222
             College Station, TX 77843-1228
Nickname: Aggies
Telephone: (979) 845-5725
Football Stadium (Capacity): Kyle Field (80,600)
Basketball Arena (Capacity): Reed Arena (12,500)
President: Dr. Ray Bowen
Athletic Director: Wally Groff
Football Coach: R.C. Slocum
Basketball Coach: Melvin Watkins
Sports Information Director: Alan Cannon
www.aggieathletics.com

Texas Tech University
Address: Box 43021
             Lubbock, TX 79409
Nickname: Red Raiders
Telephone: (806) 742-2770
Football Stadium (Capacity): Jones SBC Stadium
(50,500)
Basketball Arena (Capacity): United Spirit Arena (15,000)

Texas Tech University *(Cont.)*
President: Dr. David Schmidly
Athletic Director: Gerald Myers
Football Coach: Mike Leach
Men's Basketball Coach: James Dickey
Women's Basketball Coach: Marsha Sharp
Sports Information Director: Kent Partridge
www.texastech.com

BIG WEST CONFERENCE
Address: 2 Corporate Park, Suite 206
             Irvine, CA 92606
Telephone: (949) 261-2525
Commissioner: Dennis Farrell
Publicity Director: Mike Daniels
www.bigwest.org

Boise State University
Address: 1910 University Drive
             Boise, ID 83725
Nickname: Broncos
Telephone: (208) 426-1288
Football Stadium (Capacity) Lyle Smith Field (30,000)
Basketball Arena (Capacity): BSU Pavilion (13,000)
President: Dr. Charles Ruch
Athletic Director: Gene Bleymaier
Football Coach: Dirk Koetter
Basketball Coach: Rod Jensen
Sports Information Director: Max Corbet
www.broncosports.com

Cal Poly
Address: One Grand Avenue
             San Luis Obispo, CA 93407
Nickname: Mustangs
Telephone: (805) 756-6531
Football Stadium (Capacity): Mustang Stadium (8,500)
Basketball Arena (Capacity): Mott Gym (3,200)
President: Dr. Warren J. Baker
Athletic Director: John McCutcheon
Football Coach: Larry Welsh
Basketball Coach: Jeff Schneider
Sports Information Director: Jason Sullivan
www.gopoly.com

University of California–Irvine
Address: Intercollegiate Athletics, Crawford Hall
             903 West Peltason
             Irvine, CA 92697
Nickname: Anteaters
Telephone: (949) 824-6931
Basketball Arena (Capacity): Bren Event Center (5,000)
Chancellor: Ralph Cicerone
Athletic Director: Dan Guerrero
Basketball Coach: Pat Douglass
Sports Information Director: Bob Olson
www.athletics.uci.edu
Note: No football program.

University of California–Santa Barbara
Address: Department of Athletics
             1000 Robertson Gymnasium
             Santa Barbara, CA 93106-7211
Nickname: Gauchos
Telephone: (805) 893-3428
Basketball Arena (Capacity): Thunderdome (6,000)
Chancellor: Henry Yang
Athletic Director: Gary Cunningham
Basketball Coach: Bob Williams
Sports Information Director: Bill Mahoney
www.ucsbgauchos.com
Note: No football program.

California State University–Fullerton

Address: 800 North State College Boulevard
P.O. Box 6810
Fullerton, CA 92834-6810
Nickname: Titans
Telephone: (714) 278-3970
Basketball Arena (Capacity): Titan Gym (3,500)
President: Dr. Milton A. Gordon
Athletic Director: John Easterbrook
Basketball Coach: Donny Daniels
Sports Information Director: Mel Franks
www.sports.fullerton.edu
Note: No football program.

University of Idaho

Address: Kibbie Activities Center
P.O. Box 442302
Moscow, ID 83844-2302
Nickname: Vandals
Telephone: (208) 885-0211
Football Stadium (Capacity): Martin Stadium (37,600)
Basketball Arena (Capacity): Kibbie Dome (10,000)
President: Dr. Robert Hoover
Athletic Director: Mike Bohn
Football Coach: Tom Cable
Basketball Coach: David Farrar
Sports Information Director: Becky Paull
www.its.uidaho.edu/athletics

Long Beach State University

Address: 1250 Bellflower Boulevard
Long Beach, CA 90840-7701
Nicknames: 49ers, The Beach
Telephone: (562) 985-7565
Basketball Arena (Capacity): The Pyramid (5,000)
President: Dr. Robert C. Maxson
Athletic Director: Bill Shumard
Basketball Coach: Wayne Morgan
Sports Information Director: Steve Janisch
www.longbeachstate.com
Note: No football program.

University of Nevada–Reno

Address: Legacy Hall
Athletic Department M/S: 232
Reno, NV 89557-0110
Nickname: Wolf Pack
Telephone: (775) 784-6900
Football Stadium (Capacity): Mackay Stadium (31,545)
Basketball Arena (Capacity): Lawlor Event Center (11,200)
President: Dr. Joe Crowley
Athletic Director: Chris Ault
Football Coach: Jeff Tisdel
Basketball Coach: Trent Johnson
Interim Sports Information Director: Jamie Klund
www.nevadawolfpack.com

New Mexico State University

Address: Department of Athletics, MSC 3145
P.O. Box 30001
Las Cruces, NM 88003
Nickname: Aggies
Telephone: (505) 646-4126
Football Stadium (Capacity): Aggie Memorial Stadium (30,343)
Basketball Arena (Capacity): Pan American Center (13,071)
President: Dr. Jay Gogue
Athletic Director: Brian Faison

New Mexico State University *(Cont.)*

Football Coach: Tony Samuel
Basketball Coach: Lou Henson
Sports Information Director: David Hardee
www.nmstatesports.com

University of North Texas

Address: P.O. Box 311397
Denton, TX 76203-1397
Nickname: Eagles, Mean Green
Telephone: (940) 565-2664
Football Stadium (Capacity): Fouts Field (30,500)
Basketball Arena (Capacity): Super Pit (10,032)
President: Dr. Alfred F. Hurley
Athletic Director: Craig Helwig
Football Coach: Darrell Dickey
Basketball Coach: Vic Trill
Sports Information Director: Sean Johnson
www.unt.edu/meangreen

University of the Pacific

Address: 3601 Pacific Avenue
Stockton, CA 95211
Nickname: Tigers
Telephone: (209) 946-2472
Basketball Arena (Capacity): Alex G. Spanos Center (6,150)
President: Dr. Donald DeRosa
Athletic Director: Lynn King
Basketball Coach: Bob Thomason
Director, Athletic Media Relations: Mike Millerick
www.pacifictigers.com
Note: No football program.

Utah State University

Address: 7400 Old Main Hill
Logan, UT 84322-7400
Nickname: Aggies
Telephone: (435) 797-1850
Football Stadium (Capacity): Romney Stadium (30,000)
Basketball Arena (Capacity): The Smith Spectrum (11,000)
President: Dr. George H. Emert
Athletic Director: Rance Pugmire
Football Coach: Mike Dennehy
Basketball Coach: Stew Morrill
Sports Information Director: Mike Strauss
www.utahstateaggies.com

CONFERENCE USA

Address: 35 East Wacker Drive, Suite 650
Chicago, IL 60601
Telephone: (312) 553-0483
Comissioner: Michael Slive
Media Relations Director: Brian Teter
www.c-usa.org

University of Alabama–Birmingham

Address: Bartow Arena
617 13th Street South
Birmingham, AL 35294
Nickname: Blazers
Telephone: (205) 934-7252
Football Stadium (Capacity): Legion Field (83,091)
Basketball Arena (Capacity): Bartow Arena (8,500)
President: Dr. Ann Reynolds
Athletic Director: Gene Bartow
Football Coach: Watson Brown
Men's Basketball Coach: Murray Bartow
Women's Basketball Coach: Jeannie Milling
Sports Information Director: Grant Shingleton
www.blazers.uab.edu

University of Cincinnati
Address: 309 Lawrence Hall
Cincinnati, OH 45221-0021
Nickname: Bearcats
Telephone: (513) 556-5191
Football Stadium (Capacity): Nippert Stadium (35,000)
Basketball Arena (Capacity): Myrl Shoemaker Center (13,176)
President: Dr. Joseph A. Steger
Athletic Director: Bob Goin
Football Coach: Rick Minter
Basketball Coach: Bob Huggins
Assistant A. D. /Media Relations: Tom Hathaway
www.ucbearcats.com

DePaul University
Address: 1011 West Belden Avenue
Chicago, IL 60614
Nickname: Blue Demons
Telephone: (773) 325-7526
Basketball Arena (Capacity): Allstate Arena (18,000)
President: Rev. John P. Minogue, C.M.
Athletic Director: Bill Bradshaw
Basketball Coach: Pat Kennedy
Sports Information Director: Scott Reed
www.depaulbluedemons.com
Note: No football program.

University of Houston
Address: 3100 Cullen Boulevard
Houston, TX 77204
Nickname: Cougars
Telephone: (713) 743-9370
Football Stadium (Capacity): Robertson Stadium (33,000)
Basketball Arena (Capacity): Hofheinz Pavilion (8,479)
Chancellor and President: Dr. Arthur Smith
Athletic Director: Chet Gladchuk
Football Coach: Dana Dimel
Basketball Coach: Ray McCallum
Sports Information Director: Chris Burkhalter
www.uhcougars.com

University of Louisville
Address: Athletic Department,
Student Activities Center
Louisville, KY 40292
Nickname: Cardinals
Telephone: (502) 852-5732
Football Stadium (Capacity): Papa John's Cardinal Stadium (42,000)
Basketball Arena (Capacity): Freedom Hall (18,865)
President: Dr. John Schumaker
Athletic Director: Tom Jurich
Football Coach: John L. Smith
Basketball Coach: Denny Crum
Sports Information Director: Kenny Klein
www.uoflsports.com

Marquette University
Address: P.O. Box 1881
Milwaukee, WI 53201-1881
Nickname: Golden Eagles
Telephone: (414) 288-7447
Basketball Arena (Capacity): Bradley Center (19,150)
President: Rev. Robert A. Wild, S.J.
Athletic Director: Bill Cords
Basketball Coach: Tom Crean
Sports Information Director: John Farina
www.marquette.edu/athletics
Note: No football program.

University of Memphis
Address: 570 Normal Street, Room 203
Memphis, TN 38152-3730

University of Memphis (Cont.)
Nickname: Tigers
Telephone: (901) 678-2337
Football Stadium (Capacity): Liberty Bowl Memorial Stadium/Rex Dockery Field (62,380)
Basketball Arena (Capacity): The Pyramid (20,142)
Interim President: Ralph Faudree
Athletic Director: R.C. Johnson
Football Coach: Rip Scherer
Basketball Coach: John Calipari
Sports Information Director: Bob Winn
www.gotigersgo.com

University of North Carolina–Charlotte
Address: 9201 University City Boulevard
UNC–Charlotte
Student Activity Center
Charlotte, NC 28223-0001
Nickname: 49ers
Telephone: (704) 547-4937
Basketball Arena (Capacity): Dale F. Halton Arena (9,100)
Chancellor: James H. Woodward
Athletic Director: Judy W. Rose
Basketball Coach: Bobby Lutz
Sports Information Director: Tom Whitestone
www.charlotte49ers.com
Note: No football program.

Saint Louis University
Address: 3672 West Pine Mall Road
St. Louis, MO 63108
Nickname: Billikens
Telephone: (314) 977-2524
Basketball Arena (Capacity): Kiel Center (20,000)
President: Rev. Lawrence Biondi, S.J.
Athletic Director: Doug Woolard
Basketball Coach: Lorenzo Romar
Sports Information Director: Doug McIlhagga
www.slubillikens.com
Note: No football program.

University of South Florida
Address: 4202 East Fowler Ave., PED 214
Tampa, FL 33620
Nickname: Bulls
Telephone: (813) 974-2125
Football Stadium (Capacity): Raymond James Stadium (46,500)
Basketball Arena (Capacity): Sun Dome (10,411)
President: Judy Genshaft
Athletic Director: Paul Griffin
Football Coach: Jim Leavitt
Basketball Coach: Seth Greenberg
Sports Information Director: John Gerdes
www.gousfbulls.com

University of Southern Mississippi
Address: P.O. Box 5161
Hattiesburg, MS 39406
Nickname: Golden Eagles
Telephone: (601) 266-4503
Football Stadium (Capacity): M.M. Roberts Stadium (33,000)
Basketball Arena (Capacity): Reed Green Coliseum (8,095)
President: Dr. Horace Fleming
Athletic Director: Richard Giannini
Football Coach: Jeff Bower
Basketball Coach: James Green
Sports Information Director: M. Regiel Napier
www.athletics.usm.edu

Tulane University

Address: James Wilson Jr. Center for
Intercollegiate Athletics
New Orleans, LA 70118
Nickname: Green Wave
Telephone: (504) 865-5501
Football Stadium (Capacity): Louisiana Superdome
(69,767)
Basketball Arena (Capacity): Fogelman Arena (3,600)
President: Scott Cowen
Athletic Director: Ralph Dickson
Football Coach: Chris Scelfo
Basketball Coach: Shawn Finney
Sports Information Director: Donna Turner
www.tulanegreenwave.com

IVY LEAGUE

Address: 330 Alexander Street
Princeton, NJ 08544
Telephone: (609) 258-6426
Executive Director: Jeff Orleans
Publicity Director: Brett Hoover
www.ivyleaguesports.com

Brown University

Address: 235 Hope Street
Providence, RI 02912
Nickname: Bears
Telephone: (401) 863-2219
Football Stadium (Capacity): Brown Stadium (20,000)
Basketball Arena (Capacity): Paul Bailey Pizzitola
Memorial Sports Center (3,100)
Interim President: Sheila Blumstein
Athletic Director: David Roach
Football Coach: Phil Estes
Basketball Coach: Glen Miller
Sports Information Director: Christopher Humm
www.brownbears.com

Columbia University

Address: Dodge Physical Fitness Center
3030 Broadway
New York, NY 10027
Nickname: Lions
Telephone: (212) 854-2534
Football Stadium (Capacity): Lawrence A. Wien
Stadium at Baker Field (17,000)
Basketball Arena (Capacity): Levien Gymnasium (3,400)
President: Dr. George Rupp
Athletic Director: Dr. John Reeves
Football Coach: Ray Tellier
Basketball Coach: Armond Hill
Director of Athletic Communications: Al Langer
www.columbia.edu/cu/athletics/comm

Cornell University

Address: Teagle Hall, Campus Road
Ithaca, NY 14853-6701
Nickname: Big Red
Telephone: (607) 255-5220
Football Stadium (Capacity): Schoellkopf Field (25,597)
Basketball Arena (Capacity): Newman Arena (4,473)
President: Hunter R. Rawlings III
Athletic Director: J. Andrew Noel Jr.
Football Coach: Pete Mangurian
Basketball Coach: Steve Donahue
Sports Information Director: TBA
www.cornellbigred.com

Dartmouth College

Address: 6083 Alumni Gym
Hanover, NH 03755-3512
Nickname: Big Green

Dartmouth College (Cont.)

Telephone: (603) 646-2465
Football Stadium (Capacity): Memorial Field (20,416)
Basketball Arena (Capacity): Leede Arena (2,100)
President: James Wright
Athletic Director: Richard G. Jaeger
Football Coach: John Lyons
Basketball Coach: Dave Faucher
Sports Information Director: Kathy Slattery
www.dartmouth.edu/student/athletics/publicity

Harvard University

Address: 65 North Harvard St.
Murr Center
Boston, MA 02163
Nickname: Crimson
Telephone: (617) 495-2206
Football Stadium (Capacity): Harvard Stadium (30,898)
Basketball Arena (Capacity): Lavietes Pavilion (2,198)
President: Neil L. Rudenstine
Athletic Director: William J. Cleary Jr.
Football Coach: Tim Murphy
Basketball Coach: Frank Sullivan
Sports Information Director: John Veneziano
www.fas.harvard.edu/athletics

University of Pennsylvania

Address: Weightman Hall South
235 South 33rd Street
Philadelphia, PA 19104-6322
Nickname: Quakers
Telephone: (215) 898-6128
Football Stadium (Capacity): Franklin Field (52,593)
Basketball Arena (Capacity): The Palestra (8,700)
President: Dr. Judith Rodin
Athletic Director: Steven Bilsky
Football Coach: Al Bagnoli
Basketball Coach: Fran Dunphy
Director, Athletic Communications: Carla Schulzberg
www.upennathletics.com

Princeton University

Address: P.O. Box 71
Jadwin Gym
Princeton, NJ 08544
Nickname: Tigers
Telephone: (609) 258-3568
Football Stadium (Capacity): Princeton Stadium
(30,000),
Basketball Arena (Capacity): Jadwin Gym (7,230)
President: Harold Shapiro
Athletic Director: Gary D. Walters
Football Coach: Steve Tosches
Basketball Coach: Bill Carmody
Sports Information Director: Jerry Price
www.goprincetontigers.com

Yale University

Address: Box 208216
New Haven, CT 06520
Nickname: Bulldogs, Elis
Telephone: (203) 432-1456
Football Stadium (Capacity): Yale Bowl (64,269)
Basketball Arena (Capacity): John J. Lee
Amphitheater (3,100)
President: Richard C. Levin
Athletic Director: Tom Beckett
Football Coach: Jack Siedlecki
Basketball Coach: James Jones
Sports Information Director: Steve Conn
www.yale.edu/athletics

MID-AMERICAN CONFERENCE
Address: 24 Public Square 15th floor
             Cleveland, OH 44113
Telephone: (216) 566-4622
Commissioner: Rick Chryst
Director of Communications: Gary Richter
www.midamconf.com

Ball State University
Address: 2000 University Avenue
             Muncie, IN 47306
Nickname: Cardinals
Telephone: (765) 285-2242
Football Stadium (Capacity): Ball State University
  Stadium (21,581)
Basketball Arena (Capacity): University Arena
  (11,500)
President: Dr. John E. Worthen
Athletic Director: Andrea Seger
Football Coach: Bill Lynch
Basketball Coach: Ray McCallum
Athletic Communications Director: Joe Hernandez
www.bsu.edu/athletics

Bowling Green University
Address: Perry Stadium East
             Bowling Green, OH 43403
Nickname: Falcons
Telephone: (419) 372-2401
Football Stadium (Capacity): Doyt L. Perry Stadium
  (30,599)
Basketball Arena (Capacity): Anderson Arena (5,000)
President: Dr. Sidney A. Ribeau
Athletic Director: Paul Krebs
Football Coach: Gary Blackney
Basketball Coach: Dan Dakich
Sports Information Director: J.D. Campbell
www.bgsufalcons.com

Central Michigan University
Address: West Hall
             Mount Pleasant, MI 48859
Nickname: Chippewas
Telephone: (517) 774-3277
Football Stadium (Capacity): Kelly/Shorts
  Stadium (30,199)
Basketball Arena (Capacity): Rose Arena (5,200)
President: Michael Rao
Athletic Director: Herb Deromedi
Football Coach: Mike DeBord
Basketball Coach: Jay Smith
Sports Information Director: Fred Stabley, Jr.
www.cmuchippewas.com

Eastern Michigan University
Address: 371 Convocation Center
             Ypsilanti, MI 48197
Nickname: Eagles
Telephone: (734) 487-1050
Football Stadium (Capacity): Rynearson
  Stadium (30,200)
Basketball Arena (Capacity): Convocation Center
  (8,857)
President: Sam Kirpatrick
Athletic Director: Dr. David L. Diles
Football Coach: Jeff Woodruff
Basketball Coach: Milton Barnes
Sports Information Director: Jim Streeter
www.emich.edu/goeagles

Kent State University
Address: P.O. Box 5190
             Kent, OH 44242
Nickname: Golden Flashes

Kent State University (Cont.)
Telephone: (330) 672-2110
Football Stadium (Capacity): Dix Stadium (30,520)
Basketball Arena (Capacity): Memorial Athletic and
  Convocation Center (6,327)
President: Dr. Carol A. Cartwright
Athletic Director: Laing Kennedy
Football Coach: Dean Pees
Basketball Coach: Gary Waters
Sports Information Director: Will Roleson
www.kentstate.edu/athletics

Miami University
Address: 230 Millett Hall
             Oxford, OH 45056
Nickname: Red Hawks
Telephone: (513) 529-3113
Football Stadium (Capacity): Yager Stadium (30,012)
Basketball Arena (Capacity): Millett Hall (9,200)
President: Dr. James Garland
Athletic Director: Joel Maturi
Football Coach: Terry Hoeppner
Basketball Coach: Charlie Coles
Sports Information Director: Mike Wolf
www.redhawks.com

Ohio University
Address: P.O. Box 689
             Convocation Center
             Athens, OH 45701-2979
Nickname: Bobcats
Telephone: (740) 593-1174
Football Stadium (Capacity): Don Peden
  Stadium (20,000)
Basketball Arena (Capacity): Convocation
  Center (13,000)
President: Dr. Robert Glidden
Athletic Director: Thomas Boeh
Football Coach: Jim Grobe
Basketball Coach: Larry Hunter
Director of Sports Media Services: Heather Czeczok
www.ohiobobcats.com

University of Toledo
Address: 2801 W. Bancroft St.
             Toledo, OH 43606
Nickname: Rockets
Telephone: (419) 530-3790
Football Stadium (Capacity): Glass Bowl (26,248)
Basketball Arena (Capacity): Savage Hall (9,000)
Interim President: Dr. William Decatur
Athletic Director: Pete Liske
Football Coach: Gary Pinkel
Basketball Coach: Stan Joplin
Sports Information Director: Paul Helgren
www.utrockets.com

Western Michigan University
Address: Read Field
             Kalamazoo, MI 49008
Nickname: Broncos
Telephone: (616) 387-4138
Football Stadium (Capacity): Waldo Stadium (30,200)
Basketball Arena (Capacity): University Arena (5,800)
President: Dr. Elson Floyd
Athletic Director: Kathy Beauregard
Football Coach: Gary Darnell
Basketball Coach: Robert McCullum
Sports Information Director: Daniel Jankowski
www.wmubroncos.com

PACIFIC-10 CONFERENCE
Address: 800 S. Broadway, Suite 400
             Walnut Creek, CA 94596
Telephone: (925) 932-4411
Commissioner: Thomas C. Hansen
Publicity Director: Jim Muldoon
www.pac-10.com

University of Arizona
Address: 106 McHale Center
             Tuscon, AZ 85721
Nickname: Wildcats
Telephone: (520) 621-4163
Football Stadium (Capacity): Arizona Stadium (57,803)
Basketball Arena (Capacity): Lute Olson Court at
McHale Center (14,489)
President: Dr. Peter Likins
Athletic Director: Jim Livengood
Football Coach: Dick Tomey
Basketball Coach: Lute Olson
Sports Information Director: Tom Duddleston
www.arizcats.com

Arizona State University
Address: ICA Building, Room 105
             Tempe, AZ 85287-2505
Nickname: Sun Devils
Telephone: (602) 965-6592
Football Stadium (Capacity): Sun Devil Stadium (74,186)
Basketball Arena (Capacity): Wells Fargo Arena
(14,198)
President: Lattie F. Coor
Athletic Director: Gene Smith
Football Coach: Bruce Snyder
Basketball Coach: Rob Evans
Director, Sports Media Relations: Mark Brand
www.thesundevils.com

University of California at Berkeley
Address: 210 Memorial Stadium
             Berkeley, CA 94720
Nickname: Golden Bears
Telephone: (510) 642-5363
Football Stadium (Capacity): Memorial Stadium (75,028)
Basketball Arena (Capacity): Haas Pavilion (12,300)
Chancellor: Robert Berdahl
Athletic Director: John Kasser
Football Coach: Tom Holmoe
Basketball Coach: Ben Braun
Sports Information Director: Herb Benenson
www.calbears.com

University of California at Los Angeles
Address: P.O. Box 24044
             Los Angeles, CA 90024-0044
Nickname: Bruins
Telephone: (310) 206-6831
Football Stadium (Capacity): Rose Bowl (102,083)
Basketball Arena (Capacity): Pauley Pavilion (12,819)
Chancellor: Albert Carnesale
Athletic Director: Peter T. Dalis
Football Coach: Bob Toledo
Basketball Coach: Steve Lavin
Sports Information Director: Marc Dellins
www.uclabruins.com

University of Oregon
Address: Len Casanova Athletic Center
             2727 Leo Harris Parkway
             Eugene, OR 97401
Nickname: Ducks
Telephone: (541) 346-4481

University of Oregon (Cont.)
Football Stadium (Capacity): Autzen Stadium (41,698)
Basketball Arena (Capacity): McArthur Court (9,738)
President: David Frohnmayer
Athletic Director: Bill Moos
Football Coach: Mike Bellotti
Basketball Coach: Ernie Kent
Director of Media Services: David Williford
www.goducks.com

Oregon State University
Address: Gill Coliseum
             Corvallis, OR 97331
Nickname: Beavers
Telephone: (541) 737-3720
Football Stadium (Capacity): Reser Stadium (35,362)
Basketball Arena (Capacity): Gill Coliseum (10,400)
President: Dr. Paul Risser
Athletic Director: Mitch Barnhart
Football Coach: Dennis Erickson
Basketball Coach: Ritchie McKay
Sports Information Director: Hal Cowan
www.osubeavers.com

University of Southern California
Address: Los Angeles, CA 90089-0602
Nickname: Trojans
Telephone: (213) 740-8480
Football Stadium (Capacity): Los Angeles Memorial
  Coliseum (94,159)
Basketball Arena (Capacity): Los Angeles Sports
  Arena (15,509)
President: Dr. Steven Sample
Athletic Director: Mike Garrett
Football Coach: Paul Hackett
Basketball Coach: Henry Bibby
Sports Information Director: Tim Tessalone
www.usctrojans.com

Stanford University
Address: Arrillaga Family Sports Center
             Stanford, CA 94305
Nickname: Cardinal
Telephone: (650) 723-4418
Football Stadium (Capacity): Stanford Stadium (85,500)
Basketball Arena (Capacity): Maples Pavilion (7,391)
President: Dr. John Hennessy
Athletic Director: Dr. Ted Leland
Football Coach: Tyrone Willingham
Men's Basketball Coach: Mike Montgomery
Women's Basketball Coach: Tara Van Derveer
Director, Sports Media Relations: Gary Migdol
www.gostanford.com

University of Washington
Address: UW Media Relations
             Graves Building, Box 354070
             Seattle, WA 98195-4070
Nickname: Huskies
Telephone: (206) 543-2230
Football Stadium (Capacity): Husky Stadium (72,500)
Basketball Arena (Capacity): Bank of America Arena
at Heck Edmonson Pavilion (17,072)
President: Richard L. McCormick
Athletic Director: Barbara Hedges
Football Coach: Rick Neuheisel
Basketball Coach: Bob Bender
Sports Information Director: Jim Daves
www.gohuskies.com

Washington State University
Address: Bohler Addition
             Suite 395
             Pullman, WA 99164-1602
Nickname: Cougars
Telephone: (509) 335-2684
Football Stadium (Capacity): Martin Stadium (37,600)
Basketball Arena (Capacity): Friel Court (12,058)
President: V. Lane Rawlins
Athletic Director: Jim Sterk
Football Coach: Mike Price
Basketball Coach: Paul Graham
Sports Information Director: Rod Commons
www.wsucougars.com

SOUTHEASTERN CONFERENCE
Address: 2201 Richard Arrington Boulevard
             Birmingham, AL 35203
Telephone: (205) 458-3000
Commissioner: Roy Kramer
Publicity Director: Charles Bloom
www.sec.org

University of Alabama
Address: P.O. Box 870391
             323 Paul Bryant Drive
             Tuscaloosa, AL 35487
Nickname: Crimson Tide
Telephone: (205) 348-6084
Football Stadium (Capacity): Bryant-Denny Stadium
(83,818)
Basketball Arena (Capacity): Coleman
  Coliseum (15,043)
President: Dr. Andrew Sorensen
Interim Athletic Director: Mal Moore
Football Coach: Mike DuBose
Men's Basketball Coach: Mark Gottfried
Women's Basketball Coach: Rick Moody
Sports Information Director: Larry White
www.rolltide.com

University of Arkansas
Address: Broyles Athletic Center
             Fayetteville, AR 72701
Nickname: Razorbacks
Telephone: (501) 575-2751
Football Stadium (Capacity): Razorback Stadium
  (50,000); War Memorial Stadium (53,727)
Basketball Arena (Capacity): Bud Walton
  Arena (19,200)
Chancellor: Dr. John White
Athletic Director: Frank Broyles
Football Coach: Houston Nutt
Basketball Coach: Nolan Richardson
Sports Information Director: Kevin Trainor
www.hogwired.com

Auburn University
Address: P.O. Box 351
             Auburn, AL 36831-0351
Nickname: Tigers
Telephone: (334) 844-9800
Football Stadium (Capacity): Jordan Hare Stadium (85,214)
Basketball Arena (Capacity): Beard-Eaves Memorial
  Coliseum (13,500)
President: Dr. William V. Muse
Athletic Director: David Housel
Football Coach: Tommy Tuberville
Men's Basketball Coach: Cliff Ellis
Women's Basketball Coach: Joe Ciampi
Sports Information Director: Meredith Jenkins
www.auburn.edu/athletics

University of Florida
Address: P.O. Box 14485
             Gainesville, FL 32604
Nickname: Gators
Telephone: (352) 375-4683
Football Stadium (Capacity): Ben Hill Griffin Stadium
  at Florida Field (83,000)
Basketball Arena (Capacity): Stephen C. O'Connell
  Center (12,000)
Interim President: Dr. Charles Young
Athletic Director: Jeremy Foley
Football Coach: Steve Spurrier
Men's Basketball Coach: Billy Donovan
Women's Basketball Coach: Carol Ross
Sports Information Director: John Humenik
www.gatorzone.com

University of Georgia
Address: P.O. Box 1472
             Athens, GA 30603-1472
Nickname: Bulldogs
Telephone: (706) 542-1621
Football Stadium (Capacity): Sanford Stadium (86,117)
Basketball Arena (Capacity): Stegman Coliseum
  (10,523)
President: Dr. Michael F. Adams
Athletic Director: Vince Dooley
Football Coach: Jim Donnan
Men's Basketball Coach: Jim Harrick
Women's Basketball Coach: Andy Landers
Sports Information Director: Claude Felton
www.georgiadogs.com

University of Kentucky
Address: 23 Memorial Coliseum
             Lexington, KY 40506-0019
Nickname: Wildcats
Telephone: (606) 257-3838
Football Stadium (Capacity): Commonwealth
  Stadium (68,000)
Basketball Arena (Capacity): Rupp Arena (24,000)
President: Dr. Charles Wethington Jr.
Athletic Director: Larry Ivy
Football Coach: Hal Mumme
Basketball Coach: Orlando (Tubby) Smith
Sports Information Director: Rena Vicini
www.ukathletics.com

Louisiana State University
Address: P.O. Box 25095
             Baton Rouge, LA 70894
Nickname: Fighting Tigers
Telephone: (225) 388-8226
Football Stadium (Capacity): Tiger Stadium (80,000)
Basketball Arena (Capacity): Pete Maravich
  Assembly Center (14,164)
Chancellor: Dr. Mark Emmert
Athletic Director: Joe Dean
Football Coach: Nick Saban
Men's Basketball Coach: John Brady
Women's Basketball Coach: Sue Gunter
Sports Information Director: Michael Bonnette
www.lsusports.net

University of Mississippi
Address: P.O. Box 217
             University, MS 38677
Nickname: Rebels
Telephone: (662) 232-7522
Football Stadium (Capacity): Vaught-Hemingway
  Stadium/Hollingsworth Field (50,577)
Basketball Arena (Capacity): C.M. (Tad) Smith
  Coliseum (8,135)

University of Mississippi *(Cont.)*
Chancellor: Dr. Robert C. Khayat
Athletic Director: John Schafer
Football Coach: David Cutcliffe
Basketball Coach: Rod Barnes
Sports Information Director: Langston Rogers
www.olemisssports.com

Mississippi State University
Address: P.O. Box 5308
Mississippi St., MS 39762
Nickname: Bulldogs
Telephone: (662) 325-2703
Football Stadium (Capacity): Scott Field (40,656)
Basketball Arena (Capacity): Humphrey Coliseum (10,500)
President: Malcolm Portera
Athletic Director: Larry Templeton
Football Coach: Jackie Sherrill
Basketball Coach: Rick Stansbury
Sports Information Director: Mike Nemeth
www.mstateathletics.com

University of South Carolina
Address: Rex Enright Athletic Center
1300 Rosewood Drive
Columbia, SC 29208
Nickname: Gamecocks
Telephone: (803) 777-5204
Football Stadium (Capacity): Williams-Brice
Stadium (80,250)
Basketball Arena (Capacity): Frank McGuire
Arena (12,401)
President: Dr. John Palms
Athletic Director: Dr. Mike McGee
Football Coach: Lou Holtz
Basketball Coach: Eddie Fogler
Sports Information Director: Kerry Tharp
www.uscsports.com

University of Tennessee
Address: P.O. Box 15016
Knoxville, TN 37901
Nickname: Volunteers
Telephone: (865) 974-1212
Football Stadium (Capacity): Neyland Stadium (102,854)
Basketball Arena (Capacity): Thompson-Boling Arena
and Assembly Center (24,535)
President: J. Wade Gilley
Athletic Director: Doug Dickey
Football Coach: Phillip Fulmer
Men's Basketball Coach: Jerry Green
Women's Basketball Coach: Pat Summitt
Sports Information Directors: (M) Bud Ford,
(W) Debby Jennings
www.utsports.com

Vanderbilt University
Address: P.O. Box 120158
Nashville, TN 37212
Nickname: Commodores
Telephone: (615) 322-4121
Football Stadium (Capacity): Vanderbilt Stadium
(41,600)
Basketball Arena (Capacity): Memorial Gym (14,100)
Chancellor: E. Gordon Gee
Athletic Director: Todd Turner
Football Coach: Woody Widenhofer
Men's Basketball Coach: Kevin Stallings
Sports Information Director: Rod Williamson
www.vucommodores.com

WESTERN ATHLETIC CONFERENCE
Address: 9250 East Costilla Avenue, Suite 300
Englewood, CO 80112
Telephone: (303) 799-9221
Commissioner: Karl Benson
Publicity Director: Jeff Hurd
www.wacsports.com

Air Force
Address: 2169 Field House Drive
USAF Academy, CO 80840-9500
Nickname: Falcons
Telephone: (719) 333-2313
Football Stadium (Capacity): Falcon Stadium (52,480)
Basketball Arena (Capacity): Clune Arena (6,002)
Superintendent: Lt. Gen. John R. Dallager
Athletic Director: Col. Randall W. Spetman
Football Coach: Fisher DeBerry
Basketball Coach: Reggie Minton
Sports Information Director: David Kellogg
www.airforcesports.com

Brigham Young University
Address: 30 Smith Field House
Provo, UT 84602
Nickname: Cougars
Telephone: (801) 378-4911
Football Stadium (Capacity): Cougar Stadium (65,000)
Basketball Arena (Capacity): Marriott Center (23,000)
President: Merrill J. Bateman
Athletic Director: Val Hale
Football Coach: LaVell Edwards
Basketball Coach: Steve Cleveland
Sports Information Directors: Brett Pyne/Jeff Reynolds
www.byucougars.edu

Colorado State University
Address: McGraw Athletic Center
Moby Arena
Fort Collins, CO 80523
Nickname: Rams
Telephone: (970) 491-5300
Football Stadium (Capacity): Hughes Stadium (30,000)
Basketball Arena (Capacity): Moby Arena (8,745)
President: Dr. Albert C. Yates
Athletic Director: Tim Weiser
Football Coach: Sonny Lubick
Basketball Coach: Dale Layer
Sports Information Director: Gary Ozello
www.csurams.com

Fresno State University
Address: 5305 N. Campus Drive, Room 153
Fresno, CA 93740-8020
Nickname: Bulldogs
Telephone: (559) 278-2509
Football Stadium (Capacity): Bulldog
Stadium (41,031)
Basketball Arena (Capacity): Selland Arena (10,182)
President: Dr. John Welty
Athletic Director: Dr. Al Bohl
Football Coach: Pat Hill
Basketball Coach: Jerry Tarkanian
Sports Information Director: Steve Weakland
www.gobulldogs.com

University of Hawaii
Address: 1337 Lower Campus Road
Honolulu, HI 96822-2370
Nickname: Warriors
Telephone: (808) 956-7523
Football Stadium (Capacity): Aloha Stadium (50,000)

University of Hawaii (Cont.)
Basketball Arena (Capacity): Stan Sheriff Center (10,225)
President: Dr. Kenneth Mortimer
Athletic Director: Hugh Yoshida
Football Coach: June Jones
Basketball Coach: Riley Wallace
Sports Information Director: Lois Manin
www.uhathletics.hawaii.edu

University of Nevada at Las Vegas
Address: 4505 Maryland Parkway
             Las Vegas, NV 89154-0004
Nickname: Rebels
Telephone: (702) 895-3207
Football Stadium (Capacity): Sam Boyd Stadium (36,800)
Basketball Arena (Capacity): Thomas & Mack Center (18,500)
President: Dr. Carol C. Harter
Athletic Director: Charles Cavagnaro
Football Coach: John Robinson
Basketball Coach: Bill Bayno
Sports Information Director: Andy Grossman
www.unlvrebels.com

University of New Mexico
Address: UNM South Complex
             Albuquerque, NM 87131-0041
Nickname: Lobos
Telephone: (505) 925-5500
Football Stadium (Capacity): University Stadium (33,218)
Basketball Arena (Capacity): University Arena (18,018)
President: Dr. William Gordon
Athletic Director: Rudy Davalos
Football Coach: Rocky Long
Basketball Coach: Fran Fraschilla
Sports Information Director: Greg Remington
www.golobos.com

Rice University
Address: P.O. Box 1892 MS548
             Houston, TX 77251-1892
Nickname: Owls
Telephone: (713) 348-4034
Football Stadium (Capacity): Rice Stadium (70,000)
Basketball Arena (Capacity): Autry Court (5,000)
President: Malcolm Gillis
Athletic Director: Bobby May
Football Coach: Ken Hatfield
Basketball Coach: Willis Wilson
Sports Information Director: Bill Cousins
www.riceowls.com

San Diego State University
Address: San Diego, CA 92182-4309
Nickname: Aztecs
Telephone: (619) 594-5547
Football Stadium (Capacity): Qualcomm
  Stadium (71,400)
Basketball Arena (Capacity): Cox Arena (12,414)
President: Dr. Stephen Weber
Athletic Director: Rick Bay
Football Coach: Ted Tollner
Basketball Coach: Steve Fisher
Sports Information Director: Kevin Klintworth
www.goaztecs.com

San Jose State University
Address: One Washington Square
             San Jose, CA 95192-0062
Nickname: Spartans
Telephone: (408) 924-1217
Football Stadium (Capacity): Spartan Stadium (30,578)
Basketball Arena (Capacity): Event Center (5,000)

San Jose State University (Cont.)
President: Dr. Robert L. Caret
Athletic Director: Chuck Bell
Football Coach: Dave Baldwin
Basketball Coach: Steve Barnes
Sports Information Director: Lawrence Fan
www.sjsuspartans.com

Southern Methodist University
Address: SMU Box 0216
             Dallas, TX 75275-0216
Nickname: Mustangs
Telephone: (214) 768-2883
Football Stadium (Capacity): Gerald J. Ford Stadium
  (32,000)
Basketball Arena (Capacity): Moody Coliseum (8,998)
President: R. Gerald Turner
Athletic Director: Jim Copeland
Football Coach: Mike Cavan
Basketball Coach: Mike Dement
Sports Information Director: Chris Walker
www.smumustangs.com

University of Texas at El Paso
Address: 201 Baltimore
             El Paso, TX 79902
Nickname: Miners
Telephone: (915) 747-5347
Football Stadium (Capacity): Sun Bowl (52,000)
Basketball Arena (Capacity): Don Haskins Center (12,222)
President: Dr. Diana Natalicio
Athletic Director: Bob Stull
Football Coach: Gary Nord
Basketball Coach: Jason Rabedeaux
Sports Information Director: Jeff Darby
http://athletics.utep.edu (no www)

Texas Christian University
Address: Box 297600
             Fort Worth, TX 76129
Nickname: Horned Frogs
Telephone: (817) 257-7969
Football Stadium (Capacity): Amon G. Carter
  Stadium (44,008)
Basketball Arena (Capacity): Daniel-Meyer Coliseum (7,200)
Chancellor: Dr. Michael R. Ferrari
Athletic Director: Eric Hyman
Football Coach: Dennis Franchione
Basketball Coach: Billy Tubbs
Sports Information Director: Steve Fink
www.gofrogs.com

University of Tulsa
Address: 600 S. College
             Tulsa, OK 74104-3189
Nickname: Golden Hurricane
Telephone: (918) 631-2395
Football Stadium (Capacity): Skelly Stadium (40,385)
Basketball Arena (Capacity): Donald W. Reynolds
  Center (8,300)
President: Dr. Robert Lawless
Athletic Director: Judy MacLeod
Football Coach: Keith Burns
Basketball Coach: Buzz Peterson
Sports Information Director: Don Tomkalski
www.tulsahurricane.com

University of Utah
Address: 1825 E. South Campus Drive, Front
             Salt Lake City, UT 84112-0900
Nickname: Utes
Telephone: (801) 581-8171

University of Utah (Cont.)
Football Stadium (Capacity): Rice-Eccles Stadium (45,634)
Basketball Arena (Capacity): Jon M. Huntsman
  Center (15,000)
President: Dr. Bernie Machen
Athletic Director: Dr. Chris Hill
Football Coach: Ron McBride
Basketball Coach: Rick Majerus
Sports Information Director: Liz Abel
www.utahutes.com

University of Wyoming
Address: P.O. Box 3414
             Laramie, WY 82071-3414
Nickname: Cowboys
Telephone: (307) 766-2256
Football Stadium (Capacity): War Memorial Stadium
  (33,500)
Basketball Arena (Capacity): Arena-Auditorium (15,028)
President: Dr. Philip Dubois
Athletic Director: Lee Moon
Football Coach: Vic Koenning
Basketball Coach: Steve McClain
Sports Information Director: Kevin McKinney
www.wyomingathletics.com

INDEPENDENTS

Army
Address: Howard Road Building 639
             West Point, NY 10996
Nickname: Black Knights
Telephone: (914) 938-3303
Football Stadium (Capacity): Michie Stadium (39,929)
Basketball Arena (Capacity): Christl Arena (5,043)
Superintendent: Lt. Gen. Daniel W. Christman
Athletic Director: Rick Greenspan
Football Coach: Todd Berry
Basketball Coach: Pat Harris
Asst. Athletic Dir. for Media Relations: Bob Baretta
www.goARMYsports.com
Note: Plays football in Conference USA, basketball in
Patriot League.

East Carolina University
Address: Ward Sports Medicine Building
             Greenville, NC 27858-4353
Nickname: Pirates
Telephone: (252) 328-4600
Football Stadium (Capacity): Dowdy-Ficklen (43,000)
Basketball Arena (Capacity): Williams Arena (7,500)
Chancellor: Dr. Richard R. Eakin
Athletic Director: Michael A. Hamrick
Football Coach: Steve Logan
Basketball Coach: Bill Herrion
Asst. Athletic Dir. for Media Relations: Norm Reilly
www.ecupirates.com

Navy
Address: 566 Brownson Road, Ricketts Hall
             Annapolis, MD 21402
Nickname: Midshipmen
Telephone: (410) 293-2340
Football Stadium (Capacity): Navy-Marine Corps
  Memorial Stadium (30,000)
Basketball Arena (Capacity): Alumni Hall (5,700)
Superintendent: John Ryan, USN
Athletic Director: Jack Lengyel
Football Coach: Charlie Weatherbie
Basketball Coach: Don DeVoe
Sports Information Director: Scott Strasemeier
www.navy sports.com
Note: Plays football as independent, basketball in Patriot League.

University of Notre Dame
Address: 112 Joyce Center
             Notre Dame, IN 46556
Nickname: Fighting Irish
Telephone: (219) 631-7516
Football Stadium (Capacity): Notre Dame Stadium (80,232)
Basketball Arena (Capacity): Joyce Athletic and
  Convocation Center (11,418)
President: Rev. Edward A. Malloy, CSC
Athletic Director: Dr. Kevin White
Football Coach: Bob Davie
Men's Basketball Coach: Michael Brey
Women's Basketball Coach: Muffet McGraw
Sports Information Director: John Heisler
www.und.com

Olympic Sports Directory

United States Olympic Committee
Address: Olympic House
             1 Olympic Plaza
             Colorado Springs, CO 80909
Telephone: (719) 632-5551
CEO: Norm Blake
Managing Director for Media and Public
  Relations: Mike Moran
www.usolympicteam.com

U.S. Olympic Training Centers
Address: 1 Olympic Plaza
             Colorado Springs, CO 80909
Telephone: (719) 578-5500
Director: John Smith
Address: 421 Old Military Road
             Lake Placid, NY 12946
Telephone: (518) 523-2600
Director: Jack Favro
Address: 2800 Olympic Parkway
             Chula Vista, CA 91915
Telephone: (619) 656-1500
Director: Patrice Milkovich
www.olympic.org

International Olympic Committee
Address: Chateau de Vidy
             Case Postale 356
             CH-1007 Lausanne, Switzerland
Telephone: 41-21-621-6111
President: Juan Antonio Samaranch
Director General: Francois Carrard
www.olympic.org

Salt Lake Organizing Committee for the Olympic Winter Games
Address: 299 South Main Street, Suite 1300
             Salt Lake City, UT 84111
Telephone: (801) 212-2002
President/CEO: Mitt Romney
Director of Media Relations: Caroline Shaw
(XIX Winter Games; Feb. 8–24, 2002)
www.saltlake2002.com

U.S. Olympic Organizations

National Archery Association (NAA)
Address: 1 Olympic Plaza
          Colorado Springs, CO 80909
Telephone: (719) 578-4576
President: Norm Graham
Executive Director: George Greenway
Media Relations: Bill Kellick
www.usarchery.org

USA Badminton (USAB)
Address: 1 Olympic Plaza
          Colorado Springs, CO 80909
Telephone: (719) 578-4808
President: Don Chew
Executive Director: Dan Cloppas
Media Contact: Barb Kissick
www.usabadminton.org

USA Baseball
Address: Hi Corbett Field
          3400 East Camino Campestre
          Tucson, AZ 85716
Telephone: (520) 327-9700
President: Neil Lantz
Executive Director/CEO: Paul V. Seiler
Director of Media Relations: David Fanucchi
www.usabaseball.com

USA Basketball
Address: 5465 Mark Dabling Blvd.
          Colorado Springs, CO 80918
Telephone: (719) 590-4800
President: Russ Granik
Executive Director: Warren Brown
Assistant Executive Director for Public Relations:
  Craig Miller
www.usabasketball.com

U.S. Biathlon Association (USBA)
Address: 29 Ethan Allen Avenue
          Colchester, VT 05446
Telephone: 1 (802) 654-7833
President: Lyle Nelson
Executive Director: Stephen R. Sands
Media Contact: Mary Grace
www.usbiathlon.org

U.S. Bobsled and Skeleton Federation
Address: P.O. Box 828
          Lake Placid, NY 12946
Telephone: (518) 523-1842
President: Jim Morris
Executive Director: Matt Roy
Media and PR Director Director: Julie Urbansky
www.usabobsledandskeleton.org

USA Bowling
Address: 5301 South 76th Street
          Greendale, WI 53129
Telephone: (414) 421-9008
President: Elaine Hagin
Executive Director: Gerald Koenig
Communications Directors: Mark Miller and Marc Whitney
www.bowl.com

USA Boxing, Inc.
Address: 1 Olympic Plaza
          Colorado Springs, CO 80909
Telephone: (719) 578-4506
President: Gary Toney
Executive Director: Paul Montville
Director of PR and Media: Shilpa Bakre
www.usaboxing.org

U.S. Canoe and Kayak Team
Address: P.O. Box 789
          Lake Placid, NY 12946
Telephone: (518) 523-1855
Chairman of the Board: Helen Collins
Executive Director: TBA
Public Relations Director: Lisa Fish
www.usacanoekayak.org

USA Cycling
Address: 1 Olympic Plaza
          Colorado Springs, CO 80909
Telephone: (719) 578-4581
President: Mike Plant
Executive Director and Chief Executive Officer:
  Lisa Voight
Director of Communications: Richard Wanninger
www.usacycling.org

United States Diving, Inc. (USD)
Address: Pan American Plaza, Suite 430
          201 South Capitol Avenue
          Indianapolis, IN 46225
Telephone: (317) 237-5252
President: William Walker
Executive Director: Todd Smith
Director of Communications: Seth Pederson
www.usdiving.org

U.S. Equestrian Team (USET)
Address: Pottersville Rd.
          Gladstone, NJ 07934
Telephone: (908) 234-1251
Executive Director: Robert C. Standish
Director of Public Relations: Marty Bauman
www.uset.org

U.S. Fencing Association (USFA)
Address: 1 Olympic Plaza
          Colorado Springs, CO 80909
Telephone: (719) 578-4511
President: Don Alperstein
Executive Director: Michael Massik
Media Relations Director: Cynthia Bent
www.usafencing.org

U.S. Field Hockey Association (USFHA)
Address: 1 Olympic Plaza
          Colorado Springs, CO 80909-5773
Telephone: (719) 578-4567
President: Sharon Taylor
Executive Director: Jane Betts
Sport and Public Information Director:
  Howard Thomas
www.usfieldhockey.com

U.S. Figure Skating Association (USFSA)
Address: 20 First Street
          Colorado Springs, CO 80906
Telephone: (719) 635-5200
President: Phyllis Howard
Executive Director: John LeFevre
Communications Coordinator: Bob Dunlop
www.usfsa.org

USA Gymnastics
Address: Pan American Plaza, Suite 300
          201 South Capitol Avenue
          Indianapolis, IN 46225
Telephone: (317) 237-5050
Chairman of the Board: Sandy Knapp
President: Robert Colarossi
Director of Public Relations: Steve Penny
www.usa-gymnastics.org

USA Hockey
Address: 1775 Bob Johnson Drive
             Colorado Springs, CO 80906
Telephone: (719) 576-8724
President: Walter L. Bush, Jr.
Executive Director: Doug Palazzari
Coordinator, Media Relations: Chuck Menke
www.usahockey.com

United States Judo, Inc. (USJ)
Address: 1 Olympic Plaza Suite 202
             Colorado Springs, CO 80909
Telephone: (719) 578-4730
President: Yoshihiro Uchida
Executive Director: William Rosenberg

U.S. Luge Association (USLA)
Address: 35 Church Street
             Lake Placid, NY 12946
Telephone: (518) 523-2071
President: Doug Bateman
Executive Director: Ron Rossi
Public Relations Manager: Jon Lundin
www.usaluge.org

U.S. Modern Pentathlon Association
Address: 8610 Broadway, Suite 260
             San Antonio, TX 78217
Telephone: (210) 822-1206
President: Dr. Risto Hurme
Executive Director: Paul K. Pesthy
www.usmpa.home.texas.net

U.S. Racquetball Association
Address: 1685 West Uintah
             Colorado Springs, CO 80904
Telephone: (719) 635-5396
President: Otto Dietrich
Executive Director: Luke St. Onge
Public Relations Coordinator: Christie Hyde
www.usra.org

USA Roller Skating
Address: 4730 South Street
             P.O. Box 6579
             Lincoln, NE 68506
Telephone: (402) 483-7551
President: TBA
Executive Director: Louis Marciani
Sports Information Director: Jean Stanek
www.usacrs.com

U.S. Rowing
Address: Pan American Plaza, Suite 400
             201 South Capitol Avenue
             Indianapolis, IN 46225
Telephone: (317) 237-5656/ 1 (800) 314-4769
President: Dave Vogel
Executive Director: Frank J. Coyle
Press Contact: Brett Johnson
www.usrowing.org

U.S. Sailing Association
Address: P.O. Box 1260
             Portsmouth, RI 02871
Telephone: (401) 683-0800
President: James P. Muldoon
Executive Director: Terry Harper
Marketing Director: Walt Green
Olympic Yachting Director: Jonathan R. Harley
www.ussailing.org

USA Shooting
Address: 1 Olympic Plaza
             Colorado Springs, CO 80909

USA Shooting (Cont.)
Telephone: (719) 578-4670
President of the Board: Stevan B. Richards
Executive Director: Robert K. Mitchell
Director of Marketing: Bob Groate
www.usashooting.com

U.S. Ski and Snowboard Association
Address: P.O. Box 100
             Park City, UT 84060
Telephone: (435) 649-9090
Chairman: Jim McCarthy
President and CEO: Bill Marolt
V.P. of Communications and Media: Tom Kelly
Media Services Coordinator: Scott Flanders
www.usskiteam.com

U.S. Soccer Federation (USSF)
Address: 1801-1811 South Prairie Avenue
             Chicago, IL 60616
Telephone: (312) 808-1300
President: Robert Contiguglia
Secretary General: Dan Flynn
Director of Communications: Jim Moorhouse
www.us-soccer.com

Amateur Softball Association (ASA)
Address: 2801 N.E. 50th Street
             Oklahoma City, OK 73111
Telephone: (405) 424-5266
President: Bill Humphrey
Executive Director: Ron Radigonda
Director of Communications: Brian McCall
www.softball.org

U.S. Speed Skating
Address: P.O. Box 450639
             Westlake OH 44145
Telephone: (440) 899-0128
President: Fred Benjamin
Executive Director: Katie Marquard
Public Relations Director: Nick Paulenich
Publicity telephone: (810) 212-2350
www.usspeedskating.org

U.S. Swimming, Inc. (USS)
Address: 1 Olympic Plaza
             Colorado Springs, CO 80909
Telephone: (719) 578-4578
President: Dale Neuburger
Executive Director: Chuck Wielgus
Public Relations Director: Mary Wagner
www.usa-swimming.org

U.S. Synchronized Swimming, Inc. (USSS)
Address: Pan American Plaza, Suite 901
             201 South Capitol Avenue
             Indianapolis, IN 46225
Telephone: (317) 237-5700
President: Laurette Longmire
Executive Director: Debbie Hesse
Media Relations: Brian Eaton
www.usasynchro.org

U.S. Table Tennis Association (USTTA)
Address: 1 Olympic Plaza
             Colorado Springs, CO 80909
Telephone: (719) 578-4583
Executive Director: Ben Nisbet
President: Sheri Pittman
Director of Media and PR: Vicki Ulrich
www.usatt.org

U.S. Taekwondo Union (USTU)
Address: 1 Olympic Plaza, Suite 405
Colorado Springs, CO 80909
Telephone: (719) 578-4632
President: Sang Lee
Executive Director: R. Jay Warwick
Media and Communications Director: Cecil Bleiker
www.ustu.org

USA Team Handball
Address: 1903 Powers Ferry Road, Suite 230
Atlanta, GA 30339
Telephone: (770) 956-7660
President: Dennis Berkholtz
Executive Director: Mike Cavanaugh
www.usateamhandball.org

U.S. Tennis Association
Address: 70 West Red Oak Lane
White Plains, NY 10604
Telephone: (914) 696-7000
President: Julia Levering
Executive Director: Richard D. Ferman
Director of Communications: Andrea Jayson
www.usta.com

USA Track & Field (formerly TAC)
Address: P.O. Box 120
Indianapolis, IN 46206-0120
Telephone: (317) 261-0500
President: Patricia F. Rico
Chief Executive Officer: Craig A. Masback
Media Information Coordinator: Tom Surber
www.usatf.org

U.S. Volleyball Association (USVBA)
Address: 3595 East Fountain Boulevard, Suite I-2
Colorado Springs, CO 80910-2368
Telephone: (719) 228-6800
President: Rebecca Howard
Executive Director: Kerry Klostermann
Director of Marketing and Comm.: Lorene Graves
www.usavolleyball.org

United States Water Polo (USWP)
Address: 1685 West Uintah
Colorado Springs, CO 80904
Telephone: (719) 634-0699
President: Brett Bernard
Executive Director: Bruce J. Wigo
Scoreboard Editor: TBA
www.usawaterpolo.com

USA Weightlifting
Address: 1 Olympic Plaza
Colorado Springs, CO 80909
Telephone: (719) 578-4508
President: Brian Derwin
Executive Director and Media Contact: Jim Fox
www.usaweightlifting.org

USA Wrestling
Address: 6155 Lehman Drive
Colorado Springs, CO 80918
Telephone: (719) 598-8181
President: Bruce Baumgartner
Executive Director: Jim Scherr
Director of Communications: Gary Abbott
www.usawrestling.org

Affiliated Sports Organizations

Amateur Athletic Union (AAU)
Address: Walt Disney World Resort
P.O. Box 10000
Lake Buena Vista, FL 32830-1000
Telephone: (407) 934-7200
President: Bobby Dodd
Media Contact: Melissa Wilson
www.aausports.org

U.S. Curling Association (USCA)
Address: 1100 Center Point Drive
P.O. Box 866
Stevens Point, WI 54481
Telephone: (715) 344-1199
President: Albert M. Anderson
Executive Director: David Garber
Communications Director: Rick Patzke
www.usacurl.org

USA Karate Federation
Address: 1300 Kenmore Boulevard
Akron, OH 44314
Telephone: (330) 753-3114
President: George Anderson
www.usakarate.org

U.S. Orienteering Federation
Address: P.O. Box 1444
Forest Park, GA 30298
Telephone: (404) 363-2110
President: Chuck Ferguson
Executive Director: Robin Shannonhouse
Marketing and Public Relations VP: Sherry Litasi
Publicity telephone: (303) 694-4914
www.us.orienteering.org

U.S. Squash Racquets Association
Address: 23 Cynwyd Road
P.O. Box 1216
Bala Cynwyd, PA 19004
Telephone: (610) 667-4006
President: Eben Hardie III
Vice President: Kevin Jernigan
www.uss-squash.org

USA Trampoline and Tumbling
Address: 400 West Broadway, Suite 207
or P.O. Box 306
Brownfield, TX 79316
Telephone: (806) 637-8670
President: Paul Parilla
Executive Director: Ann Sims
www.usa-gymnastics.org

USA Triathlon
Address: 3595 East Fountain Boulevard, Suite F-1
Colorado Springs, CO 80910
Telephone: (719) 597-9090
President: Mike Highfield
Executive Director: Steve Locke
Communications Director: B. J. Hoeptner
www.usatriathlon.org

USA Waterski
Address: 799 Overlook Drive, S.E.
Winter Haven, FL 33884
Telephone: (863) 324-4341
President: Andrea Plough
Executive Director: Steve McDermeit
Public Relations Manager: Scott Atkinson
www.usawaterski.org

Miscellaneous Sports Directory

Championship Auto Racing Teams (CART)
Address: 755 West Big Beaver Road, Suite 800
        Troy, MI 48084
Telephone: (248) 362-8800
President and CEO: Bobby Rahal
Director of Publicity: Ron Richards
www.cart.com

Indy Racing League
Address: 4565 West 16th Street
        Indianapolis, IN 46222
Telephone: (317) 484-6526
President and Founder: Tony George
Manager of Media Relations: Ron Green
www.indyracing.com

Professional Sports Car Racing, Inc.
Address: 14175 Icot Blvd., Suite 300
Clearwater, FL 33760
Telephone: (727) 533-0503
Managing Director: H. Doug Robinson
Communications Director: Cindy Robinson
www.professionalsportscar.com

National Association for Stock Car Auto Racing (NASCAR)
Address: 1801 W International Speedway Blvd.
        Daytona Beach, FL 32114-1243
Telephone: (904) 253-0611
President: Bill France Jr.
Director of Communications Worldwide: John Griffin
www.nascar.com

National Hot Rod Association
Address: 2035 East Financial Way
        Glendora, CA 91741
Telephone: (626) 914-4761
President: Tom Compton
Director of Communications: Denny Darnell
www.nhra@nhraonline.com

Bowling, Inc.
Address: 5301 South 76th Street
        Greendale, WI 53129-1191
Telephone: (414) 421-0900
President & COO: David Patrick
Public Relations Manager: Barbara Weitzer
Women's Int'l Bowling Congress Exec. Director:
Roseann Kuhn
Amer. Bowling Congress Exec. Dir. Roger Dalkin

Professional Women's Bowling Association
Address: 7171 Cherryvale Boulevard
        Rockford, IL 61112
Telephone: (815) 332-5756
Tournament Director: Wyatt Slaughter
Media Director: Darlene Priscilla
www.pwba.com

Professional Bowlers Association
Address: P.O. Box 5118
        1720 Merriman Road
        Akron, OH 44334-0118
Telephone: (330) 836-5568
Commissioner: Mark Gerberich
Public Relations Director: Dave Schroeder
www.pba.com

U.S. Chess Federation
Address: 3054 Route 9 W
        New Windsor, NY 12553
Telephone: (845) 562-8350
Executive Director: George De Feis
Associate Director: Glenn Petersen
www.uschess.org

International Game Fish Association
Address: 300 Gulf Stream Way
        Dania Beach, FL 33004
Telephone: (954) 927-2628
President: Mike Leech
www.igfa.org

Ladies Professional Golf Association
Address: 100 International Golf Drive
        Daytona Beach, FL 32124
Telephone: (904) 274-6200
Commissioner: Ty Votaw
Director of Communications: Leslie King
www.lpga.com

PGA Tour
Address: 112 PGA Tour Boulevard
        Ponte Vedra Beach, FL 32082
Telephone: (904) 285-3700
Commissioner: Timothy W. Finchem
Senior VP of Communications: Bob Combs
www.pgatour.com

Professional Golfers' Association of America
Address: 100 Avenue of the Champions
        Box 109601
        Palm Beach Gardens, FL 33410-9601
Telephone: (561) 624-8400
President: Will Mann
Director of Public Relations: Julius Mason
www.pgaonline.com

United States Golf Association
Address: P.O. Box 708, Golf House
        Liberty Corner Road
        Far Hills, NJ 07931-0708
Telephone: (908) 234-2300
President: F. Morgan Taylor
Director of Communications: Marty Parkes
www.usga.org

American Greyhound Track Operators Association
Address: Seminole Greyhound Park
        2000 Seminola Blvd
        Casselberry, FL 32707
Telephone: (407) 699-4286
President: Bill Lee
Secretary and Managing Coordinator: Rob Christmas
www.agtoa.com

U.S. Handball Association
Address: 2333 North Tucson Boulevard
        Tucson, AZ 85716
Telephone: (520) 795-0434
Executive Director: Vern Roberts
Director of Public Relations: Mark Carpenter
www.ushandball.org

Breeders' Cup Limited
Address: 2525 Harrodsburg Road
        PO Box 4230
        Lexington, KY 40504
Telephone: (606) 223-5444
President: D. G. Van Clief Jr.
Media Relations Director: James Gluckson
Director of Marketing: Damon Thayer
www.breederscup.com

The Jockeys' Guild, Inc.
Address: 250 West Main Street, Suite 1820
        Lexington, KY 40507
Telephone: (859) 259-3211
President: Pat Day
National Manager and Secretary: John Giovanni
www.jockeysguild.com

Thoroughbred Racing Associations of America
Address: 420 Fair Hill Drive, Suite 1
Elkton, MD 21921
Telephone: (410) 392-9200
President: Stella Thayer
www.tra-online.coml

National Thoroughbred Racing Association
Address: 444 Madison Avenue, Suite 503
New York, NY 10022
Telephone: (212) 907-9280
VP of NTRA Communications: Chip Tuttle
www.ntra.com

United States Trotting Association
Address: 750 Michigan Avenue
Columbus, OH 43215
Telephone: (614) 224-2291
Executive Vice President: Fred J. Noe
Director of Publicity: John Pawlak
www.ustrotting.com

Iditarod Trail Committee
Address: P.O. Box 870800
Wasilla, AK 99687
Telephone: (907) 376-5155
Executive Director: Stan Hooley
Race Director: Joanne Potts
www.iditarod.com

U.S. Lacrosse
Address: 113 W University Parkway
Baltimore, MD 21210
Telephone: (410) 235-6882
Executive Director: Steven B. Stenersen
www.lacrosse.org

Little League Baseball, Inc.
Address: P.O. Box 3485
Williamsport, PA 17701
Telephone: (570) 326-1921
President & CEO: Stephen D. Keener
Communications & Marketing Director: Jud Rogers
www.littleleague.org

U.S. Polo Association
Address: 4059 Iron Works Parkway, Suite 1
Lexington, KY 40511
Telephone: (859) 255-0593
Executive Director: David Cummings
Media Contact: Merle Jenkins
www.uspolo.org

American Powerboating Association
Address: P.O. Box 377
Eastpointe, MI 48021
Telephone: (810) 773-9700
Executive Administrator: Gloria Urbin
www.APBA.org

Professional Rodeo Cowboys Association
Address: 101 Pro Rodeo Drive
Colorado Springs, CO 80919
Telephone: (719) 593-8840
Commissioner: Steve Hatchell
Director of Communications: Steve Fleming
www.prorodeo.com

U.S.A. Rugby Football Union
Address: 3595 East Fountain Boulevard
Colorado Springs, CO 80910
Telephone: (719) 637-1022
President: Anne Barry

U.S.A. Rugby Football Union *(Cont.)*
Chair, Communications Committee: Paul Mabry
Chair, Collegiate & Membership Committee: Bill Sexton
www.usarugby.org

The United Systems of Independent Soccer Leagues
Address: 14497 North Dale Mabry Highway, Ste 201
Tampa, FL 33618
Telephone: (813) 963-3909
President and A-League Commissioner: Francisco Marcos
Associate Directors of Media Relations: Scott Creighton and Gerald Barnhart
www.unitedsoccerleagues.com

Major League Soccer
Address: 110 East 42nd Street, Suite 1000
New York, NY 10017
Telephone: (212) 687-1400
Commissioner: Don Garber
Director of Communications: Dan Courtemanche
www.mlsnet.com

National Professional Soccer League
Address: 115 Dewalt Avenue NW, 5th floor
Canton, OH 44702
Telephone: (330) 455-4625
Commissioner: Steve Paxos
Director of Media Relations: Chuck Murr
wwwnpsl.com

Association of Tennis Professionals Tour
Address: 201 ATP Tour Boulevard
Ponte Vedra Beach, FL 32082
Telephone: (904) 285-8000
Chief Executive Officer: Mark Miles
VP of Comm. & Media Relations: Greg Sharko
www.atptour.org

COREL WTA Tour (Women's Tennis)
Address: 1266 East Main Street, 4th floor
Stamford, CT 06902-3546
Telephone: (203) 978-1740; (727) 895-5000
Chief Executive Officer: Bart McGuire
Director of Communications: Christopher DeMaria
www.sanexwta.com

Association of Volleyball Professionals
Address: 330 Washington Blvd., Suite 600
Marina Del Rey, CA 90292
Telephone: (310) 577-0775
President: Bill Berger
Vice President of Sales and Marketing: Jeff David
PR Director: Lara Potter
www.avptour.com

MINOR LEAGUES

Baseball (AAA)

National Association of Professional Baseball Leagues
Address: 201 Bayshore Drive S.E.
St. Petersburg, FL 33701
Telephone: (727) 822-6937
President: Mike Moore
Director of Media Relations: Jim Ferguson
www.minorleaguebaseball.com

International League
Address: 55 South High Street, Suite 202
Dublin, OH 43017
Telephone: (614) 791-9300
President: Randy Mobley
www.ilbaseball.com

MINOR LEAGUES (Cont.)

Baseball (AAA) (Cont.)

Pacific Coast League
Address: 1631 Mesa Avenue
            Colorado Springs, CO 80906
Telephone: (719) 636-3399
President: Branch Rickey
www.pclbaseball.com

Mexican League
Address: Angela Pola #16
            Col. Periodista, C.P. 11220
            Mexico D.F.
Telephone: 011-525-557-10-07
Manager of Operations: Nestor Alva Brito
President: Jose Orozco Topete
www.imb.com.mx

Hockey

American Hockey League
Address: 1 Monarch Place Suite 2400
            Springfield, MA 01144
Telephone: (413) 781-2030
President, CEO & Treasurer: David A. Andrews
Director of Hockey Operations: Jim Mill
Director of Comm. & Media Relations: Bret Stothart
www.theahl.com

International Hockey League
Address: 1395 East 12-Mile Road
            Madison Heights, MI 48071
Telephone: (248) 546-3230
President: Douglas Moss
Director of Communications: Sean Krabach
www.theihl.com

Halls of Fame Directory

National Baseball Hall of Fame and Museum
Address: P.O. Box 590/25 Main Street
            Cooperstown, NY 13326
Telephone: (607) 547-7200
President: Dale Petroskey
Vice President: Bill Haase
V.P. of Communications and Education: Jeff Idelson
www.baseballhalloffame.org

Naismith Memorial Basketball Hall of Fame
Address: 1150 West Columbus Avenue
            Springfield, MA 01105
Telephone: (413) 781-6500
COO: Don E.N. Gibson
Director of Marketing Communications: Kim Lee
www.hoophall.com

International Bowling Museum and Hall of Fame
Address: 111 Stadium Plaza
            St. Louis, MO 63102
Telephone: (314) 231-6340
Executive Director: Gerald Baltz
Communications Director: Jim Baer
www.bowlingmuseum.com

National Boxing Hall of Fame
Address: 1 Hall of Fame Drive
            Canastota, NY 13032
Telephone: (315) 697-7095
President: Donald Ackerman
Executive Director: Edward Brophy
www.ibohf.com

Professional Football Hall of Fame
Address: 2121 George Halas Drive NW
            Canton, OH 44708
Telephone: (330) 456-8207
Executive Director: John Bankert
Vice President of Public Relations: Joe Horrigan
www.profootballhof.com

LPGA Hall of Fame
Address: 100 International Golf Drive
            Daytona Beach, FL 32124
Telephone: (904) 274-6200
Commissioner: Ty Votaw
Communications Director: Leslie King
www.lpga.com

Hockey Hall of Fame
Address: 30 Young Street BCE Place
            Toronto, Ontario Canada M5E 1X8
Telephone: (416) 360-7735
Chairman: William Hay
President & COO: Jeff Denomme
VP of Marketing and Communications: Craig Baines
www.hhof.com

National Museum of Racing and Hall of Fame
Address: 191 Union Avenue
            Saratoga Springs, NY 12866
Telephone: (518) 584-0400
Executive Director: Peter Hammell
Assistant Director: Catherine Maguire
Communications Officer: Richard Hamilton
www.racingmuseum.org

National Soccer Hall of Fame
Address: Wright Soccer Campus
            18 Stadium Circle
            Oneonta, NY 13820
Telephone: (607) 432-3351
President: Will Lunn
www.soccerhall.org

International Swimming Hall of Fame
Address: 1 Hall of Fame Drive
            Fort Lauderdale, FL 33316
Telephone: (954) 462-6536
President: Dr. Samuel J. Freas
Media Contact: Preston Levi
www.ishof.org

International Tennis Hall of Fame
Address: 194 Bellevue Avenue
            Newport, RI 02840
Telephone: (401) 849-3990
Executive Vice President and Chief Operating
  Officer: Mark Stenning
Marketing Manager: Kat Anderson
www.tennisfame.com

National Track & Field Hall of Fame
Address: 1 RCA Dome, Suite 140
            Indianapolis, IN 46225
Telephone: (317) 261-0500
Chief Executive Officer: Craig Masback
Director of Communications: Jill Geer
www.usatf.org

SPORTSWOMEN *of the* YEAR

Sports Illustrated

World Cup Champion
U.S. Soccer Team

DECEMBER 20, 1999 www.cnnsi.com

MARK ABRAHAMS/PMI

Awards

Athlete Awards

Sports Illustrated Sportsman of the Year

1954	Roger Bannister, Track and Field
1955	Johnny Podres, Baseball
1956	Bobby Morrow, Track and Field
1957	Stan Musial, Baseball
1958	Rafer Johnson, Track and Field
1959	Ingemar Johansson, Boxing
1960	Arnold Palmer, Golf
1961	Jerry Lucas, Basketball
1962	Terry Baker, Football
1963	Pete Rozelle, Pro Football
1964	Ken Venturi, Golf
1965	Sandy Koufax, Baseball
1966	Jim Ryun, Track and Field
1967	Carl Yastrzemski, Baseball
1968	Bill Russell, Pro Basketball
1969	Tom Seaver, Baseball
1970	Bobby Orr, Hockey
1971	Lee Trevino, Golf
1972	Billie Jean King, Tennis
	John Wooden, Basketball
1973	Jackie Stewart, Auto Racing
1974	Muhammad Ali, Boxing
1975	Pete Rose, Baseball
1976	Chris Evert, Tennis
1977	Steve Cauthen, Horse Racing
1978	Jack Nicklaus, Golf
1979	Terry Bradshaw, Pro Football
	Willie Stargell, Baseball
1980	U.S. Olympic Hockey Team
1981	Sugar Ray Leonard, Boxing
1982	Wayne Gretzky, Hockey
1983	Mary Decker, Track and Field
1984	Mary Lou Retton, Gymnastics
	Edwin Moses, Track and Field
1985	Kareem Abdul-Jabbar, Pro Basketball
1986	Joe Paterno, Football
1987	Athletes Who Care:
	Bob Bourne, Hockey
	Kip Keino, Track and Field
	Judi Brown King, Track and Field
	Dale Murphy, Baseball
	Chip Rives, Football
	Patty Sheehan, Golf
	Rory Sparrow, Pro Basketball
	Reggie Williams, Pro Football
1988	Orel Hershiser, Baseball
1989	Greg LeMond, Cycling
1990	Joe Montana, Pro Football
1991	Michael Jordan, Pro Basketball
1992	Arthur Ashe, Tennis
1993	Don Shula, Pro Football
1994	Bonnie Blair, Speed Skating
	Johann Olav Koss, Speed Skating
1995	Cal Ripken Jr, Baseball
1996	Tiger Woods, Golf
1997	Dean Smith, College Basketball
1998	Mark McGwire, Baseball
	Sammy Sosa, Baseball
1999	U.S. Women's Soccer Team

Associated Press Athletes of the Year

	MEN	WOMEN
1931	Pepper Martin, Baseball	Helene Madison, Swimming
1932	Gene Sarazen, Golf	Babe Didrikson, Track and Field
1933	Carl Hubbell, Baseball	Helen Jacobs, Tennis
1934	Dizzy Dean, Baseball	Virginia Van Wie, Golf
1935	Joe Louis, Boxing	Helen Wills Moody, Tennis
1936	Jesse Owens, Track and Field	Helen Stephens, Track and Field
1937	Don Budge, Tennis	Katherine Rawls, Swimming
1938	Don Budge, Tennis	Patty Berg, Golf
1939	Nile Kinnick, Football	Alice Marble, Tennis
1940	Tom Harmon, Football	Alice Marble, Tennis
1941	Joe DiMaggio, Baseball	Betty Hicks Newell, Golf
1942	Frank Sinkwich, Football	Gloria Callen, Swimming
1943	Gunder Haegg, Track and Field	Patty Berg, Golf
1944	Byron Nelson, Golf	Ann Curtis, Swimming
1945	Bryon Nelson, Golf	Babe Didrikson Zaharias, Golf
1946	Glenn Davis, Football	Babe Didrikson Zaharias, Golf
1947	Johnny Lujack, Football	Babe Didrikson Zaharias, Golf
1948	Lou Boudreau, Baseball	Fanny Blankers-Koen, Track and Field
1949	Leon Hart, Football	Marlene Bauer, Golf
1950	Jim Konstanty, Baseball	Babe Didrikson Zaharias, Golf
1951	Dick Kazmaier, Football	Maureen Connolly, Tennis
1952	Bob Mathias, Track and Field	Maureen Connolly, Tennis
1953	Ben Hogan, Golf	Maureen Connolly, Tennis
1954	Willie Mays, Baseball	Babe Didrikson Zaharias, Golf
1955	Hopalong Cassidy, Football	Patty Berg, Golf
1956	Mickey Mantle, Baseball	Pat McCormick, Diving
1957	Ted Williams, Baseball	Althea Gibson, Tennis
1958	Herb Elliott, Track and Field	Althea Gibson, Tennis
1959	Ingemar Johansson, Boxing	Maria Bueno, Tennis
1960	Rafer Johnson, Track and Field	Wilma Rudolph, Track and Field
1961	Roger Maris, Baseball	Wilma Rudolph, Track and Field
1962	Maury Wills, Baseball	Dawn Fraser, Swimming
1963	Sandy Koufax, Baseball	Mickey Wright, Golf
1964	Don Schollander, Swimming	Mickey Wright, Golf
1965	Sandy Koufax, Baseball	Kathy Whitworth, Golf

Associated Press Athletes of the Year *(Cont.)*

	MEN	WOMEN
1966	Frank Robinson, Baseball	Kathy Whitworth, Golf
1967	Carl Yastrzemski, Baseball	Billie Jean King, Tennis
1968	Denny McLain, Baseball	Peggy Fleming, Skating
1969	Tom Seaver, Baseball	Debbie Meyer, Swimming
1970	George Blanda, Pro Football	Chi Cheng, Track and Field
1971	Lee Trevino, Golf	Evonne Goolagong, Tennis
1972	Mark Spitz, Swimming	Olga Korbut, Gymnastics
1973	O.J. Simpson, Pro Football	Billie Jean King, Tennis
1974	Muhammad Ali, Boxing	Chris Evert, Tennis
1975	Fred Lynn, Baseball	Chris Evert, Tennis
1976	Bruce Jenner, Track and Field	Nadia Comaneci, Gymnastics
1977	Steve Cauthen, Horse Racing	Chris Evert, Tennis
1978	Ron Guidry, Baseball	Nancy Lopez, Golf
1979	Willie Stargell, Baseball	Tracy Austin, Tennis
1980	U.S. Olympic Hockey Team	Chris Evert Lloyd, Tennis
1981	John McEnroe, Tennis	Tracy Austin, Tennis
1982	Wayne Gretzky, Hockey	Mary Decker, Track and Field
1983	Carl Lewis, Track and Field	Martina Navratilova, Tennis
1984	Carl Lewis, Track and Field	Mary Lou Retton, Gymnastics
1985	Dwight Gooden, Baseball	Nancy Lopez, Golf
1986	Larry Bird, Pro Basketball	Martina Navratilova, Tennis
1987	Ben Johnson, Track and Field	Jackie Joyner-Kersee, Track and Field
1988	Orel Hershiser, Baseball	Florence Griffith Joyner, Track and Field
1989	Joe Montana, Pro Football	Steffi Graf, Tennis
1990	Joe Montana, Pro Football	Beth Daniel, Golf
1991	Michael Jordan, Pro Basketball	Monica Seles, Tennis
1992	Michael Jordan, Pro Basketball	Monica Seles, Tennis
1993	Michael Jordan, Pro Basketball	Sheryl Swoopes, Basketball
1994	George Foreman, Boxing	Bonnie Blair, Speed Skating
1995	Cal Ripken Jr, Baseball	Rebecca Lobo, Basketball
1996	Michael Johnson, Track and Field	Amy Van Dyken, Swimming
1997	Tiger Woods, Golf	Martina Hingis, Tennis
1998	Mark McGwire, Baseball	Se Ri Pak, Golf
1999	Tiger Woods, Golf	U.S. Women's Soccer Team

James E. Sullivan Award

Presented annually by the AAU to the athlete who "by his or her performance, example and influence as an amateur, has done the most during the year to advance the cause of sportsmanship."

1930	Bobby Jones, Golf	1962	Jim Beatty, Track and Field
1931	Barney Berlinger, Track and Field	1963	John Pennel, Track and Field
1932	Jim Bausch, Track and Field	1964	Don Schollander, Swimming
1933	Glenn Cunningham, Track and Field	1965	Bill Bradley, Basketball
1934	Bill Bonthron, Track and Field	1966	Jim Ryun, Track and Field
1935	Lawson Little, Golf	1967	Randy Matson, Track and Field
1936	Glenn Morris, Track and Field	1968	Debbie Meyer, Swimming
1937	Don Budge, Tennis	1969	Bill Toomey, Track and Field
1938	Don Lash, Track and Field	1970	John Kinsella, Swimming
1939	Joe Burk, Rowing	1971	Mark Spitz, Swimming
1940	Greg Rice, Track and Field	1972	Frank Shorter, Track and Field
1941	Leslie MacMitchell, Track and Field	1973	Bill Walton, Basketball
1942	Cornelius Warmerdam, Track	1974	Rich Wohlhuter, Track and Field
1943	Gilbert Dodds, Track and Field	1975	Tim Shaw, Swimming
1944	Ann Curtis, Swimming	1976	Bruce Jenner, Track and Field
1945	Doc Blanchard, Football	1977	John Naber, Swimming
1946	Arnold Tucker, Football	1978	Tracy Caulkins, Swimming
1947	John B. Kelly Jr, Rowing	1979	Kurt Thomas, Gymnastics
1948	Bob Mathias, Track and Field	1980	Eric Heiden, Speed Skating
1949	Dick Button, Skating	1981	Carl Lewis, Track and Field
1950	Fred Wilt, Track and Field	1982	Mary Decker, Track and Field
1951	Bob Richards, Track and Field	1983	Edwin Moses, Track and Field
1952	Horace Ashenfelter, Track and Field	1984	Greg Louganis, Diving
1953	Sammy Lee, Diving	1985	Joan B.-Samuelson, Track and Field
1954	Mal Whitfield, Track and Field	1986	Jackie Joyner-Kersee, Track and Field
1955	Harrison Dillard, Track and Field	1987	Jim Abbott, Baseball
1956	Pat McCormick, Diving	1988	Florence Griffith Joyner, Track
1957	Bobby Morrow, Track and Field	1989	Janet Evans, Swimming
1958	Glenn Davis, Track and Field	1990	John Smith, Wrestling
1959	Parry O'Brien, Track and Field	1991	Mike Powell, Track and Field
1960	Rafer Johnson, Track and Field	1992	Bonnie Blair, Speed Skating
1961	Wilma Rudolph, Track and Field	1993	Charlie Ward, Football, Basketball

James E. Sullivan Award (Cont.)

1994	Dan Jansen, Speed Skating	1997	Peyton Manning, Football
1995	Bruce Baumgartner, Wrestling	1998	Chamique Holdsclaw, Basketball
1996	Michael Johnson, Track and Field	1999	Kelly and Coco Miller, Basketball

The Sporting News Sportsman of the Year

1968	Denny McLain, Baseball	1985	Pete Rose, Baseball
1969	Tom Seaver, Baseball	1986	Larry Bird, Pro Basketball
1970	John Wooden, Basketball	1987	No award
1971	Lee Trevino, Golf	1988	Jackie Joyner-Kersee, Track and Field
1972	Charles O. Finley, Baseball	1989	Joe Montana, Pro Football
1973	O.J. Simpson, Pro Football	1990	Nolan Ryan, Baseball
1974	Lou Brock, Baseball	1991	Michael Jordan, Pro Basketball
1975	Archie Griffin, Football	1992	Mike Krzyzewski, Basketball
1976	Larry O'Brien, Pro Basketball	1993	Pat Gillick and Cito Gaston, Baseball
1977	Steve Cauthen, Horse Racing		
1978	Ron Guidry, Baseball	1994	Emmitt Smith, Pro Football
1979	Willie Stargell, Baseball	1995	Cal Ripken Jr, Baseball
1980	George Brett, Baseball	1996	Joe Torre, Baseball
1981	Wayne Gretzky, Hockey	1997	Michael Jordan, Basketball
1982	Whitey Herzog, Baseball	1998	Mark McGwire, Baseball
1983	Bowie Kuhn, Baseball	1999	New York Yankees, Baseball
1984	Peter Ueberroth, LA Olympics		

United Press International Male and Female Athlete of the Year

	MEN	WOMEN
1974	Muhammad Ali, Boxing	Irena Szewinska, Track and Field
1975	Joao Oliveira, Track and Field	Nadia Comaneci, Gymnastics
1976	Alberto Juantorena, Track and Field	Nadia Comaneci, Gymnastics
1977	Alberto Juantorena, Track and Field	Rosie Ackermann, Track and Field
1978	Henry Rono, Track and Field	Tracy Caulkins, Swimming
1979	Sebastian Coe, Track and Field	Marita Koch, Track and Field
1980	Eric Heiden, Speed Skating	Hanni Wenzel, Alpine Skiing
1981	Sebastian Coe, Track and Field	Chris Evert Lloyd, Tennis
1982	Daley Thompson, Track and Field	Marita Koch, Track and Field
1983	Carl Lewis, Track and Field	Jarmila Kratochvilova, Track and Field
1984	Carl Lewis, Track and Field	Martina Navratilova, Tennis
1985	Steve Cram, Track and Field	Mary Decker Slaney, Track and Field
1986	Diego Maradona, Soccer	Heike Drechsler, Track and Field
1987	Ben Johnson, Track and Field	Steffi Graf, Tennis
1988	Matt Biondi, Swimming	Florence Griffith Joyner, Track and Field
1989	Boris Becker, Tennis	Steffi Graf, Tennis
1990	Stefan Edberg, Tennis	Merlene Ottey, Track and Field
1991	Michael Jordan, Pro Basketball	Monica Seles, Tennis
1992	Mario Lemieux, Hockey	Monica Seles, Tennis
1993	Michael Jordan, Pro Basketball	Steffi Graf, Tennis
1994	Nick Price, Golf	Bonnie Blair, Speed Skating
1995	Cal Ripken Jr, Baseball	Steffi Graf, Tennis

Note: Award not given since 1995.

Dial Award

Presented by the Dial Corporation to the male and female national high school athlete/scholar of the year.

	BOYS	GIRLS
1979	Herschel Walker, Football	No award
1980	Bill Fralic, Football	Carol Lewis, Track and Field
1981	Kevin Willhite, Football	Cheryl Miller, Basketball
1982	Mike Smith, Basketball	Elaine Zayak, Skating
1983	Chris Spielman, Football	Melanie Buddemeyer, Swimming
1984	Hart Lee Dykes, Football	Nora Lewis, Basketball
1985	Jeff George, Football	Gea Johnson, Track and Field
1986	Scott Schaffner, Football	Mya Johnson, Track and Field
1987	Todd Marinovich, Football	Kristi Overton, Water Skiing
1988	Carlton Gray, Football	Courtney Cox, Basketball
1989	Robert Smith, Football	Lisa Leslie, Basketball
1990	Derrick Brooks, Football	Vicki Goetze, Golf
1991	Jeff Buckey, Football, Track and Field	Katie Smith, Basketball, Volleyball, Track
1992	Jacque Vaughn, Basketball	Amanda White, Track and Field, Swimming
1993	Tiger Woods, Golf	Kristin Folkl, Basketball
1994	Taymon Domzalski, Basketball	Shannon Miller, Gymnastics
1995	Brent Abernathy, Baseball	Shea Ralph, Basketball
1996	Grant Irons, Football	Grace Park, Golf
1997	Ronald Curry, Football	Michelle Kwan, Figure Skating

Note: Award not given since 1997.

Profiles

Los Angeles Lakers
coach Phil Jackson

Henry Aaron (b. 2-5-34): Baseball OF. "Hammerin' Hank." Alltime leader in HR (755) and RBI (2,297); third in hits (3,771). 1957 MVP. Led league in HR and RBIs four times each, runs scored three times, hits and batting average twice. No. 44, he had 44 homers four times. Had 40+ HR eight times; 100+ RBI 11 times; .300+ average 14 times. All-Star 24 times . Career span 1954–76; jersey number retired by Atlanta and Milwaukee.

Kareem Abdul-Jabbar (b. 4-16-47): Born Lew Alcindor. Basketball C. Alltime leader points scored (38,387), field goals attempted (28,307), field goals made (15,837); second alltime blocked shots (3,189); third alltime rebounds (17,440). Won six MVP awards (1971–72, 1974, 1976–77, 1980). Career scoring average was 24.6, rebounding average 11.2. Ten-time All-Star, All-Defensive team five times. 1970 Rookie of the Year. Played on six championship teams; was playoff MVP in 1971, 1985. Career span 1969–88 with Milwaukee, Los Angeles. Also played on three NCAA championship teams with UCLA; tournament MVP 1967–69; Player of the Year two times.

Affirmed (b. 2-21-75): Thoroughbred race horse. Triple Crown winner in 1978 with jockey Steve Cauthen aboard. Trained by Laz Barrera.

Andre Agassi (b. 4-29-70): Tennis player. Won 1999 French Open to become one of five players in history who have won all four Grand Slams. Won '92 Wimbledon, '94 and '99 U.S. Opens and '95 Australian Open. Ranked No. 1 in 1995 and again in '99.

Troy Aikman (b. 11-21-66): Football QB. MVP of Super Bowl XXVII, in which he completed 22 of 30 passes for 273 yards and four TDs with no interceptions. Led Cowboys to victory in Super Bowls XXVIII and XXX. Career span since 1989 with Dallas Cowboys.

Michelle Akers (b. 2-1-66): Soccer player. Charter member of U.S. women's national team. Scored first goal ever for U.S. women's team on 8-21-85 against Denmark. Second alltime leading scorer in U.S. women's national team history. Member of Women's World Cup champion team in 1991, '99, and third-place team in '95. Member of Olympic champion team in 1996. Battles Chronic Fatigue Syndrome.

Tenley Albright (b. 7-18-35): Figure skater. Gold medalist at 1956 Olympics, silver medalist at 1952 Olympics. World champion two times (1953, 1955) and U.S. champion five consecutive years (1952–56).

Grover Cleveland Alexander (b. 2-26-1887, d. 11-4-50): Baseball RHP. Tied for third alltime most wins (373), second most shutouts (90). Won 30+ games three times, 20+ games six other times. Set rookie record with 28 wins in 1911. Career span 1911–30 with Philadelphia (NL), Chicago (NL), St. Louis (NL).

Vasili Alexeyev (b. 1942): Soviet weightlifter. Gold medalist at two consecutive Olympics in 1972, 1976. World champion eight times.

Muhammad Ali (b. 1-17-42): Born Cassius Clay. Boxer. Heavyweight champion three times (1964–67, 1974–78, 1978–79). Stripped of title in 1967 because he refused to serve in the Vietnam War. Career record 56-5 with 37 KOs. Defended title 19 times. Also light heavyweight gold medalist at 1960 Olympics.

Phog Allen (b. 11-18-1885, d. 9-16-74): College basketball coach. Seventh alltime most wins (746); .739 career winning percentage. Won 1952 NCAA championship. Spent most of his career from 1920 to '56, with Kansas.

Bobby Allison (b. 12-3-37): Auto racer. Third all-time in NASCAR victories (84) at the time of his retirement. Won Daytona 500 three times (1978, 1982, 1988). Also NASCAR champion in 1983.

Naty Alvarado (b. 7-25-55): Mexican-born handball player. "El Gato (The Cat)." Won a record 11 U.S. pro four-wall handball titles starting in 1977.

Lance Alworth (b. 8-3-40): Football WR. "Bambi" led AFL in receiving in 1966, '68 and '69. 200+ yards in a game five times in career, a record. Gained 100+ yards in game 41 times. In 1965 gained 1,602 yards receiving. Career span 1962–70 with San Diego and 1971–72 with Dallas. Elected to Pro Football Hall of Fame 1978.

Gary Anderson (b. 7-16-59): Football K. Four-time Pro Bowl kicker (1983, '85, '93, '98), was second on alltime NFL scoring list entering 2000 season. Made league record 40 consecutive FGs during 1997–98.

Sparky Anderson (b. 2-22-34): Baseball manager. Only manager to win World Series in both leagues (Cincinnati, 1975–76; Detroit, 1984); only manager to win 100 games in both leagues. Elected to Hall of Fame in 2000.

Willie Anderson (b. 1880, d. 1910): Scottish golfer. Won U.S. Open four times (1901 and an unmatched three straight, 1903–05). Also won 4 Western Opens between 1902 and 1909.

Mario Andretti (b. 2-28-40): Auto racer. The only driver in history to win Daytona 500 (1967), Indy 500 (1969) and Formula One world championship (1978). Second alltime in CART victories (52) as of retirement in Oct. 1994. Also 12 career Formula One victories. USAC/CART champion 4 times (consecutively 1965–66, 1969, 1984).

Earl Anthony (b. 4-27-38): Bowler. Won PBA National Championship six times, more than any other bowler (consecutively 1973–75, 1981–83) and Tournament of Champions two times (1974, 1978). First bowler to top $1 million in career earnings. Bowler of the Year six times (consecutively 1974–76, 1981–83). Has won 41 career PBA titles since 1970.

Said Aouita (b. 11-2-60): Track and field. Moroccan set world records in 2,000 meters (4:50.81 in 1987), and 5,000 meters (12:58.39 in 1987). 1984 Olympic champion in 5,000; 1988 Olympic third place in 800.

Al Arbour (b. 11-1-32): Hockey D-coach. Led NY Islanders to four consecutive Stanley Cup championships (1980–83). Also played on three Stanley Cup champions: Detroit, Chicago and Toronto, from 1953 to 1971.

Eddie Arcaro (b. 2-19-16, d. 11-14-97): Horse racing jockey. The only jockey to win the Triple Crown two times (aboard Whirlaway in 1941, Citation in 1948). Rode Preakness Stakes winner (1941, 1948, consecutively 1950–51, 1955, 1957) and Belmont Stakes winner (consecutively 1941–42, 1945, 1948, 1952, 1955) 6 times each and Kentucky Derby winner five times (1938, 1941, 1945, 1948, 1952). 4,779 career wins.

Nate Archibald (b. 9-2-48): Basketball player. "Tiny" only by NBA standards at 6' 1", 160 pounds. Drafted by Cincinnati in 1970. Led NBA in scoring (34.0) and assists (11.4) in 1972–73. First team, all-NBA in 1973, '75 and '76. MVP of NBA All Star game in 1981. Retired in 1984.

Alexis Arguello (b. 4-19-52): Nicaraguan boxer. Won world titles in three weight classes, featherweight, super featherweight and lightweight. Won first title, WBA featherweight, on 11-23-74 when he KO'd Ruben Olivares in 13. Career record: 88 bouts; won 64 by KO, 16 by decision; lost eight.

Henry Armstrong (b. 12-12-12, d. 10-24-88): Boxer. Champion in three different weight classes: featherweight (1937–relinquished 1938), welterweight (1938–40) and lightweight (1938–39). Career record 145-20-9 with 98 KOs (27 consecutively, 1937–38) from 1931 to 1945.

Lance Armstrong (b. 9-18-71): Cyclist. Two-time Tour de France winner (1999, '00). Two-time winner of Tour DuPont (1995, '96). Won 1993 world championships. Recovered from testicular cancer to win 1999 Tour de France title.

Arthur Ashe (b. 7-10-43, d. 2-6-93): Tennis player. First black man to win U.S. Open (1968, as an amateur), Australian Open (1970) and Wimbledon singles titles (1975). 33 career tournament victories. Member of Davis Cup team 1963–78; captain 1980–85.

Assault (b. 1943, d. 1971): Thoroughbred race horse. Horse of the Year for 1946; won Triple Crown that year. Won Kentucky Derby by 8 lengths; Preakness by a neck over Lord Boswell; and the Belmont by three lengths from Natchez. Trained by Max Hirsch.

Red Auerbach (b. 9-20-17): Basketball coach-executive. 938 career wins. Coached Boston from 1946 to 1965, winning nine championships, eight consecutively. Had .662 career winning percentage, with 50+ wins eight consecutive seasons. Also won seven championships as general manager.

Hobey Baker (b. 1-15-1892, d. 12-21-18): Sportsman. Member of both football and hockey Halls of Fame. College hockey and football star at Princeton, 1911–14. Fighter pilot in World War I, died in plane crash. College hockey Player of the Year award named in his honor.

Seve Ballesteros (b. 4-9-57): Spanish golfer. Notorious scrambler. Won British Opens in 1979, '84 and '88. Won Masters in 1980 and '83.

Ernie Banks (b. 1-31-31): Baseball SS-1B. "Mr. Cub." Won two consecutive MVP awards, in 1958–59. 512 career HR. League leader in, RBIs two times each; career batting average of .274; 40+ HR five times; 100+ RBIs eight times. Most HR by a shortstop with 47 in 1958. Career span 1953–71 with Chicago.

Roger Bannister (b. 3-23-29): Track and field. British runner broke the four-minute mile barrier, running 3:59.4 on 5-6-54.

Red Barber (b. 2-17-08, d. 10-22-92): Sportscaster. TV-radio baseball announcer was the voice of Cincinnati, Brooklyn and NY Yankees. His expressions, such as "sitting in the catbird seat," "pea patch" and "rhubarb" captivated audiences from 1934 to 1966.

Charles Barkley (b. 2-20-63): Basketball F. All-Rookie team, 1985. Led NBA in rebounding, 1987. Averaged 20+ points in seven of eight seasons with Philadelphia. 1992 Olympic team leading scorer. Traded to Phoenix before 1992–93 season, then to Houston before '96–97 season. League MVP for 1992–93 season.

Rick Barry (b. 3-28-44): Basketball F. Only player in history to win scoring titles in NBA (San Francisco, 1967) and ABA (Oakland, 1969). Second alltime highest free throw percentage (.900). Career scoring

average 23.2. Led league in free throw percentage six times, steals and scoring one time each. Averaged 30+ points 2 times, 20+ points 6 other times. Five-time All-Star. 1975 playoff MVP with Golden State. 1966 Rookie of the Year. Career span 1967–79.

Carmen Basilio (b. 4-2-27): Boxer. Won titles in two weight classes, welter and middle. Won world welter title by TKO of Tony DeMarco in 12 rounds on 6-10-55. Won and then lost middleweight title in two 15-round fights with Ray Robinson. Made three unsuccessful bids to regain middle title. *The Ring* Fighter of the Year for 1957. Career record: 78 bouts; won 26 by KO and 29 by decision; drew seven; lost 16, two by KO.

Sammy Baugh (b. 3-17-14): Football QB-P. Led league in passing six times and punting four times, a record. Also holds record for highest career punting average (45.1) and highest season average (51.0 in 1940). Career span 1937–52 with Washington. Also All-America with Texas Christian three consecutive seasons.

Elgin Baylor (b. 9-16-34): Basketball F. Fourth alltime highest scoring average (27.4), scored 23,149 points. Averaged 30+ points three consecutive seasons, 20+ points eight other times. Ten-time All-Star. 1959 Rookie of the Year. Played in 8 finals without winning championship. Career span 1958–71 with Los Angeles. Also 1958 MVP in NCAA tournament with Seattle.

Bob Beamon (b. 8-29-46): Track and field. Gold medalist in long jump at 1968 Olympics with world record jump of 29' 2½" that stood until 1991.

Franz Beckenbauer (b. 9-11-45): West German soccer player. Captain of 1974 World Cup champions and coach of 1990 champions. Also played for NY Cosmos from 1977 to 1980.

Boris Becker (b. 11-22-67): German tennis player. The youngest male player to win a Wimbledon singles title at age 17 in 1985. Won three Wimbledon titles (consecutively 1985–86, 1989), one U.S. Open (1989) and one Australian Open title (1991). Led West Germany to two consecutive Davis Cup victories (1988–89).

Chuck Bednarik (b. 5-1-25): Football C-LB. Last of the great two-way players, was named All-Pro at both center and linebacker. Missed only three games in 14 seasons with Philadelphia from 1949–62. Also All-America two times at Pennsylvania.

Clair Bee (b. 3-2-1896, d. 5-20-83): Basketball coach. Originated a 1-3-1 defense, helped develop three-second rule, 24-second clock. Won 82.7 percent of games as coach for Rider College and Long Island University. Coach, Baltimore Bullets, 1952–54. Author, 23-volume Chip Hilton series for children, 21 nonfiction sports books.

Jean Beliveau (b. 8-31-31): Hockey C. Won MVP award two times (1956, 1964), playoff MVP in 1965. Led league in assists three times, goals two times and points once. 507 career goals, 712 assists. All-Star six times. Played on 10 Stanley Cup champions with Montreal from 1950 to 1971.

Bert Bell (b. 2-25-1895, d. 10-11-59): Football executive. Second NFL commissioner (1946–59). Also owner of Philadelphia (1933–40) and Pittsburgh (1941–46). Proposed the first college draft in 1936.

James (Cool Papa) Bell (b. 5-17-03, d. 3-7-91): Baseball OF. Legendary foot speed—according to Satchel Paige could flip light switch and be in bed before room was dark. Hit .392 in games against white major leaguers. Career span 1922–46 with many teams of the Negro Leagues, including the Pittsburgh Crawfords and the Homestead Grays. Inducted in the Hall of Fame in 1974.

Lyudmila Belousova/Oleg Protopov (no dates of birth available): Soviet figure skaters. Won Olympic gold medal in pairs competition in 1964 and 1968. Won four consecutive World and European championships (1965–68) and eight consecutive Soviet titles (1961–68).

Deane Beman (b. 4-22-38): Commissioner of the PGA Tour 1974–94. Won British Amateur title in 1959 and U.S. Amateur titles in 1960 and 1963.

Johnny Bench (b. 12-7-47): Baseball C. MVP in 1970, 1972; World Series MVP in 1976; Rookie of the Year in 1968. 389 career HR. League leader in HR two times, RBI three times. Career span 1967–83 with Cincinnati. Elected to Hall of Fame in 1989.

Patty Berg (b. 2-13-18): Golfer. Alltime women's leader in major championships (16), third alltime in career wins (57). Won Titleholders Championship and Western Open 7 times each, the most of any golfer. Also won U.S. Women's Amateur (1938) and U.S. Women's Open (1946).

Yogi Berra (b. 5-12-25): Baseball C. Played on 10 World Series winners. Alltime Series leader in games, at bats, hits and doubles. MVP in 1951 and consecutively 1954–55. 358 career HR. Career span 1946–63, '65. Also managed pennant-winning Yankees (1964) and Mets (1973).

Jay Berwanger (b. 3-19-14): College football RB. Won the first Heisman Trophy and named All-America with Chicago in 1935.

Raymond Berry (b. 2-27-33): Football E. Led NFL in receiving 1958–60. In 13-season career, caught 631 passes, 68 for TDs. Career span 1955–67, all with Baltimore Colts. Later coached New England Patriots from 1984–89 with 51–41 record.

George Best (b. 5-22-46): Northern Ireland soccer player. Led Manchester United to European Cup title in 1968. Named England's and Europe's Player of the Year in 1968. Played in North American Soccer League for Los Angeles (1976–78), Fort Lauderdale (1978–79) and San Jose (1980–81). Frequent troubles with alcohol and gambling shadowed career.

Abebe Bikila (b. 8-7-32, d. 10-25-73): Track and field. Ethiopian barefoot runner won consecutive gold medals in the marathon at Olympics, in 1960 and 1964.

Fred Biletnikoff (b. 2-23-43): Football WR. In 14 pro seasons caught 589 passes for 8,974 yards and 76 TDs. In 1971 led NFL receivers with 61 catches; in '72 led AFC with 58. Career span 1965–78, all with Raiders. Elected to Pro Football Hall of Fame in 1988.

Dmitri Bilozerchev (b. 12-22-66): Soviet gymnast. Won three gold medals at 1988 Olympics. Made comeback after shattering his left leg into 44 pieces in 1985. Two-time world champion (1983, '87). At 16, became youngest to win all-around world championship title in 1983.

Dave Bing (b. 11-24-43): Basketball G. Averaged 24.8 points a game in four years at Syracuse. NBA Rookie of Year in 1967. Led NBA in scoring (27.1) in 1968. MVP NBA All Star game in 1976. In 12-year career from 1967–78, most of it with Detroit Pistons, averaged 20.3 points.

Matt Biondi (b. 10-8-65): Swimmer. Winner of five gold medals, one silver medal and one bronze medal at 1988

Olympics. Won one gold and one silver at 1992 Olympics.

Larry Bird (b. 12-7-56): Basketball F. Won three consecutive MVP awards (1984–86) and two playoff MVP awards (1984, 1986). Also Rookie of the Year (1980) and All-Star nine consecutive seasons. Led league in free throw percentage four times. Averaged 20+ points 10 times. Career span 1979–92 with Boston. Named College Player of the Year in 1979 with Indiana State. 1997–98 NBA Coach of the Year in first year as coach of Indiana Pacers.

Bonnie Blair (b. 3-18-64): Speed skater. Won gold medal in 500 meters and bronze medal in 1,000 meters at 1988 Olympics and gold medals in both events in 1992 and '94. Also 1989 World Sprint champion. Winner of 1992 Sullivan Award. *Sports Illustrated* Sportswoman of the Year, 1994.

Toe Blake (b. 8-21-12, d. 5-17-95): Hockey LW and coach. Second alltime highest winning percentage (.634) and sixth in wins (500). Led Montreal to eight Stanley Cup championships from 1955 to 1968 (consecutively 1956–60, 1965–66, '68). Also MVP and scoring leader in 1939. Played on two Stanley Cup champions with Montreal from 1932 to 1948.

Doc Blanchard (b. 12-11-24): College football FB. "Mr. Inside." Teamed with Glenn Davis to lead Army to three consecutive undefeated seasons (1944–46) and two consecutive national championships (1944–45). Won Heisman Trophy and Sullivan Award in 1945. Also All-America three times.

George Blanda (b. 9-17-27): Football QB-K. Alltime leader in seasons played (26), games played (340), points scored (2,002) and points after touchdown (943); kicked 335 field goals. Also passed for 26,920 career yards and 236 touchdowns. Tied record with 7 touchdown passes on Nov. 19, 1961. Player of the Year two times (1961, 1970). Retired at age 48, the oldest to ever play. Career span 1949–75 with Chicago, Houston, Oakland.

Fanny Blankers-Koen (b. 4-26-18): Track and field. Dutch athlete won four gold medals at 1948 Olympics, in 100-meters; 200 meters; 80-meter hurdles; and 400-meter relay. Versatile, she also set world records in high jump (5' 7¼" in 1943), long jump (20' 6" in 1943) and pentathlon (4,692 points in 1951).

Wade Boggs (b. 6-15-58): Baseball 3B. Won five batting titles (1983, consecutively 1985–88); had .350+ average five times, 200+ hits 7 times. Won World Series with 1996 Yankees. Career span 1982–99 with Boston, New York Yankees, Tampa Bay; .328 career average, 3,010 hits.

Nick Bolletieri (b. 7-31-31): Tennis coach. Since 1976, has run his Nick Bolletieri Tennis Academy in Bradenton, Fla. Former residents of the academy include Andre Agassi, Monica Seles and Jim Courier.

Barry Bonds (b. 7-24-64): Baseball OF. One of three players to top 40 homers (42) and 40 steals (40) in same season (1996). Three-time National League MVP (1990, '92, '93); Career span 1986–92 with Pirates; 1993– with Giants. Father Bobby had solid 14-year MLB career, mostly with Giants.

Bjorn Borg (b. 6-6-56): Swedish tennis player. Third alltime in Grand Slam singles titles (11—tied with Rod Laver). Set modern record by winning five consecutive Wimbledon titles (1976–80). Won six French Open titles (consecutively 1974–75, 1978–81). Reached U.S. Open final four times, but title eluded him. 65 career tournament victories. Led Sweden to Davis Cup win in 1975.

Julius Boros (b. 3-3-20, d. 5-28-94): Golfer. Won U.S. Opens in 1952 at Northwood CC in Dallas and in 1963 at The Country Club in Brookline, Mass. Also won 1968 PGA Championship at Pecan Valley CC, San Antonio, when 48 years old, making him oldest winner of a major ever. Led PGA money list in 1952 and '55.

Mike Bossy (b. 1-22-57): Hockey RW. In 1978 set NHL rookie scoring record of 54 goals, broken in 1993. Scored 50 or more each of first nine seasons, totaling 573 goals and 1,126 points in 10 seasons (1977–78 through 1986–87) with New York Islanders. Elected to Hall of Fame in 1991.

Ralph Boston (b. 5-9-39): Track and field. Long jumper won medals at three consecutive Olympics: gold in 1960, silver in '64, bronze in '68.

Ray Bourque (b. 12-28-60): Hockey D. Won Norris Trophy as NHL's top defenseman five times. Career span since1979–00 with Boston Bruins. Traded to Colorado in 2000.

Scotty Bowman (b. 9-18-33): Alltime leader in regular season wins (1,138) and in regular season winning percentage (.658). Also alltime leader in playoff wins (200). Has won eight Stanley Cups; coached Montreal, St. Louis, Buffalo, and Detroit. Won Jack Adams Award, Coach of the Year, 1976–77.

Bill Bradley (b. 7-28-43): Basketball F. Played on two NBA championship teams with New York from 1967 to '77. Player of the Year and NCAA tournament MVP in 1965 with Princeton; All-America three times; Sullivan Award winner in 1965. Rhodes scholar. U.S. Senator (D-NJ) 1979–96.

Terry Bradshaw (b. 9-2-48): Football QB. Played on four Super Bowl champions (consecutively 1974–75, 1978–79); named Super Bowl MVP two consecutive seasons (1978–79). 212 career touchdown passes; 27,989 yards passing. Player of the Year in 1978. Career span 1970–83 with Pittsburgh.

George Brett (b. 5-15-53): Baseball 3B-1B. MVP in 1980 with .390 batting average; three batting titles, in 1976, '80, '90; and .300+ average 11 times. Led league in hits and triples three times. Reached 3,000-hit mark in 1992. Career span 1973–93, with Kansas City. Career totals: 3,153 hits; 317 HR; 1,595 RBIs; batting average .305. Elected to Hall of Fame in 1999.

Bret Hanover (b. 1962, d. 1993): Horse. Son of Adios. Won 62 of 68 harness races and earned $922,616. Undefeated as two-year-old. From total of 1,694 foals, he sired winners of $61 million and 511 horses which have recorded sub-2:00 performances.

Lou Brock (b. 6-18-39): Baseball OF. Second alltime most stolen bases (938); second most season steals in modern era (118). Led league in steals eight times, with 50+ steals 12 consecutive seasons. Alltime World Series leader in steals (14—tied with Eddie Collins); hit .391 in World Series play. 3,023 career hits. Career span 1961–64 Chicago (NL), 1964–79 St. Louis.

Jim Brown (b. 2-17-36): Football FB. 126 career touchdowns; 12,312 career rushing yards. Led league in rushing a record eight times. His 5.2 yards per carry average is the best ever. Player of the Year four times (consecutively 1957–58, '63, '65) and Rookie of the Year in 1957. Rushed for 1,000+ yards in seven seasons, 200+ yards in four games, 100+ yards in 54 other games. Career span 1957–65 with Cleveland;

never missed a game. All-America in both football and lacrosse at Syracuse.

Paul Brown (b. 9-7-08, d. 8-5-91): Football coach. Led Cleveland to 10 consecutive championship games. Won four consecutive AAFC titles (1946–49) and three NFL titles (1950, consecutively 1954–55). Coached Cleveland from 1946 to 1962; became first coach of Cincinnati, 1968–75, and then general manager. Career coaching record 222-113-9. Also won national championship with Ohio State in 1942.

Avery Brundage (b. 9-28-1887, d. 5-5-75): Amateur sports executive. President of International Olympic Committee 1952–72. Served as president of U.S. Olympic Committee 1929–53. Also president of Amateur Athletic Union 1928–35. Member of 1912 U.S. Olympic track and field team.

Paul (Bear) Bryant (b. 9-11-13, d. 1-26-83): College football coach. Alltime Division I-A leader in wins (323). Won six national championships (1961, consecutively 1964–65, 1973, consecutively 1978–79) with Alabama. Career record 323–85–17, including four undefeated seasons. Also won 15 bowl games. Career span 1945–82 with Maryland, Kentucky, Texas A&M, Alabama.

Sergei Bubka (b. 12-4-63): Track and field. Ukrainian pole vaulter was gold medalist at 1988 Olympics. Only five-time world outdoor champion in any event (1983, '87, '91, '93, '95). First man to vault 20 feet, set world indoor record of 20' 2" on 2-21-93 and world outdoor record of 20' 1½", set on 9-20-92.

Buck Buchanan (b. 9-10-40): Football DT. Career span 1963–75 with Kansas City Chiefs. Elected to Pro Football Hall of Fame 1990.

Don Budge (b. 6-13-15, d. 1-26-00): Tennis player. First player to achieve the Grand Slam, in 1938. Won two consecutive Wimbledon and U.S. singles titles (1937–38), one French and one Australian title (1938).

Dick Butkus (b. 12-9-42): Football LB. Recovered 25 opponents' fumbles, third most in history. Selected for Pro Bowl eight times. Career span 1965–73 with Chicago. Also All-America two times with Illinois. Award recognizing the outstanding college linebacker named in his honor.

Dick Button (b. 7-18-29): Figure skater. Gold medalist at two consecutive Olympics in 1948, 1952. World champion five consecutive years (1948–52) and U.S. champion seven consecutive years (1946–52). Sullivan Award winner in 1949.

Walter Byers (b. 3-13-22): Amateur sports executive. First director of NCAA, served from 1952 to 1987.

Frank Calder (b. 11-17-1877, d. 2-4-43): Hockey executive. First commissioner of NHL, served from 1917 to 1943. Rookie of the Year award named in his honor.

Walter Camp (b. 4-7-1859, d. 3-14-25): Football pioneer. Played for Yale in its first football game vs. Harvard on Nov. 17, 1876. Proposed rules such as 11 men per side, scrimmage line, center snap, yards and downs. Founded the All-America selections in 1889.

Roy Campanella (b. 11-19-21, d. 6-26-93): Baseball C. Career span 1948–57, ended when paralyzed in car crash. MVP in 1951, 1953, 1955. Played on five pennant winners; 1955 World Series winner with Brooklyn Dodgers.

Earl Campbell (b. 3-29-55): Football RB. 9,407 career rushing yards; gained 1,934 yards rushing in

1980; 19 TDs rushing in 1979. Led league in rushing three consecutive seasons. Rushed for 1,000+ yards in five seasons. Scored 74 career touchdowns. Player of the Year two consecutive seasons (1978–79). Rookie of the Year in 1978. Career span 1978–85 with Houston, New Orleans. Won Heisman Trophy with Texas in 1977.

John Campbell (b. 4-8-55): Canadian harness racing driver. Alltime leading money winner with over $100 million in earnings. Leading money winner each year 1986–90.

Billy Cannon (b. 2-8-37): Football RB. Led Louisiana State to national championship in 1958 and won Heisman Trophy in 1959. Signed contract in both NFL (Los Angeles) and AFL (Houston). Houston won lawsuit for his services. Played in six AFL championship games with Houston, Oakland, Kansas City. Career span 1960–70. Served three-year jail term for 1983 conviction on counterfeiting charges.

Jose Canseco (b. 7-2-64): Baseball OF. One of three players to top 40 homers (42) and 40 steals (40) in same season (1988). AL MVP in 1988, when he also batted .307 with 124 RBIs. Career span 1985–1992 and 1997 with Oakland; 1993–94 with Texas; 1995–96 with Boston; 1998 with Toronto; 1999– with Tampa Bay.

Harry Caray (b. 3-1-17, d. 2-18-98): Sportscaster. TV-radio baseball announcer 1945–97 with St. Louis (NL), Oakland, Chicago (AL) and Chicago (NL). Achieved celebrity status on Cubs' superstation WGN by singing "Take Me Out to the Ballgame" with Wrigley Field fans.

Rod Carew (b. 10-1-45): Baseball 2B-1B. Won 7 batting titles (1969, consecutively 1972–75, 1977–78). Had .328 career average, 3,053 career hits, and .300+ average 15 times. 1977 MVP; 1967 Rookie of the Year. Career span 1967–85; jersey number (29) retired by Minnesota and Anaheim.

Steve Carlton (b. 12-22-44): Baseball LHP. Second alltime most strikeouts (4,136). Four Cy Young awards (1972, '77, '80, '82). 329 career wins; won 20+ games six times. League leader in wins four times, innings pitched and strikeouts five times each. Struck out 19 batters in one game in 1969. Career span 1965–88 with St. Louis, Philadelphia and four other teams in last two years.

JoAnne Carner (b. 4-21-39): Golfer. Won 42 titles, including U.S. Women's Opens in 1971 and '76 and du Maurier Classic in 1975 and '78. LPGA top earner in 1974 and 1982–83. LPGA Player of the Year in 1974 and 1981–82. Won five Vare Trophies (1974–75 and 1981–83).

Joe Carr (b. 10-22-1880; d. 5-20-39): Football administrator. Instrumental in forming American Professional Football Association in 1920. President of AAFA from 1922 to '39.

Don Carter (b. 7-29-26): Bowler. Won All-Star Tournament 4 times (1952, 1954, 1956, 1958) and PBA National Championship in 1960. Voted Bowler of the Year six times (consecutively 1953–54, 1957–58, 1960, 1962).

Alexander Cartwright (b. 4-17-1820, d. 7-12-1892): Baseball pioneer. Credited with setting the basic rules of baseball: bases 90 feet apart, nine men per side, 3 strikes per out and 3 outs per inning. On June 19, 1846, in what is often cited as the first baseball game, his New York Knickerbockers lost to the New York Nine 23–1 at Elysian Fields in Hoboken, NJ.

Billy Casper (b. 6-24-31): Golfer. Famed putter. Won 51 PGA tournaments. PGA Player of Year in both 1966 and '70. Won Vardon Trophy in 1960, '63, '64, '65 and '68. Won the U.S. Open twice, in 1959 at Winged Foot in Mamaronek, New York, and in 1966 in 18-hole playoff over Arnold Palmer at Olympic Club, San Francisco. Beat Gene Littler in 18 hole playoff to win 1970 Masters.

Tracy Caulkins (b. 1-11-63): Swimmer. Won 3 gold medals at 1984 Olympics. Won 48 U.S. national titles, more than any other swimmer, from 1978 to 1984. Also won Sullivan Award in 1978.

Steve Cauthen (b. 5-1-60): Jockey. In 1978 became youngest jockey to win Triple Crown, aboard Affirmed. First jockey to top $6 million in season earnings (1977). *Sports Illustrated* Sportsman of Year for 1977. Moved to England in 1979; rode Epsom Derby winners Slip Anchor (1985) and Reference Point (1987).

Evonne Goolagong Cawley (b. 7-31-51): Tennis. Won four Australian Open titles from 1974 through '77; won '71 French Open; Wimbledon in 1971 and '80, Runnerup four straight years at U.S. Open (1973–76), which she never won.

Bill Chadwick (b. 10-10-15): Hockey referee. Spent 16 years as a referee despite vision in only one eye. Developed hand signals to signify penalties. Also former television announcer for the New York Rangers.

Wilt Chamberlain (b. 8-21-36, d. 10-12-99): Basketball C. Alltime leader in rebounds (23,924) and rebounding average (22.9). Alltime season leader in points scored (4,029 in 1962), scoring average (50.4 in 1962), rebounding average (27.2 in 1961) and field goal percentage (.727 in 1973). Alltime single-game most points scored (100 in 1962) and most rebounds (55 in 1960). Second alltime most points scored (31,419) and most field goals made (12,681). Four MVP awards (1960, consecutively 1966–68); playoff MVP in 1972 and 1960 Rookie of the Year. Seven-time All-Star. 30.1 career scoring average. Career span 1959–72 with Philadelphia, Los Angeles. College Player of the Year in 1957 at Kansas.

Colin Chapman (b. 1928, d. 12-16-83): Auto racing engineer. Founded Lotus race and street cars, designing the first Lotus racer in 1948. Introduced the monocoque design for Formula One cars in 1962 and ground effects in 1978.

Julio Cesar Chavez (b. 7-12-62): Boxer. Career record through 8-3-00: 103-5-2. Held titles as junior welterweight, lightweight and super featherweight.

Gerry Cheevers (b. 12-7-40): Hockey goalie. Goaltender for Stanley Cup-winning Boston Bruins teams of 1970 and '72. In 12 seasons with Boston had 230-94-74 record with a goals against average of 2.89. Also coached Bruins from 1980–84, with 204-126-46 record. Elected to Hall of Fame 1985.

Cigar (b. 1990): Thoroughbred race horse. Tied Citation's American-record 16-race winning streak with a win on 7-13-96. Won $4 million Dubai World Cup on 3-27-96.

Citation (b. 4-11-45, d. 8-8-70): Thoroughbred race horse. Triple Crown winner in 1948 with jockey Eddie Arcaro aboard. Trained by Ben A. Jones.

King Clancy (b. 2-25-03, d. 11-6-86): Hockey D. Four-time All-Star. Coach, Montreal Maroons, Toronto. Also referee. Trophy named in his honor, recognizing leadership qualities and contribution to community.

Jim Clark (b. 3-4-36, d. 4-7-68): Scottish auto racer. Twenty-five career Formula 1 victories. Formula 1 champion two times (1963, 1965). Won Indy 500 in 1965. Named Indy 500 Rookie of the Year in 1963. Killed during competition in 1968 at age 32.

Bobby Clarke (b. 8-13-49): Hockey C. Won MVP award three times (1973, consecutively 1975–76). 358 career goals, 852 assists. Scored 100+ points 3 times. Played on 2 consecutive Stanley Cup champions (1974–75) with Philadelphia. Career span 1969 to 1984. Also general manager with Philadelphia 1984–90, Minnesota 1991–92, Florida 1993–94, and Philadelphia since 1994.

Roger Clemens (b. 8-4-62): Baseball RHP. Has struck out a record 20 batters in one game on two occasions. Won five Cy Young awards (1986, '87, '91, '97, '98), most by any pitcher. Also 1986 MVP. League leader in ERA six times, wins and strikeouts four times each. Won Triple Crown of pitching in 1997 and '98. Career span 1984–96 with Boston, 1997–98 with Toronto; 1999– with Yankees.

Roberto Clemente (b. 8-18-34, d. 12-31-72): Baseball OF. Killed in plane crash while still an active player. Had 3,000 career hits and .317 career average. four batting titles; .300+ average 13 times. 1966 MVP; 1971 World Series MVP. Twelve consecutive Gold Gloves; led league in assists five times. Career span 1955–72 with Pittsburgh.

Ty Cobb (b. 12-18-1886, d. 7-17-61): Baseball OF. Alltime leader in batting average (.366) and runs scored (2,245); second most hits (4,189); fourth most stolen bases (892). 1911 MVP and 1909 Triple Crown winner. Twelve batting titles. Had .400+ average three times, .350+ average 13 other times; 200+ hits nine times. Led league in hits seven times, steals six times and runs scored five times. Career span 1905–28 with Detroit.

Mickey Cochrane (b. 4-6-03, d. 6-28-62): Baseball C. Second highest career batting average among catchers (.320). MVP in 1928, 1934. Had .300+ average eight times. Career span 1925–37 with Philadelphia, Detroit.

Sebastian Coe (b. 9-29-56): Track and field. British runner was gold medalist in 1,500 meters and silver medalist in 800 meters at two consecutive Olympics in 1980, 1984. Set world record in 800 meters (1:41.73 in 1981) and 1,000 meters (2:12.18 in 1981). Served in Parliament after his running career.

Eddie Collins (b. 5-2-1887, d. 3-25-51): Baseball 2B. Alltime leader among second basemen in games, chances and assists; led league in fielding nine times. 3,311 career hits; .333 career average; .330+ average 12 times. 743 career stolen bases; alltime most World Series steals (14—tied with Lou Brock); alltime leader in single-game steals (6, twice). 1914 MVP. Career span 1906–30 with Philadelphia, Chicago.

Nadia Comaneci (b. 11-12-61): Romanian gymnast. First ever to score a perfect 10 at Olympics (on uneven parallel bars in 1976). Won three gold, two silver and one bronze medal at 1976 Olympics. Also won two gold and two silver medals at 1980 Olympics.

David Cone (b. 1-2-63): Baseball P. Won 20 games in 1988 and again in '98 to set ML-record for longest stretch between 20-win seasons. On Yogi Berra Day at Yankee Stadium, 7-18-99, with Berra and Don Larsen in attendance, pitched perfect game against Montreal Expos, 14th in modern major league history. Won 1994 AL Cy Young award. Career span since 1986 with Kansas City, NY Mets, Toronto and NY Yankees.

Dennis Conner (b. 9-16-42): Sailing. Captain of America's Cup winner three times (1980, '87,'88).

Maureen Connolly (b. 9-17-34, d. 6-21-69): Tennis player. "Little Mo" first woman to achieve the Grand Slam, in 1953. Won the U.S. singles title in 1951 at age 16. Thereafter lost only four matches before retiring in 1954 because of a broken leg caused by a riding accident. Was never beaten in singles at Wimbledon, winning 3 consecutive titles (1952–54). Won three consecutive U.S. singles titles (1951–53) and two consecutive French titles (1953–54). Also won Australian title (1953).

Jimmy Connors (b. 9-2-52): Tennis player. Alltime men's leader in tournament victories (109). Held men's #1 ranking a record 160 consecutive weeks, July 29, 1974 through Aug. 16, 1977. Won five U.S. Open singles titles on three different surfaces (grass 1974, clay 1976, hard 1978, consecutively 1982–83). Won two Wimbledon singles titles (1974, '82) further apart than anyone since Bill Tilden. Also won 1974 Australian Open title. Reached Grand Slam final seven other times.

Jim Corbett (b. 9-1-1866; d. 2-18-33): Boxer. "Gentleman Jim." Invented jab. Fight with Australian Peter Jackson on 5-21-1891 ruled no contest when neither could continue into 62nd round. Won heavyweight title on 9-7-1892 with a KO of John Sullivan in 21 rounds; it was first heavyweight title fight using gloves. Lost title when KO'd by Bob Fitzsimmons in 14 on 3-17-1897, then lost two bids to regain it against Jim Jeffries. Career record: 19 fights; won seven by KO and four by decision; drew two; lost four; two no decision.

Angel Cordero (b. 11-8-42): Jockey. Through October 1999, fifth alltime in wins (7,057) and seventh in earnings ($164,561,227). Led yearly earnings three times, in 1976 and 1982–83, winning Eclipse Awards in the last two years.

Howard Cosell (b. 3-25-18, d. 4-23-95): Sportscaster. Lawyer–turned–TV-radio sports commentator in 1953. Best known for his work on "Monday Night Football." His nasal voice and "tell it like it is" approach made him a controversial figure.

James (Doc) Counsilman (b. 12-28-20): Swimming coach. Coached Indiana from 1957 to 1990. Won six consecutive NCAA championships (1968–73). Career record 287-36-1. Coached U.S. men's team at Olympics in 1964, '76. Swam English Channel in 1979 at age 58.

Count Fleet (b. 3-24-40, d. 12-3-73): Thoroughbred race horse. Triple Crown winner in 1943 with jockey Johnny Longden aboard. Trained by Don Cameron.

Yvan Cournoyer (b. 11-22-43): Hockey RW. "The Roadrunner" had 428 goals and 435 assists during his 15-season career with the Montreal Canadiens. Had 25 or more goals in 12 straight seasons. Played on 10 Stanley Cup championship teams. Elected to Hall of Fame in 1982.

Margaret Smith Court (b. 7-16-42): Australian tennis player. Alltime leader in Grand Slam singles titles (24) and total Grand Slam titles (62). Achieved Grand Slam in 1970 and mixed doubles Grand Slam in 1963 with Ken Fletcher. Won 11 Australian singles titles (consecutively 1960–66, 1969–71, '73), five French titles (1962, '64, consecutively 1969–70, '73), 5 U.S. titles (1962, '65, consecutively 1969–70, '73) and three Wimbledon titles ('63, '65, '70). Also won 19 Grand Slam doubles titles and 19 mixed doubles titles.

Bob Cousy (b. 8-9-28): Basketball G. Finished career with 6,955 assists; in 1958 had 28 assists in a single game. League leader in assists eight consecutive seasons. Averaged 18+ points and named to All-Star team 10 consecutive seasons. 1957 MVP. Played on six championship teams with Boston from 1950 to 1969. Also played on NCAA championship team in 1947 with Holy Cross.

Dave Cowens (b. 10-25-48): Basketball C. After college career at Florida State, NBA co-Rookie of Year in 1971. NBA MVP for 1973. All-Star game MVP in 1973. Career span 1970–71 through 1982–83, all but the last year with the Boston Celtics. Coached Charlotte Hornets 1996–99. Named head coach of Golden State in 2000. Elected to Hall of Fame in 1991.

Ben Crenshaw (b. 1-11-52): Golfer. Legendary putter. Won Masters in 1984 and '95.

Johan Cruyff (b. 4-25-47): Dutch soccer player. Led Ajax Amsterdam to three European Cup titles, and guided the Netherlands to the 1974 World Cup final, a 2–1 loss to Germany.

Larry Csonka (b. 12-25-46): Football RB. In 11 seasons rushed 1,891 times for 8,081 yards (4.3 per carry) and 64 TDs. MVP of Super Bowl VIII, when he rushed 33 times for a then Super Bowl record 145 yards in Miami's 24–7 defeat of Minnesota. Career span 1968–74, '79 with Miami Dolphins; 1976–78 with New York Giants. Elected to Hall of Fame in 1987.

Billy Cunningham (b. 6-3-43): Basketball player and coach. Averaged 24.8 points a game at North Carolina. In nine seasons (1965–66 through 1975–76) with Philadelphia 76ers, averaged 20.8 points per game. All NBA first team 1969, '70 and '71. In eight seasons as Sixers coach went 454–196 in regular season, 66–39 in playoffs and won NBA title in 1983. Elected to Hall of Fame in 1985.

Bjørn Dæhlie (b.6-19-67): Norwegian skier. Legendary cross-country skier won a Winter Olympics–record eight gold medals over three Games from 1992 to '98. Won a total of 12 Olympic medals and more than 40 World Cup races.

Chuck Daly (b. 7-20-30): Basketball coach. Won two consecutive championships with Detroit (1989–90). Won 50+ games four consecutive seasons. Coach of 1992 Olympic team. Career span as pro coach 1983–92 with Pistons; 1992–94 with New Jersey; 1997–99 with Orlando.

Damascus (b. 1964, d. 1995): Thoroughbred race horse. After finishing third in 1967 Kentucky Derby, won the Preakness, the Belmont, the Dwyer, the American Derby, the Travers, the Woodward and others—12 of 16 starts. Unanimous Horse of the Year in 1967.

Stanley Dancer (b. 7-25-27): Harness racing driver. Only driver to win the Trotting Triple Crown two times (Nevele Pride in 1968, Super Bowl in 1972). Also won Pacing Triple Crown driving Most Happy Fella in 1970. Won The Hambletonian 4 times (1968, '72, '75, '83). Driver of the Year in 1968.

Tamas Darnyi (b. 6-3-67): Hungarian swimmer. Gold medalist in 200-meter and 400-meter individual medleys at 1988 and '92 Olympics. Also won both events at World Championships in 1986 and '91. Set world records in these events at 1991 Championships (1:59.36 and 4:12.36).

Al Davis (b. 7-4-29): Football executive. Owner and general manager of Oakland-LA Raiders since 1963.

Team has won three Super Bowl championships (1976, '80, '83). Also served as AFL commissioner in 1966, helped negotiate AFL–NFL merger.

Ernie Davis (b. 12-14-39, d. 5-18-63): Football RB. Won Heisman Trophy in 1961, the first black man to win the award. All-America three times at Syracuse. First selection in 1962 NFL draft, but became fatally ill with leukemia and never played professionally.

Glenn Davis (b. 12-26-24): College football HB. "Mr. Outside." Teamed with Doc Blanchard to lead Army to three consecutive undefeated seasons (1944–46) and two consecutive national championships (1944–45). Won Heisman Trophy in 1946. Also named All-America three times.

John Davis (b. 1-12-21, d. 7-13-84): Weightlifter. Gold medalist at two consecutive Olympics, 1948, '52. World champion six times.

Terrell Davis (b. 10-28-72): Football RB. Selected in the sixth round of '95 NFL draft, rushed for over 1,000 yards in each of his first four seasons, including a league-leading 2,008 yards in '98 to become the fourth back to break 2,000-yard barrier. Led Denver to back-to-back Super Bowl wins (1998–99) and won Super Bowl MVP award in '98.

Pete Dawkins (b. 3-8-38): Football RB. Starred at Army 1956–58. Won Heisman Trophy 1958. Was first captain of cadets, class president, top five percent of class academically and football team captain; first man to do all four at West Point. Did not play pro football. Attended Oxford on Rhodes scholarship, won two Bronze Stars in Vietnam, rose to brigadier general before leaving Army to become investment banker. Made unsuccessful run for Senate from New Jersey in 1988.

Len Dawson (b. 6-20-35): Football QB. Completed 2,136 of 3,741 pass attempts with 239 TDs. In Super Bowl I threw for one TD in 35–10 loss to Green Bay. MVP of Super Bowl IV. Career span 1957–75, the last 13 seasons with Kansas City Chiefs. Elected to Hall of Fame in 1987.

Dizzy Dean (b. 1-16-11, d. 7-17-74): Baseball RHP. 1934 MVP with 30 wins. League leader in strikeouts, complete games four times each. 150 career wins. Arm trouble shortened career after 134 wins by age 26. Career span 1930–41 and 1947 with St. Louis and Chicago Cubs.

Dave DeBusschere (b. 10-16-40): Basketball F. NBA First Team Defense six straight seasons, 1969–74. Member of NBA champion New York Knicks in 1970 and '73. Career span 1962–63 through middle of 1968–69 season with Detroit Pistons; through 1973–74 with Knicks. Youngest coach (24) in NBA history. Elected to NBA Hall of Fame in 1982.

Pierre de Coubertin (b. 1-1-1863, d. 9-2-37): Frenchman called the father of the Modern Olympics. President of International Olympic Committee from 1896 to 1925.

Oscar De La Hoya (b. 2-4-73): Boxer. Won lightweight gold medal at 1992 Olympics in Barcelona. Won lightweight, super lightweight and welterweight titles as a professional. 32–2 with 26 KO's.

Jack Dempsey (b. 6-24-1895, d. 5-31-83): Boxer. Heavyweight champion (1919–26), lost title to Gene Tunney and rematch in the famous "long count" bout in 1927. Career record 62-6-10 with 49 KOs from 1914 to 1928.

Gail Devers (b. 11-19-66): Track and field sprinter/hurdler. Won 100 at 1992 and '96 Olympics; leading 100 hurdles in '92 when she tripped over final hurdle and finished fifth. Successfully completed 100m/100h double at 1993 World Championships, winning 100 in 10.82 and 100 hurdles in American record 12.46. Also won '93 world indoor title in 60 (6.95). Battled Graves Disease.

Klaus Dibiasi (b. 10-6-47): Italian diver. Gold medalist in platform at 3 consecutive Olympics (1968, '72, '76) and silver medalist at 1964 Olympics.

Eric Dickerson (b. 9-2-60): Football RB. Alltime season leader in yards rushing (2,105 in 1984), fourth alltime most career yards rushing (13,259). Rushed for 1,000+ yards in seven consecutive seasons; 100+ yards in 61 games, including 12 times in 1984. Led league in rushing four times. Rookie of the Year in 1983. Career span 1983–93 with Los Angeles Rams, Indianapolis, L.A. Raiders and Atlanta Falcons.

Bill Dickey (b. 6-6-07 d. 11-12-93): Baseball C. Lifetime average .313. Hit 202 career home runs. Played on 11 AL All-Star teams. In eight World Series, hit five homers and 24 RBIs. Career span 1928–43 and 1946, all with the New York Yankees. Inducted to Hall of Fame 1954.

Harrison Dillard (b. 7-8-23): Track and field. Only man to win Olympic gold medal in sprint (100 meters in 1948) and hurdles (110 meters in 1952). Sullivan Award winner in 1955.

Joe DiMaggio (b. 11-25-14 d. 3-8-99): Baseball OF. "The Yankee Clipper." Tremendous all-around talent. Record 56-game hitting streak in 1941. MVP in 1939, 1941, 1947. Had .325 career batting average; .300+ average 11 times; 100+ RBI nine times. League leader in batting average, HR, and RBI two times each. Played on 10 World Series winners with NY Yankees. Career span 1936–51.

Mike Ditka (b. 10-18-39): Football TE-Coach. NFL Rookie of the Year in 1961. Named to Pro Bowl five times. Made 427 catches for 5,812 yards and 43 TDs. Career span 1961 to '72 with Bears, Eagles and Cowboys. Coach of Bears from 1982–92 with 112–68 overall record. Coach of Bears team that won Super Bowl XX, 46–10 over New England. Coach of New Orleans 1997–99. Elected to Hall of Fame 1988.

Tony Dorsett (b. 4-7-54): Football RB. Rushed for 12,739 yards on 2,936 career attempts. Rushed for 1,000+ yards in eight seasons. Set record for longest run from scrimmage with 99-yard touchdown run on Jan. 3, 1983. Scored 91 career touchdowns. Named Rookie of the Year in 1977. Career span 1977–88 with Dallas, Denver. Also won Heisman Trophy in 1976, leading Pittsburgh to national championship. Graduated as alltime NCAA leader in yards rushing and was first man to break 6,000-yard barrier (6,082).

Abner Doubleday (b. 6-26-1819, d. 1-26-1893): Civil War hero incorrectly credited as the inventor of baseball in Cooperstown, NY, in 1839.

Clyde Drexler (b. 6-22-62): Basketball G. Nicknamed "The Glide" for his smooth play. Member of U.S. "Dream Team" that won 1992 Olympic gold medal. Career span 1984–1994 with Portland Trail Blazers and 1995–98 with Houston Rockets, with whom he won his first NBA title in 1995. Head coach at University of Houston in 1998–00.

Ken Dryden (b. 8-8-47): Hockey G. Goaltender of the Year five times (1973, consecutively 1976–79). Playoff MVP as a rookie in 1971, maintained rookie status and

named Rookie of the Year in 1972. Led league in goals against average five times. Career record 258-57-74, including 46 shutouts. Career 2.24 goals against average is the modern record. Four playoff shutouts in 1977. Played on six Stanley Cup champions with Montreal from 1970 to 1979.

Don Drysdale (b. 7-23-36, d. 7-3-93): Baseball RHP. Led NL three times in strikeouts (1959, '60, '62) and once in wins (1962). Won 1962 Cy Young Award with 25–9 mark. In 1968 pitched six straight shutouts en route to major league record—broken in 1988 by Orel Hershiser—of 58 consecutive scoreless innings. Career record of 209–166, with 2,484 K's and ERA of 2.95. Career span 1956–69, all with Dodgers. Inducted into Hall of Fame 1984.

Tim Duncan (b. 4-25-76): Basketball C. Won 1998 rookie of the year award and named first-team All-NBA, only ninth rookie in league history to be so honored. First-team All-NBA and first-team All-Defensive NBA in '99, when he led Spurs to NBA title and was named Finals MVP. Career span since 1997 with San Antonio.

Roberto Duran (b. 6-16-51): Panamanian boxer. Champion in 3 different weight classes: lightweight (1972–79), welterweight (1980, lost rematch to Sugar Ray Leonard in famous "no más" bout) and junior middleweight (1983–84).

Leo Durocher (b. 7-27-05, d. 10-7-91): Baseball manager. "Leo the Lip." Said "Nice guys finish last." Managed three pennant winners and 1954 World Series winner. Won 2,008 games in 24 years. Led Brooklyn 1939–48; New York 1948–55; Chicago 1966–72; and Houston 1972–73.

David Duval (b. 11-9-71): Golfer. Set record for tour earnings in a single season with $2.6 million in 1998, when he also won Vardon Trophy for lowest scoring average (69.13). Won 1997 Tour Championship, four tournaments in 1998. Four-time all-America at Georgia Tech.

Tomás Dvorák (b. 5-11-72): Czech decathlete. Broke Dan O'Brien's seven-year-old decathlon world record by 103 points on 7-4-99 in Prague, amassing 8,994 points. Won decathlon bronze medal at Atlanta in '96.

Eddie Eagan (b. 4-26-1898, d. 6-14-67): Only American athlete to win gold medal at Summer and Winter Olympic Games (boxing 1920, bobsled '32).

Alan Eagleson (b. 4-24-33): Hockey labor leader. Founder of NHL Players' Association and its executive director from 1967–92. Pleaded guilty on 1-6-98 to three counts of fraud and theft involving players' insurance premiums; served six months on an 18-month jail sentence. Resigned from Hall of Fame 3-25-98.

Dale Earnhardt (b. 4-29-52): Auto racer. NASCAR champion 7 times (1980, 1986–87, 1990–91, 1993–94). Won 1998 Daytona 500.

Stefan Edberg (b. 1-19-66): Swedish tennis player. Won two Wimbledon singles titles (1988, '90), two Australian Open titles (1985, '87) and two U.S. Open titles (1991, '92). Led Sweden to three Davis Cup victories (consecutively 1984–85, '87).

Gertrude Ederle (b. 10-23-06): Swimmer. First woman to swim the English Channel, in 1926. Swam 21 miles from France to England in 14:39. Also won three medals at the 1924 Olympics.

Jason Elam (b. 3-8-70): Football K. Tied Tom Dempsey's 28-year-old NFL record for the longest field goal with a 63-yard boot on 10-25-98 against Jacksonville.

Hicham El Gerrouj (b. 9-14-74): Track and field. Morrocan runner broke world record in mile on 7-7-99, clocking 3:43.13 to trim 1.26 seconds from six-year-old previous record. Performance gave him four world records as of late '99: indoor mile, indoor 1,500 and outdoor 1,500.

Herb Elliott (b. 2-25-38): Track and field. Australian runner was gold medalist in 1960 Olympic 1,500 meters in world record 3:35.6. Also set world mile record of 3:54.5 in 1958. Undefeated at 1500 meters/mile in international competition. Retired at 22.

Ernie Els (b.10-17-69): South African golfer. Two-time U.S. Open winner (1994, '97); first foreign-born player to win the event twice since Alex Smith in 1910. Second at '96 British Open.

John Elway (b. 6-28-60): Football QB. First player taken in 1983 NFL draft. Topped 3,000 yards passing every season from 1985–91. One of two NFL QBs with more than 50,000 passing yards (51,475); 300 career TD passes. Famous for last-minute drives. Won back-to-back Super Bowls (XXXII and XXXII) after three previous Super Bowl losses. Career span 1983–99 with Denver Broncos.

Roy Emerson (b. 11-3-36): Australian tennis player. Second alltime in Grand Slam singles titles (12). Won six Australian titles, five consecutively (1961, 1963–67), two consecutive Wimbledon titles (1964–65) two U.S. titles (1961, '64) and 2 French titles (1963, '67). Also won 13 Grand Slam doubles titles.

Kornelia Ender (b. 10-25-58): East German swimmer. Won 4 gold medals at 1976 Olympics and 3 silver medals at 1972 Olympics.

Julius Erving (b. 2-22-50): "Dr. J." Basketball F. Fourth alltime most points scored for combined ABA and NBA career (30,026). 24.2 scoring average. Averaged 20+ points 14 consecutive seasons. 4 MVP awards, consecutively 1974–76, '81; playoff MVP 1974, '76. All-Star 9 times. Led league in scoring three times. Played on 3 championship teams, with New York (ABA) and Philadelphia (NBA). Career span 1971 to 1986. Executive VP of Orlando 1997–. Elected to Hall of Fame in 1993.

Phil Esposito (b. 2-20-42): Hockey C. "Espo." First to break the 100-point barrier (126 in 1969). 1,590 career points, 717 goals, and 873 assists. Led league in goals six consecutive seasons, points five times and assists three times. Won MVP award two times (1969, 1974). Scored 30+ goals 13 consecutive seasons and 100+ points six times. All-Star 6 times. Career span 1963–81 with Chicago, Boston, NY Rangers. General manager of NY Rangers from 1986–89.

Tony Esposito (b. 4-23-43): Hockey goalie. Brother of Phil. A five-time All Star during 16-season NHL career, almost all of it with the Chicago Blackhawks. In 886 games gave up 2,563 goals, an average of 2.92 per game. Won or shared Vezina Trophy three times. Elected to Hall of Fame in 1988.

Janet Evans (b. 8-28-71): Swimmer. Competed in 1988, '92 and '96 Olympics, winning three gold medals in '88 and one in '92. Set world record in 400-meter freestyle (4:03.85 in 1988), 800-meter freestyle (8:16.22 in 1989) and 1,500-meter freestyle (15:52.10 in 1988). Sullivan Award winner in 1989.

Lee Evans (b. 2-25-47): Track and field. Gold medalist in 400 meters at 1968 Olympics with world record time of 43.86 that stood until 1988.

Chris Evert (b. 12-21-54): Also Chris Evert Lloyd. Tennis player. Second alltime in tournament victories (157). Tied for fourth alltime in women's Grand Slam singles titles (18). Won at least one Grand Slam singles title every year from 1974 to '86. Won seven French Open titles (1974–75, 1979–80, '83, 1985–86), 6 U.S. Open titles (1975–77, 1978, 1980, 1982), three Wimbledon titles (1974, 1976, 1981) and two Australian Open titles (1982, 1984). Reached Grand Slam finals 16 other times. Reached semifinals at 52 of her last 56 Grand Slams.

Weeb Ewbank (b. 5-6-07, d. 11-17-98): Football coach. Only coach to win titles in both the NFL and AFL. Coached Baltimore Colts to classic overtime defeat of New York Giants in 1958 and New York Jets to their stunning 16–7 win over Baltimore in Super Bowl III. Career record of 134-130-7. Career span 1954–62 with Colts and 1963–73 with Jets. Elected to Hall of Fame in 1978.

Patrick Ewing (b. 8-5-62): Basketball C. 1986 Rookie of the Year with New York. 20+ points per game average in 13 of 15 seasons with Knicks. All-NBA first team 1990. Played on 3 NCAA final teams with Georgetown (1982, 1984–85); tournament MVP in 1984. All-America 3 times.

Nick Faldo (b. 7-18-57): British golfer. Three-time winner of Masters (1989–90, consecutively, 1996) and British Open 3 times (1987, 1990, 1992).

Juan Manuel Fangio (b. 6-24-11, d. 7-17-95): Argentine auto racer. 24 Formula 1 victories in just 51 starts. Formula 1 champion 5 times, the most of any driver (1951, consecutively 1954–57). Retired in 1958.

Brett Favre (b.10-10-69): Football QB. Sixth quarterback in NFL history to throw for more than 3,000 yards in five consecutive seasons. Won NFL MVP award three years in a row (1995–97). Led Packers to victory in Super Bowl XXXI. Career span 1991 with Atlanta, since '92 with Green Bay.

Bob Feller (b. 11-3-18): Baseball RHP. League leader in wins 6 times, strikeouts 7 times, innings pitched 5 times. Pitched 3 no-hitters and 12 one-hitters. 266 career wins; 2,581 career strikeouts. Won 20+ games 6 times. Served 4 years in military during career. Career span 1936–41, 1945–56 with Cleveland.

Tom Ferguson (b. 12-20-50): Rodeo. First to top $1 million in career earnings. All-Around champion 6 consecutive years (1974–79).

Enzo Ferrari (b. 2-8-1898, d. 8-14-88): Auto racing engineer. Team owner since 1929, he built first Ferrari race car in Italy in 1947 and continued to preside over Ferrari race and street cars until his death. In 68 years of competition, Ferrari's cars have won over 5,000 races.

Mark Fidrych (b. 8-14-54): Baseball RHP. "The Bird." Rookie of the Year in 1976 with Detroit. Had 19–9 record with league-best 2.39 ERA and 24 complete games. Habit of talking to the ball on the mound made him a cult hero. Arm injuries curtailed career.

Herve Filion (b. 2-1-40): Harness racing driver. Alltime leader in career wins (more than 14,000). Driver of the Year 10 times, more than any other driver (consecutively 1969–74, 1978, 1981, 1989).

Rollie Fingers (b. 8-25-46): Baseball RHP. Won 107 games in relief in his career; 341 career saves. 1981 Cy Young and MVP winner; 1974 World Series MVP. Alltime Series leader in saves (6). Career span 1968–85 with Oakland, San Diego, Milwaukee.

Bobby Fischer (b. 3-9-43): Chess. World champion from 1972 to 1975, the only American to hold title. Never played competitive chess during his reign. Forfeited title to Anatoly Karpov by refusing to play him.

Carlton Fisk (b. 12-26-47): Baseball C. Alltime HR leader among catchers (352) and second in games caught (2,226). 376 career HR, including a record 75 after age 40. Rookie of the Year in 1972 and All-Star 11 times. Hit dramatic 12th-inning HR to win Game 6 of 1975 World Series. Career span 1969–93 with Boston, Chicago (AL). Elected to Hall of Fame in 2000.

Emerson Fittipaldi (b. 12-12-46): Brazilian auto racer. Won Indy 500 in 1989 and '93. Won CART championship in 1989. Formula 1 champion 2 times (1972, 1974).

James Fitzsimmons (b. 7-23-1874, d. 3-11-66): Horse racing trainer. "Sunny Jim." Trained Triple Crown winner 2 times (Gallant Fox in 1930, Omaha in 1935). Trained Belmont Stakes winner 6 times (1930, 1932, consecutively 1935–36, 1939, 1955), Preakness Stakes winner 4 times (1930, 1935, 1955, 1957) and Kentucky Derby winner 3 times (1930, 1935, 1939).

Peggy Fleming (b. 7-27-48): Figure skater. Olympic champion 1968. World champion (1966–68) and U.S. champion (1964–68).

Curt Flood (b. 1-18-38, d. 1-20-97): Baseball OF. Won 7 consecutive Gold Gloves from 1963 to 1969. Career batting average of .293. Refused to be traded after 1969 season, challenging baseball's reserve clause. Supreme Court rejected his plea, but baseball was eventually forced to adopt free agency system. Career span 1956–69 with St. Louis.

Whitey Ford (b. 10-21-26): Baseball LHP. Alltime World Series leader in wins, losses, games started, innings pitched, hits allowed, walks and strikeouts. 236 career wins, 2.75 ERA. Alltime leader career winning percentage (.690—tied with Dave Foutz). Led league in wins and winning percentage 3 times each; ERA, shutouts, innings pitched 2 times each. 1961 Cy Young winner and World Series MVP. Career span 1950, 1953–67 with New York Yankees.

Forego (b. 1970, d. 8-27-97): Thoroughbred race horse. Horse of the Year in 1974 (won 8 of 13 starts); '75 (won 6 of 9); and '76 (won 6 of 8). Finished fourth in 1973 Kentucky Derby. Over six years won 34 of 57 starts and $1,938,957.

George Foreman (b. 1-22-48): Boxer. Heavyweight champion (1973–74). Retired in 1977, but returned to the ring in 1987. Lost 12–round decision to champion Evander Holyfield in 1991. Retired after losing to Tommy Morrison 6-7-93; returned again in 1994 at age 45 to KO Michael Moorer for heavyweight title. Also heavyweight gold medalist at 1968 Olympics.

Dick Fosbury (b. 3-6-47): Track and field. Gold medalist in high jump at 1968 Olympics. Introduced back-to-the-bar style of high jumping, called the "Fosbury Flop."

Jimmie Foxx (b. 10-22-07, d. 7-21-67): Baseball 1B. Won 3 MVP awards, consecutively 1932–33, 1938. Fourth alltime highest slugging average (.609), with 534 career HR; hit 30+ HR 12 consecutive seasons, 100+ RBI 13 consecutive seasons. Won Triple Crown in 1933. Led league in HR 4 times, batting average 2 times. Career span 1925–45 with Philadelphia, Boston.

A.J. Foyt (b. 1-16-35): Auto racer. Alltime leader in Indy Car victories (67). Won Indy 500 4 times (1961,

1964, 1967, 1977), Daytona 500 1 time (1972), 24 Hours of Daytona 2 times (1983, 1985) and 24 Hours of LeMans 1 time (1967). USAC champion 7 times, more than any other driver (consecutively 1960–61, 1963–64, 1967, 1975, 1979).

William H.G. France (b. 9-26-09, d. 6-7-92): Auto racing executive. Founder of NASCAR and president from 1948 to 1972, succeeded by his son Bill Jr. Builder of Daytona and Talladega speedways.

Dawn Fraser (b. 9-4-37): Australian swimmer. First swimmer to win gold medal in same event at 3 consecutive Olympics (100-meter freestyle in 1956, 1960, 1964). First woman to break the 1-minute barrier at 100 meters (59.9 in 1962).

Joe Frazier (b. 1-12-44): Boxer. "Smokin' Joe." Heavyweight champion (1970–73). Best known for his 3 epic bouts with Muhammad Ali. Career record 32-4-1 with 27 KOs from 1965 to 1976. Also heavyweight gold medalist at 1964 Olympics.

Walt Frazier (b. 3-29-45): Basketball G. Point guard on championship Knick teams of 1970 and '73. First team All Star in 1970, '72, '74 and '75. First team All Defense every year from 1969–1975. Averaged 18.9 points per game in 13-season NBA career. Elected to Hall of Fame in 1986.

Frankie Frisch (b. 9-9-1898, d. 3-12-73): Baseball IF. "The Fordham Flash." Led NL in hits in 1923 (223). Hit over .300 13 seasons. Scored 100+ runs 7 times. Drove in 100+ runs three times. Career .316 batting average. Career span 1919–26 with New York Giants and 1927–37 with St. Louis Cardinals' "Gashouse Gang." NL MVP in 1931. Elected to Hall of Fame in 1947.

Dan Gable (b. 10-25-48): Wrestler. Gold medalist in 149–pound division at 1972 Olympics. Also NCAA champion 2 times (in 1968 at 130 pounds, in 1969 at 137 pounds). Coached Iowa to NCAA championship 15 times (consecutively 1978–86, 1991–93 and 1995–97).

Clarence Gaines (b. 5-21-23): College basketball coach. "Bighouse." Retired after 1992–93 season with 828 career wins in 46 seasons at Division II Winston-Salem State since 1947.

John Galbreath (b. 8-10-1897, d. 7-20-88): Horse racing owner. Owner of Darby Dan Farms from 1935 until his death and of baseball's Pittsburgh Pirates from 1946 to 1985. Only man to breed and own winners of both the Kentucky Derby (Chateaugay in 1963 and Proud Clarion in 1967) and the Epsom Derby (Roberto in 1972).

Gallant Fox (b. 3-23-27, d. 11-13-54): Thoroughbred race horse. Triple Crown winner in 1930 with jockey Earle Sande aboard. Trained by James Fitzsimmons. The only Triple Crown winner to sire another Triple Crown winner (Omaha in 1935).

Don Garlits (b. 1-14-32): Auto racer. "Big Daddy." Has won 35 National Hot Rod Association top fuel events. Won 3 NHRA top fuel points titles (1975, 1985–86). First top fuel driver to surpass 190 mph (1963), 200 mph (1964), 240 mph (1973), 250 mph (1975) and 270 mph (1986). Credited with developing rear engine dragster.

Haile Gebrselassie (b. 4-18-73): Track and field. Ethiopian distance runner reclaimed the world record in the 10,000 meters on 6-1-98 in Hengelo, Neth., clocking 26:22.75, and in the 5,000, running 12:39.36 in Helsinki on 6-13-98. Won 10,000 meter gold medal in 1996 Games at Atlanta.

Lou Gehrig (b. 6-19-03, d. 6-2-41): Baseball 1B. "The Iron Horse." Second alltime in consecutive games played (2,130), leader in grand slam HR (23), third in RBI (1,995) and slugging average (.632). MVP in 1927, 1936; won Triple Crown in 1934. .340 career average; 493 career HR. 100+ RBI 13 consecutive seasons. Led league in RBI 5 times and HR 3 times. Played on 7 World Series winners with New York Yankees. Died of disease since named for him. Career span 1923–39.

Bernie Geoffrion (b. 2-16-31): Hockey RW. "Boom Boom" for his powerful slapshot. Won Hart Memorial Trophy for 1960–61. Scored 393 goals and 429 assists in 16 seasons (1950–51 through 1967–68), the first 14 with the Montreal Canadiens, the final two with the New York Rangers. Elected to Hall of Fame 1972.

Eddie Giacomin (b. 6-6-39): Hockey goalie. "Fast Eddie" led NHL goalies in games won for three straight seasons. Shared Vezina Trophy for 1970–71. In 610 games gave up 1,675 goals, a goals against average of 2.82. Career span 1965–75 with the New York Rangers and 1975–78 with Detroit Red Wings.

Althea Gibson (b. 8-25-27): Tennis player. Won 2 consecutive Wimbledon and U.S. singles titles (1957–58), the first black player to win these tournaments. Also won 1 French title (1956).

Bob Gibson (b. 11-9-35): Baseball RHP. 1968 Cy Young and MVP award winner with modern National League best ERA (1.12) and second most shutouts (13). Also 1970 Cy Young award winner. Record holder for most strikeouts in a World Series game (17); Series MVP in 1964, 1967. Won 20+ games 5 times. 251 career wins; 3,117 strikeouts. Pitched no-hitter in 1971. Career span 1959–75 with St. Louis.

Josh Gibson (b. 12-21-11, d. 1-20-47): Baseball C in Negro leagues. "The Black Babe Ruth." Couldn't play in major leagues because of skin color. Credited with 950 HR (75 in 1931, 69 in 1934) and .350 batting average. Had .400+ average 2 times. Career span 1930–46 with Homestead Grays, Pittsburgh Crawfords.

Kirk Gibson (b. 5-28-57): Baseball OF. Played on 2 World Series champions (Detroit in 1984 and Los Angeles in 1988). Hit dramatic pinch-hit HR in 9th inning to win Game 1 of 1988 series. MVP in 1988. Career span 1979–94 with Detroit, LA, KC, Pitt. Also starred in baseball and football at Michigan State.

Frank Gifford (b. 8-16-30): Football RB. NFL Player of Year in 1956 when he rushed for 819 yards and caught 51 passes. Played in seven Pro Bowls. Retired for one season after ferocious hit by Chuck Bednarik. Career span 1952–60 and 1962–64, all with New York Giants. Elected to Hall of Fame in 1977.

Rod Gilbert (b. 7-1-41): Hockey RW. Played 16 seasons, all with the New York Rangers (1960–61 through 1977–78), and had 406 goals and 615 assists. Elected to Hall of Fame 1977.

Sid Gillman (b. 10-26-11): Football coach. Developed wide-open, pass-oriented style of offense, introduced techniques for situational player substitutions and the study of game films. Won one division title with Los Angeles Rams and five division titles and one AFL championship (1963) with Los Angeles/San Diego Chargers. Career span 1955–59 Los Angeles Rams; 1960 Los Angeles Chargers; 1961–69 San Diego; 1973–74 Houston. Lifetime record 124-101-7. Also general manager in San Diego and Houston.

Pancho Gonzales (b. 5-9-28, d. 7-3-95): Tennis player. Won 2 consecutive U.S. singles titles (1948–49). In 1969, at age 41, beat Charlie Pasarell 22–24, 1–6, 16–14, 6–3, 11–9 in longest Wimbledon match ever (5:12).

Jeff Gordon (b. 8-4-71): Auto racer. Began racing go-carts and quarter midgets at age five. Youngest NASCAR Winston Cup Series champion in the modern era, having won the title at age 24 in 1995. Won at least 10 times in three straight seasons (1996–98), and won 13 times in 1998, both modern records.

Shane Gould (b. 11-23-56): Australian swimmer. Won three gold medals, one silver and one bronze at 1972 Olympics. Set 11 world records over 23-month period beginning in 1971. Held world record in five freestyle distances ranging from 100 meters to 1,500 meters in late 1971 and 1972. Retired at age 16.

Steffi Graf (b. 6-14-69): German tennis player. Achieved the Grand Slam in 1988. Won 4 Australian Open singles titles (1988–90, '94), 7 Wimbledon titles (1988–89, 1991–93, '95–96), 6 French Open titles (1987, '88, '93, '95, '96 and '99) and 5 U.S. Open titles (1988–89, '93 and '95–96). Held the No. 1 ranking a record 186 weeks; Aug. 17, 1987 through March 10, 1991. Gold medalist at 1988 Olympics. Second in alltime Grand Slam singles titles (22).

Otto Graham (b. 12-6-21): Football QB. Led Cleveland to 10 championship games in his 10-year career. Played on 4 consecutive AAFC champions (1946–49) and 3 NFL champions (1950, consecutively 1954–55). Combined league totals: 23,584 yards passing, 174 touchdown passes. Player of the Year 2 times (1953, 1955). Led league in passing 6 times. Career span 1946–55.

Red Grange (b. 6-13-03, d. 1-28-91): Football HB. "The Galloping Ghost." All-America 3 consecutive seasons with Illinois (1923–25), scoring 31 touchdowns in 20–game collegiate career. Signed by George Halas of Chicago in 1925, attracted sellout crowds across the country. Established the first AFL with manager C.C. Pyle in 1926, but league folded after 1 year. Career span 1925–34 with Chicago, New York.

Rocky Graziano (b. 6-7-22, d. 5-22-90): Boxer. Middleweight champion from 1947 to 1948. Career record 67–13. Endured 3 brutal title fights against Tony Zale, with Zale winning by KO in 1946 and 1948, and Graziano winning by KO in 1947.

Hank Greenberg (b. 1-1-11, d. 9-4-86): Baseball 1B. 331 career HR (58 in 1938). MVP in 1935, 1940. League leader in HR and RBI 4 times each. Fifth alltime highest slugging average (.605). 100+ RBI 7 times. Career span 1933-41, 1945-47 with Detroit, Pittsburgh.

Joe Greene (b. 9-24-46): Football DT. "Mean Joe." Anchored Pittsburgh's famed "Steel Curtain" defense. Selected for Pro Bowl 10 times. Played on 4 Super Bowl champions (consecutively 1974–75, 1978–79). Career span 1969 to 1981.

Maurice Greene (b. 7-23-74): Track and field. Set world record for 100 meters (9.79) on 6-16-99 in Athens.

Forrest Gregg (b. 10-18-33): Football OT/G. Played in then-record 188 straight games from 1956 through 1971. Named all-NFL eight straight years starting in 1960. Career span 1956–71, most of it with Green Bay Packers. Played on winning Packer team in first two Super Bowls. Inducted into Hall of Fame in 1977.

Wayne Gretzky (b. 1-26-61): Hockey C. "The Great One." Most dominant player in history. Alltime scoring leader in points (2,795), assists (1,910), and goals (885). Alltime single-season scoring leader in points (215 in 1986), goals (92 in 1982) and assists (163 in 1986). Has won MVP award 9 times, more than any other player (consecutively 1980-87, 1989). Led league in assists 16 times, scoring 11 times, goals 5 times. Scored 200+ points 4 times, 100+ points 10 other times; 70+ goals 4 consecutive seasons, 50+ goals 5 other times; 100+ assists 11 consecutive seasons. Playoff MVP 2 times (1985, 1988). Played on 4 Stanley Cup champions with Edmonton from 1978 to 1988. Traded to Los Angeles on Aug. 9, 1988, then to St. Louis Feb. 1996. Moved as a free agent to NY Rangers before 1996–97 season. Wore uniform No. 99, which NHL retired when Gretzky ended career after '99 season.

Bob Griese (b. 2-3-45): Football QB. Career span 1967–80 with Miami Dolphins. Played in three straight Super Bowls, 1971–73. Quarterback of 1972 Dolphin team that went 17–0. Won Super Bowl VII and VIII. In 14 seasons completed 1,926 passes for 25,092 yards and 192 TDs. Elected to Hall of Fame in 1990.

Florence Griffith Joyner (b. 12-21-59, d. 9-21-98): Track and field. Won 3 gold medals (100 meters, 200 meters, 4x100-meter relay) at 1988 Olympics; Set world record in 100 (10.49) in 1988 and in 200 (21.34) at the 1988 Olympics. Sullivan Award winner in 1988.

Ken Griffey Jr. (b. 11-21-69): Baseball OF. Hit 56 home runs in back-to-back seasons (1997–98). Hit career home run No. 300 on 4-13-98 to become, at 28 years 143 days, the second youngest to reach the milestone. Won AL MVP award in 1997, when he hit .304 with 56 HRs and 147 RBI. Father Ken Sr. starred with Cincinnati Reds in 1970s.

Archie Griffin (b. 8-21-54): College football RB. Only player to win the Heisman Trophy 2 times (consecutively 1974-75), with Ohio State. Sixth alltime NCAA most yards rushing (5,177), his 6.13 yards per carry is the collegiate record. Professional career span 1976-83 with Cincinnati; totaled 2,808 yards rushing and 192 receptions.

Lefty Grove (b. 3-6-00, d. 5-22-75): Baseball LHP. 300 career wins and fourth alltime highest winning percentage (.680). League leader in ERA 9 times, strikeouts 7 consecutive seasons. Won 20+ games 8 times. 1931 MVP. Career span 1925-41 with Philadelphia, Boston.

Tony Gwynn (b. 5-9-60): Baseball OF. 8 batting titles (1984, consecutively 1987–89, 1994–97). League leader in hits 6 times, with .300+ average 16 times, 200+ hits 5 times. Career span since 1982 with San Diego. Reached 3,000 career hits in 1999.

Walter Hagen (b. 12-21-1892, d. 10-5-69): Golfer. Third alltime leader in major championships (11). Won PGA Championship 5 times (1921, consecutively 1924-27), British Open 4 times (1922, 1924, consecutively 1928-29) and U.S. Open 2 times (1914, 1919). Won 40 career tournaments.

Marvin Hagler (b. 5-23-54): Boxer. "Marvelous." Middleweight champion (1980-87). Career record 62-3-2 with 52 KOs from 1973 to 1987. Defended title 13 times.

George Halas (b. 2-2-1895, d. 10-31-83): Football owner and coach. "Papa Bear." Alltime leader in seasons coaching (40) and second in wins (324). Career record 324-151-31 intermittently from 1920 to 1967. Remained as owner until his death. Chicago won a record 7 NFL championships during his tenure.

Glenn Hall (b. 10-3-31): Hockey goalie. "Mr. Goalie" was an All-Star goalie in 11 of his 18 seasons. Set record for consecutive games by a goaltender, with 502, and ended career with goals against average of 2.51. Won or shared Vezina Trophy three times. Career span 1952–53 through 1970–71.

Charles Haley (b. 1-6-64): Football DE. Only player in NFL history to be a member of five Super Bowl champions, two with San Francisco (1989, '90) and three with Dallas (1993, '94 and '96). Career span 1986–91 with 49ers; 1992–96 with Dallas ; 1999– 49ers.

Mia Hamm (b. 3-17-72): Soccer player. Alltime leading scorer in U.S. women's national team history. Member of Women's World Cup champion team in 1991, '99, and third-place team in '95. Member of Olympic champion team in 1996. Debuted with national team against China on 8-3-87 as its youngest player ever, at age 15.

Arthur B. (Bull) Hancock (b. 1-24-10, d. 9-14-72): Horse racing owner. Owner of Claiborne Farm, and arguably the greatest breeder in history. For 15 straight years, from 1955 to 1969, a Claiborne stallion led the sire list. Foaled at Claiborne Farm were 4 Horses of the Year (Kelso, Round Table, Bold Ruler and Nashua).

Tom Harmon (b. 9-28-19, d. 3-17-90): Football RB. Won Heisman Trophy in 1940 with Michigan. Triple-threat back led nation in scoring and named All-America 2 consecutive seasons (1939-40). Awarded Silver Star and Purple Heart in World War II. Played in NFL with Los Angeles (1946-47).

Franco Harris (b. 3-7-50): Football RB. Rushed for 12,120 yards and 91 touchdowns. Gained 1,000+ yards in 8 seasons, 100+ yards in 47 games. Scored 100 career touchdowns. Selected for Pro Bowl 9 times. Rookie of the Year in 1972. Played on 4 Super Bowl champions (consecutively 1974–75, 1978–79) with Pittsburgh. Super Bowl MVP in 1974. Holds Super Bowl record for most career rushing yards (354). Made the "Immaculate Reception" to win 1972 playoff game against Oakland. Career span 1972–83 with Pittsburgh. Elected to the Hall of Fame in 1990.

Leon Hart (b. 11-2-28): Football DE. Won Heisman Trophy in 1949, the last lineman to win the award. Played on 3 national champions with Notre Dame (consecutively 1946–47, 1949) and the Irish went undefeated during his 4 years (36-0-2). Also played on 3 NFL champions with Detroit. Career span 1950-57.

Bill Hartack (b. 12-9-32): Horse racing jockey. Rode Kentucky Derby winner 5 times (1957, 1960, 1962, 1964, 1969), Preakness Stakes winner 3 times (1956, 1964, 1969) and Belmont Stakes winner 1 time (1960).

Doug Harvey (b. 12-19-24, d. 12-26-90): Hockey D. Defensive Player of the Year 7 times (consecutively 1954-57, 1959-61). Led league in assists in 1954. All-Star 10 times. Played on 6 Stanley Cup champions with Montreal from 1947 to 1968.

Dominik Hasek (b. 1-29-65): Czech hockey G. Two-time NHL MVP (1997, 98) with Buffalo; five-time Vezina Trophy winner (1994–95, 1997–99) as top goalie in league. Led NHL with a 1.95 goals-against average in 1993–94, the first sub-2.00 GAA since Bernie Parent in 1974. Topped that with 1.87 GAA in 1998–99. Guided Czech Republic to Olympic gold medal in 1998 at Nagano. Career span 1990–92 with Chicago, since '92 with Buffalo.

Billy Haughton (b. 11-2-23, d. 7-15-86): Harness racing driver. Won the Pacing Triple Crown driving

Rum Customer in 1968. Won The Hambletonian 4 times (1974, consecutively 1976-77, 1980).

John Havlicek (b. 4-8-40): Basketball F/G. Member of Ohio State team that won 1960 NCAA title. "Hondo" averaged 20.8 points per game over 16-season NBA career, all with Boston. First team NBA All Star in 1971, '72, '73 and '74. Member of eight Celtic teams that won NBA title. Playoff MVP 1974. Elected to Hall of Fame in 1983.

Elvin Hayes (b. 11-17-45): Basketball C. 1968 *Sporting News* College Player of Year as Houston senior. Averaged 21.0 points per game over 16-season NBA career. Led NBA in scoring (28.4) in 1969 and in rebounding in 1970 (16.9 per game) and '74 (18.1). First team All-NBA in 1975, '77 and '79. Elected to Hall of Fame in 1989.

Woody Hayes (b. 2-14-13, d. 3-12-87): College football coach. Won national championship 3 times (1954, 1957, 1968) and Rose Bowl 4 times. Career record 238-72-10, including 4 undefeated seasons, with Ohio State from 1951 to 1978. Forced to resign after striking an opposing player during 1978 Gator Bowl.

Marques Haynes (b. 10-3-26): Basketball G. Known as "The World's Greatest Dribbler." Beginning in 1946 barnstormed more than 4 million miles throughout 97 countries for the Harlem Globetrotters, Harlem Magicians, Meadowlark Lemon's Bucketeers, Harlem Wizards.

Thomas Hearns (b. 10-18-58): Boxer. "Hit Man." Champion in four weight classes: welterweight, super welterweight, middleweight and light heavyweight.

Eric Heiden (b. 6-14-58): Speed skater. Won 5 gold medals at 1980 Olympics. World champion 3 consecutive years (1977-79). Also won Sullivan Award in 1980.

Carol Heiss (b. 1-20-40): Figure skater. Gold medalist at 1960 Olympics, silver medalist at 1956 Olympics. World champion 5 consecutive years (1956-60) and U.S. champion 4 consecutive years (1957-60). Married 1956 Olympic gold medalist Hayes Jenkins.

Rickey Henderson (b. 12-25-57): Baseball OF. Alltime career stolen base leader (1,334 through 1999); modern season stolen base record holder in 1982 (130). Led league in steals 11 times. 1990 MVP. Alltime most HR leading off game. Career span since 1979 with Oakland, NY Yankees, Toronto, San Diego, NY Mets, and Seattle.

Sonja Henie (b. 4-8-12, d. 10-12-69): Norwegian figure skater. Gold medalist at 3 consecutive Olympics (1928, 1932, 1936). World champion 10 consecutive years (1927-36).

Orel Hershiser (b. 9-16-58): Baseball RHP. Alltime leader most consecutive scoreless innings pitched (59 in 1988). Cy Young Award winner in 1988 and World Series MVP. Career span 1983-94, Los Angeles; 1995-97, Cleveland; 1998, San Francisco; 1999, NY Mets.

Foster Hewitt (b. 11-21-02, d. 4-22-85): Hockey sportscaster. In 1923, aired one of hockey's first radio broadcasts. Became the voice of hockey in Canada on radio and later television. Famous for the phrase, "He shoots ... he scores!"

Tommy Hitchcock (b. 2-11-00, d. 4-19-44): Polo. 10-goal rating 18 times in his 19-year career from 1922 to 1940. Killed in plane crash in World War II.

Lew Hoad (b. 11-23-34): Australian tennis player. Won 2 consecutive Wimbledon singles titles (1956-57).

Also won French title and Australian title in 1956, but failed to achieve the Grand Slam when defeated at Forest Hills by countryman Ken Rosewall.

Ben Hogan (b. 8-13-12, d. 7-25-97): Golfer. Third alltime in career wins (63). Won U.S. Open 4 times (1948, consecutively 1950–51, 1953), the Masters (1951, 1953) and PGA Championship (1946, 1948) 2 times each and British Open once (1953). PGA Player of the Year 4 times (1948, consecutively 1950-51, 1953).

Marshall Holman (b. 9-29-54): Bowler. Won 21 PBA titles between 1975 and 1988. Had leading average in 1987 (213.54) and was named PBA Bowler of the Year.

Nat Holman (b. 10-18-1896, d. 2-12-95): College basketball coach. Only coach in history to win NCAA and NIT championships in same season in 1950 with CCNY. 423 career wins, a .689 winning percentage.

Larry Holmes (b. 11-3-49): Boxer. Heavyweight champion (1978–85). Career record 67–6 with 43 KOs from 1973 to 1999. Defended title 21 times. Fought periodically after 1991, including three unsuccessful bids for the title.

Lou Holtz (b. 1-6-37): Football coach. Coached Notre Dame to national championship in 1988 with 12–0 record and a 34–21 win over West Virginia in Fiesta Bowl. Retired after 1996 season with a 216-95-7 career record. 10-8-2 career record in bowl games. Career span 1969–71 at William & Mary (13–20); 1972–75 at N.C. State (33-12-3); 1977–83 at Arkansas (60-21-2); 1984–85 at Minnesota (10–12); 1986–96 at Notre Dame (100-30-2); and 1999– S Carolina.

Evander Holyfield (b. 10-19-62): Boxer. Won heavyweight crown Oct. 25, 1990 when he beat James (Buster) Douglas in Las Vegas. Lost title to Riddick Bowe in Las Vegas on 11-13-92, regained it from Bowe one year later, then lost to Michael Moorer on 4-22-94. Defeated Mike Tyson for WBA crown on 11-9-96 to join Muhammad Ali as the only men to win the heavyweight title three times. Won rematch on 6-28-97 when Tyson was disqualified for biting Holyfield's ears. Lost title to Lennox Lewis 11-13-99.

Red Holzman (b. 8-10-20; d. 11-13-98): Basketball coach. Led New York Knicks to NBA title in 1970 and '73. NBA Coach of the Year in 1970. Member of Rochester team that won NBA title in both 1946 (in NBL) and '51. After two-year coaching stints with Milwaukee and St. Louis, coached New York Knicks from 1968–82. Elected to Hall of Fame in 1985.

Harry Hopman (b. 8-12-06, d. 12-27-85): Australian tennis coach. As nonplaying captain, led Australia to 15 Davis Cup titles between 1950 and 1969. Mentor to Lew Hoad, Ken Rosewall, Rod Laver and John Newcombe.

Willie Hoppe (b. 10-11-1887, d. 2-1-59): Billiards. Won 51 world championship matches from 1904 to 1952.

Rogers Hornsby (b. 4-27-1896, d. 1-5-63): Baseball 2B. Second alltime in career batting average (.358), won 7 batting titles, including with .424 average in 1924. 200+ hits seven times; .400+ average three times and .300+ average 12 other times. Led league in slugging average 9 times. Triple Crown winner in 1922, 1925; MVP award winner in 1925, 1929. Career span 1915–37 with St. Louis (NL), New York (NL), Boston, Chicago (NL).

Paul Hornung (b. 12-23-35): Football RB-K. Led league in scoring 3 consecutive seasons, including a record 176 points in 1960 (15 touchdowns, 15 field goals, 41 extra points). Player of the Year in 1961. Career span 1957–66 with Green Bay. Suspended for 1963 season by Pete Rozelle for gambling. Also won Heisman Trophy in 1956 with Notre Dame.

Gordie Howe (b. 3-31-28): Hockey RW. Second alltime in goals (801), first in years played (26) and games (1,767). Finished career with 1,850 points and 1,049 assists. Won MVP award 6 times (consecutively 1952–53, 1957–58, 1960, 1963). Led league in scoring 6 times, goals 5 times and assists 3 times. Scored 40+ goals 5 times, 30+ goals 13 other times, 100+ points 3 times. All-Star 12 times. Played on 4 Stanley Cup champions with Detroit from 1946 to 1971. Teamed with sons Mark and Marty in the WHA with Houston and New England from 1973 to 1979, in NHL with Hartford in 1980.

Carl Hubbell (b. 6-22-03, d. 11-21-88): Baseball LHP. 253 career wins. MVP in 1933, 1936. League leader in wins and ERA 3 times each. Won 24 consecutive games from 1936 to 1937. Struck out Ruth, Gehrig, Foxx, Simmons and Cronin consecutively in 1934 All-Star game. Pitched no-hitter in 1929. Career span 1928–43 with New York.

Sam Huff (b. 10-4-34): Football LB. Made 30 interceptions. Career span 1956–69 with New York Giants and Washington Redskins. Elected to Hall of Fame in 1982.

Bobby Hull (b. 1-3-39): Hockey LW. "The Golden Jet." Led league in goals 7 times and points 3 times. 610 career goals. Scored 50+ goals 5 times, 30+ goals 8 other times. Won MVP award 2 consecutive seasons (1965–66). Son Brett won MVP award in 1991, the only father and son to be so honored. All-Star 10 times. Career span 1957–72 with Chicago, 1973–80 with Winnipeg of WHA.

Brett Hull (b. 8-9-64): Hockey RW. Son of Bobby Hull. Won Hart Memorial Trophy for 1990–91 season. Scored Stanley Cup–winning goal for Dallas in third overtime of Game 6 against Buffalo in 1999. Career span 1986–87 with Calgary Flames; 1987–98 with St. Louis Blues; since 1998 with Dallas Stars.

Jim (Catfish) Hunter (b. 4-8-46, d. 9-9-99): Baseball RHP. 1974 Cy Young award winner. Won 20+ games 5 consecutive seasons. Led league in wins and winning percentage 2 times each, ERA 1 time. 250+ innings pitched 8 times. Pitched perfect game in 1968. Member of 5 World Series champions for Oakland and New York Yankees. Career span 1965–79.

Don Hutson (b. 1-31-13, d. 6-26-97): Football WR. Fourth alltime in touchdown receptions (99). Led league in pass receptions 8 times, receiving yards 7 times and scoring 5 consecutive seasons. Caught at least 1 pass in 95 consecutive games. Player of the Year 2 consecutive seasons (1941–42). Career span 1935–45 with Green Bay.

Hank Iba (b. 8-6-04; d. 1-15-93): College basketball coach. Coached Oklahoma A&M (which became Oklahoma State) from 1934 to 1970. Team won NCAA titles in 1945 and '46. 767 career wins is third alltime behind Dean Smith and Adolph Rupp.

Jackie Ickx (b. 1-1-45): Belgian auto racer. Won the 24 Hours of LeMans a record six times (1969, consecutively 1975–77, 1981–82) before retiring in 1985.

Punch Imlach (b. 3-15-18, d. 12-1-87): Hockey coach. 467 wins. With Toronto from 1958 to 1969. Won 4 Stanley Cup championships (consecutively 1962–64, 1967).

Miguel Induráin (b. 7-16-64): Cyclist. Won an unprecedented five consecutive Tours de France (1991–95).

Juli Inkster (b.6-24-60): Golfer. Became only the second woman ever to win all four of the LPGA's modern majors when she won the LPGA Championship on 6-27-99. Finished eagle-birdie-birdie for a 6-under 65 and a four-stroke victory. Inducted to LPGA Hall of Fame in 1999.

Bo Jackson (b. 11-30-62): Baseball OF and Football RB. Only person in history to be named to baseball All-Star game and football Pro Bowl game. 1985 Heisman Trophy winner at Auburn. First pick in 1986 NFL draft by Tampa Bay, but opted to play baseball at Kansas City. 1989 All-Star game MVP. Signed with football's LA Raiders in 1988. Retired 1994 following hip replacement surgery.

Joe Jackson (b. 7-16-1889, d. 12-5-51): Baseball OF. "Shoeless Joe." Third alltime highest career batting average (.356), with .300+ average 11 times. One of the "8 men out" banned from baseball for throwing 1919 World Series. Career span 1908–20 with Cleveland, Chicago.

Phil Jackson (b. 9-17-45): Basketball F-Coach. Coached the Lakers to the 2000 NBA Championship, his seventh as a coach. Won six titles as coach of the Chicago Bulls ('91, '92, '93, '96, '97, '98). Best winning percentage in NBA history (612-208, .746). Spent 13 years as a scrappy forward in the NBA, winning an NBA title with the Knicks in 1973.

Reggie Jackson (b. 5-18-46): Baseball OF. "Mr. October." Alltime leader in World Series slugging average (.755). 1977 Series MVP, hit 3 HR in final game on 3 consecutive pitches. 563 career HR total is sixth best alltime. Led league in HR 4 times. 1973 MVP. Alltime strikeout leader (2,597). In a 12-year period played on 10 first-place teams, 5 World Series winners. Career span 1967–87 with Oakland, Baltimore, New York and California. Inducted to baseball Hall of Fame in 1993.

Bruce Jenner (b. 10-28-49): Track and Field. Set then-world decathlon record (8,634) in winning gold medal at 1976 Olympics. Sullivan Award winner in 1976.

John Henry (b. 1975): Thoroughbred race horse. Sold as yearling for $1,100, the gelding was Horse of the Year in 1981 and 1984 and retired with then-record $6,597,947 in winnings.

Ben Johnson (b. 12-30-61): Track and field. Canadian sprinter set world record in 100 meters (9.83 in 1987). Won event at 1988 Olympics in 9.79, but gold medal revoked for failing drug test. Both world records revoked for steroid usage. Suspended for life after testing positive for elevated testosterone level at an indoor meet in Montreal on 1-17-93.

Earvin (Magic) Johnson (b. 8-14-59): Basketball G. Retired Nov. 7, 1991 after being diagnosed with HIV, the virus that causes AIDS. Returned to Lakers Feb '96 at age 36. Finished career second alltime in assists (10,141), ninth alltime in steals (358). MVP award 3 times (1987, consecutively 1989–90) and playoff MVP in 1980, '82 and '87. Played on 5 championship teams with Los Angeles since 1979. All-Star 8 consecutive seasons. League leader in assists 4 times, steals 2 times, free throw percentage once. Also won NCAA championship and named tournament MVP in 1979 with Michigan State.

Jack Johnson (b. 3-31-1878, d. 6-10-46): Boxer. First black heavyweight champion (1908-15). Career record 78-8-12 with 45 KOs from 1897 to 1928.

Jimmy Johnson (b. 7-16-43): Football coach. Led the Cowboys from 1–15 in 1989, his first season in Dallas, to a 52–17 win over the Buffalo Bills in the Super Bowl XXVII just four seasons later. Also coached Super Bowl XXVIII champion Cowboys. Head coach at Oklahoma State from 1979–83 and Univ. of Miami 1984–88. Johnson's Hurricanes won national championship in 1987. Succeeded Don Shula as Miami Dolphins coach, Jan. '96.

Michael Johnson (b. 9-13-67): Track and field sprinter. First man to win gold medals in both the 200 and 400 at the Olympics (1996). Broke17-year-old 200-meter world record (from 19.72 to 19.66) in '96 U.S. Olympic trials, then further lowered mark to 19.32 at Atlanta. Won 200 at 1991 World Championships, 400 at '93 worlds and both events at the '95 worlds. Anchored U.S. 4x400 team at 1993 World Championship to world record of 2:54.29 with fastest ever relay carry of 42.97.

Walter Johnson (b. 11-6-1887, d. 12-10-46): Baseball RHP. "Big Train." Alltime leader in shutouts (110), second in wins (416), fourth in losses (279) and third in innings pitched (5,914). His 2.17 career ERA and 3,509 career strikeouts are seventh best alltime. MVP in 1913, 1924. Won 20+ games 12 times. League leader in strikeouts 12 times, ERA 5 times, wins 6 times. Pitched no-hitter in 1920. Career span 1907–27 with Washington.

Ben A. Jones (b. 12-31-1882, d. 6-13-61): Horse racing trainer. Trained Triple Crown winner (Whirlaway in 1941). Trained Kentucky Derby winner 6 times, more than any other trainer (1938, 1941, 1944, consecutively 1948-49, 1952), Preakness Stakes winner 2 times (1941, 1944) and Belmont Stakes winner 1 time (1941).

Bobby Jones (b. 3-17-02, d. 12-18-71): Golfer. Achieved golf's only recognized Grand Slam in 1930. Second alltime in major championships (13). Won U.S. Amateur 5 times, more than any golfer (consecutively 1924-25, 1927-28, 1930), U.S. Open 4 times (1923, 1926, consecutively 1929-30), British Open 3 times (consecutively 1926-27, 1930) and British Amateur (1930). Also designed Augusta National course, site of the Masters, and founded the tournament. Winner of Sullivan Award in 1930.

K.C. Jones (b. 5-25-32): Basketball G-coach. Member of 8 straight NBA-championship Boston Celtic teams in his nine season career from 1958–59 through 1966–67. Averaged 7.4 points and 4.3 assists per game. Coached Celtics from 1983–84 through 1987–88, with 308–102 regular season record and 65–37 playoff record with NBA titles in 1984 and '86.

Robert Trent Jones (b. 6-20-06, d. 6-14-00): English-born golf course architect designed or remodeled over 500 courses, including Baltusrol, Hazeltine, Oak Hill and Winged Foot. In the mid-60s five straight U.S. Opens were played on courses designed or remodeled by Jones.

Roy Jones Jr. (b.1-16-69): Boxer. Won silver medal at the 1988 Olympics in Seoul despite dominating his South Korean opponent in the final. Decision commonly called worst in Olympic boxing history. Awarded Val Barker Trophy as outstanding boxer of '88 Games. Won titles at middleweight, super middleweight and light heavyweight as a professional.

Sam Jones (b. 6-24-33): Basketball G. Played 12 seasons with Boston Celtics (1958–69) which won NBA title every year from 1959–66, plus 1968 and '69. Averaged 17.7 points per game. Elected to Hall of Fame in 1983.

Michael Jordan (b. 2-17-63): Basketball G. "Air." Arguably greatest player of all time. Led Bulls to six NBA titles (consecutively, 1991–93; 1996–98). Retired after 1997–98 season with alltime highest regular season scoring average (31.5) and most points scored in a playoff game (63 in 1986). Guided Bulls to an NBA-record 72 wins in 1995–96. Led league in scoring a record 10 seasons; led in steals 3 times. League MVP in 1988, 1991–92, '96 and '98; Finals MVP in 1991–93 and 1996–98. Rookie of the Year in 1985. All-Star team 6 consecutive seasons, All-Defensive team 5 consecutive seasons. Career span 1984–93, 1995–98 with Chicago. Announced retirement on 10-6-93, returned in March 1995. Also College Player of the Year in 1984. Played on NCAA title team with North Carolina in 1982. Member of gold medal-winning 1984 and '92 Olympic teams.

Jackie Joyner-Kersee (b. 3-3-62): Track and field. Gold medalist in heptathlon and long jump at 1988 Olympics and in the former at the 1992 Olympics. Set heptathlon world record (7,291 points) at 1988 Olympics. Also won silver medal in heptathlon at 1984 Olympics and bronze in long jump at 1992 and '96 Olympics. Sullivan Award winner in 1986.

Alberto Juantorena (b. 3-12-51): Track and field. Cuban was gold medalist in 400 meters and 800 meters at 1976 Olympics.

Wang Junxia (b. 1963): Chinese distance runner. Broke four existing world records over six days in Sept. 1993. Broke 10,000 (29:31.78) on 9-8; ran 1500 in 3:51.92 in finishing second to countrywoman Qu Yunxia's world record of 3:50.46 on 9-11; ran 3,000 record of 8:12.19 in heats on 9-12 and lowered it to 8:06.11 on 9-13. Won gold in 5,000 and silver in 10,000 at 1996 Olympics.

Sonny Jurgensen (b. 8-23-34): Football QB. In 18 seasons completed 2,433 of 4,262 pass attempts for 32,224 yards and 255 TDs. Led NFL in passing both 1967 and '69. Career span 1957–1974 with Philadelphia Eagles and Washington Redskins. Elected to Hall of Fame in 1983.

Duke Kahanamoku (b. 8-24-1890, d. 1-22-68): Swimmer. Won a total of 5 medals (3 gold and 2 silver) at 3 Olympics in 1912, 1920, 1924. Introduced the crawl stroke to America. Surfing pioneer and water polo player. Later sheriff of Honolulu.

Al Kaline (b. 12-19-34): Baseball OF. 3,007 career hits and 399 career HR. As a 20-year-old in 1955, became youngest player to win batting title, with .340 average. Had .300+ average 9 times. Played in 18 All-Star games. Career span 1953–74 with Detroit.

Anatoly Karpov (b. 5-23-61): Soviet chess player. First world champion to receive title by default, in 1975, when Bobby Fischer chose not to defend his crown. Champion until 1985 when beaten by Garry Kasparov. Recognized by FIDE as champion in 1994.

Garry Kasparov (b. 4-13-63): Born Harry Weinstein. Chess player. World champion from 1985 to 1993 when stripped of title by FIDE. Won six-game series against IBM computer, Deep Blue, in 1996. Lost to Deep Blue in 1997.

Kip Keino (b. 1-17-40): Track and field. Kenyan was gold medalist in 1,500 meters at 1968 Olympics and in steeplechase at 1972 Olympics.

Jim Kelly (b. 2-14-60): Football QB. Led NFL in passing in 1990 (219 of 346 for 2,829 yards and 24 TDs). Led AFC in passing in 1991. In 11 seasons completed 2,874 of 4,779 attempts for 35,467 yards and 237 TDs. Career span 1983–85 with Houston Gamblers (USFL), 1986–96 with Buffalo Bills. Led Bills to four straight Super Bowls, all losses.

Kelso (b. 1957, d. 1983): Thoroughbred race horse. Gelding was Horse of the Year 5 straight years (1960-64). Finished in the money in 53 of 63 races. Career earnings $1,977,896.

Harmon Killebrew (b. 6-29-36): Baseball 3B-1B. 573 career HR total is fifth most alltime. 100+ RBI 9 times, 40+ HR 8 times. League leader in HR 6 times and RBI 4 times. 1969 MVP. 100+ walks and strikeouts 7 times each. Career span 1954-75 with Washington, Minnesota.

Jean Claude Killy (b. 8-30-43): French skier. Won 3 gold medals at 1968 Olympics. World Cup overall champion 2 consecutive years (1967-68).

Ralph Kiner (b. 10-27-22): Baseball OF. Third to Babe Ruth in alltime HR frequency (7.1 HR every 100 at bats). 369 career HR. Led league in HR 7 consecutive seasons, with 50+ HR 2 times; 100+ RBI and runs scored in same season 6 times; 100+ walks 6 times. Career span 1946–55 with Pittsburgh, Chicago (NL), and Cleveland.

Billie Jean King (b. 11-22-43): Tennis player. Won a record 20 Wimbledon titles, including 6 singles titles (consecutively 1966-68, 1972-3, 1975). Won 4 U.S. singles titles (1967, consecutively 1971-72, 1974), and singles titles at Australian Open (1968) and French Open (1972). Won 27 Grand Slam doubles titles—total of 39 Grand Slam titles is third alltime. Helped found the women's pro tour in 1970, serving as president of the Women's Tennis Association 2 times. Helped form Team Tennis.

Nile Kinnick (b. 7-9-18, d. 6-2-43): College football RB. Won the Heisman Trophy in 1939 with Iowa. Premier runner, passer and punter was killed in plane crash during routine Navy training flight. Stadium in Iowa City named in his honor.

Tom Kite (b. 12-9-49): Golfer. Led PGA in scoring average in 1981 (69.80) and '82 (70.21). PGA Player of Year in 1989, when he won a then-record $1,395,278. Shook reputation for failing to win the big ones by winning 1992 U.S. Open at windy Pebble Beach.

Franz Klammer (b. 12-3-54): Austrian alpine skier. Greatest downhiller ever. Gold medalist in downhill at 1976 Olympics. Also won four World Cup downhill titles (1975–78).

Bob Knight (b. 10-25-40): College basketball coach. Won 3 NCAA championships with Indiana in 1976, 1981, 1987. Coached U.S. Olympic team to gold medal in 1984. 763 career wins and .725 career winning percentage since 2000–01 season. Career span since 1966 with Army, Indiana. Fined and suspended for three games by Indiana University in 2000.

Olga Korbut (b. 5-16-55): Soviet gymnast. First ever to complete backward somersault on balance beam. Won 3 gold medals at 1972 Olympics.

Johann Olav Koss (b.10-29-68): Speed Skater. Norwegian won three gold medals at 1994 Olympics in Lillehammer, with world records in the 1,500, 5,000 and 10,000 meters. Won 1,500 meter gold medal and 10,000 meter silver medal in 1992 Games at Albertville.

Sandy Koufax (b. 12-30-35): Baseball LHP. Cy Young Award winner 3 times (1963, consecutively 1965-66); and MVP in 1963; World Series MVP in 1963, 1965. Pitched 1 perfect game, 3 no-hitters. League leader in ERA 5 consecutive seasons, strikeouts 4 times. Won 25+ games 3 times. Career record 165-87, with 2.76 ERA. Career span 1955-66 with Brooklyn/Los Angeles.

Jack Kramer (b. 8-1-21): Tennis player. Won 2 consecutive U.S. singles titles (1946-47) and 1 Wimbledon title (1947). Also won 6 Grand Slam doubles titles. Served as executive director of Association of Tennis Professionals from 1972 to 1975.

Ingrid Kristiansen (b. 3-21-56): Track and field. Norwegian runner is only person—male or female—to hold world records in 5,000 meters (14:37.33 set in 1986), 10,000 meters (30:13.74 set in 1986) and marathon (2:21:06 set in 1985, a record that still stands). Also won Boston Marathon 2 times (1986, 1989) and New York City Marathon once (1989).

Bob Kurland (b. 12-23-24): College basketball player. 6' 10¼" center on Oklahoma A&M teams that won NCAA titles in 1945 and '46. Consensus All America and NCAA tournament MVP in both 1945 and '46. Led nation in scoring in '46. His habit of swatting shots off rim led to creation of goaltending rule in 1945. Won gold medals in both 1948 and '52 Olympics. Turned down lucrative pro offers, playing instead for Phillips 66 Oilers AAU team.

Michelle Kwan (b. 7-7-80): Figure skater. Three-time U.S. champion (1996, '98, '99), two-time world champion (1996, '98); silver medalist in 1998 Olympics at Nagano.

Rene Lacoste (b. 7-2-05, d. 10-12-96): French tennis player. "The Crocodile." One of France's "Four Musketeers" of the 1920s. Won 3 French singles titles (1925, 1927, 1929), 2 consecutive U.S. titles (1926–27) and 2 Wimbledon titles (1925, 1928). Also designed casual shirt with embroidered crocodile that bears his name.

Marion Ladewig (b. 10-30-14): Bowler. Won All-Star Tournament 8 times (consecutively 1949–52, 1954, 1956, 1959, 1963) and WPBA National Championship once (1960). Also voted Bowler of the Year 9 times (consecutively 1950–54, 1957–59, 1963).

Guy Lafleur (b. 9-20-51): Hockey RW. Won MVP award 2 consecutive seasons (1977–78), playoff MVP in 1977. Scored 50+ goals and 100+ points 6 consecutive seasons. Led league in points scored 3 consecutive seasons, goals and assists 1 time each. 560 career goals, 793 assists. Played on 5 Stanley Cup champions with Montreal from 1971 to 1985.

Curly Lambeau (b. 4-9-1898; d. 6-1-65): Football QB and coach. Quarterback for Packers team in early 20's. Record of 212-106-21 in his 29 seasons (1921–49) as Packer coach, winning three NFL titles in 1929–31.

Jack Lambert (b. 7-8-52): Football LB. Anchored Pittsburgh's famed "Steel Curtain" defense. Selected for Pro Bowl 9 times. Played on four Super Bowl champions (consecutively 1974–75, 1978–79) with Pittsburgh from 1974 to 1984. Elected to Hall of Fame 1990.

Jake LaMotta (b. 7-10-21): Boxer. "The Bronx Bull." Subject of *Raging Bull*, movie by Martin Scorsese, starring Robert DeNiro. Won middleweight title by knocking out Marcel Cerdan in 10 on 6-16-49. Lost title to Ray Robinson, who KO'd him in 13 on 2-13-51.

Career record: 106 bouts; won 30 by KO and 53 by decision; drew 4; and lost 19, 4 by KO.

Kenesaw Mountain Landis (b. 11-20-1866, d. 11-25-44): Baseball's first and most powerful commissioner from 1920 to 1944. By banning the 8 "Black Sox" involved in the fixing of the 1919 World Series, he restored public confidence in the integrity of baseball.

Tom Landry (b. 9-11-24, d. 2-12-00): Football coach. Third alltime in wins (270). The first coach in Dallas history, from 1960 to 1988. Led team to 13 division titles, 7 championship games and 5 Super Bowls. Won 2 Super Bowl championships (1971, 1977). Career record 270-178-6.

Dick (Night Train) Lane (b. 4-16-28): Football DB. Third alltime in interceptions (68) and second in interception yardage (1,207). Set record with 14 interceptions as a rookie in 1952. Career span 1952–65 with Los Angeles, Chicago Cardinals, Detroit.

Joe Lapchick (b. 4-12-00, d. 8-10-70): Basketball C-coach. One of the first big men in basketball, member of New York's Original Celtics. Coached St. John's (1936–47, 1956–65) winning four NIT Tournaments. Coached New York Knicks, 1947–56.

Steve Largent (b. 9-28-54): Football WR. Retired as alltime leader in pass receptions (819), and TD receptions (100). 177 consecutive games with reception, 10 seasons with 50+ receptions and 8 seasons with 1,000+ yards receiving. Career span 1976–89 with Seattle. Oklahoma congressman since 1994.

Don Larsen (b. 8-7-29): Baseball RHP. Pitched only perfect game in World Series history for the NY Yankees on Oct. 8, 1956, beating the Dodgers 2–0; named World Series MVP. Career span 1953–67 for many teams.

Tommy Lasorda (b. 9-22-27): Baseball manager. Spent nearly his entire minor and major league career in Dodgers organization as a pitcher, coach and manager. Managed Dodgers 1977–96, winning 4 pennants and 2 World Series (1981, 1988). Only three men managed one baseball team longer. Named U.S. Olympic baseball coach for 2000 Summer Games.

Rod Laver (b. 8-9-38): Australian tennis player. "Rocket." Only player to achieve the Grand Slam twice (as an amateur in 1962 and as a pro in 1969). Third alltime in men's Grand Slam singles titles (11—tied with Bjorn Borg). Won 4 Wimbledon titles (consecutively 1961-62, 1968-69), 3 Australian titles (1960, 1962, 1969), 2 U.S. titles (1962, 69) and 2 French titles (1962, 1969). Also won 8 Grand Slam doubles titles. First player to earn $1 million in prize money. 47 career tournament victories. Member of undefeated Australian Davis Cup team from 1959 to 1962.

Andrea Mead Lawrence (b. 4-19-32): Skier. Gold medalist in slalom and giant slalom at 1952 Olympics.

Bobby Layne (b. 12-19-26; d. 12-1-86): Football QB. Led Detroit Lions to NFL championships in both 1952 and '53. In 1952 led NFL in every passing category. Career span 1948–62, most with the Detroit Lions. Elected to Hall of Fame in 1967.

Sammy Lee (b. 8-1-20): Diver. Gold medalist at 2 consecutive Olympics (highboard in 1948, 1952); bronze medalist in springboard at 1948 Olympics. Won the 1953 Sullivan Award. Also 1960 U.S. Olympic diving coach.

Jacques Lemaire (b. 9-7-45): Hockey C-Coach. As center for Montreal Canadiens from 1967–68 through 1978–79 was part of eight Stanley Cup winning teams. Over 12 seasons, all with Montreal, scored 366 goals and had 469 assists. Elected to Hall of Fame in 1984. Coached Canadiens 1983-85 and N.J. Devils 1993–98. Named first coach of expansion Minnesota Wild in 2000.

Mario Lemieux (b. 10-5-65): Hockey C. Won MVP award in 1988, '93, '96. Playoff MVP in 1991. Led league in points 5 seasons and goals scored 3 seasons, assists 1 season. Scored 40+ goals and 100+ points 6 consecutive seasons, including 85 goals and 199 points in 1989. Rookie of the Year in 1985. Won 1992–93 scoring title despite sitting out six weeks to receive treatment for Hodgkin's disease, a form of cancer. Sat out 1994–95 season, returned in '95–96 to lead league in scoring and become second fastest player to score 500 career goals. Career span 1984–94, 1995–97 with Pittsburgh. Awarded ownership of Penguins in a settlement in 1999.

Greg LeMond (b. 6-26-61): Cyclist. First American to win Tour de France; won event 3 times (1986, consecutively 1989–90). Recovered from hunting accident to win in 1989.

Ivan Lendl (b. 3-7-60): Tennis player. Second alltime men's most career tournament victories (94). Won 3 consecutive U.S. Open singles titles (1985–87) and 3 French Open titles (1984, consecutively 1985–86). Also won 2 consecutive Australian Open titles (1989–90). Reached Grand Slam final 9 other times.

Suzanne Lenglen (b. 5-24-1899, d. 7-4-38): French tennis player. Lost only 1 match from 1919 to her retirement in 1926. Won 6 Wimbledon singles and doubles titles (consecutively 1919–23, 1925). Won 6 French singles and doubles titles (consecutively 1920–23, 1925–26).

Sugar Ray Leonard (b. 5-17-56): Boxer. Champion in five weight classes: welterweight, junior middleweight, middleweight, super middleweight and light heavyweight. Career record 36-3-1 with 25 KOs from 1977 to 1997, including comeback loss to Hector Camacho at the age of 41. Also light welterweight gold medalist at 1976 Olympics.

Carl Lewis (b. 7-1-61): Track and field. Held world record for 100 meters 9.86; set on 8-25-91 at World Championships in Tokyo. Duplicated Jesse Owens's feat by winning 4 gold medals at 1984 Olympics (100 and 200 meters, 4x100-meter relay and long jump). Also won 2 gold medals (100 meters, long jump) and 1 silver (200 meters) at 1988 Olympics and two gold medals (long jump, 4x100 relay) at 1992 Olympics. Sullivan Award winner in 1981. Won 1996 Olympic long jump gold at age 35, giving him nine career gold medals and making him just the second track and field athlete (along with Al Oerter) to win four golds in a single event.

Nancy Lieberman-Cline (b. 7-1-58): Basketball G. Three-time All-America at Old Dominion. Player of the Year (1979, 1980). Olympian, 1976, and selected for 1980 team, but quit because of Moscow boycott. Promoter of women's basketball, played in WPBL, WABA. First woman to play basketball in a men's professional league (USBL), in 1986. Joined WNBA in 1997, retired in '98 to become GM/coach of the Detroit Shock.

Bob Lilly (b. 7-26-39): Football DT. Dallas Cowboys' first ever draft pick, first Pro Bowl player and first all-NFL choice. Made all-NFL eight times. Career span 1961–74, all with Cowboys. Elected to Hall of Fame in 1980.

Tara Lipinski (b. 6-10-82): Figure skater. In 1998 at Nagano eclipsed Sonja Henie as the youngest individual Winter Olympic champion in history when, at 15, she won the women's figure skating gold medal. Also won U.S. and world championships in 1997.

Sonny Liston (b. 5-8-32, d. 12-30-70): Boxer. Heavyweight champion from 1962 to 1964. Won title by KO of Floyd Patterson on 9-25-62. Lost title when TKO'd by Cassius Clay (Muhammad Ali) on 2-25-64 and then lost rematch on 5-25-65 when KO'd in first round. Career record: 54 fights; won 39 by KO and 11 by decision; lost 4, three by KO.

Vince Lombardi (b. 6-11-13, d. 9-3-70): Football coach. Highest alltime winning percentage (.740). Career record 105-35-6. Won 5 NFL championships and 2 consecutive Super Bowl titles with Green Bay from 1959 to 1967. Coached Washington in 1969. Super Bowl trophy named in his honor.

Johnny Longden (b. 2-14-07): Horse racing jockey. Rode Triple Crown winner Count Fleet in 1943. 6,032 wins.

Nancy Lopez (b. 1-6-57): Golfer. LPGA Player of the Year 4 times (consecutively 1978-79, 1985, 1988). Winner of LPGA Championship 3 times (1978, 1985, 1989). Member of the LPGA Hall of Fame.

Greg Louganis (b. 1-29-60): Diver. Gold medalist in platform and springboard at 2 consecutive Olympics in 1984, 1988. World champion 5 times (platform in 1978, 1982, 1986; springboard in 1982, 1986). Also Sullivan Award winner in 1984.

Joe Louis (b. 5-13-14, d. 4-12-81): Boxer. "The Brown Bomber." Longest title reign of any heavyweight champion (11 years, 9 months) from June 1937 through March 1949. Career record 63-3 with 49 KOs from 1934 to 1951. Defended title 25 times.

Jerry Lucas (b. 3-30-40): Basketball F. Star at Ohio State. *Sporting News* College Player of Year in both 1961 and '62. In 1960 member of both NCAA championship team and gold-medal winning U.S. Olympic team. Averaged over 20 points and 20 rebounds a game for college career. NBA Rookie of Year in 1964. In 11 NBA seasons averaged 17 points a game. Elected to Hall of Fame in 1979.

Sid Luckman (b. 11-21-16, d. 7-5-98): Football QB. Played on 4 NFL champions (consecutively 1940–41, 1943, 1946) with Chicago. Player of the Year in 1943. Tied record with 7 touchdown passes on Nov. 14, 1943. All-Pro 6 times. 137 career touchdown passes. Career span 1939–50. Also All-America with Columbia.

Jon Lugbill (b. 5-27-61): Whitewater canoe racer. Won 5 world singles titles from 1979 to 1989.

Hank Luisetti (b. 6-16-16): Basketball F. The first player to use the one-handed shot. All-America at Stanford 3 consecutive years from 1936–38.

D. Wayne Lukas (b. 9-2-35): Horse racing trainer. Former college basketball coach and quarter horse trainer. Trained two Horses of the Year, Lady's Secret in 1986 and Criminal Type in 1990. Won 1988 Kentucky Derby with a filly, Winning Colors. Won 1994 Preakness and Belmont with Tabasco Cat. Won all three Triple Crown races in 1995, with Thunder Gulch (Kentucky Derby and Belmont) and Timber County (Preakness). Won 1999 Derby and Preakness with Charismatic. Six-race Triple Crown winning streak ended at '96 Preakness.

Connie Mack (b. 2-22-1862, d. 2-8-56): Born Cornelius McGillicuddy. Baseball manager. Managed Philadelphia for 50 years (1901–50) until age 87. All-time leader in games (7,755), wins (3,731) and losses (3,948). Won 9 pennants and 5 World Series (1910–11, 1913, 1929–30).

Greg Maddux (b. 4-14-66): Baseball P. Won unprecedented fourth consecutive Cy Young Award in 1995, when he was 19–2 with a 1.63 ERA and led the Atlanta Braves to their first World Series title. Career span 1986–92 Chicago (NL), 1993– Atlanta.

Larry Mahan (b. 11-21-43): Rodeo. All-Around champion 6 times (consecutively 1966–70, 1973).

Frank Mahovlich (b. 1-10-38): Hockey LW. Winner of Calder Trophy for top rookie for 1957–58 season. In 18 NHL seasons with Toronto Maple Leafs, Detroit Red Wings and Montreal Canadiens, had 533 goals and 570 assists. Played for six Stanley Cup winners. Elected to Hall of Fame 1981.

Phil Mahre (b. 5-10-57): Skier. Gold medalist in slalom at 1984 Olympics (twin brother Steve won silver medal). World Cup champion 3 consecutive years (1981–83).

Joe Malone (b. 2-28-1890, d. 5-15-69): Hockey F. "Phantom Joe." Led the NHL in its first season, 1917–18, with 44 goals in 20 games with Montreal. Led league in scoring 2 times (1918, 1920). Holds NHL record with most goals scored, single game (7) in 1920.

Karl Malone (b. 7-24-63): Basketball F. "The Mailman." Eight-time first-team All-Star. All-Star MVP, 1989, 1993 (shared with John Stockton). All-Rookie team, 1986. League MVP in 1997 when he led Jazz to NBA Finals. Won a second MVP award in '99. Member of 1992 and '96 Olympic teams. Career span since 1985 with Utah.

Moses Malone (b. 3-23-55): Basketball C. Alltime leader free throws made (8,531), fifth in rebounds (16,212) and fifth in points scored (27,409). 3 MVP awards in 1979, consecutively 1982–83; playoff MVP in 1983. 4-time All-Star. Led league in rebounding 6 times, 5 consecutively. Career span 1976–95 with Houston, Philadelphia, Washington, Atlanta, Milwaukee, San Antonio.

Hermann Maier (b.12-7-72): Austrian skier. Recovered from spectacular crash in the downhill to win two gold medals at 1998 Olympics in Nagano. Won 1998 Super G, Giant Slalom and overall World Cup season titles.

Man o' War (b. 1917, d. 1947): Thoroughbred race horse. Won 20 of 21 races 1919–20. Only loss was in 1919 in Sanford Stakes to Upset. Passed up Derby but won both Preakness and Belmont. Winner of $249,465. Sire of War Admiral, 1937 Triple Crown winner.

Mickey Mantle (b. 10-20-31, d. 8-13-95): Baseball OF. Won 3 MVP awards, consecutively 1956–57 and 1962; won Triple Crown in 1956. 536 career HR. Greatest switch hitter in history. Played in 20 All-Star games. Alltime World Series leader in HR (18), RBI (40) and runs scored (42). No. 7 was a member of 7 World Series winners with NY Yankees. Career span 1951–68.

Diego Maradona (b. 10-30-60): Argentine soccer player. Led Argentina to 1986 World Cup victory and to 1990 World Cup finals. Led Naples to Italian League titles (1987, 1990), Italian Cup (1987) and to UEFA Cup title (1989). Throughout 1980s often acknowledged as best player in the world. Tested positive for cocaine and suspended by FIFA and Italian Soccer Federation for 15 months in March 1991. Failed drug test in 1994 World Cup and suspended before second round.

Pete Maravich (b. 6-22-47, d. 1-5-88): Basketball G. "Pistol Pete." Alltime NCAA leader in points scored (3,667), scoring average (44.2) and games scoring 50+ points (28, including then Division I record 69 points in 1970). Alltime season leader in points scored (1,381) and scoring average (44.5) in 1970. College Player of the Year in 1970. NCAA scoring leader and All-America 3 consecutive seasons from 1968 to 1970 with Louisiana State. Also led NBA in scoring in 1977. Averaged 20+ points 8 times. All-Star 2 times. Career span 1970–79 with Atlanta, New Orleans/Utah, Boston.

Gino Marchetti (b. 1-2-27): Football DE. Played in Pro Bowl every year from 1955 to '65, except 1958 when he broke right ankle tackling Frank Gifford in Colts' 23–17 win over the Giants. Career span 1952–66, almost all with Baltimore Colts. Inducted into Hall of Fame in 1972.

Rocky Marciano (b. 9-1-23, d. 8-31-69): Boxer. Heavyweight champion (1952–56). Career record 49–0 with 43 KOs from 1947 to 1956. Only heavyweight to retire as undefeated champion.

Juan Marichal (b. 10-24-37): Baseball RHP. 243 career wins, 2.89 career ERA. Won 20+ games 6 times; 250+ innings pitched 8 times; 200+ strikeouts 6 times. Pitched no-hitter in 1963. Career span 1960–75, mostly with San Francisco. Elected to Hall of Fame in 1983.

Dan Marino (b. 9-15-61): Football QB. Set alltime season record for yards passing (5,084) and touchdown passes (48) in 1984. Has passed for 4,000+ yards 5 other seasons. Player of the Year in 1984. Career totals: 61,361 yards passing, 420 touchdown passes, first alltime in both categories. Career span 1983–00 with Miami.

Roger Maris (b. 9-10-34, d. 12-14-85): Baseball OF. Broke Babe Ruth's alltime season HR record with 61 in 1961. Won consecutive MVP awards and led league in RBIs 1960–61. Career span 1957–68 with Kansas City, New York (AL), St. Louis.

Billy Martin (b. 5-16-28, d. 12-25-89): Baseball 2B-manager. Volatile manager was hired and fired by Minnesota, Detroit, Texas, New York Yankees (five times!) and Oakland from 1969 to 1988. Won World Series with Yankees as manager in 1977 and as player four times.

Pedro Martinez (b. 10-25-71): Baseball P. Became second pitcher to win Cy Young Awards in both leagues when he went 23–4 with a 2.07 ERA for Boston in '99. Dominican righthander went 17–8 with a 1.90 ERA and 305 strikeouts for Montreal in 1997 to win Cy Young award. First pitcher in 25 years to have more than 300 Ks and ERA below 2.00. Started '99 All-Star Game and was named MVP after striking out first four batters.

Eddie Mathews (b. 10-13-31): Baseball 3B. 512 career HR and 30+ HR 9 consecutive seasons. League leader in HR 2 times, walks 4 times. Career span 1952–68 with Milwaukee.

Christy Mathewson (b. 8-12-1880, d. 10-7-25): Baseball RHP. Third alltime most wins (373, tied with Grover Alexander) and shutouts (79); career ERA 2.13. Led league in wins 5 times; won 30+ games 4 times and 20+ games 9 other times. Led league in ERA and strikeouts 5 times each. Pitched two no-hitters. Pitched three shutouts in 1905 World Series.

Career span 1900–16 with New York. Played one game for Reds in 1916.

Bob Mathias (b. 11-17-30): Track and field. At age 17, youngest to win gold medal in decathlon at 1948 Olympics. First decathlete to win gold medal at consecutive Olympics (1948, 1952). Also won Sullivan Award in 1948.

Ollie Matson (b. 5-1-30): Football RB. Versatile runner totalled 12,884 combined yards rushing, receiving and kick returning. Scored 73 career touchdowns, including a 105-yard kickoff return on Oct. 14, 1956, the second longest ever. Career span 1952–66 with Chicago Cardinals, Los Angeles, Detroit, Philadelphia. Also won bronze medal in 400-meters at 1952 Olympics. Elected to Hall of Fame in 1972.

Roland Matthes (b. 11-17-50): German swimmer. Gold medalist in 100-meter and 200-meter backstroke at 2 consecutive Olympics (1968, 1972). Set 16 world records from 1967 to 1973.

Don Maynard (b. 1-25-37): Football WR. Retired in 1973 as the NFL's alltime leading receiver. In 15 seasons, 10 with the New York Jets, caught 633 passes for 11,834 yards and 88 TDs. Averaged 18.7 yards per catch for career. In 1967 and '68 led AFL with average of 20.2 and 22.8 yards per catch. Elected to Hall of Fame in 1987.

Willie Mays (b. 5-6-31): Baseball OF. "Say Hey Kid." MVP in 1954, 1965; Rookie of the Year in 1951. Third alltime most HR (660), with 50+ HR 2 times, 30+ HR 9 other times. Led league in HR 4 times. 100+ RBI 10 times; 100+ runs scored 12 consecutive seasons. 3,283 career hits. Led league in stolen bases 4 consecutive seasons. 30 HR and 30 steals in same season 2 times and first man in history to hit 300+ HR and steal 300+ bases. Won 11 consecutive Gold Gloves; set record for career putouts by an outfielder and league record for total chances. His catch in the 1954 World Series off the bat of Vic Wertz called the greatest ever. Career span 1951–73 with New York and San Francisco Giants, New York Mets.

Bill Mazeroski (b. 9-5-36): Baseball 2B. Hit dramatic 9th-inning home run in Game 7 to win 1960 World Series, first of only two Series' to end on a home run. Also a great fielder, won Gold Glove 8 times. Led league in assists 9 times, double plays 8 times and putouts 5 times.

Joe McCarthy (b. 4-21-1887, d. 1-3-78): Baseball manager. Alltime highest winning percentage among managers for regular season (.615) and World Series (.763). First manager to win pennants in both leagues (Chicago (NL), 1929, New York (AL), 1932). From 1926 to 1950 his teams won 7 World Series and 9 pennants.

Mark McCormack (b. 11-6-30): Sports marketing agent. Founded International Management Group in 1962. Also author of best-selling business advice books.

Pat McCormick (b. 5-12-30): Diver. Gold medalist in platform and springboard at 2 consecutive Olympics (1952, 1956). Also won Sullivan Award in 1956.

Willie McCovey (b. 1-10-38): Baseball 1B. Led NL in HRs three times (1963, '68, '69) and in RBIs twice (1968–69). 521 career homers. .270 career b.a. Hit 18 grand slams. Rookie of Year 1959. NL MVP in 1969. Career span 1959–73 and 1977–80 with San Francisco Giants, 1974–76 with San Diego Padres and 1976 with Oakland A's. Elected to Hall of Fame in 1986.

John McEnroe (b. 2-26-59): Tennis player. Won 4 U.S. Open singles titles (consecutively 1979–81, 1984) and 3 Wimbledon titles (1981, consecutively 1983–84). Also won 8 Grand Slam doubles titles. Third alltime men's most career tournament victories (77). Led U.S. to 5 Davis Cup victories (1978–79, 1981–82, 1992).

John McGraw (b. 4-7-1873, d. 2-25-34): Baseball manager. Second alltime most games (4,801) and wins (2,784). Guided New York Giants to three World Series titles and 10 pennants from 1902 to 1932.

Mark McGwire (b. 10-1-63): Baseball 1B. Broke Roger Maris's 37-year-old single-season HR record with 70 in 155 games in 1998; season also included 162 walks—tied for second most alltime—and seventh alltime best slugging pct of .752. Rookie of the Year in 1987, when he hit rookie record 49 HR. Hit 30+ HR 10 times, 40+ HR five times, 50+ HR four straight years (1996–99). Member of 1984 U.S. Olympic baseball team. Career span 1986–97 Oakland; since 1997 with St. Louis.

Denny McLain (b. 3-29-44): Baseball RHP. Last pitcher to win 30+ games in a season (Detroit, 1968); won 20+ games two other times. Won two consecutive Cy Young Awards (1968–69). Led league in innings pitched two times. Served 2½-year jail term for 1985 conviction of extortion, racketeering and drug possession. Re-entered prison in 1997 on fraud conviction. Career span 1963–72.

Mary T. Meagher (b. 10-27-64): Swimmer. "Madame Butterfly." Won three gold medals at 1984 Olympics (100-meter butterfly, 200-meter butterfly and 400-medley relay). In 1981 set world records in 100-meter butterfly (57.93) and 200-meter butterfly (2:05.96).

Rick Mears (b. 12-3-51): Auto racer. Has won Indy 500 four times (1979, '84, '88, '91) and been CART champion three times (1979, consecutively 1981-82). Named Indy 500 Rookie of the Year in 1978.

Eddy Merckx (b. 1945): Belgian cyclist. Won five Tours de France, including four in a row (1969–72).

Mark Messier (b. 1-18-61): Hockey C. Two-time Hart Trophy (MVP) winnner; won Stanley Cups with Edmonton (1984, '85, '87, '88 and '90) and NY Rangers (1994). Among top five alltime in points, top ten in goals, assists. Career span 1979–91 Edmonton, 1991–96 NY Rangers, 1997– Vancouver.

Cary Middlecoff (b. 1-6-21, d. 9-1-98): Golfer. Also a dentist. Won 40 PGA tournaments, including 1955 Masters and U.S. Opens in 1949 and '56. Won 1956 Vardon Trophy.

George Mikan (b. 6-18-24): Basketball C. Averaged 20+ points per game and named to All-Star team six consecutive seasons. Led league in scoring three times, rebounding once. Played on five championship teams in six years (1949–54) with Minneapolis. Also played on 1945 NIT championship team with DePaul. All-America three times. Served as ABA Commissioner from 1968 to 1969.

Stan Mikita (b. 5-20-40): Hockey C. Won MVP award two consecutive seasons (1967–68). 926 career assists, 1,467 career points. Led league in assists four straight seasons and points four times. 541 career goals. All-Star six times. Career span 1958–80 with Chicago.

Del Miller (b. 7-5-13; d. 8-19-96): Harness racing driver. Raced in eight decades, beginning in 1929, the longest career of any athlete. Won The Hambletonian in 1950.

Marvin Miller (b. 4-14-17): Labor negotiator. Union chief of MLB Players Association from 1966 to 1984. Led strikes in 1972 and '81. Negotiated five labor contracts that increased minimum salary and pension fund, allowed for agents and arbitration, and brought about the end of the reserve clause and the start of free agency.

Art Monk (b. 12-5-57): Football WR. Third alltime in pass receptions (940 for 12,721 and 68 TDs). 106 catches in 1984 was then NFL single season record. Career span 1980–93 with Redskins, 1993–95 with New York Jets, 1995 with Eagles.

Earl Monroe (b. 11-21-44): Basketball G. "The Pearl" played 13 seasons (1968–80) with the Baltimore Bullets and New York Knicks. NBA Rookie of Year in 1968. Member of 1973 NBA championship Knicks team. Averaged 18.8 points a game. Elected to Hall of Fame 1989.

Joe Montana (b. 6-11-56): Football QB. Second alltime highest-rated passer (92.3); fifth in completions (3,409); retired with 40,551 passing yards and 273 touchdown passes. Won 4 Super Bowl championships (1981, 1984, consecutively 1988–89) with San Francisco. Named Super Bowl MVP three times (1981, 1984, 1989). Player of the Year in 1989. Also led Notre Dame to national championship in 1977. Career span 1979–92 with San Francisco, 1993–94 Kansas City. Elected to Hall of Fame in 2000.

Carlos Monzon (b. 8-7-42, d. 1-8-95): Argentine boxer. Longest title reign of any middleweight champion (6 years, 9 months) from Nov. 1970 through Aug. 1977. Career record 89-3-9 with 61 KOs from 1963 to 1977. Won 82 consecutive bouts from 1964 to 1977. Defended title 14 times. Retired as champion.

Helen Wills Moody (b. 10-6-05, d. 1-1-98): Tennis player. Third alltime most women's Grand Slam singles titles (19). Her eight Wimbledon titles are second most alltime (consecutively 1927–30, 1932–33, 1935, 1938). Won seven U.S. titles (consecutively 1923–25, 1927–29, 1931) and four French titles (consecutively 1928–30, 1932). Also won 12 Grand Slam doubles titles.

Archie Moore (b. 12-13-16 d. 12-9-98): Boxer. Longest title reign of any light heavyweight champion (9 years, 1 month) from Dec. 1952 through Feb. 1962. Career record 199-26-8 with an alltime record 145 KOs from 1935 to 1965. Retired at age 52.

Davey Moore (b. 11-1-33; d. 3-23-63): Boxer. Won featherweight title by KO of Kid Bassey in 13 on 3-18-59. Five successful defenses of title, before losing it on 3-21-63 to Sugar Ramos who KO'd him in 10. Died two days after fight of brain damage suffered during fight. Career record: 67 bouts; won 30 by KO, 28 by decision, 1 because of foul; drew 1; lost 7, two by KO.

Noureddine Morceli (b. 2-20-70). Algerian track and field middle distance runner. Set world record for mile (3:44.39) in Rieti, Italy, on 9-5-93. Set world record for 1,500 (3:28.86) on 9-5-92. World champion at 1,500 in both 1991 and '93. Finished a shocking seventh at 1992 Olympics, but won gold medal in '96 at Atlanta. Only man ever to rank first in the world at 1,500/mile four straight years (1990–93).

Joe Morgan (b. 9-19-43): Baseball 2B. Won two consecutive MVP awards in 1975-76. Fourth alltime most walks (1,865). 689 stolen bases. Led league in walks four times. 100+ walks and runs scored eight times each; 40+ stolen bases nine times. Won five Gold Gloves. Second alltime most games played by 2nd baseman (2,527). Career span 1963–84 with

Houston, Cincinnati, San Francisco, Philadelphia and Oakland.

Willie Mosconi (b. 6-27-13; d. 9-16-93): Pocket billiards player. Won world title a record 15 straight times between 1941 and 1957. Once pocketed 526 balls without a miss.

Edwin Moses (b. 8-31-55): Track and field. Gold medalist in 400-meter hurdles at two Olympics, in 1976, '84 (U.S. boycotted '80 Games); bronze medalist at '88 Olympics. Set four world records in 400-meter hurdles (best of 47.02 set on 8-31-83). Won 122 consecutive races from 1977 to 1987. Won Sullivan Award in 1983.

Marion Motley (b. 6-5-20 d. 6-27-99): Football FB. All-time AAFC leader in yards rushing (3,024). Also led NFL in rushing once. Combined league totals: 4,712 yards rushing, 39 touchdowns. Played with four consecutive AAFC champions (1946–49) and one NFL champion (1950). Career span with Cleveland 1946–1953.

Shirley Muldowney (b. 6-19-40): Drag racer. First woman to win the Top Fuel championship, which she won three times (1977, 1980, 1982).

Anthony Munoz (b. 8-19-58): Football OT. Probably the greatest tackle ever. Made Pro Bowl a record-tying 11 times. Career span 1980–92 with the Cincinnati Bengals. Elected to Hall of Fame 1998.

Isaac Murphy (b. 4-16-1861, d. 2-12-1896): Horse racing jockey. Top jockey of his era, Murphy, who was black, won three Kentucky Derbys (aboard Buchanan in 1884, Riley in 1890 and Kingman in 1891).

Eddie Murray (b. 2-24-56): Baseball 1B. 100+ RBIs six seasons and 30+ HRs five seasons. Retired with 3,255 hits, 504 HRs and 1,917 RBI. Alltime leader in RBI by switch hitter. Career span 1977–88, '96 with Baltimore Orioles; 1989–91, '97 with Los Angeles; 1992–93 with New York Mets, 1994–96 with Cleveland; 1997 with Anaheim.

Jim Murray (b. 12-29-19; d. 8-16-98): Sportswriter. Won Pulitzer Prize in 1990. Named Sportswriter of the Year 14 times. Columnist for *Los Angeles Times* 1961–98.

Ty Murray (b. 10-11-69): Rodeo cowboy. All-Around world champion, 1989–94. Set single-season earnings record, 1990 ($213,771). Rookie of the Year, 1988. At 20 in 1989, became youngest man ever to win national all-around title.

Stan Musial (b. 11-21-20): Baseball OF-1B. "Stan the Man." Had .331 career batting average and 475 career HR. MVP award winner 1943, 1946, 1948. Fourth alltime in hits (3,630) and third in doubles (725). Won seven batting titles. Led league in hits six times, slugging average five times, doubles eight times. Had .300+ batting average 17 times, 200+ hits six times, 100+ RBI 10 times, and 100+ runs scored 11 times. 24-time All-Star. Career span 1941-63 with St. Louis.

John Naber (b. 1-20-56): Swimmer. Won four gold medals and one silver medal at 1976 Olympics. Sullivan Award winner in 1977.

Bronko Nagurski (b. 11-3-08, d. 1-7-90): Football FB. Punishing runner played on three NFL champions (1932, '33, '43) with Bears. 2,778 career yards, 1930–37 and 1943 with Chicago.

James Naismith (b. 11-6-1861, d. 11-28-39): Invented basketball in 1891 while an instructor at YMCA Training School in Springfield, Mass. Refined the game while a professor at Kansas from 1898 to 1937. Hall of Fame is named in his honor.

Joe Namath (b. 5-31-43): Football QB. "Broadway Joe." Super Bowl MVP in 1968 after he guaranteed victory for AFL. 173 career touchdown passes. Led league in yards passing 3 times, including 4,007 yards in 1967. Player of the Year in 1968, Rookie of the Year in 1965. Career span 1965–77 with NY Jets, LA Rams.

Ilie Nastase (b. 7-19-46): Romanian tennis player. "Nasty" for his unruly deportment on court. Beat Arthur Ashe to win 1972 U.S. Open title. Won 1973 French Open. Twice Wimbledon runnerup (to Stan Smith in 1972 and Bjorn Borg in '76).

Martina Navratilova (b. 10-18-56): Tennis player. Fourth alltime most women's Grand Slam singles titles (18—tied with Chris Evert). Won a record nine Wimbledon titles, including six consecutively (1978–79, 1982–87, '90). Won four U.S. Open titles (consecutively 1983–84, 1986–87), three Australian Open titles (1981, '83, '85) and two French Open titles (1982, '84). Reached Grand Slam final 13 other times. Also won 38 Grand Slam doubles titles. Her total of 56 Grand Slam titles is second alltime to Margaret Court's. Set mark for longest winning streak with 74 matches in 1984. Also won the doubles Grand Slam in 1984 with Pam Shriver. Won 109 consecutive matches with Shriver from 1983–85.

Byron Nelson (b. 2-14-12): Golfer. Won the Masters (1937, 1942) and PGA Championship (1940, 1945) two times each and U.S. Open once (1939). Won 52 career tournaments, including 11 consecutively in 1945.

Ernie Nevers (b. 6-11-03, d. 5-3-76): Football FB. Set alltime pro single game record for points scored (40) and touchdowns (6) on Nov. 28, 1929. Career span 1926–31 with Duluth, Chicago. Also a pitcher with St. Louis, surrendered two of Babe Ruth's 60 home runs in 1927. All-America at Stanford, earned 11 letters in four sports.

John Newcombe (b. 5-23-44): Australian tennis player. Won 3 Wimbledon singles titles (1967, consecutively 1970–71), two U.S. titles (1967, 1973) and two Australian Open titles (1973, 1975). Also won 17 Grand Slam doubles titles.

Pete Newell (b. 8-31-15): College basketball coach. Despite coaching only 13 seasons, 1947 through 1960, was first coach to win NIT, NCAA and Olympic crowns. Led Univ. of San Francisco to 1949 NIT title, Cal to 1959 NCAA title, and the 1960 U.S. Olympic basketball team that included Jerry Lucas, Oscar Robertson and Jerry West to gold medal. Overall collegiate coaching record of 234–123.

Jack Nicklaus (b. 1-21-40): Golfer. "The Golden Bear." Alltime leader in major championships (20). Second alltime in career wins (70). Won Masters six times, more than any golfer (1963, consecutively 1965-66, '72, '75, '86—at age 46, the oldest player to win event), PGA Championship five times (1963, '71, '73, '75, '80), U.S. Open 4 times (1962, '67, '72, '80), British Open 3 times (1966, '70, '78) and U.S. Amateur twice (1959, '61). PGA Player of the Year five times (1967, consecutively 1972–73, 1975–76). Also NCAA champion with Ohio State in 1961.

Ray Nitschke (b. 12-29-36 d. 3-8-98): Football LB. Defensive signal caller for the great Packer teams of the '60s. Voted Packer MVP by teammates after 1967 season. MVP of the 1962 NFL title game. Career span 1958–72 with Green Bay Packers.

Chuck Noll (b. 1-5-32): Football coach. Led Pittsburgh to four Super Bowl victories in six years (1975, '76, '79, '80). Retired in 1991 after 23 years and 209 wins.

Greg Norman (b. 2-10-55): Golfer. "The Shark" led PGA in winnings in 1986, '90, 1995–96. Won Vardon Trophy twice, 1989–90. Won two British Opens (1986, '93) but is almost as famous for his heartbreaking misses. Beaten at the 1986 PGA when Bob Tway holed out a sand shot and '87 Masters when Larry Mize chipped in from a downhill lie. Blew a six-stroke, third-round lead to lose to Nick Faldo by five shots at 1996 Masters. PGA Player of the Year 1996.

James D. Norris (b. 11-6-06, d. 2-25-66): Hockey executive. Owner of Detroit from 1933 to 1943 and Chicago from 1946 to 1966. Teams won four Stanley Cup championships (consecutively 1936–37, '43, '61). Defensive Player of the Year award named in his honor. Also a boxing promoter, operated International Boxing Club from 1949 to 1958.

Paavo Nurmi (b. 6-13-1897, d. 10-2-73): Track and field. Finnish middle- and long-distance runner won a total of nine gold medals at 3 Olympics in 1920, '24, '28.

Matti Nykänen (b. 7-17-63): Finnish ski jumper. Three-time Olympic gold medalist. Won 90-meter jump (1984, '88) and 70-meter jump (1988). World champion on 90-meter jump in 1982. Won four World Cups (1983, '85, 86, '88).

Dan O'Brien (b. 7-18-66): Track and field decathlete. Won world decathlon title in 1991, '93 and '95. Set world decathlon record of 8,891 in Talence, France, on 9-4/5-92, that stood for seven years. Heavily favored to win 1992 Olympic decathlon but missed making U.S. team when he no-heighted in pole vault at U.S. Olympic Trials. Won gold medal at 1996 Olympics in Atlanta.

Parry O'Brien (b. 1-28-32): Track and field. Shot putter who revolutionized the event with his "glide" technique and won Olympic gold medals in 1952 and '56, silver in '60. Set 10 world records from 1953 to 1959, topped by a put of 63' 4" in '59. Sullivan Award winner in 1959.

Al Oerter (b. 8-19-36): Track and field. Gold medalist in discus at 4 consecutive Olympics (1956, '60, '64, '68), setting Olympic record each time. First to break the 200-foot barrier, throwing 200' 5" in 1962.

Sadaharu Oh (b. 5-20-40): Baseball 1B in Japanese league. 868 career HR in 22 seasons for the Tokyo Giants. Led league in HR 15 times, RBIs 13 times, batting five times and runs 13 consecutive seasons. Awarded MVP nine times; won two consecutive Triple Crowns and nine Gold Gloves.

Hakeem Olajuwon (b. 1-21-63): Basketball C. From Nigeria. Led NCAA in field goal percentage, rebounding and blocked shots in 1984 at Houston. Alltime NBA career leader in blocked shots (3,652 through 1999–00). All-NBA First Team 1987–89, '93–94. League MVP in 1994 as he led Houston to NBA title (repeated in '95). Career span since 1985 with the Rockets. Member of 1996 U.S. Olympic team.

Merlin Olsen (b. 9-15-40): Foolball DT. Part of LA Rams "Fearsome Foursome" defensive line. Named to Pro Bowl 14 straight times. Career span 1962–76, all with LA Rams. Elected to Hall of Fame 1982.

Omaha (b. 1932, d. 1959): Thoroughbred race horse. Won Triple Crown in 1935. Trained by Sunny Jim Fitzsimmons.

Mark O'Meara (b. 1-13-57): Golfer. Won Masters and British Open in 1998. Tour rookie of the year in 1981; won 1979 U.S. Amateur.

Shaquille O'Neal (b. 3-6-72): Basketball C. Led NCAA in blocked shots in 1992, with 5.23 a game; averaged 4.58 over his 90-game, three-year career. Top pick of Orlando Magic in 1992 NBA draft. NBA Rookie of the Year 1993. Averaged 23.4 points, 13.9 rebounds and 3.5 blocked shots in first NBA season. Led league in scoring with 29.3 average in 1994–95. Member of 1996 U.S. Olympic team. Moved to LA Lakers as free agent in July 1996. Led NBA in scoring (29.7 ppg) and was named MVP of the regular season, All-Star game, and playoffs in 1999–2000.

Bobby Orr (b. 3-20-48): Hockey D. Defensive Player of the Year more than any other player, eight consecutive seasons (1968-75). Won MVP award three consecutive seasons (1970-72), playoff MVP two times (1970, '72). Also Rookie of the Year in 1967. Led league in assists five times and scoring two times. Career span 1966–77 with Boston.

Mel Ott (b. 3-2-09, d. 11-21-58): Baseball OF. 511 career HR, 1,861 RBI, .304 batting average. League leader in HR and walks six times each. 100+ RBI 9 times and 100+ walks ten times. Career span 1926–47 with New York Giants.

Jim Otto (b. 1-5-38): Football C. Number 00 started every game (308) in his 15-year career (1960–74) with the Oakland Raiders. Inducted to Hall of Fame in 1980.

Kristin Otto (b. 1966): German swimmer. Won six gold medals for East Germany at 1988 Olympics.

Jesse Owens (b. 9-12-13, d. 3-31-80): Track and field. Gold medalist in four events (100 meters and 200 meters; 4x100-meter relay and long jump) at 1936 Olympics. At the 1935 Big 10 championship set or equaled 4 world record in 70 minutes, including 100 yards, long jump, 220-yard low hurdles and 220 dash.

Alan Page (b. 8-7-45): Football DT. First defensive player to be named NFL Player of the Year, in 1972. Career span 1967–78 with Minnesota Vikings and 1978–81 with Chicago Bears. Now sits on Minnesota Supreme Court.

Satchel Paige (b. 7-7-06, d. 6-8-82): Baseball RHP. Alltime greatest black pitcher, didn't pitch in major leagues until 1948 at age 42 with Cleveland. Oldest pitcher in major league history at age 59 with Kansas City in 1965. Pitched in the Negro leagues from 1926 to 1950 with Birmingham Black Barons, Pittsburgh Crawfords and Kansas City Monarchs. Estimated career record is 2,000 wins, 250 shutouts, 30,000 strikeouts, 45 no-hitters. Said "Don't look back. Something may be gaining on you."

Se Ri Pak (b. 9-28-77): South Korean golfer. Named 1998 LPGA Rookie of the Year for a season in which she won both the first major she entered, the LPGA Championships, and the U.S. Open.

Arnold Palmer (b. 9-10-29): Golfer. Fourth alltime in career wins (60). Won the Masters four times (1958, 1960, 1962, 1964), British Open two consecutive years (1961–62) and U.S. Open (1960) and U.S. Amateur (1954) once each. PGA Player of the Year two times (1960, 1962). The first golfer to surpass $1 million in career earnings. Also won Seniors Championship two times (1980, 1984) and U.S. Senior Open once (1981).

Jim Palmer (b. 10-15-45): Baseball RHP. 268 career wins, 2.86 ERA. Won three Cy Young Awards (1973, consecutively 1975–76). Won 20+ games eight times. Led league in wins three times, innings pitched four times, ERA two times. Never allowed a grand slam HR. Pitched on six World Series teams with Baltimore, including shutout at age 20. Pitched no-hitter in 1969. Career span 1965–84.

Bernie Parent (b. 4-3-45): Hockey G. Alltime leader for wins in a season (47 in 1974). Goaltender of the Year, playoff MVP, league leader in wins, goals against average and shutouts two consecutive seasons (1974–75). Career record 270-197-121, including 55 shutouts. Career 2.55 goals against average. Tied record of four playoff shutouts in 1975. Played on two consecutive Stanley Cup champions (1974–75). Career span 1965–79 with Philadelphia.

Brad Park (b. 7-6-48): Hockey D. Seven-time All Star. In 17 seasons with the New York Rangers, Boston Bruins and Detroit Red Wings (1968–69 through 1984–85) scored 213 goals and had 683 assists. Elected to Hall of Fame 1988.

Jim Parker (b. 4-3-34): Football T/G. Winner of 1956 Outland Trophy as Ohio State senior. Blocked for Johnny Unitas. All-NFL four times at guard, four times at tackle. Career span 1957–67, all with Baltimore Colts. Inducted to Hall of Fame in 1973.

Joe Paterno (b. 12-21-26): College football coach. Third alltime in wins in Division I-A (317 through 1999—the most of any active coach at that level). Has won two national championships (1982, 1986) with Penn State since 1966. Career record 317-83-3, including five undefeated seasons. Has also won 19 bowl games.

Lester Patrick (b. 12-30-1883, d. 6-1-60): Hockey coach. Led NY Rangers to three Stanley Cup championships (1928, '33, '40). Originated the NHL's farm system and developed playoff format.

Floyd Patterson (b. 1-4-35): Boxer. Heavyweight champion two times (1956-59, 1960-62). First heavyweight to regain title, in rematch with Ingemar Johansson. Career record 55-8-1 with 40 KOs from 1952 to 1972. Also middleweight gold medalist at 1952 Olympics.

Walter Payton (b. 7-25-54, d. 11-1-99): Football RB. Alltime leader in yards rushing (16,726). Gained 1,000+ yards rushing in 10 seasons. Third alltime in rushing touchdowns (110). 125 career touchdowns. Gained a record 275 yards on Nov. 20, 1977, against Minnesota. Selected for Pro Bowl nine times. Player of the Year two times (1977, 1985). Led league in rushing five consecutive seasons. Career span 1975–87 with Chicago.

Pelé (b. 10-23-40): Born Edson Arantes do Nascimento. Brazilian soccer player. Soccer's great ambassador. Played on three World Cup winners with Brazil (1958, 1962, 1970). Helped promote soccer in U.S. by playing with NY Cosmos from 1975 to 1977. Scored 1,281 goals in 22 years.

Willie Pep (b. 9-19-22): Boxer. Featherweight champion two times (1942-48, 1949-50). Lost title to Sandy Saddler, won it back in rematch, then lost it to Saddler again. Career record 230-11-1 with 65 KOs from 1940 to 1966. Won 73 consecutive bouts from 1940 to 1943. Defended title nine times.

Gil Perreault (b. 11-13-50): Hockey C. NHL rookie of the year in 1970–71. Played 17 seasons, all with Buffalo Sabres. Scored 512 goals and had 814 assists in career. Elected to Hall of Fame in 1990.

Fred Perry (b. 5-18-09, d. 2-2-95): British tennis player. Won three consecutive Wimbledon singles titles (1934–36), the last British man to win the tournament. Also won three U.S. titles (consecutively 1933–34, '36), French title (1935) and Australian title (1934).

Gaylord Perry (b. 9-15-38): Baseball RHP. First pitcher to win Cy Young Award in both leagues (Cleveland 1972, San Diego 1978). 314 career wins, 3,534 strikeouts. 20+ wins five times; 200+ strikeouts eight times; 250+ innings pitched 12 times. Pitched no-hitter in 1968. Admitted to throwing a spitter. Career span 1962–83 with eight teams.

Bob Pettit (b. 12-12-32): Basketball F. First player in history to break 20,000-point barrier (20,880 career points scored). 26.4 career scoring average; 16.2 rebound avg. MVP in 1956, 1959; Rookie of the Year in 1955. All-Star 10 consecutive seasons. Led league in scoring two times, rebounding once. Career span 1954–64 with St. Louis.

Richard Petty (b. 7-2-37): Auto racer. Alltime leader in NASCAR victories (200). Daytona 500 winner (1964, '66, '71, consecutively 1973–74, '79, '81) and NASCAR champion (1964, 1967, consecutively 1971–72, 1974–75, '79) seven times each, the most of any driver. First stock car racer to reach $1 million in earnings. Son of Lee Petty, three-time NASCAR champion (1954, consecutively 1958–59). Retired after 1992 season.

Laffit Pincay Jr. (b. 12-29-46): Jockey. Second only to Bill Shoemaker in wins. Among the top money-winners of all time, approaching $200,000,000 in career earnings. Won five Eclipse Awards as outstanding jockey. Rode three Kentucky Derby winners; two Preakness winners; and one Belmont winner.

Scottie Pippen (b. 9-25-65): Basketball F. Won six NBA titles with Chicago Bulls (consecutively 1991–1993, and 1996–1998). Tied NBA record with seven three-pointers against Utah in Game 3 of '97 Finals. Member of 1992 and '96 gold medal–winning U.S. Olympic basketball teams. Career span 1987–99 with Chicago, 1999 Houston, since 1999 with Portland.

Jacques Plante (b. 1-17-29, d. 2-27-86): Hockey G. First goalie to wear a mask. Third alltime in wins (434) and second lowest modern goals against average (2.38). Goaltender of the Year 7 times, more than any other goalie (consecutively 1955-59, 1961, 1968). Won MVP award in 1961. Led league in goals against average eight times, wins six times and shutouts four times. Was on six Stanley Cup champions with Montreal from 1952 to 1962 and played for four other teams until retirement in 1972.

Gary Player (b. 11-1-35): South African golfer. Won the Masters (1961, '74, '78) and British Open (1959, '68, '74) three times each, PGA Championship two times (1962, '72) and U.S. Open (1965). Also won Seniors Championship three times (1986, '88, '90) and U.S. Senior Open two consecutive years (1987–88).

Sam Pollock (b. 12-15-25): Hockey executive. As general manager of Montreal from 1964 to 1978 won nine Stanley Cup championships (1965–66, 1968–69, '71, '73, 1976–78).

Denis Potvin (b. 10-29-53): Hockey D. Seven-time All Star during 15-season career (1973–74 through 1987–88), all with New York Islanders. Won Calder Trophy for 1973–74 season. Won Norris Trophy three times. Captained Islanders to four Stanley Cup championships. Elected to Hall of Fame in 1991.

Mike Powell (b. 11-10-63): Track and field. Long jumper broke Bob Beamon's 23-year-old world record at 1991 World Championships in Tokyo with a jump of 29' 4½". Won silver in 1992 Olympics.

Steve Prefontaine (b. 1-25-51, d. 5-30-75): Track and field. Distance runner killed in car accident at age 24. Held every American record from 2,000 meters to 10,000 meters at the time of his death. At age 21, finished fourth in the 5,000 at the 1972 Olympics in Munich after holding lead with less than 600 meters to go.

Annemarie Moser-Pröll (b. 3-27-53): Austrian skier. Gold medalist in downhill at 1980 Olympics. World Cup overall champion six times, more than any other skier (consecutively 1971–75, '79).

Alain Prost (b. 2-24-55): French auto racer. Alltime leader in Formula 1 victories (51). Formula 1 champion four times (consecutively 1985–86, '89, '93).

Jack Ramsay (b. 2-21-25): Basketball coach. Coached 11 seasons at St. Joseph's University, with 234–72 record. Overall record of 864–783 as NBA coach. Coach of NBA champion 1977 Portland Trail Blazers. Elected to Hall of Fame 1992.

Jean Ratelle (b. 10-3-40): Hockey C. In 21-season career (1960–61 through 1980–81) with the New York Rangers and Boston Bruins, scored 491 goals and had 776 assists. Twice won Lady Byng Trophy. Elected to Hall of Fame in 1985.

Willis Reed (b. 6-25-42): Basketball C. Played 10 seasons (1965–74), all with the New York Knicks. Career average of 18.7 points a game. NBA Rookie of Year in 1965. Playoff MVP of both Knick championship teams, in 1970 and '73. NBA MVP in 1970. Elected to Hall of Fame in 1981.

Harold Henry (Pee Wee) Reese (b. 7-23-18 d. 8-14-99): Baseball SS. Played for six pennant-winning Dodger teams. Led NL in runs scored in 1949, with 132. Elected to Hall of Fame in 1984.

Mary Lou Retton (b. 1-24-68): Gymnast. Won one gold, one silver and two bronze medals at 1984 Olympics.

Grantland Rice (b. 11-1-1880, d. 7-13-54): Sportswriter. Legendary figure during sport's Golden Age of the 1920s. Wrote "When the Last Great Scorer comes/ To mark against your name,/ He'll write not 'won' or 'lost'/ But how you played the game." Also named the 1924–25 Notre Dame backfield the "Four Horsemen."

Jerry Rice (b. 10-13-62): Football WR. Alltime leader in touchdowns (184), touchdown receptions (174), receptions (1,267), receiving yards (19,127) and in consecutive games with a TD reception (13 in 1988). Player of the Year in 1987 and led league in scoring (138 points on 23 touchdowns). Super Bowl MVP in 1989 with record 215 receiving yards on 11 catches. Also set Super Bowl record with three touchdown receptions in 1990 and in 1995. Career span since 1985 with San Francisco 49ers.

Henri Richard (b. 2-29-36): Hockey C. "The Pocket Rocket." Won 11 Stanley Cup championships with Montreal. Four-time All-Star. Career span 1955–75.

Maurice Richard (b. 8-4-21, d. 5-27-00): Hockey RW. "The Rocket." First player ever to score 50 goals in a season, in 1945. Led league in goals five times. 544 career goals. MVP in 1947. All-Star eight times. Tied playoff game record for most goals (five on March 23, 1944). Won eight Stanley Cups with Montreal 1942–59.

Bob Richards (b. 2-2-26): Track and field. The only pole vaulter to win gold medal at two consecutive Olympics (1952, 1956). Also won Sullivan Award in 1951.

Branch Rickey (b. 12-20-1881, d. 12-9-65): Baseball executive. Integrated major league baseball in 1947 by signing Jackie Robinson to contract with Brooklyn Dodgers. Conceived minor league farm system in 1919 at St. Louis; instituted batting cage and sliding pit.

Pat Riley (b. 3-20-45): Basketball coach. Most career playoff wins (155). Coached Los Angeles to four championships, two consecutively, from 1981 to 1989. 60+ wins seven times (four times consecutively), 50+ wins four other times. Coach of the Year in 1990, '93 and '97. Led New York Knicks to NBA Finals in 1994, then left three weeks later to become coach and part owner of Miami Heat.

Cal Ripken Jr (b. 8-24-60): Baseball SS-3B. Broke Lou Gehrig's record for most consecutive games played (2,131) on Sept. 5, 1995; streak ended at 2,632 games on Sept. 20, 1998. Set record for consecutive errorless games by a shortstop (95 in 1990). MVP in 1983 and '91. Rookie of the Year in 1982. Hit 20+ HRs in 10 consecutive seasons; elected to 18th All-Star game in 2000.

Glenn (Fireball) Roberts (b. 1-20-31, d. 7-2-64): Auto racer. Won 34 NASCAR races. Died as a result of fiery accident in World 600 at Charlotte Motor Speedway in May 1964. At time of his death had won more major races than any other driver in NASCAR history.

Oscar Robertson (b. 11-24-38): Basketball G. "The Big O." 9,887 career assists; 26,710 points, 25.7 ppg. MVP in 1964, All-Star nine consecutive seasons and 1961 Rookie of the Year. Led league in assists six times, free throw percentage two times. Averaged 30+ points six times in seven seasons, 20+ points four other times. Only player in history to average a season triple-double (1961). Career span 1960–72 with Cincinnati, Milwaukee. Also College Player of the Year, All-America and NCAA scoring leader three consecutive seasons from 1958 to 1960 with Cincinnati. Third all-time NCAA highest scoring average (33.8); seventh most points scored (2,973).

Brooks Robinson (b. 5-18-37): Baseball 3B. Alltime leader in assists, putouts, double plays and fielding average among 3rd basemen. Won 16 consecutive Gold Gloves. Led league in fielding average a record 11 times. MVP in 1964—led league in RBI—and MVP in 1970 World Series. Career span 1955–77 with Baltimore.

David Robinson (b. 8-6-65): Basketball C. *Sporting News* Player of the Year in 1987. Led college players in 1986 in both rebounding (13.0) and blocked shots (5.91). 1990 NBA Rookie of the Year. Led NBA in rebounding 1991 (13.0), in scoring in '94 (29.8) and in blocked shots in '92, when he was named Defensive Player of the Year. Named NBA MVP in 1995. Member of 1988, '92 and '96 Olympic teams. Career span since 1989 with San Antonio. Won NBA title with Spurs in '99.

Eddie Robinson (b. 2-13-19): College football coach. Retired with alltime college record 408 career wins through 1941–97 at Division I-AA Grambling State.

Frank Robinson (b. 8-31-35): Baseball OF-manager. Only player to win MVP awards in both leagues (Cincinnati, 1961, Baltimore, 1966). Won Triple Crown and World Series MVP in 1966. Rookie of the Year in 1956. Fourth alltime most HR (586). 30+ HR 11 times; 100+ RBI 6 times; 100+ runs scored 8 times (led league

3 times). Had .300+ batting average 9 times. Became first black manager in major leagues, with Cleveland in 1975. Career span as player 1956–76. Career span as manager 1975–77 with Cleveland; 1981–84 with San Francisco; 1988–91 with Baltimore.

Jackie Robinson (b. 1-13-19, d. 10-24-72): Baseball 2B. Broke the color barrier as first black player in major leagues in 1947 with Brooklyn Dodgers. 1947 Rookie of the Year; 1949 MVP with .342 batting average to lead league. Had .311 career batting average. Led league in stolen bases 2 times; stole home 19 times. Played on six pennant winners in 10 years with Brooklyn. Elected to Hall of Fame in 1962.

Larry Robinson (b. 6-2-51): Hockey D. Twice won Norris Trophy as NHL's top defenseman. Career span 1972–73 through 1991–92, all but the last three with the Montreal Canadiens. Member of six Montreal teams that won Stanley Cup. Awarded Conn Smythe Trophy as MVP of 1978 Stanley Cup. Coached New Jersey to Stanley Cup in 2000.

Sugar Ray Robinson (b. 5-3-21, d. 4-12-89): Born Walker Smith, Jr. Boxer. Called best pound-for-pound boxer ever. Welterweight champ (1946–51) and middleweight champ five times. Career record: 174-19-6 with 109 KOs from 1940–65. Won 91 consecutive bouts from 1943–51. Fifteen losses came after age 35.

Knute Rockne (b. 3-4-1888, d. 3-31-31): College football coach. Won national championship three times (1924, consecutively 1929–30). Alltime highest winning percentage (.881). Career record 105-12-5, including five undefeated seasons, with Notre Dame from 1918 to 1930.

Bill Rodgers (b. 12-23-47): Track and field. Won the Boston and New York City marathons four times each between 1975 and 1980.

Dennis Rodman (b. 5-13-61): Basketball F. NBA Defensive Player of the Year 1990, '91. First player to win seven consecutive rebounding titles; won NBA titles with Detroit 1989 and '90 and Chicago 1996–98. Career span 1986–93 with Detroit, '93–95 with San Antonio, '95–99 with Chicago, '99 with LA, and '00 with Dallas.

Chi Chi Rodriguez (b. 10-23-35): Golfer. Led senior money list for 1987 ($509,145). Won eight events during PGA career that began in 1960.

Art Rooney (b. 1-27-01; d. 8-25-88): Owner of Pittsburgh Steelers. Bought team in 1933 and ran it until his death in 1988. Elected to Hall of Fame in 1964.

Murray Rose (b. 1-6-39) Australian swimmer. Won three gold medals (including 400- and 1500-meter freestyle) at 1956 Olympics. Also won one gold, one silver and one bronze medal at 1960 Olympics.

Pete Rose (b. 4-14-41): Baseball OF-IF. "Charlie Hustle." Alltime leader in hits (4,256), games played (3,562) and at bats (14,053); second in doubles (746); fourth in runs scored (2,165). Had .303 career average and won three batting titles. Averaged .300+ 15 times, 200+ hits and 100+ runs scored each 10 times. Led league in hits seven times, runs scored four times, doubles five times. 1963 Rookie of the Year; 1973 MVP; 1975 World Series MVP. Had 44-game hitting streak in 1978. Played in 17 All-Star games, starting at five different positions. Career span 1963–86 with Cincinnati, Philadelphia and Montreal. Manager of Cincinnati from 1984 to 1989. Banned from baseball for life by Commissioner Bart Giamatti in 1989 for betting activities. Served five-month jail

term for tax evasion in 1990. Ineligible for Baseball Hall of Fame.

Ken Rosewall (b. 11-2-34): Australian tennis player. Won Grand Slam singles titles at ages 18 and 35. Won four Australian titles (1953, '55, consecutively 1971–72), two French titles (1953, '68) and two U.S. titles (1956, '70). Reached four Wimbledon finals, but title eluded him.

Art Ross (b. 1-13-1886, d. 8-5-64): Hockey D-coach. Improved design of puck and goal net. Manager-coach of Boston, 1924–45, won Stanley Cup, 1938–39. The Art Ross Trophy is awarded to the NHL scoring champion.

Donald Ross (b. 1873, d. 4-26-48): Scottish-born golf course architect. Trained at St. Andrews under Old Tom Morris. Designed over 500 courses, including Pinehurst No. 2 course and Oakland Hills.

Patrick Roy (b. 10-5-65): Hockey G. Won Vezina Trophy three times. Won Conn Smythe Trophy twice (1986, '93). Career span 1984–95 Montreal, '95–Colorado. Traded to Colorado by Montreal in Dec. '95, won '96 Stanley Cup with Avalanche. Second-youngest goalie to reach 300 career wins.

Pete Rozelle (b. 3-1-26, d. 12-6-96): Football executive. Fourth NFL commissioner, served from 1960 to 1989. During his term, league expanded from 12 to 28 teams. Created Super Bowl in 1966 and negotiated merger with AFL. Devised plan for revenue sharing of lucrative TV monies among owners. Presided during players' strikes of 1982, '87.

Wilma Rudolph (b. 6-23-40, d. 11-12-94): Track and field. Gold medalist in 3 events (100-, 200- and 4x100-meter relay) at 1960 Olympics. Also won Sullivan Award in 1961.

Adolph Rupp (b. 9-2-01, d. 12-10-77): College basketball coach. Second alltime in NCAA wins (876) and third highest winning percentage (.822). Won four NCAA championships: consecutively 1948–49, '51, '58. Career span 1930–72 with Kentucky.

Amos Rusie (b. 5-3-1871, d. 12-6-42): Baseball RHP. Fastball was so intimidating that in 1893 the pitching mound was moved back 5' 6" to its present distance of 60' 6". Led league in strikeouts and walks five times each. Career record 246–174, 3.07 ERA with New York (NL) from 1889–1901.

Bill Russell (b. 2-12-34): Basketball C. Won MVP award five times (1958, consecutively 1961–63, '65). Played on 11 championship teams, eight consecutively, with Boston (1957, 1959–66, 1968–69). Player-coach 1968–69 (league's first black coach). Second alltime most rebounds (21,620) and second highest rebounding average (22.5); second most rebounds in a game (51 in 1960). Led league in rebounding four times. Also played on two consecutive NCAA championship teams with San Francisco in 1955–56; tournament MVP in 1955. Member of gold medal-winning 1956 Olympic team.

Babe Ruth (b. 2-6-1895, d. 8-16-48): Born George Herman Ruth. Baseball P-OF. Most dominant player in history. Alltime leader in slugging average (.690), HR frequency (8.5 HR every 100 at bats) and walks (2,056); second alltime most HR (714), RBI (2,211) and runs scored (2,174). Holds season record highest slugging average (.847 in 1920). 1923 MVP. Had .342 career batting average and 2,873 hits. 60 HR in 1927, 50+ HR 3 other times and 40+ HR seven other times; 100+ RBI and 100+ walks 13 times each; 100+ runs scored 12 times. Second alltime most World Series HR (15), including his "called shot" off Charlie Root in

1932. Began career as a pitcher for Boston Red Sox: 94 career wins and 2.28 ERA. Won 20+ games 2 times; ERA leader in 1916. Played on 10 pennant winners, seven World Series winners (three with Boston, four with New York). Sold to Yankees in 1920 (Boston hasn't won World Series since). Career span 1914–35.

Nolan Ryan (b. 1-31-47): Baseball RHP. Pitched record 7th no-hitter on May 1, 1991. Alltime leader in strikeouts (5,714), walks (2,795). League leader in strikeouts 11 times, walks eight times, shutouts three times, ERA two times. 300+ strikeouts six times, including season record of 383 in 1973. 324 career wins. Career span 1966–93 with New York (NL), California, Houston, Texas. Elected to Hall of Fame 1999.

Jim Ryun (b. 4-29-47): Track and field. Youngest ever to run under four minutes for the mile (3:59.0 at 17 years, 37 days). Set two world records in mile (3:51.3 in 1966 and 3:51.1 in 1967) and one in 1,500 (3:33.1 in 1967). Plagued by bad luck at Olympics; won silver medal in 1968 1,500 meters despite mononucleosis; was bumped and fell in 1972. Won Sullivan Award in 1967.

Toni Sailer (b. 11-17-35): Austrian skier. Won gold medals in 1956 Olympics in slalom, giant slalom and downhill, the first skier to accomplish the feat.

Juan Antonio Samaranch (b. 7-17-20): Amateur sports executive. Since 1980, Spaniard has served as president of International Olympic Committee.

Pete Sampras (b. 8-12-71): Tennis player. First player in ATP rankings history to hold No. 1 ranking for six consecutive years. Won seventh Wimbledon title in 2000 to surpass Roy Emerson's record of 12 Grand Slam singles titles.

Joan Benoit Samuelson (b. 5-16-57): Track and field. Gold medalist in first ever women's Olympic marathon (1984). Won Boston Marathon 2 times (1979, 1983). Sullivan Award winner in 1985.

Barry Sanders (b. 7-16-68): Football RB. Alltime NCAA season leader in yards rushing (2,628 in 1988). Won Heisman Trophy in 1988 at Oklahoma State. Entered NFL in 1989 with Detroit and named Rookie of the Year. Gained 1,000+ yards rushing in each of his 10 seasons. Retired abruptly in 1999, ranked second alltime in career rushing yards (15,269). Third player to rush for over 2,000 yards (2,053 in 1997). Led league in rushing in 1990, '94 and 1996–97.

Gene Sarazen (b. 2-27-02 d. 5-13-99): Golfer. Won PGA Championship 3 times (consecutively 1922-23, 1933), U.S. Open 2 times (1922, 1932), British Open once (1932) and the Masters once (1935). His win at the Masters included golf's most famous shot, a double eagle on the 15th hole of the final round to tie Craig Wood (Sarazen then won the playoff). Won 38 career tournaments. Also won Seniors Championship 2 times (1954, 1958). Pioneered the sand wedge in 1930.

Glen Sather (b. 9-2-43): Hockey coach and general manager. As coach, third alltime highest winning percentage (.616). 464 regular season wins. Led Edmonton to 4 Stanley Cup championships (consecutively 1984–85, 1987–88) from 1979 to 1989 and 1993–94. Also played for 6 teams from 1966 to 1976.

Terry Sawchuk (b. 12-28-29): Hockey G. Alltime leader in wins (447) and shutouts (103). Career 2.52 goals against average. Goaltender of the Year 4 times (consecutively 1951–52, 1954, 1964). Led league in wins and shutouts three times and goals against average 2 times. Rookie of the Year in 1950. Tied record of four playoff shutouts in 1952. Played on four

Stanley Cup champions with Detroit and Toronto from 1949 to 1969.

Gale Sayers (b. 5-30-43): Football RB. Alltime leader in kickoff return average (30.6). Scored 56 career touchdowns, including a rookie record 22 in 1965. Led league in rushing and gained 1,000+ yards rushing 2 times. Averaged 5 yards per carry. Rookie of the Year in 1965. Tied record with 6 rushing touchdowns on Dec. 12, 1965. Career span 1965–71 with Chicago cut short due to knee injury. Also All-America 2 times with Kansas.

Dolph Schayes (b. 5-19-28): Basketball player. College star at NYU. In 1960 became first NBA player to reach 15,000 career points. Also first NBA player to play in 1,000 games. Led NBA in free throw percentage three times, and averaged .843 for his career. Over stretch of 10 years played in 706 consecutive games. Elected to Hall of Fame 1972.

Bo Schembechler (b. 4-1-29): Football coach. In 21 seasons at Michigan from 1969–89, had a 194-48-5 record. Overall college coaching record 234-65-8.

Mike Schmidt (b. 9-27-49): Baseball 3B. Won 3 MVP awards (1980, '81, '86). 548 career HR, seventh alltime. Led league in HR 8 times, slugging average 5 times and RBI, walks and strikeouts 4 times each. 40+ HR 3 times, 30+ HR 10 other times; 100+ RBI 9 times, 100+ runs scored 7 times, 100+ strikeouts 12 times and third alltime most strikeouts (1,883). 100+ walks 7 times. Won 10 Gold Gloves. Career span 1972–89 with Philadelphia. Elected to the Hall of Fame in 1995.

Don Schollander (b. 4-30-46): Swimmer. Won 4 gold medals (including 100- and 400-meter freestyle) at 1964 Olympics; won 1 gold and 1 silver medal at 1968 Olympics. Also won Sullivan Award in 1964.

Dick Schultz (b. 9-5-29): Amateur sports executive. Second executive director of the NCAA, served from 1987 to '93. Also served as athletic director at Cornell (1976–81) and Virginia (1981–87).

Seattle Slew (b. 1974): Thoroughbred race horse. Horse of the Year for 1977, when he won the Triple Crown, winning the Kentucky Derby by 1¾ lengths; the Preakness by 1½; and the Belmont by 4. In three-year career from 1976–78, won 14 of 17 starts.

Tom Seaver (b. 11-17-44): Baseball RHP. "Tom Terrific." 311 career wins. 2.86 ERA. Cy Young Award winner 3 times (1969, 1973, 1975) and Rookie of the Year 1967. Fourth alltime most strikeouts (3,640). Led league in strikeouts 5 times, winning percentage 4 times and wins and ERA 3 times each. Won 20+ games 5 times; 200+ strikeouts 10 times. Struck out 19 batters in 1 game in 1970, including the final 10 in succession. Pitched no-hitter in 1978. Career span 1967–86 with New York Mets, Cincinnati, Chicago White Sox, Boston.

Secretariat (b. 3-30-70, d. 10-4-89): Thoroughbred race horse. Triple Crown winner in 1973 with jockey Ron Turcotte aboard. Trained by Lucien Laurin.

Katja Seizinger (b. 5-10-72): German skier. Won downhill gold medals in 1994 at Lillehammer and '98 at Nagano. Won Giant Slalom bronze medal at Nagano. 1998 World Cup champion in downhill, Super G and overall. 32 World Cup victories in downhill and Super G.

Monica Seles (b. 12-2-73): Tennis player. Has won 3 consecutive French Open singles titles (1990-92), 4 Australian Open titles (1991-93, '96) and 2 U.S. Open titles (1991-92). Seles' 1993 season ended on 4-30 when she was stabbed in the back by Gunther Parche while seated during a changeover in a tournament in

Hamburg, Germany; also missed 1994 season. Returned to tennis in 1995, reached U.S. Open final.

Bill Sharman (b. 5-25-26): Basketball G. First team All Star four straight years 1956–59. Led NBA in free throw percentage every year from 1953–57, and in 1959 and '61. All Star Game MVP in 1955. NBA Coach of the Year in 1972, when his Lakers won NBA title. Elected to Hall of Fame in 1974.

Wilbur Shaw (b. 10-31-02, d. 10-30-54): Auto racer. Won Indy 500 3 times in 4 years (1937, consecutively 1939-40). AAA champion 2 times (1937, 1939). Also pioneered the use of the crash helmet after suffering skull fracture in 1923 crash.

Patty Sheehan (b. 10-27-56): Golfer. Won back-to-back LPGA championships, 1983–84. Won 1992 and '94 U.S. Women's Opens, '93 LPGA title. 1983 LPGA Player of Year. Vare Trophy winner in 1984. Qualified for Hall of Fame in 1993.

Fred Shero (b. 10-23-25, d. 11-24-90): Hockey coach. Fourth alltime highest winning percentage (.612, regular season). Led Philadelphia to 2 Stanley Cup championships (1974-75). Also coached NY Rangers. Played defense for NY Rangers, 1947–50.

Bill Shoemaker (b. 8-19-31): Horse racing jockey. Alltime leader in wins (8,833). Rode Belmont Stakes winner 5 times (1957, 1959, 1962, 1967, 1975), Kentucky Derby winner 4 times (1955, 1959, 1965, 1986—at age 54, the oldest jockey to win Derby) and Preakness Stakes winner 2 times (1963, 1967). Also won Eclipse Award in 1981.

Eddie Shore (b. 11-25-02, d. 3-16-85): Hockey D. Won MVP award 4 times (1933, consecutively 1935–36, 1938). All-Star 7 times. Played on 2 Stanley Cup champions with Boston from 1926 to 1940.

Frank Shorter (b. 10-31-47): Track and field. Gold medalist in marathon at 1972 Olympics, the first American to win the event since 1908. Olympic silver medalist in 1976 marathon. Sullivan Award winner in 1972.

Jim Shoulders (b. 5-13-28): Rodeo. Sixteen career titles. All-Around champion 5 times (1949, consecutively 1956–59).

Don Shula (b. 1-4-30): Football coach. Alltime leader in wins (347). Won 2 consecutive Super Bowl championships (1972–73) with Miami, including NFL's only undefeated season in 1972. Also reached Super Bowl 4 other times. Career span 1963–70 with Baltimore, 1970–95 Miami.

Al Simmons (b. 5-22-02; d. 5-26-56): Baseball OF. "Bucketfoot Al" for hitting stance. Named AL MVP for 1929, when he led league with 157 RBIs. Led league in batting average in 1930 (.381) and '31 (.390). Lifetime average of .334 with 307 homers. Career span 1924–44 with a variety of teams, but mostly Philadelphia A's. Elected to Hall of Fame in 1953.

O.J. Simpson (b. 7-9-47): Given name Orenthal James. Football RB. 11,236 career yards rushing. Gained 1,000+ yards rushing 5 consecutive seasons, including then-record 2,003 yards in 1973. Player of the Year 3 times (consecutively 1972–73, 1975). Led league in rushing 4 times. Gained 200+ yards rushing in a game a record 6 times, including 273 yards on Nov. 25, 1976. Scored 61 career touchdowns, including 23 in 1975. Also won Heisman Trophy with USC in 1968.

Sir Barton (b. 1916, d. 1937): Thoroughbred. In 1919, before they were linked as the Triple Crown, became

first horse to win the Kentucky Derby, the Preakness and the Belmont. Won 8 of 13 starts as 3-year-old.

George Sisler (b. 3-24-1893, d. 3-26-73): Baseball 1B. His 257 hits in 1920 season are alltime major league record. League leader in hits two times, banged out 200+ hits six times. Won two batting titles, including with .420 average in 1922; averaged .400+ 2 times and .300+ 11 other times. Had 2,812 career hits and a .340 lifetime batting average. Career span 1915–30 with St. Louis.

Mary Decker Slaney (b. 8-4-58): Track and field. American record holder in 5 events ranging from 800 to 3,000 meters. Won 1,500 and 3,000 meters at World Championships in 1983. Lost chance for medal at 1984 Olympics when she tripped and fell after contact with Zola Budd. Won Sullivan Award in 1982. Competed in 1996 Olympics at age 37.

Bruce Smith (b. 6-18-63): Football DE. Second alltime in NFL sacks. Played in four consecutive Super Bowls with the Bills (1991–94), all losses. Career span since 1985 with Buffalo.

Dean Smith (b. 2-28-31): College basketball coach. Alltime leader in wins (879); sixth alltime highest winning percentage (.776). Alltime most NCAA tournament appearances (27), reached Final Four 11 times. Won NCAA championship in 1982 and '93. Coached 1976 Olympic team to gold medal. Career span 1962–97 with North Carolina. 1997 *Sports Illustrated* Sportsman of the Year.

Emmitt Smith (b. 5-15-69): Football RB. Led NFL in rushing in 1991 (1,563 yards), '92 (1,713 and 18 TDs), and '95 (1,773). Record 25 TDs in 1995. Rushed for 108 yards in 52–17 Cowboys win over Bills in Super Bowl XXVII. Rushed for 132 yards and named MVP of Super Bowl XXVIII, a 30–13 Dallas victory over Buffalo. Career span since 1990 with Cowboys.

Ozzie Smith (b. 12-26-54): Baseball SS. "The Wizard of Oz." May be the best defensive shortstop in history. Holds alltime record for most assists in a season among shortstops (621 in 1980). Career double-play and assist leader among shortstops. 14-time All-Star. Won 13 consecutive Gold Gloves. Career span 1978–96 with San Diego, St. Louis.

Red Smith (b. 9-25-05, d. 1-15-82): Sportswriter. Won Pulitzer Prize in 1976. After Grantland Rice, the most widely syndicated sports columnist. His literate essays appeared in the *NY Herald Tribune* from 1945 to 1971 and the *NY Times* from 1971 to 1982.

Stan Smith (b. 12-14-46): Tennis. Won 39 tournaments in career, including 1972 Wimbledon in 5 sets over Ilie Nastase. Won 1971 U.S. Open over Jan Kodes and amateur version of U.S. Open in 1969. In 1970 won inaugural Grand Prix Masters. Inducted to Tennis Hall of Fame in 1987.

Tommie Smith (b. 6-5-44): Track and field. Sprinter won 1968 Olympic 200 meters in world record of 19.83, then was expelled from Olympic Village, along with bronze medalist John Carlos, for raising black-gloved fist and bowing head during playing of national anthem to protest racism in U.S.

Conn Smythe (b. 2-1-1895, d. 11-18-80): Hockey executive. As general manager with Toronto from 1929 to 1961 won seven Stanley Cup championships (1932, '42, '45, consecutively 1947–49, '51). Award for playoff MVP named in his honor.

Sam Snead (b. 5-27-12): Golfer. Alltime leader in career wins (81). Won the Masters (1949, '52, '54) and

PGA Championship (1942, '49, '51) three times each and British Open (1946). Runner-up at U.S. Open four times, but title eluded him. PGA Player of the Year in 1949. Won Seniors Championship six times, more than any golfer (1964–65, '67, '70, 1972–73).

Peter Snell (b. 12-17-38): Track and field. New Zealand runner was gold medalist in 800 meters at two consecutive Olympics in 1960, '64. Also gold medalist in 1,500 meters at 1964 Olympics. Twice broke world mile record; broke world 800 record once.

Duke Snider (b. 9-19-26): Baseball OF. Career .295 average, 407 HR and 1,333 RBIs. Hit 40+ HR five consecutive seasons and 100+ RBIs six times. Also led league in runs scored three consecutive seasons. Played on six pennant winners with the Brooklyn Dodgers. World Series total of 11 HR and 26 RBIs are NL best. Career span from 1947–64.

Sammy Sosa (b. 11-12-68): Baseball RF. Followed Mark McGwire in eclipsing Roger Maris's single-season HR mark in 1998. Lost HR race to McGwire that season but won MVP with .308 average, 66 HR, 134 runs, 158 RBIs. Career span 1989 with Texas; 1989–91 with Chicago White Sox; 1992– with Chicago Cubs.

Javier Sotomayor (b. 10-13-67): Track and field. Cuban high jumper broke the 8-foot barrier with world record jump of 8' 0" in 1989. Set current record of 8' ½" in 7-27-93 in Salamanca, Spain.

Warren Spahn (b. 4-23-21): Baseball LHP. Alltime leader in games won for a lefthander (363). 20+ wins 13 times. League leader in wins eight times (five seasons consecutively), complete games nine times (seven seasons consecutively), strikeouts four consecutive seasons, innings pitched four times and ERA three times. 1957 Cy Young award. 63 career shutouts. Pitched two no-hitters after age 39. Career span 1942–65, all but last year with Boston Braves, Milwaukee.

Tris Speaker (b. 4-4-1888, d. 12-8-58): Baseball OF. Alltime leader in doubles (792), fifth in hits (3,514) and fifth in batting average (.345). One batting title (.386 in 1916), but .375+ average six times and .300+ average 12 other times. League leader in doubles eight times, hits two times and HR and RBI one time each. 200+ hits four times, 40+ doubles 10 times and 100+ runs scored seven times. MVP in 1912. Career span 1907–28 with Boston, Cleveland.

Michael Spinks (b. 7-13-56): Boxer. 1976 Olympic middleweight champion. Brother Leon was heavyweight gold medalist. Won world light heavyweight title on 7-18-81. Defended it five times and consolidated light heavy titles with decision over Dwight Braxton on 3-18-83. Defended four more times. Won heavyweight title on 9-22-85 in decision over Larry Holmes. Lost title to Mike Tyson in 91 seconds on 6-27-88.

Mark Spitz (b. 2-10-50): Swimmer. Won a record seven gold medals (two in freestyle, two in butterfly, three in relays) at 1972 Olympics, setting world record in each event. Also won two gold medals and one silver and one bronze medal at 1968 Olympics. Sullivan Award winner in 1971.

Amos Alonzo Stagg (b. 8-16-1862, d. 3-17-65): College football coach. 314 career wins. Won national title with Chicago in 1905. Coach of the Year with Pacific in 1943 at age 81. Five undefeated seasons. Career span 1892 to 1946. Only person elected to both college football and basketball Halls of Fame. Played in the first basketball game in 1891.

Willie Stargell (b. 3-6-40): Baseball OF/1B. "Pops" achieved a 1979 MVP triple crown, winning NL regular season, playoff and World Series MVP awards. Led NL in homers in 1971 and '73. Hit 475 career homers. Drove in 1,540 runs. Had .282 career batting average. Played all 21 seasons with the Pirates. Elected to Hall of Fame in 1988.

Bart Starr (b. 1-9-34): Football QB. Played on three NFL champions (consecutively 1961–62, '65) and first two Super Bowl champions (1966–67) with Green Bay. Also named MVP of first two Super Bowls. Player of the Year in 1966. Led league in passing three times. Also coached Green Bay to 53-77-3 record from 1975 to 1983.

Roger Staubach (b. 2-5-42): Football QB. Won Heisman Trophy with Navy as a junior in 1963. Served four-year military obligation before turning pro. Led Dallas to six NFC Championships and two Super Bowl titles (1971, '77). Player of the Year and Super Bowl MVP in 1971. Also led league in passing four times. Career span 1969–79.

Jan Stenerud (b. 11-26-42): Football K. Scored 1,699 career NFL points. Converted 373 field goals in 558 attempts. Career span 1967–79 with Kansas City Chiefs, 1980–83 with Green Bay Packers and 1984–85 with Minnesota Vikings. First pure kicker inducted to Hall of Fame, 1991.

Casey Stengel (b. 7-30-1890, d. 9-29-75): Baseball manager. "The Ol' Perfesser." Managed New York Yankees to 10 pennants and seven World Series titles (5 consecutively) in 12 years from 1949 to 1960. Alltime leader in World Series games (63), wins (37) and losses (26). Platoon system was his trademark strategy, Stengelese his trademark language ("You could look it up"). Managed New York Mets from 1962 to 1965. Jersey number (37) retired by Yankees and Mets.

Ingemar Stenmark (b. 3-18-56): Swedish skier. Gold medalist in slalom and giant slalom at 1980 Olympics. World Cup overall champion three consecutive years (1976–78).

Woody Stephens (b. 9-1-13 d. 8-22-98): Horse racing trainer. Trained two Kentucky Derby winners (Cannonade, who won the 100th Derby in 1974 and Swale in 1984) and five straight Belmont winners from 1982–86, starting with 1982 Horse of the Year Conquistador Cielo.

David Stern (b. 9-22-42): Fourth NBA commissioner. Served since 1984. Oversaw unprecedented growth of league. Owners rewarded him with five-year, $40-million contract extension in 1996.

Jackie Stewart (b. 6-11-39): Scottish auto racer. Fourth alltime in Formula 1 victories (27); Formula 1 champion three times (1969, '71, '73). Also Indy 500 Rookie of the Year in 1966. Retired in 1973.

Payne Stewart (b. 1-3-57, d. 10-25-99): Golfer. Two-time U.S. Open champion (1991, '99), also won 1989 PGA Championship. Killed in plane crash.

John Stockton (b. 3-26-62): Basketball G. Alltime leader in assists (13,790) and steals (2,844). Set single-season assist record of 1,164 in 1990–91. Led NBA in assists a record nine consecutive times, 1988–96. 10-time All-Star, consecutively 1989–97, 2000. Co-MVP (with Karl Malone) of 1993 All-Star Game. Member of 1992 and '96 Olympic teams. Career span since 1984 with Utah.

Picabo Street (b. 4-3-71): Skier. Won silver medal in downhill at 1994 Olympics in Lillehammer and gold in Super G at '98 Games in Nagano. World Cup downhill champion in 1995 and '96. Nine career World Cup victories.

John L. Sullivan (b. 10-15-1858, d. 2-2-18): Boxer. Last bareknuckle champion. Heavyweight title holder (1882–92), lost to Jim Corbett. Career record 38-1-3 with 33 KOs from 1878 to 1892.

Paul Tagliabue (b. 11-24-40): Football executive. Fifth NFL commissioner, has served since 1989.

Anatoli Tarasov (b. 1918, d. 6-23-95): Hockey coach. Orchestrated Soviet Union's emergence as a hockey power. Won nine consecutive world amateur championships (1963–71) and three Olympic gold medals in 1964, '68, '72.

Fran Tarkenton (b. 2-3-40): Football QB. Hall of Famer retired with 342 touchdown passes, 47,003 yards passing, 6,467 pass attempts and 3,686 pass completions. Player of the Year in 1975. Career span 1961–78 with Minnesota, NY Giants.

Lawrence Taylor (b. 2-4-59): Football LB. Revolutionized the linebacker position. Ended 1993 season as the alltime leader in sacks. Also named to Pro Bowl a record 10 consecutive seasons. Player of the Year in 1986. Has played on two Super Bowl champions with New York Giants (1986, '90). Career span 1981–93 with Giants. Elected to Hall of Fame 1999.

Isiah Thomas (b. 4-30-61): Basketball G. Member of Indiana University team that won 1981 NCAA title. Point guard for Detroit Pistons 1982–94. All-NBA First Team 1984, '85 and '86. NBA All Star Game MVP both 1984 and '86. Led NBA in assists (13.9) in 1984–85. Fourth alltime in assists (9,061). Member of Pistons team that won NBA title in both 1989 and '90. GM of Toronto Raptors 1995–97. Named head coach of Indiana Pacers in 2000.

Thurman Thomas (b. 5-15-66): Football RB. Led AFC in rushing both 1990 (1,297 yards) and '91 (1,407). Career span since 1988-00 with Buffalo Bills. Signed with Miami Dolphins in 2000.

Daley Thompson (b. 7-30-58): Track and field. British decathlete was gold medalist at two consecutive Olympics in 1980, '84. At 1984 Olympics set world record (8,847 points) that lasted eight years.

John Thompson (b. 9-2-41): College basketball coach. Coached at Georgetown (1973–99), where he mentored Patrick Ewing, Alonzo Mourning and Dikembe Mutombo. Won NCAA title in 1984, runnerup in '82 and '85.

Bobby Thomson (b. 10-25-23): Baseball OF. Hit dramatic 9th-inning playoff home run to win NL pennant for New York Giants on Oct. 3, 1951. The Giants came from 13½ games behind the Brooklyn Dodgers on Aug. 11 to win the pennant on Thomson's three-run homer off Ralph Branca in the final game of the three-game playoff.

Jim Thorpe (b. 5-28-1888, d. 3-28-53): Sportsman. Gold medalist in decathlon and pentathlon at 1912 Olympics. Played pro baseball with New York (NL) and Cincinnati 1913–19, and pro football with several teams 1919–26. Also All-America two times with Carlisle.

Dick Tiger (b. 8-14-29; d. 12-14-71): Nigerian boxer. Born Richard Ihetu. Two-time middleweight champ, also won light heavyweight title Fighter of the Year for 1962 and '65. Elected to Boxing Hall of Fame 1974.

Bill Tilden (b. 2-10-1893, d. 6-5-53): Tennis player. "Big Bill." Won seven U.S. singles titles, six consecutively (1920–25, '29) and three Wimbledon

titles (consecutively 1920–21, '30). Also won six Grand Slam doubles titles. Led U.S. to seven consecutive Davis Cup victories (1920–26).

Ted Tinling (b. 6-23-10, d. 5-23-90): British tennis couturier. The premier source on women's tennis from Suzanne Lenglen to Steffi Graf. Also designed tennis clothes, most notably the frilled lace panties worn by Gorgeous Gussy Moran at Wimbledon in 1949.

Y.A. Tittle (b. 10-24-26): Football QB. Threw 33 TD passes in 1962 and in '63 led league in passing, completing 221 of 367 attempts for 3,145 yards and 36 TDs. Career span 1948–64, mostly with San Francisco 49ers and New York Giants. Inducted into Hall of Fame 1971.

Jayne Torvill/Christopher Dean (b. 10-7-57/ b. 7-27-58): British figure skaters. Won 4 consecutive ice dancing world championships (1981–84) and Olympic ice dancing gold medal (1984). Won world professional championships in 1985. Won Olympic ice dancing bronze in 1994.

Vladislav Tretiak (b. 4-25-52): Hockey G. Led USSR to gold medals at Olympics in 1972, '76, '84. Played on 13 world amateur champions from 1970 to 1984.

Lee Trevino (b. 12-1-39): Golfer. Won U.S. Open (1968, '71), British Open (consecutively 1971–72) and PGA Championship (1974, '84) two times each. PGA Player of the Year in 1971. Also won U.S. Senior Open in 1990. First Senior $1 million season.

Emlen Tunnell (b. 3-29-25, d. 7-23-75): Football S. Alltime leader in interception return yardage with 1,282 and second in interceptions (79). All-Pro nine times. Career span 1948–61 with New York Giants and Green Bay.

Gene Tunney (b. 5-25-1897, d. 11-7-78): Boxer. Heavyweight champion (1926–28). Defeated Jack Dempsey two times, including famous "long count" bout. Career record 65-2-1 with 43 KOs from 1915 to 1928. Retired as champion.

Ted Turner (b. 11-19-38): Sportsman. Skipper who successfully defended the America's Cup in 1977. Also owner of the Atlanta Braves since 1976 and Hawks since '77. Founded the Goodwill Games in 1986.

Mike Tyson (b. 6-30-66): Boxer. Youngest heavyweight champion at 20 years old in 1986. Held title until knocked out by James (Buster) Douglas on 2-10-90. Convicted of rape in 1992, released from prison in 1995. Lost WBA title to Evander Holyfield on 11-9-96. In one of boxing's more bizarre episodes, disqualified from rematch on 6-28-97 for biting Holyfield's ears.

Johnny Unitas (b. 5-7-33): Football QB. 47 consecutive games throwing touchdown pass (1956–60); 290 career touchdown passes; 40,239 career passing yards. Led league in touchdown passes four consecutive seasons. Player of the Year three times (1959, '64, '67). Career span 1956–72 with Baltimore, San Diego.

Al Unser Sr. (b. 5-29-39): Auto racer. Won Indy 500 four times (1970, '71, '78, '87). Retired with 39 career CART victories. USAC/CART champion 3 times (1970, '83, '85). Brother of Bobby.

Bobby Unser (b. 2-20-34): Auto racer. Won Indy 500 three times (1968, '75, '81). Retired with 35 career victories. USAC champion twice (1968, '74). Brother of Al Sr.

Harold S. Vanderbilt (b. 7-6-1884, d. 7-4-70): Sailor. Owner and skipper who successfully defended the America's Cup three consecutive times, in 1930, '34 and '37.

Glenna Collett Vare (b. 6-20-03, d. 2-2-89): Golfer. Won U.S. Women's Amateur six times, more than any golfer (1922, '25, consecutively 1928–30, '35).

Bill Veeck (b. 2-9-14, d. 1-2-86): Baseball owner. From 1946 to 1980, owned ballclubs in Cleveland, St. Louis (AL), Chicago (AL). In 1948, Cleveland became baseball's first team to draw two million in attendance. That year Veeck integrated AL by signing Larry Doby and then Satchel Paige. A brilliant promoter, Veeck sent midget Eddie Gaedel up to bat for St. Louis in 1951.

Guillermo Vilas (b. 8-17-52): Tennis. Argentine won 50 straight matches in 1977. In '77 won French Open, where he beat Brian Gottfried, and the U.S. Open, where he beat Jimmy Connors. Also won Australian Open twice, 1978–79.

Lasse Viren (b. 7-22-49): Track and field. Finnish runner was gold medalist in 5,000 and 10,000 meters at two consecutive Olympics (1972, '76).

Virginia Wade (b. 7-10-45): Tennis. Beloved in Britain, Wade won three major titles, most notably Wimbledon in 1977, its centenary year, where she triumphed over Betty Stove. Also won 1968 U.S. Open, '72 Australian Open, and doubles titles in '73 at the Australian, French and U.S. Open, all with Margaret Smith Court.

Honus Wagner (b. 2-24-1874, d. 12-6-55): Baseball SS. Had .327 career batting average, 3,415 hits and eight batting titles. Averaged .300+ 15 consecutive seasons. Led league in RBI four times, with 100+ RBI nine times. Third alltime in triples (252) and league leader in doubles eight times. 703 career stolen bases, league leader in steals five times. Career span 1897–1917 with Pittsburgh.

Grete Waitz (b. 10-1-53): Track and field. Norwegian runner has won New York City Marathon a record nine times (consecutively 1978–80, 1982–86, '88). Won the women's marathon at the 1983 World Championship.

Jersey Joe Walcott (b. 10-31-14, d. 2-25-94): Boxer. Heavyweight champion from 1951 to 1952. Won title at age 37 on fifth attempt before surrendering it to Rocky Marciano. Later became sheriff of Camden, NJ.

Doak Walker (b. 1-1-27, d. 9-27-98): Football HB. Led league in scoring two times, his first and final seasons. All-Pro five times. Played on two consecutive NFL champions (1952–53) with Detroit. Career span 1950 to 1955. Also won Heisman Trophy as a junior in 1948. All-America three consecutive seasons with SMU.

Herschel Walker (b. 3-3-62): Football RB. Won Heisman Trophy in 1982 with Georgia. Turned pro by entering USFL with New Jersey. Gained 7,000+ rushing yards and scored 61 touchdowns in three seasons before league folded. Entered NFL in 1986 with Dallas and led league in rushing yards in 1988 (1,514).

Bill Walsh (b. 11-30-31): Football coach. Led San Francisco to three Super Bowl wins, after the 1981, '84, '88 seasons. Career record with 49ers 102-63-1. Developed short-passing game. Returned to Stanford University for 1992 season.

Bill Walton (b. 11-5-52): Basketball C. College Player of the Year three consecutive seasons (1972–74). Played on two NCAA championship teams (1972–73) with UCLA; tournament MVP twice (1972–73). Sullivan Award winner in 1973. NBA MVP in 1978, playoff MVP in '77. Led league in rebounding and blocks in 1977. Career span 1974–86 with Portland, San Diego, Boston.

War Admiral (b. 1934, d. 1959): Thoroughbred race horse. A son of Man o' War, won Triple Crown and Horse of the Year honors in 1937.

Paul Warfield (b. 11-28-42): Football WR. Caught 427 passes for 8,565 yards and 85 TDs. Played on two Super Bowl-winning Miami Dolphins teams. Career span 1964–77, all with Cleveland Browns except for 1970–74 with Miami Dolphins. Inducted into Hall of Fame 1983.

Glenn (Pop) Warner (b. 4-5-1871, d. 9-7-54): College football coach. Second alltime in wins (319). Won three national championships with Pittsburgh (1916, '18) and Stanford (1926). Career record 319-106-32 with 6 teams from 1896 to 1938.

Tom Watson (b. 9-4-49): Golfer. Winner of British Open five times (1975, '77, '80, consecutively 1982–83), the Masters two times (1977, '81) and U.S. Open once (1982). PGA Player of the Year six times, more than any golfer (consecutively 1977–80, '82, '84).

Dick Weber (b. 12-23-29): Bowler. Won All-Star Tournament four times (consecutively 1962–63, 1965–66). Voted Bowler of the Year three times (1961, '63, '65). Won 31 career PBA titles.

Johnny Weismuller (b. 6-2-04, d. 1-21-84): Swimmer. Won 3 gold medals (including 100- and 400-meter freestyle) at 1924 Olympics and two gold medals at '28 Olympics. Also played Tarzan in the movies.

Jerry West (b. 5-28-38): Basketball G. 10 time All-Star; All-Defensive Team four times; 1969 playoff MVP. Led league in assists and scoring one time each. Career span 1960–72 with Los Angeles. Currently executive vice president of Lakers. Also NCAA tournament MVP in 1959. All-America two times with West Virginia. Played on 1960 gold medal-winning Olympic team.

Whirlaway (b. 4-2-38, d. 4-6-53): Thoroughbred race horse. Triple Crown winner in 1941 with jockey Eddie Arcaro aboard. Trained by Ben A. Jones.

Byron (Whizzer) White (b. 6-8-17): Football RB. Led NFL in rushing 2 times (Pittsburgh in 1938, Detroit in '40). Led NCAA in scoring and rushing with Colorado in 1937; named All-America. Supreme Court justice 1962–93.

Reggie White (b. 12-19-62): Football DE. Alltime leader in sacks. Signed with Green Bay in 1993 for $17 million over four years. Member of Green Bay's 1997 Super Bowl championship team. Career span: 1984 with Memphis Showboats (USFL), 1985–92 with Philadelphia, 1993–99 with Packers, 2000– with Carolina.

Charles Whittingham (b. 4-13-13 d. 4-20-99): Thoroughbred race horse trainer. "Bald Eagle" after losing hair to tropical disease in World War II. Led yearly earnings list for trainers from 1970–73 consecutively; in 1975; and in 1981–82 consecutively. Won three Eclipse Awards and trained two Horses of the Year (Ack Ack in 1971 and Ferdinand in '87).

Kathy Whitworth (b. 9-27-39): Golfer. Alltime LPGA leader with 88 tour victories, including six majors. Won LPGA Championship in 1967, '71 and '75. Won Titleholders Championship (extinct major) in 1965 and '66. Won Western Open (extinct major) in 1967. Won Vare Trophy every year from 1965–72, except '68. LPGA Player of Year from 1966–69 and 1971–73.

Hoyt Wilhelm (b. 7-26-23): Baseball RHP. Hall of Famer. Threw knuckleball until age 48. Alltime pitching leader in games (1,070). Career 2.52 ERA, 227 saves. Hit home run in his first at bat (never hit another) and pitched no-hitter in 1958. Career span 1952–72 with 9 teams.

Bud Wilkinson (b. 4-23-15 d. 2-9-94): Football coach. Alltime NCAA leader in consecutive wins (47, 1953–57). Won three national championships (1950, consecutively 1955–56) with Oklahoma, where he coached from 1947 to 1963. Won Orange Bowl 4 times and Sugar Bowl two times. Career record 145-29-4, including four undefeated seasons. Also coached with St. Louis of NFL in 1978–79.

Billy Williams (b. 6-15-38): Baseball OF. "Sweet Swinging." NL Rookie of the Year for 1961. Hit 426 career home runs. Drove in 1,475 runs. Lifetime average of .290. Named to six NL All Star teams. Career span 1959–74 with Chicago Cubs, 1975–76 with Oakland A's. Elected to Hall of Fame in 1987.

Ted Williams (b. 8-30-18): Baseball OF. "The Splendid Splinter." Last player to hit .400 (.406 in 1941). MVP in 1946, '49 and Triple Crown winner in 1942, '47. Sixth alltime highest batting average (.344), third most walks (2,019) and second-highest slugging average (.634). 521 career HR. League leader in batting average and runs scored six times each, RBI and HR four times each. Had .300+ average 15 consecutive seasons; 100+ RBI and runs scored nine times each; 30+ HR eight times; and 100+ walks 11 times. Lost nearly five seasons to military service. Career span 1939–42 and 1946–60 with Boston.

Hack Wilson (b. 4-26-1900; d. 11-23-48): Baseball OF. Stood 5' 6" but weighed 210. Had five incredible seasons 1926–30. Best was 1930 when he hit .356, scored 146 runs, hit a NL record 56 homers and drove in 190, which is still the major league record. Career span 1923–34 with several teams. Elected to Hall of Fame in 1979.

Dave Winfield (b. 10-3-51): Baseball OF. Drafted out of Univ. of Minnesota for both pro basketball and football. Led NL in RBIs in 1979 (118). In 1992, first 40-year-old to get 100+ RBIs, with 108. Hit clutch double to win 1992 World Series. Got 3,000th hit, off Dennis Eckersley, on 9-16-93. Career span 1973–80 with San Diego; 1981–90 with Yankees; 1990–91 with California; 1992 with Toronto; 1993–94 with Minnesota; and 1995 with Cleveland.

Major W.C. Wingfield (b. 10-16-1833, d. 4-18-12): British tennis pioneer. Credited with inventing the game of tennis, which he called "Sphairistike" or "sticky" and patented in February 1874.

Colonel Matt Winn (b. 6-30-1861, d. 10-6-49): General manager of Churchill Downs from 1904 until his death; made Kentucky Derby premier U.S. race.

Katarina Witt (b. 12-3-65): East German figure skater. Gold medalist at 1984 and '88 Olympics. Also world champion four times (consecutively 1984–85, 1987–88).

John Wooden (b. 10-14-10): College basketball coach. First member of basketball Hall of Fame as coach and player. Coached UCLA to 10 NCAA championships in 12 years (consecutively 1964–65, 1967–73, 1975). Alltime winning streak 88 games (1971–74). 664 career wins and fifth alltime highest winning percentage (.804). Career span 1949–75 with UCLA. 1932 College Player of the Year at Purdue.

Tiger Woods (b. 12-30-75): Golfer. Won three straight U.S. Junior Amateur titles (1991–93), three straight U.S. Amateur titles (1994–96), then took the PGA tour by storm, winning six of his first 21 tournaments, including the 1997 Masters. There he was the youngest winner ever, scoring a record low 270, and winning by the widest margin in tournament history, 12 strokes. 1996 *Sports Illustrated* Sportsman of the Year. Became the youngest player to win all four major

tournaments ('99 PGA, '00 U.S. Open, '00 British Open). Holds tournament record for best scores at Masters, U.S. Open, and British Open.

Mickey Wright (b. 2-14-35): Golfer. Second alltime in career wins (82) and major championships (13; tied with Louise Suggs). Won U.S. Open four times (consecutively 1958-59, 1961, 1964), LPGA Championship four times (1958, consecutively 1960–61, '63), Western Open three times (consecutively 1962–63, '66).

Kristi Yamaguchi (b.7-12-71): Figure skater. Olympic champion in 1992. Back-to-back world champion (1991–92).

Cale Yarborough (b. 3-27-40): Auto racer. Won Daytona 500 four times (1968, '77, consecutively 1983–84). 83 career victories. Also NASCAR champion three consecutive years (1976–78).

Carl Yastrzemski (b. 8-22-39): Baseball OF. "Yaz." 3,419 career hits, 452 HR. 1967 MVP and Triple Crown winner. Three batting titles, including .301 in 1968, lowest ever to win. Second alltime in games played (3,308) and fifth in walks (1,845). Career span 1961–83 with Boston.

Cy Young (b. 3-29-1867, d. 11-4-55): Baseball RHP. Alltime leader in wins (511), losses (315), innings pitched (7,354⅔) and complete games (749); fourth in shutouts (76). Had 2.63 career ERA. Pitched three no-hitters, including a perfect game in 1904. Career span 1890–1911 with Cleveland, Boston.

Steve Young (b. 10-11-61): Football QB. Highest rated passer in NFL history, with 96.8 rating. Led 49ers to victory in Super Bowl XXIX of which he was MVP. Two-time NFL MVP (1992 and '94). Career span 1984 with LA Express of the USFL, 1985–86 with Tampa Bay, and 1987–00 with San Francisco.

Robin Yount (b. 9-16-55): Baseball OF/SS. Became Brewers shortstop at 18. Won 1982 AL MVP when he hit .331 with 29 homers. 3,142 career hits. Shoulder injury caused move to outfield in 1984. Career span 1974–93, all with the Brewers. Elected to Hall of Fame 1999.

Steve Yzerman (b. 5-9-65): Hockey C. Won back-to-back Stanley Cups with Red Wings (1997, '98). Won Conn Smythe trophy in 1998. Scored 100+ points six consecutive seasons (1987–88 through 1992–93). Career span since 1983 with Detroit.

Babe Didrikson Zaharias (b. 6-26-14, d. 9-27-56): Sportswoman. Gold medalist in 80-meter hurdles and javelin throw at 1932 Olympics; also won silver medal in high jump (her gold medal jump was disallowed for using the then-illegal western roll). Became a golfer in 1935 and won 12 major titles, including U.S. Open three times (1948, 1950, 1954—a year after cancer surgery). Also helped found the LPGA in 1949.

Tony Zale (b. 5-29-13, d. 3-20-97): Boxer. Born Anthony Zaleski. "The Man of Steel." Two-time middleweight champ. Fought Rocky Graziano for title three times in 21 months, winning twice. 67-18-2 with 44 KOs. Elected to Boxing Hall of Fame 1958.

Emil Zatopek (b. 9-19-22): Track and field. Czech runner became only athlete to win gold medal in 5,000 and 10,000 meters and marathon, at 1952 Olympics. Also gold medalist in 10,000 meters at '48 Olympics.

Zinedine Zidane (b. 6-23-72): French soccer player. "Zizou." Led France to 1998 World Cup title; scored two goals in 3–0 win over Brazil in the final. Led Juventus to 1998 Italian League title and to '98 European Cup final. 1998 FIFA World Player of the Year. Led France to 2000 European Championship.

ANDY HAYT

Obituaries

Obituaries

Sid Abel, 81, hockey player. The center on the Detroit Red Wings' fabled "Production Line" (featuring Gordie Howe on the right wing and Ted Lindsay on the left), Abel won the Hart Trophy as the league MVP in the 1948–49 season. The year 2000 brought the 50 year anniversary of the Production Line which finished 1-2-3 in the NHL scoring race. Lindsay had 78 points in 69 games, Abel had 69 and Howe, 68. Old Boot Nose, as he was nicknamed, was considered a Detroit institution, having spent 32 years as a player and a coach for the Red Wings (he still ranks No.11 in all-time scoring). Abel racked up 472 points during his career (189 goals, 283 assists) in 613 games. But Gordie Howe remembered his friend even more for his strong leadership qualities. After his retirement from the NHL, Abel became a coach, general manager and hockey announcer. In Farmington Hills, MI, of cancer, February 8, 2000.

Gary Adams, 56, golf-club innovator. Known as "the father of the metal wood," Adams founded the Taylor Made Golf Co. in 1979, using his pioneering metal woods to create a leading company in the field. He also began the Founders Club Golf Co. and McHenry Metals, two other golf equipment manufacturing firms, serving as their CEO and chairman. In McHenry, IL, of cancer, January 2, 2000.

Stanley George (Frenchy) Bordagaray, 90, baseball player. Bordagaray played 11 years in the majors from 1934–45 with a lifetime batting average of .283. During the 1935 season, he became known for the flamboyant mustache he grew for a bit part in the movie *The Prisoner of Shark Island*. A few months into the season, under pressure from his coach, Frenchy finally shaved it off. Facial hair was not seen on the diamond for another three decades. Bordagaray also played with the Cardinals, the Reds and Yankees before returning to the Dodgers from 1942–45. In Port Orchard, WA, of natural causes, April 13, 2000.

Bill Bowerman, 88, track coach. Bowerman made major contributions to track and field as a coach, inventor, entrepreneur and promoter. During his 24 years as the University of Oregon's track coach, he led the Ducks to four NCAA titles, and his runners to 24 individual titles. Bowerman also served as the U.S. team's track coach during the 1972 Olympics. In the late '60s, he and Phil Knight (a former Oregon miler) pooled $500 each to cofound the Nike company. The company's first model of running shoes was designed by Bowerman and included an innovative "waffle iron" sole, still used in current designs. Bowerman is also credited with fueling America's running boom with his book on jogging and by espousing fitness for all, regardless of age. He turned Eugene, Ore., into the unofficial track capital of the U.S. (it was the site of three Olympic trials). A multimillionaire, Bowerman was also a generous donor to Oregon's athletics programs. In Fossil, OR, of natural causes, December 24, 1999.

Don Budge, 84, tennis player. With his powerful whiplash backhand, Budge was the first tennis player to win all four major championships (Australian, French, Wimbledon and United States) in one year— 1938. Only four players since then have matched his feat.

SI's Frank Deford writes:

"It's doubtful that any American athlete who survived World War II was as penalized by the conflict as was Don Budge who died last week at 84. When the war came, Budge was in his mid-20s, at the height of his powers. In 1938 he had won the Grand Slam, demonstrating a game without weakness, with a backhand that's generally considered as close to perfection as a stroke has ever been. Then he turned pro, whipped the estimable Ellsworth Vines and Fred Perry and, at that point, might well have become the finest player, before or since, to hit a tennis ball.

"The war all but shut down the sport, and Budge volunteered for the Army. One cool morning, while running an obstacle course, he tore a muscle in his right shoulder. Neither his serve nor his overhead was ever the same. Effectively his career was finished; certainly his majesty was.

"The most storied moment in tennis still belongs to Budge, though. In 1937, just before he and Gottfried von Cramm stepped onto the court in the Davis Cup semifinal at Wimbledon (the tie was held at a neutral site), Hitler telephoned Cramm. 'Ja, mein Führer,' Cramm said repeatedly into the phone. His victory would most likely have handed the Cup to Nazi Germany and kept it there throughout the war, possibly to be lost forever. But with the magnificent match in Cramm's grasp, 4–1 in the fifth set, Budge changed tactics, started taking the ball on the rise and won 6–8, 5–7, 6–4, 6–2, 8–6.

"Budge would have turned pro after that year, but he dreamed up the concept of winning the championships of the four nations that had won the Davis Cup— Australia, England, France, and the U.S. Thus did Budge create the Grand Slam. and he positively breezed. I asked him once to describe the highlights. 'You know, not a whole lot happened that year,' he said. Budge was just too good. In fact, what he remembered most about his Grand Slam was earning a private concert from the great cellist Pablo Casals after winning the French."

In Scranton, PA, of injuries sustained in a auto accident, January 26, 2000.

Jim Davis, 103, motorcycle racer. Elected to the Motorcycle Hall of Fame in Pickerington, Ohio, in 1998, Davis competed in 71 national events, riding for the Harley-Davidson and Indian factory teams in both board-track and dirt-track races. In the first event Davis ever entered, he won a pair of riding goggles and a quart of oil. In Daytona Beach, FL, of natural causes, February 6, 2000.

Tom Fears, 76, football player. Hall of Famer Fears was known as one of the first great receivers in professional football history. The former Los Angeles Rams player was a native Californian who starred on both Santa Clara's and UCLA's teams. In his first three NFL seasons (1948–50) Fears led the league in receptions. His NFL record of 18 catches in a 1950 game against Green Bay still stands. In Palm Desert, CA, from complications of Alzheimer's disease, January 4, 2000.

Colby Goodwin, 32, rodeo steer roper. While competing in the Oklahoma City National Finals steer roping competition, Goodwin's horse tripped on a piece of rope and reared, falling backward onto the steer roper from Texas. In Oklahoma City, of head injuries sustained during a rodeo, October 31, 1999.

Mitch Halpern, 33, boxing referee. Halpern refereed 51 world title fights, gaining renown after his excellent refereeing during the 1996 Evander Holyfield–Mike Tyson bout. Considered one of the best boxing referees in the world, Halpern presided over many famous bouts, among them: Johnny Tapia–Danny Romero, Holyfield–Michael Moorer II, Oscar De La Hoya–Ike Quartey, De La Hoya–Felix Trinidad, Lennox Lewis–Holyfield II, Erik Morales–Marco Antonio Berrera, and Trinidad–David Reid. In Las Vegas, of self-inflicted gunshot wounds to the head, August 20, 2000.

Kenny Irwin, 30, race car driver. A native of Indianapolis, Irwin began racing at the age of five and quickly progressed to tackle sprint cars, trucks and stock cars. By the time a practice run at the New Hampshire International Speedway ended his life, Irwin had qualified twice for the Brickyard 500. In 1996 he became the National Midget Series Champion and two years later went on to become NASCAR's 1998 Winston Cup Rookie of the Year. In Loudoun, NH, of head injuries incurred during a crash, July 7, 2000.

Robert Trent Jones Sr., 93, golf course architect. This legendary golf course architect was known for designing some of the most challenging and difficult courses in the world. Nicknamed "The Open Doctor," Jones created more than 400 courses across every continent except Antarctica and Australia. He also helped to transform golf-course architecture into a high-profile, prestigious profession, and became a steady fixture at the U.S. Open after redesigning six of their courses and building two more from scratch.

SI writes:

"[He] was one of the most prolific golf course architects in the history of the game. He designed and rebuilt more than 500 courses in 45 states and 29 countries, and was the father of the so-called heroic school of course architecture. Here are some highlights from his career, which spanned seven decades.

" *1926* As a student at Cornell, he puts together a curriculum that becomes the standard for course designers—landscape architecture, agronomy, horticulture, surveying and hydraulics.

" *1948* In building the Dunes Course in Myrtle Beach, S.C., he combines large-scale fairways and greens with multiple hazards, encouraging a high ratio of risk-reward shots. This style of design comes to be known as heroic architecture. The 13th at the Dunes—a long par-5 along a crescent-shaped water hazard—is a Jones classic.

" *1950* He dams Rae's Creek at Augusta National, transforming numbers 11 and 16 into dramatic water holes.

" *1951* Jones's renovation of Oakland Hills for the U.S. Open defines the modern major championship venue. He moves outmoded bunkers into landing areas and increases the severity of the greens. Golfers must play a longer, more aerial game.

" *1951* A profile of Jones, written by Herbert Warren Wind in the *The New Yorker*, characterizes a course architect for the first time as a highly trained creative force in the game.

" *1952* Under fire for the changes he made to the par-3

4th at Baltusrol, Jones aces the hole during a round with members and quips, 'I think the hole is eminently fair.'

" *1964* Mauna Kea in Kohala Coast was the first of the great Hawaiian resort courses. Built on 'the most challenging terrain' Jones ever saw, Mauna Kea is among the world's finest tropical courses.

" *1966* He completes his masterpiece, Spyglass Hill on California's Monterey Peninsula. The first five holes are among the finest ever built on dunesland.

" *1985* Ballybunion New, on undulating Irish linksland, is called too extreme. Jones's most generous critics call it a magnificent failure.

" *1999* Waking from a coma and finding his two course-architect sons, Rees and Robert Jr., at his bedside, Jones is told he has had a stroke. 'Do I have to count it?' he asks."

In Ft. Lauderdale, FL, of complications from a stroke, June 14, 2000.

Larry Kelly, 85, football player. Kelly was the first formal winner of the Heisman Trophy in 1936. (In 1935 Jay Berwanger of the University of Chicago had been awarded the "Downtown Athletic Club Trophy" as it was then called.) Kelly, a receiver, was awarded the Heisman after helping Yale to a 7–1 record and being named All-America. In December 1999 Kelly auctioned off his Heisman Trophy for $328,110. He was the second winner to do so—O.J. Simpson had auctioned his off in February of 1999 for $100,000 less. In Hightstown, NJ, of a self-inflicted gunshot wound, June 27, 2000.

Jonathan Kiser, 22, steeplechase jockey. Kiser was one of America's top steeplechase riders when he suffered a freak accident, falling from a rope swing at his sister's home. Known as the "Tiger Woods of the jump jockeys," Kiser was named the National Steeplechase Association's leading jockey in 1997 and 1999. He was considered a natural, a true horseman and keen strategist who had already chalked up 16 victories halfway through the season—well on his way to a third title. In Whiteford, MD, of head injuries, July 21, 2000.

Vladimir Kondrashin, 70, Soviet basketball coach. Kondrashin is best known as the coach of the 1972 Soviet Olympic team that upset the U.S. for the gold medal in one of the most controversial games ever. After an international official ordered two seconds restored to the game clock, the Soviet Union used the extra time to score the winning bucket in a dubious 51–50 win. The victory ended the U.S. team's 62-game winning streak and was the first Olympic loss for the U.S. In Moscow, of cancer, December 23, 1999.

Tom Landry, 75, football coach. Hall of Fame coach of the Dallas Cowboys for the first 29 years of the franchise, Landry led the team to five Super Bowls, winning two. Pacing the sidelines in his trademark suit and fedora, Landry won 270 games (more than any other NFL coach except George Halas and Don Shula). From 1966 to 1985, Landry's teams won 13 division titles and had winning records every season.

SI's Paul Zimmerman writes:

"Tom Landry was a New York favorite before he ever put X's and O's to paper. In 1949 he played left cornerback—defensive halfback, as it was called in those days—for the Brooklyn–New York Yankees of the old All-America Conference, and he played the position with a roughneck style that the fans loved. Picture an early-day Mel Blount, and you've got Landry. A year later folks around the NFL learned that there was a brain to go with the muscle. Landry played that season for the Giants, who were coached by Steve Owen. After watching the Browns, New York's next opponent, annihilate the defending champion Eagles in Philadelphia, Owen returned with a new defensive formation that he had devised, the 4–3. The 26-year-old Landry was the man he chose to break down the scheme on the blackboard for the team. 'He can explain it better than I can,' Owen said…Six years later, in 1956, Landry coached the defense and Vince Lombardi oversaw the offense, giving the NFL champion Giants the most dynamic pair of assistant coaches ever to grace one staff. A visitor of the Giants that season described a walk down the corridor where the coaches' offices were located. 'The first office I passed belonged to Landry,' he said. 'He was busy putting in a defense, running his projector, studying film. The next office was Vince Lombardi's. He was breaking down his own film, putting in an offense. The next office was head coach Jim Lee Howell's. He had his feet up on the desk, and he was reading a newspaper.' Upon seeing the visitor, Howell quipped, 'With guys like Lombardi and Landry in the building, there isn't much for me to do around here.'

"Landry would go on to build the Cowboys from an undermanned expansion team into an NFL power, first with a stunning array of offensive formations and maneuvers, then with a solid organizational structure. Perhaps the most unusual thing about Landry's early years in Dallas was that he devised both an offense and defense for his expansion babies. 'I realized that I couldn't beat anyone with my personnel,' he told me. 'So I had to do it with the motion and formations and gadget plays, the kind of stuff that bothered me most when I was an defensive coach.' The result was an offense that in 1962 averaged 28.4 points and finished second in the NFL in total yards, remarkable achievements for a team in only its third year.

"In 29 seasons under Landry, Dallas won two Super Bowls, played in three other title games and went 20 consecutive years with a winning record. He ranks third in career NFL victories, with 270. In his 40-year pro career Landry was vital in forging a brand of football that the NFL could hang its hat on."

In Irving, TX, of leukemia, February 12, 2000.

Fred Lane, 24, football player. Lane had been traded to the Indianapolis Colts in April. He was fatally shot by his wife, Deidra Lane, in their home.

SI writes:

"An undrafted free agent out of Lane College in Jackson, Tenn., Lane first grabbed the Panthers' attention during training camp in 1997 with his wild bursts of speed and his reckless running style. 'He's the underdog, and everybody loves the underdog,' said Dom Capers, Carolina's coach at the time. 'If you look at our team and ask who is the biggest success story, it's Fred Lane.' He earned the starting job midway through his rookie year, but by the following season things began going sour for Lane. In October 1998 he was benched for a game after he misread the Panthers' itinerary and arrived at the airport late for the team's charter flight. Lane, dressed in a suit, chased the plane as it taxied down the tarmac, his teammates watching from inside and chanting, 'Fred-dee! Fred-dee!' Said Lane: 'I guess I wasn't fast enough.' That

incident could serve as a metaphor not only for Lane's brief and troubled NFL career, one characterized by his dogged determination (he's Carolina's alltime leading rusher, with 2001 yards) but also by naiveté and immaturity."

In Charlotte, NC, of gunshot wounds, July 6, 2000.

Lucien Laurin, 88, horse trainer. Hall of Famer Laurin began his 45-year career in 1942 (after winning 161 races as a jockey). In 1972 and '73, Laurin won five of six Triple Crown races with Riva Ridge and Secretariat.

SI's William Nack writes:

"For the Canadian-born Laurin…nothing could have seemed more unlikely in the summer of 1971 than [Secretariat's] rush to glory. After all, Secretariat was an unknown yearling on a Virginia farm and Laurin had just retired as a horse trainer. He had begun as a jockey but had been suspended for three years when he was caught carrying an illegal battery—a device used to shock horses into running faster—at Narragansett Park in 1938. Laurin claimed that he had been framed, saying someone had slipped the buzzer into his pocket, but he never recovered as a rider, and in 1942 he turned to training horses. By '71 he had prepared one champion, the brilliant filly Quill, and he had saddled the winner of the 1966 Belmont Stakes, Amberoid, but they were notable exceptions in a 30-year career during which he trained a long line of mostly forgettable horses.

"At 58 he was looking forward to a long retirement when his son, Roger, also a trainer, made what turned out to be the most momentous decision of his and his father's lives. Roger was training for Penny Chenery's Meadow Stable in New York, with a promising 2-year-old, Riva Ridge, in his barn, when he accepted the job of training for the powerful Phipps family stable of horses. That left Chenery without a trainer, and when she asked the departing Roger whom she should hire, he said, 'How about my dad?'

"So she did, as her 'temporary' trainer, just as racing's Jupiter was aligning with Mars. Lucien could hardly fathom his good fortune. 'Can you believe this?' he muttered more than once. He regarded himself as the luckiest trainer who ever lived. And that was before Secretariat raced as a 2-year-old. By year's end Laurin had managed Secretariat through a brilliant campaign that ended with his being voted America's 1972 Horse of the Year.

"Secretariat's record breaking charge through the 1973 Triple Crown season transformed the formerly retired horseman into the most famous trainer on earth. Through that five-week ordeal, Laurin fretted openly. 'I wish his thing were over,' he'd say. He beamed as Secretariat roared through the stretch in the Kentucky Derby, winning what remains the fastest Derby ever run, and fairly danced into the winner's circle at Pimlico two weeks later, when the red horse won the Preakness. The night before the Belmont, I called Laurin at his Long Island home to talk about what the horse might do. 'I think he'll win by more than he's ever won by in his life,' he said, his voice rising. 'I think he'll win by 10!'

"The colt won by 31 lengths, smoking through the 1 1/2 miles in 2:24 flat, still a record, and became only the ninth Triple Crown winner—the first in 25 years—as well as the horse of the century. No wonder Laurin walked around for weeks grinning like a Cheshire cat, pinching himself and muttering incredulously at his good fortune. The Belmont was his crowning moment, propelling him on the shortest, fastest journey ever taken to the racing Hall of Fame. Riva Ridge held the door. Secretariat carried Laurin inside. He belongs with them there."

Miami, FL, of complications from hip surgery, June 26, 2000.

Bob Lemon, 79, baseball player. A Hall of Fame pitcher, Lemon played with the Cleveland Indians for 15 years. He retired in 1958 with a career record of 207–128, including seven 20-victory seasons—the most by any pitcher in Indians history. His uniform No. 21 was retired in 1998. Lemon ranks third in franchise history in victories (207), innings pitched (2,860), strikeouts (1,277), starts (350) and shutouts (31). After his retirement Lemon went on to manage eight seasons with the Kansas City Royals, Chicago White Sox and New York Yankees, compiling a 430–403 (.516) record. In Long Beach, CA, of liver complications, January 11, 2000.

Don Liddle, 75, baseball player. Liddle threw the pitch to Vic Wertz in the 1954 World Series that led to Willie Mays's famous over-the-shoulder catch in centerfield at the Polo Grounds. He had relieved pitcher Sal Maglie specifically to pitch to the left-handed Wertz. Liddle started and won Game 4 of that Series as the Giants beat Cleveland for their first championship since 1933. Liddle was 28–18 in 117 games with Milwaukee, the Giants and the St. Louis Cardinals. In Mount Carmel, IL, of lung cancer, June 5, 2000.

John Milner, 50, baseball player. Milner, nicknamed "The Hammer," was a member of National League championship teams with the Mets (1973) and Pittsburgh Pirates ('79). As a first baseman and outfielder, he spent 12 years in the majors and finished with a career batting average of .249 with 131 home runs and 598 RBIs. In East Point, GA, of cancer, January 4, 2000.

Saul Morales, 25, cyclist. A member of the Fuenlabrada team, Morales was killed during the 2000 Tour of Argentina's seventh stage, when he collided with a truck in San Juan province. The riders had been cycling on rural roads without police supervision. In Argentina, of a double cardiac arrest suffered after the accident, February, 28, 2000.

Greg Moore, 24, race car driver. A rising star in auto racing, Moore lost control of his car and slammed into a concrete retaining wall at the California Speedway during the 10th lap of the CART's Marlboro 500. In Fontana, CA, of severe head injuries, Oct. 31, 1999.

Walter Payton, 45, football player. Payton retired as (and remains) the NFL's alltime leader in career rushing yards (16,726). Nicknamed Sweetness for both his nature and his ability on the field, Payton is also the NFL's alltime leader in combined yards (rushing, receiving and returning) with 21,803. He produced 77 100-yard rushing games and ten 1,000-yard rushing seasons in his 13-year career. In 1977 he was voted the league's most valuable player. He was also a member of the Chicago Bears team that won the Super Bowl after

the 1985 season. In 1993 Sweetness was inducted into the Pro Football Hall of Fame.

SI's Peter King writes:

"The legacy that Walter Payton left the pro game was in full view last February when the New Orleans Saints were interviewing college prospects in a meeting room at the NFL scouting combine in Indianapolis. The Saints were enamored of Texas running back Ricky Williams; now they were trying to determine just how much they loved him. New Orleans coach Mike Ditka, who had coached Payton for six years with the Chicago Bears, was praying that he'd have a twice-in-a-lifetime chance to get a rusher with the perfect package of power, speed and attitude. So when the Saints' staff interviewed Williams, Ditka asked him what running backs he liked growing up.

" 'Walter Payton,' said Williams. 'Great ability. Great work ethic. Played through pain. Didn't run out-of-bounds. Won.' That was music to Ditka, who traded eight draft picks to the Washington Redskins so that he could take Williams with the fifth selection. An hour after hearing of Payton's death on Monday, Ditka's voice quavered. 'I think that Walter was the greatest player who ever lived,' he said. 'He was a power back, a speed back, a blocking back. People ask me about the play he was involved in that I remember most, and it's probably a block he threw. There's no question he was one of the best blocking backs ever.' ... It's interesting that when remembering Payton, Ditka and McMahon talked about his blocking, not the fact that he was the leading rusher in NFL history. Meanwhile, opponents recalled Payton's extraordinary running. 'In their Super Bowl year [1985], we played them at Lambeau,' says former Green Bay Packers linebacker Brian Noble. 'It was my rookie season, and we were having a great game, up 10–9 late in the fourth quarter. They had the ball at about our 30. I weighed 265 pounds, and Walter came right at me with the ball. I teed up, and there was a huge collision. I hit that man as hard as I hit anybody in my career. I knocked him back about four yards, but he stayed up and just kept going. Touchdown. I was devastated; I cost us the game. Sitting in the locker room afterward, I was ready to quit. But my teammate John Anderson put his arm around me and said, "Believe me, that's not the first time and it won't be the last time that Walter Payton breaks a tackle like that." '

"Noble sighed. 'I had some collisions in my day with great backs, big backs—William Perry, Earl Campbell, Eric Dickerson. Without question Walter was the greatest player I played against. Or saw.' Said Ditka, 'He was a coach's dream. I just stayed away from him and tried not to screw him up.' "

In Barrington, IL, of bile-duct cancer, Nov 1, 1999.

Max Patkin, 79, baseball clown. Patkin, who began his career as a minor league pitcher in the 1940s (in his best season he went 10–8 for the Wisconsin Rapids), was known as the "Clown Prince of Baseball." He was a beloved figure at minor league games for over 50 years and 4,000 games before retiring in 1996. Dressed in a baggy uniform adorned with a question mark, Patkin was known for his one-liners, umpire-teasing, pratfalls and funny faces. Playing himself, Patkin delivered a hilarious performance in the 1988 baseball film, *Bull Durham*. In Philadelphia, of complications from a ruptured aorta, October 30, 1999.

Adam Petty, 19, race car driver. Adam Petty was a rising star in NASCAR's royal family, the Pettys. He was the fourth generation of the clan to take up the sport, following his great-grandfather, Lee, his grandfather, Richard, and his father, Kyle, into racing. He made his debut at the Winston Cup in Fort Worth, Texas, coming in 40th only a few days before his great-grandfather passed away.

SI's Mark Bechtel writes:

"If there was one thing that stayed with you after meeting Adam Petty, it was this: In an era when pro athletes are getting younger and trying harder to act older, there was no mistaking the fact that Petty was 19. He had a gangly frame, a goofy grin and a goofier laugh. He was genuine, and he was charming—all of which made it especially tough to accept last Friday's news that the youngest of the racing Pettys had been killed in a crash during practice for a NASCAR Busch Series race at New Hampshire International Speedway in Loudon. His death came five weeks after that of his great-grandfather, family patriarch Lee.

"On occasion Adam's deeds belied his greenness. On the racetrack he was the youngest driver to win an American Speed Association race, at 17, and the youngest to win an Automobile Racing Club of America race, a year later. (This was to have been his second full season on the Busch circuit; he was slated to drive a full Winston Cup schedule next year.) Off the track he could display a maturity beyond his years. A few hours before he made his Winston Cup debut, at Texas Motor Speedway in April, he was sitting in his trailer talking about the tough season his father, Kyle, was having. 'I feel really bad for him because his engines just stink now,' Adam said. 'I just hope he doesn't get down on himself.'

"If that sounds like something a father would say about his son rather than vice versa, it's because Adam and Kyle's relationship was as much buddy-buddy it was child-parent. Adam spent most of his formative years at tracks or in garages, learning what it takes to be a driver. 'Growing up the way I did, I don't have a lot of close friends my age,' Adam said. 'So my dad's my best friend.'

"People say such things all the time, but if you took one look at the two of them together, you'd know just how true it was. They had practically everything in common—except, as Adam joked, 'I don't have long hair, and I'm more clean-cut.' In Victory Lane at Charlotte Motor Speedway in 1998, after Adam won his first ARCA race, Kyle was beaming as he told reporters that of all the victories the Petty clan had notched, this one made him the proudest. Asked how he felt about his dad's words of praise, Adam said, 'It makes me want to cry.'"

In Loudon, NH, of injuries sustained in a crash at New Hampshire International Speedway, May 12, 2000.

Lee Petty, 86, race car driver. Lee Petty founded a racing dynasty that yielded 271 race winners in 1,800 races and 10 NASCAR championships between himself, his son, grandson and great-grandson. He is credited with lending charisma, pedigree and humility to a new field of American sports.

SI's Mark Bechtel writes:

"Three days after Adam Petty became NASCAR's first fourth-generation driver, the patriarch of the dynasty, his great-grandfather Lee, died at age 86. But to remember Lee Petty simply as the man who begat Richard (who won an astounding 200 races), who begat Kyle (who has driven on the top stock car circuit for 22 years), who begat Adam, is to neglect the fact that in his day Lee was the best driver around.

"Lee drove the family Buick Roadmaster from Level Cross, N.C., to Charlotte on June 19, 1949, to run in the inaugural NASCAR race. His crewmen that day were his sons, 11-year-old Richard and 10-year-old Maurice. Team

Petty finished 17th. Five years later, in 1954, Lee won NASCAR's points championship, a title that was his again in '58 and '59. 'He used to take those little old Plymouths and just outthink people,' Richard has said. 'When they got him in Oldsmobiles [in 1957], he won races. He won championships. He was blowing people away.' ...

"Among Lee's 54 career wins was the 1959 Daytona 500, the first race on the 2.5-mile superspeedway. His career was effectively ended by a horrific crash on that track during a qualifying race in '61. 'It was a left turn, and we went straight,' Lee said of the incident, in which he jumped a wall and landed 150 feet away, wheels up, in a parking lot. He spent four months in the hospital with a punctured lung and broken collarbone, among other injuries, and raced only sporadically after that. In retirement he oversaw the family's racing business, Petty Enterprises, and took up golf, whittling his handicap to scratch.

" 'The Petty family is a national racing treasure,' said three-time Winston Cup champ Darrell Waltrip after Lee's death. 'When you lose part of that treasure, it's truly time to grieve.' "

In Greensboro, NC, of complications from a stomach aneurysm, April 5, 2000.

Bobby Phills, 30, basketball player. During his nine-year pro career, Phills played guard for the CBA's Sioux Falls franchise, the Milwaukee Bucks, the Cleveland Cavaliers and the Charlotte Hornets. During his senior year at Southern University, Phills was the No. 4 scorer in the country (28.4 points a game). He was universally admired for his sportsmanship and community involvement, leading "Educational Awareness" basketball training camps for 12- to 18-year-olds at his alma mater as well as founding the Bobby Phills Education Foundation. Phills was in the third year of his seven-year, $33 million contract with the Hornets. In Charlotte, NC, of injuries sustained in a head-on traffic collision, January 12, 2000.

Maurice (The Rocket) Richard, 78, hockey player. Remembered as one of the greatest players in NHL history, Richard was the first NHL player to score 50 goals in a season and the first to net 500 goals.

On December 28, 1944, after spending the day moving his family into a new house, Richard scored an NHL-record eight points (five goals, three assists) against the Detroit Red Wings. To ensure that his legend will live on (Richard also shares an NHL record of five goals in a playoff game, and has a record six playoff overtime goals), the NHL created the Maurice Richard Trophy in 1998 to honor the leading goal scorer each season.

Appearing in *SI*, Montreal hockey broadcaster Dick Irvin writes:

"The first time I saw Maurice Richard play for the Canadiens, he broke his ankle. It was December 27, 1942, and I was the 10-year-old son and namesake of the Canadiens' coach. Early in the game Richard, then a 21-year-old rookie, scored two goals, the fourth and fifth of his career, on Bruins goaltender Frank Brimsek.

"In the third period Boston defenseman Johnny Crawford leveled Richard with a heavy body check. The rookie crumpled to the ice, his right ankle broken. As an amateur Richard had fractured his left ankle and a wrist. Now another broken bone had people saying he was too brittle to play in the NHL. Obviously they had the wrong idea. Richard would go on to play 978 NHL games, score 544 goals and win eight Stanley Cups.

"A few nights before that Bruins game, Richard had

arrived for the first time in the Canadiens' dressing room at the Montreal Forum. My father told him he wouldn't be playing that night. Instead of taking the news quietly, as was expected of a rookie, Richard, in an early display of the temper that would become part of his legend, stormed out of the room, slammed the door in his coach's face and went home. His new teammates were shocked by the disrespectful outburst, but my father wasn't offended. 'That's the kind of guy I want on my team,' he told his players. Obviously he had the right idea."

In Montreal, of cancer, May 27, 2000.

Mack Robinson, 85, sprinter. A world-class athlete in a time when African-Americans received little recognition and even less support, Mack Robinson, Jackie Robinson's brother, was the silver medalist in the 1936 Olympic Games, placing a close second to Jesse Owens in the 200 meters. He later became known for his outstanding community service to the city of Pasadena.

SI writes:

"[Mack] was Jackie's older brother (by four years) and proud of it; thanks largely to his efforts a statue of Jackie was erected on the UCLA campus. He was a terrific athlete in his own right. At the 1936 Berlin Games, Robinson tied the Olympic record of 21.1 seconds in a semifinal of the 200 meters and matched that time in the final, only to finish second to the incomparable Jesse Owens, who ran 20.7 on a dirt track in light rain. Robinson had begun the '36 season as an unknown sprinter at Pasadena Junior College who needed $150 from a few local businessmen to attend the U.S. trials in New York City. There he upset 1932 Olympic 200 silver medalist Ralph Metcalfe, among others, to earn a place on the team.

"In New York and Berlin, Robinson ran in the battered spikes that he had worn throughout the college season. 'I thought I'd at least get a pair of new shoes [for making the team],' he told the *Los Angeles Times* in 1984. 'I always thought if I'd had some help, I could have beaten Jesse, or made it even closer than it was.'

"In 1938 Robinson dropped out of school and returned home to Pasadena to earn a living. For several years he swept streets, often wearing his USA Olympic sweatshirt. 'If anyone in Pasadena was proud for me other than my family and close friends, they never showed it,' he once said. Nevertheless Robinson, who moved on from street sweeping to community service, worked tirelessly in Pasadena to improve its deteriorating northwest side. In '97 he finally received recognition with the unveiling of the Pasadena Robinson Memorial. It honors both Jackie and Mack."

In Pasadena, CA, of complications from diabetes, March 12, 2000.

Aurelio Rodriguez, 52, baseball player. Rodriguez played third base from 1967 to '83, with California, Washington, Detroit, San Diego, the New York Yankees, the Chicago White Sox and Baltimore. Though his career batting average was .237, he led American League third basemen twice in fielding and was always reliable defensively. In Detroit, of injuries incurred when a car struck him, September 23, 2000.

Jack Scott, 57, sports psychologist. Considered by many to be a sports visionary, Scott played diverse roles in his lifetime: radical journalist, Oberlin College athletic director, confidant to Symbionese Liberation Army fugitive Patty Hearst, and guru to sports figures

such as basketball star Bill Walton and former NFL stars Dave Meggyesy, Chip Oliver and George Sauer. He also worked with Olympians Carl Lewis and Joan Benoit.

SI's Kenny Moore writes:

"Scott grew up a 'libertarian jock,' in Scranton, Pa., sprinted for Stanford, graduated from Syracuse in 1966, got his Ph.D. in sports psychology from California and with his wife, Micki, founded the Institute for the Study of Sport and Society. In his books *Athletics for Athletes* and *The Athletic Revolution*, Scott decried authoritarian coaching, ripped performance-enhancing drugs and the commercialization of our games, and called for including more women and minorities.

"Labeled by some as a militant nihilist, Scott was about as revolutionary as Abraham Lincoln. 'I'm not trying to do anything radical,' he'd say. 'I'm just trying to be fair.' Of course, nothing is more irksome than a fair man in a world that needs some work on the issue.

"In 1972 Oberlin College hired him to be athletic director. Scott tripled funding for women's sports and brought in three black head coaches, when few non-all-black colleges had even one. All Scott's coaches won. The Oberlin faculty objected anyway, saying Scott was causing divisions in the student body and the faculty. Scott resigned after two years...

"In 1975 he moved to Oregon and mastered the use of microcurrent therapy, which increases circulation and promotes healing. Over the years the world caught up to Jack. Title IX made women in sports commonplace. Free agency and the Amateur Athletic Act secured athletes' rights.

"And so Scott could leave us, too soon, yet having savored the fruit of his activism and the true, tested friends it won him. 'The secret of Jack is no secret at all,' said Blakely. 'He learned to forgive the blows of being vilified and the equally horrible blows of being idolized. He was always faithful. Semper fidelis. Always faithful.'"

In Los Angeles, of throat cancer, February 6, 2000.

William Edward Simon, 72, Olympics administrator. A member of the U.S. Olympic Committee for more than 30 years, Simon served as its president from 1981–85. After the financial crises of the '76 Montreal Games and the 1980 American boycott, Simon's vision and commitment were credited with saving the American Olympic movement. In the days before extensive corporate sponsorship, his training as treasurer—he had served as both Nixon's and Ford's Treasury Secretary—helped steer the USOC to the 1984 Los Angeles financial bonanza. The USOC was then able to distribute millions of dollars worth of grants to amateur U.S. sports groups. In 1991 Simon was inducted into the Olympic Hall of Fame and seven years later he announced that he would donate his entire $350 million fortune to charitable organizations, AIDS hospices and low-income educational groups. In Santa Barbara, CA, of pulmonary complications, June 3, 2000.

Karsten Solheim, 88, golf equipment designer. Solheim revolutionized golf equipment with his principle of perimeter weighting. In the 1960s, Solheim began designing putters in his garage and selling them to pros from the trunk of his car. Because of the curious sound the putters made as they struck the golf ball, he gave them the apt name of "PING." Though both the U.S. Golf Association and the PGA Tour tried to ban Solheim's game-improvement clubs—irons which used investment casting to make clubs with cavity backs—his company rallied to become extremely successful. In Phoenix, AZ, of Parkinson's disease, February 16, 2000.

Dr. John Paul Stapp, 89, rocket sledder. In 1954 U.S. Air Force Colonel Stapp became known as "the fastest man on earth" when his pioneering rocket-sled experiment accelerated him from zero to 632 mph in five seconds and back to zero in 1.4 seconds. Serving as a human guinea pig, Stapp collected data on the effects of bailing out from supersonic aircraft. His research later helped introduce crucial safety innovations such as car seatbelts. In Alamogordo, NM, of natural causes, November 13, 1999.

Sanford (Sandy) Stephens, 59, college football player. Stephens, an All-America quarterback, led the Minnesota Gophers to their only Rose Bowl victory, a 21–3 triumph over UCLA in 1962. As the university's first black quarterback, Stephens inspired the next generation of young black athletes, many of whom went on to compete for the University of Minnesota.

SI's John Rosengren writes:

"Before Martin Luther King Jr. marched on Washington, Sandy Stephens paraded in Pasadena. Stephens led Minnesota to the football national title in 1960 and to victory in the Rose Bowl the next season—the same one in which he became the first black All-America quarterback. … [He] blazed a trail that would be followed by Warren Moon and Steve McNair and made Minnesota a place to go if you were an aspiring black signal-caller. 'I wanted to play quarterback,' said Buccaneers coach Tony Dungy, who did just that for the Golden Gophers from 1973 to '76, 'and I knew that Minnesota had pretty much set the trend.'

"At the time when segregation in the South and bigotry in the North kept blacks from calling the plays for whites, Gophers coach Murray Warmath took a chance on Stephens, a four-sport star from Uniontown, Pa. The experiment wasn't an immediate success. Stephens debuted as a sophomore in 1959, and when Minnesota went 2–7, irate fans hung Warmath in effigy outside the players' dorm. But Stephens' teammates rallied behind him. 'He was full of self-confidence, and the players responded to that,' says Gophers interim athletic director Tom Moe, a receiver on the '59 team. Warmath, too, stuck by his man, in whom he saw not just a natural born leader but also at 6 feet and 215 pounds, one tough kid. 'He wouldn't put up with any abuse,' Warmath says. 'It would've taken one hell of a guy to threaten him.'

"Stephens's college heroics never translated into success as a pro. He played briefly for the Montreal Alouettes of the CFL and subsequently held jobs in banking, real estate and social work. Recently he served as an analyst on Minnesota football broadcasts, and for the past several years he had been preparing a book on the significance of his college football experience. Even if that book never makes it to print, Stephens's legacy will endure. Said Al Nuness, who captained the Gophers' basketball team in the late 1960s, 'Every African-American who wanted to be a quarterback looked up to Sandy Stephens. He's a legend among black athletes.'"

In Minneapolis, of a heart attack, June 6, 2000.

Tod Surmon, 26, wrestler. Surmon was an All-America wrestler at Stanford University. He graduated in 1996 and won the 1999 Midlands Championships in Chicago two days prior to his accident. In Las Vegas, of head wounds incurred from a fall from a light pole on the Las Vegas Strip shortly after the millennium midnight, January 1, 2000.

Derrick Thomas, 33, football player. Thomas, a linebacker, made nine Pro Bowl appearances and ranked ninth in career sacks. He was also an active humanitarian, twice recognized by the league for his off-field contributions.

SI's Michael Silver writes an open letter to young NFL fans across America:

DEAR KIDS:

"You may be too young to realize it, but a great football player died last week. As you grow up, older people will tell you that Derrick Thomas, the leopard-quick Chiefs linebacker, caused 300-pound offensive linemen to tremble with fear and literally made a star quarterback sick; that he read to more children than Mr. Rogers; that he packed a lifetime's worth of fun into a 33-year whirlwind and touched everyone lucky enough to be swept up by it. They'll also say that Thomas dedicated himself to giving kids a brighter future. I'm here to tell you that it's all true.

"On the field Thomas may have made more game-changing plays than any defender since Lawrence Taylor, and Kansas City thrived on his passion. More important, Thomas was a complex, animated person, a quick-witted, thoughtful original who whizzed through adulthood as if he were afraid he would miss something.

"The NFL's social butterfly could also sting like a bee. Two years ago, a few days before his final Pro Bowl appearance, Thomas sat at the poolside bar at the Ihilani Resort and Spa and held court before a group of NFL stars that included Chester McGlockton, the Raiders' enigmatic defensive lineman. 'Big Chester,' Thomas chirped. 'Minimum pay, minimum play. One out of every five snaps, when he feels like it, he can't be blocked.' It was a major dis, but Thomas was funny, charming and bold enough to pull it off. Finally, McGlockton startled the group by admitting, 'I *am* a dog.' Three months later Big Chester signed with the Chiefs.

"Like so many others in the NFL community, I was lucky enough to hang with DT. Over the years I saw him gather teammates like a pied piper and blow through Kansas City as if he owned the place, which he did. We drank beers with working-class Mexican-Americans in a dark alley and swapped JFK conspiracy theories over burgers and spent more time laughing than anything else.

"Kids, Thomas wasn't a saint. He was simply a good man with a huge heart and an awesome motor that never stopped. If he could talk to you now, I'm prettty sure he'd tell you to read a good book, question authority and live every day as if it were your last. And wear your seat belt.

"I'll never forget him. I hope you won't either."

In Miami, FL, from complications following a car accident, February 8, 2000.

Erik Turner, 31, football player. Turner was the second overall pick in the 1991 NFL draft. He joined the Cleveland Browns before switching to the Oakland Raiders as a free agent for the '97 season. In Thousand Oaks, CA, of complications from abdominal cancer, May 28, 2000.

Robert Wagenhoffer, 39, figure skater. The only skater ever to win junior championships in singles and pairs in the same year, Wagonhoffer went on to finish second in the 1979 pairs competition (with Vicki Heasley). He also finished second in the 1982 U.S. men's nationals. He starred and choreographed for several professional touring shows. In Torrance, CA, of complications from AIDS, December 13, 1999.

2 0 0 1   M a j o r   E v e n t s

JANUARY

Major College Bowl Games	Jan. 1 & 2
Orange Bowl/National Championship	Jan. 3
NFL Divisional Playoffs	Jan. 6 & 7
U.S. Figure Skating Championships	Jan. 13–21
NFL Conference Championships	Jan. 14
Australian Open	Jan. 22–28
Super Bowl XXXV	Jan. 28
PBA National Championship	Jan. 31–Feb. 4

FEBRUARY

Millrose Games	Feb. 4
AFC-NFC Pro Bowl	Feb. 4
NHL All-Star Game	Feb. 4
NBA All-Star Game	Feb. 11
Daytona 500	Feb. 18

MARCH

World Indoor Track & Field Championships	March 9–11
World Figure Skating Championships	March 18–25
The Players Championship	March 22–25
NCAA Women's Final Four	March 30–April 1
NCAA Men's Final Four	March 31–April 2

APRIL

Baseball Opening Day	April 2
Masters Tournament	April 5–8
Stanley Cup Playoffs Begin	April 11
Major League Soccer Season Begins	April 14
Boston Marathon	April 16
NBA Playoffs Begin	April 21

MAY

Kentucky Derby	May 5
Preakness	May 19
Indianapolis 500	May 27
Stanley Cup Finals Begin	May 29

JUNE

French Open Tennis	June 4–10
NBA Finals Begin	June 6
Belmont Stakes	June 9
U.S. Open Golf	June 14–17

JULY

Wimbledon Tennis	July 2–8
Baseball All-Star Game	July 10
British Open Golf	July 19–22

AUGUST

IAAF Track & Field Championships	Aug. 3–12
PGA Championship	Aug. 16–19
College Football Season Begins	Aug. 25

SEPTEMBER

U.S. Open Tennis	Sept. 3–9
NFL Season Begins	Sept. 9
Ryder Cup	Sept. 28–30

OCTOBER

NHL Season Begins	Oct. 3
MLS Cup	Oct. 13
World Series	Oct. 20
Breeders' Cup	Oct. 22
Women's Tennis Tour Championships	Oct. 29–Nov. 4
NBA Regular Season Begins	Oct. 30

NOVEMBER

New York Marathon	Nov. 4
Tennis Masters Cup	Nov. 12–18

DECEMBER

Heisman Trophy Presentation	Dec. 8
Major College Bowl Games Begin	Dec. 20